THE
ALL ENGLAND
LAW REPORTS

1975
VOLUME 1

EDITOR
R N G Harrison BA
of Lincoln's Inn, Barrister

LONDON
BUTTERWORTHS

ENGLAND: Butterworth & Co (Publishers) Ltd
                    London: 88 Kingsway, WC2B 6AB

AUSTRALIA: Butterworths Pty Ltd
                    Sydney: 586 Pacific Highway, Chatswood, NSW 2067
                    Melbourne: 343 Little Collins Street, 3000
                    Brisbane: 240 Queen Street, 4000

CANADA: Butterworth & Co (Canada) Ltd
                    Toronto: 2265 Midland Avenue, Scarborough, M1P 4S1

NEW ZEALAND: Butterworths of New Zealand Ltd
                    Wellington: 26-28 Waring Taylor Street 1

SOUTH AFRICA: Butterworth & Co (South Africa) (Pty) Ltd
                    Durban: 152-154 Gale Street

©

Butterworth & Co (Publishers) Ltd

1975

ISBN 0 406 85111 5

Printed in Great Britain by R J Acford Ltd, Industrial Estate, Chichester, Sussex

House of Lords

The Lord High Chancellor: Lord Elwyn-Jones

Lords of Appeal in Ordinary

Lord Reid
(retired 10th January 1975)
Lord Morris of Borth-y-Gest
(retired 10th January 1975)
Viscount Dilhorne
Lord Wilberforce
Lord Diplock

Lord Simon of Glaisdale
Lord Cross of Chelsea
Lord Kilbrandon
Lord Salmon
Lord Edmund-Davies
Lord Fraser
(appointed 13th January 1975)

Court of Appeal

The Lord High Chancellor

The Lord Chief Justice of England: Lord Widgery

The Master of The Rolls: Lord Denning

The President of the Family Division: Sir George Gillespie Baker

Lords Justices of Appeal

Sir Charles Ritchie Russell
Sir John Megaw
Sir Denys Burton Buckley
Sir David Arnold Scott Cairns
Sir Edward Blanshard Stamp
Sir John Frederick Eustace Stephenson
Sir Alan Stewart Orr

Sir Eustace Wentworth Roskill
Sir Frederick Horace Lawton
Sir Leslie George Scarman
Sir Arthur Evan James
Sir Roger Fray Greenwood Ormrod
Sir Patrick Reginald Evelyn Browne
Sir Geoffrey Dawson Lane
(appointed 31st December 1974)

Chancery Division

The Lord High Chancellor
The Vice-Chancellor: Sir John Anthony Plowman

Sir Reginald William Goff
Sir Robert Edgar Megarry
Sir John Patrick Graham
Sir Peter Harry Batson Woodroffe Foster
Sir John Norman Keates Whitford

Sir John Anson Brightman
Sir Ernest Irvine Goulding
Sir Sydney William Templeman
Sir Raymond Henry Walton
Sir Peter Raymond Oliver

Queen's Bench Division

The Lord Chief Justice of England

Sir John Percy Ashworth
Sir Aubrey Melford Steed Stevenson
Sir Gerald Alfred Thesiger
Sir Basil Nield
Sir Bernard Joseph Maxwell MacKenna
Sir Alan Abraham Mocatta
Sir John Thompson
Sir Daniel James Brabin
Sir Helenus Patrick Joseph Milmo
Sir Joseph Donaldson Cantley
Sir George Stanley Waller
Sir Hugh Eames Park
Sir Ralph Vincent Cusack
Sir Stephen Chapman
Sir John Ramsay Willis
Sir Graham Russell Swanwick
Sir Patrick McCarthy O'Connor
Sir John Francis Donaldson
Sir Geoffrey Dawson Lane
   (appointed Lord Justice of Appeal,
   31st December 1974)
Sir John Robertson Dunn Crichton
Sir Samuel Burgess Ridgway Cooke

Sir Bernard Caulfield
Sir Nigel Cyprian Bridge
Sir Sebag Shaw
Sir Hilary Gwynne Talbot
Sir Edward Walter Eveleigh
Sir William Lloyd Mars-Jones
Sir Ralph Kilner Brown
Sir Philip Wien
Sir Peter Henry Rowley Bristow
Sir Hugh Harry Valentine Forbes
Sir Desmond James Conrad Ackner
Sir William Hugh Griffiths
Sir Robert Hugh Mais
Sir Neil Lawson
Sir David Powell Croom-Johnson
Sir Tasker Watkins VC
Sir John Raymond Phillips
Sir Leslie Kenneth Edward Boreham
Sir John Douglas May
Sir Michael Robert Emanuel Kerr
Sir Alfred William Michael Davies
Sir John Dexter Stocker
Sir Kenneth George Illtyd Jones

Family Division

The President of the Family Division

Sir Charles William Stanley Rees
Sir Reginald Withers Payne
Sir Neville Major Ginner Faulks
Sir James Roualeyn Hovell-Thurlow
   Cumming-Bruce
Sir John Brinsmead Latey
Dame Elizabeth Kathleen Lane
Sir Henry Vivian Brandon

Sir Robin Horace Walford Dunn
Sir William Arthur Bagnall
Sir Alfred Kenneth Hollings
Sir John Lewis Arnold
Sir Charles Trevor Reece
Sir Francis Brooks Purchas
Sir Haydn Tudor Evans
Dame Rose Heilbron

CITATION

These Reports are cited thus:

[1975] 1 All ER

REFERENCES

These reports contain references, which follow after the headnotes, to the following major works of legal reference described in the manner indicated below—

Halsbury's Laws of England

The reference 2 Halsbury's Laws (3rd Edn) 20 para 48, refers to paragraph 48 on page 20 of volume 2 of the third edition, and the reference 2 Halsbury's Laws (4th Edn) 708, para 1535, refers to paragraph 1535 on page 708 of volume 2 of the fourth edition of Halsbury's Laws of England.

Halsbury's Statutes of England

The reference 5 Halsbury's Statutes (3rd Edn) 302 refers to page 302 of volume 5 of the third edition of Halsbury's Statutes of England.

English and Empire Digest

References are to the replacement volumes (including reissue volumes) of the Digest, and to the continuation volumes of the replacement volumes.

The reference 31 Digest (Repl) 244, 3794, refers to case number 3794 on page 244 of Digest Replacement Volume 31.

The reference Digest (Cont Vol B) 287, 7540b, refers to case number 7540b on page 287 of Digest Continuation Volume B.

The reference 28(1) Digest (Reissue) 167, 507, refers to case number 507 on page 167 of Digest Replacement Volume 28(1) Reissue.

Halsbury's Statutory Instruments

The reference 12 Halsbury's Statutory Instruments (Second Reissue) 124, refers to page 124 of the second reissue of volume 12 of Halsbury's Statutory Instruments; references to subsequent reissues are similar.

Encyclopaedia of Forms and Precedents

The reference 7 Ency Forms & Precedents (4th Edn) 247, Form 12, refers to Form 12 on page 247 of volume 7 of the fourth edition of the Encyclopaedia of Forms and Precedents.

Cases reported in volume 1

vii

Index

COMPANY—Winding-up—Compulsory winding-up—*continued*

COMPENSATION

CONDITION

CONFESSION

CONFIDENTIAL INFORMATION

CONFLICT OF LAWS

CONSIDERATION

CONTEMPT OF COURT

CROWN COURT—*continued*
Committal of offender to Crown Court for sentence – Powers of justices – Order by justices
following conviction – Compensation order – Propriety – Justices having no power to make
any order following conviction where offender is to be committed for sentence – All questions
associated with sentence to be left to Crown Court – Magistrates' Courts Act 1952, s 29.
Sentence – Commencement – Sentence to take effect from day on which pronounced unless
court otherwise directs – Ante-dated sentence – Whether court having power to direct sentence to take effect from day before day on which it is pronounced – Courts Act 1971, s 11(1).
Supervisory jurisdiction of High Court – Orders of mandamus, prohibition and certiorari – Orders
, in relation to jurisdiction of Crown Court – Meaning of 'jurisdiction' – Whether power to
make an order of certiorari when error of law shown on the face of the record – Courts Act

CURRENCY
Ship – Sale by Admiralty marshal – Sale for sum expressed in foreign currency. *See* **Admiralty**
(Appraisement and sale – Currency of sale).

DAMAGES
Fatal Accidents Acts, under. *See* **Fatal Accident.**
Interest, on. *See* **Interest.**
Nuisance. *See* **Nuisance** (Damages).
Sale of land – Breach ol contract. *See* **Sale of Land** (Contract – Breach).

DEATH
Damages in respect of. *See* **Fatal Accident.**
Fatal accident. *See* **Fatal Accident**

DEBT
Funded debt – Stamp duty. *See* **Stamp Duty** (Issue of loan capital).

DECREE NISI
See **Divorce.**

DEED
Escrow – Condition – Implied condition – Conveyance executed in anticipation of sale – Time for
completion – Reasonable inference from circumstances – Transfer executed by vendor and
delivered to his solicitor – Purchaser entitled to delivery of transfer on payment of purchase
price – Delay in completion by purchaser – Whether escrow subject to implied condition as to
time of payment – Whether condition that payment should be made promptly or within a

DEFENCE
Criminal proceedings. *See* **Criminal Law** (Defence).
Statutory – Food and Drugs Act 1955. *See* **Food and Drugs** (Defence to proceedings).

DELAY
Certiorari. *See* **Certiorari** (Delay).

DELEGATION
Agent – Implied authority – Estate agent. *See* **Estate Agent** (Delegation).

DESTRUCTION
Will. *See* **Will** (Revocation – Destruction).

DISCOVERY
Interlocutory motion – Jurisdiction – Infringement of copyright – Defendant in possession of
infringing copies – Plaintiffs seeking on motion order for disclosure of information as to
suppliers – Strong prima facie case of infringement – Jurisdiction to order discovery on
motion – Order limited to names and addresses known to defendant. **RCA Corporation v**
Production of documents – Confidence – Implied undertaking – Third party – Public interest in
disclosure of information – Implied undertaking by party obtaining discovery not to use documents for collateral purpose – Duty of third party to whom documents passed – Documents
disclosed by defendants in action passed to newspaper publishers – Action raising matters of
general public interest – Publishers proposing to publish article dealing with matters raised by
action – Article making use of information obtained from defendants' documents – Article
critical of defendants – Public interest in proper administration of justice – Whether publishers
under a duty not to use documents for purpose other than purpose for which discovery made –
Whether publishers entitled to use documents for ulterior purpose when disclosure in public
Production before commencement of proceedings – Claim in respect of personal injuries –
Medical records – Disclosure to prospective plaintiff's medical adviser only – Use of documents – Plaintiff not bound by medical expert's report – Right of plaintiff's counsel to
question expert in relation to records to determine whether a case. **Deistung v South**

DISCRETION
Certiorari – Refusal – Delay in application. *See* **Certiorari** (Delay – Discretion).

DISQUALIFICATION
Driving licence. *See* **Road Traffic** (Disqualification for holding licence).

DIVORCE

DOCUMENT

DOMESTIC WATER SUPPLY

DRINK

DRIVING LICENCE

DRIVING TEST

DUPLICITY

DURESS

DUTY

DWELLING - HOUSE

EASEMENT

INCOME TAX—*continued*

INDICTMENT

INDUCEMENT

INEQUALITY OF BARGAINING POWER

INFANT

INJUNCTION

INSPECTION

INSURANCE

SOLICITOR

SPECIFIC PERFORMANCE

SPECIMEN

STAMP DUTY

STATEMENT

STATUTE

STATUTORY NUISANCE

STATUTORY TENANT

STAY OF PROCEEDINGS

STOLEN GOODS

STREET TRADING

Cases Noted

Statutes, etc, noted

Words and Phrases

Corrigenda

[1973] 1 All ER

p 766. **MFI Warehouses v Nattrass.** Line *b* 6: for 'The advertisement complained of referred to the doors as being' read 'The advertisement complained of referred to the door gear as being'.

[1974] 3 All ER

p 859. **Re a Solicitor.** Lines *b* 3 and 4: for 'forego his benefit' substitute 'decline to act. Equally, where a client wishes to make a substantial gift inter vivos, the solicitor should not accept it unless the client has been independently advised.'

p 991. **DPP v Withers.** Line *a* 6: for 'wild' read 'wide'. Page 1005, *a* 4: for 'procrastinate' read 'procrustenate'.

p 1027. **Saunders v Soper.** Counsel for the appellant: for '*S J Burton*' read '*S J Burnton*'.

[1975] 1 All ER

p 498. **Pexton (Inspector of Taxes) v Bell.** Line *a* 3: for '30 Halsbury's Laws' read '20 Halsbury's Laws'.

p 682. **Re Coleman (deceased).** Line *c* 5: for 'does not operate' read 'does operate'.

Cumbers v Cumbers

COURT OF APPEAL, CIVIL DIVISION
LORD DENNING MR, STAMP AND ORMROD LJJ
27th JUNE 1974

Divorce – Financial provision – Lump sum order – Circumstances in which payment of lump sum should be ordered – Contribution to marriage deserving compensation – Short marriage – Separation after 18 months – Divorce by consent – Husband sole owner of house – Part played by wife in marriage deserving compensation – Award of lump sum amounting to approximately one-third of net proceeds of sale of matrimonial home.

Divorce – Separation – Financial protection for respondent – Decree nisi granted – Decree absolute although no financial provision made by petitioner – Undertaking by petitioner where desirable to make decree absolute without delay – Necessity for undertaking – Better course to withdraw application and make usual application for financial provision or property adjustment order – Matrimonial Causes Act 1973, s 10(4).

In January 1969, three months before his marriage, the husband bought a house which was conveyed into his name. He paid £600 towards the purchase price, the balance of £3,200 being raised on mortgage. After the marriage both the husband and wife went out to work. A child was born in September 1969. In November 1970 the husband left the home and in May 1971 the wife obtained a maintenance order for £5 a week for herself and £2 a week for the child. In September 1971 the husband sold the house. The net proceeds of the sale amounted to £1,600. In March 1973 the husband obtained a divorce by consent which was made absolute in September 1973. The husband remarried and used the £1,600 for the purpose of buying a new house. In proceedings for financial provision the judge ordered that, in addition to the provision for maintenance, the husband should pay the wife a lump sum of £800 to be paid by instalments and charged on the husband's new house. The husband appealed, contending that the case was not one for capital provision since the marriage had been very short and the wife had had no proprietary interest in the matrimonial home.

Held – Although the marriage had been a short one the wife had played a part in it which deserved compensation of a capital nature in addition to the income provision, which would come to an end automatically if she remarried. However £800 was too large a sum and should be reduced to £500 which would be charged on the husband's house, payable by weekly instalments, with interest at ten per cent on the amount outstanding. Maintenance should be dealt with in the Family Division and accordingly the justices' order would be replaced by an interim order in the High Court and would be subject to review on application to the Family Division. The appeal would therefore be allowed to that extent (see p 3 g to p 4 d, post).

Wachtel v Wachtel [1973] 1 All ER 829 applied.

Per Ormrod LJ. Where it is desired to obtain a decree absolute quickly it is usually better for an application under s 10 of the Matrimonial Causes Act 1973 with respect to financial provision to be withdrawn rather than be dealt with by way

of an undertaking under s 10(4).   In such cases financial matters can be more appro-   *a*
priately dealt with by way of financial provision and property adjustment orders
under ss 23 and 24 of the 1973 Act (see p 4 *e* to *h*, post).

Notes
For financial provision on granting a decree of divorce and the matters to be con-
sidered by the court in exercising its powers, see Supplement to 12 Halsbury's Laws
(3rd Edn) para 987A, 1-4.   *b*
   For the restrictions on making a decree absolute when based on a period of
separation, see ibid para 900A.
   For the Matrimonial Causes Act 1973, ss 10, 23, 24, see 43 Halsbury's Statutes (3rd
Edn) 552, 564, 566.

Cases referred to in judgments   *c*
Grigson v Grigson [1974] 1 All ER 478, [1974] 1 WLR 228, CA.
Wachtel v Wachtel [1973] 1 All ER 829, [1973] Fam 81, [1973] 2 WLR 366, CA.

Appeal
The husband, Alan James Cumbers, and the wife, Loraine Susan Cumbers, were
married on 5th April 1969.   On 18th November 1970 the husband left the wife
and on 17th May 1971 the wife obtained a maintenance order against the husband for   *d*
herself and the child of the marriage in Maldon Magistrates' Court.   On 19th March
1973 the husband obtained a decree nisi of divorce, the irretrievable breakdown of
the marriage being evidenced by two years' separation and the wife's consent to the
grant of a decree.   On an application by the husband for the decree to be made
absolute, the wife applied for financial protection under s 6 of the Divorce Reform
Act 1969, and the husband gave an undertaking that he would make such financial   *e*
provision for the wife as the court might approve.   On 27th September 1973 his
Honour Judge Buckee sitting at Southend County Court, declared that the financial
provision of which the court approved was (a) as to maintenance, continuance until
further order by the justices of payment of the sums ordered by them on 17th May
1971; (b) as to capital, payment by the husband to the wife of £800 being one-half
of the net proceeds of the matrimonial home, to be paid by instalments of not less   *f*
than £20 per month with interest at ten per cent per annum calculated on the balance
outstanding from time to time and with the grant of a sufficient security for payment,
including if need be a charge on the husband's interest in the house that he had lately
acquired and to which he had applied in whole or in part the sum of £800 previously
held by his solicitor in respect of any claim by the wife and with the promise that in
the event of default in payment of any instalment the whole unpaid balance should   *g*
become due and the charge enforceable.   The husband appealed on the following
grounds: (i) that the judge had exceeded his functions under s 6(3)(*b*) of the 1969
Act in that he was required thereunder only to approve or disapprove such financial
provision as the husband might propose to make for the wife and the child of the
family; (ii) that the financial arrangement between the husband and the wife which
the judge considered amounted to reasonable financial provision did not constitute   *h*
provision within the meaning of s 6; (iii) that the amount of financial provision which
the judge found to be reasonable was excessive having regard to all the circumstances
of the case and, in particular, the age, earning capacity, income and assets of the
parties and the duration of the marriage; (iv) that the type of provision which the
judge considered that the husband ought to make for the wife and the child of the
family, namely, provision of a capital nature, was not one which should have been   *j*
made having regard to all the circumstances of the case and, in particular, the assets
and earning capacity of the husband.   The facts are set out in the judgment of
Lord Denning MR.

Christopher Sowden for the husband.
Richard Lines for the wife.

a **LORD DENNING MR.** Mr and Mrs Cumbers were married in April 1969. Both were in their early twenties. Three months earlier, in January 1969, the husband had bought a house. It was conveyed into his name. The husband paid the deposit of it of £600. He paid it out of compensation which he had got from an accident. The balance of £3,200 was raised on mortgage with a building society. They had a child, a boy, born in September 1969. Both went out to work. But

b the marriage did not last more than about 18 months. On 18th November 1970 the husband left. In May 1971 the wife got a maintenance order against the husband from the justices—£5 a week for herself and £2 a week for the child who was with her. After a time, in September 1971, the husband sold the house. The money which was obtained on resale brought in a sum of £1,600.

In March 1973 there was a divorce. It was by consent after two years' separation,

c under s 2(1)(d) of the Divorce Reform Act 1969. In September 1973 the husband wanted it made absolute because he had formed an attachment with another woman and wished to marry her. So on 10th September 1973 it was ordered by consent that the husband be at liberty to make the decree nisi absolute forthwith. But that was only done on his undertaking that he would make such financial provision for his wife as the court may approve. That order was made by consent. So the wife

d cannot complain of it. But the recent case of *Grigson v Grigson*[1] shows that an undertaking in that form is undesirable. If the sum is not fixed beforehand, the wife is helpless. The actual financial provision ought to be fixed beforehand. Later, on 27th September 1973, the matter came before the judge for determination. He treated it as if an application had been taken out under ss 2 and 4 of the Matrimonial Property Act 1970. Neither party objected. It was a sensible way of dealing with

e it. They must be treated as consenting to it. Those sections give the judge a considerable discretion and power to order transfer of property. After reading the affidavits and hearing the parties, the judge said that the maintenance order by the justices should be continued and be dealt with by them; but he made a special order about a capital provision. He treated her as entitled to half of the equity in the house. The equity was £1,600. He ordered that she should have half of it, that is, £800.

f The husband had however already received the whole of the £1,600 and had used it in getting a new car and in getting another house for himself and his new wife. So the judge did not order him to pay the £800 at once to the wife. He ordered it to be paid by instalments of not less than £20 a month, with interest at ten per cent, and he charged it on the house which the husband had lately acquired.

Now the husband appeals to the court. It was said for the husband that this was

g not a case for capital provision at all. It was pointed out that the marriage had been very short. The wife had no proprietary right in the matrimonial home. She had no case under s 17 of the Married Women's Property Act 1882. So no part of the £1,600 should be allocated to her.

I can see the force of that argument. But, looking once again at *Wachtel v Wachtel*[2], it is important to remember that, in addition to the income provision, there should

h be, in a proper case, a capital provision. During the argument in this case Ormrod LJ pointed out that an income provision comes to an end automatically if the wife remarries. So it may sometimes be wise to make some capital provision for her which will not cease on her remarriage. That is, in a case where she has really played a part in the marriage which deserves compensation of a capital nature. It seems to me that this case is properly one in which a capital provision—a lump sum—should

j be ordered. But I think that the sum of £800 is too large. The better figure would be one-third or thereabouts. I would put it at £500, in regard to the capital provision.

Again it would not be right that the wife should be able to sell up the husband's new house. The right course would be to award her a sum of £500 to be a charge on the

---

1 [1974] 1 All ER 478, [1974] 1 WLR 228
2 [1973] 1 All ER 829, at 830, [1973] Fam 81 at 95

new house, but such charge not to be available or enforced except on further applica- *a*
tion to the court; but meanwhile interest to run at an appropriate rate which I
would suggest to be ten per cent. The husband should pay that ten per cent on the
balance outstanding by weekly instalments. He should repay the £500 gradually
as he could—by instalments to be agreed or fixed—until the £500 is discharged. So
far as maintenance is concerned, it would be better dealt with in the future by the
registrar in the Family Division here. So I would replace the justices' order by an *b*
interim order in the High Court here. It should be at present the same amount,
namely, £5 for the wife and the £2 for the child; but that that income provision
could and should be reviewed on application to the Family Division here. The
registrar is to be able to consider it in the light of all the circumstances. I would
allow the appeal to that extent accordingly.

c

STAMP LJ. I agree.

ORMROD LJ. I agree. I would just add one thing. This case is a good illustration of the difficulties which I know arise under s 6 of the Divorce Reform Act 1969
(now s 10(2)-(4) of the Matrimonial Causes Act 1973), particularly when it is desired *d*
to obtain a decree absolute quickly. The first thing to be noticed about s 6 I think
is this: it was inserted into the 1969 Act at a time when the court's powers to order
financial and other provisions were much more restricted than they are today. Now
that the court has the full powers given under the Matrimonial Proceedings and
Property Act 1970, now contained in s 23 and s 24 of the 1973 Act, the value of s 6 is
substantially diminished. In a case like this, where it is agreed by both parties that *e*
the decree absolute should be made, it would seem to be much more satisfactory
if first of all the wife did not make an application under s 6, because if she does not
make an application under that section, it does not apply at all, and it would be better
if applications under s 6 were not made except in cases where they are necessary.
If they are made and it is then agreed that the decree should be made absolute
quickly, the tidy way to deal with it, I should have thought, would be to withdraw *f*
the application under s 6 rather than try to deal with it under sub-s (3), i e the subsection dealing with undertakings, because there is no doubt that this leads to the
sort of confusion that we find in this case where no proposal was made by the husband
for the court to approve and it was in fact left to the court to say what the court
thought was appropriate. It would be very much better if these cases were dealt
with under what one might call the normal practice for dealing with maintenance *g*
and property adjustment orders under the new Act and if s 6 applications were
limited to those cases where for some special reason they were thought to have
special value. Otherwise they merely complicate the position, as this case amply
demonstrates.
   I agree with the order that is proposed.

h

Appeal allowed.

Solicitors: *Crick & Freeman*, Maldon, Essex (for the husband); *Moss & Coleman*,
Hornchurch, Essex (for the wife).

L J Kovats Esq Barrister.

a Re Turner (a bankrupt), ex parte the trustee of the bankrupt v Turner and another

CHANCERY DIVISION
GOFF J
22nd JULY 1974

b

Bankruptcy – Property available for distribution – Matrimonial home – Husband and wife joint tenants – Husband declared bankrupt – Home held by husband and wife on trust for sale – Wife entitled to half share in equity – Husband having no other assets to meet claims of creditors – Application by trustee in bankruptcy for order for sale – Husband and wife living in home – Discretion of court whether to order sale – Factors governing exercise of
c *discretion.*

The husband and wife lived together in the matrimonial home which belonged to them jointly at law and in equity, being held on the normal statutory trust for sale. The husband was adjudicated bankrupt. There were no realisable assets to meet the claims of the creditors other than the matrimonial home. The husband's
d trustee in bankruptcy moved for a declaration that he was entitled against both the husband and wife to have vacant possession of the matrimonial home and an order that it should be sold with vacant possession and that both the husband and wife should concur in the sale, the proceeds to be divided between the trustee and the wife. The trustee contended that, where there were no other assets, the court was bound to order a sale of the matrimonial home.

e **Held** – The court had a discretion whether or not to order that the trust for sale should be carried into effect and was not bound to exercise that discretion in the trustee's favour. The question for the court was not whether the trustee or the wife was being reasonable but whose voice in equity ought to prevail. In all the circumstances of the case the claim of the trustee, based on his statutory duty, was the stronger in equity and accordingly the order sought by the trustee would be
f made (see p 6 *j* to p 7 *b* and *e* and p 8 *a* and *b*, post).

Jones v Challenger [1960] 1 All ER 785 and *Re a Debtor, ex parte the Trustee v Solomon* [1966] 3 All ER 255 applied.

Notes

For the property of a bankrupt available for distribution, see 3 Halsbury's Laws
g (4th Edn) 325-330, paras 590-595, and for cases on the subject, see 5 Digest (Repl) 679-685, *5972-6037*.

Cases referred to in judgment

Boydell v Gillespie (1970) 216 Estates Gazette 1505.
Debtor, Re a, ex parte Trustee v Solomon [1966] 3 All ER 255, [1967] Ch 573, [1967] 2 WLR 172, Digest (Cont Vol B) 58, *6306a.*
h *Hardy's Trust, Re, Sutherst v Sutherst* [1970] The Times 23rd October, 114 Sol Jo 864.
Jones v Challenger [1960] 1 All ER 785, [1961] 1 QB 176, [1960] 2 WLR 695, CA, 47 Digest (Repl) 400, *3595.*

Cases also cited

D, Re, a debtor [1967] NZLR 828.
j *National Provincial Bank Ltd v Ainsworth* [1965] 2 All ER 472, [1965] AC 1175, HL.
No 39 Carr Lane, Acomb, Re, Stevens v Hutchinson [1953] 1 All ER 699, [1953] Ch 299.

Motion

By notice of motion dated 20th May 1974 the trustee of the property of the first respondent, Albert David Turner, a bankrupt, applied for (1) a declaration that the trustee, as trustee in bankruptcy of the first respondent, was entitled against the

first respondent and the second respondent, Anne Turner, the first respondent's   *a*
wife, and each of them, to vacant possession of the freehold premises known and
situate at 21 Briscoe Road, Rainham, Essex ('the property'); (2) an order that the
property be sold with vacant possession and that the first and second respondents
and each of them, as trustees for sale of the property, concur in the sale; (3) an order
that the conduct of the sale of the property be given to the trustee as trustee in
bankruptcy of the first respondent; and (4) an order that the net proceeds of sale   *b*
of the property be divided and paid to the trustee, as trustee in bankruptcy of the
first respondent, and to the second respondent in equal shares or in such shares as
the court should think fit. The facts are set out in the judgment.

Michael Crystal for the trustee.
The respondents appeared in person.
  c

GOFF J. This is one of those unfortunate cases which arise when one of the parties
to a marriage (which has proceeded normally and has not broken down) has the
misfortune to become bankrupt. That has happened in this case to the husband,
the first respondent to this motion. The applicant is his trustee in bankruptcy.
The wife is the second respondent and the matrimonial home belongs to them
beneficially and jointly. They are registered as joint owners in the proprietorship   *d*
register at the Land Registry. It has been accepted that the wife is beneficially
entitled to half the equity in the property.

There are no realisable assets to pay the creditors other than by a sale of the matrimonial home, which is held on the normal statutory trust for sale. In the circumstances, the trustee first offered the husband a number of opportunities to raise
money on the security of the property to enable the husband and wife to protect   *e*
the matrimonial home. That was a very proper attitude to take, but efforts failed,
perhaps not unnaturally, because the husband, being a bankrupt, found that it was
not possible to raise the money. The trustee, however, did not approach the matter
from the angle of seeing whether there was anything the wife could do. I do not
blame him for that; he communicated on at least one occasion with solicitors acting
for the husband and wife. I have therefore thought it right to suspend the order   *f*
in this case to give the wife an opportunity of seeing whether she can do anything to
save their position.

By his notice of motion, the trustee asks for a declaration that as trustee in bankruptcy he is entitled against husband and wife, and each of them, to have vacant
possession of their property, 21 Briscoe Road, Rainham, Essex. He also asks for an
order that the property be sold with vacant possession and that each of them should   *g*
concur in the sale. He asks further for an order that the conduct of the sale of the
property be given to him as trustee in bankruptcy, and that the net proceeds of
sale of the property be divided and paid to him, as trustee in bankruptcy of the husband, and to the wife in equal shares or in such shares as to the court shall seem fit.
I pause to say there is no reason to suppose that anything other than equal shares
would be appropriate on the facts of the case. The wife is entitled to her half, and   *h*
if on realisation of the husband's share there is not sufficient to pay the creditors,
well, so it must be; if there is a surplus after payment of all the creditors and costs
and charges of the bankruptcy, the trustee will account for that surplus to the
husband.

However, is the trustee entitled to the relief which he seeks? He has presented
his case on the basis that as the husband is bankrupt, the trust for sale should be   *j*
immediately carried into effect, and he says the court has no discretion. In my
judgment, such an argument is inconsistent with the decision of the Court of Appeal
in *Jones v Challenger*[1] and my own decision in *Re a Debtor, ex parte Trustee v Solomon*[2].

---

1 [1960] 1 All ER 785, [1961] 1 QB 176
2 [1966] 3 All ER 255, [1967] Ch 573

a I adhere to the view that I expressed in the *Solomon* case[1] that the matter is one of discretion.

The trustee then sought to argue that, even if that be so, where there is a situation involving a trustee in bankruptcy, there is only one way in which the discretion can be exercised, namely in favour of the trustee. That appears to be merely a different way of putting the same argument and equally wrong.

b It was then argued that I ought to order a sale on the facts of the case. In my judgment, the guiding principle in the exercise of the court's discretion is not whether the trustee or the wife is being reasonable but, in all the circumstances of the case whose voice in equity ought to prevail. In the *Solomon* case[1] there were factors not present in this case which compelled me to the conclusion that an order in favour of the trustee was a proper exercise of my discretion although I took into account[2]

c the important factor that the question at issue was not one between husband and wife but between the wife and trustee in bankruptcy. The trustee here has pointed out that if a sale is not ordered, there is no other way of realising the husband's interest in the property for the benefit of his creditors. He argues that where there are no other sufficient assets, one must perforce have recourse to a sale of the matrimonial home in order to satisfy creditors.

d In my judgment, there exist in equity two conflicting claims: on the one hand the wife, as part owner of the house, asks: why should she as co-owner be turned out merely because her husband, the other co-owner, is bankrupt? On the other hand, the trustee in bankruptcy says he is not only entitled to realise the husband's interest but is bound by statute to do so. As I have said, on the facts before me, there is no other reasonable alternative. If it were possible to realise the husband's beneficial

e half share, that ought to be done, but clearly that cannot be done here. However, there may be future cases where that would be the course for the trustee to pursue.

In my judgment, weighing the two conflicting claims, that by the trustee, based on his statutory duty, gives him the stronger claim, and requires me to treat his voice as the one that ought to prevail in equity. In reaching this conclusion, I am supported by the decision of Plowman J in *Boydell v Gillespie*[3]. As reported, that decision is not

f entirely satisfactory as it does not appear whether *Jones v Challenger*[4] and my case, *Re a Debtor, ex parte Trustee v Solomon*[1], were brought to his attention, and so he does not seem to have been directing his mind to the problem which the cases I have mentioned require to be answered, but, on the other hand, what he says in a case similar on its facts does assist me considerably, and supports the conclusion I have reached. He says[5]:

g 'The relief sought in the action included sale of the properties in question with vacant possession, and counsel for the defendants had gone on to submit that as regarded 25, Bellvue Road, which was the matrimonial home, an order for sale with vacant possession ought not to be made. He (counsel) had referred to a decision reported in "The Times" on October 23 last in a case called *Re Hardy's*

h *Trust*[6] where Stamp, J., had held that a wife had a right to a roof over her head to be provided by her husband, and that that being so, unless he provided some other alternative accommodation, the husband could not have the relief he sought in that case, which was an order under section 30 of the Law of Property Act 1925 to compel his wife whom he had deserted to join in a sale of the matrimonial home. That case was not this case. Here it was not the husband who was trying

j to get the wife out of the matrimonial home: it was a husband and wife who were

---

1 [1966] 3 All ER 255, [1967] Ch 573
2 [1966] 3 All ER at 264, [1967] Ch at 589
3 (1970) 216 Estates Gazette 1505
4 [1960] 1 All ER 785, [1961] 1 QB 176
5 216 Estates Gazette at 1507
6 [1970] The Times, 23rd October

united in trying to prevent the trustee under the deed of arrangement from   *a*
selling the house with vacant possession for the benefit of Mr. Gillespie's creditors.
There was no dispute in the matter as between the defendants themselves.'

Plowman J there rejected the claim of the wife to pray in aid the doctrine of *Re Hardy's
Trust*[1] and I think I ought to follow the conclusion of Plowman J and say that, in the
circumstances of this case, the wife is not entitled to pray in aid the *Jones v Challenger*[2]
line of cases, and is not entitled to deprive the husband's creditors in the bankruptcy   *b*
of their share in the matrimonial home.

I will make the order as asked but direct that my decision shall be suspended for
two months or such extended time as the parties may agree, or the court order, with
liberty to apply. If within two months the wife has proceeded substantially towards a
solution to the problem then the trustee in bankruptcy may well agree to a reasonable extension. Alternatively, if there has been no solution that the court can properly   *c*
accept, then the possession order will take effect.

Order accordingly.

Solicitors: *Clintons* (for the trustee).

                                         R W Farrin Esq   Barrister.   *d*

R v Morgan and others

COURT OF APPEAL, CRIMINAL DIVISION   Affirmed on different grounds HL
LORD WIDGERY CJ, BRIDGE AND MAY JJ   DPP v MORGAN [1975] 2 All ER 347
24th, 25th JULY, 14th OCTOBER 1974   *e*

*Criminal law – Rape – Consent of victim – Mens rea – Mistake – Belief of accused – Belief in
victim's consent – Honest and reasonable belief – Circumstances such as to indicate that
victim not consenting to intercourse – Evidential burden on accused of showing belief honest
and reasonable – Whether honest mistake a defence even though no reasonable grounds for*   *f*
mistaken belief.

M, a senior non-commissioned officer in the RAF, invited three junior members of
the RAF to his home in order to have sexual intercourse with his wife. The three
younger men, who were complete strangers to the wife, were at first incredulous but
they were persuaded to take the invitation seriously. According to the three men M
told them to expect some show of resistance from his wife but that they were not to   *g*
take that seriously as it would be a mere pretence on her part to stimulate her own
sexual excitement. That night the three men went with M to his house, removed the
wife from the bed in which she was sleeping to another room where each had intercourse with her in the presence of M. According to the wife she protested and resisted
as best she could in the circumstances. The three men were charged with raping the
wife. The judge directed the jury that the Crown had to prove that each defendant   *h*
intended to have sexual intercourse with the wife without her consent and that if he
believed that she was consenting to him having intercourse with her he would not be
guilty. He directed them that 'such a belief must be honestly held by the defendant
... and must be a reasonable belief; such a belief as a reasonable man would entertain
if he applied his mind and thought about the matter'. The defendants were convicted
and appealed, contending that the burden was on the Crown to negative honest   *j*
belief in consent and that the question whether there were reasonable grounds for the
belief was merely a factor in the evidence to be considered by the jury in deciding
whether the belief was honestly held.

---

1   [1970] The Times, 23rd October
2   [1960] 1 All ER 785, [1961] 1 QB 176

a **Held** – In order to secure a conviction for rape the Crown had to prove something more than a subjective unwillingness on the part of the victim to submit to intercourse; what had to be shown was that the circumstances in which the act of intercourse took place were such that absence of consent had been objectively demonstrated. On proof of such circumstances, which in the nature of the case must have come to the notice of the defendant, it could be presumed that he had appreciated
b their significance and was therefore aware that the victim did not consent to intercourse. That presumption cast on the defendant the evidential burden of showing that he had in fact entertained an honest and reasonable belief that the victim had given her consent before any issue as to his state of mind could arise for the jury's consideration. The mere assertion of an honest but mistaken belief in the absence of reasonable grounds for that belief was evidence of insufficient substance to raise an
c issue requiring the jury's consideration. It followed that the jury had been properly directed and the appeals would be dismissed (see p 14 *h* and *j* and p 15 *a* to *e*, post).

Notes

For rape and the defence of consent, see 10 Halsbury's Laws (3rd Edn) 746-748, paras 1436-1439, and for cases on the subject, see 15 Digest (Repl) 1009-1014, 9941-9990.

d **Cases referred to in judgment**

Bank of New South Wales v Piper [1897] AC 383, 66 LJPC 73, 76 LT 572, 61 JP 660, PC, 14 Digest (Repl) 32, 40.
R v Daly [1968] VR 257.
R v Flaherty (1968) 89 WN (Pt 1) NSW 141.
R v Flannery and Prendergast [1969] VR 31.
e R v Flattery (1877) 2 QBD 410, 46 LJMC 130, 36 LT 32, 13 Cox CC 388, CCR, 15 Digest (Repl) 1012, 9968.
R v Gould [1968] 1 All ER 849, [1968] 2 QB 65, [1968] 2 WLR 643, 132 JP 209, 52 Cr App Rep 152, CA, Digest (Cont Vol C) 249, 8591a.
R v Hornbuckle [1945] VLR 281.
R v King [1963] 3 All ER 561, [1964] 1 QB 285, [1963] 3 WLR 892, 48 Cr App Rep 17,
f CCA, Digest (Cont Vol A) 418, 8582a.
R v Prince (1875) LR 2 CCR 154, [1874-80] All ER Rep 881, 44 LJMC 122, 32 LT 700, 39 JP 676, 13 Cox CC 138, CCR, 14 Digest (Repl) 52, 181.
R v Tolson (1889) 23 QBD 168, [1886-90] All ER Rep 26, 58 LJMC 97, 60 LT 899, 54 JP 420, 16 Cox CC 629, CCR, 15 Digest (Repl) 890, 8578.
Sweet v Parsley [1969] 1 All ER 347, [1970] AC 132, [1969] 2 WLR 470, 133 JP 188, 53 Cr
g App Rep 221, HL, Digest (Cont Vol C) 671, 243bda.
Thomas v The King (1937) 59 CLR 279.
Wilson v Inyang [1951] 2 All ER 237, [1951] 2 KB 799, 115 JP 411, 49 LGR 654, DC, 33 Digest (Repl) 543, 143.
Woolmington v Director of Public Prosecutions [1935] AC 462, [1935] All ER Rep 1, 104 LJKB 433, 153 LT 232, 25 Cr App Rep 72, 30 Cox CC 234, HL, 14 Digest (Repl)
h 493, 4768.

Cases also cited

Cambridgeshire and Isle of Ely County Council v Rust [1972] 3 All ER 232, [1972] 2 QB 426, DC.
R v Smith (David) [1974] 1 All ER 632, [1974] QB 354, CA.

j **Appeals**

On 24th January 1974 in the Crown Court at Stafford before Kenneth Jones J and a jury, the appellants, William Anthony Morgan, Michael Andrew Parker, Robert McLarty and Robert Alan Michael McDonald, were convicted as follows: Morgan on counts 1 to 3 of aiding and abetting rape; Parker on counts 1 and 2 of aiding and abetting rape and on count 3 of rape; McLarty on counts 1 and 3 of aiding and

abetting rape and on count 2 of rape; McDonald on count 1 of rape and on counts *a*
2 and 3 of aiding and abetting rape. Parker, McLarty and McDonald were each
sentenced to concurrent terms of four years' imprisonment, and Morgan to 10
years' imprisonment concurrent on each of counts 1 to 3. All four appellants
appealed against their convictions. The facts are set out in the judgment of the
court.

Nicholas Budgen for Morgan.   *b*
Malcolm Ward for Parker, McLarty and McDonald.
John B Baker for the Crown.

25th July. At the conclusion of argument the court dismissed the appeals of Parker,
McLarty and McDonald and stated that it would give its reasons for doing so at a
later date. The appeal of Morgan was adjourned for further argument on a different   *c*
point.

14th October. **BRIDGE J** read the following judgment of the court. On 24th
January 1974 at Stafford Crown Court the appellants McDonald, McLarty and Parker
were severally convicted of rape on Daphne Ethel Morgan, and each was further
convicted of aiding and abetting the principal offences of rape committed by the   *d*
other two. The appellant Morgan was convicted of aiding and abetting the rapes
committed by his three co-defendants.

All have appealed against conviction by leave of the single judge. All the appeals
except Morgan's were dismissed by the court on 25th July 1974. Morgan's appeal was
adjourned for further argument on a point with which this judgment is not concerned.
We now give our reasons for rejecting the main grounds of appeal which were   *e*
canvassed before us.

The facts of the case are somewhat bizarre. The appellant Morgan was a senior
non-commissioned officer in the Royal Air Force, the other appellants younger and
junior members of that service. On the night of the offences Morgan invited the
other three to return to his house and suggested to them that they should all have
intercourse with his wife, the prosecutrix. The young men, who were complete   *f*
strangers to Mrs Morgan, were at first incredulous but were persuaded that Morgan's
invitation was intended seriously when he told them stories of his wife's sexual
aberrations and provided them with contraceptive sheaths to wear. McDonald,
McLarty and Parker also said in effect that Morgan told them to expect some show
of resistance on his wife's part but that they need not take this seriously since it was a
mere pretence whereby she stimulated her own sexual excitement. This part of the   *g*
conversation was denied by Morgan.

Mrs Morgan's account of what happened, in substance, was that she was awakened
from sleep in a single bed in a room which she shared with one of her children. Her
husband and the other men in part dragged and in part carried her out on to a landing
and thence into another room which contained a double bed. She struggled and
screamed and shouted to her son to call the police, but one of the men put a hand over   *h*
her mouth. Once on the double bed the appellants had intercourse with her in turn,
finishing with her husband. During intercourse with the other three she was continuously being held, and this, coupled with her fear of further violence, restricted
the scope of her struggles, but she repeatedly called out to her husband to tell the
men to stop.

In due course all the appellants made statements to the police, and those of Mc-   *j*
Donald, McLarty and Parker in differing degrees corroborated the general picture
of a forcible rape against clear protest and resistance on the part of the victim.

In evidence they said that in the incriminating parts of their statements words had
been put into their mouths by the police. Of the account which these three gave in
their evidence of their acts of intercourse with Mrs Morgan and of her conduct throughout the incident, it is sufficient to say that all three spoke of her manifesting her

a sexual co-operation and enjoyment in a way which could only indicate that she was consenting. Any element of resistance on her part was, according to this account, no more than playacting.

Morgan's statement to the police was equivocal, but in evidence he asserted that his wife agreed in advance to have intercourse with the three friends whom he had brought home and, in the event, indicated her pleasure in doing so. According to
b Morgan, the only protest voiced by his wife related to the fact that one of the men who had intercourse with her was not wearing a contraceptive sheath.

In summing-up the trial judge said:

> 'The crime of rape consists in having unlawful sexual intercourse with a woman without her consent and by force. By force. Those words mean exactly what they say. It does not mean there has to be a fight or blows have to be inflicted. It
c > means that there has to be some violence used against the woman to overbear her will or that there has to be a threat of violence as a result of which her will is overborne.'

Later he added:

> 'Further, the prosecution have to prove that each defendant intended to have
d > sexual intercourse with this woman without her consent. Not merely that he intended to have intercourse with her but that he intended to have intercourse without her consent. Therefore if the defendant believed or may have believed that Mrs Morgan consented to him having sexual intercourse with her, then there would be no such intent in his mind and he would be not guilty of the offence of rape, but such a belief must be honestly held by the defendant in the first place.
e > He must really believe that. And, secondly, his belief must be a reasonable belief; such a belief as a reasonable man would entertain if he applied his mind and thought about the matter. It is not enough for a defendant to rely upon a belief, even though he honestly held it, if it was completely fanciful; contrary to every indication which would be given which could carry some weight with a reasonable man.'

f And finally:

> 'But if you are satisfied, if you are sure that she did not consent, then you would have to turn to consider: Well, did the particular defendant honestly and reasonably believe that she consented? Bear in mind that it is not for him to prove that. It is for the prosecution to prove that he did not so believe.'

g It is submitted on behalf of the appellants that these passages embody a misdirection insofar as they indicate that the Crown can establish the element of mens rea necessary to support a conviction for rape if they satisfy the jury that a defendant's belief in consent by the prosecutrix, though honestly held, was not based on reasonable grounds. The correct view in law, it is urged, is that the Crown must negative honest belief in consent and that the question whether or not there were reasonable grounds
h for such a belief is no more than a factor, albeit an important factor, in the evidence to be considered by the jury in deciding whether the belief was honestly held.

The question raised by this submission is not decided by any English authority, and the only dictum to which we have been referred bearing directly on it is that of Denman J in R v Flattery[1] where he said:

> 'There may be cases where a woman does not consent in fact, but in which her
j > conduct is such that the man reasonably believes she does.'

An apparently fuller report of the same case in Cox's Criminal Law Cases[2] gives this version:

> 'There is one case where a woman does not consent to the act of connection and yet the man may not be guilty of rape, that is where the resistance is so slight and her behaviour such that the man may *bona fide* believe that she is consenting . . .'

In Australia, however, the question has been canvassed in two different jurisdictions   *a*
and, unfortunately for our peace of mind, has received conflicting answers. A series of
decisions of the Supreme Court of Victoria support the view contended for on behalf
of the appellants: *R v Hornbuckle*[1]; *R v Daly*[2]; *R v Flannery and Prendergast*[3]. But the
view taken by the Supreme Court of New South Wales would support the direction
given by the trial judge in the instant case: *R v Flaherty*[4].

To resolve the conflict it is necessary first to examine the principles underlying the   *b*
defence of mistake in the criminal law, secondly to consider how those principles
apply to the offence of rape, which although now statutory, still requires to be defined
by the common law.

A useful starting point is *R v Tolson*[5] where Cave J said:

'At common law an honest and reasonable belief in the existence of circumstances, which, if true, would make the act for which a prisoner is indicted an   *c*
innocent act, has always been held to be a good defence.'

Later Stephen J said[6]:

'. . . I think it may be laid down as a general rule that an alleged offender is
deemed to have acted under that state of facts which he in good faith and on reasonable grounds believed to exist when he did the act alleged to be an offence.'   *d*

The decision in the case that, notwithstanding a statutory prohibition in unqualified
terms, the offence of bigamy is not committed by one who honestly and reasonably,
albeit mistakenly, believes the former spouse to be dead, has been followed, and
extended to embrace other honest and reasonable mistakes affecting matrimonial
status, both in Australia (see *Thomas v The King*[7]) and here (see *R v King*[8] and *R*
Gould[9]).   *e*

R v King[8] is of particular significance for present purposes because there the court,
notwithstanding a misdirection to the jury, upheld a conviction for bigamy on the
ground that the evidence afforded no reasonable grounds for the mistaken belief
advanced by the defendant in the invalidity of a former marriage.

The language used by the judges in *R v Tolson*[10] repeatedly suggests that the defence   *f*
of honest and reasonable mistake is one to be 'proved' by the defendant. In what
circumstances and in what sense any such principle can survive in the modern law
must shortly be considered. But it is helpful first to consider two further 19th century
authorities very much in point. The discussion of principle in the judgment of Brett J
in *R v Prince*[11] is not the less valuable by reason of the fact that he dissented from the
majority on the narrow point of construction decided by that case. He considered the
significance in relation to statutory prohibitions of the presence of such words as   *g*
'knowingly', 'wilfully', and 'maliciously' and observed[12]:

' "Wilfully" is more generally applied when the prohibited acts are in their
natural consequences not necessarily or very probably noxious to the public
interest, or to individuals; so that an evil mind is not the natural inference or
consequence to be drawn from the doing of the acts. The presence of the word   *h*
requires somewhat more evidence on the part of the prosecution to make out a
prima facie case, than evidence that the prisoner did the prohibited acts. So as to

---

1   [1945] VLR 281
2   [1968] VR 257
3   [1969] VR 31
4   (1968) 89 WN (Pt 1) (NSW) 141
5   (1889) 23 QBD 168 at 181, [1886-90] All ER Rep 26 at 34
6   23 QBD at 188, [1886-90] All ER Rep at 37
7   (1937) 59 CLR 279
8   [1963] 3 All ER 561, [1964] 1 QB 285
9   [1968] 1 All ER 849, [1968] 2 QB 65
10 23 QBD 168, [1886-90] All ER Rep 26
11 (1875) LR 2 CCR 154, [1874-80] All ER Rep 881
12 LR 2 CCR at 161, 162, [1874-80] All ER Rep at 890

a   the word "maliciously", it is usual where the prohibited acts may or may not be
     such as in themselves import prima facie a malicious mind. In the same way the
     word "knowingly" is used, where the noxious character of the prohibited acts
     depends upon a knowledge in the prisoner of their noxious effect, other than the
     mere knowledge that he is doing the acts. The presence of the word calls for more
     evidence on the part of the prosecution. But the absence of the word does not
b   prevent the prisoner from proving to the satisfaction of the jury that the mens
     rea, to be prima facie inferred from his doing the prohibited acts, did not in fact
     exist.'

     Then later he said[1]:

        'What reason is there why, in like manner, a criminal mind, or mens rea, must
        not ultimately be found by the jury in order to justify a conviction, the distinc-
c   tion always being observed, that in some cases the proof of the committal of the
        acts may prima facie, either by reason of their own nature, or by reason of the
        form of the statute, import the proof of the mens rea? But even in those cases it
        is open to the prisoner to rebut the prima facie evidence, so that if, in the end, the
        jury are satisfied that there was no criminal mind, or mens rea, there cannot be a
        conviction in England for that which is by law considered to be a crime.'
d
     After a lengthy examination of authority he concluded[2]:

        'It seems to me to follow that the maxim as to mens rea applies whenever the
        facts which are present to the prisoner's mind, and which he has reasonable ground
        to believe, and does believe to be the facts, would, if true, make his acts no criminal
        offence at all.'

e   In *Bank of New South Wales v Piper*[3] Sir Richard Couch said:

        'It was strongly urged by the respondent's counsel that in order to the consti-
        tution of a crime [sic], whether common law or statutory, there must be mens rea
        on the part of the accused, and that he may avoid conviction by shewing that such
        mens did not exist. That is a proposition which their Lordships do not desire to
f   dispute; but the questions whether a particular intent is made an element of the
        statutory crime, and when that is not the case, whether there was an absence of
        mens rea in the accused, are questions entirely different, and depend upon differ-
        ent considerations. In cases when the statute requires a motive to be proved as an
        essential element of the crime, the prosecution must fail if it is not proved. On
        the other hand, the absence of mens rea really consists in an honest and reason-
        able belief entertained by the accused of the existence of facts which, if true,
g   would make the act charged against him innocent.'

     These principles must, of course, now be understood in the light of the decision in
     Woolmington v Director of Public Prosecutions[4]. Save where so provided by statute and
     save in the anomalous case of the defence of insanity (the one common law exception
     to the general rule) it is never for the accused to satisfy the jury on any issue on which
h   his guilt or innocence depends, and expressions to the contrary in the passages cited
     must be modified accordingly. But this does not mean that the principles have been
     invalidated. So long as the distinction is borne in mind between the ultimate burden
     of satisfying the jury on an issue ('the probative burden') and the initial burden of
     introducing evidence which is sufficient to raise an issue for the jury's consideration
     ('the evidential burden') the principles, appropriately modified, can sensibly and
j   reasonably continue to be applied. As Lord Diplock said in *Sweet v Parsley*[5]:

        '*Woolmington's* case[4] did not decide anything so irrational as that the prosecu-
        tion must call evidence to prove the absence of any mistaken belief by the accused

1   (1875) LR 2 CCR at 163, [1874-80] All ER Rep at 891
2   LR 2 CCR at 169, 170, [1874-80] All ER Rep at 895
3   [1897] AC 383 at 389, 390
4   [1935] AC 462, [1935] All ER Rep 1
5   [1969] 1 All ER 347 at 363, [1970] AC 132 at 164

in the existence of facts which, if true, would make the act innocent, any more *a*
than it decided that the prosecution must call evidence to prove the absence of
any claim of right in a charge of larceny. The jury is entitled to presume that the
accused acted with knowledge of the facts, unless there is some evidence to the
contrary originating from the accused who alone can know on what belief he
acted and on what ground the belief if mistaken was held. What *Woolmington's*
case[1] did decide is that, where there is any such evidence, the jury, after con- *b*
sidering it and also any relevant evidence called by the prosecution on the issue
of the existence of the alleged mistaken belief, should acquit the accused unless
they feel sure that he did not hold the belief or that there were no reasonable
grounds on which he could have done so.'

The relevant principles can perhaps be restated in the following propositions:
  1. In all crimes the Crown has both the evidential and the probative burden of *c*
showing that the accused did the prohibited act, and where that act, according to the
definition of the offence, is an act of volition, of showing that the act of the accused
was voluntary. An obvious example of a crime where the evidential burden on the
Crown is limited to these two elements is common assault.
  2. Wherever the definition of a crime includes as one of its express ingredients a
specific mental element both the evidential and the probative burden lie on the Crown *d*
with respect to that element. Typical examples are dishonesty in theft and knowledge
or belief in handling. In seeking to rebut the Crown's case against him in reference to
his state of mind the accused may and frequently does assert his mistaken belief in
non-existent facts. Of course it is right that in this context the question whether
there were reasonable grounds for the belief is only a factor for the jury's consideration in deciding whether the Crown has established the necessary mental element of *e*
the crime. This is because the issue is already before the jury and no evidential
burden rests on the accused.
  The decision of the Divisional Court in *Wilson v Inyang*[2] is to be understood in the
light of this principle. The court there rejected the argument that an acquittal by a
magistrate of a defendant charged with an offence under s 40 of the Medical Act
1858 should be reversed on appeal by case stated on the ground that the defendant *f*
had no reasonable ground for his belief that he was entitled to call himself a
'physician'. Lord Goddard CJ said[3]:

  'If he has acted without any reasonable ground and says: "I had not properly
  inquired, and did not think this or that," that may be (and generally is) very good
  evidence that he is not acting honestly. But it is only evidence.' *g*

The Act, however, under which that prosecution was brought required the prosecution to prove that the defendant acted 'wilfully and falsely'. Inevitably, therefore,
if this subjective mental element was not proved the prosecution failed.
  3. Where, however, the definition of the crime includes no specific mental element
beyond the intention to do the prohibited act, the accused may show that though he *h*
did the prohibited act intentionally he lacked mens rea because he mistakenly, but
honestly and reasonably, believed facts which, if true, would have made his act
innocent. Here the evidential burden lies on the accused but once evidence sufficient
to raise the issue is before the jury the probative burden lies on the Crown to negative
the mistaken belief. The rationale of requiring reasonable grounds for the mistaken
belief must lie in the law's consideration that a bald assertion of belief for which the *j*
accused can indicate no reasonable ground is evidence of insufficient substance to
raise any issue requiring the jury's consideration. Thus, for example, a person charged
with assault on a victim shown to have been entirely passive throughout who said he
had believed himself to be under imminent threat of attack by the victim but could

1 [1935] AC 462, [1935] All ER Rep 1
2 [1951] 2 All ER 237, [1951] 2 KB 799
3 [1951] 2 All ER at 240, [1951] 2 KB at 803

a   indicate no circumstance giving cause for such a belief would not discharge the evidential burden of showing a mistaken belief that he was acting lawfully in self-defence.

However the crime of rape be defined, the Crown clearly has the evidential burden of showing the act of intercourse, and absence of consent. The second element is, of course, something more than the subjective unwillingness of the prosecutrix. The

b   circumstances in which the act of intercourse takes place must be such that absence of consent is objectively demonstrated. This is appropriately emphasised by the presence of the words 'by force, fear or fraud' in the definition cited in Archbold[1]. That definition may not be academically comprehensive but it is eminently practical in all ordinary cases and is the definition by reference to which, as in the instant case, juries are habitually directed.

c   Has the Crown, beyond these two elements, the evidential burden of showing any and if so what degree of subjective appreciation by the accused of that which, ex hypothesi, has been objectively demonstrated, namely, absence of consent? No accepted definition of the offence suggests the need to prove such a subjective mental element. Dicta to the effect that the mens rea of rape is an intention to have intercourse without consent really carry the matter no further. They tell us that the act

d   of intercourse must be intentional, which by its nature it inevitably is, but throw no light on the state of mind required to be shown quoad absence of consent. The correct view, we think, is that on proof of the fact of absence of consent from circumstances which in the nature of the case must have come to the notice of the defendant he may be presumed to have appreciated their significance, and it is this presumption which casts on the defendant the evidential burden of showing an honest

e   and reasonable belief in consent before any issue as to his state of mind can arise for the jury's consideration.

It was for these reasons that we reached the conclusion that the passages cited from the trial judge's summing-up contained no misdirection.

Further complaint was made of a comment made by the trial judge on the defence of mistaken belief in consent. He pointed out that before the jury came to consider

f   it at all they must first have been satisfied that Mrs Morgan did not in fact consent and thus have rejected as untrue the appellants' evidence to the contrary. Then he added:

> 'You may consider—it is a matter entirely for you—it is a desperate defence to put forward, that even although you have rejected so much of their evidence that nevertheless you should have some doubt as to whether they honestly and
g   reasonably believed that she was consenting. There it is. The Defence invite you to consider that matter and you must give to it such consideration as you think it right.'

We think the trial judge's comment was a perfectly fair and legitimate one in the circumstances and find no substance in the criticism directed at it.

h   [The court then heard and rejected a further submission on behalf of Morgan.]

Appeals dismissed. Leave to appeal to the House of Lords granted, the court having certified the following to be a point of law of general public importance: 'Whether in rape the defendant can properly be convicted notwithstanding that he in fact believed that the woman consented if such belief was not based on reasonable grounds.'

j   Solicitors: *R Gwynne & Sons*, Wellington, Salop (for the appellants); *Director of Public Prosecutions*.

N P Metcalfe Esq   Barrister.

---

1   Pleading, Evidence and Practice in Criminal Cases (38th Edn, 1973), para 2871

Maunsell v Olins and another

HOUSE OF LORDS
LORD REID, VISCOUNT DILHORNE, LORD WILBERFORCE, LORD DIPLOCK AND LORD SIMON OF
GLAISDALE
9th, 10th OCTOBER, 27th NOVEMBER 1974

Rent restriction – Sub-tenancy – Determination of superior tenancy – Sub-tenancy of dwelling-house forming part of premises let as a whole on superior letting – Premises – Meaning – Buildings used for residential purposes – Farm – Farm buildings including cottage – Tenant of farm subletting cottage – Sub-tenancy protected as between tenant and sub-tenant – Termination of tenancy of farm – Whether farm 'premises' of which cottage forming part – Rent Act 1968, s 18(5).

The plaintiff owned the freehold of a farm which comprised some 106 acres. The buildings on the farm included a farmhouse and two cottages. For many years B was the tenant of the farm under a tenancy which was protected by the Agricultural Holdings Act 1948. The tenancy provided that the tenant should not underlet the farm or any part thereof except for the cottages which could be sublet only on monthly tenancies. B sublet one of the cottages to the defendant. As between B and the defendant the tenancy of the cottage was protected by the Rent Acts. Subsequently B died and his tenancy was terminated by the plaintiff who thereupon brought proceedings against the defendant for possession of the cottage. The defendant contended that he was entitled to the protection of the Rent Acts as against the plaintiff by virtue of s 18(5)ᵃ of the Rent Act 1968 in that the cottage was a dwelling-house which formed part of 'premises', i e the farm, which had been let as a whole on a superior letting and did not constitute a dwelling-house let on a protected tenancy.

Held (Lord Diplock and Lord Simon of Glaisdale dissenting) – The word 'premises' in s 18(5)(a) was to be construed as being limited to premises which, for the purposes of the 1968 Act, were treated as dwelling-houses or (per Viscount Dilhorne) as meaning buildings. Since the cottage did not form part of a dwelling-house or building which had been let as a whole on a superior letting, s 18(5) had no application and the defendant was not therefore entitled to the protection of the Rent Acts (see p 18 c g and h, p 19 d to f and j to p 20 a, p 23 e and j to p 24 c and p 25 a to c, post).
Hobhouse v Wall [1963] 1 All ER 701 approved.
Decision of the Court of Appeal [1974] 2 All ER 250 affirmed.

Notes
For protection under the Rent Acts of a sub-tenant of premises forming part of a superior letting, see 23 Halsbury's Laws (3rd Edn) 826-829, para 1611, and for cases on the subject, see 31(2) Digest (Reissue) 1100-1105, 8551-8580.
For the Rent Act 1968, s 18, see 18 Halsbury's Statutes (3rd Edn) 808.

Cases referred to in opinions
Attorney-General v HRH Prince Ernest Augustus of Hanover [1957] 1 All ER 49, [1957] AC 436, [1957] 2 WLR 1, HL, 44 Digest (Repl) 241, 647.
Beswick v Beswick [1967] 2 All ER 1197, [1968] AC 58, [1967] 3 WLR 932, HL, 12 Digest (Reissue) 49, 256.
Bracey v Read [1962] 3 All ER 472, [1963] Ch 88, [1962] 3 WLR 1194, 31(2) Digest (Reissue) 215, 1764.

---

a   Section 18(5) is set out at p 23 *g* and *h*, post

a *Cartledge v E Jopling & Sons Ltd* [1963] 1 All ER 341, [1963] AC 758, [1963] 2 WLR 210, [1963] 1 Lloyd's Rep 1, HL, 32 Digest (Repl) 401, *259*.

Central Asbestos Co Ltd v Dodd [1972] 2 All ER 1135, sub nom *Smith v Central Asbestos Co Ltd* [1973] AC 518, [1972] 3 WLR 333, [1972] 2 Lloyd's Rep 413, 13 KIR 75, HL.

Chertsey Urban District Council v Mixnam's Properties Ltd [1964] 2 All ER 627, [1964] 2 WLR 1210, 128 JP 405, 62 LGR 528, [1964] RVR 632, HL, 45 Digest (Repl) 359, *126*.

b *Cow v Casey* [1949] 1 All ER 197, [1949] 1 KB 474, [1949] LJR 565, CA, 31(2) Digest (Reissue) 1102, *8562*.

Heydon's Case (1584) 3 Co Rep 7a, 76 ER 637, 44 Digest (Repl) 203, *149*.

Hobhouse v Wall [1963] 1 All ER 701, [1963] 2 QB 124, [1963] 2 WLR 604, CA, 31(2) Digest (Reissue) 1102, *8565*.

Sherwood (Baron) v Moody [1952] 1 All ER 389, 50 LGR 180, 2 Digest (Repl) 15, *63*.

c *Whitley v Stumbles* [1930] AC 544, 99 LJKB 518, 143 LT 441, HL, 31(2) Digest (Reissue) 933, *7675*.

Appeal

The plaintiff, Nesta Gwendoline Maunsell, owned the freehold of Hallsannery Farm, Bideford, Devon. The farm included two cottages, 1 and 2 Hallsannery Cottages.
d In about 1924 the plaintiff let the farm to Ernest Beer, who continued to farm it until his death on 15th March 1971. The tenancy was protected under the Agricultural Holdings Act 1948. For some years the first defendant, Ilmars Olins, was employed by Mr Beer on the farm as a farm labourer and, with his wife, the second defendant, he occupied 2 Hallsannery Cottages as a service occupant. In 1955 the first defendant left the employment of Mr Beer and obtained employment with a firm of agricultural *e* engineers but he stayed in the cottage. Subsequently, when 1 Hallsannery Cottages, which adjoined the farmhouse, became vacant, Mr Beer granted the defendants a tenancy of that cottage unfurnished at a rent of £1 a week. The tenancy was, as between the defendants and Mr Beer, protected under the Rent Acts. On the death of Mr Beer the plaintiff served a notice to quit on his estate and in consequence the tenancy of the farm came to an end on 25th March 1973. The plaintiff, taking the view *f* that the sub-tenancy of the defendants had come to an end with the termination of the tenancy of Mr Beer, brought proceedings in the Bideford County Court for possession of 1 Hallsannery Cottages and mesne profits. On 26th July 1973 his Honour Judge Stansfield dismissed the claim holding that the defendants were entitled to the protection of the Rent Act 1968 by virtue of s 18(5) of that Act. On 21st February 1974 the Court of Appeal[1] (Edmund Davies, Cairns and Lawton LJJ) allowed an *g* appeal by the plaintiff. The defendants appealed.

Ronald Bernstein QC and *Simon Tuckey* for the defendants.
Derek Wood for the plaintiff.

LORD REID. My Lords, I have had an opportunity of reading the speech of *h* my noble and learned friend, Lord Wilberforce. I agree with it and I shall only add some further observations.

The construction of s 18 of the Rent Act 1968 is unusually difficult. Differences of opinion show that it is thought to be capable of having more than one meaning, and I regard this as ambiguous. It occurs in a consolidation Act. Draftsmen of such Acts rephrase the original statutory provisions which are to be consolidated but they *j* are well aware that it is their duty not to make any substantial alteration of the existing law and there is a very strong presumption that they have not done so. So where the consolidation Act is ambiguous it is, in my judgment, always permissible and often necessary to go back to the original Act, in this case s 41 of the Housing Repairs and Rents Act 1954.

---

1 [1974] 2 All ER 250

There can be no doubt that the primary purpose of that section was to reverse *a*
the decision in *Cow v Casey*[1]. Often a department in such circumstances takes
advantage of the opportunity to make a more extensive alteration of the law than
is necessary to reverse the decision. Often it does not. I do not think that in this
case there is any presumption in favour of either of these courses.

Then rules of construction are relied on. They are not rules in the ordinary
sense of having some binding force. They are our servants not our masters. They *b*
are aids to construction, presumptions or pointers. Not infrequently one 'rule'
points in one direction, another in a different direction. In each case we must look
at all relevant circumstances and decide as a matter of judgment what weight to
attach to any particular 'rule'.

I fully accept that a word should be given its ordinary meaning unless there is
sufficient reason to give it in the particular case a secondary or limited meaning. *c*
Here the difficult word is 'premises'. The case for the plaintiff is that it should
here be given a limited meaning, and the question as I see it is whether there is
sufficient reason for doing that. I shall not repeat the reasons adduced by my noble
and learned friend. But it appears to me that s 41 of the 1954 Act itself contains a
fairly clear pointer to the word 'premises' being intended to be limited to premises
of a residential character. *d*

Section 41 directs us to suppose that in lieu of the superior letting there had been
two lettings, one of the sublet part and one of the rest of the subjects in the superior
lease, and it further directs us to suppose (as I read the section) that the subjects of
each of these two supposed lettings were let 'for the like purposes as under the
superior letting'. If the purposes under the superior letting were residential purposes there is no difficulty—the purpose for the sublet part was in the original lease *e*
residential, it remains residential and the Rent Acts apply. But this part of the
section causes some difficulty if the purpose of the superior letting was not residential but was, say, agricultural. Suppose that a farm to be let includes several cottages
all occupied by farm workers. One would I think naturally say that the whole
original lease or 'superior letting' had only one purpose which was agricultural.
It would at least be unusual to say that it had two purposes—residential as regards *f*
the farmer's house and the cottages and agricultural as regards the land and the
other buildings. I would think that if one of the cottages is sublet to a person who
has no connection with the farm, there is a change of purpose. But the section will
not work unless it can be said that there were two purposes in the original lease so
that the purpose of letting the house and cottage was residential and not agricultural.
I do not regard this as a conclusive argument but it is I think a fairly clear indication *g*
that the draftsman did not have in mind any 'superior letting' other than a letting
for residential purposes.

Finally I think this is a typical case for the application of the 'rule' that a court, in
doubt between two constructions of a statutory provision, should lean towards that
construction which involves the least alteration of the common law.

I would dismiss this appeal. *h*

VISCOUNT DILHORNE. My Lords, I have had the advantage of reading
the speech of my noble and learned friend, Lord Wilberforce, and I agree with him
that this appeal should be dismissed.

The event which led to the enactment of s 41 of the Housing Repairs and Rents
Act 1954, now replaced by s 18(5) of the Rent Act 1968, clearly was the decision in *j*
Cow v Casey[1]. That was the 'mischief' which s 41 was designed to cure, and while
Parliament may, of course, have intended to do more than just cure the mischief,
that should not be readily assumed and I see nothing in s 41 that leads me to that
conclusion. The Agricultural Holdings Act 1948 contains a separate code for dealing

1   [1949] 1 All ER 197, [1949] 1 KB 474

a with agricultural holdings. It gives power to the Minister to make regulations dealing with the situation where a tenant of such a holding has sublet a dwelling-house on a protected tenancy, and the superior tenancy has been lawfully determined. No such regulations have been made and it would, indeed, be surprising to me if Parliament, in an Act dealing with housing and rents, had intended s 41 to apply to agricultural holdings, that no reference should be made to such a holding. Unless b the word 'premises' in s 41 of the 1954 Act and in s 18(5) of the 1968 Act is to be interpreted as applying to the subject-matter of the superior letting, whatever that subject-matter may be, the argument that those sections apply where the superior letting is an agricultural holding must fail.

'Premises' is an ordinary word of the English language which takes colour and content from the context in which it is used. A reference to Stroud's Judicial Dictionary shows this to be the case. It has, in my opinion, no recognised and established c primary meaning. Frequently it is used in relation to structures of one kind or another. No one would, I think, in the ordinary use of the English language refer to farm land as 'premises' though farm buildings may often be referred to as 'farm premises'. I do not think that it is right, when Parliament uses that word in a statute to conclude that it is intended to have the meaning that conveyancers attach to it d unless a contrary intention appears. It is for these reasons that, in my opinion, whatever may be the scope of ss 41 and 18(5), it does not extend to include a superior letting of an agricultural holding. Such a holding is not 'premises' in the sense in which that word is used in the sections.

My noble and learned friend, Lord Wilberforce, goes on to consider what the word 'premises' in these sections should be taken to mean. In my opinion, it means e 'dwelling-houses'. They are what the 1954 Act and the 1968 Act were concerned with and, in my view, the dwelling-houses which are covered by the word 'premises' are those which for the purposes of these Acts are treated as such. But if that is not right, then I think that the word should be given the slightly wider meaning of 'buildings'. It is often used in that sense. Whether it covers, as I think, dwelling-houses in the sense in which those words are used in those Acts or means buildings, f it is another thing to say that it covers acres of arable and pasture land and to say that just by the use of that one word, it is to be concluded that Parliament meant the section to encroach on the sphere of the Agricultural Holdings Act 1948.

Our task is to interpret the sections 'according to the intent of them that made it'[1]. It is not for us to decide whether a sub-tenant with a protected tenancy on a farm, the subject of the superior letting, should be placed in the same position as a sub-g tenant of a dwelling-house on a protected tenancy when that sub-tenancy has been carved out of the tenancy of a dwelling-house or other building which is not protected. That involves questions of policy and all we have to do is to decide whether the sections apply in this case. The use of the word 'premises' is not, in my opinion sufficient to justify the conclusion that Parliament intended to restrict the common law rights of the owner of the freehold of a farm.

h   Why, then, it may be asked, was the word 'premises' used in s 41? One can only speculate as to that and the wording closely follows that of the headnote in Cow v Casey[2]. The intention of Parliament could by the use of different and possibly more words have been put beyond doubt. Perhaps this is an instance where the desire for brevity in an enactment has led to litigation which might have been avoided. However this may be, in the process of consolidation, it would not, in my view, have j been right to change the word from 'premises' to something else and I accordingly attach no significance to the fact that that word is repeated in s 18(5) of the 1968 Act.

The fact that a different word or words might have been used does not lead me to

1 4 Co Inst 330
2 [1949] 1 All ER 197, [1949] 1 KB 474

the conclusion that premises in the sections covers an agricultural holding and, for *a* the reasons I have stated, I think it does not.

LORD WILBERFORCE. My Lords, the defendants claim the protection of the Rent Act 1968 in respect of their occupation of a cottage situated on a 106 acre farm in Devonshire. They are not employed on the farm. The question raised is of *b* general importance both to owners of farms and to cottage occupiers. As will be seen it is not easy to decide.

The plaintiff is the freehold owner of the farm. The main buildings are approximately in the centre of the holding and include a farmhouse and two cottages. The cottage occupied by the defendants form, together with the farmhouse itself, a semi-detached pair of dwelling-houses. The other cottage is separate, but nothing *c* in this appeal depends on any distinction between the physical situation of the one cottage or the other.

The farm was let for many years to Mr Ernest Beer on a tenancy protected by the Agricultural Holdings Act 1948. Mr Olins was employed on the farm for some time and lived in the other cottage, but in 1955 he took other employment and in 1959 Mr Beer let the cottage in question to both defendants on an unfurnished tenancy *d* for £1 a week.

On 30th April 1963 the tenancy agreement between the plaintiff and Mr Beer, which had previously been oral, was replaced by a written agreement in the standard 'short form'. Under this agreement the farm was let to Mr Beer from 25th March 1963 for one year certain and thereafter from year to year at a rent of £400 per annum. Clause 4(12) of the tenancy agreement provided that the tenant— *e*

'will reside in the farmhouse and will use the farm for agricultural purposes only and will not assign underlet or part with possession of the farm or any part thereof except the two cottages which may be sub-let on monthly tenancies.'

The defendants were, of course, already in occupation of their cottage under a sub-tenancy. The defendants continued to live in the cottage and it is not disputed that *f* they were protected tenants vis-à-vis Mr Beer.

Mr Beer died on 15th March 1971 and the plaintiff served a notice to quit on his legal personal representatives terminating the head tenancy on 25th March 1973. On 15th June 1973 she started these proceedings against the defendants for possession of the cottage. There is no doubt that at common law this claim must succeed since the defendants' subtenancy could not survive the termination of the tenancy. But *g* the defendants claimed the protection of the Rent Act 1968, s 18(5).

This claim succeeded in the county court on the ground that the cottage formed physically part of the farm buildings, a circumstance supposed to distinguish the case from *Hobhouse v Wall*[1]. On appeal to the Court of Appeal[2], this distinction was rejected and the court followed its earlier decision. The defendants in this house abandoned any attempt to distinguish this case from *Hobhouse v Wall*[1] on the facts. *h* So they are faced with the task of contending that two decisions of the Court of Appeal are wrong. It is fair to say that more than one of the learned judges, whose judgments are under review, have found difficulties in interpreting the statutory provisions, and the section is certainly one which admits, almost invites, opposing constructions.

As I have stated, the provision actually relied on is s 18(5) of the Rent Act 1968. *j* This Act is a consolidation Act so that it is legitimate to look to the origin of the subsection in question. That is to be found in s 41 of the Housing Repairs and Rents Act 1954. There are some differences in the language of these two provisions, but,

---

1   [1963] 1 All ER 701, [1963] 2 QB 124
2   [1974] 2 All ER 250

a in agreement with the Court of Appeal, I do not find them significant. I shall quote, at the present stage, the earlier section—I quote the present section later—because the next step will be to ascertain what was its legal background at the time of its enactment: it was also the section interpreted in *Hobhouse v Wall*[1]. It read as follows:

b 'Where a dwelling-house to which the Act of 1920 applies (hereinafter referred to as "the sub-let part") forms parts of premises, not being such a dwelling-house, which have been let as a whole on a superior letting, then from the coming to an end of the superior letting under the operation of the Rent Acts in relation to the sub-let part shall be the same as if in lieu of the superior letting there had been separate lettings of the sub-let part and the remainder of the premises, for the like purposes as under the superior letting, and at rents equal to the just *c* proportion of the rent under the superior letting.'

Before we try to interpret this we must look at its context. The Act in which it appears deals with two separate subjects. Part I is essentially a housing enactment dealing with slum clearance and fitness for habitation, and contains a number of amendments of Housing Acts. Part II, in which s 41 appears, is essentially rent legislation. After ten sections (ss 23-32) dealing with the increase of rents on account of *d* repairs, it proceeds from s 33 onwards to introduce some miscellaneous amendments to previous Rent Acts and also to Housing Acts. Section 41 is one of these amendments; it seems to stand by itself as an independent provision not reflecting or forming part of some wider change in policy. Rather it seems, as we know is common in rent legislation, a section of a piecemeal or patching character.

A first reading of this does not, to my mind, convey an impression of conspicuous *e* clarity, particularly as to its general scope. I think that I would not be alone in finding that the key word 'premises' invites reflection. It is true that it is a general word or, rather, a word of some generality but I know of no rule of construction which requires general words to be interpreted literally regardless of their context. If appeal is made to the principle that the plain meaning of a word should be taken, unless at least some *f* other indication appears, it must be said that a word does not necessarily have a plain meaning just because it appears to be general—certainly not such a word as 'premises'. We know that this is a word of conveyancing jargon, meaning, strictly (and pace Viscount Hailsham in *Whitley v Stumbles*[2]) everything in a deed which precedes the habendum. From this it has passed into the vernacular, at least a quasi-legal vernacular, as referring to some sort of property, but not with any precise connotation. A reference to Stroud's Judicial Dictionary shows that a number of different meanings *g* have been acquired of which the most central appears to be buildings or some kinds of buildings, but it would be far too much to say that there is any prima facie, still less any grammatical meaning from which one should start.

The appellants' main argument was that if the word is not itself a general word equivalent to property, it is given the general meaning in this subsection of any property which can be or has been let. This is said to follow from the phrase 'part of *h* premises . . . which have been let as a whole . . .' But this is a confusion of thought. A relative clause merely qualifies that to which it is relative, and does not define it or help in its definition. What kind of property (which has been let) is meant must be ascertained aliunde. I am not, myself, able to solve this problem by a simplistic resort to plain meaning. Most language, and particularly all language used in rents legislation, is opaque: all general words are open to inspection, many general words demand *j* inspection, to see whether they really bear their widest possible meaning. As Viscount Simonds said:

'For words, and particularly general words, cannot be read in isolation; their colour and content are derived from their context. So it is that I conceive it to be

---

1   [1963] 1 All ER 701, [1963] 2 QB 124
2   [1930] AC 544 at 546

my right and duty to examine every word of a statute in its context, and I use *a*
context in its widest sense, which I have already indicated as including not only
other enacting provisions of the same statute, but its preamble, the existing
state of the law, other statutes in pari materia, and the mischief which I can, by
those and other legitimate means, discern the statute was intended to remedy.'

(*Attorney-General v HRH Prince Ernest Augustus of Hanover*[1]).   *b*
    A first stage in this inspection might be to ask whether, to an ordinary man,
'premises' would be regarded as equivalent to 'land' or 'property'. I doubt very much
whether a farmer would accept the word as a description of his farm land, or whether
the local hunt would use it when asking for permission to hunt over his land. I note
with interest that the tenancy agreement of this farm does not use the word 'premises'
at all: what is let, and referred to in the covenants is 'the farm'. This tenancy agree-   *c*
ment, moreover, was made in the standard short form which applies to many holdings
all over the country.
    So the reader of this section is bound to ask himself what the word does include:
has it some lesser meaning than property or than leasehold property: is it coloured
by the references to dwelling-houses: why is it used in preference to something more
precise: is there perhaps a drafting reason for it? It certainly seems to facilitate the   *d*
later words 'the remainder of the premises'. And in the same line of thought what is
meant by 'forms part of', 'for the like purposes as under the superior letting'. In
sum, what is the section trying to do? We do not have to look far for a clue.
    In 1949 the Court of Appeal decided *Cow v Casey*[2]. That case was concerned with a
subtenancy of a dwelling-house which was not subject to the Rents Acts. The decision
was that the subtenant was not entitled as against the superior landlord to the pro-   *e*
tection of the Acts. Quite obviously s 41 was intended to deal with that situation and
to bring about the opposite result.
    My Lords, it frequently happens that legislative changes are made in order to
reverse decisions of the courts; sometimes, indeed, the courts themselves invite the
change. The decision is then the occasion of the enactment. The question may,
consequently, arise whether the new enactment is confined to dealing with the par-   *f*
ticular situation with which the court was concerned or whether it goes further and
covers a wider field, and, if so, how much wider. There is no general rule or presumption as to this. Often Parliament, or its expert advisers, may take the opportunity to
review the whole matter in principle and make broad changes. (See for example
Central Asbestos Co Ltd v Dodd[3] as to the Limitation Acts.) Legislative time is a precious
commodity and it is natural that opportunities, when they arise, will be used. Or,   *g*
and this happens in the fiscal field, the draftsman, faced with some loophole in a
taxing Act which the courts have recognised, will not merely close that particular
loophole but will use general language extending much more widely, sometimes so
as to sweep the honest and conscientious taxpayer up in the same net as the evader.
On the other hand, there may be cases where Parliament takes a narrow and piecemeal view of the matter; time may not admit of an extensive review which may   *h*
involve wide policy questions, or necessitate consultation with other interests. All
these possibilities must be taken into account by courts in assessing the legislative
intention. In performing that task here, I think that help is to be gained from setting
down the two main elements which the draftsman must have had in mind: the pre-
existing law and the decision in *Cow v Casey*[2].
    The pre-existing law is s 15(3) of the Increase of Rent and Mortgage Interest   *j*
(Restrictions) Act 1920:

---

1 [1957] 1 All ER 49 at 53, [1957] AC 436 at 461
2 [1949] 1 All ER 197, [1949] 1 KB 474
3 [1972] 2 All ER 1135, [1973] AC 518

a   'Where the interest of a tenant of a dwelling-house to which this Act applies is
determined, either as the result of an order or judgment for possession or ejectment, or for any other reason, any sub-tenant to whom the premises or any part
thereof have been lawfully sublet shall, subject to the provisions of this Act, be
deemed to become the tenant of the landlord on the same terms as he would
have held from the tenant if the tenancy had continued.'

b   The decision in Cow v Casey[1] as reported in the headnote in the Law Reports reads:

'Held, dismissing the appeal, that the dwelling-house, the subject of the original
demise, not being a dwelling-house to which the Rent Restriction Acts applied,
s. 3 of the Rent and Mortgage Interest Restrictions (Amendment) Act, 1933, did
not apply to the sub-tenancy of a part of the premises so as to protect a sub-tenant
c   from ejectment. On the determination of his sub-tenancy the defendant became
at common law a trespasser. Section 15, sub-s. 3 of the Increase of Rent and Mortgage Interest (Restrictions) Act, 1920, under which (where the interest of a tenant
of a dwelling-house to which the Act applied was determined) any sub-tenant to
whom any part of the premises had been lawfully sub-let was to be deemed to
have become the tenant of the head landlord, only applied to the case where the
d   head tenant, whose tenancy had been determined, was tenant of a dwelling-house
to which the Acts applied. The defendant accordingly was not entitled to the
protection of the Rent Restriction Acts.'

The coincidence in language between the holding in Cow v Casey[1] and s 41 conveys
to my mind a strong impression that s 41 is a section of limited effect, dealing primarily
with subleases of dwelling-houses or, at the most, with subleases of property in the
e   same field. And this fits in with the context—a section on the face of it piecemeal,
included in what is throughout housing legislation.
The effect of the change on the previous law can well be seen by looking at the
consolidation Act which now sets out the old provision and the new as two subsections
of the same section, s 18. These are:

f   '(2) Where a protected or statutory tenancy of a dwelling-house is determined,
either as a result of an order for possession or for any other reason, any sub-tenant
to whom the dwelling-house or any part of it had been lawfully sublet shall,
subject to the provisions of this Act, be deemed to become the tenant of the
landlord on the same terms as he would have held from the tenant if the tenant's
protected or statutory tenancy had continued.'

g   '(5) Where a dwelling-house—(a) forms part of premises which have been let
as a whole on a superior letting but do not constitute a dwelling-house let on a
protected tenancy; and (b) is itself let on a protected tenancy, or subject to a
statutory tenancy, then, from the coming to an end of the superior letting, this
Act shall apply in relation to the dwelling-house as if, in lieu of the superior
letting, there had been separate lettings of the dwelling-house and of the re-
h   mainder of the premises, for the like purposes as under the superior letting, and
at rents equal to the just proportion of the rent under the superior letting.'

There seems to be a relation between these two subsections. They cover similar
ground—broadly that of tenancies of dwelling-houses. There is no indication that
they extend any wider.
j   So what should 'premises' be taken to mean? One view, the narrowest view,
would be that it simply means 'dwelling-houses'. I find this, linguistically, a perfectly
possible construction: the phrase 'premises, not being such a dwelling-house' meaning
premises being a dwelling-house but not a protected dwelling-house: the exclusion
qualifies and colours the preceding generality. A less narrow view would be to say

---

1   [1949] 1 All ER 197, [1949] 1 KB 474

that 'premises' includes not only dwelling-houses in the normal popular sense, but *a*
premises, which, for the purposes of the Rent Act 1968, are treated as dwelling-houses.
Everybody knows, and the draftsman must be taken to have known, that protection
under the Rent Acts is given not merely to single, identifiable, pure dwelling-houses
or dwelling units, but also to units of a mixed character—houses let with a garden or a
yard or a garage or a paddock, houses part (even a substantial part) of which is used
for business purposes. This is, of course, an untidy situation and it means that no clear *b*
definition of a dwelling-house entitled to protection can be given. (We note that a
distinction is made between a house let together with land and land let with a house.)
But it reflects the reality of life, and the county courts are used, and skilful, at solving
what are inevitably questions of degree. We should recognise this and, as between the
narrow and the less narrow meaning, I would apply to premises the latter which
would include any premises which, as a matter of fact, applying accepted principles, *c*
would be held to be a dwelling-house for the purposes of the Act.

But the alternatives must be considered. One suggested alternative is to give to
'premises' a general meaning but to exclude from it any property forming part of an
agricultural holding. The basis for this would be that agricultural holdings have a
code of their own (see Megarry, The Rent Acts[1]) and should not be brought under the
general provisions of the Rent Acts. I see the force of this, but I think that a particular *d*
exception limited in this way would have received specific legislative mention and this
is not to be found. The only real alternative seems to me to be to give to 'premises' a
universal meaning—and that is in effect the defendants' contention. The effect of this
would be to give protection not only to subtenants of individual dwelling-houses in
the middle of agricultural holdings but to subtenants of individual dwelling-houses in
other complexes, industrial or business, or in any large estate of any kind. To do this *e*
would represent a very great enlargement of the rights of subtenants as compared
with the situation pre-1954. No doubt Parliament might think fit to take this course,
but it is obvious that a number of problems and policy considerations would arise—
quite distinct from those which relate to subtenants of 'housing properties' (I use this
expression for convenience to refer to what I think is *within* the section). An indication
that such problems exist and were recognised is to be found in the Agricultural *f*
Holdings Act 1948, s 26(1)(c) of which confers on the Minister power *by regulation* to
safeguard the interests of subtenants of agricultural holdings—a power which had
been partially, but not relevantly, exercised prior to 1954 (see *Sherwood v Moody*[2]).
Nobody can be unaware that the law relating to tenancies of agricultural land is one
of considerable political import and delicacy and I am very reluctant to believe that
the particular aspect of this law which relates to subtenancies, treated with evident *g*
circumspection in 1948, would have been dealt with in a general provision such as
appears in s 41 of the 1954 Act. I cannot finally help noticing that although the Court
of Appeal decided in 1963 (in *Hobhouse v Wall*[3]) against protection of subtenants of
premises in an agricultural holding, Parliament, normally quick enough to react in
this field, has not disturbed the decision. The changes made by the Rent Act 1965 (not
directly affecting the point at issue, but relating to agricultural tenancies) cannot *h*
affect the construction of a provision enacted in 1954.

It remains to say a few words on the judgments in the Court of Appeal. The
leading judgment is that of Upjohn LJ in *Hobhouse v Wall*[3]. The learned lord justice
clearly felt difficulty about the case, as who does not? Certainly the word 'premises'
was not clear in its meaning to him; but after a thoughtful consideration of the
issues he reached the conclusion with which, broadly, I agree. I do not read him as *j*
saying that 'premises' means 'buildings' though, as I have pointed out, the word has
been given this meaning in other contexts, but as saying that his interpretation

---

1   10th Edn (1967), pp 107, 108
2   [1952] 1 All ER 389
3   [1963] 1 All ER 701, [1963] 2 QB 124

a   would in effect cover only buildings. His reference[1], on the other hand, to 'what are essentially dwelling-houses' seems to reflect the conception which I would favour. He did not attempt any definition of 'premises', but contented himself with the negative conclusion that the section did not apply to agricultural holdings. I sympathise with his caution, but I think that now in this House, we must, unless we are to accept a universal meaning of 'premises', risk the attempt to draw a dividing line. I have

b   attempted to do so in this opinion. In the present case, Lawton LJ[2] might be taken perhaps as equating 'premises' with (conventional) dwelling-houses, but I do not think that in his reference to large Victorian houses he was using more than an illustration.

My Lords, I regret that a matter which is really one of impression should have needed so many words to dispose of but we have heard some well-balanced arguments

c   and the case is not one for quick solution. On the whole I would dismiss the appeal.

LORD DIPLOCK. My Lords, I have had the privilege of collaborating with my noble and learned friend, Lord Simon of Glaisdale, in the preparation of the speech which he will deliver. The opinion that he expresses coincides entirely with my own.

d   **LORD SIMON OF GLAISDALE.** My Lords, the following speech has been prepared in collaboration with my noble and learned friend, Lord Diplock. It expresses the opinion which we share. The appeal turns on a very short point of construction—namely, the meaning of 'premises' in s 18(5) of the Rent Act 1968. In our judgment 'premises' there means 'the subject-matter of the letting referred to' (i e the superior tenancy). We would therefore allow the appeal.

e   Ordinarily, on an issue of statutory construction—where certainty in the law is most important—we would not have ventured in a dissenting judgment beyond this point. But there seems to be difficulty in agreeing on the proper interpretation of 'premises' in s 18(5); and a number of issues of statutory construction of general importance are in question, on which we feel we would be remiss not to express an

f   opinion.

1. *The 'golden' rule of construction*
What Maxwell on Interpretation of Statutes[3] calls 'the first and most elementary rule of construction'—

g   'is that it is to be assumed that the words and phrases of technical legislation are used in their technical meaning if they have acquired one, and otherwise in their ordinary meaning.'

This 'golden' canon of construction has been so frequently and authoritatively stated that further citation would be otiose. It is sometimes put that, in statutes dealing with ordinary people in their everyday lives, the language is presumed to be used in its primary ordinary sense, unless this stultifies the purpose of the statute, or

h   otherwise produces some injustice, absurdity, anomaly or contradiction, in which case some secondary ordinary sense may be preferred, so as to obviate the injustice, absurdity, anomaly or contradiction, or fulfil the purpose of the statute: while, in statutes dealing with technical matters, words which are capable of both bearing an ordinary meaning and being terms of art in the technical matter of the legislation will presumptively bear their primary meaning as such terms of art (or, if they must

j   necessarily be modified, some secondary meaning as terms of art).
This is true as far as it goes, and it is sufficient to dispose of this appeal. If these are the two alternatives, the Rent Act 1968 deals with legal technicalities of leasehold

1   [1963] 1 All ER at 703, 704, [1963] 2 QB at 131
2   [1974] 2 All ER 250 at 255
3   12th Edn (1969), p 28

tenure on which ordinary citizens consult their lawyers, rather than with everyday   *a*
affairs; so that 'premises' must be construed presumptively in the primary sense
which it bears as a term of art (i e the subject-matter of the habendum clause of a
lease: Whitley v Stumbles[1]; Bracey v Read[2]). But, in fact, these two statutory situations—dealing with ordinary people in their everyday lives, on the one hand, and
dealing with technical branches of the law, on the other—are only two extreme
situations. Statutory language, like all language, is capable of an almost infinite   *b*
gradation of 'register'—i e it will be used at the semantic level appropriate to the
subject-matter and to the audience addressed (the man in the street, lawyers, merchants, etc). It is the duty of a court of construction to tune in to such register and so to
interpret the statutory language as to give to it the primary meaning which is appropriate in that register (unless it is clear that some other meaning must be given in
order to carry out the statutory purpose or to avoid injustice, anomaly, absurdity or   *c*
contradiction). In other words, statutory language must always be given presumptively
the most natural and ordinary meaning which is appropriate in the circumstances.
    It is essential that this 'golden' rule is adhered to. An English court of construction
must put itself in the place of the draftsman, and ascertain the meaning of the words
used in the light of all the circumstances known by the draftsman—especially the
'mischief' which is the subject-matter of the statutory remedy. But an English court   *d*
of construction cannot look at the parliamentary proceedings in order to ascertain
whether the meaning thus identified of the statutory language is what the legislature
meant to say. The canons of construction—including, first and foremost, the 'golden'
rule—constitute a code of communication between the draftsman and the court of
construction. Observing the code on his side, the draftsman will use language in such
a way that its meaning represents what Parliament means to say; and it is only by   *e*
observance of the code by the court on its own side that a divergence can be avoided
between its interpretation of what the words mean from what Parliament meant to
say.
    The subject-matter of the legislation under your Lordships' instant consideration
provides an example of what we mean by language having various 'registers'. In
popular parlance 'landlord' can mean 'innkeeper'—indeed, even 'lessee from a   *f*
brewery'. But in ordinary legal parlance, which is, we think, the appropriate register
of language in legislation dealing with rent restriction and security of leasehold
tenure, 'landlord' presumptively means 'lessor', and it would take a good deal to
displace the presumption. Similarly, in popular parlance 'premises' can mean
'building'. But in ordinary legal parlance 'premises' means 'the subject-matter of a
letting'. Or, even higher in the register, if the Rent Act 1968 is considered as dealing   *g*
with legal technicalities, 'premises' presumptively bears its most ordinary meaning
as a term of art—namely, the subject-matter of the habendum clause of the relevant
lease.

2. *Construction of consolidation Acts*
    Consolidation is not nowadays limited to mere re-enactment. Under a procedure   *h*
recommended by the Law Commissions in 1965 under the Law Commissions Act of
that year, even substantial amendments may be made in the pre-existing law, where
such are deemed by the Law Commissions to be desirable in order to secure satisfactory consolidation. Such amendments are subject to full and traditional parliamentary control. But, even short of this, by the Consolidation of Enactments (Procedure) Act 1949, ss 1(1) and 2, a consolidation Act may embody such corrections and
minor improvements as are confined to, and may be judged expedient with a view   *j*
to—

        'resolving ambiguities, removing doubts, bringing obsolete provisions into

---

1 [1930] AC 544 at 546
2 [1962] 3 All ER 472, [1963] Ch 88

a conformity with modern practice, or removing unnecessary provisions or anomalies which are not of substantial importance, and amendments designed to facilitate improvement in the form or manner in which the law is stated [including] any transitional provisions which may be necessary in consequence of such amendments . . .'

b Moreover, the very purpose of consolidation is to enact a compendious code standing on its own and making it unnecessary to scrutinize the consolidated legislation (which is, indeed, repealed in a schedule to the consolidation Act). For all these reasons it is, in our respectful submission, an incorrect approach to the construction of a consolidation Act (even one limited to re-enactment) to try to interpret it by reference to the repealed statutes which are consolidated.

c It has been generally accepted in the past that there is a presumption that Parliament does not intend by a consolidation Act to alter the pre-existing law (see Maxwell[1]; *Beswick v Beswick*[2]). How far this rule may need modification in the case of some types of consolidation under the 1949 Act or of consolidation under the 1965 procedure, and how the courts should inform themselves of the manner in which Parliament has proceeded, may have to be considered in some future case. But in any event such a presumption has no scope for operation where the actual words of the consolidation Act are not, as a matter of legal language, capable of bearing more than one meaning. The docked tail must not be allowed to wag the dog. It is only where the actual words used in the consolidation Act are ambiguous (in the sense of being fairly susceptible of bearing more than one meaning in their context and register) that recourse may be had to any difference in phraseology of the corresponding provision in the repealed enactment as an aid to their construction. Even in such a case

e the corresponding provision of the repealed enactment is capable of being an aid to the construction of the consolidation Act only if its own wording is unambiguous and its sole meaning is one of those which the words in the consolidation Act can fairly bear.

3. *The use of the 'mischief' rule*

It was suggested on behalf of the plaintiff that s 41 of the Housing Repairs and

f Rents Act 1954 was enacted to abrogate the decision in *Cow v Casey*[3]; so that its substantial re-enactment as s 18(5) of the Rent Act 1968 should be construed as if limited to dealing with *Cow v Casey*[3], thus giving a special colour to the word 'premises'. But, even were your Lordships concerned with construing s 41 of the 1954 Act and not s 18(5) of the 1968 Act, there is no such canon of construction as that suggested on behalf of the respondent. It is turning the rule in *Heydon's* case[4] on its head. The

g barons of the exchequer there resolved that, in construing an Act of Parliament, you identify the 'mischief' which the statute seeks to remedy (i e in modern parlance, the statutory objective), and so construe the statute that it advances the remedy and suppresses the mischief (i e in modern parlance, in construing the statute you bear its objective in mind). It is, in other words, a positive and not a negative canon of construction; it enjoins a liberal, and not a restrictive, approach. For a court of construction

h tion to constrain statutory language which has a primary natural meaning appropriate in its context so as to give it an artificial meaning which is appropriate only to remedy the mischief which is conceived to have occasioned the statutory provision is to proceed unsupported by principle, inconsonant with authority and oblivious of the actual practice of parliamentary draftsmen. Once a mischief has been drawn to the attention of the draftsman he will consider whether any concomitant mischiefs should

j be dealt with as a necessary corollary. What happened as a result of *Cartledge v Jopling*[5] provides an example. Your Lordships there held, drawing attention to the

---

1 Interpretation of Statutes (12th Edn, 1969), pp 20-25
2 [1967] 2 All ER 1197 at 1202, [1968] AC 58 at 73
3 [1949] 1 All ER 197, [1949] 1 KB 474
4 (1584) 3 Co Rep 7a
5 [1963] 1 All ER 341, [1963] AC 758

injustice, that, under the then existing law of limitation, a cause of action for personal *a*
injuries based on the negligence of an employer was barred notwithstanding that the
plaintiff, though knowing of the defendant's breach of duty, did not know, and could
not reasonably know, by the expiry of six years from the accrual of his cause of action,
that he had suffered injury as a result of that breach of duty. When Parliament
came (in the Limitation Act 1963) to remedy this injustice, it is clear that the draftsman immediately considered two situations which were corollaries and which it   *b*
would therefore be anomalous not to remedy at the same time—namely, first, where
the plaintiff, though knowing that he had suffered injury, did not know, and could
not reasonably know, that it was caused by breach of duty on the part of the defendant
and, secondly, where the plaintiff knew that he had suffered *some* injury as a result of
the defendant's breach of duty, but did not know, and could not reasonably know,
that it was a serious injury. All the members of your Lordships' House who heard the   *c*
appeal in *Central Asbestos Co Ltd v Dodd*[1] were agreed that the draftsmen had gone at
least as far as this beyond remedying the mischief of *Cartledge v Jopling*[2]: the difference
of opinion was as to whether the draftsman had gone further still. In other words,
the mischief which was identified in *Cartledge v Jopling*[2] can be recognised as the
occasion for the remedy afforded by the Limitation Act 1963, but did not define the
limit of the remedy which was provided.   *d*

It follows that there is no presumption that, when an Act of Parliament is amended
by a subsequent Act which has the effect of rendering inapplicable previous decisions
of courts of law as to the meaning of the legislation prior to the amendment, the
intention of Parliament was confined to making no more extensive alteration in the
law than was necessary to render those decisions inapplicable. The most that can be
said is that it may be a natural, though irrelevant, inference that it was those decisions   *e*
that originally attracted Parliament's attention to the need for *some* amendment to
the legislation.

It is true that there have been pronouncements favouring a presumption in statutory construction against a change in the common law: see Maxwell[3]. Indeed, the
concept has sometimes been (possibly without advertence) in the form that there is a
presumption against change in the law pre-existing the statute which falls for con-   *f*
struction. So widely and crudely stated, it is difficult to discern any reason for such a
rule—whether constitutional, juridical or pragmatic. We are inclined to think that it
may have evolved through a distillation of forensic experience of the way Parliament
proceeded at a time when conservatism alternated with a radicalism which had a
strong ideological attachment to the common law. However valid this particular
aspect of the forensic experience may have been in the past, its force may be questioned   *g*
in these days of statutory activism. No doubt where, in a statute whose primary
purpose manifested by its provisions taken as a whole is to effect reforms in a limited
field of law, there appear in a particular provision general words which are capable
as a matter of language of applying outside that limited field of law as well as within
it, it may be reasonable to presume that Parliament intended them to apply in that
limited field of law only. And no doubt, too, it is reasonable to look for plain words   *h*
where the abrogation of a long-standing rule of law is in question. This absolves us
from the necessity of any further discussion of the matter in the instant appeal.
Whatever subsisting scope any canon of construction may have, whereby there is a
presumption against change of the common law, it is clearly a secondary canon (see
the way it was put by our noble and learned friend, Lord Reid, in *Chertsey Urban
District Council v Mixnam's Properties Ltd*[4]—of assistance to resolve any doubt which   *j*
remains after the application of 'the first and most elementary rule of construction',

---

1   [1972] 2 All ER 1135, [1973] AC 518
2   [1963] 1 All ER 341, [1963] AC 758
3   Interpretation of Statutes (12th Edn, 1969), pp 116-122
4   [1964] 2 All ER 627 at 631, [1965] AC 735 at 751

a that statutory language must always be given presumptively the most natural and ordinary meaning which is appropriate in the circumstances. Moreover, even at the stage when it may be invoked to resolve a doubt, any canon of construction against invasion of the common law may have to compete with other secondary canons. English law has not yet fixed any hierarchy amongst the secondary canons: indeed, which is to have paramountcy in any particular case is likely to depend on all the
b circumstances of the particular case.

The rule in *Heydon's* case[1] itself is sometimes stated as a primary canon of construction, sometimes as secondary (i e available in the case of an ambiguity): c f Maxwell on Interpretation of Statutes[2] with Craies on Statute Law[3]. We think that the explanation of this is that the rule is available at two stages. The first task of a court of construction is to put itself in the shoes of the draftsman—to consider what
c knowledge he had and, importantly, what statutory objective he had—if only as a guide to the linguistic register. Here is the first consideration of the 'mischief'. Being thus placed in the shoes of the draftsman, the court proceeds to ascertain the meaning of the statutory language. In this task 'the first and most elementary rule of construction' is to consider the plain and primary meaning, in their appropriate register, of the words used. If there is no such plain meaning (i e if there is an
d ambiguity), a number of secondary canons are available to resolve it. Of these one of the most important is the rule in *Heydon's* case[1]. Here, then, may be a second consideration of the 'mischief'.

In the instant case, however, we ourselves find no reason to resort to any secondary canon.

e *4. The meaning of 'premises' in s 18(5)*

We have seen no advantage in discussing the various meanings that have been canvassed for 'premises', alternative to what we regard as its primary and true meaning in its context. We therefore content ourselves with stating why we find unacceptable the meaning which counsel for the plaintiff finally settled for—namely, 'a building used predominantly for residential purposes'. In the first place, this is not a natural meaning of 'premises', either in a popular or technical context, or in any inter-
f mediate register. It therefore involves rewriting the subsection—quite unnecessarily and inadmissibly. In the second place, in our respectful opinion, it produces absurdity and anomaly. Why should Parliament wish to protect a sub-tenant of a flat in a block containing 40 per cent office accommodation and 60 per cent residential accommodation, but not a sub-tenant where the percentages are reversed? The case provides a striking example of how disregard of 'the first and most elementary rule of construc-
g tion' can lead to the ascription of a parliamentary vagary.

Appeal dismissed.

Solicitors: *Cripps, Harries, Willis & Carter* (for the defendants); *Macfarlanes* (for the plaintiff).
h

Gordon H Scott Esq Barrister.

---

1 (1584) 3 Co Rep 7a
2 12th Edn (1969), pp 40, 96
3 7th Edn (1971), pp 94, 96

R v HM Inspector of Taxes, ex parte Frank Rind Settlement Trustees

R v HM Inspector of Taxes, ex parte Sylvia Rind Settlement Trustees

QUEEN'S BENCH DIVISION

LORD WIDGERY CJ, MILMO AND ACKNER JJ

14th, 15th OCTOBER 1974

Income tax – Appeal – Case stated – Proceedings to be heard and determined in same way as appeal – Jurisdiction of commissioners to state case – Loss of tax to Crown due to fraud, wilful default or neglect – Interest – Assessment for making good loss of tax – Application to commissioners by inspector for certificate that tax charged by assessment carries interest – Whether application a proceeding heard and determined in same way as appeal – Whether appeal lies by way of case stated against commissioners' decision to give certificate – Taxes Management Act 1970, ss 48(2), 56, 70(3), 88(1).

Income tax – Interest – Interest on overdue tax – Tax recovered for purpose of making good loss of tax due to taxpayer's fault – Loss of tax – Meaning – Delay in payment – Payment ultimately secured – Delay because of taxpayer's failure to make return in reasonable time – Whether a loss of tax – Taxes Management Act 1970, s 88(1).

Income tax – Return of income – Notice by inspector – Notice requiring person to give return of income which is not his but in respect of which he is chargeable – Notice only requiring return of certain sources of income – Validity – Whether notice must require return of all sources of income – Taxes Management Act 1970, s 8(2).

The taxpayers were trustees of a settlement created in 1962. From 1965 onwards they were in receipt of large sums of money consisting of income and chargeable gains accruing to the settlement from various sources which was paid to them gross, without deduction of tax. Acting under s 8[a] of the Taxes Management Act 1970 the inspector of taxes gave notice to the taxpayers requiring them to make returns of the trust income, sending them two forms for that purpose. One of those forms (form 1) required the recipient to make a return of income not taxed at source while the other (form R59A) required the recipient to make a return of all income from all sources. Form 1 also required the person signing it to make a declaration, in accordance with s 8(7) of the 1970 Act, that the return was to the best of his knowledge correct and complete. Form R59A did not require any such declaration to be made. After considerable delay the taxpayers gave the inspector of taxes the information that he required on the trust income and paid on account a portion of the tax to which they were assessed in respect of the income for the years 1965-66 to 1970-71. Subsequently on an application by the inspector of taxes, under ss 70(3)[b] and 88(1)[c] of the 1970 Act, the General Commissioners issued a certificate of interest on the tax charged on the ground that the assessments made on the taxpayers were for the purpose of making good to the Crown a loss of tax attributable to the wilful default or neglect of the taxpayers. In their reasons for granting the certificate the commissioners noted that the taxpayers had 'made no return of income for over five years . . .

---

a   Section 8, so far as material, is set out at p 36 g to p 37 a, post
b   Section 70(3) is set out at p 33 b and c, post
c   Section 88(1) is set out at p 32 j, post

a and allowed tax totalling over £210,000 to accumulate in their hands and so to be available for their use, and then offered a payment of only £40,000 on account for four years liability'. The taxpayers, wishing to appeal against the certificate, requested the commissioners to state a case for the opinion of the High Court under s 56 of the 1970 Act but the commissioners declined on the ground that the application under s 70(3) was not, by virtue of s 48^d, an appeal or proceeding to which s 56 applied. The *b* taxpayers applied for an order of mandamus requiring the commissioners to state a case on the ground that an application to the commissioners for a certificate under s 70(3) was a proceeding which was, within s 48(2), 'to be heard and determined in the same way as an appeal' and, therefore, one to which s 56 applied. Alternatively, the taxpayers applied for an order of certiorari to quash the commissioners' certificate on the grounds, inter alia, (a) that although payment of the tax had been delayed, *c* there had been no 'loss of tax' to the Crown, within s 88(1), and (b) that, in any event, the taxpayers could not have been guilty of neglect or wilful default in making returns since the forms given to the taxpayers by the inspector under s 8 on which to make the returns were defective in that form 1 only dealt with part of the income of the trust, whereas s 8(2) required a return of all income, and form R59A did not contain the declaration required by s 8(7).

d **Held** – (i) The reference in s 48(2) to proceedings under the Taxes Acts which were to be heard and determined in the same way as an appeal was a reference to proceedings which, in the express terms of the relevant provisions of the Acts, were to be so decided. Since there was no express provision in s 70(3) that proceedings for the award of a certificate of interest were to be heard and determined in the same way as an appeal, the commissioners had no power to state and sign a case under *e* s 56 in relation to those proceedings. Accordingly the application for an order of mandamus would be dismissed (see p 34 *f* and *g* and p 38 *f*, post).

(ii) The application for certiorari would also be dismissed for the following reasons—
(a) The expression 'loss of tax' in s 88(1) was wide enough to include, not only tax which had been lost because a taxpayer had failed to disclose a source of income on his return, but also tax the payment of which, although ultimately secured, had *f* been delayed for an excessive period because of the failure of the taxpayer to make a return within a reasonable time (see p 35 *h*, p 36 *c* and *d* and p 38 *f*, post); dictum of Stamp LJ in *Knight v Inland Revenue Comrs* [1974] STC at 166 applied.

(b) It was not a requirement of s 8(2) that a notice given by an inspector of taxes under that subsection should require the person to whom it was given to deliver a return of all the relevant income. The subsection was permissive only, its purpose *g* being to define the limits beyond which the inspector could not go. Accordingly form 1 supplied by the inspector constituted a valid requirement to make a return of income (see p 37 *g* and p 38 *f*, post).

Notes
For the right to appeal by way of case stated, see 20 Halsbury's Laws (3rd Edn) 690, 691, para 1362.
h
For interest charges on loss of tax due to taxpayer's fault, see Supplement to 20 Halsbury's Laws (3rd Edn), para 1404A.
For notice given by the inspector of taxes calling for returns of income, see 20 Halsbury's Laws (3rd Edn) 656, para 1284, and for cases on returns and assessments, see 28(1) Digest (Reissue) 540, 541, 1978-1983.
For the Taxes Management Act 1970, ss 8, 48, 56, 70, 88, see 34 Halsbury's Statutes *j* (3rd Edn) 1255, 1295, 1302, 1315, 1326.

Case referred to in judgment
Knight v Inland Revenue Comrs [1974] STC 156, CA.

Cases also cited
Clinch v Inland Revenue Comrs [1973] 1 All ER 977, [1974] QB 76, [1973] STC 155.

d Section 48 is set out at p 33 *h* and *j*, post

Royal Bank of Canada v Inland Revenue Comrs [1972] 1 All ER 225, [1972] Ch 665, 47 Tax   *a*
Cas 565.
Thurgood v Slarke (Inspector of Taxes) [1971] 3 All ER 606, 47 Tax Cas 130.
Wellington v Reynolds (Inspector of Taxes) (1962) 40 Tax Cas 209.

Motions
By notice of motion dated 25th February 1974, Samuel Conway, Philip Fisher, David   *b*
Brecher, Paula Adler and Sylvia Rind ('the taxpayers'), the trustees of the Frank
Rind settlement, applied by leave of the Divisional Court given on 19th February
1974 (i) for an order of mandamus directed to the Commissioners for the General
Purposes of the Income Tax for the division of Holborn ('the commissioners') requiring them to state a case for the opinion of the High Court pursuant to s 56 of the
Taxes Management Act 1970 on the giving by them of a certificate dated 14th August   *c*
1973 under s 88 of the 1970 Act; (ii) alternatively for an order of certiorari that the
certificate be removed into the Divisional Court and quashed. The grounds on which
the orders were sought were: (i) that the commissioners had wrongly refused to state
a case for the opinion of the High Court; (ii) that the certificate was wrong in law; and
(iii) that there was no, or alternatively insufficient, evidence to support or justify the
commissioners' findings for signing the certificate. By notice of motion dated 25th   *d*
February 1974, Samuel Conway, Philip Fisher, David Brecher and Paula Adler, the
trustees of the Sylvia Rind settlement, applied, by leave of the Divisional Court given
on 19th February 1974, (i) for an order of mandamus in the same terms as that applied
for by the trustees of the Frank Rind settlement; (ii) alternatively for an order of
certiorari, also in the same terms as that applied for by the trustees of the Frank Rind
settlement. The facts are set out in the judgment of Lord Widgery CJ.   *e*

Leolin Price QC and *C W Koenigsberger* for the taxpayers.
Patrick Medd QC and *Brian Davenport* for the Crown.

LORD WIDGERY CJ. There are two motions before us today. They raise
identical points and it is common ground between counsel that it suffices if the court   *f*
deals in terms with one. I take, therefore, the first motion concerning, as it does,
the Frank Rind settlement.
    Counsel moves on behalf of Samuel Conway and others ('the taxpayers'), who are
trustees of the Frank Rind settlement, and the relief sought is first an order of mandamus directed to the Commissioners for the General Purposes of Income Tax for
the division of Holborn in the county of London requiring them to state a case for   *g*
the opinion of the High Court of Justice pursuant to s 56 of the Taxes Management
Act 1970 on the giving by them of a certificate under s 88 of the 1970 Act, dated
14th August 1973, following a hearing by them of an application made to them as
such commissioners by an inspector of taxes under s 70(3) of the 1970 Act. The
grounds of that application are that the commissioners wrongly refused to state a
case. Alternatively, counsel moves for an order of certiorari to remove into this   *h*
court with a view to its being quashed the certificate to which I have already referred
given under s 88 of the 1970 Act.
    It is necessary to take the two applications separately, although the first does not
occupy a great deal of time. The matter arises out of s 88 of the 1970 Act. Section
88(1) provides:

    'Where an assessment has been made for the purpose of making good to the   *j*
    Crown a loss of tax wholly or partly attributable to the fraud, wilful default
    or neglect of any person, the tax charged by the assessment, or as the case may
    be such part thereof as corresponds to the part so attributable, shall carry interest
    at the precibed rate from the date on which the tax ought to have been paid
    until payment.'

a The section in its terms clearly contemplates that an assessment shall be made. The purpose of the assessment shall be the making good to the Crown of a loss of tax and that that loss shall be wholly or partly attributable to fraud, wilful default or neglect. The consequence, equally plainly stated, is that in such circumstances the tax so attributable will carry interest at the prescribed rate.

The powers, as it were, for bringing that section into effect are to be found in s 70(3):

b

'A certificate by the General or Special Commissioners that the tax or a specified part of the tax charged by an assessment specified in the certificate carries interest under section 88 of this Act from a date so specified shall be sufficient evidence of that fact in proceedings for the recovery of that interest. A certificate under this subsection shall not be given except on the application

c   of the inspector or the Board, and on any such application the person charged by the assessment (or, if he has died, his personal representatives) shall be entitled to appear and be heard.'

So what seems to be contemplated is that in a case which in the inspector of taxes' view falls within s 88, he or the board can apply for a certificate under s 70(3). When such

d an application is made, the taxpayer, the person to be affected by the certificate, is entitled to appear and be heard, and the General or Special Commissioners are required to adjudicate on the question of liability to pay interest under s 88 and to give a certificate if they are satisfied that such interest is payable.

All that happened in this case. The matter was referred to the commissioners for a certificate under s 70(3), and in this instance to the General Commissioners for

e the division of Holborn, and on 14th August 1973 they produced what purports to be a certificate of their conclusions. It is not necessary to say more about the certificate than that it follows the form of s 70(3). It sets out the date from which the interest is payable, and if that stands by itself it means that it is evidence of the obligation of the taxpayer to pay in accordance with the certificate.

The taxpayers, being dissatisfied with the conclusion of the General Commis-

f sioners on that issue, sought to take the matter to this court by means of an appeal by case stated. Section 56 of the 1970 Act provides for appeal from the commissioners to the High Court by means of special case, but that provision is only a part of what one can conveniently call the appellate machinery of the 1970 Act. Objection was taken by the commissioners that the particular proceeding before them was not an appeal, or to be treated as an appeal, for the purposes of the 1970 Act and that consequently no jurisdiction to state a case existed.

g On this aspect of the matter the commissioners have not attempted a conclusion on the merits. They have simply taken the view that on a true construction of the Act the right to appeal to the High Court by case stated does not apply to the proceedings which I have endeavoured to describe.

To find an answer to that one has to go to s 48 of the 1970 Act, which provides:

h   '(1) In the following provisions of this Part of this Act [and I pause to interpolate that in general terms those are the appellate provisions], unless the context otherwise requires—"appeal" means any appeal to the General Commissioners or to the Special Commissioners under the Taxes Act, "the Commissioners" means the General Commissioners or the Special Commissioners as the case may be.

i   '(2) The following provisions of this Part of this Act shall apply in relation to— (a) appeals other than appeals against assessments, and (b) proceedings which under the Taxes Act are to be heard and determined in the same way as an appeal, subject to the omission of section 56(9) below and to any other necessary modifications.'

The argument before us has shown that the issue on the motion for mandamus

really turns on whether the proceedings before the commissioners giving rise to the *a*
certificate under s 70(3) are proceedings which under the Taxes Acts are to be heard
and determined in the same way as an appeal.   If that phrase means that the appellate provisions are to apply to proceedings under the Taxes Acts which are conducted
in the same manner as an appeal, then of course there is a great deal to be said for
the proposition that they apply to the present case.

The proceedings under s 70(3) bear a marked resemblance to the general and *b*
appellate procedure under s 50 of the 1970 Act.   They contemplate, as I have already
indicated, a hearing.   They contemplate that the commissioners shall adjudicate
having heard both sides, and that is in substance the same kind of procedure which is
adopted for the ordinary appeals under the Act.   So if the true meaning of s 48 is
that the appeal procedure applies to any proceedings which are to be heard and
determined in the same sort of way as an appeal, then one would be minded to say *c*
that those appellate proceedings applied to the instant case.

There is, however, a strong argument the other way because, as we have shown
with the assistance of counsel, there are in fact a very large number of instances in
the Taxes Acts in which reference is specifically made to a hearing and a determination of an issue being done in the same way as an appeal.   The language is not always
exactly the same, but a few instances will serve to make good the submission that *d*
this is a common feature of the Taxes Acts.

If one looks at s 11(6) of the Income and Corporation Taxes Act 1970 one finds this
phrase: 'The Commissioners making any apportionment under this section shall
hear and determine the case in like manner as an appeal' and then it goes on to add
certain qualifications.   One has, in other words, an express reference in the section
to the proceedings being carried on in like manner as an appeal, and no doubt such *e*
proceedings would come within the terms of s 48 of the 1970 Act to which I have
referred.

One need not take time by going on to all the other instances we have been given:
ss 137(2), 138(2), 154(5) of the Income and Corporation Taxes Act 1970 and so on.
I have come to the conclusion in the end that when that phrase, or a phrase like it,
is in such common currency in these Acts, the proper conclusion is that when Parlia- *f*
ment spoke in s 48 of proceedings which under the Acts are to be heard and deter-
mind in the same way as an appeal it meant proceedings which are expressly in
the terms of the Acts to be so decided.   If that is the case, the present proceedings
are not capable of giving rise to an appeal by case stated and the commissioners
reached the right conclusion in my judgment, and accordingly the application for
mandamus in my opinion must fail.   *g*

That means that we must now consider the alternative motion for certiorari
because if the taxpayers cannot go to the High Court by case stated, then their only
course is to come before us as they have today asking that the order shall be quashed
on the basis either that it was made without jurisdiction or that it discloses an error
of law on the face of the record.

I have already described the form of the certificate which it is sought to quash. *h*
In addition to that the record, as placed before us, contains the reasons of the
commissioners stretching to some four to five closely typed pages of foolscap, and
two forms which were issued to the taxpayers requiring them to make certain returns
of the trust income or give other particulars.

It is not altogether easy to deal with reasonable brevity with the commissioners'
findings or the points of law which are said to arise out of them.   But I think it *j*
fair to summarise the commissioners' attitude in this way.   The evidence before
them showed that up to a date in May 1965 most of the trust income was income
which was paid subject to deduction of tax.   After 10th May 1965 much of the trust
income was income which was paid gross without deduction of tax.   As from that
date of course the return of the income received and due steps for payment of the
tax became of great importance.   The commissioners find, not surprisingly on the

a material before me, that over the next four or five years there was what has been
colloquially described in argument as a very considerable dragging of feet by the
taxpayers on whom the obligation to pay is said to rest. They did not make returns.
They were dilatory to say the least of it—and I am now reporting the views of the
commissioners—in attending to these matters. They accumulated this large income
which was received by them gross over a number of years, and it was some 3½ or
b four years before any sort of payment was made. Then the payment made was only
£40,000 in respect of each of the two settlements when the commissioners clearly
take the view that that was a figure which was less than justified by the
circumstances after all that delay.

In a sense one gets the pith of the commissioners' views from their very last sentence
of the reasons in which they say:

c   'The Commissioners noted that these persons of knowledge and experience
made no return of income for over five years after the 29th July 1965 and allowed
unpaid tax totalling over £210,000 to accumulate in their hands and so to be
available for their use, and then offered a payment of only £40,000 on account
for four years liability.'

d That is the sort of finding which the commissioners rely on in greater detail in the
remainder of their written reasons, and of course their written reasons were made as
a speaking order, and that entitles this court on an application for certiorari to examine
the reasons and see whether they are good in law.

Counsel for the taxpayers, to whom the court is much indebted for his assistance,
has taken five points. I find it convenient to look at those five points in a somewhat
e different order because, despite the efforts of counsel on both sides to discourage me
in taking this view, I have felt from the earliest times right up to now that the key
to the whole of this problem of whether the certificate was properly granted in law
or not is to discover the true meaning of the phrase 'loss of tax', which it will be
remembered is contained in s 88(1) of the 1970 Act.

I confess that if I were approaching this matter without any previous authority,
f and perhaps with somewhat greater experience of the subject than in fact I have,
I should have been very hesitant to accept that delay in paying tax was fairly to be
described as a loss of tax to the Revenue. It does not seem to me in my own un-
tutored mind that a loss of tax can be equated with the postponement of the payment
of tax, or, as has been said in the course of the commissioners' decision, a loss of the
use of the money presented by tax. I would, therefore, have been very happy to
g decide that loss of tax in s 88 is confined to the evasion type of case, that is to say a
case where the taxpayer deliberately conceals a portion of his income, completes his
return and has the assessment made on it without this source of income being disclosed. Then perhaps a year or so later, long after his tax affairs for the year had
been settled, there came to light this additional source of income.

I could understand, using the language in its ordinary sense, that it would be fair
h then to describe the Revenue as having lost that particular source of income for the
period in question. But I am satisfied that one cannot adopt that attitude. I am
satisfied that the expression 'loss of tax' must have a wider meaning, and I am really
compelled to take that view by a brief extract from the judgment of Stamp LJ in
Knight v Inland Revenue Comrs[1]. One need not go into the details of the Knight case[1] in
any length, but one finds Stamp LJ dealing with a submission, put forward
j coincidentally again by counsel for the Crown, which goes very close to the present
matter.

The court were very concerned with this same phrase 'loss of tax', and Stamp LJ
giving the judgment of the court said[2]:

1 [1974] STC 156
2 [1974] STC at 166,

'We accept counsel for the Crown's submission that the expression "loss *a* of tax" is not to be read as referring to a loss of tax suffered because an assessment is out of time or would be out of time unless attributable to fraud or wilful default. What is spoken of is "assessments . . . for the purpose of making good to the Crown any loss of tax attributable" etc, and we accept counsel for the Crown's submission that this means that the assessment may be made for the purpose of assessing to tax income which has not been taxed as the result of *b* the taxpayer having failed in his duty to make a return or a correct return and being tax which would have been assessed and become payable if he had made the return he should have made.'

It seems to me that looking at the matter as one of principle that that expression of view of the meaning of 'loss of tax' requires this court to treat the phrase as being wide enough to include tax the payment of which was ultimately secured but *c* the payment of which was delayed for an unreasonable time owing to the default of the taxpayer.

If it is right that that is the principle to be applied in construing this key phrase 'a loss of tax', I am unable to say that the commissioners in the instant case applied a wrong principle. Whether they got the solution right is a matter of fact and is not something which we can consider on certiorari, but it seems to me that they cannot *d* be faulted on the principle on which they have approached this phrase, and accordingly I can find no help from counsel for the taxpayers on that point, which was, I think, the fourth point in the submissions that he made before us.

The next point I would like to deal with is a very important and carefully presented argument, the essence of which is that there was no wilful default in this case and no opportunity for the commissioners finding wilful default because the only feature *e* of the case capable of being so described would be the failure on the part of the taxpayers to make a return of income.

Counsel for the taxpayers, I think, is minded to accept that if a taxpayer, having received the appropriate notice from the inspector of taxes, deliberately refuses to make a return, that is wilful default of the kind which we are considering. But he says, on the facts of this case, as apparent from the speaking order, there never was *f* a moment at which the taxpayers were obliged to make a return. If there never was a moment at which they were so obliged, it would follow no doubt that they could not be described as being guilty of default for not making it.

The argument depends primarily on s 8 of the 1970 Act, which is the section dealing with the returns and the inspector's right to require them. Subsection (2) provides: *g*

'Any person may be required by a notice given to him by an inspector or other officer of the Board to deliver to the officer within the time limited by the notice a return of income which is not his income, but in respect of which he is chargeable in any capacity specified in the notice, computed in accordance with the Income Tax Acts and specifying each separate source of income and the amount from each source.' *h*

Subsection (7) provides:

'Every return under this section shall include a declaration by the person making the return to the effect that the return is to the best of his knowledge correct and complete.'

Finally sub-s (8) provides: *j*

'In this section references to returns of income computed in accordance with the Income Tax Acts are references to returns which include, as well as all particulars relating to income from which tax has not been deducted, all particulars relating to income from which tax has been deducted before receipt, and relating to charges on income, which are required for computing total income for the *a*   purposes of the provisions of the Income Tax Acts relating to surtax or, as the case may require, to tax at the standard rate . . .'

That long sentence I think is a sufficient extract from sub-s (8) for present purposes.

Against that background it is clear from the speaking order that there were two documents sent, to take a neutral term, by the inspector to the taxpayers with a *b*   view to giving the inspector information about the trust.

The first document is one which has been referred to throughout argument as 'form 1', and that is a form similar to the one which most individual income taxpayers receive shortly after 5th April in each year. It requires the taxpayer to make the declaration reflected in s 8(7), i e that the particulars are correct. But in this instance (it may be in other instances as well) form 1 required a statement by its recipient not *c*   of all income from all sources but only income which was not taxed at source.

The other form 'form R59A', required a return of all income from all sources whether taxed at source or not, but this form did not require the person signing it to make a declaration contemplated by s 8(7).

So counsel for the taxpayers submits that in the result there never has been a single form sent by the inspector to the present applicants which complied with *d*   s 8, and thus set off, as it were, the obligation on the taxpayer to make his returns. He said that form 1 was defective because although it contained the declaration, it only dealt with part of the income of the trust, and form R59A was defective because although it contained all the income of the trust, it had not got the declaration.

It is an interesting point. Counsel for the Crown's answer on it is not to point out any specific extract from the 1970 Act which will provide the solution to the problem, *e*   but to submit that on its true construction s 8(2) is not as restrictive as counsel for the taxpayers would have us accept.

Counsel for the Crown says that is a subsection which provides the boundaries, as it were, within which the inspector can make his enquiries. Although the boundaries are wide enough to enable the inspector to ask for information as to income taxed at source as well as income not so taxed, counsel for the Crown says that one should not treat *f*   the section as requiring in every case that the information sought shall be comprehensive of all possible sources.

True the language of the section does seem to imply that what is contemplated is all income from all sources, but I am persuaded in the end by counsel for the Crown that one should regard sub-s (2) as permissive only, not mandatory, and its real purpose is to define the limits beyond which the inspector cannot go, and that the *g*   notice requiring the further income is not affected by sub-s (2) merely because it does not require all the taxpayer's relevant income to be disclosed at the same time.

Those are the two main points on certiorari, but certainly in deference to counsel for the taxpayer's argument I would wish to say a few words about the remainder. His first point was that the commissioners' decision was based on a great many irrelevancies. He points to the fact that the commissioners were obviously upset, *h*   amongst other things, at the fact that these taxpayers, when they came to make a payment on account, made a payment which the commissioners clearly thought was inadequate.

Counsel for the taxpayers says that the adequacy or inadequacy of a payment on account is neither here nor there when one is considering whether there has been a loss of tax within the meaning of s 88. I respectfully agree with him if one takes the *j*   matter in isolation   But I think the relevance of these findings in the present case is that if the commissioners concluded, as I think they could, that there had been a loss of tax, if they then moved on to see whether there had been wilful default, I think this kind of conduct and the general dragging of feet as previously described is relevant as showing the state of mind of the taxpayers. That is a matter which must be relevant on wilful default, if not in any other way.

Accordingly, although at one time I was tempted to think that the whole decision was vitiated by the commissioners having regard to a matter which they should *a* have disregarded, in the end I think that it was a matter properly within their comprehension as a factor going to the state of mind of the taxpayers.

Finally there is another submission which I doubt if I am alone in finding difficult on the basis of the restricted information which is before us in this case. Just before the relevant assessments were made the taxpayers had made substantial payments on account: £40,000 in respect of each of the two relevant settlements. Counsel *b* for the taxpayers says that even if one assumes against him that there was here a loss of tax properly recoverable by a new assessment as contemplated by s 88, yet if a payment on account had been made before the assessments were made, then the mischief had been corrected at all events in part and it was no longer competent on the inspector to make further assessments.

I find it difficult to answer this problem because the material before us does not *c* really show the relative size of the amounts charged against the payments on account, and I am certainly unable to say as a matter of law that a payment on account some three or four years after the delay began prevents the Revenue from raising assessments under s 88. It would be a very strange thing, as was pointed out in argument, if perhaps an evader of tax, who was perhaps at risk of assessment under s 88, could bring all the proceedings against him to a halt by tendering a payment on account. *d*

I am bound to say on this point that I am just not in a position to see how a principle of law has been breached on the bare facts which lie before us, and that means of course that on this ground also I am unable to support the submission of counsel for the taxpayers.

In my judgment all these four applications—two mandamus and two certiorari—must be refused. *e*

MILMO J. I agree and have nothing to add.

ACKNER J. I also agree.

Applications dismissed. *f*

Solicitors: *Brecher & Co* (for the taxpayers); *Solicitor of Inland Revenue.*

Rengan Krishnan Esq Barrister.

RCA Corporation and others v Reddingtons Rare Records *g*

CHANCERY DIVISION
GOFF J
4th OCTOBER 1974

h

Discovery – Interlocutory motion – Jurisdiction – Infringement of copyright – Defendant in possession of infringing copies – Plaintiffs seeking on motion order for disclosure of information as to suppliers – Strong prima facie case of infringement – Jurisdiction to order discovery on motion – Order limited to names and addresses known to defendant.

The plaintiffs brought an action to restrain the defendants from selling copies of *j* certain records and sound tracks in breach of copyright. They applied for interlocutory relief and in their notice of motion sought an order requiring the defendants to disclose by affidavit 'the names and addresses of all persons or companies responsible for supplying them with and to whom they had supplied . . . infringing copies'. The defendants did not appear and were not represented at the hearing of the motion.

a **Held** – The plaintiffs would clearly be entitled to discovery at the trial, provided that it was proved that there had in fact been the infringements alleged, and the court had power to grant such relief on motion as an interlocutory step in the action. Since there was strong prima facie evidence of infringement, an order for discovery would accordingly be made subject to the limitation that it extended only to the names of persons and companies known to the defendants.

b *Norwich Pharmacal Co v Comrs of Customs and Excise* [1973] 2 All ER 943 applied.

Notes

For procedure regarding discovery, see 12 Halsbury's Laws (3rd Edn) 17-21, paras 22-27, and for cases on the subject, see 18 Digest (Repl) 27-32, 206-253.

Case referred to in judgment

c *Norwich Pharmacal Co v Comrs of Customs and Excise* [1973] 2 All ER 943, [1974] AC 133, [1973] 3 WLR 164, HL; *rvsg* [1972] 3 All ER 813, [1972] 3 WLR 870, CA.

Case also cited

Orr v Diaper (1876) 4 Ch D 92.

d **Motion**

By notice of motion dated 30th September 1974 RCA Corpn, Phonogram Inc, Phonogram Ltd, MCA Records Inc and EMI Records Ltd, the plaintiffs in an action against the defendants, Reddingtons Rare Records (a firm), sought, inter alia, until judgment or further order: (1) an injunction restraining the defendants from doing without the licence of the plaintiffs any of the following acts: (a) parting with posses-

e sion power custody or control of sound recordings which were infringing copies of sound recordings and/or sound tracks associated with cinematographic films the copyright in which was vested in the plaintiffs or one or more of them or under the copyright in which the plaintiffs or one or more of them were exclusive licensees; (b) in any way altering, defacing, destroying or erasing sound recordings which were infringing copies; (c) selling or by way of trade offering or exposing for sale or dis-

f tributing for the purposes of trade sound recordings the making of which to the knowledge of the defendants constituted an infringement of the copyrights or one or more of them or would have constituted such an infringement if done in the United Kingdom; and (2) an order that the defendants make and serve in the plaintiffs' solicitors an affidavit setting forth the names and addresses of all persons or companies responsible for supplying them with and to whom they had supplied such infringing

g copies together with the date and quantities of each such supply and exhibiting to the affidavit copies of all documents in the defendants' possession, power, custody or control relating to such supply to or by the defendants.

Robin Jacob for the plaintiffs.
The defendants did not appear and were not represented.

h **GOFF J.** This is an action of a type which is very common at the moment in which the makers of gramophone records containing various kinds of what is known as 'pop music' sue defendants for selling 'pirated' copies. In the action the plaintiffs move for an injunction pending trial to restrain infringement. They have made a strong prima facie case and the defendants have not appeared to answer the case

j made against them. The plaintiffs, as I have indicated, are clearly entitled to relief on that head of their claim.

The plaintiffs are, however, in this type of case, very anxious to ascertain the source of the pirated copies so that they may take steps to establish their rights against the people who are making these records and not be confined simply to attacking retailers whom they find in various places selling the infringing records. The notice of motion therefore asks for—

'AN ORDER that the Defendants do make and serve upon the Plaintiffs' Solici- *a*
tors within 7 days of the date of the Order of this Honourable Court an affidavit
setting forth the names and addresses of all persons or companies responsible for
supplying them with and to whom they have supplied such infringing copies
together with the dates and quantities of each such supply and exhibiting to the
said affidavit copies of all documents in the Defendants' possession power custody
or control relating to such supply to or by the Defendants.'   *b*

It is clear, and the plaintiffs accept, that in any event that is too wide and must be
limited to names of persons and companies known to the defendants. But I have had
to consider the question whether the plaintiffs are entitled to relief of that nature. In
this type of case it has been granted in many instances by consent. It has never been
resisted and refused, but there is, at present, no case in which it has been sought where
the defendant has not appeared. It is clear in my judgment from the decision of the *c*
House of Lords in *Norwich Pharmacal Co v Comrs of Customs and Excise*[1] that the plaintiffs will, at the trial, be entitled to such relief, provided they prove there have in
truth been infringements, because the principle decided[2] by that case is that where a
person, albeit innocently and without incurring any personal liability, and a fortiori
if he himself is an infringer, becomes involved in the tortious acts of others, he comes
under a duty to assist one injured by those acts by giving him full information by way *d*
of discovery and disclosing the identity of the wrongdoers. For that purpose it matters
not that such involvement was the result of voluntary action or the consequence of
the performance of a duty statutory or otherwise.

The question, however, is whether such relief can be obtained on motion. There is
no authority conclusively dealing with that, but it seems to me, both on principle and
by analogy to the case cited[1], where relief was granted on an interlocutory application, *e*
that it is an order which can and, in an appropriate case, ought to be made on motion
as an interlocutory step in the action. That being so, there being in this case strong
prima facie evidence that there has been infringement, and since the defendants must
know the names of people from whom they have obtained the records, it is in my
view appropriate to make the order sought with the one limitation I have mentioned,
that it extends only to names known to the defendants.   *f*

Order accordingly.

Solicitors: *A E Hamlin & Co* (for the plaintiffs).

F K Anklesaria Esq Barrister. *g*

---

1 [1973] 2 All ER 943, [1974] AC 133
2 [1973] 2 All ER at 948, [1973] AC at 175, per Lord Reid

The Distillers Co (Biochemicals) Ltd v Times Newspapers Ltd
The Distillers Co (Biochemicals) Ltd v Phillips

QUEEN'S BENCH DIVISION

Applied in RIDDICK V THAMES BOARD
BOARD MILLS [1977] 3 All ER 677

TALBOT J

17th, 18th, 19th, 20th, 21st, 24th, 25th, 26th, 27th JUNE, 31st JULY 1974

Discovery – Production of documents – Confidence – Implied undertaking – Third party – Public interest in disclosure of information – Implied undertaking by party obtaining discovery not to use documents for collateral purpose – Duty of third party to whom documents passed – Documents disclosed by defendants in action passed to newspaper publishers – Action raising matters of general public interest – Publishers proposing to publish article dealing with matters raised by action – Article making use of information obtained from defendants' documents – Article critical of defendants – Public interest in proper administration of justice – Whether publishers under a duty not to use documents for purpose other than purpose for which discovery made – Whether publishers entitled to use documents for ulterior purpose when disclosure in public interest.

The plaintiffs secured the right to market a drug, thalidomide, in the United Kingdom. In consequence of the injuries suffered by children whose mothers had taken the drug during pregnancy the plaintiffs became involved in a number of actions brought against them by the children and their parents ('the claimants'). During the proceedings the plaintiffs disclosed on discovery approximately 30,000 documents, of which the claimants bespoke some 10,000. A chemist, P, was retained by the claimants to advise them and the claimants' solicitors handed over to him a large number of the 10,000 documents. Subsequently P entered into an agreement with the defendants, who were newspaper publishers, to sell them the documents, the copy documents and his own documents derived from them for an agreed sum. Having obtained those documents the defendants published a number of articles in their newspapers that were critical of the plaintiffs. The defendants were restrained from publishing a further article in proceedings for contempt of court[a]. The plaintiffs were supplied with a copy of that article and in consequence they became aware that the defendants were in possession of documents and material which belonged to the plaintiffs. They brought an action against the defendants and applied for an interlocutory injunction restraining the defendants from using or disclosing the documents. The defendants contended that publication of the documents would not constitute a breach of any duty which they might owe as a result of the disclosure of the documents to them by P and that in any event publication of articles based on the documents was justified in the public interest.

Held – (i) There was an implied undertaking on discovery that the documents disclosed would not be used for any collateral or ulterior purpose. Furthermore that undertaking was binding on anyone into whose hands the documents might come if he knew that the documents had been obtained by way of discovery. It was a matter of public interest that documents disclosed on discovery should not be permitted to be put to improper use and that the court should give its protection to prevent such use (see p 46 c and e, p 47 e and p 48 f to h, post); *Prince Albert v Strange* (1849) 1 Mac & G 25, *Williams v Prince of Wales Life etc Co* (1857) 23 Beav 338, *Alterskye v Scott* [1948] 1 All ER 469, *Duchess of Argyll v Duke of Argyll* [1965] 1 All ER 611 and *Fraser v Evans* [1969] 1 All ER 8 applied.

---

a   See *Attorney-General v Times Newspapers Ltd* [1973] 3 All ER 54, [1974] AC 273

(ii) The only competing right that the defendants could advance was that there *a*
was a public interest in the disclosure of the documents which overrode the public
interest in the protection of documents disclosed on discovery. Although the
thalidomide story, and any light that it could throw on the matter which might obviate
the occurrence of similar events in the future, was a matter of public interest, that
interest did not outweigh the public's interest in the proper administration of justice
which required that the confidentiality of discovery documents should be protected. *b*
Accordingly the injunction would be granted (see p 49 *h* to p 50 *b* and p 52 *a* and *b*,
post).

Notes
For the implied undertaking not to use documents produced on discovery for a
collateral or ulterior purpose, see 12 Halsbury's Laws (3rd Edn) 34, para 49, and for
cases on undertakings as to the use of documents produced, see 18 Digest (Repl) *c*
63, 494-497.
For the grant of injunctions to restrain the disclosure of confidential information,
see 21 Halsbury's Laws (3rd Edn) 395, 396, para 825, and for cases on the subject, see
28(2) Digest (Reissue) 1081-1090, 868-917.

Cases referred to in judgment   *d*
Albert (Prince) v Strange (1849) 1 Mac & G 25, 1 H & Tw 1, 18 LJCh 120, 12 LTOS 441,
   13 Jur 109, 41 ER 1171, 1 Digest (Repl) 50, 368.
Alterskye v Scott [1948] 1 All ER 469, 18 Digest (Repl) 55, 421.
Argyll (Margaret), Duchess of v Duke of Argyll [1965] 1 All ER 611, [1967] Ch 302, [1965]
   2 WLR 790, Digest (Cont Vol B) 448, 875c.
Ashburton (Lord) v Pape [1913] 2 Ch 469, [1911-13] All ER Rep 708, 82 LJCh 527, 109 *e*
   LT 381, CA, 22 Digest (Reissue) 236, 2033.
Attorney-General v Times Newspapers Ltd [1973] 3 All ER 54, [1974] AC 273, [1973]
   3 WLR 298, HL.
Beloff v Pressdram Ltd [1973] 1 All ER 241, [1973] RPC 765.
British Oxygen Co Ltd v Liquid Air Ltd [1925] Ch 383, 95 LJCh 81, 133 LT 282, 13 Digest
   (Repl) 55, 55.   *f*
Church of Scientology of California v Kaufman [1973] RPC 635.
Fraser v Evans [1969] 1 All ER 8, [1969] 1 QB 349, [1968] 3 WLR 1172, CA, Digest (Cont
   Vol C) 173, 487a.
Gartside v Outram (1856) 26 LJCh 113, 28 LTOS 120, 3 Jur NS 39, 18 Digest (Repl)
   115, 973.
Hubbard v Vosper [1972] 1 All ER 1023, [1972] 2 QB 84, [1972] 2 WLR 389, CA.   *g*
Initial Services Ltd v Putterill [1967] 3 All ER 145, [1968] 1 QB 396, [1967] 3 WLR 1032, CA,
   Digest (Cont Vol C) 564, 873h.
Jones v Pacaya Rubber & Produce Co Ltd [1911] 1 KB 455, 80 LJKB 155, 104 LT 446,
   18 Mans 139, CA, 9 Digest (Repl) 351, 2249.
S v Distillers Co (Biochemicals) Ltd, J v Distillers Co (Biochemicals) Ltd [1969] 3 All ER 1412,
   [1970] 1 WLR 114, Digest (Cont Vol C) 287, 165h.   *h*
Saltman Engineering Co Ltd v Campbell Engineering Co Ltd (1948) [1963] 3 All ER 413,
   65 RPC 203, CA, 12 Digest (Reissue) 778, 5536.
Truth and Sportsman Ltd, Re, ex parte Bread Manufacturers Ltd (1937) 37 SRNSW 242,
   54 NSWWN 98, 9 Digest (Repl) 75, *98.
Weld-Blundel v Stephens [1919] 1 KB 520, 88 LJKB 689, 120 LT 494, CA; *affd* [1920]
   AC 956, [1920] All ER Rep 32, 89 LJKB 705, 123 LT 593, HL, 45 Digest (Repl) 296, 139. *j*
Williams v Prince of Wales Life &c Co (1857) 23 Beav 338, 3 Jur NS 55, 53 ER 133, 18
   Digest (Repl) 63, 497.

Motion
By a writ issued on 2nd November 1972 the plaintiffs, The Distillers Co (Biochemicals)
Ltd, brought an action against the defendants, Times Newspapers Ltd, claiming

a (1) an injunction restraining the defendants by their servants, agents or otherwise from using or disclosing any documents or copy documents in the possession, power or custody of the defendants, their servants or agents or any of the information contained in any such documents, which (a) were documents disclosed in the discovery of documents made in the action *S v Distillers Co (Biochemicals) Ltd*[1] by the plaintiffs (as the defendants in that action), or (b) were documents which were copies

b of or based on or contained information from any of the documents referred to in (a), or (c) were documents belonging to the plaintiffs and/or in respect of the contents of which the plaintiffs were the owners of the copyright, or (d) were documents which the defendants, their servants or agents had obtained as a result of a breach or breaches of a duty of confidence owed to the plaintiffs by the person or persons from whom whether directly or indirectly the defendants, their servants or agents

c had obtained such documents, or which the defendants, their servants or agents had obtained in circumstances such that the defendants had become subject to a duty of confidence towards the plaintiffs; and (2) an order that the defendants deliver up forthwith to the plaintiffs all the documents referred to in (1) above and also forthwith deliver up to the plaintiffs or destroy all copies of any such documents in the possession, power or custody of the defendants, their servants or agents. By an

d order made on 9th January 1973 that action was consolidated with an action commenced by a writ issued on 30th November 1972 by the plaintiffs claiming similar relief against Helena May Matilda Phillips, the representative of the estate of Montague A Phillips deceased, who, the plaintiffs alleged, had obtained the documents in question as an expert in the action and had retained them in breach of the duty of confidence owed to the plaintiffs or the contents of which he had made available

e to others in breach of that duty. By notice of motion the plaintiffs applied for an interlocutory injunction against the defendants, Times Newspapers Ltd, in terms similar to the injunction claimed in the writ. The hearing and judgment were in chambers and the judgment is published with the permission of Talbot J subject to the deletion of certain passages and the substitution therefor of the words printed in square brackets. The facts are set out in the judgment.

f
John Wilmers QC and *David Sullivan* for the plaintiffs.
Brian Neill QC and *Charles Gray* for the defendants.

Cur adv vult

g 31st July. **TALBOT J** read the following judgment. In this application the plaintiffs claim an interlocutory injunction against the defendants to restrain them from using or disclosing certain documents. By their statement of claim they allege that the defendants are in possession of a number of documents or copies of documents which are the property of the plaintiffs. By reason of matters which I shall hereinafter deal with, the plaintiffs claim that the defendants are not entitled

h to publish or make use of any of these documents or of the copies.
  This action arises as a result of litigation in which the plaintiffs have been and are involved in respect of the drug thalidomide which they marketed from April 1958 until 27th November 1961. The drug was discovered by a German firm, Chemie Grunenthal, and by agreement with that firm the plaintiffs obtained the right to market it in the United Kingdom and other countries. The name they chose for

j this drug was Distaval.
  The sad and terrible results of the drug taken by pregnant women are well known to require any description from me. The result was that the plaintiffs became involved in a number of actions brought by the unfortunate children and their parents. The first writ was issued on 7th November 1962 in the action *S v*

---

1 [1969] 3 All ER 1412, [1970] 1 WLR 114

Distillers Co (Biochemicals) Ltd[1]. In the course of that action the plaintiffs disclosed *a*
on discovery some 30,000 documents of which the solicitors of the claimants (as
I will so describe the plaintiff and other claimants) bespoke some 10,000. There
was retained on behalf of the claimants in order to advise them, a chemist, Dr Phillips,
and in order to enable him to advise the claimants their solicitors handed over to
Dr Phillips a large number of the 10,000 documents bespoken by them.

The claimants' action continued on its way and the claimants were joined by a *b*
number of other plaintiffs until there were some 62 actions which eventually came
before Hinchcliffe J[1] on 19th February 1968 when a settlement was approved. I
shall deal a little later with the settlement that was arrived at on that date. In
the meanwhile it appears that Dr Phillips had entered into an agreement with the
defendants to sell to them the documents, the copy documents and his own documents derived therefrom. This agreement was made on 6th February 1968 and it *c*
appears that Dr Phillips agreed to supply to the defendants all the information
whether in documentary form or otherwise that he had in his possession in return
for which the defendants agreed to pay Dr Philips a sum totalling £5,000; it appears
that he was paid £1,000 on 19th January 1968. Later in 1968 the plaintiffs discovered
that Dr Phillips had come into possession of a number of their documents which
they had disclosed in the claimants' action and accordingly, by a letter dated 6th *d*
November 1968, the plaintiffs' solicitors wrote to Dr Phillips asking him for an
undertaking that he would not use for publication of any kind their clients' documents or dispose of such material. On 16th December 1968 Dr Phillips replied to
the plaintiffs' solicitors saying that he was quite willing to give such an undertaking
until such time as he had received advice. Dr Phillips has since died, and cannot
therefore answer such queries as arise, but of this there is no doubt that on 6th *e*
February 1968 he sold, inter alia, to the defendants, the plaintiffs' documents and
on 16th December 1968 he dissembled when he wrote the letter of that date.

Sometime in 1972, on behalf of the claimants in the actions against the present
plaintiffs, the defendants published a number of articles on this matter and in particular they wished to publish an article which features largely in the matter before
me. They had sent a copy of this article to the Attorney-General and as a result the *f*
Attorney-General moved the Divisional Court on 17th November 1972 for an injunction to prevent the defendants publishing this article on the ground that it was a
contempt of court. The Divisional Court[2] granted the injunction. It was discharged
by the Court of Appeal[3] on 16th February 1972 but restored by the House of Lords[4]
on 25th July 1973. A copy of this article was also supplied to the plaintiffs, and they
became aware that the defendants were in possession of a number of documents *g*
and material which belonged to them. On 18th October 1972 the plaintiffs' solicitors
wrote to the solicitors for the claimants asking them to take immediate steps to
obtain all the documents which they had made available to Dr Phillips, who had by
that time died. The claimants' solicitors replied on 19th October saying that they had
written to Dr Phillips on 17th April 1968 pointing out that the documents which they
had made available to him so that he could advise must not be supplied to third *h*
parties. The matter was taken up by the plaintiffs' solicitors with the defendants by
letter of 27th October; by that time the defendants had returned to the claimants'
solicitors certain documents which they had received from Dr Phillips. The plaintiffs,
however, were concerned as appears from their solicitors' letter that there should
be returned to them all documents emanating from their discovery in the claimants'
action and all copies or extracts from such documents, or that such copies or extracts *j*
should be destroyed and that no use should be made from the information supplied
to the defendants by Dr Phillips.

---

1 [1969] 3 All ER 1412, [1970] 1 WLR 114
2 [1972] 3 All ER 1136, [1972] 3 WLR 855
3 [1973] 1 All ER 815, [1973] QB 710
4 [1973] 3 All ER 54, [1974] AC 273

a   The plaintiffs then commenced the present action by writ dated 2nd November 1972. By letter dated 10th November the defendants gave an undertaking to the plaintiffs' solicitors that they would not use any of the documents the subject of the action or any information contained in the documents, save only for the purposes of taking legal advice in the proceedings.

b   The application for an injunction now comes before me because by letter dated 4th March 1974 the defendants' solicitors informed the plaintiffs that the defendants had decided that they would terminate the undertaking given in the letter of 10th November 1972.

To return to the history relevant to this matter, I mentioned that 62 actions came before Hinchcliffe J on 19th February 1968. The settlement arrived at was that the plaintiffs agreed to pay 40 per cent of the value of each claim which was subsequently *c*   arrived at. I should mention that the claimants had had the best possible advice, and at the time of the settlement mentioned before Hinchcliffe J they were advised by a number of counsel, the leader of whom was Mr Ackner, now Ackner J. For the defendants there appeared Mr Kerr, now Kerr J and other counsel and it is important to note that one of the terms of the settlement was that all allegations of negligence against the defendants were unreservedly withdrawn.

d   Since that settlement it is necessary to observe that many new writs on behalf of alleged malformed children have been issued, to the number from 1968 to 1973 of 262. It is the plaintiffs' complaint in this matter that not only have the defendants had in their possession the plaintiffs' confidential documents, which is admitted, but also that they have made use of such confidential information in order to write the article, which is also admitted. It is also pointed out by the plaintiffs that the *e*   affidavit sworn on behalf of the defendants by Mr Knightly, the author of the article, is largely based on the documents which the defendants bought from Dr Phillips. It is the plaintiffs' case that the defendants have no right to make use of their documents or of any information derived therefrom, that they are confidential documents which they were compelled to produce under an order for discovery and the court therefore should protect them. 123 of these documents are exhibits to the affidavit *f*   of Mr Knightly and they may generally be described as memoranda, reports and letters, all dealing with the drug Distaval, the name under which the plaintiffs had marketed the drug.

Perhaps the principal reason why the plaintiffs complain of the defendants' use of their material is that the defendants are unfairly critical, that they have mis-reported the documents which they have used, that they have selected information *g*   from the documents to support their criticism of the plaintiffs and that they have suppressed other material which has relevance to the matters contained in the defendants' critical article. The plaintiffs further point out that the defendants knew that Dr Phillips had been retained in the litigation by the claimants as an expert adviser, that they knew that Dr Phillips had access to the documents in question in his capacity as such adviser, that they knew that the documents were discovery *h*   documents and that it must follow that the defendants were prepared to pay and did pay for these documents and so procure a breach of confidence on the part of Dr Phillips. It seems to me, that on the evidence, all these matters have been proved. The plaintiffs therefore claim that the defendants should be restrained from making use of their confidential documents and information and furthermore that the documents are subject to copyright by virtue of s 4 of the Copyright Act *j*   1956. The defendants in support of their claim that they are entitled to make use of the information that they have derived from these documents principally allege that the publication of these documents would not constitute any breach of any duty which they might owe as a result of the disclosure to them by Dr Philips of these documents, and that in any event publication of the proposed article based on these documents is justified in the public interest. They further deny that such publication would constitute an infringement of the plaintiffs' copyright or,

alternatively, they allege that the publication would be fair dealing with a literary *a*
work within s 6(2) and (3) of the 1956 Act.

Counsel for the plaintiffs made a number of submissions. First he said that it is an
established principal that a party to litigation is under an obligation not to make
improper use of documents disclosed in an action, i e as a result of compulsory
process of law. That process, he pointed out, was in itself an invasion of a private
right to keep one's documents to oneself. Next he submitted that disclosure of *b*
such documents for purposes other than the litigation in question is an improper use.
He cited two cases and a passage in Bray on Discovery[1]. The first authority was
Alterskye v Scott[2]. In that case the defendant complained that the plaintiff had made
an improper use of documents disclosed in the action and asked for an undertaking
before making a further and better affidavit. Jenkins J said[3], and indeed it was not
disputed, that there is an implied undertaking on discovery that the documents *c*
disclosed will not be used for any collateral or ulterior purpose. Jenkins J continued[4]:

'The defendant must rely on the implied obligation not to make improper
use of the documents. If he can substantiate improper use in any particular
case, he has his remedy. He can bring that instance of alleged improper use
before the court either on proceedings for contempt, if he considers that it *d*
amounts to contempt of court, or on proceedings to restrain the conduct
complained of.'

The next case was *Williams v Prince of Wales Life &c Co*[5] in which Romilly MR
said: '. . . it is not the right of a Plaintiff, who has obtained access to the Defendants'
papers, to make them public. The Court has granted injunctions to prevent it.'

The next submissions were that anyone who himself receives such disclosed *e*
documents is under the same duty and anyone who receives such disclosed documents
can be in no better position if he knows the origin of the documents to be the product
of discovery. Counsel for the plaintiffs relied on a number of authorities for these
propositions. The first was *Lord Ashburton v Pape*[6]. In that case an action was
brought by the plaintiff to restrain the defendant from disclosing letters or copies
of them which the defendant had obtained; the defendant had obtained them from *f*
the clerk of the plaintiff's solicitors, a Mr Mockton. Swinfen Eady LJ said[7]:

'The principle upon which the Court of Chancery has acted for many years has
been to restrain the publication of confidential information improperly or
surreptitiously obtained or of information imparted in confidence which ought
not to be divulged. Injunctions have been granted to give effectual relief, that *g*
is not only to restrain the disclosure of confidential information, but to prevent
copies being made of any record of that information, and, if copies have already
been made, to restrain them from being further copied, and to restrain persons
into whose possession that confidential information has come from themselves
in turn divulging or propagating it.'

In *Prince Albert v Strange*[8] the defendant had obtained from others some impres- *h*
sions of drawings and etchings belonging to HRH Prince Albert and there was a
claim for an injunction to restrain the defendant from, inter alia, taking or making
copies and publishing a catalogue of them. Lord Cottenham LC pointed out in

---

1   (1885), p 238
2   [1948] 1 All ER 469
3   [1948] 1 All ER at 470, 471
4   [1948] 1 All ER at 471
5   (1857) 23 Beav 338 at 340
6   [1913] 2 Ch 469, [1911-13] All ER Rep 708
7   [1913] 2 Ch at 475, [1911-13] All ER Rep at 711
8   (1849) 1 Mac & G 25

j

a his judgment that the only answer was that the defendant did not know or believe that the copies had been improperly obtained, but he found they were in fact obtained in breach of trust, confidence or contract and that would entitle the plaintiff to an injunction. It is important to note that Lord Cottenham LC considered that the injunction should issue against the defendant into whose hands the impressions had come. Further assistance is gained from *Fraser v Evans*[1]. A confidential report

b made by the plaintiff to the Greek Government had been surreptitiously obtained and got into the hands of a Sunday newspaper and the plaintiffs sought an injunction to prevent publication. One of the grounds was that it was a confidential document. Dealing with this aspect, Lord Denning[2], citing *Prince Albert v Strange*[3] and *Argyll v Argyll*[4], said that those cases showed that in a proper case the court would restrain the publication of confidential information. He went on to say:

c   'The jurisdiction is based, not so much on property or on contract, but rather on the duty to be of good faith. No person is permitted to divulge to the world information which he has received in confidence, unless he has just cause or excuse for doing so. Even if he comes by it innocently, nevertheless, once he gets to know it was originally given in confidence, he can be restrained from breaking that confidence.'

d
    In *Argyll v Argyll*[4] Ungoed-Thomas J applied the principle to communications being between husband and wife and held that an injunction would be granted to restrain publication not only by the person who was party to the confidence but by other persons into whose possession that information came.
    Counsel for the plaintiffs' next proposition, which I would put as one of great

e importance, was that the protection of discovery documents is paramount in the public interest for the proper administration of justice; if discovery were to result in documents becoming public the process of discovery would be in danger. He referred here to the speeches of their Lordships in the contempt proceedings *Attorney-General v Times Newspapers Ltd*[5] in which the high importance of the proper administration of justice was stressed. Lord Reid[6] quoted Jordan CJ in *Re Truth and*

f *Sportsman Ltd, ex parte Bread Manufacturers Ltd*[7]:

       'It is of extreme public interest that no conduct should be permitted which is likely to prevent a litigant in a court of justice from having his case tried free from all matters of prejudice.'

    Lord Diplock said[8]:

g   'My Lords, in any civilised society it is a function of government to maintain courts of law to which its citizens can have access for the impartial decision of disputes as to their legal rights and obligations towards one another individually and towards the state as representing society as a whole. The provision of such a system for the administration of justice by courts of law and the main-tenance of public confidence in it are essential if citizens are to live together in

h   peaceful association with one another.'

    Of course, there has to be balanced against this public interest, other public interests, such as, in the contempt case, freedom of speech, and other matters of public concern. Counsel for the plaintiffs then went on to deal with the competing public

1 [1969] 1 All ER 8, [1969] 1 QB 349
j 2 [1969] 1 All ER at 11, [1969] 1 QB at 361
3 (1849) 1 Mac & G 25
4 [1965] 1 All ER 611, [1967] 2 Ch 302
5 [1973] 3 All ER 54, [1974] AC 273
6 [1973] 3 All ER at 61, [1974] AC at 296
7 (1937) 37 SRNSW 242 at 249
8 [1937] 3 All ER at 71, [1974] AC at 307

interests. His submission was that when one considers the need that litigants who a
made discovery should feel that their interests would be fully protected, there was
no room for a higher public interest. It is on this submission that the principal issue
between the parties lies. He referred me to *Saltman Engineering Co Ltd v Campbell
Engineering Co*[1]. In that case the defendant had come into possession of drawings
and tools for the manufacture of leather punches belonging to the plaintiffs, and the
defendants had used them for their own purposes. Lord Greene MR held that there b
was a confidential obligation in relation to the drawings as between the plaintiffs
and the defendants and he approved a formulation of the law in these terms[2]:

> 'If a defendant is proved to have used confidential information, directly or
> indirectly obtained from a plaintiff, without the consent, express or implied
> of the plaintiff, he will be guilty of an infringement of the plaintiff's rights.'
c

It is 'a fortiori', said counsel for the plaintiffs, where the defendant was compelled by
law to produce his documents in an action.

His final submissions on this part of the case related to the matters which must be
taken into account if there has to be a balancing of public interest. It was, he said,
for the defendant to show that the balance was in their favour and that there was such
a strong public interest that it outweighed the public interest that the plaintiffs rely d
on. He claimed that the court should take into account the manner in which the
defendants acquired the documents and also the use the defendants intend to make
of them and that if the use is substantially unfair to the plaintiffs the degree of public
interest diminishes, as the court cannot approve, as in the public interest, what might
amount to an attack on the plaintiffs and unfair use of their confidential material.
The court must, he submitted, take into account that the claimants in the various e
actions, having received the most expert advice based partly on all the disclosed
documents, including the advice of Dr Phillips, decided to accept the terms of settlement and absolve the plaintiffs in this action from all negligence.

These submissions can therefore be summarised as follows. (1) The plaintiffs
claim an overriding protection from publication and use of their documents which
they were compelled to disclose in the action against them. They claim this pro- f
tection involves those in whose hands the documents come, particularly where the
possession was unlawfully obtained. I do not doubt the correctness of this proposition; I do not think that on the authorities and for the proper administration of
justice it can be argued to the contrary. Those who disclose documents on discovery
are entitled to the protection of the court against any use of the documents otherwise
than in the action in which they are disclosed. I also consider that this protection g
can be extended to prevent the use of the documents by any person in whose hands
they come unless it be directly connected with the action in which they are produced.
I am further of the opinion that it is a matter of importance to the public, and therefore of public interest, that documents disclosed on discovery should not be permitted
to be put to improper use and that the court should give its protection in the right
case. h

Save as to questions of copyright and the defence of fair dealing, I consider that
the only competing right that the defendants can advance is that there is a public
interest that is so high that it overrides the public interest which protects documents
disclosed on discovery.

Before turning to this problem I will deal with the issue of confidentiality as dealt
with in a line of cases beginning with *Gartside v Outram*[3]. The proposition is that j
there are some confidential communications which should not be protected by the
courts. In this case the plaintiffs' clerk had taken documents which he alleged

1 [1963] 3 All ER 413
2 [1963] 3 All ER at 414
3 (1856) 26 LJCh 113

a showed fraudulent transactions on the part of the plaintiffs. On the question of
the confidentiality of the documents Wood V-C said[1]:

'The true doctrine is, that there is no confidence as to the disclosure of iniquity.
You cannot make me the confidant of a crime or a fraud, or be entitled to close
up my lips upon any secret which you have the audacity to disclose to me relating
b to any fraudulent intention on your part: such a confidence cannot exist.'

This question was further extensively considered in *Weld-Blundell v Stephens*[2]. In that
case a letter containing instructions to the defendant, a chartered accountant, also
contained statements defamatory of two persons. The defendant's partner carelessly
left the letter in such a place that it came into the hands of those two persons. The
plaintiff having had to pay damages for his defamation, sued the defendant for
c breach of an implied duty to keep secret the letter of instruction, and the court held
that there was such a duty. The defendant had argued that he had been under no
such duty as any such obligation would be contrary to public policy. Bankes LJ
drew a clear distinction between confidential communications as to the proposed
commission of a crime or civil wrong where there would be a duty of disclosure,
and such communications as to the fact that a crime had been committed where, as
d in the case of a solicitor and client, there would be no duty to disclose. Warrington
LJ's view is expressed thus[3]:

'On the whole I can see no reason founded on public policy or any other ground
why an agent should be at liberty to disclose evidence of a private wrong
committed by his principal.'

e Scrutton LJ found nothing contrary to public policy in an agreement to use reasonable
care not to disclose statements prima facie libellous of others, and distinguished
Gartside v Outram[4] where the court declined to exercise its equitable jurisdiction
to restrain a clerk from disclosing his employers' frauds.

The next authority which I turn to for guidance is *Initial Services Ltd v Putterill*[5]
where it was held that the exceptions to the implied obligation of a servant not to dis-
f close information or documents received in confidence extended to any misconduct of
such a nature that it ought in the public interest to be disclosed to one who had a
proper interest to receive it. Lord Denning MR[6] held that the limitation of the
exception by Bankes LJ in *Weld-Blundell v Stephens*[7] to proposed or contemplated crime
was too limited. The exception he held should extend to crimes, frauds and misdeeds
actually committed as well as those in contemplation, and disclosure must be to one
g who has a proper interest to receive the information. Later in his judgment[8],
speaking of the servant's position and what he should do if his master told him to
keep quiet, he said:

'I say nothing as to what the position would be if he disclosed it out of malice or
spite or sold it to a newspaper for money or for reward. That would indeed
h be a different matter. It is a great evil when people purvey scandalous
information for reward.'

Pausing here in my summary of the cases cited, counsel for the plaintiffs, in my
view, rightly points out that the facts of the present case are widely different. There

j 1 (1856) 26 LJCh at 114
2 [1919] 1 KB 520
3 [1919] 1 KB at 535
4 26 LJCh 113
5 [1967] 3 All ER 145, [1968] 1 QB 396
6 [1967] 3 All ER at 148, [1968] 1 QB at 405
7 [1919] 1 KB 520
8 [1967] 3 All ER at 149, [1968] 1 QB at 406

is here no crime or fraud or misdeed on the part of the plaintiffs, and in my view _a_
negligence, even if it could be proved, could not be within the same class so as to
constitute an exception to the need to protect confidentiality. But in fact counsel
for the defendants in his final address said that it was no part of the defendants' case
to say that a case of negligence against the plaintiffs would have succeeded. What
counsel submitted was that there was such a wide and vital public interest involved
that it overrode the plaintiffs' private right to confidentiality and the public interest _b_
involved in protecting documents disclosed in an action.

In _Hubbard v Vosper_[1] Lord Denning MR stated the principles already referred to
whereby confidential information will be protected and in the unusual circumstances
of that case, there were, in the view of the court, good grounds for thinking that it
was in the public interest to publish the information. This seems to me to be rather
a special case as the material was even on first view so dangerous that it was in the _c_
public interest that it should be made known.

A similar case was _Church of Scientology of California v Kaufman_[2]. Finally, there
is _Beloff v Pressdram Ltd_[3] where Ungoed-Thomas J held[4] that the authorities showed
that public interest might justify disclosure of—

> 'matters carried out or contemplated, in breach of the country's security,
> or in breach of law, including statutory duty, fraud, or otherwise destructive _d_
> of the country or its people, including matters medically dangerous to the
> public; and doubtless other misdeeds of similar gravity.'

I would say that nothing that the plaintiffs did would bring them within these
categories so as to entitle their confidential information to be published.

The question therefore is have the defendants shown that there is a competing public _e_
interest which overrides the plaintiffs' private rights and the public interest arising out of
discovery. Before embarking on a consideration of this I must consider the article.
[His Lordship then considered certain passages of the draft article, found them to be
inaccurate, and continued:] I now must consider the competing public interests
involved in this case as shown from the exhibits and affidavits. I must stress, however, that I have only to decide this on the basis of what the plaintiffs have to prove. _f_
Taking the principles from Lord Denning MR's judgment in _Hubbard v Vosper_[1],
the plaintiffs have to prove a strong prima facie claim to their right or rights, and
secondly an arguable case that the defendants have infringed their rights or are about
to infringe them. Thirdly, Lord Denning MR said[5]:

> 'In considering whether to grant an interlocutory injunction, the right course
> for a judge is to look at the whole case. He must have regard not only to the _g_
> strength of the claim but also to the strength of the defence, and then decide
> what is best to be done.'

Megaw LJ said[6]:

> 'Each case must be decided on a basis of fairness, justice and common sense _h_
> in relation to the whole of the issues of fact and law which are relevant to the
> particular case.'

Finally on this point I must remind myself of the words of Buckley LJ in _Jones v
Pacaya Rubber and Produce Co Ltd_[7]:

---

1   [1972] 1 All ER 1023, [1972] 2 QB 84   _j_
2   [1973] RPC 635
3   [1973] 1 All ER 241
4   [1973] 1 All ER at 260
5   [1972] 1 All ER at 1029, [1972] 2 QB at 96
6   [1972] 1 All ER at 1031, [1972] 2 QB at 98
7   [1911] 1 KB 455 at 457

a
'In all cases of applications for interlocutory injunctions the governing principle is that pending the settlement of the dispute between the parties the Court will as far as possible keep matters in statu quo.'

Counsel for the defendants poses this question: is the administration of justice so important that everything else has to be swept aside, and he said that if this is so these documents will be shut up for ever and there will be a bar on them, which
b
operates for ever. He points out that there has never been any public inquiry, but the fact is, apparently, that 25 members of Parliament tried to get such an inquiry and did not succeed, and there has been no such demand since. In any event, as counsel for the plaintiffs says, a public inquiry with an independent tribunal, hearing both sides, is a vastly different proposition from letting the defendants make such use of the plaintiffs' documents as they think fit.
c
Counsel for the defendants lists 16 questions which would have to be put to such an inquiry which he claims should be investigated in the public interests. They involve the general state of scientific knowledge from 1956 to 1958, the knowledge and experience of Chemie Grunenthal, the reliance placed by the plaintiffs on that company, the tests carried out by the plaintiffs and their research into medical and
d
scientific literature, the obtaining of clinical reports and whether the plaintiffs exercised influence on those making reports, the plaintiffs' knowledge at each stage, the experience and strength of their staff and their facilities, the steps taken by the plaintiffs to keep the medical profession and the people informed, whether the views of the medical and scientific staff of the plaintiffs were subordinated to the management and sales staff views, what part commercial considerations played in the mar-
e
keting and advertising, steps taken by the plaintiffs to ensure that adverse reports reached them, the date when the plaintiffs and the DCBA first learned of teratogenic births, the responsibility of a multi-national company for a subsidiary, what discussion did the plaintiffs have with the Ministry of Health and, finally, why has no public inquiry been held.

Counsel for the defendants then embarked on a detailed examination of the
f
documents in order to seek to support the need for the questions to be investigated, arguing in each case that the matter was so vital that the public interest demanded an inquiry. I do not think that it will be of assistance to me to set out in detail the nature of the documents and the way in which it is suggested they support his thesis, nor the counter arguments put forward by counsel for the plaintiffs; this would not assist the parties nor anyone else who may have to consider this judgment. In the
g
end the decision must be one which a judge reaches by considering the matter as a whole, and not by making individual decisions in respect of each point taken. [His Lordship then referred to certain of the 123 documents exhibited to Mr Knightley's affidavit and continued:] The arguments ranged over these 123 documents and what place they took in the suggested questions for inquiry. Counsel for the plaintiffs pointed out that these are not matters for public inquiry but are matters for the
h
claimants who have had these and many thousands of other documents, and who have been given the highest and most expert advice on them. No one can doubt that the thalidomide tragedy has been, is, and may well be for some time, a matter in which the public is deeply interested. What the defendants wish to do, counsel for the defendants says, is (1) to publish either a series of articles or a book based on the material they have; (2) to seek to put the material before Lord Pearson's Commis-
j
sion on Compensation for Personal Injuries; (3) to make the documents available to claimants who did not get them from the plaintiffs, e g claimants outside the country.

As to (2) and (3) the plaintiffs say that Lord Pearson's Commission has never asked for any of their documents and the claimants can get hold of the documents if they bring proceedings and obtain discovery. As to (1), the plaintiffs say that the defendants, judging from what has gone before, are not the most suitable persons to present an unbiassed examination of all the facts.

Whilst as I have said the public have a great interest in the thalidomide story *a*
(and it is a matter of public interest) and any light that can be thrown on this matter
to obviate any such happening again is welcome, nevertheless the defendants have
not persuaded me that such use that they proposed to make of the documents which
they possess is of greater advantage to the public than the public's interest in the
need for the proper administration of justice, to protect the confidentiality of discovery documents. I would go further and say that I doubt very much whether *b*
there is sufficient in the use which the defendants have proposed to raise a public
interest which overcomes the plaintiffs' private right to the confidentiality of their
documents. In any event I consider that the plaintiffs have established their right (this
is not really disputed) and have an arguable case to protect it by an injunction.

I will now deal with copyright. It is not disputed that the plaintiffs have the copyright in some of the documents. Two questions arise: (1) have the defendants shown *c*
that what they propose is fair dealing for the purposes of criticism or review under
s 6(2) of the Copyright Act 1956? (2) have the defendants shown that what they
propose is fair dealing for the purpose of reporting current events in a newspaper?
I will take number (1) first. In *Hubbard v Vosper*[1] Lord Denning MR said that
under the defence of fair dealing one may criticise not only the style of the work but
the thoughts underlying it. Counsel for the plaintiffs argues that criticisms of the *d*
plaintiffs marketing the drug is not criticism of underlying ideas; counsel for the
defendants submits to the contrary. I would think that a fair criticism of all the
ideas and events described in the documents could be fair dealing. A question
arises, however, whether such criticism would be permissible insofar as the plaintiffs'
documents might be said not to have been published. Romer J in *British Oxygen
Co Ltd v Liquid Air Ltd*[2] was of the opinion that any criticism of an unpublished work *e*
without the consent of the author would not be fair dealing. Lord Denning MR in
Hubbard v Vosper[1] thought that this went too far in that a literary work may not be
published to the world at large but it may have been circulated to such a wide circle
that it is fair dealing to criticise it publicly. For my part I doubt whether the plaintiffs' documents could be said to have been circulated so widely that, though not
published generally, it is fair dealing to criticise them. So also on s 6(3) of the 1956 *f*
Act there is the question whether the events described in the documents are current
events. I am inclined to the view that they are not despite counsel for the defendants'
argument that the effects of thalidomide are still apparent and that earlier discussion
has been prevented by the sub judice rule. In any event the plaintiffs have a right
which is not disputed and have an arguable case on 'fair dealings'.

Finally, there is the question whether an interlocutory injunction should be granted. *g*
I am strongly of the view that it should; to do so will not cause the defendants any
loss whereas not to do so might cause irreparable harm to the plaintiffs, and to use
the words of Lord Cottenham LC in *Prince Albert v Strange*[3] 'postponing the injunction
would be equivalent to denying it altogether'.

Injunction granted.   *h*

Solicitors: *Wilkinson, Kimbers & Staddon* (for the plaintiffs); *Denton, Hall & Burgin*
(for the defendants).

                                                    E H Hunter Esq Barrister.

                                                                                  j
_____

1 [1972] 1 All ER 1023, [1972] 2 QB 84
2 [1925] Ch 383
3 (1849) 1 Mac & G 25 at 47

Kenilworth Industrial Sites Ltd v E C Little & Co Ltd

COURT OF APPEAL, CIVIL DIVISION

MEGAW, LAWTON AND ORMROD LJJ

23rd OCTOBER 1974

Landlord and tenant – Rent – Review – Notice – Time limits – Failure to comply with time limits – Effect – Clause providing machinery for determination of rent for specified period of term – No other provision in lease for rent during that period – Notice to operate clause to be given by landlord within specified time limits before termination of preceding period of term – Failure of landlord to give notice within time limits – Validity of notice given subsequently.

The landlords granted the lease of factory premises to the tenants for a term of 21 years from 19th January 1968. Clause 1 provided that the rent was to be £2,980 per annum for the first five years and thereafter 'a rent to be agreed as hereinafter mentioned in clause 5 hereof'. Clause 5 provided: 'NOT more than twelve months nor less than six months before the expiration of the fifth tenth and fifteenth years of the term the Landlord shall serve upon the Tenant a notice to agree the rent of the said property for the ensuing five years ...' The clause provided for the determination of the new rent by arbitration in default of agreement and was subject to a proviso 'that any failure to give or receive such notice shall not render void the right of the Landlord hereunder to require the agreement or determination as aforesaid of a new rent'. The landlords failed to serve a notice before 18th July 1972, which was the date six months before the expiration of the first five years, but served a notice on 10th October 1972. The tenants rejected that notice, contending that the provisions of cl 5 were in essence to be regarded as being of the nature of an option and that a term should be implied into the lease that if the landlords failed within the stated time to give the notice seeking agreement or arbitration then the rent which was payable in the preceding period should continue to be the rent to be paid during the succeeding five years.

Held – There was no ground for implying such a term in the lease for it would be inconsistent with the express provisions of cll 1 and 5. The proviso to cl 5 could not be ignored, for it was not inconsistent with the opening words of cl 5, and if it was not ignored there was no reason to imply the term suggested. It was impossible to treat cl 5 as being of the nature of an option and therefore the special principles of law applicable to options, requiring strict adherence to time limits, did not apply. On the true construction of the lease it was clear that a failure by the landlords to comply with the requirement that they should serve the notice to agree the rent within a particular time did not have the effect of precluding them from validly requiring agreement or arbitration to fix the rent after that time had elapsed (see p 55 *g* to p 56 *b*, post).

Decision of Megarry J [1974] 2 All ER 815 affirmed.

Notes

For agreements to review rents subject to a time limit for giving notice, see Supplement to 23 Halsbury's Laws (3rd Edn) para 1197, and for a case on the subject, see 31(1) Digest (Reissue) 481, 3952.

Appeal

This was an appeal by the defendants, E C Little & Co Ltd ('the tenants'), against the judgment of Megarry J[1] given on 21st January 1974 whereby it was declared

---

1   [1974] 2 All ER 815, [1974] 1 WLR 1069

that on the true construction of a lease dated 19th January 1968 made between the   *a*
plaintiffs, Kenilworth Industrial Sites Ltd ('the landlords'), and the tenants, a notice
contained in a letter dated 10th October 1972 from the landlords to the tenants
operated as a valid notice to agree the rent for the second five years of the term created
by the lease for the purposes of cl 5 thereof.   The facts are set out in the judgment
of Megaw LJ.

b

Edwin Prince for the tenants.
C P F Rimer for the landlords.

MEGAW LJ. This is an appeal from the judgment of Megarry J[1] delivered on
21st January 1974. The matter arises out of an originating summons taken out
by the landlords for a declaration affecting the proper amount of rent payable under   *c*
a lease existing between the landlords and the tenants.
    The facts of the matter are short and simple.   There was a lease dated 19th January
1968 between the landlords and the tenants.   The lease concerned a property in
Farmer Ward Road, Kenilworth, in the county of Warwick, containing factory
premises.   By cl 1 of the lease it was provided that in consideration of the rent thereinafter reserved the landlords demised to the tenants the premises set out in the   *d*
schedule for the term of 21 years from 19th January 1968, the tenants paying therefor
yearly until 18th January 1973 the rent of £2,980, and thereafter 'a rent to be agreed
as hereinafter mentioned in clause 5 hereof'.   Clause 5 provides as follows:

    'NOT more than twelve months nor less than six months before the expiration
    of the fifth tenth and fifteenth years of the term the Landlord shall serve upon
    the Tenant a notice to agree the rent of the said property for the ensuing five   *e*
    years and thereupon the parties hereto shall agree a new rent as aforesaid and fail-
    ing agreement such rent shall be determined by a single arbitrator to be appointed
    by the President of the Royal Institute [sic] of Chartered Surveyors whose de-
    cision shall be binding and final on the parties hereto PROVIDED always that such
    new rent shall not be lower than the rent payable in respect of the premises
    for the last year of the term before such determination of the new rent AND   *f*
    PROVIDED always that any failure to give or receive such notice shall not
    render void the right of the Landlord hereunder to require the agreement or
    determination as aforesaid of a new rent.'

    It would seem that by inadvertence the landlords failed to give notice, as contem-
plated by the opening words of cl 5, within the period provided by those opening   *g*
words.   They ought to have given to the tenants such notice to agree the rent for
the ensuing five years not later than six months before the expiration of the fifth
year of the term.   The expiration of the fifth year of the term was at 18th January
1973; the notice therefore ought to have been given before 18th July 1972.
    In fact no notice was given purporting to be under cl 5 until 10th October 1972.
On that date the landlords sent to the tenants a notice which said: *h*

    'In accordance with your Lease, the rent is to be reviewed and the new rent
    charged from the 18th January 1973.   We propose that the new rent for the
    premises be £6,176·00 per annum.'

That, it is to be observed, was an increase from the figure of £2,980 per year provided for the first five years of the lease.   The letter went on: 'If you are not in   *j*
agreement with this figure perhaps you will instruct your Surveyor to contact the
writer.'
    On 18th October 1972 that notice was in substance rejected by the tenants who
wrote back saying:

a   'Under Clause 5 of the Lease, there is a provision for the rent to be reviewed but Notice requiring the rent to be reviewed must be served not more than 12 months nor less than 6 months before the expiration of the fifth year.'

So issue was joined, and that was the issue which was decided by Megarry J[1] in favour of the landlords. The tenants appeal to this court against that decision. The tenants say that on the true construction of the lease, taking into account cll 1 and 5,

b   the landlords had lost their right to seek agreement or, in the absence of agreement, decision by arbitration, of a new and higher rent for the second five years of the lease, because they had failed to observe the requirements of cl 5 requiring that they should serve notice on the tenants within the period stated.

It is clear on the terms of the lease, from its own express words, that the rent fixed in cl 1 was for the first five years of the lease and for those five years only. If, there-

c   fore, cl 5, for some reason or other, could not be operated, then it would seem that the consequence under the express terms of the lease would be that no rent at all would be payable, at any rate for the next five years, and possibly not for the remaining 16 years of the lease. That, however, would be to ignore altogether the second proviso to cl 5, which again appears to say, in quite clear terms, that any failure to give or receive a notice shall not render void the right of the landlords to require

d   the agreement of a new rent. That must include, as being a failure to give such a notice, a failure to give notice within the time specified in the opening words of the clause. The proviso, if it has any effect at all, is saying that, even though the time specified in the opening words of the clause may not have been observed by the landlords, and the landlords are thereby in breach of that provision of the contract, nevertheless that breach of the contract by them shall not render void their right

e   to have the new rent for the succeeding five years agreed or, in the absence of agreement, determined by arbitration.

Counsel for the tenants submits, as he submitted to the learned judge, that the provisions of cl 5 are in their essence, though not so expressed, to be treated as being an option. If the lease failed to make provision for any rent to be payable in the absence of notice being given within the proper time, then plainly there would not

f   be the alternative which would be necessary to constitute an option. But, says counsel for the tenants, it is proper and necessary to imply into this lease the provision that if the landlords fail within the stated time to give the notice seeking agreement or arbitration, then the rent which was payable in the preceding period shall continue to be the rent to be paid during the succeeding five years.

   For myself, I am quite unable to see that there is any valid basis for implying such

g   a term in this lease. It would, in my judgment, be inconsistent with the express provisions of cll 1 and 5, whether read separately or together. Moreover, the provisions of the second proviso cannot, in my judgment, be ignored, and if they are not ignored there is no reason for implying such a term.

Counsel for the tenants concedes, as I understand his argument, that if, on the true view, cl 5 is not to be regarded as being of the nature of an option, then he

h   cannot complain of the learned judge's decision. In my judgment, it is impossible to treat cl 5 as being of the nature of an option, and therefore the special principles of law which no doubt affect options, in relation to the necessity for maintaining time limits and other conditions, do not apply. Further, there is no reason for ignoring the second proviso. It is not inconsistent with the provisions of the opening words of the clause. It is, to my mind, clear on this agreement, as the learned judge held,

j   that a failure by the landlords to comply with the provisions of the opening words of cl 5 that they shall serve the notice within a particular time does not have the effect of precluding them from thereafter, outside that specified time, validly requiring such agreement or arbitration.

For those reasons, which are, I think, completely in accordance with the reasons *a*
given by the learned judge in the court below[1]—a judgment with which I entirely
agree—I have come to the conclusion that this appeal is without substance and
should be dismissed.

LAWTON LJ. I agree with the judgment delivered by Megaw LJ, and I have
nothing to add.   *b*

ORMROD LJ. I agree.

Appeal dismissed.
                                                                                       c
Solicitors: *Martin & Nicholson*, agents for *Pitt & Derbyshire*, Sutton Coldfield (for
the tenants); *White & Leonard* (for the landlords).

                                    Mary Rose Plummer Barrister.

                                                                                       d

Practice Direction

CHANCERY DIVISION   *e*

*Practice – Chancery Division – Lists – Revision of system for listing causes and matters –
Appointment of clerk of lists.*

*Practice – Chancery Division – Lists – Witness list – Allocation of cause or matter to Part 1
or Part 2 – Fixing of dates for trial – Alteration or vacation of fixed date – Settlement, with-*   *f*
*drawal or discontinuance of actions – Duty to keep clerk of lists informed of developments –
Publication of lists – Warned list.*

*Practice – Chancery Division – Lists – Non-witness list – Publication of warned list – Applica-
tions to fix dates for hearing – Duty to give clerk of lists information relevant to length
of hearing.*   *g*

Arrangement of the Chancery lists
    1. The system of listing causes and matters (hereinafter called 'actions') for
hearing by the judges of the Chancery Division is to be revised, with the object of
ensuring (a) greater flexibility, (b) the avoidance of wastage of the judges' time and
(c) greater speed.   It is not proposed to abolish Part 1 and Part 2 of the Witness List, *h*
but actions in these parts will be more readily interchangeable.   This direction has
no application to actions to be heard outside the Royal Courts of Justice.
    2. (a) Mr E S F Lee (Room 165, Royal Courts of Justice) has been appointed Clerk
of the Chancery Lists.   He will co-ordinate the hearings of actions in the Witness
and Non-Witness Lists, long procedure summonses and certain long chamber summonses.   (b) At present the appointment is experimental.   Further responsibilities *j*
may be given to the clerk of the lists as time goes on.   At present he will not be
responsible for (i) hearings in the Companies Court, the Bankruptcy Court, the Court
of Protection, the Revenue List, the Short Probate List and the Special List (for applications under RSC Ord 113), or (ii) actions governed by RSC Ord 103 (Patent Actions

---

1 [1974] 2 All ER 815, [1974] 1 WLR 1069

a etc), or (iii) chambers and procedure summonses, when the dates for hearing are fixed by the masters , and actions to be tried before masters pursuant to RSC Ord 36, r 9, or (iv) actions attended by the district registrars of Liverpool, Manchester or Preston, but he will co-operate with all others concerned with listing so that there may be no overlapping or confusion.

3. Counsel are reminded of their duty (see practice directions of 2nd April 1954[1],
b and 5th April 1972[2], para 2) to supply promptly certificates stating the length of time that the trial of any action in the Witness List is expected to occupy, and to revise them promptly should circumstances change. This is of cardinal importance to all listing. Failure to give certificates has in the past resulted in delay. In future, should any counsel fail to give his certificate within 10 days after setting down, the certificate of the other counsel instructed in the action will be accepted on
c notification of the default to the clerk of the lists.

The Witness List

4. The following directions will apply to actions set down for hearing in the Witness List:

(1) (a) When an action is set down for hearing in the Witness List it will as previously
d be allocated to the Witness List Part 1, if the provisional estimate of length of hearing, made by the Master in the order for setting down, is of over three days, and to the Witness List Part 2 if such provisional estimate is of three days or less. An action will be re-allocated to Part 1 or Part 2 if counsels' certificate of length of hearing is to the effect that, contrary to the master's provisional estimate, it is likely to last more than three days or not more than three days as the case may be. Actions in each
e part of the list will be numbered in sequence according to the dates on which they first appear in that part, and will be re-numbered on any re-allocation; and the date of setting down will be noted against each action. (b) Subject to the provisions of sub-paras (2), (3) and (4) below actions will be liable to be heard at any time after the expiration of 28 days from the date of setting down in either part of the list, or earlier if a judge or master has given a direction to that effect or if the parties agree
f and time is available.

(2) (a) Within 28 days after an action has been set down in Part 1 of the Witness List any party may give notice to the clerk of the lists and to all other parties of his intention to apply to fix a date for the trial of the action. (b) Dates for trial will not normally be fixed for actions set down in Part 2 of the Witness List, but in special circumstances this may be done on application to the clerk of the lists as in sub-para 2 (a)
g above. If the application succeeds the action will be transferred to Part 1. The judge who is appointed to try actions in Part 2 will nevertheless be in control of such actions throughout the term for which he is appointed.

(3) (a) On the hearing of an application for a fixed date the clerk of the lists may, after taking into account the wishes of the parties, the circumstances of the case and the state of Part 1 of the Witness List—(i) fix a date for the trial of the action; or
h (ii) direct that the case shall come on for trial on a specified date, subject to the actions already fixed for hearing on that date; or (iii) subject to the consent of the parties, direct that the action be marked not to come on for trial before a specified date, keeping its numerical number in the list; or (iv) subject to the consent of the parties, direct that the action is not heard without a specified number of weeks' or days' notice to the parties to be given by him. If none of these courses is taken the action
j will be liable to appear in the Warned List at any time after 28 days from setting down. (b) The clerk of the lists may alter or vacate a fixed date—(i) if any party so applies to him after giving one day's notice in writing to all other parties, or if all parties apply jointly; or (ii) if any revised estimate of length of hearing makes it

---

1 [1954] 1 All ER 946, [1954] 1 WLR 693
2 [1972] 2 All ER 599, [1972] 1 WLR 723

necessary to do so; or (iii) if any circumstances arise which make it unlikely that there *a*
will be an effective hearing on the fixed date; or (iv) if the state of the list prevents
the date previously fixed from being kept. So far as practicable the Clerk of the
Lists will not alter or vacate a fixed date without giving the parties an opportunity of
being heard.

(4) If any party is dissatisfied with any decision by the clerk of the lists, that party
may, on giving one clear day's notice in writing to the other party or parties, apply *b*
to the judge in charge of Part 1 of the Witness List to vary that decision. Such application must be made within seven days of the making of the decision by the clerk of
the lists. On the hearing of such application the judge may give such directions on
such terms as to costs or otherwise as he thinks fit.

(5) (a) When an action in the Witness List is settled, or thought likely to be settled,
or is withdrawn or discontinued, or when the estimate of length of trial is varied, it *c*
is the duty of the solicitors for the parties so to inform the clerk of the lists in writing
forthwith. (b) When such an action is settled but the parties wish to obtain an order
by consent from a master all parties must notify the clerk of the lists in writing of
that fact and the clerk of the lists will thereupon take the case out of the list and
notify the master that he has done so. The master may then make such order as
may be necessary for the disposal of the action. But nothing in this sub-paragraph is *d*
to prevent the parties from applying to the judge for an order by consent if they so
prefer.

(6) Seven days before the date for which an action is fixed for trial or, if no date
has been fixed, within seven days of the action appearing in the Warned List, the
solicitors for the plaintiff (or, if the plaintiff is in person, the solicitors for the first
named of the defendants who have appeared by solicitors) must inform the clerk *e*
of the lists (by personal attendance, writing or telephone) whether the case is likely
to run its full estimated course or is likely to be disposed of in some summary way.
In the latter event the solicitors must keep the clerk of the lists informed of any
developments in the situation immediately they occur.

(7) Any application to the judge in charge of Part 1 of the Witness List must be *f*
made at the sitting of the court or at such other time as the judge directs.

(8) (a) By the beginning of each term the clerk of the lists will publish a list showing
under separate headings the actions set down for hearing in each part of the Witness
List, with the dates, if any, fixed for hearing. (b) Subsequently at intervals of four
weeks during each term the clerk of the lists will publish a list of all actions which,
since the publication of the previous list (i) have been given fixed dates for hearing in *g*
Part 1 of the list or (ii) have been set down in either part of the list.

(9) By the beginning of each term, and subsequently on each Friday of each term,
the clerk of the lists will publish a Warned List for the following week, showing the
actions in each part of the Witness List liable to be heard during that week and the
dates (if any) fixed for hearing. Any such action for which no date has been fixed
will be liable to appear in the list for hearing without any further warning than the *h*
next day's cause list posted outside Room 136, Royal Courts of Justice each afternoon.

(10) If an action is not ready for hearing by the date it is called on for trial it will,
unless the judge otherwise directs, be put at the bottom of the list.

The Non-Witness List   *j*

5 (1) When an action is set down in the Non-Witness List the cause clerk will transmit the papers to the clerk of the lists. The action may come on for hearing at any
time after setting down as judges become available, without any warning other than
the posting of the next day's cause list outside Room 136, Royal Courts of Justice.
The clerk of the lists will nevertheless at or before the beginning of each term and on
each Friday of each term, publish a Warned List of all actions remaining in the

a Non-Witness List except such as have been stood over generally or are otherwise temporarily ineffective.

(2) Applications to fix dates for hearing of actions in the Non-Witness List may be made to the Clerk of the Lists, in accordance with para 4(3) and (4) above, substituting the judge in charge of the Non-Witness List for the judge in charge of Part 1 of the Witness List.

b (3) (a) Parties need not supply a certificate of estimated length of hearing in respect of an action set down in the Non-Witness List, but the solicitors for all parties must on request give the clerk of the lists all such information relevant to the length of hearing as he may require, and must, without any request, inform him in writing of any settlement, anticipated settlement, withdrawal or discontinuance. (b) Paragraph 4(5)(b) above also applies to actions set down in the Non-Witness List.

c
Chambers and procedure summonses
6. Reference is made to the practice direction[1] issued on 5th November 1974.

Cancellation and modification of former practice directions
7. The following practice directions are cancelled to the following extent:
d (1) Direction of 2nd April 1954[2]; the whole, except for para 2. (2) Direction of 9th March 1966[3]; the whole. (3) Direction of 9th March 1966 (sic)[4]; the whole. (4) Direction of 18th February 1969[5]; the whole, except for para 2. (5) Direction of 18th April 1969[6]; para 1 and first sentence of para 2. (6) Direction of 27th February 1970[7]; second sentence of para 1 and paras 5 and 6, and in para 4 substitute a reference to the clerk of the lists for the reference to the cause clerk, and delete the rest of the *e* paragraph. (7) Direction of 15th December 1970[8]; para 2. (8) Direction of 5th May 1972[9]; paras 1, 3 and 4. (9) Direction of 31st July 1972[10]; the whole. (10) Direction of 24th November 1972[11]; the whole. (11) Direction of 3rd May 1973[12]; the whole. (12) Direction of 16th July 1974[13]; the whole.

By the direction of the Vice-Chancellor.

f
25th November 1974

R E BALL
Chief Master

1 [1974] 3 All ER 880
2 [1954] 1 All ER 946, [1954] 1 WLR 693
3 *Practice Note* [1966] 1 All ER 916, [1966] 1 WLR 538
g 4 [1966] 2 All ER 720, [1966] 1 WLR 1125
5 *Practice Note* [1969] 1 All ER 787, [1969] 1 WLR 322
6 [1969] 2 All ER 1132, [1969] 1 WLR 1257
7 *Practice Note* [1970] 1 All ER 904; the references are to paras 2, 6, 7 and 4 respectively of the note as set out in [1970] 1 WLR 525
8 [1971] 1 All ER 64, [1971] 1 WLR 78
9 [1972] 2 All ER 599, [1972] 1 WLR 723
h 10 [1972] 3 All ER 254, [1972] 1 WLR 1194
11 [1973] 1 All ER 30, [1972] 1 WLR 1652
12 [1973] 2 All ER 422, [1973] 1 WLR 658
13 [1974] 3 All ER 177, [1974] 1 WLR 1119

Re Hennessey's Agreement
Hillman v Davison

CHANCERY DIVISION
PLOWMAN V-C
7th OCTOBER 1974

*Landlord and tenant – Residential property – Security of tenure – Statutory protection –
Agreement purporting to exclude statutory provisions void – Statute not preventing surrender
of tenancy – Surrender – Agreement to surrender in futuro – Agreement giving landlord
option to purchase residue of term in certain events – Agreement by tenant to surrender
tenancy in those events – Whether agreement to surrender tenancy in futuro void by virtue
of statute – Landlord and Tenant Act 1954, s 17.*

By an agreement in writing the landlord agreed to grant a lease to the tenant of
three rooms of a house for the term of 99 years from 25th March 1961 at a premium
and a low ground rent.   Clause 7 provided (a) that if at any time during the term the
tenant wished to vacate the premises he should forthwith give notice to the landlord
and (b) that if at any time during the term the landlord wished to sell the house with
vacant possession she should forthwith give notice to the tenant.   In either of those
events the landlord would have an option to purchase the residue of the term from
the tenant for a specified sum.   A lease was executed in pursuance of the agreement.
Subsequently the tenant, who wished to carry out certain alterations to the premises,
took out a summons seeking a declaration that the options contained in cl 7 of the
agreement were void and of no effect by virtue of s 17[a] of the Landlord and Tenant
Act 1954.   It was common ground that the plaintiff's tenancy was within the
protection of Part I of the 1954 Act.

Held – Although s 17 provided that nothing in Part I of the 1954 Act was to be construed as preventing the surrender of a tenancy, that meant an actual surrender of
the tenancy; an agreement to surrender the tenancy in futuro was caught by the
earlier provision of s 17 that the provisions of Part I were to have effect notwithstanding any agreement to the contrary.   Clause 7 constituted an agreement by the
tenant that he would, on the occurrence of certain events in the future, surrender
the tenancy.   Should the events come about which gave rise to one of the options,
the landlord would, on the exercise of that option, be entitled to vacant possession.
That implied a surrender of the tenancy in order to enable the landlord to acquire
vacant possession.   Accordingly, the options in cl 7 were void by virtue of s 17 (see
p 64 *b* to *d* and *f*, post).

Joseph v Joseph [1966] 3 All ER 486 applied.

Notes

For determination of a term of years by surrender, see 23 Halsbury's Laws (3rd Edn)
683-690, paras 1412-1419; and for contracting out of the Landlord and Tenant Act
1954, see ibid 883, para 1705.   For cases on the subject of surrender in futuro, see
31(2) Digest (Reissue) 876-877, 7275-7278.

For the Landlord and Tenant Act 1954, s 17, see 18 Halsbury's Statutes (3rd Edn)
745.

Cases referred to in judgment

De Vries v Sparks (1927) 43 TLR 448, 137 LT 441, 25 LGR 497, DC, 31(2) Digest (Reissue)
1087, 8475.

---

a   Section 17 is set out at p 62 *a*, post

a *Fenner v Blake* [1900] 1 QB 426, 69 LJKB 257, 82 LT 149, DC, 31(2) Digest (Reissue) 866, 7183.
Joseph v Joseph [1966] 3 All ER 486, [1967] Ch 78, [1966] 3 WLR 631,CA, 31(2) Digest (Reissue) 940, 7707.

Adjourned summons

b By an originating summons dated 19th April 1974, the plaintiff, Mayer Hillman, sought a declaration that, on their true construction, the options contained in cl 7 of an agreement for sale dated 26th April 1961, and made between the defendant, Brenda Trevor Davison (otherwise Degerdon), of the one part and the plaintiff of the other part, were void and of no effect. The facts are set out in the judgment.

c *W A Blackburne* for the plaintiff.
P St J Langan for the defendant.

PLOWMAN V-C. This originating summons raises a question as to the validity of certain options contained in an agreement for a lease dated 26th April 1961, made between the present defendant as vendor and the plaintiff as purchaser. The agree-
d ment was one for the grant of a lease by the defendant to the plaintiff of three rooms on the top floor of 44 Primrose Hill Road, NW3, for a term of 99 years from 25th March 1961 at a premium of £2,500 and a ground rent of £25 per year. That agreement contained the following provisions in cl 7:

'It is hereby mutually agreed by the Vendor and the Purchaser:—(a) That if
e the Purchaser shall at any time during the term granted by the said Lease wish to vacate the said premises he shall forthwith give to the Vendor notice of such his desire and the Vendor shall have an option (such option to be exercised within 3 months of the receipt of such notice) to purchase the residue of the term granted by the said Lease from the Purchaser for the sum of Two thousand five hundred pounds (£2,500) such sum to be paid as to One thousand pounds on
f the exercise of such option and as to the balance of One thousand five hundred pounds by equal half yearly instalments over two years. (b) That if the Vendor shall at any time during the term granted by the said Lease wish to sell the said building with vacant possession she shall forthwith give to the Purchaser notice of such her desire and the vendor shall have an option (such option to be exercised within 3 months of the receipt of such notice by the Purchaser) to purchase the
g residue of the term granted by the said Lease from the Purchaser for the sum of Two thousand five hundred pounds. PROVIDED THAT the exercise by the Vendor of such options shall not prejudice her rights against the Purchaser under the said Lease in respect of any antecedent breach of any of the Tenant's covenants therein contained.'

h The agreement for a lease to which I have referred was followed on 7th July 1961 by a lease which did not, however, mention the options which were contained in the agreement. The reason why this originating summons has been brought is this: that the plaintiff wants to spend a lot of money—the sum of £5,000 has been men-tioned—on doing alterations to the premises, but he wants to know what his legal position is having regard to the terms of those options before he spends that money
j on the premises. I am satisfied that in bringing these proceedings he is not motivated by any desire to repudiate the bargain into which he has entered, but has brought them for the reason I have mentioned. I should say that he offers, whatever the result of the proceedings, to pay the defendant's costs.
It is common ground that the plaintiff's tenancy is one within the protection of Part I of the Landlord and Tenant Act 1954. It is submitted on behalf of the plaintiff that the options are void as infringing s 17 of the 1954 Act. Section 17 provides:

'The provisions of this Part of this Act shall have effect notwithstanding any   *a*
agreement to the contrary: Provided that nothing in this Part of this Act shall
be construed as preventing the surrender of a tenancy.'

It was submitted by counsel for the plaintiff that while the proviso to s 17 says that
'nothing in this Part of this Act shall be construed as preventing the surrender of a
tenancy', that means an actual surrender and does not include an agreement to
surrender. He submitted that an agreement to surrender is within the earlier part   *b*
of s 17 and that both the options which were conferred by the agreement for a lease
are, in effect, agreements to surrender which are of no effect.

Counsel for the plaintiff drew my attention to analogous provisions in Part II
of the 1954 Act. Section 24 provides:

'(1) A tenancy to which this Part of this Act applies shall not come to an end   *c*
unless terminated in accordance with the provisions of this Part of this Act; and,
subject to the provisions of section 29 of this Act, the tenant under such a tenancy
may apply to the court for a new tenancy—(a) if the landlord has given notice
under section 25 of this Act to terminate the tenancy, or (b) if the tenant has
made a request for a new tenancy in accordance with section 26 of this Act.
'(2) The last foregoing subsection shall not prevent the coming to an end of a   *d*
tenancy by notice to quit given by the tenant, by surrender or forfeiture . . .'

unless certain things which are set out in the two paragraphs are found to exist.
Then s 38(1)—which is also in Part II of the 1954 Act—says:

'Any agreement relating to a tenancy to which this Part of this Act applies
(whether contained in the instrument creating the tenancy or not) shall be void   *e*
[(except as provided by subsection (4) of this section)] in so far as it purports to
preclude the tenant from making an application or request under this Part of
this Act or provides for the termination or the surrender of the tenancy in the
event of his making such an application or request or for the imposition of any
penalty or disability on the tenant in that event.'

The words in that subsection, 'purports to preclude the tenant' were construed by   *f*
the Court of Appeal in the case to which I will refer in a moment, *Joseph v Joseph*[1] as
meaning 'has the effect of precluding the tenant'. The relevant part of the headnote[2]
to *Joseph v Joseph* is:

'Three brothers, A., G. and H., traded together as partners and A. and G.
were joint tenants of the freehold of premises which they held in trust for the   *g*
partners and other persons who might become entitled to the partnership
assets. In 1956, they signed an agreement and entered into a new partnership
deed; the terms included that A. and G. would grant to the partnership a 10-year
lease of the premises from February 1, 1956. In 1958, by a written document,
the partnership was dissolved and G. and H. only continued in partnership.
Clause 6 of that document provided: "By July 31, 1960 [the partnership] will   *h*
give up possession of [the premises] and meantime will pay rent of such an
amount as will give A. per year the same as he got January, 1956, to January,
1957, for all the properties owned jointly by all three brothers". G. and H.
continued in possession of the premises after July 31, 1960, and, after G. had also
ceased to be a partner, A. brought an action seeking an order for possession
against H. and damages against his brothers for breach of the agreement to give   *j*
up possession. Thereafter H. vacated the premises and he and G. successfully
defeated the claim for damages on the ground that clause 6 had created a new

---

1   [1966] 3 All ER 486, [1967] Ch 78
2   [1967] Ch at 78, 79

a tenancy and that they were entitled to remain in possession under Part II of
the Landlord and Tenant Act, 1954. On appeal by A.: *Held*, that "purports"
in section 38(1) of the Landlord and Tenant Act, 1954, meant "has the effect of"
and, therefore, if the agreement of 1958 was an agreement to surrender the
tenancy before July 31, 1960, it had the effect of precluding the tenants from
making an application under sections 24 and 29 of the Act, and was therefore
b void'.

In the course of his judgment, Lord Denning MR said[1]:

'In case I am wrong about this, I proceed to consider the case on the assumption
that the agreement of June 23, 1958, only made variations in the old tenancy
and did not work a surrender by operation of law. In that event the old tenancy
c continued in existence after June 23, 1958, with merely an agreement to surrender
in futuro by July 31, 1960, such as took place in *Fenner* v. *Blake*[2] as explained in
FOA's GENERAL LAW OF LANDLORD AND TENANT[3]. Then the important question
arises: what happens when the tenant of business premises on a long lease
agrees to surrender them on a named date before the end of the term, but
afterwards changes his mind and declines to surrender on the named date?
d I think that the tenancy does not come to an end. It can come to an end by
"surrender" proper; see s. 24(2) of the Act. But I do not think that it comes to an
end by a mere agreement to surrender. The very agreement to surrender is
"void in so far as it purports to preclude the tenant from making an application
or request" for a new tenancy; see s. 38(1) of the Landlord and Tenant Act,
1954. The word "purports", as used in sub-s. (1) and sub-s. (2) of this section,
e does not mean "professes". It means "has the effect of". The agreement to
surrender is void, therefore, in so far as it has the effect of precluding the tenant
from applying for a new lease. Under the Rent Acts an agreement to surrender
is not effective to determine the rights of the statutory tenant; see *De Vries* v.
Sparks[4]. So also under the Landlord and Tenant Act, 1954. If the landlord
wishes to get possession, he must persuade the tenant to give notice to quit
f under s. 27; and then the tenancy will come to an end on the due date.'

In the course of his judgment Diplock LJ said[5]:

'The tenancy was one to which Part 2 of the Act of 1954 applies. That Part
of the Act does not prevent tenancies coming to an end by notice to quit given
by the tenant or by surrender or forfeiture or by the forfeiture of a superior
g tenancy (s. 24(2)). It also does not prevent a tenancy for a term of years certain
coming to an end by effluxion of time if the tenant at any time not later than
three months before the date of its expiry gives notice that he does not desire
it to be continued (s. 27(1)). The Act thus leaves the tenant at liberty to bring
a tenancy to an end in accordance with its contractual terms by notice to quit,
if it is a periodical tenancy or by a notice under s. 27 of the Act if it is a tenancy
h for a term of years certain, and in either case, with the consent of the landlord,
by surrender. In none of these events has the tenant any right to apply to the
court for a new tenancy. Can he then agree in advance with the landlord that
he will bring the tenancy to an end in one of these methods and in particular
by surrendering it at some future date before it would, apart from the Act of
1954, expire by effluxion of time? This depends on the true construction of
j s. 38(1) of the Landlord and Tenant Act 1954, which is in the following terms:

1 [1966] 3 All ER at 489, 490, [1967] Ch at 87, 88
2 [1900] 1 QB 426
3 8th Edn (1957), pp 627, 628
4 (1927) 43 TLR 448, 137 LT 441
5 [1966] 3 All ER at 490, 491, [1967] Ch at 89

[then Diplock LJ read it]. In my judgment this subsection does render void *a* any provision of an agreement between landlord and tenant whereby the tenant undertakes to do in the future any act which will have the effect under the statute of disqualifying him from applying for a new tenancy under s. 24(1) and s. 29.'

I agree with counsel for the plaintiff that that is an analogous case to the present one and I therefore agree with him that whereas s 17 of the 1954 Act says that nothing *b* in Part I is to be construed as preventing the surrender of the tenancy, that means an actual surrender of the tenancy, and an agreement to surrender the tenancy in futuro is caught by the earlier provision of s 17 saying that 'the provisions of this Part of this Act shall have effect notwithstanding any agreement to the contrary'. The question then arises: whether as a matter of construction cl 7 of the agreement for a lease is an agreement by the tenant that he will in futuro, in certain events, *c* surrender the tenancy. My answer to that is, clearly it is. If either of the events happens which give rise to an option in favour of the landlord, the landlord, on the exercise of that option, is entitled to vacant possession of the property and that, in my judgment, implies a surrender of the tenancy in order to enable the landlord to acquire vacant possession.

Counsel for the defendant submitted that there was a difference in the wording *d* of ss 38 and 17; that s 38 was framed in terms of effect, whereas s 17 was framed in terms of intent. He also submitted that one ought, if possible, to construe a statute in such a way as to leave freely negotiated commercial arrangements standing. I accept that that is so, but at the same time the provisions of the Act have to be construed in the light of the policy of the legislature in passing this legislation for the protection of tenants. If I were to give effect to the submissions of counsel for the *e* defendant, it seems to me that the result would enable a landlord to drive a coach and horses through this legislation by providing in every agreement for a lease which is within Part I of the Landlord and Tenant Act 1954, provisions such as those as are found in cl 7 of the agreement with which I am concerned. In the result, I am driven to the conclusion that the options with which I am concerned are caught by s 17 of the 1954 Act. *f*

I am asked by the originating summons to make 'A Declaration that upon their true construction the options contained in Clause 7 of an Agreement for Sale dated the 26th day of April 1961 and made between the Defendant of the one part and the Plaintiff of the other part are void and of no effect'. And I must make that declaration.

Declaration accordingly. *g*

Solicitors: *Gouldens* (for the plaintiff); *Bower, Cotton & Bower* (for the defendant).

Jacqueline Metcalfe Barrister.

a   # R v Clerkenwell Stipendiary Magistrate, ex parte Mays

QUEEN'S BENCH DIVISION

LORD WIDGERY CJ, BRIDGE AND SHAW JJ

31st OCTOBER 1974

b

Magistrates – Fine – Enforcement – Supervision order – Effect – Committal to prison in default of payment – Limitation on power where supervision order in force – Meaning of 'commit . . . to prison' – Term of imprisonment fixed for defaulter but issue of warrant of committal postponed subject to conditions – Defaulter not subject to supervision order – Effect of making supervision order subsequently – Defaulter failing to comply with conditions of postponement – Whether court bound to issue warrant of commitment despite supervision
c   *order – Magistrates' Courts Act 1952, ss 65(2), 71(6).*

In January 1971 the applicant was convicted by a magistrates' court and fined £275. He was ordered to pay that sum by instalments of £2 a week.   In 1972 he fell into arrears with the instalments.   In August 1972 the magistrates' court, acting under s 65(2)ᵃ of the Magistrates' Courts Act 1952, fixed a term of imprisonment but post-
d   poned the issue of the warrant of commitment on the terms and subject to the condition that the applicant should pay the outstanding amount at the rate of 75p per week.   By August 1974 the applicant was once more substantially in arrears with those payments.   The applicant was again brought before the court and applied for a money payment supervision order under s 71ᵇ of the 1952 Act.   The magistrate refused to consider the application on the grounds that it would, in the circumstances,
e   be futile to do so.   The applicant applied for (i) an order of mandamus requiring the magistrate to hear the application for the supervision order and (ii) an order prohibiting him from issuing any warrant of commitment in respect of the default in paying the fine until that application had been heard.   It was contended by the applicant that after an order had been made under s 65(2) it was nevertheless open to the applicant to have resort to s 71 in order to secure, by way of the limitation
f   placed on committing persons to prison under s 71(6), a variation, postponement or possible withdrawal of the order under s 65(2).

Held – The making of a supervision order under s 71 could not have the effect of further postponing the operation of a committal warrant under s 65(2) for s 71(6) had no effect where an order had already been made under s 65(2); the limitation in s 71(6) applied only to the making of an order under s 65(2) after a supervision
g   order had been made, for the words 'shall not commit him to prison' referred to the act of fixing a term of imprisonment and postponing the issue of the warrant and not to the act of issuing the warrant on default of compliance with the conditions. It followed that there was no power to vary an order which had been properly made under s 65(2) and once there had been a breach in the conditions of postpone-
h   ment the court would have no power to grant any further relief to the defaulter whether or not a supervision order under s 71 was in force.   Accordingly the magis-trate had been fully justified in coming to the conclusion that no useful purpose could be served by considering an application under s 71 and the applications for mandamus and prohibition would therefore be dismissed (see p 68 *e* and *f* and p 69 *b* to *g* and *j* to p 70 *a*, post).

j   **Notes**
For the making of an order fixing periods of imprisonment postponed subject to the payment of a weekly amount, and any power to vary such order, see 25 Halsbury's Laws (3rd Edn) 240, para 442.

---

a   Section 65(2) is set out at p 67 *j*, post
b   Section 71, so far as material, is set out at p 68 *b* to *d*, post

D

For the Magistrates' Courts Act 1952, ss 65, 71, see 21 Halsbury's Statutes (3rd Edn) *a*
240, 243.

Application
This was an application pursuant to leave given by the Divisional Court on 8th
October 1974 by Robert John Mays for (i) an order of mandamus directed to the
stipendiary magistrate (R J A Romain Esq) sitting at Clerkenwell Magistrates' Court,
requiring him to hear and determine an application by the applicant for a money *b*
payment supervision order under s 71 of the Magistrates' Courts Act 1952 in respect
of two fines of £5 and £272 in relation to which terms of imprisonment had already
been fixed and the issue of the warrant of commitment postponed on payment of
75p per week under s 65(2) of the 1952 Act and (ii) an order prohibiting the magistrate
from issuing any warrant of commitment on default in payment until after the
hearing and determination of the application under s 71. The facts are set out in the *c*
judgment of the court.

Laurence Oates for the applicant.
Harry Woolf as amicus curiae.

                                                                                      d
BRIDGE J delivered the first judgment at the invitation of Lord Widgery CJ.
In these proceedings counsel moves on behalf of one Robert John Mays for an order
of mandamus directed to the stipendiary magistrate of Clerkenwell court, requiring
him to hear and determine an application on behalf of Mr Mays for a money payment
supervision order under s 71 of the Magistrates' Courts Act 1952, and for an order
of prohibition directed to the same magistrate, prohibiting him from issuing any *e*
warrant of commitment in respect of a default in paying a fine by Mr Mays, until
after the hearing and determination of the application under s 71.
    The matter arises in this way. The applicant was convicted in the Cambridge
magistrates' court as long ago as 5th January 1972 of using a motor vehicle without
a current Ministry test certificate and of keeping a vehicle on a road without there
being an excise licence in force. He was fined £5 in respect of each of those offences. *f*
In addition, he was ordered to pay back duty of £265·75, and that back duty thereupon, under statutory provisions to which it is unnecessary to refer, became recoverable as a fine. So the situation was in effect that the applicant had been fined
£275·75. He was ordered to pay that sum by instalments at the rate of £2 a week.
    In due course, when he moved from Cambridge to London there was a transfer
of fine order which had the effect of transferring to the Clerkenwell magistrates' *g*
court the appropriate powers for the enforcement of payment of the fine. By April
1972 the applicant was in arrears with the £2 weekly instalments and some time
after that he appeared at Clerkenwell magistrates' court on a means enquiry. On
17th June being again in arrears he was again required to appear at the Clerkenwell
magistrates' court for further enquiry into his means, which took place on 26th
August 1972 and on that occasion the court, acting under s 65(2) of the 1952 Act, *h*
fixed concurrent terms of imprisonment of 14 days and six weeks respectively, with
reference to the sums due, but postponed the issue of the warrant on terms and
subject to the condition that the applicant should pay the outstanding amounts at
the rate of 75p per week. In the ensuing two years, the applicant failed to comply
with that condition, and by 22nd August 1974, whereas he should, in compliance with
the condition on which the issue of the warrant had been postponed, have paid a total *j*
of £82·25 he had in fact only paid £63; so, as will be seen, he was some 25 weekly
instalments in arrears. In an affidavit which is before the court, he sets out that in the
two years elapsing between August 1972 and August 1974, there had been a
deterioration in his financial circumstances.
    It was on 22nd August 1974 that the stipendiary magistrate of Clerkenwell had
before him the applicant's application for an order under s 71 of the 1952 Act. The

a magistrate took the view, first, that the sole purpose of the application was to secure
in effect a further postponement or variation of the terms for postponement of the
warrant committing the applicant to prison, the issue of which had been ordered
to be postponed in August 1972; secondly, that he had no jurisdiction in the circumstances to entertain an application for a money payment supervision order under
s 71 of the 1952 Act; and thirdly, that in any event if he were to entertain such an
b application, it would be futile in the circumstances because it would not provide any
means whereby, the applicant being already in default and in breach of conditions
of postponement of the warrant of commitment ordered under s 65, the issue of
that warrant could any longer be postponed.

Before turning to the submissions made by counsel before this court, it will be
convenient to refer, as shortly as I may, to the relevant legislation.   An appropriate
c starting point is s 44 of the Criminal Justice Act 1967 which, in what amounts in effect
to an amendment of the relevant provisions of the Magistrates' Courts Act 1952, now
embodies the stringent conditions which have to be observed by a magistrates'
court charged with the enforcement of fines before the court can resort to the ultimate
sanction of imprisonment in default of payment.   Section 44 provides:

d '(1) The following provisions of this section shall have effect with respect to
the issue of a warrant of commitment under Part III of the Magistrates' Courts
Act 1952 for default in paying a sum adjudged to be paid by a conviction of a
magistrates' court . . .

'(4) Where on the occasion of the offender's conviction a magistrates' court
does not issue a warrant of commitment for a default in paying any such sum
as aforesaid or fix a term of imprisonment under the said section 65(2) which is
e to be served by him in the event of any such default [and I pause to observe
that the conditions for ordering the immediate issue of a warrant or immediately
fixing a term of imprisonment, which are stringent, were not here satisfied],
it shall not thereafter issue a warrant of commitment for any such default unless
. . . (b) the court has since the conviction inquired into his means in his presence
on at least one occasion.

f '(5) Where a magistrates' court is required by the last foregoing subsection
to inquire into a person's means, the court may not on the occasion of the inquiry
or at any time thereafter issue a warrant of commitment for a default in paying
any such sum unless . . . (b) the court has considered or tried all other methods
of enforcing payment of the sum and it appears to the court that they are
inappropriate or unsuccessful.

g '(6) After the occasion of an offender's conviction by a magistrates' court, the
court shall not [with two exceptions which are immaterial] issue a warrant of
commitment for a default in paying the sum or fix such a term except at a
hearing at which the offender is present.'

It will be observed that the strict requirements of that section that there shall be at
least one occasion when the court enquires into the defaulter's means and that there
h shall be a hearing at which the defaulter is present before any warrant is ordered to
issue or any term of imprisonment is fixed in default, were here complied with,
and it is further common ground that the court duly performed its duty under
s 44(5)(b) to consider or try all other methods of enforcing payment of the fines due
from the applicant, and it must have appeared to them that they were inappropriate
or unsuccessful before the order was made under s 65(2) of the 1952 Act, to which I
j now turn.   It provides:

'Where a magistrates' court has power to issue a warrant of commitment
under this Part of this Act [which on 26th August 1972 the Clerkenwell magistrates' court had], it may if it thinks it expedient to do so, fix a term of imprisonment and postpone the issue of the warrant until such time and on such conditions, if any, as the court thinks just.'

It was in the exercise of that power, unquestionably in August 1972 a valid exercise   *a*
of that power, that the terms of 14 days and six weeks concurrent were fixed. It was
under that subsection that the issue of a warrant committing the applicant to prison
for those terms was postponed on condition that he paid the outstanding amounts at
the rate of 75p per week.

The next section to which reference must be made is s 71, the section providing
for what are referred to as money payment supervision orders. It is unnecessary   *b*
to read more than the first and sixth subsections:

'(1) Where any person is adjudged to pay a sum by a summary conviction and
the convicting court does not commit him to prison forthwith in default of
payment, the court may, either on the occasion of the conviction or on a subsequent occasion, order him to be placed under the supervision of such person
as the court may from time to time appoint.'   *c*

'(6) Where an order placing a person under supervision with respect to a sum
is in force, a magistrates' court shall not commit him to prison in default of
payment of the sum, or for want of sufficient distress to satisfy the sum, unless
the court has before committing him taken such steps as may be reasonably
practicable to obtain from the person appointed for his supervision an oral or
written report on the offender's conduct and means and has considered any   *d*
report so obtained, in addition, in a case where an inquiry is required by the
last preceding section, to that inquiry.'

The submission made on the applicant's behalf by counsel, in its amplest form, if
I understand him, is to this effect, that after an order has been made by a magistrates'
court under s 65(2) fixing a term of imprisonment in default of payment of a fine and
laying down conditions for the postponement of the issue of a warrant of commit-   *e*
ment, resort may nevertheless be had to s 71 to secure in effect by way of the limitation placed on committing persons to prison under sub-s (6) of that section an effective
variation or possible withdrawal of the order under s 65(2). Counsel concedes, as
indeed he has to because it is plain, that there is nowhere in the relevant legislation
any power conferred in terms on any court to vary the conditions imposed on an
order under s 65(2) for the postponement of the issue of the warrant of commitment   *f*
which that subsection contemplates.

Before coming to the narrower question of the precise construction of the phrase
in s 71(6) 'shall not commit him to prison' on which it may be in the last analysis
this application turns, I am bound to say at the outset that it is to my mind wholly
unacceptable that one should construe this statute in a way which would reveal
Parliament by such an extraordinary side wind and by implication introducing a power   *g*
to vary the terms of the postponed issue of a warrant under a s 65(2) order. I would
think that such an odd result was unacceptable as a matter of broad principle, but if I
had any doubts in the matter they would be effectively resolved by considering the
very different position which obtains in relation to the enforcement of sums payable
under maintenance orders. An order under s 65(2) fixing a term of imprisonment in
default of payment and postponing the issue of the warrant may be made in relation   *h*
to a sum due under a maintenance order in the same way as it may be made in
relation to a sum due as a fine, but an elaborate code is provided by the Maintenance
Orders Act 1958, providing in terms for subsequent reviews of the terms of postponement of the issue of a warrant in relation to such an order. It is s 18(1) of the
Act which provides:

'Where for the purpose of enforcing a maintenance order, a magistrates'   *j*
court has exercised its power under subsection (2) of section sixty-five of the
Magistrates' Courts Act, 1952, or this section to postpone the issue of a warrant of
commitment and under the terms of the postponement the warrant falls to be
issued,'

then, summarising the effect of the following provisions, it is not to be issued until a the party liable to be imprisoned has been notified and has had an opportunity to appear before the court, and in particular one of the powers which is conferred on the court, after it has heard from the party in default, is under sub-s (3)(b) further to postpone the issue of the warrant until such time and on such conditions, if any, as the court thinks just, or, (c) if in case of any change in the circumstances of the defendant the court considers it appropriate so to do, to order that the warrant shall not

b be issued in any event.

It is to my mind quite unthinkable that if Parliament had intended that similar powers of indefinite variation, postponement or cancellation of orders under s 65(2) should be available in relation to fines as they have expressly made available in relation to maintenance orders, that would not have been made plain in similar provisions.

c There remains the question, the narrow question, of construction; what is the meaning of the phrase 'shall not commit him to prison' which is to be found in s 71(6) of the 1952 Act. There are two alternative possibilities and they cannot, as it seems to me, both be right. The act of committing the defaulter to prison which that phrase contemplates in relation to the exercise of the powers conferred by s 65(2) is either the act of fixing the term of imprisonment and postponing the issue of

d the warrant, an act which here the court took in August 1972, or it is the act of issuing the warrant at a time when default in compliance with the conditions of postponement has taken place. It seems to me when one considers those two alternatives that it is really plain that it is the first alternative to which the language of s 71(6) is intended to apply. Considering that, for the reasons I have already sought to explain, the effective moment when the court determines the fate of the

e defaulter, subject to such locus poenitentiae as the conditions of postponement may allow him, is the moment when the s 65 order is made, it is I think clear that, where a supervision order is in force, the order fixing a term of imprisonment and postponing the issue of the warrant, should not be made without considering the supervisor's report. That is one good reason why the words 'shall not commit him to prison' should be construed as referring to that moment in time. Another equally

f good reason is that since there is no power in the court to vary the terms of the s 65 order after there has been a breach of the conditions of postponement, it would at that stage be quite futile for the court to consider a supervisor's report under s 71(6) because whatever the supervisor's report might say the court would be able to do nothing about it by way of granting any relief at that stage to the defaulter.

g For those reasons, it seems to me that the stipendiary magistrate was fully justified in the course that he took. Counsel who has addressed the court as amicus, and for whose assistance we are very grateful, has not sought to persuade us that the stipendiary magistrate was correct in the conclusion which he expressed that he had at the time when the application was made to him under s 71 no jurisdiction to entertain such an application. Both counsel submit, and as I think rightly, that technically there is jurisdiction, notwithstanding the existence of an order under

h s 65(2), to consider making a supervision order under s 71. One can visualise a situation in which the court might take the view that as well as giving a defaulter a last chance by way of conditions of postponement under s 65(2), it would be in the interests of the defaulter and perhaps his family that he should have the support and encouragement of supervision under s 71 in the hope that the supervisor would keep him up to the mark. But whether that is so or not, in a case like the present where

j the applicant has long since fallen far into arrear in failing to comply with the conditions for the postponement of the issue of the warrant under s 65, it would, as the magistrate also thought and in my judgment rightly thought, have been quite futile to have considered an application under s 71 which could have made no difference to the reality of the situation.

For those reasons, I would refuse these applications.

SHAW J. I agree.   *a*

LORD WIDGERY CJ. I agree also.

Solicitors: *W H Merricks* (for the applicant); *Treasury Solicitor.*

Jacqueline Charles Barrister.   *b*

R v Turner

COURT OF APPEAL, CRIMINAL DIVISION   *c*
LAWTON LJ, NIELD AND CANTLEY JJ
26th JULY, 17th OCTOBER 1974

Criminal law – Evidence – Admissibility – Expert evidence – Principles to be applied in determining admissibility – Evidence of psychiatrist – Evidence regarding personality of accused – Accused charged with murder – Accused seeking to call psychiatrist to support ***d*** *defence of provocation and his credibility – Admissibility of psychiatrist's evidence.*

The appellant killed his girl friend, W, in a car by battering her over the head with a hammer. At his trial on a charge of murder, his defence was provocation. He said that he had been in love with W and had understood that she was pregnant by him, but that when she had told him in the car that she had been having affairs *e* with two other men while the appellant was in prison and that the expected child was not his, he had lost his self control and had hit her with the hammer without realising what he was doing and without intending to do her any harm. After he had given his evidence, his counsel sought to call a psychiatrist (i) to help the jury to accept as credible the appellant's account of what happened and (ii) to indicate why the appellant was likely to be provoked. The judge asked to see the evidence *f* which the psychiatrist proposed to give. He was handed a report prepared by the psychiatrist and based on information provided in part by medical records and in part by the appellant, his family and friends. The psychiatrist expressed the following opinion at the end of the report: 'His homicidal behaviour would appear to be understandable in terms of his relationship with [W] which . . . was such as to make him particularly vulnerable to be overwhelmed by anger if she confirmed *g* the accusation that had been made about her. If his statements are true that he was taken completely by surprise by her confession, he would have appeared to have killed her in an explosive release of blind rage. His personality structure is consistent with someone who could behave in this way . . . since her death his behaviour would appear to have been consistent with someone suffering from profound grief . . . in the absence of formal psychiatric illness there are no indications for recom- *h* mending psychiatric treatment.' The judge refused to admit the evidence of the psychiatrist on the ground that the report contained hearsay character evidence, and was irrelevant and inadmissible. The appellant was convicted of murder. On appeal,

Held – (i) The psychiatrist's evidence was relevant in that it provided an opinion from *j* a knowledgeable person about the appellant's personality and mental make-up which could play an important part in human judgments (see p 74 *a*, post).

    (ii) The evidence was not, however, admissible, and the appeal would therefore be dismissed, for the following reasons—

    (a) An expert opinion was only necessary where the expert could furnish the court with scientific information that was likely to be outside the experience and a knowledge of the judge or jury and the psychiatrist's evidence was not necessary to tell them (a) how an ordinary person who was not suffering from mental illness was likely to react to the stresses and strains of life, and (b) what reliance they could place on the evidence of someone who was not mentally disordered (see p 74 *d* to *j*, post); *Folkes v Chadd* (1782) 3 Doug KB 157 applied.

(b) Except in very exceptional circumstances a psychiatrist's evidence could not be
b led in chief to prove the probability of the accused's veracity (see p 75 *a* to *e*, post); *Lowery v The Queen* [1973] 3 All ER 662 explained.

Notes
For admissibility of expert evidence, see 15 Halsbury's Laws (3rd Edn) 321-323, paras 587, 588, and for cases on the subject, see 22 Digest (Reissue) 559, 560, 5730-5740.

c
Cases referred to in judgment
Director of Public Prosecutions v A & BC Chewing Gum Ltd [1967] 2 All ER 504, [1968] 1 QB 159, [1967] 3 WLR 493, 131 JP 373, HL, Digest (Cont Vol C) 250, 8654ba.
Folkes v Chadd (1782) 3 Doug KB 157, 99 ER 589; *affd* (1783) 3 Doug KB 340, 99 ER 686, 22 Digest (Reissue) 567, 5812.
d *Glinski v McIver* [1962] 1 All ER 696, [1962] AC 726, [1962] 2 WLR 832, HL, 33 Digest (Repl) 431, 504.
Lowery v The Queen [1973] 3 All ER 662, [1974] AC 85, [1973] 3 WLR 235, 58 Cr App Rep 35, PC.
Myers v Director of Public Prosecutions [1964] 2 All ER 881, [1965] AC 1001, [1964] 3 WLR 145, 128 JP 481, 48 Cr App Rep 348, HL, 22 Digest (Reissue) 63, 388.

e
Cases also cited
R v Chard (1972) 56 Cr App Rep 268, CA.
R v Coney (1882) 8 QBD 534.
R v Eades [1972] Crim LR 99, CA.
R v Ives [1969] 3 All ER 470, [1970] 1 QB 208, CA.
f *R v Lupien* [1970] SCR 263.
R v McKay [1967] NZLR 139, CA.
R v Riley [1967] Crim LR 656.
R v Thompson [1917] 2 KB 630.
Toohey v Metropolitan Police Comr [1965] 1 All ER 506, [1965] AC 595, HL.

g **Appeal**
On 14th February 1974 at the Crown Court at Bristol before Bridge J and a jury the appellant, Terence Stuart Turner, was convicted of murder and sentenced to life imprisonment. He appealed against conviction on the ground that the trial judge refused to admit evidence which a psychiatrist was prepared to give in support of his defence of provocation. In addition he sought the court's leave to receive that
h evidence. The facts appear in the judgment of the court.

Arthur Mildon QC and *Mark Dyer* for the appellant.
David Calcutt QC and *John Main QC* for the Crown.

Cur adv vult

j
17th October. **LAWTON LJ** read the judgment of the court. On 14th February 1974 at Bristol Crown Court after a trial before Bridge J, the appellant was convicted of murder and sentenced to life imprisonment. He has appealed against his conviction on the ground that the judge refused to admit evidence which a psychiatrist was prepared to give in support of his defence of provocation. He has asked this court to receive that evidence.

At about midnight on 26th/27th October 1973 at Swindon whilst sitting in a motor   a
car with a girl named Wendy Basterfield, the appellant killed her by battering her
about the head and face with a hammer. Fifteen blows were struck. Very shortly
after striking these blows he went to a nearby farmhouse and told the occupants
there that he had killed his girl friend. The police were sent for. When they arrived
he said: 'I've killed my girl friend . . . I bashed her head with a hammer. I didn't
mean to do it. I didn't mean to do it, honestly.' Later when told he would be   b
arrested on suspicion of murder he said: 'I know, I know. I just kept hitting her.'

His defence was provocation. In the circumstances it could not have been any
other. The basis for this defence was that he was deeply in love with the girl, whom
he thought was pregnant by him. Whilst he was in the motor car with her he said
that she had told him with a grin that whilst he had been in prison she had been
sleeping with two other men, that she could make money in this way and that the   c
child she was carrying was not his. He claimed that he had been very upset by
what she had said. His hand had come across the hammer which was down by the
side of the seat and he had hit her with it. ' It was never in my mind', he said, 'to
do her any harm. I did not realise what I had in my hand. I knew it was heavy . . .
When I realised it was a hammer I stopped.' If the jury rejected his evidence as to
how the girl came to be killed (it was challenged by the Crown) there was no founda-   d
tion for the defence put forward. The appellant's credit as a witness was an important
issue.

After the appellant had given evidence his counsel told the judge that he wanted to
call a psychiatrist. He explained why. 'First of all', he said, 'it may help the jury
to accept as credible the [appellant's] account of what happened and, second, it
may tell them why this man was provoked.' The judge queried whether the   e
evidence of a psychiatrist was admissible on these matters. There was some discussion, at the end of which the judge said he wanted 'to see the evidence which the
psychiatrist proposed to give.' Counsel for the appellant then handed to the judge
a lengthy psychiatric report dated 2nd February 1974 which had been prepared
by a Dr Smith. It was in a form with which judges have become familiar in recent
years. At the beginning the doctor said that he had been asked to deal with various   f
matters and in particular to assess the appellant's 'personality, his present mental
state and to consider from the psychiatric point of view his emotional state and reaction at the time of the crime'. Then followed a long account of the appellant's
personality and medical history and his family background. Some of the information
had come from medical records; most of it from the appellant himself but a little
from his family and friends as is shown by the following passage: g

> 'From all accounts his personality has always been that of a placid, rather
> quiet and passive person who is quite sensitive to the feelings of other people.
> He was always regarded by his family and friends as an even-tempered person
> who is not in any way aggressive . . . In general until the night of the crime he
> seems to have always displayed remarkably good impulse control.'

This passage surprised counsel for the Crown because he knew that in November   h
1971 the appellant had been convicted of being in unlawful possession of an offensive
weapon and in May 1972 of assault with intent to rob. The appellant himself had
not put his character in issue. If the psychiatrist had given evidence in accordance
with his report, the appellant would have been put before the jury by the psychiatrist
as having a character and disposition which the Crown considered in the light of his
record he had not got. The opinion expressed at the end of this report was as follows: j

> 'At no time has this man appeared to show any evidence of mental illness
> as defined by the Mental Health Act 1959. His homicidal behaviour would
> appear to be understandable in terms of his relationship with Wendy Basterfield
> which, as I have endeavoured to outline above, was such as to make him particu-
> larly vulnerable to be overwhelmed by anger if she confirmed the accusation

a that had been made about her. If his statements are true that he was taken completely by surprise by her confession, he would have appeared to have killed her in an explosive release of blind rage. His personality structure is consistent with someone who could behave in this way. There is no demonstrable clinical evidence to suggest that brain damage or organic disease of the brain diminished his sense of responsibility at the time he killed her, and since

b her death his behaviour would appear to have been consistent with someone suffering from profound grief. Although he would obviously benefit from psychotherapeutic counselling, in the absence of formal psychiatric illness there are no indications for recommending psychiatric treatment.'

Counsel for the Crown pointed out to the judge the difficulty presented by the references in the report to the appellant's alleged disposition and character. There-

c upon the judge commented that the report contained 'hearsay character evidence' which was inadmissible. He could have said that all the facts on which the psychiatrist based his opinion were hearsay save for those which he observed for himself during his examination of the appellant such as his appearance of depression and his becoming emotional when discussing the deceased girl and his own family. It is not for this court to instruct psychiatrists how to draft their reports, but those who

d call psychiatrists as witnesses should remember that the facts on which they base their opinions must be proved by admissible evidence. This elementary principle is frequently overlooked.

Counsel for the appellant appreciated that problems would arise about character if the psychiatrist gave evidence along the lines of his report. He submitted that he would be entitled to ask the following questions: have you examined this man?

e Over what period of time did you examine him? Are you able to help the jury as to the intensity of his feelings for Wendy? Assuming what the appellant has said here in court as to the nature of the provocation is true, how would you have expected him to react? The judge did not rule specifically on these suggested questions; he directed his attention to the report and ruled that it was irrelevant and inadmissible.

Before dealing with the submission made on behalf of the appellant in this court

f we would like briefly to refer to the questions which counsel for the appellant suggested he could properly put to the psychiatrist. What he was proposing to do was to use a common forensic device to overcome objections of inadmissibility based on hearsay. The use of this device was criticised by Lord Devlin in *Glinski v McIver*[1]: he thought it was objectionable. It is certainly unhelpful. Before a court can assess the value of an opinion it must know the facts on which it is based.

g If the expert has been misinformed about the facts or has taken irrelevant facts into consideration or has omitted to consider relevant ones, the opinion is likely to be valueless. In our judgment counsel calling an expert should in examination in chief ask his witness to state the facts on which his opinion is based. It is wrong to leave the other side to elicit the facts by cross-examination.

Before this court counsel for the appellant submitted that the psychiatrist's opinion

h as to the appellant's personality and mental make-up as set out in his report was relevant and admissible for three reasons: first, because it helped to establish lack of intent; secondly, because it helped to establish that the appellant was likely to be easily provoked; and thirdly, because it helped to show that the appellant's account of what had happened was likely to be true. We do not find it necessary to deal specifically with the first of these reasons. Intent was not a live issue in this

j case. The evidence was tendered on the issues of provocation and credibility. The judge gave his ruling in relation to those issues. In any event the decision which we have come to on counsel for the appellant's second and third submissions would also apply to his first.

---

1 [1962] 1 All ER 696 at 723, [1962] AC 726 at 780, 781

The first question on both these issues is whether the psychiatrist's opinion was *a* relevant. A man's personality and mental make-up do have a bearing on his conduct. A quick-tempered man will react more aggressively to an unpleasing situation than a placid one. Anyone having a florid imagination or a tendency to exaggerate is less likely to be a reliable witness than one who is precise and careful. These are matters of ordinary human experience. Opinions from knowledgeable persons about a man's personality and mental make-up play a part in many human *b* judgments. In our judgment the psychiatrist's opinion was relevant. Relevance, however, does not result in evidence being admissible: it is a condition precedent to admissibility. Our law excludes evidence of many matters which in life outside the courts sensible people take into consideration when making decisions. Two broad heads of exclusion are hearsay and opinion. As we have already pointed out, the psychiatrist's report contained a lot of hearsay which was inadmissible. A *c* ruling in this ground, however, would merely have trimmed the psychiatrist's evidence: it would not have excluded it altogether. Was it inadmissible because of the rules relating to opinion evidence?

The foundation of these rules was laid by Lord Mansfield CJ in *Folkes v Chadd*[1] and was well laid: 'The opinion of scientific men upon proven facts', he said, 'may be given by men of science within their own science.' An expert's opinion is admissible *d* to furnish the court with scientific information which is likely to be outside the experience and knowledge of a judge or jury. If on the proven facts a judge or jury can form their own conclusions without help then the opinion of an expert is unnecessary. In such a case if it is given dressed up in scientific jargon it may make judgment more difficult. The fact that an expert witness has impressive scientific qualifications does not by that fact alone make his opinion on matters of human *e* nature and behaviour within the limits of normality any more helpful than that of the jurors themselves; but there is a danger that they may think it does.

What, in plain English, was the psychiatrist in this case intending to say? First, that the appellant was not showing and never had shown, any evidence of mental illness as defined by the Mental Health Act 1959 and did not require any psychiatric treatment; secondly that he had had a deep emotional relationship with the girl *f* which was likely to have caused an explosive release of blind rage when she confessed her wantonness to him; thirdly, that after he had killed her he behaved like someone suffering from profound grief. The first part of his opinion was within his expert province and outside the experience of the jury but was of no relevance in the circumstances of this case. The second and third points dealt with matters which are well within ordinary human experience. We all know that both men and women who *g* are deeply in love can, and sometimes do, have outbursts of blind rage when discovering unexpected wantonness on the part of their loved ones; the wife taken in adultery is the classical example of the application of the defence of 'provocation'; and when death or serious injury results, profound grief usually follows. Jurors do not need psychiatrists to tell them how ordinary folk who are not suffering from any mental illness are likely to react to the stresses and strains of life. It follows *h* that the proposed evidence was not admissible to establish that the appellant was likely to have been provoked. The same reasoning applies to its suggested admissibility on the issue of credibility. The jury had to decide what reliance they could put on the appellant's evidence. He had to be judged as someone who was not mentally disordered. This is what juries are empanelled to do. The law assumes they can perform their duties properly. The jury in this case did not need, and *j* should not have been offered the evidence of a psychiatrist to help them decide whether the appellant's evidence was truthful.

Counsel for the appellant submitted that such help should not have been rejected by the judge because in *Lowery v The Queen*[2] the Privy Council had approved of the

1   (1782) 3 Doug KB 157 at 159
2   [1973] 3 All ER 662, [1974] AC 85

a admission of the evidence of a psychologist on the issue of credibility. We had to
consider that case carefully before we could decide whether it had in any way put
a new interpretation on what have long been thought to be the rules relating to the
calling of evidence on the issue of credibility, i e that in general evidence can be called
to impugn the credibility of witnesses but not led in chief to bolster it up. In *Lowery
v The Queen*[1] evidence of a psychologist on behalf of one of two accused was admitted
b to establish that his version of the facts was more probable than that put forward by
the other. In every case what is relevant and admissible depends on the issues
raised in that case. In *Lowery v The Queen*[1] the issues were unusual; and the accused
to whose disadvantage the psychologist's evidence went had in effect said before it
was called that he was not the sort of man to have committed the offence. In giving
judgment of the Board Lord Morris of Borth-y-Gest said[2]:

c   'The only question now arising is whether in the special circumstances above
       referred to it was open to King in defending himself to call Professor Cox to
       give the evidence that he gave. The evidence was relevant to and necessary
       for his case which involved negativing what Lowery had said and put forward:
       in their Lordships' view in agreement with that of the Court of Criminal Appeal
       the evidence was admissible.'

d We adjudge *Lowery v The Queen*[1] to have been decided on its special facts. We do
not consider that it is an authority for the proposition that in all cases psychologists
and psychiatrists can be called to prove the probability of the accused's veracity.
If any such rule was applied in our courts trial by psychiatrists would be likely to
take the place of trial by jury and magistrates. We do not find that prospect
e attractive and the law does not at present provide for it.
       In coming to the conclusion we have in this case we must not be taken to be dis-
couraging the calling of psychiatric evidence in cases where such evidence can be
helpful within the present rules of evidence. These rules may be too restrictive of the
admissibility of opinion evidence. The Criminal Law Revision Committee in its
eleventh report[3] thought they were and made recommendations for relaxing them.
f The recommendations have not yet been accepted by Parliament and until they are,
or other changes in the law of evidence are made, this court must apply the existing
rules (see *Myers v Director of Public Prosecutions*[4] per Lord Reid). We have not overlooked what Lord Parker CJ said in *Director of Public Prosecutions v A & BC Chewing
Gum Ltd*[5] about the advance of science making more and more inroads into the old
common law principle applicable to opinion evidence; but we are firmly of the
g opinion that psychiatry has not yet become a satisfactory substitute for the common
sense of juries or magistrates on matters within their experience of life. The appeal
is dismissed.

Appeal dismissed.

h Solicitors: *Kinneir & Co*, Swindon (for the appellant); *Director of Public Prosecutions*.

                                        N P Metcalfe Esq Barrister.

1   [1973] 3 All ER 662, [1974] AC 85
2   [1973] 3 All ER at 672, [1974] AC at 103
j 3   Evidence (General) (1972) Cmnd 4991, paras 266-271
4   [1964] 2 All ER 881, [1965] AC 1001
5   [1967] 2 All ER 504, [1968] 1 QB 159

a

Note
Re Vidiofusion Ltd

CHANCERY DIVISION   *b*
MEGARRY J
7th OCTOBER 1974

*Company – Winding-up – Compulsory winding-up – Advertisement of petition – Error in
advertisement – Waiver – Name of company – Error in name – Trifling error – Mis-spelling
– Circumstances in which error will be waived on ground that it is very trifling.*   *c*

Notes
For the contents of an advertisement of a petition, see 7 Halsbury's Laws (4th Edn)
608, para 1018.
    For the court's power to waive irregularities, see ibid 798, para 1419, and for a case
on the subject, see 10 Digest (Repl) 885, 5888.   *d*

Cases referred to in judgment
L'Industrie Verrière Ltd, Re [1914] WN 222, 58 Sol Jo 611, 10 Digest (Repl) 885, 5888.
R v Davis (1851)20 LJMC 207,2 Den 231, T & M 557, 4 New Sers Cas 611,17 LTOS 135,
    15 JP 450, 15 Jur 546, 5 Cox CC 237, CCR, 22 Digest (Reissue) 26, 60.
R v Shakespeare (1808) 10 East 83, 103 ER 707.   *e*

Petition
On 29th July 1974 the petitioning creditors, Swift Hardman Ltd, advertised a petition
for winding-up of the company, Vidiofusion Ltd in the London Gazette and Liverpool
Daily Post. In both advertisements, the company's name appeared as 'Videofusion
Limited', instead of 'Vidiofusion Limited'. At the hearing of the petition an   *f*
application was made to waive the errors.

Robin Potts for the petitioning creditors.

MEGARRY J. I have looked into this point and propose to rule on it. The name   *g*
of this company is 'Vidiofusion Limited', and both advertisements of the petition
for winding-up were in the name of 'Videofusion Limited', with an 'e' in place of
the second 'i'. The general rule, as stated in Buckley on the Companies Acts[1], is
that an error in the name of the company as it appears in the requisite advertisements
renders them absolutely void; but this is qualified by the words 'except, perhaps, a
very trifling error in spelling, which could not mislead any one'. For this, *Re L'Indus-*   *h*
trie Verrière Ltd[2] is cited. In that case, the error which Astbury J waived lay in the
omission of the penultimate letter of 'Industrie'.
    Questions sometimes arise in this court as to what errors in spelling can be called
'very trifling'. In my judgment, if four conditions are satisfied the error should
normally be regarded as being 'very trifling', and as one that ought to be waived.
First, as indicated by Astbury J in the case cited, there should be no other company   *j*
of any similar name on the register. Second, the true name and the mis-spelt name
should bear substantially the same pronounciation. Even in the old days of strict
pleading, there was a rule as to names which were idem sonantia; an erroneous

---

1   13th Edn (1957), p 1024
2   [1914] WN 222

a   spelling would be accepted if it was idem sonans with the true spelling: see e g *R v Davis*[1] and compare *R v Shakespeare*[2]. Third, there should be no marked visual difference between the two names. If the name 'Jackson', spelled in the orthodox way, appears as 'Jaxen', the appearance is so different that I do not think that similarity of pronounciation would save it. The difference is between a spelling mistake that has to be looked for, and one that obtrudes itself. Fourth (and this will often

b   overlap the third head) the error should not materially affect the alphabetical order of the names. In some circumstances the letters C and K produce the same sound, as do F and Ph; but as initial letters their alphabetical differences materially affect indexing, and bearing in mind the importance of indexes, I do not think that such a difference could be dismissed as being very trifling.

    I am not, of course, saying that no error can be waived unless it satisfies these

c   conditions; but I think that any error that does will normally be waived. In the present case, all the conditions are satisfied, and accordingly I waive the errors and make the usual winding-up order.

    Ruling accordingly.

d   Solicitors: *Wedlake Bell,* agents for *Kent, Jones & Done,* Stoke-on-Trent (for the petitioning creditors).

                                                                F K Anklesaria Esq Barrister.

e
R v Isequilla

COURT OF APPEAL, CRIMINAL DIVISION
LORD WIDGERY CJ, BRIDGE AND MAY JJ
23rd, 24th JULY 1974

f
Criminal law – Evidence – Admissibility – Admission – Confession – Inducement – Conduct of person in authority – Conduct not improper or unjustified – Conduct such as to have effect of inducing a confession – Whether exclusion of confession on ground that it was not voluntary must be related to some improper or unjustified conduct on part of person in authority.

g   *Jury – Direction to jury – Inability to agree – Majority verdict direction given – Proper direction when jury still unable to agree.*

    Three detectives acting on information about a proposed armed robbery went to a bank where they saw the appellant sitting in the passenger seat of a car. One of the detectives jumped into the car, caught hold of the appellant and handcuffed him.

h   Another detective approached the car from the other side with a gun. Inside the car was a briefcase containing an imitation firearm and a note which read: 'Keep calm. Hand over £3,000 or I'll blow your head off'. When asked about the revolver and note, the appellant began to cry, saying: 'I won't cause any trouble. I have been very stupid.' He was taken to a police car and asked what he had been intending to do. The appellant replied: 'I was short of money and I was going to try and get some from

j   the bank.' He was cautioned and taken to a police station. At all times it was clear that the appellant was very frightened and by the time he had arrived at the police station he was completely hysterical. He was charged with, inter alia, possessing an imitation firearm and of having an article for use in connection with theft. At his trial objection

---

1   (1851) 20 LJMC 207
2   (1808) 10 East 83

was taken to the admission of the confessions. The trial judge concluded that the   *a*
detectives had acted properly and held that the confessions were admissible. The
appellant was convicted and appealed, contending (i) that, although the police officers
had acted quite properly, their conduct had been such as to amount to an inducement to confess even though that had not been their intention, and (ii) that, in any
event, the appellant's mental state had been such that he had been deprived of the
capacity to make a free choice whether to confess or not.   *b*

Held – The appeal would be dismissed for the following reasons—
  (i) The exclusion of a confession as a matter of law on the grounds that it was not
voluntary had to be related to some conduct on the part of the person in authority
which was improper or unjustified, such as the offer of an inducement (see p 82 *g* to
j, post); dicta of Lord Campbell in *R v Scott* (1856) Dears & B at 58, of Winn LJ in   *c*
R v Richards [1967] 1 All ER at 830 and *Naniseni v R* [1971] NZLR 269 applied.
  (ii) It was impossible to say that at the time of the confession the appellant's mental
state was such that his utterances were completely unreliable or that his mind was so
unbalanced that it would be unsafe to rely on them (see p 83 *j* to p 84 *a*, post).
  Observations on the proper direction to give when a majority verdict direction has
already been given and the jury are still unable to agree (see p 84 *d* to *h*, post).   *d*

Notes
For admissions or confessions made by a defendant before trial, see 10 Halsbury's
Laws (3rd Edn) 469, 470, paras 860-862, and for cases on the subject, see 14 Digest
(Repl) 468, 469, 4508-4527, 480-486, 4578-4649.
                                                                                     e

Cases referred to in judgment
Naniseni v R [1971] NZLR 269, CA.
R v Prager [1972] 1 All ER 1114, [1972] 1 WLR 260, 56 Cr App Rep 151, CA.
R v Richards [1967] 1 All ER 829, [1967] 1 WLR 653, 131 JP 283, 51 Cr App Rep 266, CA,
  Digest (Cont Vol C) 213, 4577e.
R v Scott (1856) Dears & B 47, 25 LJMC 128, 27 LTOS 254, 20 JP 435, 2 Jur NS 1096, 7   *f*
  Cox CC 164, CCR, 14 Digest (Repl) 463, 4472.

Cases also cited
Commissioners of Customs and Excise v Harz [1967] 1 All ER 177, [1967] AC 760, HL.
R v Baldry (1852) 5 Cox CC 523, CCR.
R v Booher [1928] 4 DLR 795.   *g*
R v Burnett [1944] VLR 115.
R v Northam (1968) 52 Cr App Rep 97, CA.
R v Smith [1959] 2 All ER 193, [1959] 2 QB 35.
R v Spilsbury (1835) 7 C & P 187.
R v Starecki [1960] VR 141.
R v Stroud (1911) 7 Cr App Rep 38, CCA.   *h*
R v Thompson [1893] 2 QB 12, [1891-4] All ER Rep 376.
R v Warickshall (1783) 1 Leach 263.
R v Washer (1948) 98 Can CC 218.
R v Williams [1959] NZLR 502.
R v Zavekas [1970] 1 All ER 413, [1970] 1 WLR 516, CA.   *j*
Sinclair v Regem (1946) 73 CLR 316.

Appeal and application
On 24th October 1973 at the Central Criminal Court before his Honour Judge Thomas
the appellant, Alberto Ramon Isequilla, was convicted on three counts of an indictment
which charged him with possessing an imitation firearm with intent to commit an

a indictable offence (count 2); having an article for use in connection with theft (count 3); and being carried in a motor vehicle taken without authority (count 4). On 25th October he was sentenced to four years' imprisonment on count 2, to three years' imprisonment on count 3 and to three months' imprisonment on count 4, all the sentences to run concurrently with each other. A six months' suspended sentence imposed for a two year period and passed by Bow Street Magistrates' Court on 15th

b February 1973 for an offence of theft was ordered to take effect consecutively, making 4½ years' imprisonment in all. He appealed against conviction and applied for leave to appeal against sentence. The facts are set out in the judgment of the court.

Louis Blom-Cooper QC and *Geoffrey Robertson* for the appellant.
William Denny and *B J Waylen* for the Crown

c

LORD WIDGERY CJ delivered the judgment of the court. On 24th October 1973 at the Central Criminal Court the appellant (as I shall call him on the basis that this is an appeal on a point of law) was convicted of possessing an imitation firearm with intent to commit an indictable offence; he was also convicted of having an

d article for use in connection with theft, and of being carried in a motor vehicle taken without authority: three separate offences. He was sentenced to four years' imprisonment on count 2, which was the possession of the imitation firearm, three years' imprisonment on count 3 and three months' imprisonment on count 4, all concurrent making four years in all, but a suspended sentence of six months previously imposed on him was activated consecutively to the sentence imposed for the instant

e charges, and that made a total of 4½ years. He now appeals against conviction on points of law.

The facts can be put very shortly and are somewhat exceptional. At about 9.30 am on 26th April 1973, three police officers were in a police car in Chesterfield Street in the West End. They had received information to the effect that an armed robbery was going to take place at the Midland Bank, and acting on that information they

f went to the Midland Bank in Chesterfield Street. Two of them were armed with pistols. When they were there a Triumph motor car drew up at the bank. There were two people in the car. The appellant was sitting in the passenger seat, and there was another man who was driving the car. As soon as the police officers saw the arrival of this vehicle, the two police sergeants, Sergeant Batty and Sergeant Ganley left the police car and approached the Triumph. The driver of the Triumph ran away. The

g third police officer chased him unsuccessfully and he disappears from the story at that point. When the two sergeants approached the car, which still had the appellant sitting in the passenger seat, Sergeant Batty jumped into the Triumph without ceremony, as one can understand in the circumstances, he caught hold of the appellant and put handcuffs on him at once. The explanation of that, and it is not criticised, is that he anticipated that the man in the car might be armed and he was taking no

h chances.

About this time Sergeant Ganley got out his gun with which he was armed and approached the car on the other side. The appellant reached down to a black brief case which was at his feet, and Sergeant Batty relieved him of the brief case. When the brief case was opened, two important articles were found therein; the first was an imitation revolver and the second was a note on which he had written: 'Keep calm.

j Hand over £3,000 or I'll blow your head off'. A reasonable inference from the existence of those two articles in juxtaposition was that a rather elementary raid on the bank was being planned, the gun to cover the cashier and the note to indicate what the cashier was to do. The appellant was asked by Sergeant Batty what the note and the gun were for and the appellant began to cry. I emphasise this was a very dramatic piece of action taking place up to this point in a few seconds; the sudden eruption of Sergeant Batty into the car, the putting of the handcuffs on the appellant and the approach of Sergeant Ganley with the gun. The question was put to the appellant *a* what the gun and the note were for. He then began to cry. He said: 'I won't cause any trouble. I've been very stupid.' The appellant was then taken a few yards down the road to the police car where he was asked what he had been intending to do; he then replied: 'I've been very stupid. I was short of money and I was going to try and get some from the bank. It's not a real gun, though, it's a toy.' At this moment the police officers very properly cautioned him, they told him he need not say any more unless *b* he wished to. He went on with one more sentence. He was asked how often he had done this, meaning attempting to raid a bank in this style. He said: 'Not very often, but I expect you will find out. I have been very stupid.'

At this moment he was put into the police car and taken to Vine Street police station and further questioned there, but at a very early stage after his arrival in Vine Street police station he became wholly hysterical and it was apparent to the *c* police that there was no point in asking him further questions until he calmed down. There was some indication of an oncoming hysteria before the car left Chesterfield Street, some indication of frothing at the mouth in the car at Chesterfield Street, but by the time he got to Vine Street police station his condition had deteriorated. He was, as one police officer put it, 100 per cent hysterical. He had been crying or sobbing from a very early stage in the proceedings, and the police officers recognised *d* in their evidence that he was very frightened. No one condescended to detail why he was frightened, but that he was frightened was accepted by the officers and that condition, coupled with the fact that he was sobbing and coupled with the fact he was hysterical very shortly afterwards, is much relied on in this appeal, as will appear later.

The judge was told that objection was going to be taken to the admission of the *e* confessions to which I have already referred, and a trial within a trial was held. The judge concluded that the police officers had acted properly throughout, as indeed was accepted by counsel for the appellant. He rejected any suggestion that the caution had not been applied at the appropriate time. He came to the conclusion that the confessions were admissible and they duly went before the jury.

The only ground which is really taken before us in this appeal is that in the circum- *f* stances which I have outlined the confessions should not have been admitted. This is a case which, simple though it may be, does involve a certain amount of research into the early development of the law in regard to the admission of confessions.

It has been accepted from the earliest time, both in common law and common sense, that although a confession may be the most valuable of evidence to establish guilt, if it is made voluntarily, a confession which is not made voluntarily but which *g* is induced by pressures or other influences may be and often is thoroughly unreliable. It is for that reason that from the earliest days the common law has recognised that evidence of certain confessions is not admissible as a matter of law.

It is convenient to look at least one of the earlier authorities in which this proposition is stated, *Scott's* case[1]. There the principle on which the exclusion of such confessions is based was stated by Lord Campbell CJ in these terms[2]:   *h*

'It is a trite maxim that the confession of a crime, to be admissible against the party confessing, must be voluntary; but this only means that it shall not be induced by improper threats or promises, because, under such circumstances, the party may have been influenced to say what is not true, and the supposed confession cannot be safely acted upon.'
j

I cite that as one of the many indications that the rule is formulated as being one whereby the confession is excluded if it may have been induced by improper threats or promises.

1   (1856) Dears & B 47
2   Dears & B at 58

a Another example of the same principle in application is to be found in a New Zealand case, *Naniseni v R*[1]. The statement of principle for which I refer to this case is to be found in two passages. The first reads[2]:

b
'What must appear, if a confession is to be held voluntary, is in our opinion no more and no less than that it has been made by the prisoner, his will in making it not being overborne by the will of some other person by means of some consideration such as has been mentioned above. Not that the considerations which we have enumerated are to be narrowly interpreted as constituting a necessarily exhaustive list. But the factor which is relied upon as having over-borne, or as apt to overbear, the will of the prisoner, must be found in the will of some other person, by the exertion of which his confession is induced or is deemed by the law to have been induced. The will of some other person is essential;

c the involuntariness cannot be produced from within. Such consideration as fatigue, lack of sleep, emotional strain, or the consumption of alcohol, cannot be efficacious to deprive a confession of its quality of voluntariness, except, perhaps, so far as any of these may have been brought about or aggravated by some act or omission of other persons to the end that a confession should be made.'

d
A little further on in this same report appears this passage[3]:

'It is impossible to suggest, in this case, that any degree of fatigue or stress (if indeed there were any) under which the prisoner suffered was caused in the slightest degree by any act or omission either of those in authority over him or of any other persons to the end that he should confess. We are therefore of

e opinion that the learned trial Judge properly admitted the confession . . .'

Coming back to this country, I can usefully cite a judgment of Winn LJ, a judge who was as anxious as any to uphold the principle that a confession should not be admitted unless it was clearly voluntary. I take a passage from his judgment in *R v Richards*[4] where he deals with this same principle thus:

f
'It is clear law and has been for generations in this country, for reasons which were perhaps plainer when at one time men could not give evidence on their own behalf than now, that no statement which has been induced or which may have been induced by any promise or threat made by a person in authority is admissible evidence against the maker of the statement. It is now clear, further,

g that it is immaterial, if the inducement be made by the person in authority, whether or not it has any reference to any pending charge, any pending prosecution, or any potential prosecution. Whatever be the nature of the inducement so made and however trivial it may seem to the average man to have been, such an inducement will be at least capable of rendering the statement then made inadmissible; it will have that effect unless in a given case it becomes plain

h beyond a reasonable doubt that it did not operate at all on the mind of the person to whom it was made.'

Those cases, and there are many others, all as it seems to us proceed on this basis, that to rule a confession out as being inadmissible at law it must be shown it was not voluntary in the sense that it was procured by inducement of some form, either threats or promises offered by a person in authority at the particular situation in

j which the confession was made. The rule has not, as we see it, substantially changed over the years except in the following respects. In the first place this century has

---

1 [1971] NZLR 269
2 [1971] NZLR at 274
3 [1971] NZLR at 276
4 [1967] 1 All ER 829 at 830, [1967] 1 WLR 653 at 654

probably shown a more generous attitude to the suspect in the application of the rule;   *a*
by that I mean that although the principle has remained the same, the courts have
perhaps been overgenerous in accepting as an inducement for present purposes
something which would be unlikely to induce the average man.

Furthermore, the conception of the confession being made or the inducement
offered in the presence of a person in authority has been extended to the point where
the authority in question is perhaps minimal, but the principle is not affected.   *b*

The only possible addition to the principle which one finds in the English books at
the present time is that exemplified in the recent case, *R v Prager*[1], where it is
established that interrogation by police officers if carried on to the point of oppression
may be held to have destroyed the will of the suspect who was being interrogated,
and thus prevented a subsequent confession from being treated as a voluntary confession. That is I think another example of the confession ceasing to be voluntary   *c*
because of some failure on the part of authority to observe the rules which naturally
must govern situations of this kind.

There, as we see it, the extent of this principle in the English authorities ceases,
and although counsel for the appellant has disclaimed any suggestion that his argument is attaching a new principle or significantly extending that principle, we are of
the opinion that it is. I hope to do justice to his argument, which was very clear and   *d*
covered all the ground. It really amounts to this, in his first submission, that a
confession may be required to be ruled out as being inadmissible in law if
it is prompted by words or deeds emanating from a person in authority, whether or
not the person who used the words or did the deeds necessarily directed his conduct
to obtaining a confession. Counsel for the appellant submits that in those circumstances if the words or deeds are capable of amounting to an inducement, they   *e*
should be regarded as such with the result that the resultant confession should be
excluded.

He justifies this approach with logic, if I may say so, on the basis that the underlying
thought behind all these principles is the necessity for excluding all confessions
which are not voluntary. He submits in the circumstances which I have tried to
repeat and which he has postulated, that we have again an example of a confession   *f*
which is not voluntary, therefore he says it should be excluded from being given in
evidence before the jury. He says that the fact that he does not require any kind of
impropriety on the part of those in authority is no bar to the success of this argument,
because he rejects the suggestion that the question: admissible or no? is entirely
dependent on impropriety on the part of the police or authority. He says that has
no part in the argument, and he asserts that in the circumstances he postulates it is   *g*
possible to say a resultant confession is not voluntary and that we should give effect
to that principle.

We are not able to accept that submission. In the first place we accept what counsel
for the Crown has said, which to some extent has been made out by the reference to
authority included in this judgment, that under the existing law the exclusion of a
confession as a matter of law because it is not voluntary is always related to some con-   *h*
duct on the part of authority which is improper or unjustified. Included in the phrase
'improper or unjustified' of course must be the offering of any inducement, because
it is improper in this context for those in authority to try to induce a suspect to make a
confession. Counsel for the Crown says, and we agree, that if one looks to the
authorities there is no case in the books which indicates that a confession can
be regarded as not voluntary by reason of the present grounds, unless there is some   *j*
element of impropriety on the part of those in authority. That seems to be the case,
and we can see no justification for extending the principle today.

We are confirmed in that view by the extreme difficulty which we have had in
seeing exactly how counsel for the appellant's formula, if I may so describe it, would

---

1 [1972] 1 All ER 1114, [1972] 1 WLR 260

a work, and in the extreme difficulty of defining that formula in the sort of terms which a trial judge requires to have before him if he is to conduct a trial in a proper fashion. I illustrate that by taking a piece of counsel's argument and looking at it in a little more detail. He says that in the facts of this case the violent arrest, the hand-cuffing and the presence of Sergeant Ganley with his gun all combined naturally and understandably to make the appellant extremely frightened. He says that when the
b officers put to him the two simple questions which I have already related, he might well have felt, in the background in which this was being done, that he was deprived of a free choice, and that it was necessary for him to make some kind of statement.

Counsel for the appellant, significantly in our view, recognises that that would not have been so but for Sergeant Ganley's gun; he recognises that if all that happened here was a violent arrest and a handcuffing, if that had been done in the absence of
c the gun he would have no case.

We ask ourselves what is the principle? Where is the dividing line which separates the present situation with the gun included in the scenario, and the present situation without the gun. We find it quite impossible to define any sort of principle which would separate the two instances in that way, and if there is no principle which can be discovered and no relatively simple test which can be prescribed for the benefit of
d those trial judges who have to employ it, we would be extremely reluctant to confirm the submission which counsel for the appellant makes.

He submits, and we agree with him on this, that the basis of the exclusion rule is not a disciplinary measure to keep the police in order. He says that being the case, we should not regard impropriety on the part of the police as being the open sesame to the application of this rule.

e Although we accept what he says in the first part of that argument, it does not influence us to the extent that it would be proper or appropriate to state the law in what we regard as an advanced and different form based on counsel for the appellant's argument.

That is not an end of the matter because he takes a second and related, though independent point. He submits that if one forgets about the gun and the form of the
f arrest, there is a wholly independent principle, namely that if the suspect's mental state is such that he is deprived of the capacity to make a free choice whether to confess or not, then any confession which he makes is necessarily not a voluntary confession because it was not supported by the capacity to make a voluntary choice.

This is a relatively novel submission, although it is supported by certain Common-wealth authorities and is hinted at, if no more than that, in Cross on Evidence[1] where
g the learned author says:

> 'A good deal of Commonwealth authority supports the view that a confession will be inadmissible if obtained at a time when the accused's mind was so unbalanced as to render it wholly unsafe to act upon it. There is no clear English authority on this point, but, if one of the reasons for excluding confessions is the danger that they may be untrustworthy, it would be in accordance with principle
h to exclude a confession made by someone whose mental state was such as to render his utterances completely unreliable. It is, however, difficult to formu-late a governing principle, and it is possible that, in England, the matter will be treated as one of judicial discretion.'

We would accept that summary of the position as it stands at the present time, and
j we would recognise that one must not regard Professor Cross's phrase in which he describes the suspect as being in a condition where his utterances are completely unreliable as being the sole and only test in these matters. It may be in time other tests will be developed, but however one reads that and however one seeks to antici-pate further developments of this kind, we find it quite impossible to say on the

---

1   3rd Edn (1967), pp 450, 451

evidence in this case that the mental state of the appellant at the time of the con- a
fession which amounted to no more than the fact he was sobbing and frightened and
later became hysterical was within any sort of range of the test Professor Cross had in
mind.

Of course, in an extreme case where a man is a mental defective, it would be no
doubt absolutely right to rule out evidence of his confession as being wholly unreliable.
Not only does the appellant not come in that class, he does not come anywhere near b
that class. We do not need to consider developments on that aspect of counsel for
the appellant's submission but content ourselves with saying this particular appellant
could not come within this principle however widely it was applied.

That means so far as the appeal against conviction is concerned it must be dismissed.
I pause only to make one brief reference to another point on which counsel for the
appellant invited us to express an opinion if we thought fit. It is a procedural matter c
but not without importance, and it relates to the direction which the trial judge
gave to the jury in this case when the jury failed to produce a unanimous verdict.
He, the trial judge, had given them the proper instruction at the proper stage, that
they could bring in a majority verdict if they wanted, and in respect of one count they
brought in a majority verdict but remained in disagreement on the other two which
were before them. At this stage the trial judge gave the jury a direction which has d
been given by trial judges ever since 1952, and which has obtained the approval of the
Court of Appeal, to the effect that jurors should not be stubborn and stick to their own
points of view, but should discuss the matter amongst themselves and see whether
other jurors' views were not worth looking at and proper to be adopted. Those are
my words, and not the words of the direction, but that is the sense of it. This direction was given to the jury at a stage when they had produced one majority verdict e
and were still in disagreement about the other two counts.

Counsel for the appellant says, correctly, that that direction was first approved
when majority verdicts were unheard of. He says it is inappropriate to use such a
direction now when majority verdicts are available, and particularly inappropriate to
use such a direction when the jury have already had a majority verdict direction and
indeed have produced one such verdict.   f

We do not think that this is a case in which we would seek to lay down hard and
fast rules, because we think them unnecessary. We think it obvious that if a trial
judge seeks to use the general direction to which I have referred after he has given a
majority verdict direction, he ought to adapt the language to make it suitable for the
new situation for which it was not originally designed.

We also think that before giving such a general direction at that stage, the judge g
ought to remember that to some extent the fact that majority verdicts are possible
has taken away the mischief at which the original direction was aimed; but despite all
that we are not disposed to say that it is improper for the judge to give the general
direction at the point at which it was given in this case, though we would counsel trial
judges to use some discretion in the matter and not repeat the direction in its exact
and precise terms without regard to the changing circumstances in which it is h
operative. However, the effect of the appeal so far as conviction is concerned is that
it is dismissed.

[Counsel then addressed the court on sentence].

LORD WIDGERY CJ. Whether or not the trial judge misdirected himself in
respect of the consecutive effect in each case, so far as this court is concerned we must j
consider whether the applicant should be sentenced differently, that being the word
used in the Criminal Appeal Act 1968. By way of explanation, I am pointing out that
even if the trial judge did approach this on a wrong principle in the respect to which
counsel for the applicant refers, the effect will be in any event now to ask ourselves
whether the appellant should have been sentenced differently. We think that having
regard to the gravity of this offence, despite its comparatively elementary planning,

a that the sentence of four years' imprisonment in respect of it was not a day too long and accordingly we refuse the application for leave to appeal against sentence.

Appeal against conviction dismissed. Application for leave to appeal against sentence refused. Leave to appeal to House of Lords refused.

b Solicitors: *Offenbach & Co* (for the appellant); *Solicitor, Metropolitan Police* (for the Crown).

N P Metcalfe Esq Barrister.

Warr v Warr

c
FAMILY DIVISION
BAGNALL J
16th MAY, 16th, 17th JULY 1974

Divorce – Separation – Period of separation – Computation – Period immediately preceding
d *presentation of petition – Whether day on which separation took place to be excluded in computing period of separation – Matrimonial Causes Act 1973, s 1(2)(c)(d)(e).*

The husband and wife separated at noon on 6th February 1972. During the afternoon of 6th February 1974 the wife filed a petition for divorce relying on the facts prescribed by s 1(2)(d)^a of the Matrimonial Causes Act 1973, i e that the parties had lived apart for a continuous period of at least two years immediately preceding the
e presentation of the petition and that the husband consented to a decree being granted.

Held – The day on which the separation had taken place was to be excluded when computing the periods of time specified in s 1(2)(c)(d) and (e) of the 1973 Act. Accordingly the wife had failed to prove that the statutory period had expired when she presented her petition, and the petition would therefore be dismissed (see p 92 *d*
f and *e*, p 93 *e* and *g* and p 94 *b*, post).
Re North, ex parte Hasluck [1895] 2 QB 264 and *Belfield v Belfield* [1945] VLR 231 applied.
Terry v Terry [1939] 3 All ER 546 not followed.

Notes
For the inclusion or exclusion of a day in the computation of periods of time, see
g 37 Halsbury's Laws (3rd Edn) 92, para 161, and for cases on the subject, see 45 Digest (Repl) 253-254, *198-215*.
For divorce on proof of desertion or separation for specified periods, see Supplement to 12 Halsbury's Laws (3rd Edn) para 437A, 4, 5.
For the Matrimonial Causes Act 1973, s 1, see 43 Halsbury's Statutes (3rd Edn) 541.

h **Cases referred to in judgment**
Bamford v Bamford [1956] CLY 2831.
Belfield v Belfield [1945] VLR 231, ALR 206, 27 (1) Digest (Reissue) 460, *1802.*

---

a Section 1(2), so far as material, provides: ' The court hearing a petition for divorce shall
j   not hold the marriage to have broken down irretrievably unless the petitioner satisfies
       the court of one or more of the following facts, that is to say . . . (c) that the respondent has
       deserted the petitioner for a continuous period of at least two years immediately preceding
       the presentation of the petition; (d) that the parties to the marriage have lived apart for
       a continuous period of at least two years immediately preceding the presentation of the
       petition . . . and the respondent consents to a decree being granted; (e) that the parties
       to the marriage have lived apart for a continuous period of at least five years immediately
       preceding the presentation of the petition . . .'

Chapman v Chapman [1954] 1 All ER 798, [1954] AC 429, [1954] 2 WLR 723, HL, *a*
47 Digest (Repl) 329, *2973*.
Lester v Garland (1808) 15 Ves 248, [1803-13] All ER Rep 436, 33 ER 748, 45 Digest
(Repl) 254, *211*.
North, Re, ex parte Hasluck [1895] 2 QB 264, 64 LJQB 694, 72 LT 854, 59 JP 724, 2 Mans
326, 45 Digest (Repl) 252, *197*.
R v St Mary, Warwick (Inhabitants) (1853) 1 E & B 816, 1 CLR 192, 22 LJMC 109, 21 *b*
LTOS 74, 17 JP 552, 118 ER 642, 45 Digest (Repl) 269, *375*.
R v Shropshire Justices (1838) 8 Ad & El 173, 112 ER 803, sub nom *R v Salop Justices*
3 Nev & PKB 286, 1 Will Woll & H 158, 7 LJMC 56, 45 Digest (Repl) 253, *204*.
Seaford (deceased), Re, Seaford v Seifert [1968] 1 All ER 482, [1968] P 53, [1968] 2 WLR 155,
CA, Digest (Cont Vol C) *333, 1647a*.
Terry v Terry [1939] 3 All ER 546, 27(1) Digest (Reissue) 471, *3425*.   *c*
Young v Higgon (1840) 6 M & W 49, [1835-42] All ER Rep 278, 8 Dowl 212, 9 LJMC 29,
4 JP 88, 151 ER 317, 45 Digest (Repl) 254, *214*.
Zouch v Empsey (1821) 4 B & Ald 522, 106 ER 1028, 45 Digest (Repl) 263, *299*.

Case also cited
Lawford v Davies (1878) 4 PD 61, 47 LJP 38.   *d*

Petition
The husband, Michael Warr, and the wife, Jacqueline Warr, separated on 6th February
1972. By her petition filed on 6th February 1974, the wife alleged that the marriage
had broken down irretrievably, relying on the facts prescribed by s 1(2)(*d*) of the
Matrimonial Causes Act 1973, ie that the parties had lived apart for a period of *e*
two years immediately preceding the presentation of the petition and that the
husband consented to the decree being granted. When the matter first came before
Bagnall J, the Queen's Proctor was invited to intervene in the suit and the wife was
given leave to issue a fresh petition in case she failed to prove that the parties had
lived apart for a period of two years immediately preceding the presentation of the
first petition.   *f*

Mathew Thorpe for the wife.
Gilbert Rodway for the Queen's Proctor as amicus curiae.

BAGNALL J. By her petition in this suit the wife, Jacqueline Warr, claims *g*
dissolution of her marriage and, in order to establish that the marriage has broken
down irretrievably, she relies on the combination of facts set out in s 1(2)(*d*) of the
Matrimonial Causes Act 1973. It is established to my satisfaction, by evidence and
admission, that she and her husband separated at noon on 6th February 1972 and
that they have lived apart continuously since then; also that the respondent husband
consents to the granting of a decree. The petition was issued at some time after *h*
noon on 6th February 1974. The question I have to decide is whether those facts
establish that the parties to the marriage have lived apart for a continuous period of
at least two years immediately preceding the presentation of the petition.
I quote that phrase from para (*d*) of s 1(2) of the Act, but the phrase: 'for a continuous period of at least [a stated number of] years immediately preceding the
presentation of the petition' also occur in paras (*c*) and (*e*) of s 1(2). The same phraseology in relation to the matrimonial offence of desertion appeared in s 1(1)(*a*) of *j*
the Matrimonial Causes Act 1965, and s 2 of the Matrimonial Causes Act 1937. In
s 27 of the Matrimonial Causes Act 1857 the description of desertion where it was
relevant was 'desertion, without reasonable excuse, for two years or upwards'.
I think there is no material difference in that wording from the wording in the other
Acts that I have quoted.

a   Counsel for the wife submits, first, that the separation must be treated as having occurred immediately after midnight on 6th February 1972, so that the two year period ended at midnight on 5th February 1974, and had been completed before the day on which the petition was issued. Alternatively, he submits that I should look at the actual times at which the relevant events occurred, so that the two year period ended at noon on 6th February 1974 and, the petition having been *b*   issued at a time later than noon on that day, the period of two years ended before the presentation of the petition.

When the matter first came before me I took steps to arrange that the Queen's Proctor should intervene in this suit. He did so and counsel has appeared on his instructions, in order to put all relevant submissions of law before me, and I am indebted to him for his assistance.

c   I may say at once that in my judgment counsel for the wife's alternative submission must be rejected for this reason: none of the cases which have been cited to me on statutes either in pari materia or dealing with similar matters has suggested that in a case such as this the question should be resolved by reference to precise times of day. Precise times of day have been held to be relevant in cases in which it is necessary to establish priority of time as between two conflicting parties, *d*   such as in relation to land charges or equitable interests, whether by registration or otherwise; and in such a case as *Re Seaford (decd), Seaford v Seifert*[1], where the question that arose related to the effect of the filing of an application for decree absolute after the respondent husband had died, but on the day on which that death occurred. The ratio decidendi in that case was that it was impossible for the court to dissolve by its decree a marriage which had already been brought to an *e*   end by death, or, as Russell LJ put it succinctly[2]:

'Whom God had put asunder no man could join together, even for the purpose of putting them asunder again.'

I am satisfied that that case is of no assistance on the matter which I have to decide. I do, however, add that the uncertainties and inconveniences that would arise if *f*   counsel for the wife's alternative submission were accepted are all too obvious to require to be stated.

I turn to his principal submission, in support of which he relies both on principle and on authority. As to principle, he submits that at common law the law takes no account of part of a day, in this sense, that an event which occurs during any given day is treated as creating a state of affairs which must be deemed to have had a *g*   continuous existence throughout the whole of that day. The most familiar example of this principle in operation is to be found in the rule which, until it was abrogated by s 9(1) of the Family Law Reform Act 1969, recognised that a person attained the age of 21 at the first moment of the day immediately preceding the 21st anniversary of his birth. Applying that principle, counsel submits that the two year period must be treated as having expired at the first moment of, or at any rate at some moment *h*   during, 5th February 1974, so bringing the presentation of this petition within the requirements of s 1(2)(d) of the 1973 Act.

As to authority, he relies on *Terry v Terry*[3]. In that case the question was whether a period of three years had expired immediately before 28th January 1937. Hodson J, dealing with that question at the end of his judgment, said this[4]:

i   'The terminal date from which desertion must commence would be, at the latest, Jan. 28, 1934, and I think, therefore, that the date on which the husband failed to arrive at the new business, as promised, was too late to come within the

---

1   [1968] 1 All ER 482, [1968] P 53
2   [1968] 1 All ER at 491, [1968] P at 73, 74
3   [1939] 3 All ER 546
4   [1939] 3 All ER at 548

period of 3 years. I am satisfied, however, from the conduct of the respondent, *a*
that he never really intended to rejoin his wife, and that desertion commenced
from the time when she left his mother's house, which I find to be either Jan. 27
or Jan. 28, 1934 to pack up her things with a view to settling in the new home.
The law takes no account of part of a day for such a purpose as this, and desertion
for a period of 3 years, therefore, was completed on Jan. 27, 1937, the day before
the issue of the summons.'   *b*

If Hodson J had taken a view contrary to the submission made on behalf of the wife
it would have been crucial for him to have decided as a fact that which he left as an
alternative, namely, the date on which the desertion commenced, but it is plain from
the fact that he left that as an alternative, and from his precise words, that his view
coincided with counsel for the wife's submission. It is tempting simply to follow
that decision without enquiry as completely concluding the question which I have to *c*
decide, a course which I should the more readily follow recognising that the learned
judge who decided that case had an experience of the practice of the predecessor of
this division which was unrivalled. I am, however, satisfied that I ought not to take
that course, for two reasons. First, although as appears from the report, that case
was heard on three separate days in 1939, it was undefended, so that the contrary
argument was not presented, and it is plain from the report as a whole, and from the *d*
judgment in particular, that none of the relevant authorities with which I have
been assisted were drawn to the attention of the learned judge.

I have, however, been referred to cases on other statutes in which a similar question
has arisen which are binding on me, also to persuasive authority on a statute in pari
materia which led to a contrary conclusion. There is a number of cases, both before
and after the beginning of the 19th century, dealing with the attainment of majority *e*
for the purpose of ability to make a will, or of entitlement to property, in which the
principle on which counsel for the wife relies has been applied. They are referred to
in some of the cases which I shall cite, but I do not think it necessary to refer to
them. It is, however, to be observed that, where that principle has been applied
in relation to attainment of majority, its application has invariably been to the
advantage of the person principally involved.   *f*

Counsel referred me to a further case as an example of the application of the
principle in a different context, namely, *R v St Mary, Warwick (Inhabitants)*[1]. In that
case, in order that a person might gain his settlement in the relevant parish, it was
necessary to show that he had rented and occupied a tenement for the term of one
whole year at least. He had taken a tenancy from the 30th September 1850 for one
year, had entered at noon on that day and had quitted at 4.00 pm on 29th September *g*
in the following year. Lord Campbell CJ, giving the principal judgment, said[2]:

'Any one, talking of these facts in ordinary language, would say that the pauper
occupied for a year. I would abstain from so holding, if any recognised rule or
direct decision militated against it: but really law and sense concur. The general
rule is that the law does not regard fractions of a day. Well then, here is an occu- *h*
pation which begins on the 30th of September and continues through a part of
the 29th of September following: there are therefore 365 days of occupation,
which make a legal year. Then is the case within any of the exceptions in which
it has been held that the fraction of a day may be regarded? I think not. You must
indeed regard the fraction in cases where you have to determine the rights of
contending parties, each insisting on their portion of the time: but this is not *j*
such a case.'

Lord Campbell CJ concluded[3]:

1   (1853) 1 E & B 816
2   1 E & B at 827
3   1 E & B at 828

a   'Here, by the very form of the instrument, the hiring is for one year commencing on 30th September. Was there then an occupation for that year. The occupation began on the 30th of September and ended on the 29th of September; so that, including those two days, there were 365 days, making up a whole year. It seems to me, therefore, that there was a renting for a year and an occupation for that year; and that a settlement was acquired.'

b   The other three learned judges concurred both in the reasoning and in the result. Again, it is to be observed that the view taken by the court was to the advantage of the person principally concerned.

    At the beginning of the 19th century there was an example to which I was also referred, in which the contrary view on a similar question was taken. The case is *Lester v Garland*[1]. In that case the testator's sister was required by a will to give a

c   security within a period of six months that she would not intermarry with a certain individual, and on her failure to comply with that condition her children were to forfeit part of the benefit conferred on them by the will. Grant MR said this[2]:

    'The question in this case is, whether Mrs. *Pointer* within six calendar months after the decease of her brother gave the security, required by his Will, as the condi-

d   tion, upon which her children should take the benefit of his residuary estate. He died upon the 12th of *January*, 1805, at a quarter before nine o'clock in the evening. The security required was executed upon the 12th of *July* following, about seven in the evening. Computing the time *de momento in momentum*, six calendar months had not elapsed: but it is admitted that this is not the way in which the computation is legally to be made. The question is, whether the day of Sir *John Lester's*

e   death is to be included in the six months, or to be excluded: if the day is included, she did not, if it is excluded, she did, give the required security before the end of the last day of the six months; and therefore did sufficiently comply with the condition. It is said for the Plaintiffs, that upon this subject a general rule has been by decision established; that, where the time is to run from the doing of an act, (and for the purpose of this question it must extend to the happening of an

f   event) the day is always to be included. Whatever *dicta* there may be to that effect, it is clear, the actual decisions cannot be brought under any such general rule.'

Grant MR then considered a number of authorities and went on as follows[3]:

    'It is not necessary to lay down any general rule upon this subject: but upon technical reasoning I rather think, it would be more easy to maintain, that the

g   day of an act done, or an event happening, ought in all cases to be excluded, than that it should in all cases be included. Our law rejects fractions of a day more generally than the civil law does. The effect is to render the day a sort of indivisible point; so that any act, done in the compass of it, is no more referrible to any one, than to any other, portion of it; but the act and the day are co-extensive; and therefore the act cannot properly be said to be passed, until the day is passed.'

h   Having referred to a further authority, Grant MR concluded[4]:

    'But it is not necessary to lay down any general rule. Whichever way it should be laid down, cases would occur, the reason of which would require exceptions to be made. Here the reason of the thing requires the exclusion of the day from the period of six months, given to Mrs. *Pointer* to deliberate upon the choice she

j   would make; and upon the whole my opinion is, that she has entered into the security before the expiration of the six months; in sufficient time therefore to fulfil the condition, on which her children were to take.'

1 (1808) 15 Ves 248, [1803-13] All ER Rep 436
2 15 Ves at 253, [1803-13] All ER Rep at 437
3 15 Ves at 257, [1803-13] All ER Rep at 439
4 15 Ves at 258, [1803-13] All ER Rep at 439

Again, it is to be observed that the decision reached was to the advantage of the person a
principally involved.

The contrast between those two cases provokes the question: on what principle is
it to be determined whether the phraseology with which I am concerned points to the
shorter period, as in *R v St Mary, Warwick (Inhabitants)*[1] or to the longer period, as in
Lester v Garland[2]. The answer, in my view, is to be found in the decision of the Court
of Appeal in *Re North*[3].   b

Before, however, I turn to that case I should record that I was referred to a number
of authorities in procedural matters where the question was what length of notice of
process had to be given. Examples of them are *Zouch v Empsey*[4], *R v Shropshire Justices*[5], and *Young v Higgon*[6]. I was also referred to RSC Ord 3 r 2, which, since its predecessor was introduced, has regulated these matters in relation to all forms of procedure under those rules. I was also referred to the note in the White Book[7] under c
that rule, which reads as follows:

'For example, the words "three months before the presentation of the bankruptcy petition" specified in the B.A., 1914, s 4(1)(e) as the period within which
an act of bankruptcy must have occurred, are exclusive of the date of the act of
bankruptcy but inclusive of the date of presentation . . .'
                                                                                    d

Two authorities are referred to in support of that proposition.

I am satisfied that no guidance can be obtained from the cases to which I have referred as dealing with procedural matters, that I am not entitled to make use of a
general rule contained in the Rules of the Supreme Court as an aid to the construction
of a specific statute, and that the bankruptcy cases cited in support of the note which I
have read turned on specific provisions of the Bankruptcy Act 1914 dealing with the e
interpretation of the relevant time requirement.

Re North[3] turned on a requirement of s 1 of the Bankruptcy Act 1890, the relevant
part of which is in the following terms:

'A debtor commits an act of bankruptcy if execution against him has been
levied by seizure of his goods under process in an action in any court, or in any f
civil proceeding in the High Court, and the goods have been either sold or held
by the sheriff for twenty-one days.'

The question that arose was whether the requisite 21 days had elapsed. Lord Esher
MR said[8]:

'No general rule exists for the computation of time either under the Bank- g
ruptcy Act or any other statute, or, indeed, where time is mentioned in a contract,
and the rational mode of computation is to have regard in each case to the purpose for which the computation is to be made. Notwithstanding the elaborate
array of authorities which have been cited to us, they seem on being sifted to
contain no binding rule to the effect that time must be computed according to a
hard and fast rule: that seems clear from the judgment in *Lester v Garland*[2], in h
which Sir William Grant, after a learned examination of the whole subject, laid
down what I conceive to be the wholesome view that no general rule exists. A
great deal of difficulty has been caused in the administration of the law, and
particularly of the common law, by decisions in which technical rules have been

1 (1853) 1 E & B 816
2 (1808) 15 Ves 248, [1803-13] All ER Rep 436   j
3 [1895] 2 QB 264
4 (1821) 4 B & Ald 522
5 (1838) 8 Ad & El 173
6 (1840) M & W 49
7 Supreme Court Practice 1973, vol 1, p 14, para 3/2/6
8 [1895] 2 QB at 269

a formulated which were not true—that is, were not in accordance with the facts of the case. To say that by the common law a part of a day is the whole of a day is to say something which is contrary to the truth; it is a technical rule which was imposed upon the law with the result of bringing the law into disrepute. It is immaterial whether these older decisions were right in the particular cases; if they, or any of them, laid down any general rule as to the mode of computing *b* time, that rule has been departed from in recent times, and no longer exists.'

After stating that the court must determine what was the proper mode of computing a period of time under this statute, Lord Esher MR went on[1]:

'If we construe s. 1 of the Act of 1890 according to the ordinary English meaning of the words, it enacts that certain consequences are to happen if the sheriff holds *c* for twenty-one days goods seized by him under an execution: an act of bankruptcy is committed if he holds them for that time. The ordinary meaning of the words is that he must hold them for twenty-one days, but we are told that under a technical rule of construction the section is satisfied if he holds them for twenty days and a part of a day. Which is right? It is clear to me that when the section says that a certain result is to follow if the sheriff holds the goods for twenty-one days, it *d* means twenty-one days and not twenty days and a fraction; he must hold them for twenty-one whole days. A fair rule of construction seems to be that where the computation is to be for the benefit of the person affected as much time should be given as the language admits of, and where it is to his detriment the language should be construed as strictly as possible. Here the result may be to make a man a bankrupt, which is not a benefit to him, nor necessarily to the whole of his *e* creditors. The bankruptcy law is a law of public social policy, and affects in a very detrimental manner the status of those who are brought under its operation; in old times, indeed, to make a man a bankrupt was to make him a criminal; therefore, in a Bankruptcy Act such a provision as the one in question ought to be construed as much for the debtor's benefit as possible.'

f A L Smith LJ was of the same opinion, as also was Rigby LJ. In the course of his judgment Rigby LJ said[2]:

'It is said that the law takes no account of fractions of a day; but that is not a correct statement, if it means that the law will never inquire at what time a particular event took place; for instance, a difference of five minutes in the registration of two deeds in the Middlesex Registry would be sufficient to determine a question of priorities, and the time of their respective registrations *g* would, as a matter of course, be looked at. If the doctrine is cut down to the proposition that in the computation of time the law takes no account of fractions of a day, then it means one of two things: either that the fraction of a day is to be taken as a whole day, or that it is to be excluded altogether from the calculation; it does not help us to determine in any particular case whether the part is to *h* be left out or kept in'.

Then, after referring to the judgment of Grant MR in *Lester v Garland*[3], Rigby LJ went on[4]:

'His classification of the cases shews that where the calculation is in favour of a person, the construction should be adopted which is more favourable to him. In the case of a sheriff, for instance, it is more in his favour to include the day on *j* which the act is done than to exclude it, and on that ground it is included; but where, to take another example, something has to be done which is necessary

1 [1895] 2 QB at 270
2 [1895] 2 QB at 273
3 (1808) 15 Ves 248, [1803–13] All ER Rep 436
4 [1895] 2 QB at 274

to complete a title, the first day is excluded, otherwise there would be a cutting   *a*
down of the time allowed for doing the act. In my opinion, although Sir W. Grant
did not put the proposition in so many words, his judgment leads us to the
conclusion that the question of whether the day on which the act is done is to be
included or excluded must depend on whether it is to the benefit or disadvantage
of the person primarily interested.'

The difficulty of applying the principle thus enunciated in *Re North*[1] in matrimonial   *b*
proceedings is this. In such proceedings two persons are primarily concerned. If one
adopts Lord Esher MR's words, ought one to look to the benefit of the petitioner who
desires the decree, or to the detriment of the respondent against whom a decree may
be granted? I have not overlooked that, in the present case, founded as it is on s 1
(2)(*d*) of the 1973 Act, each party desires a decree, and the adoption of the shorter
period would be for the benefit of both; but, as I have said, identical words appear in   *c*
paras (*c*) and (*e*) of the subsection, and where those are the relevant paragraphs a
decree may be granted against a protesting respondent. I have no doubt that the same
interpretation must be given to the phrase in question in each of those three paragraphs.
    If the matter were res integra my own conclusion would be that one should look to
the detriment to the respondent. Divorce involves a change of status, and to have his
status changed against his will is, I think, a quasi-penal consequence to a man com-   *d*
parable with bankruptcy or the forfeiture of an estate. An example may illustrate the
point. Suppose a man to leave his wife with the intention of never returning, at 4.00
p m on 6th February 1972; suppose then, a petition presented at 10.00 a m on 6th February 1974; and suppose finally that the husband in question returns wishing to be
reconciled at 2.00 p m on that day; in terms of true time he would not have been absent
for a full period of two years. But, if counsel for the wife's submissions prevail, he   *e*
would have no answer to an allegation that he had deserted his wife for the period
described in s 1(2)(*c*) of the 1973 Act.
    When I turn to the last case from which I must make a citation I find that it provides
support for the conclusion that I should have reached apart from authority. The case
is *Belfield v Belfield*[2], an Australian case. The phrase in the statute, the Marriage Act
1928, s 75(*a*), which there had to be construed (it being a case of desertion) was that the   *f*
respondent had, 'without just cause or excuse wilfully deserted the petitioner, and,
without any such cause or excuse, left him, or her, continuously so deserted during
three years and upwards'. Before coming to the substance of the judgment of O'Bryan
J—which was given after full argument and extensive citation of authority—I observe
that the learned judge took the view that the words 'and upwards' were equivalent to
'or more' and indicated that desertion must have continued for a complete and actual   *g*
period of three years, and he assimilated them to such expressions as 'clear days', 'so
many days at least', 'a month or more', or 'not less than'. I think, with respect to the
learned judge, that a purist might say that 'three years and upwards' required that
the period should be more than three years, whereas 'three years at least' is a phrase
that would be satisfied by the lapse of that exact period. However, I refer to that part
of the judgment only because it is plain that the learned judge was treating the phrase   *h*
with which he had to deal as identical to the phrase which is before me.
    In his reserved judgment the learned judge said[3]:

    'If time is to be measured by the calendar, and regard is had to parts of a day,
    desertion had not continued for a complete period of three years. But counsel for
    the petitioner contended that the law does not pay regard to parts of a day, and   *j*
    that the general principle of statutory construction is that in computing a period
    of time from the doing of an act or the happening of an event, the day upon which

---

1 [1895] 2 QB 264
2 [1945] VLR 231
3 [1945] VLR at 232

a   the act is done or the event happens is *primâ facie* to be included. He contends that this principle applies to this case, and that you compute the period of three years from the original act of desertion, and that in doing so you include the day upon which desertion started, viz.: the 2nd March 1942, and that, accordingly, three years' desertion was complete at midnight on 1st March 1945. In support of that proposition he cited a number of authorities.'

b   The learned judge then referred to some of the authorities on the attainment of majority and to a number of other cases, including *R v St Mary, Warwick (Inhabitants)*[1] and *Lester v Garland*[2]. He made a full analysis of the decision of the Court of Appeal in *Re North*[3] and expressed his own conclusion in these words[4]:

c   'That decision is, in my opinion, very much in point in this case. Here the statute says that the desertion must continue during three years and upwards. Is there any reason for saying that the matrimonial offence is to be deemed to be complete although desertion has not actually continued for three years? In my opinion, there is not. *In re North*[3] is an illustration of the principle that any general rule that, in computing a period of time, fixed by statute, for the doing of an act or the happening of an event, the day on which the act is done or the event *d*   happens is prima facie to be included, gives way if the context suggests otherwise, and more especially if the statute provides that at the expiration of the period there will follow forfeiture or the loss of status or liberty.'

The learned judge decided that the longer period was appropriate in that case and accordingly held that the requisite period of desertion had not been established.

e   As I have indicated in expressing my own view, I find the reasoning of O'Bryan J convincing and I agree with his conclusions. Nevertheless, counsel for the wife, in his cogent and attractive argument, submitted that I should follow *Terry v Terry*[5] and distinguish *Belfield v Belfield*[6], because, since 1st January 1971, and now under the provisions of the 1973 Act, the concept of a matrimonial offence has been abandoned and the only ground leading to a decree of divorce is that the marriage has broken down *f*   irretrievably. He recalls to mind statements of high authority that divorce is now not so much a matter of fault as of misfortune. Finally, he points out, rightly, that a respondent against whom any of the facts set out in s 1(2) of the Act is proved may still resist the grant of a decree by establishing, under s 1(4), that the marriage has not broken down irretrievably. In my judgment that distinction is unsound.

The scheme of the 1973 Act provides a respondent with two shields whereby he may *g*   resist the grant of a decree. To take two examples: desertion for two years, or continuous separation for five years, if established on the evidence, deprives a respondent of one of those shields. In my view that deprivation constitutes a penalty or detriment within the principle which seems to me to be firmly established by the decision of the Court of Appeal in *Re North*[3].

During the course of the argument reference was made to the presumption said *h*   to apply where words of a statute have been judicially construed in a decided case and then the same words are used in a subsequent statute. Parliament, it is said, must be presumed to know the law established by the cases and must therefore be presumed in the later Act to have used the words in the sense established by judicial authority. There have been differences, both in professional and in academic opinion, on the strength, and, indeed, on the existence of the presumption to which I have referred.

j

---

1   (1853) 1 E & B 816
2   (1808) 15 Ves 248, [1803-13] All ER Rep 436
3   [1895] 2 QB 264
4   [1945] VLR at 237
5   [1939] 3 All ER 546
6   [1945] VLR 231

I do not find it necessary to take time in pursuing an argument based on that pre-   a
sumption because it seems to me that, however strong or however weak the presumption may be, it does not apply where the only authority for the relevant construction
of the earlier Act is a case at first instance where the suit was undefended and full
argument on both sides was not presented.

On the whole matter I am of the opinion that I ought to follow the reasoning and
conclusion in *Belfield v Belfield*[1], and that I ought not to follow—though with the great-   b
est respect and regret—the decision in *Terry v Terry*[2].   Accordingly, I hold that the
petitioner in this case has not established that she and her husband have lived apart
for a continuous period of at least two years immediately preceding the presentation
of her petition.   It follows, also, that I agree with the decision of Mr Commissioner
Reid in *Bamford v Bamford*[3], where he reached a similar conclusion to that which I
have reached on a similar question in relation to the period of three years prescribed   c
by s 3(1) of the 1973 Act.

When the matter first came before me I gave leave to the petitioner to issue a
fresh petition in case she should be unable to succeed on her original petition.   Accordingly, treating both petitions as before me, I propose to dismiss the petition presented on 6th February 1974.   On the second petition I shall grant a decree nisi, holding
the marriage to have irretrievably broken down by reason of the facts set out in   d
s 1(2)(d) of the 1973 Act, and I certify that there is no child of the family to whom the
Act applies.

I understand that there has been a number of similar cases in which the petition has
been issued on the second anniversary of the commencement of the separation, and
that, pursuant to some of them, decrees may have been granted.   In those circumstances it seems desirable that I should record my opinion that no doubt can be cast on   e
the validity of any decree so granted.   In my judgment the petition was not a nullity.
If my view of the construction of the Act is right, the decision to grant a decree was
wrong in law, but, in the absence of an appeal, the decree stands effective according
to its terms.   If authority were required for that proposition, it is, I think, to be found
in the observations of Lord Cohen in *Chapman v Chapman*[4].

f

First petition dismissed.   Decree nisi granted on the second petition.

Solicitors: *Franks, Charlesly & Co* (for the wife); *The Queen's Proctor*.

R C T Habesch   Barrister.

g

1   [1945] VLR 231
2   [1939] 3 All ER 546
3   [1956] CLY 2831
4   [1954] 1 All ER 798 at 821, [1954] AC 429 at 474

a
Higgs and another v Nassauvian Ltd

PRIVY COUNCIL
LORD CROSS OF CHELSEA, LORD SALMON AND SIR HARRY GIBBS
14th OCTOBER 1974

b
Limitation of action – Land – Adverse possession – Acts amounting to possession – Acts tending to prove possession of part of land – Acts tending to prove possession of part tending to prove possession of whole – Land not enclosed by wall or other physical barrier – Boundaries of land known and not in dispute – Whether acts tending to prove possession of part capable of proving possession of whole.

c
The respondent claimed to be the owner of an undivided one-fourth part of or interest in a tract of land ('the tract') of some 92 acres in the Bahama Islands. The tract was for the most part arable, although some of it consisted of pine barren. It was not fenced or otherwise enclosed but the boundaries were known and not disputed. The respondent's claim was based on documentary title. The appellants,
d who also had an undivided interest in the land based on documentary title, claimed to have acquired a possessory title to the tract, on the ground that they and their predecessors in title had been in exclusive possession of the tract for more than 20 years before the proceedings were commenced, and that the respondent's title was therefore barred by the Real Property Limitation Acts 1833 and 1874, which applied to the Bahama Islands. The evidence established that the respondent and
e its predecessors in title had been out of possession during the relevant period, and that at various dates during that period the appellants' predecessors and their tenants had farmed the land, producing small crops of various kinds, particularly vegetables. It appeared that the practice of most of the farmers had been to cultivate a small area, to reap the harvest, and then to move on to another area, leaving the first to become overgrown. The evidence presented by the appellants was however impre-
f cise and lacking in detail; it was not consistent within itself and was in certain material respects contradicted by other evidence. The trial judge rejected the appellants' claim that they had acquired a possessory title by adverse possession and his decision was affirmed by the Court of Appeal of the Bahama Islands. The appellants appealed contending, inter alia, that the judge and the Court of Appeal had erred in law in that they had held that sporadic farming over portions of a large tract of land could
g never be enough to establish possession of the whole tract.

Held – Although the rule that acts which tended to prove possession of a part of a tract of land tended to prove possession of the whole did not apply to land with undefined or disputed boundaries, it did not follow that acts done on part of the land were only relevant to prove possession of the whole if the land was enclosed by
h a wall or other physical barrier. The land claimed by possession might be suffi- ciently defined in other ways. Although the tract in question was not physically enclosed its boundaries were known and undisputed and accordingly possession of the whole by the appellants might have been established by acts done on parts of it. The question was, however, one of fact and it had not been shown that the trial judge had failed to consider the question of fact which he had to decide.
j Accordingly the appeal would be dismissed (see p 101 *h* to p 102 *a* and *d e*, post).
Dictum of Lord Diplock in *Ocean Estates Ltd v Pinder* [1969] 2 AC at 23, 24, explained.

Notes
For the meaning and effect of adverse possession, see 24 Halsbury's Laws (3rd Edn) 251, 252, paras 481, 482, and for cases on the subject, see 32 Digest (Repl) 503-509, *1106-1134.*

Cases referred to in opinion   a

Clark v Elphinstone (1880) 6 App Cas 164, 50 LJPC 22, PC, 7 Digest (Repl) 329, 437.

Jones v Williams (1837) 2 M & W 326, [1835-42] All ER Rep 423, Murph & H 51, 6 LJEx
    107, 150 ER 781, 46 Digest (Repl) 365, 119.

Lord Advocate v Lord Blantyre (1879) 4 App Cas 770, HL, 32 Digest (Repl) 509, 1136.

Lord Advocate v Lord Lovat (1880) 5 App Cas 273, HL, 25 Digest (Repl) 26, 242.

Ocean Estates Ltd v Pinder [1969] 2 AC 19, [1969] 2 WLR 1359, PC, Digest (Cont Vol C)   b
    1033, 98a.

Paradise Beach and Transportation Co Ltd v Price-Robinson [1968] 1 All ER 530, [1968]
    AC 1072, [1968] 2 WLR 873, PC, Digest (Cont Vol C) 640, 1546a.

Smith v Lloyd (1854) 9 Exch 562, 2 CLR 1007, 23 LJEx 194, 22 LTOS 289, 156 ER 240,
    32 Digest (Repl) 505, 1115.

Stanley v White (1811) 14 East 332, 104 ER 630, 2 Digest (Repl) 88, 531.   c

Trustees, Executors & Agency Co Ltd v Short (1888) 13 App Cas 793, 58 LJCP 4, 59 LT 677,
    53 JP 132, PC, 32 Digest (Repl) 505, 1116.

West Bank Estates Ltd v Arthur [1967] 1 AC 665, [1966] 3 WLR 750, PC, Digest (Cont
    Vol B) 92, 463Aa.

Appeal   d

By a petition dated 23rd August 1967 and presented to the judges of the Supreme Court
of the Bahama Islands the respondent, Nassauvian Ltd, prayed that its title to two
tracts of land, one of 92·33 acres and the other of 12·52 acres, situate on the south-
western side of Harrold Road in the Western District of the Island of New Providence,
be investigated, determined and declared under the Quieting Titles Act 1959. By
an adverse claim dated 13th October 1967 Roger Charles Adderley claimed to be   e
the owner in fee simple of an undivided interest in the two tracts of land which
were the subject of the respondent's petition. By an adverse claim dated 16th
October 1967 Clotilda Eugenie Higgs claimed to be entitled to an undivided interest
in fee simple in the two tracts of land. On 29th January 1970 H C Smith J, sitting
in the Equity Side of the Supreme Court of the Bahama Islands, ordered that the
adverse claims be dismissed and that a certificate of title in the prescribed form   f
issue to the respondent for a one-fourth undivided interest in the tract of land comprising 92·33 acres and for the entire interest in the tract of land comprising 12·52
acres. The adverse claimants appealed against the judgment but Mr Adderley
subsequently, with leave, withdrew his appeal. On 5th November 1970 the Court
of Appeal of the Bahama Islands (Bourke P, Archer and Hogan JJA) dismissed Mrs
Higgs's appeal but granted leave to appeal to the Privy Council. Mrs Higgs subse-   g
quently died and her executors, Kenneth McKinney Higgs and another, were
substituted as appellants. The facts are set out in the opinion of the Board.

Gerald Godfrey QC and *Peter Millett QC* for the appellants.
Jeremiah Harman QC and *Nigel Hague* for the respondent.

                                                                                             h

SIR HARRY GIBBS. This is an appeal from a judgment of the Court of Appeal
of the Bahama Islands affirming a judgment of the Supreme Court of the Bahama
Islands (Smith J) given in favour of the respondent, Nassauvian Ltd, in proceedings
brought under the Quieting Titles Act 1959.

The proceedings were commenced by a petition presented to the Supreme Court   j
on 23rd August 1967 by the respondent which claimed to be the owner in fee simple
in possession of (1) an undivided one-fourth part of or interest in a tract of land, 92·33
acres in area, on the Island of New Providence ('Tract A'), and (2) a parcel of land
comprising 12·52 acres adjacent to Tract A ('Tract B'). The respondent's claim
to each tract of land was based on a documentary title. Adverse claims were filed
by Clotilda Eugenie Higgs and Roger Charles Adderley, stating, in each case, that

a the claimant claimed an undivided interest in fee simple in the lands the subject of the petition. These statements of the adverse claims did not reveal the real issues in the case, for although it is uncontested that the adverse claimants have an undivided interest in Tract A, their claims were not based on that fact but on the contention that they had acquired a possessory title to the lands in both tracts, and on the further assertion that the documentary titles on which the respondent relies are invalid.

b Smith J found against the adverse claimants on both issues. An appeal was brought to the Court of Appeal by both adverse claimants, but Roger Charles Adderley withdrew his appeal and has played no part in the subsequent proceedings. The decision that the respondent had established a valid documentary title was not challenged either before the Court of Appeal or before their Lordships' Board. On the question whether the adverse claimants had acquired a possessory title, the c Court of Appeal agreed with the conclusion of Smith J. Clotilda Eugenie Higgs obtained leave to appeal from the decision of the Court of Appeal but she has since died and her executors have been substituted in her place as appellants.

It does not appear to have been in contest that Tract A formed part of a larger area which was in 1873 granted to one Alliday Adderley. In 1890, the land was d conveyed to Joseph Richmond Adderley, William Campbell Adderley, Daniel Dewellmair Adderley and Sarah Ann Bain, the four children of Alliday Adderley, as tenants in common. Daniel Dewellmair Adderley died in 1934, leaving a will whereby he appointed his natural son, Frederick William Adderley, his executor and devised to his children, Richard Crowther Adderley, Clotilda Eugenie Higgs, Roger Charles Adderley and Mary Ellen Adderley—

e 'one quarter interest in the Goodman tract of land situate in the Western District of the Island of New Providence, TO HOLD the same as tenants in common and not as joint tenants, in fee simple, subject however to the life interest in the same of my natural son Frederick William Adderley.'

f Frederick William Adderley died in 1945. It is conceded that since that date Clotilda Eugenie Higgs and Roger Charles Adderley have each been entitled in possession to an undivided share of at least one-sixteenth in Tract A. Their Lordships do not find it necessary to consider whether their interest has been enlarged by succession to the shares of any of the other co-owners on their deaths, because it is clear that neither of them has any documentary title to the one-fourth interest claimed by the respondent. The title of the respondent to the undivided one-fourth interest in g Tract A is traced back to William Campbell Adderley who, as has been mentioned, became in 1890 one of the four tenants in common of the land. In 1892, the one-fourth interest of William Campbell Adderley in the land was sold and conveyed by the Provost Marshal of the Bahama Islands, acting under the authority of a writ of execution, to one James Austin Thompson. As part of their attempt to assail the documentary title of the respondent, the adverse claimants at the trial attempted h to establish that in 1890 Joseph Richmond Adderley and William Campbell Adderley had agreed to dispose of their interests to Daniel Dewellmair Adderley and Sarah Ann Bain, and that in 1892 William Campbell Adderley had no interest in the land which the Provost Marshal could sell, and, further, that the debt, the subject of the execution, had been paid, but these facts were not established and the attack on the respondent's title failed. On 2nd November 1939 the successors in title to James j Austin Thompson conveyed the interest in Tract A to the Caves Company Ltd. Some evidence was given on behalf of the adverse claimants that Tract B had also formed part of the Adderley estates, but the only conclusion possible on the whole of the evidence is that Tract B was Crown Land until 15th May 1940 when it was granted to the Caves Company Ltd. Subsequently, the undivided one-fourth interest in Tract A and the entire interest in Tract B were transferred by the Caves

E

Company Ltd to the trustees of the will of Sir Harry Oakes and by them to the *a* respondent.

The appellants' case, as originally presented, was that the adverse claimants and their predecessors in title had been in exclusive possession of the land for more than 20 years before the present proceedings were commenced in 1967, and that the title of the respondent is barred by the Real Property Limitation Acts 1833 and 1874 which were declared in force in the Bahama Islands by Acts 9 Vic c 9 and 40 Vic c 2 *b* of that colony (as it then was). However, it was conceded in argument that the limitation period fixed in respect of actions for the recovery of land brought by the Crown is 60 years (Act 36 Vic c 6 of the Bahama Islands), and that to establish a title to Tract B the appellants would have to prove that their predecessors in title had been in possession for 60 years, unless of course, a period of 20 years' possession after 15th May 1940, when the land ceased to be Crown land, could be established.   *c*

It may be accepted that the respondent's predecessors in title were not in possession of Tract A during a period of more than 20 years from the date when they first became entitled to possession by virtue of the conveyance to James Austin Thompson on 25th May 1892. Although no evidence was directed to the question whether the Crown was ever in possession of Tract B, it may be proper to infer that over a period exceeding 60 years it was not in actual possession of that tract. According to the *d* evidence it was not until 1950 and 1951 that any predecessor in title of the respondent did any act indicating possession of the lands. In those years concrete markers were erected on the lands to indicate that they belonged to the Oakes estate, which controlled a number of companies, including the Caves Company Ltd. The view was taken in the courts below that some importance could be attached to the facts that in 1937 and 1938 workmen employed by Sir Harry Oakes put a road through the *e* lands and that between 1940 and 1959 this road was blocked by employees of the Oakes companies who once each year put a barrier of stakes across it. However, in 1937 and 1938 neither Sir Harry Oakes nor any of his companies had an interest in the land—the workmen who built the road were trespassers—and there is no evidence that the barriers which were erected after the Caves Company Ltd had acquired its interest, were erected on the lands themselves; they may well have been erected *f* on adjoining lands. Accordingly it is right to say that, for many years before 1950, the persons having the documentary title did nothing to exercise their right to possession of the subject lands. However, time does not run against an owner of land simply because he is out of possession for the limitation period. The law on this point was stated by Parke B in *Smith v Lloyd*[1] in a passage cited with apparent approval in *The Trustees Executors & Agency Co Ltd v Short*[2] as follows: *g*

'... we are clearly of opinion that the statute applies not to cases of want of actual possession by the plaintiff, but to cases where he has been out of it, and another in, possession for the prescribed time. There must be both absence of possession by the person who has the right, and actual possession by another, whether adverse or not, to be protected, to bring the case within the statute.'   *h*

The crucial question in the present case therefore is whether the courts below were correct in holding that it had not been established that the appellants' predecessors in title had been in possession of the land for the required period. This question is one of fact, and there are concurrent findings of the courts below against the appellants. The settled practice of their Lordships is to decline to review the evidence for a third time where there are concurrent findings of two courts on a pure question of fact, *j* unless there has been some miscarriage of justice or violation of some principle of law or procedure. In the present case, for reasons which will appear, their Lordships think that there may have been some misapprehension of principle in the courts

1 (1854) 9 Exch 562 at 572
2 (1888) 13 App Cas 793 at 799

a below and that the Board should therefore consider for itself whether the findings made below ought to stand.

The land in question—the total area comprising both tracts—was for the most part arable although some of it consisted of pine barren. It was not fenced or otherwise enclosed. There was evidence that at various dates between 1920 and the date of the trial, the land was farmed by Daniel Dewellmair Adderley and his descendants

b and their tenants. The farms produced small crops of various kinds, particularly vegetables. The practice of most of the farmers was to cultivate a small area, to reap the harvest, and then to move on to another area leaving the first to become overgrown. There was some evidence that fruit trees were planted but it was not made at all clear where or how extensive the orchards were or how long they survived. There was also evidence that lime burning or coal burning was carried out

c on the land. Although it is unnecessary to repeat the effect of the evidence in full detail, it is desirable to refer to some of the most important parts of it. Clotilda Eugenie Higgs, who at the date of the trial was aged 79, said that her father, Daniel Dewellmair Adderley, had possession of the land from 1890 until his death in 1934. She qualified this by saying that it was her father and her aunt, Sarah Bain, who were in possession in 1890. In part, this evidence was hearsay—a circumstance which,

d under the Quieting Titles Act 1959, s 8(1) did not render it inadmissible but which of course affected its weight—since she herself did not go on the land until 1920. She said that her father farmed the land from 1920 until his death, that he was always on the land from about 1922, that he had about six tenants whom she named, and that after his death the tenants stayed on the land and worked it continuously. Although some of her general statements were to the effect that the whole of the land was in

e possession, it is clear that she cannot have meant that it was physically occupied, for she said:

'Most of the farming was on the South—now the Stapleton Gardens. There was farming also to the West. I cannot say the size of the farms. Farming was done by keeping moving through the land—no spot was ever continuously farmed. Women farmed up to 2 acres—men up to 3 acres or 4. They go back

f to the old farms for vegetables. The entire land could not be covered.'

The other adverse claimant, Roger Charles Adderley, was on the land between about 1908-1909 and 1914-1915; he said that his father had let the land to tenants who grew crops such as tomatoes and cassava. One of the tenants named by Mrs Higgs, William Knowles, gave evidence which in some material respects was at variance with that given by the adverse claimants. William Knowles said that he worked on

g the lands between 1930 and 1948. He first worked in the neighbourhood in 1912 and at that time no one worked the Adderley land. It appears from his evidence that he cultivated one small farm after another and in so doing, traversed the subject land from side to side. Another tenant, Etheline Maylock, who worked about 1½ acres from 1932 to 1942, said that during that period there were other tenants on the land.

h In apparent conflict with the evidence of these witnesses, and with that of other witnesses, to which reference will later be made, was that of Edward Knowles, who was called on behalf of the respondent, and who said that in 1937 and 1938, when the road was put through the land, he saw no farms on it. Another tenant, Dudley Johnson, worked from 1943 to 1960 partly on the subject land and partly on adjacent Crown land; he had a farm of from two to three acres and would cut and burn the

j land and then move on. Although his evidence was rather confused, he apparently meant to say that Leonard Higgs (the husband of Clotilda Eugenie Higgs) farmed most of the land and that there were in addition a number of tenant farmers. Oliver Vanstock Higgs, a son of Clotilda Eugenie Higgs, gave evidence that from 1929 or 1930, when at the age of about six he first went on to the land, both Tract A and Tract B were quite extensively farmed by his father and by tenants, some of whom planted trees. He said that he still had tenants and was still farming Tract A; indeed his

family was now farming a larger area than in the 1940s; they also had quarried *a*
the land since 1950. If accepted, his evidence would lend considerable strength
to the appellants' case, but in one respect it appeared patently unreliable. At the
time of the trial, as Smith J who inspected the lands saw, quarrying had taken the
place of the former farming, all traces of which had been completely obliterated.
Further, one of the respondent's witnesses, Samuel Plante, whose evidence the trial
judge said that he had no reason to disbelieve, visited the land in 1958 and saw no *b*
signs of farming on Tract A, although there was quarrying there; he saw no activity
at all on Tract B before 1965. Osborne Higgs, another son of Clotilda Eugenie
Higgs, said he had been on the land since the 1930s. He said that his father farmed
a vast area of the land, that he remembered six farms on the land in the
early war years and that he himself farmed about 10 acres after 1930. Another
brother, the appellant Kenneth Higgs, gave evidence (which was hearsay) that the *c*
whole of the land was used by his grandparents for money crops, that his parents
continued this type of farming until 1930, that all the land had been farmed up
to the 1930s but had since been gradually overgrown. He asserted that his family
had been in undisturbed possession but this, of course, could not have been true of
the period after 1951 when the respondent's predecessor in title entered to put the
markers on the land. Two other witnesses also gave evidence, but with little par- *d*
ticularity, that there had been farming on the land by the Higgs family and their
tenants at various times. Finally, there were tendered aerial photographs which,
according to the explanation of them given in evidence, showed that in 1943 roughly
40 per cent of the usable land in both tracts was being cultivated and that in 1958 there
was some occupation and clearing but fewer farms than in 1943.

It is clear that the evidence given on behalf of the adverse claimants would not *e*
have supported a finding that the adverse claimants and their predecessors were in
possession of Tract B for the requisite period of 60 years before 15th May 1940, and
they could not have had exclusive possession for 20 years after that date, because the
respondent's predecessor exercised its right to possession in 1951. However, if that
evidence could have been accepted in its entirety, it might have established that over
a period extending from 1920, or even earlier, until 1951, the adverse claimants and *f*
their predecessors were in actual possession of parts of Tract A and, indeed, according
to some of the assertions made, of the whole of that tract. The fact that for part of
this period—before 1934, when Daniel Dewellmair Adderley died, and after 1945,
the date of death of Frederick William Adderley, the life tenant—they were entitled
to possession as co-owners would not have prevented them from establishing a
possessory title: *Paradise Beach and Transportation Co Ltd v Price-Robinson*[1]. However, *g*
the body of evidence presented by the adverse claimants was imprecise and lacking
in detail; it was not completely consistent within itself and it was in certain material
respects contradicted by other evidence. The trial judge was not bound to accept it;
on the contrary it was open to him to take the view—which indeed has much to
commend it—that the evidence was vague, nebulous and unreliable and insufficient
to discharge the burden of proof resting on the adverse claimants. *h*

However, the judges of the Court of Appeal, in affirming the decision of the trial
judge, placed considerable reliance on the decision of their Lordships' Board in
Ocean Estates Ltd v Pinder[2], and there are passages in their judgments which suggest
that they regarded that decision, which Bourke P described as 'the locus classicus in
quieting investigations, on the question of rotational or peripatetic use of open land'
as determinative of the appeal. Although the trial judge did not expressly mention *j*
Ocean Estates Ltd v Pinder[2], some of the expressions which he used suggest that he
also may have taken the view that sporadic farming over portions of a large tract of
land could never be enough to establish possession of the whole tract. In *Ocean
Estates Ltd v Pinder*[2] the Board was concerned with a claim made by the defendant

1 [1968] 1 All ER 530, [1968] AC 1072
2 [1969] 2 AC 19

a   in that case to a possessory title to a plot of land of 144 acres on New Providence
Island, part of which was unfit for cultivation and part of which consisted of poor
quality scrub land. The defendant had grown vegetables on various small plots on
the land and had also planted some fruit trees on part of it. The defendant's method
of farming was similar to that described by some of the witnesses in the present case.
The conclusion of the Board on the matter now relevant was expressed by Lord
b   Diplock as follows[1]:

> 'On these findings, the defendant's claim that he had acquired a possessory title
> to the whole or any part of the land in suit or, what is the same thing, that the
> plaintiffs' title was extinguished must fail. So far as any claim to the whole
> parcel of land is concerned he established no dispossession of the plaintiffs or
> their predecessors in title in respect of the uncultivable swamp, and his own
c   > occupation of the cultivable scrub land was not exclusive during the period up
> to 1946 when Mr. Chipman in the right of the Chipper Orange Co. Ltd. was
> concurrently cultivating fruit trees on the land or inconsistent with the purpose
> for which the plaintiffs held the land after 1950, when they exercised powers of
> dominion over it in 1957 and 1959-60 by going on to the land for the purposes
> of inspecting and surveying it for future development. So far as concerns any
d   > claim to any individual plot which the defendant cultivated from time to time
> under his peripatetic system of market gardening, his occupation of the plot,
> though it may have been exclusive while the plot was under actual cultivation,
> was not continuous. During any period when he was not cultivating any par-
> ticular plot the owners of the land would have no continuing cause of action
> against him. When he returned to any plot, a fresh cause of action would arise
e   > and the limitation period of 20 years would start anew.'

In this passage, Lord Diplock was discussing the facts of the particular case before the
Board, and the members of the Court of Appeal were wrong in viewing it as laying
down a general principle that to establish possession of an area of land, a claimant
must show that he has made physical use of the whole of it, or as deciding that a
f   farmer can never establish possession of an area of land over parts of which he
works in rotation. It is clearly settled that acts of possession done on parts of a tract
of land to which a possessory title is sought may be evidence of possession of the
whole. In *Lord Advocate v Lord Blantyre* Lord Blackburn said[2]:

> 'And all that tends to prove possession as owners of parts of the tract tends to
> prove ownership of the whole tract; provided there is such a common character
g   > of locality as would raise a reasonable inference that if the barons possessed one
> part as owners they possessed the whole, the weight depending on the nature
> of the tract, what kind of possession could be had of it and what the kind of
> possession proved was.'

This rule is not applicable to a question of undefined and disputed boundary (*Clark v
Elphinstone*[3], *West Bank Estates Ltd v Arthur*[4]), but this does not mean that acts done
h   on part of the land are only relevant to prove possession of the whole if the land is
enclosed by a wall or other physical barrier. The property claimed by possession may
be sufficiently defined in other ways, e g where the claim is to trees in a belt of wood-
land (*Stanley v White*[5]), to the bed or foreshores of a river (*Jones v Williams*[6], *Lord
Advocate v Lord Blantyre*[7]) or to the right to fish in a river (*Lord Advocate v Lord Lovat*[8]).

j   1   [1969] 2 AC at 23, 24
2   (1879) 4 App Cas 770 at 791
3   (1880) 6 App Cas 164 at 170, 171
4   [1967] 1 AC 665 at 679, 680
5   (1811) 14 East 332
6   (1837) 2 M & W 326, [1835-42] All ER Rep 423
7   (1879) 4 App Cas 770
8   (1880) 5 App Cas 273 at 289

In the present case, although the two tracts were not physically enclosed, their *a*
boundaries were known and undisputed, and possession of the whole tracts might
have been established by appropriate evidence of acts done on parts of them. The
question was one of fact and degree and depended on a consideration of all the
circumstances of the case.

However, it does not appear from the reasons given by the trial judge that he
reached his conclusion simply in obedience to a supposed principle of law rather *b*
than by considering whether the evidence given was sufficient to make out the case
of the adverse claimants. It has already been mentioned that he indicated his acceptance of evidence contrary to some of that given on behalf of the adverse claimants
and it is obvious that he could not have accepted as correct everything that was said
by their witnesses. His concluding words:

> 'It is impossible to say on the evidence that the petitioners have been ousted *c*
> so far as the one-fourth interest they claim is concerned . . .'

suggest that the basis of his decision was that the evidence which he accepted was
insufficient to discharge the onus of proof that rested on the adverse claimants. It is
true that in those words he did not mention Tract B, but it is clear from the judgment
as a whole and from the order that he made that this was a mere slip, and in fact the *d*
evidence of possession of Tract B was weaker than that relating to Tract A. Their
Lordships have reached the conclusion that it has not been shown that the trial judge
failed to consider the question of fact which he had to decide, or that there is any
ground of interfering with his decision of that question.

For these reasons, their Lordships will humbly advise Her Majesty that the appeal
should be dismissed. The appellants must pay the respondent's costs of the appeal. *e*

Appeal dismissed.

Solicitors: *Wilson Freeman* (for the appellants); *Stephenson, Harwood & Tatham* (for
the respondent).

Gordon H Scott Esq Barrister.

f

R v Secretary of State for the Environment, ex parte Hood

QUEEN'S BENCH DIVISION
LORD WIDGERY CJ, MILMO AND ACKNER JJ   *g*
10th, 22nd OCTOBER 1974

Highway – Classification – Definitive map – Road used as a public path – Reclassification –
Special review – Presumption that public have right of way on horseback over highway classified
as road used as public path – Reclassification of roads used as public path – No right of way for
vehicular traffic – Reclassification as footpath or bridleway – Application of presumption – *h*
Whether authority bound to reclassify highway as bridleway rather than footpath – National
Parks and Access to the Countryside Act 1949, ss 27(6), 32(4)(b) – Countryside Act 1968, Sch 3,
Part III, para 9(1).

A county council prepared a definitive map under Part IV of the National Parks and
Access to the Countryside Act 1949. At the time when the map was prepared it was *j*
not clear whether the public right of way over one path which appeared on the map
included a right of way on horseback, or leading a horse, in addition to a right of way
on foot. There was no question of any other right of way over the path and therefore
it was shown on the definitive map as a 'road used as a public path', within s 27(6)*a* of

---

a Section 27(6), so far as material, is set out at p 104 *g*, post

a   the 1949 Act. Accordingly, under s 32(4)(*b*)*b* of the 1949 Act, there was a conclusive presumption that the public had a right of way on horseback, or leading a horse, over the path. Following the enactment of the Countryside Act 1968 the county council undertook a 'special review' of 'roads used as public paths', in accordance with Part III of Sch 3 to the 1968 Act. At the time of the special review there was no new evidence which showed whether or not the path in question was subject to a public right of

b   bridleway and the county council proposed that the path should be classified under para 9 (1)*c* of Part III of Sch 3 as a 'footpath' rather than a 'bridleway'. The proposal was confirmed by the Secretary of State for the Environment. The applicant moved for an order of certiorari to quash the Secretary of State's decision, contending that, since the path was conclusively presumed to be one over which the public had rights of bridleway as well as footway, it should have been classified as a bridleway.

c
Held (Ackner J dissenting) –Where on a special review under Part III of Sch 3 to the 1968 Act a path which had formerly been classified as a 'road used as a public path' could not be reclassified as a 'byway open to all traffic', the authority responsible for preparing the definitive map was entitled to determine whether a bridleway or foot-path subsisted at the relevant date and to reclassify the path accordingly. In coming

d   to that determination the authority was not bound by any presumption under s 32(4)(*b*) of the 1949 Act and accordingly was entitled, in the light of the available evidence, to reclassify the path as a footpath. The appeal would therefore be dismissed (see p 106 *h* to p 107 *a*, post).

Notes

e   For revision of maps and statements and reclassification of public footpaths, see 19 Halsbury's Laws (3rd Edn) 177, 178, paras 273, 274, and for cases on the classification of highways, see 26 Digest (Repl) 273, *23-41*, 280, *85*.

For the National Parks and Access to the Countryside Act 1949, ss 27, 32, see 15 Halsbury's Statutes (3rd Edn) 37, 44.

For the Countryside Act 1968, Sch 3, Part III, para 9, see 15 Halsbury's Statutes
f   (3rd Edn) 519.

Case referred to in judgments
Morgan v Hertfordshire County Council (1965) 63 LGR 456, CA.

Case also cited
g   *Attorney-General v Shonleigh Nominees Ltd* [1972] 2 All ER 263, [1972] 1 WLR 577, CA.

Motion for certiorari
This was an application by way of motion by Margaret Cynthia Hood for an order of certiorari to remove into the High Court for the purpose of its being quashed a decision of the Secretary of State for the Environment made by letter dated 22nd August 1973
h   whereby he confirmed the proposal of the Kent County Council that a highway shown on the definitive map prepared under Part IV of the National Parks and Access to the Countryside Act 1949 as a road used as a public path (CRF 30) should be re-classified as a footpath. The relief was sought on the following grounds: (1)(a) the Secretary of State in making his decision was not entitled to have regard to matters other than those specified in s 33(1) and (2) of the 1949 Act as amended by para 10 of
j   Part III of Sch 3 to the Countryside Act 1968; (b) the Secretary of State's decision to confirm the reclassification of the road used as a public path CRF 30 as a footpath was founded on the finding by his inspector that 'it is unlikely, in the context of this route's general situation and relationship to other rights of way, that bridle rights ever existed';

---

b   Section 32(4), so far as material, is set out at p 105 *b* and *c*, post
c   Paragraph 9(1) is set out at p 105 *j*, post

(c) that finding was not supported by any evidence to which, in accordance with the   *a*
provisions mentioned in (a) above the inspector and Secretary of State was entitled to
have regard; (2) in the absence of evidence of matters falling within the provisions
mentioned in 1(a) above, the Secretary of State was not entitled to reclassify the road
used as a public path otherwise than in accordance with the conclusive presumption
created by s 32(4)(*b*) of the 1949 Act, ie as a bridle path. The facts are set out in the
judgment of Lord Widgery CJ.   *b*

Leonard Hoffmann for the applicant.
Harry Woolf for the Secretary of State.

Cur adv vult

22nd October. The following judgments were read.   *c*

LORD WIDGERY CJ. In these proceedings counsel moves on behalf of Margaret
Cynthia Hood for an order of certiorari to remove into this court for the purpose of its
being quashed a decision of the Secretary of State for the Environment communicated
by his decision letter dated 22nd August 1973 whereby the Secretary of State confirmed
the proposal of the Kent County Council that a highway shown on the definitive map   *d*
prepared under Part IV of the National Parks and Access to the Countryside Act 1949
as a road used as a public path should be reclassified as a footpath.
    The highway in question is a short and unimportant length of path. The application
does, however, raise an important principle which is perhaps the better illustrated in
such simple, factual, circumstances.
    By s 27 of the 1949 Act county councils were required to produce draft maps of their   *e*
area showing on the map a footpath or a bridleway as might appear to the council to
be appropriate wherever in their opinion such a right of way subsisted or was reasonably alleged to have subsisted at the relevant date. By sub-s (2) a map prepared in
accordance with the last foregoing subsection shall also show thereon any way which
in the opinion of the authority carrying out the survey was at the relevant date, or was
at that date reasonably alleged to be, a road used as a public path.   *f*
    Section 27(6) defines the various ways to which the earlier subsections have made
reference. Thus:

> ' "Footpath" means a highway over which the public have a right of way on
> foot only, other than such a highway at the side of a public road; "bridleway"
> means a highway over which the public have the following but no other, rights
> of way, that is to say, a right of way on foot, and a right of way on horseback   *g*
> or leading a horse, with or without a right to drive animals of any description
> along the highway . . . "public path" means a highway being either a footpath
> or a bridleway . . . [and finally] "road used as a public path" means a highway
> other than a public path used by the public mainly for the purposes for which
> footpaths or bridleways are so used.'
                                                                                       h
    The conception of a 'road used as a public path' is a slightly unusual one. To comply
with the definition, the road in question must be a highway where the rights of the
public are not precisely defined. If it is clear that the rights of the public are confined
to those embraced by a footpath or a bridleway, and thus the path is a public path
within the several definitions, the classification must be footpath, or bridleway as
appropriate. It is only where the public rights are not clearly confined to footpath or   *j*
bridleway that resort is had to the imprecise definition of the phrase 'road used as a
public path'.
    The 1949 Act contained complicated provisions to which I need not refer in detail,
whereby the draft map produced by the county council was made open to inspection
and landowners and other interested parties were able to make representations as to
its accuracy. Eventually, the procedure contemplated by the 1949 Act produced a

a definitive, or, as one might say, a final map, and the consequences of entry of the various paths on the definitive map are shown in s 32 of the Act.

Thus by s 32(4):

b
> "A definitive map and statement prepared under subsection (1) of this section shall be conclusive as to the particulars contained therein in accordance with the foregoing provisions of this section to the following extent, that is to say—(a) where the map shows a footpath, the map shall be conclusive evidence that there was at the relevant date specified in the statement a footpath as shown on the map; (b) where the map shows a bridleway, or a road used as a public path, the map shall be conclusive evidence that there was at the said date a highway as shown on the map, and that the public had thereover at that date a right of way on foot and a right of way on horseback or leading a horse, so however that this paragraph
c shall be without prejudice to any question whether the public had at that date any right of way other than the rights aforesaid . . .'

The presumption created by s 32(4)(b) is unexpected in one particular respect. It will be remembered that in order that a road could be classified as a road used as a public path it sufficed that the rights of the public should be more extensive than a footpath
d or bridleway. It was not necessary to come within the definition that the particular road should be shown to be a bridleway because it sufficed if the public rights were more extensive than a footway without being more precisely defined. By virtue of the presumption, however, if a road were shown on the map as a road used as a public path, the effect was to establish conclusively that at the relevant date a right of way on foot *and* a right of way on horseback existed over the path. Accordingly, any road
e classified as a road used as a public path necessarily produced in practice a consequence that the public could claim a right of bridleway over that road.

The 1949 Act contains in s 33, as amended by the Countryside Act 1968, a comprehensive procedure for the revision of these maps from time to time in the circumstances set out in the section. Thus, on the occasion of any review, amendments to the map can be made in respect of occurrences happening after the last review, or, in some
f circumstances, on account of fresh evidence coming to light. I do not go into these provisions in detail because it is common ground that in the instant case nothing has happened which would justify a factual review of the provisions of this map relating to the way in question, and that the fact that doubts had arisen whether the path in question ever had rights of bridleway established by the public would not in itself justify any alteration in the original classification. In the instant case the classification
g of the way in question was 'road used as a public path', and the sole reason for altering that classification and thus creating the problem of what the new classification should be, is to be found in the Countryside Act 1968.

Part III of Sch 3 to the 1968 Act contains provision for a special review of footpath maps, and further provides that at such special review the classification 'road used as a public path' shall no longer appear.
h The interest of the applicant is in preserving this path as a path which can be used by the public with horses, and it is her contention that on the removal of the classification 'road used as a public path' there should be substituted either 'a byway open to all traffic' or 'a bridleway'. The county council, supported by the Secretary of State for the Environment, takes the view that on reclassification at the special review the proper new classification is as 'a footpath'.
j The relevant provisions of Part III of Sch 3 to the 1968 Act are as follows:

> '9.—(1) In the special review the draft revision, and the definitive map and statement, shall show every road used as a public path by one of the three following descriptions—(a) a "byway open to all traffic", (b) a "bridleway", (c) a "footpath", [the three alternatives to which I have already briefly referred] and shall no longer employ the expression "road used as a public path".'

Paragraph 10, under the cross-heading 'Test for reclassification', provides as follows: *a*

'10. The considerations to be taken into account in deciding in which class a road used as a public path is to be put shall be—(*a*) whether any vehicular right of way has been shown to exist, (*b*) whether the way is suitable for vehicular traffic having regard to the position and width of the existing right of way, the condition and state of repair of the way, and the nature of the soil, (*c*) where the way has been used by vehicular traffic, whether the extinguishment of vehicular rights of   *b* way would cause any undue hardship.'

No doubt the first question which arises when the special review is carried out, and consideration turns on a road previously classified as 'road used as a public path', is whether the correct new classification should or should not be 'byway open to all traffic'. For this purpose I find the tests laid down in para 10 sufficient and compre-   *c* hensible. There is, however, nothing in para 10 to assist in deciding whether the classification should be 'bridleway' rather than 'footway' once it has been decided that the road does not justify reclassification as 'byway open to all traffic'. Thus, although para 10 appears to be comprehensive, and to reflect all considerations, it seems to me that other considerations must be brought into play if it is clear that the road is not to be reclassified as a 'byway open to all traffic', and the issue is whether it should be a   *d* bridleway or a footway.

The argument before us is directed to this problem. The applicant who, as I have said, wishes to retain the public right to use such paths with horses, contends that since under s 32(4)(*b*) of the 1949 Act the road when classified as a road used as a public path was conclusively presumed to be a road over which the public had rights of footway and bridleway, it is said that the new classification must reflect that position   *e* and thus must be as a bridleway.

The alternative argument is that s 32(4)(*b*) of the 1949 Act merely raised an evidentiary presumption arising out of the fact that the map for the time being classified the way in question as a road used as a public path. Once that classification is removed, as it must be, under the special review, then it is contended that there is nothing left in s 32(4)(*b*) on which the evidentiary presumption can bite. Accordingly it is con-   *f* tended by the county council, and on behalf of the Secretary of State, that when classification of 'road used as a public path' is removed, the question 'footway' or 'bridleway' must be decided in the same manner as such questions were decided by the county council when preparing its original draft maps under the 1949 Act. In other words, it is contended that in deciding whether the new classification shall be 'footway' or 'bridleway' the county council, and in due course the Secretary of State, must make   *g* such determination as may appear to it to be appropriate wherever in the opinion of the county council a footpath or a bridlepath is shown to have subsisted at the relevant date.

It is further argued that no prejudice to the public will result from this approach because substantially similar provisions for reconsideration of any classification decided on by the county council will exist under the Countryside Act 1968, as they   *h* did under the 1949 Act.

In my judgment the contention for the county council and the Secretary of State is the correct one. For reasons I have already given, I cannot accept that the only matters to be taken into account on this question are those set out in para 10 of Part III of Sch 3 to the 1968 Act, nor can I accept that a presumption relating to a bridleway which flowed from the fact that that way was formerly described as a 'road used as a public   *j* path' can be in any sense conclusive of the proper classification of the way under the 1968 Act between 'bridleway' and 'footway'.

Since I feel satisfied that the Secretary of State has correctly applied the law on this point, I can see no reason why certiorari should go, and I would dismiss the application.

MILMO J.   I have had the benefit of reading in advance the judgment which Lord *a* Widgery CJ has just delivered. I agree with it and there is nothing which I can usefully add. I also would dismiss this application.

ACKNER J. I much regret that I have the misfortune of being unable to agree that the Secretary of State for the Environment reached the correct decision. The point is ultimately a short one and I will state briefly and with great diffidence my reasons.

b This will, I fear, necessitate requoting some of the statutory provisions already mentioned.

CRF 30 was a highway, shown on the definitive map prepared under Part IV of the National Parks and Access to the Countryside Act 1949 as a 'road used as a public path'. Section 27(6) of that Act defines a 'road used as a public path' as meaning a highway, other than a public path, used by the public mainly for the purpose for which footpaths or bridleways are so used. Since 'public path' is defined as a highway being either a

c footpath or a bridleway, 'a road used as a public path' is a highway where at least footpath rights must have been established. Finally, for completeness, I should add that in the same subsection 'bridleway' is defined as meaning a highway over which the public have a right of way on foot and a right of way on horseback or leading a horse. So much for the definitions.

d Section 32(4)(*b*) of the 1949 Act provides in unusually strong terms what is to be the effect of the classification of roads in the definitive or final plan, that is, the plan which eventuates after the draft and provisional plan procedure has been carried through. Under this subsection, where the definitive map shows a road used as a public path, the map shall be conclusive evidence that there was at the date specified in s 27(3) a highway as shown on the map, and that the public had thereover on that date a right of way on foot *and* a right of way on horseback, or leading a horse, but without

e prejudice to whether the public had at that date any right of way other than those rights.

In order to provide for periodical revisions of maps s 33 gave power to the authority by whom the definitive map and statement had been prepared to review the particulars having regard to certain events specified in that section which occurred at any time between the relevant dates specified in the definitive statement and such date as might be determined by the authority. The powers given by this section were very

f limited, as was somewhat dramatically established by *Morgan v Hertfordshire County Council*[1], where by a demonstrable series of errors and omissions, there was shown on the definitive map a bridle path over a strip of land in fact covered by timber trees and impassable. After ramblers had claimed the right to pass along the strip, the council told the owner that they proposed to cut down his trees and clear the way. He then applied to the court for a declaration that the map was not conclusive, but the Court

g of Appeal decided that it was and that his only remedy was to apply to the proper authority to have the special way stopped up, for there were no provisions in s 33 to enable a public right of way, once marked on the definitive map, to be deleted.

To deal with the inadequacy of the provisions of s 33 an important amendment was made by Part I of Sch 3 to the Countryside Act 1968, the very schedule on which the Secretary of State relies. By Part I of this schedule s 33 was amended so that in carrying

h out a review under s 33(1) the authority shall have regard to the discovery by the authority, in the period mentioned in that subsection, of any new evidence or of evidence not previously considered by the authority concerned, showing that there was no public right of way over land shown on the map as a public path, or as a road used as a public path. It is, however, specifically provided that the authority must not take account of this evidence if satisfied that the person prejudiced by the public right

j of way, or his predecessor in title, could have produced the evidence before the relevant date mentioned in s 33(1) and had no reasonable excuse for failing to do so.

Further, to remedy the imprecision of the definition of 'road used as a public path', special provision was made in Part III of this schedule. Paragraph 7 provides that the first review carried out by any authority after the coming into force of the Act is a special review. Paragraph 9, which is headed 'Reclassification of roads used as public

1   (1965) 63 LGR 456

paths', enlarges the scope of that review since it provides that in the special review the *a*
draft revision, and the definitive map and statement shall show every road used as a
public path by one of the three following descriptions: (a) a 'byway open to all traffic',
(b) a 'bridleway' and (c) a 'footpath', and shall not employ the expression 'road used as
a public path' to describe any way.

Paragraph 10 is entitled 'Test for reclassification' and it reads as follows:

> 'The considerations to be taken into account in deciding in which class a road *b*
> used as a public path is to be put shall be—(a) whether any vehicular right of way
> has been shown to exist, (b) whether the way is suitable for vehicular traffic
> having regard to the position and width of the existing right of way, the condition
> and state of repair of the way, and the nature of the soil, (c) where the way has
> been used by vehicular traffic, whether the extinguishment of vehicular rights of
> way would cause any undue hardship.' *c*

It is thus quite clear that the 'Test for reclassification' is of an extremely limited nature
since it relates only to whether the *first* of the three descriptions, namely, 'byway open
to all traffic' is or is not the appropriate description and provides no test whatsoever
for differentiating between a 'bridleway' or a 'footpath'. This seems to me to suggest
quite clearly that roads used as public paths are not to be downgraded beyond that
of a bridleway unless there is evidence that can be properly considered under s 33 of *d*
the 1946 Act as amended by this very schedule. After all, nothing could have been
easier than to have provided in para 10, if Parliament had so intended, that Part III of
Sch 3 was to authorise a freeranging enquiry, that in deciding whether or not a 'road
used as a public path' should be classified as a bridlepath or a footpath there were no
restrictions on the evidence that could be received, and that the conclusive evidence
provisions of s 32(4)(*b*) were no longer to operate in this regard. That this was not done *e*
in express terms is incontestable. I can find no warrant for filling this lacuna by
implying words—and many words would be required—which the draftsman of the
Act considered unnecessary. If Parliament wishes substantially to increase the powers
of an authority to interfere with or reduce public rights it must do so in clear and
unequivocal terms.

What the inspector did, as he was entitled to do, applying the three, and the only *f*
three, tests for reclassification provided in para 10 of Part III of Sch 3 to the 1968 Act,
was to conclude that the route ought not to be included on the draft revised map as a
byway open to all traffic because: (a) vehicular rights of way had not been shown to
exist, (b) the way was not suitable beyond the hospital for vehicular traffic, and (c) the
question of undue hardship did not arise.

This conclusion left unresolved whether the path should be classified as a bridlepath *g*
or a footpath. He went on to conclude, while reserving to the Secretary of State the
legal issue as to whether the provisions of s 32(4)(*b*) had been affected by Sch 3, that—

> 'it was unlikely in the context of this route's general situation and relationship
> to other rights of way, that bridle rights over existed, except, perhaps, in a general
> way over all the land included in Herne Common.'
> *h*

In his opinion the route should therefore be reclassified on the revised map as a
footpath. His recommendation so to reclassify, which was accepted by the Secretary
of State, was thus based neither on the criteria of para 10, that is on the 'test for
reclassification', nor on the basis of evidence admissible or acceptable within the
terms of s 33 of the 1949 Act as amended by the 1968 Act.

Accordingly, in my judgment the Secretary of State was not therefore entitled in *j*
such circumstances to reclassify the road otherwise than in accordance with the
conclusive presumptions created by s 32(4)(*b*) of the 1949 Act, that is, as a bridlepath,
and I would therefore have quashed the decision.

Certiorari refused.

Solicitors: *Cripps, Harries, Hall & Co* (for the applicant); *Treasury Solicitor.*

NP Metcalfe Esq   Barrister.

a
Re S (a minor) (adoption order: access)

COURT OF APPEAL, CIVIL DIVISION
CAIRNS AND BROWNE LJJ
22nd, 23rd OCTOBER 1974

b

Adoption – Welfare of infant – Severance of adopted child from natural parents – Circumstances in which adoption may be made even though child may see natural parent thereafter.

Adoption – Order – Terms and conditions – Terms and conditions which may be imposed – Access by natural parent – Jurisdiction to impose condition as to access   Condition not to
c *detract from rights and duties of adoptive parents – Exceptional circumstances justifying condition – Regulation of access – Adoption Act 1958, ss 7(3), 13(1).*

The father, who was of non-European racial origin, came to England from Singapore. In 1963 he met the mother.   Soon afterwards they began to live together as man and wife and continued to do so for more than five years.   A child, S, was born to them
d in September 1964.   In September 1969 the mother left the father, taking S with her. The father made numerous and strenuous efforts to trace them but without success. S was made a ward of court on the father's application in January 1970.   Eventually S and the mother were traced.   In July 1971 an order was made that the wardship should continue.   The judge gave care of S to the mother but allowed the father access to the child once a month at the home of mutual friends.   In October 1971
e the mother married and subsequently she applied for an adoption order in respect of S in favour of herself and her new husband.   The judge was satisfied that the adoption was in the best interests of S.   Accordingly he made the order but refused to attach to it any condition which would have allowed the father some measure of continued access.   The father appealed, asking that the adoption order be set aside or, alternatively, that it be made conditional on his having continued rights of
f access to S.   He contended that as S was then 10 years old and had had more or less constant contact with him since birth, she would always have a recollection of him and might therefore suffer a sense of deprivation if her relationship with him was completely severed; he further maintained that in view of S's mixed racial origins it was particularly desirable that she should retain a bond with her father and his family, who were people of standing in Singapore, and should have an awareness of
g her cultural and racial heritage.   At the hearing of the appeal the parties came to an agreement, in the form of a draft order for the approval of the court, whereby the father consented to an adoption order and the mother and her husband agreed to allow a court welfare officer to interview S once a year and not to raise any objection to the welfare officer giving the father information as to the child's welfare etc, acting as an intermediary with respect of arrangements for the resumption or con-
h tinuance of access by the father, and forwarding Christmas and birthday presents from the father to the child.

Held – (i) Although the whole tenor of the Adoption Act 1958 was that from the time of adoption the adoptive parents took over completely from the natural parents the role of parents of the child, the court nevertheless had jurisdiction under s 7(3)[a]
j to impose a condition relating to access in an adoption order if special circumstances made such a condition desirable, provided that such a condition did not detract from

_____

a   Section 7(3) provides: 'The court in an adoption order may impose such terms and conditions as the court may think fit, and in particular may require the adopter by bond or otherwise to make for the infant such provision (if any) as in the opinion of the court is just and expedient.'

the rights and duties of the adoptive parents under s 13(1)[b] and provided also that a *a* clearly drafted undertaking was put forward. Conditions concerning access were, however, to be imposed on an adoption order only in most exceptional cases and where they were in the interests of the minor (see p 112 *e f* and *j* and p 113 *b* and *d*, post); *Re J (a minor)* [1973] 2 All ER 410 approved.

(ii) In view of the exceptional circumstances of the case, and because it might be for the benefit of S to see her father again at some time in the future, it was right that *b* the adoption order should be made subject to the conditions set out in the draft order. Those conditions were such as not to affect the rights and responsibilities of the adoptive parents in relation to the matter of access. Accordingly, the appeal would be allowed to the extent of incorporating in the adoption order the conditions as to access in favour of the natural father which had been agreed between the parties and approved by the court (see p 112 *f* and *g* and p 113 *c* and *d*, post). *c*

Notes

For adoption orders, see 21 Halsbury's Laws (3rd Edn) 236, paras 509-510, and for cases on the subject, see 28(2) Digest (Reissue) 838-840, *1407-1414*.

For adoption in relation to illegitimacy, see 1 Halsbury's Laws (4th Edn) 350, para 615. *d*

For the Adoption Act 1958, ss 7, 13, see 17 Halsbury's Statutes (3rd Edn) 645, 650.

Cases referred to in judgments

F v S (adoption: ward) [1973] 1 All ER 722, [1973] Fam 203, [1973] 2 WLR 178 137, JP 301, CA.

G (T J) (an infant), Re [1963] 1 All ER 20, 127 JP 144, 61 LGR 139, sub nom *Re G* *e* *(infant)* [1963] 2 QB 73, [1963] 2 WLR 69, CA, 28(2) Digest (Reissue) 828, *1373*.

J (a minor), Re (adoption order: conditions) [1973] 2 All ER 410, [1973] Fam 106, [1973] 2 WLR 782, 137 JP 467.

Case also cited

E (P) (an infant), Re [1969] 1 All ER 323, [1968] 1 WLR 1913, CA. *f*

Appeal

The father, who was of non-European racial origin, came to England from Singapore. He met the mother in November 1963. He was then 31 and unmarried. The mother was 21 and had already given birth to two illegitimate children who had been adopted. Her own parents had separated when she was 16. The father *g* and mother began living together as man and wife. A child, S, was born to them in September 1964. The father and mother continued to cohabit until September 1969 when the mother left the father, taking S with her. The father made numerous and strenuous efforts to trace them but without success. The father issued a wardship summons on 8th January 1970. The mother eventually entered an appearance to that summons on 9th November 1970. The summons came before Stirling J in *h* July 1971. He ordered that the wardship should continue and that the mother should have care of the child, but he allowed the father access once a month at the home of mutual friends. In October 1971 the mother married. Her husband was in good employment and they lived, with S, in an attractive three-bedroomed house.

---

b Section 13(1) provides: 'Upon an adoption order being made, all rights, duties, obligations *j* and liabilities of the parents or guardians of the infant in relation to the future custody, maintenance and education of the infant, including all rights to appoint a guardian and (in England) to consent or give notice of dissent to marriage, shall be extinguished, and all such rights, duties, obligations and liabilities shall vest in and be exercisable by and enforceable against the adopter as if the infant were a child born to the adopter in lawful wedlock; and in respect of the matters aforesaid . . . the infant shall stand to be adopted exclusively in the position of a child born to the adopter in lawful wedlock.'

a   The father was living with another woman in accommodation comprising a bed-sittingroom with a partitioned kitchenette and bathroom. The mother applied for leave to commence proceedings for the adoption of S by herself and her husband. On 18th May 1972 Stirling J refused leave but on 8th December 1972 the Court of Appeal[1] (Davies, Megaw and Orr LJJ) allowed an appeal by the mother and granted leave. On 27th November 1973 Sir George Baker P made an adoption order in

b   favour of the mother and her husband ('the adopters'). The father appealed, seeking an order that the adoption order be set aside or, alternatively, that it be made conditional on his having continued rights of access to S.

    Anita Ryan for the father.
    Ian Romer for the adopters.
c   *Donald Rattee* for the Official Solicitor.

    CAIRNS LJ. This is an appeal by the father of an illegitimate child, a girl of ten, from an adoption order made by Sir George Baker P on 27th November 1973, in favour of the mother and a man whom she married three years ago. The father by

d   his notice of appeal asked for the adoption order to be set aside or, failing that, that the order should be conditional on his being granted access to the child. There is one reported case in which such a condition has been imposed under s 7(3) of the Adoption Act 1958. That was *Re J (a minor) (adoption order: conditions)*[2], a case which was heard by Rees J and which has some features in common with the present case.
    In this present case, when leave was sought to commence adoption proceedings, such leave was refused at first instance. There was then an appeal to this court[1], and

e   the appeal was allowed. It is in consequence of the allowance of that appeal that these proceedings were brought for an adoption order. On the hearing of the appeal from the refusal of leave, the leading judgment was given by Orr LJ. It contains a full statement of the history of the case, which relieves me of the need to recount it.
    When this present appeal was before this court yesterday counsel for the father

f   put forward a number of reasons in favour of the view that the adoption order should not have been made at all, but failed to convince the court that Sir George Baker P was wrong in making an adoption order. We were quite satisfied at the end of the argument, despite the points which were raised on behalf of the father, that it was in the interests of the child that the adoption order should stand. But we were left in considerable doubt at that stage whether or not in the very exceptional circumstances of this case, which are set out in the judgment of Orr LJ[3] to which I have referred, there

g   should be some possible opportunity for the father to have contact with the child at some time in the future. Overnight counsel for the father and for the adopters have considered the matter and have arrived at an agreed solution, subject of course to the approval of the court. It must be subject to the approval of the court, first, because the court must be satisfied that there is jurisdiction to make an order of the kind proposed; and secondly, because in the case of a minor the court always has

h   to be satisfied, whatever may be agreed between the parties, that the proposed solution is in the interests of the minor.
    I think it is right that I should read the minutes of order which have been agreed on. They are to this effect:

j   'AND the [father] by his Counsel undertaking not to communicate or attempt to communicate directly or indirectly with the minor or with the [adopters] during the minority of the minor AND the [father] by his Counsel stating that having regard to the facts recited in paragraphs (a) to (c) hereof he no longer

---

1   *F v S (adoption: ward)* [1973] 1 All ER 722, [1973] Fam 203
2   [1973] 2 All ER 410, [1973] Fam 106
3   [1973] 1 All ER at 723, 724, [1973] Fam at 205, 206

opposes the adoption of the minor by the [adopters] and that such factors are (a)   *a*
it is in the best interests of the minor that these proceedings be resolved by
agreement without a contested appeal (b) the consent of the [adopters] to the
conditions of such adoption set forth in the Schedule hereto (c) it is anticipated that
the [adopters] have due regard to the natural heritage of the [father] AND the
[adopters] by their Counsel undertaking to observe the conditions set forth in the
Schedule hereto AND the parties consenting to this order IT IS ORDERED that that   *b*
part of the Order made herein on the 27th November 1973 by the Right Honourable the President which authorised the [adopters] to adopt the minor be varied
as follows namely that the [adopters] be authorised to adopt the minor upon the
conditions set out in the Schedule hereto

THE SCHEDULE

                                                                                   c
'1. The [adopters] will on some date in December 1974 and every subsequent
December during the minority of the minor permit a Court Welfare Officer to
interview the minor at her home or school and without any other person being
present once the Court Welfare Officer is known to the child
'2. The [adopters] will raise no objection to such Court Welfare Officer: (i)
giving to the [father] such information as the Court Welfare Officer may think   *d*
fit concerning the health education and welfare of the minor (ii) acting as an
intermediary in connection with the arrangement of any resumption or continuance of access by the [father] to the minor which the [adopters] may agree to
(iii) forwarding Christmas and birthday presents from the [father] to the minor
'3. The [adopters] will keep a Court Welfare Officer informed of any change of
address they may make from time to time during such minority.'
                                                                                   e
As I have said, there is only one reported case in which a condition relating to
access has been imposed at the time of the making of an adoption order, and clearly
such a condition, if it can be imposed at all, should only be imposed in most exceptional cases. The whole tenor of the Adoption Act 1958, particularly emphasised in
s 13(1) thereof, is that from the time of the adoption the adoptive parents take over
completely from the natural parents the role of parents of the child. Clearly no   *f*
condition should be imposed which could be regarded as detracting from the rights
and duties of the adoptive parents under that subsection. But it does appear to me that
the conditions which are asked to be included in the order here are such as not to
affect the rights and responsibilities of the adoptive parents in relation to the matter
of access. I draw attention, in particular, to the words: 'resumption or continuance of
access by the [father] to the minor which the [adopters] may agree to'.   *g*
There has been some doubt whether conditions relating to access could be made
under s 7(3) of the 1958 Act. In Re G (TJ)[1] this court upheld a decision of a county court
judge refusing an adoption order, the county court judge having refused to make the
adoption order because inter alia he thought it was desirable that the child should
maintain some contact with his mother and grandparents and he took the view that
he could not properly make an adoption order subject to the condition of that con-   *h*
tact being maintained. In upholding the decision two members of this court expressed
some doubt as to the enforceability of a condition for access if one were made: see
per Ormerod and Pearson LJJ[2]. But it does not appear to me that any member of
the court meant to rule that there was no jurisdiction to impose a condition relating
to access if special circumstances made such a condition desirable and if a clearly
drafted undertaking was put forward. Pearson LJ referred expressly to the absence in   *j*
that case of any such clear draft. Here we have one.
In Re J (a minor) (adoption order: conditions)[3] Rees J gave careful consideration in his

---

1   [1963] 1 All ER 20, [1963] 2 QB 73
2   [1963] 1 All ER at 23, 32, [1963] 2 QB at 88, 102
3   [1973] 2 All ER 410, [1973] Fam 106

a   judgment to that decision[1] of the Court of Appeal, and he came to the conclusion that it did not preclude him as a matter of jurisdiction from making an adoption order subject to the conditions as to access which were before him. In deciding to make the order on those conditions he took into account a provision contained in them for the regulation of the access through the Official Solicitor. I am satisfied that the reasoning of Rees J[2] in that case was sound, and that it is open to the court to

b   make an adoption order subject to such conditions as are put forward here. While emphasising that, in my view, it is only in a most exceptional case that any conditions concerning access should be imposed, I am satisfied that it is right to impose them here, bearing in mind the provision for regulation by a court welfare officer. I would add that this view involves no criticism of the attitude which was adopted by Sir George Baker P at the time of his judgment, because, although there was a suggestion then

c   of an adoption order subject to conditions of access, the parties were then far from having arrived at such an agreement as has fortunately been arrived at now.

I am fully satisfied that in this case it is in the interests of the minor that an adoption order should be made, and should be made subject to the proposed conditions. Accordingly, I would allow the appeal to the extent of making those conditions part of the order in the manner set forth in the minutes before the court.

d

BROWNE LJ. I agree. I have no doubt that it is for the benefit of this child that the adoption order should be made as asked for. As to the conditions, Cairns LJ has said that the general principle underlying the Adoption Act 1958 is that when an adoption order is made that cuts off the child completely from its natural parents. But I entirely agree with Cairns LJ that this is a very exceptional case. The mother

e   agrees, and, as I understand it, Sir George Baker P accepted, that it may be for the benefit of the child to see her father again at some time in the future. In this respect, it seems to me that this case is like *Re J (a minor) (adoption order: conditions)*[3], the decision of Rees J to which Cairns LJ has referred.

In these circumstances I agree that for the reasons given by Cairns LJ we can, and should, impose the conditions on which the parties are agreed. Accordingly, I agree

f   with the order proposed by Cairns LJ.

Appeal allowed to the extent of incorporating in the adoption order the conditions enumerated in the judgment.

g   Solicitors: *Cecil Altman & Co* (for the father); *Dale & Newbery* (for the adopters); *Official Solicitor.*

James Collins Esq   Barrister.

---

1   [1963] 1 All ER 20, [1963] 2 QB 73
2   [1973] 2 All ER at 418, [1973] Fam at 116
3   [1973] 2 All ER 410, [1973] Fam 106

a

R v Inner London Crown Court, ex parte London Borough of Greenwich

Reversed CA [1976] 1 All ER 273

QUEEN'S BENCH DIVISION

LORD WIDGERY CJ, BRIDGE AND KILNER BROWN JJ

7th NOVEMBER 1974

b

Certiorari – Delay – Discretion – Refusal of order – Unreasonable delay by applicant – Application made within statutory time limit – Jurisdiction of court to refuse order on ground of delay – Circumstances in which order would be refused – Need to show exceptional cir cumstances – Party acting to his detriment in reliance on order sought to be quashed – RSC Ord 53, r 2(2).

c

The applicants, a local authority, passed a resolution, pursuant to para 3[a] of Part II of Sch 11 to the Gaming Act 1968, to the effect that they would not grant permits under s 49 of the Betting, Gaming and Lotteries Act 1963, as amended by the Gaming Act 1968, s 53(1) and Sch 11, Part I, in respect of premises which were not purpose built for the provision of public entertainment. H and S owned premises which were not built for that purpose. They applied to the applicants for a permit under s 49 of the 1963 Act in respect of those premises. It was their intention to use the premises wholly or mainly for the playing of prize bingo. In accordance with their resolution the applicants refused to grant a permit. H and S appealed to the Crown Court which, on 22nd October 1973, reversed the applicants' decision, holding that the premises were to be used 'wholly or mainly for the purposes of a pleasure fair consisting wholly or mainly of amusements' within para 4(2)[b] of Part II of Sch 11 to the 1968 Act and therefore, by virtue of para 4(1), the applicants' resolution had no effect in relation to the grant of permits in respect of those premises. The court granted the permit sought. The applicants gave no indication that they intended to seek an order of certiorari to quash the decision and H and S proceeded without delay with the development of the premises, incurring substantial expenditure. They had not at that time obtained planning permission but anticipated that they would do so. Permission was granted in March 1974. Meanwhile, on 19th February 1974, the applicants intimated to H and S for the first time that they might seek an order of certiorari to quash the Crown Court's decision. They obtained leave for that purpose on 5th April, shortly before the six months' time limit, prescribed by RSC Ord 53, r 2(2)[c], was due to expire. At the hearing of the application it was common ground that, in consequence of the decision in *R v Herrod, ex parte Leeds City District Council[d]*, the decision of the Crown Court was wrong in law. It was contended, however, that, in the exercise of its discretion, the Divisional Court should refuse to grant the order sought in view of the applicants' unreasonable delay in making the application.

d

e

f

g

h

Held – On the assumption that the court had jurisdiction to refuse the discretionary remedy of certiorari on the ground of delay, even though the application had been made within the six months' time limit, the circumstances in which an application would be refused on that ground would be exceptional and the party who sought to resist the application would have to make out a strong case. The applicants' delay in applying for certiorari was unjustified but the expenditure which H and S had incurred was not a consequence of that delay but of their own haste in proceeding

i

---

a   Paragraph 3, so far as material, is set out at p 116 e, post
b   Paragraph 4, so far as material, is set out at p 116 f, post
c   Rule 2(2), so far as material, is set out at p 118 c, post
d   [1974] 3 All ER 362, [1974] 1 WLR 1275

a with the development without having obtained planning permission. Accordingly there were no grounds which would justify the refusal of the remedy of certiorari and the application would therefore be granted (see p 118 *g* to *j*, p 119 *d* to *j* and p 120 *b*, post).

Notes

b For the discretionary nature of certiorari, see 1 Halsbury's Laws (4th Edn) 156-160, paras 161-167, and for cases on the subject, see 16 Digest (Repl) 450, 451, 2580-2590.

For permits for the provision of amusements with prizes, see Supplement to 18 Halsbury's Laws (3rd Edn) para 469B, 3, and for cases on the subject, see Digest (Cont Vol C) 395, 396, 316*aa*-316*e*.

For the Betting, Gaming and Lotteries Act 1963, s 49, see 14 Halsbury's Statutes

c (3rd Edn) 593.

For the Gaming Act 1968, s 53, Sch 11, Part I and Part II, paras 3, 4, see 14 Halsbury's Statutes (3rd Edn) 749, 797, 800.

Case referred to in judgment

R v Herrod, ex parte Leeds City District Council [1974] 3 All ER 362, [1974] 1 WLR 1275, DC.

d

Cases also cited

Cruse v Johnson [1898] 2 QB 91, [1895-9] All ER Rep 105, DC.

R v Aston University Senate, ex parte Roffey [1969] 2 All ER 964, [1969] 2 QB 538, DC.

R v Glamorgan Appeal Tribunal, ex parte Fricker (1917) 115 LT 930, DC.

R v Nicholson [1899] 2 QB 455, CA.

e *R v Pembrokeshire Quarter Sessions, ex parte Bennell* [1969] 1 All ER 940, [1969] 1 QB 386, DC.

R v Sheward (1880) 9 QB 741, CA.

R v Stafford Justices, ex parte Stafford Corpn [1940] 2 KB 33, CA.

R v Surrey Justices (1870) LR 5 QB 466.

f **Motion for certiorari**

This was an application by way of motion by the London Borough of Greenwich ('the applicants') for an order of certiorari to remove into the High Court for the purpose of its being quashed an order made by Judge Layton in the Crown Court sitting at Inner London Sessions House, Newington Causeway, SE1, on 22nd October 1973 whereby he allowed an appeal by Alan Hunt and Graham Smith against a g refusal of the applicants to grant a permit for the provision of amusements with prizes at premises known as 2A and 2B Woolwich New Road, Woolwich, SE18. The grounds for the application were (1) that the applicants had resolved on 29th July 1970, pursuant to para 3 of Part II of Sch 11 to the Gaming Act 1968, not to grant any permits for the provision of amusements with prizes under s 49 of the Betting, Gaming and Lotteries Act 1963 in respect of premises which were not purpose built for the h provision of public entertainment; (2) that by virtue of para 4 of Part II of Sch 11, the resolution did not have effect in relation to premises which were used or to be used for the purpose of a pleasure fair consisting wholly or mainly of amusements; (3) that on 13th August Alan Hunt and Graham Smith were refused a permit by the applicants and appealed to Inner London Crown Court on the ground that the premises the subject of the application were in law and in fact established and con- j ducted for the purposes of such a 'pleasure fair', as they were used or intended to be used for prize bingo; (4) that premises used for prize bingo, played by automatic machine or otherwise, did not constitute a 'pleasure fair' within the meaning of para 4 of Part II of Sch 11; (5) that the judge at the Crown Court had allowed the appeal on the law and the facts, the judge deciding as a matter of law that the premises were used or to be used for the purpose of a pleasure fair consisting wholly or mainly of amusements within the meaning of para 4 of Part II of Sch 11; and (6) that the

decision was wrong in law and was an improper exercise of the judge's discretion. *a*
The facts are set out in the judgment of Lord Widgery CJ.

Robin Simpson QC and *Colin Nicholls* for the applicants.
David Tudor Price for the respondent.

LORD WIDGERY CJ. In these proceedings counsel moves on behalf of the London *b*
Borough of Greenwich for an order of certiorari to bring up into this court with a
view to its being quashed an order made by His Honour Judge Layton at Inner
London Crown Court on 22nd October 1973, granting to one Alan Hunt and one
Graham Smith a permit for the provision of amusements with prizes at premises
situate at 2A and 2B Woolwich New Road, Woolwich, SE18. In fact, the applicants,
to whom the matter had come in the first instance, had declined to issue the permit *c*
which Mr Hunt and Mr Smith sought, and their decision was in effect overruled in
the Inner London Crown Court with the effect that I have mentioned.
     On 29th July 1970 the applicants passed a resolution to the effect that the council had
resolved not to grant any permits under s 49 of the Betting, Gaming and Lotteries
Act 1963, as amended, in respect of premises which were not purpose built for the
provision of public entertainment. The permit which Mr Hunt and Mr Smith *d*
sought and obtained in the Crown Court was such a permit as is referred to in that
resolution.
     The authority for passing a resolution of that kind is contained in para 3 of Part II
of Sch 11 to the Gaming Act 1968, which provides:

> 'Any local authority may pass either of the following resolutions, that is to
> say . . . (*b*) that (subject to paragraph 4 of this Schedule) the authority will *e*
> neither grant nor renew any permit in respect of premises of a class specified
> in the resolution.'

Paragraph 4(2) provides:

> 'This paragraph applies to any premises used or to be used wholly or mainly
> for the purposes of a pleasure fair consisting wholly or mainly of amusements.' *f*

That links up with para 4(1) which provides:

> 'No resolution under paragraph 3 of this Schedule shall have effect in relation
> to the grant or renewal of permits in respect of premises to which this paragraph
> applies.'

Thus, although I have reached it by rather a tortuous course, the effect of para 4 is *g*
that if the premises are used, or to be used wholly or mainly, for the purposes of a
pleasure fair, the inhibition on the grant of permits contemplated by the resolution
does not apply. If they are not to be used as a pleasure fair, then the inhibition applies
with its full force, and that is underlined, as it were, by para 6, which provides:

> 'Where an application for the grant or renewal of a permit is made to a local *h*
> authority, then if—(*a*) there is for the time being in force a resolution passed
> by that authority in accordance with paragraph 3 of this Schedule which is applic-
> able to the premises to which the application relates . . . it shall be the duty of
> the authority to refuse to grant or renew the permit.'

So again if the resolution is effective in regard to these premises, then the Crown *j*
Court's hands were equally tied and it could not make the order which it purported
to make in this case.
     Before the Crown Court the main issue was whether the premises were to be used
wholly or mainly for the purposes of a pleasure fair. What they were to be used for
wholly or mainly was the playing of prize bingo, and at a time earlier in the last
12 months there was some doubt whether premises used wholly or mainly for prize

a bingo were used wholly or mainly for the purposes of a pleasure fair within the meaning of this paragraph. But that problem was resolved, for the time being at all
events, by a decision of this court in *R v Herrod, ex parte Leeds City District Council*[1]. That
is the present authority on the point. It is to the effect that premises used wholly
or mainly for prize bingo, and for no other relevant purpose, are not used wholly
or mainly as a pleasure fair within the definition.

b   Hence the resolution passed by the applicants can bite on these premises, and
hence if the premises are not purpose built so as to come within the terms of the
resolution (and they are not) it follows that the applicants were bound to refuse the
permit and on this basis that the Crown Court was wrong to take the opposite view.
    Down to that point, on the authorities as they stand, counsel today are in agree-
ment before us. Subject to the further issue to which I turn in a moment, counsel
c for the respondent recognises that in view of the decision in *R v Herrod, ex parte
Leeds City District Council*[1] he cannot contend that this was a pleasure fair and, therefore, on the face of it the Crown Court order was made either without jurisdiction or
showing an error of law on its face, whichever is the correct view, but either of which
would result in the order being quashed by certiorari in this court.
    Counsel for the respondent, resisting the application for certiorari, puts his case
d on the principle which can be narrowly and easily stated, and it is this. He says that
it has been recognised from the beginning of time that certiorari, like the other
prerogative orders, is a discretionary remedy, and he says accordingly that even
though counsel for the applicants makes out a prima facie case for an order of certiorari on these facts, having regard to the unreasonable delay of which counsel
for the respondent says the applicants were guilty, we in our discretion should decline
e to allow the order of certiorari to go.
    The essential dates and facts on which one can judge the issue whether there has
been delay of an exceptional kind are these. The decision in the Crown Court was
on 22nd October 1973. The order included an order for costs, and on the following
day the successful parties in the Crown Court wrote to the applicants asking for their
costs. They did not get them at that time or indeed for some time afterwards, and
f nothing was said on either side at this stage as to whether an application to this court
to quash the Crown Court order was or was not likely to be made.
    There is in fact no power in these circumstances for the dissatisfied party in the
Crown Court to come to this court by case stated. That is a remedy which is specifically excluded by s 10 of the Courts Act 1971. There was, therefore, no question of
that procedure being employed. During the remaining months of 1973, following
g the order in the Crown Court, no discussion was initiated between the parties to
discover whether an application for certiorari was or was not likely to be made.
    However, in those remaining months Mr Hunt and Mr Smith were not idle be-
cause they began to acquire and equip the premises for the use of prize bingo to
which they sought to put them. They had not at this stage, incidentally, obtained
planning permission for the use of the premises for this purpose, but they had been
h successful in many similar planning appeals elsewhere in the country and had some
justifiable confidence that they would succeed on this site also. I say 'justifiable
confidence' because in fact they did succeed in obtaining planning permission on
28th March 1974.
    However I stress that they did not wait for that planning permission before pro-
ceeding to develop the premises. They went ahead, and clearly without delay, and
j by the end of 1973 they had incurred expenditure which counsel for the respondent
totalled at about £80,000. That figure includes the price of acquiring the premises
and we do not know what their resale value might be, but it also includes a number
of matters such as legal fees, shopfitting for fitting out the premises and, altogether,

---

1 [1974] 3 All ER 362, [1974] 1 WLR 1275

apart from the payment for the premises themselves, some £12,000 or more was **a**
used in the autumn of 1973 to get the premises ready.

The turn of the year came. No further relevant development took place, and
indeed there was no reference to the possibility of an application to this court to
set aside the Crown Court order until 19th February 1974. On that date, for the
first time, the developers were advised of the fact that an application to this court
was a possibility. True enough, on 5th April the applicants got leave to move for **b**
certiorari, and that brings them before this court today.

The first point to look at on counsel for the respondent's argument that there was
here unreasonable delay which disentitled the applicants to their remedy is, I think,
the provisions of the Rules of the Supreme Court about the time within which such
an application must be made. RSC Ord 53, r 2(2) provides:

'Leave shall not be granted to apply for an order of certiorari to remove any **c**
judgment, order, conviction or other proceeding for the purpose of its being
quashed, unless the application for leave is made within six months after the
date of the proceeding...'

That reads like a perfectly simple and straightforward time limit. Anyone reading
that rule might well think that as long as he acted within six months he would be all **d**
right, and if he took more than six months to make his application he would require
special leave to apply out of time. But the contention is that though six months is
there expressed as the maximum period within which the application can be made,
yet a shorter period may suffice in many cases because in the exercise of this court's
discretion it may refuse to allow an order of certiorari to go even though the time
lapse has been less than six months. **e**

For my part I have no doubt that that six months' time limit, which has been in
the rules for nearly 100 years, is generally regarded throughout the country as being
a limit within which an applicant can safely act. I think that for those who are
concerned with this branch of the law to be told this afternoon that the six months'
limit was merely a maximum, and that in any large number or variety of cases a
shorter limit had been imposed, they would be surprised, and indeed I think that one **f**
must hesitate to drive anything in the nature of a serious wedge into the limits of
RSC Ord 53, r 2, which has stood for so long and been given that accepted meaning
for so long.

But I am bound to say on the authorities which have been cited to us that there is a
great deal to be said for the proposition that, since the remedy is discretionary, the
court can, and sometimes should, impose a tighter limitation than six months. I am **g**
not sure how far it is necessary to decide the point this afternoon, but I draw attention
to the fact that in none of the authorities which we have seen today has any court
been compelled squarely to face the first question which faces us this afternoon: in
other words, the decision on whether the six months' limit can be reduced in the
court's discretion. As I say, I am not sure how far it is necessary to decide that today,
but I certainly would wish to approach this application on the footing that that limit **h**
can be reduced in appropriate cases on a principle to which I have already referred.

I think that the circumstances in which a shorter period of limitation should be
applied will be rare. I think that anyone who seeks to resist certiorari on the basis
of lapse of time when less than six months had elapsed has got to make out his case,
and make out a strong case, but I am prepared for the purposes of this judgment to
assert that, given a sufficiently strong case, the court can and should impose stricter **j**
limits on the application for certiorari.

What are the essential features of the conduct of the parties in this case? The
period which has elapsed between the Crown Court order and the giving of leave to
move for certiorari was nearly six months. During that time the applicants did
virtually nothing. I am not saying that in a critical sense because it has been explained
to us that their litigation department was very busy at the time, but they did nothing

a for practical purposes and allowed the matter to ride through the remainder of 1973 and through the early months of 1974.

On the other side Mr Hunt and Mr Smith had been showing great activity, as I have already indicated. They had committed themselves to this considerable amount of expenditure by the end of 1973. It is to be observed that in doing that they must have realised that they were running some kind of risk. To begin with, *b* they had not obtained planning permission, and that did not follow until March, so they must have been running some kind of risk in that regard.

Furthermore I think it fair to say that the local planning authority, who are the applicants in this case, would have known that planning permission had not been granted and might very well have regarded that as an indication that no further and decisive action on the part of Mr Hunt and Mr Smith would be taken at this *c* time.

Further it seems to me not irrelevant that even if the applicants had acted within a period which on any view would be reasonable, and by that I mean a period of two to three months, or something of that kind, the commitment of Mr Hunt and Mr Smith to the extent relied on would have taken place. It was all done, as I have stressed, before the end of 1973, and no one could have said that the applicants *d* were dragging their feet or being unreasonably slow in taking action if they had acted at some time in October, November or December of that year.

Accordingly, whilst the delay on the part of the applicants was unjustified, by which I mean there was no ground which required them to take six months, yet it is not easy to say that the commitment of the developers is the result of that delay. I think as a matter of common sense it is not the result of that delay and there was no *e* reason in this case for the planning authority to think that development of an expensive character was imminent having regard to the fact that they knew that no planning permission had been granted.

For all those reasons it seems to me that, if one accepts the principle for which counsel for the respondent contends, namely, that the court's discretion can and should in proper circumstances restrict the period within which certiorari can be *f* applied for, I do not think that this case, on the facts which I have indicated, is a case to which that principle can properly be applied. For those reasons I think that the order of the Crown Court was without jurisdiction and that there are no discretionary grounds which should deprive the applicants of the remedy they seek. I would say that the order should go.

g **BRIDGE J.** I agree. I feel some sympathy for Mr Hunt and Mr Smith in the predicament in which they now find themselves. But the grounds which invoke that sympathy are insufficient to afford a basis for the court, in the exercise of its discretion, to withhold the remedy sought by the applicants to which, apart from discretion, it is common ground the applicants are plainly entitled.

It is important in my judgment to take account of the fact that, as Lord Widgery CJ *h* has pointed out, the effect of s 10 of the Courts Act 1971 is that the sole remedy open to the applicants, if minded to challenge the decision of the Crown Court given against them in this matter, was to come to this court by way of an application for an order of certiorari.

Like Lord Widgery CJ, I approach this matter on the basis that delay in applying for an order of certiorari within the period of six months prescribed under RSC *j* Ord 53, r 2(2), may, as a matter of theory, certainly if coupled with other factors, provide a basis for a discretionary withholding of an order which it would otherwise be proper to make. But in a case where the remedy by way of certiorari is the only remedy available, I find it extremely difficult to visualise a situation—I am not saying that such a situation could not arise—in which delay within six months will per se, without any other factor capable of playing a part and influencing the exercise of the court's discretion, lead to a discretionary refusal to allow an order otherwise due to go.

None of the authorities to which our attention has been drawn persuades me that   *a*
the court has ever grappled with this specific point and held that delay as such
within the six months' limit provided it causes prejudice can be a ground for such a
discretionary refusal. If it can, like Lord Widgery CJ, I agree it would be only in
the rarest and most exceptional cases.

I agree that the order sought should go.

b

KILNER BROWN J. I cannot usefully add to either judgment, with both of
which I agree.

Certiorari granted.

Solicitors: *Town Clerk, London Borough of Greenwich* (for the applicants); *Phillip Ross,*
Elliston & Bieber (for the respondent).   *c*

N P Metcalfe Esq Barrister.

Kingston and another v Ambrian Investment   *d*
Co Ltd

COURT OF APPEAL, CIVIL DIVISION   Applied in GLESSING v GREEN
LORD DENNING MR, BUCKLEY AND SCARMAN LJJ   [1975] 2 All ER 696
18th, 19th, 22nd JULY 1974

e

Deed – Escrow – Condition – Implied condition – Conveyance executed in anticipation of sale
– Time for completion – Reasonable inference from circumstances – Transfer executed by
vendor and delivered to his solicitor – Purchaser entitled to delivery of transfer on payment
of purchase price – Delay in completion by purchaser – Whether escrow subject to implied
condition as to time of payment – Whether condition that payment should be made promptly
or within a reasonable time.   *f*

The plaintiffs, who were tenants of a leasehold house, proposed to purchase the
freehold of the house, as they were entitled to do under the Leasehold Reform Act
1967. The purchase price was agreed with the landlords and the required deposit
thereon was paid. In July 1970 the defendants bought the reversion to the lease
but the sale was subject to the statutory obligation to convey the freehold to the   *g*
plaintiffs, which the defendants then believed was binding on them. In April
1971 the plaintiffs executed a transfer of the house to themselves. The transfer
was then executed by the defendants and sent by them to their solicitors with a
covering letter, dated 21st April 1971, pointing out that the plaintiffs should pay
the defendants' solicitors' costs of the conveyance so that the full proceeds of sale
should be remitted to the defendants' bank. In a further letter dated 21st April   *h*
1971 the defendants wrote to their bankers that the sale to the plaintiffs would be
completed within the next few days. There were however delays in completion,
initially for a period of six weeks to 3rd June. On that date the parties agreed
that the plaintiffs should pay interest on the balance of the purchase price, as from
15th February 1971, to compensate for their delay. The plaintiffs were ready to
complete by November 1971 and asked for a completion statement which the   *j*
defendants' solicitors sent to them proposing that completion should take place on
23rd November. The plaintiffs accepted the completion statement and said that they
hoped to complete the purchase by 23rd November. But further delay ensued
because the plaintiffs wished to vary the transfer to effect a conveyance of the house
to someone other than themselves; the defendants did not, however, reply to that
suggestion. The defendants then discovered that the notice to buy the freehold

a   which had been served under the 1967 Act had not been registered as an estate contract, as required by s 5(5) of the 1967 Act. The defendants therefore refused to go on with the sale on the ground that the notice was not binding on them. The plaintiffs brought proceedings for specific performance and for delivery up of the transfer executed in April 1971 on payment of the balance of the purchase price and the costs of the transaction which they were ready to pay. The judge dismissed the

b   plaintiffs' claim holding that, although the executed transfer had been delivered by the defendants to their solicitors as an escrow, the escrow was subject to an implied condition that the plaintiffs would complete the transaction within seven days of the plaintiffs being told of the defendants' solicitors' costs and that condition had not been fulfilled. The plaintiffs appealed.

c   **Held** – It was not an implied condition of the escrow that the transaction should be completed promptly. Having regard to all the circumstances, including the fact that the escrow had to be regarded in the light of the defendants' belief at the time of execution that there was a binding contract for sale, the condition to be implied was (a) (per Buckley and Scarman LJJ) that completion should take place in due course, that being the reasonable inference which was to be drawn, in the absence of contra-

d   indications, where a conveyance was delivered by a vendor in escrow; or (b) alternatively (per Lord Denning MR and Scarman LJ) that completion should take place within a time that was reasonable in all the circumstances; the delay which had occurred was not such as to be unreasonable. Accordingly, as the plaintiffs were ready to complete by paying the balance of the purchase price and the costs of the transaction, the condition of the escrow had been fulfilled; the defendants' solicitors

e   were therefore bound to hand over the transfer to the plaintiffs on payment of the purchase price and costs and the appeal would be allowed accordingly (see p 125 *e*, p 126 *c* to *e* and *g*, p 127 *f* to *j* and p 128 *e* and *h*, post).

     Beesly v Hallwood Estates Ltd [1961] 1 All ER 90 and *Vincent v Premo Enterprises (Voucher Sales) Ltd* [1969] 2 All ER 941 applied.

f

Notes

For delivery of a deed as an escrow, see 11 Halsbury's Laws (3rd Edn) 348-351, paras 559-561, and for cases on the subject, see 17 Digest (Reissue) 255-262, 200-275.

Cases referred to in judgments

g   *Beesly v Hallwood Estates Ltd* [1961] 1 All ER 90, [1961] Ch 105, [1961] 2 WLR 36, CA; affg [1960] 2 All ER 314, [1960] 1 WLR 549, Digest (Cont Vol A) 472, 241a.

     Byrnlea Property Investments Ltd v Ramsay, Re 33 Byrne Road Balham [1969] 2 All ER 311, [1969] 2 QB 253, [1969] 2 WLR 721, [1969] RVR 183, CA, Digest (Cont Vol C) 599, 1464Ae.

h   *Phillips v Edwards* (1864) 33 Beav 440, 3 New Rep 658, 55 ER 438, 17 Digest (Reissue) 260, 248.

     Powell v London & Provincial Bank [1893] 2 Ch 555, 62 LJCh 795, 69 LT 421, 41 WR 545, 2 R 482, CA, 17 Digest (Reissue) 246, 106.

     Vincent v Premo Enterprises (Vouchers Sale) Ltd [1969] 2 All ER 941, [1969] 2 QB 609, [1969] 2 WLR 1256, CA, Digest (Cont Vol C) 293, 204a.

j   *Windsor Refrigerator Co Ltd v Branch Nominees Ltd* [1961] 1 All ER 277, [1961] 1 Ch 375, [1961] 2 WLR 196, CA; rvsg [1960] 2 All ER 568, [1961] Ch 88, [1960] 3 WLR 108, Digest (Cont Vol A) 472, 210a.

Cases also cited

Foundling Hospital (Governors & Guardians) v Crane [1911] 2 KB 367, CA.
Thompson v McCullough [1947] 1 All ER 265, [1947] KB 447, CA.

Appeal   *a*

The plaintiffs, David Kingston and John Spencer Rossdale, brought an action against
the defendants, Ambrian Investment Co Ltd, claiming specific performance of the
plaintiffs' right to have the freehold of premises known as 27 Queen's Gate Mews,
London, SW7, and an order that a transfer of the premises, executed by the plaintiffs
and the defendants, and delivered by the defendants to their solicitors, should be
handed over to the plaintiffs on payment of the balance of the purchase price and   *b*
the defendants' solicitors' costs. At the trial of the action, his Honour Judge
McDonnell, sitting at West London County Court, gave judgment on 27th July 1973
dismissing the plaintiffs' claim on the ground, inter alia, that the transfer had been
delivered by the defendants to their solicitors as an escrow on the implied condition
that the plaintiffs would complete the transaction within seven days of being told
of the amount of the defendants' solicitors' costs and the plaintiffs, having delayed   *c*
completion beyond that time, were not entitled to delivery up of the transfer. The
plaintiffs appealed. The facts are set out in the judgment of Lord Denning MR.

David Hunter QC and *Derek Turriff* for the plaintiffs.
J E Vinelott QC and *John Lindsay* for the defendants.

d

LORD DENNING MR. In 1967 Parliament passed the Leasehold Reform Act. It
came into force on 1st January 1968. It gave a tenant of a leasehold house a right to
buy the freehold provided that certain requirements were satisfied. Mrs Moreton,
a widow, was the tenant of a leasehold house who satisfied all the requirements.
The house was 27 Queens Gate Mews, SW7. It was owned by the Harrington Estate.   *e*
She held a lease of the house for 36 years from 24th June 1950 at a rent of £30 a year.
So it was a long tenancy at a low rent. The rateable value was £397. So it was under
£400. She and her husband had lived in the house as their residence for 17 years.
As she was clearly entitled to buy the freehold, Mrs Moreton asked her solicitors to
give the appropriate notice to the landlords. They gave a notice on 1st February
1968, soon after the Act came into force; but this notice was out of order owing to a   *f*
technical defect. They failed to delete some of the words in the form. It was a defect
into which many solicitors fell at that time: see *Byrnlea Property Investments Ltd v
Ramsay*[1]. But Mrs Moreton's solicitors soon found out the mistake and remedied it.
On 7th March 1968 they gave a further notice to acquire the freehold which was a
good notice. It was afterwards questioned but, so far as I can see, it was perfectly
in order. Thereupon the landlords were bound to sell the freehold to the tenant   *g*
and the tenant was bound to buy it. It was just as if there was a contract for sale
freely entered into between them: see s 5(1) of the 1967 Act. The landlords sought
to avoid it. They applied to the Minister under s 19 of the 1967 Act to allow them to
retain powers of management. This application failed. Thereupon the landlords
admitted that the tenant had a right to buy the freehold. On 4th September 1969
the landlords gave a notice in the prescribed form admitting the tenant's right: see   *h*
Sch 3, para 7 to the 1967 Act. On making this admission the landlords undoubtedly
became bound to sell the freehold to the tenant just as if there was a contract between
them. The conditions of the sale were those set out in Part I of the schedule to
the statutory regulations[2]. The landlords accepted the position. On 18th September
1969 they asked for a deposit of £90 (three times the annual rent) in accordance with
condition 1 of Part I of the schedule to the regulations[2]. The tenant duly paid that   *j*
deposit. In November 1969 the valuers for both sides agreed the price at £3,750. (I
should mention here that on 30th September 1969 Mrs Moreton died; but under the

---

1   [1969] 2 All ER 311, [1969] 2 QB 253
2   Leasehold Reform (Enfranchisement and Extension) Regulations 1967 (SI 1967 No 1879)

a 1967 Act all her rights and obligations vested in her executors: see s 5(1).) Thereupon the landlords and Mrs Moreton's executors were bound, just as if there was a concluded contract of sale for £3,750 on the statutory conditions. If the landlords had remained owners, the contract would have been completed without trouble. But the landlords did not remain owners. They determined to sell the freehold subject, of course, to the right of Mrs Moreton's executors to buy the freehold.

b Now I must mention a point which was not realised by anyone until much later. In March 1968, when the solicitors for the tenant gave the notice to buy the freehold, they made a mistake. It was the early days of the Act. They overlooked this important point; they ought to have then registered the notice as it if were an estate contract: see s 5(5). They did not do so. The result was that, if the landlords sold the house, the notice was void as against the purchaser, even though he had full

c knowledge of it. In this case no one realised this mistake for four years. Meanwhile the following events took place. In 1970 the landlords decided to sell the freehold of the house. They entered into negotiations with intending buyers called Ambrian Investment Co Ltd ('Ambrian'). The landlords told Ambrian in writing that they had admitted the right of the tenant to buy the freehold of 27 Queens Gate Mews. In April 1970 the landlords contracted to sell the reversion to Ambrian. That con-

d tract of sale expressly stated that the freehold was sold subject to this admitted right of the tenant. No doubt the buyers paid much less for the reversion on that account. On 31st July 1970 the reversion was conveyed to Ambrian and the deposit of £690 was credited to them.

The solicitors for Ambrian, the new landlords, were Lee & Pembertons, a firm of high standing. They treated the notice as good and binding on Ambrian. They

e admitted the price of £3,750. They acknowledged the receipt of the deposit. The solicitors for the tenants submitted a draft transfer for approval. Lee & Pembertons returned it duly approved. On 15th March 1971 Lee & Pembertons wrote to the tenants' solicitors saying: 'We look forward to receiving from you, as soon as possible, the engrossment for sealing by our Clients.'

Now we come to an important point of the case. It is the execution of the transfer.

f In April 1971 the tenants' solicitor had the transfer engrossed. He got it signed, sealed and delivered by the tenants (the two executors) in the presence of witnesses. Then on 5th April he sent it to Lee & Pembertons. On 19th April 1971 Lee & Pembertons wrote acknowledging the receipt of 'the engrossment of the Transfer which we are now having sealed by our Clients'. They sent it to their clients, Ambrian. They advised them that they were legally bound to convey the freehold

g of the premises to the tenants. On 21st April 1971 Ambrian executed the transfer. It showed on the face of it that it had already been duly executed by the tenants (the two executors, David Kingston and John Rossdale). Ambrian affixed on it their common seal in the presence of a director, Mr David Kirch, and the secretary of the company. Then Mr Kirch sent it back to Lee & Pembertons with this covering letter dated 21st April 1971:

h

'I return herewith the Transfer . . . I suppose all that you are entitled to collect up until completion is the ground rent on this property . . . They should of course pay your costs in connection with this purchase and you should therefore be in a position to remit the full proceeds of £3,750 to the Bank.'

j So Lee & Pembertons held the transfer duly executed by both sides. Then there was much delay in completion. It seems to have been largely due to the tenants (the two executors). They wanted to delay payment of the price of £3,750 until they sold some other property. Ambrian became restive and said that, in view of the delay, they wanted to be paid interest. On 3rd June Mr David Kirch spoke to the solicitor for the tenants and it was agreed that the tenants should pay interest at eight per cent (two per cent over bank rate) from 15th February 1971. Eventually

in November 1971 the tenants said they wished to complete and asked for a comple-   *a*
tion statement. On 15th November 1971 Lee & Pembertons sent this statement:

'Balance sale price   £3660·00
Interest on balance purchase money at 2% above
Bank Rate from 15th February 1971 to 23rd
November 1971   £220·78
          Our costs   46·00   *b*

                                                                ─────────
                                                                £3926·78.'

On 17th November 1971 the tenants' solicitor agreed the completion figures. So all
was ready for completion on 23rd November 1971.

There was, however, further delay. In December 1971 the tenants asked for a
variation. They asked that the transfer should be varied so that the property should   *c*
not be transferred into their own names but into the name of one of the beneficiaries,
Mr de Segundo. Lee & Pembertons sought to get the instructions of Ambrian.
But Ambrian never gave instructions to Lee & Pembertons. On the contrary, in
April 1972 they changed their solicitors. They took the work away from Lee &
Pembertons and entrusted it to another firm of solicitors, S Farren & Co. These
new solicitors enquired into the matter. They asked for a sight of the original notice   *d*
to buy the freehold. By mistake the tenants sent a copy of the notice of 1st February
1968, which was out of order, and did not send the notice of 7th March 1968, which
was entirely in order. The new solicitors for Ambrian said that the notice of 1st
February 1968 was of no effect. They refused to go on with the sale.

Faced with this refusal, the solicitors for the tenants brought these proceedings for
specific performance against Ambrian. They relied at first on the notice of 1st   *e*
February 1968 (mistakenly describing it as 1st February 1969). Ambrian's solicitors
pleaded that the notice of 1st February 1969 was not valid. The tenants' solicitors
then replied that they had referred to the wrong notice. They amended their claim
so as to rely on the notice of 7th March 1968. Ambrian's solicitors questioned the
validity of that notice too. They gave several reasons. On that issue the case came
on for hearing in the county court in July 1973. The judge thought that the notice   *f*
of 7th March 1968 might well have been good; but he did not find it necessary to
decide it. The reason was because on 10th July 1973, in the course of the hearing,
Ambrian discovered a new point. They were allowed to amend their defence so as to
plead it. It was this. The notice of 7th March 1968 (assuming that it was good) ought
to have been registered under the Lands Charges Act 1925 as an estate contract (see
s 5(5) of the 1967 Act) and not having been registered, it was void as against Ambrian.   *g*
This was a formidable point. It was a very technical point because, at the time of the
purchase, Ambrian were aware that the previous landlords had accepted the notice
as valid and binding. Indeed Ambrian had paid a less sum on that account. Yet,
technical as the point was, it was a good point unless it could be overcome in some
way. In order to overcome it, the tenants answered it by another technicality based
on the doctrine of escrow. They were allowed to amend so as to plead it. It arose   *h*
in this way. In the course of the hearing Ambrian had produced the transfer which
had been executed in April 1971 by both sides. The tenants said it was an escrow
and that they were entitled to have the transfer handed over to them on payment of
the purchase price and costs. They relied for this purpose on the decision of this
court in *Beesly v Hallwood Estates Ltd*[1], affirming Buckley J's decision[2].

The county court judge held that the transfer was an escrow, but he did not allow   *j*
the tenants to rely on it. He distinguished this case from *Beesly v Hallwood Estates
Ltd*[1]. He said that Ambrian had executed the transfer subject to a condition which
had not been fulfilled. He said:

───
1   [1961] 1 All ER 90, [1961] Ch 105
2   [1960] 2 All ER 314, [1960] 1 WLR 549

a   'I find that when they affixed the seal of [Ambrian] to the transfer David and Mr. Peter Kirch intended to deliver it as a Deed but they intended to deliver it conditionally not only upon the [tenants] paying the balance of the price and [Ambrian's] solicitors costs but upon their completing the transaction within *no more than seven days* of being told of the amount of such costs.'

The judge found that the condition had not been fulfilled. The transaction was not
b   completed within the seven days. The tenants could not therefore rely on the transfer or claim that it should be handed to them. The tenants appeal to this court.

The law on escrows has recently been stated in this court in *Beesly v Hallwood Estates Ltd*[1] and *Vincent v Premo Enterprises (Voucher Sales) Ltd*[2]. When a party executes a deed of transfer as an escrow, it means that he executes it subject to a condition express or implied which is thereafter to be fulfilled. As soon as the condition is
c   fulfilled the transfer becomes complete. The deed operates to transfer the title to the transferee. But if the condition is not fulfilled, the deed is not effective to make the transfer. But what is the position during the intervening time between the time when the deed is executed and the time when that condition is fulfilled? The law says that during this intervening time, the maker of the deed cannot withdraw it. He cannot recall it or repudiate it. He must await the event to see whether or not
d   the condition is fulfilled.

It is agreed here that Ambrian executed this transfer as an escrow, that is, subject to a condition. The only question is, what was the condition? The judge found that the condition was that the transaction should be completed 'within no more than seven days of being told of the amount of such costs'. Counsel for Ambrian sought to support the judgment, but he stated the condition a little differently. He said that
e   the condition was that the transaction should be completed 'promptly'.

I do not accept either of those suggested conditions. In my opinion the condition in this case was simply that the tenants should pay the purchase price and costs within a reasonable time—that is, a time which is reasonable in all the circumstances.

Take the ordinary case of a written contract of sale. Let us suppose that the vendor's solicitor sends the engrossed conveyance to the vendor asking him to
f   execute it but to leave the date blank. The vendor duly executes it by signing, sealing and delivering it. He sends it back to the solicitors, with or without a covering letter. There is a clear implication that the solicitor is not to hand over the conveyance to the purchaser except on completion, that is, except when the sums payable under the contract are paid. If completion is for some reason delayed, even for some little time, nevertheless the deed still holds good. The vendor cannot recall it so
g   long as a reasonable time has not expired. Once the sums payable under the contract are paid—or tendered—the condition is fulfilled. The solicitor can then properly hand over the conveyance in exchange for the money or a banker's draft for the amount.

Counsel for Ambrian suggested that, if completion was not had promptly, then the condition was not fulfilled and the deed was not operative at all. The result of
h   any delay, or lack of promptness, was that the solicitor had no authority to hand over the conveyance unless he got a fresh authority under seal. He quoted *Powell v London & Provincial Bank*[3], per Bowen LJ, and *Windsor Refrigerator Co Ltd v Branch Nominees Ltd*[4] by Cross J. But I think that is wrong. In such a case the solicitor for the vendor has ample authority to hand over the conveyance whenever payment is made—or tendered—of the sums payable under the contract, even though delayed
j   for some little time. No doubt there may come a time when the delay is so unreasonable or so long that the person who has executed the escrow may be released and

---

1   [1961] 1 All ER 90, [1961] Ch 105
2   [1969] 2 All ER 941, [1969] 2 QB 609
3   [1893] 2 Ch 555 at 563
4   [1960] 2 All ER 568 at 575, [1961] Ch 88 at 102

the solicitor would have no authority to hand over the conveyance: see *Beesly v*   **a**
Hallwood Estates Ltd[1] by Harman LJ[2] and by Lord Evershed MR[3]. Or the time may
come when it appears that the purchaser cannot or will not pay the money. In that
case too the escrow would be inoperative and the solicitor would have no authority
to hand it over: see the instance given by Romilly MR in *Phillips v Edwards*[4]. But
except in such or similar circumstances, the vendor is not released. The escrow,
once executed, cannot be recalled. On payment being made—or tendered—the   **b**
solicitor has authority to hand over the conveyance.

In the present case there was no contract of sale such as I have supposed. But
both parties believed there was. Both parties believed there was a valid notice to
buy the freehold which was equivalent to a contract of sale. They also believed that
it was binding on the purchasers of the reversion, either because they thought it
did not need to be registered or because they thought it had been registered. But,   **c**
whichever it was, they believed it to be binding. Such being their belief, the escrow
must be regarded as being executed in the same state of mind as if their belief had
been true. It was executed subject to the simple condition that the deed of transfer
was not to be handed over except on payment of the sums properly payable on
completion—or tender of them within a time that was reasonable in all the
circumstances.   **d**

It is true that the completion was delayed, but the delay was not excessive. The
initial period was six weeks from 21st April to 3rd June 1971. That was not unduly
long. Then on 3rd June 1971 the parties agreed that interest should run on the
purchase money at two per cent above bank rate to compensate for the past delay
from 15th April 1971 and for any further delay in the future. In those circumstances
the delay was not such as to be unreasonable in all the circumstances of the case.   **e**
It was not such as to affect the validity of the escrow. It remained binding on
Ambrian. The solicitors were bound to hand it over against payment of principal,
interest and costs. The tenants, I understand, are ready to pay those sums now.
Even though this is since action brought, it is good enough, just as in *Vincent v Premo
Enterprises (Voucher Sales) Ltd*[5]. The point did not arise until the actual hearing in
the county court. The tenants made the offer as soon as the point arose. Ambrian   **f**
must accept the money and hand over the transfer to the tenants.

I ought to mention one further point. Counsel for Ambrian suggests that the
tenants had in some way prejudiced their position by asking that the transfer be
made to Mr de Segundo. But Ambrian did not reply to the suggestion. Any delay
on that score was their own doing. So it is no bar to the claim of the tenants.

I know that all this law about escrows seems very archaic and technical, but it   **g**
has proved useful in this case—as it did in *Beesly v Hallwood Estates*[1]. It has enabled
the court to overcome a technical defence which had no merit.

I would therefore allow the appeal and hold that on tender of the appropriate sum,
the transfer should be handed over.

BUCKLEY LJ. It is common ground that the transfer which was sealed by the   **h**
defendants on or about 21st April 1971, and was then returned by the defendants to
their solicitors, Messrs Lee & Pembertons, was then delivered as an escrow; the
question is what the condition of the escrow was. Indeed as the argument for the
defendants, who are respondents to this appeal, proceeded it became clear that that
was in substance the only question for decision.

The plaintiffs say that the condition was the payment of the balance of the purchase   **j**

---

1   [1961] 1 All ER 90, [1961] Ch 105
2   [1961] 1 All ER at 94, [1961] 1 Ch at 118
3   [1961] 1 All ER at 95, [1961] 1 Ch at 120
4   (1864) 33 Beav 440 at 447
5   [1969] 2 All ER at 945, [1969] 210 QB at 620

a   price and the defendants' solicitors' costs. The defendants say the condition was that such payment should be made promptly. The learned judge found that the condition was the completion of the transaction within no more than seven days of the plaintiffs being told the amount of the costs. In his finding I think the judge went further than the evidence warranted. The documents include a letter from Mr David Kirch, a director of the plaintiff company, dated 21st April 1971 which *b*   indicates that he then contemplated that the sale would be 'completed within the next few days'. There was, I think, no other evidence to support the judge's finding. The letter is, in my opinion, quite inadequate for the purpose.

The answer to the question what the condition was accordingly depends in my opinion on inference from the circumstances. In this connection counsel for the defendants has emphasised that delivery of an escrow cannot be recalled by the *c*   deliverer and that this must be borne in mind in considering his probable intention. He contends that therefore a vendor would not execute a conveyance on sale except in the expectation of early completion, for by doing so he would put it out of his power to rescind the contract in the event of default on the part of the purchaser to complete in due time in accordance with the contractual terms, for the purchaser could at any time satisfy the condition of the escrow by paying the balance of the *d*   purchase price and costs. On this basis counsel for the defendants argues that the condition of the escrow must at least be that the purchaser shall complete the purchase within a reasonable time, that is, as counsel submits, that the anticipated timetable for completion will be adhered to subject only to reasonable modifications. With deference to counsel's able argument, this seems to me to be a very indefinite or imprecise form of condition. Unless time has been made of the essence of the *e*   contract, what timetable should the vendor reasonably anticipate? Unless the vendor has made clear to his solicitor what timetable he does anticipate, how is the solicitor to know whether the condition of the escrow has been satisfied? The test of a reasonable time would necessarily be a subjective one depending exclusively on the state of mind and intention of the vendor.

In my judgment, if a vendor executes a conveyance in anticipation of the comple-*f*   tion of a sale, the reasonable inference is that the vendor is satisfied that the sale will be satisfactorily completed in due course and that he executes the conveyance with the intention that it shall be handed to the purchaser or his solicitor on completion and thereupon become fully effective. In such a case, in my judgment, the reasonable inference with regard to the execution of the conveyance is that it is delivered in escrow conditionally on completion of the sale in due course. This *g*   inferred condition does not, in my opinion, import any time limit either by reference to a particular date or a reasonable period. If for any reason the contract is never completed, the condition will not be satisfied and the conveyance will never become effective.

But such an inference would, of course, have to give way to any sufficient contra-indications. The facts of the particular case must be considered.

h   Assuming that the plaintiffs' predecessor in title served a proper notice on the defendants' predecessor in title under the Leasehold Reform Act 1967 entitling the former to a grant of the freehold reversion, it is common ground that (a) the obligation to convey the freehold reversion is not binding on the defendants for lack of registration of the obligation under the Land Charges Act 1925 or the Land Registration Act 1925, but that (b) at all relevant times the parties were unaware of this *j*   and believed that a statutory obligation to convey the freehold reversion on payment of the appropriate purchase price and costs subsisted.

The defendants' intention when this transfer was executed must be determined in the light of what they then believed the legal position to be; not of what the true legal position was. Mr David Kirch thought that completion was imminent, and I am prepared to assume that his brother, who also countersigned the defendant company's seal, thought the same and that this view should be imputed to the defendant company. Nevertheless no step had been taken to make or purport to make time of the essence of the transaction, as it could have been under paras 6 and 10 of the Schedule to the Leasehold Reform (Enfranchisement and Extension) Regulations 1967[1], if in fact a statutory contract existed under the Act.

Although Mr David Kirch and his brother may have thought that completion was imminent on 21st April 1971, they do not seem to have worried about it unduly, for on 27th May 1971 Mr David Kirch wrote to Mr Rossdale a letter in which, while asking for immediate completion, he said: 'I would not mind if you were paying a market rate of interest . . .' On 3rd June 1971 he and Mr Rossdale orally agreed that the plaintiffs should pay interest on the balance of the purchase price as from 15th February 1971 at two per cent above bank rate. This, in my opinion, throws a measure of retrospective light on the defendants' intention when executing the transfer, for nowhere is any suggestion to be found that they or their solicitors regarded the transfer as no longer available for use on completion without redelivery by the defendants by reason of the passage of time.

On 15th November 1971 Messrs Lee & Pembertons produced a completion statement bringing into account interest at two per cent above bank rate from 15th February 1971 to 23rd November 1971, proposing completion on 23rd November 1971. On 17th November Messrs Rossdale wrote that they hoped to complete on that date. They did not in fact do so, but had they done so, there can I think be no doubt that Messrs Lee & Pembertons would have preferred the transfer sealed on 21st April 1971. They evidently did not think it necessary to get it resealed, or at least, redelivered, on the footing that the original execution in escrow no longer availed.

In my judgment there is no circumstance in this case which displaces what I have called the reasonable inference.

Counsel for the defendants has submitted that the request to the plaintiffs that the freehold should be conveyed to Mr de Segundo operated as a release of the binding effect of the escrow. I feel unable to accept this contention. The request was no more than a request or suggestion. It was not intended in any way to affect any legal relationship between the plaintiffs and the defendants and, in my judgment, it had no effect on the escrow. If in response to the request the freehold had been conveyed to Mr de Segundo, I think that the plaintiffs would have become estopped from relying on the supposed statutory obligation as requiring or the escrow as effecting a conveyance to themselves; but no such conveyance was made. In my judgment the request had no effect on the escrow.

Although counsel for the defendants has complained that the plaintiffs were wilfully dilatory in completing the supposed statutory contract, saying that they played the defendants along, he has not asserted any right to equitable relief of the kind suggested in *Beesly v Hallwood Estates Ltd*[2] in this court.

I would allow this appeal and declare the plaintiffs entitled to delivery of the executed transfer on payment of the balance of the purchase price and interest from 15th February 1971 until the date of payment and the defendants' conveyancing costs.

SCARMAN LJ. I agree with both the judgments delivered.

Appeal allowed, declaration that plaintiffs entitled to delivery of the executed transfer against payment of the purchase price of £3,750 less the deposit, with interest thereon from 15th February 1971 to date at two per cent above bank rate or the minimum lending rate, and £46 costs. Leave to appeal to the House of Lords refused.

Solicitors: *Lovell, White & King* (for the plaintiffs); *S Farren & Co* (for the defendants).

Wendy Shockett   Barrister.

---

1   SI 1967 No 1879
2   [1961] 1 All ER 90, [1961] Ch 105

a
John Mccann & Co (a firm) v Pow

COURT OF APPEAL, CIVIL DIVISION

LORD DENNING MR, ORR AND BROWNE LJJ

7th, 8th OCTOBER 1974

b *Estate agent – Delegation – Implied authority to delegate – Appointment of sub-agent – Duties requiring personal skill and competence – Agent instructed to find purchaser of property – Agent not expressly authorised to appoint sub-agent – Agent giving particulars of property to another firm of estate agents – Other firm introducing purchaser – Whether agents having implied authority to appoint other firm as sub-agents – Whether agents entitled to commission on sale.*

c
The defendant wished to secure a purchaser for a leasehold property which he owned. He instructed the plaintiffs, a firm of estate agents, to find a purchaser for the property. It was a term of the arrangement between them that the defendant would pay the plaintiffs a reasonable commission if they effected an introduction which resulted in a sale. Nothing was said about making the plaintiffs sole agents and the defendant
d considered himself free to conduct private negotiations with any prospective purchasers who might approach him directly. The plaintiffs advertised the property in the local press, describing themselves in the advertisement as 'sole agents'. They also made arrangements with another firm of estate agents, D & Co, whereby D & Co were to be sent particulars of the property. On receipt of those particulars D & Co entered the property in their books and prepared particulars on their own headed note-
e paper which they circulated to prospective purchasers. As a result of an enquiry made to D & Co, a prospective purchaser went to see the defendant. When asked by the defendant whether he had come from the plaintiffs he replied that he had not, but had come privately. Subsequently negotiations were conducted entirely between the defendant and the purchaser, and a few days later they instructed their solicitors to prepare a contract of sale. Meanwhile the defendant had informed the plaintiffs
f of the prospective sale by private treaty. Thereupon the plaintiffs suggested that they should appoint sub-agents in case the private sale fell through. The defendant agreed. After the sale to the purchaser had gone through, however, the plaintiffs discovered that the purchaser had originally been introduced by D & Co. Accordingly they claimed to be entitled to commission, alleging that D & Co were their sub-agents.

g
Held – An estate agent, in particular one who claimed to be a sole agent, did not have implied authority to appoint a sub-agent since he held a position of discretion and trust. The functions and duties of an estate agent required personal skill and competence of such a kind that he had no authority to delegate his responsibilities to a sub-agent unless he was expressly authorised to do so. The functions which
h the plaintiffs had purported to delegate to D & Co did not consist of acts of a purely ministerial character which could be carried out by any reasonably competent person, but were ones which an estate agent was bound to discharge personally in the absence of an express authorisation permitting the appointment of sub-agents. Accordingly the plaintiffs' claim failed (see p 131 *g* to *j* and p 132 *a* to *e* and *g* to *j*, post).

Mullens v Miller (1882) 22 Ch D 194 applied.

j *Burial Board of the Parish of St Margaret, Rochester v Thompson* (1871) LR 6 CP 445 distinguished.

Notes

For an agent's authority to delegate, see 1 Halsbury's Laws (4th Edn) 448-450, paras 747-752, and for cases on the subject, see 1 Digest (Repl) 444-447, 964-1000.

Cases referred to in judgment

Bentall, Horsley & Baldry v Vicary [1931] 1 KB 253, 100 LJKB 201, 144 LT 365, 1 Digest   *a*
(Repl) 606, 1967.

Burial Board of the Parish of St Margaret, Rochester v Thompson (1871) LR 6 CP 445,
40 LJCP 213, 24 LT 673, 36 JP 6, 1 Digest (Repl) 447, *995*.

Maloney v Hardy and Moorshead (1970) 216 Estates Gazette 1582; see also [1971] 2 All
ER at 630, [1971] 2 QB at 442, [1971] 2 WLR at 942, CA.

Mullens v Miller (1882) 22 Ch D 194, 52 LJCh 380, 48 LT 103, 1 Digest (Repl) 685, *2444*.   *b*

Cases also cited

Allam & Co Ltd v Europa Poster Services Ltd [1968] 1 All ER 826, [1968] 1 WLR 638.
De Bussche v Alt (1878) 8 Ch D 286, [1874-80] All ER Rep 1247, CA.

Appeal   *c*

This was an appeal by the defendant, Raymond Pow, against the judgment of his
Honour Judge Lermon QC given in the Epsom County Court on 20th September
1973, whereby the defendant was held liable to pay commission to the plaintiffs,
John McCann & Co, a firm of estate agents, in respect of the sale of a leasehold
property owned by the defendant. The facts are set out in the judgment of Lord
Denning MR.   *d*

Roger Henderson for the defendant.
Mark Tennant for the plaintiffs.

LORD DENNING MR. In August 1972 the defendant, Mr Pow, was the owner   *e*
of a flat, 18 Briarvels Court, Downshill Road, Epsom. It was a leasehold with 994
years unexpired, at a ground rent of £26 a year. Early in August he was in private
negotiation to sell it to a lady. But it was doubtful whether she would buy it. So
on 14th August 1972 he instructed the plaintiffs, John McCann & Co, a firm of estate
agents, to find a purchaser. He said that he wanted £14,350 for the flat. The
arrangement, as found by the judge, was that if the estate agents introduced someone   *f*
who purchased the flat, Mr Pow would pay them a reasonable commission.

Nothing was said about their being 'sole agents'. But Mr Pow had no other agents.
He had only instructed them. Thenceforward John McCann & Co undoubtedly
treated themselves as sole agents. They advertised the flat in the local newspapers,
with photographs, on 17th, 24th and 31st August. In these advertisements they
gave the heading 'John McCann & Co'; they described the flat, they gave the price
'£14,350 leasehold', and they added the significant words 'Sole Agents'. Mr Pow   *g*
took no exception to those advertisements. He realised that, although John McCann
& Co were sole agents, it was still open to him to deal privately himself with any
prospective purchasers, and that, if he himself secured a purchaser—without the
assistance of the estate agents—he would not be liable to pay them commission:
see *Bentall, Horsley & Baldry v Vicary*[1].

Now it appears that John McCann & Co did not keep the flat solely in their own   *h*
hands. On the very day on which Mr Pow instructed them, that is, on 14th August
1972, they sent particulars of the property to another firm of estate agents called
Douglas & Co. But they did not give Douglas & Co the vendor's name or telephone
number. Douglas & Co received the particulars on 15th August 1972. They
entered the flat in their own books with the note: 'Keys and View through John
McCann & Co'. Douglas & Co then prepared particulars on their own headed   *j*
paper 'Douglas & Co' with the price and everything copied straight from the particulars which John McCann & Co had prepared, adding at the foot: 'View by appointment through the agents, Messrs Douglas & Company as above.' Then Douglas &

1   [1931] 1 KB 253

Co circulated those particulars—as if their own—to a number of persons who they
a thought might be interested. Soon afterwards, on 29th August 1972, a Mr Rudd
called on Messrs Douglas & Co. He enquired about buying a flat. Their secretary
gave him three addresses including the flat at 18 Briavels Court. She did not know
the vendor's name and telephone number. So she rang John McCann & Co. They
gave her the name of the vendor, Mr Pow, and his number. She gave this information to Mr Rudd. It was the only way in which Mr Rudd heard of the property.
b   On the next day Mr Rudd went to see Mr Pow at the flat. Mr Pow asked him:
'Have you come from McCann's?' Mr Rudd said: 'No.' He added that he had come
privately. Thereupon Mr Pow thought that he would not be liable to pay commission
if he sold to Mr Rudd. He had no idea that any other agents were involved. The judge
expressly so found. Mr Pow and Mr Rudd then negotiated between themselves.
They agreed a price of £14,200. (I expect Mr Pow was ready to accept a lower
c figure than £14,350 because he thought he would not have to pay commission out
of it.) On 9th September 1972 each instructed solicitors to prepare the contract of
sale.
    Meanwhile, on 7th September 1970, Mr Pow went along to John McCann & Co
and told them that Mr Rudd was interested and that it was a private sale. (John
McCann & Co at that time did not know anything about Mr Rudd, as they had not
d introduced him.) John McCann & Co at that interview said that they would like
to involve sub-agents, just in case the sale to Mr Rudd fell through. Mr Pow agreed
to this. That was 7th September 1970. Soon afterwards the sale to Mr Rudd was
effected without a hitch. So there was nothing for a sub-agent to do.
    A little later John McCann & Co found out that Douglas & Co had told Mr Rudd
about the flat, and that it was through Douglas & Co that Mr Rudd had heard of it.
e John McCann & Co then claimed that they were entitled to commission. They
said that Douglas & Co were their sub-agents. John McCann & Co brought an
action in the county court for £275.50 commission. They pleaded that: 'The Plaintiffs, through their sub-agents, Douglas & Co., introduced one C. G. Rudd to the
Defendant, who thereafter purchased the said property for the sum of £14,200'.
Mr Pow acted in person. He wrote a statement in his defence. He objected to
f any payment because, he said, John McCann & Co had not introduced the purchaser
to him at all; it was private negotiation between him and Mr Rudd, and he ought
not to pay commission on it. The judge found that Mr Pow was liable for commission
and he gave judgment for £275.50.
    Now there is an appeal to this court. One point made on behalf of Mr Pow was
that Mr Rudd was not called, and that the judge admitted letters from Mr Rudd
g which were hearsay—and the rules regulating admission of them had not been
fulfilled and there ought to be a new trial. But I need not go into that point because
there is another point on which the whole case can be disposed of. It is simply this,
that at the material time John McCann & Co had no authority to appoint Douglas &
Co as a sub-agent and could not therefore rely on the introduction by Douglas & Co.
    The general rule is that an agent has no authority to appoint a sub-agent except
h with the excess or implied authority of the principal. There was no express authority
here. The question is whether or not there was implied authority at the time,
29th August, when the property was introduced by Douglas to Mr Rudd. It seems
to me that an estate agent, and certainly one who claims to be a sole agent, has no
implied authority to appoint a sub-agent. The reason is because an estate agent
holds a position of discretion and trust. Discretion in his conduct of negotiations.
j Trust in his handling of affairs. It is his duty, certainly in the case of a sole agent, to
use his best endeavours to sell the property at an acceptable price to a purchaser
who is satisfactory and who is ready and willing and able to purchase the property.
It is his duty also to take care to prepare particulars of the property accurately, and
to make no misrepresentation about it. It is his duty to receive applications, to make
appointments to view, and to negotiate the best price that can be obtained in the

circumstances. Furthermore, he is at liberty in the course of the negotiations to
receive a deposit as stakeholder, but not as agent for the vendor. Those functions *a*
and duties of an estate agent, certainly of a sole agent, require personal skill and
competence. So much so that I think an estate agent has no authority to delegate
his responsibilities to a sub-agent, unless he is expressly authorised so to do. That
is borne out by the authorities to which we have been referred this morning by counsel
for Mr Pow, such as *Mullens v Miller*[1] and *Maloney v Hardy and Moorshead*[2].

Faced with the general principle, counsel for John McCann & Co sought to avoid *b*
it by saying that Douglas & Co had a very limited kind of sub-agency. They were
only entrusted, he said, with a mere ministerial duty. Their part was only to pass
particulars to potential purchasers, leaving all the negotiations and so forth to the
principal agents, John McCann & Co. He referred to the entertaining case of *Burial
Board of the Parish of St Margaret, Rochester v Thompson*[3] where it was held that a
sexton was able to appoint a delegate to dig the grave and ring the bell because those *c*
acts could be done by any reasonably competent person. But the court said that
when it was an employment to which personal skill was essential—as a painter engaged
to paint a portrait—he could not hand it over to some one else to perform.

It seems to me that the functions entrusted to Douglas & Co were not merely
ministerial. They prepared particulars. They said that they took every care to
ensure that particulars are correct. If they had been sub-agents, Mr Pow would be *d*
liable for any misrepresentations that they made. That would be most unfair seeing
that he did not choose them and knew nothing of them. The reason why he would
not be liable is because they were not authorised sub-agents at all. So it comes to
this. The introduction of Mr Rudd was not made by the agents, John McCann & Co,
nor was it made by any authorised sub-agent. It was made by Douglas & Co, who
had no authority, express or implied, to act as sub-agents so as to bind Mr Pow or to *e*
make him liable to pay commission.

I might add just this one point. It seems to me the justice of the case is such that
Mr Pow should not be held liable. He knew that John McCann & Co claimed to be
sole agents and he knew he had not appointed anyone else as agents at all. So when
Mr Rudd came to him and said: 'I do not come from McCann's. I am negotiating
privately', Mr Pow was entitled to say to himself: 'In those circumstances I am not *f*
liable to pay agents' commission. Therefore I can negotiate free of commission
and accept a lower price'. He did so on the footing that he would not be liable for
commission. It would not be right that he should now be made to pay commission.
I think on these grounds the appeal should be allowed and judgment entered for
the defendant.

g

ORR LJ. I agree that, for the reasons given by Lord Denning MR this appeal should
be allowed on the ground that the plaintiffs in this case had no authority to appoint
Douglas & Co as sub-agents; and I would only add that there was not before the
court any evidence of a usage in the business of estate agents which would authorise the
appointment of sub-agents. Like Lord Denning MR I find it unnecessary to express *h*
any view on the other issues which arose in the case. I also would allow this appeal.

BROWNE LJ. I agree with both the judgments which have already been delivered and do not feel I can usefully add anything. I agree with the result proposed
by Lord Denning MR.

j

1 (1882) 22 Ch D 194
2 (1970) 216 Estates Gazette 1582
3 (1871) LR 6 CP 445

Appeal allowed.

a

Solicitors: *Bowles & Co*, Epsom (for the defendant); *A R Drummond & Co*, Epsom (for the plaintiffs).

James Collins Esq Barrister.

b

R v Crown Court at Leeds, ex parte City of Bradford Chief Constable

c

QUEEN'S BENCH DIVISION

LORD WIDGERY CJ, BRIDGE AND SHAW JJ

30th OCTOBER 1974

d
Licensing – Licence – Condition – Grant of licence subject to condition – On-licence – Payment required in pursuance of condition prohibited – Payment required in pursuance of condition – Meaning – Condition prohibiting supply of intoxicating liquor to persons other than holders of admission tickets purchased for not less than specified amount – Whether condition requiring payments to be made to licensee valid – Licensing Act 1964, s 4(1) (as amended by the Finance Act 1967, ss 5(1), 45(8), Sch 16, Part I).

e
Crown Court – Supervisory jurisdiction of High Court – Orders of mandamus, prohibition and certiorari – Orders in relation to jurisdiction of Crown Court – Meaning of 'jurisdiction' – Whether power to make an order of certiorari when error of law shown on the face of the record – Courts Act 1971, s 10(5).

A social club applied to justices for an on-licence in respect of premises which the
f club owned. The premises were used for playing bingo on five days a week and for dancing and other entertainment on the other two days. The justices granted the licence but made it subject to a condition, under s 4(1)[a] of the Licensing Act 1964, that on days when the premises were not being used for bingo, intoxicating liquor should only be supplied to customers who held admission tickets purchased by or for them at a cost of not less than 25p. The club appealed to the Crown Court
g which allowed the appeal on the ground that s 4(1) of the 1964 Act prohibited any payment in pursuance of a condition attached to an on-licence. On an application by the chief constable for an order of certiorari to quash the court's decision, the club contended that, even if the decision was wrong in law, the power of the Divisional Court under s 10(5)[b] of the Courts Act 1971 to make prerogative orders was limited to cases where it was alleged that the Crown Court had exceeded its jurisdiction.

h
Held – The application would be granted for the following reasons—
(i) The Crown Court's decision was based on an error of law for the payments prohibited by s 4(1) of the 1964 Act were payments made by the licensee in pursuance of a condition imposed on his licence and did not extend to payments which were to be made to the licensee by customers who patronised his premises (see p 135 g and
j h, p 137 c and j and p 138 c to e, post).
(ii) The power of the High Court under s 10(5) of the 1971 Act to exercise its super-visory jurisdiction by means of the prerogative orders 'in relation to the jurisdiction

---

a Section 4(1), as amended, is set out at p 135 f, post
b Section 10(5) is set out at p 137 e, post

of the Crown Court' was not limited to cases where the complaint was that the Crown
Court had exceeded its jurisdiction. The power extended to all circumstances *a*
which would normally be appropriate for the use of prerogative orders including
cases where there was an error of law on the face of the record (see p 137 *g* to *j* and
p 138 *e*, post); dictum of Lord Widgery CJ in *R v Crown Court at Exeter, ex parte
Beattie* [1974] 1 All ER at 1186 approved.

b

Notes
For conditions attached to the grant of justices' on-licences, see 22 Halsbury's Laws
(3rd Edn) 540, para 1068, and for cases on the subject, see 30 Digest (Reissue) 38, 39,
281-291.
    For supervisory jurisdiction of the High Court, see Supplement to 9 Halsbury's
Laws (3rd Edn), para 963D.   *c*
    For the Licensing Act 1964, s 4, see 17 Halsbury's Statutes (3rd Edn) 1064.
    For the Courts Act 1971, s 10, see 41 Halsbury's Statutes (3rd Edn) 298.

Cases referred to in judgment
R v Crown Court at Exeter, ex parte Beattie [1974] 1 All ER 1183, [1974] 1 WLR 428, DC.
R v Sussex Confirming Authority, ex parte Tamplin & Sons' Brewery (Brighton) Ltd [1937] *d*
    4 All ER 106, 157 LT 590, 101 JP 562, 35 LGR 593, DC.

Case also cited
Comrs of Customs & Excise v Curtis [1914] 2 KB 335.

e

Motions for certiorari and mandamus
This was an application by way of motion by Harry Ashworth Kitching, acting chief
constable for the city of Bradford, (a) for an order of certiorari to bring up and quash
an order made on 4th February 1974 by the Crown Court at Leeds (his Honour Judge
Beaumont and justices) whereby the court allowed an appeal by the licensee, Thomas
David Barry, of the Mecca Social Club, Bradford, against a decision of the Bradford *f*
licensing justices on 5th September 1973 that his licence should be subject to a condition
that there be no sale or supply of intoxicating liquor for consumption on the premises
except 'to persons being bona fide patrons, who hold tickets purchased by or for
them at a cost of not less than twenty-five pence'; and (b) for an order of mandamus
directed to the Crown Court at Leeds directing it to dismiss the appeal of the licensee
against the justices' decision. The facts are set out in the judgment of Lord Widgery *g*
CJ.

Quentin Edwards for the applicant.
Gilbert Gray QC and *Anton Lodge* for the licensee.

h

LORD WIDGERY CJ. In these proceedings counsel moves on behalf of one Harry
Ashworth Kitching, who is acting chief constable of the city of Bradford, for an order
of certiorari to remove into this court with a view to its being quashed a judgment
given by the Crown Court sitting at Leeds on 4th February 1974 on appeal from the
licensing justices for the city of Bradford.
    The matter arises in a perfectly simple way. Application was made by the Mecca *j*
organisation for a justices' on-licence in respect of premises at Bradford known as
the Mecca Social Club, Little Horton Lane, Bradford. The justices granted an
application for an on-licence but they subjected it to conditions, and in particular they
subjected it to a condition that during the period when the premises were not being
used for the playing of bingo there should be no sale or supply of intoxicating liquor

for consumption on the premises except to persons being bona fide patrons who hold
a admission tickets purchased by or for them at a cost of no less than 25p. The
reference to the premises not being used for the playing of bingo is explained by the
fact that these premises were used for bingo on five days of the week and used for
dancing and other entertainment on the remaining two days. The condition which
I have read was designed to operate during the last days of the week and not the period
when bingo was being played.

b   The basis of the imposition of this condition was that the justices were impressed
by the contention of the police that, unless some kind of restriction was imposed on
entry into late night licensed premises, what happens in practice is a kind of exodus
from the public houses into these premises as soon as the public houses close. The
imposition of a condition whereby nobody was to be served on these two nights unless
he bought a ticket of admission was a means of checking the movement of drinkers
c from the closed public houses to the still open Mecca Social Club. The justices
obviously thought this was a good idea in the public interest to impose this
requirement and they approved the condition accordingly.

     The matter was appealed to the Crown Court, and it came on before the learned
judge and justices sitting with him. They were of the opinion, and they expressed
it in quite positive terms, that this condition was a sound provision to include in the
d licence from the point of view of the public interest. But in the Crown Court there
appeared to the court to be a technical legal objection to the imposition of this condition, even though the court clearly thought on the merits that it ought to be imposed. So the matter comes before us on an application for certiorari, and the first
question we have to decide is whether the Crown Court were right in the view they
took of the supposed legal obstacle to the imposition of this condition.

e   The obstacle was just this. Section 4(1) of the Licensing Act 1964, which deals
with the imposition of conditions says:

     'Subject to the provisions of Part IV of this Act, licensing justices granting a
     new justices' on-licence, other than a licence for the sale of wine alone, may
     attach to it such conditions governing the tenure of the licence and any other
f   matters as they think proper in the interests of the public; but no payment
     may be required in pursuance of a condition attached under this subsection.'

     What was argued before the Crown Court, and has been argued before us today
on behalf of the Mecca organisation, is that the provision that no payment may be
required in pursuance of a condition is broken by the condition to which I have
referred, because that does not involve the payment of 25p from each customer to the
g licensee. The argument put forward by counsel for the chief constable is that no
such prohibition on the charging of an entrance fee is contained in s 4. He submits
that the kind of payment which is forbidden by the words that I have read is payment
by the licensee in pursuance of the condition imposed on his licence, and does not
extend to payments to the licensee from the customers who patronise his premises.
h If one just looks at the language of the subsection which I have read, it may be that
there is an argument on both sides, but for my part I am quite satisfied when one
looks at the history of this legislation that the argument on behalf of the
chief constable is the right one.

     For this purpose one must begin by looking at s 14(1) of the Licensing (Consolida-
tion) Act 1910, which contained provisions for payment following on the grant of a
j justices' licence. Section 14(1) provided:

     'The licensing justices, on the grant of a new justices' on-licence, may attach
     to the grant of the licence such conditions, both as to the payments to be made
     and the tenure of the licence and as to any other matters, as they think proper
     in the interests of the public [I pause there to observe that language is very
     similar to the language which I have read from s 4 of the Act of 1964] . . . (*a*) Such

conditions shall in any case be attached as, having regard to proper provision
for suitable premises and good management, the justices think best adapted for *a*
securing to the public any monopoly value which is represented by the difference
between the value which the premises will bear, in the opinion of the justices,
when licensed, and the value of the same premises if they were not licensed . . .'

That was a reference to a feature of licensing law no longer with us which is called
'monopoly value'.   It represented a payment which new licensees had to make as *b*
representing the difference in the value of their premises licensed and unlicensed
respectively.   Section 14(1)(*a*), which I have read, places on the justices the duty of
requiring such payments from new licensees as will be appropriate to secure the
monopoly value.   The section continued:

'(*b*) The amount of any payments imposed under conditions attached in pursuance of this section shall not exceed the amount thus required to secure the *c*
monopoly value.'

So the draftsman there is clearly contemplating that payments by the licensee may
be a feature of the conditions which can be attached to a licence, but that although
the justices are under a duty to obtain such payments as properly reflect the monopoly
value, there shall be no other payments.   In other words, it seems perfectly clear *d*
that the 1910 Act, when referring to the conditions involving payment, is concerned
with payment by the licensee as part of the transaction under which he gets his
licence.

Events have moved since 1910 and licensing law has been consolidated more than
once.   One can pick up the more recent version of these provisions in s 6 of the
Licensing Act 1953, which consolidated the 1910 Act and the Licensing Act 1949. *e*
Section 6 has features similar to those to which I have already referred:

'(1) Subject to the provisions of the next following section, licensing justices
shall attach to the grant of a new justices' on-licence such conditions as, having
regard to proper provision for suitable premises and good management, they
think best adapted for securing to the public any monopoly value that is repre- *f*
sented by the difference between the value that the premises will in their opinion
bear when licensed and the value of the premises unlicensed . . . [Then there is a
proviso which I need not read.]
'(2) The licensing justices may attach to the grant of a new justices' on-licence
such conditions governing the tenure of the licence and any other matters as
they think proper in the interests of the public: Provided that no payment shall *g*
be required in pursuance of a condition attached under this subsection.'

For my part I am quite satisfied that the draftsman in s 6 of the 1953 Act is seeking
to preserve the situation which prevailed under the 1910 Act.   It is a consolidating
Act and one should approach its construction in that way, and one sees there emerging
the language of the 1964 Act which we have ultimately to construe.   In my judgment
the situation under the 1953 Act was that the payments which were being referred *h*
to and prohibited were payments by the licensee.

One moves on from there to the 1964 Act, bearing in mind that by this time monopoly value had been abolished.   Accordingly when these provisions had to be
reproduced in the consolidating 1964 Act they had to be reproduced without any
reference to monopoly value, and on the face of it it seems to me that the language of
s 4 which I have read complies with that requirement and does perpetuate the *j*
situation prevailing so far as payments by the licensees are concerned.

It has been pointed out to us in argument that there are many instances in which a
person seeking to drink in premises licensed by a justices' on-licence may have to
acquire some kind of status in order to enter the premises, and may in the process of
acquiring that status have to spend money.   No one has so far suggested that the

fact that money may be spent by a customer in obtaining the status required to enter
a the premises is in any sense a breach of the terms of s 4. The point is underlined,
if underlining be required, by *R v Sussex Confirming Authority, ex parte Tamplin & Sons
Brewery*[1]. That was a case in which a bus company, having established a bus depot,
wished to provide a licensed bar on the depot for the benefit of its customers. It
invited the licensing justices when granting a licence to impose a condition that no one
should be served in this licensed bar unless he could produce a bus ticket and thus
b establish his status as a bona fide traveller. No one suggested in that case, or in my
view could have suggested in that case, that the fact that payment was required for
a bus ticket, and that a bus ticket was required in order to enter the bar meant that a
payment was being required in breach of the Licensing Acts.

This is quite a different type of case, but it seems to me when one has regard to
the history of the provision that the contention, as I have said, of the applicant is
c right and that the prohibition in regard to payments under s 4(1) is a prohibition
relating to payments *by* the licensee and not *to* the licensee.

That is sufficient to dispose of the merits of the point of law involved in the case,
but reference has been made to the jurisdiction of this court to control the Crown
Court in matters of certiorari with particular reference to the earlier decision in
R v Crown Court at Exeter, ex parte Beattie[2]. The point can be put quite briefly. Section 10
d of the Courts Act 1971 prescribes the extent to which, and the methods by which,
the High Court can supervise and control the activities of the Crown Court. In the
earlier subsections of s 10 are set out the circumstances in which appeal by case stated
is possible, but that does not apply to appeals under the Licensing Acts. When one
gets to sub-s (5) of s 10 one comes to the provisions dealing with the jurisdiction over
the Crown Court in certiorari, and the phrase used is:
e

'In relation to the jurisdiction of the Crown Court, other than its jurisdiction
in matters relating to trial on indictment, the High Court shall have all such
jurisdiction to make orders of mandamus, prohibition or certiorari as the High
Court possesses in relation to the jurisdiction of an inferior court.'

f It was argued in the *Exeter* case[2] that on its true construction that language allowed
this court to exercise its supervisory jurisdiction over the Crown Court by use of the
prerogative orders only where the complaint against the Crown Court was that it
had exceeded its jurisdiction strictly so called. I expressed the provisional view in
the *Exeter* case[3], the matter not being fully argued, that the construction of s 10(5)
was wider than that and that it gave these supervisory powers over the Crown Court
g not only in matters strictly relating to jurisdiction but also in regard to other matters
normally appropriate for use of the prerogative orders. The opportunity for argument has been given today and I understand that my brethren in this court today are
of the view that the provisional statement of the situation given by me in the *Exeter*
case[3] was the right one. Certainly I am not minded to depart from it and would
wish to take the opportunity to confirm it if in fact it does have the approval of my
h brethren sitting today.

On that footing the jurisdiction of the court to order certiorari to go is clear. It is
a simple case, in the end, of an inferior tribunal making a speaking order which contains an incorrect statement of law, and I think the order should go. I do not at the
moment, subject to argument, think that mandamus is required because the quashing
of the order of the Crown Court suffices to restore the disputed condition.

j
BRIDGE J. I agree on both points, and I add a word of my own only out of respect

---

1   [1937] 4 All ER 106
2   [1974] 1 All ER 1183, [1974] 1 WLR 428
3   [1974] 1 All ER at 1186, [1974] 1 WLR at 433

for the learned circuit judge from whose conclusion on the main point we are differing. He was referred to the legislative history of the statutes leading to the Licensing   *a*
Act 1964, but in the end approached the question of construction on the bare language,
if I may put it that way, of the relevant section in the 1964 Act. I think it was by that
approach that he fell into error.

The history of the legislation in my judgment is the key to the solution of the
problem of construction presented by the language of s 4 of the 1964 Act, and that is
apparent as soon as one appreciates that the 1953 and 1964 Acts are made under the   *b*
Consolidation of Enactments (Procedure) Act 1949 and are, therefore, presumed not
to change the law. If one starts from the Licensing Consolidation Act 1910, the
language of which I need not read because it has been read by Lord Widgery CJ, it
is really plain beyond argument that the limitation on justices' powers of imposing
conditions requiring payment was a limitation which prohibited the requirement of a
payment by a licensee of more than the monopoly value. When one comes to the   *c*
1953 Act and compares the terms of s 6(1) and (2) of that Act with the terms of s 14
of the 1910 Act again it is plain to my mind that although the drafting of the provision has been recast, its substance and effect remain unaltered. So the very
language which falls to be construed in the 1964 Act first appears in 1953 and is
language directed to prohibiting the requirement of payments by the licensee in
excess of the monopoly value. In 1959 monopoly value disappears, and in 1964   *d*
one is left with a bare requirement restricting payments being required under
conditions by the licensee.

SHAW J. I agree entirely with both judgments which have been given.
                                                                              e

Certiorari granted; application for mandamus withdrawn.

Solicitors: *Tuck & Mann & Geffen and D Jones & Co*, agents for *David Morgan*, Bradford
(for the applicant); *Willey, Hargrave & Co*, Leeds (for the licensee).   *f*

N P Metcalfe Esq Barrister.

a
Crowther v Shannon Motor Co (a firm)

COURT OF APPEAL, CIVIL DIVISION
LORD DENNING MR, ORR AND BROWNE LJJ
7th OCTOBER 1974

b

Sale of goods – Implied condition of fitness – Particular purpose – Fitness for purpose – Secondhand motor car – Engine seizing up after 2,300 miles – Replacement engine necessary – Whether car reasonably fit for purpose of being driven on road at time of sale – Sale of Goods Act 1893, s 14(1).

c The defendants, who were motor car dealers, sold a secondhand Jaguar car to the plaintiff for £390. It was then eight years old and showed 82,165 miles on the mileometer. In commending the car to the plaintiff, the defendants described it as being in excellent condition inside and out and said that, as far as the mileage was concerned it was, for a Jaguar, 'hardly run in', although those words were not treated seriously by the plaintiff. The plaintiff bought the car but, three weeks later, after he had *d* driven it 2,300 miles, the engine seized up completely. On examination it was found to be in an extremely bad condition and had to be replaced. The plaintiff brought an action for damages for breach of contract against the defendants alleging, inter alia, that the defendants were in breach of the condition implied by s 14(1)[a] of the Sale of Goods Act 1893 that the car was reasonably fit for the purpose for which it was required, namely, being driven on the road. The judge gave judgment for the plaintiff, *e* holding that 'fitness for purpose' meant, in the context of the sale of the car, 'To go as a car for a reasonable time'. The defendants appealed.

Held – While the buyer of a secondhand car should realise that defects might appear sooner or later so that minor repairs would be necessary, replacing the engine was very *f* different from a minor repair. The fact that the engine had seized up after only three weeks was evidence that, at the time of the sale, the car was not reasonably fit for the purpose of being driven on the road. Accordingly, the judge was entitled to conclude that the defendants were in breach of the implied condition under s 14(1) and the appeal would therefore be dismissed (see p 141 *a* to *g*, post).

Bartlett v Sidney Marcus Ltd [1965] 2 All ER 753 distinguished.

g
Notes
For implied terms as to fitness, see 34 Halsbury's Laws (3rd Edn), 51-54, para 77, and for cases on the subject, see 39 Digest (Repl) 544-546, 782-792.

For the Sale of Goods Act 1893, s 14, see 30 Halsbury's Statutes (3rd Edn), 14.

As from 18th May 1973 a new section was substituted for s 14 of the 1893 Act by the *h* Supply of Goods (Implied Terms) Act 1973, s 3.

Case referred to in judgment
Bartlett v Sidney Marcus Ltd [1965] 2 All ER 753, [1965] 1 WLR 1013, CA, Digest (Cont Vol B) 630, 781*a*.

j
a Section 14(1), so far as material, provides: 'Where the buyer, expressly or by implication, makes known to the seller the particular purpose for which the goods are required, so as to show that the buyer relies on the seller's skill or judgment, and the goods are of a description which it is in the course of the seller's business to supply (whether he be the manufacturer or not), there is an implied condition that the goods shall be reasonably fit for such purpose . . .'

Appeal

This was an appeal by the defendants, Shannon Motor Co (a firm), against the judg- *a*
ment of his Honour Judge Michael Lee QC in the Southampton County Court on 21st
February 1974, whereby he awarded damages of £460·37 to the plaintiff, Andrew
Brian Darby Crowther, for breach of contract. The facts are set out in the judgment of
Lord Denning MR.

J Norman Rudd for the defendants.   *b*
R Belben for the plaintiff.

LORD DENNING MR. The plaintiff, Mr Crowther, is a young man interested in
art. In 1972 he bought a secondhand motor car from the defendants who were
reputable dealers in Southampton. It was a 1964 Jaguar. He bought it on 17th July *c*
1972 for the sum of £390. The dealers commended it. They said that 'it would be
difficult to find a 1964 Jaguar of this quality inside and out'. They added that for a
Jaguar 'it is hardly run in'. Mr Crowther looked carefully at it. He took it for a trial
run. The next day it was tested by the Ministry of Transport officials. The report of
the test was satisfactory. So Mr Crowther bought the Jaguar. He did not take the
words of puff seriously. But he relied on the sellers' skill and judgment. There was *d*
clearly an implied condition under s 14(1) of the Sale of Goods Act 1893 that the car
was reasonably fit for the purpose for which he required it and which he made known
to the sellers.

That was 17th July 1972. The mileage as stated on the mileometer at that time was
82,165 miles. Mr Crowther took the car. He drove it on some long journeys. He went
up to the north of England and back. He went round Hampshire. He went over *e*
2,000 miles in it. He found that it used a great deal of oil. But he managed to drive it
for three weeks. Then on 8th August 1972, when he was driving up the M3 motorway,
it came to a full stop. The engine seized up. The car was towed into a garage. The
engine was found to be in an extremely bad condition. So much so that it had to be
scrapped and replaced by a reconditioned engine. The car was out of use for a couple
of months or so.   *f*

Mr Crowther brought an action in the county court for damages from the dealers.
He called as a witness a previous owner of the car, a Mr Hall. He gave evidence that
he had bought it from these selfsame dealers about eight months before. He had paid
them about £400 for it. He had used it for those eight months and then sold it back
in July 1972 to these very dealers. When he resold it to them he knew the engine was
in a very bad state, but he did not disclose it to them. He left them to find out for *g*
themselves. He was himself an engineer. He gave a trenchant description of the
engine:

'At the time of resale I thought the engine was clapped out. I do not think this
engine was fit to be used on a road, not really, it needed a rebore.'

The judge accepted the evidence of Mr Hall. He held that there was a breach of *h*
s 14(1) of the 1893 Act. He awarded Mr Crowther damages in the sum of £460·37
with costs. Now there is an appeal to this court by the dealers. They say there was
no justification for the finding that this car was not reasonably fit for the purpose.
The mileage when they sold it was 82,165 miles. The mileage when it 'clapped out'
was 84,519 miles. So that in the three weeks it had gone 2,354 miles.

Counsel for the dealers, who put the case very cogently before us, submitted that a *j*
car which had covered 2,354 miles must have been reasonably fit for the purpose of
driving along the road. He drew attention to a case some years ago in this court,
Bartlett v Sidney Marcus Ltd[1]. We emphasised then that a buyer, when he buys a

1 [1965] 2 All ER 753, [1965] 1 WLR 1013

a secondhand car, should realise that defects may appear sooner or later. In that particular case a defect did appear in the clutch. It was more expensive to repair than had been anticipated. It was held by this court that the fact that the defect was more expensive than had been anticipated did not mean that there had been any breach of the implied condition. But that case seems to me to be entirely distinguishable from the present case. In that case it was a minor repair costing £45 after 300 miles. Here we have a very different case. On the dealers' own evidence, a buyer could reasonably

b expect to get 100,000 miles life out of a Jaguar engine. Here the Jaguar had only done 80,000 miles. Yet it was in such a bad condition that it was 'clapped out' and after some 2,300 miles it failed altogether. That is very different from a minor repair. The dealers themselves said that if they had known that the engine would blow up after 2,000 miles, they would not have sold it. The reason obviously was because it would not have been reasonably fit for the purpose.

c Some criticism was made of a phrase used by the judge. He said: 'What does "fit for the purpose" mean?' He answered: 'To go as a car for a reasonable time.' I am not quite sure that that is entirely accurate. The relevant time is the time of sale. But there is no doubt what the judge meant. If the car does not go for a reasonable time but the engine breaks up within a short time, that is evidence which goes to show it was not reasonably fit for the purpose at the time it was sold. On the evidence

d in this case, the engine was liable to go at any time. It was 'nearing the point of failure', said the expert, Mr Wise. The time interval was merely 'staving off the inevitable'. That shows that at the time of the sale it was not reasonably fit for the purpose of being driven on the road. I think the judge on the evidence was quite entitled to find there was a breach of s 14(1) of the 1893 Act and I would therefore dismiss the appeal.

e

ORR LJ. I agree. The question whether this car was fit for the purpose of being driven on the road was in my judgment a question of fact and to an extent one of degree for the learned judge, and there was ample material before him, in particular, in the evidence of Mr Hall, a previous owner of the car, and a Mr Wise, a motor

f engineer, as to the condition in which it would have been on the date when it was bought by the plaintiff. The case differs, in my judgment, very materially from tht of *Bartlett v Sidney Marcus Ltd*[1] to which we have been referred. I would dismiss this appeal.

g **BROWNE LJ.** I agree and I agree with the reasons given by Lord Denning MR and Orr LJ.

Appeal dismissed.

h Solicitors: *Ward, Bowie*, agents for *Ewing, Hickman & Clark*, Southampton (for the defendants); *Paris, Smith & Randall*, Southampton (for the plaintiff).

James Collins Esq Barrister.

---

1   [1965] 2 All ER 753, [1965] 1 WLR 1013

R v Socialist Worker Printers and Publishers Ltd *a*
and another, ex parte Attorney-General

QUEEN'S BENCH DIVISION
LORD WIDGERY CJ, MILMO AND ACKNER JJ   *b*
16th, 17th, 18th OCTOBER 1974

Contempt of court – Witness – Interference with witness – Blackmail proceedings – Identity of witness – Disclosure – Order by judge that identity of witness should not be disclosed in court – Newspaper article – Article published after evidence given by witness – Article identifying witness – Affront to authority of court – Danger that witnesses in future blackmail ***c*** *cases might be unwilling to come forward.*

Criminal law – Practice – Evidence – Witness – Identity – Disclosure – Blackmail proceedings – Jurisdiction – Order by judge that identity of witness should not be disclosed – Whether judge having jurisdiction to make order.

d

J was tried at the Central Criminal Court on various offences relating to the procuring of women for prostitution and organising prostitution. J was also tried on two charges of blackmail, the allegation being that she had threatened two men that she would disclose their activities with the women she had procured for them unless they paid her sums of money. At the trial of the blackmail charges the judge, with the acquiescence of defence counsel, gave a direction that in his court the names of the two *e* victims of the alleged blackmail should not be disclosed but that they should instead be referred to as 'Y' and 'Z'. After Y and Z had given their evidence, the first respondent published a newspaper containing an article written by the second respondent about the blackmail proceedings which disclosed the identities of Y and Z. On a motion by the Attorney-General for an order committing the respondents for contempt, the respondents contended, inter alia, that the judge had no jurisdiction to *f* order that the names of the two witnesses should not be disclosed.

Held – (i) On the trial of a charge of blackmail, the judge had jurisdiction to order that the name of a prosecution witness should not be disclosed if there was a danger that, because the witness had something disreputable or discreditable to hide, he might *g* in the absence of such a direction, refuse to come forward (see p 149 *f* and *g* and p 150 *j* to p 151 *b* and *f*, post).
   (ii) The respondents had been guilty of contempt in publishing the article naming the two witnesses in defiance of the judge's direction for in doing so they were committing a blatant affront to the authority of the court and furthermore, if witnesses in blackmail proceedings were not adequately protected, potential witnesses in other *h* blackmail cases might be deterred from coming forward. It was immaterial that, on the face of it, the judge's order had been directed at what was to happen in the proceedings before him and did not deal in express terms with anything that was to happen outside the court (see p 147 *e,* p 148 *j* to p 149 *f* and p 151 *f,* post); *Attorney-General v Butterworth* [1972] 3 All ER 326 and *Moore v Clerk of Assize, Bristol* [1973] 1 All ER 58 applied.

j

Notes
For contempt of court by speeches or writings tending to defeat ends of justice, see 8 Halsbury's Laws (3rd Edn) 6-12, paras 8-15, and for cases on the subject, see 16 Digest (Repl) 21-41, *155-342.*

Cases referred to in judgment

a   *Attorney-General v Butterworth* [1962] 3 All ER 326, sub nom *Re Attorney-General's Application* [1963] 1 QB 696, LR 3 RP 327, [1962] 3 WLR 819, CA, Digest (Cont Vol A) 454, *395a*.

Attorney-General v Times Newspapers Ltd [1973] 3 All ER 54, [1974] AC 273, [1973] 3 WLR 298, HL.

Littler v Thomson (1839) 2 Beav 129, 48 ER 1129, 16 Digest (Repl) 30, *238*.

b   *Moore v Clerk of Assize, Bristol* [1972] 1 All ER 58, [1971] 1 WLR 1669, 136 JP 91, CA.

Scott v Scott [1913] AC 417, [1911-13] All ER Rep 1, 82 LJP 74, 109 LT 1, HL, 16 Digest (Repl) 40, *339*.

Cases also cited

Agricultural Industries Ltd, Re [1952] 1 All ER 1188, CA.

c   *Chapman v Honig* [1963] 2 All ER 513, [1963] 2 QB 502, CA.

Cleland v Cleland (1913) 109 LT 744.

R v Kray (1969) 53 Cr App Rep 412.

R v Odhams Press Ltd, ex parte Attorney-General [1956] 3 All ER 494, [1957] 1 QB 73, DC.

Motion

d   This was an application by way of motion by Her Majesty's Attorney-General to the Divisional Court of the Queen's Bench Division for an order that the respondents, Socialist Worker Printers and Publishers Ltd ('the company') and Paul Foot, the publisher and author respectively of an article published in a newspaper known as the 'Socialist Worker', be committed for contempt of court. The facts are set out in the judgment of Lord Widgery CJ.

e

The Attorney-General (S C Silkin QC), Gordon Slynn QC and *Harry Woolf* in support of the application.

Stephen Sedley for the company.

Ronald Waterhouse QC and *Michael Lewis* for Mr Foot.

f   **LORD WIDGERY CJ.** These proceedings come before the court on an application by the Attorney-General made under RSC Ord 52 whereby he asks for a committal for contempt of the two several respondents to this application: first, the Socialist Worker Printers and Publishers Ltd and, secondly, Mr Paul MacIntosh Foot, who at all material times was either the editor or the acting editor of the paper published by that company and known as the 'Socialist Worker'.

g   The ground stated by the Attorney-General in his statement in support of the application is that the company and Mr Foot were guilty of contempt of court in publishing or causing to be published in the issue of the said newspaper on 13th April 1974 an article headed 'Y, oh Lord, oh why . . .' which disclosed the identities of two prosecution witnesses in a trial then proceeding at the Central Criminal Court in which the accused was charged with offences of blackmail, contrary to s 21(1) of the

h   Theft Act 1968, and the trial judge had directed that the said witnesses be referred to by letters, in that the said publication tended and was calculated to prejudice the due administration of justice by causing victims of blackmail to fear publicity and thus deter them from coming forward in aid of legal proceedings or from seeking the protection of the law and/or by holding up to public obloquy witnesses who had given evidence in criminal proceedings.

j   The case in which this matter arose was a trial at the Central Criminal Court in the latter part of 1973 and early 1974 of a woman referred to throughout as Janie Jones. She in fact was the defendant at two trials, and of the charges against her some related to procuring women for prostitution, some to organising prostitution and in at least two instances (and they are the only two with which we are concerned) there were charges of blackmail. The allegation was that she had blackmailed two men on the

basis that she would disclose their activities with her girls unless suitable remuneration
was provided. Those two blackmail counts were part of the trial which began on or *a*
about 3rd December 1973 before His Honour Judge King-Hamilton and went on until
a date in April 1974.

When that trial began there was some discussion between the judge and counsel
whether the witnesses should have their names disclosed when they came to the box
to give their evidence, or whether they should be permitted, or required, as the case
might be, to write their names down in such a way that the names would not be *b*
communicated to the press and the public present in court. It is quite interesting to
notice at the outset that counsel for the defence, who was taking a strong line on this
question of disclosure of witnesses' names, accepted from the beginning that as far
as the complainants in the blackmail charges were concerned it would be proper for
their names to be concealed.

In the transcript counsel for the defence is shown as saying: *c*

'My Lord, in a blackmail case I would readily concede at once because the
whole purpose of anonymity in blackmail cases is if the identity of the victim is
disclosed then the blackmailer has had his way, but this is quite different.'

When he says 'this is quite different' he refers to witnesses other than the two
complainants in the blackmail case.   *d*

I say at once it surprises me not at all that counsel should have been so ready to
accept the situation in regard to the complainants in blackmail charges because all
of us concerned in the law know that for many years than any of us can remember it
has been a commonplace in blackmail charges for the complainant to be allowed to
give his evidence without disclosing his name. That is not out of any feelings of
tenderness towards the victim of the blackmail, a man or woman very often who *e*
deserves no such consideration at all. The reason why the courts in the past have so
often used this device in this type of blackmail case where the complainant has something to hide, is because there is a keen public interest in getting blackmailers convicted and sentenced, and experience shows that grave difficulty may be suffered in
getting complainants to come forward unless they are given this kind of protection.
Hence, no doubt, the ready acceptance on the part of counsel for the defence of the *f*
suggestion that the two blackmail victims should not have their names disclosed but
should be known as Mr Y and Mr Z.

No doubt fortified by that attitude on the part of counsel for the defence, the trial
judge gave a direction accordingly. He said:

'Having listened to the arguments on both sides I have come to the conclusion *g*
in the exercise of my discretion that it would not be right for the full names to
be given and for this reason I adhere to the decision which Mr Robey gave,
namely, that they, the witnesses, should be referred to by letters.'

Mr Robey was the magistrate who conducted the committal proceedings and who
had made a similar direction. Although there has been some dispute in argument as
to exactly what those words of the trial judge mean, I find it impossible to say that *h*
they have other than a very straightforward and clear meaning. It seems to me quite
clear that what he is saying is 'in my court there shall be no mention of the proper
names of these two men, but they shall instead be called Y and Z'. I do not think for a
moment the order was expressed to go beyond the four walls of the Central
Criminal Court, but within those four walls the judge is saying 'we will have no proper
names of these two men. We will have their letters instead.'   *j*

So it was, and one gathers that the trial went on in a perfectly normal way with
suitable references to Mr Y and Mr Z when required until the trial was nearly over,
indeed until 13th April 1974. At that time the judge was on the point of summing-up
and there were, therefore, a few days of the trial left. On that day there was published
the issue of the 'Socialist Worker' which contains the article said to be a contempt.

a It is not disputed by Mr Foot that he wrote the article, and it is perfectly clear to anyone who reads it, as we have read it, that he is not only criticising a system which allows the names of such witnesses as these to be concealed, but he is also quite plainly giving a name, address and certain description to two men who he says are in fact Mr Y and Mr Z.

I am not going to read the article again. It was read so far as relevant yesterday, and it suffices to note that not only does it go to the lengths which I have described, *b* but it also shows that Mr Foot knew that what was being done in the way of conceal-ment of the witnesses' names was done with the approval of the judge because he says:

'By prior arrangement with the judge, the barristers and the hacks on the press bench, the names of the gentlemen whose curious tastes led to the prosecution *c* in the first place are hidden.'

I think it sensible to observe at this point that this was a rather dangerous thing for Mr Foot to do in any event because if there be one rule about contempt of court which I should think every experienced journalist knows, it is that it is exceedingly dangerous to publish matter about parties to a pending proceeding when it is possible that that *d* publication may affect the minds of the jury. And I feel bound to say that if Mr Foot had any real concern for the law of contempt at all, he would have made it his business to see that this article was not published until the jury had returned their verdict and were no longer liable to be affected by it.

But be that as it may, it came out on 13th April and the applicant does not seek to make any point of the fact that the jury in the Janie Jones case might have been *e* affected by it. It seems highly unlikely that they would have been and the point does not deserve further mention.

The only other matter to which reference should be made is that the judge, having been told of the publication of this article, said in open court that he proposed to send the papers to the Director of Public Prosecutions, and that he did. It was his action in doing that which eventually moved the Attorney-General to make this *f* application.

Mr Foot has filed an affidavit in reply. Much of it consists of matters of fact with which I can deal more conveniently in a moment or two, but I ought to read para 3 of the affidavit because it does throw some light on his state of mind at the time. He says:

'When I wrote the article, I was not aware that any order had been made by *g* the trial judge, prohibiting the disclosure of identities of the witnesses Mr. Y and Mr. Z. My understanding was that at some stage of the trial there had been a discussion about the question of disclosure and that the judge had said he would permit the witnesses to be referred to as Mr. Y and Mr. Z. I also understand that the judge had requested the representatives of the Press who were in court not to disclose the names. In thirteen years of journalistic experience, I have always *h* believed that such requests have no legally binding effect and that it is in the dis-cretion of an editor or journalist whether or not to comply with such a request.'

What Mr Foot is referring to there, no doubt, is the fact that, quite apart from cases like the present where the court may direct that a witness's name be concealed, it is, again as we all know, a commonplace that in all sorts of litigation the judge, if he *j* thinks it right, will sometimes turn to the press and say 'perhaps you might consider not publishing that piece of evidence or not publishing that person's name' or what-ever. Of course where the matter is a simple matter of request like that, an invitation, it may very well be that it has no legal effect at all. But what was done here by the trial judge unquestionably was to give a direction and not merely an invitation.

With those simple facts in the background one can turn to look at some of the relevant law in regard to contempt of court. Lord Reid said in a recent case[1] that the law of contempt in this country is uncertain, and unhappily there is no doubt that his Lordship was entirely right in so saying. A committee[2] originally presided over by the late Phillimore LJ is no doubt going to recommend a review of this branch of the law in due course, but until we have the benefit of that committee's report we must manage as best we can with what we have.

There are many forms which contempt can take, and one very broad grouping of contempt is to say that it is normally a contempt of court to do an act calculated to interfere with the due course of justice. That means to do an act which produces as a result of real likelihood that some interference with the due course of justice will result.

There is a comparatively recent decision of the Court of Appeal on this aspect of contempt, which I have found of particular assistance in considering the present case. It is *Attorney-General v Butterworth*[3]. In that case there had been a hearing before the Restrictive Practices Court of a reference of an agreement between the Newspaper Proprietors' Association Ltd on one side and the National Federation of Retail Newsagents, Booksellers and Stationers on the other. The issue was whether a certain agreement should be declared void as being against the public interest.

In the hearing before the Restrictive Practices Court 'G', who was treasurer of the Romford branch of the federation and a branch delegate, thought that the agreement was harmful to the public and gave evidence to that effect as a witness before the court. In other words, he gave evidence against his own side, supporting the registrar's view and not the view of his own union.

When the case was over, and in fact the agreement had been held to be harmful to the public, the conduct of 'G' was investigated by his union. His conduct aroused hostility with certain members and he was called on to answer for his conduct at a special committee meeting at which his action was condemned. Then at a general meeting of the branch at which the members' voting was evenly divided on the merits of his conduct, no decision was taken. However, at two later branch meetings resolutions were passed purporting to deprive him of his office as branch delegate and treasurer.

The matter came originally before the Restrictive Practices Court by way of complaint, it being said that this was a contempt of court that this man, who had given evidence in court according to his conscience, should be penalised or victimised later for what he had done. The Court of Appeal held that there was a contempt of court in those circumstances. The interesting feature of this case is that it deals with an act calculated to interfere with the due course of justice not merely as being confined to justice in pending proceedings, but also to the possibility of an injustice following in further unidentified future proceedings.

What was said, first of all, by Lord Denning MR, giving the leading judgment, was this. Having set out the decision of the Restrictive Practices Court which was that there had been no contempt, he said[4]:

'It may be that there is no authority to be found in the books, but, if this be so, all I can say is that the sooner we make one the better. For there can be no greater contempt than to intimidate a witness before he gives his evidence or to victimise him afterwards for having given it. How can we expect a witness to give his evidence freely and frankly, as he ought to do, if he is liable, as soon as the case is over, to be punished for it by those who dislike the evidence he has given? After he has honestly given his evidence, is he to be liable to be dismissed from his employment, or to be expelled from his trade union, or to be deprived of his

---

1   *Attorney-General v Times Newspapers Ltd* [1973] 3 All ER 54 at 60, [1974] AC 273 at 294
2   See the Report of the Committee on Contempt of Court (1974), Cmnd 5794
3   [1962] 3 All ER 326, [1963] 1 QB 696
4   [1962] 3 All ER at 329, [1963] 1 QB at 719

a office, or to be sent to Coventry, simply because of that evidence which he has given? I decline to believe that the law of England permits him to be so treated. If this sort of thing could be done in a single case with impunity, the news of it would soon get round. Witnesses in other cases would be unwilling to come forward to give evidence, or, if they did come forward, they would hesitate to speak the truth, for fear of the consequences. To those who say that there is no authority on the point, I would say that the authority of LORD LANGDALE M.R. in Littler v.

b Thomson[1] in 1839 is good enough for me: ". . . if witnesses are in this way deterred from coming forward in aid of legal proceedings, it will be impossible that justice can be administered. It would be better that the doors of the courts of justice were at once closed." I have no hesitation in declaring that the victimisation of a witness is a contempt of court, whether done whilst the proceedings are still pending or after they have finished.'

c It is very important, I think, to appreciate what a big step is taken by that case. To try and influence a witness before he gives his evidence, to try and stop him from giving evidence, or to try and make him alter the evidence he gives is clearly contempt of court, and indeed if done by two or more people together it can well be an indictable conspiracy. But in that case the proceedings were over before the victimisation began.

d The case before the Restrictive Practices Court was finished and nothing which was done by the witness thereafter could affect the position, yet Lord Denning MR accepts with such gusto, one might almost say, the proposition that a contempt of court is found. He puts it, I think, on two grounds. In the first ground he is saying in effect that it is so obvious that the courts must stop this, that is to say victimisation after the event, that it must be contempt of court. It is a clear and deliberate affront

e to the authority of the court. That, I think, is the first ground on which he puts it. But he does indicate the other ground, albeit in only a sentence or two, when he says that witnesses in other cases might be affected and induced not to come forward if they heard that the witness in the first case had been victimised in this way after having given his evidence. So much for Lord Denning MR's views on the matter.

That was a strong Court of Appeal, and the next learned Lord Justice was Donovan

f LJ. He dealt with the point to which I have just referred when he said[2]:

'But it would be reading far too much into [certain cases] to regard them as impliedly recognising or asserting the principle that contempt is impossible once the case is over. The administration of justice is, after all, a continuing thing. It is not bounded by the day's cases. It has a future as well as a present. And, if somebody pollutes the stream today so that tomorrow's litigant will find

g it poisoned, will he appeal to the court in vain?'

A brief confirmation, as it were, of Lord Denning MR's opinion that in considering the allegation of contempt one can have regard to the possible effect on subsequent proceedings (proceedings following later) between different parties. Pearson LJ said the same thing even more clearly[3]:

h 'The Attorney-General has contended that, on those findings, contempt of court was established, and that the court could and should have dealt with it summarily in the exercise of the inherent jurisdiction. Counsel on behalf of the respondents has contended that the court's inherent jurisdiction to deal with contempt of court is limited to two classes of cases, namely, those in which there

j is a scandalising of the court and those in which there is prejudice to pending proceedings, and that the jurisdiction does not extend to a case in which, after the conclusion of the proceedings, some person is victimised for what he did as

1 (1839) 2 Beav 129
2 [1962] 3 All ER at 332, [1963] 1 QB at 725
3 [1962] 3 All ER at 334, [1963] 1 QB at 727, 728

witness or juror in those proceedings. In my judgment, however, such victimisation, because it tends to deter persons from giving evidence as witnesses in future *a*
proceedings and giving their evidence frankly and fully and without fear of
consequences, is an interference with the due administration of justice as a
continuing process, and does constitute contempt of court, and can be dealt with
summarily under the inherent jurisdiction.'

Counsel for the respondents, and I think perhaps particularly counsel for the com- *b*
pany, was minded to stress that this is a comparatively new case, perhaps opening up
new aspects of this branch of the law. Indeed he invited us to say that it is probably
obiter dicta anyway and we were not bound by it.

Whether that is true or not, it seems to me that we certainly ought to follow this
case, and the more so because it has been confirmed in more recent times in *Moore v
Clerk of Assize, Bristol*[1]. The headnote gives the facts[2]:   *c*

'C, a schoolgirl aged 14, gave evidence at the trial of a number of men charged
with affray. After she had completed her evidence and been released by the
judge she went to a café for a meal. There she was approached by the appellant
who reproved her for giving evidence against his brother, one of the accused, and
threatened her, clenching his fist and shouting at her. C was frightened and left
the café. The appellant was brought before the judge and sentenced to three *d*
months' imprisonment for contempt.'

This was a very clear, straightforward example of victimisation after the case was over
and when the case itself was settled once and for all, but I cite it for Lord Denning MR's
note of his own judgment in *Butterworth*[3]. He says[4]:

'The first question is whether this was a contempt. The law has been settled *e*
by *A-G v Butterworth*[3]. The court will always preserve the freedom and integrity
of witnesses and not allow them to be intimidated in any way, either before the
trial, pending it or after it. Here it was after the girl had given evidence. It is a
contempt of court to assault a witness after he has given evidence: it is also a
contempt of court to threaten him or put him in fear, if it is done so as to punish *f*
him for what he has said. There is no doubt whatever that this conduct of Colin
Moore was a contempt.'

Founding himself primarily on *Attorney-General v Butterworth*[3], and to a lesser
extent on some of the more recent cases, the Attorney-General submits that Mr Foot
and the company are guilty of contempt on the two grounds mentioned by Lord
Denning MR in the *Butterworth* case[3]. In the formal application which I have read, *g*
emphasis is certainly placed on the second of Lord Denning MR's two grounds, and
in the learned Attorney-General's address to us on Wednesday I got the impression
that he was putting that in the forefront. However, in Mr Glynn's reply yesterday he
made it perfectly clear that the Crown would seek to support this allegation on both
grounds, and I think that we should deal with it accordingly.

On the basis of *Butterworth's* case[3], and on the facts which I have recounted, it *h*
seems to me that there was a prima facie case of contempt on the part of the company
and Mr Foot when the Attorney-General concluded his submissions, and I think that
there was at that stage of the argument a prima facie case on both grounds: first, on
the ground that by publishing the names of these two witnesses in defiance of the
judge's directions the respondents were committing that sort of blatant affront on the
authority of the court to which Lord Denning MR had referred; further it seems to *j*

1   [1972] 1 All ER 58, [1971] 1 WLR 1669
2   [1972] 1 All ER at 58
3   [1962] 3 All ER 326, [1963] 1 QB 696
4   [1972] 1 All ER at 59, [1971] 1 WLR at 1670

me that the Crown at this stage had presented a prima facie case of contempt on the
a second ground because it is to my mind quite evident that if witnesses in blackmail
actions are not adequately protected, this could affect the readiness of others to come
forward in other cases.

Accordingly with the prima facie case of contempt made out, one has to turn to the
argument for the defence and see on what basis that is put forward.

Counsel for Mr Foot started with a short point. He said that the order made by
b the trial judge in this case did not extend to ordering the press not to disclose the
names of the two witnesses. That, I think, is absolutely correct, and my reading of
the trial judge's directions is that he was directing what was to happen in his court
and was not in express terms dealing with anything which was to happen outside.

But that does not in my view make any difference. The basis of the prima facie
case to which I have referred is not that the judge had made an order directly and
c expressly affecting the conduct of people outside his court. The real vice of this
publication can only be judged by imagining a person suffering blackmail, who is
trying to screw up his courage to go to the police and do something about it. He
sees in the paper that at the Central Criminal Court the judge has allowed Mr Y
and Mr Z not to give their names but to pass under those descriptions. Our potential
complainant of blackmail feels cheered by this and sees the prospect perhaps of his
d being able to bring his proceedings without disclosure of his circumstances. But
then if the next day or a few days after he sees published in the papers the names of
Mr Y and Mr Z, he would at once realise what the protection which he was hoping
for is a myth. He would say to himself, 'Even the judge cannot protect me. Look
at this case. The judge said the names were not to be given and yet they were.
Even the judge cannot protect me.' It is that aspect of the matter which is the sting
e of the allegation against the publication in this case, and it is not affected in my
judgment at all by the fact that the order was not in terms an order addressed to the
press but was an order concerned with the conduct of the trial. The publication
made the directions as to the conduct of the trial meaningless in this regard.

So I pass to what is really the main argument put forward by the respondents, and
indeed the main legal interest, if I may so describe it, in this case, because the second
f contention of counsel for Mr Foot adopted by counsel for the company is a bold one.

He submits that the trial judge had no authority in law to give the direction which
he gave. He submits that the judge had no power to say of one witness or several
that their names should be withheld and merely put down on paper. Of course
if it be right that the trial judge had no power to make the order, it would be clear
enough that the whole basis of the case of contempt would go. It is, therefore, of
g the utmost importance to decide how far counsel for Mr Foot is right on
this submission.

He starts by saying that the general rule which requires courts to be open and public—
a rule for which everyone cites the well-known decision of *Scott v Scott*[1]—in 1931—
and not held in camera, apart from certain special exceptions, applies equally to the
evidence being given in public. He says that the same evils will follow if part or
h parts of the evidence can be suppressed from the public as would follow if the court
itself was closed and the public and press were excluded altogether. He says that
both these requirements—the requirement of a public access to the court and the
requirement that the public should hear the evidence given to the court—spring
from the same roots. They both come from the age old concern of the courts of
this country that justice should be administered in public.

j I have listened to counsel for Mr Foot with care on this argument and in the end I
have come to the conclusion that I cannot accept it. To begin with, I think one must
notice in passing, at all events, that there are certain features of this type of case which
are not unlike the features of one of the well-known exceptions to the no hearing in

1 [1913] AC 417, [1911-13] All ER Rep 1

camera rule, and that is the exception which deals with cases involving secret processes. It has for long been recognised that if an action is brought in regard to a *a*
secret process and the publicity of the hearing will prevent the process from being
secret any longer and thus destroy it, that is a legitimate ground for a hearing in
camera. In a sense, as the Attorney-General submitted on Wednesday, what is
going on here is the same kind of thing. The complainant in the blackmail charge has
a secret which he shares with Miss Janie Jones, a secret which he has been paying
money to keep a secret. If by coming to court in order to see that she is charged with *b*
her offence he must give up his secret, there is, one would think, a parallel of some
consequence between the different proceedings.

The matter is conveniently summed up in the decision of *Scott v Scott*[1] in this
passage, in the judgment of Earl Loreburn:

> 'An aggrieved person, entitled to protection against one man who had stolen *c*
> his secret, would not ask for it on the terms that the secret was to be com-
> municated to all the world. There would be in effect a denial of justice.'

A man who has a secret with a defendant and no other would not seek proceedings
on the terms that the secret was to be communicated to the world. Therefore, it is,
I think, salutary to remember that this type of case is much closer to the *Scott v
Scott*[2] principle than one might think at first blush. But I do not for a moment want *d*
to give credence to the idea that blackmail charges should be tried in camera. Nothing
which I say today should be regarded as any sort of pointer in that direction at all
because I think that would be disastrous, but it is worth noting in the present argument that in some respects the necessity for protection recognised as justifying a
hearing in camera for secret processes has a parallel in this type of case.

The real reason why I think counsel for Mr Foot's argument cannot stand is be- *e*
cause there is such a total and fundamental difference between the evils which flow
from a court sitting in private and the evils which flow from pieces of evidence being
received in the way which was followed in this case. The great virtue of having the
public in our courts is that discipline which the presence of the public imposes on the
court itself. When the court is full of interested members of the public, as indeed
one can say it is today, it is bound to have the effect that everybody is more careful *f*
about what they do, everyone tries just that little bit harder and there is a disciplinary
effect on the court which would be totally lacking if there were no critical members
of the public or press present.

When one has an order for trial in camera, all the public and all the press are
evicted at one fell swoop and the entire supervision by the public is gone. Where one
has a hearing which is open, but where the names of the witnesses are withheld, *g*
virtually all the desirable features of having the public present are to be seen. The
only thing which is kept from their knowledge is the name of the witness. Very
often they have no concern with the name of the witness except a somewhat morbid
curiosity. The actual conduct of the trial, the success or otherwise of the defendant,
does not turn on this kind of thing, and very often the only value of the witness's
name being given as opposed to it being withheld is that if it is published up and *h*
down the country other witnesses may discover that they can help in regard to the
case and come forward. That, of course, is not unusual, and if the witnesses' names are
not given, it may tend to prevent other witnesses coming forward in that way.

Having said that, however, it seems to me that one cannot fairly compare the
consequences of an in camera hearing with the consequences of an open hearing with
a restriction on the names of witnesses. It seems to me quite impossible for counsel *j*
for Mr Foot to say, as he boldly does, and he must be commended for it, that there
is really no difference, and the only way in which one can achieve the kind of result
achieved here is to go the whole way and have the hearing in camera. Indeed in

1   [1913] AC at 445, [1911-13] All ER Rep at 13
2   [1913] AC 417, [1911-13] All ER Rep 1

the end I think that must be his submission: one must either satisfy the rules for
a an in camera hearing or one must go to the other extreme and have every word of
the evidence said aloud.

I do not believe that we are faced with those stark alternatives. I think that there
is a third course suitable and proper for this kind of case of blackmail where the
complainant has done something disreputable or discreditable, and has something
to hide and will not come forward unless thus protected.

b Those are the only considerations to which I find it necessary to refer, and when I
now come to the end of the argument and ask myself whether I am satisfied that the
alleged contempt has been made out in this case, I feel bound to say that it has for
the reasons which I have already given, and on both grounds: on the ground first
that it was an affront to the authority of the court following Lord Denning MR in
the *Butterworth* case[1] and secondly on the ground that, by destroying the confidence
c of witnesses in potential future blackmail proceedings in the protection which they
would get, there was an act calculated to interfere with the due course of justice.

I add one sentence, however, in conclusion, and that is to say that I have not overlooked the fact that in the course of argument some reference was made to the fact
that the courts had not given similar protection to the victim in a case of rape. It
is topical for this to be raised, because there have been some recent sayings among the
d public that perhaps the victim in a rape case should be protected in this way.

All I would say about that for my part is that there are, I think, significant differences between the complainant in blackmail and in rape respectively, but perhaps
more important is the fact that the complainant in rape has never up to now been
recognised as being entitled to this protection, and I would have thought that if it
was now to be given here it would be more proper for it to be done by Parliament
e than by the courts.

I think we should in these matters follow our existing practice unless and until
Parliament alters it, and it is the fact that we are following an existing practice by
allowing witnesses' names to be concealed which distinguish the case from one of
rape. In the end, for my part, I would say that the complaint of contempt is made
out on both grounds.
f

MILMO J. I agree with the judgment that has just been given and I feel that there is
nothing which I can usefully add to it.

ACKNER J. I also agree.

g [Counsel addressed the court on penalty.]

LORD WIDGERY CJ. We have given this matter the best consideration we can
on the information available to us. We do not overlook the fact that this case has
ventilated a somewhat dark corner of the law of contempt, but we feel bound to
recognise the fact that Mr Foot acted recklessly in this matter, and furthermore we
h cannot fail to notice that there has not been a word of withdrawal or apology through
the entire proceedings.

In those circumstances the penalty imposed will be a fine of £250 on the company
and a fine of £250 on Mr Foot.

Leave to appeal to House of Lords refused.

j
Solicitors: *Director of Public Prosecutions* (for the applicant); *Seifert, Sedley & Co* (for the
company); *Bindman & Partners* (for Mr Foot).

N P Metcalfe Esq Barrister.

1 [1962] 3 All ER 326, [1963] 1 QB 696

Applied in BARCLAYS BANK V LEVIN
BROS [1976] 3 All ER 900

Schorsch Meier GmbH v Hennin   *a*

Followed in MILIANGOS v GEORGE
FRANK [1975] 1 All ER 1076

COURT OF APPEAL, CIVIL DIVISION

LORD DENNING MR, LAWTON LJ AND FOSTER J   Considered in THE HALCYON [1975]
                                               1 All ER 882

22nd, 26th NOVEMBER 1974

Judgment – Payment of sum of money – Foreign currency – Jurisdiction to order payment *b*
of sum expressed in foreign currency – Contract – Currency of contract foreign currency –
European Economic Community – Creditor of member state entitled against debtor of another
member state to payment in own currency – Circumstances in which judgment should be
given for payment of a sum expressed in foreign currency – EEC Treaty, art 106.

The plaintiffs carried on business in West Germany as dealers in motor car parts   *c*
and accessories.   The defendant lived in England where he was engaged in the motor
trade.   In 1970 and 1971 the defendant ordered goods from the plaintiffs.   The
plaintiffs despatched the goods and invoiced the defendant for them in deutschmarks,
the currency of the contract.   The defendant paid part of the sum due but failed to
pay the balance.   On 3rd February 1972 the plaintiffs rendered a statement of account
for DM 3,756·03 for goods sold and delivered to the defendant.   At that time the   *d*
sterling equivalent of that sum was £452.   On 13th July 1973 the plaintiffs issued a
summons in the county court against the defendant.   In the county court the amount
owing was proved in deutschmarks, i e DM 3,756·03.   Between the date of invoice
and the date of the summons, however, sterling had been devalued with the consequence that at the date of judgment the value of £452 had fallen to DM 2,664.   Relying
on art 106[a] of the EEC Treaty the plaintiffs asked for judgment in deutschmarks   *e*
and declined to adduce evidence of the equivalent value in sterling.   The judge
held that art 106 had no bearing on the matter and that he could only give judgment
for value in sterling.   Accordingly he dismissed the action and the plaintiffs appealed.

Held – The appeal would be allowed for the following reasons—   *f*
    (i) (per Lord Denning MR and Foster J)   Since the courts were no longer precluded
from ordering a defendant to pay a sum of money or from granting a decree of
specific performance for the payment of a sum of money, there was no longer any
justification for the rule that judgment could only be given for a sum of money in
sterling.   Accordingly, where the currency of the contract was a foreign currency the
English courts had power to give judgment in that currency (see p 156 *d* to *h* and p 161 *h*,
post); *Beswick v Beswick* [1967] 2 All ER 1197 and *Jugoslavenska Oceanska Plovidba v*   *g*
Castle Investment Co Inc [1973] 3 All ER 498 applied; dicta of Lindley MR in *Manners*
v Pearson & Son [1898] 1 Ch at 587, of Lord Denning in *Re United Railways of the Havana*
and Regla Warehouses Ltd [1960] 2 All ER at 365 and of Salmon LJ in *The Teh Hu*
[1969] 3 All ER at 1206 not followed.
    (ii) Furthermore, the effect of art 106 of the EEC Treaty was that a creditor in one   *h*
member state of the European Economic Community was entitled to receive payment for goods supplied to a person in another member state in the currency of the
creditor's own state if that was the currency of the contract under which the goods
had been supplied.   In conformity with art 106 the English court should give
judgment in favour of a creditor of a member state in the currency of that state
or its sterling equivalent at the time of payment (see p 157 *g* and *h* and p 161 *c* to *h*,   *i*
post).
    Per Lord Denning MR.   Where judgment is given in a foreign currency the order
should be in the form: 'It is adjudged this day that the defendant do pay to the
plaintiff [the specified amount in foreign currency being the currency of the contract]

---

a   Article 106, so far as material, is set out at p 157 *f*, post

a or the sterling equivalent at the time of payment.' If the defendant fails to comply with the judgment the plaintiff should apply for leave to enforce it, filing an affidavit showing the rate of exchange at the date of the application and giving the amount of the debt converted into sterling at that date. Leave will then be given to enforce payment of that sum (see p 156 *h* to p 157 *b* and *j* to p 158 *a*, post).

Note

b For damages for breach of contract, the currency of which is a foreign currency, see 8 Halsbury's Laws (4th Edn) 424, 425, para 614.

Cases referred to in judgment

Application des Gaz SA v Falks Veritas Ltd [1974] 3 All ER 51, [1974] 3 WLR 235.
Beswick v Beswick [1967] 2 All ER 1197, [1968] AC 58, [1967] 3 WLR 932, *affg* [1966]
c   3 All ER 1, [1966] Ch 538, [1966] 3 WLR 396, CA, 12 Digest (Reissue) 49, 256.
Bulmer (H P) Ltd v J Bollinger SA [1974] 2 All ER 1226, [1974] 3 WLR 202.
Celia (Steamship) (Owners) v Owners of Steamship Volturno [1921] 2 AC 544, [1921] All ER
    Rep 110, 90 LJP 385, 126 LT 1, 15 Asp MLC 374, 27 Com Cas 46, HL; 17 Digest (Re-
    issue) 204, 753.
Crampton v Vana Railway Co (1872) LR 7 Ch AC 562, 41 LJCh 817, 13 Digest (Repl)
d   316, 1255.
Cumming v Munro (1792) 5 TR 87.
Jugoslavenska Oceanska Plovidba v Castle Investment Co Inc [1973] 3 All ER 498, [1974]
    QB 292, [1973] 3 WLR 847, [1973] 2 Lloyd's Rep 1, CA.
Manners v Pearson & Son [1898] 1 Ch 581, [1895-9] All ER Rep 415, 67 LJCh 304, 78 LT
    432, CA, 35 Digest (Repl) 201, 90.
e *NV Algemene Transport-en Expeditie Onderneming Van Gend en Loos v Nederlandse*
    Tariefcommissie [1963] CMLR 105, CJEC.
Rastell v Draper (1605) Yelv 80, Moore KB 775, 80 ER 55, sub nom *Draper v Rastal*,
    Cro Jac 88, 22 Digest (Reissue) 164, 1373.
Reading's Petition of Right, Re [1949] 2 All ER 68, sub nom *Reading v The King* [1949]
    2 KB 232; *affd* sub nom *Reading v Attorney-General* [1951] 1 All ER 617, [1951]
f   AC 507, HL, 34 Digest (Repl) 149, 1028.
Teh Hu (The), Turbo-Electric Bulk Carrier Teh Hu (Owners) v Nippon Salvage Co Ltd of
    Tokyo [1969] 3 All ER 1200, [1970] P 106, [1969] 3 WLR 1135, [1969] 2 Lloyd's Rep
    365, CA, Digest (Cont Vol C) 891, 8366b.
United Railways of the Havana and Regla Warehouses Ltd, (Re) [1960] 2 All ER 332,
    [1961] AC 1007, [1960] 2 WLR 969, HL, Digest (Cont Vol A) 232, 862a.
g *Ward v Kidswin* (1662) Latch 77, 82 ER 283.

Cases also cited

British Bank for Foreign Trade Ltd v Russian Commercial & Industrial Bank (1921) 38
    TLR 65.
Kornatski v Oppenheimer [1937] 4 All ER 133.
h

Appeal

This was an appeal by the plaintiffs, Schorsch Meier GmbH, against the judgment of his Honour Judge Perks sitting at West London County Court, made on 11th February 1974, whereby it was ordered that, although the plaintiffs' claim of DM 3,756·03 against the defendant, A R Hennin, had been established the action should be dis-
j missed on the grounds (i) that no evidence had been adduced as to the equivalent value of that amount in sterling; (ii) that the court could only give judgment for value in sterling, and (iii) that the plaintiffs were unwilling to produce evidence of the equivalent value or to have their judgment debt expressed in pounds sterling. The ground of the appeal was that the judge had misdirected himself as to the effect of art 106 of the EEC Treaty which, by the European Communities Act 1972, s 2(1),

had become directly applicable as part of the law of England. The facts are set out
in the judgment of Lord Denning MR.   *a*

Louis Blom-Cooper QC and *Derek Hene* for the plaintiffs.
The defendant did not appear and was not represented.

Cur adv vult
b
26th November. The following judgments were read.

LORD DENNING MR.

1. *Introduction*
   Here we see the impact of the Common Market on our law. No one would have   *c*
thought of it before. A German company comes to an English court and asks for
judgment—not in English pounds sterling but, if you please, in German deutschmarks.
The judge offered a sterling judgment. But the German company said, 'No. Sterling
is no good to us. It has gone down much in value. If we accepted it, we would lose
one-third of the debt. The debt was payable in deutschmarks. We want deutschmarks. We will accept no other.' The judge refused their request. He had no   *d*
power, he said, in English law to give any judgment but in sterling. The German
company appeal to this court.
   These are the facts. Schorsch Meier GmbH are dealers in motor car parts and
accessories. They have offices and workshops in Munich in the Federal Republic of
Germany. Mr Hennin lives in England. He is engaged in the motor car trade.
In 1970 and 1971 he ordered spare parts and accessories from the Germany company.   *e*
Some of the orders he gave himself when he called at the German company's offices
at Munich. Other orders he gave by telephone from England. The company
invoiced the goods to him, giving the price in deutschmarks, and despatched them to
him in England. He made some payments in cash when he was in Munich. He
made these payments in deutschmark bank notes. He also gave two cheques in
sterling; but they were dishonoured. On 3rd February 1972 the German company   *f*
rendered a statement of account to him. It was for DM 3,756·03 for goods sold and
delivered.
   The currency of the contract was clearly German. The money of account and the
money of payment was German deutschmarks. At the time when the sum became
due the rate of exchange was £1=DM 8·30. At that rate the sterling equivalent of
DM 3,756·03 was £452 sterling. Some time later sterling was devalued. As a result   *g*
£1 sterling was only worth DM 5·85.
   On 13th July 1973 the German company issued a summons in the West London
County Court for the sum of DM 3,756·03. They claimed the sum in deutschmarks.
They did not claim payment in sterling and for a very good reason. Sterling had
gone down in value. If they had claimed in sterling, they would have had to convert
the deutschmarks into sterling at the date the payment should have been made,   *h*
i e 3rd February 1972: see *Re United Railways of Havana*[1]. They would have got
judgment for only £452, which would at that time have only produced DM 2,664;
whereas if they were able to claim in deutschmarks and get judgment in deutschmarks for DM 3,756·03, the sterling equivalent would be £641. In other words, by
getting judgment in sterling, they would lose one-third of the money due to them;
whereas by getting judgment in deutschmarks they would recover the full amount.   *j*
   When the case came before the county court judge, the German company proved
the debt owing in deutschmarks, that is, DM 3,756·03. They gave no evidence of
rates of exchange. They asked for judgment in deutschmarks. They relied on the

---

1   [1960] 2 All ER 332, [1961] AC 1007

Treaty of Rome. They submitted that the rule of English law (by which an English
a court can give judgment only in sterling) is incompatible with art 106 of the treaty.
They asked the court to refer the matter to the European Court under art 177(1)(a)
of the treaty. The judge refused. He held that, applying English canons of construction, art 106 had no bearing on the rule of the common law; and that this was
so clear that no reference to the European court was required under art 177(1)(a).
The case is reported in Current Law[1].
b

2. *English law apart from the treaty*

So far as I can discover, no one has ever before asked an English court to give judgment in a foreign currency. It has always been assumed that it cannot be done.
As long ago as 1605 a merchant sold some cloth to another for 60 Flemish pounds.
He brought an action of debt in which he claimed the English equivalent, namely,
c £39 sterling. The defendant said he was not indebted in English pounds. The
court overruled his objection, and said:

> '... the debt ought to be demanded by a name known, and the Judges are
> not apprised of Flemish money; and also when the plaintiff has his judgment,
> he cannot have execution by such name; for the sheriff cannot know how to
d > levy the money in Flemish.'

See *Rastell v Draper*[2]. A few years later this was reaffirmed. In 1626 it was agreed
by all the judges that 'in the case of foreign coin, such as Flemish, one must declare
the value in English': see *Ward v Kidswin*[3] which is reported in Norman-French but
translated in the *Havana* case[4].
From that time forward it has always been accepted that an English court can only
e give judgment in sterling. Judges and textwriters have treated it as a self-evident
proposition. No advocate has ever submitted the contrary. The modern cases start
with *Manners v Pearson & Son*[5] in which Lindley MR said: 'Speaking generally, the
Courts of this country have no jurisdiction to order payment of money except in
the currency of this country.' In 1961 I was myself quite confident about it. In the
Havana case[6] I said, '... if there is one thing clear in our law, it is that the claim must be
f made in sterling and the judgment given in sterling.' In 1969 Salmon LJ was equally
confident, and he extended it to awards by arbitrators. In *The Teh Hu*[7] he said:

> 'It is well settled that an English court cannot give judgment for the payment
> of an amount in foreign currency ... Nor, in my view, can an arbitrator make an
> award in foreign currency except perhaps by agreement between the parties.'

g   In several other countries they have no such rule. Dr Mann in his book[8] gives a list
of many countries, including Germany, in which a plaintiff can claim payment of a
sum of money in a foreign currency and get judgment for it.
Why have we in England insisted on a judgment in sterling and nothing else? It is, I
think, because of our faith in sterling. It was a stable currency which had no equal.
Things are different now. Sterling floats in the wind. It changes like a weathercock
h with every gust that blows. So do other currencies. This change compels us to think
again about our rules. I ask myself: why do we say that an English court can only
pronounce judgment in sterling? Lord Reid in the *Havana* case[9] thought that it was

1   [1974] 3 CL § 24
2   (1605) Yelv 80 at 80, 81
j 3   (1662) Latch 77
4   [1960] 2 All ER at 340, [1961] AC at 1044
5   [1898] 1 Ch 581 at 587, [1895-9] All ER Rep 415 at 417
6   [1960] 2 All ER at 356, [1961] AC at 1068, 1069
7   [1969] 3 All ER 1200 at 1206, [1970] P 106 at 129
8   Legal Aspect of Money (3rd Edn, 1971)
9   [1960] 2 All ER at 345, [1961] AC at 1052

'primarily procedural'. I think so too. It arises from the form in which we used to
give judgment for money. From time immemorial the courts of common law used to   *a*
give judgment in these words: 'It is adjudged that the plaintiff *do recover* against the
defendant £X in sterling.' On getting such a judgment the plaintiff could at once
issue out a writ of execution for £X. If it was not in sterling, the sheriff would not be
able to execute it. It was therefore essential that the judgment should be for a sum of
money in sterling; for otherwise it could not be enforced.

There was no other judgment available to a plaintiff who wanted payment. It was   *b*
no good his going to a Chancery Court. He could not ask the Lord Chancellor or the
Master of the Rolls for an order for specific performance. He could not ask for an
order that the defendant do pay the sum due in the foreign currency. For the Chancery Court would never make an order for specific performance of a contract to pay
money. They would not make it for a sterling debt: see *Crampton v Vana Railway Co*[1],
and Halsbury's Laws of England[2]. Nor would they make it for a foreign currency.   *c*
In the *Havana* case[3] Lord Reid said:

> 'A plaintiff cannot sue in England for payment of dollars and he cannot get
> specific performance of a contract to pay dollars—it would not be right that he
> should.'

Those reasons for the rule have now ceased to exist. In the first place, the form of   *d*
judgment has been altered. In 1966 the common law words 'do recover' were dropped.
They were replaced by a simple order that the defendant 'do' the specified act. A
judgment for money now simply says that: 'It is this day adjudged that the defendant
do pay the plaintiff' the sum specified: see the notes to RSC Ord 42, r 1, and the
appendices. That form can be used quite appropriately for a sum in foreign currency
as for a sum in sterling. It is perfectly legitimate to order the defendant to pay the   *e*
German debt in deutschmarks. He can satisfy the judgment by paying the deutschmarks; or, if he prefers, he can satisfy it by paying the equivalent sum in sterling, that
is, the equivalent at the time of payment.

In the second place, it is now open to a court to order specific performance of a
contract to pay money. In *Beswick v Beswick*[4] the House of Lords held that specific
performance could be ordered of a contract to pay money, not only to the other   *f*
party, but also to a third party. Since that decision, I am of opinion that an English
court has power, not only to order specific performance of a contract to pay in sterling,
but also of a contract to pay in dollars or deutschmarks or any other currency.

Seeing that the reasons no longer exist, we are at liberty to discard the rule itself.
Cessante ratione legis cessat ipsa lex. The rule has no support amongst the juridical
writers. It has been criticised by many. Dicey[5] says: *g*

> 'Such an encroachment of the law of procedure upon substantive rights is
> difficult to justify from the point of view of justice, convenience or logic.'

Only last year we refused to apply the rule to arbitrations. We held that English
arbitrators have jurisdiction to make their awards in a foreign currency, when that   *h*
currency is the currency of the contract: see *Jugoslavenska Oceanska Plovidba v Castle
Investment Co Inc*[6]. The time has now come when we should say that when the currency
of a contract is a foreign currency—that is to say, when the money of account and the
money of payment is a foreign currency—the English courts have power to give
judgment in that foreign currency; they can make an order in the form: 'It is adjudged

j

1 (1872) LR 7 Ch AC 562
2 3rd Edn (1961), vol 36, p 279
3 [1960] 2 All ER at 345, [1961] AC at 1052
4 [1967] 2 All ER 1197, [1968] AC 58, HL; *affg* [1966] 3 All ER 1, [1966] Ch 538
5 Conflict of Laws (9th Edn, 1973), p 883
6 [1973] 3 All ER 498, [1974] QB 292

a this day that the defendant do pay to the plaintiff' so much in foreign currency (being the currency of the contract) 'or the sterling equivalent at the time of payment'. If the defendant does not honour the judgment, the plaintiff can apply for leave to enforce it. He should file an affidavit showing the rate of exchange at the date of the application and give the amount of the debt converted into sterling at that date. Then leave will be given to enforce payment of that sum.

b It must be remembered that if the English courts refuse to give a judgment in deutschmarks, the German company could readily find a way round it. They could bring proceedings in the German courts to get judgment there in deutschmarks for DM 3,756·03. Then they could bring that judgment over to England and register it in the High Court here. On registration here, the sum would have to be converted into sterling 'on the basis of the rate of exchange prevailing at the date of the judgment of the original court'; that is, at the rate in force at the date of the German judgment:

c see s 2(3) of the Foreign Judgments (Reciprocal Enforcement) Act 1933. By that means the company would get judgment for the full sum they now seek, i e £641 or thereabouts, and not £452.

3. *The Treaty of Rome*

d I turn now to the Treaty of Rome. It is by statute part of the law of England. It creates rights and obligations, not only between member states themselves, but also between citizens and the member states, and between the ordinary citizens themselves; and the national courts can enforce those rights and obligations: see *NV Algemene Transport-en Expeditie Onderneming Van Gend en Loos v Nederlandse Tariefcommissie*[1]. Whenever the treaty is prayed in aid, the English courts can them-

e selves interpret it, subject always to the European Court, if asked, having the last word: see the *Champagne*[2] and *Gaz*[3] cases. Counsel for the appellant relies on art 106 of the treaty. It says:

f '1. Each Member State undertakes to authorise, *in the currency of the Member State in which the creditor or the beneficiary resides*, any payments connected with the movements of goods, services or capital, and any transfers of capital and earnings, to the extent that the movement of goods, services, capital and persons between Member States has been liberalised pursuant to this Treaty ...'

In interpreting this article we need not examine the words in meticulous detail. We have to look at the purpose or intent: see the *Champagne* case[4]. There is no need to refer the interpretation to the European Court at Luxembourg. We can do it

g ourselves. It seems to me that the purpose of art 106—or one of its purposes—is to ensure that the creditor in one member state shall receive payment for his goods in his own currency—if it is the currency of the contract—without any impediment or restriction by reason of changes in the rate of exchange. The underlying principle is this: it is the duty of the debtor to pay his debt to the creditor in the currency of the contract according to its terms. If he delays and sterling depreciates, the creditor ought not to suffer loss as a result of the debtor's delay. The debtor ought to bear the

h burden of his own default. The English courts would be acting contrary to the spirit and intent of the treaty if they made a German creditor accept payment in depreciated sterling. In order to comply with the treaty, they should give judgment that the defendant do pay the stated sum in deutschmarks or its sterling equivalent at the time of payment. If the defendant fails to comply with that judgment, the plaintiff

j can apply for leave to enforce it, producing an affidavit showing the sterling equivalent

---

1   [1963] CMLR 105 at 129
2   [1974] 2 All ER 1226, [1974] 3 WLR 202
3   [1974] 3 All ER 51, [1974] 3 WLR 235
4   [1974] 2 All ER at 1237, [1974] 3 WLR at 216

at the date of his application to enforce it. Leave will then be given to enforce payment of that sterling sum.   *a*

4. *Conclusion*

This is the first case in which we have had actually to apply the Treaty of Rome in these courts. It shows its great effect. It has brought about a fundamental change. Hitherto our English courts have only been able to give judgment in sterling. In future when a debt is incurred by an English debtor to a creditor in one of the member *b* states—payable in the currency of that state—the English courts can give judgment for the amount in that money. This change will have effects, too, beyond the Common Market. It has already made us think again about our own laws. As a result, it is my opinion, that, whatever the foreign currency, be it United States dollars or Japanese yen, or any other, the English courts can give judgment in that money where it is the currency of the contract.   *c*

I would allow the appeal and adjudge that the debtor do pay to the plaintiff DM 3,756·03 or the sterling equivalent at the time of payment.

LAWTON LJ. If A sells and delivers goods to B, both justice and the law say that A should be paid the price. If B does not pay, the courts should do all in their power *d* to see that A does not lose by B's default—and it matters not that A is a trader outside the jurisdiction of this court or how the claim is based. Traders from overseas have been coming to this country for centuries. When the merchants from the Hanseatic towns and the Low Countries gathered together at Cambridge for the midsummer fair in the middle ages they would not have wanted to be paid with clipped coins which from time to time some kings put into circulation; and if the law merchant *e* enforced in the pie poudre court at that fair had made them accept clipped coins, it is probable that they would never have come again. If the judgment under appeal in this case is right, a foreign trader who has agreed in his own country—in accordance with his own law—to sell and deliver goods here and who is entitled under his contract to be paid in his own currency, must accept the modern equivalent of clipped coins, now called devalued currency. If this be so, our courts and our law will have a *f* poor reputation in the market places of the world as long as our currency is unstable.

Judges and lawyers have long thought that claims arising under foreign contracts must be for a sterling sum and that the judgment must be in sterling. A list of the judges who have said so includes the names of the most outstanding judges of the last 80 years: it starts with Lindley MR, and Vaughan Williams LJ in *Manners v Pearson & Son*[1]. It includes Lord Sumner in *Owners of Steamship Celia v Owners of Steamship* *g* *Volturno*[2]; Viscount Simonds and Lords Reid and Denning in *Re United Railways of the Havana and Regla Warehouses Ltd*[3]; and it ends with Lord Denning MR stating in *Jugoslavenska Oceanska Plovidba v Castle Investment Co Inc*[4], that the rule should be reconsidered, but he knows 'that this is not yet the law'. Before these names, if I may adopt the words of the late James Thurber, I am astonished at my own presumption in even querying what they have said. There has been no discussion in modern times *h* about the rule. It has been assumed to be the law. It must have had a beginning. What was it? Why was such a rule necessary?

If disputes about foreign exchange did arise in the middle ages—and they must have done—the surviving reports do not, so it seems, disclose what they were. The upsurge of international trade at the beginning of the 17th century which in this country led to the grant of royal charters to trading companies such as the East *j*

---

1   [1898] 1 Ch 581 at 587, 592, [1895-9] All ER Rep 415 at 417, 420
2   [1921] 2 AC 544 at 555, 556, [1921] All ER Rep 110 at 115, 116
3   [1960] 2 All ER 332 at 340, 345, 356, [1961] AC 1007 at 1043, 1052. 1069
4   [1973] 3 All ER 498 at 501, [1974] QB 292 at 299

a India Company and the Levant Company, did result in disputes about foreign exchange. The problems were practical. How did a plaintiff sue for what was due to him in a foreign currency? How did the court apprise itself of the value in English currency of a foreign currency of which neither the judge nor the jury had had any experience? The approach to these problems was pragmatic, as is illustrated by *Rastell v Draper*[1]. The plaintiff had sold to the defendant some cloth for 60 Flemish pounds to be paid on request. The plaintiff sued in the Court of Common Pleas *b* for £39, which he alleged was the equivalent in English money. The defendant moved in arrest of judgment, submitting that the plaintiff should have claimed 60 Flemish pounds, not 39 English ones. The court[2] would not accept this—

'for the debt ought to be demanded by a name known and the Judges are not apprised of Flemish money; and also when the plaintiff has his judgment, he *c* cannot have execution by such name; for the sheriff cannot know how to levy the money in Flemish.'

This was robust common sense appropriate to trading conditions in which there were no telephones, no radio, no telex and news took seven days to get to London from Paris and a month from Rome. In the end the problem was put into the strait-jacket of the forms of action. It was decided that claims for foreign currency should *d* be in detinue, not debt. The remedy for detinue was damages and they were always given in English currency: see *Ward v Kidswin*[3]. The law has worn that strait-jacket ever since. It is time it was discarded, since most of the reasoning in both *Rastell v Draper*[1] and *Ward v Kidswin*[3] is inappropriate nowadays. Our judges, especially those presiding in the Commercial Court, are familiar with foreign currencies, and under the Foreign Judgments (Reciprocal Enforcement) Act 1933 an *e* English judgment expressed in deutschmarks could be enforced in the Federal Republic of Germany and West Berlin. It is, of course, as true today as it was in 1605 that a sheriff acting under a writ of fieri facias cannot by execution raise foreign currency. All he can do by a forced sale is to provide a sum in sterling. Nowadays the conversion of foreign currency into sterling and vice versa is no longer a difficult task; and judges seldom, if ever, have to do the conversions themselves; they are *f* done for them by someone in the case making a calculation from a copy of a newspaper for the day on which the sum became payable. The forms of action have been abolished. Time has swept away nearly all the reasons why our courts were reluctant to give judgment in a foreign currency.

After the early years of the 17th century the courts seem to have been untroubled by problems of foreign exchange until the end of the 18th century. The intervening *g* period was one of rapidly expanding trade in which England was pre-eminent and sterling much sought after. Then came the American and French revolutionary wars. Trade was upset. The political and economic fortunes of nations ebbed and flowed and at the end of the 18th century the inevitable financial consequences of such changes became the concern of the courts. One such consequence was fluctuating exchange rates. As far as I can judge from the reported cases noted by Dr F A *h* Mann in his treatise, The Legal Aspect of Money[4], the judges concerned themselves with making orders which met with the justice of the case, but not with defining areas of jurisdiction. Thus in *Cumming v Munro*[5] an action was brought on a bond dated 13th July 1775 for a sum of £2,400 proclamation money of North Carolina. The defendant wanted to pay that sum into court. The application was opposed on the *j* ground that such a sum in that currency was of no value. The submission was based

---

1 (1605) Yelv 80
2 Yelv at 80, 81
3 (1662) Latch 77
4 3rd Edn (1971)
5 (1792) 5 TR 87

on the broad justice of the case and the uncertainty as to the sterling equivalent which
would have to be resolved by a jury.   It was not suggested that an English court had   *a*
no jurisdiction to make an order in any currency other than sterling.   The judgments
of the two judges, Buller and Grose JJ, dealt with the justice of the case, not
jurisdiction.

There appears to be nothing more in the reports until *Manners v Pearson & Son*[1].
The years since 1815 have been a period of great economic and financial stability and
this may well have influenced English lawyers, as Lord Denning pointed out in   *b*
Re United Railways of the Havana and Regla Warehouses Ltd[2], into thinking that sterling
was a currency (I use his quotation) 'of whose true-fixed and resting quality there is
no fellow in the firmament'[3].

In *Manners v Pearson & Son*[4] Lindley MR based the rule on jurisdiction and gave
as his reason for it, not the uncertainty which has concerned the 17th and 18th centuries judges, but the fact that an order in a foreign currency could not be enforced   *c*
by the ordinary writs of execution.   The ordinary processes, if not writs of execution,
nowadays include the legal processes of other countries which have reciprocal arrangements with the United Kingdom.   Further, the judges of that period may have
thought, as many judges have thought since (for an example see *Re United Railways
of Havana and Regla Warehouses Ltd*[5]) that a court could not make   an order for
specific performance of a contract to pay a specific sum in a foreign currency.   In   *d*
Beswick v Beswick[6] the House of Lords adjudged that an order for the specific performance of an undertaking to pay by instalments specific sums in sterling could be
made.   If such an order can be made for the payment of sterling, I can see no reason
why an order should not be made for the payment of specific sums in   a foreign
currency.   Say another case, like *Re Reading's Petition of Right*[7] occurred.   Suppose
an army officer serving in Germany, who was the holder of an imprest account,   *e*
withdrew large sums of deutschmarks, deserted to the United Kingdom and put the
stolen deutschmarks in a safe deposit.   Suppose that by the time the military police
found him sterling had been devalued against the deutschmark.   It would be an
affront to justice if our courts could only give judgment for the sterling equivalent at
the date of conversion.   Why should he not be made to deliver up the deutschmarks?   All the reasons which have been given for a chauvinistic approach to foreign   *f*
currency, with the exception of those based on the difficulty of execution by writs
and garnishee orders have become meaningless; and the consequences of adhering
to the practice of giving judgment in sterling has been to do injustice to foreign
traders and to allow defaulting British traders to get a benefit which brings discredit
on the administration of justice in this realm.

I am, however, a timorous member of this court.   I stand in awe of the House of   *g*
Lords.   I have asked myself whether counsel for the plaintiffs' submission to the
effect that there is no case binding on the court which requires us to dismiss the
appeal was sound.   He submitted that in all the cases in which reference has been
made to giving judgment in sterling the question under discussion was a different
one altogether.   That may well be so as to the specific issues raised, but in both *Owners of
Steamship Celia v Owners of Steamship Volturno*[8] and *Re United Railways of the Havana*   *h*
and Regla Warehouses Ltd[9], the approach of some of their Lordships to the specific
issues was to find out what was the real nature of the cause of action which produced

1   [1898] 1 Ch 581, [1895-9] All ER Rep 415
2   [1960] 2 All ER 332 at 356, [1961] AC 1007 at 1069
3   Julius Caesar, Act III, scene 1
4   [1898] 1 Ch at 587, [1895-9] All ER Rep at 417
5   [1960] 2 All ER at 345, [1961] AC at 1052
6   [1967] 2 All ER 1197, [1968] AC 58
7   [1949] 2 All ER 68, [1949] 2 KB 232
8   [1921] 2 AC 544, [1921] All ER Rep 110
9   [1960] 2 All ER 332, [1961] AC 1007

the claim.   See Lord Sumner's speech in *Owners of Steamship Celia v Owners of Steam-*
a *ship Volturno*[1] and the speeches of Viscount Simonds and Lord Denning in the *Havana*
case[2].   Both their Lordships in the latter case pointed out that a claim in respect of a
foreign debt was a claim in damages, not in debt.   Viscount Simonds referred to,
and approved, the case which established this proposition, *Ward v Kidswin*[3].   Jones J,
one of the judges in that case, is reported[4] as saying that—

b   'the action is properly brought in detinet alone for Hamburg money which
        is of no value and as if the action were brought for a piece of plate.'

It is disturbing to find that a rule which does injustice to a foreign trader is founded
on archaic legalistic nonsense of this kind.   It is, however, my duty to apply the law,
not to reform it.   I have reluctantly been driven to the conclusion that, subject to
c counsel for the plaintiffs' submission based on the European Communities Act 1972,
this must be deemed to have been approved and followed by the House of Lords in
Re United Railways of the Havana and Regla Warehouses Ltd[5].   Has the European
Communities Act 1972 altered the law?   The relevant provision of the Treaty of
Rome is art 106.   This article occurs in a section of the treaty which is concerned,
amongst other matters, with the maintenance of confidence in the currencies of the
d member states.   There is to be an end to barriers being erected by member states
to stop transfer of capital and earnings from one to the other.   Payments connected
with the movement of goods are to be authorised in the currency of the member
states in which the creditor resides.   Before the treaty became part of our law, a
foreign creditor who had the misfortune to have a defaulting debtor in this country
was at a serious disadvantage if he sought to get payment with the help of a judgment in our courts.   Under the judgment he could not get payment in his own
e currency, only in sterling.   This was a barrier and the law had raised it.   Article 106
requires barriers of this kind to be taken down.   As art 106 is now part of our law,
this court must apply it and the old rule is superseded.   The result is that English
law in this respect falls into line with that of the Federal Republic of Germany and
a number of other states forming part of the European Economic Community.   The
f plaintiffs may have difficulties if they try to execute the judgment in England and
they may have problems under the Exchange Control Act 1947.   As the plaintiffs in
this case have asked for a judgment in deutschmarks, I infer that there are good
business reasons for their doing so.   One reason may be that the defendant has
interests abroad.   The plaintiffs, however, must be left to extricate themselves from
the intricacies of the law relating to execution and exchange control.   It is for them
g to choose what to do.   All I have adjudged is that this judgment can be in the form
for which they have asked.
     I would allow the appeal.

FOSTER J. I agree with the judgment of Lord Denning MR and for the reasons
h which he gave.

Appeal allowed with costs in sterling in the Court of Appeal and below.

Solicitors: *Buckeridge & Braune* (for the plaintiffs).

                                                   M G Hammett Esq Barrister.

j ───

1 [1921] 2 AC 544, [1921] All ER Rep 110
2 [1960] 2 All ER at 340, 356, [1961] AC at 1043, 1044, 1069
3 (1662) Latch 77
4 In the *Havana* case [1960] 2 All ER at 340, [1961] AC at 1044   G
5 [1960] 2 All ER 332, [1961] AC 1007

Ayerst (Inspector of Taxes) v C & K (Construction) Ltd

COURT OF APPEAL

STAMP AND SCARMAN LJJ, BRIGHTMAN J

25th, 28th OCTOBER 1974

Income tax – Discontinuance of trade – Carry forward of trade losses – Company – Transfer of business by company to subsidiary company – Liquidation – Effect – Transfer of business by company in liquidation – Ownership of share capital of subsidiary company – Beneficial ownership – Creditors and contributories – Business belonging to person as trustee to be treated as belonging to persons for time being entitled to income of trust – Business belonging to company to be regarded as belonging to owners of ordinary share capital – Whether before transfer transferor company trustee of business for benefit of creditors and contributories as persons entitled to income under trust – Whether after transfer creditors and contributories beneficial owners of ordinary share capital of subsidiary company – Finance Act 1954, s 17(4)(5).

Mactrac was a limited company which carried on business as a builder and civil engineering contractor. The taxpayer company was a private limited company which had an issued share capital of £100 divided into 100 ordinary shares of £1 each. Mactrac was the registered holder of 99 of those shares and the beneficial owner of all of them. On 4th June 1962 an order was made for the compulsory winding-up of Mactrac. On 8th January 1963 the receiver and the liquidator of Mactrac sold the whole of its business as a going concern to the taxpayer company. After the sale Mactrac continued to be the registered holder of 99 of the taxpayer company's shares. The taxpayer company claimed that it was entitled to set off the unrelieved losses and capital allowances of Mactrac against its profits for the years 1962-63 and 1963-64 on the ground that, under s 17(1)[a] of the Finance Act 1954, Mactrac's business

---

a Section 17, so far as material, provides:

'(1) A trade carried on by a company, whether alone or in partnership, shall not be treated for any of the purposes of the Income Tax Acts as permanently discontinued, or a new trade as set up and commenced, by reason of a change in the year 1954-55 or any subsequent year of assessment in the persons engaged in carrying on the trade, if the company is the person or one of the persons so engaged immediately before the change and on or at any time within two years after the change the trade or an interest amounting to not less than a three-fourths share in it belongs to the same persons as the trade or such an interest belonged to at some time within a year before the change . . .

'(4) For the purposes of this section . . . (b) a trade or interest therein belonging to any person as trustee (otherwise than for charitable or public purposes) shall be treated as belonging to the persons for the time being entitled to the income under the trust; (c) a trade or interest therein belonging to a company shall, where the result of so doing is that the conditions for subsection (1) or subsection (2) of this section to apply to a change are satisfied, be treated in any of the ways permitted by the next following subsection.

'(5) For the purposes of this section, a trade or interest therein which belongs to a company engaged in carrying it on may be regarded—(a) as belonging to the persons owning the ordinary share capital of the company and as belonging to them in proportion to the amount of their holdings of that capital, or (b) in the case of a company which is a subsidiary company, as belonging to a company which is its parent company, or as belonging to the persons owning the ordinary share capital of that parent company, and as belonging to them in proportion to the amount of their holdings of that capital, and any ordinary share capital owned by a company may, if any person or body of persons has the power to secure by means of that holding of shares or the possession of voting power in or in relation to any company, or by virtue of any power conferred by the articles of association or other document regulating any company, that the affairs of the company owning the share capital are conducted in accordance with his or their wishes, be regarded as owned by the person or body of persons having that power . . .'

was not to be treated as discontinued by reason of a change in the persons carrying

a on the business. The taxpayer company contended (i) that, immediately prior to the transfer of Mactrac's business, the business had belonged to Mactrac as trustee and that the creditors and contributories of Mactrac, as the only persons interested in the assets falling to be dealt with in liquidation, were collectively 'entitled to the income under the trust' within s 17(4)(*b*), and were, therefore, to be treated as the beneficial owners of Mactrac's business; and (ii) that, after the transfer, the creditors and shareholders

b of Mactrac collectively were the beneficial owners of the ordinary shares of the taxpayer company and that accordingly, under s 17(4)(*c*) and (5)(*a*), the trade transferred to the taxpayer company was to be regarded as belonging to the creditors and shareholders of Mactrac. It was common ground that, for the purposes of s 17(5) the taxpayer company was not a subsidiary of Mactrac since the liquidation had had the effect that Mactrac ceased to be the beneficial owner of the shares in the taxpayer

c company.

Held – The creditors and shareholders of a company in liquidation were not the beneficial owners of its assets under a trust of which the company was the trustee since (a) the company, stripped of all its rights, powers and obligations in relation to its assets, could not be a trustee of those assets for the creditors and shareholders and

d (b) the creditors and shareholders, having no rights or powers even collectively to deal with a single asset of the company or to direct how it should be dealt with, were not the beneficial owners of those assets. It followed that the creditors and shareholders of Mactrac were not the beneficial owners of the taxpayer company's shares immediately after the sale of Mactrac's business to the taxpayer company. Accordingly the sale had effected a discontinuance of the business and the taxpayer

e company's claim failed (see p 165 *j*, p 166 *a* to *e* and p 167 *f*, post).

Pritchard (*Inspector of Taxes*) *v MH Builders (Wilmslow) Ltd* [1969] 2 All ER 670 approved.

Decision of Templeman J [1974] 1 All ER 676 affirmed.

Notes

f For company reconstruction not treated as a discontinuance, see 20 Halsbury's Laws (3rd Edn) 135, 136, para 238, and for cases on succession to a trade, see 28(1) Digest (Reissue) 110-114, 312-329.

For the Finance Act 1954, s 17, see 34 Halsbury's Statutes (3rd Edn) 296.

For the year 1970-71 and subsequent years of assessment, s 17(4)(5) of the 1954 Act has been replaced by the Income and Corporation Taxes Act 1970, s 253.

g **Cases referred to in judgments**

Knowles *v Scott* [1891] 1 Ch 717, 60 LJCh 284, 64 LT 135, 7 TLR 306, 10 Digest (Repl) 1047, 7257.

Oriental Inland Steam Co, Re, ex parte Scinde Railway Co (1874) 9 Ch App 557, 43 LJCh 699, 31 LT 5, 10 Digest (Repl) 903, 6137.

h Pritchard (*Inspector of Taxes*) *v M H Builders (Wilmslow) Ltd* [1969] 2 All ER 670, 45 Tax Cas 360, [1969] 1 WLR 409, 47 ATC 453, [1968] TR 429, 28(1) Digest (Reissue) 114, 328.

Cases also cited

Barleycorn Enterprise, Re, Mathias and Davies (a firm) v Down (liquidator of Barleycorn Enterprises Ltd) [1970] 2 All ER 155, sub nom Barleycorn Enterprises, Re, Mathias and

j Davies (a Firm) v Down [1970] Ch 465, CA.

Calgary and Edmonton Land Co Ltd v Dobinson [1974] 1 All ER 484, [1974] Ch 102, [1974] 2 WLR 143.

Smith v Anderson (1880) 15 Ch D 247, CA.

Wood Preservation Ltd v Prior (Inspector of Taxes) [1969] 1 All ER 364, 45 Tax Cas 112, [1969] 1 WLR 1077, CA.

Appeal

C & K (Construction) Ltd ('the taxpayer company') was a private company with an *a* issued share capital of £100 divided into 100 £1 shares.   Ninety-nine of those shares were registered in the name of another company, Mactrac Ltd ('Mactrac'), which carried on business as a builder and civil engineering contractor.   On 31st March 1962 a debenture-holder of Mactrac appointed a receiver of all the property and assets of Mactrac.   On 4th June 1962, following a creditor's petition presented to the court on 21st May 1962, an order was made for the compulsory winding-up of Mactrac *b* and a liquidator was appointed.   It was common ground that at all times until the commencement of Mactrac's liquidation Mactrac was the beneficial owner of all the shares in the taxpayer company.   By an agreement dated 18th January 1963, made between the liquidator, the receiver and the taxpayer company, the whole of the business of Mactrac was sold as a going concern to the taxpayer company.   At the date of the sale, Mactrac was still the registered holder of 99 shares in the taxpayer *c* company.   On 6th April 1964 the taxpayer company was assessed to income tax for the years 1962-63 and 1963-64 in the sum of £350 and £1,000 respectively.   The taxpayer company appealed to the Special Commissioners contending that at all material times it was a subsidiary company of Mactrac within the meaning of s 17(5) of the Finance Act 1954 and that accordingly it was entitled to set off the unrelieved losses and capital allowances of Mactrac against its own profits for the years 1962-63 *d* and 1963-64 by virtue of s 17(1) of the 1954 Act.   The commissioners upheld the taxpayer company's claims on the ground that the shareholders of Mactrac were the legal owners of the business both before the sale and after the transfer of it to the taxpayer company.   The Crown expressed dissatisfaction with that determination and required the commissioners to state a case for the opinion of the High Court. On 27th November 1973 Templeman J[1] allowed the appeal holding that the taxpayer *e* company was not a subsidiary of Mactrac within s 17(5) of the 1954 Act since at the date of the sale of Mactrac's business to the taxpayer company, Mactrac, being in compulsory liquidation, was not the beneficial owner of its shares in the taxpayer company.   The taxpayer company appealed.

C N Beattie QC and *George Bretten* for the taxpayer company   *f*
Leonard Bromley QC and *Peter Gibson* for the Crown.

STAMP LJ.   This is an appeal from an order of Templeman J.   The case is reported under the name *Ayerst (Inspector of Taxes) v C & K (Construction) Ltd*[1].   Because the facts, so far as they are known, are fully stated in the report, I need not refer to them *g* in this judgment; nor need I refer to the terms of s 17 of the Finance Act 1954 which are stated in the judgment of Templeman J.

In this appeal counsel for the taxpayer I have no doubt rightly felt unable to quarrel with the conclusion of the learned judge that Mactrac had by the effect of its liquidation ceased to be the beneficial owner of the shares in the taxpayer company, *h* which company was accordingly not a subsidiary of Mactrac at the time of the transfer of the trade.   He advanced a wholly new argument in support of the appeal, submitting that the persons carrying on Mactrac's trade as well before, as after, the sale to the taxpayer company, were, within the meaning of s 17 and by the effect of sub-ss (4)(*b*) and (4)(*c*) and sub-s (5) of the section, which were not relied on in the court below, the same persons: namely, the creditors and shareholders of Mactrac, who it *j* is submitted were collectively the beneficial owners of each of Mactrac's assets within the meaning of the section.

Counsel for the Crown did not object to the new point being raised.   The new

---

1   [1974] 1 All ER 676, [1974] STC 98

a submissions were, as I have indicated, based on the provisions of sub-ss (4)(*b*) and 4(*c*) and sub-s (5) of the section. Subsection (4)(*b*) provides:

> 'For the purposes of this section— ... (*b*) a trade or interest therein belonging to any person as trustee (otherwise than for charitable or public purposes) shall be treated as belonging to the persons for the time being entitled to the income under the trust.'

b Looking at the situation immediately prior to the transfer of Mactrac's trade, it was submitted that the trade belonged to Mactrac as trustee and that the creditors and contributories of Mactrac, as the only persons interested in the assets falling to be dealt with in the liquidation, were collectively entitled to the income under a trust. It followed, so it was submitted, that these persons were for the purposes of the section the beneficial owners of Mactrac's trade.

c Looking at the situation immediately after the transfer, reliance was placed on para (*c*) of sub-s (4) and sub-s (5) taken together. Paragraph (*c*) provides that for the purposes of the section—

> 'a trade or interest therein belonging to a company shall, where the result of so doing is that the conditions for subsection (1) or subsection (2) of this section *d* to apply to a change are satisfied, be treated in any of the ways permitted by the next following subsection.'

That takes one to sub-s (5), which provides, so far as relied on by counsel for the taxpayer company:

> 'For the purposes of this section, a trade or interest therein which belongs to a *e* company engaged in carrying it on may be regarded—(*a*) as belonging to the persons owning the ordinary share capital of the company and as belonging to them in proportion to the amount of their holdings of that capital ...'

Relying on the latter subsection, counsel submitted that after the transfer the creditors and shareholders of Mactrac collectively owned the ordinary shares of *f* the taxpayer company and that accordingly the trade transferred to the taxpayer company may for the purposes of s 17 be regarded as belonging again to the creditors and shareholders of Mactrac. So it is said the trade can be regarded as belonging to the same persons immediately after the transfer as it did, by the effect of sub-s (4)(*b*), immediately before. I emphasise in passing that the analysis of the situation immediately after the transfer so advanced depends on the proposition that, notwithstand- *g* ing that Mactrac was in liquidation, the creditors and shareholders were 'the owners of' Mactrac's shares in the taxpayer company within the meaning of sub-s (5)(*a*) and also that the reference to ownership is, by the effect of sub-s (6)(*a*), a reference to 'beneficial ownership'.

Similar submissions to those so put forward were rejected by Cross J in *Pritchard v MH Builders Ltd*[1], in circumstances not dissimilar from the facts in this case. Counsel *h* for the taxpayer company accepted that in order to succeed in this appeal he must persuade us that that case was wrongly decided.

Now, a liquidator in a liquidation has the duties imposed on him by the Companies Acts. The creditors and contributories are entitled to require him to carry out those duties and to deal with the company's assets in accordance with the statutory provisions. But I cannot equate that right with the beneficial ownership of the assets or *j* of any particular asset falling to be administered in accordance with the Acts. It does not, in my judgment, in the least follow that because a person or collection of persons have the right to have a collection of assets sold and the proceeds applied indirectly for their benefit, he or they are the beneficial owners of each asset. Basic

---

1 [1969] 2 All ER 670, [1969] 1 WLR 409, 45 Tax Cas 360

to counsel's submission is the proposition that a company in liquidation holds its
assets on trust for its creditors and contributories, and accordingly that the creditors　*a*
and contributories are the beneficial owners of those assets. Cross J, in the *Pritchard*
case[1], took the view that once a company is in liquidation, the beneficial ownership
of its assets is in suspense. With that view I whole-heartedly agree. To describe
those for whose benefit the assets of a company in liquidation fall to be administered
as beneficial owners of each of those assets is, in my judgment, a misuse of the English
language. The creditors and shareholders in such a situation have no rights or　*b*
powers, even collectively, to deal with a single asset or to direct how it shall be dealt
with.

There is some language in some of the cases—we were referred in particular to
Re Oriental Inland Steam Co[2]—to the effect that after liquidation a company's assets
are subject to a trust, which no doubt is a convenient way of saying that the assets
cease to belong to the company beneficially and become subject to the statutory　*c*
provisions contained in the Companies Acts. I share the view of Romer J in *Knowles
v Scott*[3] that a liquidator does not hold the company's property on trust for its creditors
and contributories; and the company itself, stripped as it is of all its rights, powers
and obligations in relation to the property, cannot in my judgment be a trustee of
it for the creditors and shareholders. The attempt to apply the conception of trustee
and cestui que trust to the law relating to the liquidation of companies so as to fix　*d*
a company as a trustee of its assets for its creditors and contributories must, in my
judgment, fail.

It follows, in my judgment, that the shares in the taxpayer company did not,
immediately after the transfer of the business to that company, belong to the creditors
and shareholders of Mactrac collectively, so as to bring the case within sub-s (5)(*a*)
of the section.　*e*

That, by itself, if right, would be an end of the case. There is, however, another
way of approaching the case. The conception of the creditors and shareholders
of Mactrac collectively owning the share capital of the taxpayer company according
to their respective rights and interests, in my judgment, ill accords with the concluding words of para (*a*) of sub-s (5), providing that the trade may be regarded as
belonging to the persons owning the share capital 'in proportion to their holdings　*f*
of that capital'. The latter words are no doubt included for the purpose of the
computation required to determine whether the condition of sub-s (1) that at some
time within two years from the change a three-fourths share of the trade belonged
to the same persons as it belonged to a year before the change. In the instant case
the problem is obscured by the fact that the comparison of ownership sought to be
made is between the situation existing immediately before the change and that　*g*
existing immediately afterwards. But once the conception of collective ownership
of creditors and shareholders, as counsel for the taxpayer company put it 'according
to their respective rights and interests', is introduced into the section, it would, as
I see it, be in many cases impossible to undertake the necessary enquiry. If sub-s (5)
and sub-s (4)(*b*) are designed, as I think they are, to assist in the determination of the
question whether a specified proportion of the trade belonged at some date to the　*h*
same persons as it belonged to at some other date, and if the trade were to be treated
by the effect either of sub-s (4)(*b*) or sub-s (5) as belonging at each date to the shareholders and creditors of the company in liquidation collectively according to their
respective rights and interests, I know not how the enquiry could be answered in a
case where between those two dates there had been dealings with those interests by
the creditors or shareholders or where, for example, the preferential creditors had　*j*
been paid in full. In the instant case the problem is, as I have indicated, obscured

---

1　[1969] 2 All ER 670, [1969] 1 WLR 409, 45 Tax Cas 360
2　(1874) 9 Ch App 557
3　[1891] 1 Ch 717

a because the comparison sought to be made is a comparison between the persons
owning the trade immediately before and immediately after the transfer. But it
would, in my judgment, be contrary to the scheme of the section to introduce the
conception of a single collective beneficial ownership of a fluctuating body of persons
according to their respective but unspecified and unknown rights and interests in
the assets of the company.   To do so would, as I see it, make the section unworkable.

b   Counsel for the taxpayer company attempted to deal with the difficulty by referring
to sub-s (7) of the section.   That subsection provides as follows:

> 'In determining for the purposes of this section, whether or to what extent
> a trade belongs at different times to the same persons, persons who are relatives
> of one another and the persons from time to time entitled to the income under
> any trust shall respectively be treated as a single person . . .'

c   So counsel, reiterating his submission that the creditors and shareholders are
collectively entitled to the assets, submitted that they were 'the persons from time
to time entitled to the income under any trust' and so fall to be treated as a single
person for the purposes of sub-s (1).   I can only say, with all respect to that submission, that in the context of the section it would, in my judgment, be a misuse of
d language to describe a fluctuating body of persons who were collectively entitled
as well to capital as income under a trust as persons from time to time entitled to
any income under the trust.   Even if the assets of the company in liquidation were
correctly described as held by the company on trust for the creditors and shareholders collectively—a view which I have rejected—that trust must relate to capital
and income alike.   In my judgment, sub-s (7) is clearly not directed to meet such a
case.
e   I would add, for completeness, that a similar objection applies to the construction
sought to be put on sub-s (4)(b) of the section, which likewise is concerned with
persons for the time being entitled to the income under the trust.
      For these reasons I would dismiss the appeal.

f **SCARMAN LJ.** I agree.

BRIGHTMAN J. I agree.

Appeal dismissed.   Leave to appeal to the House of Lords refused.

Solicitors: *Masons* (for the taxpayer company); *Solicitor of Inland Revenue.*

Rengan Krishnan Esq Barrister.

Barclay's Trustee v Inland Revenue Commissioners

HOUSE OF LORDS

LORD REID, LORD MORRIS OF BORTH-Y-GEST, VISCOUNT DILHORNE, LORD WILBERFORCE
AND LORD KILBRANDON

2nd, 3rd, 7th OCTOBER, 27th NOVEMBER 1974

Estate duty – Aggregation – Property in which deceased had an interest – Insurance policy – Policy subject to trust – Beneficial interest of assured – Exclusion – Policy expressed to be for benefit of assured's wife and sons – Beneficial interest in policy in event of wife and sons predeceasing assured – Whether policy to be held in trust for benefit of estate of one or other of beneficiaries – Whether assured effectively excluded from benefit of policy – Married Women's Policies of Assurance (Scotland) Act 1880, s 2 – Finance Act 1894, s 4.

The deceased desired to effect a policy of assurance on his own life under s 2ᵃ of the Married Women's Policies of Assurance (Scotland) Act 1880 in the sum of £15,000. For that purpose he entered into a contract based on a proposal form signed by him, a letter of request submitted by him to the insurance company and a letter of acceptance from the company. The letter of request stated, inter alia: 'I desire the Policy to be issued under the provisions of the Married Women's Policies of Assurance (Scotland) Act, 1880, for the benefit of: My Son . . . Stuart Lothian Barclay, whom failing My Son . . . Norman Veitch Lothian Barclay, whom failing My Wife . . . Mrs. Florence Winifred Barclay.' The deceased died shortly after the contract had been completed. The Inland Revenue Commissioners assessed his estate to duty on the basis that the proceeds of the contract of life assurance had, by virtue of s 4ᵇ of the Finance Act 1894, to be aggregated with other property passing on his death and could not be separately assessed to duty under the proviso to s 4 as property 'in which the deceased never had an interest' because he had not effectively divested himself of all interest in the policy in that if the sons had predeceased him and the wife had predeceased one or both of the sons, the right to dispose of the benefit of the policy would have reverted to him.

Held – The deceased had never had an interest in the policy for the clear intention of the deceased was that the whole of the benefit of the policy should go to one of the three persons named in the letter of request and to no one else, and that the policy should be for the 'benefit of his wife or children' within s 2 of the 1880 Act. That intention was in no way negatived by the words used in the letter of request for, on the true construction of that document, in the event of the wife and sons dying before the deceased the trustees would be bound to hold it either for the estate of the last of them to die or, if the words 'whom failing' meant that the interests of the sons were contingent on surviving the deceased, for the estate of the wife. In either case the deceased could not in his lifetime have had any interest in the policy (see p 170 j, p 171 b, p 172 d, p 173 g to p 174 a and g to p 175 b and j to p 176 a and d to f, p 177 e and j to p 178 a e and g and p 181 d to f, post).

---

a   Section 2, so far as material, is set out at p 170 c to e, post

b   Section 4 provides: 'For determining the rate of Estate duty to be paid on any property passing on the death of the deceased, all property so passing in respect of which Estate duty is leviable shall be aggregated so as to form one estate, and the duty shall be levied at the proper graduated rate on the principal value thereof: Provided that any property so passing, in which the deceased never had an interest . . . shall not be aggregated with any other property but shall be an estate by itself, and the Estate duty shall be levied at the proper graduated rate on the principal value thereof . . .'

Notes

a For aggregation in connection with life insurance and property in which the deceased never had an interest, see 15 Halsbury's Laws (3rd Edn) 63, 64, paras 125, 126.

For the Finance Act 1894, s 4, see 12 Halsbury's Statutes (3rd Edn) 461. The proviso to s 4 was repealed with savings by the Finance Act 1969, s 61(6), Sch 21, Part V, in respect of deaths on or after 16th April 1969.

b   **Cases referred to in opinions**

Cousins v Sun Life Assurance Society [1933] Ch 126, [1932] All ER Rep 404, 102 LJCh 114, 148 LT 101, CA, 27(1) Digest (Reissue) 167, *1112*.

Dickson's Trustees v Elliott 1949 SLT 359.

Galloway v Craig (1861) 4 Macq 267, 23 D 12, HL, 27(1) Digest (Reissue) 169, *655*.

Haldane's Trustees v Lord Advocate 1954 SC 156, 21 Digest (Repl) 53, *79*.

c   *Hicks v Inland Revenue Comrs* [1973] STC 406, sub nom *Hicks's Trustee v Inland Revenue* 1974 SLT 62.

Taylor v Gilbert's Trustees (1878) 5 R (HL) 217, HL.

Vandervell v Inland Revenue Comrs [1967] 1 All ER 1, [1967] 2 AC 291, 43 Tax Cas 519, [1967] 2 WLR 87, [1966] TR 315, 45 ATC 394, HL, 28(1) Digest (Reissue) 438, *1576*.

Vandervell's Trusts (No 2), Re, White v Vandervell Trustees Ltd [1974] 3 All ER 205, **d**   [1974] 3 WLR 256, CA.

Walker's Trustees v Lord Advocate 1955 SC (HL) 74, sub nom *Walker v Inland Revenue Comrs* 1955 SLT 185, [1955] TR 137, 34 ATC 135; *rvsg* 1954 SC 156, 21 Digest (Repl) 53, *79*.

Appeal

e This was an appeal from an interlocutor of the Second Division of the Court of Session as the Court of Exchequer in Scotland[1] (Lord Kissen, Lord Fraser and Lord Keith) dated 31st January 1974 refusing an appeal by the appellant, Norman Veitch Lothian Barclay, the trustee of James Barclay deceased, against an assessment to estate duty made by the Inland Revenue Commissioners on 5th January 1973 at the rate of 75 per cent on the value of a policy of life assurance issued by the Sun Life Assurance Society. **f** The facts are set out in the opinion of Lord Reid.

J P H MacKay QC and *G W Penrose* (both of the Scottish Bar) for the appellant.
W D Prosser QC, J A D Hope (both of the Scottish Bar) and *Peter Gibson* for the Crown.

Their Lordships took time for consideration.

g 27th November.   The following opinions were delivered.

LORD REID.   My Lords, James Barclay, on 22nd December 1962, submitted to the Sun Life Assurance Society a proposal for three whole life policies of £15,000 each. This was accompanied by requests one of which was in these terms:

'I desire the Policy to be issued under the provisions of the Married Women's **h**   Policies of Assurance (Scotland) Act, 1880, for the benefit of: My Son . . . Stuart Lothian Barclay, whom failing My Son . . . Norman Veitch Lothian Barclay, whom failing My Wife . . . Mrs. Florence Winifred Lothian Barclay . . .'

The other requests were similar but the beneficiaries were placed in different orders.

j This proposal was accepted and the first premiums were paid on 4th January 1963. Mr Barclay died on 31st January 1963. It is common ground that a contract was completed on payment of the first premium so that the three sums of £15,000 became payable on Mr Barclay's death. The question at issue in this case is whether estate duty falls to be paid on the basis that they must be aggregated with the rest

1   [1974] STC 320

of Mr Barclay's estate in which case the rate of duty would be 75 per cent or whether
they are to be treated as estates by themselves in which case the rate of duty would be   *a*
eight per cent.

It is clear that it was contemplated that if Mr Barclay had lived longer policies
would have been issued in terms slightly different from those in the requests, super-
seding the contract made on payment of the premium, but we are not concerned
with that. We must take the destinations set out in the requests. This case is
only concerned with the destination which I have quoted but we are entitled to bear   *b*
in mind the existence of the other two.

Section 4 of the Finance Act 1894 requires the property to be aggregated unless the
deceased 'never had an interest' in it. It is common ground that the appellant can
only succeed if he can shew that in no possible event could Mr Barclay have become
beneficially entitled to the policy. Section 2 of the Married Women's Policies of
Assurance (Scotland) Act 1880 provides by s 2:   *c*

> 'A policy of assurance effected by any married man on his own life, and expressed
> upon the face of it to be for the benefit of his wife, or of his children, or of his wife
> and children, shall, together with all benefit hereof, be deemed a trust for the
> benefit of his wife for her separate use, or for the benefit of his children, or for
> the benefit of his wife and children; and such policy, immediately on its being so   *d*
> effected, shall vest in him and his legal representatives in trust for the purpose
> or purposes so expressed, or in any trustee nominated in the policy, or appointed
> by separate writing duly intimated to the assurance office, but in trust always
> as aforesaid, and shall not otherwise be subject to his control, or form part of
> his estate, or be liable to the diligence of his creditors, or be revocable as a
> donation, or reducible on any ground of excess or insolvency . . .'   *e*

It is admitted that the effect of the request which I have quoted being incorporated
in the contract is that so long as any of the beneficiaries mentioned in it survived
Mr Barclay had no interest in the policy. The case for the Crown is that in at least
one possible event—the death of his wife followed by the deaths of the two sons
during his lifetime—Mr Barclay would have become beneficially entitled to the
policy. If that is right then the appeal fails. But the appellant maintains that even   *f*
in that event Mr Barclay would have acquired no interest in the policy. So I turn to
consider the meaning and effect of the destination in the context in which it appears.

This raises a question of vesting. If there were no vesting in anyone until Mr
Barclay's death then the Crown succeeds. It has always been said that the time of
vesting depends on the intention of the maker of the deed, derived from reading
the deed as a whole. But at one time in the interests of certainty when dealing with   *g*
destination in terms well known to the law, courts were reluctant to seek the real
intention of the testator: they deemed that he must have intended a result based on
a long series of decided cases. More recently there has I think been more flexibility
but we must still say that in the absence of any clear indication of a contrary intention
the normal meaning of a destination established by the authorities must prevail.

I agree with the Crown's contention to this extent. When a gift is payable at a   *h*
date later than the date when the deed takes effect, and it takes the form of a gift
to A whom failing to B whom failing to C the normal rule is that vesting is suspended
or delayed until the date of payment, so that if A, B and C all predecease the date of
payment none of them takes anything.

So the first question here must be whether it can be shown clearly that Mr Barclay
had a different intention. In my view it is clear from the terms of the bequest that   *j*
he intended the whole benefit of these policies to go to one or other of the three
named beneficiaries. The policies were to be issued under the provisions of the 1880
Act for the benefit of one or other of the three named beneficiaries and of no one else.
The purpose of the Act is to protect the beneficiaries against the donor's creditors.
It only affords protection to gifts to the donor's wife or children, so a gift over to

issue would not be protected.   In the case of a gift by will there may be a competition
a between the institute or conditional institute and the residuary legatee and it may be
proper to interpret strictly the gift to an institute or conditional institute.   But here
if the gifts to institute and conditional institute all failed the result would be that by
virtue of his residual right the donor himself would become entitled to the policy.
In my view it is quite clear that Mr Barclay never intended to retain any interest in
any event.   But it is possible that by unskilful conveyancing his intention has been
b defeated.   That would be so if it is not reasonably possible to construe the destination
so as to avoid the possibility of total failure of the gift.

Three constructions of the destination have been suggested, any one of which
would avoid this result, (1) vesting subject to defeasance, (2) immediate vesting in the
last survivor if two of the three beneficiaries should die during the donor's lifetime,
(3) the implication of a further conditional institution of the estate of the last
c mentioned conditional institute, the donor's wife.

There have always been two schools of thought with regard to vesting subject to defeasance.   One regard is as an anomaly introduced into the law of Scotland by this
House in *Taylor v Gilbert's Trustees*[1] and opposes any extension of the doctrine
beyond existing authorities.   The other regards it as an acceptable principle to be
applied, as all principles should be applied, to new cases which appear to call for its
d application.   I would support the view of Gloag and Henderson[2]:

> 'There are three types of cases in which the application of this doctrine is
> now definitely recognised, and beyond which it will not readily be extended.'

The key word is 'readily'.   I would not lay down hard and fast rules.   For example,
I think it at least unwise to say 'there cannot be a vested right in a conditional
e institute so long as there is an ascertained prior institute in existence' (*Dickson's
Trustees v Elliot*[3]).

In *Hicks v Inland Revenue Comrs*[4] arguments put forward in the present case were
not adduced.   I am doubtful whether the doctrine of vesting subject to defeasance
ought to have been applied.   In my view the case ought to have been decided in
favour of the trustees on grounds similar to those which I shall later explain as my
f reasons for allowing the present appeal.

The present case is so far removed from any in which the doctrine of vesting subject
to defeasance has hitherto been applied that I would not be prepared to apply it
here.

In my view there was here no immediate vesting in any of the three named beneficiaries because the donor intended that only one of the three named beneficiaries
g should take and so long as more than one of them remained the matter was still in
doubt.   But if two of them died during the donor's lifetime the doubt was resolved.
He intended to benefit one or other and there was only one left.   The only reason
for postponing vesting would then have disappeared.

In an ordinary testamentary disposition if there is no vesting a morte the presumption is that vesting is postponed until the date of payment.   Often the gift takes the
h form of a direction to pay at that date.   But even where it does not the presumption
is that survivance of the date of payment is a condition attached to the gift.   Vesting
at a date intermediate between the death of the testator and the date of payment
is certainly unusual but it is not impossible.   Professor Henderson dealt with the
matter in his book on Vesting[5] and I can see no reason why, even in the case of a
gift in a will to X in liferent, and in fees to A whom failing B, there should not be
j vesting in B on the death of A during the life of the liferenter if that will best achieve

---

1   (1878) 5 R (HL) 217
2   Introduction to the Law of Scotland (7th Edn, 1968), p 608
3   1949 SLT 359
4   [1973] STC 406
5   2nd Edn (1938), p 84

a purpose which clearly appears from the will. Normally if both A and B die before
the liferenter the fee falls into residue. But that must depend on intention presumed **a**
or expressed and presumed intention must give way to expressed intention or
intention clearly to be inferred.

There is a further element in cases like the present case. The donor is under no
obligation to go on paying premiums. If he should cease to do so it must be the
duty of the trustee who holds the policy to realise what he can. If there is a surrender
value he may surrender and get a sum of money in his hands. If at that stage there **b**
were only one of the three named beneficiaries alive I do not think that we would be
forced by the terms of the destination to hold that still there could be no vesting
until the donor's death. In other words, there is no provision explicit or to be
implied that the gift to each of the three named beneficiaries is subject to a personal
condition that he must survive the donor before he can take.

Counsel could find no authority which throws light on this matter so it appears **c**
to me that I have to choose between making the law depend on technicalities and
making it depend on the intention of the donor appearing from the relevant source.
I have no doubt that vesting in the last survivor during the lifetime of the donor
would best carry out the donor's intention and I see no technical reason to prevent
me from so deciding. If that is right then there was no possible event in which
none of the three beneficiaries would take and the beneficial right to the policy would **d**
therefore belong to the donor. So Mr Barclay never had an interest and the appeal
must succeed.

I do not propose to deal with the third ground argued for the appellant further
than to say that I would find great difficulty in supporting it.

LORD MORRIS OF BORTH-Y-GEST. My Lords, in the Court of Session[1] it **e**
was agreed between the parties that the question at issue fell to be decided on the
basis that when on 4th January 1963 there was the payment of the first premium, a
policy or contract of life assurance came into being. It was agreed that it came into
being in terms of (a) a proposal form signed by Mr James Barclay dated 27th December 1962, containing statements declared to be true and complete, (b) a form of **f**
request by Mr James Barclay to the assurance society, and (c) a letter of acceptance
from the assurance society dated 31st December 1962. It was agreed that though the
form of request was in fact unsigned it was to be accepted as having been the request
of Mr James Barclay. It was as follows:

'MARRIED WOMEN'S POLICIES OF ASSURANCE (SCOTLAND) ACT 1880

'Form of request regarding the proposal for a Life Policy in my name dated **g**
————————

'I desire the Policy to be issued under the provisions of the Married Women's
Policies of Assurance (Scotland) Act, 1880, for the benefit of: My Son . . . Stuart
Lothian Barclay, whom failing My Son . . . Norman Veitch Lothian Barclay,
whom failing My Wife . . . Mrs Florence Winifred Lothian Barclay.
'I desire to appoint—————————————————— **h**

as Trustee(s) of the moneys payable under the policy dated this——————day of
————————————196—— .
'Signature of Proposer——————————————
'Address: 966 Great Western Road,
          Glasgow W2 **j**
'T.S.
'G.R.R.
'NORMAN VEITCH LOTHIAN BARCLAY, ROCKFORT, HELENSBURGH.'

1 [1974] STC 320

It being agreed that on the terms to which I have referred there was a policy of
a assurance it becomes necessary to consider the application and effect of s 2 of the
Married Women's Policies of Assurance (Scotland) Act 1880. I turn then to the
consecutive words of that section. Was there 'a policy of assurance effected by any
married man on his own life?' Undoubtedly there was. Was it 'expressed upon
the face of it to be for the benefit of his wife, or of his children, or of his wife and
children'? The answer would appear that it was. But here there lurks an enquiry
b which must be considered. The policy which we are considering is undoubtedly
expressed on the face of it to be for the benefit of Mr Barclay's wife or of his children
or of his wife and children. No others are mentioned as being persons for whom the
policy was issued. But what would be the position if a form of request though only
mentioning a wife and children was so worded that in events that could conceivably
happen there would not be complete provision for the devolvement of the benefit of
c the policy? To that question I must return.

Continuing to apply the wording of s 2, if there was a policy of assurance effected
by a married man on his own life and expressed on the face of it to be for the benefit
of his wife or of his children or of his wife and children then the section provides that
such policy 'shall, together with all benefit thereof, be deemed a trust for the benefit
of his wife for her separate use, or for the benefit of his children, or for the benefit of
d his wife and children'. So there would by statute be a deemed trust. The section then
goes on to provide that such a policy 'immediately on its being so effected, shall vest
in him and his legal representatives in trust for the purpose or purposes so expressed,
or in any trustee nominated in the policy, or appointed by separate writing duly
intimated to the assurance office'. Nothing arises in the present case as to the
nomination or identity of the trustee or trustees of the policy.

e Having dealt with the question as to the vesting of the policy in a trustee the section
then continues with the important words 'but in trust always as aforesaid, and shall
not otherwise be subject to his control, or form part of his estate, or be liable to the
diligence of his creditors, or be revocable as a donation, or reducible on any ground of
excess or insolvency'. There follow words which by common assent have no
relevance in the present case.

f From a consideration and application of the wording of the section it seems to me
to follow that if the policy in this case was 'expressed upon the face of it to be for the
benefit of his wife, or of his children, or of his wife and children' then a trust was
deemed to have come into existence. The policy vested immediately in the trustee
or trustees. They held the policy 'in trust always' as expressed on the face of the
policy. Unless Mr Barclay was himself a trustee the policy would not 'otherwise be
g subject to his control'. It would not 'form part of his estate'. It would be property
in which he 'never had an interest' (see s 4 of the Finance Act 1894). It would not
be aggregated with property passing on his death. I think, however, that the section
contemplates the situation where what is 'expressed upon the face of' the policy deals
with the entire benefit of the policy. The section uses the words 'together with all
benefit thereof'. So the result of what is expressed on the face of the policy must be
h that all the benefit of the policy must be 'for the benefit of his wife, or of his children,
or of his wife and children'. It will not do, therefore, if the matter is so left that the
'benefit' of the policy may pass for the 'benefit' of persons other than those within
the statutory words.

On this analysis it seems to me that the present case falls to be determined on a
consideration of the meaning and effect of the form of request. It constituted the
j terms of the trust. In that request Mr Barclay definitely stated and expressed his
desire that the policy was to be issued 'under the provisions of' the 1880 Act. He
contemplated the appointment of trustees who were to be trustees for the purposes
of s 2 of the 1880 Act. The question arises whether by some inadvertence or positive
error he failed to do what he undoubedly set out to do. There is no reason to
question his expressed desire which was that the policy that he was taking out was

to be held on trust for others with no right left in him to control it. He was expressly
saying (by stating that the policy was to be issued under the provisions of the 1880
Act) that the policy was not to be a part of his estate and was not to be liable to the
diligence of his creditors. So I think that the question that arises is whether the
words that he used in his form of request must when properly construed produce
the result that he failed to create a trust in which he had no interest; and that, contrary to his intention and desire, he set up a trust which in certain eventualities did
not prescribe any recipient of the trust property with the result that it would enure
for his or for his estate's benefit.

We are, of course, not concerned with the events that actually happened. The
policy came into being on 4th January 1963; Mr Barclay was then 77; he died on
31st January 1963. There probably was no difficulty in deciding who was to benefit
under the trust. But in considering whether Mr Barclay himself ever had 'an interest'
in the trust property it becomes necessary to consider whether there could have been
circumstances under which the disposition of the trust property was not provided
for by the terms of the trust; in other words might there have been some resulting
or remaining benefit which would be beyond and outside the benefit referred to in
the words 'for the benefit of his wife, or of his children, or of his wife and children'.

The eventuality to be considered is that of the death of both sons and of the wife
in the lifetime of Mr Barclay with variations of that eventuality dependent on the
various possible dates of the various deaths.

A policy which is issued under the provisions of s 2 vests in the trustees of the
deemed trust. The policy being one of life assurance, in normal circumstances the
time when the trustee would have to determine who was to benefit would be the
time of the ending of the life assured. Thereafter the trustee would receive the sum
assured. In some circumstances the time could be the time of the receipt of a surrender value. Taking the present case the trustee in normal circumstances would
have to consider the facts as they existed on whatever date it was that Mr Barclay
died. He would then have to carry out the trust terms. Were there any possible
circumstances under which the trustee would have to pay or account for the sum
assured to the personal representatives of or as part of the estate of Mr Barclay?
Interpreting the terms of the trust the trustee would first enquire whether Mr Stuart
Lothian Barclay was alive. If he was there would be no difficulty. If he was not
then the words 'whom failing' would apply. Those words would direct the trustee
to enquire whether Mr Norman Veitch Lothian Barclay was alive. If he was then
he would take. If he was not then the benefit would not pass to his estate because
in his case, as in the case of his brother the words 'whom failing' showed that the
taking of benefit was conditional on his surviving his father. If they were both dead
then the trustee would have to hold 'for the benefit of' Mrs Barclay. In reference
to her there was no provision covered by such words as 'whom failing'. There is a
marked contrast between the presence of those words in reference to the sons and
the absence of such words in reference to her. There was therefore no provision
requiring that in her case the benefit for her was conditional on her personal survival
to the date of Mr Barclay's death.

In my view, the policy and the sum payable under the policy were, in the event of
neither son being alive at the time of Mr Barclay's death, to be for the benefit of
Mrs Barclay, and in the absence of some provision introduced by such words as
'whom failing' that meant that the trustee was to hold for the benefit of Mrs Barclay
whether she was alive or not. If she was not alive her estate would take. That
would, in such eventuality, be the way in which it would be for her benefit. (See
Walker's Trustees v Lord Advocate[1].) It would make no difference whether she had
died before the sons or after.

If in the lifetime of Mr Barclay both sons and Mrs Barclay had died and if the

1 1955 SC (HL) 74

trustees and the insurance company knew such facts the position would merely be
a that in advance of the time of Mr Barclay's death they would know what would be
the disposition of the policy money when payable. They would know that there
would have to be accounting and payment to Mrs Barclay's estate. Mr Barclay, of
course, in that state of affairs could not vary the trust disposition.

In my view, the analysis of the words of the trust leads to the conclusion that Mr
Barclay did not fail to do what he clearly intended to do. Accordingly he never
b had any beneficial interest in the trust property. I would therefore allow the appeal.

VISCOUNT DILHORNE. My Lords, I have had the advantage of reading
the speeches of my noble and learned friends, Lord Reid and Lord Wilberforce, and
I agree with them that this appeal should be allowed.

The question at issue does not arise under any testamentary disposition of the late
c Mr James Barclay or in relation to any gift made by him in his lifetime. It arises
under a contract he entered into with the Sun Life Assurance Society Ltd. On 27th
December 1962 he submitted to them a proposal for the insurance of his life for
£45,000 under three policies of £15,000 each. The proposal was accompanied by
three requests to the Society that the policies should be issued under the Married
Women's Policies of Assurance (Scotland) Act 1880 for the benefit of his wife and his
d two sons. The request with which this appeal is concerned was that the policy should
be held for the benefit of his son Stuart, 'whom failing' his son Norman 'whom failing'
his wife. The other two requests named these three beneficiaries in different orders,
one that it should be held for the benefit of his son Norman, 'whom failing' Stuart,
'whom failing' Mrs Barclay, the other for Mrs Barclay 'whom failing' Norman,
'whom failing' Stuart.

e The insurance was to commence and did commence as soon as receipt of the first
premium was acknowledged by the issue of the society's official receipt. That happened on 4th January 1963. On 31st January 1963 Mr James Barclay died. So to
determine the terms of the contract between him and the society, one can only
look at the proposal and the request that accompanied it.

While I presume that the moneys due under the policy were after Mr James
f Barclay's death paid by the society to Stuart, directly or indirectly, for we were not
told that Stuart had not survived his father, the Crown contend that the late Mr
Barclay had not divested himself of all interest in the policy for they contend that if
his sons and his wife had died during his life, the right to dispose of the benefit of
the policy would have reverted to him. If they are right, the policy moneys will
have to be aggregated with the rest of Mr Barclay's estate with the result that estate
g duty will be payable at the rate of 75 per cent. On the three policies for £45,000 the
Crown claim £33,611·46 for duty and £7,551·09 in interest, in all £41,162·55. If
this appeal succeeds duty is only payable on the policy moneys at the rate of eight
per cent.

I think that the first question to consider is to whom the society were obliged under
their contract with Mr Barclay to pay the policy moneys on his death, ignoring for
h the moment that the policy was to be issued under the Married Women's Policies
of Assurance (Scotland) Act 1880.

It is clear beyond doubt that if Stuart was alive on his father's death, the moneys
would have had to be paid to him; that if he was not then alive but his brother was,
to his brother and if both sons were then dead, to Mrs Barclay. Payment to them
was conditional on their surviving their father. Payment to her was not conditional
j on her surviving her husband. In the event of the sons failing to take, the society
were under an obligation to pay her and no one else. If she also died before the
moneys became payable, I fail to see that they had any right or were under any
obligation to pay anyone else. In that event the moneys would on her husband's
death have been payable to her executors. I cannot see that under his contract with
the society any term is to be implied that in the event of all three dying before him,

Mr Barclay had any right to require the policy to be held for the benefit of anyone
else. So if the Crown's contention depended solely on the construction to be placed   *a*
on the contract, it would, in my opinion, fail for Mr Barclay did not have and never
had under the contract an interest in the policy.

It was not disputed that s 2 of the Act of 1880 applied to the insurance effected by
Mr Barclay. Under that section the policy—

> 'shall, together with all benefit thereof, be deemed a trust for the benefit of   *b*
> his wife for her separate use, or for the benefit of his children, or for the benefit
> of his wife and children'

and the policy immediately on its being effected is to vest in him and his legal representatives in trust for the purposes stated or in other trustees nominated or appointed
by him. The section goes on to provide that the policy shall not otherwise, i e save as   *c*
trustee,

> 'be subject to his control, or form part of his estate, or be liable to the diligence
> of his creditors, or be revocable as a donation, or reducible on any ground of
> excess or insolvency . . .'

The language is clear and unambiguous. Where a policy to which the section   *d*
applies is taken out, a trust is engrafted on the contract of insurance. It is a trust
for the 'purpose or purposes expressed' in the policy. In this case that has to be
interpreted as the purposes expressed in the contract of insurance. I see nothing in
the section to justify the conclusion that by virtue of it a term has to be read into the
contract giving Mr Barclay a right in the event of his wife and sons dying before him
to give directions to the society as to the disposal of the policy moneys. Indeed, the   *e*
provision that the policy is not to be subject to his control save as trustee and is not
to form part of his estate goes far to negative any such implication.

If, on a proper construction of the contract, it was the case that the payment to
Mrs Barclay was conditional on her surviving him, then it might be said that on her
death and that of her two sons in his lifetime, there was a resulting trust in favour of
Mr Barclay or there remained in him a radical right but I cannot see that the request   *f*
in this case is open to that construction.

My approach to this is somewhat similar to that of my noble and learned friend,
Lord Wilberforce, and I do not wish to add to his observations as to the relevance of
Cousins v Sun Life Assurance Society Ltd[1] and in particular of Romer LJ's judgment.
Nor do I wish to add anything, save to say that I agree with what he has said, about
the two Scottish cases to which he referred and about the Scottish law as to vesting   *g*
subject to defeasance.

In my opinion, this appeal should be allowed.

LORD WILBERFORCE. My Lords, the claim of the Crown is for estate duty
at the rate of 75 per cent on the proceeds of a policy of assurance for £15,000 taken   *h*
out by Mr James Barclay on his life shortly before his death. The rate of 75 per cent
applies if, and only if, the policy money has to be aggregated with the rest of his
estate. The appellant, who is entitled to the policy money as trustee, claims that it
should be treated as an estate by itself as being property in which the deceased
never had an interest (Finance Act 1894, s 4). So, did Mr Barclay have an interest in
the policy money? In the events which happened he had none since he was survived   *j*
by at least one of the beneficiaries, but it is not disputed that he must be treated as
having an interest if the trusts declared by him of the money fail to exhaust the
beneficial interests in it in any event which might have happened. As in similar

---

1 [1933] Ch 126, [1932] All ER Rep 404

cases (c f *Vandervell v Inland Revenue Comrs*[1], *Re Vandervell's Trust (No 2)*[2]) this issue
a gives rise to some rather refined arguments.

The form of request signed by Mr Barclay has already been set out as have the terms of s 2 of the Married Women's Policies of Assurance (Scotland) Act 1880. Two things can be said about these. First, there is similar legislation (Married Women's Property Act 1882, s 11) in England, and similar forms of request are used. The insurance company has, in fact, its principal office in London and does business *b* throughout the United Kingdom. The law as to estate duty is common to both legal systems. Therefore, the same result ought to be produced on whichever side of the border the policy is signed and it should not depend on niceties of the two countries' trust laws. Secondly, the destination of the policy money, the subject of the trust, is fixed by a combination of request and statute—a kind of hybrid mechanism not therefore necessarily to be governed by the rules applying to private trusts. Thus, *c* the disponer's simple request, which is expressed in popular language, is given its legal effect by s 2 of the 1880 Act. The initial phrase is satisfied since the policy is effected by a married man and is expressed on its face to be for the benefit of his wife and children. By force of the following provisions of the section, the policy, together with all the benefit thereof, is 'deemed a trust for the benefit of wife and children'; it vests immediately in the nominated or appointed trustees in trust as aforesaid. *d* Then follow imperative words: it shall not otherwise (i e except as trustee) be subject to his control, or form part of his estate.

My Lords, I accept at once, as did the appellant's counsel, that if the expressed purposes do not extend to the whole policy, or to the whole beneficial interest in the policy, the statutory trust would only operate over such part or such interest as would be included in the purposes expressed. But where, as here, the expressed *e* purposes extend to the whole policy, and where the disponer's apparent intention was that wife and children should have the whole beneficial interest, the statute, in my understanding, operates in aid and, if necessary, in reinforcement of that intention.

There is one case, at least, in which this seems to be so, the case, which cannot be very uncommon, where the designated beneficiary dies before the date of payment, *f* i e (normally) before the death of the disponer. Such a case must, in one way or the other, be governed by the statutory words—either his estate must be allowed to take, and be protected, or it must not. Indeed, this case has come before the courts. In England the Court of Appeal had to consider the situation where a husband effected policies under the English Act of 1882 for the benefit of his wife named therein and the wife predeceased him (*Cousins v Sun Life Assurance Society*[3]). Reversing the decision *g* of Eve J and doubting, if not overruling, previous decisions in England and Ireland, the Court of Appeal held that the policy passed to the wife's personal representatives as part of her estate. Lord Hanworth MR said that an absolute interest was taken by her by virtue of the statute and a trust created in her favour. (It is true that the English s 11 contains a phrase 'so long as any object of the trust remains unperformed' which is not present in the Scottish enactment, but I am unable to perceive that the *h* absence of these words gives rise to any difference in result—at least any difference against the interest of his wife.) Romer LJ[4] said this:

'In the policies themselves I cannot find the remotest indication that the husband intended the wife's interest to be contingent on her surviving him. If he had so wished nothing was easier than for him to have said so in the policies *j* themselves . . . there was a trust created in favour of the named wife . . .

1   [1967] 1 All ER 1, [1967] 2 AC 291, 43 Tax Cas 519
2   [1974] 3 All ER 205, [1974] 3 WLR 256
3   [1933] Ch 126, [1932] All ER Rep 404
4   [1933] Ch at 140, [1932] All ER Rep at 410

that trust did not come to an end on her death, but persisted and remains to be
performed in favour of her personal representative.'   a

The lord justice's comment is applicable—a fortiori—to the present case, since
words of survivorship were used in relation to the sons and deliberately not used
in relation to the wife.

In Scotland there are two relevant authorities.   In *Haldane's Trustees v Lord
Advocate*[1] policies were effected by a father for the benefit of three children.   Each b
policy was for the benefit of one child if living at the date of his father's death, but, if
that child was not then living, for the benefit of such of the other two children as
should then be alive, and, if none of his three children should be living at that date,
the whole benefit of the policy was to vest absolutely in the last of such children to die.
It was held by the Second Division that if all three children predeceased the father
the benefit of each policy would vest absolutely in the last survivor.   c

In *Walker's Trustees v Lord Advocate*[2] the policies were similar to those in *Haldane's
Trustees v Lord Advocate*[1] but differed in that the final destination carried the policies
to the benefit of the estate of the last to die.   This House held that holding for his
estate of a deceased child was holding for the benefit of that child within the meaning
of s 2.

My Lords, I appreciate that the present case may be seen to differ from each of the d
three authorities I have mentioned.   It differs from *Cousins v Sun Life Assurance Society*[3]
in that here the interest of his widow is preceded by contingent gifts to the two sons
and may be said not to emerge until they are dead.   It differs from *Haldane's Trustees
v Lord Advocate*[1] and *Walker's Trustees v Lord Advocate*[2] in that the person to whom
the absolute interest is given (the named wife) might not be the last survivor, but
might be the first or second of the three to die.   But, in my opinion, the sense of these e
decisions is clear in showing that the intention of the Act is to enable a wife (or a child)
to take the benefit of a policy effected under it, provided that the donor's intention
to benefit her (or him) is not clearly limited or circumscribed, whether or not she
(or he) survives the donor and that a gift which would carry the benefit of the policy
to her (or his) estate is within the purpose of the section.

We heard an interesting argument on the Scottish law as to vesting subject to f
defeasance.   I admired its intricacies and I am willing to believe that there are difficulties under the Scottish law of gifts in defining the wife's interest under this policy
as either a vested gift, or as a gift vested subject to defeasance.   Such difficulties would
not arise in English law.   But I do not think that these specialities ought to dictate
the decision in the present case, and for that reason I do not think it is necessary
for us to reconsider *Hicks v Inland Revenue Comrs*[4] in which the argument which g
I would accept in this appeal was apparently not developed.   In my opinion, the
words of the section warrant an untechnical approach such as would best give effect
to donors' wishes, and I think that the trend of court decisions in Scotland and in
England endorses this.   I understand that all of your Lordships are in agreement
that this is the right approach, though there is some powerful support for the view
that, in the event of all the named beneficiaries predeceasing the donor, the last h
survivor or his or her estate would take.   I would say no more as to this than that a
choice between this result and that which I would—with all deference—favour
would, if necessary, have to be made in a suit between the competing beneficiaries;
it does not need to be made here and now because either solution excludes any interest
of the donor.   The appeal, in my opinion, must succeed.
                                                                                        j

---

1 1954 SC 156
2 1955 SC (HL) 74
3 [1933] Ch 126, [1932] All ER Rep 404
4 [1973] STC 406

LORD KILBRANDON. My Lords, the late Mr Barclay made provision for his
a wife and sons by taking out simultaneously with the same underwriters three policies
of assurance, which he required to be written under the terms of the Married
Women's Policies of Assurance (Scotland) Act 1880. We are concerned with one of
those policies only, namely, that which was to be issued for the benefit (to put the
provision shortly) of the assured's son Stuart, whom failing his son Norman, whom
failing his wife. We have now to decide whether the proceeds of the policy must
b be aggregated with the estate of Mr Barclay for the purposes of estate duty, or whether
they constitute a separate estate which is not so to be aggregated. That depends on
whether this policy, or its proceeds, constitutes an estate in which Mr Barclay in his
lifetime had an interest. If so, it is so aggregable. It is conceded that Mr Barclay
had an interest in the estate represented by the policy, if in any situation which could
arise during his lifetime that estate could, despite the trusts which he had imposed
c on it, have reverted to him free of those trusts. It is not necessary for me further
to resume the terms of the statutes or of the instructions given by Mr Barclay, all of
which have already been set out.

I would like to begin by looking briefly at a historical background. The 1880 Act
was passed at a time when revolutionary changes were being made in the relationship
between husband and wife, so far as this was concerned with property rights and
d obligations hinc inde. The rule as to donations inter virem et uxorem in the old law
was stated by Erskine[1] as follows:

> 'All deeds, whether granted by the wife to the husband, or by him to the wife,
> are indeed valid; but may, both by the Roman law and ours, be revoked or
> avoided by the donor, at any time of his or her life; lest either of the two spouses
e should, by ill-judged testimonies of their affection, undo themselves or their
> families.'

Fountainhall went further and applied the rule also to ante-nuptial gifts, '*inter
sponsum et sponsam in aestu amoris* . . . there being a greater eclipse of the use of
reason at that time than afterwards'. But aliter in Stair[2]. A gift to a wife which was
f revocable became, of course, available on his insolvency to the husband's creditors,
who could call on him to reverse a transaction which, while lawful, was not
necessarily permanent.

On the other hand, one of the marital duties of a husband was to provide for the
sustentation of his wife. In many spheres of life, that obligation might have been
discharged by his giving to her a share of the accommodation and aliment which
was appropriate to their own social standing. But in the case where a better provision
g was warranted, it was encouraged by the law inasmuch as it was recognised as being
irrevocable if given in good faith and not on an obviously exorbitant scale; it thus
became, in contrast to the mere donation, protected from the consequences of the
husband's indebtedness or insolvency. One of the important features of this distinction was, that a policy of insurance, taken out by a husband, who was liable in the
h premiums, the proceeds being payable to his wife, was regarded as a provision for the
benefit of the wife, not as a donation in her favour. As such, it was unattachable by
the husband's creditors, even if he may have been at the time he took out the policy
vergens ad inopiam. This was decided by the House of Lords in *Galloway v Craig*[3];
it does not appear, from the posthumous speech of Lord Campbell LC, that the fact
that the destination of the policy was to the wife and her heirs had any influence on
j the result. It is therefore, as it seems to me, impossible to accept a suggestion that
was made on behalf of the Crown, namely, that, since a primary purpose of the
Act was to provide to the wife a protected fund, little or no conclusion can be drawn,

1 An Institute of the Law of Scotland (8th Edn, 1871), bk I, tit V, para 29
2 Institutions of the Law of Scotland (5th Edn, 1832), bk I, tit IV, para xviii
3 (1861) 4 Macq 267

in an estate duty question, from the fact that the machinery adopted consisted of the
creation of a separate estate.   The Act clarified and in some sense extended the a
common law, inasmuch as a statutory policy could not be challenged for 'excess', i e
exorbitance, but it did not for the first time make it possible for a husband to make
for his wife a provision by means of a policy of assurance on his own life, which was
inaccessible to his creditors.

The controversy before us was in the end really refined to this: whether, had Mr
Barclay's wife and sons predeceased him, the policy being still in force, he could b
have called on the trustee of the policy to denude in his favour.   Would the trust
purposes have failed, leaving the radical right in him, unencumbered? If the answer
is in the affirmative, it is conceded that the policy was property in which Mr Barclay
had an interest.   It is also conceded that, in the contingency figures, the wife must
predecease at least one of the sons, otherwise she, both sons being dead, would be
left with an indefensible vested interest, on the authority of *Cousins v Sun Life* c
Assurance Society[1], which in its turn would be inconsistent with a radical right
remaining in the assured.

Such a problem, being fundamentally one of vesting, was inevitably related in
argument to the situation, illustrated in innumerable reported cases, where a
testator makes a provision in liferent, then in fee either to survivors in a class or to
successive institutes conditionally upon survivorship.   The analogy is a fair one to a d
certain extent, because the trusts such as we are here concerned with are not revocable
before the policy matures, as is a testamentary deed before the death of the grantor,
so that mors testatoris in the case of a testamentary trust is in some sense comparable
with the date of the writing of the policy.   What would in a testamentary trust be
vesting a morte testatoris becomes to that extent comparable with vesting in the
life-time of the assured.   On the other hand, the principles which the courts have e
laid down for determining the time of vesting of interests conferred mortis causa
can have no higher status than this: the court declares that the use of a particular
form of words by a testator indicates that he had the intention that a particular
result should follow.   Such a man's estate is not distributed according to judge-made
rules; it is distributed in accordance with the intention expressed by him in his testa-
ment, as that intention is deduced by the court from the language used by him therein f
and by others like him in time past.

The situation in the present controversy is special.   The truster has expressed his
intention with particularity and with reference to the language of the statute.   I
pause to observe that by our somewhat technical rules of construction or of evidence
other even clearer expressions of his intention must—what might surprise a layman
—be disregarded.   After stating the trust purposes on which the policy is to be held, g
namely, for the benefit of his sons and widow, he goes on to state purposes on which
it is not to be held, namely, that except insofar as he exercises the office of trustee,
it is not to be subject to his control or to form part of his estate.   It is difficult to
figure language more apt to declare his intention that he was to have no interest in
the policy, and it is against that declaration, contrasted with the words of any testamentary declaration with which the cases make one familiar, that one is to judge of h
the duties of the trustee of the policy in the imaginary contingency on which the
Crown are here bound to rely.

There is one difficulty in coming to a conclusion on the analogy of the testamentary
trust.   The truster, as I have explained, is to be treated as analogous to a deceased
testator.   In the contingency figured, does the fee (to which the policy has been
equiparated by analogy) vest in the representative of the last surviving son, or of the j
representative of the widow, or does it fall into intestacy? It is only if the last of those
questions be answered in the affirmative that the Crown here succeed.   The effect of a
survivorship clause or a destination-over in a testamentary disposition as postponing

---

1   [1933] Ch 126, [1932] All ER Rep 404

vesting to the time of payment is hardly in doubt. It is set out in Henderson on Vesting[1] (a work of high authority). In the present case, however, the question whether, on the emergence of a last survivor before the date of payment, vesting in him is necessarily accelerated, although survivorship of the term of payment had been made a condition of his taking, on the ground that the individuality of the last survivor is by then settled, was not properly before us, as it would have been in the kind of competition I have just envisaged. I prefer to express no opinion on it, since in the view I have formed of this appeal it is unnecessary either so to do, or to review the large number of cases which were cited to us. I will only say that, while I have no doubt of the correctness of the decision in *Dickson's Trustees v Elliot*[2], the dictum of Lord Strachan therein[3] which was relied on in *Hicks v Inland Revenue Comrs*[4] cannot be accepted as a rule to which there are no exceptions.

The view which I take of the present case is this. We have to assume that Mr Barclay is alive, predeceased by both his sons, one or both of whom was predeceased by Mrs Barclay. What, then, on that assumption would be the duty of the trustee of the policy? I will also assume in favour of the Crown, though by no means deciding, that they could not hold the policy for the benefit of the representatives of the last surviving son, since the provision to both sons was fettered by a condition of survivorship of the date of payment. On the provision for Mrs Barclay, however, there was no such fetter; if after her death the trustee could continue to hold for her benefit, I think he would be obliged to do so. It was decided in *Walker's Trustees v Lord Advocate*[5] that one of the modes in which trustees may hold a policy under the 1880 Act for the benefit of a named beneficiary, he having predeceased the date of maturity, is to hold for his estate. In my opinion, it follows that the trustees could not denude in favour of the assured, but would be obliged to hold for the wife's estate, thereby contradicting any radical right in the assured, who accordingly could not in his lifetime have any interest in the policy. This gives effect to his plainly expressed intention, and to the evident policy of the 1880 Act.

My Lords, I would therefore allow this appeal. I should add that I would have decided *Hicks v Inland Revenue Comrs*[4] differently; as was pointed out by Lord Keith in the present case, however, the argument which, in my opinion, here succeeds was not put forward in the earlier case.

Appeal allowed.

Solicitors: *Wilkinson, Kimbers & Stadden*, agents for *Nightingale & Bell*, SSC, Edinburgh, and *Tindal Oatts & Rodger*, Glasgow (for the appellant); *Solicitor of Inland Revenue.*

Gordon H Scott Esq Barrister.

1 2nd Edn (1938), pp 45-49
2 1949 SLT 359
3 1949 SLT at 359
4 [1973] STC 406
5 1955 SC (HL) 74

William Skelton & Son v Harrison & Pinder Ltd   *a*

QUEEN'S BENCH DIVISION
HIS HONOUR JUDGE FAY QC
23rd, 24th, 25th, 26th, 30th JULY 1974   *b*

Landlord and tenant – Lease – Underlease – Term of underlease – Underlease for whole term of lease operating as assignment – Reversion sufficient to support underlease – Indefinite but defeasible term – Business premises – Term continuing after date of expiry by virtue of statute – Term liable to be determined by notice – Underlease for term expiring after date of expiry of lease – Whether sufficient reversion to support underlease.   *c*

Landlord and tenant – Business premises – Continuation of tenancy – Severance of reversion – Notice to determine – Part of premises ceasing to be protected – Tenants of business premises subletting part of premises – Sub-tenants occupying part for business purposes – Sub-tenants acquiring lease from landlord of their part of premises to commence on expiry of tenants' term – Right of sub-tenants after expiry of tenants' lease to give tenants notice to quit part   *d* *of premises occupied by sub-tenants – Law of Property Act 1925, s 140(1) – Landlord and Tenant Act 1954, ss 23(1), 24(3)(a).*

The plaintiffs were lessees of a factory under a 21 year lease ('the headlease') from S which was due to expire on 26th April 1970. The plaintiffs occupied the factory for the purposes of their business. In 1962 S and the plaintiffs desired to grant to the   *e* defendants a 21 year lease of part of the factory. For that purpose it was agreed that the plaintiffs should execute an underlease of that part to the defendants for a term to expire three days before expiry of the headlease and that S would execute a lease ('the reversionary lease') to the defendants commencing on the expiry date of the headlease for the balance of the 21 years. The grant of the reversionary lease was conditional on the underlease not having been determined otherwise than by   *f* effluxion of time at the date when the reversionary lease was to commence. By mistake the documents as executed provided for the termination of the underlease and commencement of the reversionary lease on 26th May 1970 instead of 26th April 1970. The defendants went into and at all times remained in occupation of their part of the factory for the purposes of their business. On 15th October 1969 the plaintiffs served a notice on the defendants under s 25 of the Landlord and Tenant Act 1954   *g* purporting to terminate the defendants' tenancy from 24th June 1970. Without prejudice to their contention that the notice was invalid, the defendants served a counter-notice under the 1954 Act but no application to the court for the grant of a new tenancy was made. On 27th March 1972 the defendants, purporting to act as the plaintiffs' landlords under the reversionary lease, served on the plaintiffs a notice under s 24(3)(*a*)[*a*] of the 1954 Act terminating from 1st July 1972 the plaintiffs' tenancy   *h* of the part of the factory occupied by the defendants. The plaintiffs brought two actions against the defendants: in the first they claimed possession of the part occupied by the defendants, mesne profits and dilapidations and rectification of the underlease by substituting a reference to 26th April for the reference to 26th May; and, in the second, declarations that the reversionary lease had never taken effect, and that the defendants' notice under s 24(3)(*a*) was of no effect, on the ground that by virtue of   *j* Part II of the 1954 Act the headlease and underlease had continued after the dates on which they would otherwise have expired and the latter had been determined on 24th June 1970 by virtue of the notice under s 25. The defendants contended,

---

a   Section 24(3), so far as material, is set out at p 190 *e*, post

a   inter alia, that since the underlease was for a term longer than the headlease it
operated as an assignment.

Held – (i) The unrectified underlease did not take effect as an assignment for, at the
time of the underlease, the plaintiffs had a term which, although expressed as a
term certain in the instrument, would continue indefinitely by virtue of Part II of
the 1954 Act, defeasible by notice given under Part II. That indefinite but defeasible
b   reversion of the plaintiffs was sufficient to support the underlease, and, therefore,
rectification was unnecessary (see D 187 *d* to *g*, post); *Oxley v James* (1844) 13 M & W
204 applied.

(ii) The reversionary lease had taken effect on 26th May 1970 since on that date the
underlease had not expired otherwise than by effluxion of time. On coming into
effect the reversionary lease had severed the reversion on the headlease in respect of
c   that part of the factory occupied by the defendants. In consequence of that severance
the plaintiffs' tenancy of the defendants' part of the factory ceased to be one which
included premises occupied by the plaintiffs for the purposes of their business, within
s 23(1)[b] of the 1954 Act, and furthermore the defendants were entitled, under s 140(1)[c]
of the Law of Property Act 1925, to give notice to the plaintiffs in respect of that part
of the factory as if it 'had alone originally been comprised in' the headlease. Since the
d   plaintiffs did not occupy any of that part of the factory they had, on the severance
taking place, ceased to be protected under Part II of the 1954 Act. Accordingly the
notice given by the defendants under s 24(3)(*a*) was valid, the plaintiffs' interest in
the defendants' part of the factory had ceased and the plaintiffs were in occupation
pursuant to the reversionary lease. The plaintiffs' action therefore failed, save for
the claims to mesne profits and dilapidations (see p 189 *c* and *g*, p 190 *c* and *g* and
e   p 191 *j* to p 192 *d*, post); *Jelley v Buckman* [1973] 3 All ER 853 distinguished.

Notes

For notices under Part II of the Landlord and Tenant Act 1954, see 23 Halsbury's
Laws (3rd Edn) 888-890, paras 1710, 1711, and for cases on the subject, see 31(2)
Digest (Reissue) 949, 950, 7742-7745.
f   For severance of the reversion, see 23 Halsbury's Laws (3rd Edn) 660, 661, para
1380, and for cases on the subject, see 31(2) Digest (Reissue) 747-750, 6169-6192.
For the effect of an underlease for the whole term, see 23 Halsbury's Laws (3rd
Edn) 477, 478, para 1102, and for cases on the subject, see 31(1) Digest (Reissue)
181-184, 1521-1547.
For the Law of Property Act 1925, s 140, see 27 Halsbury's Statutes (3rd Edn) 556.
g   For the Landlord and Tenant Act 1954, ss 23, 24, 25, see 18 Halsbury's Statutes (3rd
Edn) 555, 557, 559, 571.

Cases referred to in judgment

Bolton (H L) (Engineering) Co Ltd v T J Graham & Sons Ltd [1956] 3 All ER 624, [1957]
1 QB 159, [1956] 2 WLR 844, CA, 31(2) Digest (Reissue) 944, 7722.
h   *Bowes-Lyon v Green* [1961] 3 All ER 843, [1963] AC 420, [1961] 3 WLR 1044, HL, 31(2)
Digest (Reissue) 941, 7712.
Cornish v Brook Green Laundry Ltd [1959] 1 All ER 373, [1959] 1 QB 394, [1959] 2 WLR
215, CA, 31(2) Digest (Reissue) 967, 7800.
Curtis v Wheeler (1830) 4 C & P 196, Mood & M 493, NP, 31(2) Digest (Reissue) 184,
1540.
j   *Dendy v Evans* [1910] 1 KB 263, [1908-10] All ER Rep 589, 79 LJKB 121, 102 LT 4, CA,
31(2) Digest (Reissue) 810, 6715.
Jelley v Buckman [1973] 3 All ER 853, [1974] QB 488, [1973] 3 WLR 585, CA.

---

b   Section 23(1), so far as material, is set out at p 190 *g*, post
c   Section 140, so far as material, is set out at p 189 *j* to p 190 *b*, post

Milmo v Carreras [1946] 1 All ER 288, [1946] 1 KB 306, 115 LJKB 278, 174 LT 223, CA, 31(1) Digest (Reissue) 183, *1531*. ***a***

Oxley v James (1844) 13 M & W 209, 13 LJEx 358, 3 LTOS 222, 153 ER 87, 31(1) Digest (Reissue) 157, *1365*.

Pike v Eyre (1829) 9 B & C 909, 4 Man & Ry KB 661, 8 LJOSKB 69, 109 ER 338, 31(1) Digest (Reissue) 187, *1579*.

Walsh v Lonsdale (1882) 21 Ch D 9, 52 LJCh 2, 46 LT 858, CA, 31(1) Digest (Reissue) 78, *594*. ***b***

Action

By a writ issued on 3rd September 1970 the plaintiffs, William Skelton & Son Ltd, brought an action against the defendants, Harrison & Pinder Ltd, claiming possession of part of factory premises which the plaintiffs had let to the defendants by an under-lease made on 8th March 1963, on the ground that the tenancy created by the under-   ***c***
lease had been determined by notice pursuant to s 25 of the Landlord and Tenant Act 1954. The plaintiffs also claimed mesne profits and damages for breach of repair-ing covenants contained in the underlease. By their amended statement of claim, the plaintiffs claimed a declaration that the habendum of the underlease ought to be construed so as to refer to 26th April 1970 in place of 26th May 1970, alternatively, an order for rectification. By a writ issued on 3rd August 1972 the plaintiffs brought a   ***d***
second action against the defendants claiming declarations (1) that a deed dated 8th March 1963 between Walter Skelton and the defendants whereby Walter Skelton had agreed to grant the defendants a lease of the same part of the factory premises to commence on 26th May 1970 had never taken effect, and (2) that a notice from the defendants to the plaintiffs purporting to terminate the plaintiffs' tenancy of the same part of the factory premises under s 24(3)(a) of the 1954 Act was of no effect.   ***e***
By their defence in the first action the defendants denied that the plaintiffs were their landlords so as to be competent to give notice under s 25 of the 1954 Act in respect of the underlease. The two actions were heard together. The facts are set out in the judgment.

f

J Finlay QC and *Bernard Marder* for the plaintiffs.
Ronald Bernstein QC and *Christopher Priday* for the defendants.

Cur adv vult

30th July. **JUDGE FAY QC** read the following judgment. These two cases, which were tried together, arise out of certain leases of a factory at 66 and 68 Waldeck Road,   ***g***
Chiswick. The factory is owned by one Walter Skelton. He was, and is, a director of a family company, William Skelton & Son Ltd, the plaintiffs in both actions. In 1949 he let the factory to his company, by a lease which I shall refer to as the headlease, for a term of 21 years from 26th April 1949. This headlease was thus due to expire in April 1970.

In 1962 Mr Skelton and the plaintiffs wished to find a tenant for part of the factory,   ***h***
comprising about one-third of its ground floor area. Negotiations took place with Harrison and Pinder Ltd, the defendants, who wished to occupy that part for their business as signmakers. The negotiations were conducted between Mr Walter Skelton on the one part, and Mr Gerald Golding, a director of the defendant com-pany, on the other part. Mr Skelton offered a 21 year tenancy. Mr Golding wanted a shorter term, but Mr Skelton insisted and got his way. He was a man of firm   ***j***
character according to Mr Golding in evidence. The parties settled on a 21 year tenancy. The matter was then passed to the solicitors for each side. One firm repre-sented both Mr Skelton and the plaintiffs. The conveyancing was complicated by the fact that the property to be let was part of the premises comprised in the head lease which had then eight years to run. Apparently the solicitors considered a surrender

by the plaintiffs of the relevant part, leaving the way clear for Mr Skelton to grant a
a 21 year lease. But this was not found to be feasible. By a letter dated 19th November
1962 the solicitors for the plaintiffs and Mr Skelton wrote:

> 'It is not possible at this stage to grant the entire term from Mr. Walter Skelton
> on a surrender of the Company's Lease, as there are intermediary incumbrances.
> There is, however, no question of the title of the Company to grant the said
> *b*   Sub-Lease.'

The alternative chosen was that there should be two instruments, first an underlease by the plaintiffs to the defendants from 1st December 1962 to a date intended
to be three days less than the plaintiffs' term under the head lease and, secondly,
a reversionary lease from Mr Skelton from a date intended to be the date of expiry
in 1970, of the headlease until 29th September 1983. The rental was £1,200 per
c annum under both instruments. These instruments, which I shall call the underlease and the reversionary lease, were duly executed and the defendants went into
occupation. The plaintiffs were, and are, in occupation of the rest of the factory
for the purposes of their printing business.

The defendants may be forgiven for having thought, at this stage, that they had
security of tenure for 21 years. Unfortunately the underlease and the reversionary
d lease contained two major blemishes. The first blemish was caused by the plaintiffs'
solicitor getting it into her head that the headlease expired on 26th May 1970 and
not, as was the fact, on 26th April 1970. Her draft underlease provided by its
habendum for a term 'until the Twenty sixth day of May 1970 (less three days)'.
The defendants' solicitor did not inspect the headlease, but assumed from the draft
that 26th May 1970 was its expiry date. The error went undetected, and the instru-
e ments, when executed, provided for an underlease to 26th May 1970, less three days,
and for a reversionary lease from 26th May 1970. These dates were of course one
month after the true expiry of the headlease. The other blemish arose from the
fact that neither solicitor spared a thought for the effect of the Landlord and Tenant
Act 1954 on the transaction.

I have seen the two solicitors concerned—Mr Leonard Dark, a partner in the
f defendants' solicitors' firm, and Miss Anne Amphlett who conducted the conveyancing on behalf of Miss Storey the principal of the firm acting for Mr Skelton and the
plaintiffs. Mr Dark said that he had no idea that the reversionary lease might be a
species of trap. He thought the two instruments had the same effect as a lease for 21
years. Miss Amphlett said, 'the fact that the Landlord and Tenant Act might nullify
the second document was not present in my mind'. She had no idea how the error
g in the date had crept in. In the letter of 19th November 1962, from which I have
already quoted, she said:

> 'We enclose herewith draft of a Sub-Lease to be granted by our clients, Wm
> Skelton & Son Ltd., who hold under a Lease which expires in 1970. Our Client,
> the Freeholder, Mr. Walter Skelton, would, however, be prepared to grant a
> *h*   direct Lease to your Clients to start at the expiration of the said term . . .
> We are not sending with this letter a draft of the Lease to be granted by the
> Freeholder to avoid delay, but the same would be substantially on the same
> terms as the draft submitted herewith.'

It was the draft of the underlease which gave Mr Dark the impression that the head
lease expired one month later than it in fact did. And, in my view, he was fully
j justified in drawing that inference from the draft and that accompanying letter.
The next matter which I need record is that the defendants were, on occasions, late
with their rent payments, and on 25th April 1969 the plaintiffs issued a writ claiming
possession, on forfeiture, for non-payment of the rent due on 25th March 1969, within
21 days. The rent and costs were paid and the action abandoned.

Now, the changeover from underlease to reversionary lease was due to take place in May 1970, but on 15th October 1969 the plaintiffs served a notice under s 25 of the Landlord and Tenant Act 1954, purporting to terminate the tenancy from the plain- *a* tiffs to the defendants on 24th June 1970. Without prejudice to the contention that the notice was invalid, the defendants served a counter-notice on 27th November 1969 stating that they were unwilling to give up possession. This is ordinarily a prelude to an application to the court for a new lease, but the defendants have not so applied. Had they done so, of course, a new lease granted by the court would have been at a current rent; and rents have risen considerably between 1962 and 1970. They *b* preferred to take their stand on the rights they thought they had under the reversionary lease.

Much later, on 27th March 1972, the defendants served on the plaintiffs a notice under s 24(3)(a) of the 1954 Act, terminating on 1st July 1972, the tenancy of the plaintiffs which— say the defendants—the plaintiffs held of them by virtue of the reversionary lease. The defendants, I may add, remain to this day in occupation of *c* their part of the factory.

The plaintiffs now bring these two actions. By the first, commenced in 1970, the plaintiffs claim possession of the premises, mesne profits and dilapidations. And, by an amendment, they claim a declaration that on the proper construction of the underlease the habendum ought to be construed and read, 'without any order for rectification', as though a reference to 26th April 1970 was substituted therein for 26th *d* May 1970, and, in the alternative, an order that the said habendum, that is to the underlease, be rectified by substituting for the reference therein to 26th May a reference to 26th April.

Under the second action, the plaintiffs claim declarations, firstly, that the reversionary lease has never taken effect; alternatively, that the notice given under s 24(3)(a) is of no effect. In outline, the plaintiffs' case is that by virtue of Part II of the *e* 1954 Act both the headlease and the underlease were continued after the expiry dates expressed in the documents; that the headlease is still in being, since nothing has occurred to determine it, and that the underlease was brought to an end on 24th June 1970, by virtue of the notice under s 25.

The defendants, on the other hand, advanced two separate lines of argument. The first is that since the underlease was for a longer term than the headlease, owing to the *f* error of a month, it operated as an assignment; that in consequence the defendants were from the outset tenants of Mr Skelton, and that the plaintiffs had no right to give the s 25 notice. The plaintiffs meet this argument by claiming rectification, alterna- tively, that, as a matter of interpretation, the word 'May' be read as 'April' in the underlease, alternatively, by asserting that the effect of Part II of the 1954 Act is to give a sufficient reversion to the plaintiffs to support the underlease so that it does not *g* have effect as an assignment. The defendants' other argument is that the reversionary lease, when it came into force, severed the reversion expectant on the plaintiffs' tenancy so that from that date the plaintiffs held the part of the factory they occupied from Mr Skelton, and the defendants' part from the defendants. This, say the defendants, takes the plaintiffs' tenancy of the defendants' part out of the protection of the 1954 Act, and opens the way for service of a notice under s 24(3)(a). In addition *h* to joining issue on the law, the plaintiffs claim to meet this point by referring to a proviso in the reversionary lease which, they say, has prevented it from coming into force at all. I will deal, in order, with these issues.

The defendants' first line of attack depends on the underlease not being rectified either by court order or by interpretation. It is the clearest possible case of mutual mistake, not less so because it originated with the plaintiffs' own solicitors. Prima *j* facie I think it is a clear case for rectification. Counsel for the defendants says, however, that no equitable remedy should be granted in this case, because the plaintiffs come to the court without the necessary clean hands. He says that Mr Skelton and the plaintiffs have been acting in concert to defeat the bargain they made, and that equity should not assist them.

I have some sympathy with this submission. In essence, the plaintiffs are seeking to
a avoid their own bargain by relying on a mistake of law; and there may be rough
justice in allowing the defendants to defeat them by relying on the other mistake as
to the date. I need not pursue this matter into these difficult regions however,
because I have reached the conclusion that even if unrectified the underlease does not
operate as an assignment. The doctrine that an underlease for longer than the
underlessor's own term operates as an assignment, was reaffirmed in *Milmo v Carreras*[1].
b In that case the underlessor had no reversion, but it was held in *Oxley v James*[2] that a
tenant from year to year has a sufficient reversion to enable him to sublet for a term
of years; see per Pollock CB[3]:

> 'It is clear, according to the cases of *Pike* v. *Eyre*[4] and *Curtis* v. *Wheeler*[5], that, if a
> tenant from year to year demises for a term of years, and the original tenancy
c   from year to year lasts beyond that term, such a demise is not an *assignment*, but
> there is a reversion, on which covenant may be maintained.'

Parke B[6] referred to the matter as the grantor not assigning the whole of his interest,
which was an indefinite period, subject to determination by notice to quit from his
landlord. Counsel for the plaintiffs submits, I think correctly, that a tenant of business
premises has a similar term for an indefinite period.
d   At the time of the underlease, in *Oxley's* case[2], the underlessor had a term which
would continue indefinitely, defeasible by notice given by either landlord or tenant.
At the time of the underlease in the present case the plaintiffs had a term which,
although expressed as a term certain in the instrument, would by operation of Part II
of the 1954 Act continue indefinitely, defeasible by notice under Part II. It is to be
observed that, even if events occurred which caused the tenancy to cease to be pro-
e tected by the Act, it would continue until terminated by notice: see s 24(3) which I
shall have to consider later.
   I can see no difference, in principle, between this kind of indefinite but defeasible
reversion, and that in *Oxley's* case[2]. It is not as though the contractual tenancy ceases
and is replaced by a new statutory tenancy. The Court of Appeal has decided that
under Part II of the 1954 Act the common law tenancy subsists, with a statutory varia-
f tion as to mode of determination (*H L Bolton (Engineering) Co Ltd v T J Graham & Sons
Ltd*[7] and *Cornish v Brook Green Laundry Ltd*[8]). For these reasons I hold that the unrectified underlease does not have effect as an assignment, and for this reason the
defendants' first line of argument fails. In these circumstances it would be idle to
consider rectification, and I shall not grant that remedy.
   I turn to the argument based on the reversionary lease. Counsel for the plaintiffs
g claims that this fails in limine because the lease never took effect; this was because it
was subject to a condition precedent which was not satisfied. Here I must mention that
although, for convenience, I have been calling this instrument a reversionary lease it
was in fact an agreement for a reversionary lease. It was by deed, and it had been
stamped with the duty appropriate to a lease. I apprehend that I must treat it as a
reversionary lease, in equity, following the well-known doctrine of *Walsh v Lonsdale*[9].
h Clause 1 reads in part:

> 'SUBJECT to a lease dated the 8th day of March 1963 and made between
> WM SKELTON & SON LTD (1) RONALD GODFREY GOLDING (2) and GERALD DENNIS

---

1   [1946] 1 All ER 288, [1946] 1 KB 306
2   (1844) 13 M & W 209
j 3   13 M & W at 214
4   (1829) 9 B & C 909
5   (1830) 4 C & P 196
6   13 M & W at 215
7   [1956] 3 All ER 624 at 626, [1957] 1 QB 159 at 168
8   [1959] 1 All ER 373 at 382, [1959] 1 QB 394 at 409
9   (1882) 21 Ch D 9

GOLDING (3) not having been terminated other than by effluxion of time and to *a*
the Agreement and other matters mentioned in Clause 2 hereof and in consideration of the Rent and Covenants hereinafter reserved and contained and on
the part of the Tenants to be paid performed and observed the Landlord hereby
agrees to demise . . .'

The material words are 'subject to a lease' (which, although inaccurately described
as to its parties, is the underlease)—subject to that lease not having been terminated *b*
other than by effluxion of time. And those words are repeated in cl 6(4) which reads:

'PROVIDED always that this Deed is subject to the said Lease dated the
day of   One thousand nine hundred and Sixty Three not having been
terminated other than by effluxion of time and if such Lease shall have been
terminated as aforesaid then this Agreement shall not take effect and everything
herein shall be null and void.'   *c*

Again, although the date is not filled in, in this carelessly drafted document, there is
no dispute that it is the underlease which is referred to. Counsel for the plaintiffs'
argument is that the writ for possession, which was issued on 25th April 1969,
represented an election by the plaintiffs to accept the forfeiture worked by non-
payment of rent, and, that from that moment, the underlease was at an end and, *d*
within the terminology of the proviso, had been terminated otherwise than by
effluxion of time; and thus the reversionary lease was avoided.

With the first part of his argument I agree; the issue of the writ signifies the lessor's
intention to determine. But what followed the service of the writ is relevant. The
defendants at once paid the overdue quarter's rent and costs, and the matter was
settled without even appearance being entered. On 30th April 1969 the defendants' *e*
solicitors wrote as follows:

'We refer to our conversation with you on the telephone this morning when
we informed you that we had been instructed by the Defendants. It appears
that the Defendants changed their Accountants recently and in so doing the fact
that the rent was due on the 25th March last was overlooked. Our Clients have *f*
no intention of avoiding their obligation. We accordingly enclose our cheque for
£311.15.0d. being as to £300.0s.0d. the arrears of rent, and £11.15.0d. the costs of
the Writ. We confirm that you informed us that in the circumstances your
Clients would not press for forfeiture and the payment would be accepted in
satisfaction of the claim and that it was unnecessary for us to enter an Appearance
to the Writ on behalf of the Defendants. Would you please acknowledge receipt *g*
of the enclosed cheque and confirm this agreement.'

On 5th May 1969 the plaintiffs' solicitors replied:

'We thank you for your letter dated 30th April and cheque. We confirm that
our clients will not press for forfeiture and that payment is accepted in satisfaction
of the claim and costs. We understand that your clients have now been in direct *h*
touch with Messrs. Skelton & Co. and that they are now arranging to pay the
rent which will be due in June by banker's order and thereafter to make a regular
monthly payment by banker's order of £100. This arrangement will be very
agreeable to our clients and they are going to let us have a copy of Messrs. Harrison
& Pinder's letter informing them of the arrangement.'

In my judgment, the effect of this settlement was to waive the forfeiture. In such a *j*
case a court could, and certainly would, have granted relief against the forfeiture, and
here the parties by their settlement are doing precisely that. Where the court grants
relief against forfeiture—I quote Woodfall[1]—'the effect is for all purposes and between

---

1   Law of Landlord and Tenant (27th Edn, 1968), vol 1, p 913, para 1959

all parties to do away with the forfeiture just as if there had never been any'. In
a *Dendy v Evans* Farwell LJ said[1]:

'The forfeiture is stopped in limine; so that there is no question of any destruction of an estate which has to be called into existence again.'

What the court can do by decree the parties can do by agreement, and I find they
have expunged the forfeiture; this point fails. Counsel for the plaintiffs also sought
b to rely on the revised arrangement mentioned in the letter which I have cited, for
rents to be payable monthly instead of quarterly, as some support for the view that
the old underlease had gone and a new one with new terms had sprung up. This
variation seems to me to be a neutral fact. Such an arrangement could equally operate
as a variation of the old lease, and I do not think it affects the matter one way or the
other. It follows that the deed containing the reversionary lease was effective on 26th
c May 1970, the day when the reversionary lease was expressed to commence. On that
date the underlease had not been determined otherwise than by effluxion of time; indeed
it had not been determined at all although a notice under s 25 was then running.
Counsel for the plaintiffs argued that one must consider the effect of the proviso as at
some later date after expiry of the notice to quit. I see no reason to do this other than
by following a line of argument which was at one time advanced, but was abandoned.
d This derived from the character of the instrument as an agreement only, and would
distinguish *Walsh v Lonsdale*[2]. Counsel for the plaintiffs, on instructions, expressly
abandoned this argument after certain correspondence had been referred to, and I say
no more about it. I hold that on 26th May 1970 the defendants became tenants of
Walter Skelton of the premises described in the reversionary lease. This does not however mean that the defendants were entitled to occupancy. As from this date there
e existed four interests in the property. At the bottom of the structure stood the defendants, occupying by virtue of their underlease not yet then determined under
Part II of the 1954 Act. Their immediate landlords were the plaintiffs who, in turn,
held from the defendants, and the defendants held from Walter Skelton, the freeholder. As regards the rest of the factory, the plaintiffs still held from Walter Skelton
under the headlease. What has happened is that the coming into force of the rever-
f sionary lease has severed the reversion expectant on the headlease so that, in popular
parlance, the plaintiffs, from that moment, had two landlords, although holding
under one lease.

I now come to the nub of counsel for the defendants' argument on this second
branch of his case. He says that the severance of the reversion as governed by s 140
of the Law of Property Act 1925 has put an end to the application of Part II of the
g 1954 Act to this part of the tenancy, and that this fact brings into play s 24(3)(*a*) of
that Act, under which effective notice to quit may be given. This is the notice which
the defendants gave to expire on 1st July 1972. As from that date, says counsel for the
defendants, the plaintiffs' interest is gone and the defendants' occupation is an occupation under what I have called the reversionary lease, but which, as from that date,
ceased to be reversionary.
h In order to deal with these submissions I must look, first, at the statutory provisions.
Section 140 of the Law of Property Act 1925 reads as follows:

'(1) Notwithstanding the severance by conveyance, surrender, or otherwise of
the reversionary estate in any land comprised in a lease, and notwithstanding
the avoidance or cesser in any other manner of the term granted by a lease as to
j part only of the land comprised therein, every condition or right of re-entry,
and every other condition contained in the lease, shall be apportioned, and
shall remain annexed to the severed parts of the reversionary estate as severed,

---

1 [1910] 1 KB 263 at 270, 271, [1908-10] All ER Rep 589 at 593
2 (1882) 21 Ch D 9

and shall be in force with respect to the term whereon each severed part is reversionary, or the term in the part of the land as to which the term has not been   *a*
surrendered, or has not been avoided or has not otherwise ceased, in like manner
as if the land comprised in each severed part, or the land as to which the term
remains subsisting, as the case may be, had alone originally been comprised in
the lease.

'(2) In this section "right of re-entry" includes a right to determine the lease by
notice to quit or otherwise; but where the notice is served by a person entitled   *b*
to a severed part of the reversion so that it extends to part only of the land
demised, the lessee may within one month determine the lease in regard to the
rest of the land by giving to the owner of the reversionary estate therein a counter
notice expiring at the same time as the original notice . . .'

I need not read s 140(3).

The effect of the first two subsections is to provide that the right to determine the   *c*
lease by a notice to quit remains annexed to the severed part of the reversionary
estate, that is the defendants' interest, in like manner as if the defendants' part of the
factory had alone originally been comprised in the lease. So the defendants are entitled
to give to the plaintiffs, in respect of the defendants' portion of the factory, whatever
notice the lease—that is the headlease as modified by Part II of the 1954 Act—permits.   *d*
Section 24(3) of the 1954 Act provides:

'Notwithstanding anything in subsection (1) of this section—(*a*) where a tenancy
to which this Part of this Act applies ceases to be such a tenancy, it shall
not come to an end by reason only of the cesser, but if it was granted for a
term of years certain and has been continued by subsection (1) of this section then
(without prejudice to the termination thereof in accordance with any terms of the   *e*
tenancy) it may be terminated by not less than three nor more than six months'
notice in writing given by the landlord to the tenant . . .'

I need not read para (*b*). The notice given in this case complied as to length with this
provision. The crux of the matter is whether the head tenancy, which was one to
which Part II of the 1954 Act applied, has ceased, quoad the defendants' part of the   *f*
factory, to be such a tenancy. Counsel for the defendants says that the severance of the
reversion has effected that cesser of protection. He says that, because by s 23(1), a
tenancy to which Part II applies—which I shall call a protected tenancy—is one—

'where the property comprised in the tenancy is or includes premises which are
occupied by the tenant and are so occupied for the purposes of a business carried
on by him or for those and other purposes.'   *g*

By virtue of the two words 'or includes' the plaintiffs initially enjoyed protection as
regards the whole factory, because they occupied a part. But now they have a separate landlord of the severed part, and of that part they occupy none. So, says counsel,
they have lost protection and the way is open for the s 24(3)(*a*) notice.

Counsel for the plaintiffs' rejoinder is to cite the recent case in the Court of Appeal,   *h*
Jelley v Buckman[1]. That was a case under the Rent Acts where land had been let
together with a dwelling-house. The reversion to the land had become severed from
the reversion to the dwelling-house. The Court of Appeal rejected the argument that,
by reason of the severance, the land had ceased to be land let together with the dwelling-house, and held that the whole still enjoyed the protection of the Rent Acts.
Stamp LJ, giving the judgment of the court said[2]: 'In our judgment, however, a   *j*
severance of the lessor's reversion by conveyance does not bring two separate tenancies
into being' and, after dealing with s 140 of the Law of Property Act 1925, he said[3]:

1   [1973] 3 All ER 853, [1974] QB 488
2   [1973] 3 All ER at 855, [1974] QB at 496
3   [1973] 3 All ER at 856, 857, [1974] QB at 498

a   'But it is one thing to say that each reversioner has rights and remedies similar
     to or even indistinguishable from the rights and remedies which he would have
     had if there had been two separate tenancies and quite another thing to say that
     this operates against the tenant and that he therefore has two tenancies; and we
     cannot read s 140 as producing the latter result. We can find nothing in the section
     to suggest for a moment that the legislature intended that following a severance
     to which the lessee was not a party, he should find himself holding part of his land
b   under one tenancy and part under another.'

     Now I see the force of counsel for the plaintiffs' contention that just as the severed
     land in *Jelley v Buckman*[1] was still let together with the remainder so here, in the
     words of s 23(1) of the 1954 Act, the tenancy is still, notwithstanding the severance,
     one which includes premises occupied for business purposes. If the question I had to
c   decide was whether the two parts of the tenancy are let together with one another, the
     matter would be concluded in the plaintiffs' favour. But that is not what I have to
     decide. The question here is whether or not the defendants may serve a s 24(3)(*a*)
     notice. There are words in s 140 of the Law of Property Act 1925 which govern notices.
     It may be significant that the 1954 Act, although it contains detailed provisions cover-
     ing some specific situations such as ss 28 and 44 as to future tenancies and reversionary
d   leases, has no specific provision as to the problem of the severed reversion. In passing
     the 1954 Act, Parliament must be taken to have had the provisions of the earlier Act
     in mind; and it may well be that the 1954 Act contains no special provision because
     the matter is adequately covered by s 140 of the 1925 Act.
     In any event s 140 clearly applies, and I must examine what it says about terminating
     a tenancy. Section 140(2) defines a 'right of re-entry' to include a right to determine a
e   lease by notice to quit or otherwise. Section 140(1) provides, among other things, that
     every right of 're-entry' shall be in force 'in like manner as if the land comprised in
     each severed part . . . had alone originally been comprised in the lease'. Some meaning
     has to be given to these words. In the light of the 1954 Act there are three situations
     affecting the method of terminating the tenancy: firstly, it may never have been pro-
     tected, in which case the rights of re-entry are those to be found in the relevant lease;
f   secondly, it may have been protected, and may have lost protection, in which case the
     right of re-entry is that provided by s 24(3)(*a*); thirdly, it may continue to be protected;
     in which case the right of re-entry is that provided by s 25.
     This cannot be the first case, since the plaintiffs enjoyed protection at one time
     because the relevant part of the factory was let together with the part they occupied.
     This may also be so because they may have, themselves, occupied this part before the
g   underlease to the defendants. Whether or not they did so was not stated in evidence.
     Can this be the last case of the three, as counsel for the plaintiffs claims? If this is
     right the defendants can only terminate by a s 25 notice, and this contemplates a
     counter-notice, and an application by the tenant for a new tenancy. But he cannot get
     a new tenancy because the court, unless the landlord agrees otherwise, can only grant
     a new lease of the holding (s 32(1)) and the holding is defined in s 23(3) as excluding
h   any property not occupied by the tenant. The plaintiffs do not occupy, and thus
     cannot obtain a new lease. While it is true that a s 25 notice would then effec-
     tually bring the tenancy to an end it is a clumsy method and does not seem to me to
     be what the Act intends s 25 to be used for. Its true use is as the opening move to-
     wards the grant of a new tenancy. But if this is the second case these difficulties
     disappear. And it is the second case, in my judgment, if full effect is allowed to be
j   given to the words in s 140(1): 'in like manner as if the land comprised in each severed
     part . . . had alone originally been comprised in the lease.'
     This is a deeming provision; one must assume a hypothetical lease of the rele-
     vant land alone. But this is not occupied by the plaintiffs, and is not protected. But

───

1   [1973] 3 All ER 853, [1974] QB 488

it once was, before the coming into force of the reversionary lease, and it seems to
me that I here find the cesser of which s 24(3)(a) speaks. For purposes other than this *a*
deeming no doubt the fact that there is but one tenancy means that the two parts of
the land are still let together. But for the purposes of rights of re-entry the deeming
provision is required to be applied. And it seems to me that I could not adopt counsel
for the plaintiffs' submission without ignoring that deeming provision. This, in my
judgment, is what distinguishes the present case from *Jelley v Buckman*[1]. Moreover it
explains why there is no special provision in the 1954 Act as to severed reversions. *b*

I should mention that the recent House of Lords case of *Bowes-Lyon v Green*[2] was
cited. The chain of leasehold interests in that case bears a startling similarity to that
in the present case. But it decided an entirely different point, and does not touch the
issues in this case.

My finding on this part of the case, therefore, is that the notice under s 24(3)(a) was
good, and that the plaintiffs' interest in the defendants' part of the factory has ceased. *c*
The defendants are in occupation pursuant to the reversionary lease. The effect of my
findings is that the plaintiffs' claims in both actions are dismissed, save as regards their
claims to mesne profits and dilapidations. The parties sensibly agreed to postpone
consideration of these until after my judgment on the major issues was known.
These two claims subsist, and in case they need to be tried I reserve them to myself.

d

Plaintiffs' claims in both actions dismissed save for the claims to mesne profits and damages.

Solicitors: *Faull, Best & Knight* (for the plaintiffs); *Jacobson, Ridley* (for the defendants).

e

Janet Harding Barrister.

---

1   [1973] 3 All ER 853, [1974] QB 488
2   [1961] 3 All ER 843, [1963] AC 420

Wolkind v Ali

QUEEN'S BENCH DIVISION

LORD WIDGERY CJ, BRIDGE AND SHAW JJ

4th NOVEMBER 1974

Approved in SIMMONS V PIZZEY [1977]
2 All ER 432

Housing – Overcrowding – Lodgings – Premises used as lodging house – Notice by local authority – Notice limiting number of persons permitted to sleep on premises – Premises subsequently ceasing to be used as lodging house – Premises used as home for members of one family – Members of family sleeping on premises exceeding number permitted by notice – Whether notice limiting number of persons permitted to sleep on premises still valid when premises no longer used as lodging house – Housing Act 1957, s 90(1)(4).

In 1967 the respondent occupied the ground and basement floors of a house. He used those premises as a lodging house. The premises comprised two rooms on the ground floor and two rooms in the basement. On 9th June the local authority served a notice on the respondent under s 90(1)[a] of the Housing Act 1957. The effect of that notice was to limit to two the number of persons who were permitted to sleep in either of the two rooms on the ground floor of the premises and to prohibit the use as sleeping accommodation of either of the two rooms in the basement. The restrictions imposed by the notice were observed by the respondent until 1973 when he was joined by his large family from abroad. From that time the premises were no longer used as a lodging house but were occupied solely by the respondent's family. On 24th July 1973 the respondent was convicted by the justices under s 90(4) of the 1957 Act of causing the ground floor rooms to be occupied otherwise than in accordance with the notice in that the front room of the ground floor was occupied as sleeping accommodation by the respondent's four sons, and the back room was so occupied by the respondent, his wife and ten year old daughter. The respondent appealed to the Crown Court and his appeal was allowed. The prosecutor appealed to the Divisional Court.

Held (Lord Widgery CJ dissenting) – Where a notice under s 90(1) of the 1957 Act had been served on the occupier of premises which were being used as a lodging house, restricting the number of persons who might be permitted to occupy those premises, the offence of contravening the notice could only be committed under s 90(4) so long as the premises continued to be premises of a kind to which s 90(1) applied, i e a house let as lodgings or occupied by members of more than one family. Since the premises had ceased to be used as a lodging house when the respondent's family came to live there, the respondent was not guilty of the offence charged and the appeal would therefore be dismissed (see p 197 *c* to *f*, post).

Notes

For the control of overcrowding in houses let as lodgings or occupied by more than one family, see 19 Halsbury's Law (3rd Edn) 614, para 992.

For the Housing Act 1957, s 90, see 16 Halsbury's Statutes (3rd Edn) 184.

Cases cited

Attorney-General v Beauchamp [1920] 1 KB 650.

Reed v Hastings Corpn (1964) 62 LGR 588, CA.

Case stated

On 24th July 1973 the justices for the Inner London Area acting in and for the petty sessional division of Thames heard two informations laid by the appellant, Jack

---

a Section 90, so far as material, is set out at p 194 *f* to *j*, post

H

Wolkind, Town Clerk, on behalf of the London Borough of Tower Hamlets. The
first information alleged that on 17th April 1973 at 15 New Road (ground floor) within *a*
the borough the respondent, Nimar Ali, having been served with a notice dated 9th
June 1967 by the Tower Hamlets borough council did unlawfully cause the ground
floor front room of the premises to be occupied as sleeping accommodation otherwise
than in accordance with the notice, contrary to s 90 of the Housing Act 1957 and s 20
of the Housing Act 1961. The second information alleged a similar offence on the
same date, but in respect of the ground floor back room of the premises. The *b*
justices found the respondent guilty of both offences and ordered him to pay a fine
of £20 in respect of each information. The respondent appealed to the Crown
Court. The appeals were heard by the court sitting at Inner London Sessions House,
Newington Causeway, London, SE1, on 19th October 1973. The appeals were
allowed and the convictions quashed. The appellant requested the court to state a
case for the opinion of the High Court. The facts are set out in the judgment of *c*
Bridge J.

J Blair-Gould for the appellant.
A Williams for the respondent.

d

BRIDGE J. This is a respondent's appeal by case stated from a decision of the
Crown Court for Inner London given on 19th October 1973 which allowed an appeal
by the respondent in this court, Mr Nimar Ali, against his conviction by a magistrates' court of an offence charged against him under the provisions of s 90 of the
Housing Act 1957 of unlawfully causing the ground floor front room of certain premises to be occupied as sleeping accommodation otherwise than in accordance with *e*
a notice which had been served on him under s 90 of the Housing Act 1957.
   It is convenient to refer at once to the relevant legislation before coming to the
facts of the case. Section 90 of the Housing Act 1957 re-enacts a provision originally
introduced into the corpus of housing legislation for the first time as s 12 of the
Housing (Repairs and Rents) Act 1954. Section 90(1) provides as follows:

   'If it appears to a local authority, in the case of a house within their district, *f*
   or of part of such a house, which is let in lodgings or occupied by members of
   more than one family, that excessive numbers of persons are being accommodated on the premises having regard to the rooms available, the local authority
   may serve on the occupier of the premises or on any person having the control
   and management thereof, or on both, a notice—(*a*) stating, in relation to any
   room on the premises, what is in the authority's opinion the maximum number *g*
   of persons by whom it is suitable to be occupied as sleeping accommodation at
   any one time, or, as the case may be, that it is in their opinion unsuitable to be
   occupied as aforesaid, and (*b*) informing him of the effect of subsection (4) of
   this section.'

Subsection (3) gives a right of appeal against the restrictions imposed by the notice *h*
to the county court. Then sub-s (4) provides:

   'Any person who has been served with a notice under this section shall be
   guilty of an offence if, after the notice has become operative,—(*a*) he causes or
   knowingly permits any room to which the notice relates to be occupied as
   sleeping accommodation otherwise than in accordance with the notice...'
                                                                                j

Subsection (5) provides the penalties for an offence committed under the section, and
sub-s (6) deals with withdrawal and re-service of notices under the section and other
such matters.
   What happened in the present case was that back in 1967 the respondent was in
occupation of the ground and basement floors of a house known as 15 New Road,

London, E1, and was at that time using those premises as a lodging house. The
a premises comprised two rooms on the ground floor and two rooms in the basement.
On 9th June 1967 the local authority, the appellant before us today, served a notice
on the respondent under s 90. The effect of that notice, which there is no doubt
conformed to and complied with the Act at the time of service, was to limit to two
persons the number of persons who could be permitted to sleep in either of the two
rooms on the ground floor of the premises and to prohibit the use as sleeping
b accommodation of either of the two rooms in the basement.

Presumably the restrictions imposed by the notice were observed by the respondent
during the period of time, some six years or more, that these premises continued to
be used by him as a lodging house. But in February 1973 that state of affairs came
to an end for the good reason that the respondent was joined by his large family
from Bangla Desh.

c On 17th April 1973, which was the date of the offence charged against him in the
information, the occupation of the premises on the ground floor and basement of
this house was such that the front room on the ground floor was occupied by four
persons, namely, the respondent's four sons, and the back room on the ground floor
was occupied again also as sleeping accommodation by three persons, the respondent,
his wife and his ten year old daughter.

d The prosecution proceeded on the footing, and succeeded before the justices at
petty sessions on the footing, that that state of affairs was in contravention of the
notice under s 90 of the 1957 Act and, therefore, represented the commission of an
offence by the respondent under s 90(4).

Before turning to the main arguments on which this appeal depends, it is right to
mention that in 1969, by s 58 of and Sch 8 to the Housing Act 1969, the provisions of
e s 90 of the 1957 Act were amended in such a way that in the amended form of the section sub-s (1) now reads: 'If it appears to a local authority, in the case of a house within
their district, which is occupied by persons who do not form a single household . . .'
For my part, however, I am not persuaded that that amendment is of any relevance
for the purposes of the present appeal since this prosecution was for the contravention
of the provisions of a notice served under, and taking effect under, the unamended
f provisions of the section as it stood before 1969.

The point in the appeal, which in the end is a very short one, is simply this. Read
literally, the language of s 90(4), according to its ordinary grammatical meaning,
and if not subject to any qualification, clearly leads to the conclusion that the respondent on the day in question, by permitting his family to occupy the ground floor
rooms of the premises in the numbers they did, was committing an offence in that he
g was knowingly permitting a room to which the 1967 notice related to be occupied
as sleeping accommodation otherwise than in accordance with the notice. That was
the basis on which the magistrates' court convicted him. That is the basis on which
we are invited by the appellant to say that his conviction should be restored.

The Crown Court on the appeal from the magistrates' court took the opposite
view. They state their opinion to that effect without elaboration, and the basis on
h which they reached their conclusion is as a matter of inference by looking at the
effect of s 90 in the context of the legislation in which it is found.

It is found in Part IV of the Housing Act 1957, which is concerned with abatement
of overcrowding, and ss 76 to 89 may be said all to be concerned with the control
of overcrowding in dwelling-houses generally. The most important provisions at
the heart of the code for the control of overcrowding which apply to any ordinary
j dwelling-house in single occupation, or dwelling-house units in single occupation,
are ss 77 and 78.

I will read s 77(1):

'A dwelling-house [and I pause to observe in passing that that, by the definition
in s 87, means "any premises used as a separate dwelling by members of the
working classes"] shall be deemed for the purposes of this Act to be overcrowded

at any time when the number of persons sleeping in the house either—(*a*) is
such that any two of those persons, being persons ten years old or more of oppo-   *a*
site sexes and not being persons living together as husband and wife, must sleep
in the same room; or (*b*) is, in relation to the number and floor area of the rooms
of which the house consists, in excess of the permitted number of persons as
defined in the Sixth Schedule to this Act.'

Sub-s (2) provides: *b*

 'In determining for the purposes of this section the number of persons sleeping
 in a house, no account shall be taken of a child under one year old, and a child
 who has attained one year and is under ten years old shall be reckoned as one-half
 of a unit.'

Then by s 78(1):   *c*

 'Subject to the provisions of this Part of this Act, if the occupier or the landlord
 of a dwelling-house causes or permits it to be overcrowded, he shall be guilty
 of an offence. . .'

The subsequent provisions of the Act to which the words 'Subject to the provisions
of this Part of this Act' draw attention provide many exemptions from liability for   *d*
a state of statutory overcrowding in a single dwelling-house which may arise in
contravention of the mathematical limitations laid down in s 77 in conjunction with
Sch 6.

It is unnecessary to go through all of them but, to take one example of what I may
call a statutory exemption, s 78(3) provides:

                                                                                  e
 'Where a dwelling-house which would not otherwise be overcrowded becomes
 overcrowded by reason of a child attaining one of the ages referred to in the last
 foregoing section, then, if the occupier applies to the local authority for suitable
 alternative accommodation or has so applied before the date when the child
 attains that age, he shall not be guilty of an offence.'

It seems to me that the Crown Court must have thought, and I think, that when   *f*
one compares the statutory code for controlling overcrowding in dwelling-houses
generally with the very different code specially provided for controlling overcrowding
in lodging houses under s 90, it is evident that the latter was never intended to apply
to any premises except for so long as they were let in lodgings or occupied by members
of more than one family.

It will be observed that under s 77 what determines the point at which the numbers   *g*
of persons sleeping in a house pass the limit and the house becomes overcrowded is a
precise mathematical criterion laid down by the Act, whereas under s 90 the criteria
to be applied in the case of lodging houses are entirely at the discretion of the local
authority, subject to appeal to the county court. Again the way in which children
under a certain age are to be treated in the calculations required to arrive at an
answer to the question, 'Is the single private dwelling house overcrowded?' is pre-   *h*
cisely laid down in s 77(2), whereas in s 90(2) again the special criteria applicable in
the case of persons under a certain age may be such as the local authority think
appropriate.

If the argument addressed to the court by counsel for the appellant were right, it
would lead to this, to my mind, remarkable and anomalous situation. A notice   .
having been served on the occupier of premises at a time when those premises   *j*
were in use as a lodging house would continue to apply so as to restrict the numbers
of persons who may be permitted to occupy those premises after it had ceased to be
a lodging house, with the result that whereas Mr Smith living in one half of a semi-
detached house in a suburban road could legitimately house his whole family in it
without committing any offence under s 78 of the 1957 Act, Mr Brown next door,

occupying a house of identical size with a family of identical size to Mr Smith's,
a would be committing a continuing offence under s 90 by reason only of the historical
accident that at some remote date in the past he had used his premises for a short
period to let out to lodgers, and during that period had been the recipient of a notice
under s 90, which the local authority had subsequently refused to withdraw. That,
to my mind, would be such an absurd situation that I am not prepared to reach the
conclusion that that was a result intended by the legislature unless compelled to do
b so by the language of the Act.

As I have said, and I appreciate the force of the argument which is based on it,
s 90(4) of the 1957 Act, if read quite literally and without qualification, does produce
that result. Nevertheless it seems to me that this is one of those cases where one
looks at a subsection in the context of the whole legislation in which it is found, and
if it is necessary to cut down the ambit of the language used in order to prevent
c absurdity or an anomaly, then the language should be cut down. The restriction
on the operation of s 90(4) to my mind which is appropriate is a restriction which
limits the ambit of that subsection so that an offence can only be committed in contravention of a notice served under s 90(1) so long as the house continues to be a house
of a kind to which s 90(1) applies; that is to say, in its unamended form, a house or
part of a house let in lodgings or occupied by members of more than one family,
d and in its amended form, a house which is occupied by persons who do not form
a single household.

For those reasons I have reached the conclusion that the Crown Court was right to
allow this appeal by the respondent from his conviction in the magistrates' court and
I would dismiss the appeal to this court.

e **SHAW J.** I agree with the judgment which has just been delivered and for the
reasons stated by Bridge J. I would only add that for myself I find some support for
the view which he has expressed in the fact that at the time the informations were
laid against the respondent the notice under s 90 in its amended form would not have
been competent at all. I, too, would dismiss the appeal.

f

LORD WIDGERY CJ. On this very short point I take the opposite view. Section
90(1) details precisely the circumstances which must exist before a notice under the
section can be served, and it is not disputed that in this case those conditions were
satisfied at the date of the service of the notice. Given that, in my judgment one
has no further occasion to come back and look at the language of s 90(1) at all.
g If the notice is a valid notice when given, and in this instance it was, its consequence,
as I see it, is to be found in s 90(4), which is in perfectly plain and unambiguous
language and contains no suggestion of the interpretation which Bridge J would
put on it.

I can appreciate the anomaly which presently exists, or which would exist, if my
view were accepted by the court, because it is true that on the local authority's sub-
h missions in this case the respondent would be subject to the more stringent restrictions by virtue of the notice having been served than to the restrictions which would
have applied under earlier sections of the Act to a single family dwelling-house.

I do not feel that Parliament necessarily applied its mind to this problem at all,
or that if it had done so, it would have taken a different view. This legislation is of a
kind which is often unenforceable unless expressed in clear terms, and I can well
j understand that Parliament might have hesitated to limit the effect of s 90(4) and
produce a situation in which a breach of the Act would or would not occur from day
to day according to the precise type of individual residing on the premises.

Under s 90(6) the local authority has power to withdraw the notice given under the
section, and the only amendment to the Act which I would like to see would be a
provision requiring the local authority to withdraw a notice once it is established that

the initial circumstances justifying its circumstances no longer apply. But in the absence of such a provision, it seems to me the language here is too strong, and for *a* my part I would allow the appeal. In fact the appeal is dismissed.

Appeal dismissed.

Solicitors: *Edward Fail, Bradshaw & Waterson* (for the appellant); *Gerston & Co* (for the respondent).   *b*

Lea Josse Barrister.

Mountford and another v Scott

COURT OF APPEAL, CIVIL DIVISION
RUSSELL, CAIRNS LJJ AND SIR JOHN PENNYCUICK
16th, 17th OCTOBER 1974

Specific performance – Option – Option to purchase freehold land – Option granted gratuitously or for token consideration – Equity will not assist a volunteer – Exercise of option by purchaser – Exercise of option constituting contract of sale for agreed sum – Sum constituting adequate consideration – Refusal of vendor to complete – Whether purchaser entitled to specific performance or confined to remedy in damages.

The defendant was the owner of a dwelling-house. He signed an agreement with the plaintiffs whereby, in consideration of the sum of £1, he granted the plaintiffs an option to purchase his house at the price of £10,000. Subsequently the plaintiffs gave notice exercising the option. The defendant refused to complete the sale and the plaintiffs brought an action for specific performance. The judge held that the plain- *f* tiffs were entitled to the order sought on the ground that an option to purchase land constituted an equitable interest in land and it was immaterial that it had been granted gratuitously or for a token payment. The defendant appealed contending, inter alia, that, since the consideration for the grant of the option was a token payment equity would not enforce the contract, and that the plaintiffs should therefore have been left to their remedy in damages.   *g*

Held – The option agreement constituted an irrevocable offer to sell and once the plaintiff had accepted that offer by exercising the option, a contract had come into being for the sale of the house for £10,000. It was that contract which the court was being asked to enforce and the fact that the consideration for the option could be described as a token consideration was irrelevant to the question of the appropriate *h* remedy under the contract of sale. The appeal would therefore be dismissed (see p 200 *j*, p 201 *b* to *e* and p 202 *f* and *g*, post).

Decision of Brightman J [1974] 1 All ER 248 affirmed on different grounds.

Notes
For options to purchase, see 23 Halsbury's Laws (3rd Edn) 470-472, paras 1090-1093, *j* and 34 ibid 206, 207, para 345, and for cases on the subject, see 31(1) Digest (Reissue) 160-170, *1403-1455* and 40 ibid 54, *347, 348.*

Case referred to in judgments
Gilchrist Vending Ltd v Sedley Hotel Ltd (1967) 66 DLR (2d) 24.

Cases also cited
a Baker v Monk (1864) 4 De J & Sm 388.
   Clark v Malpas (1862) 4 De GF & J 401, 45 ER 1238.
   Evans v Llewellin (1787) 1 Cox Eq Cas 333, 29 ER 1191.
   Fry v Lane, Re Fry, Whittet v Bush (1888) 40 Ch D 312, [1886-90] All ER Rep 1084.
   Longmate v Ledger (1860) 2 Giff 157; affd 4 De GF & J 402.
   Vivers v Tuck (1863) 1 Moo PCC NS 516, 15 ER 795, PC.
b Worthing Corpn v Heather [1906] 2 Ch 532, [1904-7] All ER Rep 530.

Appeal
By an agreement in writing dated 12th December 1971 the defendant, Calvin Scott,
granted to the plaintiffs, Frederick William Mountford and Hilda Beatrice Mountford, in consideration of the sum of £1 an option to purchase the freehold property
c known as 49 Enmore Road, South Norwood, London, SE25, at a price of £10,000.
The option was to be exercised by notice in writing to the defendant at any time
within the period of six months from the date of the agreement. On the exercise
of the option the plaintiffs were to pay to the defendant's solicitors, as stakeholders,
a deposit of £1,000, and the sale of the property was to be completed, unless otherwise agreed in writing, on the first day after the expiration of six weeks from the
d date of the exercise of the option. By letter dated 29th March 1972 the plaintiffs'
solicitors served on the defendant formal notice exercising the option. The letter
also requested the defendant to instruct his solicitors to deal with the sale of the
property, and to advise the plaintiffs' solicitors of the name and address of his
solicitors so that the deposit of £1,000 might immediately be sent to them. No reply
to the letter was received from the defendant. On 2nd May 1972 the plaintiffs'
e solicitors again wrote to the defendant referring to their previous letter and repeating
the request. No reply to that letter was received from the defendant. The defendant
subsequently denied that the agreement was binding on him and refused to perform
it or take any steps to complete the sale to the plaintiffs of the property.
   By a writ issued on 11th May 1972 the plaintiffs brought an action against the defendant claiming specific performance of the contract for the sale of the property con-
f stituted by the option agreement and the exercise in writing of the option thereby
granted by the letter of 29th March 1972 and, further or alternatively, damages for
breach of contract. On 24th May 1973 Brightman J[1] held that an option to purchase
land constituted an equitable interest in land, it being immaterial that the option
had been granted gratuitously or for a token payment; that when the option agreement had been signed, therefore, the plaintiffs had acquired an equitable interest in
g the defendant's property and that, accordingly, subject to the payment of the purchase
price, the plaintiffs were entitled to a decree of specific performance. The defendant
appealed.

Harry Narayan for the defendant.
I H Maxwell for the plaintiffs.
h

RUSSELL LJ. This case is reported below[1] and reference may be made to the
reports for the details of the case. Counsel, who has argued the case for the defendant
with courtesy and candour allied to pertinacity, has taken a number of points, some
attacking the validity of the option agreement itself, and a final point, in the alterna-
j tive, if the option agreement be valid, asserting that specific performance should not
be ordered of the contract, constituted by the exercise of the option, for sale and
purchase of the property at the price of £10,000.
   His first contention is that the option agreement was vitiated by a representation
made on behalf of the plaintiffs by Mr Sambruck on the occasion when the agreement

1 [1974] 1 All ER 248, [1973] 3 WLR 884

was signed by the defendant, the representation being to the effect that what he (the defendant) was being asked to sign was a document which he would be able to get *a* out of at any time within six weeks of its signature. The judge's finding that there was no such representation was, it was contended, against the weight of the evidence. This was indeed, with respect, a hopeless point, particularly in the absence of any transcript of evidence. The learned judge heard the evidence of Mr Sambruck and of the defendant; he preferred the evidence of Mr Sambruck where the evidence of the two diverged, and he came not only to the clear conclusion that no such representa- *b* tion had been made in any shape or form, but further that the defendant was never under any misapprehension on this point. That attack on the validity of the option agreement, in those circumstances, cannot possibly succeed.

The next attack on the validity of the option agreement was that it was an un-conscionable bargain and consequently one that a court of equity would not support. I may say at once that there was no evidence or even any suggestion that the price of *c* £10,000 was inadequate. Indeed, the defendant had successfully stuck out for £1,000 more than his neighbours. Nor, under this head, was any reliance placed on the £1 option money being inadequate consideration for the option. The suggestion mainly made really amounted I think to this, that Mr Sambruck ought to have told this house-painter with a wife and six children that he ought, before signing, to have considered whether if he sold the house he would have enough money to buy himself *d* a suitable house elsewhere. Several cases—and of this I make no complaint—on unconscionable bargains were cited to us. But, in my view, none of them assists. It is perfectly true that the defendant cannot read; but there is nothing before us to suggest that he was not intelligent, let alone that he has any weakness of mind. He speaks (according to the learned judge) and understands English perfectly well. The option agreement was explained to him by his friend and lodger, Mr Reid, *e* and I have little doubt that the whole matter of the options on this row of four houses was the subject of much discussion between the defendant and his neighbours well before he signed the final document at the price which he thought right. I can find nothing in this case remotely approaching the circumstances in which equity has been prepared to intervene under the general heading of unconscionable bargain.

The third ground of attack on the validity of the option agreement was that the *f* consideration for the grant of the option, stated and paid, namely £1, was a sum which the law would not regard as valuable consideration; therefore there was no consideration in the eye of the law to support the obligation on the defendant not to withdraw his offer for six months. This I found a startling proposition. The industry of counsel for the defendant has not been able to find any support for it in English authority; and his reliance on a Canadian case of *Gilchrist Vending Ltd v Sedley Hotel* *g* *Ltd*[1] was based on a misreading, in my view, of the decision in that case, which appears to me to suggest only that possible future obligations which could be avoided by payment of $1 were illusory as consideration.

The situation in this case, therefore, is that the option agreement was valid and effective, it constituted an irrevocable offer to sell (so that the defendant's purported rejection of any obligation in his letter in January 1972 was inoperative as a with- *h* drawal of the offer) and, on the exercise of the option, the offer to sell was accepted and the contract for sale and purchase was constituted.

The final contention for the appellant was that *that* contract should not be specifi-cally enforced, but that the purchaser should have only been awarded damages. I see no justification for that contention. If the owner of a house contracts with his eyes open, as the judge held that the defendant did, it cannot in my view be right to deny specific *j* performance to the purchaser because the vendor then finds it difficult to find a house to buy that suits him and his family on the basis of the amount of money in the proceeds of sale. It is to be observed, as to this particular case, that to the knowledge

1 (1967) 66 DLR (2d) 24

of the defendant, the purchasers were and are planning development on one site
a embracing his house together with the three other houses. It is right to say that,
after this final point had been the subject-matter of a certain amount of debate in
this court, counsel for the defendant found himself unable to pursue the point—
unable, let me say, not because he was unable to get a word in edgeways, but because
he thought in the end, after debate, that the point was not a good one. Accordingly, I
reject the contention that the judge could not or should not have ordered specific
b performance.
    But I wish to add a comment on the learned judge's approach to that last point. As I
have said, a valid option to purchase constitutes an irrevocable offer to sell during the
period stated, and a purported withdrawal of the offer is ineffective. When, therefore,
the offer is accepted by the exercise of the option, a contract for sale and purchase is
thereupon constituted, just as if there were then constituted a perfectly ordinary
c contract for sale and purchase without a prior option agreement. The court is asked
to order specific performance of that contract of sale and purchase, not to order
specific performance of a contract not to withdraw the offer; provided that the option
be valid and for valuable consideration and duly exercised, it appears to me to be
irrelevant to the question of remedy under the contract for sale and purchase that the
valuable consideration can be described as a token payment; and so also if the option
d agreement be under seal with no payment, which is what I take the learned judge to
be referring to when he refers to a gratuitous option in his judgment. While I therefore agree that a valid option to purchase constitutes an interest in the land, I do not
consider, as the learned judge appears to have thought, that that fact is necessary to
his conclusion and my conclusion on what is the appropriate remedy.
    I would, for those reasons, dismiss the appeal.
e
    CAIRNS LJ. Counsel for the defendant summarised his argument under three
headings: first, that the learned judge's finding that the defendant was not induced to
enter into the transaction by misrepresentation by Mr Sambruck on behalf of the
plaintiffs was against the weight of evidence; secondly, that the whole transaction was
an unconscionable bargain which the court will not enforce; thirdly, that the option
f agreement was not valid or, alternatively, if it was valid, then the only remedy to
which the plaintiffs were entitled was damages and not specific performance.
    As to the first of these points, the only representation relied on in this court was a
representation that the effect of the option agreement was to give either party the
right to withdraw from it within six weeks. So far as appears from the judgment,
which is the only guide we have to the evidence which was given, it is not even clear
g that the defendant stated that Mr Sambruck had said anything of the kind. The
defendant may have been resting his case wholly on his allegation, not now persisted
in, that pages of the document had been changed after he signed it. But if he did say
that such a representation had been made orally, the judge disbelieved him; and it is
impossible for this court to say that the judge was not entitled to do so. Counsel for
the defendant invited us to infer that Mr Reid, a friend of the defendant who was
h present when the agreement was signed, in explaining the matter to the defendant,
misinterpreted cl 4 of the agreement and that Mr Sambruck failed to correct it.
This is pure speculation, and it is quite impossible to say that it is supported by
evidence of weight or by any evidence at all.
    As to the second point, there is in my opinion no good ground for describing this as
an unconscionable bargain. All the 19th century cases to which counsel for the defen-
j dant referred had features which distinguished them from this one. They were cases
where a person at some disadvantage was induced to enter into a very bad bargain,
usually with no time for thought and no opportunity of getting legal advice. Here,
there was no reason to suppose that £10,000 was less than the market value of the
house. The defendant had had many weeks to consider a transaction on the lines of
what was ultimately agreed, and more than a week to consider a price of £10,000.

It had been suggested in a letter from Mr Sambruck that he might get the advice of a lawyer, and at the time of the signing of the agreement he had two friends with him, *a* one of whom explained it to him, and the whole transaction lasted over a period of about half an hour. Stress is laid by counsel for the defendant on the fact that between 12th December 1971 and 3rd January 1972 the defendant was unable to find suitable accommodation for himself and his family at a price which, with the £10,000 he was to receive, he would be able to pay. There was no duty on the part of the plaintiffs or their agent to discover what the defendant's requirements were in the way of a new *b* home, or what the cost of it was likely to be. Even assuming a degree of ignorance and lack of intelligence on the part of the defendant, which by no means follows from the fact of his illiteracy, it cannot possibly be said that the bargain was unconscionable because the defendant was not advised as to the difficulties that he might be faced with if he could not quickly find a new home within his means. It is contended that the option agreement was unconscionable, in that the defendant was paid only £1 and *c* might have to wait six months before knowing whether the plaintiffs were going to buy his house or not. But it is very difficult to put a value on an option, and I believe it to be a common practice for options to be granted for a merely nominal consideration. There was nothing unreasonable in the plaintiffs wishing to have a reasonable time to ensure that they could buy all four houses and get planning permission. No doubt the price that the defendant could have got for the house without planning *d* permission would have been much lower. At the risk of some uncertainty, there was the chance of his receiving a substantial price for the house; and I cannot regard the option agreement as being in any way unconscionable.

Then, thirdly, there was a separate contention, based on the Canadian decision[1] to which Russell LJ has referred, that the £1 consideration was no consideration in law. That was not the actual decision in the Canadian case[1] and, if it had been, it *e* would have been contrary to a mass of English authority to the effect that anything of value, however small the value, is sufficient consideration to support a contract at law. When it comes to the equitable remedy of specific performance, it is to be remembered that this only arises if the option agreement is valid. If it was valid, then it was conceded that it was irrevocable. Therefore, on 29th March 1972, when the plaintiffs exercised the option, a valid contract for sale was made. For that contract *f* there is no basis for saying that the consideration was inadequate or that for any other reason specific performance should not be ordered. Insofar as there is a difference in approach to this matter between that of the learned trial judge and that of Russell LJ, I agree with Russell LJ.

For the reasons that I have given, I too would dismiss this appeal.

g

SIR JOHN PENNYCUICK. I agree with the judgments which have been delivered, and do not wish to add anything.

Appeal dismissed.

h

Solicitors: *Suriya & Co* (for the defendant); *Hancock & Willis* (for the plaintiffs).

F K Anklesaria Esq Barrister.

1 *Gilchrist Vending Ltd v Sedley Hotel Ltd* (1967) 66 DLR (2d) 24

Esso Petroleum Co Ltd v Mardon

a

QUEEN'S BENCH DIVISION   Varied CA [1976] 2 All ER 5

LAWSON J

15th, 16th, 17th, 18th, 19th, 22nd, 23rd, 24th, 31st JULY 1974

Negligence – Duty to take care – Statement – Information or advice – Special relationship
b *giving rise to duty of care – Financial interest of adviser in advice given – Reliance on adviser's*
knowledge and expertise – Company engaged in distribution of petrol – Negotiation by
company to let new petrol station – Forecast by company of prospective petrol sales from
station – Forecast inducing tenant to enter tenancy agreement – Forecast inaccurate – Whether
company under duty of care to tenant.

c *Negligence – Duty to take care – Statement – Pre-contract negotiations – Statement made by*
one party to other in course of negotiations – Statement inducing other party to enter agree-
ment – Whether fact that statement made in course of pre-contract negotiations precluding
duty to take care in making statement.

A company engaged in the production and distribution to the public of petroleum,
owned petrol stations throughout the United Kingdom. The company had a dealer
d sales representative, L, who had 40 years' experience of that side of the business. L
was anxious for the company to acquire a site within his area for development as a
petrol station. The site lay in a busy part of a town. L attached great weight to
the custom which could be obtained at that site from 'passing trade', i e traffic coming
into and out of the town. In 1961 the representative submitted to the company a
proposal for the acquisition of the site. He estimated that the annual consumption
e of the developed petrol station would amount to 200,000 gallons a year in the second
year after development. The proposal was enthusiastically received by the company
which proceeded to acquire and develop the site. When the development had been
completed it was obvious that, because of certain physical characteristics, the petrol
station suffered from a number of deficiencies for the purpose of attracting custom
from passing traffic. Early in 1963 the company began negotiations with a prospec-
f tive tenant who was interested in acquiring a tenancy of the petrol station. The
tenant inspected the site and its deficiencies with regard to potential passing trade
were readily apparent to him. L and other representatives of the company told
the tenant that they estimated that the 'throughput' of the site in the third year
of development would be 200,000 gallons a year. The tenant indicated that in his
view 100,000 to 150,000 gallons would be a more realistic estimate but his doubts
g were quelled by L whose estimate, as L appreciated, the tenant was prepared to
accept in view of L's expertise and long experience. Because of what he had been
told about the estimated throughput in the third year the tenant agreed to take a
three year tenancy of the site. Under the agreement the tenant undertook to pay
the rent and to take all his supplies of petrol from the company at a discount on the
retail price. Despite the efforts of the tenant to make a success of the venture, the
h business did not prosper, largely because it failed to attract the passing trade.
Although in 1964 the company agreed to substitute a new tenancy at a lower rent
and revised terms as to the supply of petrol, the tenant continued to make heavy
losses. In the third year the annual throughput of petrol had risen to only 86,502
gallons. In 1966 the tenant gave up the tenancy. In proceedings by the company
for arrears of rent, the tenant counterclaimed for damages for negligence, relying
j on the statements made to him on behalf of the company in 1963 when he was
negotiating the tenancy agreement.

Held – (i) In making statements, during the course of negotiations for the tenancy
agreement, concerning the petrol station's prospects, the company owed the tenant
a duty of care for the following reasons—

(a) There was a special relationship between the company and the tenant which gave rise to the duty of care since the company had a financial interest in the advice *a* which they had given in that they knew that the tenant, in reliance on their knowledge and expertise, was seeking information which would affect his decision whether or not to enter into a tenancy agreement of which the company would have the benefit (see p 220 *d* and *e*, post); *Hedley Byrne & Co Ltd v Heller and Partners Ltd* [1963] 2 All ER 575 and dictum of Lord Diplock in *Mutual Life and Citizens Assurance Co Ltd v Evatt* [1971] 1 All ER at 160, 161, applied. *b*

(b) The fact that the statements had been made in the course of pre-contractual negotiations between the company and the tenant did not relieve the company from a duty of care in making those statements (see p 220 *g* and p 221 *h*, post); *Dillingham Construction Pty v Downs* [1972] 2 NSWLR 49 applied.

(ii) In forecasting that in the third year of operation the throughput of petrol would be 200,000 gallons the company had failed to take reasonable care for they had failed *c* to reappraise the 1961 throughput forecast of 200,000 gallons in the light of the physical characteristics of the site as they had become plain when the development had been completed in 1963 and before the tenant had begun negotiations for the tenancy. Accordingly the company was liable to the tenant for the loss and damage which he had suffered in consequence of the company's negligent statement (see p 216 *f*, p 217 *a* and p 222 *h*, post). *d*

Notes

For the circumstances giving rise to a duty to take reasonable care, see 28 Halsbury's Laws (3rd Edn) 7, 19-21, paras 4, 17, and for cases on the subject, see 36 Digest (Repl) 12-18, 34-79.

e

Cases referred to in judgment

Anderson (W B) & Sons Ltd v Rhodes (Liverpool) Ltd [1967] 2 All ER 850, Digest (Cont Vol C) 406, *199a*.

Andrews v Hopkinson [1956] 3 All ER 422, [1957] 1 QB 229, [1956] 3 WLR 732, Digest (Cont Vol A) 1161, *443b*.

Bentley (Dick) Productions Ltd v Harold Smith (Motors) Ltd [1965] 2 All ER 65, [1965] *f* 1 WLR 623, CA, Digest (Cont Vol B) 629, *559a*.

Bissett v Wilkinson [1927] AC 177, [1926] All ER Rep 343, 136 LT 97, 42 TLR 727, PC, 35 Digest (Repl) 8, *22*.

Brown v Sheen & Richmond Car Sales Ltd [1950] 1 All ER 1102, 26 Digest (Repl) 666, *34*.

Candler v Crane, Christmas & Co [1951] 1 All ER 426, [1951] 2 KB 164, [1951] 1 TLR 371, CA, 36 Digest (Repl) 17, *75*. *g*

Coats Patons (Retail) v Birmingham Corpn (1971) 69 LGR 356.

Chess (Oscar) Ltd v Williams [1957] 1 All ER 325, [1957] 1 WLR 370, CA, 39 Digest (Repl) 514, *559*.

De Lassalle v Guildford [1901] 2 KB 215, [1900-3] All ER Rep 495, 70 LJKB 533, 84 LT 549, CA, 12 Digest (Reissue) 161, *935*.

Dillingham Constructions Pty v Downs [1972] 2 NSWLR 49. *h*

Erskine v Adeane, Bennett's Claim (1873) LR 8 Ch App 756, 42 LJCh 825, 29 LT 234, 38 JP 20, 2 Digest (Repl) 50, *256*.

Hedley Byrne & Co Ltd v Heller & Partners Ltd [1963] 2 All ER 575, [1964] AC 465, [1963] 3 WLR 101, [1963] 1 Lloyd's Rep 485, Digest (Cont Vol A) 51, *1117a*.

Hill v Harris [1965] 2 All ER 358, [1965] 2 QB 601, [1965] 2 WLR 1331, CA, Digest (Cont Vol B) 477, *3302a*. *j*

Heilbut, Symonds & Co v Buckleton [1913] AC 30, [1911-13] All ER Rep 83, 82 LJKB 245, 107 LT 769, 20 Mans 54, HL, 39 Digest (Repl) 514, *355*.

Le Lievre v Gould [1893] 1 QB 491, 62 LJQB 353, 68 LT 626, 57 JP 484, 4 R 274, CA, 36 Digest (Repl) 9, *27*.

Morgan v Griffith (1871) LR 6 Ex 70, 40 LJEx 46, 23 LT 783, 12 Digest (Reissue) 160, *930*.

Mutual Life & Citizens Assurance Co Ltd v Evatt [1971] 1 All ER 150, [1971] AC 793,
a   [1971] 2 WLR 23, [1970] 2 Lloyd's Rep 44, [1971] ALR 235, PC.
Nocton v Lord Ashburton [1914] AC 932, [1914-15] All ER Rep 45, 83 LJCh 784, 111 LT
    641, 35 Digest (Repl) 57, *502*.
Oleificio Zucchi ASP v Northern Sales Ltd [1965] 2 Lloyd's Rep 496, Digest (Cont Vol C)
    855, *848c*.
Robinson v National Bank of Scotland 1916 SC (HL), 154, HL, 26 Digest (Repl) 33, **63*.
b   *Shanklin Pier Ltd v Detel Products Ltd* [1951] 2 All ER 471, [1951] 2 QB 854, [1951]
    2 Lloyd's Rep 187, 39 Digest (Repl) 579, *1030*.

Action

By a writ issued on 1st December 1966 the plaintiffs, Esso Petroleum Co Ltd, brought
an action against the defendant, Philip Lionel Mardon, claiming (1) possession of
c   premises known as Eastbank Service Station, Eastbank Street, Southport, in the
countyof Lancaster, (2) £1,133 13s 9d being the arrears of rent due under an agreement
in writing dated 1st September 1964 whereby the plaintiffs let those premises to the
defendant, and (3) mesne profits from 28th December 1966 at the rate of £101 15s 11d
per month until possession was delivered up. By his defence and counterclaim,
as subsequently amended, the defendant claimed damages. By para 6 of the amended
d   counterclaim the defendant alleged that, in order to induce him to enter into a tenancy
agreement and in consideration of him so doing the plaintiffs by their servants or
agents had represented and warranted to the defendant that the petrol-filling station,
the subject-matter of the agreement, had a potential selling capacity of 200,000 to
250,000 gallons of petrol per annum which amount would be realised before the
expiration of a tenancy agreement for a period of three years made between the
e   plaintiffs and the defendant on 10th April 1963, that the plaintiffs were experts in that
sphere of business and that the defendant could rely on those representations and
warranties. By paras 7 and 8 the defendant alleged that he had been induced to enter
into the tenancy agreements of April 1963 and September 1964 and that the representations were untrue and the warranties broken in that the filling-station only
ever had a potential throughput of 60,000 to 70,000 gallons per annum. Further or
f   alternatively, by para 8A the defendant alleged that the plaintiffs' servants or agents—

> 'knew, or ought to have known that the Defendant was relying upon them to
> exercise due care, skill and judgment in giving him information and advice
> relating to the said petrol station and its throughput potential. Accordingly the
> plaintiffs owed the Defendant a duty to exercise reasonable care in tendering
> such information and advice to him.'

g
By para 8B the defendant alleged that in breach of their duty of care the plaintiffs
had been negligent in tendering such advice and information to the defendant. By
para 9 the defendant alleged that in consequence of the plaintiffs' breaches of warranty
and misrepresentation and/or by reason of their breach of their duty of care, the
defendant had sustained damage; the moneys he had expended in equipping the
h   premises had been lost; he had traded at a loss and had lost the profits he would have
made had the petrol station been as represented and warranted; the plaintiffs had
exercised their right of forfeiture of the agreement of September 1964 and, to minimise
further loss, the defendant had been compelled to give up the premises. The facts are
set out in the judgment.

Colin Ross-Munro QC and *John Peppitt* for the plaintiffs.
j   *John Hall QC* and *Alan Rawley* for the defendant.

Cur adv vult

31st July. **LAWSON J** read the following judgment. In this case the plaintiffs,
by their writ issued on 1st December 1966, claim against the defendant, formerly
the plaintiffs' tenant of a petrol service station, showroom, offices and other premises

situated on the south side of Eastbank Street, Southport, firstly possession on the
ground of non-payment in breach of covenant of money due under the relevant *a*
tenancy agreement in respect of which breach the plaintiffs duly served a notice
under s 146 of the Law of Property Act 1925; secondly, payment of moneys due;
thirdly, the mesne profits from 28th December 1966 until possession is given. The
defendant in fact gave up possession on 7th March 1967. The moneys due have been
agreed in the sum of £483·69 and the mesne profits at £620. There is no issue
outstanding therefore on the claim and, subject to the counterclaim, £1,103.69 is *b*
due to the plaintiffs.

By way of counterclaim against the plaintiffs, the defendant claims damages,
relying on certain statements alleged to have been made to him by the plaintiffs'
employees in 1963 and 1964. His counterclaim is based on three grounds. First of all,
on misrepresentation, but it is conceded that since the transaction in this case was
dealt with long before the Misrepresentation Act 1967, and since the relief provided *c*
for in that Act in respect to innocent misrepresentation is specifically excluded in
pre-1967 cases, the defendant is not entitled to any relief in respect of this head of
counterclaim. Secondly, he counterclaims for breach of warranty by the plaintiffs
in relation to the subject-matter of the defendant's tenancy agreements. Since these
agreements were completely reduced into writing, however, the defendant's claim
is put as being for breach of a collateral agreement or collateral agreements, that is *d*
to say, an agreement or agreements entered into between the parties in relation to
the subject matter of the tenancy agreements. Thirdly, he counterclaims for damages
in negligence, in that he alleges that the plaintiffs by their employees made statements
to him in relation to the subject-matter of the tenancy agreements without taking
proper care as to the accuracy of those statements. It is the second and third heads of
the counterclaim with which I am thus concerned. As I have said, the defendant's *e*
counterclaim is based on statements allegedly made to him by various of the plaintiffs'
representatives. This happened as long ago as 1963 and 1964. Not only therefore is
there great difficulty in determining what in fact was and was not said ten or 11
years ago before the trial, but this difficulty is accentuated here by the relative absence
of contemporary records. Nevertheless some important witnesses, though not all of
them, to these oral transactions are available and have given evidence to the best *f*
of their recollection, which necessarily cannot be more than uncertain after so long
an interval. The problem is aggravated for the plaintiffs by the fact that the defence
initially failed to particularise the occasions on which the statements in question were
made or the persons by whom they were alleged to have been made on behalf of the
plaintiffs. When these particulars were sought in April 1967, they were not furnished until January 1971. In some contrast to the position of the plaintiffs is that of *g*
the defendant, who told me that he had lived with this case for years, and that
indicates to me that I have to scrutinise his evidence with very great care, because
with the best will in the world it is well known that people who have brooded on a
grievance or a claim do in fact persuade themselves that things have been said, or not
said, contrary to the facts.

The plaintiffs are a well-known company engaged in the production and distribution *h*
to the public of petroleum and allied products. They also own petrol stations throughout the country, some of which, as in the present case, are occupied by the plaintiffs'
tenants. Through these petrol stations, and other independently owned stations,
petrol is supplied to the general public. The defendant, who is now aged 49, has
since 1947 been concerned with the motor trade. From 1947 to 1949, and again for a
time in 1953, he was general manager with a company known as Ormskirk Motors *j*
where he was mainly concerned with commercial vehicle sales. From 1949 to 1952,
and again from 1953 to 1959, he was employed as a motor tour organiser and manager
by two different companies. In 1952-53 the defendant was manager of an Esso service
station in Toronto, Canada, but he returned from Canada and resumed the employment which I have earlier indicated. Finally, in 1959 he commenced his own business,

for the purpose of which he formed a limited company, as a garage owner, omnibus
a proprietor and petrol station operator at Skelmersdale in Lancashire. Ultimately his
company operated four pumps at Skelmersdale and he estimated the eventual
throughput of petrol at the rate of about 50,000 gallons a year. In 1962, for health
reasons, he decided to put the Skelmersdale business on the market, and he eventually
sold it satisfactorily early in 1963. He then returned to live in Southport. Except for
his year in Canada, he lived in Southport from 1947 to 1959, and he was thus no
b stranger to its characteristics as a town, to its population spread and character and its
traffic volumes and patterns.

   The plaintiffs had a dealer sales representative, a Mr Leitch, a gentleman with
nearly 40 years' experience of that side of the petroleum business, within whose area
at all material times until autumn 1963 fell the town of Southport. For some time
from as early as 1959, largely at Mr Leitch's instigation, the plaintiffs were interested
c in the possible acquisition of a site at Eastbank Street, a busy part of the town, and
its development as a filling station and as an additional outlet in Southport for their
petrol. Ultimately they in fact acquired this site in 1962, with the appropriate planning
permission, and developed it as a petrol station, saleroom and other premises. This
development was completed in early 1963.

   It is unnecessary to go into the early history of the acquisition of the site by the
d plaintiffs in any detail. Two matters must, however, be mentioned. The first is that
there was a planning application which was rejected in 1959, which led to an appeal
by the plaintiffs which failed. Mr Leitch gave evidence in these proceedings in support
of the need for a petrol station at Eastbank Street, at this site, his proof having been
handed in to the inspector. In the course of this trial, he was cross-examined at great
length on the proof. It indicated that Mr Leitch was at the time concerned to establish
e a substantial demand for a modern petrol station in the relevant area and to dispute
the local authority's contention that the area was adequately served by other petrol
stations to the extent that an additional output was redundant. It is clear that at this
time Mr Leitch attached great weight to the custom to be obtained from passing
trade, that is to say, traffic coming from the east and moving towards the west into
Southport, mainly coming along the road which leads from Manchester and Ormskirk
f into Southport.

   The second matter is of much greater importance. In 1961 Mr Leitch submitted to
the plaintiffs a proposal for the acquisition of the Eastbank site for which conditional
planning permission had then been granted. In this proposal Mr Leitch estimated
that the annual consumption of the developed petrol station would amount to
200,000 gallons a year in the second year after development. Accompanying this
g proposal was a sketch plan showing the location, the brand allocation and the
estimated annual throughput of all other petrol stations in a wide area of Southport.
The importance of this sketch plan and its data is that it contained information as to
throughput known to Mr Leitch and his employers in 1961 and, if updated, generally
speaking in 1963, but not known to or within the means of knowledge of the defendant; that is, the defendant knew the number and locations of the other petrol
h stations in Southport but had not, and could not have had, any detailed knowledge of
their respective consumptions. Mr Leitch's recommendation seems to have been
enthusiastically processed to the top level of the plaintiffs who acted on it, no doubt
applying their own judgment in this matter, and accepted the estimate as to throughput and in due course proceeded to acquire and develop the Eastbank Street site.

   On the completion of this development early in 1963, the plaintiffs had an area of
j approximately 920 square yards. This was laid out as shown in the plan and illustrated
by photographs, although the photographs are of much more recent origin. The
plan of the area shows Eastbank Street and the route by which traffic from the east
can approach Lord Street and the sea front in Southport, without such obstructions as
level crossings and other diversions because of the position as shown on the plan of the
railway lines and the relative absence of road bridges in the area coming from east to

west. Eastbank Street is and was at all material times a very busy street carrying a
great deal of traffic, both local and passing traffic. When I use the expression 'passing   *a*
traffic' I mean that which is coming in and moving out of Southport into other areas
in both east and west directions, and Eastbank Street also has 'bus routes.

The fundamental criticisms of the site as such are, firstly, entry and exit is provided
only through side streets, Yellow House Lane and Part Street respectively, and not
directly from or into Eastbank Street. Secondly, the improbability of eastbound
traffic in Eastbank Street utilising the site for refuelling, because firstly of the lack   *b*
of visibility of the pumps from the north side of the street until vehicles have virtually
passed out of sight. Thirdly, the problem of turning across the westbound traffic
moving in the street. Fourthly, the position of the Esso sign as shown in the photographs which made it unlikely that drivers coming east would see it before too late
to make a turn into Yellow House Lane.

The positioning of the building comprising the showroom and offices above the   *c*
south pavement of Eastbank Street, which was dictated by planning conditions and
which meant that the forecourt which constituted the petrol station was behind that
building, also obscured to a large extent the existence of the pumps from traffic,
particularly the eastbound, in Eastbank Street. That is another basic deficiency of
the site. These deficiencies are in the forefront of the defendant's case, but they are
all matters of physical layout and structure and must have been obvious and apparent   *d*
to anyone paying attention, as the defendant did, to the characteristics of the site
as it had been developed, before its operations began. From the viewpoint of a prospective tenant these things must have been quite obvious.

I accept the evidence given for the plaintiffs that initially a concern known as
'Hollands', who operated a large garage and petrol station at the junction of Virginia
Street and Scarisbrick New Road was contemplated as a potential tenant for Eastbank   *e*
Street. Hollands were in fact distributors of Esso, but their site had the disadvantage
of being situated so that, owing to the interposition of a roundabout, traffic moving
from east to west along Scarisbrick New Road and Eastbank Street would be unlikely
to use it to refuel. I find that the defendant knew at all material times that Hollands
had the business of the kind I have indicated and he was in a position to make an
assessment of their position as possible competitors with the Eastbank Street site.   *f*
The proposal to let the site to Hollands, however, fell through.

The defendant asserts that Mr Leitch introduced him as a potential tenant for the
Eastbank Street site in the course of conversation between them at Skelmersdale.
I do not accept this and prefer Mr Leitch's evidence that the first time he met the
defendant was at Manchester at the plaintiffs' district offices. However that may be,
the defendant certainly got to know of the availability of the site, and he visited it on   *g*
a number of occasions and formed a favourable assessment of its potentiality sufficient
to move him to seek the tenancy. I am satisfied that the defendant visited Manchester
early in 1963, having first seen the site, and on that occasion, or possibly a later date
in March 1963, Mr Leitch drove him there. The purpose of the visit on which he was
the driver was that the defendant should negotiate for a tenancy of the plaintiffs' site.
In the course of the drive Mr Leitch, in general conversation, told the defendant of his   *h*
very long experience in the petrol trade, and I am sure that the defendant was
impressed, as I was, by Mr Leitch as a very straightforward and careful man, as well
as by his experience. But it is clear, and I am satisfied, that at the interview which
followed—at which certainly Mr Allen of the plaintiffs, who had become late in
1962, or early in 1963, the area dealer sales manager, and Mr Leitch were present—the
defendant was told that the plaintiffs estimated that the throughput of the Eastbank   *j*
Street site, in its third year of operation, would amount to 200,000 gallons a year.
I also find that the defendant then indicated that he thought 100,000 to 150,000 gallons
would be a more realistic estimate, but he was convinced by the far greater expertise
of, particularly, Mr Leitch. Mr Allen is a far younger man and, although on his
appointment as manager for the area I am satisfied he made his own observations as to

a the potentiality of the Eastbank Street site, in the result he accepted Mr Leitch's estimate. The defendant, having indicated that he thought that a lower figure would be a more realistic estimate, had his doubts quelled by the experience of, and the estimate furnished by, Mr Leitch; and it was for that reason, I am satisfied, because of what he was told about the estimated throughput in the third year, that he then proceeded to negotiate for and obtain the grant of a three year tenancy at a rent of £2,500 a year for the first two years, rising to £3,000 yearly in the last year. The

b tenancy agreement is dated 10th April 1963. The defendant personally became the tenant under the agreement and liable to make the payments for rent and the payments for fuel supplied under the provisions of the agreement.

The defendant makes certain other allegations in his pleadings or in his evidence, or both, as to statements made to him in 1963, before 10th April 1963, the date when he entered into the agreement. I deal briefly with these. I am satisfied he was told that

c he should have a capital of £8,000 to £10,000 available and that he satisfied the plaintiffs that he met this requirement. I am sure, and I find, that he was told nothing of the plaintiffs' capital outlay on the petrol station, and I find that he was not told that the rent was fixed in relation to that outlay. I find that the only estimate or forecast given to him was of a 200,000 gallons per year throughput in the third year of operation, and I note that this is the figure which is mentioned in the defendant's first letter

d of 'complaint'—I will call it that—which is dated 17th July 1964. I find that Mr Allen did not tell him that the plaintiffs were experts and that he was only a layman. Nevertheless it is clear that from what he was told, rightly, of Mr Leitch's experience, he certainly took the view—and the plaintiffs' representatives must have appreciated, and I find they did appreciate it—that he would accept their better informed and expert estimate.

e I should have mentioned that after the Manchester meeting Mr Leitch entertained the defendant to lunch. At this lunch I find that Mr Leitch was enthusiastic as to the prospects of the site and that he expressed his confidence in the previously given forecast. I think it probable, and I find that Mr Leitch told the defendant, that it was possible that Hollands might cease distributing Esso and if that happened some trade might result from this; but I am sure that Leitch did not give any estimate as to what

f percentage of Hollands' customers for Esso would come to Eastbank Street in that event. I am satisfied that this had no influence on the defendant's decison to take his tenancy. I note again that in his letters of complaint to the plaintiffs, of which there are two, he does not complain about that matter.

This brings me shortly to state some findings of fact in the defendant's favour as at 10th April; that is to say, he was induced to, and did, enter into the tenancy agreement

g of 10th April in reliance on an estimate or forecast of potential turnover of 200,000 gallons, in the third year of that tenancy, which was one given by experts, and I find also that the plaintiffs through their representatives appreciated that the defendant did in fact so act in reliance on this estimate or forecast. This is to my mind confirmed by the defendant's first letter of complaint, dated 17th July 1964, and by what happened thereafter, to which I will come in due course. It is however essential to

h emphasise that there is no question but that the representatives of the plaintiffs concerned in this matter acted with complete honesty and genuinely believed in the validity of what was the potential throughput as stated to the defendant.

As I have said, the defendant personally signed the tenancy agreement dated 10th April 1963, and on 12th April 1963 the Eastbank Street site was opened for trading. It is clear that the business of the site, which included a not unsubstantial

j trade in good class secondhand motor cars—the defendant estimated a gross profit in this line of trade of some £1,100 in the first year of trading—was in fact carried on by the defendant's old Skelmersdale company of which he and his wife were the sole shareholders and directors. The plaintiffs contemplated that this would be the position and, although the appropriate change in name of the company was duly registered, the tenancy agreement and the succeeding agreement of 1st September 1964, to which I will come, remained in the name of the defendant alone.

The Eastbank Street site got away to a poor start as far as petrol sales and sales of ancillary goods were concerned, and it is clear that the defendant and Mr Leitch, who *a* was in close touch with the defendant until about September 1963, when he retired, were both worried about this. A combination of laudable and grim determination not to be beaten—of which the defendant perhaps possesses more than most people —and optimism as to the future moved the defendant to carry on doing his best, as I am sure he did, to build up his trade.

When Mr Leitch retired his place was taken by Mr Kinrade, whom I have heard *b* in evidence, and I have no doubt that the poor trading results of the defendant's business were the main subject of fairly regular meetings when Mr Kinrade, from the autumn of 1963, commenced calling at the site in the course of his normal duties as a dealer sales representative. I have no doubt that both the defendant and Mr Kinrade firmly believed that the forecast potential would ultimately be achieved and mutually expressed these opinions. Perhaps it is unfortunate, but I see no blame attaching to *c* the defendant in this respect, that, being the man he is, he decided to wait for the results of the first year's trading before reaching a decision as to what he should do in relation to the site. He knew that it was running at a loss, but he had not, I am sure, anticipated trading at a profit during his first year. The defendant's company's first trading year closed at 30th April and in due course, at the end of June 1964, the company's accountants produced the accounts, which on the face of them showed a *d* gross profit of some £3,000 but a startling loss of some £5,800 net. I have no doubt that the company's outgoings, which had been planned and incurred to handle a far larger volume of trade than had materialised, were the main cause of this relatively high loss. There were, I should mention, other factors which operated adversely to the defendant during this period. In particular, after the site opened, two serious competitors in selling cheaply ancillaries such as oil, parts and other goods opened up *e* business in the immediate neighbourhood of the site.

When the defendant had digested the ominous message of these accounts, he wrote what has been described in his own terms as a letter of resignation to the plaintiffs. This is the letter dated 17th July 1964. I will not read it all. After reluctantly tendering notice to quit—a course which was not in fact available to him under the tenancy agreement of 10th April 1963—in order, as he quite reasonably asserts, to avoid *f* bankruptcy and salvage what he can, he sets out at some length all the efforts he has made to establish a thriving business. I think it is right to say that I find that the poor trading results were not in any way attributable to the defendant's business methods or conduct of the site or its trade. I am satisfied that the defendant did all that he reasonably could, and indeed more, to establish the business and to build it up to attain its potential throughput by the time that throughput had been forecast. In the *g* letter the defendant then gives brief details of the throughput of petrol and the trading results over the period 12th April 1963 to June-July 1964. He appeals to the plaintiffs to find a solution to the problem and he concludes with an important passage which I will read; he says this:

'This letter sir, I assure you is most confidential, and no one is even vaguely *h* aware at this stage of my plight, therefore I trust we can arrange an amicable departure of this site without publicity to our mutual detriment. I must add finally, that I certainly would have been delighted to have been able to inform you that the site was doing the gallonage you assessed on my taking over, 200,000 gallons a year at least, but alas, to compare the figures actually done against the estimated figure is certainly one for very much concern jointly.'   *j*

This assertion relates only to a forecast throughput of 200,000 gallons per annum which was furnished, as I find, by the plaintiffs before the defendant took over the tenancy; and it is right that the defendant, in this letter, makes no other complaint of the plaintiffs' conduct or statements made by them in relation to his entering into the tenancy.

Although the plaintiffs made no written reply to this letter, it is clear, as I find,
a that the defendant's appeal did not fall on deaf ears. The ensuing events are somewhat confused, and I regret that in the face of the contemporary documents I am
unable to accept the evidence of the defendant to the effect that in August 1964 he had
a short and stormy interview, principally with Mr Allen in Manchester, in which he
complained that he had been 'sold a pup'; that Mr Allen inferred that he, the defendant, had not been running the site properly and told him that if he didn't like it he
b could get out. Mr Allen has no recollection of this interview, and I am sure that he is
an honest and reliable witness so far as his recollection of events so long ago extends,
and that if an interview of this character had taken place Mr Allen would have
recalled it and told me frankly about it. Moreover, this evidence of the defendant is
wholly inconsistent and irreconcilable with the memorandum dated 4th August 1964,
signed by Mr Allen, but probably written and signed for him by Mr Wooldridge, who
c was his assistant, who had been dealing with the Eastbank Street site and had been
present at a number of meetings between Mr Allen and the defendant.
I should say that owing to the lapse of time and the delay in furnishing the particulars to which I have earlier referred, it has been impossible to trace Mr Wooldridge
and therefore I have not had the advantage of hearing his evidence about any of these
matters. The memorandum contains a number of important statements. Mr Allen,
d or the person who signed for Mr Allen, writes an internal memorandum in which
he says, among other things:

> 'You will observe that the actual sales of the site to date are considerably less
> than what was anticipated in relation to the second year e.a.c. [estimated annual
> consumption] of 200,000 gallons p.a. [That is a reference back to the proposals of
> 1961 which contain that figure as e a c in the second year of development.] The
e > main reasons for this low throughput are the many restrictions placed on the site
> by Southport Corporation, who insisted that the service station forecourt should
> be developed at the back of the site and not with both access points on the main
> road. We feel it will take longer than normally expected to obtain a throughput
> in line with our e.a.c.'

f I have already mentioned the deficiencies resulting from the layout and physical
characteristics of the site. The memorandum proceeds:

> 'Mr Mardon is an extremely good tenant who has tried every method to
> increase the sales and profitability of the service station and we are in no way
> dissatisfied with the way he has operated this site. The attached letter from Mr.
> Mardon [of 17th July 1964] gives in detail the situation as it exists today and was in
g > fact, his letter of resignation. Following discussions with him, he does not wish
> to leave the premises, but can only carry on if our Company is prepared to reduce
> the rental and place the service station on a surcharge basis with a fixed rental
> element. Mr. Mardon has discussed this matter with his Bank Manager at the
> National Provincial Bank in Southport and they are adamant that the maximum
> fixed rental element he can afford to pay is £1,000 p.a. Even this figure in our
h > opinion is high when one takes into account that the revaluation of the rates . . .
> means an additional outgoing of £544. The success of this site as a profit making
> concern depends largely on how Mr. Mardon can cover the cost of the fixed
> rental element and rates, by making use of the car showroom and office accom-
> modation . . . It is our wish to retain Mr. Mardon as tenant of this site, as it will be
> necessary, if he does resign, to obtain a rental reduction before we will be able to
j > install any other person in this tenancy. In addition, we do not believe we can
> improve on his operation of this site which was first class in all respects.'

They then ask for the provision—

> 'as soon as possible of a surcharge table with a fixed rental element not exceed-
> ing £1,000 p.a. On this basis, Mr. Mardon considers he will be able to continue

and possibly recoup his losses although this will obviously take some considerable
time. It is felt that a business appraisal form is unnecessary in view of the detail   *a*
given in Mr. Mardon's letter.'

I emphasise the views expressed there about Mr Mardon's operation of the site, as to
which I have already made a finding, and it is quite clear that no criticism can or
could in fact have been levied against him in that respect.

The other point which is important in this internal memorandum is that, contrary   *b*
to the evidence and recollection of the defendant, it is manifest that there must have
been discussions before this internal memorandum was written, in which Mr Mardon
expressed himself as willing to pay a rent of £1,000 per year and take a tenancy on a
surcharge basis. This is important particularly in view of the allegation which has
been made about certain other representations made, it is said, to induce Mr Mardon to
enter into a tenancy agreement which is dated 1st September 1964. It is, of course,   *c*
quite clear that there had been discussions between the defendant and the plaintiffs'
representatives before this memorandum was written. It is equally clear that the
plaintiffs' representatives' suggested new rental basis for the tenancy related to the
defendant's ability to pay and the poor results thus far of the site. I am not satisfied
that in the course of these discussions the potential throughput of 200,000 gallons per
annum was mentioned except as a target which was attainable more remotely than   *d*
originally forecast. I am however satisfied that whatever was said about the 1963
forecast at this time, it had no effect upon the defendant in relation to the agreement
dated 1st September 1964 which he subsequently entered into.

These discussions were, I find, followed by a visit paid by Mr Kinrade to the Eastbank
Street site at or about the latter part of August, on which occasion Mr Kinrade
produced and handed to the defendant a document entitled 'A Business Appraisal',   *e*
the purpose of which was to establish a realistic forecast of the Eastbank Street site's
trading for the period January-December 1965. I am satisfied that this document was
not produced at the behest or for the purposes of the plaintiffs but originated from
Mr Kinrade's genuine desire to help the defendant to find a solution to the trading
problems which clearly faced him should he continue as the plaintiffs' tenant of the
site. That the plaintiffs did not require such an appraisal is clear from the internal   *f*
memorandum of 4th August 1964, part of which I have read. In fact, the matter of the
appraisal, except insofar as providing a test as to the reliability of the recollections of
Mr Kinrade and the defendant—in which respect I have no hesitation in preferring the
former's evidence to that of the latter—has little relevance to the issues of the case.
Nothing in the appraisal is relied on as constituting any matter of representation or
warranty. Specifically, it is not alleged that the defendant was induced to enter into   *g*
the agreement dated 1st September 1964, which followed the appraisal, by means of
any representation or warranty expressed or implied in the appraisal. In fact, I find,
on the basis of that internal memorandum, that the defendant, as early as 4th August
or just before 4th August, well before the appraisal came into existence, was ready and
willing to take a tenancy at the rent of £1,000 per year plus surcharge rent on the
gallons sold. The appraisal is only pleaded as constituting in one respect a particular   *h*
of the plaintiffs' alleged negligence in relation to information and advice given in
1963 and 1964. That particularised matter is that the appraisal wrongly stated the
actual throughput of petrol and the amount of certain other income items which it is
alleged related to 16½ to 17 months' trading as appropriate to a 12 months' trading
period and contrasted these figures, which were in fact figures for 16½ to 17 months,
with figures of outgoings for a period of 12 months. It is said that the calculations on
the left hand side of the appraisal were inaccurate and misleading. But even if this   *j*
were the case, I accept Mr Kinrade's evidence, firstly that it was the defendant who
provided the figures which appeared on the left hand side of the appraisal, and he
obtained these from his own books; secondly, that the only purpose of inserting on
that side the petrol sales was to reach an assessment of the proportions of the various
types of all petrol sold, which proportions could be carried forward to the right hand

a side of the appraisal which contained the forecast throughput for the 12 months of 1965. It is also to be observed that if one compares the actual expenditure on the main items of wages and rent which appear from the defendant's certified accounts for the period April 1963 to 1964, the discrepancies between those figures and those given in the appraisal are very substantial indeed. Further, the figure given for car sales and accessories on the left hand side of the appraisal is gross £460, which contrasts strikingly with the defendant's own evidence of an approximate profit of £1,100 for the 12 months'

b period under this head. The right hand side stating a profit objective which relates to the year 1965 results in an estimated net operating profit of £1,006. This is based on an estimated annual throughput of 100,000 gallons, as to the basis of which I accept Mr Kinrade's evidence, and I am satisfied that he explained the appraisal to the defendant, who appreciated the basis of the calculation.

The defendant, in his evidence, said that he entered into the September 1964

c agreement, to which I come, on the basis of this estimate of operating profit. This however is not pleaded and for that reason, and also because I am told by counsel who agree that some two years ago leave to amend the counterclaim to rely on this matter was refused in interlocutory proceedings, I do not propose to go further into the matter. The defendant also said in his evidence that, save as to the figure of £1,006 profit, he paid no regard to the appraisal and did not examine it. This being the case, it also

d reinforces my view that nothing on the left hand side of the document, which as I find contained only information which he himself had provided, misled him.

Shortly after the handing over of the appraisal, the defendant again personally entered into a new tenancy agreement. It is dated 1st September 1964 but was entered into rather later in that month. It is clear that this new agreement supersedes the three year tenancy at a rent of £2,500 for the first two years and £3,000 for the

e third year. The new agreement creates a term of one year and to continue thereafter being terminable by three months' notice to expire at the end of the first year or on the last day of any month thereafter. The yearly rent is agreed at £1,000 plus a £120 reducing rent for the lubrication bay, plus a surcharge at the rates set out in the annexed schedule, which on a consumption of 100,000 gallons per year would amount to a penny per gallon. The rental so agreed was payable monthly in arrear on the last

f day of the month. The reasons which brought the defendant to enter into this agreement did not, I find, include his reliance on the 1963 throughput forecast.

The defendant, through his company, thereafter carried on business at the East-bank Street site but there was little improvement in his trading. In accordance with his earlier determination not to be beaten, and to try to recoup his loss on the lower rental to which I have referred, the defendant persisted. It is clear that sometime in

g 1965 he formed the not unreasonable view that the solution to his problems would be for the plaintiffs to offer him the tenancy of another, more profitable site from which he could subsidise the unprofitable business at Eastbank Street. Some steps were taken in this connection but nothing concrete emerged. Eastbank Street continued a failure.

At last, following a meeting with his accountants, on 1st January 1966 the defendant

h wrote a further letter of complaint to the plaintiffs. Early in this letter he refers to the assurances as to potential which he had been given before April 1963, which he now states as a throughput of 250,000 gallons per annum in approximately two years. I am satisfied, for the reasons I have mentioned, and because I prefer Mr Leitch's and Mr Allen's evidence to that of the defendant, and looking at the defendant's own letter of July 1964, that the plaintiffs' statements related to a throughput of 200,000 gallons

j per annum in the third year. He again refers to the efforts he has made to succeed but attributes failure to the site's position—a fact of which the defendant must have been aware from a date before the negotiations with the plaintiffs began and to which he makes no reference in his letter of July 1964. I am, however, quite sure that it was this fact which played a major part in the unsatisfactory progress of the business (see the plaintiffs' internal memorandum of 4th August 1964 which confirms this). The

defendant also, in this letter, confirms that he had been hopeful of and was waiting
for an Esso 'cream' site to enable him to offset his losses at Eastbank Street, a matter   **a**
to which I have already referred. Again, the plaintiffs did not reply to this letter, but
on 8th February 1966 two of their representatives, a Mr Millyard and a Mr Jasper,
called on him to discuss their mutual problems. In the result Mr Jasper wrote a
memorandum to Mr Kinrade on 10th February 1966. It is clear that the possibility of
the defendant becoming tenant of another site was discussed and that further rental
relief to the tenant was being contemplated in respect of Eastbank Street. Unfortu-   **b**
nately this came to nothing. The defendant consulted his solicitors, who wrote to the
plaintiffs on 31st March 1966. There followed a meeting but no conclusion was
reached and the defendant continued, with no better results, to carry on at the
Eastbank Street site.

The tragic story of the wasted endeavour and financial disaster of the defendant
really ends on 28th August 1966 when, finding himself unable to pay moneys due for   **c**
petrol supplied by the plaintiffs and sold by him, and despite his genuine and reasonable belief that the plaintiffs would continue to supply him on the basis of a day-to-
day payment, he had his tanks drained and his petrol supplies cut off, and as a petrol
station he was put out of business. I am bound to say that this seems a harsh action on
the part of the plaintiffs, although there is no issue in this action concerning it and it
may well be that in law the plaintiffs were entitled to do what they did. The defendant   **d**
remained at the site doing such business as he could. On 1st December 1966 the
plaintiffs issued their writ. On 7th March 1967 the defendant yielded up possession
of the site. Shortly thereafter, in May 1967, the plaintiffs obtained another tenant for
the site, a Mr Sinclair, who remained thereafter and remains in occupation of and
operating the site.

Three matters will, I think, round off my findings as to the facts of this case. On   **e**
7th November 1967 the defendant's accountants certified the accounts of the defendant's company for the three years ending 30th April 1967. Briefly stated these
accounts disclose the following. The year ended 30th April 1965, gross profit £4,649,
net operating loss approximately £2,000; year ended 30th April 1966, gross profit
£4,082, net operating loss approximately £1,600; year ended 30th April 1967, gross
profit £1,238, net operating loss approximately £3,500. From the figures of operating   **f**
loss I have excluded depreciation and directors' remuneration, and it must also be
noted that as a petrol station Eastbank Street effectively closed down at the end of
August 1966, so that the last year's results are not comparable with the results of the
two earlier years ending 30th April 1965 and 1966.

The next point is this, that the evidence indicates that the throughput of petrol at
the Eastbank Street site was as follows: 11th April 1963 to 10th April 1964, the first   **g**
year of operation by the defendant's company, 58,375 gallons; 11th April 1964 to
10th April 1965, 83,306 gallons; 11th April 1965 to 10th April 1966, 86,502 gallons.
The period 11th April 1966 to 27th August 1966, 4½ months, 26,347 gallons. Under
Mr Sinclair, according to his agreed statement of evidence, the figures are: year 1968,
82,117 gallons; 1969, 96,318 gallons; 1970, 110,418 gallons; 1971, 101,821 gallons;
1972, 94,240 gallons; 1973, 96,265 gallons. Mr Sinclair gives no figures for the period   **h**
May-December 1967.

I have referred to the criticism of the Eastbank Street site, its layout, access, egress
and limited visibility which are mentioned in the plaintiffs' internal memorandum
4th August 1964 and much later in the defendant's letter of complaint written on
1st January 1966. I am satisfied that as a result of the site's physical characteristics the
passing trade which Mr Leitch was optimistic of attracting largely failed to materialise.   **j**
This is borne out not only by the defendant's evidence that the best part of his trade
was with regular and local customers, and this point is also made in his letter of
1st January 1966, but also by Mr Sinclair's agreed statement which concludes with the
following: 'The majority of the sales was to regular customers and sales of petrol to
casual callers was comparatively small.'

As I am now moving to the questions of law affecting the issue of liability on the
a counterclaim, it will probably be helpful if I briefly recapitulate my basic findings of
fact as to the defendant's inducement to enter into, firstly the agreement of 10th
April 1963, and secondly the agreement dated 1st September 1964. As to the former,
I find that the defendant was induced and did enter into that agreement in reliance
on the plaintiff's forecast of a 200,000 gallons throughput of petrol in the third year of
that tenancy as one provided by experts, and the plaintiffs appreciated that the
b defendant did in fact so act in reliance on the plaintiffs' statement. As to the latter,
I find that the defendant was not induced to enter into that agreement in reliance on
their earlier forecast or any repetition of that earlier forecast prior to his entering into
the agreement dated 1st September 1964. I further find that the 1963 forecast referred
to expressly or by implication contained a statement of fact, namely as to the then
potential of the site, and was not a mere expression of opinion as to what throughput
c the site might in fact achieve in the future. I further find that this statement of fact
was incorrect. Put another way, in 1963 I find that the Eastbank Street site had not a
potential throughput of 200,000 gallons in the third year or foreseeably in any year
after the third year of tenancy. The incorrectness of this statement was attributable
to the physical conditions of the site, its layout and siting, which were such as to fail
in substance to attract the attention of passing as opposed to local traffic, and it was
d plain that without a substantial contribution from passing traffic their forecast
throughput was unattainable.

For the reasons I have mentioned at the outset of my judgment, the counterclaim,
so far as it is based on innocent misrepresentation, cannot be pursued. I come first
therefore to the counterclaim based on a breach of warranty set out in para 6 of the
defendant's counterclaim as amended. In my judgment the statement as to potential
e cannot properly be treated as a warranty. I think the authorities indicate conclusively
that to constitute a warranty a statement firstly must be intended on the part of the
maker to constitute a promise which can be described as a warranty or, putting it into
common language, a statement by which the maker says 'I guarantee that this will
happen'. Secondly, to constitute a warranty a statement must be of such nature that
it is susceptible in relation to its content of constituting a clear contractual obligation
f on the part of the maker of the statement.

I have been referred to the following principal authorities. The first group is
constituted by three cases: *Morgan v Griffith*[1]; *Erskine v Adeane*[2]; *De Lassalle v Guildford*[3].
In *De Lassalle v Guildford*[3] there is a dictum as to what is said to be the decisive test
whether a statement of the kind that we have under review in this case constitutes a
warranty, a statement which I find was rejected by the House of Lords unanimously
g in a later case to which I will refer, *Heilbut, Symons & Co v Buckleton*[4]. In each of these
three cases the court held that a promise that the promisor would fulfil specific
obligations in the future on the basis of faith of which the promisee entered into a
lease was enforceable at the suit of the promisee who had entered into the lease in the
event of the promisor failing to carry out his promise. *Hill v Harris*[5] is another case
which deals with the matter on the same basis, although in that case the existence of
h a promise was negatived.

The second set of cases is constituted by a group of which the following are representative and have been cited to me: *Brown v Sheen & Richmond Car Sales Ltd*[6]; *Shanklin
Pier Ltd v Detel Products Ltd*[7]; *Oscar Chess v Williams*[8]; *Andrews v Hopkinson*[9] and

1 (1871) LR 6 Ex 70
2 (1873) LR 8 Ch App 756
j 3 [1901] 2 KB 215, [1900-03] All ER Rep 495
4 [1913] AC 30, [1911-13] All ER Rep 83
5 [1965] 2 All ER 358, [1965] 2 QB 601
6 [1950] 1 All ER 1102
7 [1951] 2 All ER 471, [1951] 2 QB 854
8 [1957] 1 All ER 325, [1957] 1 WLR 370
9 [1956] 3 All ER 422, [1957] 1 QB 229

Dick Bentley Productions Ltd v Harold Smith (Motors) Ltd[1]. In all these cases the statements which were held to or alleged to constitute warranties were statements as to the *a* existing qualities or attributes of the property which became the subject of the post-statement contract. The statement made in this case does not fall in my judgment into this category. The statement relied on here possesses none of the characteristics of the cases in the group to which I have last referred. In my judgment it cannot be said that this was intended, and I find that it was not intended, to constitute a promise on the part of the plaintiffs; nor do I find that this statement was of such a *b* nature that it was susceptible of constituting a clear contractual obligation. In other words I am satisfied that there was no intention by the plaintiffs to promise that the forecast throughput should be achieved. I cannot see how the plaintiffs could possibly implement such a promise.

The vital point, I believe, is that whether or not the potential throughput of the site was achieved at the time indicated depended largely if not exclusively on factors *c* entirely outside the control of the plaintiffs. I have been greatly helped in this part of the case by the references and citations which have been made to the case to which I referred a moment ago, *Heilbut, Symons & Co v Buckleton*[2] and particularly passages from the speeches of Lord Haldane[3], Lord Atkinson[4] and Lord Moulton[5]. I am therefore against the defendant on the issue of warranty.

On the other hand, the relevant statement was not a mere expression of opinion. *d* In that respect it is to be distinguished from a statement which was the subject of Privy Council scrutiny in the case of *Bisset v Wilkinson*[6].

I finally come to what has been the most difficult part of the case, that is, the counterclaim based on the allegations of negligence contained in para 8A of the defence and counterclaim. This involves considering two questions: firstly, in the circumstances *e* of this case did the plaintiffs owe a duty of care to the defendant in relation to the information contained in the statement which I have found was made to him in or about March 1963? Secondly, if such duty were owed, was it broken? I can deal at once with the second question. I am satisfied that the plaintiffs failed to take reasonable care in relation to the relevant statement. Their fatal error lay in the failure to reappraise the 1961 throughput forecast of 200,000 gallons in the light of the physical *f* characteristics of the site as they became plain when its development was completed in 1963 and before the defendant began negotiations for the April 1963 tenancy. Mr Leitch said, and I accept, that he was disappointed when he saw the results of the building of the showroom. He thought it was, as was the fact, blocking the visibility from Eastbank Street of part of the forecourt. He agreed that the obstruction of the view of the pumps from that street would adversely affect throughput. He also *g* conceded that the site layout was back-to-front and this adversely affected the site's potential. The same view is of course expressed in the plaintiffs' internal memorandum of 4th August 1964.

Paragraph 8B of the defence and counterclaim was amended by an addition made in the course of the trial, which refers to the alleged ignoring of the information contained in Mr Leitch's sketch plan of May 1961 to which I have referred, and the *h* further and better particulars of the plaintiffs' failure to exercise due care contain numerous and, I am sorry to say, repetitive allegations all of which apart from the allegation relating to the design and siting of the station, I find to be wholly unfounded. It is not necessary for me to deal with them in detail.

j

1   [1965] 2 All ER 65, [1965] 1 WLR 623
2   [1913] AC 30, [1911-13] All ER Rep 83
3   [1913] AC at 37, 38, [1911-13] All ER Rep at 85, 86
4   [1913] AC at 43, [1911-13] All ER Rep at 88
5   [1913] AC at 49-51, [1911-13] All ER Rep at 91, 92
6   [1927] AC 177, [1926] All ER Rep 343

My finding that the plaintiffs were in breach of duty, if one was owed to the defen-
a dant, rests and rests solely on a state of facts as to the site which were apparent to the
defendant when he began his negotiations. The plaintiffs' difficulty in relying on this
as an answer to the counterclaim based on negligence lies in the fact, which I found,
that the defendant's realistic assessment of throughput communicated to the plaintiffs' representatives was 100,000 to 150,000 gallons per annum and that he resiled
from his estimate in reliance on the plaintiffs' superior expertise, which so to speak
b 'sugared' their statement so that he relied on what they told him and not what he
himself thought.

I come back to the vital question: did the plaintiffs, in all the circumstances, owe the
defendant the duty in relation to the statement made? My answer is, Yes. The reasons
why I reach this conclusion can be summarised as follows. In *Nocton v Lord Ashburton*[1]
I understand their Lordships to be saying that a duty of care may arise in relation to a
c statement made when there are special circumstances which give rise to an implied
contract in law or to a relationship which equity would regard as fiduciary. Lord
Dunedin[2] treats this liability as an aspect of the law of negligence. That I think is an
important point because one finds very strong echoes of the same position being
taken up in the judgment of Lord Devlin in *Hedley Byrne & Co Ltd v Heller &
Partners Ltd*[3] to which I will now come. In the *Hedley Byrne* case[4], Lord Reid was
d clearly of opinion that such a duty might arise from a special relationship; and the
nature of this he indicated in two passages in his speech. In the first passage[5] he
referred to Lord Haldane's speech in *Robinson v National Bank of Scotland*[6], a case in
which Lord Haldane was virtually repeating points he had made, if that is the right
expression to use, in *Nocton v Lord Ashburton*[1]. Lord Reid said:

e   'This passage makes clear that LORD HALDANE did not think that a duty to
take care must be limited to cases of fiduciary relationship in the narrow sense of
relationships which had been recognised by the Court of Chancery as being of a
fiduciary character. He speaks of other special relationships, and I can see no
logical stopping place short of all those relationships where it is plain that the
party seeking information or advice was trusting the other to exercise such a
f   degree of care as the circumstances required, where it was reasonable for him to
do that, and where the other gave the information or advice when he knew or
ought to have known that the inquirer was relying on him.'

Then in the second passage[7] Lord Reid said this; he was again referring to Lord
Haldane who in *Robinson v National Bank*[8] had used the expression 'a contract to be
g careful':

      '...LORD HALDANE must have meant an agreement or undertaking to be
careful. This was a Scots case and by Scots law there can be a contract without
consideration: LORD HALDANE cannot have meant that similar cases in Scotland
and England would be decided differently on the matter of special relationship
for that reason. I am, I think, entitled to note that this was an extempore judg-
h   ment. So LORD HALDANE was contrasting a "mere inquiry" with a case where
there are special circumstances from which an undertaking to be careful can be
inferred.'

---

1 [1914] AC 932, [1914-15] All ER Rep 45
j 2 [1914] AC at 963, 964, [1914-15] All ER Rep at 57, 58
3 [1963] 2 All ER 575, [1964] AC 465
4 [1963] 2 All ER at 582, [1964] AC at 485, 486
5 [1963] 2 All ER at 583, [1964] AC at 486
6 1916 SC (HL) 154
7 [1963] 2 All ER at 586, [1964] AC at 492
8 1916 SC (HL) at 157

He then went on to deal with the specific facts in that case. Lord Morris of Borth-y-Gest in the *Hedley Byrne* case[1] related the duty to take care in relation to a statement *a* to what he describes as an assumption of responsibility by the maker of the statement; to which he added that the maker should be possessed of some special skill or expertise. Lord Hodson[2] contemplated that the duty of care in the making of statements might arise where there was no fiduciary relationship, as where the maker of the statement held out his skills to reinforce the acceptability of the statement; and Lord Hodson agreed[3] with the assumption of responsibility test with which Lord Morris *b* in his judgment dealt—there is one particularly cogent passage[4]. Then Lord Devlin[5] indicated that the duty of care is not limited by reference to certain types of person or sorts of situations but arose from the situations which he described[6] in his speech. He said:

'It is a responsibility that is voluntarily accepted or undertaken either generally *c* where a general relationship, such as that of solicitor and client or banker and customer, is created, or specifically in relation to a particular transaction.'

Finally Lord Pearce[7] stressed the importance of the existence of a special relationship and said:

'Was there such a special relationship in the present case as to impose on the *d* respondents a duty of care to the appellants as the undisclosed principals for whom National Provincial Bank, Ltd. was making the inquiry? The answer to that question depends on the circumstances of the transaction. If, for instance, they disclosed a casual social approach to the inquiry no such special relationship or duty of care would be assumed . . . To import such a duty, the representation must normally, I think, concern a business or professional transaction whose *e* nature makes clear the gravity of the inquiry, and the importance and influence attached to the answer.'

It seems to me that all their Lordships were all agreed that, apart from a general relationship involving fiduciary aspects such as solicitor and client, bank and customer, the special relationship from which the duty of care in the making of the statements *f* arises, is not limited to particular categories of persons or types of situations. In the Privy Council case, *Mutual Life & Citizens Assurance Co Ltd v Evatt*[8] their Lordships were divided. The majority, Lords Hodson, Guest and Diplock, appeared to limit the duty of care in the making of statements to persons who carried on or held themselves out as carrying on the business of giving advice (see the passage[9] of the majority judgment): *g*

'In their Lordships' view these additional allegations are insufficient to fill the fatal gap in the declaration that it contains no averment that the company to the knowledge of the respondent carried on the business of giving advice on investments or in some other way had let it be known to him that they claimed to possess the necessary skill and competence to do so and were prepared to exercise the necessary diligence to give reliable advice to him on the subject-matter of his *h* enquiry. In the absence of any allegation to this effect the respondent was not entitled to assume that the company had accepted any other duty towards him

---

1 [1963] 2 All ER at 588, 594, [1964] AC at 494, 502
2 [1963] 2 All ER at 598, [1964] AC at 509, 510
3 [1963] 2 All ER at 601, [1964] AC at 514   *j*
4 [1963] 2 All ER at 594, [1964] AC at 502, 503
5 [1963] 2 All ER at 610 et seq, [1964] AC at 528 et seq
6 [1963] 2 All ER at 611, [1964] AC at 529
7 [1963] 2 All ER at 617, [1964] AC at 539
8 [1971] 1 All ER 150, [1971] AC 793
9 [1971] 1 All ER at 160, 161, [1971] AC at 809

a than to give an honest answer to his enquiry nor, in the opinion of their Lordships, did the law impose any higher duty on them. This is in agreement with
the reasoning of Taylor J in the High Court of Australia with which the judgment
of Owen J is consistent.'

The *Mutual Life* case[1] was an appeal from the High Court of Australia in which the
High Court by a majority had decided that the claim of the person who had suffered
b damage as a result of relying on a mis-statement as to the financial situation of a
company disclosed a cause of action. The majority in the *Mutual Life* case[2] went
on with a substantial note of caution:

'As with any other important case in the development of the common law,
Hedley Byrne[3] should not be regarded as intended to lay down the metes and
bounds of the new field of negligence to which the gate is now opened. Those will
c fall to be ascertained step by step as the facts of particular cases which come
before the courts make it necessary to determine them. The instant appeal is an
example: but their Lordships would emphasize that the missing characteristic of
the relationship which they consider to be essential to give rise to a duty of care in
a situation of the kind in which the respondent and the company found themselves
when he sought their advice, is not necessarily essential in other situations, such as,
d perhaps, where the advisor has a financial interest in the transaction on which he
gives his advice.'

Then there is a reference made to the decision of Scott Cairns J in *W B Anderson &
Sons Ltd v Rhodes (Liverpool) Ltd*[4] which has been cited to me. A reference is made to
the American Restatement of the Law of Torts, and the passage concludes:
e
'On this, as on any other metes and bounds of the doctrine of *Hedley Byrne*[3]
their Lordships are expressing no opinion. The categories of negligence are never
closed and their Lordships' opinion in the instant appeal, like all judicial reasoning,
must be understood secundum subjectam materiam.'

f It should be said, I think, that the majority in the Privy Council approached this
matter as a decision to be made on a point of pleading, although the observations
which the court made are clearly of general application.

The minority, Lords Reid and Morris, differed from the majority view, the effect of
which—implicit in the last passage which I have read—can fairly be said to be that the
duty of care relating to statements is limited to people who are carrying on, or holding
themselves out as carrying on, the business of giving advice in relation to the subject-
g matter of the statements which they make. But, with respect, I think that this is
unduly restrictive of the duty under consideration. I much prefer the minority
reasoning of Lord Reid and Lord Morris, and I cite the following passage[5]:

'Then it was argued that an adviser ought not to be under any liability to
exercise care unless he had, before the advice was sought, in some way held
h himself out as able and willing to give advice. We can see no virtue in a previous
holding out. If the enquirer, knowing that the adviser is in a position to give
informed advice, seeks that advice and the adviser agrees to give it, we are unable
to see why his duty should be more onerous by reason of the fact that he had
previously done the same for others. And again, if the previous conduct of the
j adviser is relevant, would it be sufficient that, in order to attract new customers

1   [1971] 1 All ER 150, [1971] AC 793
2   [1971] 1 All ER at 161, [1971] AC at 809
3   [1963] 2 All ER 575, [1964] AC 465
4   [1967] 2 All ER 850
5   [1971] 1 All ER at 163, [1971] AC at 812

or increase the goodwill of existing customers, he had indicated a general willingness to do what he could to help enquirers, or must he have indicated a willing- *a*
ness and ability to deal with the precise kind of matter on which the enquirer
seeks his assistance?'

Then comes the vital test, in the minority's opinion:

    'In our judgment when an enquirer consults a businessman in the course of his *b*
business and makes it plain to him that he is seeking considered advice and
intends to act on it in a particular way, any reasonable businessman would
realise that, if he chooses to give advice without any warning or qualification, he
is putting himself under a moral obligation to take some care. It appears to us to
be well within the principles established by the *Hedley Byrne* case¹ to regard his
action in giving such advice as creating a special relationship between him and the *c*
enquirer and to translate his moral obligation into a legal obligation to take
such care as is reasonable in the whole circumstances.'

    Subject to one last point which I have to consider, I am satisfied that there was, in
the circumstances of this case, a special relationship; and this special relationship I
find to have existed, even if one applies the tests indicated by the majority in the *d*
Mutual Life case². The present was a situation in which in fact the plaintiffs did
have a financial interest in the advice they gave. This was advice which was given to
the defendant who, as they knew, was asking or seeking information and was in fact
given information which would lead him into the decision to enter into the tenancy
agreement, the benefit of which the plaintiffs as landlords would have. If one applies
the *Mutual Life* minority test, which is expressed in the passage³ which I have just *e*
read, it is clear in my judgment, subject to the final point I am now coming to, that
this was a situation in which the plaintiffs owed the defendant a duty of care.
    The last point on which the counterclaim could founder is whether the fact that
the statement was made in the context of pre-contractual negotiations between the
plaintiffs and the defendant, and from which a contract resulted, excludes the duty of
care. McNair J (obiter) in *Oleificio Zucchi v Northern Sales Ltd*⁴ did take this view; *f*
but it was quite unnecessary for him to do so, because he was dealing with a case
stated on an arbitration award in which the arbitrator found that there had been *no*
failure to take care in the making of a statement in a pre-contractual relationship
situation. It is also possible to contend that the observations of the House of Lords
in the *Hedley Byrne* case¹ assumed that statements made in pre-contractual negotiations between parties who ultimately came to contract are excluded from the duty *g*
of care principle: see, for example, what Lord Reid said in a passage in his speech in
*Hedley Byrne*⁵: 'Where there is a contract there is no difficulty as regards the contracting parties: the question is whether there is a warranty.' But there are other
relevant passages in *Hedley Byrne*¹ and, taking the speeches as a whole, in my
judgment it is not right to regard *Hedley Byrne*¹ as containing anything which
excludes the duty of care relationship in a pre-contractual negotiation situation. It *h*
seems to me that Lord Devlin's observations⁶ are a clear indication to the contrary,
because he was dealing in those passages with the situation where one has running
alongside a contractual relationship and a relationship which gives rise to a duty of
care.

j

1 [1963] 2 All ER 575, [1964] AC 465
2 [1971] 1 All ER 150 at 160, 161, [1971] AC 793 at 809
3 [1971] 1 All ER at 163, [1971] AC at 812
4 [1965] 2 Lloyd's Rep 496
5 [1963] 2 All ER at 581, [1964] AC at 483
6 [1963] 2 All ER at 602, 603, 609, [1964] AC at 516, 517, 526, 527

It is right to say there is no direct authority on this point which is binding on me.
a There was in fact a decision of Bean J in *Coats Patons (Retail) v Birmingham Corpn*[1].
But this is a decision which I find not helpful, because in that case it was conceded that
there was a duty of care situation in relation to the making of statements.

I have however been referred to *Dillingham Construction Pty v Downs*[2], an Australian
case, a decision of Hardie J sitting in the Supreme Court of New South Wales. This
question is discussed by the judge at some length. I think it is sufficient if I read
b passages from the headnote, having first said that this is a decision which was handed
down after the Privy Council had decided the *Mutual Life* case[3] in the way which has
been indicated. The facts, putting them very briefly, were that the plaintiffs had
entered into a contract to undertake certain works in a New South Wales harbour;
these works became much more difficult to carry through at the contract price,
because all sorts of snags and difficulties emerged, since there were disused coal
c workings under the harbour; the defendant knew of the existence of these workings
but nothing had been said of them to the plaintiffs. So the plaintiffs alleged, amongst
other things, that there was a duty of care on the defendant to give them this information, in the course of making statements in the pre-contractual situation, and that this
duty of care had been broken. The relevant passage in the headnote is as follows[4]:

d   'Held: (1) The policy of the common law is to uphold contracts freely made
      between parties who are at arm's length and on equal terms. The pre-contract
      relationship between such parties would not normally qualify as a special relation-
      ship of the type which, according to the doctrine of *Hedley Byrne & Co. Ltd.* v. *Heller
      & Partners Ltd*[5], would subject one or other of the parties to a duty of care in the
      assembly or presentation of facts, figures or other information as to the subject
e   matter of the contract.'

Then there is a reference to McNair J's case[6] and to two other Australian cases[7]
where the point had arisen but in which no determination was reached about it.
Then the headnote goes on:

      '(2) In the present case, in view of the very special nature of the contract and
f   the nature and extent of the specialised knowledge in the possession of the
      defendant which would have been of the utmost importance to the plaintiffs if it
      had been imparted to them, the mere fact that the parties were in a pre-contract
      relationship at the time when the duty was said to have been created
      and to have been breached, would not in itself necessarily preclude the
      application of the principle under consideration. (3) Upon a consideration of
      all relevant factors . . . there was no assumption or acceptance by the defendant,
g   in fact or law, of the task of providing the plaintiffs with accurate or full
      information . . .'

I am not going to read passages from Hardie J's judgment; they are, in my view,
accurately summarised in those passages in the headnote. I find the reasoning and the
decision in his case to be very helpful, because it does indicate a view, which I personally
h hold, that the fact that statements are made in a pre-contractual relationship does
not preclude the person to whom the statements are made from relying on the duty
of care in the making of the statements by the person who is making them.

The special features of the present case are, of course, that here was the defendant
who had himself formed what he thought a realistic estimate of the turnover of this

1   (1971) 69 KIR 356
j 2   [1972] 2 NSWLR 49
3   [1971] 1 All ER 150, [1971] AC 793
4   [1972] 2 NSWLR at 49, 50
5   [1963] 2 All ER 575, [1964] AC 465
6   *Oleificio Zucci ASP v Northern Sales Ltd* [1965] 2 Lloyd's Rep 496
7   *Presser v Caldwell Estates Pty Ltd* [1971] 2 NSWLR 471; *Morrison-Knudson International Co
    Inc v The Commonwealth* (1972) 46 ALJR 265

garage; he puts his realistic figure to the plaintiffs, who are the landlords seeking a
tenant for their premises, and he is given by them a different estimate which I find *a*
to be affected by a failure to take care in relation to its being made. I have given the
reasons why I hold that there was a failure to take care. Furthermore, the plaintiffs
must have appreciated, and I am sure they appreciated—and in fact they quite
frankly said this—that had the statement not been made the defendant would certainly
have not entered into the tenancy agreement of 10th April at the rental and on the
terms which he did.   *b*

As a matter of principle, I cannot think there is anything wrong in holding that the
duty of care in relation to the making of statements may arise in a pre-contractual
situation. For example, it is well established that a seller of goods which are dangerous,
and which are dangerous to the knowledge of the seller, can be liable to the buyer in
damages for negligence as well as in damages for breach of the contractual term in
relation to the merchantability or fitness of the goods; and the passages to which I *c*
have referred in Lord Devlin's speech in *Hedley Byrne*[1] are really on the same lines.
The theory that in some way or other the law is different in relation to negligent
mis-statements from the law concerning the circulation of dangerous things—the
theory that there is a distinction between a negligent statement and some negligence
or omission in relation to goods or chattels or land—seems to me to be harking
back to the pre-*Hedley Byrne*[1] days when the view was taken, on the basis of cases *d*
since overruled—*Le Lievre v Gould*[2] and the majority decision in *Chandler v Crane,
Christmas & Co*[3]—that there was no duty of care in relation to the making of statements. What *Hedley Byrne*[1] has done, I am quite satisfied, is to indicate that there is
really no difference between the duty of care in relation to the making of a statement
and the duty of care in relation to other situations which, if broken, might give rise to a
cause of action for damages for negligence. Of course, it may well be said, if my view is *e*
right, that I am opening the door very wide indeed and eroding the principle of
caveat emptor and the general principle that contracting parties are at arm's length.
But I fall back on what Lord Reid said in *Hedley Byrne*[4] on this point:

> 'A reasonable man, knowing that he was being trusted or that his skill and
> judgment were being relied on, would, I think, have three courses open to him. *f*
> He could keep silent or decline to give the information or advice sought: or he
> could give an answer with a clear qualification that he accepted no responsibility
> for it or that it was given without that reflection or inquiry which a careful
> answer would require: or he could simply answer without any such qualification.
> If he chooses to adopt the last course he must, I think, be held to have accepted
> some responsibility for his answer being given carefully, or to have accepted a
> relationship with the inquirer which requires him to exercise such care as the *g*
> circumstances require.'

Therefore, for those reasons I find for the defendant on his counterclaim for damages
for negligence. I am against him on the other basis of his counterclaim, but I have
indicated sufficiently, I trust, the four walls within which this liability falls. It follows
that the plaintiffs are entitled to £1,103·69, subject to setting off such damages as the *h*
defendant may be entitled to having regard to my findings on the plaintiffs' liability
on the counterclaim.

*Judgment for the plaintiffs and judgment for the defendant on the counterclaim. Defendant's
damages to be assessed.*

Solicitors: *Durrant, Piesse & Co* (for the plaintiffs); *Batchelor, Fry, Coulson & Burder,*
agents for *Bellis, Son & Ashton,* Southport (for the defendant).   *j*

E H Hunter Esq Barrister.

1 [1963] 2 All ER 575, [1964] AC 465
2 [1893] 1 QB 491
3 [1951] 1 All ER 426, [1951] 2 KB 164
4 [1963] 2 All ER at 583, [1964] AC at 486

Practice Direction

FAMILY DIVISION

Paternity – Blood test – Divorce – Guardian ad litem – Official Solicitor – Appointment of Official Solicitor as guardian ad litem where blood test likely to be directed – Appointment usually unnecessary in first instance – Circumstances in which appointment should be made.

Where the court directs the trial of a separate issue as to the paternity of a child it has been general practice at the same time to direct under r 115 of the Matrimonial Causes Rules 1973[1] that the child be separately represented, and the Official Solicitor has almost invariably been appointed as guardian ad litem.

It is now usual, whenever a question of paternity needs to be resolved, to direct the use of blood tests under RSC Ord 112 or CCR Ord 46, r 23, as the case may be. It is found in practice that the report on the blood tests often in effect disposes of the issue or dispute.

While the court should, when such a question of paternity arises, always consider the position of the child, it is not necessary, especially when blood tests are likely to be directed, for the court in the first instance to make an order appointing the Official Solicitor as guardian ad litem of the minor unless either: (a) the minor is ten years old or more; or (b) there are special circumstances making such appointment immediately desirable.

Where no order appointing the Official Solicitor is made at the time blood tests are directed, the direction for blood tests should include a provision that the proceedings be restored for further directions by the registrar when the report by the tester has been filed.

The registrar should then decide, in the light of the position following the report, whether to order that the Official Solicitor be appointed guardian ad litem of the minor. Such an order should be made, for example, where in the opinion of the court the issue as to paternity is still a live one or other aspects of the case make it desirable that the minor should be represented by the Official Solicitor.

The Registrar's Practice Direction dated 8th March 1965[2] is cancelled.

Issued by the President with the concurrence of the Lord Chancellor.

D NEWTON
Senior Registrar

20th December 1974

---

1 SI 1973 No 1972; see Rayden on Divorce (12th Edn, 1974), vol 2, p 3406
2 [1965] 1 All ER 905, [1965] 1 WLR 600

Graddage v London Borough of Haringey a

CHANCERY DIVISION
WALTON J
15th OCTOBER 1974

Housing – Notice from local authority – Validity – Challenge to validity – Appeal – Pre- b
scribed time limit – Notice invalid on its face – Unauthorised signature – Failure to appeal
against notice within time limit – Effect – Whether recipient of notice precluded from challeng-
ing validity – Whether recipient entitled to disregard notice – Housing Act 1957, ss 11(1),
37(1), 166(2).

A local authority served notices under s 9(1)^a of the Housing Act 1957 on the owner c
of two properties requiring certain works to be carried out in order to make them
fit for human habitation. The owner failed to do the necessary works. Accordingly
the local authority, in exercise of its powers under s 10 of the 1957 Act, entered the
properties and executed the works. It also carried out on each of the properties
other works which had not been specified in the s 9 notices. In order to recover the
expenses incurred in executing those works the local authority served on the owner d
notices under s 10(3)^b of the 1957 Act demanding payment. The notices were in
similar terms and stated: 'To: Work Under: Housing Act 1957, Sections 9 and 10.'
They gave details of how the total figure had been made up and were signed by the
borough treasurer. Subsequent letters from the borough treasurer indicated that
the total figures given in the demands included sums for the additional works which
had not been specified in the s 9 notices. The owner failed to pay the sums demanded. e
Some years later the plaintiff, who was the successor in title to the properties, brought
proceedings to challenge the demands on the grounds that they had not been signed
by the town clerk or his lawful deputy, as required by s 166(2)^c of the 1957 Act, and
that they included sums in respect of works not specified in the s 9 notice. The
local authority contended that, since the owner of the properties had not appealed
to the county court under s 11(1)^d of the 1957 Act against the demands within 21 f
days of service, they had become operative by virtue of s 37(1)^e of the 1957 Act.

Held – The requirement of s 166(2) that a notice or demand should be signed by the
town clerk or his deputy was mandatory and accordingly a notice or demand which
failed to comply with that requirement was invalid. Since the demands served on
the owner were invalid on their face the owner was entitled to disregard them; he g
was not compelled to appeal against them in order to be in a position to assert their
invalidity (see p 227 j to p 228 a and p 231 b c and j to p 232 a, post).
   West Ham Corpn v Charles Benabo & Sons [1934] 2 KB 253 and dictum of Salmon LJ
in *Plymouth City Corpn v Hurrell* [1967] 3 All ER at 358 applied.
   Dicta of Davies and Russell LJJ in *London Borough of Hillingdon v Cutler* [1967] 2 All
ER at 366 not followed. h
   Per Walton J. Although the local authority was not entitled to demand payment
in respect of costs incurred on work which had not been specified in the s 9 notice,
since there was nothing on the face of the demands served on the owner to indicate
that the local authority was asking for payment of such costs, the owner would only
have been entitled to challenge the validity of the demands on that ground by way of
an appeal under s 11 of the 1957 Act (see p 231 e and g to p 232 a, post). j

a Section 9(1), so far as material, is set out at p 226 g, post
b Section 10, so far as material, is set out at p 226 j to p 227 a, post
c Section 166(2) is set out at p 227 e, post
d Section 11(1), so far as material, is set out at p 227 b, post
e Section 37(1), so far as material, is set out at p 227 d, post

Notes

a For authentication of notices under the Housing Act 1957, see 19 Halsbury's Laws (3rd Edn) 586, para 947.

For the Housing Act 1957, ss 9, 10, 11, 37, 166, see 16 Halsbury's Statutes (3rd Edn) 121, 122, 125, 147, 232.

Cases referred to in judgment

b *Becker v Crosby Corpn* [1952] 1 All ER 1350, 116 JP 363, 50 LGR 444, 26 Digest (Repl) 706, 150.

Cohen v West Ham Corpn [1933] Ch 814, [1933] All ER Rep 24, 102 LJCh 305, 149 LT 271, 97 JP 155, 31 LGR 205, CA, 26 Digest (Repl) 683, 13.

London Borough of Hillingdon v Cutler [1967] 2 All ER 361, [1968] 1 QB 124, [1967] 3 WLR 246, 131 JP 361, 65 LGR 535, CA, Digest (Cont Vol C) 955, 268a.

c *Plymouth City Corpn v Hurrell* [1967] 3 All ER 354, [1968] 1 QB 455, [1967] 3 WLR 1289, 131 JP 479, 65 LGR 557, CA, Digest (Cont Vol C) 420, 15a.

R v Berkshire (Forest) Justices, ex parte Dallaire [1961] 3 All ER 1138, [1962] 2 QB 629, [1962] 2 WLR 642, 126 JP 48, 60 LGR 172, DC, Digest (Cont Vol A) 657, 150a.

West Ham Corpn v Charles Benabo & Sons [1934] 2 KB 253, [1934] All ER Rep 47, 103 LJKB 452, 151 LT 119, 98 JP 287, 32 LGR 202, 26 Digest (Repl) 685, 33.

d

Case also cited

Benabo v Wood Green Corpn [1945] 2 All ER 162, [1946] KB 38, DC.

Preliminary issue

By a writ issued on 13th April 1973 the plaintiff, Edward Stanley Graddage (as trustee

e of the S A Graddage Will Trust), brought an action against the defendants, the Council of the London Borough of Haringey ('the local authority') claiming, inter alia, a declaration that the local authority were entitled to further payment of £556·85 only in respect of works executed by it on premises known as 106 and 108, North Hill, Highgate, owned by the plaintiff, under the Housing Act 1957 and pursuant to notices served on the plaintiff's predecessor in title on 4th November 1965 and 19th

f January 1966 respectively. By their defence and counterclaim the local authority claimed declarations that it was entitled to the further payment of £2,339·86 in respect of the works. On 19th June 1974, on the summons for directions, the master ordered the trial of a preliminary issue whether certain documents served on the plaintiff's predecessor in title by the local authority, or any of them, amounted to a valid demand for payment under ss 9 and 10 of the 1957 Act. The facts are set out

g in the judgment.

David Hands for the plaintiff.
Robert Wakefield for the local authority.

h **WALTON J.** The plaintiff in this action is the present owner of two properties, 106 and 108 North Hill, Highgate. On 4th November 1965 and 19th January 1966 respectively the local authority served notices on the then owner of these premises under s 9 of the Housing Act 1957 requiring the execution of certain works. The validity of these notices is not in dispute. The owner did not do the works and the local authority, as they were entitled to do, entered the respective properties and

j executed the works. They also carried out other works not included in the s 9 notices on each of the properties. Having done so, they sought to recover the costs from the owner under their statutory powers, and it is with the documents seeking to effect that result that I am concerned in the present case. They are, first of all, notices in virtually similar terms in regard to each of the properties, addressed to a former owner of the property. The name of the property is given and it then says:

'To: Work Under: Housing Act, 1957, Sections 9 and 10.' It gives the date of completion and makes up an amount for wages and materials and so forth, and comes out *a* at the final figure. I am not particularly concerned with the exact amount of those figures. It is headed: 'Borough of Haringey J. Owen [and then his qualifications are given] Borough Treasurer.' Then there are a number of directions as to payment. Those two notices are dated 23rd May 1968 and are on what I judge to be printed forms. There is then a letter of 2nd July 1968 which has been sent by the borough treasurer, and is signed by him, to the solicitors for the then owner of the *b* property, and that letter, besides asking in substance for payment, says this: 'During the course of the works additional items' that is to say items additional to those in the original s 9 notice 'became necessary as follows' and then they are set out, there being three matters in connection with no 106 and a number of matters in connection with no 108. There is then another document of 7th August 1968 which is another letter from the borough treasurer demanding payment. There are two final appli- *c* cations of 22nd August 1968, one in respect of each of the properties bearing a printed signature of the borough treasurer. Finally there is a letter of 6th November 1968 signed by the borough treasurer. All of those quite clearly requested payment of the sums alleged to be due. It will be observed that, first of all, none of these documents is signed by the town clerk or his deputy, and, second, the sums sought to be recovered in each case include the costs of the additional works, that is to say *d* those in addition to those originally specified in the s 9 notices.

On 13th April 1973 the present proceedings were launched, the plaintiff claiming a declaration that the local authority is only entitled to be paid a very much less sum than that which it claims. In effect, he wishes to exclude the costs of the additional works. The local authority says that by failing to appeal against the demands which it alleges it has made in time, the plaintiff is now too late to *e* take the points he wishes to take, and so battle has been joined.

In these proceedings a preliminary issue has been directed by the master in the following terms:

'It is ordered that the following question be tried as a preliminary issue before the trial of this action and counterclaim, namely, whether the documents dated *f* 23rd May, 1968, 2nd July, 1968, 7th August, 1968, 22nd August, 1968 and 6th November, 1968 in paragraph 2 of the Defence referred to, or any of them, amounted to a valid demand under sections 10 and 11 of the Housing Act, 1957.'

In order to make the debate intelligible, it is necessary to bear in mind the relevant sections of the 1957 Act which are, fortunately, few. There is first of all s 9(1) which provides:

g

'Where a local authority . . . are satisfied that any house is unfit for human habitation [which was the case here], they shall, unless they are satisfied that it is not capable at a reasonable expense of being rendered so fit, serve upon the person having control of the house a notice—(*a*) requiring him, within such reasonable time, not being less than twenty-one days, as may be specified in *h* the notice, to execute the works specified in the notice . . .'

Section 10(1) provides:

'If a notice under the last foregoing section requiring the person having control of a house to execute works is not complied with, then, after the expiration of the time specified in the notice or, if an appeal has been made against the notice *j* and upon that appeal the notice has been confirmed with or without variation, after the expiration of twenty-one days from the final determination of the appeal, or of such longer period as the court in determining the appeal may fix, the local authority may themselves do the work required to be done by the notice, or by the notice as varied by the court, as the case may be.'

That, of course, is what happened here. Then s 10(3) provides:

a

'Any expenses incurred by the local authority under this section, together with interest from the date when a demand for the expenses is served until payment, may, subject as hereinafter provided, be recovered by them, by action or summarily as a civil debt, from the person having control of the house ...'

Then s 11, under the rubric right of appeal:

b

'(1) Any person aggrieved by ... (*b*) a demand for the recovery of expenses incurred by a local authority in executing works specified in any such notice ... may, within twenty-one days of the service of the notice, demand or order, appeal to the county court within the jurisdiction of which the premises to which the notice, demand or order relates are situate, and no proceedings shall be taken by the local authority to enforce any notice, demand or order in relation to

c

which an appeal is brought before the appeal has been finally determined ...
'(3) On an appeal to the county court under this section the judge may make such order either confirming or quashing or varying the notice, demand or order as he thinks fit ...'

Section 37(1) provides:

d

'Any notice, demand or order against which an appeal might be brought to a county court under this Part of this Act shall, if no such appeal is brought, become operative on the expiration of twenty-one days from the date of the service of the notice, demand or order, and shall be final and conclusive as to any matters which could have been raised on such an appeal ...'

e Finally, s 166(2) provides:

'A notice, demand or other written document proceeding from a local authority under this Act shall be signed by their clerk or his lawful deputy.'

On these facts in law, counsel for the plaintiff submits that the demands in each of them are nullities and that for two reasons: first, none of such notices is signed by the

f town clerk or his deputy as required by s 166(2) of the Act; second, the sum sought thereby to be recovered in respect of each house contains costs in respect of works which were not set out in the original s 9 notices. He then proceeds to say that the demands being nullities, he is not obliged to appeal against them, and that there is nothing in s 37 of the Act which turns an invalid notice or demand when un-appealed within the 21 days' time limit into a valid notice or demand.

g   Counsel for the local authority on the other hand, contends that the requirements of s 166(2) are purely procedural; that, accordingly, the only remedy open to the plaintiff was to appeal under s 11 and that, not having done so, by virtue of s 37 he cannot now take the point in these proceedings. He further says that whatever might be said of later demands, after the letter of 2nd July 1968 had been written by the local authority explaining that the earlier demands of 23rd May contained costs

h in relation to work additional to that included in the s 9 notice, nevertheless those two earlier demands themselves were not, on their faces, in any way invalid. Accordingly, the plaintiff not having appealed against either of those within the 21 days is not now able to question their validity on counsel for the plaintiff's second ground.

It appears to me that on both principle and authority counsel for the plaintiff is correct in his first submission. In view, however, of the extremely careful arguments

j which have been addressed to me on this matter, I must take some little time with the authorities. On principle, however, it is difficult to see that the requirements of s 166(2) are not mandatory, so that the subject who is affected thereby may not be able to see at a glance whether the notice which he has received is one which does or does not properly proceed from the local authority. He is, surely, obviously entitled to ignore any notice ostensibly served on him in exercise of the relevant statutory powers unless it bears on its face the imprimatur of the town clerk or his deputy. There would seem to be no conceivable reason why he should have to go to the *a* length of appealing against any other notice if he does not like it. His legal obligations in this regard are limited to those franked by the authority of the town clerk.

So far as authority is concerned, I begin with *Cohen v West Ham Corpn*[1]. There were two points there in issue. The first was whether the plaintiff was entitled to maintain that a notice served on him under what is now s 9 of the 1957 Act which, on its face, complied with all the necessary formalities was invalid because the council *b* had not, in fact, properly considered the matters which, under that section, it was bound to consider; two, whether, if he could show that he had, in fact, complied with the notice, the council was nevertheless entitled to enter and carry out the work it wished to carry out. The second point is of no relevance here. It was held by Maugham J and the Court of Appeal that the plaintiff's only remedy would have been to have appealed against the notice when originally served. It is to be *c* observed that there was no evidence before the court one way or the other whether the council had, in fact, properly discharged the duties laid on it by the section before issuing the notice. None of the judges in the Court of Appeal was prepared to assume, in the absence of evidence, that the council was in default, and they were unanimous as to that point being decisive. As I read their judgments, however, they were far from unanimous as to what the position would have been had there been such *d* evidence before them. Lord Hanworth MR said[2]:

'The simple point that is before this Court is whether those notices were valid or invalid. We have come to the conclusion that they were valid. Consideration must be given to ss. 17, 18 and 19 of the Housing Act [1930], also to s. 22, which enables an appeal to be made to the county court, but makes it impossible *e* to appeal after the lapse of twenty-one days from the date of the service of the notice. In the present case there was no appeal to the county court within the twenty-one days of the service of the notices, and the result is that they stand good in their terms if they are valid notices under s 17.'

He then proceeds to enquire whether they were valid notices under s 17 and came to the conclusion that they were. But his enunciation of the simple point before the *f* court as being whether those notices were valid or invalid, and particularly his use of the word 'if' towards the concluding part of that paragraph, makes it appear to me clearly that if he had not found that they were valid, he would have decided the case in favour of the plaintiff. Lawrence LJ took, I think, a different view. He said[3]:

'Be that as it may, however, even if the Council has in some way neglected its *g* duty in the present case, I am clearly of opinion that the notices were given by the Council under s. 17, and, therefore, if the owner desired to dispute the notices on the ground that they were improperly given, his proper course was to appeal against them under s. 22.'

It is to be observed, however, that he was of the opinion that the notices had, in fact, *h* been given by the council under s 17. He expressed no opinion, because the matter was not before him, as to what the consequences would have been if the notices had not borne the signature of the town clerk, and therefore the notices had been bad on their face. I do not think it is possible to assume that automatically he would have said that the notices were given by the council in those circumstances under s 17. Romer LJ expressly declined to deal with the point[4]. So there one has, as it *j* were, one to the right, one to the left, and one dead centre on the point with which

1   [1933] Ch 814, [1933] All ER Rep 24
2   [1933] Ch at 832, [1933] All ER Rep at 26
3   [1933] Ch at 835. [1933] All ER Rep at 27
4   [1933] Ch at 836, [1933] All ER Rep at 28

we are now concerned. Certainly, there is no ratio decidendi in that case which is of
a any assistance, and it was in that state of the law that *West Ham Corpn v Charles Benabo & Sons*[1] was decided. The headnote[2] in that case reads:

> 'On the default of the defendants to render fit for human habitation two blocks
> of houses, numbering twenty-three houses altogether, which were under their
> control, after proper notices served on them, the plaintiff corporation, under s. 18,
> **b** sub-s. 1, of the Housing Act, 1930, did the work themselves, and served a demand
> for payment on the defendants under s. 18, sub-s. 3, of the Housing Act, 1930.
> The claim was signed by one of the plaintiffs' officials, not the town clerk. It
> claimed two sums, one in respect of each block of houses, giving the totals of the
> different items of expenditure, labour and materials, but there was no demand
> for the expenditure on each or any house separately. On these demands being
> **c** made the defendants did not appeal to the county court under s. 22, sub-s. 1 (*b*), of
> the Act of 1930:—*Held*, that the demands were bad, firstly, in that they were not
> signed by the town clerk as directed by s. 120, sub-s. 2, of the Housing Act, 1925,
> which by s. 65, sub-s. 1, of the Act of 1930 is to be construed as one with the latter
> Act; and secondly, because they did not specify the sums spent on each separate
> house. *Held*, further, that the fact that the defendants did not appeal to the
> **d** county court did not make demands good demands, and that "demand" in s. 22,
> sub-s. 1 (*b*), of the Act of 1930 meant a valid demand. The defendants, therefore,
> were not bound to appeal to the county court.'

I may pick up the nub of the decision in the judgment of Atkinson J[3]:

> '. . . but in my view if the document called the demand is one which does not
> **e** create a legal liability to pay, it cannot subsequently create such legal liability
> because of a failure to appeal. It is quite true that s. 18, sub-s. 4, providing for the
> time from which the time limit of six months is to run, says that it is to be
> reckoned from the date of the service of the demand or, if an appeal is made
> against that demand, from the date on which the demand becomes operative.
> But I do not think that quite touches the point that there has to be a good demand
> **f** to create a legal liability. If the demand is not one which satisfies the statutory
> requirements, I cannot for my part see how a neglect to appeal can turn it into a
> good demand. A neglect to appeal certainly debars a defendant from making any
> objection to such matters as the amount, whether the work has been done, the
> reasonableness of the charges, and so on. It is quite clear that a county court judge
> must be able to deal with some such objections as are raised in this case, because
> **g** if the defendants had appealed it would have jumped to the eye of everybody
> that this was a bad notice, and I think the county court judge could have said: I
> quash it; it is a bad notice. But s. 22, sub-s. 1 (*b*), says: "Any person aggrieved by,"
> not any demand, good, bad or indifferent, but "a demand for the recovery of
> expenses incurred by a local authority in executing works specified in any such
> notice." Why is it all set out at such length? Supposing some of these houses had
> **h** been mortgaged. What is the mortgagee to do when he gets served with a demand
> of this kind? I cannot myself see that there is any obligation on a person receiving
> a demand of this sort to appeal if the demand does not come within s. 22, sub-s. 1
> (*b*). I think all statutes of this kind, which confer upon local authorities rights
> which some people think are harsh, are to be dealt with strictly, and I do not think
> I have any right practically to eliminate from that subsection words which I am
> **j** satisfied were put in to indicate the nature of the demand against which a person
> can, and indeed must, appeal.'

---

1 [1934] 2 KB 253, [1934] All ER Rep 47
2 [1934] 2 KB at 253
3 [1934] 2 KB at 264, 265, [1934] All ER Rep at 53

It has been suggested, as will be seen, that *Cohen's* case[1] should have been cited to the learned judge, but it was not, and I cannot myself see that it would have been of *a* the slightest assistance to him dealing as he was with a notice which was, on its face, a bad notice. The strict view of what is now s 166 (2) of the Housing Act 1957 taken in *Benabo's* case[2] has also been taken expressly or impliedly in several cases relating to the service of notices to quit by local authorities, for example in *Becker v Crosby Corpn*[3] and *R v Berkshire (Forest) Justices*[4]. But I do not think these cases afford any real assistance on matters of principle. It is, however, to be noticed that the provision of *b* the Housing Acts of 1925 and 1930 which were under discussion in *Benabo's* case[2] have been re-enacted by Parliament in virtually the same terms in the Housing Act 1957. That having been done in the light of the fact that *Benabo's* case[2] had been decided the way it had been, affords at any rate some argument to the effect that *Benabo's* case[2] carried out the intention of Parliament.

Counsel for the local authority relied heavily, however, on dicta of Davies and *c* Russell LJJ in *London Borough of Hillingdon v Cutler*[5] to which case I must now accordingly turn. The points on which that case was decided were completely different. Harman LJ dealt only with that, but Davies LJ said[6]:

'We have had cited to us two authorities with regard to this point, one a decision at first instance, ATKINSON, J., in *West Ham Corpn v. Charles Benabo & Sons*[2] and the *d* other a decision of this court, *Cohen v. West Ham Corpn*[1]. If it were necessary to decide this point (which, in view of the opinion which I have formed on the first point, it is not), I am bound to say that I should have thought that ATKINSON, J.'s decision in the later case could not stand in the light of the decision of this court in the earlier case, which for some extraordinary reason was not, apparently, cited to ATKINSON, J., although one of the counsel who appeared in the former case also *e* appeared in the later one.'

Russell LJ said[7]:

'I am, alternatively, inclined to think that the validity of the demolition orders could not be challenged on the ground on which they are challenged, having regard to the provisions of s. 20 and s. 37, the Housing Act 1957, to which DAVIES, L.J., has referred.' *f*

With the greatest possible respect to their authors, I think these dicta bear all the signs of not being well considered. As I have already pointed out, it just is not true to say, as Davies LJ appears to assume, that there is anything inconsistent in the actual decisions in the two cases of *Benabo*[2] and *Cohen*[1]. There is not, and it will also be borne in mind that *Cutler's* case[5], which is the case in which they were uttered, is *g* another case like *Cohen*[1] in which the orders were, on their face, good and valid and there was nothing on their face to suggest that they were anything other than good and valid. Whilst, therefore, I naturally am somewhat shaken in my views by being referred to the dicta, I do not feel constrained to follow them. I think there is a very good reason why *Cohen's* case[1] was not cited in *Benabo's* case[2], namely that it really had absolutely nothing whatsoever to do with it, and I am strengthened in the resolve *h* not to follow them by a dictum of another very formidable jurist indeed, Salmon LJ, in a case again under the Housing Act 1957, although that was not the principle point of the case, *Plymouth City Corpn v Hurrell*[8]. That was a curious case where the signature of the town clerk was a mere facsimile. At the end of the day, by virtue of the

1 [1933] Ch 814, [1933] All ER Rep 24
2 [1934] 2 KB 253, [1934] All ER Rep 47
3 [1952] 1 All ER 1350
4 [1961] 3 All ER 1138, [1962] 2 QB 629
5 [1967] 2 All ER 361, [1968] 1 QB 124
6 [1967] 2 All ER at 366, [1968] 1 QB at 138
7 [1967] 2 All ER at 366, [1968] 1 QB at 139
8 [1967] 3 All ER 354, [1968] 1 QB 455

j

Local Government Act 1933 as amended by the London Government Act 1963, it was
a held that the facsimile signature was good. In the course of the case Davies LJ not unnaturally referred to what was then the recent decision in *Cutler's* case[1] and received
the rather chilling, but in my view completely justified, reply from counsel that that
case was of no assistance, which I think was the right answer precisely because of the
differences between notices which are and those which are not bad on their face; but
the dictum to which I wish to refer is in the following words[2]:
b

'Under s. 166 (2) of the Housing Act, 1957, a notice from a local authority under
the Act of 1957 must be signed by "their clerk or his lawful deputy". That is a
mandatory requirement. Clearly the local authority cannot "duly give" a notice
under s. 9 unless that notice is signed by their clerk or his lawful deputy.'

This conclusion appears to me to be fully in line with both principle and authority
c and I am content to follow it. Accordingly, I come to the conclusion that none of the
alleged demands relied on by the local authority in this case are valid demands within
the meaning of the Housing Act 1957 and that the plaintiff need not pay to any of them
the slightest attention whatsoever.

I should be happy to leave the matter there, but in deference to the forceful and
attractive argument of both counsel, I think I ought to deal with counsel for the
d plaintiff's second basic ground of submission of invalidity, namely that the notices
were all bad because the amount thereby claimed was excessive in that it included
works not originally covered by the s 9 notices. I agree with counsel for the plaintiff
that as regards the letter of 2nd July and all subsequent notices or demands, this point
is a good and valid one. I do not think that a local authority is entitled to add to the £X
which it might conceivably properly recover under the Act £Y to which it has no title
e under the Act whatsoever and claim that an un-appealed notice in respect of £X plus
Y becomes binding on the recipient. My difficulty is, however, that pointed out by
counsel for the local authority, namely, that there is nothing on the face of either of the
notices of 23rd May to indicate any invalidity. It is not as if, for example, the sums
claimed were so utterly extravagant that anyone comparing the s 9 notice and the
demand for payment would say, 'There is a mistake here somewhere'. I have con-
f sidered whether there could be any case for dissecting the amount claimed so as to
show that, in fact, part of it was excessive, being outside the sum which can be recovered
under the statutory provision; but I cannot think of any proper way in which what is
sometimes possible (for example, when one is dealing with the statute of limitation it
is possible to dissect acknowledgments in balance sheets and things of that nature) can
be properly effected in a case such as the present. I cannot really think that those sort
g of sophisticated procedures were meant to be applied to what is intended basically to
be a very simple notice, a demand for money under the 1957 Act. I therefore think that
consistently with what appears to me to be the right line of demarcation, that is to say
between notices which are bad on their face (either for lack of compliance with the
requirement of the Act or because they are so utterly extravagant in their terms that
anyone acquainted with the property or any other relevant fact would say unhesitat-
h ingly that there must be a mistake somewhere) in which case the recipient may either
appeal if so minded, or, if of sufficiently strong nerve simply disregard them, and
those which disclose no invalidity on their face and in relation to which, in general, the
only relief to be obtained is, in my view, by way of appeal.

I therefore think at the end of the day that the two notices of 23rd May fall into the
category of those notices which, for aught that appears in them or from any of the
j surrounding circumstances immediately apparent, are good and valid and therefore
can only be challenged by an appeal. Therefore, at the end of the day, I come to the
conclusion that counsel for the plaintiff succeeds on his first point, but, had it been

---

1   [1967] 2 All ER 361, [1968] 1 QB 124
2   [1967] 3 All ER at 358, [1968] 1 QB at 465

material, would have lost on the second. I will accordingly answer the issue raised in
this action by declaring that none of the specified documents amounted to a valid   *a*
demand under ss 10 and 11 of the 1957 Act.

Declaration accordingly.

Solicitors: *Crossman, Block & Keith* (for the plaintiff); *Dennis E Wood* (for the local
authority).   *b*

Jacqueline Metcalfe Barrister.

Practice Direction   *c*

CHANCERY DIVISION

*Practice – Chambers – Chancery Division – Adjournment to judge – Application to master
for adjournment – Time limit – Applications after order pronounced but before order perfected.*

d

1. Many minor orders made by chancery masters are not drawn up but remain
recorded in their notes, available to be perfected at some future time should occasion
arise. This practice is authorised by RSC Ord 42, r 4, and is convenient but its value is
diminished if a party requires an adjournment to the judge in accordance with para 3
of the Practice Direction of 24th September 1965[1] some considerable time after the
order has been pronounced. Difficulty also arises when a request to adjourn is made   *e*
at a late stage in the drawing up of an order. The said para 3 is accordingly cancelled.

2. A party dissatisfied with a master's order should, immediately on the pronouncement of the order, apply to the master to adjourn to the judge or allow him
time to consider whether to require such an adjournment. If, however, a party omits
to make such application or has a change of mind he may, before the order is perfected but not later than seven days after it has been pronounced, apply to the master *f*
to restore the matter to his list, at the party's own expense, so that an adjournment
may be required or the matter may be considered further. The perfection of orders
will not be delayed in anticipation of any such application.

3. If no requirement to adjourn to the judge is made within the period fixed by the
master or, where no such period has been fixed, if no application to restore is made
within seven days after the order has been pronounced, the order may be perfected *g*
at the instance of any party regardless of any requirement or application made out
of time.

4. The above is without prejudice to the power of the judge or master under the
inherent jurisdiction to withdraw an order of his own motion for sufficient cause at
any time before it is perfected.

By the direction of the Vice-Chancellor.   *h*

R E Ball
18th December 1974   Chief Master

---

1 [1965] 3 All ER 306, [1965] 1 WLR 1259

a
R v Davis (Alan Douglas)

COURT OF APPEAL, CRIMINAL DIVISION
LAWTON, SCARMAN LJJ AND DUNN J
18th OCTOBER, 1st NOVEMBER 1974

b   *Criminal law – Evidence – Character of accused – Evidence against other person charged with
same offence – Evidence establishing that either accused or co-accused or both guilty of offence
charged – Accused denying guilt – Denial necessarily implicating co-accused – Whether
denial constituting 'evidence against' co-accused – Criminal Evidence Act 1898, s 1(f)(iii).*

The appellant and the co-accused visited a private house for the ostensible purpose of
c   inspecting antiques belonging to the occupier. Following the visit it was discovered
that certain articles, including a gold cross on a chain and a soup tureen, were missing.
The appellant and the co-accused were jointly charged on indictment with the theft
of those articles. In his evidence-in-chief at the trial the co-accused denied stealing the
cross and chain, and in cross-examination he stated that, shortly after the time of the
alleged theft, the appellant had showed him the cross and chain, producing it from his
d   pocket. In his examination-in-chief the appellant denied the allegation and, when
cross-examined on behalf of the co-accused, said: 'I am not suggesting [the co-accused]
took the cross and chain. As I never, and it is missing, he must have done but I am not
saying he did.' The trial judge allowed an application by counsel for the co-accused to
cross-examine the appellant about his previous convictions under s 1(f)(iii)[a] of the
Criminal Evidence Act 1898 on the ground that he had 'given evidence against
e   [another] person charged with the same offence'. The appellant and the co-accused
were both convicted of stealing the soup tureen and the co-accused alone was convicted of stealing the cross and chain. The appellant appealed against his conviction
on the ground that the judge should not have admitted evidence of his previous
convictions since a mere denial was not evidence of the kind contemplated by
f   s 1(f)(iii) of the 1898 Act.

Held – As only the appellant or the co-accused or both of them could have stolen the
cross and chain, the appellant's denial that he had done so necessarily undermined
the defence of the co-accused, for if the jury accepted the denial the co-accused stood
little chance of acquittal. It followed that the denial constituted 'evidence against' the
co-accused within s 1(f)(iii) and the appeal would therefore be dismissed (see p 235 j
g   to p 236 a and d, post).

Murdoch v Taylor [1965] 1 All ER 406 applied.
Dictum of Winn J in *R v Stannard* [1964] 1 All ER at 38 explained.

Notes
For admissibility of evidence of bad character, see 10 Halsbury's Laws (3rd Edn) 447,
h   449, paras 823, 828, and for cases on the subject, see 14 Digest (Repl) 410-412, 4008-4025.
For the Criminal Evidence Act 1898, s 1, see 12 Halsbury's Statutes (3rd Edn) 865.

Cases referred to in judgment
Director of Public Prosecutions v Merriman [1972] 3 All ER 42, [1973] AC 584, [1972] 3
WLR 545, 136 JP 659, HL.

j
   a   Section 1, so far as material, provides: '... (f) A person charged and called as a witness
       in pursuance of this Act shall not be asked, and if asked shall not be required to answer,
       any question tending to show that he has committed or been convicted of or been charged
       with any offence other than that wherewith he is then charged, or is of bad character,
       unless ... (iii) he has given evidence against any other person charged with the same
       offence ...'

Murdoch v Taylor [1965] 1 All ER 406, [1965] AC 574, [1965] 2 WLR 425, 129 JP 208, 49
Cr App Rep 119, HL, Digest (Cont Vol B) 175, 4957b.   *a*
R v Stannard [1964] 1 All ER 34, [1965] 2 QB 1, [1964] 2 WLR 461, 128 JP 224, 48 Cr App
Rep 81, CCA, Digest (Cont Vol B) 177, 5018c.

Appeal
On 15th May 1974 in the Crown Court at Chichester before his Honour Judge Cunliffe
the appellant, Alan Douglas Davis, was convicted of theft and sentenced to six months'   *b*
imprisonment. He appealed against conviction with leave of the single judge (Forbes
J). The facts are set out in the judgment of the court.

Rodger Bell for the appellant.
R A Anelay for the Crown.

c

LAWTON LJ. In May 1974 at Chichester Crown Court before his Honour Judge
Cunliffe, the appellant and his co-accused, Owen, were tried on an indictment charging
them with theft. They were alleged to have stolen a gold cross on a chain, a soup
tureen, a pair of prints and a cakestand. The judge directed the jury that there was no
case against either accused as regards the prints and no case against Owen as regards   *d*
the cakestand. On 15th May both Owen and the appellant were found guilty of stealing
the soup tureen. Owen alone was found guilty of stealing the gold cross on a chain.
Owen was sentenced to 15 months' imprisonment, the appellant to six months.
    Now, by leave of the single judge, the appellant appeals against his conviction. He
does so on two grounds: first, that as the two accused had been charged jointly with
theft, the jury could not properly find them both guilty of stealing one article and   *e*
only Owen guilty of stealing the cross on a chain; secondly, that the judge had misdirected himself by adjudging, as he did, that the appellant had given evidence against
Owen so as to make him liable to be cross-examined about previous convictions by
Owen's counsel. He was so cross-examined.
    The first ground of appeal can be disposed of shortly. In our judgment the verdict
returned by the jury was a proper one. A charge of theft made against two persons is   *f*
several as well as joint: see *Director of Public Prosecutions v Merriman*[1]. After a short
discussion, the appellant's counsel agreed that the decision in *Merriman*[1] covered this
case.
    The second ground raises a much more difficult point. In broad terms it is this:
when the evidence establishes that either A or B or both of them acting together must
have committed the crime charged and A in evidence says that B alone was guilty and   *g*
B in his evidence denies that he committed the crime, has B given evidence against A
within the meaning of the Criminal Evidence Act 1898, s 1(*f*)(iii) as construed in
Murdoch v Taylor[2]?
    The appellant and Owen were a couple of 'knockers', that is to say they went
around knocking at doors, claiming to be interested in buying antiques and taking
advantage of householders who were ignorant of the value of their possessions to buy   *h*
articles at prices well below the market prices. In this case the Crown alleged that
these two men, having gained entry to the house of an elderly lady on the pretence of
looking at some of her possessions, took advantage of her by stealing the articles
mentioned in the indictment. The circumstances were such that one or other or both
of them acting together must have stolen the gold cross on a chain. It was never
recovered. Both denied stealing it. During the course of his interrogation by the   *j*
police the appellant was asked whether he was suggesting that Owen had taken the
cross on a chain and was alleged to have answered: 'I am not suggesting he took the

1   [1972] 3 All ER 42, [1973] AC 584
2   [1965] 1 All ER 406, [1965] AC 574

a cross and chain. As I never, and it is missing, he must have done, but I am not saying he did.'

When Owen gave evidence-in-chief he denied stealing the cross on a chain. He did not then implicate the appellant in the stealing. When he was cross-examined on behalf of the Crown he did so. He alleged that when they were going away in a van, the appellant showed him the cross on a chain, producing it from his pocket. In saying this he was clearly giving evidence against the appellant whose counsel was adjudged *b* to be entitled to cross-examine him about his previous convictions.

At the end of Owen's case, the appellant gave evidence. He too had had previous convictions, one being on facts much the same as in this case. We infer from the way he gave his evidence that he was aware of the dangers which he was likely to face if he gave evidence against Owen. He had to say something about Owen's accusation against him; the jury would have thought it significant if he had not denied it. In *c* examination-in-chief he was asked whether he had shown the cross on a chain to Owen. He said: 'No, that is a pack of lies.' At the end of his examination he repeated his denial. He was cross-examined by both counsel for Owen and the Crown. Owen's counsel cross-examined him about the oral statement about Owen which he was alleged to have made to the police. In the course of answering he said:

d   'I am not suggesting he took the cross and chain. As I never, and it is missing, he must have done but I am not saying he did. If it is not in the house, who did steal it I do not know. I am not going to implicate [sic] that he stole it because I never saw him steal it. I have got no idea.'

A piece of evidence given by a police officer which when first given was only admissible against the appellant had now become evidence which the jury could consider when *e* considering the case against Owen. The extended admissibility had come about not because the appellant wanted to say anything about Owen but because the latter's counsel had made him do so.

Counsel for the Crown also cross-examined the appellant about Owen's accusation against him to which he replied: 'That is a pack of lies. As I stand here that is a pack of lies.' There then followed a submission by counsel for the Crown that he should be *f* allowed to cross-examine the appellant because in one of the answers he had given to Owen's counsel he had sought to establish his own good character. The judge refused this application. Some discussion between the judge and Owen's counsel then followed in the course of which the judge said to him: 'I thought you were going to make some application about cross-examining this witness [i e the appellant].' Counsel said that he was and referred to the appellant's statement that Owen's evidence against him *g* was a 'pack of lies'. After more discussion the judge ruled that the appellant had given evidence against Owen so as to entitle Owen's counsel to cross-examine the appellant about his previous convictions. The reason given for the ruling was that the appellant's evidence had undermined Owen's defence. The problem for us has been whether this ruling was correct. Owen's counsel took advantage of it.

h The meaning of the words 'he has given evidence against any other person charged with the same offence' in s $1(f)$(iii) of the Criminal Evidence Act 1898 was considered by the House of Lords in *Murdoch v Taylor*[1]. The following propositions were clearly established by that case: first, that what an accused person says in cross-examination is just as much a part of his evidence as what he says in examination; secondly, that 'evidence against' means evidence which supports the prosecution's case or under-mines the defence of the co-accused; and thirdly, that it is not necessary to show the *j* witness to have had a hostile intent against his co-accused.

When what happened in this case is examined against these propositions it seems clear to us that the appellant did give evidence against Owen. As only he or Owen or both of them could have stolen the cross on a chain, his denial that he had done so

---

1   [1965] 1 All ER 406, [1965] AC 574

necessarily meant that Owen had. In cross-examination, whilst trying to avoid saying
Owen had stolen these articles, he said he must have done so. In our judgment these *a*
answers would have undermined Owen's defence. We should add that we have
attached no importance to the use by the appellant of such phrases as 'pack of lies'
and 'that was dreamed up yesterday' as forms of denial. A denial in restrained language
is often more likely to undermine the evidence of a co-accused than a denial in the
language of the gutter.

It was submitted on behalf of the appellant that there was a fallacy in our reasoning *b*
because mere denials are not the kind of evidence contemplated by s 1(*f*)(iii) of the
1898 Act. This was based on an opinion expressed by Winn J in *R v Stannard*[1], approved
and adopted by Lord Donovan in *Murdoch v Taylor*[2]. It may well be that, as Winn J
put it in *Stannard*[3]—

'mere conflict between a version of fact given by one is quite insufficient to *c*
amount to evidence given by one against the other.'

Much will depend, however, on the relevance of the conflict to the issues in the case.
Here the conflict went to the very root of the case. If the jury accepted the appellant's
denial, Owen had little chance of acquittal. For his part the appellant had to make the
denial if he was to have any chance of being acquitted and in making it, by under- *d*
mining Owen's defence, he exposed himself to cross-examination about his previous
convictions, thereby severely damaging, probably destroying, such chances as he had.
Some may not find this result attractive: Lord Reid did not (see *Murdoch v Taylor*[4]).
We have to apply the law as it is. No injustice has been done in this case. Once the
appellant through his counsel had suggested that Owen was a rogue, the jury would
have wanted to know whether the pot was calling the kettle black. If they had not
been told, they might have drawn inferences which were not justified by the facts. *e*
The appeal will be dismissed.

Appeal dismissed.

Solicitors: *Registrar of Criminal Appeals*; *T Lavelle*, Lewes (for the Crown). *f*

Sepala Munasinghe Esq   Barrister.

---

1   [1964] 1 All ER 34 at 38, [1965] 2 QB 1 at 12
2   [1965] 1 All ER at 415, [1965] AC at 591
3   [1965] 2 QB at 12, cf [1964] 1 All ER at 38
4   [1965] 1 All ER at 408, [1965] AC at 583

a # Clifford Davis Management Ltd v WEA Records Ltd and another

COURT OF APPEAL, CIVIL DIVISION
LORD DENNING MR AND BROWNE LJ
b 18th, 21st OCTOBER 1974

Equity – Undue influence – Inequality of bargaining power – Assignment of copyright – Validity – Circumstances in which assignment invalid – Agreement to assign unenforceable because of inequality of bargaining power Relationship between parties – Composer of music and business manager – Manager procuring composer to enter into agreement – c *Composer not receiving independent advice – Terms of agreement manifestly unfair – Agreement requiring composer to assign to manager for nominal sum copyright in all compositions for period of ten years – Whether assignment valid.*

The plaintiff was the manager of a 'pop group'. Two members of the group, M and W, were talented composers who wanted to get their songs published. The plaintiff d persuaded them to sign publishing agreements with him. Although M and W were experienced performers and were of full age, they were not experienced in business. The agreements were in a standard form. They were long documents which had been professionally drafted. Neither M nor W received independent legal advice before signing. The agreements bound M and W for a period of five years, which could be extended for a further five years at the plaintiff's option, to e assign to the plaintiff the English and world copyright in any work composed by them. The consideration for the assignment was to be 1s per work, though royalties were payable by the plaintiff if he chose to exploit the works. M promised to deliver at least one composition a month. Under the agreements the plaintiff had the right to reject any work without payment, but even when he chose to retain a work he was under no obligation to exploit or to do anything with it. Further, the agree-f ments gave him the right to assign the copyright of the work to any third party. Subsequently the plaintiff and the group split up. The group acquired a new manager. M and W wrote new songs for the group which were recorded in an album of records. Arrangements were made for the defendants to distribute the album in England. The plaintiff brought an action in which he sought an interim injunction restraining the defendants from infringing his copyright in the songs composed by M and W g by selling, distributing or otherwise dealing with the album.

Held – The defendants had succeeded in establishing a prima facie case that the agreements between the plaintiff and M and W were unenforceable in that they had been made in circumstances in which there was inequality of bargaining power since (i) at the time when the agreements were made M and W were members of a h pop group of which the plaintiff was the manager, (ii) M and W had received no independent legal advice before signing the agreements and (iii) the terms of the agreements were manifestly unfair. It followed that there was a prima facie case that the assignments of copyright under the agreements were invalid. The plaintiff was not therefore entitled to an interim injunction (see p 240 e to p 241 e, post).

A *Schroeder Music Publishing Co Ltd v Macaulay* [1974] 3 All ER 616 and dictum of j Lord Denning MR in *Lloyds Bank Ltd v Bundy* [1974] 3 All ER at 765 applied.

Notes
For undue influence in relationship to transactions inter vivos, see 9 Halsbury's Laws (4th Edn) 174, para 298, 17 Halsbury's Laws (3rd Edn) 672-681, paras 1297-1312, and for cases on the subject, see 12 Digest (Reissue) 125-142, 687-820.

For agreements in restraint of trade, see 38 Halsbury's Laws (3rd Edn) 20, 21, paras 13, 15, and for cases on the subject, see 45 Digest (Repl) 443-449, 271-297.   *a*

Cases referred to in judgments

Esso Petroleum Co Ltd v Harper's Garage (Stourport) Ltd [1967] 1 All ER 699, [1968] AC 269, [1967] 2 WLR 871, HL, Digest (Cont Vol C) 985, *132a*.

Lloyds Bank Ltd v Bundy [1974] 3 All ER 757, [1974] 3 WLR 501, CA.

Schroeder (A) Music Publishing Co Ltd v Macaulay [1974] 3 All ER 616, [1974] 1 WLR   *b*
1308, HL; *affg* sub nom *Instone v A Schroeder Music Publishing Co Ltd* [1974] 1 All ER 171.

Interlocutory appeal

By a writ issued on 27th September 1974, the plaintiffs, Clifford Davis Management Ltd, brought an action against the defendants, WEA Records Ltd and CBS Records   *c*
Ltd, claiming (i) an injunction restraining the defendants by their servants, agents or otherwise from infringing the plaintiffs' musical and literary copyright in the compositions and writings of Anne Christine McVie and Robert Lawrence Welch by manufacturing, publishing, releasing for sale, selling, distributing or in any other manner dealing with a record album bearing the title 'Heroes are Hard to Find'; (ii) delivery up of all infringing records and all plates or other originals thereof;   *d*
and (iii) damages. On 8th October 1974 Forbes J in chambers granted the plaintiffs an interim injunction in the terms of the injunction claimed in the writ. The defendants sought to have the interim injunction discharged but the judge refused to discharge it. The defendants appealed against that refusal. The facts are set out in the judgment of Lord Denning MR.

     e

F M Drake QC and *Harold Burnett* for the defendants.
David Hunter QC and *R Neville Thomas* for the plaintiffs.

LORD DENNING MR. There is a pop group of four or five musicians called 'Fleetwood Mac'. The group take their name from two of their members, Michael   *f*
Fleetwood and John McVie. The group have formed themselves into a limited company called Fleetwood Mac Promotions Ltd. The members are the directors and shareholders of it. I will call them 'the group'. The manager of the group was Clifford Adams, known as Clifford Davis. He has now turned himself into a limited company: Clifford Davis Management Ltd. He and his wife are the sole shareholders. I will call it 'the manager'.   *g*

The manager, by a written agreement, had agreed to act as agent and manager for the group. The group was successful. They made several tours to the United States of America and were well known there. In January 1974 the manager fell out with the group or they fell out with him. He went his own way; they went theirs. On his side he formed a new group of five musicians. He called them 'Fleetwood Mac', and sent them on a tour of the United States. The original group   *h*
brought an action against the manager for passing-off. On 12th July 1974 Goff J granted an interim injunction until trial.

The original group, having broken off from their old manager, worked under new management. Two of them were talented composers. They wrote and composed new songs and put them to music. They made arrangements with well-known firms in the United States to record them and distribute the records. These firms   *j*
have made a record album called 'Heroes are Hard to Find'. It contained 11 songs. It has been released in the United States and has sold 150,000 copies. Now the firms in the United States, through their English subsidiaries, wish to release this record album for sale in England. It is very important, they say, that this should be done quickly, within two weeks—else it will lose its impact.

The old manager, Clifford Davis, now seeks to prevent this record album being
a sold in England. He claims that his company is entitled to the copyright in this
album 'Heroes are Hard to Find', even though it was produced by the group after
he ceased to have anything to do with them. He has brought this action against
the makers and distributors, through their English subsidiaries. He seeks to stop
the sale and distribution in England. The judge in chambers granted an interim
injunction. The defendants sought to have it discharged. The judge refused to
b discharge it. The defendants appeal to this court.

The words and music of the 11 songs were composed by two talented members of
the group. One of them is Christine McVie. She joined the group in July 1970.
The other was Mr Robert Welch. He joined the group in January 1971. They are
both of full age and are experienced performers and composers. But several months
after they had joined the group, the old manager got each of them to sign a publishing
c agreement with him. Mrs McVie signed hers on 1st January 1971. Mr Welch
signed his on 21st December 1972. Under each publishing agreement the manager
(that is the old manager through his self-same company) described himself as 'the
publisher'. Under each agreement, the composer was to write and compose songs.
The publisher was to be at liberty to publish them. If he did so, the composer was
to get 10 per cent of the retail price of the sheet music and 50 per cent of the royalties
d on the records. So far so good. It was fair enough. But when each of the publishing
agreements is examined, it is found to contain some amazing provisions. It gives the
publisher, alias the manager, a stranglehold over each of the composers. It does it
by means of the copyright. In every work which the composer produces over a
period of ten years, the copyright is vested in the publisher. I will not read the
agreements in full. I will summarise the provisions. (1) Each composer bound
e himself to the publisher for five years, but the publisher could extend the term at
his option for another five years, making it ten years in all. (2) The composer for
the whole of those ten years was tied hand and foot to the publisher. Whenever
he composed a work he was bound to submit it to the publisher, who at once became
entitled to the copyright in it. The composer assigned to the publisher the copyright
in every one of his works. Not only the English copyright but the copyright through-
f out the world. Each was expected to be very productive. In the case of Mrs McVie,
she promised to deliver to the publisher at least one complete musical composition
a month. (3) The publisher was not bound to publish any of the works. At any
rate, he did not give any positive undertaking to do so. All he did was to promise
Mrs McVie that he would use his best endeavours to launch her works to the fullest
extent. There was no such promise to Mr Welch; but it may perhaps be implied.
g (4) The publisher had the right for six months to reject any work without payment.
If he did not reject it, he was held to have retained it. But even when he retained
it, he was not under any positive obligation to exploit it or to do anything with it.
If he thought it was not good enough for him to publish, he could put it in a drawer
and forget about it; or he could burn it. He did not have to pay anything for it,
except that he had to pay Mrs McVie the sum of 1s and to pay Mr Welch a sum left
h blank in the form. No doubt it was also intended to be 1s. (5) The manager had
the right to assign the copyright of the works to any third party. He could assign
it to anyone he chose no matter that the assignee knew nothing about the trade or
about publishing and had not the means to publish it. The composer had no say in
it at all.

Now the question arises: is the court bound to enforce this assignment of copyright
j at the suit of the publisher alias manager? The agreement is of the same class as
the agreement considered by the Court of Appeal in *Instone v A Schroeder Musical
Publishing Co Ltd*[1], and by the House of Lords[2] only last week.

---

1   [1974] 1 All ER 171
2   Sub nom *Schroeder Music Publishing Co Ltd v Macaulay* [1974] 3 All ER 616, [1974] 1 WLR
     1308

An agreement such as this is not an agreement which is 'in restraint of trade' strictly so called. It does not preclude a man from exercising his trade at all. But *a* it is an agreement which is 'restrictive of trade' in this sense, that it requires a man to give his services and wares to one person only for a long term of years to the exclusion of all others. Lord Reid said[1] that such restrictive agreements do not normally require to be justified; but he did add the important qualification. Wherever such agreements contain—

'contractual restrictions [which] appear to be unnecessary or to be reasonably capable of enforcement in an oppressive manner, then they must be justified before they can be enforced.'

Lord Diplock[2] urged the courts to be vigilant. They should look into the provenance of such agreements. He made it clear[3] that if one party uses his superior bargaining power so as to 'exact . . . promises that were unfairly onerous', or 'to drive an unconscionable bargain', then the courts will relieve the other party of his legal duty to fulfil it. He gave this pertinent example. A strong concern prepares a new standard form containing terms which are most unfair—and dictates to the customer: 'Take it or leave it.' The customer is in a weak position. He has no real option but to accept. The courts may decline to enforce it or, at any rate, may decline to enforce *d* any term which is unfair to the customer, such as an exemption clause.

Reading those speeches in the House of Lords, they afford support for the principles we endeavoured to state at the end of last term about inequality of bargaining power. It was in *Lloyds Bank Ltd v Bundy*[4]. *Instone's* case[5] provides a good instance of those principles. The parties there had not met on equal terms. The one was so strong in bargaining power and ʳhe other so weak that, as a matter of common fairness it *e* was not right that the strong should be allowed to push the weak to the wall.

In the present case I would not presume to come to any final opinion. It is only interlocutory. But there are ingredients which may be said to go to make up a case of inequality of bargaining power. The composers can urge these points. (1) That the terms of the contract were manifestly unfair. Each composer was tied for ten years without any retaining fee and with no promise to do anything in return save *f* for a promise by the publisher to use his best endeavours. Such a promise was so general as probably to be of little use to the composer. See what Lord Reid said in *Instone's* case[6]. And the tie of ten years for a composer seems to me just as unfair as a tie of 21 years in a solus agreement for a garage: see *Esso Petroleum Co Ltd v Harper's Garage (Stourport) Ltd*[7]. (2) That the property (the copyright in every one of the works over ten years) was transferred for a consideration that was grossly inadequate. It was 1s for each work. It is true that if the publisher chose to exploit a work, he was *g* to pay royalties; but if he did not do so, he got the copyright for 1s. (3) That the bargaining power of each of the composers was gravely impaired by the position in which he or she was placed vis-à-vis the manager. Each composer was in a group which was managed by him. They wanted to get their songs published. It was their ladder to success. In order to get the songs performed—and to get them *h* published—they were dependent on the manager. Their needs and desires were dependent on his will. He could say Aye or No. He was skilled in business and finance. They were composers talented in music and song but not in business. In negotiation they could not hold their own. That is why they needed

---

1   [1974] 3 All ER at 622, [1974] 1 WLR at 1314
2   [1974] 3 All ER at 624, [1974] 1 WLR at 1316
3   [1974] 3 All ER at 623, 624, [1974] 1 WLR at 1315, 1316
4   [1974] 3 All ER 757 at 765, [1974] 3 WLR 501 at 508, 509
5   [1974] 3 All ER 616, [1974] 1 WLR 1308
6   [1974] 3 All ER at 621, 622, [1974] 1 WLR at 1313, 1314
7   [1967] 1 All ER 699, [1968] AC 269

j

a manager. (4) That undue influences or pressures were brought to bear on the
a composers by or for the benefit of the manager. The manager did not condescend
to say how the agreements came to be signed. But from the internal evidence much
can be inferred. They were cyclostyled and hence came from a stock of forms.
They were very long and full of legal terms and phrases. Hence they were drawn
up by lawyers. Some spaces had been filled in by typewriters, others left blank.
Hence done by clerks in the office. Both the composer and the publisher signed in
b the presence of the same witness. It may be inferred that the manager took a stock
form, got the blanks filled in and asked the composer to sign it without reading it
through or explaining it. One thing is clear from the evidence. The composer had
no lawyer and no legal advisers. It seems to me that, if the publisher wished to
exact such onerous terms or to drive so unconscionable a bargain, he ought to have
seen that the composer had independent advice.
c For these reasons it may well be said that there was such inequality of bargaining
power that the agreement should not be enforced and that the assignment of copyright was invalid and should be set aside. In any case, the balance of convenience
is all in favour of discharging the injunction. The defendants are responsible concerns. They are ready to keep an account of their sales. If the publisher is right, he
will be adequately compensated in damages.
d On those grounds, I would allow the appeal and discharge the injunction.

BROWNE LJ. I agree. As Lord Denning MR has said, we are dealing in this
case with an interlocutory matter. We therefore only have to be satisfied that there
is a prima facie case, that these agreements may be unenforceable. The final
e decision will, of course, be made at the trial. For the reasons given by Lord Denning
MR I am satisfied, as he is, that there is such a prima facie case.
Counsel for the defendants also raised a point about repudiation, but he was not
asked to address us on this point, which, however, remains open for the future if he
wishes to rely on it.
So far as balance of convenience is concerned, again I entirely agree with Lord
f Denning MR. I assume that the offer made in the letter from the solicitors to the
first defendants dated 1st October 1974 that all royalties arising from the sales of
this album will be paid to a suspense account and held there until the dispute has
been settled still stands.
Accordingly I agree that this appeal should be allowed and the injunction
discharged.
g

Appeal allowed; injunction discharged; undertaking given in letter of 1st October 1974
that royalties arising out of sale of album 'Heroes are Hard to Find' would be placed on a
suspense account until dispute settled, reaffirmed by counsel for the defendants.

Solicitors: *Harbottle & Lewis* (for the defendants); *Clintons* (for the plaintiffs).

Wendy Shockett Barrister.

International Tank and Pipe SAK v Kuwait Aviation Fuelling Co KSC

COURT OF APPEAL, CIVIL DIVISION

LORD DENNING MR, ORR AND BROWNE LJJ

8th, 9th OCTOBER 1974

Conflict of laws – Contract – Arbitration – Time-bar – Extension of time – Jurisdiction of English court – Contract made outside jurisdiction – Proper law of contract English law – Clause conferring right to refer disputes to arbitration within specified time limit – Arbitration procedure to be governed by foreign law – Dispute arising – Expiry of time limit under arbitration clause – Application by party to English court to extend time limit – Whether English court having jurisdiction to grant extension – Arbitration Act 1950, s 27.

By a written contract the contractors agreed to construct a new fuelling depot for the employers at the Kuwait International Airport. Both parties were companies registered in Kuwait. The contract was expressed to be subject to general conditions prepared by the International Federation of Engineers together with certain supplementary conditions of particular application. Clause 75 of the conditions provided that the contract was to be construed and operated in conformity with the laws of England and that the respective rights and liabilities of the parties were to be in accordance with the laws for the time being in force. Clause 67 made provision for the settlement of disputes by requiring them to be referred in the first place to the engineer who should give the parties written notice of his decision within 90 days. A party which was dissatisfied with the engineer's decision could submit the matter to arbitration, however, by communicating a claim to arbitration to the engineer within 90 days of receiving notice of his decision. If no such claim were made the engineer's decision was to be final and binding. Any dispute submitted to arbitration was to be settled finally under the Rules of Conciliation and Arbitration of the International Chamber of Commerce. By art 16 of those rules the arbitration procedure was to be governed by the law of procedure chosen by the parties or, failing such choice, by that of the country in which the arbitrator held the proceedings. In 1972 a dispute arose concerning certain extra asphalting carried out by the contractors. They maintained that the work represented a variation from the contract specification for which they were entitled to additional payment. The question was referred to the engineer by the contractors on 9th December 1972. On 25th January 1973 the engineer rejected the contractors' claim. There followed a period during which the parties attempted to negotiate a settlement of the dispute but on 19th April the contractors, realising that the 90 day period in which a claim to arbitration could be made would expire on 25th April, wrote to the engineer explaining the position. Their letter stated: 'Should no settlement be reached, we reserve our right to have the matters in dispute settled by arbitration in accordance with clause 67.' The employers did not accept that that letter constituted a sufficient communication of a claim to arbitration within 90 days of the engineer's decision. The contractors therefore applied to the High Court in London for an extension of time for commencing arbitration proceedings under s 27[a] of

---

a   Section 27 provides: 'Where the terms of an agreement to refer future disputes to arbitration provide that any claims to which the agreement applies shall be barred unless notice to appoint an arbitrator is given or an arbitrator is appointed or some other step to commence arbitration proceedings is taken within a time fixed by the agreement, and a dispute arises to which the agreement applies, the High Court, if it is of opinion that in the circumstances of the case undue hardship would otherwise be caused, and notwithstanding that the time so fixed has expired, may, on such terms, if any, as the justice of the case may require, but without prejudice to the provisions of any enactment limiting the time for the commencement of arbitration proceedings, extend the time for such period as it thinks proper.'

the Arbitration Act 1950 on the grounds that they would otherwise suffer undue
a hardship.   The employers contended that the court had no jurisdiction to entertain
an application under s 27 since it was possible that the arbitration would be conducted
according to the rules of procedure of the law of some country other than England.

Held – As English law was the proper law of the contract, it governed the interpretation and effect of the contract between the parties, and in particular, it governed
b the arbitration clause, even though the law governing the procedure in an arbitration
arising from the contract might be some other law.   The question whether s 27 of
the 1950 Act could be invoked to extend time for initiating a claim to arbitration was
therefore a matter to be decided according to English law since any right to go to
arbitration was a right arising under the contract and not a matter of procedure in an
arbitration which did not yet exist.   Section 27 was to be looked on as being, in effect,
c an additional statutory term written into the arbitration clause and, as such, its
interpretation, application and effect were to be governed by English law.   Accordingly, the English court had jurisdiction to grant an extension of time (see
p 246 *c* to *j* and p 247 *b* to *g*, post).
James Miller and Partners Ltd v Whitworth Street Estates (Manchester) Ltd [1970] 1 All
ER 796 applied.
d

Notes
For conflict of laws in relation to arbitration clauses in a contract, see 2 Halsbury's
Laws (4th Edn) 280, para 546, and for cases on the subject, see 2 Digest (Repl) 448,
173-175.
For the Arbitration Act 1950, s 27, see 2 Halsbury's Statutes (3rd Edn) 457.
e

Cases referred to in judgments
Liberian Shipping Corporation v A King & Sons Ltd [1967] 1 All ER 934, [1967] 2 QB 86,
[1967] 2 WLR 856, [1967] 1 Lloyd's Rep 302, CA, Digest (Cont Vol C) 24, 7c.
Miller (James) and Partners Ltd v Whitworth Street Estates (Manchester) Ltd [1970] 1 All
ER 796, [1970] AC 583, [1970] 2 WLR 728, [1970] 1 Lloyd's Rep 269, HL, Digest
f (Cont Vol C) 29, 1949a.
Rolimpex (Ch E) Ltd v Avra Shipping Co Ltd (The Angeliki) [1973] 2 Lloyd's Rep 226.

Cases also cited
Rendal (A/S) v Arcos Ltd [1937] 3 All ER 577, 58 Lloyd LR 287.
Richmond Shipping Ltd v Agro Co of Canada Ltd (The Simonburn (No 2)) [1973] 2 Lloyd's
g   Rep 145.
Tradax Export S A v Volkwagenwerk AG [1970] 1 All ER 420, [1970] 1 QB 537, CA.

Interlocutory appeal
This was an appeal by the defendants, the Kuwait Aviation Fuelling Co KSC,
against an order of Ackner J made on 14th May 1974 by which the plaintiffs, Inter-
h national Tank and Pipe SAK, were allowed an extension of 14 days from the date
of the order in which to initiate arbitration proceedings in respect of a dispute which
had arisen under a contract made between the plaintiffs and the defendants.   The
facts are set out in the judgment of Lord Denning MR.

A R Barrowclough QC for the defendants.
j *Johan Steyn* for the plaintiffs.

LORD DENNING MR.   This case arises out of some construction work at the
Kuwait International Airport.   The defendants, Kuwait Aviation Fuelling Co ('the
employers') wanted to construct a new fuelling depot.   They employed the plaintiffs,

International Tank and Pipe Co SAK of Kuwait ('the contractors'). Both companies
were registered in Kuwait. Whilst the work was being done, there was a dispute   *a*
about some asphalting. The contractors claimed to be paid for it. The employers
refused. The engineer decided against the contractors. They wished to refer it
to arbitration. But the employers said that the contractors did not make the claim
for arbitration within the permitted time. The contractors seek an extension of
time under s 27 of the English Arbitration Act 1950. The question is whether the
court has any jurisdiction to grant an extension.   *b*
     The contract was made on 24th March 1971. It was subject to the general con-
ditions prepared by the International Federation of Engineers, as amended and
supplemented by particular clauses, including this clause, cl 75:

> 'Construction of Contract: The contract shall in all respects be construed and
> operated in conformity with the laws of England and the respective rights and   *c*
> liabilities of the parties shall be in accordance with the Laws for the time being
> in force.'

The general conditions themselves contained a cl 67 about the settlement of disputes.
I will not read it in full. It is similar to provisions in our English contracts for engineering works. They are based on the fact that many questions arise which require
immediate solution. The engineer makes the decision then and there so that the   *d*
works can go ahead without delay. But his decisions can afterwards be reviewed—
and referred to arbitration—after the works are completed. In order to have such
a review, a party who is dissatisfied with the engineer's decision must give notice
within 90 days. The material parts of the clause are these:

> 'If the engineer has given written notice of his decision to the employer and   *e*
> the contractor and no claim to arbitration has been communicated to him by
> either the employer or the contractor within a period of 90 days from receipt of
> such notice, the said decision shall remain final and binding upon the employer
> and the contractor.'

So the aggrieved party is barred unless he claims arbitration within 90 days. The   *f*
clause goes on:

> 'If the engineer shall fail to give notice of his decision as aforesaid within a
> period of 90 days after being requested as aforesaid or *if either the employer or the
> contractor be dissatisfied with any such decision*, then and in any such case either the
> employer or the contractor *may within 90 days after receiving notice of such decision*
> or within 90 days after the expiration of the first named period of 90 days (as   *g*
> the case may be) *require that the matter* or matters in dispute be referred to
> arbitration as hereinafter provided.'

That means that within 90 days the party who is dissatisfied can require the matter
to be submitted to arbitration. The clause contains this final provision:

> 'All disputes or differences in respect of which the decision (if any) of the   *h*
> engineer has not become final and binding as aforesaid shall be finally settled
> under the Rules of Conciliation and Arbitration of the International Chamber of
> Commerce by one or more arbitrators appointed in accordance with the said
> Rules.'

Such being the relevant clauses, I turn to the facts of this particular case. A dispute
arose about some asphalting which had been done, on the ground that it was an   *j*
extra or variation. The contractors claimed additional payment. The employers
refused it. On 9th December 1972 the contractors wrote to the engineer asking for
a decision on the point whether it was a variation for which they were entitled to be
paid. The contractors asked for a decision within 90 days in accordance with cl 67.
The engineer gave it. On 25th January 1973 his firm wrote saying:

a

'We do not consider that the remedial work required on the asphalt paving as originally laid represents a variation to the contract.'

So there it was. The contractors' claim was made on 9th December 1973. It was rejected by the engineer on 25th January 1973. According to cl 67 the contractors had 90 days in which to communicate to the engineer their claim to arbitration. If they did not communicate it to the engineer, his decision would become final and

b binding. During the 90 days the contractors submitted details of their claim to the employers, and there were negotiations for a settlement. The 90 days were due to expire on 25th April 1973. In order to protect themselves the contractors wrote this letter on 19th April 1973:

c

'We take this opportunity of advising you that at present the dispute between ourselves and the employer is being discussed with a view to possible settlement, before proceeding to arbitration in accordance with clause 67 of the Contract "Settlement of Disputes". Should no settlement be reached, we reserve our right to have the matters in dispute settled by arbitration in accordance with clause 67.'

d There is a difference between the parties about that letter. The contractors say that that letter of 19th April was a sufficient communication of a claim to arbitration within the 90 days, and therefore they are within time under cl 67. The employers say, No, not at all. It was not a sufficient communication of a claim to arbitration. It did not require the matter in dispute to be referred to arbitration. That is a controversy on the true interpretation of cl 67. We need not rule on it today. Suffice

e it to say that the contractors were nervous about the point. They realised that the letter might not be a sufficient communication within cl 67, and that they might be barred by time. So they applied for an extension of time under s 27 of the Arbitration Act 1950. They said that undue hardship would be caused to them if the time was not extended.

This submission raises this important point of jurisdiction. Can s 27 of the 1950

f Act be invoked here? This depends on what is the law to be applied. Is it English law or some other law? The contract itself is to be construed by English law. (That appears from cl 75 which I have read.) But the arbitration is to be governed by the law of Kuwait or some other country. I say this because the arbitration is governed by the rules of the International Chamber of Commerce. (That appears from cl 67 which I have read.) And the Rules of the International Chamber of Commerce say

g in art 16 that the arbitration is governed by the rules—

'of the law of procedure chosen by the parties or, failing such choice, those of the law of the country in which the arbitrator holds the proceedings.'

Thus the parties may choose that the arbitration procedure is to be governed by the law of some country other than England. If they do not so choose, the procedure

h will be governed by the law where the arbitrator sits. That may be in Kuwait.

We reach, therefore, this point. English law governs the interpretation and effect of the contract. But the Kuwait law, or some other law, governs the arbitration procedure. This sort of difference is well known. It is recognised by the decision of the House of Lords in *James Miller and Partners Ltd v Whitworth Street Estates (Manchester) Ltd*[1]. Lord Dilhorne[2] and Lord Wilberforce[3] expressed the opinion that the law is correctly stated in Dicey and Morris[4]:

j _____

1   [1970] 1 All ER 796, [1970] AC 583
2   [1970] 1 All ER at 806, [1970] AC at 612
3   [1970] 1 All ER at 809, 810, [1970] AC at 616
4   Conflict of Laws (8th Edn, 1967), p 1048

'It cannot however be doubted that the courts would give effect to the choice of a [procedural] law other than the proper law of the contract. Thus, if parties *a* agreed on an arbitration clause expressed to be governed by English law but providing for arbitration in Switzerland, it may be held that, whereas English law governs the validity, interpretation and effect of the arbitration clause as such (including the scope of the arbitrators' jurisdiction), the proceedings are governed by Swiss law.'

b

In these circumstances the question is whether English law applies so as to enable the contractors to invoke s 27 of the Arbitration Act 1950? The learned judge held that it did. He said that the rules of the International Chamber of Commerce had not come into operation. Article 16 had not come into force because the parties had not chosen what country was to govern the procedure; and no decision had been taken as to where the arbitration should take place. So the judge thought *c* that the only law which could govern the matter was the proper law of the contract itself, which was English law. The judge may be right about this; but I should prefer to put it differently. It seems to me that English law governs a great deal of the arbitration clause. Take the interpretation of it. Suppose the arbitration clause had said the claim had to be made within three months, and then there was an argument as to whether 'months' meant lunar months or calendar months. That *d* dispute would have to be solved according to English law. Take next the very question here, that is, whether a sufficient 'communication' had been made to the engineer within 90 days. That, too, would have to be decided by English law. Similarly it seems to me that it is for English law to say whether or not s 27 of the 1950 Act can be invoked. That section says that when the terms of the agreement contain a time-bar—   *e*

'the High Court, if it is of opinion that in the circumstances of the case undue hardship would otherwise be caused . . . may, on such terms, if any as the justice of the case may require . . . extend the time for such period as it thinks proper.'

I look on s 27 as being, in effect, an additional statutory term written into the arbitra- *f* tion clause. As such, its interpretation, its application and effect are to be governed by English law. It may be that some other law will govern the procedure in the arbitration itself. It may be Kuwait law, or some other law. But that procedural law does not take effect until the arbitration has actually started, that is to say, not until the arbitrator has been properly appointed and is able to rule on the procedure to be adopted in the arbitration.   *g*

Counsel for the employers drew our attention to *Ch E Rolimpex Ltd v Avra Shipping Co Ltd (The Angeliki)*[1]. In that case Kerr J said that, when there was a time limit under the Hague Rules, it would be very rare for our courts to exercise their power under s 27 of the 1950 Act to extend the time. Counsel submitted that, when parties contracted on the form of an international agreement, the time ought not to be capable of extension by the fortuitous circumstance that the determination of the *h* matter might arise in England. I cannot accept this submission. It may be that other countries have provisions similar to s 27. In any case the parties have agreed that the contract shall be interpreted and operated in conformity with the laws of England. This means reading into it s 27 of the 1950 Act. In my opinion, therefore, the High Court has jurisdiction under s 27 to extend the time.

The next question is whether the judge was right in the circumstances to extend *j* the time. I think he was. The contractors thought that their letter of 19th April 1973 was sufficient claim to arbitration within the 90 days. Thereafter discussions for a settlement continued. It was only on 8th September 1973 that the employers

---

1 [1973] 2 Lloyd's Rep 226

took the point that the 90 days requisite had not been fulfilled. The employers
a knew perfectly well that the contractors were reserving their rights in regard to
arbitration. The employers suffered no prejudice whatever. On 3rd December
1973 the contractors applied for an extension of time under s 27. The judge, applying
Liberian Shipping Corporation v A King and Sons Ltd[1], thought that in all the circumstances undue hardship would be caused to the contractors unless the time was
extended. I agree with him. He extended the time for six weeks. It may be it
b will have to be extended further in view of the appeal. I would dismiss the appeal.

ORR LJ. I entirely agree and do not wish to add anything.

BROWNE LJ. I also agree that the appeal should be dismissed for the reasons
c given by Lord Denning MR. I only add a few words on the question of jurisdiction.
It is common ground that the proper law of a contract and the law governing the
procedure in an arbitration arising from that contract may be different. In this case
the law to be applied to the problem we have to decide is in my view the proper law
of the contract, that is, English law, in accordance with cl 75 of the contract. The
d question is whether the plaintiffs are entitled to require the defendants to go to
arbitration. If they have a right to go to arbitration, this is (and can only be) a right
arising from the contract. The first question, as Lord Denning MR has said, is whether
the plaintiffs' letter of 19th April 1973 was an effective claim or demand for arbitration
under cl 67 of the contract. In my view that is clearly a question of the construction
or operation of the contract within cl 75 and will have to be decided according to
e English law. For the purposes of this appeal, we are assuming that that letter was not
an effective claim or demand. The effect of granting an extension under s 27 of
the Arbitration Act 1950 is that the plaintiffs will be entitled to exercise their right
under cl 67 to claim arbitration although they are out of time and their right to claim
arbitration would otherwise be barred. The effect of granting an extension under
s 27 is that the engineer's decision is no longer final and binding within cl 67. In my
f view this is not a matter of procedure in the arbitration, which in fact does not yet
exist, but a matter of the operation of the contract. In my view, it is a question of
the effect of the arbitration clause, which is stated in the passage from Dicey and
Morris[2] which Lord Denning MR has already quoted and which was approved by
Lord Wilberforce in the House of Lords, in *James Miller and Partners Ltd v Whitworth
Street Estates (Manchester) Ltd*[3], to be a question to be decided in accordance with
English law, in the circumstances of this case. In my view therefore English law
g applies to this problem in accordance with cl 75 and the English courts have jurisdiction to grant an extension of time under s 27 of the Arbitration Act 1950. For this
reason, in addition to those given by Lord Denning MR, I agree that this appeal
should be dismissed.

h *Appeal dismissed. Liberty to apply for further extension of time. Leave to appeal to the
House of Lords refused.*

Solicitors: *Herbert Smith & Co* (for the defendants); *Frere, Cholmeley & Co* (for the
plaintiffs).

j   James Collins Esq Barrister.

1   [1967] 1 All ER 934, [1967] 2 QB 86
2   Conflict of Laws (8th Edn, 1967), p 1048
3   [1970] 1 All ER 796 at 809, 810, [1970] AC 593 at 616

Sun Alliance and London Assurance Co Ltd v Hayman

COURT OF APPEAL, CIVIL DIVISION
LORD SALMON, STEPHENSON LJ AND MACKENNA J
11th, 31st OCTOBER 1974

Landlord and tenant – New tenancy – Business premises – Notice by landlord to terminate tenancy – Validity – Form of notice – Prescribed form – Notice substantially to like effect – Notice informing tenant of right to apply for new tenancy within specified time limit – Notice stating that time running from receipt of notice by tenant – Prescribed form stating that time running from giving of notice by landlord – Whether notice given by landlord 'substantially to the like effect' as prescribed form – Landlord and Tenant (Notices) Regulations 1957 (SI 1957 No 1157), reg 4 – Landlord and Tenant (Notices) Regulations 1969 (SI 1969 No 1771), reg 3, Appendix I, Form 7.

The landlord of premises occupied by a tenant for business purposes purported to give the tenant a notice under s 25 of the Landlord and Tenant Act 1954 terminating her tenancy. The notice complied with all the relevant statutory provisions save that it required the tenant to notify the landlords 'within two months *after receiving* this notice' whether she would be willing to give up possession. In accordance with s 66(2)[a] of the 1954 Act the notice also contained an explanatory note stating that an application by the tenant to the court for a new tenancy 'must be made not less than 2 or more than 4 months *after receipt* of the Notice'. The tenant contended that the notice was invalid since it was not in the form prescribed by reg 4[b] of and the Appendix, Form 7, to the Landlord and Tenant (Notices) Regulations 1957, as amended and replaced by reg 3[c] of, and Form 7[d] in Appendix I to, the Landlord and Tenant (Notices) Regulations 1969, in that it referred to the relevant time limits running from the *receipt* of the landlord's notice rather than from the *giving* of the notice, and furthermore was not a form 'substantially to the like effect' as the prescribed form, within reg 4 of the 1957 regulations, since there might be a significant lapse of time between the giving of the notice by the landlords and its receipt by the tenant.

Held (MacKenna J dissenting) – The effect of s 66(4)[e] of the 1954 Act was that a notice under the provisions of the Act was both given and received when it was served in accordance with s 23(1)[f] of the Landlord and Tenant Act 1927 and therefore, in law,

---

a Section 66(2), so far as material, is set out at p 250 *b*, post

b Regulation 4, so far as material, provides: 'The Forms on the Appendix to these Regulations, or forms substantially to the like effect, shall be used for the following purposes, that is to say . . . (vii) A notice under the provisions of section 25 of the Act, being a notice terminating a tenancy to which Part II of the Act applies, shall . . . be in Form 7 . . .'

c Regulation 3, so far as material, provides: 'For Forms 7 and 9 in the Appendix to the Landlord and Tenant (Notices) Regulations 1957 as amended . . . then shall be substituted the forms so numbered in Appendix I to these Regulations.'

d Form 7, so far as material, is set out at p 250 *g* to *j*, post

e Section 66(4) provides: 'Section twenty-three of the Landlord and Tenant Act 1927 (which relates to the service of notices) shall apply for the purposes of this Act.'

f Section 23(1), so far as material, provides: 'Any notice, request, demand or other instrument under this Act shall be in writing and may be served on the person on whom it is to be served either personally, or by leaving it for him at his last known place of abode in England or Wales, or by sending it through the post in a registered letter addressed to him there . . .'

the time when the notice was given and the time when it was received were one and
a the same, i e the time of service. There was therefore no substantial difference
between the form of the landlord's notice and the prescribed form. Accordingly
the notice was valid (see p 251 *j* to p 252 *a* and *d*, p 253 *h* and p 254 *c*, post).

Notes
For the forms of notice to be served under the Landlord and Tenant Act 1954, see
b 23 Halsbury's Laws (3rd Edn) 840, 841, para 1629.
For the Landlord and Tenant Act 1927, s 23, see 18 Halsbury's Statutes (3rd Edn)
468.
For the Landlord and Tenant Act 1954, ss 25, 66, see ibid 559, 604.
For the Landlord and Tenant (Notices) Regulations 1957, reg 4, see 12 Halsbury's
Statutory Instruments (3rd Reissue) 115.
c

Cases referred to in judgments
Compagnie Continentale D'Importations v Handelsverstretung der Union der SSR in Deutsch-
land (1927) 29 Ll LR 52; *affd* (1928) 138 LT 663, 17 Asp MLC 428, 33 Com Cas 213,
30 Ll LR 140, CA, 39 Digest (Repl) 517, *587*.
Newborough (Lord) v Jones [1974] 3 All ER 17, [1974] 3 WLR 52, CA.
d *Price v West London Investment Building Society* [1964] 2 All ER 318, [1964] 1 WLR 616,
CA, 31(2) Digest (Reissue) 948, *7737*.

Appeal
The defendant, Freda Hayman ('the tenant') appealed against the decision of his
Honour Judge Lind-Smith given at the Warwick County Court on 10th December
e 1973 whereby it was adjudged that the plaintiffs, Sun Alliance and London Assurance
Co Ltd ('the landlords'), were entitled to possession of the shop and premises situate
at 32 The Parade, Leamington Spa, Warwick, which had been let to the tenant by
a lease dated 2nd June 1966 for a term of two years at a yearly rent of £1,200, and it
was ordered that the tenant give to the landlords possession of the property on
25th January 1974. On 25th January 1974 the tenant was granted a stay of execution
f of the order pending the hearing of an appeal. The tenancy was one to which Part II
of the Landlord and Tenant Act 1954 applied. The facts are set out in the judgment
of Stephenson LJ.

Anthony Dinkin for the tenant.
I A B McLaren for the landlords.
g   *Cur adv vult*

31st October. The following judgments were read.

STEPHENSON LJ. On 7th August 1972 the landlords purported to give the
h tenant notice under the provisions of s 25 of the Landlord and Tenant Act 1954
terminating her tenancy.
There is no dispute that the notice complied with all the provisions of the section
save one. It stated that the landlords would oppose an application for the grant
of a new tenancy as required by s 25(6) of the 1954 Act. It was properly served on
the tenant in compliance with s 23 of the Landlord and Tenant Act 1927 as required
j by s 66(4) of the 1954 Act. But it required the tenant 'within two months *after*
receiving this Notice to notify me in writing whether or not you will be willing to
give up possession of the premises' on 25th March 1973 and it referred to Note 2
which was in these terms:

'Part II of the Act enables the tenant, on being served with a notice in this
form, to apply to the court for an order for the grant of a new tenancy. Such

an application, however, will not be entertained unless the tenant has within
2 months after receiving the Notice terminating the tenancy notified the landlord   *a*
in writing that he will not be willing to give up possession of the premises on the
date specified in the Notice. The application must be made not less than 2
or more than 4 months *after receipt* of the notice.'

By s 25(1) and s 66(1) of the 1954 Act the landlords' notice had to be given in the
form prescribed by regulations made by the Lord Chancellor by statutory instrument,   *b*
and that form was required by s 66(2) to—

'include such an explanation of the relevant provisions of this Act as appears
to the Lord Chancellor requisite for informing persons [to be served] of their
rights and obligations under those provisions.'

The most relevant provision of the Act was s 29(3) which reads: *c*

'No application under subsection (1) of section twenty-four of this Act shall be
entertained unless it is made not less than two nor more than four months after
the giving of the landlord's notice under section twenty-five of this Act or, as the
case may be, after the making of the tenant's request for a new tenancy.'

The landlords' notice was a print, filled in and corrected in some particulars imma-   *d*
terial to this appeal, of Form 7 in the Appendix to the Landlord and Tenant (Notices)
Regulations 1954[1] made by the Lord Chancellor under s 66.   Regulation 4 provided:

'The forms in the Appendix to these Regulations, or forms substantially to the
like effect, shall be used for the following purposes, that is to say:—. . . (vii) A
notice under the provisions of section 25 of the Act . . . shall . . . be in Form 7   *e*
. . .'

Unfortunately, the 1954 regulations were no longer in force at the date of the landlords' notice. They had been repealed and repeated by the Landlord and Tenant
(Notices) Regulations 1957[2];   but Form 7 and Note 2 of the 1957 regulations had been
amended by reg 6 of the Landlord and Tenant (Notices) Regulations 1967[3], which   *f*
by reg 8 preserved from invalidity any notice served before 1st January 1968 which
complied with the requirements of the 1957 regulations.   The amended Form 7
and Note 2 were prescribed by reg 3 of the Landlord and Tenant (Notices) Regulations
1969[4] and at the date of the landlords' notice the prescribed form and note (see
Form 7 in Appendix I to the 1969 regulations) were in these terms:

'2. You are required within two months after the giving of this Notice to   *g*
notify me in writing whether or not you will be willing to give up possession
of the premises at that date.'

Note 2 is in these terms:

'Part II of the Act enables the tenant, on being served with a notice in this
form, to apply to the court for an order for the grant of a new tenancy. Such   *h*
an application, however, will not be entertained unless the tenant has within
2 months after the giving of the notice terminating the tenancy notified the
landlord in writing that he will not be willing to give up possession of the
premises on the date specified in the notice. The application must be made
not less than 2 or more than 4 months after the giving of the notice.'

j

---

1   SI 1954 No 1107
2   SI 1957 No 1157; so far as material, reg 4 of the 1957 regulations was in identical terms to
    reg 4 of the 1954 regulations
3   SI 1967 No 1831
4   SI 1969 No 1771

a The only question for the county court judge and for this court was concisely stated by him to be whether the notice in fact served on the tenant was 'substantially to the like effect' as the form of notice prescribed by the 1968 regulations which were in force at the date of the service of the notice.

The tenant's contention is that it was not. The form of notice prescribed by the 1954 regulations was, her counsel submits, not substantially to the like effect because it required her to give her counter-notice under s 24(1)(a) of the Act within two

b months *after receiving* the landlords' notice, and warned her that her application for a new tenancy would not be entertained unless she notified the landlords of her objection to giving up possession within two months *after receiving* their notice, and that she must apply for a new tenancy not less than two nor more than four months *after receipt* of the notice; whereas the notice should have stated that those times ran from the *giving* of the landlords' notice.

c The 1967-69 wording of the form of notice brings it into line with the wording of s 29(2) and (3), whereas the 1954-57 wording departs from it, as was pointed out by this court in *Price v West London Investment Building Society*[1] and recognised by the Lord Chancellor in his amendments made by the Landlord and Tenant (Notices) Regulations 1967. But neither those amendments nor the decision in *Price's* case[1] determine the question posed by the tenant in this case. The importance of the answer which

d it receives is great. If the change back to the obsolete wording has produced a form of notice which is substantially to the like effect as the new wording, the landlords' notice is good and the tenant cannot apply for a new tenancy because she is out of time; if the effect of the old wording is substantially different from the new, the notice is bad, the landlords must serve a fresh notice and she can apply for a new tenancy.

e Counsel for the tenant has rightly conceded that on the facts of this case there is no difference in time between the date when she was given notice and the date when she received it; and I think that counsel for the landlords conceded, rightly also, in my judgment, that if the judge held that he could take that fact into account in answering the question raised by the tenant, he was wrong. For, as it seems to me, what we have to do is to construe the few relevant words in the regulations and in the two forms of

f notice, and to decide whether in their ordinary significance the old words which were in fact used do mean substantially the same as the new words which should have been used. If they do not, then a notice in the old form is bad and cannot be validated because the particular tenant on whom it is served is not prejudiced by any difference in their meaning.

Counsel for the tenant submitted that there was a real difference between the giving

g of a notice and its receipt. If a tenant went away on holiday and found the notice on his return home, he would not receive it until he found it, but the landlord would have given it when it reached the tenant's home. If the notice was in the old form, the tenant on reading it with the aid of Note 2 would reasonably think that he had two months from the day he found it to go into action, whereas the true time limit was shorter by the length of his holiday and the time the notice had been at his home.

h That is at first sight a powerful argument without considering the complications introduced by supposing that he failed to find the notice on his return because it had gone under the linoleum near his door: see *Lord Newborough v Jones*[2], to which we were referred. But I have come to the conclusion that it must be rejected.

It is an argument which is provided for the tenant by the reluctance of the legisla-ture to refer simply and directly and consistently to the service of notices in the

j particular provisions of statutes and statutory instruments which prescribe notices. In my judgment, the effect of s 66(4) of the 1954 Act is that a notice under the provisions of the Act is both given and received when it is served in accordance with s 23(1) of the

---

1 [1964] 2 All ER 318, [1964] 1 WLR 616
2 [1974] 3 All ER 17, [1974] 3 WLR 52

1927 Act, and to anyone who knows the law, the time when it is given and the time
when it is received are one and the same, namely, the time of service when the giving *a*
of the notice is in law complete. There is therefore on a true construction of the old
form no material departure from the statute and no material difference from the new
form. It is a distinction without a difference. It describes the same act from the
landlord's and tenant's points of view. The giving and receiving of the notice are two
aspects of the same action and are simultaneous, like 'the giving and receiving of a
ring' in the Form of Solemnization of Matrimony in the Book of Common Prayer. *b*
The one gives, the other receives. The tenant takes what the landlord gives when he
gives it, and he need not be there to take it from the landlord. The time when this
two-sided act is done is the time when it is deemed to be done by the statutory provisions as to service. The tenant cannot say that he has not received it when the Act
says that it has been served on him. The effect which a court of law must give to the
different words in order to see whether their effect is substantially like is their true *c*
effect in the context of landlord and tenant.

These doubts, which the 1967 amendments sought to remove with 'an explanation
of the relevant provisions of the Act' which I regard as inadequate, would never have
existed if Parliament had spoken plainly of 'service' and 'served' in relation to notices
instead of 'giving' and 'given' in s 25 and the regulations. Why not a plain statement
that all notices referred to in this Act are given and received when served in accordance *d*
with s 23(1) of the Landlord and Tenant Act 1927 if it is too much trouble to repeat
the words of that section, instead of resorting to the cryptic cross-reference in s 66(4)?
But the effect is, I think, the same, and the effect of using the words 'giving' and
'receiving' in reference to notices is substantially the same.

It is said that it is hard on the tenant, who is not necessarily conversant with s 23 of
the 1927 Act to read different words in the same sense in the light of that section: *e*
the different words would, or might reasonably, have a different effect on him or her.
But if it is legitimate to look at the effect of the difference in wording on the mind of a
hypothetical tenant who is ignorant of the relevant law, the answer to that contention
is that such a tenant would not, I think, see any difference between the time of giving
the notice and the time of receiving it. To him or her a notice would not appear to be
given unless and until it was received, for instance, when found after returning from a *f*
holiday. That, it is true, would not be when it was served according to law. But, as
counsel for the landlords pointed out, this notice would not be bad simply because it
was misleading, but only if it misled in different directions; if it misled the tenant into
thinking that she could take action when in law she was out of time, it would be good
provided that it would have misled in the same way if it had been in the proper form.
That is not an attractive argument, but I see no answer to it. It does, however, *g*
provide strong support for so amending the Act and regulations, the forms and notes,
as to leave landlords and tenants in no doubt when time begins to run for and against
them.

I therefore agree with the answer given by the learned judge to the question raised
by this appeal, though for rather different reasons, and I would dismiss it.

h

MACKENNA J. The question we have to decide is whether a notice in the old form,
which speaks of 'receiving', is 'substantially to the like effect' as one which speaks of
'giving', which is the word used in the amended form. If it is, the landlords' notice was
a valid one and they succeed. If it not, they fail and the appeal must be allowed.

A notice is a notification, a making known, a communication, of some matter by *j*
one person to another, and in the ordinary way a notice is not received until the
person to whom it is to be communicated becomes aware of that matter; in other
words, he receives the notice when the matter is brought to his attention. Where the
notice is given personally, the giving and the receiving will as a rule be simultaneous;
the notice will be received at the same time as it is given. But where, as here, the law

provides that notice may be given in other ways, by leaving a document at the tenant's
a place of abode, or by sending it to him through the post, the view might reasonably be
taken that the giving and the receiving may not be simultaneous, that the notice will
be given when the document is left at the tenant's house or delivered by the postman,
but that it will not be received until the tenant actually becomes aware of its existence.
To tell a person taking that view that he must act within two months from the giving
of the notice is not the same as telling him that he must act within two months from
b its receipt. For this reason, it seems to me that the old form which uses the word
'receiving' is not substantially to the like effect as the new form which uses the word
'giving'.

In *Price v West London Investment Building Society*[1] the landlord had used the old form
which was current at the time and had sent the notice to the right address by registered post where it was signed for on 23rd March by one of the tenant's employees.
c By some mischance it did not come to the tenant's notice until 29th March. He argued
unsuccessfully that his time ran from that date, pointing to the word 'received' in
para 2 and Note 2 of the form. The argument was rejected by Danckwerts LJ in the
following passage[2] from his judgment:

> 'Another argument was based on the form and the notes[3] issued under the
> *d* provisions of s. 66 of the Landlord and Tenant Act, 1954 . . . The word "received"
> is used. A reference is plainly intended to s. 29 of the Landlord and Tenant Act,
> 1954, in which the word is not "received", but "giving". It seems to me to be
> quite plain that neither the form nor the notes can alter the provisions of the Act.
> In so far as there is an attempt to provide for a different situation from that
> contained in the sections of the Act to which I have referred, which use the word
> *e* "give", "giving" or "given", the forms and these notes [are] ultra vires, because
> the regulations [in which they are contained] can not enlarge the jurisdiction of
> the court as conferred by the Landlord and Tenant Act, 1954.'

If it had seemed to Danckwerts LJ that giving and receiving must necessarily be
simultaneous, and therefore that it made no difference which word was used in the
regulations, he would perhaps have said so. As it is, his language suggests that the
f word 'receiving' refers to 'a different situation' from the word 'giving', and it was no
doubt with these observations in mind that the Lord Chancellor amended the
regulations in 1967.

The judge decided this case against the tenant because on its particular facts the
giving and the receiving of the notice were truly simultaneous. I think that this was
wrong. If the form used was not substantially to the like effect as the prescribed
g form, the notice was invalid. It is, I think, irrelevant that on the facts of the particular
case, the giving and the receiving were simultaneous, so that it did not matter to
the tenant which words were used. The case is to be decided on a comparison of
the two forms without regard to those facts.

I would allow the appeal.

h **LORD SALMON** (read by Stephenson LJ). I entirely agree with the judgment
of Stephenson LJ and add only a few observations of my own.

According to the ordinary and natural use of English words, giving a notice means
causing a notice to be received. Therefore, any requirement in a statute or a contract
for the giving of a notice can be complied with only by causing the notice to be actually
received—unless the context or some statutory or contractual provision otherwise
j provides: see the judgment of Wright J in the *Compagnie Continentale D'Importations*
cases[4].

---

1 [1964] 2 All ER 318, [1964] 1 WLR 616
2 [1964] 2 All ER at 322, [1964] 1 WLR at 622, 623
3 I e in Form 7 in the Appendix to the Landlord and Tenant (Notices) Regulations 1957
4 (1927) 29 Ll LR 52; *affd* (1928) 138 LT 663, CA

Statutes and contracts often contain a provision that notice may be served on a
person by leaving it at his last known place of abode or by sending it to him there *a*
through the post. The effect of such a provision is that if notice is served by any of the
prescribed methods of service, it is, in law, treated as having been given and received.

I recognise that the out-of-date form of notice served in the present case may well
be misleading—but no more nor less than the amended form of notice introduced
by reg 6 of the Landlord and Tenant (Notices) Regulations 1967. (The fact that in the *b*
present case the tenant was not misled is, of course, irrelevant.) The only difference
between the two forms is that the 1967 form has the advantage of following the
exact words of the statute. The two forms are, however, 'substantially to the like
effect'. Neither, in my view, takes on a different meaning from the other because
one speaks of an act to be done 'within two months after receiving this notice' and
the other, 'within two months after giving this notice', because the ordinary and *c*
natural meaning of words make it plain that a notice cannot ordinarily be given until
it is received just as it cannot be received until it is given.

The notice is misleading in both its forms, because neither makes any reference
on its face, or states in the explanatory note accompanying it, that it has been served
in accordance with the law; and that therefore the tenant cannot be heard to say
that the notice has not been validly served on him, nor deny that it has been given *d*
to, and therefore received by him.

This is particularly alarming as s 66(2) makes it evident that the legislature recognised that the notice is likely to be served on persons who may have difficulty in
obtaining legal help and still more difficulty in understanding it by themselves.
This they could only do by ploughing through the Act until they reached the, to
them, obscure cross-reference in s 66(4) and then obtaining access to the Landlord *e*
and Tenant Act 1927 s 23. Both very unlikely contingencies. If this had not been
recognised by the legislature, there would have been no point in s 66(2) enacting
that the form of notice shall include an explanation of the relevant provisions of the
Act for the purpose of informing tenants of their rights and obligations under those
provisions. I strongly support Stephenson LJ's recommendation that the Act and
regulations, the forms and explanatory notes should be revised as soon as possible *f*
in the way he suggests. There may well be difficulty in finding parliamentary time
to amend the Act and to make the consequential amendments in the forms now.
The explanatory notes, however, particularly Note 2, could, and should, be quite
easily amended in the immediate future so that tenants shall be clearly informed
of their statutory rights and obligations when a landlord's notice under the Act is
served on them.

I would dismiss the appeal. *g*

Appeal dismissed.

Solicitors: Field & Sons, Leamington Spa (for the tenant); Russell, Livingstone, Wood &
Co, Worcester (for the landlords). *h*

A S Virdi Esq   Barrister.

a

Practice Direction

CHANCERY DIVISION

b

Practice – Chambers – Chancery Division – Masters' powers – RSC Ord 32, r 14.

1. The judges of the Chancery Division have decided that it would be proper for the chancery masters to adjudicate in Chambers on wider lines than those set out in the memorandum[1] on this subject dated 30th January 1970.

2. As has been the case hitherto, the judges have refrained from giving any direction under RSC Ord 32, r 14, that certain classes of business shall be transacted by a
c judge in person but give the following guidance to the masters as to how they should
exercise their powers under that rule. This memorandum supersedes all previous
memoranda on the subject and amendments[2] thereof.

3. The masters will continue to transact business and exercise jurisdiction to the
same extent as they did under the practice prevailing before 1955 but may make the
following additional orders:

d

(a)   For service out of the jurisdiction, in clear cases, and for substituted service of
orders made by judges on motion.

(b)   For the appointment of trustees except in cases where a trustee (not being a
trustee under disability or a judicial trustee) of a fund or property significantly
in excess of £5,000 in value is to be superseded without his consent.

e (c)   Vesting property or directing or authorising some person to assign or convey
unless there is a pending application for a new trustee which should be
determined by a judge.

(d)   Under s 59 of the Trustee Act 1925, where a trustee cannot be found.

(e)   For enquiries relating to the next-of-kin of deceased persons or beneficiaries
under wills or settlements, including special inquiries for particular persons
f   and their issue, but only in clear cases.

(f)   Approving purchases of trust property of any description by executors,
administrators or trustees, but only in clear cases.

(g)   Authorising executors, administrators and trustees to acquire (by purchase or
otherwise) property of any description the holding of which is not authorised
by the trust instrument, under s 57 of the Trustee Act 1925, s 64 of the Settled
g   Land Act 1925 or otherwise.

(h)   Authorising solicitor trustees and trust corporations to charge remuneration
for acting as trustees (in the case of corporate trustees such remuneration not
to exceed the limits prescribed by their published terms).

(i)   Under s 1(1) of the Variation of Trusts Act 1958, to the extent only of removing
protective trusts where the interest of the principal beneficiary has not failed
h   or determined.

(j)   For the administration of an estate or execution of trusts, whether the estate is
solvent or not.

(k)   Giving leave to executors, administrators and trustees to bring or defend
proceedings, or to continue the prosecution or defence of proceedings, with
indemnity for costs out of the trust estate, in plain cases.

j (l)   Approving a compromise on behalf of a person under disability where: (i)
there is a claim not involving the payment of money, or (ii) the value of that
person's interest in a fund or, if there is no fund, the maximum amount of

---

1   [1970] 1 All ER 1183, [1970] 1 WLR 762
2   See [1971] 2 All ER 215, [1971] 1 WLR 706

the claim (as certified by counsel) does not significantly exceed £5,000 (but not so as to effect any variation of trusts for the purposes of the Variation of Trusts Act 1958 in cases falling outside item (i) above).

(m)   For payment or transfer of funds out of court where a petition would have been necessary under the practice prevailing before 1955 (that is, in effect, where a devolution of trust funds has to be proved and it was not merely a question of establishing the identity or title of some particular person), but only where the value of the fund, the subject of the application, does not significantly exceed £5,000 at the date of the issue of the summons.

(n)   Appointing guardians of minors' estates, in straightforward cases, without limit of amount. The masters may in suitable cases authorise guardians to retain property out of court in the capacity of trustees, subject to appropriate safeguards.

(o)   Summary orders for specific performance under RSC Ord 86 except where it is necessary for the plaintiff to rely on acts of part performance.

(p)   Under s 50(2) and (3) of the Law of Property Act 1925, declaring land to be freed from incumbrances, and the consequential orders for which sub-s (2) provides.

(q)   Determining a rent which it would be reasonable for a tenant to pay while a tenancy continues, by virtue of s 24 of the Landlord and Tenant Act 1954, and (in clear cases where no suggestion of oppression or coercion could be made) orders under s 38(4) of that Act.

(r)   Giving leave to take proceedings under s 1 of the Leasehold Property (Repairs) Act 1938.

(s)   Giving general liberty to wards to go out of the jurisdiction, subject to appropriate safeguards.

(t)   For the appointment of a receiver.

(u)   For an injunction in the following cases: (i) in a consent order, but only if the parties are unwilling to consent to an undertaking in lieu of an injunction, and (ii) if, and only so far as, the injunction is ancillary to an order for the appointment of a receiver by way of equitable execution.

4. A master should not, without the special authority of a judge, make the following orders:

(a)   An order sanctioning any compromise, arrangement or transaction except in any of the cases specified in para 3.

(b)   An order binding persons on whom service of a notice of judgment or order for accounts and inquiries has been dispensed with.

5. Cases involving exceptional difficulties or complications should be referred to the judge as heretofore and before exercising his extended powers the master should consider in every case whether it is one in which it would be more appropriate that the judge should make the order.

6. Nothing in this memorandum is intended to derogate from the established practice under which a judge may (a) in a special case authorise a master to make any order which the judge has power to make in chambers or (b) reserve any particular matter for his own decision.

R E BALL
Chief Master
Chancery Division

18th December 1974

a

Hay and another v Hughes

COURT OF APPEAL, CIVIL DIVISION
LORD EDMUND DAVIES, BUCKLEY AND ORMROD LJJ
2nd, 3rd, 4th, 7th, 8th, 17th OCTOBER 1974

Dictum of LORD EDMUND-DAVIES at
265 applied in TAYLOR v BRISTOL
OMNIBUS CO [1975] 2 All ER 1107

Dictum of LORD EDMUND-DAVIES at
261 explained in REGAN v WILLIAM-
SON [1976] 2 All ER 241

b

Fatal accident – Damages – Assessment – Deduction from damages – Benefit resulting from death – Children – Parents killed in accident – Children deprived of mother's services in caring for them – Grandmother voluntarily taking children into her care – Whether grandmother's services in caring for children benefit resulting from death –Whether value of grandmother's services to be deducted from damages otherwise recoverable in respect of mother's death.

c

A husband and wife, then aged 28 and 24 respectively, were killed in a motor accident for which the defendant admitted liability. They left two sons aged 4½ and 2½. The wife had not at any material time been engaged in gainful employment. Her energies had been devoted exclusively to caring for the family as a wife and mother.

d

After the death of their parents the two orphan boys were taken in by their maternal grandmother who cared for them thereafter. When she took the boys into her care the grandmother neither expected nor received any payment; she intended to continue to care for the boys irrespective of whether she was paid for doing so. When the accident occurred the grandmother was aged 49 and already had substantial domestic responsibilities of her own, having three teenage children. She did not give up any paid employment in order to look after her two grandsons. In an

e

action by the administrators on behalf of the estates of the deceased, and also on behalf of the two boys under the Fatal Accidents Acts 1846 to 1959 and the Law Reform (Miscellaneous Provisions) Act 1934 the defendant contended that, in assessing the damages to which the boys were entitled under s 2[a] of the Fatal Accidents Act 1846, the grandmother's services in caring for them should be taken into account in abate-

f

ment of the financial loss suffered by the boys as a result of their mother's death, on the ground that the grandmother's services were benefits resulting from the mother's death in that they were a predictable consequence of the fatality resulting from the accident.

Held – In view of her circumstances at the time of the accident it could not have been predicted with any certainty that the grandmother would take the boys into

g

her care. Accordingly the services which the grandmother had provided and would continue to provide for the boys were benefits resulting not from the death of their mother but from the decision made by the grandmother after the accident to take them into her care. Accordingly those services were not to be taken into account in diminution of the damages recoverable on behalf of the sons in respect of their mother's death (see p 267 *d* to *f*, p 272 *f* to *h*, p 273 *c* and p 275 *c*, post).

h

Notes
For deductions from damages awarded under the Fatal Accidents Acts, see 28 Halsbury's Laws (3rd Edn) 103, 104, para 113, and for cases on the subject, see 36 Digest (Repl) 211-214, *1111-1132*.

j

For the Fatal Accidents Act 1846, s 2, see 23 Halsbury's Statutes (3rd Edn) 781.

Cases referred to in judgments
Baker v Dalgleish Steam Shipping Co Ltd [1922] 1 KB 361, 91 LJKB 392, CA, 36 Digest (Repl) 223, *1191*.

---

a   Section 2, so far as material, is set out at p 260 *d*, post

K

Berry v Humm & Co [1915] 1 KB 627, 84 LJKB 918, 36 Digest (Repl) 221, *1175*.   *a*

Buckley v John Allen & Ford (Oxford) Ltd [1967] 1 All ER 539, [1967] 2 QB 637, [1967] 2 WLR 759, Digest (Cont Vol C) 754, *1194h*.

Burgess v Florence Nightingale Hospital for Gentlewomen Management Committee [1955] 1 All ER 511, [1955] 1 QB 349, [1955] 2 WLR 533, Digest (Cont Vol A) 1202, *1117a*.

Carroll v Purcell (1961) 35 ALJ 384.

Cunningham v Harrison [1973] 3 All ER 463, [1973] QB 942, [1973] 3 WLR 97, CA,   *b* 17 Digest (Reissue) 116, *191*.

Daniels v Jones [1961] 3 All ER 24, [1961] 1 WLR 1103, CA, Digest (Cont Vol A) 1205, *1163c*.

Davies v Powell Duffryn Associated Collieries Ltd (No 2) [1942] 1 All ER 657, [1942] AC 601, 111 LJKB 418, 167 LT 74, HL, 36 Digest (Repl) 231, *1229*.

Donnelly v Joyce [1973] 3 All ER 475, [1974] 1 QB 454, [1973] 3 WLR 514, [1973] 2 Lloyd's   *c* Rep 130, CA, 17 Digest (Reissue) 117, *193*.

Franklin v South Eastern Railway Co (1858) 3 H & N 211, [1843-60] All ER Rep 849, 31 LTOS 154, 4 Jur NS 565, 157 ER 448, 36 Digest (Repl) 213, *1128*.

Goodburn v Thomas Cotton Ltd [1968] 1 All ER 518, [1968] 1 QB 845, [1968] 2 WLR 229, CA, Digest (Cont Vol C) 754, *1194ca*.

Hicks v Newport, Abergavenny & Hereford Railway Co (1857) 4 B & S 403 n, 122 ER 510,   *d* 36 Digest (Repl) 221, *1178*.

Howitt (Widow and Administratrix of Richard Arthur Howitt) v Heads [1972] 1 All ER 491, [1973] QB 64, [1972] 2 WLR 183.

Jeffrey v Smith [1970] RTR 279, CA.

Jenner v Allen West & Co Ltd [1959] 2 All ER 115, [1959] 1 WLR 554, CA, Digest (Cont Vol A) 599, *340c*.   *e*

Malyon v Plummer [1963] 2 All ER 344, [1964] 1 QB 330, [1963] 2 WLR 1213, CA, Digest (Cont Vol A) 1203, *1132b*.

Mallett v McMonagle [1969] 2 All ER 178, [1970] AC 166, [1969] 2 WLR 767, HL, [1969] 1 Lloyd's Rep 127, Digest (Cont Vol C) 292, *838a*.

Mead v Clarke Chapman & Co Ltd [1956] 1 All ER 44, [1956] 1 WLR 76, CA, Digest (Cont Vol A) 1208, *1194c*.   *f*

Monarch Steamship Co Ltd v A B Karlshamns Oljefabriker [1949] 1 All ER 1, [1949] AC 196, [1949] LJR 772, 82 Lloyd LR 137, 1949 SC (HL) 1, 1949 SLT 51, HL, 41 Digest (Repl) 362, *1549*.

Moore v Babcock & Wilcox Ltd, Rawlinson v Same [1966] 3 All ER 882, [1967] 1 WLR 481, Digest (Cont Vol B) 570, *1194g*.

Parry v Cleaver [1969] 1 All ER 555, [1970] AC 1, [1969] 2 WLR 821, [1969] 1 Lloyd's Rep   *g* 183, HL, Digest (Cont Vol C) 750, *1061e*.

Peacock v Amusement Equipment Co Ltd [1954] 2 All ER 689, [1954] 2 QB 347, [1954] 3 WLR 288, CA, Digest (Cont Vol A) 1208, *1194b*.

Pevec v Brown (1964) 108 Sol Jo 219, Digest (Cont Vol B) 570, *1194f*.

Pym v Great Northern Railway Co (1863) 4 B & S 396, [1861-73] All ER Rep 180, 2 New Rep 455, 32 LJQB 377, 8 LT 734, 10 Jur NS 199, 122 ER 508, 36 Digest (Repl) 208,   *h* *1097*.

Redpath v Belfast & County Down Railway Co [1947] NI 167, 18 Digest (Repl) 177, **902*.

Reincke v Gray [1964] 2 All ER 687, [1964] 1 WLR 832, CA, Digest (Cont Vol B) 570, *1194e*.

Shaw v Mills (7th March 1961) unreported, CA, [1961] Bar Library transcript 86, CA.   *j*

Taff Vale Railway Co v Jenkins [1913] AC 1, [1911-13] All ER Rep 160, 82 LJKB 49, 107 LT 564, HL, 36 Digest (Repl) 213, *1124*.

Thompson v Price [1973] 2 All ER 846, [1973] QB 838, [1973] 2 WLR 1037, [1973] 1 Lloyd's Rep 591.

Voller v Dairy Produce Packers Ltd [1962] 3 All ER 938, [1962] 1 WLR 960, Digest (Cont Vol A) 1205, *1163ac*.

Cases also cited

a

Blake v Midland Railway Co (1852) 18 QB 93.

Bradburn v Great Western Railway Co (1874) LR 10 Exch 1, [1874-80] All ER Rep 195.

Daish (an infant by his next friend, Albert Edward Daish) v Wauton [1972] 1 All ER 25 [1972] 2 QB 262, [1972] 2 WLR 29, CA.

Davies v Tenby Corporation [1974] The Times, 10th April.

b *Gage v King* [1960] 3 All ER 62, [1961] 1 QB 188.

Grand Trunk Railway Co of Canada v Jennings (1888) 13 App Cas 800, PC.

Haggar v de Placido [1972] 2 All ER 1029, [1972] 1 WLR 716.

Hurt v Murphy [1971] RTR 186.

Liffen v Watson [1940] 2 All ER 213, [1940] 1 KB 556, CA.

Povey v Governors of Rydal School [1970] 1 All ER 841.

c *Roach v Yates* [1937] 3 All ER 442, [1938] 1 KB 256, CA.

Schneider v Eisovitch [1960] 1 All ER 169, [1960] 2 QB 430.

Seward v The Vera Cruz, The Vera Cruz (1884) 10 App Cas 59, HL.

Wattson v Port of London Authority [1969] 1 Lloyd's Rep 95.

Appeal

d This was an appeal by the defendant, Leslie Hughes, against the judgment of Reeve J given on 24th October 1973 awarding the plaintiffs, Alfred Stanley Hay and John Toone, the administrators of the estates of Francis James Edward Hay deceased, and of his wife, Patricia Hay deceased, £16,400 damages under the Fatal Accidents Acts 1846 to 1959 (£7,900 being in respect of the death of the husband and £8,500 in respect of the death of the wife) and £2,460 interest thereon at 7½ per cent per

e annum from 17th June 1971 for two years, and £1,110·30 under the Law Reform (Miscellaneous Provisions) Act 1934 and £150 interest on £1,000 (part thereof) at 7½ per cent per annum from 17th June 1971 for two years. The defendant admitted liability for the accident and the only issue was the quantum of damages. The appeal related solely to the awards under the Fatal Accidents Acts. By a respondent's notice the plaintiffs sought to have both awards increased. The facts are set out in the

f judgment of Lord Edmund Davies.

Michael Turner QC and *Alan Taylor* for the defendant.
Charles McCullough QC and *Nigel Baker* for the plaintiffs.

Cur adv vult

g 17th October. The following judgments were read.

LORD EDMUND DAVIES. The defendant appeals from the judgment of Reeve J, dated 24th October 1973, in an action brought against him under the Fatal Accidents Acts 1846 to 1959 and the Law Reform (Miscellaneous Provisions) Act 1934. The appeal is said to raise problems in the law of damages hitherto unconsidered by

h the courts or, if considered, not always satisfactorily solved, and we have been referred to a very large number of authorities on the subject during its hearing.

The plaintiffs are the administrators of the estates of Francis Hay, deceased, and of his wife Patricia, both of whom were killed in a motor accident on 10th January 1970, for which the defendant admitted liability. The action was brought on behalf of their estates and also on behalf of their two sons, born on 29th July 1965 and 24th

j May 1967, and accordingly 4½ and 2½ years old when their parents were killed. The total award was for £20,120·30, £16,400 being in respect of the Fatal Accidents Acts claims (£7,900 relating to the death of the father and £8,500 to the death of the mother) and £1,110·30 under the 1934 Act, the balance consisting of interest. The appeal relates only to the awards under the 1846 Act, as amended, which the defendant challenges as being wrongly arrived at and excessive, while by a respondent's notice the plaintiffs seek to have both awards increased.

The relevant facts, which were set out in detail by Reeve J, may for present purposes *a*
be summarised in this way: when the fatal accident occurred, Mr Hay was nearly
29, his wife nearly 25. They lived with their children in a three bedroom house
which he had bought on mortgage. After working for some years with the National
Coal Board, he became a trainee welder in August 1969, and soon showed considerable
aptitude. His average weekly take-home pay at the time of his death was nearly
£24. His chances of promotion were good and, had they been realised he would *b*
have been earning net weekly wages of £40 by April 1973, when the case was first
heard. The learned judge accepted that this net wage would have been apportioned
within the family circle in the manner indicated by plaintiff's counsel. On this
basis he concluded that the total annual dependancy of the two boys on their father
at the date of trial was £1,100. But, recognising that, while exceeding the figure
prevailing at the date of the accident this was also less than the figure appropriate *c*
for the future, he said that he would bear those competing considerations in mind
when considering the multiplier. He eventually applied a multiplier of nine to
both claims under the Fatal Accidents Acts.

Section 2 of the 1846 Act provides that—

> 'the jury may give such damages as they may think proportioned to the injury *d*
> resulting from such death to the parties respectively for whom and for whose
> benefit such action shall be brought . . .'

The relevant facts in connection with the orphaned children's dependancy on their
father were not disputed, but the position was markedly different in respect of the
claim brought in relation to the mother's death. I quote from the words of the
learned trial judge: *e*

> 'After the death of their parents the two boys were taken in by their maternal
> grandmother (Mrs Toone) who has cared for them ever since, except for one
> and a half days at weekends and for some holiday periods when they are cared
> for by their paternal grandparents. Mrs Toone has received no payment for
> keeping the children, and she candidly admitted to me that the question of *f*
> payment never entered her head when she decided to act as mother-substitute
> for these two orphans. It is true that on the 18th March 1972 she signed a letter,
> addressed to the plaintiffs in their capacity as administrators of the estates of
> Mr and Mrs Hay, in which she stated: "I am writing to advise you that as from
> this date I am charging the estate of the above-named deceased the sum of £5
> per week in respect of each of the two children . . . This total sum of £10 is for *g*
> my time and trouble in looking after the said children." No secret has been
> made of the fact that such a letter was written on legal advice in the hope that
> the plaintiffs' case on the quantum of damages to be recovered in these pro-
> ceedings would thereby be strengthened; and Mrs Toone freely admitted that
> she intends to continue to care for the children irrespective of whether she is or
> is not paid for so doing. It is now conceded by counsel that the letter is irrelevant *h*
> to the assessment of damages. Mrs Hay was not at any material time engaged
> in gainful employment. Her energies were exclusively devoted to caring for
> the family as a wife and as a mother. The children have, by her death, been
> deprived of the full-time services of a mother.'

As the cases repeatedly remind us, the starting point must always be the wording *j*
of the Fatal Accidents Act 1846. That these two infants were 'injured' by the death
of their mother is not, in my judgment, open to doubt. Thereby they were deprived
of her services which had that pecuniary value which, ever since *Franklin v South
Eastern Railway Co*[1], has been held to be the basis of an award under the Act. What is

---

1   (1858) 3 H & N 211, [1843-60] All ER Rep 849

a contested is how the damages proportionate to that injury are to be arrived at, and the difficulty is due to the two-fold nature of the exercise involved. This was explained in *Malyon v Plummer*[1] by Diplock LJ who said:

b 'The pecuniary loss which the court has to assess is a loss which will be sustained in the future. This involves making two estimates, videlicet, (i) what benefit in money or money's-worth arising out of the relationship would have accrued to the person for whom the action is brought from the deceased if the deceased had survived but has been lost by reason of his death and (ii) what benefit in money or money's-worth (subject to certain statutory exceptions) the person for whom the action is brought will derive from the death of the deceased which would not have been enjoyed had the deceased lived. The difference between these two estimates is the measure of damages recoverable under the Fatal Accidents Acts, 1846 to 1959.'

c As to the first estimate, we begin with the undoubted fact that, by reason of her premature death, these two very young children lost the care which their 25 year old mother could reasonably have been expected to continue to bestow on them for several years to come. In *Pevec v Brown*[2] a widower claimed on behalf of himself and his infant son damages in respect of his wife's death, and contended that compensation should be awarded for loss, not of a mother's love, but for the disadvantage of the care which the child would receive from the nanny whom the father had engaged as compared with that which he would have received from his mother had she survived. The report is a very short one, but it appears that, in rejecting this submission, Megaw J adverted to the 'irrecoverability of compensation for the father's loss of the companionship of his wife' and, saying that there was no distinction in principle in relation to the child, held that no damages should be awarded in respect of any element of the child receiving less care than he would have done had his mother survived. Were it now necessary to decide the point, I am not at present convinced that I should take the same view, and it is to be noted that in *Burgess v Florence Nightingale Hospital for Gentlewomen Management Committee*[3] Devlin J expressed the view that damages should be awarded 'for what the child lost by the wife's death, both in respect of the school fees and of what she might have done for the child'. While it is undoubtedly established that damages can be awarded under the Fatal Accidents Acts only in respect of pecuniary loss and not as a solatium for injured feelings (see *Taff Vale Railway Co v Jenkins*[4], per Lord Haldane V-C, and *Davies v Powell Duffryn Associated Collieries Ltd (No 2)*[5]), so that these two children could recover nothing for the deprivation of their mother's love, yet it may sometime have to be considered whether Mr McGregor[6] is not right in saying that—

h 'it may be argued that the benefit of a mother's personal attention to a child's upbringing, morals, education and psychology, which the services of a housekeeper, nurse or governess could never provide, has in the long run a financial value for the child, difficult as it is to assess.'

Be that as it may, in the present case it was accepted by the defence that in different circumstances these children would have been entitled to damages for the quantified loss of their mother's services. Counsel for the defendant conceded that if a nanny or housekeeper had been engaged by the plaintiffs to look after these children, the

j

---

1 [1963] 2 All ER 344 at 353, [1964] 1 QB 330 at 349
2 (1964) 108 Sol Jo 219
3 [1955] 1 All ER 511 at 513
4 [1913] AC 1 at 4, [1911-13] All ER Rep 160 at 161
5 [1942] 1 All ER 657 at 665, [1942] AC 601 at 617
6 McGregor on Damages (13th Edn, 1972), para 1232

cost of employing her would be recoverable from the defendant (as in *Berry v Humm &* *a* *Co*[1] and *Jeffrey v Smith*[2]) and, furthermore, that the salary of £15 a week claimed by the plaintiffs and adopted by the learned trial judge as the estimated cost of obtaining her services could not then have been challenged.   Similarly, it is accepted that, had Mrs Toone (their grandmother) given up a paid job in order to look after her grandchildren, the administrators could have recovered in the action a sum equivalent to her losses to date and in respect of her future salary losses.   *b*

But the engagement of a nanny or housekeeper has not taken place nor is it contemplated, and the grandmother gave up no paid job, though it has already been noted that she has evinced a desire to be paid £5 a week in respect of her services to each child.   She has taken them in and looked after them 'without any thought of payment' just as she would have done had their parents died of natural causes, and she told the trial judge that she intended to care for them indefinitely in exactly *c* the same way.   As a result, they have unquestionably benefited from her care, and it is this fact which has given rise to difficulty in considering the second of the estimates referred to by Diplock LJ[3].   Counsel for the defendant has submitted that all the trial judge could properly do would be to award the plaintiffs something to cover the risk of Mrs Toone's services ceasing and hired service having to be obtained.   Then can it be truly said that Mrs Toone's services 'derive from the death of the *d* deceased'?   They would undoubtedly not have been rendered had the children not become orphans, but are those services relevant to the balancing operation involved in assessing, in the words of s 2 'the injury *resulting from such death*'?

This question has not infrequently arisen in earlier cases.   It is not easy to extract from them any test which may be universally applied nor to reconcile all the decisions.   Clearly, not all events that happen after a death can be said to have resulted *e* from it.   Thus, it has been held that no deduction should be made for rent received from lodgers whom a widow started taking in after her husband's death (*Buckley v John Allen & Ford (Oxford) Ltd*[4]); the High Court of Australia has decided that none should be made from a widow's award because she had gone out to work (*Carroll v Purcell*[5]); and in this country a similar conclusion was arrived at by Cumming-Bruce J in *Howitt v Heads*[6].   But in this case, the mother having also been killed, *f* it is said by the defendant that the position is entirely different where the grandmother works gratuitously for the two orphaned children.

Several of the earlier reported cases would now have to be decided differently. This arises from the Fatal Accidents (Damages) Act 1908 and the Fatal Accidents Act 1959, the latter providing that no deduction shall be made for a wide range of money payments following on death which would otherwise have had to be taken into *g* account.   Nevertheless the earlier cases have still to be borne in mind when considering whether a benefit received by the dependants after the death, but not consisting of the payment of money to them, is to be regarded as 'resulting from such death'.

Broadly speaking, it was considered that payments received as a result of arrangements already set up to meet the eventuality of death did so result.   Thus in *Baker v* *h* *Dalgleish Steam Shipping Co Ltd*[7] the Court of Appeal held that the fact that a widow was in receipt of a Crown pension ought, as a general rule, to be taken into consideration, notwithstanding that payments depended on the voluntary bounty of the Crown, Younger LJ saying[8] that 'their voluntary character cannot affect the value

1   [1915] 1 KB 627   *j*
2   [1970] RTR 279
3   *Malyon v Plummer* [1963] 2 All ER 344 at 353, [1964] 1 QB 330 at 349
4   [1967] 1 All ER 539, [1967] 2 QB 637
5   (1961) 35 ALJ 384
6   [1972] 1 All ER 491, [1973] QB 64
7   [1922] 1 KB 361
8   [1922] 1 KB at 380

a the plaintiffs of those payments already received', though Bankes LJ stressed[1] that 'The reasonable expectation of their continuance must, I think, be taken into account', while Scrutton LJ said[2] that regard must be had to 'the extreme probability of the Admiralty not continuing a pension if compensation could be obtained from the wrongdoer'.

But the position was and is less clear where payments are made or services having
b pecuniary value are rendered in circumstances never foreseen before the death. In *Baker v Dalgleish Steam Shipping Co Ltd*[3] all members of the Court of Appeal approved of the view expressed by Greer J in the lower court that sums subscribed by fellow workmen of the deceased would not be deductible, Younger LJ saying[4]:

c 'I conceive that normally in such cases the amount of the subscription is largely personal to the beneficiaries, and is materially affected by their merit in the eyes of the subscribers or the reverse.'

Similarly, in *Redpath v Belfast & County Down Railway Co*[5] it was held in a claim for personal injuries (which in that respect is not distinguishable from a fatal accident claim) that money received by the plaintiff from a fund subscribed to by the public in respect of a railway disaster was not deductible from what would otherwise have
d been his proper entitlement to damages. And in *Peacock v Amusement Equipment Co Ltd*[6], where the plaintiff did not benefit under the will of his deceased wife but his stepchildren (to whom his wife had bequeathed everything) voluntarily paid him a sum equivalent to one-third of the value of the estate, the Court of Appeal held that no deduction should be made from his Fatal Accident Act damages on that account. Somervell LJ said[7]:

e '... I think it would be only in very unusual circumstances that a voluntary payment would be taken into account when there was no expectation of it at the time of the death. It seems to me that that indicates for itself that there is a nova causa interviens and, therefore, the payment was not made in consequence or as a result of the death ... Of course, it would not have been made unless the
f wife had died, but I would say that it was made as the result of the stepchildren's consideration, and, perhaps, affection for their stepfather.'

In line with this was the decision of Nield J in *Voller v Dairy Produce Packers Ltd*[8] that the claims of infant daughters in respect of their father's death were not to be reduced by the fact that they had been taken into the home of their aunt after the subsequent death of their mother and were being well looked after. A similar case is *Moore v*
g *Babcock & Wilcox Ltd*[9], where proceedings under the Fatal Accidents Acts instituted by the widow of a man employed by the defendants were brought to trial in the names of her administrators, she herself having died 16 months after her husband. Their orphaned daughter was then taken into the home of an uncle, and another uncle gave her money presents from time to time. On these facts, it was submitted on behalf of the defendants that she was no worse off than she would have been had
h her father still been alive. Rejecting this submission, which he considered was based on a misunderstanding of certain observations of Jenkins LJ in *Mead v Clarke Chapman & Co Ltd*[10], which must shortly be considered, Chapman J held that the

1   [1922] 1 KB at 369
2   [1922] 1 KB at 372, 373
j 3   [1922] 1 KB 361
4   [1922] 1 KB at 380
5   [1947] NI 167
6   [1954] 2 All ER 689, [1954] 2 QB 347
7   [1954] 2 All ER at 692, [1954] 2 QB at 354
8   [1962] 3 All ER 938, [1962] 1 WLR 960
9   [1966] 3 All ER 882, [1967] 1 WLR 481
10 [1956] 1 All ER 44, [1956] 1 WLR 76

support extended to the girl by her two uncles arose fundamentally from motives a
of charity and benevolence and must be ignored, as their operative cause was not the
fact of death but the voluntary decision of the donors activated by motives of compassion towards a person in distress. I disagree with the submissions of counsel for
the defendant that these last two cases were wrongly decided.

In performing the balancing operation involved in assessing fatal accident claims,
it is established that, just as it is not necessary that the claimant should have a legal b
right to pecuniary benefits from the deceased and that it is enough that there was a
reasonable expectation of their continuance, voluntary though they may be—

'so the probability of voluntary contribution bestowed in consequence of the
death may be used to reduce the claim by showing what loss the claimant has
in fact sustained by the death. Less weight will be given to voluntary contributions than to those made under legal obligation, just because they are c
voluntary':

per Scrutton LJ in *Baker v Dalgleish Steam Shipping Co Ltd*[1]. Cases arising from the
remarriage of the widow illustrate both types of expectation. Until the passing
of the Law Reform (Miscellaneous Provisions) Act 1971, in assessing the damages
payable to a widow there had to be taken into account her prospects of remarriage d
and so acquiring the legal right to be maintained by her new husband, thereby
reducing her dependancy and, it may be, terminating it altogether (*Davies v Powell
Duffryn Associated Collieries Ltd (No 2)*[2], *Goodburn v Thomas Cotton Ltd*[3]). Accordingly,
in *Mead v Clarke Chapman & Co Ltd*[4] the second husband earning as much money as the
first, Donovan J awarded the widow damages only in respect of the period between the
death of her first husband and her remarriage. But a similar limitation in respect e
of her infant daughter was disapproved by the Court of Appeal, Singleton LJ saying[5]:

'I do not think that it is right to say that no regard should be paid to the fact
that the child has a stepfather who is kind and good to her . . . but it should not
be assumed that of necessity the position will remain the same . . . there is a
difference between a father and a stepfather, in that the father can be forced to f
support his child if he fails to do so, while the stepfather cannot. Over and
above that, when the child is getting a little older, the father may well be willing
to do something for his own child to help it forward in education or in some other
way, a burden which a stepfather might not be willing to undertake . . . I do
not consider it was right to say that no damages after the date of the second
marriage should be given in respect of the child's claim.' g

As to the submission that the acquisition of an affectionate stepfather should be
ignored in that the mother's remarriage gave her daughter no rights of maintenance
against the stepfather and that, in accordance with *Peacock v Amusement Equipment
Co Ltd*[6], the defendants could not take advantage of the stepfather's voluntary
actions in undertaking the care of his stepdaughter, Jenkins LJ said[7]:
h

'Clearly, if the father had not died, the mother could not have re-married
and the child could never have acquired a stepfather. She could not have the
advantage of being protected by her two fathers at one and the same time;
so that the financial advantage to her of the protection of the stepfather was

j

1   [1922] 1 KB at 372
2   [1942] 1 All ER 657, [1942] AC 601
3   [1968] 1 All ER 518, [1968] 1 QB 845
4   [1956] 1 All ER 44, [1956] 1 WLR 76
5   [1956] 1 All ER at 47, 48, [1956] 1 WLR at 81-83
6   [1954] 2 All ER 689, [1954] 2 QB 347
7   [1956] 1 All ER at 48, [1956] 1 WLR at 83

a   something that she could not have enjoyed but for the death of her father. In my view, there is a sufficient causal connection here to make it proper to take into account the financial consequences to the child of the re-marriage of her mother.'

For myself, I have some difficulty in following this approach and there seems force in the view expressed by Professor Street[1] that 'Only if the Court of Appeal had found that at the death it was probable that the child would be maintained by a kind stepfather would the decision be correct.' The Matrimonial Proceedings

b   (Children) Act 1958, s 1(1), provides that if a widow remarries and her children are accepted as members of the family by their stepfather, he incurs a legal obligation to maintain and educate them. But even this does not, in my judgment, mean that if a widow with a child has prospects of remarriage or has even actually remarried (as in *Reincke v Gray*[2]) the dependancy of the child thereupon terminates, for it may

c   never 'be accepted as one of the family' by the new husband, and, even if it is, the chance that it may not be as well-treated financially by the stepfather as it would have been by the natural father had he lived must be allowed for, just as it was before the 1958 Act (see *Mead v Clarke Chapman & Co Ltd*[3]).

It is for the defendant to a Fatal Accidents Acts claim to establish that there must be offset against the loss caused by the death benefits received after that death (*Baker v*

d   *Dalgleish Steam Shipping Co Ltd*[4], per Younger LJ; *Peacock v Amusement Equipment Ltd*[5] per Somervell LJ; and *Mead v Clarke Chapman & Co Ltd*[6] per Parker LJ). And there is a presumption against deducting the value of unpaid services rendered to a bereaved person. This is in conformity with the general policy against deductions evinced by the 1959 Act. The observations of Somervell LJ in *Peacock*[5] on this matter have already been referred to. In *Shaw v Mills*[7] the court took into

e   account in its assessment of damages the value of services rendered to her father by a daughter after her mother's death, Sellers LJ saying that they 'were not actually compensated for but will be out of the proceeds of these damages'. And a whole series of cases dealing with non-fatal accident claims establish that the injured plaintiff can recover the value of nursing and other services gratuitously rendered to him by a stranger to the proceedings: *Parry v Cleaver*[8] per Lord Reid, *Cunningham*

f   *v Harrison*[9] per Lord Denning MR, and *Donnelly v Joyce*[10] per Megaw LJ.

I have difficulty in reconciling the rationale of *Jenner v Alan West & Co Ltd*[11] with the increasing tendency of the courts to make no deductions for purely voluntary benefits in claims in respect of personal injuries, fatal or otherwise. A man was killed in the course of his employment at his employer's premises, and his personal representatives successfully sued them under the Fatal Accidents Acts for negligence and statu-

g   tory breaches. Before the matter came to trial the employers had made voluntary payments to the widow but there was no evidence that they had done anything of the sort before. Lord Evershed MR and Pearce LJ held that these payments had to be deducted from the widow's damages. There is nothing remarkable in that finding; such an approach is adopted frequently by the courts in respect of ex gratia payments, which are often regarded as being impliedly made simply without preju-

h   dice to any claim which may be advanced but nevertheless on the basis that they are

---

1 Principles of the Law of Damages (1962), p 181
2 [1964] 2 All ER 687, [1964] 1 WLR 832
3 [1956] 1 All ER 44, [1956] 1 WLR 76
4 [1922] 1 KB at 377
5 [1954] 2 All ER at 692, [1954] 2 QB at 354
6 [1956] 1 All ER at 49, [1956] 1 WLR at 84
7 (7th March 1961) unreported; CA; cited in Kemp and Kemp on Damages (2nd Edn, 1962), vol 2, pp 178-181
8 [1969] 1 All ER 555 at 558, [1970] AC 1 at 14
9 [1973] 3 All ER 463 at 469, [1973] QB 942 at 952
10 [1973] 3 All ER 475 at 480, [1974] 1 QB 454 at 462
11 [1959] 2 All ER 115, [1959] 1 WLR 554

to be taken into account in the event of liability being established. But that is not *a* how the court arrived at its decision. Pearce LJ said[1]:

'Had the pension come from the generosity of some third party who was in no way concerned with the accident, one might well say that it did not result from the death but from that generous impulse. Here, however, the employers paid the pension to the widow of a man whose whole working life had been spent in their service and who had met his death while working on the roof of *b* their premises. It is true that there is no evidence as to their motives or their usual practice or the machinery by which they instituted the pension ... But the chain of causation is so direct and so strong on the few facts which are known to us, and any inferences that would break or weaken that chain are so unlikely and remote that, in my view, the pension should be taken into account as "resulting" from the death.' *c*

Lord Evershed MR expressed himself similarly[2]. But, in the light of the exiguous facts, how can it be said that at the moment of death there was a reasonable expectation that the employers would act as they did? For my part, I find it impossible to hold that there was and, applying that test alone, I should have held that the payments must be ignored. *d*

The fact is that it is impossible to extract from the large number of decided cases one universal test or principle and, indeed, in *Jenner's* case[3] Pearce LJ warned against making the attempt. In *Monarch Steamship Co Ltd v A B Karlshamns Oljefabriker*[4] Lord du Parcq stressed that 'in the end what has to be decided is a question of fact, and therefore a question proper for a jury', and continued:

'Circumstances are so infinitely various that, however carefully general rules *e* are framed, they must be construed with some liberality and not too rigidly applied. It was necessary to lay down principles lest juries should be persuaded to do injustice by imposing an undue, or, perhaps, an inadequate, liability on a defendant. The court must be careful, however, to see that the principles laid down are never so narrowly interpreted as to prevent a jury, or judge of fact, *f* from doing justice between the parties. So to use them would be to misuse them.'

There was canvassed before us the question of what the position would be had these two orphaned children been taken into care of the local authority, pursuant to s 1 of the Children Act 1948. But this not having occurred, the question is not before us and does not call for consideration. Nor, in my respectful view, does *g* allusion to it assist in determining the problem now being considered, for, as Buckley LJ said in the course of counsel's submissions, the fact that faute de mieux these children might have been taken into care does not affect the situation where, as here, they are not.

How would a jury have regarded this case? Would they have accepted the defendant's invitation to say that, in the events which have occurred, either (a) no loss *h* measurable in money terms had been suffered by the dependant children by reason of the death of their mother, or, (b) alternatively, that the services already rendered by the grandmother are 'benefits resulting from the death' and should therefore be taken into account, with the result that all the children were entitled to recover was something to safeguard them against the contingency that, for one reason or another, her services might cease to be available? Or, as the plaintiff's counsel at the trial *j* and before us contended, would they say that, by reason of their mother's death, the

1 [1959] 2 All ER at 125, [1959] 1 WLR at 565, 566
2 [1959] 2 All ER at 126, 127, [1959] 1 WLR at 568, 569
3 [1959] 2 All ER at 124, [1959] 1 WLR at 565
4 [1949] 1 All ER 1 at 19, [1949] AC 196 at 232

a children had lost her services which, had their father not also died, would have been
replaced by a paid housekeeper, and that compensation should therefore be assessed
by reference to the probable cost of so doing; that damages should be calculated on
this notional basis even though the children were in fact housed and cared for by the
gratuitous services of their grandmother; and that these services were not benefits
'resulting from the death' and therefore do not require to be brought into account?

b   As to (a) counsel for the defendant has urged that, there is no reported case where
the replacement of a deceased wife's services not having taken place or been contemplated (unlike *Berry v Humm & Co*[1]), the court has awarded damages for the
pecuniary loss of those services and that this lack of precedents is due to the obvious
absence of any right to recover such damages. I disagree. In my judgment, the
fact that a widower decided to manage for himself after the death of his wife would
c not disentitle him to sue for and recover damages for the pecuniary loss he had nevertheless sustained. And, in the same way, the fact that the orphaned children here
have incurred no expense in engaging a housekeeper to look after them does not
destroy or diminish that right to be compensated which the defendant concedes
would be theirs had such expense actually been incurred or had the grandmother
given up a paid job in order to look after them. As to (b), in my judgment, while
d the need for the grandmother's care undoubtedly arose from the mother's death,
the view which a reasonable jury would be likely to adopt would be that the children
benefited not as a result of their mother's death but simply because the grandmother
had taken it on herself to render them services. At the time of their mother's
death it was anyone's guess what would happen to them and the defendant had not
discharged the onus of establishing that at that time there was a reasonable expecta-
e tion that the grandmother would act as she subsequently did. Then aged 49, she already
had substantial domestic responsibilities of her own (she had three teenage children
and she too lived in a three-bedroom house) and it would not have been surprising
had she decided against adding to them. In my judgment, it would be an unreasonable conclusion were a jury or judge of fact to hold that, because she was moved by
their plight to act as she did, her generous action fell within s 2 of the 1846 Act.

f   For these reasons I hold that the learned judge rightly came to the conclusion that
the grandmother's services should be ignored in calculating the financial loss sustained
by the children as a result of the death of their mother.

      In relation to the children's dependency on their father, the defendant makes
no criticism of the learned judge's award of £7,900, save in relation to a figure of £604
per annum adopted by him in respect of the provision of a house and such additional
g items as fuel, power and repairs. It is said that, having regard to the family budget
at the time of death and the fact that the children did not occupy the whole house
£604 is an excessive figure. I restrict myself to saying that I do not regard this
criticism as well founded.

      As to their dependency on the mother, the defendant accepts that if the approach
of the learned judge was right and if the appropriate test is what it would cost to
h engage a nanny-housekeeper the £8,500 he awarded cannot be effectively attacked.

      On the other hand, the plaintiffs attack both awards on the ground that a multiplier
of 12 should have been applied, instead of the figure of nine adopted, but I see no
reason to differ from the finding of the learned judge on this point. The plaintiffs
also attack as inadequate the multiplicand of £1,000 adopted in relation to the
mother's death. They say that this figure ignored the cost of a housekeeper's main-
j tenance and that £234 per annum should have been added therefor; that the judge
omitted the cost of engaging a substitute housekeeper for a fortnight in each year
(£42); and that, having done this sum, he unwarrantably reduced the annual total
of £1,099 arrived at to a round figure of £1,000. In the result, so it is submitted,
there was a shortfall of £375 per annum, to which the multiplier of 12 contended for

---

1 [1915] 1 KB 627

should be applied. Such criticisms are in my judgment ill founded. The editors   *a*
of Clerk and Lindsell[1] are right in saying that, although some arithmetical calculations are necessarily involved in the assessment of the loss in such cases as the present,
much of the calculation must be in the realm of hypothesis. As Holroyd Pearce LJ
said in *Daniels v Jones*[2], arithmetic is a good servant but a bad master. The loss
suffered by the dependants must be assessed as best they can in the light of their
particular facts. But, having done his arithmetic, there comes a stage when the judge   *b*
has to stand back and look at the result. When he does, he should bear in mind the
wise words of Willmer LJ who said in the last mentioned case[3]: 'In what is essentially
a jury question the over-all picture is what matters. It is the wood that has to be
looked at, and not the individual trees.' I think the trial judge sought to do that in
the present case. I also think that, after prolonged reflection, he did it well, and I
would not disturb his awards either separately or in their totality.   *c*
    In the result I would dismiss both the appeal and the cross-notice.

BUCKLEY LJ. The Fatal Accidents Act 1846, s 2, invests a jury with the duty of
awarding such damages as they may think proportioned to the injury to the claimant
resulting from the death which occasions the claim. Although this function is now   *d*
performed by a judge in place of a jury, the question remains what is commonly
called a jury question, that is to say, a question which is to be answered not in a
narrowly legalistic or analytical way but in a commonsense way after giving due
weight to careful consideration of all the relevant facts.
    It has long been established that only injuries capable of evaluation in monetary
terms can found claims for damages under the section (see, for example, *Franklin v*   *e*
South Eastern Railway Co[4]), but the loss need not be a monetary loss: a loss of services
capable of being valued in pecuniary terms will suffice (*Berry v Humm & Co*[5]), as
also will the loss of reasonable expectation at the time of death of future financial
benefits from the deceased (*Taff Vale Railway Co v Jenkins*[6]) or, as must follow, the
reasonable expectation of services in the future capable of evaluation in monetary
terms. But an injury which cannot be so evaluated, such as grief or humiliation,   *f*
cannot found a claim (*Franklin v South Eastern Railway Co*[4]).
    In the present case Mr and Mrs Hay's children doubtless suffered grievously in a
variety of ways in consequence of their parents' death in the accident which has
occasioned this action. They have lost the benefits and happiness it was to be expected they would derive as they grew up from the companionship of their father
and mother. They have lost parental love. They have lost the joys of a happy   *g*
home. These losses cannot be assessed in monetary terms and so cannot support
a claim for damages. They have lost the financial support of their father, the breadwinner of the family, and with it they have lost the family home which he provided
and maintained for them, including its furnishings and ancillaries, such as the family
motor car and the provision of all those things which he provided for them to maintain them in the style in which that home was conducted. These losses can be   *h*
evaluated in financial terms and accordingly can support a claim for damages.
Although damages cannot be recovered for the loss of their mother's love, they can
be recovered for the loss of those services capable of being valued in terms of money
which she would have rendered to them as their mother had she survived. About

                                                                  j

1   Torts (13th Edn, 1969), para 430
2   [1961] 3 All ER 24 at 28, [1961] 1 WLR 1103 at 1110
3   [1961] 3 All ER at 30, [1961] 1 WLR at 1113
4   (1858) 3 H & N 211, [1843-60] All ER Rep 849
5   [1915] 1 KB 627
6   [1913] AC 1, [1911-13] All ER Rep 160

a these matters there is no dispute in this action, but there is dispute about how the losses capable of evaluation should be valued.

I shall call the monetary value which it is proper to be put on these losses capable of valuation the children's gross loss. Its ascertainment is not the end of the matter, for it is common ground that, where a dependant of a deceased person has suffered a gross loss of this nature as a result of the deceased's death by a fatal accident, any

b benefit which the dependant has secured in consequence of the same death may, if it can be valued in money terms, have to be taken in abatement of the gross loss. It was contended in the present case that, had there been no member of their family willing to give the children a home and had they been taken into the care of a local authority and placed with foster parents at the public expense, no damages would have been recoverable because the children would have been provided without expense to them with a substitute home and substitute parental care. As I under-

c stand counsel for the defendant's argument, he says that either the children could not in these circumstances be shown to have suffered any loss (that is to say, they would not have suffered any injury within the meaning of the section) or their gross loss would be shown to have been wholly abated by gains accruing to them as the result of the accident in consequence of their being taken into the care of a local

d authority as homeless orphans. The children were not taken into public care. The occasion for that never arose because their maternal grandmother, Mrs Toone, took them into her home and has ever since cared for them as if they were her own children. Counsel for the defendant contends that in these circumstances again the children cannot be shown to have suffered any loss or alternatively that the benefits which have accrued to them in this way must be set off against their gross loss in assessing

e the damages, if any, recoverable in this action. Counsel for the plaintiffs on the other hand contends that these benefits are not such as should be taken in abatement of the gross loss—he says that they are irrelevant to the assessment of the recoverable damages.

The question to be asked can be simply stated. How much worse off financially were the children as the result of their parents' deaths than they would have been if their father and mother had not been killed? It is less easily answered. Four

f problems have been discussed in the course of the argument. First, did the judge value the children's gross loss in relation to their father rightly? Secondly, did the judge value the children's gross loss in relation to their mother rightly? Thirdly, ought the grandmother's services to be brought into account? And fourthly, was the judge justified in adopting a multiplier of nine years?

In relation to the first of these questions figures were placed before the judge analys-

g ing the probable expenditure of the Hay family, had Mr and Mrs Hay survived, on the basis that Mr Hay's expendable income would have been of the order of £40 per week, which as was common ground, was the amount of take-home pay which he would have been earning at the date of the trial if his career had not been interrupted by the accident. These figures were broken down into amounts representing how much of this income would have been expended exclusively for the benefit of

h Mr Hay, how much of it would have been expended exclusively for the benefit of Mrs Hay, how much would have been expended exclusively for the benefit of the children and what balance would have been expended for the general benefit of the family collectively. In this way of a total expendable income of £2,080 per annum £520 was attributed to the father, £420 to the mother, and £496 to the two children, leaving a balance of £644 (which the judge and everyone else, misled by an arithme-

j tical error in the table of figures before the court, assumed to be £673) attributable to expenditure for the family generally. No question now arises with regard to the £496. The learned judge discounted the figure of £673 by £69 and proceeded on the basis that the children were worse off in respect of expenditure that would have been made for the benefit of the family generally to the extent of £604, making with the £496 a total sum of £1,100 a year by which the children were worse off in consequence of the loss of their father. Counsel for the defendant disputes the propriety of

dealing with the general family expenditure in this way. He contends that the figure of a
£674 should have been apportioned to the father, the mother and each of the children
in the fractions one-third, one-third, one-sixth and one-sixth respectively. The
learned judge, rightly, in my opinion, regarded this as a wholly unrealistic approach.
Each boy, he said, lived in a whole house, not in one-sixth of a house. The children
have lost the enjoyment of a home, not a fraction of a home. The cost of providing
a substitute home for the children of a similar quality to the house provided by their b
parents and capable of accommodating them and a substitute mother would not be
greatly less than the cost of their family home would have been had their parents
survived. In my judgment the learned judge's approach to this part of the problem
was realistic and reasonable.

As regards the value to be placed on the mother's services, the only evidence
put before the court was that of a Mrs Baxter, a proprietress of an employment c
agency. Her evidence was that at the time of the trial it would have been difficult
to find any woman who would go and live in such a house as the family home to
look after two children aged five and seven and to perform the duties of a mother at
less than £15 per week. Founding himself on this figure, and making an addition in
respect of the cost of providing substitute care when the substitute mother would
take time off, and making allowance for the cost of National Insurance contributions, d
the learned judge arrived at a figure of £1,000 per annum as representing the value
of the services which the mother would have provided had she survived. The
learned judge added the figures of £1,100 and £1,000 together and multiplied the
result by nine arriving at a sum of £18,900 from which he deducted £2,500 representing the net values of the estates of the deceased parents including damages
recovered under the Law Reform (Miscellaneous Provisions) Act 1934, thus arriving e
at a sum of £16,400 which with interest thereon he awarded as damages under the
Fatal Accidents Act 1846.

In my judgment counsel for the defendant's argument that in consequence of the
fact that the grandmother is voluntarily affording maternal care to the two children
they are not shown to have suffered any injury as a result of the loss of their mother
cannot be sound. If it were sound, it seems to me that it might equally well be argued f
that, since their grandmother is also providing them with a home and their keep they
have suffered no loss as a result of the death of their father. But it would surely be
necessary at least to compare and take into account the comparative qualities of the
services and benefits afforded in these respects by the parents in their lifetime and by
the grandmother since the parents' death. In my judgment, the proper approach is
first to place a valuation on those losses which the children have suffered in consequence g
of the death of their parents and then to set against those losses any benefits which it is
proper to take into account as benefits that have come to them as the result of the
accident. If that is the right approach, counsel for the defendant does not dispute the
validity of the figures adopted by the learned judge for the purposes of his calculations.

Counsel for the plaintiffs on the other hand says that the judge in arriving at the
figure of £1,000 a year for the mother's services has adopted too low a figure in that he h
omitted to bring into the calculation anything for the cost of the substitute mother's
board and for the provision of other care during an annual holiday for the substitute
mother, and on account of his having rounded the total calculated figure down by £99
a year. In these respects counsel for the plaintiffs says the judge's figure of £1,000 fell
short by £375, which, when multiplied by an appropriate multiplier, would make a
substantial difference to the amount of damages. It is true that the learned judge did j
not take these two matters (board and holidays) explicitly into account, but there
were other things going the other way which he also did not take explicitly into
account, such for example as the amount of assistance and relief which a substitute
mother might expect to receive from the children's grandparents, both maternal and
paternal, and other relations. Moreover, it must be borne in mind that in making
such an assessment as this arithmetic cannot provide a means of arriving at an exact

a amount but merely a method of checking the reasonableness of the proposed award. I see no reason to interfere with the figure of £1,000, and the less so since the judge by excusably overlooking the arithmetical error to which I have referred may have adopted a slightly larger figure in respect of the loss of the father's support than he would otherwise have done.

I now come to the question whether what Mrs Toone has done should be taken into

b account in abatement of the children's gross loss. Counsel for the defendant has contended that the principle can be stated thus: if immediately before the death which occasions a claim there was a reasonable expectation that any benefit which in fact thereafter enures would arise in the event of the death occurring, then this benefit should be taken into account in abatement of any gross loss. Counsel for the defendant relies in this connection on the evidence of Mrs Toone to the effect that if her daughter

c and son-in-law had died at any time from any cause she would have taken their children into her home as their grandmother who loved them and would have wished to care for them. Counsel for the defendant consequently says that it was wholly predictable that if both Mr and Mrs Hay were killed Mrs Toone would look after the children as if they were her own. What has happened in this respect was accordingly a predictable consequence of the fatality which resulted in the deaths of Mr and Mrs

d Hay, so that the benefits resulting to the children ought to be taken into account in considering the extent of the injury they suffered as a result of the deaths.

Counsel for the plaintiffs on the other hand says that the cases establish no clear principle on which it should be decided whether a benefit accruing to a dependant of a deceased person after the death should be treated as abating any injury suffered by the dependant as a result of the death. He says that one must look at the words of the

e section, which are in wide terms, and decide on the facts of the particular case whether the benefit ought fairly to be regarded as abating the injury. He relies strongly on the remarks of Pearce LJ and of Lord Evershed MR in *Jenner v Allen West & Co Ltd*[1] and on *Daniels v Jones*[2].

Counsel for the plaintiffs also points out that a strange anomaly would flow from the defendant's argument. If only one parent had been killed in the accident, there

f could be no doubt that damages would be recoverable under the Fatal Accidents Act 1846, on behalf of both the surviving parent and the children, whereas, according to the defendant's argument, in the event which happened of both parents being killed no or only very small damages are recoverable. Nobody doubts that, if the dependants inherit property from the deceased, this is a benefit so directly resulting from the death of the deceased that it should be taken into account under the section. On the

g other hand the gift by a deceased mother's children of one third of her estate to their stepfather in *Peacock v Amusement Equipment Co Ltd*[3] was, I think, a benefit of a kind which any juryman would say should not be treated as reducing the injury he had suffered by reason of his wife's death. It was a windfall which, it is true, would not have occurred but for her death. It resulted from an act of generosity on the part of her children subsequent to her death. But there may obviously be many cases in which it

h is difficult to draw the line—for example, a voluntary pension granted to a dependant after the death, the proceeds of contributions from fellow employees of the deceased, a fund similarly provided by friends or relations, a grant from a disaster fund, a compassionate gift. Similar difficulty may arise where the benefit is not monetary but in the form of services, such as voluntary nursing care. Questions have also arisen in respect of moneys received by the dependant as the result of accident or life insurances

j and as to the effect on the recoverable damages of the fact or possibility of a widow remarrying, as well when the claimant is the widow herself as where the claimant is a child of hers.

---

1 [1959] 2 All ER 115 at 124, 126, [1959] 1 WLR 554 at 565, 568
2 [1961] 3 All ER 24, [1961] 1 WLR 1103
3 [1954] 2 All ER 689, [1954] 2 QB 347

It is not surprising that in cases of such a variety of kinds judges have used different a language in different cases. In some judgments attention has been directed to whether the benefit was to be accurately regarded as resulting from the death. In such cases consideration has been given to causation. In others the court has approached the problem from the point of view of what should be regarded as reasonably to have been expected to follow the event of the death.

For it to be proper to take a post-obit benefit into account in limitation or reduction b of an injury suffered by reason of a death, there can be no doubt, I think, that there must be some association between the death and the receipt of the benefit, but the cases clearly establish that this need not be a direct causal link, a causa causans. See for example *Mead v Clarke Chapman & Co Ltd*[1], where the remarriage of the widow of the deceased was not the direct consequence of his death, although she could not have remarried had her first husband still been alive. Jenkins LJ there considered[2] that c there was 'a sufficient causal connection'. And this was held to affect the damages recovered by the deceased's children notwithstanding that at that time a stepfather was under no legal obligation to maintain stepchildren, even if he accepted them into his family.

We have been referred to a considerable number of reported cases decided either under the Fatal Accidents Acts or in personal injuries cases in which questions of this kind d or analogous questions have arisen, but I do not think that I need to refer to them. Lord Edmund Davies has already mentioned a number of them. In my opinion counsel for the plaintiffs is justified in saying that it is not possible to discover from them any established principle by which we should decide whether the benefits which Mrs Toone has conferred and is conferring on her grandchildren should be taken into account in the present case. The question remains, in my opinion, a jury question in the sense e indicated at the beginning of this judgment, and must be answered accordingly in the way which seems fair in the light of all the circumstances of the case. The learned judge asked himself this question: 'Do the services which Mrs. Toone has already provided and will continue to provide for the two children constitute benefits resulting from the death of their mother?' He answered it in the negative.

To my mind Mrs Toone's evidence, to which I have already referred, which was f given with hindsight, really amounts to no more than this, that in the event of Mr and Mrs Hay becoming for any reason unable to provide and care for their children she as the children's grandmother would have wished to do her best to fill their parents' place. Whether in any given circumstances she would have been able to do so, or, even if able, would in fact have done so, must be dependent on what the circumstances might be when the event occurred. Mrs Toone's health, or her commitments to other g dependant members of her family, or her financial or domestic situation might have rendered her incapable of doing as she would have liked to do; or some other member of the children's family, either on their mother's side or their father's, might have been in a better position to care for them. In my judgment, it is more realistic to say that Mrs Toone's services to her grandchildren resulted from a decision made by her on her own initiative after the accident than that they resulted from Mr and Mrs Hay's h deaths in the accident. Counsel for the plaintiffs put the point neatly and epigrammatically when he said that generosity does not result from death.

I doubt if it is very useful to try to find analogies in cases where the facts are very different, but it seems to me that Mrs Toone's services are more similar in quality to the subscriptions of fellow employees (see *Baker v Dalgleish Steam Shipping Co Ltd*[3]) than to the voluntary pension from the Crown with which that case was concerned or j the voluntary pension in *Jenner v Allen West & Co Ltd*[4]. Contributions to a workshop

---

1 [1956] 1 All ER 44, [1956] 1 WLR 76
2 [1956] 1 All ER at 48, [1956] 1 WLR at 83
3 [1922] 1 KB 361 at 369, 380
4 [1959] 2 All ER 115, [1959] 1 WLR 554

a   whip-round would, I think, normally be properly attributed to a desire by the contributors, conceived after the death, to relieve the needs of the widow or orphaned children of the dead man, whereas a widow's pension, albeit voluntary, is by its nature fairly obviously related to her dead husband's past services to the payer and is thus connected with matters dating from before the death and is likely to have been associated with the circumstances in which the deceased died.

b   In *Jenner's* case[1], in a passage already cited by Lord Edmund Davies, Pearce LJ contrasted a pension provided by the generosity of a third party who was in no way connected with the accident and a pension paid by employers to the widow of an employee who has died in consequence of an accident in the course of his employment.

In my judgment, the learned judge was fully entitled on the evidence in the present case to answer the question which he asked himself as he did, from which it follows

c   that, in my judgment, he rightly treated Mrs Toone's care of the children as conferring no benefit on them which ought to be taken into account in diminution of the damages recoverable in this action.

I would only add to the discussion of this part of the case that the decision in *Mead's* case[2] strikes me as somewhat anomalous. That a claim to damages on behalf of children in respect of their father's death should be liable to abatement on account of

d   the possibility or the event of their mother's contracting a second marriage of which no prospect existed at the date of the death seems to me a strange proposition. It must, I think, have flowed from the fact that it had become established that the widow's own claim was until 1971 liable to abatement in respect of such prospect of remarriage as she might have. This proceeded on the basis that on her remarriage any claim in respect of her earlier dependancy on her former husband must have ceased, since she

e   could not claim to be entitled to be treated as dependant on two husbands at one time. From this it was perhaps not a long step to hold that the children of a dead father could no longer claim for loss of dependancy on him when they had become de facto dependant on a stepfather. The position in respect of the widow's claim has now been altered by statute (Law Reform (Miscellaneous Provisions) Act 1971, s 4) but no similar change has been made in the law in respect of a claim by a widower or a child.

f   See in this connection *Jeffrey v Smith*[3] and *Thompson v Price*[4]. This may be thought to call for consideration by the legislature.

There only remains the question of the multiplier. The learned judge assumed that each child would remain dependant until the age of 18½, which resulted in an average period of 15 years' dependancy for each. On this footing he adopted a multiplier of nine. Counsel for the defendant has suggested that this is too high because, he says, it

g   does not take account of the fact that the boys' need for a substitute mother's care will decrease as they grow older. We cannot tell to what extent, if at all, the judge took this factor into account. Counsel for the plaintiffs says that the boys would be likely to remain dependant until the age of 20 and that consequently the average period of dependancy should be taken at more than 15 years, so that a multiplier of nine is too low. There seems to me to be little, if any, evidence to support this. I should be most

h   unwilling to upset the learned judge's decision in this respect, unless he could be shown to have proceeded on some clearly mistaken basis of fact or erroneous principle. Neither party has persuaded me of this and accordingly I do not think that the learned judge's decision in this respect should be disturbed.

For these reasons I am of opinion that both this appeal and the cross-appeal fail and I agree that each should be dismissed.

j

---

1   [1959] 2 All ER at 125, [1959] 1 WLR at 565, 566
2   [1956] 1 All ER 44, [1956] 1 WLR 76
3   [1970] RTR 279
4   [1973] 2 All ER 846, [1973] QB 838

ORMROD LJ. The main issue in this appeal is whether or not the fact that Mrs a
Toone, the children's maternal grandmother, has voluntarily assumed the responsibility of bringing them up, should be taken into account in assessing the extent of the
injury which they have sustained as a result of the death of their mother.

Leaving aside for the moment the large volume of authority which has been cited
to us by counsel on both sides, and looking only at the wording of the statutory
provision which created this cause of action, namely, s 2 of the Fatal Accidents Acts b
1846, which permitted the jury to 'give such damages as they may think proportioned
to the injury, resulting from such death . . .', it would appear that Parliament intended
the jury to make a comparison between the position of the dependants before and after
the relevant death, and award damages 'proportioned' to the difference, excluding
of course, benefits acquired after, but independently of the death. This in fact was the
interpretation adopted by the courts from the beginning. (See *Hicks v Newport*, c
Abergavenny & Hereford Railway Co[1], *Pym v Great Northern Railway Co*[2] and many
other cases.) This principle was reaffirmed by the House of Lords in *Davies v Powell
Duffryn Associated Collieries Ltd (No 2)*[3], in which Lord Macmillan said:

> '. . . the damages to be awarded to a dependant of a deceased person under the
> Fatal Accidents Acts must take into account any pecuniary benefit accruing to that
> dependant in consequence of the death of the deceased. It is the net loss on balance d
> which constitutes the measure of damages.'

Lord Wright said[4]:

> 'The actual pecuniary loss of each individual entitled to sue can only be as-
> certained by balancing on the one hand the loss to him of the future pecuniary e
> benefit, and on the other any pecuniary advantage which from whatever source
> comes to him by reason of the death.'

This principle, however, has been so seriously eroded by subsequent legislation that,
today, little remains of it. Already by the 1908 Act Parliament had excepted sums
payable on the death of the deceased under insurance policies. The 1959 Act went much
further, excepting a very wide class or classes of benefits, including pensions; and the f
1971 Act directed the court, in the case of widows, to ignore all benefits arising from
remarriage or the prospect of remarriage. All that is left of the balancing process
appears to be benefits arising from the estate of the deceased and, in the case of
children, from their stepfather's liability to maintain them: *Mead v Clarke Chapman &
Co Ltd*[5], *Reincke v Gray*[6], and *Thompson v Price*[7]. *Daniels v James*[8] suggests that even
in cases where the benefit arises from the estate, the court will not be unduly in- g
fluenced by arithmetical calculations. The courts themselves have further restricted
the classes of benefit which are to be taken into account by construing such phrases as
'resulting from' or 'in consequence of' the death, restrictively. (See, for example,
Peacock v Amusement Equipment Co Ltd[9] and *Redpath v Belfast & County Down Railway
Co*[10], *Voller v Dairy Produce Packers Ltd*[11], and *Moore v Babcock & Wilcox Ltd*[12].)
h

---

1 (1857) 4 B & S 403 n
2 (1863) 4 B & S 396, [1861-73] All ER Rep 180
3 [1942] AC 601 at 609
4 [1942] 1 All ER at 662, [1942] AC at 612
5 [1956] 1 All ER 44, [1956] 1 WLR 76
6 [1964] 2 All ER 687, [1964] 1 WLR 832
7 [1973] 2 All ER 846, [1973] QB 838
8 [1961] 3 All ER 24, [1961] 1 WLR 1103
9 [1954] 2 All ER 689, [1954] 2 QB 347
10 [1947] NI 167
11 [1962] 3 All ER 938, [1962] 1 WLR 960
12 [1966] 3 All ER 882, [1967] 1 WLR 481

a   In the light of this history, the court ought, in my judgment, to hesitate to extend the balancing principle to classes of benefit which are not directly covered by authority which is binding on it. Accordingly, I think there is a great deal of weight in counsel for the plaintiff's primary submission that this court should not, as a matter of policy, bring into account the benefits provided to these children by Mrs Toone. I accept also his submission that it is impossible to formulate in general terms any test which will

b   satisfactorily discriminate between benefits to be taken into account and those to be ignored. Attempts to do so using phrases such as 'resulting from' or 'in consequence of' lead to sterile debates on causation, and have produced results in the reported cases which are difficult, if not impossible, to reconcile one with another. Counsel for the defendant's suggestion that benefits, of which there can be said to have been a reasonable expectation at the time of death, should be included in the balancing

c   process, in practice, also fails. It is difficult to see why a benefit from a stepfather should reasonably be expected, and a benefit from a fund raised by subscriptions from fellow employees, which is quite a common practice, should not be expected.

     I, therefore, conclude that in the present state of the law it would be wrong to bring into account the benefit which these children are deriving from their grandmother, and that the learned judge was right to exclude it from his calculations. It seems to me,

d   however, to follow from this, that it is necessary to avoid putting an inflated value on the pecuniary loss sustained by the children. Loss of the services of a wife and mother is a grievous loss on any view, but I am not convinced that the current cost of a notional housekeeper is necessarily a reliable guide in this most difficult exercise. No question on this point arises in this appeal but it would have been helpful to have had evidence, if it were available, of the cost of providing a foster home for these

e   children. So far as the cross-appeal is concerned the learned judge was right, in my judgment, to ignore such items as the notional cost of feeding the notional house-keeper and of providing notional substitutes for her holidays. To include such items would be to make the valuation still more artificial and unreal.

     Looking at the learned judge's final figure, and bearing in mind Lord Diplock's observations about annuity values in his speech in *Mallett v McMonagle*[1], I would not

f   interfere with the multiplier of nine which the learned judge decided to apply. I would therefore dismiss the appeal and the cross-appeal.

Appeal and cross-appeal dismissed. Leave to appeal to House of Lords refused.

Solicitors: *Robert Walters & Co*, Birmingham (for the defendant); *Field, Fisher &*

g   *Martineau*, agents for *Moss, Toone & Dean*, Loughborough (for the plaintiffs).

Mary Rose Plummer   Barrister.

---

1   [1969] 2 All ER 178 at 191, [1970] AC 166 at 177

Dyson v Ellison

a

QUEEN'S BENCH DIVISION
LORD WIDGERY CJ, MAIS AND CROOM-JOHNSON JJ
14th NOVEMBER 1974

b

Road traffic – Disqualification for holding licence – Two previous convictions endorsed on licence within previous three years – Evidence of previous convictions – Appeal to Crown Court – Appeal against sentence only – Offence involving obligatory endorsement – Driving licence endorsed by justices – Duty of Crown Court to order production of driving licence for endorsement – Duty of court to examine licence for purpose of determining whether disqualification should be ordered – Road Traffic Act 1972, ss 93(3), 101(4).

c

Where a defendant is convicted by justices of a road traffic offence involving obligatory endorsement and, following conviction, the defendant's driving licence is produced to the court for endorsement in accordance with s 101(4)[a] of the Road Traffic Act 1972, it is the duty of the court to have regard to any endorsements already on the licence for the purpose of determining whether, in view of previous convictions disclosed by the endorsements, the defendant should be disqualified from holding a driving licence under the provisions of s 93(3)[b] of the 1972 Act. Where, on conviction of an offence involving obligatory endorsement, the defendant appeals to the Crown Court against sentence only, the appeal is by way of a rehearing and it is the duty of the Crown Court also to require production of the defendant's licence for endorsement and for the purpose of determining whether he should be disqualified (see p 278 h and j, and p 279 b to g, post).

d

e

Notes

For disqualification and endorsement of driving licences, see 33 Halsbury's Laws (3rd Edn) 638-644, paras 1080-1089, and for cases on the subject, see 45 Digest (Repl) 117-120, 398-430.

For the Road Traffic Act 1972, ss 93, 101, see 42 Halsbury's Statutes (3rd Edn) 1744, 1753.

f

Case stated

This was an appeal by way of a case stated by the Crown Court (Mr Recorder Muscroft and justices) at Bradford in respect of its adjudication sitting on appeal from justices for the city of Bradford.

On 20th March 1973, on an information preferred by the prosecutor, James Arthur Ellison, the defendant, John Thomas Dyson pleaded guilty before the justices to a charge of unlawfully driving a motor vehicle on a restricted road at a speed exceeding 30 m p h contrary to ss 71 and 78A of the Road Traffic Regulation Act 1967.

On 6th April 1973 the justices ordered: (a) that the defendant should pay a fine of £12; (b) that particulars of the offence should be endorsed on his driving licence; and (c) that, pursuant to s 93(3) of the Road Traffic Act 1972, he be disqualified from

g

h

---

a   Section 101(4) is set out at p 278 f and g, post
b   Section 93(3) provides: 'Where a person convicted of an offence involving obligatory or discretionary disqualification has within the three years immediately preceding the commission of the offence been convicted on not less than two occasions of any such offence and particulars of the convictions have been ordered to be endorsed in accordance with section 101 of this Act, the court shall order him to be disqualified for such period not less than six months as the court thinks fit, unless the court is satisfied, having regard to all the circumstances, that there are grounds for mitigating the normal consequences of the conviction and thinks fit to order him to be disqualified for a shorter period or not to order him to be disqualified.'

j

a holding or obtaining a driving licence for a period of six months. Pursuant to s 94(2) of the Road Traffic Act 1972 the period of disqualification was suspended pending the hearing of an appeal by the defendant.

On 6th April 1973 the defendant by his solicitors gave notice of appeal against so much of the sentence as ordered that he be fined £12 and disqualified from driving for six months. The notice specified that the general grounds of the appeal were *b* that the sentence was too severe. No other ground was specified. On 8th June 1973 the defendant's appeal was heard in the Crown Court at Bradford. The defendant's counsel explained that the disqualification had been imposed under the 'totting-up' procedure. The recorder pointed out that there was no evidence before him as to the defendant's previous convictions. Counsel for the prosecutor informed the recorder that the police had no record of minor motoring offences. He did not indicate that *c* the defendant's driving licence was available or invite him to look at it but simply called Pc Cranswick to give evidence. The constable, who was present to give evidence of the defendant's antecedents, had no knowledge and gave no evidence of the defendant's previous convictions. He did however indicate that there would be convictions endorsed on the defendant's driving licence. The recorder was of the opinion that the prosecutor had not supplied evidence of those convictions and *d* that accordingly there was no evidence on which the court could or ought to have ordered the defendant to be disqualified from holding or obtaining a driving licence pursuant to s 93(3) of the 1972 Act. The recorder concluded, therefore, that he had no alternative but to allow the appeal.

Accordingly the Crown Court allowed the appeal to the extent that the period of disqualification was removed. No legal arguments on either side were heard and *e* no authorities were cited. The question for the opinion of the High Court was whether the recorder should have asked if the defendant's driving licence was available and if so called for its production.

Andrew Pugh for the prosecutor.
The defendant did not appear and was not represented.

f

LORD WIDGERY CJ. This is an appeal by case stated from the Crown Court at Bradford in respect of an adjudication on an appeal from the justices for the city of Bradford.

What had happened by way of history was this. On 20th March 1973 the defendant *g* pleaded guilty before the justices to a charge of unlawfully driving a motor vehicle on a restricted road at a speed exceeding 30 m p h contrary to ss 71 and 78A of the Road Traffic Regulations Act 1967. The case came before the justices on 6th April 1973. They ordered that the defendant be fined £12 and that his licence be endorsed; and pursuant to s 93(3) of the Road Traffic Act 1972 they applied the totting-up procedure and disqualified him from holding or obtaining a driving licence for a *h* period of six months. He appealed to the Crown Court against his sentence only, and the only ground which he specified was that his sentence was too severe. The matter came before the learned recorder sitting in the Crown Court on 8th June 1973 and nothing was put before him by way of proof of the earlier and qualifying offences which would be the basis of the justices' order for disqualification on totting-up. It is exceedingly difficult to know exactly what happened in the Crown *j* Court, and I cannot go further with confidence than to say that the recorder took the objection that he had no evidence on which to conclude that this was a case for totting-up at all.

Of course what is intended to happen on occasions of this kind is that the earlier offences which form the foundation of the totting-up will normally be proved (at all events prima facie) by reference to the endorsements on the defendant's licence. One need not go further for that proposition than s 101(1) of the Road Traffic Act 1972,

which prescribes that where a person is convicted of an offence of the kind which the *a*
section describes as an 'offence involving obligatory endorsement', the court shall
order that particulars of the conviction and, if the court orders him to be disqualified,
particulars of the disqualification, shall be endorsed on any licence held by him; and
particulars of any conviction or disqualification so endorsed may be produced as
prima facie evidence of the conviction or disqualification.

So evidently Parliament intended that the elementary and normal method of *b*
proving the qualifying offences would be by looking at the driver's licence to see
what endorsements the licence carried. But for some reason, which we cannot
discover on the material before us, the licence does not seem to have been before
the recorder. Accordingly he decided that he had no evidence on which to support
the totting-up disqualification. He allowed the appeal to the extent of disallowing
the disqualification, but otherwise allowed the justices' order to stand. The case *c*
is brought to us, and the question for the opinion of the court is whether the recorder
should have asked if the defendant's driving licence was available and, if so, called
for its production.

If we still had to consider whether this particular man was going to be disqualified,
we should have a very considerable task on our hands owing to the form in which
the case has been stated, but counsel for the prosecutor has assured us that there is *d*
no intention of asking us in this court to restore the disqualification after all this lapse
of time. So we are really being asked by the prosecutor to give an answer to the
legal problem to which I have referred because apparently it is one where an authoritative ruling would be appreciated, and would be of assistance to the police hereafter.
I think in all the circumstances we ought to endeavour to do just that.

What is the problem? As I say, if the licence is produced before the court, refer- *e*
ence to its endorsements, if any, will prima facie satisfy the requirements to be proved
in totting-up, but the problem seems to be how you get the licence before the court
in certain circumstances. Section 101(4) of the 1972 Act is designed to deal with
this very problem. It provides:

'A person who is prosecuted for an offence involving obligatory endorsement
and who is the holder of a licence, shall either—(a) cause it to be delivered to *f*
the clerk of the court not later than the day before the date appointed for the
hearing, or (b) post it, at such a time that in the ordinary course of post it would
be delivered not later than that day, in a letter duly addressed to the clerk and
either registered or sent by the recorded delivery service, or (c) have it with
him at the hearing; and if he is convicted of an offence and the court makes an
order under subsection (1) above the court shall require the licence to be produced *g*
to it for endorsement.'

That provision, operating in the court of first instance, namely, the magistrates'
court, should in my judgment work in this way. The charge being one which
involves an obligatory endorsement on conviction, the justices first of all proceed
to the question of conviction or no. If they decide to convict, then it being an obliga- *h*
tory endorsement case, they order an endorsement under sub-s (1), and the moment
they have taken those two steps they can call for the licence and look at it. Having
called for the licence and looked at it, they can then take whatever action is appropriate in regard to any endorsements which an inspection of the licence reveals.

In saying that they can do that, I am not in the least put off by the terms of the
section which say that the requiring of the licence to be produced shall be for endorse- *j*
ment. Maybe it is. That may be the initial excuse for requiring it to be produced,
but once it is before the court, then its evidential value to support the earlier convictions seems to be clear enough. That is the situation in the magistrates'
court.

Next we are in the Crown Court. Appeal to the Crown Court against sentence is a
rehearing just like any other appeal from the justices to the Crown Court, and it is

a   a rehearing from conviction onwards. In other words, the court should take the matter up, as it were, at the moment when the conviction is announced and then proceed to fix the sentence on a rehearing basis. The conviction having been entered in the magistrates' court and not being appealed against, the conviction is effective in the Crown Court from the moment when the hearing begins. The Crown Court should, in compulsory endorsement cases, order an endorsement under s 101(1).

b   In saying that, I am not oblivious to the fact that there may be a standing endorsement in existence ordered by the magistrates' court. That is another matter. The Crown Court in my judgment should go through the sentencing procedure on a rehearing basis without regard to the existing order in the magistrates' court. Having, therefore, decided, as it must, in the Crown Court to order an endorsement, then the Crown Court should ask for the licence—demand it, if you like—and then, that

c   licence being inspected and showing the previous convictions, the totting up procedure can be followed.

I think that is the only way to make sense of this section, and it is strictly in parallel with the Criminal Appeal Act 1968 which enjoins the Court of Appeal, Criminal Division, when dealing with an appeal against sentence to ask itself, 'Should this man be sentenced differently?' I think the Crown Court on an appeal against sentence

d   again is asking itself 'Should this man be sentenced differently?' The only way in which one can decide that is to decide how he ought to be sentenced and then see to what extent, if at all, it differs from the order made in the court below. If it differs to a significant degree, then the appeal should be allowed to that extent.

Accordingly in the present instance my view of the problem of law put before us is that it should be answered in this way, that on the opening of the appeal, the

e   conviction standing, the court should have ordered the obligatory endorsement, which was on any view inescapable in this case, and should then have called for the licence. Having called for the licence, the problems which in fact arose before the Crown Court would, I hope, not arise at all.

It is not necessary for us to allow the appeal. Indeed I think the right thing is that it should be dismissed, but that will not affect, I hope, any assistance which this

f   judgment may give to recorders sitting in the Crown Court hereafter.

MAIS J. I agree.

CROOM-JOHNSON J. I agree.

g
Appeal dismissed.

Solicitors: *Tuck & Mann & Geffen* and *T D Jones & Co*, agent for *David Morgan*, Bradford (for the prosecutor).

Jacqueline Charles Barrister.

a

Reiterbund v Reiterbund

COURT OF APPEAL, CIVIL DIVISION

MEGAW, ORMROD LJJ AND CUMMING-BRUCE J

28th, 29th OCTOBER 1974

b

Divorce – Separation – Five year separation – Decree nisi – Refusal – Grave financial hardship – Social security benefits – Relevance – Loss of chance of widow's pension – Right to supplementary benefit of similar amount to pension – Duty of husband to maintain wife irrelevant in situation where husband assumed to be dead – Entitlement to social security benefits to be taken into account – Matrimonial Causes Act 1973, s 5.

c

The parties were married in 1942. In 1956 they separated and lived apart thereafter. In February 1971 the husband petitioned for dissolution of the marriage relying on the fact prescribed by s 1(2)(e)[a] of the Matrimonial Causes Act 1973, i e that the parties had lived apart for a continuous period of five years immediately preceding the presentation of the petition. The wife, relying on s 5[b] of the 1973 Act, opposed the petition on the ground that a decree would cause grave financial hardship to her in that d she would lose her pension rights as a married woman. The wife lived on supplementary benefits of £7.75 a week out of which she paid £4.55 for her keep to a charitable institution that was looking after her. For some time she had required psychiatric help as an in-patient at a mental hospital and, although she was employed at a day-centre earning £1 a week, she was unable to seek other than a sheltered form of employment from which she could not earn enough for her keep if not assisted by e private charity. It was likely that she would in the future remain incapable of earning her own living and would have to continue to rely on external sources of support. The husband was himself a poor man dependent for the most part on state benefits and that situation was unlikely to change in the future. He had chronic bronchitis and was a registered disabled person. He made a few pounds from time to time in casual activities but he had no substantial income or disposable capital. At the date of f the hearing the husband was aged 54 and the wife 52. The judge found that if he granted a decree and the husband predeceased the wife before she reached the age of 60, she would lose a widow's pension but that she would in any event be entitled to a retirement pension on attaining the age of 60. He held that, although the loss of the chance of acquiring a widow's pension would constitute financial hardship within s 5, the wife had failed to prove that the hardship would be grave. He further held that g the wife would not in any event suffer grave financial hardship since the supplementary benefits to which she would be entitled would not be less than the widow's pension. The wife appealed contending, inter alia, that in determining whether she would suffer grave financial hardship the court was not entitled to take into account her right to social security benefits.

h

Held – Since the loss of the wife's right to a widow's pension would only occur in the event of the husband's death, there was no reason to ignore the wife's right to social security benefits in determining whether the loss would constitute grave financial hardship for, the husband being dead, there could be no question of public funds being used to relieve him of his duty to maintain her. It followed that, in the particular circumstances where there was no prospect of the wife entering gainful employment j which would reduce her right to supplementary benefits, the grant of a decree would not cause the wife any financial hardship since in the event of the husband predeceasing the wife before she reached the age of 60, the sums that she would receive from

---

a   Section 1(2), so far as material, is set out at p 282 *a*, post
b   Section 5 is set out at p 282 *b* to *e*, post

a public funds in the form of supplementary benefits would be not less than those which she would otherwise receive in the form of a widow's pension. The appeal would therefore be dismissed (see p 286 *a* to *g* and p 288 *j* to p 289 *b* and *g*, post).

Dictum of Sir George Baker P in *Dorrell v Dorrell* [1972] 3 All ER at 348 disapproved.

Per Curiam. Each case must depend on its own facts and the right of a respondent to receive supplementary benefits would not necessarily be a determinant, or even a *b* relevant, factor in deciding whether the respondent would suffer grave financial hardship in the event of a decree being granted (see p 286 *g* and *h*, and p 289 *b* and *g*, post).

Decision of Finer J [1974] 2 All ER 455 affirmed.

Notes

c For the refusal of a decree on the ground of hardship, see Supplement to 12 Halsbury's Laws (3rd Edn) para 437A, 6, and for cases on the subject, see 27(1) Digest (Reissue) 361, 362, 2638-2644.

For the Matrimonial Causes Act 1973, ss 1, 5, see 43 Halsbury's Statutes (3rd Edn) 541, 548.

d **Case referred to in judgments**
Dorrell v Dorrell [1972] 3 All ER 343, [1972] 1 WLR 1087.

Cases also cited
Ashley v Ashley [1965] 3 All ER 554, [1968] P 582, DC.
Brickell v Brickell [1973] 3 All ER 508, [1973] 3 WLR 602, CA.
e *Grigson v Grigson* [1974] 1 All ER 478, [1974] 1 WLR 228, CA.
Mathias v Mathias [1972] 3 All ER 1, [1972] Fam 287, CA.
Parker v Parker [1972] 1 All ER 410, [1972] Fam 116.
Talbot v Talbot [1971] The Times, 19th October.
Wilson v Wilson [1973] 2 All ER 17, [1973] 1 WLR 555, CA.

f **Appeal**
This was an appeal by the wife, Bessie Reiterbund, against the order of Finer J[1] made on 18th February 1974 whereby he granted the husband, Solomon Reiterbund, a decree nisi of divorce having been satisfied that the parties had lived apart for a continuous period of at least five years immediately preceding the presentation of the petition. The facts are set out in the judgment of Megaw LJ.

g John Samuels for the wife.
Norman Primost and Mordecai Levene for the husband.

MEGAW LJ. This is an appeal from the judgment and order of Finer J[1] made on 18th February 1974 whereby it was decreed that the marriage of the petitioner, Mr Solomon Reiterbund, and the respondent, Mrs Bessie Reiterbund, should be dissolved.
h For simplicity, I shall refer to the petitioner as 'the husband' and to the respondent as 'the wife'. The wife appeals to this court, asking that the decree nisi should be set aside and that the petition should be dismissed, or that a new trial should be ordered. The appeal is concerned with the question of the defence of 'grave financial hardship' under s 5 of the Matrimonial Causes Act 1973. The relevant provisions are well known, but I should perhaps read the more immediately relevant provisions.
j Section 1 of that Act provides:

'(1) Subject to section 3 below, a petition for divorce may be presented to the court by either party to a marriage on the ground that the marriage has broken down irretrievably.

---

1 [1974] 2 All ER 455, [1974] 1 WLR 788

'(2) The court hearing a petition for divorce shall not hold the marriage to have *a* broken down irretrievably unless the petitioner satisfies the court of one or more of the following facts, that is to say—. . . (e) that the parties to the marriage have lived apart for a continuous period of at least five years immediately preceding the presentation of the petition . . .'

Section 5 provides for refusal of decree in what are called 'five year separation *b* cases' on grounds of grave hardship to the respondent. Section 5 reads:

'(1) The respondent to a petition for divorce in which the petitioner alleges five years' separation may oppose the grant of a decree on the ground that the dissolution of the marriage will result in grave financial or other hardship to him and that it would in all the circumstances be wrong to dissolve the marriage. *c*
'(2) Where the grant of a decree is opposed by virtue of this section, then—(a) if the court finds that the petitioner is entitled to rely in support of his petition on the fact of five years' separation and makes no such finding as to any other fact mentioned in section 1(2) above, and (b) if apart from this section the court would grant a decree on the petition, the court shall consider all the circumstances, including the conduct of the parties to the marriage and the interests of those *d* parties and of any children or other persons concerned, and if of opinion that the dissolution of the marriage will result in grave financial or other hardship to the respondent and that it would in all the circumstances be wrong to dissolve the marriage it shall dismiss the petition.
'(3) For the purposes of this section hardship shall include the loss of the chance of acquiring any benefit which the respondent might acquire if the marriage *e* were not dissolved.'

The husband and wife were married on 18th January 1942. The husband was then 22 years of age, and the wife was 20. So, when the petition was heard and decided by Finer J in the beginning of 1974, the husband was 54 and the wife was 52. There were two children of the marriage, but they are both now adults, the younger of them *f* being some 24 years of age. The parties separated in 1956. In August 1956, on the wife's complaint of desertion by the husband, a stipendiary magistrate made an order for the husband to pay £5 a week for the wife's maintenance and 15s a week for each child. I doubt whether very much was paid under that order, even before 1959; and in 1959 payments ended. In 1958 the husband brought divorce proceedings, alleging cruelty on the part of the wife. After a contested hearing, those proceedings were *g* dismissed.

The husband's petition in the proceedings out of which this appeal arises was filed on 18th February 1971. The husband asserted irretrievable breakdown of the marriage, relying, and relying only, on para (e) of s 2(1) of the Divorce Reform Act 1969 (which is now s 1(2)(e) of the Matrimonial Causes Act 1973): that is, that the parties had lived apart for a continuous period of five years immediately preceding the service of the *h* petition. The wife's answer relied on s 5 of the 1973 Act (as it now is). Initially, she relied, not only on 'grave financial', but also on 'other', hardship. The 'other' hardship was that divorce was anathema to the wife, on religious and moral grounds. That plea was expressly abandoned at the outset of the hearing before the learned judge, and we are not concerned with it.

The issue which the judge had to decide was the issue of grave *financial* hardship. *j* That issue was raised in the wife's answer to the petition dated 17th June 1971. The relevant part of that document is para 8 which reads:

'If a decree of dissolution is granted to the Petitioner the Respondent will lose her pension rights as a married woman, and, in the future, as a widow under the prevailing regulations of the Department of Health and Social Security.'

a   The evidence before the learned judge was indeed, as he has said in his judgment, 'distinctly exiguous'. So far as concerns the wife, the judge said[1]:

'The wife lives on supplementaty benefits at the rate, as at 2nd November 1973, of £7.75 weekly. A letter from her solicitors dated 23rd August 1972 states that out of the then payment of £6 a week for supplementary benefit she paid £4.55 a week for her keep to a charitable institution that was looking after her,

b   and was earning up to £1 a week for working during the day for a day-centre. She had no savings or capital, and her clothing was largely provided by the charity. The answer filed in June 1971 alleges that the wife has for some time required psychiatric treatment as an in-patient in a mental hospital and, although now employed at a day-centre, is unable to seek other than a sheltered form of employment from which she could not earn enough for her keep if not assisted by

c   private charity. All this leaves her precise current circumstances rather obscure, but I am satisfied (and it has never been contested by the husband, who, indeed, himself asserts that his wife was mentally disturbed when he left her) that the wife is, and will in the future, remain incapable of earning her own living, and will have to continue to rely on external sources of support.'

d   As regards the husband, the learned judge went in some detail into such evidence as was indeed before him. The conclusion which the learned judge expressed as to the husband's circumstances was[2]:

'On the whole of the evidence, including the agreed documents, I find that the husband is himself a poor man, dependent for the most part on support from state benefits, and not very likely to be able to break out of that situation in the future.'

e   I should perhaps add that there was material on which the court could conclude that the husband had suffered from indifferent health and that he had had chronic bronchitis. He had been issued with a certificate of registration under the Disabled Persons (Employment) Acts 1944 and 1958. According to the judge, he made a few pounds from time to time in casual activities, but he certainly had no substantial income, and he had no disposable capital at all. The judge referred to the fact that there had been

f   no attempt by the Supplementary Benefits Commission to seek to enforce the maintenance order against the husband after payments had stopped, and the judge inferred that the commission had taken the view that the husband was too poor to be worth pursuing.

The learned judge was concerned, and as I think rightly concerned, at the lack of proper evidence as to matters relating to the husband, and as to matters relating to

g   the wife, which would have been relevant to the assessment of the wife's entitlement to benefits which she would, in certain contingencies, lose if the divorce were to take place. It was such contingent losses on which she was relying before the learned judge to establish grave financial hardship. In saying that, it is right that one should appreciate the difficulties that face the advisers of a party in a case such as this in obtaining the evidence, or information which can be converted into evidence, on various matters

h   which may well be relevant for the purpose of establishing the case.

Before the learned judge, the somewhat obscure assertions which I have read in para 8 of the wife's answer were interpreted as referring to the contingent loss by the wife, if she were divorced, of two different types of benefit. The first of those was retirement pension when the wife would be over the age of 60. I need not consider, I think, any of the matters which were argued before the learned judge and dealt

j   with in his judgment in respect of retirement pension, because in this court counsel for the wife did not contend that any contingent loss which the wife might suffer as a result of a divorce would continue after she attained the age of 60. So, we are concerned in this appeal with the risk of the loss of a widow's pension, a loss which, if it

---

1 [1974] 2 All ER at 458, [1974] 1 WLR at 791
2 [1974] 2 All ER at 459, [1974] 1 WLR at 792

came into existence, would cease when the wife became 60. What is involved? If *a* there were no divorce, and if (i) the husband died at any time between the date of the divorce decree and the date of the wife's 60th birthday (a total period of some eight years), and if (ii) the wife was surviving when the husband died, then the wife would be entitled to receive a widow's benefit for the period between the husband's death and her 60th birthday, or her earlier death. If, on the other hand, the divorce decree stood, the wife would not receive a widow's benefit for any such period, even if the circum- *b* stance arose of the husband predeceasing the wife during those eight years. She would receive something else, namely, a greater sum in the form of supplementary benefit; but for the moment I propose to leave that out of account altogether, as Finer J did in reaching what he described as his 'first conclusion'.

The learned judge's first conclusion, so far as is relevant for the purposes of this appeal, was[1]:

c

'My first conclusion may, on the basis of the preceding discussion, be thus stated. If I grant the husband a decree and he dies within the next eight years or so, before the wife is 60 years of age, she will have lost a widow's pension before becoming eligible for a retirement pension . . . A divorce will therefore cause a hardship to the wife within the meaning of s 5(3) of the 1973 Act, but I do not consider that she has sufficiently proved that the hardship is a grave one.'   *d*

As I understand it, the learned judge was finding that 'a divorce will therefore cause hardship' on the assumption, which he is making at the moment, of disregarding the question of supplementary benefit. There was the contingency of the loss of a widow's pension, and that the learned judge accepted as being a hardship which would be caused by the divorce even though it was only a contingency. Quite clearly, *e* having regard to s 5(3) of the 1973 Act, which I have read, the judge was right to take into account the contingencies—risks of loss.

Counsel for the wife contends that the learned judge's conclusion, that the hard-ship relating to the potential loss of the contingent pre-60 widow's pension was not shown to be 'grave', was caused by a failure on the part of the learned judge to take into account a relevant fact which was in evidence. It appears that the judge thought *f* that there was no evidence before him as to the amount of the widow's benefit, if any, to which the wife would have been entitled if the husband had died, say, imme-diately before the pronouncement of the decree. In particular, I think, as I read his judgment, the learned judge felt that he was being asked to walk in the dark, because the amount of the widow's benefit would depend on the husband's contribution record, and there was no evidence as to that fact except the inference which the *g* learned judge was able to draw from the facts that were before him that the husband had paid at least 156 national insurance contributions. In his judgment the learned judge said[2], 'On the other hand, I have no material from which to determine the amount of the widow's pension she risks losing.'

However, counsel for the wife has referred us to letters in the agreed bundle of correspondence, and we are told, and of course accept, that the facts stated in those *h* letters were, by express or tacit agreement between the parties, accepted as being correct. By letter dated 25th September 1972 the wife's solicitors asked the Depart-ment of Health and Social Security, amongst other questions, the question what would be the amount of pension which the wife should receive as a widow, in the event that her husband were to die forthwith. The answer to that letter from the Department of Health and Social Security dated 2nd February 1973 said: '. . . I would like to inform *j* you that, as a widow, Mrs Bessie Reiterbund would receive benefit as follows (assuming her husband were to die forthwith) . . .' Then there is set out the widow's allowance for 26 weeks, and the possibility of a widow's supplementary allowance for 26 weeks:

---

1   [1974] 2 All ER at 461, 462, [1974] 1 WLR at 795
2   [1974] 2 All ER at 460, 461, [1974] 1 WLR at 794

a I need not read that because nothing turns on it in this appeal. Then the letter goes on: 'After that [that is, after 26 weeks] she would receive Widow's Pension at £6·75 and any increase for dependent children (rates as above).' (Of course, no question of dependent children arises.)

So, it does seem to me that there was material on which the learned judge could find that the potential widow's benefit (apart from the 26 weeks' allowance, which I b think it is agreed has to be ignored) would have been at the rate of £6·75 a week up to the age of 60. Of course, that amount might increase, and so no doubt would other benefits at the same time.

Let it be assumed, in favour of the wife, that the learned judge did, indeed, for some reason, omit to take into account that piece of evidence. I have considerable doubt whether the taking of it into account would, or ought to, have made any c difference to the judge's first conclusion—the absence of sufficient proof of *grave* financial hardship (still ignoring for the moment the question of the receipt of supplementary benefit).

Let me say at this point that I reject completely a submission made by counsel for the wife that the word 'grave' in this context means no more than 'greater than de minimis'. ('De minimis' is, of course, the Latin tag used to express the meaning d 'wholly trivial', or 'of no practical significance'.) 'Grave', in this context, has its ordinary meaning. If it were necessary (which I doubt) to use other words to provide guidance as to its meaning, I would offer the words 'important' or 'very serious'. I would reject also counsel for the wife's submission, made later in his argument, that somehow or other the meaning of the word 'grave' in the phrase 'grave financial hardship' is affected by the fact that one who relies as a defence on the provisions of s 5 of the 1973 e Act has to persuade the court, not merely of the existence of grave financial or other hardship, but also that it would in all the circumstances be wrong to dissolve the marriage.

What is the nature and extent of the chance that a financial loss will be suffered (still forgetting for the moment supplementary benefit) if the wife is divorced? She was 52. The period within which the various factors must coincide, in order that she f would have obtained the benefit if not divorced and therefore would lose the benefit if divorced, is limited to eight years. If the husband does not die within the eight years, there is no loss. True, the husband has been in ill-health (I have referred to chronic bronchitis); but I do not think that the learned judge can be faulted for holding[1], on the evidence before him (as he did expressly hold) that it is 'a circumstance which can be regarded as very likely' that the wife will be over 60 when the g husband dies. Again, of course, it is more likely than not, in the absence of evidence of physical ill-health of the wife, that she will survive to the age of 60 and beyond. But there is a chance that she will not. If she predeceased her husband, then, again, there would be no loss of widow's benefit.

However, let me assume for this purpose, though I am not to be taken as so deciding, that, apart from the relevance of supplementary benefit, there would be ground h here for holding that the potential loss of widow's benefit was such as to warrant the description 'grave financial hardship'. Making that assumption, I should nevertheless hold that this appeal fails, on the second ground set out in Finer J's judgment.

We were referred to a passage in the judgment of Sir George Baker P, in *Dorrell v Dorrell*[2]. There, Sir George Baker P appears to have taken the view that supplementary benefit or other social security benefit ought, as a matter of principle, to be j ignored in deciding the question of 'grave financial hardship' under s 5 of the 1973 Act. I am far from sure that Sir George Baker P was indeed intending to state that as being a principle. The facts in *Dorrell v Dorrell*[3] were different from the facts with which we

---

1 [1974] 2 All ER at 461, [1974] 1 WLR at 794
2 [1972] 3 All ER 343 at 348, [1972] 1 WLR 1087 at 1093
3 [1972] 3 All ER 343, [1972] 1 WLR 1087

are here concerned, and, it may be, materially different. But, if and insofar as anything *a* which was said in that case ought to be construed to mean that, on facts such as exist in the present case, the fact and the amount of supplementary benefit must be ignored in assessing financial hardship under s 5, I would respectfully disagree. I agree with Finer J's conclusion that, on the facts of the present case, there cannot be grave, or indeed any, financial hardship to the wife, by reason of the divorce decree, because, in the event of her husband's death during the next eight years following *b* the divorce (the only period now alleged to be relevant), while the wife would lose the contribution from public funds consisting of the widow's benefit, she would be entitled to a larger contribution from public funds consisting of supplementary benefit. That, as I understand it, is the undoubted and admitted fact in this case. If there were no divorce, and the husband died before the wife reached 60, she would have been entitled to a widow's pension of £6.75, plus, no doubt (on the present *c* scale) a further £1 of supplementary benefit, and, no doubt, payment of rent. That would not come from the husband, for he is, on this hypothesis, dead, but it would come from public funds. Why should it be said that there is hardship to the wife— grave financial hardship—when, the divorce having taken place, and the husband having died, the wife gets precisely the same amount from the public funds, though from a different account in the public funds? *d*

I do not see that there is grave, or any, hardship to the wife in this contingency— which is the only contingency relied on as potentially creating hardship. Nor do I see how the fact that the payment comes from one public fund rather than another could be a relevant factor or could lead to the conclusion that the fact that the wife would receive such payment should be ignored in considering the question of financial hardship. It must be borne in mind that, on the facts of this case, on the letter from *e* the department which I have read and on which the wife so strongly relies in this appeal, it is apparent that the necessary contributions of the husband for the purpose of providing the widow's benefit had already been paid before a divorce decree was pronounced.

With all respect, I think the position here is quite different from that which prevails, rightly, in my view, as decided in a number of cases, in respect of the assessment of *f* the proper amount of a periodic order for maintenance to be paid by a husband. The husband's means are relevant. It would be wrong that social security benefits to the wife should reduce his liability at the expense of the state. But in a case such as the present one is looking at potential hardship on the hypothesis that the husband is dead, and that the benefit in question to the wife will in any event come from public funds, and that in fact she will not be one penny the worse off because of the decree. *g*

I wish to make it clear that what I have said has been said in relation to the facts of this particular case. We were invited to consider various hypothetical cases. I do not find it useful so to do. I do not intend to suggest, and I hope that nothing which I have said would be taken to suggest, that the existence, or the amount, of supple- mentary benefit, in lieu of widow's pension, would always, and necessarily, be a determinant, or even a relevant, factor in deciding the question of grave financial *h* hardship for the purposes of s 5 of the 1973 Act. For example, as Finer J pointed out in his judgment, there might well be a case—though on the facts it is not this case—in which the receipt of the widow's benefit would have carried with it the right of substantially greater outside earnings, without diminishing the entitlement to benefit, than would be the case in respect of supplementary benefit. Again, it may be, though it would be wrong to express a concluded view on a question which does not arise, *j* that if the potential widow's pension were greater in amount than the potential supplementary benefit, the latter might not fall to be taken into account at all in the consideration of financial hardship under s 5. Those are all questions which may arise and may have to be considered when the facts of the case require the decision of those questions. All that I say now is that, in my view, on the facts of this case it would be impossible to say that there had been shown grave financial hardship to the wife *a* having regard to the only contingency which is relied on as showing the potential existence of that loss, and by reason of the fact that she would not in fact suffer any financial loss whatever if that contingency were to arise.

We were addressed by counsel for the wife on questions of public policy and on questions of the relevance of the Fatal Accidents Acts. With great respect to counsel's submissions, I am unable to find that there is anything in any of those submissions *b* which is of help in this case.

With regard to public policy, I should perhaps say that on the question of the source of the benefits counsel for the wife contended that it should be regarded as contrary to public policy to enlarge the number of persons who are required to have recourse to supplementary benefit rather than to contributory funds. Let us see in this context what that argument on public policy is. It is, apparently, that, where *c* Parliament has provided a defence on the ground of grave financial hardship, that defence should be extended to a case where in fact the defending spouse would suffer no financial hardship, and that that extension should be made to what Parliament has provided because of a view of public policy relating to the question whether it is desirable that a person should be required or encouraged to have recourse to one fund or another. That argument does not appeal to me.

d   I would dismiss the appeal.

ORMROD LJ. I agree. In my judgment the learned judge below was right on both the grounds on which he based his judgment; and I would like at the outset of this judgment to express my gratitude to him for his extremely lucid summary of the relevant provisions relating to widow's pension, retirement pension, and social *e* security or supplementary benefit. He is, of course, himself an expert in this field; and his summary has enabled me to see the issues very much more clearly than I am sure I would have been able to do without it.

The case as it was presented to the learned judge below seems to have been put on the general proposition which is often put forward—that, as a result of the divorce, the wife would lose her widow's pension. The first thing to be noticed about the *f* learned judge's judgment, I think, in this context, is the distinction which he draws, and which is now accepted as entirely valid, between the widow's pension, properly so called, and the retirement pension; because, as he fully demonstrates and counsel for the wife now accepts, after the wife has reached the age of 60 the dissolution of her marriage will not have any adverse effect on her retirement pension situation, on the facts of this case. On the other hand, the learned judge pointed out the different *g* considerations which concern the widow's pension, the widow's pension being a pension which is payable on widowhood and, on facts like these at any rate, which becomes absorbed in the retirement pension at the age of 60. In practice in this case the only way in which the wife can establish grave financial hardship is by relying on the loss to her of the chance of obtaining a widow's pension; that is, a potential loss of income between the date when her marriage is dissolved and her 60th birthday, *h* which in practice in this case is a period of eight years.

I accept for the purpose of the argument, as I am bound to by the terms of s 5(3), that the loss of the chance of acquiring a benefit is included in the word 'hardship'. I would for my part hesitate to conclude that Parliament was saying that all losses of chances of acquiring benefit must necessarily be 'hardship'; but the word 'hardship' in sub-s (2), as sub-s (3) says, 'includes the loss of the chance'. In other words, loss of *j* chances of acquiring pension or other benefits is a matter which the courts must take into account in calculating and assessing whether or not there is grave financial hardship.

So the question here is, what will this wife lose in the event of her marriage being dissolved? Leaving aside supplementary benefit altogether, it is said that her potential loss if her husband dies within the next eight years and she survives him will be a sum of £6·75 a week widow's pension. The learned judge I think overlooked the fact that that one figure was definitely stated in the evidence before him—and it *a* seems to have been about the only one that was clear and definite. But I do not think that the fact that he was uncertain as to the quantum of the widow's pension in this case affects the principle or the substance of the judgment in any way; because what the learned judge had to do (still leaving supplementary benefit out of account) was to assess what were the chances of this wife suffering this loss of a widow's pension. He had virtually no material before him on which he could make anything but a *b* guess as to that. All he knew was the ages of these two people, both in their early 50s, and the fact that the husband suffered from chronic bronchitis. So he had no means of making a prognosis as to the likelihood of the husband surviving or as to the likelihood of the wife surviving, about whom there was no evidence whatever. He took the view, and in my judgment reasonably, that on that material, and dealing with people of that age, and in the absence of any strong evidence to the contrary, it *c* was very unlikely that the husband would die during the eight years following the divorce. Consequently, the chance that the wife would suffer any financial loss or hardship during those eight years was remote; and that to me is equivalent to finding that she failed to prove grave financial hardship. It would, in my judgment, be quite ridiculous, in such a speculative situation as this, to refuse this man a divorce. Logically, I suppose, over the next eight years or as she approaches her 60th birthday, the poten- *d* tial hardship on her becomes progressively less. But the court must make its finding as to what the real risks are. If there were evidence that the husband's life expectancy was very short, I could well understand the learned judge coming to a different view— again leaving the supplementary benefit out of consideration. But in the present state of the evidence in this case, any finding of grave financial hardship on the basis of the evidence put before the court by the respondent would be absurd, in my *e* judgment.

I now turn to the second point. That is, as the learned judge put it, that if he were wrong in his assessment on the 'grave financial hardship' question on the bare facts of the case, then it would be necessary and proper for him to take into account the wife's position in relation to supplementary benefit. I think he was right about that also. *f*

Counsel for the wife had the advantage of having a decision of Sir George Baker P in *Dorrell v Dorrell*[1] in his favour. In a short passage Sir George Baker P simply said this, in relation to a submission which had been made to him about taking into account certain social security benefits[2]:

> 'This is a novel argument but I am not disposed to accept it for I do not think it can be right. I think you have to look at the position of this lady, quite apart *g* from social security. That is my understanding of the law which has been applied in these courts for many years in relation to magistrates' orders.'

I think it is clear from the report itself that the relevant cases dealing with magistrates' orders were not in fact cited to Sir George Baker P, and it is my impression that the matter was not at all fully argued before him. If one takes the facts of the present *h* case, they turn out to be these. In the event that the husband dies during the next eight years and the marriage is still subsisting, the widow (as she would be then) would receive £6·75, plus any increments subsequently ordered by the government, by way of widow's pension, and, by way of supplementary benefit, such sum as brought her up to whatever is the going rate for supplementary benefit at the time. If, on the other hand, her marriage had been dissolved, she would continue to receive *j* precisely the same sum (at the time when it was before the learned judge the sum of £8·25) from social security. So that she would be in precisely the same financial position as to income whether her marriage was dissolved or whether it was not.

1 [1972] 3 All ER 343, [1972] 1 WLR 1087
2 [1972] 3 All ER at 348, [1972] 1 WLR at 1093

a Counsel on her behalf submits that as a matter of law the court should ignore her social security benefits. Why, I am unable to understand; but he submits that this is the law. A law which produces the paradox that a woman who is in precisely the same financial position before and after the dissolution of her marriage has yet suffered, in law, grave financial hardship as a result of the divorce, requires no elaboration on my part to demonstrate its absurdity. What possible sense could there be in supporting such a paradox? There is in fact nothing in the report of *Dorrell v Dorrell*[1] to suggest *b* that such a situation as this was put before Sir George Baker P before he made the observations which I have cited; and had he had this in mind I venture to think that his judgment would have gone the other way. Equally it would be quite wrong, in my judgment, to lay it down as a proposition of law that in all cases under s 5 the court must take into account the wife's potential social security benefits. Each case must, it seems to me, depend on its own facts. Megaw LJ has already referred to the position of *c* a wife who is in fact not earning very much but working. It is clear from the summary that Finer J gave that such a wife could be worse off if she were dependent on the supplementary benefit than if she were drawing the widow's pension or a retirement pension, because each of these different kinds of benefit has a different 'disregard' figure. That is just one example of balancing the situation. Another may be facts like those in *Dorrell v Dorrell*[1] itself, because at the end of the judgment in that case *d* Sir George Baker P adjourned the case to give the husband an opportunity of putting forward some financial proposal to compensate for the loss of the £2 a week local government pension which the wife ran the risk of losing. It may well be that where a husband can make financial provision for the loss of a chance of the widow's pension the court will require him to do so, without taking into account the fact that the social security is the longstop at the end to protect the wife from destitution. I merely *e* mention these matters to show that it is essential to keep an open mind in these cases. This court and the Family Division deal with human people with human problems, and it is vitally important, in my judgment, that their lives should not be complicated unnecessarily by what I might call highly theoretical lawyers' points.

In conclusion, I would just say this. I doubt whether it does anybody any kindness *f* to try to dress up very understandable, strongly-felt, feelings about the undesirability of a divorce into a supposed grave financial hardship. I do not think it is kind to anybody to do that; and so, speaking for myself, 'grave financial hardship' means what it says. The purpose of s 5 is to protect husbands and wives against grave financial hardship as a result of marriages being dissolved without their consent after five years' separation. While it is most important that that provision should not be whittled away, it is equally important that it should not be used as a method of whittling *g* away the rights of other people to get a divorce after five years' separation.

I agree that this appeal should be dismissed.

CUMMING-BRUCE LJ. I agree.

h *Appeal dismissed.*

Solicitors: *Stanley Sovin* (for the wife); *Herbert Oppenheimer, Nathan & Vandyk* (for the husband).

Mary Rose Plummer   Barrister.

j _____

1 [1972] 3 All ER 343, [1972] 1 WLR 1087

L

Colin Smith Music Ltd v Ridge

COURT OF APPEAL, CIVIL DIVISION
CAIRNS, LAWTON LJJ AND BRIGHTMAN J
30th OCTOBER 1974

Rent restriction – Statutory tenant – Occupation of dwelling-house as his residence – Occupation on behalf of tenant by wife or mistress – Mistress having borne children to statutory tenant – Tenant leaving premises permanently – Mistress remaining in occupation – Tenant executing surrender –Whether mistress continuing to occupy premises on behalf of tenant – Whether mistress entitled to rely on statutory tenancy – Rent Act 1968, s 3(1).

V and the defendant, a divorced woman, lived together as husband and wife in premises of which V was the statutory tenant. The defendant had two children by V and two children from her previous marriage. In July 1973 V left the defendant with no intention of returning. On 9th August he signed a deed of surrender of his tenancy and the landlords claimed possession against the defendant on the ground that she was a trespasser from 9th August onwards. The judge held that V had a protected tenancy in the premises which could be ended only by a judgment against him or by actual surrender and delivery up of possession by him; accordingly he held that as V had left the defendant in possession to provide accommodation for herself and the children, he had not given up possession when he left but remained a statutory tenant by virtue of s 3(1)[a] of the Rent Act 1968. On appeal,

Held – V had ceased to be a statutory tenant of the premises since he no longer occupied the premises 'as his residence', within s 3(1)(a) of the 1968 Act. The position of the mistress of a statutory tenant was not analogous to that of a wife and it could not be said that a mistress who had borne the tenant children occupied premises on his behalf, after he had left the premises permanently and surrendered them to his landlord. It followed that the defendant was a mere licensee and as such could not claim the protection of the Rent Acts. The landlords were therefore entitled to possession and the appeal would be allowed (see p 293 b to p 294 b, post).
Brown v Brash [1948] 1 All ER 922 and *Thompson v Ward* [1953] 1 All ER 1169 applied.
Hawes v Evenden [1953] 2 All ER 737 distinguished.

Notes
For the nature of a statutory tenancy, see 23 Halsbury's Laws (3rd Edn) 805-808, para 1586, and for cases on the subject, see 31(2) Digest (Reissue) 976-997, 7841-7964.
For the Rent Act 1968, s 3, see 18 Halsbury's Statutes (3rd Edn) 788.

Cases referred to in judgments
Brown v Brash [1948] 1 All ER 922, [1948] 2 KB 247, [1948] LJR 1544, CA, 31(2) Digest (Reissue) 984, 7905.
Brown v Draper [1944] 1 All ER 246, [1944] KB 309, 113 LJKB 196, 170 LT 144, CA, 31(2) Digest (Reissue) 986, 7915.
Hawes v Evenden [1953] 2 All ER 737, [1953] 1 WLR 1169, CA, 31(2) Digest (Reissue) 992, 7946.
Middleton v Baldock [1950] 1 All ER 708, [1950] 1 KB 657, CA, 31(2) Digest (Reissue) 1079, 8445.

---

a   Section 3(1), so far as material, provides: 'Subject to sections 4 and 5 below—(a) after the termination of a protected tenancy of a dwelling-house the person who, immediately before that termination, was the protected tenant of the dwelling-house shall, if and so long as he occupies the dwelling-house as his residence, be the statutory tenant of it . . .'

a *Thompson v Ward* [1953] 1 All ER 1169, [1953] 2 QB 153, [1953] 2 WLR 1042, CA, 31(2)
   Digest (Reissue) 1029, 8170.
   Wabe v Taylor [1952] 2 All ER 420, [1952] 2 QB 735, CA, 31(2) Digest (Reissue) 1122,
   8700.

Case also cited

b *Richards v Dove* [1974] 1 All ER 888.

Appeal
The plaintiffs, Colin Smith Music Ltd, appealed against a decision of his Honour
Judge Forrest at the Weston-super-Mare County Court on 20th February 1974 where-
by he dismissed the plaintiffs' claim against the defendant, Frances Paula Ridge, for
c possession of premises known as First and Second Floor Flat, The Bank House,
High Street, Worle, Weston-super-Mare. The facts are set out in the judgment of
Cairns LJ.

Patrick Talbot for the plaintiffs.
C Gosland for the defendant.

d

CAIRNS LJ.   This appeal raises interesting points under the Rent Act and the court
has had the benefit of a very helpful argument from counsel on both sides.
   The appeal comes from a decision of Judge Forrest, sitting at the Weston-super-
Mare County Court, by which he refused an order for possession. The premises
e concerned are the upper part of a building called The Bank House, High Street,
Worle, Weston-super-Mare.
   The plaintiffs, by their particulars of claim, claimed possession against the defendant
on the ground that she was a trespasser from 9th August 1973 onwards. By her defence
the defendant asserted that she was a joint weekly tenant with one Venn and was
protected by the Rent Act. In further and better particulars she said the joint weekly
f tenancy had been created by an oral agreement made in 1969 between one Fry, who
was a former owner of the premises, on the one hand, and herself and Venn on the
other.
   The evidence given for the plaintiffs was given by a Mr Joyner, who said that he and
his wife had bought the premises in March 1973 at a time when Venn was the tenant;
there was a rent book which showed Venn as sole tenant. Mr Joyner was a director
g of the plaintiff company, and the purpose of buying the premises was to use the shop
which was on the ground floor as a music shop and to use the upper part of the
premises as a residence for the manager. They got Mr Venn to sign a deed of surrender
on 9th August 1973 and immediately after that the Joyners conveyed the premises to
the plaintiffs.
   The defendant gave evidence that she was a divorced woman who had lived with
h Venn from 1968 onwards; she already had two children of her own and they lived
with her and Venn. Then, from September 1969 the couple lived, not being married
to one another, as husband and wife at the flat with which we are concerned here
and they continued to live together until nearly the end of July 1973; during that time
two further children were born to the defendant, who were fathered by Venn. On
28th July 1973 Venn left her with no intention of returning.
j The learned judge held that Venn had a protected tenancy which could be terminated only by a judgment against him or by surrender and actual delivery up of
possession by him. The judge said that Venn had left, leaving the defendant in
possession, to provide accommodation for herself and the children. Accordingly, the
judge held that he had not given up possession.
   Really, the whole matter boils down to the question of whether or not, in the
circumstances that I have outlined, Venn had given up possession; or, to put it in the

statutory language under s 3(1)(a) of the Rent Act 1968, whether he had ceased to   *a*
occupy the premises as his residence, because it is only so long as he occupies the
premises as his residence that he is a statutory tenant and it would only have been if
he had continued to be a statutory tenant that the defendant could be there otherwise
than as a trespasser.

It is clear from a number of cases decided in this court that the mere physical
absence of the tenant from the premises in which he is a protected tenant does not   *b*
remove protection from him. A number of the cases which have been decided,
particularly *Brown v Draper*[1], are cases where a wife was left in possession; the position
of a mistress left in possession was first considered, so far as appears from the reports,
in *Brown v Brash*[2]. That was a decision of this court in which the judgment of the court
was delivered by Asquith LJ. It was a case where a mistress had been left in occupation
of the premises, but had in fact left at the time when the landlord was seeking posses-   *c*
sion. These passages in the judgment of the court are I think material to the present
case. Asquith LJ said[3]:

'We are of opinion that a "non-occupying" tenant *prima facie* forfeits his status
as a statutory tenant. But what is meant by "non-occupying"? The term clearly
cannot cover every tenant who, for however short a time, or however necessary
a purpose, or with whatever intention as regards returning, absents himself   *d*
from the demised premises. To retain possession or occupation for the purpose
of retaining protection the tenant cannot be compelled to spend 24 hours in all
weathers under his own roof for 365 days in the year. Clearly, for instance, the
tenant of a London house who spends his weekends in the country, or his long
vacation in Scotland, does not necessarily cease to be in occupation. Nevertheless,
absence may be sufficiently prolonged or uninterrmittent to compel the inference,   *e*
prima facie, of a cesser of possession or occupation. The question is one of fact and
of degree. Assume an absence sufficiently prolonged to have this effect: The
legal result seems to us to be as follows [and then five propositions follow, of
which the material ones are the first two:] (1) The onus is then on the tenant to
repel the presumption that his possession has ceased. (2) To repel it he must, at
all events, establish a *de facto* intention on his part to return after his absence . . .   *f*
Apart from authority, in principle possession in fact (for it is with possession in
fact and not with possession in law that we are here concerned) requires not
merely an *"animus possidendi"* but a *"corpus possessionis"*, viz., some visible state
of affairs in which the *animus possidendi* finds expression.'

And a reference was made to the person left in possession being there as a 'caretaker'   *g*
pending the return of the tenant.

That case was applied by this court in the later decision of *Thompson v Ward*[4]. There
a tenant had installed his mistress in a house of which he was tenant. After he had
lived with her for some time his contractual tenancy was determined by the
landlord. Later he left, leaving his mistress behind. Some time later he brought an
action for possession against her, claiming to be a statutory tenant. He obtained an   *h*
order for possession in the county court but this was set aside on appeal. Evershed
MR, giving the leading judgment, cited a passage from the judgment in *Brown v
Brash*[5] and said[6]:

'Counsel for the plaintiff further contended that, since the defendant's presence
on the premises must be attributed to a licence given by the plaintiff, it followed   *j*

1 [1944] 1 All ER 246, [1944] KB 309
2 [1948] 1 All ER 922, [1948] 2 KB 247
3 [1948] 1 All ER at 925, 926, [1948] 2 KB at 254, 255
4 [1953] 1 All ER 1169, [1953] 2 QB 153
5 [1948] 1 All ER at 925, [1948] 2 KB at 254
6 [1953] 1 All ER at 1174, [1953] 2 QB at 164

a   that the plaintiff was still in possession, so to speak, in the person of his licensee. Again, I think that for the purposes of these Acts such a conclusion would be in conflict with the reasoning of ASQUITH, L.J., in *Brown v Brash*[1]. In the passage which I have already cited he makes it, in my judgment, clear that, in order that a statutory tenant may be said to retain possession through the medium of an occupying licensee, the latter must be his licensee "with the function of pre-

b   serving the premises for his own ultimate home-coming".'

On the basis of those decisions it appears to me that a licensee left in possession by a protected tenant when he himself leaves, and leaves with the intention of remaining permanently away from the premises, no longer has the protection of the Rent Acts.

Counsel for the defendant cites *Middleton v Baldock*[2]. That appears again to have

c   been a decision which depended wholly on the relationship of husband and wife. The same is true of another case which counsel for the defendant cited, *Wabe v Taylor*[3]. Counsel seeks to say that in these days possession by a mistress who has borne children to the protected tenant is analagous to possession by a wife; but in my view that is not so.

Counsel for the defendant drew an interesting comparison with the position of a

d   mistress who, with her children, was residing in the house with the protected tenant up to the time of his death. It was held in *Hawes v Evenden*[4] that she was a member of the family of the protected tenant for the purpose of succeeding to the protection of the Act after his death; but that of course depends on the construction to be placed on the word 'family' in the Act and I do not find it of real assistance in this case.

It appears to me that the defendant could only succeed here if it were laid down as

e   a general principle that any person who has a licence from the protected tenant to reside would continue to have the protection notwithstanding the surrender by the protected tenant to his landlord, notwithstanding his permanently leaving the premises without any intention at all to come back.

In my view it cannot be the intention of the legislature in using the expression 'so long as he'—that is, the tenant—'occupies the dwelling-house as his residence' that

f   protection should be extended in that way.

With all respect to the learned county court judge here, I think he came to the wrong conclusion and I would allow the appeal and make an order for possession in favour of the plaintiffs.

LAWTON LJ. In my judgment the starting point for deciding what is the right

g   order in this case is to look at the status of the defendant when she and Mr Venn were cohabiting together. She was not his wife, so she did not enjoy the special position recognised by the common law for wives; she was his lodger; she was in the house by his leave and licence. He was under no legal obligation to her. In respect of the children he had had by her, she was entitled to look to him for money payments, but she was not entitled to call on him to provide them with a home.

h   When the cohabitation stopped in the summer of 1973, Mr Venn left the premises never intending to return; of that there is no doubt. He left before the protected tenancy had come to an end. It follows, on the face of it, that he never had a statutory tenancy within the meaning of s 3 of the Rent Act 1968.

It has been submitted that he did get the benefit of a statutory tenancy through the defendant, his mistress and lodger. He could only get that statutory tenancy if he

j   had, through her, notionally been residing in the premises himself. On the authorities a wife occupies the house on behalf of her husband, so as to confer a statutory tenancy

---

1   [1948] 1 All ER 922, [1948] 2 KB 247
2   [1950] 1 All ER 708, [1950] 1 KB 657
3   [1952] 2 All ER 420, [1952] 2 QB 735
4   [1953] 2 All ER 737, [1953] 1 WLR 1169

on him. There is nothing in the authorities which justifies this court, or any other a
court, adjudging that a mistress in her capacity as a lodger, or indeed in any other
capacity, is in any position analogous to that of a wife. I find it unnecessary to review
the authorities because it seems to me clear on principle that the Act does not protect
those who are mere licensees of the tenant.

For those reasons I would allow this appeal.

                                                                                  b

BRIGHTMAN J. I agree with the judgments that have been delivered.

Appeal allowed; order for possession.

Solicitors: *Reed & Reed*, agents for *Hall, Ward & Fox*, Weston-super-Mare (for the
plaintiffs); *Stiddard & Chew*, Weston-super-Mare (for the defendant).   c

                                          A S Virdi Esq   Barrister.

                                                                                  d

Evans v Sant

QUEEN'S BENCH DIVISION
LORD WIDGERY CJ, BRIDGE AND SHAW JJ
1st NOVEMBER 1974
                                                                                  e

*Building – Working places regulations – Safety of working places – Duty of employer –
Working places so far as practicable to be made and kept safe – Made safe – Working place
safe having regard to permanent equipment and normal activities carried on there – Equipment
brought on to premises temporarily for particular purpose – Equipment creating a source of
danger – Whether rendering place of work unsafe for purpose of regulations – Construction f
(Working Places) Regulations 1966 (SI 1966 No 94), reg 6(2).*

The appellant, a civil engineering contractor, was engaged by a water board to lay a
water main alongside a road. The work was carried out by three of the appellant's
employees. Once the main had been laid it was necessary to test it to see whether it
could contain the pressure of water which it was designed to carry. For that purpose a g
length of pipe ('the test head') was inserted into the end of the pipeline which was to be
tested. The test head was laid in the trench. On to the other end of the test head was
screwed a cap ('the test cap'). The test cap had a hole in the middle into which was
fixed a length of steel pipe which passed through 90 degrees and ran to ground level
where it was connected to a pressure gauge and stop valve which was in turn connected by means of a rubber hose to a pump. The water pressure required for the test h
and the consequent thrust on the test cap were considerable. The normal means of
preventing the thrust from blowing off the test cap, and the test head from rising,
was to wedge it against a solid object. About 14 inches from the test cap was a
concrete block. The employees filled the gap with hardcore which they rammed
down hard. They also partly filled the trench on top of the test head with loose earth.
The loose earth was inadequate for its purpose, however, and as the pressure built up j
in the test head the employees saw the earth moving. They realised that the thrust
was causing the test head to rise. Before they could take effective steps to stop it, the
test head was blown out of the end of the pipeline and thrown a distance of 15 feet. In
order to avoid being struck by it one of the employees ran on to the adjacent road
where he was knocked down and killed by a passing car. The appellant was convicted
on an information which alleged that he was an employer of workmen undertaking

a   operations or works to which s 127 of the Factories Act 1961 and the Construction (Working Places) Regulations 1966 applied and that the place of work at which the deceased employee worked 'was not so far as reasonably practicable made safe' as required by reg 6(2)*ᵃ* of the 1966 regulations, contrary to reg 3(1)(*a*) of those regulations and s 155(2) of the 1961 Act.

b   **Held** – Where a place of work, having regard to the equipment permanently there and the activities normally carried out there, was safe, the mere fact that a piece of equipment brought on to it temporarily for a particular purpose produced an element of danger did not render the place unsafe for the purposes of reg 6(2) of the 1966 regulations. Accordingly the appeal would be allowed and the conviction quashed, for the source of danger arising from the pressure on the test head did not cause the

c   place where the deceased had been working to be one which had not been 'made safe' within reg 6(2) (see p 301 *e* to *j* and p 302 *a* to *e*, post).

Notes

For safety regulations for building and construction, see 17 Halsbury's Laws (3rd Edn) 125-128, para 206, and for cases on the subject, see 24 Digest (Repl) 1075-1080,

d   326-373.

For the Factories Act 1961, ss 127, 155, see 13 Halsbury's Statutes (3rd Edn) 526, 550.

For the Construction (Working Places) Regulations 1966, regs 3, 6, see 8 Halsbury's Statutory Instruments (2nd Reissue) 301, 304.

Cases referred to in judgment

e   *Higgins v Lyons & Co Ltd* (1941) 85 Sol Jo 93, 24 Digest (Repl) 1066, *276*.

Latimer v AEC Ltd [1953] 2 All ER 449, [1953] AC 643, [1953] 3 WLR 259, 117 JP 387, 51 LGR 457, HL, 24 Digest (Repl) 1065, *267*.

Levesley v Thomas Firth & John Brown Ltd [1953] 2 All ER 866, [1953] 1 WLR 1206, 51 LGR 571, CA, 24 Digest (Repl) 1065, *268*.

Woods v Power Gas Corpn Ltd (1969) 8 KIR 834, CA.

f

Case also cited

Stanley v Concentric (Pressed Products) Ltd (1971) 11 KIR 260, CA.

Case stated

This was an appeal by way of a case stated by the justices for the petty sessional

g   division of Ross-on-Wye in the county of Hereford in respect of their adjudication as a magistrates' court sitting at the Court House, Cantilupe Road, Ross-on-Wye, on 18th October 1973.

On 2nd July 1973 an information was preferred by the respondent, Frederick Alan Sant, one of Her Majesty's inspectors of factories, against the appellant, Thomas Evans, that he on 14th March 1973 at St Leonards on the A466 Hereford to Monmouth Road

h   in the county of Hereford was an employer of workmen undertaking operations or works to which s 127 of the Factories Act 1961 and the Construction (Working Places) Regulations 1966 applied and the place of work at which an employed person, namely Patrick Joseph Doherty, worked was not so far as reasonably practicable made safe as required by reg 6(2) of the 1966 regulations and contrary to reg 3(1)(*a*) of the 1966 regulations whereby he was guilty of an offence as provided by s 155(2) of the 1961

j   Act.

At the hearing of the information the justices found the following facts. The appellant was a civil engineering contractor. On 14th March 1973 the appellant, by his employees, was engaged, pursuant to a contract between himself and the Herefordshire Water Board, in laying a mains water pipe line. The line of the pipeline lay along

---

a   Regulation 6 is set out at p 298 *j* to p 299 *a*, post

the A466 road (Monmouth to Hereford). The work of laying the pipeline was being *a* carried out by three employees of the appellant, Patrick Joseph Doherty, John Leslie Smith and Michael John Price. Mr Doherty was the foreman of the three employees and was an experienced foreman with several years' experience of laying and testing water mains. As part of the work it was necessary to carry out a pressure test on a section of pipeline. A pressure test consisted of filling the section of pipeline with water under a specified pressure and leaving it under that pressure for a specified length of *b* time. The pressure test was being carried out on 14th March 1973 by Mr Doherty and Mr Smith. In order to carry out the pressure test, a length of piping about six feet long (called a 'test head') was inserted into the end of the pipeline section in question. The test head was laid in a trench approximately 18 inches wide and three feet deep. The nearest edge of the trench to the main road was about five feet from the edge of the carriageway. On to the other end of the test head from that which was inserted *c* into the pipeline, was a screwed cap (called the 'test cap'). The test cap had a hole in the middle into which was fixed a length of one inch diameter steel pipe which passed through 90 degrees and ran to ground level where it was connected to a pressure gauge and stop valve. A one inch diameter rubber hose connected the stop valve to a pump which was used for pumping water into the pipeline. The pressure required for the pressure test was 220 lbs per square inch. That would result in a thrust of *d* approximately 2¾ tons on the test cap. The normal means of preventing the thrust from blowing the test cap off or from blowing the test head out of the pipeline was by wedging it against a solid object, such as a timber sleeper dug well into the sides of the trench or concrete block so positioned as to distribute the thrust over an area of earth. The test head had also to be prevented from moving upwards during testing by reason of thrust. Mr Doherty and Mr Smith did not use a timber sleeper to act as a *e* thrust block, although they could have done so if they had wished. About 14 inches away from the test cap, there was a concrete block securing pipes running in the other direction. Mr Doherty and Mr Smith filled this 14 inch gap with hardcore which they rammed hard down. They partly filled the trench on top of the test head with loose backfilling. The process of building up the required pressure for the test lasted some hours. At about 1.10 pm the pressure had reached approximately 200 lbs per square *f* inch. Mr Doherty and Mr Smith were both standing in the vicinity of the gauge between the trench and the road. They saw the earth above the test head moving and realised that (as was the fact) the thrust was causing the test head to rise. They threw some more earth and tarmac into the trench but this did not stop the movement of the test head. Almost immediately afterwards they realised that the test head was going to blow off. Mr Smith ran towards the pump in order to stop it but, before he *g* reached it, the test head blew out of the end of the pipeline. The test head was thrown a distance of approximately 15 feet. If the test head had been securely fixed both laterally and vertically it would not have blown off. Mr Doherty and the other employees concerned could have securely fixed it against lateral movement by means of a sleeper. There was a conflict of evidence whether the use of hardcore rammed between the test head and the existing concrete block was satisfactory to prevent *h* lateral movement, but it was unnecessary for the justices to decide the point because: (a) the movement which did occur was vertical, and (b) the backfilling on the top of the test head should have been, but was not, rammed down adequately. The appellant had not supervised Mr Doherty or his other employees concerned in any way in connection with the laying and testing of the pipeline. He visited them once a week only in order to pay wages. He considered that the responsibility for supervising lay with *j* the Herefordshire Water Board. Neither Mr Doherty nor Mr Smith had, while employed by the appellant, carried out an identical pressure test. When, or immediately before, the test head blew off Mr Doherty ran into the road and was killed by impact with a passing vehicle on the far side of the road from the trench. There were warning signs in the road on each side of the site where the test was taking place and an arrow indicating that the traffic should keep to the other side of the road. There

a were no cones to prevent traffic from passing close to the trench. The appellant left
to Mr Doherty as foreman the responsibility for using, erecting and placing any traffic
signs or traffic lights which he considered necessary for the safety of the operation in
hand. Traffic lights were available at the site on 14th March 1973 but were not in
use on that day although they had been used on previous days.

b It was contended by the appellant (a) that the place of work was safe as far as was
reasonably practicable and that reg 6(2) of the Construction (Working Places) Regulations 1966 had not therefore been contravened; (b) that if, which was not admitted,
the requirements of reg 6(2) of the 1966 regulations had been contravened, such contravention was brought about by reason only of a contravention of an employed
person's, in this case Mr Doherty's, duties imposed by the 1966 regulations or by s 143
of the Factories Act 1961; (c) that if there had been a contravention of the 1966 regula-
c tions or a breach of the duties imposed by s 143 of the 1961 Act by an employed person,
in this case Mr Doherty, the respondent had failed to show that such contravention
arose because of the appellant's failure to take all reasonable steps to prevent it;
(d) that if, which was not admitted, the method of testing the pipeline was in any way
unsafe, such unsafe system of work did not make the place where Mr Doherty was
working unsafe.

d It was contended by the respondent (a) that the method of preparing the site, the
test head and the pipeline was unsatisfactory in that inadequate measures were taken
to prevent the test head from moving when test pressures were applied; (b) that the
unsatisfactory and unsafe method of testing the pipeline made the place of work
unsafe and that all reasonably practicable steps to make it safe had not been taken;
(c) that the place of work had been made unsafe by the lack of cones on the road in the
e vicinity of the trench when the testing of the pipeline was being carried out.

The justices were of the opinion that the case had been proved and accordingly, the
appellant was fined £150 together with costs of £35·45.

Piers Ashworth QC and *J Playford* for the appellant.
Peter Scott for the respondent.

f
LORD WIDGERY CJ. This is an appeal by case stated by justices for the county of
Hereford sitting as a magistrates' court at Ross-on-Wye. The hearing took place on
18th October 1973 and the business before the court was an information preferred by
the respondent against the appellant that the appellant on 14th March 1973 at an
address in Herefordshire being an employer of workmen undertaking operations or
g works to which s 127 of the Factories Act 1961 and the Construction (Working Places)
Regulations 1966 applied and the place of work at which an employed person, namely
Patrick Joseph Doherty, worked was not so far as reasonably practicable made safe as
required by reg 6(2) of the 1966 regulations.

The justices convicted the appellant of that offence, and the appellant accordingly
appeals by case stated, which means that the appellant is seeking the opinion of the
h court on a point of law arising in the proceedings. I feel bound to say at once that the
point of law could not conceivably be identified by anyone reading the text, and it
would be of considerable assistance if more attention had been paid initially to the
way in which the case was stated in that regard. But I am satisfied that, with the
assistance of counsel, we have isolated the point of law the decision of the court on
which can be conclusive of the issue.

j The facts are found with great clarity and considerable detail so far as the general
narrative and description of the scene is concerned, and I shall put them quite shortly.
The appellant, as a civil engineering contractor, had undertaken to lay a water main
for the Herefordshire Water Board. The actual laying of the main was carried out by
three workmen: Doherty, Smith and Price, of whom Mr Doherty, an experienced
man, was the foreman.

The time had come when the main was laid and when it had to be tested; that is to

say it had to be tested to see if it could contain the pressure of water which it was *a*
designed to carry. For that purpose a system of testing apparently well known and
understood was employed in this manner. First of all there was brought to the site of
the main, which was alongside a highway in Hereford, a thing called a 'test head',
which was a length of pipe about six feet long, which could be, and was, inserted into
the end of the section of pipe to be tested. The test head was laid in a trench 18 inches
wide and three feet deep and so laid, as I understand it, in order that it could physically *b*
be inserted into the end of the main itself. On the end of the test head, remote from
the main, there was something which was called a 'test cap', which was a cap screwed
on to the test head. Then there were devices which I need not endeavour to explain
whereby the pressure in the main could be monitored so that as pumping took place
and pressure was built up, it was possible to see what pressure was being contained in
the main.   *c*
    It is quite obvious that when the required pressure was produced in the main (a
pressure of 220 lbs per square inch) a very heavy force would be exerted on the test
cap, and it was well recognised that precautions would have to be taken in order to
prevent the test cap from being blown out by the pressure built up in the main.
Normal engineering practice, as the justices find, would have been to locate the test
cap against something solid such as a block of concrete inserted in the trench or some *d*
other resistant material which would prevent the pressure from blowing the cap off.
It was also recognised that some steps would have to be taken to prevent the test
head from rising vertically from its bed under the pressure. In other words, it was
necessary to guard against a lateral movement of the test head or a vertical movement,
either of which with high pressure in the main might have produced disaster.
    The method employed under Mr Doherty's direction to guard against this danger *e*
was not to use a block of concrete or a sleeper or anything of that kind, but since there
was already a concrete block about 14 inches away from the test cap, the method
employed was to fill that space with hardcore, which was rammed down hard. What
seems to have been omitted was adequate precaution to prevent the test head rising
vertically. All that was done there was that certain hardcore was put on the top of the
head but in insufficient quantity or insufficiently well impacted to prevent the head *f*
from rising.
    The test began. Some hours passed whilst pressure was being built up in the pipe,
and at about 1.10 p m on the day in question, when the pressure was up to about 200
lbs per square inch, it was observed by the three men standing at the side of the
equipment that the earth was beginning to move around the test head. This, of course,
meant that something had gone wrong, and indeed that imminent danger might arise. *g*
An attempt was made to turn off the pump in order to prevent the pressure from
increasing, but before the pump could be turned off, the test head blew out of the
main. It was carried some 15 feet as a result of pressure behind it, and Mr Doherty,
seeking to escape from the consequences of the accident which was imminent, ran on
to the adjacent highway and was knocked down and killed by a passing car.
    Arising out of those facts and without our being given any views which the justices *h*
formed on the technical issues in this case, we are asked to say by the appellant that
the conviction was wrong and that the events to which I have referred could not result
in a situation in which the employer, the appellant, was criminally responsible under
the statute for having failed so far as reasonably practicable to make safe the workplace
of these men.
    The actual provision under which the charge was laid is reg 6 of the Construction *j*
(Working Places) Regulations, 1966. It provides:

    '(1) Without prejudice to the other provisions of these Regulations, there shall,
    so far as is reasonably practicable, be suitable and sufficient safe access to and
    egress from every place at which any person at any time works, which access and
    egress shall be properly maintained.
    '(2) Without prejudice to the other provisions of these Regulations, every place

a   at which any person at any time works shall, so far as is reasonably practicable, be made and kept safe for any person working there.'

The issue between the parties on the principal point in this appeal can be put quite shortly. The prosecution maintain, as they maintained, I think, below, that the presence of this test head, insufficiently secured in its bed and containing, as it did, a very high pressure of water, caused the place where these men were working to be unsafe.

b   Looking at the whole picture, the actual ground on which the work had been done, the equipment with which it was being done and the consequences of the manner in which it was being done, it is said by the prosecution that you have here a place which is unsafe. Of course if one simply asks oneself: was Mr Doherty safe standing by the side of this imminent disaster? the answer would quite readily be returned that he was unsafe.

c   The argument for the appellant is that one must distinguish in these matters between a danger which is a danger arising from the place qua place, and a danger arising from the particular operation which at the moment in question is being carried on in that place. Counsel for the appellant submits that if one looked at the place before the operation began, there was nothing about it which would indicate that it was in any way unsafe, and he says that the place does not fail to be made and

d   kept safe within the meaning of the regulation merely because the operation carried on on it on that day is one which produces a potential danger to those who are working in that place.

There is the issue, clear cut for all to see, and strangely enough it seems to be an issue which has never been decided before. There is little authority on the point, but in looking at it one has to remember that the precise language of the Factories Acts and

e   the regulations made under them has varied from time to time, and one must bear in mind and have regard to the actual statutory provisions on which the various judgments were based.

The first case to which we have been referred is *Higgins v J Lyons & Co Ltd*[1]. That is a case in which it was alleged that the means of access to a place of work was unsafe within the meaning of the then current regulations, regulations which in this regard

f   were not dissimilar from the present. The simple facts of the case were that a girl employed in a large premises occupied by J Lyons & Co Ltd was moving through those premises on her way back from lunch. She was making her way back to the office in which she worked and was doing so through her employers' premises. She passed through a yard for the purpose of getting back to her office, and as she went through the yard a truck carrying some 15 cwt of flour was being pushed towards her

g   by two employees. The negligence of the two employees resulted in the girl being injured by this truck, and the question arose as to whether in those circumstances she had been provided with a safe means of access back to her office. The Court of Appeal held that the fact that a truck was negligently operated in the means of access did not in itself prevent the means of access from being safe. Clauson LJ, giving the leading judgment, said:

h
        'It was admitted that the plaintiff and the persons pushing the lorry were in common employment. Accordingly mere negligence was not *ad rem*. But the plaintiff said that there had been a breach of s.26(1) of the Factories Act, 1937. The deputy county court judge found that the defendants had committed a breach of the Act. There was no evidence that they did. It was a perfectly simple position.

j   There was a yard with a footpath round it. There was no trap and nothing wrong with the yard. Someone was using the yard negligently, but that fact alone did not justify the deputy county court judge in finding that there had been a breach of the subsection. The appeal must be allowed.'

I find that a helpful authority, although the language is somewhat different, and

1   (1941) 85 Sol Jo 93

certainly helpful to the appellant in this case because it is at all events an example of   *a* the proposition that if the place qua place was safe, it does not cease to be a safe place because somebody happens to be conducting himself negligently in it at the material time.

The next case to which I propose to refer is *Levesley v Thomas Frith & John Brown Ltd*[1]. This was a case again dealing with means of access, and the obligation imposed by the relevant legislation was that the means of access should be maintained in a safe con-   *b* dition. The evidence showed that for a short period articles had been allowed to stand on the defined means of access in such a way as might give rise to danger to those who sought to use it; and although no one criticised the means of access itself (it was perfectly properly made and laid down initially) it was said, and held by the learned trial judge, that the means of access was not maintained in a safe condition because these articles for a short period were lying on it.   *c*

Denning LJ, dealing with the section which required that the means of access should be provided and maintained in a safe state, said[2]:

> 'The proper interpretation is to read "safe" with "provided" so that the section reads in this way: There shall be provided a safe means of access (such as scaffolding, staging or so forth) and, such a means having been provided, it must there- after be "maintained", i.e., maintained in the way defined in s. 152(1), viz.,   *d* maintained in an efficient state, in efficient working order, and in good repair. *Latimer's* case[3] shows that this obligation to "maintain" should not be used so as to put an excessive obligation on the employer ... The obligation is not an abso- lute obligation to maintain safety, but a relative obligation to maintain efficiently. Once a safe means of access is provided, such as a passage or gangway, the occupier is not responsible for every temporary obstruction (such as a patch of oil or   *e* slipperiness) which may, through some accident or mischance, occur in it. If he has an efficient system to keep it clean and free from obstruction, that is all that can be reasonably demanded of him.'

I remind myself that the language is somewhat different, and whereas in our regulation the obligation in regard to the place of work is that it be kept safe, in *Levesley's* case[1]   *f* the obligation was that it be maintained, a word which had a statutory meaning in the Act. But I find it very difficult to believe that 'kept safe' in our regulation has any significant difference from 'maintained' in the legislation under consideration in *Levesley's* case[1], and that seems to me to go some way—perhaps not very far—in support of the proposition of the appellant in this case.

Finally I would refer to some obiter dicta of Winn LJ in *Woods v Power Gas Corpora-*   *g* *tion Ltd*[4]. This was a case on reg 7 of the Construction (General Provisions) Regulations 1961[5], and the terms of the regulation were these:

> '(1) Sufficient safe means of access and egress shall so far as is reasonably prac- ticable be provided and maintained to and from every place at which any person has at any time to work and every such place shall so far as is reasonably practicable   *h* be made and kept safe for any person working there.
>
> '(2) Where work cannot safely be done (a) on or from the ground or from part of a building, or other permanent structure there shall be provided (b) and maintained either *scaffolds* (c) or where appropriate ladders or other means of support, each of which shall be suitable and sufficient for the purpose.'

I draw particular attention to the fact that in para (1) which I have already read we   *j*

1   [1953] 2 All ER 866, [1953] 1 WLR 1206
2   [1953] 2 All ER at 869, [1953] 1 WLR at 1210
3   *Latimer v AEC Ltd* [1953] 2 All ER 449, [1953] 3 WLR 259
4   (1969) 8 KIR 834
5   SI 1961 No 1580

a have a reference to the working place being made and kept safe in the same language as in our present regulation.

Winn LJ, at the end of his judgment, delivered himself of some general observations about the meaning to be attached to the words in the regulation such as 'access', 'egress', 'ground' etc. He said[1]:

b 'But I think that, having regard to the juxtaposition of the provisions of sub-regulation (2) with those of sub-regulation (1), which relate to safe means of access and egress and safety of a place of work, the whole concept is that the means of access, and egress, the place of work, or the ground, part of a building or permanent structure, referred to respectively in sub-regulations (1) and (2) of regulation 7 shall be safe in themselves, *qua* access, *qua* egress, *qua* place, *qua* ground, *qua* building, *qua* permanent structure. Not all ground is safe to stand on. Ground *c* may slip away. It may give in by caving in, collapsing. Parts of a building may not be stable. They may collapse in the course of, for example, demolition of an old decrepit building. Similarly, in the case of means of access or means of egress, such means may be safe or unsafe in themselves. They may be slippery. They may tend to collapse or slip away, as distinct from having a slippery surface. In each case, in my suggested approach to this regulation, it is the safety or lack of safety *d* of the place which is relevant as the primary consideration.'

Although, as I have indicated, that is not an observation on the self-same regulation with which we are concerned, it was dealing with a regulation in virtually identical terms, and I am much attracted by Winn LJ's approach in that he says that the quality of access, egress, place etc, shall be considered qua access, egress or place respectively.

e I think that the guiding light in our approach to the problem before us today is to say that in deciding whether the place of work was made safe, it is the place qua place that we look at, and not the place qua operation carried on on the place. That does not mean of course that in deciding whether the place is made safe one has total disregard for the activities which go on in the place itself. The safety of the place depends not simply on the construction of the floor or the solidity of the walls, but it also depends *f* in some degree on the nature of the operations carried on therein. Insofar as there is permanent equipment in the place, then its safety can in my judgment reflect on the safety of the place. Insofar as there are activities carried on in the place which are constant, regular and recurring, I can well see that they may have their impact on the question of whether the place has been made safe.

But where, as in the present instance, you start with a place safe in every degree, *g* and the only thing which renders it unsafe is the fact that equipment brought on it for a particular operation, and being used for a particular operation on a particular day, produces an element of danger, it seems to me that that is not enough to justify the allegation, certainly in criminal proceedings, that the place itself had not been made safe.

It seems to me that if the justices had instructed themselves on those lines, they *h* would have been bound to hold that the source of danger arising from the pressure in the test head was not an element which would cause the place to be other than a safe place; and, if they had come to that conclusion, then I think they would have been bound to dismiss this information quite apart from the number of other points which have been raised, though not fully argued, before us today.

On the face of the case stated it might be said to be possible that the justices had *j* reached their conclusion not on the matters to which my judgment has been directed, but on the very much narrower point, namely, that insufficient steps had been taken to mark off the working place from the highway and thus to give adequate protection to the workmen from the dangers of the highway. I can well see that a failure to mark off the working place from the highway might be the production of an unsafe

---

1 (1969) 8 KIR at 841

working place, but the prosecution (and I think quite rightly) have not asked us to   *a*
consider the possibility that the justices may have been moved by those considerations
to reach the conclusion which they did.

Approaching the matter on the footing that they tested this by asking themselves
whether the dangerous process made the place a dangerous place, I think that they
reached a conclusion untenable in law, and I would allow the appeal and quash the
conviction.   *b*

BRIDGE J. I entirely agree and I would only add this. It seems to me clearly right
that a line must be drawn, when considering whether or not a breach of reg 6(2) of the
Construction (Working Places) Regulations 1966 has been established, between a
danger on the one hand, arising from the condition of the place as such, and a danger
on the other hand, arising essentially from some activity carried on at the place in   *c*
question.

I should hesitate to make any attempt to lay down a comprehensive test to distinguish in practice between those two different situations. I can envisage great
difficulties in relation to particular sets of facts in saying exactly where the line
should be drawn and exactly on which side of the line a particular case might fall.
It must be largely a question of fact and degree. But I have no hesitation in agreeing   *d*
with Lord Widgery CJ in concluding that on the facts of this case the dangers which
arose from the high pressure of water introduced into the test head, and the absence
of suitable precautions to prevent the escape of that pressure, fall on the side of the
line which is favourable to the appellant, and I agree that the appeal for those reasons
should be allowed.
                                                                                      e

SHAW J. I also agree.

*Appeal allowed. The court refused leave to appeal to the House of Lords but the following
point of law was certified as being of general public importance: 'Whether (and to what
extent) a place of work can for purposes of reg 6(2) of the Construction (Working Places)*   *f*
Regulations 1966 be made unsafe by an unsafe system of work therein.'

Solicitors: *Stevensons,* agents for *Rowberry, Morris & Co,* Gloucester (for the appellant);
Solicitor for the Department of Employment.

Lea Josse Barrister.

National Transit Insurance Co Ltd v Customs and Excise Commissioners

QUEEN'S BENCH DIVISION

LORD WIDGERY CJ, MELFORD STEVENSON AND WATKINS JJ

5th DECEMBER 1974

Value added tax – Supply of goods or services – Supply of services – Supply for a considera-
tion – Meaning of 'consideration' – Expenses – Reimbursement – Principal and agent –
Sum paid by principal to agent towards cost of agent's expenses incurred on behalf of principal
– Whether sum paid a consideration for services supplied by agent – Finance Act 1972, s 5(2).

Value added tax – Exemptions – Insurance – Provision of insurance of any description –
Meaning of 'provision of insurance' – Whether limited to the provision of insurance cover –
Whether including the settling of claims – Finance Act 1972, Sch 5, Group 2, Item 1.

The taxpayer company carried on business as an insurer. Under an agreement
between a large number of insurance offices the taxpayer was a member of a committee which acted on behalf of members in effecting insurance policies for the Road
Haulage Executive. The committee had the right to receive premiums, issue policies,
and to settle and pay claims, the proceeds of the business being divided rateably among
members in accordance with the agreement. The committee had authority to
delegate its responsibility in a particular area to any one of its members. The
committee arranged that when an insurer settled a claim on behalf of the committee
the insurer was entitled to a credit of £4. The credit was not intended to
be economic but to be as fair as possible between all those concerned and to be a
contribution towards expenses incurred in handling the claim. The taxpayer was
assessed to value added tax on the sum of £4 which it had received for settling a
claim on behalf of the committee. The taxpayer appealed contending, inter alia,
(i) that the sum of £4 did not constitute a 'consideration' for the supply of services
within s 5(2)[a] of the Finance Act 1972 but was merely a reimbursement of expenses;
(ii) that, alternatively, the settling of the claim by the taxpayer constituted the
'provision of insurance' within Item 1[b] of Group 2 of Sch 5 to the 1972 Act and was
not therefore a taxable supply of services. The tribunal dismissed the appeal. On
appeal,

Held – The appeal would be dismissed for the following reasons—
(i) The tribunal were entitled to find that in the circumstances the credit of £4
was not the equivalent of reimbursing an agent for costs incurred on behalf of his
principal and could therefore properly be described as a consideration within s 5(2)
of the 1972 Act (see p 306 *j* to p 307 *a* and p 308 *e* and *f*, post).

(ii) The words 'provision of insurance' in Item 1 of Group 2 meant the provision of
insurance cover, i e the effecting of a contract of indemnity, and did not include the
settling of a claim made under such a contract. The sum of £4 had not therefore
been paid for the 'provision of insurance' and was not therefore consideration for
an exempt supply (see p 308 *d* to *f*, post).

Notes

For value added tax on the supply of services for a consideration, see Supplement to
33 Halsbury's Laws (3rd Edn) para 479B, 4.

---

a Section 5(2), so far as material, provides: 'Supply of goods includes all forms of supply . . .
    but supply of services does not include anything done otherwise than for a consideration.'

b Item 1 reads: 'The provision of insurance of any description.'

For the exemption from value added tax in relation to insurance, see ibid, para *a* 479B, 10.

For the Finance Act 1972, s 5, Sch 5, Group 2, Item 1, see 42 Halsbury's Statutes (3rd Edn) 167, 222.

Appeal

This was an appeal by National Transit Insurance Co Ltd ('the taxpayer') against a decision of a value added tax tribunal (chairman Neil Elles Esq) sitting at London *b* on 1st May 1974 affirming a decision of the Customs and Excise Commissioners communicated to the taxpayer in a letter dated 18th January 1974 whereby it was determined that the following supplies of services by the taxpayer were liable to value added tax: (i) handling a claim in respect of damage to 400 cartons of eggs reported to the Road Haulage Insurers' Committee on 13th April 1973 by Pickfords International Ltd, the alleged consideration received by the taxpayer for that service *c* being £4; (ii) handling a claim notified to the taxpayer on 12th April 1973 by Pick-fords International Ltd from British Aluminium Ltd in respect of one case of aluminium in transit to Belfast, the alleged consideration received by the taxpayer for that service being £4. The facts are set out in the judgment of Lord Widgery CJ.

C Potter QC and *P Lawton* for the taxpayer.   *d*
Harry Woolf for the commissioners.

LORD WIDGERY CJ. This is an appeal by the National Transit Insurance Co Ltd against the decision of a value added tax tribunal sitting at London on 1st May 1974 whereby the tribunal determined a liability for payment of value added tax by the appellants in regard to the receipt by the appellants of the sum of £4, the *e* circumstances of such receipt being apparent in a moment.

I would like to begin by complimenting the tribunal on the form of judgment in this case. It is extremely clear, in good sequence, descriptive and, as far as I can judge, accurate, and so much so that I find it possible, instead of trying to find my own words to describe the issues which arise in this case, to take liberal portions of the judgment below and adopt them as my own. *f*

The background appears in the judgment in these words:

'Road Transport was partially nationalised in 1949 and as a result of this the insurance market had to cope with the Road Haulage Executive and there arose a need to reorganise and rationalise insurance relating thereto. Accordingly on 1st January 1951 an agreement ("the 1951 Agreement") was entered into between a large number of insurance offices and Lloyds Underwriters all of *g* whom are collectively referred to in the Agreement as the "Insurers". The Road Haulage Executive was referred to in the Agreement as "the Insured" and the individuals severally appointed by the Insurers as the "Road Haulage Insurers Committee" was referred to in the Agreement as "the Committee". A detailed system of administration was brought into being by the 1951 Agreement. The insurers acting together vested in the Committee the consideration *h* of proposals for insurance, the fixing of the rates of premium and the acceptance, renewal, modification and discontinuance thereof. Under Clause 1(a) thereof any acceptance by the Committee of a proposal was to be accepted on behalf of the Insurers severally and rateably according to the proportions of each class of business set against the name of each Insurer in the second column of the Schedule thereto or such other proportions as might be substituted. They also *j* vested in the Committee the receipt of premiums and the settling, adjustment, compromising, allowance and payment of claims.'

All that means, in a sentence or two, is that consequent on the amalgamation of a large number of road haulage operations into the one nationalised entity, a similar rationalisation of the insurance cover was required. The device, as the tribunal say,

a   was the setting up of this committee and the individual insurers appointing the committee as their agent to conduct and run the business for them.   The committee had a right to receive premiums, issue policies, settle claims and pay claims, and indeed, apart from the fact that at the end of each period, I think of three months, there was a final reckoning and an apportionment amongst the parties of amounts due to them, the committee were responsible for organising and running the insurance
b   work involved.

In addition to the provisions of the contract noted in the tribunal's decision, I would also draw attention to two other matters.   In the first place it was provided that the committee itself should not be entitled to any remuneration although it was entitled to be indemnified by the insurers rateably.   One finds that in para 10 of the agreement.

c   Further, by para 1(p) of the agreement provision was made whereby the committee could delegate its responsibility under the agreement to chosen individuals as it thought fit.   This was no doubt to prevent the business being handled centrally by one unmanageably large organisation, and the committee took advantage of the power in para 1(p) to appoint one of the insurers themselves, preferably the larger, to act in any given area and any specific field of insurance under the title
d   of a 'service point'.

Thus one has the taxpayers, National Transit Insurance Co Ltd, playing, as it were, a dual role in that not only is it one of the insurers on whose behalf the committee was appointed, but it is also a service point, and as such it is responsible for handling claims which arise in its area or field of business, even though the claims are not claims under its own policies.

e   The first question which arises, indeed all the questions which arise in this case are concerned with a test sum of £4, and the tribunal describe the way in which this comes into relevance in the following way.   They say:

'Pursuant to its powers under the Agreement the Committee after discussion with all those concerned has made the following arrangements for dealing with expenses incurred in handling claims.'

f   I pause to observe that as a service point the taxpayer is concerned with the handling of claims.   The tribunal go on:

'Each Service Point is entitled to a credit of £4·00 for every claim which it handles.   Originally in 1951 this was £3, and we find as a fact that this credit (known generically as a "handling fee") was never intended to be economic,
g   but was intended to be as fair as possible as between all those concerned, and to be a contribution towards expenses incurred in dealing with these matters.'

The dispute, as I say, centres around that £4 credited in the way described in the tribunal's conclusion, and the way it comes before us is simply this.   The Commissioners of Customs and Excise took the view that when each service point, including
h   the taxpayer, settled a claim on behalf of the insurers generally (I pause to observe of course it would be on behalf of the insurers generally, the committee merely being an agent or conduit pipe connecting the insurers to the insured person) and received a credit of £4 in respect of that settlement, then according to the contention of the Commissioners of Customs and Excise, there was there a supply of a taxable service within the meaning of the Finance Act 1972 for a consideration, namely, £4 which
j   was credited.

The provisions of the 1972 Act which give rise to the payment of value added tax are becoming well known, and I do not propose to refer to them all, but it is important to bear in mind, having regard to the form of the argument in this case, that no tax is payable on the supply of a service unless the service is rendered for a consideration.   One gets that from s 5(2) of the 1972 Act.

Accordingly, in order to sustain the commissioners' argument in the present

instance it is necessary, amongst other things, to demonstrate that the £4 is a con-   a
sideration for present purposes. Furthermore, no value added tax is chargeable
unless the supply in question, whether of goods or services, is by a taxable person in
the course of a business carried on by him. Hence in order to sustain the commissioners' argument in the present instance it is necessary as well to show that the
supply of the service by the service point was a supply in the course of a business
carried on by that insurer.   b
    Those being the main issues involved, and I turn to the remaining ones later on,
I can pass on to see in what language the tribunal disposed of this claim, although
before I do so, in deference to counsel for the taxpayer's own contentions, I ought to
say that in opposition to the contention of the commissioners to which I have already
referred he submits to us, first, that there was no consideration in respect of this
alleged supply of a service; secondly, that it was not in the course of a business   c
carried on by the service point; and also another matter to which I will come later,
if he is wrong on those two points, that the supply was an exempt supply.
    To take the first two points first and the language used by the tribunal to deal
with them: I have already read the tribunal's findings of fact in which they say that
this payment of £4 was never intended to be economic but was intended to be as
fair as possible and a contribution towards expenses incurred.   d
    Having heard the argument on both sides, the tribunal deal with the matter in
this way:

> 'For each claim handled the [taxpayer] is allowed a handling fee of £4·00,
> which is credited to its account in the quarterly settlement as between all the
> relevant Insurers which is effected through the Committee. Despite the super-
> ficial attraction of treating the activities undertaken by the Insurers, the Com-   e
> mittee and the [taxpayer] as though they were one insurance company, and of
> looking at the end result, instead of what was actually done step by step, we are
> driven to the conclusion on the facts before us that a separate service is supplied
> by the [taxpayer] for a consideration which, whether or not it is aptly termed a
> handling fee, is quantified in the sum of £4·00 per claim handled. It was con-
> tended by [counsel for the taxpayer] with some force that some part of this   f
> service in reality relates to self supply, and self supply of a service is not a taxable
> supply . . .'

Then there is further reference to the contention put before the tribunal on behalf
of the taxpayer.
    Counsel for the taxpayer criticises the decision of the tribunal and takes, as I have   g
indicated, as his first point that the £4 is not a consideration for present purposes. He
says that it is only a book entry and does not involve the actual transfer of cash from
one person to another. But in a much more formidable argument, as it seems to me,
he contends that a consideration for present purposes means some kind of remuneration or reward, and that one would not regard a service as being supplied for a consideration if all that the supplier was doing was getting his out-of-pocket payments.   h
    I confess this point has given me more than a little trouble in the course of the
hearing, and I am glad in a sense that we do not have today to decide what the position
would be in a simple case in which the only consideration of any kind passing was
the reimbursement to an agent of expenses which he had incurred on behalf of
his principal, but that is not this case.
    It seems to me here that when one looks at the basis of the fixing of the £4 sum it   j
is not intended to be, nor do the tribunal find it intended to be, a reimbursement of
expenses as such. It seems to me to be a kind of compounded fee which is payable
to the service point in respect of each and every claim which it handles and settles,
regardless of whether the actual expense exceeds or falls short of the figure of £4,
or indeed amounts to anything at all.
    In my judgment the tribunal were entitled to find on what is really a mixed point

a of law and fact that in the circumstances of the present instance the credit allotted of £4 per claim settled was not the equivalent simply of reimbursing an agent for the costs incurred on behalf of his principal and could fairly and properly be described as a consideration for present purposes.

The second argument put forward by counsel for the taxpayer in regard to the chargeability of this sum is a contention that the payment, if payment it was, was
b not made by the taxpayer in the course of its business, and if that is right, of course it is enough to exclude the payment from the net of value added tax.

I confess that on this point I have never really had any inclination to accept the argument put forward because it seems to me to be too clear for argument that when the taxpayer provides the service of settling the claims it is doing so in the course of its business.

c What is its business? It is an insurer. It has also taken on itself the responsibility under the agreement of 1951 to act as a service point for other insurers as well. Perhaps it is fair to describe that as an addition to its business activities; perhaps it is not. But when it comes to settle a claim on behalf of itself and the other insurers who have joined in the agreement, it seems to be beyond argument that that should be a service supplied in the course of its business.

d I have listened with care to counsel for the taxpayer's contentions on this point. He made much of the fact that if, as he submitted, two solicitors were in partnership with one another each would supply services for the other, yet any money received would not be regarded as received in the course of a business carried on by the recipient. I think that may be so, but it seems to me to be a wholly artificial example unrelated to the problems which face us.

e In the simple arguments in our case on this point I can see no possible ground for saying that the service was supplied otherwise than in the course of a business carried on by the taxpayer.

So I come to the third and last point which has been raised in regard to this matter, and that is a contention taken by counsel for the taxpayer, only if he has failed on both of his first principal submissions, that the supply of this service was an exempt
f supply under Sch 5, Group 2, Item 1, to the 1972 Act. This schedule contains a number of exemptions, and in Group 2, Item 1, the exemption described is: 'The provision of insurance of any description.' In other words, what it means is that if the service alleged to be taxable is the provision of insurance of any description, it ceases to be taxable because it is taken out of the scope of the tax by the exemption.

Counsel for the taxpayer contends that the provision of insurance is not confined
g to the issuing of the policy or to the continuance in force of the policy, but extends up to and includes the day when the policy matures for whatever reason it matures and the actual claim is examined, settled and paid. He says that the insurers are supplying the service of the provision of insurance right through that period and accordingly the service of checking and settling the claim is all under the umbrella, as it were, of the provision of insurance.

h What the tribunal thought about that was as follows. They said:

'It remains then to be considered whether the service supplied by the [taxpayer] in handling the claim is an exempt service within the meaning of Group 2 of Schedule 5 to the Finance Act 1972. The insurance is collectively provided by the Insurers of the Insured under the 1951 Agreement, but what are the limits of the description "the provision of insurance"? and does this term include the
j handling of claims? In the view of the majority of us ... the term "insurance" has the meaning ascribed to it in Webster's Dictionary under the definition numbered 2(b), "coverage by contract whereby for a stipulated consideration one party undertakes to indemnify or guarantee against loss by a specified contingency or peril ..." The handling of claims appears to us to be an integral part of providing the indemnity itself after the contingency has arisen against

which the insurance is effected. It is true that this forms part of the normal *a* business undertaken by an insurance company: it is also true that the consideration or premium paid by the Insured for the insurance appears to have been costed by the Committee to include the estimated average cost of meeting claims in the relevant class of business, including the estimated cost of handling claims, and also an element of profit for the Insurer. None the less we hold that what is provided by the Insurer for the premium is the coverage against specified *b* perils and we do not consider that the manner in which the premium is costed is relevant to the point which we have to decide. Insurance is a contract to indemnify and, once this has been effected we consider that the term in Group 2 of Schedule 5 "the provision of insurance" has been exhausted. The actual indemnity may never be called on and, in our view, if and when the relevant contingency arises the handling of the claim for the indemnity by the [taxpayer] *c* against the Insurers is separate and distinct from the provision of the insurance as such.'

I feel disposed to accept not only that conclusion but also its reasoning. I agree with the conception, supported by the majority of the tribunal, that the provision of insurance means the provision of cover, and does not include as part of the service the settlement of a claim by the insurers on their own behalf or on behalf of other insurance companies, and accordingly it seems to me that the tribunal were entirely right in rejecting the argument that the supply of this service was an exempt supply in Item 1 of Group 2 of Sch 5.

For all those reasons, and thinking, as I do, that the tribunal was entirely right in its conclusions, I would dismiss the appeal. *e*

MELFORD STEVENSON J. So would I.

WATKINS J. I agree.

f

Appeal dismissed.

Solicitors: *Theodore Goddard & Co* (for the taxpayer); *Solicitor, Customs and Excise.*

N P Metcalfe Esq Barrister.

Davies v Customs and Excise Commissioners

QUEEN'S BENCH DIVISION

LORD WIDGERY CJ, MAIS AND CROOM-JOHNSON JJ

13th NOVEMBER 1974

Value added tax – Value of supply of goods or services – Determination of value – Supply for consideration in money – Payment for goods by means of cash vouchers – Vouchers issued by company – Taxpayer accepting vouchers from customers in exchange for goods – Taxpayer entitled to reimbursement from company of cash value of vouchers less an agreed commission due to company – Whether goods supplied in exchange for vouchers supplied for a consideration in money – Whether tax to be charged by reference to the value of the goods supplied less amount of commission due to company – Finance Act 1972, ss 9(1), 10(2).

The taxpayer carried on business as a retail draper. He had an arrangement with a company whereby he would accept 'checks', i e vouchers bearing a face value, issued by the company and presented by customers in exchange for goods supplied in his shop. The company reimbursed the taxpayer the amount of the checks received by him subject to a deduction of $13\frac{3}{4}$ per cent which represented a commission from the taxpayer to the company in respect of customers introduced by means of the company's checks. The taxpayer was assessed to value added tax under the Finance Act 1972, ss 9(1) and 10[a], on the total cash value of goods paid for by means of the company's checks. The taxpayer claimed that for the purposes of the charge to VAT he was entitled to deduct from the cash value of such goods the amount of the commission paid to the company.

Held – Payment by one of the company's checks was a cash payment and s 10(2) of the 1972 Act was therefore applicable. The transaction between the taxpayer and the customer was in every way similar to a contract for the sale of goods; only the method of payment was different. It followed that, for the purposes of VAT, the value of the goods supplied was the amount which, with the addition of the tax chargeable, equalled the face value of the check presented by the customer by way of payment. The taxpayer had, therefore, been properly assessed by the commissioners (see p 311 *a c d f* and *j*, post).

Notes

For the value of a supply of goods or services, see Supplement to 33 Halsbury's Laws (3rd Edn) para 479B, 8.

For the Finance Act 1972, ss 9, 10, see 42 Halsbury's Statutes (3rd Edn) 172, 173.

Appeal

This was an appeal by John Joseph Davies ('the taxpayer') trading as Peter Sogood, against a decision of a value added tax tribunal sitting at the Birmingham Tribunal Centre on 20th May 1974 affirming a decision of the Commissioners of Customs and Excise contained in a letter dated 10th October 1973. The facts are set out in the judgment of Lord Widgery CJ.

The taxpayer appeared in person.

Harry Woolf for the commissioners.

LORD WIDGERY CJ. This matter comes before the court by way of an appeal from a value added tax tribunal which, on 20th May 1974, dismissed an appeal to the tribunal by Mr Davies, who is now in turn the appellant in this court.

The fact that the appeal comes from a value added tax tribunal indicates the

---

a   Section 10, so far as material, is set out at p 311 *e*, post nature of the matters with which we are concerned. The facts are these. The *a* contention put forward by the taxpayer is really a contention about a variety of principles which he says are either wrong or wrongly applied in relation to the administration of this tax, and much of the paperwork which has been generated in this case has been due to the fact that only at a late stage was the issue applied to a single transaction so that it was possible to look at it and test the arguments of the taxpayer in relation to that transaction.   *b*

In brief, the background is this. The taxpayer is a drapery retailer, and he has an arrangement with a number of check companies (which is the simplest way of putting it), which are organisations which issue checks of a certain face value, which checks can be used in the appropriate and suitable shops for payment of goods on sale in the shops; and more specifically in relation to this shop of the taxpayer there was at all material times an agreement between the shopkeeper under a *c* business name, but it was the taxpayer in substance, on the one hand, and the Provident Clothing & Supply Co Ltd ('Provident') on the other. The terms of the agreement were that the taxpayer would act on authorities issued by the company in the form of checks and cash vouchers and supply to the holder of such checks and vouchers any of the goods or services offered for sale from his premises and charge the same to the account of Provident at normal retail prices.   *d*

The purpose of that is clear enough. Customers of Provident who acquired their checks can use them in the taxpayer's shop as though they were cash, and the obligation on the taxpayer is to charge Provident customers who come armed with these checks at normal retail prices which he would charge anybody else. But in some respects the customers who come to the taxpayer via Provident are less attractive than those who by their own way go from the street, because having charged *e* customers only at normal retail prices, Provident proceeded to take 13¾ per cent from the amount of reimbursement which they would normally pay to the taxpayer when he submitted the check for payment. Thus, as a consideration for the services which Provident gives him, he is receiving on the sales to Provident customers 13¾ per cent less than he would have received had the sale been to a cash customer who walked into the shop.   *f*

That agreement was made in 1970 before value added tax was ever thought of, and the taxpayer says, and I have no doubt that he is right, that it has worked very well and very successfully, and he had no trouble in regard to the carrying on of business with Provident in that way. But of course VAT has come on to the scene, and undoubtedly it has created considerable problems for this kind of trader. One can illustrate the problem by reference to the particular transaction which was *g* eventually isolated and made the subject of the tribunal's decision before the matter came to us.

The transaction was a very simple one. There were six gentlemen's handkerchiefs, and they were sold over the counter for £1·02. On an ordinary sale to an ordinary member of the public the customer would pay £1·02, and of that, some 9p would be VAT and the taxpayer would have to account for it to the Customs and *h* Excise in the ordinary way. In other words, the £1·02 was an inclusive price, inclusive of VAT and on an ordinary sale the taxpayer would get 93p and would have to surrender 9p as VAT to the Revenue.

In fact this was not an ordinary sale; it was a sale to a Provident customer, so he took Provident checks to the value of £1·02, exactly the same price as an ordinary customer would pay, and when he submitted those checks to Provident for payment *j* he received from Provident not £1·02 but 88p. The reason for that was by virtue of the agreement to which I have referred Provident were entitled to deduct 13¾ per cent of the face value of the checks when making payment to the taxpayer. He contends that in those circumstances he received only 88p in cash and that he should not be required to account for VAT on a notional sale at a net figure of 93p when in fact all he received was 88p from Provident.

a This simple transaction has given rise to arguments at great length, many of which have gone up to what I venture with respect to think were blind alleys. Consideration has been given to the question of whether a Provident customer acquiring goods through the Provident check is giving cash or something other than cash as a consideration. The point may be of some importance. From my point of view I am quite confident that the customer who presents the Provident check is paying cash

b and not consideration other than cash.

Another question which has been raised by the taxpayer this time is that the sale of the goods from his shop is not a sale to the customer who comes in and selects them but is a sale to Provident. He argues that because he is paid by Provident, Provident is his customer, and that the whole matter should be viewed on the footing that he is supplying the goods to Provident.

c Again from my point of view I can see no substance either in law or common sense for that proposition. It seems to me that the transaction between the taxpayer and his customer is in every way similar to a final contract of sale of goods, save that the method of payment is different. As I suggested to the taxpayer when he was putting forward his argument, I said that if the goods had been defective, it seems clear enough that the customer would have brought them back to the taxpayer and would not have

d taken them to Provident. That is only a pointer to the fact that this is in my judgment a normal commercial sale from the taxpayer to the customer who comes into his shop.

Those being the circumstances, we find in s 9 of the Finance Act 1972 the provisions which determine how a supply of goods or services is to be valued for the purposes of VAT. Reference is made in s 9(1) to the provisions of s 10 as being relevant for

e this purpose. Section 10 is in these terms:

'(1) For the purposes of this Part of this Act the value of any supply of goods or services shall be determined as follows.

'(2) If the supply is for a consideration in money its value shall be taken to be such amount as, with the addition of the tax chargeable, is equal to the consideration . . .'

f That means in this case there being a sale to the customer for cash as I have already in my opinion indicated, the supply for VAT purposes is to be treated as being of such amount as with the addition of the tax chargeable is equal to £1·02; in other words the value of the supply is 93p and the difference of 9p is the VAT which has to be accounted for by the retailer.

If one stops at that point, I can see no further problems in the case as far as this

g simple example is concerned, and I think, with deference to the taxpayer, that he is not endeavouring to say that the conclusion of the tribunal in this specific instance was wrong, but he is eloquently describing to us the difficulties which retail traders have when dealing with VAT, and particularly when they also deal with provident societies and the like who issue these check forms.

I say with sincerity that he has my sympathy because the problems are obviously

h acute, and it may be that Parliament will find a way out of some of them, but this court is not here to make new laws. This court is only here concerned to say whether the tribunal's view was right that on this simple sale of six handkerchiefs the taxpayer was accountable to the Customs for 9p. I think he was and I would dismiss the appeal accordingly.

j **MAIS J.** I agree.

CROOM-JOHNSON J. I agree.

Appeal dismissed.

Solicitor: *Solicitor, Customs & Excise.*

N P Metcalfe Esq Barrister,

Revell Fuels Ltd v Customs and Excise Commissioners

QUEEN'S BENCH DIVISION
LORD WIDGERY CJ, BRIDGE AND KILNER BROWN JJ
6th, 7th NOVEMBER 1974

Value added tax – Relief – Goods held at commencement of April 1973 – Goods on which purchase tax or other duty paid – Deduction as input tax of purchase tax or duty paid – Goods deemed to be held on material date by taxpayer – Goods supplied to taxpayer before that date and not by then supplied by him – Goods supplied to taxpayer before material date – Goods subsequently destroyed before material date – Whether goods deemed to be held by taxpayer on material date – Finance Act 1973, s 4(1)(6).

The taxpayer company was registered for the purposes of value added tax under the Finance Act 1972. On 19th March 1973 the taxpayer company held a large quantity of unused goods for the purpose of sale in the course of its business, on which purchase tax had been paid. On that day the premises where the goods were held were destroyed by fire and the entire stock was lost. The taxpayer company claimed a rebate under s 4(1)[a] of the Finance Act 1973 for the purchase tax which it had paid. It contended that it had satisfied the requirements of s 4(1) since, under s 4(6)[b], the goods were to be deemed to have been held by it at the beginning of April 1973 in that they had been supplied to the taxpayer company before the end of March 1973 and had not by then been supplied by it.

Held – The purpose of s 4(6) was to prescribe the conditions which had to be fulfilled if goods which were in existence at the beginning of April 1973 were to comply with the requirement of s 4(1) that they should then be held by the person claiming relief for sale in the course of his trade. The conditions prescribed by s 4(1) and (6) were framed on the basis that the goods in question did in fact exist at the beginning of April 1973. Goods which had perished before then were not, therefore, eligible for relief under s 4(1). Accordingly the taxpayer company's claim failed (see p 315 *a* to *c* and *e* to *h*, post).

Notes

For the deduction of input tax, see Supplement to 33 Halsbury's Laws (3rd Edn) para 479B, 3.

For the Finance Act 1973, s 4, see 43 Halsbury's Statutes (3rd Edn) 389.

Appeal

This was an appeal by Revell Fuels Ltd (trading as British Fuel Co) ('the taxpayer company'), against the decision of a value added tax tribunal sitting at Pudsey on 5th March 1974 dismissing an appeal by the taxpayer company against the refusal of the Commissioners of Customs and Excise to allow the taxpayer company to include the sum of £17,615 in its value added tax return as an amount to be deducted as input tax by virtue of s 4 of the Finance Act 1973. The facts are set out in the judgment of Bridge J.

P G Whiteman for the taxpayer company.
Harry Woolf for the commissioners.

---

a   Section 4(1), so far as material, is set out at p 314 *c* to *e*, post
b   Section 4(6) is set out at p 314 *h* and *j*, post

a **BRIDGE J** delivered the first judgment at the invitation of Lord Widgery CJ. This is an appeal under the Tribunals and Inquiries Act 1958 from the decision of a value added tax tribunal sitting at Pudsey given on 5th March 1974, dismissing an appeal by the taxpayer company from the refusal of the Commissioners of Customs and Excise to allow the taxpayer company a rebate or reduction of tax in the sum of £17,615 claimed by the taxpayer company to be due under the provisions of s 4 of
b the Finance Act 1973.

The facts, which were undisputed, can be very shortly stated. The taxpayer company is a trader which, on 19th March 1973, held in stock at certain supermarket premises in Hull a large and valuable quantity of goods intended in due course to be sold by the taxpayer company in the course of its business, which goods had suffered purchase tax in the sum of £17,615, the amount in dispute in this appeal. On that
c date, 19th March 1973, the premises in question were destroyed by fire and the stock of goods was totally destroyed in that fire.

The system of taxation known as value added tax was introduced by the Finance Act 1972 and came into operation on 1st April 1973. Before going to the provisions of s 4 of the Finance Act 1973, on which in the last analysis this appeal turns, it is necessary to say a very few words about the general structure of the value added
d tax system under the 1972 Act.

Value added tax is a tax charged on the supply of goods or services. We are concerned in this case solely with goods, so nothing more need be said about services. Only certain categories of goods attract the tax, but a person who carries on business in supplying goods of those categories is a taxable person, and when he supplies goods that is a taxable supply. The supply of goods by a taxable person attracts the tax
e notwithstanding that the person to whom that supply is made is not the ultimate consumer, but is another trader somewhere along the chain, who resells the goods supplied to him or uses them in the course of his business. That being so, the 1972 Act introduces what are called 'input tax' and 'output tax' with the object of ensuring that tax which is paid by a trader on goods supplied to him may be deducted from tax which he is liable to pay when he supplies those goods on to a third party or
f supplies other goods on to a third party having used in the course of his business the goods supplied to him.

This is effected by s 3 of the 1972 Act, sub-s (1) of which provides:

> 'The following tax (in this Part of this Act referred to as "input tax"), that is to say—(*a*) tax on the supply to a taxable person of any goods or services for the purpose of a business carried on or to be carried on by him; and (*b*) tax paid
g > or payable by a taxable person on the importation of any goods used or to be used for the purpose of a business carried on or to be carried on by him; may, at the end of any prescribed accounting period, be deducted by him, so far as not previously deducted and to the extent and subject to the exceptions provided for by or under this section, from the tax chargeable on supplies by him (in this section referred to as "output tax").'
h

It is also necessary, as will appear when I come to look at s 4 of the 1973 Act, to take careful note of the provisions of s 7 of the 1972 Act, which embodies certain technical and, in a sense, artificial rules for determining the moment at which a supply is deemed to have taken place, which is referred to as the 'tax point', the point of time at which tax becomes payable.
j Section 7(2) of the 1972 Act provides:

> 'Subject to the following provisions of this section, a supply of goods shall be treated as taking place—(*a*) if the goods are to be removed, at the time of the removal; (*b*) if the goods are not to be removed, at the time when they are made available to the person to whom they are supplied; (*c*) if the goods (being sent or taken on approval or sale or return or similar terms) are removed

before it is known whether a supply will take place, at the time when it becomes *a* certain that the supply has taken place, but not later than twelve months after the removal.'

Then sub-ss (4) and (5), which I need not read in extenso, have this effect, that if an invoice in relation to goods supplied is issued either before the time of supply determined as under sub-s (2), or within 14 days thereafter, then the date of the issue of the invoice becomes the notional date of supply and supersedes the date which would *b* otherwise be appropriate under the rules provided by sub-s (2). I also refer in passing to the circumstances that a somewhat similar artificial rule is adopted by s 47 in relation to the time of importation of goods.

Bearing those provisions in mind, I turn to the provisions of s 4 of the 1973 Act. That provides by sub s (1):

c
'Where the Commissioners of Customs and Excise are satisfied that purchase tax or a duty to which this section applies was charged on or in respect of goods or on or in respect of parts or ingredients of goods which at the beginning of April 1973 were unused and held by a taxable person for sale in the course of his business, then—[subject to certain administrative conditions] an amount determined or arrived at in accordance with subsection (2) of this section to *d* take account of the tax or duty charged may ... be included in the return made by the taxable person under Part I of the Finance Act 1972 for the first prescribed accounting period or, with the sanction of the Commissioners, in such a return made for a later period and shall, if so included, be treated for the purposes of that Part as an amount to be deducted as input tax.'

The object of that provision is plain. The value added tax system when it came *e* into operation on 1st April 1973 took the place of the old purchase tax system, and if under the old system a trader had paid purchase tax on goods which he held in stock at the beginning of April 1973, and which on being supplied after that date by him in the course of his business would attract value added tax, such a provision as one finds in s 4 was necessary in order to avoid double taxation, and that is what this *f* provision is intended to achieve.

The argument for the taxpayer company in this court is, as it has been both in making its claim to the commissioners and before the value added tax tribunal, to the effect that, notwithstanding that the goods destroyed in the fire on 19th March 1973 no longer existed at the beginning of April of that year, nevertheless, by reference to certain later provisions of this section, they are in a position to claim that those goods were at the beginning of April 1973 'unused and held by a taxable person for *g* sale in the course of his business'. Accordingly it claims to be entitled to deduct the £17,615 purchase tax paid on those goods as input tax from its first return for value added tax purposes of tax due from it.

At first blush the argument seems a somewhat far-fetched one, but before reaching a conclusion about it, one has to look at s 4(6) of the 1973 Act, which is in these terms: *h*

'For the purposes of this section goods shall be deemed to be held by a person at the beginning of April 1973 if, and only if, they were—(*a*) produced by or supplied to him in the United Kingdom; or (*b*) imported by him; before the end of March 1973 and had not then been supplied by him; and any question whether goods were supplied by or to or were imported by any person before the end of March 1973 shall be determined as, under sections 7 and 47 of the *j* Finance Act 1972, it falls to be determined for the purposes of the charge to value added tax.'

The argument of counsel for the taxpayer company is a very short one. Indeed the point is very short. He says that if one looks at the language of this subsection, it applies quite literally to the taxpayer company's situation in relation to the goods *a*   destroyed by fire because those goods had been supplied to the taxpayer company before the end of March 1973, and by the end of March 1973 the goods had not been supplied by the taxpayer company.

In my judgment the argument is quite untenable when one looks at the object of sub-s (6) and, having considered that object, returns to consider its effect in relation to sub-s (1). The object of sub-s (6) in my judgment is plain. If s 4 is to operate as

b   intended as a protection against double taxation where necessary, and only where necessary, then the question whether goods are to be treated as held by the taxpayer at midnight on 31st March 1973 has to be determined not by reference to his physical possession at that moment, but by reference to the artificial and technical rules relating to the moment of supply or importation to which I drew attention under ss 7 and 47 of the 1972 Act. The question whether goods at the critical moment

c   are held by the taxpayer depends on whether they have been notionally supplied to him before that date, and whether they were notionally supplied by him after that date, quite irrespective of the question whether he then had them physically in his possession.

Thus, for instance, goods would be treated as being held by the taxpayer at the beginning of April 1973 if they had been invoiced to him before that date notwith-

d   standing that they had not been delivered by that date. Conversely, they would be treated as not being held by him on that date if he had invoiced them to a third person before that date, but not delivered them until after 1st April.

Bearing those considerations in mind, which arise from an examination of the purpose of sub-s (6), one may accordingly return to sub-s (1) to see what is its proper construction. It seems to me quite clear under sub-s (1) that before a deduction

e   as input tax of an amount paid by way of purchase tax can be allowed, it must be shown that three conditions are satisfied as at the beginning of April in relation to the goods which have suffered purchase tax. They are, first, that those goods should be unused; secondly, that they should be held by the taxpayer in the sense provided by sub-s (6), that is to say notionally held on the basis that the date falls between the notional dates of supply to and supply by the taxpayer, not by

f   reference to his physical possession; thirdly and finally, the goods must satisfy the condition that on that date they are so held by the taxpayer for sale in the course of his business.

Each of those conditions clearly presupposes that the goods are in existence. At the beginning of April the goods in relation to which the taxpayer company's claim is made did not exist. The commissioners in my judgment were right to refuse to allow the deduction claimed and the value added tax tribunal to confirm that view.

g   I would dismiss this appeal.

KILNER BROWN J. I agree.

h   **LORD WIDGERY CJ.** I agree also.

Appeal dismissed.

Solicitors: *Herbert Oppenheimer, Nathan & Vandyk* (for the taxpayer company); *Solicitor, Customs and Excise.*

N P Metcalfe Esq   Barrister.

Watkinson v Barley   *a*

QUEEN'S BENCH DIVISION
LORD WIDGERY CJ, MAIS AND CROOM-JOHNSON JJ
19th NOVEMBER 1974

Road traffic – Driving with blood-alcohol proportion above prescribed limit – Evidence –
Provision of specimen – Breath test – Device – Instructions for use – Strict compliance with **b**
instructions not essential to validity of test – Smoking – High concentration of tobacco smoke
liable to affect result of test – Instructions stating that smoking should not be permitted
immediately before test – Defendant having been smoking shortly before test – No evidence
that smoking affected result of test – Validity of test.

The respondent, who was driving a car on the wrong side of a main road, was stopped by   **c**
the police and asked to take a breath test. He agreed and walked from his car to the police
car to take the test. When he left his car, he was, to the knowledge of the police, smoking
a cigar, which he extinguished before reaching the police car.   The Alcotest 80 device
used by the police for the purpose of the test was accompanied by the manufacturers'
instructions which stated, inter alia: 'A high concentration of tobacco smoke tends   **d**
to colour the re-agent brown.   Smoking during or immediately prior to the test
should not therefore be permitted.'   The breath test was positive and the respondent
was arrested. A subsequent laboratory test showed that his blood contained 186
milligrammes of alcohol per 100 millilitres of blood.   The respondent was charged
with driving a motor vehicle having consumed alcohol in such a quantity that the
proportion thereof in his blood exceeded the prescribed limit, contrary to s 6(1) of
the Road Traffic Act 1972.   The justices upheld a submission by the respondent that   **e**
the breath test was invalid on the ground that, by allowing the respondent to take
the test so soon after he had finished smoking, the police had failed to comply with
the manufacturers' instructions.   Accordingly they dismissed the information and
the prosecutor appealed.

Held – A breath test would be invalidated by a failure to comply with manufacturers'   **f**
instructions only if it could be shown that the failure had affected the result of the
test adversely to the accused.   Where it was quite evident that the volume of smoke
left in a driver's mouth and lungs was not sufficient to be capable of being described
as a 'high concentration', the fact that he had smoked before the test, or at all, became
completely irrelevant.   In the circumstances it was impossible to contend that
when the respondent took the test there had been such a residual concentration of   **g**
tobacco smoke in his lungs and mouth as to affect the test in the manner envisaged in
the manufacturers' instructions.   Accordingly the appeal would be allowed and the
case remitted to the justices to continue the hearing (see p 319 *c* and *j* to p 320 *a* and
d e, post).

Note   **h**
For the relevance of the manufacturers' instructions as to the use of a device approved
for the purposes of a breath test, see Supplement to 33 Halsbury's Laws (3rd Edn)
para 1061A, 4, and for cases on the subject, see Digest (Cont Vol C) 936, 937, *322aa-*
322bb.

Cases referred to in judgment   *j*
Darnell v Portal [1972] RTR 483, (1972) 136 JP 717, DC.
Director of Public Prosecutions v Carey [1969] 3 All ER 1662, [1970] AC 1072, [1969]
    3 WLR 1169, 134 JP 59, [1970] RTR 14, HL, Digest (Cont Vol C) 936, *322aa.*

Case also cited
Gill v Forster [1970] RTR 372, DC.

a **Case stated**
This was an appeal by way of a case stated by justices for the county of Lincoln Parts of Kesteven acting in and for the petty sessional division of Spitalgate in respect of their adjudication as a magistrates' court sitting at Grantham on 7th March 1974.

On 24th January 1974 an information was preferred by the appellant, Charles Watkinson, against the respondent, Henry John Barley, that he on 8th December
b 1973 in the parish of Barrowby drove a motor car on the Great North Road having consumed alcohol in such quantity that the proportion thereof in his blood as ascertained from a laboratory test for which he subsequently provided a specimen exceeded the prescribed limit of 80 milligrammes per 100 millilitres at the time he provided the specimen, namely his blood contained not less than 186 milligrammes of alcohol per 100 millilitres of blood, contrary to s 6(1) of, and Sch 4, Part 1 to, the
c Road Traffic Act 1972. The following facts were found: (a) At 11.05 p m on 8th December 1973 the respondent drove a motor car in a northerly direction in the fast lane of the southbound carriageway of the A1 road at Barrowby, Lincolnshire, when two police officers in uniform caused him to stop whereupon the respondent got out of his car. (b) The respondent was unsteady on his feet and his breath smelt of alcoholic drink. (c) One of the police officers required the respondent to give a
d sample of breath for a test and the respondent sat in the rear seat of a police patrol car whilst giving a sample using the Alcotest 80 device. The test was positive, and he was arrested. (d) When the respondent got out of his car he was smoking a cigar to the actual knowledge of both police officers. (e) The time which elapsed between the respondent getting out of his car and his arrest following the positive breath test was about three minutes. (f) The respondent extinguished his cigar at some
e point in time between getting out of his car and getting into the police patrol car for the breath test to be administered. (g) After his arrest the respondent was taken to Grantham police station where a second breath test was administered and found to be positive. (h) The respondent provided a specimen of his blood in response to a requirement made by a police officer which was taken by a medical practitioner and divided into three parts one of which was offered to the respondent and another
f of which was later analysed and found to contain not less than 186 milligrammes of alcohol in 100 millilitres of blood.

It was contended on behalf of the respondent in a submission that the respondent had no case to answer, that the initial breath test was not conducted properly in that to the actual knowledge of the police officer conducting the test the respondent had been smoking immediately before the test was administered and hence that the
g power of arrest did not arise and all that followed it was unlawful.

It was contended on behalf of the appellant that the second breath test was properly conducted and was positive whereupon the requirement to provide a specimen of blood, the taking of that specimen and its subsequent analysis to show a level in excess of the prescribed limit was lawful.

The justices were referred to *Director of Public Prosecutions v Carey*[1] and in particular
h to part of the opinion of Viscount Dilhorne[2] and to the manufacturers' printed instructions for the use of the Alcotest 80 breath testing kit reproduced in Wilkinson's Road Traffic Offences[3] and in particular to the words: 'Smoking during or immediately prior to the test should not therefore be permitted.'

The justices were of the opinion that the evidence adduced by the prosecution being uncontradicted entitled them to make their findings of fact without hearing
j such evidence as the respondent might wish to adduce and to uphold the submission made on his behalf that since the respondent had been smoking immediately prior to the initial breath test being administered to the actual knowledge of the police

---

1 [1969] 3 All ER 1662, [1970] AC 1072
2 [1969] 3 All ER at 1670, [1970] AC at 1086
3 7th Edn (1973), pp 168, 169

officer administering it, the test was invalid hence invalidating the subsequent steps.　*a*

The question for the opinion of the high court was whether smoking to the actual knowledge of the police officer administering the breath test immediately prior to the breath test being administered in contravention of the instructions of the manufacturers of the Alcotest 80 kit invalidated the test.

Igor Judge for the appellant.　　　　　　　　　　　　　　　　　　　　　　　*b*
F B Smedley for the respondent.

LORD WIDGERY CJ. This is an appeal by case stated by justices for the county of Lincoln sitting as a magistrates' court at Grantham on 7th March 1974. There was before them an information laid by the appellant against the respondent that the respondent, on 8th December 1973, had driven a motor car on a road at a time　*c* when there was contained in his blood a higher proportion of alcohol than that permitted by the Road Traffic Act 1972. The justices, as will appear in a moment, accepted a submission of no case to answer and accordingly dismissed the information.

The facts found so far as are relevant are these. At 11.05 p m on 8th December 1973 the respondent was driving a motor car on the A1 road but unhappily driving on the wrong side of the road. He was, therefore, proceeding in a northerly direction　*d* on that part of the road reserved for traffic travelling to the south. Not surprisingly, the police took an interest in him, stopped him and when he got out of his car his breath smelt of alcohol. One of the police officers quite properly required him to give a sample of breath for a breath test, and the respondent, having got out of his own car, walked over to the police car, which must have been fairly near, although one does not know exactly how near, and sitting in the rear of the police car he gave a　*e* sample of breath using the Alcotest 80 device. The test was positive and he was arrested.

So far the facts give rise to no comment. The point comes next. When the respondent got out of his car he was smoking a cigar and both police officers observed this. The time which elapsed between the respondent getting out of his car and his arrest following the positive breath test was about three minutes. The respondent　*f* had extinguished his cigar at some point in time between getting out of his car and getting into the police car for the breath test to be administered.

The point which arises out of this is, that amongst the instructions which are issued by the manufacturers of the Alcotest device are two in regard to smoking. The short instructions, which appear on the lid of the box in which the device is contained, say, amongst other things, 'Smoking during or immediately prior to the　*g* test should not be permitted'. In a pamphlet which is in the box is this observation: 'A high concentration of tobacco smoke tends to colour the re-agent brown. Smoking during or immediately prior to the test should not therefore be permitted.'

I am left in no doubt, having read those two brief instructions from the manufacturers, that what they are saying is this, that a high concentration of tobacco smoke passed through the crystals into the bag is apt to turn the crystals brown. If the　*h* crystals turn brown, then it may be difficult to discover whether they simultaneously turn green, which is after all the outward and visible sign of excessive alcohol in the blood. So the manufacturers are saying this, and really no more than this: 'Since a high concentration of tobacco smoke tends to colour the re-agent brown, make sure that a high concentration of tobacco smoke is not allowed to go through the crystals into the bag.'

On the facts which I have stated it was submitted by the advocate for the respondent that he had no case to answer. Although the precise nature of his argument is not altogether clear from the case, what he must have been saying was, that by allowing the respondent to take a test so shortly after he had extinguished his cigar, there was a failure to comply with the instructions issued by the manufacturers. The argument must have been that on the facts of the present case the respondent *a*   was still smoking at a time which could be described as during or immediately prior to the test. The next step in the argument must have been that if the manufacturers' instructions were not meticulously adhered to, the test was vitiated, and if there was no valid test, then of course there could be no further proceedings.

The justices were referred, albeit I think a little briefly, to the opinion of Viscount Dilhorne in *Director of Public Prosecutions v Carey*[1]. That was another case about a

b   driver who had been smoking when stopped by the police with a view to his being subjected to a breath test, and their Lordships' speeches contain a great deal of extremely important and valuable material to assist in deciding the extent to which, and the manner in which, the manufacturers' instructions must be taken into account when deciding whether a valid breath test has been administered or not. Suffice it to say for present purposes that *Carey*[1] decides that mere proof of non-compliance

c   with the manufacturers' instructions does not of itself invalidate the test. It must be shown, in my judgment, that the failure to comply with the manufacturers' instructions, if failure there be, is a failure which could adversely affect the driver. If it is apparent that departure from the instructions could not affect the result of the test adversely to the driver, then no further reference to a failure to comply with the instructions need be made.

d   In the present instance the point had arisen in another case apart from *Carey*[1], *Darnell v Portal*[2]. There the driver of the motor car had been smoking prior to the imposition of the test. In the judgment given by myself[3] I turned to consider why the manufacturers make this recommendation in regard to smoking at all, because it seemed to me then, and it seems to me now, that one cannot construe the reference to smoking immediately prior to the test or during the test unless you know why

e   smoking can affect the test. I made the observation in *Darnell v Portal*[2] that the only reason why smoking should be regarded as relevant at all in my judgment would be because of the possibility that cigarette smoke might contaminate the sample and thus render it unreliable. I said[3]:

> *f*   'If that is the right approach, then in this case there was ample opportunity to clear his lungs between the stubbing out of the cigarette on the defendant's own evidence and the moment when the test was actually taken. It will be recalled that the parties moved to the police car, the breath test equipment was assembled, the test was taken, and that was all done on any view after the cigarette had been stubbed out in the defendant's ashtray.'

On the footing that after an interval of that kind, short though it was, the possi-

g   bility of smoke contaminating the sample had been eliminated, the case was sent back to the justices in order that they might continue the hearing.

What we were not told in *Darnell's* case[2] but have had pointed out to us today is the phrase which I have already read from the manufacturers' instructions explaining why smoking is a relevant factor in these matters, and it will be remembered that what the manufacturers say is this: 'A high concentration of tobacco smoke tends

h   to colour the re-agent brown'. That which I have guessed at in *Darnell's* case[2] is now clearly the real reason why smoking becomes a relevant factor, and in my judgment in considering what the manufacturers mean by saying that 'Smoking during or immediately prior to the test should not be permitted', one has to remember that that is the mischief which they are seeking to avoid.

Accordingly, as it seems to me, if in the individual case it is quite evident that the

j   volume of smoke left in the driver's lungs was not sufficient to be capable of being described as a high concentration, to borrow the words of the manufacturers, the fact that he had smoked prior to the test or at all becomes completely irrelevant.

---

1   [1969] 3 All ER 1662, [1970] AC 1072
2   [1972] RTR 483
3   [1972] RTR at 487

In the present instance it seems to me to be beyond argument that, when he stubbed
out his cigar whilst he was walking between the two cars, he then got into the back   *a*
seat of the police car and he then took the test, it is quite impossible to contend that
at that time there was the sort of residual concentration of tobacco smoke in his lungs
and mouth to create the difficulty which the manufacturers have referred to in
their instructions.

I very much hope that this case will set to rest any tendency to argue further on   *b*
the precise meaning of the phrase 'smoking during or immediately prior to the test',
and will discourage advocates appearing for defendants in circumstances of this kind
from putting forward this kind of argument when it is quite clear that at the time
when the test was taken there was insufficient tobacco smoke in the defendant's
lungs and mouth to permit of a high concentration of such smoke entering the test
bag. Only in those cases does it seem to me that a non-compliance with the manu-   *c*
facturers' regulations has occurred at all, and only in those circumstances would it
be appropriate to consider the more detailed instructions on this subject contained in
the speeches in *Carey's* case[1].

In this case, within the meaning of the phrase 'smoking during or immediately
prior to the taking of the test', I would say that the justices could not on the material
before them reach the conclusion that the appropriate concentration of smoke was   *d*
available. It seems to me that the whole reference to smoking is a false trail in this
case. A submission of no case should never have been made. It should not have been
acceded to. The appeal will have to be allowed and the case will go back to the justices
for them to continue the hearing.

MAIS J. I agree.   *e*

CROOM-JOHNSON J. I agree.

Appeal allowed.   *f*

Solicitors: *Norton & Hamilton*, Grantham (for the appellant); *Routh, Stacey & Co*,
agents for *Maples & Son*, Spalding (for the respondent).

Jacqueline Charles   Barrister.

g

1   [1969] 3 All ER 1662, [1970] AC 1072

a   # Robinson v Collins

CHANCERY DIVISION
PENNYCUICK V-C
16th JULY 1974

b   *Intestacy – Appropriation by personal representatives – Surviving spouse – Matrimonial home – Valuation – Date of valuation – Right of surviving spouse of intestate to require appropriation of matrimonial home in or towards satisfaction of spouse's interest in intestate's estate – Valuation of home for purpose of appropriation – Whether home to be valued at date of intestate's death or date of appropriation – Administration of Estates Act 1925, s 41 – Intestates' Estates Act 1952, Sch 2, para 1(1).*

c

Where the surviving husband or wife of an intestate exercises the power conferred by para 1(1)ᵃ of Sch 2 to the Intestates' Estates Act 1952 to require the personal representatives of the intestate, in the exercise of their powers under s 41ᵇ of the Administration of Estates Act 1925, to appropriate the intestate's interest in a dwelling-house in which the surviving husband or wife was resident when the intestate died, in or towards

d   satisfaction of any absolute interest of the husband or wife in the intestate's estate, the value at which the dwelling-house is to be appropriated for that purpose is the value thereof at the date of appropriation and not at the date of the intestate's death (see p 325 *d* to *f*, and p 326 *a* to *c*, post).
       Talbot v Talbot [1967] 2 All ER 920 distinguished.

e   **Notes**
For the right of the surviving spouse of an intestate to acquire the matrimonial home, see 16 Halsbury's Laws (3rd Edn) 397, 398, para 767.
       For statutory power of appropriation, see 16 Halsbury's Laws (3rd Edn) 372, para 721, and for cases on the subject, see 24 Digest (Repl) 645-648, *6373-6391*.
       For valuation for the purposes of appropriation, see 16 Halsbury's Laws (3rd Edn)

f   374, para 724.
       For the Administration of Estates Act 1925, s 41, see 13 Halsbury's Statutes (3rd Edn) 66.
       For the Intestates' Estates Act 1952, Sch 2, para 1, see 13 Halsbury's Statutes (3rd Edn) 130.

g   **Cases referred to in judgment**
Charteris, Re, Charteris v Biddulph [1917] 2 Ch 379, 86 LJCh 658, 117 LT 391, CA, 47 Digest (Repl) 369, *3309*.
Gollin's Declaration of Trust, Re, Turner v Williams [1969] 3 All ER 1591, [1969] 1 WLR 1858, Digest (Cont Vol C) 1048, *3192a*.
Talbot v Talbot [1967] 2 All ER 920, [1968] Ch 1, [1967] 3 WLR 438, CA, Digest (Cont Vol

h   C) 1060, *427a*.

Case also cited
Heath, Re, Heath v Widgeon [1907] 2 Ch 270.

j   **Adjourned summons**
By para 3 of an originating summons dated 27th November 1973, the plaintiff Carol Robinson ('the daughter'), an administratrix of the estate of Alfred Henry Robinson ('the intestate'), who died on 6th May 1972, and the intestate's only daughter, sought

---

a   Paragraph 1, so far as material, is set out at p 323 *j* to p 324 *a*, post
b   Section 41, so far as material, is set out at p 322 *j* to p 323 *b*, post

the determination by the court of the following question: whether on an appropriation by the personal representatives of the intestate's fee simple in 2 Shelton Gardens, *a*
Ruddington (the 'matrimonial home') in consequence of a requirement made by the
defendant, Mavis Joy Collins ('the widow'), the intestate's lawful widow and the other
administratrix of the intestate's estate, in exercise of the powers conferred on her by
para 1 of Sch 2 to the Intestates' Estates Act 1952, the value at which the matrimonial
home was to be appropriated in or towards satisfaction of the fixed sum of £8,750,
payable to the widow out of the intestate's residuary estate, was (a) the value at the *b*
date of the intestate's death, or (b) the value at the date on which the widow exercised
the right conferred on her under para 1 of Sch 2 to the 1952 Act, or (c) the value at the
date of appropriation, or (d) the value at some other and if so what date. The facts
are set out in the judgment.

J A Moncaster for the daughter.   *c*
Brian Parker for the widow.

PENNYCUICK V-C. This originating summons raises a single question as to the
terms on which a surviving spouse is entitled to acquire a matrimonial home on an
intestacy. The summons arises in the matter of the estate of Alfred Henry Collins, *d*
to whom I will refer as 'the intestate'. He died on 6th May 1972. He had been married
some two months earlier, that second marriage revoking a will it is said he had made in
favour of his only daughter. The intestate left surviving his second wife and
his daughter.
    His estate was sworn at £11,493 net. The exact figure is not important. The widow
had, under the law as it stood at the death of the intestate, a first charge of £8,750 on
the estate, the balance being held as to half for her for life, with remainder to the *e*
daughter and the second in trust for the daughter. The estate included a freehold
house, 2 Shelton Gardens, Ruddington, in the county of Nottingham, which was their
matrimonial home. The house was sworn for probate at £4,200. It is now stated to be
of the value of £8,000, or thereabouts.
    The short question is: at what value is the widow entitled to have that property *f*
appropriated towards satisfaction of her charge of £8,750? The daughter maintains
that the value will be the value of the property as at the date of appropriation. The
widow contends that the value is the value as at the date of death.
    There was considerable correspondence between the parties' solicitors before this
summons was issued, but a good deal of that correspondence was on matters which in
the event are not now relevant. The summons raises a single effective question,
which is in these terms: *g*

> 'THAT it may be determined whether upon any such appropriation as aforesaid
> [that is an appropriation of the house towards the £8,750] (whether already
> made or to be made) [I interpose to say that the appropriation has not in fact yet
> been made] the value at which the said dwellinghouse is to be appropriated in or
> towards satisfaction of the said fixed net sum is:—(a) the value thereof at the *h*
> date of the Intestate's death, or . . . (c) the value thereof at the date when the
> personal representatives appropriate the same . . .'

There are two other alternatives mentioned, for which neither party contends. It is
not necessary to refer further to the evidence filed in this summons. The question
before me is entirely one of law.   *j*
    It will be convenient at this stage to read the statutory provisions which are relevant
to the present question. The Administration of Estates Act 1925, s 41 provides:

> '(1) The personal representative may appropriate any part of the real or personal
> estate, including things in action, of the deceased in the actual condition or state
> of investment thereof at the time of appropriation in or towards satisfaction of

a any legacy bequeathed by the deceased, or of any other interest or share in his property, whether settled or not, as to the personal representative may seem just and reasonable, according to the respective rights of the persons interested in the property of the deceased ...

'(3) For the purposes of such appropriation, the personal representative may ascertain and fix the value of the respective parts of the real and personal estate and the liabilities of the deceased as he may think fit, and shall for that purpose *b* employ a duly qualified valuer in any case where such employment may be necessary; and may make any conveyance (including an assent) which may be requisite for giving effect to the appropriation ...'

Then s 46(1) of the 1925 Act, which has subsequently been replaced by a different provision, reads:

c
'The residuary estate of an intestate shall be distributed in the manner or be held on the trusts mentioned in this section, namely:—(i) If the intestate leaves a husband or wife (with or without issue) the surviving husband or wife shall take the personal chattels absolutely, and in addition the residuary estate of the intestate (other than the personal chattels) shall stand charged with the payment *d* of a net sum of one thousand pounds, free of death duties and costs [to provide the husband or wife with interest].'

The last-mentioned provision has been superseded twice: first by the Intestates' Estates Act 1952, s 1:

'(1) As respects a person dying intestate after the commencement of this Act *e* sections forty-six, forty-seven and forty-eight of the Administration of Estates Act, 1925 (hereafter in this Part of this Act referred to as the "principal Act"), shall have effect subject to the amendments set out in this section.

'(2) For paragraph (i) of subsection (1) of the said section forty-six (which relates to the disposition of the residuary estate of an intestate leaving a surviving spouse) there shall be substituted the following paragraph—"(i) If the intestate *f* leaves a husband or wife, then in accordance with the following Table: ... If the intestate ... (2) leaves issue ... the surviving husband or wife shall take the personal chattels absolutely and, in addition, the residuary estate of the intestate (other than the personal chattels) shall stand charged with the payment of a net sum of five thousand pounds, free of death duties and costs, to the surviving husband or wife with interest thereon ..."'

g
That section has again been superseded, but before leaving the 1952 Act I will refer to the section under which the surviving spouse has a right to acquire the matrimonial home. Section 5 of the 1952 Act provides:

'The Second Schedule to this Act shall have effect for enabling the surviving *h* husband or wife of a person dying intestate after the commencement of this Act to acquire the matrimonial home.'

Then para 1(1) of Sch 2 to the 1952 Act, which is headed 'Rights of Surviving Spouse as respects the Matrimonial Home', provides:

j
'Subject to the provisions of this Schedule, where the residuary estate of the intestate comprises an interest in a dwelling-house in which the surviving husband or wife was resident at the time of the intestate's death, the surviving husband or wife may require the personal representative, in exercise of the power conferred by section forty-one of the [Administration of Estates Act 1925] (and with due regard to the requirements of that section as to valuation) to appropriate the said interest in the dwelling-house in or towards satisfaction of any absolute

interest of the surviving husband or wife in the real and personal estate of the
intestate . . .'   *a*

Then paragraph 3(2):

'A notification in writing under paragraph (c) of the foregoing sub-paragraph
shall not be revocable except with the consent of the personal representative; but
the surviving husband or wife may require the personal representative to have
the said interest in the dwelling-house valued in accordance with section forty-   *b*
one of the principal Act and to inform him or her of the result of that valuation
before he or she decides whether to exercise the right.'

Paragraph 5:

'(1) Where the surviving husband or wife is one of two or more personal   *c*
representatives, the rule that a trustee may not be a purchaser of trust property
shall not prevent the surviving husband or wife from purchasing out of the estate
of the intestate an interest in a dwelling-house in which the surviving husband or
wife was resident at the time of the intestate's death.
'(2) The power of appropriation under section forty-one of the principal Act
shall include power to appropriate an interest in a dwelling-house in which the   *d*
surviving husband or wife was resident at the time of the intestate's death partly
in satisfaction of an interest of the surviving husband or wife in the real and personal estate of the intestate and partly in return for a payment of money by the
surviving husband or wife to the personal representative.'

Finally, the Family Provision Act 1966, s 1:

e

'(1) In the case of a person dying after the coming into force of this section,
section 46(1) of the Administration of Estates Act 1925, as amended by section 1
of the Intestates' Estates Act 1952 and set out in Schedule 1 to that Act, shall apply
as if the net sums charged by paragraph (i) on the residuary estate in favour of a
surviving husband or wife were as follows, that is to say,—(a) under paragraph
(2) of the Table (which charges a net sum of £5,000 where the intestate leaves   *f*
issue) a sum of £8,750 or of such larger amount as may from time to time be
fixed by order of the Lord Chancellor . . .'

£8,750 was the sum in force at the date of the intestate's death.
  Leaving aside the statutory provisions as to the matrimonial home, there can be no
doubt that where a personal representative exercises the statutory power of appropriation under s 41 of the 1925 Act he must do so at the value of the property appro-   *g*
priated as at the date of appropriation. See as to this the note in Wolstenholme and
Cherry[1]: 'The value of appropriated securities should be taken as at the of date
appropriation.'   The case there cited, Re Charteris[2], contained the statement by
Swinfen Eady LJ[3].

'Upon that proposition being communicated to the solicitors for the plaintiff   *h*
they objected to the appropriation. They pointed out that their client, Colonel
Richard Charteris, was entitled to have 230,000l in cash, or the value thereof, as at
the date of appropriation; that almost all the securities comprised in the list had
dropped in value since February 21, 1915, the date of the death, and some of them
considerably, and that if their client liked to invest in any of these securities he
should do so on the basis of present prices. In other words, they raised the point   *j*
that the value of the securities appropriated should be the value as at the date of

---

1 Conveyancing Statutes (13th Edn, 1972), vol 5, p 74
2 [1917] 2 Ch 379
3 [1917] 2 Ch at 386

appropriation, and not as at the date of the testatrix's death. In my opinion that contention was well founded; and upon that point being raised by the plaintiff's advisers the executors took the opinion of counsel with regard to the appropriation, and, having taken it, they sent a copy of it to the plaintiff's advisers.'

If further citation is needed on this point, see Re Gollin's Declaration of Trust[1], where Buckley J, said[2]:

'... I must treat the transfer which was made to the first defendant in 1947 as a transfer to her of property of a certain cash value, that is to say, the then existing value of the stocks transferred on account of her true interest in the fund.'

The point is sometimes put by treating the appropriation as a notional sale of the appropriated assets to the beneficiary, the legacy to the beneficiary being applied in discharge of the purchase price on the sale. This is a rule of administration too well-established to require further discussion.

The question, however, then arises whether a different date should be taken, namely the date of death instead of the date of appropriation, where the appropriation is made pursuant to an exercise by the surviving spouse of the statutory right conferred by Sch 2 to the 1952 Act. It seems to me that on the terms of that statutory provision the answer to this question is plainly in the negative. Schedule 2 to the 1952 Act imports the provision for appropriation contained in s 41 of the 1925 Act, and indeed adds the bracketed words 'and with due regard to requirements of that section as regards valuation'. The only distinction in this connection is that under the 1952 Act the spouse may mandatorily require the personal representative to exercise the power of appropriation, whereas under the 1925 Act the personal representative has a discretion whether to exercise the power or not. There is, however, no hint in Sch 2 to the 1952 Act that the appropriation is to be carried out on some basis different from that applicable in any other case where the personal representative makes an appropriation under s 41 of the 1925 Act and it seems to me that whatever is the appropriate date for valuing the appropriated assets under s 41 must equally be imported into an appropriation made pursuant to the requirement of the spouse under Sch 2 to the 1952 Act. That was the contention of counsel for the daughter and I accept it.

Counsel for the widow contended that, notwithstanding that in the ordinary case under s 41 of the 1925 Act, the value of the appropriated assets must be taken at the date of the appropriation, in this particular case of an appropriation under Sch 2 to the 1952 Act the value must be taken as at the date of death. He relied principally on the point that under Sch 2 the widow has a right to insist on an appropriation, and then he equated this position with that in which a beneficiary had an option to purchase an asset at the death of the testator or life tenant. He relied on Talbot v Talbot[3] in the Court of Appeal, which was the case of an option given by a testator to two of his sons to purchase the farms in which they lived together with some land which went with them 'at a reasonable valuation'. And it was held that the relevant date for the valuation was the date of death, because it was then that the rights of the option beneficiaries accrued: see Harman LJ[4]:

'The valuation is to be made, according to [the order appealed from], as at the death of the testator. There is no appeal about that, and it is justified, I feel, because the right to have the land by the exercise of the option accrued at that date ...'

---

1   [1969] 3 All ER 1591, [1969] 1 WLR 1858
2   [1969] 3 All ER at 1592, [1969] 1 WLR at 1861
3   [1967] 2 All ER 920, [1968] Ch 1
4   [1967] 2 All ER at 923, [1968] Ch at 13

It seems to me, however, that the short answer to that contention is that the 1952 Act did not confer on the surviving spouse an option to purchase. What the 1952 Act does, *a* read in conjunction with the 1925 Act, is to confer a right on the surviving spouse to have the matrimonial home appropriated in or towards satisfaction of a fixed sum charged on the estate, that fixed sum being in the nature of an absolute interest. That being the position, I can see no valid reason for departing from the general rule applicable to appropriation under s 41 of the 1925 Act. If Parliament had intended that the appropriation should take effect retrospectively as at the date of death, one would *b* have expected this result to be achieved by plain words. The words actually used are quite inept to achieve such a result. No injustice is involved in this conclusion. There is no reason that I can see why the widow rather than the other next-of-kin should benefit from rising house prices or indeed, in the contrary case, less familiar in the circumstances of today, suffer from a fall in house prices.

I conclude that I must answer the question in para 3 of the summons in accordance *c* with alternative (c), i e the value thereof at the date when the personal representatives appropriate the same.

Determination accordingly.

Solicitors: *Caporn, Campbell, Clare & Clare*, agents for *George Shelton & Co*, Hucknall *d* (for the daughter); *Peacock & Goddard*, agents for *H J Hallam & Co*, Nottingham (for the widow).

                                        Evelyn Budd Barrister.

e

Somerset County Council v Kingscott

QUEEN'S BENCH DIVISION
LORD WIDGERY CJ, MAIS AND CROOM-JOHNSON JJ   *f*
15th, 18th NOVEMBER 1974

Criminal law – Compensation – Compensation order – Children and young persons – Court's power to order parent or guardian to pay compensation instead of child or young person – Parent or guardian conducing to commission of offence by neglecting to exercise due care or control over child or young person – Local authority guardian of child – Test for determining g whether local authority guilty of neglect conducing to commission of offence – Child placed in care of local authority pursuant to care order – Authority placing child in community home – Home not a secure penal institution – Purpose of home to rehabilitate children – Child absconding from home and committing offence – Whether authority having conduced to commission of offence by neglecting to exercise due care or control of child – Children and Young Persons Act 1933, s 55 (as amended by the Criminal Justice Act 1972, s 64(1), Sch 5). *h*

Three boys, aged 12, 13 and 14, were committed to the care of the appellant, a local authority, under the Children and Young Persons Act 1969. The boys were required by the authority to reside at a community home. While at the home the boys absconded and committed certain offences of breaking and entering and stealing. The boys were charged and convicted of the offences and a large number of similar offences were *j* also taken into consideration. The justices gave each boy a conditional discharge so that he could return to the home. Thereupon the justices, in purported exercise of their powers under s 55(1)[a] of the Children and Young Persons Act 1933, considered

---

a Section 55, as amended and so far as material, is set out at p 330 *f* and *g*, post

whether the authority, as guardian of the boys, should be ordered to pay compensa-
a tion to the victims of the offences. They found that the home was not constructed as,
nor was it capable of being, a penal institution; that the chief aim of the home was the
rehabilitation of the boys sent there, but that 'the staff regard "protection of the
public" as an important part of their work'; and that the boys 'were cared for in a
proper and professional manner and in accordance with normally accepted practice
in institutions of this kind'. The justices concluded, however, that the authority had
b conduced to the commission of the offences by 'neglecting to exercise due care and
control over the boys', the reasons given for that conclusion being (i) that the boys had
committed the offences in question, (ii) that, on balance, the chief interest of the staff
at the home had been in the boys' rehabilitation 'to the detriment of the members of
the Public who had suffered from their depredations', and (iii) that the boys had been
allowed to play in the grounds of the home without being watched. Accordingly the
c justices ordered the authority to pay compensation. The authority appealed.

Held – In determining whether a local authority had been guilty of neglect conducing
to the commission of offences, within s 55(1) of the 1933 Act, the justices were required
to apply the same test as in the case of an individual parent or guardian, i e to determine, as a question of fact, whether in the light of the individual circumstances of each
d case, e g the disturbed character of the child in question, the authority had exercised a
proper degree of care and control. In particular the justices were bound to ask, not
whether the authority ought to have been provided with better facilities for controlling
absconders, but whether the authority had made a sensible and responsible use of
facilities which existed or which were in its power to provide (see p 332 *b* to *h* and
p 333 *g* and *h*, post).
e   (ii) The facts found by the justices could not possibly lead to the conclusion that the
local authority had been guilty of neglect conducing to the commission of the offences.
The mere fact that the offences had been committed could not support the conclusion
that the authority had been guilty of neglect; furthermore, since the home was not a
secure penal institution, the boys could not be kept under perpetual supervision, nor
was there material on which it could be held that the boys' escapes had been attributable
f to any breach of duty to the public on the part of the authority. Accordingly the
appeal would be allowed (see p 333 *b* to *h* and p 334 *e* to *g*, post).

Notes
For the court's power to order a parent or guardian to pay compensation, see 10
g Halsbury's Laws (3rd Edn) 516, para 940.
    For the Children and Young Persons Act 1933, s 55, see 17 Halsbury's Statutes (3rd
Edn) 473.

Case referred to in judgment
Dorset Yacht Co Ltd v Home Office [1969] 2 All ER 564, [1969] 2 QB 412, [1969] 2 WLR
h 1008, CA; *affd* [1970] 2 All ER 294, [1970] AC 1004, [1970] 2 WLR 1140, [1970] 1 Lloyd's
Rep 453, HL, Digest (Cont Vol C) 731, *133b*.

Cases also cited
R v Croydon Juvenile Court Justices, ex parte Croydon London Borough Council [1973] 1 All
ER 476, [1973] QB 426.
j *Somerset County Council v Brice* [1973] 3 All ER 438, [1973] 1 WLR 1169.

Case stated
This was an appeal by way of case stated by the justices for the county of Gloucestershire acting in and for the petty sessional division of the city of Gloucester in respect
of their adjudication as a magistrates' court sitting at Gloucester on 13th February 1974.

1. On 13th December 1973 an information was preferred by the respondent, William Herbert Stephen Kingscott, police inspector, against two boys, Andrew (aged *a* 13) and Ian (aged 12), that on 15th November 1973, having entered as trespassers the dwelling-house of John Thomas Allin at 17 Gratton Way, Hucclecote, in the county of Gloucester, they stole two cigarette lighters, an alarm clock, two torches, £10 in money and other property valued at £32·57 belonging to Mr Allin, contrary to s 9(1)(b) of the Theft Act 1968.

2. On 13th December 1973 an information was preferred by the respondent against *b* Andrew and Ian that on 18th November 1973, having entered as trespassers the dwelling-house of Sylvia Dilys Neale at 26 Church Lane, Barnwood, in the county of Gloucester, they stole a silver bracelet, a clock, a magnifying glass, £7 in money and other property valued at £24 belonging to Sylvia Neale, contrary to s 9(1)(b) of the 1968 Act.

3. On 31st December 1973 an information was preferred by the respondent against *c* a third boy, Michael (aged 14), and Ian that on 2nd December 1973, having entered as trespassers the dwelling-house of David Michael Blake at 70 Pickwick Road, Corsham, in the county of Wiltshire, they stole £13 in money, a gold chain and locket, a gold watch and other property valued at £106 belonging to Mr Blake, contrary to s 9(1)(b) of the 1968 Act.

4. On 31st December 1973 an information was preferred by the respondent against *d* Michael and Ian that on 2nd December 1973, having entered as trespassers the dwelling-house of Silvanus Arthur Harris, 12 Bradford Road, Corsham, in the county of Wiltshire, they stole a paper knife, a quantity of cigarettes and other property valued at £5·43 belonging to Mr Harris, contrary to s 9(1)(b) of the 1968 Act.

5. On 13th February 1974 the justices heard the information and found the following facts: (a) The informations were properly preferred and the three boys were guilty of *e* the offences contained therein. (b) Ian was guilty of a further 21 offences of burglary which he asked the justices to take into consideration when passing sentence on him. Andrew was similarly guilty of 15 further offences of burglary which he likewise asked the justices to take into consideration, and Michael was guilty of a further eight offences of burglary which he likewise asked the justices to take into consideration when passing sentence on him. (c) At all material times the appellant, Somerset *f* County Council, was the guardian of the three boys in respect of whom care orders had been made and the boys were required to reside at Eagle House School, Church Street, Bathford, in the county of Somerset, from which they had absconded on two occasions in November and December 1973 at the times when the various offences were committed. (d) Eagle House School was a community home controlled by the appellant and provided residential treatment for children in the care of local author- *g* ities from the south west region of England and Wales. Normal school education was provided for boys aged between nine and 15 years by experienced staff in which capacity one Maurice Dobbs had been continuously employed for 17 years, the last six of which as headmaster. (e) Boys who were admitted to Eagle House all exhibited serious signs of disturbed behaviour, and Ian, born on 14th October 1961, Andrew, born on 5th January 1960, and Michael, born on 24th October 1959, were all boys who *h* came to Eagle House from broken homes. (f) Ian first went to Eagle House in January 1973 following a care order made by the Gloucester city juvenile court, Andrew was made the subject of a care order in August 1972 and went to Eagle House in September of that year and Michael first went to Eagle House in March 1970 by virtue of an approved school order which became a care order in January 1971. He was discharged from the school in May 1972 and readmitted in June 1973. (g) Ian was the eldest of six *j* children who between them had three fathers. He had never been able to get on well with his current stepfather and having regard to his mother's preoccupation with her own problems and to other factors beyond his control, Ian had never had an effective mother or father figure from whom he could gain the securities and values so important to children of all ages. He therefore tended to act out his problems in the form of

delinquent behaviour and his abscondings were illustrations of that reaction. (h) Andrew
a was a child of divorced parents who found it hard to place faith in any adult. He had
been attending special schools since he was ten years of age. He had been the subject
of psychotherapy and had begun to form meaningful relationships with Eagle House.
(i) Michael's mother died when he was three and he was a sad and rootless child. The
children's home, in whose care he was after leaving Eagle House in 1972, found him
impossible to control and, when he returned to the school in June 1973, he was in a
b highly disturbed state. Thereafter some headway had been made with him. (j)
Eagle House was not constructed as, nor was it capable of being, a penal institution.
The aim of the school, which had Home Office approval, was to endeavour to make
the boys live as normally as possible, and any security of the kind invoked for example
at Borstal institutions or prisons would have had a deleterious effect on their long-
term treatment. The school comprised a Georgian house and converted outbuildings
c bounded at the front by a six foot wall and gate. At the back some three acres of
sloping grounds were not securely fenced. The non-teaching staff of eight (of whom
three were on duty at any one time) aimed to permit the 25 boys to live as normally as
possible and to make them feel emotionally secure so that they did not desire to
abscond. The staff did not overtly oversee the boys' every activity and it was considered desirable that they should from time to time be allowed to play in the grounds
d without their being watched. (k) Although the chief aim of the school was the rehabilitation of the boys, the staff regarded the 'protection of the public' as an important part of their work. If a boy absconded or failed to return from home leave the
police were notified. And when, in November and December 1973, Ian, Andrew and
Michael absconded, the police were immediately notified. (l) The boys were cared
for in a proper and professional manner and in accordance with normally accepted
e practice in institutions of that kind. (m) The Home Office would not have considered
transferring the boys to a community home which contained more secure provision.
The staff of Eagle House carried out their instructions and duties as defined above.
The records of the three boys were not exceptional for schools of that kind.
6. It was contended on behalf of the appellant that the court should impose sentences on the three boys which would make possible their immediate return to Eagle
f House and that as the appellant had not conduced to the commission of the offences
by neglecting to exercise due care and/or control over the children they should not be
ordered to pay damages.
7. The justices were referred to *Dorset Yacht Co Ltd v Home Office*[1].
8. The respondent did not reply to the appellant's contentions.
9. The justices, being of the opinion that it was desirable to allow the three boys to
g return to Eagle House, granted each of them a conditional discharge for a period of
two years. The justices were also of the opinion that the appellant had conduced to the
commission of the offences by neglecting to exercise due care and control over the
boys. The reasons given by the justices for that opinion were as follows:

'(i) On 15th and 18th November, Andrew and Ian were in Gloucester and
h stealing. On 2nd December 1973, Michael and Ian were in Corsham and stealing.
Each boy admitted other offences and wished them to be taken into consideration.
These facts impelled us to the conclusion that the Appellants were not exercising
due care and control in their capacity as guardians of these boys.
'(ii) As directed in *Dorset Yacht Co Ltd v Home Office*[1] we weighed on the one
hand the public interest of protecting neighbours and their property from the
depradations of escaping trainees and on the other hand the public interest of
j promoting their rehabilitation, and were of the opinion that in these cases the
chief interest of the staff of the Appellants' school had been in their rehabilitation
to the detriment of the members of the Public who had suffered from their
depradations.
'(iii) The boys were allowed to play in the grounds without being watched.'

1 [1969] 2 All ER 564, [1969] 2 QB 412

10. Accordingly the justices ordered the appellant to pay the total sum of £134·49 by way of compensation to the occupiers of the burgled premises.   *a*

Donald Farquharson QC and *C T Drew* for the appellant.
R Ashton for the respondent.

LORD WIDGERY CJ. This is an appeal by case stated by the justices for the   *b* county of Gloucester sitting as a magistrates' court in Gloucester on 13th February 1974. On that occasion there were before them a number of informations laid against three youths, who I will call Andrew, now aged 14, Ian, now aged 13, and Michael, now aged 15. The informations related to a variety of offences concerned with breaking and entering and stealing on which these young men had been engaged.

At the material time, by which I mean at the time when the offences were com-   *c* mitted, all three youths were subject to care orders, made under the Children and Young Persons Act 1969, which had placed each of the individuals in the care of the appellant. At the relevant time again they were required to reside at a community home called Eagle House School, which is described in the case as being controlled by the appellant.

Having found all the charges proved, and having taken into account a large number   *d* of similar offences, the justices gave each of the youths a conditional discharge so that they could return to Eagle House. But in purported exercise of their powers under s 55 of the Children and Young Persons Act 1933, as amended, the justices also ordered the appellant council to pay a total sum of £134·49 by way of compensation to the occupiers of the burgled premises, and it is in regard to that order that the appeal is brought to this court today.   *e*

Section 55(1), as amended, and omitting irrelevant words, reads as follows:

'Where a child or young person is charged with any offence for the commission of which a fine . . . or a compensation order may be made . . . if the court is of opinion that the case would be best met by the imposition of a fine . . . or the making of such an order, whether with or without any other punishment, the   *f* court may in any case, and shall if the offender is a child, order that the fine, compensation . . . be paid by the parent or guardian of the child or young person instead of by the child or young person, unless the court is satisfied that the parent or guardian cannot be found or that he has not conduced to the commission of the offence by neglecting to exercise due care or control of the child or young person.'   *g*

The facts so far as relevant are these. As I have already said, the boys at the material time were at Eagle House School, and it is not disputed before us that the appellant council was the guardian of these boys for the purposes of s 55. The boys had been at Eagle House for some time. They absconded on two occasions in November and December 1973, and it was during these abscondings that the offences were committed.   *h*

At Eagle House the appellant provides residential treatment for children in the care of the local authorities from the south west region of England and Wales. Normal school education is provided for boys aged between nine and 15 years by experienced staff in which capacity one Maurice Dobbs has been continuously employed for 17 years, the last six of which as headmaster.

The boys who are admitted to Eagle House all exhibit serious signs of disturbed   *j* behaviour, and each of the three to whom I have referred came from a broken home. The justices then go on to give a good deal of detail about the history of these indivi- dual boys, about the family difficulties from which they have suffered before they were taken into the care of the appellant, and the justices refer to such facts as that Andrew is the child of divorced parents, who finds it hard to place faith in any adult.

I do not find it necessary to deal with those parts of the justices' findings in further
a   detail.

In para 5(i) of their findings, however, one comes to something directly relevant to
the present appeal. The justices find that Eagle House is not constructed as nor is it
capable of being a penal institution. The aim of the school, which has Home Office
approval, is to endeavour to make the boys live as normally as possible, and any
security of the kind invoked for example at Borstal institutions or prison would have
b   a deleterious effect on their long-term treatment. These, I stress, are all findings of
fact by the justices. In sub-para (i) they go on to say:

> 'The School comprises a Georgian house and converted outbuildings which are
> bounded at the front by a six foot wall and gate. At the back some three acres of
> sloping grounds are not securely fenced. The non-teaching staff of eight (of whom
c   three are on duty at any one time) aim to permit the twenty-five boys to live as
> normally as possible and to make them feel emotionally secure so that they do
> not desire to abscond. The staff do not overtly oversee the boys' every activity and
> it is considered desirable that they should from time to time be allowed to play
> in the grounds without their being watched.'

d   In sub-para (k) they say:

> 'Although the chief aim of the school is the rehabilitation of the boys, the
> staff regard "protection of the public" as an important part of their work. If
> a boy absconds or fails to return from home leave the police are notified.'

In the instant case, when the boys absconded, the police were immediately notified.
The justices further say in sub-para (1): 'The boys were cared for in a proper and
e   professional manner and in accordance with normally accepted practice in institutions
of this kind.' They make some reference to the fact that the Home Office would not
have contemplated transferring the boys to more secure accommodation, but I
hesitate to pay any attention to that because it is not very clear how the justices
have reached a conclusion of that kind.

As I have said, it is not disputed that the appellant was the guardian of these three
f   boys for the purposes of s 55 of the 1933 Act, and the justices, when they came to their
conclusions on this matter—and when I say 'their conclusions' I mean their conclusions on the issue as opposed to their findings of fact—they gave the following
judgment:

> 'We were also of the opinion that the Appellants had for the following reasons
g   conduced to the commission of the said offences by neglecting to exercise due
> care and control over the said boys.'

They then give their reasons:

> '(i) On 15th and 18th November, Andrew and Ian were in Gloucester and
> stealing. On 2nd December 1973, Michael and Ian were in Corsham and stealing.
h   Each boy admitted other offences and wished them to be taken into consideration.
> These facts impelled us to the conclusion that the Appellants were not exercising
> due care and control in their capacity as guardians of these boys.
> '(ii) As directed in the *Dorset Yacht Co Ltd v Home Office*[1] we weighed on the one
> hand the public interest of protecting neighbours and their property from the
> depradations of escaping trainees and on the other hand the public interest of
j   promoting their rehabilitation, and were of the opinion that in these cases the
> chief interest of the staff of the Appellants' school had been in their rehabilitation
> to the detriment of the members of the Public who had suffered from their
> depradations.
> '(iii) The boys were allowed to play in the grounds without being watched.'

1   [1969] 2 All ER 564, [1969] 2 QB 412

The appellant says that these reasons are unsupported by evidence, and show that the justices had misdirected themselves as to the nature of the authority referred *a* to and as to the meaning of 'neglect' in the section.

When the section was first passed in 1933, Parliament was concerned principally with the parent or guardian who was a private individual. Applying the section to those circumstances, the question which arose involved no problem with the construction of the section and no vestige of any legal difficulties at all, because in relation to a private individual the question posed for the justices in s 55 is a very homely one *b* for which they are admirably equipped to deal, because the justices had only to ask themselves whether the particular parent or guardian had shown neglect in the due care of the child, and whether that neglect had conduced to the offences. The justices would have applied what one might describe as 'the good parent standards' and asked themselves, using their ordinary common sense knowledge of how children are brought up, whether there had been neglect of the kind specified in the statute *c* or not. I cannot see how in those happy days any vestige of a legal issue or problem could possibly have arisen out of the section.

I have no doubt that in applying the section to a private individual the justices should, and would, have regard to the individual circumstances of the case. By that I mean justices, in good sense, would recognise that a widow controlling six young children could hardly achieve the same standard of supervision which is possible in *d* a single-child family with both parents alive. That is only an example of the fact that in applying the principle of the good parent test they would have to have regard to the difficulties or advantages of the individual parent.

When one turns to consider the multiplying number of instances in which the parent or guardian referred to is not an individual but is a local authority, as in the present instance, I think that exactly the same principle must be applied. *e*

Counsel for the appellant has helpfully taken us through all the relevant legislation, but the net result, as it seems to me, is that the authority is given the power and duty necessary to enable it to bring up the child as a good parent would bring it up, and, therefore, as I have said, I think the principle is the same whatever the character of the parent or guardian in question. But, of course, as in the case of the private individual parent, the local authority must again have its responsibility tested in the *f* light of the individual circumstances of the case. For example, the degree of control necessary should reflect such things as the disturbed character of the children, the potential danger to the public if they absconded and the facilities available at the school for the purpose of keeping them under control.

This does not in any way depart from what I have said that the principle is the same. It merely emphasises that you must apply the principle to the circumstances *g* prevailing at the time. In such cases the justices should in my judgment bear in mind that high policy decisions, such as whether the perimeter should consist of unclimbable fences or not, are matters for the Home Office and not for them. They should not find the authority guilty of neglect merely because they think that greater facilities for controlling absconders might have been provided, or should have been provided, by a higher authority. The justices are primarily concerned with whether *h* the school authorities have made a sensible and responsible use of the facilities existing on the ground or within their powers to provide.

In the present case the justices' findings of fact are not critical of the school. I come to their reasons in a moment, but their findings of fact, which I have read, are not in the main critical. They say that the school has an experienced headmaster and apparently adequate staff. The findings of fact recognise both that the school cannot *j* be made a penal institution and that the staff show regard for the protection of the public. Even so, if the justices had merely said that they were not satisfied about the matters mentioned in s 55 of the 1933 Act, and given no reasons, it may be that we should not have been able to disturb those conclusions. In fact, however, the justices have given reasons, and if these will not bear examination, then their conclusions cannot stand.

I turn, therefore, to examine the reasons. The first, it will be remembered, merely
a records the fact that Andrew and Ian were in Gloucester on two days, and Michael
and Ian were in Corsham on one day, as the justices put it, 'stealing'. To say that
that shows that there was neglect in control is really to beg the question. What
the justices have to consider is whether overall there was neglect which caused these
boys to be out absconding, stealing, and in my judgment they cannot reach that conclusion merely by repeating, as it were, the symptoms of the disease. If there had
b been numerous abscondings by the same children, of course different factors might
arise, but I do not see how the simple fact that these children had absconded in
itself answers the question of whether there was neglect conducive to their absconding.

The third reason again one can dismiss quite briefly. It was that the boys were
allowed to play in the grounds without being watched. One asks oneself: 'Why
shouldn't they?' Bearing in mind that this was not, and never attempted to be, a
c fully secure establishment and the fences at the back of the house were not unclimbable, unless the boys were being watched every moment of their lives, the opportunity
to abscond was bound to exist. Again the justices had to ask themselves whether
there was neglect in this instance, and the fact that they were not always under
supervision day and night does not seem to me to be an adequate reason, because
that standard seems intolerably and impossibly high when regard is had to the
d justices' own reason.

Finally, they refer in their second reason to *Dorset Yacht Co Ltd v Home Office*[1].
This is a case which is concerned with the obligation of the authorities responsible
for penal institutions towards the public generally. Although it is helpful to remind
oneself, as counsel for the appellant has reminded us, of the principles there applicable,
I do not find that it helps very much in this case.

e In this case we are concerned with whether there was neglect conducing to the
particular offences, and in view of the findings of fact I find the reasoning given in
the justices' second reason to be contradictory to those findings. They find, as I
have pointed out, that this could not be made a penal institution. They find that
the staff had the protection of the public in mind. There seems to me to be absolutely no material in the case, when one has regard to the justices' findings of fact,
f which could possibly make sense, if I may use the phrase, of the conclusions which
they reached in the second paragraph.

Accordingly, in this case, which I confess I have not found an altogether easy one,
I think that the submissions of the appellant should prevail and that the appeal
should be allowed and the compensation orders quashed.

g **MAIS J.** I agree. I find the findings of fact by the justices somewhat inconsistent;
and their reasons for stating that the appellant neglected to exercise due care and
control over these particular boys are not to my mind supported by the facts as
found.

h **CROOM-JOHNSON J.** I also agree. I would like to add one or two points.
The justices have a mandatory duty in the case of children, and discretionary in the
case of young persons, under s 55 of the Children and Young Persons Act 1933 to
order the guardian to pay a fine, compensation order or costs unless they are satisfied
that the guardian has not conduced to the commission of the offence by neglecting
to exercise due care or control of the child or young person. 'Control' was inserted
j into the section by amendment in 1969: Children and Young Persons Act 1969,
Sch 5.

Under the Children and Young Persons Act 1969, the guardian, in this case the
appellant, Somerset County Council, does have a duty to the child in its care or

---

1   [1969] 2 All ER 564, [1969] 2 QB 412

under its control. The duty under s 55 of the 1933 Act I think can be described as the
duty owed to the public on the part of the justices to see whether due care and control *a*
has been exercised, which to me implies also that there must be a duty in the guardian to do likewise. The duties which the guardian has may, of course, conflict,
particularly in cases where the guardian is a public authority, like the appellant.

For the good of the child, there must be some risks taken to let it develop its
personality or its sense of responsibility. On the other hand, one can visualise
cases where the duty to the child is discharged, but not that which is owed towards *b*
the public.

The test by which the duty to the public is measured may well be a strict one,
certainly in those cases where a child is not a first offender when he comes before the
magistrates' court for the relevant offence. But in my view it would not of itself
be enough, when consideration for making an order under s 55 is before the justices,
that the public authority, being the guardian, should simply be able to say to the *c*
justices: 'This was a normally run school, and well run of its type.' I think that the
evidence would have to go further and satisfy the justices that the particular child
which has been before the court for this offence has also been sufficiently supervised,
for if the child is very disturbed, or prone to violence or other criminal acts, some form
of strict supervision may prove to be necessary. This kind of evidence, one may think,
is easy to give and difficult to challenge, but this is the kind of instance in which *d*
assistance should be given to the court where the justices have to make up their minds
whether to make an order under s 55. I would hope that the prosecution in a case
like this would certainly regard it as part of their duty to help the court by testing the
evidence that was given, as in this case, where a good deal of evidence appears to have
been given as to the way in which the school was run and its physical layout and
protection and so on. I hope that the prosecution would not say that this was *e*
a matter only going to penalty which did not concern them.

I entirely agree with Lord Widgery CJ's analysis of the reasons which the justices
gave. So far as the findings of fact are concerned, there was one other finding which
I should like to refer to. After the finding that the staff regards protection of the
public as an important part of their work, the justices went on to make another
finding, saying that 'The staff of Eagle House carried out their instructions and *f*
duties' as defined in para 5(k).

They went on and said: 'The records of the three boys are not exceptional for
schools of this kind.' I think that finding was sufficient to justify saying here that
there was before the court in fact the necessary material that the three boys concerned did not require any exceptional form of supervision and, therefore, on the
general supervision which was given to the boys at the school, that the appellant *g*
had not conduced to the commission of the offences by neglecting to exercise due
control of the three boys.

I agree with Lord Widgery CJ's judgment as to the allowing of this appeal.

Appeal allowed. Compensation orders quashed.

h

Solicitors: *Sharpe, Pritchard & Co*, agents for *S E Harwood*, Taunton (for the appellant);
G R Archer, Chief Prosecuting Solicitor for Gloucestershire (for the respondent).

Lea Josse Barrister.

a Raymond Lyons & Co Ltd v Metropolitan Police Commissioner

QUEEN'S BENCH DIVISION
LORD WIDGERY CJ, THOMPSON AND MAIS JJ
b 27th NOVEMBER 1974

Police – Property in possession of police – Delivery to owner – Power of magistrates' court to order property to be delivered to person appearing to court to be owner – Owner – Meaning – Application by person having good title save against true owner by virtue of possession – True owner untraceable – Whether applicant 'owner' – Police (Property) Act 1897, s 1(1)
c (as amended by the Criminal Justice Act 1972, s 58).

A youth went to a jewellers' shop, produced a ring and asked for it to be valued. The shop assistant and the manager suspected that the ring had been stolen and they told the youth to come back later after it had been valued. The youth gave a name and address, but never returned. On valuation the ring was found to be worth £3,500.
d The jewellers informed the police and handed the ring over to them for the purpose of their investigations into the suspected offence. The owner of the ring could not be traced. Accordingly, the jewellers applied under s 1(1)*a* of the Police (Property) Act 1897 for an order that the police should deliver the ring to them, claiming that they were the owners, within s 1(1), in that when the ring came into their possession they had acquired a title to it which was good against the whole world save for the true
e owner.

Held – The word 'owner' in s 1(1) was to be given its ordinary popular meaning, i e the person who was entitled to the goods in question and not simply the person who happened to have them in his hands at any given moment. The jewellers were not the owners in that sense and accordingly were not entitled to an order under
f s 1(1) (see p 338 *b c* and *h*, post).
  Per Curiam. The summary procedure under the 1897 Act is not intended to be used in cases involving difficult questions on title but only in straightforward cases where there is no difficulty of law and the matter is clear (see p 338 *e* to *h*, post).

Notes
g For property in possession of the police, see 30 Halsbury's Laws (3rd Edn) 90-91, para 152.
  For the Police (Property) Act 1897, s 1, see 25 Halsbury's Statutes (3rd Edn) 280.

Cases cited in argument
Armory v Delamirie (1722) 1 Stra 505.
h Marsh v Police Commissioners [1944] 2 All ER 392, [1945] KB 43, CA.
R (Curtis) v Louth County Justices (1916) 50 ILT 191.

Case stated
This was an appeal by way of a case stated by justices for the South East London Commission Area acting in and for the petty sessional division of Croydon in respect of
j their adjudication as a magistrates' court sitting at Croydon on 12th July 1974.
  On 7th June 1974 a complaint was preferred by the appellants, Raymond Lyons & Co Ltd, against the respondent, the Metropolitan Police Commissioner, that certain property, namely, a three stone diamond ring, had come into the possession of the

---

a Section 1(1), as amended and so far as material, is set out at p 337 *d*, post

metropolitan police in connection with their investigation of a suspected offence and
the appellants applied for an order for the delivery of the ring to them.   *a*

The justices found the following facts. (a) At all material times the appellants
carried on business as retail jewellers at a shop at 1030 Upper Level, Whitgift Centre,
Croydon. (b) At lunch time on 29th November 1973 a youth entered the shop and asked
for a valuation of a ring which he produced and handed to a shop assistant. Subsequently
it was ascertained that the ring was worth about £3,500. The youth stated that he
was Mr Peter of 6 Godding Avenue, Wallington, Surrey. The shop assistant and her   *b*
manager reasonably suspected that the ring was stolen, because of the youth's age
and the high value of the ring. The youth was told that it was necessary to retain the
ring to value it. He was given a receipt for the ring which he left with the appellants.
He was asked to return in about an hour. (c) The manager immediately telephoned
the police station, Croydon, and shortly after two police officers arrived and waited
for the youth. The police officers kept observation in the shop for three days but the   *c*
youth never returned. On 29th November the ring was handed to the police officers
by the appellants and thereafter it remained in the possession of the metropolitan
police. (d) Police officers made enquiries at 6 Godding Avenue, Wallington and
ascertained that the youth did not live there and was not known there. (e) The justices
were satisfied that the ring had come into the possession of the metropolitan police in
connection with their investigation of a suspected offence. (f) The police circulated   *d*
information about the ring to police stations and to insurance companies, and on 15th
December 1973 it was shown in a television programme entitled 'Police Five', but no
third party established ownership or pursued a claim to ownership. (g) The employees
of the appellants, namely their manager and shop assistant, had acted with com-
mendable propriety and were instrumental in taking the ring from the youth and
placing it in the possession of the metropolitan police; despite this conduct on the   *e*
part of the appellants' employees, the appellants did not appear to be the owners of
the ring. The owner was some other person who could not be ascertained. (h) If the
regulations with respect to unclaimed property made by the Secretary of State
pursuant to s 2(1) of the Police (Property) Act 1897 were applied to the case, the
consequences were likely to be as follows: (i) the ring would be sold by public auction
in about January 1975; (ii) the appellants would be notified of the time and place   *f*
of the auction; and (iii) half of the net proceeds of sale would be paid to the appellants.

It was contended by the appellants that they were the owners of the ring within
the meaning of s 1(1) of the 1897 Act.

The appellants did not appear to the justices to be the owners of the ring and as the
owner could not be ascertained the order which seemed meet was to direct that the
ring should be dealt with in accordance with the regulations with respect to unclaimed   *g*
property.

Giles Harrap for the appellants.
Raymond Sturgess for the respondent.

h

LORD WIDGERY CJ. This is an appeal by case stated by justices for the South
East London Commission Area sitting as a magistrates' court at Croydon on 12th
July 1974.

I pause to observe, before going into the merits of the case, the relevant dates
which are somewhat more encouraging than some in this court. The complaint was
preferred on 7th June, the hearing was on 12th July, the case was stated on 21st   *j*
October and actually comes before the court on 27th November, which is a time scale
very much nearer to that which we hope to achieve in future than we have often
achieved in the past. But enough of that and back to the substance of the matter.

Before the justices on the date in question was a complaint by Raymond Lyons &
Co Ltd, who sought from the justices an order under the Police Property Act 1897,

whereby there should be delivered up to them a ring, the immediate history of
a which had been as follows.

On 29th November 1973 a youth came into the shop of Messrs Lyons, who are
jewellers, produced a ring and asked for a valuation. It was subsequently discovered
that the ring was a valuable one worth £3,500. The youth gave a name and address,
but the shop assistant and the manager, both suspecting that he had not come by
the ring by honest means, told him that he would have to come back shortly after
b the ring had been valued, and on his leaving the shop they rang up the police. In fact
the young man never returned and has never been seen again, and the ring in the
hands of the appellants remained there until they handed it over to the police that
same day on the footing that the police needed it for the purpose of their enquiries.
The justices say, and there is no doubt about it, that the ring came into the possession
of the metropolitan police in connection with their investigation of a suspected
c offence.

Efforts have been made to get the true owner of the ring to come forward and
claim it, but all has been to no avail. So the ring is physically in the possession of the
police, and the proceedings below were designed to enable the jewellers to obtain
possession from the police.

d If one looks at s 1(1) of the Police (Property) Act 1897 it is in these terms:

> 'Where any property has come into the possession of the police in connexion
> with their investigation of a suspected offence . . . a court of summary jurisdiction
> may, on application either by an officer of police or by a claimant of the property,
> make an order for the delivery of the property to the person appearing to the
> magistrate or court to be the owner thereof, or, if the owner cannot be ascer-
e > tained, make such order with respect to the property as to the magistrate or
> court may seem meet.'

Section 1(2) preserves the right of any person for a period of six months to bring a
civil action to assert any rights of property which he may have in goods which have
reached the hands of the police in the circumstances stated in s 1(1). So that even if
an attempt to obtain possession via the magistrates' court is unsuccessful, a person
f claiming to be the true owner of the goods has his civil remedy as long as he pursues
it without unreasonable delay. Section 2(1) of the 1897 Act goes on to provide:

> 'A Secretary of State may make regulations for the disposal of property which
> has come into the possession of the police under the circumstances mentioned in
> this Act in cases where the owner of the property has not been ascertained and
g > no order of a competent court has been made with respect thereto.'

Thus as a final provision there is the power to make regulations which will determine
the issue in cases where the justices are unable to do it under the terms of s 1.

The argument below was extremely short. On behalf of the appellants it was
said that they were the owners at the relevant time for the purposes of s 1. The argu-
h ment in a little more detail was to the effect that when the ring came into their
possession they had a good title to it as against the whole world save for the true
owner, and that possession of that kind valid against the world except the true owner
is ownership for the purposes of s 1. The justices equally clearly rejected that
argument and based their conclusions on such rejection because they say:

j > 'The appellants did not appear to us to be the owner of the ring and as the owner
> could not be ascertained the order which seemed meet was to direct that the
> ring should be dealt with in accordance with the said regulations with respect
> to unclaimed property.'

So the difference, as it were, between the argument put forward by the appellants
today and the justices' conclusions is very clear to see. Counsel contends that the

appellants were the owners for the purposes of the section; the justices thought they
were not. The only question, as I see it, which we really have to decide is which of   *a*
those views is the right one.

I have listened to counsel for the appellants' argument and would readily accept
that in certain circumstances the word 'owner' can have a meaning different from the
ordinary popular meaning. The popular meaning of 'owner' is a person who is
entitled to the goods in question, a person whose goods they are, not simply the
person who happens to have them in his hands at any given moment. I have little   *b*
doubt that in s 1 'owner' is to be given that ordinary popular meaning, which lay
justices would naturally give to it, using the word in the ordinary layman's sense. I
think that that conclusion is underlined by the fact that the draftsman is distinguishing
between 'possession' and 'ownership' because the section, it will be remembered,
began with the phrase 'where any property has come into the possession of the
police'.   *c*

The justices in this case asked themselves whether the jewellers, who had received
custody of this ring in the manner which I have described, were to be regarded as
owners for the purpose of the section. They thought not; I think they were right. I
do not think that the appellants were owners in the ordinary popular sense at all.

Once one reaches that conclusion, then it is clear to me that this appeal will have to
be dismissed, but I must say one further word in answer to counsel for the appellants'   *d*
argument, where he recommended our giving the word 'owner' a wider meaning in
order that this summary process for the return of goods in police possession would be
more widely used.

The view which I take of this case will perhaps prevent any unnecessary or unacceptable wider user of the section. But I think it worthwhile pointing out that
there is a very close parallel between this summary procedure and the summary   *e*
procedure now exercised by all criminal courts under the Criminal Justice Act 1972
to make compensation to injured persons as part of the disposal of a criminal case.
It has been said over and over again that the latter summary procedure is not to be
used in difficult cases involving tricky questions of title or large sums of money. It is
much better that the civil courts should handle disputes of that kind. What is intended
both in regard to compensation orders and orders under the Police (Property) Act   *f*
1897 in my judgment is that in straightforward, simple cases where there is no difficulty of law and the matter is clear, the justices should be able to make a decision
without involving the expense of civil proceedings. But I would actively discourage
them from attempting to use the procedure of the Act in cases which involve a real
issue of law or any real difficulty in determining whether a particular person is or is
not the owner. I would dismiss this appeal.   *g*

THOMPSON J. I agree.

MAIS J. I agree.
  h
Appeal dismissed.

Solicitors: *David Alterman & Sewell* (for the appellants); *Solicitor, Metropolitan Police.*

N P Metcalfe Esq   Barrister.

Fletcher v London (Metropolis) Licensing Planning Committee

COURT OF APPEAL, CIVIL DIVISION   Reversed HL [1975] 2 All ER 916
LORD DENNING MR, CAIRNS LJ AND SIR JOHN PENNYCUICK
25th OCTOBER 1974

Licensing – Certificate of non-objection – Grant of certificate by licensing planning committee – Duty of committee to try to secure that number nature and distribution of licensed premises accord with local requirements – Nature of licensed premises – Meaning – Club premises – Admission to membership of club – Delay between application for and admission to membership – Application for licence containing condition that delay should be 24 hours – Committee refusing to grant certificate unless period increased to 48 hours – Whether period of delay affecting nature of licensed premises – Whether committee having jurisdiction to refuse certificate on that ground – Licensing Act 1964, s 119(2).

The applicant was employed by a company which ran numerous clubs, each of which was licensed for gaming limited to the playing of bingo under the Gaming Act 1968. One of the clubs, which was also licensed to sell intoxicating liquor, was situated in London which was a licensing planning area within Part VII of the Licensing Act 1964. The licence for that club was in the name of the applicant. The terms of the licence included a restriction against the admission of new members without a delay of at least two days from the date of their application for membership. The applicant wished to obtain a new licence limiting the delay after application for membership to 24 hours, the minimum required for bingo clubs by s 20(5) of the 1968 Act. The London (Metropolis) Licensing Planning Committee, however, refused to grant a certificate of non-objection to a new licence containing such a condition. The applicant appealed to the Divisional Court for an order of mandamus directing the committee to hear and determine the application according to law, on the ground that the committee had considered matters outside its jurisdiction under s 119(2)[a] of the 1964 Act. The Divisional Court granted the order sought, holding that the difference between a delay of 24 hours and one of two days was a matter affecting the conduct and not the 'nature' of the licensed premises within s 119(2). The committee appealed.

Held – It was not possible to draw a distinction between the nature and the conduct of licensed premises for the conduct of the premises might well affect their nature. The length of time between application for and admission to membership of a licensed club might have a direct effect on the type of members who were admitted to the club and therefore on its nature. Accordingly the matter was one which was within the purview of the committee under s 119(2). The appeal would therefore be allowed (see p 341 *h* to p 342 *a c* and *f* to p 343 *a*, post).

R v London (Metropolis) Licensing Planning Committee, ex parte Baker [1970] 3 All ER 269 doubted.

Notes
For general duties of licensing planning committees, see 22 Halsbury's Laws (3rd Edn) 643, para 1353.

For the Licensing Act 1964, s 119, see 17 Halsbury's Statutes (3rd Edn) 1168.

Case referred to in judgments
R v London (Metropolis) Licensing Planning Committee, ex parte Baker [1970] 3 All ER 269, [1971] 2 QB 226, [1970] 3 WLR 758, 134 JP 662, DC, 30 Digest (Reissue) 21, *132.*

---

a   Section 119(2) is set out at p 341 *d*, post

Case also cited

Kennedy v Birmingham Licensing Planning Committee [1972] 2 All ER 305, sub nom *R v* **a**
Birmingham Licensing Planning Committee, ex parte Kennedy [1972] 2 QB 140, CA.

Appeal

By a motion dated 17th July 1973 the applicant, James Stephen Grant Fletcher, applied
for an order of mandamus directing the London (Metropolis) Licensing Planning
Committee ('the committee') to hear and determine according to law the application **b**
of the applicant for the grant to him of a certificate of non-objection to the grant of
a new on-licence in respect of premises known as the Top Rank Club situated at 60
Wandsworth High Street, SW18. On 4th February 1974 the Divisional Court of the
Queen's Bench Division (Lord Widgery CJ, Boreham and May JJ) granted the order
sought. The committee appealed. The facts are set out in the judgment of Lord
Denning MR. **c**

David Tudor Price for the committee.
Jarlath Finney for the applicant.

LORD DENNING MR. Rank Leisure Services Ltd run about 50 clubs. One of
them is the Top Rank Club at 60 Wandsworth High Street, London. It has a licence **d**
for the playing of bingo. If a person wants to become a member—so as to play bingo
—he must apply in person in writing and at least 24 hours must elapse before he is
admitted. That is a statutory provision contained in the Gaming Act 1968, ss 12(3)
and 20(5). For other gaming clubs—for games other than bingo—the time is 48 hours.

Now the company want to be able to sell intoxicating liquor in this bingo club. For
this purpose it has to have a licence under the Licensing Act 1964. It wishes the 24 hour **e**
rule to apply to this licence also, so that a person can, after waiting 24 hours, not only
play bingo but also drink intoxicating liquor.

If this club were granted an intoxicating liquor licence—with only a 24 hour condition—it would be an entirely new departure for clubs in London. The practice in
London for the last 70 years has been that, in order to supply intoxicating liquor, a
club must have a rule that there is a '48 hour' interval between nomination of a **f**
member and his admission. This practice has been reinforced by statute: see s 28(1)(*g*)
of the Licensing Act 1902, s 95(1)(*g*) of the Licensing Act 1910, s 144(1)(*g*) of the Licensing
Act 1953, and s 41 of the Licensing Act 1964. But in the present case the Top Rank
Club seek to break down that practice so far as regards bingo clubs. They wish to
obtain justices' licenses for their bingo clubs with a '24 hour' condition instead of a '48
hour' condition. Outside London they have been successful in getting '24 hour' **g**
conditions on licenses for bingo clubs. But in London they have not so far been
successful.

It is only since 1961 that a club has been enabled to hold a justices' licence. But so
far as London is concerned, a club has to pass a preliminary test before it can even
apply for a justices' licence. It has to go before a special committee called the licensing
planning committee. This is because London is a licensing planning area within Part **h**
VII of the Licensing Act 1964. This committee has the task of considering the applications for justices' licenses and seeing whether they should be objected to or not. If
the committee objects to the grant of a licence, that is the end of the matter. The
applicant cannot get a justices' licence at all. If the committee does not object, it
grants a certificate of non-objection. Armed with that certificate, the applicant has
to go before the licensing justices. They will then grant or refuse a licence as they **j**
think fit and subject to such conditions as they think fit.

In this case the club has only got as far as the preliminary test. It applied to the
committee for a certificate of non-objection. The committee said that it was
unwilling to grant a certificate unless the applicant was ready to accept the 'usual'
club conditions. These were:

'1. Intoxicating liquor may be sold only to members of the Club meeting at
the within mentioned premises for consumption by those members and their
bona fide guests.

'2. No person shall be admitted to membership of the said Club without an
interval of at least 2 days between nomination or application for membership
and admission . . .

'3. No "Off" Sales.'

So the 'usual' conditions include a 'two-day' interval. The committee was prepared
to give to the bingo club a certificate of non-objection if the applicant accepted that
'two-day' interval. But otherwise it would not grant the applicant a certificate.
The Top Rank Club challenge this rule. They say that the committee has gone
outside its powers. It has no right, it is said, to require a 'two-day' condition.

The powers and duties of the committee are to be found in the 1964 Act. Section
119(2) says:

'It shall be the duty of every licensing planning committee to review the
circumstances of its area and to try to secure, after such consultation and negotiation as it may think desirable, and by the exercise of the powers conferred on it
by this Part of this Act, that the number, nature and distribution of licensed
premises in the area, the accommodation provided in them and the facilities
given in them for obtaining food, accord with local requirements, regard being
had in particular to any redevelopment or proposed redevelopment of the area.'

The Top Rank Club submits that the 'two-day' rule is not the concern of the committee. They say that it does not affect the 'nature' of licensed premises; and that it
only affects the 'conduct' of persons within it; and that on that account it does not
come within the purview of the committee. They rely on the decision of the Divisional
Court in *R v London (Metropolis) Licensing Planning Committee, ex parte Baker*[1]. That
case concerned the Warner Theatre at Leicester Square. That is a cinema. The
committee wanted the manager to accept a condition that no intoxicating liquor
would be sold when the premises were being used for continuous performance. In
other words, the committee was agreeable to liquor being sold during an interval,
but not during continuous performance. The Divisional Court held that the committee had no right to suggest any such condition. Lord Parker CJ said[2]:

'For my part try as may be I am quite unable to see that such a matter had got
anything to do with the number, the nature, or the distribution of licensed
premises . . . It is not a matter going to the nature of the premises but going to
the conduct of those premises, something which is, as it seems to me, entirely a
matter for the licensing justices and quite extraneous to the considerations and
duties of the licensing planning committee.'

In the present case Lord Widgery CJ applied that direction to the present case. He
held that the '24 hour' or '48 hour' rule was a matter which did not affect the nature
of the licensed premises, but only the conduct of it. He held that the committee was
not entitled to take it into account.

I am afraid that I take a different view from the Divisional Court in those two cases.
I do not think it is possible to draw a distinction between the 'nature' of the licensed
premises and the 'conduct' of them. A club may get its nature—its character—from
the way it is conducted. If it admits anyone to membership on application—without
any waiting period—it may become the haunt of casual passers-by and strangers. If
it only admits to membership after a two day interval, it will attract the steady
inhabitants of the place and their friends. If it admits on an entrance fee of 1s, it will

---

1   [1970] 3 All ER 269, [1971] 2 QB 226
2   [1970] 3 All ER at 272, [1971] 2 QB at 229

have a different nature from what it would on an entrance fee of £5. Such matters seem to me to affect the nature of the licensed premises and to be within the purview *a* of the committee. I find myself in entire agreement with the reasons given by the chairman, Judge Cassels. He said:

'It was our view that whereas it was within the applicant's rights to have only a 24 hour interval as qualifying time for Bingo, separate and distinct considerations arose if the applicant sought in addition a Justices' Club licence to supply intoxi- *b* cating liquor to members and their guests. It seemed to us that the nature of the licensed premises was affected by a diminution of the usual waiting period in the case of licensed clubs.'

I must say that seems to me a very sensible interpretation. I think the committee was entitled to take the view it did. I would therefore allow the appeal and reject the *c* application for mandamus.

CAIRNS LJ. I agree that the appeal should be allowed. Like Lord Denning MR I have some doubt as to the correctness of the decision in *R v London (Metropolis) Licensing Planning Committee, ex parte Baker*[1], but whether or not that case was rightly *d* decided, I am quite satisfied that in this case the committee was entitled to treat the matter which was in issue here as a matter affecting the nature of the premises and therefore that it was entitled to refuse to grant the certificate of non-objection. Counsel for the applicant has pointed out that this club had had a licence for the supply of alcoholic liquor to members for some time, and that the only new feature that was being introduced was a change in the rules under which the time to elapse *e* between the application for membership and admission to membership was 24 hours instead of 48 hours; and he says that that is not a change in the nature of the premises. Counsel contends that in connection with this matter of the times between applica- tion and admission to membership the only thing that should properly be taken into account was whether it was a genuine club or not. I am not of that opinion. I take the view that a club which has what I may call the 24 hour condition is a club of a different nature from that which has the 48 hour condition. I therefore form the *f* opinion that the decision of the Divisional Court here was wrong and this appeal should be allowed accordingly.

SIR JOHN PENNYCUICK. I too would allow this appeal. The Divisional Court based its decision entirely on the view that the committee, in considering the nature *g* of these premises, took into account as a factor, namely, the difference between 24 and 48 hours, as the qualifying time for admission of a member, which was extraneous in that it related to the conduct rather than the nature of the premises. It seems to me that that is putting an unduly narrow meaning on the word 'nature'. This word 'nature' is one of wide import. Admittedly it is not in the present context confined to the physical condition of the premises; but extends, at any rate to some extent, to the *h* character of the activities carried on on those premises. It was, however, contended that the word relates only to certain limited categories of those activities, in particular on or off licence, what liquor is supplied on the premises, whether the premises are open to the public or to members only. But I do not think one should stop at that point in considering the nature of the premises. The nature of the premises must depend more generally on the kind of activities carried on on the premises; and it *j* seems to me that one important and relevant factor in considering those activities is the type of members who are admitted. The type of member may vary very con- siderably according to period of admission, e g whether it is 24 or 48 hours. That

---

1   [1970] 3 All ER 269, [1971] 2 QB 226

becomes apparent if one considers a qualifying period of one hour only. I think the
a length of this qualifying period is a relevant factor in considering the nature of the
premises.

Appeal allowed. Leave to appeal to the House of Lords refused.

b Solicitors: *Sharpe, Pritchard & Co* (for the committee); *Routh, Stacey, Pengelly & Boulton* (for the applicant).

M G Hammett Esq   Barrister.

c

Rukat v Rukat

COURT OF APPEAL, CIVIL DIVISION
d MEGAW, LAWTON AND ORMROD LJJ
24th, 25th OCTOBER 1974

Divorce – Separation – Five year separation – Refusal – Grave financial or other hardship – Hardship other than financial hardship – Whether necessary to establish that hardship would be grave – Divorce Reform Act 1969, s 4.

e
The husband, a Pole, and the wife, a Sicilian, were married in Southern Italy in
March 1946. Both were of the Roman Catholic faith. Shortly after the marriage they
came to England where their daughter was born in May 1947. In December 1947 the
wife returned to Sicily with the daughter intending to return later but the husband
wrote telling her not to come back as he had fallen in love with another woman.
f The parties did not cohabit after that date. In February 1970 the husband's mistress
died and the wife came to England with the intention of reconstituting the marriage.
She obtained work in a hospital and continued in that employment thereafter. The
wife failed to effect a reconciliation and in September 1972 the husband presented a
petition for divorce under s 2(1)(e)[a] of the Divorce Reform Act 1969 relying on five
years' separation. The wife filed an answer opposing the grant of a decree under
g s 4[b] of the 1969 Act on the ground that she would suffer grave hardship if the marriage
were dissolved. The allegation of hardship was based on religious and social grounds.
During the 25 years that the wife had lived with her parents in Sicily she had kept up
the pretence that the marriage was subsisting. The trial judge found that the wife's
belief that she would not find it possible to go back to Sicily because of the hostile
attitude which would be adopted towards her if she were divorced was a sincere
h belief but he also found that there would be no greater hardship, inconvenience or
social distress to the wife in respect of a decree of divorce than there had been over
all the years in relation to what must have been known to anybody who had any
interest in the wife, i e that she had in fact for many years been living apart from her
husband. Accordingly he granted the husband a decree nisi finding that no grave
hardship had been established by the wife. On appeal the wife contended that, on
j the true construction of s 4, where a respondent sought to establish that she would
suffer hardship other than financial hardship in the event of a decree being granted,
it was not necessary to show that the hardship would be grave.

---

a Section 2(1), so far as material, is set out at p 344 *j*, post
b Section 4, so far as material, is set out at p 345 *a* to *d*, post

Held – The adjective 'grave' in the phrase 'grave financial or other hardship' in s 4
applied not only to financial but also to other hardship. In all the circumstances *a*
the judge was fully entitled to come to the conclusion that the wife had failed to
establish that she would suffer grave hardship if a decree were granted. Accordingly
the appeal would be dismissed (see p 345 *g* and *h*, p 350 *j* to p 351 *a*, p 352 *f* and p
353 *d*, post).

Notes   *b*
For the refusal of a decree on the ground of hardship, see Supplement to 12 Halsbury's
Laws (3rd Edn) para 437A, 6, and for cases on the subject, see 27(1) Digest (Reissue)
361, 362, *2638-2644.*
        For the Divorce Reform Act 1969, ss 2 and 4, see 40 Halsbury's Statutes (3rd Edn)
770, 773.
        As from 1st January 1974, ss 2 and 4 of the 1969 Act have been replaced by ss 1 and 5 *c*
of the Matrimonial Causes Act 1973.

Cases referred to in judgments
Dorrell v Dorrell [1972] 3 All ER 343, [1972] 1 WLR 1087.
Parghi v Parghi [1973] The Times, 8th May, 4 Fam Law 82.
Parker v Parker [1972] 1 All ER 410, [1972] Fam 116, [1972] 2 WLR 21.   *d*

Cases also cited
Allan v Allan (1973) 4 Fam Law 83.
Banik v Banik [1973] 3 All ER 45, [1973] 1 WLR 860, CA.
Brickell v Brickell [1973] 3 All ER 508, [1973] 3 WLR 602, CA.
Magor and St Mellons Rural District Council v Newport Corporation [1951] 2 All ER 839, *e*
        [1952] AC 189, HL.
Mathias v Mathias [1972] 3 All ER 1, [1972] Fam 287, CA.

Appeal
This was an appeal by the wife against the order of Hollings J made on 22nd February
1974 whereby he granted the husband a decree nisi of divorce under s 2(1)(e) of the *f*
Divorce Reform Act 1969. The facts are set out in the judgment of Megaw LJ.

S Seuffert QC and *Valerie Pearlman* for the wife.
Julian Priest QC and *Andre de Moller* for the husband.

MEGAW LJ. This is an appeal from an order of Hollings J made on 22nd February *g*
1974 by which he granted a decree nisi of divorce to the husband. The wife appeals
against that decree nisi of divorce and asks that this court should set it aside. The
issue which arises on the appeal stems from provisions of the Divorce Reform Act
1969, now included in the Matrimonial Causes Act 1973. It is desirable that I should
at the outset read the two provisions of that Act which are relevant to the appeal. *h*
Section 1 provides:

> 'After the commencement of this Act the sole ground on which a petition for
> divorce may be presented to the court by either party to a marriage shall be that
> the marriage has broken down irretrievably.'

Section 2(1) provides: *j*

> 'The court hearing a petition for divorce shall not hold the marriage to have
> broken down irretrievably unless the petitioner satisfies the court of one or
> more of the following facts, that is to say— . . . (e) that the parties to the marriage
> have lived apart for a continuous period of at least five years immediately
> preceding the presentation of the petition.'

Then comes s 4 (now s 5 of the 1973 Act). Subsection (1) reads:

> 'The respondent to a petition for divorce in which the petitioner alleges any such fact as is mentioned in paragraph (e) of section 2(1) of this Act may oppose the grant of a decree nisi on the ground that the dissolution of the marriage will result in grave financial or other hardship to him and that it would in all the circumstances be wrong to dissolve the marriage.'

Subsection (2) provides:

> 'Where the grant of a decree nisi is opposed by virtue of this section, then,—(a) if the court is satisfied that the only fact mentioned in the said section 2(1) on which the petitioner is entitled to rely in support of his petition is that mentioned in the said paragraph (e), and (b) if apart from this section it would grant a decree nisi, the court shall consider all the circumstances, including the conduct of the parties to the marriage and the interests of those parties and of any children or other persons concerned, and if the court is of opinion that the dissolution of the marriage will result in grave financial or other hardship to the respondent and that it would in all the circumstances be wrong to dissolve the marriage it shall dismiss the petition.'

The petition of divorce by the husband in the present case alleged, and alleged only, grounds set out in s 2(1)(e) of the 1969 Act. In consequence, the provisions of s 4 of that Act became relevant. As matters have developed, the only issue which remains is whether the learned judge ought, under the provisions of s 4, to have dismissed the petition on the ground that the granting of the decree would have resulted in grave other hardship to the wife and that in all the circumstances it would be wrong to dissolve the marriage.

I shall deal immediately with the only question of construction of the Act which has been raised. I can deal with it independently of the facts, to which I shall refer in a moment. Counsel for the wife, with the leave of this court, has amended the grounds set out in his notice of appeal to include the ground that, on the true construction of s 4(1) and (2) of the 1969 Act, the adjective 'grave' in the phrase 'grave financial or other hardship' applies only to *financial* and not to *other* hardship. That submission was not put forward in the court below. The learned judge was invited to deal and did deal with the matter on the basis that, on the true construction of s 4, the adjective 'grave' applied to 'other' hardship as well as to 'financial' hardship. For myself, I am satisfied that there is no doubt whatever, on the true construction of the section, that the adjective 'grave' should be treated as applying, not merely to financial but also to other hardship. It was so decided by Cumming-Bruce J in *Parker v Parker*[1]. It may be that the expression of view there by the judge was obiter. Whether or not it was obiter, it is not, of course, binding on this court. There is no subsequent decision, either of this court or any other court, which gives any reason to cast doubt on the view there expressed by Cumming-Bruce J. In my judgment it is plainly right, as a matter of ordinary construction, that the phrase 'will result in grave financial or other hardship' cannot, taking full account of the context, be treated as meaning 'will result in grave financial hardship or will result in other hardship which is not necessarily grave'. I therefore proceed on the basis that the learned judge was right in the criterion which he applied in his judgment in the court below, which indeed was at that stage wholly unchallenged. Before the defence of s 4 is available, where it is not a question of financial hardship that is in issue, the court must be satisfied that there is shown grave other hardship; and in addition the court must be satisfied that in all the circumstances, even if there be grave other hardship, it would be wrong to dissolve the marriage.

---

1 [1972] 1 All ER 410, [1972] Fam 116

I shall now set out the relevant facts out of which this litigation arises. The wife is
an Italian lady. When I say that, I am not expressing any view as to what her nation-   **a**
ality, in the strict sense of the word, is at the moment because we have had no evidence or information whatsoever on that point. It is, however, plain that she was
born as an Italian in Italy, in that part of Italy which is the island of Sicily. On 3rd
March 1946 she married the husband at Loreto, in Southern Italy. She married in a
Roman Catholic church. Both parties were of that faith. The husband was a member
of the Polish Forces, born in Poland; he was serving with General Anders's Forces in   **b**
Italy, and no doubt it was there that the parties had met. A short time after the
marriage the parties came to England. The husband was with the Polish Resettlement
Corps. In May 1947, in England, a daughter was born.

In December 1947, after that relatively short stay in England, the wife returned to
her home in Palermo, in Sicily, where her parents live. She took the daughter with
her. When she had gone to Italy she had apparently understood that it was only for a   **c**
temporary separation, but the husband thereafter told his wife not to come back.
The husband told the wife (I suppose by correspondence) that he had fallen in love
with another woman.

In 1953 the husband presented a petition in England for dissolution of the marriage.
The wife, having come to hear of the petition, managed to trace where her husband
was then living in England, and she came to England for the first time since she had   **d**
gone back to Italy in December 1947. She saw her husband. She persuaded him to
abandon the divorce petition. Her evidence was that when she saw her husband he
indicated that his love for her was rekindling and that he was minded to have her back
in order that the marriage might be re-established as a proper marriage, with the
husband and wife living together; but he wished to have, as he told his wife, a short
time in which, quietly and decently, to get rid of the woman with whom he had been   **e**
living, and so he suggested that his wife should return to Italy and come back with the
child in the spring. The wife went back to Sicily, hoping to return in the spring. Then
came a letter from the husband in which he said that he did not love her any more.
Thereafter for a period he sent her some instalments of money, but that stopped
about the year 1960.

So the years went on until 1970. The husband was living in England; the wife was   **f**
living in Sicily. In 1970 the wife started proceedings in England under s 22 of the
Matrimonial Causes Act 1965 (as it then was), asking for maintenance. She says that
the reason why she took that step was that her daughter was then at the stage of
going to a university and she thought it right that she should have money from her
husband to help in that respect. Nothing came of those proceedings. In February
1970, apparently, the husband's mistress died.   **g**

In May 1972 the wife came back to England again. She came back to try to re-
constitute the marriage. After about 1½ months in this country she took work in a
hospital and, as I understand it, she has continued in that work since then, continuing
to live in this country. She failed to persuade her husband towards a reconciliation.
In September 1972 the husband started proceedings under s 2(1)(e) of the Divorce
Reform Act 1969. At first those proceedings were undefended, but ultimately the   **h**
wife, with leave, filed an answer to the petition, relying on s 4 of the 1969 Act, the
provisions of which I have already read. The amended answer asserted:

'9. That the [husband] well knew and knows that the [wife] finds the prospect
of divorce an anathema to her on religious and moral grounds in that she is a
Roman Catholic.   **j**
'10. She further says that because of the social structure of the area in which
she lives in Italy and has always lived a divorce would cause serious repercussions
as to her position and that of the child of the family.
'11. That if a decree of divorce is pronounced she would not be accepted in her
community in Sicily, that she will be unable to return to live in Sicily where her

a   property and where her parents and child live and further that the position of
    the child of the family and any grandchildren would be jeopardised.'

At the hearing before Hollings J, a somewhat unusual course was followed. When it
came to the defence, instead of the wife giving evidence first, counsel said that she
proposed to take the unusual course of calling first another witness. That course was
acceded to by the learned judge, and the first witness for the wife was called. That
b   witness was Father Rossi. Let me say at once, in view of certain comments that I
shall have to make on the evidence, that there is no suggestion, and could be no
suggestion, of any sort against the integrity of Father Rossi, or any suggestion that he
was not trying in every possible way to do his duty in helping the court by his evidence.
The evidence which he was invited to give, and which he did his best to give, was
evidence relating to social conditions in Italy, and particularly in Sicily. It was directed
c   towards supporting the contentions, which I have already read, set out in the wife's
answer. Father Rossi did give such evidence, some of it somewhat dramatic, in
relation to what might happen in Sicily if the wife were divorced by the husband and
if that divorce became known. It was, for example, suggested that in such cases in
Sicily it might be that indignant relatives of the wife might go so far as to shoot the
husband.

d   I do not propose to go in any detail into the evidence given by Father Rossi, because
it emerged that he, though no doubt he was Italian-born and no doubt he had lived
for a substantial period in Italy, had left Italy in 1949 to go to Africa, that he had been
in Africa more or less continuously until 1970, and that then he had come to England,
and apparently his residence had been in England since then. True, during his time
in Africa, and no doubt during his time in England, he had gone back to Italy on not
e   infrequent occasions; but it was perfectly clear that he had not had his residence in
Italy, in the sense of any habitual residence, since 1949, a quarter of a century before
he was called to give evidence of social conditions in Italy. But it went further than
that. The essence of the evidence that he was invited to give was in relation to conditions in Sicily; and one of the things which he put forward in his evidence was that
Sicily was substantially different in its social conditions and outlook even from
f   Southern Italy. It emerged that Father Rossi had never in his life been in Sicily.

In those circumstances, it is perhaps not surprising that the learned judge felt it
difficult to attach any great weight to the evidence of Father Rossi, and that indeed
is clear from what the learned judge said before he reviewed the evidence given by
Father Rossi in the judgment.

Further, since Father Rossi was called to give evidence before the wife had given
g   her evidence, his evidence could not be related to any factual matters which might
subsequently emerge on the wife's examination and cross-examination.

As a result of the evidence of Father Rossi, it would seem that the learned judge
was anxious that there should be evidence of Italian law, because questions had arisen
about Italian legislation regarding divorce. The relevance of that, I suppose, would be
said to be that, if the Italian law contains provisions for divorce that were, at any rate
h   broadly, comparable to the provisions of the English legislation with which we are
here concerned, it might be somewhat surprising if the wife would be regarded as a
social outcast in Sicily as a result of a divorce having been granted in England on
legislation which is comparable with the law prevailing in Italy. However that may
be, as a result a witness, expert in Italian law, was called on behalf of the husband.
He was Mr Wall, who is a practising member of the English Bar and who, according
j   to his qualifications, quite clearly has experience in Italian law. He has chambers in
Milan. He undoubtedly has visited Italy on frequent occasions. He is conversant with
Italian law. He has been in Sicily on more than one occasion. The evidence which Mr
Wall gave on Italian law was related to the divorce law, and he proved (and I do not
think there was any challenge to it) that, I think it was in 1970, the Italian legislature
had enacted a law there. According to Mr Wall, that legislation provided for divorce

on broadly the same grounds as those with which we are here concerned in English
law, namely, the existence of de facto separation for a period of years. The period of *a*
years which, according to Mr Wall, was broadly the relevant period was some five
years. However, when Mr Wall was giving his evidence he was cross-examined and
asked questions thereafter by the learned judge in relation, not to Italian law, but to
Italian social conditions, as to such matters as the likelihood that persons in Palermo
would discover the existence of an English decree of divorce and what the consequences would be if they did. Again, with very great respect, I find difficulty—and *b*
this is no criticism whatever of Mr Wall, who was doing his best to answer questions
that were put to him—in seeing how that evidence could be of very much weight or
assistance.

The learned judge, it is right to say, did, I think, find himself able to gain some
assistance from the evidence of Mr Wall. In his judgment, the learned judge, having
reviewed at considerable length the evidence given by Mr Wall, dealt with the ques- *c*
tion to what extent would a 'stigma' attaching to a wife because of a divorce be
increased as compared with the 'stigma', whatever it might be, that would attach
to her because she had in fact been separated from her husband for many years. The
learned judge's view on that, based on what he was told by Mr Wall, was this:

'He said that given the facts of this case he would not say that there is a significant increase in the effect of the result of divorce upon [the wife], though possibly *d*
there would be some increase.'

The evidence of the wife, called, as I say, after these two witnesses had been called,
was given through an interpreter. That no doubt was necessary. No doubt the wife
had difficulty in understanding or speaking the English language. It is, I think,
unfortunate that the evidence as given through the interpreter was not evidence *e*
directly translated, and it seems to me, in reading that evidence, that there was at
any rate the possibility of misunderstanding arising. In the ordinary way, when an
interpreter has to be used, counsel's questions ought to be directed to the witness
as though there were no interpreter there, in the form of words which would be used
to a witness who was going to answer in English, and should not be directed to the
interpreter, referring to the witness as 'he' or 'she'; and the witness's answer ought to *f*
be given by the interpreter interpreting the answer directly as given: where the first
person is used by the witness, in the first person—not, 'She [in this case] did so-and-so',
or, 'She thought so-and-so', but to translate the answer of the witness 'I', which no
doubt is the form in which the witness gave it in the Italian language. I do think that
there is a real danger that some confusion may have arisen here. But there is nothing,
unfortunately, that we can do about that at this stage. *g*

In the evidence given by the wife, after she had described the events which I have
summarised in relation to the history of the marriage, she went on to deal in her
examination-in-chief with the problems to which reference was made in her answer.
I think it would be desirable here to read the whole of the relevant passage in her
evidence relating to that matter in examination-in-chief:

'Q. Mrs Rukat, how old are your parents now? A. 76 her father, 72 her mother. *h*
[That, of course, is the answer as given by the interpreter.]
'Q. Do they know you are separated from your husband? [There is no answer
recorded immediately to that question. The learned judge said:] I would have
thought the answer could have been Yes or No to this question.'

It is apparent, therefore, that what happened was that the witness was giving a
lengthy answer to the interpreter and the learned judge, before that answer was *j*
perhaps completed and before it was interpreted, had intervened to say: 'Well,
cannot she answer in the first instance "Yes" or "No"?' The judge having said that—
we do not know, of course, from the transcript whether there was further communication from the interpreter to the wife, or further answer by the wife to the interpreter
—the next thing that is recorded is:

a

'A. The answer is No. The answer is Yes and No. They do understand there is something but she reckons it is such a tragedy for them at their age to admit separation complete fully that she has always done her best to hide it from them, but they do feel there is something.'

The evidence goes on:

b

'Q. [by the learned judge] If there was a divorce would she tell her parents? A. She thinks she might; she feels she would be forced to tell them; she would have to tell them, but it would be the end for them.'

Then, after an adjournment—the wife, not surprisingly, feeling something of a strain—the examination was resumed by counsel for the wife. She goes on:

c

'Q. Mrs Rukat, I am sorry to have to ask you this but what would your parents think about a divorce? A. She says her parents know she is perfectly blameless but even so the suffering on their part would be tremendous.

'Q. What about if a divorce is made against her in England, what effect would that have on her daughter? A. Her daughter knows as well as her parents do that she is absolutely innocent of this thing but even so it would be a great shock

d

to her and she would also lose all of the love she has for her father because she, the daughter, has hope herself that in the last moment things could get better.

'Q. Is your daughter married? A. Yes.

'Q. Would a divorce have any effect on any grandchildren that might be born? A. She says technically yes but it would have bad repercussions not even on her daughter's children [I think that must be, 'not only on her daughter's children']

e

but on her husband because he is starting now to become a magistrate and this sort of thing can be damaging in that part of the world.

'Q. What about the position if a divorce is made against her with her friends? A. She prefers to die in England.

'Q. [the judge] Rather than? A. Go back a divorced woman.

'Q. [counsel for the wife] What effect would she think a divorce would have on

f

her friends; would they accept her or not? A. For her friends as well as for her relatives she would be a woman full of guilt.

'Q. [the judge] A guilty woman? A. A guilty woman, a very guilty woman.

'Q. She would be considered a guilty woman? A. Yes.

'Q. [counsel for the wife] Has she told people in Sicily that she and her husband have in fact been separated for 26 years? A. She has been a good actress.

g

'Q. [the judge] She has been a good actress meaning what? A. She says that in as much as she has always hidden the situation; if you want to hear the whole story of how she managed to cover up you can hear it. [Then counsel for the wife said:] I do not propose to ask that, my Lord. [Then the wife was asked what her religion was, and the answer was:] Roman Catholic.

'Q. And your husband? A. Roman Catholic.

'Q. In the time in which you lived together did you and he follow the Roman

h

Catholic religion? A. Yes.

'Q. Were you both devout Roman Catholics? A. Yes, they were devout Catholics and the local priest was their greatest friend.

'Q. [the judge] This is in England? A. In England, a Polish priest.'

j

The learned judge, in dealing with the wife's evidence, accepted fully and entirely her honesty and sincerity as a witness. He paid high tribute more than once to the wife. It is sufficient for that purpose, I think, if I read a passage which appears in the transcript of the judgment:

'. . . substantially in every case where there is a conflict between the evidence of the [husband] and the [wife] I prefer the evidence of the [wife]. While I am dealing with this aspect let me say this. I have found her throughout this case a most sincere woman who has quite evidently not only been seeking to tell me *a* the truth about the facts but also seeking to tell the truth about her emotions and the effect of various matters on her and her friends and relations.'

On the basis of that evidence, which I have tried to summarise in that way and which the learned judge summarised much more fully, what conclusions did the learned judge come to that are relevant on the question of 'grave other hardship'? *b* As I understand his judgment, the conclusion to which he came was, in effect: 'I fully accept the sincerity of the wife. I fully accept that at the moment she feels that if this decree of divorce were made absolute she would not feel it right or possible to go back to Sicily because of the attitude that would be adopted towards her there.' The learned judge had accepted, as I understand it, that that is an honest statement of her attitude, reflected in the answer I have read that she would die in England. On *c* the other hand, the learned judge has held that the evidence as to the reality of those fears or apprehensions is, if I may put it this way, hopelessly weak. There is really in the evidence no basis or substance for the suggestion, either that anybody in Palermo or Sicily would be likely to know about the decree of divorce or that, if they did know, after she had explained that this was a decree which involved no fault on her part whatever, these fears or apprehensions that she had as to the social conditions that *d* would apply in Palermo could really have any substance. Moreover, the learned judge has taken the view that there is no reason why there should be substantially any greater hardship or inconvenience or social distress to the wife in respect of the decree of divorce, if it be made, than there has been over all the years in relation to what must have been known to anybody in Palermo who had any interest in the wife: that is, that she has in fact for many many years been living apart from her husband, *e* he in England, she in Sicily. The learned judge, I think, was entitled on the evidence, such as it was, to come to the conclusion that there would be no substantial increase in any social distress by reason of the one as compared with the other, and that is even on the assumption that the fact that the wife had been divorced became known in Italy. But why should it become known? We have here no evidence whatever as to whether or not this English decree would, as a matter of Italian law, be given effect to in Italian *f* law and, therefore, whether there would be any legal consequences of any sort on the status of one who was living in Italy. Moreover, as appears from the evidence which I have read, the wife, according to her own evidence, which the judge has accepted as entirely truthful, has sought to conceal from her parents over all these 25 years the fact that something had gone wrong with the marriage. There is no reason offered in the evidence why that concealment, which has been with some degree of success *g* applied to the fact of separation, should not equally be applied to the fact of the divorce. The wife's evidence (I need not read the passage again) as to what she would feel obliged to do, if a decree of divorce were pronounced, in relation to telling her parents, is indeed very weak and, if I may say so, unconvincing. By that I do not mean that she was being untruthful; but no reason was offered why she would really feel it necessary to distress her parents—if it was going to distress them—by telling them *h* of the divorce, or why she would make it known to other persons, when she had not felt it necessary to disclose to them, over all the 25 years, that the marriage had factually broken down by separation.

I regard the judgment of the learned judge here as a very careful judgment, with a careful review of evidence in a case where the nature of the evidence was not at all easy. I regard the conclusions expressed by the learned judge as being conclusions to *j* which he was most clearly entitled to come on the evidence, and on the basis of those conclusions he was entitled as a matter of law to express the result which he ultimately did express: first, that there is here no 'grave other hardship' established, and secondly, that, even if there were, it would not be right, in the circumstances of the case, to refuse a decree. Accordingly, I would dismiss the appeal.

LAWTON LJ.   This appeal has given me some concern, for two reasons.   The
a evidence in the case and the finding of the learned judge show that this wife feels that
she has suffered a grave injustice. I can understand why. She is a Roman Catholic.
She comes from Sicily, where most people are of the same religion. She has almost
certainly been instructed in her youth about the sacramental nature of marriage; and
it may well be that she has been inspired by the mystical language in the Epistle to
the Ephesians which is said to justify that view of marriage. It is likely that marriage
b means much more to her than it does to most people in this country, indeed to most
people in Western Europe. It is always sad when a court has to come to a finding which
appears to the unsuccessful litigant to inflict a grave injustice.

The second reason why I feel concern about this appeal is this. The Divorce Reform
Act 1969, under which the appeal comes before the court, has now been in operation
a few years. As far as counsel knows, and as far as I know, no one has yet succeeded in
c a defence under that part of s 4 of the 1969 Act under which this wife comes to this
court for help; and I have asked myself the question whether the courts may not have
whittled away the defence provided by Parliament by setting far too high a standard
of proof.

One has to start, I think, by looking at the context in which the phrase 'grave financial or other hardship' occurs. The word 'hardship' is not a word of art. It follows that
d it must be construed by the courts in a common sense way, and the meaning which is
put on the word 'hardship' should be such as would meet with the approval of ordinary
sensible people. In my judgment, the ordinary sensible man would take the view
that there are two aspects of 'hardship'—that which the sufferer from the hardship
thinks he is suffering and that which a reasonable bystander with knowledge of all
the facts would think he was suffering. That can be illustrated by a homely example.
e The rich gourmet who because of financial stringency has to drink vin ordinaire with
his grouse may well think that he is suffering a hardship; but sensible people would
say he was not.

If that approach is applied to this case, one gets this situation. The wife undoubtedly
feels that she has suffered a hardship; and the learned judge, in the passages to which
Megaw LJ has referred, found that she was feeling at the time of the judgment that
f she could not go back to Sicily. That, if it was genuine and deeply felt, would undoubtedly be a 'hardship' in one sense of that word. But one has to ask oneself the
question whether sensible people, knowing all the facts, would think it was a hardship.
On the evidence, I have come to the conclusion that they would not, and for this
reason. The wife has been separated from her husband now since 1947. She returned
in that year to Sicily. She has been living in Palermo with her mother and father. Her
g relatives have been around her; they must have appreciated that something had gone
wrong with the marriage. I make all allowances for the undoubted fact that many
male Sicilians leave their country to work elsewhere, and wives may be left alone for
months and years on end. Nevertheless, 26 years is a very long time; and such evidence as there was before the learned judge was to the effect that it was almost
inevitable that her family and those who knew her would have appreciated that
h there was something wrong. There would be some social stigma attached to that;
she might be thought to have failed as a wife. But she has lived that down; and the
fact that there had been a divorce in some foreign country would add very little to
the stigma.

In those circumstances, it is very difficult to see how it can be said on the evidence
that her present emotional rejection of Palermo as her home can in any real sense be
j regarded as 'hardship'. In my judgment she is bound to be drawn there by the
presence of her aged parents and her daughter, seemingly happily married. It
follows, first, that she has not proved her case and, secondly, that this is not a case
in which anyone could say that the trial judge had whittled down the defence given
by s 4 of the 1969 Act.

I too take the view that this appeal must be dismissed.

ORMROD LJ. I agree. In my judgment the learned judge approached this case
in an impeccable manner. Section 4 of the Divorce Reform Act 1969 must, in my view,   *a*
be read in its context. It is a section which appears in an Act which entirely alters the
conceptual basis of divorce in this country. It is quite plain from s 1 of the Act that
from that time onwards the basis of dissolution of marriage is the irretrievable
breakdown of the relationship between the spouses, and so clearly the whole policy
of Parliament was, and is, to create a state of affairs where, once the real relationship
of husband and wife between the parties has gone, and gone for good, the legal   *b*
relationship of husband and wife should as far as possible be removed or dissolved so
as to bring the legal situation into line with the factual situation. But Parliament did
not go quite so far because in s 2 it limits in a rather curious way the powers of the court
by prescribing in effect what evidence the court must have before it could come to a
conclusion that a marriage had irretrievably broken down, and consequently Parliament prescribed the well-known five 'facts' or situations. In this case we are concerned   *c*
with the last of those, that is, five years' separation—the strongest possible evidence,
one would have thought, that the factual relationship between husband and wife
had permanently broken down. But Parliament decided to include s 4, to provide a
defence in certain limited circumstances, mainly with an eye on wives who might
suffer great hardship at the hands of unfaithful husbands who were able to take
advantage of the five year separation to get a divorce which the wives could otherwise   *d*
have withheld.

So s 4 was passed; and it is important, I think, to look at s 4 a little closely. Reading
it as a whole it comes to this, that where the defence of grave financial or other
hardship is put forward by a respondent the court shall begin (sub-s (2)) by considering—

> 'all the circumstances, including the conduct of the parties [as we now know   *e*
> from a recent case in this court, the word 'conduct' is used widely] and the
> interests of those parties and of any children or other persons concerned, and if
> the court is of opinion that the dissolution of the marriage will result in grave
> financial or other hardship to the respondent and that it would in all the circum-
> stances be wrong to dissolve the marriage it shall dismiss the petition.'
>   *f*

In my view, what that amounts to is this. The court has first to decide whether there
was evidence on which it could properly come to the conclusion that the wife was
suffering from grave financial or other hardship; and 'other hardship' in this context,
in my judgment, agreeing with Megaw and Lawton LJJ, must mean other *grave*
hardship. If hardship is found, the court then has to look at the second limb and
decide whether, in all the circumstances, looking at everybody's interests, balancing   *g*
the respondent's hardship against the petitioner's interests in getting his or her freedom, it would be wrong to dissolve the marriage. That being so, it is not, I think,
perhaps so surprising as Lawton LJ feels that this type of defence has not succeeded. In
the first place, my impression at any rate is (I have no details of it) that this is a defence
which is very rarely used by practitioners. The financial hardship may be different,
but even that can be so easily cured now, under the wide powers of the Matrimonial   *h*
Property and Proceedings Act 1970, that it must be extraordinarily difficult to establish
financial hardship in any circumstances today. So far as my experience goes, the only
other type of 'grave hardship' that has been advanced is the sort of matter that has
been put forward in this case, which is a mixed religious-social type of ground. Certainly that is true of the cases that have been cited to us, and I do not know of any others.

In those circumstances, what is the right way to approach it? The onus is clearly   *j*
on the respondent to establish *grave* hardship of some kind. Clearly (and I entirely
agree in this with Latey J in *Parghi v Parghi*[1]) each case must be looked at on its own facts,
because the court is concerned with whether or not the wife is going to suffer hardship,

---

1   [1973] The Times, 8th May

a   so to that extent it is subjective—subjective in the sense that it has to be looked at through the eyes of the wife. But that does not mean to say that even when a perfectly truthful and perfectly sincere respondent gives evidence to the effect that he or she will suffer various kinds of hardship in consequence of the divorce the court is obliged to accept their ipse dixit. It seems to me quite clear that, as the judge found in this case that the wife was entirely sincere, he had to go on and judge the reality of her apprehension; and when she said, as she did in evidence, that she did not think she

b   could go back to Sicily if she were divorced and she would rather die in England, he had to consider not only whether that was a perfectly sincere statement, made in the sense that she believed it as she said it, but also whether there was any real likelihood that after the divorce she would in fact believe that she could not go back to Sicily. To consider that, he obviously had to have evidence about conditions in Sicily—social conditions, customs and so forth—and to balance that evidence against her

c   apprehension. That I think is exactly what the learned judge did in this case.

In approaching this type of case, in my experience, it is very important to remember that with the most honest and sincere witnesses who are in a highly emotional state, as no doubt the wife was in this case, the borderline between fantasy and reality may be very difficult to draw, not only for her but for the tribunal that is trying the case. In my judgment the learned judge here assessed the situation very sympathetically

d   to the wife; he arrived at a conclusion with which for my part I agree and which I cannot believe could be seriously challenged. I accordingly agree with the order proposed by Megaw LJ and would dismiss this appeal.

I would only add this. The learned judge did not in fact go on to consider the 'conduct' matter because at the time he was relying on *Dorrell v Dorrell*[1]; but had he had to go on and consider that at the instance of the other party, I would have been

e   extremely surprised if he had come to any other conclusion than that the interests of the parties as a whole, certainly on facts like these, required the court to dissolve this marriage. Making all allowances for the sacramental views of some people, to keep in existence a marriage which has been dead for 25 years requires, in my judgment, a considerable amount of justification.

f   *Appeal dismissed.*

Solicitors: *Howard, Kennedy & Rossi* (for the wife); *Martin & Nicholson* (for the husband).

Mary Rose Plummer   Barrister.

---

1   [1972] 3 All ER 343, [1972] 1 WLR 1087

Greater London Council v Jenkins   *a*

COURT OF APPEAL, CIVIL DIVISION
LORD DIPLOCK, CAIRNS AND BROWNE LJJ
23rd, 24th OCTOBER 1974

b

Land – Recovery of possession – Summary proceedings – Order for possession – Land occupied solely by persons who entered into or remained in occupation without licence or consent – Persons entering into possession with licence or consent but remaining in possession after licence terminated – Availability of summary procedure – Discretion of court – Licence granted for substantial period – Whether court has a discretion to prevent use of summary procedure where licensee holds over after termination of licence – CCR Ord 26, r 1(1).   *c*

A local authority made an arrangement with an organisation ('SCH') whereby the authority made available to SCH houses which had been acquired for demolition and replacement in pursuance of redevelopment schemes, in order that they might be used as temporary accommodation by students and homeless persons until the authority was ready to begin demolition work. Those 'short-life' properties were *d* occupied by SCH and its nominees under a licence granted by the authority to SCH. It was a term of the licence that the premises were to be vacated and returned to the authority when they were required for demolition. One such property was handed over to SCH by the authority in January 1972. SCH put the appellant into occupation of the property in the spring of 1973. As a result of a series of postponements of the authority's development plans for the area in which the property lay, the licence *e* given to SCH was progressively extended until 31st May 1974. Following discussions between the authority and SCH on 17th July 1974, the authority wrote two letters to SCH, on 26th July and 8th August, in which it indicated that it would require vacant possession of the premises by 1st September 1974. On 14th August, however, the authority made an application to the county court for a possession order under the summary procedure provided for by CCR Ord 26, r 1(1)[a]. The judge found *f* that the licence granted to SCH had been finally terminated on 31st May 1974 and that the appellant had therefore become a trespasser by the time the proceedings were instituted. Accordingly he granted an order for possession. On appeal,

Held – (i) Where an applicant who brought proceedings for possession under CCR Ord 26 succeeded in establishing that the respondent had been let into possession *g* of land belonging to the applicant under a licence but had remained in occupation after the licence had been terminated without the applicant's consent, the court had no discretion to refuse to allow the summary procedure to be used, even where the respondent had been in occupation under the licence for a substantial period; it was bound to grant an order for possession in such circumstances (see p 356 c, p 358 j and p 359 b and h, post); dictum of Pennycuick V-C in *Bristol Corpn v persons* *h* *unknown* [1974] 1 All ER at 596 disapproved.

(ii) On the true construction of the letters of 26th July and 8th August the authority had extended the appellant's licence to remain in possession until 1st September. Accordingly, since the proceedings had been commenced on 14th August, they were premature for at that date the appellant was not in occupation without the licence

j

---

a Rule 1(1) provides: 'Where a person claims possession of land which he alleges is occupied solely by a person or persons (not being a tenant or tenants holding over after the termination of the tenancy) who entered into or remained in occupation without his licence or consent or that of any predecessor in title of his, the proceedings may be brought by originating application in accordance with the provisions of this Order.'

of the authority.   The appeal would therefore be allowed (see p 358 *c* to *f* and *h* and
a p 359 *f* and *h*, post).

Notes
For actions for the recovery of land, see 32 Halsbury's Laws (3rd Edn) 370-377, paras
590-606, and for cases on the subject, see 38 Digest (Repl) 908-938, *986-1280*.

b **Cases referred to in judgments**
Bristol Corpn v persons unknown [1974] 1 All ER 593, [1974] 1 WLR 365, 72 LGR 245.
Minister of Health v Bellotti [1944] 1 All ER 238, [1944] KB 298, 113 LJKB 436, 170 LT
    146, CA, 11 Digest (Repl) 581, *163*.
Winter Garden Theatre (London) Ltd v Millenium Productions Ltd [1947] 2 All ER 331,
    [1948] AC 173, [1947] LJR 1422, 177 LT 349, HL, 45 Digest (Repl) 201, *83*.
c

Cases also cited
Barnes v Barratt [1970] 2 All ER 483, [1970] 2 QB 657.
Crane v Morris [1965] 3 All ER 77, [1965] 1 WLR 1104.
Luganda v Service Hotels Ltd [1969] 2 All ER 692, [1969] 2 Ch 209.
Manchester Corpn v Connolly [1970] 1 All ER 961, [1970] 1 Ch 420.
d *Thompson v Park* [1944] 2 All ER 477, [1944] KB 408.
Wykeham Terrace, Brighton, Sussex, Re [1971] Ch 204, [1970] 3 WLR 649.

Appeal
This was an appeal by Alan Jenkins against an order made by his Honour Judge
Leslie, sitting in the Bloomsbury and Marylebone County Court on 13th September
e 1974, whereby, on an application by the Greater London Council ('the GLC') under
CCR Ord 26, r 1, to which the appellant and other persons, including persons un-
known, were respondents, it was ordered that the GLC recover possession of land
known as 11 Elgin Avenue, London, W9.   The facts are set out in the judgment of
Lord Diplock.

f *Lord Gifford* for the appellant.
Benjamin Levy for the GLC.

LORD DIPLOCK. This is an appeal from an order for recovery of possession of
premises known as 11 Elgin Avenue in the Paddington area.   It was made on 13th
September 1974 by the judge of the Bloomsbury and Marylebone County Court
g under the special procedure for the recovery of land permitted by CCR Ord 26,
which corresponds with RSC Ord 113.   The application under that order was made
on 14th August 1974.   The appellant had gone into occupation of the premises in
the spring of 1973, and it is common ground that when he went into occupation he
did so as a licensee of the owners of the premises, the Greater London Council.   The
h date of 14th August 1974 is a significant date in this case, because, in my view, the
respondent's right to the order depended on whether or not his licence to occupy
the premises had expired by the time that the proceedings started.
    I may mention briefly, in order to get it out of the way, a submission made on
behalf of the appellant that the procedure under CCR Ord 26 was not available in cases
where a person remains on as a trespasser after the determination of a licence which
j he had previously held to remain on the land.   That submission was really based on
a note[1] which appears in the current Supreme Court Practice making a suggestion
to that effect.
    The matter was dealt with in *Bristol Corpn v persons unknown*[2], where Pennycuick

1 Supreme Court Practice 1973, vol 1, p 1481, para 113/1-8/2
2 [1974] 1 All ER 593, [1974] 1 WLR 365

V-C had occasion to construe the corresponding rule, which is in identical words, in RSC Ord 113. The relevant words of CCR Ord 26, r 1(1) read thus: *a*

'Where a person claims possession of land which he alleges is occupied solely by a person or persons . . . who entered into or remained in occupation without his licence or consent . . .'

Pennycuick V-C pointed out that it is clear beyond a peradventure that this order *b* applies to cases where a person who is alleged to be a trespasser was previously on the premises by licence.

In the course of his judgment in that case Pennycuick V-C did suggest that the judge or the court had a discretion whether to permit this summary procedure to be used in cases where there had been, as in this case clearly, a licence to occupy originally. For my part, I am unable to see that the court has any discretion to prevent a plaintiff *c* using this procedure where the circumstances are those described in the rule. So, while agreeing, as I do, with Pennycuick V-C's construction of the rule, I personally would disagree that the court has any discretion to prevent the use of this procedure where circumstances are such as bring them within its terms.

I turn then to what is the real point in this case, and for that purpose I must say briefly what are the relevant facts. The appellant was let into occupation of the *d* premises by a body which is a registered charity known as Students Community Housing, of which the appellant, on being let into possession, became a member. The Students Community Housing (which I shall call 'SCH') is a body which makes arrangements, among other things no doubt, for the use for occupation of houses which have been acquired by local authorities—in this case the Greater London Council ('the GLC')—for the purpose of demolition and replacement by modern *e* housing or by other buildings. These houses have to be acquired some time before the opportunity for demolition and reconstruction arises, and they are known familiarly as 'short-life properties'.

In August 1971 the GLC entered into an arrangement with SCH for the use of short-life property for temporary accommodation for students and for homeless persons. The terms on which the GLC agreed to let the SCH and their nominee occupy such *f* property under licence are set out in a letter of 2nd August 1971. It is only necessary for me to refer to three of the terms. The first was that SCH undertook to repair the buildings at their expense and render them fit for habitation. The second was that there should be no rehousing liability caused to the GLC. The third I will read verbatim:

'That the premises be vacated and returned to the Greater London Council *g* when they are required for demolition. In this connection the importance of the Council being given vacant possession by the date requested, cannot be stressed too highly, since serious financial consequences could result from the Council's inability to make a site available for redevelopment by the contractual date.'

It was made clear that the arrangement applied to all short-life property that was *h* subsequently made available to SCH in a letter of 2nd September 1971 which pointed out that—

'any properties offered to you under the short-life arrangements are offered to you on the terms and conditions as laid down in my letter of 2nd August 1971.'

The property, 11 Elgin Avenue, was handed over to SCH under this arrangement *j* in January 1972 and SCH and those whom SCH put into occupation became licensees of the GLC on the terms of those two letters to which I have already referred.

At the time of the letters in 1971 it appears to have been expected that the development would take place within a year of the houses being licensed to SCH. But it became apparent that delay seemed to be inevitable in development schemes and

that period might be exceeded. On 23rd June 1972 an additional term was put on the
a agreement under which a licence was given to SCH, which was—

'that Associations should inspect annually their holdings of G.L.C. short-life properties (including those handed over within the preceding three months) and let the Council know that an inspection has been carried out and that properties are in a reasonable state of repair.'

b A licence granted to SCH of short-life property, including that of Elgin Avenue, was thus, in my view, a contractual licence; and it is also, in my view, clear law that when a contractual licence has been granted a person who has been on the premises under the licence cannot be treated as a trespasser until a reasonable time after notice that the licence has been or will be withdrawn. That is clearly laid down in *Winter Garden Theatre (London) Ltd v Millenium Productions*[1], a case in the House of Lords. What is a *c* reasonable time depends on all the circumstances of the case, and where the licence has been to occupy premises for residential purposes the reasonable time has reference to enabling the licensee to have an opportunity of taking his effects away from the property. That was again a matter which was decided by authority binding on the court in *Minister of Health v Bellotti*[2].

That being the law applicable to the situation of the appellant, the sub-licensee of *d* SCH, the question in this case is whether or not the licence was withdrawn and reasonable opportunity given to the licensee to remove his effects by the time that the proceedings were started on 14th August.

Elgin Avenue was part of a development scheme in which there seem to have been a number of progressive postponements, and at various times what counsel for the appellant has described as 'deadlines' were given to SCH as to the date at which vacant *e* possession of the premises would be required. The first of them was 31st July 1973; the second was 28th February 1974; and the third 31st May 1974. I need not go into those in detail. Suffice it to say that, as a result of discussion, the licence was extended at any rate to the last of those dates. The GLC, as is evident from all the correspondence, took a sympathetic view towards the need for making the utmost use of this accommodation until the last possible date, and so extended it from time to time as *f* the possibility of getting the development started faded more and more into the future.

The last deadline given up to this time was, as I say, 31st May 1974. Subsequently to that there were discussions between representatives of the GLC and representatives of SCH and another body which had been formed by licensees and by squatters in this neighbourhood, and as a result of the final discussions (to which it is not necessary *g* to refer), which were held on 17th July, a letter was written by Mr Eden, who was, I think, the vice-chairman of the housing committee, in which he referred to the discussions which had taken place. There had apparently been some attempt on the part of the SCH to extract from the GLC an undertaking that vacant possession of the property would not be required until alternative accommodation had been provided by the GLC to those who were in occupation of it.

h At the hearing before the learned county court judge, apparently, an attempt was made to prove that there had been an agreement to that effect. But the learned judge held that there had been no such agreement at that meeting; and, indeed, the existence of such agreement is wholly inconsistent with the subsequent correspondence, and in particular the letter of 26th July. There is, however, an important paragraph at the end of that letter. It said this:

j 'At our meeting I sought your help in our getting vacant possession of the Elgin Avenue properties by 1 September. This remains our target. All the possible arrangements described above for helping SCH and MHS & TA members are dependent upon our receiving your co-operation in achieving this.'

1   [1947] 2 All ER 331, [1948] AC 173
2   [1944] 1 All ER 238, [1944] KB 298

That was followed shortly afterwards, on 8th August, by another letter, addressed
in fact to the other body, but clearly intended to be directed to them as agents of the *a*
appellant here. I will read the last two paragraphs:

'Other short-life properties have been offered to SCH/MHS and TA [that is the
other body] and you have the opportunity to accept them subject to your agreeing
to the Council's standard conditions and to vacant possession of the Elgin Avenue
properties being given to the Council by 1 September 1974. These conditions *b*
which were made clear by me at our meeting on 17 July were subsequently
confirmed in my letter of 26 July. With the letter sent to all occupiers and the
notices given to SCH, everyone has had reasonable notice for the properties to
be vacated by 1 September and we cannot change this deadline. It is not a date
arbitrarily fixed but one that is related to commencement of construction in
December.'   *c*

In my view, a recipient of that letter would be entitled reasonably to understand
that his licence to continue in occupation of the property in question, which included
11 Elgin Avenue, was extended until 1st September. And if it was extended until 1st
September, there are two reasons why the application for an order for possession on
14th August was 17 days too soon. The first is that in law the appellant was entitled to *d*
remain there until 1st September. In my view, having been given the advance warning
that by 1st September the premises must be vacated, he would not have been entitled
to any further delay after that under the rule of law that a reasonable notice to
terminate the licence must be given. The second reason is a technical reason under the
terms of the order itself. I have read its words previously, and it is plain that the
application cannot be made until the persons who are made respondents to it have
either entered into or remained in occupation without this licence. So long as the *e*
licence is continued, then the application under the summary proceedings order is
premature.
    So this appeal, in my view, is entitled to succeed, but to succeed only on the tech-
nical ground that the application for the order for possession was made about two
weeks too soon. It may perhaps discourage the GLC from behaving in the humane *f*
and, if I may say so, admirable way in which they have sought to do their best for the
unfortunate people whom shortage of accommodation has driven to use this kind of
accommodation. I fear that they will have to be a little more careful in future.
    Perhaps I should say this. In deference to the learned county court judge, and per-
haps not unnaturally, the case before him appears to have been fought on the grounds
of an attempt to establish an agreement that they could stay in occupation until new
housing accommodation had been found by the GLC. One can well understand why *g*
as a matter of tactics that should be put in the forefront of the argument before the
county court judge, as it was put in the forefront of the argument before us.
    In the result, the position now is that, 1st September having expired, there would
seem no reason why a similar application should not be made to recover possession of
this property. But, the former application having been premature, this appeal must *h*
be allowed and the order of the learned county court judge for possession must be
set aside.

CAIRNS LJ. In my view it is impossible so to construe CCR Ord 26, or the corresponding RSC Ord 113, as to exclude from either order a trespasser who has previously *j*
been a licensee of any particular class. I agree with the actual decision of Pennycuick
V-C in *Bristol Corpn v persons unknown*[1]. But in the course of his judgment in that case
he said[2]:

---

1   [1974] 1 All ER 593, [1974] 1 WLR 365
2   [1974] 1 All ER at 596, [1974] 1 WLR at 369

'Let me say at once that this order will no doubt not be utilised nor an order
a   made under it in the case envisaged in the note [that is the note in the White
Book[1] to which Lord Diplock has referred], namely, where there has been a
grant of a licence for a substantial period and the licensee holds over after the
determination of the licence.'

With respect to Pennycuick V-C, that opinion, expressed obiter, appears to me one
b   which it would be difficult to sustain. It may well be that a local authority or other
responsible landlord would be reluctant to use this summary procedure against a
former licensee with whom good relations have been maintained over a long period.
But if the procedure is adopted, I do not consider that there is any discretion for the
court to say: 'I shall not make an order for possession, because I do not think this is
the sort of defendant against whom the procedure should be used.'
c   The other issue I have found one of considerable difficulty. It may well be that the
officers of the GLC, and perhaps the chairman and vice-chairman of the housing
development committee as well, thought that the licence had been finally determined
on 31st May 1974 or earlier, and that the references in the later letters to 'vacant
possession being given on 1 September' meant no more than that that was the date by
which the council considered it essential that their legal right to possession should be
d   given effect. On the whole, however, I think that the reasonable construction of the
passages in the letters of 26th July and 8th August, which Lord Diplock has read, is
that the licence was extended to 1st September.
The learned county court judge found that the licence was finally terminated on
31st May and that no licence was granted thereafter to anybody to occupy the premises.
Counsel for the GLC has contended that this was a finding of fact, and has pointed out
e   that in this appeal it is not open to the appellant to appeal on a matter of fact. If the
learned judge meant by his finding only that nothing that was said at the meeting
on 17th July was by way of extending the licence or granting a fresh licence, his
finding is no obstacle to the conclusion which I reach on the construction of the letters.
If he meant that no extension is to be found in the letters, that is a matter of construction, and therefore of law, and I respectfully disagree with the learned judge.
f   If the licence was extended to 1st September, it had not been terminated before
proceedings were issued, and whether or not such issue had the effect of terminating
the licence, I do not consider that it can be said that the appellant in this case had
remained in occupation without the consent of the landlord at the time of the application. I am quite unable to follow the contention put forward here by counsel for the
GLC that in some way CCR Ord 5, r 6, or CCR Ord 15, r 1, enables him to overcome
g   this difficulty.
In fairness to the learned judge, it should be observed that, so far as appears from
his judgment, he was not asked to consider whether the GLC could succeed in their
application even if the licence had been extended to 1st September, and therefore
that the further matters that arose on the basis that there had been such extension
were apparently not discussed before him.
h   I agree that the appeal should be allowed.

BROWNE LJ. I also agree that the appeal should be allowed, and I feel that I
cannot usefully add anything to what Lord Diplock and Cairns LJ have already said,
with which I entirely agree.

j   *Appeal allowed. Order in county court set aside.*

Solicitors: *The Paddington Law Centre* (for the appellant); *Solicitor to the Greater London
Council.*

James Collins Esq   Barrister.

---

7   Supreme Court Practice 1973, vol 1, p 1481, para 113/1-8/2

R v Robinson (Adeline)

a

COURT OF APPEAL, CRIMINAL DIVISION
JAMES LJ, PHILLIPS AND MAY JJ
11th NOVEMBER 1974

Criminal law – Autrefois acquit – Autrefois convict – Acquittal or conviction – Verdict of b
jury – Jury agreed on verdict – Verdict not formally delivered to court – Jury discharged
before delivery of verdict – Accused tried again on same charge – Whether agreement of jury
at first trial sufficient to found plea of autrefois acquit or convict.

The appellant was charged on an indictment containing seven counts. The jury
retired to consider their verdict and returned to announce that, save for one count, c
they had disagreed on all the counts against the appellant. The trial judge discharged
the jury before they had time to specify the count against the appellant on which
they had agreed. The judge ordered the appellant to be retried on all seven counts.
At the second trial the judge overruled a plea by the appellant of autrefois acquit or
convict. The appellant was convicted on three counts and appealed. d

Held – In order to sustain a plea of autrefois convict or autrefois acquit, an accused
had to show that on a former occasion there had been a verdict delivered by the jury
to the court. Since no formal verdict had been delivered by the jury to the court at
the first trial, there had been no conviction or acquittal of the appellant. Accordingly
the appellant could properly be put in charge of a second jury for the same offences e
and the appeal would be dismissed (see p 366 b to f, post).
R v Charlesworth (1861) 1 B & S 460 and *Winsor v R* (1866) 7 B & S 490 explained.

Notes
For the delivery of the verdict of a jury, see 10 Halsbury's Laws (3rd Edn) 427, 428,
para 789, and for cases on the subject, see 14 Digest (Repl) 349-351, *3390-3418.* f
  For autrefois convict or acquit, see 10 Halsbury's Laws (3rd Edn) 405-407, paras
736-738, and for cases on the subject, see 14 Digest (Repl) 378-379, 390-393, *3700-3711,*
3786-3819.

Cases referred to in judgment
Conway & Lynch v R (1845) 5 LTOS 458, 7 ILR 149, 1 Cox CC 210, 14 Digest (Repl) 370, g
  2237.
R v Beadell (1933) 24 Cr App Rep 39, CCA, 14 Digest (Repl) 580, *5799.*
R v Charlesworth (1861) 1 B & S 460, 31 LJMC 25, 5 LT 150, 25 JP 820, 8 Jur NS 1091,
  9 Cox CC 44, 121 ER 786, 14 Digest (Repl) 390, *3789.*
R v Lester (1938) 27 Cr App Rep 8, CCA, 14 Digest (Repl) 380, *3719.*
R v Lewis (1909) 78 LJKB 722, [1908-10] All ER Rep 654, 100 LT 976, 73 JP 346, 22 Cox h
  CC 141, 2 Cr App Rep 180, CCA, 14 Digest (Repl) 346, *3354.*
R v Randall [1960] Crim LR 435, CCA.
R v Yeadon & Birch (1861) Le & Ca 81, 31 LJMC 70, 5 LT 329, 26 JP 148, 7 Jur NS 1128,
  9 Cox CC 91, CCR, 14 Digest (Repl) 359, *3496.*
Winsor v R (1866) LR 1 QB 390, 7 B & S 490, 35 LJMC 161, 14 LT 567, 30 JP 374, 12 Jur
  NS 561, sub nom *R v Winsor* 10 Cox CC 327; *affg* (1866) LR 1 QB 289, 10 Cox CC 276, j
  14 Digest (Repl) 370, *3590.*

Cases also cited
O (an infant), Re [1971] 2 All ER 744, [1971] Ch 748, CA.
R v Starkie [1922] 2 KB 295, CCA.

Appeal

a On 5th November 1973 at the Central Criminal Court before his Honour Judge King Hamilton QC the appellant, Adeline Ione Robinson, on an indictment containing seven counts, was convicted of wounding with intent (count 2), attempted unlawful wounding (count 4) and wounding with intent (count 5); she was acquitted on the other counts. She was not sentenced but on 28th November 1973 was ordered to enter into her own recognisances in the sum of £10 to appear for judgment if called
b on within five years. The appellant appealed against conviction on the ground that the judge had erred in law in not acceding to a submission of autrefois convict or acquit made on her behalf. The facts are set out in the judgment of the court.

W T Williams QC and *Stephen Solley* for the appellant.
Robert Harman QC and *F P L Evans* for the Crown.

c

JAMES LJ delivered the following judgment of the court. This is an appeal against conviction on a point of law. The appellant, Adeline Ione Robinson, was convicted on 5th November 1973 at the Central Criminal Court after a trial before his Honour Judge King Hamilton.

d The facts giving rise to the charges that were preferred relate to as long ago as 23rd September 1972. On that date police raided premises on which it was believed there might be breaches of the licensing laws taking place. The evidence was that various officers found drugs and according to them found drugs in the possession of the appellant's husband. The attention of the police to the appellant's husband resulted in the appellant herself intervening, and intervening in a way that resulted in certain officers receiving injuries. The appellant's husband was charged with possessing
e drugs. The appellant herself was charged with nine offences in all, including two charges of attempting to murder police officers and alternatives of lesser offences, such as wounding with intent or attempting to wound with intent.

Having regard to the narrow compass of the matter before this court, there is no need to go into the facts giving rise to the charges any further, or indeed to recite any more of the proceedings than that which immediately follows. On 19th July 1973
f at the Central Criminal Court, after a trial that lasted, we were told, some 17 days, before his Honour Judge Clarke, the appellant's husband was acquitted on a charge of possessing a dangerous drug. The jury stated that they had not been able to reach a verdict in respect of the appellant herself, save on one count. The trial had proceeded on seven of the nine counts in which she was named.

It is relevant to recite precisely what occurred after the jury had been out for nearly
g five hours and after they had received directions as to the circumstances of returning a majority verdict. They came back into court and the foreman announced: 'We have reached a verdict on two counts, my Lord.' The judge then remarked: 'Oh, that is all?' and the foreman replied: 'Yes'. The jury then indicated that they had agreed on the first count against the appellant's husband and the judge said: 'Very well, I will take that verdict.' Then the following exchanges took place:
h
'*The clerk of the court:* Mr Foreman, have you reached a verdict on which at least ten of you are agreed on the first count of this indictment?
'*The foreman of the jury:* We have.
'*The clerk;* Do you find the [appellant's husband], Gladstone Alexander Robinson, guilty or not guilty?
j '*The foreman:* We find him not guilty.
'*Judge Clarke:* And you have been unable to reach a verdict in respect of any of the other counts, except one of them?
'*The foreman:* Yes, my Lord.
'*Judge Clarke:* Very well, I shall discharge you from giving a verdict in respect of the counts involving [the appellant] and her case will be tried again.'

The transcript that follows is agreed to be in error, but everyone concerned agrees as to how it should read, namely:

'[Counsel for the Crown]: I am only wondering whether the verdict on which they are agreed . . .

'Judge Clarke: No, I think the best thing is for the matter to be dealt with again. It is only fair for the whole thing concerned; that is the situation concerning [the appellant].'

So it came about that in November 1973 the appellant was at the Central Criminal Court facing the same seven charges in relation to which the former jury had been discharged.

At the outset of the proceedings before his Honour Judge King Hamilton, counsel who led for the defence of the appellant submitted a plea in bar of a former acquittal or former conviction. That plea was the subject of a long and detailed argument, including references to leading authorities, textbooks and also to decided cases of earlier days and of more modern times. The trial judge overruled the submission, and ruled that there had been no previous acquittal or previous conviction, because there had been no verdict of the jury which had been returned. The submissions made to the judge are the same submissions that have been made to this court by counsel for the appellant, and it is his submission to us that the judge misdirected himself in law in the ruling that there had been no former acquittal or conviction.

The position was indeed a curious one, and the researches of learned counsel have not been able to produce any authority in which this precise situation has arisen or indeed in which this precise situation has been canvassed in argument or adverted to in the judgment.

It is accepted that a trial judge has got a discretion in the exercise of which he can discharge a jury in whose charge the accused has been placed. It is counsel for the appellant's submission that there comes a time when that discretion no longer exists. It is said that once the jury have reached their verdict, then the court has no discretion in the matter, but must accept the verdict that the jury have reached. The step in the proceedings which involves the foreman of the jury announcing to the court the decision arrived at by the jury is argued before us to be a matter of form and not of substance. It is argued that the jury are given the duty of considering the evidence and arriving at a conclusion on it, and that once the jury have arrived at a conclusion that is their verdict on which they have agreed, and once they have agreed on their verdict the court is bound to accept it.

One must remember in this connection that the oath taken by the juryman is to try the issues joined between the Queen and the accused, and to give a true verdict according to the evidence.

At the trial in the course of the submissions made to his Honour Judge King Hamilton, it would appear that reference was made to a number of definitions of the word 'verdict'. In the course of his ruling, the trial judge recites some of these definitions. For instance in Wharton's Law Lexicon[1] it is defined as: 'Determination of a jury declared to a judge.' In Tomlins's dictionary[2] 'verdict' is defined as: 'The answer of the jury given to the Court concerning a matter of fact in any cause committed to their trial.' In an American authority, Bouvier's dictionary[3], the definition is: 'The decision made by a jury and reported to the court.' In another American authority, that of Black[4], it is defined as: 'a true declaration.'

Counsel for the appellant has invited our attention to those authorities which support the proposition that once a jury has returned a verdict then the court has no

---

1   14th Edn (1938)
2   4th Edn (1835)
3   8th Edn, 3rd Rev (1914)
4   4th Rev Edn (1968)

jurisdiction to refuse to accept it. *R v Yeadon & Birch*[1] and *R v Lester*[2] are the cases
a particularly referred to in the course of argument. There are others in the books as
well which show that once the jury has returned a verdict, then the judge cannot say
'I will not have it', provided, of course, it is a verdict that is not ambiguous and provided it is a verdict that can properly be returned on the indictment they have been
considering. But counsel for the appellant said, although that in origin is the situation,
it by no means follows that up to the time that the jury return the verdict there still
b exists the discretion under which the jury can be discharged. His argument, almost
an assertion if I may be permitted to say so, is that it is common sense that once the
jury have agreed to reach their verdict, then that discretion which is vested in the
judge no longer exists.

To support that proposition, although no authority precisely in point can be cited,
counsel does cite and relies on *Winsor v R*[3] and *R v Charlesworth*[4]. It is unnecessary to
c cite from *Winsor v R*[5] in any detail, but from that which is said in the course of the
judgment of Blackburn J, and in particular the passage I am going to cite now, counsel
for the appellant says there is authority supporting, not directly but indirectly, the
proposition which he contends before us. The passage reads[6]:

> 'When the jury have once found a verdict of conviction or acquittal, the matter
d > becomes *res adjudicata*, and after that there can be no further trial. If, when the
> jury have found the verdict, the Court were to issue process for the purposes of
> summoning another jury to try it over again, and award process upon the same
> indictment to try the whole matter over again, that would be erroneous, and in
> such a case the proper remedy would be to bring a writ of error, the error being,
> that whereas there was an acquittal or a conviction, which terminated the whole
e > matter, process had issued to a fresh jury. If, instead of proceeding in that way,
> a second indictment were found, it would be necessary that the prisoner should
> plead *autrefois acquit*, or *autrefois convict*, as the case might be, and that would raise
> the point, and the question would then be, had the matter been so determined
> by the jury as to pass into *res adjudicata*, and had it become a matter that was not
> to be tried again?'

f In that passage counsel draws attention to the use of the words 'the jury have once
found', and it is his submission that in *Winsor v R*[3] the language of Blackburn J,
and indeed the language of Cockburn CJ, is such as to show that the court in that case
was looking at the matter in a broad sense, and not restricting consideration to the
position in which there had been a pronouncement of the verdict in court and information to the court being stated by the foreman of the jury. It is to be observed
g that immediately prior to using the words which I have cited, Blackburn J does say[6]:
'. . . that the jury should proceed to give a verdict upon the issue of guilty or not guilty.'
If one looks at his judgment as a whole, and if one looks at the judgment of Mellor J[7],
one finds that the words 'finding', 'found' and so forth are really related to
the pronouncement, the giving of the verdict to the court.

In *R v Charlesworth*[4] counsel for the appellant relies on a passage which reads[8]:
h
> 'The second question presents even greater difficulty in the way of the defen-
> dant. Assuming that the Judge had not this power, or that he exercised it im-
> properly, the question is, whether what he has done amounts to an acquittal of

---

1   (1861) Le & Ca 81
j 2   (1938) 27 Cr App Rep 8
3   (1866) LR 1 QB 289, 10 Cox CC 276
4   (1861) 1 B & S 460
5   LR 1 QB 289
6   10 Cox CC at 315
7   10 Cox CC at 321
8   1 B & S at 506

the defendant, and entitles him to have judgment entered up as if he had been
acquitted. On this I can add nothing to the conclusive reasoning of Crampton J. *a*
in *Conway and Lynch* v. *The Queen*[1] on which so much observation has been made.
There is no instance of such a plea as this, except in this case and that. It may be
said with truth that may be because, since the practice established in the time
of Lord Holt, juries have not been discharged, and therefore the occasion for such
a plea has not presented itself. On the other hand, the only pleas known to the
law of England to stay a man from being tried on an indictment or information *b*
(and we must consider this as if it was a fresh information, and the defendant had
pleaded to it the facts stated on the record) are the pleas of autrefois acquit and
autrefois convict, and it is clear that this statement of facts amounts to neither.
It is said that a man is not to be tried twice, and is not a second time to be put in
jeopardy; and that that applies equally to this case as to a case where a man has
been convicted or acquitted. In that I cannot concur; and the reasoning of Cramp- *c*
ton J. is conclusive on that subject. When we talk of a man being twice tried, we
mean a trial which proceeds to its legitimate and lawful conclusion by verdict;
and when we speak of a man being twice put in jeopardy, we mean put in
jeopardy by the verdict of a jury; and he is not tried nor put in jeopardy
until the verdict is given. If that is not so, then in every case of a defective verdict
a man could not be tried a second time; and yet it is well known that, though a *d*
jury have pronounced upon the case, yet, if their verdict be defective, it will not
avail the party accused in the event of his being put on his trial a second time.
Therefore, in my humble judgment (though it is not necessary to decide the
point), as at present advised, I cannot come to the conclusion that there has been,
in this case, a trial, or that the accused has been put in jeopardy, or put in the
position, either in fact or in law, of a man who has been once acquitted, and who, *e*
having been once acquitted, cannot be put on his trial a second time.'

Restating his argument in the light of that case, counsel argues that this appellant
had been put in peril and, as he would put it, released from that peril at the moment
that the jury agreed on their verdict, and that in those circumstances it would be
wrong to put the appellant in peril a second time, as in fact Judge Clarke ordered. *f*

As an alternative to his main proposition that Judge Clarke exceeded his jurisdiction in discharging the jury after the jury had told him they had arrived at their
verdict, counsel for the appellant argues that there was an improper exercise of
judicial discretion by Judge Clarke in his ruling that the jury should be discharged.

On either basis, the argument is this, that once the jury in the first trial had arrived
at their verdict, whether it be a verdict of guilty or not guilty, on the one count on *g*
which they had agreed, the appellant was entitled to know that verdict and have it
pronounced in court, and to know where she stood. Whether it be an excessive jurisdiction or a wrongful and improper exercise of judicial discretion, the conduct of the
trial judge, Judge Clarke, on that first trial was such as to deprive the appellant of
the opportunity of having that verdict pronounced. It is said, and rightly said, that
there was no fault on the part of the appellant. The position was that the judge took *h*
it into his own hands and made the decision which precluded the pronouncement
and recording of the jury's verdict. Therefore the position should be equated to the
situation which would have been present had the jury been allowed, as they should
have been allowed, to pronounce their verdict.

On that argument, therefore, there was a decision of the jury, which was either
a decision of guilty or not guilty on one count, and no one can tell, never would be *j*
able to tell, which decision it was, because the judge prevented that decision being
given. If that is the situation, it is said, it would be wrong to place this appellant in
charge of the jury, so that she is in peril of a conviction a second time, and that applies

---

1 (1845) 7 ILR 149 at 165

a to all the seven counts, because no one can say which count it was on which the jury had said they had reached agreement. It is argued, in those circumstances it is an injustice and crucially unfair to the appellant that she should have to stand her trial again.

In the way the argument developed in this court, we permitted junior counsel to follow senior counsel for the appellant. He invited our attention to the line of authorities which dealt with the proposition that an appellate court cannot entertain the

b proposition that it should interfere with the exercise of a discretion whereby the judge discharges a jury. There have been a number of cases in which the Court of Criminal Appeal have said that the exercise of discretion discharging a jury is a matter with which the Court of Criminal Appeal has no jurisdiction to deal. R v Lewis[1] is the case that is usually cited. Channell J gave the judgment of the court. It was a case in which there had been a date for trial that was fixed and witnesses were called on that

c date, but owing to the absence of other witnesses, the prosecution's case was not as strong as they would have liked it to be and they asked for an adjournment. The chairman granted that request and discharged the jury. In giving the judgment of the court, Channell J said[2]:

d 'The question in this case is one of law, and it is whether the appellant was entitled to say at his trial on April 30th that the jury were improperly discharged on April 20th. That question has been before the Courts in the most solemn form possible, namely, on a writ of error. [Then he referred to the judgment of Crampton J in Conway & Lynch v R[3] and said:] That judgment, which was a dissenting judgment, was approved in R v Charlesworth[4] and Winsor v R[5]. It lays down the law in plain terms, namely, that the discharging of a jury is entirely

e within the discretion of the judge.'

At the conclusion of the judgment he said[6]:

'That is the rule on which judges have acted and on which we think we ought to act, but we have no jurisdiction to deal with this matter.'

f Junior counsel's argument in particular drew our attention to the fact that in R v Lewis[1], the court relied on the decision in Winsor v R[5], to which reference has already been made in this judgment, and counsel argues, cogently, that the ratio of the decision not to interfere with the exercise of the discretion in Winsor v R[5] was that a court of error, which was the nature of the court dealing with the matter of Winsor v R[5], had no jurisdiction to interfere with what was a question of fact or mixed law and fact at

g the best, and not a question of error on the face of the record. He argues that R v Lewis[1] is based on an authority which does not entirely support the proposition for which R v Lewis[1] is cited. Let it be said that R v Lewis[1] has been followed in subsequent cases, and in particular it was adverted to in R v Randall[7], and was also referred to in R v Beadell[8].

h Be that as it may, in dealing with this matter of discretion and the effect of an improper use of discretion, a different situation now arises in view of the Criminal Appeal Act 1968, in s 2(1) of which conditions under which this court can and shall interfere with a conviction are laid down. But this is not an appeal from the decision of Judge

1   (1909) 2 Cr App Rep 180, [1908-10] All ER Rep 654
j 2   2 Cr App Rep at 181, [1908-10] All ER Rep at 654
3   (1845) LTOS 458, 7 ILR 149
4   (1861) 1 B & S 460
5   (1866) LR 1 QB 390
6   2 Cr App Rep at 182, cf [1908-10] All ER Rep at 655
7   [1960] Crim LR 435
8   (1933) 24 Cr App Rep 39 at 43

Clarke to discharge the jury. This is an appeal from the decision of his Honour Judge King Hamilton on a matter of law overruling the submission of formerly convicted *a* or formerly acquitted. In our judgment Judge King Hamilton was right to reject the submission of counsel for the appellant, and the reasons that he gave for his rejection of the submissions appear to this court to be the right reasons.

In our judgment, in order to sustain a plea of autrefois convict or autrefois acquit, the accused must show that there has been on a former occasion a verdict of the jury which is given to the court. It is not sufficient to say: 'Well, the jury announced that *b* they had reached a decision on one or any or all the counts and then were discharged from giving their verdicts.' A conviction or acquittal arises at the proper conclusion of the matter, and there is no conclusion of the matter until the verdict is given to the court. This is more than a matter of form. It is a matter of substance. The jury cannot send a message to the judge in his room saying what they have decided on and what they have agreed. They have to come back into court formally and their verdict has *c* to be given formally in the presence of the accused person, unless for some reason he decides to absent himself from being present. So it is a matter of substance.

In this particular case the jury were discharged at what must be the very last moment of time at which the judge had discretion in the exercise of which he could discharge them. All that remained to be done, if he had not discharged them, was to ask them what their verdict was. It is not for us to speculate what operated on *d* the mind of his Honour Judge Clarke in deciding to discharge the jury. The exercise of that discretion calls in all the circumstances for great care to ensure that fairness is done, and when we say fairness, we mean fairness to the Crown and to the defence. It is not for us to say whether he was right or wrong. We have to determine, as a matter of law, whether there was a conviction or an acquittal in the trial before Judge Clarke which could be a bar to the proceedings before Judge King Hamilton. We *e* find there was no verdict given to the court. There being no verdict given to the court, there was no conviction and no acquittal, and the appellant could properly be put in charge of a second jury for the same offences.

For those reasons, without embarking on any review of the many authorities that have dealt with the problems in this field but not on the precise issue, this appeal must be dismissed.   *f*

Appeal dismissed.

Solicitors: *Peter Kandler* (for the appellant); *Director of Public Prosecutions.*

N P Metcalfe Esq   Barrister.

a   # H v H (financial provision: remarriage)

FAMILY DIVISION

SIR GEORGE BAKER P

3rd, 4th APRIL, 13th JUNE 1974

b *Divorce – Financial provision – Matters to be considered by court when making order – Remarriage of parties – Lump sum payment – Financial needs, obligations and responsibilities of parties – Wife having remarried man of substantial means – Wife entitled to lump sum by reason of contribution to welfare of family – Whether amount affected by financial circumstances of wife following remarriage – Matrimonial Causes Act 1973, s 25(1)(b).*

c *Divorce – Financial provision – Matters to be considered by court when making order – Contribution by each of the parties to welfare of family – Contribution by wife in bringing up children – Application of concept of earning to domestic situation – Wife leaving husband and children – Wife's contribution to family welfare in bringing up children incomplete – Effect on wife's entitlement to share in family assets – Matrimonial Causes Act 1973, s 25(1)(f).*

d The parties were married in December 1957 and had four children born in 1963, 1964, 1966 and 1967. In December 1972 the wife left the husband and went to live with the co-respondent. An agreed joint custody order was made under which the husband obtained care and control of the children with access to the wife. The husband obtained a decree nisi of divorce which was made absolute in May 1973. The husband remarried in July 1973 and the wife married the co-respondent in the following December. At that time the husband had an income of some £20,500 a year. The

e value of the former matrimonial home, where the husband was living with the children, was assessed at £65,000. He also owned another property, which was let, valued at £7,000 and shares worth some £7,000. He also had two bank overdrafts amounting to £40,000 secured by the title deeds of the matrimonial home. The husband's new wife had no income or assets and the husband had the financial responsibility of bringing up and educating the four children. The co-respondent

f had an income of about £14,000 and capital of some £50,000. The wife's capital was between £7,000 and £9,000. She and the co-respondent were living in a house which had been acquired in their joint names with a child born to them in 1974. The wife applied for a property adjustment order claiming that the former matrimonial home should be held in trust for the parties in equal shares until the youngest child attained its 18th birthday, or alternatively, that she should receive a lump sum

g payment of £17,000. In support of her claim, it was argued for the wife that by reason of her contributions to the welfare of the family she had earned an accrued right to participate in the division of the family assets by virtue of s 25(1)(f)[a] of the

---

a Section 25(1), so far as material, provides: 'It shall be the duty of the court in deciding whether to exercise its powers [to make certain financial provision or property adjust-

h ment orders] in relation to a party to the marriage and, if so, in what manner, to have regard to all the circumstances of the case including the following matters, that is to say— (a) the income, earning capacity, property and other financial resources which each of the parties to the marriage has or is likely to have in the foreseeable future; (b) the financial needs, obligations and responsibilities which each of the parties to the marriage has or is likely to have in the foreseeable future; (c) the standard of living enjoyed by the family before the breakdown of the marriage; (d) the age of each party to the marriage and

j the duration of the marriage; . . . (f) the contributions made by each of the parties to the welfare of the family, including any contribution made by looking after the home or caring for the family; . . . and so to exercise those powers as to place the parties, so far as it is practicable and, having regard to their conduct, just to do so, in the financial position in which they would have been if the marriage had not broken down and each had properly discharged his or her financial obligations and responsibilities towards the other.'

Matrimonial Causes Act 1973, and that her marriage to a wealthy man should
not affect such right nor have any bearing on her accrued entitlement.   *a*

Held – (i) Although a wife's prospects of remarriage should not affect her entitlement to a lump sum award, the fact of remarriage, which did not admit of
speculation, was something which the court was bound to consider by virtue of
its statutory duty under s 25(1) 'to have regard to all the circumstances of the case'
and in particular, under s 25(1)(*b*), to have regard to the financial needs of the parties   *b*
in the foreseeable future.   For that purpose the fact that the wife's new husband
was a wealthy man was a relevant factor (see p 371 *c* and *e* to *g*, post); *Wachtel v
Wachtel* [1973] 1 All ER 829 and dicta of Bagnall J in *Jackson v Jackson* [1973] 2 All ER
at 399 and in *Harnett v Harnett* [1973] 2 All ER at 601 applied; *Trippas v Trippas* [1973]
2 All ER 1 distinguished.
     (ii) In all the circumstances it would be unjust to order the husband to pay a lump   *c*
sum and unjust that the wife should receive a lump sum for the probable benefit of
her new family.   So far as the wife's share in the matrimonial home was concerned,
if she was to be regarded as having earned that share by her contribution in looking
after the home and caring for the family, account had to be taken of the fact that she
had left that job unfinished.   Any payment would put her in a better financial
position than if the marriage had continued.   In the circumstances the wife was   *d*
entitled to one-twelfth of the unencumbered value of the house, her entitlement to
to rank after the charges for the bank overdrafts and not to be payable until the
youngest child was 18 (see p 373 *c* and *e* to *h*, post).

Notes
For the matters to be considered by the court in relation to financial provision, see   *e*
Supplement to 12 Halsbury's Laws (3rd Edn) para 987A, 4.
     For the Matrimonial Causes Act 1973, s 25, see 43 Halsbury's Statutes (3rd Edn) 567.

Cases referred to in judgment
B v B [1974] The Times, 9th April.
Buckley v John Allen & Ford (Oxford) Ltd [1967] 1 All ER 539, [1967] 2 QB 637, [1967]   *f*
     2 WLR 759, Digest (Cont Vol C) 754, *1194h*.
Chamberlain v Chamberlain [1974] 1 All ER 33, [1973] 1 WLR 1557, CA.
Goodburn v Thomas Cotton Ltd [1968] 1 All ER 518, [1968] 1 QB 845, [1968] 2 WLR 229,
     CA, Digest (Cont Vol C) 754, *1194ca*.
Harnett v Harnett [1973] 2 All ER 593, [1973] Fam 156, [1973] 3 WLR 1; *affd* [1974]
     1 All ER 764, [1974] 1 WLR 219, CA.   *g*
Hector v Hector [1973] 3 All ER 1070, [1973] 1 WLR 1122, CA.
Jackson v Jackson [1973] 2 All ER 395, [1973] Fam 99, [1973] 2 WLR 735.
Marsden (J L) v Marsden (A M) [1973] 2 All ER 851, [1973] 1 WLR 641.
Mesher v Mesher [1973] The Times, 13th February, [1973] Bar Library transcript 59, CA.
S v S [1973] The Times, 11th December.
Trippas v Trippas [1973] 2 All ER 1, [1973] Fam 134, [1973] 2 WLR 585, CA.   *h*
Wachtel v Wachtel [1973] 1 All ER 829, [1973] Fam 72, [1973] 2 WLR 366, CA.
White v White [1972] Bar Library transcript 54A, CA.

Cases also cited
Griffiths v Griffiths [1974] 1 All ER 932, [1974] 1 WLR 1350, CA.
Kowalczuk v Kowalczuk [1973] 2 All ER 1042, [1973] 1 WLR 930, CA.   *j*

Summons
The marriage of the husband and the wife was dissolved by a decree of divorce which
was made absolute in May 1973.   The wife applied for an order that the former
matrimonial home be settled on trust for her and her husband in equal shares until

a their youngest child, aged six, came of age, or alternatively for a lump sum payment of £17,000. Judgment was given in open court after a hearing in chambers.

Joseph Jackson QC and *Neil Taylor* for the wife.
Bruce Holroyd Pearce QC and *Mathew Thorpe* for the husband.

Cur adv vult

b 13th June 1974. **SIR GEORGE BAKER P** read the following judgment. For convenience I shall refer to the parties as the husband, the wife and the co-respondent, although the husband has remarried and the wife has married the co-respondent. The husband aged 44 is a director of a bank; the co-respondent aged 34 is a solicitor. The wife is 37. The main question for decision is the effect of the wife's remarriage to a man of means, with her new home conveyed in their joint names, on her claim for the settle-*c* ment of the former matrimonial home, in trust, until the youngest child is 18, in equal shares, or alternatively for a lump sum of £17,000.

The parties married in December 1957 and parted finally in December 1972 when the wife went to live with the co-respondent after 15 years of married life. The decree absolute was granted on 15th May 1973. It is agreed that the conduct of the parties is not a relevant issue. The wife miscarried in 1958 and again in 1959. The *d* first child, a girl, was born in March 1963 (now ten), the second, a boy, in December 1964 (now eight), the third, a girl, in March 1966 (now seven) and the fourth, a boy, in July 1967 (now six). There is an agreed order for joint custody with care and control to the father. The present homes are very close and access arrangements have been made. The children live at the former matrimonial house which the wife accepts should not be sold for the next 12 years. The agreement also envisages *e* their being taken on holiday by their mother at her expense but there is a dispute, which I think is immaterial, about how much of the holidays are spent with her.

The husband remarried on 10th July 1973. The wife married the co-respondent on 5th December 1973 and they have a child born on 6th February 1974. His two children aged eight are living with his former wife.

The wife does not suggest that she has any property rights in the sense of a legal *f* interest, or a beneficial interest arising from a joint tenancy, under s 17 of the Married Women's Property Act 1882 or by virtue of improvements under s 37 of the Matrimonial Proceedings and Property Act 1970. Her case is that she has contributed to the welfare of the family, including looking after the home and caring for the family: see s 25(*f*) of the Matrimonial Causes Act 1973; that in the 15 years of marriage she bore the four children, was a wife and mother, and in the early days washed, *g* ironed, cooked for and looked after a paying guest; that with the husband she decorated a flat they had early in the marriage and part of a house they had in 1963; that she cleaned the stairs and bathroom of a tenanted house the husband owns, and that she gardened and supervised decoration and workmen. Under the new law such contributions can and must be adequately recognised on the division of the family assets, either as a moral claim, or as an accrued right, a beneficial interest, *h* already in existence at the end of the marriage earned by her contribution: see Lord Denning MR in *Wachtel v Wachtel*[1]. Counsel for the wife rightly points out that continuing financial provision orders (see the sidenote to s 28 of the 1973 Act) end on remarriage, but that a property adjustment order can be made after remarriage. The sole prohibition, contained in s 28(3) of the 1973 Act, is that a party to a remarriage shall not be entitled to apply for a financial provision order, and the *j* courts have consistently held that that means 'make a new application'. An application which has already been made can be pursued: see *Jackson v Jackson*[2], *Marsden v Marsden*[3] and *B v B*[4].

---

1 [1973] 1 All ER 829 at 841, [1973] Fam 81 at 96
2 [1973] 2 All ER 395, [1973] Fam 99
3 [1973] 2 All ER at 855, [1973] 1 WLR at 646
4 [1974] The Times, 9th April

This must, he submits, be because a proprietary right has already accrued as a result of the wife's contribution under s 25(*f*). She has earned that right and re- *a* marriage only affects that right by making it unenforceable if a claim, that is an application for its recognition, has not already been made. If such a claim has been made it would be imposing a penalty on the wife to hold, in the absence of a statutory provision, that her right ends with remarriage.

Counsel for the husband submits that this is a misconceived claim and that the wife has no entitlement in law or justice because of (1) her remarriage to this co- *b* respondent and (2) an agreement of 4th January 1973. I can dispose briefly of the agreement. I accept the husband's evidence that there had been discussions at the end of 1972 between husband, wife and co-respondent in which money was mentioned; that the wife had said she wanted nothing from the husband and the co-respondent had said something to the effect that it was a pity the proceeds of the sale of some ICI shares owned by the wife had been used to buy curtains rather than on *c* the house, in which event she would have had a share. I am also satisfied that the wife saw her solicitor about divorce on 28th November 1972 and was advised, but she did not see him again until 27th March 1973. The agreement of 4th January 1973 was the result of a clause by clause discussion between husband and wife alone. The husband wrote it; the wife copied it. She had no advice; he had read for the Bar but was never called. She was to remove her personal property and he was to *d* pay her half the value of the remainder of the contents less his personal property 'in order that [the former matrimonial home] shall remain home for our children'. He was also to pay the value of the ICI shares, which he has done. The wife was concerned primarily about the children and I accept that she did not intend to give up any claim she might have in the house. The husband may have thought that he was securing the house for the children but there is clearly no estoppel. In *e* any event the agreement was reached before judgment was delivered in *Wachtel v Wachtel*[1] on 8th February 1973 and I doubt if legal advice at that time would have been able to forecast accurately the possibilities. I therefore disregard the agreement.

On the effect of remarriage, many cases have been cited to me and critically examined but most are of little help. *White v White*[2] was a decision under the old law. In that case the wife had married the co-respondent and Lord Denning MR said he *f* was the one who should maintain her. It was cited in *Wachtel v Wachtel*[1] but not referred to in the judgments. It is no longer authoritative. In *Wachtel v Wachtel*[1] Lord Denning MR dealt with remarriage thus[3]:

'*Remarriage*

'In making financial provision, ought the prospects of remarriage to be taken *g* into account? The statute says in terms that periodical payments shall cease on remarriage: see s 7(1)(*b*). But it says nothing about the prospects of remarriage. The question then arises: ought the provision for the wife to be reduced if she is likely to remarry? So far as the capital assets are concerned, we see no reason for reducing her share. After all, she has earned it by her contribution in looking after the home and caring for the family. It should not be *h* taken away from her by the prospect of remarriage. In *Buckley v John Allen & Ford (Oxford) Ltd*[4] Phillimore J showed that it was a guessing game, which no judge was qualified to put his—or her—money on. His observations were disapproved by this court in *Goodburn v Thomas Cotton Ltd*[5]. But they have been vindicated by Parliament.'

j

1 [1973] 1 All ER 829, [1973] Fam 72
2 [1972] Bar Library transcript 54A
3 [1973] 1 All ER at 841, [1973] Fam at 96
4 [1967] 1 All ER 539 at 542, [1967] 2 QB 637 at 645
5 [1968] 1 All ER 518, [1968] 1 QB 845

a
Lord Denning MR was careful to deal with the prospects, the likelihood, of remarriage. He said nothing of the fact of remarriage in relation to capital assets. It is said that the passage is obiter and its guidance is not binding on me, but in a reserved judgment given in chambers on 27th March 1972 allowing an appeal by a wife against a lump sum award of £350,000 I had myself said:

b
'It would be strange, indeed repugnant, if, in the face of s 4 of the Law Reform (Miscellaneous Provisions) Act 1971, which prohibits the court from taking into account a widow's remarriage or prospects of remarriage in assessing damages in respect of the death of her husband, this court had to embark on an enquiry into this lady's prospects of remarriage before deciding on the lump sum.'

c
In *Trippas v Trippas*[1] the wife was living with another man whom she might marry. That did not affect her entitlement. The prospect, chance or hope of remarriage is I think irrelevant, but the fact of remarriage, which does not admit of speculation, is in my judgment something which the court must consider in the course of its statutory duty under s 25 'to have regard to all the circumstances of the case'.

d
This accords with Bagnall J's view in *Jackson v Jackson*[2] that the wife's intervening marriage is a factor to be weighed with all the others in a particular case, and with at least part of Latey J's conclusion in *S v S*[3] reached after reviewing *Mesher v Mesher*[4], *Hector v Hector*[5] and *Chamberlain v Chamberlain*[6] (an appeal against his decision was dismissed) that the following emerges as guidance:

'4 If the wife has remarried (or is going to remarry) her financial position on remarriage must be considered. If it is guess work whether she will or will not remarry prospective remarriage should be ignored. [The brackets are mine.]'

e
To ignore remarriage entirely would be to ignore the financial needs of the parties in the foreseeable future: see s 25(1)(b).

It seems to me that the real problem in any particular case is to decide how to translate a new marriage into money. How is it to be regarded and what part is it to play in the financial provision? Counsel for the wife argues that a wife who remarries a poor man should get no more, and therefore a wife who remarries a rich man gets no less. I do not accept this submission. Remarriage to a poor man would reflect in her financial resources and financial needs, and would probably result in her receiving the full share of what she had earned. Equally, marriage to a wealthy man has a bearing on her financial needs and resources just as her own capital would be taken into account, for as Bagnall J said in *Harnett v Harnett*[7], 'Where the wife has some capital that must be taken into account in determining what she should be given by the husband.' The Matrimonial Causes Act 1973, s 25(1) gives the court the widest possible power to achieve the statutory object, namely—

g
'to place the parties, so far as it is practicable and . . . just to do so, in the financial position in which they would have been if the marriage had not broken down . . .'

h
First, in my opinion, justice must be done in all cases not only in those in which conduct is relevant. That is a matter of construction. Then, it is not the wife alone who is to be placed in the same position but 'the parties'. Too often the husband's position tends now to be disregarded. In the present case I find that the husband,

j
1 [1973] 2 All ER 1, [1973] Fam 134
2 [1973] 2 All ER 395 at 399, [1973] Fam 99 at 104
3 [1973] The Times, 11th December
4 [1973] The Times, 13th February, [1973] Bar Library transcript 59
5 [1973] 3 All ER 1070, [1973] 1 WLR 1122
6 [1974] 1 All ER 33, [1973] 1 WLR 1557
7 [1973] 2 All ER 593 at 601, [1973] Fam 156 at 164

having remarried a lady of 29 with no income or assets and having to bring up and
educate four young children, is near enough in the same financial position as he   *a*
would have been if the marriage had not broken down.

I now turn to consider what that position is. He has a salary of £20,000 per annum
and about £500 per annum from rents and dividends. The former matrimonial
home was bought by him in 1968 for £25,500 as the perfect home for the children.
Substantial improvements were carried out. There is a valuation of Messrs John D
Wood & Co dated 28th March 1974 of £75,000 if a pending appeal against a refusal   *b*
of planning permission is dismissed and £70,000 if it is granted. There is also a
valuation dated January 1974 by a chartered surveyor of £65,000 and £50,000. The
value has been taken for the purposes of this case as £65,000. The husband has two
accounts with his bank one of which is designated 'house purchase account'. It is
overdrawn to the limit of £20,000. Of this £9,718 arose from house improvements
and £6,516 from accumulated overdraft interest, of which it is submitted for the   *c*
wife, only a half should be charged against the house. His other account was overdrawn £20,358 in August 1973 (limit £20,000). Both accounts are secured by the
title deeds of the property. Only a part of the overdraft interest will in future be
allowable against tax. The household effects are valued at £4,505 but half of this
sum has already been paid to the wife.

In 1954 the husband bought freehold property in London for £800 as an invest-   *d*
ment. It is let. Its value is agreed as £7,000 or £16,000 with vacant possession;
of course capital gains tax will be payable. He has personal effects worth about
£3,000 and a bank account with the National Westminster with an average overdraft
of £1,000. He pays the present school fees of £300 a term. The boys are to go to
a public school. Then he owns shares valued on 13th November 1973 at £8,054 but
said now to be about £6,000. I accept that the 9,487 shares in Magnox Ltd are   *e*
practically valueless. Finally the husband has an interest in a share incentive scheme
operated by his bank. He has bought a partly paid share but he cannot exercise
his option to pay the balance of the striking price for five years from allotment, and
then only if the share price has increased over 50 per cent. He cannot sell his rights,
at least as long as he works for the bank, and now the Chancellor of the Exchequer's
proposals have at least cast a large question mark over the profitability of the scheme.   *f*
I find it impossible and unreal to regard his interest as a capital asset.

To summarise his capital position he can be treated broadly as having
£35,000-£40,000 made up as follows:

	£	
Matrimonial home	65,000	
Property in London	7,000	*g*
Shares	7,000	
	79,000	
Less two overdrafts	40,000	
	39,000	*h*

The answer to the argument that only one overdraft is material and one has to look
at the position at decree absolute, is: I do so and find that then (15th May 1973) the
house purchase account was overdrawn £20,000 and the other by £19,384.

Turning next to the co-respondent: he has an income of about £14,000 per annum   *j*
gross which, after tax, will not be very greatly less than that of the husband. I do
not think that it is necessary or desirable for me to go into his capital position in
detail. Suffice it to say that I have studied his lengthy affidavit in his own matrimonial proceedings, and have regard to his oral evidence before me which I accept.
I find that, as he said, he has capital, after allowing for capital gains tax, of approximately £50,000. There are some uncertainties. The wife and her counsel were

prepared to accept that the co-respondent's capital position is roughly the same as
a the husband's.   I find he is better off.   On any view his capital position is no worse.
Now the wife: the present house, where she lives with the co-respondent, was
bought in January 1973 for £65,000 total, of which the house and garden was put
by him into their joint names.   £35,000 was for adjoining plots which are to be sold at,
he hopes, a profit.   The house is therefore worth £30,000 plus £4,000 spent on it by
the co-respondent.   The equity is probably about £14,000 although there is no
b very clear evidence.   She is also a beneficiary under her grandfather's will subject
to life interests.   Her interest is valued at the present day at £2,250.   I disregard the
payment to her for her share of the furniture and the £1,000 for curtains bought with
the proceeds of the ICI bonds.   She can fairly, I think, be treated as having notional
capital of £7,000-£9,000.

In these circumstances, and with due regard to them all, I think, first, that it is
c unjust and impracticable to make the husband pay a lump sum.   He cannot raise
more money on the house, he has to pay for the four children and he has little other
capital.   Only a few years ago this case might have resulted in heavy damages against
the co-respondent.   Lord Denning MR said in *Wachtel v Wachtel*[1]:

d 'Take a case like the present when the wife leaves the home and the husband
stays in it.   On the breakdown of the marriage arrangements should be made
whereby it is vested in him absolutely, free of any share in the wife, and he alone
is liable for the mortgage instalments.   But the wife should be compensated
for the loss of her share by being awarded a lump sum.   It should be a sum
sufficient to enable her to get settled in a place of her own, such as by putting
down a deposit on a flat or a house.   It should not, however, be an excessive
e sum.   It should be such as the husband can raise by a further mortgage on the
house without crippling him.'

She needs no flat or house and I think most people would find it distasteful and unjust
that a lump sum should be given to a wife for the probable benefit of the new family.
But, she says, she has earned a share, and will accommodate her first family by
f allowing it to remain with them till the youngest is 18.   She now says that share
should be one-third of the house.   If the concept of earning is to be applied to a
domestic situation, then it should be applied with all its normal consequences.   One
is that if the job is left unfinished you do not earn as much.   A builder agrees to
build four houses.   He goes off to a job which he prefers to do, leaving them in
varying stages of completion.   Leaving aside any question of special contractual
g terms, the best he could hope to receive is the value of work actually done, remembering also that the owner has to have the work completed.   Is there any difference
between four houses and four children?   I think not.   Any payment will in fact put
her in a better financial position than if the marriage had continued and I would give
her one-twelfth of the unencumbered value of the house (at present £65,000) her
entitlement to rank after the present charges for the bank overdrafts and not to be
h payable until the youngest child is 18.

The final form of the order will have to be agreed or be the subject of further
argument; in any event no notice as required by r 74(4)(c) of the Matrimonial Causes
Rules 1973 has yet been given to the bank.

Order accordingly.

j
Solicitors: *Theodore Goddard & Co* (for the wife); *Charles Russell & Co* (for the husband),

R C T Habesch Esq   Barrister.

---

1   [1973] 1 All ER 829 at 840, 841, [1973] Fam 81 at 96

LTSS Print and Supply Services Ltd v London *a* Borough of Hackney and another

QUEEN'S BENCH DIVISION

LORD WIDGERY CJ, BRIDGE AND SHAW JJ

4th, 5th NOVEMBER 1974

Reversed CA [1976] 1 All ER 311

Applied in LAMB v SEC OF STATE [1975] 2 All ER 1117

Town and country planning – Enforcement notice – Effect – Reversion to earlier lawful use – Purpose for which land may be used without planning permission – Purpose for which land could lawfully have been used if development enforced against had not been carried out – Established use – Use unlawful at its inception but no longer liable to enforcement action by **c** *reason of lapse of time – Whether permission required for that use after service of enforcement notice – Town and Country Planning Act 1971, s 23(9).*

In s 23(9)[a] of the Town and Country Planning Act 1971 (which provides that, where an enforcement notice is served in respect of any development of land, planning per- **d** mission is not required for the use of that land for a purpose for which it could law- fully have been used if the development had not been carried out) the reference to lawful use includes a use which although unlawful at its inception cannot be the sub- ject of enforcement action because it was established before the end of 1963 (see p 376 *f* and *h*, p 377 *a* and p 378 *a b* and *e*, post).

Quaere. Whether the reference to lawful use in s 23(9) includes a use established **e** after 1963 and therefore not immune from enforcement action (see p 378 *b* and *c*, post).

Notes

For development for which permission is required, see 37 Halsbury's Laws (3rd Edn) 269-272, para 370, and for cases on the subject, see 45 Digest (Repl) 335-340, *33-35*.

For the Town and Country Planning Act 1971, s 23, see 41 Halsbury's Statutes **f** (3rd Edn) 1608.

Case cited

Petticoat Lane Rentals Ltd v Secretary of State for the Environment [1971] 2 All ER 793, [1971] 1 WLR 1112, DC.

g

Appeal

This was an appeal by LTSS Print and Supply Services Ltd under s 246 of the Town and Country Planning Act 1971 against a decision of the second respondent, the Secretary of State for the Environment, contained in a letter dated 10th April 1974, on an appeal by Frederick A Jones (Wholesale) Ltd against an enforcement notice **h** dated 6th December 1972 and served by the first respondents, the London Borough of Hackney, on the appellants and others. Frederick A Jones (Wholesale) Ltd went into liquidation before the Secretary of State's decision was given. The facts are set out in the judgment of Lord Widgery CJ.

Alistair Dawson for the appellants.   **j**
Harry Woolf for the Secretary of State.
The first respondents were not represented.

---

a Section 23(9) is set out at p 376 *e*, post

LORD WIDGERY CJ. This matter comes before the court in the shape of an appeal
under s 246 of the Town and Country Planning Act 1971 against a decision of the Secretary of State for the Environment contained in his decision letter dated the 10th
April 1974 and relating to an enforcement notice served by the Borough of Hackney
on, amongst others, the present appellants in respect of a piece of land at 138 Kings-
land Road, E2. The enforcement notice recited that the land was being used for the
sale of furniture without the grant of planning permission and required that sale of
furniture to be discontinued. The Secretary of State inserted the word 'retail' before
'sale', but otherwise allowed the enforcement notice to stand.

The case has been argued economically by counsel on both sides, and in the end
the issues which remain for us are simple and short. The background facts of the case
are that the appeal site had been used in 1961 and for some time thereafter by a
business dealing in veneers and plywood. This was mainly wholesale trade, but the
public could enter and buy offcuts of plywood.

When this firm left the site some two or three years after 1961 the site was taken
over by a firm of timber importers, and there was no evidence before the inspector
at the inquiry held in this case that they made retail sales to the public. The timber
importers left in 1969, and for some time in 1971 the greater part of the appeal
premises was used for displaying furniture for retail sale to the public which was
delivered to customers subsequent to purchase. From October 1972 all available
floor space was used for discount sales of furniture to the public, who could take away
their purchases when paid for.

There was no dispute between the parties that the established use of the premises
at least up to 1969 was as a wholesale warehouse within Class X of the Town and
Country Planning (Use Classes) Order 1963[1].

So there is the history in a nutshell. You have an activity in the form of wholesale
storage with some element of sales, and it is common ground between the parties
that the established use was as a wholesale warehouse. You then get the more immediate activity sought to be restrained, which is the selling of furniture retail to customers who come to the premises. The Hackney borough council, taking the view
that that change was a material change carried out without permission, served the
enforcement notice in question.

The Secretary of State sets out the history almost in the words which I have given.
He then goes on in para 8 of his decision letter to a long enquiry into the meaning of
the word 'warehouse'. I for my part find nothing to complain about in this consideration of the meaning of the word 'warehouse', although I do not intend by that
to commit myself to the acceptance of every proposition the paragraph contains. In
particular, the Secretary of State discusses 'discount selling', 'cash and carry', 'storage'
and phrases like that, which to my mind are imprecise and which may have more than
one meaning. But his general description of activities implicit in the phrase 'warehouse', and indeed 'wholesale warehouse', I find quite unobjectionable. Therefore,
it comes as no surprise in para 9 to discover that the Secretary of State upholds the
inspector in thinking there was a material change of use which required
permission, which permission had not been obtained.

Later on the Secretary of State proceeds to consider whether planning permission
should nevertheless be granted on the merits of the matter. He does that because
under the 1971 Act, as indeed some of its predecessors, where an enforcement notice
is upheld, the Secretary of State does go on to consider whether planning permission
should nevertheless be granted for the activity in question. The purpose of that is to
make it unnecessary to have a second and separate application. He went on, therefore,
to consider the merits of the planning application which arise in such a case.

The argument before the inspector at the inquiry on the merits was as follows.
First of all, it was contended by the appellants, or those representing them at the

---

1   SI 1963 No 708

inquiry, that the established use of this site was as a wholesale warehouse, and there
was no argument about that. It was contended by the appellants that within that *a*
definition, and having regard to the provisions of Class X of the Town and Country
Planning (Use Classes) Order, it would be open to the appellants to open on this site,
without planning permission, a retail cash and carry grocery business. That, it was
said, would result in more traffic than was occasioned by the retail furniture business
presently carried on on the site, and so it was contended that on the merits it would
be a proper thing for the Secretary of State to authorise the furniture sales use.   *b*

One must remind oneself all the time that the application for planning permission
is assumed to be an application for furniture selling. The reference to a grocery
business was merely an in terrorem proposition put forward by the appellants to
indicate what other and less attractive activity would follow if they were not allowed
to sell furniture.

In deciding whether or not permission for the furniture selling would or would not *c*
be better in the interests of the environment than use as a wholesale warehouse, the
Secretary of State was undoubtedly entitled to consider the resultant traffic produced
by those two alternatives. In other words, it was perfectly proper for him, if he
thought fit when deciding whether or not to authorise the furniture sales, to ask
himself what the alternative was and how far the alternative would be more or less
suitable. Had he asked himself what the alternative was, he would in my judgment *d*
have been referred, or would have referred himself, to s 23(9) of the 1971 Act, which
provides:

'Where an enforcement notice has been served in respect of any development
of land, planning permission is not required for the use of that land for the
purpose for which (in accordance with the provisions of this Part of this Act) it *e*
could lawfully have been used if that development had not been carried out.'

I think that means, and plainly was intended to mean, that if an enforcement notice
is served and the present activity is to be discontinued, the landowner or occupier can
revert to any use which would have been lawful or permitted under the terms of
the 1971 Act.   *f*

In the present instance, since it was accepted by all that the use before development
was a use as a wholesale warehouse, the landowner was entitled under s 23(9) to go
back to the use as a wholesale warehouse, and that was the alternative activity which
the Secretary of State should have had regard to if he was making the comparison to
which I have referred.

I feel reinforced in the view that that is the proper meaning of s 23(9) by the different *g*
treatment of a similar point which one finds in s 23(5) and (6). There it is, I think, clear
that, when considering what is the normal use of the land, one must have regard to
the use which was begun otherwise than in contravention of the provisions of the Act
or in contravention of previous planning control. A somewhat looser reference is
contained in s 23(9) where the reference, as I have said, is merely to 'lawful use'. I
think that that subsection permits the return to any use which could be carried on at *h*
the time of the development enforced against without breach of the terms of the
planning Acts and without there being any risk of enforcement action being taken
against him. The Secretary of State has not taken that view. In para 11 of his decision
letter he has said:

'It is pointed out that an established use is not a lawful use of land for the *j*
purposes of Section 23(9) of the 1971 Act, it is merely a use which at a certain time
becomes immune from enforcement action. Once an established use has been
materially changed to another use involving development, it is considered that
the established use has been abandoned and there is no right to revert to the
established use, which in this case was use as a wholesale warehouse.'

With deference to the Secretary of State, I think that was wrong. I think there was a
a right here to revert to the established use as a wholesale warehouse. But did it make
any difference? It seems highly improbable that it did. When I say 'it', I refer of course
to this error on the part of the Secretary of State.

The inspector, giving his reasons for refusing planning permission on the merits,
obviously contemplated the amount of traffic which might be generated by the
established use, and thought that it would not be greatly in excess of that already
b involved. He then gave strong and particular grounds for saying that this land was
unsuitable for the present use (the furniture selling use) which was the only use for
which planning permission was deemed to be sought.

I find it very unlikely, to put it no higher than that, that the Secretary of State, in
considering the inspector's reasons, was influenced by the error of law which he had
made earlier in his decision letter. He sets out, that for the reasons given by the
c inspector it is not proposed to grant planning permission for the continuation of the
use enforced against, and it may very well be that his decision is quite unaffected by
the error in the construction of s 23(9) to which I have referred.

However, it seems to me right, as Shaw J pointed out in argument, that, if there is
any possibility that the Secretary of State was influenced by this error, he should be
given the opportunity of saying so and making whatever adjustments are required.
d I would allow this appeal on the very narrow ground that it may be that the decision
of the Secretary of State was influenced by the error of law to which I have referred
and I think it appropriate the matter should go back to him for reconsideration in
the light of the judgments in this court.

e **BRIDGE J.** I entirely agree in the order proposed by Lord Widgery CJ, and in the
reasons he has given for arriving at his conclusions, subject to one very limited and
narrow qualification as to the precise application of the provisions of s 23(9) of the Town
and Country Planning Act 1971.

I think that in planning law doubt has been felt for some years as to the precise
circumstances in which in different situations a right to revert to an earlier use of
f land arises. Broadly, as it seems to me, there are three kinds of situation in which
this question can arise.

The first familiar situation is where land, having been used for purpose A, is used
for a different purpose, purpose B, either in pursuance of a permission to change
from A to B or without any such permission. But in the second case the planning
authority takes no steps to require the discontinuance of use B. In those two situations,
g which in law produce a similar result, a reversion from use B to use A, contrary to
what at one time used to be thought to be the law, requires planning permission
because it is a material change of use.

That being so, Parliament in the 1971 Act (both these provisions have, I think, in
principle been in this legislation since 1947) has had to make special provision for a
right to revert in two situations: one, after the grant of temporary planning permission,
h and two, after the service of an enforcement notice.

The provisions of s 23(5) and (6), to which Lord Widgery CJ has referred which deal
with the right to revert to an earlier use after the expiry of a temporary planning
permission, are clear beyond doubt. The only earlier use to which the right to revert
applies is a use itself commenced either before the 1947 Act came into operation or
with permission under the Act. An earlier use on which a temporary permitted use
j has supervened, which was itself begun in contravention of the provisions of the
legislation, does not attract a right to revert, even though it might itself have become
immune from the possibility of enforcement by the passage of time long before the
temporary permission was granted.

But the quite different language of s 23(9), which deals with the right to revert to
an earlier use after the service of an enforcement notice requiring discontinuance of

an offending use, produces quite a different result. I am entirely satisfied in the
circumstances of this case that a use, here the wholesale warehouse use, established   *a*
before the end of 1963, and therefore long since immune from liability to enforcement
before the offending retail furniture use began, was a use for which this land could
lawfully have been used if the retail furniture use had never begun within the meaning of the phrase 'could lawfully have been used' in sub-s (9). So far, therefore, I am
entirely in agreement with Lord Widgery CJ.

The only point on which, as I said at the outset of this judgment, I would wish to   *b*
reserve my opinion is the situation that would arise if use A was commenced after
the end of 1963, was continued for some years, and then displaced by use B. If the
planning authority then serves an enforcement notice requiring discontinuance of
use B, is there a right to revert to use A, which does not itself require permission as a
material change of use? Without wishing to decide the point today, because it is not
before us, I would keep that point open. I would think that it is at least very arguable *c*
in the circumstances I have indicated that use A is a use which could lawfully have
been continued if use B had not supervened possibly because no enforcement notice
has ever been served in respect of it. In a sense it may perhaps be said that the point
is academic, because the right to revert to use A, if I am right in the view that that
might be a proper construction of the Act, would of course itself always be subject
to the possibility that a further enforcement notice could be served after the reversion *d*
to require the discontinuance of use A, which ex hypothesi having begun after the end
of 1963, would still be susceptible to enforcement procedure.

SHAW J. I propose to say nothing further than to agree with the course proposed
by Lord Widgery CJ.   *e*

Appeal allowed.

Solicitors: *Kingsley, Napley & Co* (for the appellants); *Treasury Solicitor.*
                                                                                        f
Lea Josse Barrister.

a R v Liverpool City Council, ex parte Liverpool Taxi Fleet Operators' Association

QUEEN'S BENCH DIVISION
LORD WIDGERY CJ, MELFORD STEVENSON AND WATKINS JJ
4th DECEMBER 1974

b

Public authority – Meeting – Admission of public – Resolution to exclude public – Reason for exclusion – Special reason arising from nature of business or of proceedings – Accommodation for public at place of meeting – Lack of accommodation – Reasonable provision made to accommodate public – Unexpectedly large numbers wishing to attend meeting – Resolution by body to exclude all members of public rather than select some to fill available seats – Whether
c *a reason 'arising from the nature of [the] business or of the proceedings' – Whether resolution valid – Public Bodies (Admission to Meetings) Act 1960, s 1(2).*

Public authority – Meeting – Admission of public – Resolution to exclude public – Reason for exclusion – Special reason stated in the resolution – Failure of body to state reason in resolution – No-one suffering injury in consequence of failure – Whether requirement the reason
d *be stated in resolution mandatory or directory – Whether resolution valid – Public Bodies (Admission to Meetings) Act 1960, s 1(2).*

A local authority issued a public notice stating that a committee of the authority would meet on a specified date to review the issue of licences for taxi cabs. Anyone wishing to make representations to the committee was invited to attend. The appli-
e cants, who were representatives of most of the taxi cab owners within the district of the local authority, did not wish to make representations to the committee but they did want to attend the meeting and hear the evidence being given. The room set aside for the meeting had 55 seats and 41 were taken by members and officers of the local authority wishing to sit on the committee or attend the meeting. The meeting excited a great deal of public interest and when it was due to take place there were
f more than 40 people waiting outside the room. The committee chairman decided that in view of the numbers it would be impossible either to admit all the public who wished to attend or to choose some people to fill the remaining seats. The chairman also felt that the people making applications for licences should be heard in the absence of those who wished to make competing applications. The committee accepted the chairman's views and accordingly passed a resolution under s 1(2)ᵃ of
g the Public Bodies (Admission to Meetings) Act 1960 excluding the public from the meeting 'in view of the limitations of available space and in order that the business of the Committee may be carried out satisfactorily'. At the meeting the committee decided to authorise the grant of an increased number of licences to operate within the local authority's area. Subsequently the local authority resolved to adopt the decisions of the committee. The applicants moved for an order of certiorari to quash
h that resolution on the ground that the committee's resolution to exclude the public from its meeting under s 1(2) of the 1960 Act was invalid and therefore the proceedings at the meeting were in breach of s 1(1) of the 1960 Act as extended by the Local Government Act 1972, s 100.

Held – The application would be refused for the following reasons—
j (i) Both reasons adopted by the committee for deciding to exclude the public were valid reasons under s 1(2) of the 1960 Act. Where a public body had made reasonable arrangements to accommodate the public wishing to attend one of its meetings but in the event so many people wished to attend that it was quite impossible to accommodate them all, that would be a special reason 'arising from the nature of [the]

---

a Section 1, so far as material, is set out at p 382 *j* and p 383 *b* and *c*, post

business or of the proceedings', within s 1(2), justifying a decision of the committee, arrived at honestly and fairly, that the only solution would be to exclude all members *a* of the public. Alternatively the second reason for excluding the public, i e that it was desirable that individual applicants should be heard in the absence of competing applicants, was a valid one (see p 383 *h* to p 384 *b* and *h j*, post).

(ii) The requirement of s 1(2) that the reasons for excluding the public should be stated in the resolution was directory and not mandatory. Accordingly, if the only valid reason for excluding the public had been to allow applicants to be heard in the *b* absence of competing applicants, the fact that that reason had not been stated in the resolution would not have had the effect of invalidating the resolution automatically and in those circumstances the resolution would only be set aside by the Divisional Court if it could be shown that someone had suffered a significant injury in consequence of the irregularity; no such injury had been shown in the instant case (see p 384 *d* to *j*, post).   *c*

Notes

For admission to public meetings, see Supplement to 24 Halsbury's Laws (3rd Edn) para 852B.

For the Public Bodies (Admission to Meetings) Act 1960, s 1, see 19 Halsbury's Statutes (3rd Edn) 835.   *d*

Case referred to in judgments

Liverpool Taxi Owners' Association, Re [1972] 2 All ER 589, sub nom *R v Liverpool Corporation, ex parte Liverpool Taxi Fleet Operators' Association* [1972] 2 QB 299, [1972] 2 WLR 1262, 136 JP 491, 70 LGR 387, CA.   *e*

Motions for prohibition, mandamus and certiorari

This was an application by way of motion by the Liverpool Taxi Fleet Operators' Association for the following orders: (a) an order of prohibition prohibiting the respondents, Liverpool City Council ('the corporation') and its committees and sub-committees from acting on a resolution of the corporation dated 9th October *f* 1974 affirming and approving a resolution of the Highways and Environment Committee of the Corporation dated 18th September 1974 which related to the issue of taxi cab licences and from issuing any such licences over and above those authorised by the resolutions passed by the special sub-committee of the Environmental Health and Protection Committee of the corporation appointed to consider matters relating to hackney carriage and private hire vehicles on 23rd November 1973 and pro- *g* hibiting the corporation by its committees and sub-committees from taking any steps or making any directions towards the issue of any such further licences; (b) an order of mandamus directed to the corporation and the Highways and Environment Committee thereof commanding them and each of them (1) to admit the applicants as members of the public to committee meetings of the Highways and Environment Committee when that committee was considering matters relating to taxi cabs *h* except on such occasions as the public were lawfully excluded therefrom; (2) to revoke all such taxi cab licences as had been issued by or on behalf of the corporation pursuant to its resolution of 9th October 1974 approving and affirming the resolutions of the Highways and Environment Committee of 18th September 1974; (c) an order of certiorari to remove into the court and quash the resolutions of the corporation of 9th October 1974 and further to remove and quash the resolutions of the Highways *j* and Environment Committee of 18th September 1974 relating to taxi cab licences. The facts are set out in the judgment of Lord Widgery CJ.

Charles James for the applicants.
Alan Booth for the corporation.

LORD WIDGERY CJ. In these proceedings counsel moves on behalf of the Liver-
a pool Taxi Fleet Operators' Association for a variety of forms of relief under the
prerogative orders. More especially, and in my judgment central to his motion, is
an application for an order of certiorari to remove into this court with a view to its
being quashed a resolution of the Liverpool City Council ('the corporation') dated
9th October 1974, the effect of which was to authorise the grant of an increased
number of hackney carriage licences to operate within the city boundaries.

b   The substantial ground for the relief sought is that the committee meeting leading
up to the decision of the corporation on 9th October 1974 was itself held in breach of
the provisions of the Public Bodies (Admission to Meetings) Act 1960 in that it is
alleged the public were not admitted to the relevant committee meeting as required
by that Act.

          There is a certain history to this application. I mention it very briefly because it
c seems to me to have no real bearing on the issue which is before the court. A very
similar matter was before this court, and subsequently the Court of Appeal, in *Re
Liverpool Taxi Owners' Association*[1]. That was a case which again had raised the vexed
issue of whether there should be additional hackney carriage licences in Liverpool,
this being a matter of very considerable interest to those whose livelihood depends
on obtaining and retaining licences to operate such cabs, and indeed to those who
d already operate such cabs and who wish to be protected against unfair competition
by an undue increase in the number. In the matter which was before the court in
1972 it was laid down that the corporation in exercising their undoubted jurisdiction
to grant or withhold the grant of licences were required to act fairly, and in
particular were required to give interested parties an opportunity of making
representations before any decision in regard to the grant of new licences was taken.

e   Further intervention by this court occurred as recently as July 1974 because the
corporation, being minded to alter the number of hackney carriage licences, and
mindful of the directions of this court and the Court of Appeal in 1972[1], had invited
representations before embarking on their decision but unhappily had not made
that invitation sufficiently all embracing to bring in all those who were interested,
and accordingly an application for prohibition in this court on 19th July to prohibit
f the corporation from acting on the then current resolution was successful because the
corporation conceded that it was in the wrong and the resolution then made by the
corporation was duly set aside.

          It is in the autumn of 1974 that the corporation make their third attempt to deal
with this problem and they began by publishing a public notice dealing with their
plans. The notice went out on or about 14th August and it says in the plainest terms,
g it being a notice in the public press, that the corporation are proposing to review the
present issue of licences for taxi cabs. It recognises in terms that the corporation are
under a duty to hear representations before reaching a conclusion and invites all
those who wish to make representations to attend at a meeting of the Highways and
Environment Committee to be held on 18th September 1974.

          If I may pause there, so far so good. The corporation appear to be following to
h the letter the lessons which they have learnt, if I may say so without giving offence,
in the two previous proceedings before us here. The notice of course came to the
attention of the applicants, who are a representation of a very large number of taxi
drivers in Liverpool. In the first instance the applicants seem to have been minded
to appear at the committee meeting fixed for 18th September and to make representations. But in the end they decided that they would not make representations,
j but they informed the corporation that they wished to attend the meeting in order to
listen to the representations which were made by other people.

          So one comes to the meeting of 18th September. It is at this meeting that the
resolution was passed, which on adoption by the corporation on 9th October becomes

---

1 [1972] 2 All ER 589, [1972] 2 QB 299

the resolution under attack in the present case. On 18th September the room set
aside for the meeting of the committee had 55 seats. When those concerned began *a*
to assemble it became apparent that there were 22 members of the corporation who
wished to sit on the committee on that day, or at least to be present on that day.
That in itself was some indication of how keen is the interest in this matter in Liverpool. In addition to the 22 members of the corporation who wanted seats there were
17 officials. One feels bound to say that seems rather a large number of officials,
but it is not for us in this court to decide what was or was not necessary in that respect. *b*
There were also two police officers. So of the original 55 seats, 41 were absorbed in
that way, leaving only 14 vacant. Those 14 had to serve for the claims of the press,
the public and those individuals who were making representations to the committee.

It is not difficult to understand that the number of seats was clearly inadequate for
that purpose: all the more so, because when the meeting was about to start there
were something like 40 people outside waiting to come in being either members of *c*
the public or interested persons minded to make representations or otherwise
concerned to be present. There were 40 of them there, coming to deal with a subject
on which, as I have said, feelings ran high.

The decision as to what to do in that event fell on Mrs Jones, who was the chairman
of the committee, and she tells us in her affidavit what the position was. She said that
having regard to the numbers to which I have already referred it was clear that it *d*
was not possible to throw the meeting open to members of the public in the ordinary
sense of the word. There just was not room for that purpose. Again there was no very
obvious way in which individual members of the public could be selected to occupy
such seats as there were. This was not a case where there was a public gallery set
aside and marked out for use as such, and it was not a case where there was an orderly
queue of people from whom the first six or eight, or whatever number it was, could *e*
be taken. If there had been an indication to the assembled 40 outside that there were
14 seats, the possibility of an ugly rush was clear enough.

But not only that, in Mrs Jones's mind there were strong reasons for saying in this
case that each person coming forward to make his representations about the issue
should be entitled to make those representations to the committee not in the presence
of others making conflicting representations. Whether that was a sensible point of *f*
view or not is not for us to comment on, but I am bound to say that I see no reason
at all why that should be regarded as other than a tenable conclusion in the rather
unusual facts and circumstances of this case.

Having regard to all those matters, Mrs Jones put it to the committee and the
committee agreed that the public should be excluded from the meeting but the
press should be allowed to attend. No doubt Mrs Jones thought there would probably *g*
be room for the press, and this on the face of it, it may be, was a perfectly sensible
compromise. But be that as it may, the committee adopted Mrs Jones's suggestion
on those lines and the resolution makes reference to that fact. It is resolution 101 of
the relevant committee on the 18th September, and it says:

'Exclusion of Public. Resolved that members of the public, with the exception *h*
of the Press, be excluded from the meeting during consideration of the following
item in view of the limitations of available space and in order that the business
of the Committee may be carried out satisfactorily.'

That is the reason recorded in the minutes for the exclusion of the public. The
contention that these proceedings were irregular, and irregular to the point that the
resolution should be set aside, is entirely based on the provisions of the 1960 Act *j*
to which I have already referred. Section 1(1) provides:

'Subject to subsection (2) below, any meeting of a local authority or other body
exercising public functions, being an authority or other body to which this Act
applies, shall be open to the public.'

The expression 'body' there does include, as counsel have been kind enough to
a agree, this committee by virtue of the extension of the 1960 Act produced by s 100 of
the Local Government Act 1972. So the committee was a body within the meaning
of that subsection and thus required to open its proceedings to the public subject to
s 1(2) of the 1960 Act, which s 1(2) says:

b
> 'A body may, by resolution, exclude the public from a meeting (whether
> during the whole or part of the proceedings) whenever publicity would be
> prejudicial to the public interest by reason of the confidential nature of the
> business to be transacted or for other special reasons stated in the resolution and
> arising from the nature of that business or of the proceedings; and where such a
> resolution is passed, this Act shall not require the meeting to be open to the
> public during proceedings to which the resolution applies.'

c
So under s 1(2) it is permissible for the committee to resolve to exclude the public
for special reasons stated in the resolution and arising from the nature of that business,
that is to say the business of the body or of the proceedings.
The first question I think we have to decide here is whether the public really were
excluded or not in this particular case. It is, I think, important to stress that authori-
d ties arranging committee meetings and other meetings to which the 1960 Act applies
must have regard to their duty to the public. That means they must have regard
when making the arrangements for the committee meeting to the provision of
reasonable accommodation for the public. If a committee was minded to choose to
meet in a very small room and turned round and said 'We cannot have the public in
because there is no room', it would be acting in bad faith and it would not be beyond
e the long arm of this court. The committee must in the first instance so organise its
affairs as to recognise its obligation to the public. But of course if the interest in the
matter is unexpectedly great, if the estimates of persons attending are proved to be
too low, and if the accommodation reasonably allotted to the public is filled up,
then other members of the public will be excluded but not excluded by order of the
committee; they will be excluded for the simple reason that no more can get in the
f space provided.
If that situation is reached, it is wrong to speak of the exclusion of the public at all
in the context in which we use the phrase in this case, but in my judgment that was
not this case, and I am moved to that conclusion most by the fact that the committee
themselves did not regard this as a case in which the public were only turned back
because the last seat had gone. The last seat indeed had not gone. The committee
g quite deliberately decided to exclude the public, and their conduct must be justified,
if at all, under the terms of s 1(2) of the 1960 Act.
Next I turn to consider what was the reason which prompted the exclusion order
and we cannot do better than take the account given by Mrs Jones. Indeed I think
that is the only source to which one can go. As I read her affidavit, extracts from which
I have already given, there were really two reasons in her mind somewhat overlapping
h and perhaps slightly confusing each other because they do overlap.
I think she was mindful of the fact that with only a minimum number of seats
available there was no practical way in which the public could be selected to come
and occupy those seats. Insofar as that was her reason, and later the reason of the
committee which adopted her suggestion, I would have thought that was a perfectly
good reason under s 1(2). It would not be a case of a body declining to face up to its
j responsibility and provide accommodation for the public. It would be a case of a
body which found that its arrangements, apparently sensibly made, had been swamped
by the number of people who sought to attend. If in those circumstances the committee said 'The only way out of this is to keep all the members of the public out', and
if they took that view fairly and honestly, then I think that that would be a reason
arising from the nature of the business or the proceedings within the meaning of s 1(2).

But, equally, as it seems to me, the second reason which Mrs Jones put forward is a valid one as well. The second reason, it will be remembered, was that it was desirable *a* that individual applicants should be heard in the absence of competing applicants. That seems to me to be a conclusion which could properly be reached by this committee if so minded, and indeed there is a hint of something rather like that in s 1(3), a subsection to which I need not refer in detail.

Accordingly, if the committee had said either separately or in addition to their first reason that they wanted to exclude the public in order that individual applicants *b* could be individually heard, I would have thought that could be regarded as a special reason arising from the nature of the business or the proceedings within the terms of s 1(2).

So it seems to me that the acceptable reasons were there and that they were the reasons which caused Mrs Jones to give the committee the advice she did and caused the committee to adopt the resolution which it adopted. *c*

The only remaining stumbling block is whether those reasons have been correctly stated in the minute as required by the section. I have read the minute and insofar as the reason was based on lack of available space that reason is mentioned in the minute. But insofar as the refusal of admission to the public was based on the desire to hear applicants individually, then in my judgment that reason cannot be discovered from the terms of the minute itself. It seems to me that the expression 'that the *d* business of the committee may be carried out satisfactorily', is too vague to meet the requirement of the statute where it insists that reasons for this kind of decision be given. Therefore I would be bound to say that looked at by themselves those words did not adequately show as a reason why the committee thought that individual applicants should be individually heard.

Accordingly, the final question which has to be decided is whether, given adequate *e* reasons, the decision of the committee becomes irregular, whether as a nullity or otherwise by reason of the failure properly to state the reasons in the resolution.

At this point I think that one must distinguish between statutory provisions which are clearly imperative or mandatory and those which are merely directory. In my opinion the requirement that the reasons shall be stated in the resolution is a purely directory requirement. The effect of that is that the resolution does not automatically *f* become a nullity by reason of the failure to state the reasons within its terms. It stands unless and until set aside by this court, and it would not be set aside by this court unless there were good reasons for setting it aside on the footing that someone had suffered a significant injury as a consequence of the irregularity. No such injury is suggested in this case, and it seems to me therefore that the corporation has perhaps at long last produced a resolution on this subject which is not subject to attack in *g* this court. For the reasons I have given I would refuse the application.

MELFORD STEVENSON J. I agree. I would only add this. I regard it as a possible approach to this case that the phrase in the resolution 'in order that the business of the committee may be carried out satisfactorily', although loosely and vaguely drafted, might be read as a special reason set out in circumstances in which *h* the author of the resolution might well need to particularise all the circumstances that are to be gathered from Mrs Jones's affidavit. Whether that approach is right or wrong, it does not matter because I would agree with the whole of Lord Widgery CJ's judgment.

WATKINS J. I agree and have nothing to add. *j*

Application refused.

Solicitors: *Markbys*, agents for *Layton & Co*, Liverpool (for the applicants); *K M Egan*, Liverpool (for the Corporation).

N P Metcalfe Esq Barrister.

a
Re Beesley (Audrey), ex parte Beesley (Terence Jack) v The Official Receiver and others

b
CHANCERY DIVISION
GOULDING AND WALTON JJ
11th NOVEMBER 1974

Bankruptcy – Annulment – Application to annul adjudication – Application by person interested – Meaning of 'person interested' – Spouse of bankrupt – Whether spouse a 'person interested' merely by reason of his or her matrimonial status – Bankruptcy Act 1914, s 29(1).

c

For the purposes of s 29(1)[a] of the Bankruptcy Act 1914, which empowers the court to annul an adjudication in bankruptcy on the application of 'any person interested', the spouse of a bankrupt is not, merely by reason of his or her matrimonial status, a 'person interested' (see p 386 b to d, p 387 b and j and p 388 d to g, post).

d
Re Roehampton Swimming Pool Ltd [1968] 3 All ER 661 applied.

Notes
For applications to annul adjudication orders, see 3 Halsbury's Laws (4th Edn) 260-261, para 457, and for cases on the subject, see 4 Digest (Repl) 201-203, *1802-1829*.
For the Bankruptcy Act 1914, s 29, see 3 Halsbury's Statutes (3rd Edn) 77.

e **Cases referred to in judgments**
Roehampton Swimming Pool Ltd, Re [1968] 3 All ER 661, [1968] 1 WLR 1693, Digest (Cont Vol C) 124, *7948c*.
No 39 Carr Lane, Acomb, Re, Stevens v Hutchinson [1953] 1 All ER 699, sub nom *Stevens v Hutchinson* [1953] Ch 299, [1953] 2 WLR 545, 21 Digest (Repl) 781, *2652*.

f **Cases also cited**
Smith v Hancock [1894] 2 Ch 377, CA.
Stanger, Re, ex parte Geisel (1883) 22 Ch D 436, CA.
Wood and Martin (Bricklaying Contractors) Ltd, Re [1971] 1 All ER 732.

Appeal
g
By notice of appeal dated 26th June 1974 and by a supplementary notice of appeal dated 1st October 1974, the appellant, Terence Jack Beesley, the husband of Audrey Beesley ('the bankrupt') against whom an adjudication order had been made in 1971, gave notice to (1) Triton Engineering (Sales) Ltd, the petitioning creditor, through their solicitors, (2) the Official Receiver, (3) the trustee in bankruptcy and (4) the registrar of the Croydon County Court, of the appellant's intention to appeal to the Divisional Court in Bankruptcy against the decision of the registrar on 19th June 1974
h to dismiss an application by the appellant for the annulment of the adjudication order on the ground that the appellant was not affected personally by the bankrupt's bankruptcy in any way so far as his property or any pecuniary interest or title of his was concerned, and was therefore not a 'person interested' within s 29(1) of the Bankruptcy Act 1914. The facts are set out in the judgments.

j
The appellant appeared in person.
Christopher Bathurst for the Official Receiver.
The trustee in bankruptcy appeared in person.
Michael Crystal for the petitioning creditor.

---

a   Section 29(1) is set out at p 386 c, post

o

GOULDING J.   This is an appeal against a decision of the registrar of the Croydon   *a*
County Court.   The registrar dismissed an application made by the present appellant,
whose wife was adjudicated bankrupt in the latter part of 1971.   The appellant
applied for the annulment of his wife's bankruptcy pursuant to s 29 of the Bankruptcy
Act 1914.   The court below held that he was not a person entitled to make the
application, and dismissed it on that ground.   Accordingly, we have to decide that
short point on s 29 before there is any question of going into the merits of the demand   *b*
to annul the bankruptcy.
     Section 29(1) reads as follows:

> 'Where in the opinion of the court a debtor ought not to have been adjudged
> bankrupt, or where it is proved to the satisfaction of the court that the debts of
> the bankrupt are paid in full, the court may [and now come the critical words],
> on the application of any person interested, by order annul the adjudication.'   *c*

     The short point is, therefore, is the appellant a 'person interested' within s 29?
Since no special legal relationship other than that of matrimony is alleged, I formulate
it in the more general way, is a husband a 'person interested'   for the purpose of
applying that his wife's bankruptcy be annulled?
     The appellant appears before us in person, and although he has presented his case   *d*
with clarity and moderation, he has not, of course, the advantage that counsel have
of general knowledge of the law.   I should wish to make it clear at once that there
is in my view a good deal that could be said on his side in the matter, and I have
tried to give it full consideration in my mind.
     It cannot in my view reasonably be suggested that when Parliament included, first
in the Bankruptcy Act 1883 and then in the Bankruptcy Act 1914 in revising the law,   *e*
these same words providing for 'the application of any person interested', it intended
to open the door to persons having an interest based on family sentiment or similar
feelings alone.   Thus, for my part, I disagree with the suggestion made in very
tentative language in the 17th[1] and 18th[2] editions of Williams on Bankruptcy, but
not, we were told by counsel, in earlier editions, that a 'person interested' might
possibly include a relative desiring to clear the family name.   *f*
     However, it does not necessarily follow that a 'person interested' must show a
specific interest in the sense of an interest in some particular claim, contract, or the
like.   The more difficult question, as I think it is, is whether the matrimonial status
that exists between a husband and a wife is of itself sufficient to give him an interest
within the meaning of the section in the status of his wife as a bankrupt or a person
not bankrupt.   *g*
     There is no doubt that the mere relationship of husband and wife is regarded by
the law for certain purposes as giving the one an interest in the status or assets of
the other.   For example, the law recognises that each spouse has an insurable interest
in the life of the other without limit of amount, and also, where the spouses are living
together an insurable interest to a proper value in the possessions of the other.   Again,
a husband is liable to maintain his wife at common law, and each spouse is liable   *h*
to contribute to the maintenance of the other under the Social Security Acts.   Again,
if one spouse dies the other has, in the case of intestacy, a right to a considerable part
of the estate of the deceased and, if not provided for because of dispositions by will, a
right to come to this court and ask for the will to be altered under the Inheritance
(Family Provision) Act 1938.   Not to elaborate matters, one has also to remember
that under present legislation in case the marriage is dissolved, the matrimonial   *j*
court has a very large discretion in redistributing the property of the spouses between
them as it thinks fit.
     If this were a newly enacted statute without historical background, and if I had no

1   (1958), p 150
2   (1968), p 160

guidance in reported cases on other sections in other statutes, I might well have
a thought that where Parliament used so broad a phrase as 'on the application of any
person interested' it would give each spouse a right to apply for the annulment of
the other's bankruptcy under that comprehensive wording. The survey of relations
in the law between husband and wife which I have briefly given is enough to show that
it would be no answer to that sort of argument to say that in the present case, as is
the fact, the husband is bankrupt, so that his own assets at a certain date vested in his
b trustee in bankruptcy.

In the end, however, three considerations persuade me that the words must bear a
narrower meaning in this context. I want to make it perfectly clear that for my part
all I seek to decide is whether mere matrimonial status is enough to make one spouse
interested in the affairs of the other for the purposes of s 29. Nothing that I say
is to be taken as throwing any light on a case where, for example, there is a subsisting
c or pending order or application for maintenance, or the like. I leave those special
circumstances entirely out of consideration. I am dealing simply with the question
of matrimonial status.

The first and strongest reason which persuades me to reject the appeal is this.
The Bankruptcy Act 1883, which for present purposes contains the legislation still
in force, and the Married Women's Property Act 1882, which founded the modern
d status of married women, came into force near enough at the same time. In the
more than 90 years that have elapsed there is apparently no record of any case in
which an application of this kind has been made to the court. Counsel have clearly
devoted a good deal of industry to searching the books, and bankruptcy cases are
generally well reported. Accordingly, it appears to me that the profession, at a
time when the intention of Parliament in originally enacting these words may have
e been clearer than it is now, by tacit agreement probably rejected such arguments
as have been addressed to us. I would think very carefully before approving an
application for which there is no precedent after so long a period.

Secondly, I conceive that to give one spouse merely as such the right to intervene in
the bankruptcy affairs of the other is not a necessary facility, and might be easily
abused. I must not be thought to go all the way with counsel who have addressed
f us on behalf of the Official Receiver and the petitioning creditor. It is very easy,
when a novel form of application is being considered, to paint an exaggerated picture
of the width of the door that would be opened and the possible unpleasant things
that would come through it. But it is, I think, true to say that a bankrupt, male or
female, has ample facilities under the 1914 Act for making his or her own application,
if necessary with the advice and assistance of his or her spouse. There is no real
g necessity for the spouse to be entitled to do so independently. Further, the courts
might be burdened with a multiplicity of applications in this branch of the law where
economy of administration is of the first importance.

Thirdly, we have been referred to a decision of Megarry J on s 352 of the Companies
Act 1948 under the name *Re Roehampton Swimming Pool Ltd*[1]. Megarry J in that case,
like Upjohn J in the earlier case of *Stevens v Hutchinson*[2], was disposed to give a rather
h restricted meaning, compared with my first ideas, to the term 'person interested'
in statutory enactments. I think, therefore, that those cases are of some guidance to
us, even though the subject-matter is a little different, and point the same way as
the other considerations I have mentioned.

Accordingly, for my part, although not without some hesitation, I have come to
the conclusion that the appellant's application was rightly dismissed by the county
j court, and his appeal here ought to be dismissed also.

WALTON J. This is a somewhat disquieting case in that we are told that the
bankrupt, the wife, has only one creditor and the proof of that creditor has now been

1   [1968] 3 All ER 661, [1968] 1 WLR 1693
2   [1953] 1 All ER 699, [1953] Ch 299

rejected by the trustee in bankruptcy. Therefore, as I say, it is a somewhat dis- *a*
quieting case, and I have a great deal of sympathy with the bankrupt's husband, the
appellant. He says that there has been here a miscarriage of justice. But, of course,
one must bear in mind that in fact the proof has been rejected. One assumes that
the petitioning creditor will appeal against that rejection, and in those proceedings
it will be decided finally Aye or Nay whether there are any really serious debts, or any
debts at all, of the bankrupt wife.   *b*

However, although one starts out with a certain amount of sympathy for the husband in his application, a certain amount of that sympathy vanishes when one dis-
covers that he was offered the opportunity in the court below of the application
being transferred into the name of the wife and made in the name of the wife, and
that offer was refused. Although there might very well be difficulties in the way,
because she had in fact at an earlier stage applied for a discharge from bankruptcy on *c*
2nd July 1973 which was refused on 18th July, nevertheless, if the facts had been
sufficiently strong there is no doubt that the court could have made the order sought
on her application. However, that offer or opportunity having been turned down,
as Goulding J has said the simple point for us is whether the husband is a 'person
interested' merely by virtue of being a husband.

I think one can see that that cannot be the right solution, because if he is merely *d*
interested as a husband and has no other interest, pecuniary or financial, at all,
what is supposed to happen if he takes one view and his wife takes another view?
Is one to have the bankruptcy court used as a forum for domestic squabbles along those
lines? Quite clearly that cannot be right. Therefore I think one has to come on
to the conclusion that the husband can only make such an application when he has
an interest which is not necessarily the same as that of the wife. Of course, if he has *e*
a financial or pecuniary interest in his wife's bankruptcy, as he may very well have,
then that will be a sufficient foundation for him having an interest, but otherwise,
in my judgment, No.

Therefore, like Goulding J, I think that this court ought to follow *Re Roehampton
Swimming Pool Ltd*[1], a very similar point arising under the companies' legislation and
not the bankruptcy legislation. Therefore for my part also I would dismiss the *f*
appeal on this point.

Once again I should like to emphasise, as Goulding J has emphasised, that both of
us are merely saying that mere matrimonial status is not a sufficient foundation for
the necessary interest under s 29(1) of the 1914 Act, leaving quite open what other
relationships between husband and wife might in proper circumstances be a
foundation for the necessary interest.   *g*

Appeal dismissed. Application for leave to appeal dismissed.

Solicitors: *Treasury Solicitor* (for the Official Receiver); *Furley, Page, Fielding &
Pembrook*, Canterbury (for the petitioning creditor).

Evelyn Budd   Barrister.

1   [1968] 3 All ER 661, [1968] 1 WLR 1693

a
Metropolitan Property Holdings Ltd v Finegold and others

QUEEN'S BENCH DIVISION
LORD WIDGERY CJ, MAIS AND CROOM-JOHNSON JJ
b 20th NOVEMBER 1974

Rent restriction – Rent – Determination of fair rent – Scarcity element – Assumption that number of persons seeking to become tenants of similar dwelling-houses in locality not substantially greater than number available in locality – Locality – Meaning – Amenity available in particular area – Amenity creating excessive demand for similar flats and houses in that
c *area – No general scarcity of similar flats and houses – Whether deduction to be made in assessing fair rent on account of scarcity element in particular area created by existence of amenity – Rent Act 1968, s 46(1)(2).*

The landlords owned flats in St John's Wood, London, which were let on regulated tenancies. In St John's Wood there was a school for the children of American families living in London. In consequence the landlords' flats, and other flats and houses
d which were near the school, were particularly attractive to American families, and therefore the market rental values of those flats and houses were higher than they would otherwise have been. For the same reason there was an element of scarcity in that more Americans wished to come and live in that part of St John's Wood than the available accommodation would permit. Proceedings were brought before a rent
e assessment committee of the London Rent Assessment Panel for the purpose of determining the fair rents of the landlords' flats under Part IV of the Rent Act 1968. In coming to its decision the committee took account of the presence of the American school, in accordance with s 46(1)[a] of the 1968 Act, as one of the circumstances affecting the rental value of the landlords' flats. The committee, however, also found that the presence of the school had had the effect of reducing the available accommodation
f in the immediate locality of the school and accordingly held that they were required, under s 46(2)[b] of the 1968 Act, to disregard the consequential scarcity element in the rental values of the landlords' flats and therefore to make a deduction for the purpose of determining the fair rents. The landlords appealed against the rents determined by the committee on that basis.

g **Held** – Amenity advantages which could increase the fair rent under s 46(1) did not result in a set-off under s 46(2) merely because the amenity advantages of a particular house or district had attracted more people than could live there. The test for scarcity of accommodation under s 46(2) was to be applied over a wide locality, i e a really substantial area. A local scarcity caused by a particular amenity was too limited for consideration under s 46(2). Accordingly, the appeal would be allowed and the case
h remitted to the committee for reconsideration (see p 392 *f* and *g*, p 393 *a* to *c*, p 394 *c* to *h* and p 395 *a* to *c*, post).

Notes
For the determination of fair rents by the rent assessment committee, see Supplement to 23 Halsbury's Laws (3rd Edn) para 1571B, 2.
j For the Rent Act 1968, s 46, see 18 Halsbury's Statutes (3rd Edn) 835.

Case referred to in judgments
Palmer v Peabody Trust [1974] 3 All ER 355, [1974] 3 WLR 575, DC.

---

a Section 46(1) is set out at p 392 *c*, post
b Section 46(2) is set out at p 392 *j*, post

Appeal

The appellants, Metropolitan Property Holdings Ltd, owned a block of flats known *a*
as South Lodge, Grove End Road, St John's Wood, London, NW8, and flats 8, 14, 15,
35, 39, 42, 51, 55, 60, 61, 64, 65, 66, 74, 77, and 83, which formed part of that block and
of which the respondents, W Finegold and 16 others, were the tenants. On 19th
January 1973 the appellants objected to fair rents in respect of the flats registered by
the rent officer for the Westminster registration area and effective from various dates
and its objection was referred to the London Rent Assessment Panel a committee of *b*
which ('the third committee') was convened for 14th and 15th May 1973. Before the
third committee the appellants called two witnesses, the assistant area manager
employed by the appellants' managing agents and Jon Arthur Derisley, a surveyor
experienced in rental values of residential properties and conversant with the
workings of the rent regulation provisions of the Rent Act 1968. Evidence was given
by Mr Derisley to the effect that, in his opinion, a fair rent for the purposes of the *c*
1968 Act was the market rent less any deduction necessary to exclude the amount
by which that rent had been inflated by excess demand caused by shortage of accommodation; that such demand was, however, distinct from excess demand attributable
to the amenities of the particular flat or area; that there was not a great deal of scarcity
in the locality, i e St John's Wood, of the class and type of accommodation similar to
the flats; that there had, however, been a high increase in rental values in St John's *d*
Wood over the previous two or three years; that one of the factors which had caused
that had been the opening of the American school known as Eyre Court, which had
been provided for the use of the children of American families; that in consequence
living accommodation within the area having reasonable access to the school had
become much sought after; that the overall result had been an increase in market
values in the St John's Wood area which anyone else desiring living accommodation *e*
in the area had had to compete with. It was Mr Derisley's view that a large proportion
of the demand for accommodation in that locality was due to a particular desire of
people to live in that part of London and that that demand was attributable to amenity
as distinct from demand generated by shortage of rented accommodation. In his
evidence on behalf of ten of the respondents, John A Wagstall, chartered surveyor,
agreed with Mr Derisley's valuations of the market rents and further agreed that *f*
scarcity of high quality and large flats was less than it was for smaller and lower quality
flats.

The reference was the third which had been made to the London Rent Assessment
Panel objecting to fair rents determined by the rent officer in respect of flats in the
same block. In the second reference the decision had been given by a committee
('the second committee') on the 16th August 1972 and was based on the grounds (i) *g*
that the rent officer had made his determinations before the decision by a committee
('the first committee') on the first reference dated 23rd November 1971; (ii) that, in
any event, the decision on the first reference was wrong and ought not to be relied
on because of internal inconsistencies as disclosed in Mr Derisley's proof of evidence
as submitted to the second committee; (iii) that the deductions for the supposed *h*
excess demand attributable to scarcity of rented accommodation exceeded that
properly referable to such scarcity.

The appellants' case before the third committee was (1) that the rent officer had
followed the decision of the first committee, the decision of the second committee
not having been given, and (2) that the second committee in their decision had not
correctly interpreted and applied the amenity point and that, therefore, the determinations of fair rents made by them fell below the market rents by a degree that *j*
the appellants considered wrong for flats of the quality of the subject flats. In their
decision on the third reference the third committee did not accept as valid the
appellants' criticism of the decision of the second committee.

On 16th July 1973 the third committee determined that the following should be
registered as the fair rents under the 1968 Act: flat 8—£1,150; flat 14—£1,300; flat 15—

a
£900; flat 35—£1,150; flat 39—£1,180; flat 42—£1,125; flat 51—£1,325; flat 55—£1,355; flat 60—£1,325; flat 61—£1,355; flat 64—£1,275; flat 65—£1,180 flat 66—£1,240; flat 74—£1,350; flat 77—£1,350; flat 83—£1,210. The appellants appealed against that decision seeking an order that the assessments be set aside and that the questions as to what rents ought to be registered in respect of the flats under the 1968 Act be remitted to a committee of the London Rent Assessment Panel for rehearing and determination. The grounds of the appeal were (1) that the third committee had
b
decided as a matter of construction of s 46(2) of the 1968 Act that the word 'locality' comprised an area substantially wider than the St John's Wood area, but they had failed properly to apply the subsection as so construed, for, if they had properly applied it, it would necessarily have followed that the presence of a particular amenity within a smaller area could not significantly affect the availability of accommodation throughout the wider area; and (2) that the surveyor acting for the ten respondents
c
had agreed with the appellants' surveyor's valuations of market rents arrived at by reference to lettings of other comparable flats, and had further agreed that those market rental values were substantially increased by the presence of the American school, but the committee had failed to give intelligible reasons for fixing as the fair rents figures very substantially below the market rents.

d
Ronald Bernstein QC and *M Singh* for the appellants.
Harry Woolf as amicus curiae.
The respondents did not appear and were not represented.

e
LORD WIDGERY CJ. This is an appeal by Metropolitan Property Holdings Ltd brought under the Tribunals and Inquiries Act 1958 against the decision of a committee of the London Rent Assessment Panel given on 16th July 1973 and affecting a large number of flats belonging to the appellants in a block known as South Lodge in St John's Wood. The appellants complain that in reaching their conclusions as to the fair rents of each of these several flats the committee misdirected itself in its application of s 46 of the Rent Act 1968.
f
Before I deal with the merits of the matter, it is convenient to take up a point made by counsel as amicus curiae on behalf of rent assessment committees in general, that there ought to be some recognised practice as to the type of documents put before the court in cases of this kind. It is the fact, and I do not say this in any critical sense, that the paper produced and put before us in this case has greatly exceeded that which was necessary; and it may be necessary in the future to issue a practice direction to
g
put the matter on a formal basis. Meanwhile, I accept and confirm counsel's submission that one ought in general in these cases to be able to deal with the point of law raised by having before the court the notice of motion, the reasons for the decision of the committee and such features of the evidence put before the committee as are necessary to develop the point of law. If that approach had been made in the present case, it would, I feel sure, have resulted in a considerable saving in time, money and typing.
h
But to return to the issue. The flats in question, as I have said, are in St John's Wood, and there was recently built in St John's Wood a substantial school restricted in its entry to the children of American families in London. The result of that school being built has undoubtedly rendered this part of St John's Wood far more attractive to American families than it might otherwise have been because of the facility of the
j
education of their children which this school provides. Although there is no specific finding to this effect on the part of the committee, it is a reasonable inference, I think, from the material which has been put before us that the presence of this school has almost certainly put up the market rental values of flats and houses in the neighbourhood. And it may be, although again there is no specific finding to this effect, that this has produced locally an element of scarcity in the sense that more Americans

want to come and live in St John's Wood and have the facility of having their children
educated at that school than the accommodation vacant and to let in St John's Wood   *a*
would permit. I think it only right to approach the problem on the footing that both
those assumptions are good, namely, that the school in its own immediate surroundings has produced an increase in the number of Americans and, secondly, it may well
have produced an element of scarcity, or accentuated an element of scarcity which
previously existed.

The bone of contention between the parties is this, that applying their minds to   *b*
s 46 of the 1968 Act, the rent assessment committee has reached the conclusion that
the presence of the school has produced an element of scarcity of the kind mentioned
in s 46(2) and has thought it right, in fixing the fair rents of these flats, to make a
deduction, and one can go no further than that, on account of that scarcity.

To see why that contention is put forward and what the answer to it might be, one
has to look at the section itself. It is quite short. Section 46(1) provides: *c*

'In determining for the purposes of this Part of this Act what rent is or would
be a fair rent under a regulated tenancy of a dwelling-house, regard shall be had,
subject to the following provisions of this section, to all the circumstances (other
than personal circumstances) and in particular to the age, character and locality
of the dwelling-house and to its state of repair.'   *d*

I would observe on that straightaway that that seems to be saying in Parliamentary
language that one must have regard to the sort of factors which tend to push rents up
or down on the market. One must have regard to the age of the premises, and that
may have an effect up or down according to whether the premises are old or modern.
One must have regard to their character and their locality. Their locality is important   *e*
because a house situate in pleasant surroundings, and with the advantage of local
amenities, may very well command a higher rent than an identical house in a less
attractive setting.

Looking for a moment at the American school to which I have referred, if the
committee took the view that the presence of that school made the houses in the
surrounding area, and in particular these flats, more attractive, and thus likely to   *f*
command more rent, then so far as s 46(1) is concerned the fair rent ought to reflect
that factor. In other words, looking for the moment only at sub-s (1), any
amenity (as the word has been used frequently in this argument), any advantage
which the premises inherently have, either in their construction, their nature, their
scale, their situation, their proximity to a school, a zoo or a theatre, whatever it may
be, all those factors which would tend in the market to increase the rental, are factors   *g*
to be taken into account by the committee in fixing the fair rent. To what extent
they are taken into account is, of course, the duty of the committee to decide, but
that these are matters which are eligible for consideration is beyond doubt. At this
point, as I have already said, the presence of the American school would, on the face
of it, tend to put up the fair rent because it would be an amenity making the premises
more attractive.   *h*

Then one comes to s 46(2) which provides:

'For the purposes of the determination it shall be assumed that the number
of persons seeking to become tenants of similar dwelling-houses in the locality on
the terms (other than those relating to rent) of the regulated tenancy is not
substantially greater than the number of such dwelling-houses in the locality   *j*
which are available for letting on such terms.'

This is the provision which is intended to eliminate what is popularly called 'scarcity
value' from the fair rent fixed by the committee, and it is a provision which has given
rise to a great deal of difficulty in practice.

I think that before one begins to consider the difficulties, and before one begins to
a consider the section in detail, one must have clearly in mind what Parliament's
obvious intention was in including this provision in the Act. It seems to me that what
Parliament is saying is this: if the house has inherent amenities and advantages, by all
means let them be reflected in the rent under s 46(1); but if the market rent would be
influenced simply by the fact that in the locality there is a shortage, and in the locality
rents are being forced up beyond the market figure, then that element of market
b rent must not be included when the fair rent is being considered. Parliament, I am
sure, is not seeking to deprive the landlord of a proper return on the inherent value
and quality of his investment in the house, but Parliament is undoubtedly seeking to
deprive a landlord of a wholly unmeritorious increase in rent which has come about
simply because there is a scarcity of houses in the district and thus an excess of demand
over supply.

c Bearing that in mind, one turns to the point in the committee's decision which is
under attack in this appeal and indeed the point on which counsel as amicus curiae
has usefully made submissions on their behalf. The committee have come to the
conclusion and expressed it in more than one way that the presence of the American
school has created a local scarcity of premises. When I say 'local', I deliberately do not
attempt at this stage to define it further. But what was in the committee's mind
d undoubtedly was that the attraction of the school has produced a local scarcity of
houses, and that there is consequently in the premises now under review all the
elements contained in s 46(2) of a scarcity which ought to be eliminated when the
fair rent is assessed.

I find the committee's views on this somewhat difficult to follow, I must confess,
and indeed to get them fully one has to go back to what they said in an earlier case
e in which the same issue was raised. In the ordinary way one would not think it right
to consider an earlier case when deciding a later, but it is useful here because, as has
been shown, some light is thrown on the working of the committee's mind on this
point.

In a letter of 5th January 1973, giving an explanation of the committee's views in
f the earlier case, one finds this passage:

> 'The Committee accepted that there is a substantial amenity value in the St.
> John's Wood area but it is satisfied that there is a considerable degree of "scarcity"
> within section 46(2) of the Rent Act 1968. In the Committee's opinion the matters
> relied on by [counsel for the appellants] as constituting evidence of "scarcity"
> do not constrain it to limiting the difference between market rents and fair rents
g > merely to the extent reflected in the valuations made by Mr. Derisley. The
> Committee considers in the light of its own general knowledge and experience
> and having regard to the evidence and its inspection of the property that the
> rents determined by it properly reflect both "amenity" and "scarcity".'

I pause there to say so far so good, but the next paragraph is illuminating:

h > 'The American School is undoubtedly an amenity for those wishing their
> children to attend it but the Committee considers that the presence of the school
> tends to limit accommodation in the area available to tenants in general and thus
> to create an element of "scarcity".'

It is because I have read that paragraph in the course of the argument that I venture
j to say that the Committee seem to be acting on a supposedly very local scarcity
created by the presence of the American school.

In their decision in the instant case one gets a clear touch of the same reasoning in
this paragraph:

> 'The Committee does not accept [counsel for the appellants'] contention that
> the Committee in 1972 was wrong in attributing an element of scarcity to the

presence of the American School. The Committee accepts that "locality" for the purposes of Section 46(2) is very substantially wider than The St. John's Wood *a* area. It is of the opinion that, within this wider area, the American School must to some extent reduce available accommodation similar to that in South Lodge.'

Again emphasis is laid on the effect of the school in its immediate locality. For the reasons which I have already given, I do not think that Parliament was concerned with this kind of local scarcity when s 46 was passed. If one is looking for the unearned, *b* unmeritorious increase in rent which might accrue to landlords if s 46(2) had never been passed, one must, I think, take a very much wider sweep than the sort of area to which the committee seems to have applied its mind in this case. Of course if you look at half a dozen streets round the American school, you may well find a scarcity. As you go out to a greater radius round the school, then the effect of the school is less and less. But, as I emphasised, we are not looking at the effect of the school as such; *c* we are looking for scarcity in the locality which results from an excess of demand over supply.

It seems to me, with all deference to the committee, that they have somewhat lost sight of the fact that the sort of scarcity we are concerned with is a broad, overall, general scarcity affecting a really substantial area, and they wrongly focussed their attention on the extremely limited area which would not, I think, qualify as a 'locality' *d* for the purposes of s 46(2) of the 1968 Act.

What should be done? What can we add which may be of some assistance in the future? I think that committees will find their consideration of s 46 somewhat easier if they start with the propositions clearly in mind that amenity advantages which can increase the fair rent under s 46(1) do not result in a set-off under s 46(2) merely because the amenity advantages of a particular house or district attract more people *e* than can live there. The test on scarcity is to be taken over the locality as a whole, and that, as I emphasised, is a broad area.

What area? We have been referred to *Palmer v Peabody Trust*[1] where, dealing with the word 'locality' in s 46(1) of the 1968 Act, I said[2] that the exact extent of the locality was something which was primarily for the committee to fix. I would repeat that in regard to the fixing of the locality under s 46(2), but at the risk of repetition, I do *f* emphasise that when the committee fix the locality for the purpose of deciding whether there is an overall scarcity or not, they must pick a really large area, an area that really gives them a fair appreciation of the trends of scarcity and their consequences.

It may be, although I would not for a moment attempt to define the limits of the area precisely, that when operating s 46(2) committees will be well advised to draw *g* their inspiration from the area with which they are familiar in their work. Of course different parts of the country require different considerations, but there will be many instances in practice where the most reliable area for the committee to choose on which they are likely to achieve the most accurate result is the area from which their work regularly and normally comes.

However, to return to this case, it seems to me that the committee have erred in, *h* I say at once, the one relatively small respect which I have tried to describe, and I think that the matter must be reconsidered in the light of that error.

The question arises whether this matter should go back to the committee in order that they might reconsider the point for themselves, or whether it should go to an entirely new committee. Whilst I hear and respect counsel for the appellants' submissions that from the litigant's point of view it is always somewhat unsatisfactory *j* to go back to the original tribunal, it is the fact that we constantly do that in this court, particularly in regard to magistrates' courts when some relatively small error

---

1   [1974] 3 All ER 355, [1974] 3 WLR 575
2   [1974] 3 All ER at 360, [1974] 3 WLR at 581

a has been made and all that is necessary is for the court to look again at the point on which they were in error.

I think that when one has regard to all the work which has been done in this case, the inspections by the committee, and all the other matters, that the proper thing to do here would be to allow the appeal and send the case back to the committee to review their approach to s 46(2) in the light of the judgments of this court.

b **MAIS J.** I agree.

CROOM-JOHNSON J. I agree.

Appeal allowed.

c Solicitors: *D J Freeman & Co* (for the appellants); *Treasury Solicitor.*

N P Metcalfe Esq   Barrister.

d

Ellis v Burton

QUEEN'S BENCH DIVISION
LORD WIDGERY CJ, MAIS AND CROOM-JOHNSON JJ
e 14th NOVEMBER 1974

Criminal law – Assault – Dismissal of charge – Assault so trifling as not to merit any punishment – Hearing on the merits – Plea of guilty – Facts outlined to justices by prosecution – Whether a hearing of the case 'upon the merits' – Whether justices having jurisdiction to
f *dismiss charge – Offences against the Person Act 1861, s 44.*

The complainant laid an information against the defendant charging him with assault. At the hearing the defendant pleaded guilty and the solicitor for the complainant outlined the facts to the justices. The justices decided to dismiss the information under s 44[a] of the Offences against the Person Act 1861 on the ground that it was 'so trifling as not to merit any punishment'. The complainant appealed.
g

Held – Since the defendant had pleaded guilty there had been no hearing of the case by the justices 'upon the merits', within s 44, and accordingly they had no jurisdiction to dismiss the complaint. Accordingly the appeal would be allowed, a conviction entered and the defendant granted an absolute discharge (see p 398 *a* to *f*, post).
h   *Reed v Nutt* (1890) 24 QBD 669 applied.

Notes
For the requirement that the court should hear a case 'on the merits' before dismissing a complaint of assault, see 10 Halsbury's Laws (3rd Edn) 745, para 1435.
For the Offences against the Person Act 1861, s 44, see 8 Halsbury's Statutes (3rd
j Edn) 164.

Case referred to in judgments
Reed v Nutt (1890) 24 QBD 669, 59 LJQB 311, 62 LT 635, 54 JP 599, 17 Cox CC 86, DC, 33 Digest (Repl) 235, 657.

a Section 44 is set out at p 396 *h* and *j*, post

Cases also cited

Henry v Geoprosco International Ltd [1974] The Times, 28th June.   *a*
R v Harrington (1864) 9 LT 721, 28 JP 485.

Case stated

On 28th December 1973 an information was laid before the justices for the west
central division of the Inner London area by the complainant, Mark Ellis, by his
father and next friend, Peter Ellis, alleging that the defendant, Vic Burton, had   *b*
unlawfully assaulted and beaten the complainant on 27th December 1973. The
justices heard the information on 22nd February 1974. The defendant pleaded guilty
to the assault. The justices decided to dismiss the information under s 44 of the
Offences against the Person Act 1861 At the request of the complainant the justices
stated a case for the opinion of the High Court. The facts are set out in the judgment
of Lord Widgery CJ.   *c*

Evan Stone for the complainant.
Mark Strachan for the defendant.

LORD WIDGERY CJ. This is an appeal by case stated by justices for the west   *d*
central division of the Inner London area in respect of their adjudication as a magistrates' court sitting at Downshire Hill, Hampstead, on 22nd February 1974.
    Before the justices on that occasion was the defendant who had been charged with
assault and battery against the complainant. The defendant before the justices pleaded
guilty to the assault, and the facts were then outlined by the solicitor for the complainant in this form. I need not go into them in detail.   *e*
    The complainant was a boy of 10 years of age. He lives with his family in a house
near that occupied by the defendant. There had been a certain amount of irritation
caused by the children of one family to the members of the other family, and this
culminated on 27th December 1973 when the complainant was playing with other
boys and riding his bicycle in a mews in an area near the houses respectively occupied
by the complainant and the defendant, when the defendant appeared and told the   *f*
boys to shut up. He grabbed the complainant by the hair, put his fist up to his face
and said: 'If you swear at my wife or are horrible to my children again, your parents
won't be able to help you, and I am always around.' He tugged the complainant's
hair and then let go. No real harm was done because the justices were told that the
only physical damage caused was a temporary reddening of the skin.
    The justices accepted the facts as outlined by the prosecuting solicitor and, being in *g*
possession of a plea of guilty by the defendant, there was nothing more for them to do
except to determine how the defendant should be dealt with. There was then drawn
to their attention the provisions of s 44 of the Offences against the Person Act 1861.
That section provides:

> 'If the justices, upon the hearing of any such case of assault or battery [I   *h*
> pause to say that is any such case as is mentioned in the preceding section] upon
> the merits, where the complaint was preferred by or on behalf of the party
> aggrieved, under either of the last two preceding sections [ss 42, 43], shall deem
> the offence not to be proved, or shall find the assault or battery to have been
> justified, or so trifling as not to merit any punishment, and shall accordingly
> dismiss the complaint, they shall forthwith make out a certificate under their   *j*
> hands stating the fact of such dismissal, and shall deliver such certificate to the
> party against whom the complaint was preferred.'

The importance of that certificate is, of course, that under s 45 of the 1861 Act the
issue of a certificate is a' bar to further civil proceedings. It was suggested to the
justices in this case that they could dispose of the matter under s 44, notwithstanding

that the defendant had pleaded guilty. The alternative which was submitted to the
a justices was that there should be an absolute discharge of the defendant.
The justices were obviously conscious of the importance of their decision on this
point. They took the advice of their clerk. Their clerk told them that they could
take, as a matter of law, either of the suggested courses, that is to say to dismiss the
information under s 44, or to award an absolute discharge. They considered the
matter and decided that they would act under s 44, and accordingly they dismissed
b the summons relying on that authority.

The complainant comes here today, appearing by his father as his next friend, and
represented by counsel, to say that on the facts which I have outlined there was no
jurisdiction to operate s 44 so as to enable the information to be dismissed. The
argument put forward by counsel is that s 44 can only be used where there has been
a hearing before the justices on the merits. He says that one does not have a hearing
c on the merits if all that has happened is that the defendant has pleaded guilty and the
facts have been outlined to the justices before they proceed to deal with the offence.
The submission is that 'on the merits' here involves a hearing with the witnesses
being present and heard by the justices, and that only when the hearing has taken
that form can a certificate be issued.

Of course if that is right, it follows that the proper course for the defendant, odd
d though it may seem to have been, would be for him to have pleaded not guilty and
then to have opened the door for the justices, having heard all the evidence, to make
an order under s 44 if they thought fit. But it is said that since he pleaded guilty, it
would be very strange for the justices nevertheless to have power to dismiss the
information, and the contention is that they had no such power because on a plea of
guilty with no investigation of the merits, there was no opportunity to operate the
e section.

Reliance is placed on one authority, *Reed v Nutt*[1]. It was on the same section with
which we are concerned, i e s 44 of the 1861 Act. In the judgment reference is made to
two earlier cases on an earlier statute which contains a provision somewhat like s 44,
save that the words 'on the merits' do not appear. On that earlier statute it had
always been held that where a summons for assault exists and the complainant does
f not appear to pursue his complaint at the hearing, then the justices could operate
the equivalent provisions of s 44 to grant a certificate, although there had been in
no sense a hearing at all and what had happened was that the information was
dismissed for want of prosecution.

Lord Esher MR, having described the situation prevailing before 1861, as I have
endeavoured to describe it, said[2]:
g
'Coming to the later Act [of 1861], we find that the language of s. 44 is in a very
important respect different; it gives a like power to justices to grant a certificate
of dismissal; but it is to be exercised "upon the hearing of any such case of assault
or battery *upon the merits*." How are those additional words "upon the merits"
to be interpreted? Can we say that the new section which contains them means
h the same thing as the old section where they were omitted? Speaking for myself,
I cannot help thinking that the strict interpretation which had been placed on
s. 27 of the [Offences against the Person Act 1828] had been brought to the attention of the Legislature, and that those words were advisedly inserted, the intention being that if the dispute between the parties were really fought out upon
the hearing of the summons and the charge dismissed, the certificate should be
j given and should bar all further proceedings, but that if the charge were withdrawn, so that there was no real trial, it should be left open to the person who
had laid the information to be remitted to his common law rights and to maintain an action for the assault notwithstanding the dismissal of his complaint.'

1 (1890) 24 QBD 669
2 24 QBD at 673

That view is adopted by Lord Coleridge CJ giving the second judgment in that case[1].   *a*

That seems to me to cover the whole field in which we have to reach a conclusion. The emphasis placed by Lord Esher MR on a 'real trial' and the matter being thoroughly gone into are the keys to the characteristics of a hearing which amounts to a hearing on the merits for present purposes. Just as the fact that when a summons is dismissed for want of prosecution there is not a hearing on the merits, so it seems to me that if the case is disposed of on a plea of guilty again one cannot say there has   *b* been a hearing on the merits. I would not pretend for a moment that the results are entirely logical, and we have been assisted by argument of counsel for the defendant to show some of the illogicalities which will result. But I have no doubt, speaking for myself, that since *Reed v Nutt*[2], one cannot regard a disposal of the matter otherwise than after a thorough going into of the evidence by the justices as being a disposal on the merits for present purposes.   *c*

Accordingly I would say that the justices were wrong in law in issuing their certificate, and in dismissing the complaint. They should enter a conviction and they should not grant a certificate. Since it seems unnecessary to send the matter back to the justices for them to carry out those acts, I would myself think it right for this court itself to impose the appropriate penalty, which I think would be an absolute discharge.   *d*

MAIS J. I agree.

CROOM-JOHNSON J. I agree. This appeal seems to me to be highly technical.   *e* If there had been a hearing on the merits, the justices could have deemed the offence not to be proved if they thought fit and then dismissed the information. But I agree with Lord Widgery CJ that a hearing on the merits does involve proof of the complaint other than on the mere confession of the defendant. In those circumstances the justices acted without jurisdiction.

I would agree with Lord Widgery CJ that the appropriate penalty here would be   *f* an absolute discharge, which, under s 13 of the Powers of Criminal Courts Act 1973, should be deemed not to be a conviction.

Appeal allowed.

Solicitors: *Victor J Lissack* (for the appellant); *Ewett Price & Primhak* (for the   *g* respondent).

Jacqueline Charles Barrister.

---

1   (1890) 24 QBD at 674
2   24 QBD 669

a
Wykes and others v Davis and another

COURT OF APPEAL, CIVIL DIVISION
BUCKLEY, BROWNE LJJ AND MACKENNA J
28th, 29th, 30th OCTOBER, 8th NOVEMBER 1974

b
Agriculture – Agricultural holding – Notice to quit – Validity – Non-compliance with notice to remedy breaches of agreement – Effectiveness of notice to remedy – Reasonable period specified for remedying breaches – More than one breach specified in notice – Notice specifying seven months as period to remedy breaches – Insufficient period to remedy all breaches – Meaning of 'reasonable period . . . to remedy any breach' – Whether notice valid if specified period is not a reasonable one in which to remedy all the breaches although reasonable for remedying some – Agricultural Holdings Act 1948, s 24(2)(d) – Agriculture (Miscellaneous Provisions) Act 1963, s 19(1).

c

The landlords were the owners of agricultural land held by the tenants on a yearly tenancy. On 26th January 1973 the landlords gave the tenants a notice in writing in the prescribed form[a] pursuant to s 24(2)(d)[b] of the Agricultural Holdings Act 1948 and s 19(1)[c] of the Agriculture (Miscellaneous Provisions) Act 1963 requiring them to
d remedy within seven months certain breaches of the tenancy agreement by carrying out works of repair, maintenance and replacement. The tenants failed to carry out two of the works required within the seven month period. Accordingly, on 29th August 1972, the landlords served the tenants with notice to quit on the ground of their failure to comply with the notice to remedy. The tenants claimed that the notice to remedy was invalid and that their failure to comply with it could not there-
e fore be relied on by the landlords as a ground for terminating the tenancy. The dispute was submitted to arbitration. The arbitrator found as a fact that while the period of seven months was a reasonable one in which to carry out one of the works which the tenants had failed to accomplish, it was not a reasonable time in which to carry out the other. The arbitrator sought the opinion of the court on the question of law whether, on the true construction of s 24(2)(d) of the 1948 Act and s 19(1) of
f the 1963 Act, the notice to remedy given on 26th January 1973 was 'invalid on the ground that the period specified in the notice was not a reasonable period in which to remedy all of the breaches specified in the notice, although it was a reasonable period in which to remedy some of the breaches'.

Held – The reasonableness of the period within which a tenant was required to
g remedy the breach or breaches alleged in a notice to remedy was to be judged in relation to all the work required to be done. If more than one breach was required to be remedied the period had to be such as would allow reasonable time to remedy all the specified breaches, and if the period specified was not a reasonable one for remedying all the breaches the notice was invalid. A notice to remedy could not be treated as if it only required a tenant to remedy such breaches as he reasonably could
h within the specified period so as to be pro tanto valid. The notice to remedy of 26th January 1973 was, therefore, invalid and could not be relied on by the landlords (see p 404 d to f, p 407 e f and j to p 408 b and e, p 409 f g and j and p 410 a and b, post).
Shepherd v Lomas [1963] 2 All ER 902 applied.

Notes
j For notices to remedy in relation to agricultural holdings, see 1 Halsbury's Laws (4th Edn) 575, 576, para 1055, and for cases on notices to quit, see 2 Digest (Repl) 8-13, 18-52.

---

a   See the Agriculture (Forms of Notice to Remedy) Regulations 1964 (SI 1964 No 707)
b   Section 24(2), so far as material, is set out at p 401 h, post
c   Section 19(1), so far as material, is set out at p 401 j to p 402 b, post

For the Agricultural Holdings Act 1948, s 24, see 1 Halsbury's Statutes (3rd Edn) 707.
For the Agriculture (Miscellaneous Provisions) Act 1963, s 19, see ibid 776.   *a*

Cases referred to in judgments
Britt v Buckinghamshire County Council [1963] 2 All ER 175, [1964] 1 QB 77, [1963] 2 WLR
    722, 127 JP 389, 14 P & CR 318, 61 LGR 223, [1963] RVR 215, CA.
Fox v Jolly [1916] 1 AC 1, 84 LJKB 1927, 113 LT 1025, HL, 31(2) Digest (Reissue) 823,
    6841.   *b*
Pannell v City of London Brewery Co [1900] 1 Ch 496, 69 LJCh 244, 82 LT 53, 31(2) Digest
    (Reissue) 824, 6842.
Price v Romilly [1960] 3 All ER 429, [1960] 1 WLR 1360, Digest (Cont Vol A) 15, 70b.
Shepherd v Lomas [1963] 2 All ER 902, [1963] 1 WLR 962, CA, Digest (Cont Vol A)
    15, 70c.

Cases also cited   *c*
French v Elliot [1959] 3 All ER 866, [1960] 1 WLR 40.
Hopley v Tarvin Parish Council (1910) 74 JP 209.
Horsey Estate Ltd v Steiger [1899] 2 QB 79, [1895-9] All ER Rep 515, CA.
Price v West London Investment Building Society [1964] 2 All ER 318, [1964] 1 WLR 616,
    CA.   *d*

Appeal
This was an appeal by the tenants, Eric Albert John Davis and Margaret Burnham
Davis, his wife, against a judgment of his Honour Judge Pratt given on 11th July 1974
at Barnstaple County Court whereby on a case stated for the opinion of the court by
an arbitrator under the Agricultural Holdings Acts it was adjudged that the correct
answer to the final question stated by the arbitrator, i e whether on a true construction   *e*
of s 24(2)(d) of the Agricultural Holdings Act 1948 and s 19(1) of the Agriculture
(Miscellaneous Provisions) Act 1963 the notice to remedy dated 26th January 1973,
served by the respondents, Norman Gordon Wykes, William Lloyd Baxendale,
Peter Baring and Ronald Christie Price, the trustees of the Christie Estate ('the landlords'), on the tenants, was invalid, was No.   The facts are set out in the judgment   *f*
of Buckley LJ.

Alan Fletcher for the tenants.
Derek Wood for the landlords.

                                                                   Cur adv vult

8th November.   The following judgments were read.   *g*

BUCKLEY LJ.   This is an appeal from a judgment of his Honour Judge Pratt
on 11th July 1974 on a case stated by an arbitrator for the opinion of the court under
the Agricultural Holdings Act 1948 as amended by the Agriculture (Miscellaneous
Provisions) Act 1963.   The arbitrator submitted two questions of law for the opinion
of the court with only one of which we are concerned.   It is this: *h*

   'On a true construction of s. 24 (2) (d) of the Agricultural Holdings Act 1948,
   and s. 19 (1) of the Agriculture (Miscellaneous Provisions) Act 1963 was the notice
   to remedy [given on 26th January 1973] invalid on the ground that the period
   specified in the notice was not a reasonable period in which to remedy all of the
   breaches specified in the notice, although it was a reasonable period in which to   *j*
   remedy some of the breaches?'

The learned judge answered that question in the negative, holding in effect that the
notice was valid in part, although invalid as to part.
   The appellants are yearly tenants of two farms in Devon known as Saunton Barton
and East Saunton Farms, comprising some 500 acres, under an agreement of 29th May

a 1969. The year of the tenancy ends on 29th September. The respondents are the landlords. I shall refer to the parties as 'the tenants' and 'the landlords' respectively.

On 26th January 1973 the landlords by their agent gave the tenants notice in the prescribed form required by s 19(1)(a) of the 1963 Act requiring them to remedy within seven months from the date of service of that notice the breaches of which particulars were set out in the notice. The terminal date of that notice, which was 26th August 1973 or thereabout, was such as to allow the landlords time to serve notice to **b** quit on the tenants before 29th September 1973 so as to terminate the tenancy at 29th September 1974. On 29th August 1973 the landlords served the tenants with notice to quit the farms on 29th September 1974 on the ground of their failure to comply with the notice to remedy.

The tenants did not dispute their liability to carry out any of the remedial works specified in the notice to remedy. These works were listed in the schedule to the notice **c** to remedy, which is headed in accordance with the prescribed form: 'Particulars of Breaches of Terms or Conditions of Tenancy'. They were grouped under three headings; first, 'Dilapidations to Hedges & Banks', under which heading work was required to be carried out on nine separate hedges or banks; secondly, 'Dilapidations to Field Surfaces', under which heading work was required to be done in five fields; thirdly, 'Dilapidations to Gates', under which heading work was required on gates in **d** nine fields. By 26th August 1973 the tenants had done all the work required by the notice except (1) they had not repaired all the 'growth banks' mentioned under the first heading, and (2) they had not fully cleaned one field of couch.

The arbitrator made two important findings of fact. He found that the period of seven months specified in the notice to remedy was not a reasonable time in which to repair all the growth banks because, according to the rules of good husbandry, this **e** type of work was to be carried out during the winter months; and he found that the period of seven months specified in the notice to remedy was a reasonable time within which to eradicate the couch from the field which was still to some extent infested at 26th August 1973.

The tenants contend that in these circumstances the notice to remedy was wholly invalid, because seven months was not a reasonable period in which to carry out all **f** the work required by it. The landlords contend that the notice was valid, notwithstanding the first of the two findings which I have mentioned, to the extent of all the works required by the notice with the exception of the repair of the growth banks.

The question to be determined is rightly formulated as a question of construction of s 24(2)(d) of the 1948 Act and of s 19(1) of the 1963 Act. Section 24(1) of the 1948 Act provides that where a tenant is given notice to quit an agricultural holding he may **g** give a counter-notice to the landlord, whereupon, subject to the provisions of sub-s (2), the notice to quit shall not have effect unless the Minister (now the Agricultural Land Tribunal) consents to the operation thereof. Subsection (2), so far as material for present purposes, was originally enacted in the following terms:

'The foregoing subsection shall not apply where . . . (d) at the date of the **h** giving of the notice to quit the tenant had failed to comply with a notice in writing served on him by the landlord requiring him . . . within a reasonable time or within such reasonable period as was specified in the notice to remedy any breach by the tenant that was capable of being remedied of any term or condition of his tenancy which was not inconsistent with the fulfilment of his responsibilities to farm in accordance with the rules of good husbandry, and it is stated in the notice **j** to quit that it is given by reason of the matter aforesaid . . .'

By s 19(6) of the 1963 Act, s 24(2)(d) of the 1948 Act was amended by deleting the words 'within a reasonable time or'. Section 19(1) provides:

'For the purposes of paragraph (d) of section 24 (2) of the Agricultural Holdings Act 1948 . . . (a) a notice requiring the tenant to remedy a breach of any term or

condition must be in the prescribed form and must specify the period within
which the breach is to be remedied; (b) where such a notice in the prescribed   a
form requires the doing of any work of repair, maintenance or replacement, any
further notice requiring the doing of any such work and served on the tenant less
than twelve months after the earlier notice shall be disregarded, unless the
earlier notice was withdrawn with his agreement in writing; (c) a period of
less than six months shall not be treated as a reasonable period within which
to do any such work . . .'   b

Subsections (2), (3) and (4) of that section enable the Lord Chancellor to make regulations and to prescribe forms by statutory instrument subject to annulment by
resolution of either House of Parliament. This power includes power to prescribe
different forms for the purposes of s 19(1)(a). The form appropriate to the present
case was prescribed by the Agriculture (Forms of Notices to Remedy) Regulations   c
1964[1]. It was adopted in the present case. It is headed: 'Notice to tenant to remedy
breach of tenancy agreement by doing work of repair, maintenance or replacement'.
It provides for identifying the holding in respect of which the notice is given, and the
tenants to whom it is addressed, and then proceeds in the following terms:

'1. I hereby give you notice that I require you to remedy within [blank] months   d
from the date of service of this Notice the breaches whereof particulars are given
below of the terms or conditions of your tenancy, being breaches which are
capable of being remedied of terms or conditions which are not inconsistent with
the fulfilment of your responsibilities to farm the holding in accordance with the
rules of good husbandry. 2. The Notice requires the doing of the work of repair,
maintenance or replacement specified below. 3. This Notice is given in accor-   e
dance with section 24 (2) (d) of the Agricultural Holdings Act 1948, and section
19 (1) of the Agriculture (Miscellaneous Provisions) Act 1963. Failure to comply
with it within the period specified above may be relied on as a reason for a notice
to quit under section 24 (2) (d) of the Agricultural Holdings Act 1948. 4. Your
attention is drawn to the Notes following the signature to this Notice.'

There then follows the schedule, headed in the manner I have already mentioned,   f
which contains spaces for indicating the term or condition of tenancy alleged to have
been contravened in each case and particulars of the breach alleged and the work
required to remedy it. A marginal note is printed opposite to para 1 of the notice
relating to the words 'within [blank] months'. The note is in these terms:

'This period must be a reasonable period for the tenant to remedy the breaches   g
and must in any event be not less than six months.'

At the foot of the space left to contain the schedule there are some explanatory notes
which I do not think it necessary for me to read.
    The tenants contend that the natural meaning of the statutory language is such that
the landlord must serve a notice allowing a reasonable period for all the work speci-   h
fied in it to be completed. In this connection they rely by way of analogy on decisions
under the Conveyancing Act 1881, s 14, now superseded by the Law of Property Act
1925, s 146. They contend that the language of those sections is very similar to the
language of s 24(2)(d) of the 1948 Act as originally enacted, and they say that, if a landlord had served a notice under that section requiring works to be done within a
reasonable time without specifying any particular period, a reasonable time would not   j
have been held to have elapsed until the expiration of a sufficient period to allow of the
completion of all the works required by the notice. They say that it would be illogical if a different principle or construction were to be adopted in a case in which the

---

1   SI 1964 No 707

a landlord chose to specify the period. They contend that the 1963 amendment cannot have been intended to alter the effect of the words 'within such reasonable period as was specified in the notice' drastically to the advantage of the landlord. They say that it is for the landlord to decide what works he shall require by the notice, and that it is for him to determine what period he thinks will be sufficient to enable the tenant to complete all those works. In this situation, counsel for the tenants says, the land-lord is in control of the position and is not exposed to any difficulty, embarrassment **b** or hardship, while the tenant is free, as he should be, to decide how and in what order he will tackle the works which he is required to carry out.

Counsel for the landlords has placed much emphasis on the inconvenience which he submits would arise from adopting the tenants' argument. He points out that under the Agriculture (Notices to Remedy and Notices to Quit) Order 1964[1], art 5(3), a tenant who does not contest his liability to do the required works need not dispute **c** the validity of the notice to remedy on any other ground until after a notice to quit has been served. Suppose in the case of a yearly tenancy expiring on the September quarter day in each year a landlord were to serve a six months' notice to remedy early in March to expire in the following September before the end of the current tenancy year. The tenant, if he did not dispute liability, would be under no obligation to assert the invalidity of the notice on the ground that the period allowed was unreasonable **d** until after a notice to quit had been served. In the following September the landlord serves a notice to quit and the tenant thereupon disputes the validity of the notice to remedy. If the tenants' contention succeeds, upwards of six months have been wasted and the landlord would be precluded by s 19(1)(b) of the 1963 Act from serving a new notice to remedy until the following March. The notice to remedy which he would then serve would have to allow a reasonable period for the works to be done, **e** which ex hypothesi would be more than six months. He would consequently be unable to serve a notice to quit before the next September quarter day. Instead of being able to terminate the tenancy at about 18 months after his original notice to remedy, the landlord would be unable to recover possession of the holding until some 42 months from that date. The landlord cannot himself initiate arbitration on the reasonableness of his notice to remedy. Counsel for the landlords says that **f** this state of affairs would enable a tenant to continue in default under his obligations with impunity.

In answer to this counsel for the tenants says that, in any ordinary case, the alterna-tive remedy of forfeiture would at all times be available to the landlord, subject to the possibility of the tenant obtaining relief from forfeiture.

Counsel for the landlords contends that where a notice to remedy specifies a period **g** which is reasonable as regards some of the works comprised in the notice, but un-reasonable as regards others, the notice is invalid in respect of the latter works, but valid in respect of the former, and can be severed so that the bad does not infect the good. The tenant can at any time require arbitration of the question to what extent the notice is a good one. He ought not to be allowed to remain in default in respect of obligations in relation to which a good notice has been served merely because the **h** notice has also included works for which no reasonable time has been allowed.

On the language of s 24(2)(d) of the 1948 Act counsel for the landlords contends that the words 'any breach' should be construed, as he says, distributively; so that the question to be asked in any case would be whether the notice requires the tenant to remedy any breach within a reasonable period and, if so, whether the tenant has in fact remedied that breach within that period. If the tenant has not done so, counsel **j** for the landlords says that the landlord is entitled to serve a notice to quit based on that default, whatever may be the position with regard to any other works specified in the notice to remedy.

The learned judge approached the construction of the subsection in this way:

---

1   SI 1946 No 706

'On a strict construction of the words quoted the period stated in the notice
for remedying the breaches (assuming there are more than one breach) is to be a   *a*
reasonable period for remedying *all* the breaches.   Therefore a notice specifying
a period reasonable for remedying some but not all of the breaches is not a notice
in accordance with the section.   But there is a less strict construction of these
quoted words namely that the period stated in the notice is to be a reasonable
period for remedying each of the breaches.   Therefore a notice specifying a
period reasonable for remedying some but not all of the breaches is valid as   *b*
regards the breaches for which a reasonable time has been given and invalid as
regards the other, i e the notice is not void in toto.'

Before discussing any authorities I will consider the language of the subsection.
It is to be observed that the condition precedent of an effective notice to quit under
s 24(2)(*d*) is that the tenant shall have failed to comply with a notice.   The words   *c*
which follow are words describing the notice, not words defining the condition.   The
notice is to be one by which the landlord requires the tenant within a reasonable
period to remedy any breach by the tenant of any term or condition of his tenancy.
It is common ground that it is open to a landlord to include more than one breach in
one notice.   So the words 'any breach' must be read as equivalent to 'any breach or
breaches'.   It may be that the words 'reasonable period' should also be read as   *d*
equivalent to 'reasonable period or periods', but that does not arise for determination
in this case.   It seems to me that the use of the word 'any' in this context merely
signifies that the landlord may select what breach or breaches he chooses to specify
in the notice.   By what then is the reasonableness of the period to be measured?
It must surely be by reference to the length of time required to remedy the breach
or breaches in question.   If more than one breach is required to be remedied, it   *e*
seems to me that the period must be such as will reasonably allow time to remedy all
the specified breaches.   If this is right, a notice comprising a number of breaches will
not be such a notice as is described in the subsection unless it allows a reasonable
period within which to remedy all of them.   If the notice is not such as to satisfy
the description in the subsection, failure to comply with it cannot satisfy the condition
for an effective notice to quit.   That is the construction which the learned judge   *f*
described as a 'strict construction'.   He, however, preferred the 'less strict construction'.   In arriving at that conclusion the learned judge was largely influenced
by the circumstance that he thought that the strict construction would, for reasons
which I have already indicated, throw a burden on a landlord and give a bonus to
a tenant which seemed to him unreasonable and unfair.

The effect of these two constructions can perhaps best be demonstrated by an   *g*
illustration.   Suppose that a landlord serves a notice to remedy in which he complains
of nine breaches which he requires the tenant to remedy.   Suppose that eight of
those breaches could all be remedied within six months, but that one could not be
remedied in less than 12 months.   If the notice were to specify seven months as the
period within which the necessary works were to be done, would the notice be entirely
ineffective, or would it be effective in relation to the eight breaches but ineffective in   *h*
relation to the ninth?   On the strict construction the notice would be wholly bad.
On the less strict construction it would be bad only as regards the ninth breach. But
now suppose that in a similar case any one of the nine breaches could reasonably
be remedied within two months, but circumstances are such that all nine could not
reasonably be remedied in less than 12 months.   In these circumstances, could a
notice requiring the tenant to remedy the breaches within seven months be good?   *j*
On the strict construction it would not, but on the less strict construction it would
seem that it would be wholly good, notwithstanding that the tenant would almost
certainly be unable to comply with it.   The learned judge seems to have considered
that this would have occasioned a difficulty for the tenant of a theoretical rather than
a practical kind, because he could at once apply for arbitration under art 5 of the 1964

Order to have the question of the reasonableness of the period determined; but if
a the reasonableness of the period is to be measured in relation to individual breaches
and not in relation to all the specified breaches taken together, it is difficult to see
how the arbitrator could in such a case decide in relation to which breaches the notice
should be treated as valid and in relation to which it should be treated as invalid.

We were referred to cases in which it has been decided under the Conveyancing Act
1881, s 14, that a notice requiring true breaches to be remedied, and also requiring
b the tenant to remedy a matter in respect of which he was not in fact in breach, was
not invalidated by the latter circumstance (*Pannell v City of London Brewery Co*[1]) and
that a notice which specified certain breaches with sufficient particularity would not
be invalidated by the fact that other alleged breaches were referred to in the notice
with insufficient particularity (*Fox v Jolly*[2]). I, for my part, do not find these authorities of great assistance in the present case. The landlords here did not require the
c tenant to carry out any work which he was not liable to do. It may be said that the
landlords failed to give any effective notice in respect of the dilapidations to hedges
and banks because seven months was not a reasonable period within which those
works could be completed, but this is not a defect of the same kind as reliance on a
non-existent obligation nor, for reasons which I will explain, do I think that it is
a defect of a similar kind to failure to specify alleged breaches with sufficient parti-
d cularity. There is, in my opinion, an important difference between the Conveyancing Act 1881, s 14(1), and the subsection with which we are directly concerned
in this case. As I have already pointed out, the condition for an effective notice to
quit under the latter subsection is a fail on the part of the tenant to comply with a
notice. Under s 14(1) of the 1881 Act the condition precedent for forfeiture of a
lease was the failure of the lessee within a reasonable time after a notice to remedy a
e breach complained of in the notice. Under that subsection the question to be asked
is whether a lessee has failed to remedy a breach and has been required to remedy
that breach by a notice given at a sufficient interval before. What else may have
been contained in the notice, whether justifiably or unjustifiably, is irrelevant to
the answer to that question. It follows, I think, that a notice given under that section
in respect of a number of breaches is capable of operating as a separate notice in
f respect of each of those breaches. This is not, however, in my opinion, the case under
s 24(2)(*d*) of the 1948 Act.

In *Price v Romilly*[3] Diplock J had to consider what amounted to compliance with a
notice served under s 24(2)(*d*) of the 1948 Act. The notice to remedy in that case had
specified seven distinct works required to be done. At the expiry of the period
limited by the notice the tenant had not done the work comprised in the first of
g these seven items. The tenant contended that a partial failure to comply with the
notice was insufficient to satisfy the subsection. Diplock J disposed of this argument
by saying[4]: 'It seems to me that, if he has not remedied it and remedied it completely, he has failed to comply with the notice.' In some closing observations the
learned judge referred to the fact that the arbitrator had found as a fact that one of
the seven breaches was not capable of being remedied within the time stated in the
h notice. He mentioned this only to negative an argument that it was not apparent
whether the arbitrator had considered whether or not the notice gave a reasonable
time for doing the work. It does not appear that the question whether this circumstance might have invalidated the entire notice was canvassed. In *Shepherd v
Lomas*[5] Harman LJ[6] referred to this part of Diplock J's judgment, pointing out that

j
1 [1900] 1 Ch 496
2 [1916] 1 AC 1
3 [1960] 3 All ER 429, [1960] 1 WLR 1360
4 [1960] 3 All ER at 431, [1960] 1 WLR at 1362
5 [1963] 2 All ER 902, [1963] 1 WLR 962
6 [1963] 2 All ER at 907, [1963] 1 WLR at 974

if the argument of the tenant in *Shepherd v Lomas*[1] was right the notice in *Price v Romilly*[2] would have been invalid; but Harman LJ pointed out that the point was not *a* taken before Diplock J.

In *Shepherd v Lomas*[1] the court was concerned with a case in which the landlord served a notice to remedy in respect of a number of breaches of covenant in connection with some of which the landlord was under an obligation to provide materials for carrying out the repairs, and with some he was under no such obligation. The landlord did not deliver the necessary materials until too late to make it possible for *b* the tenant to carry out the required repairs within the period limited by the notice. When the time expired, the tenant had carried out none of the repairs for which the landlord was obliged to provide materials; he had also failed to carry out much of the work for which the landlord was not bound to provide materials. The landlord served a notice to quit and the case went to arbitration under the 1948 Act. The *c* arbitrator made this finding:

'. . . that the period of time specified in the notice was reasonable in respect of the breaches for the remedy of which the landlords were not required to supply any materials and was unreasonable with regard to those for the remedy of which the landlords were liable to provide materials.'

d

The Court of Appeal reached the conclusion that, properly interpreted, this finding meant that the period was reasonable in respect of the first group (where no materials were required), and that it would also have been reasonable in respect of the second group (where materials were required), provided always that the landlord did his part and supplied the materials, but that in the events that happened the period turned out to be unreasonable for the second group because of the landlord's failure *e* to provide the materials. Lord Denning MR said[3]:

'So interpreting the finding, I do not think that the notice to remedy breaches was void ab initio. It was good in the beginning, because six months was reasonable for all the breaches, not only the first group but also the second group, seeing that it could fairly be assumed that the landlords would do their part and *f* fulfil their covenant to provide the materials.'

He then made a passing reference to *Pannell v City of London Brewery Co*[4] and *Fox v Jolly*[5] and proceeded as follows[6]:

'So, also, it seems to me that under the Agricultural Holdings Act, 1948, even though some of the matters that are specified in the notice turn out not to be *g* breaches, or the tenant afterwards is excused from performing some of them, the landlord is still entitled to rely on the others. It follows that, in this case, although the tenant was excused from remedying the second group of breaches (because the landlords did not provide materials), nevertheless he ought to have remedied the first group. He was not entitled to ignore the whole notice and do nothing.'

h

Towards the end of his judgment Lord Denning MR said[6]:

'I would only add this: in considering what is a reasonable time for any of the breaches, the arbitrator should always take into account the rest of the breaches

j

1   [1963] 2 All ER 902, [1963] 1 WLR 962
2   [1960] 3 All ER 429, [1960] 1 WLR 1360
3   [1963] 2 All ER at 904, [1963] 1 WLR at 970
4   [1900] 1 Ch 496
5   [1916] 1 AC 1
6   [1963] 2 All ER at 905, [1963] 1 WLR at 971

specified in the notice. It may often be quite reasonable for the tenant to post-
a pone some work until other work has been done; or to wait until he has men
to spare for the task; or to abide a suitable season. The time specified ought to
be time to do them all.'

Harman and Pearson LJJ expressed similar opinions, the latter saying[1]:

b 'The effect of that notice was not to impose any new obligation to remedy
breaches but to prepare the way for the landlord to serve an effective and operative notice to quit if the tenant failed to comply with the notice which required him
to remedy the breaches within a period of six months. That notice, when it was
served, was a good and valid notice. It was at that time reasonable to specify six
months as the period within which all those breaches had to be rectified.'

c Having reached the conclusion which they did about the arbitrator's finding, the
court did not have to consider in that case whether, if the time specified in the notice
had not been a reasonable time for remedying some one breach referred to in the
notice, the notice to remedy would have been wholly ineffective; but, in my opinion,
it is an inescapable inference from their judgments that if they had not interpreted
the finding in the way in which they did they would have held the notice to be bad
d and wholly ineffective. I am inclined to think that we are bound by the decision in
Shepherd v Lomas[2] to adopt what has been called the strict construction, but, however
that may be, I am of opinion that that is the true meaning and effect of the subsection.
On a proper reading of the language the condition of a valid notice to quit is not that
the tenant shall have failed to remedy any breach alleged in a notice to remedy
within the period specified in that notice, but that the tenant shall have failed to
e comply with the notice. Compliance with the notice to remedy must involve compliance with all the legitimate requirements of it. It may be that, if some alleged
breach was not in truth a breach of the tenant's obligations, the fact that the time for
compliance specified in the notice would not allow a reasonable period for the work
required to remedy that alleged breach would not invalidate the notice; but nothing
of that kind arises here, where the tenants have not disputed liability to do any of the
f required works. If that is the right view of what is involved in compliance and failure
to comply, it necessarily follows, in my opinion, that the reasonableness of the period
within which the tenants are required to remedy the breach or breaches alleged
in the notice must be judged in relation to all the work required to be done. The
same reasoning would, I think, have applied before the 1963 amendment to a case
in which the landlord by a notice to remedy required a tenant to remedy a number of
g breaches within a reasonable time without specifying any particular period for
compliance. In such a case the landlord could not, in my opinion, have served an
effective notice to quit on the ground of non-compliance until a reasonable period
within which to remedy all the breaches had elapsed or, perhaps, until it had become
manifest that the tenant would not be able to remedy all the breaches within such
a period from the date of the notice to remedy. It does not seem to me, therefore,
h that the amendment can be said to have had any effect on the true interpretation
of the words 'within such reasonable period as was specified'.

Counsel for the tenants presented an argument to us in support of the strict construction based on the terms of the prescribed form of notice to remedy, and, in
particular, on the marginal note to para 1 of that form which I have read. I do
not find it necessary to deal with that argument because, in my judgment, the true
j interpretation of the subsection is clear without any assistance which might otherwise
have been available from the form or the note. So I need not consider whether any
such assistance could be invoked in this case. The subsection is not, in my judgment,

---

1   [1963] 2 All ER at 907, [1963] 1 WLR at 974
2   [1963] 2 All ER 902, [1963] 1 WLR 962

susceptible of the construction contended for by the landlords without some violence to the language.   Since the so-called strict construction does not, in my opinion, do *a* any violence to the language, and since it leads, as it seems to me, to a reasonable interpretation and result, it must, in my judgment, be preferred.

For these reasons I would hold that this appeal succeeds.   I would amend the learned judge's order to declare that the question referred to at the outset of this judgment should be answered affirmatively, to the effect that the notice to remedy dated 26th January 1973 was invalid on the ground that the period specified in it was *b* not a reasonable period in which to remedy all the breaches specified in the notice.

BROWNE LJ.   I have had the advantage of reading the judgment which has been delivered by Buckley LJ and the judgment which is going to be delivered by MacKenna J.   I agree that, for the reasons they give, this appeal should be allowed, *c* with the consequences stated by Buckley LJ.

The notice to remedy in this case (dated 26th January 1973) specified a single period of seven months as the period within which the landlords required the tenants to remedy all the considerable number of breaches specified in the notice.

The arbitrator found that on the expiry of the notice on 26th August 1973 the tenants had carried out all the works specified in the notice, except that they had not *d* repaired all the growth banks and that one field 'was still to a greater or less degree infested with couch'; that the period of seven months specified in the notice was not a reasonable time in which to repair all the growth banks, and that the period of seven months was a reasonable time within which to eradicate the couch.

Where, as here, the notice to remedy specifies a single period for remedying a number of breaches, I agree, for the reasons given by Buckley LJ, that on the true *e* construction of s 24(2)(*d*) of the 1948 Act and s 19(1) of the 1963 Act that period must be a reasonable period for remedying *all* the breaches specified in the notice and that if the period allowed is not a reasonable one for remedying *all* the breaches, the notice is invalid.   In my judgment, we are also bound by the decision of this court in *Shepherd v Lomas*[1] so to hold.   As Buckley LJ has said, I think, 'it is an inescapable inference . . . that if [the court] had not interpreted [the arbitrator's] finding in *f* the way they did they would have held the notice to be bad and wholly ineffective'.

I would only add two things: (a) I have a good deal of sympathy with counsel for the landlords' point that if a tenant is guilty of two breaches, one of which could be remedied in six months, but the other of which could not be remedied in less than 12 months, it is unreasonable that the tenant should be allowed 12 months to remedy the former.   Counsel suggested that by a properly drafted notice or notices different *g* periods could validly be specified in respect of different breaches, but that point does not arise in this case and I express no opinion about it; (b) on the view we take of the true construction of the statutory provisions, counsel for the tenants' suggestion that the provisions of the Agriculture (Forms of Notices to Remedy) Regulations 1964, including the marginal note in the schedule, can be taken into account as an aid to the construction of the statute does not arise.   So I will only say that I should hesitate *h* for a very long time before accepting that argument.   It seems to me that *Britt v Buckinghamshire County Council*[2], on which he relied, was a most exceptional case, dealing with a most exceptional statutory provision.   The statute there in question (the Town and Country Planning Act 1947, s 33 (2)) in effect gave the Minister power to amend the statute by regulations, and the regulations, when made, became part of the statute: see Harman[3] and Pearson LJJ[4], both of whom emphasised the *j* exceptional position in that case.

1   [1963] 2 All ER 902, [1963] 1 WLR 962
2   [1963] 2 All ER 175, [1964] 1 QB 77
3   [1963] 2 All ER at 179, [1964] 1 QB at 88
4   [1963] 2 All ER at 182, [1964] 1 QB at 92

MACKENNA J. Section 24(2) of the Agricultural Holdings Act 1948 provides a
a number of exceptions to sub-s (1) which, as the general rule, renders ineffective a
landlord's notice to quit in cases where the tenant has served a counter-notice. In
the present case the landlord relied on sub-s (2)(*d*), as amended by the 1963 Act,
which, omitting inessential words, is in these terms:

> '... at the date of the giving of the notice to quit the tenant had failed to
> *b* comply with a notice in writing served on him by the landlord requiring him
> ... within such reasonable period as was specified in the notice to remedy any
> breach by the tenant that was capable of being remedied of any term or con-
> dition of his tenancy which was not inconsistent with the fulfilment of his
> responsibilities to farm in accordance with the rules of good husbandry ...'

We are required to construe these provisions, in particular the words 'within such
c reasonable period as was specified in the notice'.

The general effect is clear enough. The landlord must prove that at the date of
the notice to quit there had been a failure by his tenant to comply with a notice
which fulfilled the requirements of the subsection. What then are those requirements? The notice must be in writing and it must have been served by the landlord
on the tenant. The notice must state the landlord's complaint. He is not limited
d to complaining of a single breach. He may complain of breaches in the plural.
The breaches must be of terms and conditions of the tenancy, and the terms must be
such that the tenant's observance of them would have been consistent with the rules
of good husbandry. And lastly, the notice must specify a period which is reasonable
for some purpose. The question is, for what purpose? Must it be, as the tenant in
our case contends, a reasonable period in which to do the whole of the remedial
e work which the notice properly requires him to do, so that if it is too short for that
purpose the notice is bad? Or will the notice be pro tanto a good one, if the landlord
can prove that the period was long enough for the tenant to remedy at least one of
the stated breaches, and that the tenant failed to remedy that breach, which is the
landlord's contention?

During the argument the meaning of the word 'any' in the expression 'any breach'
f was discussed. I do not think that there is any doubt about its meaning. In this
context it means 'every'. Where the notice mentions more than one breach, the
tenant will be required to remedy every one of those mentioned, and if he omits to
remedy any of them within the prescribed reasonable period, he will have failed to
comply with the notice.

As the notice will require the tenant to remedy all the breaches complained of,
g it would seem that the period specified must be reasonable for the whole of the work.
There are two different ways in which a period might be unreasonable. (a) It might
not be sufficient to remedy all the breaches taken together, though each breach could
be separately remedied within the period. For example, the notice might require a
tenant to repair gates and to eradicate weeds—two separate obligations—within
period of six months. If that period were long enough to do either job separately,
h but not long enough to do them both together, it would be unreasonable. (b) It
might not be sufficient to remedy one breach taken by itself, though long enough to
remedy the other, as, in the case I have supposed, if the six months were enough for
the gates but not for the weeds. In this case, too, the specified period would be an
unreasonable one.

What then is the effect of the landlord's specifying an unreasonable period? The
j effect, in my opinion, is to make his notice invalid. If the period is, in either of the
ways I have described, unreasonably short, the notice imposes no obligation on the
tenant and he may disregard it with impunity.

The landlord argues that a notice stating several breaches and specifying a single
period for remedying all of them can be treated as if it were a series of notices each
stating a single breach and specifying the same period for remedying it. If the period

is reasonable for remedying any one of the breaches, the composite notice is, it is argued, pro tanto valid, and the tenant who has failed to comply with the valid *a* part loses the protection of the Act. I find this argument unacceptable. The notice requires the tenant to remedy *all* the breaches. To treat it as if it required him to remedy just one of them, or even some of them, is to change its character. Answering the argument in other words, I would say that in deciding whether the specified period is reasonable, it is impossible to disregard any of the breaches which the tenant is required to remedy within that time. It is impossible to treat the notice as if it *b* only required him to remedy such breaches as he reasonably can within the specified period.

This conclusion is, I believe, supported by the judgments of Lord Denning MR and Pearson LJ in *Shepherd v Lomas*[1]. I must examine at a little length the facts of that confusing case.

The landlord has served on the tenant a notice requiring him to remedy 30 breaches *c* and specifying six months for the whole of the work. It was the landlord's obligation to provide the materials for remedying some, but not all, of these breaches. By the end of the six months the tenant had done only part of the work for which he himself had to find the materials, and none of the work for which the landlord was to provide the materials. These had not been provided by the landlord until near the end of the six months. A notice to quit was served and an arbitration followed. *d* One of the points was whether the specified period of six months was a reasonable one. On this point the arbitrator found:

'. . . that the period of time specified in the notice was reasonable in respect of the breaches for the remedy of which the landlords were not required to supply any materials and was unreasonable with regard to those for the remedy of *e* which the landlords were liable to provide materials.'

The arbitrator stated two questions for the opinion of the county court: (a) whether on the facts which he had found the notice was void ab initio; and if not, (b) whether the tenant's failure to remedy the breaches for which a reasonable time had been specified (namely, those for which he had to find the materials himself) was a failure *f* to comply with the notice within the meaning of the subsection. The county court judge answered both questions in the landlord's favour. He decided that the notice was not void ab initio, and that the tenant's failure to remedy the breaches for which a reasonable time had been specified was a failure to comply with the notice.

Lord Denning MR interpreted the arbitrator's finding to mean that the period of six months specified for the whole of the work was reasonable at the time when the *g* notice was given, but that, because of the landlord's failure to provide the materials, it had become unreasonable for those parts of the work for which his materials were needed. The judgment continued[2]:

'So interpreting the finding, I do not think the notice to remedy breaches was void ab initio. It was good in the beginning because six months was reasonable *h* for all the breaches, not only the first group but also the second group, seeing that it could fairly be assumed that the landlords would do their part and fulfil their covenant to provide the materials. So the answer to the first question: "Was the notice void ab initio?" is: "No".'

The reasoning presupposes that the notice would have been invalid if the specified period had been too short for any part of the work. A passage later in the judgment *j* confirms this view[3]:

---

1 [1963] 2 All ER 902, [1963] 1 WLR 962
2 [1963] 2 All ER at 904, [1963] 1 WLR at 970
3 [1963] 2 All ER at 905, [1963] 1 WLR at 971

a 'I would only add this: in considering what is a reasonable time for any of the breaches, the arbitrator should always take into account the rest of the breaches specified in the notice. It may often be quite reasonable for the tenant to postpone some work till other work has been done; or wait until he has men to spare for the task; or to abide a suitable season. The time specified ought to be time to do them all. In this very case, the arbitrator might have found that, having regard to the total amount of work required, the term specified for the first group was

b unreasonable. But he has not done so; he has found it was reasonable. We are bound by that finding, which means that the notice was good in respect of those breaches; and, it not having been complied with, the notice to quit was good.'

Pearson LJ reasoned in the same way. Initially it was a valid notice, as the period of six months was a reasonable one for rectifying all the breaches. Presumably, if

c it had been reasonable for rectifying only part of the work, it would not have been valid.

I have not found it easy to understand the judgment of Harman LJ in that case. Counsel for the tenant's argument, which he describes in one passage[1] as 'formidable', was, I think, the argument that the six months given to do the thirty jobs was insufficient because of their number, and this argument failed because it had not been raised

d before the arbitrator. What Harman LJ describes in a later passage[2] as 'counsel for the tenant's point', must, I think, have been a different argument from the earlier one, and was presumably the argument that the time was too short for doing that part of the work for which the landlord should have provided the materials. Harman LJ in rejecting this argument pointed out that in the earlier case of *Price v Romilly*[3] (where the point we are considering was not argued or discussed by the judge) the landlord had

e succeeded, even though the time specified by him had been too short for remedying one of the breaches, and it was clearly Harman LJ's view that the decision was right on those facts. I find it difficult to reconcile the two passages of Harman LJ's judgment unless it was his view that the landlord may fail where the time is unreasonably short for repairing all the breaches together though long enough to remedy each separately (the 'formidable argument'), but succeeds where the time is too short for

f remedying one of them ('counsel for the tenant's point'). If that is the explanation of the two passages, I do not think that the distinction is a sound one.

I have considered the cases cited to us under s 14 of the Conveyancing Act 1881. I do not find that they give us any clear guidance in construing the 1948 Act and I do not refer to them.

For these reasons I would allow the appeal and amend the learned judge's order

g as proposed by Buckley LJ.

Appeal allowed. Leave to appeal to the House of Lords granted.

Solicitors: *Parker, Garrett & Co* (for the tenants); *Freshfields* (for the landlords).

James Collins Esq   Barrister.

---

1 [1963] 2 All ER at 906, [1963] 1 WLR at 972
2 [1963] 2 All ER at 907, [1963] 1 WLR at 974
3 [1960] 3 All ER 429, [1960] 1 WLR 1360

Harris Simon & Co Ltd v Manchester City Council

a

QUEEN'S BENCH DIVISION
LORD WIDGERY CJ, MAIS AND CROOM-JOHNSON JJ
12th NOVEMBER 1974

b

Case stated – Appeal from Crown Court – Jury verdict – Appeal by way of case stated – Appeal not rehearing – Question only whether error of law on facts stated in case – Need to show error of law in direction to jury or that verdict of jury perverse – Power of highway authority under local Act to stop up highway – Right of person aggrieved by stopping-up order to lodge objection in Crown Court – Objection to be allowed if jury find objector to be a person aggrieved – Finding of jury that objector a person aggrieved one which a reasonable jury could come to – Manchester General Improvement Act 1851, ss 46, 47, 48 – Courts Act 1971, s 10.

c

A highway authority was authorised by the Manchester General Improvement Act 1851 to stop up highways. The highway authority passed a resolution to stop up two streets, and served the proper notices in accordance with s 46 of the 1851 Act. The objector used those streets for access to a private right of way leading to his premises. Accordingly he lodged an objection to the resolution with the Crown Court in accordance with s 47ᵃ of the 1851 Act. His appeal was heard by a judge sitting with a jury in accordance with s 48ᵇ of the 1851 Act. The objector gave evidence that he would be prejudiced by the highway authority stopping up the streets despite the alternative arrangements offered. In answer to questions put to them by the judge, the jury found (i) that the streets were unnecessary for public thoroughfare and (ii) that the objector would be 'aggrieved or injured' by the stopping up. In view of the answers the judge allowed the objector's appeal as required by s 48 of the 1851 Act. The highway authority appealed to the High Court by case stated, contending that the case should be reheard as a civil appeal and the jury's verdict set aside on the ground that it was not supported by the evidence.

d

e

f

Held – By virtue of s 10ᵉ of the Courts Act 1971, an appeal under the 1851 Act against the decision of the Crown Court could only be by way of case stated on the ground that it was wrong in law or was in excess of jurisdiction. It was not an appeal by way of rehearing but a form of consultation with the court to obtain an answer on a point of law in the same way as an appeal by way of case stated by justices. There was no error of law in the judge's direction to the jury, and the jury's verdict was not perverse in the sense that it was a conclusion which no reasonable jury could have reached. Accordingly the appeal would be dismissed (see p 416 *j* to p 417 *j* and p 418 *a*, post).

g

Bracegirdle v Oxley [1947] 1 All ER 126 applied.

h

Notes
For the right to appeal by way of case stated from the Crown Court on a point of law, see Supplement to 9 Halsbury's Laws (3rd Edn) para 963D.

For the Courts Act 1971, s 10, see 41 Halsbury's Statutes (3rd Edn) 298.

---

a   Section 47, so far as material, is set out at p 414 *b*, post
b   Section 48, so far as material, is set out at p 414 *d* and *e*, post
c   Section 10, so far as material, provides:
     '(2) Any decision as respects which this subsection has effect may be questioned by any party to the proceedings on the ground that it is wrong in law or is in excess of jurisdiction.
     '(3) The decision shall be questioned by applying to the Crown Court to have a case stated by the Crown Court for the opinion of the High Court.'

j

Cases referred to in judgments

a *Bracegirdle v Oxley* [1947] 1 All ER 126, [1947] KB 349, [1947] LJR 815, 176 LT 187, 111 JP 131, 45 LGR 69, DC, 33 Digest (Reissue) 312, *1360*.

Mechanical & General Inventions Co Ltd and Lehwess v Austin and the Austin Motor Co Ltd [1935] AC 346, [1935] All ER Rep 22, 104 LJKB 403, 153 LT 153, HL, 51 Digest (Reissue) 863, *4134*.

b
Cases also cited

Benmax v Austin Motor Co Ltd [1955] 1 All ER 326, [1955] AC 370, HL.

Metropolitan Railway Co v Wright (1886) 11 App Cas 152, [1886-90] All ER Rep 391, HL.

Montgomerie & Co Ltd v Wallace-James [1904] AC 73, [1900-3] All ER Rep 926, HL.

c **Case stated**

This was an appeal by way of case stated by the Crown Court at Manchester in respect of its adjudication sitting with a jury at Crown Square, Manchester on 12th, 13th November 1973.

By a resolution dated 13th January 1973 the appellant, Manchester City Council ('the highway authority'), resolved, under the provisions of the Manchester General *d* Improvement Act 1851, to stop up certain streets in the city of Manchester, namely Briddon Street (from Nightingale Street to Brewery Street) and Brewery Street (from Briddon Street to Back Ducie Street).

The respondent, Harris Simon & Co Ltd ('the objector'), as a person thinking himself to be aggrieved by the resolution, lodged objection thereto with the Crown Court at Manchester. His appeal was heard by a judge and jury, under the provisions *e* of s 47 of the 1851 Act. At the conclusion of the evidence the jury was directed to give a special verdict by answering the following questions in accordance with the requirements of s 47:

'(a) Are Briddon Street (from Nightingale Street to Brewery Street) and Brewery Street (from Briddon Street to Back Ducie Street) unnecessary for public thorough-
f fare? If the answer to (a) is 'no', then, (b) Would the stopping up of these streets be beneficial to the public? (c) Will the [objector] be injured or aggrieved by the stopping up of these streets?'

The jury answered Yes to both questions (a) and (c) and accordingly judgment was entered for the objector.

The questions for the opinion of the High Court were: (1) was the verdict of the *g* jury perverse and/or against the weight of evidence? and (2) should the judgment of the Crown Court be sustained, or should it be certified in pursuance of the Manchester Improvement Act 1865 that the streets in question had been duly stopped up by the highway authority in the exercise of the powers vested in them by the 1851 Act?

h *Simon Fawcus* for the highway authority.
The objector did not appear and was not represented.

LORD WIDGERY CJ. This is an appeal by case stated by the Crown Court at Manchester in respect of an adjudication in a somewhat unusual jurisdiction. The *j* matter arises in this way. By virtue of the Manchester General Improvement Act 1851, power is given to the highway authority to stop up highways under a procedure prescribed in that Act. The sections dealing with this power begin at s 45, which states the power in general terms. Section 46 contains matters of procedure concerning the notices which have to be served on interested parties in the event of the highway authority being minded to exercise the power to which I have referred.

Section 46 also contains reference to an appeal which may be possible where the
highway authority proposes to stop up a highway.   *a*

The nature of the appeal is described in s 47 and provides:

> 'That it shall be lawful for any Person who may think that he would be
> aggrieved by the altering, diverting, stopping up, or inclosing of any such Street,
> Court, Alley, Way, or Passage as aforesaid, within Four Months after the making
> of the said Order, to appeal against the same to the Court of Quarter Sessions for   *b*
> the Borough, upon giving Ten Days Notice in Writing of such Appeal, together
> with a Statement in Writing of the Grounds thereof to the Council . . .'

Further procedural provisions are made on those lines.

Section 48 is the one which prescribes the issues which such an appeal will raise
and how they are to be determined, and it is, as I have already said, a provision   *c*
somewhat unconventional in its form. It says:

> 'That in case of such Appeal the Court of Quarter Sessions of the Borough shall,
> for the Purpose of determining whether such Street, Court, Alley, Way, or
> Passage shall be altered, diverted, stopped up, or inclosed, or whether the Party
> appealing would be thereby injured or aggrieved, empannel a Jury of Twelve   *d*
> disinterested Men out of the Persons returned to serve as Jurymen at such
> Quarter Sessions; and if, after hearing the Evidence produced before them, the
> said Jury shall return a Verdict that such Street, Court, Alley, Way, or Passage is
> unnecessary, or may beneficially to the Public be altered, diverted, stopped up,
> or inclosed, and that the Party appealing would not be injured or aggrieved
> thereby, then the said Court shall dismiss such Appeal . . .'   *e*

The section goes on to provide that in the event of a jury reaching a contrary decision
on those questions that the appeal shall be allowed instead.

The facts are somewhat difficult to discover because the case has found no facts as
such at all. It may be that the judge sitting with the jury creates real practical difficulties about finding facts in conventional form, and we have, therefore, thought it   *f*
right with the assistance of counsel for the highway authority to look at the plan
which was before the court below to get some idea of the nature of the ways which
the corporation sought to stop up. They are shown as being rights over the street
called Brewery Street and a street called Briddon Street. These two streets, approaching each other at right angles, form alternative means of access to a private right of
way enjoyed by the objector, Mr Simon, leading through to premises occupied by   *g*
him and fronting on to Jubilee Street.

At the present moment, therefore, before any stopping up takes place, the objector
has two routes whereby he can approach his private right of way and thence through
the private way leading to his premises where he is a furniture manufacturer. The
two alternative routes, as I say, are Briddon Street and Brewery Street, and it is those
streets which the highway authority sought to stop up and in respect of which they   *h*
made the appropriate procedural steps under the 1851 Act.

The objector, as I have said he was entitled to do, appealed to the Crown Court and
the issue debated before the Crown Court judge and jury was whether the objector
should or should not be regarded as a person who would be injured or aggrieved by
virtue of the stopping up. As I will point out in a moment, that was not the only
question for the jury, but it was, I think, the central question, and understandably   *j*
enough counsel for the highway authority, both in leading evidence for the highway
authority and in cross-examination of the objector, was endeavouring to play down, if
I may use that word without giving offence, the consequences which the stopping-up
would have on the objector, and the objector was resolutely asserting that he would
nevertheless be aggrieved.

What had been proposed for his benefit was that on his losing his public right of
a way over Briddon Street and Brewery Street he should be given a private right of way
by agreement in lieu. However, it was part of the scheme for those who were going to
develop the land in the event of the stopping up of the highway that both Brewery
Street and Briddon Street should be equipped with gates which could be locked so as
to obstruct all passage along those roads. Arrangements of a complicated nature were
described in the evidence before the court below as to the provision of keys, either
b personally to the objector, or in the hands of a janitor who would be in attendance
on the gates so as to make sure that the gates could be opened whenever the objector
wished his vehicles to go through.

I say without hesitation that, having listened to counsel, I can well understand that
the highway authority thought that the inconvenience which would result, or the
injury which would result, to the objector would be very small indeed if facilities
c for the opening of the gates were made in accordance with the arrangement to which
I have referred.

But not so the objector. Appearing in person before the Crown Court he roundly
asserted that he would be inconvenienced as a result of what was proposed. I read
one or two of his answers merely to give the general gist of what he was saying.
d At one point in the transcript of evidence he said:

> 'As you see, our only access to the ground floor is through Brewery Street and
> Briddon Street. You have heard that Boddingtons Breweries plan to erect fences
> with gates and locks to the streets, and provide us with a key.'

Then he must have turned to the jury because the transcript goes on:

e > 'Members of the jury, I ask you "Would you like to unlock a pair of large gates
> before you could gain access to your home?"'

Then he gives one or two references which may well be irrelevant to other citizens
and other objectors, and he wound up by saying:

f > 'We have had free access to our premises for over 75 years, and I would like
> the position to remain so. That is all I have to say, your Honour.'

He was cross-examined by counsel for the highway authority and went over much
the same ground again. A question of some interest is to be found where counsel
says:

g > 'Can I now leave that aspect of the matter and turn to deal with another
> matter? I am now asking you about whether it is going to injure you, and what I
> suggest to you is that your firm will be in no worse position than they are at the
> moment if you have an agreement giving you a right of way, a right of access, to
> your premises along Briddon Street and along Brewery Street, and if incorporated
> into that agreement there are conditions as to what times of day the gates shall
h > be kept open or manned. If you have a legally binding agreement of that sort,
> would you, your firm, be any worse off than they are now?'

The objector replied: 'Yes, of course.' 'How?' said counsel. The objector answered:
'It would be an encumbrance, wouldn't it, to open the gates?' He goes on in a number
of other instances to make the point that he has had a free right of access as a member
of the public down these roads heretofore and that in his view the new arrangement
j with the gates and keys would be an encumbrance, or at all events it would be an
obstacle.

When all that evidence had been heard the judge summed up to the jury and he
invited them to return a special verdict, giving them three questions which could be
answered, and, as will be seen, the three questions are based on the language of
s 48 of the 1851 Act which I have read. The first question he asked the jury to decide

was: 'Are Briddon Street . . . and Brewery Street . . . unnecessary for public thorough-
fares?' If the answer to that is 'No', then the second question is: 'Would the stopping   *a*
up . . . be beneficial to the public?' Thirdly: 'Would [the objector] be injured or
aggrieved by the stopping up of these streets?'

The jury retired and returned with a special verdict, answering question (a) in
the affirmative, that is to say that the streets were unnecessary for a public thoroughfare. The jury gave no answer to question (b), which they had been told was one
which would arise only if their answer to question (a) was negative, and in regard to   *b*
question (c) they again brought in an affirmative answer, in other words that the
objector would be injured or aggrieved by the stopping up of these streets. That
verdict meant that the appeal must be allowed and the stopping up order will not
take effect.

It is with a view to reversing that conclusion that counsel appears on behalf of the
highway authority today. The first question of course is to decide what jurisdiction   *c*
we have, and the Crown Court having displaced Quarter Sessions it has not been suggested, and I see no reason to suggest, that the provisions of the 1851 Act are affected
by the passing of the Courts Act 1971, save only that the tribunal becomes the Crown
Court judge with a jury rather than the chairman of Quarter Sessions with a jury,
as no doubt he would have been before.

Given that the Crown Court has that jurisdiction, the methods of appeal against a   *d*
decision of the Crown Court are to be found in s 10 of the Courts Act 1971 and in
particular it is possible to appeal to this court against a finding of the Crown Court
within the jurisdiction in question if the appeal is on the ground that the decision
below was wrong in law or in excess of jurisdiction. An appellant who seeks to come
to this court alleging that the decision below was wrong in law or in excess of jurisdiction may do so by case stated, and that explains why a case has been stated for our   *e*
opinion today.

I have, in dealing with the outline of the facts, strayed far beyond the confines of
the case. The case does not include as part of it the evidence which was heard below,
but the court de bene esse has allowed counsel to read some of that evidence, and
indeed has read some of it itself. I do not think that any injustice would be done in the
present instance by treating the case as effectively raising a question for the con-   *f*
clusion of this court, and the question is whether the verdict of the jury was perverse
and/or against the weight of the evidence.

Counsel submits that the propriety or otherwise of the jury's verdict in this civil
case should depend on the same sort of considerations as apply when an appeal is
brought in the civil jurisdiction of the Court of Appeal from a judge sitting in a civil
case. He has shown us a number of useful and relevant authorities, and I think that   *g*
I need do no more than refer to the last of them, which is *Mechanical & General
Inventions Co Ltd and Lehwess v Austin and the Austin Motor Company*[1]. The headnote
under the heading: 'Principles which should guide an appellate Court in reviewing
the verdict of a jury', is in these terms:

> 'When it is decided that a case is to be tried by a jury, that tribunal is the only   *h*
> judge of the facts, and no appellate tribunal can substitute its finding for that of
> the jury. The appellate Court has a revising function to see, first, whether there is
> any evidence in support of the issue found by the jury; and, secondly, whether the
> verdict can stand as being one which reasonable men might have come to. If
> on the latter question it is obvious that no verdict for the plaintiff on all the
> available evidence could be supported, the Court may save the waste of time in
> ordering a new trial . . .'   *j*

Thus in one formulation or another counsel has invited us to say that the real test

---

1   [1935] AC 346, [1935] All ER Rep 22

here is whether the jury's conclusions, particularly on question (c), were conclusions
a which reasonable men might have come to.

For my part I do not think that that is the right approach to this problem at all.
The authorities cited all relate to a right of appeal in the nature of a rehearing which
is the sort of right of appeal considered in those cases. The right of appeal given by
s 10 of the 1971 Act by way of case stated is not a right of appeal by way of rehearing.
Like any other appeal by case stated, it is a form of consultation with this court to
b obtain an answer on a point of law, and there is clearly no jurisdiction for us to concern ourselves with this matter at all unless it can be said that the decision of the court
below is wrong in law or in excess of jurisdiction.

I think perhaps that the present situation is unique. None of us in court today has
been able to think of a case in which a decision of a jury is open to appeal by case
stated on a point of law, and it may be that this is a unique situation. But be that as it
c may, as counsel says, unique or no, we must face it, and for my part I think that in
this unusual procedure there are really only two ways in which an error of law could
be said to arise of such a kind and arising in such circumstances as to justify the
interference of this court under the powers in s 10 of the Courts Act 1971.

The first way in which an error of law might arise would be if the judge when
charging the jury had himself made such an error. Then I have no doubt it would be
d possible to bring an appeal to us in the form the present appeal is brought alleging as
the error of law a misdirection in law by the presiding judge. The second, and I
think the only, alternative would be if it could be said of the verdict of the jury that it
was perverse in the true sense, namely, that it was a conclusion which no reasonable
jury could have reached.

That is the test which this court applies on appeal by case stated from magistrates,
e and I see no reason why it should not apply on an appeal by case stated from a jury
in the rare circumstances in which such an appeal has to be considered. I think it
would be quite wrong to apply the looser test submitted for by counsel for the highway authority because the whole concept of an appeal by rehearing is foreign to the
procedure of an appeal by case stated. I would, therefore, adopt in the present
instance what I might call the magistrates' test based on *Bracegirdle v Oxley*[1] rather
f than the one urged by counsel.

If that is the way to approach it, if the question is: 'Was the conclusion of the jury
on question (c) a conclusion which no reasonable jury could have arrived at?' I am
bound to say that I think that it was not. It seems to me that the 12 disinterested
persons so thoughtfully provided for by the terms of the Manchester Act of 1851
might very well have been impressed by the objector's argument that he was losing
g something. He was losing an unrestricted right and he was receiving a restricted right.
I am certainly not prepared to say that no reasonable jury, having heard the proceedings in this case, could have come to the conclusion that the objector was
aggrieved. That being the case, it seems to me that the appeal to this court is bound
to fail with the result that the stopping up order will not be carried into effect.

h
MAIS J. I agree.

CROOM-JOHNSON J. I agree. However the first two questions which had to be
put to the jury were answered, once the jury had found that the objector was going
j to be aggrieved at the stopping up of the streets, then the appeal had to be allowed
and the stopping up order could not take effect.

There is no definition in the Act of 1851 of what is meant by 'aggrieved' and it was
essentially a matter for the jury. Having in mind that what the objector was going

---

1   [1947] 1 All ER 126, [1947] KB 349

P

to lose was an absolute right of way, which arose in circumstances not entirely clear
from the evidence, which would be substituted by a restricted right, it was entirely   *a*
within the power of the jury, giving a proper verdict, to come to the conclusion which they did. I agree with the judgment which Lord Widgery CJ has given.

Appeal dismissed.

Solicitors: *Church, Adams, Tatham & Co*, agents for *Cobbetts*, Manchester (for the   *b*
highway authority).

Jacqueline Charles Barrister.

c

EMI Ltd and others v Pandit

CHANCERY DIVISION

TEMPLEMAN J

5th DECEMBER 1974

Approved in ANTON PILLER v MANU-
FACTURING PROCESSES [1976] 1 All
ER 779

d

*Practice – Preservation of subject-matter of cause of action – Inspection – Interlocutory motion
– Ex parte application – Documents and property on premises controlled by respondent –
Order requiring respondent to permit applicants to enter premises for purpose of inspection
etc – Circumstances in which order will be made ex parte – Danger that in default of an order
applicants might be deprived of a remedy in the action – Danger that if notice of motion given   *e*
documents and property might be destroyed – Action for infringement of copyright – Order
requiring defendant to permit plaintiffs to enter defendant's premises for purposes of inspection, photographing of documents and property and removal of infringing copies – RSC Ord 29,
r 2.*

The plaintiffs, who owned the copyright in certain sound recordings of Indian music,   *f*
brought an action against the defendant for infringement of copyright and passing-
off. They obtained an interlocutory injunction restraining the defendant from parting
with infringing material, from selling such material and from passing-off. They also
obtained an interlocutory order that the defendant should make and serve on the
plaintiffs' solicitors a sufficient affidavit setting forth the names and addresses of all
persons or companies responsible for supplying him with, or to whom he had supplied,   *g*
such infringing copies, and that he should exhibit to the affidavit copies of all documents in his possession, power, custody or control relating to the supply to or by him.
In purported compliance with that order, the defendant swore an affidavit stating that
only one person, whom he named, with a post office box address in Dubai, had been
responsible for supplying him with infringing material; that he had no documents in
his possession, except a letter, a copy of which he exhibited and which purported   *h*
to be a statement by one of the plaintiffs saying that they had granted copyrights to
the company which had been producing the infringing material. The affidavit
went on to state that the defendant had supplied the infringing material to two
persons only, whom he named and who were already known to the plaintiffs. The
plaintiffs subsequently obtained evidence which indicated that the defendant's
affidavit was untrue, that he had forged the letter exhibited, and that the probability   *j*
was that there existed infringing material and evidence at the defendant's address
which were vital to the plaintiffs' case. Accordingly they appplied ex parte for an
order under RSC Ord 29, r 2(1) and (2)ᵃ, that such persons as might be duly authorised
by the plaintiffs be at liberty forthwith to enter the defendant's premises between

---

a   Rule 2, so far as material, is set out at p 421 *h* and *j* and p 422 *a*, post

specified hours for the following purposes: inspecting and photographing prerecorded tapes and other infringing material, and invoices, bills and other documents and correspondence which were relevant to the action; removing infringing articles, and inspecting, photographing and testing typewriters, since the plaintiffs suspected that the typewriter which had been used to carry out the alleged forgery was one belonging to the defendant which might still be on the premises. The plaintiffs were apprehensive that if they served notice on the defendant of the application, as required by RSC Ord 29, r 2(5), he would destroy or remove from the premises all relevant documents and articles and that the plaintiff would be effectively debarred from obtaining further relief in the action.

Held – (i) The court had jurisdiction to make an order giving the plaintiffs substantially the relief which they claimed. Such an order would only be made on an ex parte application in exceptional circumstances where it plainly appeared that justice required the intervention of the court in that, in default of such an order, the plaintiffs might be substantially deprived of a remedy. The order would only be granted on terms which safeguarded the defendant, as far as possible, and which narrowed the relief so far as it might otherwise cause harm to the defendant (see p 422 b and c, p 423 e and p 424 b to d, post).

(ii) In the circumstances an order giving substantially the relief claimed would be made on the ex parte application since the plaintiffs had established that, if notice of the application were given to the defendant it would almost certainly result in the immediate destruction of the articles and information to which they were entitled and which they sought. The order would however be in the form of a mandatory injunction requiring the defendant to allow the plaintiffs to enter premises occupied or used by the defendant between reasonable hours to inspect, identify and photograph infringing material and other articles to which they were entitled, to remove infringing copies and to inspect and test all typewriters and photographic machines (see p 422 c and p 424 d to p 425 c, post).

United Company of Merchants of England, trading to the East Indies v Kynaston (1821) 3 Bli 153 and *Hennessey v Rohmann, Osborne & Co* (1877) 36 LT 51 applied.

Notes

For inspection and preservation of property, see 21 Halsbury's Laws (3rd Edn) 419, para 879, and for cases on the subject, see 28(2) Digest (Reissue) 1125, *1234-1242*.

Cases referred to in judgment

A & M Records Inc v Darakdjian (1974) unreported.
EMI Ltd v Khazan (1974) unreported.
Hennessey v Rohmann, Osborne & Co (1877) 36 LT 51, [1877] WN 14, 28(2) Digest (Reissue) 1125, *1238*.
Morris v Howell (1888) 22 LR Ir 77, 28(2) Digest (Reissue) 1125, *694*.
Pall Europe Ltd v Microfiltrex Ltd (1974) unreported.
United Company of Merchants of England, trading to the East Indies v Kynaston (1821) 3 Bli 153, 4 ER 561.

Motion

This was an application, ex parte, by (1) EMI Ltd, (2) EMI Records Ltd, (3) the Gramophone Company of India Ltd, (4) Polydor of India Ltd, and (5) Polydor Ltd, the plaintiffs in an action against Kishorilal Narshi Pandit for alleged infringement of copyright and passing off. By their application the plaintiffs sought an order that the defendant, whether by himself, his servants, agents or any of them or otherwise howsoever should permit such persons not exceeding three as might be duly authorised by the plaintiffs and members or employees not exceeding two of the plaintiffs'

solicitors to enter forthwith premises known as 150 Nedham Street, Leicester, or such
parts thereof as should be occupied or used by the defendant at any hour between *a*
8 o'clock in the forenoon and 9 o'clock in the evening for the purpose of (a) inspecting
and photographing any of the following: (i) prerecorded tapes, (ii) labels for use
with the prerecorded tapes, (iii) packaging for the prerecorded tapes, (iv) invoices,
bills, and other documents relating to the purchase, sale, importation, ordering or
distribution of prerecorded tapes and parts therefor, (v) invoices, bills, and other
documents relating to the manufacture of prerecorded tapes, (vi) all correspondence *b*
passing between the defendant and the third plaintiffs; (b) removing into the plaintiffs' solicitors' custody all prerecorded tapes which were infringing copies of sound
recordings the copyright in which was vested for the time being in the plaintiffs or in
one or more of them or under the copyright in which the plaintiffs or one or more of
them were for the time being exclusive licensees; and (c) inspecting, photographing
and testing all typewriters or photographic reproducing machines. The facts are *c*
set out in the judgment.

Hugh Laddie for the plaintiffs.

TEMPLEMAN J. This is an ex parte application for an unusual order, which will *d*
only be made in unusual circumstances. The plaintiffs own the copyright in certain
sound recordings of Indian music and in the action claim injunctions against the
defendant restraining him from infringing their copyright and from passing-off,
an order for delivery up of infringing material, an order requiring the defendant to
give discovery of suppliers and customers of infringing material, an order for production of documents and, finally, damages for infringement of copyright, passing-off *e*
and conversion.

On 22nd March 1974 Plowman J made an interlocutory order. That took the form
of an injunction against the defendant until judgment or further order from parting
with infringing material, from selling infringing material, from passing-off and,
finally, there was an order in these terms:

> '. . . that the Defendant do within 7 days after service upon him of this Order *f*
> make and serve upon the Solicitors for the Plaintiffs a sufficient Affidavit setting
> forth the names and addresses of all persons or companies responsible for
> supplying him with or to whom he has supplied such infringing copies and do
> exhibit to such Affidavit copies of all documents in his possession power custody
> or control relating to such supply to or by him.' *g*

The defendant, in purported compliance with that order, swore an affidavit on 3rd
April 1974, and he said that the only person responsible for supplying him with
infringing material was a gentleman called Hajisayed, with a convenient post office
box address in Dubai. He said that he had no documents in his possession, except
a letter dated 20th February 1973, a copy of which he exhibited and which purported
to be a statement by one of the plaintiffs saying that they had granted copyrights to *h*
the Hindustan Music Corpn. The affidavit went on to say that the defendant had
supplied the infringing material only to two persons, whom he named, and who were
already known to the plaintiffs. That was all.

The plaintiffs have now produced evidence to show that affidavit of the defendant
is, putting it shortly, a pack of lies, that he forged the letter which he exhibited, that
the defendant has been engaged in an expensive, extensive and quite deliberate *j*
course of dealing in infringement of the plaintiffs' copyright and that there must be,
or have been in existence, many more documents than the defendant discloses in his
affidavit.

The defendant has been operating from an address in Leicester and it is quite clear
that if the plaintiffs now seek further relief and they serve notice on the defendant of

the relief which they seek, then the horse will rapidly leave the stable, if he has not
a gone already, and the plaintiffs will be effectively debarred from obtaining further
relief. It also seems clear from the evidence that there have been and may well be
still on the premises documents which are vital to the plaintiffs if they are to prove
their case at the trial and which, more particularly, and more importantly, will be
vital to the plaintiffs if they are to calculate and prove damages in the course of the
enquiry into damages which they seek.

b   The plaintiffs are thus driven to make an ex parte application. I am satisfied that
the information on which they now apply to me has only recently come to their
knowledge and that it is only now that they are able to demonstrate with great force
what they say is the falsity of the defendant's affidavit and the probability that there
existed and exists infringing material and evidence at the defendant's address, which
are vital to the plaintiffs. The application being, as I have said, necessarily ex parte,
c it may be that the defendant has an answer to the allegation which the plaintiffs now
make in the affidavits which I have read, unlikely though that seems to me at present.
That means that I must of course be very careful to protect the defendant and to see
that the relief which is now sought is proper relief and is no wider than is necessary.

     The order sought by the plaintiffs appears, to misuse a current popular phrase,
to be draconian. The draft seeks an order that such persons as may be duly authorised
d by the plaintiffs be at liberty to enter forthwith the premises at Leicester, which
are named, at any hour between eight o'clock in the forenoon and nine o'clock in
the evening, for certain specified purposes. Those purposes include the inspection
and photographing of prerecorded tapes and other infringing material and of invoices, bills and other documents and correspondence which are relevant to the
action, also for the purpose of removing infringing articles and, finally, for the purpose
e of inspecting, photographing and testing typewriters, that last relief being sought
because it is thought that the typewriter which actually carried out the alleged forgery
was a typewriter belonging to the defendant and may still be on the premises.

     Whatever the justification and authority for such an order, I would be very slow
to authorise what appears, at first blush, to be a trespass of property and invasion
of privacy. The plaintiffs, perceiving this difficulty, offered to give an undertaking
f that they would not forcibly enter on the premises, but it seemed to me that it
would be better if the order of the court were perfectly plain and if it granted no
more relief than would be the combined effect of the order which the plaintiffs seek
together with an undertaking mitigating its rigour. I am prepared, subject to
authority and the rules justifying this course and subject to suitable safeguards, to
make an order on the defendant to allow the plaintiffs to enter on premises in which
g he is in occupation for the purposes specified by the plaintiffs. This order will not
involve forcible entry but would make the defendant liable for contempt proceedings
if he disobeyed the order.

     I turn to see the justification for the substance of the order which the plaintiffs now
seek. Counsel for the plaintiffs referred me to RSC Ord 29, r 2. Paragraph (1) of
that rule provides:
h

> 'On the application of any party to a cause or matter the Court may make
> an order for the detention, custody or preservation of any property which is the
> subject-matter of the cause or matter, or as to which any question may arise
> therein, or for the inspection of any such property in the possession of a party
> to the cause or matter.'

j
It is clear that the infringing material and other items which the plaintiffs specify
in their application fall within that paragraph. Paragraph (2) provides:

> 'For the purpose of enabling any order under paragraph (1) to be carried out
> the Court may by the order authorise any person to enter upon any land or
> building in the possession of any party to the cause or matter.'

That in terms is as draconian as the order which the plaintiffs seek, but the rule is mitigated by para (5), which provides: *a*

'An application for an order under this rule must be made by summons or by notice under Order 25, rule 7.'

In the normal course of events, a defendant will have notice of the relief which is sought against him in the exercise of the powers given by this rule and will be able   *b* to come along to the court and to give reasons why the order should not be made or why, if it is made, particular safeguards should be included. Nevertheless, in my judgment, if it appears that the object of the plaintiffs' litigation will be unfairly and improperly frustrated by the very giving of the notice which is normally required to protect the defendant, there must be exceptional and emergency cases in which the court can dispense with the notice and, either under power in the rules to dispense   *c* with notice or by the exercise of its inherent jurisdiction, make such a limited order, albeit ex parte, as will give the plaintiffs the relief which they would otherwise be unable to obtain. In the present case I am satisfied that, if notice were given to the defendant, that would almost certainly result in the immediate destruction of the articles and information to which the plaintiffs are entitled and which they now seek.   *d*

In *The United Company of Merchants of England, trading to the East Indies v Kynaston*[1], the House of Lords upheld an order on the occupier of warehouses to permit inspection by the rector of the parish so that the premises could be valued for the purpose of calculating tithe. Lord Redesdale[2] adverted to the argument, which could be put forward in the present case by the defendant, namely:

'... that this is a private dwelling-house, and that the occupier is entitled to   *e* exclusive possession,—that no adverse entry can be made but by lawful authority —and that the Court of Chancery has no authority to order that an entry should be allowed. As to the first ground of objection, it does not directly apply to the case, because the order is, not directly to compel, but, upon the party, that he shall permit inspection.'   *f*

Pausing there, as I have indicated, the order which I propose to make in the present case would similarly be upon the party to permit inspection. Then Lord Redesdale continued:

'The objection that the Court has no power, is the material ground of Appeal. If it be true that it has no such power, there are many cases in which there must   *g* be a total defect of justice.'

Then, after citing the practice of courts in the past, Lord Redesdale said[3]:

'What was the origin of the power of the Court, it might be difficult to determine. It now stands upon usage, and is not confined to cases precisely similar to those which have preceded, but is adapted to emergencies to make the juris-   *h* diction of the Court effectual ... In this case the substantial question is, whether such a power in the Court is not necessary for the purposes of justice.'

All those observations apply to the case which is now before me. In that case in the House of Lords due notice had been given. The order for inspection was made after judgment in the action. Lord Redesdale referred to an earlier case[4] where,   *j*

---

1 (1821) 3 Bli 153
2 3 Bli at 162
3 3 Bli at 165
4 *Earl of Lonsdale v Curwen* (1799) 3 Bli 168

a as he said[1], 'the order was made before the decree, and upon a question where the rights of the parties were uncertain'. Thus there is authority for the proposition that there is inherent jurisdiction to enable inspection to take place both before judgment and in what may be called the interlocutory stage, but in the case to which I have referred notice was possible and notice was given.

In *Hennessey v Rohmann, Osborne & Co*[2] however, in an action for passing off brandy, an order was sought under what then was RSC Order LII, r 3, for an injunction and *b* for an order—

'that some proper person might be authorized by the Court to enter upon the defendants' warehouse or other premises belonging to or used by them, and there inspect such cases and bottles and take samples of the contents of such cases and bottles.'

c In the argument[3] it is made quite clear that the order for inspection was made ex parte. Malins V-C said[3] that he had never made an order of that nature ex parte and should not do so, except in a case of emergency; he considered that the circumstances of the case warranted him in making an immediate order for inspection of the premises.

d So that is authority that in an emergency an ex parte order can be made. Counsel produced a copy of the relevant RSC Ord 52, r 3, which it appears is for the present purposes indistinguishable from the present Ord 29, r 2, and satisfied me that in the same way as Ord 29 makes provision for summons or notice, so similar provision was made in Ord 52, r 3, and, therefore, the case is not to be distinguished on that ground.

Finally, to complete the 19th century, in *Morris v Howell*[4], under a similar rule the *e* plaintiff was given leave to inspect a ship lying in a harbour on which it was alleged that certain timber, part of the subject-matter of the action, had been placed.

From the terms of RSC Ord 29 and from the authorities which I have quoted, it seems to me that I have jurisdiction to make an order which will give these plaintiffs substantially the relief which they seek. Of course in the present case I must bear in mind that the order is ex parte, that the premises are unknown to this extent that *f* I cannot know at the moment whether they are office premises or a private dwelling-house, or whether they belong to the defendant, or what the position is and I must bear in mind that an order is sought not only which will enable the plaintiffs to send their representatives to ask to be allowed entry, but also to enable them to go through documents and correspondence to see if they can find infringing articles or evidence.

There is some modern, unreported, authority in point. By an order dated 21st May *g* 1974 in *A & M Records Inc v Aram Darakdjian*[5] Foster J, in the course of a similar action, made an order authorising persons authorised by the plaintiffs and a member of the plaintiffs' solicitors to enter forthwith certain premises, between certain specified hours, for purposes which are indistinguishable from those which are sought now, save for the relief sought with regard to the typewriters. That was an order made by Foster J after the motion had been treated as the trial of the action and *h* while the plaintiffs were still pursuing their remedies of claiming an enquiry which would lead to damages. On 3rd July 1974 Foster J made a similar order in *EMI Ltd v Khazan*[5], before the action had been commenced, on the usual terms that the plaintiffs would issue their writ so as to put their tackle in order.

Finally, by an order made on 28th October 1974 in *Pall Europe Ltd v Microfiltrex Ltd*[5], Goff J also made a similar order in the course of interlocutory proceedings. Thus

j

1   (1821) 3 Bli at 166
2   [1877] WN 14
3   [1877] WN at 14
4   (1888) 22 LR Ir 77
5   Unreported

there is authority for an order substantially in the terms which the plaintiffs seek
at any stage of the action. I am informed that by reason of the speed required in those   *a*
three cases and the time of day at which they were heard, it was not possible for
considered judgments to be given and I have been requested to go into this particular
application in some detail. I think it right to stress that, in my judgment, the kind
of order which is sought now can only be justified by a very strong case on the evidence   *b*
and can only be justified where the circumstances are exceptional to this extent, that
it plainly appears that justice requires the intervention of the court in the manner
which is sought and without notice, otherwise the plaintiffs may be substantially
deprived of a remedy. The order will only be granted on terms which safeguard
the defendant, as far as possible, and which narrows the relief so far as it might
otherwise cause harm to the defendant.

    In essence, the plaintiffs are seeking discovery, but this form of discovery will   *c*
only be granted where it is vital either to the success of the plaintiffs in the action or
vital to the plaintiffs in proving damages; in other words, it must be shown that
irreparable harm will accrue, or there is a high probability that irreparable harm may
accrue to the plaintiffs, unless the particular form of relief now sought is granted to
them.

    With that I turn now to consider the details of the order which, after helpful   *d*
discussion with counsel, I have resolved to make.

    First of all, there is the usual undertaking by the plaintiffs by their counsel—

    'to abide by any Order this Court may make as to damages in case this Court
    shall hereafter be of opinion that the Defendant shall have sustained any by   *e*
    reason of this Order which the Plaintiffs ought to pay.'

I shall then order—

    'that the Defendant whether by himself, his servants, agents or any of them
    or otherwise howsoever shall permit such persons not exceeding three as may   *f*
    be duly authorised by the Plaintiffs and members or employees not exceeding
    two of the Plaintiffs' solicitors to enter forthwith the premises known as [and
    then the address is given in Leicester] or such parts thereof as shall be occupied
    or used by the Defendant at any hour between 8 o'clock in the forenoon and 9
    o'clock in the evening . . .'

    An order in that form does not justify any unlawful entry. It imposes on the   *g*
defendant a mandatory injunction ordering him to allow the plaintiffs to enter. It
limits the persons who shall be allowed in to those whom counsel has satisfied me
are necessary in the present case to inspect, identify and photograph infringing
materials and other articles to which the plaintiffs are entitled. It does not order an
entry on premises unless they are in the occupation or use by the defendant, so that   *h*
the rights of other persons who may be interested in the property are fully protected
and, finally, it lays down reasonable hours for the exercise of the power which is
granted by this order.

    Then the order continues by specifying the purposes and the only purposes for
which the plaintiffs are to be allowed to enter the premises. The first is that they may
enter for the purpose of inspecting and photographing—   *j*

    '(i) pre-recorded tapes (ii) labels for use with the said pre-recorded tapes (iii)
    packaging for the said pre-recorded tapes (iv) invoices bills and other documents
    relating to the purchase sale importation ordering or distribution of pre-recorded
    tapes and parts thereof (v) invoices bills and other documents relating to the
    manufacture of pre-recorded tapes [and lastly]: (vi) all correspondence passing
    between the Defendant and [certain of the plaintiffs].'

a That limits the object of the entry to the infringing materials, which belong in any event to the plaintiffs, by virtue of being infringing material, and to the documents which are vital to their case for the purposes of discovery.

The second purpose for which the entry may be obtained is for the removal of all prerecorded tapes which are infringing copies of sound recordings, the copyright in which is vested for the time being in the plaintiffs. The removal is restricted to property which belongs to the plaintiffs under copyright law, by virtue of being
b infringements of their copyright. Finally, this entry is permitted for the purpose of 'Inspecting photographing and testing all typewriters or photographic reproducing machines'. That in the present instance is granted, because the very strong evidence as to the forgery can be strengthened or dispelled by testing the defendant's typewriter, which it is thought was the machine by which the forgery was carried out.

c Then, as a separate injunction, I shall order that the defendant be restrained until trial or further order whether by himself or his servants or agents, in the usual form, from in any way altering, defacing or destroying or removing from the premises or distributing or selling any of the articles and documents referred to in the earlier part of the order, without leave of the court or the consent of the plaintiffs. The first part of the order is to compel the defendant to give discovery of the infringing material and typewriters and the second part of the order restrains him from making
d away with or destroying them.

So far as the typewriters are concerned, RSC Ord 29, r 3, enables the court, where it considers it necessary or expedient for the purpose of obtaining full information or evidence in any cause or matter, to authorise or require any sample to be taken of any property which is the subject-matter of the cause or matter or as to which any question may arise therein, any observation to be made on such property or any
e experiment to be tried on or with such property. There again the order incorporates provisions with regard to notice, but on the authorities and for the reasons which I have outlined, the fact that notice cannot for obvious reasons be given in this case does not, in my judgment, debar me from making an order in these unusual circumstances.

f *Order accordingly.*

Solicitors: *A E Hamlin & Co* (for the plaintiffs).

Jacqueline Metcalfe   Barrister.

Re Manual Work Services (Construction) Ltd   *a*

CHANCERY DIVISION
MEGARRY J
7th, 8th OCTOBER 1974

b

Company – Winding-up – Compulsory winding-up – Advertisement of petition – Amendment – Readvertisement – Petitioner at hearing seeking order for winding-up subject to supervision of court instead of compulsory winding-up – All creditors represented at hearing supporting application – Substantial body of creditors not before court – Whether readvertisement of petition necessary.

c

A creditor by his petition prayed that a company be wound up by the court under the Companies Act 1948 'or that such other order may be made in the premises as shall be just'. The company had over 300 creditors with debts totalling nearly £200,000. The petition was duly advertised, the advertisement stating simply that it was a petition for the winding-up of the company and saying nothing about any other relief. At the hearing, the petitioner, with the concurrence of the creditors on the list, *d* numbering some 34 in all with claims totalling over £115,000, applied for an order for the winding-up to continue subject to the supervision of the court instead of a compulsory winding-up order.

Held – Where a petition for a compulsory order had been advertised, and at the hearing the petitioner asked for a supervision order only, the petition ought as a *e* general rule to be readvertised, for the differences between winding-up by the court and winding-up subject to supervision were very great and the latter gave the company's creditors less protection. Although the court had a discretion to dispense with readvertisement, the only proper course, having regard to the number of creditors (some with substantial claims) who were not represented, was for the creditors generally to be given due warning of the actual order sought by the petitioner. *f* Accordingly the petition should be readvertised (see p 427 *h* to p 428 *d* and *g h*, post).

Note

For readvertisement of petition, see 7 Halsbury's Laws (4th Edn) 609, para 1019, and for cases on the subject, see 10 Digest (Repl) 886, 5898-5903.   *g*

Cases referred to in judgment

Civil Service Brewery Co, Re [1893] WN 5, 37 Sol Jo 194, 10 Digest (Repl) 1120, 7776.
National Whole Meal Bread and Biscuit Co, Re [1891] 2 Ch 151, 60 LJCh 350, 64 LT 285, 10 Digest (Repl) 886, 5902.
New Morgan Gold Mining Co, Re [1893] WN 79, 37 Sol Jo 441, 10 Digest (Repl) 1120, *h* 7775.
New Oriental Bank Corpn, Re [1892] 3 Ch 563, 62 LJCh 63, 67 LT 87, 10 Digest (Repl) 1114, 7726.
United Bacon Curing Co, Re [1890] WN 74, 10 Digest (Repl) 1119, 7773.
Waterproof Materials Co, Re [1893] WN 18, 37 Sol Jo 231, 10 Digest (Repl) 1051, 7283.

j

Petition

This was a petition by Kevin Docherty, trading as Surveying Associates, for an order that Manual Work Services (Construction) Ltd ('the company') be wound up by the court under the provisions of the Companies Act 1948 or 'that such other order may be made in the premises as shall be just'. The facts are set out in the judgment.

Charles Bonney for the petitioner and supporting creditors.
a *Stephen Hunt* for the opposing creditors.
Philip Heslop for the liquidator.

MEGARRY J. In this case, on 2nd January 1974, the company passed a special resolution that it should be wound up voluntarily. On the same day there was a
b meeting of creditors of the company who, the petition alleges, unanimously agreed that the voluntary winding-up was unacceptable by reason of the company's general indebtedness. The fact that there was a unanimous agreement to this effect is to some extent controverted in the affidavits, but it seems plain that at least a substantial number of the creditors took the view that the voluntary winding-up should not be accepted. On 15th March a creditor presented a petition praying that the company
c should be wound up by the court under the Companies Act 1948, 'or that such other Order may be made in the premises as shall be just'. This petition was duly advertised, the advertisements stating simply that it was a petition for the winding-up of the company, with nothing said about any other relief. After various adjournments, the petitioner has now, with the support of all the supporting and opposing creditors on the list, asked that instead of making the usual compulsory winding-up order,
d the court should make an order that the winding-up should continue subject to the supervision of the court. In those circumstances, the question has arisen whether the petition, duly amended, ought to be readvertised.
The authorities are not in an altogether happy state. In some cases the court has dispensed with readvertisement: see, for example, *Re United Bacon Curing Co*[1] and *Re Civil Service Brewery Co*[2]; and *Re Waterproof Materials Co*[3] may be in the same
e category. On the other hand, readvertisement was required in *Re New Oriental Bank Corpn*[4] and in *Re New Morgan Gold Mining Co*[5]. In cases so shortly reported as most of these are, it is not easy to perceive what the principle is. I have found some assistance in *Re National Whole Meal Bread and Biscuit Co*[6], where Kekewich J said[7]:

'I take it that the intention of the rules as to the advertising of winding-up
f   petitions is that the petition which is heard shall be advertised—that is to say, that which is advertised and that which is heard shall be substantially the same petition.'

I am not entirely sure that this accords exactly with what the judge said on the next page of the report, but nevertheless it seems to me to be a clear and intelligible statement of principle.
g   What appears to be the most recent reported authority on the subject is contained in a *Practice Note*[8]. There, Buckley J, whose learning in these matters was, of course, pre-eminent, said:

'. . . where a petition for a compulsory order had been advertised, and at the hearing the petitioner asked for a supervision order only, the petition ought as a general rule to be re-advertised. This appeared to be the practice more recently
h   adopted, the reason for it apparently being that persons who would be satisfied with a compulsory order would not take the trouble to appear if they thought such an order would be made, but might appear and object to a supervision order only being made.'

j 1 [1890] WN 74
     2 [1893] WN 5
     3 [1893] WN 18
     4 [1892] 3 Ch 563
     5 [1893] WN 79
     6 [1891] 2 Ch 151
     7 [1891] 2 Ch at 152
     8 [1902] WN 77

That statement, if I may say so, carries very considerable weight.

The court is naturally reluctant to expose the petitioner and others to the delay *a* that readvertisement would produce. It has not been suggested in this case that there is any objection to readvertisement other than the delay and, no doubt, the expense involved. But the question for me is, I think, whether it is right to make a supervision order where the only relief advertised and appearing in the cause list as being sought is a winding-up order. The differences between winding-up by the court and winding-up subject to supervision are, of course, very great. A glance at Sch 11 to the Companies *b* Act 1948 gives some indication of this. In general, winding-up under supervision is a voluntary liquidation with some important but not very extensive safeguards for those concerned, such as the requirement of quarterly reports to the court, protection against actions against the company, and the opportunity to make applications to the court. The two processes are, in substance, very different indeed.

I say nothing about a case in which all the creditors are before the court, for there *c* is no question of that here. The creditors listed as supporting a winding-up order are over 20 in number, with claims of over £40,000, while those listed as opposing the order are some 14 in number, with claims of over £75,000. Even though they all now join in supporting the petitioning creditor's application for a supervision order, they by no means represent the whole body of creditors. A statement of affairs at the end of November 1973 shows that there are over 300 creditors, with debts totalling *d* nearly £200,000. It is therefore plain that there are many creditors, some with substantial claims, who are not represented before me.

It has been said in argument that the greater includes the less, and so on a petition for a winding-up order the lesser relief of a supervision order may be granted. That, however, is not the point. What matters is not what appears to the company, but what relief and protection is accorded to the creditors. If they are told that the relief *e* being sought is the relief which will afford them all the greatest measure of protection, namely, a compulsory winding-up order, is it right, without forewarning to them, to seek an order which protects them less? No doubt any of those who felt strongly enough on the matter could, after a supervision order had been made, petition for a compulsory order, but that of course involves the time and trouble of commencing new proceedings instead of merely attending the hearing of an existing petition and *f* urging that a particular course of action should be taken. It has also been said that the court has a discretion in these matters and that this is a case in which that discretion should be exercised so as to dispense with readvertisement. It may indeed be that there will be cases in which the court will consider it right to exercise such a discretion, perhaps where it is satisfied that substantially the entire body of creditors is before the court or has received due warning in one form or another of the proposed *g* course of action; but those circumstances do not exist in the present case. It seems to me that the only fair course is for the creditors generally to be given due warning of the actual order which the petitioner now seeks. I therefore hold that the petition in this case should be amended to show the relief now being sought, and that the petition, as so amended, should be readvertised.

h

Order accordingly.

Solicitors: *Wedlake Bell*, agents for *G R Smith & Co*, West Bromwich (for the petitioner and supporting creditors); *James Beauchamp*, Birmingham (for the opposing creditors and the liquidator).

F K Anklesaria Esq   Barrister.

a

Crane Fruehauf Ltd v Inland Revenue Commissioners

Applied in IRC v UFITEC GROUP [1977] 3 All ER 924

COURT OF APPEAL

RUSSELL, STAMP AND SCARMAN LJJ

29th, 30th, 31st OCTOBER, 16th DECEMBER 1974

b Stamp duty – Relief from duty – Reconstruction or amalgamation of companies – Acquisition of shares in existing company – Consideration for acquisition issue of shares in transferee company in exchange for shares in existing company – Consideration consisting as to not less than 90 per cent in issue of shares in transferee company – Issue of shares – Meaning – Shares issued subject to a condition requiring shareholders in existing company to transfer them to third party in exchange for cash – Whether consideration consisting in the issue of shares to shareholders in existing company – Whether necessary that shares should be issued to c shareholders in existing company unconditionally – Finance Act 1927, s 55(1) (as amended by the Finance Act 1928, s 31).

On 1st September 1967 Crane Fruehauf Ltd ('Crane') entered into an agreement with Boden Trailers Ltd ('Boden') and the Boden shareholders, under which Crane agreed to acquire the whole of the ordinary share capital of Boden, which consisted d of 4,900,000 shares of 1s each. The consideration for the acquisition was to be the allotment of 18 fully paid ordinary shares of 2s each in Crane and the payment of £1 in cash in exchange for every 49 shares in Boden making a total of 1,800,000 ordinary shares and £100,000 cash. It was an express term of the agreement that, if required to do so by Fruehauf International Ltd ('FIL'), a company which held one-third of the share capital in Crane, the vendors of the Boden shares were to transfer to FIL one-third of the Crane shares ('the FIL shares') to which they were entitled under the e agreement, at £1 per share, making 600,000 shares for £600,000. The option was exercisable by FIL by notice in writing and on 20th September FIL duly gave notice requiring the Boden shareholders to transfer the 600,000 FIL shares. On 12th October Crane increased its nominal share capital by the creation of 1,800,000 shares with a view to the acquisition of the Boden shares. On the same date the acquisition of f the Boden shares by Crane and the purchase of the FIL shares by FIL were completed in that order. Crane registered the new 1,800,000 shares in the names of the Boden shareholders, delivered to them the share certificates relating thereto and paid £100,000. The Boden shareholders delivered to Crane the transfers and share certificates relating to the Boden shares. Then the Boden shareholders delivered to FIL executed transfers of and share certificates relating to the FIL shares and g received the £600,000 from FIL. Crane claimed relief under s 55(1)[a] of the Finance

<hr>

a Section 55(1), as amended and so far as material, provides: 'If in connection with a scheme for the reconstruction of any company or companies or the amalgamation of any companies it is shown to the satisfaction of the Commissioners of Inland Revenue that there exist the following conditions, that is to say—(a) that . . . the nominal share capital of a company has been increased; (b) that the company (in this section referred to as "the transferee com-h pany") . . . has increased its capital with a view to the acquisition . . . of not less than ninety per cent of the issued share capital of, any particular existing company; (c) that the consideration for the acquisition (except such part thereof as consists in the transfer to or discharge by the transferee company of liabilities of the existing company) consists as to not less than ninety per cent thereof—(i) . . . (ii) where shares are to be acquired, in the issue of shares in the transferee company to the holders of shares in the existing company in exchange for the shares held by them in the existing company; then, subject to the j provisions of this section,—(A) The . . . amount by which the capital of the transferee company has been increased . . . shall, for the purpose of computing the stamp duty chargeable in respect of that capital, be treated as being reduced by either—(i) an amount equal to the amount of the share capital of the existing company . . . or the amount to be credited as paid up on the shares to be issued as such consideration as aforesaid . . . whichever amount is the less; and (B) Stamp duty under the heading "Conveyance or Transfer on Sale" in the First Schedule to the Stamp Act, 1891, shall not be chargeable on any instrument made for the purposes of or in connection with the transfer of the . . . shares . . .'

Act 1927 from capital duty on the increase of its nominal capital and from transfer
duty on the transfers of shares on the grounds that both had arisen in connection with   *a*
a scheme for the amalgamation of the companies and that the consideration for the
acquisition of the Boden shares consisted as to not less than 90 per cent thereof in
the issue of 1,800,000 ordinary shares of 2s each in Crane.

Held – Since it was Crane itself that, by its contract with the Boden shareholders, had   *b*
imposed on them the option in favour of FIL and with it the obligation, should FIL
exercise the option, to receive £600,000 instead of 600,000 shares, the consideration
for the acquisition of Boden shares by Crane could not be truly regarded, as to the
600,000 shares in Crane, as consisting in the issue of those shares to the Boden shareholders, within s 55(1)(c)(ii) of the 1927 Act; the consideration was not simply 'the
issue of shares' but the issue of shares subject to an obligation to transfer them to FIL   *c*
for cash should FIL exercise the option. What the Boden shareholders had in effect
acquired under the contract was no more than a right to receive £600,000 from FIL.
It followed that the consideration by Crane for the acquisition of Boden shares did
not consist as to not less than 90 per cent thereof in the issue of shares in Crane to
the Boden shareholders, and accordingly Crane was not entitled to the relief claimed
(see p 433 *h* to p 434 *a* and *c j*, p 435 *g* to *j*, p 436 *a* to *c* and p 438 *b e* and *f*, post).   *d*
Per Stamp LJ. The reference in s 55(1)(c)(ii) to 'the issue of shares . . . to the holders
of shares in the existing company' must be construed as a reference to a condition
that the shares are issued to those holders beneficially and not as nominees (see
p 435 *h* and p 436 *d*, post).
Decision of Templeman J [1974] 1 All ER 811 affirmed.

e

Notes
For relief from companies capital duty and transfer stamp duty on reconstruction
or amalgamation, see 7 Halsbury's Laws (4th Edn) 866-868, paras 1556-1558, and for
cases on the subject, see 10 Digest (Repl) 1101, 1102, 7612, 7613.
For the Finance Act 1927, s 55, see 32 Halsbury's Statutes (3rd Edn) 229.

f

Cases referred to in judgments
Brotex Cellulose Fibres Ltd v Inland Revenue Comrs [1933] 1 KB 158, [1930] All ER Rep 595,
    102 LJKB 211, 148 LT 116, 10 Digest (Repl) 1101, 7612.
Central and District Properties Ltd v Inland Revenue Comrs [1966] 2 All ER 433, [1966]
    1 WLR 1015, 45 ATC 169, [1966] TR 147, HL, Digest (Cont Vol B) 99, 2720*a*.
Lever Brothers Ltd v Inland Revenue Comrs [1938] 2 All ER 808, [1938] 2 KB 518, 107   *g*
    LJKB 669, 159 LT 136, CA, 9 Digest (Repl) 420, 2720.
Parway Estates v Inland Revenue Comrs (1958) 45 Tax Cas 135, 37 ATC 164, [1958] TR
    193, CA.

Cases also cited   *h*
Murex Ltd v Inland Revenue Comrs [1933] 1 KB 173.
Tillotson (Oswald) Ltd v Inland Revenue Comrs [1933] 1 KB 134, [1932] All ER Rep 965.

Appeal
The appellant, Crane Fruehauf Ltd ('Crane'), incorporated in 1950, had an authorised
capital of £600,000 divided into 6,000,000 ordinary shares of 2s each. Another com-   *j*
pany, Boden Trailers Ltd ('Boden'), incorporated in 1954, had an authorised capital
of £500,000 divided into 10,000,000 shares of 1s each, of which 4,900,000 had been
issued and fully paid. Both Crane and Boden carried on business as manufacturers
of semi-trailers. Fruehauf International Ltd ('FIL') was a shareholder of Crane,
holding at all relevant times approximately 33⅓ per cent of its issued share capital.

On 1st September 1967 Crane entered into an agreement for amalgamation ('the
a agreement') with directors and shareholders of Boden (together called 'vendors').
Under the agreement Crane offered to acquire the whole of the issued share capital
of Boden as from 31st March 1967 ('the date of sale') on the basis of 18 fully paid
ordinary shares of 2s each in Crane plus £1 in cash in exchange for every 49 shares
in Boden, making a total consideration of 1,800,000 such ordinary shares and £100,000
cash. Acceptance of the offer by the directors and shareholders of Boden was to
b be in the terms of a form of assent and transfer annexed to the agreement. It was
an express term of the agreement that if so required by FIL, the vendors should on
completion be bound to sell to FIL, and FIL should purchase, at £1 per share, 600,000
of the new ordinary shares ('the FIL shares') in Crane, to be allotted and issued to
the vendors. On 20th September 1967 FIL, by notice in writing, made a requisition
of the 600,000 FIL shares from the vendors. Meanwhile, between 1st September
c and 22nd September forms of assent and transfer in the form provided for by the
agreement were executed by all the shareholders of Boden in respect of their holdings
of shares in Boden and were handed over to the directors of Boden. On 12th October
Crane increased its nominal share capital by the creation of 1,800,000 shares with a
view to the acquisition of the Boden shares. On the same date, the acquisition of the
Boden shares and the purchase of the FIL shares by FIL were completed in that
d order. Crane registered the new 1,800,000 shares in the names of the Boden shareholders, delivered to them share certificates relating thereto and paid £100,000. The
Boden shareholders delivered to Crane the transfers and share certificates relating
to the Boden shares. The Boden shareholders then delivered to FIL executed
transfers of and share certificates relating to the FIL shares and received the £600,000
from FIL. Crane claimed relief under s 55(1) of the Finance Act 1927 from capital
e duty on the statement of increase of its nominal capital and ad valorem stamp duty
on documents effecting the transfers to Crane of the issued share capital of Boden.
The respondents, the Inland Revenue Commissioners ('the commissioners'), dis-
allowed the claim and assessed the statement of increase of nominal capital to capital
duty at the rate of 10s for every £100 on the £180,000, and the transfer document to ad
valorem stamp duty at the rate of 10s for every £50 or fractional part of £50 of the con-
f sideration moving from Crane for transfer to it of the 4,900,000 issued shares of Boden.
In computing the value of the consideration, however, the commissioners took the
market value of the Crane shares as at 12th October 1967, the first day of dealings
therein on the London Stock Exchange, which was 33s 9d per share. Being dissatisfied
with the assessments made, Crane, for the purpose of an appeal to the High Court,
required the commissioners to state and sign a case setting forth the questions on
g which the court's opinion was required and the assessments made by the commissioners. On 21st December 1973 Templeman J[1] affirmed the commissioners'
assessments, holding that, although the agreement between Crane and Boden of
1st September 1967 was a scheme for amalgamation and that the consideration for
the acquisition of shares in Boden consisted in the issue of shares in Crane to Boden
shareholders 'in exchange for the shares held by them' in Boden, the transaction
h did not comply with s 55(1)(c) of the 1927 Act, and Crane was not entitled to the relief
claimed, since the condition imposed by s 55(1)(c) was only satisfied where the acquisition was in exchange for shares and not for shares subject to a contract to sell or an
option to purchase imposed by the acquirer as a condition of the acquisition. Crane
appealed.

j C N Beattie QC and Richard Sykes for Crane.
Michael Wheeler QC and Peter Gibson for the commissioners.

---

1   [1974] 1 All ER 811, [1974] STC 110

Cur adv vult

a

16th December. The following judgments were read.

RUSSELL LJ. This case is reported below[1]. The questions for decision in connection with exemption from capital duty on the increase of 1,800,000 2s shares in Crane Fruehauf Ltd ('Crane') and in connection with exemption from ad valorem stamp duty on the transfers to Crane of the issued share capital of Boden Trailers Ltd *b* ('Boden') under s 55 of the Finance Act 1927, are as follows: (1) Was there a scheme for the amalgamation of Crane and Boden? (2) If the answer is Yes, then in connection with that scheme, (a) Did Crane increase its capital with a view to the acquisition by Crane of the issued share capital of Boden? (b) Did the consideration for the acquisition by Crane of the Boden shares consist as to not less than 90 per cent thereof in the issue of shares in Crane to the holders of shares in Boden in exchange for the shares in Boden *c* held by those holders?

The commissioners contend first that there was no scheme for the amalgamation of Crane and Boden. Alternatively, they contend that the increase in Crane capital, if in connection with a scheme for the amalgamation of Crane and Boden, was not or was not solely with a view to the acquisition by Crane of the issued share capital of Boden. Further, the commissioners contend that in the circumstances of the case the *d* consideration for the acquisition by Crane of the Boden shares was not truly 1,800,000 shares in Crane plus £100,000 but in reality 1,200,000 shares in Crane plus £100,000 plus a vendor's lien on 600,000 Crane shares for £600,000, which of course would reduce the share content of the consideration to below 90 per cent.

Further, the commissioners contend that in the circumstances of the case the 600,000 shares in Crane which inevitably would be transferred immediately to Fruehauf *e* International Ltd ('FIL') were not to be regarded as having been 'issued' to the Boden shareholders, notwithstanding that in respect also of these shares the Boden shareholders had been placed on the Crane register as holders thereof and certificates in their favour had been issued by Crane.

Further, the commissioners contend that the issue of the 1,800,000 Crane shares to the Boden shareholders was not, or not solely in exchange for, the Boden shares, but *f* also in exchange for the Boden shareholders having committed themselves to sell 600,000 of the Crane shares to FIL at a price, which proved to be below market price on completion, of £1 each. This contention is perhaps the same as the contention about what was the consideration, but expressed differently.

I have set these out as the contentions of the commissioners, but it must of course be borne in mind that throughout it is for Crane to bring itself within the exemptions. *g*

Now the substance of the matter is reasonably clear. Those responsible for the undertakings and activities of Crane and Boden came to the conclusion that it would be advantageous that those undertakings should be under one command, a situation which would be achieved if Boden were to become a 100 per cent subsidiary of Crane. There would be various methods by which this could be achieved, but naturally and sensibly a method was sought by which advantage could be taken of the exemptions *h* afforded by s 55 of the 1927 Act. If there were simply an increase in Crane capital of 1,800,000 shares for issue to Boden shareholders and with it (plus £100,000) all the Boden shares were acquired, there could be no doubt (subject to a point reserved by the commissioners for a higher court) that 'amalgamation' must involve dissolution of one of the companies. But FIL held about one-third of the issued share capital of Crane and thus as a practical matter could block the increase in Crane share *j* capital and thus the scheme. FIL was not prepared to concur in the increase unless a means could be found to secure that FIL could retain its position, after the increase in capital had been issued, of owning about one-third of the Crane issued share

1   [1974] 1 All ER 811, [1974] STC 110

capital. Hence the arrangements and transactions that were ultimately carried
a through, the primary object and effect being to achieve the unification of control of
both undertakings, but with provision for the acquisition by FIL from Boden shareholders of one-third of the Crane shares to be issued to Boden shareholders—that is
to say 600,000 at a cash price of £1 (which was a proper price when the arrangements
were made) in order to preserve the FIL proportion of Crane issued share capital so
that FIL would not block the scheme. It is perhaps convenient to note here that ad
b valorem duty on the transfers of the 600,000 shares in Crane by Boden shareholders
was exigible and paid. Those shares have been referred to as 'the FIL shares'.

Templeman J decided all points in favour of Crane except the question what was
the consideration for the acquisition by Crane of the Boden shares. He concluded
that the consideration for the acquisition of the shares in Boden by Crane was not the
issue of 1,800,000 shares in Crane plus £100,000, but the issue of 1,200,000 shares and
c a further 600,000 shares subject to the right of FIL to acquire the latter for £600,000,
plus the £100,000. From this he concluded that part of the consideration was in effect
the sum of £700,000 and the other part only 1,200,000 shares, which was outside the
conditions required for exemption.

I am content to agree with Templeman J on those aspects of the case on which he
was in favour of Crane without elaborating his reasons. Thus there was a scheme for
d the amalgamation of Crane and Boden; Crane increased its nominal capital by
1,800,000 shares in connection with that scheme and with a view to the acquisition of
the whole issued share capital of Boden; and the 1,800,000 new Crane shares were
issued to the Boden shareholders in exchange for the Boden shares. This leaves the
major question whether the consideration for the acquisition of the Boden shares
consisted as to not less than 90 per cent thereof of shares in Crane. The offer and the
e only offer that was made by Crane to the Boden shareholders was one which, on
acceptance by them, bound them to an option in favour of FIL to sell the 'FIL shares'
to FIL at £1 a share. What truly was the consideration that the Boden shareholders
were to receive for their Boden shares under their bargains with Crane? It was not, it
seems to me, simply 1,800,000 shares plus £100,000. Rather it was 1,200,000 shares
plus £100,000, plus 600,000 shares subject to an immediate obligation (which the very
f mechanics of the transaction made inescapable) and right to receive £600,000; and
this situation was procured by Crane in the bargain offered by Crane to the Boden
shareholders. If the Boden shareholders were asked what they were getting for their
shares by accepting Crane's offer, they would correctly as a matter of substance say
that they were getting 1,200,000 shares in Crane plus £100,000 plus £600,000.

It is, I think, correct to say that if, prior to the bargain between Crane and the Boden
g shareholders, FIL had contracted separately with the Boden shareholders that if Crane
should acquire the Boden shares in exchange for 1,800,000 shares in Crane plus
£100,000, the Boden shareholders would sell 600,000 of those Crane shares, when
issued, to FIL at £1 each, then the consideration for the acquisition of the Boden shares
would have been 1,800,000 shares plus £100,000, notwithstanding that the Boden
shareholders had committed themselves in advance to sell 600,000 of them to FIL, and
h consequently on registration would acquire no more than an unpaid vendor's lien for
£600,000. But the method adopted was other than that. It was Crane itself that, by
its bargain with the Boden shareholders, imposed on them the option in favour of
FIL and with it the obligation (should FIL exercise the option) to receive £600,000
instead of 600,000 shares. The strings were attached by Crane as an essential part of
the scheme for amalgamation. In those circumstances, I conclude that the considera-
j tion for the acquisition of the Boden shares by Crane cannot be truly regarded, as to
the 600,000 shares in Crane, as consisting of the issue of those shares. To that extent
the consideration which Crane procured should reach the Boden shareholders was in
the event no more than a right to receive £600,000 from FIL. It was pointed out in
argument that the £600,000 received by the Boden shareholders was the consideration
for shares in Crane; but it does not appear to me that this is inconsistent with the

proposition that the consideration for the acquisition of Boden shares was as to 600,000
Crane shares not simply the issue of them to Boden shareholders.   *a*

If in order to maintain the one-third position of FIL in Crane the latter had issued
600,000 of the new 1,800,000 capital to FIL for £600,000 cash, and acquired all the
Boden shares for 1,200,000 in shares plus £700,000 in cash, the effect would have been
exactly the same as that which was aimed at and desired by Crane, and quite plainly
the section would not have applied. What was procured in fact by Crane by its
agreement with the Boden shareholders conferred on the Boden shareholders as   *b*
consideration for the acquisition of the Boden shares no different rights, as a matter of
substance, than would have been conferred on them as such consideration had the
procedure last mentioned been adopted.

It will be observed from what I have said, in particular in regard to the situation had
the Boden shareholders bound themselves previously simply to FIL, that a feature
essential to my conclusion is that it was Crane itself that by contract with the Boden   *c*
shareholders attached the string to the 600,000 shares. Consequently, on the main
point in the case, I would hold that the conditions of s 55 of the 1927 Act were not
shown to have been complied with, and I would dismiss the appeal.

There remains the secondary point. On the basis that the taxpayer was not entitled
to relief under s 55, the commissioners assessed the ad valorem duty on the transfers
of the Boden shares on the footing that the whole of the 1,800,000 Crane shares   *d*
fell to be treated and valued pursuant to s 55 of the Stamp Act 1891 as part of the
consideration for the transfers.

Before Templeman J it was conceded, however, that the 600,000 FIL shares which
were subject to the option ought not to be brought into the computation at their
market value, but that £600,000 ought to be substituted therefor as part of the
consideration.   *e*

On the basis that Crane was not entitled to relief under s 55 of the 1927 Act it was
submitted on behalf of Crane, as well in this court as before Templeman J, that the
appropriate dates for valuing the 1,200,000 Crane shares, being part of the consideration
for the transfer of the Boden shares within s 55 of the 1891 Act, were the respective
dates on which the transfers of the Boden shares were signed by the holders. Section
6 of the Stamp Act 1891 provides that where an instrument is chargeable with ad   *f*
valorem duty in respect of any stock (which includes shares)—

> 'the duty shall be calculated on the value, on the day of the date of the instru-
> ment . . . of the stock or security according to the average price thereof.'

At the respective dates when the Boden shareholders signed the transfers of their
shares the Crane shares had not been issued and accordingly, so the argument ran,   *g*
s 6 had no application and the value of the Crane shares ought to be taken to be the
issue price attributed to those shares in the books of Crane. Templeman J rejected
these submissions, taking the view that until the issue of the Crane shares on 12th
October 1967 each of the transfers of the Boden shares was in escrow conditional on
the issue of the Crane shares. The date of the several transfers was accordingly 12th
October 1967, on which date each share could have been sold for the stock exchange   *h*
price. In my judgment, Templeman J came to a correct conclusion for the reason
which he gave. I would, however, add this. Where s 6 of the 1891 Act does not apply,
the commissioners must do the best they can and, if it were correct that the transfers
were executed prior to the issue of the Crane shares, the market value of the latter at
the moment of their issue plus the cash payable to the vendors would in my view be a
good indication of the amount or value of the consideration for the transfers.   *j*

Accordingly, on this subsidiary point also, I would dismiss the appeal.

STAMP LJ (read by Scarman LJ). I agree. As has been indicated in more than one
judgment where s 55 of the Finance Act 1927 has fallen to be considered, the section

is designed to secure exemption from stamp duties to the extent therein specified
a where, as the result of an amalgamation of the businesses of more than one company,
the businesses remain in substance owned by the same persons.

Such a result may be achieved in two classes of case. In the first class of case the
result may be achieved by a transaction whereunder the business of one of the
companies is acquired by the other company ('the transferee company') in return for
an issue of shares in the transferee company to the transferor company or to its
b shareholders. If, as will normally be the case, the shares in the transferee company so
issued are of a value equal to the value of the business transferred, the shareholders of
the two companies will after the transaction have an interest in the two businesses
which have become one having a value corresponding to the value of their former
interests in the separate businesses. And if then it is shown that the transferee company
was to be registered or had been incorporated or had increased its capital with a view
c to the acquisition of the business it acquired, and the transaction is not otherwise
complicated, relief from stamp duty which would otherwise be payable will to the
extent specified in the section be accorded. The condition of the section (see sub-s (1)
(*b*)), namely that the transferee was to be registered or had been incorporated with a
view to the acquisition of the undertaking, will have been satisfied. And so will the
condition (see sub-s (1)(*c*)(i)) that the consideration for the acquisition consists in the
d issue of shares to the company from whom the undertaking is acquired (the 'existing
company' spoken of in the section) or to the holders of the existing company's shares.

A similar result will be achieved in the second class of case, where the transferee
company acquires the shares of the existing company in exchange for shares in the
transferee company issued to the shareholders of the existing company. Again, if the
value of the shares so issued corresponds to the value of the shares transferred, the
e shareholders of the two companies will after the transaction have, through their
holding in the transferee company, an interest in the two businesses equivalent to
their former interests in the separate businesses.

It is apparent that if the consideration for the acquisition consists not of shares in the
transferee company but exclusively of money, the result will be quite different. The
two businesses will not continue to be, as Rowlatt J put it in *Brotex Cellulose Fibres Ltd*
f *v Inland Revenue Comrs*[1], 'in the old hands but under the domination' of the transferee
company. The business of the existing company will, on the contrary, be in new hands
and to the extent that the consideration for the acquisition consists in part of cash
(or a consideration not consisting of shares in the transferee company) the business
will pro tanto not be in the old hands; something will have gone from the shareholders in the existing company and found its way into the hands of the shareholders
g in the transferee company.

The condition in para (*c*) of sub-s (1) is designed to prevent the latter result providing
that where, as here, shares in the existing company are to be acquired, the consideration for the acquisition of the shares must consist as to not less than 90 per cent 'in the
issue of shares in the transferee company to holders of shares in the existing company'.
If, however, the condition was satisfied by an issue of shares to the holders of shares in
h the existing company on the terms that the holders of the new shares should become
nominees for another, the condition would not secure the situation which it was
designed to secure. What is contemplated is an issue of shares to the holders of shares
in the existing company as beneficial owners, and sub-s (1)(*c*) must, in my judgment,
be construed accordingly; otherwise, the businesses will not be in the same hands.

Much of the argument in this case proceeded on the footing that it is enough in
j order to satisfy sub-s (1)(*c*) to show that the consideration for the acquisition consists
as to 90 per cent in the issue of shares in the transferee company without regard to the
terms on which the shares are issued, and much of the argument turned on the
question whether the FIL shares were part of the consideration for the transfer. I am

---

1   [1933] 1 KB 158 at 171, [1930] All ER Rep 595 at 602

prepared to assume that consideration for the transfer included the issue of the FIL shares on the terms that the Boden shareholders should sell them to FIL. The *a* question, however, still remains whether the FIL shares were, within the meaning of the paragraph, the subject of an issue of shares 'to the holders of shares' in Boden. That at the moment of issue of the FIL shares the holders of the shares in Boden became bound under the terms of the scheme to sell them to FIL cannot be doubted. And so as from the moment of their issue FIL became the equitable owners of them (see, for example, *Parway Estates v Inland Revenue Comrs*[1]). Similarly, the *b* Boden shareholders never acquired the equitable ownership of the FIL shares. These consequences had been secured not by the effect of a separate bargain between FIL and the Boden shareholders but had at the moment of the issue become part and parcel of the scheme as it was always intended that they should. The submission of Crane would not be different if the so-called option had extended over the whole of the new issue, so that by the very terms of the scheme the Boden shareholders would *c* have parted with all their shares in Boden and acquired no beneficial interest in the amalgamated businesses. To construe the condition in sub-s (1)(c) so as to bring such a scheme within the exemption would be to ignore its purpose and intent. In my judgment, the reference in sub-s (1)(c)(ii) to 'the issue of shares . . . to the holders of shares in the existing company' must, consistently with the purpose of the paragraph, be construed as a reference to a condition that the shares are issued to those holders *d* beneficially and not as nominees.

I would dismiss the appeal.

SCARMAN LJ. Section 55 of the Finance Act 1927 provides relief from capital and transfer stamp duty in the case of reconstructions or amalgamations of companies. *e* The section is now nearly 50 years old. It has been described in successive editions of Sergeant on Stamp Duties as 'one of the longest and most complicated sections in revenue legislation'. This description has, however, been dropped from the 6th edition—perhaps because the legislative activity of Parliament over the years has produced worthy rivals.

The section remains a formidable challenge to the advisory skills of solicitors and *f* accountants, and a problem for judges. But the test of time has proved useful. Distinguished judges have analysed it with care and declared with authority its general intendment. Rowlatt J had to consider the section in its early years. In *Brotex Cellulose Fibres Ltd v Inland Revenue Comrs*[2] he said that he approached the question of compliance or not with the section—

'with the idea—I do not say that it is to guide one too far—that when a company *g* is reconstructed or amalgamated, in substance one expects to find the property in the old hands but under the domination of the new company.'

In *Lever Brothers Ltd v Inland Revenue Comrs*[3] Greene MR made the same point when, discussing sub-s (1)(c)(ii), he said[4]:

'The object of that [i e the condition required by the subsection] is to confine *h* the relief to cases where the shareholders are remaining substantially the same.'

The purpose of the section is to give relief from capital duty and transfer stamp duty when there exists for the reconstruction of any company or companies or the amalgamation of any companies a scheme which does not require either the creation of fresh capital or a transfer of interest. A tolerance of 10 per cent is, however, allowed; *j*

---

1   (1958) 45 Tax Cas 135
2   [1933] 1 KB 158 at 171, [1930] All ER Rep 595 at 602
3   [1938] 2 All ER 808, [1938] 2 KB 518
4   [1938] 2 All ER at 809, [1938] 2 KB at 524

if the element of new capital or transfer is kept within this limit, all is well. If, subject
a to this tolerance, a scheme merely reconstructs or amalgamates that which already
existed unreconstructed or as separate entities, the section provides relief from the
two types of duty. But if a scheme for amalgamation introduces new capital or
includes a substantial transfer of shares to a new shareholder, it would appear, on
general grounds, to be a scheme outside the purview of the section and not entitled
to the relief provided by the section; for then the shareholding does not remain
b substantially the same, nor does the property remain 'in the old hands'.

Two questions invariably arise when relief is claimed. The first is whether a scheme
for reconstruction or amalgamation has been shown to exist. If it has, then the
second question is whether in connection with the scheme the conditions imposed
by the section also exist. An affirmative answer to each question is needed to establish
the case for relief from duty.

c Templeman J held that the scheme was a scheme for amalgamation because it
brought together in one company, Crane Fruehauf Ltd (the appellants, 'Crane'), the
share capital of two companies, Crane and Boden Trailers Ltd (hereinafter called
'Boden'). He held that it was nonetheless an amalgamation because it also included
a transfer of Crane shares by the Boden shareholders to Fruehauf International Ltd
('FIL'). I agree with his analysis and conclusion. Although 'amalgamation' is a tech-
d nical term in the sense that it is frequently used by technicians in the field of company
law, it is not a legal term of art; it has no statutory definition. It is frequently used to
describe a merging of the undertakings of two or more companies into one undertaking. Such a merger can be achieved in several ways; and the resultant one undertaking may become that of one of the companies concerned or of a new company
altogether. In the present case the scheme contemplated the amalgamation of the
e Crane and Boden undertakings into one by the issue to the Boden shareholders of
Crane shares in exchange for their Boden shares. On its completion the Boden and
Crane separate undertakings were united in the one undertaking of Crane.

This being the intention and effect of the scheme, it cannot lose its character of
amalgamation merely because in the events that happened, and as envisaged by the
scheme, the Boden shareholders were obliged to sell, and did at once sell, one-third
f of their new Crane shares to FIL. There still existed only one undertaking comprising
the two that had existed before the scheme.

Having held, in my judgment correctly, that there was a scheme for amalgamation,
Templeman J turned his attention to the conditions that have to be shown to exist if
relief from duty is to be obtained. The scheme was for an amalgamation by acquisition of shares; and all the Boden shares were to be acquired by Crane. So far so good.
g The condition imposed by s 55(1)(b) of the 1927 Act was met. Subsection (1)(c)(ii)
requires that the consideration for the acquisition of the shares consist, as to not less
than 90 per cent thereof, in the issue of shares in the acquiring company.

Was this condition as to the nature of the consideration met? What was the consideration for the acquisition by Crane of the Boden shares? This is the crucial question
raised by the appeal. If, as Crane contends, it was the issue of the Crane shares and
h £100,000 cash, the section applies and the adjudicated instruments (namely, the
statement of increase of Crane's nominal capital and the share transfers to the Boden
shareholders) are relieved from stamp duty. But if the consideration included some
further feature the result of which was that the issue of the Crane shares amounted to
less than 90 per cent of the consideration, the section does not apply and Crane's case
for relief fails (though there remains for decision the question as to the amount of
duty payable).

j Our attention was directed to the decision of the House of Lords in *Central and
District Properties Ltd v Inland Revenue Comrs*[1]. Though there was some disagreement
between their Lordships, I am prepared to accept that we should treat the decision as

---

1 [1966] 2 All ER 433, [1966] 1 WLR 1015

requiring us to read the section as meaning that the consideration must move from
the acquiring company, i e Crane. I agree with Templeman J that part of the con-   *a*
sideration in this case was an issue of shares by Crane to the Boden shareholders in
exchange for their Boden shares. The consideration certainly included one further
element, £100,000 in cash payable by Crane to the Boden shareholders; but this was
within the 10 per cent tolerance allowed by the section. Did the consideration moving
from Crane include any further element?

In my judgment, it did. Crane was not prepared to offer the new issue of shares to   *b*
the Boden shareholders without imposing a condition that, if FIL opted, FIL could
obtain, on payment of £600,000, the immediate transfer from the Boden shareholders
of one-third of their newly-allotted and registered Crane shares. The Boden shareholders were not, therefore, being offered a 'straight swop', to use Templeman J's
expressive phrase[1], but something else—an issue of shares, as to two-thirds unconditionally but as to one-third with a string attached, for the acceptance of which they   *c*
were to be paid £600,000 cash. They accepted the offer; the option was exercised, as
all knew it would be, and they received, on the final completion of the scheme, two-
thirds of the new issue of shares and £700,000 (£100,000 from Crane, £600,000 from
FIL). The fact that, because of the market movement in Crane shares, the offer turned
out to be less valuable than an offer of all the new issue unconditionally does not
detract from the fact that it was the offer which Crane made and they accepted. The   *d*
fact that Crane was constrained to make the offer because without the condition FIL
could and would have blocked the scheme is also irrelevant; it is merely the reason
why the offer was what it was, and not something different. The fact that Crane did
not have to find the £600,000 is also irrelevant. Crane proposed a scheme, accepted by
the Boden shareholders, under which the Boden shareholders did not part with the
new shares until the sum of £600,000 was paid by FIL. The cash did not move from   *e*
Crane; but the offer which secured the cash did, and was accepted. In my judgment,
the totality of the offer made by Crane and accepted by Boden was the consideration
moving from Crane in exchange for the Boden shares. Since the total offer included
an element other than the issue of shares which was worth more than 10 per cent of
the value of the whole, the condition which the section imposes as to the nature of the
consideration has not been shown to exist. Duty is therefore payable on the adjudicated   *f*
instruments.

This conclusion is consistent with the general intendment of the section; for the
effect of the scheme was to substitute a new shareholder, FIL, for the old Boden
shareholders so far as concerned one-third of the Boden share capital amalgamated
into the new undertaking. Not all the property therefore remained 'in the old hands'.

I agree with Russell LJ's judgment on the question of quantum. Accordingly, I   *g*
agree that the appeal should be dismissed.

Appeal dismissed.

Solicitors: *Stephenson, Harwood and Tatham* (for Crane); *Solicitor of Inland Revenue.*

h

Rengan Krishnan Esq   Barrister.

---

1   [1974] 1 All ER 811 at 821, [1974] STC 110 at 120

a # Customs and Excise Commissioners v Thorn Electrical Industries Ltd

QUEEN'S BENCH DIVISION
LORD WIDGERY CJ, THOMPSON AND MAIS JJ
b 25th NOVEMBER, 5th DECEMBER 1974

Value added tax – Supply of goods or services – Time of supply – Supply of goods on hire – Retrospective effect of statute introducing value added tax – Agreement for hire made and goods supplied under agreement before statute coming into operation – Agreement providing for periodic payments – Power of commissioners to make regulations providing for time of
c *supply where goods 'are supplied' for consideration payable periodically – Commissioners making regulations – Regulations providing for goods supplied under hire agreement to be treated as being supplied on each occasion payment of hire received – Regulations applying to goods supplied under hire agreement made before statute coming into force – Whether regulation ultra vires – Finance Act 1972, s 7(2)(8) – Value Added Tax (General) Regulations 1972 (SI 1972 No 1147), reg 14(1).*

d
On 19th July 1972 Mrs F entered into a written agreement with the respondents whereby she agreed to hire a television set. The agreement provided that Mrs F should pay a monthly rental in advance. The respondents installed the television set in Mrs F's house on the following day. Thereafter Mrs F made the monthly rental payments in accordance with the agreement. On 27th July the Finance
e Act 1972, which introduced value added tax, received the Royal Assent. The Act came into force on 1st April 1973. The television set was still in Mrs F's house during April, May and June 1973 and thereafter and she continued to make the monthly rental payments under the agreement of 19th July 1972. The Customs and Excise Commissioners determined that the monthly payments made after 1st April were chargeable to value added tax in that, by virtue of reg 14(1)[a] of the Value Added Tax
f (General) Regulations 1972, made by the commissioners under the powers contained in s 7(8)[b] of the 1972 Act, the television set was to be treated as having been successively supplied to Mrs F on the occasions when the payments of hire were received by the respondents. The respondents appealed, contending that the matter was governed by s 7(2)[c] of the 1972 Act under which the supply had taken place when the television set was installed; that s 7(8) was not applicable since that subsection was
g not to be construed as having a retrospective effect but as applying only to cases where goods 'are supplied' after the coming into force of the Act; and that the 1972 regulations were therefore to be treated as being ultra vires to the extent that they imposed a charge to value added tax on payments under an agreement for hire made before the 1972 Act had come into force. The value added tax tribunal allowed the respondents' appeal and the commissioners appealed.

h
Held – The appeal would be allowed for the following reasons—
(i) The provisions of s 7(2) of the 1972 Act had been expressly made subject to the following provisions of s 7, in particular s 7(8), because s 7(2) did not appropriately provide for transactions, such as those with which s 7(8) was concerned, where the time of supply had to be determined in a situation where the consideration for which
j goods had been supplied was a periodic payment. The date on which the goods had first been supplied was not material to that situation. The use of the present

---

a   Regulation 14(1) is set out at p 444 *d* and *e*, post
b   Section 7(8) is set out at p 443 *j* to p 444 *a*, post
c   Section 7(2) is set out at p 443 *c* and *d*, post

tense, 'are supplied', in s 7(8) indicated a continuing and subsisting state of affairs to which s 7(2) could not sensibly or appropriately be applied and for which it was *a* considered necessary to empower the commissioners to make provision as to what should be substituted as the 'time of supply'. Mrs F's hiring was within the power of the commissioners under s 7(8) to provide for by regulations and the regulations which they made were not therefore ultra vires (see p 445 *g* to *j* and p 446 *b*, post).

(ii) Since the meaning of the words in s 7 was clear there could be no presumption against them having a retrospective effect. In any event, on its true construction *b* s 7(8) was not retrospective for, although the payments of hire arose out of an agreement that antedated the 1972 Act, tax was only chargeable on payments made after the Act had come into force (see p 448 *e* and *f*, post); *Re Pulborough School Board Election* [1891-94] All ER Rep 831 and *R v General Commissioners of Income Tax for Wallington, ex parte Fysh* (1962) 40 Tax Cas 225 distinguished.

c

Notes

For the time of supply of goods and services for the purposes of value added tax, see Supplement to 33 Halsbury's Laws (3rd Edn) para 479B, 5.

For the Finance Act 1972, s 7, see 42 Halsbury's Statutes (3rd Edn) 169.

Cases referred to in judgment   *d*

Master Ladies Tailors Organisation v Minister of Labour and National Service [1950] 2 All ER 525, 66 (pt 2) TLR 728, 34 Digest (Repl) 104, 726.

Pulborough School Board Election, Re, Bourke v Nutt [1894] 1 QB 725, [1891-94] All ER Rep 831, 63 LJQB 497, 70 LT 639, 58 JP 572, 1 Mans 172, 9 R 395, CA, 4 Digest (Repl) 12, 26.

R v General Commissioners of Income Tax for Wallington, ex parte Fysh (1962) 40 Tax Cas *e* 225, [1962] TR 393, 41 ATC 415, DC, Digest (Cont Vol A) 912, 1685*c*.

R v Inhabitants of St Mary, Whitechapel (1848) 12 QB 120, 3 New Sess Cas 262, 17 LJMC 172, 11 LTOS 473, 116 ER 811, 44 Digest (Repl) 285, 1144.

Solicitor's Clerk, Re A [1957] 3 All ER 617, [1957] 1 WLR 1219, DC.

West v Gwynne [1911] 2 Ch 1, 80 LJCh 578, 104 LT 759, CA, 44 Digest (Repl) 287, 1172.   *f*

Cases also cited

Attorney-General v Wilts United Dairies (1921) 37 TLR 884, CA.

Cape Brandy Syndicate v Commissioners of Inland Revenue [1921] 1 KB 64.

Pratt, Re, ex parte Pratt (1884) 12 QBD 334.

Reed International Ltd v Commissioners of Inland Revenue [1974] 1 All ER 385, [1974] Ch 351.   *g*

St Aubyn v Attorney-General [1951] 2 All ER 473, [1952] AC 15, HL.

Ward v British Oak Insurance Co Ltd [1932] 1 KB 392, 101 LJKB 240, CA.

Appeals

This was an appeal by the Commissioners of Customs and Excise against the decision of a value added tax tribunal given on 12th February 1974 in an appeal under s 40 *h* of the Finance Act 1972, whereby it was decided that value added tax could not be charged on supplies made by Radio Rentals Ltd and other companies in a group of companies of which the respondents' company, Thorn Electrical Industries Ltd, was the representative member for the purposes of s 21 of the 1972 Act, of television sets delivered to customers before 27th July 1972 under contracts of hire which continued on and after 1st April 1973, and that an assessment for tax in a sum of £463,780 *j* for the period of three months ended 30th June 1973 be discharged. The grounds of appeal were: (i) that the tribunal had erred in law in failing to construe the words 'are supplied' in s 7(8) of the 1972 Act as descriptive of a process continuing or state of affairs existing at or after 27th July 1972 when the 1972 Act received the Royal Assent; (ii) that the tribunal, whilst correctly recognising that the word 'supplied' in

the phrase 'goods supplied on hire' in s 7(8)(*a*) was used in a descriptive sense referable
a to a continuing process, erred in law in holding that the power conferred by s 7(8) to
make regulations was limited in respect of the supply of goods on hire to cases where
the supply was first made on or after 27th July 1972; (iii) that the construction adopted
by the tribunal of the words 'are supplied' in s 7(8) was inconsistent with, or would
create anomalies if applied to, ss 42 and 48 of the 1972 Act and the Value Added Tax
(Television Rental) Order 1972[1]; (iv) that on the true construction of the 1972 Act
b value added tax was intended to be charged on the consumption of goods and
services on or after 1st April 1973, and a construction of s 7(8) that permitted a charge
to tax in respect of goods supplied under a contract of hire for a period continuing on
or after that date, whether or not the contract was entered into and the goods were
first supplied before 27th July 1972, accorded with that intention and should be
adopted; (v) that the tribunal had erred in law in directing itself that the rule against
c giving a statute a retrospective operation should be applied so as to disallow a construction of s 7(8) that would permit a charge to tax in respect of goods first supplied
before 27th July 1972 under a contract of hire entered into before that date, when
such charge to tax would attach only to consideration paid on or after 1st April 1973
in respect of a period of hire continuing on or after the latter date. The other respondents to the appeal were British Relay Ltd and Visionhire Ltd. The facts are
d set out in the judgment of the court.

The Solicitor-General (Peter Archer QC), Christopher Staughton QC and *Peter Gibson* for
   the commissioners.
John M Rankin QC and *J Rogers* for Thorn Electrical Industries Ltd.
George B Graham QC and *P Whiteman* for British Relay Ltd.
e *George B Graham QC* and *G R Bretten* for Visionhire Ltd.

Cur adv vult

5th December.   **THOMPSON J** read the following judgment of the court at the
invitation of Lord Widgery CJ.   These appeals by the Commissioners of Customs and
f Excise come before us on appeal from the decision of the Value Added Tax Tribunal
given on 12th February 1974. By its decision that Tribunal allowed the appeals of the
several respondents before us against assessments to VAT made by the commissioners. Before us, as before the Tribunal, it was agreed that the matter at issue
is the same in all four appeals and we have accordingly done, as the Tribunal did, and
have confined ourselves to the facts in the Thorn assessment relating to the case of
g Mrs Beryl Freeman.
   All four appeals—

> 'relate to television sets hired-out, delivered and installed under agreements
> entered into before 27th July 1972 and which thereafter remained continuously
> on hire to the same persons.'

h
It was not and is not contended that there is any material difference between the
hire agreements to which the several appeals relate.
   The Tribunal found that on 19th July 1972 Mrs Freeman entered into a written
agreement to hire a colour television set on terms and conditions set out in the
agreement.   By these she was required to and did pay on signing the agreement an
j initial rental of £21·60, being three months' rent at £7·20 per month, and in the
remaining nine months of the first year a rental of £7·20 a month payable in advance.
After the first 12 months the monthly rent reduced to £7 per month in advance
during the next 12 months and thereafter the agreement provided that the monthly

---

1   SI 1972 No 2033

rent payable in advance should be at the lesser rates specified in the agreement.
The Tribunal further found: a

'The conditions set out in the agreement (inter alia) conferred upon Mrs
Freeman the right to terminate the agreement by one month's notice expiring
on a payment date on or after 12 months from the date thereof, conferred upon
[the hiring company] a right in certain specified circumstances to terminate
the agreement, and conferred upon [the hiring company] the right to increase   b
the payments due by Mrs. Freeman any time after 12 months from the date
thereof. The conditions also required [the hiring company] to service the
television set on reasonable notice and request, but empowered [them] to replace
the television set with another. The . . . documents also disclose that [the hiring
company] delivered a colour television set . . . to Mrs B Freeman and installed
it at her house on the 20th July, 1972.'   c

The Tribunal inferred—

'that since such date such television set has remained continuously on hire
to Mrs Freeman under the said agreement and that during the period from the
1st April 1973 to the 30th June 1973 [the hiring company] received from her three
payments of £7·20 each as the monthly rentals under that agreement.'   d

That which the Tribunal inferred is admitted as fact before us.
    On 27th July 1972 the Finance Act 1972 received the Royal Assent. Part I of that
Act has as its subject-matter Value Added Tax. The commencement section, s 47,
provides in its first subsection: 'Tax shall not be charged on any supply or importation taking place before 1st April 1973.'   e
    The relevant dates for the problem raised in these appeals are accordingly: agree-
ment 19th July 1972; set installed 20th July 1972; Finance Act enacted 27th July 1972;
commencement date 1st April 1973; set still at Mrs Freeman's house during April,
May and June 1973 and thereafter.
    The contention of the commissioners is that VAT is chargeable in respect of the
hiring to Mrs Freeman for the months of April, May and June in 1973. The commis-   f
sioners submit that on a true construction of the relevant provisions of the 1972
Act there was a supply of goods, namely the television set, in each of these months.
The contention of the respondents, which found favour with the Tribunal, was that
on a true construction of the provisions of the Act the goods were supplied to Mrs
Freeman before the Finance Act 1972 was enacted and that VAT accordingly never
became chargeable in respect of her hiring.   g
    We turn now to the provisions of the Finance Act 1972 which provided as follows:

'1.—(1) A tax, to be known as value added tax, shall be charged in accordance
with the provisions of this Part of this Act on the supply of goods and services
in the United Kingdom (including anything treated as such a supply) and on the
importation of goods into the United Kingdom.
'(2) The tax shall be under the care and management of the Commissioners . . .   h
'2.—(1) Except as otherwise provided by this Part of this Act the tax shall be
charged and payable as follows.
'(2) Tax on the supply of goods or services shall be charged only where—
(a) the supply is a taxable supply; and (b) the goods or services are supplied by
a taxable person in the course of a business carried on by him; and shall be
payable by the person supplying the goods or services . . .   j
'5.—(1) The following provisions apply for determining for the purposes of
this Part of this Act what is a supply of goods or services.
'(2) Supply of goods includes all forms of supply and, in particular, the letting
of goods on hire and the making of a gift or loan of goods; but supply of services
does not include anything done otherwise than for a consideration.

'(3) Where a person produces goods by applying to another person's goods a treatment or process he is treated as supplying goods and not as supplying services.

'(4) The supply of any form of power, heat, refrigeration or ventilation is a supply of goods and not of services . . .'

The remaining subsections of s 5 do not appear material to the problem before us and we pass over s 6, which deals with self-supply, to s 7 the sidenote to which is 'Time of supply':

'7.—(1) The following provisions of this section shall apply for determining the time when a supply of goods or services is to be treated as taking place for the purposes of the charge to tax.

'(2) Subject to the following provisions of this section, a supply of goods shall be treated as taking place—(a) if the goods are to be removed, at the time of the removal; (b) if the goods are not to be removed, at the time when they are made available to the person to whom they are supplied; (c) if the goods (being sent or taken on approval or sale or return or similar terms) are removed before it is known whether a supply will take place, at the time when it becomes certain that the supply has taken place, but not later than twelve months after the removal.

'(3) Subject to the following provisions of this section, a supply of services shall be treated as taking place at the time when the services are performed.

'(4) If, before the time applicable under subsection (2) or subsection (3) of this section, the person making the supply issues a tax invoice in respect of it or if, before the time applicable under paragraph (a) or (b) of subsection (2) or subsection (3) of this section, he receives a payment in respect of it, the supply shall, to the extent covered by the invoice or payment, be treated as taking place at the time the invoice is issued or the payment is received.

'(5) If, within fourteen days after the time applicable under subsection (2) or subsection (3) of this section, the person making the supply issues a tax invoice in respect of it, then, unless he has notified the Commissioners in writing that he elects not to avail himself of this subsection, the supply shall (notwithstanding the preceding provisions of this section) be treated as taking place at the time the invoice is issued.

'(6) The Commissioners may, at the request of a taxable person, direct that subsection (5) of this section shall apply in relation to supplies made by him (or such supplies made by him as may be specified in the direction) as if for the period of fourteen days there were substituted such longer period as may be specified in the direction.

'(7) Where goods are deemed to be supplied by virtue of paragraph 1 of Schedule 2 to this Act or section 6 of this Act, the supply shall be treated as taking place when they are applied or used as mentioned in that paragraph or section.'

We come now to sub-s (8) the construction and application of which are at the heart of the problem raised by these appeals. It is in these terms:

'(8) The Commissioners may by regulation make provision with respect to the time at which, notwithstanding the preceding provisions of this section, a supply is to be treated as taking place in cases where goods or services are supplied for a consideration the whole or part of which is determined or payable periodically or at the end of any period or where goods are supplied for a consideration the whole or part of which is determined at the time when the goods are appropriated for any purpose; and any such regulations may provide—(a) for treating goods supplied on hire for any period as being successively supplied on hire for successive parts of that period; and (b) for treating services supplied for any period as being successively supplied for successive parts of that period.'   *a*

Subsection (9), which is the final subsection of s 7, need not detain us, being concerned merely to define for the purposes of the section the expression 'tax invoice'.

On 1st August 1972, in exercise of the powers conferred on them by various sections of the 1972 Act, including s 7(8) just recited, the commissioners made the Value Added Tax (General) Regulations 1972.   *b*

The part of these regulations which is relevant to these appeals is Part IV, 'Time of Supply'. Regulations 13 and 14 are the important ones. Regulation 13 reads:

> 'In this Part of these Regulations—"agreement to hire" means an agreement for the bailment of goods for hire and includes leases of goods and rental agreements, but does not include an agreement under which the bailee has an option to buy the goods or under which the property in the goods passes to the bailee,   *c* nor does it include hire-purchase agreements, credit-sale agreements or conditional sale agreements, as defined in the Hire-Purchase Act 1965, the Hire-Purchase (Scotland) Act 1965 or the Hire-Purchase Act (Northern Ireland) 1966.'

Regulation 14 reads:

   d

> '(1) Subject to paragraph (2) of this Regulation, where goods are or have been supplied under an agreement to hire, they shall be treated as being successively supplied on hire for successive parts of the period of the agreement, and each of the successive supplies shall be treated as taking place when a payment under the agreement is received or a tax invoice relating to the supply is issued by the supplier, whichever is the earlier.
>
> '(2) Where goods are supplied [parenthetically we note the present tense]   *e* under an agreement to hire which provides for periodical payments and the supplier at or about the beginning of any period not exceeding 1 year issues a tax invoice containing the following particulars—(a) the date on which each payment is to become due in the period; (b) the amount payable (excluding tax) on each date; and (c) the rate of tax in force at the time of the issue of the tax   *f* invoice and the amount of tax chargeable in accordance with that rate on each payment, they shall be treated as being successively supplied on hire for successive parts of the period of the agreement, and each of the successive supplies shall be treated as taking place when a payment becomes due or is received, whichever is the earlier.'

So far as these regulations are concerned it is common ground that the transaction   *g* with Mrs Freeman and all the transactions to which the present appeals relate arise from an agreement to hire within the meaning of reg 13. Furthermore it is not, as we understood it, disputed by the respondents that reg 14(1) would apply to all the relevant transactions if (and this *is* disputed by the respondents) it was within the powers conferred on the commissioners by s 7(8) of the 1972 Act to make a regulation in the terms of reg 14(1). The debate accordingly has been concerned with the true   *h* construction of s 7(8) of the 1972 Act.

The contention on behalf of the respondents, which prevailed in their appeals before the Tribunal, is that in such a case as that of Mrs Freeman the time of supply was when the television set was installed in her house, that is on 20th July 1972, seven days before the Finance Act 1972 became law. The respondents submit that s 7(2) governs the matter and defines when the 'supply of goods is to be treated as taking place'.   *j* It is further submitted that though the introductory words of sub-s (2) are 'Subject to the following provisions of this section', none of the following provisions has any application. In particular, it is submitted that the power given to the commissioners by sub-s (8) to make provision by regulation does not, on the true construction of the subsection, extend to empower the commissioners to make regulations applicable

to such a hiring as that of Mrs Freeman and the other hirers to whose cases the appeals
a relate.

The respondents' attack on the commissioners' interpretation of sub-s (8) directs
attention to the use of the present tense in the phrase 'in cases where goods or services
are supplied' and in effect submits that these words are to be understood as confined
to cases where goods or services are *hereafter* supplied. The respondents submit that
the natural and ordinary meaning of the words used leads to that conclusion but they
b further submit that even if the words used are capable of more than one interpretation
they should be understood in the sense for which they contend, since to do otherwise
would be to give a retrospective and a retroactive effect to unclear words in a fiscal
provision. The respondents further submit that since the power to make provision
by regulation given by sub-s (8) is not confined to agreements to hire but is wide
enough to extend to hire-purchase and credit sale agreements, we should not in
c construing the subsection fall into the error of thinking that such agreements as these
appeals relate to are the sole subject-matter of sub-s (8).

For the commissioners it is contended that reg 14 was made within the authority
conferred on the commissioners by s 7(8) of the 1972 Act and that Mrs Freeman's
hiring and all the hirings in the four appeals are affected by the provision substituted
for the general provision in s 7(2). They call attention to the opening words of
d sub-s (2): 'Subject to the following provisions of this section', and to the words in
sub-s (8): 'notwithstanding the preceding provisions of this section.' They therefore
submit that sub-s (2) offers no impediment to the power of the commissioners by
regulation to make provision with respect to the time at which a supply is to be
treated as taking place. The commissioners can so provide, the argument continues,
'in cases where goods or services are supplied for a consideration the whole or part
e of which is determined or payable periodically . . .' The goods here were, they
submitted, not supplied only on a specific occasion—when the set was installed on
20th July—but are continuously supplied while the set remains in Mrs Freeman's
house under the hiring agreement of 19th July in the same way that power, heat,
refrigeration and ventilation are supplied and by s 5(4), already recited, the supply
of such commodities constitutes a supply of goods and not of services. In the case
f of certain kinds of goods and certain kinds of agreements under which goods are
supplied the supply cannot sensibly be regarded as a once and for all event and it is
for such cases that sub-s (8) gives the commissioners the power to substitute a provision more relevant than s 7(2) for determining the time when the supply in such
cases is to be treated as taking place. 'Supplied' cannot in all cases sensibly be equated
with 'delivered'. The date of the inception of the supply is immaterial for the
g exercise of the power under s 7(8). What matters is that currently goods are being
supplied under an arrangement involving continuity and periodic payment.

The true view of s 7 and the part sub-s (8) has to play in the tax arrangement we
believe to be as follows. What may be called the basic rule appears in sub-s (2).
That is appropriate for many, maybe for most, transactions on which the tax is to be
chargeable. There are however transactions for which sub-s (2) does not appro-
h priately provide. Subsection (2) itself acknowledges that fact and intimates that
its application and operation are subject to what follows in later subsections. Subsection (8) is one such. It deals with the way in which the time of supply may be
determined in a situation in which the consideration for which goods are supplied is a
periodic payment. In our judgment the date on which the goods were first supplied
is not material to this situation or to the way in which it may be dealt with by the
j commissioners. We do not ascribe to the use of the present tense, 'are supplied',
the meaning or significance contended for by the respondents. We consider the
tense indicative of a continuing and subsisting state of affairs to which sub-s (2) could
not sensibly or appropriately be applied and for which it was considered necessary to
empower the commissioners to make provision as to what should be substituted as
the 'time of supply'.

In sub-s (8)(a) it is provided that the regulations which the commissioners are empowered to make may provide—

'for treating goods supplied on hire for any period as being successively supplied on hire for successive parts of that period . . .'

In our judgment that is consonant with the interpretation we put on the meaning and purpose of sub-s (8).

In our judgment Mrs Freeman's hiring and the other similar ones in the four appeals are within and not outside the power of the commissioners to provide for by regulations and the regulations they have made are not in our judgment ultra vires.

Two further related matters should be mentioned. First, the Tribunal was impressed and greatly influenced to reach the conclusion it did by two decisions which were cited on behalf of the present respondents. The first of these decisions was *Re Pulborough School Board Election*[1]. In that case a Mr Nutt, who had been adjudicated bankrupt under the Bankruptcy Act 1869, was in April 1893 elected to the School Board for Pulborough. A petition was thereafter presented for a declaration that his election was void on the ground that he was at the time an undischarged bankrupt and that s 32 of the Bankruptcy Act 1883 provided:

'Where a debtor is adjudged bankrupt he shall, subject to the provisions of this Act, be disqualified for . . . (e) Being elected to . . . the office of . . . member of a school board . . .'

The majority in the Court of Appeal held that the 1883 Act had no retrospective effect and, since Mr Nutt had not been adjudged bankrupt under that Act but under the 1869 Act, he was not disqualified by the terms of s 32 of the 1883 Act.

The other case is *R v General Commissioners of Income Tax for Wallington, ex parte Fysh*[2]. That was a tax case in which the Divisional Court held that the interest provisions contained in s 58 of the Finance Act 1960 did not apply to assessments made prior to the passing of that Act. The assessment to tax had been made in 1958. The opening words of s 58 of the Finance Act 1960 were: '(1) Where an assessment is made . . .' The Divisional Court held that the prima facie conclusion that an assessment which had been made two years previously was not caught by s 58 was not displaced on their true construction by other provisions in the Finance Act 1960. A passage in the judgment of MacKenna J[3] may usefully be quoted as bearing also on the second matter with which we shall shortly deal:

'The General Commissioners for the Wallington Division have held that the provisions do not apply in such a case; and, in my judgment, their decision was right. Upon the general principle which denies retrospective effect to legislation, Section 58 can apply only to assessments made after the commencement of the Finance Act 1960, unless the Statute clearly provides to the contrary. Section 58 does not do so. Section 44 provides that the provisions of Part III, in which Section 58 is found, shall have effect in relation to any year of assessment, whether ending before or after the commencement of the Act. That means that an assessment made in respect of assessment years ending before the commencement of the Act will not be, for that reason, outside Section 58. It does not mean that Section 58 will apply even to an assessment made before the commencement of the Act. The assessment must be made after the Act; and, if it is, it will still be covered by Part III even though the assessment years were over before the Act began. That is the effect of Section 44(1) which is relevant to Section 58(1).

1   [1894] 1 QB 725, [1891-94] All ER Rep 831
2   (1962) 40 Tax Cas 225
3   40 Tax Cas at 228

a   In other words, Section 44(1) gives retrospective effect only partially to the provisions of Part III; and that which has not been given is essential to the Crown's
success in this motion.'

The second matter to be mentioned is the argument that to construe s 7(8) of the
1972 Act in the way which the commissioners contended for is to give words in a fiscal
provision retrospective effect against which it is submitted there is a presumption.
b   As to that, we say first that if the meaning of words in an enactment is clear, there is no
presumption against them having a retrospective effect if that is indeed the result
they produce. Secondly, we say, that the effect of the construction for which the
commissioners contend is not retrospective in the sense of imposing a tax on monthly
payments paid before the Act was passed or even on monthly payments made after
the Act was passed but before 1st April 1973. It is of course true that from 1st April
c   1973 the tax would become chargeable on the monthly payments, though the agreement under which they were paid antedated the passing of the Act. In that sense
only does the commissioners' construction of the Act have a retrospective effect.

Is there then any presumption against a construction which in that sense had a
retrospective effect? On the respondents' contention that the commissioners'
construction would involve retrospectivity and retroactivity and should therefore
be avoided because of the legal presumption the Solicitor-General in reply referred
d   us to Maxwell on Interpretation of Statutes[1]:

'If, however, the language or the dominant intention of the enactment so
demands, the Act must be construed so as to have a retrospective operation,
for "the rule against the retrospective effect of statutes is not a rigid or inflexible
rule but is one to be applied always in the light of the language of the statute and
e   the subject-matter with which the statute is dealing"[2]. Those situations in
which Acts will be construed so as to have a retrospective operation will be
discussed later in this chapter. Before the presumption against retrospectivity is
applied, a court must be satisfied that the statute is in fact retrospective. In the
words of Craies on Statute Law[3], a statute is retrospective "which takes away or
impairs any vested right acquired under existing laws, or creates a new obligation,
f   or imposes a new duty, or attaches a new disability in respect to transactions or
considerations already past". Other statutes, though they may relate to acts
or events which are past, are not retrospective in the sense in which the word is
used for the purposes of the rule under consideration.'

The Solicitor-General took us through the cases cited by Maxwell in illustration of
the proposition in its text. These are R v Inhabitants of St Mary, Whitechapel[4], Master
g   Ladies Tailors Organisation v Minister of Labour and National Service[5], Re a Solicitor's
Clerk[6].

In the second of these cases Somervell LJ[7] repeated and adopted and with necessary
adaptation applied what Lord Denman CJ had said in R v Inhabitants of St Mary,
Whitechapel[8]:

h   '. . . we have before shewn that the statute is in its direct operation prospective,
as it relates to future removals only, and that it is not properly called a retrospective statute because a part of the requisites for its action is drawn from time
antecedent to its passing.'

---

1   12th Edn (1969), p 216
2   See Carson v Carson and Stoyek [1964] 1 All ER 681 at 686, [1964] 1 WLR 511 at 517, per
j   Scarman J
3   6th Edn (1963), p 386
4   (1848) 12 QB 120
5   [1950] 2 All ER 525, 66 (pt 2) TLR 728
6   [1957] 3 All ER 617, [1957] 1 WLR 1219
7   [1950] 2 All ER at 527, 66 (pt 2) TLR at 730
8   12 QB at 127

Re a Solicitor's Clerk[1] was a decision of the Divisional Court, and a quotation from the judgment of Lord Goddard CJ[2] is apposite:

     a

'This appellant was convicted of larceny in 1953 of property which belonged neither to his employer nor to a client of his and he accordingly contends that to apply the provisions of the Act of 1956 to a person convicted before that Act came into operation would be to make its operation retrospective. In all editions of Maxwell on the Interpretation of Statutes it is stated that it is a fundamental rule of English law that no statute should be construed to have a retrospective operation unless such a construction appears very clearly in the terms of the Act or arises by a necessary or distinct implication and this passage has received judicial approval by the Court of Appeal; see *West* v. *Gwynne*[3] (per Kennedy L.J.). In my opinion, however, this Act is not in truth retrospective. It enables an order to be made disqualifying a person from acting as a solicitor's clerk in the future and what happened in the past is the cause or reason for the making of the order; but the order has no retrospective effect. It would be retrospective if the Act provided that anything done before the Act came into force or before the order was made should be void or voidable or if a penalty were inflicted for having acted in this or any other capacity before the Act came into force or before the order was made. This Act simply enables a disqualification to be imposed for the future which in no way affects anything done by the appellant in the past. Accordingly in our opinion the disciplinary committee had jurisdiction to make the order complained of and the appeal fails.'

     b

     c

     d

As to these two further related matters we would add only this. We do not find in the decisions in the *Pulborough* case[4] or *Ex parte Fysh*[5] any impediment to the construction for which the commissioners contend and which we consider the correct construction. Each of these cases was concerned with a once and for all event: in one case a bankruptcy adjudication, in the other an assessment to tax. In neither was there an uncompleted and continuing transaction.

     e

So far as the argument on retrospectivity is concerned in our judgment that has no application here both because we consider the meaning of the words in s 7(8) of the 1972 Act is clear and also because on the authorities the effect of those words is not to produce a retrospective result within the area of the presumption properly defined and understood.

     f

For the reasons we have given in our judgment the decision of the Tribunal was wrong and this appeal will be allowed.

Appeals allowed; decision of the commissioners restored; certificate granted under Administration of Justice Act 1969, s 12, for purposes of an application for leave to appeal to the House of Lords.

     g

Solicitors: *Solicitor of Customs and Excise; John Harte and Son* (for Thorn Electrical Industries Ltd); *Nicholson, Graham & Jones* (for British Relay Ltd); *Norton, Rose, Botterell & Roche* (for Visionhire Ltd).

     h

Lea Josse Barrister.

---

1 [1957] 3 All ER 617, [1957] 1 WLR 1219
2 [1957] 3 All ER at 619, [1957] 1 WLR at 1222
3 [1911] 2 Ch 1 at 15
4 [1894] 1 QB 725, [1891-94] All ER Rep 831
5 (1962) 40 Tax Cas 225

     j

R v Bicester Justices, ex parte Unigate Ltd

QUEEN'S BENCH DIVISION
LORD WIDGERY CJ, BRIDGE AND SHAW JJ
5th NOVEMBER 1974

Food and drugs – Defence to proceedings – Contravention due to act or default of third party – Information laid by defendant against third party – Time limit – Information against defendant laid within six months of commission of offence – Information against third party laid more than six months after commission of offence – Whether proceedings against third party barred – Whether defendant entitled to rely on act or default of third party as defence – Magistrates' Courts Act 1952, s 104 – Food and Drugs Act 1955, s 113(1).

On 26th May 1973 a firm of food retailers sold a package of rancid butter to a customer in one of their branches. On 16th October an information in respect of that sale was laid against the retailers by a public health inspector alleging an offence under s 2(1) of the Food and Drugs Act 1955 in that the food was not of the quality demanded by the purchaser. On 28th December the retailers laid an information under s 113(1)ᵃ of the 1955 Act against the applicants alleging that the contravention of s 2 had been due to the act or default of the applicants. The applicants sought an order prohibiting the justices from proceeding with the trial of the second information on the ground that the information against them had been laid more than six months after the commission of the offence and therefore outside the time limit prescribed by s 104ᵇ of the Magistrates' Courts Act 1952. The retailers contended that the time limit did not apply to the second information and that the third party remained liable so long as the original information was not barred.

Held – The information against the applicants was barred under s 104 of the 1952 Act since it had been laid more than six months after the date of the commission of the offence. It was however an effective defence under s 113(1) of the 1955 Act for the retailers to prove that the applicants had been responsible for the contravention and that defence was not time-barred. Accordingly the order of prohibition would be granted (see p 451 *d* and *e*, p 452 *a b* and *j* and p 453 *b* and *c*, post).

Malcolm v Cheek [1947] 2 All ER 881 applied.

Notes
For the time limit of six months between the commission of an alleged offence and the issue of an information, see 25 Halsbury's Laws (3rd Edn) 164-166, para 299, and for cases on the subject, see 33 Digest (Repl) 205-207, 441-445.

For the Food and Drugs Act 1955, ss 2, 113, see 14 Halsbury's Statutes (3rd Edn) 21, 108.

For the Magistrates' Courts Act 1952, s 104, see 21 Halsbury's Statutes (3rd Edn) 273.

Case referred to in judgment
Malcolm v Cheek [1947] 2 All ER 881, [1948] 1 KB 400, [1948] LJR 388, 112 JP 94, 46 LGR 26, DC, 25 Digest (Repl) 112, *331*.

Application
This was an application by Unigate Ltd ('Unigate') for an order directed to the justices for the petty sessional division of Bicester in the county of Oxford prohibiting them from further proceeding with the trial of the applicants on an information laid by Fine

---

a Section 113(1) is set out at p 451 *a* and *b*, post
b Section 104, so far as material, is set out at p 450 *h*, post

Fare Ltd ('Fine Fare') on 28th December 1973 pursuant to s 113(1) of the Food and Drugs *a*
Act 1955. The facts are set out in the judgment.

Kenneth Wheeler for Unigate.
R Neville Thomas for Fine Fare.

BRIDGE J gave the first judgment at the request of Lord Widgery CJ. In these *b*
proceedings counsel moves on behalf of Unigate for an order of prohibition directed
to the Bicester justices to prevent them from further proceeding with the trial of the
applicants on an information laid by Fine Fare against the applicants pursuant to
s 113(1) of the Food and Drugs Act 1955.

The history of the matter was as follows. On 26th May 1973 Fine Fare Ltd sold
some butter. On 16th October 1973 a public health inspector laid an information in *c*
the Bicester magistrates' court against Fine Fare Ltd in respect of that sale of butter
on 26th May 1973, alleging that it was a sale to the prejudice of the purchaser, a Mrs
McCormack, because the butter, being rancid, was not of the quality demanded by
the purchaser, in contravention of s 2 of the Food and Drugs Act 1955.

The summons was served on Fine Fare Ltd on 18th October 1973, but it was not
until 28th December 1973 that Fine Fare Ltd laid an information against Unigate *d*
pursuant to s 113 of the 1955 Act, alleging that the contravention charged against
them was due to the act or default of Unigate.

When the matter came before the magistrates' court on 24th June 1974 a preliminary point was taken on behalf of Unigate that the information bringing them into
the proceedings was ineffective to render them liable to be convicted, and that the
court had no jurisdiction to proceed against them on the ground that the information *e*
under s 113 had been laid outside the limitation period prescribed by s 104 of the
Magistrates' Courts Act 1952, that is to say more than six months after 26th May 1973,
the date of the alleged offence by Fine Fare of which Unigate were liable to be convicted under the provisions of s 113 if the s 113 procedure was effective as against
them.

The justices, having heard submissions on the point, were minded to proceed with *f*
the hearing on the basis that they had jurisdiction and that Unigate's submission on
the time limit was ill-founded. But when told that it was desired to test the matter in
this court, they naturally and properly adjourned sine die so that the present
application for an order of prohibition could be made.

It is surprising that this point, which one might have thought could arise quite
commonly in practice, has never arisen before and there is no authority on it, although *g*
this legislation has been on the statute book at least since 1938. It is convenient to
turn at once to the relevant statutory provisions. Section 104 of the Magistrates'
Courts Act 1952 provides:

'Except as otherwise expressly provided by any enactment, a magistrates'
court shall not try an information or hear a complaint unless the information *h*
was laid, or the complaint made, within six months from the time when the
offence was committed, or the matter of complaint arose . . .'

In the Food and Drugs Act 1955 it is quite clear that no express provision is made for a
special period of limitation different from that prescribed by s 104 of the 1952 Act in
relation to proceedings against what it will be convenient to call third parties under *j*
s 113 of the 1955 Act. Indeed that absence of express provision is emphasised by the
presence of express provisions varying the six months' limit in relation to some types
of prosecution under the 1955 Act which are to be found in s 108, but which it is
unnecessary to read because they are not material in themselves to the present
judgment.

One comes then to s 113(1), which is in these terms:

a   'A person against whom proceedings are brought under this Act shall, upon
         information duly laid by him and on giving to the prosecution not less than three
         clear days' notice of his intention, be entitled to have any person to whose act or
         default he alleges that the contravention of the provisions in question was due
         brought before the court in the proceedings; and if, after the contravention
         has been proved, the original defendant proves that the contravention was due
b   to the act or default of that other person, that other person may be convicted of
         the offence, and, if the original defendant further proves that he has used all due
         diligence to secure that the provisions in question were complied with, he shall
         be acquitted of the offence.'

It is to be observed that by s 113(3) where the prosecuting authority is reasonably
satisfied that an offence committed by one party was due to the act or default of some
c other person, they are empowered to proceed immediately by way of information
against the third party without prosecuting the initial offender.

It seems to me clear that there are three possible solutions to this problem, and
only three. One possibility is that the six months' limitation does not apply to an
information against a third party, so that such an information, laid out of time, is
effective for all purposes. A second possibility is that it is wholly ineffective, so that
d unless the defendant lays his information within the six months the special defence
provided by s 113 ceases to be available to him. The third possibility, which counsel
for Unigate invites us to adopt as the correct construction of the statute, is that whilst
the laying of the third party information after the expiry of six months from the
date of the offence does not deprive the original defendant of the protection of s 113,
it is nevertheless ineffective to render the third party liable to conviction.

e   For my part I confess at the outset that I do not find any of those three alternatives
wholly satisfactory. Objection can be made, both in principle and on the ground of
the difficulty of fitting them into the statutory language, to any one of the three, but
I have come to the conclusion that it is the third course, the middle course, which
provides the right solution.

I arrive at that conclusion partly by process of elimination in considering the
f extremely unsatisfactory aspects of the other two alternatives. It is really unthinkable,
and indeed no submission has been made to us in support of the view, that the passage
of six months before the original defendant has the opportunity to serve an information on the third party under s 113 should deprive him of the protection of the section.
Clearly a situation could arise in which the prosecutor only laid his information
against the defendant on the last day of the six months' period so that the defendant
g would first hear about the matter at a time when it was too late for him to lay a
timely information under s 113 against the third party.

On the other hand, to hold that the third, fourth, fifth or subsequent parties
remain liable to conviction under the operation of this provision, no matter how long
the delay from the time of the events which constitute the alleged contravention to
the time when the intention to prosecute him is brought to the notice of the third or
h subsequent party, is unsatisfactory for at least two solid reasons. One is that there
seems no ground in principle, unless the statute makes it clear by unambiguous
language, why a party liable to prosecution should lightly be held to have been
deprived of the protection of the six month limitation period which s 104 of the
Magistrates' Courts Act 1952 prescribes. Secondly, it seems to me that one could only
adopt this solution of the problem by doing some violence to the language of the two
j statutes read together. The provisions of s 113 certainly refer to the step which brings
the third party before the court as an information, and it is clearly a separate information, a different information from that which instituted the proceedings. It is difficult
to see how the third party can be convicted pursuant to that information without the
justices trying the information; but that is precisely what s 104 of the 1952 Act says
they may not do when the information is laid after the expiry of six months from the
date of the offence.

What then of the third solution to the problem which presents itself, the conclusion that when the information is laid outside the period of six months from the date of the offence the defendant is entitled to the protection of s 113, albeit that the third party is not at risk of being convicted.

I am fortified in the conclusion that that is not an unreasonable solution of the problem by a decision of this court in 1947 in *Malcolm v Cheek*[1], which at least establishes in principle that a situation may arise in which the defence made available by this section may be effective for a defendant's purpose even though there is no possibility of convicting the third party. It is unnecessary to recite the facts of the case. It is sufficient to say that an offence under the predecessor[2] to the 1955 Act had been charged against a publican. Under the provision of the earlier Act corresponding to s 113 of the 1955 Act the publican laid an information against a barman in his employ, alleging that it was the barman's act or default which had caused the contravention of the statute. But when the matter came before the magistrates' court the barman was not present because it had not proved possible to serve him with the necessary summons. The stipendiary magistrate took the view, although the third party was not before the court, that the defendant was not deprived of the defence under the section, and on appeal by the prosecutor to this court the magistrate's view was confirmed. It is sufficient to read one paragraph from the leading judgment of Lord Goddard CJ[3]:

'. . . it is not the conviction of the other person which is made a condition precedent to the defence being effective to the defendant. The section says: "that other person may be convicted of the offence." If the magistrate refused, under the provision of the Probation of Offenders Act, to proceed to conviction, there would be no conviction, but nevertheless, although there was no conviction, it seems to me the defence provided by the section would be available to the original defendant.'

He goes on to point out that the original defendant in the case had done everything which it was necessary for him to do, and indeed in the circumstances had done everything which it was possible for him to do to avail himself of the special defence. The fact that the defendant could not be found in order to be brought before the court and so become liable for conviction was not to prevent the defendant's defence from prevailing if he proved that his contravention was indeed due to the other's default, and further proved that he had used all due diligence.

Although the two situations are not the same, there is some parallel between that situation and the situation where the information laid under s 113 of the 1955 Act by the defendant alleging the default of the third party cannot be, or is not, laid until after the six month period from the commission of the offence has lapsed.

Counsel for Fine Fare Ltd, although from his client's point of view this solution is as acceptable no doubt as the solution which would render the third party liable to conviction despite the lapse of time, has submitted that this reading of the section is unsustainable because he says that an information which is laid out of time in relation to the magistrates' court would be wholly ineffective and therefore would not entitle the defendant to have the third party brought before the court. He submits that that is a condition precedent to the defendant's right to set up the defence under this section.

I think there is some force in that submission, but, as I said at the outset, I do not see any one of the three alternatives available which has the happy result of resolving every discord into song. This is, as I say, the least unsatisfactory conclusion and for those reasons I would say that the order of prohibition sought should go.

---

1 [1947] 2 All ER 881, [1948] 1 KB 400
2 Food and Drugs Act 1938
3 [1947] 2 All ER at 883, [1948] 1 KB at 407

a **SHAW J.** I agree with the judgment of Bridge J, and in particular with the observation that has fallen from him as to the unsatisfactory alternatives which present themselves in seeking to reconcile the provisions of s 113 of the Food and Drugs Act 1955 with the requirements of s 104 of the Magistrates' Courts Act 1952.

On the whole it seems to me that a construction which preserves the defence provided by s 113 of the 1955 Act to the original defendant, and yet does not deny to *b* the subject the protection given by the limitation on proceedings under the 1952 Act, is, if tenable, not only expedient but just. The solution of the problem propounded by Bridge J appears to me to satisfy all these requirements and I entirely agree with it.

LORD WIDGERY CJ. I agree with both judgments and have nothing to add.

c *Application granted.*

Solicitors: *Scott, Son & Chitty,* Epsom (for Unigate); *Johnson and Gaunt,* Banbury (for Fine Fare).

Jacqueline Charles Barrister.

d

Re Clark (a bankrupt), ex parte the trustee of
e # the property of the bankrupt v Texaco Ltd

CHANCERY DIVISION
WALTON J
21st, 22nd, 28th OCTOBER 1974

f *Bankruptcy – Trustee in bankruptcy – Duty to act fairly – Duty not to take advantage of third party's mistake – Enrichment of estate at third party's expense – Claim by trustee against third party for recovery of sums paid by bankrupt after receiving order and before adjudication – Third party ignorant of bankruptcy proceedings – Third party supplying goods to bankrupt – Sums paid by bankrupt in part payment for goods supplied – Estate having benefited from goods supplied – Claim by trustee to recover sums paid to third party –*
g *Third party not entitled to submit proof of debt and having no effective remedy for recovery of price of goods delivered – Whether trustee should be allowed to recover sums paid.*

On 21st May 1969 the debtor signed an agreement with a petrol company ('Texaco') under which he was licensed to carry on business at a petrol station belonging to Texaco on the terms that he paid a licence fee of £7 10s per week and obtained all his *h* requirements of motor fuel and oil from Texaco. Subject to those obligations he was entitled to retain the whole of the profits, or obliged to defray the loss, arising from the operations. Texaco were, however, only prepared to deliver petrol on a 'cash sale' basis but the debtor was permitted to pay by cheque. In July bankruptcy proceedings were started against the debtor by a third party. On 7th November a receiving order was made. Texaco had no knowledge of the bankruptcy proceedings and on the same *j* day they delivered 3,800 gallons of petrol to the debtor and received in payment a cheque for £1,123 drawn on the petrol station's bank account which was operated on the sole signature of the debtor. The account was £767 overdrawn on 7th November but on 12th November, when the cheque was cleared, it had a credit balance of £277 immediately before the clearance. On 13th November a further delivery of petrol was made and Texaco received a similar cheque for £1,183 in payment. The cheque was cleared on 18th November when, immediately before clearance, the account

was in credit in the sum of £260. On 20th November a third delivery of petrol was ⟨a⟩
made and a cheque for £1,123 was given in payment. That cheque was dishonoured
by the bank. Shortly afterwards the Official Receiver, who until then had known
nothing of the transactions between the debtor and Texaco, intervened. When he
did so the bank account had a credit balance of some £205 and there was a stock of
petrol and oil at the petrol station worth £718. At all material times Texaco had
been completely ignorant of the bankruptcy. The trustee in bankruptcy brought ⟨b⟩
proceedings against Texaco claiming repayment of the sums of £1,123 and £1,183
paid to Texaco by the debtor on the ground that, by virtue of ss 18(1), 37(1) and 38(2)(a)
of the Bankruptcy Act 1914, those sums formed part of the property of the debtor
vesting in his trustee.

Held – The trustee was not entitled to recover the sums paid to Texaco since (i) the
assets of the debtor's estate had been enriched to the extent of £972 by the conversion ⟨c⟩
of an overdraft of £767 into a credit balance of £205 during the relevant period at
the expense of Texaco in consequence of the transactions of which the payments to
Texaco formed part; (ii) Texaco would not be entitled to submit a proof of debt in
respect of the price of the petrol delivered, and (iii) in all the circumstances it could
not be regarded as fair to allow the estate to take the whole benefit of the sale price
of the petrol whilst repudiating all obligation to pay for it, for to do so would enable ⟨d⟩
the trustee to extract funds from Texaco which did not form part of the assets of
the bankrupt's estate at the commencement of the bankruptcy (see p 457 c, p 458 a b
and e to g, p 459 a and p 461 h to p 462 f, post).

Ex parte James (1874) 9 Ch App 609, *Ex parte Whittaker* (1875) 10 Ch App 446, *Re Tyler*
[1904-7] All ER Rep 181, *Re Regent Finance and Guarantee Corpn Ltd* [1930] WN 84,
Re Gozzett [1936] 1 All ER 79, dictum of Lord Keith of Avonholm in *Government of* ⟨e⟩
India, Ministry of Finance (Revenue Division) v Taylor [1955] 1 All ER at 300 and *Re
Wyvern Developments Ltd* [1974] 2 All ER 535 applied.

Re Wigzell [1921] 2 KB 835 and *Scranton's Trustee v Pearse* [1922] 2 Ch 87 distinguished.

Per Walton J. It is not a necessary requirement for the operation of the rule in
Ex parte James[a] that there should be an identifiable fund, or an identifiable piece of ⟨f⟩
property, on which the doctrine can operate, unless there is comprehended in that
requirement the right, where necessary, to dissect a bank account into its component
parts (see p 459 c to f, post).

Notes
For the application of the rule in *Ex parte James*, see 3 Halsbury's Laws (4th Edn) 289,
para 524, and for cases on the subject, see 4 Digest (Repl) 226-229, *2028-2046*. ⟨g⟩

Cases referred to in judgment
Cohen v Mitchell (1890) 25 QBD 262, 59 LJQB 409, 63 LT 206, 7 Morr 207, CA, 5 Digest
(Repl) 787, *6675*.
Dewhurst, ex parte, Re Vanlohe (1871) 7 Ch App 185, 41 LJBcy 18, 25 LT 731, 5 Digest
(Repl) 789, *6697*. ⟨h⟩
Government of India, Ministry of Finance (Revenue Division) v Taylor [1955] 1 All ER 292,
[1955] AC 491, [1955] 2 WLR 303, sub nom *Re Delhi Electric Supply & Traction Co Ltd*,
34 ATC 10, HL, Digest (Cont Vol A) 217, *7b*.
Gozzett, Re, ex parte Messenger & Co Ltd v The Trustee [1936] 1 All ER 79, 80 Sol Jo 146,
CA, 4 Digest (Repl) 228, *2040*.
Hall, Re, ex parte the Official Receiver [1907] 1 KB 875, 76 LJKB 546, 97 LT 33, 14 Mans 82, ⟨j⟩
CA, 4 Digest (Repl) 413, *3692*.
James, ex parte, Re Condon (1874) 9 Ch App 609, [1874-80] All ER Rep 388, 43 LJBcy 107,
30 LT 773, 5 Digest (Repl) 887, *7383*.
Phillips, Re [1914] 2 KB 689, 83 LJKB 1364, 21 Mans 144, 5 Digest (Repl) 680, *5981*.

a   *Re Condon, ex parte James* (1874) 9 Ch App 609, [1874-80] All ER Rep 388 a *Regent Finance and Guarantee Corpn Ltd, Re* [1930] WN 84, 69 LJ 283, 169 LTJo 305, 10 Digest (Repl) 918, *6274*.

Scranton's Trustee v Pearse [1922] 2 Ch 87, [1922] All ER Rep 764, 91 LJCh 579, 127 LT 698, [1922] B & CR 52, CA, 4 Digest (Repl) 228, *2038*.

Stokes, Re, ex parte Mellish [1919] 2 KB 256, [1918-19] All ER Rep 1179, 88 LJKB 794, 121 LT 391, [1918-19] B & CR 208, 5 Digest (Repl) 790, *6703*.

b *Tapster v Ward* (1909) 101 LT 503, 53 Sol Jo 503, CA, 5 Digest (Repl) 727, *6289*.

Thellusson, Re, ex parte Abdy [1919] 2 KB 735, [1918-19] All ER Rep 729, 88 LJKB 1210, 122 LT 35, [1918-19] B & CR 249, CA, 4 Digest (Repl) 227, *2035*.

Tyler, Re, ex parte the Official Receiver [1907] 1 KB 865, [1904-7] All ER Rep 181, 76 LJKB 541, 97 LT 30, 14 Mans 73, CA, 4 Digest (Repl) 228, *2041*.

Warren, Re, Wheeler v Mills [1938] 2 All ER 331, [1938] Ch 725, 107 LJCh 409, 159 LT 17,

c [1938-39] B & CR 1, DC, 4 Digest (Repl) 187, *1705*.

Wells v Wells [1914] P 157, 83 LJP 81, 111 LT 399, CA, 3 Digest (Repl) 371, *241*.

Whittaker, ex parte, Re Shackleton (1875) 10 Ch App 446, 44 LJBcy 91, 32 LT 443, 5 Digest (Repl) 740, *6403*.

Wigzell, Re, ex parte Hart [1921] 2 KB 835, 90 LJKB 897, [1921] B & CR 42, CA, 4 Digest (Repl) 227, *2036*.

d *Wyvern Developments Ltd, Re* [1974] 2 All ER 535, [1974] 1 WLR 1097.

Cases also cited

Clifton Place Garage Ltd, Re [1970] 1 All ER 353, [1970] Ch 477, CA.

Hone, Re, ex parte the trustee v Kensington Borough Council [1950] 2 All ER 716, [1951] Ch 85.

e *Opera Ltd, Re* [1891] 2 Ch 154.

Russian Commercial and Industrial Bank, Re [1955] 1 All ER 75, [1955] Ch 148.

Sandiford (No 2), Re, Italo-Canadian Corpn Ltd v Sandiford [1935] Ch 681, [1935] All ER Rep 364.

Wilson, Re, ex parte Salaman [1926] Ch 21.

f **Motion**

By notice of motion dated 9th November 1973, Norman Harold Davies, the trustee in bankruptcy of Albert George Clark ('the bankrupt'), sought the following relief: (1) a declaration that a payment of £1,123 10s 10d (£1,123·54) made by the bankrupt to the respondents, Texaco Ltd ('Texaco'), on or shortly after 7th November 1969,

g and a payment of £1,182 14s 2d (£1,182·71) made by the bankrupt on or shortly after 13th November 1969, were void against the trustee under s 37(1) of the Bankruptcy Act 1914 in that they had been made after the bankrupt had committed an act of bankruptcy to which the trustee's title related back; and (2) an order that Texaco repay the sums of £1,123·54 and £1,182·71. The facts are set out in the judgment.

h

M K I Kennedy for the trustee.
David Graham for Texaco.

Cur adv vult

j 28th October. **WALTON J** read the following judgment. The facts in the present case are simple, and are not disputed. On 5th July 1969 a bankruptcy notice was, with some difficulty, served on Albert George Clark, whom it will be convenient to call 'the bankrupt'. He did not comply with the requirements of that notice, and on 12th August 1969 a bankruptcy petition founded thereon was duly presented to this court. A receiving order was duly made on 7th November 1969. There was then, unfortunately, an industrial dispute in being, which affected the printing of

the London Gazette, and the order was consequently not gazetted until 21st
November 1969. Nothing, however, turns on this.

Sometime earlier the same year, namely on 21st May 1969, the bankrupt had
signed a licence agreement with the respondents, Texaco Ltd ('Texaco') under the
terms of which he was licensed to carry on business at a petrol filling and service
station belonging to Texaco, on the terms that he paid a modest licence fee of £7 10s
(old currency) per week, and obtained all his requirements of motor fuels and oils
from Texaco. Subject to these obligations, he was entitled to retain the whole of
the profits—and correspondingly obliged to defray the whole of any loss—arising
from his operations. The garage in question was known as the Commercial Road
Service Station, and it was situate at 516 Commercial Road, London, E1.

There was no real evidence before me as to the earlier history of the bankrupt's
trading at this garage, but at some date before the story commenced Texaco had
withdrawn all credit facilities; they were only prepared to deliver, at any rate
petrol, on a 'cash sale' basis. This, apparently, extended to payment by cheque,
whether by definition or concession I am unable to say. Thus, on the very same day
that the receiving order was made (but of course in contemplation of law subsequent
thereto: see Re Warren[1]) Texaco made a delivery of 3,800 gallons of petrol, and
received in payment a cheque for £1,123 10s 10d. This cheque (and the other two
cheques hereinafter referred to) was drawn on an account in the name of 'Commercial
Road Service Station' with Lloyds Bank Ltd, but it was obviously operated on the
sole signature of the bankrupt. This account was £766 15s 5d overdrawn at the
commencement of business on 7th November 1969, but various sums were credited
thereto between 7th and 12th November, on which day the cheque was cleared, so
that, immediately prior to such clearance there was a credit balance of £276 17s 8d
in the account. The cheque was therefore met partly out of the balance of £276 17s 8d
and by a technical loan from the bank of £846 13s 2d, in which sum the account
finished up in debit on that day.

A week later, on 13th November 1969, Texaco made another delivery, this time
of some 4,000 gallons, and again received a similar cheque, dated that day, in the sum
of £1,182 14s 2d in payment. This cheque was again delayed in presentation; it
was cleared on 18th November by means of the then credit in the account (£260 10s)
and another overdraft facility from the bank of £922 4s 2d.

A week after that, on 20th November, a further delivery of petrol was made, and
again a similar cheque was given in payment, this time for £1,123 10s 2d. On the
following day a cheque for £30 was given by the bankrupt to Texaco in respect of a
month's licence fees. Both these cheques were dishonoured by the bank, and these
sums have never been paid to Texaco. Shortly thereafter, the Official Receiver, who
knew nothing about these transactions, intervened, and when he did so there was a
credit balance of some £205 14s 3d in the account, and a stock of about £700 worth
of petrol on the premises. A tripartite agreement was entered into on 10th December 1969 between a representative of the Official Receiver's department, a representative of Texaco and a Mr Jenkins, whereunder Mr Jenkins was to be given a
licence to carry on business at the premises on the same terms as the bankrupt, and
Mr Jenkins was to pay to the Official Receiver the sum of £718 in respect of the
stocks of petrol and oil on the premises. Mr Jenkins appears to have sold the stocks
and disappeared without paying the agreed £718.

Now in all of this, Texaco appears to have been completely blameless. They
knew nothing of the bankrupt's bankruptcy at any material time. They finished up
by having delivered some £3,429·76 (new currency) worth of petrol and having been
paid only some £2,306·25 in respect thereof. Their commerce with the bankrupt
had also been very beneficial so far as his estate is concerned, in that (a) a debit

---

1   [1938] 2 All ER 331, [1938] Ch 725

a   balance of £766 15s 5d on the bankrupt's account with Lloyds Bank Ltd has been converted into a credit of £205 14s 3d (parenthetically I note that the trustee in bankruptcy has in fact recovered from the bank the sum of £972 9s 8d, being the *total* affirmative movement on the account over the period we are now considering); (b) a stock of some £718 worth of petrol and oil became part of the estate of the bankrupt. It cannot, of course, for this purpose matter that the realisation of these

b   stocks did not, in the event, prove beneficial to the estate. This has nothing to do with Texaco. It is, however perhaps, fair to notice that probably there were some stocks at the premises on 7th November 1969, so that the force of this observation is rather less than it might, given different circumstances, have been.

Finally, it is to be observed that the addition to the estate to which I have already referred is without any corresponding claim against the estate in the present bank-

c   ruptcy: see Bankruptcy Act 1914, s 30(3). Texaco have a theoretical remedy against the bankrupt by making him bankrupt a second time, but quite obviously this is a wholly unreal remedy, when the present estimated deficiency as regards the present bankruptcy is £3,556.

This being the state of affairs, the trustee in bankruptcy has launched the present motion which seeks the following relief:

d   '(1) A declaration that a payment of £1,123. 10. 10d. (£1,123·54) made by the above named Bankrupt to the Respondents on or shortly after the 7th November 1969 and a payment of £1,182. 14. 2d. (£1,182·71) made by the said Bankrupt on or shortly after the 13th November 1969 are void against the Applicant as such Trustee under the provisions of Section 37(1) of the Bankruptcy Act 1914 in that they were made after the said Bankrupt had committed an act of bankruptcy

e   to which the title of the Applicant as such Trustee relates back. (2) An Order that the Respondents do repay the said sum of £1,123·54 and the said sum of £1,182·71. (3) Costs. (4) Further or other relief.'

Counsel for the trustee puts his case very simply. He says, and says truly, that by virtue of the Bankruptcy Act 1914, s 18(1), which provides that on adjudication all

f   the property of the bankrupt vests in his trustee, s 37(1), which provides when the bankruptcy commences, and s 38(2)(*a*), which provides that the property of the bankrupt divisible amongst his creditors includes all property which might be acquired by him before his discharge, even though the moneys represented by the two cheques in question were acquired by the bankrupt after the date of the receiving order, they are part of the property of the bankrupt vesting in his trustee, and there-

g   fore Texaco are bound to pay them over to his clients, unless counsel for Texaco can successfully rely on the principle of *Ex parte James*[1].

Counsel for the trustee points out that there are some exceptions to the general rule that all property automatically vests in the trustee—including, in particular, the provisions of s 47 giving statutory effect to the decision of the Court of Appeal in *Cohen v Mitchell*[2] whereunder a bankrupt can dispose of all property which he disposes

h   of bona fide and for value if it is property acquired by him after he has been adjudicated bankrupt, but that there is no similar protection during what has been described as the 'twilight' period between the receiving order and adjudication. Counsel for the trustee also called my attention to all the other possible exceptions (see the Bankruptcy Act 1914, ss 45 and 46, and the Bankruptcy (Amendment) Act 1926, s 4) for the purpose of correctly demonstrating that none of those exceptions

j   applies. This position was accepted by counsel for Texaco, and consequently the sole, but extremely difficult and important question which I have to answer is: ought the doctrine laid down in *Ex parte James*[1] ('the rule') to be applied in the present case so as to deny the trustee relief to which, according to the letter of the statute,

---

1   (1874) 9 Ch App 609. [1874-80] All ER Rep 388
2   (1890) 25 QBD 262

he is plainly entitled? Stating the matter in very broad terms indeed for the moment,   *a*
and deliberately using for the purpose unemotive language, the rule provides that
where it would be unfair for a trustee to take full advantage of his legal rights as
such, the court will order him not to do so, and, indeed, will order him to return
money which he may have collected. For the rule to operate, it is clear that certain
conditions must be present.

(1) The first is that there must be some form of enrichment of the assets of the   *b*
bankrupt by the person seeking to have the rule applied. I take this condition
from a passage in the speech of Lord Keith of Avonholm in *Government of India,
Ministry of Finance (Revenue Division) v Taylor*[1]. (I observe incidentally, since counsel
for Texaco has some responsibility in the matter, that in Halsbury's Laws of England,
title Bankruptcy[2], it is stated that 'all the cases are examined' in that passage: I can
find no such examination in my copy of the law reports.)   *c*

As this is a universal feature of all the cases in which the rule has been applied, I
do not think that any further citation of authority is called for. I would, however,
observe that the doctrine of two of the cases on which counsel for Texaco placed
some reliance, namely, *Ex parte Dewhurst, Re Vanlohe*[3] and *Cohen v Mitchell*[4], has
nothing to do with enrichment in any shape or form. The doctrine in those cases,
which has received statutory recognition in the Bankruptcy Act 1914, s 47, is based   *d*
on the theory that until the trustee in bankruptcy actually intervenes, the bankrupt
has a qualified property in anything which he acquires after the bankruptcy. It is
quite impossible in my view for the courts to extend this principle, which in its origins
could quite easily have been used to cover property acquired in the twilight period,
which did not then exist, in view of the express wording of s 47 itself restricting this
to the period after adjudication. It is fair to say that counsel for Texaco placed but   *e*
faint reliance on these two cases; in my judgment they do not assist his argument
in any way.

(2) Returning to the conditions for the application of the rule, it is, I think, clear
that except in the most unusual cases the claimant must not be in a position to submit
an ordinary proof of debt. I think that this is exemplified by the decisions in *Ex
parte Whittaker, Re Shackleton*[5] which was admitted by Bacon CJ to be an exceedingly   *f*
hard case, and *Re Gozzett, ex parte Messenger & Co Ltd v the Trustee*[6]. Although the
basis for this has never been expressly formulated, I think that the underlying reason
is obviously that to give effect to the rule would conflict with the mandatory rateable
division of the estate between all the bankrupt's creditors. The rule is not to be used
merely to confer a preference on an otherwise unsecured creditor, but to provide relief
for a person who would otherwise be without any.   *g*

It is true that in *Re Regent Finance and Guarantee Corpn Ltd*[7] Maugham J applied the
rule in a company case where a proof of debt would have lain. As to that it may be
observed that there is no similar difficulty in the case of companies to that which
confronts Texaco in the present case, and also that, reading the case as a whole, it is
impossible not to see that the learned judge regarded the £400 ordered to be repaid
to the applicants as being in effect their own money throughout, merely sent by the   *h*
company in liquidation as agents for them to the vendors of the vehicle they intended
to purchase, so that when the liquidator got it back from the vendors, the money he
got back was not in any real sense of the word the company's own money. Their
money was the £100 they were to get for effecting the deal, and that (and a further
£100) they had got anyway.

1   [1955] 1 All ER 292 at 300, [1955] AC 491 at 512, 513   *j*
2   4th Edn, vol 3, para 524, note 3
3   (1871) 7 Ch App 185
4   (1890) 25 QBD 262
5   (1875) 10 Ch App 446
6   [1936] 1 All ER 79
7   [1930] WN 84

a (3) The third, and crucial, test for the application of the rule is, I think, capable of
being stated simply as follows. If, in all the circumstances of the case, an honest man
who would be personally affected by the result would nevertheless be bound to
admit: 'It's not fair that I should keep the money; my claim has no merits', then the
rule applies so as to nullify the claim which he would otherwise have.

(4) Finally, for completeness, I should observe that when the rule does apply, it
b applies only to the extent necessary to nullify the enrichment of the estate; it by no
means necessarily restores the claimant to the status quo ante. Thus, to take the
clearest possible example of this, in *Re Regent Finance and Guarantee Corpn Ltd*[1], the
claimants had actually paid over a sum of £600 to the company, but they only got
back their 'own money' component of £400 less the sum which was in the company's
account anyway, namely £49 4s 2d.

c I should also add that counsel for the trustee, who argued his case most attractively,
submitted that there was another requirement which was universally present,
namely that there must be an identifiable fund on which the doctrine can operate:
the claimant, in other words, must be able to point to a specific fund which he says
is his. Counsel for Texaco suggested that perhaps 'identifiable piece of property'
would be a better generalisation. As to this, I am not satisfied that this is a necessary
d requirement for the operation of the rule (see *Wells v Wells* per Swinfen Eady LJ[2]),
at any rate unless there is comprehended in that requirement the right, where
necessary, to dissect a bank account into its component parts. If this is conceded,
I think that any such requirement becomes of no great assistance in any particular
case. In any event, even if counsel for the trustee is right on that point in
relation to a claimant making a claim against the trustee, it is a little difficult to see
e how it could ever operate when the trustee is making a claim against the claimant,
who is simply saying: 'Listen to my story as to how I came to get paid and judge
whether I ought to be asked to repay.'

Summarising the cases then, it seems to me that in *Ex parte James*[3] itself the court
was saying that it was certainly not fair that a trustee in bankruptcy should seek to
retain moneys which had been paid to him purely under a mistake of law. In *Re
f Tyler, ex parte the Official Receiver*[4] a policy belonging in theory to the trustee was to
his knowledge kept up by the wife of the bankrupt. Buckley LJ dealt with the matter
in terms which appear to me to be exactly consistent with the way I would approach
the ambit of the rule. He said[5]:

g 'He [that is the trustee in bankruptcy] knew in 1901 that there were policies
and that the wife was paying the premiums on those policies. Knowing that,
he allowed those payments to go on from 1901 to 1906. In 1906 the life dropped.
Under these circumstances, looking beyond rights enforceable in a Court of Law
or Equity, the real fact is that the policy moneys payable in 1906 originated from
and owed their existence to the premiums which the wife to the knowledge of
the trustee had paid, and it would be grievously unfair, and contrary to natural
h justice between man and man, that whereas she kept up the policy yet when the
life dropped somebody else should take the money. She may not have an
enforceable claim, but as matter of justice it cannot be right, when the time
comes for the payment of the moneys due on the policy, to allow the trustee to
turn round and say "I knew you were keeping down the premiums, but I shall
take the policy moneys, and you shall go without the money you have paid."
j That is not consistent with justice, and no high-minded man would do it.'

1 [1930] WN 84
2 [1914] P 157 at 166, 167
3 (1874) 9 Ch App 609, [1874-80] All ER Rep 388
4 [1907] 1 KB 865, [1904-7] All ER Rep 181
5 [1907] 1 KB at 874, [1904-7] All ER Rep at 185

In *Re Hall, ex parte the Official Receiver*[1] some mortgagees had advanced money to   *a*
the bankrupt on a mortgage, and after his bankruptcy they tried to assist him to
arrive at a composition with his creditors. They paid the creditors 4s in the £, a total
of £158, and then sought to add that sum to their mortgage. The estate of the debtor
had in no wise been benefited by what they had done, and so I think an essential
requirement for the application of the rule was missing. As Vaughan Williams LJ
said[2]:   *b*

'Mr. Ringwood, in putting the case in the only way in which it could be put,
said that the estate had benefited by the payment of this 4s. I do not see it
myself...'

This was even clearer if, as I think the whole court thought was probably the case,
the mortgagees were in law subrogated to the rights of the creditors whom they had   *c*
paid off. *Tapster v Ward*[3], *Re Phillips*[4] and *Re Stokes, ex parte Mellish*[5] were all again
very like *Re Tyler*[6] save that it was the bankrupt himself who had made the payments
on the policy, and his executors who claimed to be repaid the premium. The trustee,
however, knew nothing of the circumstances at all, the policy not having been disclosed by the bankrupt. Clearly, there was no reason at all why the trustee should
not claim the policy; there was nothing unfair about that. Any unethical conduct   *d*
was on the part of the bankrupt himself. *Re Thellusson, ex parte Abdy*[7] is, I suppose,
the most extreme of the cases in which the rule has been applied. Basically, the
claimant lent money to the bankrupt to enable him to pay a pressing creditor, not
knowing that he had committed an act of bankruptcy or that a petition against him
was pending. The loan was made the day after, unknown to both of them, a receiving
order had been made. The Court of Appeal held that, as the loan would not have   *e*
been made had the lender known the facts, and as he had no other real remedy
(Atkin LJ was particularly scathing about this and the point was also emphasised by
Younger LJ in the case next to be cited), it fell within the class of cases where the
court would direct its officer[8]—

'to pursue a line of conduct which an honest man actuated by motives of   *f*
morality and justice would pursue, although not compellable thereto by legal
process.'

In other words, they regarded it as unfair that the trustee should seek to retain a
loan made for a purpose which could not, having regard to the bankruptcy, be
fulfilled. Had it been made even slightly before the bankruptcy, of course, the
situation would have been different. This case is undoubtedly the highwater mark   *g*
of the exercise of the jurisdiction in relation to the rule. Doubts have subsequently
been cast on some of the dicta contained therein, which is why I have simply taken
the bald facts.

In *Re Wigzell, ex parte Hart*[9] after the receiving order the sum of £165 was paid into
the bankrupt's bank account, and he drew £199 out. It was held that the bank had
to refund the £165 without being able to claim credit for any part of the £199, in   *h*
the absence of evidence that any of it had gone to pay off the bankrupt's debts. It is
quite clear, I think, on the facts, that there was no enrichment of the estate. This was

1   [1907] 1 KB 875
2   [1907] 1 KB at 878
3   (1909) 101 LT 503   *j*
4   [1914] 2 KB 689
5   [1919] 2 KB 256, [1918-19] All ER Rep 1179
6   [1907] 1 KB 865, [1904-7] All ER Rep 181
7   [1919] 2 KB 735, [1918-19] All ER Rep 729
8   [1919] 2 KB at 743, [1918-19] All ER Rep at 730
9   [1921] 2 KB 835

a the view of Salter J in the Divisional Court, and Scrutton LJ[1] in the Court of Appeal commended his judgment. But even if one overlooks that fact, there was no particular feature in that case which made it unfair for the trustee to rely on his legal rights. It is true that advertisement of the receiving order had been stayed, but this was nothing to do with the trustee. It finally remains to observe on that case that if it did indeed cause any injustice that has now been put right by Bankruptcy (Amendment)

b Act 1926, s 4.

In *Scranton's Trustee v Pearse*[2] a trustee sued to recover betting losses of the bankrupt which the latter had discharged by cheque from the defendant bookmaker. The latter claimed that it was unfair for the trustee to recover these sums, in exercise of the statutory right which he then had. Astbury J thought that he ought to apply the rule; the Court of Appeal disagreed, holding that such a case was not one in which

c the question of the application of the rule properly arose at all. It is a little difficult to see how even the most optimistic of bookmakers could hope to characterise the exercise of a statutory right to recover betting losses as unfair. Moreover, as it seems to me, as there had been no enrichment of the estate (on the contrary, ex necessitate rei the very reverse) the doctrine did not apply on that ground alone.

I have already mentioned *Re Regent Finance and Guarantee Corporation Ltd*[3]. The

d simple question there was, could it be fair for the liquidator to retain moneys which were to all practical intents and purposes the purchase money which the claimant had paid to the ultimate vendor through the company—against the background of the fact that if the company had, in fact, passed on the whole of the £500 purchase price to the vendors, as it had undertaken to do, the claimant would have obtained their omnibus? Only one answer could conceivably be given to that question.

e Finally, in *Re Wyvern Developments Ltd*[4] as an alternative ground for his judgment in that case, that the Official Receiver was bound to keep his promise to join in a conveyance of land in fulfilment of a contract of sale by a person who had a lien thereover, Templeman J said[5]:

'It is quite true that Gresham and Winter are not seeking recoupment, but there undoubtedly would be enrichment of the assets of the insolvent company

f Wyvern at the expense of Winter if, by dint of a refusal by the Official Receiver to perform his promise, supported by an order made by me, Winter lost a contract under which it is to buy land for £16,000, when the present value of the land, if Mrs Goldstein is a genuine purchaser, is £35,000. In my judgment, these are extreme circumstances and I see no reason why *Ex parte James*[6] should not apply or be extended if necessary to allow the Official Receiver to comply with

g an express promise made by him in the circumstances in which he was placed.'

Once again, it would simply not be fair to allow the official receiver to back out of his promise in all the circumstances of that case. Having now dealt with all the cases on *Ex parte James*[6] which were cited to me and which turned out, on analysis, to be cases in which the rule was, or was not, as such, applied, I turn to the facts of this

h particular case. The question as I feel it ought to be posed is simply: 'Is it fair that the trustee should recover the amount of these two cheques from Texaco?' As matters now stand, as a result of the activities of Texaco, the estate has benefited to an extent of £972 9s 8d. Texaco are out of pocket to the tune of some £1,123 10s 2d, in respect of which they have no right of proof whatsoever. If the claim of the trustee is allowed, the estate will have been benefited to an extent of £3,278 16s 8d, and

j

1 [1921] 2 KB at 863
2 [1922] 2 Ch 87, [1922] All ER Rep 764
3 [1930] WN 84
4 [1974] 2 All ER 535, [1974] 1 WLR 1097
5 [1974] 2 All ER at 543, 544, [1974] 1 WLR at 1105
6 (1874) 9 Ch App 609, [1874-80] All ER Rep 388

Texaco will be out of pocket to the tune of some £3,429 15s 2d for which they will   *a*
again have no right of proof in the current bankruptcy. Can this be fair? I have no
hesitation in answering that it is not. The situation would amount to the estate
taking the whole of the benefit of the sale price of the petrol whilst repudiating all
obligation to pay for it, even via a proof of debt.

I note that counsel for Texaco, in the exercise of an admirable discretion, has not
sought any stage in the case to seek to claim payment out of the estate of the amount   *b*
of the last cheque. I express no opinion whether he would have any prospect of
establishing any such claim, but his expressed disclaimer of any such intent does,
I think, enable me to take a very broad view of the whole of the transactions. Left
as they are, the estate gains quite substantially, and Texaco loses a not inconsiderable
sum. Give effect to the trustee's legal claims, and the estate gains dramatically and
Texaco's losses increase threefold. I cannot think that in all these circumstances any   *c*
dispassionate observer would not say: 'Well, I don't know what the legal technicalities
are, but it is obviously much fairer to all concerned to leave the matter as it is than
to force Texaco to repay money which, had they not have thought it had been
properly paid to them, would not have attracted the deliveries of petrol.'

There is, I think, one final consideration, not so far as I am aware referred to in any
of the cases, and possibly peculiar to the present case. The object of the property   *d*
vesting provisions of the Bankruptcy Act 1914 is obviously to ensure that the bankrupt's
estate is not dissipated away, but is kept together for the ultimate benefit of his
creditors. If, during the twilight period, the bankrupt trades at a profit for the benefit
of his estate, it is hard to see why he should only be allowed to do so on terms that
the other party to such trade is on a hiding to nothing. Obviously, such a person takes
many risks, and may not be able, at the end of the day, to prove for any claims he may   *e*
have. But if he trades on a ready money basis, and the net result of the bankrupt's
efforts is beneficial so far as the estate is concerned, as happened here, it does seem
somewhat greedy for the trustee in bankruptcy to seek to extract not funds which
actually formed part of the estate at the commencement of the bankruptcy, but
something which never did, from the unfortunate trading partner of the bankrupt.
Everything must depend on its own particular facts, but on the facts of the present   *f*
case, I think that our dispassionate observer would accuse the trustee of opening his
mouth too wide; and *that* is not fair.

I ought perhaps here, in justice to counsel for the trustee, to notice his final argument, which was that, if I were minded to apply the rule, I should not do so to the
full amount of the two cheques, but only to the extent to which the estate has, in
fact, benefited, namely, £972 9s 8d. I regret that I failed to follow the argument,   *g*
because if I allowed the trustee's claim to proceed to any extent, the figure of
£972 9s 8d would be increased. I shall leave that argument there.

In the result, treating the motion before me as a motion for directions, I direct the
trustee to take no proceedings whatsoever to recover the amount of the two cheques
therein referred to, or any part or parts thereof, from Texaco.

h

*Motion treated as application for directions; trustee directed to take no proceedings to recover
amount of two cheques or any parts thereof from Texaco.*

Solicitors: *A Kramer & Co* (for the trustee); *Stephenson, Harwood & Tatham* (for Texaco).

Jacqueline Metcalfe   Barrister.

a   R v Arrowsmith

COURT OF APPEAL, CRIMINAL DIVISION
LAWTON LJ, MOCATTA AND CANTLEY JJ
3rd, 4th DECEMBER 1974

b   *Criminal law – Indictment – Duplicity – Incitement to disaffection – Endeavouring to seduce*
      member of armed forces from his duty or allegiance to Crown – Count alleging defendant had
      endeavoured to seduce members of forces from 'duty or allegiance' – Whether count bad for
      duplicity – Incitement to Disaffection Act 1934, s 1 – Indictment Rules 1971 (SI 1971 No 1253),
      r 7.

c   *Criminal law – Defence – Mistake – Mistake as to consequences of committing offence –*
      Defendant distributing leaflets to members of armed forces – Leaflets encouraging troops to
      desert or to refuse to obey orders if posted to Northern Ireland – Director of Public Prosecu-
      tions refusing to consent to prosecution for incitement to disaffection – Defendant mistakenly
      believing consent would not be given to prosecution for distributing leaflets on future occasions
      – Whether mistaken belief a defence to prosecution for subsequent distribution of leaflets.
d
      The appellant and others distributed leaflets to troops stationed at an army camp
      urging them to desert or to refuse to obey orders if they were posted to Northern
      Ireland. She was arrested and a report was made to the Director of Public Prosecutions
      ('the DPP') with a view to prosecution under the Incitement to Disaffection Act 1934.
      The DPP did not however give his consent and so, under s 3(2)ᵃ of the 1934 Act, no
e   prosecution under that Act could take place. The appellant's solicitor was merely
      informed by the DPP of his decision; no indication was given of what action the DPP
      would take should the appellant distribute the leaflets to troops on any future occasion.
      Shortly afterwards the appellant was found distributing the leaflets to troops at
      another army post. The DPP gave his consent to a prosecution under the 1934 Act
      and accordingly the appellant was committed for trial on an indictment containing
f   two counts: (1) endeavouring to seduce a member of Her Majesty's forces from his
      duty or allegiance to Her Majesty, contrary to s 1ᵇ, and (2) possession of a document of
      such a nature that the dissemination thereof among members of Her Majesty's forces
      would constitute an offence under s 1, contrary to s 2(1)ᶜ. She was convicted on each
      count and sentenced to 18 months' imprisonment on each, the sentences to run
      concurrently. She appealed against conviction on the grounds, inter alia, that the
g   counts were bad for duplicity in that they had failed to specify whether she was being
      charged with an offence relating to seducing servicemen from their duty to the Crown
      or from their allegiance, and that she had a lawful excuse for distributing the leaflets
      in that she had been led to believe that the DPP would not give his consent to a
      prosecution under the 1934 Act for distributing the leaflets. She also applied for leave
      to appeal against sentence.
h
      Held – (i) The appeal against conviction would be dismissed for the following reasons—
           (a) Section 1 of the 1934 Act created a single offence which was committed by any-
      one who endeavoured to seduce members of the forces with a particular intent. The
      intent might either be to seduce them from their duty or from their allegiance or
      from both. In any event it was permissible to state the intent in the alternative under

---

j   *a*   Section 3(2) is set out at p 467 *e*, post
      b   Section 1 is set out at p 468 *g*, post
      c   Section 2(1), so far as material, provides: 'If any person, with intent to commit . . . or pro-
           cure the commission of an offence under section one of this Act, has in his possession or
           under his control any document of such a nature that the dissemination of copies thereof
           among members of His Majesty's forces would constitute such an offence, he shall be guilty
           of an offence under this Act.'

r 7^d of the Indictment Rules 1971^e. It followed that the counts against the appellant *a*
were not bad for duplicity (see p 469 *j* and p 470 *c* and *d*, post).

(b) The appellant was not entitled to rely on the defence of mistake, for her belief
that the DPP would not give his consent to a prosecution was not a mistake about
the facts constituting the offence but about the possible consequences of committing
it (see p 471 *e* and *h*, post).

(ii) Although in principle the sentence which the appellant had received was amply *b*
justified, it was possible that she might have inferred from the DPP's original decision
not to give his consent to a prosecution and his failure to give a warning about her
future conduct, that she would not be prosecuted if she repeated her conduct. Since
in those circumstances she might feel that she had been treated unfairly and since it
was necessary that justice should appear to have been done, the application for leave
to appeal against sentence would be granted and the terms of imprisonment reduced *c*
so as to allow for her immediate release (see p 472 *f* to *h*, post).

Notes

For incitement to mutiny and disaffection among HM Forces, see 10 Halsbury's Laws
(3rd Edn) 572-574, paras 1062, 1063; and for cases on the subject, see 15 Digest (Repl)
781, 7332-7335.

For mistake as a defence to a criminal charge, see 10 Halsbury's Laws (3rd Edn) *d*
284, 285, para 525, and for cases on the subject, see 14 Digest (Repl) 51, 52, *178-181*.

For the Incitement to Disaffection Act 1934, ss 1, 2, see 8 Halsbury's Statutes (3rd Edn)
312.

Cases referred to in judgment

Brutus v Cozens [1972] 2 All ER 1297, [1973] AC 854, [1972] 3 WLR 521, 136 JP 636, 56 Cr *e*
App Rep 799, HL.

Cambridgeshire and Isle of Ely County Council v Rust [1972] 3 All ER 232, [1972] 2 QB 426,
[1972] 3 WLR 226, 136 JP 702, 70 LGR 444, DC.

Joyce v Director of Public Prosecutions [1946] 1 All ER 186, [1946] AC 347, 115 LJKB 146,
174 LT 206, 31 Cr App Rep 57, HL, 14 Digest (Repl) 140, *1030*.

Prairie Schooner News Ltd v Powers (1970) 1 CCC (2d) 251, 75 WWR 585. *f*

R v Solanke [1969] 3 All ER 1383, [1970] 1 WLR 1, 134 JP 80, 54 Cr App Rep 30, CA,
Digest (Cont Vol C) 254, *8924a*.

Surrey County Council v Battersby [1965] 1 All ER 273, [1965] 2 QB 194, [1965] 2 WLR 378,
129 JP 116, 63 LGR 152, DC, Digest (Cont Vol B) 443, *2328a*.

Cases also cited

Howell v Falmouth Boat Construction Ltd [1951] 2 All ER 278, [1951] AC 837, HL; *affg* *g*
[1950] 1 All ER 538, [1950] 2 KB 16, CA.

R v Burns (1886) 16 Cox CC 353.

R v Foley, R v Chandler, R v Randle (1967) 52 Cr App Rep 123, CA.

R v Surrey Quarter Sessions, ex parte Lilley [1951] 2 All ER 659, [1951] 2 KB 749, DC.

Wong Pooh Yin (alias Kwang Sin, alias Kar Sin) v Public Prosecutor [1954] 3 All ER 31, *h*
[1955] AC 93, PC.

Appeal

Patricia Arrowsmith appealed against her conviction on 20th May 1974 at the Central
Criminal Court before his Honour Judge Abdela QC of endeavouring to seduce a

---

d Rule 7 provides: 'Where an offence created by or under an enactment states the offence to *j*
    be the doing or the omission to do any one of any different acts in the alternative, or the
    doing or the omission to do any act in any one of any different capacities, or with any one
    of any different intentions, or states any part of the offence in the alternative, the acts,
    omissions, capacities or intentions, or other matters stated in the alternative in the
    enactment or subordinate instrument may be stated in the alternative in an indictment
    charging the offence.'

e SI 1971 No 1253

a   member of her Majesty's Forces from his duty or allegiance to her Majesty, contrary to s 1 of the Incitement to Disaffection Act 1934 (count 1) and with possessing a document of such a nature that the dissemination of copies thereof among members of her Majesty's Forces would constitute an offence contrary to s 1 of the 1934 Act, contrary to s 2(1) of that Act (count 2). She was sentenced to concurrent terms of 18 months' imprisonment. The appellant also applied for leave to appeal against

b   sentence. The facts are set out in the judgment of the court.

John Platts-Mills QC and *R B Tansey* for the appellant.
Michael Coombe for the Crown.

LAWTON LJ delivered the following judgment of the court. On 20th May 1974
c   at the Central Criminal Court, after a trial before his Honour Judge Abdela QC, the appellant was convicted on two counts of an indictment. The first charged her as follows: endeavouring to seduce a member of Her Majesty's forces from his duty or allegiance to Her Majesty, contrary to s 1 of the Incitement to Disaffection Act 1934. Count 2 charged her with possessing a document of such nature that the dissemination of copies thereof among members of Her Majesty's forces would constitute an offence

d   contrary to s 1 of the 1934 Act, the offence itself being contrary to s 2(1) of the 1934 Act. She was sentenced to 18 months' imprisonment on each count, the sentence to run concurrently. She now appeals to this court against her conviction on points of law. She applies for leave to appeal against her conviction on grounds of mixed fact and law, and she also applies for leave to appeal against her sentence. Her application for leave to appeal against sentence is granted.

e   The facts out of which this appeal arises are as follows. At Warminster in Wiltshire, there is an army centre. It consists of a school of infantry, a command workshop and married quarters. It was said at the trial that somewhere in the Warminster area in September 1973 there was a batallion of an Irish regiment. During the afternoon of 22nd September 1973 Warrant Officer Laidlaw, who was the orderly officer of the day, as a result of certain information received by him, and after consultation with

f   the civil police, went with two other soldiers to a block of flats in the married quarter area occupied by serving soldiers and their families. On getting there he saw two people, one of whom was the appellant, go into a block of flats. He followed, and found the pair of them on the top floor putting leaflets through some doors. He told them that they were on military property, and that they must stop delivering their leaflets, and leave. The appellant gave him her name, referred to a case at Colchester,

g   and said the Director of Public Prosecutions had ruled that the leaflet was in order. She refused to go. Another man and another woman were found nearby distributing the same leaflets.

The civilian police at Warminster were informed; two officers arrived. According to these police officers, the appellant handed to each of them a copy of the leaflet, saying something to the effect that it had been seen by the Director of Public Prosecu-

h   tions who had ruled that it was not subversive literature and that 'as they had been found not guilty at Colchester' they did not regard themselves as committing any offence.

After argument and various warnings, the appellant said 'If you are not going to arrest us, I shall go on delivering'. She walked off and was seen to put a leaflet into the door of one of the flats. She was about to put another one into another flat, when

j   one of the police officers arrested her for conduct likely to cause a breach of the peace. She resisted arrest and sat on the pavement. She was eventually carried to the police car and conveyed to the police station. When arrested, 95 leaflets, similar to the ones which she had handed to the police constables, were taken from her. She admitted that she had drafted part of the leaflet in question.

It is necessary now to make some reference to Colchester and the Director of Public Prosecutions. This appellant is, and has been for many years, a convinced pacifist.

She is opposed to any use of force, whether by the military or anybody else. She has *a* campaigned in support of her views and on occasions she has come into conflict with the law over them. She is opposed to the presence of the armed forces in Northern Ireland as a means of bringing peace to that troubled area. She helped with the drafting of this leaflet, which was intended to be given to soldiers.

It purports to be published by an organisation called The British Withdrawal from Northern Ireland Campaign, and an address in the London area is given. It is headed *b* 'Some information for British soldiers'. It starts off by giving what purport to be two quotations from statements made by British soldiers who have already deserted from the army. It then goes on as follows:

> 'We are aware that there are British soldiers who are leaving the army, or who want to because of British policy in N. Ireland. We are glad about this and hope many more will do so. We have therefore compiled this fact-sheet giving *c* information about various methods of quitting the British armed forces, hoping it may prove useful.'

Then it goes on to the first heading 'Going absent without leave' which is divided into four numbered paragraphs. The first has a sub-heading 'Sweden', and purports to give information as to what help a soldier, going absent without leave, can expect *d* to get if he goes to Sweden. He is told that on arrival he will get legal advice and social help. Then comes a paragraph with a sub-heading 'Eire'. Readers of the leaflet are advised that it may be dangerous to go to Eire as a deserter. The next paragraph has a sub-heading 'Britain'. It points out the difficulties which may arise if a soldier goes absent without leave in Britain. He may, for example, find difficulty over employment and accommodation, and will have to keep moving in order to avoid the police. The final sub-heading is 'Other countries' and the readers are warned *e* that as far as is known, other countries are not offering sanctuary for British deserting soldiers. All this is useful information for a soldier who is contemplating deserting in order to avoid service in Northern Ireland.

On the other side of the leaflet comes a paragraph headed 'Conscientious objection', and points out that soldiers nowadays can get themselves discharged from the army *f* on conscientious grounds and indicates what the army will not accept as conscientious grounds—another useful piece of information. Then there is a heading 'Discharge on other grounds'. Under it comes information setting out in detail the present regulations whereby those who have not been warned of a posting to Northern Ireland or elsewhere overseas can buy themselves out of the army. It is clear from this section of the leaflet that those who drafted it are very familiar indeed with army regulations. They are not ignorant people who do not know how the army works. *g*

Then comes a paragraph with a heading 'Open refusal to be posted to Northern Ireland'. In our judgment this is the part of the leaflet which is the most mischievous. It is in these terms:

> 'A soldier who publicly stated that he refused to serve in N. Ireland, whatever the consequences, would be taking a courageous stand. He would be setting an *h* example to other soldiers: strengthening their resolve to resist the Government's disastrous policy. Better still, if a group of soldiers made this announcement simultaneously it would make a great impact on public opinion, both inside and outside the army. Such an action could lead to Court Martial and imprisonment. But soldiers who believe, as we do, that it is wrong for British troops to be in N. Ireland are asked to consider whether it is better to be killed for a cause you do *j* not believe in or to be imprisoned for refusing to take part in the conflict. All soldiers who intend to refuse to be posted to N. Ireland are asked to inform the BRITISH WITHDRAWAL FROM NORTHERN IRELAND CAMPAIGN, so that their brave actions can receive as much publicity and have as much effect as possible. WE WHO ARE DISTRIBUTING THIS FACT-SHEET TO YOU HOPE THAT, BY ONE MEANS OR ANOTHER, YOU WILL AVOID TAKING PART IN THE KILLING IN NORTHERN IRELAND.'

a This leaflet is the clearest incitement to mutiny and to desertion. As such, it is a most mischievous document. It is not only mischievous but it is wicked. This court is not concerned in any way with the political background against which this leaflet was distributed. What it is concerned with is the likely effects on young soldiers aged 18, 19 or 20, some of whom may be immature emotionally and of limited political understanding. It is particularly concerned about young soldiers who either come

b from Ireland or who have family connections with Ireland; there are probably a large number of them in the British army. These young soldiers are encouraged to desert on learning of a posting to Northern Ireland and to mutiny. If they mutiny, they are liable to be sentenced by court-martial to a very long term of imprisonment, and if they desert, they must expect to get a sentence of at least 12 months' detention. For immature women like this appellant to go round military establishments dis-

c tributing leaflets of this kind amounts to a bad case of seducing soldiers from both their duty and allegiance.

There is, however, a history to this leaflet, which we find a disturbing one. The appellant is not the only person who has been distributing it. She was helped at Warminster by at least one other woman, probably more, and a man. The evidence established that a friend of this appellant in Scotland had been distributing this

d leaflet in military establishments there. Some time in the late summer 1973 the appellant herself distributed these pamphlets at Colchester, which is a military centre. She was seen there by the Colchester police distributing these pamphlets to soldiers; they thought that they ought to intervene and they did. They arrested her for insulting behaviour contrary to the Public Order Act 1936. They took the leaflets from her and told her that she would be reported to the Director of Public Prosecu-

e tions. Reporting her to the Director of Public Prosecutions before a charge was preferred was necessary because of the provisions of the Incitement to Disaffection Act 1934. Section 3(2) of that Act is in these terms: 'No prosecution in England under this Act shall take place without the consent of the Director of Public Prosecutions.' According to the appellant, her friend in Scotland had been told that he would be reported with a view to prosecution under this Act. To whom he would have been

f reported is not clear.

The Colchester police did make a report to the Director of Public Prosecutions. A hearing was fixed at Colchester Magistrates' Court for 14th September 1973. The appellant took legal advice. Her solicitor was concerned to know whether there was going to be a charge under the Incitement to Disaffection Act 1934. Some time about 7th September 1973 he telephoned the office of the Director of Public Prosecutions for information as to what was going to happen. He was told that the Director of

g Public Prosecutions did not propose to give his consent. On 7th September 1973 the Director of Public Prosecutions wrote to the appellant's then solicitor in these terms:

h 'Dear Sirs, *Re: Patricia Arrowsmith* With reference to the recent telephone call from your Mr Rose-Smith, I have to inform you that the Director has decided not to consent to proceedings against your client under the Incitement to Disaffection Act, 1934. The prosecution of the existing charge will be in the hands of the Chief Constable of Essex and Southend-on-Sea.'

As a result of that letter, the only matter which the justices had to concern themselves with was the charge under the Public Order Act 1936. Having regard to the decision of the House of Lords in *Brutus v Cozens*[1] it was not surprising that the justices

j adjudged that merely handing a leaflet of this kind to a soldier did not amount to insulting behaviour under the 1936 Act. Accordingly the appellant was acquitted.

She claimed at her trial in this case that the incidents at Colchester led her to believe that the Director of Public Prosecutions did not regard this leaflet as subversive. There was nothing in the letter to indicate that. The letter was merely a statement

---

1 [1972] 2 All ER 1297, [1973] AC 854

that the Director of Public Prosecutions did not intend to consent to a prosecution in   *a*
respect of the distribution of this leaflet in Colchester, which is another matter
altogether. I have mentioned these facts in some detail because it is necessary to have
them before us for the purpose not only of conviction, but of sentence too.

In due course the appellant was brought before the justices in the Warminster area.
The prosecution were represented by one of the members of the Director of Public
Prosecution's staff. He told the justices that the director was willing to consent to   *b*
summary trial. The appellant, however, elected to be tried by a jury. This matter is
of importance in relation to sentence, because the 1934 Act provides, in s 3(1), as
follows:

> 'A person guilty of an offence under this Act shall be liable, on conviction on
> indictment to imprisonment for a term not exceeding two years or to a fine not
> exceeding two hundred pounds, or on summary conviction to imprisonment   *c*
> for a term not exceeding four months or to a fine not exceeding twenty pounds,
> or (whether on conviction on indictment or on summary conviction) to both
> such imprisonment and fine.'

An argument can be put forward that the fact that the Director of Public Prosecutions was willing to consent to a summary trial was some indication that he, a public   *d*
officer, representing the Crown in criminal matters, did not regard this offence as
serious. How he could have been of that opinion, if he ever was, surprises this
court.

The appellant, no doubt on advice and after due consideration, elected to go for
trial. She was in due course committed for trial at the Central Criminal Court.
There the facts were not much in dispute. Such dispute as there was arose from   *e*
the inferences to be drawn from the facts. The way the Crown put their case against
the appellant can be summarised as follows. It was not sought to say that there was
no defence in law to this charge, as might perhaps have been said, as I will explain
later in this judgment, but that such belief as she had as to the effect of the Director
of Public Prosecution's decision on 7th September 1973 not to give his consent was a
material matter to be taken into consideration when the jury came to consider   *f*
whether she had the intent which it is necessary in order to establish to prove charges
under ss 1 and 2 of the Incitement to Disaffection Act 1934. The trial proceeded on
that basis and the trial judge summed up on that basis. In due course the jury
convicted and the trial judge passed the sentence which I have already indicated.

Grounds of appeal have been clearly and succinctly set out by counsel. I will
deal with them one by one. It was said that both counts in the indictment were bad   *g*
for duplicity. The basis of that argument was this. Section 1 of the 1934 Act is in
these terms:

> 'If any person maliciously and advisedly endeavours to seduce any member
> of [Her] Majesty's forces from his duty *or* allegiance to [Her] Majesty, he shall
> be guilty of an offence under this Act.'   *h*

The reference in the statute to 'duty or allegiance' is reproduced by reference in
s 2 because that section is concerned with the possession of documents having the
effect of seducing any member of Her Majesty's forces from his duty or allegiance.
Counsel for the appellant pointed out that the words 'maliciously and advisedly
endeavours to seduce any member of Her Majesty's forces' in the 1934 Act, have been
taken from the Incitement to Mutiny Act 1797. That Act was passed shortly after   *j*
the Nore mutiny in that year. It is necessary now to turn to the 1797 Act and the
relevant section is headed: 'Any person who shall attempt to seduce any sailor or
soldier from his duty or incite him to mutiny . . . to suffer death', and the terms of
it are as follows:

> '. . . any person who shall maliciously and advisedly endeavour to seduce any

a person or persons serving in [Her] Majesty's forces by sea or land from his or their duty *and* allegiance to [Her] Majesty . . .'

and then the rest of the section deals with other matters. I shall come back to one of those other matters later in this judgment.

Counsel for the appellant based his submission on the transposition of the words 'their duty and allegiance' from one Act to the other; in the course of it the con-

b junctive had been put into the disjunctive. Counsel argued that that must have been done for a reason. That argument appears to us to be sound. Counsel then built up this argument, that in law there must be a distinction between seducing a soldier from his duty and seducing him from his allegiance. If a girl persuaded her boy friend serving in the army to disregard the sergeant major's legitimate order to get his hair cut, that may be seducing him from his duty, but it is a long way from

c seducing him from his allegiance to the Crown. In these circumstances, anyone charged with this offence ought to know whether he is being charged with seducing a member of the armed forces from his duty or whether he is being charged with seducing him from his allegiance. In other words, said counsel, there are two offences in one, whereas the indictment charged only one offence. He tried to support his argument by saying that there are members of the armed forces who may

d be under a duty to the Crown as members of those forces, but who owe no allegiance to the Crown.

As this was a startling submission, we thought it necessary to look into it in some detail, in order to ensure, if it is right, that everyone knows about it; and if it is wrong, that this argument is never put forward again.

The basis for it was the statutory method of enlisting soldiers into the armed forces.

e The relevant provisions are now to be found in the Army Act 1955. Section 2 of that Act deals with the method of enlisting into the armed forces, and sub-s (2) sets out the procedure for enlisting a person into the regular forces by reference to Sch 1 to the Act. That schedule is headed 'Procedure for attestation'. Paragraph 1 deals with various warnings which a recruiting officer should read to the prospective recruit. Then the schedule goes on as follows, in para 3:

f
'He shall then ask that person to make and sign the declaration set out in the attestation paper as to the truth of the answers and shall administer to him the oath of allegiance as set out in the attestation paper.'

It follows that if that procedure is adhered to, as it should be, then, subject to what I am going to say in a moment, everybody in the armed forces will take the oath

g of allegiance. There is, however, an exception for aliens who serve in the armed forces. That is provided by s 21 of the 1955 Act which ends as follows:

'[The Defence Council] may by regulations provide that in such cases as may be prescribed by the regulations it shall not be necessary to administer the oath of allegiance to an alien on his enlistment . . .'

h It follows, submitted counsel for the appellant, that there may be soldiers in the army who have not taken the oath of allegiance.

He also called our attention to the fact that amongst those who are subject to military law, there may even be British subjects who have not taken the oath of allegiance, because s 18(2) provides that if a prospective recruit on going to a recruiting office takes the modern equivalent of the Queen's shilling by accepting a small

j advance of pay, he thereby becomes subject to military law.

On the basis of these provisions of the 1955 Act, it was submitted that two offences under s 1 of the Incitement to Disaffection Act 1934 can be committed and that an accused should know whether he is being charged with seducing soldiers from their duty or from their allegiance.

This submission has no foundation in law. A man owes allegiance to the Crown, whether he has taken the oath of allegiance or not. If ever there was any doubt

about it, it has been resolved by the decision of the House of Lords in *Joyce v Director*   *a*
of Public Prosecutions[1]. In the leading speech, which was delivered by Lord Jowitt LC,
it was said[2]:

> 'Allegiance is owed to their Sovereign Lord the King by his natural-born sub-
> jects; so it is by those who, being aliens, become his subjects by denisation or
> naturalisation (I will call them all "naturalised subjects"); so it is by those
> who, being aliens, reside within the King's realm.'   *b*

On any view an alien serving in the British army and stationed in England is residing
in the Queen's realm. Anyone in the armed forces of the Crown who wears the
Queen's uniform and takes the Queen's pay, is within the protection of the realm.
Nobody could be more within the protection of the Queen than one of her serving
soldiers.

I now approach the matter on the basis of general principle. What is the offence   *c*
created by statute? It is that of seducing members of the forces from doing various
things. In other words it is the act of seducing with a particular intent which is the
offence, and the intent may be to seduce from duty or from allegiance or both. It
follows on principle that no question of duplicity arises in this case. If there was any
doubt on principle, which there is not, the matter is now completely and finally
dealt with by r 7 of the Indictment Rules 1971 made under the Indictments Act 1915.   *d*
There is nothing in the duplicity point at all.

I turn now to the next ground of appeal, which is as follows: 'The learned judge
misdirected the Jury in Law as to the meaning [in the context of this Act] of "maliciously". It is necessary to consider what the learned judge did say about the word
'maliciously'; he invited the jury's attention to this word in the indictment, and went
on as follows: it 'does not bear the meaning of ill-will or spite at all. It means   *e*
something which is wilful or intentional: deliberate. Here it means "wilfully and
intentionally to do an unlawful act . . .".' That is the normal direction given as to
the meaning of the word 'maliciously' which occurs in a large number of statutes,
mostly from the Victorian period.

It was said by counsel for the appellant that it did not bear that meaning in this   *f*
case, because of its origins in the Incitement to Mutiny Act 1797. It was submitted
that that Act was concerned with much graver offences than the Incitement to
Disaffection Act 1934. It was concerned with conduct which was seditious. Indeed
the word 'traitorous' is used in the earlier Act. In those circumstances it should be
equated with concepts of sedition. We do not agree. We can see no reason at all
why in the 1934 Act the word 'maliciously' should not bear the same meaning as it
does in many other statutes. In our judgment the trial judge gave a correct direction   *g*
in law.

The next ground of appeal was as follows:

> 'The learned judge failed to direct the jury in law that lawful excuse was a
> defence to both counts; secondly, that the appellant's belief that she was acting
> lawfully, would be such a defence; thirdly, that her honest, perhaps mistaken   *h*
> mis-interpretation of the Director of Public Prosecution's letter would amount
> to lawful excuse for her conduct, and thus to a defence.'

The words 'lawful excuse' do not appear in s 1 of the Incitement to Disaffection
Act 1934. It is difficult to conceive how anyone could have a lawful excuse to incite
soldiers to desert or to mutiny. It was submitted that the words 'lawful excuse'
should be read into the Act by necessary implication.   *j*

The basis for that submission was the decision of this court in *R v Solanke*[3]. That
case was a very different one on its facts; it was concerned with a charge of uttering

---

1   [1946] 1 All ER 186, [1946] AC 347
2   [1946] 1 All ER at 189, [1946] AC at 366
3   [1969] 3 All ER 1383, [1970] 1 WLR 1

a a letter, which threatened to kill or murder somebody.   It was based on s 16 of the Offences against the Person Act 1861: the word 'maliciously' comes in that section. In the course of giving the judgment of the court in that case Salmon LJ said[1]:

'So long as the sender acts intentionally with full knowledge of the contents of the letter and without lawful excuse, it is unnecessary to look for an ulterior evil motive.'

b Counsel for the appellant's submission was that if in a charge under s 16 of the Offences against the Person Act 1861 the words 'without lawful excuse' should be read into the Act, so they should be in the Act now under consideration.   In our judgment no special significance is to be attached to Salmon LJ's words 'without lawful excuse' because our understanding is that all that Salmon LJ was saying was c that in a charge under s 16, the ordinary common law defences are open to the person charged.   One of the defences which is always open, unless the offence is an absolute one, is that of mistake.   It follows on the same principle that in this parti-cular case it was open to the appellant to say, if she was so minded, that she acted as she did as a result of a mistake.

It is necessary to see what kind of mistake, if any, she made.   A mistake as to the d law would not avail the appellant except perhaps in mitigation of sentence.   Only a mistake as to the facts will provide a defence.   What was she mistaken about, if she was mistaken about anything?   All she could have been mistaken about, on the strength of the Director of Public Prosecution's letter, was that she was not likely to be prosecuted if she once again distributed these pamphlets.   The matter being investigated by the court was whether she had committed the offence charged. e She had made no mistake whatsoever about the facts constituting the offence charged. She knew what was in the leaflets because she had helped to draft them.   She had gone to Warminster intending to distribute these leaflets among soldiers and their families, and she had done so.   A belief that she would not be prosecuted, in our judgment, would have been no defence in law at all.

Overnight our attention was drawn to an article in the current number of the f Criminal Law Review[2] by Mr A J Ashworth.   We are grateful to him for the informa-tion which he has collected together and analysed in an article entitled 'Excusable Mistake of Law'.   Amongst that material is an interesting case from the Manitoba Court of Appeal, which has considerable bearing on this case.   I quote[3]:

'These points [that is these problems about excusable mistakes of law] may be illustrated by reference to the Canadian case of *Prairie Schooner News Ltd and* g   *Powers*[4]   One of the defences to charges of possessing obscene written matter for the purpose of publication was mistake: D believed that the magazines were not criminally obscene because the Canadian Customs Department, which had the power to prevent the importation of any matter "of an immoral or indecent character", had allowed them to be imported.   But the Manitoba Court of Appeal pointed out that the Customs Department applied a different h   test and not the test of "obscenity" under the Criminal Code, so that there was no warrant for D's inference.'

That seems to us to be very near this case, because such mistake as the appellant made has got nothing to do with the facts constituting the offence.   It has merely got something to do, or may have something to do, with the consequences of committing the offence, which is a different matter altogether.

j The way I have dealt with the problem so far is not, however, the way counsel for the Crown dealt with it at the trial.   He could have dealt with it in that way.   He

1 [1969] 3 All ER at 1385, [1970] 1 WLR at 4
2 [1974] Crim LR 652
3 [1974] Crim LR at 660
4 [1970] 1 CCC (2d) 251

invited the judge to leave mistake to the jury. The submission of counsel for the *a* appellant has been that the judge did not leave this issue adequately, or alternatively, fairly, to the jury.

With counsel's assistance, we have gone through the summing-up very carefully indeed. We have come to the conclusion that the issue of the nature and extent of the appellant's belief was left to the jury. In our judgment the summing-up was fair. It was an admirable summing-up and no valid criticism of it can be made on *b* the ground of either inadequacy or unfairness.

I turn now to the problem of sentence, which has caused us considerable anxiety. On a number of occasions in the past the courts have had to consider the effect of mistake as to law. Fairly recently there have been cases in which people have found themselves in the dock for doing something which an official had advised them it was permissible to do: *Surrey County Council v Battersby*[1] is one example. More *c* recently there was the case of *Cambridgeshire and Isle of Ely County Council v Rust*[2].

Textbook writers have commented on the position which arises when people are led into a breach of the law by something which has been said by someone in authority or by a lawyer. Counsel for the appellant invited our attention to some passages on this topic in the well-known work[3] by Professor Glanville Williams.

In this case the person in authority was the Director of Public Prosecutions. What *d* he did was not to take any action in respect of previous distributions of this pamphlet, and to say by his letter of 7th September that he was not going to give his consent to a prosecution. What effect ought this inaction have on sentence? It is difficult to believe that this well-educated and intelligent appellant did not appreciate what she was doing. She must have known that she was inciting mutiny and desertion. The story which she put forward at the trial, that she was merely giving information *e* to those in the services who were already disaffected, was an insult to the intelligence of the jury who were trying her. Nevertheless, as a result of the Director of Public Prosecution's decision, she may have thought that she could continue, with immunity, doing what she had done. I want to say in the clearest possible terms in this case, that her conduct was unlawful. Had there not been the complication arising from the Director of Public Prosecutions' decision, this court would have had no hesitation *f* whatsoever in saying that every day of that 18 months' prison sentence was deserved. If anybody thinks because of the course we are going to take that light sentences are appropriate in this class of case, they should think otherwise.

It is, however, one of the principles of the administration of justice in this country that not only should justice be done (and justice would have been done to this woman by a long sentence), but it must appear to be done. The appellant may have drawn *g* the inference from the Director of Public Prosecutions' inaction and decision that nothing would happen to her if she went on distributing these leaflets. We have looked carefully to see whether there is any evidence that she was warned that if there was a repetition of her conduct, she could not expect the Director of Public Prosecutions to remain inactive. There was no such warning. It follows, we think, that she has got some grounds for thinking that she has not been treated fairly. *h*

Having said what I have, it remains for me to say that in the interests, not of justice but of the appearance of justice, the appropriate order for this court to make is that the sentence be quashed and a sentence be substituted which will allow for this appellant's immediate release.

Appeal against conviction dismissed. Sentence varied.

Solicitors: *Bowling & Co* (for the appellant); *Director of Public Prosecutions.*   *j*

N P Metcalfe Esq Barrister.

---

1 [1965] 1 All ER 273, [1965] 2 QB 194
2 [1972] 3 All ER 232, [1972] 2 QB 426
3 Criminal Law, The General Part (2nd Edn), 1961

a

O'Moran and others v Director of Public Prosecutions
Whelan and others v Director of Public Prosecutions

b

QUEEN'S BENCH DIVISION

LORD WIDGERY CJ, MELFORD STEVENSON AND WATKINS JJ

11th DECEMBER 1974

c
Public order – Uniforms in connection with political objects – Prohibition – Uniform – Meaning – Single article of clothing – Article worn by each member of group to indicate that they are together and in association – Black beret – Whether single article capable of constituting 'uniform' – Whether necessary that article should cover whole or most of body – Public Order Act 1936, s 1(1).

d
Public order – Uniforms in connection with political objects – Prohibition – Wearing of uniform to signify wearer's association with political organisation or with promotion of political objects – Evidence that uniform signifies association with political organisation – Evidence that uniform used in past to signify such association – Evidence that group assembling together wore uniform to indicate such association – Public Order Act 1936, s 1(1).

e
About 300 people assembled at Hyde Park intending to march to Downing Street and thence to the Embankment. The march had been organised by the 'Provisional Sinn Fein' and certain other groups. The Provisional Sinn Fein was an organisation which had been formed to further the republican cause in Ireland. The march was intended as a protest against internment in Northern Ireland. As the march was beginning to form up the organiser on behalf of the Provisional Sinn Fein distributed banners in the Irish national colours among the crowd. Black berets from a box were
f
also distributed and a number of persons, including the appellants, placed the black berets on their heads. One of the appellants took up position carrying an Irish tricolour flag at the front of the march and a number of other persons, all wearing black berets and carrying flags of the provinces of Ireland, formed up behind him as a colour party. Behind the colour party a number of persons also wearing black berets took up position, carrying banners which bore the caption 'Provisional Sinn
g
Fein'. Banners of other Irish and left wing political movements were also being carried. As the march moved off there were many people wearing black berets in or with the colour party or near the banners of the Provisional Sinn Fein. The appellants were arrested and charged with wearing in a public place a uniform signifying their association with a certain political organisation, called 'Provisional Sinn
h
Fein', contrary to s 1(1)[a] of the Public Order Act 1936. At the trial evidence was given that for about four years the black beret had been worn at such demonstrations and signified association with the Provisional Sinn Fein. The appellants were convicted. On appeal the questions arose whether a black beret was, by itself, capable of constituting a 'uniform', and if so, whether there was sufficient evidence that it signified association with a political organisation.

j
Held – The appeals would be dismissed and the convictions affirmed for the following reasons—

(1) Where a particular article of clothing was worn by each member of a group of individuals to indicate that they were together and in association, that article could

---

a Section 1 (1), so far as material, is set out at p 480 c, post properly be regarded as uniform, within s 1 (1), without any proof that it had been *a* used as such. Subject to the de minimis rule, there was no necessity that the article should cover the whole or the major part of the body. In the alternative it was open to the prosecution to establish that the article of clothing was a uniform by showing that it had been commonly used by members of a political organisation. Accordingly the magistrate was entitled to conclude that the black berets constituted 'uniform', within s 1 (1) (see p 480 *h* to p 481 *b* and p 483 *d* and *f* to *h*, post).   *b*

(2) It was open to the prosecutor to prove that a uniform signified the wearer's association with any political organisation or promotion of a political object in one of two ways: (i) by evidence that the uniform in question had in the past been used as the uniform of a political organisation; for that purpose it was not necessary to specify the particular organisation; it was sufficient to show that it had been associated with a political organisation capable of identification in some manner; alternatively (ii) *c* by evidence that a group of persons assembling together had worn uniform to indicate their association with each other and, furthermore, by their conduct had indicated that the uniform associated them with other activity of a political character. In the circumstances, the issuing of banners carrying political slogans and black berets to persons taking part in the demonstration was ample evidence that the berets were being worn to signify the wearers' association with a political organisation or with the *d* promotion of a political object (see p 481 *c* to *f* and p 483 *e* and *g*, post).

Notes

For wearing political uniforms, see 10 Halsbury's Laws (3rd Edn) 579, 580, para 1077.

For the Public Order Act 1936, s 1, see 8 Halsbury's Statutes (3rd Edn) 327.

e

Cases stated

O'Moran and others v Director of Public Prosecutions

This was an appeal by way of a case stated by William Edward Charles Robins Esq, one of her Majesty's metropolitan stipendiary magistrates, in respect of his adjudication as a magistrate sitting at Old Street Magistrates' Court on 29th July 1974.   *f*

1. (i) On 17th June 1974 informations were laid by the respondent, the Director of Public Prosecutions, against each of the eight appellants, Seamus O'Moran, Egan McCormack, John Lynch, Brian O'Reilly, Michael Hayes, Patrick Currie, Ronald Currie and Patrick Murray, alleging that on 7th June 1974 and again on 8th June 1974 they had committed offences against s 1(1) of the Public Order Act 1936. Her Majesty's Attorney-General consented to the proceedings as required by that section. The *g* summonses issued against each appellant alleged that he in respect of each day, at the public places alleged, 'wore uniform signifying his association with a political organisation or with the promotion of a political object', contrary to s 1(1) of the 1936 Act. (ii) The magistrate heard the evidence on 29th July 1974 and submissions by counsel on both sides, and convicted all the appellants of both offences. He fined each appellant £20 on the first summons with £10 costs and £40 on the second *h* summons.

2. After hearing the evidence the magistrate found the following facts: (1) On Friday 7th June 1974 relatives and friends of Michael Gaughan, a man who had died in prison in the Isle of Wight, conveyed his body to Cricklewood. The hearse containing Gaughan's coffin arrived at Cricklewood in north London at about 7.45 p m. (2) The eight appellants then took up positions in two parallel files of four in front of the hearse. Thereafter they marched in military style, executing a slow march, in front of the hearse *j* from The Crown Hotel, Cricklewood Broadway, to Kilburn railway station. From that point they continued to march in the same style and formation in front of the coffin which was then borne on the shoulders of pall bearers to the Church of the Sacred Heart in Quex Road. During the march the other appellants responded to military commands given by the appellant, Seamus O'Moran, who referred to them

a as 'party' or 'colour party' in giving his commands. (3) Each appellant was dressed in a similar, but not identical, fashion. In particular each man wore a black or very dark blue beret, dark glasses, black roll-necked pullovers and other very dark clothing. (4) After the coffin had been taken into the church, Chief Inspector Wass of the Metropolitan Police took the name of each appellant and warned him that he would be reported for wearing a political uniform. None of the appellants replied

b except the appellant, Patrick Murray, who at first insisted on replying only in Gaelic but ultimately said in English: 'One of my comrades has died.' (5) On Saturday, 8th June 1974, at about 10 a m the eight appellants were seen by Chief Inspector Wass to emerge from a house in Quex Road dressed in the same manner as on the previous day. The chief inspector warned them that in his view they were breaking the law but none of them replied. (6) At 10.40 a m the coffin containing the remains of Michael Gaughan was brought to the front porch of the Church of the Sacred Heart. All the

c appellants stood in front of the coffin in military formation and style while a speaker delivered an oration first in Gaelic and then in English. The speaker made references to the Irish republican movement and described himself as one of the leaders of that movement. After this address an Irish tricolour flag was placed on the coffin and a black beret similar to those worn by the appellants was placed on the flag. (7) At the

d conclusion of the address the appellants marched in the same military style as on the previous day in front of the coffin which was carried to the State Cinema, Kilburn. As on the previous day the appellants responded to military style commands and were accompanied by a piper playing a lament. Their march was again watched by a tense and emotional crowd. The appellants were very solemn, absolutely orderly throughout, completely dignified and did nothing to inflame the emotions of a crowd

e of 5,000 to 6,000. The only adverse reaction was from one man who sounded his motor horn. (8) The magistrate heard and accepted as true the evidence of a police sergeant in the Ceremonial Division at Cannon Row police station named Sergeant Garnham. He said: (i) He had attended many demonstrations concerned with the situation in Northern Ireland in central London. (ii) At those demonstrations he had frequently seen banners with the words 'Sinn Fein', which was an Irish political organisation,

f written on them. He agreed that Sinn Fein was not the same as the 'Irish Republican Army' ('the IRA'). (iii) On many occasions the persons immediately around the banners or carrying them had been wearing black berets. Sometimes orange, white and green armbands were worn with the word 'Provisional' written on them. Sometimes lapel badges and Easter lilies were worn. (iv) On the last two occasions that he had attended such demonstrations he had seen dark glasses worn and predomin-

g antly dark clothing worn with black berets. (v) Whereas there had been a considerable variety of dress worn by demonstrators on the occasions he had witnessed, the common factor, or most favoured piece of dress, had been the black beret. He accepted that on the day previously black berets and dark clothing had been the predominant dress at a demonstration by Greek Cypriots and that black berets were habitually worn by French onion sellers. (vi) The traditional uniform feature of the IRA of

h which he was aware was green berets and could include combat jackets. He had never dealt with the IRA, only Sinn Fein.

3. The appellants called no evidence but counsel on their behalf submitted: (1) that there was not sufficient evidence that the appellants were wearing uniform, there being differences in dress between them; (2) that the political organisation alleged or concerned had not been sufficiently identified in the evidence; (3) that

j the summonses were bad for duplicity in that both the limbs of the subsection were alleged, and the prosecution had not elected whether the 'uniform' signified association with a political organisation or whether it signified association with the promotion of a political object; and (4) that there was no evidence that the dress worn was the uniform of any political organisation, let alone the one specified by the Crown, i e the IRA. The magistrate was told that there had been no decision by any superior court on any of those matters under s 1 of the 1936 Act but he was referred

to journals reporting decisions of magistrates' courts prior to 1939, and to dictionary   a
definitions of the word 'uniform'.

4. Counsel for the respondent submitted: (1) that it was not necessary to show
that the entire outer clothing of each appellant was identical in order to establish
that they were wearing a 'uniform'; the uniform appearance of the appellants justified the conclusion that they had been wearing a uniform; (2) that it was unnecessary
to identify exactly which political organisation was concerned; it was well known   b
that Irish republican organisations had many divisions and 'splinter groups', and it
was sufficient under the section if the prosecution satisfied association with a political
organisation without identifying it further, although conceding that if he needed to
specify it would be the IRA; (3) that there was no duplicity in the summonses; often
a uniform would signify both association with a political organisation and with the
promotion of a political object; if its association with either were proved the offence   c
was committed; in this case there was both association with an Irish republican
political organisation and a demonstration of rejection or contempt for United
Kingdom Authority.

The magistrate was of the opinion: (1) that he had to construe 'uniform' in a
common sense way. It was a question of fact and of degree whether the dress
amounted to a uniform; he concluded that, despite minor differences of apparel,   d
the appellants were wearing a distinctive garb of uniform character which was
intended to be recognised as such and was a 'uniform' within the meaning of the
section; (2) that on the facts found it had been proved that the uniform was intended
to and did signify association with an Irish republican political organisation; he was
particularly impressed by the evidence relating to the placing of the tricolour and of
the black beret on the coffin; the magistrate considered that it was not necessary   e
for the prosecution to identify the political organisation further or to give it an exact
title; he also considered that the uniform signified association with a political object,
namely the rejection or defiance of the government of the United Kingdom; (3) that
the summonses were not bad for duplicity as the essential feature of the offence was
the wearing of uniform in a public place.

The questions for the opinion of the High Court were: (1) Was the dress worn   f
capable of being a uniform and was the common denominator, the black beret, a
uniform within the meaning of s 1(1) of the 1936 Act? (2) Was it necessary under that
subsection for the prosecution to prove exactly which political organisation was
concerned? (3) Were the summonses bad for duplicity? (4) Was the evidence of
Sergeant Garnham relevant to the issue before the magistrate? (5) Did a uniform
appearance justify a conviction under s 1(1) of the 1936 Act?   g

Whelan and others v Director of Public Prosecutions
This was an appeal by way of case stated by Kenneth John Heastey Nichols, one of
Her Majesty's metropolitan stipendiary magistrates, in respect of his adjudication
as a magistrate sitting at Lambeth Magistrates' Court on 19th and 20th November
1974.

On 11th August 1974 each of the appellants, Patrick Whelan, Joseph King, Peter John   h
McCaffrey, Padraig O'Siotcain, William John McGrath, John McCluskey, Thomas
McAhon, Michael Joseph Francis McGrath, Bernard Mulvey, James Mannion, William
Wilson, Georgina Mary Barham, together with two other persons named Margaret
Mary Crowley and James Henry De Vere, were arrested and charged with an offence
contrary to s 1(1) of the Public Order Act 1936. Her Majesty's Attorney-General
consented to the proceedings against each defendant as required by the section. After   j
certain amendments had been permitted, without defence objection, the charge
against each appellant alleged that he or she:

'Did on the 11th day of August 1974 in a public place called Speaker's Corner,
W2, wear a uniform signifying his association with a certain political organisation
called "Provisional Sinn Fein",'

a contrary to s 1 of the 1936 Act.   After hearing the evidence and submissions by counsel on both sides the magistrate convicted all the appellants of the offence but acquitted Margaret Mary Crowley and James Henry De Vere.   In the case of William John McGrath he imposed a sentence of three months' imprisonment suspended for two years and fined him £50 with £15 costs.   In the cases of the remaining 11 appellants he fined each of them £50 with £15 costs and bound over all 12 appel-

b lants in the sum of £150 to be of good behaviour and to keep the peace for the next two years.

After hearing the evidence the magistrate found the following facts: (1) On Sunday, 11th August 1974, shortly before 3 p m, a group of approximately 300 persons had gathered at Speaker's Corner intending to march to Downing Street to hand in a petition and then to the Embankment.   The march was planned by the Political

c Hostages Committee, the Provisional Sinn Fein and other groups as a protest on the anniversary of internment in Northern Ireland.   (2) As the march was beginning to form up the principal organiser on behalf of the Provisional Sinn Fein, known to the police as Brian Highstead, was seen to be distributing banners in the Irish national colours amongst the crowd. A distribution of black berets from a box was also taking place and at the same time a number of persons were seen to be placing black berets

d on their heads.   The appellant William John McGrath removed a brown trilby hat from his head and replaced it with a black beret and took up position carrying an Irish tricolour flag at the front of the march.   A number of other persons then formed up in line behind him carrying the flags of the provinces of Ireland, and together formed a colour party, all of them wearing black berets. Behind the colour party persons also wearing black berets took up position carrying banners which

e bore the captions 'Provisional Sinn Fein' and the names of various branches of that movement.   Banners of other Irish and left wing political movements were also being carried. (3) While the march was forming up a police officer in uniform, Chief Inspector Cooksley, using a loud hailer warned the marchers that the wearing of political uniforms was a criminal offence. He told them that that included the black berets and sun-glasses and asked the marchers to remove their berets, telling

f them that they would be arrested if they did not do so.   The chief inspector made that announcement three times but each announcement was received with hostility and apparent dissent. After the third such announcement Brian Highstead addressed the marchers over his loud hailer and said words to this effect:

'Supporters of the Political Hostages Campaign, we have been warned by the fascist police that anyone wearing the black beret will be arrested before he

g leaves the park. You know what to do. You know what the beret means to the Provisionals.'

That statement was greeted with sounds of assent from the marchers who kept their black berets on. (4) Chief Inspector Cooksley then dropped back some 200 yards and as the march moved forwards towards him there were many persons wearing black berets marching in or with the colour party or near the banners of the Provisional Sinn

h Fein.   Chief Inspector Cooksley then issued a final warning over his loud hailer, instructing the marchers to remove their berets or they would be arrested.   The marchers refused to remove their berets and all the appellants were then arrested, together with Margaret Mary Crowley and James Henry De Vere, and charged with wearing political uniforms. (5) Each of the appellants wore or carried the following items relevant to the charge:

j

Whelan	black beret and flag;
King	black beret;
McCaffrey	black beret and banner;
O'Siotcain	black beret and banner;
W J McGrath	black beret, dark glasses, black pullover, dark blue two piece suit, black shoes and Irish tricolour flag;

McCluskey	black beret and flag;	*a*
McAhon	black beret, dark glasses and 13 Sinn Fein membership cards;	
M J McGrath	black beret, dark glasses, black pullover, IRA badge and a banner;	
Mulvey	black beret;	
Mannion	black beret and banner;	*b*
Wilson	black beret and IRA badge;	
Miss Barham	black beret.	

(6) The magistrate accepted the evidence of Sergeant Garnham as true in respect of the following relevant matters.   (i) Since 1968 as an officer in the Ceremonial Office at Cannon Row he had attended many Irish demonstrations in London.   *c* (ii) The black beret had first started to appear on such demonstrations in 1970 or 1971 and since that time had appeared in increasing numbers and signified association with the Provisional Sinn Fein.   (iii) The black beret was a part of the full uniform of the Provisional Sinn Fein and the dress worn by the appellant William John McGrath was dress which the sergeant recognised as the full uniform.   The sergeant did not recognise the black beret as a full political uniform.   (iv) The names of the   *d* appellants O'Siotcain and William John McGrath had been taken at a demonstration on 9th June 1974 because they had been wearing black berets on that occasion.   They had not been prosecuted over that matter although there would have been no evidential difficulty in doing so.   (7) The magistrate accepted as true the admissions made by the prosecution that: (i) letters had been sent on behalf of the Commissioner of Police to the two appellants O'Siotcain and William John McGrath on 8th August   *e* 1974 informing them that after careful consideration the commissioner had decided to take no action against them in respect of their conduct on 9th June 1974; (ii) the eight men who had been convicted of wearing uniforms at Gaughan's funeral service on 7th and 8th June 1974 had all been wearing a black or very dark blue beret, dark glasses, black roll-necked pullovers and other very dark clothing. (8) Of the appellants three only gave evidence, namely McAhon, Mulvey and Miss Barham; in   *f* relation to them: (1) the magistrate did not believe McAhon's denial that he had been wearing a beret at the time that he was arrested and found that he had been; he accepted that he was one of the organisers of Sinn Fein and that berets were being handed out on behalf of that organisation; (2) the magistrate was prepared to accept Mulvey's evidence that he was not a member of the Sinn Fein but he found, as he himself said, that he had put on the black beret in order to show his sympathy with   *g* the Provisional Sinn Fein, and his association with them; (3) the magistrate did not believe Miss Barham's denial that the officer who had arrested her had asked her to take off the beret and had only arrested her when she said: 'I will not remove my beret'; he found that she also had put on the beret in order to signify her association with the Provisional Sinn Fein.

Counsel on behalf of all the appellants except Mulvey submitted: (i) that 'uniform'   *h* meant in the section the whole or substantially the whole of a person's outer clothing; (ii) that a single item such as a beret could not in ordinary language be described as a uniform; and (iii) that the letters sent by the commissioner on 8th August to two of the appellants showed that a black beret at that time had not been thought by the authorities to amount to a uniform and that it was of vital importance that the criminal law should be clear and certain and not arbitrarily administered.

Counsel for the appellant Mulvey adopted those submissions but also drew the   *j* magistrate's attention to other cases decided under s 1 of the 1936 Act by magistrates. In all of those cases he submitted there had been uniformity in substantially all the outer clothing of the convicted persons.

Counsel for the respondent drew the magistrate's attention to the preamble to the 1936 Act and the purpose of the section and submitted: (i) that whether or not a dress was 'uniform' within the meaning of the section was a question of fact to be decided in all the circumstances of each case; (ii) that the proper test was whether at least one item of clothing had been worn which was of a sufficiently substantial nature as to be clearly visible to onlookers and which was identifiable as being an item of clothing of the same pattern, colour and material as had been adopted by a body of persons to signify association with a political organisation.

b   The magistrate was of the following opinion: (1) that whether or not a particular dress amounted to a uniform was a question of fact to be decided in all the circumstances of the case; (2) that an independent bystander, seeing the approach of a group of marchers wearing identical headgear under the banners of the Provisional Sinn Fein, would conclude that it was their uniform; (3) that in view of all the evidence, particularly that of Sergeant Garnham, the black beret on 11th August 1974 was a c uniform which signified the association of those who wore it with the Provisional Sinn Fein; (4) that he should dismiss the charge against Miss Crowley because he was not satisfied that she had worn a black beret; similarly that he should discharge De Vere because, although he was satisfied that De Vere was wearing a black beret at the march and distributing IRA badges, he accepted De Vere's evidence that he wore a black beret as his usual headdress and had not adopted it for this occasion in d order to signify his association with the Provisional Sinn Fein.

The questions for the opinion of the High Court were: (1) Did the term 'uniform' in s 1(1) of the 1936 Act necessarily imply the whole or the majority of a person's outer clothing? (2) Was the magistrate justified on the facts found in concluding that a single item of dress, namely a beret, did amount to a uniform within the meaning of the section?

e *Michael West* for the appellants in the first appeal.
D Altaras for the appellants in the second appeal.
David Tudor Price for the respondent.

LORD WIDGERY CJ. The court will deal first with the case of O'Moran. This f is an appeal by case stated coming from Mr Robins, one of Her Majesty's Metropolitan Stipendiary Magistrates, in respect of his adjudication when sitting at Old Street Magistrates' Court on 29th July 1974. On that date each of the appellants was convicted of an offence under s 1(1) of the Public Order Act 1936, the information alleging that he wore uniform signifying his association with a political organisation or with the promotion of a political object, contrary to s 1(1) of the 1936 Act.

g   The facts found so far as relevant are these. On the 7th June 1974 relatives and friends of a man called Gaughan, who had died in prison in the Isle of Wight, brought his body to Cricklewood. The hearse containing the body arrived in Cricklewood at about 7.45 p m. The eight appellants took up positions in two parallel files of four in front of the hearse and thereafter they marched in military style, executing a slow march, in front of the hearse from the Crown Hotel, Cricklewood Broadway, to Kilburn railway station. Thereafter they marched in the same formation in front h of the coffin, which was borne on the shoulders of pall bearers, until it reached the Church of the Sacred Heart in Quex Road.

Each of the appellants was dressed in a similar but not identical fashion. Each man wore a black or very dark blue beret, dark glasses, black roll-necked pullover and other very dark clothing. The court was supplied with colour photographs of the j scene which fully bear out that description of the clothing being worn by the men in question.

On the following day, 8th June, at about 10 a m the eight appellants appeared again in Quex Road dressed as on the previous occasion. The chief inspector who saw them warned them that they were breaking the law, but this did not discourage them, and at 10.40 a m a coffin containing the remains of Gaughan was brought to the front porch of the church where due honours were paid to it by the appellants standing in military formation and style while a speaker delivered an oration first in Gaelic and then in English. The speaker made references to the Irish republican movement and described himself as one of the leaders of that movement, and after this address an Irish tricolour flag was placed on the coffin and a black beret similar to those worn by the appellants was placed on the flag. Thereupon the cortege marched off and a tense and emotional group was present to watch.

It is right to say that, although it has no direct bearing on the charge, the eight men behaved with dignity, there was no disorder and they did nothing to inflame the emotions of the group beyond any such reactions as could be generated by what I have described in regard to their actions and dress.

The question arises whether in those circumstances the magistrate acted within the law in finding that the charges were proved. I go back to the section itself which creates the offence, s 1(1):

'Subject as hereinafter provided, any person who in any public place or at any public meeting wears uniform signifying his association with any political organisation or with the promotion of any political object shall be guilty of an offence ...'

There is no difficulty here about the fact that whatever was done by these eight men was in a public place, and we have to consider, I think, word by word the terms of the prohibition, the breach of which gives rise to the alleged offence here.

The section, as will be remembered, refers to a person in a public place wearing uniform. 'Wearing', in my judgment, implies some article of wearing apparel. I agree with the submission made in argument that one would not describe a badge pinned to the lapel as being a uniform worn for present purposes. In the present instance, however, the various items relied on, such as the beret, dark glasses, the pullovers and the other dark clothing, were clearly worn and therefore satisfy the first requirement of the section.

The next requirement is that that which was worn was a uniform, so one has to consider the meaning of that word. It seems to me that in deciding whether a person is wearing a uniform different considerations may apply according to whether he is alone or in company with others. If a man is seen walking down Whitehall wearing the uniform of a policeman or a soldier, it is unnecessary to prove that that is uniform of any sort because it is so universally recognised or known as being the clothing worn by a member of the Metropolitan Police or the Army, as the case may be, that it is described as uniform on that account, and judges can take judicial notice of the fact that it is uniform in that sense.

If a man was seen walking down Whitehall wearing a black beret, that certainly would not be regarded as uniform unless evidence were called to show that that black beret, in conjunction with any other items appropriate to associate it, had been used and was recognised as the uniform of some body.

In other words, the policeman or the soldier is accepted as wearing uniform without more ado, but the isolated man wearing a black beret is not to be regarded as wearing a uniform unless it is proved that the beret in its association has been recognised and is known as the uniform of some particular organisation, proof which would have to be provided by evidence in the usual way.

In this case of course the eight men in question were together. They were not seen in isolation. Where an article such as a beret is used in order to indicate that a group of men are together and in association, it seems to me that that article can be regarded as uniform without any proof that it has been previously used as such. The simple fact that a number of men deliberately adopt an identical article of attire justifies in my judgment the view that that article is uniform if it is adopted in such a way as to show that its adoption is for the purposes of showing association between the men in question. Subject always to the de minimis rule, I see no reason why the article or articles should cover the whole of the body or a major part of the body, as was argued at one point, or indeed should go beyond the existence of the beret by itself.

a   In this case of course the articles did go beyond the beret. They extended to the pullover, the dark glasses and the dark clothing, and I have no doubt at all in my own mind that those men wearing those clothes on that occasion were wearing uniform within the meaning of the Act.

Evidence has been called in this case from a police sergeant to the effect that the black beret was commonly used, or had been frequently used, by members of the *b*   IRA, and I recognise that it is possible to prove that an article constitutes uniform by that means as well. But what I stress, first of all, is that it is not necessary to prove previous use of the article as uniform if it is clear from the activities of the accused on the day in question that they were adopting a similar style of dress in order to show their mutual association one with the other.

The next point, and perhaps the most difficult problem of all, is the requirement *c*   of the section that the uniform so worn shall signify the wearer's association with any political organisation. This can be done in my judgment in two ways. The first I have already referred to. It is open to the prosecution, if they have the evidence and wish to call it, to show that the particular article relied on as uniform has been used in the past as the uniform of a recognised association, and they can by that means, if the evidence is strong enough, and the court accepts it, prove that the black beret, *d*   or whatever it may be, is associated with a particular organisation. In my judgment it is not necessary for them to specify the particular organisation because in many instances the name of the organisation will be unknown or may have been recently changed. But if they can prove that the article in question has been associated with a political organisation capable of identification in some manner, then that would suffice for the purposes of the section.

e   Alternatively, in my judgment the significance of the uniform and its power to show the association of the wearer with a political organisation can be judged from the events to be seen on the occasion when the alleged uniform was worn. In other words it can be judged and proved without necessarily referring to the past history at all because in my judgment if a group of persons assemble together and wear a piece of uniform such as a black beret to indicate their association one with the other, *f*   and furthermore by their conduct indicate that that beret associates them with other activity of a political character, that is enough for the purposes of the section.

Applying that to the instant case, the wearing of the uniforms described shows, first, the association of these men amongst themselves, and then one looks to see what they are doing, and one finds that they are taking an active part in a funeral service associated with a member of the Irish republican movement, and at which *g*   there is delivered an address which can hardly have been otherwise than of a political character. If you look at the picture as presented outside the church in Quex Road that morning, you would find these men in uniform and in a uniform which associated them with the other activities then going on. If one examined what those activities were, it would become abundantly clear that they were activities of an organisation of a political character. Thus the chain of responsibility under the section would be *h*   complete.

This was very largely the way in which the magistrate approached this problem. He gave as his opinion:

> 'That I must construe "uniform" in a commonsense way. It was a question of fact and of degree as to whether the dress amounted to a uniform. Looking at *j*   the photographs, in particular, I concluded that, despite minor differences of apparel, the appellants were wearing a distinctive garb of uniform character which was intended to be recognised as such and was a "uniform" within the meaning of the Section.'

I agree that it was a matter of fact and degree, and I cannot fault the magistrate's approach in that sentence. He goes on to give as his second opinion:

'That on the facts found it had been proved that the uniform was intended to *a*
and did signify association with an Irish Republican Political organisation. I was
particularly impressed by the evidence relating to the placing of the tricolour
and of the black beret upon the coffin. I considered that it was not necessary for
the prosecution to identify the political organisation further or to give it an exact
title. I considered also that the uniform signified association with a political
object, namely the rejection or defiance of the government of the United *b*
Kingdom.'

I have some reservations about the last sentence contained in that passage, but otherwise it seems to me to be a wholly proper approach to the problem.

Turning finally to the questions which are submitted for the opinion of this court,
the first one is:

c

'Was the dress worn capable of being a uniform and was the common
denominator, the black beret, a uniform within the meaning of Section 1(1) of
the Public Order Act of 1936?'

I have already given sufficient reasons for my conclusion that it undoubtedly was.
The second question is:

d

'Is it necessary under this subsection for the prosecution to prove exactly which
political organisation is concerned?'

The answer is No.

We are further asked whether the evidence of Sergeant Garnham, who it will be
remembered spoke of previous use of the black beret as a badge of those sympathetic
to the Irish republican interest, was relevant to the issue before the court. The
answer to that is Yes, because it is permissible, as I have already explained, to prove
the significance of the uniform by reference to its previous employment if the prosecution have evidence to that effect and wish to employ it either alone or in conjunction
with any other evidence.

In my judgment the appeals in the case headed by Seamus O'Moran are all to be *f*
dismissed.

The second case concerned again a number of appellants, each of whom was convicted of an offence under s 1(1) of the Public Order Act 1936, the terms of which
have already been read in connection with the preceding case.

The relevant facts here were that on 11th August 1974, shortly before 3 p m a group
of approximately 300 people had gathered at Speaker's Corner intending to march
through London and eventually to get to the Embankment. The march was planned, *g*
the magistrates find—

'by the Political Hostages Committee, the Provisional Sinn Fein and other
groups as a protest on the anniversary of internment in Northern Ireland.'

The findings of fact go on:

h

'As the march was beginning to form up the principal organiser on behalf of
the Provisional Sinn Fein, known to the police as Brian Highstead, was seen to be
distributing banners in the Irish National colours amongst the crowd. A distribution of black berets from a box was also taking place and at the same time
a number of persons were seen to be placing black berets on their heads.'

When the distribution of black berets and the Irish tricolour flag had taken place *j*
a line was formed of persons carrying flags of the provinces of Ireland, forming a
colour party, all of whom were wearing black berets. Behind the colour party were
other persons wearing black berets and carrying banners which bore the captions,
'Provisional Sinn Fein' and the names of various branches of that movement.

When the police informed the intending marchers through loud hailers that a

a breach of the law was being committed by the wearing of political uniforms, Brian
Highstead, using his own loud hailer and addressing his followers, said:

> 'Supporters of the Political Hostages Campaign, we have been warned by the
> fascist police that anyone wearing the black beret will be arrested before he
> leaves the Park. You know what to do. You know what the beret means to the
> Provisionals.'

b

That statement was greeted with sounds of assent.

The appellants in question in the case which is before the court today were all
wearing black berets. They were all involved in the march in some aspect or another.
Several of them, though not all of them, carried flags or banners of the kind to which
I have referred.

c Faced with the same kind of issue as faced the magistrate in the previous case, the
magistrate in the instant case, Mr Nichols, sitting at Lambeth, formed this opinion:

> '(1) That whether or not a particular dress amounted to a uniform was a
> question of fact to be decided in all the circumstances of the case. (2) An indepen-
> dent bystander, seeing the approach of a group of marchers wearing identical
> headgear under the banners of the Provisional Sinn Fein, would conclude that it
> was their uniform.'

d

I am entirely in agreement with what the magistrate had said there. Whether or
not a particular article of dress is to be described as a uniform must depend on all
the circumstances of the case. For reasons I have already given, I see no difficulty
whatever in saying that a uniform can consist of nothing more than a black beret.
e When one looks at the circumstances of this case, of 300 people forming up to march,
carrying banners with political slogans, and being issued with black berets which
were clearly intended to be worn to show an association between the marchers and
those who carried the banners, it seems to me in those circumstances that there can
be no doubt that an offence under the Act was committed.

Indeed counsel for the appellants in the second appeal did not in this case really
f attempt to argue any point against the conviction except his submission that a beret
by itself was not enough to justify the appellation of uniform for the purposes of this
Act.

As I say, I would reserve the case of de minimis but apart from that I see no reason
why a beret in itself, if worn in order to indicate association with a political body,
should not be a uniform for present purposes. Accordingly in this case also I would
g dismiss all the appeals.

MELFORD STEVENSON J. I agree.

WATKINS J. I agree.

h

Appeals dismissed.

Solicitors: *Cripps, Harries, Willes & Carter,* agents for *Jonas, Grove & Co,* Birmingham
(for the appellants in the first appeal); *Bowling & Co* (for the appellants in the second
appeal); *Director of Public Prosecutions.*

N P Metcalfe Esq Barrister.

Reed International Ltd v Inland Revenue Commissioners

COURT OF APPEAL

MEGAW, STAMP AND ROSKILL LJJ

9th, 10th OCTOBER, 13th NOVEMBER 1974

Stamp duty – Issue of loan capital – Meaning of 'loan capital' – Funded debt – Meaning of 'funded debt' – Characteristics of funded debt – Conversion of short-term debt into long-term debt – Repayment to be financed by creation of sinking fund or appropriation of funds for redemption – Company reducing capital by cancelling shares held by another company – Consideration for cancellation creation of debt in favour of other company – Debt of long duration bearing interest at regular intervals – Whether debt a 'funded debt' – Finance Act 1899, s 8(1)(5).

Stamp duty – Issue of loan capital – Meaning of 'loan capital' – Capital raised which has character of borrowed money – Raising of capital – Company reducing capital by cancelling shares held by other company – Consideration for cancellation creation of debt in favour of other company – Whether creation of debt constituting raising of capital – Finance Act 1899, s 8(1)(5).

A company ('Reed') made an offer to acquire all the ordinary shares of another company ('IPC') which Reed did not already own. At the time of the offer IPC Services Ltd ('IPCS'), a wholly owned subsidiary of IPC, held over 15,000,000 ordinary shares in Reed. In order to prevent a situation arising in which a subsidiary would be holding shares in its holding company, contrary to the provisions of s 27 of the Companies Act 1948, it was proposed, with the consent of IPCS, as a condition of the offer, that IPCS's holding of over 15,000,000 ordinary shares in Reed should be cancelled. That was to be effected by a special resolution reducing Reed's ordinary share capital to the appropriate extent and also by reducing the share premium account by £21,000,000. But in order to protect the creditors of IPC and IPCS that resolution also proposed the creation of indebtedness by Reed in favour of IPCS of over £36,000,000. The debt was to carry interest at 10½ per cent per annum and was not to be discharged so long as any existing preference shares in Reed and any existing debt or liability of Reed remained outstanding. It was common ground that many years would pass before any part of that new debt could be discharged by Reed. In due course all necessary resolutions were passed and orders made giving effect to the proposals for the take-over of IPC. The question then arose whether the creation of the debt by Reed to IPCS constituted an issue of loan capital by Reed, within the meaning of the Finance Act 1899, s 8(1)[a], so as to attract stamp duty. It was contended by the Inland Revenue Commissioners that the debt constituted 'loan capital', within s 8(5)[b] of the 1899 Act, on the grounds (i) that being long term and interest bearing it was a 'funded debt' or (ii) that it was 'capital raised ... which ... has the character of borrowed money'.

Held (Stamp LJ dissenting) – The creation of the debt by Reed was not an issue of loan capital for the following reasons—

(i) A debt was not to be regarded as a funded debt simply because it had some degree of permanence. It was the character of the debt which determined whether or not it was a funded debt. The fact that it arose from a conversion of a short term debt into a long term one, that its repayment was to be financed by the creation of a

---

a Section 8(1) is set out at p 488 *a*, post

b Section 8(5) is set out at p 488 *b* to *d*, post

a sinking fund or by any special appropriation of funds of a particular kind allocated for the purposes of its redemption, were but some of the attributes to be taken into consideration in determining whether the debt had the character of a funded debt. The debt created by Reed in favour of IPCS did not have sufficient of those attributes and accordingly was not a funded debt within s 8(5) of the 1899 Act (see p 493 *c g* and *h*, p 496 *g* and p 497 *c* and *f*, post); *Attorney-General v South Wales Electrical Power*
b *Distribution Co Ltd* [1920] 1 KB 552 explained.

(ii) The operation involving the creation of the debt could not be said to have raised capital, for the capital represented by the shares cancelled had already been raised when those shares were originally subscribed for. It followed that the debt did not represent 'capital raised' which had the character of borrowed money, within s 8(5) (see p 494 *b* and *c* and p 497 *g*, post).

c   Decision of Pennycuick V C [1974] 1 All ER 385 reversed.

Notes
For the duty on loan capital, see 6 Halsbury's Laws (3rd Edn) 488, para 944.
For the Finance Act 1899, s 8, see 32 Halsbury's Statutes (3rd Edn) 206. Section 8 has been repealed by the Finance Act 1973, ss 49(2), 59(2), Sch 22, Part V, with effect from
d 1st January 1973.

Cases referred to in judgments
Attorney-General v South Wales Electrical Power Distribution Co [1920] 1 KB 552, 89 LJKB 145, 122 LT 417, CA; *affg* [1919] 2 KB 636, 121 LT 382, 35 TLR 701, 10 Digest (Repl) 1286, 9089.
e *Canadian Eagle Oil Co Ltd v R, Selection Trust Ltd v Devitt (Inspector of Taxes)* [1945] 2 All ER 499, [1946] AC 119, 27 Tax Cas 205, 114 LJKB 451, 173 LT 234, HL, 28(1) Digest (Reissue) 299, 1026.
Studholme v South Western Gas Board [1954] 1 All ER 462, [1954] 1 WLR 313, 25 Digest (Repl) 516, 3.

f **Cases also cited**
London and India Docks Co v Attorney-General [1909] AC 7, HL.
Attorney-General v Regent's Canal and Dock Co [1904] 1 KB 263, CA.

Appeal
In February 1970 the appellants, Reed International Ltd ('Reed'), sent to the shareholders of International Publishing Corporation Ltd ('IPC') an offer to acquire the
g entire share capital of IPC not already owned by Reed in consideration of the issue of shares and unsecured loan stock in Reed. At the date of the offer 15,168,652 ordinary shares of £1 each in Reed were held by International Publishing Corporation Services Ltd ('IPCS'), a wholly owned subsidiary of IPC. On 26th March 1970 the Reed company passed a special resolution in the following terms:

h   'THAT subject to fulfilment of all the conditions to which the Offer on behalf of this Company dated 27th February, 1970 to acquire Ordinary Shares of International Publishing Corporation Limited (or any revised Offer in that behalf) is subject (except the condition that the reduction of capital and share premium account to be effected by this Resolution shall have taken effect) and subject to IPC Services Limited consenting to the said reduction in accordance with the terms of this Resolution the capital of the Company be reduced from £62,825,609
j   ... to £47,656,957 ... and that the share premium account be reduced from £72,360,514 to £51,124,401 by cancelling the 15,168,652 Ordinary Shares of £1 each beneficially owned by IPC Services Limited and by cancelling £21,236,113 of the share premium account and so that in consideration of such cancellation the Company shall become indebted to IPC Services Limited in the sum of £36,404,765 carrying interest at the rate of 10¼ per cent. per annum calculated

as from 1st April, 1970 payable half-yearly on 31st March and 30th September *a*
in each year provided that so long as there shall remain outstanding any Preference Shares of the Company in issue at the date of the passing of this Resolution
no part of the principal of such indebtedness shall be discharged without the
consent (given in accordance with the provisions of the Articles relating to
modification of class rights) of the holders of each class of such Preference Shares
and that provided that so long as there shall remain outstanding against the Com- *b*
pany any debt or liability which if the date of the passing of this Resolution
were the commencement of a winding up of the Company would be admissible
in proof against the Company no part of the principal of such indebtedness
shall be discharged without the consent of every person entitled to any such
debt or claim for the time being outstanding and that subject to and upon the
aforesaid reduction of capital taking effect the capital of the Company be in- *c*
creased to its present amount of £62,825,609 by the creation of 15,168,652 Un-
classified Shares of £1 each and further increased to £106,884,984 by the
creation of 44,059,375 Ordinary Shares of £1 each with a view to the acquisition
of not less than 90 per cent. of the issued share capital of International Publishing
Corporation Limited.'

At the date of the passing of the resolution there were outstanding four classes of *d*
preference shares of which two were redeemable and two irredeemable. Under the
articles of association of Reed neither class of redeemable preference shares was
bound to be redeemed at any particular date. Debts of Reed at the date of the
passing of the resolution included £10,000,000 secured debenture stock not ultimately
redeemable until the year 1995 and £16,259,882 unsecured loan stock not ultimately
redeemable until the year 2001. The reduction was sanctioned by the court on 27th *e*
April and took effect on 6th May. By an originating summons dated 1st October
1972, to which the Inland Revenue Commissioners were the defendants, Reed sought
the determination, inter alia, of the question whether the liability of Reed to IPCS of
£36,404,765, resulting from the special resolution passed by Reed and sanctioned by
the court, was 'loan capital' within the meaning of s 8 of the Finance Act 1899. On
13th November 1973, Pennycuick V-C[1] held that the liability of Reed to IPCS was a *f*
'funded debt' within s 8(5) of the 1899 Act since it was a capital liability, bore interest
and was of indefinite duration and that the creation of the debt therefore constituted
an issue of 'loan capital', within s 8(1) of the 1899 Act, which attracted liability to
stamp duty. His Lordship rejected a contention that the expression 'funded debt'
was limited to a debt which had been constituted by the operation of funding an
antecedent obligation. Reed appealed against that decision on the ground that the *g*
judge had erred in law in holding that 'funded debt' within s 8(5) did not require any
pre-existing debt or liability. By a respondent's notice the Crown asked that the
decision should be affirmed on the additional ground that Reed's liability to IPCS
was 'capital raised . . . which . . . has the character of borrowed money' within s 8(5)
of the 1899 Act.
                                                                                        h

C N *Beattie* QC and R S *Nock* for Reed.
Leonard Bromley QC and *Peter Gibson* for the Crown.

                                                                    Cur adv vult

13th November. The following judgments were read.
                                                                                        j

ROSKILL LJ read the first judgment at the invitation of Megaw LJ. Early
in 1970 the appellants, whom I shall call 'Reed', made a take-over bid for all the
ordinary shares of International Publishing Corporation, whom I shall call 'IPC',

---

1   [1974] 1 All ER 385, [1974] 2 WLR 679, [1974] STC 1

a which Reed did not already own. Another company, IPC Services Ltd, whom I shall call 'IPCS', was at that time a wholly-owned subsidiary of IPC. IPCS then owned over 15,000,000 ordinary shares in Reed. The terms of Reed's offer are contained in the circular letter dated 27th February 1970, issued by S G Warburg & Co Ltd on behalf of Reed. The offering letter correctly stated that if the offer became unconditional, as it ultimately did, IPCS would become a subsidiary of Reed. It was feared

b that in that event s 27 of the Companies Act 1948, which precludes a subsidiary from holding shares in its parent company, would or might be infringed. Accordingly it was proposed, with the consent of IPCS, as a condition of the offer, that that company's holding of over 15,000,000 ordinary shares in Reed should be cancelled, this being effected by a special resolution reducing Reed's ordinary share capital to the appropriate extent and also by reducing the share premium account by £21,000,000.

c The terms of the proposed special resolution need not be set out in detail in this judgment. But in order to protect the creditors of IPC and IPCS this resolution also proposed the creation of indebtedness by Reed in favour of IPCS of over £36,000,000. This figure was fixed by reference to the market value of these shares based on the middle market quotation of 48s per share on 18th February 1970. This was the date on which the proposed terms were first announced. The debt was to carry

d interest at 10½ per cent per annum. The special resolution further provided, inter alia, that, so long as any existing preference shares in Reed and any existing debt or liability of Reed remained outstanding, no part of this newly created indebtedness should be discharged. This provision was clearly made for the benefit of Reed's preference shareholders and creditors and would involve, as was common ground in the argument before us, the passage of many years before any part of this

e new debt could be discharged by Reed.

  In due course all necessary resolutions were passed and orders made giving effect to the proposals for the take-over which I have outlined. The question then arose whether the creation of this debt constituted an issue of 'loan capital' by Reed so as to attract stamp duty within the meaning of s 8 of the Finance Act 1899, as later amended. Reed's solicitors (Messrs Allen & Overy) advised Reed that it did not

f constitute an issue of loan capital. But having regard to the penalty provisions of sub-s (4) of s 8, on 15th October 1970 Messrs Allen & Overy wrote to the Controller of Stamps inviting his concurrence with their view. On 28th October 1970 the Controller disagreed. He asked for payment of the duty. This request was repeated on 1st December 1970. Messrs Allen & Overy demurred on 2nd December 1970 advancing further arguments. On 15th December 1970 the Controller adhered to

g his view. We were told that in order to avoid serious penalties the stamp duty was paid. On 1st October 1971 the present summons was issued on behalf of Reed to have this difference of opinion resolved by the court. By that summons Reed sought the appropriate declarations against the Inland Revenue Commissioners. The matter came before Pennycuick V-C[1], who on 13th November 1973 determined the matter against Reed. He gave judgment for the commissioners. Reed now appeal

h against that judgment and invite this court to reverse Pennycuick V-C's decision.

  The question for determination can be simply stated: namely, whether the creation of this new indebtedness by Reed in favour of IPCS was an issue by Reed of 'loan capital'. This turns on the application of s 8 of the Finance Act 1899, properly construed, to the agreed facts already outlined. I therefore begin by setting out the provisions of s 8. The most relevant provisions for present purposes are sub-ss (1),

j (2) and (5), and in particular sub-s (5), which contains an exhaustive definition of 'loan capital'. Section 8 has been amended on various occasions since 1899[2], but since those amendments are presently irrelevant (save as to rate of duty) I can take the relevant text of the subsection from the statute in its original form:

---

1 [1974] 1 All ER 385, [1974] 2 WLR 679, [1974] STC 1
2 See Sergeant on Stamp Duties (6th Edn, 1972), p 183

'(1) Where any local authority, corporation, company, or body of persons *a* formed or established in the United Kingdom propose to issue any loan capital, they shall, before the issue thereof, deliver to the Commissioners a statement of the amount proposed to be secured by the issue.

'(2) Subject to the provisions of this section every such statement shall be charged with an ad valorem stamp duty of two shillings and sixpence for every hundred pounds and any fraction of a hundred pounds over any multiple of a *b* hundred pounds of the amount proposed to be secured by the issue, and the amount of the duty shall be a debt due to Her Majesty . . .

'(5) In this section the expression "loan capital" means any debenture stock, county stock, corporation stock, municipal stock, or funded debt, by whatever name known, or any capital raised by any local authority, corporation, company, or body of persons formed or established in the United Kingdom, which is *c* borrowed, or has the character of borrowed money, whether it is in the form of stock or in any other form, but does not include any county council or municipal corporation bills repayable not later than twelve months from their date or any overdraft at the bank or other loan raised for a merely temporary purpose for a period not exceeding twelve months, and the expression "local authority" includes any county council, municipal corporation, district council, *d* dock trustees, harbour trustees, or other local body by whatever name called.'

The punctuation of the phrase 'which is borrowed, . . . money' is taken from the Queen's Printer's copy of the statute.

The contentions of the parties were twofold. It was contended for the Crown, first, that any long-term debt, and particularly any long-term interest-bearing debt, *e* was a 'funded debt' and therefore 'loan capital' within the definition, and it was not an essential prerequisite of a 'funded debt' that it should have been created as part of the operation of converting short-term debt into long-term or permanent debt, as it is sometimes called. It was contended for the Crown, secondly, and in any event, that the creation of this debt was 'capital raised . . . which . . . has the character of borrowed money'. It was not argued for the Crown that it was 'capital raised . . . *f* which is borrowed . . . money'.

It was contended for Reed that this debt was not 'funded debt'. Initially counsel for Reed contended that there could not be a 'funded debt' within the meaning of that phrase in s 8(5) because there was here no conversion of short-term debt into long-term or permanent debt—indeed there had never been any pre-existing debt in any accurate sense of that word which was susceptible of conversion into long-term or *g* permanent debt. Subsequently, however, in reply, counsel for Reed somewhat modified the full breadth of his original submission and accepted that there might be a 'funded debt' within sub-s (5) without there being any conversion operation of the type just mentioned, as, for example, where a debt was created which was to be redeemed through the mechanism of the creation of a sinking fund into which payments specially appropriated for this purpose were to be made for the purpose of *h* redemption. But, even granting this concession, counsel maintained that the debt here in question was not a 'funded debt' because there was neither any conversion operation nor the creation of any sinking fund or of anything akin to a sinking fund. As to the Crown's second contention, counsel for Reed contended that the creation of this debt was not a raising of capital at all and still less was it a raising of capital which had the character of borrowed money. *j*

Pennycuick V-C, as I have already stated, gave judgment for the Crown. He accepted the contention on behalf of the Crown on the first point. He did not find it necessary to deal with the second. In his judgment he said[1]:

---

1   [1974] 1 All ER 385 at 390, [1974] 2 WLR 679 at 684, [1974] STC 1 at 6

a   'A funded debt is simply any debt possessing certain characteristics. Such a debt may be created by the process of funding a pre-existing obligation, but is not necessarily so created; it may come into existence without there being any pre-existing obligation.'

In his judgment he had earlier referred to a number of dictionary definitions of 'fund', both as a noun and as a verb, and of 'funding' as well as of 'funded'[1]. I
b shall consider those definitions hereafter in more detail. It is to be observed that, although the phrase 'funded debt' appears in sub-s (5) as part of the definition of 'loan capital', the phrase itself is nowhere defined in the subsection, thus leaving it open to the courts to determine on the facts of any particular case whether the debt there in question is or is not a 'funded debt'. It is also to be observed that this court is here concerned with the phrase used in a statute enacted in 1899, 75 years
c ago. There have been in the intervening period great changes in the methods and means adopted in the City of London and elsewhere of borrowing money and creating capital. That is a matter of common knowledge. Money markets in general and the new issue market in particular do not stand still. A host of methods of borrowing money exist today which did not exist in 1899, and what might be regarded as a 'funded debt' today might not have been so regarded in 1899, if only because a parti-
d cular type of financial operation was not then known or was not then regularly used. In his judgment Pennycuick V-C said[2]:

'I threw out the suggestion at one point in the argument that this [i e the phrase "funded debt"] might conceivably be a term of art on which expert evidence would be admissible, but neither side was disposed to follow up that
e   suggestion and in fact there is no expert evidence. I do not doubt they were quite right in taking that attitude.'

I greatly hesitate to disagree, but it seems to me that Pennycuick V-C's initial sugges-tion may well have been right and that it would have been useful for the court to have had the benefit of expert evidence as to what type or types of operation are
f today regarded in the City of London as 'funding' and what types of creation of debt are today regarded as the creation of 'funded debt'. However this may be, and I express no final view on this matter, Pennycuick V-C's suggestion, as I have already said, was not accepted, and the court has therefore to construe the crucial two words and then to apply the agreed facts to them unaided by any expert evidence but fortified—if that be the right word—by such help as dictionaries may give. In such
g cases it behoves the court not to trespass outside the strict limits of what can properly be regarded as judicial knowledge.

There is no authority directly in point. There is but one authority which is in-directly relevant though others (as I respectfully think irrelevant) were drawn to our attention, especially on behalf of the Crown. Decisions on the meaning of the word 'funds' in cases arising on wills seem to me to be of no assistance at all and I say no
h more about those cases.

In addition to the Oxford English Dictionary, we were referred to Dr Johnson's Dictionary (1755) and to Webster's Dictionary (1928). I hope it is no disrespect to Dr Johnson's memory to say that his magnum opus with its reference to famous poets and writers of the late 17th and early 18th century is to my mind of no help in construing the language used by the draftsman of a Finance Act enacted in 1899, whilst the definitions in Webster's really add nothing to those in the Oxford English
j Dictionary.

I turn to those definitions, pausing only to observe, first, that the relevant volume was published in 1901 (two years after the relevant statute was enacted) and secondly,

---

1 [1974] 1 All ER at 390, [1974] 2 WLR at 683, 684, [1974] STC at 6
2 [1974] 1 All ER at 389, [1974] 2 WLR at 683, [1974] STC at 5

that the 1972 supplement to that dictionary contains additional entries relating to the   *a*
word 'fund' in its use both as a noun and as a verb.   These additions are, however,
not directly relevant.   The relevant entries in the Oxford English Dictionary in
the volume published in 1901 were drawn to Pennycuick V-C's attention and are
set out in his judgment[1].   I venture to repeat them so far as they are relevant, for
they are of immediate importance.   I take first the relevant meaning of 'fund' as
a noun: 'A stock or sum of money, especially one set apart for a particular purpose'.   *b*
I turn next to the relevant entry regarding the word 'fund' when used as a verb:
'originally to provide a "fund" . . . for the regular payment of the interest on (an
amount of public debt); hence, to convert (a floating debt) into a more or less per
manent debt at a fixed rate of interest'.   The adjective 'funded' is given this first
meaning: 'of a debt or stock; That has been made part of the permanent debt of
the state, with provision for the regular payment of interest at a fixed rate.'   Finally   *c*
I refer to the definition of 'funding'.   This definition is: 'The action of the verb
Fund (sense 1); conversion of a floating debt into a permanent one.'

   Much reliance was placed by the Crown on the definition just quoted of 'fund' as a
noun; and Pennycuick V-C accepted this argument.   There is nothing in that
definition, it was said—and Pennycuick V-C so held—which suggested that it was an
essential part of the meaning of the word as a noun that it incorporated the concept   *d*
of conversion of short-term debt into long-term or permanent debt.   This is, of
course, perfectly correct so far as the relevant dictionary definition goes.   But it
seems to me, with respect, to be a legitimate criticism of this contention that the court
is not here concerned with the word 'fund' used as a noun but with the word 'funded'
as a participial adjective derived from the verb 'to fund', and that in construing the
word 'funded' in the context of 'funded debt' it is not right only to rely on a meaning   *e*
attaching to the noun 'fund' without considering as at least of equal and perhaps
of greater importance the use of the word 'fund' as a verb.

   Pennycuick V-C reached his conclusion as a matter of the construction of the
critical phrase apart from the single relevant authority.   I think, with respect, that this
approach was entirely correct.   That authority is only directly relevant if it compels
or at least suggests a conclusion different from that at which the court would arrive   *f*
as a matter of construction apart from authority.   Nonetheless, since, as will shortly
appear, this court in that case did have regard, in part at least, to what would seem
from internal evidence to have been the same dictionary definition (though the
source is not stated in the judgment of Lord Sterndale MR[2]) it is convenient to consider it next.   The authority is *Attorney-General v South Wales Electrical Power Distribution Co*[3].   The question there was whether the issue under special statutory powers   *g*
of 'deferred warrants' by the defendants in respect of payment of outstanding interest
on their debenture stock was the creation by them of a 'funded debt' and therefore
an issue by them of 'loan capital' within s 8(5).   In passing it is to be observed that
the headnote in both reports[3] is not quite accurate.   Both courts had no difficulty in
rejecting the Crown's claim for duty.   Each learned counsel before us relied on
certain selected passages from the judgments in support of his argument.   It is   *h*
important to realise that these were extempore or all but extempore judgments.
They were dealing with facts far removed from those of the present case, namely
provision for the deferred payment of overdue interest by the issue of deferred
warrants.   They were dealing with no other point.   Language used by the learned
judges concerned must therefore be related to the subject-matter of the case and not
construed as if it were the language of a statute.   The most important passage in   *j*
the judgment of Rowlatt J is[4]:

1   [1974] 1 All ER at 390, [1974] 2 WLR at 683, 684, [1974] STC at 6
2   [1920] 1 KB 552 at 555
3   [1919] 2 KB 636, [1920] 1 KB 552
4   [1919] 2 KB at 641, 642

a   'The contention on behalf of the Crown is that it [that is the issue of the deferred warrants in question] comes within the words "funded debt" in that subsection. It is not easy to give an exhaustive definition of "funded debt". The expression is most often used in connection with national or municipal issues, where a liability for interest or for a short-term floating debt is converted into long-term debt bearing interest. When one is dealing with a transaction of
b   that description it is immaterial to consider whether the original debt which thus becomes "funded" resulted from a liability for interest or from any other liability, nor would one have to consider what was done with the money which was raised in this way. In my opinion a long-term debt is a "funded debt". But when it is sought to apply the term "funded debt" to a transaction of a company like the defendant company, a difficulty arises. I do not think that
c   the origin of the debt is a material consideration, and the fact that the issue owed its existence to a default in the payment of debenture interest would not, in my opinion, prevent the company from converting the debt into a funded debt. But, under this scheme, the debt in question, both principal and interest, is payable out of the revenue of the company, so long as the company is a going concern. I have come to the conclusion that that fact prevents it being a funded
d   debt.'

In the Court of Appeal Lord Sterndale MR said[1]:

'It has been rightly said that there is no definition in law of "funded debt", and I do not intend to attempt to give one which is in any way exhaustive; I merely intend to deal with the expression "funded debt" so far as is necessary
e   for the purpose of this case. I did take the trouble to see what definitions were given for the general public in the best dictionaries and I found this definition of "fund" as a verb: "to provide a fund, hence to convert a floating debt into a more or less permanent debt at a fixed rate of interest." I also found the following definition of "funded": "That which has been made part of the permanent debt of the State with provision for regular payment of interest at a fixed rate."
f   Of course, this definition overlooks the fact that it need not be a debt of the State at all; it may be a debt of a company as well as that of the State. I do not mean to say that those definitions are exhaustive or complete in every respect, but I think they are substantially correct, and at any rate sufficiently substantially correct for the purposes of this case. There must be something of the operation which is mentioned in that definition of the word "funded"; there
g   must be a making of something into a permanent debt with provision for regular payment of interest at a fixed rate, and when once we have arrived at the fact, as in my opinion we have in this case—namely, that this was a mere postponement of the payment of overdue interest on condition of paying interest on that overdue interest, what is called a warrant, which sets out the right to payment at a postponed date with the specified interest—we have arrived at something
h   which does not come within any definition that can be framed of "funded debt." It is not converting a floating debt of any sort into a permanent or long-term debt; it does not in any way, it seems to me, come within that expression.'

Atkin LJ said[2]:

'To my mind a funded debt involves at any rate this conception—namely,
j   the substitution for short obligations of a series of obligations more or less permanent and uniform in character—and it appears to me that this series of postponements for varying short periods coupled with the indefinite attributes

1   [1920] 1 KB at 555, 556
2   [1920] 1 KB at 559

which attach to them, cannot in any sense be said to be the equivalent of funding   *a*
these obligations for the payment of interest.'

Younger LJ said[1]:

'... it appears to me that it would be straining the language of the statute
to an impossible point to suggest that this statutory moratorium, or, if you like,
forbearance to sue for money that had become due, was ... the funding of a   *b*
debt. I entirely agree with the analysis ... which [Lord Sterndale MR] has
given in his judgment.'

Counsel for the Crown naturally placed great reliance on the single sentence in
the judgment of Rowlatt J[2]: 'In my opinion a long term debt is a "funded debt".'
But Pennycuick V-C[3], as I venture to think correctly, said that he derived no help
from that single sentence. Counsel for Reed equally naturally placed much reliance   *c*
on the passage which I have quoted from the judgment of Atkin LJ[4], which in some
respects can be said to be differently based from the judgments of Lord Sterndale MR
and Younger LJ. But none of the learned judges concerned was attempting to
define 'funded debt'. They were dealing with a specific set of facts, and for my part
I suggest that the succinct sentence in Rowlatt J's judgment[2], so much relied on by   *d*
counsel for the Crown, might properly be somewhat expanded by paraphrasing it
as meaning 'For there to be a funded debt, the debt in question must at least be a
long-term debt'. But I do not think that Rowlatt J meant in this part of his judgment
to hold, either that there could not be a 'funded debt' within the subsection unless it
arose from a conversion operation, or that it was enough to constitute a 'funded
debt' within the subsection that the debt in question was a long-term debt. To have   *e*
held either would have been inconsistent with his express disclaimer of giving an
exhaustive definition, a disclaimer in which he was expressly joined by Lord Sterndale
MR.

Whilst, therefore, respect must be paid to this decision, I do not regard it as of
more than marginal assistance in resolving the present dispute and, like Pennycuick
V-C, I venture to doubt whether it supports the conclusion at which he arrived or   *f*
militates against the correctness of that conclusion.

Counsel for the Crown, however, reinforced his argument in this court by certain
references to the phrase 'funded debt' in the Stamp Act 1891, to which the attention
of Pennycuick V-C was not drawn. He pointed out that s 14 of the Finance Act 1899
provided that that Act was to be construed together with the 1891 Act. Counsel
drew our attention to the provision in Sch 1 to the 1891 Act granting a general exemption from all stamp duty in respect of 'transfers of shares in the Government or   *g*
Parliamentary stocks or funds'. He also drew our attention to the use of the phrase
'funded debt' in the definition of 'stock' in s 122 and of 'stock certificate' in s 108, in
the context of 'capital stock or funded debt' in the former section and of the creation
of various kinds of stock or 'funded debt' in the latter, and to the repeated use of the
phrase 'stock or funded debt' in the provision for composition of stamp duty by   *h*
(inter alia) county councils in s 115(1)(3) and (6) and in the first part of Sch 2. He
pointed out that these were clear uses of the phrase 'funded debt' in relation to
county council, corporation and company stocks irrespective of whether such stocks
arose from a conversion or other funding operation. If, he argued, there was no
reason, when construing these provisions in the 1891 Act, for importing the concept
of conversion of an antecedent short-term debt, there was no reason suddenly to   *j*
introduce that conception when construing s 8(5) of the 1899 Act, which, as already
stated, has to be construed together with the 1891 Act.

1   [1920] 1 KB at 561
2   [1919] 2 KB at 642
3   [1974] 1 All ER 385 at 392, [1974] 2 WLR 679 at 686, [1974] STC 1 at 8
4   [1920] 1 KB at 559

a The answer seems to me to lie in the fact that the phrase in s 8(5) has to be construed in its context. That context includes an antithesis between what one might call long-term loan capital and short-term borrowings. All long-term capital such as debenture stock and corporation stock attracts duty. But long-term loan capital does not escape duty merely because it results from a funding operation converting short-term to long-term capital though the exemption for short-term borrowing is

b preserved.

Counsel for the Crown also contended that if a court had to construe the phrase 'secured debt' it would not seek to ascertain the reason why security had been taken from the debtor, nor what the antecedent relationship of the parties had been. It is, he said, the characteristics of the debt which matter, not its antecedents. By parity of reasoning, he contended that in construing the phrase 'funded debt' any antecedent liability

c of the debtor was equally irrelevant. But, with respect, this analogy is not exact. The phrase has to be construed as a whole. In considering whether a particular debt is or is not a 'funded debt', it is the character of the debt which has to be considered. The antecedents of the debt are but one of the matters for consideration in determining that character and, as I have already said, I do not think conversion from short-term to long-term debt is the sole relevant criterion.

d Pennycuick V-C has treated 'funded debt' as synonymous with the creation of any long-term interest-bearing capital obligation. With profound respect, if this view be right it is not easy to see what loan capital would not in any event fall within some other part of the definition in s 8(5) without the necessity for adding the special provision regarding 'funded debt'. The addition of the word 'funded' to 'debt' must add something to the word 'debt' beyond 'long-term', especially having regard

e to the exemption accorded to short-term borrowing. As I have already said, I venture to think it wrong, in construing the word 'funded', to ignore the dictionary meaning of 'fund', whether used as a verb or as a noun, and also the definition of 'funding'. I think the word 'funded' must be construed in its proper context with proper regard to the meanings of the words both 'fund' and 'funding'. Accordingly I have reached the conclusion that, although I cannot agree with the broad submission

f of counsel for Reed that there cannot under any circumstances be a 'funded debt' unless there is some conversion of some antecedent liability by way of debt, I do accept his narrower submission that the creation of this debt was not in any accurate sense of the phrase the creation of a 'funded debt'. It seems to me that this debt created by Reed in favour of IPCS did not have sufficient of the requisite attributes of a 'funded debt' as I think that phrase must be construed. This debt did not

g arise from any conversion operation. Nor was any sinking fund created, nor was repayment of this debt to be financed by the creation of any sinking fund or by any special appropriation of funds of a particular kind allocated for the purposes of its redemption. Like Rowlatt J and like this court in the *South Wales* case[1], I decline to attempt any exhaustive definition of 'funded debt', but I am satisfied that it is not enough that the debt is both long-term and interest-bearing to bring it within that

h phrase. This conclusion is sufficient to resolve the first point in the appellants' favour.

With profound respect, therefore, to Pennycuick V-C and to Stamp LJ, whose judgment I have had the privilege of reading in advance, I feel myself compelled to differ from them on this part of the case.

Some reliance was placed on certain passages in a judgment of Lynskey J in *Studholme v South Western Gas Board*[2]. I do not find it necessary to consider those passages

j for I do not find them of assistance in this case. The actual decision was on other grounds and I would only add that I respectfully question the relevance of the argument founded on s 8(5) of the 1899 Act advanced in that case, for I cannot see how it

1 [1920] 1 KB 552
2 [1954] 1 All ER 462, [1954] 1 WLR 313

can be relevant, in construing a provision for remuneration in a service agreement   *a*
entered into in 1938, to have regard to the provisions of that subsection of a statute
enacted in 1899.
   This appeal must, therefore, be allowed unless the Crown can succeed on the second
point. Was this 'capital raised which . . . has the character of borrowed money'?
Counsel for Reed contended that neither condition was satisfied. Counsel for the
Crown said that the phrase must be construed as a whole. No doubt both parts of   *b*
the phrase have to be construed together. For my part, I cannot see how any capital
was raised by this operation. As Stamp LJ pointed out during the argument, the
capital represented by the shares cancelled had already been raised when those shares
were originally subscribed for. Those shares were cancelled and indebtedness
equivalent to the market value of those shares at the date of cancellation was created
in favour of the shareholders. I am unable to see how this can fairly be said to be a   *c*
raising of capital. Reed was no better off on capital account when the operation
was complete. Their capital had not been increased in any way. I think, therefore,
that the Crown's second argument fails in limine. Further, whatever may be meant
by the phrase 'the character of borrowed money', I am unable to see that the creation
of this indebtedness had in any way that character. A similar argument was advanced
in the *South Wales* case[1], but the judgments on that point do not assist in the solution   *d*
of this part of the present appeal. In my judgment, therefore, the Crown fail to
make good either of their two contentions. In the result, with great respect to
Pennycuick V-C, I would allow this appeal and grant Reed the declarations sought in
the originating summons.

STAMP LJ. That the expression 'a funded debt'—I have purposely added the   *e*
indefinite article 'a' which is not found in s 8 of the Finance Act 1899—read in isolation,
is open to more than one construction, can hardly be doubted. But read by itself
and divorced from its context it would, I think, signify a debt which had pre-existed
as an unfunded debt. A debt which had arisen in the course of trade or other activities and which by agreement between debtor and creditor had been converted into
an obligation to pay, not on demand or at a future date ascertained by reference to   *f*
the terms of the trading contract, but by reference to some agreement beween debtor
and creditor and carrying interest in the meantime, would have one characteristic at
least of 'a funded debt'. Whether it would also require the characteristic that some
fund was designated or was to be set up to service the payment of capital or interest,
I do not find it necessary to consider, because I am persuaded that in the context of
s 8 of the Finance Act 1899 'funded debt' need not have that characteristic.   *g*
   I add, before turning to consider the meaning of the expression 'funded debt',
appearing, without the indefinite article 'a', in s 8(5) of the Finance Act 1899, that
although I was, until a late stage of the submissions made on behalf of the Crown,
disposed to accept the view expressed by Atkin LJ in *Attorney-General v South Wales
Electrical Power Distribution Co*[2] that 'funded debt' involved the conception of a
substitution for short-term obligations of more permanent obligations, I accept the   *h*
submission of counsel for the Crown that as a matter of English the expression
'funded debt' does not of necessity involve that conception. In this regard I find
the analogy of 'secured debt' convincing. The word 'funded', like the word 'secured',
may in the context in which it appears be no more than indicative of the characteristics of the debt and not of its history. Moreover, it is, I think, more easy to construe the
word 'funded' as not importing the conception of substitution or conversion where, as   *j*
here, you find the expression 'funded debt' used without the indefinite article and in
a collocation of terms and language none of which is in the least concerned with, or
can involve the necessity of, that conception.

---

1 [1920] 1 KB 552
2 [1920] 1 KB at 559

a   Here in s 8 the expression 'funded debt' does not appear in isolation. Section 8 is concerned with a proposal to issue 'loan capital', and in my judgment it would be wrong to construe the definition of 'loan capital' without at least bearing in mind that which falls to be defined. Nor is it permissible to construe one of the expressions found in the definition of 'loan capital' without regard to the other expressions used in that definition and the definition as a whole. And in the end it is not necessary to

b   define the words 'funded debt' but to determine whether, applying proper principles of construction, the debt in the instant case, reading s 8 as a whole, falls within that description.

The following considerations appear to me material in considering whether, as Pennycuick V-C held, 'funded debt' is a description of any long-term debt or whether the expression has the more limited meaning the taxpayer would put on it.

c   It is to be noted that the definition of 'loan capital', whatever meaning you attach to the expression 'funded debt', is about as wide a definition of 'loan capital' as you could frame. It embraces any debenture stock, county stock, corporation stock, municipal stock or funded debt, by whatever name known, and it goes on to elaborate that description to cover any capital 'raised . . . which is borrowed or has the character of borrowed money'.

d   Secondly, it is to be noted that the several descriptions appearing in the definition overlap. If a company proposes to issue (I quote the words of sub-s (1)) 'debenture stock' to secure a borrowing, what is proposed to be issued will fall within both limbs of the definition. A company which 'proposes to issue' 'funded debt'—whatever meaning you give to that expression—will, if it is proposing to raise capital to be secured by the issue, likewise fall within both limbs of the subsection. It is

e   to be observed, moreover, and in approaching the construction I attach great importance to this consideration, that, however narrow a meaning you give to the expression 'funded debt', a company which is proposing to raise capital and secure its repayment by an issue of 'funded debt' will fall within the latter part of the definition clause.

Thirdly, it is to be observed that s 112 of the Stamp Act 1891 had imposed a charge of stamp duty on the share capital of limited liability companies, and reading s 8 of

f   the 1899 Act as a whole, I would, subject to any limitation imported by the use of the word 'funded', regard the later section as designed to bring into charge at a lower rate the loan capital, whether secured (see s 8(3)) or unsecured, of such a company and of the other bodies referred to in the later section, subject only to the exclusion of the short-term borrowing referred to at the end of the section and to the relief from duty accorded by sub-s (3) where mortgage stamp duty has been paid.

g   Fourthly, all the categories of loan capital specified in the definition of that term are concerned with capital having the character of borrowed money without any such limitation or qualification as is sought to be attached to the expression 'funded debt' on behalf of the taxpayer. It is not, for example, required of debenture stock or corporation stock that in order to fall within the definition it must either replace a trade or other existing liability in debt or that it should contain terms for the

h   funding of the debt which it constitutes or evidences. I ask the rhetorical question, why in the world the legislature should have required 'other debt' to possess either of these characteristics! A company which proposes to issue 'debenture stock' will fall within the charge whether or not the stock is issued in substitution for a trade or other debt or debts repayable on demand and whether or not the stock is issued on the terms that something in the nature of a 'fund' is set aside or is to be set aside or

j   provided to service the debt secured by the stock. It would be anomalous if the proposal 'to issue loan capital' in the shape of long-term debt not divided into stock was in a different case.

Fifthly, if the taxpayer's construction is correct, a corporation which proposed to issue loan capital with no fund to service it in the form of stock in satisfaction of a liability other than a debt would have been subject to the charge—corporation stock is specifically mentioned in s 8(5)—whereas a corporation which proposed to satisfy the liability by the creation of debt not divided into stock would have escaped it. In the context of the proposal 'to issue loan stock' found in s 8(1) and the collocation of the terms 'debenture stock, corporation stock, municipal stock or funded debt', defining loan capital, the expression 'funded debt' ought not, in my judgment, to receive the restricted meaning which the taxpayer would put on it. It ought not to receive a construction which, if applied to debenture stock, county stock etc, would limit the scope of those descriptions. Nor, having regard to the width of the definition of loan capital in other respects, should it receive a construction which would take some debt otherwise properly described as 'loan capital' outside the ambit of the charge.

I am assisted to my conclusion by the terms of the definition of 'stock' in s 122 of the Stamp Act 1891 which 'includes . . . any share . . . in the capital stock or funded debt of any council, corporation, company or society'. There, 'capital stock' or 'funded debt' are used in the same breath, and I can see no reason to attach to the words 'funded debt' characteristics not found in a debt constituted by an issue of 'stock'. I would in that definition treat the words 'funded debt' as meaning no more nor less than 'debt' similar to and including a debt represented by loan stock but not necessarily divided into stock transferable in the books of the body issuing it. By the effect of s 14 of the Finance Act 1899, that Act is to be construed together with the 1891 Act. And the expression 'funded debt' in s 8 of the later Act, following as it does 'debenture stock, county stock, corporation stock', ought in my judgment to receive a construction which will bring within it stock which, in the words of s 8(1), 'any . . . company or body of persons . . . propose to issue', and as embracing debt not divided into stock.

Of course, one cannot reject the word 'funded' as mere surplusage, but I read it in the context to connote more or less permanent debt and as used to exclude debt arising automatically in the ordinary course of business or other activities, and, perhaps, other miscellaneous debt not having the character of loan capital.

I have anxiously considered whether, consistently with *Attorney-General v South Wales Electrical Power Distribution Co*[1] it is open to this court to come to this conclusion. I have, however, had the advantage of reading, in draft, the judgment Roskill LJ has delivered and I agree with the opinion he expresses regarding that case.

Taking the same view as Pennycuick V-C, it is not necessary for me to express a view upon the Crown's alternative argument based on the second limb of s 8(5).

I would dismiss the appeal.

MEGAW LJ. I have reached the same conclusions as Roskill LJ, substantially for the same reasons. It is not in dispute that there is here a debt. The question is whether it is a 'funded debt' within the meaning properly to be given to those words in their context at the time when they were used by Parliament in the Finance Act 1899. The relevant provision is a taxing provision. On authority (see, for example, *Canadian Eagle Oil Co Ltd v R* per Viscount Simon LC[2]) the burden rests on the Crown, if they are to succeed, to show, looking fairly at the language used, without anything to be read in or implied, that the debt here in question was a 'funded debt'.

In order to determine whether a debt is a 'funded debt' within the Act, it is necessary to consider what is the characteristic, or what are the characteristics, introduced by the addition of the adjective 'funded' to the noun 'debt'. No one has suggested that 'funded' is to be ignored as being surplus verbiage, adding nothing. If it did not add some additional quality or characteristic, a debt would always be a funded debt: which is absurd.

The submission of counsel for the Crown before us was that the characteristic, and the only characteristic, of a funded debt, as distinguished from a debt simpliciter, *a*   is that 'the debt must have some degree of permanence'. At another stage the characteristic was expressed as being 'long-term', so that a 'funded debt' would mean 'a long-term debt'. The debt must also, counsel submitted, be 'of a capital nature, not of a revenue or an income nature'. But that quality or characteristic, he said, does not stem from the presence of the adjective 'funded'; it stems from the fact that the definition is a definition of 'loan capital'. So we can forget that, when we

b   consider the limitation introduced by the word 'funded'. Further, counsel expressly disclaimed the submission that interest-bearing was a necessary characteristic of a funded debt. He went on to say that where, as here, the debt is interest-bearing, that is a sign of its being a funded debt. However, I do not think that for present purposes we are concerned with signs which are not essential characteristics.

So the question is whether, within the meaning of the 1899 Act, a debt is to be

c   regarded as a funded debt simply because it has some degree of permanence. With great respect to those who think differently, I find myself unable to accept that this is so, or was so when that Act was passed in 1899. Why, etymologically or for any other reason, should the word 'funded' mean only 'having some degree of permanence' or 'long-term'? If that was Parliament's intention, why did it not use such a phrase as long-term? Moreover, why, on that basis, say 'funded' at all, when

d   the concluding words of the relevant subsection are specifically directed to excluding short-term debts?

I would, with great respect to those who think otherwise, accept the view expressed by Atkin LJ, already quoted by Roskill LJ, in *Attorney-General v South Wales Electrical Power Distribution Co Ltd*[1]:

e
> 'To my mind a funded debt involves at any rate this conception—namely, the substitution for short obligations of a series of obligations more or less permanent and uniform in character . . .'

The debt with which we are concerned is not within that conception. Therefore, in my opinion, it is not a funded debt within the statute.

While the strict ratio decidendi of the decision of this court in the case cited may

f   well be narrower, I think that each of the judgments therein is inconsistent with the view that a debt is a funded debt merely because it possesses the characteristic of a degree of permanence, or is 'long-term'. Something more is required. It is for the Crown to show what the 'something' is, and to show that this debt possesses it. They have not done so.

On the other submissions on behalf of the Crown, as to 'capital raised . . . which . . .

g   has the character of borrowed money', I agree entirely with the view expressed by Roskill LJ.

I would allow the appeal.

Appeal allowed. Leave to appeal to House of Lords granted.

h   Solicitors: *Allen & Overy* (for Reed); *Solicitor of Inland Revenue.*

Rengan Krishnan Esq   Barrister.

---

1   [1920] 1 KB at 559

a

Pexton (Inspector of Taxes) v Bell and another

CHANCERY DIVISION
WALTON J
28th NOVEMBER 1974

b

Capital gains tax – Settlement – Settled property – Termination of life interest – Deemed disposal of assets forming part of settled property – Life interest in part of settled property – Part in which life interest subsists to be treated as being property under a separate settlement – Part – Meaning – Life interest in share of settled fund – Assets forming fund not appropriated by trustees to separate shares – Death of person having life interest in one-quarter share in fund – Whether deemed disposal of all the assets forming fund or only one-quarter thereof – Finance Act 1965, s 25(4)(12).

c

The testator had four daughters. Under a settlement contained in his will, they were each entitled to a life interest in one-quarter share of the trust fund which consisted mainly of stocks and shares. One of the daughters died. At the time of *d* her death, the trustees of the will had not separated out the daughters' shares, and so there was a single fund applicable to those shares. The Crown claimed that since there had been no appropriation of the deceased daughter's share of the fund, she could not be said to have a life interest in only part of the fund, within s 25(12)[a] of the Finance Act 1965, but had an interest in each and every asset thereof and that, accordingly, capital gains tax was assessable on the basis that, on her death, all the *e* assets forming the trust were, under s 25(4) of the 1965 Act, deemed to have been disposed of and reacquired by the trustees for a consideration equal to their market value.

Held – The daughter's life interest in one-quarter share of the trust fund was a life interest in only 'part' of the trust fund, within s 25(12), for the word 'part' in that *f* subsection meant a fraction and not a part which had been separated out from the rest of the fund. Accordingly capital gains tax was to be assessed on the basis that, by virtue of s 25(12), there had been a disposal of only one-quarter of the securities forming the fund (see p 503 *e g* and *j* and p 504 *c*, post).

Notes

g

For capital gains tax in relation to life interests in part of settled property, see Supplement to 30 Halsbury's Laws (3rd Edn) para 3062.

For the Finance Act 1965, s 25, see 34 Halsbury's Statutes (3rd Edn) 884.

Cases cited

h

Fraser v Murdoch (1880) 6 App Cas 855, HL.
Kidson (Inspector of Taxes) v Macdonald [1974] 1 All ER 849, [1974] 2 WLR 566, [1974] STC 54.
Marshall, Re, Marshall v Marshall [1914] 1 Ch 192.
Skinner v Attorney-General [1939] 3 All ER 787, [1940] AC 350, HL.

j

Case stated

1. At a meeting of the Commissioners for the Special Purposes of the Income Tax Acts held on 5th June 1973, William Harbutt Chatterton Bell and Bernard Colbourne

---

a Section 25, so far as material, is set out at p 502 *f g* and *h*, post

a ('the trustees'), as trustees of James Colbourne Will Trust, appealed against an assessment to capital gains tax for the year 1968-69 in the sum of £10,000.

2. Shortly stated the question for decision was whether on the death of a person who was entitled under a will to a life interest in a one-fourth share of a settled fund (no appropriation of investments within that fund having been made) the trustees of the will were deemed under s 25(4) of the Finance Act 1965 to have disposed of the *b* whole of the settled fund or, by virtue of s 25(12) of the 1965 Act of only a one-fourth share thereof.

[Paragraph 3 listed the documents which were admitted before the commissioners.]

4. The following facts were admitted between the parties. (a) James Colbourne died on 1st April 1929. (b) By his will he created a settlement in favour of his nine children. The residuary estate was left to trustees and they were directed to hold *c* the net proceeds thereof in trust for such of his sons as attained the age of 25 and for such of his daughters as attained the age of 21 or married. The share of each of the daughters was directed to be retained by the trustees who were to hold each such share separately in trust to invest it and to pay the daughter the income of it for life. The first codicil to the will provided that one son of the testator, Linser, was not to have an absolute share in the estate but a settled share. (c) The will contained *d* the following provisions:

'I DIRECT my Trustees to stand possessed of my Trust Property UPON TRUST for all or such one or more of my nine children now living as shall survive me and being sons have attained or shall live to attain the age of twenty five years or being daughters have attained or shall live to attain the age of twenty one *e* years or be married. NEVERTHELESS I DIRECT that in case any son of mine shall die in my lifetime leaving issue who shall be living at my decease the share to which such son so dying would if living at my decease have been entitled shall not lapse but shall be held by my Trustees UPON TRUST for the child if only one or for all the children equally as tenants in common if more than one of my same son so dying who being a son or sons shall attain the age of twenty one years or *f* being a daughter or daughters shall attain that age or be married AND I FURTHER DECLARE that in case any daughter of mine shall die in my lifetime leaving issue who shall be living at my decease the share of each such daughter in my Trust Property shall go and devolve according to the Trusts hereinafter contained as if my same daughter had survived me and had died immediately after me NEVERTHELESS as to the share of every daughter of mine in my Trust Property I DIRECT *g* that the same shall not be paid to her but shall be retained by my Trustees UPON THE TRUSTS hereinafter declared concerning the same that is to say:— AS TO THE SHARE of every such daughter separately UPON TRUST to invest the same pursuant to the clause concerning investments hereinafter contained AND UPON FURTHER TRUST to pay the income of such share and the investments thereof for the time being (which are hereinafter referred to as "the portion of *h* my same daughter") to my same daughter without power of anticipation during her life and from and after her decease AS to the capital and future income of the portion of my same daughter UPON TRUST for all or such one or more of the issue of my same daughter including grand-children and more remote issue born in her lifetime for such interests and in such shares and subject to such limitations as my same daughter shall by Will or Codicil appoint And in default of and *j* subject to any such appointment UPON TRUST for her child if only one or for all her children equally as tenants in common if more than one who being a son or sons shall attain the age of twenty one years or being a daughter or daughters shall attain that age or be married But if no object of the preceding trusts shall acquire an absolutely vested interest in the portion of my same daughter then I DIRECT that the portion of my same daughter shall go and devolve to and be held UPON TRUST for the person or persons who at my decease would have

been entitled thereto under the Trusts hereinbefore contained if my same *a*
daughter had died in my lifetime childless.'

(d) The first codicil (which was the only material codicil) had the effect of requiring
weekly payments to be made to the testator's son Linser out of the income of his
share (the balance of its income not so used being accumulated) and of empowering
the trustees to distribute capital to him out of the share at their discretion.   On his *b*
death the capital and accumulations not so distributed were to accrue equally to
the other shares.   (e) The nine children of the testator were Ethel Stiles, Frances
Colbourne, James Colbourne, Horace Colbourne, Gladys Roberts, Linser Colbourne,
Margaret Bridgman, Christine Hudson and Bernard Colbourne.   (*f*) On the death
of Mrs Stiles in 1938 one-eighth of her share in the settlement went to each of the
settled shares of Miss Frances Colbourne, Mrs Roberts, Mrs Bridgman, Mrs Hudson
and the son Linser, and the remainder thereof went to the other surviving sons and *c*
the personal representatives of a deceased son.   Part of Linser's share was transferred
to him in his lifetime in exercise of the trustees' powers.   Of the rest, one-seventh
accrued on his death to each of the settled shares of Miss Frances Colbourne, Mrs
Roberts, Mrs Bridgman and Mrs Hudson, and the other three-sevenths went absolutely to the other sons or their personal representatives.   (g) Mrs Bridgman who
died in 1962 exercised her power of appointment in her will in the following terms: *d*

'IN EXERCISE of the power for this purpose given to me by the Will of my said
late father James Colbourne dated the Twenty-fourth day of November One
thousand nine hundred and twenty-six and proved in the Principal Probate
Registry on the Twenty-seventh day of May One thousand nine hundred and
twenty-nine and of every or any other power enabling me in this behalf I HEREBY *e*
APPOINT that the Trustees or Trustee for the time being of the said Will shall
from and after my death stand possessed of the investments and property
subject to the trusts thereof and over which I have a power of appointment by
Will Upon trust to pay the income thereof to my said daughter Pauline May
Simonds during her life and after her death to hold the capital and income
thereof in trust for the child or children (if any) of my said daughter born in *f*
my lifetime who shall attain the age of twenty-one years and if more than one
in equal shares Provided that if my said daughter shall predecease me leaving a
child or children her surviving who shall attain the age of twenty-one years then
I appoint that the Trustees or Trustee for the time being of the said Will shall
stand possessed of the said investments and property then subject to the trusts
thereof and over which I have such power of appointment as aforesaid as to *g*
both the capital and income thereof for such child or children of my said daughter
and if more than one in equal shares.'

(h) Immediately before Mrs Roberts's death on 24th February 1969 the daughters'
shares were the only funds remaining in settlement, and part of the original trust
fund had been appropriated to them collectively (the daughters' fund).   The sons *h*
or their personal representatives had under the relevant trusts and powers become
absolutely entitled to the remaining part of the original trust fund and the assets
appropriated to this remaining part had been paid or transferred to them.   The
daughters' fund was a single fund not appropriated into shares.   Each daughter's
settled share was a one-fourth share of this fund and the net income from the fund
was divided and paid to Mrs Roberts, Miss Frances Colbourne, Mrs Hudson and *j*
Pauline May Simonds (the daughter of Mrs Bridgman) in equal shares subject to
small deductions arising from expenses attributable to particular shares.   The fund
consisted of stocks and shares quoted on the London Stock Exchange, secured loans
and a building society deposit.   (i) The point at issue in this appeal arose as a result
of the death of Mrs Roberts, and the computations of liability based on the rival
contentions were as follows:

a

A *On basis that trustees' contentions are correct*
  Total gains on securities held on behalf of settled shares of
    four daughters—
      As agreed   £8,245

b

  One fourth representing
    Mrs Gladys Roberts's share   £2,061
  Available relief under ss 24(2) and 25(5) of the Finance
    Act 1965   £4,831

  Assessable gains   £ NIL

c

B *On basis that Inspector of Taxes' contentions are correct*
  Total gains as above   £8,245
  Available relief as above   £4,831

  Assessable gains   £3,414 at 30%

d

                                        £1,024·20

5. It was contended on behalf of the trustees that: (a) on a proper construction of the relevant provisions of the will and codicil of James Colbourne deceased the late Mrs Roberts had a life interest in a fractional part of the property settled under that will; (b) within the meaning of s 25(12) that interest was a life interest in income and there was no right of recourse to, or to the income of, the remainder of the settled property, that is to say, the property so settled other than the fractional part in which Mrs Roberts had a life interest; (c) accordingly for the purposes of s 25(4) the part of the settled property in which Mrs Roberts's life interest had subsisted should while it subsisted be treated as being settled property under a separate settlement; and (d) in accordance with the appropriate computation set out in para 4(i) above the assessment appealed against should be discharged.

6. It was contended on behalf of the Crown that: (a) as no appropriation of the daughters' fund had been made before her death, Mrs Roberts had a life interest in the whole of that fund, that is to say, in each and every asset that formed part thereof; (b) she could not be said to have had a life interest in only part of the daughters' fund within the meaning of s 25(4)(12) as she had an interest in each and every asset thereof; (c) even if she did have a life interest in part of the daughters' fund within the meaning of the said subsections, sub-s (12) could not apply as she had a right of recourse to the income of the remainder thereof; (d) accordingly, on the death of Mrs Roberts all the assets forming part of the daughters' fund were deemed under s 25(4) to have been disposed of and reacquired by the trustees for a consideration equal to their market value; (e) the assessment appealed against should be reduced to £3,414 in accordance with the relevant computation set out in para 4(i) above.

7. The commissioners who heard the appeal preferred the arguments addressed to them on behalf of the trustees. They therefore allowed the appeal and discharged the assessment.

8. The Crown immediately after the determination of the appeal declared their dissatisfaction therewith as being erroneous in point of law and on 4th July 1973 required the commissioners to state a case for the opinion of the High Court pursuant to the Taxes Management Act 1970, s 56.

Peter Gibson for the Crown.
P W E Taylor for the trustees.

WALTON J. This is an appeal by the Crown against a decision of the Special *a* Commissioners in the matter of capital gains tax. The relevant facts are of the simplest. Mrs Roberts had a life interest in one-quarter of the daughters' fund established under her father's will. At the relevant time, just before she died—and she died on 24th February 1969—the income from that fund was divisible between four people, in fact in equal shares, and she was one of them. I think that the testator really had intended all his daughters' shares to be separated out and dealt with *b* separately, because he provided by his will that the shares of every such daughter were to be held separately on various trusts. But, be that as it may, I have to take the matter as I find it, and the matter was that the trustees of his will had not separated out the funds and there was a single fund applicable to the daughters' settled share. It was of that fund, as I say, that she was a life tenant of a quarter share. *c*

The point at issue between the parties is very simple. It is whether, on the death of Mrs Roberts, there is to be a deemed disposal for the purpose of capital gains tax of the whole of the securities forming the daughters' fund or only of one-quarter thereof. Of course, the different solutions produce different amounts of capital gains tax. In the case of the trustees' contention, that in fact it is only one-quarter of the fund that is deemed to be disposed of, it is agreed that there will in fact be no *d* capital gains tax payable. On the other hand, if the Crown's contention that the whole of the fund be deemed to be disposed of is correct, the capital gains tax will be in the sum of £1,024·20.

Now I intend to deal with this on a very narrow basis because I think it can be dealt with on a very narrow basis, although the debate has very properly and very sensibly ranged far and wide. I think it is first of all necessary to say that the capital gains tax *e* legislation applicable is to be found in the Finance Act 1965. There were some amendments to the sections made before Mrs Roberts died, but I do not think they affect anything that I have to decide. 'Settled property' is defined in s 45 of the 1965 Act as, for present purposes, 'any property held in trust other than property' which is held in trust merely in the guise of a nominee. In relation to settled property the governing section is s 25, and it is two subsections of s 25 which give rise to the *f* debate in the present case. The first one is sub-s (4) which provides:

> 'On the termination at any time after 6th April 1965 of a life interest in posses-sion in all or any part of settled property, all the assets forming part of the settled property, except any which at that time cease to be settled property, shall be deemed for the purposes of this Part of this Act at that time to be disposed of and immediately reacquired by the trustee for a consideration equal to their *g* market value.'

That is the subsection which the Crown says applies. Then there is sub-s (12) which provides:

> 'If there is a life interest in a part of the settled property and, where that is a *h* life interest in income, there is no right of recourse to, or to the income of, the remainder of the settled property, the part of the settled property in which the life interest subsists shall while it subsists be treated for the purposes of [various subsections, including sub-s (4)] as being settled property under a separate settlement.'

That is the subsection which the taxpayer says applies, taking the view that the word *j* 'part' therein includes a fraction, in this case one-quarter.

The first point made by counsel for the Crown is that sub-s (12) is a relieving section and that it is therefore for the trustees to show clearly that they fall within it. Counsel for the trustees says that sub-s (12) is not, properly construed, a relieving subsection; it is a subsection which is part of the whole structure of the provisions of s 25. He

a
says that it is not in any sense a relieving subsection; it merely has to be applied in order to see what the effects of the section are. If anything turns on that—and I do not think in fact that anything does—I should have preferred the submissions of the trustees.

It is to be observed that sub-s (12) is a rather oddly drafted subsection in many ways. It starts off, as I have already read, 'If there is a life interest in a part of the settled property and, where that is a life interest in income . . .' I think it is accepted by all

b
parties that that does not really mean precisely what it says. It is not a life interest in income; it is a life interest producing income. Then the subsection goes on, 'there is no right of recourse to, or to the income of, the remainder of the settled property . . .', then various things shall happen. Of course, those words, 'there is no right of recourse to, or to the income of, the remainder of the settled property', would more naturally apply to an annuity, and do not apply to a mere income interest.

c
However, counsel for the trustees and I both thought at the same point of time of a possible explanation which would account for there being these words, which at first sight do not appear very appropriate to a life interest. That explanation is this, that one might very well find a type of provision under which somebody who is entitled to a share in the income of a trust fund might nevertheless be entitled to have that

d
income interest made up to a fixed figure, in the event of it falling below that particular fixed figure, out of the income of the remainder of the settled property, and the possibility of that kind of provision would make it sensible to include those words in sub-s (12).

The real point at issue between the parties is, I think, an extremely narrow one. It is whether the word 'part' in the phrase 'in a part of the settled property' in sub-s

e
(12) includes a fractional share, in this particular case one-quarter, and I really have no hesitation at all in saying that it does. One of the meanings of the word 'part' as given in the Oxford English Dictionary is 'fraction', the full scope of this portion of the definition being: ' A portion, division, section, element, constituent, fraction, fragment, piece.' It appears to me that 'a part' very easily comprises, and in its natural meaning comprises, a fraction.

f
Indeed, I think that that is in a sense self-evident if one goes back to s 25(4). Subsection (4) starts off: 'On the termination at any time after [the relevant date] of a life interest in possession in all or any part of settled property . . .' Now, what was the situation here? The situation here was that Mrs Roberts was certainly not possessed at the time of her death of her life interest in possession in all the settled property. That would be an absurd suggestion. She was entitled to a life interest in possession in part of the settled property; namely, a one-quarter share. So it

g
seems to me that, on the natural meaning of sub-s (4), the charging section, which the Crown certainly say charges her 'part', must include of its very nature a fraction. Therefore, it seems to me that when one gets to sub-s (12), 'part' there also must mean 'fraction'. Really, on that very short ground, I would come to the conclusion that this appeal falls to be dismissed.

h
Counsel for the Crown argued that the word 'part' in s 25(12) meant something different from a fraction or a share; it meant either a completely separated out part or a particular bit; for example, a house or a field, or something of that nature, forming part of the settled property. But I am afraid that, in spite of the valiant effort by counsel for the Crown to maintain to the contrary, I think that his argument really proves too much. It seems to me that if, by 'part', you mean a separated out

j
part, then when you come to apply sub-s (4) the settled property in question is the separated out part, or alternatively the portion of the trust fund which, though not a fraction, is somehow distinct from it, as a field or house. Thus you do not require the provision relating to a part at all—it would become otiose.

Counsel for the Crown sought to counter that by saying that if you had a partial appropriation so that you had a one-quarter share separated out but not the three-quarters separated out, then the situation would be that, if one of the life tenants of

one of the fractions which was not separated out died, one would then have sub-s (4) *a*
applying so as to make the whole of the three-quarters which have not been
separated out deemed to be disposed of for the purpose of capital gains tax. It
seems to me that that is really a very odd use of these two subsections.

It seems to me that that was not what was contemplated at all, and that one is still
in the same dilemma and difficulty, because here the unseparated out three-quarters
would then be the settled property—and not a part of the settled property—because *b*
the life interest would have had no connection with the separated out quarter. So I
do not think counsel for the Crown's counter-attack advances his position at all.

Accordingly it seems to me that the argument of counsel for the Crown proves
too much; if he were correct, as I see it, there would not be any necessity for s 25(12)
at all.

Therefore, on those two short grounds, but especially the first one—namely, that *c*
the word 'part' in my judgment properly includes and was obviously, so far as I can
see having regard to the way in which sub-s (4) was framed, intended to include a
fraction—the case for the trustees appears to me to be established, and the appeal
of the Crown equally, in my view, is doomed to failure.

Appeal dismissed. *d*

Solicitors: *Solicitor of Inland Revenue; Stanleys & Simpson, North*, agents for *Chapman,
Baker & Wilson*, Brighton (for the trustees).

Rengan Krishnan Esq Barrister.

e

American Cyanamid Co v Ethicon Ltd

HOUSE OF LORDS

LORD DIPLOCK, VISCOUNT DILHORNE, LORD CROSS OF CHELSEA, LORD SALMON AND LORD *f*
EDMUND-DAVIES

12th, 14th NOVEMBER 1974, 5th FEBRUARY 1975

*Injunction – Interlocutory – Principle governing grant – Prima facie case – Serious question
to be tried – Unnecessary for applicant to establish prima facie case – Open to court to consider whether on balance of convenience interlocutory relief should be granted provided* *g*
claim not frivolous or vexatious.

*Injunction – Interlocutory – Principle governing grant – Balance of convenience – Matters to
be considered by court in determining whether balance of convenience lies in favour of granting
or refusing relief.*

A company ('Cyanamid') registered a patent in the United Kingdom for the use as *h*
absorbable surgical sutures of filaments made of a particular kind of chain polymer
known as 'a polyhydroxyacetic ester' ('PHAE'). The sutures were of a kind that
disintegrated and were absorbed by the human body once they had served their
purpose. The priority date of the patent was 2nd October 1964. At that date the
absorbable sutures commonly in use were made from catgut. A rival company *j*
('Ethicon') were the main suppliers of catgut sutures in the United Kingdom. Cyanamid introduced their patented product in 1970 and by 1973 had captured some 15
per cent of the United Kingdom market for absorbable surgical sutures. In order
to meet the competition from Cyanamid, Ethicon proposed to introduce their own
artificial suture ('XLG'). The chemical substance of which PHAE was made was a
homopolymer whereas the substance of which XLG was made was a copolymer. In

a March 1973 Cyanamid brought a quia timet action against Ethicon, claiming an injunction to restrain a threatened infringement of their patent by supplying XLG sutures to the surgeons in the United Kingdom, and gave notice of motion for an interlocutory injunction. At the hearing of the motion a large body of conflicting affidavit evidence was advanced by both parties on the issue whether the use of XLG as an absorbable surgical suture would constitute an infringement of Cyanamid's

b patent. The patent judge held that on the available evidence Cyanamid had made out a strong prima facie case against Ethicon and that on a balance of convenience an interlocutory injunction, on an undertaking in damages by Cyanamid, should be granted to maintain the status quo between the parties pending the trial of the action. On appeal, the Court of Appeal reversed that decision on the grounds that on the evidence Cyanamid had not made out a prima facie case of infringement and

c that there was a well established rule of law that a court was precluded from granting an interlocutory injunction or from considering the balance of convenience between the parties unless the evidence adduced at the hearing of the application satisfied the court on the balance of probabilities that, at the trial, the plaintiff would succeed in establishing his right to a permanent injunction. Cyanamid appealed.

d **Held** – The appeal would be allowed and the order of the patent judge restored for the following reasons—

(i) The grant of interlocutory injunctions for infringement of patents was governed by the same principles as those in other actions. There was no rule of law that the court was precluded from considering whether, on a balance of convenience, an interlocutory injunction should be granted unless the plaintiff succeeded in establish-

e ing a prima facie case or a probability that he would be successful at the trial of the action. All that was necessary was that the court should be satisfied that the claim was not frivolous or vexatious, i e that there was a serious question to be tried (see p 508 *j* to p 509 *a*, p 510 *b* to *d* and *f* and p 512 *f* to *j*, post).

(ii) The affidavit evidence showed that there were serious questions to be tried and that it was therefore necessary that the balance of convenience should be considered.

f The factors which the judge had properly taken into account in considering the balance of convenience were that Ethicon, which had a dominant position in the market for absorbable surgical sutures, had not yet put XLG sutures on the market whereas Cyanamid were in the course of establishing a growing market in PHAE sutures in competition with Ethicon's catgut sutures; if Ethicon were allowed to market XLG sutures, Cyanamid, if ultimately successful in proving infringement,

g would have lost its chance of continuing to increase its share in the total market for absorbable sutures. There were no grounds for interfering with the judge's assessment of the balance of convenience or with the discretion that he had exercised in granting the injunction (see p 511 *g* to p 512 *j*, post).

Observations on the matters which are to be considered in determining whether the balance of convenience lies in favour of granting or refusing interlocutory relief

h (see p 510 *f* to p 511 *f*, post).

Notes

For the principles governing the grant of interlocutory injunctions, see 21 Halsbury's Laws (3rd Edn) 364-366, paras 763-766, and for cases on the subject see 28(2) Digest (Reissue) 968-980, 67-161.

j For interlocutory injunctions to restrain infringement of patent, see 29 Halsbury's Laws (3rd Edn) 105, para 216, and for cases on the grounds for granting or refusing interlocutory injunctions, see 26 Digest (Repl) 979-987, 3229-3317.

Cases referred to in opinions

Donmar Productions Ltd v Bart (1964) [1967] 2 All ER 338, [1967] 1 WLR 740, Digest (Cont Vol C) 174, 731a.

Harman Pictures NV v Osborne [1967] 2 All ER 324, [1967] 1 WLR 723, Digest (Cont   *a*
Vol C) 174, 731*b*.
Hubbard v Vosper [1972] 1 All ER 1023, [1972] 2 QB 84, [1972] 2 WLR 389, CA.
Jones v Pacaya Rubber and Produce Co Ltd [1911] 1 KB 455, 80 LJKB 155, 104 LT 446,
18 Mans 139, CA, 28(2) Digest (Reissue) 982, 172.
Preston v Luck (1884) 27 Ch D 497, 33 WR 317, CA, 28(2) Digest (Reissue) 1061, 781.
Smith v Grigg Ltd [1924] 1 KB 655, 83 LJKB 237, 130 LT 697, 41 RPC 149, CA, 46 Digest   *b*
(Repl) 199, 1324.
Wakefield v Duke of Buccleuch (1865) 12 LT 628, 6 New Rep 288, 11 Jur NS 523; *subse-
quent proceedings* (1866) 36 LJCh 179, (1870) LR 4 HL 377, HL, 28(2) Digest (Reissue)
1134, 1335.

Appeal   *c*
This was an appeal by American Cyanamid Co ('Cyanamid') against an order of the
Court of Appeal (Russell, Stephenson LJJ and Foster J), dated 5th February 1974,
allowing an appeal against an order of Graham J, dated 30th July 1973, whereby
Cyanamid were granted an interlocutory injunction against the respondents, Ethicon
Ltd ('Ethicon'), restraining them from infringing Cyanamid's letters patent 1,043,518.
The facts are set out in the opinion of Lord Diplock.   *d*

Andrew J Bateson QC and *David Young* for Cyanamid.
Stephen Gratwick QC and *G D Paterson* for Ethicon.

Their Lordships took time for consideration.

5th February. The following opinions were delivered.   *e*

LORD DIPLOCK. My Lords, this interlocutory appeal concerns a patent for
the use as absorbable surgical sutures of filaments made of a particular kind of chain
polymer known as 'a polyhydroxyacetic ester' ('PHAE'). These are sutures of a kind
that disintegrate and are absorbed by the human body once they have served their   *f*
purpose. The appellants ('Cyanamid'), an American company, are the registered
proprietors of the patent. Its priority date in the United Kingdom is 2nd October
1964. At that date the absorbable sutures in use were of natural origin. They were
made from animal tissues popularly known as catgut. The respondents ('Ethicon'),
a subsidiary of another American company, were the dominant suppliers of catgut
sutures in the United Kingdom market.   *g*
     Cyanamid introduced their patented product in 1970. The chemical substance of
which it is made is a homopolymer, i e all the units in the chain, except the first and
the last ('the end stabilisers'), consist of glycolide radicals. Glycolide is the radical
of glycolic acid, which is another name for hydroxyacetic acid. By 1973 this product
had succeeded in capturing some 15 per cent of the United Kingdom market for
absorbable surgical sutures. Faced with this competition to catgut, Ethicon who   *h*
supplied 80 per cent of the market were proposing to introduce their own artificial
suture ('XLG'). The chemical substance of which it is made is not a homopolymer
but a copolymer, i e although 90 per cent by weight of the units in the chain consist
of glycolide radicals, the remaining ten per cent are lactide radicals which are
similar in chemical properties to glycolide radicals but not identical in chemical
composition.   *j*
     Cyanamid contend that XLG infringes their patent, of which the principal claim is
'A sterile article for the surgical repair or replacement of living tissue, the article
being readily absorbable by living tissue and being formed from a polyhydroxyacetic
ester'. As is disclosed in the body of the patent, neither the substance PHAE nor the
method of making it into filaments was new at the priority date. Processes for manufacturing filaments from PHAE had been the subject of two earlier United States

a patents in 1953 (Lowe) and 1954 (Higgins). The invention claimed by Cyanamid thus consisted of the discovery of a new use for a known substance.

On 5th March 1973 Cyanamid started a quia timet action against Ethicon for an injunction to restrain the threatened infringement of their patent by supplying sutures made of XLG to surgeons in the United Kingdom. On the same day they gave notice of motion for an interlocutory injunction. Voluminous affidavits and exhibits were
b filed on behalf of each party. The hearing of the motion before Graham J lasted three days. On 30th July 1973 he granted an interlocutory injunction on the usual undertaking in damages by Cyanamid.

Ethicon appealed to the Court of Appeal. The hearing there took eight days. On 5th February 1974 the Court of Appeal gave judgment. They allowed the appeal and discharged the judge's order. Leave to appeal from that decision was granted
c by your Lordships' House. It was estimated that the hearing in this House of the appeal at which leave to adduce more affidavit evidence was to be sought would last 12 days.

The question whether the use of XLG as an absorbable surgical suture is an infringement of Cyanamid's patent depends on the meaning to be given to the three words 'a polyhydroxyacetic ester' in the principal claim. Cyanamid's contention is that at
d the date of publication of the patent those words were used as a term of art in the chemistry of polymerisation not only in the narrower meaning of a homopolymer of which the units in the chain, apart from the end stabilisers, consisted solely of glycolide radicals but also in the broader meaning of a copolymer of which up to 15 per cent of the units in the chain would be lactide radicals; and that what was said in the body of the patent made it clear that in the claim the words were used in this
e wider meaning.

Ethicon's first contention is that the words 'a polyhydroxyacetic ester' in the principal claim bear the narrower meaning only, viz that they are restricted to a homopolymer of which all the units in the chain except the end stabilisers consist of glycolide radicals. In the alternative, as commonly happens where the contest is between a narrower and a wider meaning in a patent specification, they attack the validity of
f the patent, if it bears the wider meaning, on the grounds of inutility, insufficiency, unfair basis and false suggestion. These objections are really the obverse of their argument in favour of the narrower construction. They are all different ways of saying that if the claim is construed widely it includes copolymers which will not have as surgical sutures the characteristics described in the body of the patent. Ethicon also attack the validity of the patent on the ground of obviousness.

g Both Graham J and the Court of Appeal felt constrained by authority to deal with Cyanamid's claim to an interlocutory injunction by considering first whether, on the whole of the affidavit evidence before them, a prima facie case of infringement had been made out. As Russell LJ put it in the concluding paragraph of his reasons for judgment with which the other members of the court agreed—

h 'If there be no prima facie case on the point essential to entitle the plaintiff to complain of the defendant's proposed activities, that is the end of the claim to interlocutory relief.'

'Prima facie case' may in some contexts be an elusive concept, but the sense in which it was being used by Russell LJ is apparent from an earlier passage in his judgment. After a detailed analysis of the more conflicting expert testimony he said:
j
'I am not satisfied on the present evidence that on the proper construction of this specification, addressed as it is to persons skilled in the relevant art or science, the claim extends to sterile surgical sutures produced not only from a homopolymer of glycolide but also from a copolymer of glycolide and up to 15 per cent of lactide. That is to say that I do not consider that a prima facie case of infringement is established.'

In effect what the Court of Appeal was doing was trying the issue of infringement *a*
on the conflicting affidavit evidence as it stood, without the benefit of oral testimony or
cross-examination.   They were saying: 'If we had to give judgment in the action now
without any further evidence we should hold that Cyanamid had not satisfied the
onus of proving that their patent would be infringed by Ethicon's selling sutures
made of XLG.' The Court of Appeal accordingly did not find it necessary to go into
the questions raised by Ethicon as to the validity of the patent or to consider where *b*
the balance of convenience lay.

Graham J had adopted the same approach as the Court of Appeal; but, on the
same evidence he had come to the contrary conclusion on the issue of infringement.
He considered that on the evidence as it stood Cyanamid had made out a 'strong
prima facie case' that their patent would be infringed by Ethicon's selling sutures
made of XLG. He then went on to deal briefly with the attack on the validity of *c*
the patent and came to the conclusion that on the evidence before him none of the
grounds of invalidity advanced by Ethicon was likely to succeed. He therefore felt
entitled to consider the balance of convenience. In his opinion it lay in favour of
maintaining the status quo until the trial of the action. So he granted Cyanamid
an interlocutory injunction restraining Ethicon from infringing the patent until the
trial or further order.   *d*

The grant of an interlocutory injunction is a remedy that is both temporary and
discretionary. It would be most exceptional for your Lordships to give leave to
appeal to this House in a case which turned on where the balance of convenience lay.
In the instant appeal, however, the question of the balance of convenience, although
it had been considered by Graham J and decided in Cyanamid's favour, was never
reached by the Court of Appeal. They considered that there was a rule of practice *e*
so well established as to constitute a rule of law that precluded them from granting
any interim injunction unless on the evidence adduced by both the parties on the
hearing of the application the applicant had satisfied the court that on the balance
of probabilities the acts of the other party sought to be enjoined would, if committed,
violate the applicant's legal rights. In the view of the Court of Appeal the case which
the applicant had to prove before any question of balance of convenience arose was *f*
'prima facie' only in the sense that the conclusion of law reached by the court on
that evidence might need to be modified at some later date in the light of further
evidence either detracting from the probative value of the evidence on which the
court had acted or proving additional facts. It was in order to enable the existence
of any such rule of law to be considered by your Lordships' House that leave to
appeal was granted.   *g*

The instant appeal arises in a patent case. Historically there was undoubtedly a
time when in an action for infringement of a patent that was not already 'well
established', whatever that may have meant, an interlocutory injunction to restrain
infringement would not be granted if counsel for the defendant stated that it was
intended to attack the validity of the patent.

Relics of this reluctance to enforce a monopoly that was challenged, even though *h*
the alleged grounds of invalidity were weak, are to be found in the judgment of
Scrutton LJ as late as 1924 in *Smith v Grigg Ltd*[1], but the elaborate procedure for the
examination of patent specifications by expert examiners before a patent is granted,
the opportunity for opposition at that stage and the provisions for appeal to the
Patent Appeal Tribunal in the person of a patent judge of the High Court, make the
grant of a patent nowadays a good prima facie reason, in the true sense of that term, *j*
for supposing the patent to be valid, and have rendered obsolete the former rule of
practice as respects interlocutory injunctions in infringement actions. In my view the
grant of interlocutory injunctions in actions for infringement of patents is governed

---

1   [1924] 1 KB 655 at 658

a by the same principles as in other actions. I turn to consider what those principles are.
   My Lords, when an application for an interlocutory injunction to restrain a
defendant from doing acts alleged to be in violation of the plaintiff's legal right is
made on contested facts, the decision whether or not to grant an interlocutory
injunction has to be taken at a time when ex hypothesi the existence of the right or
the violation of it, or both, is uncertain and will remain uncertain until final judgment
b is given in the action. It was to mitigate the risk of injustice to the plaintiff during
the period before that uncertainty could be resolved that the practice arose of granting
him relief by way of interlocutory injunction; but since the middle of the 19th century
this has been made subject to his undertaking to pay damages to the defendant for
any loss sustained by reason of the injunction if it should be held at the trial that the
plaintiff had not been entitled to restrain the defendant from doing what he was
c threatening to do. The object of the interlocutory injunction is to protect the plaintiff
against injury by violation of his right for which he could not be adequately compensated in damages recoverable in the action if the uncertainty were resolved in
his favour at the trial; but the plaintiff's need for such protection must be weighed
against the corresponding need of the defendant to be protected against injury
resulting from his having been prevented from exercising his own legal rights for
d which he could not be adequately compensated under the plaintiff's undertaking
in damages if the uncertainty were resolved in the defendant's favour at the trial.
The court must weigh one need against another and determine where 'the balance of
convenience' lies.
   In those cases where the legal rights of the parties depend on facts that are in
dispute between them, the evidence available to the court at the hearing of the
e application for an interlocutory injunction is incomplete. It is given on affidavit
and has not been tested by oral cross-examination. The purpose sought to be achieved
by giving to the court discretion to grant such injunctions would be stultified if the
discretion were clogged by a technical rule forbidding its exercise if on that incomplete
untested evidence the court evaluated the chances of the plaintiff's ultimate success
in the action at 50 per cent or less, but permitting its exercise if the court evaluated
f his chances at more than 50 per cent.
   The notion that it is incumbent on the court to undertake what is in effect a
preliminary trial of the action on evidential material different from that on which
the actual trial will be conducted, is, I think, of comparatively recent origin, though
it can be supported by references in earlier cases to the need to show 'a probability
that the plaintiff is entitled to relief' (Preston v Luck[1] per Cotton LJ) or 'a strong
g prima facie case that the right which he seeks to protect in fact exists' (Smith v Grigg
Ltd[2] per Atkin LJ). These are to be contrasted with expressions in other cases indicating
a much less onerous criterion, such as the need to show that there is 'certainly a case to
be tried' (Jones v Pacaya Rubber and Produce Co Ltd[3] per Buckley LJ) which corresponds
more closely with what judges generally treated as sufficient to justify their considering the balance of convenience on applications for interlocutory injunctions, at any
h rate up to the time when I became a member of your Lordships' House.
   An attempt had been made to reconcile these apparently differing approaches to
the exercise of the discretion by holding that the need to show a probability or a
strong prima facie case applied only to the establishment by the plaintiff of his right,
and that the lesser burden of showing an arguable case to be tried applied to the
alleged violation of that right by the defendant (Donmar Productions Ltd v Bart[4] per
j Ungoed Thomas J, Harman Pictures NV v Osborne[5] per Goff J). The suggested distinction between what the plaintiff must establish as respects his right and what he

1   (1884) 27 Ch D 497 at 506
2   [1924] 1 KB at 659
3   [1911] 1 KB 445 at 457
4   [1967] 2 All ER 338 at 339, [1967] 1 WLR 740 at 742
5   [1967] 2 All ER 324 at 336, [1967] 1 WLR 723 at 738

must show as respects its violation did not long survive. It was rejected by the Court *a* of Appeal in *Hubbard v Vosper*[1]—a case in which the plaintiff's entitlement to copyright was undisputed but an injunction was refused despite the apparent weakness of the suggested defence. The court, however, expressly deprecated any attempt to fetter the discretion of the court by laying down any rules which would have the effect of limiting the flexibility of the remedy as a means of achieving the objects that I have indicated above. Nevertheless this authority was treated by Graham J *b* and the Court of Appeal in the instant appeal as leaving intact the supposed rule that the court is not entitled to take any account of the balance of convenience unless it has first been satisfied that if the case went to trial on no other evidence than is before the court at the hearing of the application the plaintiff would be entitled to judgment for a permanent injunction in the same terms as the interlocutory injunction sought.

Your Lordships should in my view take this opportunity of declaring that there is no such rule. The use of such expressions as 'a probability', 'a prima facie case', or 'a strong prima facie case' in the context of the exercise of a discretionary power to grant an interlocutory injunction leads to confusion as to the object sought to be achieved by this form of temporary relief. The court no doubt must be satisfied that the claim is not frivolous or vexatious; in other words, that there is a serious *d* question to be tried.

It is no part of the court's function at this stage of the litigation to try to resolve conflicts of evidence on affidavit as to facts on which the claims of either party may ultimately depend nor to decide difficult questions of law which call for detailed argument and mature considerations. These are matters to be dealt with at the trial. One of the reasons for the introduction of the practice of requiring an under- *e* taking as to damages on the grant of an interlocutory injunction was that 'it aided the court in doing that which was its great object, viz abstaining from expressing any opinion upon the merits of the case until the hearing' (*Wakefield v Duke of Buccleuch*[2]). So unless the material available to the court at the hearing of the application for an interlocutory injunction fails to disclose that the plaintiff has any real prospect of succeeding in his claim for a permanent injunction at the trial, the court *f* should go on to consider whether the balance of convenience lies in favour of granting or refusing the interlocutory relief that is sought.

As to that, the governing principle is that the court should first consider whether if the plaintiff were to succeed at the trial in establishing his right to a permanent injunction he would be adequately compensated by an award of damages for the loss he would have sustained as a result of the defendant's continuing to do what was *g* sought to be enjoined between the time of the application and the time of the trial. If damages in the measure recoverable at common law would be adequate remedy and the defendant would be in a financial position to pay them, no interlocutory injunction should normally be granted, however strong the plaintiff's claim appeared to be at that stage. If, on the other hand, damages would not provide an adequate remedy for the plaintiff in the event of his succeeding at the trial, the court should *h* then consider whether, on the contrary hypothesis that the defendant were to succeed at the trial in establishing his right to do that which was sought to be enjoined, he would be adequately compensated under the plaintiff's undertaking as to damages for the loss he would have sustained by being prevented from doing so between the time of the application and the time of the trial. If damages in the measure recoverable under such an undertaking would be an adequate remedy and the *j* plaintiff would be in a financial position to pay them, there would be no reason this ground to refuse an interlocutory injunction.

---

1   [1972] 1 All ER 1023, [1972] 2 QB 84
2   (1865) 12 LT 628 at 629

a   It is where there is doubt as to the adequacy of the respective remedies in damages available to either party or to both, that the question of balance of convenience arises. It would be unwise to attempt even to list all the various matters which may need to be taken into consideration in deciding where the balance lies, let alone to suggest the relative weight to be attached to them. These will vary from case to case.

Where other factors appear to be evenly balanced it is a counsel of prudence to
b   take such measures as are calculated to preserve the status quo. If the defendant is enjoined temporarily from doing something that he has not done before, the only effect of the interlocutory injunction in the event of his succeeding at the trial is to postpone the date at which he is able to embark on a course of action which he has not previously found it necessary to undertake; whereas to interrupt him in the conduct of an established enterprise would cause much greater inconvenience to him
c   since he would have to start again to establish it in the event of his succeeding at the trial.

Save in the simplest cases, the decision to grant or to refuse an interlocutory injunction will cause to whichever party is unsuccessful on the application some disadvantages which his ultimate success at the trial may show he ought to have been spared and the disadvantages may be such that the recovery of damages to which he would
d   then be entitled either in the action or under the plaintiff's undertaking would not be sufficient to compensate him fully for all of them. The extent to which the disadvantages to each party would be incapable of being compensated in damages in the event of his succeeding at the trial is always a significant factor in assessing where the balance of convenience lies; and if the extent of the uncompensatable disadvantage to each party would not differ widely, it may not be improper to take into
e   account in tipping the balance the relative strength of each party's case as revealed by the affidavit evidence adduced on the hearing of the application. This, however, should be done only where it is apparent on the facts disclosed by evidence as to which there is no credible dispute that the strength of one party's case is disproportionate to that of the other party. The court is not justified in embarking on anything resembling a trial of the action on conflicting affidavits in order to evaluate the
f   strength of either party's case.

I would reiterate that, in addition to those to which I have referred, there may be many other special factors to be taken into consideration in the particular circumstances of individual cases. The instant appeal affords one example of this.

Returning, therefore, to the instant appeal, it cannot be doubted that the affidavit evidence shows that there are serious questions to be tried. Graham J and the Court
g   of Appeal have already tried the question of infringement on such affidavit evidence as was available and have come to contrary conclusions. Graham J has already also tried the question of invalidity on these affidavits and has come to the conclusion that the defendant's grounds of objection to the patent are unlikely to succeed, so it was clearly incumbent on him and on the Court of Appeal to consider the balance of convenience.

h   Graham J did so and came to the conclusion that the balance of convenience lay in favour of his exercising his discretion by granting an interlocutory injunction. As patent judge he has unrivalled experience of pharmaceutical patents and the way in which the pharmaceutical industry is carried on. Lacking in this experience, an appellate court should be hesitant to overrule his exercise of his discretion, unless they are satisfied that he has gone wrong in law.

j   The factors which he took into consideration, and in my view properly, were that Ethicon's sutures XLG were not yet on the market; so they had no business which would be brought to a stop by the injunction; no factories would be closed and no workpeople would be thrown out of work. They held a dominant position in the United Kingdom market for absorbable surgical sutures and adopted an aggressive sales policy. Cyanamid on the other hand were in the course of establishing a growing market in PHAE surgical sutures which competed with the natural catgut sutures

marketed by Ethicon. If Ethicon were entitled also to establish themselves in the
market for PHAE absorbable surgical sutures until the action is tried, which may not a
be for two or three years yet, and possibly thereafter until the case is finally disposed
of on appeal, Cyanamid, even though ultimately successful in proving infringement,
would have lost its chance of continuing to increase its share in the total market in
absorbable surgical sutures which the continuation of an uninterrupted monopoly
of PHAE sutures would have gained for it by the time of the expiry of the patent in b
1980. It is notorious that new pharmaceutical products used exclusively by doctors
or available only on prescription take a long time to become established in the
market, that much of the benefit of the monopoly granted by the patent derives
from the fact that the patented product is given the opportunity of becoming
established and this benefit continues to be reaped after the patent has expired.

In addition there was a special factor to which Graham J attached importance.
This was that, once doctors and patients had got used to Ethicon's product XLG in c
the period prior to the trial, it might well be commercially impracticable for Cyanamid to deprive the public of it by insisting on a permanent injunction at the trial,
owing to the damaging effect which this would have on its goodwill in this specialised
market and thus on the sale of its other pharmaceutical products.

I can see no ground for interfering in the learned judge's assessment of the balance d
of convenience or for interfering with the discretion that he exercised by granting
the injunction. In view of the fact that there are serious questions to be tried on which
the available evidence is incomplete, conflicting and untested, to express an opinion
now as to the prospects of success of either party would only be embarrassing to the
judge who will have eventually to try the case. The likelihood of such embarrassment
provides an additional reason for not adopting the course that both Graham J and
the Court of Appeal thought they were bound to follow, of dealing with the existing e
evidence in detail and giving reasoned assessments of their views as to the relative
strengths of each party's cases.

I would allow the appeal and restore the order of Graham J.

VISCOUNT DILHORNE. My Lords, I have had the advantage of reading the f
speech of my noble and learned friend, Lord Diplock. I agree with it and that this
appeal should be allowed and the order of Graham J restored.

LORD CROSS OF CHELSEA. My Lords, for the reasons given by my noble
and learned friend Lord Diplock in his speech, which I have had the advantage of g
reading in draft, I would allow this appeal.

LORD SALMON. My Lords, I agree with the opinion of my noble and learned
friend Lord Diplock, and for the reasons he gives I would allow the appeal and
restore the order of Graham J. h

LORD EDMUND-DAVIES. My Lords, for the reasons given by my noble and
learned friend, Lord Diplock, I would also allow this appeal.

Appeal allowed.

j

Solicitors: *Allen and Overy* (for Cyanamid); *Lovell, White and King* (for Ethicon).

Gordon H Scott Esq   Barrister.

a

Bassett v Bassett

COURT OF APPEAL, CIVIL DIVISION
MEGAW, ORMROD LJJ AND CUMMING-BRUCE J
6th, 7th NOVEMBER 1974

b *Injunction – Husband and wife – Matrimonial home – Exclusion of spouse from matrimonial home – Divorce proceedings pending – Balance of hardship – Circumstances making it impossible or intolerable for wife to live in same house as husband – Wife looking after child of family – Need to provide home for wife and child – No suitable alternative accommodation for wife and child – Marriage relationship having broken down completely – Hostility between parties – Matrimonial home too small to allow parties to live there separately – No*
c *evidence that husband would have difficulty in finding alternative accommodation – Whether wife entitled to injunction excluding husband from home.*

The parties were married in September 1970 when the husband was 31 and the wife 24. They had one child, born in February 1973. The matrimonial home was a small two roomed flat. The husband had been previously married and had a son.
d In May 1974 he brought his son, then aged 15, to live in the matrimonial home, although there was no bedroom for him. In June the wife left, taking her baby with her. She went to live with her parents in grossly overcrowded conditions. In July she returned to the matrimonial home but finally left on 3rd September. Shortly afterwards she filed a petition for divorce on the ground that the husband had behaved in such a way that she could not reasonably be expected to live with him. The
e husband was proposing to file an answer in the same terms. The wife applied for an order to exclude the husband from the matrimonial home and an injunction against molestation. According to the wife, she had been the victim of at least two serious assaults in December 1973 and July 1974, had been ordered to leave the home on 3rd September and had left because she was frightened of what her husband would do to her if she disobeyed him. She stated that she was afraid to go back.
f The husband denied all the wife's allegations and said that she had no reason to fear him, but he offered no alternative suggestion why she had left to live in such acutely uncomfortable conditions elsewhere. There was no evidence from the husband that he would have any special difficulty in finding suitable accommodation for himself if the order asked for by the wife were to be made. The judge granted the injunction sought. The husband appealed.

g

Held – (i) When dealing with an application to reject a spouse from the matrimonial home, particularly where it was clear that the marriage had already broken down, the court should think essentially in terms of homes, especially for the children, and then consider the balance of hardship likely to be caused by the making of such an order against the hardship likely to be caused by refusing it; the court should be
h careful not to underestimate the difficulties of finding somewhere to live bearing in mind that the break would have to be made in the relatively near future and that property rights as between the spouses were of comparatively minor importance. If the circumstances were such that a workable scheme could be arranged so that the spouses could live together more or less separately in the matrimonial home pending the final determination of their respective interests in it, the situation would
j not be an 'impossible' one, nor would the wife require 'protection'. Where an 'impossible' situation did exist, the sooner it was ended the better. Delay in such cases might be a serious denial of justice and sometimes a grave failure on the part of the court to exercise its protective powers (see p 519 c to e, p 520 h and p 521 c d and h to p 522 c, post).

(ii) The appeal would be dismissed for, on the facts, it could properly be said to

s

be 'impossible' or 'intolerable' that the wife should be required to live in the flat
with the husband in view of the extremely restricted accommodation there and the *a*
relationship between the parties; the alternative accommodation at the wife's
parents' home clearly offered no solution and there was no evidence that the husband
would find it impossible to obtain other accommodation for himself (see p 518 *f g*
and *j* to p 519 *c* and *f* and p 521 *g* to p 522 *c*, post).

Hall v Hall [1971] 1 All ER 762 and Phillips v Phillips [1973] 2 All ER 423 explained.

b

Note
For the grant of injunctions in divorce proceedings, see 12 Halsbury's Laws (3rd Edn)
477, para 1067, and for cases on the subject, see 27(2) Digest (Reissue) 936, 937, 7549-
7565.

Cases referred to in judgments   *c*
Akingbehin v Akingbehin (1964) 108 Sol Jo 520, CA.
Hall v Hall [1971] 1 All ER 762, [1971] 1 WLR 404, CA, 27(1) Digest (Reissue) 299,
2242.
Mamane v Mamane (1974) 4 Fam Law 87, [1974] Bar Library transcript 66A, CA.
Phillips v Phillips [1973] 2 All ER 423, [1973] 1 WLR 615, CA.
Wachtel v Wachtel [1973] 1 All ER 829, [1973] Fam 72, [1973] 2 WLR 366, CA.   *d*

Interlocutory appeal
This was an appeal by the husband, Terence George Bassett, against an order made
by his Honour Judge Phelan in chambers dated 18th October 1974 whereby he
ordered the husband to leave the matrimonial home by 28th October 1974 and
granted an injunction until further order restraining him thereafter from returning *e*
to, entering or attempting to enter or loitering near the premises and also against
assaulting, molesting, threatening or otherwise interfering with the wife, Sylvia
Frances Bassett, or the child of the family, pending divorce proceedings. The facts
are set out in the judgment of Ormrod LJ.

Elizabeth Lawson for the husband.   *f*
Thomas Coningsby and *David Van Hee* for the wife.

ORMROD LJ delivered the first judgment at the invitation of Megaw LJ. This
is an appeal from an order made by his Honour Judge Phelan on 18th October 1974,
whereby he ordered the respondent husband to vacate the matrimonial home at
116 Powerscroft Road, London, E5, on or before 28th October, and went on to grant *g*
an injunction restraining him from returning to, entering or attempting to enter or
loitering near 116 Powerscroft Road and also against assaulting, molesting, threatening
or otherwise interfering with the wife or the child of the family. That order was
stayed by this court by the judge himself in order to give the husband an opportunity to appeal
to this court, which he now does.

In his notice of appeal the husband took the point at first that the judge was wrong *h*
to deal with the matter on affidavit evidence only and without hearing oral evidence.
However, it transpired at an early stage of the hearing of the appeal that in fact no
application had been made to the judge to adjourn the matter to enable cross-
examination to take place, and indeed no notice had been given requesting the attendance of any of the deponents at the hearing for the purpose of cross-examination.
So that point is clearly not open to the husband on this appeal and I say no more *j*
about it except that too much should not be made of it in cases like this. There are
cases where there is a conflict of evidence over a fact or facts which are crucial to the
decision of the case, and in such cases cross-examination may well be essential if
justice is to be done. There are other cases, and this is one of them, in which practically every word of the wife's affidavit is challenged, yet there is sufficient material

which is common ground to enable the court to reach a proper decision. In such
a cases the delay caused by resolving a mass of disputed fact by oral evidence may be
quite unjustified and in itself productive of injustice.

The basic facts of this case can be set out quite briefly. The parties were married
on 19th September 1970. At that time the husband was 31 years of age and the wife
was 24. He had been previously married and that marriage had been dissolved.
They had one child who was born on 21st February 1973. They lived at first, as
b I understand it, with the husband's mother, but they later obtained a small two
roomed flat at the address mentioned in the order, 116 Powerscroft Road. The
two of them went to live there, together with the baby.

The marriage, according to the wife, was extremely unhappy, for a variety of
reasons, all of which the husband disputes. In May 1974 the husband's son by his
first marriage, a boy of 15 years of age, now 16, was brought by the husband to live
c in the flat, although of course there was no bedroom available for him. The reason
for that apparently was that his mother, with whom he had hitherto been living,
was about to get married again and was moving to live in Leicester. The boy
did not want to go with her to Leicester, and so the father took him in. The reason
why the boy did not want to go to Leicester appears quite clearly from the father's
evidence, namely, that the boy's friends, and particularly his girl friend, live in
d London. It was suggested by counsel for the husband at one time that some serious
question about the continuity of his education was the reason for his staying in London
and not going to Leicester, but the father in his affidavit makes nothing of that
point and I rather doubt whether in this case education was comparable in importance
to the convenience of this young man and his girl friend. At any rate, he came to
live in this flat, clearly creating a situation of great overcrowding. Although there
e is no evidence as to this, the coincidence in time is probably significant, because the
wife in fact left for the first time in June. There is a complete conflict of evidence
between husband and wife as to why she left in June; but she left, taking the child
with her, and went to live with her own parents in circumstances of extreme difficulty. She had to share a bedroom with a sister and another woman, sharing a
single bed with her sister and having this 18 month old child in the room with the
f three of them, a condition of such discomfort that it is difficult to avoid the inference
that she must have had strong reasons for leaving home and putting herself, and
of course her family, into such a position. At any rate they must have been reasons
which seemed very strong to her.

There is an issue whether the husband asked her to come back or what happened, but she did return in July and brought the baby back and resumed life in this
g two roomed flat with the husband and his son. There was a quarrel—I think this
is common ground—on 22nd July, at a time when her mother was in hospital, but
they continued to live in the flat until 3rd September when, again in circumstances
which are in issue, the wife left again and left finally. Very shortly after leaving she
filed her petition. It is only necessary to say this about the petition: it is based on
the ground that the husband had behaved in such a way that she could not reasonably
h be expected to continue to live with him. The substance of her allegations is of a
very familiar pattern—a mixture of aggressive behaviour including some acts of
violence by the husband, drinking too much, and constant quarrelling over housekeeping money—in fact a picture, if it is true, of an oppressive husband in a variety
of different ways, a pattern which is familiar to all of us who have had much experience in the Family Division. The wife also took out a summons asking for the relief
j which the learned judge gave her, namely, that she wanted to go back to the matrimonial home with the baby and without the husband. She took out a summons
asking for the injunction which I have mentioned. She swore an affidavit in support
of that application which sets out briefly the history of the marriage, and I need not
refer to it any more because all the matters which to my mind are relevant are
common ground, and I have mentioned them all.

In reply to that the husband filed an affidavit in which he denied seriatim each paragraph of the petition and each allegation made in the wife's affidavit, except the *a* facts, which of course he could not deny, of separation and so on. He offers virtually no explanation for the break-up of this marriage except to say that the wife when she was a girl sustained a severe head injury which, he suggests, may have accounted for her behaviour; and he goes on to say that the final quarrel arose over her taking money of his. Otherwise he produces no explanation at all as to why she should leave and go and live in such acutely uncomfortable conditions elsewhere. He does *b* not say in his affidavit anything about his own difficulties about finding alternative accommodation; nor did his affidavit contain any suggestion whatever that, so far as he is concerned, this marriage is still viable. In fact, in answer to a question from the court, counsel for the husband told us that he was waiting for a legal aid certificate to enable him to file an answer which would contain a cross-prayer for divorce on the ground that the wife had behaved in such a way that he could not reasonably be *c* expected to live with her. It is thus clear that this marriage has totally broken down. The husband made no proposals about the wife and child except by implication that they should come back pending the hearing of this suit, which might be a long time, perhaps a year or so, ahead; and he made no offer of anything except an undertaking not to molest. So it was a very uninviting proposal so far as the wife was concerned. Indeed it is quite plain that his one object was to exclude her from this *d* flat. He does not believe for a moment that she is going to come back while he is there, anyway.

On that state of the evidence, counsel for the husband submitted that the wife had failed to bring herself within what counsel called the 'principles' of *Hall v Hall*[1] and *Phillips v Phillips*[2]. For my part, I doubt whether either of those cases can be said to lay down anything which could be dignified by the term 'principle'. I think *e* they both contain, if I may say so with respect, statements of commonsense. In *Hall v Hall*[3] Lord Denning MR said:

> 'But I would like to say that an order to exclude one spouse or the other from the matrimonial home is a drastic order. It ought not to be made unless it is proved to be impossible for them to live together in the same house. It is *f* difficult to draw the line, as is shown by a case which came before this court in 1964, *Akingbehin v Akingbehin*[4]. There was a difference of opinion in the court. The majority of the court thought that unpleasantness and inconvenience was not a sufficient ground for ordering one spouse out. I agree. Such an order ought not to be made unless the situation is impossible. I would add that it is important as well to have regard to the interests of the children. In the ordinary *g* way, the longer they can be brought up together in one house with their parents, the better for them.'

In regard to the last sentence, it does not appear that Lord Denning MR was visualising a situation such as we have here, where the marriage is about to be dissolved quite shortly. Sachs LJ agreeing, said[5]: *h*

> 'It is, of course, impossible to lay down general rules as to when orders evicting a spouse from the home should be made. It is, however, right on each occasion to remind oneself that the remedy which is being sought is indeed a drastic one. It is equally well to remind oneself, as was stated by Willmer and Russell LJJ in *Akingbehin v Akingbehin*[4] that the essence of the matter for consideration is *j*

1 [1971] 1 All ER 762, [1971] 1 WLR 404
2 [1973] 2 All ER 423, [1973] 1 WLR 615
3 [1971] 1 All ER at 764, [1971] 1 WLR at 406
4 (1964) 108 Sol Jo 520
5 [1971] 1 All ER at 765, [1971] 1 WLR at 407

a normally to determine whether such an order is necessary for the protection of the spouse. (Of course, that does not rule out those occasionally outstanding instances when such an order is necessary in the interests of the children; that can be an independent point.) It is naturally difficult, as regards the interests of a wife, or indeed a husband, to imagine a case where both sides continue to reside under the same roof during the pendency of divorce proceedings, and there is no tension between them. It is equally obvious that that tension may

b be hard on either or both the parties; but that of itself is not normally sufficient to warrant the order.'

Sachs LJ earlier in his judgment commented on an important aspect of this type of case when he referred to what he called 'the indicia of tactical manoeuvres' and I will come back to that later.

c   In *Phillips v Phillips*[1] Edmund Davies LJ, essentially following *Hall v Hall*[2], pointed out[3] that it would be a misunderstanding of *Hall v Hall*[2] to think that it referred only to protection from physical assault, and he adopted the 'impossible' phrase of Lord Denning MR and added some other words of his own to describe the conditions which he felt it would be necessary to establish. Stephenson LJ agreed with that judgment and said[4]:

d   'This case demonstrates to me that there may be cases where the same right of a divorced wife is destroyed in the same way. I am ready to accept for the purposes of this case the more restricted principle that no court ought to make such an order as we are asked to make unless it is proved to be necessary for the protection of the health, physical or mental, of the divorced wife or any child of the marriage living with her. She cannot be allowed to gain sole occupation

e   of the house for which he pays by scraping the bottom of the barrel to find complaints against her husband's past conduct or even its continuation since the decree absolute.'

Those are the two cases to which we were referred, together with another one, *Mamane v Mamane*[5], to which I do not think it is necessary to make special reference.

f   In my judgment, all the adjectives and phrases used in the judgments in those two cases must be read in the context of the facts of the respective cases. To order a spouse to leave the matrimonial home is, of course, a drastic order, in that it is likely to occasion hardship of some degree, varying in gravity from case to case. But it has to be borne in mind, in my judgment, that to refuse to make such an order may have no less drastic results, if the consequence of refusing to make an order is to

g   inflict severe hardship on the unsuccessful spouse. It is also necessary, I think, particularly in these days, to have regard to the state of the marriage relationship. If, as in this case, the relationship has completely broken down—as I have already said, the wife is petitioning on the ground that the husband's behaviour is so unreasonable that she could not reasonably be expected to live with him, and the husband is proposing to file an answer in the same terms—the hardship may be considerably

h   less on the spouse who is required to leave, because sooner or later the question of the occupancy of the matrimonial home will have to be decided and one or other of the spouses will be leaving in any event.

Counsel for the husband admitted in the course of her submissions to us that after the decree nisi in this case there was a strong probability, on the present facts, that the wife would in fact obtain the use of this flat as a house for herself and the child.

j

1 [1973] 2 All ER 423, [1973] 1 WLR 615
2 [1971] 1 All ER 762, [1971] 1 WLR 404
3 [1973] 2 All ER at 426, [1973] 1 WLR at 618
4 [1973] 2 All ER at 428, 429, [1973] 1 WLR at 621
5 (1974) 4 Fam Law 87

So the effects of an order made on this application will still be drastic but they will
only be felt by this husband sooner rather than later.   This does not, of course, mean,   *a*
and I should be very sorry if anything that I say was interpreted to mean, that a wife
can expect to be able to turn the husband out of the matrimonial home merely by
filing a petition and applying to the court. Certainly Sachs LJ's observations on
tactics must always be remembered.   There are cases, well known to us all, in
which an application like this has been made for purely tactical reasons, to put
pressure of one sort or another on the husband; if such is the fact there can be no   *b*
stronger ground for refusing such an application.   It may be that, if the wife's case
simply depends on tensions and unhappiness, which are inevitable when the break-up
of the marriage relationship is in its final stages, again the court may well refuse to
make the order.   Similarly, if there is some prospect that the marriage is not in
fact breaking up; one spouse may feel that there is still some chance of success in
reconciliation, in which case the court will be slow to order the parties to live apart;   *c*
but it should not necessarily refuse to do so even so.

So far as the so-called 'principle' is concerned, the element of protection of a spouse
has always played an important part in the decisions of this court in this class of case.
In my judgment, 'protection' must not be interpreted too narrowly.   It is clear from
Phillips v Phillips[1] that it has never been limited to protection in a physical sense,
that is, from violence or apprehension of violence.   It goes much further.   When the   *d*
court is confronted, as it is in this case, with a wife who has left the home with her
18 month old baby and has gone to stay in grossly overcrowded conditions with her
parents, the court must look for some explanation of that fact.   In this case the wife
says that she is frightened of her husband.   He denies it and says that she has no reason
to fear him.   But, as I have already pointed out, he makes no alternative suggestion
as to why she left.   The case here might, of course, have been wholly different if there   *e*
was some reason to think that perhaps the wife was associating with another man,
or was so immature that she would run back to her mother at the slightest provocation.   But in the absence of some such explanation, it is difficult to believe that any
woman would put herself or her family to the discomfort that this lady has done
without good reason.   If there is good reason, prima facie she needs the protection of
the court—not to save her from physical violence or of direct threat to herself but to   *f*
enable her to have somewhere where she can make a home for her child.

The husband in this case, as I have already mentioned, has not advanced any
evidence to show his own accommodation difficulties, and my conclusion is that,
using the test in *Hall v Hall*[2] and *Phillips v Phillips*[1], it is fair to say that the situation
would be 'impossible' or 'intolerable' for this wife if she were required to return to
live in that flat with her husband and his son.   *g*

Hall v Hall[2], on the facts, was a totally different case, because it was the case of a
professional couple living in a six bedroomed house, the husband being away at his
office most of the day.   Plainly, in the absence of evidence amounting to proof of
'impossible' behaviour by him, no one could come to the conclusion that the situation
of that family was 'intolerable' or 'impossible'.

The *Phillips*[1] situation was quite unusual.   The parties had already been divorced,   *h*
and the real issue was which of them was to be entitled to continue to occupy the
council flat in which they were still living after decree absolute.   It is not a case which
is very applicable to such a situation as this.

As I have said, I think the position is properly described as 'impossible' so far as
this case is concerned, and I am quite satisfied on the facts that the husband here has
adopted a thoroughly hostile attitude towards his wife.   One only has to look at the   *j*
tone of his affidavit in reply to hers and at the fact that he has drawn up what amounts
to an 'order of battle', with supporting witnesses filing a mass of affidavits at this

1   [1973] 2 All ER 423, [1973] 1 WLR 615
2   [1971] 1 All ER 762, [1971] 1 WLR 404

early stage. He is also making no proposal about the son, whom he obviously intends
a should remain in the flat. If the wife were to return to this very limited accommodation, the only way that she could keep out of close and regular contact with her
husband and this boy is to keep out of the flat virtually altogether. That conclusion
is totally independent of all the specific allegations by the wife of misbehaviour which
are in issue in the affidavits. Hence nothing is to be gained by determining where
the truth lies between the story deposed to by the wife and that deposed to by the
b husband: the facts which are common ground speak for themselves.

The only remaining question, and to my mind the most important consideration,
is the effect that such an order as this will have on the husband. Will he be rendered
homeless? The son's position, I think, is less important. He is only there basically for
his own convenience. But the court has in substance, I think, to balance the hardship
likely to be caused by the making of such an order against the hardship likely to be
c caused by refusing it. On the facts here there is nothing to suggest that the husband
will find it impossible to get some other place to live; and equally the wife's position
can only be described as desperate. My conclusion is that the court, when it is dealing
with these cases, particularly where it is clear that the marriage has already broken
down, should think essentially in terms of homes, especially for the children, and then
consider the balance of hardship as I have indicated, being careful not to under-
d estimate the difficulties which even single men have these days in finding somewhere
to live, bearing in mind that the break will have to be made in the relatively near
future and that property rights as between the spouses are of comparatively minor
importance. Obviously, if the circumstances are such that a workable scheme can
be arranged so that the spouses can live more or less separately in the matrimonial
home pending the final determination of their respective interests in it, the situation
e will not be 'impossible' within the meaning of the cases, nor will the wife require 'protection'. But where an impossible situation does exist, the sooner that it is ended the
better. Delay in these cases may be a serious denial of justice, and sometimes a grave
failure on the part of the court to exercise its 'protective' powers.

Consequently, in my judgment the learned judge was right in the conclusion to
which he came and was right to make the order which he did. I would dismiss this
f appeal.

CUMMING-BRUCE J. I agree, and only add some words of my own because I
am aware, as a matter of experience, in cases where injunctions are sought to expel
a spouse from the matrimonial home, that passages from the judgments previously
delivered in this court are frequently quoted without adequate regard to the facts
g of the cases with which this court was on each occasion concerned. The effect has been
that the right to an injunction is liable to be mistakenly regarded as unduly restricted
and circumscribed.

The relevant facts which are not in issue in the present case may be summarised as
follows. The wife has to look after a child of the family aged 20 months. She is living
with the baby at her parents' flat. In the basement there, there is a kitchen and a
h living room. On the ground floor there are two bedrooms, one of which is used by
the wife's parents, and the other shared by the wife, an older woman and the baby,
and for a time also by the wife's 17 year old sister. This accommodation is not suitable
to enable the wife adequately to discharge her duty to bring up the child. At the
matrimonial home live the husband and his 16 year old son, the child of his previous
marriage, who arrived in June 1974, when his mother, with whom he had been living,
j moved to Leicester. The boy wanted to stay in London, and the father wishes to keep
him in the matrimonial home as all the boy's friends are in London, and in particular
his girl friend, and the boy wishes to live there with his father. The accommodation
consists of a kitchen, sitting room, toilet and bathroom in the basement, and one
bedroom on the first floor. The husband proposes that his wife and baby should
return home, but is insistent that his 16 year old son should continue to stay there.

The difficulties of finding accommodation in London are well known; but there is no evidence from the husband to suggest that he would have any special difficulty in *a* finding accommodation for himself if he had to leave, and there appears no reason save the boy's desire to stay with his London friends why he should not live with his mother in Leicester.

The learned judge was placed in the difficulty that the parties had agreed that he should decide the case on the evidence in the affidavits, a situation which is commonly encountered in applications pending suit. Neither party had given notice to the other *b* that any deponents should attend for cross-examination. The evidence was dramatically conflicting. According to the wife, she had been the victim of at least two serious assaults, in December 1973 and July 1974, had been ordered to leave the home on 3rd September, and that she left because she was frightened of what her husband would do to her if she disobeyed him. She deposed that she was afraid to go back. Her evidence was corroborated in material particulars by four deponents. The *c* evidence of the husband was a complete denial of all his wife's allegations, and he alleged that his wife was mentally unstable and had invented all her allegations. His denial of the wife's allegations was supported by six deponents.

The learned judge expressed his finding in these words:

> 'There have been no less than thirteen affidavits before the Court; three of *d* those are by the parties, the others are largely by friends and relations and are by way of corroboration. Doing the best I can, dependent upon affidavit evidence, I find that the wife's evidence here is more reliable, and I find that the corroboration of her evidence is on the whole more satisfactory.'

The learned judge applied the test laid down in *Hall v Hall*[1] and said:

> '. . . I have to be quite satisfied . . . that this is not just a situation of unpleasantness or tension but that there is a very appreciable risk that if these parties were to be living together there would be a risk of violence and that living apart is necessary for the protection of the wife. [He added later:] I am also bearing in mind the fact that at present the wife is living with this child in quite unsatisfactory accommodation [which he described].' *f*

Counsel for the husband attacked the learned judge's application of the test in *Hall v Hall*[1] and submitted that on any view there had been no violence since 22nd July, that the wife had lived with her husband thereafter until 3rd September without any untoward event, that he had given an undertaking to the court not to molest the wife, and that there was no evidence since the undertaking was given which would justify an inference of an intent on the part of the husband to commit a breach of his *g* undertaking; but, for the reasons stated by Ormrod LJ these criticisms are not made out.   There was ample material in the affidavits to found the learned judge's conclusion.

In my view, the approach of the court to these cases of application to expel a spouse from the matrimonial home should be strictly practical, having regard to the realities *h* of family life. Where a mother is looking after a child or children, it is necessary to examine with the utmost care whether it is really practicable for the husband and wife to continue to live in the matrimonial home. In *Hall v Hall*[1] there was a large and lovely house in Surrey with six bedrooms, dining room, drawing room, study, playroom and so forth. The husband was a chartered accountant who went to London daily to work. While the case was pending, in spite of the background of marital dispute, there was a finding that the children had a normal family Christmas. Lord *j* Denning MR said that this was a civilised couple who do not break out into violence. It was in this context that Lord Denning MR said that an order to exclude one spouse or the other from the matrimonial home was a drastic order which should not be

made unless it is proved to be impossible for them to live together in the same house.
As Sachs LJ said, there was no risk to the wife of real difficulties occurring which
required an order for her protection, and it was not at all necessary in the interests
of the children.

In *Phillips v Phillips*[1] Edmund Davies LJ[2] suggested that the question for the court
in that case was: has it been established that the conditions which now prevail in the
matrimonial home are such as to make it quite intolerable for the wife and her 14 year
old son to continue to share with the husband a small house of three bedrooms, a
living room and kitchen? He regarded that question as the same as the question
whether it was impossible for the parties to live together in the same house. Stephenson
LJ[3] accepted for the purpose of the case that no court ought to make such an order
unless it is proved to be necessary for the protection of the health, physical or mental,
of the wife or a child living with her. I do not understand him to suggest that that is
to be regarded as a comprehensive test which would necessarily be appropriate in
every case.

I extract from the cases the principle that the court will consider with care the
accommodation available to both spouses, and the hardship to which each will be
exposed if an order is granted or refused, and then consider whether it is really
sensible to expect a wife and child to endure the pressures which the continued
presence of the other spouse will place on them. Obviously inconvenience is not
enough. Equally obviously, the court must be alive to the risk that a spouse may be
using the instrument of an injunction as a tactical weapon in the matrimonial conflict.
Further, though property rights are relevant, they probably assume a good deal less
importance today than they did before this court explained in *Wachtel v Wachtel*[4] the
scope for property adjustment orders after a decree of divorce, as it is now a common
feature of dissolution proceedings for the property rights eventually to be adjusted
so as to give priority to the accommodation of the spouse who is looking after the
children.

In proceedings pending suit it is unlikely that the court will be able to predict who
will be living in the matrimonial home after all the problems of custody, finance and
property adjustment have been determined. Where there are children, whom the
mother is looking after, a major consideration must be to relieve them of the psychological stresses and strains imposed by the friction between their parents, as the long-
term effect on a child is liable to be of the utmost gravity. This factor ought to weigh
at least as heavily in the scales as the personal protection of the parent seeking relief.

I would add that in the present case we were told that the husband himself is going
to pray for dissolution on the ground that his wife's behaviour has been such that he
cannot reasonably be expected to live with her. When one considers the extremely
restricted accommodation in this matrimonial home, that factor is also a circumstance
relevant to the question whether they can really be required to live together until
the final determination of their rights after decree absolute.

For those reasons, and those given by Ormrod LJ, I would dismiss this appeal.

MEGAW LJ. I agree with both the judgments which have already been delivered,
both in respect of the principle which is applicable and the considerations which are
relevant in an application of this nature, and also as to their bearing on the decision
of this particular case.

There are three matters related to the facts and circumstances of the particular
case which I regard as being of substantial relevance to the decision here. First, the
evidence as to the accommodation in the matrimonial home showed quite clearly,

---

1   [1973] 2 All ER 423, [1973] 1 WLR 615
2   [1973] 2 All ER at 426, [1973] 1 WLR at 618
3   [1973] 2 All ER at 428, [1973] 1 WLR at 621
4   [1973] 1 All ER 829, [1973] Fam 72

in my view, that it would be intolerable that the husband and his 16 year old son   *a*
and the wife and the 20 month old child should live in that accommodation when
their relationship to one another is such as it unfortunately now clearly is. I repeat, as
it now clearly is, whatever the reason and wherever the fault. That is the sad fact,
whether the affidavit evidence of the husband and those who have deposed on his
behalf is wholly right and that of the wife and those who have deposed on her behalf
is wholly wrong, as to the causes of the wife having left the home and as to the events   *b*
which led up to it; or whether, on the other hand, the affidavit evidence of the wife
and of those who have deposed on her behalf is right; or whether the truth lies
between the two. Therefore, someone must go. Otherwise the court would be
refusing to provide a remedy for an intolerable situation

Secondly, the evidence as to the accommodation available to the wife and the child
at the wife's parents' home is such as to indicate that that does not provide a solution.   *c*

Thirdly, there was no evidence on behalf of the husband that he would have
difficulty in finding suitable accommodation for himself and his son, if the order asked
for by the wife were to be made. It may be that there is, or would be, in fact such
difficulty—perhaps grave difficulty. But the judge had to deal with this application
on the evidence; and we on appeal are not entitled to go outside the evidence.

I should say a word also as to the second ground put forward in the first notice of   *d*
appeal. That is phrased in this way:

> 'That the Learned Judge was wrong in law in deciding disputed issues of fact
> on the basis of conflicting affidavit evidence only without hearing the oral
> evidence of the parties and their witnesses, whereby substantial wrong or
> miscarriage of justice has been occasioned.'
                                                                                              e

As to that, it will be sufficient to say that there was no application for cross-examination of any of the deponents, nor any application for an adjournment for that purpose.
I do not say that by way of criticism of any decision made by anyone concerned with
the case. I do not say that, if such an application had been made, it would, or should,
have been granted. That question does not arise for decision. I agree with the observations made by Ormrod LJ as to certain general considerations on that question. But,   *f*
however that may be, the fact is that in this case no such application was made and,
therefore, the learned judge was bound to reach a decision on the affidavit evidence.
He could not say 'I will not decide this issue which I have been asked to decide'. He
was bound to decide it on such evidence as he had. Hence, a complaint on behalf of
the husband that the judge was wrong to decide that issue without oral evidence could
not prevail.   *g*

Counsel for the husband invited us also to say that the learned judge was wrong
in granting an injunction against the husband in respect of restraining him from
molesting the wife. Counsel said that it would have been appropriate here that, as
the husband had offered an undertaking in that respect, the undertaking should have
been accepted. I do not agree. I think that the learned judge was right to grant the
injunction in that respect also.   *h*

I agree that the appeal should be dismissed.

*Appeal dismissed: Order below varied by inserting, after the words 'is hereby granted
restraining him', the words 'without the consent of the petitioner'. Leave to appeal to the House
of Lords refused.*
                                                                                              j

Solicitors: *Clinton, Davis & Co* (for the husband); *Trott & Gentry* (for the wife).

Mary Rose Plummer   Barrister.

Anderson and Heeley Ltd v Paterson

QUEEN'S BENCH DIVISION

LORD WIDGERY CJ, BRIDGE AND SHAW JJ

5th NOVEMBER 1974

Road traffic – Licence – Goods vehicle – Operator's licence – Exemption – Cases in which licence not required – Tower wagon – Vehicle on which only goods carried are those required in connection with work on which tower wagon ordinarily used as such – Meaning of 'tower wagon' – Vehicle used solely as mobile tower enabling overhead work to be done – Transport Act 1968, s 60(1)(2) – Goods Vehicles (Operators' Licences) Regulations 1969 (SI 1969 No 1636), reg 3, Sch 1, para 20.

Road traffic – Goods vehicle plating and test certificates – Exemption – Tower wagon – Meaning – Vehicle into which there is built any expanding or extensible contrivance – Contrivance designed for facilitating erection, inspection, repair or maintenance of overhead structures or equipment – Vehicle not constructed or adapted for use nor used for conveyance of loads except contrivance and articles used in connection therewith – Vehicle used for erection of street lighting – Converted goods vehicle – Body removed from chassis – Extensible contrivance fitted behind car with platform for carrying tools and equipment – Vehicle used to carry concrete pillars intended to form part of street lights – Whether vehicle a 'tower wagon' – Vehicles (Excise) Act 1971, Sch 4, para 9(1) – Goods Vehicles (Plating and Testing) Regulations 1971 (SI 1971 No 352), reg 4(2), Sch 2, Item 6.

In the course of their business as street lighting contractors, the appellants used a converted van for the erection of street lamps. That van had been reconstructed by having the body removed from the chassis and an extensible contrivance fitted behind the cab. The remaining space was filled by a low side platform to carry tools and equipment. The appellants were engaged by a local authority to erect street lamps. For that purpose they used the platform of the vehicle to carry concrete pillars which were to be part of the street lamps, as well as their tools and equipment. The respondent laid informations on behalf of the local licensing authority against the appellants for using a goods vehicle (a) in connection with their business without holding an operator's licence, contrary to s 60(1)ᵃ of the Transport Act 1968; and (b) without a current goods vehicle test certificate, contrary to s 46(2) of the Road Traffic Act 1972. The appellants contended that the vehicle had been reconstructed as a 'tower wagon', within para 9(1)ᵇ of Sch 4 to the Vehicles (Excise) Act 1971, and so by s 60(2)(b) of the 1968 Act and para 20ᶜ of Sch 1 to the Goods Vehicles (Operators' Licences) Regulations 1969, was exempt from the requirement to hold an operator's licence, and by reg 4(2)ᵈ of, and Item 6ᵉ of Sch 2 to, the Goods Vehicle (Plating and Testing) Regulations 1971, was exempt from the requirement of having a current test certificate. The justices held that the van was not a tower wagon, within para 9(1)

---

of Sch 4 to the 1971 Act, since the adaptation of the van had not terminated its suitability as a goods vehicle but had merely decreased it, and the concrete lighting   *a*
pillars which the van had been carrying were not 'articles used in connection' with the
extensible contrivance. Accordingly the justices convicted the appellants of both
offences. On appeal,

Held – The appeal would be dismissed for the following reasons—
(i) The definition of 'tower wagon' in Sch 4 to the 1971 Act was not applicable to that   *b*
expression in para 20 of Sch 1 to the 1969 regulations which was therefore to be construed in its ordinary, accepted meaning, i e a vehicle the sole function of which was
its use as a mobile tower enabling overhead work to be done in such places as it fell
to be executed, subject to the provision in para 20 that tools and equipment used in
connection with the work to be done from the vehicle could be carried without
destroying the vehicle's character as a tower wagon. The appellants' vehicle was   *c*
not a tower wagon in that sense but a goods vehicle with an extensible contrivance
incorporated into its structure as had been demonstrated by the fact the vehicle had,
at the material time, been carrying the concrete pillars (see p 527 *e f* and *g* to p 528 *a*
and *e*, post).
(ii) Further the vehicle was not a 'tower wagon' within Item 6 of Sch 2 to the 1971
regulations and Sch 4 to the 1971 Act since the vehicle had been used (irrespective of   *d*
any question of construction or adaptation) for the carriage of a load, i e the concrete
pillars, which could not be regarded as articles 'used in connection with' the
expanding or extensible contrivance (see p 528 *c* to *f*, post).

Notes
For exemptions from the requirement of an operator's licence, see Supplement   *e*
to 33 Halsbury's Laws (3rd Edn) para 1251A, 3.
For the plating and testing of goods vehicles, see ibid, para 1333B.
For the Transport Act 1968, s 60, see 28 Halsbury's Statutes (3rd Edn) 708.
For the Vehicles (Excise) Act 1971, Sch 4, para 9, see 41 Halsbury's Statutes (3rd Edn)
473.
For the Road Traffic Act 1972, s 46, see 42 Halsbury's Statutes (3rd Edn) 1692.   *f*

Cases cited
Hawes Freight Co Ltd v Hammond [1962] 3 All ER 950, [1963] 1 QB 275.
Taylor v Mead [1961] 1 All ER 626, [1961] 1 WLR 435.

Case stated
This was an appeal by way of a case stated by the justices for the petty sessional   *g*
division of Dewsbury in the West Riding of the county of York in respect of their
adjudication as a magistrates' court sitting at Dewsbury on 22nd February 1974.
On 9th November 1973 Ernest Wurzal, on behalf of the Licensing Authority
Yorkshire Traffic Area, preferred against the appellants, Anderson and Heeley Ltd,
the following information: (a) that they on 7th July 1973 at Mirfield were guilty of   *h*
an offence under Part V of the Transport Act 1968, by using a goods vehicle within
the meaning of that Act, to wit, a motor vehicle number 8430 YG, in contravention
of s 60 of the 1968 Act, in that they did unlawfully use the vehicle as a goods vehicle
on a road there situate called Water Royd Lane for the carriage of goods in connection
with the trade or business of street lighting contractors carried on by them, they not
being the holders of a licence under Part V of the 1968 Act in respect of the vehicle,   *j*
contrary to s 60 of the 1968 Act; (b) that they on 7th July 1973 at Mirfield were guilty
of an offence under the Road Traffic Act 1972 in that they did use on a certain road
called Water Royd Lane a goods vehicle number 8430 YG, being a goods vehicle of
a class required by the Goods Vehicles (Plating and Testing) Regulations 1971[1] to

1   SI 1971 No 352

have been submitted for a goods vehicle test, there being no goods vehicle test
a certificate in force for the vehicle at that time, contrary to s 46(2) of the 1972 Act.

The following facts were found: (i) The appellants carried on the business of street
lighting contractors and on 7th July 1973 whilst acting as such in pursuance of a contract
with Mirfield Council were engaged on the erection of street lighting in Water Royd
Lane. (ii) The appellants' employee, Brian Firth, was the driver in charge of the
vehicle registered number 8430 YG. At the material time the said vehicle was station-
b ary and Mr Firth was engaged in the erection of street lighting in pursuance of the
contract. (iii) The registration book for the vehicle disclosed that it had originally been
registered on 8th February 1962 as a Bedford van with an unladen weight of 3 tons,
1 cwt, 56 lbs with a taxation class 'goods' and that that registration particular was
amended on 23rd February 1971 by deleting the description 'goods' and inserting
the description 'tower wagon'. (iv) The appellants had shortly before 23rd February
c 1971 altered the construction of the vehicle by removing the body and fitting immediately behind the cab of the vehicle an extensible contrivance known as a 'Hiab
loader' and by rebuilding between the Hiab loader and the rear of the vehicle a low
side platform. (v) The weight of the Hiab loader was approximately 15 cwts. The
unladen weight of the vehicle, including the Hiab loader, was 3 tons 12 cwts and the
vehicle was a heavy goods vehicle. (vi) On 7th July 1973 the platform of the vehicle
d was carrying a concrete lighting pillar and various tools and the vehicle was drawing
a cement mixing machine for use in the erection of lighting pillars. Articles carried
on the said vehicle were connected with the erection and/or maintenance of street
lighting. (vii) The vehicle was displaying a vehicle excise licence exemption disc
bearing the description 'street lighting'. (viii) Although the platform of the vehicle
was capable of carrying any goods which could be placed on it and the Hiab loader
e could be used for lifting items on and off the platform the appellants used the platform
solely for carrying articles consisting of tools, equipment and materials used by them
in connection with the erection and maintenance of street lighting. (ix) The Hiab
loader was used by the appellants for various purposes in connection with their work
and in particular was used for lifting lamp standards on and off the vehicle; for lifting
lamp standards into position and holding them upright until the concrete round the
f base had set sufficiently; for raising and lowering maintenance personnel by means of
a basket attachment. (xi) In 1969 the appellants had made an application to the goods
vehicle centre at Swansea for an appointment for plating and testing of a similar
vehicle and received the reply dated 14th April 1969 which was produced to the court
and which stated that this vehicle was an exempted vehicle. (xii) The appellants were
not the holders of an operator's licence authorising the use of the vehicle on 7th July
g 1973. (xiii) No goods vehicle test certificate was in force in respect of the vehicle on
that date.

It was contended on behalf of the appellants: (a) the construction and use of the
vehicle complied with the description of a 'tower wagon' contained in the Vehicles
(Excise) Act 1971, Sch 4 para 9(1); (b) the construction and use of the vehicle at the
material time was exempt from the requirements of the operator's licence by virtue
h of ss 60(2)(b) and 91 of the Transport Act 1968 and para 20 of Sch 1 to the Goods
Vehicles (Operators' Licences) Regulations 1969[1]; and (c) the construction and use of
the vehicle at the material time was exempt from the requirement of a plating and
testing certificate by virtue of s 46(5)(b) of the Road Traffic Act 1972 and para 6 of the
Goods Vehicles (Plating and Testing) Regulations 1971.

4. It was contended on behalf of the respondent (a) that the vehicle in question at
j the material time was not a tower wagon within para 20 of Sch 1 to the 1969 regulations; (b) that although the tower wagon was not expressly defined in para 20 of Sch 1
to the Goods Vehicles (Operators' Licences) Regulations 1969 the court should apply
the definition of tower wagon contained in para 9 of Sch 4 to the Vehicles (Excise) Act
1971; (c) that, while it was accepted that the goods being carried at the material time

1   SI 1969 No 1636

were in connection with the work on which the vehicle was ordinarily used, the
vehicle in its adapted state was nonetheless suitable for the conveyance of other loads; *a*
and (d) that accordingly the appellants were not entitled to exemption under para 20
of Sch 1 to the 1969 regulations and they were guilty of both offences.

The justices decided that the construction and use of the said vehicle at the material
time did not fall within the exemption provisions because: (a) the vehicle was originally constructed for the conveyance of loads and its adaptation by the appellants had
decreased but not terminated its suitability for this purpose; and (b) although the *b*
vehicle was being used in that connection with the lighting pillars they were not used
in connection with the vehicle. Accordingly they convicted the appellants of both
offences.

G W Humphries for the appellants.
Harry Woolf for the respondent.   *c*

SHAW J delivered the first judgment at the invitation of Lord Widgery CJ.
This is an appeal by way of case stated by the justices for the petty sessional division
of Dewsbury in respect of their adjudication on two informations against the appellants arising from their user of a vehicle in connection with their contract with a
street lighting authority for the installation of street lighting. The justices convicted *d*
the appellants in both cases.

The first information alleged that the appellants had contravened s 60 (1) of the
Transport Act 1968 by using a goods vehicle in connection with their business when
they did not hold an operator's licence as required by that subsection. The second
information alleged that on the same occasion the appellants were in breach of the
requirements of the Goods Vehicles (Plating and Testing) Regulations 1971 in that no *e*
goods vehicle test certificate was in force for the vehicle. It was not in dispute that
the appellants did not hold an operator's licence and that no test certificate had been
issued in relation to the vehicle. The question raised by the appeal is whether the
vehicle came within the scope of exemptions afforded both in regard to operators'
licences and to test certificates when the vehicle concerned is a tower wagon.

It is convenient before turning to the facts found by the justices to look at the *f*
provisions giving rise to the exemptions relied on. In regard to operators' licences,
s 60 (2)(*b*) of the Transport Act 1968 enacts that the requirements of sub-s (1) shall
not apply 'to the use of a vehicle of any class specified in regulations'. The relevant
regulations are the Goods Vehicles (Operators' Licences) Regulations 1969 made under
Part V of the 1968 Act. Regulation 3 provides that s 60(1) of the Act shall not apply
to the use of a vehicle of any class specified in Sch 1 to the regulations. Paragraph 20 *g*
of that schedule dispenses with the requirement of an operator's licence in the case
of—

> 'A tower wagon or trailer drawn by a tower wagon, provided in each case the
> only goods carried on the vehicle are such as are required for use in connection
> with the work on which the tower wagon is ordinarily used as such.'
                                                                              h
No definition of a 'tower wagon' is to be found either in the 1968 Act or in the regulations made thereunder.

As to the test certificate, there is an exoneration from its requirement by reg 4(2)
of the Goods Vehicles (Plating and Testing) Regulations 1971, which provides that
nothing in those regulations shall apply to a goods vehicle of any of the classes of
vehicle specified in Sch 2. Item 6 of that schedule exempts from the operation of the *j*
regulations: 'Tower wagons as defined in Schedule 4 to the 1971 Act.' The Act referred
to is the Vehicles (Excise) Act 1971 and the definition referred to is in para 9(1) of Sch 4
and reads thus:

> ' "tower wagon" means a goods vehicle—(*a*) into which there is built, as
> part of the vehicle, any expanding or extensible contrivance designed for

a   facilitating the erection, inspection, repair or maintenance of overhead structures or equipment; and (b) which is neither constructed nor adapted for use nor used for the conveyance of any load, except such a contrivance and articles used in connection therewith'.

The facts found by the justices so far as material may be summarised as follows. The appellants carried on the business of street lighting contractors and on the
b   occasion when the use of the vehicle gave rise to the two informations it was being used in connection with a contract made with the Mirfield council, which was a street lighting authority, for the erection of street lamps. The vehicle had been originally a normal goods vehicle but it had been reconstructed some time early in 1971. The body had been removed from the chassis. In its place there had been fitted immediately behind the cab an extensible contrivance called a Hiab loader. In place of the original
c   deck there had been built a low side platform which, so the justices found, diminished but did not extinguish the capacity of the vehicle to carry goods.

At the time of the offences alleged by the informations there was being carried on the platform a concrete pillar or pillars which were to be part of the street lamps, and also various tools and equipment. The vehicle was also drawing a cement mixing machine. All these various items were to be used in connection with the erection of
d   the pillars as part of the street lighting.

A further and, as it seems to me, irrelevant and immaterial finding by the justices was that some years ago the appellants had sought an appointment for a test in respect of a similarly constructed vehicle and had been informed that it was an exempted vehicle. This is a matter which might go to penalty for infringement but cannot be decisive of the questions raised or offer any assistance in deciding them.
e   Before the justices it was submitted on behalf of the prosecution that the statutory definition of a tower wagon in regard to questions arising under the Vehicles (Excise) Act 1971 and the Goods Vehicles (Plating and Testing) Regulations 1971, made in the same year, was applicable also to any question arising under the Road Transport Act 1968 and the Goods Vehicles (Operators' Licences) Regulations 1969. This was an untenable and ill-founded proposition, but no argument was advanced before the
f   justices on behalf of the appellants to counter it. Not surprisingly, but unfortunately, the justices acceded to the proposition propounded for the prosecutor and decided the question of exemption as a tower wagon in regard to each of the informations on the basis of the statutory definition which is applicable only in regard to the second information.

It is therefore necessary to look at the matter afresh in the light of the justices'
g   findings of fact. In deciding whether the use of the vehicle concerned did not call for the holding of an operator's licence because it was a 'tower wagon', one has to construe that description in its ordinary popular and generally accepted sense. If trade custom or understanding conferred a special character on tower wagons, there would have to be evidence to prove it. None was adduced in that regard before the justices. What then is the ordinary popular meaning to be attributed to the descriptive phrase 'tower
h   wagon'? It seems to me that it must connote a mobile tower enabling overhead work to be done in such places as it falls to be executed. Moreover, this must be its sole function. If, for example, its construction is such as to make it also usable for the carriage of general goods, it is not merely a tower wagon but something more than and different from a tower wagon. The only qualification of this construction is implicit in para 20 of Sch 1 to the Goods Vehicles (Operators' Licences) Regulations 1969,
j   namely, that tools and equipment used in connection with the work to be done from the tower wagon may be capable of carriage on it without destroying its character as a tower wagon. On this basis, which is that on which in my view the justices should have founded their decision in relation to the first information, the vehicle was not a tower wagon. It was a goods vehicle with an extensible contrivance incorporated in its construction. That it was so is demonstrated by the justices' finding that apart from

tools and equipment the vehicle was at the material time carrying also a concrete
pillar to be erected as a lamp standard. It follows that, albeit the justices approached *a*
the question in the wrong way, they nonetheless arrived on the facts found by them
at the correct conclusion so far as the first information was concerned.

What of the second information and the effect of the exemption of tower wagons
as defined in the Vehicles (Excise) Act 1971? In the two paragraphs which contain the
definition a number of essential characteristics are incorporated. Those demanded by
para (*a*) appear to exist in the vehicle concerned, that is to say there is built into it an *b*
expanding or extensible contrivance for facilitating the erection, etc, of overhead
structures or equipment. Paragraph (*b*), however, is more complicated. The overall
requirement is that it must not be constructed or adapted for use for the conveyance
of any load. Whether a vehicle is so constructed or adapted may often be a difficult
matter to determine. But it is unnecessary to deal with that esoteric question in the
present case. The last essential requirement in the statutory definition is that the *c*
vehicle should not actually be used (irrespective of any question of construction or
adaptation) for the conveyance of any load, except the expanding or extensible
contrivance and articles used in connection therewith. It follows that unless concrete
pillars to be erected as lamp standards come within the category of 'articles used in
connection with' the contrivance, the vehicle was not, certainly in the circumstances
of its use at the material time, a tower wagon. In my judgment by no stretch of *d*
language can a concrete pillar to be erected as a lamp standard be regarded as an
article used in connection with the Hiab loader.

The justices came to the right conclusion and in this case by the right road. I would
dismiss the appeal in regard to both the informations.

e

BRIDGE J. I agree.

LORD WIDGERY CJ. I agree also.

Appeal dismissed.   *f*

Solicitors: *Jacques & Co* agents for *Backhouse-Forbes*, Blackburn (for the appellants);
Treasury Solicitor.

Jacqueline Charles   Barrister.

Microbeads AC and another v Vinhurst Road Markings Ltd

COURT OF APPEAL, CIVIL DIVISION
LORD DENNING MR, ROSKILL LJ AND SIR JOHN PENNYCUICK
7th, 8th NOVEMBER 1974

Sale of goods – Implied undertaking – Warranty as to quiet possession – Warranty that the buyer shall have and enjoy quiet possession – Interference with possession by title paramount – Title paramount not in existence at date of sale – Sale of machinery – Application by third party for patent – Complete specification published after sale of machinery – Patentee's rights having retrospective effect – Seller and buyer unaware of patent at date of sale – Action by patentee against buyer for infringement of patent by using machinery – Action constituting interference with buyer's possession – Whether seller in breach of warranty as to quiet possession – Sale of Goods Act 1893, s 12(2).

An English company ('the patentee') held a patent for apparatus for applying markings on roads. The application for the patent was filed on 28th December 1966. The complete specification was filed on 28th December 1967. After the Patent Office had made various examinations the complete specification was published on 11th November 1970. Letters patent were granted to the patentee on 12th January 1972. Under the Patents Act 1949, ss 13(4) and 22, it was only after the publication of the complete specification that the patentee had any rights or privileges in respect of the patent, and only after letters patent had been granted that the patentee could institute proceedings for infringement. Meanwhile, between January and April 1970 (i e before the publication of the complete specification of the patent) the defendants bought some road marking machines and accessories from the plaintiffs. Neither the defendants nor the plaintiffs were aware of the patent or that the use of the machines might infringe any patent. The machines proved to be unsatisfactory and the defendants did not pay the balance of the price. In November 1970 the plaintiffs brought an action against the defendants for the unpaid balance and damages. The defendants put in a defence alleging that the machines were not reasonably fit for the purpose for which they had been sold. In 1972 the patentee brought an action against the defendants for using the machines in breach of their patent. Thereupon the defendants amended their defence in the plaintiffs' action and set up the infringement as a defence and counterclaim. The trial of a preliminary issue was ordered on the question whether the defendants had been in breach of contract by virtue of s 12(1)[a] or s 12(2) of the Sale of Goods Act 1893. The judge held that at the time of sale the plaintiffs had had a right to sell the machines to the defendants and therefore they were not in breach of the condition implied by s 12(1). He further held that, as there could only be a breach of the warranty implied by s 12(2) if there was a defect in the plaintiffs' title at the time of sale, the plaintiffs were not in breach of the implied warranty since the sale had taken place before the complete specification had been published. The defendants appealed.

Held – Although the defendants could not avail themselves of s 12(1) since they had acquired a perfectly good title to the machines, they were nevertheless entitled to rely on s 12(2) since that subsection implied a warranty that the defendants 'shall have and enjoy' quiet possession in the future and not merely at the time of sale. No exception could be implied into s 12(2) either in relation to disturbance by someone

---

a Section 12, so far as material, is set out at p 532 *a*, post

with a title paramount or in relation to a title paramount which had only come into
existence after the time of sale. The proceedings by the patentee constituted a dis-   *a*
turbance of the defendants' possession and therefore a breach of the warranty implied
by s 12(2). The appeal would therefore be allowed (see p 532 *a b* and *h* to p 533 *a c*
and *d*, p 535 *d e* and *g* to p 536 *a d* and *h* and p 537 *b*, post).

   Niblett Ltd v Confectioners' Materials Co Ltd [1921] 3 KB 387 and dictum of Lord Greene
MR in *Mason v Burningham* [1949] 2 All ER at 144, 145 applied.

b

Notes
For implied undertakings as to title, see 34 Halsbury's Laws (3rd Edn) 46, 47, para 72.
   For the Sale of Goods Act 1893, s 12, see 30 Halsbury's Statutes (3rd Edn) 13.
   For the Patents Act 1949, ss 13, 22, see 24 Halsbury's Statutes (3rd Edn) 564-565, 576.
   As from 18th May 1973 a new section has been substituted for s 12 of the Sale of
Goods Act 1893 by the Supply of Goods (Implied Terms) Act 1973, s 1.   *c*

Cases referred to in judgments
Howell v Richards (1809) 11 East 633, 103 ER 1150, 17 Digest (Reissue) 452, *2142.*
Jones v Lavington [1903] 1 KB 253, 72 LJKB 98, 88 LT 223, CA, 31(1) Digest (Reissue)
   353, *2806.*
Mason v Burningham [1949] 2 All ER 134, [1949] 2 KB 545, [1949] LJR 1430, CA 39,   *d*
   Digest (Repl) 590, *1110.*
Monforts v Marsden (1895) 12 RPC 266.
Niblett Ltd v Confectioners' Materials Co Ltd [1921] 3 KB 387, [1921] All ER Rep 459, 90
   LJKB 984, 125 LT 552, CA, 39 Digest (Repl) 527, *648.*

Cases also cited   *e*
Bristol-Myers Co v Beecham Group Ltd [1974] 1 All ER 333, [1974] AC 646, HL.
Williams v Burnett (1845) 1 CB 402, 14 LJCP 98.

Interlocutory appeal
The plaintiffs, Microbeads AG and Alfred Ehrismann AG, brought an action against   *f*
the defendants, Vinhurst Road Markings Ltd, claiming, inter alia, payment of the
price of goods sold by the plaintiffs to the defendants between January and April 1970.
In 1972 Prismo Universal Ltd, holders of a patent over the goods, brought an action
against the defendants alleging infringement of the patent. Accordingly the defendants, pursuant to an order of MacKenna J made on 11th January 1973, amended their
defence and counterclaim to allege breaches of s 12(1) and (2) of the Sale of Goods Act
1893 on the part of the plaintiffs. The plaintiffs sought an order that the point of law   *g*
raised by the amendment be tried as a preliminary issue. On 24th May 1973 Master
Ritchie refused to make the order sought but, on appeal, Milmo J in chambers on 4th
July 1973 ordered that the point be tried as a preliminary issue. On 18th December 1973
Mars-Jones J directed that judgment should be entered for the plaintiffs in the preliminary issue and declared that there had been no breach of contract on the part of
the plaintiffs under either s 12(1) or s 12(2) of the 1893 Act having regard to the dates   *h*
of filing and publication of the complete specification and of the grant of letters
patent to Prismo Universal Ltd. The defendants appealed. The facts are set out in
the judgment of Lord Denning MR.

William Macpherson QC and *Edwin J Glasgow* for the defendants.
A Rogers for the plaintiffs.   *j*

LORD DENNING MR.   This case raises a new and interesting point on the sale
of goods. The defendants, an English company ('Vinhurst'), bought some special
machinery from the plaintiffs, a Swiss company. They used the machines for making

white lines on roads. Two or three years later another English company, who owned
a a patent, came along and said that these machines infringed their patent. They
sought an injunction to prevent the use of the machines. Have the English company,
who bought the machines, a cause of action against the Swiss company who sold them?
The dates are important. I will start with the owners of the patent. They are an
English company, Prismo Universal Ltd ('Prismo'), who carry on business near
Crawley in Sussex. They hold a patent for an apparatus for applying markings on
b roads. It is done by the machine which carries a spray gun and a quantity of thermo-
plastic material. This gun sprays the material on to the roads so as to make a white
and yellow line.

For some time the invention was kept secret. The application for a patent was
filed on 28th December 1966. The complete specification was filed on 28th December
1967. The Patent Office made their various examinations. Eventually, on 11th
c November 1970, the complete specification was published. It was on that date that
it became open to the world to learn about it. It was only after that date that the
patentee had any right or privileges in respect of it: see ss 13(4) and 22 of the Patents
Act 1949. On 12th January 1972 letters patent were granted to Prismo in respect of the
invention. It was only then the patentee was entitled to institute proceedings for
infringement: see s 13(4) of the 1949 Act.
d Now, before that invention was made public, Vinhurst bought some road marking
machines and accessories from the Swiss company. These machines were sold and
delivered to Vinhurst between January and April 1970, that is some months before
the Prismo specification was published in November 1970. The price of the machines
and accessories was nearly £15,000, of which Vinhurst paid £5,000, leaving the £10,000
balance to be paid. The buyers, Vinhurst, did not know anything about the patent.
e They had no idea that the machines might be infringing machines. They took them
in good faith and used them. But they found the machines very unsatisfactory. They
were dissatisfied. They did not pay the balance of the price.

On 30th November 1970 the sellers, the Swiss company, sued Vinhurst for the
balance of £10,000 owing for the machines. At first Vinhurst put in a defence saying
that the machines were not reasonably fit for the purpose of marking roads.
f But then in 1972 Prismo came down on Vinhurst and said these machines (supplied
by the Swiss company) infringed their patent. Thereupon Vinhurst amended their
defence so as to set up the infringement as a defence and counterclaim. The point
was set down as a preliminary issue. The judge found that the sellers, the Swiss
company, were not guilty of a breach of contract in this respect. The buyers appeal to
this court.
g The preliminary issue was directed on these assumptions: (1) that the letters patent
were valid; (2) that the machines sold by the Swiss company to Vinhurst were such
as to fall within the scope of the claims in the specification; (3) that the property in each
of the machines was to pass prior to November 1970. On those assumptions the point
of law was whether there was any breach of contract on the part of the Swiss company
under s 12(1) or s 12(2) of the Sale of Goods Act 1893 having regard to the dates of
h filing and publication of the specification and of the grant of the patent.

Before the judge most of the discussion was on s 12(1). It says that there is an
'implied condition on the part of the seller that . . . he has a right to sell the goods . . .'
That means that he has, *at the time of the sale*, a right to sell the goods. The words 'a
right to sell the goods' mean not only a right to pass the property in the machines to
the buyer, but also a right to confer on the buyer the undisturbed possession of the
j goods: see *Niblett Ltd v Confectioners' Materials Co Ltd*[1] by Atkin LJ. Now, at the time
of the sale in January 1970 the Swiss company were able to confer those rights. They
had made the machines out of their own materials and they could undoubtedly pass
the property in them to the buyers. Moreover there was no one at that time entitled

---

1 [1921] 3 KB 387 at 402, [1921] All ER Rep 459 at 464

to disturb their possession. There was then no subsisting patent. The specification
had not been published. No one could sue for infringement. The buyers could, at a
that time, use the machines undisturbed. So I agree with the judge that there was no
breach of s 12(1).

Now I turn to s 12(2). It says that there is an 'implied warranty that the buyer shall
have and enjoy quiet possession of the goods'. Taking those words in their ordinary
meaning, they seem to cover this case. The words 'shall have and enjoy' apply not
only to the time of the sale but also to the future; 'shall enjoy' means in the future. b
If a patentee comes two or three years later and gets an injunction to restrain the use
of the goods, there would seem to be a breach of the warranty. But it is said that
there are limitations on the ordinary meaning such limitations being derived from
the civil law (as suggested by Benjamin on Sale[1]) or from conveyancing cases.

One such limitation is said to follow from the words of Lord Ellenborough CJ in
Howell v Richards[2] when he said: c

'The covenant for title is an assurance to the purchaser, that the grantor has
the very estate in quantity and quality which he purports to convey, viz. in this
case an indefeasible estate in fee simple. The covenant for quiet enjoyment is an
assurance against the consequences of a defective title, and of any disturbances
thereupon.' d

Counsel for the Swiss company said that Lord Ellenborough CJ there meant a defective
title existing at the time of the sale. The covenant, he said, did not apply to a defective
title which only appeared some time after the sale. The defect here appeared after
the sale; it entered in November 1970 when the complete specification was published.

The other limitation, derived from the conveyancing cases, was that the covenant
for quiet enjoyment protected the purchaser or tenant only from the acts or operations e
of the vendor or lessor and those claiming under him, but not against the acts or
operations of those claiming by title paramount: see *Jones v Lavington*[3]. Counsel for
the Swiss company submitted that that conveyancing rule applied to s 12(2) also. Here
the claim by the patentee was by title paramount.

There is one case which supports this contention. It is a decision of Lord Russell of f
Killowen CJ in 1895 when he was on the Northern Circuit. It is *Monforts v Marsden*[4].
But that case was disapproved by this court in *Niblett Ltd v Confectioners' Materials Co
Ltd*[5] and must be taken to be overruled. Afterwards in *Mason v Burningham*[6] Lord
Greene MR made it clear that the conveyancing cases should not be applied to s 12 of
the Sale of Goods Act 1893. He said:

'It is to be observed that in the language used in the Sale of Goods Act, 1893, g
s. 12(2), there is no exception for any disturbance by title paramount. The words
are as I have quoted them, "that the buyer shall have and enjoy quiet possession
of the goods." I invited counsel for the defendant to refer us to any authority
that would justify the insertion into that statutory phrase of an exception in the
case of disturbance by title paramount, but he was unable to do so, and, in the
absence of any authority, I can only express my opinion that the statute means h
what it says and is not to have any such gloss put on it.'

I would follow the guidance of Lord Greene MR. Even if the disturbance is by title
paramount—such as by the patentee coming in and claiming an injunction to restrain
the use of the machine—there is a breach of the implied warranty under s 12(2).

j

1 9th Edn (1974)
2 (1809) 11 East 633 at 642
3 [1903] 1 KB 253
4 (1895) 12 RPC 266
5 [1921] 3 KB 387, [1921] All ER Rep 459
6 [1949] 2 All ER 134 at 144, 145, [1949] 2 KB 545 at 563

a   But the main point of counsel for the Swiss company before us—a point which the judge accepted—was that the defects of title must be present *at the time of the sale.* That is why so much turned on the date of publication, 11th November 1970. After that date the Swiss company, could by taking reasonable steps, have known that their machines were infringing machines and that they could not have a right to use them. So, if they had sold after 11th November 1970, they would be in breach of s 12(2) and of s 12(1) also. But counsel for the Swiss company says that before that date the Swiss

b company may have been perfectly innocent. Nothing had been published about this patent. The machines were sold in January and April 1970. There was no defect in title existing at the time of the sale. Accordingly counsel submitted there was no breach of s 12(2).

I cannot accept this submission. It means putting a gloss on s 12(2) by introducing a qualification which is not there. It seems to me that when the buyer has bought

c goods quite innocently and later on he is disturbed in his possession because the goods are found to be infringing a patent, then he can recover damages for breach of warranty against the seller. It may be the seller is innocent himself, but when one or other must suffer, the loss should fall on the seller; because, after all, he sold the goods and if it turns out that they infringe a patent, he should bear the loss. In the present case Prismo sue for infringement now and stop the buyer using the

d machines. That is a clear disturbance of possession. The buyer is not able to enjoy the quiet possession which the seller impliedly warranted that he shall have. There is a breach of s 12(2) of the 1893 Act.

I would therefore allow the appeal and I will answer the preliminary question accordingly.

e

ROSKILL LJ. I would begin, if I may, by expressing my appreciation to counsel for the plaintiffs for his admirable argument, which loses none of its merit by its lack of success. It is ironic that the first occasion on which in recent years this court has had to consider s 12(2) of the Sale of Goods Act 1893 should be one year after that section has been amended by Parliament by the Supply of Goods (Implied

f Terms) Act 1973. The amended text of s 12 will be found in Benjamin on Sale[1]. But the matters to which this appeal gives rise took place long before that amendment; and we have to determine what Lord Denning MR has called—rightly, if I may respectfully say so—a novel point with reference to the unamended language of s 12(2) even though our decision may not affect many other cases in the future. It is indeed, as Lord Denning MR has remarked, strange that there is so little authority

g on the meaning and scope of s 12(2). That is I think because, as the cases show, almost all of them have arisen in circumstances in which the aggrieved plaintiffs either successfully maintained a claim or at least tried to enforce a claim for breach of s 12(1), alleging against the vendors some defect in title. In those cases and in particular the case decided by Lord Russell of Killowen CJ (*Monforts v Marsden*[2]) the claims under sub-s (1) and sub-s (2) were closely linked. In that case, Lord

h Russell of Killowen CJ first held that there had been no breach of s 12(1). In the later case of *Niblett Ltd v Confectioners' Materials Co Ltd*[3], this court, then consisting of Bankes, Scrutton and Atkin LJJ, held that Lord Russell of Killowen CJ had been wrong in so holding. In *Monforts v Marsden*[2] Lord Russell of Killowen CJ went on to consider the plaintiff's claim under sub-s (2) and rejected the claim. If his reasoning for rejecting the claim under sub-s (1) had been right (contrary to what this court

j later held) one can readily understand the reasoning which then led to his rejection of the related claim under sub-s (2). But in the *Niblett* case[3] two members of this

1   9th Edn (1974), para 2405
2   (1895) 12 RPC 266
3   [1921] 3 KB 387, [1921] All ER Rep 459

court did not find it necessary to express a view on the meaning of sub-s (2) because
they held that the plaintiffs were manifestly entitled to succeed in their claim under *a*
sub-s (1), Atkin LJ, having, in the passage to which Lord Denning MR has referred,
made certain observations on the scope of sub-s (2), to which I shall refer later.
Finally, on this part of the case, there is the passage to which Lord Denning MR has
already referred in the judgment of Lord Greene MR in *Mason v Burningham*[1],
in which Lord Greene MR said that there was no justification for the introduction of
a gloss on the language of that statute by reading into it some exception in the case *b*
of disturbances of quiet possession by title paramount.   Ultimately the solution of
the present appeal must depend on the construction of those few words in sub-s (2).
      Whatever the historical origin of sub-s (2) and whether Sir Mackenzie Chalmers
when he drafted sub-s (2) had in mind the decision in *Howell v Richards*[2], and in
particular the passage[3] where Lord Ellenborough CJ said:
                                                                                             c
      'The covenant for quiet enjoyment is an assurance against the consequences,
      of a defective title, and of any disturbances thereupon.   For the purpose of
      this covenant, and the indemnity it affords, it is immaterial in what respects,
      and by what means, or by whose acts the eviction of the grantee or his heir
      takes place'
                                                                                             d
—or whether he had in mind civil law on the subject must remain one of the un-
solved mysteries of legal history.   As Lord Denning MR has said, we are not concerned with the historical origin of sub-s (2).   We are concerned with that subsection
as it appeared in the 1893 Act until that Act was recently amended.   The question
must be resolved as a question of construction together with such help as one can get
from the authorities which have been cited.   Those authorities are twofold: text- *e*
books and decided cases.   I would say a few words about the textbooks, because in
his judgment Mars-Jones J quoted Mr Goldblatt QC, who appeared below for the
defendants, as follows:

      'Mr Goldblatt has rightly said that many writers consider that section 12(1)
      and (2) of this Act cover much the same ground.'
                                                                                             f
I asked counsel for the defendants in this court who were the 'many writers', but
he was unable to help.   We have been referred only to two (or perhaps I should say
three) such writers.   The first and second are the editors of the 8th edition[4] of
Benjamin on Sale.   This edition had the advantage of being edited by the late Finne-
more J and the present James LJ.   In a passage—and this passage does not appear in the
earlier editions—the learned editors said[5]:   *g*

      'But this remedy [that is the remedy under sub-s (2)] does not seem to be of
      much value in English law, which already implies a condition of *title*, and where
      a buyer has also a remedy by action of trespass or trover.   Under the civil law
      (from which s. 12(2) is borrowed) the warranty against eviction gave a very
      necessary and practical remedy, as the seller did not profess to transfer ownership, *h*
      but only undisturbed possession.'

      The learned editors then quote a passage from Lord Russell of Killowen CJ's
judgment in *Monforts v Marsden*[6].   It is a little unfortunate that the passage contains
an incorrect quotation, because it is quoted as: 'It [that is the subsection] is *little*
                                                                                             j

1   [1949] 2 All ER 134 at 144, 145, [1949] 2 KB 545 at 563
2   (1809) 11 East 633
3   11 East at 642
4   (1950)
5   Page 682
6   (1895) RPC at 269

[sic] more than a covenant for the title', whereas when one looks at the text of Lord
a Russell of Killowen CJ's judgment, it reads: 'It is *a little* [sic] more than a covenant
for title'. Furthermore that passage was apparently written, or was at least published,
in 1950, after *Mason v Burningham*[1] was decided in 1949, but without reference to
Lord Greene MR's judgment in that case which I have already mentioned. The
weight which I would otherwise attach to that passage must be somewhat lessened by
these two matters. The third writer is Professor Atiyah in his book on Sale of Goods[2]
b where the learned author says much the same as was said earlier in the 8th edition[3]
of Benjamin:

> 'It is not easy to see what additional rights this [that is sub-s (2)] confers on
> the buyer over and above those conferred by Sect. 12(1).'

With the greatest respect to those expressions of opinion, I find myself unable to
c agree with them. Subsection (1) is dealing only with questions of defects of title.
I ventured to point out yesterday that sub-s (1) implies a *condition* as to title. Subsection (2), on the other hand, is expressed to be a *warranty*—the remedy for a breach
of which will sound only in damages. When one looks at the language of sub-s (2),
it is plain that it is looking forward to some future time after title has passed from the
seller to the buyer; whereas sub-s (1) is related to defect of title at the time of sale.
d As this court said in *Niblett's* case[4], sub-s (1) covers (inter alia) the position where some
third party is entitled as of right to stop the sale, so that the intending seller cannot
transfer a good title to his intending buyer. But sub-s (2) is concerned with the
problem where, although (as in the present case) a good title was passed to the
buyer, the buyer's right to quiet possession is for some reason subsequently interfered
with. It seems to me that the underlying purposes of sub-s (1) and of sub-s (2) are
e therefore different.

Further, the remedies for breach of sub-s (1) are—or at least may be—different
from the remedies for breach of sub-s (2). A breach of the condition implied by
sub-s (1) may give the aggrieved buyer a right to rescind, to recover the purchase
price (if paid), or to refuse to pay it (if not paid), and also to claim damages (if suffered),
or he may elect to treat the breach of condition as breach of warranty and only claim
f damages. But a breach of the warranty implied by sub-s (2) can never give to the
aggrieved buyer more than a remedy in damages.

It follows that in my view these two subsections create and were intended to create
independent rights and remedies for an aggrieved buyer according to whether it is
the implied condition or the implied warranty which is broken. Of course, in many
cases—and the three cases already referred to are examples of this—a plaintiff com-
g plaining of a breach of sub-s (1) may also be able to complain of a breach of sub-s (2).
But that is not necessarily always the case and the present is an example of a case
where there was no breach of the former but there was (in my view at least) a breach
of the latter subsection. I think the learned judge was entirely right to reject the
claim founded on sub-s (1) because the defendants acquired a perfectly good title to
the machines the price of which is claimed from them. But I think counsel for the
h plaintiffs is wrong in his argument that there cannot be a breach of sub-s (2) without a
breach of sub-s (1) as to title. I reach that conclusion for two reasons. First, as a matter
of construction, I see no justification for reading into the language of the subsection
the gloss or limitation for which counsel for the plaintiffs contended. I do not think
any of the decided cases supports his contention except *Monforts v Marsden*[5], and
that, as already stated, was later held to have been wrongly decided. Secondly, I
j find myself in complete and respectful agreement with what Lord Greene MR said

---

1   [1949] 2 All ER 134, [1949] 2 KB 545
2   4th Edn (1974), p 49
3   (1950)
4   [1921] 3 KB 387, [1921] All ER Rep 459
5   (1895) 12 RPC 266

in *Mason v Burningham*[1] on the matter, and I also agree with the relevant passage in the 9th edition of Benjamin[2].

It follows that (with all respect) I find myself unable to agree with passages quoted from the 8th edition of Benjamin[3] and from Professor Atiyah's book[4], and with the note in Halsbury's Laws of England[5] to which we have been referred this afternoon, notwithstanding that that note apparently had the authority of Diplock J (as he then was). The note reads:

'The distinction between the condition as to title and the warranty of quiet possession is similar to that between a covenant for title and one for quiet enjoyment. The former is an assurance by the grantor that he has the very estate in quantity and quality which he purports to convey; the latter is an assurance to the grantee against the consequences of a defective title and of any disturbance thereupon.'

The learned editors refer to *Howell v Richards*[6], to which I have just referred. Some reliance was also placed by counsel for the plaintiffs on the passage already referred to in the judgment of Atkin LJ in *Niblett's* case[7]. I would only say as to that, with the utmost respect, that for once Atkin LJ expressed himself with less than his usual precision and accuracy. In the result, therefore, like Lord Denning MR, I have reached the conclusion that, whilst the learned judge was right in rejecting the proposed defence based on s 12(1), he was wrong in rejecting the proposed defence under s 12(2). It is true that because of the retrospective effect of certain of the provisions of the Patents Act 1949, this is a most unusual case. But I venture to think that it is one example of the type of case—and there may well be others—for which sub-s (2), as distinct from sub-s (1), was intended to deal. I would therefore answer the relevant question asked of the court in the preliminary issue in the affirmative; but I would add to that answer that it is given not because of the defence sought to be raised under sub-s (1), but because of the defence sought to be raised under sub-s (2). Without expressing any view whatever on the point, I can see that the extent of the remedy in damages (if any) may be different if it is claimed under sub-s (2) rather than under sub-s (1).

I would therefore allow the appeal to that extent.

SIR JOHN PENNYCUICK. I agree with both the judgments which have been delivered.

The learned judge was I think clearly right in holding that s 12(1) of the Sale of Goods Act 1893 is inapplicable here, and I need say no more about that. Section 12(2) is, however, in a very different position, though the two subsections may overlap. I will read the opening words of s 12 again:

'In a contract of sale, unless the circumstances of the contract are such as to show a different intention, there is . . . (2) an implied warranty that the buyer shall have and enjoy quiet possession of the goods . . .'

It is, I think, quite impossible to imply into sub-s (2) an exception for interference by someone with a title paramount. Contrast in this respect the implied covenant for quiet enjoyment contained in the Law of Property Act 1925 and its predecessor, the Conveyancing Act 1891. The distinction is clearly drawn by Lord Greene MR

---

1   [1949] 2 All ER 134, [1949] 2 KB 545
2   (1974), para 277
3   8th Edn (1950), p 682
4   Sale of Goods (4th Edn, 1974), p 49
5   3rd Edn, vol 34; p 47, note (*s*)
6   (1809) 11 East 633
7   [1921] 3 KB at 401, [1921] All ER Rep at 464

a   in *Mason v Burningham*[1] and, in particular, in the passage which Lord Denning MR has already read:

> 'I can only express my opinion that the statute means what it says and is not to have any such gloss put on it.'

So far the present case is I think covered by the authority of that case.

b   It remains, however, to consider whether the title paramount, giving the right to interfere, must be in existence at the date of the sale. That was in fact the position in all the cases that have been cited. But again I do not think that such a limitation on the words of the subsection can be implied. The covenant for quiet possession looks forward, and I can see no justification for cutting down sub-s (2) by a qualification of this kind. Lord Greene MR's words are equally applicable here. In argument a number of illustrations were given, some exotic, in which sub-s (2) could not *c*   reasonably be expected to apply. It seems to me that insofar as the scope of sub-s (2) is to be cut down, it must be under the opening words of the section, namely, 'unless the circumstances of the contract are such as to show a different intention'. It will be for the court to consider in any of these cases—which are likely to be rare—whether those words are sufficient to take the particular case out of the ambit of sub-s (2).

d   This is a context in which one of two innocent parties must suffer. It seems to me the 1893 Act throws the loss on the vendor, and really there is not much more to be said. I do not think any assistance is to be derived from such research as counsel have been able to make into the historical origins of s 12; and in particular to my mind Roman law does not throw even a flickering light on the construction of the section.

e   I would allow this appeal.

ROSKILL LJ. May I just add to what I said earlier and express my agreement with what Sir John Pennycuick has said about the possible limitations on sub-s (2) by reason of the words 'unless the circumstances of the contract are such as to show a different intention'. I had intended to say that but I omitted to say it.

f

Appeal allowed.

Solicitors: *Rendall & Co* (for the defendants); *Frere, Cholmeley & Co* (for the plaintiffs).

M G Hammett Esq Barrister.

1 [1949] 2 All ER 134 at 144, 145, [1949] 2 KB 545 at 563

Oppenheimer v Cattermole (Inspector of Taxes) *a*
Nothman v Cooper (Inspector of Taxes)

HOUSE OF LORDS
LORD HAILSHAM OF ST MARYLEBONE, LORD HODSON, LORD PEARSON, LORD CROSS OF
CHELSEA AND LORD SALMON *b*
26th, 27th, 28th, 29th MARCH, 5th NOVEMBER, 13th DECEMBER 1973, 6th, 7th, 11th
NOVEMBER 1974, 5th FEBRUARY 1975

*Income tax – Double taxation – Relief Nationality – Remuneration and pensions payable
out of public funds of one of contracting parties – Taxpayer required to be national of both
contracting parties to qualify for relief – Federal Republic of Germany – Taxpayer British* *c*
*subject and German national by birth – Taxpayer a Jew – Taxpayer having emigrated
to England before second world war – Taxpayer deprived of German nationality by German
government decree during war – Basic Law of Federal Republic enacted on basis that wartime
decree void – Basic Law requiring person deprived of nationality by wartime decree to apply
for renaturalisation – Taxpayer not having applied – Whether taxpayer a German national
for purpose of tax relief under double taxation convention – Double Taxation Relief (Taxes* *d*
on Income) (Federal Republic of Germany) Order 1967 (SI 1967 No 25), Sch, art IX(2).

*Nationality – Enemy alien – Deprivation of nationality – Recognition by English courts –
Deprivation by decree of enemy state in wartime – Public policy precluding recognition of
change of status – Recognition once war terminated – War terminating as soon as fighting
ceases.* *e*

*Nationality – Enemy alien – Naturalisation during war – Alien becoming naturalised British
subject – Compatability of allegiance to Crown with allegiance to enemy state – Whether
alien ceasing in English law to be national of enemy state on naturalisation.*

*Conflict of laws – Foreign law – Recognition – Seizure of property – Legislation violating
human rights – Legislation depriving section of citizen body selected on racial grounds of* *f*
*property – Legislation also depriving them of nationality – Whether English courts should
refuse to recognise validity of legislation.*

The taxpayer was born in Germany in 1896 and was therefore a German national by
birth. He was a Jew and for many years was a teacher at a Jewish orphanage in
Bavaria. In 1939, after a period of detention in a concentration camp under the Nazi *g*
regime, he came to live in England where he remained during the war. A German
decree enacted on 25th November 1941 provided, inter alia: 'A Jew loses his German
citizenship (a) if at the date of entry into force of this regulation, he has his usual
place of abode abroad . . .' The decree also provided for the confiscation of the
property of Jews thus deprived of their nationality and for the use of that property
'to further aims connected with the solution of the Jewish problem'. Hostilities *h*
between the United Kingdom and Germany ceased on 8th May 1945. On 24th May
1948 the taxpayer became a British subject by naturalisation. The German nationality law of 1913 provided that a German who had neither his habitual residence
nor his permanent abode in Germany lost his nationality when he acquired a
foreign nationality if such acquisition was made on application by him unless he had
the written permission of the competent authority of his native country to retain his *j*
nationality. In May 1949, on the founding of the Federal Republic of Germany, a Basic
Law was enacted which, by art 116(2)[a], provided that former German citizens who
had been deprived of their German nationality during the period from 1933 to 1945,

---

a Article 116 is set out at p 560 *f* to *h*, post

were to be 'renaturalised' on application and, furthermore, were to be considered
a as not having been deprived of their nationality if they took up residence in Germany
after 8th May 1945 and did not express any wish to the contrary. The taxpayer,
however, remained resident in the United Kingdom. The war between the United
Kingdom and Germany officially ended on 9th July 1951. In 1953 the Federal Government of Germany awarded the taxpayer, as an employee of a Jewish religious community, a pension from 1st October 1952 to compensate for his persecution under the
b Nazi regime. He was given a second pension by the German authorities in 1961
when he attained the age of 65. Both pensions were payable out of public funds of
the Federal Republic. In 1968 the German Federal Constitutional Court held that
art 116 of the Basic Law had been formulated on the assumption that the 1941 decree
'was void ab initio' but that the effect of art 116(2) was that 'persecutees'
who had acquired a foreign nationality could regain their nationality by taking up
c residence in Germany or by making an application but that for persecutees who had
not acquired a foreign nationality the effect of art 116(2) was that the German state
'does not treat them as Germans unless they assert their German nationality by
taking up residence or making an application'. The taxpayer was assessed to income
tax in respect of the pensions paid to him by the German government for each of
the years of assessment 1953-54 to 1967-68 inclusive. The taxpayer, who had con-
d tinued to be resident in the United Kingdom during those years and had made no
application to be renaturalised under art 116(2) of the Basic Law, appealed against
the assessments, claiming exemption under double taxation conventions concluded
between the United Kingdom and Germany in 1954 and 1964. Under the provisions
of each of those conventions, which were set out in the schedule to statutory instruments of 1955 and 1967[b], the pensions were exempt from United Kingdom income
e tax if during the relevant years the taxpayer was a 'national' both of the United
Kingdom and Germany, but they were not exempt if he was a national of the United
Kingdom only. The taxpayer contended that during the relevant years of assessment
he had retained his German nationality since (i) the 1941 decree could not be recognised
by English law, (ii) the 1913 nationality law had not operated to deprive him of his
German nationality when he became a British subject in 1948, and (iii) after the
f enactment of art 116(2) of the Basic Law he continued to be a German national even
though, in default of an application for renaturalisation, he was not treated as such by
the German state.

Held – The question whether under German law the taxpayer had retained his
German nationality was to be determined by the English courts as a question of fact.
g The evidence showed that, on the assumption that the taxpayer had not lost his
German nationality on becoming a naturalised British subject in 1948, he had nevertheless lost it in May 1949 when the Basic Law was enacted. Since he had neither
applied for renaturalisation nor taken up residence in Germany during the relevant
years of assessment, he was not treated by German law as a German national and no
distinction could be drawn between a person who was not a German national and a
h person who was in law 'not treated' as a German national; it was, furthermore,
immaterial that the taxpayer had an automatic right to acquire German nationality
on application or on returning to live in Germany. It followed that the taxpayer was
not, during the relevant years of assessment, a German national and accordingly
was not entitled to relief under the relevant conventions (see p 554c and d, p 556c and g,
p 557 a, p 562 b to g, p 564 j and p 572 j to p 573 c, post).

j   Per Curiam. (i) The English courts will only refuse to recognise a change in the
status of an enemy alien effected under the law of the enemy country during wartime
so long as the war subsists. Once the war is over the courts will recognise and give

---

b See the Double Taxation Relief (Taxes on Income) (Federal Republic of Germany) Order
1955 (SI 1955 No 1203), Sch, art IX(1), and the Double Taxation Relief (Taxes on Income)
(Federal Republic of Germany) Order 1967 (SI 1967 No 25), Sch, art IX(2)

effect to the change. For that purpose 'wartime' is to be regarded as coming to an
end when fighting ceases and not as continuing until the United Kingdom government   *a*
declares officially that the state of war is over (see p 553 *g*, p 556 *g*, p 557 *a*, p 565 *c* and
f to *h* and p 570 *d*, post); *R v Home Secretary, ex parte L* [1945] KB 7 and *Lowenthal v
Attorney-General* [1948] 1 All ER 295 explained.

(ii) Where a national of an enemy state becomes a British subject by naturalisation
in time of war it does not follow that he thereby ceases to be a national of the enemy
state (see p 555 *f* to *h*, p 556 *g*, p 557 *a*, p 569 *a* and p 570 *d*, post).   *b*

(iii) The fact that legislation by which a foreign state deprives a man of his status as
a citizen of that state can be described as 'confiscatory' does not necessarily entail the
consequence that English law should deem him to remain a citizen of that state for
the purpose of deciding whether or not he is entitled to property in England, his right
to which depends on his being or not being a citizen of that state at some point in time
(see p 553 *g*, p 556 *g*, p 557 *a*, p 566 *d* to *f* and p 570 *d*, post).   *c*

Per Lord Hodson, Lord Cross of Chelsea and Lord Salmon (Lord Hailsham of St
Marylebone and Lord Pearson dissenting). Legislation enacted by a foreign state, such
as the 1941 decree, which takes away without compensation from a section of the
citizen body singled out on racial grounds all their property on which the state can
lay its hands and, in addition, deprives them of their citizenship is contrary to international law and constitutes so grave an infringement of human rights that the   *d*
English courts ought to refuse to recognise it as law at all (see p 556 *j* to p 557 *a*, p 566 *g*,
p 567 *a* to *g*, p 570 *j* to p 571 *a* and p 572 *c d* and *f*, post).

Decision of the Court of Appeal [1972] 3 All ER 1106 affirmed on different grounds.

Notes

For double taxation relief, see 20 Halsbury's Laws (3rd Edn) 455, para 855, and for   *e*
cases on the subject, see 28(1) Digest (Reissue) 454, 455, 1636-1638.

For alien enemies, see 4 Halsbury's Laws (4th Edn) 458, para 950, and for cases on the
subject, see 2 Digest (Repl) 212-215, 259-288.

For the recognition of foreign decrees effecting seizure of property, see 8 Halsbury's
Laws (4th Edn) 446, para 663, and for cases on the subject, see 11 Digest (Repl) 325,
19, 20.   *f*

Cases referred to in opinions

Aksionairnoye Obschestvo A M Luther v James Sagor & Co [1921] 3 KB 532, 90 LJKB 1202,
125 LT 705, CA, 11 Digest (Repl) 325, 19.

Colquhoun v Brooks (1899) 14 App Cas 493, [1886-90] All ER Rep 1063, 59 LJQB 53, 61 LT
518, 54 JP 277, 2 Tax Cas 490, HL, 17 Digest (Reissue) 345, 1130.   *g*

Foulsham v Pickles [1925] AC 458, [1925] All ER Rep 706, 94 LJKB 418, 133 LT 5, 9 Tax Cas
261, HL, 28(1) Digest (Reissue) 358, 1307.

Frankfurther v W L Exner Ltd [1947] Ch 629, [1948] LJR 553, 177 LT 257, 11 Digest (Repl)
612, 422.

Helbert Wagg & Co Ltd, Re, Re Prudential Assurance Co [1956] 1 All ER 129, [1956] 1 Ch
323, [1956] 2 WLR 183, 2 Digest (Repl) 267, 609.   *h*

Kramer v Attorney-General [1923] AC 528, HL, 2 Digest (Repl) 23, 354.

Lowenthal v Attorney-General [1948] 1 All ER 295, 64 TLR 145, 36 Digest (Repl) 848, 1962.

Novello & Co Ltd v Hinrichsen Edition Ltd [1951] 2 All ER 457, [1951] Ch 1026, [1951] TLR
645, CA, 13 Digest (Repl) 95, 363.

Paley (Princess Olga) v Weisz [1929] 1 KB 718, 98 LJKB 465, 141 LT 207, CA, 11 Digest
(Repl) 612, 421.   *j*

R v Home Secretary, ex parte L [1945] KB 7, 114 LJKB 229, 2 Digest (Repl) 215, 288.

R v Vine Street Police Station Superintendent, ex parte Liebmann [1916] 1 KB 268, [1914-15]
All ER Rep 393, 85 LJKB 210, 113 LT 971, 80 JP 42, 2 Digest (Repl) 324, 13.

Stoeck v Public Trustee [1921] 2 Ch 67, 90 LJCh 386, 125 LT 851, 11 Digest (Repl) 324, 13.

United States of America, ex rel Schwarzkopf v Uhl (1943) 137 Fed R (2d) 898.

Weber, Ex parte [1916] 1 AC 421, 85 LJKB 944, 114 LT 214, 80 JP 249, 25 Cox CC 258, HL;
affg [1916] 1 KB 280, [1916] 85 LJKB 217n, 113 LT 968, CA, 2 Digest (Repl) 214, 279.

Appeals

Oppenheimer v Cattermole (Inspector of Taxes)

At a meeting of the Commissioners for the Special Purposes of the Income Tax Acts held on 19th January 1970 Meier Oppenheimer appealed against assessments to income tax in the sum of £800 for each of the years 1953-54 to 1967-68 inclusive. Shortly stated the question for the commissioners' decision was whether certain pension payments received by Mr Oppenheimer from German public funds qualified for exemption from income tax under the terms of the double taxation relief conventions made between the United Kingdom and the Federal Republic of Germany. The commissioners heard evidence from Dr Ernst Josef Cohn, a Doctor of Laws of the University of Breslau, formerly Professor of Law at the university, and an Honorary Professor of Laws in the University of Frankfurt-am-Main.

As a result of the evidence both oral and documentary adduced before the commissioners they found the following facts proved or admitted: (1) Mr Oppenheimer was born in Germany in 1896. From 1919 to 1938 he was a teacher at a Jewish orphanage at Fürth, Bavaria. On his release in December 1938 from a period of detention in the concentration camp at Dachau he resumed teaching until, in April 1939, he emigrated to England where he had since resided. He became a naturalised British subject in 1948. The certificate of naturalisation issued to the taxpayer showed in the particulars relating to him 'Nationality German'. (2) In 1953 Mr Oppenheimer was notified by the German Federal Department for Compensation to Employees of Jewish Religious Communities that he had been awarded a pension (the 'first pension') with effect from 1st October 1952. In April 1961 he attained the age of 65 and was awarded a pension (the 'second pension') under the provisions of s 25(1) of the 'Angestelltenversicherungsgesetz in der Fassung vom 23.2.1957 (A.V.G.)' with effect from 1st April 1961, from which date the first pension was abated by 87·8 per cent. The provisions of s 25(1) of the AVG provided:

'An insured person who has reached the age of 65 shall receive a retirement pension, on condition that the qualifying period has been completed.'

Both the first pension and the second pension were payable out of public funds of the Federal Republic of Germany. (3) The evidence given by Dr Cohn, which was accepted, was to the following effect: (a) by a decision of the Federal German Constitutional Court given in 1968, which was binding on all Federal German courts by virtue of a subsequent decree of the Federal German Government, the decree of 25th November 1941 was absolutely void ab initio; (b) that decision had no retrospective effect; (c) the German nationality law of 22nd July 1913 remained in force (with certain amendments not relevant for present purposes) and was unaffected by the decision; (d) in his opinion, under German law, if the taxpayer had not lost German nationality under the decree of 25th November 1941 he lost it under the German nationality law of 22nd July 1913 on being naturalised a British subject in 1948.

No dispute arose regarding figures, and the only question for the commissioners' decision was whether or not the pension payments made to Mr Oppenheimer were exempt from United Kingdom income tax (for the years 1953-54 to 1959-60) by virtue of para (1) of art IX of the convention between the United Kingdom and the Federal Republic of Germany for the avoidance of double taxation which was set out in the schedule to the Double Taxation Relief (Taxes on Income) (Federal Republic of Germany) Order 1955[1] and (for the years 1960-61 to 1967-68) by virtue of para (2) of art IX of the similar convention set out in the schedule to the Double Taxation Relief

---

1 SI 1955 No 1203

(Taxes on Income) (Federal Republic of Germany) Order 1967[1]. It was common
ground that, for the aforementioned exemptions to apply, it would require to be   *a*
shown (i) that when he received the pension payments Mr Oppenheimer (who was
admittedly a national of the United Kingdom at the material times) was also a German
national, and (ii) that the pension payments fell within the description 'Remuneration,
including pensions, paid, in respect of present or past services or work . . .' In regard
to the question whether Mr Oppenheimer was a German national at the material
times, 'national' in the context in which it appeared in art IX of each of the conventions   *b*
was not defined in either convention. Having regard to the terms of art II (3) of each
convention, it was agreed before the commissioners that the question fell to be
determined according to English law. It was not in dispute that Mr Oppenheimer was
a German national from birth until at least 25th November 1941. On that date there
was promulgated, with immediate effect, a decree of the then National Socialist
Government of Germany depriving of German citizenship Jews whose usual place of   *c*
abode was outside Germany—a class which included Mr Oppenheimer.

It was contended on behalf of Mr Oppenheimer: (1) that Mr Oppenheimer's loss or
purported loss of German citizenship under the decree could not be recognised by the
English courts, and that, whatever the position might have been under German law,
under English law Mr Oppenheimer remained a German national after 25th November 1941 on the grounds that: (a) English law did not recognise a change of status in its   *d*
nationals brought about by a decree of a foreign enemy state in wartime, and/or (b)
English law would not give effect as far as it related to matters in this country to a
penal and confiscatory decree of a foreign country; (2) that payments made to Mr
Oppenheimer by way of both the first pension and the second pension fell within the
description 'Remuneration, including pensions, paid in respect of present or past
services or work . . .'; (3) that the payments were exempt from tax under the provisions   *e*
of art IX of the conventions.

It was contended on behalf of the Crown: (1) that under English law the question
whether an individual was a national of a foreign state fell to be determined by
reference to the municipal law of that state; (2) that so far as the English courts were
concerned questions of foreign law were questions of fact; (3) that even if Mr Oppenheimer did remain a German national after 25th November 1941, which was not   *f*
admitted, he ceased to be such on applying for and acquiring British nationality in 1948
(not having, prior to the acquisition, applied for and been granted the written permission of the competent German authority to retain his German nationality) by
virtue of the German nationality law of 22nd July 1913; (4) that payments made to
Mr Oppenheimer by way of the second pension did not fall within the description
'Remuneration, including pensions, paid, in respect of present or past services or   *g*
work . . .'; (5) that no exemption was due in respect of payments made to the taxpayer
by way of either the first pension or the second pension under the provisions of art IX
of the conventions; (6) that the appeal should fail in principle and should be adjourned
for the agreement of figures.

The commissioners who heard the appeal took time to consider their decision and
gave it in writing on 18th February 1970 as follows: *h*

'1. These appeals are made against assessments for the years 1953/54 to 1967/68,
inclusive, in respect of certain pension payments received by [Mr Oppenheimer]
from German public funds under two awards made to him in 1953 (with effect
from 1st October, 1952) and 1961 respectively. It is not contended before us that
the said receipts do not constitute income for Income Tax purposes and the first   *j*
question for our decision is whether or not the receipts are exempt from tax in
[Mr Oppenheimer's] hands under Article IX of the Convention set out in the
Schedule to the Double Taxation Relief (Taxes on Income) (Federal Republic of

---

1   SI 1967 No 25

a Germany) Order, 1955 (S.I., 1955 No. 1203) and the similar Article of the Convention set out in the Schedule to the corresponding Order of 1967 (S.I., 1967 No. 25).

'2. Having considered the evidence adduced before us and the arguments advanced to us we hold that these appeals fail. We find from that evidence that under German law [Mr Oppenheimer] ceased to be a German national not later than 4th June, 1948, when he became a national of the United Kingdom. We hold

b that under English law [Mr Oppenheimer] was not a German national certainly from 4th June, 1948, when he became a national of the United Kingdom. Whatever may have been their effect in determining the nationality of [Mr Oppenheimer] under English law between 25th November, 1941 and 4th June, 1948, we hold that the decisions in *R v Home Secretary, ex parte L*[1] and *Lowenthal v A-G*[2] do not require us to hold that [Mr Oppenheimer] was a German national after 4th

c June, 1948. [Mr Oppenheimer] is not therefore entitled, in our view, to relief under Article IX of the Conventions on the footing that throughout the relevant years he was at one and the same time a German national and a national of the United Kingdom.

'3. In view of this determination we do not need to deal with the Crown's argument that in any event [Mr Oppenheimer] was not entitled to the exemption

d claimed in respect of the payments he received under the 1961 award because those payments were not "Remuneration, including pensions, paid, in respect of present or past services or work" within Article IX of the Conventions.

'4. We leave figures to be agreed between the parties on the basis of this our decision in principle.'

e Figures were subsequently agreed between the parties and on 30th June 1970 the commissioners adjusted the assessments accordingly.

Mr Oppenheimer appealed against that decision. On 21st December 1971 Goulding J[3] allowed the appeal and remitted the assessments to the commissioners for adjustment or discharge, holding that Mr Oppenheimer was both a German and British national during the relevant years of assessment on the grounds (i) that the 1941 decree

f could not be recognised since an enemy decree made during wartime and purporting to make enemy nationals stateless would not be recognised by the English courts; (ii) that accordingly Mr Oppenheimer remained a national of Germany for the purposes of English law; and (iii) that since the 1941 decree was, however, effective in German law to deprive him of his German nationality, the nationality law of 1913 could not operate to deprive him of German nationality in 1948 for, at the time when

g he acquired British nationality, he was not in German law a German national. The Crown appealed against that decision and, on 20th July 1972, the Court of Appeal[4] (Lord Denning MR, Buckley and Orr LJJ) reversed the decision of Goulding J holding that during the relevant years of assessment Mr Oppenheimer was a national of the United Kingdom only on the following grounds: (i) (by Buckley and Orr LJJ) that, although so long as the war continued, English courts could not recognise a wartime

h decree made by an enemy state which purported to deprive its citizens of their enemy nationality, once the state of war had terminated, the courts were bound to recognise the change of status brought about by such a decree if the decree was still valid and effective under the law of the former enemy state, and that, accordingly, following the conclusion of the peace treaty with Germany on 9th July 1951, the English courts were bound to recognise the 1941 decree as having deprived Mr Oppenheimer of his

j German nationality; and (ii) (by Lord Denning MR) that Mr Oppenheimer had lost

---

1   [1945] KB 7
2   [1948] 1 All ER 295
3   [1972] 2 All ER 529, [1972] Ch 585
4   [1972] 3 All ER 1106, [1973] Ch 264

his German nationality on becoming a British subject in 1948 when the United
Kingdom and Germany were still at war for, at such a time, allegiance to both coun-　*a*
tries was incompatible and, by applying for naturalisation, Mr Oppenheimer had
accepted the repudiation by the German authorities in 1941 of their obligation to
protect him by depriving him of his German nationality. Mr Oppenheimer appealed
to the House of Lords.

Sir Elwyn Jones QC and *M Englard* for Mr Oppenheimer.　　　　　　　　　*b*
John Vinelott QC and *Patrick Medd* for the Crown.

Their Lordships took time for consideration.

13th December 1973. The following opinions were delivered.

c

LORD HAILSHAM OF ST MARYLEBONE LC.　My Lords, I have had the
opportunity of reading the speech of my noble and learned friend, Lord Cross of
Chelsea, and, for the reasons he gives, I agree the cause be remitted back to the Special
Commissioners for further consideration.

LORD HODSON.　My Lords, I agree with the terms of the order proposed by my　*d*
noble and learned friend, Lord Cross of Chelsea.

LORD PEARSON.　My Lords, I have had the advantage of reading the opinion of
my noble and learned friend, Lord Cross of Chelsea, and I agree that for the reasons
which he has given an order should be made in the terms which he has proposed.

e

LORD CROSS OF CHELSEA.　My Lords, the question at issue in this appeal
is whether the appellant, Mr Oppenheimer, is liable to pay United Kingdom income
tax for the tax years 1953-54 to 1967-68 inclusive on certain pension payments which
he received during those years from German public funds. Mr Oppenheimer, who is
a Jew, was born in Germany in 1896. From 1919 to 1939 he taught at a Jewish orphanage　*f*
in Bavaria but in 1939, after having been detained for a short period in a concentration
camp, he succeeded in leaving Germany and coming to this country where he has
lived ever since. In 1948 he applied for and was granted a certificate of naturalisation
and became a British subject. As a former employee of a Jewish religious community
he has been since 1953 in receipt of a pension payable out of the revenues of the
German Federal Republic. Conventions with regard to double taxation relief were　*g*
made between the United Kingdom and the Federal Republic in 1954 and 1964 and
made law in this country by the Double Taxation Relief (Taxes on Income) Federal
Republic of Germany Orders 1955 and 1967. Article IX(1) of the former convention
—which Mr Oppenheimer contends is applicable to the first seven assessments in
dispute—runs as follows:

h

> 'Remuneration, including pensions, paid in respect of present or past services
> or work out of public funds of one of the Contracting Parties shall be exempt from
> tax in the territory of the other Contracting Party, unless the individual concerned
> is a national of that other Party without being also a national of the first mentioned
> Party.'

Article IX(2) of the second convention which Mr Oppenheimer contends is applicable　*j*
to the other eight assessments is to the same effect. Mr Oppenheimer is, of course,
undoubtedly a national of this country and the Crown admits for the purpose of this
case that the pensions in question fall within the description in the Conventions. The
point at issue is whether the appellant was in the years of assessment not only a
British subject but also a German national. Dr Cohn, an expert in German law called

by the Crown, gave evidence before the commissioners, to whom Mr Oppenheimer
a had appealed against the assessments made on him, which the commissioners
understood to be to the following effect: (1) The German nationality law of 22nd July
1913 provides that a German who is neither domiciled nor permanently resident in
Germany loses his nationality on acquiring a foreign nationality unless he has the
previous written permission of the appropriate German authority to retain it. (2) A
decree of 25th November 1941, enacted by the 'Nazi' government during the war,
b provided that a Jew of German nationality who had his usual place of abode abroad
when the decree came into force should lose his nationality forthwith. (3) By a
decision of the Federal German Constitutional Court given in 1968 the decree of 25th
November 1941 was held to be absolutely void ab initio but nevertheless that decision
had no retrospective effect. (4) In Dr Cohn's opinion, if Mr Oppenheimer had not lost
his German nationality under the decree of 25th November 1941 he lost it under the
c nationality law of 22nd July 1913 on becoming naturalised as a British subject in 1948.

The commissioners accepted the evidence of Dr Cohn, and held that Mr Oppenheimer ceased to be a German national at latest on 4th June 1948, when he became a
British subject. They therefore confirmed the assessments. At the request of the
appellant they stated a case for the opinion of the court which came before Goulding
J[1] who reversed their decision. He held first that English law would not recognise the
d decree of 25th November 1941 as having any effect with regard to Mr Oppenheimer
since it purported to alter during wartime the nationality of someone who was then
an enemy alien and, secondly, that Mr Oppenheimer had not lost his German
nationality by the law of 22nd July 1913, since under German law he had already
ceased to be a German national before he became a British subject—although our
law regarded him as still a German national. The respondents appealed to the Court
e of Appeal[2] (Lord Denning MR, Buckley and Orr LJJ) who reversed the decision of
Goulding J and restored that of the commissioners. Lord Denning MR held that whatever the position might be under German law English law would not regard an enemy
alien whom it allowed to become naturalised as a British subject during wartime as
continuing thereafter to be a national of the enemy country as well as a British subject.
Buckley and Orr LJJ based their judgments on a different ground—namely, that
f although English law would not recognise a change in the status of an enemy alien
effected by the alien's domestic law during wartime, that non-recognition only lasted
so long as the state of war lasted, and that consequently when the state of war between this country and Germany came to an end, our law would recognise that Mr
Oppenheimer had been deprived of his status as a German national by the decree of
25th November 1941. Mr Oppenheimer appealed to this House from the decision
g of the Court of Appeal and the appellate committee heard arguments from both
sides on the basis of the findings as to German law made by the commissioners and
set out in the stated case. But before we reported our views to the House we became
aware that there were grounds for thinking that the findings of the commissioners as
to the relevant German law might have been based on inadequate material and that,
in particular, art 116(2) of the Constitution of the Federal Republic enacted in 1949
h before the years of assessment might have a bearing on the point to be decided. We
therefore put the appeal back into the list for further argument and, as a result of the
discussion which then ensued, it became clear—and was accepted by counsel on both
sides—that the case ought to be sent back to the commissioners for further findings
as to the relevant German law. I would, therefore, propose that an order be made in
the following terms:
j
'That this case be and the same is hereby remitted back to the Commissioners
for the Special purposes of the Income Tax Acts for further consideration, and

---

1   [1972] 2 All ER 529, [1972] Ch 585
2   [1972] 3 All ER 1106, [1973] Ch 264   T

with a Direction that they amend the Case Stated by finding on further consideration of the evidence already adduced and on consideration of any further evidence   *a*
the parties may adduce and taking into account any relevant decisions of the
German Courts and their necessary implications and any other provision of
German law (*a*) whether for the purposes of German municipal law [Mr Oppen-
heimer] was deprived of his German citizenship by the Decree of 25th
November, 1941; (*b*) if [Mr Oppenheimer] was not deprived of his German
citizenship by the said Decree whether for the purposes aforesaid he was deprived   *b*
of German citizenship by the German Nationality Law of 22nd July, 1913, on
being naturalised a British subject on 24th May, 1948, and taking into account his
Oath of Allegiance on 4th June, 1948; (*c*) if the appellant was deprived of German
citizenship by the said Decree or by the said German nationality law at any time
prior to the assessment years whether (i) his German citizenship was re-instated
or deemed to be re-instated by the Constitution of the Federal Republic or by   *c*
any legislation or judicial decision or under any other provision of German law,
or (ii) his German citizenship would have been re-instated at any time before or
during the relevant years of assessment if he had applied for German citizenship
under Article 116 of the Grundgesetz 1949.
  'AND IT IS FURTHER ORDERED, that the said Commissioners do report the amended
Case to this House.'   *d*

LORD SALMON. My Lords, I agree with my noble and learned friend, Lord Cross
of Chelsea.

Order accordingly.
                                                                            e

  The following supplementary case was stated by the commissioners under the
direction of the House of Lords.
  [Paragraph 1 recited the order made by the House of Lords and continued:] Of the
two commissioners who heard Mr Oppenheimer's appeal on 19th January 1970 one
has since retired from the public service and was not available to carry out the direction   *f*
of the House of Lords. One of the parties was not prepared to consent to the proceedings being continued before the continuing commissioner under the terms of s 45(3) of
the Taxes Management Act 1970. With the agreement of both parties to the appeal,
the proceedings were continued with the continuing commissioner and another
commissioner.
  2. At a further meeting of the commissioners held on 29th April to 3rd May 1974
inclusive, the order of 13th December 1973 was read, and evidence heard from Dr   *g*
Franz Paul Jaques, a member of the English Bar, a practising German lawyer and a
Doctor of Law of the University of Hamburg together with further evidence from
Dr Ernst Josef Cohn and the observations of counsel on all the evidence adduced
before the commissioners.
  [Paragraph 3 listed the documents produced before the commissioners.]
  4. As a result of the evidence both oral and documentary adduced before the   *h*
commissioners the following facts were proved or admitted:

Background information
  (a) (i) The basis of the German law relating to nationality is the 1913 law which in s 17
thereof sets out grounds for loss of nationality and in art 25 thereof provides for loss of
German nationality by the reason of the acquisition of a foreign nationality.   *j*
This law is hereinafter referred to as 'the nationality law'. (ii) The Nazis came
into power in Germany in 1933 and in July of that year there was passed a law
which gave the government power by decree to deprive of their German nationality
individuals considered undesirable. Under that law numerous Germans were
individually deprived of German citizenship. In 1935 there was enacted another act

which created two classes of citizens, those of German or kindred blood and,
a secondly, all others. This act enabled the German government by decree to deprive
of their nationality citizens in the second class. The 1941 decree or 11th Ordinance
was made under the 1935 legislation. (iii) The Nazis surrendered to the Allied Powers
on 8th May 1945, and shortly thereafter the 1941 decree was repealed by Allied
Military Government legislation. It is generally accepted by German lawyers that
this repeal by the appropriate occupying authority was without any retrospective
b effect. (iv) Between 1945 and 1948 the governments of the various German lander in
the United States zone of occupation of Germany passed a uniform law whereunder
expatriates resident in the respective lander were given the right to apply to have their
expatriation declared null and void. (v) The new constitution of the Federal Republic
of Germany was promulgated as the Basic Law on 23rd May 1949. (vi) By a declaration
dated 9th July 1951 the government of the United Kingdom declared that the state of
c war between the United Kingdom and Germany had ended. (vii) There is a presumption in German law that German civilians who went missing during the Second
World War or who were sent to concentration camps and never came out had died
on 8th May 1945 the day on which the German armed forces surrendered to the Allied
forces. (viii) The Constitutional Court is the supreme court in Germany in relation
to matters affecting the constitution as enacted in the Basic Law. Its jurisdiction is set
d out in art 93 of that law. The decisions of the Constitutional Court are declaratory and,
therefore, retrospective. A decision of the Constitutional Court declaring a Federal
statute valid or invalid must be published in the official gazette and when published
has the force of a statute. Other decisions of the Constitutional Court (for instance
those interpreting the Constitution) do not have the force of a statute but all govern-
mental agencies and all courts are nonetheless bound not only by the decision but by
e the principle on which it is based. That part of the reasoning of the Constitutional
Court which is not essential to its decision is not binding on other courts but in practice
is normally followed. (ix) In 1948 when the appellant was applying for British nationality conditions in Germany were such that he could not have effectively made application under the nationality law for the written permission of the competent authority
to retain his German nationality. (x) The following terms are used in succeeding
f paragraphs: 'expatriate' or 'persecutee', a German affected by a decree made under the
Nazi legislation of 1933 or 1935; hence 'expatriation' and 'expatriated'; Germany, the
Federal Republic of Germany; art 116, art 116 of the Basic Law.

(b) It was agreed between the parties to the appeal that before considering what
answers should be given to the questions posed to the commissioners it was desirable
to consider the decisions of the German courts. Those decisions were all concerned
g with various matters affecting the rights and liabilities of expatriates. As they made
plain, the question of the proper treatment of those individuals under the law was a
peculiarly sensitive one for the new German state. It was anxious on the one hand to
restore to the expatriate the nationality which the Nazis had purported to take away,
but it was not disposed on the other hand to force such restoration on an unwilling
recipient. That somewhat ambivalent attitude finds expression in the various cases
h and makes them neither easy of reconciliation nor productive of clear principles of
general application.

(c) The commissioners considered the relevant decisions: (i) They were referred to
two decisions of the Federal Constitutional Court. The later of those two decisions,
the 1968 decision, dealt with a German Jewish refugee who had emigrated to Amsterdam shortly before the Second World War, had apparently been deprived of his
j German nationality by the 1941 decree and had subsequently been deported from
Amsterdam in 1942. Since nothing was known of his fate thereafter, he was presumed
to have died on 8th May 1945 in accordance with the relevant compensation law. The
question which fell to be decided was whether he had died a German national, or
without nationality. As the commissioners understood the evidence of the expert
witnesses three points decided by the Constitutional Court formed part of the binding

ratio decidendi of that case: (a) that the 1941 decree was void ab initio; (b) that art
116(2) was not directly applicable to persecutees who died before 8th May 1945; and   *a*
(c) that German nationality should be forced on persecutees who died before 8th May
1945, as little as on those who died after that date; only if there were any concrete
indications showing that the persons in question, knowing that they could return to a
free, democratic and lawful Germany—a Germany governed by the rule of law—
would not have wanted to make use of that possibility, was it to be assumed that they
wished to renounce their German nationality. In relation to those points there was   *b*
substantial agreement between the witnesses; divergence between their views
emerged when it came to reconciling the 1968 with the 1958 decision and applying
art 116(2) to persecutees who survived 8th May 1945. In the course of the decision of
the Constitutional Court in the 1968 case the following passage occurred following a
reference to and citation of art 116(2):
                                                                                       c
    'In formulating this article the constitutional legislator proceeded from the
    assumption that the [1941 decree] was void ab initio. This means that the
    persecutees have never lost their German nationality by virtue of the expatria-
    tion. They may of course have lost it for some other reason, especially through
    acquisition of a foreign nationality. The effect of article 116(2) of the Constitution
    in such a case is that even these persons can regain German nationality by taking   *d*
    up residence in the Federal German Republic or by making an application.
    For persecutees who have not acquired a foreign nationality the effect of article
    116(2) is that notwithstanding the fact that they did not lose their German
    nationality by expatriation the German State does not treat them as Germans
    unless they assert their German nationality by taking up residence or making
    an application. Thus far article 116(2) gives effect to the idea that no persecutee   *e*
    should have German nationality forced upon him against his will.'

Following that passage and a review of the legislative history of art 116 there occurs
a further passage on which the views of the witnesses diverged:

    'The persecutees who died before 8 May 1945 cannot be treated differently   *f*
    from those who survived the coming into force of the Basic Law. Both groups
    were victims of the national-socialist regime. There is no good reason for
    differentiating between them with regard to the consequences arising from
    "expatriation". Even in the case of persecutees affected by the [1941 decree]
    who died before 8 May 1945, it must be borne in mind that they may have wanted
    to renounce their German nationality.'
                                                                                       g
Dr Jaques approached those passages on the basis that it was fundamental to the
decision of the Constitutional Court that the 1941 decree was void ab initio and had
not deprived the persecutees affected by it of their German nationality. In the case
of a persecutee who died before the Basic Law took effect, in the absence of the
clearest possible evidence of an intention to renounce German nationality, he had
to be taken to have died a German since nothing had occurred to deprive him of his   *h*
German nationality. The reference to persecutees who survived being entitled to
similar treatment implied that they, too, retained their German nationality since
nothing had occurred to deprive them of it. Assertion of German nationality in
one of the ways contemplated in art 116(2) would be no more than declaratory.
Article 116(2) could not itself be said to have deprived the persecutees of their German
nationality since its purpose was indemnificatory: it was certainly not the function   *j*
of art 116(2) to give effect to the National Socialist legislation declared by the Constitutional Court to be void ab initio. The principle of not forcing German nationality
on a persecutee against his will was to be met by the state not considering a persecutee
as a German national until he himself took one of the simple steps identified in art
116(2) to assert his German nationality. Dr Cohn took a different view. In the

passage cited he considered that what the Constitutional Court was saying with
a regard to persecutees who survived was that, notwithstanding the fact that they did
not lose their German nationality by virtue of the 1941 decree which was void, nonetheless the German state would not treat them as being Germans unless they relied
on their nationality by residence or application. It had been suggested that they
retained a kind of shadowy, theoretical or 'half' nationality. But Dr Cohn preferred to interpret the words used somewhat differently. The Constitutional Court
b did not say that surviving persecutees still possessed German nationality. It only said
that they did not lose it through the expatriation which the 1941 decree purported
to effect. Though not in the position of having lost their nationality, they no longer
currently had it unless they established residence or made application. Any other
conclusion would result in German nationality being forced on them. The Constitutional Court was in effect saying to such persecutees, although you have not been
c expatriated, unless you assert your nationality you are deemed not to be Germans.
The furthest Dr Cohn felt himself able to go in expressing the matter in English
terms was to say that a persecutee in the position of Mr Oppenheimer could not be
said to have been deprived of his German nationality by the 1941 decree, but, having
survived 23rd May 1949 and not having established residence in Germany or made
application under art 116(2) he was treated as if he had been so deprived.
d   (ii) The relevance of the 1958 decision of the Constitutional Court, on which the
views of Dr Jaques and Dr Cohn also diverged, was in relation to the question whether
if Mr Oppenheimer still had German nationality when he applied for British nationality in 1948, he then lost it by virtue of the nationality law of 1913 which provided
in effect that a non-resident German lost his German nationality if he acquired a
foreign nationality without first obtaining permission to retain his German nationality.
e The 1958 case concerned a German Jewish refugee who abandoned his residence in
Germany in 1934, settled in the United States of America, was expatriated in 1938,
was granted United States nationality in 1946, and in 1948 returned to live in Germany.
He claimed to be a German national by virtue of the second sentence of art 116(2).
The following passage occurred in the course of the decision of the Constitutional
Court:
f
> 'The appellant's expatriation for racial reasons in 1938 is therefore by Article
> 116(2), second sentence, of the Basic Law deemed not to have taken place. Accord-
> ing to the clear wording and meaning of this provision he did not lose his German
> nationality by the expatriation. The loss of this nationality can also not be
> derived from (or based on) his naturalisation in the United States of America in
g > 1946 by virtue of Section 17 number 2 and Section 25(1) of the Nationality Act
> [of 1913]; those provisions presuppose that the person concerned enjoyed the
> effective possession of German nationality at the time when he acquired
> a foreign nationality. That is not the case if at the material time he was
> not in a position to rely on his German nationality; for, if an expatriation
> pronounced *before* that time is only declared invalid by a law enacted *after*
h > that time, then the person in question had no reason at the material time to
> take the legal consequences of the acquisition of a foreign nationality under the
> German Nationality Law into consideration. A contrary view would also have
> the effect of frustrating the indemnificatory purpose of Article 116(2), second
> sentence, of the Basic Law and would result in the person in question being
> treated by his home country in a manner contrary to good faith.'

j The 1958 case concerned a refugee who had returned to live in Germany. If he had
in fact acquired residence in Germany and had indicated no contrary intention, he
was clearly entitled to be treated under the second sentence of art 116(2) as never
having been deprived of his nationality. Dr Jaques, however, regarded the decision
as having a wider application. He thought it to be an absolute and clear-cut authority
for the proposition that the acquisition of a non-German nationality by a persecutee

prior to 23rd May 1949 did not result in loss of his German nationality by virtue of
s 25 of the nationality law of 1913. He understood the last sentence of the above   a
quoted passage to mean that to hold that s 25 of the nationality law of 1913 applied
to such a persecutee would not only frustrate the indemnificatory purpose of art
116(2) but also—and quite independently—be contrary to 'good faith' which is a paramount and well-defined principle of German law comparable to the concept of
equity in English law, which made it inappropriate to apply the nationality law to a   b
citizen who would have no cause to consider the consequences of his application for
foreign nationality and who, moreover, at the relevant time would have been unable
to obtain permission to retain his German nationality had he recognised the need to
do so. Dr Jaques saw no conflict between what he regarded as the authoritative
finding of one division of the Constitutional Court in 1958 and the comments of the
other division in 1968 that persecutees who had not lost their German nationality
by virtue of the purported expatriation 'may of course have lost it for some other   c
reason, especially through acquisition of a foreign nationality', because this was true
of persecutees who had acquired a foreign nationality after 23rd May 1949. He did
not think it possible that the court in 1968 intended to overrule the 1958 decision.
Dr Cohn, on the other hand, took a different view of the passage cited from the 1958
decision. At the date when that decision was made the effect of art 116(2) was
thought to be that it brought about a retrospective regrant of German nationality to   d
a refugee who returned and took up residence in Germany. In 1958 it was still
generally thought that the expatriations of 1941 were legally effective notwithstanding the abrogation of the 1941 decree by the Allied Military Government legislation.
The question which the court had then to decide was whether the effect of s 25 of
the nationality law of 1913 was that the German nationality retrospectively regranted
was nonetheless lost by the intervening event of the refugee having acquired United   e
States citizenship. Article 116(2), second sentence, the Constitutional Court said,
had an indemnificatory purpose: in other words, it was to be retrospective in its
effect. The retrospective effect must counter the effect of s 25 of the nationality
law of 1913. That case, Dr Cohn explained, was the only decision dealing with a
returning persecutee retrospectively granted German nationality. The court
was concerned only with the question whether art 116(2) overruled the nationality   f
law of 1913 in the case of expatriates returning to Germany and it answered this
question in the affirmative. As to the passage in the 1968 decision which referred to
persecutees who might have lost their German nationality through acquisition of a
foreign nationality, Dr Cohn found nothing inconsistent between this passage and the
1958 decision. In the 1968 decision the meaning of the comment was that a persecutee, who had not lost his German nationality by reason of the 1941 decree would as   g
a rule lose it if he subsequently acquired a foreign nationality. The significance
of art 116(2) for such a persecutee was that even he could recover his German
nationality by taking up residence in Germany or applying for a regrant.

(iii) In addition to the 1958 and 1968 decisions of the Constitutional Court the
commissioners were referred to two decisions of the Berlin District Court, the 'Hong   h
Kong dentist's decision' of 1968 and the 'mental incapacity decision' of 1971, to a
decision of the Berlin Court of Appeal, the 'Luxembourg decision' of 1970, and to a
decision of the Supreme Court, the 'Dutch decision' of 1962. In the latter case the
Supreme Court held that the 1941 decree had never been law and was void ab initio.
However, by virtue of the fact that the unlawful laws and decrees of the Nazis were
actually applied within the sphere of power of the Nazis to the legal relationships of
those concerned, factual conditions were created which could not simply be treated   j
as if they had never happened. The court therefore recognised the validity of a
declaration of death made by a foreign court which could have had jurisdiction only
on the footing that the deceased expatriate had lost his German nationality, although
on the correct view of the law the expatriate had not lost his German nationality by
his expatriation. In the Luxembourg case the Court of Appeal dealt with the case of

a persecutee who died in October 1945, after 8th May 1945 but before the coming into
a force of the Basic Law. Following the 1968 decision of the Constitutional Court the
Berlin Court of Appeal held that such a persecutee was not deprived of his German
nationality by the 1941 decree but was to be taken to have retained it in the absence
of any concrete indication that he wanted to relinquish German nationality. In
the 1971 decision of the Berlin District Court that principle was extended to a persecutee who died in England in 1956 but who by reason of mental incapacity could not
b exercise his intention to comply with one of the sets of facts provided for in art 116(2).
The court held the application of art 116(2) to be excluded since it could be applied
only to those cases in which the persons in question had a chance to make known
their intention by complying with one or other of the sets of requirements referred
to in the article. The commissioners understood the implication of those last two
decisions to be that art 116(2) applied to a persecutee who survived the coming into
c force of the Basic Law and was thereafter in a position to avail himself of one or
other of the means of asserting German nationality indicated by the article. Dr
Jaques was constrained to agree that it was implicit in these decisions that in the case
of a persecutee who was not mentally incapacitated when the Basic Law was adopted,
one could look simply to art 116(2) to see whether or not he was a German national.
He stopped short, however, of accepting any suggestion that the Basic Law could be
d treated as a ground for loss of nationality. Dr Cohn took the view that it was implicit
in what was said in those cases about the application of art 116(2) that a persecutee
who survived the coming into force of the Basic Law and enjoyed full capacity did
not have German nationality unless he reapplied for it or returned to live in Germany.
The 1968 decision of the Berlin District Court dealt with a persecutee who died in
Hong Kong in 1954. The court held that he died a German national notwithstand-
e ing that he had made no application under art 116(2). In reaching that conclusion
the court in terms disagreed with the reasoning of the 1968 decision of the
Constitutional Court:

> 'This division is not able to accept this interpretation of the law, which is based
> on the wording of Article 116(2) and its legislative history. Nationality is a
f > membership in a state and in accordance with the dominant view constitutes a
> legal quality, a legal status of a person ... If it is true that the persecutees whose
> case was covered by the [1941 decree] never lost German nationality by virtue
> of their expatriation ... then a loss can also not have taken place by virtue of the
> rule contained in Article 116(2). It is incompatible with the dominant view that
> nationality is a legal quality that a refugee who has not acquired a foreign nation-
g > ality is not considered as having lost his German nationality and yet is not to be
> treated by the German State as a German national so long as he has not by
> taking up residence or applying for naturalisation (viz under Article 116(2))
> asserted (or relied on) his German nationality.'

Dr Jaques took the view that in this passage the members of the court were criticising
the 1968 decision of the Constitutional Court but that the District Court's decision, to
h the effect that a persecutee who neither adopted a foreign nationality nor decided
against German nationality had to be treated in the same way as those who did not
survive the coming into force of the Basic Law and accordingly had to be treated as a
German national unless he clearly evinced a contrary intention, was consistent with
what had been said by the Constitutional Court. Dr Cohn, however, was of the
view that the District Court clearly understood the 1968 decision of the Constitutional
j Court and deliberately deviated from it. Insofar as the 1968 decision of the Constitutional Court dealt with the position of persecutees who survived the coming into
force of the Basic Law the principles stated by the court were not essential to its
decision and were therefore strictly not binding on the Berlin District Court.

(d) In the light of what he took to be the German law having regard to the cases
mentioned Dr Jaques answered the question whether for the purposes of German

municipal law Mr Oppenheimer had been deprived of his German citizenship by the 1941 decree with a firm, No, Dr Cohn found the matter too complex for a simple *a* answer, Yes or No. By the 1968 decision of the Constitutional Court the 1941 decree was held to be invalid and as not depriving Mr Oppenheimer of his German citizenship. But on the coming into effect of the Basic Law Mr Oppenheimer was no longer treated by the German state as a German national unless he applied for a regrant of his nationality or returned to Germany, and it followed that from then on he was no longer a German national. The effect of the 1968 decision taken in conjunction with *b* the 1941 decree and art 116(2) was that from 23rd May 1949 Mr Oppenheimer had been effectively deprived of German nationality. To the second question,

> 'If [Mr Oppenheimer] was not deprived of his German citizenship by the said Decree whether for the purposes aforesaid he was deprived of German citizenship by the German Nationality Law of 22nd July, 1913, on being naturalised a British *c* subject on 24th May, 1948, and taking into account his Oath of Allegiance on 4th June 1948',

Dr Jaques again gave the simple answer, No. Dr Cohn's answer was that although Mr Oppenheimer had not been deprived of his German citizenship by the 1941 decree, he was by virtue of having been naturalised as a British subject and having taken the oath of allegiance in 1948, no longer effectively a German national unless he *d* either returned to Germany or was regranted German nationality. So far as Dr Jaques was concerned there was no question of Mr Oppenheimer having lost his German nationality and therefore no question of his citizenship being reinstated. Dr Cohn considered that nothing had occurred by which Mr Oppenheimer's citizenship had been reinstated but that it would have been reinstated if he had returned to Germany or had applied under art 116(2). *e*

5. The commissioners made the following findings:

> 'On considering the whole of the evidence of the two expert witnesses and the cases which were cited and explained to us, it seems to us that the question put to us as to [Mr Oppenheimer] being "deprived" of his German citizenship is precisely the question to which the German Courts have carefully and de- *f* liberately avoided giving an answer. The reasons for this avoidance are twofold: on the one hand the Courts were concerned that nothing should be said which might suggest that the [1941 decree] was valid—it was void ab initio. On the other, it was inappropriate to fasten on expatriates the German nationality of which the [1941 decree] had purported to deprive them unless they gave some indication that they would welcome its retention. In the case of those who had *g* never had an opportunity to indicate a preference, in the absence of concrete proof to the contrary it was to be assumed that they would have welcomed retention. In the case of those who survived and could evince a wish one way or the other, the German State would not recognise the expatriates as German nationals without their taking the first step. For these same reasons we find ourselves unable to answer the questions as framed with a simple "Yes" or *h* "No". We prefer the approach of Dr Cohn to that of Dr Jaques on grounds of consistency and because we think that it reconciles the decisions cited to us. Accordingly, we answered the questions put as follows:
> '(a) [Mr Oppenheimer] was not deprived of his German citizenship by the Decree of 25 November 1941. The effect of the Decree and of Article 116(2) of *j* the Basic Law was that in the relevant assessment years for the purposes of German municipal law [Mr Oppenheimer] was not regarded as having German nationality unless and until he chose to assert it by returning to Germany to live or by making application.
> '(b) When [Mr Oppenheimer] was naturalised a British Subject, and subsequently took the Oath of Allegiance, the German Nationality Law of 22 July

1913 applied so that [Mr Oppenheimer], if and so far as he was a German national at that time, ceased to be a German national, subject, however, to his being able to avail himself of the opportunity afforded by Article 116(2) of the Basic Law of asserting his German nationality and thereby securing recognition as a German national.

'(c) (i) Nothing occurred prior to the assessment years which had the effect of reinstating [Mr Oppenheimer's] German citizenship, or which otherwise resulted in his being treated as a German national for the purposes of German municipal law.   (ii) Had he applied at any time before or during the relevant assessment years under Article 116(2), (as he did subsequently), [Mr Oppenheimer] would thereafter have been treated as a German national for the purposes of German municipal law.'

Nothman v Cooper (Inspector of Taxes)

Miriam Nothman appealed against the decision of the Court of Appeal[1] (Lord Denning MR, Buckley and Orr LJJ) dated 20th July 1972 allowing an appeal by the Crown against an order of Goulding J dated 21st December 1971 whereby, on a case stated by the Special Commissioners, he reversed the decision of the commissioners dated 27th January 1970, on an appeal by Miss Nothman against assessments to income tax under Sch D in respect of profits described as 'German pension' for the years 1953-54 to 1964-65 inclusive, that payments received by the taxpayer were not exempt from income tax under the double taxation agreements concluded between the United Kingdom and the Federal Republic of Germany.   The main issue raised in Miss Nothman's appeal was the same as that raised in Mr Oppenheimer's appeal, but, by a respondent's notice before the Court of Appeal, Miss Nothman had sought to uphold the decision of Goulding J on certain alternative grounds which had been rejected by him.   The facts are set out in the opinion of Lord Cross of Chelsea.

Sir John Foster QC and *M Englard* for Mr Oppenheimer.
Miss Nothman appeared in person.
John Vinelott QC and *Patrick Medd QC* for the Crown.

Their Lordships took time for consideration.

5th February.   The following opinions were delivered.

LORD HAILSHAM OF ST MARYLEBONE. My Lords, I have had the advantage of reading in draft the illuminating opinion about to be delivered by my noble and learned friend, Lord Cross, and since in almost everything I agree with it my own opinion can be correspondingly short.

The decisive point in this case is whether, during the assessment years, the appellant, Meier Oppenheimer, was a dual national possessing the German nationality (which had been his by birth) in addition to the British nationality which he acquired by naturalisation in 1948.   If this question is answered affirmatively he can claim the advantage of art IX of the double taxation agreements[2] between this country and the Federal Republic in respect of the pension he receives from them.   Otherwise his appeal fails.   It is true that under the terms of the agreements the question must be decided by English law (see art II(3)), but English law requires as a rule that the question of foreign nationality falls to be decided according to the municipal law of

---

1   [1972] 3 All ER 1106
2   Set out in the Schedules to the Double Taxation Relief (Taxes on Income) (Federal Republic of Germany) Order 1955 (SI 1955 No 1203) and the Double Taxation Relief (Taxes on Income) (Federal Republic of Germany) Order 1967 (SI 1967 No 25)

the foreign state concerned. (See *Stoeck v Public Trustee*[1].) According to English law that municipal law is a question of fact.   *a*

It is, of course, the case that Russell J, in the course of *Stoeck v Public Trustee*[2], accepted that in exceptional cases English law might attribute a particular foreign nationality to persons who might not in fact possess it, as may have been done in *Ex parte Weber*[3] and *R v Vine Street Police Superintendent, ex parte Liebman*[4]. These, however, were cases in which a person who had never acquired British nationality was classed as an enemy alien in time of war owing to his continuing connection with the enemy   *b* state. I can see no reason for invoking such exceptional considerations here. It is also true that in time of war English law will for certain purposes disregard changes of status made by the enemy state during the war: cf *R v Home Secretary, ex parte L*[5], *Lowenthal v Attorney-General*[6]. But I agree with the Court of Appeal[7] that this particular doctrine no longer applies after the end of hostilities.

It appears quite clearly from the supplemental case that Mr Oppenheimer's   *c* status for the assessment years in the municipal law of the Federal Republic depends on art 116(2) of the Grundgesetz or Basic Law as construed in the light of the decisions of the Constitutional Court, e g in 1968. The commissioners have found as a fact that in the assessment years Mr Oppenheimer was not regarded as a German citizen according to German law, unless he applied for it which he had not done during the assessment years, and I can see no reason for disputing this finding. On the contrary,   *d* were I to attempt the task on the basis solely of art 116(2) and the German decisions exhibited to the case I would reach the same conclusion. In arriving at their own conclusion the commissioners enjoyed in addition the oral evidence on this point of two German lawyers. The case below was argued largely on the question whether English courts would recognise the infamous decree of the National Socialist regime of 25th November 1941, which purported to deprive the appellant of his German   *e* nationality on the ground that he was a Jew. Goulding J[8] upheld the appellant's contention on the grounds stated in *R v Home Secretary, ex parte L*[5] and *Lowenthal v Attorney-General*[6] which were cited before him. But, as I have said, I agree with the Court of Appeal[9] that this ground, founded on the public policy of a belligerent United Kingdom, continued only during the continuance of the state of war between this country and Germany. In the light of the supplemental case, the opinion of   *f* Buckley and Orr LJJ that the National Socialist decree, for all its discriminatory character, was effective to deprive Mr Oppenheimer of his citizenship cannot be supported, since the effect of the 1968 decision of the Constitutional Court, and the findings of the commissioners can now be seen to contradict this possibility. The position is governed by the present Federal Law and not by the National Socialist decree, and the conflicting considerations which led the Federal legislature to adopt   *g* the particular solution contained in art 116(2) of the Grundgesetz are adequately stated by the Constitutional Court in their 1968 decision, and in the commissioners' finding. It is clear that the Federal legislature did not recognise the National Socialist decree, but sought to deal with a difficult practical problem on humane and reasonable lines which left persons in the position of the appellant outside German nationality unless and until they applied to receive it. The position would have been the   *h* reverse had Mr Oppenheimer gone to live in Germany. In that case the law of the Federal Republic would have presumed that he wished to be recognised as a national

---

1   [1921] 2 Ch 67; see especially p 87
2   [1921] 2 Ch 67
3   [1916] 1 AC 421; *affg* [1916] 1 KB 280   *j*
4   [1916] 1 KB 268, [1914-15] All ER Rep 393
5   [1945] KB 7
6   [1948] 1 All ER 295
7   [1972] 3 All ER 1106 at 1114, [1973] Ch 264 at 274, 275
8   [1972] 2 All ER 529, [1972] Ch 585
9   [1972] 3 All ER at 1114, [1973] Ch at 274, 275

ab initio unless he unequivocally expressed a wish to the contrary. What would
a have been the decision in English law had the point fallen to be decided at a point
of time before the Grundgesetz came into operation or if the Constitutional Court
had reached a different conclusion in 1968, is, perhaps fortunately for us, academic.
The arguments for and against are set out in the article[1] in the Law Quarterly Review
which led directly or indirectly, to the remission of the case to the commissioners.
I would prefer to express no concluded opinion on it. But I do point out, with the
b author of the article above referred to, that only in a relatively small proportion of
cases is the possession of dual nationality an advantage to the possessor. There would
seem small value in adding hardship to injustice in order to emphasise the cruel
nature of the injustice. I quite see the force of the argument contained in the opinions
of my noble and learned friends Lord Cross and Lord Salmon to the effect that the
validity of a law cannot depend on its effects on individuals. But with due respect
c to that argument, foreign municipal law is not a question of law but of fact, and the
only way known to English law of disregarding an unpleasant fact is to create
the legal fiction that it does not exist. I do not think that such fictions always serve
a useful purpose, and where they do, among the criteria would certainly be included
the effect of the proposed fiction on individuals but not, I venture to think, the distasteful nature of the facts. It may well be that English law will not give a single and
d unequivocal answer to the problems raised by the unjust and discriminatory legislation of a foreign country. (See for instance *Aksionairnoye Obschestvo A M Luther Co v James
Sagor & Co*[2]; *Princess Olga Paley v Weisz*[3]; and cf also *Frankfurther v W L Exner Ltd*[4] and
Novello & Co Ltd v Hinrichsen Edition Ltd[5].) American law appears to have fallen
short of rejecting the National Socialist decree, at least when the consequences of
doing so would have been the internment of the propositus. (See *United States of
e America, ex rel Schwarzkopf v Uhl*[6].) The fact remains that, for the purposes of the
case before us, the National Socialist decree falls to the ground, the Constitutional
Court of the Federal Republic having declared it, for the purposes of the municipal
law as from the first 'unrecht' and not law, and we cannot do other than hold that
it was invalid.

The remaining judgment in the Court of Appeal was that of Lord Denning MR[7],
f who based his reasoning on the effect in English law of the application of Mr
Oppenheimer for British naturalisation in 1948. With great respect to Lord Denning
MR I do not find this reasoning convincing. It proceeds on the basis, which is contrary
to *Stoeck v Public Trustee*[8], that English law can decide who is and who is not a German
national, and appears to assume that the coexistence of British and enemy alien
nationality is an impossibility. But this is not so (cf *Kramer v Attorney-General*[9]).
g Quite apart from this I find it impossible to apply the doctrine of election or renuncia-
tion which is appropriate enough in the law of contract to questions of national status
in the absence of a statute to that effect and, even if I were able to do so, I would not
be prepared to decide this case on the basis of any election either by Mr Oppenheimer
or the Crown unless the conduct relied on as establishing election were absolutely
unequivocal; and I am not persuaded that in 1948 either the Crown or Mr Oppen-
h heimer were fully aware that Mr Oppenheimer had any surviving rights in his
nationality of origin which he could select to renounce.

---

1 F A Mann, The Present Validity of Nazi Nationality Laws (1973) 89 LQR 194
2 [1921] 3 KB 532
j 3 [1929] 1 KB 718
4 [1947] Ch 629
5 [1951] 2 All ER 457, [1951] Ch 1026
6 (1943) 137 Fed R (2d) 898
7 [1972] 3 All ER at 1111, [1973] Ch at 271
8 [1921] 2 Ch 67
9 [1923] AC 528

The commissioners have found that if they were wrong about their decision on the National Socialist decree, Mr Oppenheimer would nevertheless have lost his nationality under German law by virtue of the so-called Delbruck law of 1913 when he applied for British naturalisation in 1948. The Crown indicated that, if it were necessary, they would seek to support this finding of fact. We did not hear the Crown fully on this. But I would wish expressly to reserve any opinion on this point. Not only is it difficult to reconcile this position with the 1958 decision of the Constitutional Court, but one seems to enter a strange looking-glass world if one were compelled to hold that Mr Oppenheimer lost a nationality which no one at the time believed he possessed, and which he himself almost certainly did not then wish to retain, simply because he did not ask permission to retain it from authorities who did not then exist, and who, if they had existed, would almost certainly have refused the application on the ground that they had no jurisdiction to grant it.

In my view the appeal fails on the ground that I have stated. The supplementary case establishes that in the assessment years Mr Oppenheimer is not to be regarded as a German national.

I turn now to the second appeal, that of *Nothman v Cooper*. In this case also I agree with the opinion expresssed by my noble and learned friend, Lord Cross of Chelsea, and it follows that in my opinion this appeal must be dismissed. Miss Nothman conducted her own appeal with conspicuous courtesy and ability. She accepted expressly that on the principal matter of contention her case stood or fell with the appeal of Mr Oppenheimer. By leave of your Lordships she also raised a number of other points which she had argued below, but had disclaimed hitherto as matters she desired to place before the House of Lords. These points are (1) that the 'pension' she received was not income, but a payment by way of compensation for a frustrated career, and so not assessable to British tax even if her sole nationality were British; (2) that the payments were purely voluntary and therefore in the nature of gifts, and (3) that the source of income was not a foreign possession within the meaning of income tax law as defined in *Colquhoun v Brooks*[1] and *Foulsham v Pickles*[2]. I desire to say nothing about these points except that I agree with the opinions of Lord Cross of Chelsea in this House and of Goulding J[3] and Lord Denning MR[4] on them.

LORD HODSON. My Lords, for the reasons given by my noble and learned friend, Lord Cross of Chelsea, with which I am in complete agreement, I would dismiss these appeals.

Since the case has, in the end, been argued on a different basis from that which obtained in the Court of Appeal,[5] it is not strictly necessary to consider the reasons given by the members of that court in connection with the notorious 1941 decree. My noble and learned friend, Lord Pearson, has, however, expressed in the opinion which he has prepared a position which in effect confirms that taken by the majority of the Court of Appeal, expressed by Buckley LJ[6] in the following passage:

'... the answer to the question whether or not the person is a national or citizen of the country must be answered in the light of the law of that country however inequitable, oppressive or objectionable it may be.'

I do not agree that this is a correct view of the relevant international law and as at present advised am of opinion that Lord Cross's approach, consistent with that of

1   (1899) 14 App Cas 493, [1886-90] All ER Rep 1063
2   [1925] AC 458, [1925] All ER Rep 706
3   [1972] 2 All ER 529, [1972] Ch 585
4   [1972] 3 All ER at 1112
5   [1972] 3 All ER 1106, [1973] Ch 264
6   [1972] 3 All ER at 1113, [1973] Ch at 273

Dr Martin Wolff in his work on Private International Law[1], is to be preferred. The
a courts of this country are not in my opinion obliged to shut their eyes to the shocking
nature of such legislation as the 1941 decree if and when it falls for consideration.

LORD PEARSON. My Lords, I have had the advantage of reading the opinion
prepared by my noble and learned friend, Lord Cross of Chelsea, and I agree that
b these two appeals should be dismissed for the reasons given by him.

On the other hand, I am not able to agree with my noble and learned friend as to
the conclusion which should have been reached if the relevant German law had
consisted, as we thought it did, simply and solely of the 1941 decree and the 1913
law. When a Government, however wicked, has been holding and exercising full
and exclusive sovereign power in a foreign country for a number of years, and has
c been recognised throughout by our Government as the government of that country,
and some legislative or executive act of that government, however unjust and discriminatory and unfair, has changed the status of an individual by depriving him
of his nationality of that country, he does in my opinion effectively cease to be a
national of that country and becomes a stateless person unless and until he has
acquired some other nationality (as the appellant Oppenheimer did in this case).
d Suppose then that the wicked government is overthrown. I do not think it would
be right for the courts of this country on their own initiative to disregard that person's
change of status, which in fact had occurred and deem that it never had occurred.
A decision on that fictitious basis might be no kindness to the person concerned, who
might be quite content with his new status and unwilling to have his former status
artificially restored to him. The problem of effecting any necessary rectification of
e the position created by the unjust decree of the wicked government is a problem for
the successor government of the foreign country, and we know that in the present
case the problem was dealt with by the successor government of West Germany
by its Basic Law of 1949. But if the successor government had not dealt with the
problem, I do not see that the courts of this country would have had any jurisdiction
to restore to the person concerned his lost nationality of the foreign country. There
f is the rule of public policy that our courts may refuse to recognise in war time a
change of nationality of an enemy alien, but that rule would cease to apply at the
end of the war, which would be at latest when the war was officially declared to be
at an end.

I would dismiss the appeals.

g

LORD CROSS OF CHELSEA. My Lords, the question at issue in the appeal
Oppenheimer v Cattermole is whether the appellant, Mr Oppenheimer, is liable to pay
United Kingdom income tax for the tax years 1953-54 to 1967-68 inclusive on certain
pension payments which he received during those years from German public funds.
Mr Oppenheimer, who is a Jew, was born in Germany in 1896. From 1919 to 1939
h he taught at a Jewish orphanage in Bavaria but in 1939, after having been detained
for a short time in a concentration camp, he succeeded in leaving Germany and
coming to this country where he has lived ever since. On 4th June 1948 he was
granted a certificate of naturalisation and became a British subject. As a former
employee of a Jewish religious community he has been since 1953 in receipt of a
pension payable out of the revenues of the German Federal Republic. Conventions
j with regard to double taxation relief were made between the United Kingdom and
the Federal Republic in 1954 and 1964 and made law in this country by the Double
Taxation Relief (Taxes on Income) (Federal Republic of Germany) Orders 1955[2]

---

1 2nd Edn (1950), p 129
2 SI 1955 No 1203

and 1967[1]. Article IX(1) of the former convention—which Mr Oppenheimer contends is applicable to the first seven assessments in dispute—runs as follows: *a*

Remuneration, including pensions, paid, in respect of present or past services
or work, out of public funds of one of the Contracting Parties shall be exempt
from tax in the territory of the other Contracting Party, unless the individual
concerned is a national of that other Party without being also a national of the
first-mentioned Party.'   *b*

Article IX(2) of the Second Convention which Mr Oppenheimer contends is applicable
to the other eight assessments is to the same effect. Mr Oppenheimer is, of
course, a national of this country and the Crown admits for the purpose of this case
that the pensions in question fall within the description in the conventions. The
point at issue is whether Mr Oppenheimer was in the years of assessment not only a   *c*
British subject but also a German national.

Article II(3) of the 1954 convention states that in the application of its provisions by
one of the contracting parties any term not defined therein shall unless the context
otherwise requires have the meaning which it has under the laws in force in the territory
of that party relating to the taxes which are the subject of the convention. There is
a similar provision in the 1967 convention and neither convention contains any defini-   *d*
tion of the term 'a nation'. Accordingly the question whether Mr Oppenheimer
was a German national during the years of assessment has to be determined by
English law. But as Russell J pointed out in *Stoeck v Public Trustee*[2], English law
refers the question whether a person is a national of another state to the municipal
law of that state—though it may in certain circumstances 'deem' a person to be a
national of that state although he is not in fact a national of it. The Special Commis-   *e*
sioners to whom Mr Oppenheimer appealed against the assessments made on him
by the respondent inspector of taxes heard evidence from Dr Cohn, an expert in
German law called by the Crown, and in the light of it found that under German
law Mr Oppenheimer ceased to be a German national not later than 4th June 1948
when he became a national of the United Kingdom. At the request of Mr Oppenheimer, the commissioners stated a case for the opinion of the court and in view of   *f*
the subsequent history of this case, it is important to set out what was the material
to which, according to the case stated, Dr Cohn referred them and what was their
understanding of the effect of his evidence in relation to it. First they had before
them and exhibited to the case parts of a decree made on 25th November 1941 by
the National Socialist government providing that a Jew of German nationality who
had his usual place of abode abroad when the decree came into force should lose his   *g*
nationality forthwith. Secondly, they had before them and exhibited to the case
part of the German nationality law of 22nd July 1913, which provides that a German
who has neither his natural residence or permanent abode in Germany loses his
nationality on acquiring a foreign nationality unless he had the previous written
permission of the appropriate German authority to retain it. Thirdly, the case
states that Dr Cohn gave evidence to the following effect: *h*

'(a) by a decision of the Federal German Constitutional Court given in 1968,
which is binding upon all Federal German courts by virtue of a subsequent decree
of the Federal German Government, the decree of 25th November 1941 (Exhibit
"A") was absolutely void ab initio; (b) the said decision had no retrospective
effect; (c) the German nationality law of 22nd July 1913 (Exhibit "B") remains   *j*
in force (with certain amendments not relevant for present purposes) and was
unaffected by the said decision; (d) in his opinion, under German law, if [Mr

a   Oppenheimer] had not lost German nationality under the decree of 25th November, 1941, he lost the said nationality under the German nationality law of 22nd July 1913, on being naturalised a British subject in 1948.'

Two points are to be particularly noted, *first*, that, whether or not Dr Cohn referred to it in his evidence, the case stated makes no reference to art 116 of the Constitution of the Federal German Republic enacted in 1949 which, as will hereafter appear, is of
b   vital importance in this case and, *secondly*, that the case stated attributes to Dr Cohn the opinion that in the 1968 decision the Federal German Constitutional Court held that the 1941 decree was ab initio but that nevertheless the decision had no retrospective effect.   It is clear from the evidence given by Dr Cohn on a later occasion that the commissioners who signed the original case stated must have misunderstood the evidence which he was giving with regard to the 1968 decision.   As a result of
c   the absence from the case of any mention of art 116 and the presence in it of the statement that the 1968 decision had no retrospective effect the case was argued in the High Court[1] and in the Court of Appeal[2] and on the first occasion before this House on the footing that the only material to be considered in order to decide whether or not Mr Oppenheimer was a German national during the years of assessment was (a) the 1941 decree and (b) the 1913 law.   The case came first before Gould-
d   ing J[1] who reversed the decision of the Special Commissioners. He held first that English law would not recognise the decree of 25th November 1941 as having any effect with regard to Mr Oppenheimer since it purported to alter during wartime the nationality of someone who was then an enemy alien and, secondly, that Mr Oppenheimer had not lost his German nationality by the law of 22nd July 1913 since under German law he had already ceased to be a German national before he
e   became a British subject—although our law regarded him still as a German national. The Crown appealed to the Court of Appeal[2] (Lord Denning MR, Buckley and Orr LJJ) who reversed the decision of Goulding J[1] and restored that of the commissioners. Lord Denning MR held that whatever the position might be under German law English law would not regard an enemy alien who had been naturalised as a British subject during wartime as continuing thereafter to be a national of the enemy country
f   as well as a British subject.   Buckley and Orr LJJ based their judgments on a different ground—namely, that although English law would not recognise a change in the status of an enemy alien effected by the alien's domestic law during wartime, that non-recognition only lasted so long as the state of war lasted, and that consequently when the state of war between this country and Germany came to an end, our law would recognise that Mr Oppenheimer had been deprived of his status as a German
g   national by the decree of 25th November 1941.   Mr Oppenheimer appealed to this House from the decision of the Court of Appeal and the appellate committee heard arguments from both sides on the basis of the findings as to German law made by the commissioners and set out in the case stated. But before we reported our views to the House we became aware from an article by Dr F A Mann on 'The Present Validity of Nazi Nationality Laws' in the Law Quarterly Review[3] that the findings of
h   the commissioners as to the relevant German law were almost certainly based on inadequate material.   We therefore put the appeal back into the list for further argument and, as a result of the discussion which then ensued, it became clear—and was accepted by counsel on both sides—that the case ought to be sent back to the commissioners for further findings as to the relevant German law. This House therefore made an order in the following terms. [His Lordship then read the order[4]
j   and continued:] Pursuant to this order the Special Commissioners held a meeting on 29th April to 3rd May 1974, at which they heard further evidence from Dr Cohn

1   [1972] 2 All ER 529, [1972] Ch 585
2   [1972] 3 All ER 1106, [1973] Ch 264
3   (1973) 89 LQR 194
4   See pp 545, 546, ante

and also evidence from Dr Jaques, another expert on German law, who was called on
behalf of the appellant.   In the course of their evidence the witnesses as well as   *a*
referring to the 1941 decree and the 1913 law also referred to art 116 of the Basic
Law for the Federal Republic of Germany promulgated on 23rd May 1949, and to six
decisions of various German courts including two decisions—one given in 1958 and
the other in 1968—of the Federal Constitutional Court which is the Supreme Court
in Germany in relation to the interpretation of the Basic Law—the latter decision
being the decision referred to in the original case stated.   Translations of art 116   *b*
and of the relevant parts of all these decisions were attached to the supplementary
case which the commissioners stated in pursuance of the order of the House.   This
case further contains a full statement of the views expressed by Dr Cohn and Dr
Jaques respectively on the legal questions which arise.

Shortly after the collapse of the Nazi regime in May 1945, the 1941 decree was
repealed by Allied Military Government legislation.   It is, however, generally   *c*
accepted by German lawyers that this repeal had no retrospective effect.   When
the newly established Federal Republic of Germany came to frame its constitution it
had to decide what persons were to be its nationals.   This was a difficult and delicate
question for several different reasons.   In the first place—and this, of course, is the
aspect of the matter with which we are concerned in this case—it had to decide what
to do about those persons who had been deprived of their German nationality   *d*
by Nazi legislation.   On the one hand the new Germany was anxious not to appear
to treat the 1941 decree as valid in any way; but on the other hand it had to face the fact
that many of those affected by it had made their homes abroad and had no intention
of returning to Germany, and that such persons, many of whom had become naturalised in other countries, might well not welcome having German nationality which
they thought they had lost thrust on them without their consent.   Other problems   *e*
which the framers of the Basic Law had to face but which are of no relevance in this
case were, of course, the status in the Federal Republic of those 'Germans' who had
taken refuge there in the later stages of the war and of the 'Germans' in the Soviet
Zone of occupation.   At this point it will be convenient to refer to art 116 of the
Basic Law.   It runs as follows:

f

'(1) A German person within the meaning of this Basic Law is, subject to further
legal provisions any person who possesses German nationality or has been admitted into the sphere of the German Reich according to the position on 31st
December 1937 as a refugee or exile, member of the German people or as the
spouse or descendant of such a person.

'(2) Former German citizens who were deprived of their German nationality   *g*
between the 30th January 1933 and 8th May 1945 for political, racial or religious
reasons, and their descendants, are to be renaturalised on application. They
shall be considered as not having been deprived of their nationality, provided
that they have taken up their residence in Germany since 8th May 1945 and have
not expressed any wish to the contrary.'

It is, of course, with para (2) that we are concerned.   Reading the translation   *h*
simply as a piece of English without the aid of a German lawyer or of German decisions I would have interpreted it as saying that the Nazi legislation must be taken
as having effectively deprived those falling within its terms of their German nationality unless they had returned to live in Germany after the war, and had not expressed
a wish not to be German nationals.   On the other hand, those still abroad could
regain the German nationality which they had lost whenever they wished by applying   *j*
for it to the appropriate authority.   Mr Oppenheimer, though he has now made
such an application, did not make it until after the years of assessment with which we
are concerned.

Accordingly if the meaning of art 116(2) was what I have suggested—and it appears
that for some time after 1949 it was widely thought in Germany that that was its

true meaning—it would be clear that he was not a German national in the years of
a assessment.   It would also be clear that the 1913 law could have had no application
in his case since he would not have been a German national when he was naturalised
here.   But the 1968 decision of the Federal Constitutional Court shows that it is wrong
to interpret art 116(2) as saying—even if only by implication—that the Nazi legislation
had deprived anyone of his German nationality.   The court in that case had to decide
whether someone affected by the 1941 decree who died before the end of the war—
b i e 8th May 1945—and had not been naturalised in another country died a German
national or a stateless person.   It held that he died a German national because the
1941 decree was 'to so intolerable a degree irreconcilable with justice that it must be
considered to have been void ab initio'.   It was common ground between Dr Cohn
and Dr Jaques that this decision had retrospective effect and that in the light of it the
appellant remained a German national notwithstanding the 1941 decree, at least
c until he became a British subject in 1948.

Accordingly the questions to be decided were (1) did he lose his German nationality
under the 1913 law when he became a British subject, and (2), if he did not, did he lose
it in 1949 by reason of the enactment of art 116 of the Basic Law?   Dr Cohn answered
both these questions in the affirmative while Dr Jaques answered them in the negative.   The commissioners preferred the views of Dr Cohn on both points and since
d foreign law is a question of fact it might be argued that the view taken by the commissioners was binding on us even if we disagreed with it—unless indeed it was one
which we thought no one could reasonably entertain.   But in a case of this sort it
would, I think, be unfortunate if we were obliged to give effect to a view as to the
relevant foreign law which we thought to be wrong and we did in fact hear a full
argument from counsel for Mr Oppenheimer in support of the opinion of Dr Jaques.
e I propose therefore to proceed on the footing that it is open to us to decide the questions at issue for ourselves but for reasons which will hereafter appear I shall assume
in favour of Mr Oppenheimer that he did not lose his German nationality on becoming
naturalised here in 1948 and confine myself to the question whether he lost it by
reason of the enactment of the Basic Law in 1949.   The passage in the judgment of
the Federal Constitutional Court in the 1968 case which deals with the position of
f persons affected by the 1941 decree who were alive when the Basic Law took effect
ran as follows:

'In formulating this article the constitutional legislator proceeded from the
assumption that the [1941 decree] was void ab initio.   This means that the
persecutees have never lost their German nationality by virtue of the expatriation.   They may of course have lost it for some other reason, especially through
g acquisition of a foreign nationality.   The effect of article 116(2) of the Constitution in such a case is that even these persons can regain German nationality by
taking up residence in the Federal German Republic or by making an application.   For persecutees who have not acquired a foreign nationality the effect
of article 116(2) is that notwithstanding the fact that they did not lose their
German nationality by expatriation the German State does not treat them as
h Germans unless they assert their German nationality by taking up residence or
making an application.   Thus far article 116(2) gives effect to the idea that no
persecutee should have German nationality forced upon him against his will.'

If one looked simply at the language of art 116(2)—in particular at the word 'renaturalised'—the first sentence quoted above might be difficult to justify.   But
j the Federal Constitutional Court supported its interpretation by reference to the
views expressed during the preparation of the law by members of the committee
of the Parliamentary Council responsible for its wording.   The part of the quoted
passage which is, of course, particularly relevant for present purposes is the sentence:

'For persecutees who have not acquired a foreign nationality [and I am assuming that Mr Oppenheimer's naturalisation here in 1948 can be disregarded] the

effect of article 116(2) is that notwithstanding the fact that they did not lose their
German nationality by expatriation the German State does not treat them as *a*
Germans unless they assert their German nationality by taking up residence or
making an application.'

The effect of Dr Cohn's evidence was that no distinction could sensibly be drawn
between not being treated as a German by the German state and not being a German
and that accordingly Mr Oppenheimer, assuming that he was a German national *b*
immediately before 23rd May 1949, ceased then to be a German national until he
either applied to become a German national again or took up residence in Germany.
The effect of Dr Jaques's evidence on the other hand was that art 116 of the Basic Law
could not be taken to have deprived anyone of his German nationality and that
Mr Oppenheimer continued to be a German national after the enactment of the Basic
Law although he would not be recognised as such by the German authorities unless *c*
he applied to be recognised or took up residence.

Applying my mind as best I can to the problem of interpreting art 116(2) of the
Basic Law in the light of the 1968 decision of the Federal Constitutional Court I prefer
—as did the commissioners—the view of Dr Cohn to the view of Dr Jaques. I find the
conception of a man being by German law a German national but at the same time
not being by German law treated or recognised as a German national very hard to *d*
grasp and although it may look at first sight odd that a man who had not lost his
German nationality by the 1941 decree should lose it in 1949 under the operation of
the Basic Law, this apparent oddity disappears if one bears in mind the conflicting
considerations which the framers of the Basic Law had to try to reconcile. On the one
hand they were unwilling to admit that the 1941 decree had ever been part of the law
of Germany but at the same time they did not wish to thrust German nationality on *e*
people who did not want it. As a compromise—if one reads the Basic Law as the
Federal Constitutional Court read it—they drew a line at the date of the enactment
of the Basic Law. Up to that date people who fell within the scope of the 1941 decree
retained their German nationality unless they had given some positive indication
that they rejected it; but after the date of the coming into force of the new constitution
it was up to the persons concerned to give some positive indication that they wished *f*
to be nationals of the new Germany either by living there or by applying for German
nationality.

That Dr Cohn's reading of the 1968 decision is the right one is, I think, confirmed
by two decisions of other German Courts dealing with persons affected by the 1941
decree who died after the enactment of the Basic Law. The first (called in argument
the 'mental defective' case), was decided by the Berlin District Court in 1971. The *g*
question to be decided was whether a German Jew who left Germany in 1933 to settle
in this country and died here in 1956 in a psychiatric institution died a German
national. He had not been naturalised here and from before the date of the enactment
of the Basic Law until the date of his death he had been continuously under mental
disability. The court held that as he had never been able to apply his mind to the
question whether or not to apply for German nationality under the provisions of art *h*
116(2) he remained clothed with his original German nationality of which the 1941
decree had not deprived him. 'Article 116(2)', to quote a passage from the judgment—

'can be applied only to those cases in which the persons in question have or
have had the possibility of making known their intention by complying with
one or other of the set of requirements referred to'.
j

It is however implicit in the decision that had the propositus not been mentally
incapable on 23rd May 1949 he would have lost his German nationality on that date.
It might, I suppose, be argued that the conception of a 'possibility of making known
their intention' included not only mental capacity but also actual knowledge of the
terms of art 116(2) and that no one should lose his German nationality under the

a   article until the lapse of a reasonable time for making his application after the date
when he became aware of the terms of the article; but such an interpretation might
obviously give rise to disputes of fact which would be very hard to resolve and it is not
surprising that, so far as the evidence before us goes, it has never been advocated by
anyone.

The other decision (called in argument 'the Hong Kong Dentist' case) was decided
by the Berlin District Court in 1968. The 'propositus' in that case was a Jewish dentist
b   who left Germany in 1937 and eventually settled in Hong Kong where he died in 1954.
He never became naturalised in any other country and according to Dr Cohn's view
of the meaning of the 1968 decision of the Federal Constitutional Court he died a
stateless person since he had not applied for German nationality after the enactment
of the Basic Law. The District Court held that he died a German national
because there was no evidence that he had done anything to show that he wished
c   to renounce his German nationality. But as I read the decision this was not because
the court interpreted the 1968 decision of the Federal Constitutional Court differently
from Dr Cohn but because it thought that the Constitutional Court had been wrong
to draw a line at the date of the enactment of the Basic Law and to say that, whereas
up to that date 'persecutees' were German nationals unless they had done something
to show that they wished to renounce German nationality, after that date they ceased
d   to be German nationals unless and until they took steps to acquire German nationality.
The District Court may have been entitled to take a different view on this point from
the Federal Constitutional Court since in the 1968 decision the point at issue was the
status of persons within the scope of the 1941 decree who had died before the end of
the war and what the court said about those who were alive when the Basic Law was
enacted was only an obiter dictum; but I think that we should follow any views
e   expressed by the Constitutional Court on the meaning of the Basic Law even if not
part of the ratio decidendi unless they conflict with dicta of the same court in other
cases. For these reasons I think that even if one assumes that Mr Oppenheimer did
not lose his German nationality when he became naturalised in this country in 1948 he
ceased to be a German national from 23rd May 1949 until he applied to become a
German national after the years of assessment.

f   Logically, of course, the question whether Mr Oppenheimer lost his German
nationality when he became a British subject in 1948 comes before the question
whether he lost it on the coming into force of the Basic Law—for it is common ground
that if he ceased to be a German national on naturalisation here in 1948 he did not
become one again until he applied under art 116(2) after the years of assessment. At
first sight the passage from the 1968 decision quoted above would seem to point con-
g   clusively to the view that he did lose his German nationality in 1948 by the operation
of the 1913 law. The court after saying that 'the persecutees' had not lost their German
citizenship by their expatriation under the 1941 decree went on to say, 'They may of
course have lost it for some other reason, especially through acquisition of a foreign
nationality'. But against this one has to set what was said by the Federal Constitutional
Court itself in a decision in 1958 on which Dr Jaques strongly relied. The propositus
h   there was a German Jew who emigrated to the United States of America in 1934;
became naturalised as an American citizen in 1946; later returned to live in Germany
and had never evinced any intention not to be a German national. In 1956 the Munich
Court of Appeal issued a provisional extradition warrant against him on the request
of the Swiss Government in respect of criminal offences of which he was accused but
the Federal Constitutional Court quashed the order on the ground that he was a
j   German national. After pointing out that he had not lost his German nationality by
the Nazi legislation the court dealt with the effect of his naturalisation in the United
States of America as follows:

'The loss of this nationality can also not be derived from (or based on) his
naturalisation in the United States of America in 1946 by virtue of Section 17

number 2 and Section 25(1) of the Nationality Act [of 1913]; those provisions
presuppose that the person concerned enjoyed the effective possession of German
nationality at the time when he acquired a foreign nationality. That is not the
case if at the material time he was not in a position to rely on his German nationality; for, if an expatriation pronounced *before* that time is only declared invalid
by a law enacted *after* that time, then the person in question had no reason at the
material time to take the legal consequences of the acquisition of a foreign
nationality under the German Nationality Law into consideration. A contrary
view would also have the effect of frustrating the indemnificatory purpose of
Article 116(2), second sentence, of the Basic Law and would result in the person
in question being treated by his home country in a manner contrary to good faith.'

That case differs, of course, on its facts from this case because the appellant there had
returned to live in Germany whereas Mr Oppenheimer has not done so. But though
the second reason for their conclusion given in the last sentence of the quoted passage
would not apply here the first reason is expressed in general terms which would
appear on their face to apply to Mr Oppenheimer's naturalisation as much as to that
of the appellant in that case. We did not hear a full argument from counsel for the
Crown on this branch of the case and it may be that he would have convinced me that
there is no inconsistency between what is said as to the effect of naturalisation in another country before the enactment of the Basic Law in the 1958 and 1968 decisions respectively. But as it is I prefer to leave open the question whether had Mr Oppenheimer
died between 4th June 1948 and 23rd May 1949 he would have been a German national
at the date of his death and to rest my decision on the point that, having survived the
enactment of the Basic Law, he ceased thereupon to be a German national until he
applied to be one.

Counsel for Mr Oppenheimer further submitted that even if contrary to his main
argument his client was not, after the enactment of the Basic Law, a German national
in the fullest sense of the word, the right which he undoubtedly possessed to become
a German national whenever he wished placed him in such a special position that
English law—which under the tax conventions is the law to be applied—should
regard him as having been a German national during the years of assessment. For
this he relied on the decision in *Weber's* case[1]. Weber was born in Germany in 1883.
He left that country in 1898 and after living for two or three years in South America
came to this country about 1901 and was still living here when the authorities
interned him in 1915. He applied for a writ of habeas corpus on the ground that he
was not an 'enemy alien' but a 'stateless person'—having lost his German nationality
either (a) under German laws of 1870 and 1873 by reason of his continuous residence
outside Germany for ten years or more or (b) under s 26 of the 1913 law (already
mentioned) on attaining the age of 31 on 30th January 1914—that being the latest
date on which he was liable for military service in peace time. The courts were not
satisfied that it would be right to regard him as other than an 'enemy alien' since
although he might have lost any rights which a German national had against the
German state it appeared that he was still under an obligation to serve in the German
army in time of war and further that he could claim to be 'renaturalised' as of right
if he returned to Germany. I do not think that that case assists Mr Oppenheimer.
It is one thing to say that a right to claim German nationality at will constitutes a
sufficient link with Germany to justify the authorities in treating a man as an 'enemy
alien' at a time when this country is at war with Germany and quite another thing
to say that our law ought to treat a man who has such a right as a German national
for the purposes of these tax conventions although by German law he is not a German
national. For these reasons I think that the Oppenheimer appeal fails and should
be dismissed.

1   [1916] 1 AC 421; *affg* [1916] 1 KB 280

As the members of the Court of Appeal in giving their judgments proceeded—
a through no fault of their own—on a wholly false view of the German law applicable
to this case the reasons which they gave for dismissing the appeal are, strictly speaking,
irrelevant. In particlar, of course, the shocking character of the 1941 decree on which
so much of the argument in the courts below and in the first hearing before us centred ceases to have any bearing on the case when once one appreciates that the
problem posed by that decree was tackled by the Federal Republic before the years of
b assessment in the Basic Law of 1949. But as the judgments below[1] have been
reported and I do not in all respects agree with them I shall state as briefly as I can
what conclusion I would have reached if the relevant German law had consisted,
as we thought that it did, simply and solely of the 1941 decree and the 1913 law.

There are four arguments to be considered. The first ran as follows: (A) at the
outbreak of the war in 1939 Mr Oppenheimer, who was then undoubtedly a German
c national resident in this country, became an 'enemy alien'; (B) *R v Home Secretary,
ex parte L*[2] and *Lowenthal v Attorney-General*[3] show that the courts of this country
will not recognise a change in the status of an 'enemy alien' effected during the war
under the law of the enemy country; and (C) this non-recognition does not end with
the war. The first two steps in the argument are plainly right but the third is, I think,
wrong. In reaching the conclusion that our courts should continue to refuse recogni-
d tion to the change of nationality effected by the 1941 decree even after the end of the
war because it was a change effected during the war Goulding J was to some extent
influenced by the character of the decree[4], but the character of the decree has no
relevance to this argument. The refusal of our courts to recognise a change in the
status of an 'enemy alien' effected during war time is not confined to changes effected
by laws passed by the enemy state during the war and may operate to deny recogni-
e tion to changes effected by legislation of a wholly unobjectionable character. For
example, if under a law of the enemy state passed before the war a female national
loses her nationality on marrying a national of another state a female national of the
enemy state who was living in this country and married during the war a national of
this or of some third country would be regarded by our courts as remaining an
'enemy alien' even after her marriage so long as the war continued, at all events
f so far as regards matters connected with the conduct of the war. But there is no
reason in sense or logic why our courts should continue to regard her as a national
of the former enemy state for any purpose after the end of the war although by the
law of that state she is no longer a national of it. I agree with Buckley and Orr LJJ
that the doctrine of public policy in question merely suspends recognition during
wartime. I would add however that I incline to think that 'during wartime' for this
g purpose should be interpreted in a common sense way as 'until the end of the
fighting'. It appears to have been assumed in the courts below that the relevant date
would be not 8th May 1945 but 9th July 1951, when the Government of this country
declared that the state of war had ended. The man in the street would have been
very surprised to be told in 1950 that we were still at war with Germany; and as at
present advised I can see no reason why the suspension of recognition of changes of
h nationality should be artificially extended in this way. It is not clear from the report
of *Lowenthal v Attorney-General*[3] whether the relevant date was 28th April 1944
when the summons under s 18 of the Patents and Designs Acts was issued or some
date after 8th May 1945. If the latter was the case I doubt whether the decision was
right.

The second ground on which it was argued that English law should deem Mr
j Oppenheimer to have remained a German national notwithstanding the 1941 decree

1 [1972] 3 All ER 1106, [1973] Ch 264; *rvsg* [1972] 2 All ER 529, [1972] Ch 585
2 [1945] KB 7
3 [1948] 1 All ER 295
4 [1972] 2 All ER at 537, [1972] Ch at 595

was that the decree was 'confiscatory'. 'Confiscatory legislation' is a somewhat vague phrase which is sometimes used to cover not only expropriation with no or only *a* inadequate compensation but also compulsory acquisition for full compensation. But it is clear that if foreign legislation on its true construction purports to divest the owner of particular property here of his title to it our courts will not give effect to the transfer even if the foreign legislation provides for full compensation. I cannot see, however, how this rule could have assisted Mr Oppenheimer here. Even if one regards his status as a German national as being a bundle of rights and duties those *b* rights and duties were not themselves locally situate here. The right to claim exemption from United Kingdom tax given to him by the convention if he was a German national at the relevant time was no doubt situate here. In the same way if a testator who died in 1953 had left him a legacy if he was *not* a German national at the date of his death the right to claim the legacy if he could fulfil the condition would have been a right situate here. If the 1941 decree deprived him of his German *c* nationality in the eyes of English law that no doubt would entail the consequence that his position with regard to rights then existing or subsequently arising in this country which were dependent on his being or not being a German national would have been changed by the decree; but I do not think that the fact that the legislation by which a foreign state deprives a man of his status as one of its nationals can be described as 'confiscatory' necessarily entails the consequence that our law should *d* deem him to remain a citizen of that state for the purpose of deciding whether or not he is entitled to property rights in this country. Suppose, for example, that it was the law of Ruritania that any Ruritanian citizen who was convicted of treason by a Ruritanian court should forfeit all his property wherever situate to the Ruritanian state and should also cease to be a citizen of Ruritania. Our courts would certainly refuse to entertain an action by the Ruritanian state to obtain possession of the *e* traitor's property here; but I can see no sufficient reason why we should continue to regard him as a Ruritanian citizen for the purpose of deciding whether or not he was entitled to property here, his right to which depended on his being or not being a Ruritanian citizen at some point of time.

The third ground on which it was argued that English law should pay no regard to the 1941 decree was that it was contrary to international law. In his judgment *f* Buckley LJ says[1]:

'. . . the answer to the question whether or not the person is a national or citizen of the country must be answered in the light of the law of that country however inequitable, oppressive or objectionable it may be.'

With all respect I cannot agree that that is the law. If a foreign country purported *g* to confer the benefit of its protection on and to exact a duty of allegiance from persons who had no connection or only a very slender connection with it our courts would be entitled to pay no regard to such legislation on the ground that the country in question was acting beyond the bounds of any jurisdiction in matters of nationality which international law would recognise. In this respect I think that our law is the same as that of the United States as stated by the Circuit Court of Appeals *United States of* *h* *America, ex rel Schwarzkopf v Uhl*[2]. Schwarzkopf who was then an Austrian national came to the United States in 1936 with the intention of living there permanently. By a decree of 3rd July 1938 the German state—which had annexed Austria on 13th March 1938—purported to make him a German citizen and on 9th December 1941 he was arrested by the American authorities as a German citizen under a presidential decree made in view of the imminence of war between the United States and Ger- *i* many. The court held in reliance on a number of authorities referred to in the judgment that the German decree of 3rd July 1938, so far as it purported to impose

---

1 [1972] 3 All ER at 1113, [1973] Ch at 273
2 (1943) 137 Fed R (2d) 898

German nationality on persons who at that time had no connection with Germany,
a must be disregarded by the American courts. It may be said, perhaps, that though
international law sets limits to the jurisdiction of sovereign states so far as concerns
the granting of nationality it sets no limits whatever to their power to withdraw it.
I am not prepared to accept that this is so. I think for example that Martin Wolff[1],
may well be right in saying that if a state withdraws its citizenship from some class
of its citizens living within its borders to which it has taken a dislike and would be
b glad to be rid, other states are not obliged to regard such people as 'Stateless'.
Counsel for the Crown was prepared to concede that this might be so; but he pointed
out that the 1941 decree was only aimed at persons who had already left Germany
for good and that emigration was a common and well-recognised ground for the
withdrawal of nationality. This is, of course, true, and if the decree had simply
provided that all Germans who had left Germany since Hitler's advent to power with
c the intention of making their homes elsewhere should cease to be German nationals
it may be that our courts would have had to recognise it even though many of those
concerned were not in truth voluntary emigrants but had been driven from their
native land. But the 1941 decree did not deprive *all* 'emigrés' of their status as German
nationals. It only deprived *Jewish* emigrés of their citizenship. Further, as the later
paragraphs of the decree show, this discriminatory withdrawal of their rights of
d citizenship was used as a peg on which to hang a discriminatory confiscation of their
property. A judge should, of course, be very slow to refuse to give effect to the
legislation of a foreign state in any sphere in which, according to accepted principles
of international law, the foreign state has jurisdiction. He may well have an inadequate understanding of the circumstances in which the legislation was passed and his
refusal to recognise it may be embarrassing to the branch of the executive which is
e concerned to maintain friendly relations between this country and the foreign country
in question. But I think—as Upjohn J thought (see *Re Helbert Wagg & Co Ltd*[2])—
that it is part of the public policy of this country that our courts should give effect
to clearly established rules of international law. Of course on some points it may
be by no means clear what the rule of international law is. Whether, for example,
legislation of a particular type is contrary to international law because it is
f 'confiscatory' is a question on which there may well be wide differences of opinion
between Communist and capitalist countries. But what we are concerned with
here is legislation which takes away without compensation from a section of the citizen
body singled out on racial grounds all their property on which the state passing the
legislation can lay its hands and, in addition, deprives them of their citizenship.
To my mind a law of this sort constitutes so grave an infringement of human rights
g that the courts of this country ought to refuse to recognise it as a law at all. There
are no doubt practical objections to adopting that course with this law, for in many,
if not most, cases the persons affected by the 1941 decree would not have wished to
remain German nationals. Dr Mann in his article[3] quotes several cases in which
courts in different countries, while characterising the 1941 decree as 'atrocious' or
'barbarous' have yet given effect to it for this reason. But it surely cannot be right
h for the question whether the decree should be recognised or not to depend on the
circumstances of the particular case. Moreover, in some cases—as for instance where
the propositus is dead and what is in issue is the law to be applied to the devolution
of his estate—it might be impossible to say which law he would have wished to
govern the matter. If one held—as I would have held—that Mr Oppenheimer
remained a German national in the eyes of our law notwithstanding the 1941 decree
j the further question would have arisen whether in the eyes of our law he lost his
German nationality in 1948 under the law of 1913, although by German law as it

1 Private International Law (2nd Edn, 1950), p 129
2 [1956] Ch 323 at 334
3 (1973) 89 LQR 194

then was he was not a German national when he was naturalised here. It would
not, however, have been necessary for me to form a view of my own on this point   *a*
since counsel for the Crown was prepared to accept as correct the view expressed
by Goulding J in the following words[1]:

'. . . I cannot see that the non-recognition of one foreign law on grounds of
public policy either demands or justifies imputing to a later foreign law an
operation which, on its true construction in its own system, it evidently could   *b*
not have.'

Finally it is necessary to consider the reason given by Lord Denning MR[2] for
allowing the appeal from Goulding J[3]. It was, as I understand it, that even if Mr
Oppenheimer was a German national by German law in the years of assessment
English law, which is the law to be applied in construing the convention, would not
regard him as a German national as well as a British subject in view of the circum-   *c*
stances in which he became a British subject. Our law is, of course, familiar with the
concept of dual nationality—indeed the relevant part of the tax convention
proceeds on the footing that a man may be at one and the same time a British subject
and a German national—and the English law which is to be applied in deciding
whether or not Mr Oppenheimer was a German national at the relevant time is not
simply our municipal law but includes the rule which refers the question whether   *d*
a man is a German national to the municipal law of Germany. Of course, the fact
that our law recognises that a man as well as being a British subject is also a German
national does not in the least affect either his rights or his duties as a British subject.
Consequently, in time of war between the countries concerned a man with dual
nationality may find himself in a very unenviable position. As Viscount Cave pointed
out in *Kramer v Attorney-General*[4] he may be forced to fight in the British army   *e*
and yet have his property confiscated under the peace treaty as the property of a
German national.

Lord Denning MR was not, I am sure, intending to deny any of this; but he thought
that the particular circumstances in which Mr Oppenheimer became a British subject
made it impossible for him thereafter to be considered by our law as having German
nationality whatever German law might say on the point. His judgment, as I read   *f*
it, contains two different reasons for this conclusion—though they are not, if I may say
so, very clearly distinguished. The first depended on the character of the 1941 decree.
By it—the argument runs—Germany repudiated its obligations to Mr Oppenheimer
and he accepted the repudiation by applying for British citizenship, so that even if
the 1941 decree were to be declared 'void ab initio' by German law he would be in the
eyes of English law precluded from asserting that he had remained a German   *g*
national. For my part I cannot accept that concepts drawn from the law of contract
can be imported in this way into the law of nationality. The second reason was a
more general one—namely, that if the Secretary of State grants a certificate of
naturalisation to a national of a country with whom this country is then at war
English law will deem him to have thereupon lost his previous nationality for good
whatever the law of the foreign country may say. If a certificate of naturalisation   *h*
is granted in peace time Lord Denning MR would, I think, accept that the man in
question would in the eyes of English law retain his other nationality if he did so by
the law of the other country. But he considered that the conception of an enemy
alien being granted a certificate of naturalisation in war time and still remaining
thereafter in the eyes of our law under a duty of allegiance to the enemy Sovereign
as well as to the Queen of England was an impossible one and that accordingly   *j*

---

1   [1972] 2 All ER at 538, [1972] Ch at 596
2   [1972] 3 All ER at 1111, [1973] Ch at 271
3   [1972] 2 All ER 529, [1972] Ch 585
4   [1923] AC 528 at 532

after the grant our law would regard him as having only a single nationality—
a namely, British nationality—even after the end of the war. I do not myself see any
need to draw a distinction between naturalisation in time of peace and naturalisation
in time of war. In either case the man in question comes under a duty of allegiance
to the Queen which is not affected in any way by the fact—if it be a fact—that by the
law of the foreign country in question he remains a national of it.

   In the result, therefore, if the relevant German law had been what we assumed it
b to be when the appeal was first argued I would have been in favour of allowing it;
but in the light of the German law as we now know it I would, as I have said, dismiss it.

   I turn now to consider the appeal *Nothman v Cooper*. Miss Nothman was born in
1915 in Frankfurt. She went to a grammar school and obtained distinction in mathematics. As she was a Jewess she could not go to Frankfurt University but she took a
teacher's training course at a Jewish teachers' training college where she passed an
c examination in March 1936. During the next three years she held various teaching
posts in the dwindling and persecuted Jewish community in Germany and eventually—
in April 1939—came to this country. The Crown accepts for the purposes of this appeal
that she has become a British subject. Under a law enacted in 1951 by the Federal
Government of Germany former public servants who had suffered injury in their
careers through the 'Nazi' persecution became entitled to apply for compensation
d (Wiedergutmachung). Article 31(d)(1) of the law provided that former employees of
Jewish communities or public organisations who had or but for the persecutions
would have attained a right to retirement benefits against their employers should be
entitled from 1st October 1952 onwards to pension payments on the basis of their
former salary payments. In 1956 Miss Nothman was awarded as from 1952 a basic
monthly compensation under this article. She was assessed to United Kingdom income
e tax in respect of the payments which she received in the tax years 1953-54 to 1964-65
inclusive on the footing that they were income arising from possessions out of the
United Kingdom. She appealed to the Special Commissioners against the assessments
arguing (1) that she was a German national in the years in question and therefore
exempt from United Kingdom income tax under the tax conventions previously
mentioned and (2) that for various reasons the payments which she received were not
f subject to United Kingdom tax. The commissioners held that she was liable to United
Kingdom tax and this decision was upheld both by Goulding J[1] and the Court of
Appeal[2]. On her appeal to this House Miss Nothman, who presented her case with
ability and courtesy, was prepared on the first point to adopt the arguments which
had been submitted by counsel for Mr Oppenheimer; but on the second point she
addressed to us—as she had to the court below—several arguments with which it is
g necessary to deal. In the first place she pointed out that the payments in question
were not really pension payments at all but were in truth compensation for having
been deprived of the opportunity of following her chosen career. They were therefore
in the nature of damages and should not be treated as income payments. But the
payments, even if not properly described as 'pension' payments, are not instalments
of any ascertained capital sum, and I cannot see any more than could the commis-
h sioners or the courts below why they are not received by Miss Nothman as income.
Her second contention was that the payments were not assessable to tax because they
were 'voluntary payments'. It is, of course, true that she received them because the
Federal Republic decided of its own volition to do something towards making good
to persons in the position of Miss Nothman the wrong done to them by the Nazi
government, and no doubt what the Federal Republic has given it could if it wished
j take away. But the payments which Miss Nothman receives under the law while it
is in force cannot be regarded as a series of voluntary gifts. Then she argued that the
payments were not income from a 'foreign possession' but those words mean simply

---

1   [1972] 2 All ER 529, [1972] Ch 585
2   [1972] 3 All ER 1106, [1973] Ch 264

income derived from a source outside the United Kingdom and I think that Miss
Nothman's rights under the German law in question constitute such a source. Finally *a*
Miss Nothman referred us to s 22(1) of the Finance Act 1961 which says:

> 'Annuities payable under the law of the Federal German Republic relating to
> the compensation of victims of National-Socialist persecution, being annuities
> which under any such law relating to the taxation of such compensation are
> specifically exempted from tax of a character similar to that of income tax, shall *b*
> not be regarded as income for any income tax purposes.'

Unfortunately, however, as Miss Nothman admits, the German authorities have not
granted to the payments being made to her any 'specific exemption' from tax—
although according to her they ought, consistently with their approach in other cases,
to have exempted them.

In the result, therefore, I think as the courts below thought that the decision of the *c*
commissioners in Miss Nothman's case was correct and that her appeal must also be
dismissed.

LORD SALMON. My Lords, I am in entire agreement with all the views expressed
in the speech of my noble and learned friend Lord Cross of Chelsea. I wish to add
only a few observations of my own. *d*

The original case stated made no mention of art 116(2) of the Basic Law enacted by
the Federal German Republic in 1949. Neither your Lordships at the first hearing of
this appeal, nor the Court of Appeal[1], nor Goulding J[2], had any opportunity of
considering this vitally important enactment. Accordingly, in the courts below and
at the first hearing before your Lordships, the appeal was necessarily conducted on
the basis that the principal point for decision was whether or not our courts were *e*
bound to recognise the Nazi decree of November 1941 as effective in English law to
deprive Mr Oppenheimer of his German nationality. On that basis, I was unhesitatingly in favour of allowing the appeal. The relevant parts of the Nazi decree read as
follows:

> 'Clause 2   *f*
> 'A Jew loses German citizenship (a) if at the date of entry into force of this
> regulation he has his usual place of abode abroad, with effect from the entry into
> force of this decree; (b) if at some future date his usual place of abode is abroad,
> from the date of transfer of his usual place of abode abroad.
> 'Clause 3
> '(a) Property of Jews deprived of German nationality by this decree to fall to *g*
> the State. (b) such confiscated property to be used to further aims connected with
> the solution of the Jewish problem.'

The expense of transporting large numbers of men, women and children, in all about
six million, even without heat, food or sanitary arrangements, must have been
considerable. So no doubt was the expense of erecting, equipping and staffing con- *h*
centration camps and gas chambers for their extermination. Evidently, the Nazis
considered it only natural that the confiscated assets of those who had been lucky
enough to escape the holocaust should be used to finance it.

The Crown did not question the shocking nature of the 1941 decree, but argued
quite rightly that there was no direct authority compelling our courts to refuse to
recognise it. It was further argued that the authorities relating to penal or confiscatory *j*
legislation, although not directly in point, supported the view that our courts are
bound by established legal principles to recognise the 1941 decree in spite of its nature.
The lack of direct authority is hardly surprising. Whilst there are many examples in

1   [1972] 3 All ER 1106, [1973] Ch 264
2   [1972] 2 All ER 529, [1972] Ch 585

the books of penal or confiscatory legislation which according to our views is unjust
a the barbarity of much of the Nazi legislation, of which this decree is but an example,
is happily unique. I do not consider that any of the principles laid down in any of the
existing authorities require our courts to recognise such a decree and I have no doubt
that on the grounds of public policy they should refuse to do so.

I recognise that it is particularly within the province of any state to decide who are
and who are not its nationals. If a foreign state deprives one of its nationals of his
b nationality, *as a rule*, our courts will follow the foreign law and hold that the man in
question shall be treated as not being a national of that foreign state. That principle
was restated by Russell J in *Stoeck v Public Trustee*[1]. Russell J recognised, however,
that circumstances could arise in which a man might be treated as a national of a
foreign state for the purpose of English law although he was not a national of that
state according to its own municipal law. I do not suppose that in 1921 it would have
c been possible for anyone to be sufficiently imaginative or pessimistic to foresee
anything like the decree of 1941. But had Russell J been able to do so, he might well
have concluded that there could be nothing which could afford a stronger justification
for English law treating a man as a German national in spite of the fact that by German
law he had lost his German nationality.

The principle normally applied by our courts in relation to foreign penal or con-
d fiscatory legislation was correctly stated by Goulding J[2]. The comity of nations
normally requires our courts to recognise the jurisdiction of a foreign state over all its
own nationals and all assets situated within its own territories. Ordinarily, if our
courts were to refuse to recognise legislation by a sovereign state relating to assets
situated within its own territories or to the status of its own nationals on the ground
that the legislation was utterly immoral and unjust, this could obviously embarrass
e the Crown in its relations with a sovereign state whose independence it recognised and
with whom it had and hoped to maintain normal friendly relations. In *Aksionairnoye
Obschestvo A M Luther v James Sagor & Co*,[3] the Soviet Republic by a decree passed
in June 1918 declared all mechanical sawmills of a certain capital value and all wood-
working establishments belonging to private or limited companies to be the property
of the Soviet Republic. In 1919 agents of the Soviet Republic seized the plaintiff's mill
f in Russia and the stock of wood it contained. In 1920 the Soviet Republic sold a
quantity of this stock to the defendants who imported it into England. The plaintiffs
claimed a declaration that they were entitled to this stock on the ground that the 1918
decree of confiscation was so immoral and contrary to the principles of justice as
recognised by this country that our courts ought not to pay any attention to it. It was
held however that as the government of this country had recognised the Soviet
g Government as the de facto Government of Russia prior to the 1918 decree,
neither the decree nor the sale of the wood to the defendants in Russia could be
impugned in our courts. The reasons for this decision are illuminating, since they
illustrate one of the important differences between the present case and the host of
other cases (of which the *James Sagor* case[3] is an example) in which foreign penal or
confiscatory legislation has been considered in our courts. Scrutton LJ said[4] :
h
'But it appears a serious breach of international comity, if a state is recognized
as a sovereign independent state, to postulate that its legislation is "contrary to
essential principles of justice and morality." Such an allegation might well with
a susceptible foreign government become a casus belli; and should in my view
be the action of the Sovereign through his ministers, and not of the judges in
j reference to a state which their Sovereign has recognized . . . Individuals must
contribute to the welfare of the state, and at present British citizens who may

1 [1921] 2 Ch 67 at 82
2 [1972] 2 All ER at 534, [1972] Ch at 592
3 [1921] 3 KB 532
4 [1921] 3 KB at 558, 559

contribute to the state more than half their income in income tax and super tax, and a large proportion of their capital in death duties, can hardly declare a *a* foreign state immoral which considers (though we may think wrongly) that to vest individual property in the state as representing all the citizens is the best form of proprietary right. I do not feel able to come to the conclusion that the legislation of a state recognized by my Sovereign as an independent sovereign state is so contrary to moral principle that the judges ought not to recognize it.'

b

The alleged immorality of the Soviet Republic's decree of 1918 was different in kind from the Nazi decree of 1941. The latter was without parallel. But even more importantly, England and Russia were not at war in 1918 whilst England was at war with Germany in 1941—a war which, as Goulding J points out, was presented in its later stages as a crusade against the barbarities of the Nazi regime of which the 1941 decree is a typical example. I do not understand how, in these circumstances, it *c* could be regarded as embarrassing to our Government in its relationship with any other sovereign state or contrary to international comity or to any legal principles hitherto enunciated, for our courts to decide that the 1941 decree was so great an offence against human rights that they would have nothing to do with it.

It is for these reasons that I respectfully disagree with the finding of Buckley LJ, in which Orr LJ concurred, that our courts would have been obliged to recognise the *d* decree of 1941 as effective to deprive Mr Oppenheimer of his German nationality. It has been said that this decree conferred a positive benefit on many of those whom it deprived of their German nationality. This may be so but there is no such finding in the case stated and it is not permissible to travel outside the case to explore these possibilities. In any event, I doubt whether the question whether an enactment is so great an offence against human rights that it ought not to be recognised by any *e* civilised system of law can depend on its impact on the facts of any particular case.

Mr Oppenheimer was exempt from English income tax in respect of his German pension if, but only if, he had a German as well as an English nationality during the tax years in question. He undoubtedly had no German nationality at the relevant period because of the decree of 1941—if that decree was effective to prevent him from being treated in English law as a German national. As I have, however, already *f* indicated, the decree in my judgment should not be recognised by our courts as having any effect in English law for any purpose. Although this view would have entitled Mr Oppenheimer to succeed on the case as originally stated, it is of no avail to him on the case as now restated.

The findings in the case, as restated, relating to German law, and in particular to art 116(2) of the Basic Law of 1949, throw an entirely new light on this appeal. It is *g* now clear that during the tax years in question, Mr Oppenheimer's nationality under German municipal law did not in any way depend on the decree of 1941. Indeed, by enacting the Basic Law of 1949, the German Federal Republic cleansed German municipal law of its contamination by the Nazis and did everything possible to rectify the injustice which the Nazi decrees had perpetrated. The German Federal Government were careful, however, not to thrust German nationality on anyone *h* against his will if the decree of 1941 had purported to deprive him of it. The Basic Law accordingly enabled anyone affected by the decree who wished to be a German national to be 'renaturalised' and treated for all purposes as a German national by German municipal law. Such a person had only to apply, at any time, for German nationality and his application would automatically be granted. Alternatively if he returned to and resided in Germany without declaring a wish not to be a German *j* national he would be regarded, in German law, as a German national. If he did neither of these things, it would be assumed that he did not wish to be a German national and his wish would be respected. In such circumstances, German law would treat him as not being a German national—which as the commissioners have found in the restated case would mean that, in German law, he was not a German

national. Mr Oppenheimer did not return to Germany, nor did he make any applica-
a tion under art 116(2) until after the tax years in question. Had he made any such
application at any time between those years and 1949, he would immediately from
the date of his application have been regarded by German municipal law as a German
national and therefore also treated in English law as a German national. It was not
the odious Nazi decree of 1941 but his own failure to apply in time under the benevo-
lent art 116(2) of the Basic Law enacted in 1949 which deprived him of exemption
b from United Kingdom income tax for the tax years in question.

My Lords, I would accordingly dismiss Mr Oppenheimer's appeal. I would also, for
the reasons given by my noble and learned friend Lord Cross of Chelsea dismiss
Miss Nothman's appeal.

Appeals dismissed.

c
Solicitors: *Rayner & Co* (for Mr Oppenheimer); *Solicitor of Inland Revenue.*

Gordon H Scott Esq Barrister.

d

Deistung v South Western Metropolitan Regional Hospital Board

COURT OF APPEAL, CIVIL DIVISION
e LORD DENNING MR, CAIRNS LJ, SIR JOHN PENNYCUICK
24th, 25th OCTOBER 1974

Discovery – Production of documents – Production before commencement of proceedings –
Claim in respect of personal injuries – Medical records – Disclosure to prospective plaintiff's
medical adviser only – Use of documents – Plaintiff not bound by medical expert's report –
f *Right of plaintiff's counsel to question expert in relation to records to determine whether a*
case.

Where hospital notes and records are disclosed to a medical expert selected by a
person who is a prospective plaintiff in an action for personal injuries the plaintiff is
not entitled to see them, nor are his legal advisers. The plaintiff is not bound by the
report made by the medical expert on the basis of those documents. The report is to
g be regarded as one made by a potential witness for the plaintiff and if the plaintiff or
his legal advisers feel that the report needs further explanation or reconsideration
they may take it up with the expert. That may be followed by a conference between
counsel and the expert at which counsel may ask further questions in order to determine whether the plaintiff has a case. In answering the questions the expert may refer
to the hospital notes and records without showing them to counsel (see p 575 *d* to *f*,
h post).

Note
For discovery before commencement of proceedings, see Supplement to 12 Halsbury's
Laws (3rd Edn) para 2A.

Case referred to in judgment
j *Davidson v Lloyd Aircraft Services Ltd* [1974] 3 All ER 1, [1974] 1 WLR 1042, CA.

Cases also cited
Dunning v Board of Governors of the United Liverpool Hospitals [1973] 2 All ER 454, [1973]
1 WLR 586, CA.
Shaw v Vauxhall Motors Ltd [1974] 2 All ER 1185, [1974] 1 WLR 1035, CA.

Appeal

By an originating summons dated 15th February 1974 the plaintiff, Janet Deistung (a   *a*
minor suing by her next friend, Otto Martin Karl Herbert Deistung), sought an order
under RSC Ord 24, r 7A(1), that the defendants, South Western Metropolitan Regional
Hospital Board ('the hospital board'), disclose to the plaintiff all records held by the
hospital board, their servants or agents in relation to the treatment of the plaintiff at
the Worthing Hospital, Lyndhurst Road, Worthing, between 18th October and 22nd
November 1972.   On 20th March 1974 Master Ritchie refused to make the order   *b*
sought.   The plaintiff appealed to a judge in chambers.   On 13th May 1974 Bristow J
allowed the appeal and made the order.   The hospital board appealed.   The facts are
set out in the judgment of Lord Denning MR.

Thomas Bingham QC and *Peter Scott* for the hospital board.
Margaret Puxon for the plaintiff.   *c*

LORD DENNING MR.   This is an application for the disclosure of documents
before an action has been started.   It is made under s 31 of the Administration of
Justice Act 1970.   Janet Deistung is a young girl aged 12 years.   In 1974 she had treatment in the Worthing Hospital.   Her father thinks that the hospital were negligent.
On her behalf he seeks to have discovery of the notes and records of the hospital.   *d*
The hospital are ready and have always been ready to show the notes and records to
her medical advisers for them to make a report; but they do not wish them to be
shown to the girl, her father or their lawyers.   That is what has happened so far.   The
hospital have disclosed the notes and records to a medical adviser chosen by the father
and his solicitors.   He is a Mr R R Kendrick FRCS.   On 11th May 1973 he wrote a
report which gives the history and his opinion.   I will read it in full: *e*

'Janet was admitted to Worthing Hospital on 18th October 1972 with abdomi-
nal pain and vomiting since eating sausages on 15th October. Her father had also
eaten some and had suffered from similar but milder symptoms. She was very
dehydrated. She was seen by the House Surgeon who commenced treatment for
the dehydration. At 2.00 p.m. a needle inserted into the right lower abdomen
revealed brownish fluid. She was seen by Mr Price the Surgical Registrar at 3.00   *f*
p.m. who suspected a ruptured ectopic pregnancy. She was seen by a Gynae-
cologist at about 5.00 p.m. He did not suspect a gynaecological cause for her
illness. At laparotomy shortly afterwards no surgical abnormality was found.
She continued in negative balance and an X-ray suggested duodenal obstruction
and on 3rd November 1972 laparotomy was carried out by Mr Martin, the Con-
sultant Surgeon in charge of Janet. Again no specific surgical anomaly was found.   *g*
She made no real progress and could not be kept on a positive fluid balance by
mouth. On 21st November 1972 she was transferred to Great Ormond Street
Hospital where she quite quickly settled down on a graduated bland diet and was
discharged home after 10 days. She has since apparently made a full recovery.
'*Opinion*: Her history and treatment by the House Surgeon was accurate and
prompt. I think it was very unwise of the Surgical Registrar to diagnose an   *h*
ectopic pregnancy and especially to inform the father of his suspicion, without
first carrying out a pregnancy test, which could be performed in the laboratory
within a few minutes—however this omission is counteracted by the fact that a
Specialist Gynaecological opinion was obtained during the afternoon. Perhaps
the possibility of food poisoning was not sufficiently taken into account before the
first laparotomy was performed, but in every other respect the fact that two   *i*
laparotomies were carried out, unnecessarily as it turned out and doubtlessly
with distressing scarring in a girl of her years, cannot in any way be classified as
negligent. Her post-operative convalescence was protracted and full of set backs
but, again, in my opinion, can in no way be classified as negligent.
'R. R. KENDRICK, F.R.C.S.'

On receiving that report, the father and his advisers felt it was not sufficient. They asked for the notes or the records of the hospital to be shown to the legal advisers and, if need be, to her father and the girl herself. And so they made this application for the purpose. Bristow J made the order. He made it on 13th May 1974. He said:

'. . . it seems to me that what the Applicant is entitled to, if the applicant is entitled to anything, is the joint consideration of the raw material by the Legal
Advisers and the Medical Experts together.'

On the very next day in this court we had the case of *Davidson v Lloyd Aircraft Service Ltd*[1]. I feel sure that if the judge had had that case before him he would have come to a different conclusion.

But apart from that, as a result of the discussion in this court, the matter has been elucidated a great deal. At the beginning, counsel for the plaintiff, who is advising
the girl's father, seems to have thought that the plaintiff was limited to the report of Mr Kendrick, that the plaintiff was bound by it and could not go further. But counsel for the hospital board agreed that the plaintiff was not so limited. It is, I think, to be regarded as a medical report made by a potential witness for the plaintiff. If the plaintiff or his lawyers feel that the report needs further explanation—or that they would like Mr Kendrick to reconsider his opinion—they can write him a letter. This
can be followed by a conference with counsel such as counsel often does have with an expert witness. At such a conference counsel can ask further questions so as to see whether or no there is a reasonable and probable case. In answering the questions the medical expert can refer to the notes and records which he has received from the hospital—without any need to show them to the plaintiff or the advisers. In that way all that is necessary will be done. At any rate, all that is necessary at this stage:
s 31 of the 1970 Act and the rules under it make it clear that an order for discovery should only be made if it is necessary at that stage, and, I would add, necessary in the interests of justice. In the circumstances of this case it is not necessary. I would allow the appeal accordingly.

CAIRNS LJ. I agree and have nothing to add.

SIR JOHN PENNYCUICK. I agree and have nothing to add.

Appeal allowed.

Solicitors: *C H Brown* (for the board); *Lovell, Son & Pitfield*, agents for *Anderson, Longmore & Higham*, Petworth (for the plaintiff).

M G Hammett Esq   Barrister.

1 [1974] 3 All ER 1, [1974] 1 WLR 1042

Practice Direction   *a*

CHANCERY DIVISION

Practice – Chambers – Chancery Division – Setting down for trial – Delay – Failure to set case down for trial by date specified in order – Effect – Review by master.

b

Practice – Chambers – Chancery Division – Orders – Master's orders to be made in master's name only – Order under judge's name only if made by judge.

Delays in setting down

1. There is often considerable delay in setting cases down for hearing. Though orders for trial and adjournments of originating summonses into court to the Witness List or the Non-Witness List specify a time within which the case is to be set down, the time limit is frequently exceeded and it is difficult for the court to refuse an application to set down out of time unless an opposing party has applied to dismiss for want of prosecution. These delays are frequently the fault of the professional advisers rather than the fault of the litigants themselves.

c

2. In future the master will keep a note of every date by which he has ordered a   *d* case to be set down in the Witness List or the Non-Witness List. If there is no setting down by that date and no written consent, signed on behalf of all parties, to defer the setting down for some specific reason, he will call before him the party whose duty it is to set down and require him to explain the delay. He will thenceforth keep the matter under continuous review until the case is set down and may, if he thinks fit, call for the attendance of all opposing parties so that they may be aware of the   *e* situation.

3. It follows that the parties should apply for realistic time limits when obtaining orders for setting down or adjournment into court.

Judges' names on masters' orders

4. The name of the judge responsible for chambers work in the group to which a   *f* master is attached will no longer appear on an order made by that master. If a judge's name appears on an order it will indicate that the order was made by the judge in person. The group will continue to be included in every order.

By the direction of the Vice-Chancellor.

R E BALL

31st January 1975   Chief Master *g*

a

Re Lubin, Rosen and Associates Ltd

CHANCERY DIVISION

MEGARRY J

21st, 22nd, 25th OCTOBER 1974

b

Company – Winding-up – Compulsory winding-up – Secretary of State's petition – Secretary of State taking view that it is expedient in the public interest that company be wound up – Just and equitable ground – Company already subject to voluntary winding-up – Need to satisfy court that it is just and equitable that company be wound up compulsorily – Compulsory winding-up opposed by creditors – Whether additional burden on Secretary of State to satisfy court that voluntary winding-up cannot be continued with due regard to interests of creditors

c

and contributories – Companies Act 1948, s 224(2) – Companies Act 1967, s 35(1).

Company – Winding-up – Liquidator – Duty of liquidator – Voluntary winding-up – Duty not to take steps which appear to be designed to secure support for himself or be discouraging to creditors who take contrary view.

d

A company was registered as a private company on 19th January 1971 to carry on the business of developing land. Shortly after its incorporation it became engaged in the development of land in Spain by the erection of blocks of flats. The flats were to be sold to members of the public on terms which required the purchaser to pay a substantial proportion of the purchase price before completion of his flat. The purchase moneys paid in advance were used to finance the building of the flats. Only one of the four blocks was eventually completed. Most of the flats in the second and third

e

blocks had been sold, but the company was unable to finance further building work. In 1973 the Secretary of State authorised an investigation into the company's affairs under s 109 of the Companies Act 1967. Following the investigation the company passed a resolution on 26th July 1974 for its voluntary winding-up and appointed a liquidator for that purpose. On 15th August a creditors' meeting confirmed the appointment of the liquidator and appointed a committee of inspection, although on

f

9th August the Secretary of State had presented a petition for a compulsory winding-up order pursuant to s 35(1)*a* of the Companies Act 1967 to supersede the voluntary winding-up. The petition, having described the company's activities, alleged that at no time had the company had sufficient paid up capital to finance those activities, that since April 1973 the company had been insolvent and unable to pay its debts, a fact which had been well known to the directors since January 1974, but that the company

g

had nevertheless continued to trade. The petition concluded by alleging that the the company was insolvent and unable to pay its debts and that in the circumstances it was just and equitable that it should be wound up. On 15th August the liquidator sent all creditors a report and statement of affairs. The report referred to only four creditors in a meeting of over 300 people having voted against confirming the credi-

h

tors' voluntary winding-up. It then stated that in order that the Secretary of State's petition could be opposed in the courts a form was being enclosed 'for you to sign and forward' to the company's solicitors. The form instructed the solicitors 'to oppose

---

j   *a*   Section 35(1), so far as material, provides: 'If, in the case of any body corporate liable to be wound up under the [Companies Act 1948], it appears to the Board of Trade from any report made under section 168 (inspectors' report) of that Act or from any information or document obtained under Part III of this Act or section 18 or 19 of the Protection of Depositors Act 1963 that it is expedient in the public interest that the body should be wound up, the Board may, unless the body is already being wound up by the court, present a petition for it to be so wound up if the court thinks it just and equitable for it to be so wound up . . .'   ʊ

the making of a compulsory winding-up order against the company'. In the event the   *a*
petition was opposed by 198 creditors with claims of over £540,000. Most, if not all, of
the opposing creditors were, however, purchasers of flats who had at one time been
given some grounds for hoping that under a voluntary winding-up some of the flats
might still be completed. At the hearing of the petition it was contended on behalf of
the company and opposing creditors that, under s 224(2)[b] of the Companies Act 1948,
ir was necessary for the Secretary of State to satisfy the court that the voluntary
winding-up could not be continued with due regard to the interests of the creditors   *b*
and contributories.

Held – A compulsory winding-up order would be made for the following reasons—
    (i) Where the Secretary of State petitioned under s 35 of the 1967 Act for the
compulsory winding-up of a company which was already being wound up volun-   *c*
tarily or subject to supervision, it was only necessary for the Secretary of State to show
that it was 'just and equitable', within s 35(1) of the 1967 Act and s 222(f) of the 1948 Act,
that the company should be wound up compulsorily. Section 224(2) of the 1948 Act
did not impose on the Secretary of State the additional burden of satisfying the court
that the voluntary winding-up or winding-up subject to supervision could not be
continued with due regard to the interests of the creditors or contributories for, on its   *d*
true construction, s 224(2) applied only in cases where a petition was presented by the
Official Receiver and not where a petition was presented by a person, such as the
Secretary of State, authorised to do so under the other provisions of s 224. Accordingly
the existence of the voluntary winding-up was merely one of the circumstances to be
considered in deciding whether it was just and equitable that a winding-up order
should be made (see p 581 f to p 582 d, post).   *e*
    (ii) Notwithstanding the existence of a voluntary winding-up and the opposition of
the creditors, it was just and equitable that the company should be wound up having
regard to the circumstances and in particular to the fact (a) that the petition had been
presented, not by a creditor, but by the Secretary of State pursuant to investigations
by him which indicated that it was expedient in the public interest that the company
should be wound up, and (b) that there were circumstances of suspicion which made it   *f*
highly desirable that the winding-up should be conducted by the court with all the
safeguards which that provided, including the investigation of any suspected offences
(see p 582 f to h and p 583 b and e, post).
    Per Megarry J. (i) It is undesirable for a voluntary liquidator to take steps which
appear to be designed to secure support for himself and be discouraging to creditors
who take a contrary view. A voluntary liquidator ought not even to give the   *g*
appearance of being one-sided in such matters (see p 580 j, post).
    (ii) A petition presented by the Secretary of State under s 35(1) of the 1967 Act is in a
somewhat different category from a petition presented by a creditor or contributory,
since the latter petition in their own interest as a class whereas the Secretary of State
petitions under a special statutory provision which comes into operation only when it
appears expedient to him in the public interest that the company should be wound up.   *h*
In such a case the court, without abdicating any of its judicial and discretionary powers,
ought to give weight to the Secretary of State's views (see p 583 f to h, post).

Notes
For proceedings arising out of inspectors' report, see 7 Halsbury's Laws (4th Edn) 577,   *j*
para 975.
    For the Companies Act 1948, s 224, see 5 Halsbury's Statutes (3rd Edn) 293.
    For the Companies Act 1967, s 35(1), see ibid 579.

---

b Section 224(2) is set out at p 581 d and e, post

Cases referred to in judgment

a *Attorney-General (on the relation of Hornchurch District Council) v Bastow* [1957] 1 All ER 497, [1957] 1 QB 514, [1957] 2 WLR 340, 121 JP 171, 55 LGR 122, 8 P & CR 168, 28(2) Digest (Reissue) 962, 39.

Swain (J D) Ltd, Re [1965] 2 All ER 761, [1965] 1 WLR 909, CA, Digest (Cont Vol B) 112, 5813b.

b *Vuma Ltd, Re* [1960] 3 All ER 629, [1960] 1 WLR 1283, CA, Digest (Cont Vol A) 187, 5819a.

Petition

This was a petition by the Secretary of State for Trade for an order that Lubin, Rosen and Associates Ltd ('the company') be wound up by the court under the provisions of the Companies Acts 1948 to 1967 or that such other order be made as should seem to
c the court just. The petition was not supported by any of the creditors. It was opposed by the company and by 198 creditors with claims of over £540,000. The facts are set out in the judgment.

Andrew Morritt for the petitioner.
John Vallat for the company and opposing creditors.
d
Cur adv vult

25th October. **MEGARRY J** read the following judgment. This is a petition by the Secretary of State for Trade for a compulsory winding-up order under the Companies Act 1967, s 35. The company was incorporated on 19th January 1971 with a capital of
e 5,000 £1 shares which are now fully paid. The petition states that on 12th June 1973 and on 15th July 1974—

'the Secretary of State for Trade and Industry and the Secretary of State for Trade respectively in pursuance of the powers conferred on him by Section 109 Companies Act 1967 authorised George Ronald Winn, one of his officers, to
f require the Company to produce to him forthwith any books or papers which he might specify. From the information and documents obtained in pursuance of the powers conferred by Part III Companies Act 1967 it appears to Your Petitioner that it is expedient in the public interest that the Company should be wound up. Since shortly after its incorporation the Company has been and still is engaged in the development of land at Los Arenales, Alicante in the Republic of Spain by the erection thereon of blocks of flats and the sale of such flats to members of the
g public on terms which required such a purchaser to pay a substantial proportion of the purchase price before completion of his flat. At no time has the Company had a paid up share capital sufficient to finance its said activities. Since 30th April 1973 the Company has been and now is insolvent and unable to pay its debts as the directors of the Company Paul Lubin and Maurice Rosen well knew at
h all times since 22nd January 1974.'

The petition then goes on to state that notwithstanding the facts specified the company has continued to trade and that there are certain circumstances specified in the petition relating to the trading activities of the company which require investigation by a liquidator. The petition concludes by alleging that the Company is insolvent and unable to pay its debts, and that in the circumstances it is just and
j equitable that the company should be wound up.

There are four blocks of flats in Spain in question. The first block was completed and the flats were duly conveyed by the company to the purchasers. Of the second block, some 70 to 80 per cent of the building work has been completed. In the third block there is apparently nothing more than the foundations, while the fourth block has not yet been begun. Most of the flats in the second and third blocks have been sold.

The purchasers who have paid much of the price and yet have not obtained their flats are in a sad plight. 20 per cent of the price became due by the time the company *a* signed the contract and a further 25 per cent and then 35 per cent was payable at quarterly intervals, making 80 per cent in all. The final 20 per cent was payable only on the production of the architects' certificate of completion. Some of the purchasers have not paid all that was due from them, but it is quite plain that the company's capital was wholly inadequate for the projects that it undertook, and that these pro- jects were being financed by the payments in advance made by the purchasers. Sharp *b* and continuous increases in building costs in Spain, coupled with delays caused by the requirements of the local authority, and so on, have made it plainly impossible for the company to complete its proposals. Various attempts were made to find a way of escape, including an attempt to persuade all the purchasers who had not obtained their flats to pay an increase of 35 per cent above their contract price, but these attempts have failed.   *c*

After an investigation had been made by Mr Winn, on 26th July 1974 the company passed a resolution for its voluntary winding-up and appointed Mr Phillips liquidator. On 15th August the creditors' meeting confirmed Mr Phillips's appointment and appointed a committee of inspection. The Secretary of State's petition was filed on 9th August 1974, and the main affidavit in support is an affidavit sworn by Mr Winn on 27th August and filed on 30th August. Before me, Mr Morritt appeared for the *d* petitioner, and Mr Vallat for the company and the opposing creditors, 198 in number, with claims of over £540,000. It is accepted on all hands that the company must be wound up, but the question is whether the voluntary liquidation should be superseded by the making of a compulsory winding-up order. Many problems face any liquidator, not least the tangled questions that arise from most of the assets of the company being in Spain, and problems of Spanish law, some of which have been touched on but *e* not explored before me.

Now a petition which is not supported by any creditors but is opposed by so many, with claims of so large a value, is one that, prima facie, has a formidable obstacle in its way. However, there are certain special features about this opposition. First, it is obvious that the creditors did not have before them Mr Winn's affidavit. This, which is critical of the directors in a number of respects, contains much information which *f* in all probability was not put before the creditors' meeting; there is at least no evi- dence to show that all of these matters were fully put before the creditors. Second, on 15th August 1974 the liquidator sent all creditors a two-page report and a statement of affairs. The report refers to only four creditors in a meeting of over 300 people having voted against confirming the creditors' voluntary winding-up with Mr Phillips as liquidator and a committee of inspection. It then says this: *g*

> 'In order that the petition of the compulsory winding up of the company can be opposed in the courts, a Form is enclosed herewith for you to sign and forward to Messrs. Pritchard Englefield & Tobin of 23, Great Castle Street, Oxford Circus, W1N 8NQ. You will incur no cost in relation to this.'

The form enclosed says simply: *h*

> 'I/We the undersigned, being creditors of the above company in the sum of £ hereby instruct you to oppose the making of a compulsory winding-up order against the company.'

Neither the four creditors at the meeting who supported the compulsory winding- up nor any other creditors who were not present but took a similar view are catered *j* for, either in the shape of having a form on which to express their wishes, or any assurance about costs. Let me say at once that it seems undesirable for a voluntary liquidator to take steps such as these, which appear to be designed to secure support for himself and be discouraging to the creditors who take a minority view. A voluntary liquidator ought not even to give the appearance of being one-sided in such matters.

a A liquidator who does this at least exposes himself to the comment that he does not seem to have a full appreciation of his position; and counsel for the company was constrained to accept that this part of the circular was indeed open to criticism. The result is that the weight to be attached to the apparently large body of opposing creditors must in some degree be diminished.

Now there was a basic difference of view as to the law between counsel for the petitioner and counsel for the company in relation to cases where, as here, the Secre-
b tary of State seeks a compulsory winding-up order. Counsel for the petitioner contended that the whole question was whether or not it is 'just and equitable' within the Companies Act 1967, s 35(1) and the Companies Act 1948, s 222(f) for the company to be compulsorily wound up. Section 310 of the 1948 Act deals with petitions by creditors and contributories for the compulsory winding-up of a company in voluntary liquidation, and requires that on a petition by a contributory the court should
c be satisfied that the rights of the contributories will be prejudiced by the voluntary winding-up; but this says nothing about petitions by the Secretary of State. Section 346 of the 1948 Act does no more than provide that 'the court may . . . have regard to the wishes of the creditors . . .', and this does not affect the basis, which is one of what is just and equitable. Section 224(1) of the 1948 Act shows that petitions can be presented by any creditor or contributory or by the Secretary of State. Subsection (2) provides as follows:

d
'Where a company is being wound up voluntarily or subject to supervision in England, a winding-up petition may be presented by the official receiver attached to the court as well as by any other person authorised in that behalf under the other provisions of this section, but the court shall not make a winding-up
e order on the petition unless it is satisfied that the voluntary winding up or winding up subject to supervision cannot be continued with due regard to the interests of the creditors or contributories.'

That, however, merely enables the Official Receiver to petition if there is a voluntary winding-up or winding-up subject to supervision, and does not affect the Secretary of
d State. Accordingly, none of these provisions affected the matter, and so the question was simply whether or not it was just and equitable to make a winding-up order. Thus ran the argument.

To these contentions counsel for the company demurred. He pointed to the phrase 'as well as by any other person authorised in that behalf under the other provisions of this section' which appears in s 224(2), and said that (as is indeed the case) the Secretary of State, in place of the Board of Trade, was a person who was authorised by sub-s
f (1)(d) of the section; thus he too was subject to the burden of showing that the voluntary winding-up 'cannot be continued with due regard to the interests of the creditors or contributories', and this imposed on him a far greater burden than a mere 'just and equitable' clause. Counsel for the petitioner's reply was that the Secretary of State was not 'any other person' within the phrase in sub-s (2) for the purposes of being subjected to this heavier burden; and this accords with notes appearing in
g Buckley's Companies Acts[1], and Halsbury's Laws of England[2], which state that sub-s (2) seems to be limited to the Official Receiver. In a sense, the argument of counsel for the company proves too much. The 'any other person' clause must include not only the Secretary of State but also any creditor or contributory, so that all, on counsel's argument, are subject to the same high burden; yet that is not consistent with s 310 relating to the right of creditors and contributories to petition for a winding-up order
j despite a voluntary winding-up. The right way to read sub-s (2), said counsel for the petitioners was to treat the 'any other person' clause parenthetically. Subsection (1) does not mention the Official Receiver but gives creditors and contributories the

1   13th Edn (1957), p 468
2   4th Edn, vol 7, p 601

general right to petition for a compulsory winding-up order. Subsection (2) then
brings in the Official Receiver, who is not given any general right to petition but only a   *a*
right to petition if the company is already being wound up voluntarily or under supervision. In conferring this right, the draftsman, seeking to make it plain that if a company is being wound up voluntarily or subject to supervision it is not the Official
Receiver alone who can petition but also any other person authorised to petition,
included the phrase beginning 'as well as any other person'; but, this saving paren-
thesis ended, the subsection continues with the second part beginning 'but the court',   *b*
which applies only to a petition presented solely by the Official Receiver. Counsel
for the petitioner also stressed that unlike a creditor or contributory the Secretary of
State was not able to petition on all the grounds set out in s 222 but only on the 'just
and equitable' ground which s 35(1) of the 1967 Act makes applicable unless the
body is already being wound up by the court, an exception which does not include a
voluntary winding-up.   *c*

In its essence, it seems to me that counsel for the petitioner's argument is right, and
I accept it. The existence of a voluntary winding-up is, of course, one of the circumstances to be considered in deciding whether or not it is just and equitable to make a
compulsory winding-up order, but I do not think it is more than that. Counsel for the
company referred me to *Re J D Swain Ltd*[1], where the Court of Appeal affirmed the
decision of Pennycuick J in dismissing a petition for a compulsory winding-up order   *d*
which was opposed by the great majority of creditors in number and value. There,
the petition was presented before the voluntary liquidation had been resolved on, and
so in that respect it was a stronger case than this, where the petition was presented
after the resolution had been passed. However, I observe that Harman LJ[2] referred
to *Re Vuma Ltd*[3], where the court made a compulsory winding-up order against the
majority view, and said, 'There were circumstances of suspicion in that case which   *e*
made an order desirable'. Furthermore, as counsel for the petitioner contended,
where a petition is presented by a creditor seeking to exercise a class right, the view
of the majority of his class has a potency which does not exist where the petition is presented not by a creditor but by the Secretary of State, after he has reached the conclusion that it is expedient in the public interest that the company should be wound
up. It seems to me that the very fact that the Secretary of State has reached such a   *f*
conclusion is a factor which, without being in any way decisive, ought to be given
appropriate weight by the court. Counsel for the petitioner also referred me to
Palmer's Company Law[4], where it is said:

> 'The court is invested with a wide jurisdiction in the interests of commercial
> morality; and if the facts disclose a strong prima facie case for investigation into   *g*
> the formation or promotion of the company, or the issue of debentures by it, the
> court will make a compulsory order irrespective of creditors' opposition.'

Now in the present case counsel for the petitioner contends that from the affidavit
of Mr Winn emerges substantial evidence of fraudulent trading and other activities
which ought to be enquired into with a strong hand. He accepted that under the
Companies Act 1948, s 334, there is provision for a voluntary liquidator to report   *h*
apparent offences to the Director of Public Prosecutions; but he said (as is the case)
that the provisions of this section lacked the force of s 236. In the case of a compulsory
winding-up order, that section imposes on the Official Receiver a duty to submit a
preliminary report to the court as to the cause of the failure of the company and
whether further enquiry is desirable, inter alia, in relation to the failure of the company or the conduct of its business; and there is also provision for further reports as to   *j*
frauds. The case before me has the peculiarity, too, that most if not all of the creditors

1   [1965] 2 All ER 761, [1965] 1 WLR 909
2   [1965] 2 All ER at 763, [1965] 1 WLR at 912
3   [1960] 3 All ER 629 [1960] 1 WLR 1283
4   21st Edn (1968), pp 742, 743

a   of the company who oppose the making of a compulsory order are purchasers of flats, who at least at one time were given some grounds for hoping that under a voluntary winding-up at least some of the flats might still be completed. I appreciate, as counsel for the company urged, that there is at least some urgency in taking prompt steps in Spain to protect the interests of all concerned, and that there might be some delay in taking these steps if a compulsory winding-up order supersedes the voluntary liquida-

b   tion. But I do not think that this consideration, or indeed anything else that counsel for the company has so persuasively urged on me, outweighs the consideration that where there are circumstances of suspicion, as there undoubtedly are in this case, it is highly desirable that the winding-up should be by the court, with all the safeguards that this provides, including the investigation of any suspected offences.

In this case, the investigation by the Secretary of State preceded the resolution for a voluntary winding-up. Where the results of that investigation lead the Secretary of

c   State to the conclusion that is expedient in the public interest that the company should be wound up, and he accordingly presents a petition for a compulsory order, I do not think that the passing of a resolution for a voluntary winding-up shortly before the Secretary of State presents his petition, and the subsequent confirmation of that resolution, ought to be allowed to put the voluntary winding-up into an entrenched position, as it were, which can be demolished only if the Secretary of State can demon-

d   strate that the process of voluntary winding-up will be markedly inferior to a com- pulsory winding-up. The Secretary of State may, of course, reach the conclusion that a voluntary winding-up will suffice, and so not proceed with his petition; but if he does proceed, then in my judgment the question is essentially whether, in all the cir- cumstances of the case (including, of course, the existence of a voluntary winding-up and the views of the creditors), it is just and equitable for the company to be wound

e   up compulsorily. In addition to the suspicion of offences, the presence of foreign com- plications such as exist in this case, and the differences between the interests of the disappointed purchasers and those of any other creditors, seem to me to make it both just and equitable that this winding-up should be conducted with the full authority and resources of the court. I shall therefore make the usual compulsory order.

I would add this, in amplification of something that I have already mentioned. It

f   seems to me that a petition presented by the Secretary of State under s 35 of the 1967 Act is in a somewhat different category from a petition presented by a creditor or contributory. Creditors and contributories petition in their own interests as mem- bers of a class; under the section the Secretary of State petitions under a special statutory provision which comes into operation only when it has appeared to him that it is expedient in the public interest that the company should be wound up. The

g   Secretary of State is necessarily acting not in his own interests but in the interests of the public at large. Though there are many differences, it seems possible to contend that there is at least some analogy with the attitude of the court to the Attorney- General in relator proceedings: see *Attorney-General v Bastow*[1]. But however that may be, it is clear that s 35 puts the Secretary of State in the position of acting in the public interest; and when a high officer of state whom Parliament has entrusted

h   with these functions has reached the conclusion that his duty requires him to petition for the winding-up of a company, I think that the court, without in the least abdicating any of its judicial and discretionary powers, ought to give special weight to his views. At the same time I wish to make it clear that my decision rests on the grounds that I have already set out, without the aid of this amplification, which was not debated during argument. I nevertheless mention it as it may be of assistance in other cases,

j   and in any event it serves to reinforce the conclusion that I reach without its aid.

Order for compulsory winding-up.

Solicitors: *Treasury Solicitor; Pritchard Englefield & Tobin* (for the company and the opposing creditors).

F K Anklesaria Esq Barrister.

1   [1957] 1 All ER 497, [1957] 1 QB 514

Horsler and another v Zorro

CHANCERY DIVISION
MEGARRY J
10th, 24th, 31st OCTOBER 1974

Sale of land – Contract – Breach – Damages – Rescission – Claim for rescission and damages for breach of contract – Order for rescission and enquiry as to damages – Plaintiff not entitled to more than nominal damages where contract rescinded – Plaintiff entitled to payment of such sums as would restore him to position in which he would have been if contract had not been made – Reference in order to 'damages' to be construed accordingly.

On 28th June 1971 the defendant contracted to sell his freehold house to the plaintiffs for £4,000. The date for completion was 26th July 1971. Subsequently the defendant refused to proceed with the sale. On 30th November 1971 the plaintiffs issued a writ against him, claiming specific performance or, alternatively, damages for breach of contract. However, on 4th April 1972 the plaintiffs' solicitors informed the defendant's solicitors that their clients did not intend to press proceedings for specific performance but wished to recover their deposit and to look for a property elsewhere. The defendant's solicitors returned the deposit on 17th April. On 16th May the plaintiffs amended their writ by deleting the claim for specific performance. Instead they claimed rescission and damages for breach of contract. On 1st June 1972 the master made an order which, so far as material, read: 'And it *appearing* that the Defendant has repudiated the contract of sale . . . It is *ordered* that the said contract be rescinded And it is *ordered* that the following Inquiry be made that is to say 1 An Inquiry what sum of money ought to be allowed and paid to the Plaintiffs by way of damages for the non-performance by the Defendant of the said contract And it is *ordered* that the amount of the said damages be certified . . .' The defendant did not appeal against that order. The master's certificate was made on 10th June 1974, assessing the damages at £3,000, being the difference between the contract price for the house and its value on the date when the order for rescission and an enquiry as to damages was made. That assessment was made on the basis that, where damages were awarded in substitution for specific performance, the award was not limited to the difference between the contract price and the value of the house at the date of breach. The defendant applied for the master's order to be discharged.

Held – (i) Since the plaintiffs had abandoned their claim for specific performance, they were not entitled to damages in lieu of specific performance. Furthermore, since the plaintiffs had elected to rescind the contract, they were precluded from claiming damages, other than nominal damages, for breach of contract. The basis on which the damages had been computed was therefore untenable and the master's certificate should be discharged accordingly (see p 587 j to p 588 c and h to p 589 a, post).

(ii) Since the plaintiffs had elected for rescission, a strict construction of the word 'damages' in the order of 1st June 1972 would necessarily lead to the result that the quantum of damages certified, apart from a nominal award for breach of contract, would be nil. However, a party who rescinded a contract was not thereby deprived of all right to monetary payment, and reasonable effect should be given to the order by construing the word 'damages' as a reference to those sums which a plaintiff would be entitled to recover where the contract had been rescinded, i e such sums as would restore him to the position in which he would have been had the contract never been made. The case would therefore be adjourned to chambers for the master to hold an enquiry as to damages on that limited basis (see p 594 b to e, p 595 b to d and p 596 e, post).

Notes

For the damages which a purchaser of land may recover for breach of contract, see 34

Halsbury's Laws (3rd Edn) 334-336, paras 567, 568, and for cases on the subject, see 40
a Digest (Repl) 284-291, *2358-2439*.
For the date by reference to which damages are measured, see 11 Halsbury's Laws
(3rd Edn) 237, 238, para 405.
For the right of a purchaser to rescind on default by the vendor, see 34 Halsbury's
Laws (3rd Edn) 328-330, paras 557, 558.

b **Cases referred to in judgment**
Abram Steamship Co Ltd v Westville Shipping Co Ltd [1923] AC 773, [1923] All ER Rep 645,
    93 LJPC 38, 130 LT 67, HL, 35 Digest (Repl) 71, *648*.
Bain v Fothergill (1874) LR 7 HL 158, [1874-80] All ER Rep 83, 43 LJEx 243, 31 LT 387,
    39 JP 228, HL; *affg* (1870) LR 6 Exch 59, Ex Ch, 17 Digest (Reissue) *122, 222.*
Barber v Wolfe [1945] 1 All ER 399, [1945] Ch 187, 114 LJCh 149, 172 LT 384, 40 Digest
c   (Repl) 240, *2016*.
Bryant & Barningham's Contract, Re (1890) 44 Ch D 218, 59 LJCh 636, 63 LT 20, CA, 40
    Digest (Repl) 253, *2121*.
Grant v Dawkins [1973] 3 All ER 897, [1973] 1 WLR 1406, 27 P & CR 158.
Hargreaves & Thompson's Contract, Re (1886) 32 Ch D 454, 56 LJCh 199, 55 LT 239, CA, 40
    Digest (Repl) 229, *1894*.
d *Harold Wood Brick Co Ltd v Ferris* [1935] 2 KB 198, [1935] All ER Rep 603, 104 LJKB 533,
    153 LT 241, CA; *affg* [1935] 1 KB 613.
Henty v Schröder (1879) 12 Ch D 666, 48 LJCh 792, 40 Digest (Repl) 239, *1994*.
Hutchings v Humphrey (1885) 54 LJCh 650, 52 LT 690, 40 Digest (Repl) 239, *1995*.
Jackson v De Kadich [1904] WN 168, 48 Sol Jo 687, 40 Digest (Repl) 239, *1998*.
Lee v Soames (1888) 59 LT 366, 36 WR 884, 40 Digest (Repl) 121, *945*.
e *Lowe v Hope* [1969] 3 All ER 605, [1970] Ch 94, [1969] 3 WLR 582, 20 P & CR 857, Digest
    (Cont Vol C) 866, *2051a*.
Mussen v Van Dieman's Land Co [1938] 1 All ER 210, [1938] Ch 253.
Public Trustee v Pearlberg [1940] 2 All ER 270, [1940] 2 KB 1, 109 LJKB 597, CA, 40 Digest
    (Repl) 102, *772*.
Reese River Silver Mining Co Ltd v Smith (1869) LR 4 HL 64, 39 LJCh 849, HL, 10 Digest
f   (Repl), 959, *6597*.
Robinson v Harman (1848) 1 Exch 850, [1843-60] All ER Rep 383, 18 LJEx 202, 13 LTOS
    141, 154 ER 363, 17 Digest (Reissue) 89, *40*.
Stockloser v Johnson [1954] 1 All ER 630, [1954] 1 QB 476, [1954] 2 WLR 439, CA, 20
    Digest (Repl) 548, *2565*.
Whittington v Seale-Hayne (1900) 82 LT 49, 16 TLR 181, 31(1) Digest (Reissue) 421, *3340*.
g *Wroth v Tyler* [1973] 1 All ER 897, [1974] Ch 30, [1973] 2 WLR 405, 25 P & CR 138.

Cases also cited
Gainsford v Carroll (1824) 2 B & C 624, 107 ER 516.
Lesters Leather & Skin Co Ltd v Home & Overseas Brokers Ltd [1948] WN 437, CA.
Owen v Routh and Ogle (1854) 14 CB 327, 139 ER 134.
h *Shepherd v Johnson* (1802) 2 East 211, 102 ER 349.
Startup v Cortazzi (1835) 2 Cr M & R 165, 150 ER 71.

Summons
This was an application by Titus Zorro, the defendant in an action by the plaintiffs,
John Richard Horsler and Dorothy Helen Horsler, for an order that the certificate of
j Master Dyson dated 10th June 1974 be discharged or varied. The facts are set out in
the judgment.

The defendant appeared in person.
Colin Rimer for the plaintiffs.

Cur adv vult

31st October. **MEGARRY J.** This is an unhappy case which involves points of
law of some importance to conveyancers. By a contract dated 28th June 1971 the *a*
defendant contracted to sell his freehold house, 38 Talma Road, London, SW2, to the
plaintiffs for £4,000; and 26th July 1971 was stated to be the date for completion.
The property was subject to a mortgage to Goulston Finance Corporation Ltd (which
I shall call 'Goulston'), and on 8th July the defendant's solicitors received a letter from
Goulston stating that the amount required to redeem the mortgage on 26th July
would be £3,601·70. On 12th July the defendant's solicitors wrote to the defendant to *b*
point out that after providing for the agents' commission, costs and certain other
matters he would be left with a balance of under £100. The defendant then failed to
proceed with the sale, and on 30th November 1971 the plaintiffs issued a writ against
him, claiming specific performance, alternatively damages for breach of contract,
and a declaration that they were entitled to a lien for the deposit and interest thereon,
and for any damages and costs. They then issued a summons seeking to add Goulston *c*
as parties, and on 4th February 1972 they issued a further summons claiming an order
for specific performance under RSC Ord 86.
    Before these summonses came on for hearing, an important event occurred. On
16th May 1972 the plaintiffs amended their writ. The claim for specific performance
was deleted and instead they claimed rescission; and in the second prayer, which
began 'Alternatively, damages', the word 'Alternatively' was deleted. From the *d*
claim for a lien the words relating to the deposit and interest were deleted. At that
stage the action accordingly became one in which, apart from the lien, the plaintiffs
simply claimed rescission and damages; and this is a difficult combination. In that
state of affairs both summonses came on for hearing before the master on 1st June
1972. On the summons to add Goulston no order was made, save that the plaintiffs
should pay Goulston's costs. The order made on the hearing then continued: *e*

> '*And it appearing* that the Defendant has repudiated the contract for sale dated
> 28th June 1971 in the said Writ of Summons mentioned *It is ordered* that the said
> contract be rescinded.'

The order then proceeded to direct an enquiry as to what sum of money ought *f*
to be allowed and paid to the plaintiffs 'by way of damages for the non-performance
by the Defendant of the said contract', with an order that the amount of damages be
certified and that the defendant pay the plaintiffs the damages within 14 days of the
certificate being served on him. For the moment I abstain from comment on that
order, save to say it was duly perfected on 25th July 1972, and there has been no appeal
from it.
    There was then a long gap. In the autumn of 1973 certain other steps were taken, *g*
but I can come forward to 10th June 1974, when the master's certificate was made.
This certifies the damages at £3,149·23, consisting of two items. The first is £3,000,
being the difference between the contract price for the house and its value on 1st June
1972 when the order for rescission and an enquiry as to damages was made. The
second item is £149·23, being the taxed costs payable by the plaintiffs to Goulston in *h*
accordance with the order of 1st June 1972. The matter now comes before me on a
summons by the defendant to discharge or vary the master's certificate, the summons
stating the grounds as being—

> 'Because when I asked the master to use the evidence in my file with him,
> before given his decision the master says that they are irrelevant. But these *j*
> can not be so.'

The file in question is before me, and I shall refer to it shortly.
    As may be inferred from the grounds stated in the defendant's summons, the
defendant appears in person: the plaintiffs are represented by Mr Rimer. When the
matter came before me initially on 10th October, I had great difficulty in ascertaining

any coherent grounds that the defendant had for discharging or varying the master's
a certificate. I had read all the papers in his file the night before, even though they
were not supported by any affidavit and so technically were not in evidence; and
counsel for the plaintiffs very properly did not make any objection on this score. I
also read the affidavits filed on behalf of the plaintiffs, and the other documents. In
the defendant's file was some correspondence in the autumn of 1971 between solicitors
then acting for the defendant, Goulston, Goulston's solicitors, and two Members of
b Parliament. The essence of the complaint made by the defendant's solicitors was that
Goulston were proposing to charge the defendant with the interest due over the
whole 15 years' term of the mortgage, even though the defendant was seeking to
repay the loan after only five years. If this in fact was the case and the matter was
brought before the courts, I think they would know how to deal with it. However,
before the end of July Goulston had offered the defendant a reduction of £570 in
c the figure for redemption, diminishing that figure from £3,601·70 to £3,031·70;
but the defendant nevertheless did not proceed with the sale to the plaintiffs.

I pause there. The defendant may well have some cause of complaint; indeed,
he displayed a crusading zeal against Goulston in particular, and also against men
whom he said were making money without working for it. But no claim for relief
against Goulston is before me, and Goulston are not even a party to these proceedings.
d The defendant made a contract to sell the house to the plaintiffs, and it is nothing to
do with them that the defendant then found the contract less advantageous to him
because of Goulston's claim against him. Furthermore, the defendant refused to
continue with the contract even after Goulston had reduced their claim by £570. It
follows that in my judgment the defendant's grievances against Goulston provide no
reason why the plaintiffs should not succeed in their claim against the defendant.
e On the other hand, there are plainly considerable legal and equitable difficulties in
the plaintiffs' path as their claim now stands.

At the initial hearing before me, I made repeated attempts to explain this to the
defendant; but he would have none of it. I attempted to persuade him to seek legal
aid, but he firmly rejected my endeavours. One difficulty was that he kept on inter-
rupting my attempts at explanation, despite repeated warnings to him not to do so,
f and finally a warning as to contempt. Very soon, however, he was shouting me down
again, and so I left the Bench, returning only when my officers had succeeded in
quieting him down. He was plainly in contempt, but I imposed no penalty, as when
I returned to court he very properly apologised. It is indeed difficult to help those
who so determinedly resist all attempts at help, and in the end I adjourned the case
for a fortnight, partly in the hope that on reflection the defendant would seek to
g obtain the legal assistance that was so plainly desirable. Another reason for the
adjournment lay in the difficulties in which counsel for the plaintiffs found himself; for
until I drew his attention to the court's copy of the writ, he had no idea that the writ
had been amended on 16th May 1972, and he was not prepared with the relevant
authorities. At the same time, the defendant has plainly been in breach of his contract,
and from first to last he has put forward nothing by way of justification for that
h breach. If he did not want to sell the house at the contract price because so little
would be left over after paying off the mortgage, he ought not to have made the
contract; and it can be no justification for a breach that the vendor subsequently finds
that he has made a bad bargain. Nevertheless, the course which the plaintiffs have
pursued have created serious difficulties for them.

One point was obviously this. The damages had been awarded on the basis of
j Wroth v Tyler[1], being the difference between the contract price and the value of the
property at the date not of the breach but of the order. Yet such an award is based on
the jurisdiction conferred by Lord Cairns's Act[2] which arises when damages are

---

1 [1973] 1 All ER 897, [1974] Ch 30
2 Chancery Amendment Act 1858, s 2

awarded in substitution for specific performance; and in this case the claim for
specific performance had disappeared when the amendment was made on 16th May   a
1972, before the order for rescission and damages was made.   There are obvious
difficulties in awarding damages as a substitute for what is not even claimed. Another
point, even more fundamental, was this.   If a vendor repudiates the contract, the
purchaser may accept the repudiation, treat the contract as at an end, and sue for
damages for breach of contract.   On the other hand, the purchaser may chose to rescind
the contract, in which case the parties will be as far as possible restored to their   b
positions before the contract was made.   In the latter case, however, it is difficult
to see how the purchaser can in the same breath seek to treat matters as if the contract
had not been made and yet claim damages for the breach of it: see, e g, _Barber v
Wolfe_[1].

   To that I should add that in the defendant's file of papers there is a letter from the
plaintiffs' solicitors to the defendant's solicitors, dated 4th April 1972, stating that the   c
plaintiffs do not intend to press proceedings for specific performance, but intend to
recover their deposit and look for another property; and the solicitors ask for the
return of the deposit which the defendant's solicitors held as stakeholders. The letter
said nothing about damages.   On 17th April the defendant's solicitors wrote to the
plaintiffs' solicitors returning the whole of the deposit, except for £25 in the hands of
another, and saying that they would seek to get this released as well.   Quite apart   d
from the amendment to the writ, by that date the plaintiffs had firmly embarked
on a course of seeking not to enforce the contract but simply to recover the deposit.
The amendment to the writ made a month later was in line with this.

   During the adjournment, my clerk arranged for an experienced registrar of this
Division to see the defendant, in the hope that he could persuade the defendant to
obtain legal aid or some other form of legal assistance, or that at least he could make   e
the defendant understand, in more informal surroundings than in court, the nature
that the proceedings had assumed; but the registrar has reported that although he
spent at least half an hour with the defendant, 'I do not feel that anything constructive
was achieved'. The defendant also sent me a two-page letter dated 15th October 1974.
In it he says: 'I will need no legal aid as the judge suggested because I do not have to be
a lawyer to tell the truth'; and there is very little in the letter or in anything the   f
defendant said in court that has any bearing on what I have to decide.   In legal proceedings the truth is not enough unless it is both relevant and supported by the
appropriate law.   Counsel for the plaintiffs has very properly drawn my attention to
certain authorities that may assist the defendant, and has presented the plaintiffs'
case temperately yet cogently.   I have read every document that the defendant asked
me to read, some of them a number of times, and in reply to my question the defen-   g
dant assured me, more than once, that there were no other affidavits or other documents that he wished me to read.   It is difficult to see what more could be done to
help a litigant so incapable of helping himself and so obstinate in his refusal to accept
aid in obtaining legal assistance.

   I now turn to the issues.   First, I must consider the master's certificate, which in his
summons the defendant seeks to discharge or vary.   Counsel for the plaintiffs found   h
himself unable to attempt to support the certificate.   On the basis that damages are
to be awarded, the basis adopted in the certificate is plainly untenable.   The whole
foundation of _Wroth v Tyler_[2] damages is that they are awarded under the jurisdiction
conferred by Lord Cairns's Act 1858 in substitution for specific performance; and as
I have mentioned, when in this case the master came to make his certificate, specific
performance was no longer even being claimed by the plaintiffs.   Counsel for the   j
plaintiffs also had no contention to put forward that damages on this footing could be
awarded at common law.   In _Wroth v Tyler_[3] I left this point open, and I leave it open

---

1   [1945] 1 All ER 399, [1945] Ch 187
2   [1973] 1 All ER 897, [1974] Ch 30
3   [1973] 1 All ER at 919, [1974] Ch at 57

now. I shall say something more later. For the moment I do no more than hold that,

a as conceded, the certificate cannot stand, and must be discharged. I may add that originally the plaintiffs appear to have based their claim to damages on the cost of purchasing an alternative residence, a flat in Camberwell Grove, SE5, and despite my efforts the defendant devoted some time to attempts to discuss this alternative. However, it plainly does not arise, as the certificate was based not on the cost of the flat but on the changed value of the house.

b   That brings me to the second question. The unappealed order of 1st June 1972 directing an enquiry as to damages still stands. Counsel for the plaintiffs naturally asked that if the question of damages is to be referred back to chambers for a further enquiry, it should go back with a direction as to the basis on which damages are to be assessed. The basis of assessment for which he contended was that of the difference between the contract price and the value of the house, not at the date of the breach

c or the date of the order, but at the date when the plaintiffs abandoned their claim for specific performance and claimed damages. Initially he contended for the date of the amendment to the writ, namely, 16th May 1972, but he then readily accepted that there might be an earlier date, such as that of the letter of 4th April 1972 that I have mentioned, whereby the plaintiffs' solicitors informed the defendant's solicitors that the plaintiffs were not proceeding with their claim for specific performance but

d would recover their deposit and seek another dwelling. It may indeed be that there is no great difference in the value of the house at the date the master took, 1st June, and its value on 16th May or 4th April; but that, of course, is a matter of evidence.

This second question plainly embraces two distinct parts. First, there is the question whether, on the facts of this case, any damages at all can be recovered. Only if that question is answered Yes does the second point arise, that of the basis on which the

e damages ought to be assessed. I therefore begin with the first of these points. On this, counsel for the plaintiffs' sheet anchor was the order of 1st June 1972, which he accepted was unusual in its terms. As I have already stated, there is the recital of it having appeared that the defendant 'has repudiated' the contract, and then 'It is ordered that the said contract be rescinded'. I think that I should now quote the remainder of the relevant parts of the order in full:

f
    'And it is ordered that the following Inquiry be made that is to say 1 An Inquiry what sum of money ought to be allowed and paid to the Plaintiffs by way of damages for the non-performance by the Defendant of the said contract And it is ordered that the amount of the said damages be certified And it is ordered that the Defendant do within fourteen days after service upon him of the Certificate in answer to the said Inquiry pay to the Plaintiffs what shall be certified to be due
g   to them in respect of such damages.'

Before discussing this order any further, I think that I should first attempt to summarise the basic principles involved. I need not discuss so-called anticipatory breaches of contract, and I can confine myself to the cases where the time for performance of a contract for the sale of land is long past, both at law and in equity, and

h one party has long been refusing to perform any of his obligations under the contract. First, in those circumstances the other party has a choice. He—

    'may, at his election, either rescind the contract and sue for restitution to his former position, or affirm the contract and sue either for damages for the breach or for specific performance of the agreement':

j Williams, The Contract of Sale of Land[1], adding the qualification that the innocent party cannot rescind if by his act restitutio in integrum has become impossible. If the innocent party elects to rescind he cannot then recover damages for the loss of his bargain, because he cannot in the same breath say that the contract should be set aside and the parties restored to their former positions and also that the contract

---

1 (1930), p 119

should be treated as still being in force, and the party in breach made to pay damages for breach of the contract. The innocent party need not elect forthwith, and may, *a* of course, claim inconsistent remedies in the alternative; but if he obtains judgment on one footing, that is a conclusive election: see the third head below.

I have already mentioned the leading modern authority, *Barber v Wolfe*[1]; and counsel for the plaintiffs also referred me to *Lowe v Hope*[2] as being in principle to the same effect. I need not discuss the older cases, such as the decision of Jessel MR in *Henty v Schröder*[3], that of North J in *Hutchings v Humphrey*[4], and that of Farwell J in *b* *Jackson v De Kadich*[5]. In each of these there is a clear statement of the principle. But I should mention briefly the decision of the Court of Appeal in *Public Trustee v Pearlberg*[6]. This shows that a party to a contract cannot rescind it while an action of his claiming specific performance of it and damages is in existence, for the two remedies are inconsistent with each other. If the claim for specific performance and damages is abandoned, there may then be rescission (per Luxmoore LJ[7]); *c* but I do not think the reverse process is possible, for once a contract has been rescinded it is at an end, and there cannot very well be a decree for the specific performance of a contract which no longer exists.

Second, the process of rescission is essentially the act of the party rescinding, and not of the court. Of course, if matters are disputed, the dispute may have to be determined by the court, and until the decision is given it will not be known whether *d* or not there has been a proper and effectual rescission; but that does not mean that there is no rescission until the court speaks. I think that this appears plainly from the speech of Lord Hatherley LC in *Reese River Silver Mining Co Ltd v Smith*[8] where he says that the agreement—

> subsists until rescinded; that is to say, in this sense—until rescinded by the *e* declaration of him whom you have sought to bind by it, that he no longer accepts the agreement, but entirely rejects and repudiates it.'

Lord Hatherley LC added[8] that the expression 'until rescinded' did not mean that—

> 'the rescission must be an act of some Court of competent authority, and that, until the rescission by that Court of competent authority takes place, the *f* agreement is subsisting in its full rigour.'

As Lord Atkinson observed in *Abram Steamship Co Ltd v Westville Shipping Co Ltd*[9] Lord Westbury and Lord Cairns seem to have approved Lord Hatherley's statement; and Lord Atkinson's view, in the *Abram* case[10], is to the same effect. Lord Hatherley's use of the word 'repudiate' is unlikely to confuse: the word must obviously be read *g* in its context. In *Lee v Soames*[11] it was held in terms that a contract for the sale of land was rescinded on 8th November 1887, the date of a letter whereby one of the parties purported to rescind the contract. Of course, applications to the court are often made because consequential relief is sought, whether as part of the restitutio in integrum or otherwise; and although the older forms of order were sometimes expressed as being an order that the contract 'be rescinded' (see Seton's Judgments *h*

---

1   [1945] 1 All ER 399, [1945] Ch 187
2   [1969] 3 All ER 605, [1970] Ch 94
3   (1879) 12 Ch D 666
4   (1885) 54 LJCh 650
5   [1904] WN 168   *j*
6   [1940] 2 All ER 270, [1940] 2 KB 1
7   [1940] 2 All ER at 280, [1940] 2 KB at 18
8   (1869) LR 4 HL 64 at 73
9   [1923] AC 773 at 784, [1923] All ER Rep 645 at 649, 650
10   [1923] AC at 781-783, [1923] All ER Rep at 648-650
11   (1888) 36 WR 884

and Orders[1]), I think the more modern, and preferable, practice is to make a declaration that the contract 'ought to be rescinded': see Atkin's Court Forms[2]. Indeed, I would have thought that at least in some cases a declaration that the contract had been rescinded on such-and-such a date might be better still.

Third, once a party has elected between on the one hand affirming the contract and claiming specific performance or damages, and on the other hand rescinding the contract, he cannot retract his decision. Once judgment has been given on one footing, it is too late to proceed on the other footing. To this there is the exception that the defendant's failure to comply with an order for specific performance gives the plaintiff a fresh opportunity of claiming rescission if he prefers this to enforcing the judgment. I shall not set out the authorities, which are collected in Williams's Contract of Sale of Land[3].

Fourth, although the word 'rescind' has a fairly precise meaning, I readily accept that the word is not invariably used with the same meaning. Thus in a contract it may be used with whatever meaning the contract gives it. If, for instance, the parties to the contract agree to 'rescind' it on certain terms, I see no reason why those terms should not contain an agreement for the payment of some sums by one to the other, which may or may not be called 'damages'. Again, a contract may contain provisions which confer a unilateral power of 'rescission' on certain terms in certain events; and if that unilateral power is properly exercised, the consequences of doing so will be as stated in the contract, including the payment of any 'damages' for which it provides. In truth, the meaning of the term 'rescission' in a contract, like that of any other term, is whatever the contract gives it. See, for instance, *Mussen v Van Diemen's Land Co*[4]; and consider also *Stockloser v Johnson*[5]. In the case before me, however, nobody has relied on, or even mentioned, any provision of the contract relating to rescission; and when the word 'rescind' is used otherwise than in a contract, and particularly in a formal document such as a writ or order of the court, I think it will usually, at all events, bear its normal meaning, related to restitutio in integrum and so on. I cannot in the present case find in the writ or order a sufficient context to show that 'rescission' is not used in its ordinary sense.

In this connection I must, I think, refer to the difficult case of *Harold Wood Brick Co Ltd v Ferris*[6] which counsel for the plaintiffs cited to me. There, a purchaser of land failed to complete. In those circumstances a clause in the contract gave the vendor the right to forfeit any deposit, rescind the contract, and resell. In fact, in the events which occurred the contract did not make any deposit payable, and none was paid. The vendor gave the purchaser notice that he rescinded the contract and was proceeding to resell, and also that he held the purchaser responsible in damages. At first instance[7] Swift J explained and distinguished *Henty v Schröder*[8] and *Hutchings v Humphrey*[9], and held that the vendor was entitled to damages notwithstanding rescission. The Court of Appeal[6] affirmed this decision, but on different grounds. Slesser and Roche LJJ both reserved all questions arising on the contractual right to rescind, the clause on which the argument before Swift J appears to have been solely based[10]. Greer LJ discussed the contractual right to rescind but based his judgment 'mainly, if not exclusively', on the terms of another clause in the contract[11]. All

---

1   7th Edn (1912), pp 347, 2218
2   2nd Edn, vol 18, pp 301, 302
3   (1930), p 121
4   [1938] 1 All ER 210 at 215, [1938] Cr 253 at 260
5   [1954] 1 All ER 630, [1954] 1 QB 476
6   [1935] 2 KB 198, [1935] All ER Rep 603
7   [1935] 1 KB 613
8   (1879) 12 Ch D 666
9   (1885) 54 LJCh 650
10   [1935] 2 KB at 208, [1935] All ER Rep at 608
11   [1935] 2 KB at 205, [1935] All ER Rep at 606

three members of the court appear to rest their decision on there having been a repudiation of the contract by the purchaser in his failing to complete on the date *a* for which time had been made of the essence of the contract, and on the vendor having accepted this as a repudiation by suing him for damages for breach of the contract. There is some difficulty in ascertaining what view was taken of the notice of rescission. Greer LJ seems to treat it as having been given under the clause of the contract, for he speaks[1] of the clause as saying 'that there shall be, what otherwise there could not be, a rescission by the other party'; the words 'what otherwise there *b* could not be' have their own difficulties. Slesser LJ[2] merely refers to the argument submitted to Swift J as being one based on the vendor 'having elected to proceed under that clause', whereas on the same page[2] Roche LJ says flatly that the vendor—

> 'did not require to nor did he avail himself of the stipulations in that clause. He proceeded on his common law right irrespective of that clause.'   *c*

There are other difficulties in the case, too.

In *Barber v Wolfe*[3], Romer J treated the *Harold Wood* case[4] as being merely a case of a claim for damages by a party to a contract who had accepted the repudiation of it by the other party; and he said that it did not appear to him that there was a principle deducible from the case sufficient to displace the long series of authorities *d* which bound him. The principle of the *Harold Wood* case[4] might, I suppose, be expressed in something like the following manner: 'If a purchaser of land repudiates the contract, the vendor's right to accept the repudiation and sue him for damages for breach of contract remains unaffected even if, after the repudiation but before action brought, the vendor sends the purchaser a notice which purports to rescind the contract but also states that the purchaser will be held responsible in damages for *e* any loss occasioned by his breach of agreement. Quaere how far, if at all, this depends on the existence of a contractual right to rescind.' That, of course, is very far from being a principle decisive of the case before me, where the letter of 4th April 1972 (which elected not to proceed with specific performance) said nothing about damages, the writ was amended to claim rescission in lieu of specific performance, and an order has been made for rescission and an enquiry as to damages. *f*

Now in the present case, when the writ was issued on 30th November 1971 the contractual date for completion was over four months past, and the defendant was persisting in his refusal to carry out the contract. Nevertheless, the plaintiffs made no election to rescind at that stage, for the writ had claimed specific performance and alternatively damages, and said nothing about rescission. The plaintiffs were then relying on alternative forms of relief in respect of a contract which they were *g* treating as still subsisting. There is evidence that by March 1972 it had become clear to the plaintiffs that the total then due under the mortgage exceeded the contractual price; and *Grant v Dawkins*[5] had not then been decided. In that case, it will be remembered, Goff J held that in similar circumstances the purchaser could obtain specific performance and also recover damages equal to the amount by which the money due under the mortgage exceeded the contract price, subject to a limitation *h* there stated. Not knowing that the law was later to be laid down in this way, the solicitors to the plaintiffs in the present case wrote their letter of 4th April 1972. I have already mentioned that letter but I think I should read it in full:

> 'We write to advise that our clients do not intend to press proceedings against Mr. Zorro for specific performance of the contract but now intend to recover   *j*

---

1   [1935] 2 KB at 205, [1935] All ER Rep at 606
2   [1935] 2 KB at 208, [1935] All ER Rep at 608
3   [1945] 1 All ER 399 at 400, 401, [1945] Ch 187 at 190, 191
4   [1935] 2 KB 198, [1935] All ER Rep 603
5   [1973] 3 All ER 897, [1973] 1 WLR 1406

their deposit and look for another property elsewhere. Accordingly we require

a   you to forward to us the deposit held by you as stakeholder under the conditions of sale. Mr. Zorro is held liable for our clients' costs but, in all the circumstances, we can see no effective way of proceeding in regard to these and do not propose to formulate them at this stage. We would be grateful to hear from you without delay since our clients desire to use the deposit money immediately.'

b   Apart from anything that can be made of the reference to costs, that letter, as I have said, makes no reference to damages, and plainly amounts to an intimation that the plaintiffs were regarding the contract as being at an end. They were accepting the defendant's repudiation of the contract, and electing to restore the status quo ante at least to the extent of recovering the deposit. If the contract was no more, then they were entitled to their deposit back: but its return in this manner is hardly

c   consistent with treating the contract as still being in existence despite the defendant's default.

Then came the amendment of the writ on 16th May, deleting any claim for specific performance and making for the first time a claim for rescission, with the claim for damages no longer being expressed in the alternative. It was on the basis of the writ in that state that the order of 1st June was made. As I have mentioned, the order re-

d   cited that it appeared that the defendant had repudiated the contract. I pause there. The recital is entirely correct, but of course it does not say what action the plaintiffs have elected to take in respect of the defendant's repudiation. The next sentence in the order is, however, '*It is ordered* that the said contract be rescinded'. Again I pause. These words make it explicit that the path chosen by the plaintiffs is the path of rescission, which, indeed, accords with their amended writ. For the reasons

e   that I have given, the form of wording in the order may be regarded as being a somewhat elliptical way of recognising that on 4th April the plaintiffs had elected to rescind the contract. The authorities that I have mentioned show that there is certainly no need (even if it is correct) to treat an order for rescission as relating back to the plaintiffs' decision to rescind, for rescission is the act of a party and not of the court. The better course seems to be to treat the order for rescission as recognising the validity

f   of the decision to rescind that had already been made. At all events, the order of 1st June plainly states that what the plaintiffs have done is to rescind the contract, so that one way or another the contract was at an end at the latest by 1st June.

Finally, there is the order for the enquiry as to damages. When it was suggested that the answer to the question of what damages ought to be paid might be: 'Nil, because the contract has been rescinded', counsel for the plaintiffs' comment was

g   that such an answer would be simplistic. I am not sure that counsel for the plaintiffs' comment was not itself somewhat simplistic, in the sense in which I think he was using the word. That sense must, I think, differ from the meaning given by the Shorter Oxford English Dictionary, where 'simplistic' is given as the adjective from 'simplist', which means 'one who studies simples; a herbalist'. The American usage (see Funk and Wagnall's New Standard Dictionary) is that the word means

h   (inter alia) 'characterized by a simplicity that is inadequate to explain', and this meaning, like so much else, has probably crossed the Atlantic. The fact remains that on 1st June 1972 the order was made that the contract 'be rescinded'; and on that date either the contract was rescinded, or else a prior rescission was confirmed by the court. I appreciate, as counsel for the plaintiffs emphasised, that the order of the court is one that has been perfected, and that no appeal against it has been made. Further-

j   more, doubtless any breach of contract gives rise to a claim for at least nominal damages. Yet apart from that I cannot see that the order for an enquiry as to damages which next follows amounts to an order that on the enquiry some sum must be found to be due. At the enquiry it may be found that on the facts there is no valid claim for damages; and it may also be found that as a matter of law some heads of claim are not recoverable. It also seems to me that on such an enquiry the scope of the enquiry must be limited by the ambit of the substantive order that has been made.   An enquiry as to damages is an enquiry as to the damages payable in respect *a* of the particular tort or breach of contract or other matter in respect of which judgment has been entered.   Here, the matter for enquiry is what ought to be allowed and paid to the plaintiffs by way of damages in respect of the defendant not performing a contract which they have rescinded.

Although there seems to me to be considerable force in the argument that the quantum of damages to be certified must, apart from a nominal award, be nil, I *b* think that I ought to attempt to give reasonable effect to the whole of this unfortunate order, unappealed as it is, and see whether the words ordering an enquiry as to damages can be made to operate in some way other than by requiring an enquiry that is foredoomed to produce a nil certificate.   I think that the answer, or an answer, may lie along the following lines.   It seems to be clearly established that a party who rescinds a contract for the sale of land is not thereby deprived of all right to any *c* monetary payment.   Subject to one qualification, he is entitled, so far as possible, to be restored to his former position in the same way as if the contract had never been made, so far as relates to any obligations of the contract that he has discharged: see *Whittington v Seale-Hayne*[1].   The qualification relates to the deposit, which forms a pledge of performance: for a vendor who rescinds may nevertheless (subject to Law of Property Act 1925, s 49(2)) retain any deposit already in his hands, though he *d* cannot sue to recover any part of the deposit which has not been paid to him: *Lowe v Hope*[2].   Apart from the special position of the deposit, the right of a party who rescinds to be restored to his former position includes the right, if he is the purchaser, to recover his expenses of investigating title, and doubtless the right, if he is the vendor, to recover his expenses of deducing title: see Williams's Contract of Sale of Land[3] and Williams's Vendor and Purchaser[4].   *e*

These passages refer to *Lee v Soames*[5], which I have already mentioned, as being a case in which a purchaser who sued for rescission 'appeared to have recovered his expenses of investigating title, erroneously described as damages'.   In that case, Kekewich J ended his judgment by holding that the contract had been rescinded, and saying that the claim asked for a declaration of the validity of the rescission of the contract, and for repayment of the deposit with interest.   He then added[6]: 'Any- *f* thing more comes by way of damages.   The case of *Bain v. Fothergill*[7] lays down exactly how the damages are to be arrived at.'   The other report of the case[8] is shorter and less explicit.   I am not at all sure that I understand the references to damages, as none seem to have been claimed.   However, in view of the reference to *Bain v Fothergill*[7], it may be that the purchaser was held to be entitled to his expenses of investigating title as a consequence of his having validly rescinded the *g* contract.   At all events, in a case of rescission the judge spoke of damages; and in the absence of any term of convenient brevity for describing the monetary payments to which a party rescinding may be entitled, it is easy to see how the term 'damages' could be applied to them.

The point may be illustrated by reading *Re Bryant & Barningham's Contract*[9] with *Re Hargreaves & Thompson's Contract*[10].   In the former case[11] Kay J referred to *h*

---

1   (1900) 82 LT 49
2   [1969] 3 All ER 605, [1970] Ch 94
3   (1930), p 122
4   4th Edn (1936), p 1005
5   (1888) 36 WR 884   *j*
6   36 WR at 885, 886
7   (1874) LR 7 HL 158, [1874-80] All ER Rep 83
8   (1888) 59 LT 366
9   (1890) 44 Ch D 218
10 (1886) 32 Ch D 454
11 44 Ch D at 222

the latter case as being one in which 'the contract was rescinded'. Yet in that latter
a case, which was decided on a vendor and purchaser summons, all three members
of the Court of Appeal spoke of the costs of investigating title, which they awarded
to the purchaser, as being 'damages': see per Cotton LJ[1], per Lindley LJ[2] ('all such
damages as interest and expenses of investigating the title, which, although they are
called damages, are matters rather for computation and taxation than for an inquiry'),
and per Lopes LJ[3], saying that no doubt interest and the costs of investigating the
b title 'are matters in the nature of damages . . .' In those circumstances, it seems to
me that it must at least be permissible to read the reference to damages in the order
of 1st June 1972 in this case as having been a reference to such damages, or matters
in the nature of damages, as are appropriate in a case where the contract has been
rescinded, and not as being an order for the assessment and payment of full damages
for loss of the bargain, or what Farwell J in *Whittington v Seale-Hayne*[4] called
c 'damages pure and simple'. The usage may not satisfy a purist, but I am concerned
with working out a difficult order; and in my judgment I can best give effect to it
in all its parts by holding, as I do, that the references in it to damages are references
to such sums, whether by name of damages, or of indemnity, or of restitution or
otherwise, as may properly be awarded in respect of a contract that has been rescinded.
That at least seems preferable to treating the reference to damages as altering the
d meaning of 'rescission'. The plaintiffs have already recovered their deposit, so that
that item does not arise, but they may have incurred expenses in carrying out their
obligations under the contract, and to these they are entitled. On the other hand,
they can claim nothing for loss of their bargain in respect of the contract that they
have rescinded. In saying this, I bear in mind, as I have borne in mind throughout,
that this is a case in which the defendant has without any sufficient cause refused to
e carry out a contract that proved to be advantageous to the plaintiffs, and that they
are failing to get the damages to which they would otherwise be entitled by reason of
what seem to be procedural errors on their side. Yet I must give effect both to
principle and to the authorities; I cannot with propriety cast overboard the plaintiffs'
procedural difficulties merely because if they had done something different they
could have recovered more. A judgment for rescission is a judgment for rescission,
f and I cannot denature it merely because an enquiry as to damages is also ordered.
For long the law students' adage has been 'You can't both rescind and claim damages',
and that warning remains, subject only to the claim for limited damages, or a limited
sum in the nature of damages, which can be recovered. The defendant may indeed
account himself fortunate in the result.
    That suffices to dispose of the case, and I do not intend to extend an over-long
g judgment by any detailed consideration of what does not arise for decision. Out
of courtesy to counsel for the plaintiffs, however, I think that I should say something
about the main point on which he founded an extended argument. On the footing
that the plaintiffs were entitled to damages for the loss of their bargain (a footing that
I have rejected) counsel contended, as I have said, that the damages should be assessed
not as at the date fixed for completion nor as at a reasonable time thereafter, but as
h at the date when the plaintiffs abandoned their claim for specific performance and
resolved to claim damages; and this date was at latest when the writ was amended
on 16th May 1972, and might be earlier, e g at the date of their solicitors' letter of
4th April 1972. He contended that the rule that damages would be assessed as at
the date of the breach was not an inflexible rule, and he put before me a number of
cases, mostly concerned with the sale of goods. He conceded that the authorities
j on the sale of land all appeared to take the date as being the date of the breach.
The main thrust of his argument was that the plaintiffs were under a duty to mitigate

1   (1886) 32 Ch D at 457
2   32 Ch D at 459
3   32 Ch D at 460
4   (1900) 82 LT at 51

damages, and that as obtaining specific performance would prevent there being any damages, they ought not to be penalised if, on discovering that specific performance would be fruitless or impracticable, they then abandoned their claim for specific performance and attempted to cut their losses by suing for damages.

As I have indicated, *Wroth v Tyler*[1] touched on the point of damages at common law. In that case there is an observation[2] that the rule requiring damages at common law to be ascertained as at the date of the breach did not seem to be inflexible, and that the rule was one that might on occasion fail to carry out the principle which Parke B enunciated in *Robinson v Harman*[3] of putting the injured party in the same situation with respect to damages as if the contract had been performed. I see no reason for resiling from what was said there. Furthermore, I can see some force in the view that where a purchaser who has been claiming specific performance abandons that claim and instead seeks damages, he thereupon ceases to treat the land as property in which he has a specific interest and treats it instead as a mere commodity, to be replaced by as near an equivalent as possible, thereby producing some analogy with a disappointed purchaser of goods, who at least in theory can at once purchase equivalent goods on the market. Nevertheless, in the present case, where the point has been argued on one side only, and in any case, on the view that I take, does not arise for decision, I do not think that it would be right for me to attempt to carry the point any further, especially as the argument is by no means free from difficulties. Accordingly, I say nothing more on the subject, save to thank counsel for the plaintiffs for his careful argument.

In the result, therefore, for the reasons that I have given, I discharge the master's certificate, and I adjourn the case back into chambers for the master to hold the enquiry as to damages directed by the order of 1st June 1972. I direct that those damages, if any, be assessed on the limited basis that I have indicated.

I must add this. After I had reserved judgment, I found it necessary to consider many authorities that had not been discussed in argument. I therefore think that counsel for the plaintiffs and, for that matter, the defendant, ought to be given an opportunity of applying, if so desired, to be allowed to put forward further argument before the order is perfected. Subject to that, the order will be as I have stated.

Order accordingly, neither party having applied to put forward further argument.

Solicitors: *Harbottle & Lewis* (for the plaintiffs).

F K Anklesaria Esq Barrister.

---

1   [1973] 1 All ER 897, [1974] Ch 30
2   [1973] 1 All ER at 919, [1974] Ch at 57
3   (1848) 1 Exch 850 at 855, [1843-60] All ER Rep 383 at 385

a

Salford City Council v McNally

QUEEN'S BENCH DIVISION

Affirmed HL [1975] 2 All ER 860

LORD WIDGERY CJ, MELFORD STEVENSON AND WATKINS JJ

19th DECEMBER 1974

b

Nuisance – Statutory nuisance – Nuisance order – House subject to clearance order – House acquired by local authority for purpose of demolition – Demolition postponed on ground house could be rendered capable of providing accommodation adequate for time being – Tenant of house preferring complaint against authority alleging statutory nuisance – Complaint proved – Whether justices bound to make nuisance order – Whether authority can

c *be compelled to carry out repairs rendering house of more than adequate standard for time being – Public Health Act 1936, s 99 – Housing Act 1957, s 48.*

A local authority, in pursuance of its powers under the Housing Act 1957, declared an area within its boundaries to be a clearance area on the ground that the houses within that area were unfit for human habitation. The authority then purchased the

d houses in that area under the compulsory powers contained in s 43 of the 1957 Act. The authority, however, in exercise of its powers under s 48(1)[a] of the 1957 Act, resolved to postpone the demolition of those houses which it had acquired under the compulsory purchase order and which in its opinion could be rendered capable of providing accommodation of a standard which was adequate for the time being. A tenant of one of those houses subsequently preferred a complaint against the authority under

e s 99[b] of the Public Health Act 1936 alleging that a statutory nuisance had arisen and continued to exist at the house which she occupied and that the authority had made default in failing to abate the nuisance. The magistrate found the complaint proved and accordingly made a nuisance order against the authority requiring them to abate the nuisance within two months. The authority appealed, contending that when a local authority had postponed demolition of houses under s 48 of the 1957

f Act it was only required to render the houses capable of providing accommodation of a standard which was adequate for the time being and was excused from complying with the provisions of the 1936 Act insofar as those provisions required the accommodation to be of a standard which was more than adequate for the time being.

Held – When a person who had brought a complaint under s 99 of the 1936 Act

g succeeded in proving his case the justices were bound to make a nuisance order notwithstanding that the house was one to which a resolution under s 48 of the 1957 Act applied. The appeal would therefore be dismissed (see p 603 *f* to *j*, post).

Notes

For statutory nuisances outside London, see 31 Halsbury's Laws (3rd Edn) 367-369,

h para 546, and for cases on the subject, see 36 Digest (Repl) 272, 273, 241-254.

For the power of abatement of statutory nuisances, see 31 Halsbury's Laws (3rd Edn) 363, para 540.

For the Public Health Act 1936, s 99, see 26 Halsbury's Statutes (3rd Edn) 275.

For the Housing Act 1957, ss 43, 48, see 16 Halsbury's Statutes (3rd Edn) 151, 158.

j **Case referred to in judgments**

Nottingham Corpn v Newton, Nottingham Friendship Housing Association Ltd v Newton [1974] 2 All ER 760, [1974] 1 WLR 923, 72 LGR 535, DC.

---

a Section 48(1) is set out at p 601 *b* and *c*, post

b Section 99 is set out at p 600 *c* and *d*, post

Case stated

This was an appeal by way of a case stated by the stipendiary magistrate for the   a
city of Salford in respect of his adjudication as a magistrates' court sitting at Salford
on 16th April 1974.

On 21st March 1974 a complaint was preferred by the respondent, Brenda McNally,
being a person aggrieved under s 99 of the Public Health Act 1936, against the appellants, Salford City Council, stating that on 1st February 1974 a statutory nuisance
contrary to s 92 of the 1936 Act had arisen and continued to exist at 20 Johnson Street,   b
Salford, and the appellants, being the owners of the property on which the nuisance had
arisen, had been informed of the existence of the nuisance by letters from the respondent dated 1st February 1974 and 26th February 1974 specifying the defects complained
of, i e accumulation of refuse, dampness, defective sanitary fittings, unsealed drains
allowing egress of rats, defective windows and/or doors, leaking rainwater goods,
leaking roof, defective drainage, defective plasterwork and defective floors and that   c
the appellants had made default in failing to abate the nuisance.

The following facts were found.   (a) At all material times the respondent was the
occupier of the premises known as 20 Johnson Street, Salford, and the appellants
were the owners thereof for the purposes of the 1936 Act.   (b) When the magistrate
inspected the premises, the following defects existed: there was rising damp and
perished plaster, the rear door was rotted and unhinged, there was severe dampness   d
in the first floor and the water closet pipe was cracked and insanitary.   By reason of
those defects, the premises were in such a state as to be prejudicial to health, or a
nuisance and therefore constituted a statutory nuisance under s 92 of the 1936 Act.
(c) On 1st March 1967 the appellants, as part of their extensive slum clearance programme and acting under the powers conferred on them by s 42 of the Housing
Act 1957, declared a number of areas in the Lower Broughton district of the city of   e
Salford to be clearance areas.   On the same date, the appellants, in pursuance of
their powers under s 43 of the 1957 Act, made the City of Salford (Lower Broughton
Clearance Areas nos 2F and 2G) Compulsory Purchase Order 1967.   The order applied
to 407 properties of which 406, including 20 Johnson Street, were properties included
in the clearance areas as houses unfit for human habitation.   (d) By letter dated 8th
March 1968, the then Minister of Housing and Local Government confirmed the   f
compulsory purchase order (with certain modifications which did not affect 20 Johnson
Street).   (e) Since the clearance areas were areas where the number of unfit dwelling-
houses liable to demolition was so large that it would be many years before all the
occupiers could be rehoused and the dwelling-houses demolished, the appellants,
in exercise of their powers under s 48 of the 1957 Act, deferred for a period of seven
years the demolition of the dwelling-houses in the compulsory purchase order   g
being dwelling-houses which in the opinion of the appellants were or could be
rendered capable of providing accommodation of a standard adequate for the time
being.

The appellants contended that, on a true construction of s 48 of the 1957 Act, a
local authority which had deferred demolition of dwelling-houses already declared
to be unfit was required only to render the houses capable of providing accommo-   h
dation of a standard adequate for the time being and was excused from complying
with the terms of ss 92, 93 and 94 of the 1936 Act insofar as those sections required
a standard of accommodation higher than adequate for the time being; that 20 Johnson Street in its existing state was capable of providing accommodation of a standard
adequate for the time being and that a nuisance order should not be made against
the appellants.   j

The respondent contended that the provisions of ss 92, 93 and 94 of the 1936 Act
were mandatory and that the 1957 Act did not affect the operation of the 1936 Act,
particularly having regard to s 188 of the 1957 Act.   She further contended that,
having found the facts set out above, the magistrate was bound to make a nuisance
order against the appellants.

a
The magistrate was of the opinion (a) that, having found the facts set out above, he was bound to make a nuisance order against the appellants, and (b) that the terms of s 48 of the 1957 Act did not excuse the appellants from their duties under the 1936 Act. He accordingly made a nuisance order against the appellants requiring them within two months of the date of the order to abate the statutory nuisance described above.

b
Raymond Sears for the appellants.
B A Hytner QC and *Donald Hart* for the respondent.

LORD WIDGERY CJ. This is an appeal by case stated by one of Her Majesty's stipendiary magistrates for the city of Salford in respect of his adjudication as a magis-
c
strates' court at Salford on 16th April 1974. Before him on that date was a complaint preferred by the respondent, Mrs McNally, as being a person aggrieved under s 99 of the Public Health Act 1936. The complaint was made against the appellants, who are the local authority for the city of Salford, and stated that on 1st February 1974 a statutory nuisance contrary to s 92 of the 1936 Act had arisen and continued to exist at 20 Johnson Street, Salford, and the appellants being the owners of the
d
property on which the nuisance had arisen, had been informed of the existence of the nuisance by letters from the respondent dated 1st February and 26th February 1974 specifying the defects complained of, namely, accumulation of refuse, dampness, defective sanitary fittings, unsealed drains allowing egress of rats, defective windows and/or doors, leaking rainwater goods, leaking roof, defective drainage, defective plasterwork and defective floors.
e
The complaint was made by Mrs McNally pursuant to s 99 of the 1936 Act, and before I turn to s 99 I should briefly review the scheme of that Act in regard to nuisance rendering premises unfit for habitation.
Section 92 of the 1936 Act defines as 'statutory nuisance' a number of factors, one of which is that the premises are in such a state as to be prejudicial to health or a nuisance. Where a statutory nuisance is alleged to exist, the local authority, if
f
satisfied of its existence, may under s 93 serve what is called an abatement notice on the person by whose act, default or sufferance a nuisance arises or continues. On the service of that abatement notice if no action is taken in accordance with the notice to abate the nuisance, then by s 94 the matter can be referred to the court. Indeed s 94(1) is in these terms:

g
'If the person on whom an abatement notice has been served makes default in complying with any of the requirements of the notice, or if the nuisance, although abated since the service of the notice, is, in the opinion of the local authority, likely to recur on the same premises, the authority shall cause a complaint to be made to a justice of the peace, and the justice shall thereupon issue a summons requiring the person on whom the notice was served to appear
h
before a court of summary jurisdiction.'

Thus what is contemplated in the ordinary situation, if one may so describe it, by the 1936 Act is that the local authority, being apprised of the existence of a statutory nuisance, serve an abatement notice. If it is complied with, well and good. If it is not, then the local authority follow the matter up by making complaint to a court of summary jurisdiction.
j
In s 94(2) we find a direction to the court of summary jurisdiction how it is to deal with such a situation:

'If on the hearing of the complaint it is proved that the alleged nuisance exists, or that although abated it is likely to recur on the same premises, then, subject to the provisions of subsections (4) and (5) of this section the court shall make an order (hereafter in this Act referred to as "a nuisance order") for either, or both, of the following purposes—(a) requiring the defendant to comply with all or *a* any of the requirements of the abatement notice, or otherwise to abate the nuisance, within a time specified in the order, and to execute any works necessary for that purpose . . .'

At this point one may well ask where does Mrs NcNally come into the matter and how is it that the council of the city of Salford are parties to the proceedings. *b* The answer is that in this instance the owners of the property were the city of Salford and Mrs NcNally was the occupier. Section 99 provides what has been described in argument before us as a short cut whereby, in the absence of action taken by the local authority, a person aggrieved may take action for him or herself. Section 99 says:

'Complaint of the existence of a statutory nuisance under this Act may be made to a justice of the peace by any person aggrieved by the nuisance, and *c* thereupon the like proceedings shall be had, with the like incidents and consequences as to the making of orders, penalties for disobedience of orders and otherwise, as in the case of a complaint by the local authority, but any order made in such proceedings may, if the court after giving the local authority an opportunity of being heard thinks fit, direct the authority to abate the nuisance.'

That is why in this case the complaint is laid by Mrs NcNally and not, as would *d* generally be contemplated by the earlier sections, by the authority itself.

This is another case, of which there have been a number recently, where the provisions of the 1936 Act, to which I have briefly referred and the purpose of which is to prevent people from living in houses which are not fit for human habitation, have come in some measure into conflict with parallel legislation in the Housing Acts. *e*

The relevant Housing Act for present purposes is that of 1957, and that Act contains not only general provisions charging local authorities with the duty of providing houses for those who need to be housed in their area, but it also provides comprehensive machinery whereby local authorities can clear areas which have out of date housing with a view to those houses being replaced by up to date dwellings. The procedure is laid down in detail to an extent that I need not follow in those *f* provisions of the 1957 Act which are contained in Part III headed 'Clearance and Re-Development'.

A local authority has power to declare an area a clearance area on the ground that the houses in the area are unfit for human habitation. So one starts with the approach to the 1957 Act by bearing in mind that it is concerned with houses which are unfit and it is concerned with the removal of the houses which are unfit within the provision *g* there specified.

Having declared the area to be a clearance area, s 43 provides that the housing authority may deal with the situation, either by requiring the owners of the houses to demolish them, or, alternatively, by acquiring houses and demolishing the houses itself. The second method, I think, as we all know, is the one which is more generally favoured at the present time. The fact that the Act is concerned with unfit houses *h* in which people should not continue to live to the prejudice of their health is underlined by the sense of urgency in the matter which is injected by s 47. That provides that following on the making of the clearance order—

'a local authority who have under this Part of this Act purchased any land comprised in, or surrounded by, or adjoining, a clearance area shall, so soon as may be, cause every building thereon to be vacated and shall deal with *j* that land in one or other of the following ways, or partly in one of these ways and partly in the other of them, that is to say—(a) they shall demolish every building thereon before the expiration of six weeks from the date on which it is vacated, or before the expiration of such longer period as in the circumstances they deem reasonable . . .'

I say a sense of urgency because, understandably, when dealing with unfit houses
a Parliament was minded to see that the unfit houses were removed as speedily as
possible. However from 1954 onwards[1] an additional provision has been included
in this code and now finds itself in s 48(1) of the 1957 Act:

> 'Notwithstanding anything in the foregoing provisions of this Part of this
> Act a local authority by whom an area has been declared to be a clearance area
> may postpone, for such period as may be determined by the authority, the
b > demolition of any houses on land purchased by or belonging to the authority
> within that area, being houses which in the opinion of the authority are or can
> be rendered capable of providing accommodation of a standard which is adequate
> for the time being, and may carry out such works as may from time to time be
> required for rendering or keeping such houses capable of providing such
c > accommodation as aforesaid pending their demolition.'

It seems to me, looking at that section in isolation for the moment, that it is clearly
intended to provide a qualification to s 47. Despite the note of urgency which s 47
injects into this matter, s 48 is recognising that there will be occasions when authorities
just cannot act as fast as that. It accepts and justifies as a principle that the local
authority may postpone the actual demolition of houses provided they are able
d by patching them up to keep them up to the standard defined by the section, which
is inevitably a lower standard than that which is contemplated by the Public Health
Act 1936 to which I have referred.

Before I turn to the facts of the instant case it is, I think, helpful to refer next to
the only recent authority on this subject and one which perhaps covers a number
of the points which the instant problem raises. It is *Nottingham Corpn v Newton*[2],
e a decision of this court. Anyone who is concerned hereafter to deal with these problems
in detail can read the decision in the *Nottingham* case[2] for himself, and I do not therefore
propose to burden this judgment by extensive quotations from it. Suffice it to say,
the situation which arose in the *Nottingham* case[2] was in many respects similar to the
present. Again there were houses where statutory nuisance existed because the
houses were unfit for human habitation. Again the initiative was taken by one of
f the occupiers of those unfit houses under s 99 of the 1936 Act. Again (and when I
say 'again', reference to the instant case will soon bear this out) there was on the
face of it a conflict between the two Acts, because in the *Nottingham* case[2] the local
authority had declared a clearance area, had made a clearance order and were well
advanced towards obtaining a compulsory purchase order which would enable
them to clear the area as owners. They had not reached the stage of a compulsory
g purchase order, but they were, as it were, well on the way. When the occupier of
one of the houses took action under s 99 and the case therefore came before the
magistrates' court, it was argued, and, if I may say so, argued with some force, that
it was uneconomic and contrary to common sense that a house of this kind should
be put into a state which would satisfy the 1936 Act, and then perhaps be demolished
within a few months thereafter. Thus the justices were faced with the problem
h of whether in a case in which the house is liable to be demolished in the near future
there can be any obligation on the landlord to make the house habitable for the
purposes of the 1936 Act. The justices in the *Nottingham* case[2] read the sections to
which I have already referred, and they decided it was their duty under s 99 to make
a nuisance order requiring the abatement of the nuisance, if in the fact statutory
nuisance was proved before them. It was proved before them and so they made
j the order. The Nottingham Corporation appealed to this court raising issues similar,
as will be seen, to those raised in the present case.

The decision in the *Nottingham* case[2] was this: that where the essentials of a statutory nuisance had been proved before the magistrates so that they were satisfied

---

1 See the Housing Repairs and Rents Act 1954, s 2(1)
2 [1974] 2 All ER 760, [1974] 1 WLR 923

that a statutory nuisance existed, they were, as the section said, bound to make a nuisance order. However it was pointed out by this court that, although bound *a* to make a nuisance order, they had considerable tolerance in deciding precisely how many of the complaints, and which complaints, required to be remedied, and also the time within which that remedy should be supplied. This court made it perfectly clear that justices faced with this situation, although bound to make an order under the Act, can use their common sense and are entitled to take into account all the circumstances, and thus avoid the expenditure of public money *b* unnecessarily in a case where the house is likely to be pulled down shortly in any event.

I have quoted from the *Nottingham* case[1] at some length because it has, as I have said, a very similar background to the present case. I will turn now to the facts as found by the magistrate. He finds that at all material times Mrs NcNally was the occupier of the house, 20 Johnson Street, Salford, and that the appellants were the *c* owners. The appellants had proceeded to the point of acquiring the title to the premises under a compulsory purchase order. The magistrate inspected the premises and found a number of defects existing. For example, there was rising damp, perished plaster, the rear door was rotted, there was severe dampness in the first floor and the water closet pipe was cracked and insanitary. By reason of those defects he found that the premises were in a condition prejudicial to health and therefore *d* were a nuisance for the purpose of the 1936 Act. He then goes on to deal with the council's plans for this area in terms of redevelopment under the Housing Act 1957. He records that

'On the 1st March 1967, the Appellants, as part of their extensive slum clearance programme, and acting under the powers conferred on them by Section 42 of *e* the Housing Act 1957 declared a number of areas in the Lower Broughton district of the City of Salford to be clearance areas. On the same date, the Appellants, in pursuance of their powers under Section 43 of the Housing Act 1957, made [a compulsory purchase order for the acquisition of the area in which Mrs McNally's house exists].'

Since the clearance areas were areas where a large number of unfit properties were *f* liable to be demolished, or so large, says the magistrate, that it would be many years before all the occupiers could be rehoused and the dwelling-houses removed, the appellants in exercise of their powers under s 48 of the 1957 Act deferred for a period of seven years the demolition of the dwelling-houses in the compulsory purchase order being dwelling-houses which in the opinion of the appellants were or could be rendered capable of providing accommodation of a standard adequate for the *g* time being. There it will be seen is the first, and perhaps the only real, distinction between this case and the *Nottingham* case[1], because in this case the local authority had proceeded to the point of resolving to postpone demolition in accordance with their undoubted powers under s 48 of the 1957 Act.

Then the magistrate goes on to deal with the arguments which had been put *h* before him. He was supplied with a copy of a report of the *Nottingham* case in The Times[2], which was a comparatively full report. Having found the premises, that is to say Mrs McNally's house, unfit for human occupation, he concluded that he was bound to make a nuisance order. I pause there to say on the face of it by that decision in the *Nottingham* case[1] he was so bound. He went on to conclude that the resolution under s 48 did not excuse the appellants from their duties under the 1936 Act. He *j* made the nuisance order, and he asks us in effect whether he was right in law in so doing.

Thus in the end it seems to me the only question we have to decide is this: given

---

1 [1974] 2 All ER 760, [1974] 1 WLR 923
2 [1974] The Times, 11th April

that the decision in the *Nottingham* case[1] is right (and no one has attacked it in this
a court; indeed we would normally regard ourselves as being bound by it anyway),
the background situation here is that the house was unfit for human habitation, it
was in a condition prejudicial to health, the magistrate found it to be in that condition
and regarded himself as bound to make a nuisance order requiring the abatement of
the nuisance.   On the face of it, following the *Nottingham* case[1], that was entirely
correct.

b   The question is: does the resolution under s 48 make any difference?   Counsel
for the appellants has argued manfully to support the contention that it does.   Let
me say at once that there is a great deal of common sense in the submissions made
on behalf of the appellants that s 48 should make a difference.   I entirely agree
with counsel for the appellants when he says that s 48 is a recognition by Parliament
that there will be occasions when people have to live perhaps for some time in houses
c which are not up to the standard of fitness for human habitation laid down in the
1936 Act.   I agree with him that that is a situation which Parliament may well have
contemplated and indeed is really part of the background to s 48.

What I find it impossible to say is that the effect of s 48 is to remove, as it were, the
normal Public Health Act standard of fitness for habitation in cases where a nuisance
within the Public Health Act arises.   If it had been Parliament's intention to apply a
d lower standard of fitness in cases within s 48, it would gave been the simplest thing
in the world to say so.   Nothing would have been easier than to say that where s 48
applies, then a house which complies with the standard there laid down should not
be regarded as unfit for the purposes of the Public Health Act 1936.   But what in fact
Parliament said was just the opposite.   Under s 188 of the 1957 Act one finds this:

e   'All powers given by this Act shall be deemed to be in addition to and not in
derogation of any other powers conferred by Act of Parliament, law, or custom,
and such other powers may be exercised in the same manner as if this Act had
not passed, and nothing in this Act shall exempt any person from any penalty
to which he would have been subject if this Act had not passed . . .'

If one gives these words their ordinary meaning, they can only mean one thing,
f and that is that nothing in the 1957 Act is to affect the standards of suitability for
occupation already prescribed by the 1936 Act.   I am driven to the conclusion that,
whether or not this is a wholly satisfactory solution, the position in law at the present
time is that an individual occupier of a house unfit for human habitation can initiate
proceedings under s 99 of the 1936 Act and on proving his case can require the magistrate to make a nuisance order, and that notwithstanding the fact that the house is a
g house to which a resolution under s 48 of the 1957 Act applies.

Having reached that conclusion, I do not think there is anything more to be said.
No doubt the existence of the s 48 resolution is one of the factors which will affect
the magistrates' court when dealing with this difficult type of question, but that it
is more than a factor and having such weight as the magistrate thinks right and no
more, I find it impossible to say.   Although the magistrates' opinion as stated in his
h case is not in wholly satisfactory terms, I feel satisfied that he was shown an adequate
report of the *Nottingham* case[1], and that he did take into account all the circumstances
before him in reaching the conclusion he reached.

In those circumstances it seems to me therefore that there is nothing we can do
but dismiss the appeal.

j **MELFORD STEVENSON J.** I agree.

WATKINS J. I agree.

Appeal dismissed.   Leave to appeal to the House of Lords refused but the court certified that

1   [1974] 2 All ER 760, [1974] 1 WLR 923

the following point of law of general public importance was involved in the decision: 'Whether it is a lawful defence for a housing authority in proceedings brought against it by virtue of either s 93 or s 99 of the Public Health Act 1936 to prove that the house, the subject of the complaint, is one occupied by reason of s 48 of the Housing Act 1957 and maintained to the standard under s 48.'

Solicitors: *Sharpe, Pritchard & Co*, agents for *G F Bannister*, Salford (for the appellants); *Davis, Hope & Furniss*, Glossop (for the respondent).

Jacqueline Charles Barrister.

Re Kayford Ltd

CHANCERY DIVISION
MEGARRY J
4th OCTOBER 1974

Trust and trustee – Creation of trust – Personalty – Intention – Manifestation of intention to create trust – Company – Moneys paid by customers in advance for goods – Oral arrangement made by company to place moneys in special bank account – Arrangement made on professional advice – Purpose to protect customers in view of possible insolvency of company – Whether sufficient manifestation of intention to create trust in favour of customers.

The company carried on a mail-order business. Customers either paid the full purchase price or a deposit when ordering goods. By November 1972 the company was in financial difficulties. Being concerned for the customers of the company who had sent and were sending money for goods, the company took advice on how the customers might be protected in the event of the company becoming insolvent. They were advised by accountants to open a separate bank account to be called 'Customers' Trust Deposit Account' into which all further sums of money sent by customers for goods not yet delivered should be paid, so that, should the company be forced into liquidation, those sums could be refunded to the customers who had sent them. The company accepted that advice and on 27th November 1972 its managing director gave instructions by telephone to the company's bank. Instead of opening a new account, however, he agreed to use a dormant deposit account in the company's name for that purpose. The account had a credit balance of £47·80. On 8th December discussions were held about putting the company into liquidation. On 11th December the accountants were told of the oral account arrangements with the bank and realised that their advice had not been precisely carried out. They advised that the oral arrangements be confirmed in writing. On the same day the company resolved to go into liquidation. The letter to the bank was sent on the following day, and the words 'Customer Trust Deposit account' were then added to the name of the account. In the liquidation proceedings the question arose whether the sums of money paid into the bank account were held on trust for those who had sent them or whether they formed part of the general assets of the company.

Held – In the circumstances a trust had been created. All the requisites of a valid trust of personalty were present and the company had manifested a clear intention to create a trust since, from the outset, the whole purpose of what had been done had been to ensure that the moneys sent remained in the beneficial ownership of those who had sent them. Although payment into a separate banking account was a useful (though by no means conclusive) indication of an intention to create a trust, there was nothing to prevent the company from binding itself by a trust even if there were no effective

banking arrangements. Accordingly the moves were held in trust for those who
a had sent them (see p 607 *a* to *f*, post).

Note
For the constitution of an express trust, see 38 Halsbury's Laws (3rd Edn) 830-836,
paras 1388-1402, and for cases on the subject, see 47 Digest (Repl) 22-33, *93-172*.

b **Case referred to in judgment**
Nanwa Gold Mines Ltd, Re, Ballantyne v Nanwa Gold Mines Ltd [1955] 3 All ER 219, [1955]
1 WLR 1080, Digest (Cont Vol A) 165, *866a*.

Case also cited
Barclays Bank Ltd v Quistclose Investments Ltd [1968] 3 All ER 651, [1970] AC 567, HL;
c *affg* sub nom *Quistclose Investments Ltd v Rolls Razor Ltd* [1968] 1 All ER 613.

Adjourned summons
By an originating summons dated 10th October 1973, as subsequently amended, the
applicants, Arthur William Wainwright and David Alexander Wild, the joint liquidators of Kayford Ltd, sought, inter alia, the following relief: (i) a declaration whether
d the principal moves amounting to £37,872·45 together with interest thereon held to
the credit of the company on deposit account 90667670 with the branch of National
Westminister Bank Ltd situated at Newton Heath, Manchester, were held (a) as part
of the general assets of the company or (b) on trust for those persons who had paid to
the company the respective moves which made up the total of £37,872·45 in proportion to the amounts paid by such persons, or (c) on other and if so what trusts; (ii)
e an order that Clive Philip Joels ('the representative beneficiary') be appointed to
represent on trust those persons who had paid to the company the respective moves
which made up the total of £37,872·45. The facts are set out in the judgment.

Allan Heyman QC and Eben Hamilton for the joint·liquidators.
M K I *Kennedy* for the representative beneficiary.
f

MEGARRY J. This case arises on a summons taken out on 10th October 1973 by
the joint liquidators of Kayford Ltd which is in voluntary liquidation: I shall call it 'the
company'. The summons relates to a sum of £37,872·45, with interest thereon,
standing to the credit of the company in a deposit account at a bank. A further £47·80,
g with interest thereon, is also in that bank account. The company carried on a mail-
order business in bedding quilts, stretch covers for chairs and so on. The customers
either paid the full price in advance, or paid a deposit. In January 1972 the company
was experiencing difficulties in getting supplies, and it entered into an arrangement
with a manufacturing company named Monaco Manufacturing (Household Textiles)
Ltd, which I shall call 'Monaco'.
h   After an advertising campaign by the company in August 1972, similar to previous
campaigns, money came in for goods, but the company found itself unable to obtain
supplies to meet all the orders. By November 1972 Monaco, which by then was the
company's chief supplier, was in serious difficulties, after the company had already
provided financial support to Monaco to the extent of some £80,000. Mr Kay, the
managing director of the company, was becoming concerned for the customers of the
j company who had sent and were sending money for goods. On 22nd November
Monaco told the company that Monaco would have to go into liquidation unless it
received further financial support. If this happened it would affect not only the
company's ability to deliver the goods but also its solvency. The next day, 23rd
November, ·Mr Kay saw the company's accountants, who advised him to consult
accountants specialising in matters of insolvency; and the same day Mr Wainwright of

such a firm was consulted. He advised that a separate bank account should be opened
by the company, to be called a 'Customers' Trust Deposit Account', and that all   *a*
further moneys paid by customers for goods not yet delivered should be paid into
this account and withdrawn only when the goods had been delivered. The object of
doing this was so that if the company had to go into liquidation, these sums of money
could and would be refunded to those who had paid them. This advice was accepted.
On Monday, 27th November, Mr Kay gave instructions to the bank manager by
telephone. He and the manager agreed that a dormant deposit account in the com-   *b*
pany's name, with £47·80 to its credit, should be used for this purpose: and this was
done. The £37,872·45 with which I am concerned consists of money thus received,
together with the interest on it.

There is not much more to relate. On 6th December Monaco ceased to make
deliveries. On 8th December Mr Kay saw the company's solicitors to consider putting
the company into liquidation. On 11th December he saw Mr Wainwright, who then   *c*
discovered that his advice had not been precisely carried out. Mr Wainwright suggested that Mr Kay should at once write to the bank confirming the oral arrangements
that had been made; and on 12th December Mr Kay did this. On the day before, 11th
December, the company had resolved to go into voluntary liquidation, and meetings
were convened for 9th January 1973.

The question for me is whether the money in the bank account (apart from the   *d*
dormant amount of £47·80 and interest on it), is held on trust for those who paid it, or
whether it forms part of the general assets of the company. Counsel for the joint
liquidators, one of whom is in fact Mr Wainwright, has contended that there is no
trust, so that the money forms part of the general assets of the company and so will
be available for the creditors generally. On the other hand, there is a Mr Joels, who
on 12th December paid the company £32·20 for goods which have not been delivered;   *e*
and counsel for him seeks a representation order on behalf of all others whose
moneys have been paid into the bank account, some 700 or 800 in number. I make
that order. Counsel for the representative beneficiary, of course, argued for the
existence of an effective trust. I may say at the outset that on the facts of the case
counsel for the joint liquidators was unable to contend that any question of a fraudulent preference arose. If one leaves on one side any case in which an insolvent company   *f*
seeks to declare a trust in favour of creditors, one is concerned here with the question
not of preferring creditors but of preventing those who pay money from becoming
creditors, by making them beneficiaries under a trust. I should add that I had some
initial doubts about whether Mr Joels was the most suitable representative beneficiary,
in view of the date when he paid his money, and whether counsel for the joint liquidators, in representing Mr Wainwright (as well as the other joint liquidator), was not   *g*
to some degree committed to arguing against the efficacy of the course that Mr
Wainwright had advised; but discussion has allayed these doubts.

Now there are clearly some loose ends in the case. Mr Kay, advised to establish a
'Customers' Trust Deposit Account', seems to have thought that it did not matter
what the account was called so long as there was a separate account; and so the
dormant deposit account suggested by the bank manager was used. The bank   *h*
statement for this account is before me, and on the first page, for which the title is
simply 'Deposit account Kayford Limited', nearly £26,000 is credited. The second
and third pages have the words 'Customer Trust Deposit account' added after the
previous title of the account; and Mr Joels's payment was made after these words had
been added. Mr Kay also left matters resting on a telephone conversation with the
bank manager until he wrote his letter of 12th December to the bank. That letter   *j*
reads: 'We confirm our instructions regarding the opening of the Deposit account for
customer deposits for new orders'; and he then makes some mention of other accounts
with the bank. The letter goes on: 'Please ensure the Re-opened Deposit account is
titled "Customer Trust Deposit account".' Then he gives the reference number and
asks for confirmation that this has been done. Nevertheless, despite the loose ends,

a when I take as a whole the affidavits of Mr Wainwright, Mr Kay and Mr Hall (the bank manager) I feel no doubt that the intention was that there should be a trust. There are no formal difficulties. The property concerned is pure personalty, and so writing, though desirable, is not an essential. There is no doubt about the so-called 'three certainties' of a trust. The subject-matter to be held on trust is clear, and so are the beneficial interests therein, as well as the beneficiaries. As for the requisite certainty of words, it is well settled that a trust can be created without using the

b words 'trust' or 'confidence' or the like: the question is whether in substance a sufficient intention to create a trust has been manifested.

In *Re Nanwa Gold Mines Ltd*[1] the money was sent on the faith of a promise to keep it in a separate account, but there is nothing in that case or in any other authority that I know of to suggest that this is essential. I feel no doubt that here a trust was created. From the outset the advice (which was accepted) was to establish a trust account at

c the bank. The whole purpose of what was done was to ensure that the moneys remained in the beneficial ownership of those who sent them, and a trust is the obvious means of achieving this. No doubt the general rule is that if you send money to a company for goods which are not delivered, you are merely a creditor of the company unless a trust has been created. The sender may create a trust by using appropriate words when he sends the money (though I wonder how many do this, even

d if they are equity lawyers), or the company may do it by taking suitable steps on or before receiving the money. If either is done, the obligations in respect of the money are transformed from contract to property, from debt to trust. Payment into a separate bank account is a useful (though by no means conclusive) indication of an intention to create a trust, but of course there is nothing to prevent the company from binding itself by a trust even if there are no effective banking arrangements.

e Accordingly, of the alternative declarations sought by the summons, the second, to the effect that the money is held in trust for those who paid it, is in my judgment the declaration that should be made. I understand that questions may be raised as to resorting to the interest on the moneys as a means of discharging the costs of the summons; on that I will, of course, hear argument. I should, however, add one thing. Different considerations may perhaps arise in relation to trade creditors; but here I

f am concerned only with members of the public, some of whom can ill afford to exchange their money for a claim to a dividend in the liquidation, and all of whom are likely to be anxious to avoid this. In cases concerning the public, it seems to me that where money in advance is being paid to a company in return for the future supply of goods or services, it is an entirely proper and honourable thing for a company to do what this company did, on skilled advice, namely, to start to pay the

h money into a trust account as soon as there begin to be doubts as to the company's ability to fulfil its obligations to deliver the goods or provide the services. I wish that, sitting in this court, I had heard of this occurring more frequently; and I can only hope that I shall hear more of it in the future.

Representation order and declaration accordingly.

j

Solicitors: *Boxall & Boxall*, agents for *Jackson, Harris & Co*, Manchester (for the joint liquidators and the representative beneficiary).

F K Anklesaria Esq Barrister.

---

1 [1955] 3 All ER 219, [1955] 1 WLR 1080

Re Argentum Reductions (UK) Ltd   *a*

CHANCERY DIVISION
MEGARRY J
10th, 11th DECEMBER 1974

Company – Winding-up – Compulsory winding-up – Disposition of• property by company   *b*
after commencement of winding-up – Validation by court – Application to court for order
validating disposition – Locus standi of applicant – Shareholder – Shareholder not a party to
disposition – Whether shareholder entitled to apply to court for order – Companies Act 1948,
s 227.

A shareholder of a company which is being wound up by the court is entitled to apply   *c*
to the court for an order under s 227[a] of the Companies Act 1948 validating a disposition of property made by the company after the commencement of the winding-
up, even though the shareholder is not a party to that disposition (see p 611 *f* to *j*, post).

Notes
For the retrospective effect of winding-up orders, see 7 Halsbury's Laws (4th Edn)   *d*
698, para 1209.
    For the Companies Act 1948, s 227, see 5 Halsbury's Statutes (3rd Edn) 297.

Cases referred to in judgment
Shaw (John) & Sons (Salford) Ltd v Shaw [1935] 2 KB 113, [1935] All ER Rep 456, 104
    LJKB 549, 153 LT 245, CA, 9 Digest (Repl) 504, *3322.*
Marshall's Valve Gear Co Ltd v Manning Wardle & Co Ltd [1909] 1 Ch 267, 78 LJCh 46,   *e*
    100 LT 65, 15 Mans 379, 9 Digest (Repl) 718, *4760.*

Cases also cited
Levy (AI) (Holdings) Ltd, Re [1963] 2 All ER 556, [1964] Ch 19.
Operator Control Cabs Ltd, Re [1970] 3 All ER 657.   *f*

Motion
On 8th November 1974 Iris Patricia Jenkins presented a contributory's petition for
the winding-up of Argentum Reductions Ltd ('the company'). By notice of motion
dated 4th December 1974, to which Mrs Jenkins and Haydn Griffith Jenkins, a director
of the company, were respondents, Raymond Glenn McAllister, Jean Louise   *g*
McAllister and the company applied for an order that payments made out of the
company's bank account at Barclays Bank Ltd at Ludlow for the purpose of paying
debts of the company incurred after the date of the application in the ordinary
course of business should not be avoided by virtue of s 227 of the Companies Act 1948.
The facts are set out in the judgment.

     h

N F Merriman for Mr McAllister, Mrs McAllister and the company.
Robin Potts for Mr and Mrs Jenkins.

MEGARRY J. The point that arises on this motion is that of the locus standi
requisite for making an application under the Companies Act 1948, s 227. That
section is short, and contains no express provision about who can apply. It runs as   *j*
follows:

    'In a winding up by the court, any disposition of the property of the company,
    including things in action, and any transfer of shares, or alteration in the status

---

a   Section 227 is set out at letter *j*, supra

a 　of the members of the company, made after the commencement of the winding up, shall, unless the court otherwise orders, be void.'

So far as relevant, the facts which both sides have accepted for the purposes of this motion are as follows. There are 95 'A' shares in the company in question. 48 are owned by Mrs McAllister and 47 by Mrs Jenkins. The 'A' shares carry votes, whereas the remaining five shares are 'B' shares which carry no votes and are owned by a lady

b 　who does not come into the matter. The two directors of the company are Mr McAllister and Mr Jenkins, the respective husbands of the shareholders. Both couples, I was told, are Canadians. Mr and Mrs Jenkins both live in Canada, while Mr McAllister lives in England and has been running the company. The company's business, I understand, consists in the main of extracting silver from waste photographic materials. Mrs McAllister is also at present believed to be in Canada, but on

c 　each side there are arrangements by means of powers of attorney and proxies which enable those who cannot exercise their powers in person to do so indirectly.

There is now an unhappy state of deadlock on the board of the company; and each 'A' shareholder supports her own husband. On 8th November 1974 Mrs Jenkins presented a contributory's petition to wind up the company. This came on for hearing on 2nd December and was adjourned to 16th December. In the meantime,

d 　notice of motion was given on 4th December for an order that payments out of the company's bank account for the purpose of paying debts incurred after the date of the application in the ordinary course of business should not be avoided by virtue of s 227. That notice of motion was expressed to be given on behalf of Mr McAllister, Mrs McAllister and the company, and Mr Merriman appears for all three of them. For Mr and Mrs Jenkins, Mr Potts takes the preliminary objection that none of those

e 　for whom Mr Merriman appears has any locus standi to make the application, so that the motion must be dismissed. If that objection fails, then it is accepted that, subject to the overriding discretion of the court, an order should be made over 16th December, when the matter will come before the court again; and I was informed that the terms of that order have been agreed. The one question is thus that of locus standi.

f 　The point is one which, I was told, appears to be devoid of any direct authority. I will take each of the parties in turn. First, there is the company. Here the question is strictly not one of locus standi (though for brevity one may use the term), for it is accepted on all hands that the company may apply under the section. The question is really one of authority, in that Mr Potts contends that Mr Merriman has no authority to make any application in the name of the company. Mr Potts's contention

g 　was simplicity itself. The company has no managing director: the only two directors are in complete disagreement with each other: there has been no resolution of the directors that the company should apply under s 227: therefore nobody can have authorised the company to make any application under the section.

Mr Merriman's answer was that Mr McAllister was managing director of the company de facto, though not de jure, and that as such he was entitled to authorise

h 　an application in the name of the company. His tacit authority as de facto managing director clearly extended to the day-to-day running of the company's affairs: s 227 was now impeding that day-to-day running of the company's affairs; and his authority must be taken to extend to seeking in the name of the company to remove the impediment. He supported this contention by reference to Mrs McAllister's position as majority shareholder, and said that as such she could authorise her husband to

j 　make the application in the company's name. Mr Potts had contended that no meeting of the company could be held since Mrs Jenkins would not attend any meeting and so there would not be the necessary quorum of two: but, said Mr Merriman, *Marshall's Valve Gear Co Ltd v Manning Wardle & Co Ltd*[1] sufficiently answered that.

1　[1909] 1 Ch 267

In that case, three of the four directors of the company refused to sanction certain legal proceedings by the company. The other director, who held a simple majority *a* of shares in the company, had commenced the action in the name of the company. Neville J dismissed a motion by the other three directors, brought in the name of the company, to strike out the company's name as plaintiff and to dismiss the action on the ground that the company's name had been used without authority. The judge observed[1] that it would be useless to call a meeting of the company to ascertain the wishes of the shareholders, as the wishes of the majority were perfectly well known, *b* and that, contract apart, the majority of shareholders had the ultimate control of the company's affairs, and were entitled to decide whether or not an action in the company's name should proceed. That in essence, it was contended, was the situation in the present case, where Mrs McAllister, with her 48 shares, could always out-vote Mrs Jenkins, with her 47.

Mr Potts's reply was that *Marshall's* case[2] was at best of highly doubtful authority. *c* He referred me to the text and supporting authorities in Buckley's Companies Acts[3]. Put shortly, this passage is to the effect that, apart from fraud, where the articles have (as they have in this case) confided the control of the company's affairs to the directors, the shareholders, even if unanimous, cannot give directions to the directors as to what they are to do, or overrule their decisions. The shareholders may, of course, alter the articles or remove the directors, provided this is done in the appropriate *d* way; but while the directors are in the saddle, in the saddle they remain. It is another matter where there is fraud or mala fides in the directors: and a footnote suggests that *Marshall's* case[2] might be supported on this ground. In that case, I may say, the three opposing directors were personally interested in the patent which was the subject of the disputed legal proceedings.

Now there are ways in which the deadlock in the case before me might be resolved. *e* The refusal of Mrs Jenkins to attend any company meeting might be met if a successful application were to be made under s 135 of the 1948 Act, and the court ordered the holding of a meeting of the company, with a direction that one person present in person or by proxy should be deemed to constitute a meeting. Steps might be taken to remove Mr Jenkins as a director, or to appoint another director. These matters would, however, take a little time, and here I am concerned with a company *f* which is carrying on a business and has been struck by s 227, one of the usual consequences of which is that its bank account is frozen. If one accepts to the full that the shareholders cannot reverse a decision of the directors, or compel them to do what they do not want to do, one does not necessarily reach the conclusion that where the directors are in deadlock as to a course of action, the majority of the shareholders are powerless to come down on one side or the other. Nevertheless, there are deep *g* waters here; one has only to look at *John Shaw & Sons (Salford) Ltd v Shaw*[4] to see that. Furthermore, I have not been referred to any of the other authorities cited in the passage in Buckley[5] that I have mentioned: the matter, of course, has merely been argued on motion. I propose therefore to postpone any further consideration of the point until I have considered the other two heads. I accordingly turn to Mrs McAllister, the majority shareholder. *h*

Mr Potts contended that where the petition for winding up the company was brought by a contributory and not by a creditor, the only proper applicants under s 227 were either the company itself or else the other party to the transaction in question, or someone claiming a proprietary interest under him. Thus if the company sold property to a purchaser who then mortgaged it, Mr Potts accepted that the purchaser *j*

---

1   [1909] 1 Ch at 272
2   [1909] 1 Ch 267
3   13th Edn (1957), p 860
4   [1935] 2 KB 113, [1935] All ER Rep 456
5   Companies Acts (13th Edn, 1957), p 860

and the mortgagee could both apply under the section. But he contended that a
a shareholder in the company, as such, has no such right. However, he subsequently
accepted that a shareholder could apply under the section in relation to a transfer of
shares or alteration in the status of the members of the company, though not, he
said, in relation to any disposition of the property of the company. He agreed that
on the face of the section there was no restriction on those who could apply, but he
contended that the restriction which he urged was implicit. He emphasised that
b where there was a deadlock, those concerned could seek the appointment of a
provisional liquidator, and he offered to concur in such an appointment; and he
added that it would be wrong for one of the factions in a deadlock to be given the
benefits of an order under s 227 when instead that faction ought to be seeking the
appointment of a provisional liquidator.

I return to the section. The statutory material is exiguous. There are simply the
c words 'unless the court otherwise orders', set in their context. The affairs of companies are almost infinitely various, and where the legislature has refrained from
putting any express limit on those who may seek an order from the court, I would be
slow to attempt to spell out any implied limit which reaches beyond the ordinary
limits imposed by the courts on almost any application, namely, that the applicant
must have some discernible interest in the matter. The courts are not places for
d those who wish to meddle in things which are no concern of theirs, just for the
pleasure of interfering, or of proclaiming abroad some favourite doctrine of theirs, or
of indulging a taste for forensic display. Furthermore, it will be observed that the
section itself renders void three separate classes of transaction. They are (a) 'any
disposition of the property of the company, including things in action'; (b) 'any
transfer of shares'; and (c) 'any . . . alteration in the status of the members of the
e company'. It is plain, as Mr Potts accepts, that if a member of the company wishes
to apply in respect of (b) or (c), he may do so: in such a case the words 'unless the
court otherwise orders' embrace the shareholder. Yet if the member wishes to
apply in respect of (a), Mr Potts contends that the self-same words 'unless the court
otherwise orders' will not include the shareholder.

I cannot see why this should be so. To a shareholder, and not least to a majority
f shareholder, it may be a matter of great concern, as closely affecting the value of
his shares, that certain transactions should be saved from being invalidated. True,
the shareholder as such will usually be no party to the transaction, and so it can be
said that his interest in validating it is not direct but only indirect: yet an indirect
interest may be of great value and importance. Why should a person with an interest
to protect, even if it is indirect, be driven from the court when neither the Act nor the
g Rules give any indication that he should be excluded? Where the company is able
to apply to the court but chooses not to do so, the question of the weight to be
attached to an application made by a person with an indirect interest is another
matter: I am here concerned only with the right to apply. Furthermore, I do not
see why, in companies where there is a state of potential deadlock, it should be open
to one of the factions, by making the potential deadlock actual, to render it impossible
h for an application to validate a disposition under s 227 to be made except by the
other party to that disposition, or those claiming under him. Of course, if the shareholder has the locus standi to seek an order, the jurisdiction in a case of deadlock
must be exercised with a proper care: but it is a very different matter to say that the
shareholder cannot even apply.

Accordingly, in my judgment a shareholder has a sufficient locus standi to make an
j application under s 227 for the validation of dispositions. Mr Potts's preliminary
point accordingly fails as regards Mrs McAllister. I therefore need not decide whether
on the facts of this case the application by the company is validly made. Similarly I
need not decide whether Mr McAllister, who is merely a director, has a sufficient
locus standi; indeed, very little was said about him in argument. As at present
advised, I am not disposed to dismiss his claims to any locus standi as summarily as

I think Mr Potts would.   A director may have himself carried through the particular
disposition in question, and if the company is deadlocked and can make no application   *a*
the director might properly consider that he has a duty to the company to attempt to
validate a disposition which the other party to it may be ready indeed to leave as
having been struck down by the section.   However, as I have said, I do not need to
decide the point as to Mr McAllister, and I do not do so. I hold that Mrs McAllister, as
a shareholder, has a sufficient locus standi to apply under s 227, and that Mr Potts's
objection to the motion accordingly fails.   *b*

Order accordingly.

Solicitors: *Prentis, Seagrove & Co*, agents for *Cove & Co*, Birmingham (for Mr McAllister,
Mrs McAllister and the company); *Hancock & Willis* (for Mr and Mrs Jenkins).

c

F K Anklesaria Esq Barrister.

V L Skuce & Co (a firm) v Cooper   *d*

COURT OF APPEAL, CIVIL DIVISION
BUCKLEY, BROWNE LJJ AND BRIGHTMAN J
2nd, 3rd, 12th DECEMBER 1974

Hire-purchase – Agreement – Copies – Requirements as to copies – Power of court to dispense   *e*
with requirements – Duty to deliver or send copy of agreement to hirer – Agreement signed
elsewhere than at appropriate trade premises – Duty to send by post second statutory copy
within seven days – Power to dispense with requirement where second statutory copy sent
to hirer but not within seven days – Sent – Meaning – Second statutory copy handed to
hirer personally outside period of seven days – Whether copy 'sent' to hirer – Whether court
having power to dispense with requirement that second statutory copy be sent by post within   *f*
seven days – Hire-Purchase Act 1965, ss 9(3), 10(2).

The defendant entered into a hire-purchase agreement with the plaintiff firm in
respect of an electric typewriter.   The agreement was signed at premises other than
'appropriate trade premises' within s 58(1) of the Hire-Purchase Act 1965.   The defendant paid a small deposit initially but thereafter paid only two out of the 24 monthly   *g*
instalments due under the agreement.   Having first given the defendant the necessary statutory notice to terminate the agreement, the plaintiffs brought an action
for the recovery of the typewriter and arrears of instalments or, alternatively, for
the unpaid balance of the hire-purchase price.   Up to the time when the action was
to be heard the plaintiffs had failed to comply with the requirement of s 9(3)^a of the
1965 Act that a 'second statutory copy' of the hire-purchase agreement should be   *h*
sent by post to the defendant within seven days of the making of the agreement.
In his defence the defendant claimed that, by virtue of s 5^b of the 1965 Act, the
plaintiffs were not entitled to recover the typewriter because of their failure to comply
with s 9(3).   On the day of the hearing, however, the proprietor of the plaintiff firm
sought to remedy their default under s 9(3) by handing the second statutory copy
to the defendant at court.   At the hearing the judge offered the defendant an adjourn-   *j*
ment which would have allowed him to serve a notice of cancellation of the hire-
purchase agreement within four days of receiving the second statutory copy in

---

a Section 9(3) is set out at p 615 *g*, post
b Section 5, so far as material, is set out at p 614 *g* and *h*, post

accordance with s 11 of the 1965 Act. That offer was declined. The judge held that
_a_ as the plaintiffs had 'sent' the second statutory copy, within s 10(2)ᶜ of the 1965 Act,
he had power under s 10(1) to dispense with the requirements of s 9(3) on being
satisfied that the defendant had not been prejudiced by the failure to comply with
those requirements. He concluded that the defendant had not been prejudiced by
the plaintiff's failure to comply with s 9(3), since he could have determined the
agreement at any time. Accordingly he dispensed with the requirements of s 9(3)
_b_ and gave judgment for the plaintiffs. The defendant appealed.

Held – The word 'sent' in s 10(2) comprehended any effective means of ensuring
that the document in question reached the hirer's hands. Accordingly, the second
statutory copy had effectively been 'sent' to the defendant when it was handed to
him by the plaintiffs. The judge was therefore entitled to exercise the discretion
_c_ given him by s 10(1) to dispense with the requirements of s 9(3) insofar as a failure to
comply with them would otherwise have barred the plaintiffs' claim. The appeal
would therefore be dismissed (see p 617 _d g_ and _h_, p 618 _d_ and _e_ and p 619 _c_ to _e_, post).

Notes
_d_ For the statutory requirements as to the delivery of copies of a hire-purchase agreement to the hirer, see Supplement to 19 Halsbury's Laws (3rd Edn) para 848B.
For the Hire-Purchase Act 1965, ss 5, 9, 10, 11, 58, see 30 Halsbury's Statutes (3rd
Edn), 65, 69, 70, 107.
The Hire-Purchase Act 1965 is to be repealed by the Consumer Credit Act 1974,
s 192(4), Sch 5, as from a date to be appointed. For provisions governing the duty to
_e_ supply copies of agreements under the 1974 Act, see ss 62 and 63 of that Act.

Cases cited
Department of Agriculture for Scotland v Goodfellow 1931 SC 556.
Kenilworth Industrial Sites Ltd v E C Little & Co Ltd [1974] 2 All ER 815, [1974] 1 WLR
1069; *affd* p 53, ante, CA.
_f_ *Jarvis v Hemmings* [1912] 1 Ch 462.
Manchester Diocesan Council For Education v Commercial and General Investments Ltd
[1969] 3 All ER 1593, [1970] 1 WLR 241.
Newborough (Lord) v Jones [1974] 3 All ER 17, [1974] 3 WLR 52, CA.
Poyser and Mills' Arbitration, Re [1963] 1 All ER 612, [1964] 2 QB 467.
Sharpley v Manby [1942] 1 All ER 66, [1942] 1 KB 217, CA.
_g_ *Stephens v Cuckfield Rural District Council* [1960] 2 All ER 716, [1960] 2 QB 373, CA.

Appeal
This was an appeal by the defendant, Barry Cooper, against the judgment of his
Honour Judge Davison in the Walsall County Court on 2nd May 1974 whereby it
was ordered that the plaintiffs, V L Skuce & Co (a firm), should recover from the
_h_ defendant £84 arrears of monthly instalments due under a hire-purchase agreement
in respect of an electric typewriter entered into between the plaintiffs and the defendant on 1st December 1972 at premises other than 'trade premises' within the meaning
of the Hire-Purchase Act 1965, and that the defendant should deliver the typewriter
to the plaintiffs. The facts are set out in the judgment of Buckley LJ.

_j_ The defendant appeared in person.
George Newman for the plaintiffs.

Cur adv vult

_c_ Section 10, so far as material, is set out at p 615 _j_ to p 616 _a_, post

12th December. **BUCKLEY LJ** read the following judgment. This appeal raises
a question of construction on the Hire-Purchase Act 1965, which I think is difficult. *a*
On 1st December 1972 the defendant, Mr Cooper, entered into a hire-purchase agreement with the plaintiff firm in respect of an electric typewriter for a total hire purchase price of £318·50, payable as to £12·50 by a cash deposit and, as to the balance
of £306, by 24 monthly payments of £12 payable on the first day of each month
commencing 1st January 1973, and one payment of £18. It is common ground (1)
that the agreement is a hire-purchase agreement; (2) that it was signed by the defen- *b*
dant at a place other than appropriate trade premises as defined by s 58(1) of the 1965
Act; and (3) that the plaintiffs failed to comply with s 9(3) of that Act. In addition
to the cash deposit of £12·50 the defendant paid £10 in January 1973 and £14 in May
1973, but has otherwise made no payments under the agreement. By a letter dated
9th November 1973 the plaintiffs' solicitors, on their behalf, wrote to the defendant
giving formal notice to terminate the agreement, and calling for the return of the *c*
typewriter and payment of the arrears due under the agreement. On 26th November
1973 the plaintiffs commenced this action in the Walsall County Court, in which
they claimed return of the typewriter and £108 arrears. This figure was later reduced by agreement to £84. Alternatively the plaintiffs claimed £282, the unpaid
balance of the hire purchase price. On 28th January 1974 the defendant served a
defence, in para 5 of which he alleged that the plaintiffs were not entitled to enforce *d*
the agreement or to recover the typewriter on account of their failure to comply
with the requirements of s 9(3) of the 1965 Act. The defence was accompanied by a
counterclaim for damages for slander, but that has not been pursued in the county
court.

By way of remedying the default under s 9(3) of the 1965 Act, so far as possible,
Mr Skuce, the proprietor of the plaintiff firm, handed the 'second statutory copy' of *e*
the agreement to the defendant on the day of the hearing in the county court. The
learned judge came to the conclusion that this satisfied the condition of s 10(2) of the
1965 Act, and that accordingly the dispensing power contained in s 10(1) was available
to him. In the exercise of his discretion under the last-mentioned subsection he
dispensed with the requirement contained in s 9(3) for the purposes of this action.
He gave judgment for the plaintiffs for the recovery of the typewriter and £84 arrears, *f*
with costs. From that judgment the defendant appeals. The primary question in the
appeal is whether in the circumstances the agreement was enforceable by the plaintiffs,
which turns on the question whether the learned judge was entitled to dispense with
compliance with s 9(3) and was justified in doing so. Section 5 of the 1965 Act, so far
as relevant to the present case, provides:

g

> '(1) Where goods are let under a hire-purchase agreement . . . then (subject
> to the exercise of any power of the court under section 10 of this Act) the owner . . .
> shall not be entitled to enforce the agreement unless . . . (b) the requirements
> of . . . section 9 of this Act, are complied with.
>
> '(2) Where by virtue of the preceding subsection the owner . . . is not entitled
> to enforce an agreement . . . (c) if it is a hire-purchase agreement . . . the owner . . . *h*
> shall not be entitled to enforce any right to recover the goods from the hirer . . .'

Sections 6 and 7 contain requirements relating to cash price and the contents and form
of agreement to which I need not refer. Section 8 relates to cases in which the agreement is signed at appropriate trade premises. Although this is not such a case, it is,
I think, desirable to refer to the terms of that section. So far as they are referable
to hire purchase agreements, they are as follows: *j*

> '(1) The requirements of this section, in relation to an agreement which is
> signed by the hirer . . . at appropriate trade premises, are that copies are delivered
> or sent to the hirer . . . in accordance with the following provisions of this section.
>
> '(2) If either—(a) the agreement is signed by or on behalf of all other parties

a immediately after it is signed by the hirer . . . and a copy of the agreement is there and then delivered to him, or (*b*) the agreement having been signed by or on behalf of all other parties before it is signed by the hirer . . . a copy of the agreement is delivered to him immediately after he signs the agreement, and (in either case) the copy so delivered complies with the requirements of any regulations made under section 32 of this Act, the delivery of that copy shall be taken to have fulfilled the requirements of this-section in relation to that
b agreement.

'(3) If, in a case not falling within paragraph (*a*) or paragraph (*b*) of the last preceding subsection,—(*a*) either—(i) the relevant document was presented, and not sent, to the hirer . . . for his signature, and immediately after he signed it there was delivered to him a copy of that document in the form in which it then was, or (ii) the relevant document was sent to the hirer for his signature,
c and at the time when it was sent there was also sent to him a copy of that document in the form in which it then was, and (*b*) in either case, a copy of the agreement is delivered or sent to the hirer . . . within seven days of the making of the agreement, then, if each copy delivered or sent to the hirer . . . as mentioned in paragraph (*a*) or paragraph (*b*) of this subsection complies with the requirements of any regulations made under section 32 of this Act, the delivery or
d sending of those copies shall be taken to have fulfilled the requirements of this section in relation to that agreement.

'(4) In this and the next following section "the relevant document" means the document which, on being signed by the hirer . . . and by or on behalf of all other parties to the agreement, became the hire-purchase agreement . . .'

e Section 9 relates to cases where the hirer signs elsewhere than at appropriate trade premises. So far as referable to a hire-purchase agreement, it is in the following terms:

'(1) The requirements of this section, in relation to an agreement which is signed by the hirer . . . at a place other than appropriate trade premises, are that copies are delivered or sent to the hirer . . . in accordance with the following
f provisions of this section.

'(2) A copy of the relevant document (in this Part of this Act referred to as "the first statutory copy") must be delivered or sent to the hirer . . . as follows, that is to say—(*a*) if the relevant document is presented, and not sent, to the hirer . . . for his signature, a copy of that document, in the form in which it then is, must be delivered to him immediately after he signs it; (*b*) if the relevant
g document is sent to the hirer . . . for his signature, a copy of that document, in the form in which it then is, must be sent to him at the time when that document is sent.

'(3) Within seven days of the making of the agreement, a copy of the agreement (in this Part of this Act referred to as "the second statutory copy") must be sent by post to the hirer . . .'

h
I need not read sub-ss (4), (5) and (6) which contain other requirements relating to the first and second statutory copies. Section 10, so far as relevant, is in the following terms:

'(1) Subject to the following provisions of this section, if in any action the court is satisfied that a failure to comply with any of the requirements specified
j in sections 6 to 9 of this Act has not prejudiced the hirer . . . and that it would be just and equitable to dispense with the requirement, the court may, subject to any conditions that it thinks fit to impose, dispense with that requirement for the purposes of the action.

'(2) The power conferred by the preceding subsection shall not be exerciseable in relation to the requirement specified in section 9(3) of this Act except where the second statutory copy has been sent to the hirer . . . but not within the period of seven days of the making of the agreement . . .'

Section 11 confers on a hirer who has signed the relevant document in some place other than appropriate trade premises a right to serve a notice of cancellation at any time after he has signed the relevant document and before the end of the period of four days beginning with the day on which he receives the second statutory copy. Such a notice has the effect of rescinding the agreement.

It is clear that on account of the plaintiffs' failure to comply with s 9(3) the agreement in the present case is unenforceable by the plaintiffs under s 5 unless the dispensing power under s 10 is available and can properly be exercised. The first question, therefore, is whether that power is available, having regard to the terms of s 10(2). It can only be available if in the circumstances the second statutory copy of the agreement was 'sent to the hirer' after the expiration of the period of seven days from the making of the agreement. The answer to this question must depend on the proper meaning to be attributed to the word 'sent' in s 10(2).

In these sections a variety of expressions are used to describe handling documents in various circumstances: 'there and then delivered to him' (s 8(2)(a)); 'delivered to him immediately after he signs' (s 8(3)(a)(i), and see s 9(2)(a)); 'presented, and not sent, to the hirer for his signature' (s 8(3)(a)(i), s 9(2)(a)); 'sent to the hirer for his signature' (s 8(3)(a)(ii), s 9(2)(b)); 'sent' (s 8(3)(a)(ii), s 9(2)(b), s 10(2)); 'delivered or sent to the hirer within seven days' (s 8(3)(b)); 'within seven days . . . sent by post to the hirer' (s 9(3)).

A clear distinction is drawn between a document being presented for signature and one being sent for signature. There is also a distinction drawn between a document being delivered and one being sent. It seems to me that the draftsman has consistently used the terms 'presented' and 'delivered' where the act is one which must take place when the hirer and the person presenting or delivering the document are physically present together at the place where the act is done: he has used the term 'sent' where this is not the case, and in s 8(3)(b) he has used the words 'delivered or sent' where it may or may not be the case that the hirer and the person delivering or sending are face to face. The purpose of all these provisions is clearly to ensure that the hirer receives the copy or copies of the agreement at the particular stage or stages of the transaction indicated in the sections. The significance of receipt by the hirer of the second statutory copy is very clear from s 11. It is quite irrelevant to that purpose whether a copy of the agreement is handed to him, placed on his desk, put through his letter box or sent to him by post, except that perhaps, where the document is not handed to the hirer, a question might arise whether the other party must prove that it actually reached the hirer's hands.

It is not clear to me why in s 9(3) the legislature required the second statutory copy to be sent by post. Two explanations have been suggested to us: first, that this is for the advantage of the owner under the Interpretation Act 1889, s 26, which provides that where an Act of Parliament requires any document to be sent by post, then, unless the contrary intention appears, services of the document shall be deemed to have been effected by posting it properly addressed and stamped and, unless the contrary is proved, to have been effected when it would be delivered in the ordinary course of post; secondly, that the requirement is associated with the 'cooling-off period' recommended by the Committee on Consumer Protection in their Report[1] in the case of hirers who sign hire purchase agreements elsewhere than at appropriate trade premises (see Goode, Hire Purchase Law and Practice[2]). Neither explanation appears to me to be very convincing. It is not easy to see why the assistance of the Interpretation Act 1889, s 26, should have been considered appropriate in the case of a sending under s 9(3), but not in the case of any other sending, under s 8 or 9,

_____

1 (July 1962) Cmnd 1781
2 2nd Edn (1970), p 13

and particularly a sending under the parallel requirement in s 8(3)(*b*). On the other
a hand, the benefit of the cooling-off period, which, as I understand, was designed to
protect hirers from the effect of high pressure 'doorstep' salesmanship by giving
them a locus poenitentiae in the form of a period for reflection uninfluenced by any
pressure from the owner or his representatives, is achieved by the fact that under
s 11(2) the hirer has four days after receiving the second statutory copy within which
to decide whether to serve a notice of cancellation. The requirement to send that
b document by post could only have the incidental effect of extending that period
by at least about 24 hours.

However, the fact that s 9(3) requires a sending by post in a case where the agreement is not signed at appropriate trade premises, whereas s 8(3)(*b*) permits a sending
by any means when the agreement is signed at appropriate trade premises, is some
indication that s 9(3) was intended to form part of the protection afforded for the
c first time by the Hire-Purchase Act 1964 to hirers who signed agreements elsewhere
than at appropriate trade premises. The amendments of the 1938 Act effected by
the 1964 Act were all consolidated into the 1965 Act, which was a consolidating Act.
The problem in the present case accordingly really stems from the 1964 Act, but the
terms of that Act are somewhat complicated and it is consequently more convenient
and just as appropriate to consider the relevant provisions in the 1965 Act, as I have
d done in this judgment.

Nowhere else in ss 8 or 9 is any document required to be sent by post. No doubt a
document sent by post would be 'sent' within the meaning of the sections; but so
also, in my opinion, would a document sent by the hand of a messenger or put into
the hirer's letter box by the owner of the goods which are the subject-matter of the
agreement.

e It was suggested to us that the words 'by post' in s 9(3) were merely permissive,
although the remainder of the requirement was mandatory, and that the owner
could comply with the subsection by sending the copy by any means provided that
it reached the hirer. For my part, I find difficulty in accepting this. The words 'must
be sent by post' seem to me to be too positive.

In s 10(2) the expression 'sent to the hirer' is used, not 'sent by post to the hirer'
f as in s 9(3). It is contended that, since s 10(2) is dealing specifically with dispensing
with the requirement of s 9(3), 'sent' must here import the mode of sending required
by s 9(3). I do not agree. The draftsman has throughout these sections been careful
in his choice of the words used to describe the transmission of a document. If he
had meant in s 10(2) to describe the exceptional mode of sending required by s 9(3),
I would have expected him to use the same language as is used in that subsection.
g Moreover, the exception under s 10(2) only applies to a document sent after the seven
days referred to in s 9(3) have expired. There is no conflict between the two provisions if 'sent' in s 10(2) is interpreted as including sending by any means, whereas
sending under s 9(3) is required to be by post. If the object, or one of the objects,
of s 9(3) is to ensure that the cooling-off period is not too short, the default of the
owner in sending the second statutory notice within seven days will already have had
h the consequence of extending the cooling-off period and any further extension of it by
requiring a sending by post after the end of that period seems unnecessary for the
hirer's protection. Accordingly, in my judgment, on the true construction of s 10(2),
'sent' in that subsection includes sending by any means. Mr Cooper suggested that
the exclusion from the exception in s 10(2) of a case where the second statutory copy
was 'sent' otherwise than by post within seven days of the making of the agreement
j supported his contention that 'sent' in s 10(2) meant only sending by post. I think
this is an anomaly, but, in my view, it cannot alter what in my view is the true
construction of s 10(2).

The learned judge was of the opinion that what occurred at the county court on
the day of the hearing constituted a sending of the second statutory copy to the defendant by the plaintiffs. What happened was that before the hearing began Mr Skuce

handed a second statutory copy of the agreement, which was in proper form, to
the defendant personally. The defendant allowed it to drop from his hand to the   *a*
floor. The plaintiffs' solicitor then dropped the document into the defendant's brief
case. The defendant says that this may have constituted delivery of the document,
but not sending it.

As I have already indicated, the clear purpose of the various requirements to deliver
and send copies is to ensure that the hirer receives those documents (see s 11(2)).
Provided he receives the documents at the required times, it can make no practical   *b*
difference whether they are handed to him or reach him as a result of transmission
by some other means. The draftsman has been careful to use the word 'deliver'
where the occasion when transmission is required to take place is such that the
transmission would be by hand on the spot. Elsewhere he has used the word 'send',
but this does not involve holding that a document may not be 'sent' within the
the meaning of these sections by a method of transmission which involves manual   *c*
delivery to the hirer. If Mr Skuce had sent his solicitor to hand the second statutory
copy to the defendant, I feel no doubt that the document would have been 'sent'
within the meaning of s 10(2). Why, I ask myself, should it be regarded as in any
way a less satisfactory mode of getting the document into the defendant's hands if
it is taken to him and given to him by Mr Skuce personally? It seems to me that no
good reason can be suggested. In my judgment, any effective mode of ensuring   *d*
that the document reaches the hands of the hirer is comprehended in the expression
'has been sent to the hirer' in s 10(2). Accordingly, I agree with the view of the
learned judge that the second statutory copy of the agreement was in the present
case 'sent' to the defendant, though not within the period of seven days of the
making of the agreement.

In these circumstances, the next matter for consideration is whether the judge   *e*
was right in dispensing with compliance by the plaintiffs with s 9(3). The judge
held that the defendant had not been prejudiced by the default except for the costs
of bringing the action. The defendant contends that he has been prejudiced, first,
because under the judgment he has been charged £12 per month arrears, and
secondly, because the learned judge ordered that he should pay the plaintiffs' costs.
As to the arrears, these do not arise from the plaintiffs' default under s 9(3). The   *f*
defendant could have determined the agreement at any time, in which case the
instalments would have ceased to run, and, since no figure was inserted in para 2
under the heading 'Right of Hirer to Terminate Agreement' in the agreement, he
would have been liable for any subsisting arrears only. I will discuss the position
as to costs in a moment.

Had he chosen to do so, the defendant could have sought an adjournment before   *g*
delivery of judgment to afford him the period for cancellation allowed by s 11.
At the hearing the defendant was offered an adjournment for this purpose by the
judge and declined it. He told us that he did so because he was anxious to obtain
the judge's decision without delay on the facts before the court. It does not seem to
have occurred to him that in consequence of this he would be likely to be held to
have elected not to give any notice of cancellation or to have waived his right to do   *h*
so. On 5th May, 1974 the defendant purported to serve a notice of cancellation on
the plaintiffs. The defendant, with our leave, put this document before this court.
It is suggested that its effect, if any, is not a matter for present decision, but I think
we ought to consider what effect, if any, it has on the present state of affairs. I am
unable to see how it can have the effect of nullifying the judgment, as the defendant
suggested. The judgment must stand unless and until it is set aside. In view of the   *j*
fact that the defendant consented to judgment being delivered on 2nd May, 1974
and did not avail himself of the offered adjournment, any attempt to set the judgment
aside must, in my judgment, be doomed to failure. Accordingly the purported
notice of cancellation is, in my opinion, ineffective.

The learned judge ordered the defendant to pay the plaintiffs' costs. In doing *a* so, it seems to me, with deference to him, that the judge paid insufficient attention to the fact that, until the second statutory copy of the agreement had reached the defendant, the plaintiffs had no enforceable cause of action. The judge may have thought, as I do, that there was no merit in the defendant's case. Nevertheless, the defendant was entitled to rely on the provisions of the Act, and, until he received the second statutory copy, he had a perfect defence. Moreover, if he is to be condemned to pay the plaintiffs' costs, it appears to me that he has in *b* that respect been prejudiced by the plaintiffs' default under s 9(3), or, at any rate, by the late remedying of it. In my judgment, the proper order as to costs would have been that the plaintiffs should pay the defendant's costs down to the time when the second statutory copy was handed to him and that the defendant should pay only any costs of the plaintiffs in the county court which may have been incurred after that time. If this alteration be made in the order for costs below, I agree with *c* the learned judge that the defendant has not been prejudiced by the plaintiffs' failure to comply with s 9(3), and that compliance with that subsection should in the circumstances be dispensed with.

For these reasons, I would dismiss this appeal, save as to the order for costs, which I would vary in the way I have indicated.

d

BROWNE LJ. I entirely agree, and there is nothing which I feel I can usefully add.

BRIGHTMAN J. I also agree.

e

Appeal dismissed, save as to order for costs below, to be varied so that plaintiffs pay defendant's costs down to the time when the second statutory copy was handed to defendant, and defendant to pay plaintiffs' costs below incurred after that time. Defendant to pay two-thirds of plaintiffs' costs of appeal.

Solicitors: *Williams & Cole*, Walsall (for the plaintiffs).

James Collins Esq   Barrister.

R v Willis

COURT OF APPEAL, CRIMINAL DIVISION
LAWTON LJ, MOCATTA AND CANTLEY JJ
2nd, 17th DECEMBER 1974

Criminal law – Sentence – Buggery – Commission of buggery by man with boy under age of sixteen – Imprisonment – Appropriate term of imprisonment – Factors to be taken into account – Aggravating and mitigating factors.

On 8th May 1974 the appellant, who was 24 years old, went to a place where to his knowledge small boys were accustomed to play. The boys who were playing there invited the appellant to join in a game in which they undressed in the sight of one another. After some horseplay the appellant committed buggery with one of the boys who was aged eight. He was charged and released on bail. On 6th June, whilst on bail, he committed an indecent assault on a nine year old boy whom he had met casually. At his trial the appellant pleaded guilty to both offences and asked for seven other similar offences of indecent assault committed between 1st April and 5th June on boys of approximately the same age to be taken into consideration. The appellant had two previous convictions for indecent assault on girls aged about ten. The appellant lived at home and was unemployed. He was of dull intelligence and was very immature. He was not, however, sub-normal and was not suffering from any mental disorder. The judge sentenced the appellant to five years' imprisonment for buggery and three years for indecent assault, both sentences to run concurrently. On appeal against sentence,

Held – (i) Buggery committed with boys under the age of 16 was a serious offence and the younger the boy the more serious the offence. In the absence of very strong mitigating factors the proper sentence was one which would result in immediate loss of liberty. The appropriate sentencing bracket for the rare cases in which there were no aggravating or mitigating factors was from three to five years, the place in the bracket depending on age, intelligence and education (see p 622 *g* and *h*, post).

(ii) In the appellant's case there were both aggravating and mitigating factors which had to be weighed against each other: he was suffering from a personality disorder, was dull witted and still a young man; furthermore the offence of buggery had been committed in circumstances in which he was presented with an opportunity which he did not have the will power to resist; against those mitigating factors were other factors which showed that he was a danger to small boys. Accordingly the appropriate sentence was one that was likely to keep him out of trouble for a fairly long period and give him enough time to mature mentally if he was ever to do so. The sentences passed on him were the appropriate ones to achieve that result and the appeal would therefore be dismissed (see p 624 *d* to *g*, post).

Observations on the principal aggravating and mitigating factors which may need to be taken into account in determining the appropriate sentence for a person convicted of buggery with a boy (see p 622 *j* to p 624 *d*, post).

Note

For unnatural offences, see 10 Halsbury's Laws (3rd Edn) 669, 670, paras 1280, 1281, and for cases on the subject, see 15 Digest (Repl) 899, 900, 8665-8686.

Appeal

On 9th September 1974 in the Crown Court at Canterbury, before his Honour Judge Streeter, the appellant, Peter Charles Willis, pleaded guilty to two counts in an

a indictment: (1) buggery with a boy aged eight; and (2) indecent assault on a boy aged nine. After asking for seven similar offences of indecent assault on young boys to be taken into consideration, he was sentenced to five years' imprisonment on count 1 and to three years' imprisonment concurrent on count 2, making five years in all. He appealed against his sentence with leave of the single judge. The facts are set out in the judgment of the court.

b A S Hockman for the appellant.
The Crown was not represented.

At the conclusion of the argument the court intimated that the appeal would be dismissed, and that the reasons for the dismissal would be given at a later date.

c

17th December. **LAWTON LJ** read the following judgment of the court. This is an appeal, by leave of the single judge, against sentences totalling five years' imprisonment passed on the appellant by his Honour Judge Streeter at the Crown Court at Canterbury on 9th September 1974. The appellant had pleaded guilty to buggery with a boy aged eight, for which he was sentenced to five years, and with **d** an indecent assault on a boy aged nine, for which he was sentenced to a concurrent term of three years. He asked for seven other offences of indecent assault on small boys to be taken into consideration.

The buggery took place in the following circumstances. The appellant, who is now 24, has for some time been leading an aimless life. (He is said to be of dull intelligence but he is not sub-normal.) He is suffering from no mental disorder **e** within the Mental Health Act 1959. He is, however, said to have a personality disorder. He is immature, untruthful and irresponsible. He has no appreciation of the damaging effects his deviant sexual behaviour may have on the personalities of the other persons involved. For some months before he committed the offences under review in this case he had roamed around the area where he lived, doing no work and leaving both his parents and welfare officers in constant fear as to what **f** trouble, not necessarily criminal, he was going to get into next.

On 8th May 1974, in the course of his roamings, he went to a place known as The Sluice at St Mary's Bay in Kent. He had been there before and knew the place was frequented by small boys who played and fished there. On the day of the offence one of the boys said to him: 'Do you want to join our club?' One of the activities of the members was undressing in sight of one another. The boys were aged between **g** eight and 13. The younger ones may have reached the stage of development when they were becoming interested in their own bodies and the elder ones may have been prurient; but there was nothing to suggest that any of them were actively encouraging the appellant to commit homosexual acts with them. The appellant joined in their undressing activities. After some horseplay he buggered one of the youngest boys. Something of what had been going on was seen by passers-by. **h** Enquiries started. The appellant was interviewed by the police the next day. He admitted the buggery; he was charged and released on bail.

Whilst on bail on 6th June he went to a fair at Rye. He there got into conversation with a boy aged nine. He started some horseplay with him during which he committed an indecent assault. The boy told his father what had happened. Thereupon the father seized hold of the appellant. The police were sent for. The appel- **j** lant admitted the indecent assault, which had taken the form of fondling the boy's buttocks and penis. The offences taken into consideration had been committed between 1st April and 5th June 1974. The boys involved were about the same ages as the boys named in the indictment and the indecent assaults were of the same kind as that charged in the indictment.

The appellant had two previous convictions for indecent assault, both in 1969 and on girls aged about ten. For the first offence he was fined; for the second he was put on probation. He was examined by psychiatrists in December 1970 and again in April 1971. Following his arrest for the offences in this case he was examined yet again, this time by Dr Cleobury. He reported to the Crown Court that the appellant posed problems, not of treatment but of management. He found no indications that psychiatric treatment would be of much help.

This case presented Judge Streeter with a difficult sentencing problem. The experience of this court is that judges differ considerably in the way they deal with this kind of case. The single judge suggested that this court might think this an appropriate occasion for giving some guidance to judges. We will try to do so; but we wish to stress that our experience has been that these cases tend to differ widely in their facts. Nothing we say in this judgment should be taken as a desire on our part to put judges into sentencing strait-jackets.

One of the difficulties which judges have in sentencing offenders of this type is their own reactions of revulsion to what the accused has been proved to have done. Right-thinking members of the public have the same reactions and expect the judges in their sentences to reflect public abhorrence of the graver kinds of criminal homosexual acts. There is a widely held opinion that homosexual offences involving boys lead to the corruption of the boys and cause them severe emotional damage. Judges of experience are often of this opinion because when considering homosexual offences they are frequently told in pleas of mitigation that the accused was made an homosexual as a result of being involved when a boy in homosexual acts by a man.

Judicial experience is not lightly to be disregarded, but it must be weighed against other sources of information; and the main one is the Report of the Departmental Committee on Homosexual Offences and Prostitution which was presented to Parliament in 1957[1] and has become known as the Wolfenden Report. Many of its recommendations have been given statutory force, notably in the Sexual Offences Act 1967 which provided that, subject to exceptions, a homosexual act in private should not be an offence. The most important exception relates to participating persons who have not attained the age of 21. This reflects the desire of Parliament to protect the young, even from themselves. The younger a participating party is, the greater the need for protection. The revised punishments for homosexual acts in the 1967 Act provided for this since, although the punishments prescribed in the Sexual Offences Act 1956 were reduced, life imprisonment was retained for buggery with a boy under the age of 16. It follows, so it seems to us, that judges should always regard buggery with boys under the age of 16 as a serious offence—and the younger the boy the more serious the offence.

Notwithstanding the provisions of s 14 of the Criminal Justice Act 1972, it would seem inappropriate in a case in which there were no strong mitigating factors to pass a sentence which did not result in immediate loss of liberty or with a loss of liberty for only a few months or a year or so. In our judgment the sentencing bracket for offences which have neither aggravating nor mitigating factors is from three to five years; and the place in the bracket will depend on age, intelligence and education. Few offences, however, have neither aggravating nor mitigating factors. Many have both. When this happens the judge has to weigh what aggravates against what mitigates.

It may be helpful if we indicate what we believe to be the main aggravating factors, but we must not be taken to be making an all-embracing list or to be setting them out in order of importance.

(1) *Physical injury to the boy.* This may come about as a direct result of penetration. The Wolfenden Report thought this was very rare[2]; but it does sometimes occur in boys under the age of ten; and when it does the victim may be left for life with an

---

1   (1957) Cmd 247
2   See para 85

embarrassing disability. Much more common is the case in which the offender has
a used violence to overcome the boy's resistance. This is a dangerous form of violence
as it is used under the driving force of lust and may be maintained with fatal results
if the boy struggles strongly. Offenders who use violence should be discouraged from
repetition by severe sentences.

(2) *Emotional and psychological damage.* Judges should not assume that either of
these forms of damage is a probable result for a boy who has been the victim of
b buggery or that being buggered when young causes homosexuality to develop later
in life[1]: these are possible results depending on the make-up of the boy rather than
on the physical act itself. Paragraph 86 of the Wolfenden Report ended as follows:

> 'On the question of more general emotional or moral damage, our medical
> witnesses regarded this as depending more on the surrounding circumstances,
c > including the kind of approach made and the emotional relationships between
> the partners, than on the specific nature of the homosexual act committed.'

(3) *Moral corruption.* Although the act of buggery itself probably does not predispose
a boy towards homosexuality, that which leads up to the act may do so as, for example,
by gifts of money and clothes and the provision of attractive outings and material
d comforts. In our experience enticements of this kind can be very corrupting indeed
when the boys are young adolescents.

(4) *Abuse of authority and trust.* Those who have boys in their charge must not
abuse their positions for the sake of gratifying their deviant sexual urges. If they do
so, they must expect to get severe sentences. The factor of deterrence comes in here.
All who have charge of the young must be made to appreciate through the sentences
passed by the courts that society will not tolerate abuses of trust in this respect.
e We turn now to the main mitigating factors.

(1) *Mental imbalance.* The Wolfenden Report rejected the theory that homosexuality
was a disease[2] Some psychiatrists try to persuade judges that it is and that its physical
manifestations should be regarded as symptoms of the disease, rather than as breaches
of the criminal law. Parliament has considered all these matters and has decided that
f some kinds of homosexuality (buggery is one) should be criminal offences. There is
no justification for judges taking any other view. The Wolfenden Report recognised,
however, that in some cases homosexual offences do occur as symptoms in the course
of recognised mental or physical illness and cited as an example senile dementia[3].
When such cases are identified by satisfactory medical evidence, judges will want to
pass sentences which do not result in immediate committal to prison.

(2) *Personality disorders.* Men suffering from such disorders do not come within the
g purview of the Mental Health Act 1959 unless the disorder is so gross that it amounts
to psychopathy. The types of disorder may vary: at one end of the scale there is
the mentally immature adult who is in the transitional stage of psycho-sexual development; he can be helped to grow up mentally. At the other end are those with severely
damaged personalities, such as the obviously effeminate and flauntingly exhibitionist
individuals and the deeply resentful anti-social types. Probably nothing can be done
h for these individuals; but their pitiable condition calls for understanding and mercy.
Offenders with personality disorders do, however, present a difficult sentencing
problem. At present little can be done by either doctors or welfare workers for most
of them; they require management rather than treatment. If they cannot be managed,
either because they do not want to be or are mentally incapable of accepting management, they may become a danger to boys when at large in society. In such cases,
j the public are entitled to expect the courts to keep this class of offender away from
boys, in really bad cases for indefinite periods.

---

1 See para 98
2 See para 30
3 See para 30, and for more details the note by Drs Curran and Whitby at p 72 of the report

(3) *Emotional stress.* Many people have homosexual dispositions which they control as successfully as those of us who are orientated heterosexually. The Wolfenden *a* Committee found that there was no good reason to suppose that at least in the majority of cases homosexual acts are any more or less resistible than heterosexual acts[1]. Nevertheless it is a matter of both judicial and medical experience that latent homosexuals who have controlled their urges for years will give away under stress or unexpected and powerful temptation. The stress may come from the loss of a supporting parent or wife or of a job thought to be secure. The unexpected and powerful *b* temptation may come from a depraved homosexual who sets out to seduce someone whom he recognises as having the same urges as he himself has. It is a saddening and disturbing experience for judges to find, as many have, that the wicked seducer was an adolescent boy. When an accused who has kept his homosexuality under control for a long time begins committing offences either because of some precipitatory stress or exceptional temptation, the case may call for a measure of leniency.   *c*

Much the same approach is appropriate in cases of indecent assault on boys; but it must be remembered that in these cases it is not the label of indecent assault which is important but the nature of the act. In many cases it amounts to no more than putting a hand on or under clothing in the region of the testicle or buttocks. Such cases are not serious. In some the assault may take the form of a revolting act of fellatio, which is as bad as buggery, maybe more so. Sentences should reflect the *d* seriousness of the act constituting the indecent assault.

When the facts of this case are considered against the general principles to which we have referred we find both aggravating and mitigating factors. The appellant is suffering from a personality disorder: he is dull witted and he is still a young man. It cannot be said that the boys tempted him; but the circumstances in which he came to commit buggery presented him with an opportunity which he had not the will *e* power to resist. As against these mitigating factors there are a number which go to show that he is a danger to small boys. He committed some of the indecent assaults whilst he was on bail. His previous convictions for assaults on girls show that he gives way to his sexual urges whenever opportunity offers. He seems to have no aim in life except the gratification of his immediate desires and to be incapable of understanding the effect of his actions on others. In our judgment when the danger to small boys is balanced against the mitigating factors, the result indicates that the *f* appropriate sentence is one which is likely to keep the appellant out of trouble for a fairly long period and give him enough time to mature mentally, if he ever is going to do so. In our judgment the sentences passed on him by Judge Streeter achieved this result. It was for these reasons that we dismissed the appeal.

Appeal dismissed.   *g*

Solicitor: *Registrar of Criminal Appeals* (for the appellant).

N P Metcalfe Esq Barrister.

---

1 See para 33

Stephenson (Inspector of Taxes) v Barclays Bank Trust Co Ltd

CHANCERY DIVISION
WALTON J
2nd, 3rd DECEMBER 1974

Capital gains tax – Settlement – Beneficiary becoming absolutely entitled to all assets forming part of settled property – Deemed disposal and reacquisition of assets by trustees – Two or more beneficiaries – Beneficiaries jointly absolutely entitled as against trustees – Meaning of 'jointly' – Meaning of 'absolutely entitled' – Power to direct how assets shall be dealt with – Beneficiaries sui juris and collectively entitled to require transfer of trust funds subject to trustees' rights of indemnity – Trusts continuing – Beneficiaries having no power so long as trust continues to direct how trustees should manage investments – Particular assets of fund to which each beneficiary entitled not identifiable – Beneficiaries entitled as tenants in common and not joint tenants – Whether beneficiaries jointly absolutely entitled as against trustees to all assets forming trust fund – Finance Act 1965, ss 22(5), 25(3) – Finance Act 1969, Sch 19, para 9.

Capital gains tax – Settlement – Beneficiary becoming absolutely entitled to all assets forming part of settled property – Beneficiary absolutely entitled as against trustee – Entitlement subject to satisfying any outstanding charge, lien or other right of trustee to resort to assets for payment of duty, taxes, costs or other outgoings – Outgoings – Rights of trustee limited to personal right of indemnity – Not including right to resort to income for payment in respect of another beneficial interest – Finance Act 1969, Sch 19, para 9.

By his will dated 24th November 1939, the testator, after appointing the trustees to be executors and trustees thereof, bequeathed to his wife an annuity of £600 per annum for her life to commence from his death and to each of his three daughters an annuity of £300 per annum for their widowhoods to commence respectively from the dates of the deaths of their respective husbands. The will contained a direction to the trustees to appropriate a fund to answer the annuities with power to resort to the capital of the appropriated fund in case the income thereof proved insufficient. Any surplus income from the fund, and the ultimate capital, was to fall into and form part of the income or capital of the residuary estate which the testator disposed of on an accumulation trust, in the events which happened, for a period of 21 years from his death, and then on trust for all his grandchildren living at his death who should attain the age of 21 years, in equal shares. The will directed the trustees to invest the funds forming the residuary estate in any investment authorised by the will with power to change those investments for others of a like nature. By a codicil to the will made on 24th June 1940, the annuitants were confined to the income of the residuary estate, but any surplus income was to be treated as a reserve fund applicable for payment of the annuities of the daughters. The testator died on 19th April 1944. Probate of his will and codicil was granted on 28th August 1944 to the trustees. In 1948 one of the daughters was widowed. The testator's widow died in 1951. On 28th October 1952 R, the elder of the two grandsons of the testator living at his death, attained the age of 21; on 13th April 1955 C, the younger of the two grandsons, did likewise. In 1959 and 1963 the other two daughters of the testator became widows. On 18th April 1965 the accumulation period ended. On 27th January 1969 all those concerned with the residuary estate, i e the trustees, R, C and the three daughters, entered into a deed of family arrangement whereunder a fund was appropriated to answer the daughters' annuities, the trustees advanced a sum to R and C for the purpose of buying additional income for the daughters,

and the daughters confirmed that on the appropriation being effected, the trustees
and the estate and effects of the testator other than the appropriated fund should　*a*
be immediately released from all claim (if any) by and liability to the daughters or
any of them to the intent that the trustees might then forthwith transfer the remainder of such estate and effects to R and C.　The trustees had already acquired
the investments which were to form the appropriated fund and accordingly the
deed, insofar as it released the estate from the daughters' claims, took effect immediately on execution.　The trustees did not, however, immediately transfer the residuary　*b*
estate to R and C but continued to hold that fund.　The trustees were assessed to
capital gains tax on the basis that, on 27th January 1969, when the deed of family
arrangement became operative, R and C had 'jointly' become 'absolutely entitled'
to the balance of the residuary estate, within s 22(5)^a of the Finance Act 1965, and
Sch 19, para 9^b, to the Finance Act 1969, and that consequently the trustees were
deemed, under s 25(3)^c of the 1965 Act, to have disposed of the residuary estate and　*c*
immediately reacquired it in their capacity as trustees for a consideration equal to
its market value.　The Special Commissioners allowed an appeal by the trustees,
holding that R and C were not to be regarded as being 'absolutely entitled', within
para 9 of Sch 19 to the 1969 Act, since, so long as the residuary estate was held on the
trusts of the testator's will, neither R nor C had power to direct the trustees how to
manage the investments and therefore they had no power to 'direct how [the assets　*d*
of the residuary estate] shall be dealt with'.　On appeal by the Crown the trustees
contended, inter alia, that the phrase 'jointly . . . entitled' in s 22(5) did not apply to
beneficial tenants in common of pure personalty, and that beneficiaries only became
absolutely entitled to the assets forming the estate when the assets were actually
distributed to them.　Alternatively, they contended that R and C had become
absolutely entitled on 13th April 1955 when C reached the age of 21 since the right of　*e*
the annuitants to have their annuities paid out of the income of the residuary estate
was merely 'a charge, lien or other right of the trustees to resort to the [trust assets]
for payment of . . . outgoings', within Sch 19, para 9, to the 1969 Act.

Held – The appeal would be allowed for the following reasons—
　(i) The phrase 'charge, lien or other right of the trustees' in para 9 of Sch 19 to the　*f*
1969 Act referred to the trustees' personal right of indemnity against the trust funds
and was not apt to cover another beneficial interest arising under the same instrument.　Accordingly R and C had not become absolutely entitled before the deed
of family arrangement came into operation (see p 635 *h* to p 636 *c*, post).
　(ii) There was no basis for the contention that two or more beneficiaries would not
become 'absolutely entitled', within s 22(5) of the 1965 Act, to the trust assets until　*g*
the date of distribution.　The scheme of the legislation was that two or more beneficiaries were to be regarded as jointly and absolutely entitled to the trust assets
where, subject to the trustees' rights of indemnity, the beneficiaries collectively, in
the same interest, i e concurrently or as tenants in common, were entitled to require
the trustees to transfer all the trust assets to the beneficiaries themselves in their
respective shares, or to their nominees, and to give the trustees an absolute discharge　*h*
therefor.　It was immaterial that it was impossible to say before distribution which
particular assets each beneficiary had become absolutely entitled to and also immaterial that, as long as the trust continued, the beneficiaries would not be entitled
to direct the trustees how to manage the investment of the trust funds (see p 637 *c* to
g and p 638 *a* to *h*, post); *Kidson (Inspector of Taxes) v Macdonald* [1974] 1 All ER 849
applied.　　　　　　　　　　　　　　　　　　　　　　　　　　　　　　　　　　*j*
　(iii) It followed that, when the deed of family arrangement was executed, R and C
became, for the purposes of capital gains tax, jointly absolutely entitled as against

---

a　Section 22(5) is set out at p 634 *d* and *e*, post
b　Paragraph 9 is set out at p 634 *j* to p 635 *a*, post
c　Section 25(3) is set out at p 634 *h*, post

a the trustees of the grandfather's will trusts to the remaining residue of the estate not thereby appropriated to answer the daughters' annuities, within s 22(5) of the 1965 Act and Sch 19, para 9, to the 1969 Act, and that, by virtue of s 25(3) of the 1965 Act, there had been a deemed disposal of the residuary estate (see p 639 c and d, post).

Notes

b For capital gains tax in relation to settled property, see 5 Halsbury's Laws (4th Edn) 23, 59, paras 45, 115.

For the Finance Act 1965, ss 22, 25, see 34 Halsbury's Laws (3rd Edn) 877, 884.

For the Finance Act 1969, Sch 19, para 9, see ibid 1227.

Cases referred to in judgment

Brockbank, Re, Ward v Bates [1948] 1 All ER 287, [1948] Ch 206, [1948] LJR 952, 47 Digest (Repl) 142, *1041*.

c *Kidson (Inspector of Taxes) v Macdonald* [1974] 1 All ER 849, [1974] 2 WLR 566, [1974] STC 54.

Marshall, Re, Marshall v Marshall [1914] 1 Ch 192, [1911-13] All ER Rep 671, 83 LJCh 307, 109 LT 835, CA, 47 Digest (Repl) 369, *3310*.

Weiner's Will Trusts, Re, Wyner v Braithwaite [1956] 2 All ER 482, [1956] 1 WLR 579, d 47 Digest (Repl) 237, *2084*.

Cases also cited

Coller's Deed Trusts, Re, Coller v Coller [1937] 3 All ER 292, [1939] Ch 277, CA.

Hardin v Masterman [1896] 1 Ch 351, [1895-9] All ER Rep 695, CA.

Leconfield Estate Co v Inland Revenue Comrs [1970] 3 All ER 273, 46 Tax Cas 325, [1970] 1 WLR 1133.

e *Tomlinson (Inspector of Taxes) v Glyn's Executor & Trustee Co* [1970] 1 All ER 381, [1970] Ch 112, 45 Tax Cas 600, CA.

Case stated

1. At a meeting of the Commissioners for the Special Purposes of the Income Tax Acts held on 11th June 1973, the respondents, Barclays Bank Trust Co Ltd, as f trustees of Sir Richard Winfrey deceased ('the testator'), appealed against an assessment to capital gains tax for the year 1968-69 in the sum of £10,000.

2. Shortly stated the question for decision was whether on the execution of a deed of family arrangement and release dated 27th January 1969 the two grandsons of the testator became absolutely entitled to settled property as against the respondents within the meaning of s 25(3) of the Finance Act 1965.

g [Paragraph 3 listed the documents proved or admitted before the commissioners.]

4. The following facts were admitted between the parties: (i) By his will dated 24th November 1939 the testator, then of Castor House, Castor, in the county of Northampton, appointed his son Richard Pattinson Winfrey and Barclays Bank Trust Co Ltd ('the trustees') to be the executors and trustees of his will. So far as relevant the will provided as follows:
h

'5. I BEQUEATH the following annuities (free of duty) (a) To my said Wife an annuity of Six hundred pounds per annum for her life to commence from my death and (b) To each of my three Daughters Ellen Willson Lucy Eades and Ruth Agutter annuities of Three hundred pounds per annum for their respective widowhoods to commence respectively from the dates of the deaths of their j respective Husbands and I declare that each annuity shall be considered as accruing from day to day but to be paid by equal half yearly payments the first payment to be made at the end of six calendar months from the same becoming due and I direct my Trustees to set apart as soon as conveniently may be and invest with power to vary investments a sum the income whereof when invested shall be sufficient at the time of investment to pay the said Annuities and to

pay such of the said annuities as are then payable accordingly with power to
resort to the capital of the appropriated fund whenever the income shall be   *a*
insufficient and until such sum shall be so appropriated I charge my residuary
personal estate with the said annuities but after appropriation my residuary
estate shall thereby be discharged from the said annuities Subject to the payment
of the said annuities the appropriated fund or so much thereof as shall not be
resorted to to make up a deficiency of income shall fall into and form part of my
residuary estate and any surplus income of the appropriated fund shall be   *b*
applied in the same manner as income of my residuary estate . . .

'7 (a) I DEVISE AND BEQUEATH the residue of my real and personal estate (herein
called my Residuary Estate) unto my Trustees upon Trust that my Trustees shall
sell call in and convert into money the same or such part thereof as does not
consist of money with power to postpone such sale calling in and conversion
for such a period as my Trustees without being liable to account may think proper   *c*
and so that any reversionary interest be not sold until it falls into possession
unless my Trustees see special reason for sale.   (b) MY TRUSTEES shall out of the
money to arise from the sale calling in and conversion of my Residuary Estate
and out of my ready money pay my funeral and testamentary expenses death
duties (including legacy and succession duty) and debts and shall also pay or
provide for the legacies and annuities hereby or by any codicil hereto bequeathed   *d*
but so that all legacies and annuities and the duty on all legacies and annuities
bequeathed free of duty shall be paid primarily out of my personal estate.
(c) MY TRUSTEES shall invest the residue of the said money in their names or
under their control in or upon any of the investments hereby authorised with
power for my Trustees at discretion to change such investments for others of a
like nature.   (d) MY TRUSTEES shall stand possessed of the said investments   *e*
and any part of my Residuary Estate remaining unconverted and the investments
for the time being representing the same (hereinafter called the Trust Fund) and
of the annual income thereof Upon the trusts following that is to say Upon
Trust to retain and accumulate the same at compound interest by investing the
resulting income thereof in any investments hereby authorised with power from
time to time to vary such investments at discretion until the decease of the   *f*
surviving beneficiary under this my Will (other than grandchildren or remoter
issue of mine) or the expiration of Twenty-one years from my death (whichever
period shall be the shorter) but so that no part of such fund shall be invested in
the purchase of land and then upon trust for all my Grandchildren living at my
death who shall attain the age of Twenty-one years in equal shares and the
issue of any such Grandchildren of mine who may have died in my lifetime   *g*
leaving issue who shall survive me and attain the age of Twenty-one years such
issue to take and if more than one equally between them the share of my estate
their parent would have taken if such parent had survived me and attained a
vested interest . . .'

(2) By a codicil dated 24th June 1940 to his will the testator provided as follows: *h*

'When I signed my last Will I could not foresee all the dire consequences of
War! Today the French Nation has collapsed and what may happen to us is
in the lap of the gods! Already the State is taking more than half my Income
and much heavier taxation must follow. The four Newspaper Companies
from which most of my income is derived are hit very hard. My salaries from   *j*
them cease at my death. This being so I must modify my bequests and give
my Trustees increased powers.

'1. That whilst I wish my wife to receive £600 a year, I now provide that if
the yearly income from my estate does *not* reach that sum, then the annuity
must be limited to whatever the yearly income provides.

'2. With regard to the Annuities to my daughters. If they should become
a   payable during my Wife's life and the income from my estate does not exceed
£600 a year, my Trustees are to suspend payment until my Wife passes out,
after that they are to limit the sums paid to my daughters to such sums as can
be met out of the *annual income* of my estate, each daughter to share alike.

'3. If during my Wife's life and afterwards there is a surplus of income, it
shall be treated as a reserve and used when required to make up any deficiency
b   in the sums required to pay the annuities to my daughters.'

(3) The testator died on 19th April 1944 and his will and the codicil thereto were duly
proved on 28th August 1944 by the executors and trustees named in the will. At
the date of the hearing before the commissioners, the executors and trustees ('the
trustees') were the trustees of the will and the codicil. (4) The testator's wife men-
c   tioned in the will and codicil ('the wife') survived him and died on 7th August 1951.
(5) The testator's three daughters mentioned in cl 5 of the will ('the annuitants')
all survived him and at the date of the hearing were still living, all being widows,
their respective widowhoods having commenced on the following dates: Ellen
Willson, 19th May 1959; Lucy Eades, 22nd December 1963; Ruth Agutter, 22nd
January 1948. (6) The testator had two grandchildren and no more namely Richard
d   John Winfrey ('Richard') and Francis Charles Winfrey ('Charles'). Richard and
Charles were both living at the testator's death and had attained the age of 21 years,
Richard on 28th October 1952 and Charles on 13th April 1955. (7) An annuity
of £600 per annum was paid to the wife out of the annual income of the testator's
residuary estate from the testator's death for the remainder of her life. Annuities
of £300 per annum were paid to each of the annuitants out of the annual income of
e   the residuary estate from the commencement of their respective widowhoods until
the arrangements mentioned in the following sub-paragraphs were made. Until such
time the balance of the annual income of the residuary estate was dealt with as
follows: up until June 1967 sums were advanced to Richard and Charles amounting
to £6,196 each and the balance of the surplus income was accumulated and invested
in a fund ('the accumulated income fund'); since June 1967 the whole of the income
f   had been distributed equally between Richard and Charles. (8) In accordance with
the terms of cl 7(d) of the will the trust therein declared to retain and accumulate
the income of the residuary estate came to an end on the expiry of 21 years from the
testator's death. (9) On 27th January 1969 a deed of family arrangement and release
('the deed') was made between the trustees of the first part, Richard and Charles of
the second part, and the annuitants of the third part. By the deed it was recited that
g   the deed was supplementary to the will and the codicil; that the wife had survived
the testator and died on 7th August 1951; that the annuitants had survived the testator and were all widows and had not remarried; that they had from the dates of
the deaths of their respective husbands been in receipt of annuities of £300 per annum
each in accordance with the terms of the will; that the period of 21 years mentioned
in cl 7(d) of the will quoted above had ended on 18th April 1965; that the testator
h   had two grandchildren, Richard and Charles, and no more living at his death;
that the trustees had completed the administration of the testator's estate and then
held the residuary estate of the testator on trust to pay the annuities bequeathed to
the annuitants and subject thereto on trust for Richard and Charles absolutely;
that doubts had arisen about the effect of the codicil on the direction in cl 5 of the will
to set apart and invest a sum to pay the annuities; that the trustees with the consent
j   of Richard and Charles were desirous of resolving those doubts and of distributing
the estate save insofar as it might be necessary to retain a fund to satisfy the annuities;
that Richard and Charles were desirous of making further provision for the annuitants
by the purchase of an annuity for each of them of £600 per annum in addition to the
annuities provided by the will; and that the parties thereto had agreed to execute
the deed to give effect to such arrangements and to release the trustees from liability.
By the deed it was provided, inter alia, as follows:

'1. The Trustees will forthwith purchase with trust funds now subject to the terms of the Will the sum of TWENTY THOUSAND POUNDS (nominal) 5½% Treasury *a* Stock 2008/2012 and will set apart the same as a separate fund under the Will and use the income thereof to pay such of the annuities bequeathed by the Will of the testator as may from time to time be payable to each of the annuitants in satisfaction of the respective annuities given by the Will.

'2. The Trustees shall forthwith raise from the remaining trust funds now subject to the terms of the Will and advance to Richard and Charles such sums *b* as may be necessary to enable them to purchase from Norwich Union Life Assurance Society or such other Insurance Company of repute as they may select annuities of Six hundred pounds per annum for each annuitant (which Richard and Charles hereby respectively agree to do).

'3. The annuitants will at the request of Richard or Charles complete such proposal form or proposal forms in respect of annuities so to be purchased as *c* aforesaid as may reasonably be required for enabling Richard and Charles to effect the same.

'4. The annuitants and each of them hereby jointly and severally confirm that on the making by the Trustees of the investment hereinbefore referred to and its appropriation to satisfy their annuities under the Will the Trustees and the estate and effects of the testator other than such investment shall be immedi- *d* ately released from all claims (if any) by and liability to the annuitants or any of them to the intent that the Trustees may then forthwith transfer the remainder of such estate and effects to Richard and Charles.'

(10) Pursuant to the deed the sum of £20,000 (nominal) 5½ per cent Treasury Stock referred to therein was set apart and at the date of the hearing before the commis- *e* sioners was retained by the trustees for the purposes therein mentioned; and with sums of £14,889 17s 0d advanced to them by the trustees pursuant to cl 2 of the deed Richard and Charles purchased annuities of £600 per annum for each of the annui- tants. At the date of the hearing before the commissioners the trustees held the remainder of the residuary estate on trust for Richard and Charles in equal shares absolutely and were paying the income thereof to Richard and Charles accordingly. *f* (11) On 14th February 1972 the inspector of taxes, in pursuance of para 12 of Sch 10 to the Finance Act 1965, assessed the respondents to capital gains tax for the year 1968-69 in the sum of £10,000 on the basis that, on the occasion when the deed was made, there had, for the purposes of s 25(3) of the 1965 Act, been a deemed disposal of the balance of the residuary estate remaining after the appropriation of the said £20,000 (nominal) 5½ per cent Treasury Stock and payment of the said advances of £14,889 *g* as a result of which capital gains estimated at £10,000 had accrued.

5. It was contended on behalf of the respondents: (1) that so long as Richard and Charles were interested as beneficial tenants in common of the residuary estate all the assets comprised therein remained settled property for the purposes of Part III of the 1965 Act; (2) in the alternative: (i) that Richard and Charles had become absolutely entitled as against the trustees to the residuary estate when they respectively attained *h* the age of 21 and (ii) that in any event Richard and Charles had become absolutely entitled as against the trustees to the accumulated income fund 21 years after the testator's death when the accumulation period under cl 7(d) of the will expired; (3) that accordingly Richard and Charles did not on the occasion when the deed was entered into become absolutely entitled as against the trustees to any settled property (or alternatively to the accumulated income fund); and (4) that the assessment under *j* appeal should be discharged.

6. It was contended on behalf of the Crown: (1) that Richard and Charles on the occasion when the deed was made (but not at any earlier time) had become absolutely entitled as against the trustees within the meaning of s 25(3) of the 1965 Act, to settled property, namely, the balance of the residuary estate (including the accumulated

income fund) of the testator remaining after the appropriation of the said £20,000
a (nominal) 5½ per cent Treasury Stock and payment of the said advances of £14,889;
(2) that by virtue of s 25(3) there was on that occasion a deemed disposal by the
trustees to themselves of the balance of the residuary estate; (3) that capital gains
had accrued to the trustees in respect of that deemed disposal; (4) that the assessment
to capital gains tax which was under appeal should be upheld in principle, leaving
figures to be agreed.
b   [Paragraph 7 listed the cases[1] cited to the commissioners.]
    8.   The commissioners took time to consider their decision and gave it in writing
on 16th July 1973 as follows:

    '1.   On this appeal against an assessment to Capital Gains Tax made for the
    year 1968-69 the question for our determination is whether on the occasion when
c   the Deed of Family Arrangement and Release dated 27th January, 1969 (herein-
    after called the "Deed supplemental to the Will") was entered into Richard
    John Winfrey (hereinafter called "Richard") and Francis Charles Winfrey (herein-
    after called "Charles") became absolutely entitled as against the trustees within
    the meaning of Section 25(3) of the Finance Act, 1965, to settled property, namely
    the residuary estate of the late Sir Richard Winfrey and income therefrom
d   remaining after the trustees had set aside certain Treasury Stock pursuant to the
    said Deed to satisfy annuities given by the deceased's Will (or alternatively so
    much thereof as was not held as an Accumulated Income Fund), with the result
    that there was then for the purposes of that tax a deemed disposal within the
    said subsection.
    '2.   By declaratory provisions enacted in paragraph 9 of Schedule 19 to the
e   Finance Act, 1969, (below the cross-heading "Distinction between trustees of
    settled property and bare trustees") references in Part III of the Finance Act,
    1965, to any asset held by a person as a trustee for another person absolutely
    entitled as against the trustees are required to be construed as references to a
    case where that other person has the exclusive right, subject only to satisfying
    any outstanding charge, lien or other right of the trustees to resort to the asset
    for payment of duty, taxes, costs or other outgoings, to direct how that asset
f   shall be dealt with.   It was common ground between the parties that these
    provisions, being declaratory in form, took effect retrospectively.
    '3.   We think it convenient to consider in the first place the question whether
    (as was contended on behalf of the [respondents] alternatively) the annuities
    payable were, prior to the Deed supplemental to the Will being entered into,
    bequests within the scope of the words in the said paragraph 9 commencing
g   with the words "subject only" and ending with the word "outgoings" (herein-
    after called "the 'subject only' phrase").   As to this, it is, we think, material
    to note that that paragraph relates to references to any asset held by a person as
    trustee for another person absolutely entitled "as against the trustee".   Given
    this context, we are of opinion that in construing the "subject only" phrase the
    words following the words "other right" should be read as qualifying the words
h   "outstanding charge, lien or other right", and not merely in the words "other
    right".   Further, it seems to us that if this is so the annuities, while prior to the
    Deed supplemental to the Will charges against annual income of the estate,
    did not come within the scope of the "subject only" phrase.   In the first place
    we think that in construing that phrase the ejusdem generis rule applies, and that

---

j 1 *Berkeley, Re, Inglis v Berkeley (Countess)* [1968] 3 All ER 364, [1968] Ch 744, CA; *Brockbank,*
    Re, Ward v Bates [1948] 1 All ER 287, [1948] 1 Ch 206; *Coller's Deed Trusts, Re, Coller v Coller*
    [1937] 3 All ER 292, [1939] Ch 277; *Hardin v Masterman* [1896] 1 Ch 351, [1895-9] All ER
    Rep 695; *Leaconfield Estate Co v Inland Revenue Comrs* [1970] 3 All ER 273, 46 Tax Cas 325,
    [1970] 1 WLR 1133; *R v Special Comrs of Income Tax, ex parte Shaftesbury Homes and Arethusa*
    Training Ship [1923] 1 KB 393, 8 Tax Cas 367, [1922] All ER Rep 637, CA.

while the word "outgoings" is of wide import the annuities were not in view of
the said rule outgoings within the scope of that word in the expression "payment *a*
of duty, taxes, costs or other outgoings". Even, however, if this were not so the
annuities would, we think, still not be within the scope of the "subject only"
phrase by reason of their not being a charge of the trustees "to resort to the asset"
(as distinct from to income) for payment of them.

'4. If we are right so far it is, we think, evident that prior to the Deed supplemental to the Will being entered into Richard and Charles were not, having regard *b*
to the terms of the said paragraph 9, persons who had as respects the settled
property become absolutely entitled as against the trustee within the meaning
of that expression in Part III of the Finance Act, 1965. We thus have to consider
whether in these circumstances Richard and Charles did or did not become, on
the occasion when the said Deed was entered into, absolutely entitled as against
the trustee to such property, taking account in this connection of the declaratory *c*
provisions contained in the said paragraph 9 as to the construction of references
to any asset held by a person as trustee for another person absolutely entitled as
against the trustee.

'5. If they so wished, Richard and Charles as tenants in common at that point of
time could have taken steps to have the residuary estate transferred to themselves.
They did not, however, take this course, and the property accordingly continued *d*
to be held in trust, the trustees distributing the whole of the income equally
between Richard and Charles. The trustees would not, however, appear to
have become then bare trustees merely distributing income and having no
other duties of any kind to perform. They were, it would seem, empowered
as hitherto to exercise the discretion conferred on them by Clause 7(c) of Sir
Richard Winfrey's Will to change investments, and it is, we think, evident that *e*
Richard and Charles could not have arrogated to themselves the right to direct
the trustees how on such a matter the assets should be dealt with. This being
so, it seems to us that Richard and Charles still did not have the exclusive right,
subject only to matters falling within the ambit of the "subject only" phrase, to
direct how the assets in question should be dealt with, unless (and there is in
our view no sufficient warrant for this) the words "dealt with" are interpreted *f*
as having in the context in which they occur not their full ordinary meaning but a
more limited sense. Accordingly Richard and Charles did not in our view on
the occasion when the Deed supplemental to the Will was entered into become
"absolutely entitled as against the trustee" to any settled property, within the
narrow scope of the words cited as they fall to be construed having regard to
the declaratory provisions contained in the said paragraph 9. *g*

'6. The appeal, therefore, succeeds on that account and we hereby discharge
the assessment against which it was made.'

9. Immediately after the determination of the appeal the Crown declared their
dissatisfaction therewith as being erroneous in point of law and on 6th August 1973
required the commissioners to state a case for the opinion of the court. *h*

10. The question of law for the opinion of the court was whether the commissioners were right in holding that on the occasion when the deed was made Richard
and Charles did not become absolutely entitled as against the trustees to any settled
property, within the meaning of s 25(3) of the 1965 Act.

Nicolas Browne-Wilkinson QC and *Peter Gibson* for the Crown. *j*
J P Lawton for the respondents.

WALTON J. By his will dated 24th November 1939, the late Sir Richard Winfrey,
after appointing his son, Richard Pattinson Winfrey, and the respondents to be
executors and trustees thereof, inter alia: (i) bequeathed to his widow an annuity

of £600 per annum to commence from his death; (ii) bequeathed to each of his
a three daughters, Ellen, Lucy and Ruth, annuities of £300 per annum for their respective widowhoods to commence respectively from the dates of the deaths of their
respective husbands, with a direction for appropriation of a fund to answer the
annuities with power to resort to the capital of the appropriated fund in case the
income should prove insufficient.   Any surplus income thereof, and the ultimate
capital, was to fall into and form part of the income or capital or residue.   He dis-
b posed of his residuary estate on an accumulation trust (in the events which happened)
for the period of 21 years from his death and then on trust for all his grandchildren
living at his death who should attain the age of 21 years in equal shares, with certain
substitutional provisions and an ultimate gift over with which I am not concerned.

   The outbreak of war appears to have had a very devastating immediate effect on
the testator's fortunes, because he made a codicil to this will on 24th June 1940 as a
c result of which, putting it shortly, the annuitants were confined to the income of
the residuary estate but any surplus income was to be treated as a reserve fund applicable for payment of the annuities to the daughters.   The testator died on 19th April
1944.   Probate to his will and codicil was granted on 28th August of that year to the
executors therein named.   Four years later the daughter Ruth was widowed.   The
testator's widow died in 1951.   On 28th October 1952, the elder of the two grandsons
d of the testator living at his death attained the age of 21; on 13th April 1955, the
younger of the two did likewise.   In 1959 Ellen was widowed; in 1963 Lucy was
widowed.   On 18th April 1965, the accumulation period ended.

   Finally, on 27th January 1969, all those concerned with the residuary estate—the
trustees, the two grandchildren and the three widowed daughters—entered into a
deed of family arrangement whereunder a fund was appropriated to answer the
e daughters' annuities, the trustees advanced a sum to the two grandchildren for the
purpose of being used to buy additional income for the daughters, and thereby
the daughters confirmed that on the appropriation being effected the trustees and
the estate and effects of the testator other than the appropriated fund should be
immediately released from all claims (if any) by and liability to the daughters or
any of them to the intent that the trustees might thence forthwith transfer the
f remainder of such estate and effects to the two grandchildren.   In fact, the trustees
had, prior to the date of this deed, already acquired the investment which was to
form the appropriated fund, so that, immediately on its execution, the last clause
to which I have referred took immediate effect.   The trustees did not, however,
immediately transfer the residuary estate to the two grandchildren in equal shares,
or at all, and so far as I am aware the trustees are still holding that fund.

g   On these simple facts the question arises whether, as a result of the operation of
the provisions in the deed of family arrangement, capital gains tax became payable
by the trustees, as on a deemed disposal of the whole (or, alternatively, so much
thereof as did not consist of land or, just possibly, as did not consist of land and
mortgage debts) of the remaining residuary estate which thereafter the trustees
held on trust for the two grandchildren in equal shares absolutely.   It is argued by
h counsel for the Crown that it did; and by counsel for the respondents that it did
not for a variety of reasons with which I must deal in detail later.

   The matter ultimately turns on a very few provisions of the capital gains tax
legislation, which I think I should set out.   First of all, s 19(1) of the Finance Act 1965
reads:

   'Tax shall be charged in accordance with this Act in respect of capital gains,
j   that is to say chargeable gains computed in accordance with this Act and accruing
   to a person on the disposal of assets.'

   Subsection (3) of that section reads:

   'Subject to the said provisions, a tax, to be called capital gains tax, shall be
   assessed and charged for the year 1965-66 and for subsequent years of assessment

in respect of chargeable gains accruing in those years, and shall be so charged in accordance with the following provisions of this Part of this Act.'   *a*

Section 20(1):

'Subject to any exceptions provided by this Act, a person shall be chargeable to capital gains tax in respect of chargeable gains accruing to him in a year of assessment during any part of which he is resident in the United Kingdom, or during which he is ordinarily resident in the United Kingdom.'   *b*

Section 22(1):

'All forms of property shall be assets for the purposes of this Part of this Act, whether situated in the United Kingdom or not, including—(a) options, debts and incorporeal property generally, and (b) any currency other than sterling, and (c) any form of property created by the person disposing of it, or otherwise coming to be owned without being acquired.'   *c*

Section 22(5):

'In relation to assets held by a person as nominee for another person, or as trustee for another person absolutely entitled as against the trustee, or for any person who would be so entitled but for being an infant or other person under disability (or for two or more persons who are or would be jointly so entitled), this Part of this Act shall apply as if the property were vested in, and the acts of the nominee or trustee in relation to the assets were the acts of, the person or persons for whom he is the nominee or trustee (acquisitions from or disposals to him by that person or persons being disregarded accordingly).'   *d*

    e

Section 25(1):

'In relation to settled property, the trustees of the settlement shall for the purposes of this Part of this Act be treated as being a single and continuing body of persons (distinct from the persons who may from time to time be the trustees), and that body shall be treated as being resident and ordinarily resident in the United Kingdom unless the general administration of the trusts is ordinarily carried on outside the United Kingdom and the trustees or a majority of them for the time being are not resident or not ordinarily resident in the United Kingdom . . .'   *f*

Then there is a proviso to that subsection which I need not read.

Then, I think it is convenient to refer to s 45(1) for the definition of 'settled property', which, with a certain exception which is not material for present purposes, is defined as meaning 'any property held in trust other than property to which section 22(5) of this Act applies . . .' Then, still in s 25 of the Act, sub-s (3):   *g*

'On the occasion when a person becomes absolutely entitled to any settled property as against the trustee all the assets forming part of the settled property to which he becomes so entitled shall be deemed to have been disposed of by the trustee, and immediately reacquired by him in his capacity as a trustee within section 22(5) of this Act, for a consideration equal to their market value.'   *h*

Finally, there is a section which was not in fact passed until after the events with which we are concerned but which, as it is a declaratory provision, is accepted on all hands to be of retrospective effect. It is to be found in the Finance Act 1969, Sch 19, para 9, which reads: *j*

'It is hereby declared that references in Part III of the Finance Act 1965 [and then I omit some words which have been repealed] to any asset held by a person as trustee for another person absolutely entitled as against the trustee are *a* references to a case where that other person has the exclusive right, subject only to satisfying any outstanding charge, lien or other right of the trustees to resort to the asset for payment of duty, taxes, costs or other outgoings, to direct how that asset shall be dealt with.'

The first question which arises is: at what point of time did or will the two grand-children become absolutely entitled as against their trustees to the residuary estate?

b There have been suggested the following points of time: (i) by counsel for the respondents, 13th April 1955, when the younger of the two grandchildren attained the age of 21; (ii) by counsel for the Crown, 27th January 1969, when the deed of family arrangement was executed; (iii) by counsel for the respondents, the date or dates on which there is made an actual distribution of the residuary estate between the two grandchildren. This last submission was, in point of fact, the ground on which

c the Special Commissioners found in the trustees' favour. The Crown had assessed them to capital gains tax for the year 1968-69 (in accordance with the second date indicated above) in the sum of £10,000. This is in fact an estimated sum, and no actual computations have yet, so far as I am aware, been made.

The trustees appealed to the commissioners against this assessment, and they allowed the appeal. Their reasons are stated as follows[1]:

d   'If they had so wished, Richard and Charles [they are the two grandchildren] as tenants in common could at that point of time [that being the date of execution of the deed of family arrangement] have taken steps to have the residuary estate transferred to themselves. They did not, however, take this course, and the property accordingly continued to be held in trust, the trustees distributing the whole of the income equally between Richard and Charles. The trustees

e   would not, however, appear to have become then bare trustees merely distri-buting income and having no other duties of any kind to perform. They were, it would seem, empowered as hitherto to exercise the discretion conferred on them by Clause 7(c) of Sir Richard Winfrey's Will to change investments, and it is, we think, evident that Richard and Charles could not have arrogated to themselves the right to direct the trustees how on such a matter the assets

f   should be dealt with. This being so, it seems to us that Richard and Charles still did not have the exclusive right, subject only to matters falling within the ambit of the "subject only" phrase, to direct how the assets in question should be dealt with, unless (and there is in our view no sufficient warrant for this) the words "dealt with" are interpreted as having in the context in which they occur not their full ordinary meaning but a more limited sense. Accordingly Richard

g   and Charles did not in our view on the occasion when the Deed supplemental to the Will [i e the deed of family arrangement] was entered into become "abso-lutely entitled as against the trustee" to any settled property, within the narrow scope of the words cited as they fall to be construed having regard to the de-claratory provisions contained in [para 9 of Sch 19 to the Finance Act, 1969].'

h From their decision the Crown has appealed to the High Court, and the matter comes before me accordingly. I shall now return to the three possible dates in order. As regards the suggested date of 13th April 1955—which is, of course, only counsel for the respondents' alternative submission—this submission rests on equating the charge on the income of the residuary estate of the three annuities to the widowed daughters with the word 'outgoings' in the Finance Act 1969, Sch 19, para 9. Counsel

j for the respondents cited to me authority to show that the word 'outgoings' was a word of the widest possible signification. I would agree with that, but one has to look at the word here in the context in which it is found. I cannot think that the right of the annuitants to have their annuities paid out of the income of the residuary

---

1 See p 632, ante

estate is a charge, lien or other right of the trustees within the meaning of that phrase
as so found in para 9. It appears to me quite clear that the subject-matter to which   *a*
para 9 is directed is the prevention of a situation where the taxpayer was able to say,
and say truly, that he was not 'absolutely entitled against the trustees' because the
trustees had some personal right of indemnity, of resorting to the trust funds, which
took priority over the rights of the person otherwise absolutely entitled. It does not
appear to me to be in any way apt language for use in the case of another beneficial
interest arising under the same instrument as the beneficial interest of the person   *b*
said to be absolutely entitled as against the trustees. Such a person is not 'absolutely
entitled as against the trustees', whatever that phrase means, for the obvious reason
that he does not, subject only to the excepted rights of the trustees, hold the
entirety of the beneficial interest in the fund. That beneficial interest is divided
between the annuitant and the other person, and he by himself is not entitled to the
entirety of the beneficial interest.   *c*

Counsel for the respondents strove very hard to persuade me that the annuitants—
the daughters of the testator—were only in the position of chargees, but this will not
do. The trust fund was the whole of the assets in the hands of the trustees, and that
fund was the source from which the annuities were paid. Any reference to annuities
being 'charged' on the capital or income of a fund only relates to indicating that part
of the fund out of which they are to be paid, and their priority over other interests   *d*
in the fund. Per contra, where there is a genuine charge to an outsider—say, a
mortgage of some description—on a proper analysis the trust asset is the equity of
redemption only in the mortgaged asset. This is the crucial distinction.

I now approach the second date—namely, when the deed of family arrangement
was executed—stressing once again that, having regard to its provisions, any appropriation out of the annuity fund was effected uno ictu therewith. If the concept of a   *e*
person being beneficially entitled as against a trustee stood alone, there would, I
think, be little difficulty in the concept. But it does not stand alone, because in the
Finance Act 1965, s 22(5), one finds the additional words 'or for two or more persons
who are or would be jointly so entitled', the 'would be' being a reference to infancy
or disability. Now it was decided by Foster J in *Kidson (Inspector of Taxes) v Macdonald*[1], that the word 'jointly' was to be read in the sense of 'concurrently, or in   *f*
common', and was not to be confined to the strict joint tenancy—that is, a tenancy
with benefit of survivorship—as known to English conveyancers. Whilst this point
is only one in the foothills, as it were, of the argument, counsel for the respondents
did not like this decision in any way and submitted thereon, first, that it was a decision
relating to a trust for sale of land where the two joint tenants were such legally and
beneficially, and that there is no reason to suppose that Foster J would have intended *g*
his decision to apply to pure personalty, which constitutes the bulk of the present
remaining residuary estate. As a final measure, if necessary, he submitted that that
case was wrongly decided.

I reject both of these submissions. It appears to me perfectly clear that, although
the ratio decidendi of that case arises out of the consideration that the ordinary
English conveyancing concept of a joint tenancy in real property is unknown north   *h*
of the Border, whilst the same statutory provisions apply indifferently either side of
it, nevertheless the decision is a perfectly general one as to the scope of the relevant
phrase in s 22(5), and is in no wise confined to real property. The arguments as to
the generality of the meaning of 'jointly' would have been precisely the same whatever the subject-matter of the trust. As regards the soundness of the decision as a
whole, although technically I am not strictly bound to follow it, it appears to me that, *j*
even if I had thought the decision logically dubious, I ought to follow a decision of
Foster J on a novel point otherwise untouched by authority. But I go much further
than that. The reasoning of the learned judge in that case appears to me to be well

1   [1974] 1 All ER 849, [1974] 2 WLR 566, [1974] STC 54

a   founded and, were the matter res integra, such as I should have hoped myself to reproduce.

I now turn to a consideration of the phrase 'absolutely entitled as against the trustee', which is now of course fairly closely defined in the Finance Act 1969, Sch 19, para 9. It is there defined as meaning that the person concerned—

b   'has the exclusive right, subject only to satisfying any outstanding charge, lien or other right of the trustees to resort to the asset for payment of duty, taxes, costs or other outgoings, to direct how that asset shall be dealt with.'

Now it is trite law that the persons who between them hold the entirety of the beneficial interests in any particular trust fund are as a body entitled to direct the trustees how that trust fund is to be dealt with, and this is obviously the legal territory from which that definition derives. However, in view of the arguments advanced to me c   by counsel for the respondents, and more particularly that advanced by him on the basis of the decision of Vaisey J in *Re Brockbank*[1], I think it may be desirable to state what I conceive to be certain elementary principles. (1) In a case where the persons who between them hold the entirety of the beneficial interests in any particular trust fund are all sui juris and acting together ('the beneficial interest holders'), they are entitled to direct the trustees how the trust fund may be dealt with. (2) This d   does not mean, however, that they can at one and the same time override the pre-existing trusts and keep them in existence. Thus, in *Re Brockbank*[1] itself the beneficial interest holders were entitled to override the pre-existing trusts by, for example, directing the trustees to transfer the trust fund to X and Y, whether X and Y were the trustees of some other trust or not, but they were not entitled to direct the existing trustees to appoint their own nominee as a new trustee of the existing trust. By so e   doing they would be pursuing inconsistent rights. (3) Nor, I think, are the beneficial interest holders entitled to direct the trustees as to the particular investment they should make of the trust fund. I think this follows for the same reasons as the above. Moreover, it appears to me that once the beneficial interest holders have determined to end the trust they are not entitled, unless by agreement, to the further services of f   the trustees. Those trustees can of course be compelled to hand over the entire trust assets to any person or persons selected by the beneficiaries against a proper discharge, but they cannot be compelled, unless they are in fact willing to comply with the directions, to do anything else with the trust fund which they are not in fact willing to do. (4) Of course, the rights of the beneficial interest holders are always subject to the right of the trustees to be fully protected against such matters as duty, taxes, costs or other outgoings; for example, the rent under a lease which the trustees g   have properly accepted as part of the trust property.

So much for the rights of the beneficial interest holders collectively. When the situation is that a single person who is sui juris has an absolutely vested beneficial interest in a share of the trust fund, his rights are not, I think, quite as extensive as those of the beneficial interest holders as a body. In general, he is entitled to have transferred to him (subject, of course, always to the same rights of the trustees as I h   have already mentioned above) an aliquot share of each and every asset of the trust fund which presents no difficulty so far as division is concerned. This will apply to such items as cash, money at the bank or an unsecured loan, stock exchange securities and the like. However, as regards land, certainly, in all cases, as regards shares in a private company in very special circumstances (see *Re Weiner's Will Trusts*[2]) and possibly (although the logic of the addition in facts escapes me) mortgage debts (see *Re j   Marshall*[3] per Cozens-Hardy MR) the situation is not so simple, and even a person with a vested interest in possession in an aliquot share of the trust fund may have

---

1   [1948] 1 All ER 287, [1948] Ch 206
2   [1956] 2 All ER 482, [1956] 1 WLR 579
3   [1914] 1 Ch 192 at 199, [1911-13] All ER Rep 671 at 674

to wait until the land is sold, and so forth, before being able to call on the trustees
as of right to account to him for his share of the assets.   *a*

It is, I think, in the light of these elementary propositions that one can understand
the forces which have shaped the definitions in the present instance. The scheme of
the capital gains tax legislation is to treat all assets alike, and it would be extremely
curious if, by reason of the different natures of the assets when a person became
entitled to an aliquot share of a trust fund, some were treated one way and some
another way for the purposes of that tax. I appreciate that counsel for the respondents *b*
says that his solution—not becoming absolutely entitled until actual distribution—
would produce a result which treated all assets alike, but it appears to me, for reasons
which I shall elaborate later, that this is not the intent of the legislation at all.

I think that the definition has been framed, therefore, with the following points
in view. (i) The elimination of the trustees' rights of indemnity, because otherwise
it would be possible to postpone the payment of capital gains tax indefinitely by *c*
keeping alive what might be a very small right indeed. (ii) The elimination of any
question as to what were the assets to which a person has become absolutely entitled
in the commonest of all cases, namely, where the trust fund ultimately vests in possession in various persons in various shares. Of course, if, in the event, vesting takes
place at different times, it appears to me inescapable that the question may still arise.
(iii) The definition says 'jointly'; it does not say 'together'. I think this is because *d*
it is intended to comprise persons who are, as it were, in the same interest. This is
a point which was alluded to by Foster J in *Kidson v Macdonald*[1]. If property is settled
upon A for life with remainder to B, A and B are 'together' entitled absolutely as
against the trustees, but they are not so entitled 'jointly', 'concurrently', or 'as tenants in common'. (iv) Finally, of course, the definition is so framed as to require the
person who becomes absolutely entitled to be able to give the trustees a good *e*
discharge. In a sense, this is the reverse of the penny of absolute entitlement.

It follows from the foregoing, of course, that I entirely reject the submission of
counsel for the respondents that the date of becoming absolutely entitled is the date
of actual distribution. I do so for a number of reasons. The first is because this is
not what the Act says at all. If actual distribution was to be the test, this must be
the test even for a single individual, and the Act would then surely have mentioned *f*
that as the crucial date. After all, absolute entitlement, however one defines it,
provided the definition is a rational one, must antedate distribution. There is, however,
so it seems to me, an even more compelling argument in that the definition of 'absolutely entitled' to be found in the Finance Act 1969, Sch 19, para 9, presupposes that
such absolute entitlement takes place at a time when the fund is still in the hands
of the trustees, because otherwise the reference to 'satisfying any outstanding charge' *g*
etc would be completely otiose. On an actual transfer of the property there can
be no question of 'satisfaction' so far as the transferred property is concerned; and,
at any rate in the normal case of settled property, any 'lien' of the trustees is a possessory lien only and is lost as soon as the trust property is handed over. It therefore
appears to me quite clear that the legislature contemplated a point of time quite
distinct from the date of actual transfer as the date of a person becoming 'absolutely *h*
entitled' to trust property.

I therefore conclude, after this perhaps too elaborate inspection of the whole position,
that on the execution of the deed of family arrangement the two grandchildren
became absolutely entitled as against the trustees to the whole of the remaining
assets of the residuary estate, with the result that s 22(5) of the Finance Act 1965,
applies. This, however, is not the charging section. The charging section is s 25(3), *j*
and this section is framed in the singular. The Crown say that, bearing particularly
in mind the cross-reference to s 22(5) therein contained, it cannot possibly be read
as confined to a single person becoming absolutely entitled, but must embrace

---

1   [1974] 1 All ER at 858, [1974] 2 WLR at 574, [1974] STC at 63

a 'persons' as well as 'a person' so becoming entitled, and they refer to the Interpretation Act 1889, s 1, in this connection. Counsel for the respondents, on the other hand, stoutly maintains that this section applies only to a single individual becoming so entitled, and says that it is not sufficient for the Crown to seek to rely on the Interpretation Act 1889 because, in order to make good their argument, they will have to read into that subsection not only the plural as well as the singular but also the words 'jointly' after the plural 'persons'. I see the force of that argument, but I
b am not persuaded thereby. I see no necessity to read in anything more than the plural, and the cross-reference to s 22(5) then, as it seems to me, explains the sense in which the plural is to be understood.

Thus the conclusion of the whole matter appears to me to be that when the deed of family arrangement was executed the two grandchildren became, for the purposes of capital gains tax, jointly absolutely entitled as against the trustees of their grand-
c father's will trusts to the remaining residue of the estate not thereby appropriated to answer their aunts' annuities within the meaning of the Finance Act 1965, s 22(5), and the Finance Act 1969, Sch 19, para 9, and that, consequent thereon, the trustees are, by virtue of s 25(3), deemed for the purposes of capital gains tax to have disposed of the whole of such remaining residue and immediately reacquired the same in their capacity as trustees for a consideration equal to its market value. I have already
d indicated the figure of £10,000 is purely notional, and the actual figures will now remain to be worked out by the parties.

I have been supplied with a schedule of the assets forming part of the residuary estate as at 27th January 1969, and, although there are no valuations in regard to any of the assets, it would appear from a brief inspection thereof that, apart from a farm and 21 acres of land and about £3,000 out on mortgage, the vast bulk of the assets
e are shares quoted on the stock exchange. As a practical matter, any moneys out on mortgage are not capable of producing a capital gain, although they may possibly produce a capital loss in certain circumstances. So for practical purposes, if one excludes the land, on any footing each of the grandchildren has become absolutely entitled as against the trustees to one half of those shares, with the inevitable consequence of a charge to capital gains tax in relation thereto, even if one were to accept
f the argument of counsel for the respondents on s 25(3) being confined to the singular.

However, he did put forward a further argument to the effect that in such a case that subsection would not apply, because for the purposes of capital gains tax a holding of shares was a single entity, and for this he relied on the Finance Act 1965, Sch 7, para 2(1), which reads as follows:

g   'Any number of shares of the same class held by one person in one capacity shall for the purposes of this Part of this Act be regarded as indistinguishable parts of a single asset (in this paragraph referred to as a holding) growing or diminishing on the occasions on which additional shares of the class in question are acquired, or some of the shares of the class in question are disposed of.'

h I think this whole argument is misconceived. Schedule 7 is introduced by s 22(9) for the purposes of the computation of capital gains tax, not for the purposes of somehow making it impossible to regard a person as becoming absolutely entitled to that fraction of a composite holding to which he is, as a matter of equity, properly entitled. I see no difficulty at all in reading s 25(3) in the case, for example, where as here, one of the grandchildren has become on any footing absolutely entitled to
j one half of a larger parcel of shares as follows: 'On the occasion when one of the grandchildren has become absolutely entitled to any settled property [namely, here, one half of the trustees' holding of shares in X Ltd] as against the trustees, all the assets forming part of the settled property to which he becomes so entitled [namely, the said one half of the shares] shall be deemed to have been disposed of by the trustees and immediately reacquired by them in their capacity as trustees, etc.'

I point this out only because it appears to me that the economic content of this whole case, so far as the taxpaying trustees are concerned, is really very small: it is *a* limited to such tax as is payable in respect of a few small parcels of unquoted shares and the land, at the most. Be that as it may, however, I have no hesitation in coming to the conclusion that the main case presented by counsel on behalf of the Crown is correct, and that this appeal must be allowed.

Appeal allowed. Case remitted to the Special Commissioners to determine assessment in *b* *accordance with the judgment of the court.*

Solicitors: *Solicitor of Inland Revenue;* Greenwoods, Peterborough (for the respondents).

Rengan Krishnan Esq Barrister.

c

Practice Direction

d

CHANCERY DIVISION

Practice – Chambers – Chancery Division – Masters' powers.

1. In view of the amendment to RSC Ord 99, r 4, effected by the Rules of the *e* Supreme Court (Amendment) Order 1975[1], which comes into force on 1st March 1975, the judges of the Chancery Division have agreed that further powers in relation to proceedings under the Inheritance (Family Provision) Act 1938 may properly be exercised by the chancery masters.

2. Paragraph 3 of the memorandum on the powers of the chancery masters dated 18th December 1974[2] is amended with effect from 1st March 1975 by the *f* addition of the following item:

'(v) Under s 2 of the Inheritance (Family Provision) Act 1938, as amended, extending the time within which an application for reasonable provision may be made under that Act, and under s 4A of that Act, for interim maintenance.'

R E BALL *g*
Chief Master
21st February 1975 Chancery Division

1 SI 1975 No 128
2 Page 255, ante, [1975] 1 WLR 129

R v London Borough of Tower Hamlets, ex parte Kayne-Levenson and another

COURT OF APPEAL, CIVIL DIVISION
LORD DENNING MR, LORD DIPLOCK AND LAWTON LJ
25th, 26th, 27th, 28th NOVEMBER, 20th DECEMBER 1974

Street trading – Licence – Qualification to hold licence – Person already holding licence for another pitch – Whether trader entitled to apply for licence for another pitch – Whether borough council having power to grant trader licences to operate separate pitches at the same time – London County Council (General Powers) Act 1947, s 21(1) (as substituted by the London County Council (General Powers) Act 1962, s 33).

Street trading – Licence – Application – Competing applications – Discretion of borough council to choose between competing applications – Adoption of waiting list – Power of borough council to give preference to applicants not already holding licence for another pitch in area – London County Council (General Powers) Act 1947, s 21(1) (as substituted by the London County Council (General Powers) Act 1962, s 33).

Street trading – Licence – Refusal – Right of appeal – What constitutes refusal – Competing applications for licence – Council deciding to put application on waiting list – Council unable to accede to application because of lack of available space – Decision to place applicant on waiting list constituting a refusal – Duty of council to issue notice of refusal and to inform applicant of right of appeal – London County Council (General Powers) Act 1947, ss 21(3)(b), 25(1).

Street trading – Licence – Application – Nominated relative – Relative nominated by licence holder as person to whom he desires licence to be granted in event of licence holder's death – Timeous application by relative following death of licence holder – Duty of council to grant licence to relative unless grounds for refusal specified in statute – London County Council (General Powers) Act 1947, s 21(2A) (as inserted by the London County Council (General Powers) Act 1962, s 33).

Street trading – Licence – Refusal – Grounds for refusal – Applicant unsuitable to hold a licence – Unsuitability – Applicant holding licence for another pitch in same area – Whether rendering applicant 'unsuitable' to hold licence – London County Council (General Powers) Act 1947, s 21(3)(a).

For some years Mrs L held an annual licence from the respondent borough council for street trading at pitch 1 in Goulston Street in the Petticoat Lane market. She ran the pitch with the help of her son, Harold, and his wife. Harold also held an annual licence for another pitch (pitch 107) in the market. In her applications for renewal of the licence in 1969 and 1970, Mrs L, in accordance with s 21(1)[a] of the London County Council (General Powers) Act 1947, nominated Harold as being a relative associated with or dependent on the business carried on at pitch 1, to whom she desired her licence

---

a Section 21(1), as substituted and so far as material, provides: 'A person requiring an annual licence or the renewal of an annual licence shall make application in writing to the borough council and shall in such application state . . . (d) the street or streets in which he intends so to sell or expose or offer for sale and the nature and type of any receptacle which he intends to use in connection with any sale or exposure or offer for sale; and may specify the name and address of a relative of his who is associated with, or dependent upon, the business of street trading in respect of which the application is made and to whom he desires the licence to be granted in the event of his death.' Y

to be granted in the event of her death. In the application form for 1971 onwards the borough council incorporated a note stating that a nominated relative should not be a *a* person holding a current licence in the market. In consequence of that note Mrs L omitted Harold's name from her applications for 1971 and 1972 and no other relative was nominated to succeed her. In 1972 a daughter, Samantha, was born to Harold, and Mrs L, in her application for 1973, nominated Samantha as the relative to succeed to her licence. Mrs L was granted a licence for pitch 1 expiring on 31st December 1973. She died, however, on 13th February 1973. On 23rd February, within the time per- *b* mitted under s 21(2A)[b] of the 1947 Act to a nominated relative to apply for the deceased relative's licence, Harold's wife applied in Samantha's name for the licence for pitch 1. That application was refused by the council under s 21(3)(a)[c] on the ground that Samantha was not a suitable person to hold a licence because of her age. The council notified Samantha, in accordance with s 37[d] of the London County Council (General Powers) Act 1958, that she had the right to appeal to a magistrates' court. *c* An appeal was lodged on Samantha's behalf. In June 1973, no licence for pitch 1 having been granted, Harold and his wife made separate applications in their own names for the annual licence for pitch 1 expiring on 31st December 1973. Harold's application was rejected by the council on the ground that, since he already held a current licence, he was not entitled under the 1947 Act to another. The council did not issue a formal notice of refusal, taking the view that his application was not a valid *d* application but merely a request to vary the conditions of his existing licence to include pitch 1, and that there was no right of appeal against the refusal of such a request. The council operated a system of waiting lists for pitches in popular streets in the market and when an applicant who was not a nominated relative, and who held no other current licence in the area, applied for a pitch in one of those streets it was the practice of the council to place him at the bottom of the waiting list; when a pitch *e* fell vacant it was first offered to the person at the top of the list; if he refused it, it was offered to the next person on the list; a person who refused two successive offers was removed from the list. The application by Harold's wife was placed on the waiting list for pitches in Goulston Street. Again the council did not issue a formal notice of refusal; they informed Harold's wife that, although the application had not been refused, it might be some time before it was dealt with. Harold and his wife applied to *f* the Divisional Court for orders of mandamus requiring the council to hear and determine their applications according to law. The court held that the applications had in effect been refused but granted orders directing the council to issue formal notices of refusal and to notify the applicants of their right to appeal. The council appealed.

Held – (i) (Lord Denning MR dissenting) There was nothing in the 1947 Act to prevent *g* a street trader from applying for separate annual licences to operate individual pitches at the same time or to prohibit the borough council from granting a trader separate licences (see p 652 *g*, p 655 *g* and *j* to p 656 *b*, post).

(ii) However, where the applicants for a vacant pitch did not include a nominated relative, the council, in the exercise of their discretion to choose between competing *h* applicants, were entitled to adopt a policy whereby preference was given to applicants who did not hold a current licence for another pitch in the area. Furthermore where competing applications for a vacant pitch were made by more than one person who

---

b Section 21(2A) is set out at p 651 *c* and *d*, post
c Section 21(3), so far as material, is set out at p 649 *h*, post   *j*
d Section 37, so far as material, provides: 'When any decision of a borough council under
    Part IV (Regulation of street trading) of the London County Council (General Powers)
    Act 1947 . . . is notified to any person and that person has a right to appeal to a magistrates'
    court against that decision by virtue of any provision in the said Act of 1947 . . . the borough
    council shall at the same time notify that person in writing—(i) that if he is aggrieved by
    the decision he may appeal to a magistrates' court . . .'

a did not already hold a current licence for another pitch, the council were entitled to operate a waiting list. Placing an applicant on the waiting list was, however, tantamount to refusing to grant his application on the ground specified in s 21(3)(*b*) of the 1947 Act, i e that there was insufficient space available. It followed that in such cases the applicant should be given formal notice of refusal and be told of his right to appeal under s 25(1) of the 1947 Act, even though the decision to grant a licence to one of competing applicants was an administrative decision which could not be successfully

b challenged on appeal unless there were grounds for certiorari such as want of natural justice (see p 646 *h*, p 647 *f* and *g*, p 648 *a* and *b*, p 650 *d e* and *j*, p 651 *g*, p 652 *b* and *c* and p 656 *b c* and *g*, post).

(ii) Where however a timeous application was made by a nominated relative, the council were bound to grant a licence to that applicant, by virtue of s 21(2A), unless

c there were grounds for refusing the application under s 21(3) or s 24(5). The mere fact that the nominated relative already held an annual licence for another pitch in the area did not render him 'unsuitable', within s 21(3)(*a*), to hold the additional licence, for the word 'unsuitable' referred to personal unsuitability, although (per Lord Diplock and Lawton LJ) inability to exercise adequate supervision over his employees at the other pitch might render him 'unsuitable'. It followed that the

d council were not entitled to prohibit the nomination of a relative under s 21(1) merely because he held a current annual licence for another pitch and they had been wrong to incorporate the notice to that effect on their application forms (see p 646 *j* to p 647 *a*, p 649 *j* to 650 *b*, p 651 *e* and *f* and p 656 *h* and *j*, post).

(iv) The council's decision (a) not to grant Harold's application and (b) to place his wife's application on the waiting list amounted in each case to a refusal of the application for an annual licence for pitch 1 which gave each of them a right of appeal under

e s 25(1). The council should therefore have issued formal refusals and, in accordance with s 37 of the 1958 Act, should have notified the applicants of their right of appeal. The omission to do so was not a mere technicality; it was deliberate and based on an erroneous view of the law. Accordingly, the Divisional Court were entitled to grant orders of mandamus and there was no ground for interfering with their decision.

f The appeal would therefore be dismissed (see p 645 *g*, p 653 *e* and *g*, p 654 *b* and p 655 *a*, post).

Notes
For annual licences for street trading and the grounds on which an annual licence may be refused, see 33 Halsbury's Laws (3rd Edn) 587-589, paras 999, 1000; for appeals against decisions of a council, see ibid 593, para 1006, and for cases on the subject,

g see 26 Digest (Repl) 482-484, 1684-1700.

For the London County Council (General Powers) Act 1947, ss 21, 25, see 20 Halsbury's Statutes (3rd Edn) 268, 273.

For the London County Council (General Powers) Act 1958, s 37, see ibid 395.

Cases referred to in judgments

h Perilly v Tower Hamlets Borough Council [1972] 3 All ER 513, [1973] 1 QB 9, [1972] 3 WLR 573, 136 JP 799, 70 LGR 474, CA.

R v Thames Magistrates' Court, ex parte Greenbaum (1957) 55 LGR 129, CCA, 26 Digest (Repl) 482, 1692.

Stepney Borough Council v Schneider (1960) 124 JP 401, 58 LGR 202, DC.

Appeal

j The applicants, Harold Kayne-Levenson and Shirley Marina Eileen Kayne-Levenson, applied for orders of mandamus directed to the respondents, the mayor, alderman and burgesses of the London Borough of Tower Hamlets ('the borough council'), requiring them to hear and determine according to law two applications, each dated 7th June 1973, made by each applicant for a street trading licence to trade at pitch 1 in Goulston Street in the London Borough of Tower Hamlets. On 2nd May 1974 the

Divisional Court of the Queen's Bench Division (Lord Widgery CJ, Ashworth and
Bristow JJ) held that the borough council had heard and determined the applications *a*
and in effect refused them, but that they had failed to issue formal notices of refusal of
the applications including notification of a right of appeal against the refusal. Accordingly, in each case, the court made an order directing that, unless the borough council
were prepared to allow the application and grant a licence, they should forthwith
transmit to the applicant a notice of decision which was to include an intimation of the
applicant's right of appeal. The borough council appealed. The facts are set out in *b*
the judgment of Lord Denning MR.

James Comyn QC and *John Blair-Gould* for the borough council.
Colin Ross-Munro QC and *M Fitzmaurice* for the applicants.

Cur adv vult

20th December. The following judgments were read.   *c*

LORD DENNING MR. Old Mrs Annie Levenson had one of the best pitches in
the street market called Petticoat Lane. It was pitch 1. She ran it with the help of her
son Harold and his wife Shirley. She had an annual licence for the pitch which was
granted by the borough council. But she was getting on in years and the question
was: what was to happen to the pitch on her death? By statute[1] she was entitled to *d*
nominate a relative to succeed her. In her application for each of the years 1969 and
1970 she nominated her son Harold. But in her application for the year 1971 she nominated no one. The reason was because the borough council stated on the form:
'The relative so specified should NOT be a person holding a current licence in the Tower
Hamlets area.'

Now old Mrs Levenson's son Harold did hold a licence for another pitch. He held a *e*
licence for pitch 107. So old Mrs Levenson did not nominate him. And she could not
nominate his wife Shirley because a daughter-in-law does not come within the category
of 'relatives' entitled to succeed.

Likewise in her application for the following year, 1972, old Mrs Levenson nominated no one to succeed, and for the same reasons. But on 27th September 1972 her
son and his wife had a baby daughter, Samantha. This baby was a *grand-daughter* of *f*
the old lady and did come within the category of 'relatives' entitled to succeed. So on
10th October 1972, when old Mrs Levenson applied for a renewal of pitch 1, she
nominated her grand-daughter Samantha.

Four months later, on 13th February 1973, old Mrs Levenson died. On 23rd February 1973 Samantha's mother applied in *Samantha's* name for pitch 1. Someone at
the town hall told her that Samantha was too young to be a licence-holder.   *g*

On 13th and 27th March 1973 Harold wrote to the borough council suggesting that
his wife should run pitch 1 for Samantha until she was old enough to become a licence-
holder. As an alternative Harold asked if he could transfer his own pitch 107 to his
partner, Mr Bluoch, and then be entitled to apply for his mother's pitch, 1.

On 28th March 1973 the borough council refused Samantha's application and sent a
formal letter of refusal on which they notified Samantha that she could appeal to the *h*
magistrates' court. That notification was made necessary by statute: see s 37 of the
London County Council (General Powers) Act 1958. Samantha's father then went to
solicitors. They duly gave notice of appeal on her behalf to the magistrates' court.
They also wrote to the borough council asking for their reasons for refusing Samantha's
application. The council replied saying that: (1) she was not 'associated with or
dependent upon' the business carried on by old Mrs Levenson; and (2) that, in the *i*
opinion of the council, she was unsuitable to hold a licence.

In June 1973 Harold and his wife—each of them—applied for a licence for pitch 1.
Their solicitor wrote telling the council that if a licence were granted to either of

---

1 London County Council (General Powers) Act 1947, s. 21(1), as substituted by the London
  County Council (General Powers) Act 1962, s 33

them, they would not proceed with the appeal on behalf of Samantha. So they
a applied to the magistrates for an adjournment of Samantha's appeal. This was granted
pending the determination by the council of the application by Harold and his wife.
The council did not grant the applications by Harold and his wife. The correspondence shows that their reasons were that 'as Mr. Kayne-Levenson already holds a
licence, another licence cannot be granted to him', and that 'the application of Mrs.
Kayne-Levenson has been placed on the waiting list', but it was added that, as 'there
b is currently a very long list of applicants for licences in Goulston Street, it will probably
be some time before Mrs. Kayne-Levenson's application can be dealt with'.

The solicitors for Harold and his wife wrote to the council on 19th November 1973
saying that no formal refusals had been received to their request, and asked for formal
refusals so that they could appeal to the magistrates' court; and then the appeals of
Samantha and Harold and his wife could be heard at the same time. On 22nd Novem-
c ber 1973 the council's solicitors replied saying that the applications had not been
refused, that Harold's application was not valid as he was already the holder of a
current licence, and therefore could not be granted another licence, and that his wife's
application had not been refused, as she had been put on the waiting list.

Thereupon the solicitors for Harold and his wife applied for a mandamus requiring
the borough council to determine their application according to law. The Divisional
d Court held that the council had determined the applications—in that they had, to
all intents and purposes, refused them—but that the council had failed in their
statutory duty in that they had failed to issue a formal notification of refusal to the
applicants. The Divisional Court ordered that 'they should forthwith notify in writing
their refusal according to law'.

The borough council appeal to this court.
e
1. The decision of the Divisional Court

Counsel for the borough council submitted that, so long as Samantha's appeal was
still pending before the magistrates' court, it was not reasonably practicable for the
borough council to give any decision on the applications by Harold and his wife. He
pointed out that, if Samantha's appeal were allowed and the magistrate granted her a
f licence for pitch 1, it would be impossible for the council to grant a licence to Harold
and his wife for the same pitch.

This was a new point not taken below or in the notice of appeal. We allowed it to
be raised. But it is a bad point. The solicitors for Harold and his wife wanted to appeal
to the magistrates' court. They wanted their appeals to be heard at the same time as
Samantha's so that the magistrate would have all the applications before him together.
g That was a very sensible suggestion. If adopted there would be no risk of any conflict.
I think the borough council ought to have acceded to it. They had already decided
not to grant the applications by Harold and his wife. They ought to have issued formal
refusals so that they could appeal and bring on their appeals at the same time as
Samantha's.

I agree with the Divisional Court on this point and would dismiss the appeal. But
h during the course of the case many points were argued on which the parties desired
the opinion of the court. So we will try to give them.

2. One trader, one licence, one pitch at a time

The borough council have a rule whereby a street trader is only entitled to one
licence for one pitch at a time. They regard this as a positive law to be derived from
j the London County Council (General Powers) Act 1947 as interpreted in *R v Thames
Magistrates' Court, ex parte Greenbaum*[1]. This raises a nice point of interpretation. The
key to it is to be found, I think, in the use made by the draftsman of the singular and
the plural. He does not apply the general rule laid down in the Interpretation Act 1889
that the singular includes the plural. When this draftsman intends the singular, he uses

the singular. When he intends the plural, he uses the plural. Thus you will find
him, time and again, using the words 'street or streets', 'class or classes', 'day or *a*
days', and 'time or times'. In contrast, he uses the singular only in 'a person', 'a relative', 'a holder of an annual licence', or 'the position or place'. Again, when he uses
the word 'person', he clearly does not include a body corporate.

With this in mind, I turn to read the 1947 Act as a whole, together with the amending Act, the London County Council (General Powers) Act 1962. It is clear to my
mind that a street trader's licence is purely personal to him. It is an annual licence *b*
for one year only; but it may be regularly renewed so long as nothing untoward
occurs. At the same time, he should not be given a prescription to conduct it as he
pleases. He can only hold one licence. He cannot hold two. The holder cannot hold
it jointly with anyone else. He cannot assign or transfer it to anyone else. Nor can he
sublet it or part with it to another. He cannot dispose of it by will. He must himself
conduct the business personally, though he may employ any other person to assist *c*
him. If he dies, the licence dies with him. It cannot survive to a partner or joint
owner. All that he can do is to nominate a relative to whom he desires the licence to
be granted on his death; and then it must be a relative who is associated with the
business, or dependent on it. Furthermore, the Act, as I read it, when dealing with a
stationary trader, contemplates that he shall only conduct his business at one pitch
at a time. *d*

Seeing that the licence is so personal, the 1947 Act only allows the holder to conduct
his business at one pitch at a time. He is not allowed to conduct it at two pitches at
the same time. This follows from the way in which s 21(5)(*a*) is worded. It enables
the borough council to prescribe 'the position or place in any such street' at which the
licensee may sell his wares. The draftsman deliberately uses the singular 'the position
or place'. It is to be *one* position or place. The draftsman avoids the plural. He does *e*
not say 'position or positions', or 'place or places'. He says too 'in any such street'.
When he is thinking of a stationary trader, he says 'street'. But when he is thinking
of peripatetic traders (as in the opening words of s 21(5)(*a*)), he uses 'street or streets'.
But when it comes to the days and times on which the holder can sell, the draftsman
uses the plural 'day or days' and 'time or times'. So it follows that the borough council
may prescribe *one* pitch for one day and time, and *another* pitch for another day and *f*
time: but *not* two pitches for the same day at the same time. That is the way in which
the borough council have interpreted and applied the Act. For instance, in the present
case old Mrs Levenson originally had a prescription for pitch 1 on Sundays and pitch
3 on Mondays to Saturdays, but afterwards it was varied so as to exclude no 3. Such
being the way in which the borough council have interpreted and applied the Act,
I would be reluctant to interpret it differently, especially as they attach much import- *g*
ance to it: and, after all, they are the persons to whom Parliament has entrusted the
administration of the Act.

So my conclusion can be stated shortly: one trader, one licence, one pitch at a time.
I regard this as a positive rule; but in any case it is a rule which the council may adopt
as a matter of policy in their administration of the Act. And this I gather is the view
of Lord Diplock and Lawton LJ. *h*

3. *Nomination of a relative*

In 1971, however, the borough council carried that rule too far. On every application for a licence, they told the applicant that he might specify a relative to succeed,
but then added these words, and underlined them:

> 'The relative so specified should NOT be a person holding a current licence in *j*
> the Tower Hamlets area.'

It was because of these words that old Mrs Levenson did not specify her son Harold.

Now, I think those added words were wrong. They are not warranted by the
statute. The holder of a licence is entitled, as of right, to specify 'a relative of his who

is associated with the business or dependent on it': see s 21(1) of the 1947 Act. So old
a Mrs Levenson was entitled, as of right, to specify her son Harold, who helped her in
the business. If she had done so, then on her death, he would be entitled to be granted
an annual licence in respect of her pitch 1. He was in no way unsuitable to hold it.
'Unsuitable' in s 21(3)(a) refers to personal unsuitability. The fact that Harold, her
son, already held another licence for pitch 107 would not make him 'unsuitable' to
hold a licence for his mother's pitch 1. All that it meant was that he might have to
b give up his pitch 107, because, on the rule I have stated, he ought not to have two
pitches at one and the same time. This could easily be managed either by varying his
old licence so as to prescribe pitch 1 in place of pitch 107, or, alternatively, by waiting
until the end of the year when he could be granted an annual licence for pitch 1, but
not for pitch 107.
       Seeing that old Mrs Levenson was misled by the note on the form—which was
c wrongly worded—it is clear that the position should be rectified. The form should be
treated as if she had specified her son Harold, in which case he would be entitled to
an annual licence for pitch 1. He would not be entitled to retain, at the same time,
his licence for pitch 107. But his wife could, no doubt, apply for that pitch; and the
council in their discretion grant it to her, or they could refuse it.
       We were glad to hear that in the circumstances the council are likely to grant Harold
d pitch no 1 for the ensuing year.

4. *The application of a non-relative*
       When there is no relative who is entitled to the pitch, there may be many applicants
for it. How is the borough council to decide between them? *Stepney Borough Council v
Schneider*[1] said: 'first come, first served.' But that case was overruled by this court in
e *Perilly v Tower Hamlets Borough Council*[2]. We said they ought to consider the merits of
each case, but other things being equal, they could say 'first come, first served'.
Applying this principle, suppose the council decide in favour of *one* of the applicants
and grant the pitch to him. They notify the other applicants that their applications
are refused, and that they may appeal to the magistrates' court. Suppose that all or
any of them appeal? What is the magistrate to do? He cannot grant the licence to any
f of them; for this simple reason, that the council have already granted it to the successful applicant. The magistrate has no jurisdiction to take away his grant; and he
cannot grant a licence to another for the same pitch. It was so held in *Greenbaum's*
case[3]. This means that, when the borough council have validly granted an annual
licence to one applicant, the disappointed applicants can never appeal successfully.
In short, the decision to grant a licence is an administrative decision which cannot be
g successfully challenged, unless there is a want of natural justice or other ground for the
interference of the High Court.

5. *The waiting list*
       In this state of affairs, the borough council have taken this course: they have a
number of applicants for one pitch; they grant the licence to one, and put the others
h on the 'waiting list'. They write to each of the unsuccessful applicants and tell him
that his name will be placed on the 'waiting list'. This 'waiting list' is a list of applicants
for a pitch in that street. Names are added in order of date. Then when any pitch in
that street becomes vacant, it is offered to the names in that list. If the first one does
not want it, it is offered to the next, and so forth. If any applicant refuses it twice,
he goes down to the bottom of the list. The waiting list for some streets is so long that
j a person may have to wait for years before he will be offered a pitch in it.
       It appears that, in practice, when the borough council put a name on a waiting list,

---

1   (1960) 124 JP 401
2   [1972] 3 All ER 513, [1973] 1 QB 9
3   (1957) 55 LGR 129

they do not treat it as a refusal, and accordingly they do not give him formal notification, or tell him that he can appeal.   *a*

I see no objection to the council keeping a waiting list or operating it as they do. It is a convenient piece of administration. But I think they should alter their form of notification. To put an applicant on the waiting list is tantamount to a refusal. They should treat it as such and tell him so. It is a refusal on the ground that there is no space available: see section 21(3)(*b*) of the 1947 Act. They should notify him that it is a refusal and tell him of his right to appeal. This is of little use to him. But they can *b* soften the blow by telling him that his name will be put on the waiting list.

Conclusion

The borough council of Tower Hamlets is entrusted with the administration of the street traders in Petticoat Lane. Parliament has evolved rules and procedures which appear to work well. The great majority of these are warranted by the statutory provisions, and I do not think the courts should interfere with them. But there are a *c* few instances where the existing practice should be modified. On this being done, I trust there will be no further need for litigation. I would dismiss the appeal.

LORD DIPLOCK (read by Lord Denning MR). The need for a licence to engage *d* in street trading stems from s 17(1) of the London County Council (General Powers) Act 1947, which makes it an offence to do so without a licence. It is in the following terms:

> 'Subject to the provisions of this Part of this Act it shall be unlawful for any person—(*a*) to engage in street trading in or from a stationary position in any street within a borough; or (*b*) to engage in street trading in any designated street *e* whether or not in or from a stationary position; unless that person is authorised to do so by a street trading licence.'

The subsection contemplates two kinds of trading: from a stationary position or pitch and peripatetic trading. There is nothing in this subsection to suggest that any person is restricted to a single licence. Indeed it would appear to suggest that a person may hold separate licences for peripatetic and stationary trading and may hold *f* these for different streets and for different pitches in a single street.

Licences may be of two kinds, temporary and annual. It is only with the latter that the instant case is concerned. They are governed by s 21 of the 1947 Act as substantially amended in 1957 and 1962. The contents of an annual licence are dealt with in sub-s (5) which reads as follows:

> 'An annual licence shall be in a form prescribed by the Secretary of State and *g* may prescribe—(*a*) the street or streets in which and the position or place in any such street at which the licensee may sell or expose or offer for sale articles or things under the authority of the licence; (*b*) the class or classes of articles or things which the licensee may so sell or expose or offer for sale provided that no article of food shall be classed with any commodity not being an article of food; *h* (*c*) the day or days on which and the time or times at or during which the licensee may sell or expose or offer for sale articles or things as aforesaid; (*d*) the nature and type of any receptacle which may be used by the licensee in connection with any sale or exposure or offer for sale and the number of such receptacles which may so be used; and on any occasion of the renewal of an annual licence the borough council may vary such prescriptions.'   *j*

It provides for various types of licences distinguished from one another by the restrictions ('prescriptions') which are imposed on the place, time and kind of trading which they authorise. Prescriptions under (*a*) permit of the issue of such peripatetic and pitch licences; prescriptions under (*c*) permit licences to be confined to particular trading days and hours.

a Section 21(1) deals with the application for an annual licence. It specifies the particulars which the application *must* contain. These include particulars corresponding to the prescriptions that may be imposed under sub-s (5)(*b*) and (*d*) and the street or streets in which the applicant intends to trade; but there is no mandatory requirement that it should include particulars corresponding to prescriptions under paras (*a*) or (*c*).

b In particular, there is no requirement that the applicant should state whether his application is for a peripatetic or a pitch licence or, if the latter, whether it is for a particular pitch. It cannot, however, reasonably be inferred from this that Parliament intended to debar an applicant from confining his application to a particular pitch. It must have been notorious in 1947 that the value of pitches as trading points in any street might vary widely as between one another according to their location in the street. An applicant might well consider that whereas the pitch at which he wished

c to trade would be worth the fees and charges to which he would be liable under ss 23 and 26, a pitch in a less favourable location in the same street could not be used by him for trading otherwise than at a loss. It cannot be supposed that Parliament intended to force on an applicant a pitch that he did not want.

These considerations were in my view sufficient to make it plain, even before the amendment of the section, that although an applicant was not bound to specify the

d pitch he wanted, he was entitled to do so and to confine his application to a particular pitch. They are reinforced by the new sub-s (2A) added by the 1962 Act which grants special rights to nominated relatives of deceased licence holders. This refers in terms to an application for the 'grant [of] an annual licence in respect of the position or place' at which the deceased licensee is entitled to trade.

Furthermore I see nothing in the subsection to prevent a person from applying for more than one pitch whether in the same street or in different streets or from doing

e so either by a single application for more than one pitch or by separate applications for each pitch.

A licence is personal to the licensee but covers persons employed by him to assist him in the conduct of his business (s 28). An annual licence expires on 31st December of the year in which it was first granted. It can be renewed, but a fresh application by

f the holder is needed (s 21(6)). The 1947 Act had no express provision for the voluntary surrender of a licence before the date of its expiration; but a reference to surrender was added by the 1957 Act after the decision of the Court of Appeal in *R v Thames Magistrates' Court, ex parte Greenbaum*[1].

Section 21(2) places on the borough council a prima facie obligation to grant or renew an annual licence as soon as reasonably practicable after the receipt of the

g application. The only grounds on which they can refuse to do so, except where a pitch has become vacant as the result of the death of a licensee, are those set out in sub-s (3). The grounds that are relevant for the purposes of the instant case are:

'(*a*) the applicant or licensee is on account of misconduct or for any other sufficient reason in their opinion unsuitable to hold such a licence; or (*b*) the space available in the street or streets to which the application relates or which is or are

h prescribed by the licence is at the date of such application or becomes at any time after the grant of such licence insufficient to permit of the applicant or licensee engaging therein in any street trading or in the particular street trading proposed to be or actually carried on by him without causing undue interference with or inconvenience to traffic in such street or streets . . .'

j Paragraph (*a*) is in my view confined to the personal unsuitability of the applicant to engage in street trading of the kind or at the place for which he seeks a licence. The borough council are not, in my view, entitled by this paragraph to give effect to an undiscriminating policy applicable to all street traders of limiting them to a single pitch even though there is vacant space for them at the other pitches for which they

1 (1957) 55 LGR 129

have applied. This does not mean that if on an application by a particular individual for an additional pitch the council may not refuse his application on the ground of his *a* unsuitability, if they are of opinion that his commitments at his other pitches would prevent his exercising adequate supervision over his employees at the additional pitch or—although it seems unlikely that this would occur in practice—if they are of opinion that he would thereby acquire an undesirable monopoly of trade in the area concerned.

Paragraph (*b*) deals with refusals of applications on the ground of shortage of space *b* in the street or streets to which the application relates. There are two circumstances in which this ground for refusal may arise where the application is confined to a particular pitch. The first is where at the time of the application that pitch is already occupied by the holder of a current annual licence. In the context of a statute authorising street trading, the expression 'traffic' should, in my view, be construed to embrace all kinds of legitimate use of the street, including its use by street traders for pursuing *c* their lawful activities, even though this involves their occupying a stationary position for substantial periods. So where application is made for a pitch which is already occupied, the borough council are entitled to refuse it—and in practice must do so as long as the existing licence continues.

The other circumstances in which this ground for refusal may be applicable is where a particular pitch is vacant and there are concurrent applications for it by more than *d* one applicant. It was held by this court in *Greenbaum's* case[1] that the selection between competing applicants is a matter of administrative discretion to be exercised by the borough council and that the manner of its exercise was not subject to appeal to petty sessions under s 25 of the 1947 Act, though no doubt it would be subject to certiorari if the council had taken into consideration matters which the statute on its true construction did not allow them to take into consideration or had failed to take into *e* consideration matters that they should.

This decision, given at a time when the s 21 contained no sub-s (2A), which gives priority to a nominated relative of a deceased licence holder for a pitch which has become vacant on his death, in my view, is still correct as respects selection between competing applicants where there is none who falls within the new priority class. Parts of the reasoning in *Greenbaum's* case[1] are in my view invalidated by the subse- *f* quent amendments to the Act. These I will deal with later; but the underlying reason for rejecting a construction of the Act which would entitle unsuccessful applicants for a particular pitch to appeal to the magistrate against the grant of a licence for that pitch to the successful applicant is that Parliament must be presumed not to have intended the words it used to bear a meaning of which the practical consequences would be unjust and contrary to the manifest purpose of the Act. The promoters of *g* the legislation, which is a private Act, must have known that there might be many applicants for a profitable pitch in a popular street market when it fell vacant, and only one could be successful. If each of the unsuccessful applicants, whose numbers might run into scores, had a right of appeal to the magistrate, the magistrate would have to hear them all at hearings to which the successful applicant would not be a party. Since there would be no appeal by the successful applicant, the magistrate *h* would have no power under s 25 to cancel the licence to him granted by the council; so the only effective order he could make in any of the appeals would be to confirm the council's refusal. Two rival traders cannot trade simultaneously from the same pitch without risk of disorder.

Faced with concurrent applications for the same pitch, the council, 'as soon as reasonably practicable' after their receipt, must first decide which one to grant. *i* They should refuse the other applications on ground (*b*). Although in theory the un-successful applicants would have a right of appeal against the refusal, the only course open to the magistrate would be to confirm the refusal.

---

1 (1957) 55 LGR 129

a   Although the council have a wide discretion to follow any policy which they think fair and reasonable and conducive to the orderly allocations between competing applicants for vacant pitches for which the demand is greater than the supply, their discretion is now fettered in the case of applicants who fall within the priority class created by the amendments to s 21 introduced by the 1962 Act. This amendment authorised an applicant for an annual licence to nominate in his application form a relative of his associated with or dependent on the business of street trading in respect

b   of which the application was made, to whom he desired the licence to be granted in the event of his death. A new sub-s (2A) defined the rights of such a nominated relative as follows:

> '(a) When the holder of an annual licence who has specified the name and address of a relative to whom he desires the licence to be granted dies the borough
>
> c   council shall not (except as provided in paragraph (b) of this subsection) grant an annual licence in respect of the position or place in a street at which the deceased licensee was entitled to sell or expose or offer for sale articles or things under the authority of his licence until the expiration of ten days from the date of the death of the licensee; (b) If during the said period of ten days the person specified by the deceased licensee, when making application for the licence, as the relative to
>
> d   whom he desired the licence to be granted in the event of his death makes application for the grant of an annual licence in respect of the position or place available in the street the borough council shall, save as provided by the next following subsection or by subsection (5) of section 24 (For preventing interference with traffic) of this Act, grant an annual licence to that person.'

e   The borough council has no discretion to refuse a timeous application by a nominated relative except on specific grounds, of which the only one relevant to the instant case is personal unsuitability under s 21(3)(a); since ex hypothesi the pitch is vacant at the time of the application and the ground of lack of space under s 21(3)(b) is not applicable. As I have already indicated, the mere fact that the nominated relative already holds a licence for another pitch does not constitute unsuitability within the meaning of s 21(3)(a), unless there are special circumstances such as his inability

f   to exercise adequate supervision over his employees at the additional pitch if it were granted to him.

In exercising their discretion to choose between competing applicants, *where there is none who falls within the priority class*, the council may adopt any policy they consider to be fair and reasonable and conducive to the orderly allocation of vacant pitches for which the demand is greater than the supply. In the exercise of their discretion I see

g   no reason why they should not as a general rule give preference to applicants for a particular pitch who do not hold a current licence for some other pitch within their area. Nor do I see any objection to their having recourse to a system involving the operation of a waiting list such as is used by the Tower Hamlets borough council for applicants who do not already hold a current licence for another pitch.

Under this system separate waiting lists are kept for each street where the demand

h   for pitches is greater than the supply, but not for any individual pitches in the street. For popular streets the waiting list runs into hundreds. When an applicant who holds no current licence applies for the first time for a pitch in a popular street, whether the application is for a particular pitch or generally for any vacant pitch in the street, he will not get it unless he is within the priority class or had analogous claims to succeed to a pitch becoming vacant on the death of a relative or surrendered by a

j   relative who has become too old or ill to continue to trade there. Instead he will be put at the bottom of the waiting list for the street. Whenever a pitch to which there is no priority claim falls vacant in that street it is first offered to the person who is at the top of the waiting list. If he refuses, it is offered to the next person on the list. A person who refuses two successive offers is removed from the waiting list.

This system was introduced in 1973 to avoid the abuses that had resulted from the application of the rigid rule requiring vacant pitches to be granted to the applicant who was first in point of time. This rule had been laid down by the Divisional Court in *Stepney Borough Council v Schneider*[1] and was overruled in *Perilly v Tower Hamlets Borough Council*[2]. The waiting list system is now well known and accepted as fair by street traders in the Tower Hamlets area. So an applicant who, on applying for an annual licence for a particular vacant site in a popular street, is told that his name has been put on the waiting list, will rightly understand this as a refusal of the annual licence for which he has applied, since, being at the bottom of the waiting list, there would be no prospect of his being offered any annual licence during the current year.

The confusion that has given rise to the instant proceedings is a consequence of the borough council's treating applicants in the priority class as subject to an overriding rule that a person may hold one licence only, whether the rule be one of law, as they contend, or alternatively a rule which it lies in their discretion to impose.

The contention that it is a rule of law is based on the judgments of the members of the Court of Appeal in *Greenbaum's* case[3]. In that case a popular pitch had fallen vacant in Goulston Street—there were 28 applicants for it. Two of them, Greenbaum and Gritzman, each had a current annual licence for another pitch in the same street. They did not want two pitches, but at that time the Act contained no provision for surrender of a current licence. So each applied for a 'transfer' from his existing pitch to the vacant pitch. The borough council granted the licence for the vacant pitch to Greenbaum—Gritzman's application they refused. He appealed to the magistrate. The magistrate allowed the appeal and ordered the council to issue the licence to Gritzman. Greenbaum, who was not a party to Gritzman's appeal, applied for certiorari to quash the magistrate's order. The Court of Appeal regarded both applications as being in substance applications for a variation of the prescription in a current licence prescribing the position or place at which the licensee was permitted to trade. The council's decision on Gritzman's application they treated as a refusal to vary a prescription in a current licence. From this refusal no right of appeal was granted by s 25(1) of the 1947 Act. So the magistrate had no jurisdiction to entertain Gritzman's appeal. That was the common ratio decidendi of all three members of the Court of Appeal. The court was not called on to consider what the position would have been if Gritzman, instead of seeking a transfer of his current licence from one pitch to another, had applied for a new licence for the vacant pitch to be held concurrently with his licence for his existing pitch. There are observations in the judgments from which an inference might be drawn that members of the court were of opinion that s 21 in its unamended form contemplated only one annual licence for each trader and did not provide for the grant to a single trader of separate licences for individual pitches. These observations were, however, obiter. Their underlying reasoning has, in my view, become inapplicable owing to the subsequent amendments to the Act to which I have previously referred. As the Act now stands I see nothing in it to prevent a street trader from applying for separate annual licences for individual pitches nor to prohibit the borough council from granting them.

Greenbaum's case[3] was decided before the 1962 amendments to s 21 created the priority class of nominated relatives of a deceased licence holder. It can be no authority for the proposition that the borough council have any discretion to refuse a timeous application by an applicant within this class for a separate licence for the pitch which has become vacant on the death of his relative, except on one of the grounds specified in s 21(3).

Applying these principles to the facts of the instant case, the trouble started in 1970 when the council incorporated in the application form a note to the effect that a nominated relative 'should NOT be a person holding a current licence in the Tower

---

1   (1960) 124 JP 401
2   [1972] 3 All ER 513, [1973] 1 QB 9
3   (1957) 55 LGR 129

Hamlets area'. This note caused old Mrs Levenson, who wished to nominate her son
a Harold (the first applicant) and had done so in previous applications forms, to omit
his name and eventually, in her application form for the annual licence current at the
time of her death in 1973, to substitute the name of Harold's baby daughter Samantha.
On Mrs Levenson's death, a timeous application for an annual licence for the current
pitch was made in the name of Samantha, then a few months old. This application
was refused on the ground that, owing to her tender age, Samantha was not a suitable
b person to hold the licence. From this refusal an appeal was entered in Samantha's
name to the Thames Street magistrate. It is still pending, and in the meantime no
annual licence has been granted for the pitch.

After Samantha's appeal had been lodged both Harold and his wife (the second
applicant) made separate applications in their own names for the licence. The borough
council could have deferred their decision on these two applications on the ground
c that it was not reasonably practicable to grant a licence for the pitch until Samantha's
appeal had been determined.

However, they did not do this. Their decision was communicated to the applicants
by a letter of 12th June 1973. As respects Harold's application they said:

d 'We herewith enclose copies of the documents that you ask for. With regard
to the Application by Mr. Kayne-Levenson, as Mr. Kayne-Levenson already holds
a licence another licence cannot be granted to him, although the Prescription of
the Licence which he holds can be varied at the end of this year to include Pitch
1 Goulston Street in the Prescription of that licence.'

I agree with the Divisional Court that this was clearly a refusal of the first applicant's
application for an annual licence current until 31st December 1973.
e As respects the wife's application they said:

'With regard to the Application of Mrs. Kayne-Levenson this has been placed
on the waiting list, and will be considered by the Committee in due course.
The Committee will not be meeting before the 15th June.'

f This was supplemented by a letter of 8th August 1973 where it was said:

'With regard to your letter of the 11th July, and our subsequent telephone
conversation, Mrs. Kayne-Levenson's application has been placed on the waiting
list, and as there is currently a very long list of applicants for licences in Goulston
Street, it will probably be some time before Mrs. Kayne-Levenson's application
can be dealt with.'

g For the reasons already stated in connection with the way in which the waiting list
is operated, I agree with the Divisional Court that this too was a refusal of the second
applicant's application for an annual licence current until 31st December 1973.

Section 37 of the London County Council (General Powers) Act 1958 requires a
borough council, on notifying an applicant of its decision to refuse him an annual
licence, to notify him at the same time that if he is aggrieved by the decision he may
h appeal to a magistrates' court. The borough council did not do this to either of the
applicants. It was in respect of this omission that the Divisional Court made orders
of mandamus.

Mandamus is a discretionary remedy and the omission might in other circumstances
have been regarded as no more than a technicality if the applicants themselves knew
of their right of appeal. But the borough council were taking the line in which they
j have persisted in both the Divisional Court and this court, that neither applicant had
any right of appeal—Harold on the ground that his application was for the variation
of a prescription in his current annual licence and that on the authority of *Greenbaum's*
case[1] no appeal lay from their refusal to do this; his wife on the ground that putting

1 (1957) 55 LGR 129

her at the bottom of the waiting list did not amount to a decision to refuse her the
annual licence for which she had applied. So the omission to notify the applicants of   *a*
their right of appeal to a magistrate was no mere technicality. It was deliberate and
based on alleged grounds of substance which have now been held to be erroneous in
law. I see no grounds for interfering with the exercise by the Divisional Court of
their discretion to grant mandamus to each of the applicants.

Heavy costs have already been incurred in clarifying the law applicable in the
circumstances of this case. It would be a pity if the litigation were to continue. The   *b*
sensible way of dealing with the situation would be for Harold to make an application
for an annual licence for the vacant pitch for the year ending 31st December 1975,
together with an application to renew his current licence for his existing pitch. But
for his mother having been misled by the notice on the application forms between
1970 and 1973 Harold would have been her nominated relative and entitled to an
additional licence for the vacant pitch on her death. It is not suggested that there are   *c*
any reasons personal to him which make him unsuitable to be licensed to trade from
two pitches and it lies within the borough council's discretion to grant him for 1975
an annual licence for the vacant pitch to which he would have been entitled on his
mother's death in 1973 but for their own mistaken view of the law. Samantha's
appeal to the magistrate could then be withdrawn; and there would be no need for the
second applicant to make any application.   *d*

LAWTON LJ. Beyond Aldgate Pump, some five hundred yards to the east of the
City of London boundary, there is a knot of narrow streets known as Petticoat Lane.
There has been a street market there for at least 200 years. One of the reasons why
that market started in that place was probably because trading there was outside the   *e*
strict control which the Lord Mayor and the Court of Aldermen have long maintained over the markets within the city. Such control as there was in the early days
would have been that of the Middlesex justices. From the time of the local government changes in the 19th century it has been that of Stepney Borough Council and
its successors, the London Borough of Tower Hamlets ('the borough council').

There has to be some control over street markets. Without control there would be   *f*
traffic chaos; nuisances would arise from litter and garbage; there would be disorder
arising from over-vigorous competition for pitches and the activities of racketeers
trying to manipulate the trading for their own dishonest purposes, and the pitches
would become disposal points for stolen goods. The borough council are, and long
have been, aware of the need for control and of their duty to the public to ensure that
control is maintained. The attraction of this market for Londoners and its world-wide   *g*
reputation as a place tourists should visit brings large crowds to it, particularly on
Sundays. This in turn means first that those who have pitches in the market do well
financially; secondly, that a licence to trade there is a valuable asset; and, thirdly, that
anyone who can acquire a number of licences is likely to be able to have the power and
influence in the market itself, and elsewhere, which wealth can bring. The borough
council do not want to have traders in the market who because of their financial   *h*
strength are able to get others to do what they want. They have worked out a policy
for controlling the market.

Two aspects of their policy have been under discussion in this appeal, namely,
their refusal ever to allow any one trader to operate two pitches on the same day and
their operation of a waiting list for applicants for licences. The council have submitted
that, on the proper construction of their statutory powers, they are entitled, indeed   *j*
bound, to restrict trading in the way they have and that their waiting list policy is a
matter of administration and should not be subject to the supervision of the courts.
The applicants for relief by way of mandamus have countered this by submitting
that the council have misconstrued their statutory powers which, so it is said, do allow
a trader to operate more than one pitch on the same day and that the operation of the

a waiting list policy gives applicants for licences who are put on such a list a statutory right of appeal to a magistrate because of the act of putting a name on such a list is a refusal of the grant of a licence.

I am doubtful whether, as a matter of discretion, mandatory orders should have been made in this case, for a reason which I will give later, but as the Divisional Court did make them and both Lord Denning MR and Lord Diplock approve what was done, I do not dissent. Both parties to this appeal, however, want more than a bare b decision. The borough council want to know how to exercise their statutory powers in relation to this market and others in their area—and so do other councils having the same statutory powers. The two applicants want to know what their rights are under the statutory powers. As Lord Denning MR and Lord Diplock differ on some aspects of this case, although in agreement as to the order which this court should make, it may be helpful if I give my opinion on the main points which arise.

c In my judgment the borough council's policy of refusing ever to allow any one trader to operate two pitches on the same day is based on a misconstruction of the London County Council (General Powers) Act 1947, as amended. The Act envisages four categories of street traders: existing street traders, registered street traders, traders under annual licences and traders under temporary licences. An existing street trader is an individual who, at any time before the date on which a street becomes a d designated street, has regularly and lawfully traded in that street, and as an existing street trader he is entitled to carry on trading for a limited time (see ss 15 and 18). A registered street trader is an existing street trader who has registered with the borough council pursuant to the provisions of s 19. For the purposes of registration such a trader has to give notice to the borough council of 'the street in which and the position or place in that street at which he has regularly engaged in street trading', and is regis- e tered in respect of that position or place (see s 19(2) and (4)). A registered street trader is entitled—

'to engage and continue to engage in street trading to the like extent and in the like manner as if he held an annual licence granted and annually renewed by the borough council and as if the particulars registered in relation to him . . . were the f prescriptions of such licence . . .'

(see s 19(6)). It follows, as it seems to me, that a registered street trader can only enjoy his rights as such in respect of one 'position or place'. Save in one respect, he can trade in the same manner as the holder of an annual licence, but he is a different class of licensee. Whereas an annual licensee 'may employ any other person to assist him in the conduct of his business without any further street trading licence being required' g (see s 28), a registered street trader can only employ members of his family (see the proviso to s 19(6)).

The particulars which an existing street trader is required to give to obtain registra-tion (s 19(2)) are different from those which an applicant for an annual licence has to give (see s 21(1)). The latter does not have to specify a position or place in a particular street. What he is required to do is to state the street or streets in which he intends to h trade. If the licence is granted, it will 'prescribe' the street or streets (once again the plural) and the position or place in any such street at which the licensee may trade: see s 21(5)(a). An annual licence can be limited in the ways set out in s 21(5), with the result that it can prescribe a particular pitch on a particular day and a different pitch on another day. But if, as the borough council contended, an annual licence can only be granted to an individual for one pitch on one day, I find it impossible to give any j meaning to the word 'streets' in both s 21(1)(d) and s 21(5)(a). If Parliament had intended the Act to give effect to a policy of 'one licence, one pitch, one person', I should have expected s 21(1) to require applicants to state the street in which they intended to trade and the licence to prescribe the position or place in *the* street in which the holder was entitled to trade. Section 21(5)(a) has the words, 'the position in any *such* street', which refer back to 'street or streets'. I would construe this phrase as meaning that if the licence applies to two or more streets, the position or place of trading in each can be specified. I have found the construction of s 21 to be very difficult *a* and have been attracted by the desirability of a construction which would put the holder of an annual licence on the same basis of 'one licence, one pitch, one person' as a registered street trader holds his licence. In my judgment the use of the word 'streets' in s 21 makes such a construction impossible.

An applicant can only be refused a licence on one of the grounds specified in s 21(3). Lack of available space (see s 21(3)(*b*)) is probably the most usual ground of refusal, *b* since a borough council cannot accommodate more than one trader at a time on any one pitch. Where there are a number of applicants for a pitch, the borough council has to choose between them. Whom to choose must always be difficult, and in the case of a choice made by a committee of a borough council, whatever it is, some unsuccessful applicants are likely to criticise it on grounds of favouritism, political bias or even alleged corruption. In order to be fair to applicants and probably to *c* save councillors from criticism, the borough council have established a waiting list policy. This has been described fully by Lord Diplock in his judgment. He has approved it. So do I, and for the same reasons as he has given.

A borough council may also refuse an application for an annual licence, or the re- newal of one, if 'the applicant or licensee is on account of misconduct or for any other sufficient reason in their opinion unsuitable to hold such a licence' (s 21(3)(*a*)). *d* If misconduct is the ground for refusal, the acts said to be misconduct will have to be specified and identified to the applicant (s 21(4)); but if the applicant is considered unsuitable 'for any other sufficient reason', what matters is the honest opinion of those members of the borough council who have the task of deciding. They must apply their minds to the suitability of each applicant, but, in my judgment, there is nothing in the Act to stop them following guidelines. They would, for example, be *e* entitled to have a *general* policy to the effect that men over 65 should not normally be granted licences or have renewals; but care would have to be taken not to exclude *all* men over 65 merely because they were that age. There should be enough flexibility in the policy to allow an exception for the vigorous, healthy man over 65 who was still able to cope with the hurly-burly of a street market and to work in bad weather. The councillors who deal with these applications must be taken to know the markets *f* under their supervision. One street market may be quiet and trouble free; another may be a haunt of thieves, receivers, spielers and tricksters. In the former case one competent woman could probably control the whole market, whereas in the latter most traders might find difficulty in controlling their own pitches properly and only a man of outstanding and dominating personality could control properly more than one pitch. If the appropriate committee of the borough council considers that trading *g* conditions in Petticoat Lane are such that it would be difficult for most men to control properly more than one pitch at a time, in my judgment they are entitled to have as a guideline a policy of 'one man, one licence'; but they must be prepared to consider the suitability of an applicant who claims that he could control properly two or more pitches at the same time.

A borough council must, however, grant, subject to s 21(3), an annual licence to a *h* nominated relative even though the nominee is already the holder of an annual licence for the same street. The rights of the nominated relative are set out in s 21(2A). There is nothing in the Act which excludes the holder of an annual licence for the same street, or any other street, because he is such, from enjoyment of the rights conferred by the Act on a nominated relative. The borough council were wrong to exclude Mr Kayne-Levenson from nomination by his mother merely because he held *j* an annual licence for another pitch. The only grounds on which they could have re- fused his application for an annual licence for his mother's old pitch are those set out in s 21(3). Had they thought that because of his personality he could not control two pitches at the same time, they could have put him to an election as to which one he wanted to control.

a The confusion which has arisen in this case stems from the borough council's mistaken opinion about nominated relatives. Had they not made the mistake they did, Mr Kayne-Levenson would have been granted as of right an annual licence for his mother's pitch; but for the reasons given above he might have had to elect whether he wanted to retain his old licence or take up his new one.

b As a result of the council printing what they did on the back of their form to be used for the renewal of annual licences after 1970, the late Mrs Levenson, in October 1972, nominated her baby granddaughter, Samantha, for the purposes of s 21(2A). As long as that child is able to claim her rights to a grant, the council cannot grant an annual licence to any other applicant for Mrs Levenson's old pitch. An application for the grant of an annual licence was made in Samantha's name and was refused on two grounds, one being that she was unsuitable to hold a licence by reason of her age.

c An appeal against this refusal was made to the Thames magistrates pursuant to s 25. This appeal was listed on 14th December 1973; but on that day an application was made to that court to adjourn the hearing of the appeal generally because Mr and Mrs Kayne-Levenson intended to start these proceedings forthwith. This application was granted.

d The jurisdiction to make mandatory orders is discretionary and the court should not make such orders if nothing effective can be done if they are made. The orders made by the Divisional Court in favour of Mr and Mrs Kayne-Levenson will enable them to know why their applications for annual licences were refused and to get ready to appeal to the Thames Magistrates' Court against the refusals; but their appeals cannot be heard until Samantha's appeal has been disposed of, either by adjudication or withdrawal. Neither can be granted an annual licence so long as Samantha's right to take the grant of an annual licence is in being. She may be

e adjudged by the magistrates' court to be unsuitable because of her age; but infancy is not a legal bar to the holding of an annual licence; it is a discretionary one to be applied on the evidence. Had I been sitting at first instance I should have adjudged that Mr and Mrs Kayne-Levenson had started these proceedings too soon: they should have waited until Samantha's appeal was out of the way. As her parents they could

f have got rid of it either by withdrawing it or letting the magistrates' court make an order. The borough council did not take this point before the Divisional Court, which in the exercise of its discretion made the order. As the legal right in question was established, it is too late now to challenge the exercise of discretion.

Once Samantha's appeal has been disposed of, the council will be able to allot Mrs Levenson's old pitch to one of the many applicants for it. As Mr Kayne-Levenson would have jumped the queue of applicants had not the council made the mistake

g referred to earlier in this judgment, they may think it right—and I personally hope they will—to put him into the position he would have been in but for their mistake.

I concur on the dismissal of the appeal.

Appeal dismissed.

Solicitors: *Edward Fail, Bradshaw & Waterson* (for the borough council); *Tringhams* (for the applicants).

Wendy Shockett Barrister.

z

Attorney-General's Reference (No 2 of 1974)   *a*

COURT OF APPEAL, CRIMINAL DIVISION
LORD WIDGERY CJ, MELFORD STEVENSON AND WATKINS JJ
12th, 20th DECEMBER 1974

Road traffic – Driving with blood-alcohol proportion above prescribed limit – Evidence –   *b*
Provision of speci:nen – Breath test – Administration – Duty of constable to act bona fide to
obtain true indication of proportion of alcohol in blood – Manufacturers' instructions attached
to device – Constable ignorant of instructions – Failure to comply with instructions liable to
affect result of test – Constable acting bona fide – Validity of test.

Road traffic – Driving with blood-alcohol proportion above prescribed limit – Evidence –   *c*
Provision of specimen – Breath test – Device – Instructions for use – Strict compliance with
instructions not essential to validity of test – Smoking – High concentration of tobacco smoke
liable to affect result of test – Instructions stating that smoking should not be permitted
immediately prior to test – Meaning of 'immediately prior to' – High concentration only likely
if driver inhales through cigarette and at once exhales into bag – Sufficient compliance with
instructions if driver has adequately cleared tobacco smoke from lungs before taking test.   *d*

A van which was being driven erratically was stopped by two police officers, one of
whom required the driver to provide a specimen of breath for a breath test. The
driver was smoking. The constable was ignorant of the manufacturers' instructions
on the Alcotest (R)80 equipment which stated: 'A high concentration of tobacco smoke
tends to colour the reagent brown. Smoking during or immediately prior to the test
should not therefore be permitted.' Nevertheless, it was the constable's practice to   *e*
request drivers not to smoke before providing a specimen of breath for a breath test.
Within two minutes of being stopped the driver was asked to provide a specimen of
breath. He did so and the test proved positive. The driver was arrested and taken to
a police station. He failed without reasonable excuse to provide a laboratory test
specimen and accordingly was charged with an offence under s 9(3) of the Road Traffic
Act 1972. On a submission of no case to answer the judge directed the jury that the   *f*
circumstances were such that they would have to conclude that the driver was
smoking immediately before the test.   The judge further directed them that
although it was sufficient if the police officer had been doing his best to comply with
the manufacturers' instructions, he could not be said to have been doing his best if he
did not know of them. Having considered that point the judge decided that there
was no case to answer since the breath test had not been properly administered and   *g*
so the arrest and all later proceedings were vitiated. On a reference by the Attorney-
General under s 36 of the Criminal Justice Act 1972, the court's opinion was sought on
the question 'Whether a breath test is invalid where a constable administering the
alcotest, acting bona fide but in ignorance of the manufacturer's instructions, fails to
delay the giving of the test to a driver who he knows has been smoking very shortly
before but not actually at the time of the test'.   *h*

Held – The requirement that the suspect should not be permitted to smoke immediately before the test was one which went to the accuracy of the test, because failure to
comply with it could affect the colour of the crystals in such a way as to make it
difficult or impossible to determine whether the crystals had been coloured by any
alcohol in the suspect's breath as well. If the defendant had been smoking immed-   *j*
iately before the test the police officer must have been able to see what was happening.
The fact that the police officer was acting bona fide could not excuse his lack of
knowledge of the manufacturers' instructions. Accordingly in those circumstances the
test was invalid (see p 662 *h* to p 663 *a* and *e* to *g*, post).

Director of Public Prosecutions v Carey [1969] 3 All ER 1662 explained.

a   Per Curiam. Only in a very limited number of cases does the fact that the defendant was smoking have any relevance to the question whether the breath test has been properly administered. The manufacturers' reference to smoking 'immediately' before the test must be treated as meaning smoking at a time so proximate to the test that a sufficiently high concentration of tobacco smoke is still retained in the driver's lungs and is thus liable to be transmitted to the test bag. Such a high con-centration is only likely to be achieved if the suspect inhales through his cigarette
b   and at once exhales into the bag. Accordingly the trial judge should have left to the jury the issue whether the driver had been smoking immediately before the test, and if the jury had been satisfied that the driver had adequately cleared the tobacco smoke from his lungs before he took the test, the question posed by the reference would not have arisen (see p 661 *h* to p 662 *c*, post).

c   **Notes**
For the requirements of a breath test under the Road Traffic Acts, relevance of the manufacturers' instructions as to the use of a device approved for the purposes of a breath test, see Supplement to 33 Halsbury's Laws (3rd Edn) para 1061A, and for cases on the subject, see Digest (Cont Vol C) 936, 937, 322aa-322bb.
d   For the Criminal Justice Act 1972, s 36, see 42 Halsbury's Statutes (3rd Edn) 129.
For the Road Traffic Act 1972, s 9, see 42 Halsbury's Statutes (3rd Edn) 1651, 1660.

Cases referred to in judgment
Director of Public Prosecutions v Carey [1969] 3 All ER 1662, [1970] AC 1072, [1969] 3 WLR 1169, 134 JP 59, HL; *rvsg* sub nom *Webber v Carey* [1969] 3 All ER 406, [1969] 1 WLR
e   1351, 133 JP 633, 54 Cr App Rep 119, [1970] RTR 14, DC, Digest (Cont Vol C) 936, 322aa.
Watkinson v Barley p 316, ante, [1975] 1 WLR 70, DC.

Cases also cited
Darnell v Portal [1972] RTR 483, DC.
f   *Gill v Forster* [1970] RTR 45, DC.
Rendall v Hooper [1970] 2 All ER 72, [1970] 1 WLR 747, DC.

Reference
This was a reference by the Attorney-General under s 36 of the Criminal Justice Act
g   1972 for the opinion of the Court of Appeal, Criminal Division, on a point of law which had arisen in a case in which the defendant had been acquitted on a charge of failing, without reasonable excuse, to provide a specimen for a laboratory test, contrary to s 9(3) of the Road Traffic Act 1972. The facts are set out in the judgment of the court.

Donald Farquharson QC and *C J E Gardner* for the Attorney-General.
h   *Gordon Slynn QC* and *Donald Anderson* as amici curiae.

Cur adv vult

20th December. **LORD WIDGERY CJ** read the following judgment of the court. This matter comes before the court on a reference from Her Majesty's Attorney-
j   General under s 36 of the Criminal Justice Act 1972. By this reference the opinion of the court is sought on a point of law arising out of an acquittal before the Crown Court of a defendant on a charge of failing to provide a specimen contrary to s 9(3) of the Road Traffic Act 1972. The acquitted defendant has not exercised his rights to take part in the proceedings before this court, and no further reference to him is proper in view of the necessity of preserving his anonymity.

The facts of the case for the purposes of this reference may be taken to be the following. Two police constables were on duty in uniform when they saw a van being driven by the defendant erratically and in excess of the speed limit. They stopped the van, the first police constable on speaking to the defendant had reasonable cause to suspect him of having alcohol in his body, and required him to provide a specimen of breath for a breath test. The first police constable was unaware of the instruction of the manufacturer of the breath test equipment that:

'A high concentration of tobacco smoke tends to colour the reagent brown. Smoking during or immediately prior to the test should not therefore be permitted',

but it was his practice to request drivers not to smoke before providing a specimen of breath for a breath test, because he felt it was in the driver's interest not to do so. The defendant was to the knowledge of the first police constable smoking a cigarette at the time when the requirement was made, and the first police constable, in accordance with his practice, requested the defendant to put out his cigarette. It was not established by the evidence precisely when the defendant stopped smoking, but it was during the period of two minutes between the making of the requirement and the provision of the specimen of breath. The breath test proved positive and the defendant was arrested.

From the time that the defendant was stopped until his arrest the first police constable had acted fairly and conducted the breath test bona fide, in particular establishing by enquiry that the defendant had not consumed any alcohol in the preceding 20 minutes. The defendant was taken to a police station where he took a second positive breath test and thereafter without reasonable excuse failed to provide a specimen for a laboratory test, contrary to s 9(3) of the Road Traffic Act 1972.

In the Crown Court at the conclusion of the evidence for the prosecution a submission was made that there was no case to answer because the police officer had not complied with the instructions of the manufacturer of the Alcotest (R)80 equipment quoted above, namely, that smoking during or immediately prior to the test should not be permitted.

In giving his ruling on this submission the Crown Court judge addressed the jury as follows:

'You will remember that yesterday we heard evidence from Constable Taylor —who I expect you will agree was obviously a very reliable police officer—who was taking the test. In the course of his evidence he did say, first of all, that the [defendant] would have been smoking up to just before the breath test was administered, and secondly, you will remember that he said that although he was aware of the fact that a man should not be smoking while the test is actually carried out he apparently was not aware of the instructions which are printed on a piece of paper pasted inside the lid and therefore did not know that they not only said that the person should not be smoking during the test but also that he should not be smoking immediately before the test. There has been some scope for argument as to what is meant by "immediately before". You may remember that the evidence was really very uncertain about that. Clearly it looks as though it could not have been an interval of more than about two minutes, probably it was very much less, between the time when he was told to stub that cigarette out and the time when he was told to blow into the bag. Whatever this period [if], giving this man the benefit of the doubt, it was in those circumstances impossible to come to the conclusion that he was smoking at a time that is outside whatever is meant by the words "immediately before", you would have to conclude that he was smoking immediately before the test was administered.'

Having reached this conclusion, the trial judge went on to consider whether this failure to comply with the manufacturer's instructions vitiated the test. He had been

referred to the decision of the House of Lords in *Director of Public Prosecutions v Carey*[1],
a   the general effect of which was that a failure to comply with the manufacturer's
instructions did not necessarily vitiate the test if the police constable in question had
acted genuinely in an attempt to obtain an accurate result from the test, and had not
been guilty of mala fides or negligence.

   Nevertheless, in the instant case, the trial judge considered that the effect of non-
compliance with the manufacturer's instructions had vitiated the test. He said:

b
   'Now, here we are faced with a situation a little unfortunate, namely, that the
   police officer (as I remind you) did not have those instructions in his mind. He
   does not seem to have even read the instructions that there should be a prohibition on smoking immediately before. Therefore it is a question of whether
   the officer can be said to be doing his best to comply with the instructions when
   he has never read those instructions and therefore cannot be doing his best to
c   comply with them. I think you will agree that the officer was trying to do his
   best to be fair but the question I have to consider is whether he was doing his best
   to comply with the instructions and I have been driven to the conclusion with
   regard to the argument we have heard in your absence that in fact the position is
   that this officer cannot be said to have been doing his best to comply with the
d   instructions when he did not know of them. That is an unfortunate matter but
   nevertheless the fact remains that I am driven to that conclusion and I have had
   to consider where my function lies and where your function lies.'

   Having considered this point, the trial judge decided that it was for him to rule that
there was no case to answer because the breath test in his view had not been properly
conducted and thus the subsequent arrest and all later proceedings were vitiated.
e   In reaching his conclusions whether the smoking in question was to be treated as
being 'immediately prior' to the test, and thus contrary to the manufacturer's instructions, the trial judge did not have the advantage of reading a judgment in the
Divisional Court given on 19th November 1974 in *Watkinson v Barley*[2]. In that case the
court was required to consider what was the purpose of the manufacturer's prohibition
in regard to smoking, and how far an understanding of that purpose would explain
f   the significance of the words 'immediately before'.

   It was pointed out that from the manufacturer's instructions themselves it appears
that the only relevance which smoking may have to the taking of a breathalyser test
is that if a high concentration of tobacco smoke is allowed to enter the bag, the reagent
may turn brown and thus make it more difficult accurately to decide whether the
reagent has also reacted to the presence of alcohol in the blood.
g   It is however to be noticed that only where a high concentration of tobacco smoke
may have entered the bag does this problem arise, and in consequence, as the court
pointed out, there must be comparatively few cases in which the quantity of smoke in
the suspect's lungs at the relevant time is of the high concentration required for this
purpose. Whether or not in a particular case the concentration of smoke is sufficient
to turn the crystals brown must be decided by the tribunal of fact, but where the trial
h   takes place before judge and jury it is clearly the responsibility of the judge to stress
the fact that only a high concentration is relevant for present purposes, and to point
out that in the case of a suspect smoking a cigarette such a high concentration is not
likely to be achieved unless he inhales through his cigarette and at once exhales the
product into the bag. In other words, if there is an interval in which he can have two
or three normal inhalations of breath this would usually be sufficient to reduce the
j   concentration of smoke in his lungs to a quantity insufficient to affect the reagent.
   Once this point is grasped it becomes obvious that only in a very limited number of
cases does the fact that the suspect was smoking have any relevance to the question
at all. The manufacturer's reference to smoking 'immediately' before the test must

---

1   [1969] 3 All ER 1662, [1970] AC 1072
2   [1975] 1 All ER 316, [1975] 1 WLR 70

be treated as meaning smoking at a time so proximate to the test that a sufficiently *a*
high concentration of tobacco smoke is still retained in his lungs and thus liable to be
transmitted to the test bag.

In the instant case we think that the trial judge was wrong in refusing to leave to
the jury the question of whether the suspect had been smoking immediately before
the test. He should have left this issue to the jury and he would have been wise to go
to some pains to explain to the jury that it is not the trace of tobacco lingering in the *b*
lungs and mouth which is likely to create the appropriate concentration, and that
such a concentration can hardly be achieved in practice unless there is an inhalation of
tobacco smoke from the cigarette transmitted almost instantly into the bag itself and
not dispersed by normal breathing actions meanwhile. If the jury had been satisfied
that the defendant had adequately cleared the tobacco smoke from his lungs before he
took the test, the second point dealt with by the learned trial judge would not arise *c*

It is however in relation to this second point that the Attorney-General desires the
opinion of the court, and the question which he asks us to answer is expressed in these
terms:

> 'Whether a breath test is invalid where a police constable administering the
> alcotest, acting bona fide but in ignorance of the manufacturer's instructions,
> fails to delay the giving of the test to a driver who he knows has been smoking *d*
> very shortly before but not actually at the time of the test?'

As has been pointed out, this question becomes relevant only on the assumption that
the jury are not satisfied that the quantity of smoke in the suspect's lungs was insufficient to affect the accuracy of the test. We therefore proceed to consider the situation
which would arise on that basis. *e*

This in turn requires a closer look at the decision in *Director of Public Prosecutions v
Carey*[1]. The general effect of that decision is, as we have already stated, that a failure
to comply with the manufacturer's instructions for the use of the Alcotest (R)80 does
not necessarily vitiate the test provided that the police officer has genuinely attempted
to use the equipment properly to obtain a fair and accurate result, and has not been
negligent in the course of so doing. *Director of Public Prosecutions v Carey*[1] was primarily *f*
concerned with the manufacturer's instruction that a period of 20 minutes should be
allowed to elapse between the occasion when the suspect last had an alcoholic drink and
the moment when the test is administered. It was incidentally concerned with such
questions as whether the police officer is under a duty to ask the suspect whether he
has had a drink within that period, and it touched on the question of whether a breath
test could be said to have been validly taken where the manufacturer's instruction *g*
with regard to the method of inflating the test bag had not been followed.

An important feature of the instant case is that the conduct of the defendant in
regard to smoking was clear for the police officer to see, and the true failure, if there
was one, to prevent the defendant from smoking at a time too proximate to the test
was due to the constable's ignorance of the precise nature of the manufacturer's
instructions. Where the nature of the failure to comply is clear to be seen by the police *h*
officer we do not think that he can excuse himself from obeying those instructions
merely by saying that he was unaware that the instructions existed. Whilst anxious
not to impose additional burdens on police officers, we are quite unable to accept the
proposition that a failure to comply with the instructions can be justified merely
because the police officer has never read them or become acquainted with them in
other ways. *j*

Accordingly, it seems to us very difficult to introduce the conception of bona fides
into a situation such as the present. However bona fide the officer may have been, if
in fact there was a departure from the manufacturer's instructions, a departure which
might have had some effect on the accuracy of the test, we do not think that any

---

1 [1969] 3 All ER 1662, [1970] AC 1072

argument based on bona fides can excuse the officer from a failure to inform himself
a of the particular nature of the manufacturer's requirements.

In the speeches in *Director of Public Prosecutions v Carey*[1] there are several dicta which support this view. Thus Viscount Dilhorne referred to what we may call the smoking requirement in these terms[2]:

> 'The instructions placed no obligation on the police officer to enquire whether
> *b* he had been smoking immediately prior to the test. Exactly what is meant by
> "immediately before" and the word "shortly" in the finding of the justices that
> the respondent had been smoking shortly before the test I do not know. Police
> officers can observe for themselves whether a person is smoking when he is
> stopped and whether he smokes thereafter. If he is smoking, or there is reasonable
> cause for supposing that he has been recently, then, to comply with the instruc-
> *c* tions, the carrying out of the test should be delayed.'

Similarly, Lord Diplock said[3]:

> 'The requirements of the Act are satisfied provided first, that the device used
> is of a type approved by the Secretary of State, and, secondly, that the test is
> conducted and its results are evaluated bona fide by the constable carrying out the
> *d* test. He must accordingly comply with any instructions for the use of the device
> which to his knowledge in the circumstances in which the breath test is carried
> out need to be observed in order that the device may give a reliable indication
> whether or not the proportion of alcohol in the blood of the person to whom the
> test is administered exceeds the prescribed limit. If he does not, the test carried
> *e* out by him is not a "breath test" within the meaning of the Act because it is not
> carried out for the defined purpose.'

Applying this dictum to the facts of the present case we think, first, that the requirement with regard to smoking is a requirement which can go to the accuracy of the
test result because it can affect the colour of the crystals in such a fashion as to make it
difficult, or perhaps worse, to determine whether the crystals have been coloured by
f any alcohol in the suspect's breath as well. Secondly, if the suspect was smoking
immediately prior to the test in accordance with the restricted meaning which we
give to those words, it is apparent that the police officer must have been able to see
what was happening. Accordingly, the only excuse open to the police officer is that
he was unaware of the manufacturer's requirement.

At the present stage reached in these matters we do not think that that should be an
acceptable answer, and although the bona fides of the police officer may excuse his
g lack of knowledge of some fact or circumstance concerning the test, we do not think
that it can excuse a lack of knowledge of the instructions themselves. We would
accordingly answer the question posed in this reference in the affirmative.

Determination accordingly.

h

Solicitors: *Director of Public Prosecutions* (for the Attorney-General); *Treasury Solicitor.*

N P Metcalfe Esq Barrister.

---

1 [1969] 3 All ER 1662, [1970] AC 1072
j 2 [1969] 3 All ER at 1670, [1970] AC at 1086
3 [1969] 3 All ER at 1678, [1970] AC at 1095

Inland Revenue Commissioners v Montgomery *a*

CHANCERY DIVISION
WALTON J
9th, 10th DECEMBER 1974

Followed in O'BRIEN v BENSON'S
HOSIERY [1977] 3 All ER 352

Capital gains tax – Insurance policies – Rights of insured under policy of insurance – Rights **b**
not constituting asset on disposal of which gain may accrue – Capital sum derived from assets
insured – Deemed disposal of assets – Assignment of insured's rights in consideration of
capital sum – Insurance of property against damage by fire – Property damaged by fire – Sum
due under policy agreed with insurers – Right to receive that sum assigned to third party for
payment of capital sum to insured – Whether capital sum 'derived' from property insured –
Whether rights of insured an asset on the disposal of which no gain accrued – Finance Act **c**
1965, s 22(3), Sch 7, para 10(1)(2) (as amended by the Finance Act 1966, s 43, Sch 10, para 11).

The taxpayer was appointed one of three trustees under the will of his father who died
in 1961. The trust property included certain real property in Belfast. In 1962 the
trustees took out policies of insurance covering that property against loss or damage by
fire. In August 1968 the property was extensively damaged by fire. Subsequently the **d**
trustees and the insurance company agreed the amount payable under the policies
in respect of the damage at £75,192. The trustees then put into effect a scheme
whereby they assigned their rights under the policies to G for a consideration of
£75,192. In November 1968 the insurance company paid the agreed amount to G. On
16th August 1971 the taxpayer, as the first-named trustee, was assessed to capital gains
tax for the year 1968-69 in the sum of £50,000. The taxpayer appealed to the Special **e**
Commissioners who allowed the appeal holding that, under Sch 7, para 10(1)[a], to the
Finance Act 1965, the £75,192 received by the trustees from G did not fall to be taken
into account in the computation for the purposes of capital gains tax. The Crown
appealed, contending that the sum paid to the trustees was a 'capital sum . . . derived
from assets', i e the real property held by the trustees, within s 22(3)[b] of the Finance
Act 1965 and that accordingly the trustees were liable to capital gains tax in respect **f**
of that sum under Sch 7, para 10(2), to the 1965 Act.

Held – The capital sum paid by G to the trustees was derived from the sale of the
rights under the policies. It was not legitimate to trace its derivation further by
saying that, because the rights under the policies were derived from the real property,
the capital sum paid to the trustees was also derived from that source. The capital **g**
sum was not therefore 'derived' from the property assets, within s 22(3). In any event
the operation of s 22(3) was expressly made subject to the 'exceptions in this Part of
the Act' which included the exception in para 10(1) of Sch 7. Under para 10(1) the rights
of the trustees under the insurance policies did not constitute an asset on the disposal
of which a capital gain could accrue. The taxpayer was not therefore liable to capital
gains tax and the appeal would be dismissed (see p 669 g, p 670 g to j and p 672 b and c, **h**
post).

Notes

For treatment of capital sums derived from assets for the purposes of capital gains
tax, see 5 Halsbury's Laws (4th Edn) 19, para 38, and for the treatment of insurance
policies for capital gains tax purposes, see ibid 39, para 80.   **j**

For Finance Act 1965, s 22, Sch 7, para 10, see 34 Halsbury's Statutes (3rd Edn) 877,
956.

---

a Paragraph 10, as amended and so far as material, is set out at p 669 *e* to *g*, post
b Section 22(3) is set out at p 668 *j* to p 669 *a*, post

Cases referred to in judgment

a   *Harmel v Wright (Inspector of Taxes)* [1974] 1 All ER 945, [1974] 1 WLR 325, [1974] STC 88.

Thomson *(Inspector of Taxes) v Moyse* [1960] 3 All ER 684, [1961] AC 967, 39 Tax Cas 291, [1960] 3 WLR 929, 39 ATC 322, [1960] TR 309, HL, 28(1) Digest (Reissue) 299, *1023.*

Case also cited

b   *Pott's Executors v Inland Revenue Comrs* [1951] 1 All ER 76, [1951] AC 443, 32 Tax Cas 211, HL.

Case stated

1. At a meeting of the Commissioners for the Special Purposes of the Income Tax Acts held on 20th June 1973, Robert Montgomery ('the taxpayer'), as trustee of Dr Edwin Montgomery deceased ('the testator'), appealed against an assessment to capital gains
c   tax made on him for the year 1968-69 in the sum of £50,000.

2. Shortly stated the question for decision was whether by virtue of Sch 7, para 10(1), to the Finance Act 1965, certain moneys paid in the manner appearing below were exempt from capital gains tax; or whether rather the payment of those moneys gave rise to capital gains tax liability by virtue of Sch 7, para 10(2), to, and s 22(3) of, the 1965 Act.

d   [Paragraph 3 listed the documents which were proved or admitted before the commissioners.]

4. The following facts were admitted between the parties. (1) By his will dated 14th March 1958 the testator, after appointing the taxpayer, Margaret Joyce Greene, a daughter of the testator, and Robert McComb Machenry to be his executors and trustees, devised and bequeathed all his real and personal property to the executors
e   and trustees appointed in his will on trust to pay his funeral and testamentary expenses and Crown debts and to hold the balance ('the trust property') on the trusts therein declared ('the specified trusts'). The testator's will gave the trustees thereunder power to sell any leasehold or freehold property vested in them. (2) On 6th July 1961 the testator died without having revoked his will. At the time of his death, the testator held, subject to certain charges and leases, the interest comprised in a fee
f   farm grant dated 21st March 1885 and made to the late Rev Robert Montgomery, the testator's father. At the time of the testator's death that interest comprised the lands and buildings situated at and known as 2/11 Shaftesbury Square and 2/4 Donegall Pass, Belfast ('the buildings'), the same being held forever subject to an adjusted yearly rent of £194·38. (3) On 14th December 1961, probate of the testator's will was granted forth out of the Principal Probate Registry to the executors named therein.
g   (4) On 23rd March 1962 the taxpayer, Mrs Greene and Mr Machenry, as the then trustees under the testator's will, effected with the Alliance Assurance Co Ltd ('the company') two policies of insurance ('the policies') in relation to the buildings. The policies bore the numbers 11246878 and 11246879 and provided cover in respect of destruction or damage occasioned by or consequent on fire (in the case of policy 11246879 for loss of rent). (5) By virtue of a deed of appointment made on 10th June
h   1968, Margaret Summerhayes, a niece of the testator was appointed as trustee of the testator's will in place of Mr Machenry. At all material times thereafter the trustees for the purposes of the testator's will were the taxpayer, Mrs Greene and Mrs Summerhayes hereafter collectively referred to as 'the trustees'. (6) On 12th August 1968, at the time of the fire referred to below, the trustees still held, as part of the trust property on the specified trusts, the same interest in the said fee farm grant which had been held
j   by the testator at his death, subject only to the charges and leases then outstanding. On that date the buildings were extensively damaged by fire as a result of which only one of them remained standing, the others having all been completely gutted. At the time of this fire the policies were still in force. (7) Between 8th November and 26th November 1968 inclusive the following events all occurred: (i) On 8th November 1968 the trustees sent to Geoffrey Robert Alexander Greene, husband of Mrs Greene,

a letter the terms of which are set out on p 667, post. (ii) On 9th November 1968 the trustees sent to the company two notices. The notice relating to policy 11245878 was in the following terms:

> 'Subject to your approval and to the terms and conditions of the Policy we hereby agree to accept the sum of Seventy Thousand Three Hundred and Thirty Pounds—in full satisfaction and discharge of all claims under the above Policy occasioned by or consequent upon the Fire which occurred at on the buildings of 2-11 Shaftesbury Square, Belfast, on or about the thirteenth day of August, 1968. We declare that there are no other Insurances effected on the said property by us or by any other person except as above mentioned,'

The notice relating to policy 112468/9, relating to loss of rent, was in similar terms with the substitution of £4,862 for £70,330. (iii) On 13th November 1968 Mr Greene credited to the trustees' account at the Bank of Ireland, Donegall Place, Belfast, the sum of £75,192. (iv) On 14th November 1968 the trustees sent to the company a notice in the following terms:

> 'We hereby give you notice that we have assigned to Geoffrey Robert Alexander Greene of 27, Kingsway Gardens, Belfast, all our rights under the above policies and we direct that the sum of £75,192. 0. 0. payable thereunder shall be paid to the credit of his account with Northern Bank Limited, Victoria Square, Belfast.'

(v) The company paid to the credit of Mr Greene's account at the Northern Bank Ltd, Victoria Square, Belfast, on 19th November 1968, the sum of £60,153·60; and on 26th November 1968, the sum of £15,038·40, i e in total the sum of £75,192. (8) By deed of conveyance dated 29th April 1969, the trustees sold to one Herbert Henry for the sum of £37,500 their then interest in the lands and premises then comprised in the fee farm grant and covenanted to pay an annuity of £200 per annum to one Dolly Dobbs. That annuity, the only charge currently outstanding in respect of the trust property, had been created by the will of Margaret Montgomery, the testator's mother. (9) By notice of assessment issued on 16th August 1971 a capital gains tax assessment in the the sum of £50,000 for the year ending 5th April 1969 was raised, under the Finance Act 1965, Sch 10, para 12(1), against the taxpayer as the first named trustee in the testator's will. Notice of appeal dated 10th September 1971 was given against that assessment.

5. It was contended on behalf of the taxpayer that: (a) the sum of £75,192 credited to the trustees' bank account and the sums totalling that amount credited to Mr Greene's bank account were none of them 'capital sums received under a policy of insurance' within the meaning of s 22(3)(b) of the 1965 Act, or 'sums received under a policy of insurance' within the meaning of para 10(2) of Sch 7 to that Act; (b) the agreed facts disclosed no disposal of assets for the purpose of Part III of the 1965 Act, no sums derived from such assets and, accordingly, no chargeable gain chargeable to tax under s 19 of the 1965 Act.

6. It was contended on behalf of the Crown that: (a) having regard to the facts referred to at para 4(7) above and agreed between the parties, and to the nature of the scheme disclosed by those facts, it was the trustees themselves who fell to be regarded as having received the total sum of £75,192 paid by the company under the policies so that the same total sum of £75,192 qualified as 'sums received [by the trustees] under a policy of insurance' within the meaning of para 10(2), of the 1965 Act; alternatively the £75,192 paid by Mr Greene to the trustees so qualified; (b) alternatively, if, contrary to contention (a), there was no receipt by the trustees 'under a policy of insurance', there was such a receipt by Mr Greene in respect of the total sum of £75,192 paid by the company to him; and, that being so, the para 10(2) of the 1965 Act still applied since, in terms, those provisions were sufficiently wide to cover a receipt of moneys paid under a relevant policy of insurance by a third party other than

the person sought to be assessed; (c) consequently, para 10(2) applying, the exempting
a   provisions of para 10(1) of Sch 7 to the 1965 Act were excluded; and by virtue of para
10(2) (and in any event) there was, for the purposes of s 22(3), a capital sum of £75,192
derived from the assets involved; (d) accordingly there was a disposal of those assets
by the trustees in accordance with s 22(3); (e) the chargeable gain accruing on the
disposal was therefore chargeable under s 19 of the 1965 Act.

   [Paragraph 7 listed the cases[1] referred to before the commissioners.]

b   8. The commissioners who heard the appeal decided to allow it since they preferred
the arguments advanced on behalf of the trustees. They were unable to infer, insofar
as it was a question of fact, or to hold, insofar as it was a question of law, that the
trustees had received sums under a policy of insurance within the meaning of para
10(2) of Sch 7 to the 1965 Act. The commissioners left figures to be agreed on the basis
of their decision in principle.

c   9. Figures were agreed between the parties on 27th September 1973, and on 16th
October 1973 they adjusted the assessment accordingly.

   10. Immediately after the determination of the appeal the Crown declared their
dissatisfaction therewith as being erroneous in point of law and on 22nd October 1973,
required the commissioners to state a case for the opinion of the High Court pursuant
to the Taxes Management Act 1970, s 56.

d   On 22nd November 1974 the taxpayer gave notice pursuant to RSC Ord 91, r 7,
that at the hearing of the appeal, he would, in addition to the contentions set out in
para 5 of the case stated, put forward the following contentions: (i) that the sum of
£75,192 paid by Mr Greene to the trustees was a sum paid in respect of the rights of an
insured under a policy of insurance and accordingly was specifically exempted from
the charge to capital gains tax by virtue of the provisions of para 10(1) of Sch 7 to the
e   1965 Act; (ii) that neither the sum so paid to the trustees nor the sums totalling
£75,192 credited to Mr Greene's bank account constituted the receipt by the trustees
of a sum derived from assets for the purposes of s 22(3) of the 1965 Act by virtue of
the provisions of para 10(1) of Sch 7 to the 1965 Act.

Nicolas Browne-Wilkinson QC and *Peter Gibson* for the Crown.
f   *P G Whiteman* for the taxpayer.

WALTON J. Immediately prior to 8th November 1968 the situation out of which
this appeal has arisen was as follows. The taxpayer and two other persons, as trustees
of the estate of the late Dr Edwin Montgomery, deceased, held certain real property
in Belfast; that property had been insured against damage by (inter alia) fire; a dis-
g   astrous fire had taken place; and the trustees were in a position to agree the amount
of the claim which they had under the relevant policies with the insurance company
in the sum of £75,192.

   On the 8th November 1968 solicitors acting for the trustees sent to a Mr Greene, the
husband of one of the trustees, a letter in the following terms:

h   'We act on behalf of the above-named trustees. Our clients have recently
      agreed settlement of a fire claim under the above policies arising out of the recent
      fire at Shaftesbury Square and we are enclosing herewith copies of the relevant
      policies and acceptances. Our clients have instructed us that they are prepared to
      assign to you all their rights under the above policies for the sum of £75,192. If
      you wish to accept this offer the above sum should be credited to our clients'
j   account with the Bank of Ireland, Donegall Place, Belfast, and our clients will
      then give written notice to the insurance company of the assignment and direct
      the money payable under the policies to be paid to you or as you may direct.'

---

1   *Ayrshire Pullman Motor Services and Ritchie v IR Comrs* (1929) 14 Tax Cas 754; *R v Clyne,
   ex parte Harrap* [1941] VLR 200

Enclosed therein were two acceptances by the trustees of offers made on behalf of the insurers to settle their claims in the precise sum I have already mentioned. Acceptances *a* in these terms were on the following day sent to the insurance company itself, and on 13th November 1968 Mr Greene accepted the offer contained in the letter of 8th November 1968 by causing the named sum to be credited to the trustees' account at the Bank of Ireland, Donegall Place, Belfast. Notice of the assignment to Mr Greene was then given to the insurance company by a letter dated 14th November 1968. In due course the company paid two sums totalling the £75,192 to Mr Greene, and *b* the trustees subsequently disposed of their fire-damaged property.

Notice of an assessment was issued on 16th August 1971 against the taxpayer as the first-named trustee in relation to capital gains tax in the sum of £50,000 for the year ending 5th April 1969 under the Finance Act 1965, Sch 10, para 12(1). Notice of appeal dated 10th September 1971 was given against this assessment, and at the hearing of the appeal the real question at issue was whether the sum of £75,192 so received by the *c* trustees from Mr Greene fell to be taken into computation for the purposes of capital gains tax or not, the trustees maintaining that it did not and the Crown maintaining that it did. The Special Commissioners preferred the arguments put forward on behalf of the trustees, and they allowed the appeal accordingly. Figures were then agreed between the parties on 27th September 1973 as to the proper amount of any chargeable gain, and on 16th October 1973, the commissioners adjusted the assessment *d* accordingly. From this decision the Crown appeals to the High Court.

In order to understand the rival contentions it is, I think, essential to refer to some of the provisions of the Finance Act 1965 as follows. Part III thereof deals with capital gains tax, and s 19(1) reads:

> 'Tax shall be charged in accordance with this Act in respect of capital gains, *e* that is to say chargeable gains computed in accordance with this Act and accruing to a person on the disposal of assets.'

Section 19(3):

> 'Subject to the said provisions, a tax, to be called capital gains tax, shall be assessed and charged for the year 1965-66 and for subsequent years of assessment *f* in respect of chargeable gains accruing in those years, and shall be so charged in accordance with the following provisions of this Part of this Act.'

Section 22(1):

> 'All forms of property shall be assets for the purposes of this Part of this Act, whether situated in the United Kingdom or not, including—(a) options, debts and incorporeal property generally . .' *g*

Section 22(2):

> 'For the purposes of this Part of this Act—(a) references to a disposal of an asset include, except where the context otherwise requires, references to a part disposal of an asset, and (b) there is a part disposal of an asset where an interest or right *h* in or over the asset is created by the disposal, as well as where it subsists before the disposal, and generally, there is a part disposal of an asset where, on a person making a disposal, any description of property derived from the asset remains undisposed of.'

Section 22(3):

> 'Subject to subsection (6) of this section [and, interposing there, that deals with *j* matters of security], and to the exceptions in this Part of this Act, there is for the purposes of this Part of this Act a disposal of assets by their owner where any capital sum is derived from assets notwithstanding that no asset is acquired by the person paying the capital sum, and this subsection applies in particular to— (a) capital sums received by way of compensation for any kind of damage or

a injury to assets or for the loss, destruction or dissipation of assets or for any depreciation or risk of depreciation of an asset, (b) capital sums received under a policy of insurance of the risk of any kind of damage or injury to, or the loss or depreciation of, assets, (c) capital sums received in return for forfeiture or surrender of rights, or for refraining from exercising rights, and (d) capital sums received as consideration for use or exploitation of assets.'

b Section 22(9):

'The amount of the gains accruing on the disposal of assets shall be computed in accordance with Part I of Schedule 6 to this Act, and subject to the further provisions in Schedules 7 and 8 to this Act, and in this section "capital sum" means any money or money's worth which is not excluded from the consideration taken into account in the computation under the said Part I of Schedule 6 to this
c Act.'

Section 25(2):

'A gift in settlement, whether revocable or irrevocable, is a disposal of the entire property thereby becoming settled property notwithstanding that the donor has some interest as a beneficiary under the settlement and notwithstanding
d that he is a trustee, or the sole trustee, of the settlement.'

Schedule 7, para 10(1), as amended by the Finance Act 1966:

'. . . neither the rights of the insurer nor the rights of the insured under any policy of insurance, whether the risks insured relate to property or not, shall constitute an asset on the disposal of which a gain may accrue.'
e
Sub-paragraph (2):

'Notwithstanding sub-paragraph (1) above, sums received under a policy of insurance of the risk of any kind of damage to, or the loss or depreciation of, assets are for the purposes of this Part of this Act, and in particular for the purposes
f of section 22(3) of this Act, sums derived from the assets.'

Sub-paragraph (3):

'In this paragraph "policy of insurance" does not include a policy of assurance on human life.'

The rival contentions thus emerge with clarity. Counsel for the taxpayer says
g simply that rights under a policy of insurance are an 'asset' from the point of view of capital gains tax: see s 22(1)(a). This asset was disposed of by the trustees to Mr Greene, and by the express provisions of Sch 7, para 10(1), although this was a disposal of such asset by the trustees, no chargeable gain accrued as a result thereof. To this counsel for the Crown says that he accepts completely that no gain accrued on the assignment of the rights under the policy of insurance, but he says that this is not an
h end of the matter. He says that under and by virtue of s 22(3) the sum paid to the trustees by Mr Greene was a 'capital sum' derived from 'assets'—namely, the real property held by the trustees—and that accordingly there has been a disposal of such assets by the trustees, with the inevitable capital gains tax consequences.

Counsel for the taxpayer retorts that s 22(3) is wholly inapplicable, first, because it is expressly made subject 'to the exceptions in this Part of this Act', and that means
j it is subject to the express specific provisions of Sch 7, para 10(1); secondly, because on the true construction of s 22(3) that subsection applies only to a case where there is no asset acquired by the person paying the capital sum, and here Mr Greene did acquire an asset, namely, the rights under the policy; and, thirdly, because in any event the provisions of Sch 7, para 10(1), are specific and must be taken to override, if there is any conflict between them, the general provisions of s 22(3).

Leaving aside for the moment counsel for the taxpayer's two specific objections to
the application of s 22(3), can counsel for the Crown fairly maintain that the sum   *a*
paid by Mr Greene to the trustees was 'derived' from 'assets' held by the trustees,
namely, the real property? He thought he derived some support for the view that
he could from the decision of the House of Lords in *Thomson v Moyse*[1], and more
particularly the speech of Lord Radcliffe therein[2]. That case was very far removed
from the present case. It concerned the applicability of various provisions of the
Income Tax Act 1918 relating to income generated abroad being received in the   *b*
United Kingdom, and the actual decision was that the complicated series of transactions
whereby the taxpayer caused his foreign income to be remitted to the United Kingdom did not serve to disguise the plain, obvious and elementary fact that what was
being remitted to the United Kingdom was his foreign income, any more than there
would have been any real doubt if the taxpayer had used his foreign income to buy
bars of chocolate, brought them to the United Kingdom, and then sold them here.   *c*
What Lord Radcliffe actually said was as follows[2]:

> 'To take the Act first. There is nothing in Case IV about bringing anything in.
> When r. 2 is invoked, the computation in respect of income from foreign
> securities depends simply on the question what is the amount of sums which have
> been or will be received in the United Kingdom in the year of assessment. No   *d*
> doubt proper construction of those words requires that the sums computable
> must be sums "of" the income, by which I would understand "sums of money
> derived from the application of the income to achieving the necessary transfer".
> But that is all. If sterling sums are received and are so attributable, that is enough
> for liability.'

It is because he chose to use the single word 'derived' that counsel for the Crown cited the
case to me; but Lord Radcliffe was not interpreting that word as found in a statute; he
was expounding the effect of quite different words. I accordingly find that case, and
the case which he also cited to me of *Harmel v Wright*[3]—a decision on the same provisions by Templeman J, in which the only novelty was that the chain of transactions
in which the income was transmogrified from one protean form to another was even   *f*
longer than in *Thomson v Moyse*[1]—of no assistance for present purposes whatsoever.

What, in the context of s 22(3) of the 1965 Act, does 'derived' mean? The relevant
dictionary meaning of 'derivation' is to trace or show the origin, and that is what I
think it means here. There is no doubt that the capital sum here actually paid to the
trustees derived, on Mr Greene's side, either from his own private resources or, possibly,
from moneys borrowed by him for the purpose of acquiring the trustees' rights under   *g*
the policies. Certes, these moneys can in no way be said to be 'derived' from any
assets belonging to the trustees. On the other hand, there is no doubt at all but that
the only reason they were paid to the trustees was in exchange for the disposal of their
rights under the policies, which rights are quite obviously, from the point of view of
s 22(3), 'derived' from the underlying real property of the trustees. Is it right to trace
the derivation back in this way? In my view it is not. It appears to me quite clear that   *h*
the capital sum paid by Mr Greene was derived from the sale of the rights under the
policies, and that it is not right to go back any further. If it were legitimate to embark
on the exercise of tracing the derivation of assets back in the manner of an abstract of
title, I do not know where the line could ever properly be drawn. I think that one
must ask the simple question, 'From what asset of the trustees was the capital sum of
£75,192 they received derived?', and the simple answer is that it was derived from the   *j*
assignment of their rights under policies of insurance.

---

1 [1960] 3 All ER 684, [1961] AC 967, 39 Tax Cas 291
2 [1960] 3 All ER at 692, [1961] AC at 995, 39 Tax Cas at 335
3 [1974] 1 All ER 945, [1974] 1 WLR 325, [1974] STC 88

That, of course, is sufficient to dispose of this appeal, but I also think there is merit
a in the other submission of counsel for the taxpayer. Looking closely at s 22 and its
various subsections, it appears to me that the true application of s 22(3) is confined to
cases where no asset is acquired by the person paying the capital sum. One must look
first at s 22(1)(*c*) to see the extreme width of the conception of what are assets for the
purpose of capital gains tax. From this definition, it is quite clear that if the person
paying the capital sum to the disponor receives anything at all in exchange therefor
b which can be said to be a form of property, the simple and universal rule applies that
there is here a disposal of assets for some consideration, and capital gains tax is exigible
accordingly.

Then, s 22(2)(*a*) makes it quite clear that 'disposal' includes 'part disposal', and this
is defined, as it has to be, very widely indeed. Down to the end of this subsection it
appears to me that all cases where the person paying the capital sum has received
c anything at all which could possibly be regarded as an asset have been covered.
Hence, as I view the scheme of the section, when one moves on to sub-s (3) one is
moving on to a case where the person paying the capital sum receives no asset, for
whatever reason, but nevertheless the capital sum is to be taken into account for the
purposes of capital gains tax. This appears to me quite plain from the words 'notwithstanding that no asset is acquired by the person paying the capital sum'. There would
d be no conceivable necessity for enacting that there is a disposal of assets by their owner
where any capital sum is derived from assets in a case where an asset is acquired by
the person paying the capital sum. This is already covered in the preceding two
subsections read together.

Counsel for the Crown argued to the contrary, founding himself on s 25(2), where
the same word 'notwithstanding' is used. I do not think this helps him very much.
e As I read that subsection, its purpose is not to provide a general charging section for
settled property—if assets are disposed of to trustees either on trust for A absolutely
or on the trusts of a settlement there can be no question but that quite apart from this
subsection there is a disposal of them—but to quiet three possible doubts as to quantum. The first is whether there is a complete disposal if there is a revocable settlement;
the second is whether there is a disposal of the whole if a beneficial interest is reserved
f to the settlor in the settlement; and the third is of what there is a disposal if a person
disposes of the property to himself, or to himself and others, but as trustee. I find
the use of the word 'notwithstanding' in this context perfectly simple and straightforward.

But in s 22(3), which has of course a quite different scheme, and where, for the
reasons I have already indicated, I would have expected it to be dealing with a case
g where no capital asset was being acquired by the person paying the capital sum, I
do not think it is permissible to read 'notwithstanding' as 'whether or not': it is used
in a quite different sense. Had there been a comma before the word, then one might
have had to think again as to the true construction of it as a whole. However, I think
that the examples given of matters to which the subsection applies, in particular in
paras (*a*) to (*d*) thereof, all, with one single conceivable exception, show conclusively
h that the draftsman was thinking of capital sums which did not attract corresponding
assets. The sole exception is the word 'surrender' in para (*c*), which, if it stood alone,
could very well apply to cases where a person effected a surrender by way of assignment of a right which then merged in some other right, so that the person paying the
capital sum actually received the right surrendered. Having regard to the examples
as a whole and its direct connection with the word 'forfeiture', I do not consider that
j that word is here used in that sense. It is, I think, used in the sense in which, for
example, a tenant protected under Part II of the Landlord and Tenant Act 1954 may
agree to surrender his rights to his landlord in exchange for a sum of cash. The
landlord acquires no asset as a result, merely an enhancement of the value of his
existing asset.

Further, although counsel for the Crown would not accept this, I find it extremely difficult to think that the framers of para 10(1) of Sch 7 really intended to produce the result that, although there was an apparent exception from capital gains tax when *a* rights under a policy of insurance were assigned, the person making the assignment was nevertheless not saved anything by way of tax at all in that very transaction itself because the very next moment the Revenue could turn round and say: 'Oh, yes, of course there is no capital gains tax on the assignment of the policy rights, but there is nevertheless tax to pay on precisely and exactly the same amount because the consideration for the assignment must be regarded as a capital sum derived from the *b* underlying assets.' At the very least, one would have expected the introduction of the words, 'subject always to any charge for duty under section 22(3)', but there are no such words to be found. On the contrary, s 22(3) is expressly made subject to 'the exceptions in this Part of this Act', which include the provisions of para 10, so that if, contrary to my view, s 22(3) is otherwise capable of applying, it is to be read subject to the exception therein contained, and not vice versa. *c*

Accordingly, at the end of the day I have come to the conclusion that the contentions of the taxpayer are to be preferred, and this appeal must be dismissed accordingly. I realise that this is a most inconvenient conclusion to have reached, but the taxpayer has fairly brought himself within the scope of an exempting provision and the Crown has not succeeded in fairly bringing him within the scope of a charging provision. *d*

Appeal dismissed.

Solicitors: *Solicitor of Inland Revenue*; *Penningtons*, Godalming (for the taxpayer).

Rengan Krishnan Esq Barrister. *e*

Re Everest (deceased)

f

FAMILY DIVISION
LANE J
20th NOVEMBER 1974

Will – Revocation – Destruction – Partial destruction – Lower half of first page of will cut away by testator – Effect to excise clause setting out trusts on which residue to be held – Will other- *g* *wise complete and properly executed – Whether partial destruction indicating intention to revoke will – Whether will should be admitted to probate in mutilated state.*

Having executed a will in June 1958 the testator lodged it with his bank. He withdrew it in August 1960 in order to amend certain provisions but never returned it. Two days after his death in September 1973 his widow found the will among his papers. *h* The lower half of the first page had been cut away. In the will the testator gave certain chattels to his widow for life with directions that after her death the chattels should form part of his residuary estate. Then he devised and bequeathed his real estate and the residue of his personal estate to the bank, which he had appointed as executor and trustee, on certain trusts which could not be ascertained because they were set out in that part which had been cut away. In all other respects the will was *i* complete and was properly executed and attested. The executors sought to admit to probate the will as it stood.

Held – Although in consequence of the mutilation there were no instructions as to the trust which the testator had set up, the mutilation was not such as to give rise to a an inference that it had been done with the intention of revoking the will in toto. The proper inference was that the testator had intended that either his widow should inherit as on intestacy or that some other provision should be substituted which had never been done. Accordingly the will would be admitted to probate in its mutilated state (see p 674 c f and g, post).

Re Woodward (1871) LR 2 P & D 206 applied.

b **Notes**

For the law relating to revocation of wills by partial destruction and mutilation, see 39 Halsbury's Laws (3rd Edn) 895, 896, paras 1363, 1365, and for cases on the subject, see 48 Digest (Repl) 196-198, 205, 206, *1719-1747, 1821-1838*.

Case referred to in judgment

c Woodward (John), Re (1871) LR 2 P & D 206, 40 LJP & M 17, 24 LT 40, 35 JP 216, 48 Digest (Repl) 196, *1722*.

Motion

This was an application by Lloyds Bank Ltd ('the executor') for an order that the will dated 16th June 1958 of George Peter Nussey Everest deceased be admitted to probate.
d The facts are set out in the judgment.

Dennis Levy for the executor.

LANE J. This is a motion to admit to probate a will of 16th June 1958 of the de-
e ceased, George Peter Nussey Everest. The facts are these. On 16th April 1956 the deceased made a valid will, of which a copy is before me. It was drawn up by his solicitors. He deposited it for safe-keeping with his bank, Lloyds Bank at Storrington. On 6th May 1958 he withdrew it. A memorandum card of the bank in relation to that withdrawal reads in this way:

f   'He took away his will, which he proposed to draw up again omitting any benefits to one niece who has come into money.'

On 16th June 1958 he took to the bank a new, typed will which was executed then and there—the bank manager and a bank clerk being the witnesses. Thereupon a further entry was made on the memorandum card to which I have just referred thus:

g   '16.6.58. Executed a new will in office, which he had prepared himself from his old will.'

On 1st August 1960 the deceased withdrew this second will from the bank and did not return it thereto. On 11th September 1973 he died. Two days later his widow and a family friend commenced to sort out his papers; they found the will of 16th June 1958, in respect of which probate is now sought. It was in a used Lloyds Bank
h window envelope bearing a postmark of 24th March 1970. So far all appears to be in order, yet two matters require further consideration. First, the address given as that of the testator is the address which was correctly given as his in the 1956 will, whereas he ceased to live there in August of that year. The inference which I draw is that the deceased asked some unknown person to copy the 1956 will, subject to some alteration perhaps relating to the niece referred to in the bank memorandum I have
j mentioned, but that he omitted to request that the address at the head of the will should be changed. This inference I draw from the facts that the 1958 will was not typed out by his solicitors, for it is on paper of a make which they did not use, and that the deceased did not possess a typewriter and could not type. Had either his solicitors, or he himself, done the typing, presumably his address would have been correctly given.

The second and more important matter for consideration is this: when the will was found it had had the lower half of the first page cut away, obviously with a pair of scissors; what now remains of it contains the usual revocation clause, which of course effectively disposes of the 1956 will; the appointment of Lloyds Bank as the executor and trustee; a gift of his personal chattels to his wife for life, with a direction that she insure the same, and a provision that after her decease the goods and chattels are to fall into and form part of the testator's residuary estate. There is further a devise and bequest of all the real estate and the residue of the personal estate to the bank on trust; but on what trust does not appear, for that must have been contained in the part which has been cut away. What remains continues with a declaration concerning authorised investments, a clause concerning the statutory power of appointment of new trustees, and the signature of the testator and also the attestation.

In my view, the conclusion which is properly to be drawn here is that it was the testator himself who cut off the missing part of the will. His widow, in her affidavit evidence, denied that she had ever seen, or even knew of, the document before it was found following the death of her husband. The mutilation is not such as to raise an inference that it was done animo revocandi of the whole will. I have been referred by counsel for the executors to Re Woodward[1]. I need only read the headnote:

> 'On the death of deceased a will was found in an iron chest, in which the deceased kept important papers. It had been written on the first sides of seven sheets of brief-paper, and had been signed by the deceased and witnesses on each sheet and at the end. The first seven or eight lines had been cut and torn off, but in other respects the will was complete:—Held, that from the mere cutting or tearing off the beginning of the will without other circumstances, it could not be inferred that the deceased intended to revoke the whole will, and that it must be admitted to probate in its incomplete state.'

It seems to me that what the testator intended was that the clauses to which I have referred as still existing should stand but that either his widow should inherit as under an intestacy, or that other provisions should be substituted for those excised, which was never done. These are perhaps matters of speculation. What is important is that even though there be no instructions as to the trust which he set up, there is sufficient remaining of the will to satisfy me that he intended that what remained should be effective. And I am of opinion that it would be wrong to refuse to give effect to the testator's wishes, insofar as these are determinable from what remains of his will. Accordingly, I order that probate issue of the will, mutilated as it is.

Order accordingly.

Solicitors: *Bischoff & Co*, agents for *Fitzhugh, Eggar & Port*, Brighton (for the executor).

R C T Habesch Esq Barrister.

---

1   (1871) LR 2 P & D 206

a
Re Coleman (deceased)
Coleman v Coleman and others

CHANCERY DIVISION
MEGARRY J
b   14th, 15th NOVEMBER 1974

Will – Revocation – Marriage – Will expressed to be made in contemplation of a marriage not subject to revocation – Requirement that will should be made in contemplation of a marriage – Gift in will expressed to be made in contemplation of a marriage – Other gifts containing no such expression – No explicit statement that will itself made in contemplation of a marriage –
c   *Whether sufficient expression that will made in contemplation of a marriage – Law of Property Act 1925, s 177.*

Will – Revocation – Marriage – Will expressed to be made in contemplation of a marriage not subject to revocation – Contemplation of a marriage – Gift to named person described as 'my fiancée' – Whether gift expressed to be made in contemplation of a marriage – Law of Property
d   *Act 1925, s 177.*

By cll 2 and 3 of a will dated 10th September 1971 the testator made certain pecuniary and specific bequests and a specific devise 'unto my fiancée Mrs. Muriel Jeffrey'. Clause 1 appointed executors and trustees and by cl 4 the testator gave the residue of his estate to trustees on trust for sale for such of his only brother and sister as
e   survived him and in equal shares if (as occurred) both survived him. Clause 5 was a substitution clause for residue which did not take effect and the final clause, cl 6, was a professional charging clause. On 18th November 1971 the testator married the fiancée named in his will. He died a year later without making a fresh will. In proceedings for probate of the 1971 will the question arose whether under s 18 of the Wills Act 1837 that will had been revoked on the testator's marriage or whether it was
f   saved by s 177[a] of the Law of Property Act 1925 as a 'will expressed to be made in contemplation of a marriage'. At the hearing evidence was adduced de bene esse that the testator had made the will to guard against the possibility of his dying before the marriage took place and that he had intended to make a fresh will following the marriage.

g   **Held** – (i) The evidence adduced as to the testator's intention at the time when the will was made was inadmissible; the question was one of construction, it being the duty of the court to determine whether the words of the will on their true construction satisfied the language of s 177 on its true construction (see p 683 *a* and *c*, post).
    (ii) In order to comply with s 177, the fact that the will had been made in contemplation of a marriage had to be sufficiently expressed in the will itself; it was not
h   necessary, however, that an intention on the part of the testator that the will was to remain in operation should be established. Since the word 'fiancée' not only described an existing state of affairs but also contemplated a change in that state of affairs, a testamentary gift to a named person described in the will as being the testator's 'fiancée' would normally express a sufficient contemplation of marriage to that person for the purposes of s 177 (see p 679 *f*, p 680 *d* and *e*, p 682 *d* and p 683 *c*, post).
j   (iii) For s 177 to apply, however, it was the will, and not merely some gift in it, which had to be expressed to be 'made' in contemplation of a marriage. In the absence of an explicit statement that the will itself was made in contemplation of a marriage, a will which contained beneficial dispositions which could not be described

---

a Section 177 is set out at p 677 *a*, post

as trivial or immaterial, and which lacked any expression of such a contemplation, could not be described as a 'will' made in contemplation of a marriage. It followed that a the testator's will had been revoked by his subsequent marriage since the residuary gifts in cl 4 could not be described as being trivial or immaterial and in relation to them no contemplation of a marriage was expressed (see p 680 f to j, p 681 c to f and p 683 d and e, post).

Re Langston [1953] 1 All ER 928 and Burton v McGregor [1953] NZLR 487 explained. b

Notes

For wills in contemplation of a marriage, see 39 Halsbury's Laws (3rd Edn) 888, para 1351, and for cases on the subject, see 48 Digest (Repl) 162, 1424 et seq.

For the Wills Act 1837, s 18, see 39 Halsbury's Statutes (3rd Edn) 867.

For the Law of Property Act 1925, s 177, see 27 Halsbury's Statutes (3rd Edn) 598. c

Cases referred to in judgment

Burton v McGregor [1953] NZLR 487, 48 Digest (Repl) 162, *620.

Chase, Re [1951] VLR 477, [1951] ALR 1025, 48 Digest (Repl) 162, *618.

Davis (deceased), In the estate of [1952] 2 All ER 509, [1952] P 279, 48 Digest (Repl) 216, 1928.

Gray, In the estate of (1963) 107 Sol Jo 156. d

Hamilton, Re [1941] VLR 60, 47 Argus LR 52, 48 Digest (Repl) 162 *616.

Knight, Re (1944) unreported.

Langston, Re [1953] 1 All ER 928, [1953] P 100, [1953] 1 WLR 581, 48 Digest (Repl) 162, 1426.

Natusch, Pettit v Natusch, Re [1963] NZLR 273, 48 Digest (Repl) 162, *621.

Pilot v Gainfort [1931] P 103, 100 LJP 60, 145 LT 22, 48 Digest (Repl) 162, 1424. e

Public Trustee v Crawley [1973] 1 NZLR 695.

Sallis v Jones [1936] P 43, [1935] All ER Rep 872, 105 LJP 17, 154 LT 112, 48 Digest (Repl) 162, 1425.

Re Taylor [1949] VLR 201, [1949] ALR 863, 48 Digest (Repl) 162, *617.

Action f

By a writ issued on 26th November 1973 the plaintiff, Leonard Bob Coleman, claimed that the court should pronounce in solemn form for the will made by Herbert Frederick Coleman ('the testator') on 10th September 1971, naming the plaintiff and the third defendant, Douglas Lines, as executors and trustees. The plaintiff contended that the will had not been revoked by the testator's marriage on 18th November 1971 to the first defendant Muriel Coleman ('the widow') since the will had been expressed to be g made in contemplation of that marriage. The plaintiff and the second defendant, Barbara Lucy Allebon, were beneficiaries named in the will. The first defendant counterclaimed that the court should pronounce against the alleged will propounded by the plaintiff on the ground that the will had been revoked by the testator's marriage. The facts are set out in the judgment.

h

E G Nugee for the plaintiff.
Maurice Swift for the widow.
The second and third defendants did not appear and were not represented.

MEGARRY J. This action arises on a will dated 10th September 1971 whereby j the testator, who was a widower some 60 years old, left certain property to Mrs Muriel Jeffery, the first defendant. Rather over two months later, on 18th November 1971, the testator married the first defendant; and nearly a year later, on 8th November 1972, he died. I shall call the first defendant 'the widow'. It is common ground that by the Wills Act 1837, s 18, the marriage revoked the will unless the Law of Property Act 1925, s 177, saved it. Section 177 reads as follows:

a
'(1) A will expressed to be made in contemplation of a marriage shall, notwithstanding anything in section eighteen of the Wills Act, 1837, or any other statutory provision or rule of law to the contrary, not be revoked by the solemnisation of the marriage contemplated.
'(2) This section only applies to wills made after the commencement of this Act'.

b
The plaintiff, who is the only brother of the testator, and the third defendant, a solicitor, are the executors of the will, the plaintiff being beneficially entitled under the will to half the residue. The plaintiff propounds the will for proof in solemn form, contending that s 177 saved it. The widow contends that s 177 does not apply, so that the will was revoked and the testator died intestate; and she counterclaims that the court should pronounce against the will. The second defendant is the only sister of

c
the testator, and is beneficially entitled to the other half of the residue. The one question is whether the will falls within s 177. The second and third defendants have taken no part in the argument, which has been conducted by counsel for the plaintiff and counsel for the widow. As may be inferred from this statement of facts, the widow will receive under the intestacy more than she would take under the will. The estate, I gather, approaches in value the limit of £40,000 to which, in the absence

d
of issue, a widow is absolutely entitled under an intestacy, whereas what she would take under the will would be worth rather less than half of this.
The will was professionally drafted. It is simple in form. It begins by revoking all former wills and testamentary dispositions, and then cl 1 appoints the plaintiff and the third defendant as executors and trustees, and defines the term 'my Trustees'. Clause 2 runs:

e
'I give and bequeath unto my fiancée Mrs. Muriel Jeffery of 20 Mallicot Close Litchfield: (a) all my personal chattels as defined by Form 2 of the Statutory Will Forms 1925; (b) my stamp collection; and (c) the legacy or sum of five thousand pounds.'

Clause 3 states:

f
'I give devise and bequeath unto my said fiancée Mrs. Muriel Jeffery my freehold dwelling house and premises number 13 Churchill Road Rugby aforesaid absolutely'.

Clause 4 gives the residue to the trustees on trust for sale for such of the plaintiff and the second defendant as survive him, and in equal shares if (as occurred) both survive

g
him. Clause 5 is a substitution clause for residue which did not take effect, and cl 6 is a professional charging clause. That is all. The case accordingly turns in the main on the words 'unto my fiancée Mrs. Muriel Jeffrey' in cl 2, and 'unto my said fiancée Mrs. Muriel Jeffery' in cl 3. Do these expressions suffice to show that the will was 'expressed to be made in contemplation of' the marriage that in fact took place and so satisfy s 177?

h
There is a substantial body of authority on the section, or on similar provisions, and I have been carefully taken through the cases. They may be classified under three heads. First, there are the 'general contemplation' cases. In these, the will merely expressed a contemplation of marriage in general, so that the will could not be said to have been made 'in contemplation of a marriage' within the section. 'Marriage' and 'a marriage' are two different concepts; and this is emphasised by the concluding

j
words of the section, 'the solemnisation of the marriage contemplated'. Thus in *Sallis v Jones*[1], the last sentence of the will stated that 'this will is made in contemplation of marriage', and Bennett J held that this did not satisfy the section. In *Re Hamilton*[2] the will made certain detailed dispositions by a long clause beginning 'Should I

---

1 [1936] P 43, [1935] All ER Rep 872
2 [1941] VLR 60

marry prior to my death', and Lowe J held that this did not satisfy a statutory provision substantially similar to s 177. These decisions, if I may say so, seem plainly *a* right, and neither side suggested the contrary, though counsel for the plaintiff did point out that the detailed clause in Re Hamilton¹ appeared to relate to the particular woman whom the testator later married, and that this might have been said to remove the defect of generality. However, I need consider these cases no further, as they do not seem to provide any real assistance in the present case.

Second, there are the 'wife' cases, where in the will the testator describes as his *b* 'wife' someone who is not in fact married to him. In the earliest of these cases, Pilot v Gainfort², a gift to X 'my wife' was held to satisfy the section. The testator's wife had disappeared three years before he began to live with X, six years before he made his will, and seven years before he married X. Lord Merrivale P held³ that the testator had made his will 'At a time when his marriage was obviously within the contemplation of the testator, if he could validly contract it . . .' He said that the section *c* 'prescribes that the solemnization of his marriage shall not revoke his will made in contemplation of that marriage . . .' and that 'the will was in contemplation of the subsequent marriage and practically expresses that contemplation . . .' It will be observed that these statements seem to give little emphasis to the statutory requirement that the will should be 'expressed to be made' in contemplation of the marriage, as distinct from there being a mere factual contemplation of it; and as counsel for the *d* widow observed, there is some difficulty in discerning the exact sense in which the word 'practically' is used. The word 'wife', too, may be said to be an expression of the present rather than a contemplation of the future. For reasons of social conformity or otherwise a man may well describe a woman as his wife even if he has no intention whatever of marrying her. On grounds such as these, in Re Taylor⁴ O'Bryan J refused to follow Pilot v Gainfort², and held that when the testator married X, whom he had *e* previously described in his will as 'my wife' X, that marriage was not 'a marriage in contemplation of which' the will had been 'expressed to be made'.

Then there is Re Gray⁵. There the will gave everything to 'my wife' X, whom the testator had previously 'married' bigamously. Many years later X executed a will benefiting the testator. Some while later the testator discovered that his wife was still living, and X then learned for the first time of her existence. However, the wife *f* died shortly afterwards and the testator then married X. Within a year X died, and a month later the testator died. Sir Jocelyn Simon P held that s 177 saved neither will. When X executed her will, she did not contemplate marrying the testator, as she believed that she was already married to him; and when the testator executed his will he was unlikely to have had it in mind to tell X the truth when his wife died and then go through a second ceremony of marriage with X. The case is very shortly *g* reported, and one may doubt whether the full reasoning emerges. Certainly the report gives some impression that the actual intentions of the testator and X were being considered rather than the intentions expressed in their wills; but this may well have been part of the process of attaching a meaning to the words 'my wife' X, and so on. These three cases do not bear directly on the case before me, but I think they at least indicate that the courts are not at present inclined to spell out of a bare *h* reference to 'my wife' X an expressed contemplation of marrying X. Certainly I do not think that a testator who is in fact married to X could possibly be regarded as expressing an intention to marry her again merely because he describes her in his will as 'my wife X'; and yet, as an expression, 'my wife X' is precisely the same whether or not the testator is in fact married to X.

j

---

1 [1941] VLR 60
2 [1931] P 103
3 [1931] P at 104
4 [1949] VLR 201
5 (1963) 107 Sol Jo 156

The third and most relevant category of cases consists of those where the will
a refers to a named person as 'my fiancée', or uses words having an equivalent effect.
There are four of these cases, and in all save one it has been held that the statute was
satisfied. The earliest case is *Re Knight*[1], briefly mentioned in *Re Langston*[2]. There the
testator's will gave all his property to X 'my future wife', and this was held to be a
sufficient expression of contemplation of marriage to X to save the will from revocation by the testator's subsequent marriage to X. The next case is *Re Chase*[3]. There
b the gift was of two-thirds of the testator's net estate to X 'my fiancée at present travelling to Australia on board the S.S. Stratheden due in Fremantle on the 8th June
1948', and the will was made on June 6, 1948, two days before the arrival date for X.
On those facts Herring CJ held that the testator's marriage to X on 24th June 1948, was
'a marriage in contemplation of which' the will was 'expressed to be made'. Then
there is *Re Langston*[4] itself. There the testator gave his entire estate 'unto my fiancée'
c X, whom he appointed sole executrix. Davies J followed and applied *Re Knight*[5].
He said[6] that the proper test was 'Does the testator express the fact that he is contemplating marriage to a particular person?' He applied that test, and held that it
was satisfied.

The next case was decided some six weeks after *Re Langston*[4], and on the other side
of the world. In *Burton v McGregor*[7] the testator gave his whole estate 'unto my
d fiancée' X, and Adams J held that the will was not 'expressed to be made in contemplation of a marriage'. As one might expect from a jurist of Sir Francis Adams's standing, his reserved judgment contains the most substantial discussion of the subject to be
found in the cases. He expressed his concurrence with the views expressed by O'Bryan
J in *Re Taylor*[8] about *Pilot v Gainfort*[9], and he then discussed *Re Chase*[3] at some length.
He said[10] that he agreed that the question was one of construction of the language
e used in the will, and that extrinsic evidence was admissible in order to identify X
and show that she was in fact the testator's fiancée. But he held that extrinsic evidence
was not admissible merely for the purpose of ascertaining the testator's intention
and showing that the will was made in contemplation of a marriage. That contemplation, he said[10], 'must in order to comply with the statute, be sufficiently expressed
in the will itself'. With that, I would respectfully agree. I shall have to return to the
f question of evidence later. Adams J then both distinguished and dissented from the
decision in *Re Chase*[3]. The will in that case had words in it relating to X's impending
arrival in Australia which were lacking in the case before him; and in that latter
case the question was whether the mere description 'my fiancée' was enough. He
held that it was not. The testator might have been intending to provide for X only
while she remained his fiancée, and the judge regarded the word 'fiancée' as a mere
g word of description such as 'mother' or 'wife'. He held that it was going too far to
hold that the statute was satisfied 'merely because the word "fiancée" signifies that
the testator intends to marry the person so described'. The learned judge further
held[11] that the statutory language meant that the will must be made in contemplation of the marriage 'in the sense that the testator contemplated and intended that
the will should remain in operation notwithstanding the marriage'. I shall return to
h

---

1   (1944) unreported
2   [1953] 1 All ER 928 at 930, [1953] P 100 at 103
3   [1951] VLR 477
4   [1953] 1 All ER 928, [1953] P 100
j 5   (1944) unreported
6   [1953] 1 All ER at 929, [1953] P at 102
7   [1953] NZLR 487
8   [1949] VLR 201
9   [1931] P 103
10   [1953] NZLR at 491
11   [1953] NZLR at 492

this point later. For these reasons, he held that the statute was not satisfied, and so
the will was not saved from being revoked by the marriage of the testator to X.   a

It is plain from what I have said that there is a marked divergence between *Re
Langston*[1] and *Burton v McGregor*[2], each decided in ignorance of the other: and while
counsel for the plaintiff strongly relied on the former, counsel for the widow equally
strongly relied on the latter. One other case was mentioned briefly, *Re Natusch*[3],
but the point there was quite different, and I agree with the view that it provides no
help on the question before me.   b

I think that before I say anything further about the cases, I should return to the
expressions used in the will, and the words of the section, and say what they appear
to me to mean. First, the testamentary expressions to be construed consist of bequests
'unto my fiancée Mrs. Muriel Jeffery' and a devise 'unto my said fiancée Mrs Muriel
Jeffery'. 'Fiancée' is a word which means a woman who is engaged to be married, or
is betrothed, and 'my fiancée' must mean a woman engaged to be married to the   c
speaker. When a man speaks of 'my fiancée' he is speaking of 'the woman to whom I
am engaged to be married'. It seems to me that in ordinary parlance a contemplation
of marriage is inherent in the very word 'fiancée'. The word 'wife' is a word which
denotes an existing state of affairs, and one that will continue until death, or, these
days, divorce: but I do not think that it could reasonably be said that there inheres
in the word 'wife' any contemplation of a change of that state of affairs, whether by   d
death or divorce. 'Fiancée' seems to me to be quite different, in that it not only describes an existing state of affairs but also contemplates a change in that state of affairs.
No doubt some engagements last a long time, and others are broken off: but the normal future for an engagement is its termination by marriage, or perhaps I should
say its sublimation into marriage. Provided the 'contemplation' is real, I cannot see
that it makes much difference whether or not there is any particular degree of immi-   e
nence about the marriage. Accordingly in my judgment, unless curtailed by the
context, a testamentary reference to 'my fiancée X' per se contemplates the marriage
of the testator to X, as well as describing an existing status.

Second, the statutory expression to be construed is 'a will expressed to be made in
contemplation of a marriage'. Given a contemplation of the marriage, that has to be
expressed in relation to the making of the will. The words 'will' and 'made' must be   f
given due weight. It is the will, and not merely some gift in it, that must be expressed
to be 'made' in contemplation of a marriage. The statute is not framed in terms of a
will 'in which a contemplation of a marriage is expressed', or a will 'containing a
disposition expressed to be made in contemplation of a marriage'. It is the will itself,
which I think must mean the will as a whole and not just bits of it, that must be
'expressed to be made' in contemplation of a marriage. An expression to this effect   g
may appear simply enough if a clause is inserted which states 'This will is made in
contemplation of my marriage to X', or contains some such words. That, of course,
was not done in the present case. But I do not think that this is the only way of
achieving the result. If each beneficial disposition made by the will is expressed to be
made in contemplation of the testator's marriage to X, then it seems to me that the
will as a whole must have been expressed to be made in contemplation of that   h
marriage. What governs all the parts of a will must govern the will as a whole.
I do not have to decide whether the absence of any such expressed contemplation
from some non-beneficial provision, such as an appointment of executors, would
prevent the section from applying; at present I would doubt it.

On the other hand, where some of the beneficial dispositions in the will lack any
expression of such a contemplation, I find it difficult to see how it can be said that the   i
'will' is expressed to be made in contemplation of a marriage. To take an example

---

1   [1953] 1 All ER 928, [1953] P 100
2   [1953] NZLR 487
3   [1963] NZLR 273

that I put to counsel for the plaintiff in argument, if in cl 17(e) of a will disposing of an
a estate of £100,000 the testator left £100, or a gold ring, or something of the sort, to
'my fiancée Mary', but made no other provision for her, one could certainly say that
the testator had expressed a contemplation of marriage to Mary in the will, and also
in making that bequest; but it would be extravagant to say that the will was 'a will
expressed to be made in contemplation of a marriage'. Counsel for the plaintiff was
constrained to accept this: but his reply was that it sufficed if in substance, or to any
b substantial degree, the will was expressed to be made in contemplation of a marriage.
The £100 or a gold ring he dismissed as being in the nature of de minimis: but he
said that if, as in the present case, the provision made by the will for the fiancée was
substantial, then the section was satisfied.

I do not think that this can be right. Under the section one is concerned not with what
the testator actually contemplated, but what contemplation is 'expressed' in the will.
c If that contemplation relates not to the will as a whole but only to part of it, then even
if that part is substantial I do not see how it can be said that it is the will which is
expressed to be made in that contemplation. No doubt with the aid of the Interpretation Act 1889, s 1(1)(b), the expression 'a will' in the singular may be read as including
'wills' in the plural; but I know of nothing which in the present context would allow
the expression 'a will' to be read as including 'bits of a will'. In my judgment, 'a
d will' means the whole will, and not merely parts of it, even if they are substantial;
and the will that is 'made' is of necessity the whole will. It may indeed be that merely
trivial parts can be ignored, so that 'a will' can be read as being 'the whole of a will,
or substantially the whole of a will': but I cannot regard 'any substantial part of a
will' as being 'a will'. In my view, the question to ask is, 'Was the will as a whole expressed to be made in contemplation of the particular marriage that has been
e celebrated?'

If that is right, as I think it is, it disposes of this case; for nobody could dismiss the
residuary gifts as being merely trivial or immaterial, and in relation to them no
contemplation of the marriage is expressed. In my judgment, the will before me is
not 'a will' which is expressed to be 'made' in contemplation of a marriage, even
though it contains provisions which are expressed to be made in such contemplation.
f There remains, however, the question how far this view is consonant with the
authorities, and especially with Re Langston[1]. As I have mentioned, the test propounded
in that case[2] was 'Did the testator express the fact that he was contemplating
marriage to a particular person?' If all that Parliament required was something in
the will which showed that when the testator made it he was contemplating a particular marriage, thereby demonstrating that he had the marriage in mind when he
g made his dispositions, I do not see why Parliament did not speak simply in terms of
requiring the will to express such a contemplation. Instead, Parliament used the
stricter and more specific language which requires that the 'will' should be 'expressed
to be made' in that contemplation. If, of course, one accepts the test laid down in Re
Langston[2] and applies it to the present case, the answer must be that the test is satisfied, whereas on the test that I have suggested the mere expression of such a contempla-
h tion in some of the dispositions made by the will, without more, would not suffice.
However, one must remember that Re Langston[1] was argued only by the applicant
(the other parties consenting), and that in any case the will in fact gave the whole of
the testator's estate to his named fiancée. By reason of that fact, the application of
the test that I have suggested would have produced the same result in Re Langston[1]
as the test applied by Davies J. In other words, I would respectfully agree with his
j decision, though for somewhat different reasons. I would similarly agree with the
result in Re Knight[3].

---

1   [1953] 1 All ER 928, [1953] P 100
2   [1953] 1 All ER at 929, [1953] P at 102
3   (1944) unreported

Burton v McGregor[1] was also a case in which the will gave the testator's entire estate to his fiancée. The decision appears to rest on two grounds. First, 'fiancée' was held to **a** be a word which merely described a present status without also importing the necessary contemplation of marriage. On this, I would respectfully prefer to follow the view taken by Davies J in *Re Langston*[2], a case which was not, of course, before Adams J. I would also follow the view on this point expressed by Herring CJ in *Re Chase*[3], though since the contemplation there related only to a gift of two-thirds of the testator's estate, I would with respect question whether the will as a whole was **b** expressed to have been made in contemplation of the marriage.

Second, in *Burton v McGregor*[4], as I have indicated, it was held that the statutory language required it to be established 'that the will was made in contemplation of the marriage in the sense that the testator contemplated and intended that the will should remain in operation notwithstanding the marriage;' in the absence of explicit words, what must be sought 'is an expression of such contemplation and intention'. **c** Counsel for the widow at first endeavoured to support this view, but in the end he strove no longer. With all due respect, the requirement of the statute seems to me to be single and not double: one must not confuse the conditions for the section to operate with the result when it does not operate, or read into the statute words which are not there. All that the statute requires is that the will should be 'expressed to be made in contemplation' of the marriage in fact celebrated. Where **d** this is the case, the result is that the will remains in operation despite the marriage; but I cannot see that there is any requirement that an intention to produce this result must be established. In my view, an expression of the necessary contemplation in the will suffices to preserve it from revocation by the marriage, however ignorant or muddle-headed the testator may have been about the consequences of expressing the intention. I leave on one side, of course, cases of fraud, accident, mistake and the **e** like which might affect the validity of provisions in the will.

I am aware that the cases do not appear to have discussed the point that I have been examining, and I have therefore considered whether I ought to reserve my judgment. However, I have had the benefit of a full and careful deployment of the authorities, for which I must thank counsel for the plaintiff in particular, and I have heard ample argument on their significance. Indeed, more appears to have been put before me **f** than has been put before any of the courts in the other cases. I therefore do not think that I need take further time for consideration.

There is one further point that I should mention. Counsel for the widow sought to tender the viva voce evidence of Mr Lines, the third defendant, who drafted the will for the testator. Counsel for the plaintiff contended that such evidence was inadmissible on the point, which was merely one of construing the will and the statute. **g** After some discussion, counsel for the plaintiff very sensibly accepted that the best course to pursue was to do what had been done in a number of previous cases, and that was to hear the evidence de bene esse, while preserving for him his full right to object to its admissibility. This was done. The evidence was to the effect that in giving instructions for his will the testator was concerned to make provision for his fiancée until the marriage took place, but that he had said that he intended to **h** make a new will as soon as he was married, in view of Mr Lines's advice to him that he ought to do so because his will would be revoked by the marriage. The testator had told Mr Lines of the case of a relation of his who had died intestate, leaving a fiancée who had received nothing under the intestacy; and this the testator regarded as being unjust, and wished to avoid in his own case. In fact, the testator never made another will. **j**

---

1 [1953] NZLR 487
2 [1953] 1 All ER 928, [1953] P 100
3 [1951] VLR 477
4 [1953] NZLR 487 at 492

In my judgment, none of this evidence is admissible. The question is one of con-
a struction: the court must determine whether the words of the will, on their true
construction, satisfy the language of the section, on its true construction. For this
purpose I cannot see how evidence of what the testator told his solicitor he wanted, or
what his solicitor advised him, can possibly be admissible. The evidence is not evidence that is tendered merely for the purpose of identifying the widow, or proving the
marriage, or for some other admissible factual purpose. This view, though left open
b in *Sallis v Jones*[1], seems to me to be fully supported by *Re Hamilton*[2], by *Re Taylor*[3],
and by *Burton v McGregor*[4] in the passage that I have mentioned; and I do not think
that *Re Davis*[5] provides any real assistance on the point. If I am wrong in this, then I
cannot see anything in the evidence to alter the conclusion that I have reached without
its aid; indeed, it would reinforce it.

Finally, I may summarise my views as follows. First, the operation of the section is
c a matter of construction on which extrinsic evidence of intention or purpose is inadmissible. Second, a testamentary gift to a named person described in the will as
being the testator's fiancée will normally express a sufficient contemplation of marriage
to that person for the purposes of the section. Such a gift to a person described in the
will as being the testator's wife may well not satisfy the section, though the point
does not arise here, and I decide nothing on it. Third, for the section to apply the will
d must contain an expression which sufficiently shows that the will as a whole was made
in contemplation of the particular marriage celebrated. Fourth, expressions in the
will which merely show that parts of the will were made in contemplation of the
marriage celebrated will not suffice unless those parts amount at least to substantially
the whole of the beneficial dispositions made by the will.

For the reasons that I have given I hold that the will before me was revoked by the
e testator's marriage and that the section did not save it. I therefore pronounce in
solemn form against the will, and hold that the testator died intestate.

Order accordingly.

24th February 1975. *Note by Megarry J.* I have now come on *Public Trustee v Crawley*[6].
f There, Mahon J followed *Burton v McGregor*[7] in preference to *Re Langston*[8], and
considered some of the other authorities put before me. He held that where by his
will a testator had given all his property to 'my fiancée' X, the will, though showing
that a marriage was contemplated, had nevertheless failed to establish that it had
been made in contemplation of that marriage. Whatever effect this decision, if cited,
might have had on my reasoning, I do not see how it could have altered the result in
g the case before me. But the decision is plainly of relevance in construing the statute,
and I add this note so that it will not be overlooked.

Solicitors: *Bolton & Lowe*, agents for *Michael Prior & Co*, Birmingham (for the plaintiff);
Brown, Turner, Compton Carr & Co (for the widow).

h   F K Anklesaria Esq Barrister.

---

1 [1936] P 43 at 46, [1935] All ER Rep 872 at 874
2 [1941] VLR at 61
3 [1949] VLR at 202
4 [1953] NZLR at 491
j 5 [1952] 2 All ER 509, [1952] P 279
6 [1973] 1 NZLR 695
7 [1953] NZLR 487
8 [1953] 1 All ER 928, [1953] P 100

Re New Finance & Mortgage Co Ltd (in liquidation)

CHANCERY DIVISION
GOULDING J
28th JUNE, 8th JULY, 17th JULY 1974

Company – Memorandum of association – Objects clause – Construction – Objects to carry on business inter alia as 'merchants generally' – Meaning of 'merchant' – Retail trading – Company taking lease of petrol station – Company selling motor fuel by way of retail trade – Whether company carrying on business as 'merchants generally'.

Company – Memorandum of association – Objects clause – Construction – Objects to carry on business inter alia as 'concessionaires' – Meaning of 'concessionaire' – Company obtaining lease of petrol station from petrol company – Company agreeing to obtain all its supplies of motor fuel from lessors – Whether lease and trading relationship with lessors constituting a concession – Whether company carrying on business as 'concessionaires'.

Under sub-cl (a) of the objects clause of the memorandum of association of a company, the objects of the company were stated to be: 'To carry on business as financiers, capitalists, concessionaires, bankers, commercial agents, mortgage brokers, financial agents and advisers, exporters and importers of goods and merchandise of all kinds, and merchants generally.' The company carried on the business of a petrol filling and service station proprietor on premises held under an underlease from the applicants. The underlease contained a tie clause whereby the applicants bound themselves to supply to the company and the company bound itself to buy from the applicants, the whole of the company's requirements of motor fuel for sale at the premises, and the applicants in return allowed the company a rebate on the price of the motor fuel. In the course of its business the company sold by way of retail trade motor fuel, lubricants, spare parts and accessories for motor vehicles, sweets and tobacco. The company went into voluntary liquidation. The applicants lodged a proof in the winding-up founded on a judgment debt for motor fuel sold and delivered to the company. The liquidator rejected the proof on the ground that the debt had been incurred in the course of ultra vires trading. The applicants sought to reverse the liquidator's decision, contending that the company's main activity of retail trade in motor fuel and other goods could properly be described as carrying on the business either of 'concessionaires' or of 'merchants generally' within the meaning of sub-cl (a) of the objects clause.

Held – (i) Neither the underlease nor the trading relationship it provided constituted a concession by the applicants and the position of the word 'concessionaires' in sub-cl (a) between 'capitalists' and 'bankers' militated against its extension to the company's retail trading venture. Accordingly the company's business at the premises could not be described as that of 'concessionaires' within the meaning of sub-cl (a) and the applicants' proof could not be justified by reference to the word 'concessionaires' in the subclause (see p 686 g to j, post).

(ii) On their true construction, the words 'and merchants generally' in sub-cl (a) extended to all purely commercial occupations whether by way of wholesale or retail trading and therefore an authorisation to carry on business as 'exporters and importers of goods and merchandise of all kinds, and merchants generally, was wide enough to cover the company's business as proved by the evidence. Accordingly the liquidator's decision would be reversed and the applicants' proof allowed (see p 686 j to p 687 b and p 689 e to j, post).

Note

^a For the construction of objects clauses, 'see 7 Halsbury's Laws (4th Edn) 421, 422, para 703, and for cases on the subject, see 9 Digest (Repl) 81-83, *340-353*.

Cases referred to in judgment

Crown Bank, Re (1890) 44 Ch D 634, 59 LJCh 739, 62 LT 823, 9 Digest (Repl) 81, *344*.

Hamond v Jethro (1611) 2 Brownl 97, 123 ER 836, 30 Digest (Reissue) 350, *699*.

^b Josselyn v Parson (1872) LR 7 Exch 127, 41 LJEx 60, 25 LT 912, 36 JP 455, 30 Digest (Reissue) 351, *700*.

Lovell & Christmas Ltd v Wall (1911) 104 LT 85, CA, 45 Digest (Repl) 508, *964*.

Randell v Block (1893) 38 Sol Jo 141, 31(1) Digest (Reissue) 390, *3107*.

Adjourned summons

^c By summons dated 12th April 1973, the applicant, Total Oil Great Britain Ltd ('Total'), which had lodged a proof in the winding-up of the company, New Finance and Mortgage Co Ltd, applied for an order that the decision of the liquidator of the company in rejecting the applicants' proof for the sum of £23,748·39 be reversed and the applicants' proof be admitted in full. The facts are set out in the judgment.

^d *Oliver Weaver* for Total.

Gavin Lightman for the liquidator.

Cur adv vult

^e 17th July. **GOULDING J** read the following judgment. The facts of this case are very simple but they give rise to a linguistic problem that I have found difficult. It is raised by a summons in the winding-up of a company named New Finance and Mortgage Co Ltd. The company was incorporated in England with an authorised capital of £5,000 on or about 20th January 1956. Its memorandum of association contains an objects clause of which I shall now read those parts that may be material. The clause is numbered as usual cl 3 of the memorandum of association and it begins ^f as follows:

'The objects for which the Company is established are:—(a) To carry on business as financiers, capitalists, concessionaires, bankers, commercial agents, mortgage brokers, financial agents and advisers, exporters and importers of goods and merchandise of all kinds, and merchants generally. (b) To advance and borrow money, negotiate loans, and lend money for any purpose or object, with or without security, including the lending of money to finance hire purchase agreements in respect of any property or assets.'

I omit as irrelevant for present purposes sub-cll (c) and (d), but I should read sub-cl (e):

^h 'To apply for, purchase, or otherwise acquire any patents, licences or concessions which may be capable of being dealt with by the Company, or be deemed to benefit the Company and to grant rights thereout.'

I can now go to the last numbered sub-clause, sub-cl (s):

'To do all such other things as are incidental or conducive to the attainment of ^j the above objects or any of them.'

And then cl 3 ends with the following not unfamiliar declaration:

'It is declared that the foregoing sub-clauses shall be construed independently of each other and none of the objects therein mentioned shall be deemed to be merely subsidiary to the objects contained in any other sub-clause.'

It is not suggested that the concluding paragraph has any application to the ranking
of objects listed in one and the same subclause, it operates only as between two or *a*
more subclauses.

The company for some time carried on the business of a filling and service station
proprietor at Yiewsley and at Richmond, both in the outer suburbs of London. It
traded under the name NFM Garages. It held the premises at Yiewsley under an
underlease dated 22nd January 1968 for 21 years less one day from 21st December
1966 at substantial yearly rents. The underlease was granted to the company by *b*
Total Oil Great Britain Ltd to whom I shall refer shortly as 'Total'. The lease
contained a tie clause whereby Total bound itself to supply to the company, and the
company bound itself to purchase from Total, the whole of the company's requirements of motor fuel for sale at the premises, Total in return allowing the company a
specified rebate on the price of the motor fuel. Total also obtained certain rights
touching the sale of lubricants on the premises. Total did not accept any restriction *c*
on its freedom to supply competing businesses in Yiewsley or elsewhere. It would
seem that Total also had some interest in the premises at Richmond, but I have not
been asked to examine the evidence on that matter.

In the course of its business the company sold to the motoring public by way of
retail trade motor fuel, lubricants, spare parts and accessories for motor vehicles,
sweets and tobacco. There is also evidence that the company bought and sold *d*
motor cars.

Pursuant to a resolution dated 13th June 1972 the company is being wound-up
voluntarily. Total has lodged a proof in the winding-up founded on a judgment debt
of £23,748·39 for goods sold and delivered, namely, motor fuel delivered to the
company both at Yiewsley and at Richmond. The liquidator of the company, acting
on the advice of counsel, has rejected Total's proof on the ground that the debt was *e*
incurred in the course of trading which was ultra vires. He has rejected the proofs of
other creditors for the like reason. Total, by this summons, asks the court to reverse
the liquidator's decision. All the material events took place before the entry of the
United Kingdom into the European Communities, and it is therefore unnecessary to
consider the effect of the European Communities Act 1972.

So I have to decide whether the company's business was intra vires or ultra vires. *f*
It is common ground that that depends on whether the company's main activity of
retail trading in motor fuel and other goods can properly be described as carrying on
the business either of concessionaires or of merchants within the meaning of sub-cl
(a) of the objects clause. If it can, any relevant subsidiary activities of the company can
no doubt be justified under sub-cl (s) of the clause as incidental or conducive to such
retail trading. *g*

In my judgment the business was not that of concessionaires within sub-cl (a).
The word is used in various contexts to indicate the holder of something that can be
called a concession. It is contended that here the company's lease, or the trading
relationship for which it provided, constituted a concession by Total; and that in
exploiting such concession the company was carrying on the business of a concessionaire. I doubt whether any ordinary user of the English language, whether lawyer or *h*
businessman, would find that argument convincing. I also think that the position
of the word 'concessionaires' in sub-cl (a) between 'capitalists' and 'bankers', militates
against its extension to the company's retail trading venture. The appearance of the
word 'concessions' in sub-cl (e) has also been relied on in argument, but I question
whether it throws any light on the interpretation of 'concessionaires' in sub-cl (a).

Since I find that Total cannot justify its proof by reference to 'concessionaires', I *j*
turn to the alternative contention: was the company carrying on business as a merchant within the meaning of the phrase '. . . to carry on business as . . . exporters and
importers of goods and merchandise of all kinds and merchants generally'?

My first impression, when the summons was opened by counsel, was clearly in
favour of Total. I thought the word 'merchant' in its general sense meant any trader

a who buys and sells to make a profit. I regarded it as a term contrasted in political economy with 'manufacturer' on the one hand and with 'financier' on the other. When I first entered the profession of the law it was not uncommon for a small shop-keeper to describe himself in formal documents as a merchant, and while there was a touch of grandiloquence about the addition I never supposed it to be untrue or verbally unapt. (Compare the observations of Chitty J in *Randell v Block*[1].)

b Counsel for the liquidator put forward a narrower construction. He submitted that in sub-cl (a) of the company's objects clause the reference to 'merchants generally' covers only wholesale trades. I will deal first with two arguments for the narrower construction that are founded on context.

Counsel for the liquidator emphasised first of all the importance of the company's name and referred me to *Re Crown Bank*[2]. In the present case, the name New Finance and Mortgage Co Ltd suggests a moneylending business, or something

c closely allied to it. But as soon as one looks at the very first subclause in the objects clause, sub-cl (a), one sees that the authorised business goes far beyond the merely financial. To rely successfully on the company's name counsel must contend that it points to a distinction in interpreting sub-cl (a), so that some one or more of the businesses there first mentioned are to be taken as the true primary object of the company, all that follows being relegated to an ancillary and subordinate role. The

d first three terms in the subclause are, however, so imprecise, and the residue so various, that in my judgment such a construction is not possible. The truth is that the entire objects clause is too loosely drawn to be of any real value to subscribers or to persons dealing with the company. In *Re Crown Bank*[2] North J, rightly or wrongly, looked at a prospectus and at a circular issued to shareholders as putting a construction on the memorandum of association and showing the meaning of the parties and the

e words they used. I have nothing of that sort to guide me here and I cannot get enough help out of the name alone. The argument would have had more force if sub-cl (b) of the objects clause had preceded sub-cl (a) and the final declaration as to independent objects had been omitted.

Secondly, counsel for the liquidator invited me to apply the ejusdem generis canon of construction to sub-cl (a). He felt unable to confine all the nine species there

f enumerated within a single genus, but proposed two genera, 'financiers' on the one hand and 'wholesale dealers' on the other. To my mind that is a somewhat con-torted taxonomy. Assuming the term 'merchants' to be ambiguous, the argument at its strongest will only restrict it to 'wholesalers' if the other species of the com-mercial genus is clearly limited in that way. But that other species is in fact open to the same question as the species 'merchants'. Would it have been ultra vires the

g company if carrying on an export and import business to have exported English books and magazines to individuals ordering them by post from abroad, or to have imported wine in bulk and sold it at a retail establishment? In my judgment, those questions are as open as the one that I have to decide. The ejusdem generis principle does not help me.

The real force of counsel's argument in favour of the narrower construction, and it

h is formidable, is supplied by the New English Dictionary and its abbreviated editions. The New English Dictionary[3] itself begins its definition of the substantive 'merchant' as follows:

'A. . . . . 1. One whose occupation is the purchase and sale of marketable commodities for profit; originally applied *gen.* to any trader in goods not manu-

j factured or produced by himself; but from an early period restricted (*exc. Sc.* and *dial.*: see d) to wholesale traders, and *esp.* to those having dealings with foreign

---

1 (1893) 38 Sol Jo 141
2 (1890) 44 Ch D 634
3 (1908) Vol VI

countries. Often with defining word, indicating the class of goods dealt in, as in *coal—, corn—, spirit—, wine-merchant*, etc. (some of which combinations are *a* frequently applied to retail traders), or the countries traded with, as *East India, Turkey merchant.*'

Among the examples given under that part of the definition is one from Jowett's well-known translation of Plato's Dialogues, published in 1875: 'The importers and exporters, who are called merchants,' and another from a publication of 1881: 'He was *b* not a merchant. He had never been engaged in foreign trade.' Further on in the definition we find the s (d) referred to in what I have already read, which reads: 'd. A shopkeeper. Now only *Sc., north. dial.*, and *U.S.*' Among the various examples given in that section is one from De Quincey's autobiography of 1845: 'My father was a merchant; not in the sense of Scotland, where it means a retail dealer . . . but in the English sense.' The volume of the New English Dictionary from which I have read *c* extracts was published in 1908.

The oldest judicial authority cited by counsel on the meaning of 'merchant' was a passage in *Hamond v Jethro*[1]. It is there reported of the Common Bench in Trinity term 1611 that—

'it was agreed by all the Justices, that by the Law of Merchants, if two Merchants joyn in Trade, that of the increase of that, if one dye, the other shall not *d*
have the benefit by survivor: See *Fitzherberts Natura Brevium, Accompt*, 38 Ed. 3.
And so of two Joynt Shop-keepers, for They are Merchants: for as *Coke* saith,
there are four sorts of Merchants, that is, Merchant Adventurers, Merchants
Dormants, Merchants Travelling, and Merchants Residents, and amongst them
all there shall be no benefit by survivor. *Jus accrescendi inter Mercatores locum*
non habet.'   *e*

The authority of that passage as a matter of law is incontestable. On the meaning of words I think it is now too remote to be a safe guide to recent usage.

A later decision to which I have been referred is *Josselyn v Parson*[2]. Counsel for Total cited it in support of the wider construction for which he contends. The court there held that a condition not to travel for any porter, ale or spirit merchant was not *f* broken by travelling for a brewer. Bramwell B said[3]:

'. . . that a merchant of or in an article is one who *buys and sells* it, and not the
manufacturer selling. A wine grower is not a wine merchant; even a wine importer is not called a wine merchant, but a wine importer.'

Pigott B was of the same opinion. I do not think that case helps counsel for Total *g* very much, for the Court of Exchequer was not really confronted with the term 'merchant' in its general signification. The same applies to the observations of Eve J in *Lovell & Christmas Ltd v Wall*[4].

Dictionaries of different date that I have examined are by no means uniform in their interpretation of the term 'merchant'. Dr Johnson in 1755 defined a merchant as 'one who trafficks to remote countries'. Webster's Dictionary, of North American *h* origin, as reprinted in London in 1832, has the following entry:

'1. A man who trafficks or carries on trade with foreign countries, or who
exports and imports goods and sells them by wholesale. 2. In *popular usage*, any
trader, or one who deals in the purchase and sale of goods.'

Skeat's Dictionary of 1882, a great favourite in its day, says simply: 'Merchant, a *j* trader', but it is fair to remark that Professor Skeat was much more interested in the

---

1   (1611) 2 Brownl 97
2   (1872) LR 7 Exch 127
3   LR 7 Exch at 129
4   (1911) 103 LT 588 at 591

a derivation than in the meaning of words. A later edition of Webster in 1890 contains the following definition:

> 1.   One who traffics on a large scale, especially with foreign countries; a trafficker; a trader. [Item 2 is irrelevant.] 3. One who keeps a store or shop for the sale of goods; a shopkeeper. (*U.S. & Scot.*)'

b Finally, Chambers's Dictionary in the edition of 1972 defines a merchant as 'a trader, esp. wholesale: a shopkeeper'. Chambers may be suspect because of its Scottish origins, but the current edition is careful to distinguish Doricisms where they occur and does not qualify the definition that I have just read.

In my own experience, the word 'merchant' is now rarely used without qualification, except in the economic sense already mentioned where it distinguishes the trader from any other species of entrepreneur, for example, a manufacturer. Where it
c is qualified it may signify, according to the qualification, either a wholesale or a retail trader. Thus coal merchants and wine merchants, as the New English Dictionary recognises, are commonly retailers. A provision merchant may be a wholesaler but frequently is, or at any rate was in my youth, much the same as a retail grocer. A paper merchant on the other hand is commonly a wholesaler; paper is sold retail by
d a stationer. Sometimes it is necessary to indicate expressly the limits of the term by the word 'wholesale' or 'retail'. For example, in the London Yellow Pages Classified telephone directory I find a heading of 'Fish Merchants—Wholesale,' the retailers being classed as 'Fishmongers'. There are other groups, such as builders, merchants who are in a sense retailers, but retailers to a special section of the public carrying on a particular trade.

Having surveyed the history and use of the word 'merchant' to the extent I have
e indicated, I must turn back to the company's memorandum of association and apply my own judgment to the language it contains. I see no justification in current or historical usage for supposing that the reference to 'merchants' was inserted to cover wholesalers in domestic trade. The real choice, as I see it, is either to read the words: '. . . and merchants generally,' as adding nothing to the preceding reference to
f '. . . exporters and importers of goods and merchandise of all kinds'; or, on the other hand, to extend them to all purely commercial occupations. The former follows Dr Johnson's old definition; the latter embraces all the current uses of 'merchant' in different contexts.

On the whole, it is the latter that I prefer, and not only because it coincides with my first impression. Even in this memorandum of association I should be slow to dismiss words as unnecessary surplusage; and I also think that the word 'generally'
g here points to a wide construction of the word that precedes it.

In my judgment, therefore, an authorisation to carry on business as 'exporters and importers of goods and merchandise of all kinds, and merchants generally' was wide enough to cover the company's business as proved by the evidence. I must, accordingly, reverse the liquidator's decision and allow Total's proof.

h *Liquidator's decision reversed and proof allowed.*

Solicitors: *Denton, Hall & Burgin* (for Total); *Stones, Porter & Co* (for the liquidator).

Evelyn M C Budd   Barrister.

AA

Smirk v Lyndale Developments Ltd

a

COURT OF APPEAL, CIVIL DIVISION
CAIRNS, LAWTON LJJ AND WALTON J
5th NOVEMBER 1974

b

Landlord and tenant – Surrender of tenancy – Surrender on grant of new tenancy – Agreement – Inference of agreement to surrender tenancy and substitute new tenancy – Weekly tenancy – Transfer of reversion to new landlord – New landlord giving tenant new rent book – Terms stated in rent book differing in some respects from terms stipulated by previous landlord – New rent book stating that house let on terms stated where such terms not inconsistent with existing tenancy – Rent unchanged – Whether terms in new rent book supporting inference of agreement – Whether agreement to substitute new tenancy.

c

The plaintiff was granted a weekly tenancy of a dwelling-house and land in 1955 by his employers, the British Railways Board. He was issued with a rent book which stated, inter alia, that the house was 'let to the tenant in consequence of his employment' by the board but contained no requirement that the tenant should vacate the premises if he gave up his work. The rent book also contained a provision that, with the tenant's authority, rent was payable by deduction from his wages unless for any reason (e g sickness) they were paid by some other method. Soon after the plaintiff had taken possession he began to cultivate a strip of land forming part of waste land at the back of the house which also belonged to the board. By 1960 the plaintiff had taken effective possession of the strip. In 1968 the defendants bought the freehold of the tenant's house as well as the waste land from the board. They bought the house subject to the existing tenancy. The defendants distributed a new rent book to the plaintiff which contained the condition that 'these premises are let on the following terms (where such terms are not inconsistent with an existing tenancy) . . .' The terms were substantially the same as those made by the board. The differences were: (i) the period of notice to terminate the tenancy by either side was increased from one to four weeks (four weeks being the minimum period that was required to evict a tenant following the enactment of the Rent Act 1957); and (ii) the plaintiff was prohibited from keeping birds or animals and from taking in paying guests without the defendants' consent. The rent remained unchanged. The plaintiff continued to cultivate the strip of land until 1971 when the defendants began to make preparations to develop the waste land. The plaintiff sought a declaration that he had a good possessory title to the strip or alternatively that he held it as an extension of the locus of his tenancy. Pennycuick V-C[a] dismissed both claims holding, inter alia, that, although the plaintiff would have been entitled to a declaration that he held the strip as an extension of the locus of his tenancy against the board, that tenancy had been terminated and a new tenancy created when the defendants distributed the new rent book. The plaintiff appealed.

d

e

f

g

h

Held – The distribution of the new rent book did not amount to an agreement to surrender the existing tenancy and substitute a new one. The terms contained in the new rent book were common form terms and, even if they provided evidence of an agreement, they did no more than show an agreement to vary the terms of the existing tenancy. The only inference that could be drawn from the terms set out in the new rent book was that the plaintiff was to continue on much the same terms as he had when the board had been his landlords. The plaintiff was therefore entitled to a declaration that he had extended the locus of his tenancy to include the

j

---

a   strip and the appeal would be allowed accordingly (see p 694 *j*, p 695 *a* to *j* and p 696 *a* to *c e f* and *j*, post).

Joseph v Joseph [1966] 3 All ER 486 applied.

Decision of Pennycuick V-C [1974] 2 All ER 8 reversed in part.

Note

b   For the surrender of a tenancy by operation of law, see 23 Halsbury's Laws (3rd Edn) 685-687, paras 1414, 1415, and for cases on the subject, see 31(2) Digest (Reissue) 860-869, 7134-7208.

Cases referred to in judgments

Joseph v Joseph [1966] 3 All ER 486, [1967] Ch 78, [1966] 3 WLR 631, CA, 31(2) Digest (Reissue) 940, 7707.

c   Tabor v Godfrey (1895) 64 LJQB 245, 31(2) Digest (Reissue) 925, 7637.

Cases also cited in argument

Braithwaite & Co Ltd v Elliott [1946] 2 All ER 537, [1947] KB 177, CA.

Bungalows (Maidenhead) Ltd v Mason [1954] 1 All ER 1002, [1954] 1 WLR 769, CA.

d   **Appeal**

By a writ issued on 14th June 1973, the plaintiff, George Frederick Smirk, claimed a declaration that he had good possessory title to land at the rear of 191 and 193 Victoria Road, Woolston, in the city and county of Southampton, or alternatively a declaration that he held that land as an extension of his tenancy of 191 Victoria Road. The plaintiff also claimed an injunction restraining the defendants, Lyndale Developments

e   Co (an unlimited company sued as Lyndale Developments Ltd), from entering on the land or interfering with the occupation, use or enjoyment of the land by the plaintiff. The defendants counterclaimed for possession on the ground that they owned the land and the plaintiff had not acquired a good title against them. On 5th December 1973 Pennycuick V-C[1] dismissed the plaintiff's claim and granted the defendants an order for possession. The plaintiff appealed. The facts are set out in the judgment

f   of Lawton LJ.

Jack Hames QC and David Ritchie for the plaintiff.

Roger A Cooke for the defendants.

g   **LAWTON LJ** gave the first judgment at the invitation of Cairns LJ. This is an appeal from a judgment of Pennycuick V-C[1] given on 5th December 1973 whereby he dismissed the plaintiff's claim and, on the defendants' counterclaim, ordered that the plaintiff should give possession to the defendants of land situate at the rear of 191 and 193 Victoria Road, Woolston, in the city and county of Southampton. The plaintiff by his statement of claim alleged that since 13th November 1955 he had

h   been, and was, the tenant of the defendants and their predecessors in title in respect of the dwelling-house and land known as 191 Victoria Road, Woolston and that he held that land under a weekly tenancy at a rent of £1·56 per week and that that tenancy was controlled under the Rent Acts. He claimed in the action a declaration that he had a good possessory title to the land; alternatively, a declaration that he held part of the land at the back of these premises as an extension of the locus

j   of his tenancy of 191 Victoria Road.

It is pertinent to see what the defence, as delivered, was. It started by saying that para 1 of the statement of claim was admitted; that means that at the time the case came on for trial the defendants were admitting that the plaintiff was and had been a tenant of these premises under a weekly tenancy since 1955. The inference

---

1   [1974] 2 All ER 8, [1974] 3 WLR 91

I would draw is that they were admitting that the plaintiff's tenancy was, at the time
when they delivered their defence, the same tenancy as had been created by their *a*
predecessors in title in 1955. The case proceeded on that basis right up to the very
end, when Pennycuick V-C raised a point which is the point in this appeal.

The claim came about in the following circumstances: the plaintiff is, and has been
for many years, an engine driver employed by British Railways. In 1955 British Railways granted him a tenancy of 191 Victoria Road; they granted him that tenancy
in consequence of his employment. They issued him with a rent book on the cover *b*
of which his tenancy was described as a service one. After giving particulars of the
British Transport Commission officers, agent and so on (particulars which are
required by statute) the rent book went on to provide as follows:

> 'This dwelling is let to the tenant in consequence of his employment, and in
> accordance with written authority given by the tenant the rent will be deducted *c*
> from his salary or wages and no receipt will be given in this rent book in respect
> of rent so deducted. If, however, for any reason (e.g. sickness) payments of rent
> are made by the tenant by some other method, receipts for such payments will
> be entered herein.'

There were also set out in the rent book the terms on which he held the tenancy.

The plaintiff was and is a keen gardener and at the bottom of his house in Victoria *d*
Road there was some waste land belonging to British Railways. He decided that he
would put this land to some useful purpose. There was some evidence that during
the war years it had been used as allotments. From about the year 1955 onwards the
plaintiff and his wife cultivated some of the land at the back of no 191. Pennycuick
V-C found as a fact that from 1960 onwards the plaintiff had occupied a defined strip
of land at the back of his house and that the circumstances in which he was using that *e*
land were such as to give him a possessory title as against his landlords. The plaintiff
also, from some time after about 1960 cultivated and enclosed the land at the back
of no 193 Victoria Road, but Pennycuick V-C found that he had not had that under
his control, or in his possession for a long enough period to enable him to claim a
possessory title. So this appeal is concerned with the possessory title which the
plaintiff was claiming in respect of the land at the back of 191 Victoria Road. *f*

In 1967 British Railways decided to sell the waste land together with a number of
houses, including no 191, and they put the property up for auction in October of that
year. It was knocked down to the defendants and in due course conveyed to them
by a conveyance dated 10th January 1968. They bought the property subject to the
existing tenancies of the houses in Victoria Road. They knew that the tenancy of the
plaintiff's house had started in the year 1955 or thereabouts and was a controlled one. *g*

Having acquired the waste land and the houses, the defendants had to collect the
rents. As I have already said, when the plaintiff first took possession of his house
his rent was deducted from his wages as a railwayman; this could not of course go on
after the sale of the property to the defendants. Both they and their tenants wanted
some kind of record relating to the paying of rent. As the rent was payable on a
weekly basis they were under a statutory obligation to provide their tenants with rent *h*
books. According to such evidence about this as was given—and not very much
was given—somebody on behalf of the defendants (I use the word used by Pennycuick V-C in his judgment) 'distributed' rent books. One of the books so distributed
went to the plaintiff.

The book was in a common form, but the conditions of tenancy set out in the book
were in some respects different from those which had been in the British Railways' *j*
rent book. The first condition was as follows:

> 'These premises are let on the following terms (where such terms are not
> inconsistent with an existing tenancy) NO VARIATION OF THESE TERMS WILL BE
> ACCEPTED BY THE LANDLORD UNLESS IT IS IN WRITING SIGNED BY HIM OR HIS
> AUTHORISED AGENT.'

Then followed a lot of what one might call common form terms of tenancy. They
a were in some respects, as I have indicated already, different from the terms set out
in the British Railways rent book, and counsel for the defendants has called our
attention to these differences; first, that the notice that could be given by either side
to terminate the tenancy was increased from one week to four weeks. Not much
importance can be attached to that because between the time when British Railways
issued their rent book to the plaintiff and the time when the defendants (again using
b the words used by Pennycuick V-C) distributed a new rent book, the Rent Act 1957
had been passed, the effect of which was to require four weeks' notice to evict a
tenant. Secondly the defendants, by their conditions of tenancy, prohibited the
plaintiff from keeping any birds or animals in his house. The third difference was
that the new rent book prohibited lodgers and paying guests without the prior consent of the landlord. Finally, the new rent book of course made no provisions with
c regard to deducting rent from the plaintiff's wages. One of the problems in this
appeal has been whether those changes in the terms of tenancy were such as to make
a real difference to the tenancy, so as to bring into existence a new tenancy and not,
as was submitted by the plaintiff's counsel, a mere variation of the existing tenancy.
   After these rent books had been distributed, the plaintiff paid his rent in the
ordinary way; entries were made in the rent book and as far as the plaintiff was
d concerned he probably did not see any change except that he had new landlords.
He went on cultivating the land at the back of no 191. He got apprehensive early in
1973 when he saw bulldozers at work on the waste land; they had been brought in
by the defendants, who wanted to develop the waste land. That led to an application
to this court for an injunction. Undertakings were given pending the trial of the
action. When the action came on[1], it was fought out on both sides on the issue
e whether the plaintiff had a good possessory title in respect of either the land at the
back of no 191 or the land at the back of no 193, or both. Because the case was fought
on that basis, Pennycuick V-C was required to consider in detail the law relating
to encroachments by tenants on the land of their landlords. Pennycuick V-C described
the law as in something of a tangle[2]. He untangled it in a way which has met with
the approval of both the plaintiff's and defendants' counsel; on that aspect of this
f case there has been no dispute and for my part I accept Pennycuick V-C's statement
of the law as being correct.
   What happened, however, was this: at the very end of the case, when counsel were
actually addressing Pennycuick V-C, he called their attention to the position in law
which would arise if there had been a change of tenancy at about the time when
the defendants distributed new rent books. The point which he raised with counsel
g was a pertinent one for this reason: on the law as untangled, if the plaintiff had
established a possessory title to the land at the back of 191 Victoria Road, the effect
of such a title would have been that the landlords could not have evicted him from
that land, but the plaintiff's title would not have extended beyond the period of his
own tenancy. In other words, he could not sell that land or otherwise dispose of it;
he held it because it was part of his tenancy and when his tenancy came to an end he
h would have to give it up. Pennycuick V-C asked the question whether, when the
new rent books were distributed, the tenancy which had been increased in area by
encroachment had come to an end? It was understandable that Pennycuick V-C
should raise this question because the plaintiff's tenancy had been described as a
service tenancy, a somewhat loose term. Pennycuick V-C would have had in mind
the difference between a service occupancy and a service tenancy, but it seems to me
j probable that the legal consequences of service tenancies led him to enquire of
counsel what the effect of the changeover in 1968 would have been. As a result of
this, counsel had to address him on the basis of the little evidence there was in the

1   [1974] 2 All ER 8, [1974] 3 WLR 91
2   [1974] 2 All ER at 12, [1974] 3 WLR at 94

case about the changeover from British Railways to the defendants as landlords and, as I have already said, the only evidence seems to have been a statement on behalf *a* of the defendants that the new rent books had been 'distributed'. Neither counsel invited his attention to the admission as to the plaintiff's tenancy made in the defence.

Pennycuick V-C, having heard submissions on that matter, dealt with the change of tenancy point in this way[1]:

'I should next mention the alternative claim that the plaintiff holds the blue *b* plot or alternatively the pink plot [the blue plot was the plot at the back of no 191 and the pink plot was the plot at the back of no 193] as an extension of the locus of his tenancy of 191 Victoria Road. On the facts the plaintiff would it seems to me be entitled to that relief as regards the blue plot if the tenancy under British Railways were still subsisting: that is to say, the presumption would be that he had taken possession of the blue plot by way of addition to the subject-matter *c* comprised in the tenancy under British Railways',

and then he referred to an authority, *Tabor v Godfrey*[2] which supports that proposition. He went on:

'It seems to me, however, that the break in the tenancy necessarily negates this claim. Whatever accrued or accruing right the plaintiff may have had to *d* include the blue plot in his tenancy from British Railways, this right must have determined with his tenancy under British Railways, and obviously no new right can have accrued against [the defendant] during the short time in which [the defendant has] been his landlord. There can be no ground for treating a period of two different tenancies as continuous for the present purposes. Contrast the position where a possessory title is acquired by successive squatters or *e* against successive freeholders. The tenant, so long as the presumption applies, can do no more than acquire an addition to the subject-matter of the tenancy and his interest in that additional subject-matter must necessarily determine together with his interest in the original subject-matter.'

So the problem in this appeal has been: was there a determination of the original *f* tenancy? It has been submitted on behalf of the plaintiff that there was not, and on behalf of the defendants that there was, and that has been the sole issue which we have had to consider.

Counsel has submitted on behalf of the plaintiff that there was no such determination. The plaintiff had gone into possession as a weekly tenant; his tenancy had never been determined by notice to quit; all that had happened was that in 1968 *g* a new rent book had been handed to him by the defendants and he had gone on paying his rent as before. That, said counsel, is not enough to bring about a change in tenancy. He pointed out that the law relating to changes in the nature of a tenancy has been long established, and it comes to this: either it is by an express agreement, or by a surrender and grant of a new tenancy by operation of law. It was never suggested in this case that there had been an express agreement for a new tenancy. *h* So the defendants, submitted counsel, had to rely on a surrender and regrant by operation of law. Counsel called our attention to the authorities on this matter. In my judgment it is unnecessary to go into them; they are well known and the principles have long been established. Before there can be a surrender by operation of law there must be something in the nature of an agreement and that agreement must amount to more than a mere variation of the terms of an existing tenancy. *j* It was said on behalf of the plaintiff that there is no direct evidence here of an agreement of any kind; and that an agreement cannot be inferred merely from the fact that a landlord hands a rent book to a tenant. Of course, a good deal depends on

---

1   [1974] 2 All ER at 20, [1974] 3 WLR at 103
2   (1895) 64 LJQB 245

the circumstances: at the beginning of a weekly tenancy it may well be that the
a handing of a rent book to a tenant amounts to some evidence that the tenant is
accepting the tenancy on the terms set out in the rent book; but if the tenancy
has been subsisting for many years when a new rent book in replacement of an old
one is handed to the tenant, it seems to me that that is wholly insufficient to justify
the inference that there has been an agreement to do anything. These rent books
are common form documents; very often they serve no purpose other than the
b ministerial one of providing a record of rent that has been paid. I find it impossible
in this case to see where there is any evidence of an agreement; but even if the handing
over of a new rent book provides some evidence of an agreement, in my judgment
it would do no more than show a variation of the terms of the original tenancy.

As I said earlier in this judgment, the new terms started off by saying that they
were not to have effect if they were inconsistent with the terms of the existing tenancy.
c In other words, the parties were contemplating that the existing tenancy would
continue and this, so the authorities seem to show, and in particular the decision of
this court in *Joseph v Joseph*[1], is a material factor. Then it was submitted that the new
terms which I have listed showed such a substantial variation from the existing terms as
to lead to an inference that there was an intention to grant a new one. For my part
I do not find the variation substantial at all; all of them are common form terms.
d The one term which was altered when the new landlords took over was that which
related to the deduction of rent from wages. The original tenancy, however, contemplated that circumstances might arise, for example illness, in which it would be
impossible to deduct the rent from wages. Further, the original tenancy did not
require the tenant to vacate the premises if he gave up his work with British Railways; when he gave up that work he was entitled to stay on in the house subject
e to the possibility that the landlords might be able to get possession under Sch 1 to the
Rent and Mortgage Restrictions Act 1933. There was no great change there.

In my judgment the issue in this case is really one of mixed fact and law. There
was no dispute between counsel as to what the law was relating to the surrender and
regrant of a tenancy; the only dispute has been as to the inference which can properly
be drawn from what happened when the new rent book was distributed. For my
f part I am unable to draw the inference which Pennycuick V-C drew. I would draw
the inference that the landlords intended the plaintiff to continue as tenant
on much the same terms as he had when British Railways were his landlords. The
consequence of that in law, as is now agreed by counsel, is that as long as he is
tenant he can go on tending the garden at the back of no 191, but when he ceases to
be a tenant he will have to give that up.
g I would allow this appeal.

WALTON J. I entirely agree with everything that has fallen from Lawton LJ;
I would not add anything except for the fact that we are differing from Pennycuick
V-C on one very small point in what was otherwise a very powerful and useful
judgment. I need not rehearse the facts that Lawton LJ has rehearsed, but as far
h as I am concerned I can see no ground whatsoever for the implication of any new
agreement between the landlord and the tenant from the combination of circumstances on which reliance was placed, namely the change of landlord, the delivery of
the new form of rent book and the payment of rent thereunder.

So far as the change of landlord is concerned, that by itself could have no conceivable effect on the tenancy. The delivery of the book might have had, if it could
j be considered as an offer made by the landlord and accepted by the tenant; I shall
deal with that in a moment. So far as the payment of rent is concerned, the tenant
quite obviously, in changed circumstances, had actually to pay rent instead of having
it deducted from his wages by British Rail; but obviously, in meat or in malt he had

1   [1966] 3 All ER 486, [1967] Ch 78

to pay the rent somehow. So that circumstance by itself seems to me to be completely immaterial.

I do not think that the rent book can ever conceivably have been even intended as an offer. Of course, when one is starting a tenancy and a rent book is delivered, that is very frequently the only evidence there is as to the agreed terms, and if the tenant accepts a rent book at the commencement of the tenancy which starts off 'The premises are let on the following terms', that is obviously some evidence as to what those terms are. But when, there being already a tenancy in being, a new rent book is delivered starting off 'These premises are let on the following terms', that is not to my mind the language of an offer in any circumstances.

But I think the matter goes further than that, because even if it was an offer and could be construed as an offer, contrary to its wording, it seems to me that there is no act performed by the tenant which could conceivably be construed as being an acceptance of that offer. I ask rhetorically: what did the tenant do? He remained on the premises where he was, paying the rent he was supposed to be paying. It is trite law that silence never amounts to acceptance of an offer; it cannot possibly do so. Therefore it seems to me that there is nothing to be got out of the delivery of a rent book.

But even supposing I am wrong on that, and supposing that somehow the obligation was placed on the tenant when he got the rent book to look through it and see whether it contained an offer that was inconsistent with the terms of his previous tenancy, on which, I suppose, he could complain immediately to the landlord, the tenant need read no further than the first sentence: 'These premises are let on the following terms where such terms are not inconsistent with an existing tenancy', and the tenant would say to himself: what need have I to read further? I have an existing tenancy; these terms may or may not be inconsistent with its terms but that does not really matter; because the terms of my existing tenancy prevail. Also, I think in fact that those parenthetical words, 'where such terms are not inconsistent with an existing tenancy', can be utilised as a powerful reinforcement of the argument that this is not an offer anyway, because if it was an offer I again ask rhetorically: what was the purpose of putting in those parenthetical words?

Finally, even if I am wrong on both those points, before one could get to the doctrine of a surrender and regrant by operation of law, one would have to find that the alterations made by the new terms were sufficiently serious to necessitate one applying that doctrine. What are the circumstances here? Even giving absolutely literal effect to every single one of the terms set out in the rent book, the three basic essentials of the lease remain the same. The term was a weekly term before, and it still is a weekly term; the rent was so much, and the rent has not been changed; the premises were 191 Victoria Road, and the premises remain unchanged. In other words the skeleton of the lease remains exactly the same as it always has been. There may be a few more clothes put on, a cap here or a handkerchief tucked into the pocket there, but it is the same; there has been no fundamental change. Therefore to my mind, the doctrine of a regrant necessitating a surrender by operation of law has no conceivable application here.

For those reasons I entirely agree with the order proposed by Lawton LJ.

CAIRNS LJ. I agree that this appeal must be allowed. I agree entirely with the reasons for that conclusion as given in the judgments of both Lawton LJ and Walton J and although we are differing from the result at which Pennycuick V-C arrived, I cannot usefully add anything to what has already been said.

Appeal allowed.

Solicitors: *Lovell, Son & Pitfield,* agents for *Paris, Smith & Randall,* Southampton (for the plaintiff); *Riders,* agents for *G H Fowler, Shaw & Holloway,* Brighton (for the defendants).

A S Virdi Esq   Barrister.

a

Re X (a minor) (wardship: restriction on publication)

FAMILY DIVISION

LATEY J

23rd, 30th OCTOBER, 5th NOVEMBER 1974

b

COURT OF APPEAL, CIVIL DIVISION

LORD DENNING MR, ROSKILL LJ AND SIR JOHN PENNYCUICK

18th DECEMBER 1974

Ward of court – Jurisdiction – Protection of ward – Freedom of publication – Publication of
c *matter likely to be harmful to ward – Jurisdiction of court to restrain publication – Ward a*
schoolgirl of 14 – Ward psychologically fragile and highly strung – Ward's father dead –
Defendants proposing to publish book describing father's depraved sexual activities – Book
likely to be seen by ward – Public interest in freedom to publish true information – Whether
court having jurisdiction to restrain publication – Whether order should be made.

d X, a girl, was born in 1960. Her parents were divorced about six months after her
birth. X's father travelled widely until his death abroad in 1967. The mother brought
up X. In 1970 the mother married the plaintiff. X was psychologically fragile and
highly strung. She was brought up to respect the memory of her father. A friend
of X's father ('the author') wrote a book, the first chapter of which described X's father's
private life. If true, the author's account showed that X's father had been a man who
e was utterly depraved in his sexual activities, who indulged in sordid and degrading
conduct, who was obscene and drank to excess. The book was ready for publication
in 1974. Shortly before the proposed publication date, the plaintiff saw a copy of the
book and was afraid that after publication X would see it. He feared that such an
account of her father would be grossly damaging psychologically to so sensitive a
child. The plaintiff asked the defendants, the author and his publishers, to delete
f or revise the first chapter. They refused and so he applied to the court for an order
making X a ward of court and for an injunction restraining publication of the book so
long as it contained the offending passages. The judge held that the duty to protect
minors against injury gave the court unlimited powers in the exercise of its wardship
jurisdiction and that, although that duty was to be balanced against its duty to protect
freedom of publication, the danger to X was so grave that the publication of the
g offending passages in the book should be barred. Accordingly the judge made X a
ward of court for her protection and granted an injunction restraining publication of
the book until the first chapter had been rewritten in a form acceptable to the plaintiff
or the court. The defendants appealed.

Held – The rights of free speech and free publication were at least as important as the
h rights of individuals whether adults or minors. The freedom of publication was
limited by the rules of law in certain respects and the court should hesitate to interfere
further with that freedom. Although no limits to the wardship jurisdiction of the
court had been drawn, the case was not a suitable one for extending that jurisdiction
to infringe on the freedom to publish true information, for the interests of X could not be
allowed to prevail on the wider interest in the freedom of publication. Accordingly
j the appeal would be allowed (see p 704 *b* and *f* to *h*, p 705 *d f* and *j* and p 706 *b* and *f* to
p 707 *c* and *f*, post).

Per Sir John Pennycuick. The court was not bound by s 1ᵃ of the Guardianship of
Minors Act 1971 to regard the welfare of X as the first and paramount consideration
since neither the custody nor the upbringing of X was in question (see p 707 *e*, post).

---

a   Section 1, so far as material, is set out at p 707 *d*, post

Notes

For the court's jurisdiction over wards of court, see 21 Halsbury's Laws (3rd Edn)   *a*
216, 217, paras 478, 479, and for cases on the subject, see 28(2) Digest (Reissue) 911-916,
2220-2248.

For the Guardianship of Minors Acts 1971, s 1, see 41 Halsbury's Statutes (3rd Edn)
762.

Cases referred to in judgments   *b*

*A (an infant), Re, Hanif v Secretary of State for Home Affairs, Re S (N) (an infant), Singh v
Secretary of State for Home Affairs* [1968] 2 All ER 145, sub nom *Re Mohamed Arif
(an infant), Re Nirbhai Singh (an infant)* [1968] Ch 643, [1968] 2 WLR 1290, CA, Digest
(Cont Vol C) 19, *157ra.*

Iredell v Iredell (1885) 1 TLR 260, 28(2) Digest (Reissue) 923, *2324.*

Official Solicitor v K [1963] 3 All ER 191, [1965] AC 201, [1963] 3 WLR 408, HL, 28(2)   *c*
Digest (Reissue) 912, *2233.*

Powel v Cleaver (1789) 2 Bro CC 499.

R v Ensor (1887) 3 TLR 366, 32 Digest (Repl) 227, *2467.*

R v Topham (1791) 4 Term Rep 126, 100 ER 931, 32 Digest (Repl) 227, *2465.*

Wellesley v Wellesley (1828) 2 Bli NS 124, [1824-34] All ER Rep 189, 1 Dow & Cl 152,   *d*
4 ER 1078, HL; *affg* sub nom *Wellesley v Duke of Beaufort* (1827) 2 Russ 1, 5 LJOS Ch
85, 38 ER 236, 28(2) Digest (Reissue) 808, *1260*

Cases also cited

Basset's Case (1557) 2 Dyer 136a.

Beaufort (Duke) v Berty (1721) 1 PW 703.   *e*

Heath v Crealock (1873) LR 15 Eq 257.

J v C [1969] 1 All ER 788, [1970] AC 668, HL.

L, Re [1968] 1 All ER 20, [1968] P 119, CA.

Ramsbotham v Senior (1869) LR 8 Eq 575.

S v S, W v Official Solicitor [1970] 3 All ER 107, [1972] AC 24, HL.

Scott v Scott [1913] AC 417, [1911-13] All ER Rep 1, HL.   *f*

Summonses

This was an application by the plaintiff, the stepfather of X, a girl aged 14, for an order
that X be made a ward of court. The plaintiff further applied for an injunction to
restrain the defendants, the publishers and author of a book, from publishing the
book in question so long as it contained certain passages. The hearing was in chambers   *g*
but judgment was given in open court. The facts are set out in the judgment.

Bryan Anns QC, Lionel Swift and *David Vaughan* for the plaintiff.
Frederic Reynold for the defendants.

                                                                         Cur adv vult   *h*

5th November. **LATEY J** read the following judgment. This case concerns recourse
to the wardship jurisdiction in wholly novel circumstances. Because it does so it is
of some public importance and for that reason the judgment is being given in open
court. I have tried to frame the judgment in terms which give no indication of the   *i*
identities of the book concerned, its author, its publishers, the ward's dead father or
above all the ward herself. Whether or not I have succeeded, it is within the spirit
and purpose of the judgment and the orders I have made and am about to make in
chambers that there should be no public speculation in the media about those
identities.

The ward is a girl of 14 years of age. Her father died some years ago. I shall refer

to the child as X. A book has been written and is on the point of publication. The
a book begins with a short chapter about the child's father. In it there are several
explicit descriptions of the father's alleged sexual predilections and behaviour. They
are described in the author's affidavit filed in the summons as 'somewhat extravagant'
and elsewhere as 'bizarre'. Others might regard them, as revolting, or, as the plaintiff
in his affidavit describes them, as 'salacious and scandalous'.

The child's mother has remarried. The child's stepfather, the plaintiff, first heard
b of the book within a day or so before the date scheduled for publication, when friends
who had been sent copies for review told him about it, expressing their disgust and
sympathy. He obtained a copy, and in agreement with his wife, X's mother, moved
immediately, instructing solicitors, taking counsel's advice and applying to make the
child a ward of court and for an injunction restraining the publication of the book so
long as it contains the offending passages. If it be relevant the offending passages are
c all in the first short chapter of eight pages. The rest of the book is unaffected. I made
interim orders and the case has since been fully argued in chambers. In opposing the
application the defendants, the author and publishers, have rejected proposals that
this short chapter should be deleted or re-written.

The questions for decision are, first, whether in circumstances of this kind recourse
to the wardship jurisdiction can ever be appropriate. Secondly, if it can be, is it right
d that the court should exercise its powers in the circumstances of this particular case?

Counsel for the defendants was at first disposed to argue that the case is outside the
limits of the wardship jurisdiction. Later, after the authorities had been gone through
at length, he accepted that the jurisdiction is wide enough and said that the question
is whether an exercise of the jurisdiction would be appropriate. That, in my view,
states the basic question accurately. Before coming to those questions I must say
e something about what the evidence proves. To review it at length might give indications of identities which might defeat the orders I am making. I summarise it briefly.

X is 14. She is a very sensitive child. The family doctor, who has been her doctor
for ten years, says that she is rather more vulnerable emotionally than most children
and is psychologically fragile and highly strung. If she were to read this chapter or
hear about it from others it would be psychologically grossly damaging to her.
f Another witness says the effect of it on her would be appalling. Counsel, whose able
presentation of the defendants' case (that is to say of the author and publishers) was
all the more persuasive for being realistic, does not dispute this. Then there is evidence
on both sides of the likelihood or otherwise of what is written coming to X's knowledge.
I will return to that important point later.

On the first of the two questions already stated, it is argued for the defendants,
g first, that because the wardship jurisdiction has never been involved in any case
remotely resembling this, the court, though theoretically having jurisdiction, should
not entertain the application, but bar it in limine. I do not accept that contention.
It is true that this jurisdiction has not been invoked in any such circumstances. I do
not know whether they have arisen before or, if they have, whether anyone has
thought of having recourse to this jurisdiction. But I can find nothing in the authori-
h ties to which I have been referred by counsel or in my own researches to suggest that
there is any limitation in the theoretical scope of this jurisdiction; or, to put it another
way, that the jurisdiction can only be invoked in the categories of cases in which it has
hitherto been invoked, such as custody, care and control, protection of property,
health problems, religious upbringing, and protection against harmful associations.
That list is not exhaustive. On the contrary, the powers of the court in this particular
j jurisdiction have always been described as being of the widest nature. That the
courts are available to protect children from injury whenever they properly can is no
modern development. For example, in Chambers on Infancy[1] the matter is
summarised in this way:

---

1   (1842), p 20

'The general rule and object on which the Court acts, and has always in view both as to the person and property of the infants, is to direct that which is most *a* for their benefit. "The jurisdiction is not profitable to the crown, but for the benefit of infants themselves who must have some common parent" which dictum[1], it will be observed, is consistent with the notion that the Court acts in this case as parens patriae. And the Court will interfere not merely on the ground of an injury actually done, or attempted against the infant's person or property; but also if there be any likelihood of such an occurrence, or even an *b* apprehension or suspicion of it. The jurisdiction is exercised sometimes by way of punishment on such as have done any act to the prejudice of the infants, but it is more usefully exercised to restrain persons from doing anything to disparate infants where the act has not been completed.'

In Halsbury's Laws of England[2] it is put this way: *c*

'An infant does not possess full legal competence. Since he is regarded as of immature intellect and imperfect discretion, English law, while treating all the acts of an infant which are for his benefit on the same footing as those of an adult will carefully protect his interests and not permit him to be prejudiced by anything to his disadvantage.'   *d*

That statement is based on the authorities reaching as far back as 1557[3].
In *Wellesley v Duke of Beaufort*[4] Lord Eldon LC said:

'. . . and it has always been the principle of this Court, not to risk the incurring of damage to children which it cannot repair, but rather to prevent the damage being done . .'   *e*

In a later passage he said[5]:

'. . . more especially, whether it belongs to the King, as *parens patriae*, having the care of those who are not able to take care of themselves, and is founded on the obvious necessity that the law should place somewhere the care of individuals who cannot take care of themselves, particularly in cases where it is clear that *f* some care should be thrown round them.'

In *Wellesley v Wellesley*[6] Lord Redesdale said:

'The jurisdiction, I conceive, extends to the case of the person as far as is necessary for protection and education.'   *g*

And Lord Manners said[7]:

'There was an observation of Mr. Brougham on the subject, that the juris- diction could not exist, because you could not ascertain the limits of it. That objection applies to every case where there is a discretion in the judge; where the result of the facts is not a question of law, but a question of discretion. It is therefore impossible to say what are the limits of that jurisdiction; every case *h* must depend upon its own circumstances.'

What then are the origin and function of the wardship jurisdiction? In my under- standing they are these. All subjects owe allegiance to the Crown. The Crown has a

---

1 *Powel v Cleaver* (1789) 2 Bro CC 499 at 501   *j*
2 3rd Edn, vol 21, p 134
3 *Basset's Case* (1557) 2 Dyer 136a
4 (1827) 2 Russ 1 at 18
5 2 Russ at 20
6 (1828) 2 Bli NS 124 at 136, [1824-34] All ER Rep 189 at 194
7 2 Bli NS at 142, 143, [1824-34] All ER Rep at 196

duty to protect its subjects. This is and always has been especially so towards minors,
a that is to say now, the young under the age of 18. And it is so because children are
especially vulnerable. They have not formed the defences inside themselves which
older people have, and therefore, need especial protection. They are also a country's
most valuable asset for the future. So the Crown as parens patriae delegated its
powers and duty of protection to the courts. These powers and that duty so derived
are not the creation of any statute and are not limited by any statute. They are there,
b in my understanding, to protect the young against injury of whatever kind from
whatever source. So if X is in peril it is wholly right and proper to invoke those powers
to protect her.

Then, it is contended for the defendants, if these powers are called on in a novel
category of case the court should walk warily and circumspectly before exercising them.
I agree. The decisions whether or not to confirm or continue a wardship and what
c orders to make are always within the court's discretion. The implications must be
weighed. In this case, the publishers urge, and understandably urge, that there may
be wide implications concerning the freedom to publish if orders of the kind asked for
are made. Of course, in other categories of case there may well be overriding considerations of various kinds in the public interest such as there were in *Re A (an infant),
Hanif v Secretary of State for Home Affairs*[1]. Again, I would think it unlikely that the
d court would make a wardship order when a child was brought in as a vehicle to
achieve some ulterior objective—a commercial one, for example. Again, suppose a
man who has children was charged with some particularly serious and unpleasant
offence. I would think it unlikely, save perhaps in a very exceptional case, that the
court would make the children wards of court in order to restrain the press from
reporting the proceedings because of course there is the overriding public interest
e that justice should be administered openly, and that means that there should be fair
reporting of the proceedings, save in a very few limited classes of case where there is
an even more important public interest that there should be no publication. So it is
one thing that the powers exist; it is another thing whether they should be exercised.

In this context, the argument for the defendants is that if the powers exist in this
kind of case, as in my judgment they clearly do, they should never be exercised because
f to exercise them would curb the freedom of publication. This, in my judgment,
is putting it far too high. Certainly the court should be wary and circumspect. But
there is no reason in principle why the court should not protect a child in a proper
case and every reason why it should. I stress the words 'in a proper case'. There may
not be many such and in my view the publishers' properly voiced fears of the wider
effects on publishers and publications generally are probably exaggerated, if not
g indeed unfounded.

The evidence is that the elimination or rewriting of the offending chapter would be
very expensive. I accept that evidence. It is argued that this should influence the
court not to make the orders asked for. If by that it is meant that if there is substantial
expense the court should never make an order I reject the argument. If what is
meant is that expense is a factor to be weighed with all other relevant factors I accept
h it, but not to the extent that expense should ever outweigh a real danger of grave
harm to a child. It might tip the scales where the harm envisaged is a harm but not a
serious one. The factors have to be balanced as described in *Official Solicitor v K*[2].

What then are the requirements to be established before the court exercises its
powers and makes orders? In my judgment they are these: (1) It must be shown that
the real, the genuine, object of the application is to protect the child. There is no
j question about that in this case and the defendants do not suggest that there is any
doubt. (2) There must be no overriding public interest the other way. In my judgment, there is none in this case. There may from time to time be cases where a

---

1   [1968] 2 All ER 145, [1968] Ch 643
2   [1963] 3 All ER 191, [1965] AC 201

proposed publication has to be withdrawn. There is nothing approaching a general
or wide curb on publication. The freedom to publish is one of the most important *a*
freedoms and the courts are jealous to preserve it. But that does not mean that an
occasional individual publication should not be barred to protect a child from serious
injury. (3) There must be a likelihood of substantial injury to the child if the publication or its contents come to its notice. In this case there is no dispute about this.
The injury to X's emotional psychological health would be very grave indeed. (4)
There must be a real danger of the offending passages or their contents coming to the *b*
knowledge of the child. For the defendants it was at first argued that there must be
an overwhelming or very strong probability. This, in my judgment, is putting it too
high and counsel for the defendants on reflection agreed. An illusory or minimal
danger would not, in my judgment, suffice. But where the resulting injury would be
very grave, as in this case, a real risk of knowledge is quite enough to call for protection.
Both counsel accepted that the risk must be significant and no more.   *c*

There is evidence on each side about the risk. In a sense this inevitably consists of
conflicting opinions though they are supported by facts and reasons. In this judgment
I cannot say more about this evidence without giving indications of identities. It is
there and it speaks for itself if the case is considered on appeal. My conclusion on the
evidence is that there is a very real and substantial danger that the passages or their
contents may come to X's knowledge.   *d*

It follows that the requirements are established and the appropriate orders will be
made. The orders themselves will not be published because to do so would be to
disclose the identities. Their effect is to bar the publication not of the book but of the
offending passages in the first chapter. It will be sufficient that the first chapter is
omitted or rewritten in a form acceptable to the plaintiff or, if that cannot be agreed,
in a form acceptable to the court.   *e*

I must stress that this case is not in any way concerned with whether or not there is
obscenity. Nor is it concerned with censorship though that may be the incidental
result. It is concerned and concerned solely with the protection of a child from the
danger of grave injury.

Finally, I want to make it plain that the plaintiff has demonstrated beyond any room
for doubt that he is moved solely by the wish to protect the child; and that the   *f*
defendants, in writing and printing this book, have acted in perfectly good faith.
They had no realisation of any danger of injury to X, far less any intention of injuring
her. Since those facts have come to their knowledge they have argued, as they are
entitled to do, that they should be free to carry on with the publication but in the
meanwhile have done all they can to make the interim orders effective.

g

Wardship order made; injunction granted.

Solicitors: *Oswald, Hickson, Collier & Co* (for the plaintiff); *Bindman & Partners* (for the
defendants).

R C T Habesch Esq Barrister. *h*

Interlocutory appeal

Pursuant to the leave of Latey J the defendants appealed against the order restraining
the defendants from publishing certain passages in the book in question on the
grounds (i) that the order was in the circumstances of the case not an appropriate
nor a proper exercise of the court's wardship jurisdiction and (ii) that the judge had *j*
erred in finding on the basis of affidavit evidence that there was a real and substantial
danger that the offending passages contained in the book might come to the knowledge
of the ward.

Brian Neill QC and *Frederic Reynold* for the defendants.
Bryan Anns QC and *Lionel Swift* for the plaintiff.

LORD DENNING MR. This case concerns a girl now aged 14. I will not mention
a her name because it is undesirable that it should come to her notice.
The girl was born in June 1960. About six months later her parents were divorced.
In December 1967 her father died. In November 1970 her mother remarried. The
child has been at a boarding school but she is now at a day school. In October 1974 a
book was about to be published. It had been reviewed in one periodical prior to
publication. In the first chapter there were passages which described the child's
b father who had died seven years before. He was said to be—

'a man whose manner of life and death were so strange and outrageous that I
did not dare write more about him for fear of distressing his relatives'.

There follow passages in which incidents were described of the father's private life. If
true, they showed him to be a man who was utterly depraved in his sexual activities,
c who indulged in sordid and degrading conduct, and who was obscene and drank to
excess.
When the girl's mother and her stepfather, the plaintiff, learned that this book was
to be published, they were afraid that the child might get it and read it and be much
damaged by it. They asked the publishers to withdraw the publication of the book;
d but they refused. Their solicitors asked the publishers to delay publication, but still
they refused. The stepfather took legal advice as to whether there was any means at
law of stopping publication. In the result the stepfather applied for the girl to be
made a ward of court and asked in her interest for an injunction to restrain the
publication of the book.
The application came before Latey J. He found that there was a very real and
substantial danger that the passages in the book about the girl's father might come to
e the girl's knowledge. He accepted the evidence of the family doctor that she is a very
sensitive child, that she is rather more vulnerable emotionally than most children and
is psychologically fragile and highly strung. If she were to read this chapter or hear
about it from others, it would be psychologically grossly damaging to her. And
another witness said that the effect on her would be appalling. The judge reviewed
the authorities on the jurisdiction to protect wards of court. He held that it was wide
f enough to enable him to protect this child. He made an order restraining the
publication of the offending passages.
Now there is an appeal to this court. We were told that it would be quite easy for the
publishers to eliminate the offending passages. It would only cost £180. Furthermore, the child's relations are so anxious to protect her that they are ready to pay
£1,000 to get the passages removed. But the publishers refused. They object in
g principle to removing the passages.
The jurisdiction of the court in regard to wards of court is derived from the Court
of Chancery. It was exercised by that court when there was property belonging to
the infant to be taken care of. But since 1949 it can be exercised whenever an order
is made by the court making a child a ward of court: see s 9 of the Law Reform
(Miscellaneous Provisions) Act 1949. No limit has ever been set to the jurisdiction.
h It has been said to extend 'as far as necessary for protection and education': see Wellesley v Wellesley[1] by Lord Redesdale. The court has power to protect the ward from
any interference with his or her welfare, direct or indirect. But no case has ever come
before the court that is anywhere like this one. The nearest is Iredell v Iredell[2] where a
Roman Catholic priest insisted on seeing a girl of 16, contrary to her father's wishes, so
as to induce her to adhere to the Roman Catholic faith. The judge found that the
j priest, in the name of religion, was trying to teach her to disobey her father and to
have no communication with her father. The judge granted an injunction against the
priest. We were told too of an unreported case where the Official Solicitor obtained

---

1   (1828) Bli NS 124 at 136, 137, [1824-34] All ER Rep 189 at 194
2   (1885) 1 TLR 260

an injunction to restrain the publication of an advertisement. But it is of no help. The point is thus a new one. On the one hand, there is the freedom of the press to consider; on the other hand, the protection of a young child from harm. The judge seems to have balanced the one against the other and to have held that the interest of the child shall prevail.

If the function of the judges was simply a balancing function—to balance the competing interests—there would be much to be said for this view. To quote some of the adjectives used about the passages in the book, they are: 'bizarre', 'salacious', 'scandalous' and 'revolting'. It is difficult to see that there is any public interest to be served by their publication. But this is where freedom of speech comes in. It means freedom, not only for the statements of opinion of which we approve, but also for those of which we most heartily disapprove. Take some aspects of the law which are relevant in this very case. For instance, is there any remedy in the law of defamation? Suppose the mother of the child were to bring an action for defamation on the ground that the passages were untrue and a gross libel on her dead husband. Many might think she should be able to prevent the publication, especially as it would bring such grief and distress to his relatives and, in addition, emotional damage to his child. But the law of defamation does not permit any such proceeding. It says simply that no action lies for a libel on a dead man; on the ground that on balance it is in the public interest that no such action should lie: see R v Topham[1]; and R v Ensor[2]. Again, is there any remedy in the law as to infringement of privacy? Suppose the dead man were still alive. The passages describe conduct by him which was done in private and which he would wish to keep private and not disclosed to anyone except his close friends. They expose his depravity to the view of the whole world. He could not sue for libel; or, if he did, he would fail because the words are true. But could he sue for infringement of privacy? Many might think that he should be able to do so; he should be able to prevent his public exposure. But again, as I understand it, it would be difficult to give him any remedy. We have as yet no general remedy for infringement of privacy; the reason given being that on balance it is not in the public interest that there should be, see the Report of a Committee on Privacy in 1972[3].

The reason why in these cases the law gives no remedy is because of the importance it attaches to the freedom of the press; or, better put, the importance in a free society of the circulation of true information. The metes and bounds of this are already staked out by the rules of law. The law of libel stops that which is untrue on living persons. The law of contempt stops that which is prejudicial to a fair trial. The law of obscenity stops that which tends to deprave and corrupt. It would be a mistake to extend these so as to give the judges a power to stop publication of true matter whenever the judges—or any particular judge—thought that it was in the interests of a child to do so.

It is on this account that I do not think the wardship jurisdiction should be extended so as to enable the court to stop publication of this book. The relatives of the child must do their best to protect her by doing all they can to see that the book does not come into her hands. It is a better way of protection than the court can give. In my opinion it would be extending the wardship jurisdiction too far and infringing too much on the freedom of the press for us to grant an injunction in this case. I would allow the appeal and discharge the injunction.

ROSKILL LJ. I agree that this appeal must be allowed. I venture to add to the judgment which Lord Denning MR has just delivered for three reasons. First, I greatly hesitate on a matter of this kind to differ from so experienced a judge as

1   (1791) 4 Term Rep 126
2   (1887) 3 TLR 366
3   (1972) Cmnd 5012, paras 651-653

Latey J. Secondly, I regard the case as one of wide general importance. Thirdly, no
a one who has read both the allegedly offending passages in chapter one of this book
and the affidavits and the supplementary statement by the mother put in this
morning, can feel other than the greatest sympathy for the mother and the stepfather,
the plaintiff, and fully appreciate as every parent must appreciate, their natural
anxiety as to the possible effects on this child of the publication of these stories about
her father (even assuming them to be true), a father whom and whose memory she
b was brought up to respect and indeed to revere and who died in distant parts some
seven or eight years ago. All that is perfectly true; and one has to add to that the
uncontradicted evidence from the mother, a doctor and a lady who had this child in
her care when she was at boarding school, of the likely psychological damage which
would follow should these stories come to her knowledge. I should have thought it
was obvious, having regard to the educational environment of the child and the
c occupation of her mother and the plaintiff, that it would be likely that, if the injunction
is revoked and the book is published, she will become aware of these stories in one
form or another. It is therefore in one sense a strong case for parents legitimately to
seek the protection afforded by the court on the ground that the child is a ward. But
that is far from being the only issue involved. There is in this country—and it is right
that it should be restated in the clearest terms and never more so than at this stage in
d the 20th century—a right of free speech and a right of free publication. That right is at
least as important—some may think more important—as the right of individuals,
whether adults or minors, whether wards or not. Of course, that right of free publication has long been circumscribed. It was fought for right through the 17th, 18th and
19th centuries. It has developed so as to become one of the liberties which it is the
duty of the court to protect. It was enshrined in a number of late 18th century stat-
e utes, some of which are still on the statute book. But inevitably with the passing of
time and as current necessities have from time to time required, that liberty has been
circumscribed. Lord Denning MR has given some examples. There are others that
come to mind. One is the Official Secrets Act; another the statutory prohibition of the
publication of certain types of legal proceedings, as, for example, those involving
children. There are common law restrictions on freedom of publication, such as the
f law of defamation and the law relating to contempt of court—a currently controversial
topic. Another restriction is the law relating to obscenity—another controversial
topic. Those are but a few examples. There are therefore limits on freedom of
publication. But within those limits there is such freedom. Sometimes, of course, the
freedom may be sought to be exercised at the risk of payment of damages for defamation or of prosecution, as, for example, for obscenity. Sometimes the current law,
g if infringed, may lead to a prohibition on publication. Sometimes such a prohibition
may follow the exercise of common law or statutory rights by an aggrieved person.
So there is today no complete freedom of publication.

The allegedly offending paragraphs in chapter 1 appear in a book—I have read the
whole book—chapter 1 should not be read in isolation—which I regard as a serious
study of the depravity brought about by war and in particular by the war which is the
h subject of the book. Opinions may differ greatly about these passages. Some
may deplore their taste. Opinions differ greatly on questions of taste and always will.
But subjective judgments on taste have no place in the courts. The sole question here
is whether or not the interests of this child should be allowed to prevail over the
greater—as some may think—interests of freedom of publication. It is sought to
impose a restriction on publication by use of the wardship jurisdiction. For my own
j part, I would agree with counsel for the plaintiff that no limits to that jurisdiction have
yet been drawn and it is not necessary to consider here what (if any) limits there are to
that jurisdiction. The sole question is whether it should be exercised in this case. I
would also agree with him that the mere fact that the courts have never stretched out
their arms so far as is proposed in this case is in itself no reason for not stretching out
those arms further than before when necessary in a suitable case. There is never

a precedent for anything until it has been done once. He has cited a number of
instances in the last 50 years where the arm of the law has been stretched further   *a*
than before for the protection of infants. One is the use of blood tests in appropriate
cases. Another is the non-publication to parents of confidential reports made to the
courts by the Official Solicitor concerning their children. But what some might
regard as deficiencies in the law of defamation or in the law in relation to privacy—I
say nothing on the question whether there is a cause of action in respect of infringement of privacy—cannot in my view be made good by resort to wardship procedure.   *b*
However much one may sympathise with the mother and the plaintiff in the present
case, I cannot accept the argument that the interests of the child should be allowed to
prevail over the wider interests of freedom of publication, whatever may be thought
about the merits or demerits of the passages objected to.

I would add these few further observations. Counsel for the plaintiff has told us that
the plaintiff in an open letter has offered to pay for the deletion of the offending   *c*
passages. He suggested that the most objectionable of these passages are few in numbers and that the pages on which they appear could easily be taken out and replaced
by the appropriate technical process. For my part I do not think the rights or wrongs
of the present appeal can be determined by reference to whether it would be
difficult or easy to delete the offending passages. I regard this case as one to be
decided on the question of principle; and, so considering it, I take the view that   *d*
Latey J's order cannot be supported. The learned judge, after reviewing the history of
the jurisdiction in wardship cases, said[1]:

> 'These powers and that duty so derived are not the creation of any statute and
> are not limited by any statute. They are there, in my understanding, to protect
> the young against injury of whatever kind from whatever source. So if X is in   *e*
> peril it is wholly right and proper to invoke those powers to protect her.'

With the greatest respect to the judge, I venture to think that those words are too
wide. That is tantamount to saying that in every case where a minor's interests are
involved, those interests are always paramount and must prevail. As counsel for the
plaintiff rightly said, the court is required to do a difficult balancing act. Both sides of
the case have been put before us. I think the scale is tipped heavily in favour of the   *f*
defendants and against the plaintiff. I would therefore allow the appeal.

SIR JOHN PENNYCUICK. I also would allow the appeal. It may well be, and I
have no doubt it is so, that the courts, when exercising the parental power of the
Crown, have, at any rate in legal theory, an unrestricted jurisdiction to do whatever   *g*
is considered necessary for the welfare of a ward. It is, however, obvious that
far-reaching limitations in principle on the exercise of this jurisdiction must exist.
The jurisdiction is habitually exercised within those limitations. It would be quite
impossible to protect a ward against everything which might do her harm. In particular, the jurisdiction must be exercised with due regard to the rights of outside parties
whether such rights arise at common law or by contract or otherwise. By 'outside   *h*
parties' I mean those not in a family or personal relation to the ward. The court must
hold a proper balance between the protection of the ward and the rights of outside
parties. Specifically, it seems to me, the court must hold a proper balance between the
protection of the ward and the right of free publication enjoyed by outside parties
and should hesitate long before interfering with that right of free publication. It
would be impossible and not I think desirable to draw any rigid line beyond which the   *j*
protection of a ward should not be extended. The distinction between direct and indirect interference with a ward is valuable, though the borderline may be blurred. I
am not prepared to say that the court should never interfere with the publication of

1   See p 701, ante

matter concerning a ward. On the contrary, I think in exceptional circumstances the
a court should do so. On the other hand, the court would I think hardly ever prevent
publication of a book merely—I stress merely—on the ground that it would bring to
the knowledge of the ward facts which would be harmful to the ward. Latey J's
statement of the law is I think correct, but he does not lay sufficient emphasis on the
limitations with which the courts should exercise this jurisdiction.

No decision has been cited in which the court has interfered in at all comparable
b circumstances affecting the rights of outside parties. Nor, so far as my own experience
goes, in its exercise of this wardship jurisdiction in the Chancery Division when it
possessed that jurisdiction, has a comparable application ever been made to the court
—much less has such an application succeeded. Cases have been cited to us which
show that the court has from time to time extended the sphere of the exercise of this
jurisdiction. I do not think, however, that the exercise of the jurisdiction should be
c extended in the direction of interfering with the rights of outside parties.

We were referred to the familiar s 1 of the Guardianship of Minors Act 1971:

> 'Where in any proceedings before any court (whether or not a court as defined
> in section 15 of this Act)—(*a*) the custody or upbringing of a minor; or (*b*) the
> administration of any property belonging to or held on trust for a minor, or the
> *d* application of the income thereof, is in question, the court, in deciding that
> question, shall regard the welfare of the minor as the first and paramount
> consideration . . .'

That provision has been the subject of a number of decisions of the highest authority.
It seems to me that the words 'the custody or upbringing of a minor' do not cover the
issue in this present case, namely, the publication of this material. I do not think
e either the custody or the upbringing of the minor is in question within the meaning of
s 1. If it were, then I think the court would be bound by statute to regard the welfare
of the minor as the first and paramount consideration in deciding the question. On
the other side, the wording of s 1 throws I think considerable light on the sphere within
which the court in practice should exercise its jurisdiction.

The facts of the present case are I think very far indeed from warranting interfer-
f ence with the freedom of publication enjoyed by the defendants. I feel great sympathy
with the parents of this child; but that is not enough. One can only hope that this
child will in fact suffer no harm from the information which I fear will almost
inevitably come to her from this book.

g *Appeal allowed. Leave to appeal to the House of Lords refused.*

Solicitors: *Bindman & Partners* (for the defendants); *Oswald, Hickson, Collier & Co* (for
the plaintiff).

M G Hammett Esq   Barrister.

Inland Revenue Commissioners v Goodwin
Inland Revenue Commissioners v Baggley

COURT OF APPEAL, CIVIL DIVISION　　　　　Affirmed HL [1976] 1 All ER 481

RUSSELL, STAMP AND SCARMAN LJJ

5th, 6th, 7th, 8th NOVEMBER 1974, 29th JANUARY 1975

Surtax – Tax advantage – Counteracting – Transaction in securities – Transaction carried out for bona fide commercial reasons – Commercial reasons – Meaning – Transactions carried out for purpose of perpetuating family control of business – Family company – Bonus issue of redeemable preference shares – Issue to provide funds for estate duty purposes and thereby avoid loss of family control of company on death of major shareholders – Redemption of shares resulting in tax advantage – Whether issue and redemption of shares 'carried out ... for bona fide commercial reasons' – Finance Act 1960, s 28(1).

In 1935 a company was formed to carry on a family business. The company remained a family company, the issued share capital, consisting of ordinary shares, being owned by the taxpayer, his father and his uncle. Neither the father nor the uncle was in good health and it was feared that, on their deaths, the need to find sufficient sums of money to pay estate duty would lead to a forced sale of shares in the company with a consequent loss of family control. In order to provide against that possibility the company in 1951 increased its capital by the creation of preference shares, which were intended to be redeemable on three months' notice after 12 months, and by capitalisation of an appropriate amount from its profit and loss account. The company made a bonus issue of the preference shares to the existing shareholders. In 1958 the directors sought advice on a public flotation of ordinary shares in order to secure for the existing shareholders, from a sale of a proportion of their holdings, sufficient funds to meet prospective estate duty liabilities, and also to enable the company, by means of a stock exchange quotation, to obtain access to capital markets. It was then discovered that, because of a technical defect, the preference shares issued in 1951 were not redeemable. As the whole scheme for a public flotation was at risk if the supposedly redeemable 1951 preference shares were not replaced, the company capitalised a sum from its general reserve and applied that sum in part to paying up newly created redeemable preference shares; the sum was also applied in part to paying up newly created ordinary and deferred ordinary shares. The preference shares were redeemable at the company's option after 30th April 1963. The deferred ordinary shares were to rank pari passu as one class with the ordinary shares 12 months after the redemption of the preference shares. A proportion of the ordinary shares were to be offered to the public was to be made out of the ordinary shares. The deferment of the redemption of the preference shares was to facilitate the public flotation. A proportion of the redeemable preference shares was issued to the taxpayer who transferred them to his wife. In 1963 those shares were redeemed by the company for cash. The Crown took steps against the taxpayer under s 28 of the Finance Act 1958 in order to counteract the tax advantage which he had received in consequence of (i) the resolution of the company in 1958 to capitalise its reserve and apply that sum in the bonus issue of redeemable preference shares to shareholders; (ii) the issue to the taxpayer of a portion of those shares, and (iii) the receipt by his wife in 1963 of cash on the redemption of those shares. The Special Commissioners allowed an appeal by the taxpayer, holding that, by virtue of s 28(1)[a],

---

a　Section 28(1), so far as material, provides: 'Where—(a) in any such circumstances as are mentioned in the next following subsection, and (b) in consequence of a transaction in securities or of the combined effect of two or more such transactions, a person is in a position to obtain, or has obtained, a tax advantage, then unless he shows that the transaction or transactions were carried out either for bona fide commercial reasons or in the ordinary course of making or managing investments, and that none of them had as their main object, or one of their main objects, to enable tax advantages to be obtained, this section shall apply to him in respect of that transaction or those transactions ...

a the section did not apply to the taxpayer since it was not a main object of the relevant transactions to enable tax advantages to be obtained and they had been carried out for 'bona fide commercial reasons' in that the main object of the creation and issue of the 1958 redeemable preference shares was to cure the defect in the 1951 issue and the redemption of those shares was essentially the second half of the operation began in 1958, replacing the 1951 issue. Walton J[b] allowed an appeal by the Crown, holding that, as the 1958 and 1963 transactions had been carried out for the same purpose as the

b 1951 transaction, i e to secure the retention of family control of the company, they had been carried out for financial and not, therefore, for 'commercial' reasons. The taxpayer appealed.

Held – Even if the basic reason for a transaction could be described as 'financial' it did not follow that it was not therefore 'commercial'. If the directors of a company

c were of the view that the retention of family control was important for the future prosperity of the company's business, either in the context of company-customer relationships or of employer-employee relationships, and therefore took steps to ensure the retention of family control of the business, it could properly be said that those steps had been taken for 'commercial reasons'. It could be inferred that experienced commissioners in arriving at their conclusion had such considerations in

d mind and the appeal would therefore be allowed (see p 715 b to j and p 716 b and c, post).

Decision of Walton J [1973] 3 All ER 545 reversed.

Notes

For the cancellation of tax advantages, see the Supplement to 20 Halsbury's Laws

e (3rd Edn) para 276A, 1, and for cases on the subject, see 28(1) Digest (Reissue) 489-494, *1753-1762*.

For the Finance Act 1960, s 28, see 40 Halsbury's Statutes (3rd Edn) 447.

For 1970-71 and subsequent years of assessment s 28 of the 1960 Act has been replaced by the Income and Corporation Taxes Act 1970, ss 460, 461.

f **Cases referred to in judgment**

Bulmer v Inland Revenue Comrs [1966] 3 All ER 801, [1967] Ch 145, 44 Tax Cas 1, [1966] 3 WLR 672, 45 ATC 293, [1966] TR 257, 28(1) Digest (Reissue) 433, *1561*.

Inland Revenue Comrs v Brebner [1967] 1 All ER 779, [1967] 2 AC 18, 43 Tax Cas 705, [1967] 2 WLR 1001, 46 ATC 17, [1967] TR 21, 1967 SC (HL) 31, HL, 28(1) Digest (Reissue) 490, *1755*.

g *Inland Revenue Comrs v Hague, Hague v Inland Revenue Comrs* [1968] 2 All ER 1252, [1969] 1 Ch 393, 44 Tax Cas 619, [1968] 3 WLR 576, 47 ATC 217, [1968] TR 193, CA, 28(1) Digest (Reissue) 490, *1756*.

Inland Revenue Comrs v Parker [1966] 1 All ER 399, [1966] AC 141, 43 Tax Cas 396, [1966] 2 WLR 486, 45 ATC 1, [1966] TR 1, HL, 28(1) Digest (Reissue) 490, *1754*.

h **Cases also cited**

Ransom (Inspector of Taxes) v Higgs [1973] 2 All ER 657, [1973] STC 330, [1973] 1 WLR 1180, CA, rvsd [1974] 3 All ER 949, [1974] 1 WLR 1594, [1974] STC 539, HL.

Sun Life Assurance Society v Davidson, Phoenix Assurance Co v Logan [1957] 2 All ER 760, [1958] AC 184, 37 Tax Cas 330, HL.

j **Appeals**

The Inland Revenue Commissioners served a notice dated 5th May 1969 in accordance with s 28(3) of the Finance Act 1960 on John Goodwin, notifying him of the adjustments which, in the commissioners' opinion, were necessary to counteract the tax

---

b [1973] 3 All ER 545

advantages obtained or obtainable by Mr Goodwin in consequence of the following transactions:

    '1.   the special resolution of R. Goodwin & Sons (Engineers) Ltd. (hereinafter called "the company") on 18th August 1958 to capitalise the sum of £171,095, part of the company's general reserve, and, inter alia, to apply part of that sum to paying up in full 44,525 6% redeemable cumulative preference shares of £1 each, such shares (a) to be distributed amongst the holders of the ordinary shares in the company in the proportions specified in the resolution and (b) to carry rights including the company's right, on giving due notice, to redeem them on or at any time after 30th April 1963;

    '2.   the issue to you, on or about 18th August 1958, pursuant to the aforesaid special resolution, of 13,355 of the aforesaid redeemable preference shares and the transfer of those shares from you to your wife, Mrs. Patricia H. Goodwin, on or about 1st September 1958;

    '3.   the receipt by your wife on or about 30th April 1963 of £13,355 by way of redemption of her holding of 13,355 of the aforesaid redeemable preference shares.'

A notice in similar terms was also served on Frank Baggley relating to the same resolution of the company, the shares issued, and subsequently redeemed, being issued to the trustees of a settlement in which Mr Baggley's wife had the sole absolute interest. Mr Goodwin and Mr Baggley appealed to the Commissioners for the Special Purposes of the Income Tax Acts against those notices and, on 10th June 1972, the commissioners allowed both appeals, holding that s 28 of the 1960 Act did not apply to Mr Goodwin or Mr Baggley since the transactions in question had been carried out for bona fide commercial reasons and none of them had as their main object, or one of their main objects, to enable tax advantages to be obtained. Immediately after the determination of the appeals the Crown, being dissatisfied therewith as being erroneous in point of law, required the commissioners to state cases for the opinion of the High Court. On 9th July 1973 Walton J[1] allowed the Crown's appeal holding, inter alia, that the transactions in question has not been carried out for bona fide commercial reasons. Accordingly it was ordered that the notices dated 5th May 1969 served on Mr Goodwin and Mr Baggley be restored. Mr Goodwin and Mr Baggley appealed against that judgment on the grounds, inter alia: (i) that the conclusions of the commissioners were justifiable in law and no way inconsistent with the evidence; (ii) that the judge had been wrong in construing the word 'commercial' and the word 'financial' as mutually exclusive and, therefore, wrong in holding that the motives of the parties had been financial but not commercial; and (iii) that even if the transactions in question did not come within the scope of the expression 'carried out . . . for bona fide commercial reasons' they did fall within the scope of the expression 'in the ordinary course of making or managing investments' in s 28(1) of the 1960 Act. The facts are set out in the judgment of the court.

Michael Nolan QC and *Stephen Oliver* for Mr Goodwin and Mr Baggley.
D C Potter QC and *Brian Davenport* for the Crown.

Cur adv vult

29th January.   **RUSSELL LJ** delivered the following judgment of the court. These appeals are from decisions of Walton J[1] on appeals by way of case stated by the Crown from decisions of Special Commissioners. The main point in both cases is the same, and an additional point is taken in the Goodwin case.

---

1   [1973] 3 All ER 545, [1974] 1 WLR 380, [1973] STC 456

a The cases stem from assessments made on the taxpayers by way of counteraction or cancellation of tax advantages under s 28 of the Finance Act 1960 in respect of the year 1963-64. In the Baggley case, the relevant transactions relied on were: (1) the resolution of the company on 18th August 1958 to capitalise inter alia £44,525 of the company's general reserve and apply that sum in the bonus issue to ordinary shareholders of the six per cent redeemable preference shares of that nominal amount in certain proportions, such shares being redeemable at the option of the company after
b 30th April 1963; (2) the issue accordingly to a trustee for Mrs Baggley of 4,450 of those shares; and (3) the receipt by the trustee of £4,450 on redemption on 1st May 1963 of those shares.

In the case of Mr Goodwin the relevant transactions relied on were: (1) the same resolution to create and issue redeemable preference shares; (2) the issue to Mr Goodwin on 18th August 1958 of 13,355 of those shares and the transfer by him to
c his wife on 1st September 1958; (3) the receipt by his wife on 1st May 1963 of £13,355 on the redemption of those shares. As to (2), in fact the shares were allotted to Mr Goodwin and renounced by him in favour of his wife as a gift; but it was agreed that that machinery made no difference.

On the main point, stated shortly, the question is whether the taxpayer establishes (i) that the transactions were carried out either (a) for bona fide commercial reasons
d or (b) in the ordinary course of making or managing investments, and also establishes (ii) that none of the transactions had as their main object, or one of their main objects, to enable tax advantages to be obtained. In each case the Special Commissioners concluded that the transactions were carried out for bona fide commercial reasons, and also that none of them had as the, or a, main object to enable tax advantages to be obtained.

e The history of these redeemable preference shares starts in 1951. The business of the company was that of engineers and iron and steel founders, originally established in 1883 by the great-grandfather of Mr Goodwin and Mrs Baggley and his sons. It was throughout a family business. In 1935 the company was formed and took over the business; it remained a family company. At 1951 the issued share capital was 8,905 £1 ordinary shares; of these 40 per cent belonged to Mr Goodwin's father,
f J S Goodwin, and to trustees of family settlements made by J S Goodwin; 30 per cent belonged to Mr Goodwin's uncle, Frank Goodwin, and to trustees of family settlements made by Frank Goodwin; and 30 per cent belonged to Mr Goodwin. Under one of Frank's settlements 890 shares were held by the trustee for Mrs Baggley, his daughter, absolutely. Neither J S Goodwin nor Frank Goodwin was in very good health and the family were anxious lest on their respective deaths money for
g estate duty on their actual holdings of respectively 867 and 892 shares and perhaps also on the shares in their settlements (which were still vulnerable as gifts inter vivos) could only be made available by finding purchasers for shares in the company from outsiders. It is we think clear from the findings that the family was anxious to retain the maximum possible percentage control of the shares in the company consistent with what was envisaged as a possible or probable future offer to the public
h of 30 per cent of the share capital of the company, for which offer the condition of the company was not then suitable. Accordingly, in 1951 the company increased its capital by £45,000 by the creation of 45,000 six per cent preference shares intended to be redeemable by the company on three months' notice after 12 months and by capitalisation of £44,525 from profit and loss account made a five for one bonus issue thereof to the holders of ordinary shares.
j As to this transaction, the commissioners found as follows[1]:

'The main object of the 1951 bonus issue was to provide protection against the possibility that in the event of the death of either J. S. Goodwin or Frank Goodwin (father and uncle, respectively, of [Mr Goodwin]), who were directors of

---

1 [1973] 3 All ER at 547, [1973] STC at 458

and large shareholders in the Company at that time both in bad health, the
necessity to find considerable sums of money for payment of estate duty would   *a*
lead to a forced sale of ordinary shares leading to loss of 70% control of the
Company by the Goodwin family. At the same time a number of family settlements of shares were made by J. S. and F. Goodwin including the settlement on
Mrs. H. M. Baggley . . . The possibility of a flotation in 1951 was considered but
rejected because of the Company's recent profit record and plant expansion for
the future.'   *b*

Further in their reasons, para 10(7), they stated[1]:

'It is not controverted, in evidence or argument before us, that the main
object of the 1951 issue was to provide against the possibility that in the event of
the death of either Mr. J. S. Goodwin or Mr. F. Goodwin the necessity of raising
large sums to pay estate duty might lead to the break-up of family control of   *c*
the company.'

They held that the main object of the 1951 bonus preference share issue was a bona
fide commercial one and that the obtaining of a tax advantage was not a main object.
   In 1958 the directors sought advice on a public flotation of ordinary shares. The
first object, as found by the commissioners was that of providing the family from a   *d*
sale to the public of a proportion of their holdings with funds available to meet
prospective estate duty liabilities, and a secondary object of obtaining a stock exchange
quotation with the attendant advantage of access to the capital issues market to
provide possible funds for further expansion of the company's trade.
   After a good many varying suggestions, the scheme evolved for a public flotation
was as follows, accepted by the Goodwin family and trustees of the settlements: *e*
(1) acquisition by the company of the outstanding 71 per cent shareholding in a company ('Akron') so as to make it a 100 per cent subsidiary; (2) the 1951 bonus issue of
preference shares to be made irredeemable for a period of some five years to enable
expanding trade to replace the substantial sum (some £130,000) of working capital
required for the Akron acquisition; (3) half the ordinary shares in the company to
be converted into deferred ordinary shares, the offer to the public to be made out   *f*
of the unconverted ordinary shares; the deferred ordinary shares to remain as such
until after the redemption of the 1951 preference shares.
   At this late stage it was discovered that owing to a technical defect in their creation
the 1951 preference shares were not redeemable. As the commissioners say[2], the
reaction of all concerned was one of 'crisis'. After consultations—

'it was decided that the situation should be remedied by putting all the   *g*
holders of the [preference] shares into the position in which they would have
been if [the 1951 issue] had not been defective.'

This was done first by converting the 1951 preference shares into deferred ordinary
shares. The company then capitalised the sum of £171,095 from its general reserve
and applied that sum in paying up at par: (a) 44,525 out of 45,000 newly-created £1   *h*
six per cent redeemable preference shares; (b) 81,095 of previously unissued (6,095)
and newly-created ordinary shares (75,000); (c) 45,475 previously unissued (475) and
newly-created (45,000) deferred ordinary shares: the 475 representing the converted
unissued 1951 preference shares.
   The capital structure of the company for the purpose of the public flotation was
thus: issued ordinary £90,000, of which a proportion (£54,000) was to be offered to   *j*
the public; issued deferred ordinary shares, 90,000; issued six per cent redeemable
preference shares, 44,525; unissued redeemable preference shares, 475.

---

1   [1973] 3 All ER at 553, [1973] STC at 464
2   [1973] 3 All ER at 548, [1973] STC at 459

a The redeemable preference shares were redeemable at the company's option after 30th April 1963. The deferred ordinary shares were to rank pari passu as one class with the ordinary shares only after 12 months from the redemption of the preference shares. (We have for simplicity ignored subdivision of £1 shares into 2s shares.)

In this connection the commissioners remarked[1]:

b 'There were five trustee holdings of shares aggregating around half of the ordinary and preference share capital, and any scheme other than a restoration of the status quo would have been difficult to get agreed by all the beneficiaries and trustees involved.'

c By 'restoration of the status quo' was meant, of course, the putting of the 1951 preference shareholders in the situation of redeemability within a measurable time. We can well understand the view thus expressed by the commissioners. Trustees of a settlement might on the one hand well be prepared on behalf of their beneficiaries to adopt a scheme for partial public flotation which involved acquisition of the Akron company with postponement of expected redemption of six per cent preference shares and some acceptance of deferred ordinary shares, but on the other hand jib

d at a scheme which left preference shares irredeemable.

On 30th April 1963 the 44,525 of the 1958 redeemable preference shares were redeemed for cash, and in due course the deferred ordinary shares became ordinary shares. The commissioners stated[2] that this redemption was 'in order to implement the bargain made with the public in 1958'. This must be a misconception as stated: there was no obligation towards the public ordinary shareholders to redeem the

e preference shares, who indeed had been offered the carrot that the preference shares would not be redeemed for about five years and that the deferred ordinary shares would not rank for dividend until after the redemption. We think what is meant by the phrase is that what was done was that which was envisaged in the offer to the public; though it is true to say that in rehearsing the contentions for the taxpayer in para 7(2) of the case stated[3] there occurs again the phrase—'the object of the re-

f demption . . . being, in effect, to implement the bargain [of 1958] made with the public . . .' Moreover, from para 10(9)[4] it appears that this expression comes from evidence given. As we have already indicated, the commissioners formed the view that the main object of the creation and issue in 1951 of the preference shares was to avoid the necessity of break-up of family control of the company due to the exigencies of estate duty, that this was a bona fide commercial reason for that issue, and that the

g obtaining of a tax advantage was not a main object.

The commissioners, in para 10(8)[4], concluded on the evidence that the main object of the creation and issue of the 1958 redeemable preference shares was to cure the unknown defect in the 1951 issue—to restore the status quo in that respect—and that this restoration, quite apart from the concurrent public flotation, afforded a bona fide commercial reason and that the obtaining of a tax advantage was not a main reason.

h So far as the redemption of the 1958 issue of preference shares is concerned, the commissioners in their reasons (para 10(9) of the case[4]) said that this was essentially the second half of an operation begun in 1958, replacing the 1951 issue. But for the projected flotation, the 1951 issue would probably have been redeemed in 1958 or 1959; the deferment of redemption until 1963 was decided on to facilitate the public flotation—a bona fide commercial reason—and that the redemption

j itself—

---

1 [1973] 3 All ER at 549, [1973] STC at 460
2 [1973] 3 All ER at 550, [1973] STC at 461
3 [1973] 3 All ER at 551, [1973] STC at 462
4 [1973] 3 All ER at 554, [1973] STC at 465

'was carried out for bona fide commercial reasons, in order (as it was expressed
in evidence) to implement the bargain made with the public in 1958.'   a

They expressed themselves as satisfied that the obtaining of a tax advantage was not
a main object of the 1963 redemption.

We turn to the judgment of Walton J. He dealt with the matter purely on the
question of bona fide commercial reasons, understanding (mistakenly we are told)
that the taxpayer no longer relied alternatively on the ordinary course of manag- b
ment of investments (as to which there had been no finding by the commissioners),
and that the Crown no longer contended that a main object was the obtaining of a
tax advantage.

So far as the 1951 creation and issue of the assumed redeemable preference shares
was concerned, Walton J considered that the commissioners erred in law in forming
the view that when the sole object of that creation and issue was to preserve family c
control of the company and its business it was within the ambit of 'bona fide commercial reasons'. He took the view that the reasons behind the creation and issue
were properly to be labelled 'financial' and not 'commercial'. So far as the 1958
'restoration of the status quo' was concerned, the judge found no radical alteration
from the reasons for the 1951 transaction; and in his view the 1963 redemption
followed in due course, correctly saying that it was not done to implement any d
bargain with the public, though the postponement of redemption might have been
based on commercial reasons as promoting a successful flotation.

The learned judge did not find much assistance from the cases cited to him. Nor
do we. *Inland Revenue Comrs v Brebner*[1] was a case in which there was ample reason
for the view that if the steps were not taken the business of the company, in the
continuation of which the actors were both directly and indirectly much interested, e
would come to an end: there is a passage in the opinion of Lord Upjohn[2] which
Walton J perhaps took to indicate that the Special Commissioners would have been
well entitled to take the view that such would *not* constitute commercial reasons;
but in fact all that was said was that the commissioners might have concluded (but
did not) that there were two separate chapters in the transactions, the first for com-
merical reasons and the second with as its main object the obtaining of a tax f
advantage.

Bulmer v Inland Revenue Comrs[3] was a case indicating that the expression 'bona fide
commercial transaction' was used judicially to describe something lacking an
element of bounty, in determining whether there was a 'settlement'. It does not we
think help, though it indicates, as one would expect, that there can be a bona fide
commercial transaction with the obtaining of a tax advantage as a main object.
Inland Revenue Comrs v Hague[4] was indeed such a case. It was assumed that the g
commissioners found bona fide commercial reasons; but they also found a main
object of obtaining a tax advantage, which finding the taxpayer failed to upset.
On the 'commercial' point, there was involved a reorganisation and rationalisation
of the company's cotton mills business, and a substantial proportion of the shareholders were pressing for a liquidation and distribution. What actually was done h
was a capitalisation of profits by the issue of bonus shares followed by reduction of
capital by repayment out of assets surplus to the company's needs.

Inland Revenue Comrs v Parker[5] was a case in which accumulated profits were
distributed in 1953 in the form of paid-up debentures, in order that on the death of
a shareholder money might be made available to meet death duties, particularly
as the shares of one holder might be valued on an assets basis. The debentures were j

1   [1967] 1 All ER 779, [1967] 2 AC 18, 43 Tax Cas 705
2   [1967] 1 All ER at 783, [1967] 2 AC at 29, 43 Tax Cas at 717
3   [1966] 3 All ER 801, [1967] Ch 145, 44 Tax Cas 1
4   [1968] 2 All ER 1252, [1969] 1 Ch 393, 44 Tax Cas 619
5   [1966] 1 All ER 399, [1966] AC 141, 43 Tax Cas 396

redeemed in 1961. It was not contended by the taxpayer that there were involved
a any bona fide commercial reasons. The arguments were concerned with other
matters. And we do not think that the lack of contention on the part of the taxpayer
is really significant in the present case; the facts found there were different.

We agree that one should start with the 1951 transaction as part of the whole
picture, and in considering the reasons for it the failure to achieve redeemability must
of course be ignored. Basically, the motive or reason as found by the commissioners
b was the retention of family control of the company and its business. Were the
commissioners guilty of misconstruction of the phrase 'for bona fide commercial
reasons' in the statute in holding that such a reason could be commercial? Or was
the conclusion such that no body of commissioners properly instructed in the law
could arrive at it? Walton J considered the reason to be 'financial' and *therefore* not
'commercial', an approach which we do not find persuasive. It is not unknown for
c the prosperity of a business to depend in part on the very fact that it is an old-estab-
lished family business and continues as such under family control and management,
both in the context of company-customers relationships and of the employer-
employees relationship. Had the commissioners stated in terms that the reasons for
hoping to retain family control were because of its value under those headings, we
do not think that their finding that these were bona fide commercial reasons could
possibly have been faulted. And we see no reason why they should be taken as
d having ignored in 'family control' those considerations when concluding that there
were bona fide commercial reasons behind the intended 1951 transaction.

Both the commissioners and the judge in substance worked onwards through the
transactions of 1958 and 1963 from their opposing standpoints as to 1951—that nothing
in point of reasons was really changed. We consider that there were changes in the
e circumstances that, if anything, lent support to the presence in 1958 of bona fide
commercial reasons. It is true that the threat to family control by the need to meet
estate duty was much lessened by 1958; though, in considering motives of the actors,
this aspect may not have been fully appreciated in the atmosphere of crisis. On the
other hand, by the time the defect in the 1951 issue was discovered, plans for the
public flotation were well under way, with a view in part, as the commissioners
d found, to the advantage of the company and its business. As we have already indicated, the whole scheme for public flotation was, in the view of the commissioners,
at risk if the supposedly redeemable 1951 preference shares were not replaced and,
to the extent of the acquisition for £95,000 of 50 per cent of the Akron shares, the
scheme had already been carried out in April 1958, before the defect in the 1951
preference shares was discovered in June 1958. In all the circumstances, we are not
f prepared to disagree with the conclusion of the commissioners that the transactions
in 1958 in relation to redeemable preference shares were carried out for bona fide
commercial reasons.

So far as concerns the redemption in 1963, we have already indicated that this was
not properly described as an implementation of the bargain made with the public in
1958. Rather was it a fulfilment of the expectation of the trustees and other share-
g holders on the basis of which the scheme of public flotation went through. But the
redemption as a transaction cannot in our view be regarded in isolation. As Walton J
said, the redemption was in gremio the 1958 issue of the shares and, had he taken the
view that the 1958 transactions were carried out for bona fide commercial reasons,
we have no doubt that he would have considered that label equally appropriate
to the redemption in 1963. We so consider it.

j As we have indicated, the judge did not deal with the question whether the transactions or any of them had as a main object to enable tax advantages to be obtained.
The commissioners answered the question in the negative. This is essentially a
matter of subjective fact, and we are quite unable to accept the Crown's contention
that this was a finding at which the commissioners could not reasonably arrive.

In those circumstances, it is not necessary to arrive at a conclusion on the question

whether the transactions or any of them were also carried out in the ordinary course
of making or managing investments, supposing that such a finding is not inconsistent   *a*
with the finding as to commercial reasons.   Nor is it necessary to pronounce on the
secondary point in relation to the Goodwin shares: but it is right to say on this
that we found ourselves sufficiently in agreement with Walton J's views thereon as
not to call on the Crown to answer the taxpayer's contention.

We add a general observation.   The main points for decision in this case—the
objects and reasons of and for the transactions in question—are pre-eminently questions   *b*
of fact (and indeed of subjective fact) for determination by the commissioners with
expertise in this sort of field, and in the rarest case should a court find itself able to
disagree with them.

We accordingly allow the appeals with such consequential orders as will restore
the order of the Special Commissioners cancelling the notices in question.

                                                                                            c

Appeal allowed.   Leave to appeal to the House of Lords refused.

Solicitors: *Waltons & Co*, agents for *Pinsent & Co*, Birmingham (for Mr Goodwin and
Mr Baggley); *Solicitor of Inland Revenue.*

                                    Rengan Krishnan Esq   Barrister.
                                                                                            d

Courtney and Fairbairn Ltd v Tolaini Brothers (Hotels) Ltd and another   *e*

COURT OF APPEAL, CIVIL DIVISION
LORD DENNING MR, LORD DIPLOCK AND LAWTON LJ
28th NOVEMBER 1974

Contract – Formation – Certainty of terms – Term fundamental to contract – Price – No   *f*
agreed method of ascertaining price – Building contract – Price to be settled by negotiation –
Agreement 'to negotiate fair and reasonable contract sums' —Whether a concluded contract.

Contract – Validity – Contract to negotiate – Agreement that fundamental term of contract
should be negotiated – Agreement supported by consideration – No agreement to refer
negotiations to third party – Building contract – Price – Price to be negotiated by parties – No   *g*
method of ascertaining price – No provision for failure of negotiations –Whether contract to
negotiate enforceable.

A company represented by T wished to develop a site by building a motel, filling
station and hotel.   T got into touch with C, a property developer who was well
placed to obtain finance for the development.   At a meeting between T and C it was   *h*
proposed that C should introduce someone to finance the development and that T
should employ the company which C represented to construct the buildings.   After
that meeting C wrote a letter to T, dated 10th April 1969, stating that he was in a
position to introduce to T someone who had access to the necessary finance for the
development; C also pointed out that his commercial interest in the matter was that
of a building contractor. The letter continued: 'Accordingly I would be very happy to   *j*
know that, if my discussions and arrangements with interested parties lead to . . . a
financial arrangement acceptable to both parties you will be prepared to instruct
your Quantity Surveyor to negotiate fair and reasonable contract sums in respect of
each of the three projects as they arise. (These would, incidentally be based upon
agreed estimates of the net cost of work and general overheads with a margin for

profit of 5%) which, I am sure you will agree, is, indeed reasonable.' On 28th April T
wrote to C: 'In reply to your letter of the 10th April, I agree to the terms specified
therein, and I look forward to meeting the interested party regarding finance.'   C
introduced a person willing to provide finance for the development. T instructed his
quantity surveyor to negotiate with C as to the price for the building works, but
agreement with C on the price could not be reached and the negotiations broke
down. T then instructed contractors other than C's company to carry out the development. C's company brought an action in which they claimed a declaration that there
was an enforceable contract to employ them as builders for the development and that
T's company were in breach of contract in employing other building contractors.

Held – The letters did not give rise to any enforceable contract between T's company
and C's company because—
   (i) The price was a matter which was fundamental to the contract. Accordingly
there could be no binding contract unless the price had been agreed, or there was an
agreed method of ascertaining the price which was not dependent on negotiations
between the parties. The letters did not contain any agreement on the price, nor did
they provide for any method for ascertaining the price; they amounted to no more
than an agreement to negotiate fair and reasonable contract sums (see p 719 e g and j
to p 720 a and e to g, post).
   (ii) A contract to negotiate even though supported by consideration was not a contract known to the law since it was too uncertain to have any binding force and no
court could estimate the damages for breach of such an agreement (see p 720 b f and
g, post); dictum of Lord Wright in *Hillas & Co Ltd v Arcos Ltd* [1932] All ER Rep at 505
disapproved.

Notes

For incomplete agreements, see 9 Halsbury's Laws (4th Edn) 139, para 261, and for the
requirement of certainty, see ibid 148, para 266, and for cases on the subject, see
12 Digest (Reissue) 24-26, 13-23.
   For the formation of a building contract, see 4 Halsbury's Laws (4th Edn)
571-574, paras 1130-1135, and for cases on the subject, see 7 Digest (Repl) 388-340, 5-16.

Cases referred to in judgments

Hillas & Co Ltd v Arcos Ltd [1932] All ER Rep 494, 147 LT 503, 38 Com Cas 23, HL,
   39 Digest (Repl) 448, 34.
Mountford v Scott [1974] 1 All ER 248, [1973] 3 WLR 884, *affd* p 198, ante, [1975] 2 WLR
   114, CA.

Cases also cited

Brown v Gould [1971] 2 All ER 1505, [1972] Ch 53.
National Coal Board v Galley [1958] 1 All ER 91, [1958] 1 WLR 16, CA.
Smith v Morgan [1971] 2 All ER 1500, [1971] 1 WLR 803.

Interlocutory appeal

This was an appeal by the first defendants, Tolaini Brothers (Hotels) Ltd, with leave
of Shaw J, against the order of Shaw J made on 12th March 1974, the parties having
agreed to proceed only on the preliminary question whether there was concluded any
enforceable agreement between the plaintiffs, Courtney and Fairbairn Ltd, and either
the first defendants or the second defendants, The Thatched Barn Ltd, and if yes, who
were the parties to the agreement and what were its terms Shaw J declared that there
was a binding and enforceable contract between the plaintiffs and the first defendants
created by letters written on 10th April 1969 by Mr Courtney on behalf of the plaintiffs to Mr Sydney Tolaini and the reply thereto of 28th April 1969 written by Mr
Sydney Tolaini on behalf of the first defendants, the terms of which were, inter alia,

contained in those letters; and he ordered that the plaintiffs' action claiming that the
defendants were in breach of contract and an enquiry as to damages, alternatively that   *a*
the plaintiffs were entitled to a reasonable sum for services rendered to the defendants
and an enquiry into such sum, should be transferred to an official referee for final
determination. The facts are set out in the judgment of Lord Denning MR.

David Sullivan for the first defendants.
John Dyson for the plaintiffs.   *b*

LORD DENNING MR. The question in this case is whether two letters give rise
to a concluded contract.

Mr Tolaini wanted to develop a site in Hertfordshire. It was The Thatched Barn
Hotel together with five acres of land. He got in touch with a property developer,
a Mr Courtney. It appears that Mr Courtney was well placed to obtain finance for   *c*
building development. He was also a building contractor himself. The two met and
discussed ways and means at the office of Mr Sacks, an architect. The proposal was
that Mr Courtney should introduce someone to provide the money and lend it to Mr
Tolaini. Mr Tolaini was to develop the site by building a motel and other things.
But he was to employ Mr Courtney or his company to do the construction work.
After the meeting, on 10th April 1969, Mr Courtney wrote to Mr Tolaini this letter: *d*

> *'Re: Thatched Barn Hotel*
> '. . . I am now in a position to introduce you to those who: (a) are interested in
> your proposals, (b) have access to the necessary finance . . .
> 'I think I should mention, at this point, that my commercial interest in this
> matter is that of a Building Contractor. I am interested in it due to the fact that   *e*
> Mr Sacks, whom I have known for some years, is aware that I work for a number
> of large investing and development concerns, and thought it possible that I might
> be in a position to be of service to you.
> 'You will understand, therefore, that in addition to making myself useful to
> you, my objective is to build the three projects mentioned, namely, the Motel, the   *f*
> Filling Station, and the future Hotel, or other development, on the "Green Belt"
> area of your site. [Then follow these important words:] Accordingly I would be
> very happy to know that, if my discussions and arrangements with interested parties
> lead to an introductory meeting, which in turn leads to a financial arrangement
> acceptable to both parties you will be prepared to instruct your Quantity Surveyor
> to negotiate fair and reasonable contract sums in respect of each of the three projects
> as they arise. (These would, incidentally be based upon agreed estimates of the net   *g*
> cost of work and general overheads with a margin for profit of 5%) which, I am
> sure you will agree, is indeed reasonable.'

On 21st April 1969 there was a meeting between the parties at the Thatched Barn
Hotel. Mr Courtney said he wanted to have something in writing from Mr Tolaini
before he went further. Accordingly Mr Tolaini did write a letter on 28th April 1969,   *h*
in the terms:

> 'In reply to your letter of the 10th April, I agree to the terms specified therein,
> and I look forward to meeting the interested party regarding finance.'

Those are the two letters on which the issue depends. But I will tell the subsequent
events quite shortly. Mr Courtney did his best. He found a person interested who   *j*
provided finance of £200,000 or more for the projects. Mr Tolaini on his side appointed
his quantity surveyor with a view to negotiating with Mr Courtney the price for the
construction work. But there were differences of opinion about the price. And nothing
was agreed. In the end Mr Tolaini did not employ Mr Courtney or his company to do
the construction work. Mr Tolaini instructed other contractors and they completed

the motel and other works. But then Mr Tolaini took advantage of the finance which
a Mr Courtney had made possible, but he did not employ Mr Courtney's company to
do the work. Naturally enough, Mr Courtney was very upset. He has brought this
action in which he says that there was a contract by which his company were to be
employed as builders for the work, and it was a breach of contract by Mr Tolaini or
his company to go elsewhere and employ somebody else. Mr Courtney's company
claimed the loss of profits which they would have made if they had been employed as
b builders for this motel. At the trial the parties agreed to proceed only in the following
question:

> 'Whether there was concluded any enforceable agreement in law between the
> Plaintiff and the Defendants or one of them, and if yes, who were the parties to
> the agreement and what were its terms'.

c
Shaw J heard the evidence on the point, both as to the initial interview and as to the
circumstances in which Mr Courtney's company were not employed to do the work.
He held that there was an enforceable agreement. He found that the parties were
Mr Courtney's company and Mr Tolaini's company; and that the terms were, inter
alia, contained in the letters of 10th and 28th April 1967 which I have read. He said in
d his judgment that the letters—

> 'gave rise to a binding and enforceable contract whereby the Defendants
> undertook to employ the Plaintiffs . . . to carry out the work referred to in [Mr
> Courtney's letter of 10th April 1969] at a price to be calculated by the addition of
> 5% per cent to the fair and reasonable cost of the work and the general overheads
> relating thereto.'

e
I am afraid that I have come to a different view from the judge. The reason is
because I can find no agreement on the price or on any method by which the price was
to be calculated. The agreement was only an agreement to 'negotiate' fair and reasonable contract sums. The words of the letter are 'your Quantity Surveyor to *negotiate*
fair and reasonable contract sums in respect of each of the three projects as they arise.'
f Then there are words which show that estimates had not yet been agreed, but were
yet to be agreed. The words are: 'These [the contract sums] would, incidentally be
based upon agreed estimates of the net cost of work and general overheads with a
margin for profit of 5%.' Those words show that there were no estimates agreed and
no contract sums agreed. All was left to be agreed in the future. It was to be agreed
between the parties themselves. If they had left the price to be agreed by a third person
g such as an arbitrator, it would have been different. But here it was to be agreed
between the parties themselves.
Now the price in a building contract is of fundamental importance. It is so essential
a term that there is no contract unless the price is agreed or there is an agreed method
of ascertaining it, not dependent on the negotiations of the two parties themselves.
In a building contract both parties must know at the outset, before the work is started,
h what the price is to be, or, at all events, what agreed estimates are. No builder and no
employer would ever dream of entering into a building contract for over £200,000
without there being an estimate of the cost and an agreed means of ascertaining the
price.
In the ordinary course of things the architects and the quantity surveyors get out the
specification and the bills of quantities. They are submitted to the contractors. They
j work out the figures and tender for the work at a named price; and there is a specified
means of altering it up or down for extras or omissions and so forth, usually by means
of an architect's certificate. In the absence of some such machinery, the only contract
which you might find is a contract to do the work for a reasonable sum or for a sum to
be fixed by a third party. But here there is no such contract at all. There is no
machinery for ascertaining the price except by negotiation. In other words, the price

is still to be agreed. Seeing that there is no agreement on so fundamental a matter as the price, there is no contract.   **a**

But then this point was raised. Even if there was not a contract actually to build, was not there a contract to negotiate? In this case Mr Tolaini did instruct his quantity surveyor to negotiate, but the negotiations broke down. It may be suggested that the quantity surveyor was to blame for the failure of the negotiations. But does that give rise to a cause of action? There is very little guidance in the book about a contract to negotiate. It was touched on by Lord Wright in *Hillas & Co Ltd v Arcos Ltd*[1] where he said: 'There   **b** is then no bargain except to negotiate, and negotiations may be fruitless and end without any contract ensuing.' Then he went on[1]:

> '. . . yet even then, in strict theory, there is a contract (if there is good considera-tion) to negotiate, though in the event of repudiation by one party the damages may be nominal, unless a jury think that the opportunity to negotiate was of some   **c** appreciable value to the injured party.'

That tentative opinion by Lord Wright does not seem to me to be well founded. If the law does not recognise a contract to enter into a contract (when there is a funda-mental term yet to be agreed) it seems to me it cannot recognise a contract to negotiate. The reason is because it is too uncertain to have any binding force. No court could   **d** estimate the damages because no one can tell whether the negotiations would be successful or would fall through; or if successful, what the result would be. It seems to me that a contract to negotiate, like a contract to enter into a contract, is not a con-tract known to the law. We were referred to the recent decision of Brightman J about an option, *Mountford v Scott*[2]; but that does not seem to me to touch this point. I think we must apply the general principle that when there is a fundamental matter   **e** left undecided and to be the subject of negotiation, there is no contract. So I would hold that there was not any enforceable agreement in the letters between the plaintiff and the defendants. I would allow the appeal accordingly.

LORD DIPLOCK. I agree and would only add my agreement that the dictum—for it is no more—of Lord Wright in *Hillas & Co Ltd v Arcos Ltd*[1] to which Lord   **f** Denning MR has referred, though an attractive theory, should in my view be regarded as bad law.

LAWTON LJ. I agree with both the judgments which have been delivered.

          g
Appeal allowed. Action dismissed.

Solicitors: *Pollards*, Boreham Wood, Hertfordshire (for the first defendants). *Doyle, Devonshire, Box & Co* (for the plaintiffs).

Wendy Shockett   Barrister.   **h**

---

1   [1932] All ER Rep 494 at 505, 147 LT 503 at 515
2   [1974] 1 All ER 248, [1973] 3 WLR 884

Re Bushnell (deceased)
Lloyds Bank Ltd and others v Murray and others

CHANCERY DIVISION

b GOULDING J

3rd, 4th DECEMBER 1974

Charity – Education – Political object – Promotion of settlor's own theories by educational means – Trust for 'advancement and propagation of teaching of Socialised Medicine' – Direction to further 'knowledge of Socialist application of medicine' and to demonstrate that c 'full advantage of Socialised medicine can only be enjoyed in a Socialist State' – Lectures to be given on 'Socialised health and medicine' – Publication and distribution of literature on or connected with 'Socialised medicine' – Whether educational purpose – Whether trust charitable.

Charity – Charitable trust – Validity – Date of ascertainment – Public benefit – Trust established by will – Trust coming into operation after termination of prior interest – Whether d validity as charitable trust to be determined by reference to the law and character of the objects of the trust as at date of testator's death or at date when trust coming into operation.

The testator died in 1941. By his will made in 1940 he bequeathed the residue of his estate to the plaintiffs as executors and trustees on trusts for conversion and investment. The will directed the plaintiffs to hold the residuary fund on trust to pay the e income thereof to his wife during her life and after her death on trust to pay the capital and income to four unincorporated associations which were to be called the 'endowment trustees'. He directed that the fund should be used by the endowment trustees for 'the advancement and propagation of the teaching of Socialised Medicine' in accordance with and subject to conditions set out in 13 clauses in the will. Clauses 1-5 set up the first scheme for the application of the income of the fund. Under f cl 1 the fund was to be administered by managers constituted and appointed by the endowment trustees. Under cl 4 the managers were to apply the income of the fund 'towards furthering the knowledge of the Socialist application of medicine to public and personal health and well-being and to demonstrating that the full advantage of Socialised Medicine can only be enjoyed in a Socialist State by' various means such as engaging lecturers to give addresses, or publishing literature, on socialised g medicine. Clause 5 provided that the addresses, literature and other means of information should deal with some aspect of the subject in accordance with specified principles, which included the requirement that it was to be 'made evident that . . . a Socialised Medical Service can only operate effectively in a Socialised State that is a state in which all production is planned for use and happiness of the Community by the State and not for profit by the individual'. Clause 6 provided that if at any time the h endowment trustees were satisfied that it was impracticable or impossible to carry out the trust set out in cll 1-5 they should give to the managers three months' notice of their intention to determine the payments or authorities to the managers and at the end of that period the trust should come to an end. Clauses 7-13 contained the provisions of a second trust by which the fund was to be applied after the termination of the first trust under cl 6. Under cl 7 the managers were to apply the fund to provide j educational facilities for 'the teaching of the principles and practice of Socialised health and medicine as defined in the primary trusts' by buying or hiring premises and equipping with books and other educational materials. Under cl 8 the premises were to be free and open to the public, and the exhibits and activities therein were to be for the purpose 'of the education and co-operation of the public in the practice of socialised health and medicine'. Clause 9 provided, inter alia, that the premises should contain a

BB

room or hall where addresses were to be given daily by lecturers of socialist principles, and that the premises could also be used for lectures on simple anatomy, mother and *a* child welfare and hygiene, diet and other similar subjects advantageous to the primary objects of the trust. Provision was made for an institute to be set up at the premises acquired which would co-operate with national medical and educational services to make the value of the knowledge of health, its creation and preservation, clear to the public. The testator's widow died in 1972. The plaintiffs sought the determination of the question whether, on the true construction of the will and in the events that *b* had happened, the trusts thereby declared to take effect after the death of the testator's widow took effect as valid charitable trusts.

Held – (i) The first trust to be established by the will was not charitable for the following reasons—

(a) The requirement in the first trust that the fund was to be used for the advance- *c* ment and propagation of the teaching of socialised medicine, that the managers were to further the knowledge of the socialist application of medicine to public and personal health and well-being and to demonstrate that the full advantage of socialised medicine could only be enjoyed in a socialist state, and that the lecturers and authors of commissioned books were to deal with socialised medicine in accordance with the very detailed and rigid principles in cl 5, revealed that the testator was trying to *d* promote by education his own theory of 'socialised medicine' rather than to educate the public to choose for themselves, starting from neutral information, whether to support or oppose what the testator called 'socialised medicine'. Accordingly, the essential object of the first trust was political and not an educational one (see p 729 *f* to p 730 *a*, post); *National Anti-Vivisection Society v Inland Revenue Comrs* [1947] 2 All ER 217 and *Re Hopkinson* [1949] 1 All ER 346 applied. *e*

(b) The question whether a trust set up by a will was charitable because it was of public benefit stood or fell by the law and character of the objects of the trust at the date of the testator's death. Accordingly, although the first trust was one to promote a state health service, the fact that Parliament had, after the testator's death, set up a state health service could not be relied on as demonstrating that a state health service was for the public benefit (see p 730 *c d* and *g* and p 731 *c*, post); *Scottish Burial Reform f and Cremation Society Ltd v Glasgow City Corpn* [1967] 3 All ER 215 distinguished.

(ii) The second trust also failed for the following reasons—

(a) The language used in cl 6 could not apply to the event which had actually occurred, i e the first trust proving, for legal reasons, to be void ab initio. In any event the provisions of cl 6 made the second trust a contingent one. Accordingly, since the operation of cl 6 might occur at any time when the endowment trustees *g* found that the first trust had become 'impracticable or impossible', the second trust was void for perpetuity even if it were charitable (see p 731 *e* and *f*, post).

(b) Furthermore, since cl 7 required that the instruction for which the second trust made provision was to be of the principles defined in the first trust and cl 9 required the lecturers to be persons 'of socialist principles', the second trust too was essentially aimed to promote a political object even though some of the activities referred to *h* were of purely educational character (see p 733 *b* and *c*, post).

Notes

For trusts for educational purposes, see 5 Halsbury's Laws (4th Edn) 322-327, paras 522-527, and for cases on the subject, see 8(1) Digest (Reissue), 257-266, *112-158*.

For trusts for political purposes, see 5 Halsbury's Laws (4th Edn) 354, para 558, and *j* for a case on the subject, see 8(1) Digest (Reissue), 261, *142*.

Cases referred to in judgment

Bonar Law Memorial Trust v Comrs of Inland Revenue (1933) 49 TLR 220, 17 Tax Cas 508.
Bowman v Secular Society Ltd [1917] AC 406, [1916-17] All ER Rep 1, 86 LJCh 568, 117 LT 161, HL, 8(1) Digest (Reissue) 302, 427.

Hood, Re, Public Trustee v Hood [1931] 1 Ch 240, [1930] All ER Rep 215, 100 LJCh 115, 143
a   LT 691, CA, 8(1) Digest (Reissue) 259, *133*.
Hopkinson (deceased), Re, Lloyds Bank Ltd v Baker [1949] 1 All ER 346, 65 TLR 108, 8(1)
    Digest (Reissue) 261, *142*.
Income Tax Special Purposes Comrs v Pemsel [1891] AC 531, [1891-4] All ER Rep 28, 61
    LJQB 265, 65 LT 621, 55 JP 805, 3 Tax Cas 53, HL, 8(1) Digest (Reissue) 236, *1*.
McDougall (Arthur) Fund, Re the trusts of the, Thompson v Fitzgerald [1956] 3 All ER 867,
b   [1957] 1 WLR 81, 8(1) Digest (Reissue) 313, *533*.
National Anti-Vivisection Society v Inland Revenue Comrs [1947] 2 All ER 217, [1948] AC 31,
    [1947] LJR 1112, 177 LT 226, 28 Tax Cas 351, HL, 8(1) Digest (Reissue) 238, *3*.
Scottish Burial Reform and Cremation Society Ltd v Glasgow City Corpn [1967] 3 All ER 215,
    [1968] AC 138, [1967] 3 WLR 1132, 132 JP 30, [1967] RA 272, 1967 SC (HL) 116, HL,
    Digest (Cont Vol C) 69, *375a*.
c   *Scowcroft, Re, Ormrod v Wilkinson* [1898] 2 Ch 638, [1895-9] All ER Rep 274, 67 LJCh 697,
    79 LT 342, 43 Sol Jo 11, 8(1) Digest (Reissue) 259, *132*.
Spensley's Will Trusts, Re, Barclays Bank Ltd v Staughton and others [1954] 1 All ER 178,
    [1954] Ch 233, [1954] 2 WLR 145, CA, 8(1) Digest (Reissue) 308, *482*.

Cases also cited
d   *Baddeley v Inland Revenue Comrs* [1953] 2 All ER 233, [1953] Ch 504, CA.
Bailey, Re, Barrett v Hyder [1951] 1 All ER 391, [1951] Ch 407, CA.
Berry v St Marylebone Corpn [1957] 3 All ER 677, [1958] Ch 406, CA.
Pare v Clegg (1861) 29 Beav 589.
Pinion (deceased), Re, Westminister Bank Ltd v Pinion [1964] 1 All ER 890, [1965] Ch 85, CA.
Russell v Jackson (1852) 10 Hare 204.
e   *Villers-Wilkes, Re, Bower v Goodman* (1895) 72 LT 323.
Wightwick's Will Trusts, Re, Official Trustees of Charitable Funds v Fielding-Ould [1950] 1
    All ER 689, [1950] Ch 260.

Adjourned summons
By an originating summons dated 31st October 1973, the plaintiffs, Lloyds Bank Ltd,
f   Leslie Theodore Hilliard and Charles Murton Holmes, the executors and trustees of
the will dated 28th September 1940 of Frank George Bushnell deceased, who died on
14th October 1941, sought the determination of, inter alia, the question whether on the
true construction of the will and in the events that had happened the trusts thereby
declared to take effect after the death of the testator's widow (a) took effect as valid
charitable trusts for the advancement and propagation of the teaching of socialised
medicine, (b) took effect as valid charitable trusts for the purposes of a Model Workers
g   Health Institute Museum and Centre for Health Hygiene, (c) took effect on charitable
trusts under a general charitable intent disclosed in the will, (d) took effect on charitable trusts by reason of the Charitable Trusts (Validation) Act 1954, or (e) failed for
uncertainty. perpetuity, impracticability, or for any other reason. The defendants
were (1) David Stark Murray, a member of the executive committee of the Socialist
h   Medical Association (mentioned in the will); (2) Robin Page Arnot, (3) Jack
Gaster and (4) the Hon Wogan Phillips Baron Milford, the trustees of the Marx
Memorial Library (mentioned in the will under its former name of 'Marx Memorial
Library and Workers School'); (5) Nicholas Murton Holmes, an executor of the
testator's widow, Eleanor Murton Bushnell deceased, who died on 16th May 1972; (6)
Robert Bushnell and (7) Nancy Phillips, a nephew and niece respectively of the testator
j   who were beneficially interested in any property of the testator not disposed of by his
will, and (8) the Attorney-General. The facts are set out in the judgment.

Philip Rossdale for the plaintiffs.
Gavin Lightman for the first, second, third and fourth defendants.
Christopher Heath for the fifth, sixth, and seventh defendants.
Charles Aldous for the Attorney-General.

GOULDING J. The testator in this case was Frank George Bushnell, who was a
doctor of medicine and lived near Woking. He made his will on 28th September 1940   *a*
and died on 14th October 1941. By his will he set up a trust fund on terms that his
widow should have the income during her life. She died on 16th May 1972. Consequently, it has become necessary for the court now to decide on the validity, and if
valid on the mode of operation, of the provisions which the testator made to deal with
the fund after Mrs Bushnell's death.

The will is a long document and I shall have to read a great deal of it to make the   *b*
arguments in the case and my decision on them intelligible. It may be helpful if I first
of all show the general scheme of the will.

The testator began by appointing three executors and trustees, namely, the plaintiffs
in the present proceedings. He bequeathed his household goods and effects to his wife
absolutely, and then gave all the residue of his estate to the plaintiffs on trusts of a
usual character for conversion and investment of the proceeds. He then directed the   *c*
plaintiffs, or otherwise the trustees for the time being of his will, to hold the residuary
fund—

> 'UPON TRUST to pay the income thereof including income from any part of my
> unconverted estate which may be accrued or accruing due but not actually paid
> at my death to my said Wife Eleanor Murton Bushnell during her life and after   *d*
> her death IN TRUST as to both the capital and income thereof to pay the same to
> the Socialist Medical Association the Haldane Society the Labour Research
> Department and the Marx Memorial Library and Workers School (hereinafter
> called "the Endowment Trustees") and the receipt of such Endowment Trustees
> or the survivor or survivors of them shall be a sufficient discharge unto my
> Trustees for all moneys so paid to them as aforesaid and I DIRECT that such Fund   *e*
> shall be used by the Endowment Trustees for the advancement and propagation
> of the teaching of Socialised Medicine . . . in accordance with and subject to the
> following conditions namely [then follow numbered clauses].'

I stop there to observe that the four bodies appointed as endowment trustees are all
of them unincorporated associations. I also observe that the phrase 'the advancement   *f*
and propagation of the teaching of Socialised Medicine' is one that qualifies most or all
of what follows. Certainly it governs cll 1-5. I shall not yet read those clauses. They
set out a number of what the testator called 'conditions', in accordance wherewith
the endowment trustees were to discharge their functions. I shall call the scheme
set up by cll 1-5 'the first trust'. For the moment I will observe only that under the
first trust the application of the income of the trust fund was to be made not directly   *g*
by the endowment trustees, who held the fund, but by certain individuals termed
'managers'.

Having set out the detailed provisions of the first trust, the testator continued in cl 6
as follows:

> 'IF at any time hereafter the Endowment Trustees are satisfied that it is im-   *h*
> practicable or impossible to carry out the Trusts hereinbefore declared con-
> cerning the Fund subsequent to the death of my said Wife or if for any other
> reason whatever the Endowment Trustees are satisfied that the said trusts are
> not being carried out in the manner prescribed then I DIRECT that the Endowment
> Trustees shall give to the Managers at least three months' notice in writing of
> their intention to determine the payments or authorities to the Managers and   *j*
> upon the expiration of such period the Trust hereinbefore declared shall come to
> an end and whereupon the Endowment Trustees shall stand possessed of the
> Fund or so much thereof as shall remain unexpended IN TRUST to pay the income
> thereof for ever to the Managers without being liable to see to the application
> thereof and with the like power to give orders for the dividends interest and other

a   income of the Fund to be paid direct to the banking account of the Managers as aforesaid.'

Clauses 7-13 then contain provisions by which, after cl 6 has operated, the fund is to be applied. The scheme constituted by those later provisions I shall call 'the second trust'. There remain eight further clauses in the will—cll 14-21. They contain administrative provisions regarding the managers and the endowment trustees, and also

b   some administrative powers for the plaintiffs or their successors in office as general trustees of the will. I think the only one of those administrative clauses at the end of the will which was referred to in argument was cl 18, which provides: 'THE statutory power of appointing new Trustees shall apply to the Endowment Trustees.'

That being the scheme of the will, I propose to enquire first into the validity of the first trust, and having dealt with that to examine, if and so far as necessary, the

c   further directions of the testator. I proceed, therefore, to read or summarise the clauses containing the first trust.

Clause 1 provides:

> 'The Fund shall be administered by Eleven Managers who shall be constituted and appointed within six months of the death of the survivor of myself and my said Wife by the Endowment Trustees who shall so far as practicable and in their
>
> d   unfettered opinion desirable select such Managers as follows:—(a) The Council Executive Committee or other Governing Body of each of the following Institutions or Associations namely:—The Haldane Society, The Socialist Medical Association, The Marx Memorial Library and Workers School, The Labour Party, The Independent Labour Party and Guild of Youth, The National Council of Labour Colleges, The Fabian Society, The University Labour Federation, Labour Research
>
> e   Department, The United Hospitals Socialist Association and The Womens Co-operative Guild Shall be asked to put forward a nominee or nominees for the office of Manager and the Endowment Trustees may appoint one manager for each of the said Associations from the said nominees but shall not be bound to make all or any such appointments. (b) If for any reason it is not practicable or in the opinion of the Endowment Trustees desirable for any Manager to be
>
> f   appointed as aforesaid then the Endowment Trustees shall appoint to fill such place any person (chosen from the Governing Bodies concerned) whom they may in their absolute discretion think fit. If no such person will accept appointment the Endowment Trustees may appoint any person for the vacancy in question.'

g   Clause 2 prescribes the range of securities in which the endowment trustees are to invest the fund, and I need not read it. Clause 3 is as follows:

> 'THE Endowment Trustees shall hold the Fund UPON TRUST to pay the income thereof for ever to the Managers without being liable to see to the application thereof and in particular may give orders for the dividends interest and other income of the Fund to be paid direct to the banking account of the Managers.'

h   Clause 4 contains the substantive provisions of the first trust:

> 'THE Managers shall apply the income of the Fund so received by them as aforesaid from the Endowment Trustees towards furthering the knowledge of the Socialist application of Medicine to public and personal health and well-being and to demonstrating that the full advantage of Socialised Medicine can only be
>
> j   enjoyed in a Socialist State by the following means:—(a) BY engaging from time to time lecturers and speakers to give addresses and lessons in Great Britain on socialised health and medicine at such places and at such times and upon such conditions as the Managers shall in their absolute discretion determine. The lecturers and speakers shall be duly qualified medical practitioners dentists pharmacists or health or sanitary inspectors qualified midwives radiologists

biologists or other such suitable persons as the Managers shall select and such
lectures shall be given free to the public and all Socialist workers. (b) By printing *a*
publishing and distributing for sale or free distribution such books pamphlets
leaflets or other literature on or connected with Socialised Medicine and up-to-
date educational facilities such as pictorial posters diagrams models statistics
lantern slides films plays radio slogans and advertisements visits to places of
health and medical interest and the purchase or hiring of premises equipped
for such addresses and meetings as the Managers shall determine.'   *b*

The directions of cl 4 are then subjected to certain further requirements by cl 5. I
point out, as it has been much dwelt on in argument, that the auxiliary verb 'must'
appears a great many times in the contents of cl 5. I would also observe, so as to
explain the way I read it, that in my judgment the full-stop which appears in the
middle of sub-cl (a) of cl 5 must, to make grammatical sense, be read as if it were a *c*
comma, and that sub-cl (h) appears grammatically to be one with the preceding
sub-clause.

With those comments, I proceed to read cl 5:

'ALL such lectures lessons books and literature and other means of information
shall deal with some aspect of Socialised Medicine in accordance with the following
principles:—(a) That in as much as any Socialised Medical Service must be able to *d*
determine and regulate all measures possible for the planned creation and
maintenance of the health of the community and the economic security and full
maintenance thereof including the proper working hours and working conditions
and rest hours and holidays and recreation centres in all trades industries and
professions and must be able to make effective recommendations for the proper
manufacture preservation and distribution of food and housing and must have *e*
absolute powers for the prevention and treatment of communicable industrial
and other epidemic and endemic and other diseases and must have absolute and
adequate powers for the protection of expectant mothers mothers of young
children infant children and adolescent youths and the care and after care of
patients as well as many other special powers for regulating the common life of
the community and preserving the health of the individual. It must be made *f*
evident that such a Socialised Medical Service can only operate effectively in a
Socialised State that is to say in a state in which all production is planned for use
and happiness of the Community by the State and not for profit by the individual.
(b) That any Socialised Medical Service must be free and available to every member
of the community and must be a service and function of the State itself to the
community. (c) That all branches and particularised parts of any such Socialised *g*
Medical Service must be under the unified control of a State Department of
Public Health and that the State through this Department must maintain and
pay for an efficient and complete organisation for the maintenance of health as
well as for the treatment of disease and that this organisation must include
within a single network State Hospitals Sanatoria Rest Homes Recreation
Centres Nursery and Open Air Schools or Preventoria especially for children *h*
"contacts" with open tuberculosis Health Centres and Maternity and Con-
sultative Clinics and that the State through its department of Public Health must
maintain an adequate and properly unified supply throughout the whole Country
of specialists consultants and domiciliary practitioners who must be fully supported in the carrying out efficiently of their offices and functions by the Health
Authorities. (d) That in order that any such State Department of Public Health *j*
may be constantly maintained adequate to the changing and developing needs of
the community from time to time such a Socialised Medical Service must set up
and include within the State Department of Public Health adequate machinery
(including workers and medical workers) through which the community may
voice its criticism comments and suggestions especially as to the elimination of

a
autocratic bureaucracy and may effectively make its needs felt. (e) That any such State Department of Public Health must be able to maintain obtain and use the finest human material in its service wherever it may find it without distinction of class race or religion and must therefore provide complete medical education and training for all workers of either sex in all branches and sections of the State Department of Public Health. (f) That any such State Department of Public Health must in order to maintain a standard of medical knowledge and practice

b
including medical clinical and scientific research and the maintenance of the health of air water soil agriculture and animals commensurate with the developing social and industrial practice of the community maintain and pay for complete and adequate research stations and laboratories in every department of public health. (g) That any such State Department of Public Health must provide for the constant universal education of the public by health and hygiene education

c
and culture institutes and Museums fully equipped in all up-to-date methods and adequate and available for the whole population especially at health centres and clinics in the practice of the principles underlying public and personal hygiene and the encouragement of all to work actively for health and (h) Free socialised training from which the profit making system or motive will be eliminated for all workers in the Medical or "Associated Medical" services before and after

d
graduation.'

In such comprehensive terms the testator declared what I have called his first trust. The obvious attack which it invites is the assertion that the objects for which it was set up are not in law charitable purposes. For if the purposes are not charitable then it is clear in my view that the first trust must fail, both because it is designed to go on

e
for ever—and therefore would fall foul of the rule against perpetuities—and also because no individual beneficiaries are ascertained and so the purposes can only be enforced by the court if within the ambit of charity.

The attack developed along two lines. The question mostly argued, put concisely, is whether the essential or dominant purpose of the first trust is education or a political object. It is well known that trusts for what the courts term in this context 'political

f
objects' cannot be supported as legal charities. A leading case on that aspect of the matter is *Bowman v Secular Society Ltd*[1] where Lord Parker of Waddington said[2]:

'. . . but a trust for the attainment of political objects has always been held invalid, not because it is illegal, for every one is at liberty to advocate or promote by any lawful means a change in the law, but because the Court has no means of judging whether a proposed change in the law will or will not be for the public

g
benefit, and therefore cannot say that a gift to secure the change is a charitable gift. The same considerations apply when there is a trust for the publication of a book. The Court will examine the book, and if its objects be charitable in the legal sense it will give effect to the trust as a good charity . . . but if its object be political it will refuse to enforce the trust . . .'

h
The testator died in the year 1941, and it is common ground that for the purpose of this particular objection the matter must be tested as at his death. In my judgment, there is no doubt that in this country in 1941 the establishment of a state health service, or of anything that could fairly be identified with the testator's scheme of 'socialised medicine', required major legislative changes, and a trust for that purpose would accordingly fail as one for a political object. It is, however, maintained that on a

j
fair reading of the first trust it is not in essence or in dominant purpose a trust to promote or bring about the establishment of a state health service, but is a trust to inform the medical profession and the lay public about the character and advantages

---

1   [1917] AC 406, [1916-17] All ER Rep 1
2   [1917] AC at 442, [1916-17] All ER Rep at 18

of such an organisation of medicine, so that they, the profession and the public, can lend their efforts to promoting, or indeed to resisting, such a reform as they may *a* think fit when fully acquainted with the arguments. Thus it is said the true character of the first trust is not political but educational, and as such it is a good charity.

The existence of some political motive is not necessarily fatal to a good charitable trust. Counsel for the first four defendants, in supporting the validity of the first trust, referred me, among other authorities, to the speech of Lord Normand in *National Anti-Vivisection Society v Inland Revenue Comrs*[1]:　　*b*

'A society for the prevention of cruelty to animals, e.g., may include, among its professed purposes, amendments of the law dealing with field sports or with the taking of eggs or the like. Yet it would not, in my view, necessarily lose its right to be considered a charity, and if that right were questioned, it would become the duty of the court to decide whether the general purpose of the *c* society was the improvement of morals by various lawful means including new legislation, all such means being subsidiary to the general charitable purpose. If the court answered this question in favour of the society, it would retain its privileges as a charity. But if the decision was that the leading purpose of the society was to promote legislation in order to bring about a change of policy towards field sports, or the protection of wild birds, it would follow that the *d* society should be classified as an association with political objects and that it would lose its privileges as a charity. The problem is, therefore, to discover the general purposes of the society and whether they are in the main political or in the main charitable. It is a question of degree of a sort well known to the courts.'

A test propounded in such general terms is, perhaps, easier to state than to apply. *e* But the books fortunately contain a number of reported judgments in which it has been necessary for the court to determine whether what from one point of view is an educational trust is so bound up with the promotion of a political object that the general purpose, or main purpose, of the trust can only be regarded as political. I may mention briefly three of those. The first was the decision of Finlay J, in a revenue case, *Bonar Law Memorial Trust v Comrs of Inland Revenue*[2]. That related to the college at *f* Ashridge connected with the Conservative Party, and the relevant trust was to cause the house and gardens and park—

'to be used for the purposes of an educational centre or college for educating persons in economics, in political and social science, in political history with special reference to the development of the British Constitution and the growth and expansion of the British Empire and in such other subjects as the governing *g* body may from time to time deem desirable.'

In that case, having regard to the way the trust was expressed and to the character of the governing body itself, which as appears from what I have just read could determine the subjects of instruction without, apparently, any overriding limitation, the judge decided that the trust could not be considered as one for educational *h* purposes only, and accordingly was not charitable as regards income tax.

Then there was the decision of Vaisey J in *Re Hopkinson (deceased)*[3]. There a gift had been made by will for the advancement of adult education with particular reference, but without limiting the trustees' general discretion in applying the fund for adult education, to the education of men and women of all classes on the lines of the Labour Party's memorandum headed 'A Note on Education in the Labour Party'. That is *j* only a summary of the leading trust, and the learned judge held that it was a trust for

1　[1947] 2 All ER 217 at 239, [1948] AC 31 at 76
2　(1933) 17 Tax Cas 508
3　[1949] 1 All ER 346

the attainment of political objects and not charitable. The judge put the problem

a that he had to decide in this way[1]:

'In my judgment, there are two ways of reading the words which I have quoted. They may be read, first, as equivalent to a general trust for the advancement of adult education which, standing alone, would admittedly be charitable, the super-added purpose being treated merely as a rough guide to be followed or as

b a hint to be taken as to the kind of adult education which the testator had in mind, the strictly educational main purpose always being adhered to, or, secondly, they may be read as indicating that the first part is to be taken as a general direction and the second part beginning with the words 'with particular reference to" as the particular direction dominating the whole of the trust. The second of these alternative views seems to me to be the right one.'

c   The third of this group of cases is *Re the Trusts of the Arthur McDougall Fund*[2]. The decision was that of Upjohn J. He was dealing with a trust established by a deed inter vivos, and the provisions of the deed declared purposes which can fairly be described as promoting education in the subject of political science and allied branches of enquiry. There was nothing prescribing political opinions of any kind, or the attainment of any political object, in the trusts themselves, but the trustees were

d required to be members of, and could be removed by, the Proportional Representation Society. On those facts, the learned judge had no difficulty in deciding that the trust was a good charity. It is clear from that and other authorities that the choice of trustees does not convert an otherwise educational trust into one for political purposes, because the trustees, whoever they are, are bound to carry out the directions of the founder of the trust, and are subject to the control of the Attorney-General and the

e courts in doing so.

I need not, I think, review the other authorities cited in support of the first trust. They included such well-known cases as *Re Scowcroft*[3], followed by the Court of Appeal in *Re Hood*[4], which show that a certain degree of mingling or association with a political object is by no means fatal to a primary object that is clearly charitable in law.

f   I now seek to apply the test appearing from the cases, particularly from what Lord Normand[5] said, for that is the formulation chiefly relied on by counsel for the first four defendants, to the words of the testator's will in the present case. I am quite unable to avoid the conclusion that the main or dominant or essential object is a political one. The testator never for a moment, as I read his language, desired to educate the public so that they could choose for themselves, starting with neutral

g information, to support or oppose what he called 'socialised medicine'. I think he was trying to promote his own theory by education, if you will by propaganda, but I do not attach any importance to that word. He starts off in the very beginning of the first trust by saying that the fund is to be used 'for the advancement and propagation of the teaching of Socialised Medicine', and then in cl 4 not only are the managers to further 'the knowledge of the Socialist application of Medicine to public and

h personal health and well-being', but they are also to demonstrate 'that the full advantage of Socialised Medicine can only be enjoyed in a Socialist State'. Then again all lecturers and authors of books commissioned by the trust are to deal with some aspect of socialised medicine in accordance with the very detailed and rigid principles laid down by the testator himself in sub-cll (a) to (h) of cl 5, all of which I have read.

j   Accordingly, on that branch of the argument I conclude that the first trust cannot

1   [1949] 1 All ER at 348, 349
2   [1956] 3 All ER 867, [1957] 1 WLR 81
3   [1898] 2 Ch 638, [1895-9] All ER Rep 274
4   [1931] 1 Ch 240, [1930] All ER Rep 215
5   [1947] 2 All ER at 239, [1948] AC at 76

be supported as an educational trust. Just as Vaisey J thought of the trust in *Re Hopkinson (deceased)*[1], which I have cited, so I think here that the directions regarding *a* the principles of socialised medicine are to be taken as dominating the whole of the trust.

In the later stages of the argument it was suggested that, even though not supportable as an educational trust, for the reasons I have just given, the first trust could be upheld as a valid charitable trust within the fourth or miscellaneous head of the well-known classification in *Income Tax Special Purposes Comrs v Pemsel*[2]. The *b* point was mainly developed by counsel for the Attorney-General, though adopted and supported by counsel for the first four defendants also. The way the argument was put is this. Let it be that the trust is one for the setting-up of a state health service. If immediately after the testator's death the court had had to enquire whether such a health service would be for the public benefit, it would have been unable to answer the question because, as Lord Parker said in *Bowman v Secular Society Ltd*[3], the *c* court cannot judge of the desirable or undesirable character of proposed changes in the law. Today, however, when after the death of the testator's widow the question becomes ripe for decision, Parliament has brought into being a state health service, thereby demonstrating, in a manner which the court is bound to accept, an opinion that such an institution is for the public benefit. Accordingly, a trust for the promotion of a state health service must today be accepted by the court as charitable because *d* it is beneficial to the public, and beneficial in a way, namely, the promotion of public health, which is within the spirit and intendment of the Statute of Elizabeth I, namely, the Charitable Uses Act 1601. I hope I do not misrepresent the argument of counsel for the Attorney-General in putting it thus.

That way of looking at the matter derived some support, it was suggested, from a case in the House of Lords, *Scottish Burial Reform and Cremation Society Ltd v Glasgow* *e* *City Corpn*[4]. That was a rating case. The question was whether the appellant company was entitled to partial exemption from rates on the ground that its objects were charitable purposes. The objects of the appellant company were: '(a) To promote reform in the present method of burial in Scotland . . . (b) To promote inexpensive and at the same time sanitary methods of disposal of the dead . . .', in particular cremation, and so on. I should add that for the purpose of the rating statute in question, the law of charity that had to be applied was that of England and not of Scotland, *f* although the appeal was a Scottish one. More than one of the noble and learned Lords who made speeches allowing the appeal there relied on the Cremation Act 1902 as showing that whatever might have been the case in 1890, when the appellant company was incorporated, yet in the 1960s the provision of crematoria was clearly for the public benefit. *g*

In my judgment, that appeal was dealing with an entirely different problem. It did not matter there whether the company's objects at the time of its incorporation had been charitable or not. The question was: were they charitable in the year in respect of which the particular rates were levied? That is quite different from the problem of a trust set up by will which must, in my view, stand or fall by the character of the objects at the date of the testator's death. *h*

The argument for the Attorney-General ran into an additional difficulty which counsel foresaw, namely, that the testator's purposes went far beyond anything that Parliament has hitherto approved, because he, the testator, was aiming at a socialised medical service within the setting of a socialist state of the fullest character where alone, he thought, a socialised medical service could operate effectively. Counsel proposed to deal with that difficulty by saying that the requirement of a socialist *j*

1   [1949] 1 All ER 346
2   [1891] AC 531, [1891-4] All ER Rep 28
3   [1917] AC at 442, [1916-17] All ER Rep at 18
4   [1967] 3 All ER 215, [1968] AC 138

state could be rejected and the residue of the testator's first trust validated by refer-
a ence to the Charitable Trusts (Validation) Act 1954. Counsel did not read the provisions of the 1954 Act, but on briefly referring to it during the short adjournment,
it appeared to me from s 1(1) that the 1954 Act could only operate if—

> 'consistently with the terms of the provision, the property could be used
> exclusively for charitable purposes, but could nevertheless be used for purposes
> *b* which are not charitable'.

On that I would only say that I am at least very doubtful whether it would be possible
consistently with the terms of the will to advocate the health service as it exists in
this country at the present time and go no further. However, I do not mean to express
a decided opinion on that point because the ground on which I reject the argument
based on the fourth head of *Pemsel's*[1] case is that the matter has to be decided accor-
c ding to the facts and law as they stood at the death of the testator. The first trust
accordingly fails.

I must now look again at cl 6 of the will. It will be remembered that cl 6 brought
the second trust into operation. It reads as follows:

> 'IF at any time hereafter the Endowment Trustees are satisfied that it is im-
> *d* practicable or impossible to carry out the trusts hereinbefore declared concerning
> the Fund subsequent to the death of my said Wife or if for any other reason
> whatever the Endowment Trustees are satisfied that the said trusts are not being
> carried out in the manner prescribed . . .'

then according to cl 6 the endowment trustees were to give three months' notice to
the managers and the first trust would come to an end on the expiration of that period.
e In my judgment, that language cannot apply to the event which has actually
occurred, namely, the first trust proving for legal reasons invalid ab initio. The
language is simply not apt to meet that event. If I am wrong on that, I am further of
the view that the provisions of cl 6 make the second trust a contingent one. Accordingly, since the operation of cl 6 may occur at any time when the endowment trustees
find that the first trust has become 'impracticable or impossible', the second trust is
f also invalid for perpetuity even if charitable. The case in that respect would be similar
to *Re Spensley's Will Trusts*[2].

I ought, however, in case both the reasons I have given are wrong, to examine
whether the second trust is intrinsically of a charitable quality, or whether it fails for
the same reasons as the first trust, even if cl 6 is free from the vice that I have suggested.
I must, therefore, now read cll 7-13 of the will:

g
> '7. THE Managers shall then apply the income of the Fund so received by them
> as aforesaid from the Endowment Trustees for the purpose of providing educa-
> tional facilities for the teaching of the principles and practice of Socialised health
> and medicine as defined in the primary trusts in the form of suitable premises to
> be hired or purchased and equipped with books printed matter pictorial posters
> *h* diagrams statistics models cinema films lantern slides a stage for health plays or
> displays or any other form of teaching that the Managers may consider desirable
> or convenient.'

I would draw attention there in passing to two things. One is that what the managers
are to provide are 'educational facilities for the teaching of the principles and practice
of Socialised health and medicine'. The second is that the principles and practice to
j be taught are those defined in the primary trusts. That I take to be a reference to the
principles set out in cl 5.

The will continues:

---

1 [1891] AC 531, [1891-4] All ER Rep 28
2 [1954] 1 All ER 178, [1954] Ch 233

'8. THE premises so acquired as aforesaid will form a Model Workers Health Institute Museum and Centre for Health Hygiene and will be free and open to *a* all workers and the public. The exhibits in such premises and the activities carried on therein will be intended specifically for the education and co-operation of the public in the practice of socialised health and medicine and any exhibits may be kept on the said premises permanently or lent out for educational tours in this as in other countries in the absolute discretion of the Managers.

'9. SUCH premises should be situated in a district readily accessible to the *b* working population and should contain a large room or hall where daily addresses could be given to the public free at hours and of duration convenient to the workers by such teachers or lecturers as may be selected by the Managers from Medical or "Associated Medical" or lay workers of socialist principles, and such other rooms as may be available wherein the exhibits shall be disposed as for example in bays as in the London School of Hygiene and Tropical Medicine *c* Museum and elsewhere and one of such rooms shall be used for the purpose of a reading and research centre and library of Socialised medicine medical industrial and labour sociology school and dwellings hygiene health surveys and any other aspect of socialism applied to health as the Managers may from time to time decide. The rooms can be used for instructions in simple anatomy and physiology mother and child welfare hygiene diet cancer tuberculosis Rheuma- *d* toid arthritis preventive inoculation blood transfusion and such other subjects of a similar nature as the Managers may from time to time deem necessary or advantageous to the carrying out of the primary objects of the trust. A stage should be provided in the large room or hall for the acting of health plays or for the showing of cinema films and lantern slides.'

On cl 9 I would remark that the second trust, unlike the first trust, requires the *e* teachers or lecturers themselves to be persons of socialist principles. I would also remark that some of the activities envisaged in cl 9 appear to be intrinsically free from any political quality whatever, namely, instructions in simple anatomy and other subjects. It has been pointed out, however, that those instructions are not obliga- tory, but merely a permissive use of the trust property, introduced as they are by the *f* words, 'The rooms can be used', in contrast to the preceding sentence where the phrase is, 'one of such rooms shall be used'.

The will continues:

'10. THE Staff should consist of a paid curator if possible one with experience of similar institutions in the U.S.S.R. or elsewhere but who need not necessarily be a doctor and if the Managers so feel it desirable they may appoint visiting *g* lecturers and an honorary socialist medical and lay committee to manage the Institution.

'11. THE provision and upkeep of the premises exhibits and equipment would be made from the Endowment Funds and such other sources as may be available including the hire of the Hall and other lecture rooms to the Socialist Medical Association or other Socialist bodies. *h*

'12. THE Exhibits to be shown in the said premises will fall under the following heads:—(a) Statistical as for example charts showing the incidence of disease, death rates and results of treatment. (b) Pictorial by means of posters photo- graphs or other means showing the causes and prevention of disease the organisa- tion of the health and medical and dental services and their liaisons with the workers and the public and of medical and health centres as well as physical educa- *j* tion and such other matters as the Managers shall decide. (c) Models (preparation or other methods) illustrating hospitals sanatoria rest homes recreation centres and clinics specimens showing adequate diets methods of prevention of industrial and other diseases and the early diagnosis of infectious communicable and other diseases their prevention and after care. (d) Preparations and other methods

of dealing with the early diagnosis of infectious and communicable diseases and
a   their prevention and after care.

'13. THE Institute or museum would co-operate fully with the medical
"Associated Medical" maternity hospital dental and educational services and
with voluntary workers in bringing the value of the knowledge of health and
how to create and preserve it to the public.'

b   Once again it appears to me that the main intention or dominant purpose is not
educational, in spite of the purely educational character of some of the activities
referred to.   As in the case of the first trust, so in my judgment the second trust is
essentially aimed at the promotion of a political object.   That is shown eloquently
in my view by the provisions of cl 7, which require the teaching under the second
trust to be of the principles defined in the first trust, and so carry one straight back
c   to cl 5.   It also appears from the test of opinion that I have already pointed out in
cl 9, namely, the requirement that teachers and lecturers are to be persons of socialist
principles.   Accordingly, in my judgment the second trust fails for the same reasons
as the first trust.

The Attorney-General did not contend that on that view any general charitable
intention could be found in the will.   Nor was the Charitable Trusts (Validation)
d   Act 1954 invoked, except in the limited connection with which I have already dealt.

I will, therefore, answer question 1 of the originating summons by declaring that
on the true construction of the will of the testator the trusts thereby declared to take
effect after the death of his widow are not charitable trusts, and accordingly are void
for want of ascertainable beneficiaries and also for perpetuity.

e   *Declaration accordingly.*

Solicitors: *Blyth, Dutton, Robins, Hay,* agents for *Ross & Son,* Horley (for the plaintiffs);
Forsyte, Kerman & Phillips (for the first defendant); *Gasters* (for the second, third and
fourth defendants); *Royds, Barfield,* agents for *Marsh & Ferriman,* Worthing (for the
f   fifth, sixth and seventh defendants); *Treasury Solicitor* (for the Attorney-General).

Evelyn M C Budd   Barrister.

Randall v Plumb (Inspector of Taxes)   *a*

CHANCERY DIVISION

WALTON J

4th, 6th DECEMBER 1974

Capital gains tax – Computation of chargeable gains – Contingent liabilities – Option –   *b*
Consideration paid for option – Consideration repayable in certain events – Option to
purchase land – Consideration to be treated as part payment of purchase price in event of
option being exercised – Exercise of option dependent on obtaining planning permission –
Purchaser entitled to repayment of consideration in event of failure to obtain planning per-
mission – Whether contingent liability of grantor of option to repay consideration to be taken
into account in computing capital gain – Whether contingent liability to be disregarded subject   *c*
to adjustment in event of consideration becoming repayable – Finance Act 1965, Sch 6, paras
14(5), 15.

The taxpayer owned and farmed certain land. On 19th May 1966 he entered into
an agreement with a company whereby the company deposited £25,000 with the
taxpayer in consideration for the grant of an option, exercisable at any time within
a period of 20 years from the date of the agreement, to purchase for £100,000 an   *d*
area of 60 acres of sand and gravel-bearing land forming part of the taxpayer's land.
If the company exercised the option, the deposit of £25,000 was to be treated as
part payment of the purchase price. The company was entitled to repayment of
the £25,000 if at any time after ten years the company, not having obtained planning
permission for the extraction of sand, gravel and hoggin from the land, gave the
taxpayer not less than one year's notice requiring repayment. Furthermore, if the   *e*
company had not obtained the planning permission within 20 years, then at any
time after that period, the sum of £25,000 became payable to the company forthwith
on written notice to the taxpayer requiring repayment. The taxpayer was assessed
to capital gains tax on the sum of £25,000 on the basis that that sum was a gain
accruing on the disposal of an asset, i e the option. The taxpayer appealed against that   *f*
assessment. At the date of the hearing the company had not made any application
for planning permission to extract sand, gravel etc from the land. The Special Commissioners affirmed the assessment. On appeal by the taxpayer, the Crown contended
(i) that the existence of the contingency that the taxpayer might be obliged to repay
the £25,000 in whole or in part was to be disregarded altogether in computing the
gain since it was not one of the contingencies which were expressly provided for by
para 14(5)[a] or 15[b] of Sch 6 to the Finance Act 1965; (ii) alternatively, that the contingent   *g*
obligation to repay the sum in whole or in part was 'a contingent liability . . . in respect
of . . . [an] obligation assumed as vendor of land, or of any estate or interest in land',
within para 15(1)(b) of Sch 6, and therefore, under para 15(1) no allowance was to
be made for the liability in the computation subject to an appropriate adjustment
under para 15(2) in the event of the liability becoming enforceable.   *h*

Held – (i) The obligation to return a deposit was not the kind of obligation assumed
by a person 'as vendor of land' envisaged by para 15(1)(b); at the highest it was assumed
as an incident of the contract under which he was hoping to become, but would
never in the actual circumstances become, the vendor (see p 741 *e* to *g*, post).
   (ii) It followed that the contingency was not one which was expressly provided for in
para 14 or para 15 of Sch 6. The conclusion to be drawn from that was not, however,   *j*
that the contingency should be disregarded altogether but the opposite, i e that
it was one which had at once to be taken into account (if it could be taken into account

---

a Paragraph 14(5) is set out at p 739 *j*, post
b Paragraph 15, so far as material, is set out at p 740 *a* to *c*, post

as a matter of valuation) in establishing the amount of the consideration received by the taxpayer. Accordingly the case would be remitted to the commissioners to determine the value of the option taking into account the taxpayer's contingent liability to return the deposit (see p 740 *g* to *j*, p 741 *h* and p 742 *e*, post).

Notes

For computation of capital gains on the disposal of assets subject to a contingent liability, see 5 Halsbury's Laws (4th Edn) 80, para 161.

For the Finance Act 1965, Sch 6, paras 14, 15, see 34 Halsbury's Statutes (3rd Edn) 938, 939.

Cases referred to in judgment

London and South Western Railway Co v Gomm (1882) 20 Ch D 562, [1881-5] All ER Rep 1190, 51 LJCh 530, 46 LT 449, CA, 37 Digest (Repl) 81, 203.

Morley (Inspector of Taxes) v Tattersall [1938] 3 All ER 296, 22 Tax Cas 51, 108 LJKB 11, 159 LT 197, CA, 28(1) Digest (Reissue) 34, 139.

Cases also cited

Coren v Keighley (Inspector of Taxes) [1972] 1 WLR 1556, 48 Tax Cas 370.

Howe v Smith (1884) 27 Ch D 89, [1881-5] All ER Rep 201, CA.

Potters v Loppert [1973] 1 All ER 658, [1973] 1 Ch 399.

Case stated

1. At a meeting of the Commissioners for the Special Purposes of the Income Tax Acts held on 12th February 1974, Robert William Randall ('the taxpayer') appealed against an assessment to capital gains tax for the year 1966-67 in the sum of £25,000.

2. Shortly stated the question for decision was whether the whole or any part of a sum of £25,000 which was deposited with the taxpayer pursuant to an agreement dated 19th May 1966 made between the taxpayer and the Summerleaze Gravel Co Ltd ('the company') in consideration for the grant of an option to purchase and which was repayable by the taxpayer in certain contingencies on the grantee giving notice requiring repayment and the option then terminating, was a gain accruing on the disposal of an asset within the meaning of ss 19(1) and 22(9) of, and Sch 6 to, the Finance Act 1965.

3. The taxpayer gave evidence before the commissioners.

[Paragraph 4 listed the documents proved or admitted before the commissioners.]

5. As a result of the evidence both oral and documentary adduced before them, the commissioners found the following facts proved or admitted. (a) The taxpayer had been a farmer since 1936. He lived at Hyde Farm, Maidenhead and farmed both Hyde Farm and Temple Park Farm. The freehold of Temple Park Farm was purchased by his father in 1941 and given to the taxpayer who at all material times was the owner of the freehold thereof until by a deed of gift dated 5th April 1967 he transferred the freehold to himself and his wife and son as tenants in common in equal shares. The freehold of Hyde Farm was purchased by the taxpayer in 1968. The taxpayer subsequently farmed both farms in partnership with his wife and son. (b) By cl 1 of the agreement of 19th May 1966 it was agreed that

'1. THE Company will on the signing hereof deposit with [the taxpayer] the sum of Twenty Five Thousand Pounds and in consideration thereof the Company shall have the option at any time during the period of Twenty years from the date hereof subject as hereinafter mentioned of purchasing at the price of One Hundred Thousand Pounds (the said sum of Twenty-five Thousand Pounds being in part payment of the said purchase price) the fee simple of ALL THOSE pieces or parcels of land being part of Ordnance No. 64 31 and 34 on the Ordnance Survey Map for the Parish of Hurley in the County of Berks and having an area of Sixty Acres or thereabouts as the same is for the purpose of better identification edged red on the plan annexed hereto and numbered 1 TOGETHER

with the right to search for win work get and carry away the sand gravel and
hoggin (if any) lying in or under the surface of the said land PROVIDED ALWAYS *a*
that if the permission referred to in Clause 3 hereof shall be granted in relation
to part only of the said land then the Company shall have the option at any
time during the said period of Twenty years of purchasing such part of the said
land but in any case in areas of not less than Fifteen acres at a price which shall
be equal to the fraction of One Hundred Thousand Pounds which the said part
is of the whole of the said land (a similar fraction of the said sum of Twenty-five *b*
thousand pounds being treated as in part payment of such purchase price)'.

Clause 3 of the agreement gave the company the sole authority to apply during
the 20 years for planning permission to develop the land by the extraction of sand,
gravel or hoggin. By cl 4 of the agreement, during the 20 year period or until repayment of the £25,000 as provided for in cl 10, the taxpayer would not apply for *c*
planning permission to develop the land. By cl 10(i), if at any time after ten years
the company had not then obtained planning permission for the development of
the property by the extraction therefrom of sand, gravel and hoggin, it should be
entitled on giving the taxpayer not less than one year's notice to repayment of the
£25,000. By cl 10(ii) if the company had not obtained the said permission within
20 years, then at any time after that period the sum of £25,000 should be payable *d*
to the company forthwith on written notice to the taxpayer requiring the same.
The land referred to in cl 1 was the same land referred to in cl 4. (c) The agreement
related to an area of some 60 acres of land running parallel to the Thames between
Marlow and Temple Lock. It was known that there was gravel on the land and the
company wished to make test borings. Out of the 60 acres, 50 acres were workable.
At no time up to the hearing before the commissioners had the company made *e*
an application for permission to develop the land. (d) By a supplemental agreement
of 28th November 1973 made between the taxpayer, his wife and his son of the one
part and the company of the other part and which recited that the parties of the
first part were now tenants in common in equal shares of the freehold land referred
to in the principle agreement by virtue of the deed of gift of 5th April 1967, the period
of 20 years referred to in cll 1, 3, 4, 10(ii) and 14 of the agreement was extended by *f*
ten years and the period of ten years referred to in cl 10(i) of the agreement was
extended by five years. (e) By a legal charge also of 28th November 1973 made
between the taxpayer, his wife and his son of the one part and the company of the
other part the taxpayer, his wife and his son covenanted, inter alia, to pay to the
company the sum of £25,000 as provided by the principal agreement and the supplemental agreement and they also charged by way of legal mortgage all of the freehold *g*
land with the payment of that sum in accordance with their covenant. (f) The taxpayer dealt with the £25,000 by transferring £15,000 into his farming account and
investing the remaining £10,000 in securities. The taxpayer, his wife and son were in
sole control of the way in which the £25,000 was dealt with from May 1966 to the
date of the hearing. The taxpayer was aware that the sum of £25,000 might have
to be repaid to the company at any time after the period of ten years prescribed *h*
in cl 10(i) of the principal agreement and extended to 15 years by the supplemental
agreement if the company had not by then obtained planning permission for the
extraction of sand, gravel and hoggin.

6. It was contended on behalf of the taxpayer: (a) that on the true construction
of the agreement the consideration for the grant of the option was not the sum of
£25,000 but the deposit of that sum with the taxpayer by way of loan free of interest; *j*
(b) that the taxpayer was not absolutely entitled to the sum of £25,000 until the
option was exercised (in that event, it was conceded, the £25,000 would be so
assessable) but that until planning permission was granted and the option exercised
by the company the sum of £25,000 was repayable to the company.

7. It was contended by the Crown: (a) that in entering into the agreement, the
taxpayer had disposed of an asset, because (i) he granted an option for the purchase

of his land, which by virtue of para 14(1) of Sch VII to the Finance Act 1965 fell to be
a treated as the disposal of an asset, and (ii) he had derived a capital sum (£25,000) from
such option and in return for surrendering or refraining from exercising certain
rights in respect of such land within the meaning of s 22(3) of the 1965 Act; (b) that
in computing the amount of the gain accruing on the disposal of the asset under
s 22(9), no part of the £25,000 fell to be excluded from the consideration taken into
account in such computation by any provision of Part I of Sch 6 to the 1970 Act;
b and that, in particular, the contingent obligation to repay the sum of £25,000 did
not afford a ground for any part thereof to be so excluded; (c) that accordingly
the whole of the £25,000 was a gain accruing on the disposal of an asset for the
purposes of capital gains tax, and was a chargeable gain.
[Paragraph 8 noted the cases referred to[1].]
9. The commissioners took time to consider their decision and gave it in writing
c on 11th March 1974, dismissing the appeals. The decision is set out at pp 195, 196, post.
10. Immediately after the determination of the appeal the taxpayer declared
his dissatisfaction therewith as being erroneous in point of law and on 12th March
1974 required the commissioners to state a case for the opinion of the High Court.

Peter Rees QC and D J T Parry for the taxpayer.
d *Martin Nourse QC and Donald Rattee* for the Crown.

Cur adv vult

6th December. **WALTON J** read the following judgment. On 19th May 1966
the taxpayer, the then owner of a farm known as Temple Park Farm, Hurley, in
e the county of Berkshire, entered into an agreement with the Summerleaze Gravel Co
Ltd ('the company') relating to the grant of a certain option which, so far as material,
was in the following terms:

'1. THE Company will on the signing hereof deposit with [the taxpayer] the
sum of Twenty Five Thousand Pounds and in consideration thereof the Company
f shall have the option at any time during the period of Twenty years from the
date hereof subject as hereinafter mentioned of purchasing at the price of
One Hundred Thousand Pounds (the said sum of Twenty-five Thousand Pounds
being in part payment of the said purchase price) the fee simple of [summarising
it, part of the farm]'.

Clause 3:
g
'AT any time during the said period of Twenty years from the date hereof
subject as hereinafter mentioned the Company shall have the sole full licence
and authority to apply such permission either on its own behalf or in the name
of [the taxpayer] (but at its own cost and expense in every respect) for permission
under the Town and Country Planning Acts at present or at any time during
h the said period in force to develop the said land by the extraction therefrom of
sand or gravel or hoggin'.

Clause 4:

'DURING the said period of Twenty years or until repayment of the said sum of
Twenty-five Thousand pounds as provided for in Clause 10(i) hereof [the tax-
j payer] will not at any time apply for or concur in any application for permission

---

1 *Jay's the Jewellers Ltd v Inland Revenue Comrs* [1947] 2 All ER 762, 29 Tax Cas 274; *Morley v
Tattersall* [1938] 3 All ER 296, 22 Tax Cas 51; *Orr Ewing (John) v John Orr Ewing* (1882) 8 App
Cas 822; *Potters v Loppert* [1973] 1 All ER 658, [1973] Ch 399; *Radio Pictures Ltd v Inland
Revenue Comrs* (1938) 22 Tax Cas 106; *Stanley v Inland Revenue Comrs* [1944] 1 All ER 230,
[1944] 1 KB 255, 26 Tax Cas 12; *Tetley v Wanless* [1866] LR 2 Exch 21

under the Town and Country Planning Acts at present or at any time during the said period in force to develop the said land edged red on Plan No. 1 SAVE *a* only and in as far as such application or concurrence may be necessary under the last preceding clause hereof'.

Clause 5:

'THE option shall be exercised by the Company giving to [the taxpayer] written notice of its intention to exercise such option and the purchase shall be completed *b* in accordance with the National Conditions of Sale (17th. Edition) except that the rate of interest shall be Two per cent above the Bank Rate in force at the date of the said Notice'.

Clause 10(I):

'IF the Company shall not then have obtained Planning Permission for the *c* development of the said property by the extraction therefrom of sand gravel and hoggin or any of them it shall be entitled at any time after the expiration of the period of Ten years from the date hereof on giving to [the taxpayer] not less than one year's notice in writing to repayment of the said sum of Twenty-five Thousand Pounds or of such part thereof as shall then remain after taking account *d* of such part as shall have been dealt with under paragraph 1 hereof but without any interest thereon and upon repayment of such sum the option hereby granted shall absolutely cease and determine'.

Clause 10(ii):

'IF the company shall not have obtained the said permission within Twenty *e* years from the date hereof or such extended period under the provision of paragraph 14 hereof then at any time after the said period of Twenty years or such extended period as aforesaid whichever shall be the longer the said sum of Twenty-five Thousand Pounds or such part thereof as shall then remain after taking account of such part as shall have been dealt with under paragraph 1 hereof shall be payable to the Company forthwith upon written notice to [the *f* taxpayer] requiring the same but without any interest thereon'.

Finally, for completeness, cl 14:

'THE period of Twenty years referred to herein shall be extended to one month after the determination of any Planning Application or Appeal which shall be pending at the expiration of such period but so that such period shall not in any *g* event exceed Twenty four years fom the date hereof subject however to paragraph 10(i) hereof'.

Since the making of that agreement there has been an alteration in the ownership of the farm, and agreements supplemental to this agreement have been entered into. However, it was not submitted to me either by counsel for the taxpayer or by *h* counsel for the Crown that either of these circumstances affected the question presently for decision in any manner.

Arising out of the existence of this agreement, an assessment was made on the taxpayer for capital gains tax in the sum of £25,000, being the sum mentioned in cl 1 of the agreement. He appealed against that assessment to the Special Commissioners, and on 12th February 1974 they upheld the assessment, their reasons being *j* stated as follows:

'under the Agreement of 19 May 1966 the [taxpayer] received £25,000 by way of deposit and part payment of the sum of £100,000 which would become payable if [the company] obtained planning permission. The sum of £25,000 was repayable if [the company] had not obtained planning permission after *a* the expiration of 10 years. In *Morley v Messrs Tattersall*[1] it was held that sums which were never Messrs Tattersall's property and might be repayable did not fall to be included in the computation of a taxpayer's income for income tax purposes; and by parity of reasoning it was contended that the £25,000 was not within the charge to capital gains tax. In our view, liability to capital gains tax turns on different principles. The Finance Act 1965 charges gains where a capital sum is derived from assets and subsection (9) of section 22 defines "capital

b sum" as money which is not excluded from the charge by Part I of Schedule 6. We can find nothing in Schedule 6 which excludes any part of the £25,000 from the scope of section 22. The [taxpayer] was under a contingent liability to repay that sum but it does not fall within the description of any of the matters headed "Contingent liabilities" in paragraph 15 of the 6th Schedule, nor do any of the other provisions of Part I apply. We hold that the £25,000 is a capital sum within

c section 22(9). The grant of the option constituted the grant of an interest in land and we have accordingly considered whether the provisions of section 22(6) apply. The [taxpayer] did not in our view transfer such interest by way of security. He granted the option but created no charge to secure it. In our view, the registration of a land charge Class C(iv) under the Land Charges Act 1925 is not a transfer by way of security by the [taxpayer] but an act of the grantee taken to

d protect his interest in the land. By section 22(1)(*a*) an option is treated as an asset and by section 22(3) there is deemed to be a disposal where a capital sum is derived from assets. Inasmuch as the sum in question arose by virtue of the grant out of the [taxpayer's] freehold estate, it was derived from an asset of the [taxpayer's]. It also, in our view, falls within section 22(3)(*a*) by reason of the fact that it depreciated the asset, (namely the freehold estate) of the [taxpayer].

e We dismiss the appeal and confirm the assessment.'

The real question which, at the end of the day, divides the two parties to this appeal can be shortly stated: for the purposes of assessing the capital gains tax which is admittedly payable by the taxpayer in consequence of the above agreement, is it or is it not proper to take into account in order to determine the consideration

f (within the meaning of the capital gains tax legislation) which he received thereunder his contingent liability to repay this sum of £25,000 in certain events? There is a great deal of agreement as to the law applicable. As is well known, capital gains tax bites on all disposals of assets, of whatever nature, and included in the disposal of an asset is the grant of an option, either because the word 'options' in s 22(1)(*a*) of the Finance Act 1965 includes an option being granted by the grantor, as well as an

g option being received by the grantee, or else because of the express provisions of para 14 of Sch 7 to the 1965 Act, which in turns provides that the grant of an option is the disposal of an asset, namely, the option.

So far so good. The next step is the computation of the capital gain, and this, by reason of s 22(9), is dealt with in Sch 6. There are in that schedule just two provisions relating to contingencies, and it is round these provisions that most of the argument

h has raged. These are, first of all, para 14(5):

'In the computation under this Schedule consideration for the disposal shall be brought into account without any discount for postponement of the right to receive any part of it and, in the first instance, without regard to a risk of any part of the consideration being irrecoverable or to the right to receive any part of the consideration being contingent; and if any part of the consideration so

j brought into account is subsequently shown to the satisfaction of the inspector to be irrecoverable, such adjustment, whether by way of discharge or repayment of tax or otherwise, shall be made as is required in consequence.'

---

1 [1938] 3 All ER 296, 22 Tax Cas 51

Then, para 15:

'(1) In the first instance no allowance shall be made in the computation under this Schedule—(a) in the case of a disposal by way of assigning a lease of land or other property, for any liability remaining with, or assumed by, the person making the disposal by way of assigning the lease which is contingent on a default in respect of liabilities thereby or subsequently assumed by the assignee under the terms and conditions of the lease, (b) for any contingent liability of the person making the disposal in respect of any covenant for quiet enjoyment or other obligation assumed as vendor of land, or of any estate or interest in land, or as a lessor, (c) for any contingent liability in respect of a warranty or representation made on a disposal by way of sale or lease of any property other than land. '(2) If it is subsequently shown to the satisfaction of the inspector that any such contingent liability has become enforceable, and is being or has been enforced such adjustment, whether by way of discharge or repayment of tax or otherwise, shall be made as is required in consequence.'

Logically, I think I should first consider the contention of the Crown, which was accepted by the Special Commissioners and urged on me with a certain amount of enthusiasm by junior counsel for the Crown, but with markedly less enthusiasm by leading counsel for the Crown himself, to the effect that, having regard to the structure of paras 14(5) and 15, only those contingencies which are therein referred to are to be given any weight whatsoever, and if there is any contingency outside the scope of those provisions under which any part of the consideration paid might fall to be repaid by the person who disposed of the asset, the existence of such contingency must be altogether disregarded for the purposes of capital gains tax. I find this an extraordinary submission. It is not disputed that among the contingencies for which provision is made in para 15, with consequential provision for adjustment of the tax position if the contingency in fact occurs, are some contingencies which are extremely remote; for example, the breach of a covenant for quiet enjoyment by the landlord. Yet it is solemnly submitted that a very real contingency such as the contingency for repayment in the present case, if it does not fall within the terms of para 15(1), must be disregarded altogether notwithstanding that, as a result of its actually happening, the taxpayer would have to repay the whole of the £25,000 and have actually in his hand nothing but notional interest thereon for the period until repayment is effected, and that in those circumstances there is no provision for any adjustment of the tax position whatsoever.

I cannot accept this submission for one moment. I draw precisely the opposite conclusion; namely, that unless the contingency is one which is expressly mentioned in one or other of these sub-paragraphs, in which case the contingency is to be disregarded but justice will be done to the taxpayer if the contingency actually turns out the wrong way by an adjustment of tax, it must (if it can as a matter of valuation) be taken at once into account in establishing the amount of the consideration received by the taxpayer, this being the only possible method of arriving at a figure for the amount of the consideration which truly reflects the contingency to which the matter is subject. Of course, this will not do ideal justice, or even such justice as an adjustment to the tax actually paid will effect, because obviously the valuation of the contingency must lie between the extremes of its happening and its not happening, whereas finally it will either happen or not happen; but this is a chance which may redound to the advantage or to the disadvantage of either party.

Junior counsel for the Crown also urged on me a variant of the above argument, which he based on para 14(5), to the effect that the way in which 'the consideration' was approached in that subparagraph (as being the total monetary consideration, no matter how far deferred the payment and no matter how contingent the payment is) showed that it was not contemplated that any relief would be given for contingencies whatsoever, save as expressly provided. Again, I do not think that this *a* follows at all. It appears to me that the way in which contingencies are approached when one is looking at what I may call the positive side of the consideration where there are both positive and negative sides affords no guide whatsoever to the correct way in which the negative side ought to be approached; and, as the effect of adopting this argument would be that which I have already indicated, involving a quite monstrous and unnecessary injustice to the taxpayer, I decline to construe the legislation in that manner.

b This leaves for consideration as the next matter the Crown's second submission, namely, that which says that the present situation is covered by the precise wording of para 15(1)(b). In view of my decision on the Crown's first argument, I see no necessity to approach this paragraph with any particular views as to the width or narrowness of its provisions in mind. Certes, if I had reached a different conclusion on the first point I should then have been disposed to approach it with an inclination to

c give it as broad a scope as possible in order to provide as far as possible an intelligibly just scheme of taxation. But, as I say, I do not feel I need approach it in any such manner.

Approaching this subparagraph, then, with no particular preconceptions as to its scope, how does the matter stand? The crucial wording from the point of view of this case is as follows:

d

> '. . . no allowance shall be made in the computation under this Schedule . . . for any contingent liability of the person making the disposal in respect of any . . . obligation assumed as vendor of land, or of any estate or interest in land . . .'

Can it fairly be said in the present case that the taxpayer's obligation to repay the

e £25,000 in whole or in part is an obligation assumed by him in the capacity stated? Counsel for the Crown says that the answer is in the affirmative, since an option is an interest in land: see *London and South Western Railway Co v Gomm*[1]. It appears to me, however, that the obligation to return a deposit is not the kind of obligation assumed by a person as vendor of land to which this subparagraph is intending to refer. I think an obligation of the general nature of returning a deposit is not assumed

f by a person as vendor of land but, at the highest, as an incident of the contract under which he is hoping to become, but will never in the actual circumstances become, the vendor. It appears to me that this is miles away from the only kind of obligation actually mentioned—a covenant for quiet enjoyment—which is an incident of the completed relationship. 'As intending but disappointed now never to be vendor' is it not the same thing as 'vendor'.

g It was, of course, indeed questioned by counsel for the taxpayer whether, notwithstanding that this provision can be tortured to include an option, it really was intended so to do, for the simple reason that a complete code in respect of options is to be found in para 14 of Sch 7, containing in sub-para (8) a specific reference to deposits, albeit only forfeited deposits. I note this submission for the record, but I do not find it necessary to place any reliance on it for present purposes.

h I therefore reach the conclusion that there are no special provisions in Sch 6 which require the contingency of repayment in the present case to be disregarded. Accordingly, it appears to me that the exercise which now falls to be carried out is that the value of what the taxpayer obtained for the grant of the option under the agreement falls to be ascertained; that is to say, the right to an immediate deposit of £25,000 with the incident that it may fall to be repaid under the provisions of

j cl 10(i) or (ii) thereof. It has been tacitly assumed by both parties that this is a valuation exercise which it is possible to carry out, and so I think I am bound to remit the matter to the Special Commissioners in order that the figure may be determined unless agreed by the parties. It has, however, occurred to me that the valuation exercise

---

1 (1882) 20 ChD 562, [1881–5] All ER Rep 1190

may be one which those skilled in the art or mystery of valuation will say cannot
be effected. In that case, there is a very simple route open so far as I can see, although *a*
I have not yet heard any argument on the matter, in the provisions of s 22(4)(*b*),
whereunder a person's acquisition of an asset and the disposal of it to him are for the
purposes of the 1965 Act to be taken to be for a consideration equal to the market
value of the asset where he acquires the asset wholly or partly for a consideration
which cannot be valued. So that, if the strict valuation exercise proves impossible
to carry out, the Special Commissioners will then have to determine what was the *b*
market value of the option granted on 19th May 1966, on the basis that whatever
sum was to be paid for it was to be retained by the taxpayer in any event, but would,
if the option was exercised in whole or in part, go towards the purchase price.

This possibility throws some light, I think, on the general problem of contingent
liabilities, and may explain the genesis of para 15. It would, I think, be quite impossible
for a valuer to value the liability under a covenant for quiet enjoyment; but if one *c*
then tells him to value the property disposed of to which it is incident, he will un-
doubtly have to assume when valuing it that it has all the usual incidents, including
the usual covenant for quiet enjoyment, particularly of course in the case of a lease.
Hence one can see why these and similar matters are taken right outside the scope
of the consideration; otherwise, the valuers would be asked to value the property
to which they relate under s 22(4)(*b*) on an entirely false basis. If this is the true ex- *d*
planation of para 15, it reinforces my view that its contents shed no light on the
problem of contingent liabilities generally.

For the foregoing reasons, therefore, I propose to remit the case to the Special
Commissioners with the directions I have indicated above.

Appeal allowed. Case remitted to the Special Commissioners to determine value of the option. *e*

Solicitors: *Cartwright, Cunningham* (for the taxpayer); *Solicitor of Inland Revenue.*

Rengan Krishnan Esq Barrister.

R v Gilbert   *f*

COURT OF APPEAL, CRIMINAL DIVISION
JAMES LJ, PHILLIPS AND MAY JJ
15TH NOVEMBER, 5TH DECEMBER 1974

*Crown Court – Sentence – Commencement — Sentence to take effect from day on which
pronounced unless court otherwise directs – Ante-dated sentence – Whether court having* *g*
*power to direct sentence to take effect from day before day on which it is pronounced – Courts
Act 1971, s 11(1).*

Section 11(1)[a] of the Courts Act 1971, which provides that a sentence imposed on an
offender by the Crown Court shall take effect from the beginning of the day on which
it is imposed 'unless the court otherwise directs', does not empower the court to order *h*
that the sentence shall commence on a day earlier than the day on which it is
pronounced (see p 747 *h* and p 748 *a*, post).

Notes
For commencement of sentence, see 10 Halsbury's Laws (3rd Edn) 493, para 899, and
for cases on the subject, see 14 Digest (Repl) 617, 618, 6144-6166.
For the Courts Act 1971, s 11, see 41 Halsbury's Statutes (3rd Edn) 299.   *j*

Cases referred to in judgment
R v Crockett (1929) 21 Cr App Rep 164, CCA, 14 Digest (Repl) 617, 6163.
R v Hatch (1930) 22 Cr App Rep 83, CCA, 14 Digest (Repl) 618, 6164.

a Section 11(1) is set out at p 743 *h*, post

a   *R v McLean* [1911] 1 KB 332, 80 LJKB 309, 103 LT 911, 75 JP 127, 22 Cox CC 362, 6 Cr App Rep 26, CCA, 14 Digest (Repl) 557, *5481*.

R v O'Neill and Hughes (11th March 1967) unreported.

R v Roberts (1929) 21 Cr App Rep 69, CCA, 14 Digest (Repl) 617, *6162*.

Wilkes v R (1769) 4 Bro Parl Cas 360, [1558-1774] All ER Rep 570, Wilm 322, 2 ER 244, sub nom *R v Wilkes* 4 Burr 2527, 19 State Tr 1075, HL, 14 Digest (Repl) 375, *3674*.

b **Application**

On 1st February 1974 the appellant, Arthur Ernest Gilbert, was convicted at the Royal Court of Jersey of 25 offences which included offences of forgery and obtaining goods by false pretences. He was sentenced to a total of two years' imprisonment. On 2nd July 1974 at Havant Magistrates' Court he pleaded guilty to one charge of theft, one of forgery and two charges of obtaining by deception. He was committed c   for sentence to the Crown Court at Portsmouth under s 29 of the Magistrates' Courts Act 1952. On 26th July the appellant was sentenced by the Crown Court (his Honour Judge McClellan and justices) to three years' imprisonment in respect of the charges for which he had been committed concurrent with one another and concurrent with the sentence which he was already serving. In addition it was stated that the sentence imposed by the Crown Court was to run from the date on which the sentence of two d   years' imprisonment had been passed by the Royal Court of Jersey, ie from 1st February 1974. The appellant applied for leave to appeal against sentence.

G Harrap for the appellant.

A Collin as amicus curiae.

e

At the conclusion of argument the court stated that leave would be granted, the appeal allowed and that the reasons for the court's decision would be given at a later date.

15th December. **JAMES LJ** delivered the following judgment of the court. This f   judgment is an extension of that delivered on 15th November 1974. On that date this court allowed the appellant's appeal against sentence. We then decided that there was not and never had been power vested in the courts to order that a sentence should commence at a time earlier than the date on which it was pronounced and said that we would state our reasons for that decision at a later date. This we now proceed to do.

g   The Courts Act 1971 came into operation on 1st January 1972. The Act abolished courts of assize and courts of quarter sessions. Section 4(1) provided: 'There shall be a Crown Court in England and Wales which shall be a superior Court of Record.' Unlike courts of assize and courts of quarter sessions, which exercised jurisdiction only during the continuance of the particular assize or sessions, the Crown Court has a continuous jurisdiction which commenced on 1st January 1972. The sittings of the h   Crown Court are not divisible in relation to periods of time.

Section 11(1) of the Courts Act 1971 reads:

> 'A sentence imposed, or other order made, by the Crown Court when dealing with an offender shall take effect from the beginning of the day on which it is imposed, unless the court otherwise directs.'

j   Counsel for the appellant argues that the words 'unless the court otherwise directs' confer the power to order that a sentence shall commence at a date after the day on which it is pronounced or at an earlier date. He submits that the only limitation on that power is that the sentence cannot be ordered to commence at a date earlier than the commencement of the court's jurisdiction, 1st January 1972. If this is the correct construction of s 11(1), it follows that in passing sentence the court can say on 26th July:

'The sentence is imprisonment for three years commencing on 1st February last.'
It is argued that, although the court could fulfil the same intention as to length of *a*
sentence by passing a sentence of imprisonment for a shorter term commencing on
the day sentence is pronounced, the power to order a sentence to commence at an
earlier date is both useful and of practical importance. It is useful because, in a case
in which the defendant has been in custody for a period which does not count towards
the sentence, the court can, by ante-dating the sentence, avoid any sense of grievance
on the part of the defendant in circumstances in which sentence has been delayed *b*
through no fault of his. The answer to that argument is that any sense of grievance
can be avoided by the choice of words in which the sentence is expressed. That the
power may be of practical importance is illustrated by reference to 'Remission' under
the Prison Act 1952: a sentence of three years' imprisonment passed on 1st January
but expressed to commence one year earlier will result, on the basis of full remission,
in an earlier date of release than would a two year sentence commencing on the day of *c*
pronouncement.

Counsel for the appellant supports his argument by reference to the former practice of courts of quarter sessions and of assize. This practice was to treat sentences
passed, and orders made, by the court as having been passed, or made, on the first
day of the sessions or, in the case of assizes, on commission day. The practice was
founded on the legal fiction that the business of the court was completed within the *d*
compass of one day.

One result of this fiction was that the period spent in custody between the first day
and the date on which sentence was actually passed was included in the sentence.
The practice in relation to quarter sessions became subject to the provisions of s 12 of
the Stipendary Magistrates Act 1858, which reads:
                                                                                  e
'Every Sentence pronounced by any Court of General or Quarter Sessions or
adjourned Sessions of the Peace shall take effect from the Time of the same being
pronounced, unless the Court otherwise directs.'

After the passing of the Act it seems that the practice of the courts of quarter sessions
varied. Some courts, at least, clung to their ancient practice and under rules of court,
or otherwise, continued to treat sentences and orders as being passed or made on the *f*
first day of the sessions. Reference to this is made in the report of the Interdepartmental
Committee on the Business of the Criminal Courts[1].

The Criminal Justice Administration Act 1962, s 17(1) provided:

'A sentence imposed by a court of assize shall take effect from the beginning
of the day on which it is imposed, unless the court otherwise directs.'
                                                                                  g
It is to be observed that in both the 1858 Act and the 1962 Act the words 'unless the
court otherwise directs' are the same as those in the Courts Act 1971. Section 17(2) of
the 1962 Act made provision, within certain limitations, for the treatment of sentences
as being reduced by the period of time spent in custody before sentence. The present
position is governed by the Criminal Justice Act 1967, s 67, and it is clear that in cases
within that section there is no need for a power to ante-date the commencement of a *h*
sentence.

Turning to the position at common law, there is little to be gleaned from the authorities. Some assistance can be derived from *R v Wilkes*[2]. Wilmot CJ gave the answer to
the third question submitted to the judges for their opinion in these terms[3]:

'That a judgment of imprisonment against a defendant, to commence from *j*
and after the determination of an imprisonment to which he was before sentenced
for another offence, is good in law.'

1   (1960-61) Cmnd 1289, para 250
2   (1770) 19 State Tr 1075, [1558-1774] All ER Rep 570
3   19 State Tr at 1136

In the course of his reasoning leading to that answer Wilmot CJ said[1]:

> 'In general, the language of all judgments for offences, respects the time of giving the judgment',

and then[2]:

> 'We cannot explore any mode of sentencing a man to imprisonment, who is imprisoned already, but by tacking one imprisonment to the other . . . . It is shaping the judgment to the particular circumstances of the case; and the necessity of postponing the commencement of the imprisonment, under the second judgment, arises from the party's own guilt, which had subjected him to a present imprisonment . . .'

There are, however, two cases in the reports which are said on behalf of the appellant to be instances in which the Court of Criminal Appeal did vary a sentence and did order that the substituted sentence should commence at a date earlier than the date on which the original sentence was passed. The first is *R v McLean*[3]. In that case the appellant was convicted at Reading of housebreaking and sentenced to three years' penal servitude. Before sentence was passed, he informed the judge that he already stood committed for trial in Hertfordshire for arson and asked for that offence to be taken into consideration when he was sentenced. He was subsequently tried at the Hertfordshire Assizes for the arson and sentenced to five years' penal servitude to run concurrently with the three years.

He appealed against that sentence of five years. The appellant conducted his own appeal. It appears that his only argument was that the sentence passed at Reading took into account the offence of arson. The only argument for the Crown was directed to the desirability of clarifying the principles on which a court should act when invited to take offences into consideration. There was no citation of any statute or of any relevant authority. The judgment delivered by Lord Alverstone CJ contains this passage[4]:

> 'Dealing with this particular case, as the appellant admitted at Reading that he was guilty of the charge of arson, and asked the judge to take that into consideration, and that in fact was done, we think that the appellant should have the benefit of the state of things at Reading, and that his sentence should be reduced to one of three years' penal servitude, to run from October 13th, which was the date of the sentence at Reading.'

The inescapable conclusion is that the Court of Criminal Appeal did in that case substitute an ante-dated sentence. The court did so in order to put the appellant into the position in which he was entitled to be having regard to the fact that at Reading Lawrence J had taken into consideration the offence for which the appellant was later sentenced.

The second case is that of *R v Roberts*[5]. The appellant argued, in person, that in circumstances in which the recorder at the Central Criminal Court had postponed passing sentence on him to the session following that in which he was convicted, in order that he might be called as a witness in another case, his sentence should run from the first day of the session in which he was convicted. Counsel for the Crown agreed with the appellant's argument. The report reads[6]:

---

1 (1770) 19 State Tr at 1132
2 19 State Tr at 1134
3 [1911] KB 332, 6 Cr App Rep 26
4 6 Cr App Rep at 27
5 (1929) 21 Cr App Rep 69
6 21 Cr App Rep at 69

'The court [Lord Hewart CJ, Avory and Shearman JJ] took this view. *Sentence reduced.'*   *a*

The court was not referred to any statutory provision or any authority. We do not read this case as one in which the court exercised a power to ante-date a sentence. The normal course of proceedings would have been a sentence imposed on the date of conviction and the Court of Criminal Appeal held that the unusual circumstances in which sentence was not then passed ought not to postpone the date from which the *b* sentence would ordinarily have run.

We are confirmed in this understanding of *R v Roberts*[1] by the fact that Lord Hewart CJ and Avory J were both members of the court which heard *R v Crockett*[2] only ten months later. The appellant was sentenced to three years' penal servitude, to commence on the expiration of a sentence to which he was then subject, at Oxfordshire Quarter Sessions. In the following month, at Gloucester Quarter Sessions, he was *c* sentenced to three years' penal servitude to commence on the date on which he had been sentenced at Oxfordshire Quarter Sessions. The appellant appealed against both sentences. He appeared in person. The Crown was not represented. The short report does not mention any statute or previous case. The judgment of Lord Hewart CJ reads[3]:

d

'We think that the proper course is that the sentence of three years' penal servitude passed at the Oxfordshire Quarter Sessions should stand, but should date from the date of those sessions, and that the sentence passed at Gloucester City Sessions, which the Recorder had no power to ante-date, should be amended so as to be a sentence of three years' penal servitude commencing from the date of Gloucester City Sessions . . .'   *e*

There are two more cases to which we would refer. In *R v Hatch*[4] the court dismissed an application for leave to appeal against sentence but substituted a sentence of 15 months' imprisonment to date from 1st October for a sentence of 18 months' imprisonment passed on 1st October but expressed to commence on the 11th July previous thereto. The headnote to the short report reads[5]: 'The Court below cannot *f* ante-date a sentence before the first day of the sessions.' There was no appearance on behalf of the appellant or the Crown.

The second case is the unreported case of *R v O'Neill and Hughes*[6] heard in this court. In the course of the judgment Fenton Atkinson J said of the recorder of Derby 'he passed sentences of 18 months purporting to back-date the commencement of these sentences to 28th September 1966, which in fact he had no power to do'. The Court *g* substituted sentences for a lesser term commencing on the date on which the original sentences were passed, 1st December 1966, in order to 'give effect to what the learned recorder was really intending to do'.

In Archbold[7], *R v Crockett*[1] was cited as authority for the statement:

'A sentence cannot be ante-dated so as to run from an earlier date than the *h* first day of the sessions at which it is passed.'

That passage is omitted from the current edition[8], in which s 11(1) of the Courts Act

---

1   (1929) 21 Cr App Rep 69
2   (1929) 21 Cr App Rep 164   *j*
3   21 Cr App Rep at 164
4   (1930) 22 Cr App Rep 83
5   22 Cr App Rep at 83
6   11th March 1967
7   Criminal Pleading, Evidence and Practice (37th Edn, 1969), para 634
8   38th Edn (1973)

1971 is set out without comment. In Halsbury's Laws of England[1] *R v Crockett*[2] is
a similarly referred to but *R v Roberts*[3] is also cited as authority for ante-dating a
sentence beyond the first day of the sessions of the court in exceptional circumstances.

Counsel for the appellant relies on that statement of the law in support of his
argument that the words 'unless the court otherwise directs' empowered courts of
assize and courts of quarter sessions to ante-date a sentence to the first day of the
sittings in which the sentence was passed. He contends that without those saving
b words every sentence of quarter sessions would have taken effect at the time of
pronouncement and every sentence passed at assize would have commenced at the
beginning of the day on which it was imposed. He then argued that by use of the same
words in the Courts Act 1971, Parliament has conferred power on the Crown Court to
ante-date its sentences and orders to the first day of the sittings of that court, namely
1st January 1972.

c   We are unable to accept this argument as valid. The words 'unless the court
otherwise directs' were necessary in the Acts of 1858 and 1962 in order to preserve the
common law power to the court to impose a sentence, or make an order, taking effect
in future. Consideration of the authorities, apart from *R v McLean*[4] which can be
explained on the basis that the ante-dating of the sentence was effected per incuriam,
leads us to the conclusion that courts of assize and quarter session did not have power
d to ante-date their sentences. If their were such a power there would have been no
need to resort to the legal fiction under which sentences were ordered to run from the
first day. There was, and there is today, no need for the existence of a power to ante-
date in order to fulfil the intention of the court in relation to sentence. The cases of
R v Crockett[2], *R v Hatch*[5], and *R v O'Neill and Hughes*[6] reveal in our judgment a settled
understanding that in law there was no such power prior to the passing of the Courts
e Act 1971. Unless the wording of the Courts Act 1971 compels us to take a different
view, it is, we think, too late to disturb that settled understanding on the basis of an
argument that *R v Crockett*[2] does not support it and that *R v McLean*[4] and *R v Roberts*[3]
are authorities to the contrary.

Counsel appearing as amicus curiae, in his careful argument, has pointed out the
difficulties which would follow if the courts exercised a power to ante-date a sentence
f of imprisonment. We refer only to examples. The Prison Act 1952, s 25(1), makes
provision for the grant of remission of part of the sentence, on the ground of industry
and good conduct, to a person serving a sentence of imprisonment. The difficulty of
implementing that provision in the circumstances of an ante-dated sentence is self-
evident. Under s 25(2)[7] a person under the age of 21 at the commencement of his
sentence could be released on licence in lieu of being granted remission. By ante-dating
g the sentence the court could bring the prisoner within that provision in a case to
which it would not otherwise have applied. Another example is to be found in the
operation of release on parole licence under the provisions of the Criminal Justice
Act 1967.

In our judgment the words of s 11(1) of the 1971 Act do not give to the Crown Court
any greater powers in relation to the date from which sentences are made to run than
h existed by virtue of the same words used in the earlier Acts. Even on the assumption
(which we are not prepared to make) that the Acts of 1858 and 1962 created a power to
ante-date a sentence to the first day of the particular assize or session, it would not in
our judgment be justifiable to construe the same words in the 1971 Act as conferring a
general power to ante-date sentences to a date not earlier than 1st January 1972.

j 1   3rd Edn, vol 10, p 493, para 899
  2   (1929) 21 Cr App Rep 164
  3   (1929) 21 Cr App Rep 69
  4   [1911] 1 KB 332
  5   (1930) 22 Cr App Rep 83
  6   11th March (1967) unreported
  7   Repealed by the Criminal Justice Act 1967, s 103(2), Sch 7, Part I

It is for these reasons that we allowed the appeal and substituted a sentence to run
from the day on which sentence was passed.   *a*

Appeal allowed; sentence varied.

Solicitors: *Registrar of Criminal Appeals; Treasury Solicitor.*

Sepala Munasinghe Esq Barrister. *b*

Pepys v London Transport Executive   *c*

COURT OF APPEAL, CIVIL DIVISION
LORD DENNING MR, ROSKILL LJ AND SIR JOHN PENNYCUICK
4th, 5th NOVEMBER 1974

d

*Lands tribunal – Costs – Discretion – Order that costs of one party be borne by other party –
Claim for compensation – Acquisition of land – Unconditional offer by acquiring authority –
Offer rejected – Tribunal rejecting claim for compensation – Order by tribunal that authority
pay claimant's costs before date of offer – Jurisdiction to make order – Discretion to be exer-
cised judicially – Special reasons for order to be stated – Lands Tribunal Act 1949, s 3(5) –
Land Compensation Act 1961, s 4(1).*

e

Between 1966 and 1968 the London Transport Executive ('the executive') was engaged
on the construction of an underground railway. The railway passed 70 feet below a
house which was bought by the claimant in 1967 for £14,000. In order to excavate
beneath the house the executive had acquired an easement from the previous owner.
The grant of the easement contained a clause whereby the owner of the house retained *f*
a right to compensation for any injurious affection to the house by reason of the
working of the railway provided the claim was made within two years of its opening.
In 1970 the claimant wished to sell the house. An offer of £18,000 was made by a
potential purchaser. The purchaser, however, subsequently withdrew the offer
because he thought the noise from the railway was so bad. In September 1970 the
claimant put in a claim for compensation on the ground that the trains running *g*
underneath had affected the value of the house because of the noise and vibration.
In December 1970 she sold her house for £15,850, and claimed the difference of
£2,150 as compensation for the injurious affection to the house. The executive denied
that the railway had diminished the value of the property. The case was heard by the
Lands Tribunal in May 1973. Before the hearing the executive made a sealed offer.
The claimant did not, however, accept the offer. In the event she lost her case because *h*
she was unable to prove that the purchase price of £15,850 was lower than it would
have been but for the railway. Following the decision, the member of the tribunal
caused the sealed offer to be opened. The member then stated that the claimant had
been offered unconditionally an amount of £500 and continued: '. . . accordingly the
acquiring authority will pay the claimant her costs of the reference up to the date of
the sealed offer'. He ordered the claimant to pay the executive's costs from the date *j*
of the offer. The executive appealed against the order for costs, contending that,
under s 4(1)[a] of the Land Compensation Act 1961, the tribunal had no jurisdiction to
award to a claimant costs incurred before the date of the sealed offer.

---

a Section 4(1) is set out at p 752 *f* to *h*, post

Held – (i) By virtue of s 3(5)[b] of the Lands Tribunal Act 1949 the tribunal had a general
a   discretion as to costs incurred before an unconditional offer was made by the acquiring
authority. The effect of s 4(1) of the 1961 Act was only to preclude the tribunal from
awarding the claimant costs incurred after the offer had been made. Accordingly the
tribunal had jurisdiction to order the acquiring authority to pay the pre-offer costs
of a claimant who only succeeded in getting something less than the offer (see p 751
f to h, p 752 j and p 754 f, post).

b   (ii) The tribunal's discretion as to pre-offer costs was a judicial discretion and so had
to be exercised judicially. Since it was very unusual for a successful party to have to
pay the costs of the party who had lost, it should never be done except for very special
reasons and when it was done the tribunal should state its reasons. Accordingly the
appeal against the order in respect of costs before the written offer would be allowed
since there were no reasons for awarding the pre-offer costs against the authority,
c   and the reasoning of the tribunal on which the award had been based was erroneous
(see p 751 j, p 752 c and d, p 753 c e and h and p 754 d and g, post); dicta of Devlin J in
Smeaton Hanscomb and Co Ltd v Sassoon I Setty, Son & Co (No 2) [1953] 2 All ER at 1591
and of Lord Goddard CJ in *Lewis v Haverfordwest Rural District Council* [1953] 2 All ER
at 1599 approved; dictum of Harman LJ in *Hood Investment Co Ltd v Marlow Urban
District Council* (1964) 15 P & CR at 232 disapproved.
d

Notes
For the circumstances in which cases are in the discretion of the Lands Tribunal,
see 8 Halsbury's Laws (4th Edn) 175, para 244.
    For the Lands Tribunal Act 1949, s 3, see 6 Halsbury's Statutes (3rd Edn) 196.
    For the Land Compensation Act 1961, s 4, see ibid 242.
e

Cases referred to in judgments
Hood Investment Co Ltd v Marlow Urban District Council (1964) 15 P & CR 229, [1963]
    RVR 454, CA.
Knight v Clifton [1971] 2 All ER 378, [1971] 1 Ch 700, [1971] 2 WLR 564, CA, 28(2) Digest
f   (Reissue) 1143, *1448*.
Lewis v Haverfordwest Rural District Council [1953] 2 All ER 1599, [1953] 1 WLR 1486, 52
    LGR 44, 2 Digest (Repl) 720, *2329*.
Smeaton Hanscomb & Co Ltd v Sassoon I Setty, Son & Co (No 2) [1953] 2 All ER 1588,
    [1953] 1 WLR 1481, 2 Digest (Repl) 720, *2328*.
Wooton v Central Land Board [1957] 1 All ER 441, [1957] 1 WLR 424, 121 JP 137, 55 LGR
g   84, 8 P & CR 121, CA, 45 Digest (Repl) 373, *186*.

Case stated
The claimant, Elizabeth Olga Pepys, referred to the Lands Tribunal a claim for
compensation arising out of the grant of an easement by the claimant's predecessor in
title to the appellants, the London Transport Board (subsequently the London
h   Transport Executive), dated 9th March 1966, to use part of the subsoil beneath 33
Gibson Square, Islington, London, N1 for the purpose of constructing and using a
tunnel and other work. 33 Gibson Square was purchased by the claimant in 1967.
The consideration paid for the grant of the easement was £24. By cl 2 of the grant the
consideration was to be exclusive of any claim for compensation for—

        'any injurious affection to any land house or buildings of the grantor by reason
j   of the working of the railway of the Board where constructed in tunnel (including
        the working of lifts escalators and any other works in connection with the said

---

b   Section 3(5) provides: 'Subject to the following provisions of this section, the Lands Tribunal
    may order that the costs of any proceedings before it incurred by any party shall be paid by
    any other party and may tax or settle the amount of any costs to be paid under any such
    order or direct in what manner they are to be taxed.'

railway) PROVIDED that no claim for any such compensation as aforesaid shall
be made except within two years from the date of the opening of the said railway   *a*
for public traffic.'

The railway line was opened for public traffic on 1st December 1968 and a formal notice
of claim for compensation for injurious affection was made by the claimant in September 1970. Shortly before the hearing of the claim the appellants lodged a sealed
offer. The offer was rejected by the claimant. On 28th June 1973 the tribunal rejected   *b*
the claim for compensation. The tribunal then opened the sealed offer and found that
the claimant had been offered unconditionally an amount of £500. The tribunal
thereupon ordered the appellants to pay the claimant her costs of the reference up
to the date of the sealed offer and the claimant to pay the costs of the appellants as
as from the date of that offer. The appellants, being aggrieved by the decision of the
tribunal so far as it related to costs and desiring to question the same as being erroneous   *c*
in point of law, duly applied to the tribunal pursuant to the proviso to s 3(4) of the
Lands Tribunal Act 1949 to state and sign a case for the decision of the Court of Appeal.
The tribunal having stated and signed a case the appellants appealed against the order
on the ground that the tribunal had no power either under s 4(1) of the Land Compensation Act 1961 or at all to order the appellants to pay the costs of the claimant up
to the date of the sealed offer. The facts are set out in the judgment of Lord Denning   *d*
MR.

Kenneth Bagnall QC and *Jonathan Gaunt* for the appellants.
The claimant did not appear and was not represented.

LORD DENNING MR. In the years from 1966 to 1968 a new underground line   *e*
was being constructed as an extension of the Victoria Line. It went 70 ft below the
ground in Islington. It passed below a house, 33 Gibson Square, Islington, which was
the property of the claimant, Dr Elizabeth Olga Pepys. She bought her house on 7th
February 1967 at a price of £14,000. At that time the line was under construction.
On 1st December 1968 the line was open for public traffic. In order to do the work,
the appellants, London Transport Executive ('the executive'), acquired from the   *f*
previous owner an easement. It contained a clause by which the owner of the house
retained a right to compensation in respect of any injurious affection to the house by
reason of the working of the railway, provided that the claim was made within two
years from the opening. That clause enured for the benefit of Dr Pepys. In June 1970
Dr Pepys was appointed to a post in Cambridge and decided to sell the house. In
August 1970 a proposed purchaser, a Mr Matthews, offered £18,000 for the house   *g*
subject to contract; but on a later visit he thought the noise was so bad that he
withdrew his offer.

In September 1970 Dr Pepys put in a claim for compensation on the ground that
the trains running underneath had affected the value of the property because of the
noise and vibration. In December 1970 Dr Pepys sold the house to a Mr Tablenow.
The price was only £15,850. Dr Pepys said that she had lost the difference of £2,150   *h*
owing to the injurious affection to the house. The executive said that the house had
not diminished in value. The noise from this underground railway was, they said,
no worse than the noise from a passing lorry. They said that very few people had
claimed compensation for injurious affection. Only 10 or 12 claims were received,
and of them only three were still active at the time of the hearing. In other words,
most people put up with the noise and made no claim.   *j*

Just before the hearing in May of 1973 the executive put in a sealed offer. They
wanted to dispose of the claim. We now know that the sealed offer was £500. Dr
Pepys did not accept it. She went on with the claim. Unfortunately she lost. The
reason was because she could not prove that the purchase price of £15,850 was any
less because of the noise and vibration. The member of the Lands Tribunal said:

a '. . . no evidence was adduced that the eventual purchase at £15,850 was a price discounted by reason of noise . . . It is for the claimant to establish that the market value of the subject house has been depreciated by the running of the trains and this she has failed to do.'

Dr Pepys lost. It was on a point of fact. So she had no ground for appeal. That was the end of the case on compensation.

b   Now a question arises about the costs. The member of the tribunal said:

'Having read the decision in this matter and having then caused a sealed offer lodged by the acquiring authority to be opened, I find that the claimant had been offered unconditionally an amount of £500; accordingly the acquiring authority will pay the claimant her costs of this reference up to the date of the sealed offer,
c   and the claimant will pay the costs of the acquiring authority as from the date of the sealed offer . . .'

The executive were upset by that order as to costs. They had won the case. Yet they had been ordered to pay the costs of Dr Pepys up to the date of the offer being put in They wrote a letter to the president of the Lands Tribunal asking whether
d this was a slip. The Lands Tribunal said No: it was a matter in the discretion of the tribunal and it was not to be altered. Thereupon the executive asked for a case to be stated about the costs. The member has stated a case in these words:

'The question upon which the decision of the Honourable Court is desired is whether I properly ordered the Acquiring Authority to pay the Claimant her
e   costs of this Reference up to the date of the sealed offer having regard to the provisions of Section 4 of the Land Compensation Act 1961.'

The first point is whether the tribunal has any discretion as to the costs *before* the sealed offer. Under the Lands Tribunal Act 1949, s 3(5), the Lands Tribunal is given general discretion as to costs. But there is a rule which takes away that discretion in
f cases to which the provisions of s 4(1), (2) and (3) of the Land Compensation Act 1961 apply. It was submitted to us by counsel for the executive that under the section the tribunal has only a discretion as to the costs *after* the date of the sealed offer, but that it has no discretion as to the costs *before* the date of the sealed offer. He submits that a claimant is not entitled to any costs *before* the sealed offer, even though he or she is awarded a sum of compensation. He admits that his submission is contrary to
g the practice of the tribunal. If the claimant is awarded a sum which is *less* than the sealed offer, the practice is for the claimant to be awarded the costs *up to* the date of the sealed offer; but from that date onwards the authority gets the costs. It seems to me that the present practice is well justified by the statutory provisions. The general direction given in s 3(5) of the 1949 Act applies to the costs *before* the sealed offer. Section 4(1), (2) and (3) of the 1961 Act would apply to the costs *after* the sealed offer.
h   The second point is how the discretion should be exercised in a case like the present where the claimant has failed altogether. We have been referred to a number of cases starting with *Wootton v Central Land Board*[1], and finally *Knight v Clifton*[2]. The cases show that the discretion is to be judicially exercised, and that it is usually exercised in this way: that if the plaintiff fails, he has normally to bear his own costs and often to pay the costs of the other side. Sometimes each side is left to bear its own
j costs. But it is exceedingly rare for a successful defendant to have to pay the costs of a plaintiff who has failed. This should never be done except for very special reasons; and in that case the tribunal ought to state its reasons for so exceptional a course.

---

1 [1957] 1 All ER 441, [1957] 1 WLR 424
2 [1971] 2 All ER 378, [1971] 1 Ch 700

This is borne out by what Lord Goddard CJ said in *Lewis v Haverfordwest Rural District Council*[1]:   *a*

'Those words "judicially exercised" are always somewhat difficult to apply, but they mean that the arbitrator must not act capriciously and must, if he exercises his discretion to refuse the usual order, show a reason connected with the case and one which the court can see is proper.'

I am aware that in *Hood Investment Co Ltd v Marlow Urban District Council*[2] Harman LJ   *b*
said:

'The President, being appealed to for reasons, wisely gave none, and I think he was entitled to keep his counsel on that matter.'

But that was, I think, a mistake. It seems to me that if a tribunal is departing from the   *c*
ordinary exercise of discretion—in so exceptional a way—it ought to give its reasons. The same would apply to an arbitrator. Even a judge of the High Court ought to do so, though no appeal lies except with his leave.

No reasons have been adduced, and it seems to me that none exists, whereby the executive in this case should have been ordered to pay Dr Pepys's costs. The order in that respect should not stand. The only part of the order which should stand is that   *d*
from the date of the sealed offer being communicated Dr Pepys should pay the costs. I was glad to hear from counsel for the executive that in the special circumstances of this case the executive would not propose to enforce any order for costs against Dr Pepys. But on the point of principle I think the appeal should be allowed.

ROSKILL LJ. I entirely agree with the judgment of Lord Denning MR. As the   *e*
points which have been argued before us on behalf of the appellants are of general importance, I would venture to add some words of my own to what Lord Denning MR has said. Counsel for the appellants sought to argue in the first instance that there was no jurisdiction in the Lands Tribunal to make the order complained of. His argument rested on what he contended was the true construction of the latter part of s 4(1) of the Land Compensation Act 1961. That subsection provides as follows: *f*

'Where either—(a) the acquiring authority have made an unconditional offer in writing of any sum as compensation to any claimant and the sum awarded by the Lands Tribunal to that claimant does not exceed the sum offered; or (b) the Lands Tribunal is satisfied that a claimant has failed to deliver to the acquiring authority, in time to enable them to make a proper offer, a notice in writing of the amount claimed by him, containing the particulars mentioned in subsection   *g*
(2) of this section; the Lands Tribunal shall, unless for special reasons it thinks proper not to do so, order the claimant to bear his own costs and to pay the costs of the acquiring authority so far as they are incurred after the offer was made or, as the case may be, after the time when in the opinion of the Lands Tribunal the notice should have been delivered.'   *h*

Counsel for the appellants' argument, if I understood it correctly, was that the words in those last lines from 'so far as they were incurred' down to 'should have been delivered' govern only the immediately preceding phrase, 'to pay the costs of the acquiring authority'. With respect to that argument, I cannot think it is right as a matter of construction. I think those last words govern both the limb which deals with the claimant bearing his own costs and the limb which deals with the claimant   *j*
having to pay the costs of the acquiring authority. Accordingly, counsel for the appellants' argument on this first point cannot be sustained.

1 [1953] 2 All ER at 1599, [1953] 1 WLR 1486 at 1487
2 (1964) 15 P & CR 229 at 232

His second submission was that the discretion as to costs exercised by the member
a was wrongly exercised as a matter of law. The question is whether he properly
ordered the appellants to pay the claimant's costs down to the date of the sealed
offer. That involves consideration of his reasons for so doing. His apparent reason is
set out in the decision as follows:

b
> 'Having read the decision in this matter and having then caused a sealed offer
> lodged by the acquiring authority to be opened, I find that the claimant has been
> offered unconditionally an amount of £500; accordingly the acquiring authority
> will pay the claimant her costs of this reference up to the date of the sealed
> offer . . .'

I need not read the rest.

The offending word, if I may use that phrase, is 'accordingly'. It appears to have
c been the view of the member that because the claimant had been offered the sum of
£500, which she had refused, she was entitled to have her costs up to the date of the
sealed offer made by the appellants, although in the end she recovered nothing. In
my judgment the member was wrong in law in reaching that conclusion. However
much one may sympathise with Dr Pepys, I can see no difference between her position
and that of any other unsuccessful litigant. Suppose, for example, a plaintiff in a
d running down case who has suffered injury brings an action. The defendant pays,
say, £1,000 into court but contests liability. The plaintiff refuses the £1,000, fights the
action on liability and loses. It may be the judge has difficulty in making up his mind.
It may be the judge has sympathy for the plaintiff. But in the end the harsh fact
remains that the plaintiff has lost. Much as a court may sympathise with the
unsuccessful party, the successful party is entitled to have his taxed costs paid unless
e there are reasons which justify the normal rule not being followed. I therefore look
to see whether there are any reasons in this case which justify the normal rule not
being followed. Like Lord Denning MR I can find none. The solicitor for the appellants
took up this matter with the Lands Tribunal. On 16th July 1973 the registrar of the
Lands Tribunal wrote a long letter to the appellants' solicitor defending, if I may use
that phrase, the decision of the member on costs. On the second page of that letter
f he said:

> 'It is not for the registrar to interpret the Decisions of the Tribunal but I
> suggest that the above extracts [he had quoted a number of extracts from the
> decision] read in the context of the Decision as a whole, indicate that the claim
> failed for lack of pertinent evidence adduced: nowhere in the decision do I see
> any finding or suggestion by the Tribunal that a claim for injurious affection was
g misconceived or outside the legal remedies open to the claimant.'

With respect to the registrar, I cannot follow this. This passage seems to me to
suggest that a litigant who fails because he or she has failed to call the necessary
evidence to prove his or her case is in some privileged position, not only in not having
to pay costs, but being in some way entitled to receive costs from the successful party.
h This is in my judgment wrong in principle. Accordingly I can see no justification here
for the conclusion which the member has reached in regard to costs and of which
complaint is made.

There remain two other points. First, at the end of his argument counsel for the
appellants contended that in any event the discretion of the Lands Tribunal in relation
to what I will call 'pre-sealed offer costs' was limited and that it was not entitled to
j exercise the discretion prima facie accorded by r 53 of the Lands Tribunal Rules,
except in cases to which the provision of sub-ss (1), (2) and (3) of s 4 of the Land Compensation Act 1961 apply. With respect, those last subsections only apply, as I have
already pointed out, to costs incurred after the date of the sealed offer. In relation to
'pre-sealed offer costs', the Lands Tribunal, in my judgment, had complete discretion.
But that discretion must be judicially exercised. I am glad to think that that view is in

line with what we have been told is the long established practice of the Lands Tribunal. Secondly, as I have already said, the member did not give any sufficient reasons for *a* his decision on the 'pre-sealed offer' costs. In *Hood Investment Co Ltd v Marlow Urban District Council*[1] Harman LJ stated that it was unnecessary, where there was an appeal by case stated to this court from the Lands Tribunal on a question of costs, for the reasons for a special order as to costs to be stated. With great respect to Harman LJ, I cannot agree, and I venture to think his judgment, as Lord Denning MR has said, went too far. In that case this court did not have its attention drawn to the decisions *b* in *Smeaton Hanscomb & Co Ltd v Sassoon I Setty Son & Co (No 2)*[2] and *Lewis v Haverfordwest Rural District Council*[3], respectively decided by Devlin J and Lord Goddard CJ on consecutive days in December 1963. In the former case Devlin J said[4]:

> 'I think, also, that it would be very proper and convenient that any arbitrator who is making an award in the form of a Special Case and who is departing from *c* the usual order that costs follow the event should set out in the Case the grounds which have caused him to depart from the usual order. That will enable the court which is reviewing his decision to be fully informed on the matter which has influenced him, and it will not have to speculate from the nature of the case itself.'

In *Lewis v Haverfordwest Rural District Council*[5] Lord Goddard CJ said that he agreed *d* with what Devlin J had said. I respectfully agree with both decisions, and I think it should be the practice that where an arbitrator or the Lands Tribunal or any other tribunal is asked to state a special case on costs, the reason why a special order has been made should be clearly stated so that then the court will know whether there was material which justified the special exercise of the discretion in a particular way. If there was no material to justify the special exercise of the discretion in the *e* particular way in question, then generally speaking that discretion will have been wrongly exercised. If there was such material, then the discretion will have been correctly exercised.

For those reasons, as well as those stated by Lord Denning MR, I would allow the appeal. I would answer the question for the decision of this court in the negative.
f

SIR JOHN PENNYCUICK. I agree with the judgments which have been delivered. I would only say this. I agree that if the Lands Tribunal has awarded costs to an unsuccessful claimant, it ought to state reasons. But I would emphasise that in the present case, as was pointed out by Roskill LJ, the tribunal did in fact give a reason, but that reason is a bad one. I refer to the passage in the decision[6] quoted by Roskill LJ *g* and in particular the word 'accordingly'. The fact that the acquiring authority has caused an unconditional offer to be made which was not accepted by the claimant is clearly not in itself a good reason for ordering the acquiring authority to pay the claimant's costs up to the date of the offer.

Appeal allowed.
h

Solicitors: *G S M Birch* (for the appellants).

M G Hammett Esq Barrister.

j

1 (1964) 15 P & CR 229 at 232
2 [1953] 2 All ER 1588, [1953] 1 WLR 1481
3 [1953] 2 All ER 1599, [1953] 1 WLR 1486
4 [1953] 2 All ER at 1591, [1953] 1 WLR at 1487
5 [1953] 2 All ER at 1599, [1953] 1 WLR at 1487
6 See p 753, ante

a **Inland Revenue Commissioners v Joiner**

COURT OF APPEAL, CIVIL DIVISION

Affirmed on different grounds HL
[1975] 3 All ER 1050

STAMP, SCARMAN LJJ AND BRIGHTMAN J

23rd, 24th, 25th OCTOBER, 12th DECEMBER 1974

b *Surtax – Tax advantage – Transaction in securities – Transaction relating to securities – Liquidation of company – Distribution of surplus assets in course of liquidation – Distribution to shareholders – 'Securities' including shares – Whether distribution to shareholders a 'transaction . . . relating to' their shares – Whether a 'transaction in securities' – Income and Corporation Taxes Act 1970, ss 460, 467(1).*

c The taxpayer owned 75 per cent of share capital of a prosperous family company. The trustees of a family trust owned the remaining 25 per cent. The company possessed substantial assets representing accumulated and undistributed profits not needed as working capital for the conduct of the company's business. With the object of extracting those assets from the company the taxpayer, with the consent of the trustees as minority shareholders, put the company into voluntary liquidation. A d liquidator was appointed who promptly sold the company's business to another company, also controlled by the taxpayer. The liquidator then paid off such debts as the company had to meet and, pursuant to an agreement previously reached between the taxpayer and the trustees, distributed the surplus assets to them in the same proportion as their shareholdings. The Board of Inland Revenue served a notice on the taxpayer under s 460(3)*ᵃ* of the Income and Corporation Taxes Act 1970 e for the purpose of counteracting the tax advantage which the taxpayer had obtained in consequence of the distribution of the assets in the course of the liquidation. The taxpayer contended that s 460 did not apply to him since the distribution, being a step taken in the course of the liquidation of a company, was not a 'transaction in securities', within ss 460(1) and 467(1)*ᵇ* of the 1970 Act, but an integral part of the process of liquidation.

f **Held** – The distribution of surplus assets to shareholders in the course of a liquidation was a transaction relating to their shares and so a transaction 'relating to securities'

---

a Section 460, so far as material, provides:
 '(1) Where . . . (b) in consequence of a transaction in securities or of the combined effect of two or more such transactions, a person . . . has obtained. a tax advantage, then unless g he shows that the transaction or transactions were carried out either for bona fide commercial reasons or in the ordinary course of making or managing investments, and that none of them had as their main object, or one of their main objects, to enable tax advantages to be obtained, this section shall apply to him in respect of that transaction or those transactions . . .
 '(2) Subject to section 468(3) below, for the purposes of this Chapter a tax advantage obtained or obtainable by a person shall be deemed to be obtained or obtainable by him h in consequence of a transaction in securities or of the combined effect of two or more such transactions, if it is obtained or obtainable in consequence of the combined effect of the transaction or transactions and of the liquidation of a company.
 '(3) Where this section applies to a person in respect of any transaction or transactions, the tax advantage obtained or obtainable by him in consequence thereof shall be counteracted by such of the following adjustments . . . on such basis as the Board may specify by j notice in writing served on him as being requisite for counteracting the tax advantage so obtained or obtainable . . .'
b Section 467(1), so far as material, provides: 'In this Chapter . . . "securities"—(a) includes shares . . . "transaction in securities" includes transactions, of whatever description, relating to securities, and in particular—(i) the purchase, sale or exchange of securities, (ii) the issuing or securing the issue of, or applying or subscribing for, new securities, (iii) the altering, or securing the alteration of, the rights attached to securities.'

within s 467(1) for (i) shares were 'securities' under s 467(1); (ii) the word 'transaction'
included a unilateral act; and (iii) a distribution by a liquidator to shareholders gave   *a*
effect to the rights attaching to their shares (or to an agreed variation of those rights)
and therefore 'related' to the shares. It followed that the tax advantage obtained by
the taxpayer had been obtained 'in consequence of a transaction in securities' and
therefore s 460 applied to him (see p 758 *f* and *g* and p 760 *d*, post).

Decision of Goulding J [1973] 2 All ER 379 affirmed.

                                                                                    b

Notes
For counteracting tax advantages and the meaning of transaction in securities, see
Supplement to 20 Halsbury's Laws (3rd Edn) para 276A, and for cases on the subject,
see 28(1) Digest (Reissue) 489-494, *1753-1762*.

For the Income and Corporation Taxes Act 1970, ss 460, 467, see 33 Halsbury's
Statutes (3rd Edn) 591, 600.   *c*

Cases referred to in judgment
Greenberg v Inland Revenue Comrs, Tunnicliffe v Inland Revenue Comrs [1971] 3 All ER
    136, [1972] AC 109, 47 Tax Cas 240, [1971] 3 WLR 386, [1971] TR 233, HL, 28(1)
    Digest (Reissue) 492, *1759*.
Inland Revenue Comrs v Parker [1966] 1 All ER 399, [1966] AC 141, 43 Tax Cas 396,   *d*
    [1966] 2 WLR 486, 45 ATC 1, [1966] TR 1, HL, 28(1) Digest (Reissue) 490, *1754*.
Kirkness (Inspector of Taxes) v John Hudson & Co Ltd [1955] 2 All ER 345, [1955] AC 696,
    36 Tax Cas 28, [1955] 2 WLR 1135, 34 ATC 142, [1955] TR 145, 48 R & IT 352, HL,
    28 Digest (Reissue) 463, *1668*.
St Aubyn (L M) v Attorney-General (No 2) [1951] 2 All ER 473, [1952] AC 15, 30 ATC
    193, HL, 21 Digest (Repl) 49, *199*.   *e*

Cases also cited
Inland Revenue Comrs v Brehner [1967] 1 All ER 779; [1967] 2 AC 18, 43 Tax Cas 705, HL.
Inland Revenue Comrs v Burrell [1924] 2 KB 52, 9 Tax Cas 27.
Inland Revenue Comrs v Horrocks, Inland Revenue Comrs v Wainwright [1968] 3 All ER
    296, 44 Tax Cas 645, [1968] 1 WLR 1809.   *f*
Moriarty v Evans Medical Supplies [1957] 3 All ER 718, [1958] 1 WLR 66, 37 Tax Cas
    540, HL.

Appeal
At all material times the taxpayer, Albert G Joiner, owned 75 per cent of the shares
in A G Joiner & Son Ltd ('the old company'), the remaining 25 per cent being owned *g*
by the trustees of his father's settlement. In addition the taxpayer also owned 75
per cent of the shares in another company, Auto-Components and Engineering Co
Ltd ('the new company'), while 25 per cent of the shares therein were owned by the
trustees of his own settlement. On 10th April 1964 an agreement ('the liquidation
agreement') was made between the taxpayer, the trustees of his father's settlement
and Aubrey Frederick Christlieb, one of the trustees. That agreement, having   *h*
recited the parties' intent that the old company should be liquidated and that Mr
Christlieb should be appointed liquidator, provided how the principal assets of the
old company were to be valued for the purpose of intended sale to the new company and for the purpose of distribution to the members of the old company. Under
the agreement the taxpayer undertook to procure the new company to issue an
unsecured loan note in an agreed form to the liquidator in payment of the sale price. *j*
It was also agreed that in the distribution of the old company's assets, certain freehold property and certain marketable securities should be allocated to the taxpayer,
with consequential provisions for adjusting the division of assets between him and the
trustees in the correct proportion of three to one. The liquidation agreement was
carried into effect immediately, the old company going into voluntary liquidation

a
on the same day. The new company immediately took over its business, and the taxpayer in due course received, apart from certain freehold property and investments, a substantial sum of cash as his share of the old company's assets. In effect the taxpayer received a 75 per cent share of the old company's accumulated profits as a capital sum in the winding-up. On 16th November 1970 the Board of Inland Revenue issued a notice to the taxpayer under s 460(3) of the Income and Corporation Taxes Act 1970 specifying the adjustments which were requisite for counteracting the

b
tax advantage which had been obtained by the taxpayer on the basis that it had been obtained in consequence of a 'transaction in securities' within s 467(1) of the 1970 Act. The taxpayer appealed and on 4th January 1972 the Commissioners for the Special Purposes of the Income Tax Acts allowed the appeal and cancelled the notice. The Crown expressed its dissatisfaction with the commissioners' decision and required them to state a case[1] for the opinion of the High Court. On 22nd March 1973 Goulding

c
J[1] allowed the Crown's appeal, holding that the taxpayer had obtained a tax advantage in consequence of the liquidation agreement and that the liquidation agreement was a 'transaction in securities' within s 467(1) of the 1970 Act. The taxpayer appealed.

d
F Heyworth Talbot QC and *Andrew Potez* for the taxpayer.
Nicolas Browne-Wilkinson QC, *Patrick Medd QC* and *Brian Davenport* for the Crown.

Cur adv vult

e
12th December. **SCARMAN LJ** read the following judgment of the court. Section 460 of the Income Tax Act 1970 strikes at tax avoidance: it reproduces s 28 of the Finance Act 1960, as amended. Anyone who, in the circumstances specified in the section, obtains, or puts himself into a position to obtain, a tax advantage in consequence of a 'transaction in securities', may find himself subjected to action by the Board of Inland Revenue designed to counteract the advantage.

f
This appeal raises a point of importance on the interpretation of the section. Does the term which is fundamental for the operation of the section, 'transaction in securities', include a distribution of surplus assets made to a shareholder in the course of a company's liquidation? ('Surplus' means, in this context, after payment of debts and repayment of capital.) If it does, the taxpayer's case collapses, as his counsel recognised at the very outset of his argument; if it does not, it becomes necessary to consider in detail the facts and the parties' opposing analyses of the facts, as indeed Goulding J[1] did, when he allowed the Crown's appeal against the decision of the

g
Special Commissioners in favour of the taxpayer.
There is no need to state all the facts: they are succinctly set out in the judgment of Goulding J[1]. Suffice it for us to mention that Mr Joiner, the taxpayer, owned 75 per cent of the share capital of the family company which was engaged in the manufacture of component parts for the motor industry; trustees of a family trust owned the remaining 25 per cent of the share capital. The company had prospered; and it

h
possessed substantial assets representing accumulated and undistributed profits not needed as working capital for the conduct of the company's business.
With the object of extracting these assets from the company the taxpayer, with the consent of the minority shareholders, put the company into liquidation. It was a members' voluntary winding-up; a liquidator was appointed and promptly sold the company's business to another company, also controlled by the taxpayer. The

j
liquidator then paid off such debts as the company had to meet, and distributed the assets to the shareholders. The distribution was, in fact, pursuant to an agreement previously reached between the taxpayer and the family trustees; but this agreement

---

1   [1973] 2 All ER 379, [1973] 1 WLR 690, [1973] STC 224

did not vary the proportions of their respective entitlements, which corresponded
exactly to their shareholding.   *a*

It was admitted that the taxpayer had obtained a tax advantage—the avoidance
of the tax that would have been suffered had the accumulated profits been distributed by the company as dividends. It was also common ground that the immediate
cause of the tax advantage was the distribution of assets in the course of the liquidation. Was this distribution a transaction in securities? Counsel for the taxpayer
submitted that it was not. He argued that the distribution, being a step taken in the   *b*
course of the liquidation of a company, was outside s 460: it was not a transaction
in securities but an integral part of the process of liquidation, and he relied on s 460(2)
of the section as showing, by implication, that an act done in the course of liquidation
is not such a transaction.

Section 460 confers on the board the duty to counteract a tax advantage obtained
or obtainable in consequence of a transaction in securities: the sections that follow   *c*
it (ss 461-468) amplify and explain its terms, and also set up machinery to safeguard
the taxpayer. The language of these sections is of great width, and the House of Lords
has consistently refused to limit their scope by judicial interpretation: see *Inland
Revenue Comrs v Parker*[1] and *Greenberg v Inland Revenue Comrs*[2].

Section 467(1) contains an indication, but not a definition, of the meaning of the
term 'transaction in securities': it says that ' "transaction in securities" includes trans-   *d*
actions, of whatever description, relating to securities', and then particularises a
number of transactions which are included. It contains no reference to the liquidation
of a company. If it does anything, this indication extends the meaning of the term;
for it shows that the term does include transactions 'relating to' securities. Counsel
for the taxpayer, however, comments that, had it been the intention of Parliament to
include within the meaning of the term the liquidation of a company, nothing could   *e*
have been easier than to have said so; instead, the subsection goes no further than to
specify a number of transactions which, even if they had not been mentioned, would
obviously have been transactions in securities. He relies strongly, therefore, on the
absence of any reference to the liquidation of a company in this statutory indication
of the meaning of 'a transaction in securities'.

In our judgment, a distribution of surplus assets to shareholders in the course of   *f*
a liquidation is a transaction relating to securities, unless it can be shown that Parliament has expressly, or by necessary implication, excluded it. The steps in our reasoning can be stated very shortly: first, shares are securities (s 467(1)); secondly, the
word 'transaction' includes a unilateral act (for example, in *Parker's* case[1], the redemption of a debenture, and in *Greenberg's* case[2], the part payment of a price); thirdly,
a distribution by a liquidator to shareholders gives effect to the rights attaching to   *g*
their shares (or an agreed variation of these rights), and therefore relates to the shares.

Does the fact that the distribution is a step in the liquidation of a company make all
the difference? The statute does not say so in terms; its language is wide enough to
include such a distribution; and the House of Lords has made it plain that the courts
are not to cut down the width of the language used. We are in the realm of tax
avoidance; and a main object of the present transaction was the avoidance of tax.   *h*
When these provisions (originally s 28 of the Finance Act 1960) were introduced, the
intention of Parliament was to give them a wide range so that they might be proof
against the ingenuity of the tax avoider and his advisers. Safeguards were provided,
but they do not depend on tight drafting or limiting definitions. The taxpayer can
escape, even though he has obtained a tax advantage, if he can show that the transaction or transactions were carried out for bona fide commercial reasons or in the   *j*
ordinary course of making or managing investments. A taxpayer who has in mind
a transaction or transactions which will confer on him a tax advantage may seek from

---

1   [1966] 1 All ER 399, [1966] AC 141, 43 Tax Cas 369
2   [1971] 3 All ER 136, [1972] AC 109, 47 Tax Cas 240

the Revenue a prior clearance; and, if he gets it, that is the end of the matter (s 464).

a A taxpayer who certifies by statutory declaration that a transaction is outside the scope of these provisions is safe from counteraction by the Revenue, unless the board refers the case to a tribunal and the tribunal declares that there is a prima facie case against him (s 460(6)(7)). Even thereafter, he still has the opportunity of satisfying the Special Commissioners that his main object was not tax avoidance but a bona fide commercial one.

b There is, therefore, nothing so unjust or oppressive in the operation of the section as to lead one to doubt whether Parliament really intended its language to have the width that on a literal interpretation it clearly has. Parliament has made clear the means it has chosen to obviate injustice and oppression—means which do not require limitations to be put on the language of the sections.

Counsel for the taxpayer seeks to meet this reasoning by a historical argument.

c When s 28 of the 1960 Act was enacted, it contained no reference to company liquidation. We were told that the tribunal, to whom reference could be made to determine whether or not there was a prima facie case of tax avoidance, never did find such a case when a liquidation had intervened. Counsel for the Crown told the House of Lords in *Greenberg's* case[1] that the tribunal had held that a tax advantage obtained in consequence of the combined effect of a transaction in securities and the liquidation

d of a company did not fall within s 28(1). However, it may be significant that this view of the tribunal, and indeed the amendment to meet the difficulty of the view, preceded the decisions in the *Parker*[2] and *Greenberg* cases[3].

The amendment to meet the difficulty was s 25(5) of the Finance Act 1962, which is now reproduced in s 460(2) of the Income Tax Act 1970. It reads as follows:

e 'Subject to section 468(3) below, for the purposes of this Chapter a tax advantage obtained or obtainable by a person shall be deemed to be obtained or obtainable by him in consequence of a transaction in securities or of the combined effect of two or more such transactions, if it is obtained or obtainable in consequence of the combined effect of the transaction or transactions and of the liquidation of a company.'

f How, counsel for the taxpayer asks, could Parliament have so enacted, unless its intention in 1960 had been to exclude the liquidation of a company, and steps taken in the course of liquidation, from the ambit of s 28? He submits, quite simply, that, using the subsection as a guide to the interpretation of the earlier legislation, one must infer that Parliament did not intend to include a distribution of surplus assets to shareholders in the course of a liquidation as itself a transaction in securities; by

g providing that a liquidation should not break the chain of causation, Parliament showed clearly that a liquidation was not itself a transaction in securities.

We think the submission is unsound. First, a later enactment may be used as an aid to the interpretation of an earlier only if the court thinks the earlier provision is ambiguous: *Kirkness v John Hudson & Co Ltd*[4]. In our opinion the earlier provision

h was wide, but not ambiguous. And we are precluded by authority, as well as by our own view of the section read as a whole, from imposing a limitation on the words of Parliament which does not necessarily arise from the words themselves.

Secondly, the subsection is a 'deeming' provision. Parliament uses this device from time to time, and not always for the same reason. As Lord Radcliffe said in *St Aubyn v Attorney-General (No 2)*[5]:

j

1 [1972] AC 109 at 132
2 [1966] 1 All ER 399, [1966] AC 141, 43 Tax Cas 396
3 [1971] 3 All ER 136, [1972] AC 109, 47 Tax Cas 240
4 [1955] 2 All ER 345, [1955] AC 696, 36 Tax Cas 28
5 [1951] 2 All ER 473 at 498, [1952] AC 15 at 53

'The word "deemed" is used a great deal in modern legislation. Sometimes
it is used to impose for the purposes of a statute an artificial construction of a   a
word or phrase that would not otherwise prevail. Sometimes it is used to put
beyond doubt a particular construction that might otherwise be uncertain.
Sometimes it is used to give a comprehensive description that includes what is
obvious, what is uncertain and what is, in the ordinary sense, impossible.'

There being more than one possible explanation for the addition in 1962 of this   b
'deeming' provision, it would be wrong to draw any inference from it as to the
meaning of the earlier provision.

Thirdly, the draftsman was careful to warn judges against using the subsection as
a clue to the meaning of the earlier enactment. In s 25(7) of the 1962 Act (now s 468(3)
of the 1970 Act) we are warned that nothing in s 25(5) should be taken to prejudice
the operation of s 28 of the 1960 Act in respect of any transaction carried out before   c
10th April 1962.

For these reasons, we do not accede to the invitation of counsel for the taxpayer to
look to s 460(2) as a guide to the meaning of the term 'transaction in securities' when
used in sub-s (1). In our judgment, therefore, a distribution of surplus assets to shareholders in the course of the liquidation of a company is, for the purpose of s 460(1) of
the 1970 Act, a transaction in securities. Accordingly, we dismiss the appeal. Had it   d
been necessary to rule on the grounds on which Goulding J[1] decided the case against
the taxpayer, we would have agreed with him; but, in our view, it is unnecessary to
go so far. The appeal fails on the point which counsel for the taxpayer consistently
recognised was fatal to his case, if decided against him, and it is therefore dismissed.

Appeal dismissed. Leave to appeal to the House of Lords.   e

Solicitors: *Underwood & Co* (for the taxpayer); *Solicitor of Inland Revenue.*

Rengan Krishnan Esq Barrister.

f

R v Goodson

COURT OF APPEAL, CRIMINAL DIVISION
SCARMAN, JAMES LJJ AND BOREHAM J   g
23rd JANUARY 1975

*Jury – Retirement – Separation after being given in charge of bailiff – Juror leaving juryroom –
Discharge of juror – Verdict given by remaining jurors – Accused convicted – Discharge of
juror depriving accused of one potential supporter – Whether whole jury should have been
discharged – Whether verdict should be quashed.*   h

The appellant was charged with several offences to which he pleaded guilty and was
also charged with burglary to which he pleaded not guilty. After the jury had retired
to consider their verdict, one of the jurors was given permission by the jury bailiff
to leave the jury room. He was subsequently found making a telephone call. The
juror was prevented from returning to the jury room. The jury returned and the   j
court was informed of what had happened. The recorder decided that although the
juror's absence was an irregularity, no material prejudice would be suffered by the
appellant if the trial continued with a jury of only 11 members. Accordingly, under

---

1 [1973] 2 All ER 379, [1973] 1 WLR 690, [1973] STC 224

a the provisions of s 1 of the Criminal Justice Act 1965, he discharged the juror who had made the telephone call. The jury retired and reached a verdict of guilty on the charge of burglary. The appellant appealed against conviction.

Held – A material irregularity had occurred which had deprived the appellant of one potential supporter. The irregularity had left room for speculation and consequently a possibility of injustice to the appellant. The appropriate course would have
b been to discharge the whole jury. Accordingly the appeal would be allowed and the conviction quashed (see p 762 *h* to p 763 *a*, post).

Notes
For misconduct of juror, see 23 Halsbury's Laws (3rd Edn) 31, para 62, and for cases on the subject, see 14 Digest (Repl) 346, 3356-3358.
c

Cases referred to in judgment
R v Ketteridge [1915] 1 KB 467, [1914-15] All ER Rep 482, 84 LJKB 352, 112 LT 783, 79 JP 216, 24 Cox CC 678, 11 Cr App Rep 54, CCA, 14 Digest (Repl) 346, 3358.
R v Alexander (2nd November 1973) unreported.

d **Appeal**
This was an appeal by Sean Eric Goodson against his conviction for burglary in the Crown Court at Norwich on 13th May 1974 before Mr Recorder Ives and a jury. The facts are set out in the judgment.

R C Cox for the appellant.
e *G C Parkins* for the Crown.

JAMES LJ delivered the following judgment of the court. On 13th May 1974, in the Crown Court at Norwich, Sean Eric Goodson, the appellant, pleaded guilty to an offence of burglary and pleaded guilty to two offences of unlawful possession of
f firearms. He was convicted by a jury of one further charge of burglary and was sentenced to terms of imprisonment on his pleas of guilty and that conviction, which sentences are matters which are not immediately involved in this judgment. He appeals against conviction for burglary by leave of the single judge and the short point, taken out of a number of grounds of appeal submitted, is that there was a material irregularity in the course of the trial, the result of which should be that this conviction
g should be quashed. There is no need in the circumstances to cite the details of the offence of burglary, which was alleged to have taken place on 13th December 1973, involving the taking of jewellery and other articles from a house of a Mr and Mrs Mason in Norfolk while those persons were absent from their home in hospital.

The material irregularity related to the conduct of one of the jurors after the jury had retired at the end of the summing-up to consider their verdict. It appears that the
h jury having retired at 3.38 pm, about, or just over, an hour later, counsel appearing for the Crown, in going to make a telephone call, went to a telephone booth only six or seven feet away from the door of the jury room in a public corridor, where he recognised a member of the jury in the course of using the telephone. The jury bailiff was present observing that which was taking place. Counsel, rightly if we may say so, informed the court of what he had observed and rightly took steps which resulted in
j that juryman not returning to the jury room.

The jury returned just over an hour later. At that time the court, having been informed of the incident to which I have referred, investigated what had taken place by asking the juror a number of questions. The facts elicited appeared to be these. The juror desired to speak to 'people' on the telephone. He had, by inference, spoken to the jury bailiff and obtained the jury bailiff's permission to do so. He had left the

other jurors in the jury room and had spoken to 'people' on the telephone but what- *a*
ever was said by him or to him had not been communicated to the remaining 11
jurors for the very reason that prosecuting counsel had taken steps which prevented
that occurring. It may be said with certainty in this particular case that there was an
irregularity, in that a member of the jury had separated himself from the remainder
of the jury and had been in communication with other persons before the jury had
returned their verdict in the court. It can also be said with certainty that that irregularity had not resulted in the other 11 jurors having knowledge of what had taken *b*
place between their fellow member and any other person to whom he spoke.

In those circumstances the recorder invited counsel for the Crown to address him
as to the course that ought to be followed. Counsel submitted that the recorder had
power under s 1 of the Criminal Justice Act 1965 to discharge the individual juror and
to allow the trial to proceed to verdict, that juror having been discharged. Counsel
then appearing for the appellant argued to the contrary and submitted to the recorder *c*
that the appropriate course in those circumstances was to discharge the whole jury
which would have meant, of course, a new trial.

The recorder was faced with not only an irritating situation but a difficult situation.
He was reminded of the authority of *R v Ketteridge*[1] and in the end, in the ruling which
he had to give without any great and mature reflection on the matter, he said:
d

> 'What are the interests of justice? I do not think that there is any material
> prejudice that can be thought up as a real thing which either or any one of the
> three defendants will suffer if the trial continues with a jury of 11 and I think
> the public interest and the interests of justice coincide and therefore I do now
> formally discharge Mr Michael Denny from any further service on the jury.'

The trial then proceeded and the remaining 11 jurors who had been present in court *e*
listening to arguments on this incident returned verdicts on counts in respect of which
they acquitted the accused. They had not reached a verdict on the count which is the
subject-matter of this appeal and they retired again, after a further short direction,
for some five minutes or so and then returned the verdict of guilty.

Before us counsel for the Crown has reiterated his careful and persuasive submission *f*
based on s 1 of the Criminal Justice Act 1965. Counsel for the appellant argued that
s 1 of the 1965 Act is not a section which governs the situation in this case and that a
proper construction of that Act would lead to the conclusion that the court had no
power to discharge this particular juror in those circumstances. We do not find it
necessary on the facts of this particular case to consider the construction of that
statutory provision. We are faced here with what is conceded on all hands to be a
material irregularity. Such an irregularity occurred in *R v Alexander*[2] which was *g*
before this court on 2nd November 1973. In that case the court, finding an irregularity,
decided that it was so minimal and trivial as not to justify any interference with the
verdict of the jury.

In this case when one looks at the facts, as has been pointed out in the course of
argument, this is clear: that the appellant was deprived of the voice of one juryman *h*
in the jury room in the consideration of the verdict from which the appeal is made.

From what has been said in argument it is quite clear that there is abundant room
for speculation and where there is room for speculation there is, we think, room for
possible injustice, possible injustice to the appellant in respect of this conviction. That
being so, although we have every sympathy for the recorder in his decision, made
closely on the events, that it was appropriate to discharge the one juror and to continue with the proceedings, having had greater opportunity for consideration, we are *j*
satisfied that the appropriate course in this case was that the whole jury should have
been discharged.

---

1 [1915] 1 KB 467, [1914-15] All ER Rep 482
2 (2nd November 1973) unreported

In those circumstances the material irregularity is one that we find must result in
a the quashing of the conviction on count 1 of the indictment and for those reasons this
appeal is allowed.

Appeal allowed. Conviction quashed.

Solicitors: *Registrar of Criminal Appeals* (for the appellant); *J V Bates*, Norfolk (for the
b Crown).

Sepala Munasinghe Esq Barrister.

c # Cherwell District Council v Thames Water Authority

HOUSE OF LORDS
d LORD WILBERFORCE, VISCOUNT DILHORNE, LORD DIPLOCK, LORD KILBRANDON AND LORD
SALMON
14th JANUARY, 5th MARCH 1975

*Water supply – Duty of statutory water undertakers – Duty to provide domestic supply to
new buildings – Duty on request by owner of land on which buildings to be erected – Power
of undertakers to require owner to make contribution to cost of laying necessary mains –
e 'Necessary mains' – Meaning – Request by landowner for supply of water to new houses –
Construction of trunk main necessary to bring water to houses – Trunk main required for
purpose of supplying water to existing consumers in addition to proposed new houses –
Right of undertakers to require council to make contribution to cost of laying trunk main –
Water Act 1945, s 37 (as amended by the Water Act 1948, s 14(4), and the Housing Act
f 1949, s 46).*

A borough council ('the council') owned two sites in the borough on which they
proposed to build houses. There were no existing water mains from which water
for domestic use could be supplied to either site. The council, acting under s 37(1)[a]
of the Water Act 1945, requested the statutory water undertakers ('the board')
to supply water to the proposed new houses. At that time the source of water supply
g for the borough was water pumped from the River Cherwell into a service reservoir. That source, however, was becoming inadequate for the growing demand.
To supplement it the board proposed to extract water from the Thames and convey
it by a 27 inch trunk main to the existing service reservoir for the purpose of supplying the whole borough. The board in purported exercise of their power under
proviso (a) to s 37(1) required the council to make a contribution to the construction
h and laying of the 27 inch trunk main on the ground that it was a 'necessary main'
within proviso (a) in that its construction was necessary to bring water to, inter
alia, the council's proposed new houses. The council denied that they were liable to
make any such contribution on the ground that a trunk main was not capable of
constituting a 'necessary main' within proviso (a).

j **Held** – The word 'necessary' in proviso (a) to s 37(1) was applicable only to new
mains which were needed for no other purpose than to convey water from a starting
point, to which a supply of water was already being brought in existing works belonging to the undertakers, to a point at which it was practicable to connect by service

a Section 37 is set out at p 768 *j* to p 769 *g*, post

pipes the new buildings in respect of which the requisition had been made. It followed
therefore that, although in certain circumstances a trunk main might be a 'necessary'   *a*
main, the 27 inch trunk main was not such a main for, when completed, it would
supply water not only to the new houses but also to the general body of consumers
(see p 765 *d* to *f*, p 770 *a* to *e* and p 771 *e* to *h*, post).

Per Curiam. When a court is called on to construe a statute it must not allow
itself to be deflected from its task of deciding what the language of the statute means
by any agreement made between parties which involves, either expressly or by   *b*
implication, some assumption as to that meaning. On such occasions the function
of the court is to reach its own unfettered decision (see p 765 *d* to *f*, p 767 *b* and p 771
g and *h*, post).

Decision of the Court of Appeal sub nom *Banbury Borough Council v Oxfordshire
and District Water Board* [1974] 2 All ER 928 reversed.

Notes   *c*
For the duty of statutory water undertakers to provide domestic supply of water
for new buildings, see 39 Halsbury's Laws (3rd Edn) 402, 403, para 618.

For the Water Act 1945, s 37, Sch 3, see 39 Halsbury's Statutes (3rd Edn) 108, 135.
Section 37 has been further amended by the Water Act 1973, s 11(7), and Sch 8, para
53(4), as from 1st April 1974.   *d*

Appeal
The plaintiffs, Cherwell District Council (formerly the Banbury Borough Council)
('the council'), were the municipal authority of the borough of Banbury and as such
were empowered to construct dwellings in the borough or elsewhere pursuant to
the Housing Acts 1957 to 1969. Pursuant to those powers the council proposed to
erect four bungalows, twelve flats and warden's accommodation at Penrose Close off   *e*
Penrose Drive and sixteen bungalows at Ruscote, both in the borough of Banbury.
The defendants, Thames Water Authority (formerly the Oxfordshire and District
Water Board) ('the board'), were the statutory body empowered pursuant to the
Water Acts 1945 and 1948 to supply water to an area known as Oxfordshire and
District, which comprised, in addition to the borough of Banbury, the city of Oxford,
the boroughs of Abingdon, Chipping Norton and Woodstock, the urban districts   *f*
of Bicester, Thame and Witney, the rural districts of Banbury, Chipping Norton,
Ploughley and Witney, the rural district of Abingdon except certain parishes, the
rural district of Bullington except certain parishes or parts of parishes, and the rural
district of Farringdon except the parish of Kingston Lisle. Pursuant to s 37 of the
Water Act 1945, as amended by s 46 of the Housing Act 1949, the council, being
owners of land at Penrose Drive on which they proposed to erect buildings for   *g*
which a supply of water for domestic purposes would be needed, enquired of the
board, being the statutory water undertakers within whose limits of supply the
land was situated, by a letter dated 18th June 1971, as to a supply of water to the
proposed buildings, involving the laying of the necessary mains for that purpose.
By a letter dated 22nd July 1971, the board stated that the estimated cost of laying
the mains required to serve the development at Penrose Drive was £1,434, made   *h*
up as to £1,060 in respect of mains indicated in red on a plan of the site and its immediate surroundings and £374 in respect of a contribution towards a 27 inch diameter
trunk main between the outskirts of Woodstock and Banbury. Pursuant to s 37
of the 1945 Act, as amended, the council, being, owners of land at Ruscote on which
they proposed to erect buildings for which a supply of water for domestic purposes
would be needed, enquired of the board, being the statutory water undertakers   *j*
within whose limits of supply the land was situated, by a letter dated 25th June 1971
as to a supply of water to the proposed buildings, involving the laying of the necessary
mains for that purpose. By a letter dated 22nd July 1971 the board stated that the
estimated cost of laying the mains required to serve the development at Ruscote
was £1,227 made up as to £875 in respect of mains indicated in red on a plan of

the site and its immediate surroundings and £352 in respect of a contribution towards
a the 27 inch diameter trunk main between the outskirts of Woodstock and Banbury.
The trunk main had not been constructed, and could not be constructed within
three months of the date of the letters of 22nd July 1971.

By an originating summons dated 21st December 1971, as amended on 16th October
1972 pursuant to an order of Master Lubbock, the council, relying on the facts set
out above, sought the determination of the question whether the board could lawfully
b demand the sums of £374 and £352 as contributions in respect of the 27 inch diameter
trunk main. On 11th May 1973 Mocatta J[1] answered the question in the negative
and declared that the trunk main was not a necessary main for the purpose of proviso
(a) to s 37(1) of the 1945 Act. On 8th May 1974 the Court of Appeal[2] (Edmund Davies
and Stephenson LJJ, Sir Gordon Willmer dissenting) allowed an appeal by the board.
The council appealed to the House of Lords.
c

Gerald Moriarty QC and *Anthony J Anderson* for the council.
Michael Mann QC and *H D Donovan* for the board.

Their Lordships took time for consideration.

d 5th March. The following opinions were delivered.

LORD WILBERFORCE. I have had the benefit of reading in advance the speech
prepared by my noble and learned friend Lord Diplock. I agree with it and would
allow the appeal and answer the question raised in the originating summons in the
e manner contained in the judgment dated 11th May 1973 of Mocatta J.

VISCOUNT DILHORNE. I have read the speech of my noble and learned
friend Lord Diplock. I agree with it. The question raised in the originating summons
should be answered as he proposes.

f

LORD DIPLOCK. My lords, in 1971, the Banbury Borough Council (the predecessors of the Cherwell District Council) proposed to build on land they owned
at two sites in the borough, dwellings for which a supply of water for domestic use
would be needed. The borough of Banbury was within the limits of supply of the
Oxfordshire and District Water Board (the predecessor of the Thames Water Authority),
g who were the statutory water undertakers for that area. At neither of the sites
were there existing water mains from which a supply of water for the new buildings
could be obtained. This would require the laying of new mains.

At the time the source of supply for the borough was water pumped from the
River Cherwell into a service reservoir. This source, however, was becoming inadequate for the growing demand. To supplement it the board proposed to extract
h water from the Thames near Woodstock and convey it by a 27 inch trunk main to
the existing service reservoir at Banbury.

Being desirous of exercising their right under s 37 of the Water Act 1945 to require a water board to lay mains from which a supply of water to the proposed
new buildings could be obtained, the council asked the board how much the board
would require them to undertake to pay under the provisions of that section. In
j reply, the board quoted a figure which comprised two elements: (1) the cost of
laying the new mains which would be needed in the immediate vicinity of the sites,
and (2) a contribution towards the cost of the proposed new 27 inch trunk main

---

1   [1973] 3 All ER 257, [1973] 1 WLR 984
2   [1974] 2 All ER 929, [1973] 1 WLR 984

conveying water from the Thames to the existing service reservoir for supplying
the whole of the borough of Banbury.   *a*

The total cost of laying the new trunk main was of the order of a million pounds.
The contribution towards this total demanded in respect of the two sites was small,
viz £374 for one and £352 for the other. It appears to have been based upon the
estimated proportion of the total gallonage of water passing through the trunk
main which would be supplied to the buildings on those particular sites.

The council accepted their liability for the first element, viz the cost of laying the   *b*
new mains in the immediate vicinity of the two sites, but contended that the Water
Board were not entitled under the section to demand any contribution from them
towards the cost of the proposed 27 inch trunk main.

By originating summons of 21st December 1971, the council sought a declaration—

> 'whether the Defendants [sc the board] can lawfully demand the said sums   *c*
> of £374 and £352 as contributions in respect of the said 27-inch diameter trunk
> main, or at all.'

The actual amount at stake was small, but both the parties wished to have settled
a question of principle as to the construction of s 37 of the Water Act 1945. In the
belief that it would facilitate this, leading counsel for the two parties before the
commencement of the hearing of the summons before Mocatta J[1] agreed as follows: *d*

> 'We agree that the single issue between the parties is whether a trunk main
> is in law capable of falling within the phrase "necessary mains" as employed
> in proviso (*a*) to section 37(1). We further agree that, if the answer to that ques-
> tion is "yes", then no further question arises either as to whether the Woodstock-
> Banbury trunk main is in fact a necessary main or as to whether the proportion   *e*
> of the cost attributed to the [council's] development is correct. In other words
> the simple answers "yes" or "no" are each equally conclusive of the action.'

In my view, the effect of this agreement is to substitute for the question raised
in the originating summons, which was the actual question at issue between the
parties, a broader and purely hypothetical question which the court should not
have entertained. The result in the instant case has been unfortunate. The agree-   *f*
ment assumes that if, upon the true construction of the section, the expression 'necessary mains' is capable of including any trunk main at all, the 27 inch trunk main
conveying water from the Thames to the service reservoir at Banbury must be
included in that expression. It thus diverts the court from a consideration of the
meaning of the expression 'necessary' as descriptive of the mains to which the section
applies, by purporting to exclude as a possible answer to the question raised in the   *g*
originating summons that although in some circumstances a trunk main may be
a 'necessary main' within the meaning of the section, the 27 inch trunk main from
Woodstock to Banbury is not.

In the result, the only question argued at the original hearing before Mocatta J[1] and
in the Court of Appeal[2] was the hypothetical question: 'Aye or No, does the expression "necessary mains", upon a true construction of the section, exclude all trunk   *h*
mains?' In his reasons for judgment, Mocatta J dealt only with this hypothetical
question. He answered it 'Aye'. In the Court of Appeal, too, the reasons given by
the majority (Edmund Davies and Stephenson LJJ[2]) dealt only with the hypothetical
question. They answered it 'No'. Nevertheless, the formal order of the Court of
Appeal answered the actual question raised by the originating summons. It declared—

> 'that in regard to the requirement made by the [board] in respect of the   *j*
> proposed buildings of the [council] at Penrose Drive and Ruscote in the Borough
> of Banbury the 27 inch diameter trunk main to be laid by the Water Board

---

1   [1973] 3 All ER 257, [1973] 1 WLR 984
2   [1974] 2 All ER 929, [1974] 1 WLR 848

a between the outskirts of Woodstock and their service reservoir at Banbury is a necessary main for the purposes of proviso (a) to section 37(1) of the Water Act 1945'.

It was only Sir Gordon Willmer[1] who directed his mind to the actual question. He was of opinion that the 27 inch main was not a 'necessary main' within the meaning of proviso (a) to s 37(1) of the Water Act 1945. I think that he was right.

b   A court that is called on to construe a statute in order to determine an issue between parties to litigation must not allow itself to be deflected from its task of deciding what the language of the statute means by any agreement between those parties which involves, expressly or by implication, some assumption as to that meaning. On such a matter the constitutional function of a court as the interpreter of the written law compels it to reach its own unfettered decision. This House would be c failing in its duty if it confined itself to the hypothetical question dealt with in the judgments of Mocatta J and the majority of the Court of Appeal, and treated the answer to that question as conclusive of the actual question raised in the originating summons—as was done in the order made by the Court of Appeal. In the view I take as to the true construction of the statute, to do this would provide no useful guidance as to the application of the Act to other cases. It could only lead to con- d fusion. It might positively mislead. I turn then to the question of construction unfettered by any agreement between counsel for the parties as to its meaning, or as to its effect in the particular circumstances of the instant case.

The Oxfordshire and District Water Board was constituted by an order made by the Minister under s 9 of the Water Act 1945. The order incorporated, with some immaterial exceptions, the provisions of Sch 3 to the 1945 Act, which is a modernised e version of clauses formerly contained in the Waterworks Clauses Acts 1847 and 1863. The relevant powers and duties of the board are thus to be found in Part IV of the body of the Act (which includes s 37) and in Sch 3.

There is an interpretation section, s 59, in the body of the 1945 Act, but a more comprehensive one is contained in cl 1 of Sch 3. (To avoid confusion between sections of the Act which bear the same number as sections in Sch 3, I refer to the latter as f 'clauses'.) The definitions that are relevant to the construction of s 37 appear for the most part only in cl 1, but it is not, and in my view cannot be, disputed that where expressions there defined are used in the body of the Act the same meaning is to be ascribed to them.

The only definitions which I find it necessary to cite are 'main', 'trunk main' and 'supply of water in bulk':

g   ' "main" means a pipe laid by the undertakers for the purpose of giving a general supply of water as distinct from a supply to individual consumers and includes any apparatus used in connection with such a pipe';
     ' "trunk main" means a main constructed for the purpose of conveying water from a source of supply to a filter or reservoir, or from one filter or reservoir to another filter or reservoir, or for the purpose of conveying water in bulk from h   one part of the limits of supply to another part of those limits, or for the purpose of giving or taking a supply of water in bulk';
     ' "supply of water in bulk" means a supply of water for distribution by the undertakers taking the supply'.

'Main' is thus a genus of water pipe of which 'trunk main' is a species embracing j four sub-species which have the common characteristics that they are pipes con- veying water in bulk to some place such as a reservoir from which it is distributed by the undertakers. It is convenient to refer to mains which are not trunk mains as 'distribution mains', as has been done in the courts below.

The scheme of the 1945 Act and Sch 3 as respects the rights of owners and occupiers

1 [1974] 2 All ER at 937, [1974] 1 WLR at 858

of existing premises to demand and receive from statutory water undertakers a supply of water for domestic purposes is this: (1) Where there are existing mains which *a* are capable of being reached by a service pipe from the premises the owner or occupier is entitled to demand to be connected with the main and to receive a supply of water for domestic purposes, on payment or tender of the water rate. That part of the service pipe that lies between the main and the boundary of the street in which the main is laid is to be laid by the undertakers; the remainder by the owner or occupier of the premises. He must pay the cost of the undertakers of laying their *b* part of the service pipe and connecting it to the main: but no part of the cost of the main itself can be demanded of him. Even if the capacity of the existing main is insufficient to provide his premises with a constant supply at adequate pressure (as the undertakers are obliged to do by cl 39) they cannot demand any payment towards the cost of replacing the existing main by one of greater capacity or of any other measures required to enable them to fulfil this obligation. (See cll 30, 40 and *c* 41.) (2) Where premises are in an area in which there are no existing mains capable of being reached by service pipes from those premises, the owners or occupiers of such premises may combine together to require the water undertakers to lay 'the necessary mains'. The undertakers must comply with this requirement if the requisition is made by owners or occupiers of premises in respect of which the water rates payable annually will, in the aggregate, be not less than one-eighth of the cost of *d* providing and laying the necessary mains (cl 29). This right, which corresponds with a former provision of the Waterworks Clauses Acts, has been supplemented by a new provision, contained in the body of the Water Act 1945. In cases where there are not sufficient owners or occupiers of premises in the area to qualify them to make a valid requisition themselves, s 36 authorises a local authority to undertake to make good to the undertakers for a maximum period of twelve years the *e* deficiency (if any) between the water rates payable annually in respect of premises in the area and the one-eighth of the cost of providing and laying the necessary mains. On such an undertaking being given, the water undertakers are obliged to lay the necessary mains and to bring water to the area. Although when the new mains have been laid the owner or occupier of any premises in the area must pay the cost of laying a service pipe connecting them with the premises, no contribution *f* may be demanded of him towards the cost of laying the new mains or of bringing water to them. His liability is confined to paying the annual water rate levied upon him in common with all other consumers of water for domestic purposes.

Prior to the Water Act 1945, an owner of land had no statutory right to require water undertakers to lay new mains for the supply of water for domestic purposes to a building which he proposed to erect but had not yet erected. All that he could *g* do was to complete the building and hope that when it was completed he, either alone or in combination with owners or occupiers of other premises in the same area, would qualify by reason of the aggregate rateable value of the premises to make a requisition upon the undertakers under the provision of the Waterworks Clauses Act corresponding to cl 29 of Sch 3 to the Water Act 1945. The Public Health Act 1936, however, made it impracticable to build houses in reliance on this hope alone. *h* Section 137 of that Act compelled a local authority to reject plans for new houses unless they were satisfied that a supply of wholesome water sufficient for the domestic purposes of their occupants would be provided.

Section 37 of the Water Act 1945 was a new provision designed to deal with this situation. Minor amendments were made to it by the Housing Act 1949, s 46; but I do not think that these affect the meaning of the expression 'necesssary mains' *j* which was also in the section before it was amended. It is sufficient to cite it only in its amended form:

'(1) Where an owner of land proposes to erect thereon buildings for which a supply of water for domestic purposes will be needed, he may require any

statutory water undertakers within whose limits of supply that land is situated
to construct any necessary service reservoirs, to lay the necessary mains to such
point or points as will enable the buildings to be connected thereto at a reasonable
cost and to bring water to that point or those points, and thereupon the undertakers shall, subject as hereinafter provided, comply with that requisition:
Provided that the undertakers before complying with a requisition under this
subsection—(a) may require the owner to undertake to pay in respect of each
year a sum amounting to one-eighth of the expense of providing and constructing the necessary service reservoirs and providing and laying the necessary
mains (less any amounts received by the undertakers in respect of water supplied,
whether for domestic or non-domestic purposes, in that year from those mains)
until the aggregate amount of water rates payable annually in respect of the
buildings when erected and in respect of any other premises connected with
the said mains at the rates for the time being charged by the undertakers equals
or exceeds such sum as aforesaid or until the expiration of a period of twelve
years, whichever first occurs; and (b) except where the owner is a local or
public authority, may also require him to deposit with the undertakers as security for payment of the said annual sums, such sum, not exceeding the total
expense of constructing the service reservoirs and providing and laying the mains,
as the undertakers may require.

(2) The undertakers shall pay inerest at the prescribed rate or, if no rate is
prescribed, at four per cent. per annum on any sum in their hands by virtue
of a requirement under paragraph (b) of the proviso to the last foregoing subsection, and shall, on the request of the owner of the land, appropriate out of
that sum any amount due under the undertaking referred to in paragraph
(a) of the said proviso and shall, when the said undertaking is finally discharged,
repay to the owner any sum remaining in their hands as aforesaid.

'(3) Any question arising under subsection (1) of this section as to the point
or points to which mains must be taken in order to enable buildings to be connected thereto at a reasonable cost shall, in default of agreement, be determined
by the Minister.

'(4) If the undertakers, after receipt of a requisition under subsection (1) of
this section and after tender to them of any undertaking or deposit which they
may require in accordance with that subsection, do not before the expiration
of three months (or, where a question has, before that time, been referred to
the Minister under the last foregoing subsection, before the expiration of three
months from the date when the Minister notifies the undertakers of his decision,
if that period expires later) comply with the requisition, they shall, unless they
show that the failure was due to unavoidable accident or other unavoidable
cause, be guilty of an offence against this Act.'

'Mains' is, by virtue of its definition in the 1945 Act, a generic term which prima
facie includes trunk mains as well as distribution mains, unless the context in which
it appears makes it clear that it was used in some more restricted meaning. In s 37
(as also in cl 29) the only express restriction upon its generally is that the mains
must be 'necessary'. This is, in my view, the keyword in the section for the purposes
of deciding the actual question raised by the originating summons. It poses immediately the question: 'Necessary for what?'

The section pre-supposes, first, that there are no existing mains bringing water
to points at which it would be practicable at reasonable cost to connect the proposed
buildings to those mains by service pipes. If there were, there would be no need
for any requisition. Once the building was erected the owner would be entitled
to require the connection to be made under cl 30, without any liability to contribute
to the cost previously incurred by the undertakers in laying the existing mains or
to the cost of replacing them by mains of greater capacity to meet the additional
demand resulting from the connection of the newly erected building to them.

Secondly, the section pre-supposes that there will be a supply of water in bulk
capable of being brought to the new mains by the undertakers, which if it is not *a*
already available to them it is their duty to procure without demanding from the
requisitioner any contribution to the cost of doing so.

So the 'necessary mains' with which the section deals are confined to new mains
to be laid by the undertakers in a street or other place where there are no existing
distribution mains and to start from a point to which a supply of water is already
being brought in existing works belonging to the undertaker; and the answer to *b*
the question: 'Necessary for what?' is: necessary in order to convey the water from
that starting point to points at which it would be practicable to connect the proposed
buildings to those mains by service pipes, and for no other purpose.

The section contemplates that as well as 'necessary mains' there may be 'necessary
service reservoirs' to be constructed. Ex hypothesi these must lie between the starting point to which a supply of water is already being brought in existing works *c*
belonging to the undertakers and the new distribution mains to which the proposed
new buildings will be connected. The new main which will carry water from that
starting point to the service reservoir may well fall within the definition of 'trunk
main'; and if the new trunk main and the new service reservoir will serve no other
purpose than to convey water from that starting point to the new distribution main
or mains to which the proposed buildings in respect of which the requisition has *d*
been made will be connected it would, in my view, fall within the expression 'necessary mains'. For in the context of s 37 I would construe 'necessary' as applicable to
new mains and service reservoirs provided for that purpose only and not to mains
or reservoirs which will also serve some other purpose of the undertakers in connection
with the supply of water to existing consumers or to potential new consumers *e*
whose water will not be brought to them through the new distribution main or
mains.

To ascribe any wider meaning to the word 'necessary' where it appears in s 37—
or, in a similar context, in cl 29—would, in my view, conflict with the general scheme
of the 1945 Act for allocating the cost of works between the proceeds of the annual
water rate payable by the general body of consumers of water for domestic purposes
and charges additional to the water rate imposed on particular consumers. Once *f*
works have been constructed by the undertakers which bring a supply of water
to an existing distribution main, the cost of additions or improvements to any of
those works lying between the ultimate source of the supply and service pipes connected with that main, which are needed to meet increased demand for water, must
be provided for out of the proceeds of the annual water rate or loans serviced out
of the proceeds of that rate. No additional charge may be imposed on the indivi- *g*
dual consumers who benefit from particular additions or improvements, even where
they are new customers whose exercise of their right under cl 30 to have their premises
connected to an existing main has caused the increased demand. The 1945 Act thus
appears to accept as a general principle that new consumers as well as old are entitled
to the benefit of additions and improvements to existing works rendered necessary
by increased demand for water for domestic purposes which they themselves have *h*
caused; and that they cannot be required to make any individual contribution to
the cost of those additions or improvements beyond what is payable by them by
way of the annual water rate in common with consumers who may derive no such
benefit.

It would seem to conflict with that principle that an exception should be made
in respect of additions or improvements to works lying between the ultimate source *j*
of supply and the point to which water had already been brought by the undertakers, merely because the supply to the new consumer involved, in addition to
the laying of service pipes, the laying of a new distribution main beyond that point
to a point in the vicinity of the premises for which the water was required.

Moreover, there are specific indications in s 37 itself that this was not intended.

Although in the instant case the board have restricted their demand to requiring
a the council to undertake to pay annually only a minute proportion of the one-eighth
of the the total cost of laying the 27 inch trunk main from the Thames to the existing
service reservoir at Banbury, there is nothing in the section to compel them to do
so if that main is included in the expression 'necessary main'. They could have demanded an undertaking extending to one-eighth of the total cost of the 27 inch
trunk main and, if the requisitioner had not happened to be a local authority, they
b could have required him to deposit as security a sum equal to that total cost.

Again, the method of calculating the sums payable in each year pursuant to the
undertaking appears to contemplate that all the works to which the undertaking
relates (whether mains or service reservoirs) will serve to supply with water a single
identifiable group of consumers liable to pay water rates in respect of water supplied
from such of the works as are mains. There is no provision for allocating the total
c cost of the necessary service reservoirs and the necessary mains between the cost
of reservoirs on the one hand and the cost of mains on the other or between one
main and another, so as to enable account to be taken of the water rates payable
by one group of consumers in calculating the requisitioner's liability in respect
of one part of the works and those payable by another group of consumers in calculating their liability in respect of another part of the work. The calculation envisaged
d by the section provides only for the assessment of the aggregate cost of works of
which it can be predicted that *all* the mains included in them will serve to supply
water to the same group of identifiable consumers and none will serve to supply
water to other groups as well.

In the instant case it is common ground that the 27 inch trunk main, when completed, would serve to supply water to the general body of consumers of water
e for domestic purposes as well as to the proposed new buildings that were the subject
of the contemplated requisition. How small a part the necessity to supply water
to these buildings played in creating the need to provide the new trunk main is
indicated by the minute proportion of the total cost of it that the board thought it
equitable to ascribe to the council as requisitioners in respect of those buildings.
That the 27 inch trunk main would serve such other purposes as well, in my view,
f precludes its being a 'necessary main' within the meaning of s 37 of the Water Act
1945. I would answer the only question raised in the originating summons accordingly
and would allow the appeal.

LORD KILBRANDON. My Lords, I have had the advantage of reading the
g speech prepared by my noble and learned friend Lord Diplock. I agree with him
that the question raised in the originating summons should be answered in the
negative. It would not be right to attempt to answer the question relating to all
trunk mains in general and in all circumstances, which was unfortunately substituted
for the question which was in issue between the parties.

h

LORD SALMON. My Lords, I, too, have had the advantage of reading in advance
the speech of my noble and learned friend Lord Diplock, and agree with him that
the originating summons should be answered in the negative.

Appeal allowed.
j

Solicitors: *Jaques & Co* (for the council); *Lewin, Gregory, Mead & Sons* (for the board).

Gordon H Scott Esq Barrister.

St Edmundsbury and Ipswich Diocesan Board of Finance and another v Clark (No 2)

COURT OF APPEAL, CIVIL DIVISION

RUSSELL, ORR LJJ AND SIR JOHN PENNYCUICK

15th, 18th, 19th, 20th, 21st, 22nd, 25th NOVEMBER, 18th DECEMBER 1974

Easement – Right of way – Reservation in conveyance – Construction of reservation – Construction with reference to surrounding circumstances – Reservation of 'right of way' simpliciter – Words ambiguous – Examination of surrounding circumstances essential to resolve ambiguity – Circumstances at date of conveyance indicating that way used and suitable for use on foot only – Reservation to be construed as being right of way on foot only and not including a right of way with vehicles.

Easement – Right of way – Creation – Reservation in conveyance – Execution and regrant by purchaser not required – Whether reservation taking effect by way of regrant by purchaser – Law of Property Act 1925, s 65(1).

By a conveyance dated 31st December 1945 certain land, which adjoined and completely surrounded a church and its churchyard, was conveyed by the Church authorities to the defendant 'subject . . . to a right of way over the land coloured red on the [plan annexed to the conveyance] to and from' the church. The 'land coloured red' consisted of a 30 yard strip leading from a public highway up to the churchyard. The strip was the only defined access way to the church; inside the churchyard it continued as a path leading up to the church porch. The strip was wide enough for vehicles, including lorries, to drive along it and in 1945 its surface was sufficiently firm and even for them to do so. There was no evidence, however, that before 1946 the strip had ever been used by vehicles. At the time of the conveyance the strip gave no indication of being a roadway but looked like a somewhat derelict pathway. Subsequently the defendant erected gates at the end of the strip near the public highway so that it became impossible to approach the churchyard otherwise than on foot. The plaintiffs, the diocesan board of finance and the parochial church council, claimed that under the reservation contained in the conveyance they were entitled to a right of way with or without vehicles over the strip of land. Accordingly they brought an action against the defendant claiming a mandatory injunction for the removal of the gate and an injunction restraining obstruction. The judge held that the words 'right of way' in the conveyance had to be considered in the light of the circumstances which prevailed at the date of the conveyance and that on that basis the right of way was limited to a right to pass on foot only. He further held that if the ambiguity in the words 'right of way' could not otherwise be resolved the words were to be construed against the Church authorities, as vendors, since, following the enactment of s 65(1)[a] of the Law of Property Act 1925, the reservation of a right of way was no longer effected by way of a regrant by the purchaser and therefore there was no justification for construing the reservation against the purchaser on the basis that he was the grantor of the right of way. Accordingly the judge dismissed the action. The parochial church council appealed, contending, inter alia, that the proper approach to the construction of the conveyance was to construe the words of the instrument in isolation, and then to look at the surrounding circumstances in order to see whether they cut down the prima facie meaning of the words.

Held – The appeal would be dismissed for the following reasons—

(i) The words of a conveyance containing the reservation of a right of way were to

---

a Section 65(1) is set out at p 780 d, post

be construed according to their natural meaning in the document as a whole in the
a light of the surrounding circumstances. It was not until the instrument and the
surrounding circumstances had been considered in conjunction that the process of
construction was concluded. Only in cases where the words of reservation were
wholly unambiguous could the surrounding circumstances be ignored. Since the
reservation in the 1945 conveyance was in the loosest terms, consisting simply of the
words 'right of way', it was essential that there should be an examination of the
b surrounding circumstances. Those circumstances were questions of fact for the trial
judge. He had construed the conveyance correctly in accordance with the surrounding circumstances and had reached a proper conclusion thereon (see p 779 d and h to
p 780 a and p 784 b to d, post); Cannon v Villars [1874-80] All ER Rep 597 applied.

(ii) The question whether in a conveyance subject to a right of way there was any
presumption either as against the vendor or the purchaser only fell to be considered
c when a court was unable on the material before it to reach a sure conclusion on the
construction of a reservation. Since a sure conclusion had been reached no question
of any presumption arose (see p 780 c, post).

Per Curiam. The only change in the law made by s 65(1) of the Law of Property
Act 1925 is that for the reservation of an easement to be effective it is no longer
necessary that the conveyance of the legal estate out of which the reservation is made
d should be executed by the purchaser. Under s 65(1) the reservation continues to
operate by way of a regrant even though there is not in terms any purported regrant
by the purchaser (see p 780 h to p 781 b and f and p 782 c and d, post); Johnstone v
Holdway [1963] 1 All ER 432 applied; Cordell v Second Clanfield Properties Ltd [1968]
3 All ER 746 dissaproved.

Decision of Megarry J [1973] 3 All ER 902 affirmed.

e
Notes

For reservations in a conveyance, see 12 Halsbury's Laws (4th Edn) 656, para 1531,
and for cases on exceptions and reservations, see 17 Digest (Repl) 388, 389, 1918-1935.

For the construction of an instrument against a grantor, see 1 Halsbury's Laws
(4th Edn) 606, para 1472, and for cases on the subject, see 17 Digest (Repl) 298-302,
f 1028-1090.

For the reservation of an easement in a conveyance, see 12 Halsbury's Laws (3rd
Edn) 533, 536, 537, paras 1158, 1163, 1164, and for cases on the subject, see 19 Digest
(Repl) 25, 26, 102, 103, 107-112, 613-615.

For the Law of Property Act 1925, s 65, see 27 Halsbury's Statutes (3rd Edn) 445.

g
Cases referred to in judgment

Bulstrode v Lambert [1953] 2 All ER 728, [1953] 1 WLR 1064, 17 Digest (Repl) 301, 1078.
Cannon v Villars (1878) 8 Ch D 415, [1874-80] All ER Rep 597, 47 LJCh 597, 38 LT 939,
    42 JP 516, 19 Digest (Repl) 116, 716.
Cordell v Second Clanfield Properties Ltd [1968] 3 All ER 746, [1969] 2 Ch 9, [1968] 3 WLR
    864, 19 P & CR 848, 17 Digest (Reissue) 432, 1937.
h Johnstone v Holdway [1963] 1 All ER 432, [1963] 1 QB 601, [1963] 2 WLR 147, CA, Digest
    (Cont Vol A) 496, 144a.
Keefe v Amor [1964] 2 All ER 517, [1965] 1 QB 334, [1964] 3 WLR 183, CA, Digest (Cont
    Vol B) 231, 721a.
Mason v Clarke [1954] 1 All ER 189, [1954] 1 QB 460, [1954] 2 WLR 48, CA; rvsd [1955]
    1 All ER 914, [1955] AC 778, [1955] 2 WLR 853, HL, 25 Digest (Repl) 374, 48.
j Robinson v Bailey [1948] 2 All ER 791, CA, 19 Digest (Repl) 117, 721.

Cases also cited

Ballard v Dyson (1808) 1 Taunt 279.
British Railways Board v Glass [1964] 3 All ER 418, [1965] Ch 538, CA.
Gregg v Richards [1926] 1 Ch 521, CA.
Kain v Norfolk [1949] 1 All ER 176, [1949] Ch 163.

May v Belleville [1905] 2 Ch 605.

Stenquil Investments Ltd v Hicklin (23rd February 1966) unreported, [1966] Bar Library　a
Transcript 42A, CA.

Thellusson v Liddard [1900] 2 Ch 635.

Todrick v Western National Omnibus Co Ltd [1934] Ch 561, [1934] All ER Rep 25, CA

Appeal

This was an appeal by the Parochial Church Council of the Parish of Iken, Suffolk,　b
against an order of Megarry J[1], dated 26th July 1973, whereby he dismissed an action
brought by St Edmundsbury and Ipswich Diocesan Board of Finance and the parochial
church council against the respondent, Gabriel Bertram Clark, claiming (i) an order
that Mr Clark forthwith take down and remove all obstructions put up by him on an
access way leading from the highway known as Church Road or Church Lane at
Iken to the churchyard and church of the parish of St Botolph, Iken; (ii) an injunction　c
restraining him from erecting any new obstruction on the access way, and (iii) damages
for trespass. Megarry J granted Mr Clark a declaration that the plaintiffs were not
entitled to remove the gates and posts erected by Mr Clark on the access way without
his consent or that of his successor in title. The facts are set out in the judgment of the
court.

　　　　　　　　　　　　　　　　　　　　　　　　　　　　　　　　　　d

John Vinelott QC and *Spencer G Maurice* for the parochial church council.

Jeremiah Harman QC, *Gavin Lightman* and *Alan Boyle* for Mr Clark.

　　　　　　　　　　　　　　　　　　　　　　　　　Cur adv vul

18th December. **SIR JOHN PENNYCUICK** delivered the following judgment of　e
the court. This is an appeal from an order of Megarry J[1] dated 26th July 1973. The
plaintiffs in the action are St Edmundsbury and Ipswich Diocesan Board of Finance
and the Parochial Church Council of the Parish of Iken. The defendant is Mr Gabriel
Bertram Clark. Summarily, the action is concerned with the extent of a right of way
over a 30 yard long strip of land leading to Iken churchyard over former glebe land
conveyed by the Bishop of St Edmundsbury and Ipswich to Mr Clark in 1945, the　f
plaintiffs claiming that this is a right of way for all purposes and Mr Clark claiming
that it is a right of way on foot only. Megarry J decided this issue in favour of Mr Clark.
The present appeal is by the parochial church council only. In the course of a full and
careful judgment Megarry J, who had visited the site, made meticulous findings of
fact concerning the site and the user of the strip. On such extracts from the evidence
as have been read to us these findings appear to us to be unexceptionable, and we　g
propose in this judgment to quote from them at length rather than attempt to
paraphrase them. The findings should be read in conjunction with certain large-scale
maps based on the 25 inch ordnance survey which were before the court. We will
first quote Megarry J's finding concerning the lay-out of the site[2]:

> 'Iken is a small and somewhat scattered village some four miles inland from　h
> Aldeburgh. The church stands rather apart from the rest of the village, on the
> south-east bank of the River Alde, which at this point is flowing north and then
> east. The church and its churchyard are rather under an acre in extent. They
> adjoin the former rectory, a substantial house with seven bedrooms, outbuildings
> and so on. With its grounds and the former glebe, the total area is some 23 acres.
> The approach to this complex is by a narrow public highway known as "Church　j
> Lane", running north for some 600 yards from its junction (at Church Corner)
> with an unclassified road which runs in a generally east and west direction.

1　[1973] 3 All ER 902, [1973] 1 WLR 1572
2　[1973] 3 All ER at 907, [1973] 1 WLR at 1576

a   Church Lane comes to an end nearly 300 yards before reaching the banks of the Alde where it flows eastwards: and it is at this northern end of Church Lane that the main area of dispute is located. For reasons that will appear, the church authorities put up the whole of their land, save the church and churchyard, for sale by auction on 31st July 1945. The defendant was the successful bidder, and the contract was duly completed by two conveyances dated 31st December 1945. The land bought by the defendant begins some 100 yards up Church Lane, and
b   consists of the whole of the area on the west of the lane, between the lane and the river, up to the north end of the lane, and also the whole of the headland north of the top of the lane where the river bends round to the east. The church and churchyard are wholly surrounded by the land bought by the defendant. At the northern end of the lane, there is a way that leads from the lane to the church porch. This is about 100 yards long. It runs north-west in a more or less straight
c   line. For the first third of its length the way traverses what, subject to a contention of the plaintiffs, is plainly the defendant's land; and this third is the "disputed strip", the principal bone of contention. In due course I shall return to the details of this disputed strip. The remaining two-thirds of the way is within the church-yard, and, being admittedly church property, comes into the dispute only indirectly.'

d   The sale to Mr Clark was completed by a conveyance dated 31st December 1945. The parties are the bishop (selling as such since the living of Iken was vacant), the Governors of Queen Anne's Bounty (joining to receive the purchase money) and Mr Clark. The parcels are described as follows:

e   'As the same are more particularly described in the Schedule hereto and are for the purposes of identification only more particularly delineated on the map or plan annexed hereto and thereon coloured blue TO HOLD unto the Purchaser in fee simple Subject to the rights of the Coal Commission under the provisions of the Coal Act 1938 and to all rights of way water light and other easements (if any) and to all duties and payments ecclesiastical or civil affecting the same and to the covenants hereinafter contained And subject also to a right of way over
f   the land coloured red on the said plan to and from St. Botolphs Church.'

This wording is by common consent inappropriate for the reservation of a new right of way. But it was accepted at the hearing before Megarry J that its effect was to convey the disputed strip to Mr Clark together with the surrounding land subject to a reservation of a right of way over the disputed strip. It should perhaps be mentioned that the disputed strip forms part of ordnance survey 439, which com-
g   prises Church Lane itself, and that ordnance survey 439 is not mentioned in the schedule to the conveyance, but we doubt if anything now turns on this circumstance. The sole outstanding issue, as we have indicated, is the extent of the right of way reserved by the words which we have quoted from the conveyance.

We will next quote Megarry J's findings concerning the condition of the disputed strip at the date of the 1945 conveyance[1]:
h

'With that in mind, I turn to the physical circumstances in the present case existing at the time of the conveyance to Mr Clark in 1945. Church Lane was then undoubtedly a road, narrow and less well surfaced than it is at present, but still a road, and beyond dispute a public highway. At the northern end of Church Lane the disputed strip and then the church path ran out of it in an approximately straight line in a north-westerly direction, at an angle of about
j   135 degrees. The disputed strip comprised the first 33 yards or thereabouts, and the church path the other 60 yards or so. That much is not disputed in any real degree; but thereafter there is much conflicting evidence, about which I must say something.'

1   [1973] 3 All ER at 926, [1973] 1 WLR at 1596

After referring to a number of photographs which were in evidence, Megarry J
proceeded[1]:   *a*

'With all that in mind, and more, I find the following facts. At the time of
the conveyance to Mr Clark in 1945, the junction between the disputed strip and
the northern end of Church Lane consisted of a hard surface capable of being used
by vehicles. Anyone who travelled northwards up Church Lane would find
the road curving away to the left, towards the church, through something like a   *b*
gap in the hedge on the west side of Church Lane. This gap was a little to the
south of the line of the church path and the rest of the disputed strip. There
was no gate there. The road also widened out a bit at that point, so that one
could to some extent go straight on for a very short distance before reaching a
dead end. If one bore to the left, towards the church, one very soon reached the
north way, running approximately north and south, and so at an angle to the   *c*
line towards the church. This first section of the disputed strip, between the
general line of the western edge of Church Lane and the eastern edge of the
north way, was a mere seven yards long, or thereabouts. Road maintenance
men, repairing Church Lane, did some maintenance work there, and traces of
tar could be found a little beyond, in the first stretch of the disputed strip short
of the crossroads formed by that strip and the north way.'   *d*

Megarry J then referred to the erection by Mr Clark of a field gate and wicket gate
at the south end of the disputed strip in 1947 and the moving back of those gates
towards the church by a few yards in 1948, and proceeded[2]:

'Once the north way had been crossed, however, the terrain for those approaching the church was different. The north-westerly two-thirds of the disputed   *e*
strip lay between chestnut trees, three on the south-west and two on the north-
east. Two of these trees stood opposite each other on each side of the disputed
strip where it ended, just outside the churchyard, and two more some 13 yards
away, opposite each other on each side of the disputed strip and not far from the
crossroads formed by the disputed strip and the north way. The remaining
tree was on the south-west side of the disputed strip, on the edge of the crossroads,   *f*
about seven yards south-east of the nearer tree of the nearer pair. The pair next to
the churchyard stood some 11 to 13 feet apart. Measurements made in my
presence show that today at waist height the trees are 12 feet eight inches apart;
at ground level the trunks are 11 feet nine inches apart, but from exposed root
to exposed root they are ten feet four inches apart. The pair of trees nearer
to the crossroads are a little closer together, though not by more than about   *g*
15 inches. Between the trees at the end of 1945 there ran a path, consisting
mainly of trodden earth. It was covered with rotting leaves, and was a little
"dished", in that it was lower in the centre than at the sides. Beneath the
leaves there seems to have been some gravel or shingle, and perhaps some sand;
but however well covered the path may have been before the war, by 1945 the
covering was irregular and concealed. It gave no indication of being a roadway,   *h*
and looked like a somewhat derelict pathway. The width of the path was
difficult to perceive and at the end of 1945 was probably indeterminate, with no
defined edges and showing little more than the track made by the feet of those
who had used it most recently: but even with the leaves and debris removed,
I do not think that there was anything that could be recognised as a path which
was wider than four feet or four feet six inches. At the north-west end of the   *j*
disputed strip there was a gate between two gateposts. The gateposts, which
appear in photographs taken in 1947, were of a distinctive type, each with a knob

1 [1973] 3 All ER at 926, [1973] 1 WLR at 1596, 1597
2 [1973] 3 All ER at 927, 928, [1973] 1 WLR at 1597, 1598

shaped like an acorn on top of it. Viewed looking towards the church, these posts stood approximately in the middle of the gap between the pair of chestnut trees closest to the churchyard. This segment of the churchyard was (and still is) enclosed by a line of yew bushes, running in a gentle curve. There was a gap of about three feet between the nearest pair of chestnut trees and the line of these yew bushes, the trees thus plainly standing outside the churchyard. The gateposts stood in line between the line of the yew bushes and the line of the nearest chestnut trees. Exact measurements are not possible, but I think I can indicate the position best by notionally proceeding up the chestnut path towards the church, and reaching the pair of chestnuts nearest the church. First, one may take an imaginary line which forms a tangent to the tree trunks on the side nearest the church. Next, about a foot further on or perhaps a little more, one would come to the line of the gate between the two gateposts, which stood, of course, closer together than the tree trunks. Then, about two feet further on, or perhaps a little less, one would come to the line of the roots of the yew bushes forming the approximate boundary of the churchyard. These roots left a gap nearly as wide as the gap between the tree trunks, and so wider than the gap between the gateposts; but branches of the yew bushes projected, and so to some extent narrowed the gap on the line of the yew bushes, and also diminished the gap between the gateposts and the roots of the yew bushes. Anyone who preferred to do so had room to go to and fro from the church not between the gateposts, but outside either gatepost, in the gap between the gatepost and the projecting yew branches, perhaps to some extent brushing those branches aside. As I have said, exact measurements are not possible, but even if the line of the gates was closer to the line of the roots of the yew hedge than I have indicated, I am satisfied that the gates were appreciably outside the churchyard, and stood on rectory land that is now Mr Clark's. The gate itself hung on the more northerly gatepost, that is, the right-hand one, looking at the church.'

Megarry J goes on to recount the collapse of the right-hand gatepost at the churchyard end about 1946, the moving of the gate itself to the left of the left-hand gatepost and the erection by Mr Clark in 1952 of a new pair of gateposts and gates, five feet wide in all, by way of gift to the church, in the same central position as the former gateposts, but rather nearer the church, a fraction outside the line of the roots of the yew-hedge. Megarry J then proceeded[1]:

'Inside the churchyard, there was the church path itself, continuing the line of the chestnut avenue up to the church porch. There are different accounts of the width of the church path, and it may well have varied from time to time, according to whether or not the grass creeping in from the sides, together with daffodils and other plants, were left alone or were removed. Today, from raised edge to raised edge, it is at most about seven feet six inches to eight feet wide, and rather under six feet between such substantial growth of bulbs and grass as there is on each side. In 1945, it was, I think, overgown and in a narrower state, a little wider than the path in the chestnut avenue, but probably little more than five feet wide. It had a gravel surface in rather better condition than the path in the chestnut avenue. Immediately in front of the church porch there is a gravelled area, roughly rectangular in shape. Today, it is rather larger than it was in 1945, when it was something of the order of two or three yards by three or four yards. Certainly it was not large enough for any vehicle (except conceivably a "mini" car) to turn round in without risking encroaching on the grass and graves.'

He next deals with evidence of vehicular use at the time of the conveyance or prior thereto. It should be mentioned that in 1942 the land east of Church Lane

1   [1973] 3 All ER at 928, [1973] 1 WLR at 1599

had been taken over as a battle training area, so one must go back a few years in order to find normal conditions. His findings are as follows[1]:

'Finally, there is the evidence as to the vehicular use of the disputed strip at the time of the conveyance, or prior thereto. Some evidence was given of cars, large and small, being driven up to the church porch before and during the war; but this was admittedly infrequent, and in any case I found it impossible to reconcile this evidence with the physical facts and with other evidence which I accept. The witnesses were speaking of what had occurred 30 years ago, and in that time it is easy enough for events to have become blurred or muddled in the memory. The cars may have stopped in Church Lane instead of going to the porch, or one church may have become confused in recollection with another; and there may be many other explanations. There was also evidence of hearses turning into the first few yards of the disputed strip and halting in the north way; but that, of course, fell far short of the remainder of the disputed strip between the chestnuts. At all events, I found the evidence of vehicular use of the chestnut avenue and church path unconvincing at the time, and even less convincing after the rest of the evidence had been put before me. I have no hesitation in rejecting in toto the whole of the evidence relating to cars using the path between the chestnuts and the church path before 1946. I do not think that the evidence on this was dishonest; but I feel sure that it was confused and mistaken. There is evidence of some vehicular use after the collapse of one of the gateposts, as, for instance, when the church was restored. But such use was comparatively rare, intermittent, and effected only with difficulty, due to the narrowness of the ways; and in any case it cannot affect the construction of the conveyance in 1945.'

The last two sentences which we have read gave rise to considerable discussion. At first sight they read like a finding that there was some vehicular use, albeit rare. The evidence was of user in connection with repairs to the church in 1948 and 1951-52. An examination of this evidence shows it to be outstandingly unacceptable, and we think it more likely that Megarry J was simply putting this evidence out of account rather than accepting it.

We will next refer briefly to the period between 1945 and the issue of the writ in this action in 1971. The church had fallen into disrepair during the war and was reconsecrated in 1952. We have already mentioned the erection by Mr Clark of his own gates to the south end of the disputed strip. Of the gates at the south end, the field gate was kept permanently locked; the wicket gate was kept permanently open. In 1968 a fire caused great damage to the church. The disputed strip was used for bringing up materials by way of first-aid to the church, very properly without objection by Mr Clark. If and when the church comes to be rebuilt, much larger quantities of materials will have to be brought up somehow. For some years the church authorities and Mr Clark lived in amity, but disputes arose, culminating in certain incidents in 1971. We have been asked by both counsel to refrain from expressing any views as to rights and wrongs of those disputes apart from the legal issue before us, and we gladly comply with this request. Indeed, we have no information concerning these disputes apart from that issue.

The writ in this action was issued on 26th July 1971. The statement of claim as originally delivered raised a number of issues, including a claim that the diocesan board of finance is the owner of the disputed strip, but this claim was abandoned at the hearing. So far as now material, the claim is for a mandatory order for removal of the gates at the south end of the disputed strip and an injunction restraining obstruction, this claim being made on the footing of an allegation that the parochial

---

1 [1973] 3 All ER at 928, 929, [1973] 1 WLR at 1599

church council is entitled under the 1945 conveyance to a full free and uninterrupted
a right of way with or without vehicles of all kinds over the disputed strip for all
purposes connected with the church or churchyard.   The defence consists of denials
on the basis of an admission that there is a public right of way on foot over the disputed strip to the church for all purposes connected therewith, including the maintenance and repair of the same and the carriage of coffins.   There is a claim and a
counter-claim for damages with which we are not now concerned.
b   The hearing extended over 30 days in March, April and May 1973.   Some 40
witnesses were called and, as we have said, Megarry J visited the site.   A considerable part of the hearing was occupied with matters of dispute with which we are not
now concerned.   Megarry J gave his judgment on 26th July 1973, dismissing the action,
with a number of ancillary declarations and directions.
     On the appeal to this court, as we have indicated, the diocesan board of finance
c dropped out and the appeal was limited to a single issue, namely, the extent of the
right of way over the disputed strip, i e in effect whether this is a vehicular right of
way or a right of way on foot only.
     Before reading Megarry J's conclusion, we will deal shortly with two matters of
law which figured largely in his judgment and were fully argued before us.   First,
what is the proper approach on the construction of a conveyance containing the
d reservation of a right of way?   We feel no doubt that the proper approach is that
on which the court construes all documents; that is to say, one must construe the
document according to the natural meaning of the words contained in the document
as a whole, read in the light of surrounding circumstances.   In *Cannon v Villars*[1] this
principle was applied by Jessel MR to rights of way in a passage which has often
been quoted and never, so far as we are aware, questioned.   He said[2]:

e

     '. . . the grant of a right of way *per se* and nothing else may be a right of foot-
     way, or it may be a general right of way, that is a right of way not only for people
     on foot but for people on horseback, for carts, carriages, and other vehicles.
     Which it is, is a question of construction of the grant, and that construction will
     of course depend on the circumstances surrounding, so to speak, the execution
f   of the instrument.   Now one of those circumstances, and a very material circum-
     stance, is the nature of the *locus in quo* over which the right of way is granted.
     [Then, after certain illustrations, he went on:] *Prima facie* the grant of a right of
     way is the grant of a right of way having regard to the nature of the road over
     which it is granted and the purpose for which it is intended to be used; and both
     those circumstances may be legitimately called in aid in determining whether
g   it is a general right of way, or a right of way restricted to foot-passengers, or re-
     stricted to foot-passengers and horsemen or cattle, which is generally called a
     drift way or a general right of way for carts, horses, carriages and everything
     else.'

     Counsel for the parochial church council contended that the proper method of
h construction is first to construe the words of the instrument in isolation and then look
at the surrounding circumstances in order to see whether they cut down the prima
facie meaning of the words.   It seems to us that this approach is contrary to well-
established principle.   It is no doubt true that in order to construe an instrument
one looks first at the instrument and no doubt one may form a preliminary impression on such inspection.   But it is not until one has considered the instrument and
j the surrounding circumstances in conjunction that one concludes the process of
construction.   Of course, one may have words so unambiguous that no surrounding
circumstances could affect their construction.   But that is emphatically not the

1   (1878) 8 Ch D 415, [1874-80] All ER Rep 597
2   8 Ch D at 420, 421, [1874-80] All ER Rep at 599

position here, where the reservation is in the loosest terms, i e simply 'right of way'. Indeed, those words call aloud for an examination of the surrounding circumstances and, with all respect, the contention of counsel for the parochial church council, even if well founded, seems to us to lead nowhere in the present case. We do not think a few words quoted from the judgment of Lord Greene MR in *Robinson v Bailey*[1], when read in their context, lend support to this contention.

Second is the maxim 'Omnia praesumuntur contra proferentem' applicable against the vendor or against the purchaser where there is a conveyance subject to the reservation of a new right of way? In view of the full discussion of this question by the learned judge, and of the fact that we do not agree with his conclusion, we think it right to deal fairly fully with it. But it is necessary to make clear that this presumption can only come into play if the court finds itself unable on the material before it to reach a sure conclusion on the construction of a reservation. The presumption is not itself a factor to be taken into account in reaching the conclusion. In the present case we have indeed reached a sure conclusion, and on this footing the presumption never comes into play, so that the view which we are about to express on it is not necessary to the decision of the present case.

The point turns on the true construction of s 65(1) of the Law of Property Act 1925 which enacts as follows:

'A reservation of a legal estate shall operate at law without any execution of the conveyance by the grantee of the legal estate out of which the reservation is made, or any regrant by him, so as to create the legal estate reserved, and so as to vest the same in possession in the person (whether being the grantor or not) for whose benefit the reservation is made.'

Formerly the law was that on a conveyance with words merely reserving an easement, the easement was held to be created, provided that the purchaser executed the conveyance, without the necessity for words of regrant. The law treated the language of reservation as having the same effect as would the language of regrant though there was not in terms a regrant, and in those circumstances regarded the purchaser as the proferens for present purposes. This was a relaxation of the strict requirements for the creation of an easement. (An easement could be created without execution by the purchaser of a conveyance by reference to the Statute of Uses, once s 62 of the Conveyancing Act 1881 removed the technical objection that that statute could not operate to create an easement. This method disappeared with the repeal of the Statute of Uses in the 1925 property legislation, and is not of direct relevance to the present problem: though it is part of the background to the abolition by s 65 of the Law of Property Act 1925 of the need for execution of the conveyance by the purchaser.)

Section 65 must be read in the light, therefore, of two aspects of the preceding law. First: that previously the law was sufficiently relaxed from its prima facie stringency to permit the language of mere reservation to have the effect of a regrant though it was not in truth a regrant by its language. Second: that for this purpose the purchaser must execute the conveyance if an easement was to be created; that is to say, although a regrant in terms was not required. Against that background, are the words in s 65 'without . . . any regrant by' the purchaser to be regarded as altering the law so that the purchaser is no longer to be regarded as the relevant proferens? Or are they to be regarded as merely maintaining for the avoidance of doubt the situation that had been already reached by the development of the law, i e that mere words of reservation could be regarded as having the same effect as would the language of regrant though without there being in terms any purported regrant by the purchaser? We would, apart from authority, construe the words in the latter sense, so

1   [1948] 2 All ER 791 at 795

a that the only relevant change in the law is the absence of the requirement that the
purchaser should execute the conveyance.   We read the section as if it were in effect
saying that whereas an easement could be created by mere words of reservation
without any words of regrant by the purchaser, provided that the purchaser executes
the conveyance, hereafter the easement can be created by mere words of reservation
without any words of regrant by the purchaser even if he does not execute the conveyance; it is not to be said that in the latter event the previous relaxation of the
b strict law has disappeared, so that the language of the conveyance must be more than
the mere language of reservation.   It will be observed that that view keeps in line,
on the relevant point, a post 1925 conveyance executed by the purchaser, which is
apparently not touched by s 65, and one which is executed by him.

The above is our view apart from authority.   What then of authority?   We
start with the fact that Sir Benjamin Cherry, architect of the 1925 property legisla-
c tion, made no reference to this suggested change of principle in the law in the first
edition of Wolstenholme and Cherry's Conveyancing Statutes[1] after the 1925
property legislation.   Further, in more than one case since 1925, judges of high
authority took it for granted that the old principle still prevailed: see *Bulstrode v
Lambert*[2]; *Mason v Clarke* in the Court of Appeal[3] and in the House of Lords[4].
In these cases the contrary was not argued and the judicial statements are not of
d binding authority.   But in *Johnstone v Holdway*[5] (in the Court of Appeal) Upjohn LJ,
giving the judgment of the court, not only in terms restated the old principle but
made it part of the ratio decidendi of his judgment.   He said—

'that the exception and reservation of the mines and minerals was to the
vendor, that is the legal owner, but the exception and reservation of the right
e of way was to the company, the equitable owner.   If the reservation of a right of
way operated strictly as a reservation, then as the company only had an equitable
title, it would seem that only an equitable easement could have been reserved;
but it is clear that an exception and reservation of a right of way in fact operates
by way of regrant by the purchaser to his vendor, and the question, therefore,
is whether as a matter of construction the purchaser granted to the company a
f legal easement or an equitable easement.'

The opposing view was expressed by Megarry J in *Cordell v Second Clanfield Properties Ltd*[6] (on motion and without being referred to *Johnstone v Holdway*[7]) and in
the present case (after a full review of the authorities, including *Johnstone v Holdway*[7]).
He distinguishes *Johnstone v Holdway*[7] as a decision based on mistake and states his own
g conclusion in the following words[8]:

'The fair and natural meaning of s 65(1) seems to me to be that if a vendor
reserves an easement, the reservation is to be effective at law without any actual
or notional regrant by the purchaser, and so without the consequences that
flow from any regrant.   At common law, the rule that a reservation of an ease-
h ment was to be construed against the purchaser depended solely on the notional
regrant.   Apart from that, the words of reservation, being the words of the
vendor, would be construed against the vendor in accordance with the general

j 1   11th Edn (1925-27)
2   [1953] 2 All ER 728 at 731, [1953] 1 WLR 1064 at 1068, per Upjohn J
3   [1954] 1 All ER 189 at 192, [1954] 1 QB 460, at 467, per Denning LJ
4   [1955] 1 All ER 914 at 915, 916, [1955] AC 778 at 786, per Viscount Simonds
5   [1963] 1 All ER 432 at 436, [1963] 1 QB 601 at 612
6   [1968] 3 All ER 746 at 750, [1969] 2 Ch 9 at 15
7   [1963] 1 All ER 432, [1963] 1 QB 601
8   [1973] 3 All ER at 921, [1973] 1 WLR at 1591

principle stated in Norton on Deeds[1], just as an exception or a reservation
of a rent would; it was the fiction of a regrant which made reservation of *a*
easements stand out of line with exceptions and reservations in the strict sense.
With the statutory abolition of the fictitious regrant, reservations of easements
fall into line with the broad and sensible approach that it is for him who wishes
to retain something for himself to see that there is an adequate statement of
what it is that he seeks to retain; and if after considering all the circumstances
of the case there remains any real doubt as to the ambit of the right reserved, *b*
then that doubt should be resolved against the vendor. Accordingly, in this
case I hold that the words "subject also to a right of way over the land coloured
red on the said plan to and from St Botolphs Church" in the 1945 conveyance
should, if their meaning is not otherwise resolved, be construed against the
Church authorities and so in favour of Mr Clark.'

c

We see much force in this reasoning. But we find it impossible to accept Megarry
J's analysis of the decision in *Johnstone v Holdway*[2]. We are not prepared to infer
from the report that experienced and responsible counsel misrepresented the terms
of s 65 to the court and that the judge based his decision on the terms of the section
as so misrepresented. It follows that the decision in *Johnstone v Holdway*[2] is binding
on this court and that we ought to follow it.   *d*
We now return to the present case. Megarry J expressed his conclusion in the
following terms[3]:

'In those circumstances, I have to consider the effect of a reservation in 1945
of "right of way over the land coloured red on the said plan to and from St.
Botolphs Church", the width of that land being nine feet. Neither the chestnut *e*
path nor the church path had been used by vehicles; each was wide enough to
take at any rate vehicles of modest width, but neither was surfaced in such a
way as to indicate vehicular use; neither was wide enough for a vehicle to turn
round in; the terminus ad quem, the space in front of the church porch, was
not large enough to permit the turning round of any save the smallest vehicles
without risk to the grass and graves of the churchyard, a matter of natural con- *f*
cern to church authorities; and above all, the gate and gateposts stood so as to
prevent any vehicle ever reaching the church path, on land which the church
authorities were conveying and not reserving. A conveyance may, of course,
as in *Keefe v Amor*[4], sufficiently indicate that the dominant owner is to be entitled
to insist on the removal of any physical constriction of the way; but I can see no
such indication here. If "right of way" means "right of way on foot", every *g*
word of the reservation could take effect: foot passengers could indeed pass
over the land coloured red and go to and from the church. But if "right of way"
meant "right of way with or without vehicles" and so on, I cannot see how the
words "with ... vehicles" could be given any sensible effect. No vehicle could
ever reach the beginning of the church path while the two gateposts stood, and
they stood on Mr Clark's land. Even if a vehicle had driven right up to the gate, *h*
it would still have been a foot or two short of the beginning of the church path.
Having driven that far on an unsuitable surface the vehicle must of necessity
have backed out. I do not see how such movements could fairly be said to
constitute the exercise of a right of way "to and from St Botolphs Church". In
those circumstances, construing the conveyance against the vendors, as I have held
that I should, it seems to me that there is only one answer, namely, that no *j*

---

1 2nd Edn (1928), pp 127-134
2 [1963] 1 All ER 432, [1963] 1 QB 601
3 [1973] 3 All ER at 929, [1973] 1 WLR at 1599, 1600
4 [1964] 2 All ER 517, [1965] 1 QB 334

vehicular way was reserved. That result seems to me to be achieved whether I may first resort to the physical circumstances as an aid to construing the reservation, or whether I must construe it first and then look to those physical circumstances, though only for the purposes of ascertaining whether the ambit of the way apparently reserved by the words is to be restricted. In my judgment, the way is for pedestrians only, and not for vehicles. If I am wrong about construing a reservation against the grantor, my conclusion is not so unhesitating. Nevertheless, on balance I think the result is the same. True, the gate was by by the churchyard and not between the highway and the entrance to the disputed strip, so that it did not bar access to the way: but it nevertheless made it impossible for vehicles either to reach the church or even to reach the commencement of the church path. This, coupled with the narrowness and condition of the way, seems to me sufficient to restrict the ambit of the right of way "to and from St. Botolphs Church" to a pedestrian access. The contention is not so strong, but it is strong enough. Accordingly, on this alternative footing, I would reach the same conclusion.'

We find Megarry J's comment on the presumption rather perplexing. We should have thought that on his assessment of the surrounding circumstances there was no such doubt as could bring the presumption into play one way or the other. Be that as it may, is there any sufficient ground for reaching a different conclusion?

Counsel for Mr Clark stressed the factors mentioned by Megarry J and referred to evidence in more general terms to the effect that the disputed strip did not look like a road and that one would not think of taking a car along it.

Counsel for the parochial church council relied, above all, on the undoubted facts that the disputed strip is wide enough—nine feet from tree root to tree root—for cars, including lorries, to drive along it without difficulty and that its surface in 1945 was sufficiently firm and even for them to do so. This is an important factor, but far from conclusive. One may well have a strip of land capable of being used by cars but not adapted or appropriate for the passage of cars.

Counsel for the parochial church council relied on another factor which seemed to us of importance, namely, that from time to time building materials would have to be taken to the church and there was no other route available. One would certainly expect the parties to have had this consideration in mind in 1945, when the church was in rather a dilapidated condition. They could not, of course, have foreseen the 1968 fire.

We mention at this point, in order to avoid misunderstanding, that if there is no right of way for vehicles over the disputed strip, the Church authorities may have a vehicular right of way of necessity to the church for the purpose of taking up building materials and the like. This possibility does not arise on the pleadings; but if there be such, it is open to Mr Clark to select any reasonably convenient line, and he has in fact offered a longer vehicular way round to the north of the church for the repairs.

There was some evidence as to the use of a small part of the disputed strip by hearses. But this did not, we think, turn out to be a factor of much importance. No serious difficulty arises in carrying a coffin over this short stretch and it would in any event be met at the entrance to the churchyard and carried into the church. Nor did any point arise as to weddings. In a parish of this size, neither weddings nor funerals are of frequent occurrence. The ordinary churchgoer, arriving by car or on foot, would be negligibly inconvenienced by a few yards extra walk.

Counsel for the parochial church council sought to discount the gate at the churchyard end by pointing out its poor condition in 1945. This is a valid point so far as it goes. Obviously a broken-down wooden gate is of less significance than, for instance, a solid iron barrier. But the gate remains, to our mind, a factor of the first importance. Counsel for the parochial church council referred to cases in which it was held that the owner of a dominant tenement, having once established his right of way, is entitled to remove an obstacle which obstructs it: see *Bulstrode v Lambert*[1]; *Keefe v Amor*[2] in the Court of Appeal. But that does not mean that the existence of the obstruction *a* at the time of the reservation is any the less an important factor in determining whether the right of way has been established at all.

Counsel for the parochial church council advanced an argument to the effect that the gate at the churchyard end, even in its 1945 position, should be regarded as forming part of the boundary between the churchyard and Mr Clark's land, the boundary line forming a slight bow at this point. We think this argument is quite unmain- *b* tainable. Megarry J found that the gate was appreciably outside the direct line of the boundary hedge and the existence of the bow is pure speculation.

Having considered to the best of our ability all the matters which have been put before us, we feel no doubt that Megarry J reached the right conclusion. The surrounding circumstances are a matter of fact lying pre-eminently within the province of the judge who heard the witnesses and visited the site; and, as we have said, we see *c* no ground on which Megarry J's findings of fact can be impugned. The construction of the conveyance is a matter of law to be determined in accordance with the surrounding circumstances as so found. Apart from his view on the presumption, Megarry J seems to us to have stated the law correctly and on his finding of the surrounding circumstances we think he reached the proper conclusion, and we do not think we could usefully elaborate it. It should be observed that although he formed a view on *d* the presumption favourable to Mr Clark, the conclusion, though less unhesitating, would have been the same.

Accordingly, we dismiss the appeal.

Appeal dismissed.   *e*

Solicitors: *Finnis, Christopher Foyer & Co* (for the parochial church council); *Cameron, Kemm, Nordon & Co* (for Mr Clark).

Gordon H Scott Esq Barrister.
                                                                                                    f

1 [1953] 2 All ER 728, [1953] 1 WLR 1064
2 [1964] 2 All ER 517, [1965] 1 QB 334

R v Donnelly

a

COURT OF APPEAL, CRIMINAL DIVISION
JAMES LJ, TALBOT AND MICHAEL DAVIES JJ
14th JANUARY 1975

b *Road traffic – Disqualification for holding licence – Test of competence to drive – Disqualification until driving test retaken – Circumstances not disclosing lack of competence by driver – Whether test should be ordered – Road Traffic Act 1972, s 93(7).*

Section 93(7)[a] of the Road Traffic Act 1972 is not a punitive provision but is intended to protect the public against incompetent drivers. Accordingly the court should
c only exercise its power under s 93(7) to require a person convicted of an offence involving disqualification to pass a driving test where, because of his age, infirmity or the circumstances of the offence, there is reason to suspect that he may not be a competent driver (see p 787 *b to d*, post).

Notes
d For the disqualification of an offender until he passes a driving test, see 33 Halsbury's Laws (3rd Edn) 640, para 1082.
For the Road Traffic Act 1972, s 93, see 42 Halsbury's Statutes (3rd Edn) 1744.

Case referred to in judgment
Ashworth v Johnson [1959] Crim LR 735, QS.
e

Application
On 4th October 1974, in the Crown Court at Kingston-upon-Thames before his Honour Judge Finlay QC, the applicant, Paul Donnelly, pleaded guilty to driving a motor vehicle with a blood-alcohol concentration above the prescribed limit. He was fined £200 with six months' imprisonment in default, and was disqualified from
f driving for 21 months and thereafter until he had taken a driving test. He applied for leave to appeal against sentence. The court treated the hearing of the application as the hearing of the appeal. The facts are set out in the judgment.

S O'Malley for the applicant.
The Crown was not represented.
g

TALBOT J delivered the following judgment of the court at the invitation of James LJ. This is an application for leave to appeal against sentence. On 4th October at Kingston-upon-Thames Crown Court, the applicant pleaded guilty to an offence of driving a motor vehicle with a blood alcohol concentration above the prescribed limit.
h The learned judge who presided fined him £200 with six months' imprisonment in default, disqualified him from driving for a period of 21 months and added, under the powers contained in s 93(7) of the Road Traffic Act 1972, an order that the applicant must pass a test of competence before he commences to drive. In addition his licence was endorsed and he was ordered to pay the sum of £44·60 prosecution costs.
The facts of the matter as appear from the evidence of two police officers were these.
j On 16th January 1974 at 2.00 am, these two police officers were in a patrol car when

---

a Section 93(7), so far as material, provides: 'Where a person is convicted of an offence involving obligatory or discretionary disqualification the court may, whether or not he has previously passed the test of competence to drive prescribed under this Act, and whether or not the court makes an order under the foregoing provisions of this section, order him to be disqualified until he has, since the date of the order, passed that test . . .'   DD

they saw a Ford Capri motor car being driven along Queen's Road from Weybridge   *a*
to Horsham. At a junction they noticed that it braked very sharply and then turned
right without any signal being given. So the police car then followed. They managed
to catch up with it. It was driven into a narrow road, a road which was described by
the police officers as very twisty, but in fact having seen the Ordnance Survey plan of
this area with a scale of six inches to a mile, the road is not twisty, though there are
two or three sharp angle turns. But the road is narrow, being about 14 feet wide.
The Capri was driven along the centre of the road at a speed of about 40 mph. The   *b*
officers said that there were a number of private driveways coming on to this narrow
road. They eventually caught up with the Capri motor car, which of course was
driven by the applicant, when it reached his home.

When the applicant was spoken to, the officers noticed that he had been drinking.
The breathalyser test was applied, and as a result of the necessary procedures, it was
discovered that he had in his blood 229 milligrammes of alcohol per 100 millilitres of   *c*
blood.

This applicant is 52 years of age, a married man, and until recently, we are told by
counsel, he had been in a job as a chartered accountant, but he has now left that firm
and is seeking other similar employment. It appears that he has been driving
for a period of some 25 years, and that he has no previous convictions whatsoever. In
those circumstances counsel has submitted that the fine of £200 was excessive, as was   *d*
the period of 21 months' disqualification. He pointed out the short journey; it appears
from the Ordnance Survey map to be a distance of some 1½ miles. He pointed out that
the offence occurred in the early hours of the morning, when there was no other
traffic about. He pointed out that the whole journey only lasted some three or four
minutes. This offence, counsel told us, arose from drink which the applicant had
taken at a committee meeting of the local golf club. He told us, and we accept it of   *e*
course, that there was no anticipation that drink would be taken, it was not intended
to be a drinking session, but in fact because of somebody's birthday, drink was
produced and the applicant came to take too much to drink.

The learned judge pointed out, perfectly rightly, that what the applicant had done
was to take almost three times more than the permitted quantity and that it was—
and he rightly described it as such—a grossly excessive amount. Indeed he went so far   *f*
as to say that perhaps in some cases with excessive amounts like that, the court might
have to consider the question of a custodial sentence.

However, this applicant, as I have said, has an excellent driving record, and the
circumstances were such as I have outlined in this judgment. In those circumstances
what the court has first to address its mind is to the question of fine. This applicant
was a gentleman earning, we are told, in his last employment some £10,000. It is not   *g*
suggested that the fine was disproportionate to his means. This court has reached the
conclusion that it would not be right, nor does the court find it right, to say that that
amount of £200 was excessive.

I turn now to the question of disqualification. It is perfectly true that where excessive
amounts of alcohol are taken so that the driver has a great excess in his blood stream,
the period of disqualification will get longer than the statutory period of 12 months.   *h*
It is in some ways difficult to fault the learned judge's view in this case. But this
court has felt it right to pay particular attention to the very excellent driving record
of this applicant and the fact that the whole period when he was at the wheel was not
more than three minutes, the distance was short and there was no suggestion that there
was any traffic in the town, and it is able to say that in those circumstances while the
period of disqualification should be more than 12 months, it does not feel it right that   *j*
it should have gone as far as 21 months. The court therefore proposes to reduce that
period of disqualification by six months to 15 months.

That leaves the further question relating to the order that he should take a test of
competence to drive. Looking through the facts of the matter, this court can find no
reason why the court should have ordered such a test to be taken. The object of the

enactment of s 93(7) of the Road Traffic Act is to test drivers who may become dis-
a qualified and who may for some reason show some lack of competence or that some
efficiency relating to their driving should be further tested.

This question, it was said by Michael Davies J, has arisen before. Counsel for the
applicant during the adjournment has found one of the cases in which it did arise:
Ashworth v Johnson[1]. It is in fact a decision of Waller J when he was the recorder of
Sheffield City Quarter Sessions. In dealing with this very question and referring to the
b powers which were then contained in s 6(3) of the Road Traffic Act 1934, he said[2]—

'that the powers of the court under section 6(3) of the 1934 Act should be used
in respect of people who are growing old or infirm or who show in the circumstances of the offence some kind of incompetence which requires looking into.
These powers were to be contrasted with the powers of disqualification for a
c specified period which was part of the penalty imposed by the court. Section 6(3)
on the other hand, was not a punitive section, but was intended as a section for
the protection of the public against incompetent drivers.'

This court agrees with the observations there expressed, and also says that s 93(7) of
the 1972 Act is not a punitive section. In those circumstances, there being, so far as the
court can see, no reason for questioning the competence of the applicant, there could
have been no reason to order the applicant to pass a further test. As far as that order
d is concerned, it will be quashed.

Accordingly we grant leave to appeal, and with the consent of counsel treat this
application as the appeal. The order of the Crown Court will be varied so as to vary
the period of disqualification to 15 months and quash the order for a test to be taken.

e *Application granted; appeal allowed in part; sentence varied.*

Solicitors: *Braby & Waller* (for the applicant).

Sepala Munasinghe Esq Barrister.

d

Bone and another v Seale

COURT OF APPEAL, CIVIL DIVISION
STEPHENSON, SCARMAN AND ORMROD LJJ
f 25th, 26th NOVEMBER 1974

*Nuisance – Damages – Measure of damages – Smell – Loss of amenity – Non-pecuniary
damage – Smell from neighbouring pig farm interfering with plaintiffs' enjoyment of property
– Nuisance continuing intermittently for period of over 12½ years – Analogy with damages for
loss of amenity in personal injury cases – Award of damages at £500 a year – Whether
g award excessive.*

In 1955 the defendant bought a farm which thereafter he ran as a pig farm. The
two plaintiffs were the owners of neighbouring properties. In 1958 the plaintiffs
brought an action to restrain the defendant from committing a nuisance by the smell
of his pig farm. The smell was caused by the storing of pig manure and the boiling
j of pig swill. A consent order was made whereby the plaintiffs were awarded £200
damages and the defendant gave an undertaking to take certain steps to minimise
the discharge of smells from the farm. Despite the changes made by the defendant
in the way he ran his farm, and to some extent because of the increase in his pig herd

1   [1959] Crim LR 735
2   [1959] Crim LR at 736

from 300 in 1955 to over 700, those changes did not reduce the offensive smells. In
the intervening years there were repeated complaints to the local authority by the   *a*
plaintiffs and others.   In December 1968 the plaintiffs brought an action claiming an
injunction to restrain the defendant from carrying on the business of pig farming so
as or in such manner as by the discharge of noxious and offensive vapours or smell
or otherwise to cause a nuisance to the respective properties of the plaintiffs, and
damages for nuisance and injury to property.   The trial judge found that the
smell caused by the boiling swill and the accumulation of pig manure was so offen-   *b*
sive as to constitute an intolerable nuisance and that the nuisance was a serious
nuisance which had come and gone by day and by night over a period of some 12½
years. He held, however, that the plaintiffs had failed to prove diminution in the value
of their property as a result of the persistent smell. He granted an injunction and
awarded each of the plaintiffs £6,324·66 damages at the rate of £500 per annum over
the period of 12½ years for loss of amenity from the smell. The defendant appealed,   *c*
contending, inter alia, that the award of damages was too high.

Held – The award of £6,000 for loss of amenity because of the smell was an entirely
erroneous estimate of the damage sustained by the plaintiffs.   Although no direct
comparison could be drawn with the damages awarded in personal injury cases, the
sort of damages awarded in such cases for loss of the sense of smell showed that an   *d*
award calculated at the rate of £500 a year for nuisance by smell was altogether out of
proportion to the damage suffered.   Accordingly the appeal against the quantum
of damages would be allowed and an award of £1,000 for each plaintiff substituted
(see p 793 *e* to p 794 *b* and *h* to p 795 *c e f* and *j* to p 796 *a*, post).
    Dictum of Greer LJ in *Flint v Lovell* [1934] All ER Rep at 202, 203 applied.

e

Note
For damages for nuisance, see 28 Halsbury's Laws (3rd Edn) 164, 165, paras 234-238,
and for cases on the subject, see 36 Digest (Repl) 325, 326, *693-699*.

Cases referred to in judgments   *f*
Aldred's Case (1610) 9 Co Rep 57b, 77 ER 816.
Flint v Lovell [1935] 1 KB 354, [1934] All ER Rep 200, 104 LJKB 199, 152 LT 231, CA,
    17 Digest (Reissue) 227, *988*.
Halsey v Esso Petroleum Co Ltd [1961] 2 All ER 145, [1961] 1 WLR 683, Digest (Cont
    Vol A) 1214, *108b*.
Hinz v Berry [1970] 1 All ER 1074, [1970] 2 QB 40, [1970] 2 WLR 684, CA, 17 Digest   *g*
    (Reissue) 147, *391*.
McCarthy v Coldair Ltd [1951] 2 TLR 1226, 95 Sol Jo 711, 50 LGR 85, CA, 24 Digest
    (Repl) 1065, *272*.
West (H) & Son Ltd v Shephard [1963] 2 All ER 625, [1964] AC 326, [1963] 2 WLR 1359,
    HL, Digest (Cont Vol A) 1191, *1053c*.

Case also cited   *h*
Davies v Powell Duffryn Associated Collieries Ltd (No 2) [1942] 1 All ER 657, [1942] AC
    601, HL.

Appeal
This was an appeal by the defendant, David Seale, against the judgment of Walton J
given on 19th October 1973 whereby he granted an injunction restraining the defen-   *j*
ant from doing (whether by himself or by his servants workmen or agents or any
of them or otherwise howsoever) the following acts or any of them, i e carrying
on or permitting to be carried on on Holmes Farm, Betchworth, Surrey, the business
of farming so as or in such manner as by the discharge of noxious or offensive vapours
or smells or otherwise to cause a nuisance or injury to the plaintiffs, Stanley Arthur

Bone and Alan Watson Johnstone White, or either of them or to their properties
a respectively known as Little Coombe, Betchworth, and Ronda, Pebble Hill Road,
Betchworth, and ordered the defendant to pay to each of the plaintiffs the sum of
£6,324·66 being damages at the rate of £500 per annum from 24th February 1961
down to and including 19th October 1973. The operation of the injunction was
suspended until after 18th January 1974. The facts are set out in the judgment of
Stephenson LJ.
b

R N Titheridge QC and *Michael Mark* for the defendant.
J A R Finlay QC and *Alan Boyle* for the plaintiffs.

STEPHENSON LJ.   This is an appeal from a judgment of Walton J, given on
c 19th October 1973, by which he granted an injunction restraining the defendant, Mr
Seale—

'from doing (whether by himself or by his servants workmen or agents or any
of them or otherwise howsoever) the following acts or any of them that is to say
carrying on or permitting to be carried on upon Holmes Farm, Betchworth,
Surrey, the business of farming so as or in such manner as by the discharge of
d noxious or offensive vapours or smells or otherwise to cause a nuisance or injury
to the Plaintiffs or either of them or to their said properties respectively known as
"Little Coombe", Betchworth aforesaid and Ronda, Pebble Hill Road, Betchworth aforesaid BUT the operation of this Injunction is to be suspended until after
18th January 1974. AND IT IS ORDERED that the Defendant do pay to each of the
Plaintiffs the sum of Six thousand three hundred and twenty four pounds and
e sixty six pence being damages at the rate of Five hundred pounds per annum
from 24th February, 1961 down to and including 19th October 1973',

and he ordered the defendant to pay the plaintiffs the costs of the action.
The history of this matter is a long one, but I think it can be shortly summarised. In
1946 the plaintiff Bone went to live at Little Coombe, Betchworth; in January 1954,
f the plaintiff White went to live at Ronda in the same village. In 1955 the defendant
bought Holmes Farm. Holmes Farm lies just to the north-west of Mr Bone's house,
Little Coombe, and to the south-east of Mr White's premises, Ronda. There is,
between Mr White's premises and Holmes Farm, a small house, or cottage, called
Whiteholm, but he is very nearly as near to the farm buildings of Holmes Farm
as is Mr Bone. Holmes Farm was run by the defendant after his arrival in 1955 as
g a pig farm, and when he first came there the evidence is that he had something
like 300 pigs, not more. The farm included a large field, Ordnance Survey no 2373,
to the east of Ronda and to the north and north-east of Little Coombe.
From a fairly early period, as the judge found, Mr White and the defendant got
across one another; it appears that the reason why they got across one another was
principally, if not entirely, the smell that came from the defendant's farm.
h As early as 1958 Mr Bone and Mr White, the plaintiffs in this action, joined with a
Mr Ribchester, who lived across the other side of the road at the premises then called
Quaintways, but now called Pebble Hill Cottage, due west of the defendant's pig-
geries at Holmes Farm, in an action against the defendant for an injunction to restrain
him from committing a nuisance by the smell of his pig farm, and for damages. Mrs
Ribchester was substituted for Mr Ribchester as their co-plaintiff, apparently because
j she was the owner of Quaintways, and Mr Ribchester has died since that action was
brought.
The complaint made in that action was that in particular the defendant had caused—

'such discharge of vapours and smells . . . by the following acts or some or one
of them that is to say:— . . . (ii) storing or permitting to accumulate pig dung or
manure on the said farm; (iii) boiling pig swill on the said farm',

or in the buildings, so as to cause annoyance and discomfort to the plaintiffs. There
was also an allegation that the noxious vapours or smells coming from those sources   *a*
were dangerous to the health of the plaintiffs and occupiers of those properties. That
action never came to trial; it was settled, and settled on terms which are of some
importance.

By a consent order before Danckwerts J, dated 17th November 1959, the court
ordered the defendant to pay to the plaintiffs, all three of them, £200 in all by way of
damages in full satisfaction of all claims arising in the action; that order was made   *b*
on the plaintiffs and defendant by their counsel consenting to the order and on the
defendant by his counsel undertaking three things that he would not do; undertaking
that he—

> 'will not (whether by himself or by his servants or agents or any of them or
> otherwise howsoever) do the following acts or any of them that is to say (1) store   *c*
> pig manure on the Defendant's property Holmes Farm, Betchworth, Surrey at
> any point within 100 yards of the present boundaries of the properties known as
> "Little Coombe" . . . "Quaintways" . . . and "Ronda", . . . Betchworth aforesaid . . .
> (2) boil pig feed stuffs on Holmes Farm aforesaid otherwise than with the use of
> either (a) an Airwick apparatus (the same to be maintained in effective working
> order) or (b) some other effective apparatus or equipment and (3) conduct any   *d*
> pig farming and other farming carried on at Holmes Farm aforesaid except in
> such a manner as and after taking such steps as may be reasonably necessary
> to minimise the discharge of vapour and smells therefrom.'

Those three undertakings and that small sum of damages was the agreed result of
that first action and, as the learned judge said in his judgment, the effect of that was   *e*
that the plaintiffs won the war, but they lost the peace treaty and lost it badly. They
lost it badly because the smell, putting the matter shortly, continued to be offensive
to the plaintiffs; and indeed, they took legal advice and took the defendant to court to
commit him to prison for breach of the first undertaking. As the judge pointed out,
they were in obvious difficulty in proving a breach of the second undertaking, because
the defendant was using Alamast, which was as effective or ineffective as Airwick,   *f*
but they had no such difficulty in proving a breach of the first undertaking; indeed,
the defendant admitted the breach of the first undertaking and moved his manure
back within the limit of 100 yards from the boundary fixed by the undertaking,
apologising to the court and avoiding going to prison. That was in February 1961.

The plaintiffs' case is that since those abortive proceedings in 1961, things have not
got any better and that although there have been changes made by the defendant in   *g*
the way in which he has run his farm, those changes have not improved the situation
or, by and large, reduced the offensive smells which interfere with their enjoyment of their properties, Little Coombe and Pebble Hill Cottage, as Quaintways is
now called.

The main change in the position has been that the number of pigs kept by the
defendant at Holmes Farm has grown from something like 300 to 700; one witness   *h*
put it as high as 800, but the judge found that it was 700. It is true, as the learned
judge found, that the defendant has made certain changes in the way in which he has
dealt with pig manure; that is to say, after complaints from the local authority he
did burn the huts in which pigs were kept very near the boundary of Little Coombe
and cleaned the place up. He also took certain steps, not, it was said, with a view
to minimising smell but for other reasons; however that may be, he did take *j*
certain steps with regard to the swill of which the plaintiffs had complained. Those
steps involved first of all—I think they were all taken in 1966—replacing the previous
method of boiling swill in several tanks by a method which required boiling it in one
tank only; then a change in the method of delivering the swill to the pigs by piping it
instead of carrying it by buckets; and he also slowed down the process of boiling,

fast boiling apparently being more smelly than slow boiling of the swill, and he
a boiled once a day only instead of twice.

In spite of these changes, and perhaps to some extent because of the increase in the
number of pigs, there were, over the intervening years, repeated complaints to the
local authority, of which it is not necessary for me to go into any great detail. Two
consecutive officers from the local authority, a Mr Atkinson and a Mr Ayling, were
called in. Mr Atkinson impressed the judge; Mr Ayling did not. Mr Ayling took over
b from Mr Atkinson in 1966. Mr Atkinson and Mr Ayling were mainly concerned
with the question whether the way in which the pig farm was carried on constituted
a public health nuisance; in other words, was it a danger to the health of the neighbourhood? The learned judge held that Mr Atkinson's test of a public health nuisance
was whether it was a nuisance that caused risk of infection, and he never found anything going on in that pig farm which caused infection or danger to the health of the
c neighbourhood. Mr Ayling was led to formulate, perhaps unwisely, a higher test.
His test apparently was that nothing in the way of smells was a nuisance to public
health unless it so nauseated the smeller that he vomited. The learned judge did not
find that a very helpful test; whatever its value as a test of what was a nuisance contrary
to the Public Health Acts, it did not help the judge to decide whether the smells that
were present constituted a nuisance in the sense in which the law uses that word,
d namely something which interferes with the reasonable enjoyment of property.
But that there was a smell, which annoyed and offended not only the two plaintiffs
but others, including their families and visitors, is of course amply corroborated by
the fact that the public health service inspectors were being called in repeatedly to
come in and look at, and no doubt to smell, what went on at Holmes Farm.

In 1967 a public health notice was served on the defendant in respect of these huts,
e to which I shall return; having made changes in the way in which the swill was boiled
in 1966, as a result of action by the local authority he removed these huts in 1967 or
early 1968. Apparently he also ploughed up some fields.

In spite of what was done this action was brought by the plaintiffs against the defendant on 12th December 1968; in the action the plaintiffs' claim is, as it was when they
had joined with Mrs Ribchester in 1958, a claim for an injunction—
f

> 'to restrain the defendant from carrying on or permitting to be carried on upon
> his farm Holmes Farm, Betchworth, Surrey, the business of pig farming so as or
> in such manner as by the discharge of noxious or offensive vapours or smells or
> otherwise to cause a nuisance or injury to the respective properties of the plain-
> tiffs or to the plaintiffs respectively or the members of the plaintiffs' respective
g
> families',

and there is a claim for damages for nuisance and injury to property.

In the course of the statement of claim, the plaintiffs set out the previous proceedings,
the writ of 19th September 1958, the consent order of 17th November 1959 and an
order on a motion before Pennycuick J of 24th February 1961 that the defendant
should be committed to prison which was in effect not ordered to be carried out; and
h para 9 of the statement of claim went on in this way:

> 'Notwithstanding the undertaking on the part of the Defendant incorporated
> in the said Order dated 17th November, 1959 the Defendant has since the date of
> the Order dated 24th February, 1961 hereinbefore mentioned carried on the said
> business of pig farming at Holmes Farm aforesaid in such manner that at all
j material times since the date of the Order last mentioned or alternatively during
> very many periods amounting in the aggregate to the greater part of the period
> between the date last mentioned and the issue of the Writ herein the Defendant
> has wrongfully discharged or permitted to be discharged from the Defendant's
> said property over the said respective properties of the Plaintiffs noxious or
> offensive vapours or smells.'

Then particulars were given; they are particulars which I think it is unnecessary for me to read, but they did put the claim really under two heads of smell. One was the *a* smell from the accumulated urine and excreta of the pigs and the other was the smell from the boiling pig swill. Those are at any rate the two main heads of complaint, and the plaintiffs allege, as they alleged in the previous action, that those matters caused annoyance and discomfort to them and that the vapours or smells were not only noxious but dangerous to the health of the occupiers of the plaintiffs' properties; and as I have said, in their statement of claim, as well as in this injunction, they *b* sought to restrain this continued nuisance. The allegations are there particularised, and there were further claims of interference with physical well-being, sleep and so on, and of the smell of a bonfire, which do not figure in this appeal.

The learned judge tried this case for seven days in October 1973; the evidence on both sides extended over five days, concluding on 12th October. On 18th October the judge gave his reserved judgment in the terms that I have already set out. Against *c* that judgment this appeal has been brought by a notice dated 21st January 1974, which sets out in considerable detail the grounds of this appeal.

They can be summarised under three heads: [His Lordship, after referring to *Aldred's Case*[1], held that the first ground of appeal, a plea of res judicata, failed. He then considered the second ground of appeal, i e that the finding of the judge that there had been an intolerable nuisance by smell over the years was against the *d* weight of the evidence. Having summarised the evidence his Lordship said:] There was a considerable weight of evidence, making every allowance for hypersensitivity and making every allowance for exaggeration, that these two sources, boiling swill and the accumulation of pig manure, were so offensive as to constitute an intolerable nuisance over the years. It was an intermittent nuisance; it was a nuisance which no doubt those who had to live with it tended to exaggerate. But it was a nuisance; it *e* was a serious nuisance, coming and going by day and by night, over a period of something like 12½ years.

There was evidence which it is difficult to reconcile with the evidence of witnesses called by the plaintiffs (of whom one, as I have said, was on subpoena); but I think the learned judge was entitled to find that on a balance of probability, accepting as honest the evidence that was given by the plaintiffs and their witnesses, there was a nuisance *f* and that the defendant really went on his way untroubled, as the judge put it, taking the line that if he used Alamast in the boiling of the swill he had done all he could and if the smell went on after that he could not help it; he could not do any more, he had to run his pig farm; he had done what the local authority required him to do about the huts, but pigs will urinate and defecate and he did his best to clear pig manure away; if it was offensive to the neighbours, he really could not do any more about it. *g* That, as I understand it, is the effect of the evidence that was very carefully reviewed by the learned judge, and as I said, that is not enough to acquit the defendant; he created and continued a nuisance and it seems to me that on the second ground, as on the first, this appeal must fail.

On the third ground, that the damages awarded by the judge were far too high, it seems to me that this court has a very difficult task to perform. It has to ask *h* itself: what is the measure of damages for a nuisance of this kind? I start by considering whether there is really any authority which gives us, or which would have given the learned judge, any guidance. The only authority which has been cited in this court is the decision of Veale J in *Halsey v Esso Petroleum Co Ltd*[2]. That was a very different case of an unfortunate plaintiff living in Fulham who had to put up with smells, vibration and noise, by day and night, to an extent which very seriously interfered *j* with his comfort and convenience over a period of something like five years. In 1961 the learned judge gave him, for all that, damages of £200. I do not think it could be

---

1   (1610) 9 Co Rep 57b
2   [1961] 2 All ER 145, [1961] 1 WLR 683

a suggested that that was a high figure, even in those days; if it had not been coupled with an injunction, it might well have been higher.

Is there any other guide to which we can turn in considering whether the judge's figure of over £6,000 for each of these plaintiffs is the right sort of figure? It is a figure which I think struck each member of this court rather as the figure in *McCarthy v Cold-air Ltd*[1] struck Denning LJ, and led us to say to ourselves something like: 'Good gracious me—as high as that!'

b That figure of over £6,000 for what is a nuisance and is offensive but no more—something which is rightly described as a nuisance—does seem at first blush to be a very high figure, and counsel for the defendant has asked us to say that it is a figure which is so high that this court cannot uphold it. We accept the test long ago laid down by Greer LJ in *Flint v Lovell*[2]. In that case Greer LJ said[3]:

c   'I think it right to say that this Court would be disinclined to reverse the finding of a trial judge as to the amount of damages merely because they think that if they had tried the case in the first instance they would have given a lesser sum. In order to justify reversing the trial judge on the question of the amount of damages it will generally be necessary that this Court should be con-vinced either that the judge acted upon some wrong principle of law, or that

d   the amount awarded was so extremely high or so very small as to make it, in the judgment of this court, an entirely erroneous estimate of the damage [sic] to which the plaintiff is entitled.'

That test was repeated by Lord Pearson, with the agreement of Lord Denning MR and Sir Gordon Willmer, in *Hinz v Berry*[4], to which counsel for the plaintiffs also referred.

e It is difficult to find an analogy to damages for interference with the enjoyment of property. In this case, efforts to prove diminution in the value of the property as a result of this persistent smell over the years failed. The damages awarded by the learned judge were damages simply for loss of amenity from the smells as they affected the plaintiffs living on their property; and of course their enjoyment of their own property was indirectly affected by these smells inasmuch as it affected their

f visitors and members of their families. The nearest analogy would seem to be the damages which are awarded almost daily for loss of amenity in personal injury cases; it does seem to me that there is perhaps a closer analogy than at first sight appears between losing the enjoyment of your property as a result of some interference by smell or by noise caused by a next door neighbour, and losing an amenity as a result of a personal injury. Is it possible to equate loss of sense of smell

g as a result of the negligence of a defendant motor driver with having to put up with positive smells as a result of a nuisance created by a negligent neighbour? There is, as it seems to me, some parallel between the loss of amenity which is caused by personal injury and the loss of amenity which is caused by a nuisance of this kind. If a parallel is drawn between those two losses, it is at once confirmed that this figure is much too high. It is the kind of figure that would only be given for a serious and

h permanent loss of amenity as the result of a very serious injury, perhaps in the case of a young person. Here we have to remember that the loss of amenity which has to be quantified in pounds and pence extends over a long period—a period of 12½ years—but it must not take account of any future loss.

Doing the best I can, and not adopting (although I am not saying that it was not helpful) the approach that the learned judge made, of finding an annual sum and then

j multiplying it by the period over which the nuisance is being continued, I think the

1   [1951] 2 TLR 1226
2   [1935] 1 KB 354, [1934] All ER Rep 200
3   [1935] 1 KB at 360, [1934] All ER Rep at 202, 203
4   [1970] 1 All ER 1074, [1970] 2 QB 40

sort of figure that ought to have been awarded by the learned judge in this case in
respect of inconvenience, discomfort and annoyance caused by these offensive smells *a*
on and off over the years from February 1961 to October 1973, is the round sum of
£1,000 to each plaintiff.

I would therefore dismiss the appeal insofar as it relates to the judgment and the
injunction, and I would allow it insofar as it relates to the award of damages, varying
the award of damages to the sum of £1,000 in each case.

b

SCARMAN LJ. I agree and will add a few words, only on the one issue on which
we are differing from the trial judge, namely the issue as to the measure of damages
to be awarded to the two plaintiffs.

The judge awarded to each plaintiff the sum of £6,324·66 damages for nuisance by
smell. There was no pecuniary loss; there was no damage to property and no injury *c*
to health; in those circumstances damages were wholly at large and were to be
awarded for a non-pecuniary loss analogous to loss of amenity in personal injury
litigation.

Nuisance is a wrong to property, but it is well recognised that even when there is
no physical damage to property it may cause annoyance, inconvenience and discomfort to the occupier of the property in his enjoyment of it. As Mr McGregor says *d*
in his work on Damages[1]:

> 'When there is a claim for damages in respect of non-pecuniary loss caused by
> nuisance, recovery of damages is allowable and may be regarded as part of the
> normal measure of damages.'

In such a case as this, therefore, we are thrown back to general principles.   *e*

What is the relevant general principle? I think it is that to which Lord Morris of
Borth-y-Gest referred in the course of his speech in *H West & Son Ltd v Shephard*[2].
That was a case of very severe personal injury, but, speaking of the difficulty of
awarding damages where there is no financial yardstick, he said simply[3]: 'All that
judges and courts can do is to award sums which must be regarded as giving reasonable
compensation.'   *f*

Such is the principle, but the difficulty remains: what is reasonable? As Stephenson
LJ has mentioned, there is very little guidance in the case law. In *Halsey v Esso Petroleum Co Ltd*[4], to which Stephenson LJ has referred, Veale J considered £200 appropriate
damages for what, on reading the case, one would think was a gross interference with
comfort and enjoyment of property over a period of five years or thereabouts.
Nevertheless, there is in that case an indication of what one learned judge thought *g*
appropriate in a case of nuisance by noise and smell in 1961, and, unless it can be
said that his estimate was itself wholly erroneous, it is something we must bear in
mind when attempting to adopt a consistent legal pattern in the assessment of
damages at large.

Where else can one go to for assistance as to what is reasonable? As Stephenson LJ
has indicated, it is appropriate to go to personal injury litigation and to note the sort *h*
of figure that judges award for the element of loss of amenity. It is difficult to be
precise in such matters, and I think not helpful to refer to specific cases. But the
indications, both from one's own experience and from such works as have collated
damages in these cases, are that £6,000 for 12 years' discomfort in a matter of smell is
out of all proportion to awards for comparable loss of amenity in that class of case.

It is not, I think, possible to say that we must adopt, or seek to adopt, any rigid *j*
standard of comparison between a nuisance case and personal injury litigation.

1   13th Edn (1972), para 1063
2   [1963] 2 All ER 625, [1964] AC 326
3   [1963] 2 All ER at 631, [1964] AC at 346
4   [1961] 2 All ER 145, [1961] 1 WLR 683

Nevertheless, overall the law ought to remain consistent when it is dealing with
a analogous situations.

I find, therefore, both in Veale J's decision and in the general approach of judges to
the loss of amenity element in damages in personal injury litigation, some indication
that the damages awarded in this case were unreasonable.

But that in itself cannot be enough to entitle this court to disturb the award of the
trial judge. We have to go as far as Stephenson LJ has mentioned when he quoted the
b well-known passage from the judgment of Greer LJ in *Flint v Lovell*[1]. Was there here
an entirely erroneous estimate of the damage sustained by the two plaintiffs? This
must be a matter of impression—impression derived from experience and a general
knowledge of the way in which the law handles analogous claims.

One must bear in mind also a further general principle, that, when one is removed
from the world of pecuniary loss and is attempting to measure damages for non-
c pecuniary loss, an element in reasonableness is the fairness of the compensation to be
awarded. There must be moderation; some attention must be paid to the rights of
the offending defendant as well as to the rights of the injured plaintiff.

Approaching this question of impression with those principles at the back of my
mind, I ask myself the question: in the circumstances of this case was this award of
£6,000 odd to the plaintiffs an entirely erroneous estimate of the damage sustained?
d There was an intolerable nuisance but it was only a nuisance; it was endured admittedly for 12 years but it was intermittent. Clearly it varied in intensity and sometimes
it was wholly absent; these variations depended on the direction of the wind and the
change of the seasons.

At the end of the day, as at the beginning of the day, I find myself saying that the
sum awarded is altogether too much. If an appeal court, when damages are at large,
e reaches that conclusion, then in my judgment it must interfere; it must set aside
the award as being an entirely erroneous estimate, and substitute a figure which
accords with the reasonable requirements of the facts of the case.

When I get that far, I agree with Stephenson LJ that the appropriate figure is £1,000
for each plaintiff. It must of course be remembered that this figure is solely in respect
of past events; for in a nuisance action no damages are awarded in respect of the
f future, save in the exceptional case where they are a substitute for an injunction.

ORMROD LJ. I agree, and would only add a few words on the third point.

It is not a case, or a question, of making anything approaching a precise or accurate
comparison between damages awarded in one set of circumstances and damages
awarded in another; in my judgment that type of comparison is more misleading
g than anything else. All one can do in a particular set of circumstances is to look at
what sort of figures are awarded in other cases, and in that way get some sense of the
order of magnitude which the sum of damages ought to follow, bearing also in mind
the questions of reasonableness and fairness, which in this type of case I think are
extremely important.

h I doubt whether Greer LJ's addition of the adverb 'wholly' to 'erroneous', adds much
to the task of an appellant appealing against an award of damages. I am tempted to
agree with Diplock LJ's description of it as a vituperative adverb.

I think, looking at this case as a whole, that the award of the learned judge of
damages at the rate of £500 a year, is entirely out of proportion to the damage
suffered by the plaintiffs in this case. It amounts to an enormous sum over 12 years,
j although of course one has to consider the value of their houses and the value of their
pleasure in their houses.

I have no hesitation in saying that the sum awarded was erroneous to such an extent
that it requires the interference of this court and, for the reasons that have been given

---

1   [1935] 1 KB 354 at 360, [1934] All ER Rep 200 at 202, 203

by Stephenson LJ, I agree with the figure proposed of £1,000 to each plaintiff. I do not, in agreeing that figure, necessarily relate it on any precise basis to the damages *a* awarded in personal injury cases; all one can do is to look at them and keep them at the back of one's mind in arriving at this sort of figure.

I agree that the appeal should be allowed in the way proposed by Stephenson LJ.

Appeal dismissed so far as it related to the judgment and injunction; appeal allowed so far as it related to the award of damages. Judgment varied to award damages of £1,000 to each *b* *plaintiff.*

Solicitors: *V H Baker & Co* (for the defendant); *Atkins, Walter & Locke*, Dorking (for the plaintiffs).

Mary Rose Plummer Barrister.

c

Hopwood v Cannock Chase District Council

COURT OF APPEAL, CIVIL DIVISION   *d*
CAIRNS, STEPHENSON LJJ AND BRIGHTMAN J
10th DECEMBER 1974

Landlord and tenant – Repair – Implied covenant – Short lease of dwelling-house – Duty of landlord to keep in repair the structure and exterior of the dwelling-house – Exterior – Meaning – Yard behind house – Paving slabs in yard – Yard not a means of access to the *e* *house – Whether slabs part of 'exterior' of house – Housing Act 1961, s 32(1)(a).*

The plaintiff was the widow of the tenant of a dwelling-house owned by the defendants. The letting was one to which s 32 of the Housing Act 1961 applied. The house was some 16 feet in width and had a yard at the back. The yard consisted of a concrete area, adjoining the house and going out from the back of the house about five feet, *f* and then a row of paving slabs, across the full width of the house, and next to them, on the far side, another concrete slab between two and three feet across. Beyond the yard was a garden. The ordinary means of access to the house was from the front of the house, although there was a way out from one side of the yard into an alley or lane and also a way through from the yard into the yard of the adjoining house. The plaintiff came out of the back door of the house and walked diagonally across the first *g* concrete slab, but tripped and fell on the edge of one of the paving slabs and injured her knee. The paving slab was an inch and a half lower than the concrete. The defendants admitted that that part of the premises was, to their knowledge, out of repair. The plaintiff claimed damages against the defendants for breach of the duty of care, under s 4(1)[a] of the Occupiers' Liability Act 1957, in respect of the damages arising from their failure to carry out the obligation to keep the structure and exterior of the *h* house in repair under s 32(1)(a)[b] of the 1961 Act. The judge dismissed the claim, holding that the row of slabs was not part of the 'structure or exterior' of the house within s 32(1)(a). On appeal,

Held – The question whether the slabs formed part of the 'exterior' of the house *j* within s 32(1) was a question of fact and degree. In all the circumstances, and in particular in view of the fact that the yard, of which the slabs formed part, could not properly be described as being necessary to the house as a means of access to it, the

---

a   Section 4(1) is set out at p 798 *c*, post
b   Section 32(1), so far as material, is set out at p 797 *j*, post

a   judge was fully justified in coming to his conclusion. The appeal would therefore be dismissed (see p 800 *a* to *h*, post).

Brown v Liverpool Corpn [1969] 3 All ER 1345 distinguished.

Notes

For the liability of the landlord to repair implied in short leases of dwelling-houses, see Supplement to 23 Halsbury's Laws (3rd Edn) para 1253A.

b   For the Occupiers' Liability Act 1957, s 4, see 23 Halsbury's Statutes (3rd Edn) 797.

For the Housing Act 1961, s 32, see 16 Halsbury's Statutes (3rd Edn) 351.

Case referred to in judgments

Brown v Liverpool Corpn [1969] 3 All ER 1345, CA, 31(2) Digest (Reissue) 599, 4876.

c   **Appeal**

This was an appeal by the plaintiff, Enid Violet Hopwood, against the judgment of his Honour Deputy Judge Lewis sitting in the Stafford County Court on 22nd February 1974 dismissing the plaintiff's claim against the defendants, Cannock Chase District Council (formerly Rugeley Urban District Council), for damages for personal injuries. The facts are set out in the judgment of Cairns LJ.

d

Malcolm Potter for the plaintiff.

Frank Chapman for the defendants.

e   **CAIRNS LJ.** This is an appeal from a decision of deputy Judge Lewis sitting at Stafford on 22nd February 1974; he had before him an action by the plaintiff, the widow of the tenant of one of the defendants' houses, a house at 57 Newman Grove, Rugeley. It was an action for damages for personal injuries which the plaintiff suffered when she fell in the back yard of the house and injured her knee.

The house is a terraced house; it is some 16 feet in width and at the back of it there is a little yard consisting first of a concrete area adjoining the house for the full width *f*   of the house and probably about five feet going out from the back of the house; then there is a row of nine paving slabs, again across the full width of the house; then next to them, on the other side, another concrete area, a rather narrower one, perhaps between two and three feet wide. Then, still further away from the house, is a garden.

At the time the plaintiff had come from the back door of the house and she had *g*   walked diagonally across the first concrete area; she was intending to go and have a chat with her neighbour at the next house. But when she came to one edge of the paving slabs—it is not clear whether it was the first edge that she came to or the second edge going up on to the other piece of concrete—but at one of those two places she tripped and fell; and it was common ground that there was a difference in height between the concrete and the paving slab of an inch and a half, the paving slab being *h*   lower than the concrete. It was found by the learned judge that the defendants, by their servants, well knew of this condition.

The judge had however to consider whether there was any obligation on the defendants to keep this part of the premises in repair. He held that there was no such obligation, and he gave judgment for the defendants, though he assessed the damages in case there should be a successful appeal.

j   The plaintiff's case was founded on s 32 of the Housing Act 1961 which contains in sub-s (1) this provision:

'In any lease of a dwelling-house, being a lease to which this section applies, there shall be implied a covenant by the lessor—(a) to keep in repair the structure and exterior of the dwelling-house (including drains, gutters and external pipes) . . .'

I need not consider (*b*) but it is convenient to refer to one of the definitions contained
in s 32(5), namely the definition of the words 'lease of a dwelling-house' which words   *a*
are defined to mean: 'a lease whereby a building or part of a building is let wholly or
mainly as a private dwelling'; and 'the dwelling-house' means 'that building or part of
a building'.

The plaintiff's case depended on whether there was an obligation on the defendants
to repair this part of the premises, it being acknowledged that they were out of repair
and it being found that they knew they were out of repair; it was conceded that   *b*
if the obligation to repair was established, the plaintiff was entitled to succeed by
reason of the provisions of s 4(1) of the Occupiers' Liability Act 1957 which provides:

> 'Where premises are occupied by any person under a tenancy which puts on
> the landlord an obligation to that person for the maintenance or repair of the
> premises, the landlord shall owe to all persons who or whose goods may from   *c*
> time to time be lawfully on the premises the same duty, in respect of dangers
> arising from any default by him in carrying out that obligation, as if he were
> an occupier of the premises and those persons or their goods were there by his
> invitation or permission (but without any contract).'

The learned judge said this in the course of his judgment: 'It is of course plain that
it is not the whole of the letting that can compose the exterior'—he used that word   *d*
because, as I have already quoted, the obligation relates to the repair of the structure
and the exterior of the dwelling-house. The judge went on:

> 'One has to draw the line somewhere, it is a pretty close run thing. After
> considerable thought, I think that the line must fall on the other side. Steps and
> part of the front door are exterior—an integral part. A row of slabs not even   *e*
> path to the back door—they were no doubt used by the Plaintiff and her husband
> but not sensibly in the structure or exterior. I am fortified by the thought that
> the Act requires a duty to repair—nothing wrong with the slabs in themselves—
> repair should not include raising slabs.'

With regard to that last sentence it was not a point taken by counsel for the defen-   *f*
dants, and in this court he has not sought to support it. Clearly, if there is an obligation
to keep what I may call for convenience this back yard in repair, then the obligation
would run to the length of requiring the landlords not merely to have sound slabs,
but to have the slabs kept in proper position. That sentence, however, was not the
basis of the judge's judgment; it was something which he wrongly thought fortified
the view that he came to on other grounds.

In reaching his decision, he founded himself on the only reported case as far as we   *g*
know that has been decided under this provision; it is the decision of the Court of
Appeal in *Brown v Liverpool Corpn*[1]. That was a case in which the house had a path
running to steps which went up to the road, the house being at a lower level than the
road, and the plaintiff met with an accident on those steps. The question was whether
the landlords had a duty under s 32 to keep those steps in repair, and the question   *h*
that had to be considered in that case, as in this one, was: did they form part of the
structure or exterior of the building?

Danckwerts LJ, giving the first judgment, first easily reached the conclusion that
they did not form part of the structure and then went on in this way[2]:

> 'On the other hand it seems to me equally clear that the 7 feet of flagstones and
> the steps up do form part of the exterior of the dwelling-house. They are attached   *i*
> in that manner to the house for the purpose of access to this dwelling-house, and
> they are part of the dwelling-house which is necessary for the purpose of

1   [1969] 3 All ER 1345
2   [1969] 3 All ER at 1346

a anybody who wishes to live in the dwelling-house enjoying that privilege. If they have not means of access of some sort they could not get there, and these are simply the means of access. The steps are an outside structure, and therefore, it seems to me that they are plainly part of the building, and, therefore, the covenant implied by s. 32 of the Act of 1961 fits and applies to the obligations of the landlords in this case'.

b Salmon LJ agreed; he said[1]:

'I do not think that this case is by any means free from difficulty, or, indeed, from doubt. I do not wish to lay down any general principle of law or any general proposition as to the construction of the Housing Act 1961, or as to the meaning of the words "building" or "dwelling-house". I base my judgment on the particular facts of this case.'

c

Then, after referring to the main facts and quoting s 32(5) of the 1961 Act he went on[1]:

'In the particular circumstances of this case I think it proper to regard the house, with the short concrete path and steps leading to it, as being one unit. Together they formed one building and were, therefore, "the dwelling-house". It is con-
d ceded by the defendant corporation that the steps and the path were demised with the house. It seems to me that the path and steps must be an integral part of the building, otherwise it would be impossible for the building to be used as a dwelling-house for it would have no access. On that narrow ground I think that the judgment of the learned county court judge can be supported. I also think that an alternative way of putting the matter would be to say that, on the facts here, that short concrete path and those four steps were part of the exterior of the
e dwelling-house. Whichever way it is put—whether it is put in that way or whether one says that, looking at the facts, the path, steps and house are all part of the building which was let as a private dwelling-house—it would follow that the plaintiff is entitled to succeed.'

f Sachs LJ, after quoting s 32(5), said[2]:

'For my part I have no doubt but that, as counsel for the plaintiff has correctly conceded, the definition given to "the dwelling-house" was intended to and does exclude from the ambit of the landlord's liability those parts of the demise that are not part of the building itself. In particular, to my mind, there would normally be excluded from the ambit of those liabilities a garden or a pond, and
g likewise the fences round or a gate leading to such a garden or pond. Similarly, there would normally be excluded the steps leading into the garden from a road . . . The question, accordingly, is whether, in this particular case, the 7 feet approach with the steps at the end of it really was part of the exterior of the terrace building or whether that 7 feet pathway and the steps down into it were simply part of a means of traversing a garden. That seems to me—as, indeed,
h counsel for the plaintiff rightly contended—to be a question of degree, and a very close run thing at that.'

Then, after quoting a clause of the conditions of tenancy, he said[3]:

'In the end, however, I have come to the conclusion that the learned county court judge adopted the right approach and did treat this question as one of
j degree and fact. He referred specifically to the point that this concrete path was "only 7 feet long", and it seems to me that on the evidence he was entitled to

1 [1969] 3 All ER at 1346
2 [1969] 3 All ER at 1347
3 [1969] 3 All ER at 1347, 1348

come to the conclusion which he reached on this question of fact, i.e., that in all
the circumstances the steps formed part of the building.'   *a*

One matter on which all three members of the court founded their judgments was
that in that case the path and steps formed an essential part of the means of access to
the house, in that it was the only way in. In this case that certainly was not so; the
ordinary means of access to the house was from the front of the house and to my
mind it is very doubtful whether this yard could be regarded as a means of access to   *b*
the house at all. It is true that there was a way out from one side of the yard, apparently into an alley or lane, this house being at the end of the terrace of houses; and
there was also a way through from the yard into the corresponding yard of the
adjoining house. But that is very far from saying, as could be said in *Brown's* case[1],
that it was necessary to the house as the means of access to it.

Sachs LJ in *Brown's* case[1] went no further than to say that there were materials on   *c*
which it was open to the county court judge to reach the conclusion that he did.
Here, the county court judge has reached the opposite conclusion; he did I think
approach it as a question of degree and of fact, and it appears to me that the facts were
such as entitled him to reach that conclusion. I should be prepared to go still further
and say that, treating it as Danckwerts and Salmon LJJ did, as a matter of law and
construction of the section, in my view the section cannot be extended beyond what   *d*
was held in *Brown's* case[1] to include a yard of this kind.

For these reasons I would dismiss this appeal.

STEPHENSON LJ. I agree. Were it not for the decision of this court in *Brown's*
case[1], I should have regarded this as a plain case and should not have agreed with the   *e*
judge that it was a 'pretty close run thing'. In my judgment this concrete yard, including this line of paving slabs across it, could not legitimately be described as included in the structure or exterior of this dwelling-house. Nothing in s 32(1) or in
s 32(5) of the Housing Act 1961 enables me to give those words any special meaning;
nor am I compelled to stretch or strain them by the language of the lords justices in
Brown's case[1] in which they expressed their successful struggle to uphold the just   *f*
decision of the county court judge to give that injured tenant damages on the special
facts of that case.

Whatever the exterior of a dwelling-house or building may cover and whether or
not the phrase has a wider connotation in the section than in an ordinary covenant to
repair, I am not persuaded by counsel for the plaintiff's excellent argument that it
extends to the yard where this plaintiff was injured.   *g*

I would therefore dismiss this appeal.

BRIGHTMAN J. I agree.

Appeal dismissed.
        h

Solicitors: *Allan Jay & Co*, agents for *Hand, Morgan & Owen*, Rugeley (for the plaintiff).
Hollinshead & Moody, Tunstall, Stoke-on-Trent (for the defendants).

                                        Mary Rose Plummer Barrister.

1   [1969] 3 All ER 1345

a # C & J Clark Ltd v Inland Revenue Comrs

COURT OF APPEAL
STAMP AND SCARMAN LJJ AND SIR ERIC SACHS
21st, 22nd OCTOBER, 17th DECEMBER 1974

b *Income tax – Close company – Apportionment of income – Apportionment for surtax – Apportionment among participators – Addition to income to be apportioned – Amounts of annual payments to be deducted in arriving at company's distributable income – Covenanted donations to charity – Trading company – Prohibition on apportionment in absence of shortfall assessment – Whether prohibition applying to amounts of annual payments deducted in arriving at company's distributable income – Whether covenanted donations to charity may*
c *be apportioned even though no shortfall assessment – Finance Act 1965, s 78(2)(4) (as amended by the Finance Act 1966, s 27, Sch 5, para 10(1)).*

The taxpayer company, a close company for the purposes of corporation tax, was also a trading company. During the accounting period from 6th April 1966 to 31st December 1966, it paid, under the provisions of a deed of covenant, a total sum
d of £53,354 as a donation to a charitable trust. In November 1967 the inspector of taxes confirmed that no action would be taken under the Finance Act 1965, s 77, and accordingly no assessment was made on the taxpayer company in respect of a shortfall in distributions in the relevant accounting period. In December 1968, however, the Revenue issued a notice to the taxpayer company, apportioning the sum of £53,354 among the participators of the company for the purposes of surtax
e under s 78(2)[a] of the 1965 Act. The Special Commissioners affirmed the apportionment but Megarry J[b] allowed an appeal by the taxpayer company. The Crown appealed contending that s 78(2) was to be construed as requiring an apportionment to be made of amounts deducted in respect of annual payments in arriving at the taxpayer company's disposable income, on the ground that it would be anomalous if, in the case of a trading company, such an apportionment was only to be made if in
f addition to making such payments, the company had withheld from distribution more than the amount necessary for its business.

Held – It was clear from the language of s 78(2) and (3) that, in the case of a close company which was a trading company, sub-s (2) did not come into play unless there had been an apportionment of the income of the company amongst the participators

g _____

a Section 78, as amended and so far as material, provides:
'(1) Subject to the provisions of this section, the income of a close company for any accounting period may for purposes of surtax be apportioned by the Board among the participators, and any amount apportioned to a close company (whether originally or by one or more sub-apportionments under this provision) may be further apportioned among the participators in that company; and on any such apportionment section 249 of the
h Income Tax Act 1952, as adapted by this section, shall apply as it applied on an apportionment of a company's income under Chapter III of Part IX of that Act.
'(2) For purposes of an apportionment under this section, there shall be added to the amount of income to be apportioned any amounts which were deducted in respect of annual payments in arriving at the company's distributable income for the accounting period and which in the case of an individual would not have been deductible or would have been treated as his income in computing his total income for surtax . . .
j '(4) Subject to subsections (2) and (3) above, an apportionment shall not be made under this section of a company's income for an accounting period unless an assessment is made on the company under section 77 of this Act in respect of a shortfall in its distributions for that period, and the amount apportioned shall be the amount of the shortfall taken into account in making that assessment . . .'
b [1973] 2 All ER 513, [1973] 1 WLR 905, [1973] STC 299

under s 78(1).   Under s 78(4), however, there could be no apportionment of income
under s 78(1) until there had been an assessment in respect of the company's shortfall   *a*
in distributions under s 77.   Accordingly, since there had been no shortfall assessment
on the taxpayer company in respect of the relevant accounting period, there could
be no apportionment of the covenanted donation to charity amongst the participators
of the company (see p 804 *j* to p 805 *c* and *f j*, p 808 *b* to *d* and p 809 *f*, post).
   Decision of Megarry J [1973] 2 All ER 513 affirmed.

b

Notes
For apportionment provisions in relation to close companies, see Supplement to
20 Halsbury's Laws (3rd Edn) para 2044.
   For the Finance Act 1965, ss 77, 78, see 45 Halsbury's Statutes (2nd Edn) 620, 621.
For 1970-71 and subsequent years, ss 77 and 78 of the 1965 Act have been replaced
respectively by ss 289-290 and ss 296-298 of the Income and Corporation Taxes Act   *c*
1970.   In relation to accounting periods ending after 5th April 1973, ss 289-290 and
ss 296-298 of the 1970 Act have been repealed by the Finance Act 1972, ss 94, 134 and
Sch 28, Part VI, and replaced by Sch 16 to the 1972 Act.   For the power to apportion
amounts deducted in respect of certain annual payments, see para 3 of Sch 16 to the
1972 Act.

d

Cases referred to in judgments
Ayrshire Employers Mutual Insurance Association Ltd v Inland Revenue Comrs 1944 SC 421,
   27 Tax Cas 331; *affd* [1946] 1 All ER 637, 1946 SC (HL) 1, 175 LT 22, HL, 28(1) Digest
   (Reissue) 138, *414*.
Cape Brandy Syndicate v Inland Revenue Comrs [1921] 1 KB 64, 12 Tax Cas 358, 90 LJKB
   113, 125 LT 108; *affd* [1921] 2 KB 403, 90 LJKB 461, CA, 28(1) Digest (Reissue) 586,   *e*
   2172.
Coathew Investments Ltd v Inland Revenue Comrs [1966] 1 All ER 1032, [1966] 1 WLR 716,
   43 Tax Cas 301, 45 ATC 85, [1966] TR 81, HL; *affg* sub nom *Inland Revenue Comrs v
   Coathew Investments Ltd* [1965] 1 All ER 954, 1 WLR 583, 44 ATC 13, [1965] TR 17,
   CA, 28(1) Digest (Reissue) 524, *1918*.
Kirkness (Inspector of Taxes) v John Hudson & Co Ltd [1955] 2 All ER 345, [1955] AC 696,   *f*
   [1955] 2 WLR 1135, 36 Tax Cas 28, 34 ATC 142, [1955] TR 145, 48 R & IT 352, HL,
   28(1) Digest (Reissue) 463, *1668*.
Mangin v Inland Revenue Comrs [1971] 1 All ER 179, [1971] AC 739, [1971] 2 WLR 39,
   [1970] TR 249, PC, 28(1) Digest (Reissue) 543, **1322*.
Stenhouse Holdings Ltd v Inland Revenue Comrs (1970) 46 Tax Cas 670, 49 ATC 8, [1970]
   TR 9.

g

Cases also cited
Chamberlain v Inland Revenue Comrs [1945] 2 All ER 351, 28 Tax Cas 88, CA.
Greenberg v Inland Revenue Comrs [1971] 3 All ER 136, [1972] AC 109, 47 Tax Cas 240,
   HL.

h

Appeal
The taxpayer company, C & J Clark Ltd ('the company'), a close company for the
purposes of corporation tax, was also a trading company.   In the accounting period
from 6th April 1966 to 31st December 1966, the company made payments totalling
£53,354 to a charitable trust in accordance with the provisions of two deeds of covenant dated 22nd July 1960 and 26th May 1961.   Those payments were covenanted
donations to charity within the meaning of s 52(4) of the Finance Act 1965, and were   *j*
accordingly treated, for corporation tax purposes, as charges on income under the
provision of that section.   On 28th November 1967 the inspector of taxes confirmed
that no action was proposed to be taken under s 77 of the Act and accordingly no
assessment had been made on the company under that section in respect of the
relevant accounting period.   On 17th December 1968, however, the Inland Revenue

a Commissioners issued a notice to the company that in accordance with the provisions of s 78 of the Finance Act 1965, the income of the company for the relevant accounting period in the amount of £53,354 had been apportioned for the purposes of surtax amongst the participators of the company. On appeal the Special Commissioners decided that the apportionment was in principle valid, and left figures to be agreed. On 30th March 1973 Megarry J[1] allowed the company's appeal, holding that the only function of s 78(2) was to make an addition to the income to be apportioned if an *b* apportionment had been made under s 78(1), and that by virtue of s 78(2) there could be no apportionment under s 78(1) unless there had been a shortfall assessment under s 77. The Crown appealed.

John Balcombe QC, Patrick Medd QC and *Brian Davenport* for the Crown.
Michael Nolan QC and *Peter Whiteman* for the company.
c

Cur adv vult

17th December. The following judgments were read.

d **STAMP LJ.** This is an appeal from a judgment and order of Megarry J[1] allowing an appeal of the taxpayer company, C & J Clark Ltd, from a decision of the Special Commissioners. Because the case is reported below I need not set out the facts or the issues which fall to be determined on this appeal.

I ought, however, to emphasise at the outset that the payments here in question made by this close company, which is a trading company, were 'a covenanted donation *e* to charity' within s 52(4) of the Finance Act 1965 and were accordingly treated for corporation tax purposes as charges on the income of the company deductible in computing the income for the purposes of that tax. I should, perhaps, also emphasise that the payments if made by an individual would not have been allowable in computing his total income for surtax purposes. The Crown seeks by the process of apportionment to add the amounts in appropriate proportions to the surtaxable *f* income of the shareholders.

It is common ground that prior to the Finance Act 1965 covenanted payments such as are here in question made by a company under the control of not more than five persons (I will call it a close company, though it was not so called in those days) could, if the company was an investment company, be apportioned among its members so as to make the members liable to surtax in respect of those payments. As I *g* understand it, you could not so organise your affairs through the medium of such a company as to escape the ambit of surtax on payments under covenant made by the company to charity which would not be allowable as deductions in computing your income for the purposes of surtax if you yourself had made the payments under covenant. Under s 262 of the Income Tax Act 1952 the income of such a company was liable to be treated as the income of its members and so apportioned among *h* them for surtax purposes however much or however little had been distributed and (by the effect of sub-s (2) of that section) no deductions were allowable in computing the income of the company so apportionable which would not have been allowable in computing the income of an individual. The shareholders of a close company which was a trading company were not similarly vulnerable, for there was no provision in the case of such a company for disallowing in computing its income *j* deductions not allowable in computing an individual's income.

The introduction of corporation tax by the Finance Act 1965 brought with it a new situation regarding income tax. The broad effect of s 77 of that Act was that if there was what was called a shortfall in a close company's distributions, i e the amount,

---

1　[1973] 2 All ER 513, [1973] 1 WLR 905, [1973] STC 299

if any, by which the distributions fell short of what was called the required standard,
a charge of income tax (in effect) was placed on the company on an amount equal to   *a*
the shortfall.   The required standard was, subject to certain limitations, the distributable income of the company, but, in the case of a trading company, less such
amount as could not be distributed without prejudice to the requirements of the
company's business.   So, if a trading company distributed all the income which it
could distribute without prejudice to its business, it in general fell outside the section.
There were complicated provisions for limiting the required standard.   In approach-   *b*
ing the construction of s 78 it is to be emphasised first that s 77 was concerned with the
avoidance of the charge of income tax, imposed by s 47 of the 1965 Act, by the withholding of distributions, and second that a trading company which retained no more
than the amount of its distributable income necessary for its business requirements
was outside it.

Section 78 was concerned with surtax.   In the cases to which it applied it brought   *c*
into operation, by the effect of the concluding words of sub-s (1), the provisions of
s 249 of the Income Tax Act 1952 (as amended) so as to attract surtax on the amount
apportioned to a surtax payer.   Section 78(1) is expressed in general terms permitting
the whole of the income of close companies—investment companies and trading
companies alike—to be apportioned for surtax purposes.   The limitation on the
generality of sub-s (1) is found in sub-s (4), precluding any apportionment unless an   *d*
assessment is made under s 77 and providing, before its amendment, that the amount
apportioned should be the amount of that assessment.   So, if you stop there, there
could be no apportionment for surtax purposes in respect of a trading company
which had withheld from distribution no more than the amount of its distributable
income necessary for its business and which was accordingly immune from an income
tax assessment under s 77.   Such a trading company would thus be in a similar   *e*
position as regards surtax apportionments as it was prior to the 1965 Act.   An investment company, on the other hand, by the effect of s 78(3), was liable to an apportionment, if the Board saw reason for it, of the whole of its income up to the required
standard notwithstanding the absence of any shortfall; and, because sub-s (4) is
expressed to be subject to sub-s (3), notwithstanding the absence of an assessment
under s 77.   *f*

Whatever be the effect of sub-s (2) which is subject to the controversy in this case,
it is clear that once there is an apportionment in respect of either a trading or investment company, there falls to be added—and there is no discretion in the matter—
'to the amount of income to be apportioned' any amounts which were deducted in
respect of annual payments in arriving at the company's distributable income.   So,
if a trading company withheld from distribution more than the amount necessary   *g*
for its business requirements, that amount plus the last-mentioned amounts was
apportionable.   The question for determination is whether sub-s (2) operates as
well in the case of a trading company which has not withheld more than is necessary
for its business.

Because the argument of the Crown, if not founded on, is supported most strongly
by an argument based on anomaly, it is convenient to refer at once to the suggested   *h*
anomaly.   What is said is that it would be anomalous if a trading company which had
withheld from distribution more than the amount necessary for its business should be
liable to have these covenanted sums added to the amount apportionable, but that a
trading company which had distributed all that its business requirements permitted
should not be liable.   But I am not sure that it is correct to describe the situation as
anomalous.   It might have been said that under the pre-1965 legislation it was anomalous   *j*
that a trading company, which had failed to distribute a reasonable amount of its
income and was perhaps being used by its shareholders for the purpose of making payments which would not have been deductions in computing their total income for surtax
purposes if they had made them themselves, should be free from an apportionment
of its covenanted sums, whereas an investment company which had distributed the

whole of its income should be liable to an apportionment of its covenanted sums. And

a when it came to the 1965 Act it may have been thought that a trading company should still be in a better position in this regard, provided it had distributed all the income not required for the purpose of its business (and so had at least to that extent shown an absence of intent to protect its shareholders from a surtax assessment), than a company which had not done so.

But, however anomalous one may regard the effect of the distinction, the court

b is not at liberty to force a construction of clear language to correct even a clear anomaly. And I am afraid one will always find that taxing Acts of such complexity as that with which we are here concerned appear to produce anomalies. Were it not so, there would, I think, be fewer amending provisions. Counsel for the Crown in the court below, argued, as I read the judgment of Megarry J[1], that today one must not make too literal an approach to the construction of a statute. That argument

c was repeated in this court. I need not pursue it, because I am not persuaded that in favour of the Crown the provisions of a taxing Act ought to have put on them a construction which would alter their natural meaning and so enlarge the ambit of the tax imposed. Of course, in construing a particular section of an Act of Parliament you must read and consider the effect of the Act as a whole and each and every part of it. That was the process adopted by Lord Reid in *Stenhouse Holdings Ltd v Inland*

d *Revenue Comrs*[2] in determining against the Crown that a too literal construction of the language of a particular section would defeat the intention of the legislature as shown by a reading of other provisions of the Act. But that does not mean that you should in favour of the Crown, to use Megarry J's words, distort the language used in order to avoid an effect which you may think the draftsman would have avoided if he had thought about it. If here it had been intended to surtax share-

e holders of a trading company in respect of the annual payments with which sub-s (2) is concerned irrespective of what, if any, distributions had been made, I would have expected the draftsman to say so in clear terms. Nothing could have been easier.

Megarry J subjected the language of s 78 to a most careful and exhaustive analysis and, because I find that analysis convincing and detect no flaw in it, I agree with his conclusion that sub-s (2) of the section does not come into play unless there is to be

f an apportionment of income. I would only add to his reasoning, which I adopt, and in deference to an argument addressed to this court that, although it is true that you may as a matter of arithmetic add an amount to nil, to add an amount to an amount which is not subject to apportionment is as difficult as to add salt to an unmade omelette.

The conclusions of Megarry J do not, in my view, introduce such an obvious anomaly

g as would permit the court, if the section was fairly open to two alternative constructions, to prefer that which avoided the anomaly. But even supposing there was an obvious or certain anomaly or error, the language of the section is too clear to permit a construction which would correct it. To do so would be to usurp the functions of Parliament.

The Crown sought to rely on s 94 and Sch 16 of the Finance Act 1972 as an aid to the

h construction of s 68 of the 1965 Act. Since s 94 was clearly intended to amend the earlier section, I do not think it assists the Crown, and I do not find it necessary to restate the limits within which a court may look at a subsequent Act for the purpose of construing an earlier one: see *Kirkness v John Hudson & Co Ltd*[3].

I would dismiss the appeal.

i **SCARMAN LJ.** I agree that the income for the relevant period of this trading company, the respondents in this court, cannot be apportioned among its participators

---

1   [1973] 2 All ER 513 at 521, [1973] 1 WLR 905 at 912, [1973] STC 299 at 307
2   (1970) 46 Tax Cas 670
3   [1955] 2 All ER 345, [1955] AC 696, 36 Tax Cas 28

for the purposes of surtax. But I do so with regret because I believe that Parliament intended to confer on the Revenue a power to apportion in circumstances such *a*
as the present case. The difficulty arises from the weak drafting of s 78 of the Finance Act 1965. Subsection (1) empowered the Board of Inland Revenue, for the purposes of surtax, to apportion the income of a closed company among the participators. The power is 'subject to the provisions of this section'. The provisions of the section that define the income available for apportionment are sub-ss (2), (3) and (4) (together with Part II of Sch 18). The particular drafting weakness with which we are now *b*
concerned is in sub-ss (2) and (4). Subsection (2) requires that for the purposes of an apportionment under the section there shall be added to the amount of the income to be apportioned the amount of deductions in respect of annual payments such as covenanted donations to charity. Subsection (4) (as amended) has two limbs: it provides first that there shall be no apportionment unless an assessment is made on the company under s 77 of the Act in respect of a shortfall in its distributions; and, *c*
secondly, that the amount apportioned shall be the amount of the shortfall taken into account in making the assessment. Clearly the draftsman had to reconcile the two subsections. He chose to do so by the opening words of sub-s (4), 'Subject to subsections (2) and (3) . . .' These are the critical words. What do they mean? We are not directly concerned with sub-s (3): suffice it to say that it was necessary to exclude the operation of both limbs of sub-s (4) when faced with a situation to *d*
which sub-s (3) applied. The problem is how to reconcile sub-ss (4) and (2). If sub-s (4) is to be read as wholly excluded by its opening words from a sub-s (2) situation, there is nothing to prevent the apportionment of the whole of the company's income; for sub-s (1) applies to the whole of a company's income unless a later part of the section restricts its application. Yet plainly it was the intention of the section read as a whole that, in the case of a trading company, there should be a limit on the income to *e*
to be apportioned, namely the shortfall in distributions plus any deductions of the sort specified in sub-s (2). There is therefore much to be said for the taxpayer's contention that, so far as a trading company is concerned, sub-s (4) remains operative so as to prevent an apportionment unless an assessment has been made on the company in respect of a shortfall in its distributions and is excluded only in so far as it provides that the amount apportioned shall be no more than the amount of the *f*
shortfall. But, if it be right to interpret sub-s (4) as requiring an assessment of shortfall to be made even when under sub-s (2) payments such as covenanted donations to charity have to be added to the income to be apportioned, a different sort of anomaly arises. On this construction of the subsection, a company may saddle itself with a heavy burden of covenanted donations and avoid an apportionment, provided it distributes up to the standard required by s 77 the meagre income it *g*
leaves itself. This would be as much an avoidance of tax as if, instead of burdening itself with covenanted donations to charity, it had decided not to distribute its income. The participators in the company would succeed in being charitable at public expense —one of the mischiefs which legislation such as sub-s (2) is intended to prevent.

Faced with this choice of interpretations, each of which in one respect or another defeats the purpose of the enactment, I have no hesitation in asserting that the court *h*
must choose the interpretation which favours the taxpayer. In such a situation it is for the Crown to show that a taxing statute imposes a charge on the person sought to be taxed—a principle once described by Lord Normand as 'that last refuge of judicial hesitation': see *Ayrshire Employers Mutual Insurance Association Ltd v Inland Revenue Comrs*[1]. In *Stenhouse Holdings Ltd v Inland Revenue Comrs*[2], Lord Reid commented on the drafting of the Finance Act 1965; he thought that 'the prolixity *j*
and obscurity' of many of its provisions indicated hasty preparation and inadequate revisal. The drafting of s 78 certainly bears all the marks of drafting under pressure

---

1   (1944) 27 Tax Cas 331 at 344
2   (1970) 46 Tax Cas 670 at 683

a without sufficient opportunity for revisal. Fortunately, its drafting flaws have now been corrected by amending legislation: Finance Act 1972, s 94, Sch 16.

It was suggested in argument that the 1972 amendment might assist in resolving the ambiguity of the 1965 section. Suffice it to say that by 1972 the law had been radically transformed: it is not possible to draw inferences from this amendment as to the meaning of s 78 of the 1965 Act.

I would, therefore, also dismiss the appeal.
b

SIR ERIC SACHS. Upwards of a dozen times in the course of the hearing I read and re-read the provisions of the first four subsections of s 78 of the Finance Act 1965, having due regard also to the provisions of s 77 of that Act as well as to others called to our attention. When so doing, it was my endeavour to put myself in the place of an average solicitor or company secretary called on to advise a trading close
c company with reasonable directors who had posed the question 'What is the position of the company as regards charitable covenants?' In essence, of course, that question was whether any sums disbursed under those covenants would become subject to apportionment taxation. In putting myself in this situation I had in mind that passage in the speech of Lord Simonds in the *Hudson* case[1] where he refers to the right of a citizen to order his affairs on the basis of those provisions in an Act of Parliament
d that are plain.

It seems to me that, if and insofar as any provisions of a modern Finance Act can be said to be reasonably plain, that solicitor would have come to the conclusion that money paid under those covenants would not attract apportionment taxation unless there had been a shortfall in the company's distribution. In other words, unless the company was retaining in its coffers more of its profits than was reasonable (see
e s 77(2)), no such taxation would be attracted. In that behalf he would have properly taken into account the apparent prohibition under sub-s (4) against making apportionments unless there had been a shortfall assessment and in addition those words in sub-s (3), 'even if there has been no shortfall', which are carefully aimed solely against companies which are *not* trading companies.

If that solicitor happened to be versed in the history of taxation law he would have
f been entitled, in reinforcement of his conclusion, also to take into account the fact that up to 1965 trading close companies were entitled without suffering special taxation to contribute to charities to the same full degree as public trading companies —and that at all material times the Revenue had taken a sterner line in such matters against investment close companies than against trading close companies. Indeed, towards the end of his helpful address, counsel for the Crown referred to the fact that
g to this day 'investment close companies continue to be more severely treated than trading close companies' in such matters.

In making this initial approach to the issue before us in what may be an unorthodox way, I have deliberately refrained from intricate examination of all the various possible conflicting meanings that could attach to individual words and phrases in a complex piece of fiscal legislation. After all, when two completely contrasting views
h on the relevant effect of those four subsections have been adopted respectively by experienced commissioners and by a learned judge, it seems appropriate to get back to the simple question, 'What impression do they convey to those who have to use them as a guide to action?' I would respectfully add my endorsement to the much-cited (compare per Lord Donovan in *Mangin's* case[2]) and wise words of Rowlatt J in *Cape Brandy Syndicate v Inland Revenue Comrs*[3]:
j
'. . . in a taxing Act one has to look merely at what is clearly said. There is no room for any intendment. There is no equity about a tax. There is no

---

1   [1955] 2 All ER at 351, [1955] AC at 713, 36 Tax Cas at 63
2   [1971] 1 All ER 179 at 182, [1971] AC 739 at 746
3   [1921] 1 KB 64 at 71, 12 Tax Cas 358 at 366

808 All England Law Reports [1975] 1 All ER

presumption as to a tax. Nothing is to be read in, nothing is to be implied.
One can only look fairly at the language used.'

The pros and cons of the detailed and often necessarily convoluted arguments that
were before us lavished on the phraseology of the relevant statutory provisions have
already been fully canvassed judicially, so that no useful purpose would be served by
going over the same ground again—especially as my own approach is based on a
broad impression. Suffice it to say that if and insofar as such analysis is deemed
essential I, too, would find myself in general agreement with the judgment of
Megarry J.

In particular I find myself unable as regards sub-s (4), when read as a whole, to find
any obstacle to my impression arising from the opening words, 'Subject to subsections (2) and (3)'. Even if this were an immaculately drafted quartette of subsections,
that inability would persist. Moreover, having listened to the all round chorus of
sympathy expressed here for hard-pressed draftsmen of financial statutes and the
concomitant recognition of the impact of that pressure on these specific subsections,
I find it difficult to see how one can both recognise the effect of that pressure and yet
proceed to analysis as if it did not exist. For instance, suggestions that it would have
made a difference had those opening words read 'Subject to subsections (3) and (2)'
instead of 'Subject to subsections (2) and (3)', had little appeal to me.

One additional point seems worth record and perhaps comment. On explicit
instructions from the Board of Inland Revenue, counsel for the Crown, withdrawing
to some extent a previous submission, put forward the Board's view that the word
'may' in sub-s (1) gave the Board an absolute discretion, without providing any
criteria whatsoever, as to whether to make an apportionment, and also that once they
decided to make one, they were bound to make it in respect of all apportionable
income—having no discretion to apportion any fraction of it. It was indeed their
practice, it was stated, to apportion the whole of all charitable covenant disbursements both of trading and of investment close companies if they made any apportionment at all. There was no allowance for the fact that many trading companies
reasonably contribute to charities related to their trades. Asked what criteria were
in fact applied as to whether or not to make an apportionment, counsel for the Crown
replied that 'the consequences of so doing, for instance the quantum of recoverable
tax involved, were relevant'. On behalf of the Board, he expressed unwillingness to
state further criteria.

If that view of the Board is correct, it means not only that the criterion of 'shortfall'
goes for trading close companies, but that no criterion at all for the exercise of the
discretion to tax has been indicated by Parliament. It seems at least arguable that a
construction of fiscal provisions leading to such a result should be avoided if there
is available an alternative construction under which the basis for imposing a tax
liability has been decided by the legislature and—above all—that basis is ascertainable
by the taxpayer.

Moreover, the Crown's submissions on construction in substance produce a claim
that all the undistributed income of all close companies must, save in what the Board
regards as special circumstances, be apportioned insofar as it exceeds the 'required
standard' of permissible retentions as defined in s 77(2). If Parliament had so intended, then this quartette of subsections would surely have taken a different and
far simpler form. Whether Parliament would have approved of the taxpayer being
given no clue as to what were relevant special circumstances is perhaps also
questionable.

Against the factors which thus weigh in favour of the taxpayer there were two
salient points strongly pressed on behalf of the Revenue. First, the passage in the
judgment of Harman LJ in *Coathew Investments v Inland Revenue Comrs*[1] relating to

---

1 [1965] 1 All ER 954 at 958, 43 Tax Cas 301 at 312, [1965] 1 WLR 583 at 595

a taxpayers 'having the advantage of getting the state to pay most of the bounty they dispensed' was used to found an argument that by 1965 in fiscal statutes concerning close companies the courts should assume an intention to impose taxation on all charitable covenants—with no distinction between trading and investment companies, and further that this assumed intention should here be used not only to resolve any ambiguity but to override an otherwise reasonable construction of the provisions of s 78.   Secondly, that for the covenant disbursements to attract tax only if the 'short-
b fall' trip-wire operated was so lacking in logic as to produce an absurd anomaly and an opening for abuses.

As to the first point it is, however, perhaps worth remembering that the extent of donations by taxpayers to charities depends as a rule greatly on the amount of their disposable income.   So every Chancellor of the Exchequer has in his turn to determine how far he will for the benefit of the Revenue adopt measures the sub-
c stantial effect of which may in the end be to deprive taxpayers of kudos but charities of cash.   In this connection the history of taxation up to 1965 so favours trading close companies, in contrast to investment companies, that there seems little reason here to attribute a taxing intendment against them of such clarity as to override the factors weighing in favour both of the taxpayer and of charities on this issue.

The second point—that in certain unusual circumstances anomalies could arise—
d again does not seem of such weight that it warrants upsetting the natural meaning of the relevant provisions of s 78.   As to potential abuse—if it had at the time really been considered to be likely on a material scale, a natural course for the Revenue to adopt would have been in simple language to ensure that all close company charit-able disbursements were automatically taxed.   It is also perhaps only fair to observe that in this particular case no suggestion was made on behalf of the Revenue that
e there had been anything in the nature of an abuse by the taxpayers of the relevant provisions if construed in the way urged on their behalf; indeed, though charitable disbursements to the order of £50,000 in a single year may seem large if one looks only at the sum disbursed, that figure has to be put in perspective against the capitalisation of some £5,000,000 and the fact that the Board, after considering the company's accounts, did not make a shortfall assessment.

f Accordingly, the two points so cogently stressed for the Revenue do not in my judgment outweigh the factors telling in favour of the taxpayer.   I agree that this appeal should be dismissed.

Appeal dismissed.

g Solicitors: *Solicitor of Inland Revenue; Slaughter & May* (for the company).

Rengan Krishnan Esq Barrister.

Black-Clawson International Ltd v Papierwerke *a* Waldhof-Aschaffenburg AG

HOUSE OF LORDS

LORD REID, VISCOUNT DILHORNE, LORD WILBERFORCE, LORD DIPLOCK AND LORD SIMON
OF GLAISDALE   *b*

14th, 15th, 16th, 17th, 18th, 21st, 22nd OCTOBER 1974, 5th MARCH 1975

Conflict of laws – Foreign judgment – Conclusiveness in English proceedings – Recognition of judgment as conclusive between the parties in proceedings founded on same cause of action – Reliance on judgment by way of defence   Foreign judgment dismissing action by plaintiff – Judgment based on limitation period and not on merits of claim – Plaintiff bringing proceedings *c in English courts founded on same cause of action – Whether defendant entitled to rely on foreign judgment by way of defence – Whether judgment to be recognised as conclusive between parties – Foreign Judgments (Reciprocal Enforcement) Act 1933, s 8(1).*

Statute – Construction – Aids to construction – Report – Report of committee presented to Parliament – Committee recommending legislation – Report giving statement of existing law – *d Draft bill appended to report – Report containing commentary on draft bill – Commentary indicating that clause in draft bill intended to state but not alter common law – Draft bill enacted without alteration – Whether reference may be made to report to determine mischief which statute intended to cure – Whether reference may be made to report for a direct statement as to meaning of statute – Foreign Judgments (Reciprocal Enforcement) Act 1933, s 8(1).*   *e*

The Foreign Judgments (Reciprocal Enforcement) Act 1933 was passed by Parliament on 13th April 1933 following a report[a] presented to Parliament by a committee appointed by the Lord Chancellor to consider, inter alia, what legislation was necessary for the purpose of enabling conventions made with foreign countries for the mutual enforcement of judgments to become effective or for the purpose of securing recipro- *f* cal treatment from other countries. The committee consisted of eminent lawyers. The report contained a statement of the existing law relating to the enforcement of foreign judgments in the United Kingdom as the committee understood it. The report recommended legislation which would lay down the conditions under which, in return for reciprocal treatment, the judgments of foreign countries should be enforced but which would 'not depart from the substantive principles of the common *g* law applicable to foreign judgments in general'. Annexed to the report was a draft bill and a commentary thereon, which stated that cl 8 of the draft bill contained provisions 'with regard to the recognition of foreign judgments as final and conclusive between the parties as regards the question therein adjudicated upon. It is entirely in accordance with the Common Law . . .' Clause 8 of the draft bill was in terms which were identical to s 8[b] of the 1933 Act as subsequently enacted. *h*

In 1961 the plaintiffs, an English company, entered into a contract to sell to a German company certain machines to be installed in the latter's factory in West Germany. It was agreed that the price should be paid by 20 bills of exchange drawn by the English company and accepted by the German company, and payable by a bank in London between 1963 and 1967. As the result of a merger in 1970 the German company's rights and liabilities were acquired by the defendants, another German *j* company. The defendants had no assets or place of business in England. On 24th August 1972 the plaintiffs commenced proceedings against the defendants in the

a   Report of the Foreign Judgments (Reciprocal Enforcement) Committee (chairman: Sir F A Greer) (1932) Cmd 4213

b   Section 8 is set out at p 816 *d* to *h*, post

District Court of Munich, claiming the amount due on two of the bills of exchange
a which had fallen due in September 1966 but had been dishonoured. Realising, however, that the action might be barred under the German three year limitation period,
the plaintiffs, on 29th August, obtained leave to issue a writ in the High Court claiming
against the defendants the amount due on the same two bills,'and to serve notice of the
writ out of the jurisdiction. In November 1972 the Munich court dismissed the plaintiffs' claim on the ground that it was time-barred. Expert evidence showed that in
b German law that decision did not affect the existence of the plaintiffs' right but merely
barred the remedy. In August 1973 the plaintiffs served notice of their writ. The defendants applied for an order that the English proceedings be set aside on the ground that,
under s 8(1) of the 1933 Act, the judgment of the Munich court was to be recognised as
conclusive between the parties in the English proceedings. Talbot J held that the
Munich judgment did not bar the plaintiffs' claim and, in the exercise of his discretion,
c he refused to set aside the proceedings. The Court of Appeal[c] allowed the defendants'
appeal, holding that s 8(1) applied not only to judgments in favour of a plaintiff but
also to judgments in favour of a defendant dismissing a plaintiff's claim and that, since
the plaintiffs' claim was founded on the same cause of action as the German proceedings, the judgment of the Munich court was conclusive against the plaintiffs under
s 8(1) and therefore barred their claim. After the decision of the Court of Appeal the
d Munich Court of Appeal allowed an appeal by the plaintiffs against the judgment of
the District Court. The defendants proposed to appeal to the German Federal
Supreme Court. In the meantime the plaintiffs appealed to the House of Lords against
the Court of Appeal's decision.

Held (Lord Diplock dissenting) – Reference to the report of the committee pre-
e sented to Parliament indicated that, insofar as s 8(1) was ambiguous, it had not been
enacted by Parliament with the intention of altering the common law. Accordingly a
foreign judgment was only conclusive under s 8(1) as regards the matters therein
adjudicated on. The matter adjudicated on in the German judgment was the question
whether the German period of limitation applied. The judgment had not adjudicated
on the question whether the plaintiffs had a right of action or whether that right had
f been extinguished. Accordingly the German judgment did not, under s 8(1), preclude
the appellants from proceeding with their action in the English courts. The appeal
would therefore be allowed and the matter remitted to the Queen's Bench Division
with a direction to stay the proceedings pending the decision of the German Federal
Supreme Court (see p 817 *j* to p 818 *a*, p 824 *g* and *h*, p 825 *g* to *j*, p 826 *g* to p 827 *b*,
p 830 *c* to p 831 *e*, p 832 *a* to *h*, p 846 *c* to p 847 *b* and *d* and p 848 *b* to *e*, post).
g   *Harris v Quine* (1869) LR 4 QB 653 applied.
    Per Viscount Dilhorne, Lord Diplock and Lord Simon of Glaisdale (Lord Reid
dissenting). Section 8(1) of the 1933 Act applies not only to foreign judgments in
favour of a plaintiff or counterclaimant but also to a judgment in favour of a defendant
dismissing a plaintiff's claim (see p 820 *c* to *e*, p 833 *f* and p 848 *a*, post).
    Per Curiam. Where there is ambiguity in a statute the court may have regard to
h the report of a committee presented to Parliament containing proposals for legislation which resulted in the enactment of the statute, in order to determine the mischief
which the statute was intended to remedy. However (per Lord Reid and Lord
Wilberforce, Viscount Dilhorne and Lord Simon of Glaisdale dissenting) it is not
permissible to look at such a report for a direct statement of what the proposed
enactment means, even though the report sets out a draft bill which is subsequently
j enacted without alteration (see p 814 *f* to *h*, p 822 *a* and *f* to p 823 *b* and *f* to *j*, p 828
d e and *j*, p 836 *b* to *f*, p 843 *b* to *d* and *g*, p 844 *b g* and *h*, p 845 *h* to p 846 *a* and p 847 *f*
to p 848 *a*, post).
    Decision of the Court of Appeal [1974] 2 All ER 611 reversed.

c   [1974] 2 All ER 611

Notes

For the conclusiveness of foreign judgments in English proceedings, see 8 Halsbury's *a*
Laws (4th Edn) 483, 499, paras 734, 767.

For the matters which are not legitimate aids to the construction of a statute, see
36 Halsbury's Laws (3rd Edn) 410, 411, paras 621-623.

For the Foreign Judgments (Reciprocal Enforcements) Act 1933, s 8, see 6 Halsbury's
Statutes (3rd Edn) 372.

b

Cases referred to in opinions

Assam Railways and Trading Co Ltd v Inland Revenue Comrs [1935] AC 445, [1934] All ER
Rep 646, 103 LJKB 583, 152 LT 26, 18 Tax Cas 509, 28(1) Digest (Reissue) 457, *1647*.

Battus v Aberdeen Steam Trawling & Fishing Co Ltd [1933] AC 402, [1933] All ER Rep
52, 102 LJPC 33, 149 LT 169, 18 Asp MLC 384, 38 Com Cas 279, HL, 42 Digest (Repl)
696, *4468*.   *c*

Bernardi v Mottenx (1781) 2 Doug KB 575, 99 ER 364, 11 Digest (Repl) 526, *1391*.

Blunt v Blunt [1943] 2 All ER 76, [1943] AC 517, 112 LJP 58, 169 LT 33, HL, 27(1) Digest
(Reissue) 565, *4119*.

Bondholders Securities Corpn v Manville [1933] 4 DLR 699, [1933] 3 WWR 1, 9 Digest
(Repl) 688, **1989*.

Carvell v Wallace (1873) 9 NSR 165, 11 Digest (Repl) 554, **950*.   *d*

Casanova, Auraldi & Co v Meier & Co (1885) 1 TLR 213, DC, 6 Digest (Repl) 410, *2904*.

Courtauld v Legh (1869) LR 4 Exch 126, 187, 38 LJEx 124, 20 LT 496, 2 Digest (Repl)
586, *1168*.

*Eastman Photographic Materials Co v Comptroller-General of Patents, Designs and Trade-
marks* [1898] AC 571, 67 LJCh 628, 79 LT 195, 15 RPC 476, HL, 229, *478*.

Evans v Bartlam [1937] 2 All ER 646, [1937] AC 473, 106 LJKB 568, 157 LT 311, HL, 50 *e*
Digest (Repl) 169, *1458*.

Godard v Gray (1870) LR 6 QB 139, 40 LJQB 62, 24 LT 89, 11 Digest (Repl) 522, *1360*.

Gorham v Bishop of Exeter E F Moore (1852 Edn), p 462, 19 Digest (Repl) 414, *2217*.

Gundry v Pinniger (1852) 1 De GM & G 502, [1843-60] All ER Rep 403, 21 LJCh 405,
18 LTOS 325, 16 Jur 488, 42 ER 647, 49 Digest (Repl) 794, *7467*.

Harris v Quine (1869) LR 4 QB 653, 10 B & S 644, 38 LJQB 331, 20 LT 947, 11 Digest *f*
(Repl) 554, *1601*.

Hawkins v Gathercole (1855) 6 De GM & G 1, 3 Eq Rep 348, 24 LJCh 332, 24 LTOS 281,
19 JP 115, 1 Jur NS 481, 43 ER 1129, 19 Digest (Repl) 440, *405*.

Heatons Transport (St Helens) Ltd v Transport and General Workers Union [1972] 3 All ER
101, [1973] AC 15, [1972] 3 WLR 431, 14 KIR 48, HL.

Heydon's Case (1584) 3 Co Rep 7a, Moore KB 128, 76 ER 637, 21 Digest (Repl) 652, *1424*. *g*

Hoystead v Taxation Comr [1926] AC 155, [1925] All ER Rep 56, 95 LJPC 79, 134 LT 354,
PC, 21 Digest (Repl) 249, *330*.

Huber v Steiner (1835) Bing NC 202, 1 Hodg 206, 2 Scott 304, 132 ER 80, 6 Digest (Repl)
409, *2902*.

Kingston's (Duchess of) Case (1776) 1 East PC 468, [1775-1802] All ER Rep 623, 1 Leach
146, 20 State TR 355, HL, 21 Digest (Repl) 225, *225*.   *h*

Letang v Cooper [1964] 2 All ER 929, [1965] 1 QB 232, [1964] 3 WLR 573, [1964] 2 Lloyd's
Rep 421, CA, 41 Digest (Repl) 421, *653*.

Maunsell v Olins [1975] 1 All ER 16, [1974] 3 WLR 835, HL; *affg* [1974] 2 All ER 250,
[1974] 1 WLR 830, CA.

National Assistance Board v Wilkinson [1952] 2 All ER 255, [1952] 2 QB 648, 116 JP 428,
50 LGR 454, Digest (Cont Vol A) 673, *630a*.   *j*

National Provincial Bank Ltd v Ainsworth [1965] 2 All ER 472, [1965] AC 1175, [1965] 3
WLR 1, HL, Digest (Cont Vol B) 343, *621l*.

Osenton (Charles) & Co v Johnston [1941] 2 All ER 245, [1942] AC 130, 110 LJKB 420, 165
LT 235, HL, 51 Digest (Repl) 681, *2840*.

Pedersen v Young [1964] ALR 798, Digest (Cont Vol B) 127, **477b*.

Povey v Povey [1970] 3 All ER 612, [1972] Fam 40, [1971] 2 WLR 381, DC.

a *Prean v Simmonds* [1971] 3 All ER 237, [1971] 1 WLR 1381, HL.

R v West Riding of Yorkshire County Council [1906] 2 KB 676, 75 LJKB 933, 95 LT 248, 70 JP 451, 4 LGR 992, CA; *rvsd sub nom Attorney-General v West Riding of Yorkshire County Council* [1907] AC 29, HL, 44 Digest (Repl) 201, *140*.

Ricardo v Garcias (1845) 12 Cl & Fin 368, 9 Jur 1019, 8 ER 1450, HL, 11 Digest (Repl) 530, *1422*.

b *River Wear Comrs v Adamson* (1877) 2 App Cas 743, [1874-80] All ER Rep 1, 47 LJQB 193, 37 LT 543, 42 JP 244, 13 Asp MLC 521, HL, 17 Digest (Reissue) 297, *639*.

Rookes v Barnard [1964] 1 All ER 367, [1964] AC 1129, [1964] 2 WLR 269, [1964] 1 Lloyd's Rep 28, HL, Digest (Cont Vol B) 217, *13a*.

Ross Smith v Ross Smith [1962] 1 All ER 344, [1963] AC 280, [1962] 2 WLR 388, HL, Digest (Cont Vol A) 243, *1067b*.

c *Shenton v Tyler* [1939] 1 All ER 827, [1939] Ch 620, 108 LJCh 256, 160 LT 314, CA, 22 Digest (Reissue) 458, *4579*.

Shiloh Spinners Ltd v Harding [1973] 1 All ER 90, [1973] AC 691, [1973] 2 WLR 28, HL.

Thoday v Thoday [1964] 1 All ER 341, [1964] P 181, [1964] 2 WLR 371, CA, Digest (Cont Vol B) 365, *4179a*.

Warner v Buffalo Drydock Co (1933) 67 Fed R 2d 540, 291 US 678.

d *Western Coal & Mining Co v Jones* (1946) 27 Cal 2d 819, 167 P 2d 719, 164 ALR 685 (SC Cal).

Appeal

By an order dated 29th August 1972 Master Elton gave the appellants, Black-Clawson International Ltd, leave to issue a writ against the respondents, Papierwerke Waldhof-
e Aschaffenburg AG, and to serve notice of the writ on them at 8201 Raubling Reden-felden, or elsewhere in West Germany. Notice of the writ was served on the respondents on 14th August 1973. By a summons dated 3rd September 1973 the respondents applied for an order that Master Elton's order, the writ issued pursuant to the order, the service of notice of the writ and all subsequent proceedings be set aside. On 6th December Master Bickford-Smith in chambers ordered that the respondents' appli-
f cation be dismissed and on 15th February 1974 Talbot J in chambers dismissed an appeal by the respondents against that order. The respondents applied to the Court of Appeal for leave to appeal against the order of Talbot J. The Court of Appeal[1] (Lord Denning MR, Megaw and Scarman LJJ) granted leave and, on 19th March 1974, allowed the appeal. The appellants appealed, by leave of the Court of Appeal. The facts are set out in the opinion of Viscount Dilhorne.

g

Conrad Dehn QC and *Peter Scott* for the appellants.
Anthony Lincoln QC, Stanley Brodie and *D T Donaldson* for the respondents.

Their Lordships took time for consideration.

h 5th March. The following opinions were delivered.

LORD REID. My Lords, the main question at issue in this case is the proper interpretation of s 8 of the Foreign Judgments (Reciprocal Enforcement) Act 1933. The facts are not in dispute: they have been set out by my noble and learned friends and I shall not repeat them. It is sufficient to say at this point that the respondents, a
j German company, were sued by the appellants in Germany in respect of dishonoured bills of exchange. The action was dismissed as being time barred without any enquiry into the merits. The German period of limitation is shorter than in England and the appellants now seek to raise the same question here. The main issue in this case is

---

1 [1974] 2 All ER 611, [1974] QB 660

whether s 8 entitles the respondents to rely on the German judgment as conclusive
on the merits.   *a*

In this case it appears to me to be unusually important to consider as aids to construction all other material which the law allows us to look at, and I shall first state my view
on that matter. We often say that we are looking for the intention of Parliament, but
that is not quite accurate. We are seeking the meaning of the words which Parliament
used. We are seeking not what Parliament meant but the true meaning of what they
said. In the comparatively few cases where the words of a statutory provision are   *b*
only capable of having one meaning, that is an end of the matter and no further
enquiry is permissible. But that certainly does not apply to s 8.

One must first read the words in the context of the Act as a whole, but one is entitled to go beyond that. The general rule in construing any document is that one
should put oneself 'in the shoes' of the maker or makers and take into account relevant
facts known to them when the document was made. The same must apply to Acts of   *c*
Parliament subject to one qualification. An Act is addressed to all the lieges and it
would seem wrong to take into account anything that was not public knowledge at
the time. That may be common knowledge at the time or it may be some published
information which Parliament can be presumed to have had in mind.

It has always been said to be important to consider the 'mischief' which the Act was
apparently intended to remedy. The word 'mischief' is traditional. I would expand it   *d*
in this way. In addition to reading the Act you look at the facts presumed to be
known to Parliament when the Bill which became the Act in question was before it,
and you consider whether there is disclosed some unsatisfactory state of affairs which
Parliament can properly be supposed to have intended to remedy by the Act. There
is a presumption which can be stated in various ways. One is that in the absence of
any clear indication to the contrary Parliament can be presumed not to have altered   *e*
the common law farther than was necessary to remedy the 'mischief'. Of course it
may and quite often does go farther. But the principle is that if the enactment is
ambiguous, that meaning which relates the scope of the Act to the mischief should
be taken rather than a different or wider meaning which the contemporary situation
did not call for. The mischief which this Act was intended to remedy may have been
common knowledge 40 years ago. I do not think that it is today. But it so happens   *f*
that a committee including many eminent and highly skilled members made a full
investigation of the matter and reported some months before the Act was passed[1].

I think that we can take this report as accurately stating the 'mischief' and the law
as it was then understood to be, and therefore we are fully entitled to look at those
parts of the report which deal with those matters.

But the report contains a great deal more than that. It contains recommendations,   *g*
a draft Bill and other instruments intended to embody those recommendations, and
comments on what the committee thought the Bill achieved. The draft Bill corresponds in all material respects with the Act so it is clear that Parliament adopted the
recommendations of the committee. But nevertheless I do not think that we are
entitled to take any of this into account in construing the Act.

Construction of the provisions of an Act is for the court and for no one else. This   *h*
may seem technical but it is good sense. Occasionally we can find clear evidence of
what was intended, more often any such evidence, if there is any, is vague and uncertain. If we are to take into account evidence of Parliament's intention the first
thing we must do is to reverse our present practice with regard to consulting Hansard.
I have more than once drawn attention to the practical difficulties that would involve
but the difficulty goes deeper. The questions which give rise to debate are rarely those   *j*
which later have to be decided by the courts. One might take the views of the promoters of a Bill as an indication of the intention of Parliament but any view the promoters may have had about questions which later come before the court will not

---

1 Report of the Foreign Judgments (Reciprocal Enforcement) Committee (1932) Cmd 4213

often appear in Hansard and often those questions have never occurred to the promo-
a ters. At best we might get material from which a more or less dubious inference might
be drawn as to what the promoters intended or would have intended if they had
thought about the matter, and it would I think generally be dangerous to attach
weight to what some other members of either House may have said. The difficulties
in assessing any references there might have been in Parliament to the question before
the court are such that in my view our best course is to adhere to present practice.

b If we are to refrain from considering expressions of intention in Parliament it
appears to me that a fortiori we should disregard expressions of intention by committees or royal commissions which reported before the Bill was introduced. I may
add that we did in fact examine the whole of this report—it would have been difficult
to avoid that—but I am left in some doubt as to how the committee would have
answered some of the questions which we have now to answer, because I do not think
c that they were ever considered by the committee.

The committee in para 2 set out the fact that, whereas we accept foreign judgments
as conclusive, foreign courts do not in effect recognise English judgments, so that a
successful plaintiff here has to fight his case over again on the merits. They regarded
this as a substantial grievance. This could be avoided by making conventions with
foreign countries, but the committee say that there were two difficulties. First
d technically we do not enforce the foreign judgment as such, and second that our law
depends on case law and is not formulated in the statute book. There is nowhere in
the report any suggestion of any complaint, grievance or difficulty with regard to
British or foreign judgments in favour of the defendant, and I think that it is quite
clear that they did not consider that there was any 'mischief' with regard to such
judgments which required the intervention of Parliament.

e Moreover when they set out the existing law as they understood it, they do so in a
way which was entirely correct if one only has regard to a judgment in favour of the
plaintiff or a judgment for costs in favour of a successful defendant, but was clearly
not correct with regard to a judgment dismissing the plaintiff's action. A committee
of such eminence could not have been mistaken about the law so the only possible
inference is that the committee intended only to deal with plaintiffs' judgments.

f The difficulty with regard to judgments for defendants is that an action may be
dismissed for a variety of reasons: the case may have been decided against the plaintiff
on the merits or for some quite different reason such as a time bar or some other
preliminary plea. That matter was dealt with by a strong court in *Harris v Quine*[1]
when it was held that dismissal of an action in the Isle of Man because of a short
period of limitation which did not destroy the plaintiff's right but merely made it
g unenforceable, was not a bar to subsequent proceedings in England on the same cause
of action.

There is not much reference to the case in subsequent authorities but it was noted
in the textbooks and in the 60 odd years which elapsed before the committee's report
there is no indication of any disapproval of it. But the committee never mentioned it
or its subject-matter. The only possible inference is that they did not think it relevant
h to their enquiry.

It has been said that it would be strange that the Act should only deal with judgments in favour of a plaintiff and omit dealing with judgments in favour of a defendant.
Looking to the matters which I have dealt with I do not find that in the least strange.

It is clear that the Act did not intend to codify the whole law as to the effect of
foreign judgments. Section 8(3) is only one proof of that. So I approach s 8 with the
j expectation that it has a limited scope.

I now turn to the Act. Clearly its principal purpose—dealt with in Part I—was to
facilitate the enforcement here of rights given by foreign judgments to recover sums
of money. Besides rights given to plaintiffs in foreign actions, such rights might be

---

1   (1869) LR 4 QB 653

given to defendants on counterclaims or under orders for costs in favour of a successful
defendant. These I may call plaintiffs' judgments. But Part I has no application to **a**
defendants' judgments which entitle them to nothing, but merely protects them
against claims made against them. It would I think be a misuse of language to say
that such a judgment can be enforced. It can only be used as a shield or defence.

I think that s 8 is ambiguous so this is a case where it is permissible to look at the
long title. It states that the Act makes provision for the enforcement here of certain
foreign judgments, for facilitating the enforcement abroad of judgments given here **b**
and 'for other purposes in connection' with 'the matters aforesaid'. The matters
aforesaid all refer to plaintiffs' judgments which are enforceable. I do not see here
any indication of an intention to deal with judgments which are not enforceable.

Section 8 is in Part II under the heading 'Miscellaneous and General'. I do not think
that the other sections in Part II throw any light on its scope. The first question which
arises is whether s 8 has any application at all to defendants' judgments. There is **c**
provision in the Act for severence and no doubt it applies to those parts of defendants'
judgments which entitle the defendant to some remedy. But does the section apply
at all to a judgment or part of a judgment which merely absolves the defendant or
dismisses the action against him? Looking to all the matters I have mentioned they
seem to me to make it probable that s 8 was not intended to deal with such judgments
at all. Section 8 provides as follows: **d**

'(1) Subject to the provisions of this section, a judgment to which Part I of this
Act applies or would have applied if a sum of money had been payable thereunder,
whether it can be registered or not, and whether, if it can be registered, it is
registered or not, shall be recognised in any court in the United Kingdom as
conclusive between the parties thereto in all proceedings founded on the same **e**
cause of action and may be relied on by way of defence or counterclaim in any
such proceedings.

'(2) This section shall not apply in the case of any judgment:—(a) where the
judgment has been registered and the registration thereof has been set aside
on some ground other than—(i) that a sum of money was not payable under the
judgment; or (ii) that the judgment had been wholly or partly satisfied; or (iii) **f**
that at the date of the application the judgment could not be enforced by execution in the country of the original court; or (b) where the judgment has not been
registered, it is shown (whether it could have been registered or not) that if it
had been registered the registration thereof would have been set aside on an
application for that purpose on some ground other than one of the grounds specified in paragraph (a) of this subsection. **g**

'(3) Nothing in this section shall be taken to prevent any court in the United
Kingdom recognising any judgment as conclusive of any matter of law or fact
decided therein if that judgment would have been so recognised before the passing
of this Act.'

I find the first few lines very obscure. The section sets out to deal with a judgment
to which Part I applies 'or would have applied if a sum of money had been payable **h**
thereunder'. A plaintiff's judgment may order specific performance or it may be
merely a declaration. It is easy to apply these words in such cases. But I find it extremely difficult to apply them to defendants' judgments. The essence of such a
judgment is that the defendant has succeeded and that he has no liability to pay or do
anything. No sum of money could possibly have been payable under such a judgment.
It is only by putting an unnatural meaning on these words that defendants' judgments **i**
can be brought within the section at all.

I cannot believe that good draftsmen—as this committee certainly were—would
have employed such an obscure expression if the intention had been to deal with
defendants' judgments. It was argued that it throws us back to s 1(2) which is in these
terms:

a
'Any judgment of a superior court of a foreign country to which this Part of this Act extends, other than a judgment of such a court given on appeal from a court which is not a superior court, shall be a judgment to which this Part of this Act applies, if—(a) it is final and conclusive as between the parties thereto; and (b) there is payable thereunder a sum of money not being a sum payable in respect of taxes or other charges of a like nature or in respect of a fine or other penalty;

b
and (c) it is given after the coming into operation of the Order in Council directing that this Part of this Act shall extend to that foreign country.'

Subsection (3) provides:

'For the purposes of this section, a judgment shall be deemed to be final and conclusive notwithstanding that an appeal may be pending against it, or that it may still be subject to appeal, in the courts of the country of the original court.'

c
It is said that the effect of these obscure words in s 8(1) is to make the section apply to all judgments which would come within the terms of s 1(2) if condition (b) were omitted. Besides the fact that this would be a very odd way of bringing in another section of the Act that cannot be right. If (b) is omitted then s 1(2) would apply to every kind of judgment including judgments on status, family matters and in rem. No one suggests that s 8 was meant to deal with them. I am not at all clear what

d
meaning the respondents would attach to those obscure words if mere reference back to s 1(2) will not do.

Then it is said that the references in the last lines of s 8(1) to defence and counterclaim shew that the section must have been intended to deal with defendants' judgments. I do not agree. It is necessary to look closely at the preceding words in the section. It makes judgments to which it applies conclusive 'in all proceedings founded

e
on the same cause of action'. I think that cause of action normally means a right alleged to flow from the facts pleaded. But often cause of action is used to denote those facts, for example, a statute may provide that the cause of action must arise within a particular area: that must mean the facts and not the right.

Here I think it must mean the facts. Suppose that the defendant abroad raises proceedings here on the same facts as those in the foreign case. If cause of action meant

f
right only, one person has the cause of action and the section would not apply at all because the proceedings here would not be founded on the same cause of action. That could not have been intended.

But if cause of action refers to the facts there is no difficulty in applying this part of the section even if the section has no application to defendants' judgments. A successful plaintiff abroad is entitled to disregard his foreign judgment and sue here again on

g
his original right because a right does not merge in a foreign judgment. It might pay him to do that because he thinks that he could get here an even more favourable judgment than he got abroad. But this section would prevent that. The original defendant could plead the foreign plaintiff's judgment as a defence to prevent the plaintiff's attempt to do better for himself here. Similarly if the successful plaintiff abroad held an unsatisfied foreign judgment and he were sued here in some other

h
cause of action, he could counterclaim in respect of his unsatisfied foreign judgment. So there is ample scope for the operation of the last part of the subsection even if the section applies solely to plaintiffs' judgments.

I am therefore of opinion that s 8 has no application to the present case and does not entitle the respondents to rely on the foreign judgment on a preliminary point to prevent enquiry into the merits here. If further justification for my view be needed,

j
it would I think be unjust if a foreign judgment on a preliminary point were in itself sufficient to prevent enquiry into the merits here.

I may add that if it were held that the section does apply to defendants' judgments, I would, perhaps with difficulty, agree with those of your Lordships who think that the appellants should succeed. Then the respondents maintain that *Harris v Quine*[1] was

---

1   (1869) LR 4 QB 653   E.E

wrongly decided. I am clearly of opinion for reasons given by your Lordships that the   a
decision was right.

Finally I agree with your Lordships in the matter of discretion. I would therefore
allow the appeal.

VISCOUNT DILHORNE. My Lords, under a contract made in December
1961 the appellants agreed to sell paper making machinery to a German company,   b
whose rights and liabilities were acquired by the respondents as a result of a merger
in 1970. It will be convenient to refer to both companies as the respondents. The price
to be paid was £1,210,162. As part payment of the purchase price the respondents
accepted 20 bills of exchange drawn on them by the appellants. Each bill had a face
value of £48,406 and was drawn, negotiated and payable in London. Two bills were
to mature every six months between August 1963 and February 1968. In 1965 the   c
respondents complained of delays in delivery and of defects in the machinery delivered.
This was referred to arbitration and despite the time that has elapsed, that arbitration
has not yet been concluded and is not likely to be for a considerable time. Thereafter
the respondents refused to honour any of the bills which matured.

Two bills which had been dishonoured when presented by Barclays Bank by whom
they had been discounted, were the subject of litigation in this country and in Ger-   d
many. The bank's claim was strenuously resisted at every stage. When judgment was
given in this country for the bank, it was not satisfied. When the bank sought to
enforce the judgment in Germany, that was resisted on the ground that the respondents had had no opportunity of stating their case. This plea was finally rejected by the
Federal Supreme Court of Germany on 25th March 1970.

In view of the difficulties that the bank had encountered in getting payment of the   e
amounts due on these two bills, when two bills due for payment on 31st August 1966
were dishonoured, the bank called on the Export Credit Guarantee Department to
implement a guarantee they had given to the bank and that department in turn
called on the appellants to implement their undertaking to indemnify the department
against any moneys the department had to pay the bank. In accordance with their
agreement with the bank, the appellants bought these bills in August 1972 and so   f
became holders of them for value.

In the same month, on 24th August 1972 the appellants began proceedings against
the respondents in the District Court of Munich. Five days later the appellants applied
ex parte in this country for leave to issue a writ against the respondents claiming the
amount due on the two bills and interest and also asking leave to serve notice of the
writ on the respondents in Germany. They feared that the proceedings in Germany   g
might be held to be time barred in Germany; and if the writ were not issued, their
claim would shortly have become statute-barred in this country. They were given
the leave for which they asked. On 30th November 1972 the District Court of Munich
dismissed the appellant's claim, holding that under German law the applicable
period of limitation was three years and so that the appellants' claim was time-barred.
Notice of the issue of the writ was served on the respondents on 14th August 1973.   h
The respondents did not enter an appearance but by summons sought an order that
the writ, service of notice thereof and all subsequent proceedings thereon should be
set aside. The master refused to make that order and the respondents' appeal to
Talbot J, the judge in chambers, was dismissed. The respondents then appealed to
the Court of Appeal[1] which gave judgment in their favour on 19th March 1974. On
27th March 1974 the Munich Court of Appeal allowed the appellants' appeal against   j
the decision of the District Court on the ground that the English period of limitation,
namely six years, was applicable to their claim. The Appeal Court referred the case
back to the District Court for continuation of the proceedings and in those proceedings

---

1   [1974] 2 All ER 611, [1974] QB 660

the respondents are entitled to put forward any defence they may have to the claim.

a The respondents have appealed against the decision of the Munich Court of Appeal to the Federal Supreme Court but that appeal has not yet been heard.

In the Court of Appeal the respondents put forward a new point based on s 8(1) of the Foreign Judgments (Reciprocal Enforcement) Act 1933, and it was on this ground that the court (Lord Denning MR, Megaw and Scarman LJJ) allowed the appeal. The long title of that Act reads as follows:

b

'An Act to make provision for the enforcement in the United Kingdom of judgments given in foreign countries which accord reciprocal treatment to judgments given in the United Kingdom, for facilitating the enforcement in foreign countries of judgments given in the United Kingdom, and for other purposes in connection with the matters aforesaid.'

c Part I of the Act is headed 'Registration of Foreign Judgments' and is directed to securing the enforcement of foreign judgments in this country. Part II is headed 'Miscellaneous and General'. Section 8 is the first section in this Part and reads as follows:

'(1) Subject to the provisions of this section, a judgment to which Part I of this *d* Act applies or would have applied if a sum of money had been payable thereunder, whether it can be registered or not, and whether, if it can be registered, it is registered or not, shall be recognised in any court in the United Kingdom as conclusive between the parties thereto in all proceedings founded on the same cause of action and may be relied on by way of defence or counterclaim in any such proceedings.

e '(2) This section shall not apply in the case of any judgment: . . . (*a*) where the judgment has been registered and the registration thereof has been set aside on some ground other than: (i) that a sum of money was not payable under the judgment; or (ii) that the judgment had been wholly or partly satisfied; or (iii) that at the date of the application the judgment could not be enforced by execution in the country of the original court; or (*b*) where the judgment has not *f* been registered, it is shown (whether it could have been registered or not) that if it had been registered the registration thereof would have been set aside on an application for that purpose on some ground other than one of the grounds specified in paragraph (*a*) of this subsection.

'(3) Nothing in this section shall be taken to prevent any court in the United Kingdom recognising any judgment as conclusive of any matter of law or fact *g* decided therein if that judgment would have been so recognised before the passing of this Act.'

The judgments to which Part I of the Act applies are defined in s 1(2) and (3) of the Act which read as follows:

'(2) Any judgment of a superior court of a foreign country to which this Part *h* of this Act extends, other than a judgment of such a court given on appeal from a court which is not a superior court, shall be a judgment to which this Part of this Act applies, if—(*a*) it is final and conclusive as between the parties thereto; and (*b*) there is payable thereunder a sum of money, not being a sum payable in respect of taxes or other charges of a like nature or in respect of a fine or other penalty; and (*c*) it is given after the coming into operation of the Order in Council directing that this Part of this Act shall extend to that foreign country.

j '(3) For the purposes of this section, a judgment shall be deemed to be final and conclusive notwithstanding that an appeal may be pending against it, or that it may still be subject to appeal, in the courts of the country of the original court.'

Such a judgment may be registered if it has not been wholly satisfied and if it is not one which could not have been enforced by execution in the country of the original court. If a judgment of a foreign court is registered, then for the purposes of execution, *a* it is not competent to a party to apply for the registration to be set aside or such an application has been finally determined, the registered judgment is to be of the same force and effect as a judgment originally given by the registering court. Proceedings may be taken on it as if it were a judgment of that court and the judgment is to carry interest as if it were a judgment of that court (s 2(2)).

Part I of the Act only applies to judgments under which a sum of money is payable. *b* Section 8(1) applies to all judgments to which Part I applies and also to judgments to which that Part does not apply but would have applied if money had been payable under them, that is to say judgments which are final and conclusive and given after the order in council applying Part I to the foreign country concerned has been made (s 1(2)(*a*) and (*c*)).

I cannot therefore see that there is any ground for concluding, as was contended by *c* the appellants, that s 8(1) only applies to judgments which can be enforced. Section 8(1) does not deal at all with enforcement. That is dealt with in Part I. As it was not disputed that in this case s 1(2)(*a*) and (*c*) were satisfied, in my opinion the judgment of the District Court of Munich was one to which s 8(1) applies. That subsection goes on to provide that such a judgment shall be recognised in any court in the United Kingdom as 'conclusive between the parties thereto', and to state when it is to be so *d* recognised, namely 'in all proceedings founded on the same cause of action'. It concludes by saying that it may be relied on by way of defence or counterclaim in any such proceedings. The subsection does not expressly state of what the judgment is to be conclusive and the controversy in this appeal is as to that.

In *Thoday v Thoday*¹ Diplock LJ said that there were two species of estoppel per rem judicatam. The first, which he called 'cause of action estoppel' was that which pre- *e* vents a party to an action from asserting or denying, as against the other party, the existence of a particular cause of action, the non-existence or existence of which has been determined by a court of competent jurisdiction in previous litigation between the same parties. The second, which my noble and learned friend called 'issue estoppel' arises where in previous litigation one of the matters in issue between the *f* parties has already been decided by a competent court.

Lord Denning MR in the Court of Appeal held² that s 8(1) dealt with 'cause of action estoppel' and s 8(3) with 'issue estoppel'; and that as the proceedings in England would be founded on the same cause of action as those in Germany, the judgment in Germany was to be treated as conclusive. That judgment did not decide that money was not owed by the respondents to the appellants but that it was not recoverable, owing to the German period of limitation. Nevertheless, in Lord Denning MR's view *g* s 8(1) operated to prevent the appellants from suing in this country on the same cause of action even though the period of limitation under English law had not expired.

Megaw LJ and Scarman LJ³ held that s 8(1) displaced the common law as to the enforcement and recognition of foreign judgments, and agreed that the judgment of the German court prevented proceedings being instituted in this country. *h*

The contrary view advanced by the appellants was that the judgment of the foreign court was only made conclusive by s 8(1) as to the matters decided therein and so was conclusive only on the question whether the limit imposed by German law on the time within which actions must be instituted applied and barred the action.

Although since 1964 the use of the expressions 'cause of action estoppel' and 'issue *j* estoppel' has become common, I do not think that that division into two species of estoppel per rem judicatam was recognised in 1933 or that those expressions were then

---

1   [1964] 1 All ER 341 at 352, [1964] P 181 at 197
2   [1974] 2 All ER at 615, [1974] QB at 672
3   [1974] 2 All ER at 618, 623, 624, [1974] QB at 676, 681, 682

used. If that be right, it would indeed be singular if Parliament had then intended
a s 8(1) only to apply to 'cause of action estoppel' and s 8(3) only to 'issue estoppel'.
In this connection I think the way in which s 8(3) is drafted is illuminating. If that
section was intended to cover issue estoppel, I would not have expected it to commence
with the words 'Nothing in this section shall be taken to prevent . . .' That is a formula
frequently used in statutes when a provision is inserted ex abundanti cautela. Its use
in s 8(3) leads me to the conclusion that s 8(3) was not intended to cover issue estoppel
b as a distinct species of res judicata but was inserted to ensure that the Act did not by
s 8(1) reduce the recognition given by the courts of this country under the common
law to foreign judgments. It follows that s 8(1) was not intended, if this be so, to cover
only one species of estoppel per rem judicatam.

Our attention was drawn to the fact that the Foreign Judgments (Reciprocal
Enforcement) Act 1933 was passed by Parliament on 13th April 1933 shortly after the
c Report of a Committee called the Foreign Judgments (Reciprocal Enforcement)
Committee[1] had been presented to Parliament. That was done in December 1932.
The committee had been appointed by the then Lord Chancellor and its chairman was
Greer LJ. It had among its members many very eminent lawyers. To its report were
annexed a draft of conventions to be entered into with foreign countries and a draft
bill, cl 8 of which was in precisely the same terms as s 8 of the Act.

d The question was debated to what extent could recourse be had to the committee's
report as an aid to the construction of s 8. Ever since Heydon's Case[2] it has been recognised that there are, in connection with the interpretation of statutes, four questions
to be considered: (1) what was the common law before the making of the Act; (2)
what was the mischief or defect for which the law did not provide; (3) what remedy
Parliament had provided, and (4) the reason for the remedy (see Eastman Photographic
e Materials Co v Comptroller-General of Patents[3]). In that case Lord Halsbury LC cited a
passage[4] from the report of commissioners appointed to enquire into the duties,
organisation and arrangements of the Patent Office in relation to trade marks and
designs. That passage not only referred to what the existing law was but also to what
the commissioners thought it ought to be; and after citing it, Lord Halsbury LC
said[5]:
f
'My Lords, I think no more accurate source of information as to what was the
evil or defect which the Act of Parliament now under construction was intended
to remedy could be imagined than the report of that commission.'

Many instances were cited in the course of the argument where the courts have had
regard to the reports of such commissions or committees; e g in Rookes v Barnard[6]
g and Heatons Transport (St Helens) Ltd v Transport and General Workers Union[7] to the
Report of the Royal Commission on Trade Unions and Employees' Associations
1965-1968[8], in National Provincial Bank Ltd v Ainsworth[9] to the Report of the Royal
Commission on Marriage and Divorce[10] and in Letang v Cooper[11] to the Report of the
Tucker Committee on the Limitation of Actions[12]. Other instances could be cited and,
despite the observations of Lord Wright with which Lord Thankerton agreed in
h

---

1   (1932) Cmd 4213
2   (1584) 3 Co Rep 7a
3   [1898] AC 571
4   [1898] AC at 574
5   [1898] AC at 575
j   6   [1964] 1 All ER 367, [1964] AC 1129
7   [1972] 3 All ER 101, [1973] AC 15
8   Cmnd 3623
9   [1965] 2 All ER 472, [1965] AC 1175
10   (1956) Cmd 9678
11   [1964] 2 All ER 929, [1965] 1 QB 232
12   (1949) Cmd 7740

Assam Railways and Trading Co Ltd v Inland Revenue Comrs[1], it is now, I think, clearly
established that regard can be had to such reports. In that case counsel had sought to   *a*
refer to recommendations of the Royal Commission on Income Tax of 1920 and to
argue that the Finance Act 1920 followed those recommendations. The House did not
allow him to do so, Lord Wright saying[2]:

> '. . . on principle no such evidence for the purpose of showing the intention,
> that is the purpose or object, of an Act is admissible; the intention of the Legisla-   *b*
> ture must be ascertained from the words of the statute with such extraneous
> assistance as is legitimate: as to this, I agree with Farwell L.J. in *Rex* v. *West Riding
> of Yorkshire County Council*[3] where he says "I think the true rule is expressed with
> accuracy by Lord Langdale in giving the judgment of the Privy Council in the
> *Gorham Case* in Moore 1852 edition[4] 'We must endeavour to attain for ourselves
> the true meaning of the language employed'—in the Articles and Liturgy—   *c*
> 'assisted only by the consideration of such external or historical facts as we may
> find necessary to enable us to understand the subject matter to which the instru-
> ments relate, and the meaning of the words employed' " . . . It is clear that the
> language of a Minister of the Crown in proposing in Parliament a measure which
> eventually becomes law is inadmissible and the Report of Commissioners is even
> more removed from value as evidence of intention, because it does not follow   *d*
> that their recommendations were accepted.'

Despite these observations, in *Shenton v Tyler*[5] Greene MR cited a recommendation
of the Common Law Commissioners of 1852 saying that it was accepted by the
legislature and embodied in the Evidence Amendment Act 1853.

The task confronting a court when construing a statute is to determine what was
Parliament's intention. In a perfect world the language employed in the Act would   *e*
not be capable of more than one interpretation but due in part to lack of precision of
the English language, often more than one interpretation is possible. Then, to enable
Parliament's intention to be determined, as I understand the position, one may have
regard to what was the law at the time of the enactment and to what was the mischief
at which it was directed.

That one can look at such reports to discern the mischief is now, I think, established   *f*
but there is a difference of opinion as to what may be looked at in such reports. Can
one have regard to the recommendations of the committee or commission? Where a
draft bill is attached to the report, as is now frequently the case, and was the case in
this instance, can one refer to the terms of the draft bill when they have been enacted
without material alteration by Parliament? Can one refer to the notes on the clauses
of the draft bill appended to it by the committee, and in the present case to the terms   *g*
of the draft conventions prepared by the committee and attached to their report? Is it
legitimate to make use of such parts of a report as an aid to the construction of the
Act? In my opinion it is. The reason why one is entitled to consider what was the
mischief at which the Act was aimed is surely that that will throw a revealing light
on the object and purpose of the Act, that is to say the intention of Parliament; and,
applying Lord Halsbury's observations[6] cited above, what more accurate source of   *h*
information both as to the law at the time and as to the evil or defect which the Act
was intended to remedy can be imagined than the report of such a committee, or for
that matter, the reports of the Law Commission.

The contrary view seems to impose on judges the task of being selective in their

j

---

1   [1935] AC 445, [1934] All ER Rep 646
2   [1935] AC at 458, [1934] All ER Rep at 655
3   [1906] 2 KB 676
4   Page 462
5   [1939] 1 All ER 827 at 833, [1939] Ch 620 at 629
6   *Eastman Photographic Materials Co v Comptroller-General of Patents* [1898] AC 571 at 574

reading of such reports. What part may they look at and what not? Have they to stop
a reading when they come to a recommendation? Have they to ignore the fact, if it
be the fact, that the draft bill was enacted without alteration? To ignore what the
committee intended the draft bill to do and what the committee thought it would
do? I think not. I think so to hold would be to draw a very artificial line which serves
no useful purpose. What weight is to be given to a committee's recommendations is
another matter. That may depend on the particular circumstances. If the report of
b the committee merely contains recommendations, while I think that regard can be
had to them, little weight may be attached to them as it may not follow that Parliament has accepted them. Parliament may have decided to go further or not as far.
But where, as here, a draft bill is attached to the report, then one can compare its
provisions with those of the Act and if there is no difference or no material difference
in their language, then surely it is legitimate to conclude, as Greene MR did in *Shen-*
c *ton v Tyler*[1], that Parliament had accepted the recommendation of the committee
and had intended to implement it. In such a case that recommendation becomes as it
did in *Eastman Photographic Materials Co v Comptroller-General of Patents*[2] the most
accurate source of information as to the intention of Parliament.

Of course, it may be that the language used in the draft bill and in the Act is defective and does not carry out the committee's and Parliament's intention. Regard must
d be had to that possibility, however remote it may be. In *Letang v Cooper*[3] Lord
Denning MR said:

> 'It is legitimate to look at the report of such a committee [the Tucker Com-
> mittee on the Limitation of Actions], so as to see what was the mischief at which
> the Act was directed. You can get the facts and surrounding circumstances from
> the report, so as to see the background against which the legislation was enacted.
e > This is always a great help in interpreting it. But you cannot look at what the
> committee recommended, or at least, if you do look at it, you should not be
> unduly influenced by it. It does not help you much, for the simple reason that
> Parliament may, and often does, decide to do something different to cure the
> mischief.'

f While I respectfully agree that recommendations of a committee may not help
much when there is a possibility that Parliament may have decided to do something
different, where there is no such possibility, as where the draft bill has been enacted
without alteration, in my opinion it can safely be assumed that it was Parliament's
intention to do what the committee recommended and to achieve the object the
committee had in mind. Then, in my view the recommendations of the committee
g and their observations on their draft bill may form a valuable aid to construction
which the courts should not be inhibited from taking into account.

It does not follow that if one can have regard to the whole of a committee's report,
one ought also to be able to refer to Hansard to see what the Minister in charge of a
bill has said it was intended to do. In the course of the passage of a bill through both
Houses there may be many statements by Ministers, and what is said by a Minister in
h introducing a bill in one House is no sure guide as to the intention of the enactment,
for changes of intention may occur during its passage. But when a bill is drafted by
such a committee as that in this case and enacted without alteration, then, I repeat, in
my opinion it is legitimate to have regard to the whole of the committee's report,
including the terms of the draft bill attached to it, to the committee's notes on its
clauses and to the draft conventions annexed to the report, for they constitute a most
j valuable guide to the intention of Parliament.

---

1 [1939] 1 All ER at 833, [1939] Ch at 629
2 [1898] AC 571
3 [1964] 2 All ER at 933, [1965] 1 QB at 240

The report of the committee begins with a summary of the committee's recommendations and the reasons therefor. They were primarily concerned with securing *a* that English judgments should be recognised and enforced in foreign countries without the case having to be fought again on the merits in a foreign court. To that end conventions had to be entered into with foreign countries and the committee had ascertained that some foreign countries would be willing to allow judgments to be enforced 'on similar conditions to those on which we enforce theirs, provided that those conditions are defined in a Convention'. They pointed out that there were two *b* difficulties in the way of concluding such conventions: (i) that under the then existing procedure foreign judgments were not enforced as such, and (ii) 'The principles on which English courts accept foreign judgments as conclusive depend on case law and are not to be found formulated in the Statute Book'. Their aim was, they said, to remove these difficulties; and, they said, so far as the position in England was concerned, the change they proposed involved 'no radical alterations of the present *c* position'. Paragraph 4 of their report appears under the heading 'The Present Position. (i) Recognition and enforcement of foreign judgments in England', and reads as follows:

'Under English common law a foreign judgment (other than a judgment given in a criminal or fiscal matter), although it does not operate in England to *d* merge the original cause of action, is, provided that certain reasonably well-defined conditions are satisfied, recognised as conclusive between the persons who were parties to the proceedings in the foreign court as regards the question therein adjudicated* upon, and can be relied upon by any of the said parties or their privies, if further proceedings are brought in England by any other such party or his privy in respect of the same cause of action.' *e*

To this paragraph there was the following footnote:

'*The words "question adjudicated upon" refer to the actual decision (the operative parts of the judgment) as opposed to the grounds or reasoning upon which it may be based, in the course of which other points of law or fact may have been incidentally decided as preliminaries (necessary or otherwise) to the final *f* conclusion. The authorities on the effect of foreign judgments in English law are not very numerous. They appear, however, clearly to justify the statement of the position given above though it may be that this statement is slightly too narrow. This statement is in any case only intended to apply to judgments in ordinary proceedings *in personam*.'

The wording of this paragraph closely resembles that of s 8(1) of the Act and the *g* passages in the report to which I have referred establish, in my opinion, that by Part I of the bill the committee sought to secure that certain foreign judgments were capable of being enforced as such in English courts and by s 8 to state in a statute the principles on which English courts recognise foreign judgments as conclusive. There is nothing to be found in these passages or elsewhere in the report to support the contention that it was the committee's intention to alter or depart in any way from *h* the principles on which English courts had under the common law regarded foreign judgments as conclusive.

Paragraph 10 of the report states the reasons in the committee's view for 'the present failure' of foreign courts to recognise and enforce British judgments and the steps necessary to remedy that position. In para 10(*b*) they say: *j*

'The whole of the English procedure, including the conditions required for the recognition of a foreign judgment as conclusive, depends upon rules of Common Law only. There is always a natural tendency for the foreign court to suppose that such Common Law rules are too indefinite to be applied as rigidly as the provisions of a statute or a code, and that they are largely discretionary . . .'

The Report continues:

a

'Therefore, in the case of these countries, in practice . . . the conclusion of an international convention—containing reciprocal obligations for the recognition and enforcement of judgments which will be made binding as part of the municipal law of the foreign country together with the statement of our own rules in statutory form—appears to be the only manner by which anything like reciprocal

b   treatment can be secured in the matter of the recognition and enforcement of British judgments.'

And in para 16 the report states:

'It was, however, desirable that such legislation, in laying down the conditions under which, in return for reciprocal treatment, the judgments of foreign coun-

c   tries should be enforced, should not depart from the substantive principles of the common law applicable to foreign judgments in general.'

In para 23 the committee emphasised the manner in which the draft bill and rules on the one hand and the draft conventions on the other had been prepared 'concurrently with and in the light of each other, so as to render the arrangements pro-

d   posed in connexion with foreign judgments in the United Kingdom consistent with the conventions, and vice versa.'

One annex (Annex IV(6)) to the report contains a draft convention with Germany. Article 3 thereof deals with the recognition of judgments and art 3(2) provides that a judgment which is recognised—

e

'shall be treated as conclusive as to the matter thereby adjudicated upon in any further action between the parties . . . and as to such matter shall constitute a defence in a further action between them in respect of the same cause of action.'

No such convention was entered into with Germany until 1961 and art III(4) of that convention corresponds with art 3(2) of the draft. In their notes on the clauses of the draft bill (Annex V, para 13) the committee says:

f

'Clause 8 [now s 8 of the 1933 Act] contains the provisions of the Bill with regard to the recognition of foreign judgments as final and conclusive between the parties as regards the question therein adjudicated upon. It is entirely in accordance with the position at Common Law [as explained in para 4 of the report] and clause 8(3) [s 8(3) of the 1933 Act] saves the existing Common Law rules in any cases where the rule laid down by the Act may be narrower in operation than

g   the Common Law.'

The report thus shows, in my opinion beyond any question of doubt, that it was not the committee's intention by cl 8 to make any change in the existing common law rules as to recognition of foreign judgments; that cl 8(3) was inserted ex abundanti cautela and that cl 8(1) was only intended to operate to make a judgment conclusive

h   between the parties as to the matter thereby adjudicated on. Unfortunately the report was not brought to the attention of the Court of Appeal.

Parliament by enacting cl 8 without alteration must, in my opinion, have intended to implement the intentions of the committee and I can see no ground for holding that they did not effectively do so. What then was the question adjudicated on by the District Court of Munich on 30th November 1972? It was not that no money was

j   owed by the respondents to the appellants. The expert evidence in this case made it clear that the appellants' right to payment was not extinguished by that decision. It was not a judgment 'on the merits', an expression used not infrequently by lawyers, and used by the committee in para 1 of their report and one to which I must confess I have no difficulty in attaching a meaning. It was a decision that the German period of limitation applied and that the appellant's claim was consequently time-barred.

In these circumstances what was the position at common law. That was in my opinion clearly settled by the decision in *Harris v Quine*[1]. There it was held that a Manx statute which provided a three year period of limitation barred the remedy but did not extinguish the debt and that proceedings to recover the debt, though time-barred in the Isle of Man, could be brought in this country. In the course of his judgment Blackburn J said[2]:

'. . . it was said the plea . . . would shew that the Manx court had determined the matter, and that the matter ought not to be litigated again in the courts of this country; and, no doubt, wherever it can be shewn that a court of competent jurisdiction has decided the matter, the plaintiff is estopped from disputing the decision, or litigating the matter in another court, while the decision of the first court remains unreversed. But, in the present case, all that the Manx court decided was, that in the courts of the Isle of Man the plaintiffs could not recover.'

So here all that the German court decided was that in the German courts the appellants could not recover.

It was contended that this case was wrongly decided. I found that argument entirely unconvincing. It is a decision which has stood unchallenged since 1869. It was submitted that the committee must when preparing their report have overlooked it. I cannot accept that. It is a decision cited in Dicey's Conflict of Laws[3] without any adverse comment and in the first edition[4] of that work as authority for the proposition that—

'. . . it is not an answer to an action in England if it be . . . a judgment which, though it decides the cause finally in the country where it is brought, does not purport to decide it on the merits, e.g., if it is given in favour of the defendant on the ground that the action is barred by a statute of limitations.'

If the 1933 Act had not been passed, then under the common law, in the light of this decision, proceedings by the appellants in England would not have been barred by the decision of the Munich court. As in my opinion s 8 of the Act was intended to and does preserve the common law position without alteration, the respondents' claim that that decision prevents proceedings in England must be rejected.

In the Court of Appeal[5] some importance was attached to the concluding words of s 8(1), that the judgment is to be recognised as conclusive between the parties in all proceedings founded on the same cause of action and 'may be relied on by way of defence or counterclaim in any such proceedings'. Res judicata may be relied on by way of defence but the need to provide that it may be relied on by way of counter-claim founded on the same cause of action is somewhat obscure. Whatever its content be, the inclusion of the reference to a counterclaim does not, in my view, answer the question or throw a light on the answer to the question of what is a judgment to be recognised as conclusive. In my opinion, though the words 'of the matter adjudicated upon' are not in s 8(1), though they were in the draft convention and in para 4 of the report, nevertheless the language of that subsection provides that a judgment to which the subsection applies is to be conclusive of what it decides and not of what it does not decide. And the judgment of the Munich court did not decide that money was not owing by the respondents to the appellants. It was not a decision on the merits of the appellants' claim.

I would therefore allow the appeal. But the position has changed since the Court of Appeal's decision. The judgment of the Munich court has been reversed and that judgment reversing it is now under appeal.

1   (1869) LR 4 QB 653
2   (1869) LR 4 QB at 658
3   9th Edn (1973), p 1059
4   (1896), p 422
5   [1974] 2 All ER 611, [1974] QB 660

a In these circumstances while leave should be given to issue the writ and to serve notice thereof on the respondents, thereafter there should be a stay pending the decision of the Federal Supreme Court and with liberty to apply after the decision of the court has been given. I can see that formidable arguments may be advanced, if the Federal Supreme Court upholds the reversal of the decision of the Munich court, for saying that the appellants, having chosen the German courts as the forum and as the case can then be heard on its merits, should not in the exercise of discretion be b allowed at the same time to proceed in the courts of this country. But it is not necessary or desirable to express any opinion on that now.

For the reasons I have stated, in my opinion this appeal should be allowed.

LORD WILBERFORCE. My Lords, this appeal is essentially concerned with the interpretation of s 8(1) of the Foreign Judgments (Reciprocal Enforcement) Act 1933. c From the facts which have been fully stated I select those necessary for our decision.

1. The present action is brought on two bills of exchange drawn by the appellants and accepted by a predecessor in business of the respondents—it is not disputed that the respondents have succeeded to any liability on these bills. The proper law of these bills is English law. The German proceedings were brought by the appellants against the respondents on these same bills after dishonour.

d 2. Action on the bills in England is not, we must assume, barred by the English Limitation Act 1939.

3. In Germany, a three year period of limitation applies to bills of exchange. If the German period is applied to the bills, action on them is barred by German law. The question litigated in Germany, on which the German courts have differed, is whether in proceedings before a German court the German period does apply. The e basis of the affirmative decision of the District Court of Munchen is (briefly) that limitation is, under German law, classified as a matter of substance, not of procedure; that as the proper law of the bills is English law, this involves the application by a German court of English law; that under English law limitation is regarded as a matter of procedure; that, applying the doctrine of renvoi (accepted by the German court), reference back has to be made to the lex fori, i e German law, so that the f proceedings were barred.

4. According to expert evidence, German law, though classifying limitation as a matter of substance, did not, in relation to the subject-matter of dispute, extinguish the right, but did affect the remedy. As this point is crucial, I quote certain passages from the evidence filed on behalf of the respondents:

g 'In German law what is described in England as the limitation of actions does not extinguish the right. Nonetheless such limitation is a matter of substance, not of procedure.' [Dr F A Mann.]

'The completion of the limitation affects the substantive quality of the right. Notwithstanding the limitation, it is true the right remains in existence. Its effect, however is weakened by the fact that the obligor is entitled permanently to refuse h performance.' [Professor Hefermehl, commenting on the German Civil Code, s 222, cited by Dr F A Mann.]

'. . . the position is that, while the debts under the bills are not extinguished, the defendants are under no duty to pay them because they have a permanent answer to them'. [Dr F A Mann.]

j 5. The judgment of the District Court of Munchen, dated 30th November 1972, is in evidence. It consists of a single document containing (i) a dispositive part, (ii) a statement of facts, (iii) grounds for the decision. The dispositive part states 'The suit is dismissed'. The grounds for decision set out fully the grounds in law for holding that the claim is barred by the German law as to limitation. I mention this point because the respondents contend that the 'judgment' to be recognised under the 1933 Act is the dispositive provision dismissing the suit and nothing more.

After this preface I come to the 1933 Act. It is in two parts. Part I contains provisions for the enforcement of foreign judgments by registration. Part II contains *a* miscellaneous and general provisions starting with s 8, which deals with recognition. The question for decision is whether, and if so to what extent, s 8(1) applies to the present situation. There are two issues. The first is whether the subsection applies at all to foreign judgments dismissing a suit, i e in favour of a defendant: the appellants' contention is that it only applies to judgments which could, if certain other elements existed (e g an order to pay money), be enforceable under Part I. The second issue *b* is for what purpose and to what extent a foreign judgment is 'conclusive'. The appellants' contention is that it is to be conclusive as to any matter adjudicated on, but no further. Since in this case all that was adjudicated on was that the plaintiffs have no remedy in Germany on the bills, by reason of the expiry of the German limitation period, recognition of this fact does not prevent the appellants from suing in England. I shall deal first with the second point.   *c*

My Lords, we are entitled, in my opinion, to approach the interpretation of this subsection, and of the 1933 Act as a whole, from the background of the law as it stood, or was thought to stand, in 1933 and of the legislative intention. As to these matters the report to which my noble and learned friend, Lord Reid, has referred is of assistance. He has set out in his opinion the basis on which the courts may consult such documents. I agree with his reasoning and I only desire to add an observation of my *d* own on one point. In my opinion it is not proper or desirable to make use of such a document as a committee or commission report, or for that matter of anything reported as said in Parliament, or any official notes on clauses, for a direct statement of what a proposed enactment is to mean or of what the committee or commission thought it means: on this point I am in agreement with my noble and learned friend Lord Diplock. To be concrete, in a case where a committee prepared a draft bill and *e* accompanies that by a clause by clause commentary, it ought not to be permissible, even if the proposed bill is enacted without variation, to take the meaning of the bill from the commentary. There are, to my mind, two kinds of reason for this. The first is the practical one, that if this process were allowed the courts would merely have to interpret, as in argument we were invited to interpret, two documents instead of one—the bill and the commentary on it, in particular Annex V, para 13. The second *f* is one of constitutional principle. Legislation in England is passed by Parliament, and put in the form of written words. This legislation is given legal effect on subjects by virtue of judicial decision, and it is the function of the courts to say what the application of the words used to particular cases or individuals is to be. This power which has been devolved on the judges from the earliest times is an essential part of the constitutional process by which subjects are brought under the rule of law—as distinct *g* from the rule of the King or the rule of Parliament; and it would be a degradation of that process if the courts were to be merely a reflecting mirror of what some other interpretation agency might say. The saying that it is the function of the courts to ascertain the will or intention of Parliament is often enough repeated, so often indeed as to have become an incantation. If too often or unreflectingly stated, it leads to neglect of the important element of judicial construction; an element not confined to a *h* mechanical analysis of today's words, but, if this task is to be properly done, related to such matters as intelligibility to the citizen, constitutional propriety, considerations of history, comity of nations, reasonable and non-retroactive effect and, no doubt, in some contexts, to social needs.

It is sound enough to ascertain, if that can be done, the objectives of any particular measure, and the background of the enactment; but to take the opinion, whether of a *j* Minister or an official or a committee, as to the intended meaning in particular applications of a clause or a phrase, would be a stunting of the law and not a healthy development.

In this light I can state in summary form the considerations to which the report brings me in interpreting the Act. First, the objective of the Act is clear: it was to

secure the enforcement by other countries of English judgments, mainly money
a judgments, on principles similar to those on which foreign judgments were recognised in England. Second, the Act was to be based on and to follow with minimal
departures the common law. Third, the Act was to state in statutory form the general
principles on which foreign judgments (to which the Act applied) would be recognised in English courts. Fourth, the Act, a draft of which was annexed to the report,
and which the eventual statute adopted with negligible variation, was prepared in the
b contemplation that bilateral conventions would be entered into with foreign states,
with a view to securing reciprocity of treatment. It is made clear that negotiations had
taken place with the Belgian, French and German governments: draft conventions
had been prepared and are annexed to the report: the Act was intended to operate
on and in aid of these conventions. (The convention with Germany was not, in fact,
signed until 1960 and was given effect to by statutory instrument[1]; but it followed
c closely the draft scheduled to the report.) Fifth, it is relevant to notice that the
committee included a number of persons of acknowledged competence, and indeed
distinction, in the field of private international law, who must be taken to be familiar
with established rules and decided cases.

One of the rules, which they must be taken to be aware of, relates to the distinction
made in English private international law between matters of substance and matters
d of procedure, and, within that, the classification of limitation as a matter of procedure.
Classification of limitation as procedural means that in proceedings in an English
court, English law, as the lex fori, will apply its domestic law as to limitation and will
not apply foreign limitation provisions even if the foreign law is the proper law, unless,
at least, they extinguish the right. This principle has been part of English law since,
at any rate, *Huber v Steiner*[2]. I quote the well-known statement of principle by
e Tindal CJ[3]:

'The distinction between that part of the law of the foreign country where a
personal contract is made, which is adopted, and that which is not adopted by
our English courts of law, is well known and established; namely, that so much of
the law as affects the rights and merit of the contract, all that relates 'ad litis
f decisionem', is adopted from the foreign country; so much of the law as affects
the remedy only, all that relates 'ad litis ordinationem' is taken from the 'lex
fori' of that country where the action is brought.'

Huber v Steiner[2] was not itself a case involving a foreign judgment, but the question
arises immediately whether the same principle applies. The answer to this can only
g be affirmative. If English law applies its own limitation provisions to a foreign
obligation, even where there is evidence that action on that obligation would (or
would not) be barred by the limitation provisions of the proper law of that obligation,
it would seem inevitably to follow that English law should not recognise a foreign
judgment to the same effect—more precisely should treat the foreign judgment as a
decision as to the remedy procedurally available, or not available, in the foreign court
h and nothing more. Exactly that was in fact decided in 1869 by *Harris v Quine*[4].
Cockburn CJ[5] treated the matter as concluded by *Huber v Steiner*[2]:

'. . . the law being as I have stated, there is no judgment of the Manx court
barring the present action, as there was no plea going to the merits, according to
the view which we are bound to take of the Manx statute of limitations, and

j

1   Reciprocal Enforcement of Foreign Judgments (Germany) Order 1961 (SI 1961 No 1199)
2   (1835) Bing NC 202
3   Bing NC 202 at 210
4   (1869) LR 4 QB 653
5   LR 4 QB at 657

the issue which the Manx court decided in favour of the defendant is not the
same issue as is raised in the present action.'

Blackburn J[1]:

'But it was said the plea, if amended according to the facts, would shew that
the Manx court had determined the matter. ... But ... all that the Manx court
decided was, that in the courts of the Isle of Man the plaintiffs could not recover.'

We see here, in the judgment of Cockburn CJ, a reference to a plea going 'to the
merits'. This expression, whether related to pleas or to judgments, is a familiar
one in English law: any practitioner would use it —even if it is not always understood.
It is used in many well-known authorities: see *Ricardo v Garcias*[2]; *Godard v Gray*[3];
and in writers of authority: see Foote[4]; Dicey[5]; Story's Commentaries on the
Conflict of Laws[6]. See also American Law Institute (Restatement—Second) Conflict
of Laws, s 110[7]: 'A judgment that is not on the merits will be recognised in other
states only as to issues actually decided.' All of what was said in *Harris v Quine*[8]
applies directly to the present case, and unless the respondents can escape from
the force of this authority, must conclude the appeal against them. They had,
basically, two arguments. First they contended that *Harris v Quine*[8] was wrongly
decided, or at least that it stood alone and ought not to be followed. I regard this
this as a hopeless contention. It may be true that, as regards this subject-matter,
Harris v Quine[8] is the only English reported case where a foreign judgment and its
recognition was involved. But as I have shown it represents a logical and inevitable
consequence of *Huber v Steiner*[9] and other cases and is merely an application of a
principle too firmly established to be now put in question. *Harris v Quine*[8] has been
cited often enough in English and Commonwealth cases. See *Casanova, Auraldi
& Co v Meier & Co*[10]; *Carvell v Wallace*[11]; *Bondholders Securities Corpn v Manville*[12];
Pedersen v Young[13], sometimes, I must say, irrelevantly, but it has never been doubted.
The principle is well recognised by Courts of authority in the United States of America,
Warner v Buffalo Drydock Co[14]; *Western Coal and Mining Coy v Jones*[15] and see the
Restatement quoted above. As at the year 1933, then, *Harris v Quine*[8] was un-
doubtedly good law.

Secondly, and more substantially, the appellants say that *Harris v Quine*[8] is superseded by s 8(1) of the 1933 Act: this was in effect the view of the Court of Appeal[16].

Before looking at the language of the subsection, it may be useful to consider
what this contention involves. It involves the proposition that a well-established
principle of English law, namely, that to obtain recognition, a foreign judgment
must be on the merits and not be based merely on a 'procedural' provision of the
lex fori, is swept away in favour of a new principle that a foreign judgment, on whatever grounds it proceeds, is conclusive for all purposes, so long at least as the same

---

1 (1869) LR 4 QB at 658
2 (1845) 12 Cl & Fin 368 at 377, 389, 390
3 (1870) LR 6 QB 139 at 150
4 Private International Jurisprudence (4th Edn, 1914)
5 The Conflict of Laws (3rd Edn, 1922), p 455
6 8th Edn (1833), s 76
7 (1971), vol 1, pp 324, 325, s 110
8 LR 4 QB 653
9 (1835) Bing NC 202
10 (1885) 1 TLR 213
11 (1873) 9 NSR 165
12 [1933] 4 DLR 699
13 [1964] ALR 798
14 (1933) 67 Fed R 2d Cir 540
15 (1946) 27 Cal 2d 819
16 [1974] 2 All ER 611, [1974] QB 660

'cause of action' is involved, or the same facts. If one accepts that the presumption is
a against changes in the common law and that this presumption is fortified in the
present case by the report of 1932, if one accepts moreover that the principle under
consideration was perfectly well known and understood in 1932, it was to be expected
that on this point the common law would only be changed by a clear and express
provision. Yet what is relied on is the word 'conclusive' coupled with a reference
to 'cause of action'. I return to these words later. What, one could ask, could be the
b purpose of the change? Why should this Act make a judgment conclusive as to
something it never decided? Why, to take the present case, should a foreign judgment
be conclusive on a matter whose proper law is English, and accepted as English
by the foreign court, when that foreign law itself does not destroy the right, but
only limits the remedy it will grant? For English law to abolish the distinction
between substance and procedure, or to classify limitation as substance, might be
c an intelligible objective, but short of this, and leaving the distinction and classification
intact, to change the effect of a judgment is something that, at the least, requires
explanation.

Some suggestion was made that to extend the recognition of foreign judgments
might be desired on grounds of reciprocity: but I cannot understand this. There
was no evidence that foreign courts grant or would grant the wider recognition
d argued for by the respondents and in any case reciprocity was to be achieved by the
proposed conventions. There is nothing in this alleged principle—one of uncertain
extent—which assists either way in the interpretation of the Act.

I find then, so far, no intelligible reason for supposing the common law to be
changed. But the respondents say the words of the section are clear—clear words
must be given effect to—conclusive means conclusive and that is that. This, however,
e I cannot accept. In the first place one has to ask, '*What* is conclusive?' The section says
the 'judgment'—so what is 'the judgment'? The respondents say that the judgment
is the dispositive—'the suit is dismissed'. If this is contained in a self-contained document, as in the English practice, one may not look beyond it. If in a comprehensive
document, as in the German practice, only that part of it which states the disposition
is the judgment, not the whole of the judgment showing what was decided or
f adjudicated on. But there is no warrant for this limitation. The courts in this country,
when faced with a foreign judgment, whether in favour of the plaintiff or the defendant, in English proceedings, invariably look at the whole matter: the order
made; the reasons; the nature of the rival claims, resorting if necessary to extrinsic
evidence to explain them and to expose the reality. They do not confine themselves
to the fact of the record, or to the formal order. It must be remembered that at
g common law foreign judgments do not give rise to an estoppel by record. If relied
on by a plaintiff in an English court, they are so as obligations, which the defendant
ought to discharge: so the nature of the obligation must be made known and if
necessary explained. If they are relied on by a defendant as a bar in English proceedings, the nature of the bar must be enquired into, from an inspection of the matter
adjudicated on. *Harris v Quine*[1] itself is an example of this. One can cite many
h passages of authority:

'In general, in pleading a foreign judgment you produce it with the proceedings
to shew it is a judgment between the same parties and on the same matters.'

(*Ricardo v Garcias*[2] per Lord Lyndhurst LC.)

'Every plea of a former judgment in bar ought to set forth so much, at least,
j of the judgment as would shew that it was final and conclusive on the merits.'

(Ibid[3] per Bethell arg.)

1   (1869) LR 4 QB 653
2   (1845) 11 Cl & F 368 at 387
3   11 Cl & F at 389

'No one contends that the judgment and the proceedings should be set out
in full, but we should have such a description of them as would enable us to   *a*
know what was decided.'

(Ibid[1] per Lord Brougham.) So, in my opinion, to say that in a case such as the present
the English court must stop at the first line of the German judgment and ignore the
rest is irrational and out of line with what the courts do. And then 'conclusive':
conclusive of or as to what? The respondents say 'conclusive that the cause of action   *b*
on which the foreign proceedings were brought no longer exists'. But the subsection
does not say this: the words 'in all proceedings founded on the same cause of action'
merely describes the occasion on which the conclusiveness arises. There is nothing
here—and, I add in passing, nothing in Part I of the Act—to indicate that the conclusiveness is to extend, irrespective of what the judgment decided, to the whole
of the cause of action. Why should we give to the judgment a greater force than it   *c*
receives by the law of the country where it is given? Certainly the law of Germany
does not say that the cause of action does not exist.

In my opinion, therefore, an interpretation of both 'judgment' and 'conclusive'
which would require courts in this country to examine the judgment, see what
it decided, and hold it conclusive as a judgment and for what it adjudicates, is both
open on the language and is entirely consistent with the common law. To quote   *d*
another leading authority: 'As to whatever it meant to decide, we must take it
as conclusive' (*Bernardi v Motteux*[2] per Lord Mansfield).

The appellants finally relied strongly on the wording of s 8(3) of the 1933 Act.
I agree with my learned and noble friend Lord Simon of Glaisdale in the reasons
he has given why this subsection is of no assistance and shall not repeat them in words
of my own.   *e*

In my opinion, if this case had arisen at any time between 1869 and 1933 there could
be no doubt how it would have been decided. I see no reason why the 1933 Act should
be understood as intending to bring about a different result. The language of s 8(1)
does not so compel. The German judgment would be conclusive for what it decided
and for nothing more. The appellants' claim has not been decided on the merits, and
they should be allowed to pursue it. This being my conclusion on the second point,   *f*
it is not necessary to decide the first. I prefer to reserve my opinion on whether s 8(1)
applies to defendants' judgments.

There remains finally the question of residual discretion, and I must say that the
situation now existing is unfortunate. This House is called on to decide this matter
before it knows how the German proceedings will finally terminate. It is not in a position
effectively or with knowledge to exercise such discretion as the courts ought to exercise.   *g*
In my opinion, if a majority of your Lordships disagree with the legal position taken
by the Court of Appeal[3], the appeal should be allowed. But I suggest that the present
proceedings should be stayed, with liberty to apply after determination of the final
appeal in Germany and that the matter then be brought afresh, if the appellants so
desire, before the master to decide whether they should be allowed to continue their
action here. Obviously this House cannot now foresee all the contingencies. If the   *h*
respondents' appeal in Germany is allowed by the Federal Supreme Court and the
matter is restored to where it was when this case was before the Court of Appeal, then,
if your Lordships take a different view of the law from the Court of Appeal, there
would appear to be—ceteris paribus—a strong case for allowing the appellants to
continue with their action here. If, on the other hand, the respondents' appeal in
Germany is dismissed—so that the appellants in one way or another can proceed in   *j*
Germany—then the conditions on which the plaintiffs should (if at all) be allowed to

1 (1845) 11 Cl & F at 394
2 (1781) 2 Doug KB 575 at 581
3 [1974] 2 All ER 611, [1974] QB 660

sue the defendants also in this country would require examination. I do not think that
a this House can at the present stage offer any useful guidance as to the manner in
which that could be decided.

LORD DIPLOCK. My Lords, if the effect of the interpretation given by the
majority of this House to s 8(1) of the Foreign Judgments (Reciprocal Enforcement)
b Act 1933 were confined to the United Kingdom, I should content myself with recording my respectful dissent and my agreement with the interpretation unanimously
placed on it by the Court of Appeal[1]. But the Act is designed to facilitate the reciprocal enforcement of the judgments of foreign courts in the United Kingdom and of the
judgments of United Kingdom courts in foreign states. It makes provision enabling
and requiring English, Scots, and Northern Irish courts to comply with obligations
c which the United Kingdom government has assumed in international law towards
the governments of those foreign states with which it has entered into conventions 'for
the recognition and enforcement of judgments in civil and commercial matters'. So
the consequences of your Lordships' decision on this matter will not be confined to
the municipal law of the United Kingdom. It may have repercussions in international
law and in the municipal law of those foreign states with which conventions have been
d made. This emboldens me to state briefly why I am unable to accept either of the
constructions of s 8(1) which commend themselves to those of your Lordships who
consider that the interpretation placed on it by the Court of Appeal was wrong. In a
sentence the question that divides us is: 'Did s 8 of the 1933 Act alter the common law
as it had been stated by the Court of Queen's Bench in 1869 in *Harris v Quine*[2]'?
   All three members of the Court of Appeal[1] thought that it did. They reached this
e conclusion by looking at the actual words of the section. They considered that the
meaning of those words was plain and unambiguous. For my part I find their reasoning
convincing. I would not seek to improve on the way in which it is put in the judgment
of Scarman LJ. I am content to adopt it as my own. I would, however, supplement it
with three brief comments.
   First, I can see no warrant for confining the application of the section to judgments
f in favour of a plaintiff or counterclaimant. Since it applies only to 'proceedings
founded on the same cause of action' as that disposed of by the foreign judgment,
such proceedings ex hypothesi must be brought by a party who was the plaintiff
in the foreign action against a party who was the defendant in that action. The
reference to reliance on the foreign judgment 'by way of defence' in my view clearly
indicates that the section does apply to foreign judgment in favour of defendants.
   Secondly, if there had not been the reported, albeit isolated, case of *Harris v Quine*[2]
g which had been mentioned without adverse comment in the standard textbooks
on English private international law, I venture to think that it never would have
occurred to any English lawyer that the actual words of s 8(1) were to be understood
as drawing any distinction between, on the one hand, foreign judgments given in favour
of a defendant on the ground that the plaintiff's cause of action was time-barred
under the domestic law of the foreign court, and, on the other hand, all other foreign
h judgments given in favour of plaintiffs or defendants on any other ground. If it
were posssible to discern from its provisions taken as a whole that the Act was intended to apply only to foreign judgments given 'on the merits'—a phrase which I
find elusive as a term of art, but which I take it would exclude judgments given
on the ground of non-compliance with a procedural rule of the foreign court or
j on some other ground which would be classified in English private international
law as governed by the lex fori—this might justify construing the word 'judgment'
in the same restricted sense in s 8(1). But it is clear from s 4(1)(a)(iii) that, provided
the defendant has had due notice of the proceedings, a foreign judgment by default

---

1 [1974] 2 All ER 611, [1974] QB 660
2 (1869) LR 4 QB 653

obtained against him by the plaintiff is enforceable under Part I of the Act, notwithstanding that it has been given on what is solely a procedural ground governed   *a*
by the lex fori and is not a judgment which can be described as being 'on the merits'.
So the distinction sought to be drawn is peculiar to judgments in favour of a defendant on the ground that the plaintiff's cause of action was time-barred under the
domestic law of the foreign state, and must be derived as a matter of construction
from the words of s 8 itself. For my part, I am unable to discern any suggestion
of that distinction in those words.   *b*

Thirdly, the word 'conclusive' is, in my view, used in the section in the same meaning as in the phrase 'final and conclusive as between the parties thereto' which is
used in s 1(2)(*a*) as descriptive of foreign judgments to which Part I of the Act applies.
This is incorporated by reference into s 8(1) itself. So I would answer the question
'Conclusive of what?' by saying that it is conclusive of that of which the foreign
judgment is conclusive in the country of the foreign court. Whatever else the foreign   *c*
judgment does, its dispositive or operative part must embody a decision of the
foreign court on the ultimate question whether the plaintiff is entitled to the remedy
he claimed that the court ought to grant him against the defendant as redress for
the facts that he relied on as constituting his cause of action. So, in a subsequent
action brought in an English court by the same plaintiff against the same defendant
founded on the same facts and claiming the same remedy the foreign judgment   *d*
is at the very least conclusive of the question whether or not the plaintiff is entitled to
that remedy.

In the course of reaching its ultimate decision disposing of the plaintiff's claim
to the remedy he seeks, the foreign court may have incidentally decided other matters
of fact or law essential to the plaintiff's claim to be entitled to the remedy or to
the defendant's answer to that claim. Whether decisions of this kind will be em-   *e*
bodied in the same document which contains the dispositive or operative part of
the foreign judgment will depend on the practice followed by the foreign court;
and the conclusiveness attaching to such incidental decisions in subsequent litigation
in the country of the foreign court between the same parties but not founded on
the same cause of action, will depend on the extent to which the foreign system
of law incorporates a principle similar to the English doctrine of issue estoppel.   *f*
The English doctrine of issue estoppel, though it did not acquire that name until
later, was well known in 1933. It had been brought into prominence in the recent
case of *Hoystead v Taxation Comr*[1]. It is based on public policy and s 8(3) of the Act
preserves it as respects foreign judgments, whether or not the system of law of the
foreign country incorporates a similar principle.

Section 8(1), however, in contrast to s 8(3), applies only to proceedings founded   *g*
on the *same* cause of action as that for which the plaintiff claimed a remedy in the
foreign action. If the judgment in the foreign court contains, as it must, the ultimate
decision of the foreign court disposing of the plaintiff's claim to the remedy he seeks,
the conclusiveness of this decision cannot, in my view, be rendered inconclusive
by any failure of the foreign court to reach decisions on incidental matters of fact   *h*
or law which it considers unnecessary for the purpose of disposing of the plaintiff's
claim to the remedy he sought—even though, if the same remedy had been sought
in an action brought in England, the English court would have considered it necessary
to decide those incidental matters.

The attention of the Court of Appeal had not been drawn to the Report of the
Foreign Judgments (Reciprocal Enforcement) Committee which had been presented   *j*
to Parliament in December 1932. To that report there was annexed a draft bill
of which the wording was almost identical with that of the Act which received the
Royal Assent in April 1933. Also annexed was a commentary and explanation of

---

1   [1926] AC 155, [1925] All ER Rep 56

the draft bill. It is apparent from the committee's comments on cl 8, which is re-
a produced verbatim by s 8 of the Act, that they did not consider that it made any
alteration to the common law. The membership of the committee included experts
in private international law who must have been aware of the decision in *Harris v
Quine*[1]; I would therefore accept the inference that the committee did not realise
that the language that they had recommended for cl 8 would have the result of
altering the common law as to the effect given by English courts to judgments
b of foreign courts in favour of defendants which were based solely on the ground
that the plaintiff's remedy was time-barred under the domestic law of the foreign
state. On the other hand it would, in my view, be quite unrealistic to suppose that
the members of either House of Parliament who voted on the bill gave any thought,
either individually or collectively, to the decision in *Harris v Quine*[1] or to the effect
of cl 8 on it. The most that can be inferred is that those who took the trouble to
c read the small print on p 64 of Annex V to the report were not aware that it would
alter the existing common law in any way.

I do not, however, understand that any of your Lordships go so far as to suggest
that a court is entitled to put a strained construction on the words of s 8 in order
to give them the effect the committee thought that they had, if this would involve
departing from their plain and natural meaning. It is for the court and no one else
d to decide what words in a statute mean. What the committee thought they meant
is, in itself, irrelevant. Oral evidence by members of the committee as to their opinion
of what the section meant would plainly be inadmissible. It does not become
admissible by being reduced to writing.

What is suggested is that recourse may be had to the report as an aid to construction
in order to ascertain, first, what the existing law was understood to be on the subject-
e matter of the Act; and, secondly, what was the mischief for which Parliament
intended to provide a remedy by the Act.

As regards the first of these purposes for which recourse may be had to the report,
the Act deals with a technical subject-matter—the treatment to be accorded by
courts in the United Kingdom to judgments of foreign courts. The expressions
f used in it are terms of legal art which were in current use in English and Scots law
at the time the Act was passed. In order to understand their meaning the court
must inform itself as to what the existing law was on this technical subject-matter. In
order to do this it may have recourse to decided cases, to legal text-books or other
writings of recognised authorities, among whom would rank the members of the
committee. Their report contains a summary of the existing law, as they understood it. As such it is part of the material to which the court may have recourse
g for the purpose of ascertaining what was the existing law on the subject-matter of
the Act. There is, however, no real doubt as to what it was.

As regards recourse to the report for the purpose of ascertaining the mischief
for which Parliament intended to provide a remedy by the Act, this is based on
the so-called 'mischief' rule which finds its origin in *Heydon's Case*[2] decided under
the Tudor monarchy in 1584. The rule was propounded by the judges in an age
h when statutes were drafted in a form very different from that which they assume
today. Those who composed the Parliaments of those days were chary of creating
exceptions to the common law; and, when they did so, thought it necessary to
incorporate in the statute the reasons which justified the changes in the common
law that the statute made. Statutes in the 16th century and for long thereafter
in addition to the enacting words contained lengthy preambles reciting the partic-
j ular mischief or defect in the common law that the enacting words were designed
to remedy. So, when it was laid down, the 'mischief' rule did not require the court

1 (1869) LR 4 QB 653
2 (1584) 3 Co Rep 7a

to travel beyond the actual words of the statute itself to identify 'the mischief and defect for which the common law did not provide', for this would have been stated a in the preamble. It was a rule of construction of the actual words appearing in the statute and nothing else. In construing modern statutes which contain no preambles to serve as aids to the construction of enacting words the 'mischief' rule must be used with caution to justify any reference to extraneous documents for this purpose. If the enacting words are plain and unambiguous in themselves there is no need to have recourse to any 'mischief' rule. To speak of mischief and of remedy is to b describe the obverse and the reverse of a single coin. The former is that part of the existing law that is changed by the plain words of the Act; the latter is the change that these words made in it.

The acceptance of the rule of law as a constitutional principle requires that a citizen, before committing himself to any course of action, should be able to know in advance what are the legal consequences that will flow from it. Where those consequences c are regulated by a statute the source of that knowledge is what the statute says. In construing it the court must give effect to what the words of the statute would be reasonably understood to mean by those whose conduct it regulates. That any or all of the individual members of the two Houses of the Parliament that passed it may have thought the words bore a different meaning cannot affect the matter. Parliament, under our constitution, is sovereign only in respect of what it expresses d by the words used in the legislation it has passed.

This is not to say that where those words are not clear and unambiguous in them-selves but are fairly susceptible of more than one meaning, the court, for the purpose of resolving—though not of inventing—an ambiguity, may not pay regard to author-itative statements that were matters of public knowledge at the time the Act was passed, as to what were regarded as deficiencies in that branch of the existing law e with which the Act deals. Where such statements are made in official reports com-missioned by government, laid before Parliament and published, they clearly fall within this category and may be used to resolve the ambiguity in favour of a meaning which will result in correcting those deficiencies in preference to some alternative meaning that will leave the deficiencies uncorrected. The justification of this use of such reports as an aid to the construction of the words used in the statute is that f knowledge of their contents may be taken to be shared by those whose conduct the statute regulates and would influence their understanding of the meaning of ambiguous enacting words.

My Lords, I do not think that the actual words of s 8 of the 1933 Act are fairly susceptible of any other meaning than that ascribed to them by the Court of Appeal. So I see no need to look at the report of the committee; but much of the argument g in this House has been devoted to a meticulous verbal analysis of everything that the committee said in it. For my part this recourse to the report for the purpose of ascertaining what was the 'mischief' for which Parliament intended to provide a remedy by the Act has only served to confirm me in the view that s 8 should be construed as the Court of Appeal construed it.

The mischief was said by the authors of the report to be that foreign courts did h not, in effect, recognise judgments of English courts as conclusive. The reason for this was the difficulty in convincing foreign courts that reciprocal treatment was accorded to their own judgments in the United Kingdom. The causes of the diffi-culty were said to be: (1) the lack of any provision in the English legal system for the direct enforcement of foreign judgments for sums of money by execution rather than by action; and (2) the dependence of the English recognition of foreign judgments j on unwritten rules of common law which foreign courts suspected of being indefinite and discretionary as compared with written law embodied in a code or statute.

These were the reasons why, in the committee's view, the only manner of securing reciprocal treatment by foreign countries in the matter of the recognition and enforcement of British judgments was by—

'the conclusion of an international convention—containing reciprocal obligations for the recognition and enforcement of judgments which will be made binding as part of the municipal law of the foreign country *together with the statement of our own rules in statutory form* . . .'

The conclusion that I would draw from this is that in the committee's view the Act would fail in its purpose of inducing foreign states to enter into such conventions unless, as well as amending the existing law by providing a method of obtaining direct execution of foreign judgments for money sums, it also embodied a comprehensive written statement of at least the minimum effect which courts in the United Kingdom were required to give to judgments of courts of foreign states with which reciprocal conventions had been concluded—such written statement to be in substitution for the written rules of the common law and to obviate the necessity of resorting to an examination of previous judicial decisions on this topic. That, after all, is what the lawyers of the three countries with whom informal negotiations had already been conducted, France, Germany and Belgium, understood as being the purpose of a code. Yet the construction which commends itself to the majority of your Lordships can only be arrived at by going beyond the actual wording of the Act and resorting to an examination of previous judicial decisions and specifically the decision in *Harris v Quine*[1]. To do this is to perpetuate one of the very mischiefs which, according to the committee, it was the purpose of the proposed bill to remedy.

Annexed to the report were draft treaties with France, Germany and Belgium providing for the reciprocal enforcement and recognition of judgments of superior courts of the high contracting parties. Article 3 in each of these treaties, like cl 8 of the draft bill, dealt with the recognition of judgments, as distinct from their direct enforcement by execution. The final paragraph of that article stated what was meant by the 'recognition' of a judgment which the high contracting parties mutually undertook to grant to judgments of one another's superior courts. It was to the obligation to be assumed by the United Kingdom government under this article that s 8(1) of the 1933 Act was intended to give statutory effect. The paragraph was in the following terms:

'The recognition of a judgment under paragraph (1) of this article means that such judgment shall be treated as conclusive as to the matter thereby adjudicated upon in any further action between the parties (judgment creditor and judgment debtor) and as to such matter shall constitute a defence in a further action between them in respect of the same cause of action.'

There are differences of phraseology between this provision of the treaties and s 8(1) of the Act. What is significant for my present purpose is that the treaty says that the judgment shall be treated as conclusive *as to the matter thereby adjudicated upon* whereas the words I have italicised are omitted from s 8(1). These additional words may be ambiguous in themselves, but the committee (some of whose members are said to have negotiated the draft treaties with representatives of the foreign governments concerned) explained in a footnote to para 4 in the body of the report what they meant by this phrase:

'The words "question adjudicated upon" refer to the actual decision (the operative parts of the judgment) as opposed to the grounds or reasoning upon which it may be based, in the course of which other points of law or fact may have been incidentally decided as preliminaries (necessary or otherwise) to the final conclusion.'

While this on the one hand would appear to limit the 'matter adjudicated upon' to the decision of the ultimate question dealt with by the dispositive or operative

---

1 (1869) LR 4 QB 653

part of the judgment, viz whether or not the plaintiff was entitled to the remedy
that he claimed that the court ought to grant him against the defendant as redress   *a*
for the facts that he relied on as constituting his cause of action; it would, on the other
hand, bind the United Kingdom government to treat the decision of that ultimate
question as conclusive whatever might be the grounds or reasoning on which it
was based.

In construing a treaty recourse may be had, in public international law, to the
travaux preparatoires for the purpose of resolving any ambiguity in the treaty;   *b*
and it would appear from the history of the negotiations contained in the body of
the report that the report itself might be regarded as forming part of the travaux
preparatoires. If this was so, recourse to the report would in my view clearly lead
to the conclusion that the high contracting parties in using the phrase 'matter adjudicated upon' had undertaken to treat as conclusive the dispositive or operative
part of the judgment.   *c*

Where an Act of Parliament is passed to enable or to require United Kingdom
courts to give effect to international obligations assumed by Her Majesty's Government under a treaty, it is a well-established rule of construction that any ambiguity
in the words of the Act should be resolved in favour of ascribing to them a meaning
which would result in the performance of those international obligations—not in
their breach. For this additional reason recourse to the report serves to confirm me   *d*
in the view that s 8 should be construed as the Court of Appeal construed it.

LORD SIMON OF GLAISDALE.   My Lords, the appellants ('Black-Clawson'),
an English company, became holders in due course of two bills of exchange accepted
by the predecessor in title of the respondents ('Papierwerke') but dishonoured by   *e*
Papierwerke. The bills were drawn, negotiated and payable in England. Black-
Clawson became their holders only shortly before action on them in England would
have become time-barred by effluxion of six years from their acceptance. Papierwerke
is a German company without any assets in England, its principal assets being in
Germany; and, by the German law of limitation of actions, the time for suing on
a bill of exchange is three years. Although it is a slight over-simplification, for the   *f*
purpose of this appeal it can be stated that, according to the expert evidence, in
German law effluxion of the period of limitation bars the remedy (as in England)
without extinguishing the right (as it does in Scotland). Whether a German court
should, in an action on the bills, apply the English limitation period of six years
or the German limitation period of three years depends on the appropriate choice-
of-law rule in German private international law; this is a question to which different
answers have been returned at first instance by the District Court in Munich and   *g*
on appeal by the Bavarian Court of Appeal, and which now awaits decision by the
German Federal Supreme Court. In view of the doubt whether an action on the
bills in Germany would be held to be time-barred, Black-Clawson, though starting
such an action, tried to preserve a fall-back position in England. Before the effluxion
of six years from the date of acceptance they applied ex parte in England for, and   *h*
obtained, leave to issue a writ against Papierwerke and to serve it on them in Germany.
Since Black-Clawson's German action was proceeding, they gave no notice to Papierwerke of the issue of the English writ. On 30th November 1972 the Munich District
Court dismissed Black-Clawson's claim on the bills. The court held that, under
German private international law, the relevant limitation period was the German
one of three years, not the English of six years, with the result that Black-Clawson's   *j*
claim was time-barred. The judgment handed down was in three parts. The first
(headed 'Final Judgment') has in argument conveniently been called 'the dispositive
part'. This stated in translation:

'I. The suit is dismissed.
'II. The Plaintiff shall bear the cost of the dispute.

'III. The judgment is provisionally enforceable. [Then followed provisions permitting the Plaintiff to avert compulsory execution by providing security].'

The second part of the judgment handed down (headed 'Facts') was a statement of the facts of the case and the issues. The third part of the judgment handed down (headed 'Grounds for the Decision') made it clear that the action was dismissed on the ground that it was time-barred under what was held to be the relevant German choice-of-law rule.

Though Black-Clawson appealed against this judgment to the Bavarian Court of Appeal, they now gave notice to Papierwerke of the issue of the English writ. Papierwerke countered by a summons to set aside the English writ and all proceedings in pursuance thereof. The master dismissed Papierwerke's summons to set the writ aside. Papierwerke appealed to Talbot J, who on the authority of *Harris v Quine*[1], in the knowledge of the pending appeal to the Bavarian Court of Appeal, and in the exercise of his discretion, dismissed Papierwerke's appeal.

In *Harris v Quine*[1] the plaintiffs were attorneys in the Isle of Man and were retained by the defendant to conduct a suit in the courts of the Isle of Man. The plaintiffs subsequently sued for their fees in the Isle of Man; but the Manx court held that their claim was time-barred by the Manx statute of limitations, under which the relevant period was three years. The plaintiffs then sued in England within the six-year English limitation period. It was held by a powerful court that, as the Manx statute barred the remedy only and did not extinguish the debt, the judgment of the Manx court was no bar to the English proceedings. Cockburn CJ said[2]:

'. . . there is no judgment of the Manx court barring the present action, as there was no plea going to the merits . . . and the issue the Manx court decided in favour of the defendant is not the same issue as is raised in the present action.'

Blackburn J said[3]:

'. . . all that the Manx court decided was, that in the courts of the Isle of Man the plaintiffs could not recover. If the plaintiffs could have shewn, as was attempted in *Huber v Steiner*[4], that the law of the Isle of Man extinguished the right as well as the remedy, and this had been the issue determined by the Manx court, that would never have been a different matter.'

Lush J said[3]:

'Had the Manx statute of limitations . . . extinguished the right after the limited time and not merely barred the remedy, there would have been good ground for defence in this court. But the Manx law is like our statute of limitations, and bars the remedy only; and all that was decided in the Manx court was, that the action could not be maintained here.'

Hayes J concurred. The decision has beeen cited in successive editions of Dicey's The Conflict of Laws as authority for the words 'on the merits' italicised by me in the proposition that[5]:

'A foreign judgment *in personam* . . . is a good defence to an action in England for the same matter when either—(1) the judgment was in favour of the defendant and was final and conclusive *on the merits*; or . . .'

---

1 (1869) LR 4 QB 653
2 LR 4 QB at 657
3 LR 4 QB at 658
4 (1835) Bing NC 202
5 Dicey and Morris, The Conflict of Laws (9th Edn, 1973), p 1058, r 194; cf (1st Edn, 1896), p 422, r 100

Such was the decision which Talbot J followed and the rule which he applied. He *a*
held that the decision of the Munich District Court was not final and conclusive
'on the merits'; it merely decided, like the judgment of the Isle of Man court in
Harris v Quine[1] that the plaintiff's remedy was time-barred in the foreign court.

Papierwerke appealed to the English Court of Appeal[2]. In addition to argument
on the proper exercise of the discretion to allow the English writ to stand, which they
had urged before the master and Talbot J, Papierwerke put forward a new point
to the Court of Appeal. This was based on s 8(1) of the Foreign Judgments (Recip- *b*
rocal Enforcement) Act 1933. It was argued on behalf of Papierwerke that this subsection had abrogated the decision of *Harris v Quine*[1]. The Court of Appeal allowed
the appeal. So far as discretion was concerned Lord Denning MR doubted[2] whether
it would be a case for leave to serve a writ out of jurisdiction. Megaw LJ said[3]:

> 'On the arguments presented before Master Bickford-Smith and Talbot J, *c*
> their decisions were in my opinion right, including their exercises of the discretion
> under RSC Ord 11, r 1.'

Scarman LJ said[4]:

> 'If the judge was correct in law in holding that the German judgment was *d*
> not "res judicata", I do not think that his exercise of discretion can be successfully
> challenged in this court.'

But the Court of Appeal was unanimous in holding that s 8(1) of the 1933 Act had
modified the rule in *Harris v Quine*[5], and had rendered the judgment of the Munich
District Court conclusive against any cause of action on the bills by Black-Clawson *e*
in this country.

Shortly after the English Court of Appeal had given judgment, the Bavarian
Court of Appeal gave their judgment. They allowed Black-Clawson's appeal, holding
that the limitation period according to German private international law was the
English period of six years not the German period of three years. The judgment of
the Bavarian Court of Appeal is under appeal to the German Federal Supreme Court. *f*
Black-Clawson have appealed to your Lordships against the judgment of the English
Court of Appeal, in order to safeguard themselves in case the Federal Supreme
Court reinstates the judgment of the Munich District Court.

The appeal to your Lordships raises two main issues: first, what is the proper
interpretation to be given to s 8(1) of the 1933 Act, in particular in relation to *Harris
v Quine*[1]; and, secondly, how far the discretion exercised by Talbot J can be reviewed *g*
in an appellate tribunal.

I confess, my Lords, that when I first read s 8 of the 1933 Act I was under an immediate and powerful impression that the Court of Appeal must be right. It seemed
obvious that sub-s (1) was dealing with cause-of-action estoppel and sub-s (3) with
issue estoppel. If so, the judgment of the Munich District Court did not merely
determine an issue between the parties relating to the operation of the German *h*
law of limitation of action; it dismissed Black-Clawson's action founded on the bills;
and such judgment would have to be recognised in any court in the United Kingdom
as conclusive in all proceedings founded on the same cause of action, i e liability
arising from acceptance of bills.

But though the foregoing was my first and strong impression, I soon realised that I
was looking at s 8 with 1974 eyes and interpreting it in 1974 terms; and that in so doing *j*

---

1   (1869) LR 4 QB 653
2   [1974] 2 All ER 611, [1974] QB 660
3   [1974] 2 All ER at 616, [1974] QB at 673
4   [1974] 2 All ER at 621, [1974] QB at 679

I was falling into fundamental error. Contemporanea expositio est fortissima
a in lege. The concepts of cause-of-action and issue estoppel were not developed by
1933 (there is, for example, no reflection of the distinction in the notes to *The Duchess
of Kingston's Case*[1] in the authoritatively edited 1929 edition of Smith's Leading Cases),
and could not possibly be what Parliament and the draftsman then had in mind.
My initial response had been scarcely less anachronistic than if I had attempted to
interpret Magna Carta by reference to *Rookes v Barnard*[2].
b   The matter was, in my judgment put beyond doubt when your Lordships looked,
de bene esse, at the report of the Greer Committee on Reciprocal Enforcement
of Foreign Judgments[3]. This was the report of a committee of lawyers (practising,
official and academic) of high distinction and of great expertise in private international law. Its terms of reference were:

c   'To consider (1) what provisions should be included in conventions made
        with foreign countries for the mutual enforcement of judgments on a basis
        of reciprocity, and (2) what legislation is necessary or desirable for the purpose
        of enabling such conventions to be made and to become effective, or for the
        purpose of securing reciprocal treatment from foreign countries.'

d   The report discussed the prevailing law and the various problems which stood
in the way of reciprocal enforcement of judgments. It annexed conventions which
had been officially negotiated in draft with three foreign countries (Belgium, France
and Germany), and which could be carried into effect if appropriate legislation
were enacted in this country. It drafted and annexed (Annex I) a suitable draft bill,
cl 8 of which corresponds exactly with s 8 of the 1933 Act. Annex V contains a
commentary on the draft bill. Paragraph 13 of Annex V reads[4]:
e
        'Clause 8 contains the provisions of the bill with regard to the recognition
        of foreign judgments as final and conclusive between the parties *as regards the
        question therein adjudicated upon. It is entirely in accordance with the position at Common
        Law* (as explained in paragraph 4 of the Report), and Clause 8(3) saves the existing
        Common Law rules in any cases where the rule laid down by the Act may be
f   narrower in operation than the Common Law.' [My italics.]

Annex IV(b) was a draft Convention with Germany. Article 3 dealt with reciprocal
recognition of judgments. Paragraph 2 reads[5]:

        'The recognition of a judgment under paragraph (1) of this article means
        that such judgment shall be treated as *conclusive as to the matter thereby adjudicated
        upon* in any further action between the parties (judgment creditor and judgment
g   debtor) and as to such matter shall constitute a defence in a further action between
        them in respect of the same cause of action.' [My italics.]

There was similar provision in the draft conventions with France[6] and Belgium[7].
    If this material and that cited by my noble and learned friends is available to a
h court of construction, it is plain beyond doubt (if there could have been any doubt)
that Parliament (insofar as it legislated in the light of the report) did not have in
legislative contemplation the modern concepts of issue and cause-of-action estoppel;
it also shows that Parliament did not mean to abrogate the rule in *Harris v Quine*[8].

1   (1776) 1 East PC 468, [1775-1802] All ER Rep 623
j 2   [1964] 1 All ER 367, [1964] AC 1129
3   (1932) Cmd 4213
4   Page 64
5   Page 46
6   Page 54
7   Page 38
8   (1869) LR 4 QB 653

The Court of Appeal apparently was not asked to look at the report. The first questions which arise in this appeal are therefore whether your Lordships, as a court of   *a*
statutory construction, are entitled to examine the Greer report, and, if so, for what
purpose or purposes; the answers to these questions should indicate how much
of the material which has been cited from it by my noble and learned friends and
myself is available as an aid to construction. This raises some fundamental issues
relating to statutory construction.

Courts of construction interpret statutes with a view to ascertaining the intention   *b*
of Parliament expressed therein. But, as in interpretation of all written material,
what is to be ascertained is the meaning of what Parliament has said and not what
Parliament meant to say. This is not a self-evident juristic truth. It could be urged
that in a parliamentary democracy, where the purpose of the legislature is to permit
its electorate to influence the decisions which affect themselves, what should be
given effect to is what Parliament meant to say; since it is to be presumed that it   *c*
is this that truly reflects the desired influence of the citizens on the decision-making
which affects themselves. To this, however, there are three answers. First, in interpretation of all written material, the law in this country has set great pragmatic
store on limiting the material available for forensic scrutiny: society generally
thereby enjoys the advantages of economy in forensic manpower and time.   By
concentrating on the meaning of what has been said, to the exclusion of what was   *d*
meant to be said, the material for scrutiny is greatly reduced. Specifically, experience
in the United States has tended to show that scrutiny of the legislative proceedings
is apt to be a disappointingly misleading and wasteful guide to the legislative intention.
Secondly, interpretation cannot be concerned wholly with what the promulgator
of a written instrument meant by it: interpretation must also be frequently concerned
with the reasonable expectation of those who may be affected thereby. This is most   *e*
clearly to be seen in the interpretation of a contract: it has long been accepted
that the concern of the court is, not so much with the subject-matter of consent
between the parties (which may, indeed, exceptionally, be entirely absent), as with
the reasonable expectation of the promisee. So, too, in statutory construction, the
court is not solely concerned with what the citizens, through their parliamentary
representatives, meant to say; it is also concerned with the reasonable expectation   *f*
of those citizens who are affected by the statute, and whose understanding of the
meaning of what was said is therefore relevant. The sovereignty of Parliament
runs in tandem with the rule of objective law. Thirdly, if the draftsman uses the
tools of his trade correctly, the meaning of his words should actually represent
what their promulgator meant to say. And the court of construction, retracing
the same path in the opposite direction, should arrive, via the meaning of what   *g*
was said, at what the promulgator meant to say.

There are, however, two riders to be noted in relation to this last consideration.
First, draftmen's offices, government departments, houses of parliament and courts
of justice are all manned by fallible human beings; with the result that the court's
exposition of the meaning of what Parliament has said is inherently liable to differ
from what Parliament meant to say. The object of the parliamentary and forensic   *h*
techniques should be to minimise such liability to error; so that artificial rules
which stand unnecessarily in the way (i e which cannot be used as a code of communication) should be eliminated. Secondly, most words in the English language have
a number of shades of meaning. Even the bright isolating rays of the draftsman's
technical skills—his juxtapositions and differentiations—are rarely sufficient in
themselves to pick out without any posssibility of mistake by a court of construction   *j*
the exact shade of meaning intended, to the exclusion of a penumbra of other possible meanings. The draftsman therefore needs the full co-operation of the court of
construction: they must be tuned in on the same wavelength. In order to understand the meaning of the words which the draftsman has used to convey what
Parliament meant to say, the court must so far retrace the path of the draftsman

as actually to put itself in his position and that of Parliament. The expositio must
a be both contemporanea and eodem loco. All this is merely the counterpart of what
my learned and noble friend, Lord Wilberforce, said in *Prenn v Simmonds*[1], in relation
to the interpretation of another class of written material:

> 'The time [has] long passed when agreements, even those under seal, were
> isolated from the matrix of facts in which they were set and interpreted purely
b > on internal linguistic considerations.'

I can see no reason why a court of construction of a statute should limit itself in
ascertaining the matrix of facts more than a court of construction of any other written
material. A public report to Parliament is an important part of the matrix of a
statute founded on it. Where Parliament is legislating in the light of a public report
I can see no reason why a court of construction should deny itself any part of that
c light and insist on groping for a meaning in darkness or half-light. I conclude therefore that such a report should be available to the court of construction, so that the
latter can put itself in the shoes of the draftsman and place itself on the parliamentary
benches—in much the same way as a court of construction puts itself (as the saying
goes) in the armchair of a testator. The object is the same in each case, namely,
to ascertain the meaning of the words used, that meaning only being ascertainable
d if the court is in possession of the knowledge possessed by the promulgator of the
instrument.

Halsbury's Laws of England states[2]:

> 'Reference may not be made for the purpose of ascertaining the meaning
> of a statute to the recommendations contained in the report of a Royal Commis-
e > sion or of a departmental committee or in a White Paper which shortly preceded
> the statute under consideration because it does not follow that such recommend-
> ations were accepted by the legislature. On the other hand, reports of commis-
> sions preceding the enactment of a statute may be considered as showing the
> facts which must be assumed to have been within the contemplation of the
> legislature when the statute was passed.'

f
As regards the first sentence of this passage, I find unconvincing the reason given for
non-reference; I should have thought that, in general, recourse to the statute itself
will make it immediately apparent whether or not the recommendation has been
accepted by the legislature. I would wish to leave open for consideration in a later
case where the point is crucial whether this statement is correct. As regards the second
sentence, the critical questions in the instant case are whether such a report (here
g the Greer report) may be looked at in order to ascertain, first, what was the 'mischief'
which the provision falling for construction was designed to remedy, secondly,
what was believed by Parliament to be the pre-existing law, and, thirdly, where a
draft bill is annexed to the report in the same terms as the statute falling for construction, the opinion expressed by the committee as to the effect of its provisions.

h The first question is, then, whether the Greer report can be looked at in order
to ascertain what was the 'mischief' which Parliament was seeking to remedy. 'Mischief'
is an old, technical expression; but it reflects a firmly established and salutary rule
of statutory construction. It is rare indeed that a statute can be properly interpreted
without knowing what was the legislative objective. It would be trespassing on
your Lordships' patience were I to repeat what, in collaboration with my noble
and learned friend, Lord Diplock, I said about this matter in *Maunsell v Olins*[3].
j At the very least, ascertainment of the statutory objective can immediately eliminate
many of the possible meanings that the language of the Act might bear; and, if

---

1 [1971] 3 All ER 237 at 239, [1971] 1 WLR 1381 at 1383, 1384
2 3rd Edn, vol 36, p 411, para 622
3 [1975] 1 All ER 16 at 27-29, [1974] 3 WLR 835 at 847-849

an ambiguity still remains, consideration of the statutory objective is one of the means of resolving it.

The statutory objective is primarily to be collected from the provisions of the *a* statute itself. In these days, when the long title can be amended in both Houses, I can see no reason for having recourse to it only on case of an ambiguity—it is the plainest of all the guides to the general objectives of a statute. But it will not always help as to particular provisions. As to the statutory objective of these, a report leading to the Act is likely to be the most potent aid; and, in my judgment, it would be mere obscurantism not to avail oneself of it. There is, indeed, clear and high *b* authority that it is available for this purpose.

In *River Wear Comrs v Adamson*[1], Lord Blackburn said:

> 'In all cases the object is to see what is the intention expressed by the words used. But, from the imperfection of language, it is impossible to know what that intention is without inquiring farther, and seeing what the circumstances were with reference to which the words were used, and what was the object, *c* appearing from those circumstances, which the person using them had in view.'

In *Eastman Photographic Materials Co Ltd v Comptroller-General of Patents*[2] the Earl of Halsbury LC cited this passage[1] from Lord Blackburn's speech specifically as authority for looking at the report of a commission in the light of which Parliament had enacted the statute which fell for construction in the *Eastman* case. Lord Halsbury LC said[3]: *d*

> '. . . I think it desirable . . . to say something as to what sources of construction we are entitled to appeal to in order to construe a statute. Among the things which have passed into canons of construction recorded in *Heydon's Case*[4], we are to see what was the law before the Act was passed, and what was the mischief or defect for which the law had not provided, what remedy Parliament *e* appointed, and the reason of the remedy.'

Lord Halsbury LC then cited[5] at length from the report of the commission dealing with the law pre-existing the Act which fell for construction and with its defects; and added[6]:

> '. . . I think no more accurate source of information as to what was the evil or *f* defect which the Act of Parliament now under construction was intended to remedy could be imagined than the report of that commission.'

Lord Halsbury LC also cited Turner LJ in *Hawkins v Gathercole*[7] as further authority. I am therefore of opinion that the Greer report is available to your Lordships in construing the 1933 Act, by way of helping to show what facts were within the know- *g* ledge of Parliament and what was the defect in the pre-existing law which called for parliamentary remedy.

Ascertainment of a defect in the law presupposes ascertainment of the law which contains the defect. But, for purposes of statutory construction, is it the pre-existing law, as correctly determined, which is relevant or what that law was understood to be?

There may be a communis error as to the law. This is a source of law until it is *h* corrected (see Broom's Legal Maxims[8]). Indeed, a legal error may well be held

---

1 (1877) 2 App Cas 743 at 763, [1874-80] All ER Rep 1 at 11
2 [1898] AC 571 at 575, 576
3 [1898] AC at 573
4 (1584) 3 Co Rep 7a　　　　　　　　　　　　　　　　　　　　　　*j*
5 [1898] AC at 574
6 [1898] AC at 575
7 (1855) 6 De GM & G 1 at 21
8 10th Edn (1939), p 86

a to be too inveterate for correction (see, e g, *Ross Smith v Ross Smith*[1]). Once it is accepted that the purpose of ascertainment of the antecedent defect in the law is to interpret Parliament's intention, it must follow that it is Parliament's understanding of that law as evincing such a defect which is relevant, not what the law is subsequently declared to be. On reflection, I do not think that my hesitation on this point in *Povey v Povey*[2] was justified. See also *Barras v Aberdeen Steam Trawling and Fishing Co*[3].

b There is another canon of construction, which I shall have to cite later in greater detail, to which, for the same foregoing reasons, it is Parliament's understanding of the law which is relevant, rather than the law in an abstract juridical correctitude. This is the canon whereby the courts will presume that Parliament would use clear words if the intention were to abrogate a long-standing rule of law; though, no doubt, courts of construction will be readier to apply this presumption if satisfied *c* that the rule in question is juridically well-founded and if its framers carry weight in the law; whereas, on the other hand, the presumption will be weaker if the rule has been authoritatively questioned.

My Lords, I have spoken of 'Parliament's' understanding of the law. Of course, a settlor, a testator, the parties to a contract, or individual members of Parliament, may not know the relevant law. It is the draftsman of the instrument in question *d* who knows the law (or is presumed to do so); and his knowledge, so far as forensic interpretation is concerned, is irrebuttably imputed to the person for whom he is drafting. The draftsman knows the legal effect that the person for whom he is drafting wants to bring about; and he will draft accordingly, against his understanding of the prevailing law, and using as a code of communication to the courts of construction various canons of construction. Few testators will have heard of the rule in *e* *Gundry v Pinniger*[4]. But few draftsmen of wills will be ignorant of the rule so that when the words 'next of kin' appear in a will there is a strong though rebuttable presumption that the draftsman used them to denote those who would be the testator's next of kin *on his death*, and an irrebuttable presumption that the draftsman so used them in order to produce the legal effect desired by the testator. Similarly, many members of Parliament do not know the legal rule that when *f* the word 'child' is used in a legal instrument, it is presumptively taken to mean a legitimate child; but the draftsman of the statute does know this; and a court of construction will conclude that his usage was to carry into legal effect what Parliament desired. So again, few members of Parliament in 1933 will have known of the rule in *Harris v Quine*[5], but few, if any, members of the Greer committee, which drafted cl 8 of the draft bill, will have been ignorant of it. I have pointed out *g* that this rule had been cited in successive editions of Dicey without question. It had been followed in the Commonwealth and in the United States. No one had suggested that it was wrongly decided. It made good sense: any other rule would make the foreign judgment conclusive as to more than it actually decided. The legal knowledge of the Greer committee as draftsmen of the 1933 Act must be ascribed to Parliament in its enactment.

h Quite apart from the irrebuttable ascription to Parliament of a draftsman's knowledge of the law in relation to which Parliament is legislating, in my view a report like that of the Greer committee can also be looked at independently like any other work of legal authority in order to ascertain what was conceived to be the prevailing state of the law.

The most difficult question in this appeal, to my mind, arises out of the modern

j

---

1   [1962] 1 All ER 344, [1963] AC 280
2   [1970] 3 All ER 612, [1972] Fam 40
3   [1933] AC 402, [1933] All ER Rep 52
4   (1852) 1 De GM & G 502, [1843-60] All ER Rep 403
5   (1869) LR 4 QB 653

practice of annexation to a report to Parliament of a draft bill with a commentary on it. Is such a commentary available to a court construing the ensuing statute? *a*

My Lords, before turning to this question, may I venture to summarise what aids to construction your Lordships obtain from the Greer report irrespective of its commentary on the draft bill? (1) *Harris v Quine*[1], although not cited by name, was part of the antecedent common law; (2) negatively, the rule in *Harris v Quine*[1] was not regarded as a defect requiring remedy; (3) positively, the conventions negotiated in draft, and for which the statute was required for legal implementation, *b* reflected, and thereby endorsed, the rule in *Harris v Quine*[1]; (4) a provision such as the subsequent s 8(1) of the 1933 Act might well be restrictive of the common law; if therefore such a provision were enacted as part of the codification of the common law it would require a saving clause (such as the subsequent s 8(3)): although this was specifically stated in the commentary, it sufficiently appears from the body of the report. *c*

The foregoing, however, although going far to showing that s 8(1) was not meant to abrogate the rule in *Harris v Quine*[1], is not absolutely conclusive when it comes to interpretation. It unfortunately happens, occasionally, that a statutory provision has an unlooked-for effect. Such a situation is sometimes described in the phrase, 'Whatever Parliament was aiming at, it hit such-and-such a target fair and square'. If the words of s 8 can only be read as abrogating the rule in *Harris v Quine*[1], why *d* then, it must be so, however little that was the legislative objective. After all, the first and most elementary (and, I would add, salutary) rule of construction is that the words of a statute must be read in the most natural sense which they bear in their context. But I do not myself so read s 8. There is, in fact, ambiguity inherent in it; it lies in the word 'judgment'. This word in its context is capable of meaning either the 'dispositive' part of the court's pronouncement only, or the whole of *e* such pronouncement including the grounds of judgment. If 'judgment' in s 8(1) refers only to the 'dispositive' part of the pronouncement of the court, I think that it would inevitably follow that *Harris v Quine*[1] has been abrogated: an action on the bills has been dismissed, and that is an end of it. But if 'judgment' embraces also the grounds of the decision, all that is 'conclusive between the parties' is what the whole 'judgment', including its grounds, has decided. In the instant case that *f* was that Black-Clawson's claim was time-barred in Germany. If, as I think, 'judgment' is so ambiguous, the ambiguity must be resolved. There are, in fact, three canons of construction available here for its resolution.

The first is that clear and unmistakeable words will be required for the abrogation of a long-standing rule of common law: see Maxwell on Interpretation of Statutes[2].

'It is a well established principle of construction that a statute is not to be *g* taken as affecting fundamental alteration in the general law unless it uses words that point unmistakeably to that conclusion.'

(Devlin J in *National Assistance Board v Wilkinson*[3].) The rule in *Harris v Quine*[1] was such a long-standing rule of law as is appropriate for the application of this canon: and any ambiguity must be resolved in such a way that the rule in *Harris v Quine*[1] *h* is not abrogated.

Secondly, consideration of the legislative objective is available and required, not only to place a court of construction in the shoes of the draftsman, but also to resolve any ambiguity: see *Maunsell v Olins*[4]. It was no part of the legislative objective to abrogate the rule in *Harris v Quine*[1]; so that the construction which does not have that effect should be preferred. *j*

---

1 (1869) LR 4 QB 653
2 12th Edn (1969), p 116
3 [1952] 2 All ER 255 at 260, [1952] 2 QB 648 at 661
4 [1975] 1 All ER at 29, [1974] 3 WLR at 849

Thirdly, there is a presumption against a change of terminological usage: ' . . . it
a is a sound rule of construction to give the same meaning to the same words occurring
in different parts of an act of parliament . . .' (Cleasby B in *Courtauld v Legh*[1]). A
fortiori when the words occur in the same section of an Act. 'Judgment' in sub-s (3)
can only be read in its wider sense, as including the grounds of decision; it cannot
be limited to the 'dispositive' part of the judgment ('any matter of law or fact decided
therein'). There is therefore a presumption that 'judgment' in sub-s (1) is also not
b so limited.

For all these reasons this does not seem to me to be a case where it can be said
that, whatever Parliament was trying to do, it succeeded, however inadvertently,
in abrogating the rule in *Harris v Quine*[2].

It remains to consider, in this context, s 8(3). I hope that I have sufficiently indicated
that the report in itself, without necessity of recourse to the commentary, indicates
c the objective of this subsection: namely, that it was inserted as a saving provision
and by way of reassurance. I should, I think, in any event, have surmised from the
use of the common drafting formula, 'Nothing in this section shall be taken to prevent
. . .', that the subsection was inserted ex abundanti cautela, and was not intended
as a substantive provision to deal with issue estoppel in contradistinction to cause-
of-action estoppel dealt with in s 8(1).

d My conclusion is therefore that, regardless of the draft bill and the commentary
thereon, the Greer report is available as an aid to construction in such a way as to
make it clear that it was not the intention of Parliament in s 8(1) to abrogate the rule
in *Harris v Quine*[2]. It is, thus, strictly, unnecessary to decide whether the commentary on the draft bill is also available as an aid to construction. But the technique
of a draft bill with commentary is so common nowadays in reports to Parliament
e as to excuse, I hope, some expatiation on the matter. The argument against recourse
to such a commentary is that if what Parliament or parliamentarians (or, indeed,
any promulgators of a written instrument) think is the meaning of what is said is
irrelevant, so must be the opinion of any draftsman, including the draftsman of a
bill annexed to a report to Parliament. But I confess that I find this less than conclusive. In essence, drafting, enactment and interpretation are integral parts of the
f process of translating the volition of the electorate into rules which will bind themselves. If it comes about that the declared meaning of a statutory provision is not
what Parliament meant, the system is at fault. Sometimes the fault is merely a
reflection of human fallibility. But where the fault arises from a technical refusal
to consider relevant material, such refusal requires justification. The commentary
on a draft bill in a report to Parliament is not merely an expression of opinion—
g even if it were only that, it would be an expression of expert opinion, and I can see
no more reason for excluding it than any other relevant matter of expert opinion.
But actually it is more: that experts publicly expressed the view that a certain draft
would have such-and-such an effect is one of the facts within the shared knowledge of Parliament and the citizenry. To refuse to consider such a commentary, when
Parliament has legislated on the basis and faith of it, is for the interpreter to fail
h to put himself in the real position of the promulgator of the instrument before
essaying its interpretation. It is refusing to follow what is perhaps the most important clue to meaning. It is perversely neglecting the reality, while chasing shadows.
As Aneurin Bevin said: 'Why gaze in the crystal ball when you can read the book?'
Here the book is already open; it is merely a matter of reading on. Certainly, a
court of construction cannot be precluded from saying that what the committee
j thought as to the meaning of its draft was incorrect. But that is one thing; to dismiss,
out of hand and for all purposes, an authoritative opinion in the light of which
Parliament has legislated is quite another.

---

1 (1869) LR 4 Exch 126 at 130
2 (1869) LR 4 QB 653

So, as at present advised, I think that your Lordships would have been entitled, if necessary, to consider the commentary of the Greer committee on the draft bill.   *a*

The only other matter that I need add in this part of the case is that I agree with those of my noble and learned friends who hold that s 8 is not limited to plaintiffs' judgments.

In my view, therefore, Talbot J was correct in following *Harris v Quine*[1], and in holding that he had a discretion whether to allow the writ to stand. After he had given judgment, Black-Clawson's appeal from the decision of the Munich District *b* Court to the Bavarian Court of Appeal was heard and determined. It was argued that this was a new facter, showing a commitment to the proceedings in Germany which would make it inequitable to allow a fall-back position in England. But Talbot J exercised his discretion in the knowledge that such an appeal was pending; so it is no new factor permitting an appellate tribunal to substitute its own exercise of discretion for that of the judge in chambers. Unless the discretion has been *c* exercised in legal or factual error, an appellate court should not other than exceptionally interfere with the judge's discretion unless it is seen on other grounds that his decision might well result in injustice being done: *Evans v Bartlam*[2]; *Charles Osenton & Co v Johnston*[3]; *Blunt v Blunt*[4]; *Shiloh Spinners Ltd v Harding*[5]. I respectfully agree with Megaw and Scarman LJJ that there are no grounds in the instant case for interfering with the exercise of discretion by the judge in chambers. I would *d* therefore allow the appeal.

On the other hand, I cannot accede to the contention on behalf of Black-Clawson that they should be at liberty to pursue their remedy in England even if the Federal Supreme Court should decide in their favour. I therefore agree with the order proposed by my noble and learned friends, Lord Wilberforce and Viscount Dilhorne.   *e*

Appeal allowed. Cause to be remitted to the Queen's Bench Division with a direction that future proceedings be stayed pending the decision of the West German Federal Supreme Court, with liberty to apply.

Solicitors: *Slaughter & May* (for the appellants); *Herbert Smith & Co* (for the repondents). *f*

Gordon H Scott Esq Barrister.

---

1   (1869) LR 4 QB 653
2   [1937] 2 All ER 646, [1973] AC 473
3   [1941] 2 All ER 245 at 250, [1942] AC 130 at 138
4   [1943] AC 517 at 526, 527
5   [1973] 1 All ER 90 at 105, [1973] AC 691 at 728

Wallersteiner v Moir (No 2)
Moir v Wallersteiner and others (No 2)

COURT OF APPEAL, CIVIL DIVISION
LORD DENNING MR, BUCKLEY AND SCARMAN LJJ
15th, 16th, 17th JULY, 11th, 12th, 13th, 14th, 15th NOVEMBER 1974, 29th JANUARY 1975

Interest – Damages – Award of interest – Equitable jurisdiction – Simple or compound interest – Fiduciary duty – Breach – Misappropriation of funds by person in fiduciary position – Company director – Funds used for purpose of commercial transaction – Presumption that profit made by wrongdoer out of use of funds – Rate of interest – Loans obtained from company by director to purchase shares in company – Judgment against director in respect of transaction – Court entitled to award compound interest with yearly rests – Rate of interest one per cent above bank rate or minimum lending rate.

Company – Shareholder – Minority shareholder – Representative action – Costs – Indemnity – Action brought in shareholder's name – Action brought in order to redress wrongs against company committed by majority shareholder – Action brought without company's authority – Action in substance a representative action – Circumstances in which minority shareholder entitled to indemnity against company in respect of costs – Sanction of court – Procedure to be followed in order to obtain indemnity.

Company – Shareholder – Minority shareholder – Representative action – Legal aid – Persons entitled to legal aid – Action brought by minority shareholder in his own name – Action brought to redress wrongs against company shareholders – Action in substance a representative action – Persons entitled to legal aid not including body corporate – Whether minority shareholder entitled to legal aid – Legal Aid Act 1974, s 25.

Solicitor – Costs – Contingency fee – Fee payable only in event of party being successful in action – Contingency fees in general unlawful as being contrary to public policy – Exceptions – Company – Minority shareholder's action – Action in shareholder's own name – Action to redress wrongs against company committed by majority shareholder – Action in substance a representative action – Liability of minority shareholder to heavy costs – Right of indemnity against company – Whether contingency fee agreement between minority shareholder and legal advisers permissible.

The plaintiff was a minority shareholder in a public company, HB Ltd; B & Co Ltd was a subsidiary of HB Ltd. The defendant was the majority shareholder in HB Ltd and was a director of both companies; he also controlled other concerns in the United Kingdom and abroad. The plaintiff discovered that the defendant had been guilty of misconduct in managing the affairs of both companies in that, inter alia, he had procured loans from each company by means of a transaction ('the circular cheque transaction') by which moneys of the companies had been applied for the defendant's benefit to enable him to purchase shares in HB Ltd. The Board of Trade refused to hold an enquiry into the matter and the plaintiff was prevented by the defendant from raising the matter at shareholders' meetings. The only way, therefore, in which the plaintiff could get redress for the wrongs done to the companies was by bringing an action in the courts. The defendant brought an action for libel against the plaintiff, in respect of statements made by the plaintiff concerning the defendant's conduct of the companies' affairs. By way of counterclaim to that action the plaintiff sought declarations that the defendant was guilty of wrongs done to both companies and orders that the defendant pay specified sums to the companies including a sum in respect of the circular cheque transaction. In the counterclaim the plaintiff sued in his

FF

own name and made HB Ltd and B & Co Ltd parties to the counterclaim. The
defendant's action for libel was dismissed for want of prosecution. In default of *a*
delivery of a defence to the plaintiff's counterclaim the plaintiff obtained from the
Court of Appeal*ᵃ* final judgment on the counterclaim against the defendant for
£234,773 'with interest' in respect of the circular cheque transaction, and interlocutory judgment on the counterclaim for damages to be assessed by a judge in
respect of another transaction. However the defendant was given leave by the court
to defend on the remaining issues in the counterclaim provided he submitted a *b*
defence to the court within a specified time. Further, the defendant sought leave to
appeal to the House of Lords against the judgments given against him on the counterclaim. The plaintiff had exhausted his own funds in fighting the litigation for over ten
years, and contributions from the other minority shareholders in HB Ltd had also
been exhausted. The plaintiff was fearful that, should he be unsuccessful in the
matters outstanding in the litigation, i e the enquiry into damages on the interlocutory *c*
award, the remaining issues on the counterclaim and the possible appeal to the House
of Lords, he might be ordered to pay the defendant's costs himself. Even if he were
to win on those issues, any benefit from the proceedings would go to HB Ltd and
B & Co Ltd and not to the plaintiff whose only benefit might be that his few shares
would appreciate in value. Moreover the plaintiff was likely to incur considerable
costs in enforcing the existing judgments on the counterclaim since the defendant was *d*
in Germany. The plaintiff had been refused legal aid on the ground that it was
unreasonable for him to receive it in the circumstances of the case, and had unsuccessfully appealed against that refusal. In that situation the plaintiff applied to the Court
of Appeal for assistance with regard to the future costs of the litigation. The question
also arose whether the court had power to award interest on the final judgment for
£234,773 on the counterclaim, and if so whether the interest should be simple or *e*
compound.

Held – (i) The court had power under its equitable jurisdiction to award interest
whenever a trustee, or anyone else in a fiduciary position, such as a director of a
company, misused money which he controlled in his fiduciary capacity for his own
benefit. Where the money had been used for the purpose of a transaction of a commercial character, the court should assume, in the absence of evidence to the contrary, *f*
that the transaction had been profitable to the wrongdoer and should award compound interest to give adequate compensation for the profit assumed to have been
made by him. From the nature of the defendant's operations in commercial companies it could be presumed that he had put the money from the circular cheque
transaction to profitable use. Accordingly it was a proper case for the court to award
compound interest with yearly rests on the judgment for £234,773, and the court *g*
would do so at the rate of 1 per cent above bank rate or the minimum lending rate in
operation from time to time (see p 855 *g* to p 856 *b* and *d*, p 863 *d* to *j*, p 864*c* and *fg*,
p 865*a*, p 870 *g* and *h* and p 871 *c*, post); *Atwool v Merryweather* (1867) LR 5 Eq 464 and
dicta of Lord Hatherley LC in *Burdick v Garrick* (1870) 5 Ch App at 241, 242 and of Lord
Herschell in *Bray v Ford* [1896] AC at 51 applied.

    (ii) It was open to the court in a minority shareholder's action to order that the *h*
company should indemnify the plaintiff against the costs incurred in the action.
Where the wrongdoers themselves controlled the company, a minority shareholder's
action brought to obtain redress, whether brought in the plaintiff's own name or on
behalf of himself and the other minority shareholders, and even though brought
without the company's authority, was in substance a representative action on behalf
of the company to obtain redress for the wrongs done to the company. Accord- *j*
ingly, provided that it was reasonable and prudent in the company's interest for the
plaintiff to bring the action and it was brought by him in good faith, it was a proper
exercise of judicial discretion or (per Lord Denning MR) in accordance with the

---

a   [1974] 3 All ER 217, [1974] 1 WLR 991

a principles of equity, that the court should order the company to pay the plaintiff's costs down to judgment whether the action succeeded or not. The costs should be taxed on a common fund basis. Although as a general rule a plaintiff should apply at the commencement of the action for sanction to proceed with it, in the circumstances the court would authorise the plaintiff to proceed with the prosecution of the outstanding issues on the counterclaim down to the close of discovery after which he should obtain further directions of the court; and he would be indemnified by HB

b Ltd and B & Co Ltd for all the costs which he had incurred in the past, and would reasonably incur in the future down to and including discovery, over and above those which he recovered from the defendant (see p 858 *c* and *g* to p 859 *c*, p 862 *f* and *h*, p 868 *g* to p 869 *b*, p 870 *b* and *c* and p 871 *f* and *h*, post); *Re Beddoe* [1893] 1 Ch 547 applied.

c (iii) As a minority shareholder's action was a representative action on behalf of the company, the plaintiff in such an action was not entitled to legal aid for, by virtue of s 25 of the Legal Aid Act 1974, the 'persons' entitled to legal aid did not include a body corporate and, if the plaintiff were given legal aid, it would mean that the company on behalf of whom he sued would receive legal aid indirectly. Accordingly the plaintiff was not entitled to legal aid (see p 859 *g*, p 860 *a*, p 865 *h* and *j*, p 866 *b* and *d* and p 871 *e*, post).

d (iv) Contingency fees, i e fees payable to the plaintiff's lawyers only if the plaintiff were successful in the proceedings, were unlawful by the law of England on the ground that they were contrary to public policy, and no exception to that rule was recognised. Accordingly (Lord Denning MR dissenting), since the rule against contingency fees was a rule of law, the court should not introduce into that law an exception to permit contingency fees in the case of a minority shareholder's action. In

e any event (per Buckley and Scarman LJJ) neither public policy nor justice required an exception to the rule against contingency fees in the case of a minority shareholder's action since the plaintiff, having obtained the court's sanction to conduct the counterclaim, had a full indemnity for his costs against the company (see p 860 *g* and *h*, p 861 *ac* and *h*, p 867 *g*, p 868 *b* and *c*, p 872 *cf* and *g* and p 873 *c* and *d*, post); dictum of Lord Esher MR in *Pittman v Prudential Deposit Bank Ltd* (1896) 13 TLR at 121

f applied.

Observations on the procedure to be followed where a minority shareholder wishes to bring an action in a representative capacity on behalf of the company and to be indemnified by the company on a common fund basis in respect of the costs of the action (see p 859 *d* to *f*, p 869 *e* to *j* and p 871 *j*, post).

g **Notes**

For claims for interest generally, see 11 Halsbury's Laws (3rd Edn) 304, para 493; for payment of interest by a trustee, see 38 Halsbury's Laws (3rd Edn) 1048, 1049, paras 1812-1814, and for cases on the subject, see 47 Digest (Repl) 481-485, 4322-4373.

For representative actions by a shareholder, see 7 Halsbury's Laws (4th Edn) 460, 461, paras 770-772, and for cases on the subject, see 9 Digest (Repl) 714-724, 4730-4806.

h For solicitors' remuneration for contentious business generally, see 36 Halsbury's Laws (3rd Edn) 106, 107, 125, 126, paras 141, 167-169.

Cases referred to in judgments

Armory v Delamirie (1722) 1 Stra 505, [1558-1774] All ER Rep 121, 93 ER 664, 3 Digest (Repl) 67, 83.

i *Attorney-General v Alford* (1855) 4 De GM & G 843, 3 Eq Rep 952, 24 LTOS 265, 1 Jur NS 361, 43 ER 737, 47 Digest (Repl) 482, 4388.

Attorneys & Solicitors Act 1870, Re (1875) 1 Ch D 573, 45 LJ Ch 47, 43 Digest (Repl) 143, 1283.

Atwool v Merryweather (1867) LR 5 Eq 464n, 37 LJCh 35, 9 Digest (Repl) 659, 4362.

Beddoe, Re, Downes v Cottam [1893] 1 Ch 547, 62 LJCh 233, 68 LT 595, 2 R 223, CA, 47 Digest (Repl) 241, 2127.

Bray v Ford [1896] AC 44, [1895-9] All ER Rep 1009, 65 LJQB 213, 73 LT 609, HL, 17
Digest (Reissue) 217, 882.   *a*
Broom (Brown) v Hall (1859) 7 CBNS 503, 34 LTOS 66, 141 ER 911, 1 Digest (Repl) 622,
2062.
Burdick v Garrick (1870) 5 Ch App 233, 39 LJCh 369, 47 Digest (Repl) 485, *4365*.
Burland v Earle [1902] AC 83, 71 LJPC 1, 85 LT 553, 9 Mans 17, PC, 9 Digest (Repl) 564,
3727.
Cook v Deeks [1916] 1 AC 554, 85 LJPC 161, 114 LT 636, PC, 9 Digest (Repl) 488, *3211*.   *b*
East Pant du United Lead Mining Co Ltd v Merryweather (1864) 2 Hem & M 254, 5 New
Rep 166, 10 Jur NS 1231, 13 WR 216, 71 ER 460, 9 Digest (Repl) 608, *4038*.
Foss v Harbottle (1843) 2 Hare 461, 67 ER 189, 9 Digest (Repl) 662, *4382*.
Hardoon v Belilios [1901] AC 118, 70 LJPC 9, 83 LT 573, PC, 9 Digest (Repl) 210, *1328*.
Jones v Foxall (1852) 15 Beav 388, 21 LJCh 725, 51 ER 588, 47 Digest (Repl) 484, *4350*.
Keech v Sandford (1726) Sel Cas Ch 61, [1558-1774] All ER Rep 230, 2 Eq Cas Abr 741,   *c*
Cas *temp* King 61, 25 ER 223, 47 Digest (Repl) 104, *749*.
Knott v Cottee (1847) 2 Ph 192, 8 LTOS 462, 41 ER 915, 47 Digest (Repl) 56, *403*.
Mason v Harris (1879) 11 Ch D 97, 48 LJCh 589, 40 LT 644, 9 Digest (Repl) 715, *4745*.
Menier v Hooper's Telegraph Works (1874) 9 Ch App 350, 43 LJCh 330, 30 LT 209, 9 Digest
(Repl) 659, *4367*.
Neville v London Express Newspapers Ltd [1917] 2 KB 564, 86 LJKB 1055, 117 LT 598, CA;   *d*
rvsd on other grounds [1919] AC 368, [1918-19] All ER Rep 61, HL, 9 Digest (Repl) 670,
4433.
Pettman v Keble (1850) 9 CB 701, 19 LJCP 325, 15 Jur 38, 137 ER 1067, 1 Digest (Repl) 622,
2061.
Pittman v Prudential Deposit Bank (Ltd) (1896) 13 TLR 110, 41 Sol Jo 129, CA, 8(2) Digest
(Reissue) 509, *126*.   *e*
Regal (Hastings) Ltd v Gulliver [1942] 1 All ER 378, HL, 9 Digest (Repl) 523, *3447*.
Richardson, Re, Ex parte St Thomas's Hospital (Governors) [1911] 2 KB 705, 80 LJKB 1232,
105 LT 226, 18 Mans 327, CA, 5 Digest (Repl) 726, *6285*.
Simpson & Miller v British Industries Trust Ltd (1923) TLR 286.
Solicitor, A, Re, Ex parte Law Society [1912] 1 KB 302, [1911-13] All ER Rep 202, 81 LJKB
245, 105 LT 874, DC, 43 Digest (Repl) 437, *4634*.   *f*
Steeden v Walden [1910] 2 Ch 393, [1908-10] All ER Rep 380, 79 LJCh 613, 103 LT 135,
28(2) Digest (Reissue) 889, *1974*.
Trepca Mines Ltd, Re, (Application of Radomir Nicola Pachitch (Pasic)) [1962] 3 All ER 351,
[1963] Ch 199, [1962] 3 WLR 955, CA, Digest (Cont Vol A) 3, *777a*.
Vyse v Foster (1872) 8 Ch App 309, 42 LJCh 245, 27 LT 774; *affd* (1874) LR 7 HL 318,
HL, 47 Digest (Repl) 421, *3773*.   *g*
Williams v Lister & Co (1913) 109 LT 699, CA, 1 Digest (Repl) 620, *2048*.

Cases also cited
Barclay Re, Barclay v Andrew [1899] 1 Ch 674.
Cremer v General-Carriers SA [1974] 1 All ER 1, [1974] 1 WLR 341.
Dominion Coal Co Ltd v Maskinonge Steamship Co Ltd [1922] 2 KB 132.   *h*
FMC (Meat) Ltd v Fairfield Cold Stores Ltd [1971] 2 Lloyd's Rep 221.
Gath v Howarth (1884) WN 99.
Gordon v Gonda [1955] 2 All ER 762, [1955] 1 WLR 885, CA.
Hill v Archbold [1967] 3 All ER 110, [1968] 1 QB 686, CA.
Jefford v Gee [1970] 1 All ER 1202, [1970] 2 QB 130, CA.
Johnson v R [1904] AC 817, PC.   *j*
London, Chatham & Dover Railway Co v South Eastern Railway Co [1893] AC 429, HL.
Marsh v Jones (1889) 40 Ch D 563, CA.
Martell v Consett Iron Co Ltd [1955] 1 All ER 481, [1955] 1 Ch 363, CA.
Newall v Tunstall [1970] 3 All ER 465, [1971] 1 WLR 105.
Nishina Trading Co Ltd v Chiyoda Fire & Marine Insurance Co Ltd [1968] 3 All ER 712,
[1968] 1 WLR 1325.

R v Haslemere (Inhabitants) (1862) 3 B & S 313.

a *Waite v Redpath Dorman Long Ltd* [1971] 1 All ER 573, [1971] 1 QB 294.

Williams Radman's Microble Killer Co Ltd v Leather [1892] 1 QB 85.

Interlocutory appeal

Hartley Baird Ltd was a substantial public company of long standing. H J Baldwin & Co Ltd was a subsidiary of Hartley Baird Ltd. Eighty per cent of Hartley Baird Ltd's

b issued share capital was owned by Camp Bird Finance Ltd and the remainder by members of the public. Camp Bird Finance Ltd was also a public company but in 1962 its affairs were under the control of a Mr John Dalgleish who held a power of attorney authorising him to act on its behalf. The shares in Hartley Baird Ltd held by Camp Bird Finance Ltd were subject to a charge in favour of an insurance company. On 30th March 1962 Mr Dalgleish, on behalf of Camp Bird Finance Ltd entered into an

c agreement with the plaintiff to sell to the Rothschild Trust its shares in Hartley Baird Ltd for £518,787. The Rothschild Trust was a concern registered in Liechtenstein and controlled by the plaintiff, William Kurt Wallersteiner ('Dr Wallersteiner'). The purchase price was to be paid in two parts: (i) by procuring the payment of £284,982 direct to Hartley Baird Ltd in relief of Camp Bird Finance Ltd's indebtedness to Hartley Baird Ltd in that sum; (ii) by paying the balance of £233,805 direct to Camp

d Bird Finance Ltd. On 14th April Dr Wallersteiner and Mr Dalgleish wrote letters purporting to vary the terms of the agreement as to the payment of the purchase price. On 29th May they executed an assignment whereby Camp Bird Finance Ltd assigned its beneficial interest in its shares in Hartley Baird Ltd to a nominee for the Rothschild Trust. The assignment recited that the consideration for the shares 'has been duly paid or satisfied'. On the same day Dr Wallersteiner and his associates were

e appointed directors of Hartley Baird Ltd. The Rothschild Trust did not in fact procure the payment to Hartley Baird Ltd of the £284,982; the trust entered themselves in their books as debtors to Hartley Baird Ltd and took credit against Camp Bird Finance Ltd as having paid that sum. The balance of £233,805 was not paid in cash but was treated as being cancelled by means of contra-accounts, consisting principally of commissions claimed by various Liechtenstein concerns controlled by the plaintiff

f in respect of sales executed on behalf of Camp Bird Finance Ltd, including a commission on the sale of the Hartley Baird Ltd shares. Dr Wallersteiner also took steps to pay off the charge on the Hartley Baird Ltd shares; £125,000 was required by Camp Bird Finance Ltd for that purpose. Dr Wallersteiner proposed to sell certain shares which he owned to Hartley Baird Ltd and arranged for Hartley Baird Ltd to pay £50,000 as a deposit on the proposed purchase. That sum was paid into an account belonging to a

g company ('IFT') controlled by Dr Wallersteiner and registered in the Bahamas. Dr Wallersteiner obtained a further £75,000 from other sources and lent the total sum of £125,000 to Camp Bird Finance Ltd which paid off the charge to the insurance company. Meanwhile the proposed sale of shares to Hartley Baird Ltd had fallen through; however the £50,000 was not repaid; it was treated as a loan to IFT which gave a bill of exchange for that sum guaranteed by the Rothschild Trust. In September 1962,

h in order to discharge the indebtedness to Hartley Baird Ltd of £284,982 for which the Rothschild Trust had undertaken responsibility, arrangements were made whereby Camp Bird Finance Ltd drew cheques in favour of Hartley Baird Ltd for that sum on a merchant bank controlled by Dr Wallersteiner; Hartley Baird Ltd drew cheques on the same bank for the same amount in favour of IFT; and IFT drew a cheque on the same bank for the same amount in favour of Camp Bird Finance Ltd. The sum paid

j by Hartley Baird Ltd was said to be by way of a loan to IFT bearing interest at one per cent over bank rate to be paid by eight equal yearly instalments commencing a year later and guaranteed by the Rothschild Trust. In the event IFT paid Hartley Baird Ltd some of the instalments but the balance of £234,773 was not paid.

    Those transactions, and certain others into which Hartley Baird Ltd entered subsequently, came to the attention of the defendant, MJG Moir ('Mr Moir'), a shareholder

in Hartley Baird Ltd, who made statements to the press and applied to the Board
of Trade to investigate Hartley Baird Ltd's affairs. In 1967 Dr Wallersteiner arranged *a*
for IFT to make a bid for the remaining 20 per cent of the shares in Hartley Baird
Ltd. On 31st March 1967 Mr Moir issued a circular to shareholders in Hartley Baird
Ltd stating that 'those manoeuvres look distinctly fraudulent. This bid . . . represents the culmination of a series of unlawful activities in your company's affairs
since control of it was acquired in 1962 by [Dr Wallersteiner] . . .' On 10th April
Dr Wallersteiner issued a writ for libel against Mr Moir with a statement of claim *b*
indorsed. On the following day Mr Moir delivered a defence. Neither pleading was
satisfactory in form and they were followed by various interlocutory proceedings.
Eventually, on 27th March 1969, Mr Moir served a full and detailed defence and
counterclaim. Hartley Baird Ltd and HJ Baldwin & Co Ltd were joined with Dr
Wallersteiner as defendants to the counterclaim. The document claimed that Dr
Wallersteiner was guilty of fraud, misfeasance and breach of trust. It dealt in detail *c*
with the payment of the inter-company indebtedness of £284,982 by means of the
circular cheque transaction and the £50,000 lent to IFT and other matters. Dr Wallersteiner failed to deliver a reply or defence to counterclaim. In October 1969 he served
a request for further and better particulars covering 32 pages. In June 1971 Mr Moir
produced the particulars. Dr Wallersteiner took no further steps. However at
company meetings between 1968 and 1971 he refused to allow any discussion of his *d*
conduct of Hartley Baird Ltd's affairs on the ground that, in view of the pending libel
action, the matter was sub judice. In June 1972 Mr Moir applied for the dismissal of
the libel action for want of prosecution and for judgment in default of defence on the
counterclaim, under RSC Ord 19, rr 7(1) and 8. Thereupon Hartley Baird Ltd sought
leave to put in a reply and defence to counterclaim. The defence consisted merely of
a general denial of Mr Moir's allegations, with no reference to Mr Moir's particulars. *e*
The master refused leave for it to be served and gave judgment for Mr Moir on the
counterclaim. He refused, however, to dismiss the libel action. On appeal, Geoffrey
Lane J, on 26th July 1973, in chambers dismissed the libel action for want of prosecution and, in the absence of any effective defence, gave judgment on the counterclaim
which included declarations that Dr Wallersteiner had been guilty of fraud, misfeasance and breach of trust and ordered him to pay to Hartley Baird Ltd sums of £215,334, *f*
£50,000, £24,687, £100,000, £65,380 and £6,247 in all cases with interest and to HJ
Baldwin Ltd £19,443 with interest.

Dr Wallersteiner appealed and on 21st May 1974 the Court of Appeal[1] (Lord
Denning MR, Buckley and Scarman LJJ) varied the order of Geoffrey Lane J made on
the counterclaim in default of defence, gave final judgment on the counterclaim
against Dr Wallersteiner for £234,773, with interest, in respect of the circular cheque *g*
transaction, and gave interlocutory judgment on the counterclaim in respect of
another loan transaction for damages to be assessed by a judge. The Court of Appeal
also varied the order by omitting the declarations. On the remaining issues of the
counterclaim the court gave Dr Wallersteiner leave to defend provided that a draft
defence was submitted for the court's approval within 28 days. The court intimated
that at a later date it would hear argument whether the interest on the final award on *h*
the counterclaim should be single or compound; and that it would also hear argument on an application by Mr Moir with regard to the future costs of the litigation.
On 15th July 1974 the appeal came before the court for further hearing on the questions of the draft defence to the counterclaim, the interest on the final award and Mr
Moir's future costs. At the end of that hearing the court reserved judgment on the
question of interest, and adjourned Mr Moir's application regarding future costs *j*
for further argument on behalf of the Law Society. The application regarding future
costs came before the court for further argument on 11th November 1974 and at the

---

1   [1974] 3 All ER 217, [1974] 1 WLR 991

a end of that hearing the court reserved its judgment. The facts material to the questions of interest and future costs are set out in the judgment of Lord Denning MR.

John Beveridge and *Oliver Thorold* for Mr Moir[1].
Anthony Lincoln QC and *Peter Sheridan* for Dr Wallersteiner.
Michael Lyndon-Stanford and *William Charles* for Hartley Baird Ltd and H J Baldwin & Co Ltd.

b *Peter Webster QC* and *Mark Potter* as amici curiae.

Cur adv vult

29th January.   The following judgments were read.

LORD DENNING MR.

c PART I
INTEREST

When we gave judgment in May 1974[2] each of us said that Dr Wallersteiner was to pay the sums *with interest*. But it is now suggested that we made a mistake in ordering Dr Wallersteiner to pay any interest.   His counsel asserted that we had no power to award interest save under s 3(1) of the Law Reform (Miscellaneous Provisions) Act

d 1934: and that section, he said, did not apply to the present case. It applied only to 'proceedings tried in any court of record'; and here there were no proceedings 'tried'. The judgment we gave was a judgment in default of pleading; and that, he says, did not involve a trial. He relied on a note in the White Book to RSC Ord 6 r 2[3], which says:

e '... interest under this section can only be awarded in proceedings that are "tried", and therefore cannot be awarded on a judgment obtained in default of appearance or defence or failure to comply with an order or the rules, nor presumably in proceedings under O. 14, but in such cases the plaintiff may ask for final judgment for the principal sum, and for interlocutory judgment for the interest to be assessed, by analogy with an assessment of damages.'

f I think that that note may be putting too narrow a construction on the word 'tried'. It seems to me that, after all the evidence and arguments which were had in this case, it could well be said that those were proceedings 'tried' in a court of record. Similarly with proceedings under RSC Ord 14.   But it is unnecessary to go into this for this simple reason: we did not order interest to be paid under the 1934 Act, but under the equitable jurisdiction of the court. Equity now prevails in all courts; and equity

g was in the habit of awarding interest when it was considered equitable to do so. In some cases it awarded simple interest; in others compound interest, i e with yearly rests.

The principles on which the courts of equity acted are expounded in a series of cases of which I would take the judgment of Romilly MR in *Jones v Foxall*[4]; of Lord Cranworth LC in *Attorney-General v Alford*[5]; of Lord Hatherley LC in *Burdick v Garrick*[6];

h of Sir W M James LJ in *Vyse v Foster*[7]. Those judgments show that, in equity, interest is never awarded by way of punishment. Equity awards it whenever money is misused by an executor or a trustee or anyone else in a fiduciary position—who has misapplied the money and made use of it himself for his own benefit. The court presumes—

j 1 Mr Moir appeared in person during part of the hearing in July 1974 relating to the interest issue.
2 [1974] 3 All ER 217 at 241, 251, 255, 256, [1974] 1 WLR 991 at 1017, 1028, 1033, 1034
3 The Supreme Court Practice 1973, vol 1, p 38, para 6/2/7A
4 (1852) 15 Beav 388
5 (1855) 4 De G M & G 843 at 851
6 (1870) 5 Ch App 233 at 241, 242
7 (1872) LR 8 Ch App 309 at 333

'that the party against whom relief is sought has made that amount of profit which persons ordinarily do make in trade, and in those cases the Court directs *a* rests to be made [i e compound interest]':

see *Burdick v Garrick*[1] by Lord Hatherley LC. The reason is because a person in a fiduciary position is not allowed to make a profit out of his trust; and, if he does, he is liable to account for that profit or interest in lieu thereof.

In addition, in equity interest is awarded whenever a wrongdoer deprives a com- *b* pany of money which it needs for use in its business. It is plain that the company should be compensated for the loss thereby occasioned to it. Mere replacement of the money—years later—is by no means adequate compensation, especially in days of inflation. The company should be compensated by the award of interest. That was done by Sir William Page Wood V-C (afterwards Lord Hatherley) in one of the leading cases on the subject, *Atwool v Merryweather*[2]. But the question arises: should it be *c* simple interest or compound interest? On general principles I think it should be presumed that the company (had it not been deprived of the money) would have made the most beneficial use open to it, cf *Armory v Delamirie*[3]. It may be that the company would have used it in its own trading operations; or that it would have used it to help its subsidiaries. Alternatively, it should be presumed that the wrongdoer made the most beneficial use of it. But, whichever it is, in order to give adequate *d* compensation, the money should be replaced at interest with yearly rests, i e compound interest.

Applying these principles to the present case, I think we should award interest at the rate of 1 per cent per annum above the official bank rate or minimum lending rate in operation from time to time and with yearly rests.

e

PART II

FUTURE COSTS

1 *Mr Moir's anxiety as to future costs*

This case has brought to light a serious defect in the administration of justice. Mr Moir is a shareholder in a public company. He discovered that Dr Wallersteiner had been guilty of grave misconduct in the management of the company's affairs. He *f* tried every known way to get an enquiry held. He applied many times to the Department of Trade to appoint an inspector, but that department put him off. They suggested that he had a remedy in the courts. He applied to the ombudsman, but he could do nothing. He raised the matter at shareholders' meetings, but was abruptly cut off. The only way in which he has been able to have his complaint investigated is by action in these courts. And here he was come to the end of his tether. He has fought this case for over ten years on his own. He has expended all his financial *g* resources on it and all his time and labour. He has received contributions from other shareholders but these are now exhausted. He has recovered judgment for over £250,000 against Dr Wallersteiner. It may be difficult to get the money out of Dr Wallersteiner, but if it is obtained, not a penny of it will go into Mr Moir's pocket. It will all go to benefit the companies Hartley Baird and Baldwins. Yet the *h* litigation is by no means finished. There is yet to be fought: (i) an enquiry into the damages suffered by Hartley Baird in respect of the £50,000 transaction; (ii) the remaining issues on the counterclaim on which Dr Wallersteiner seeks to put in a defence; and (iii) an appeal to the House of Lords, if leave is obtained. There is also (iv) the cost of enforcing the existing judgment against Dr Wallersteiner. He is in Germany and it may cost much time and expense to get anything out of him. Mr Moir *j* tells us—and I have no doubt it is true—that he has not any money left with which to pay the costs in further matters. He is fearful, too, that, if he should lose on them or

---

1 (1870) LR 5 Ch App at 242
2 (1867) LR 5 Eq 464n at 468, 469
3 (1722) 1 Stra 505, [1558-1774] All ER Rep 121

a   any of them, he may be ordered to pay personally the costs of Dr Wallersteiner on them. Even if he wins all the way through, no part of it will redound to his own benefit. It will all go to the benefit of Hartley Baird and Baldwins. His few shares might appreciate a little in value, but that is all. In this situation he appeals to this court for help in respect of the future costs of this litigation. If no help is forthcoming, all his efforts will have been in vain. The delaying tactics of Dr Wallersteiner will have succeeded. Mr Moir will have to give up the struggle exhausted in mind, body

b   and estate.
    We felt the force of these points. So keenly indeed that we asked the Law Society to help. They instructed Mr Peter Webster as amicus curiae. He analysed the legal position in a most illuminating manner. We are much indebted to him. He took us through the three ways in which it was suggested that Mr Moir could be protected: (1) indemnity from the company; (2) legal aid; and (3) contingency fee. As the dis-

c   cussion proceeded, it appeared very necessary to be clear as to the nature of Mr Moir's counterclaim. He is a minority shareholder seeking to redress a wrong done to the company.

    2 The derivative action
    It is a fundamental principle of our law that a company is a legal person, with its

d   own corporate identity, separate and distinct from the directors or shareholders, and with its own property rights and interests to which alone it is entitled. If it is de-frauded by a wrongdoer, the company itself is the one person to sue for the damage. Such is the rule in *Foss v Harbottle*[1]. The rule is easy enough to apply when the company is defrauded by outsiders. The company itself is the only person who can sue. Likewise, when it is defrauded by insiders of a minor kind, once again the com-

e   pany is the only person who can sue. But suppose it is defrauded by insiders who control its affairs—by directors who hold a majority of the shares—who then can sue for damages? Those directors are themselves the wrongdoers. If a board meeting is held, they will not authorise proceedings to be taken by the company against them-selves. If a general meeting is called, they will vote down any suggestion that the company should sue them themselves. Yet the company is the one person who is

f   damnified. It is the one person who should sue. In one way or another some means must be found for the company to sue. Otherwise the law would fail in its purpose. Injustice would be done without redress. In *Foss v Harbottle*[2] Wigram V-C saw the problem and suggested a solution. He thought that the company could sue 'in the name of someone whom the law has appointed to be its representative'. A suit could be brought—

g   'by individual corporators in their private characters, and asking in such character the protection of those rights to which in their corporate character they were entitled'.

    This suggestion found its fulfilment in the *Merryweather* case[3], which came before Page Wood V-C on two occasions[4] It was accepted in that case that the minority

h   shareholders might file a bill asking leave to use the name of the company[5]. If they showed reasonable ground for charging the directors with fraud, the court would appoint the minority shareholders as representatives of the company to bring pro-ceedings in the name of the company against the wrongdoing directors. By that means the company would sue in its own name for the wrong done to it. That would

j   1   (1843) 2 Hare 461
    2   2 Hare at 491, 492
    3   (1867) LR 5 Eq 464n
    4   *East Pant du United Lead Mining Co Ltd v Merryweather* (1864) 2 Hem & M 254 and *Atwool v Merryweather* (1867) LR 5 Eq 464
    5   See 2 Hem & M at 259, LR 5 Eq at 467, 468

be, however, a circuitous course, as Lord Hatherley LC said himself, at any rate in cases where the fraud itself could be proved on the initial application.　　　　　*a*

To avoid that circuity, Lord Hatherley LC held that the minority shareholders themselves could bring an action in their own names (but in truth on behalf of the company) against the wrongdoing directors for the damage done by them to the company, provided always that it was impossible to get the company itself to sue them. He ordered the fraudulent directors in that case to repay the sums to the company, be it noted, with interest[1]. His decision was emphatically approved by　*b* this court in *Menier v Hoopers' Telegraph Works*[2]; and *Mason v Harris*[3]. The form of the action is always 'AB (a minority shareholder) on behalf of himself and all other shareholders of the Company' against the wrongdoing directors and the company. That form of action was said by Lord Davey to be a 'mere matter of procedure in order to give a remedy for a wrong which would otherwise escape redress': see *Burland v Earle*[4]. Stripped of mere procedure, the principle is that, where the wrong-　*c* doers themselves control the company, an action can be brought on behalf of the company by the minority shareholders, on the footing that they are its representatives, to obtain redress on its behalf. I am glad to find this principle well stated by Professor Gower in his book on companies[5] in words which I would gratefully adopt:

> 'Where such an action is allowed the member is not really suing on his own　*d* behalf nor on behalf of the members generally, but on behalf of the company itself. Although . . . he will have to frame his action as a representative one on behalf of himself and all the members other than the wrongdoers, this gives a misleading impression of what really occurs. The plaintiff shareholder is not acting as a representative of the other shareholders but as a representative of the company . . . in the United States . . . this type of action has been given the　*e* distinctive name of a "derivative action," recognising that its true nature is that the individual member sues on behalf of the company to enforce rights derived from it.'

As it happens in the present case the formula has been discarded. The counterclaim by Mr Moir was prepared by a careful, learned and skilful member of the bar, Mr William Stubbs. It is not headed 'on behalf of himself and all the other shareholders'.　*f* It is just headed 'M. J. G. Moir, plaintiff on counterclaim'. The two companies were made parties by being added to the counterclaim. The prayer is: 'Mr Moir counterclaims for' several declarations of wrongs done to the two companies, and orders on Dr Wallersteiner to pay specified sums to the two companies, and that he pay the costs of Mr Moir and the two companies. No objection has been taken to that form of proceeding. No suggestion has been made that it should be amended. Quite right.　*g* Let it stand as it is. It is in accord with principle. Mr Moir sues in his own name but in reality on behalf of the companies: just as an agent may contract in his own name but in reality on behalf of his principal.

3 Indemnity

Now that the principle is recognised, it has important consequences which have　*h* hitherto not been perceived. The first is that the minority shareholder, being an agent acting on behalf of the company, is entitled to be indemnified by the company against all costs and expenses reasonably incurred by him in the course of the agency. This indemnity does not arise out of a contract express or implied, but it arises on the plainest principles of equity. It is analogous to the indemnity to which a trustee is　*j*

1　(1867) LR 5 Eq at 469
2　(1874) 9 Ch App 350
3　(1879) 11 Ch D 97
4　[1902] AC 83
5　Modern Company Law (3rd Edn, 1969), p 587

entitled from his cestui que trust who is sui juris: see *Hardoon v Belilios*[1]; *Re Richardson*[2].
a Seeing that, if the action succeeds, the whole benefit will go to the company, it is only just that the minority shareholder should be indemnified against the costs he incurs on its behalf. If the action succeeds, the wrongdoing director will be ordered to pay the costs: but if they are not recovered from him, they should be paid by the company. And all the additional costs (over and above party and party costs) should be taxed on a common fund basis and paid by the company: see *Simpson & Miller v*
b *British Industries Trust Ltd*[3]. The solicitor will have a charge on the money recovered for his taxed costs, because it will have been recovered through his instrumentality: see s 73 of the Solicitors Act 1974.

But what if the action fails? Assuming that the minority shareholder had reasonable ground for bringing the action—that it was a reasonable and prudent course to take in the interests of the company—he should not himself be liable to pay the costs of the
c other side, but the company itself should be liable, because he was acting for it and not for himself. In addition, he should himself be indemnified by the company in respect of his own costs even if the action fails. It is a well-known maxim of the law that he who would take the benefit of a venture if it succeeds ought also to bear the burden if it fails. Qui sentit commodum sentire debet et onus. This indemnity should extend to his own costs taxed on a common fund basis.
d In order to be entitled to this indemnity, the minority shareholder soon after issuing his writ should apply for the sanction of the court in somewhat the same way as a trustee does: see *Re Beddoe, Downes v Cottam*[4]. In a derivative action, I would suggest this procedure. The minority shareholder should apply ex parte to the master for directions, supported by an opinion of counsel, as to whether there is a reasonable case or not. The master may then, if he thinks fit, straightaway approve the continu-
e ance of the proceedings until close of pleadings, or until after discovery or until trial (rather as a legal aid committee does). The master need not, however, decide it ex parte. He can, if he thinks fit, require notice to be given to one or two of the other minority shareholders—as representatives of the rest—so as to see if there is any reasonable objection. (In this very case another minority shareholder took this very point in letters to us.) But this preliminary application should be simple and in-
f expensive. It should not be allowed to escalate into a minor trial. The master should simply ask himself: is there a reasonable case for the minority shareholder to bring at the expense (eventually) of the company? If there is, let it go ahead.

4 *Legal Aid*

g Another consequence of the principle—that a minority shareholder sues on behalf of the company—is that he cannot get legal aid even though he is a poor man. Legal aid is only available for a 'person', and in this context 'person' does not include a body of persons corporate or unincorporate so as to authorise advice or assistance or legal aid to be given to such a body: see s 25 of the Legal Aid Act 1974. If a minority share-holder were given legal aid, it would mean that indirectly the company would receive
h legal aid. That would clearly be contrary to the intendment of the statute.

Apart from that objection, there was a further objection. Until recently these pro-ceedings were 'partly in respect of defamation'. Dr Wallersteiner sued for libel. Mr Moir pleaded justification in many paragraphs which he simply repeated in the counterclaim. So long as the claim for libel remained, legal aid could not be granted: see the Legal Aid Act 1974, Sch 1, Part II, para 1. Now that the claim for libel has been
j dismissed, that objection may no longer apply. But there is this further objection.

---

1 [1901] AC 118
2 [1911] 2 KB 705
3 (1923) 39 TLR 286
4 [1893] 1 Ch 547 at 557, 558

It would appear that any advantage to Mr Moir himself would be trivial, seeing that
he holds so few shares: see the Legal Aid (General) Regulations 1971[1], r 5(13)(a).   *a*

In any case, Mr Moir has applied for legal aid and has been refused on the ground
that 'it appears unreasonable that he should receive it in the particular circumstances
of the case': see s 7(5) of the 1974 Act; and reg 7(f) of the 1971 regulations; and he has
appealed unsuccessfully. The result is that legal aid is not available.

5 Contingency fee   *b*

English law has never sanctioned an agreement by which a lawyer is remunerated
on the basis of a 'contingency fee', that is that he gets paid the fee if he wins, but not if
he loses. Such an agreement was illegal on the ground that it was the offence of
champerty. In its origin champerty was a division of the proceeds (campi partitio).
An agreement by which a lawyer, if he won, was to receive a share of the proceeds was
pure champerty. Even if he was not to receive an actual share, but payment of a   *c*
commission on a sum proportioned to the amount recovered—only if he won—it
was also regarded as champerty: see *Re Attorneys and Solicitors Act 1870*[2] by Jessel
MR; *Re A Solicitor*[3]. Even if the sum was not a proportion of the amount recovered,
but a specific sum or advantage which was to be received if he won but not if he lost,
that, too, was unlawful: see *Pitmann v Prudential Deposit Bank Ltd*[4] by Lord Esher MR.
It mattered not whether the sum to be received was to be his sole remuneration, or   *d*
to be an added remuneration (above his normal fee), in any case it was unlawful if it
was to be paid only if he won, and not if he lost.

That state of the law has been recognised by Parliament. In a series of Solicitors
Acts from 1870 to 1974, a solicitor may make any agreement he likes with his client
as to his remuneration save that—

          e

'nothing [herein] . . . shall give validity to . . . (b) any agreement by which a
solicitor retained or employed to prosecute any action, suit or other contentious
proceeding, stipulates for payment only in the event of success in that action,
suit or proceeding . . .[5]'

Now for recent changes. In 1967, following proposals of the Law Commission,
Parliament abolished criminal and civil liabilities for champerty and maintenance,   *f*
but subject to this important reservation in the Criminal Law Act 1967, s 14(2):

'The abolition of criminal and civil liability under the law of England and Wales
for maintenance and champerty shall not affect any rule of that law as to the
cases in which a contract is to be treated as contrary to public policy or otherwise
illegal.'   *g*

It was suggested to us that the only reason why 'contingency fees' were not allowed
in England was because they offended against the criminal law as to champerty; and
that, now that criminal liability is abolished, the courts were free to hold that contingency fees were lawful. I cannot accept this contention. The reason why contingency
fees are in general unlawful is that they are contrary to public policy as we understand   *h*
it in England. That appears from the judgment of Lord Esher MR in *Pittman
v Prudential Deposit Bank*[6]:

'In order to preserve the honour and honesty of the profession it was a rule of
law which the Court had laid down and would always insist upon that a solicitor

          j

1   SI 1971 No 62
2   (1875) 1 Ch D 573 at 575
3   [1912] 1 KB 302, [1911-13] All ER Rep 202
4   (1896) 13 TLR 110
5   See the Solicitors Act 1974, s 59(2)(b)
6   13 TLR at 111

a could not make an arrangement of any kind with his client during the litigation which he was conducting so as to give him any advantage in respect of the result of that litigation.'

Seeing that the general rule is one of public policy, it is preserved by s 14(2) of the 1967 Act. It is so treated in the Solicitors' Practice Rules 1936-1972[1]. Rule 4, so far as material, says:

b '(1) "contingency fee" means any sum (whether fixed or calculated either as a percentage of the proceeds or otherwise howsoever) payable only in the event of success in the prosecution of any action, suit or other contentious proceeding...
'(3) A solicitor who is retained or employed to prosecute any action, suit or other contentious proceeding shall not enter into any agreement or arrangement to receive a contingency fee in respect of that action, suit or other contentious
c proceeding'.

In my opinion, those rules accurately state the general rule as to contingency fees. But r 5 gives the Council of the Law Society power to waive it in writing in any particular case or cases. The question arises: is a derivative action an appropriate case for waiver? But before doing this, it is instructive to turn to the United States and
d Canada for their views as to contingency fees.

6 The United States and Canada

In most of the United States and Canada, an agreement for a contingency fee is permissible, not only in derivative actions, but in all cases where the client is poor and his chances of success uncertain. This is seen as a way in which justice can be done.
e Otherwise a poor man would be without redress in the courts. If the lawyer was only ready to act on the terms : 'Win or lose, you must pay my fees', the client would have to go away sorrowful. But if the lawyer is ready to act on the terms 'It will cost you nothing. If we win, I will get a percentage of the damages. If we lose I will charge you nothing', the client is content. Nay, what is more, he is happy. Especially as in the United States the loser is not liable to pay the costs of the other side except to a very
f small extent. It is realised that the contingency fee has its disadvantages. It may stimulate lawyers to take on unworthy claims, or to use unfair means to achieve success. But these disadvantages are believed to be outweighed by the advantage that legitimate claims are enforced which would otherwise have to be abandoned by reason of the poverty of the claimant. The courts themselves are in a position to control any abuses. They can limit the amount of the fee which the lawyer is allowed
g to charge.

These are powerful arguments, but I do not think they can or should prevail in England, at any rate not in most cases. We have the legal aid system in which, I am glad to say, a poor man who has a reasonable case can always have recourse to the courts. His lawyer will be paid by the state, win or lose. If the client can afford it, he may have to make a contribution to the costs. Even if he loses, he will not have to pay
h the costs of the other side beyond what is reasonable—and this is often nothing. So the general rule is, and should remain in England, that a contingency fee is unlawful as being contrary to public policy.

7 An exception for England

Although public policy is against contingency fees in general, the question remains
j whether a derivative action should be an exception. There are strong arguments that it should be. Let me take a typical case. Suppose there is good ground for thinking that those in control of a company have been plundering its assets for their own benefit. They should be brought to book. But how is it to be done? and by whom?

---

1 Made by the Council of the Law Society and approved by the Master of the Rolls under the Solicitors Act 1957, s 25

By raising it at a meeting of shareholders? Only to be voted down. By reporting it to
the Board of Trade? Only to be put off, as Mr Moir was. At present there is nothing *a*
effective except an action by a minority shareholder. But can a minority shareholder
be really expected to take it? He has nothing to gain, but much to lose. He feels
strongly that a wrong has been done—and that it should be righted. But he does not
feel able to undertake it himself. Faced with an estimate of the costs, he will say:
'I'm not going to throw away good money after bad'. Some wrongdoers know this
and take advantage of it. They loot the company's funds knowing there is little risk *b*
of an action being brought against them.

What then is to be done? The remedy, as I see it, is to do as is done in the United
States—to permit a solicitor to conduct a derivative action on the basis of a contingency
fee. It should be subject to proper safeguards. The action should not be started except
on an opinion by leading counsel that it is a reasonable action to bring in the interests
of the company. The fee should be a generous sum—by a percentage or otherwise— *c*
so as to recompense the solicitor for his work—and also for the risk that he takes of
getting nothing if he loses. The other side should be notified of it from the very
beginning; and it should be subject to the approval of the Law Society and of the
courts. With these safeguards I think that public policy should favour a contingency
fee in derivative actions—for otherwise, in many cases, justice will not be done—and
wrongdoers will get away with their spoils. *d*

8 *The present case*
    When we gave judgment on 21st May 1974[1], we gave Dr Wallersteiner leave to
defend on the remaining matters, provided that he submitted a satisfactory defence
to the counterclaim, within 28 days. He did not do so within that time. But he has
since submitted a defence to them. It is not very satisfactory, but we will overlook *e*
its defects. We will allow him to submit it.

On 21st May 1974 Dr Wallersteiner applied before us for leave to appeal to the
House of Lords. We refused it. He did not petition the House from our refusal. When
this case was argued before us again, we were told that he had decided not to appeal
to the House. But he has since changed his mind. He again is asking for leave to appeal.
I would refuse this latest request also. He has been guilty of delaying tactics which are *f*
quite intolerable. No further delays of any kind should be permitted.

It is quite reasonable for Mr Moir to continue with all the future proceedings in
this case. I do not think he need make any formal application to a master at this
stage. He should go on until after discovery is concluded. We have seen sufficient to
sanction his continuance at the expense of the two companies until after discovery.
He should then apply to a master for directions. If discovery is not given, or not *g*
promptly given, he should apply likewise to a master for directions so as to get the
case on for trial as soon as may be. Meanwhile the solicitor should do everything that is
reasonable to get some money out of Dr Wallersteiner. Mr Moir has already succeeded in obtaining judgment of over £250,000 and interest. As and when those sums
are recovered from Dr Wallersteiner, his solicitors will have a first charge on them
for all the costs they have incurred. Mr Moir himself should be indemnified by the *h*
companies for all the costs he has incurred in the past and will reasonably incur in the
future (over and above those which he recovers from Dr Wallersteiner). I trust that
with this assurance he and his solicitors will be prepared to continue with the case.
It is in the public interest that they should do so.

I would go further. I would allow Mr Moir to arrange with his lawyers for them to
conduct the future proceedings on the basis of a contingency fee, subject to the per- *j*
mission, first of the Council of the Law Society and next of the courts. But Buckley
and Scarman LJJ do not think this is open to us. So he must be content with an
indemnity from the two companies.

---

1 [1974] 3 All ER 217, [1974] 1 WLR 991

BUCKLEY LJ. We now have to deal with four distinct matters in this case: first, *a* what interest, if any, should be included in the judgment in default of defence on Mr Moir's counterclaim which we awarded on 21st May 1974[1]; secondly, what order, if any, the court should now make in respect of any costs Mr Moir may have incurred since that date or may incur hereafter in this matter; thirdly, whether Dr Wallersteiner should be subjected to any further conditions in connection with this court allowing his defence to the counterclaim to proceed, notwithstanding that he was 15 *b* days out of time in complying with a time condition in that respect imposed by this court on 21st May 1974; and, lastly, whether we should accede to Dr Wallersteiner's renewed application for leave to appeal to the House of Lords.

Interest

On 21st May 1974 we said that judgment should be entered in default of defence on *c* the counterclaim for a sum of £234,773 and interest. We did not then hear any detailed argument whether it was proper that that judgment should include interest. We have now heard considerable argument on that aspect of the case, and in particular on the question whether the Law Reform (Miscellaneous Provisions) Act 1934, s 3, is applicable to this case. It is, however, in my opinion unnecessary for us to decide that question because, as I agree, the equitable jurisdiction to award interest is available *d* here.

It is well established in equity that a trustee who in breach of trust misapplies trust funds will be liable not only to replace the misapplied principal fund but to do so with interest from the date of the misapplication. This is on the notional ground that the money so applied was in fact the trustee's own money and that he has retained the misapplied trust money in his own hands and used it for his own purposes. Where *e* a trustee has retained trust money in his own hands, he will be accountable for the profit which he has made or which he is assumed to have made from the use of the money. In *Attorney-General v Alford*[2] Lord Cranworth LC said:

> 'What the Court ought to do, I think, is to charge him only with the interest which he has received, or which it is justly entitled to say he ought to have received, or which it is so fairly to be presumed that he did receive that he is *f* estopped from saying that he did not receive it.'

This is an application of the doctrine that the court will not allow a trustee to make any profit from his trust. The defaulting trustee is normally charged with simple interest only, but if it is established that he has used the money in trade he may be charged compound interest. See *Burdick v Garrick*[3] per Lord Hatherley LC, and Lewin on *g* Trusts[4], and the cases there noted. The justification for charging compound interest normally lies in the fact that profits earned in trade would be likely to be used as working capital for earning further profits. Precisely similar equitable principles apply to an agent who has retained monies of his principal in his hands and used them for his own purposes (*Burdick v Garrick*[5]).

The application of this rule is not confined to cases in which a trustee or agent has *h* misapplied trust funds or a principal's property, nor is it confined to trustees and agents. It was enunciated by Lord Herschell in *Bray v Ford*[6] in these terms:

> 'It is an inflexible rule of a Court of Equity that a person in a fiduciary position ... is not, unless otherwise expressly provided, entitled to make a profit; he is not allowed to put himself in a position where his interest and duty conflict.'

j
1 [1974] 3 All ER 217, [1974] 1 WLR 991
2 (1855) 4 De GM & G 843 at 851
3 (1870) 5 Ch App 233 at 241
4 16th Edn (1964), p 226
5 (1870) 5 Ch App 233
6 [1896] AC 44 at 51

A well-known example of the operation of the rule is *Keech v Sandford*[1] where a trustee of leasehold property obtained a renewal of a lease in his own name. He has held *a* to be a constructive trustee of the renewed lease for the infant beneficiary under the trust, notwithstanding that the lessors had refused to renew the lease for the benefit of the infant beneficiary. The rule has also been applied in many instances to directors of companies who have obtained benefits for themselves by abuse of their position as directors. One such case is *Cook v Deeks*[2], which, like the present case, was an action by a minority shareholder. Three directors of a company obtained a contract in their *b* own names to the exclusion of the company. They were held to be trustees of the benefit of the contract for the company. Numerous other cases relating to directors of companies will be found collected in a note in Lewin on Trusts[3]; and see Buckley on the Companies Acts[4].

There is no doubt that the relationship between a director of a company and that company is a fiduciary one of such a kind as to attract the operation of this doctrine: *c* *Regal (Hastings) Ltd v Gulliver*[5]. Such was Dr Wallersteiner's relationship with the two defendant companies, Hartley Baird and Baldwins. By acts of commission and omission as a director of those companies he procured the carrying out of the circular cheque transaction. By that transaction moneys of the defendant companies were applied for his benefit in connection with the purchase of the Hartley Baird shares in the manner described in the judgments of this court of 21st May 1974. The fact that *d* the moneys did not actually pass through Dr Wallersteiner's own hands is immaterial. He so conducted himself as a director that he benefited at the companies' expense. The fact that the extent of his own personal interest in the 'consortium' for whom the shares are alleged to have been bought has not been made clear is also, in my opinion, immaterial. To the extent that any part of these moneys may have been applied for the benefit of anyone other than Dr Wallersteiner, the court should, in my opinion, *e* treat him as having used his own money for that purpose and as having retained the companies' money in his own hands (compare *Knott v Cottee*[6]).

There has been no investigation of what profit, whether in the form of dividends or otherwise, Dr Wallersteiner has secured by the acquisition of the Hartley Baird shares. The transaction was, however, clearly one of a commercial character, and in the absence of evidence to the contrary the court should assume that it has been *f* profitable to him. Accordingly it is, in my opinion, equitable that the judgment awarded against him should include interest as a conventional measure of the profit he is to be taken to have made. Considering the nature of Dr Wallersteiner's operations as a financier and as a dealer in and manipulator of large shareholdings in commercial companies, it is in my opinion right to treat the investment in shares of Hartley Baird as made by him in the course of that business and as calculated to be *g* commercially valuable to him in the prosecution of that business. I accordingly agree that this is a case in which it is proper to charge compound interest with yearly rests.

Counsel for Hartley Baird and Baldwins suggested that compound interest should be awarded on the ground that the moneys were working capital of the defendant companies. I feel unable to accept this argument. In cases of this kind interest is not, as I understand the law, given to compensate for loss of profit but in order to ensure as *h* far as possible that the defendant retains no profit for which he ought to account. In any case, I do not think that it has been established that these moneys did constitute working capital for trading operations. As I understand the facts, Hartley Baird is, at least in the main, a holding company.

j

1 (1726) Sel Cas Ch 61, [1558-1774] All ER Rep 230
2 [1916] 1 AC 554
3 16th Edn (1964), p 193
4 13th Edn (1957), p 865
5 [1942] 1 All ER 378
6 (1847) 2 Ph 192

a In earlier days when interest rates were more stable than they are at present, the rate of interest used in such a case was 5 per cent per annum. In the conditions of the present time I think it would be right to award interest at 1 per cent per annum above the official bank rate or minimum lending rate in operation from time to time.

Costs

b A plaintiff in a minority shareholder's action is personally liable to his own solicitor for costs and is exposed to the risk of being ordered to pay the taxed costs of any defendant. His position in this respect is precisely the same as that of any other litigant, notwithstanding that the plaintiff in a minority shareholder's action normally has no cause of action of his own but is suing on a cause of action vested in a defendant company.

Counsel for Mr Moir has urged that litigation of this kind is always, or at least more often than not, likely to be complicated and costly. Certainly that is true of the present c case.

The position of a plaintiff in such an action is anomalous. Possibly the nearest analogy is that of a trustee who sues to protect his trust estate but has no personal interest in the relief sought, but this analogy is far from being an exact one. At law the cause of action would be vested in the trustee. He is, or may be, under a duty to bring the action; and provided that he has acted properly, he is entitled in equity to d be indemnified against all his costs out of the trust assets. In the case of a minority shareholder's action, that the plaintiff is allowed to sue in his own name on a cause of action vested in the company is purely a procedural device to get over the difficulty that as a practical matter no authority can be obtained to bring the action in the company's name. The minority shareholder, although he may be fully justified in instituting the action, is under no duty to do so; and he has no right or power to recoup e his costs out of the company's assets without the assistance of an order of the court. The fruits of any judgment recovered in such an action belong to the company, but the expenses of recovering them, except so far as they may be recovered from some other party, fall not on the company but on the plaintiff. If the action fails the plaintiff is at risk of being ordered to pay the defendant's costs as well as his own.

These are considerations which are calculated to deter a minority shareholder from f suing a fraudulent or oppressive majority. It is, I consider, clearly undesirable that in such a case a minority shareholder should be inhibited in this way. The question is how the court can best dispel or minimise the inhibition. Three possible approaches have been discussed in this case: first, some form of legal aid; secondly, the adoption of contingency fees; and, thirdly, a procedural innovation enabling a minority shareholder plaintiff to apply to the court before issuing his writ or at an early stage in the g action for an order certifying that he is acting reasonably and in the company's interests in bringing the action, in anticipation that the company will eventually be ordered to pay any costs for which he becomes liable in the course, or as a consequence, of so acting.

The Legal Aid Act 1974 makes no provision specifically for legal aid in a minority shareholder's action. It is not surprising that its provisions, which are intended to be h of general application, are ill-adapted to the circumstances of so anomalous a form of action. Legal aid is not available under the Act to any body of persons corporate or unincorporated (see the definition of 'person' in s 25). So, if the action had been brought in the company's name, it would be impossible to obtain legal aid. In my opinion, it is clear that a minority shareholder plaintiff sues as representing the company, notwithstanding that in form he sues on behalf of himself and all other shareholders. j The cause of action is the company's and not that of any one or more shareholders, nor of all the shareholders collectively. In effect, the plaintiff is permitted by the court to sue as the agent, albeit unauthorised, of the company, rather like the next friend or guardian ad litem of a party under a disability. It may be said, therefore, that it would be strange that someone in the position of an agent for a principal who is not eligible for legal aid should himself be eligible. Moreover, there may be other shareholders, not included in the majority or controlling body of shareholders whose conduct is sought to be impugned, who might equally well have brought the action or might be joined as plaintiffs in it and may be ineligible for legal aid on account of their means. It seems undesirable that the particular minority shareholder selected to act as plaintiff should be chosen on the basis of his eligibility for legal aid.

If, as I think, it is right to regard the plaintiff in a minority shareholder's action as suing in a representative capacity, his personal resources are to be disregarded (Legal Aid (General) Regulations 1971[1], reg 5(9)). In such a case regard is presumably to be had to the identity and resources of the party or parties or the estate or fund whom he represents. In the present case I consider that Mr Moir sues on the counterclaim as the representative of Hartley Baird and Baldwins, two companies neither of which is entitled to legal aid. If, however, he is to be treated as suing on behalf of the general body of shareholders in those companies, or on behalf of the minority shareholders as a body, I cannot suppose that they as a body could be entitled to legal aid. I would prefer to leave undecided whether they should be regarded as an unincorporated body of persons within the meaning of the definition of 'person' in s 25 of the 1974 Act. They might alternatively be regarded as 'persons concerned jointly with or having the same interest as the applicant' within reg 5(12) of the 1971 regulations. If they should be so regarded, it seems highly unlikely that a legal aid certificate could be obtained in the present case, even if Mr Moir personally, if he were suing only on his own behalf, might qualify for legal aid.

In my opinion counsel for Mr Moir is right in suggesting that an action of this kind is outside the purview of the 1974 Act, although I would for the time being reserve the question whether this would be so where the company has only two or three shareholders—a company of the kind sometimes described as a quasi-partnership—and is, apart from any property which may be recoverable in the action, of very little financial substance, and the plaintiff's resources are such as would make him eligible for legal aid if he were suing on a cause of action of his own.

Before leaving the question of legal aid I should say that I feel unable to accept the contention of Mr Moir's counsel that Mr Moir is not suing on his counterclaim only in a representative capacity because of the possible effect of the success of his claim on the value of his shares in the companies: see reg 5(9) of the 1971 regulations. Mr Moir is not seeking any relief on the counterclaim in his own right. Any effect which success on the counterclaim might have on the value of his shares is, I think, too remote to make the counterclaim other than a purely representative action: moreover any such effect would inevitably be trivial (see reg 5(13)(a)).

If legal aid be not available, counsel for Mr Moir urges that some other means must be sought to prevent plaintiffs in such actions from being deterred from bringing such cases before the courts. Counsel for Mr Moir submits with force that it would be most unwholesome if minority shareholders were discouraged from bringing fraud or oppression to light and seeking a remedy for fear of being beggared by costs. It is on this ground that counsel for Mr Moir contends that in this class of action contingency fees should be regarded as acceptable. A contingency fee, that is, an arrangement under which the legal advisers of a litigant shall be remunerated only in the event of the litigant succeeding in recovering money or other property in the action, has hitherto always been regarded as illegal under English law on the ground that it involves maintenance of the action by the legal adviser. Moreover, where, as is usual in such a case, the remuneration which the adviser is to receive is to be, or to be measured by, a proportion of the fund or of the value of the property recovered, the arrangement may fall within that particular class of maintenance called champerty.

Under the Criminal Law Act 1967, ss 13 and 14, maintenance and champerty have ceased to be either criminal or tortious, but without prejudice to questions of public policy. Counsel for Mr Moir suggests that, for reasons which I have already indicated,

---

1   SI 1971 No 62

public policy actually requires that contingency fees should be permitted in cases of
a minority shareholder plaintiffs.

Contingency fee agreements are countenanced and frequently resorted to in the
United States, where there is no system of legal aid at public expense. Their use is
often explained as justified by the need for a system which opens the doors of justice
to litigants too poor to risk defeat in expensive litigation. Particularly it seems that
contingency fees are often agreed in litigation analogous to our minority shareholder's
b actions. Counsel for Mr Moir submits with force that, if legal aid is not available here
in that type of action, similar considerations to those operating in the United States of
America indicate that contingency fee agreements in such actions here would be in
the public interest.

At the present time contingency fees are prohibited in this country (r 4(3) of the
Solicitors' Practice Rules 1936–72, made by the Council of the Law Society as approved
c by the Master of the Rolls under the Solicitors Act 1957, s 28[1]). Although under r 5
of those rules the Council of the Law Society has power to waive compliance with any
of the rules in any particular case or cases, that power is unlikely to be exercised, and
indeed does not seem to be designed to be exercised, in respect of a complete class of
actions.

There is another important difference between our system of dealing with costs in
d litigation and the American system. In this country a successful litigant normally
recovers his taxed costs from his opponent under an order of the court. United States
courts do not order one party to pay another party's costs.

Under a contingency fee agreement the remuneration payable by the client to his
lawyer in the event of his success must be higher than it would be if the lawyer were
entitled to be remunerated, win or lose: the contingency fee must contain an element
e of compensation for the risk of having done the work for nothing. It would, it seems
to me, be unfair to the opponent of a contingency fee litigant if he were at risk of
being ordered to pay higher costs to his opponent in the event of the latter's success in
the action than would be the case if there were no contingency fee agreement. On
the other hand, if the contingency fee litigant were to lose the action, his opponent's
right to recover costs against him should not in fairness be affected by the fact that
f the former party has a contingency fee agreement. Consequently under our system
of what are sometimes called indemnity costs a contingency fee litigant would in the
event of success have to bear a heavier burden of fees, irrecoverable from his opponent,
than he would otherwise do, while remaining exposed to the risk of being ordered to
pay his opponent's taxed costs in the event of his failure. The arguments in favour of
a contingency fee system are accordingly a good deal less cogent here than they are in
g the United States of America.

I do not think it possible to confine consideration of the introduction of contingency
fees in this country to minority shareholders' actions. I believe that there would be
found to be other litigants who could make out as good a case for this sort of treatment,
although maybe on different grounds, and perhaps with different countervailing
considerations. Before such a system were introduced to our legal regime careful
h consideration would have to be given to its public policy aspect. Notwithstanding
the help we have received from counsel, this does not appear to me to be a suitable
occasion for attempting to investigate that aspect in depth and for arriving at a final
conclusion on it. We should not, I think, make any declaratory judgment in this
respect which we have no power to implement. It may, however, be worthwhile to
indicate briefly the nature of the public policy question. It can, I think, be summarised
j in two statements. First, in litigation a professional lawyer's role is to advise his client
with a clear eye and an unbiased judgment. Secondly, a solicitor retained to conduct
litigation is not merely the agent and adviser to his client, but also an officer of the
court with a duty to the court to ensure that his client's case, which he must, of course,

---

1   See now the Solicitors Act 1974, s 31

present and conduct with the utmost care of his client's interests, is also presented and
conducted with scrupulous fairness and integrity. A barrister owes similar obligations. *a*
A legal adviser who acquires a personal financial interest in the outcome of the litigation may obviously find himself in a situation in which that interest conflicts with
those obligations. See in this connection *Neville v London Express*[1] and *Re Trepca
Mines Ltd (Application of Radomir Nicola Pachitch (Pasic))*[2].

This is not something which can be dealt with by judicial orders, directions or rules.
We cannot constrain any solicitor to accept a retainer on a contingency fee basis, nor *b*
can we require the Law Society to alter its rules. The matter is, indeed, one which,
in my opinion, would require comprehensive consideration by a body such as the Law
Commission, the Lord Chancellor's Law Reform Committee or a specially appointed
committee before any change were made on these lines; and any change must be
effected by an alteration in the relevant professional rules of etiquette or by legislation. Accordingly the suggestion that recourse might be had in this case to contingency *c*
fees is not, in my judgment, a suggestion which we can adopt. In any case, in my
opinion, public policy does not require its adoption if another solution of the problem
is available.

So I come to the third possible approach mentioned earlier. Counsel for Mr Moir,
pointing to the Supreme Court of Judicature (Consolidation) Act 1925, s 50 and to
RSC Ord 62, r 4(1), suggests that we should now make an order protecting Mr Moir *d*
against being ordered to pay the costs of any other party in this matter in any event.
I have never known a court to make any order as to costs fettering a later exercise of
the court's discretion in respect of costs to be incurred after the date of the order. I
cannot think of any circumstances in which such an order would be justified. It seems
to me to be undesirable to fetter judicial discretion in respect of future costs. If Dr
Wallersteiner were to succeed on some or all of the issues which are now awaiting *e*
trial, the trial judge appears to me to be the proper person to decide whether justice
requires that Dr Wallersteiner should recover any of his costs from Mr Moir or any
other party. We should not, in my opinion, attempt to prejudge that question.

But there are circumstances in which a party can embark on litigation with a confident expectation that he will be indemnified in some measure against costs. A
trustee who properly and reasonably prosecutes or defends an action relating to his *f*
trust property or the execution of the trusts is entitled to be indemnified out of the
trust property. An agent is entitled to be indeminfied by his principal against costs
incurred in consequence of carrying out the principal's instructions (*Broom (Brown) v
Hall*[3]; *Pettman v Keble*[4]; *Williams v Lister & Co*[5]). The next friend of an infant plaintiff is prima facie entitled to be indemnified against costs out of the infant's estate
(*Steedon v Walden*[6]). It seems to me that in a minority shareholder's action, properly *g*
and reasonably brought and prosecuted, it would normally be right that the company
should be ordered to pay the plaintiff's costs so far as he does not recover them from
any other party. In all the instances mentioned the right of the party seeking indemnity to be indemnified must depend on whether he has acted reasonably in bringing
or defending the action, as the case may be. See, for example, as regards a trustee
Re Beddoe[7]. It is true that this right of a trustee, as well as that of an agent, has been *h*
treated as founded in contract. It would, I think, be difficult to imply a contract of
indemnity between a company and one of its members. Nevertheless, where a
shareholder has in good faith and on reasonable grounds sued as plaintiff in a minority

1   [1919] AC 368 at 382 et seq, [1918-19] All ER Rep 61 at 67 et seq   *j*
2   [1962] 3 All ER 351 at 355, 358, [1963] Ch 199 at 219, 255
3   (1859) 7 CBNS 503
4   (1850) 9 CB 701
5   (1913) 109 LT 699
6   [1910] 2 Ch 393, [1908-10] All ER Rep 380
7   [1893] 1 Ch 547

shareholder's action, the benefit of which, if successful, will accrue to the company and
a only indirectly to the plaintiff as a member of the company, and which it would have
been reasonable for an independent board of directors to bring in the company's
name, it would, I think, clearly be a proper exercise of judicial discretion to order the
company to pay the plaintiff's costs. This would extend to the plaintiff's costs down to
judgment, if it would have been reasonable for an independent board exercising the
standard of care which a prudent businessman would exercise in his own affairs to
b continue the action to judgment. If, however, an independent board exercising that
standard of care would have discontinued the action at an earlier stage, it is probable
that the plaintiff should only be awarded his costs against the company down to that
stage.

There is a well-established practice in Chancery for a trustee who has it in mind to
bring or defend an action in respect of his trust estate to apply to the court for direc-
c tions (see Re Beddoe[1]). If and so far as he is authorised to proceed in the action, the
trustee's right to be indemnified in respect of his costs out of the trust property is
secure. If he proceeds without the authority of an order of the court, he does so at his
own risk as to costs. It seems to me that a similar practice could well be adopted in a
minority shareholder's action. In the case of a trustee, if there is no pending action
for the administration of the trust, the application is made by way of originating
d summons in the matter of the trust, to which at least one beneficiary must be joined
as a defendant. If the opposite party in the action, or the proposed action, is a beneficiary, he is also joined as a defendant to the summons. This enables him to place
any materials he wishes before the court and makes the court's order binding on him
as a beneficiary; but it is not the practice that he should be present in chambers when
the matter is debated, and he is not furnished with the evidence on which the court is
e asked to act[2]. In a minority shareholder's action the defendant will necessarily be a
member of the company and so might be regarded as analogous for the present purpose to a beneficiary defendant in a trustee's action. After issuing his writ a minority
shareholder plaintiff could apply by summons in the action for directions whether
he should proceed in the action and, if so, to what stage without further directions. I
think that such an application should in the first instance be made ex parte. In a
f relatively simple case the court may feel able to deal with the matter without joinder
of any other party. When the summons comes before the court, directions could be
given as to whether the company or another minority shareholder or the defendants
or any of them or anyone else should be made respondents and whether any respondent should be appointed to act in a representative capacity for the purposes of the
summons. The court might at this stage think it desirable to require the plaintiff to
g circularise or convene a meeting of other minority shareholders and to place their
views, so far as ascertained, before the court. The summons should be supported by
affidavit evidence of any relevant facts, to which instructions to counsel and his
opinion thereon should be exhibited. The respondent or respondents to the summons
(if any) would also be permitted to file evidence. The evidence of other parties would
not be disclosed to the defendants in the action unless the court so directed, and the
h defendants, if made respondents to the summons, would not be permitted to be
present when the merits of the application were discussed. On the effective hearing
of the summons the court would determine whether the plaintiff should be authorised to proceed with the action and, if so, to what stage he should be authorised to
do so without further directions from the court. The plaintiff, acting under the
authority of such a direction, would be secure in the knowledge that, when the costs
j of the action should come to be dealt with, this would be on the basis, as between
himself and the company, that he has acted reasonably and ought prima facie to be
treated by the trial judge as entitled to an order that the company should pay his costs,

---

1   [1893] 1 Ch 547
2   Supreme Court Practice 1973, vol 1, pp 1236, 1237, para 85/2/5

which should, I think, normally be taxed on a basis not less favourable than the common fund basis, and should indemnify him against any costs he may be ordered to *a*
pay to the defendants. Should the court not think fit to authorise the plaintiff to
proceed, he would do so at his own risk as to the costs. A procedure on these lines
could, I think, be adopted without any amendment of or addition to the rules of court,
although it might well be thought desirable that an appropriate rule should be made.
In the present case I think that we should here and now authorise Mr Moir to proceed
with the prosecution of the outstanding issues on his counterclaim down to the close *b*
of discovery or until further order in the meantime. He will in this way obtain the
greatest measure of immunity from future costs down to that stage of the proceedings
which, I think, the court can give him. When that stage is reached, the position can be
further considered in chambers.

Any outstanding costs down to the present time can be dealt with by today's order.
c

Conditions for being permitted to defend the counterclaim

By the order of this court on 21st May 1974 Dr Wallersteiner was permitted to
defend the remaining issues on the counterclaim on condition that he served a defence
which was satisfactory in form not later than 31st July 1974. No such defence was in
fact served until 15th August 1974. Dr Wallersteiner then served a defence which can,
in my opinion, be accepted as being in a satisfactory form. Counsel for Mr Moir has *d*
suggested that, having been 15 days out of time, Dr Wallersteiner should not be
allowed to rely on this defence except on the condition that he should seek no order
against Mr Moir in respect of any future costs. In my opinion, it would be wrong for
us to impose such a condition. The delay was short and no one was prejudiced by it.
I think that Dr Wallersteiner should be permitted to rely on this defence without any
further condition being imposed on him. *e*

Appeal to the House of Lords

Dr Wallersteiner has renewed his application for leave to appeal to the House of
Lords. I would again refuse leave.
f

SCARMAN LJ.   I have had the advantage of reading the judgments already
delivered, and am, therefore, in a position to avoid going over ground already covered.

PART I—INTEREST

I agree that we have power under the equitable jurisdiction of the court to include *g*
interest in the judgment entered against Dr Wallersteiner. This judgment we have
already said is to be for £234,773 and interest, but at the time we had not heard
argument as to the propriety of including interest. The principle on which equitable
interest is awarded was stated by Lord Hatherley LC in *Burdick v Garrick*[1] and has
been frequently applied to situations in which there was a fiduciary relationship at
the time when the money was appropriated. In *Atwool v Merryweather*[2] interest was *h*
awarded to a company on money recovered for it in a minority shareholder's action.

There is, therefore, ample authority to support the claim made by Mr Moir on
behalf of the companies to interest from the date on which the companies made their
loan to IFT—a loan which in default of defence this court has accepted was instigated
by Dr Wallersteiner in breach of his duty as a director.

The question whether the interest to be awarded should be simple or compound *j*
depends on evidence as to what the accounting party has, or is to be presumed to
have, done with the money. As Lord Hatherley LC said in *Burdick v Garrick*[1]:

---

1   (1870) 5 Ch App 233 at 241
2   (1867) LR 5 Eq 464n

a '... the Court does not proceed against an accounting party by way of punishing him for making use of the Plaintiff's money by directing rests, or payment of compound interest, but proceeds upon this principle, either that he has made, or has put himself into such a position as that he is to be presumed to have made, 5 per cent., or compound interest, as the case may be.'

b Dr Wallersteiner was at all material times engaged in the business of finance. Through a complex structure of companies he conducted financial operations with a view to profit. The quarter million pounds assistance which he obtained from the two companies in order to finance the acquisition of the shares meant that he was in a position to employ the money or its capital equivalent in those operations. Though the truth is unlikely ever to be fully known, shrouded as it is by the elaborate corporate structure within which Dr Wallersteiner chose to operate, one may safely presume c that the use of the money (or the capital it enabled him to acquire) was worth to him the equivalent of compound interest at commercial rates with yearly rests, if not more. I, therefore, agree that he should be ordered to pay compound interest at the rates, and with the rests, proposed by Lord Denning MR and Buckley LJ. This being a case for equitable interest, no question arises as to interest under s 3 of the Law Reform (Miscellaneous Provisions) Act 1934. I therefore express no opinion as to the d true construction of sub-s (1) of that section.

PART II—COSTS

Legal aid

e I agree that legal aid is not available to a plaintiff in a stockholder's derivative action (to use the apt American description of a minority shareholder's action brought to obtain redress for the company). The contrary view would be inconsistent with the intendment of the statute: see the definition of 'person' in s 25 of the Legal Aid Act 1974.

An indemnity

f I agree that it is open to the court in a stockholder's derivative action to order that the company indemnify the plaintiff against the costs incurred in the action. I think that the principle is the same as that which the court applied in *Re Beddoe*[1] which concerned the costs incurred by a trustee in an action respecting the trust estate. The indemnity is a right distinct from the right of a successful litigant to his costs at the discretion of the trial judge; it is a right which springs from a combination of factors: g the interest of the company and its shareholders, the relationship between the shareholder and the company, and the court's sanction (a better word would be 'permission') for the action to be brought at the company's expense. It is a full indemnity such as an agent has who incurs expense in the authorised business of his principal. As a general rule, I would expect an application for leave to bring proceedings at the expense of the company to be made at the commencement of the action: but, h as Lindley LJ in *Beddoe's* case[2] recognised in relation to a trustee's action on behalf of the trust estate, if at the end of the case the judge should come to the conclusion that he would have authorised the action had he been applied to, he can even then allow the plaintiff his costs on a full indemnity basis against the company. In my opinion, Mr Moir should have his indemnity not only against costs already incurred by him on behalf of the two companies but also against costs to be incurred up to and including discovery, after which he should obtain the further directions of the court. j I agree that the procedure proposed by Buckley LJ would be suitable and should be adopted until such time as a rule of court is made which covers the situation.

1 [1893] 1 Ch 547
2 [1893] 1 Ch at 557

The contingency fee

I cannot take the further step proposed by Lord Denning MR, namely that the court *a*
should declare that, subject to the approval of the Law Society, it would be proper in
this case to permit Mr Moir to employ a solicitor on the basis of a contingency fee. A
contingency fee for conducting litigation is by the law of England champerty and, as
such, contrary to public policy. This is law of longstanding. It has been frequently
declared by the courts. In the comparatively recent case of *Re Trepca Mines Ltd*
(Application of Radomir Nicola Pachitch (Pasic))[1], the Court of Appeal reaffirmed it, *b*
Lord Denning MR using these words[2]:

> 'I pause here to say that they [i e the agreements in the case] were both clearly
> champertous agreements . . . They were clearly unlawful and not capable of
> being enforced in England.'

It is to be noted that the rule does not depend on solicitors' practice or their prac- *c*
tising rules, but on public policy. As Lord Esher MR put it in the passage quoted by
Lord Denning MR from *Pittman v Prudential Deposit Bank (Ltd)*[3], the courts laid down
the rule 'in order to preserve the honour and honesty of the profession'.

Times have changed since 1896, and indeed in one significant respect since 1963,
when *Trepca Mines Ltd*[1] was decided. The maintenance of other people's litigation is
no longer regarded as a mischief: trade unions, trade protection societies, insurance *d*
companies and the state do it regularly and frequently. The law has always recognised that there can be lawful justification for maintaining somebody else's litigation;
today, with the emergence of legal aid, trade unions, and insurance companies, a
great volume of litigation is maintained by persons who are not parties to it.

As Pearson LJ remarked in *Trepca Mines Ltd*[4] champerty is a species of maintenance.
The law, may, therefore, recognise exceptions to its illegality: and Lord Denning MR *e*
proposes that an exception should be recognised in the case of a stockholder's derivative action. There is, however, no trace of any such an exception in the books. This is
not surprising. It would be strange if the company could be compelled to pay a
percentage of the moneys it recovers in the action to the plaintiff's solicitor without
its consent; for the order proposed by Lord Denning MR does not and cannot depend
on the consent of the company which is, ex concessis, in the control of the defendant. *f*

Secondly, there is no need for the exception. Justice can be done without resort to
it. We are giving Mr Moir the court's sanction for the conduct by him of the counterclaim on behalf of the two companies, the effect of which is that he has a full indemnity for his costs. Of course, this is not complete protection; for instance, one or both
of the companies concerned might become insolvent; but this is a risk often faced by
litigants in all sorts of cases. Ought this court now to introduce into the law the *g*
exception proposed by Lord Denning MR? I think not.

Counsel, who at our invitation and on the instructions of the Law Society has
presented submissions on the question as amicus curiae (thereby helping the court
immensely), has made the Law Society's position abundantly clear: they believe that
the implications of creating the exception proposed by Lord Denning MR calls for
further study. I agree. The exception, if it is to come, could have repercussions which *h*
in this, or indeed any litigation, the courts cannot fully probe, analyse, or assess. It is
legislative, not forensic work. This was clearly the view of the Law Commission when
it reported[5] on maintenance and champerty in 1966.

The Law Commission reported in favour of abolishing the criminal offences of
maintenance and champerty, and tortious liability in respect of them, but described

1   [1962] 3 All ER 351, [1963] Ch 199
2   [1962] 3 All ER at 354, [1963] Ch at 218
3   (1896) 13 TLR 110 at 111
4   [1962] 3 All ER at 359, [1963] Ch at 226
5   Proposals for Reform of the Law Relating to Maintenance and Champerty; Law Commission
    No 7

j

the question of allowing contingency fees in litigation as a big question 'upon which the
a professional bodies as well as the public must have further time for reflection before
any solutions can or should be formulated' (para 19 of the report). When Parliament
passed legislation to give effect to the Law Commission's proposals, it was careful to
preserve the existing law insofar as it declared contracts of maintenance or champerty
to be illegal: Criminal Law Act 1967, s 14(2).

Although I could have wished to have seen by now some results from 'the further
b study' of contingency fees which the Law Commission recommended (para 20), the
delay in the matter (which may or may not be inevitable, I do not know) is no excuse
for the court attempting to do the work of the legislature.

One final point. I am not impressed with the argument based on r 5 of the Solicitors'
Practising Rules 1972. The rule empowers the Council of the Law Society to waive in
writing a practising rule in a particular case or cases. Since the prohibition of a solicitor
c from conducting his client's litigation on a contingency fee basis is made part of the
practising rules (r 4), it is said that it can be waived by action taken under r 5. Waiving
a practice rule is one thing; changing the law is quite another matter. We are faced
with a rule of law recognised as such by the Court of Appeal. If on a consideration of
the law we were able to say it permits of an exception, then no doubt the Law Society
could waive its rule, if it thought fit. But, if, as I think, the present state of the law
d recognises no such exception, we are in no position either to invite the Law Society to
waive its rule or to hold that such a waiver could introduce into the law an exception
which otherwise would not exist.

PART III—CONCLUSIONS

My conclusions on the points now before us for decision are: (1) that compound
e interest, at the rates and with the rests proposed by Lord Denning MR, should be
included in the judgments obtained by Mr Moir for the benefit of the companies; (2)
that Mr Moir have the leave of the court to prosecute his counterclaim at the expense
of the two companies to the extent and subject to the limitations proposed by Buckley
LJ; (3) that it would be unlawful for a solicitor to accept a retainer from Mr Moir to
conduct this litigation on a contingency fee basis; (4) that Dr Wallersteiner have leave
f to deliver a defence to counterclaim on the conditions proposed by Buckley LJ; I
agree with his reasoning on this point; (5) that the orders for party and party costs to
date be as proposed by Lord Denning MR; (6) that the application for leave to appeal
to the House of Lords be refused, for the reasons given by Lord Denning MR.

Order that compound interest at the rate of 1 per cent per annum over bank rate or the mini-
g *mum lending rate for the time being in operation with yearly rests as from the time the original*
indebtedness arose to be included in the judgment for £234,773 in default of defence. Mr Moir
to have leave to proceed with the prosecution of the counterclaim down to the close of discovery
or until further order at the expense of Hartley Baird Ltd and H J Baldwin & Co Ltd. Order
for costs in Mr Moir's favour against Dr Wallersteiner on the interest issue. Costs of Mr
Moir's application for future costs to be paid by the companies. Leave granted on conditions
h *to Dr Wallersteiner to deliver defence to counterclaim. Leave to appeal to the House of Lords*
on the issue of contingency fees refused. Dr Wallersteiner's renewed application for leave to
appeal to the House of Lords against the judgment of 21st May 1974 refused.

Solicitors: *Bates, Wells & Braithwaite* (for Mr Moir); *Michael Sears & Co* (for Dr Wallersteiner); *David Alterman & Servell* (for Hartley Baird Ltd and H J Baldwin & Co Ltd);
j *The Law Society.*

Wendy Shockett Barrister.

Lewis v MTC (Cars) Ltd   *a*

COURT OF APPEAL, CIVIL DIVISION
RUSSELL, STAMP LJJ AND SIR JOHN PENNYCUICK
24th, 27th JANUARY 1975

Landlord and tenant – Notice to quit – Business premises – Power of landlord to give notice – **b**
Notice specifying date for termination of tenancy – Notice by head landlord – Notice to sub-
tenant – Notice specifying date for termination before date on which mesne landlord's tenancy
due to expire – Whether notice valid – Landlord and Tenant Act 1954, ss 25(3) (4), 44(1)
(as amended by the Law of Property Act 1969, s 14(1)).

A owned the freehold of certain premises. A granted B a lease of the premises which   **c**
was due to expire on 23rd December 1968. B did not occupy the premises, but granted
a sub-lease to C which was due to expire on 20th December 1968. C occupied the
premises for business purposes. After the two expiry dates had passed B continued to
pay rent to A as a yearly tenant and C, who remained in occupation of the premises,
continued to pay rent to B as a statutory tenant under Part II of the Landlord and
Tenant Act 1954. On 13th November 1972 A gave B notice to quit so that B's tenancy   **d**
terminated on 23rd December 1973. On 21st November 1972 A gave notice to C in the
prescribed form under s 25 of the 1954 Act to terminate C's sub-tenancy on 31st May
1973. C remained in occupation however and from the end of May until 23rd December, when B's contractual tenancy came to an end, continued to pay at the customary
rate sums by way of rent to B. In an action for possession by A against C it was contended by C (i) that, under s 25(3) or s 25(4)^a, A had no power to serve a notice which   **e**
purported to terminate C's tenancy on a date earlier than the expiry of B's contractual
mesne tenancy; and (ii) that, even if the notice were valid, A was not entitled to possession because C, by paying rent to B between 31st May and 23rd December 1973, had
acquired a new contractual tenancy protected by the 1954 Act.

Held – (i) Neither sub-s (3) nor sub-s (4) of s 25 was relevant to a situation where the   **f**
tenant's contractual rights had come to an end and the tenancy had continued by
virtue of the 1954 Act; the purpose of those provisions was to prevent the overriding
of contractual rights in the tenant in occupation. At the date when the notice was
given A was the competent landlord, by virtue of s 44^b of, and Sch 6, para 3^c to, the

---

a   Section 25, so far as material, is set out at p 876 *d* and *f*, post   **g**
b   Section 44(1), as amended, provides:
      'Subject to the next following subsection, in this Part of this Act the expression "the
      landlord", in relation to a tenancy (in this section referred to as "the relevant tenancy"),
      means the person (whether or not he is the immediate landlord) who is the owner of that
      interest in the property comprised in the relevant tenancy which for the time being fulfils
      the following conditions, that is to say—
            (*a*) that it is an interest in reversion expectant (whether immediately or not) on the   *h*
      termination of the relevant tenancy, and
            (*b*) that it is either the fee simple or a tenancy which will not come to an end within
      fourteen months by effluxion of time and, if it is such a tenancy, that no notice has been
      given by virtue of which it will come to an end within fourteen months or any further
      time by which it may be continued under section 36(2) or section 64 of this Act,
      and is not itself in reversion expectant (whether immediately or not) on an interest which   *j*
      fulfils those conditions.'
c   Paragraph 3, so far as material, provides: '(1) Any notice given by the competent land-
      lord . . . to terminate the relevant tenancy, and any agreement made between that landlord
      and the tenant as to the granting, duration, or terms of a future tenancy, . . . shall bind the
      interest of any mesne landlord notwithstanding that he has not consented to the giving of
      the notice or was not a party to the agreement . . .'

1954 Act, to give a notice to C under s 25 which was binding on C's immediate landlord
a B (see p 876 *bc* and *h* to p 877 *c* and p 878 *g*, post).

(ii) It could not be inferred that a new contractual lease had arisen between B and C merely because in the period from 31st May until 23rd December 1973 C had continued to pay rent to B. C, whose contractual tenancy had terminated in December 1968, had thereafter held over in possession not because of any continuation of the contractual tenancy or by reason of a new tenancy from year to year but because of the
b provisions of the 1954 Act whereby the tenancy continued for an uncertain time. The payment of rent by C to B after 31st May 1973 was not to be attributed to a new sub-tenancy for those payments had been solely because of the statutory continuation of C's tenancy (see p 878 *a* to *e* and *g*, post); dictum of Denning LJ in *Marcroft Wagons Ltd v Smith* [1951] 2 All ER at 277 applied.

Decision of Templeman J [1974] 3 All ER 423 affirmed.
c

Notes

For landlord's notice to terminate business tenancy, see 23 Halsbury's Laws (3rd Edn) 889-890, para 1711, and for cases on the validity of a notice to quit, see 31(2) Digest (Reissue) 946-949, 7732-7741.

For the Landlord and Tenant Act 1954, ss 25, 44, Sch 6, see 18 Halsbury's Statutes
d (3rd Edn) 559, 587, 606.

Case referred to in judgments

Marcroft Wagons Ltd v Smith [1951] 2 All ER 271, [1951] 2 KB 496, CA, 31(2) Digest (Reissue) 989, 7929.

e
Appeal

This was an appeal by the defendants, MTC (Cars) Ltd, against an order of Templeman J[1], dated 14th June 1974, whereby it was ordered that the defendants give to the plaintiff, Mabel Jenny Lewis, on or before 12th July 1974, possession of premises at 4, 4a, 5, 6, 7 and 8 Ledbury Mews North, London, W11, and that there be an
f enquiry as to what sum the defendants should pay to the plaintiff by way of mesne profits from 23rd December 1973 to the date of delivery of possession. The facts are set out in the judgment of Russell LJ.

Michael Essayan for the plaintiff.
John Stuart Colyer for the defendants.
g

RUSSELL LJ.   The facts in this case which was heard below before Templeman J,[1] are very shortly these. The plaintiff, whom I will label 'A', is the freeholder of the business premises in question. B had a term of years expiring on 23rd December
h 1968; and C, who is the defendant, had a sub-term expiring on 20th December 1968, and was in occupation of the premises for its business purposes. B's tenancy was outside the scope directly of the Landlord and Tenant Act 1954, since B was not in occupation.

After the expiry of their contractual terms, B and C continued to pay their respective rents to A and B. In those circumstances, B became tenant of A as a yearly tenant, or tenant from year to year. C, however, remained in occupation and paying
j rent to B, not as a yearly sub-tenant of B, but, by virtue of the 1954 Act, on a statutory continuation of that sub-tenancy. A, on 13th November 1972, gave to B due notice to quit, determining B's yearly contractual tenancy on 23rd December 1973. On 21st

---

1   [1974] 3 All ER 423

November 1972 A gave to C notice, in the form prescribed by the statute, to determine C's sub-tenancy on 31st May 1973, which is of course a date prior to the termi-   *a*
nation of B's mesne tenancy. The defendant, C, contends that that notice is ineffective
under the statute.

It was not disputed before us that A was, under the 1954 Act, a landlord competent
to serve a s 25 statutory notice on C when he did so, notwithstanding the existence at
the time of the notice of the mesne tenancy of B. Further, it is not disputed that the
notice complied with s 25(2), in that it was given not less than six months nor more than   *b*
twelve months before the termination date that was specified therein, which was
31st May 1973. It is however asserted in the first instance that there was no power to
serve a notice under s 25 with a termination date earlier than the expiry of the
contractual mesne tenancy of B.

Section 25(3) and (4) are in my view the statutory provisions, and the only statutory provisions, which govern or control, in the case of all tenancies, what termination   *c*
date may be specified in a s 25 notice. Subsection (3) is in these terms:

> 'In the case of a tenancy which apart from this Act could have been brought
> to an end by notice to quit given by the landlord—(*a*) the date of termination speci-
> fied in a notice under this section shall not be earlier than the earliest date on
> which apart from this Part of this Act the tenancy could have been brought to an   *d*
> end by notice to quit given by the landlord on the date of the giving of the notice
> under this section . . .'

Paragraph (*b*) is not here material. Subsection 3(*a*) in my view deals with any case in
which there is a contractual periodic tenancy, and in 'periodic tenancy' I include also
a tenancy for a fixed term with a special power to determine it prematurely. It is of   *e*
course to be observed that in the case of a periodic tenancy, that tenancy would
continue to exist as a common law contractual tenancy, because the Act prevented
its termination by ordinary notice to quit. Subsection (4) is in these terms:

> 'In the case of any other tenancy, a notice under this section shall not specify a
> date of termination earlier than the date on which apart from this Part of this
> Act the tenancy would have come to an end by effluxion of time.'   *f*

That subsection controls the date of termination that may be specified in the s 25
notice in the case of any tenancy other than that which I have conveniently labelled
as a periodic tenancy; that is to say, every case in which there is a contractual tenancy
not within sub-s (3), that is to say, a tenancy for a term certain. If at the date of the
s 25 notice the contractual tenancy is still in existence, then the date of termination   *g*
to be specified must not be earlier than the end of that term. But what of a case in
which the fixed term of the tenancy has expired and the tenancy only continues by
force of the Act? It seems to me really quite plain that neither sub-s (3) nor sub-s (4)
directly contains any provision controlling the date of termination that may be
specified in the s 25 notice. Those subsections appear to me to be designed to recognise
and prevent the overriding of contractual rights in the tenant in occupation and are   *h*
not directed to the situation where those contractual rights have come to an end and
only the artificial continuation of the tenancy exists under the statute. In my view,
in such a case, as I have indicated, the Act imposes no fetter on the date of termination
to be specified in the notice. It only requires, under sub-s (2), that the date of the
notice be appropriately related in point of time with the selected termination date.

Now it may—and at first sight would—appear strange that by a s 25 notice (in the   *j*
present case given by A to C) the sub-tenancy of C from B can in effect be terminated
by A's action without reference to C's mesne landlord B; that is to say, before the end
of B's contractual head tenancy. Is B to be, for example, deprived of his profit rental
while remaining liable for rent to A under the headlease? It appears to me that this
situation is covered, and indeed exactly envisaged, elsewhere in the Act. In this case,

a A was only in a position to give a s 25 notice to C because of the relatively short interest of B in reversion to C's tenancy once the notice to quit had been given to B. This is under s 44 of the 1954 Act. Section 44 applies the provisions of Sch 6 to a case such as the present, where the immediate landlord B is not the freeholder. I do not propose to read the details of Sch 6; but under para 3 of that schedule the acts of A as the competent landlord (able to give, therefore, a s 25 notice) are made binding on the intermediate landlord B; and by para 4, if the mesne landlord B has not consented to the

b acts of A, he will be entitled to compensation from A for any loss that may be caused to him. It seems to me that those provisions deprive what appears to me to be the plain result of the language of s 25 of the strangeness or oddity that without them might have occurred to the ordinary common law or indeed equity mind. Accordingly in my judgment, the judge was quite correct in concluding that the date specified in the s 25 notice could not in law be criticised.

c That left for him a secondary point taken by the defendant C, which was based on the fact that after the end of May 1973 and up to the date in December 1973, when B's contractual tenancy from year to year came to an end, C continued to pay at the customary rate sums by way of rent to B. This, it was contended, must be taken as involving the creation after the end of May 1973 of a new contractual lease between B and C. It is accepted by counsel for the plaintiff that if that was the true conclusion,

d then the s 25 notice which had been given to C by A would necessarily lose its effect and the new sub-tenancy from B to C (whether it be regarded as periodic or whether it be regarded as for a period ending in December 1973) would bring C back into the protection of the 1954 Act, and all would need to be done again.

So the question is: what was the effect of C continuing to pay sums by way of rent after the date in May and up to the date in December? Is it the proper inference that

e this was the creation of a new tenancy? In my judgment, that is not the proper conclusion. Here was C, whose contractual tenancy had come to an end in December 1968. C remained there, paying rent at the same rate thereafter, not because there was any contractual tenancy as such still in existence, not because a new tenancy from year to year was being created by the continuation of payment of the rent under the sub-tenancy, but because of the statutory provision that the tenancy should continue

f for (if I may so phrase it) a term uncertain. At any time during the period after 1968 nobody could conceive for a moment that the continued payment of rent by C to B was something which could be regarded as the creation of a new contractual tenancy.

Reliance was placed on a phrase used in answers—statutory answers, if I may coin a phrase—on the part of B in November 1973, as indicating that the proper inference was that there was a creation of a new tenancy after May 1973 because B used this

g phrase in answer to the question:

'If you have a sub-tenant I hereby require you to state [this is the statutory form[1]] . . . (ii) if the sub-tenancy is for a fixed term, what is the term, or, if the sub-tenancy is terminable by notice, by what notice it can be terminated . . .'

h The answer was: 'The sub-tenants are holding over under a sub-lease dated 5th July 1968 for a term of years expiring on the 20th December 1968.' That was the answer that was given on 1st November 1973. Reliance was placed by counsel for the defendants on the phrase 'The sub-tenants are holding over' under the 1968 lease as indicating that the true inference was that there was created after May 1973 a new tenancy. But, as I remarked in the course of debate, if that phrase had been used at any time

j prior to May 1973 by B, it would have been a perfectly natural phrase to use, having regard to the fact that the sub-tenancy of C had come to an end on 20th December 1968 and C was still there by force of the Act.

---

1 See the Landlord and Tenant (Notices) Regulations 1957 (SI 1957 No 1157), Appendix, Form 13

It is quite plain that if you find one person in occupation paying sums by way of rent quarterly or half-yearly to another person, ordinarily speaking it is a right *a* conclusion that there is a relationship between them of contractual landlord and tenant; but, of course, the circumstances may show that there is no justification for such an inference. At any time prior to the end of May 1973 there could not have been any justification for the inference that a contractual sub-tenancy was being created anew from B to C; and the reason for that was exactly and precisely the fact that there was no need for such a contractual tenancy to be spelled out of the act of payment *b* and receipt of rent. It would be quite contrary to the views and the attitudes being taken, quite correctly, by C that the statute protected him. It is abundantly plain that, after the service of the s 25 notice on C, C (the defendant) maintained—and, indeed, before us he still sought to maintain, on the first point—that the s 25 notice was a thoroughly bad one. If it were a thoroughly bad one, then indeed C would be perfectly entitled to assert that he was protected by the Act and, being protected by *c* the Act, naturally he would continue to pay, not by force of a new tenancy, but by force of the statutory protection, rent at the old rate to B as long as B remained the owner of the reversion.

I do not see any justification for attributing the payment and receipt of rent after May 1973 to a creation of a new sub-tenancy in the circumstance that it was being asserted by C himself that what he was doing was simply paying the sums which he *d* would be obliged to pay on the footing of what can be described as a statutory continuation of a tenancy. It seems to me that there is no justification for the conclusion, either in fact or in law, that a new tenancy is to be derived from that fact. It seems to me that we may aptly quote (although it was a rent restriction case) a passage from the judgment of Denning LJ in *Marcroft Wagons Ltd v Smith*[1]:

e

'If the acceptance of rent can be explained on some other footing than a contractual tenancy, as, for instance, by reason of an existing or possible statutory right to remain, then a new tenancy should not be inferred.'

Although that was not in the context which we have now, it seems to me that it is an extremely sound approach which can be applied to the instant case.

For those reasons, which I fear are substantially mere repetition of what the learned *f* judge has more compactly said, I would uphold his decision and dismiss the appeal.

STAMP LJ. I agree.

SIR JOHN PENNYCUICK. I agree. I only wish to stress that counsel for the *g* defendants in terms accepted (I do not suggest otherwise than for good cause) that para (*a*) of s 25(3) has no application here. For that reason, I do not express any view on the construction of that paragraph, which caused me a little difficulty.

Appeal dismissed. Leave to appeal to the House of Lords refused.   *h*

Solicitors: *Underwood & Co* (for the plaintiff); *Goodman, Derrick & Co* (for the defendants).

Gordon H Scott Esq Barrister.

---

1 [1951] 2 All ER 271 at 277, [1951] 2 KB 496 at 506

a

R v Brogan

COURT OF APPEAL, CRIMINAL DIVISION
SCARMAN, JAMES LJJ AND BRISTOW J
6th FEBRUARY 1975

b

Crown Court – Committal of offender to Crown Court for sentence – Powers of justices – Order by justices following conviction – Compensation order – Propriety – Justices having no power to make any order following conviction where offender is to be committed for sentence – All questions associated with sentence to be left to Crown Court – Magistrates' Courts Act 1952, s 29.

c

Justices who commit an offender to the Crown Court for sentence under s 29[a] of the Magistrates Courts' Act 1952 have no power to impose any order, such as a compensation order, subsequent to conviction. Accordingly, when committing for sentence justices must be scrupulously careful to leave all questions associated with sentence to the Crown Court (see p 880 *g* to *j* and p 881 *c* and *e*, post).

d

Notes

For the powers of a magistrates' court when committing a defendant to the Crown Court for sentence, see 25 Halsbury's Laws (3rd Edn) 226-229, paras 421-423.

For the Magistrates' Courts Act 1952, s 29, see 21 Halsbury's Statutes (3rd Edn) 215.

Case referred to in judgment

e

R v Surrey Quarter Sessions, ex parte Commissioners of Police of the Metropolis [1962] 1 All ER 825, [1963] 1 QB 990, [1962] 2 WLR 1203, 126 JP 269, DC, Digest (Cont Vol A) 394, 6018a.

Application

f

On 11th June 1974 before the Marylebone stipendiary magistrate, the applicant, Mary Brogan, was convicted of various offences of dishonesty. The magistrate made a compensation order against the applicant and committed her to the Crown Court for sentence under s 29 of the Magistrates Courts' Act 1952. On 1st August 1974 his Honour Judge MacLeay sitting in the Crown Court for Inner London sentenced the applicant to two years' imprisonment. She applied for leave to appeal against sentence. The facts are set out in the judgment of the court.

g

The applicant did not appear and was not represented.

h

SCARMAN LJ delivered the following judgment of the court. On 11th June 1974, at the Marylebone magistrates' court, the applicant, now applying for leave to appeal against sentence, was convicted of uttering a forged cheque to the value of £56, stealing a chequebook, obtaining £20 by means of a forged instrument and was committed for sentence under s 29 of the Magistrates' Courts Act 1952. At the time that the stipendiary magistrate committed her to the Crown Court for sentence he made a compensation order of £30 in favour of the Post Office. A question does arise

j

---

a   Section 29, so far as material, provides: 'Where on the summary trial . . . of an indictable offence . . . a person who is not less than seventeen years old is convicted of the offence, then, if on obtaining information about his character and antecedents the court is of opinion that they are such that greater punishment should be inflicted for the offence than the court has power to inflict, the court may . . . commit him . . . to [the Crown Court] for sentence . . .'

whether that was a proper order for the magistrate to have made but certainly it is an
order which is incapable of being challenged on appeal in this court. She was com- *a*
mitted for sentence to the Inner London Crown Court and ultimately sentenced to
two years' imprisonment imposed in respect of each offence to run concurrently.
Nine other offences were taken into consideration.

The facts were these. The chequebook had been despatched to a customer but was
never in fact received by the customer. On 9th April 1974 a cheque taken from that
book and drawn in the sum of £56 was used to open a National Savings Bank account *b*
at the Queensbury branch post office. An account was opened in the name of Mrs
Mead. Later the cheque was returned marked 'chequebook stolen', but by that time
two withdrawals had been made from the savings bank account for £10 and £20
respectively.

In June the applicant was interviewed and admitted that she had used the cheque to
open an account and had made withdrawals totalling £30. She said she had no ex- *c*
planation as to why she had been doing it and that she had torn up all the rest of the
cheques in the chequebook to stop her doing it again.

The nine offences taken into consideration were committed between the end of March
and the middle of May 1974. They were offences of dishonesty similar in character to
those in relation to which she was committed for sentence. There was an offence of
stealing a cash dispenser card, an offence of obtaining a National Savings Bank deposit *d*
book by a forged instrument and an offence of obtaining £10 on some seven occasions
each by a forged instrument. The dreary story of this woman's dishonest career
stands out clearly from the brief recital that I have given of the offences that were
under consideration when she was sentenced.

She herself is 59 years of age, a married woman separated from her husband, with
one daughter. She has been for years continually in and out of prison for offences of *e*
dishonesty. There are 12 previous convictions for dishonesty on her record and she
was released from her last imprisonment in February 1974 and, as I have already
recited, by April she was in the business of dishonesty again.

We have had the benefit of reading a full social enquiry report and we have also seen
a medical report from Dr Jacobson. An up-to-date prison report has been obtained
from which, sadly enough, it is perfectly clear that really this woman is happier in the *f*
institutional atmosphere of a prison than she is subject to the somewhat chilling
breezes of life in freedom. There is nothing that can be said by way of challenge to
the sentence of imprisonment imposed on this woman and the application must
therefore be refused.

I now pass to the disturbing feature of the case and one which is of some importance
in the administration of the law. This woman, as I have already mentioned, was *g*
committed for sentence under s 29 of the Magistrates' Courts Act 1952; at the same
time the magistrate imposed a compensation order. Whatever their legal powers are
—as to that I shall have a few words to say later—it is undesirable that magistrates
who are committing for sentence under s 29 should themselves impose a compensation order. A compensation order can be made only in the circumstances which are
set out in ss 35-38 of the Powers of Criminal Courts Act 1973, and one of the matters *h*
that has to be considered by the court in making a compensation order is the means
of the offender so far as known to the court. It is not desirable for a compensation
order to be made except at the time of sentence, i e final disposal of the offender.
There is an important relationship between the sentence of the court and the desirability or otherwise of making a compensation order. It is also very important that,
if a sentence is to be reviewed, the reviewing court should be able to look also at the *j*
compensation order.

Look now what has happened in this case. We are unable to review the compensation order because it was made by the magistrate. The Crown Court when imposing
sentence was itself unable to deal with the compensation order. The result is that,
that which should be regarded as a whole, the sentence and the ancillary orders

linked with it, has been split into separate parts: and not all those parts can be
a reviewed as a whole by the Court of Appeal.

A compensation order is not part of the sentence of the court strictly speaking; it
is an order analagous to an order for restitution of property and, when made by the
Crown Court, the Court of Appeal can annul or vary the order pursuant to s 30 of the
Criminal Appeal Act 1968, and s 36(1) of the Powers of Criminal Courts Act 1973.
The fact that care has been taken by the legislature to ensure that the Court of Appeal,
b when dealing with sentence, can also review a compensation order indicates that
Parliament was concerned to avoid the mischief of a compensation order being
incapable of review when sentence is under appeal in this court.

Though we have heard no argument, we think it clear that magistrates who commit
an offender under s 29 of the Magistrates' Courts Act 1952 have no power to impose
any order subsequent to conviction. The section provides that, where on summary
c trial a person is convicted of an offence, if on obtaining certain information the court
is of the opinion that there is a case for greater punishment than the court itself has
power to inflict, 'the court may, instead of dealing with him in any other manner,
commit him in custody to [the Crown Court] for sentence . . .'

As long ago as 1962 Lord Parker CJ in *R v Surrey Quarter Sessions, ex parte Commissioner of Police of the Metropolis*[1], commented:

d
'. . . in the case of a committal under s 29 of the Magistrates' Courts Act 1952,
a committal is alternative to dealing with the prisoner in any other way.'

Any doubts that may have survived should have been laid to rest by s 56(5) of the
Criminal Justice Act 1967, which provided that, when there is a committal, the
powers of the magistrates' court should be exercised not by that court but by the
e Court of Assize or Quarter Sessions (now the Crown Court).

Magistrates must, therefore, be scrupulously careful, when committing for
sentence, to leave all questions associated with sentence to the Crown Court.

Application refused.

Jacqueline Charles   Barrister.

---

1 [1962] 1 All ER 825 at 827, [1963] 1 QB 990 at 994

The Halcyon the Great   *a*

QUEEN'S BENCH DIVISION (ADMIRALTY COURT)
BRANDON J
4th, 21st, 26th NOVEMBER, 6th DECEMBER 1974

Admiralty – Appraisement and sale – Currency of sale – Jurisdiction of Admiralty marshal –   *b*
Commission to cause ship to be sold for the highest price obtainable – Sale in foreign currency –
Whether marshal having jurisdiction to sell ship for sum expressed in foreign currency –
RSC Ord 75, r 23(2), Appendix B, Form 13.

Practice – Funds in court – Payment of money into court – Lodgment of money – Money –
Foreign currency – Payment into court without conversion into sterling – Jurisdiction of court   *c*
to order that sum be placed in foreign currency deposit account – Treasury consent under
exchange control regulations – Admiralty Court – Proceeds of sale of ship – Sale for sum
expressed in foreign currency – Circumstances in which court will order that proceeds of sale
be paid into court and placed into deposit account without conversion – Administration of
Justice Act 1965, s 4(1) – Supreme Court Funds Rules 1927 (SR & O 1927 No 1184), r 33(1).
d

The owners of a crude oil carrier, a limited company, went into compulsory liquidation. In a mortgage action in rem against the ship, the Admiralty Court made an
order for the ship's appraisement and sale by the Admiralty marshal pending suit and
a commission for her appraisement and sale was issued. It was expected that the ship,
if sold for US dollars, would fetch between $20 million and $30 million. Hambros
Bank Ltd, the first and second mortgagees, intended to bring a claim against the ship   *e*
for about $11½ million. The plaintiffs were the third, fourth and fifth mortgagees;
their claim was for at least $14 million. National Westminster Bank Ltd, the sixth
mortgagees, had a claim, arising out of mortgage transactions largely in sterling,
for over £10 million. The plaintiffs made an interlocutory application for orders
that the vessel be sold by the marshal for a price payable in US dollars and that the
price received on sale should be paid into and held until further order in a dollar   *f*
account at the Bank of England to be opened in the marshal's name. The plaintiffs
alleged that (i) if the marshal invited offers in dollars as well as sterling, he would be
likely to obtain a higher price; (ii) if there were a sale in dollars and the proceeds of
sale were, without prior conversion into sterling, placed and retained in a dollar
account, the fund so created would be protected from the risk of depreciation of
sterling against the dollar during the period of its retention; and (iii) since the   *g*
currency of the mortgage transaction was dollars, the plaintiffs would be entitled, if
their claim succeeded, to judgment in dollars which could most simply be satisfied
out of the dollar fund.

Held – (i) Since the form of appraisement and sale prescribed by RSC Ord 75, r 23(2)ᵃ,
and Appendix B, Form 13ᵇ, required the marshal 'to cause the [ship] to be sold for the   *h*
highest price that can be obtained for it', he had authority without any order or
direction of the court to sell it for a price in foreign money, for the word 'sell' as
generally used in the law relating to the sale of goods included selling for a price in
foreign currency and, furthermore, to limit the word to selling for a price in sterling
only might be inconsistent with the requirement to obtain the highest price (see p 886
e to *g* and p 888 *b*, post).   *j*
    (ii) The word 'money' in the provisions of s 4(1)ᶜ of the Administration of Justice

---

a Rule 23, so far as material, is set out at p 885 *b* and *c*, post
b Form 13 is set out at p 885 *d* and *e*, post
c Section 4(1), so far as material, is set out at p 588 *g*, post

Act 1965 and r 33(2)^d of the Supreme Court Funds Rules 1927 relating to the 'payment
a of money' into court and 'the lodgment of money', was to be construed in its ordinary
and natural meaning, i e as including money in a foreign currency. Accordingly the
marshal could lawfully pay the dollar proceeds of sale into court without first converting them into sterling provided that Treasury consent had been obtained under
the Exchange Control Act 1947 and an order of the court had been made authorising
such payment (see p 886 *j*, p 887 *a* to *c* and p 888 *c*, post).
b   (iii) Where dollar proceeds of sale had been paid into court, the court had jurisdiction,
provided the necessary exchange control permission had been obtained, to order that
those proceeds be placed in a dollar deposit account (see p 887 *d* and *j* to p 888 *d*, post).
(iv) Since the plaintiffs had an arguable case that, if their claim succeeded, they
would be entitled to judgment in dollars, and since the judgment in dollars which the
plaintiffs and the other mortgagees would in that event obtain, might well equal or
c exceed the amount of the fund created by the sale of the ship, there were good reasons
for ordering that, should a sale be made in dollars, the proceeds should be paid into
court without conversion and placed in a dollar deposit account out of which judgment
in dollars, if given, could be satisfied directly. Orders would therefore be made
accordingly (see p 889 *f* to *h* and p 890 *a* and *b*, post); *Schorsch Meier GmbH v Hennin*,
p 152, ante, considered.
d

Notes
For the appraisement and sale of an arrested ship, see 1 Halsbury's Laws (4th Edn)
287, paras 453, 454, and for cases on the subject, see 1 Digest (Repl) 203, 204, *911-920*.
For the lodgment of funds in court, see 30 Halsbury's Laws (3rd Edn) 357, 358,
para 663.
e   For the Administration of Justice Act 1965, s 4, see 7 Halsbury's Statutes (3rd Edn)
748.

Cases referred to in judgment
Manners v Pearson & Son [1898] 1 Ch 581, [1895-9] All ER Rep 415, 67 LJCh 304, 78
LT 432, CA, 35 Digest (Repl) 201, 90.
f *Miliangos v George Frank (Textiles) Ltd* (4th December 1974) unreported.
Schorsch Meier GmbH v Hennin p 152, ante, [1974] 3 WLR 823, [1975] 1 Lloyd's Rep 1, CA.
United Railways of the Havana and Regla Warehouses Ltd, Re [1960] 2 All ER 332, sub nom
Tomkinson v First Pennsylvania Banking and Trust Co [1961] AC 1007, [1960] 2 WLR
969, HL, Digest (Cont Vol A) 231, *862a*.

g **Cases also cited**
Attorney-General for Ontario v Daly [1924] AC 1011, PC.
Cap Bon, The [1967] 1 Lloyd's Rep 543.
Kornatzki v Oppenheimer [1937] 4 All ER 133.
*Teh Hu, The, Owners of the Turbo-Electric Bulk Carrier Teh Hu v Nippon Salvage Co Ltd of
Tokyo* [1969] 3 All ER 1200, [1970] P 106, CA.
h

Motion
The plaintiffs, Bankers Trust International Ltd, were creditors of the defendants, Court
Line Ltd (in liquidation), for the sum of US $14 million secured by three mortgages
together with interest on the defendants' ship, Halcyon the Great. The plaintiffs
were third, fourth and fifth mortgagees, the first and second mortgagees were Hambros
j Bank Ltd and the sixth mortgagees were National Westminster Bank Ltd. The court
made an order on 4th November 1974 for the appraisement and sale of the ship by
the Admiralty marshal pendente lite. The plaintiffs made an interlocutory application
with the consent of the first and second mortgagees and the defendants by their

----

d Rule 33(2) is set out at p 885 *h*, post

liquidator, and without objection by the sixth mortgagees, for orders that the ship might be sold for a price payable in US dollars and that the amount of the price *a* received by the marshal be paid into and held until further order or such other provision for securing and preserving the fund as the court might think fit. The facts are set out in the judgment.

Gordon Slynn QC and *David Grace* for the plaintiffs and Hambros Bank Ltd. *Nicholas Phillips* as amicus curiae.   *b* NationalWestminster Bank Ltd and the defendants were not represented.

BRANDON J. The court has before it applications by plaintiffs in a mortgage action in rem against the ship Halcyon the Great. The court has already, on an earlier application by the plaintiffs, made an order for the appraisement and sale of the ship *c* by the Admiralty marshal pending suit, and the plaintiffs have, since that order and in pursuance of it, caused a commission for appraisement and sale to be issued.

If the ordinary procedure in such cases were to be followed, the Admiralty marshal, whose duty it is to execute the commission, would sell the ship for a price in sterling and, having done so, would pay the proceeds of sale into court, where they would be placed in a sterling deposit account bearing interest at a prescribed rate and retained *d* there until the time for payment out arrived. The plaintiffs, however, are not content that this ordinary procedure should be followed in this case, but wish it to be varied in a number of important respects. First, they wish the Admiralty marshal to sell the ship, or anyhow be free to sell the ship if the opportunity offers, for a price in US dollars rather than in sterling. Second, they wish the Admiralty marshal, following a sale in dollars, to pay the proceeds of sale into court without first converting them *e* into sterling. And, third, they wish the proceeds of sale, after they have been paid into Court in that form, to be placed in a separate dollar deposit account until the time for payment out arrives. They apply accordingly to the court to make such further orders, or give such directions to the Admiralty marshal, as may be appropriate to achieve these ends.

In support of their applications the plaintiffs rely on the following principal matters. *f* First, that, if the Admiralty marshal invites offers for the ship in dollars as well as sterling, he is likely to obtain a higher price for her. Second, that, if there is a sale in dollars and the proceeds of sale are, after payment into court without prior conversion into sterling, placed and retained in a dollar account, the fund so created will be protected from the risk of depreciation of sterling against the dollar during the period of its retention. Third, that, since the currency of the mortgage transactions out of *g* which the plaintiffs' claim in the action arises is dollars, they will be entitled, on the assumption that their claim succeeds, to a judgment in dollars, and such a judgment can most simply and beneficially be satisfied out of the dollar fund. In this connection they rely on the recent decision of the Court of Appeal in *Schorsch Meier GmbH v Hennin*[1].

The applications so made raise a number of novel questions for decision as follows: *h* (1) Can the Admiralty marshal lawfully sell the ship for a price in dollars? (2) If so, can he lawfully pay the dollar proceeds of sale into court without first converting them into sterling? (3) If so, can the dollar proceeds, after such payment into court, be lawfully placed and retained in a dollar deposit account? (4) If these things can lawfully be done, does it need any order or direction of the court to enable them to be done? (5) If so, should the court, in the particular circumstances of the present case, make *j* whatever order, or give whatever direction, is needed?

In order to answer these questions it is necessary to examine, firstly, the relevant rules of the Supreme Court; secondly, the relevant provisions of Part I of the Administration of Justice Act 1965, which governs the lodgment and subsequent application of

1   [1975] 1 All ER 152, [1974] 3 WLR 823

funds in the Supreme Court; and, thirdly, the relevant parts of the Supreme Court
a Funds Rules 1927, which are by s 7(3) of the 1965 Act to have effect as if they had been
made under that section.

I examine first the rules of the Supreme Court relating to sales in Admiralty actions
in rem. RSC Ord 75, r 23, provides:

b
'(1) A commission for the appraisement and sale of any property under an
order of the Court shall not be issued until the party applying for it has filed a
praecipe in Form No. 12 in Appendix B.

'(2) Such a commission must, unless the Court otherwise orders, be executed
by the marshal and must be in Form No. 13 in Appendix B . . .

'(4) The marshal shall pay into Court the gross proceeds of the sale of any
property sold by him under a commission for sale . . .'

c
The commission for appraisement and sale, in the form so precribed, is addressed by
Her Majesty to the Admiralty marshal and, in the case of a ship A to be sold by
private treaty, which is the method of sale normally employed by him today, reads
as follows:

d
'WHEREAS in this action the Court has ordered [the ship A] to be appraised and
sold. WE hereby authorise and command you to choose one or more experienced
persons and to swear him or them to appraise the said [ship A] according to the
true value thereof, and such value having been certified in writing by him or them
to cause the said [ship A] to be sold by [*private treaty*] for the highest price that
can be obtained for it, but not for less than the appraised value unless the Court on
your application allows it to be sold for less. AND WE further command you,
e
immediately upon the sale being completed, to pay the proceeds thereof into
Court and to file the certificate of appraisement signed by you and the appraiser
or appraisers, and an account of the sale signed by you, together with this
commission.'

f
I examine next the provisions of the 1965 Act and of the 1927 rules, which relate to
the payment of money into court, both generally and in the particular case of proceeds of sale of property under arrest in Admiralty actions in rem. In doing so I shall
confine myself to such provisions and rules as apply to actions which are not
proceeding in a District Registry.

Section 4(1) of the 1965 Act provides:

g
'The payment of money into the Supreme Court shall . . . be effected by paying
it into the Bank of England to the credit of the Accountant General's account . . .'

Rule 29(1) of the 1927 rules contains certain general provisions with regard to the
procedure for paying money into court which it is not necessary to set out. Rule 33(2),
as amended, deals with the particular case here under consideration and provides:

h
'Directions for the lodgment of money representing the proceeds of any sale
effected by the Admiralty Marshal shall be issued by the Accountant-General
upon receipt of a request from the Admiralty Marshal in Form No. 24 A.'

Form 24A reads:

j
'The Accountant-General is hereby requested to issue a direction to the Bank
to receive for the above-mentioned ledger credit the sum of £____ being the
gross proceeds of sale of ____.'

I examine finally the provisions of the 1965 Act and of the 1927 rules, which relate to
the placing and investment of money after payment into court. Section 6(1) of the
1965 Act provides:

'Save in a case in which it is provided by an order of the court that it shall not be
placed or invested as mentioned in the following provisions of this subsection, and *a*
subject to any provision to the contrary made by rules made under the next
following section, a sum of money in the Supreme Court . . . (*a*) may, if the
court so orders, be dealt with in such of the following ways as may be specified
in the order, namely: (i) it may be placed, in accordance with rules so made, to a
deposit account or a short-term investment account . . . (*b*) shall, if no order is
made with respect to it under the foregoing paragraph, be dealt with as follows:— *b*
(i) . . . it shall be placed, in accordance with rules made under the next following
section, to a deposit account . . .'

The procedure with regard to money placed in a deposit account under paras (*a*)
and (*b*) of s 6(1) is governed by rr 73, 74, 76, 77, 79 and 80 of the 1927 rules. I do not
think it necessary to set out these rules here, but I can, I think, fairly summarise their *c*
effect by saying that the terms of four of those rules, namely rr 74, 76, 77 and 79,
are consistent with the deposit account concerned being an account in sterling, and
prima facie at any rate inconsistent with its being an account in any other currency,
such as dollars.

I return now to the questions which I stated earlier were raised by the plaintiffs'
applications and I shall consider each in turn in the light of the statutory provisions *d*
and rules which I have set out, or the effect of which I have summarised, above.

(1) *Can the Admiralty marshal lawfully sell the ship for a price in dollars?*
This depends in the first place, as it seems to me, on the true construction of the
prescribed form of commission for appraisement and sale. That not only authorises
but requires the Admiralty marshal, in effect, to sell the ship for the highest price *e*
which he can obtain. The word 'sell' as generally used in the English law of sale
of goods includes selling for a price in foreign money as well as a price in sterling, and
I do not see why the same word, as used in the prescribed form of commission, should
be given any narrower meaning. Indeed to give it a narrower meaning, by limiting it
to selling for a price in sterling, might in particular cases be inconsistent with the
expressed purpose that the highest price is to be obtained.

On such information as I have I do not believe that any Admiralty marshal has ever *f*
in the past sold property under arrest in an action in rem for a price in any currency
other than sterling. Moreover the standard conditions of sale presently approved for
use by him provide for offers to be made in sterling only. Nevertheless, on the true
construction of the prescribed form of commission, I am of opinion that it permits the
Admiralty marshal, if he thinks fit in order to obtain the best price in any particular *g*
case, to invite offers and to sell the property for a price in foreign currency as well as
sterling.

Since I am of that opinion, it is not necessary to consider whether, if the prescribed
form of commission did not permit the Admiralty marshal to proceed in this way,
RSC Ord 75, r 23(2), would empower the court to vary the terms of the commission so
as to give him such permission. The wording of r 23(2) is ambiguous, and, since it is *h*
not necessary, I shall not express any opinion on the point.

(2) *Can the Admiralty marshal lawfully pay dollar proceeds of sale into court without first
converting them into sterling?*
The first point to observe with regard to this is that, assuming such payment-in
to be otherwise permissible, it would appear to require the consent of the Treasury
under the Exchange Control Act 1947. Subject to such consent being obtained, however, *i*
is such payment-in permissible? This depends, as it seems to me, on whether there
is anything in the relevant provisions of the 1965 Act or of the 1927 rules, which
expressly or impliedly prohibits such payment-in being made.

In my judgment there is not. It is true that form 24A, prescribed for use by the
Admiralty marshal when requesting directions from the Accountant-General for the

lodgment of proceeds of sale under r 33(2) of the 1927 rules, contains the symbol for
a sterling immediately before the blank space left for insertion of the amount sought to
be paid in. This indicates, I think, what I should in any case have assumed, that the
form was expected to be used in relation to sterling proceeds only. I do not, however,
consider that it would be right to infer from this evidence of expectation that it was intended to prohibit the payment-in of proceeds in some other currency. In this connection I think it is right to say that the word 'money', in its ordinary and natural meaning,
b includes money in a foreign currency as well as money in sterling. It should also be
observed that foreign securities may in certain circumstances be lodged in court under
the relevant statutory provisions and rules, and that, when they are, the dividends on
them, which are payable in foreign currency, become receivable by the Accountant-
General. It follows that the payment into court of foreign currency, and its receipt on
behalf of the court by the Accountant-General, is not without precedent.
c   For these reasons I am of opinion that, subject to any necessary exchange control
permission, the Admiralty marshal, where he has sold property for a price in a
foreign currency, can lawfully pay the proceeds of sale into court without first
converting them into sterling.

d (3) *Can dollar proceeds of sale, after payment into court, be lawfully placed and retained in
a dollar deposit account?*
      Here again the first point to observe is that, assuming such placing to be otherwise
permissible, it would appear to require the consent of the Treasury under the
Exchange Control Act 1947. The question to be answered is therefore whether, subject
to such consent being obtained, such placing is otherwise permissible.
      This depends, primarily at any rate, on the true construction of s 6(1) of the 1965
e Act and the relevant rules of the 1927 rules. I have set out earlier the material parts of
s 6(1) and summarised the effect of rr 74, 76, 77 and 79 of the 1927 rules. While the
matter is not altogether easy, I have come to the conclusion that, having regard to the
effect of those rules, as stated by me earlier, the only kind of deposit account to which
money paid into court can be placed, either pursuant to an order of the court under
para (*a*) of s 6(1), or in the absence of such order under para (*b*) of the subsection,
f is a deposit account in sterling, and that it is not possible for such money to be placed,
under either of these two paragraphs, to a deposit account in a foreign currency.
      On the footing that that view about what can and cannot be done under paras (*a*)
and (*b*) of s 6(1) is correct, it becomes necessary to consider the effect of the proviso
at the beginning of s 6(1). The material words are:

g   'Save in a case in which it is provided by an order of the court that it shall not
       be placed or invested as mentioned in the following provisions of this subsection...'

These words necessarily involve a power in the court to make a negative order that
money paid into court shall not be invested in the manner provided for in paras (*a*)
and (*b*) of s 6(1). It is for consideration, however, whether they also imply, or recognise by implication, a further power in the court to make a positive order that such
h money shall be invested in some alternative manner. There are two difficulties
about implying such further power. The first difficulty is that, if the legislature had
intended to give it, one would have expected the words in the proviso following
'order of the court' to be 'that it shall be placed or invested otherwise than as mentioned' rather than what they are. The second difficulty is that, if such a power is
implied, it appears to give the court a wholly unfettered discretion with regard to
j alternative placing or investment. In answer to those points it can be argued with
force that it would be unreasonable to suppose that the legislature would empower
the court to prohibit money being placed or invested as provided in paras (*a*) and (*b*),
without at the same time empowering it to direct some alternative way of placing or
investing it.
      Having considered the matter carefully, I have reached the conclusion that s 6(1)

either gives the court power by implication to order money to be placed or invested in other ways or, at the least, recognises by implication an inherent power in the court, *a* as master of its own practice and procedure, to do so.

For these reasons I am of opinion that, if the court so orders but not otherwise and subject to any necessary exchange control permission, dollar proceeds can lawfully, after payment into court, be placed to a dollar deposit account.

(4) *Is any order or direction of the court needed?* *b*

So far as a sale by the Admiralty marshal in dollars is concerned, I do not consider, since I have held that such a sale is authorised by the prescribed form of commission for appraisement and sale, that any order or direction is required. A declaration to that effect would, however, be helpful.

So far as both the payment into court of dollar proceeds without prior conversion into sterling and also the placing of such proceeds after payment into court to a dollar *c* deposit account are concerned, it seems to me that an order of the court is needed. Without an order with regard to the first matter the Admiralty marshal might not know whether he was obliged to convert the proceeds into sterling before payment-in or not. As to the second matter an order is clearly required to take the case out of the provisions of paras (*a*) and (*b*) of s 6(1) of the 1965 Act.

d

(5) *Should the court, in the particular circumstances of this case, grant the declaration and make the order needed?*

I do not consider that there is any problem about granting a declaration that the Admiralty marshal is entitled, if he thinks fit in order to obtain the highest price, to sell the ship for a price in dollars. Assuming that the view which I have formed on the matter is right, the granting of such a declaration involves no more than stating the *e* law applicable in all cases of sale by the Admiralty marshal in actions in rem.

It seems to me, however, that the court should not go further and make an order that, in the event of a dollar sale, the proceeds should be paid into court without prior conversion into sterling and after such payment-in be placed to a dollar deposit account, without good reasons, founded on the facts of the particular case, for doing so. I turn therefore to examine more closely the relevant features of the present case. *f*

These features can, I think, be conveniently summarised as follows: (a) The ship, which is a VLCC[1], if sold for dollars, is expected to fetch between $20 million and $30 million. (b) The plaintiff's claim against the ship, arising out of mortgage transactions in dollars, is for at least $14 million. (c) Hambros Bank Ltd intend to bring a claim against the ship, also arising out of mortgage transactions in dollars, for about $11½ million. (d) National Westminster Bank Ltd may bring a further claim against *g* the ship[2], arising out of mortgage transactions largely in sterling, for over £10 million. (e) Hambros Bank Ltd are first and second mortgagees, the plaintiffs are third, fourth and fifth mortgagees, and National Westminster Bank Ltd are sixth mortgagees, and their claims rank for priority accordingly. (f) The defendant company, Court Line Ltd, is in compulsory liquidation. It is unlikely to defend the claim of Hambros Bank Ltd at all, or that of the plaintiffs to any great extent. (g) Hambros Bank Ltd and the *h* defendant company by its liquidator consent to the plaintiffs' applications, and National Westminster Bank Ltd do not object to them.

I stated earlier the three principal matters put forward by the plaintiffs in support of their applications. The third matter was that they were entitled, if their claim succeeded, to a judgment in dollars, and I said that they relied in that connection on the recent decision of the Court of Appeal in *Schorsch Meier GmbH v Hennin*[2]. It is *j* now necessary to say something about that decision, which presents certain difficulties.

The claim in that case was by a West German motor manufacturer against an

---

1   I e a very large crude carrier
2   Page 152, ante, [1974] 3 WLR 823

English motor dealer for the price of goods sold and delivered. By the terms of the
a contract of sale the price was payable in West German marks. The plaintiff brought
his action in the West London County Court and asked for a judgment in marks. The
county court judge, while willing to give the plaintiff a judgment in sterling, refused to
do so in marks, on the ground that it was an established rule of English law that an
English court could only give judgment for the payment of money in sterling. The
plaintiff appealed to the Court of Appeal, which reversed the decision and gave the
b plaintiff an order for the payment of money in marks.

The Court of Appeal based its decision on two grounds. The first ground, as to
which the court was unanimous, was that the rule of English law followed by the
county court judge had been abrogated, as between nationals of member states of the
European Community, by art 106 of the Treaty of Rome, to which domestic effect
had been given in the United Kingdom by the European Communities Act 1972.
c The second ground, as to which one member of the court dissented, was that, as a
consequence of the rule having been abrogated by statute in the European field, it
should be regarded as abrogated also in all other fields.

The second part of this decision, if followed, would entitle the plaintiffs in the
present action, and also Hambros Bank Ltd in their intended action, to judgments in
dollars. In a still more recent case, however, *Miliangos v George Frank (Textiles) Ltd*[1],
d Bristow J declined to follow the second part of the Court of Appeal's decision on the
ground that it was given without that court hearing argument on the other side and
was inconsistent with earlier binding decisions of the Court of Appeal and the House
of Lords, in particular *Manners v Pearson & Son*[2] and *Re United Railways of the Havana
and Regla Warehouses Ltd*[3]

I do not think that it is necessary, on these interlocutory applications relating to
e what are procedural matters only, to decide whether it is the duty of this court, when
it comes to apply the substantive law, to follow the majority decision of the Court of
Appeal in *Schorsch Meier GmbH v Hennin*[4], or to decline to follow it for the reasons
given by Bristow J in *Miliangos v George Frank (Textiles) Ltd*[1]. It may be that the solution
to the problem will by then have been supplied by another decision of the Court of
Appeal or by a decision of the House of Lords.

f   It is, in my view, sufficient to say that, having regard to the majority decision of the
Court of Appeal, which is prima facie binding on this court, the plaintiffs have at least
an arguable case that they and Hambros Bank Ltd will be entitled, if their claims
succeed, to judgments in dollars, and I approach the question how I should exercise
my discretion on the plaintiffs' present applications on that basis.

Proceeding on that basis, and assuming that the arguable case to which I have referred
g succeeds, the two judgments in dollars, which the plaintiffs and Hambros Bank Ltd
would on that assumption obtain, might well equal or exceed the amount of the
fund created by the sale of the ship. In these circumstances it seems to me that there
are good reasons of a practical nature for ordering that, if a sale is made in dollars,
the proceeds should be paid into court without conversion and placed to a dollar
deposit account out of which judgments in dollars, if given, can be satisfied directly.
h These reasons, which would exist in any case, are reinforced by the risk of depreciation of sterling in relation to dollars during the period for which the fund is likely to
remain in court. Had the recent decision of the Court of Appeal not been given,
however, so that the plaintiffs and Hambros Bank Ltd had no arguable case that they
were entitled to judgments in dollars, I am not sure whether the mere facts (a) that the
transactions sued on were dollar transactions and (b) that the risk of depreciation
j   which I have mentioned existed, would by themselves justify the making of a special

1   (4th December 1974) unreported
2   [1898] 1 Ch 581, [1895-9] All ER Rep 415
3   [1960] 2 All ER 332, [1961] AC 1007
4   Page 152 ante, [1974] 3 WLR 823

order that the fund, if created in dollars, should be paid into court without conversion
and placed to a dollar deposit account, although I think that they might possibly do   *a*
so. It is not necessary, however, in the situation which exists, to express a concluded
view on that question, and I shall not therefore do so.

For the reasons which I have given I shall, in principle, accede to the plaintiffs'
applications. I have already made a declaration with regard to the Admiralty marshal
being permitted to sell for a price in dollars, and I should like to hear counsel on the
precise form of the further order now to be made.   *b*

Order accordingly.

Solicitors. *Linklaters & Paines* (for the plaintiffs); *Norton, Rose, Botterell & Roche* (for
Hambros Bank Ltd); *Treasury Solicitor.*
                                                                                         c

N P Metcalfe Esq Barrister.

R v Davies   *d*

COURT OF APPEAL, CRIMINAL DIVISION
LORD WIDGERY CJ, SCARMAN LJ AND ASHWORTH J
16th, 17th JANUARY 1975
                                                                                         e
*Criminal law – Murder – Provocation – Acts amounting to provocation – Acts of person
other than victim – Whether acts of other person capable of amounting to provocation –
Homicide Act 1957, s 3.*

The appellant married in 1970. The marriage was happy until the wife met S in 1972
and began to associate with him. The appellant was extremely resentful and   *f*
jealous. On one occasion he displayed a gun to his wife and threatened to kill S. The
wife left the matrimonial home shortly afterwards and went to stay first with her
parents and then with different friends. The appellant continued to threaten his wife
on various occasions with firearms. In January 1973 the appellant went to look for his
wife. He had a shotgun with him. In the course of his search he saw S walking towards
the library where the wife worked. He followed S, carrying the gun. The wife came   *g*
out of the library and the appellant went up to her, called her name and shot her.
He was charged with murder and at his trial raised the defence of provocation. The
judge directed the jury that provocation was an act or series of acts done by the victim,
or words uttered by her, to the appellant which would have caused in a reasonable
person, and actually caused in the appellant, 'a sudden and temporary loss of self-
control rendering the [appellant] so subject to passion as to make him for the moment *h*
not master of his mind'. He further left the question of provocation to the jury on the
footing that they could review the whole course of the wife's conduct through the
year 1972 and decide whether the appellant had been provoked to kill her. The
appellant was convicted of murder and appealed on the ground that the judge had
misdirected the jury in that he had in effect excluded from their consideration the
question whether S's conduct constituted provocation.   *j*

Held – Following the enactment of s 3[a] of the Homicide Act 1957, which had laid
down a new test for provocation, the jury, in determining whether an accused had

---

a   Section 3 is set out at p 895 *j* to p 896 *a*, post

a been provoked, were entitled to consider whether acts or words emanating from a person other than the victim had been such as to provoke a reasonable man to do as the appellant had done. It followed that there had been a technical misdirection by the judge. The matter had, however, been left to the jury in such a way that they could not have failed to have taken the actions of S into account. Accordingly there had been no miscarriage of justice and the appeal would be dismissed under the proviso to s 2 of the Criminal Appeal Act 1968 (see p 896 *g* and *h* and p 897 *c* to *j*, post).

b

Notes

For provocation see 10 Halsbury's Laws (3rd Edn) 710-713, paras 1362, 1363, and for cases on the subject, see 15 Digest (Repl) 940-943, 9009-9042.

For the Homicide Act 1957, s 3, see 8 Halsbury's Statutes (3rd Edn) 461.

c
Cases referred to in judgment

R v Brown [1972] 2 All ER 1328, [1972] 2 QB 229, [1972] 3 WLR 11, 56 Cr App Rep 564, CA.

R v Duffy [1949] 1 All ER 932, CCA.

R v Roche (16th October 1972) unreported

d R v Simpson (1915) 84 LJKB 1893, [1914-15] All ER Rep 917, 114 LT 238, 25 Cox CC 269, 11 Cr App Rep 218, CCA, 15 Digest (Repl) 941, 9018.

R v Twine [1967] Crim LR 710.

Cases also cited

Parker v R [1964] 2 All ER 641, [1964] AC 1369, PC.

e Phillips v R (1969) 53 Cr App Rep 132, PC.

R v Hall (1928) 21 Cr App Rep 48.

Appeal

On 21st June 1973 the appellant, Peter John Brinley Davies, was convicted in the Crown Court at Maidstone before Caulfield J and a jury on charges of arson and murder. He *f* appealed against the conviction for murder. The facts are set out in the judgment of the court.

Donald Farquharson QC and *Anthony Wilcken* for the appellant.
Anthony McCowan QC and *Anthony Hidden* for the Crown.

g

LORD WIDGERY CJ delivered the judgment of the court. On 21st June 1973 at the Crown Court of Maidstone before Caulfield J and a jury this appellant was convicted on count 1 of arson and on count 2 of murder. He was sentenced to seven years' imprisonment in respect of the arson and life imprisonment in respect of the murder, and the only matter with which this present judgment is concerned is his *h* appeal against the conviction for murder.

The point is a short and interesting one. The appellant killed his wife by shooting in the presence of her lover. The only issue which raised itself in the court below was whether the charge should have been reduced to manslaughter on account of provocation. The contention of the appellant is that in directing the jury as to provocation the learned judge excluded provocation from any source other than from the victim, *j* that is to say other than the wife. The question for us is whether that exclusion was justified or not.

We do not propose to set out the history of the matter in any great detail because, although its general impact is important, the detail is not. Suffice it to say that the appellant and his wife were both at all material times in their early twenties and were employed at the public library at Rochester as librarians. They met in that way.

They married in August 1970 and for at least two years the marriage appears to have been a perfectly happy one.

However, in 1972 there came on the scene a man called Terry Stedman, who worked, as we understand, in the town clerk's department of the same local authority, and who met these two young people in that connection. Almost from the outset it seems clear that the wife was strongly attracted by Stedman and for a period during 1972 Stedman seems to have conducted a campaign of seduction of the wife to the extreme resentment, understandably, of the appellant.

As early as 4th October 1972 we find the appellant upset, jealous and showing his wife a gun, as he said, 'to frighten her'. We find at the same sort of time that he has threatened to the wife that he is going to kill Stedman, although in his evidence he said that was a bluff. For whatever reasons, those or others, Mrs Davies, the wife, left the matrimonial home some time in October, and after a number of stays elsewhere, she went to stay with her parents, who lived in Newbury.

The appellant went down to Newbury on 11th October and there was further by-play with a gun or guns, whether real or imitation perhaps does not matter unduly at that stage, and on 14th October the appellant went to the length of breaking into his father-in-law's house in the middle of the night, going into the bedroom where the wife was sleeping and displaying what was undoubtedly at that stage a real Browning pistol with ammunition and generally indicating that somebody's life was threatened; whether his, Stedman's or the wife's perhaps matters little at this stage.

The police were called following this incident. The appellant was taken into custody and charged with offences relating to his breaking-in and possession of the firearm. He was then bailed on condition that he did not molest his wife.

By 21st December, when the appellant was still on bail, he had been dismissed by the local authority as a result of these charges, and on the evening of 29th December he went to the house of some mutual friends of himself and his wife where at that time the wife was staying. He saw her going into the house with Stedman at about 11.10 pm and he saw Stedman leave at about 1.00 am. He had in his car at that time no less than 17 cans of petrol, and following the disappearance of Stedman at about 1.00 am he proceeded to spread the petrol round the house in which his wife was staying and then set fire to it. Fortunately no great damage was done, and indeed what he seems to have done is not so much set fire to the house as produce a ring of fire round the house; but it was a very frightening and disgraceful episode on any view.

The appellant made himself scarce after this incident, and we next find him in the Channel Islands on 23rd January 1973 where he bought a double-barrelled shotgun and 50 rounds of ammunition to suit it. His evidence was that at that time he wanted the shotgun for the purpose of killing himself, but the Crown, not surprisingly having regard to the evidence as a whole, contended that he bought the shotgun with a view to killing his wife and that this was all part of a premeditated attack which followed on 30th January.

On that day, 30th January, we find the appellant back in Rochester making a somewhat morbid tour of some of the addresses with which he and his wife had previously been concerned, and on the evening of 30th January one comes to the matters which are really vital in this case because it was on that evening that the killing occurred.

It will save time, and perhaps be more helpful, if I deal with the events of the evening of 30th January by reference to the evidence which was given by the appellant at the trial, when he was asked about his movements. Counsel examining him said:

'Q. And where did you go then? A. Watts Avenue.
'Q. Why did you go there? A. My wife had stayed there when she first came to Rochester. I just wanted to think as well. I did not want to shoot myself.
'Q. At this point in time, where was the shotgun? A. On the back seat of the car.
'Q. Was it assembled? A. Yes.

'*Q.* It was, as it were, ready for use? *A.* It was not loaded, but it had only to be
loaded.

'*Q.* What if anything did you want to do in connection with your wife? *A.* Well
all the time I was coming there I wanted to see her.

'*Q.* It might be suggested, I do not know, that you had come to Rochester with
a gun in order to kill your wife? *A.* No, I came to see my wife. I would have
killed myself if I had seen her and she had just not wanted anything to do with
me, but as I say, when I sat in Watts Avenue I began to lose my nerve to do it.

'*Q.* And where did you go from Watts Avenue? *A.* I drove into St. Margaret's
Street, which goes down past the Cathedral to the traffic lights. I intended then
to go to my brother Roger's [I pause there to stress that phrase because the story
being told was that he was not proposing at that stage to go and find his wife,
but rather to go to his brother Roger's house], but I did not know what he could
do for me, but I was just in a position where I could not do anything for myself
any more. When I came to the traffic lights I turned left towards Rochester
Bridge. As I came round that corner, I saw Terry Stedman.

'*Q.* Is that the corner near the library? *A.* Yes.

'*Q.* You came along in the car and you saw Mr. Stedman; in what direction was
he going? *A.* He was rounding the corner, there is a public house there.

'*Q.* About how far was he from the library? *A.* 30 yards, I am not sure how far
it is.

'*Q.* Was he going in the direction of the library, or away from it? *A.* He was
going to the library. He was carrying a briefcase, wearing an overcoat, he looked
worried for some reason, I do not know why.

'*Q.* What effect had it, if any, on you? *A.* It made me angry.

'*Q.* In what way? *A.* It all welled up in me somehow. I knew I had to go round
there and confront them or something, do something about it.

'*Q.* What was it in your mind that Stedman was going to do? *A.* Meet my wife.

'*Q.* And what did you do? *A.* I drove along the High Street, turned into Corporation Street, which would bring me to the library car park.

'*Q.* And did you drive into the library car park? *A.* Yes.

'*Q.* Did you get out of the car? *A.* Yes.

'*Q.* Did you have anything with you? *A.* Yes, I took the gun with me.

'*Q.* Why did you take the gun? *A.* Because it had to be something final. It had
to be something decisive, whether it was my own death, I do not know, I know it
was a reckless situation. I was angry, I was feeling sick, shaking, it is hard to put
into words how I was feeling, but everything that had happened over the last
few months just came up inside me.

'*Q.* And where did you go then? *A.* I got out of the car, I walked towards the
library, across the grass. The lights were on in both the offices.

'*Q.* It would have been evening time, and it had been dark for some hours?
A. An hour or two, yes.

'*Q.* And as you came up towards the office, what happened? *A.* I saw Jennifer
[the wife] go into the chief librarian's office, Mr Marsh's office, walk through the
adjoining door into the secretary's office, and as she came through, I went to
meet her. She stepped outside the door.

'*Q.* At that stage, how were you holding the gun? *A.* Like that [demonstrating].

'*Q.* What, if anything, was your intention to do with the gun? *A.* I did not know
what my intention was then.

'*Q.* I want you now to tell the jury what happened, if you can, without any
interruption from me. Tell your recollection of what happened? *A.* I stepped from
the grass to meet Jennifer as she came through the door, she was outside the door
pulling it to, and I spoke to her. I said, "Jennifer", and she was obviously surprised because I had come up behind her. She made some noises of surprise and,

then she said, "What", and she turned to look at me, to see who was there. She
recognised me, I suppose, then she saw the gun. She stepped backwards two or   *a*
three paces, and as she did so she said, "No, no", and then she gave a little scream,
and then I shot her. I saw a black mark here [indicating], just below the right
breast. She seemed to be thrown backwards and upwards against the desk that
was behind her, and then she just slithered down on to the floor lying on her back,
and then she started to moan seemingly as she breathed.

    'Q. Why did you shoot her? A. Why?   *b*

    'Q. Yes. A. At the time, I suppose to kill her.'

    The judge, when directing the jury on the issue of provocation, adopted the classic
formula deriving from Devlin J in *R v Duffy*[1], a formula which to the knowledge of
every member of this court has been quoted in virtually every provocation case since   *c*
that date. The judge referred to Devlin J's formula in a number of places, but perhaps
the most convenient is where he said this:

    'Provocation is some act or series of acts done, applying it to this case, by the
    dead woman to the accused, or words uttered by the dead woman to the accused,
    or both acts and words, which would cause in any reasonable person, and actually   *d*
    causes in the accused a sudden and temporary loss of self control rendering the
    accused so subject to passion as to make him for the moment not master of his
    mind.'

    It is to be observed in that direction that the judge is restricting the provocative
conduct to the acts or deeds of the dead woman, and by implication he is excluding   *e*
from the eligible provocative conduct anything done or said by Stedman. It is, as I
have already said, at this point that he is alleged to have erred.

    It is very difficult to understand why the judge made his direction in that form
unless in fact the case was being run by the defence on the footing that only the acts
of the wife were relevant for present purposes.

    Counsel whose assistance we have had for the appellant today was not in the court   *f*
below and obviously cannot help in that regard. Counsel for the Crown and his
junior, who were in the court below, are handicapped by the lapse of time and also
by the destruction of their notebooks, but they have the recollection that the defence
were running this case on the footing that it was only the conduct of the wife which had
to be considered on this issue. We make that observation because it is very strange
that a judge of experience should give a direction as he did, three or four times in the   *g*
course of his summing-up, and that if he had wrongly understood the line which
was being taken by the defence that he should not at least have been corrected at
some stage.

    In particular, the jury came back with a question about provocation which was
answered in similar terms to those which I have already read out, and at that stage
one would have thought that if the judge had misunderstood the way in which the   *h*
case was being put, he would have been corrected. In fact he was not, and one is left
with the view that the overwhelming probability is that the direction which he gave
was consistent with the way in which the case had been run by the defence. However
that does not necessarily end the matter and I must return to it later.

    One must now consider the arguments which have been put forward on the correct-
ness or otherwise of that direction. There is some authority for the proposition that   *j*
before the Homicide Act 1957 acts could not amount to provocation for present purposes unless they were done by the deceased. The earliest case in which reference is

---

1   [1949] 1 All ER 932

a made to that is *R v Simpson*[1]. We do not find it necessary to refer to the detail of the case at all and refer to it merely for a passage in the judgment of Lord Reading CJ. There he said[2]:

> 'No authority has been cited to support the proposition that provocation by one person, followed by the homicide by the person provoked of another person, is sufficient to reduce such homicide to manslaughter. There is no such authority.'

b It is perhaps not surprising that there is such a dearth of authority on this point because in the very nature of things the likelihood is that the person provoked will turn on his provoker, and therefore in most instances one does find that the provocation comes from the person who is killed. But that is the observation of Lord Reading CJ, so far as it takes the matter, in *R v Simpson*[1].

Much more recently we have the view of Lawton J in *R v Twine*[3]. That was a case *c* decided in 1967 after the Homicide Act 1957. But Lawton J is recorded as having expressed the view that until the Homicide Act 1957 the defendant could only rely on conduct as opposed to words, and furthermore that at common law provocation was some act or series of acts done by a man to the defendant which would cause in any reasonable person a loss of self-control. Thus Lawton J is clearly accepting that before the 1957 Act the provocation had to be supplied, as it were, by the victim in *d* order that it might be relevant at all.

The matter was again touched on in this court in an unreported decision, *R v Roche*[4]. The transcript has been provided by the registrar. Wien J, giving the judgment of the court, said:

> 'It is certain law that there are three elements involved in provocation where it is raised as an issue, firstly, that there was provocation whether by something said or done by the person killed, secondly, by provocation an accused person has lost his self-control, and thirdly, that the provocation was of such a nature that it could cause any reasonable person to lose his self-control in such circumstances.'

No reference was made to the 1957 Act, and no doubt Wien J was there stating what the court took to be the view of the common law, and it is to be observed that so far *f* as the report goes it supported the view that provocation had to come from the deceased and not from elsewhere.

Of the textbooks Smith and Hogan[5] comes out positively in support of the common law view to which I have referred. The learned authors say:

> 'Provocation, with the one exception discussed below, was, at common law, something done *by the dead man to the accused*.'

g It may not be necessary, indeed it is not strictly necessary in view of what follows in this judgment, for us to reach a concluded view on this point; but it is certainly our opinion that the statement in Smith and Hogan[5] is right and that at common law provocation was restricted to acts done by the victim.

But whatever the position before 1957, it has now to be considered in the light of *h* the Homicide Act of that year. It will be remembered that this was an Act making detailed amendments in the law relating to homicide. Section 3 deals with provocation in these terms:

> 'Where on a charge of murder there is evidence on which the jury can find that the person charged was provoked (whether by things done or by things said or by both together) to lose his self-control, the question whether the provocation was *j* enough to make a reasonable man do as he did shall be left to be determined by

---

1 (1915) 11 Cr App Rep 218, [1914-15] All ER Rep 917
2 11 Cr App Rep at 220, [1914-15] All ER Rep at 917, 918
3 [1967] Crim LR 710
4 (16th October 1972)
5 Criminal Law (3rd Edn, 1973), p 235

the jury; and in determining that question the jury shall take into account everything both done and said according to the effect which, in their opinion, *a* it would have on a reasonable man.'

There has been some debate in this case as to the extent to which that section amended the common law in regard to provocation. It seems tolerably clear that it makes two amendments at any rate. First of all it allows words as opposed to acts to be considered as provocative for present purposes, and secondly it seems to provide in the plainest terms that any reference to the reaction of a reasonable man to the *b* provocation supplied is something which must be determined by the jury and cannot be determined by the judge.

Does it go further than that? Counsel for the Crown submits, 'No'. He submits that there is nothing in the section which affects the common law rule that provocation has to come from the victim. This is a point which has arisen in this court before. It is to be observed that the reasonable man test, if one may so describe it, prescribed by *c* the section is quite different from the reasonable man test prescribed by Devlin J. In *R v Duffy*[1] in Devlin J's direction, both in regard to the particular accused and in regard to the hypothetical reasonable man, the question was whether the provocation did or would cause a loss of self-control which would prevent the individual from being the master of his mind.

Reading s 3 of the 1957 Act, it is quite apparent that a different test is applied *d* because there one has to consider whether a reasonable man would act as he did, that is to say would act as the accused had done. The explanation for that difference is in fact supplied by the earlier authority in this court, *R v Brown*[2]. I find it unnecessary to make detailed reference to the case, save to say that in that case this court accepted that the reasonable man test prescribed by the statute was a new test intended to reflect not only whether the reasonable man would lose his self-control, *e* but also whether the reasonable man would have retaliated in a similar way.

The relevance of that of course is that before 1957 there was a further and independent rule relating to the question of whether the reaction was reasonable having regard to the provocation. In *R v Brown*[2] it is decided that the effect of s 3 is to embrace as it were, both the question of loss of self-control and the question of reasonable retaliation in a single question to the jury, namely, whether a reasonable man would *f* do as the appellant did.

In view of that it seems quite clear to us that we should construe s 3 as providing a new test, and on that test that we should give the wide words of s 3 their ordinary wide meaning. Thus we come to the conclusion that whatever the position at common law, the situation since 1957 has been that acts or words otherwise to be treated as provocative for present purposes are not excluded from such consideration merely *g* because they emanate from someone other than the victim.

Accordingly, counsel for the appellant is entitled to say that there was on the evidence of his client material on which the court could have found that he had lost his self-control as a result of seeing Stedman approaching his wife in the manner which he had described in his evidence. That being so, one is driven to the view that there was at all events a technical misdirection by the learned judge in that his *h* direction to the jury, which I have already read, by implication excludes any conduct of Stedman as coming within the sphere of provocation.

What is the consequence of that? It has been suggested albeit somewhat faintly, that since it is quite clear that the judge's direction was consistent with the way in which the case was being run by the defence, that no miscarriage of justice has occurred. Counsel for the appellant counters that by stating the well-known principle *j* that it is for the judge to leave the proper issues to the jury, even if counsel fails to do so. We must accept, and do accept, that counsel in stating that principle is absolutely right.

---

1   [1949] 1 All ER 932
2   [1972] 2 All ER 1328, [1972] 2 QB 229

a We would like to add this however. It is of great assistance to the trial court, and indeed to the administration of justice, that counsel agree among themselves to eliminate unnecessary difficulties or to shorten the proceedings. Where the judge has been guilty of a misdirection which was itself inspired by the action of defence counsel it may be exceedingly difficult for anyone seeking to upset the conviction to say that a miscarriage of justice has occurred. The judge is to be encouraged to promote the efficiency in the administration of justice which the co-operation of counsel will *b* produce. Therefore although it cannot be said that his misdirection, if misdirection it be, is excluded merely because it was supported by counsel, it will follow that before a miscarriage of justice is found in such circumstances a strong case has to be made out.

What is the position here? The argument of counsel for the appellant I have already recited. Was there a miscarriage of justice in these circumstances arising out of the *c* form of the learned judge's direction? We think that there was not and the result in this case which we are going to reach is to dismiss the appeal by applying the proviso to s 2 of the Criminal Appeal Act 1968.

The reasons why we think it is a proper case for the proviso are these. The judge, again we understand at the request of defence counsel, left the question of provoca- tion to the jury on the footing that they could review the whole course of conduct of *d* the wife right through that turbulent year of 1972 and decide whether the appellant had been provoked to kill her within Devlin J's test. It has been pointed out rightly that that was really too generous a direction from the point of view of the appellant because in all cases of provocation the vital question in the end must hinge on the loss of self-control and the causes of that loss. The background is material to provocation as the setting in which the state of mind of the appellant must be adjudged.

e Because it was left in that way it was quite impossible, we think, for the jury to distinguish the separate actions of the wife from the actions of Stedman. The two were complementary one to the other. The provocative conduct is summed up by the fact that the wife was leaving the husband at Stedman's enticement, and we can regard the wife's conduct and Stedman's conduct for present purposes as being two sides of the same penny and inseparable one from the other.

f This is particularly illustrated when one comes to the final act outside the library on the night of 30th January. There you have the wife coming down the library steps to greet her lover. You have the lover approaching from the opposite side of the road to meet the wife. The jury have decided that the wife's conduct was not pro- vocative for present purposes, and we ask ourselves rhetorically how could any reason- able jury, which was satisfied that the wife's conduct was not provocative, find that the *g* conduct of Stedman could be provocative. It seems to us that such a conclusion would be quite impossible, and accordingly we have no hesitation in saying that the simple failure to regard Stedman's presence and movements on the night of 30th January as being matters which amounted to provocation could not have affected the jury in this case, or indeed have appeared to any reasonable jury as amounting to provocation. We have little doubt in the end that what the jury decided in this case *h* was that it was a premeditated killing and not a question of provocation at all.

For the reasons which I have already given the appeal will be dismissed and the conviction must stand, the proviso being applied. Our understanding is that on the conclusion being reached on the murder charge nothing further is sought to be submitted in regard to the charge of arson.

j *Appeal dismissed.*

Solicitors: *Kingsley, Napley & Co* (for the appellant); *Director of Public Prosecutions*

Jacqueline Charles Barrister.

Payne-Collins v Taylor Woodrow Construction Ltd

QUEEN'S BENCH DIVISION

O'CONNOR J

15th NOVEMBER 1974

Fatal accident – Person for whose benefit action may be brought – Relations of deceased – Wife or husband – Divorce – Wife divorced from deceased – Whether divorced wife a person for whose benefit action may be brought – Fatal Accidents Act 1846, s 2.

The words 'wife' and 'husband' in s 2^a of the Fatal Accidents Act 1846 mean a person to whom the deceased was married at the time of his or her death. Accordingly a divorced wife of the deceased is not a person for whose benefit an action can be brought under the Fatal Accidents Acts 1846 to 1959.

Notes

For the persons for whose benefit an action may be brought under the Fatal Accidents Acts, see 23 Halsbury's Laws (3rd Edn) 37, 38, para 32, and for cases on the subject, see 36 Digest (Repl) 208, 209, *1098-1105*.

For the Fatal Accidents Act 1846, s 2, see 23 Halsbury's Statutes (3rd Edn) 781.

Case cited in judgment

Dickinson v North Eastern Railway Co (1863) 2 H & C 735, 3 New Rep 130, 33 LJEx 91, 9 LT 299, 159 ER 304, 36 Digest (Repl) 209, *1103*.

Interlocutory appeal

By a writ issued on 12th October 1973, Brenda Payne-Collins ('the widow'), the widow and administratrix of the estate of Robert Henry Payne-Collins deceased, brought an action against the defendants, Taylor Woodrow Construction Ltd, claiming, as administratrix of the deceased's estate, damages under the Law Reform (Miscellaneous Provisions) Act 1934 on behalf of the estate and under the Fatal Accidents Acts 1846 to 1959 on behalf of herself and Marion Anne, Susan Lane and Daryl Robert, the deceased's three children by an earlier marriage to Dorothy Payne-Collins ('the divorced wife') which had been dissolved by a decree absolute in October 1967. The widow alleged that on 3rd July 1971 the deceased had sustained personal injuries from which he had subsequently died, in consequence of the defendants' breaches of regs 10(1)(a), 11(2)(4)(5) and 29 of the Construction (Lifting Operations) Regulations 1961[1], of regs 6 and 7 of the Construction (Working Places) Regulations 1966[2] and/or the negligence of the defendants in and about their employment of the deceased at a site at Seaton Carew, Co Durham. On 27th June 1974 Master Warren in Chambers ordered that an issue be tried without pleadings between the divorced wife as plaintiff and the widow as defendant to decide, inter alia, whether at the date of the deceased's death the divorced wife was his dependant; and that the issue be tried at or after the trial of the action between the widow and the defendants as the trial judge might direct. The widow appealed against that order. The appeal was heard in chambers but judgment was given in open court.

Leslie Joseph for the widow.
Peter Duckworth for the divorced wife.
Hugh Carlisle for the defendants.

---

a Section 2, so far as material, is set out at p 899 *d*, post
1 SI 1961 No 1581
2 SI 1966 No 94

a **O'CONNOR J.** This is an appeal from an order of Master Warren made in chambers; and I have adjourned the judgment into open court as a matter of principle has been raised in it.

In this action the plaintiff, as a widow and administratrix of the estate of Robert Henry Payne-Collins, claims damages under the Fatal Accidents Acts 1846-1959 from the defendants. In the statement of claim she appears as a dependant, as do three *b* children of the deceased. They were in fact children of the deceased by a previous marriage. The deceased had been married to another lady, Dorothy Payne-Collins ('the divorced wife'), the marriage having started in May 1953 and the decree absolute of divorce being made in October 1967; and she had the custody of the three children, who are named as dependants in the statement of claim. She was also entitled to money under a magistrates' court order, and it is unnecessary to enquire as to how far *c* that order had been complied with. In due course she took out a summons effectively asking that she should be joined as a dependant in the Fatal Accidents Acts action commenced by the plaintiff. Section 2 of the Fatal Accidents Act 1846 defines the persons for whose benefit the action can be brought:

d   '. . . every such action shall be for the benefit of the wife, husband, parent, and child of the person whose death shall have been so caused . . .'

And by s 5 of the 1846 Act, which is the construction section, apart from the normal matters of masculine gender denoting feminine gender and the singular the plural, the word 'parent' shall include father, mother, grandfather and grandmother, and the word 'child' shall include son, daughter, grandson and granddaughter. There is no *e* mention of any relationship which may exist for a divorced wife.

As early as 1863, in *Dickinson v North Eastern Railway Co*[1], the court decided that a bastard is not a 'child' within s 2 of the 1846 Act. That matter was put right by the Law Reform (Miscellaneous Provisions) Act 1934, s 2(1) of which in its unamended form declared:

f   '. . . a person shall be deemed to be the parent or child of the deceased person notwithstanding that he was only related to him illegitimately or in consequence of adoption . . .'

In 1959, the Fatal Accidents Act 1846 was further amended extending the classes of dependants, and s 1 of the Fatal Accidents Act 1959 reads:

g

     'The persons for whose benefit or by whom an action may be brought under the Fatal Accidents Act, 1846, shall include any person who is, or is the issue of, a brother, sister, uncle or aunt of the deceased person.'

h And then there are provisions for deducing any relationship for the purposes of the Act of an adopted person.

Once again Parliament has made no provision for including a divorced husband or wife as a person for whose benefit the action can be brought. The master ordered that the issue should be tried at or immediately after the trial of the main action. In my judgment that is in error, because it is quite plain, on the law as it stands at the *j* moment, that the divorced wife of the deceased is not a person for whose benefit this action can be brought and, therefore, she is not entitled to be included as a dependant whose damage falls to be assessed.

---

1 (1863) 2 H & C 735

There was, in addition, a suggestion that there are two other children by another
woman who has not sought to appear. Nothing is known about them, and, in my *a*
judgment, there are no grounds whatever for including any further dependants in
this action The appeal will accordingly be allowed.

Appeal allowed.

Solicitors: *W H Thompson*, Stanmore (for the widow); *T E Rudling & Co*, Thetford (for *b*
the divorced wife); *Blount, Petre & Co* (for the defendants).

E H Hunter Esq Barrister.

c

R v Bracknell Justices, ex parte Griffiths

Affirmed sub nom R v BRACKNELL
J.J, EX PARTE GRIFFITHS HL [1975]
QUEEN'S BENCH DIVISION   2 All ER 881

LORD WIDGERY CJ, MELFORD STEVENSON AND WATKINS JJ   *d*

19th, 20th DECEMBER 1974, 16th JANUARY 1975

*Mental health – Protection in respect of acts done in pursuance of statute – Civil or criminal
proceedings – Leave – Requirement of leave to bring proceedings – Patient in hospital – Act of
nurse exercising duty of controlling patients – Act of nurse in exercise of duty not expressly
provided for in statute – Patient alleging assault by nurse – Whether alleged assault done or* *e*
*purportedly done 'in pursuance of' statute – Whether leave required to bring criminal
proceedings – Mental Health Act 1959, s 141(1)(2).*

The applicant was a male nurse in the special hospital at Broadmoor. P was a patient
in the hospital, having been committed there under s 72 of the Mental Health Act 1959, *f*
following a life sentence imposed on him for murder. P preferred an information
against the applicant alleging that he had assaulted P, contrary to s 42 of the Offences
against the Person Act 1861. According to P's evidence his family had been visiting
him at the hospital; when the time came for visitors to go the applicant had approached
him and having said, 'Come on you', had punched him on the shoulder. The applicant
was convicted by the justices and given a conditional discharge. He applied for an order *g*
of certiorari, contending that the alleged assault was an act purportedly done 'in pursuance of' the 1959 Act, within s 141(1)[a] of that Act and that accordingly the conviction
was a nullity in that the prosecution had been brought without leave of the High
Court as required by s 141(2).

Held – Section 141 was not limited to acts done, or purported to be done, in pursuance *h*
of functions specifically provided for in the terms of the 1959 Act itself. Accordingly
where a male nurse was on duty and exercising his functions of controlling the patients
in the hospital, acts done, or purportedly done, in pursuance of such control, were
acts within the scope of s 141. It followed, therefore, that in the absence of leave under
s 141(2) the conviction was a nullity and the application would be granted (see p 903
b to g, post).   *j*

Per Curiam. Where an information is laid before a magistrate against a member of
the staff of a special hospital and it appears on its face to be in order, the magistrate is
not bound to raise the issue of s 141 of the 1959 Act, although it would be sensible and

---

a   Section 141, so far as material, is set out at p 901 *j* to p 902 *c*, post *a* instructive for the magistrate to draw the informant's attention to that section (see p 903 *h* to p 904 *a*, post).

Notes

For the protection of persons purporting to act under the Mental Health Act 1959, and the necessity for the leave of the High Court before any proceedings against them may be taken, see 29 Halsbury's Laws (3rd Edn) 435, 436, para 847.

b For the Mental Health Act 1959, s 141, see 25 Halsbury's Statutes (3rd Edn) 160.

Cases cited

Attorney-General v Times Newspapers Ltd [1973] 3 All ER 54, [1974] AC 273, HL.
R v Quick [1973] 3 All ER 347, [1973] QB 910, CA.

c
Application

This was an application by Elvet Griffiths for an order of certiorari to bring up and quash a decision of the Bracknell justices sitting at Bracknell on 19th November 1974 whereby they convicted the applicant of an assault, contrary to s 42 of the Offences Against the Person Act 1861, on Alan Roy Pountney, a patient in a hospital committed
d under s 72 of the Mental Health Act 1959 following a life sentence for murder. The facts are set out in the judgment of the court.

Gordon Slynn QC and *Peter Slot* for the applicant.
Louis Blom-Cooper QC and *Alan Newman* for the respondent.
Harry Woolf as amicus curiae.

e
Cur adv vult

16th January. **LORD WIDGERY CJ** read the following judgment of the court. In these proceedings counsel moves on behalf of one Elvet Griffiths for an order of certiorari to bring up into this court for the purposes of its being quashed an order
f made by the Bracknell magistrates sitting at Bracknell on 19th November 1974 whereby they determined that the applicant should be given a conditional discharge for two years following his conviction on an information that the applicant had assaulted one Alan Roy Pountney, contrary to s 42 of the Offences against the Person Act 1861. The alleged offence occurred on 24th May 1974, at which time the applicant was a male nurse in the special hospital at Broadmoor, and Pountney was a patient in
g the hospital having been committed there under s 72 of the Mental Health Act 1959, following a life sentence imposed on him for murder.

On the day in question visitors were admitted to the hospital, and at 4.00 p m the time came for the visitors to withdraw and for the patients to return to their quarters. According to Pountney he was saying goodbye to his family when the applicant approached him and said: 'Come on you.' Pountney then says that he received a
h punch on the shoulder, which nearly caused him to lose his balance, and when he looked round the applicant said: 'I'm talking to you.' Pountney says that he was very much upset by the incident, as were his family, and that he sought the advice of a solicitor with the result that a private prosecution was instituted. The effect of the prosecution has already been stated.

No one in the course of those proceedings below referred to s 141 of the Mental
j Health Act 1959, and the question before us is concerned solely with the effect of that section on the events which I have outlined. The section provides as follows:

'(1) No person shall be liable, whether on the ground of want of jurisdiction or on any other ground, to any civil or criminal proceedings to which he would have been liable apart from this section in respect of any act purporting to be done in

pursuance of this Act or any regulations or rules thereunder, or in pursuance of
anything done in, the discharge of functions conferred by any other enactment on   *a*
the authority having jurisdiction under Part VIII of this Act, unless the act was
done in bad faith or without reasonable care.

'(2) No civil or criminal proceedings shall be brought against any person in any
court in respect of any such act without the leave of the High Court, and the High
Court shall not give leave under this section unless satisfied that there is substantial ground for the contention that the person to be proceeded against has   *b*
acted in bad faith or without reasonable care.

'(3) This section does not apply to proceedings for an offence under this Act,
being proceedings which, under any provision of this Act, can be instituted only
by or with the consent of the Director of Public Prosecutions . . .'

Although, as I have said, no point was taken under this section in the course of the   *c*
hearing in the court below, it is now contended on behalf of the applicant that the
proceedings brought against him were criminal proceedings in respect of an act
purporting to be done in pursuance of the 1959 Act. It is common ground that the
consent of the High Court was not obtained to the institution of the proceedings, and
it is further common ground that if such permission was necessary in the circumstances
of this case the proceedings below were a nullity and the order can be quashed. The   *d*
sole question therefore is whether these proceedings came within the ambit of s 141(1)
so as to make the leave of the High Court necessary.

In its long title the Mental Health Act 1959 is described thus:

'An Act to repeal the Lunacy and Mental Treatment Acts, 1890 to 1930, and the
Mental Deficiency Acts, 1913 to 1938, and to make fresh provision with respect to   *e*
the treatment and care of mentally disordered persons and with respect to their
property and affairs; and for purposes connected with the matters aforesaid'.

The Act contains no less than 154 sections and includes comprehensive and often
novel provisions as to the circumstances in which mental patients can be detained, and
the establishments in which they will be detained. There is no doubt that the respon-   *f*
dent was detained in Broadmoor in the sense that he was not there of his own volition,
and it is further clear from the Act as a whole that when patients are so detained the
object of their detention is that they shall receive treatment for their particular
mental disability. Although the Act deals comprehensively with the circumstances in
which and the method by which an effective detention order can be made, and deals
in some detail with the management and control of the patient's property, it does not,   *g*
perhaps understandably, deal specifically with the powers of nurses in the hospital, or
the detailed control of the patients who are inmates for the time being. There can,
however, in my judgment be no doubt that the conception of detention and treatment
necessarily implies that the staff at the hospital, including the male nurses, can, and
on occasion must, use reasonable force in order to ensure that control is exercised over
the patients. The first and substantial issue in this case is whether a nurse exercising   *h*
control in this manner is doing an act, or purporting to do an act, 'in pursuance of' the
1959 Act.

The contention of counsel on behalf of Pountney is that the protection afforded by
s 141 is limited to acts done or purported to be done in pursuance of functions specifically provided for in the terms of the Act itself. Thus he says that s 141 protects those
who sign certificates or make orders for detention and those who dispose of the   *j*
patient's property. He contends however that when due regard is had to the necessity
of keeping the courts open to all citizens as far as possible, the true construction of s 141
excludes the day-to-day domestic affairs of the hospital, and the actions of persons
such as the male nurses who are carrying out their functions in the course of their
duty.

Counsel for the applicant contends for a wider construction of the section. He
a submits that when a male nurse is carrying out his duties as such in the hospital, the
acts which he does are either acts done, or at least purported to be done, in pursuance
of the Act so as to bring them within the protection of s 141. He rightly says that this
is a point of great importance because in the very nature of things patients in mental
hospitals frequently make unfounded charges against the staff who control them, and
he submits that in s 141 Parliament was giving the controlling staff in the hospital the
b necessary protection from legal proceedings which the requirement of consent of the
High Court implies.

On this fundamental question I prefer the argument of counsel for the applicant.
In my judgment where a male nurse is on duty and exercising his functions of controlling the patients in the hospital, acts done in pursuance of such control, or purportedly in pursuance of such control, are acts within the scope of s 141, and are thus
c protected by the section. If one considers this principle in relation to an alleged
assault by a nurse on a patient, three possible situations arise. First, if the truth of the
matter is that the nurse used no more force than was reasonably necessary to exercise
control, no criminal offence is committed at all. No question here arises of the nurse
having done any act for which the nurse would have been liable to criminal proceedings apart from s 141. The second possible situation is that whilst purportedly
d exercising control over the patient the nurse uses more force than was reasonably
necessary. Apart from s 141 the nurse would be civilly and possibly criminally responsible in respect of the use of such excessive force. However, since this would be an act
purportedly done in pursuance of the 1959 Act, the nurse would have a defence under
s 141, and would also have the protection of the necessity for the leave of the High
Court before the proceedings were begun. The third possibility is that the alleged
e assault was committed at a time when the male nurse was not on duty, or in circumstances in which the act could clearly not be justified as an act of control within the
terms of the nurse's duty. For example, if a nurse lay in wait for a patient in order to
have revenge for some supposed grievance, and made an attack on the patient which
could in no sense be said to be an act done in the course of his control as a nurse, then
it would seem to me that the offence would not be one protected by s 141(1) and that
f no question of the leave of the court would arise.

Applying these principles to the facts of this case, it seems to me that the nurse was
entitled to the protection of the section. He was exercising his functions to control the
patients when he was calling on them to say goodbye to their families and make their
way back to their quarters. His defence to the charge was that he had not struck the
patient but had merely put out his arm to separate the patient from his family, there
g being some reluctance on his part to leave his family. On any view the incident
happened when the nurse was on duty and when he was purportedly exercising his
functions as a nurse. Accordingly, he could claim the protection of the section and
since the leave of the High Court was not obtained the proceedings were a nullity.

That is sufficient to dispose of this case, but since there has been reference in
argument to some of the practical difficulties which may arise under s 141, it may be
h helpful if I express some views on these matters.

When an information is laid by a private prosecutor it is of course the function of the
magistrate who considers the information, and who is asked to issue a summons, to see
whether on the face of it the matter comes within the jurisdiction of his court. If the
information on its face is within the jurisdiction of the court, and in other respects it is a
case in which a summons would be issued, the magistrate should proceed with the
j issue of the summons. The mere fact that he recognises that the informant is a patient
at a hospital, and that the intended respondent is a member of the staff, is not in
itself a matter which puts the magistrate on enquiry as to whether leave has been
granted under s 141. It would be sensible and constructive for the magistrate to draw
the attention of the informant to s 141 if it appears that it may be relevant, but I
would not put the obligation of the magistrate higher than that. In short, he looks at

the information before him, and if it appears to be a matter in which his court has jurisdiction, and the information is in other respects satisfactory, he ought to issue the *a* summons, and leave the respondent to raise the issue of s 141 at the hearing if he chooses to do so.

If the respondent raises the objection to jurisdiction provided by the section, the magistrates may or may not at that stage be in a position to decide whether the act complained of was or was not done in pursuance of the 1959 Act in accordance with the principles which I have tried to lay down. It is however always within the juris- *b* diction of justices to enquire whether they have jurisdiction to try the case before them, and in circumstances such as these the justices ought to continue the hearing despite the objection until they have reached the stage at which the facts are sufficiently clear for them to reach a conclusion on this point. If at that point they decide that the section does not apply, they will complete the hearing and the matter can be tested if necessary by way of appeal. If, on the other hand, the justices conclude that the *c* section does apply, and that the proceedings before them cannot continue, they will discontinue the proceedings accordingly and leave the disappointed prosecutor to move for mandamus if so advised.

So far as the present proceedings are concerned, however, the absence of the consent of the High Court rendered the proceedings below a nullity, and, in my opinion, certiorari should go to quash the decision. *d*

Application allowed.

3rd February 1975. Their Lordships certified the following point of law to be of general public importance and gave leave to appeal to the House of Lords: 'Whether *e* an alleged criminal assault by a nurse on duty and in the course of exercising functions of controlling a patient in a mental hospital, established under the National Health Service Reorganisation Act 1973, may be an Act purporting to be done in pursuance of the Mental Health Act 1959 so as to attract the provisions of s 141 of that Act.'

Solicitors: *Victor Mishcon & Co* (for the applicant); *Brain & Brain*, Reading (for the *f* respondent); *The Solicitor, Department of Health and Social Security* (for the amicus curiae).

Jacqueline Charles Barrister.

a

R v Richardson (John)

COURT OF APPEAL, CRIMINAL DIVISION
JAMES, ORMROD LJJ AND PARK J
9th, 10th DECEMBER 1974

Overruled in METROPOLITAN POLICE
COMR v CURRAN [1976] 1 All ER 162

Not followed in R v CURRAN [1975]
2 All ER 1045

b Road traffic – Driving with blood-alcohol proportion above prescribed limit – Evidence –
Failure to supply specimen – Specimen for laboratory test – Accused suspected of driving
vehicle involved in accident – Accused arrested following failure to supply specimen for breath
test – Accused alleging that he had not been driving at time of accident – Accused refusing to
supply specimen for laboratory test – Accused charged with failing to supply specimen without
reasonable excuse – Whether fact that there was reasonable cause to believe accused was
c driving sufficient to prove offence – Whether necessary to prove accused had in fact been
driving or attempting to drive – Road Traffic Act 1972, ss 8(2), 9(3).

The appellant was identified to a police officer as the driver of a motor vehicle which
had been involved in an accident. The officer suspected him of having alcohol in his
d body and required him to provide a specimen of breath for a breath test pursuant to
s 8(2)[a] of the Road Traffic Act 1972. The appellant failed to provide the specimen and
so was arrested pursuant to s 8(5). He was taken to the police station. There he refused
to provide a specimen of breath, urine or blood. Accordingly he was charged with
failing, without reasonable excuse, to provide such a specimen, contrary to s 9(3)[b] of
the 1972 Act. At the trial the appellant's defence was that he had not been the driver
of the motor vehicle in question at the time of the accident and had remained silent to
e shield the driver. The recorder ruled that where the Crown relied on s 8(2) as authorising an officer to require a specimen, an offence under s 9(3) did not depend on
whether the accused had been driving or attempting to drive at the time of the
accident but merely on whether the officer had had reasonable cause to believe that
he had been doing so. Accordingly he directed the jury that the question whether the
f appellant had been driving was irrelevant to their considerations. On that basis the
jury convicted the appellant. On appeal,

Held – Although the officer must have had reasonable cause to believe that the
appellant had been driving or attempting to drive at the time of the accident before
he could lawfully require him to provide a specimen under s 8(2), that was not suffi-
g cient for the purpose of a prosecution under s 9(3). In order to prove an offence under
s 9(3), the Crown had to establish that the appellant had been driving or attempting
to drive at the relevant time. Accordingly, the recorder's direction was wrong in law
and the appeal would be allowed (see p 909 c and e to h, post).

Notes
h For failure to provide specimen of blood or urine for laboratory test without reasonable excuse, see Supplement to 33 Halsbury's Laws (3rd Edn) para 1061A, 8.
For the Road Traffic Act 1972, ss 8, 9, see 42 Halsbury's Statutes (3rd Edn) 1651, 1655.

Case referred to in judgment
R v Downey [1970] RTR 257, CA.

j
Case also cited
R v Gortat & Pirof [1973] Crim LR 648.

---

a   Section 8(2), so far as material, is set out at p 907 g, post
b   Section 9(3) is set out at p 908 b, post

Appeal

On 10th April 1974 in the Crown Court at Bristol, before Mr Recorder Owen Thomas *a*
QC, the appellant, John Richardson, was convicted of failing to provide a specimen for
a laboratory test, contrary to s 9(3) of the Road Traffic Act 1972. The appellant was
fined £50, with three months' imprisonment in default, and disqualified from driving
for 12 months. He appealed against conviction and sentence. The facts are set out in
the judgment of the court.

b

R John Royce for the appellant.
Anthony Cox for the Crown.

Cur adv vult

10th December. **JAMES LJ** delivered the following judgment of the court. On 10th
April 1974 at the Crown Court Bristol, the appellant was convicted of failing to provide *c*
a specimen for a laboratory test, contrary to s 9(3) of the Road Traffic Act 1972. His
appeal against that conviction involves a question of law, but leave to appeal was in
fact given by the single judge.

At about 11.00 p m on 30th August 1973 a white Mercedes motor car, being driven
along Denmark Street in Bristol, collided with a parked vehicle. The Mercedes
stopped on its offside of the road in another street, Pipe Lane. The driver of another *d*
motor car, Mr Mayne, who heard the noise of the collision and followed the Mercedes
car, saw the appellant get out of that car from the front passenger side door on to the
road and walk away. He next saw the appellant standing in a recessed doorway. He
spoke to police officers who were nearby and identified the appellant as the person who
had got out of the Mercedes car.

The appellant made no answer to the police officer's questions. The police officers, *e*
from their observation of the appellant, suspected that he had alcohol in his body.
One of the officers told the appellant that he was suspected of having been the driver
of a motor vehicle when it was involved in an accident and of having alcohol in his
body, and required the appellant to provide a specimen of breath for a breath test.
The appellant did not provide the specimen and he was arrested. He was taken to a
police station. All the necessary prerequisites for the lawful requirement of a specimen *f*
to be provided for a laboratory test were satisfied. The appellant refused to provide a
specimen of breath, and urine or blood. The particulars of the offence on the indictment
as it was originally drafted, read as follows:

> 'On the 30th day of August 1973 in the City and County of Bristol, having
> driven a motor vehicle on a road, having been arrested under Section 8 sub- *g*
> section 4, of the Road Traffic Act 1972, and having been required at a Police
> Station by a constable to provide a specimen for a laboratory test, you did without
> reasonable excuse fail to provide such a specimen.'

During the course of the trial it became apparent that the appellant's defence was
that he had not been driving or attempting to drive the car at the time of the accident.
The Crown successfully applied for the particulars of the offence to be amended by *h*
striking out the words 'having driven a motor vehicle on a road' on the ground that it
was not an ingredient of the offence that the accused had in fact been driving and the
words were surplusage. As the defence objection to the amendment had been
overruled, a new trial was ordered.

On arraignment on the amended indictment, counsel for the appellant moved to
quash the indictment on the ground that it was defective in that an essential ingredient *j*
of the offence, namely that the accused had been driving or attempting to drive at the
time when the accident happened, was not alleged in the particulars of offence. The
motion to quash was refused. The recorder ruled that in a case in which the Crown
relied on s 8(2) as authorising an officer to require a specimen of breath, the question
whether the accused was in fact driving was irrelevant to an offence under s 9(3), the

issue being whether a police officer had reasonable cause to believe that the accused
a was driving or attempting to drive at the time of the collision.

The defence of the appellant was that a Mr Lowther was the driver of the Mercedes
at the time when the accident occurred. He had remained silent when questioned by
the police, in order to shield Mr Lowther. Mr Lowther had disappeared. The defence
did not contend that the appellant had a reasonable excuse for the failure to provide
a specimen. It appears that the Crown were prepared to concede that the assertion
b by a motorist in these circumstances that he had not been driving or attempting to
drive, could constitute a reasonable excuse if a jury found the fact to be that he was
not driving or attempting to drive at the relevant time. This view was not shared by
the defence, and as a 'reasonable excuse' was not advanced, this issue was not left to
the jury.

The recorder directed the jury in clear terms that the question whether in fact
c the appellant was driving or attempting to drive was irrelevant to their considerations and that the issue which they had to decide was whether Pc Lumsden had
reasonable cause to believe that the appellant was driving at the relevant time. On
this basis it was almost inevitable that the jury would convict. After the jury returned
the verdict, the recorder proceeded to decide himself the question of fact, was the
appellant driving or attempting to drive in the light of the evidence which he had
heard. He decided that the appellant was driving at the time of the accident and
d passed sentence on him on that basis.

Counsel for the appellant argues in support of the appeal that the indictment was
defective, and that the recorder ought to have quashed it. His main argument,
however, is that the direction of the recorder which removed from the jury the issue
whether the appellant was driving at the time of the accident was wrong in law. He
e argued that, in order to prove the offence under s 9(3), the Crown must establish, in a
case in which the request for the first specimen of breath was made under the power
given by s 8(2), not only that the police officer had reasonable cause to believe that the
accused was driving, but also that he was driving or attempting to drive at the time of
the accident.

Counsel for the Crown argues that the words of the statute are clear and do not, in
f relation to the offence under s 9(3), require proof that the accused was in fact driving
or attempting to drive. He argues that this subsection is designed to catch the person
who, without reasonable excuse, obstructs the police in the collection of evidence,
which procedure is authorised by the Act. The necessary safeguard is in the words
which provide that the officer requiring the first breath specimen shall have reasonable cause to believe that the person had been driving or attempting to drive. This
g was the submission which found favour with the recorder.

The pattern of this part of the 1972 Act is well known. Sections 8 and 9 make
provision for the obtaining of evidence by which an offence under s 6 can be proved.
Section 8(1) relates to requiring a breath test from a person who is driving or attempting to drive a vehicle on a road. Section 8(2) makes provision for requiring a breath
test in circumstances in which there has been an accident. In such circumstances the
h police officer may not be able to ascertain with certainty who was driving at the time
of the accident. So far as is relevant for present purposes, s 8(2) reads:

> 'If an accident occurs owing to the presence of a motor vehicle on a road or
> other public place, a constable in uniform may require any person who he has
> reasonable cause to believe was driving or attempting to drive the vehicle at the
> time of the accident to provide a specimen of breath for a breath test . . .'

j Section 8(5) reads:

> 'If a person required by a constable under subsection (1) or (2) above to provide
> a specimen of breath for a breath test fails to do so and the constable has reason-
> able cause to suspect him of having alcohol in his body, the constable may arrest
> him without warrant except while he is at a hospital as a patient.'

So there is power to arrest if the officer has reasonable cause to believe the person arrested to have been driving at the relevant time. If the officer's belief is shown to *a* have been mistaken, that does not make the arrest unlawful.

By s 9(1), a person who has been arrested under s 5(5) or s 8, may be required to provide a specimen for a laboratory test. Section 9(3) reads:

'A person who, without reasonable excuse, fails to provide a specimen for a laboratory test in pursuance of a requirement imposed under this section shall be *b* guilty of an offence.'

Counsel for the appellant argues that that subsection must be read together with s 177 of, and Sch 4, Part I, to the Act. Section 177 reads thus, so far as it is relevant:

'(1) Part I of Schedule 4 to this Act shall have effect with respect to the prosecution and punishment of the offences against the provisions of this Act specified in *c* column I of that Part of that Schedule or regulations made thereunder (of which the general nature is indicated in column 2 thereof). . .'

Then there are supplementary provisions with reference to the Schedule.

Turning to Part I of the schedule, there is a reference to the provisions in s 9(3) in these terms: in column 1 the subsection is quoted; in column 2 the general nature of *d* the offence is recited: 'Failing to provide a specimen of blood or urine for a laboratory test.'; under mode of prosecution in column 3, it is set out that it can be prosecuted summarily or on indictment; then in column 4 it recites the maximum punishment thus: '(i) Where it is shown that at the relevant time (as defined in Part V of this Schedule) the offender was driving or attempting to drive a motor vehicle on a road or other public place . . .' and then are set out the maximum consequences by way of *e* punishment; '(ii) Where in any other case it is shown that at that time the offender was in charge of a motor vehicle on a road or other public place . . .', then the punishment is set out appropriate for a summary conviction. Then further punishments are set out against conviction on indictment. Under 'Disqualification' there are entries; under 'Endorsement' there is recorded that it is obligatory. That follows a conviction of an offence under s 9(3). In column 7, 'Additional provisions', the schedule *f* provides that ss 181 and 183 and para 3 of Part IV of the schedule apply to this offence. Only s 181 has any bearing on this matter. That relates to admission of evidence by certificate as to who was driving or using a vehicle on a road at a particular time or place.

The ancestry of s 9(3) and the reference to that subsection in Sch 4 to the 1972 Act, is to be found in s 3(3) of the Road Safety Act 1967, which reads: *g*

'A person who, without reasonable excuse, fails to provide a specimen for a laboratory test in pursuance of a requirement imposed under this section shall be guilty of an offence, and—(a) if it is shown that at the relevant time he was driving or attempting to drive a motor vehicle on a road or other public place, he shall be liable to be proceeded against and punished as if the offence charged were an offence under section 1(1) of this Act; and (b) in any other case, if it is shown that *h* at that time he was in charge of a motor vehicle on a road or other public place, he shall be liable to be proceeded against and punished as if the offence charged were an offence under section 1(2) of this Act.'

Counsel for the appellant argues that the words 'a person' with which sub-s (3) commences, are to be construed as a person who is within either (a) or (b), and therefore *j* it is only a person who is shown to have been driving or attempting to drive, or a person who is shown to have been in charge of a motor vehicle at the relevant time who can be guilty of an offence under that subsection. The wording of the subsection is not free from ambiguity, as was pointed out in argument, but we have no doubt that that is the construction we ought to place on it. If it were otherwise, a person could be

a guilty of an offence under that subsection for which offence no procedure for prosecution and no maximum punishment is provided by the Act. Counsel for the
appellant then argues that the change effected by the Road Traffic Act 1972 in this
respect is merely to take the procedure for prosecution and the punishment provisions out of the subsection creating the offence, and to place them in a different part
of the Act. Despite the persuasive argument of counsel for the Crown to the contrary,
we think that this is a valid argument and that s 9(3) of the 1972 Act must be read
b together with the part of Sch 4 to that Act which refers to the subsection. When this
is done, the result is that the Act provides that the offence under the subsection is
committed only by a person who was driving or attempting to drive at the relevant
time, or, in any other case, by a person who is shown to have been in charge of a motor
vehicle.

The construction of the Act for which the Crown contends would result in a situa-
c tion in which a person could be convicted of the offence of failing to provide a specimen for a laboratory test in circumstances in which he had not been driving or
attempting to drive. On conviction that person would be liable to suffer punishment
not restricted by the provision of the Act. His licence would necessarily have to be
endorsed. We do not believe that the words of the statute achieve that result. Counsel
for the Crown argues that such a result would not follow if, as he contends, the fact
d that the person required to provide the specimen was not in fact driving or attempting
to drive at the relevant time was a reasonable excuse for failing to provide the specimen
and a defence to a charge under s 9(3). The difficulty about that argument is that as
appears from the judgment of Widgery LJ in *R v Downey*[1], an assertion in such a
case as the present, by the person from whom the specimen is required, that he was
not driving at the time of the accident, could not be a reasonable excuse for failing to
e provide the specimen if there was statutory justification for making the requirement,
irrespective of whether or not he had in fact been driving at that time.

In our judgment there is a distinction to be drawn in this case between (a) what
must be established in order to prove that a lawful requirement to provide a specimen
for a laboratory test was made, and (b) what must be proved to establish the offence
of failing to provide such a specimen contrary to s 9(3). The reasonable cause to
f believe that the accused was driving or attempting to drive at the time of the accident
is sufficient to support the first request for a breath specimen and, with the added reasonable cause to suspect alcohol in the body, the subsequent arrest, and, if the correct
procedure is followed, the final requirement of a specimen for a laboratory test. But
when it comes to proving the offence, in our judgment the Crown must prove, if this
is challenged, that the accused was in fact driving or attempting to drive at the time of
g the accident. In the ordinary case this will present no difficulty, as evidence forming
the basis of reasonable cause to believe he was driving will, at least, give rise to the
inference that he was in fact driving. There was a misdirection of the jury in that an
essential ingredient of the offence was withdrawn from their consideration.

There is no need for us to deal with the ground that the indictment was defective.
We did not hear argument on it at any length. Suffice it to say that so far as the court
h is aware, it is not the common practice, nor does it appear to be necessary, in setting
out the particulars of an offence under s 9(3), to include a recitation of all the steps
preliminary to the requirement of the specimen and the refusal without reasonable
excuse.

It is for these reasons that we allow the appeal.

j *Appeal allowed. Conviction quashed.*

Solicitors: *Registrar of Criminal Appeals; Chief Prosecuting Solicitor*, Bristol.

F K Anklesaria Esq   Barrister.

---

1   [1970] RTR 257 at 259, 260

R v Munisamy

a

COURT OF APPEAL, CRIMINAL DIVISION

SCARMAN, JAMES LJJ AND BRISTOW J

7th FEBRUARY 1975

Dictum of JAMES LJ at 912 applied
in R v MEDWAY [1976] 1 All ER 527

Criminal law – Appeal – Abandonment of appeal – Application to withdraw notice of abandonment – Bad legal advice – Accused acting under fundamental mistake in consequence of ***b*** *advice – Abandonment of appeal in consequence of mistake – Whether notice of abandonment should be treated as a nullity.*

An appellant cannot, in the strict sense, withdraw a notice of abandonment of an appeal against conviction or sentence; what he can do is to put before the court sufficient facts to satisfy the court that the abandonment was a nullity. Where the ***c*** appellant has been given bad legal advice the court will only treat his notice of abandonment as a nullity if it is satisfied that, in consequence of the advice, the appellant was acting under a fundamental mistake when he purported to give the notice (see p 911 *b* and *c* and p 912 *c* and *d*, post).

R v Moore [1957] 2 All ER 703 applied.

Dictum of Winn LJ in *R v Sutton (Philip)* [1969] 1 All ER at 929 explained.   ***d***

Notes

For abandonment of appeal, see 10 Halsbury's Laws (3rd Edn) 535, para 984. For the Criminal Appeal Act 1968, see 8 Halsbury's Statutes (3rd Edn) 687.

Cases referred to in judgment

e

R v Moore [1957] 2 All ER 703, [1957] 1 WLR 841, 41 Cr App Rep 179, CCA, Digest (Cont Vol A) 394, 6093*b*.

R v Pitman (1916) 12 Cr App Rep 14, CCA, 14 Digest (Repl) 613, 6089.

R v Sutton (Philip) [1969] 1 All ER 928, [1969] 1 WLR 375, 53 Cr App Rep 269, 133 JP 298, CA, Digest (Cont Vol C) 235 6093*d*.

Application

f

This was an application by Chinnapa Munisamy for leave to withdraw a notice dated 11th September 1974 of abandonment of appeal against a sentence of eight months' imprisonment, with a compensation order in the sum of £250, imposed on him at the Central Criminal Court on 10th July 1974. The facts are set out in the judgment of the court.

g

The applicant did not appear and was not represented.

JAMES LJ delivered the following judgment of the court. This is yet another case where the court has before it an application for leave to withdraw an abandonment of an appeal.

On 10th July 1974, at the Central Criminal Court, the applicant pleaded guilty to an ***h*** offence of wounding. He was sentenced to eight months' imprisonment, and the court made a compensation order in the sum of £250. On 29th July he applied for leave to appeal against both conviction and sentence. That against conviction was not effective, but that against sentence was supported by counsel's opinion. On 11th September his application in respect of sentence was refused by the single judge. On 2nd October the applicant lodged a notice on form 14 notifying the court that he had ***j*** abandoned all proceedings in the court. Then on 31st December 1974 he wrote to the registrar asking for leave to withdraw his notice of abandonment.

The case is a somewhat unusual one. Clearly one of the matters in relation to sentence, which was of considerable concern to the applicant, was the fact that a compensation order in the amount I have mentioned had been made. The advice that he *a* received from counsel did not deal with that aspect of the court's order at all. There is a letter received by the registrar from the solicitors then acting for the applicant, the third paragraph of which contains a reference to the compensation order, saying that the order was made 'to be not more than £250 to be fixed by magistrates'. That clearly was unlikely to have been the form of the order of the court. As a result of that letter, enquiries were made by the registrar, and it was found the compensation order was in fact in its proper form.

b   Enquiries of the solicitors also revealed that they did not give the applicant any advice whatsoever in respect of his application insofar as it referred to the compensation order, but the basis of the advice that was tendered was that, having regard to the passage of some months, he had served so much of his sentence that it was perhaps not worth while pursuing the application. It is in those circumstances that the applicant, having now served his custodial sentence, points out to the court the difficulties *c* in which he is placed in relation to the compensation order.

    The court, being faced with repeated applications of this kind, will wish to bear in mind that which was said by Lord Goddard CJ in *R v Moore*[1]:

> 'An examination of the cases[2] has shown that, except in one case at any rate, the court have only allowed notice of abandonment to be withdrawn if they are
> *d* satisfied that there has been some mistake. No doubt if a case could be made out that a prisoner had in some way or another been fraudulently led or induced to abandon his appeal, the court in the exercise of their inherent jurisdiction would say that the notice was to be regarded as a nullity; but where there has been a deliberate abandonment of an appeal, in the opinion of the court there is no power or right to allow the notice of abandonment to be withdrawn and the
> *e* appeal reinstated because, the appeal having been dismissed, the court have exercised their powers over the matter and are functus officio. Accordingly, the court will not entertain applications for the withdrawal of notices of abandonment unless something amounting to mistake or fraud is alleged, which, if established, would enable the court to say that the notice of abandonment should be regarded as a nullity.'

f

That we understand still to be the correct exposition of the principle under the Criminal Appeal Act 1968.

    Since that date there have been a number of other cases before the court where applications of this nature have been made, and in particular *R v Sutton*[3]. In that case the judgment was given by Winn LJ in these terms[4]:

g
> 'This is an application to withdraw a notice of abandonment. The court is receiving a great many of these applications in modern times, far too many, and it is perhaps desirable that it should be understood that the court will not entertain any such application for leave to withdraw a notice of abandonment unless it is shown affirmatively that something amounting to a mistake or to fraud can
> *h* be shown, with a solid foundation for the allegation . . .'

Winn LJ then referred to *R v Moore*[5]. But we would refer particularly to the words at the end of the judgment[6]:

---

1 [1957] 2 All ER at 703, [1957] 1 WLR 841 at 842
j 2 See e g *R v Van Dyn* (1932) 23 Cr App Rep 150 and *R v Pitman* (1916) 12 Cr App Rep 14, where the court said that in the absence of 'special circumstances' leave to withdraw notice of abandonment of appeal would be refused
3 [1969] 1 All ER 928, [1969] 1 WLR 375
4 [1969] 1 All ER at 928, [1969] 1 WLR at 376
5 [1957] 2 All ER 703, [1957] 1 WLR 841
6 [1969] 1 All ER at 929, [1969] 1 WLR at 377

'The purpose of delivering a judgment at all in this case instead of simply dismissing the application is to emphasise once again that the court will not *a* entertain these applications for leave to withdraw notices of abandonment unless it is apparent on the face of such an application that some grounds exist for supposing that there may have been either fraud, or at any rate bad advice given by some legal adviser, which has resulted in an unintended, ill-considered decision to abandon the appeal.'

b

Those words just cited on their face value seem to go beyond the words of Lord Goddard CJ in *R v Moore*[1]. But we do not think that Winn LJ was referring to bad advice in the sense of wrong advice. Indeed it would be very difficult to assess whether advice that was given was wrong or right. It may appear to be right at the time it was given, but wrong in the light of knowledge obtained thereafter. What Winn LJ was saying was there had to be something so defective in the information given to the *c* applicant that the court could say: 'Well, in this particular case there was such a fundamental mistake in the mind of the applicant when he purported to abandon, that his act of abandonment may be properly treated by the court as a nullity.'

In a sense the expression that has been used and is now well established, namely 'withdraw abandonment', is not strictly accurate. One cannot in the strict sense withdraw a notice of abandonment. What one can do is put before the court sufficient *d* facts to satisfy the court that the abandonment is falsified and rendered a nullity.

Turning to the facts of the case here, there is no suggestion of fraud involved. But we are quite satisfied that in the act of abandonment the applicant was acting under a fundamental mistake at least as to the situation in relation to the compensation order. In those circumstances his abandonment can properly be treated as a nullity. We so rule and decide. His application can come forward. If he wants to renew his *e* application, he must do so within the next 14 days.

Application granted.

Sepala Munasinghe Esq   Barrister.

---

1   [1957] 2 All ER 703, [1957] 1 WLR 841

a
Lynch v Director of Public Prosecutions for Northern Ireland

Distinguished in ABBOTT v THE QUEEN [1976] 3 All ER 140

Dictum of LORD SIMON at 941 disapproved in R v BELFON [1976] 3 All ER 46

HOUSE OF LORDS

b LORD MORRIS OF BORTH-Y-GEST, LORD WILBERFORCE, LORD SIMON OF GLAISDALE, LORD KILBRANDON AND LORD EDMUND-DAVIES

18th, 19th, 20th, 21st, 25th, 26th, 27th NOVEMBER 1974, 12th MARCH 1975

Criminal law – Duress – Defence – Murder – Accused charged with murder as principal in second degree – Accused alleging that he had acted under threat of death or serious bodily *c* *injury – Whether open to accused to plead duress as a defence to the charge.*

The appellant and two others were charged with the murder of a police constable in Northern Ireland. The case against the appellant was that he was a principal in the second degree in that, although he had not done any of the shooting which had resulted in the constable's death, he had driven three armed men to a place near *d* where the policeman was stationed and, after the shooting, had driven the three men away again. At his trial the appellant raised the defence of duress. He alleged that he had been ordered by M, a member of the IRA who was well known as a ruthless gunman, to participate in the events which had led to the crime. There was evidence that M was a man whom it would be perilous to disobey, that he had given his instructions in a manner which indicated that he would tolerate no disobedience and *e* that, in consequence, the appellant was afraid that if he disobeyed M he would be shot. The judge directed the jury to consider whether the appellant had been aware of the nature of the enterprise and had known that death or violence was the likely outcome. He decided, however, not to leave to the jury the question whether the appellant had been compelled by duress to participate in the events which had led to the shooting, taking the view that, as a matter of law, the defence of duress was not *f* available on a charge of murder. The appellant was convicted. On appeal,

Held (Lord Simon of Glaisdale and Lord Kilbrandon dissenting) – On a charge of murder it was open to a person accused as a principal in the second degree to plead duress, i e that he had carried out the acts constituting the alleged offence under the threat of death or serious bodily injury, as a defence to the charge. Accordingly *g* appeal would be allowed and a new trial ordered (see p 917 *c* and *d*, p 924 *d* *f* and *g*, p 927 *d*, p 929 *f*, p 930 *d* and *f* and p 956 *h* to p 957 *d* and *g*, post).

R v Crutchley (1831) 5 C & P 133, *Attorney-General v Whelan* [1934] IR 518, dictum of Widgery LJ in *R v Kray* (1969) 53 Cr App Rep at 578, *R v Hudson* [1971] 2 All ER 244 and *State v Goliath* 1972 (3) SA 1 applied.

R v Brown and Morley [1968] SASR 467 not followed.

h Dictum of Lord Denman CJ in *R v Tyler and Price* (1838) 8 C & P at 620, 621 and of Lord Goddard CJ in *R v Bourne* (1952) 36 Cr App Rep at 128 disapproved.

Quaere. Whether the defence of duress is available to a person charged with murder as a principal in the first degree (see p 918 *g* and *h*, p 927 *d*, p 929 *f*, p 930 *f* and p 956 *c* and *d*, post).

j **Notes**

For duress as a defence to a criminal charge, see 10 Halsbury's Laws (3rd Edn) 290, 291, paras 538-540, and for cases on the subject, see 14 Digest (Repl) 74-76, 346-361.

Cases referred to in opinions

Attorney-General v Whelan [1934] IR 518, CCA.

HH

Adams v Adams (Attorney-General intervening) [1970] 3 All ER 572, [1971] P 188, [1970] 3 WLR 934, Digest (Cont Vol C) 81, 26f. **a**

Barton v Armstrong (5th December 1973) unreported, PC.

Baudains v Richardson [1906] AC 169, 75 LJPC 57, 94 LT 290, PC, 48 Digest (Repl) 68, 477.

Earl and Countess of Somerset's case (1616) 1 State Trials 28.

HM Advocate v Dingwall (1867) 5 Irv 466, 14 Digest (Repl) 69, *259*.

HM Advocate v Higgins 1914 SC (J) 1, 14 Digest (Repl) 68, *250*.

Hyam v Director of Public Prosecutions [1974] 2 All ER 41, [1974] 2 WLR 607, HL. **b**

Knuller (Publishing, Printing and Promotions) Ltd v Director of Public Prosecutions [1972] 2 All ER 898, [1973] AC 435, [1972] 3 WLR 143, 136 JP 728, HL.

Lang v Lang [1954] 3 All ER 571, [1955] AC 402, [1954] 3 WLR 762, 119 JP 368, PC, Digest (Cont Vol A) 724, 2899a.

Madzimbamuto v Lardner-Burke [1968] 3 All ER 561, [1969] 1 AC 645, [1968] 3 WLR 1229, PC, Digest (Cont Vol C) 80, 26c. **c**

M'Growther's Case (1746) Fost 13, 18 State Tr 391, 14 Digest (Repl) 74, 350.

Morgans v Launchbury [1972] 2 All ER 606, [1973] AC 127, [1972] 2 WLR 1217, [1972] RTR 406, [1972] 1 Lloyd's Rep 483, HL.

National Coal Board v Gamble [1958] 3 All ER 203, [1959] 1 QB 11, [1958] 3 WLR 434, 122 JP 453, 42 Cr App Rep 240, DC, Digest (Cont Vol A) 336, 647a.

Oldcastle's Case (1419) 1 Hale PC 50, 14 Digest (Repl) 74, 349. **d**

R v Axtell (1660) Kel 13, 5 State Tr 1146, 14 Digest (Repl) 74, 353.

R v Bourne (1952) 36 Cr App Rep 125, CCA, 14 Digest (Repl) 353, 3423.

R v Brown and Morley [1968] SASR 467.

R v Crutchley (1831) 5 C & P 133, 1 Nev & MMC 282, 172 ER 909, 14 Digest (Repl) 74, 347.

R v Dudley and Stephens (1884) 14 QBD 273, [1881-5] All ER Rep 61, 54 LJMC 32, 52 LT 107, 49 JP 69, 15 Cox CC 624, CCR, 14 Digest (Repl) 75, 359. **e**

R v Farduto (1912) 10 DLR 669.

R v Fegan (1974) unreported.

R v Gill [1963] 2 All ER 688, [1963] 1 WLR 841, 127 JP 429, 47 Cr App Rep 166, CCA, Digest (Cont Vol A) 335, 361a.

R v Hudson, R v Taylor [1971] 2 All ER 244, [1971] 2 QB 202, [1971] 2 WLR 1047, 135 JP 407, CA. **f**

R v Hurley and Murray [1967] VR 526.

R v Kray [1969] 3 All ER 941, [1970] 1 QB 125, [1969] 3 WLR 831, 133 JP 719, 53 Cr App Rep 569, CA, Digest (Cont Vol C) 196, 2238b.

R v Purdy (1946) 10 Journal of Criminal Law 182.

R v Shiartos (1961) unreported.

R v Smyth [1963] VR 737. **g**

R v Steane [1947] 1 All ER 813, [1947] KB 997, [1947] LJR 969, 177 LT 122, 111 JP 337, 32 Cr App Rep 61, 45 LGR 484, CCA, 14 Digest (Repl) 33, 47.

R v Stratton (1779) 1 Doug KB 239, 99 ER 156, 21 State Tr 1045, 14 Digest (Repl) 75, 358.

R v Tyler and Price (1838) 8 C & P 616, 173 ER 643, 14 Digest (Repl) 85, 479.

Rossides v R [1957] Crim LR 813, PC.

Sephakela v R [1954] High Commission Territories LR 60, PC. **h**

State v Goliath 1972 (3) SA 1.

State v Hercules 1954 (3) SA 826.

Subramaniam v Public Prosecutor [1956] 1 WLR 965, PC, Digest (Cont Vol A) 522, *495a*.

Thomas v R (1937) 59 CLR 279.

Warner v Metropolitan Police Comr [1968] 2 All ER 356, [1969] 2 AC 256, [1968] 2 WLR **j** 1303, 132 JP 378, 52 Cr App Rep 373, HL, Digest (Cont Vol C) 182, 95d.

Wingrove v Wingrove (1885) 11 PD 81, 55 LJP 7, 50 JP 56, 23 Digest (Repl) 127, 1314.

Appeal

Joseph Lynch appealed against the order of the Court of Criminal Appeal in Northern

Ireland (Lowry CJ, Curran LJ and O'Donnell J) dated 27th June 1974 dismissing his
a appeal against his conviction for murder at the Belfast City Commission before
Gibson J and a jury on 20th June 1972. The facts are set out in the opinion of Lord
Morris of Borth-y-Gest.

C M Lavery QC and *D Magill* (both of the Northern Ireland Bar) for the appellant.
J B E Hutton QC and *W A Campbell QC* (both of the Northern Ireland Bar) for the
b respondent.

Their Lordships took time for consideration.

12th March. The following opinions were delivered.

c **LORD MORRIS OF BORTH-Y-GEST.** My Lords, the appellant was charged,
together with two others named Bates and Whelan, with having, on 28th January
1972, murdered one Raymond Norman Carroll who was a police constable. The
killing took place in Belfast. The trial, which was before a learned judge and a jury,
began on 12th June 1972 and concluded on 20th June 1972. On that latter date the
jury returned unanimous verdicts of guilty against the appellant and against Bates.
d They were sentenced to life imprisonment. Whelan, who was said by the prosecution to have been an accessory before the fact, was acquitted at the close of the case
for the Crown.

The case against the appellant was that he was a principal in the second degree. He
had not done any of the actual shooting which killed the police constable. The case
against him was that he had aided and abetted the killing. The learned judge in his
e summing-up gave careful directions to the jury as to what has to be proved before an
accused person can be found guilty of murder by having aided and abetted. Save as to
one matter to which I will later refer it was not submitted in this House that the
directions given were erroneous and we were not invited to consider them. The
main contention of the appellant and one of the main lines of his defence at the trial
was that all he had done had been done under duress and that he was entitled to be
f acquitted.

The course followed at the trial was that the evidence was given, and was not excluded, which could form the factual basis on which the plea of acting under duress
could be presented. The appellant hinself gave evidence. When all the evidence in
the case was concluded submissions in law were made to the learned judge, in the
absence of the jury, in regard to the applicability of duress as a defence in the case of
g one charged with murder as a principal in the second degree. The learned judge
ruled for reasons which he gave that in such a case the defence of duress was not
available. He therefore withdrew from the jury the question whether the appellant
had been compelled by duress to participate in the events which culminated in the
shooting of Pc Carroll. It followed that if duress was not available as a defence there
was no need for the learned judge to consider or to discuss or to direct the jury as to
h certain aspects of the matter that might on the footing of its availability have become
relevant. Where duress is in issue many questions may arise such as whether threats
are serious and compelling or whether (as on the facts of the present case may specially
call for consideration) a person the subject of duress could reasonably have extricated
himself or could have sought protection or had what has been called a 'safe avenue of
escape'. Other questions may arise such as whether a person is only under duress as a
j result of being in voluntary association with those whom he knew would require
some course of action. In the present case, as duress was not left to the jury, we
naturally do not know what they thought of it all.

It was not in contest that if in a criminal case a defence of duress is open, and if as
an issue it is raised, the burden of proof which rests on the prosecution then includes
the burden of proving that the accused did not act under duress.

The appellant appealed to the Court of Criminal Appeal. He appealed on four grounds. Of the two which were pursued the first was that the learned judge was *a* wrong in law and misdirected the jury by telling them that duress cannot be a defence to murder. The second, which is not before us, was that there had been misdirection on a question of corroboration. The appeal was heard by Lowry CJ, Curran LJ and O'Donnell J. On 27th June the appeal was dismissed. In a reasoned judgment containing a valuable review of decided cases, Lowry CJ set out the conclusions (shared by all three members of the court) which led them to hold that duress cannot be *b* accepted as a defence to murder. In giving judgment the court recorded that they had given consideration to one aspect of the case that had not been argued. It raised a point concerning the intention which must be proved before there can be a conviction of aiding and abetting. On this one point O'Donnell J delivered a dissenting opinion.

The court certified that two points of law of general public importance were involved in their decision. The second related to the aspect of the case above mentioned *c* The court gave leave to appeal. The two points are as follows:

'(1) On a charge of murder is the defence of duress open to a person who is accused as a principal in the second degree (aider and abettor)?
'(2) Where a person charged with murder as an aider and abettor is shown to have intentionally done an act which assists in the commission of the murder *d* with knowledge that the probable result of his act, combined with the acts of those whom his act is assisting, will be the death or serious bodily injury of another, is his guilt thereby established without the necessity of proving his willingness to participate in the crime?'

The facts as described or asserted by the appellant can be briefly summarised. *e* Many of them had been set out in a signed statement which he had made to the police. He said that while at his house he had received a message that one Sean Meehan required his presence. It was in the forefront of his case that Sean Meehan was and was known to be both a member of the Irish Republican Army and a ruthless gunman. The appellant had not previously known Meehan personally but had known of him. He said that what Meehan asked to be done had to be done. 'You have no other *f* option. I firmly believe that I would have been shot for defying him.' So he went with the messenger to an address in Belfast and there saw Meehan and two other men. Meehan, he said, had a rifle in his hand. After it was learned that the appellant could drive a car he was told to go with another man named Mailey (who had a small automatic gun) and seize a car. They went away. Mailey held up a car and ordered its driver to get out. The appellant was told to drive the car to the address *g* where Meehan had remained. The appellant did so. He parked the car and was told that he would not be doing any more driving. So he returned to his own house. Some half-hour later the messenger returned and told the appellant that Meehan wanted him. He went to the same house as before. Meehan, Bates, Mailey and another man were there. Meehan who had a rifle told the appellant that he was to drive the car which he then did after Mailey (who had a gun in his pocket) had got in *h* beside him and after Bates and Meehan had got into the back. Meehan, Bates and Mailey had combat jackets and balaclava helmets. The appellant was told to go to a particular road. He asked Meehan what he was going to do and was told: 'Bates knows a policeman.' Following directions given to him he drove past a garage (at which point Bates said: 'That's him') and then stopped near to the garage. Meehan told him to stay there. The other three pulled up their woollen helmets and left the *j* car and ran across the road. Then there were a number of shots fired in quick succession. The three men came running back to the car and got into it. The appellant was told to drive on—which he did. They returned to their starting point.

Witnesses gave evidence that the three men got out of the car driven by the appellant moved swiftly towards the service bay of the garage where Pc Carroll was doing work on his own car; that shots were fired; that the constable was fatally wounded; that the three men made off towards the waiting car which was then driven away.

The learned judge directed the jury fully in regard to the matters which the prosecution had to prove. I need not refer to them or elaborate them. It is sufficient for present purposes to proceed on the basis or assumption that the verdict of the jury shows that they were satisfied that the appellant participated actively in an enterprise with knowledge that death or serious injury was intended by those whom he accompanied to be its outcome.

So the question presents itself whether the issue of duress should have been left to the jury. If on the facts the conclusion could be that the appellant only participated to the extent that he did because he was forced to participate should he be held guilty? There are two aspects of the question, viz, (a) whether there was evidence on which it would be open to a jury to say that there was duress and (b) if there was, and if a jury considered that there had been duress, whether duress can avail as a defence to a charge which is presented as a charge of murder.

It is important to remember that in this case we are concerned with an alleged principal in the second degree, and that the particular points of law which are raised are framed in reference to an aider and abettor. We are concerned with duress in the form of threats (either expressly made or by conduct indicated) to kill the person threatened or to cause serious personal physical injury to him. I limit my decision to the facts of the present case. The view of the learned judge at the trial was that duress is not available as a defence to a charge of murder; he considered that he was precluded by the weight of authority from holding that it could be and, furthermore, he concluded that the defence was no more available in the case of a principal in the second degree than in the case of a principal in the first degree.

Counsel for the Crown indicated that they would have been prepared to embark before us on an examination of the evidence with a view to making a submission that the evidence did not have the weight which would warrant a finding that there was duress; they would then have submitted that in any event there could be an application of the proviso. The Court of Appeal have however held, as expressly stated in their judgment, that there was on the facts a clear issue as to duress. In view of this it would in my view have been quite inappropriate for us to go beyond the issues of law which are raised. At the same time it is to be remembered, as I have indicated, that the facts as to duress have not been considered by the jury and that because the learned judge withdrew the issue he naturally found it unnecessary to deal with various questions which would have been or might have been most pertinent had the matter been left for the consideration of the jury.

In a series of decisions and over a period of time courts have recognised that there can be circumstances in which duress is a defence. In examining them and more particularly in approaching the issue raised in this appeal the question naturally presents itself—why and on what basis can duress be raised? If someone acts under duress—does he intend what he does? Does he lack what in our criminal law is called mens rea? If what he does amounts to a criminal offence ought he to be convicted but be allowed in mercy and in mitigation to be absolved or relieved from some or all of the possible consequences?

The answer that I would give to these questions is that it is proper that any rational system of law should take fully into account the standards of honest and reasonable men. By those standards it is fair that actions and reactions may be tested. If then someone is really threatened with death or serious injury unless he does what he is told to do is the law to pay no heed to the miserable agonising plight of such a person? For the law to understand not only how the timid but also the stalwart may in a moment of crisis behave is not to make the law weak but to make it just. In the calm of the courtroom measures of fortitude or of heroic behaviour are surely not to be demanded when they could not in moments for decision reasonably have been expected even of the resolute and the well disposed.

In posing the case where someone is 'really' threatened I use the word 'really' in *a* order to emphasise that duress must never be allowed to be the easy answer of those who can devise no other explanation of their conduct nor of those who readily could have avoided the dominance of threats nor of those who allow themselves to be at the disposal and under the sway of some gangster-tyrant. Where duress becomes an issue courts and juries will surely consider the facts with care and discernment.

In my view the law has recognised that there can be situations in which duress can be put forward as a defence. Someone who acts under duress may have a moment of *b* time, even one of the utmost brevity, within which he decides whether he will or will not submit to a threat. There may consciously or subconciously be a hurried process of balancing the consequences of disobedience against the gravity or the wickedness of the action that is required. The result will be that what is done will be done most unwillingly but yet intentionally. Terminology may not however much matter. The authorities show that in some circumstances duress may excuse and may therefore *c* be set up as a special defence.

A tenable view might be that duress should never be regarded as furnishing an excuse from guilt but only where established as providing reasons why after convic-tion a court could mitigate its consequences or absolve from punishment. Some writers including Stephen[1] have so thought. It is however much too late in the day, having regard to the lines of authority, to adopt any such view. But apart from this— *d* would such an approach be just? I think not. It is said that if duress could not be set up as a defence there would be difficulties in the way of bringing evidence of the relevant facts and circumstances before the court. I am not greatly impressed by this. A judge could ensure that after a conviction full opportunity would be given to adduce all material evidence. If however what a person has done was only done because he acted under the compulsion of a threat of death or of serious bodily injury it would *e* not in my view be just that the stigma of a conviction should be cast on him. As Blackstone put it[2]:

'. . . it is highly just and equitable that a man should be excused for those acts which are done through unavoidable force and compulsion.'

The law must, I think, take a common sense view. If someone is forced at gun point *f* either to be inactive or to do something positive—must the law not remember that the instinct and perhaps the duty of self-preservation is powerful and natural? I think it must. A man who is attacked is allowed within reason to take necessary steps to defend himself. The law would be censorious and inhumane which did not recog-nise the appalling plight of a person who perhaps suddenly finds his life in jeopardy unless he submits and obeys. *g*

The issue in the present case is therefore whether there is any reason why the defence of duress, which in respect of a variety of offences has been recognised as a possible defence, may not also be a possible defence on a charge of being a principal in the second degree to murder. I would confine my decision to that issue. It may be that the law must deny such a defence to an actual killer, and that the law will not be irrational if it does so. *h*

Though it is not possible for the law always to be worked out on coldly logical lines there may be manifest factual differences and contrasts between the situation of an aider and abettor to a killing and that of the actual killer. Let two situations be supposed. In each let it be supposed that there is a real and effective threat of death. In one a person is required under such duress to drive a car to a place or to carry a gun to a place with knowledge that at such place it is planned that X is to be killed by *j* those who are imposing their will. In the other situation let it be supposed that a person under such duress is told that he himself must there and then kill X. In either

---

1   History of the Criminal Law of England (1883), vol 2, pp 107, 108
2   Commentaries on the Laws of England (1766), vol 4, p 27

situation there is a terrible agonising choice of evils. In the former to save his life
a the person drives the car or carries the gun. He may cling to the hope that perhaps X
will not be found at the place or that there will be a change of intention before the
purpose is carried out or that in some unforeseen way the dire event of a killing will
be averted. The final and fatal moment of decision has not arrived. He saves his own
life at a time when the loss of another life is not a certainty. In the second (if indeed
it is a situation likely to arise) the person is told that to save his life he himself must
b personally there and then take an innocent life. It is for him to pull the trigger or
otherwise personally to do the act of killing. There, I think, before allowing duress as
a defence it may be that the law will have to call a halt. May there still be force in
what long ago was said by Hale[1]?

c   'Again, if a man be desperately assaulted, and in peril of death, and cannot
otherwise escape, unless to satisfy his assailant's fury he will kill an innocent
person then present, the fear and actual force will not acquit him of the crime
and punishment of murder, if he commit the fact; for he ought rather to die
himself, than kill an innocent.'

Those words have over long periods of time influenced both thought and writing but
I think that their application may have been unduly extended when it is assumed
d that they were intended to cover all cases of accessories and aiders and abettors.
   Writers on criminal law have generally recorded that whatever may be the extent
to which the law has recognised duress as a defence it has not been recognised as a
defence to a charge of murder (see Russell on Crime[2], Kenny's Outline of Criminal
Law[3], Glanville Williams's Criminal Law[4], Smith and Hogan's Criminal Law[5]).
   It may be a matter for consideration whether the offences of being accessory before
e the fact to murder and of aiding and abetting murder might not be constituted as
separate offences involving a liability to the imposition of life imprisonment but not
as a mandatory sentence.
   I fully appreciate that, particularly at the present time, situations may arise where
the facts will be much less direct and straightforward than those which, as examples,
I have described. I see no advantage in giving illustrations of them. They will be
f situations presenting greater difficulties of fact than those presented in the present
case. But where there have been threats of the nature that really have compelled a
person to act in a particular way and he has only acted because of them I think that
the approach of the law should be to recognise that the person may be excused in
the cases that I have supposed.
   It is most undesirable that in the administration of our criminal law cases should
g arise in which, if there is a prosecution leading to a conviction, a just conclusion will
only be attained by an exercise thereafter of the prerogative of granting a pardon. I
would regret it, therefore, if on an application of legal principles such cases could arise.
Such principles and such approach as will prevent them from arising would seem to
me to be more soundly based.
   I do not propose to refer to all the cases which were most helpfully cited to us.
h They show the range of the offences in respect of which it has been accepted that
duress is a possible defence. In some of the cases obiter dicta are to be found as to the
exceptions to the general rule. Treason and murder have been said to be possible
exceptions. Yet as to treason such cases as *Oldcastle's Case*[6], or *M'Growther's Case*[7],

---

j   1 Pleas of the Crown (1800) vol 1, p 51
     2 12th Edn (1964), p 90
     3 19th Edn (1966), p 70
     4 2nd Edn (1961), p 759
     5 3rd Edn (1973), pp 164-168
     6 (1419) 1 Hale PC 50
     7 (1746) Fost 13

or *R v Stratton*[1], or *R v Purdy*[2] show that in some circumstances the defence may avail.

In *R v Crutchley*[3], where the charge was of breaking a threshing machine, evidence was given that the accused had against his will been compelled to join a mob from which he ran away at the first opportunity: he was acquitted.

I do not find much assistance in the report of *R v Tyler and Price*[4]. Though the two accused took part in the killing of the deceased and though they urged that they were induced from a fear of personal violence to themselves to join and continue to with Thom, who was a religious fanatic of unsound mind, there are many indications which suggest that in company with very many others they had joined Thom's assemblage because they were attracted by the claims and promises that he made. It would seemingly have been easy for them to detach themselves. It was against such a background that Lord Denman CJ in summing up is reported to have said[5] that the law was 'that no man, from a fear of consequences to himself, has a right to make himself a party to committing mischief on mankind'. Without analysing the expressions used it would not be appropriate to treat what was said as being a comprehensive statement of principle.

In *Attorney-General v Whelan*[6] there was a charge of receiving goods knowing them to have been stolen. A special question was left to the jury as follows[7]: 'In receiving the money did Peter Whelan act under threat of immediate death or serious violence?' The jury answered, 'Yes'. The trial judge then held that duress was not a defence but went in mitigation of punishment. On the basis that there was a conviction he passed a suspensory sentence. On appeal to the Court of Criminal Appeal it was held that the conviction should be quashed and a verdict of acquittal entered. Murnaghan J[8] delivering the judgment of the court said the matter had to be approached from the standpoint of general principle.

> 'It seems to us that threats of immediate death or serious personal violence so great as to overbear the ordinary power of human resistance should be accepted as a justification for acts which would otherwise be criminal.'

The court went on to say, obiter, that the general rule was subject to limitations, and that 'the commission of murder is a crime so heinous that murder should not be committed even for the price of life', so that even the strongest duress would not be a justification. There was an indication that there might be other heinous crimes within the same category. No consideration was however given to the position in a murder charge of a principal in the second degree. The court added that where the 'excuse' of duress applied (and perhaps their word 'excuse' was happier than their word 'justification') it must be the case that[8]—

> 'the overpowering of the will was operative at the time the crime was actually committed, and, if there were reasonable opportunity for the will to reassert itself, no justification can be found in antecedent threats.'

In *R v Gill*[9] it was recognised in the Court of Criminal Appeal that duress could be a defence where there were charges of conspiracy to steal and larceny. The defence

---

1 (1779) 1 Doug KB 239
2 (1946) 10 Journal of Criminal Law 182
3 (1831) 5 C & P 133
4 (1838) 8 C & P 616
5 8 C & P at 620
6 [1934] IR 518
7 [1934] IR at 521
8 [1934] IR at 526
9 [1963] 2 All ER 688, [1963] 1 WLR 841

had been left to the jury who had convicted. On appeal what came under considera-
a tion was the way in which the jury had been directed. The court gave a clear ruling
as to the onus of proof resting on the prosecution. In dealing with that matter the court
referred with approval to what had been said in an unreported case, *R v Shiartos*[1],
where the charge was one of arson and where Lawton J had told the jury that if
what the accused did 'he did at pistol point and in fear of his life, he is entitled to be
acquitted'.

b   Among those who were charged when, in respect of two murders, Kray and others
came up for trial in 1969[2], was a man Anthony Barry. The case against him was that he
was an accessory before the fact to one of the murders and the Crown relied primarily
on his having carried a gun from one place to another knowing that one of the accused
(who was convicted of murder) intended to use it in a projected murder. Barry
admitted that he had carried a gun but said that it was a gun that would not work and
c which was not the instrument of the killing that took place; but further as to whatever
he did, he pleaded that he had acted under duress being in fear for the safety of himself and his family if he failed to carry out what he was ordered to do. It was accepted
by counsel concerned that duress could be a defence in the case of one charged with
being an accessory before the fact of murder. Barry gave evidence of threats and
other evidence was given. Barry was acquitted. On appeal by those who were con-
d victed one contention was that a joint trial of several persons in respect of two murders
had been wrongly ordered. The evidence given in laying the foundation of Barry's
defence of duress had been, in the nature of things, damaging to other accused. On
behalf of one of them the line of argument was as follows: duress (though not available in murder to a person charged as a principal) is available to one charged as an
accessory provided that there was no alternative to submission to the threats and that
e Barry had had such an alternative and so had no viable defence of duress; the result
was that evidence which was prejudicial to other accused had been wrongly allowed.
On behalf of another accused it was accepted that Barry's line of defence was open to
him and that evidence in support of it could be given, but it was contended that the
evidence that had been given exceeded the limits that could be allowed. In the
course of giving reasons why those contentions failed, Widgery LJ said in the Court of
f Appeal[3]:

> 'We are further satisfied that Barry had a viable defence on the basis left to the
> jury by the learned judge, namely, that by reason of threats he was so terrified
> that he ceased to be an independent actor, and that the evidence of violent conduct
> by the Krays which Barry put before the Court was accordingly relevant and
g admissible.'

I think that the learned judge in that case did direct the jury on the basis that if
Barry acted under the compulsion of effective threats the result would be that he
would cease to be an independent actor for the reason that he would have no independent will of his own. There was no occasion in that case to have sustained legal
h argument or analysis whether this would mean that there should be an acquittal
because there was no mens rea or whether it would mean that duress if it existed was a
special defence which could result in an acquittal.

A later English case was that of *R v Hudson*[4]. Two girls, one aged 19 and the other
17, when charged with perjury, admitted that they had given false evidence in earlier
court proceedings but said that they had decided so to do because of threats that had
j been made to them. When they had arrived in court on the earlier occasion their

---

1   (1961)
2   See *R v Kray* [1969] 3 All ER 941, 53 Cr App Rep 569
3   53 Cr App Rep at 578
4   [1971] 2 All ER 244, [1971] 2 QB 202

previously formed resolve to tell lies was strengthened when they saw in court one of those who had threatened them. It might well be thought that when someone was *a* actually in a court of law in order to give evidence and was in the presence of a judge and jury, with police in attendance in the court, there would be opportunity to seek protection from the influence and effect of previous threats. That line of thought evidently weighed with the judge at the perjury trial for he directed the jury (who convicted the two girls) that in the circumstances the defence of duress did not avail. That ruling, however, as was held in the Court of Appeal, was not correct. The con- *b* victions were quashed. The matter should have been left to the jury. The Court of Appeal pointed out[1] that—

'it is always open to the Crown to prove that the accused failed to avail himself of some opportunity which was reasonably open to him to render the threat ineffective, and that on this being established the threat in question can no longer *c* be relied on by the defence. In deciding whether such an opportunity was reasonably open to the accused the jury should have regard to his age and circumstances, and to any risks to him which may be involved in the course of action relied on.'

As the defence had not been left to the jury it is impossible to know what the jury *d* would have thought of it. The case merely decides that the judge at the perjury trial—

'should have left the jury to decide whether the threats had overborne the will of the appellants at the time when they gave the false evidence'.

Though reference was there made to the will of the appellants being 'overborne' I do not think that this involved the question whether they did or did not intend to tell *e* lies. They had deliberately decided before they went to the first court that they would do so. They intended to do so. The issue for the jury in the perjury case would have been whether the threats were so real and were at the relevant time so operative and their effect so incapable of avoidance that having regard to all the circumstances the conduct of the girls could be excused.

It is not without interest to note that in the judgment of the Court in *Hudson's* *f* case[2] (which was prepared by Widgery LJ who had delivered the judgment in *Kray's* case[3]) the view was expressed[4] that it was clearly established that duress provides a defence in all cases subject only to two possible exceptions, viz, (a) possibly not in the the case of treason, and (b) possibly not in the case of 'murder as a principal'. The actions of Barry in *Kray's* case[3] as an accessory before the fact would not seem to differ very materially from the actions of the appellant in the present case as one who *g* aided and abetted.

I see no reason to question the law as laid down in *R v Dudley and Stephens*[5], the authority of which will in my view be in no way disturbed if duress is held to be a possible defence in the case of someone charged with having aided and abetted the commission of murder.

We were referred to many other decisions. The decision of the Privy Council in *h* *Subramaniam v Public Prosecutor*[6], in an appeal from the Supreme Court of the Federation of Malaya, turned on the rejection of evidence relating to questions of duress that were governed by provisions in the penal code and in the emergency regulations. The charge in that case concerned the unlawful possession of ammunition. In another

j

1 [1971] 2 All ER at 247, [1971] 2 QB at 207
2 [1971] 2 All ER 244, [1971] 2 QB 202
3 [1969] 3 All ER 941, 53 Cr App Rep 569
4 [1971] 2 All ER at 246, [1971] 2 QB at 206
5 (1884) 14 QBD 273, [1881-5] All ER Rep 61
6 [1956] 1 WLR 965

Privy Council case, *Sephakela v R*[1], questions were raised in regard to compulsion being a defence in a case of murder. The actual decision of the Board was that the evidence fell short of what was necessary in law to establish such a defence. There was no suggestion that compulsion could never be a defence. But having regard to the state of the evidence no occasion arose for the Board to enter on a full examination of principle.

In the Quebec case of *R v Farduto*[2] the result was determined by the application of sections of the criminal code. One section provided that a person was a party to and guilty of an offence who did an act for the purpose of aiding a person to commit the offence. The accused had a razor; P threatened the accused that he would be shot unless he gave his razor to him (P); the accused did so; P used it in killing someone then present. So under the section above referred to the accused was charged with murder. Had he a defence? The answer was No; another section of the code while providing that compulsion by threats of immediate death or grievous bodily harm could be 'an excuse' made exceptions in the case of a number of offences which included murder, piracy, attempting to murder, assisting in rape, robbery, causing grievous bodily harm and arson. That section of the code was said to stem from the report of the Royal Commissioners in England which seemed to proceed on the basis that duress ought not to be allowed as a defence in the case of crimes of a heinous character. A consideration of the case last referred to leads me to the view that it could not be just to lay it down that in no circumstances, whatever they were, could duress ever be a defence to a charge of aiding and abetting a murder.

We were referred to the provisions contained in certain other criminal codes. In some of these, while it is laid down that a person is exempted from responsibility if he commits an offence under the compulsion of threats of death or of grievous bodily harm, the provisions are made inapplicable in regard to certain offences including that of murder. Some of these codes though enacted at varying dates are based on suggestions made in this country nearly a century ago. Where there is no operative legislative enactment I do not think that the vital force of the common law need be anchored to the thoughts which may then have been expressed.

We were referred to the provisions of s 37 of the Criminal Justice Act (Northern Ireland) 1945 which gives a defence to a wife who proves that she acted in the presence of and under the coercion of her husband but which make an exception of murder and treason; the question arises whether an indication is given that Parliament regarded the analogous defence of duress as never being available in the case of these two crimes. But surmise as to what may have been thought in 1945 cannot yield us any positive answer to our present problem and ought not to compel us to give any particular answer. Nor can we know whether the separate position of aiders and abettors was specially considered.

A recent case of much interest is that of *R v Brown and Morley*[3] in South Australia in 1968. Morley killed a lady and the case against Brown was that he was a principal in the second degree since though he was not present in the room where the killing took place he had taken part in planning the killing and had rendered some surprisingly minor assistance to disguise the noise that Morley might make in approaching the room. Brown as well as Morley was convicted. Brown's case was that all that he did was done under duress by reason of threats made to him by Morley. The majority of the Supreme Court in dismissing the appeal considered that duress did not excuse Brown for any acts which constituted taking an active part in an arrangement for the killing of the lady. Bray CJ dissented. In a closely reasoned judgment, the persuasive power of which appeals to me, he held that it was wrong to say that no

---

1   [1954] High Commission Territories LR 60
2   (1912) 10 DLR 669
3   [1968] SASR 467

type of duress can ever afford a defence to any type of complicity in murder though
he drew a line of limitation when he said[1]:   *a*

'I repeat also that as at present advised I do not think duress could constitute a
defence to one who actually kills or attempts to kill the victim.'

Another case which repays study is that of *State v Goliath*[2].

Having regard to the authorities to which I have referred it seems to me to have
been firmly held by our courts in this country that duress can afford a defence in   *b*
criminal cases. A recent pronouncement was that in the Court of Appeal in 1971 in
the case above referred to (*R v Hudson*[3]). The court stated that they had been referred to a large number of authorities and to the views of writers of text books. In
the judgment of the court delivered by Lord Parker CJ and prepared by Widgery LJ
the conclusion was expressed that[4]—
                                                                                      c
'it is clearly established that duress provides a defence in all offences including
perjury (except possibly treason or murder as a principal) . . .'

We are only concerned in this case to say whether duress could be a possible defence
open to Lynch who was charged with being an aider and abettor. Relying on the help
given in the authorities we must decide this as a matter of principle. I consider that   *d*
duress in such a case can be open as a possible defence. Both general reasoning and
the requirements of justice lead me to this conclusion.

The second certified point of law would seem on a first study of it to raise questions
closely allied to those raised under the first: that would appear to be so when the
question of the necessity to prove 'willingness' to participate is raised. In regard to
the matters discussed in the judgments on this second point I am content to say that   *e*
I am in general agreement with the conclusion reached by the majority as expressed
in the judgment of Lowry CJ. The words 'aid' and 'abet' are, I think, synonymous.
If in the present case the jury were satisfied that the car was driven towards the garage
in pursuance of a murderous plan and that the appellant knew that that was the plan
and intentionally drove the car in execution of that plan he could be held to have
aided and abetted even though he regretted the plan or indeed was horrified by it.   *f*
However great his reluctance he would have intended to aid and abet. But if that
intention and all that he did only came about because of the compulsion of duress of
the nature that I have described he would, in my view, have a defence.

The question arises as to what is the proper course to follow. The appellant did
not have the opportunity of having his defence of duress considered. I think that he
should have it. His conviction should be quashed but having regard to all the circumstances I consider that the interests of justice require that there should be a retrial.   *g*
I would remit the case to the Court of Criminal Appeal to make the appropriate
order.

I would allow the appeal accordingly.

LORD WILBERFORCE. My Lords, the appellant has been convicted, after a   *h*
joint trial with two other persons before a judge and jury, of the murder of a police
constable in Belfast. He was sentenced to life imprisonment. The case against him,
which the jury must have accepted, was that he drove three men equipped with arms
combat jackets and balaclava helmets, in a car to a place near where the constable
was stationed; that the three men left the car and shot the constable, after which
they returned to the car and were driven away by the appellant. The appellant had   *j*

---

1 [1968] SASR at 499
2 1972 (3) SA 1
3 [1971] 2 All ER 244, [1971] 2 QB 202
4 [1971] 2 All ER at 246, [1971] 2 QB at 206

a previously been summoned by messenger to a back room where the three men were, one armed with a rifle and another with an automatic gun. There he was given orders, first to 'hi-jack' a car, which together with an armed man he did, and later to drive it. The charge was treated at the trial as one of aiding and abetting and the jury was accordingly directed to consider whether the appellant was aware of the nature of the enterprise and knew that death or violence was likely to be the outcome. They must be taken to have found that he did.

b One of the men in the room and in the car was Sean Meehan, as to whom evidence was given that he is a well-known and ruthless gunman. The appellant and one of the two persons accused with him, William Bates, gave evidence that Meehan was the kind of person whom it would be perilous to disobey and who, on the occasion in question, gave his instructions to them in a manner which indicated that he would tolerate no disobedience. Both the appellant and Bates testified to their fear of Meehan

c and their clear view that disobedience of his instructions would cause them to be shot.

The trial judge, after hearing argument, decided not to leave to the jury the question whether the appellant had been compelled by duress to participate in the events which led to the shooting. He took the view that as a matter of law a defence of duress is not available on a charge of murder. The Court of Criminal Appeal upheld this

d decision; O'Connell J dissented to the extent that, in his opinion, the defence of duress is admissible when the charge is one of aiding and abetting. Thus the appellant has been denied the opportunity of having a defence based on duress considered by the jury.

It is clear that a possible case of duress, on the facts, could have been made. I say 'a possible case' because there were a number of matters which the jury would have

e had to consider if this defence had been left to them. Among these would have been whether Meehan, though uttering no express threats of death or serious injury, impliedly did so in such a way as to put the appellant in fear of death or serious injury; whether, if so, the threats continued to operate throughout the enterprise; whether the appellant had voluntarily exposed himself to a situation in which threats might be used against him if he did not participate in a criminal enterprise (the appellant

f denied that he had done so); whether the appellant had taken every opportunity open to him to escape from the situation of duress.

In order to test the validity of the judge's decision to exclude this defence, we must assume on this appeal that these matters would have been decided in favour of the appellant.

What then, does exclusion of the defence involve? It means that a person, assumedly

g not himself a member of a terrorist group, summoned from his home, with explicit or implied threats of death or serious injury at gunpoint, to drive armed men on what he finds to be a criminal enterprise, having no opportunity to escape, but with the certainty of being shot if he resists or tries to get away, is liable to be convicted of murder. The same would be true of a bystander in a street, or an owner of a car, similarly conscripted, once it is shown that he, or she, knew the nature of the enter-

h prise. One may multiply examples of the possible involvement of persons, whom the normal man would regard as without guilt, under threats of death or violence, in violent enterprises—examples unfortunately far from fanciful at this time. Does the law require all these to be charged with murder and call for their conviction? It would be our duty to accept such a law if it existed, but we are also entitled to see if it does.

j Does then the law forbid admission of a defence of duress on a charge of murder whether as a principal in the first degree or as a principal in the second degree or as an accessory? Consistently with the method normal in the development of the common law, an answer to this question must be sought in authority, and in the principles on which established authority is based. I look first at the principle. The principle on which duress is admitted as a defence is not easy to state. Professor

Glanville Williams[1] indeed doubts whether duress fits in to any accepted theory; it may, in his view, stand by itself altogether outside the definition of will and act. The *a* reason for this is historical. Duress emerged very early in our law as a fact of which account has to be taken, particularly in times of civil strife where charges of treason were the normal consequence of defeat, long before the criminal law had worked out a consistent or any theory of 'mens rea' or intention. At the present time, whatever the ultimate analysis in jurisprudence may be, the best opinion, as reflected in deci- *b* sions of judges and in writers, seems to be that duress per minas is something which is superimposed on the other ingredients which by themselves would make up an offence, i e on the act and intention. 'Coactus volui' sums up the combination: the victim completes the act and knows that he is doing so; but the addition of the element of duress prevents the law from treating what he has done as a crime. One may note—and the comparison is satisfactory—that an analogous result is achieved in a civil law context: duress does not destroy the will, for example, to enter into a *c* contract, but prevents the law from accepting what has happened as a contract valid in law (see the Privy Council case of *Barton v Armstrong*[2] and the judgments in the Supreme Court of New South Wales).

If then it is correct that duress is an additional element which comes into play, and excuses, after act and intention have been manifested, it follows that analysis of 'intention' in the criminal law will not of itself assist in determining the scope of the *d* defence of duress. The most recent and probably the most profound analysis of the element of 'intention' in relation to murder is to be found in the opinions in this House in *Hyam v Director of Public Prosecutions*[3] and these were much cited in argument. But they do not help us here. Whatever she did, or intended, Mrs Hyam did volun- tarily and willingly. The analysis of her conduct and mental state must have been different if a gunman with a loaded weapon had been behind her and dictating her *e* action. Correspondingly, in a case such as the present, where duress may be involved, to invite a jury to make their decision merely on the appellants' intention, as that word is used in Hyam, is to stop half way and to omit a vital ingredient in his action. In the *Hyam*[3] sense he may have had the necessary intention to involve him as an aider and abettor but his intention may have been produced by threats which he could not resist. *f*

I referred above to judicial decisions; it is certainly the case that, in recent years, and subsequently to Stephen's History of the Criminal Law of England (and in spite of that eminent author's views[4]), the defence of duress has been judicially admitted in relation to a variety of crimes: inter alia, treason, receiving, stealing, malicious damage, arson, perjury. In all of these crimes there would have to be proved, in addition to an actus reus, an element of intention. Yet this defence has been admitted. This makes *g* it clear beyond doubt, to my mind, that if the defence is to be denied in relation to murder, that cannot be because the crime of murder—as distinct from other crimes— involves the presence of intention; it must be for some other reason. If the propo- sition is correct at all that duress prevents what would otherwise constitute a crime for attracting criminal responsibility, then that should be correct whatever the crime.

What reason then can there be for excepting murder? One may say—as some *h* authorities do (cf *Attorney-General v Whelan* per Murnaghan J[5], *R v Hurley and Murray* per Smith J[6]) that murder is the most heinous of crimes: so it may be, and in some circumstances, a defence of duress in relation to it should be correspondingly hard to establish. Indeed, to justify the deliberate killing by one's own hand of another human being may be something that no pressure or threat even to one's own life which can *j*

1 Criminal Law (2nd Edn, 1961), p 751
2 (5th December 1973) unreported
3 [1974] 2 All ER 41, [1974] 2 WLR 607
4 (1883), vol 2, pp 107, 108
5 [1934] IR 518 at 526
6 [1967] VR 526 at 543

be imagined can justify—no such case ever seems to have reached the courts. But if

a one accepts the test of heinousness, this does not, in my opinion, involve that all cases of what is murder in law must be treated in the same way. Heinousness is a word of degree, and that there are lesser degrees of heinousness, even of involvement in homicide, seems beyond doubt. An accessory before the fact, or an aider or abettor, may (not necessarily must) bear a less degree that the actual killer: and even if the rule of exclusion is absolute, or nearly so in relation to the latter, it need not be so in

b lesser cases. Nobody would dispute that the greater the degree of heinousness of the crime, the greater and less resistable must be the degree of pressure, if pressure is to excuse. Questions of this kind where it is necessary to weigh the pressures acting on a man against the gravity of the act he commits are common enough in the criminal law, for example with regard to provocation and self-defence: their difficulty is not a reason for a total rejection of the defence. To say that the defence may be admitted in

c relation to some degrees of murder, but that its admission in cases of direct killing by a first degree principal is likely to be attended by such great difficulty as almost to justify a ruling that the defence is not available, is not illogical. It simply involves the recognition that by sufficiently adding to the degrees, one may approach an absolute position.

So I find no convincing reason, on principle, why, if a defence of duress in the crimi-

d nal law exists at all, it should be absolutely excluded in murder charges whatever the nature of the charge; hard to establish, yes, in case of direct killing so hard that perhaps it will never be proved; but in other cases to be judged, strictly indeed, on the totality of facts. Exclusion, if not arbitrary, must be based either on authority or policy. I shall deal with each.

As to authority, this has been fully examined by others of your Lordships and I shall

e not duplicate the process. The stream is reasonably clear if not deep. I do not think it open to controversy (i) that a defence of duress is known to English law and has been so known since the 14th century (in one form or another it seems to be admitted in all common law and civil law jurisdictions); (ii) that the defence is admitted in English law as absolving from guilt, not as diminishing responsibility or as merely mitigating the punishment. Some authors do indeed suggest the latter, at least in

f relation to homicide (cf East's Pleas of the Crown[1]) and there may be a case (not an answerable case) for saying, generally, that this ought to be the law. It clearly, however, is not the law and, particularly where sentence is mandatory, whether of death or life imprisonment, Parliamentary action would be necessary if proof of duress were to operate on the sentence. It would also be necessary if duress were to be admitted as diminishing responsibility; (iii) that there is no direct English judicial

g authority against its application to charges of murder. There is the judgment of Lord Coleridge CJ in the 'necessity' case of *R v Dudley and Stephens*[2]; there are obiter dicta (*Attorney-General v Whelan*[3], *R v Steane*[4], *R v Bourne*[5]), some of eminent judges, in favour of exclusion, but these follow the writers, who in turn follow Hale. That great writer—and the same is true of Stephen—would recognise that legal thought and practice has moved far since his time. Indeed it is significant that the reason he

h gives for excluding the defence of duress to charges of treason, murder or robbery is that[6]—

> 'the law has provided a sufficient remedy against such fears by applying himself to the courts and officers of justice for a writ or precept *de securitate pacis*.'

---

j
1   (1803), p 225
2   (1884) 14 QBD 273, [1881-5] All ER Rep 61
3   [1934] IR at 526
4   [1947] 1 All ER 813 at 816, [1947] KB 997 at 1005
5   (1952) 36 Cr App Rep 125 at 128
6   Pleas of the Crown (1800), vol 1, p 50

Even if this argument was ever realistic, he would surely have recognised that reconsideration of it must be required in troubled times. That the defence may be *a*
admissible in cases of murder other than as a principal was indicated by the Court of
Appeal presided over by Lord Parker CJ in a judgment prepared by Widgery LJ in
R v Hudson[1]. That judgment was a considered judgment after relevant authorities
had been fully cited; (v) that there are two cases in which the defence of duress has
arisen in relation to charges of murder not being murder by a principal of the first
degree. The first is *R v Kray*[2]. This case is fully analysed by my noble and learned *b*
friend Lord Morris of Borth-y-Gest and is somewhat incomplete as an authority.
But the defence was admitted, and had it not been, much of the evidence in the case
would have been inadmissible. Quite apart from the present appeal I should be most
reluctant to cast doubt on it. That, as I understand it, was a case of an accessory
before the fact but it is difficult to see any logical distinction between a case where a
man is forced to carry a gun and a case where a man is forced to drive a killer—each *c*
to the scene of the crime. The other was an unreported case recently tried (by judge
alone) in Northern Ireland (*R v Fegan*[3]) also involving an involuntary car driver. The
charge seems to have been one of aiding and abetting an attempted murder or pos-
siblity of attempted murder, which would make it a stronger case, and the defence
was admitted. On the other side is *R v Tyler and Price*[4] in which Lord Denman CJ
is reported to have charged the jury in terms more widely expressed than was *d*
necessary and in which the facts could not, properly regarded, be considered as
amounting to duress.

Outside the United Kingdom there is the important authority of *R v Brown and
Morley*[5], a case of aiding and abetting murder. A majority of the Supreme Court of
South Australia held the defence of duress not admissible, in effect on grounds of
public policy. But there is an impressive judgment of Bray CJ in dissent. He fully *e*
examines the authorities, from Hale onwards, and concludes that they do not establish
that duress is no defence in any circumstances. I quote one paragraph[6]:

> 'The reasoning generally used to support the proposition that duress is no
> defence to a charge of murder is, to use the words of *Blackstone* cited above, that
> 'he ought rather to die himself, than escape by the murder of an innocent'. *f*
> Generally speaking I am prepared to accept this proposition. Its force is obviously
> considerably less where the act of the threatened man is not the direct act of
> killing but only the rendering of some minor form of assistance, particularly
> when it is by no means certain that if he refuses the death of the victim will be
> averted, or conversely when it is by no means certain that if he complies the death
> will be a necessary consequence. It would seem hard, for example, if an innocent *g*
> passer-by seized in the street by a gang of criminals visibly engaged in robbery
> and murder in a shop and compelled at the point of a gun to issue misleading
> comments to the public, or *an innocent driver compelled at the point of a gun to
> convey the murderer to the victim*, were to have no defence. Are there any authorities
> which compel us to hold that he would not?'

Events have shown that the learned judge's hypothetical examples were not *h*
fanciful. Two decisions of the Privy Council, *Sephakela v R*[7] and *Rossides v R*[8] are
certainly not authorities against the defence: the former indeed seems to assume that it
exists in relation to murder.

---

1 [1971] 2 All ER 244, [1971] 2 QB 202
2 [1969] 3 All ER 941, 53 Cr App Rep 569   *j*
3 (1974)
4 (1838) 8 C & P 616
5 [1968] SASR 467
6 [1968] SASR at 494
7 [1954] High Commission Territories LR 60
8 [1957] Crim LR 813

State v Goliath[1] on the other hand is a clear decision that compulsion can constitute
a a defence on a charge of murder. The judgment of Rumpff J contains a thorough
comparative examination of the law of many countries and systems. I quote the
following passage as a statement of principle:

'When the opinion is expressed that our law recognises compulsion as a defence
in all cases except murder, and that opinion is based on the acceptance that
b acquittal follows because the threatened party is deprived of his freedom of
choice, then it seems to me to be irrational, in the light of developments which
have come about since the days of the old Dutch and English writers, to exclude
compulsion as a complete defence to murder if the threatened party was under
such a strong duress that a reasonable person would not have acted otherwise
under the same duress. The only ground for such an exclusion would then be
c that, notwithstanding the fact that the threatened person is deprived of his
freedom of volition, the act is still imputed to him because of his failure to
comply with what has been described as the highest ethical ideal. In the application of our criminal law in the cases where the acts of an accused are judged
by objective standards, the principle applies that one can never demand more from
an accused than that which is reasonable, and reasonable in this context means,
d that which can be expected of the ordinary, average person in the particular
circumstances. It is generally accepted, also by the ethicists, that for the ordinary
person in general his life is more valuable than that of another. Only they who
possess the quality of heroism will intentionally offer their lives for another.
Should the criminal law then state that compulsion could never be a defence to a
charge of murder, it would demand that a person who killed another under
e duress, whatever the circumstances, would have to comply with a higher standard than that demanded of the average person. I do not think that such an
exception to the general rule which applies in criminal law, is justified.'

The conclusion which I deduce is that although, in a case of actual killing by a first
degree principal the balance of judicial authority at the present time is against the
f admission of the defence of duress, in the case of lesser degrees of participation, the
balance is, if anything, the other way. At the very least, to admit the defence in such
cases involves no departure from established decisions.

Finally, I ought perhaps to refer to some Commonwealth codes: there are several
which may be relevant. The Criminal Codes of Canada (art 7), of New Zealand (art
24), of Tasmania (s 20(1)), of Queensland (art 31(4)), while admitting a defence of
g compulsion by threats, exclude it in cases of murder. However, they also exclude it
in the case of a long list of other crimes—longer than is found in Hale—e g in Canada,
treason, piracy, assisting in rape, forcible abduction, robbery, causing bodily harm,
arson. These codes follow the report of the English Criminal Law Commissioners of
1879[2] which, under the influence of Stephen, prepared a draft code. It is stated in
Note A to page 10 that the section (23) on compulsion has been framed to express
h 'What we think is the existing law, and what at all events we suggest ought to be the
law', but it was not adopted in England, and as regards some at any rate of the listed
offences did not represent the law at the time and certainly does not now represent
the law as it is. The authority quoted as regards murder is, as usual that of Hale[3]:
'he ought rather to die himself than kill an innocent'.

In the same category, perhaps, is a provision (also found in English law) in the law
of Northern Ireland, The Criminal Justice Act (Northern Ireland) 1945, s 37 (cf the
j Criminal Justice Act 1925, s 47). This provides:

---

1   1972 (3) SA 1
2   (1879) C 2nd series 2346
3   Op cit, p 51   II

'Any presumption of law that an offence committed by a wife in the presence of her husband is committed under the coercion of the husband is hereby abolished, but on a charge against the wife for any offence other than treason or murder it shall be a good defence to prove that the offence was committed in the presence of, and under the coercion of, the husband.'

This section has given me some difficulty for it seems to reflect a Parliamentary opinion that murder and treason are exceptions to the defence of coercion; and if so it may seem difficult to differentiate the case of duress.

But there is considerable obscurity as to the meaning of this provision. A leading writer says of it that it raises an almost insoluble problem of interpretation and states that it may be regarded as an incomplete statement of the common law which still exists to supplement its deficiency[1]. As a guide to the principle on which duress should be admitted as a defence to a charge of the various degrees of murder, such light as it shed is too dim to read by. I conclude that these statutory provisions leave the common law of this country untouched.

The broad question remains how this House, clearly not bound by any precedent, should now state the law with regard to this defence in relation to the facts of the present case. I have no doubt that it is open to us, on normal judicial principles, to hold the defence admissible. We are here in the domain of the common law; our task is to fit what we can see as principle and authority to the facts before us, and it is no obstacle that these facts are new. The judges have always assumed responsibility for deciding questions of principle relating to criminal liability and guilt and particularly for setting the standards by which the law expects normal men to act. In all such matters as capacity, sanity, drunkeness, coercion, necessity, provocation, self-defence, the common law, through the judges, accepts and sets the standards of right-thinking men of normal firmness and humanity at a level which people can accept and respect. The House is not inventing a new defence; on the contrary, it would not discharge its judicial duty if it failed to define the law's attitude to this particular defence in particular circumstances. I would decide that the defence is in law admissible in a case of aiding and abetting murder, and so in the present case. I would leave cases of direct killing by a principal in the first degree to be dealt with as they arise.

It is said that such persons as the appellant can always be safeguarded by action of the executive which can order an imprisoned person to be released. I firmly reject any such argument. A law, which requires innocent victims of terrorist threats to be tried for murder and convicted as murderers, is an unjust law even if the executive, resisting political pressures, may decide, after it all, and within the permissible limits of the prerogative, to release them. Moreover, if the defence is excluded in law, much of the evidence which would prove the duress would be inadmissible at the trial, not brought out in court, and not tested by cross-examination. The validity of the defence is far better judged by a jury, after proper direction and a fair trial, than by executive officials; and if it is said that to allow the defence will be to encourage fictitious claims of pressure I have enough confidence in our legal system to believe that the process of law is a better safeguard against this than enquiry by a Government department.

I would allow the appeal and answer the first certified question in the affirmative. This involves no more than saying that a defence of duress was admissible in law. Since, as I have explained, that defence has yet to be made good in fact, and since a number of elements have to be proved to a jury's satisfaction, I would, under ss 13 and 38 of the Criminal Appeal (Northern Ireland) Act 1968 order a new trial and remit the case to the Court of Criminal Appeal for directions to be given under s 14 of the Act.

---

1 Glanville Williams, Criminal Law (2nd Edn, 1961), p 759

LORD SIMON OF GLAISDALE.

a

I

My Lords, the first question that arises is whether duress is a defence to a charge of murder as a principal in the second degree. The law has never recognised such a defence; and there is considerable authority that duress, and closely cognate juridical concepts (such as 'necessity' and 'coercion'), do not extend to being defences to a charge of murder as a principal—if, indeed, to murder in any degree of participation. But it is

b argued on behalf of the appellant, first, that the law has already recognised duress as a defence to some crimes, and that there is no logical reason for its limitation; and, secondly, that a criminal law which exacts sanctions against persons who are terrorised into performing prohibited acts is both making excessive demands on human nature, and is also imposing penalties in circumstances where they are unjustified as retribution and irrelevant as deterrent.

c   Before turning to examine these considerations, it is convenient to have a working definition of duress—even though it is actually an extremely vague and elusive juristic concept. I take it for present purposes to denote such [well-grounded] fear, produced by threats, of death or grievous bodily harm [or unjustified imprisonment] if a certain act is not done, as overbears the actor's wish not to perform the act, and is effective, at the time of the act, in constraining him to perform it. I am quite un-

d certain whether the words which I have put in square brackets should be included in any such definition. It is arguable that the test should be purely subjective, and that it is contrary to principle to require the fear to be a reasonable one. Moreover, I have assumed, on the basis of *R v Hudson*[1], that threat of future injury may suffice, although Stephen[2] is to the contrary. Then the law leaves it also quite uncertain whether the fear induced by threats must be of death or grievous bodily harm, or

e whether threatened loss of liberty suffices: cases of duress in the law of contract suggest that duress may extend to fear of unjustified imprisonment; but the criminal law returns no clear answer. It also leaves entirely unanswered whether, to constitute such a general criminal defence, the threat must be of harm to the person required to perform the act, or extends to the immediate family of the actor (and how immediate?), or to any person. Such questions are not academic ones in these days when

f hostages are so frequently seized. Is it worse to have a pistol thrust into your back and a grenade into your hand, or to have your child (or a neighbour's child) seized by terrorists and held at peril until you have placed in a public building a parcel which you believe to contain a bomb?

       I shall have to consider such situations in another connection in a moment. As of now I refer to them to demonstrate the uncertainty of the proffered rule of law in

g critical and far from fanciful situations. Surely, certainty in the law is hardly less important in the rules which exonerate from criminal responsibility than in those which impose it. Candid recognition, at the outset, of the vague and amorphous nature of the proffered rule should have at least three consequences: first, to cast doubt on whether there is, or should be, any general defence of duress; secondly, to encourage exploration whether the law has not other means of mitigating its rigours

h towards those who commit prohibited acts under threats which call for far more than ordinary courage to resist; and, thirdly, to cause hesitation before, in deference to logic, extending the defence beyond where it has been heretofore recognised.

       And not only do your Lordships meet with uncertainty at the very outset of your enquiry, you also meet with anomaly. Where so little is clear, this at least seems to be established: that the type of threat which affords a defence must be one of human

j physical harm (including, possibly, imprisonment), so that threat of injury to property is not enough. The criminal law (see *M'Growther's Case*[3]) is here at one with the law

---

1   [1971] 2 All ER 244, [1971] 2 QB 202
2   Digest of the Criminal Law (1877) note to art 10
3   (1746) Fost 13

of contract. But a threat to property may, in certain circumstances, be as potent in overbearing the actor's wish not to perform the prohibited act as a threat of physical *a* harm. For example, the threat may be to burn down his house unless the householder merely keeps watch against interruption while a crime is committed. Or a fugitive from justice may say, 'I have it in my power to make your son bankrupt. You can avoid that merely by driving me to the airport'. Would not many ordinary people yield to such threats, and act contrary to their wish not to perform an action prohibited by law? Faced with such anomaly, is not the only answer, 'Well, the law *b* must draw a line somewhere; and, as a result of experience and human valuation, the law draws it between threats to property and threats to the person'. But if an arbitrary line is thus drawn, is not one between murder and traditionally lesser crimes equally justifiable? How can an arbitrary line drawn between murder as a principal in the first degree and murder as a principal in the second degree be justified either morally or juridically? Faced with anomaly and uncertainty, may it not be *c* that a narrow, arbitrary and anomalous general defence of duress, negativing the crime, is far less acceptable in practice and far less justifiable in juristic theory than a broadly based plea which mitigates the penalty?

Any sane and humane system of criminal justice must be able to allow for all such situations as the following, and not merely for some of them. A person, honestly and reasonably believing that a loaded pistol is at his back which will in all probability *d* be used if he disobeys, is ordered to do an act prima facie criminal. Similarly, a person whose child has been kidnapped, and whom as a consequence of threats he honestly and reasonably believes to be in danger of death or mutilation if he does not perform an act prima facie criminal. Or his neighbour's child in such a situation. Or any child. Or any human being. Or his home, a national heritage, threatened to be blown up. Or a stolen masterpiece of art destroyed. Or his son financially ruined. Or his savings *e* for the old age of himself and his wife put in peril. In other words, a sane and humane system of criminal justice needs some general flexibility, and not merely some quirks of deference to certain odd and arbitrarily defined human weaknesses. In fact our own system of criminal justice has such flexibility, provided that it is realised that it does not consist only in the positive prohibitions and injunctions of the criminal law, but extends also to its penal sanctions. May it not be that the infinite variety of *f* circumstances in which the lawful wish of the actor is overborne could be accommodated with far greater flexibility, with much less anomaly, and with avoidance of the social evils which would attend acceptance of the appellant's argument (that duress is a general criminal defence), by taking those circumstances into account in the sentence of the court? Is not the whole rationale of duress as a criminal defence that it recognises that an act prohibited by the criminal law may be morally innocent? Is *g* not an absolute discharge just such an acknowledgment of moral innocence? Nor should one even stop short at the sentence of the court. Does not our system of criminal justice extend more widely still—to the discretion of prosecutors, to the exercise of the prerogative of mercy, to the operations of the parole board?

I spoke of the social evils which might be attendant on the recognition of a general defence of duress. Would it not enable a gang leader of notorious violence to confer *h* on his organisation by terrorism immunity from the criminal law? Every member of his gang might well be able to say with truth, 'It was as much as my life was worth to disobey'. Was this not in essence the plea of the appellant? We do not, in general, allow a superior officer to confer such immunity on his subordinates by any defence of obedience to orders; why should we allow it to terrorists? Nor would it seem to be sufficient to stipulate that no one can plead duress as a defence who had put himself *j* into a position in which duress could be exercised on himself. Might not his very initial involvement with, and his adherence to, the gang be due to terrorism? Would it be fair to exclude a defence of duress on the ground that its subject should have sought police protection, were the police unable to guarantee immunity, or were co-operation with the police reasonably believed itself to be a warrant for physical

retribution? (If *Hudson*[1] is to be taken as a growing point for this part of the law, it
a suggests that the impossibility of recourse to the police is not a necessary precondition
for the defence of duress.) In my respectful submission your Lordships should hesitate
long lest you may be inscribing a charter for terorists, gang-leaders and kidnappers.

As Stephen pointed out, coercion lies at the very basis of the criminal law itself.
The criminal law is itself a system of threats of pains and penalties if its commands
are disregarded. Is it to abdicate because some subject institutes a countervailing
b system of threats? The answer might well be a reluctant 'Yes', if the only alternative
were to require something more than ordinary human nature can reasonably be
expected to bear. But is that the only alternative? Are prosecutors bound to indict?
Have English courts no power and duty to reflect moral guilt in the sentence? (I shall
deal later with murder, where the penalty is a fixed one.)

c   II
A principal difficulty in this branch of the law is the chaotic terminology, whether
in judgments, academic writings or statutes. Will, volition, motive, purpose, object,
view, intention, intent, specific intent or intention, wish, desire; necessity, coercion,
compulsion, duress—such terms, which do indeed overlap in certain contexts, seem
frequently to be used interchangeably, without definition, and regardless that in
d some cases the legal usage is a term of art differing from the popular usage. As if
this were not enough, Latin expressions which are themselves ambiguous, and often
overlap more than one of the English terms, have been freely used—especially
animus and (most question-begging of all) mens rea.

But before I embark on what I regard as a necessary examination of some of these
terms, I venture to note that the law accepts generally two concepts as axiomatic
e even though acknowledging that metaphysicians and psychologists have amongst
themselves divergent views on the subject. The first concept which the law accepts
generally as a datum is that of the conscious mind. Of course, the law recognises that
exceptionally the mind may be absent, as with a person of very severely subnormal
mentality. And, of course, the law does not deny the existence of subconscious
psychic activity—indeed, its use of punishment as a deterrent is directed as much to
f halting action on the verge of consciousness as to instituting a utilitarian debate in the
conscious and reasoning mind whereby the pleasures and pains consequent on prohibited action are weighed against each other. But it remains generally true that it is
of conscious and provable mental processes that the law takes cognizance. Significant
among them is foresight of consequences.

Largely concomitant with this first datum, the law also accepts generally as an
g axiom the concept of the free human will—that is a potentiality in the conscious mind
to direct conscious action—specifically, the power of choice in regard to action. Even
the most devout predestinarian puts off his theology when he puts on his legal robe.
The law may be an ass, but it is not Buridan's ass. The term of art used by the law to
denote a person's physical movement actuated by his will is an 'act'. Of course, here
again, the law recognises that there will be exceptions, where a person has no freedom
h of choice. The classic example is where A by irresistible physical force directs B's
hand holding a knife to stab C: this is not B's 'act'. So, too, the law recognises that
there may be such lack of understanding as to preclude a choice in regard to action. Thus
the law recognises that a child may lack sufficient understanding to be able to exercise conscious choice: our criminal law presumes irrebuttably that a child under ten,
and rebuttably that a child between ten and 14, is incapable, through lack of under-
j standing, of having sufficient power of choice to be criminally responsible. Presumably
experience has shown that it is expedient to draw an arbitrary line somewhere; and
that, drawn here, justice is done in the generality of cases: the exceptional cases below
the age of ten can be lumped and those above the age of 14 can be safely left to the

---

1 [1971] 2 All ER 244, [1971] 2 QB 202

discretionary power of the courts in sentencing or of the Home Secretary in advising
as to the prerogative of mercy, or to the review powers of the parole board. The law *a*
has found that an arbitrary line mitigated by discretionary powers provides the most
satisfactory solution. Then, again, there may be physical movements which are not
the subject of choice—cases of so-called 'automatism'. On the other hand, exceptionally the criminal law will exert its sanctions although the accused exercised no choice:
this arises in crimes of absolute liability, where the act (involving the will) of an
employee may be imputed to his employer. Such cases, being exceptional, are not *b*
relevant to your Lordships' instant enquiry. The general basis of criminal responsibility
is the power of choice involved in the axiomatic freedom of the human will.

'Volition' I take to be synonymous with 'will' (i e the power of directing action by
conscious choice); so that an 'act' is a voluntary physical movement, and an involuntary
physical movement is not an 'act'.

With this submission that the law accepts as data the concepts of mind and will, I *c*
can approach my understanding of some of the other terms used in this branch of
the law. The first group of terms (motive, purpose, intent, desire, wish etc) all, I
think, have reference to various modes and degrees of foresight of the consequences
which generally ensue from an act.

Although I have tried to define and analyse them for myself, it would be inappropriate and presumptuous to inflict a jurisprudential essay in an appeal of this sort. *d*
It will be, I hope, sufficient if I note six matters. First, *intention* and *specific intent*
(although I myself much prefer Smith and Hogan's[1] terminology of *ulterior intent*) are
terms of art: the other terms are used in their ordinary senses (*intent*, although I
think, a legal term of art, in the main coincides with general usage). Secondly, an
intention to bring about a consequence of an act can co-exist with a *desire* that such
consequence should not ensue (*Lang v Lang*[2]). Thirdly, a *wish* is a particular instance *e*
of *desire*. Fourthly, therefore, an *intention* to perform an act with foreseen consequences can co-exist with a *wish* not to perform the act or that its consequences
should not ensue (this is crucial in considering the juridical effect of duress). Fifthly,
motive is used in two senses: first, that psychic state which induces a person to act in a
certain way by influencing his volition (internal motive); secondly, a contemplated
result or object, the desire of which tends to influence volition (external motive): *f*
they are like magnet and needle. In the context of duress, fear is the internal motive,
avoidance of injury the external motive. Motive is generally irrelevant to the positive
prohibitions and injunctions of the criminal law, though of great importance when it
comes to the sentence of the court. The motive of fear (or avoidance of injury) is,
therefore, like any other motive, on general principle irrelevant to whether a crime
has been committed; and therefore in principle duress should not be a general *g*
defence to crime. (This was Stephen's view on principle[3].) Lastly, actus reus and mens
rea are misleading terms; since (other than exceptionally) a mental state is not
criminal without an accompanying act and an act is not criminal without some
accompanying mental element. Both terms have, however, justified themselves by
their usefulness; and I shall myself employ them in their traditional senses—namely,
actus reus to mean such conduct as constitutes a crime if the mental element involved *h*
in the definition of the crime is also present (or, more shortly, conduct prohibited by
law); and mens rea to mean such mental element, over and above volition, as is
involved in the definition of the crime.

III

For the second group of terms I go back to the legal axiom of the freedom of the *i*
will. A key concept is *necessity*. Dr Johnson defined 'Free Will' as 'The power of

---

1 Criminal Law (3rd Edn, 1973), p 303
2 [1954] 3 All ER 571, [1955] AC 402
3 Digest of the Criminal Law (1877), note to art 10

directing our own action without restraint by necessity or fate', a definition repeated
a by the Oxford English Dictionary. Dr Johnson was, of course, speaking in meta-
physical or theological terms. But his definition seems to me to be equally relevant in
law. An action constrained by true necessity is one made without true choice of action;
it is therefore not a product of the will of the person so constrained, and is therefore
not an 'act'. Quidquid necessitas cogit, defendit, wrote Lord Hale[1]: that may be lawfully done which cannot be forborne. It has never been doubted that this is, in general,
b sound law.

Unfortunately *necessity* has not be confined juridically to this true and accurate
sense. This is probably due to the fact, that, as well as the legal maxim 'legem non
habet necessitas' (which comes from St Augustine, not from the rational civilians),
there was a popular saying, 'Need has no law'. So *necessity* came to be used, most
misleadingly, to denote a situation where circumstances faced a person, not with no
c choice at all, but with the choice between two evils; so that he could hardly be blamed
if he chose the lesser. The classic case was the pulling down of another man's house
to prevent a fire spreading. The legal dilemma was a real one so long as criminal
offences were of absolute liability (i e before the concept of mens rea became developed) and punishments inflexible; and some such rule may well have been desirable
then. But the resulting confusion, and its juridical sterility, can be strikingly seen in
d Bacon's treatment of the concept, which he quotes[2] in the form 'Necessitas inducit
privilegium quoad jura privata': in the field of private law necessity imparts privilege.
The first oddity is that Bacon draws the line between private and public law not, as
one might expect, between the civil and the criminal law, but towards one end of the
criminal law—namely, between murder (which is, somewhat anachronistically, lex
privata) and treason (which is lex publica). On such a basis Bacon could assert:

e
> 'Necessity is of three sorts, necessity of conservation of life, necessity of obe-
> dience, and necessity of the act of God or of a stranger. First of conservation of
> life, If a man steale viands to satisfie his present hunger, this is no felony nor
> larceny. So if divers bee in danger of drowning by the casting away of some boat
> or barge, & one of them get to some plancke, or on the boats side to keepe himselfe
f > above water, and another to save his life thrust him from it whereby he is drowned;
> this is neither *se defendendo* nor by misadventure, but justifiable.'

Of course, if all this were the law, the instant appellant's case would be plausible;
duress could be seen as a reflection of a general doctrine of criminal exoneration
based on the 'necessity' of conservation of one's own life even at the expense of
another's. But Bacon's statements certainly cannot stand today. It is, in fact, in public
g law that 'necessity' has received recognition for some purposes, being based on an
implied mandate from the lawful sovereign to a usurper to govern, in order to avoid
the greater evil of anarchy (see Grotius, De Jure Belli ac Pacis[3], *Madzimbamuto v
Lardner-Burke*[4], *Adams v Adams (Attorney-General intervening*[5])). But it has been
decisively rejected in the criminal law generally. It is certainly not the law that what
would otherwise be the theft of a loaf ceases to be criminal if the taker is starving.
h Morally, there is a world of difference between a man who steals to satisfy his children's hunger and a man who steals to satisfy his own cupidity; but the moral distinction is marked, not by the provision of some eccentric defence in the positive law,
but by the discretion of the court in its sentence. And Bacon's 'necessity of conservation of life', with his example of the 'necessity' of pushing a shipwrecked man off a
j boat's side in order to secure his place, was called in aid on behalf of the appellants in

---

1 Pleas of the Crown (1800), vol 1, p 54
2 Maxims (1636), p 25, reg 5
3 Book 1, ch 4, s xv, para 1
4 [1968] 3 All ER 561 at 575, 577, 579, 581, 584, [1969] 1 AC 645 at 726, 729, 732, 736, 740
5 [1970] 3 All ER 572, [1971] P 188

the famous and terrible case of *R v Dudley and Stephens*[1]. The two accused were in a
ship's boat without food or water; they killed and ate the ship's boy, who was with   *a*
them. The accused would otherwise probably have died before they were picked up
and the boy would probably have died before them. At the time of the homicide
there was no appreciable chance of saving life except by killing someone for the
others to eat. Their conviction for murder was upheld on appeal, though the sentence
was respited.

Attempts have been made to explain this case away; but the appellant's argument   *b*
rested on Bacon's 'necessity of conservation of life'; and the rejection of any such
doctrine was, in my view, the ratio decidendi. Unless some distinction can be drawn
in principle between 'necessity' and duress, as defences to a charge of murder, the
instant appellant can, I think, only succeed if *R v Dudley and Stephens*[1] is overruled—
unless, indeed, a distinction is to be drawn in these regards between principals in the
first and second degrees.   *c*

In my opinion no distinction can be based on the degree of participation. I have
already rehearsed the arguments in support of the concept of duress as a defence
(the absence of moral blameworthiness and the inappropriateness of punishment in
such circumstances); there are no different arguments relating to 'necessity' as a
defence: and none affords any ground for distinguishing between principals in the
first or second degrees respectively. It is, with all respect, irrational to say, 'The man   *d*
who actually pulls the trigger is in a class by himself: he is outside the pale of any
such defence as I am prepared to countenance'. He cannot on any sensible ground be
put in a class by himself: the man who pulls the trigger because his child will be
killed otherwise is deserving of exactly the same consideration as the man who merely
carries the gun because he is frightened. Moreover, in general, as Smith and Hogan
state in this very connection[2]:   *e*

> 'The difficulty about adopting a distinction between the principal and secon-
> dary parties as a rule of law is that the contribution of the secondary party to
> the death may be no less significant than that of the principal.'

So the question must be faced whether there is a sustainable distinction in principle   *f*
between 'necessity' and duress as defences to a charge of murder as a principal. In
the circumstances where either 'necessity' or duress is relevant, there is both actus
reus and mens rea. In both sets of circumstances, there is power of choice between two
alternatives; but one of those alternatives is so disagreeable that even serious infraction of the criminal law seems preferable. In both the consequence of the act is
intended, within any permissible definition of intention. The only difference is that   *g*
in duress the force constraining the choice is a human threat, whereas in 'necessity'
it can be any circumstance constituting a threat to life (or, perhaps, limb). Duress is,
thus considered, merely a particular application of the doctrine of 'necessity': see
Glanville Williams's Criminal Law[3]. In my view, therefore, if your Lordships were
to allow the instant appeal, it would be necessary to hold that *R v Dudley and Stephens*[1]
either was wrongly decided or was not a decision negativing 'necessity' as a defence   *h*
to murder; and, if the latter, it would be further incumbent, I think, to define 'necessity' as a criminal defence, and lay down whether it is a defence to all crimes, and if
not why not. It would, in particular, be necessary to consider Hale's dissent from
Bacon as to the starving man stealing a loaf of bread. It would be a travesty of justice
and an invitation to anarchy to declare that an innocent life may be taken with
impunity if the threat to one's own life is from a terrorist but not when from a natural   *j*
disaster like ship- or plane-wreck.

---

1 (1884) 14 QBD 273, [1881-5] All ER Rep 61
2 Criminal Law (3rd Edn, 1973), p 166
3 (2nd Edn, 1961), p 760

a In my respectful submission such questions—why, if duress is available as a defence to a principal in the second degree, it should not also be available to a principal in the first degree; and what is the difference in principle between 'necessity' and duress that should make the latter but not the former a defence to murder—cannot simply be shrugged off by an assertion that one's judgment goes no further than the facts instantly under consideration. One of the tests of the validity of a legal rule is to see whether its implications stand up to examination. A refusal to submit a rule to such *b* an examination can only be justified if anomaly is considered as a positive virtue in the law.

IV

Bacon's second class of 'necessity' was the necessity of obedience. Smith and Hogan state[1]:

c   '. . . it is safe to assert that it is not a defence for D merely to show that the act was done by him in obedience to the orders of a superior, whether military or civil.'

But the law for a long time recognised (and this was Bacon's principal example) a defence by a wife, in relation to certain crimes committed in her husband's presence, *d* that she acted in obedience to his orders. The fiction of the law, raising a strong presumption, was that she thereby acted under his coercion (it was this presumption that led Mr Bumble, with his domestic experience to the contrary, to call the law an ass); and the doctrine went by the technical name of *coercion*.

'Coercion' in its popular sense denotes an external force which cannot be resisted and which impels its subject to act otherwise than he would wish. In this popular *e* sense it comes into the law of probate (where it goes by a misleading technical name) as invalidating the execution of a testamentary instrument. The mental state has been thus described: if the testator could speak his mind he would say, 'This is not my wish, but I must do it' (*Wingrove v Wingrove*[2]; see also *Baudains v Richardson*[3] 'must' being used in a popular sense, not as involving absolute absence of choice). Though threats are not necessary to constitute coercion in the law of probate, it will be noted *f* that the state of mind is precisely that produced by duress. It was this state of mind which was presumed by the law to be that of a wife performing certain acts prohibited by law in the presence of her husband; and the law held her to be thereby excused.

Both the doctrine itself and its limitations are of crucial significance in relation to duress. As early as Bracton's De Legibus[4] the doctrine was held not to apply to 'heinous deeds' (atrocioribus): see Professor Thornes's edition for the Selden Society. *g* Hale stated[5] specifically that it did not apply to murder or treason, citing *The Earl and Countess of Somerset's Case*[6] in respect of murder—the Countess being an accessory. The Report of the Committee on the Responsibility of Wife for Crimes committed under the coercion of husband[7] stated that the presumption applied to all felonies except murder. The exceptions of treason and murder were given specific statutory endorsement when the *presumption* of coercion was abolished by s 47 of the Criminal *h* Justice Act 1925, the *doctrine* being otherwise affirmed:

'Any presumption of law that an offence committed by a wife in the presence of her husband is committed under the coercion of the husband is hereby abolished, but on a charge against a wife for any offence other than treason or murder

---

j 1 Op cit, p 170
2 (1885) 11 PD 81
3 [1906] AC 169
4 (1567) p 151b
5 Op cit, vol 1, p 54
6 (1616) 1 State Tr 351
7 (1922) Cmd 1677

it shall be a good defence to prove that the offence was committed in the presence
of, and under the coercion of, the husband.'   *a*

(The Criminal Justice Act (Northern Ireland) 1945 is in similar terms.) The exact
scope and effect of this provision, and its interrelationship with the doctrine of duress,
are obscure in the extreme; and different interpretations have been proffered,
without any consensus emerging. But two things at least are clear: first, Parliament
recognised 'coercion' as a subsisting defence in law; and, secondly, Parliament refused   *b*
to recognise it as a defence to charges of treason or murder, without differentiating
between degrees of participation. Since 'coercion' was defined neither by the antecedent law nor by the statute, I take it that it is used in its ordinary sense, as it is in the
law of probate, and which I have just discussed. The state of mind produced, and which
excuses from liability, is thus the same for both 'coercion' and duress—namely, 'This
is not my wish, but I must do it'—and in both the constraint is due to external human   *c*
pressure. The difference lies, first, in the method of pressure (for duress it is limited
to threats, whereas for 'coercion' it extends to any force overbearing the wish); and,
secondly, that there is authority to the effect that duress is a defence to certain types
of treason, whereas 'coercion' is not. But neither of these differences justifies any
differentiation between 'coercion' and duress of a defence to murder: and the two
concepts (duress and 'coercion') are, indeed, habitually treated by jurists as cognate.   *d*
If, therefore, 'coercion' constitutes no defence to a charge of murder, it would be
anomalous were duress to do so.

V

That duress should not negative criminal responsibility, but go to mitigation of the
penalty, is suggested by its operation in other systems and branches of law. The great
classical jurist, Paulus, discusses the doctrine, presumably in relation to the damnosa   *e*
hereditas. Under the title 'Acts done through Fear', he is reported as follows[1]:

> 'If I have accepted an inheritance under the influence of fear, I am of opinion
> that I become heir, because, although, if I had been free, I should have refused,
> yet I did consent, though under compulsion (*coactus volui*). But the Praetor will
> give me relief.'   *f*

(The praetor exercised an equitable jurisdiction to relieve from the ordinary legal
consequences of a transaction.) I do not cite this merely for its antiquarian interest.
So contemporarily aware a writer on the criminal law as Professor Glanville Williams[2]
quotes the phrase coactus volui as descriptive of the mental state of an actor under
duress according to our criminal law. I hope, indeed, to have demonstrated that duress
is not inconsistent with act and will, the will being deflected not destroyed; so that   *g*
the intention conflicts with the wish—a legal situation correctly described by the
phrase coactus volui. The actor under duress has performed an act which is capable of
full legal effect; if he is to have relief it should be discretionary. Translated into terms
of criminal law, he is guilty of the crime, but he may at discretion be relieved against
its potential penal consequences when it comes to sentencing.
    Similarly with duress in the English law of contract. Duress again deflects, without   *h*
destroying, the will of one of the contracting parties. There is still an intention on his
part to contract in the apparently consensual terms; but there is coactus volui on his
side. The contrast is with non est factum. The contract procured by duress is therefore
not void: it is voidable—at the discretion of the party subject to duress.

VI   *j*

My Lords, I have ventured so far to deal with the policy of any sane and humane
system of criminal justice as regards the problem which faces your Lordships, and

---

1 Digest, IV, ii, 21.5
2 Op cit, p 751

with its juristic implications. But, of course, no discussion can have any claim to
a adequacy which does not extend to the authorities. Fortunately, I am absolved from
reviewing them in detail, since that has been done by my noble and learned friends.
My only misgiving is that such an impressive muster should be sent packing so
ignominiously. Poor Hale, poor Blackstone; wretched Russell and Kenny; poor,
poor Lord Denman. But at least they are in good company. There are all those famous
jurists, headed by Stephen, who drew up the draft code of 1879[1] under the fond
b belief that they were codifying the common law. And all those framers of the
Commonwealth codes, and the commentators on them, under the same illusion. And
Americans too. They are like the denizens of the first circle of Hell, who, for all their
wisdom and virtue, lived in such benighted times as to have forfeited salvation. So,
too, these great lawyers are too eminent to go altogether unacknowledged: they are
recognised with a courtly bow, but their words are lost in the gale of juristic change.
c For, in truth, their voices were unanimous that duress is no defence to murder.
What is to be set against them? A dissenting judgment of Bray CJ[2], which boggles
at murder as a principal in the first degree and adds (almost alone) attempted murder
to the exception. A case[3] of accessory before the fact where the issue was virtually
uncontested. A passing reference in a Privy Council case[4] where the point did not
fall for decision. One unreported trial in England and another in Northern Ireland.
d A judgment in Roman-Dutch law[5]. If the first question for your Lordships' consideration is to be answered Yes, it is overturning the consensus of centuries. I am all
for recognising frankly that judges do make law. And I am all for judges exercising
this responsibility boldly at the proper time and place—that is, where they can feel
confident of having in mind, and correctly weighed, all the implications of their
decision, and where matters of social policy are not involved which the collective
e wisdom of Parliament is better suited to resolve (see *Morgans v Launchbury*[6]). I can
hardly conceive of circumstances less suitable than the instant for five members of an
appellate committee of your Lordships' House to arrogate to ourselves so momentous
a law-making initiative. I have had the advantage of reading the speech prepared by
my noble and learned friend, Lord Kilbrandon; and I entirely agree with it—especially
what he has said about this aspect of the appeal.
f   I would add, as regards new law-making, that the cognate defences of 'necessity'
and 'coercion' also do not extend to murder—the latter by recent statutory reinforcement.

VII

A sane system of criminal justice does not permit a subject to set up a countervailing system of sanctions nor by terrorism to confer criminal immunity on his gang.
g A humane system of criminal justice does not exact retribution from those who
infringe the substantive provisions of its code under stresses greater than ordinary
human nature can bear, nor attempt, by making an example of them, to deter those
who in the nature of things are beyond deterrent. A sane and humane system of
criminal justice is sufficiently flexible to reconcile such considerations, and to allow
for all their infinite degrees of interaction. I have ventured to suggest that our own
h system of criminal justice is capable of such sanity and humanity—provided always
that it is recognised to extend beyond the mere injunctions and prohibitions and
immunities of the substantive criminal code.
There is, however, an apparent exception to such flexibility. This is constituted
where a crime has a fixed penalty—specifically, murder with its fixed penalty of life

j
1   (1879) C 2nd series 2345
2   In *R v Brown and Morley* [1968] SASR 467
3   *R v Kray* [1969] 3 All ER 941, 53 Cr App Rep 569
4   *Sephakela v R* [1954] High Commission Territories LR 60
5   *State v Goliath* 1972 (3) SA 1
6   [1972] 2 All ER 606 at 610, [1973] AC 127 at 136, 137

imprisonment. It is true that prosecutors have a discretion whether to indict; but such discretion is hardly real in the circumstances which fall for your Lordships' *a* instant consideration. It is true that the Home Secretary can advise exercise of the royal prerogative of mercy, and that the Parole Board can mitigate the rigour of the penal code; but these are executive not forensic processes, and can only operate after the awful verdict with its dire sentence has been pronounced. Is a sane and humane law incapable of encompassing this situation? I do not believe so.

An infraction of the criminal code under duress does not involve that the conduct *b* is either involuntary or unintentional. The actor is therefore responsible for his act. But his responsibility is diminished by the duress: his is no longer actus volui, but coactus volui. Provocation operates similarly to diminish the responsibility, transmuting the great crime of murder to the lesser crime of manslaughter with no fixed penalty.

The English common law evolved the concept of provocation. Since the Homicide *c* Act 1957 the provocation may originate in a third party, making the doctrine even closer to that of duress. The Scottish common law evolved another concept of diminished responsibility for homicide (*HM Advocate v Dingwall*[1]). In my judgment the English common law is well capable of accommodating duress under the concept of diminished responsibility reducing murder to manslaughter. This was the way duress was treated in the South African case of *State v Hercules*[2]; and it seems to me *d* to be the conception of duress in relation to homicide which has greatest juridical cogency.

As for duress in relation to treason, it seems to me generally to fit more aptly into the doctrine of 'necessity' in public law which I have already referred to; otherwise falling to be dealt with, where appropriate, by amnesty and pardon (as in *M'Growther*[3] and other cases after the 1745 rebellion). I need only note that one particular class of *e* treason—being a participant in the death of the lawful sovereign—was treated as if it were murder, no defence of duress being allowed: *R v Axtell*[4] (it is significant that the accused would have been only a principal in the second degree of murder).

VIII

Your Lordships have therefore, as it seems to me, three courses open: (1) to approve *f* of the various cases where duress has been allowed to be a defence negativing the crime, and then extend the doctrine to the crime of murder as a principal; (2) to overrule the cases where duress has been allowed to be a defence negativing the crime, leaving duress as a matter of mitigation of sentence in crimes other than homicide, and in homicide as a defence reducing murder to manslaughter; (3) to affirm the cases where duress has been allowed to be a defence negativing the crime, *g* but to refuse to extend it to murder as a principal.

I have, I hope, sufficiently indicated the juridical, practical and constitutional considerations which have caused me decisively to reject the first course.

Were it not for two considerations I would strongly urge your Lordships to adopt the second course. The first such consideration is that the Parliament of Great Britain in 1925 and the Northern Irish Parliament as recently as 1945 affirmed the existence *h* of the strictly cognate concept of 'coercion' as a general defence available to married women who commit what would otherwise be criminal offences (except murder or treason) in the presence of their husbands. These seem to me to have been policy decisions by Parliament with implications as to both the existence and limitations of the defence of duress: they should be respected by the courts, which should leave it to Parliament to alter, develop or confirm the existing law as so advised. This is strongly *j*

---

1 (1867) 5 Irv 466
2 1954 (3) SA 826
3 (1746) Fost 13
4 (1660) Kel 13

reinforced by the second consideration. This branch of the law is closely bound up
a with matters of policy relating to public safety. Such matters are far more fitly
weighed in Parliament on the advice of the executive than developed in courts of law.
In fact, the law of duress is currently subject to the examination of the Law Commission (see Working Paper No 55), which will shortly be reporting to Parliament.
In these circumstances, I have no doubt that the proper course for your Lordships is
merely to accept the law as it has heretofore developed, and to declare that the
b defence of duress is not available to a person accused of murder as a principal. I
would therefore answer the first certified question, No.

IX

The second certified question reads:

c   '(2) Where a person charged with murder as an aider and abettor is shown to
have intentionally done an act which assists in the commission of the murder with
knowledge that the probable result of his act, combined with the acts of those
whom his act is assisting, will be the death or serious bodily injury of another, if
his guilt thereby established without the necessity of proving his willingness to
participate in the crime?'

d The words 'willingness to participate in the crime' exemplify what I ventured to
describe as chaotic and confusing terminology in this branch of the law. Counsel for
the appellant spelt it out in words that identified the real point at issue—namely,
whether the crime of aiding and abetting requires proof of a 'specific intent' to further
the aim of the principal offender. I have already indicated that I prefer Smith and
Hogan's[1] terminology of 'ulterior intent'; it is more illuminating as well as less
e ambiguous, since it highlights that the definition of certain crimes requires a mens
rea which goes beyond foresight of the actus reus. An example is wounding with
intent to do grievous bodily harm. The actus reas is the wounding; and the prosecution must start by proving a corresponding mens rea—namely, that the accused
foresaw the wounding as a likely consequence of his act. But this crime is defined in
such a way that its mens rea goes beyond foresight of the actus reas; so that the prose-
f cution must in addition prove that the accused foresaw that the victim would, as a
result of the act, probably be wounded in such a way as to result in serious physical
injury to him. The issue involved in the second certified question is whether the
crime of aiding and abetting another to commit a crime similarly requires proof of a
mens rea which goes beyond the actus reus.

I find myself entirely convinced by the judgment delivered by Lowry CJ on
g behalf of the majority of the court on this issue. I would merely emphasise that the
majority did not hold that the crime of aiding and abetting a crime required no proof
of mens rea: they held that the mens rea did not involve a 'specific intent'.

I respectfully agree. As regards the actus reus, 'aiding' and 'abetting' are, as Smith
and Hogan[2] note, synonymous. But the phrase is not a pleonasm; because 'abet'
clearly imports mens rea, which 'aid' might not. As Devlin J said in *National Coal*
h *Board v Gamble*[3]:

'A person who supplies the instrument for a crime or anything essential to its
commission aids in the commission of it; and if he does so knowingly and with
intent to aid, he abets it as well and is therefore guilty of aiding and abetting.'

j The actus reus is the supplying of an instrument for a crime or anything essential for
its commission. On Devlin J's analysis the mens rea does not go beyond this. The act
of supply must be voluntary (in the sense I tried to define earlier in the speech), and

1   Criminal Law (3rd Edn, 1973)
2   Op cit, p 93
3   [1958] 3 All ER 203 at 207, [1959] 1 QB 11 at 20

it must be foreseen that the instrument or other object or service supplied will probably be used for the commission of a crime. The definition of the crime does not *a* in itself suggest any ulterior intent; and whether anything further in the way of mens rea was required was precisely the point at issue in *Gamble's* case[1]. Slade J thought the very concept of aiding and abetting imported the concept of motive. But Lord Goddard CJ and Devlin J disagreed with this. So do I. Slade J thought that abetting involved assistance or encouragement, and that both implied motive. So far as assistance is concerned, this is clearly not so. One may lend assistance without any motive, *b* or even with the motive of bringing about a result directly contrary to that in fact assisted by one's effort. The failure to commit Grouchy's corps at Waterloo was of great assistance to Wellington, but this was hardly Napoleon's motive in his handling of the corps. As for encouragement, at most it is only one way of abetting.

May I add a word or two about *R v Steane*[2], which was much pressed on your Lordships? The offence charged was doing an act likely to assist the enemy with intent to *c* assist the enemy. The accused had taken part in enemy broadcasts. He alleged that he had done so in consequence of violence towards himself and of threats to himself and his family. It was a hard case; but in several ways it seems to me to be an unsatisfactory authority. The judgment proceeded on the assumption that the onus of proof of duress lay on the accused; but cf *R v Gill*[3]. The offence charged is difficult to classify as to its mens rea. It might be misleading to call it an 'ulterior intent', since *d* the mens rea went no further than the actus reus. Perhaps this is a case where 'specific intent' is justified for all its ambiguity. But the mens rea involved does not seem to admit of the approach adopted in *Hyam v Director of Public Prosecutions*[4]. I think that the 'intent' in *Steane's* case[2] should probably be construed as the mental element involved in performing an act with the object that a particular consequence should ensue—i e virtually, motive or purpose. But it seems to have been assumed that *e* motives cannot be mixed, and that proof of one purpose excludes all others; whereas an ultimate purpose of saving himself and his family was perfectly compatible with an immediate purpose of assisting the enemy—as a necessary step towards the ultimate purpose. I think the court really in silence construed 'intent' as 'desire'. I do not suggest that the actual decision was wrong; but I would support it on the alternative ground that, when a person is placed in an unusual and stressful situation, *f* it is unsafe to assume, even prima facie, that he intends the natural and probable consequence of his acts; so that the direction to the jury was misleading and inadequate. However that may be, I do not think that *R v Steane*[2] suffices to call for an answer to the second question in favour of the appellant.

I would therefore answer the second question, Yes; and I would dismiss the appeal.

g

LORD KILBRANDON. My Lords, the learned trial judge directed the jury to the effect that the defence of duress is not available as exculpation in a charge of murder, whether the accused has been charged as a principal in the first or in the second degree. In my opinion, that direction correctly stated the law as it then stood and now stands. It is my misfortune that while I agree with those of your Lordships *h* who consider that the law is in a very unsatisfactory state, and is in urgent need of restatement, I remain convinced that the grounds on which the majority propose that the conviction of the appellant be set aside involve changes in the law which are outside the proper functions of your Lordships in your judicial capacity. If duress per minas has never been admitted as a defence to a charge of murder, and if the proposal that it should now be so admitted be approved, it seems to me that your *j*

---

1 [1958] 3 All ER 203, [1959] 1 QB 11
2 [1947] 1 All ER 813, [1947] KB 997
3 [1963] 2 All ER 688, [1963] 1 WLR 841
4 [1974] 2 All ER 41, [1974] 2 WLR 607

Lordships, in countenancing a defence for many years authoritatively (though not in
a your Lordship's House) denied, would be doing what, in the converse, was firmly and
properly disapproved in *Knuller* (*Publishing, Printing and Promotions*) *Ltd v Director of
Public Prosecutions*[1]. Instead of, for reasons of public policy, declaring criminal for the
first time conduct until then not so described, your Lordships would be for the first
time declaring the existence of a defence to a criminal charge which had up to now
by judges, text writers, and law teachers throughout the common law world, been
b emphatically repudiated.

I am putting the matter in this way, because I want to emphasise in the comparatively brief observations I have to make that since, first, in my opinion, the learned
judge's charge was right, and secondly that the substance of the law which he laid
down is hard to defend, we are therefore in the realm of law reform; in my judgment
it is an impermissible, or at least an undesirable, mode of law reform to use the
c occasion of an appeal in a decided case for the purpose of declaring that changing
conditions and enlarging opinions have rendered the ratio decidendi of the lower
court obsolete and therefore susceptible of being set aside. This is perhaps a technical
way of looking at the matter. But there is a much wider aspect. It seems to me to be
clear that the effect of the opinions of the majority of your Lordships would be to
change what has during many generations of judges, teachers, practitioners and
d students been regarded as the common law. If they were all wrong, I can imagine
no more plausible justification for that rather dubious brocard communis error facit
ius. It would in my opinion be a necessary preliminary to the reform of that generally
accepted version of the common law that consultations, on a far wider basis than
discussions among lawyers, including the arguments of counsel before the highest
tribunal, should have taken place and been seriously considered. If there is one
e lesson which has been learned since the setting up of the Law Commissions it is this,
that law reform by lawyers for lawyers (unless in exceptionally technical matters)
is not socially acceptable. An alteration in a fundamental doctrine of law, such as this
appeal proposes, could not properly be given effect to save after the widest reference
to interests, both social and intellectual, far transcending those available in the
judicial committee of your Lordship's House. Indeed general public opinion is
f deeply and properly concerned. It will not do to claim that judges have the duty—
call it the privilege—of seeing to it that the common law expands and contracts to
meet what the judges conceive to be the requirements of modern society. Modern
society rightly prefers to exercise that function for itself, and this it conveniently does
through those who represent it in Parliament. And its representatives nowadays
demand, or should demand, that they be briefed by all those who can qualify an
g interest to advise them. The fascinating discussions of policy which adorn the speeches
of your Lordships—and to which I intend to make a short and undistinguished
addition—are themselves highly illustrative of what I mean. They may perhaps be
taken as the ultimate in the distillation of legal policy-opinion, but that is not enough.
I will not take time to enumerate the various other disciplines and interests whose
views are of equal value in deciding what policy should inform the legislation, neces-
h sary if reform of the law is really called for, giving effect to the defence of duress per
minas in all crimes including murder. In the absence of such consultations I do not
think it would be right to decide an appeal in such a way as to set aside the common
understanding of the law.

I will say a word only as to the law as presently understood, because thorough
examinations of the history and progression of the doctrine have already been made.
j The content of duress I will look at briefly later on, insofar as that is necessary. Duress
is recognised as a defence to crime. It has never been laid down judicially as a matter
of decision that murder is an exception to that rule, though many judges have expressed the opinion that it is. The whole weight of opinion in common law jurisdiction has always been to that effect. For sheer economy of citation I will select two

1   [1972] 2 All ER 898, [1973] AC 435

examples only, one academic, the other judicial. Professor Kenny in his Outlines of Criminal Law[1]—I quote from the 12th edition since it was prepared by him—says, 'It [sc duress *per minas*] certainly will not excuse murder.' This is what the master must have taught Cambridge law students over many years. I will select as my second authority that of Bray CJ in *R v Brown and Morley*[2], since in his dissenting opinion he allows, as I myself would not, duress as a defence to a charge of murder as a principal in the second degree. He says[3]: 'As at present advised I do not think duress could constitute a defence to one who actually kills or attempts to kill the victim.'

I do not think the fact that duress may excuse treason is relevant: see *M'Growther's Case*[4] on the argument that treason is an even graver crime than murder. I do not agree with that. The crime of treason always seems grave to an injured or threatened executive. But no one would classify George Washington or Flora Macdonald—undoubted traitors—as heinous criminals.

Your Lordships have examined the Commonwealth and other codes which were cited to us. It is true that the framers took the opportunity to include among the crimes to which duress will not be available as a defence some, other than murder, which would not be so included in a restatement of the present law of England. But it seems perfectly clear that the framers, when they so classified the crime of murder, did so because they thought they were, in that respect at least, giving effect to accepted English law. If this appeal be allowed I think it will have to be taken that they, like Professor Kenny, and many others, were under a misapprehension.

The next aspect of the matter leads me to the little I have to say on policy. The difference between the defence of duress, which comes from coercion by the act of man, and that of necessity, which comes from coercion by the forces of nature, is narrow and unreal. Counsel for the appellant was, in my opinion, right to concede that if his argument succeeded, *R v Dudley and Stephens*[5] must be held to have been wrongly decided. It seems clear that, if the argument for the appellant is sound, the judge in that case ought to have directed the jury that in law the defence of necessity was available, and to have taken a plain verdict of 'guilty' or 'not guilty'. If that be so it will then become essential, at some time or other, to decide how far the doctrine of necessity is to extend. Unless, for example, want is to be allowed to excuse theft, a strange situation would arise. Suppose that in the instant case the accused had acted under the threat of violence to his family. Then, although if he had taken a loaf from a supermarket to feed his starving children he would have been a thief, he is guiltless if, for his family's safety, he kills the father of Pc Carroll's children. Again, it is impossible not to be deeply impressed by the circumstances, dramatically figured by your Lordships, which are especially liable to occur at this moment in Northern Ireland; the coercion of otherwise law-abiding citizens could, under present law, turn them into unwilling murderers. On the other hand, if the present law be altered, coercion will be a good defence to one who, at the behest of a mafia or IRA boss, places a bomb in an aircraft and 250 people are killed. It is more likely, too, that the accused will have assisted by preparing and delivering the bomb knowing its intended use; in that case the question would be, is coercion a good defence to murder as a principal in the second degree or as accessory? This situation was long ago foreseen. The closing passage of the judgment in *R v Dudley and Stephens*[5] points out that, if the defence were a good one, the strongest man on board the boat might have eaten his way through all the crew, killing them one by one, and after his rescue have been held guiltless. How many may a man kill in order to save his own life? I pose such a question for the purpose of suggesting that it cannot be answered in this place. It

1 (12th Edn, 1926), p 74
2 [1968] SASR 467
3 [1968] SASR at 499
4 (1746) Fost 13
5 (1884) 14 QBD 273

a raises issues, some legal, others social, even more ethical, on which the public will clamour to be heard. It would probably be necessary, too, to lay down that coercion would not avail one who, e g took orders from the head of the gang of which he was a voluntary member. Such a provision figures in the codes; I do not see how it could become part of English law save by legislation. In short, the policy questions are so deeply embedded in the legal doctrines we are being asked to review that we may be in danger of reforming the law on an inadequate appreciation of public needs and
b public opinion. What would purport to be a judgment declaratory of the common law would in reality be a declaration of public policy.

On the question whether it is possible, in this context, to distinguish between the defences open to a principal in the first degree and then open to a principal in the second degree I have had the advantage of seeing the speech of my noble and learned friend Lord Simon of Glaisdale. I agree with him that no distinction can be made; I
c would accordingly agree with the majority in R v Brown and Morley[1]. As regards R v Kray[2], it is possible, though hardly satisfactory, to distinguish it on the ground that the defence was there said, there being no party to the case with an interest to argue the contrary, to be available to an accessory, not to a principal in any degree. I will leave the case by saying that if, as I hope, the examination of this doctrine, already begun by the Law Commission, is to be pursued to legislation, the case may
d therein be further considered with a view to fitting it into any proposed code. In the meantime, it does not affect the present appeal.

On the view which I have taken, it is not truly necessary to go into the meaning of the word duress, that is, the sense in which it may exhibit an admissible defence to crime. Our learned forebears who used the word knew what they meant by it, and they were capable of expressing themselves as clearly as we can do. But I must
e confess to great difficulty in seeing how, in a reformed situation (by which I mean a situation in which all crimes are treated as regards duress in the same way) duress should exculpate rather than mitigate. The effect of a threat on its recipient may be said to be to reduce his constancy, so that he is forced to do what he knows to be wrong and would not have done unless he had been threatened. He is not like the infant or the insane, who are disqualified or disabled from forming a criminal inten-
f tion. He has decided to do a wrong thing, having balanced in his mind, perhaps unconsciously, the consequences to himself of refusal against the consequences to another of acquiescence. But the agonising nature of the decision he has to make may render it impossible for a civilised system of criminal law to hold him fully responsible for what followed from that decision. Much of our difficulty in assessing his responsibility at law stems from the 'black-or-white' nature of that unfortunate
g expression mens rea, which is none the better for concealing itself 'in the decent obscurity of a learned language'. Our minds, whatever we are doing, are neither wholly wicked nor wholly virtuous. To elaborate on that proposition would be to encourage the wrong kind of debate. But the practical importance, for present purposes, is that the decision of the threatened man whose constancy is overborne so that he yields to the threat, is a calculated decision to do what he knows to be wrong, and
h is therefore that of a man with, perhaps to some exceptionally limited extent, a 'guilty mind'. But he is at the same time a man whose mind is less guilty than is his who acts as he does but under no such constraint. The law must give effect to that distinction.

This would be easy except in a charge of murder, whether against a principal in the first or the second degree, or against an accessory before the fact, on all of
j whom the court has always, on conviction, been obliged to impose the extreme penalty of the law. It seems to me probable, therefore, that if the solution ultimately found is the allowing of duress, or necessity, as defences to all crimes, in the sense

1   [1968] SASR 467
2   [1969] 3 All ER 941, [1970] 1 QB 125

only of mitigating penalty, and if murder is to continue as a crime visited on conviction with a mandatory sentence, it would be perfectly reasonable, for the reasons I *a*
have indicated, to make duress or necessity grounds for declaring diminished responsibility, so that in cases of murder where the defence was established a verdict of
manslaughter would be returned and the penalty left at large.

An example of merely antiquarian interest is provided by the law of Byrthynsak
or Burdingsek in Scotland. According to the Regiam Majestatem[1]: 'Be the law of
burdingsek na man sould be hanged for sae meikill of stollen meat as he may bear in *b*
ane seck upon his back.' Hume[2] points out that the law did not operate to exculpate
from theft, but to avoid the capital penalty, where necessity had coerced a man into
dishonesty.

There can be no doubt that the remedy proposed would require legislation. The
doctrine of diminished responsibility was introduced judicially into the common law
of Scotland (*HM Advocate v Dingwall*[3]) not without some expressions of disagreement, *c*
a late example of which is to be seen in the charge to the jury by Lord Johnston in
HM Advocate v Higgins[4]. But when it was decided to make this doctrine part of the
law of England also, it was by statute (Homicide Act 1957, s 2) that that was done. I
cannot suppose that the extension of the doctrine, in the sense I have suggested,
could be effected by judicial decision.

In the result, accordingly, I would answer the first question certified in the negative. *d*
As regards the second, I am entirely satisfied by the reasoning of Lowry CJ, which I
would desire to adopt. I would therefore refuse this appeal.

LORD EDMUND-DAVIES. My Lords, of the two points of law certified by the
Court of Criminal Appeal in Northern Ireland as properly calling for consideration *e*
by this House, the second had not been raised by the accused in his appeal to that
court but arose in the course of the hearing and led to O'Donnell J's arriving at a
conclusion different from that of Lowry CJ and Curran LJ as to the proper outcome
of the appeal.

Having regard to the view I have formed as to the correct answer to question 1, in
my judgment none is strictly called for in relation to question 2. But, as it does *f*
indeed raise a point of law of general public importance which was developed at
length before this House, it would, I think, be unsatisfactory were I to give no indication of the conclusion I have arrived at in relation to it. I can, however, do that with
brevity. In my judgment, question 2 calls for a negative answer, and it is sufficient
for me to say that I respectfully adopt in this regard the reasons advanced by Lowry
CJ. *g*

Question 1, which all three members of the Court of Criminal Appeal answered
in the negative, is: 'On a charge of murder is the defence of duress open to a person
who is accused as a principal in the second degree (aider and abettor)?' While the facts
of the instant case narrow the issue now calling for determination, its consideration
has inevitably led this House to examine wider questions both of strict law and of
public policy. That examination, in its turn, has disclosed a jurisprudential muddle *h*
of a most unfortunate kind, and one's sympathy is with the learned trial judge and
with the appellate court who were confronted by it.

The facts of the case have already been related in the speeches of my noble and
learned friends. I restrict myself to quoting a passage from the judgment of Lowry
CJ:

'It was . . . proved that, before the date of the shooting six policemen had *j*
already been murdered in the Ardoyne area, which was a stronghold of the

1   (Skenes translation, 1609) Bk 4, tit 16
2   Commentaries, I, 55
3   (1867) 5 Irv 466
4   1914 SC (J) 1

Provisional I.R.A. and where the appellant lived, and that Sean Meehan was a well known and ruthless gunman, and the appellant and Bates gave evidence that Meehan was the kind of person whom it would be perilous to defy or disobey and who, on the occasion in question, gave his instructions in a manner which indicated to them that he would tolerate no disobedience. There was no evidence of a direct threat by Meehan or any other person against the life or personal safety of the appellant or any member of his family but both the appellant and and Bates testified to their fear of Meehan and their clear view that their disobedience of his instructions would cause them to be shot.'

Lowry CJ proceeded to consider the various submissions of the prosecution that the available evidence did not constitute a triable issue fit to go to the jury on the plea of duress. The court accepted that 'mere apprehension' of death or serious bodily injury is not enough, and that 'the duress must be constraint exercised by one person on another'. But they added:

'The constraint . . . can be implied, as well as express, and, once there is evidence that A. has somehow caused B. to fear for himself or his family, it is a question of fact whether the reasonable possibility of this having occurred has been disproved by the Crown. We consider that the evidence in this case raised a question for the jury whether Meehan impliedly threatened the appellant with death or serious bodily injury.'

The court next considered the submission of the Crown that—

'the defence of duress is not available to an accused who voluntarily joins in a criminal enterprise and is afterwards subjected to threats of violence in order to ensure that he does not withdraw, even if the enterprise becomes more gravely criminal than the accused foresaw.'

This may well have been an echo of Stephen's History of the Criminal Law of England[1] that—

'If a man chooses to expose and still more if he chooses to submit himself to illegal compulsion, it may not operate even in mitigation of punishment. It would surely be monstrous to mitigate the punishment of a murderer on the ground that he was a member of a secret society by which he would have been assassinated if he had not committed murder.'

But, in the light of Lynch's police statement and his evidence that at no time was he a member of the IRA or any other organisation, and in the absence of any prosecution evidence to the contrary, the appellate court not surprisingly held that the point did not arise for consideration and expressly reserved it for determination if on any future occasion it became relevant.

As to the imminence of the threat of death or serious bodily injury, and the Crown's submission that the plea of duress is never available if the accused has not taken advantage of an opportunity to escape from its influence, Lowry CJ said:

'We consider it to be a question of fact (assuming duress to be a proper issue for the jury) whether the Crown could successfully invoke this principle, bearing in mind that if the effect of the threat is felt at the material time, this is enough to keep duress in issue: R v Hudson[2], Subramaniam v Public Prosecutor[3]. The same authorities are relevant to the immediacy of the threat, because the question

1   (1883), vol II, p 108
2   [1971] 2 All ER 244, [1971] 2 QB 202
3   [1956] 1 WLR 965

is not when the threats are made, but whether they overbore the will of the accused at a material time.'　　　　　　　　　　　　　　　　　　　　　　　　*a*

Having thus considered the main elements of duress, and having apparently adopted the subjective test of the effect on the mind of this appellant of the alleged implied threat, Lowry CJ concluded:

> 'There was, in our opinion, on the facts a clear issue of duress in this case, and therefore the question in this appeal as to whether duress may afford a defence *b* to a person accused of murder as a principal in the second degree is material.'

It is manifestly impossible to arrive at an acceptable answer to that question without first examining the rasion d'être and limits of the plea of duress, and that I diffidently proceed to attempt.

c

I. SHOULD DURESS BE A DEFENCE TO ANY CRIME?

In *R v Tyler and Price*[1] Lord Denman, CJ said[2]:

> '. . . the law, is that no man, from a fear of consequences to himself, has a right to make himself a party to committing mischief on mankind . . . It cannot be too often repeated that the apprehension of personal danger does not furnish any *d* excuse for assisting in doing an act which is illegal.'

It has been said that, despite the unqualified nature of these observations, they must be read as applying only to the murder charge then being tried. But, over 40 years later, Stephen wrote in his History of the Criminal Law[3]:

> 'Criminal law is itself a system of compulsion on the widest scale. It is a collec- *e* tion of threats of injury to life, liberty, and property if people do commit crimes. Are such threats to be withdrawn as soon as they are encountered by opposing threats? The law says to a man intending to commit murder, If you do it I will hang you. Is the law to withdraw its threat if someone else says, If you do not do it I will shoot you? Surely it is at the moment when temptation to crime is strongest that the law should speak most clearly and emphatically to the con- *f* trary. It is, of course, a misfortune for a man that he should be placed between two fires, but it would be a much greater misfortune for society at large if crimi- nals could confer impunity upon their agents by threatening them with death or violence if they refused to execute their commands. If impunity could be so secured a wide door would be opened to collusion, and encouragement would be given to associations of malefactors, secret or otherwise. No doubt the moral guilt *g* of a person who commits a crime under compulsion is less than that of a person who commits it freely, but any effect which is thought proper may be given to this circumstance by a proportional mitigation of the offender's punishment. These reasons lead me to think that compulsion by threats ought in no case whatever to be admitted as an excuse for crime, though it may and ought to operate in mitigation of punishment in most though not in all cases.'　　　　　*h*

Well, such an approach at least makes for neatness. No matter how terrifying the circumstances which have impelled a man (and which, indeed, might well have impelled *most* men) to transgress the criminal law, he must be convicted. Crutchley[4] should therefore have been convicted of malicious damage during the threshing machine riots, even though he had been compelled by a mob to strike a blow at *j*

1　(1838) 8 C & P 616
2　8 C & P at 620, 621
3　Op cit, pp 107, 108
4　*R v Crutchley* (1831) 5 C & P 133

threshing machines. Instead, his defence of duress was upheld. The trouble about
a such neatness is that it may work intolerable injustice in individual cases, for, as
Professor Glanville Williams has observed[1]:

> '*Crutchley*[2] was a case where justice demanded not merely a mitigation of
> punishment, but no punishment at all; nor would there have been any sound
> reason for registering even a technical conviction.'

b Apart from the obloquy involved in the mere fact of conviction, in the nature of
things there can be no assurance that even a completely convincing plea of duress will
lead to an absolute discharge. And even the exercise of the Royal prerogative involves
the notion that there must have been a degree of wrongdoing, for were it otherwise
no 'pardon' would be called for. Furthermore, as the appellants' counsel cogently
submitted, if duress is excluded at the trial, it may well be that (unlike in the present
c case) no evidence on the point will be given, and there would accordingly be no
satisfactory means of deciding whether the plea had any substance. In such circumstances, a decision by the Home Secretary adverse to the accused might understandably be regarded as unsatisfactory, for he might well have concluded that duress had
not been made out rather than that the prosecution had established its unacceptability,
which is indisputably the correct approach.
d Stephen himself cannot be acquitted of contributing to the lack of neatness and
consistency in this branch of the law. He was a member of the Royal Commission
whose draft criminal code of 1879[3]—that is, four years before his History appeared—
purported to express 'what we think is the existing law, and what at all events we
suggest ought to be the law'. Section 23 provided that:

e
> 'Compulsion by threats of immediate death or grievous bodily harm . . . shall
> be an excuse for the commission of any offence other than high treason . . .
> murder, piracy, offences deemed to be piracy, attempting to murder, assisting
> in rape, forcible abduction, robbery, causing grievous bodily harm and arson . . .'

These exceptions are substantially greater than those of Hale[4], who excepted only
f treason, murder and robbery. Of the several writers quoted to us, none (save Stephen)
goes so far as to assert that duress neither affords nor should afford a defence to *any*
criminal charge. Similarly, each of the many codes cited follows the pattern of providing that duress is a defence to all crimes save a specified few, while s 2.09 of the
American Law Institute's Model Penal Code excludes the plea of duress from *no*
criminal charge and in this respect resembles s 40 of the German Draft Penal Code of
g 1962.

II. WHEN IS THE PLEA OF DURESS AVAILABLE?

Despite the views of old (and not so old) writers, there has been for some years an
unquestionable tendency towards progressive latitude in relation to the plea of duress.
Thus, it may be invoked in some types of treason (*R v Purdy*[5]), in receiving (*Attorney-
h General v Whelan*[6]), in stealing (*R v Gill*[7]), in malicious damage (*R v Crutchley*[8]), in
arson (*R v Shiartos*[9], noted in *R v Gill*[7]), in unlawful possession of ammunition

---

1 Criminal Law (2nd Edn, 1961) p 755
2 *R v Crutchley* (1831) 5 C & P 133
j 3 (1879) C 2nd series 2345
4 Pleas of the Crown (1800) vol 1, p 50
5 (1946) 10 Journal of Criminal Law 182
6 [1934] IR 518
7 [1963] 2 All ER 688, [1963] 1 WLR 841
8 (1831) 5 C & P 133
9 (1961) unreported

(*Subramaniam v Public Prosecutor*[1]), and in perjury (*R v Hudson*[2]). Indeed, in the last-mentioned case, Lord Parker CJ said[3]:   *a*

'. . . it is clearly established that duress provides a defence in all offences including perjury (except possibly treason or murder as a principal) if the will of the accused has been overborne by threats of death or serious personal injury so that the commission of the alleged offence was no longer the voluntary act of the accused.'   *b*

But, as in some types of treason, complicity in murder has, at least until recent times, been put into a category of its own. Hale said[4]:

'If a man be desparately assaulted, and in peril of death, and cannot otherwise escape, unless to satisfy his assailant's fury he will kill an innocent person then present, the fear and actual force will not acquit him of the crime and punish-   *c* ment of murder, if he commit the fact; for he ought rather to die himself, than kill an innocent . . .'

And in upholding the plea of duress in answer to a receiving charge, Murnaghan J said in *Attorney-General v Whelan*[5]:

'. . . murder is a crime so heinous that murder should not be committed even   *d* for the price of life and in such a case the strongest duress would not be any justification.'

And in this context, one should not overlook the eloquent observations of Lord Coleridge CJ in *R v Dudley and Stephens*[6] in relation to the defence of necessity:

'It must not be supposed that in refusing to admit temptation to be an excuse   *e* for crime it is forgotten how terrible the temptation was; how awful the suffering; how hard in such trials to keep the judgment straight and the conduct pure. We are often compelled to set up standards we cannot reach ourselves, and to lay down rules which we could not ourselves satisfy. But a man has no right to declare temptation to be an excuse, though he might himself have yielded to it, nor allow compassion for the criminal to change or weaken in any manner the   *f* legal definition of the crime.'

But even this seemingly clear stream has been made opaque by the decision in *R v Kray*[7], where Barry, one of the accused, was charged with being an accessory before the fact to the murder of one McVitie. The Crown's case was that Barry had carried to a certain destination a gun which he well knew Reginald Kray intended to   *g* use to murder MvVitie. Barry admitted these allegations, but pleaded that he had so acted on order of the Krays, because he feared for the safety of himself and his family if he disobeyed them. Objections were raised to the admissibility of certain parts of Barry's evidence, but counsel both for the Krays and for the Crown conceded that duress was available to a person charged (as Barry was) with being an accessory before the fact to murder, though not to a person charged as a principal. In dismissing the   *h* Krays' appeal against conviction for murder, Widgery LJ said[8]:

'We are . . . satisfied that Barry had a viable defence . . . that by reason of threats

1 [1956] 1 WLR 965
2 [1971] 2 All ER 244, [1971] 2 QB 202   *j*
3 [1971] 2 All ER at 246, [1971] 2 QB at 206
4 Op cit, p 50
5 [1934] IR at 526
6 (1884) 14 QBD 273 at 288, [1881-5] All ER Rep 61 at 67, 68
7 [1969] 3 All ER 941, 53 Cr App Rep 569
8 53 Cr App Rep at 578

a   he was so terrified that he ceased to be an independent actor, and that the evidence of violent conduct by the Krays which Barry put before the Court was accordingly relevant and admissible.'

The question that immediately arises is: can a distinction properly be made between the action of Barry in carrying the murder weapon to the scene of the crime and the action of Lynch in driving Meehan and his criminal colleagues to and from the scene

b   of the shooting and waiting around the corner while the murdering was being committed? Can the styling of the one 'accessory before the fact' and the other 'principal in the second degree' of itself make any difference to their criminality? If both acted in terror of imminent death or grave injury, should the one go scot free and the other be convicted of murder and receive the mandatory sentence of life imprisonment? Professor J C Smith has little doubt how these questions should be answered[1]:

c   'A party who is absent may in fact have played a more significant role in the killing than one who is present and, if both were acting under duress, it would be wrong that the former should be able to rely on that defence and the latter not . . . If duress is once admitted as a possible defence to an accessory, then it is difficult to find a logical limit to the availability of the defence.'

d   III. WHAT IS THE BASIS OF THE PLEA OF DURESS?

Of the two theories regarding the nature of the plea of duress canvassed below and before this House, I prefer the view of Professor Glanville Williams[2] that:

        'True duress is not inconsistent with act and will as a matter of legal definition, the maxim being *coactus volui*. Fear of violence does not differ in kind from fear of

e   economic ills, fear of displeasing others, or any other determinant of choice; it would be inconvenient to regard a particular type of motive as negativing will.'

The alternative theory advanced ('Theory 2') is that, as a result of his will being overborne by threats of grave violence, the transgressor never forms the criminal intent necessary to constitute the offence with which he is charged, whatever be its nature,

f   which would thus exculpate an actual killer who would otherwise be a principal in the first degree to murder. In my judgment, this will not do. Duress is properly to be regarded as a plea in confession and avoidance, and I respectfully adopt the view of Lowry CJ that—

        'Apart altogether from philosophical argument, it seems clear that the defendants *Whelan*[3], *Gill*[4], *Subramaniam*[5], and *Hudson*[6] intentionally received

g   stolen goods, stole, took possession of ammunition and committed perjury, even though the reason that they did so was that their respective wills were overborne by threats. Their *prima facie* criminal acts were the result of a conscious choice, although that choice was made unwillingly and because of the threats to which they were subjected.'

h   At the end of the day, the defence of duress is probably best evaluated without reference to its supposed relation to either actus reus or mens rea, for, in the words of Professor Turpin[7], 'not every morally exculpatory circumstance has a necessary bearing on these legal ingredients of crime'.

---

j   1 'A Note on Duress' [1974] Crim LR 351
     2 Criminal Law (2nd Edn, 1961), p 751
     3 [1934] IR 518
     4 [1963] 2 All ER 688, [1963] 1 WLR 841
     5 [1956] 1 WLR 965
     6 [1971] 2 All ER 244, [1971] 2 QB 202
     7 [1972] CLJ 205

It follows that certain observations of Lord Goddard CJ in *R v Bourne*[1] cannot, in my judgment, be accepted. The appellant sought to upset his conviction for aiding and abetting his wife to have carnal knowledge of a dog, she having testified that she had been so terrorised into submission that she acted entirely against her will. Assuming that, had she been charged as the principal offender, the wife could have pleaded duress, Lord Goddard CJ said[2]:

'It means that she admits that she has committed the crime but prays to be excused from punishment for the consequences of the crime by reason of the duress, and no doubt in those circumstances the law would allow a verdict of Not Guilty to be entered. [He added that the plea of duress was available to the wife] not as showing that no offence had been committed, but as showing that she had no *mens rea* because her will was overborne by threats of imprisonment or violence so that she would be excused from punishment.'

But, as Professor J Ll J Edwards has pointed out[3] it is now well established that where duress applies it must lead to a clean acquittal unless disproved. Professor Cross[4] has also made the comment that the wife in fact and in law committed the actus reus with the mens rea required by the definition of the crime of bestiality, so that Lord Goddard CJ's observation that 'she had no *mens rea*' must be regarded as having been employed 'to describe an actor whose will was overborne in circumstances which rendered his conduct excusable'.

Why 'excusable'? The law makes a concession to human weakness to the extent of allowing a verdict of manslaughter to be returned even through an accused person unlawfully and maliciously killed, if he was provoked to the extent now indicated in s 3 of the Homicide Act 1957. But he will not be excused so as to be acquitted entirely. And if the charge is other than murder, provocation (however great) can operate only by way of mitigation of punishment and would not of itself, for example, justify a verdict of guilty of contravening s 20 of the Offences Against the Person Act 1861 on a charge of causing grievous bodily harm with intent contrary to s 18 of that Act. But if, on the trial of the graver charge, a plea of duress prevailed, it should, on the authorities, result in a complete acquittal, as the Supreme Court of Victoria held in *R v Smyth*[5]. In *Attorney-General v Whelan* Murnaghan J said[6]:

'It seems to us that threats of immediate death or serious personal violence so great as to overbear the ordinary power of human resistance should be accepted as a justification for acts which would otherwise be criminal.'

Save for the substitution of 'excuse' for 'justification', we were told, and were referred to, nothing more helpful than that, and the difficulty in reconciling such a view with the words of Lord Coleridge CJ, when dealing in *Dudley and Stephens*[7] with the defence of necessity is as obvious as it is great.

IV. WHY SHOULD DURESS NOT BE AVAILABLE IN MURDER?

If the circumstances are such that 'the ordinary power of human resistance' is overborne, why should they not render excusable even the unlawful killing of an innocent person? Several reasons have been advanced for asserting that no duress, however terrible, can save such a participator in unlawful killing as the appellant from being convicted of murder. One of these has already been referred to and is epitomised by

1   (1952) 36 Cr App Rep 125
2   36 Cr App Rep at 128
3   (1953) 69 LQR 226
4   Ibid 354 et seq
5   [1963] VR 737
6   [1934] IR at 526
7   (1884) 14 QBD at 288, [1881-5] All ER Rep at 67, 68

the observation of Lord Coleridge CJ, in *Dudley and Stephens*[1] that: 'To preserve
a one's life is generally speaking a duty, but it may be the plainest and the highest duty
to sacrifice it.' Such an approach was elaborately dealt with in *State v Goliath*[2] where
the Appellate Division held that on a charge of murder compulsion can be a complete
defence. In giving the majority judgment, Rumpff JA developed the submission of
defence counsel that, 'The criminal law should not be applied as if it were a blue print
for saintliness, but rather in a manner in which it can be obeyed by the reasonable
b man', by saying:

> 'It is generally accepted . . . that for the ordinary person in general his life is
> more valuable than that of another. Only those who possess the quality of
> heroism will intentionally offer their lives for another. Should the criminal law
> then state that compulsion could never be a defence to a charge of murder, it
c > would demand that a person who killed another under duress, whatever the
> circumstances, would have to comply with a higher standard than that demanded
> of the average person. I do not think that such an exception to the general rule
> which applies in criminal law is justified.'

It has also to be remembered that lack of 'heroism' may not necessarily be selfishly
d self-directed, for the duress exerted may well extend to and threaten the lives and
safety of others, and, as has been said, '. . . when a third person's life is also at stake even
the path of heroism is obscure'[3]. That these are not idle considerations is demonstrated by *R v Hurley and Murray*[4] where the wife of one of two accused (charged
with having been accessories after the fact to the felony of escape) was already a hostage
of the oppressors. In such circumstances, what, it may be asked, is the nature of the
e 'heroism' which the law may properly demand?

A second ground advanced in support of the proposition that duress affords no
defence in murder is said to have public policy as its basis. Murder, it is rightly said,
is a crime so grave that no facilities should be afforded to the murderer to escape conviction and punishment. It is then added that duress is a plea easy to raise and that
(the onus to destroy it being on the prosecution) it may prove impossible to rebut it,
f however dark the suspicion that it is not well founded, and that in this way the
murderer may well escape retribution. But this is true of many other pleas which
extenuate or even extinguish criminal culpability—drunkenness for example, as
destroying criminal intent, or an alibi which may serve to eliminate criminal involvement of any kind—and no course is open other than to repose confidence in the
tribunal of fact to discharge its duty of scrutinising with care the evidence adduced. In
g this respect, the risk of a miscarriage of justice by a guilty man being acquitted is no
greater in murder trials than in those other cases in which the plea of duress is, on the
authorities, clearly available, despite their gravity—for example, even in attempted
murder, where an intent actually to kill is an essential ingredient. Nor should the
present grave state of affairs prevailing in Northern Ireland, to which prosecuting
counsel very understandably referred, lead this House to arrive at a conclusion
h different from that which would be proper were Ireland trouble-free. Those who fear
that by accepting the appellant's submission on duress an easy road is opened for
bogus defences would do well to have in mind the observations of Dixon J in *Thomas
v R*[5], cited with approval by Lord Reid in *Warner v Metropolitan Police Comr*[6].

A further ground advanced in the present case is that, while both s 47 of the Criminal

j
1 (1884) 14 QBD 273 at 287, [1881-5] All ER Rep 61 at 67
2 1972 (3) SA 1
3 Wechsler and Michael, 'A Rationale of the Law of Homicide' (1937) 37 Col LR 738
4 [1967] VR 526
5 (1937) 59 CLR 279 at 309
6 [1968] 2 All ER 356 at 362, [1969] 2 AC 256 at 274

Justice Act 1925 and s 37(1) of the Criminal Justice Act (Northern Ireland) 1945 provide a defence to a wife charged with a criminal offence if she proves that it was *a* committed in the presence of, and under the coercion of, her husband, such a defence does not extend to treason or murder. It is accordingly said that, Parliament having so recently rendered coercion unavailable in those two instances, it would be incongruous, to say the least, were the courts now to hold that duress could excuse murder; and this seemingly led Lowry CJ to say in the present case:

> 'We appreciate the force of counsel's appeals to logic and morality but consider *b* that only Parliament can alter what we conceive to be the relevant law.'

But as to the 1925 Act, I favour the view of Professor Glanville Williams that 'The Act can be regarded as merely an incomplete statement of the common law, and the common law still exists to supplement its deficiency', and the same may be said of the Northern Ireland Act of 1945. Smith and Hogan[1] have pointed out that coercion *c* is a wider defence than duress ('because', as the Solicitor-General said during the debate on the Bill[2], 'coercion imports coercion in the moral, possibly even in the spiritual realm, whereas compulsion imports something only in the physical realm'), and that the 1925 Act renders it available to wives in addition to the general defence of duress. It would therefore not be right to say that, because Parliament has withheld the wider defence of coercion from charges of complicity in murder, the narrower *d* defence of duress should also be unavailable in a murder trial.

Prosecuting counsel urged on this House that, even were we to regard it as possibly appropriate to allow duress as a defence to murder, we should leave the matter to be dealt with by Parliament, and in this context invoked certain observations of the Lord Chancellor in *Hyam v Director of Public Prosecutions*[3]. But my noble and learned friend Lord Hailsham of St Marylebone was there dealing with a topic (the criminal intent *e* necessary to constitute murder) on which authoritative pronouncements have several times been made by this House, whereas the questions certified in the present appeal have never hitherto been considered here and, as far as I am aware, have never even been the subject of obiter dicta. We are therefore called on for the first time to make an unfettered decision on a point of pure common law in accordance with basic common law principles. In these circumstances, with respect, I find it quite unacceptable to *f* hold that, were this House otherwise inclined to adopt a view favourable to the appellant, it should dismiss his appeal and, presumably, any other appeals of a like kind until the legislature dealt with the matter.

I therefore turn at long last to consider whether, as the learned trial judge thought, 'The whole weight of judicial writing is against the availability of duress as a defence on a charge of murder', and whether, if so, that should lead this House to the same *g* conclusion. The speeches of my noble and learned friends amply illustrate the frequency with which judges in this country have observed that duress does not extend as a defence to murder, but, with but one solitary exception, these observations were all obiter dicta, being made in cases where murder was not charged. The one exception cited to this House is *R v Tyler and Price*[4], where two men accused of murder sought to excuse their participation in the act of killing performed by one *h* Thom on the ground of duress. I quoted at an earlier stage the widely expressed observations of Lord Denman CJ[5] in charging the jury, and they amount to a direction that duress was no defence. But, as Professor Glanville Williams has pointed out[6]:

> '... the same result could have been reached in *Tyler*[4] even if murder is not

---

1 Criminal Law (3rd Edn, 1973), p 169
2 Parl Deb H of C (1925) 188, col 875
3 [1974] 2 All ER 41 at 47, [1974] 2 WLR 607 at 613
4 (1838) 8 C & P 616
5 8 C & P at 620, 621
6 Op cit, p 759

excepted from the defence of duress. There appears to have been no evidence
a that Tyler went in fear of death (which would be the minimum necessary to
justify murder); nor was any attempt made to show that Tyler could not escape
from the gang. Also, the evidence seemed to show that Tyler had voluntarily
joined a criminal organisation knowing of its purpose; and one who does this has
no cause for complaint if he is debarred from the defence of duress in respect of
threats afterwards made to him.'

b
One would therefore prefer to have a more clear-cut decision before concluding that
in no circumstances is duress available in murder, and the decision of the Court of
Criminal Appeal in *R v Kray*[1] has to be borne in mind. Professor Glanville Williams
has said[2] that in *Sephakela v R*[3], where the charge was one of ritual murder, 'the
Privy Council assumed that duress was a defence . . .' But I respectfully agree with
c Lowry CJ in the present case that the Board made no such assumption and expressly
reserved their opinion on the point. It has further to be observed that the Privy
Council was there enunciating the Roman-Dutch law prevailing in Basutoland.

In *R v Brown and Morley*[4] the majority of the Supreme Court of South Australia
held that a principal in the second degree who performs an act which he intends to be
in furtherance of a proposed murder which is in fact carried out cannot be excused by
d reason of his having acted under the compulsion of threats by his co-accused (the
actual killer) against himself, his wife and his parents. But Bray CJ differed from the
majority on, as he put it, 'the question of the legal effect of duress as a defence to a
charge of minor participation in murder . . .' and, in the course of an illuminating
review of the relevant material, judicial and otherwise, said[5],

'. . . the authorities which show that duress may be a defence to some types of
e treasonable act do not necessarily prove to my mind that it is a defence to all
types of treasonable act. If this is so, then conversely it may be that authorities
which say or appear to say that duress is not a defence to murder generally do
not necessarily prove that it is not a defence to any conceivable type of complicity
in murder, however minor.'

f And then, taking a hypothetical example which has striking similarity to the defence
presented in the present case, Bray CJ said[6]:

'It would seem hard . . . if an innocent passer-by seized in the street by a gang of
criminals visibly engaged in robbery and murder in a shop and compelled at the
point of a gun to issue misleading comments to the public, or an innocent driver
compelled at the point of a gun to convey the murderer to the victim, were to
g have no defence. Are there any authorities which compel us to hold that he
would not?'

Continuing his review, he observed en route[7]:

'. . . in my view, the direction of the learned judge that threats can never be an
h excuse for the taking of an active part in murder, such as coughing to disguise the
approach of the murderer, was too wide.'

His conclusion was that[8]:

---

1   [1969] 3 All ER 941, [1970] 1 QB 125
j 2   Op cit, p 753
3   [1954] High Commission Territories LR 60
4   [1968] SASR 467
5   [1968] SASR at 493
6   [1968] SASR at 494
7   [1968] SASR at 497
8   [1968] SASR at 499

'. . . the trend of the later cases, general reasoning, and the express authority of the Privy Council in *Sephakela's Case*[1] prevent the acceptance of the simple *a* proposition that no type of duress can ever afford a defence to the type of complicity in murder. I repeat also that, as at present advised, I do not think duress could constitute a defence to one who actually kills or attempts to kill the victim.'

It appears to me, with respect, that the reliance placed by Bray CJ on *Sephakela's* *b* *Case*[1] is misplaced, though I concur when he says that[2]:

'There is nothing, in my view, in *Sephakela's Case*[1] to prevent us from holding that there can be circumstances in which duress can be a defence to a person charged with murder as a principal in the second degree.'

Such was the role of Lynch, and this House is accordingly not now called on to deal *c* with the reservation of Bray CJ in relation to a person who under duress 'actually kills or attempts to kill the victim'. As to the actual killer, while I naturally seek to refrain from prejudging future cases, I think it right to say that I agree with the observation of Smith and Hogan[3] that:

'The difficulty about adopting a distinction between the principal and second- *d* ary parties as a rule of law is that the contribution of the secondary party to the death may be no less significant than that of the principal.'

And as to attempted killing, it is to be noted that in *R v Fegan*[4] MacDermott J held in Northern Ireland that duress *is* available on a charge of aiding and abetting in attempted murder, the Crown having conceded the point, and that in the present case Lowry CJ expressed the view that such is the law. The 1972 decision of the *e* Appellate Division of the South African Supreme Court in *State v Goliath*[5], that duress (or compulsion) may constitute a defence to a murder charge has already been referred to, but it does not appear to have been cited to the appellate court in the present case.

CONCLUSION

Having considered the available material to the best of my ability, I find myself *f* unable to accept that any ground in law, logic, morals or public policy has been established to justify withholding the plea of duress in the present case. To say, as Murnaghan J did, in *Attorney-General v Whelan*[6] that: 'Murder is a crime so heinous that . . . in such a case the strongest duress would not be any justification,' is, with respect, to beg the whole question. That murder has a unique gravity most would regard as not open to doubt, but the degree of legal criminality or blameworthiness *g* involved in participation therein depends on all the circumstances of the particular case, just as it does whenever the actus reus and the mens rea necessary to constitute any other offence is established. In homicide, the law already recognises degrees of criminality, notwithstanding that unlawful killing with malice aforethought has unquestionably taken place. In non-homicidal cases, the degree of criminality or blame- *h* worthiness can and should be reflected in the punishment meted out, a course which the mandatory life sentence for murder prohibits. And in relation to *all* offences ('except possibly treason and murder as a principal', as Lord Parker CJ said in *R v Hudson*[7]), a person committing them is entitled to be completely acquitted if at

---

1   [1954] High Commission Territories LR 60   *j*
2   [1968] SASR at 496
3   Op cit, p 166
4   (1974) unreported
5   1972 (3) SA 1
6   [1934] IR at 526
7   [1971] 2 All ER 244 at 246, [1971] 2 QB 202 at 206

the material time he was acting under the threat of death or serious bodily harm.
a Professor J C Smith has rightly observed that[1]:

> 'To allow a defence to crime is not to express approval of the action of the
> accused person but only to declare that it does not merit condemnation and
> punishment.'

b For the reasons I have sought to advance, I can find no valid ground for preventing
the appellant Lynch from presenting the plea of duress, and I would therefore be for
allowing his appeal. By doing so, I consider that this House would be paying due
regard to those 'contemporary views of what is just, what is moral, what is humane',
which my noble and learned friend, Lord Diplock, described in *Hyam v Director of
Public Prosecutions*[2] as constituting 'the underlying principle which is the justification
for retaining the common law as a living source of rules binding on all members of
c contemporary society in England'.

We were invited by prosecuting counsel to apply, if necessary, the proviso to s 9(1)
of the Criminal Appeal (Northern Ireland) Act 1968 on the ground that so unsatisfactory was the evidence of duress that no miscarriage of justice resulted from its
having been withdrawn from the jury. But, for my part, I find that invitation impossible of acceptance, and this particularly in the light of the opinion expressed by
d Lowry CJ that the available evidence raised 'a clear issue of duress'.

There remains to be considered the application of the prosecution pursuant to
s 13(1) of the 1968 Act that, in the event of the appeal being allowed (as I think it
should), a new trial be ordered. Unlike s 7(1) of the Criminal Appeal Act 1968, that
provision does not restrict the power to order a retrial to cases where further evidence
has been received, but enables that course to be followed wherever 'it appears to the
e court that the interests of justice so require'. Lynch has been in custody certainly
since his conviction on 20th June 1972, and it has therefore to be borne in mind that he
has been incarcerated for a substantial period. But a dreadful crime was committed,
the appellant on his own showing played a substantial and vital part in its accomplish-
ment, and the interests of justice require that all criminally responsible therefor
should be duly punished. Despite the passage of time, in my judgment those interests
f require that the appellant be now afforded the opportunity of having considered by a
court the defence of duress on which he sought a verdict at his initial trial. It would be
undesirable for me to say more than that I consider that there are certain features of
that defence which call for the most careful scrutiny. I would therefore be for
ordering a new trial pursuant to s 13 and would remit the case to the Court of Appeal
of Northern Ireland so that, pursuant to s 14(2), they may make such orders in relation
g to the retrial as appear necessary or expedient, the appellant being ordered to remain
in custody meanwhile.

Appeal allowed; new trial ordered.

h Solicitors: *Simons, Muirhead & Allan*, agents for *P J McGroy*, Belfast (for the appellant);
Director of Public Prosecutions for Northern Ireland.

Gordon H Scott Esq   Barrister.

---

1   [1974] Crim LR 352
2   [1974] 2 All ER at 65, [1974] 2 WLR at 631

a

Secretary of State for Trade v Markus

HOUSE OF LORDS

LORD WILBERFORCE, VISCOUNT DILHORNE, LORD DIPLOCK, LORD KILBRANDON AND LORD

SALMON   b

10th, 11th FEBRUARY, 19th MARCH 1975

Criminal law – Inducement to invest money – Fraudulent inducement – Inducement to take
part or to offer to take part in prescribed arrangement – Inducement resulting in victim
offering to take part in arrangement – Inducement also resulting in victim taking part following
acceptance of offer – Whether separate offences – Whether commission of one offence preclu- c
ding commission of the other – Prevention of Fraud (Investments) Act 1958, s 13(1)(b) (as
amended by the Protection of Depositors Act 1963, s 21(1)).

Criminal law – Jurisdiction – Fraudulent inducement to invest money – Inducement to take
part in prescribed arrangement – Inducement made to investor overseas – Inducement d
resulting in investor completing written application to take part in arrangement – Applica-
tion sent to company in England to be processed – Investor authorising steps to be taken on
his behalf in England for the purpose of processing the application – Whether investor in-
duced 'to take part . . . in [an] arrangement' in England – Whether offence of fraudulently
inducing investor to take part committed in England – Prevention of Fraud (Investments)
Act 1958, s 13(1)(b) (as amended by the Protection of Depositors Act 1963, s 21(1)). e

A trust known as Agri-Fund ('the fund') was established in Panama with the ostensible
object of investing its capital in food-producing industries. The intention was that
members of the public should be invited to invest in the fund by purchasing share
units. The fund was managed by a Panamanian corporation of which the appellant
was a director. The organisation which sold share units in the fund was run by a f
company with offices in London. The appellant was also a director of that company.
The London company directed its efforts to obtaining investments from people
abroad, principally in West Germany. Salesmen in West Germany called on prospective investors at their homes and showed them a brochure containing a glowing
account of the fund's prospects and persuaded them to complete application forms for
share units in the fund. Applications were addressed to the London company. A g
prospective investor, having completed and signed an application form for shares in
the fund, gave the salesman a cheque made out to a German bank, or a share certificate in another fund together with a power of attorney in favour of the London
company authorising it to cash the certificate and receive the proceeds on the investor's
behalf. The documents were then sent by the salesmen to the London office for
processing. Where payment for the shares was made by cheque the London company h
sent it to a bank in Switzerland to be placed to the company's credit. Where payment
was made by a share certificate, the certificate together with the power of attorney
was sent to the Swiss bank for encashment. The application by the prospective
investor was not accepted until the London company had been notified that the
money had been credited to its account in Switzerland. The London company would
subsequently send a confirmatory letter to the investor followed by a certificate for j
the appropriate number of shares in the fund. The letter and the certificate were
despatched either direct to the investor by post from London or to the salesman in
Germany to give to the investor personally. The fund was in fact an entirely bogus
one and the statements in the brochure were both false and fraudulent. The appellant
was charged with 'conniving at a corporation fraudulently inducing the investment

of money', contrary to ss 13(1)(b)[a] and 19[b] of the Prevention of Fraud (Investments)
a Act 1958, in that he had connived at the fraudulent inducement by the Panamanian
corporation through the London company of a resident of West Germany 'to take
part in an arrangement' of a kind prescribed by s 13(1)(b) by means of the false
statements contained in the brochure. The appellant was convicted and appealed,
contending that all the acts of the person induced had taken place in West Germany
and that accordingly he had not connived at the commission of any offence within
b the jurisdiction of the English courts.

Held (Viscount Dilhorne dissenting) – The appeal would be dismissed for the following
reasons—
   (i) Section 13(1)(b) created two separate offences, i e inducing a person to 'take part'
in an arrangement and inducing a person to 'offer to take part' in an arrangement,
c but those offences were not mutually exclusive in the sense that where the facts
disclosed the commission of one of them it necessarily followed that the other had
not been committed. Accordingly the fact that a person was guilty of inducing another
'to . . . offer to take part' in a prescribed arrangement did not prevent him from being
guilty also of inducing the other 'to take part . . . in' such an arrangement should the
offer be accepted. The appellant had therefore been properly charged with conniving
d at an inducement to 'take part' in an arrangement (see p 960 *f*, p 965 *d* to *f* and *h* and
p 967 *d* and *e*, post).
   (ii) Furthermore the offence in question had been committed within the jurisdiction
of the English courts. Although the victims of the offences had done nothing involving
their physical presence in England, a person could 'take part' in arrangement through
other persons acting on his behalf. There was ample evidence of things done on behalf
e of the victims in England, e g the processing of their applications for shares in the
fund, which amounted to 'taking part' in arrangements within s 13(1)(b) (see p 960 *f*
and p 966 *a* to *e* and *j* to p 967 *e*, post); *R v Ellis* [1899] 1 QB 230 applied.
   Decision of the Court of Appeal, Criminal Division sub nom *R v Markus* [1974] 3
All ER 705 affirmed.

f **Notes**
For fraudulent inducements to invest money, see 36 Halsbury's Laws (3rd Edn)
577-579, para 928.
   For the limits of criminal jurisdiction, see 10 Halsbury's Laws (3rd Edn) 316-318,
paras 577-579, and for cases on the subject, see 14 Digest (Repl) 145-149, 1074-1123.
   For the Prevention of Fraud (Investments) Act 1958, ss 13, 19, see 22 Halsbury's
g Statutes (3rd Edn) 980, 990.

Cases referred to in opinions
Board of Trade v Owen [1957] 1 All ER 411, [1957] AC 602, [1957] 2 WLR 351, 121 JP 177,
41 Cr App Rep 11, HL, Digest (Cont Vol A) 341, 1100a.
R v Ellis [1899] 1 QB 230, 68 LJQB 103, 79 LT 532, 62 JP 838, 19 Cox CC 210, CCR, 14
h Digest (Repl) 148, 1112.

Appeal
On 6th November 1973 in the Central Criminal Court before his Honour Judge
Lawson QC, the appellant, Edward Jules Markus, was convicted, inter alia, on one

j
---
a Section 13(1), as amended and so far as material, is set out at p 964 *h* to 965 *a*, post
b Section 19 provides: 'Where any offence under this Act committed by a corporation is
   proved to have been committed with the consent or connivance of any director, manager,
   secretary or other officer of the corporation, he, as well as the corporation, shall be deemed
   to be guilty of that offence and shall be liable to be proceeded against and punished
   accordingly.'

count of conspiring to defraud and on eight counts of conniving at a corporation
fraudulently inducing the investment of money by false representations, contrary to   *a*
ss 13(1)(*b*) and 19 of the Prevention of Fraud (Investments) Act 1958. The last eight
counts alleged that the appellant, being a director of Agricultural Investment Corpn
SA and of First National Investment Corpn SA and of Agri-International SA and of
Agri-International (UK) Ltd, had connived at the fraudulent inducement by Agricultural Investment Corpn SA through its agents First National Investment Corpn SA
and Agri-International SA and Agri-International (UK) Ltd of certain named persons   *b*
to take part in an arrangement to invest sums of money in Agri-Fund (the investment
being an arrangement with respect to property other than securities, the purpose or pretended purpose of which was to enable those persons to participate in the profits alleged
to be likely to arise from the holding of Agri-Fund) by misleading, false or deceptive
representations that Agricultural Investment Corpn SA was genuinely carrying on an
honest business and that moneys invested in Agri-Fund were immediately redeemable   *c*
at the option of the investor. The appellant was sentenced to seven years' imprisonment in respect of each of those counts to run concurrently with each other and with
terms of imprisonment imposed on him in respect of certain other offences, making
seven years' imprisonment in all. The appellant appealed against both conviction
and sentence. On 23rd July 1974 the Court of Appeal, Criminal Division[1] (Lord
Widgery CJ, Bridge and May JJ) dismissed the appeal against conviction but sub-   *d*
stituted a sentence of five years' imprisonment. The court refused leave to appeal to
the House of Lords but certified that the decision involved a point of law of general
public importance. On 5th November 1974 the appeal committee of the House of
Lords gave leave to appeal. The facts are set out in the opinion of Viscount Dilhorne.

Montague Waters QC and *John Nutting* for the appellant.   *e*
W A B Forbes QC and *Timothy Walker* for the Crown.

Their Lordships took time for consideration.

19th March. The following opinions were delivered.   *f*

LORD WILBERFORCE. My Lords, I have had the benefit of reading in advance
the speech of my noble and learned friend Lord Diplock. I agree that the appeal
should be dismissed.

VISCOUNT DILHORNE. My Lords, the appellant was convicted at the   *g*
Central Criminal Court on 6th November 1973 on 12 counts. The first charged him
with conspiracy to cheat and defraud such persons as might be induced to invest in
'Agri-Fund' by false pretences and fraudulent devices. Eight charged him with
conniving at a corporation fraudulently inducing the investment of money in Agri-
Fund, contrary to ss 13(1)(*b*) and 19 of the Prevention of Fraud (Investments) Act 1958
(as amended by the Protection of Depositors Act 1963, ss 1 and 21): one with conniving   *h*
at a corporation attempting fraudulently to induce the investment of money in
Agri-Fund, contrary to those sections, and two with conniving at the distribution of
circulars, contrary to ss 14(1) and 19 of that Act.
　　The appellant operated from 44 Green Street, London, through a number of
companies. He was at all material times a director of a Panamanian company called
Agricultural Investment Corpn SA ('AICSA') and a director or chief executive of   *j*
First National Investment Corpn SA, of Agri-International SA and of Agri-International (UK) Ltd. Those companies acted as agents for AICSA which had its
headquarters at 44 Green Street.

1　[1974] 3 All ER 705

A prospectus was printed by AICSA. It described Agri-Fund as 'A new concept in
a mutual funds, or as they are also called, investment trusts' and represented that
AICSA was genuinely carrying on an honest business and that moneys invested in
'Agri-Fund' were immediately redeemable at the option of the investor. Salesmen in
West Germany were employed to try to induce, with the aid of the prospectus,
persons in that country to offer to subscribe to one or other of two plans. One was
called the 'Fully Paid Plan' and a subscriber to that made only one payment; the
b other was called the 'Beneficial Payment Plan' and provided for the payment by the
subscriber of instalments. No effort was made to induce persons in this country to
offer to subscribe, and all the charges preferred against the appellant relate to the
inducement or the attempted inducement of persons in West Germany who were not
British nationals to offer to subscribe.

The salesmen had with them a form for the person they approached to complete
c and sign. The form began with the words 'I hereby apply for the Plan described
below'. The applicant then had to complete the form showing which Plan he had
selected and the amount he was willing to subscribe. The application was addressed
to the First National Investment Corpn SA at 44 Green Street, London and, when
completed, was handed to the salesman with, in some cases, a cheque for the amount
to be subscribed, and in other cases with an IOS share certificate and a completed
d form of assignment of the IOS shares. We were not told how many of the counts on
which the appellant was convicted related to cases in which the salesman had been
given an IOS share certificate and a form of assignment, and how many cases in which
cheques were given. The completed forms, cheques and IOS certificates were sent
by the salesman to 44 Green Street, and there 'processed'. It was only after the
cheques had been banked in a Swiss bank account and after the IOS certificates had
e been cashed and the proceeds banked in Switzerland that confirmation, followed
later by a share certificate, was sent to the subscriber.

Section 13(1) of the Prevention of Fraud (Investments) Act 1958, as amended, made
it an offence for any person by misleading, false or deceptive statements, etc to
induce or to attempt to induce another person—

f   '(*a*) to enter into or offer to enter into [an agreement of the kind specified] or
       (*b*) to take part or offer to take part in any arrangements with respect to property
       other than securities [being arrangements of the kind described in the subsection]
       or (*c*) to enter into or offer to enter into an agreement',

the purpose or pretended purpose of which was to secure a profit on the fluctuations
in the value of any property other than shares.
g   Unlike the offence of obtaining money by false pretences and many other offences,
the obtaining of money or other property as the result of the inducement was not an
ingredient of the offences created by this section. All that has to be proved is that by
false statements, etc a person has been induced to do one of the acts specified in paras
(*a*), (*b*) and (*c*). Once it is proved that such an act has been induced, the offence is
complete. Where the charge is of attempting to induce such an act, then the nature
h of the act which it sought to induce has to be determined.

In this case all the acts of the person induced took place in West Germany, and it
was consequently contended for the appellant at the trial, before the Court of Appeal[1]
and in this House that he had not connived at the commission of any offence to which
the laws of this country apply.

Judge Lawson at the Central Criminal Court on a submission of no case, ruled that
j if the inducement was to make an offer, there was no offence committed in this
country, but that as acceptance of the offer took place in this country, an element
of the offence was committed in this country and so there was jurisdiction to try the
appellant. His appeal to the Court of Appeal was dismissed, Lord Widgery CJ

1   [1974] 3 All ER 705

holding¹ that the applicant for shares in Agri-Fund did not take part in the Agri-Fund arrangements until his application had been received in London and had been *a*
processed and so that the offences were committed in England. The Court of Appeal
certified that the following question:

'Whether upon the true construction of s 13(1)(*b*) of the Prevention of Fraud
(Investments) Act 1958 (as amended by the Protection of Depositors Act 1963,
ss 1 and 21) the offence of fraudulently inducing a person to offer to take part *b*
in an arrangement with respect to property other than securities is an offence
separate and distinct from the offence under the same paragraph of fraudulently
inducing a person to take part in an arrangement with respect to such property
so that if the facts disclose the former offence it is not open to the prosecution to
charge the latter offence by reason of the subsequent acceptance of the victim's offer',

c

was a point of law of general public importance but refused leave to appeal to this
House. The appellant now appeals, with the leave of this House, and advances the
same contentions as in the Court of Appeal.

In my opinion s 13(1)(*b*) creates a number of separate offences. In each case it is
necessary to prove that by a false statement etc a person was induced to do certain
acts. If he was induced to enter into an agreement of the kind described that is one *d*
offence; if he was induced to offer to enter into such an agreement that is a separate and
distinct offence. Similarly, if he was induced to enter into an arrangement of the sort
described, it is one offence and if he was induced to offer to enter into such
an arrangement, it is another.

Section 13, both before and after its amendment, requires one to consider what it
was that the victim was induced to do. As the section did not make it an ingredient *e*
of the offence that money or property should be obtained as the result of the inducement, cases such as *R v Ellis²*, where the English court was held to have jurisdiction
when the property was obtained in England though the false pretences were made in
Scotland, are of no assistance. In that case the crime was not completed until the
goods were obtained. In cases under s 13 the offence is complete when a person has
been induced to act in one of the ways mentioned. True it is that a subscriber to *f*
Agri-Fund did not take part in the Agri-Fund arrangements until his offer had been
accepted and processed, but that does not appear to alter the offence committed. In
every case, as I see it, the section requires consideration of what the victim was induced
to do, and what the perpetrators of the fraud did thereafter is in my view irrelevant.

The draftsman of s 13 had, once it was decided not to make the obtaining of money
or property an ingredient of the offences created by that section, not merely to provide *g*
that inducement to enter into an agreement or arrangement was sufficient. If he had
only done that, the object of the section could easily have been avoided by inducing a
person only to offer to enter into such an agreement or arrangement. Here the only
acts the victims were induced to do were performed in West Germany and on those
acts being done, the offences were complete.

In my opinion not only are the offences created by s 13 separate and distinct but *h*
they are also mutually exclusive. A man cannot at one and the same time enter
into an agreement or arrangement and offer to enter into one. If it is sought to apply
the description of 'result crime' to the offences created, the result is the act of the
victim, not as in *R v Ellis²*, the obtaining of goods.

That the signing and completion of the application form and the handing of it with
a cheque or an IOS share certificate and form of assignment to the salesman con- *j*
stituted an offer to take part in an arrangement coming within s 13(1)(*b*) appears to
have been the view both of the trial judge and of the Court of Appeal. Taking part

---

1 [1974] 3 All ER at 713
2 [1899] 1 QB 230

a in such an arrangement is a very indefinite expression, and counsel for the appellant contended, and I think rightly, that if what the victims had done amounted to taking part, then the taking part was also in Germany.

As no acts were done by the subscribers in this country in my opinion the appellant did not commit any offence against the laws of this land. In this House it was argued, though it does not appear to have been argued in the Court of Appeal, that would-be subscribers to Agri-Fund authorised one or other of the companies which acted as agents for AICSA to act on their behalf. When the subscriber handed a cheque to the salesman I can see no grounds for saying that he appointed the salesman or anyone in England to act as his agent. Only in the cases where an IOS certificate and a completed form of assignment of the shares to which it related was handed over does it appear to me that an argument can be advanced that the subscriber appointed anyone to act on his behalf. The form authorised the receipt by Agri-International of the cash realised in respect of the IOS shares and while it is headed 'Declaration of Assignment' and contains the words 'power of attorney', it appears only to have operated to authorise the sale of the shares and for payment therefor to the company. As I have said, one does not know which, if any, counts relate to cases where IOS certificates and a form of assignment were handed over. Only in relation to such cases could such an argument be advanced.

Even if it were established in relation to some of the counts that the subscribers had appointed agents to act for them in London, I do not think that that would suffice to give the courts of this country jurisdiction as, in my opinion, the offence is complete when the subscriber has been induced to offer to enter into such an arrangement.

On any view the appellant's conviction on count 1 should, in my opinion, be quashed, for there the charge was of conspiracy to cheat and defraud such persons as might be induced to invest in Agri-Fund, and the case for the prosecution was that the persons who might be induced to invest in Agri-Fund were citizens of Western Germany and this House decided in *Board of Trade v Owen*[1] that a conspiracy made in this country to cheat and defraud persons abroad is not an offence cognisable in our courts.

I appreciate that if this appeal is allowed the consequence will be that the appellant escapes the punishment he deserves. The decision of this House in *Board of Trade v Owen*[1] had a similar consequence, but the fact that that will be the consequence, should not lead to anything other than a strict construction of this penal statute. I cannot see that there is any valid ground for concluding that the offence completed by a person being induced to offer to enter into such an arrangement can be converted by subsequent acts of those engaged in the fraud into a different and distinct offence.

For these reasons in my opinion this appeal should be allowed.

LORD DIPLOCK. My Lords, the appellant played a leading part in running a gigantic international swindle known as Agri-Fund. This was a trust established in Panama to invest its capital in food-producing industries. The fund was managed by a Panamanian company, Agricultural Investment Corpn SA, of which the appellant was a director, but the organisation charged with selling units in the fund to the public was run from offices in London, at first by a Luxembourg company, First National Investment Corpn SA, and later by an English company, Agri-International (UK) Ltd. (I shall refer to both these companies as 'the London company'.) The appellant was a director of both of them and took the major role in managing them. Although the sales organisation was run from London, its efforts were directed to obtaining investments from people abroad, principally in West Germany, through the activities of a large team of salesmen, many of whom had previously been engaged in selling units in another well-known off-shore fund, IOS, which had by then fallen on evil

1 [1957] 1 All ER 411, [1957] AC 602

days. There was no evidence of any attempt to induce anyone in England to invest in Agri-Fund.   *a*

The method of operation was for the salesmen in Germany to call on prospective investors at their homes, where they showed them a glossy brochure containing a glowing account of the prospects of the fund and persuaded them to fill up an application form for share units in Agri-Fund which was addressed to the London company in England. There were two kinds of investment available, a 'Fully-Paid Plan' and a 'Beneficial Payment Plan' under which an initial payment of 20 per cent was made and   *b* the balance was payable by monthly instalments over a period of ten years. The brochure bore a conspicuous notice that all correspondence was to be addressed to the London company at its London office, and the application form contained an acknowledgement of receipt of the brochure and a provision that it should form part of the contract to be entered into on acceptance of the application. It is not disputed that the statements in the brochures about the fund were false and fraudulent to the   *c* knowledge of the appellant.

Many of the investors approached by the salesmen had previously invested in the IOS fund. As soon as the prospective investor had been persuaded to sign the application form, the salesman got him to hand over a cheque made out to the order of a German bank for the price of the units applied for or, more frequently, to hand over the certificate for his shares in the IOS fund together with a power of attorney in favour   *d* of the London company authorising it to cash the certificate and to receive the proceeds on the investor's behalf.

Having obtained these documents, the salesman forwarded them to the London company at its London office for 'processing'. If payment had been made by cheque, the London company then sent the cheque by an indirect route to be ultimately credited to its account in a Swiss bank. If payment was to be made by means of a   *e* certificate for IOS shares, the share certificate and the power of attorney were sent to Switzerland for encashment by IOS. A cheque in favour of the London company for the amount due was sent by IOS to the London company in England, who then sent this cheque to its own bank in Switzerland to be credited to its account. Whichever method of payment was used, the application by the would-be investor was not accepted until the London company had been notified that the money had been   *f* actually credited to its account in Switzerland. The London company then sent by post to the applicant a confirmation form which bore the date on which this process had been completed. The confirmation form was followed shortly after by a certificate for the appropriate number of share units in Agri-Fund, which was either sent direct to the investor by post from London or forwarded to the salesman in Germany to hand over to the investor personally.   *g*

The appellant was tried and convicted at the Central Criminal Court on a large number of counts, of which it is only necessary to refer to those which charged an offence under ss 13(1)(b) and 19 of the Prevention of Fraud (Investments) Act 1958. Section 19 provides that where an offence under the Act is committed by a corporation any director of the corporation who connives at the offence shall be deemed to be guilty of it, as well as the corporation itself. Section 13(1)(b) of the Act in its amended   *h* form reads as follows:

'13. *Penalty for fraudulently inducing persons to invest money*—(1) Any person who, by any statement, promise or forecast which he knows to be misleading, false or deceptive, or by any dishonest concealment of material facts, or by the reckless making (dishonestly or otherwise) of any statement, promise or forecast which is   *j* misleading, false or deceptive, induces or attempts to induce another person . . .
(b) to take part or offer to take part in any arrangements with respect to property other than securities, being arrangements the purpose or effect, or pretended purpose or effect, of which is to enable persons taking part in the arrangements (whether by becoming owners of the property or any part of the property or

otherwise) to participate in or receive profits or income alleged to arise or to be
a   likely to arise from the acquisition, holding, management or disposal of such
property, or sums to be paid or alleged to be likely to be paid out of such profits
or income or . . .'

His appeal against conviction was dismissed by the Court of Appeal[1] who certified
that the following point of law of general importance was involved in their decision:
b

'Whether upon the true construction of s 13(1)(b) of the Prevention of Fraud
(Investments) Act 1958 (as amended by the Protection of Depositors Act 1963,
ss 1 and 21) the offence of fraudulently inducing a person to offer to take part in
an arrangement with respect to property other than securities is an offence
separate and distinct from the offence under the same paragraph of fraudulently
c   inducing a person to take part in an arrangement with respect to such property
so that if the facts disclose the former offence it is not open to the prosecution to
charge the latter offence by reason of the subsequent acceptance of the victim's
offer.'

This is a short point of construction. The offence of inducing another person to
d   take part in any arrangements of the kind described in s 13(1)(b) is clearly a separate
and distinct offence from that of inducing another person to offer to take part in any
such arrangements. The use of the conjunction 'or' shows that they are alternative
offences; but not that to have committed one precludes the possibility of subsequently
committing the other. In many cases the actual taking part in the arrangements by
the victim of the fraudulent inducement will have been preceded by an offer by him
e   to take part and will have resulted from an acceptance of that offer. The question
posed by the Court of Appeal[1] is whether, in such a case, where the person charged
is the person who fraudulently induced the victim to make the offer, he cannot be
charged with fraudulently inducing the victim to take part in the arrangements
despite the fact that this was both the actual and the intended consequence of the
inducement. When stated in this form the question itself invites the answer, No. No
f   plausible reason has been suggested for ascribing to the words of the statute a meaning
which would have so absurd a result. In statutes which make acts done with the
intention of achieving a particular result punishable as crimes it is a common practice
to provide that there shall be alternative offences depending on the stage to which the
offender has managed to get towards achieving that result.

I do not find it credible that Parliament, by doing this, should have intended that
g   an offender who has actually succeeded in achieving the proscribed result should not
be charged with that offence because at some intermediate stage he had done something which, if he had been stopped then, would have constituted one of the alternative
offences.

So I would answer the question that was certified, No. This, however, is not sufficient to dispose of the appeal; for lurking behind the question of construction of the
h   statute lies a question whether the particular facts of this case which I have summarised
disclose any offence that is punishable under English law.

To answer this question in the instant case does not, in my view, call for any wide-
roving enquiry into the territorial ambit of English criminal law. The offences with
which the appellant was charged were 'result-crimes' of the same general nature as
the offence of obtaining goods on credit by false pretences which was the subject of
j   the charge in R v Ellis[2]. That case is well-established authority for the proposition that,

---

1   [1974] 3 All ER 705
2   [1899] 1 QB 230

in the case of what is a result crime in English law, the offence is committed in England
and justiciable by an English court if any part of the proscribed result takes place in   *a*
England.

The proscribed result in the instant case is the taking part in the arrangements
by the victim of the fraudulent inducement. So if anything the victim did in England
amounted to taking part in the arrangements, the offence was committed in England
and is justiciable in this country.

To decide whether anything that the victims did in England amounted to taking   *b*
part in the arrangements involves a further question of construction of the Act, viz,
what is meant by 'take part in any arrangements'. Taking part in arrangements is
not confined to a single act which can only be done at a single point of time. Depending
on the nature of the arrangements, it may include a whole variety of acts done over a
period. The nature of the arrangements dealt with in s 13(1)(*b*) is that they should be
arrangements with respect to property other than securities and that their pretended   *c*
purpose or effect should be to enable persons taking part in them to participate in or
receive profits or income alleged to arise or to be likely to arise from the acquisition,
holding, management or disposal of such property. Anything that a person does to
enable him to participate in or receive such profits or income thus constitutes taking
part in the arrangements.

That a person may take part in arrangements through other persons acting on his   *d*
behalf is not disputed. It is not necessary that everything should be done by him in
person. In the instant case, although the victims did nothing in England that involved
their physical presence here there is, in my view, ample evidence of things done on
their behalf in England which amount to taking part in the arrangements within the
meaning of s 13(1)(*b*). The management of the scheme for inducing investors to apply
for share units in Agri-Fund and issuing them with their share certificates which pur-   *e*
ported to entitle them to participate in the profits of the fund, was centred at the
London office of the London company, and the whole process of verifying the applications and issuing the share units was carried out there. The salesmen in Germany
had no authority from the London company to accept offers from would-be investors
to purchase share units in Agri-Fund. In order to enable prospective investors to take
part in the arrangements by acquiring share units in Agri-Fund, it was necessary for   *f*
their application forms and their cheques or IOS certificates to be forwarded on their
behalf to London. In the case of IOS certificates it was also necessary for these to be
despatched by the London office to Switzerland, again on their behalf under the
express authority conferred by the power of attorney; and for the cheque from IOS
for the proceeds of encashment of the certificates to be received in London by the
London company on their behalf under the same power of attorney, by virtue of   *g*
which the cheque remained the investor's property until the proceeds had been
credited to the London company's bank account in Switzerland and the certificates
for share units in Agri-Fund had been issued. The share unit certificates which created
the investor's title to participate in the profits of the fund were issued in London.
Monthly payments due under the beneficial payments plan had to be sent by the
investor to the London office of the London company. Any correspondence by   *h*
prospective or actual investors dealing with their investment had to be addressed by
them to the London company at its London office, and delivered there. Since such
letters from investors would not be acceptances of contractual offers that had been
made by post by the London company, the English legal fiction that the post office
acts as agent of the addressee in receiving the letter containing an acceptance, at the
place where it is posted, would not apply to them. In delivering correspondence by   *j*
investors at the London office the post office would be acting as agent of the addressor.

Such of these steps in the processing of an investor's application for share units in
Agri-Fund as were undertaken on his behalf at the London office of the London company amount to a taking part in the arrangements there by him. I am unable to
accept the argument that everything that was done after the would-be investor had

handed the application form and cheque or IOS certificate to the salesman in Germany
a was done by the London company on its own behalf or as agent for the Agricultural
Investment Corporation SA, and that none of the things that were done in London
were done as agent for the investor. This seems to me to fly in the face of the actual
evidence in the case. It is inconsistent with the limited authority given by the London
company to the salesmen in Germany, and is contradicted by the documentary
evidence of which I need only single out for special mention the power of attorney
b in favour of the London company in respect of the encashment of the IOS share
certificates.

I would therefore hold that, by what was done on their behalf in London, investors
who acquired shares in the Agri-Fund did take part there in the arrangements and
that the offence of fraudulently inducing them to do so was accordingly committed
in England and justiciable here.

c   I would dismiss this appeal.

LORD KILBRANDON. My Lords, I have had the advantage of reading the
speech prepared by my noble and learned friend Lord Diplock. I agree that the
d appeal should be dismissed for the reasons which he gives.

LORD SALMON. My Lords, I too, have had the advantage of reading the speech of
my noble and learned friend Lord Diplock and, for the reasons he gives, I would
dismiss the appeal.

e
Appeal dismissed.

Solicitors: *Anthony Leader & Co* (for the appellant); *Solicitor, Department of Trade.*

Gordon H Scott Esq Barrister.

Amoco Australia Pty Ltd v Rocca Bros Motor Engineering Co Pty Ltd

PRIVY COUNCIL

LORD MORRIS OF BORTH-Y-GEST, LORD CROSS OF CHELSEA, LORD KILBRANDON, LORD SALMON AND LORD EDMUND-DAVIES

28th, 29th, 30th, 31st OCTOBER, 4th, 5th NOVEMBER 1974, 27th JANUARY 1975

Trade – Restaint of trade – Agreement – Election – Lease – Lease containing covenant in restraint of trade – Covenant by lessee – Election between observing covenant and surrendering lease – Whether lessee should be put to election.

Trade – Restraint of trade – Agreement – Separate agreements – Lease and underlease – Single transaction – Estoppel – Underlease unenforceable as containing covenants in restraint of trade – Enforceability of lease – Provision in lease asserting that it was independent of any other contract, lease or agreement between parties – Lease by dealer of site of petrol filling station to petrol company – Underlease by petrol company to dealer – Underlease unenforceable as containing petrol tie in restraint of trade – Whether lease unenforceable – Whether dealer estopped from asserting that lease unenforceable

The appellant ('Amoco') was a refiner and distibutor of petroleum products and the respondent ('Rocca') was a motor engineering company incorporated for the purpose of carrying on business as a service station proprietor. On 19th June 1964 Amoco and Rocca entered into an agreement whereby (a) Rocca was to build a motor service station on vacant land, (b) the building was to be constructed almost entirely at Rocca's expense but Amoco was to be responsible for providing the station with the necessary plant and equipment, (c) after the station had been built Rocca was to grant Amoco a lease of the premises for 15 years at a rent of £1 per annum plus a sum of 3d per gallon for all petrol delivered for sale to the station by Amoco, (d) Amoco was then to grant an underlease of the station premises to Rocca for the term of 15 years less a day at a rent of £1 per annum, (e) the lease and underlease when executed were to be annexed to the agreement. On 19th May 1966 the lease and underlease were duly executed. Clauses 18 and 19 of the lease provided (a) that the lease was not dependent or contingent on any other contract, lease or agreement between Amoco and Rocca and was completely independent of any other transaction between the parties and (b) that the lease embodied the entire agreement between Amoco and Rocca. By cl 3(*g*), (*h*) and (*i*) of the underlease Rocca covenanted (*g*) to carry on the business of a petrol filling station and not to cease carrying on that business during the currency of the underlease without the written consent of Amoco; (*h*) to purchase exclusively from Amoco all petroleum and oil products required for sale and not to purchase or use any other such products, provided Amoco were able to supply them, and (*i*) to buy a minimum of 8,000 gallons of petrol and 140 gallons of motor oil a month from Amoco during the currency of the underlease. The lease and underlease were registered under the Real Property Act of South Australia. In 1971 Rocca, having tried unsuccessfully to re-negotiate the terms of its agreement with Amoco, started negotiations with a rival oil company. On 16th November 1971 Rocca began to remove Amoco's petrol pumps and to replace them with those of the other oil company. Amoco commenced proceedings against Rocca and the trial of certain agreed issues was ordered. The issues were, inter alia, whether the covenants or any of them in the underlease were an unreasonable restraint of trade and unenforceable; if so, whether the whole underlease was void; if so, whether the lease also was void. On 12th April 1972 the judge held that the covenants in the underlease were not an unreasonable restraint of trade. On 7th August 1972 the Full Court of the

Supreme Court of South Australia reversed that decision, holding that the covenants
a in the underlease went beyond what was reasonably necessary for the protection of
Amoco. On 11th October 1973 the High Court of Australia by a majority affirmed the
judgment of the Full Court. Amoco appealed to the Privy Council contending (i) that
even if cl 3(*g*), (*h*) and (*i*) were deleted from the underlease on the ground that they
were an unreasonable restraint of trade, it was nevertheless possible to effect a severance of the underlease so that the remainder of its terms were left in force; (ii) that
b where a lease, as opposed to a contract, contained a covenant in restraint of trade the
covenantor should be put to election whether to surrender the lease or to perform the
covenant despite its unenforceability and that Rocca should therefore be put to their
election with regard to the underlease, and (iii) that even if the underlease were void
the headlease nevertheless remained in force.

c **Held** – The appeal would be dismissed for the following reasons—
(i) It was impossible to sever cl 3 (*g*), (*h*) and (*i*) from the underlease because those
clauses contained the very essence of the underlease to Rocca, in that the effect of
those provisions was that Amoco, having paid for the installation of pumps and other
equipment, could require Rocca to buy petrol from Amoco and run a service station
on the premises. It was inconceivable that any petrol company would grant a dealer
d a lease at a nominal rent without imposing any obligation to buy petrol from it (see
p 977 *e* and *f*, post).
(ii) There was no difference between an unenforceable promise contained in a contract
and one contained in a lease. Once it was established that a covenant was an unreasonable
restraint of trade there was no ground for drawing a distinction, with regard to the
consequences, between provisions in contracts and covenants in leases. Even where
e severance was possible, a party to a lease who had entered into a covenant which was
in restraint of trade and who was forced to elect between observing the unenforceable
restraint and surrendering the lease would in fact be under pressure to observe a
promise which public policy said he should be free to disregard. In any event no
question of election could arise because the covenants in the underlease were not
severable and furthermore Rocca wished to surrender the underlease provided the
f headlease also ceased to have effect (see p 978 *c* to *g*, post); dictum of Lord Reid in *Esso
Petroleum Co Ltd v Harper's Garage (Stourport) Ltd* [1967] 1 All ER at 708 explained.
(iii) The headlease could not remain in force if the underlease were eliminated
since it was impossible to regard the two leases as being separate dispositions of
property. It was clear from the initial agreement between the parties that the two
leases were parts of a single commercial transaction under which Rocca was to obtain
g petrol at a rebate price from Amoco which in turn was to obtain a trade tie in return
for its investment in Rocca's service station. The statements to the contrary in the headlease were untrue, the statements having been inserted to strengthen Amoco's trade
tie over Rocca; no estoppel could operate against Rocca since it would have the effect
of deterring Rocca from asserting that the trade tie was unenforceable on the grounds
of public policy. It followed that the headlease was also unenforceable (see p 978 *g* to p
h 979 *a*, post).

Notes
For agreements in restraint of trade and conditions for severance of such agreements,
see 38 Halsbury's Laws (3rd Edn) 20, 53, paras 13, 62, and for cases on the subject, see
45 Digest (Repl) 443-449, 271-297.

j **Cases referred to in opinion**
Attwood v Lamont [1920] 3 KB 571, [1920] All ER Rep 55, 90 LJKB 121, 124 LT 108, CA, 45
Digest (Repl) 442, 263.
Bennett v Bennett [1952] 1 All ER 413, [1952] 1 KB 249, [1952] 1 TLR 400, CA; *affg* [1951]
1 All ER 1088, [1951] 2 KB 572, [1951] 1 TLR 873, 211 LT 333, Digest 27(2) (Reissue)
917, 7338.

Brooks v Burns Philp Trustee Co Ltd (1969) 121 CLR 432.
Esso Petroleum Co Ltd v Harper's Garage (Stourport) Ltd [1967] 1 All ER 699, [1968] AC *a*
269, [1967] 2 WLR 871, HL, Digest (Cont Vol C) 985, *132a*.
Kelly v Koshga (1959) 358 US 516.
Mason v Provident Clothing & Supply Co Ltd [1913] AC 724, [1911-13] All ER Rep 400,
82 LJKB 1153, 109 LT 449, HL; *rvsg* sub nom *Provident Clothing & Supply Co Ltd v
Mason* [1913] 1 KB 65, CA, 45 Digest (Repl) 445, *279*.
Petrofina (Gt Britain) Ltd v Martin [1966] 1 All ER 126, [1966] Ch 146, [1966] 2 WLR *b*
318, CA; *affg* on different grounds [1965] 2 All ER 176, [1965] Ch 1073, [1965] 2
WLR 1299, Digest (Cont Vol B) 701, *130a*.

Appeal

On 16th November 1971 the appellant, Amoco Australia Pty Ltd, issued a writ in the
Supreme Court of South Australia claiming interlocutory injunctions against the *c*
respondent, Rocca Bros Motor Engineering Co Pty Ltd, in respect of alleged breaches
of the covenants contained in a memorandum of an underlease from the appellant to
the respondent executed on 19th May 1966. On 18th November 1971 Wells J granted
the appellant an interlocutory injunction against the respondent pending the determination whether or not certain covenants contained in the underlease were unenforceable as being in unreasonable restraint of trade. Wells J subsequently made an *d*
order dispensing with pleadings and directed that the action be tried on agreed issues
between the parties. On 12th July 1972 Wells J held that the agreed question whether
the covenants contained in the underlease were an unreasonable restraint of trade
and thus unenforceable should be answered in the negative. On 7th August 1972 the
Full Court of the Supreme Court of Australia (Bray ACJ, Hogarth and Walters JJ)
reversed the judgment of Wells J, holding that the covenants contained in the under- *e*
lease went beyond what was necessary for the protection of the appellant. On 11th
October 1973 the High Court of Australia (McTiernan ACJ, Walsh and Gibbs JJ,
Menzies and Stephen JJ dissenting) dismissed an appeal by the appellant against
that decision. On 20th February 1974 the appellant was granted leave to appeal to the
Privy Council on the issues: (a) whether, if the covenants contained in the underlease
to the respondent were unenforceable, the whole of the underlease was void; (b) *f*
whether, if the underlease was void, the lease granted by the respondent to the
appellant was also void. The facts are set out in the opinion of the Board.

Leolin Price QC with *G de Q Walker* and *David Angel* (both of the South Australian Bar)
for the appellant.
Francis Robert Fisher QC and *Robin Rhodes Millhouse* (both of the South Australian Bar) *g*
for the respondent.

LORD CROSS OF CHELSEA. This is an appeal by special leave from a
judgment of the Full Court of the Supreme Court of South Australia dated 18th
January 1974. The appellant is a company incorporated in the Australian Capital *h*
Territory which carries on business in the Commonwealth as a refiner and distributor
of petroleum products. The respondent was incorporated in South Australia in
February 1964 with the object of carrying on business in that state as a service station
proprietor. On 19th June 1964 the respondent and the appellant entered into an
agreement in writing under which: (a) the respondent was to build a service station
on vacant land at Para Hills (at that time a newly developing suburb north of Adelaide) *j*
in accordance with agreed plans and specifications; (b) the building was to be constructed at the respondent's expense (save for certain painting which was to be carried
out by the appellant) but the appellant was to equip the service station by providing
and installing plant and equipment at the appellant's expense which were to be lent
to the respondent on the terms of an equipment loan agreement to be executed by

the parties; (c) on completion of the service station the respondent was to grant to the
a appellant a lease of the premises for a term of 15 years from the date of such completion or 31st March 1965 (whichever should be the earlier) with a right for the
appellant to terminate on notice at the expiration of the first ten years of the term
at a rent of £1 per annum plus a sum calculated at the rate of 3d per gallon for all
petrol delivered for sale to the premises by the appellant. (d) the appellant was to
grant an underlease of the premises to the respondent for the said term less one day
b at a yearly rent of £1; (e) the lease and underlease were to be in the forms annexed
to the agreement with such modifications as the parties should agree on.

The service station, which was built by the respondent at the cost of about £12,000,
was opened on 10th December 1964, the appellant having previously installed its
equipment thereon at the cost of $7,775.

The land on which the station was built had been purchased before the date of the
c agreement by one of the members of the Rocca family. It was transferred by him
into the name of the respondent in July 1965 and on 19th May 1966 the lease and
underlease contemplated by the agreement were executed by the parties substantially
in the terms of the forms annexed thereto.

By the lease the respondent leased to the appellant the land on which the service
station was built 'together with all buildings, improvements, equipment, fixtures
d and appliances owned or controlled by the Lessor and located thereon or on some
part thereof or to be erected or installed by the Lessor thereon' for a term commencing on 30th November 1964 and ending on 30th November 1979 subject to the
'powers, provisos, conditions, covenants, agreements and restrictions' thereinafter
set out. Clause 1 provided that the lessee should pay to the lessor as rental for the
demised premises (A) £1 a year and (B) a sum equal to 3d per gallon on all petrol
e delivered by the lessee to the demised premises for sale. By cl 3 the lessee covenanted to pay the rent thereby reserved and to yield up the demised premises at the
determination of the lease. The lease further provided by cl 4 (h) that the lessee should
have power at any time without the consent of the lessor to assign or sublet the
demised premises; and by cl 9 that the lessee could determine the lease after the
expiry of the first ten years of the term on giving the lessor three months' notice in
f writing. Clause 18 and 19 were in the following terms:

'18. The Lessor and the Lessee agree that this Lease is not in consideration for
or dependent or contingent in any manner upon any other contract, lease or
agreement between them and that the terms, rental or other provisions of said
Lease are not intended by said parties to be tied in with any other such contract,
g lease or agreement, but on the contrary this Lease and all of its provisions are
entirely and completely independent of any other transaction or relationship
between the parties.

'19. This Lease embodies the entire agreement between the parties hereto
relative to the subject matter hereof, and shall not be modified, changed or
altered in any respect except in writing and in the event of any termination of this
h Lease pursuant to any right reserved by the Lessee herein, all liability on the part
of the Lessee for payment of rent shall cease and determine upon payment of
rent proportionately to the date of such termination of this Lease.'

By the underlease the appellant subleased the premises demised by the lease to the
respondent for the term of 15 years less one day from 30th November 1964 at the
j rental therein provided and subject to the powers, provisos, conditions, covenants,
agreements and restrictions therein contained. Clause 1 provided that the respondent
should pay the appellant as rent £1 a year. Clause 3 contained a number of covenants
by the respondent; (a) was a covenant to pay the rent; (e) a covenant not to assign
or sublet; (g) (h) and (i) were in the following terms:

'(g) To carry on and conduct in a proper manner in and upon the demised premises during all lawful trading hours the business of a petrol service station only and not to use same for any other business or purpose whatsoever and not *a* during the continuance of this lease to cease to carry on the said business without the prior written consent of the Lessor.

'(*h*) To purchase exclusively from the Lessor all petrol, motor oil, lubricants and other petroleum products required for sale on the demised premises and not directly or indirectly to buy, receive, use, sell, store or dispose of or permit to be bought, received, used, sold, stored or disposed of at or upon the demised premises *b* or any part thereof any petroleum products not actually purchased by the Lessee from the Lessor provided that the Lessor is able to supply same.

'(*i*) To purchase at least 8,000 gallons of petrol and at least 140 gallons of motor oil from the Lessor in every month during the term of this lease.'

Clause 4 contained a number of further agreements between the parties including *c* the following:

'(*a*) The Lessor agrees to sell to the Lessee and deliver to the demised premises at the Lessor's usual list prices to resellers at the time and place of delivery, the Lessee's entire requirements of petroleum products. Delivery shall be made in quantities of not less than the Lessee's average weekly requirements calculated over the immediately preceding six weeks. Deliveries may be made at any such *d* time or times as the Lessor may in its absolute discretion determine and the Lessee shall pay the Lessor in cash for products delivered at the time of delivery of such products.

'(*b*) In the event of the Lessor being unable for any reason whatsoever which is, in the sole opinion of the Lessor, beyond its control to supply petroleum products as required under this lease, the obligation to supply such petroleum products *e* shall be suspended for the period during which the Lessor is unable so to supply and the Lessee shall be at liberty to supply himself from other sources with sufficient petroleum products but only until such time as the Lessor shall notify him that it is prepared to resume such supply and the Lessee shall not hold out or offer for sale such other petroleum products as the products of the Lessor.

'(*c*) Nothing in this lease shall impose any obligations upon the Lessor to sell or *f* supply any such petroleum products to the Lessee until he shall have paid for any such products already supplied to him by the Lessor and otherwise observed and performed the terms and conditions of this lease, nor shall a refusal on the part of the Lessor so to supply products be deemed a breach of this lease so as to release the Lessee from his obligations hereunder to purchase exclusively from the Lessor . . . *g*

'(*f*) That the Lessee [sic] may, upon the expiration of this lease or upon its sooner termination or cancellation, remove any and all equipment, tools, container or machinery belonging to the Lessee [sic] and placed or installed by the Lessee [sic] upon the leased premises . . .

'(*h*) That this lease and the rights of the Lessee hereunder are subject to all the terms and conditions of the lease under which the Lessor is entitled to the demised *h* premises and the Lessee will not do or suffer to be done upon the demised premises any act, matter or thing which if done or suffered to be done by the Lessor would constitute a violation of any of the said terms and conditions and if for any reason whatsoever the Lessor's tenure of the demised premises is determined or surrendered, cancelled or otherwise terminated, this lease and the term hereby created shall automatically determine simultaneously therewith without notice *j* or further act of the Lessor or the Lessee and without any liability on the part of the Lessor.'

The lease and underlease were duly registered under the Real Property Act of South Australia. By two agreements made between the parties on 15th September

1969 it was provided that in consideration of the appellant making at its expense
a certain additions and alterations to the demised premises and increasing the rebate
provided for in the lease from 3d—that is to say 2·5 cents—per gallon to 4 cents per
gallon the terms of the lease and underlease should each be extended for a further
five years.

In 1971 the respondent having tried unsuccessfully to re-negotiate the terms of its
agreement with the appellant entered into negotiations with a rival oil company and
b on 12th November wrote a letter to the appellant requiring it to remove its pumps
and signs from the premises by 11.00 a m on the 15th November 1971, stating that in
default it would remove them itself. On 16th November the respondent began to repaint
the service station and to replace the appellant's petrol pumps with pumps belonging
to the rival company and on the same day the appellant issued a writ against the
respondent claiming injunctions restraining the respondent from breaking various
c covenants in the underlease in particular those imposing the trade tie. The appellant
took out a summons for interlocutory relief and on 18th November Wells J made an
order based on various undertakings so as to maintain the state of affairs existing
before 16th November pending the determination of the question whether or not the
trade tie was enforceable. In December he made a further order dispensing with
pleadings and directing that the action should proceed on the basis of the following
d agreed issues:

'1. Is the [respondent] entitled to assert that the covenants contained in
Memorandum of Underlease No. 2775160 or any of them are in restraint of trade,
and unenforceable?

'2 Are the covenants contained in Memorandum of Underlease No. 2775160 or
any of them an unreasonable restraint of trade and unenforceable?

e '3. If the covenants in Memorandum of Underlease No. 2775160 or any of them
are unenforceable is the whole of the said Memorandum of Underlease void?

'4. If the said Memorandum of Underlease is void is Memorandum of Lease
No. 2775159 also void?

'5. All questions of consequential relief for either party arising from the
resolution of the above issues shall be referred for later consideration.'

f
In a full and careful judgment delivered on 12th April 1972 Wells J reviewed the law
as to restraint of trade and the evidence which had been called on each side. Applying
the law to the facts as he found them the conclusion at which he arrived was that even
assuming—contrary to his own opinion—that the respondent was entitled to assert
that the covenants in the underlease or any of them were unenforceable as in restraint
of trade the restraints were reasonable and that accordingly issue 2 must be answered
g in the negative. It followed, of course, that issues 3, 4 and 5 did not arise.

The respondent appealed from this judgment to the Full Court (Bray CJ, Hogarth
and Walters JJ) which on 7th August 1972 reversed it and answered issues 1 and 2 in
the affirmative. Bray CJ expressed his conclusion in the following words:

'The conclusion I have reached is that the covenants in the underlease go
h beyond what was reasonably necessary for the protection of [the appellant].
Certainly [the appellant], in my view, has not shown the contrary and the onus is
on it. A shorter term would, in my view, have been adequate to afford ample
protection to its proprietary interest in its investment; and a shorter term or less
onerous covenants or both would, in my view, have been adequate to protect its
commercial interests. I do not decide that a restraint for a shorter term but
j containing these covenants would necessarily be bad; or that a restraint for
fifteen years with less onerous covenants, particularly when there was some
provision for review and possible escape for [the respondent] at some point
during the term, would necessarily be bad. All I decide is that, in my view, this
restraint for this term with these covenants is unenforceable. That makes it
unnecessary to consider the question of public interest.'

After saying that the answers to issues 1 and 2 were 'Yes' he added:

'These affirmative answers are of necessity ambiguous because of the alternatives in each question between the covenants as a whole and any of them severally, but no other answers can be given since the question of severability has not yet been argued.'

Hogarth J and Walters J delivered judgments concurring with that of the Chief Justice.

The appellant appealed to the High Court of Australia from the judgment of the Full Court on issues 1 and 2 and on 11th October 1973 that court dismissed the appeal by a majority (McTiernan ACJ, Walsh and Gibbs JJ, Menzies and Stephen JJ dissenting). Walsh J—in whose judgment McTiernan ACJ concurred—expressed his conclusion in the following words:

'The question is whether or not the Full Court was in error in holding that the second issue should receive an affirmative answer. In my opinion, it was not in error . . . A decision upon the question of resonableness depends upon a judgment the reasons for which do not admit of great elaboration. In my opinion it was not shown that the restrictions placed upon [the respondent] did not go beyond what was adequate for the protection of [the appellant's] interests. It is not in doubt, in my opinion, that [the appellant] was entitled in the circumstances to obtain the benefit of a trade tie in aid of recoupment of its investment and in aid of the trading interests arising out of its agreement to supply its product to [the respondent]. The question is whether or not the terms of the tie, considered in conjunction with the covenants to which I have referred, was greater than was reasonably necessary. In my opinion it was. At all events its reasonableness was not established. In his judgment Bray CJ said: "The conclusion I have reached is that the covenants in the underlease go beyond what was reasonably necessary for the protection of [the appellant]. Certainly [the appellant], in my view, has not shown the contrary and the onus is on it. A shorter term would, in my view, have been adequate to afford ample protection to its proprietary interest in its investment; and a shorter term or less onerous covenants or both would, in my view, have been adequate to protect its commercial interests." I find myself in agreement with that statement, subject to the qualification that in my opinion the same conclusion would have been correct even if the covenants (other than the exclusive trade tie) had been less onerous.'

The most important passages in the judgment of Gibbs J are the following:

'In deciding upon the reasonableness of the restraint it is not possible to regard the length of the tie apart from the provisions of the covenants—all must be considered together. Perhaps it should be said that some covenants found objectionable in other similar cases do not appear in the present case. For example, there is no covenant giving [the appellant] the right to fix the price at which [the respondent] might sell its products. Further, it is expressly provided (by cl 4 (a)) that [the appellant] will sell to [the respondent] at its usual list prices. It is true that [the appellant] if so minded might sell at a discount to a competing retailer and it is also true that cl 4 (b) gives [the appellant] power to suspend supply in certain circumstances, but I do not regard these provisions as of cardinal importance. The covenants which seem to me most to require further mention, apart from cl 3 (h) which binds [the respondent] to buy exclusively from [the appellant], are the following. The obligation cast on [the respondent] by cl 3 (i) to purchase a specified minimum gallonage of petrol and motor oil would not have been unreasonable had it enured only for a short period, since the evidence shows that the gallonage fixed (at least that of petrol) was by no means excessive. However, if over a long term the business of the service station declined, the covenant could impose an unreasonable burden on [the respondent]. However, the most onerous of the covenants in the underlease is cl 3 (*g*) which requires [the respondent] to carry on the business of a petrol service station for the whole period of fifteen years unless [the appellant] releases it from this obligation. Perhaps cl 3 (*e*), which prevents [the respondent] from assigning, subletting or otherwise parting with possession of the demised premises should also be mentioned in this connection. It may be assumed that [the appellants'] consent to an assignment or sublease could not be unreasonably withheld, but there might be practical difficulties in finding a person willing to take an assignment or sublease on terms which included cl 3 (*g*), particularly if the business got into difficulties. It is true that provisions in the form of cl 3 (*g*) are not uncommonly inserted in leases of various descriptions. However, as I have already indicated, the clause was not inserted in the present case by an owner of land to protect his interests when he leased it, but for the purpose of imposing a restriction on the owner itself. Moreover, the long period of the underlease renders the possible operation of the clause unduly harsh. During the period of fifteen years, trade at the service station could become quite unprofitable for a variety of reasons, including some of those mentioned by Diplock LJ in *Petrofina (Gt Britain) Ltd v Martin*[1]: "Better or cheaper products may be discovered. New or improved highways may divert the motor traffic from passing the filling station, other filling stations may be opened in the vicinity—even by the appellants themselves." However, [the respondent] is obliged to carry on the business even if it is trading at a loss. It was said that in practice [the appellant] would be likely to release [the respondent] from its obligation if in fact the business became unprofitable, but the interests of [the appellant] might well be served by maintaining the service station as an outlet for its products as long as it could, notwithstanding that [the respondent] was making an inadequate profit or even trading at a loss.

'After full consideration of all the circumstances, I have reached the conclusion that it has not been shown that a tie for fifteen years on the terms of the underlease was reasonably necessary to protect the interests of [the appellant]. On the one hand, the great changes that might occur in the space of fifteen years could render the covenants intolerably burdensome on [the respondent] and the effect of inflation during that period might well greatly reduce the value of the fixed rebate which formed an important part of the consideration receivable by [the respondent]. On the other hand, there is nothing whatever to show that a tie for fifteen years was necessary to ensure for [the appellant] the stable outlet and economical system of distribution at which it was entitled to aim. Further, it was not shown that [the appellants'] outlay—even taking it as $18,955—could not be recouped with profit in a shorter period.'

As the decision of the Full Court on issues 1 and 2 had been affirmed by the High Court the other issues arose for determination and it was agreed between the parties with the assent of Wells J and the Full Court that, instead of going back to the judge of first instance, these issues should be determined by the Full Court constituted as before. That court gave judgment on issues 3 and 4 on 10th December 1973. As appears from the judgments to which reference has been made, the vice in the underlease as it stood was in the opinion of the Full Court and the High Court the cumulative effect of a number of covenants restricting the respondent's freedom to trade and a term as long as fifteen years. It would not, of course, have been possible for the Full Court on the further application to remedy the position by shortening the term but either party could have submitted that even though the term could not be shortened the covenants in restraint of trade could be 'severed' and not all of them treated as unenforceable. In order to decide whether 'severance' was possible it would have

---

1   [1966] 1 All ER 126 at 143, [1966] Ch 146 at 189

been necessary for the Full Court—which, of course, had available all the evidence given before Wells J—first to decide which of the covenants in restraint of trade must *a* go and which, if any, could still stand; whether, for example, if covenant 3(*h*) was deleted, covenants 3(*g*) and 3(*i*) would or would not constitute unreasonable restraints. Having identified the covenants which would have to go the court would then have had to decide whether what was left of the underlease could remain on foot or whether the whole underlease should be treated as at an end. It is clear from the terms of their judgments on issues 1 and 2 that all three members of the Full Court *b* realised that when issues 3 and 4 came to be debated they might be called upon to pronounce on the question of severance; but in fact they were not asked to do so since at that stage neither side wanted the underlease to remain on foot. What was argued by the appellant on the fresh application was that the underlease was unen-forceable in toto but that the lease remained in full force and effect. Bray CJ, in whose judgment Hogarth J concurred, and Walters J both emphasised in their judgments *c* that counsel for the appellant never suggested that the underlease might be left standing shorn of some of its covenants. The main argument for the respondent on the other hand was that not only the underlease but also the headlease was unen-forceable in toto. It is true that its counsel submitted—very much as a 'second best'— that if his main argument failed then the underlease should remain on foot with any offending covenants deleted, but the court did not find it necessary to give any formal *d* decision on the question of severance since it accepted the respondent's main argument. At the same time it is clear enough that the members of the court did not think that this was a case in which, if it had been necessary to decide the point, severance would in fact have been possible, indeed Walters J said this in terms. On the question argued before it the Full Court had no doubt that the headlease must share the same fate as the underlease. Both were integral parts of the same transaction; the statements to *e* the contrary in cll 18 and 19 of the lease were untrue; and as public policy was involved the respondent was not estopped from asserting that they were untrue. But for the fact that the lease and underlease were registered and that, by virtue of that fact, legal estates in the land were vested in the lessee and underlessee respectively, the court would have declared that both instruments were void. As it was it answered issues 3 and 4 as follows: *f*

    '3. The Memorandum of Underlease is not void, but neither party thereto can enforce any of the covenants in it against the other.

    '4. The Memorandum of Lease is not void, but neither party thereto can enforce any of the covenants in it against the other.'

Counsel for the appellant suggested in his argument before the Board that in its *g* order the Full Court meant by the word 'covenants' only such obligations as were expressly so described in the two instruments. Their Lordships have no hesitation in rejecting this suggestion. They have no doubt that the Full Court meant to declare unenforceable all obligations contained in or arising out of the execution of the lease and the underlease as opposed to their registration; on the other hand they left over to be dealt with under issue 5 all questions arising out of the continued existence of *h* the two bare estates.

On its appeal to the Board counsel for the appellant adopted a totally different approach from that taken on its behalf before the Full Court for he placed in the fore-front of his argument the contention that cl 3(*h*) of the underlease (which was, he submitted, the only offending covenant) should be treated as deleted and that the underlease shorn of that covenant should be left standing. This change of front places *j* their Lordships in a position of some difficulty. The point that the covenants in the underlease could be severed was never strictly speaking 'abandoned' by the appellant since it never took it and the point was in a sense before the Full Court in the shape of the subsidiary argument on behalf of the respondent. On the other hand it is not a pure point of law such as their Lordships would normally allow to be taken before a them even if it had not been taken below since it depends on a finding of fact which the Full Court has not made. It does not in the least follow that if the Full Court had found it necessary to give a decision on the question of severance it would have held on the evidence which was before it that the deletion of cl 3(h) would have sufficed to make the remainder of the underlease unobjectionable. It might well have held that not only cl 3(h) but also cl 3(g) and (i) or one or other of them would have to be deleted and their Lordships who have not the evidence before them have no means of

b reaching any conclusion of their own on the point. In the end counsel for the appellant was constrained to admit that this was so; but he submitted that even on the assumption that cl 3(g) (h) and (i) were all deleted the rest of the underlease should still be left standing. Their Lordships have no hesitation in rejecting this submission.

As Kitto J remarked in *Brooks v Burns Philp Trustee Co Ltd*[1], 'Questions of severability are often difficult'. The answer depends on the intention of the parties as disclosed by

c the agreement into which they have entered; but generally, of course, they have not foreseen that one or more of the provisions in their agreement will be unenforceable. Various tests have been formulated which might not in every case lead to the same result, e g is that which is unenforceable 'part of the main purport and substance' of the clause in which it appears? (per Lord Moulton in *Mason v Provident Clothing & Supply Co Ltd*[2]); does the deletion 'alter entirely the scope and intention of the

d agreement'? (per Lord Sterndale MR in *Attwood v Lamont*[3]); does the deletion of the covenant in question 'leave the rest of the deed a reasonable arrangement between the parties'? (per Denning LJ in *Bennett v Bennett*[4]); does what is left constitute an 'intelligible economic transaction in itself . . . even though it furnished the occasion for' the unenforceable restraint? (*Kelly v Kosuga*[5]). But whatever test be applied the answer must, their Lordships think, be the same in this case. It is inconceivable that

e any petrol company would grant a dealer a lease at a nominal rent of a site on which it had spent a substantial sum in installing pumps and other equipment without imposing on the dealer any obligation to buy petrol from it or even to carry on the business of a petrol station on the demised premises. Clause 3(g) (h) and (i) was the heart and soul of the underlease. It is, of course, true that the appellant—perhaps because it had little faith in the point on which it rested its case in the Full Court—

f now thinks that it is to its advantage to affirm the continued existence of the underlease even though shorn of those three subclauses; but that fact has no bearing on the question at issue. Their Lordships would only add on this aspect of the case that they must not be taken to be expressing any view—one way or the other—on what the position with regard to 'severability' would have been if it had been established on the facts that the only provision in the underlease which had to be excised in order to

g make the rest unobjectionable from the point of view of restraint of trade was cl 3(h).

At this point their Lordships must refer to a submission made by counsel for the appellant based on some words used by Lord Reid in his speech in *Esso Petroleum Co Ltd v Harper's Garage (Stourport) Ltd*[6]. One of the documents to be considered in that case was a mortgage of the petrol station in question by its owner to the oil company in

h consideration of a loan. The mortgage provided, inter alia, (A) that the loan should be repaid by annual instalments spread over twenty-one years and (B) that during the term of the mortgage the owner of the petrol station would buy petrol exclusively from the oil company. The owner contended that the covenant was an unreasonable restraint of trade and expressed his willingness—indeed claimed the right—to repay

j 1 (1969) 121 CLR at 438
2 [1913] AC at 745, [1911-13] All ER Rep at 411
3 [1920] 3 KB at 580, [1920] All ER Rep at 61
4 [1952] 1 All ER at 421, [1952] 1 KB at 261
5 (1959) 358 US 516 at 521
6 [1967] 1 All ER at 708, [1968] AC at 299

the loan forthwith notwithstanding the provision for repayment by instalments. It appears that the question must have been mooted in argument whether the owner could have insisted on the unenforceability of the trade tie contained in the mortgage while at the same time taking advantage of the right which it gave him to repay the loan by instalments for Lord Reid touched on that point in the following words[1]:

> 'I am prepared to assume that, if the respondents had not offered to repay the loan so far as it is still outstanding, the appellants would have been entitled to retain the tie.'

The appellant argued that what was true of a mortgage—which takes effect by way of lease to the mortgagee—must also be true of an ordinary lease and that where a lease contains a covenant which is unenforceable as being in restraint of trade the covenantor—in this case the respondent—most elect either to give up the lease or to perform the covenant notwithstanding its unenforceability.

It is clear—as counsel indeed conceded—that no such election is required of the covenantor when the unenforceable promise is contained in a bare contract. Provided that the unenforceable part is severable the rest of the contract remains in force and either party can rely on its terms. It would be odd if the position should be different when the promise in question is contained in a lease. The fact that a covenantor has obtained and will continue to enjoy benefits under the relevant agreement which formed part of the consideration for the covenant which he claims to be unenforceable is no doubt pro tanto a reason for holding that the covenant is not in unreasonable restraint of trade. But once it is held that it is in unreasonable restraint of trade, there seems to be no reason for drawing any distinction with regard to the consequences between provisions in contracts and covenants in leases. If in a case where severance was possible the party who had entered into a covenant in a lease which was unenforceable because it was in unreasonable restraint of trade was forced to make the election suggested by counsel he would be put under pressure to observe a promise which public policy said he should be free to disregard. Lord Reid was not expressing any opinion on the point and as at present advised their Lordships do not think that the assumption which he was prepared to make was justified. But even if the appellant was right in saying that had the covenants been severable the respondent would have been put to his election either to observe the unenforceable restraint or to give up the lease its case would not be advanced in the least since the covenants are not severable and the respondent has always been willing—indeed anxious—to give up the underlease provided that the headlease also disappears from the scene.

Finally their Lordships turn to consider whether the headlease can remain on foot if the provisions of the underlease disappear. On this point again they have no doubt that the Full Court reached the right conclusion. It is not possible to regard the two leases as separate dispositions of property. The agreement of 19th June 1964 shows clearly that they were parts of a single commercial transaction under which the respondent was to get a supply of petrol at an agreed rebate and the appellant a trade tie with security for its investment in the station. The statements to the contrary in cll 18 and 19 of the headlease are simply untrue and it may well be that they were inserted in order to strengthen the position of the appellant in the event of the validity of the trade tie in the underlease being challenged. If there was no question of public policy in the case then no doubt the respondent would be estopped from denying that the headlease was independent of the underlease but if there was such an estoppel here it would deter the respondent from asserting that the trade tie was unenforceable on grounds of public policy, since, as Bray CJ points out, its position if the underlease went but the headlease remained in force would be far worse than if it acquiesced in the trade tie and retained the benefit of the underlease. On this aspect of the matter their Lordships agree entirely with the passages in the judgments of

1   [1967] 1 All ER at 708, [1968] AC at 299

a Taylor J and Owen J in *Brooks v Burns Philp Trustee Co Ltd*[1] to which Bray CJ and Walters refer in their judgments.

In the result therefore their Lordships will humbly advise Her Majesty that the appeal be dismissed and that the appellant pay to the respondent its costs of it. The question whether the bare legal estates must remain on the register and if so whether the parties enjoy or are subject to any, and if so what, rights and obligations by reason of the mere fact of registration will have to be decided—in default of agreement—
b with any other questions arising under issue 5.

Appeal dismissed.

Solicitors: *Blyth, Dutton, Robins, Hay* (for the appellant); *Slaughter & May* (for the respondent).

c   Gordon H Scott Esq Barrister.

d # Coney v Choyce and others
Ludden v Choyce and others

CHANCERY DIVISION
TEMPLEMAN J
e 26th, 29th, 30th, 31st JULY 1974

Education – School – Establishment or discontinuance of school – Proposals – Public notice – Manner of giving notice – Procedural requirements – Failure to comply with requirements – Effect – Substantial compliance – Information concerning proposals brought to attention of those affected by proposals – No prejudice caused by failure to comply with regulations –
f *Failure to post notice at or near any main entrance to school – Whether procedural requirements directory or mandatory – Whether failure to comply with requirements rendering Secretary of State's approval of proposals invalid – Education Act 1944, ss 13(3), 99 – County and Voluntary Schools (Notices) Regulations 1968 (SI 1968 No 615), reg 2.*

g Following much discussion by the education authorities, proposals were put forward to reorganise the Roman Catholic schools in a number of neighbouring towns on a single 'three-tier' basis. Those proposals were discussed at public meetings, in newsletters and in churches over a period of three years. Letters were sent by the education authorities explaining the proposals. The defendants, who were the managers and governors of the schools affected, submitted the proposals to the Secretary of State in accordance with s 13(2)[a] of the Education Act 1944 and took steps to give the requisite
h public notice under s 13(3)[b] of the 1944 Act, as amended by the Education (Miscellaneous Provisions) Act 1953, s 16, in accordance with the requirements of reg 2[c] of the County and Voluntary Schools (Notices) Regulations 1968, by publishing notices in a newspaper circulating in the area served by the schools, by posting it in conspicuous places within that area and by posting it at or near the main entrance to the schools in
j question. In consequence of those steps information concerning the proposals, and what was to be done by those who wished to object, was widely circulated in the area.

---

1   (1969) 121 CLR at 444, 482
a   Section 13(2), as amended and so far as material, is set out at p 982 *d*, post
b   Section 13(3), as amended and so far as material, is set out at p 982 *e*, post
c   Regulation 2, so far as material, is set out at p 982 *j* to 983 *a*, post

However in the case of two schools the regulations were not fully complied with in that no notice was posted at or near the main entrance to either of those schools. *a* Within the time limit of two months prescribed by s 13(3), a petition signed by about 287 people was presented setting out five grounds of objection to the proposals. The Secretary of State, having received the petition, considered the proposals and purported to approve them. C, the parent of a child affected by the proposals, subsequently realised that the technical requirements of the 1968 regulations might not have been complied with and so made representations to the Secretary of State *b* claiming that, because of the non-compliance, the proposals should not be allowed to go forward. The Secretary of State, however, came to the conclusion that enough had been done to publicise the proposals and that, in those circumstances, there was no reason why they should not go ahead. C and D, as parents of children affected by the proposals, brought actions against the defendants claiming a declaration that the Secretary of State's approval was invalid, and an injunction restraining the defendants *c* from carrying out the proposals. The defendants contended, inter alia, that, even if there had been breaches of the 1968 regulations, the plaintiffs' only remedy was by way of a complaint to the Secretary of State under s 99(1)*d* of the 1944 Act.

Held – Considering the general object of the procedural requirements prescribed by reg 2 of the 1968 regulations, i e that notice should be given to a representative number *d* of people of what their rights were, those requirements were to be treated as directory rather than mandatory. Since there had been no substantial prejudice suffered by those for whose benefit the requirements had been introduced, the breach was to be treated as a mere irregularity which had not had the effect of rendering the Minister's approval of the proposals invalid. In the alternative the Minister was entitled, on complaint being made under s 99 of the 1944 Act, to take the view that there had been *e* substantial compliance with the regulations and therefore that no declaration of default under s 99 should be made. It followed that, on either ground, the action should be dismissed (see p 989 *a* to *e g* and *h* and p 990 *d* and *e*, post).

Notes
For proposals for the establishment and discontinuance of schools, see 13 Halsbury's *f* Laws (3rd Edn) 606, 607, paras 1265-1267.
    For the Education Act 1944, ss 13, 99, see 11 Halsbury's Statutes (3rd Edn) 169, 248.

Case referred to in judgment
Bradbury v London Borough of Enfield [1967] 3 All ER 434, [1967] 1 WLR 1311, 132 JP 15, 66 LGR 115, CA, Digest (Cont Vol C) 312, *103a*.   *g*

Cases also cited
Buckoke v Greater London Council [1971] 2 All ER 254, [1971] Ch 655, CA.
Byrne v Herbert [1965] 3 All ER 705, [1966] 2 QB 121.
Clark v Epsom Rural District Council [1929] 1 Ch 287.
Cumings v Birkenhead Corpn [1971] 2 All ER 881, [1972] Ch 12, CA.   *h*
Glynn v Keele University [1971] 2 All ER 89, [1971] 1 WLR 487.
Herring v Templeman [1973] 2 All ER 581.
Legg v Inner London Education Authority [1972] 3 All ER 177, [1972] 1 WLR 1245.
London Passenger Transport Board v Moscrop [1942] 1 All ER 97, [1942] AC 332, HL.
Padfield v Minister of Agriculture, Fisheries and Food [1968] 1 All ER 694, [1968] AC 997, HL.   *j*
Pasmore v The Oswaldtwistle Urban District Council [1898] AC 387, [1895-9] All ER Rep 191, HL.
R v Senate of the University of Aston, ex parte Roffey [1969] 2 All ER 964, [1969] 2 QB 538, DC.

---

d   Section 99(1), as amended and so far as material, is set out at p 989 *f*, post

a *R v Westminister Betting Licensing Committee, ex parte Peabody Donation Fund (Governors)*
[1963] 2 All ER 544, [1963] 2 QB 750, DC.
Russian Commercial and Industrial Bank v British Bank for Foreign Trade Ltd [1921] 2 AC
438, [1921] All ER Rep 329, HL.
Thorne Rural District Council v Bunting [1972] 1 All ER 439, [1972] Ch 470.
Watt v Kesteven County Council [1955] 1 All ER 473, [1955] 1 QB 408, CA.
Wood v London Borough of Ealing [1966] 3 All ER 514, [1967] Ch 364.

b

Motion
By a writ issued on 29th October 1973, the first plaintiff, Francis Coney, brought an
action against the Rev Benjamin Choyce, the Rev James McGhie, the Rev Christopher
O'Brien, the Rev Joseph Wakefield, Alfred John Burton, Hubert Joseph Bell, Cecil V
Berry, Muriel Fielding, Madeline Grunnill, James W Maloney, Robert Joseph Torton,
c Joseph Sydney Warden and Albert Wheat (governors of the Worksop Robert Ludlam
Roman Catholic Secondary School), and the Rev Benjamin Choyce, the Rev Joseph
Wakefield, Raymond Christian, Charles Frederick Cooly, Muriel Maloney, and
Eileen Phipps (managers of the Worksop St Mary's Roman Catholic Primary School).
By notice of motion dated 8th March 1974 the first plaintiff sought an order that, until
trial or further order, the defendants whether by themselves, their officers, servants
d or agents or otherwise howsoever, might be restrained from altering the age range of
the Worksop Robert Ludlam Roman Catholic Secondary School and from altering
the age range of the Worksop St Mary's Roman Catholic Primary School and from doing
any other act or thing in furtherance of their proposals for altering the age range of
those schools or otherwise for the purpose of making any such alteration.
By a writ issued on 29th October 1973 the second plaintiff, Bernard Francis Ludden,
e brought a similar action against the defendants, the governors of the Worksop
Robert Ludlam Roman Catholic Secondary School, and against the Rev James McGhie,
the Rev Mother Carmel, Sydney Fowler, Michael McShary, Jessie Parker and Stella
Smedley (managers of the Boughton St Joseph's Roman Catholic Primary School). By
notice of motion dated 8th March 1974 the second plaintiff sought orders similar to
those claimed by the first plaintiff in the case of Boughton St Joseph's Roman Catholic
f Primary School and the Worksop Robert Ludlam Roman Catholic Secondary School.
The plaintiffs were parents of children affected by the proposals with regard to the
three schools. The motions were heard together and, by consent, the hearing was
treated as the trial of the respective actions. The facts are set out in the judgment.

Jack Hames QC and *Charles Fay* for the plaintiffs.
g *R J Harvey QC*, *Roger Shawcross* and *Andrew Mier* for the defendants.

TEMPLEMAN J. This, as counsel for the plaintiffs said, is an important case and I
would have preferred to reserve my judgment but, because of the present state of the
term and because the parties must know where they stand, I am obliged to give
h judgment straight away.
    The present dispute arises out of proposals to reorganise Roman Catholic schools in
Mansfield, Worksop, Newark and Boughton in Nottinghamshire, on comprehensive
lines and on a three tier basis. Roman Catholic children in Worksop now attend the
local St Mary's School from the age of five to 11, and then the local Robert Ludlam
School until they are 16. Roman Catholic children in Boughton now attend the local
j St Joseph's School from five to 11, and then they too go on to Robert Ludlam. Under
the terms of the reorganisation, which affects children over a wide area of north
Nottinghamshire and not only children of Worksop and Boughton, Roman Catholic
children in Worksop will go to St Mary's School between the ages of five and nine,
then to Robert Ludlam between nine and 13, and finally they will go to a new comprehensive school, which has been specially built for the purpose, 16 miles away at

Mansfield; and that will offer them education between the ages of 13 and 18. Roman Catholic children in Boughton will go to St Joseph's between five and nine, then to *a* St Bede's in Mansfield between nine and 13, and then they, too, will enter the new comprehensive school at Mansfield.

These proposals were put forward after much discussion by the education authorities in 1969. They were discussed at public meetings, in newsletters and in churches, between 1969 and January 1972. Letters were sent by the education authorities to parents explaining the proposals. Anyone likely to be affected by the proposals *b* should have been aware of their nature and effect and received opportunities to voice disapproval to the education authorities, the church authorities, and local government elected representatives.

That, however, is not enough. Parliament requires that proposals with regard to education must be approved by the Secretary of State for Education and Science, and objectors must have an opportunity to make their views known to the Secretary of *c* State before he comes to a decision.

St Mary's School, the Robert Ludlam School and St Joseph's School are voluntary schools. Proposals for the alteration of ages for pupils eligible for admission involve significant changes in the character of those schools, and s 13(2) of the Education Act 1944, as amended provides:

d

'. . . where the managers or governors of . . . a voluntary school intend to make any significant change in the character . . . of the school, they shall after consultation with the authority submit proposals for that purpose to the Secretary of State.'

Section 13(3) provides:

e

'[The managers or governors] shall forthwith give public notice of the proposals in the prescribed manner, and . . . any ten or more local government electors for the area . . . may within two months after the first publication of the notice submit to the Secretary of State objections to the proposals . . .'

By s 13(4), Parliament provides for the third stage: *f*

'Any proposals submitted to the Secretary of State under this section may be approved by him after making such modifications therein, if any, as appear to him to be desirable . . .'

The defendants, who are between them managers and governors of St Mary's School, the Robert Ludlam School and St Joseph's School, submitted proposals to the *g* Secretary of State and claim to have given the requisite public notice on 1st January 1972. The Secretary of State purported to approve the proposals on 12th September 1972. The plaintiffs, who are parents of children who will be affected by the proposals with regard to St Mary's School, the Robert Ludlam School, and St Joseph's School, contend that the defendants did not give the prescribed public notice in the prescribed manner; and that in consequence the purported approval of the Secretary *h* of State is a nullity and the defendants should be restrained from giving effect to those proposals.

The manner of giving public notice is prescribed by reg 2 of the County and Voluntary Schools (Notices) Regulations 1968[1], and so far as is relevant notice must be given—

j

'(a) by publishing the notice in at least one newspaper circulating in the area served . . . by the school; (b) by posting the notice in some conspicuous place or places within that area; (c) . . . by posting the notice at or near any main entrance

---

a   to the school; and (d) in such other manner, if any, as appears ... to be desirable
       for giving publicity to the notice.'

       I find that the notice with regard to St Mary's School, Worksop, was (a) pub-
lished in the Nottinghamshire Evening Post on the 1st January 1972; (b) affixed to the
notice board of St Mary's Church, Worksop; (c) posted on the inside of the main
front door of St Mary's School in January and February 1972. So far as (d) is con-
b cerned, Father O'Keefe, who was the parish priest of St Mary's Church, Worksop, at
the relevant time said that on one Sunday at about the time of display of the notice he
devoted the sermon time at all three masses at St Mary's Church to a detailed
explanation of the proposed changes:

       'I remember this clearly because at the evening mass on that Sunday an unusual
c   incident occurred in that a gentleman attempted to heckle me while I was
       speaking about these matters.'

In oral evidence he repeated and made plain that the whole parish was in a turmoil
about these proposals. But it is not suggested that he actually read out the notice or
the full terms of it when he gave his homilies.
d   I find that the notice with regard to the Robert Ludlam School was (a) published in
the Nottinghamshire Evening Post on 1st January 1972; (b) exhibited in the St Mary's
Church, Worksop; and (c) sent to the headmaster in January 1972 without instructions,
so that he did not know he ought to display the notice until January 1973, when he
did post it at or near the main entrance.
       I find that the notice with regard to St Joseph's School, Boughton, was (a) published
in the Nottinghamshire Evening Post on 1st January 1972; and (b) affixed inside St
e Joseph's Church, Ollerton, that being the Roman Catholic church for Boughton and
Ollerton; (c) not posted at or near any main entrance to the school, again I think
because the headmistress did not know of the necessity; but (d) in the case of Boughton
there is evidence that in the first fortnight of February there was issued a newsletter
or mission letter from the church, which was delivered to all the households, whether
Roman Catholic or otherwise, in the area covered by the church, and that newsletter
f reproduced the notice. As far as Boughton was concerned there was in practice
effective saturation of the area; and so far as Worksop was concerned, whatever the
technical merits or demerits of the methods adopted, I have no doubt that the
proposals were very widely known and people knew what to do if they objected.
       Before 1st January 1972 copies of the public notices were sent to head teachers and
managers and governors of over 37 schools in Nottinghamshire, and were displayed on
g parish notice boards inside or outside churches in areas affected by the proposals. As
I have said, the proposals were not confined to Worksop and Boughton, but affected a
large area. There is no doubt that genuine and strenuous efforts were made to
disseminate information concerning the proposals and the rights of objection.
       One of the results of the publicity was that on 14th February 1972 the plaintiff,
Mr Coney, joined with other parents to form the Worksop, Carlton and Ollerton
h Catholic Action Committee, which was formed (and still exists) to co-ordinate opposition to the proposals for reorganisation of the schools in North Nottinghamshire. On
28th February 1972, within the time limit provided by the notice, there was a petition.
It was headed: 'Education Acts 1944 to 1968. Sections 13(3).' So it is quite clear that
those petitioners knew what they were up to, the legal foundation for their petition
and what their rights were. The petition set out:
j

       'We, the undersigned, being parents of children currently attending Catholic
       Schools in Worksop and Ollerton and or electors of the said areas, hereby object
       to the proposed establishment of the new Roman Catholic Upper School at
       Westfield Lane, Mansfield, Nottinghamshire, and the consequent re-organisation
       of existing R.C. Schools, both primary and secondary, on the following grounds...'

It is clear that those petitioners recognised that this was a scheme, the centre and pivot of which was the erection of a new school at Mansfield, the establishment of which *a* would have reverberations throughout the North Nottinghamshire areas concerned. The petition continued with these grounds of objection:

'1. that due regard has not been given to the amount of travel involved for Ollerton children of 9+ years of age, who would have a daily return journey of 20 miles, and the travelling distance (some 50 miles return) for children of 13+ *b* who live in the Carlton/Langold area north of Worksop. 2. because of No. 1 above, children will have little or no opportunity to participate fully in the social life afforded by Schools. 3. two good Catholic secondary schools already exist in Mansfield and Worksop respectively, and we see no need to be heavily bur- dened financially with the establishment of a third secondary school, (proposed Upper School) when both the existing secondary schools could be developed, at *c* least on an 11-16 comprehensive basis, to serve their respective catchment areas; which, in the case of the Worksop school, could continue to include not only Worksop, but also Ollerton, Carlton, Langold, Retford, (recently hived off and re-routed to Cantley, Doncaster), and the small area of Derbyshire adjacent to Worksop. 4. discrimination. We want for our children a system of education which is similar to that enjoyed by all other children in the area, i.e., infant— *d* primary (5-11) with transfer to secondary education at 11+ on a non-selective basis. 5. parents of many children, because of the distances involved, would find it extremely difficult, and perhaps impossible to get to a particular school for any purpose.'

That petition set out very clearly five obviously cogent grounds of objection. It was *e* of course for the Secretary of State to determine whether, having regard to those objections, the proposals should be approved. Although I heard a good deal of evi- dence, I have not heard of any additional ground of objection which really adds to those five. The petition ended with the usual list of signatories and their addresses, from Worksop, Carlton, New Ollerton and Boughton, Langold, Newark and Edwin- stowe, and there were in sum about 287 signatures. *f*

If one asks whether in reality people knew what was going on, powerful evidence is put in by the plaintiffs themselves that in a relatively small area a praiseworthy number of 287 persons took the trouble to join together and send up a reasoned and detailed objection, all exercising their rights under s 13(3) of the 1944 Act. The Min- ister must know that petitions are only representative; and that for every person who signs there may be two or three or more who do not sign, because they do not know *g* or because they are too idle or they are away for the weekend, or something of that sort. Education is not a question purely of head counting.

Mr Coney, one of the plaintiffs, states that he first became aware that the proposals had not, as is now contended, been given the prescribed manner of publication, in the course of a meeting which took place at the Department of Education and Science on 28th November 1972. That, of course, was after the Minister, having received that *h* petition in February, gave approval on 12th September 1972. At that stage, the battle for the soul of the Minister had been fought by the objectors and lost. The Minister had taken a time over it; had received the petition, considered the proposals, and given approval. It appears that at a meeting of the Department of Education and Science, when I imagine reasons were still being urged on the Minister why she should retract or not follow up the approval, Mr Coney got an idea that the technical requirements *j* of the 1968 regulations might not have been carried out. Perfectly properly, he made further enquiries. He made representations to the Secretary of State claiming that the regulations had not been complied with and therefore the proposals ought not to be allowed to go forward. And he did this not only himself but through a Member of Parliament, and by solicitors who referred to the possibility of legal proceedings. I

have no doubt that he acted with the help and on behalf of the committee which had
a been formed to fight the proposals.

On 4th April 1973 the Ministry wrote saying this:

'On the information available the Secretary of State, as advised, concludes that
there is no reason to believe that local government electors affected by the
proposals were denied adequate information for the purpose of exercising their
b rights under Section 13 of the Education Act as amended.'

The Minister, having heard representations about failure to comply with the
regulations, came to the conclusion that enough had been done to publicise the
proposals and tell people what their rights were, and in those circumstances there was
no reason, the Minister thought, rightly or wrongly, why the proposals should not go
ahead.

c Early in May 1973 Mr Coney's solicitors wrote to school governors, managers and
others, stating they had instructions to issue a writ unless the reorganisation was
abandoned, but the writ was not in fact issued until 29th October 1973, and a notice
of motion for interlocutory relief was not issued until 8th March 1974. It has been
agreed to treat the motion which came on before me as trial of the action. The facts
concerning the other plaintiff, Mr Ludden, are not for present purposes materially
d different.

The objects of s 13(3) of the 1944 Act are to ensure that the public are aware of the
proposals and of their rights to object to the Secretary of State; that is a preliminary
to ensuring that objections reach the Secretary of State for his consideration before he
decides the fate of the proposals. He cannot decide to approve the proposals unless he
has in front of him the objections which can fairly be raised against them. The objects
e of s 13(3) were in my judgment achieved. The notices were well publicised. A petition
of 287 persons from a small part of the affected area shows great efficiency on the part
of those who organised it.

It was not really contended that further and more effective grounds of opposition
could have been deployed if more notices had been served or posted up in more
places. It was, and is, strenuously contended that if the notices had appeared in more
f or different newspapers, and had been displayed at more or different places, then the
number of objectors would have been substantially increased, and that this would or
might have affected the mind of the Secretary of State. The largest claims are made,
as not unnaturally and frequently happens, about what is thought to be public
opinion. But in my judgment, this is wishful thinking unsupported by convincing
evidence. In the light of the wide and effective publicity which was achieved, and in
g the light of the history of the proposals, and of the objections, and of the evidence in
this case—a good deal of which I have not had occasion to mention in detail and shall
not be able to do so—I am satisfied that more notices in more or different places
would not have unearthed a significantly greater number of objectors.

In the case of Mr Coney, one and only one person gave evidence that he did not
know of his rights; but then it appeared that his evidence was not impressive because
h he was the person who had heckled the priest in the middle of his sermon, and that in
fact his interruption in church created a stir. There must have been people who came
up and said: 'We don't agree with this either. What can we do about it?' In the case
of Mr Ludden there are two and only two people who say they did not know of their
rights.

The 1968 regulations are not designed to see that everybody knows. If they were,
j they would provide for different publicity. Suppose, for example, a notice is put up at
the town hall, that it is published in the local paper, and that it is posted at the school,
thus complying with the Regulations. There must in the area of Worksop be a large
number of citizens who go more frequently to the football ground and the public
house than the town hall, who have children none of whom is over the age of five,
and who read the Daily Mirror and nothing but the Daily Mirror. Those persons

probably never go near the particular places where the 1968 regulations have been
fulfilled and the notice has been put up. The regulations are not designed to bring *a*
the matter home to everybody. If that were required there would have to be the
town crier, or perhaps on the local radio announcements every quarter of an hour.
What the Regulations require is that notice should be published in a manner
designed to show a representative number of people what their rights are, and leave
to them the organisation of others. In fact that is obviously what happened in this
case. Some people, I think a great number, saw the notice. They organised the *b*
Parents Association. No doubt they went around and said: 'Have you heard this
monstrous proposal which has been going on for years; now it is coming to a head,
and if we are going to do anything about it we have got to write to the Minister. Will
you sign a petition?'

In my judgment these regulations are not to be regarded in the light of regulations
which are intended, if the proposals and the approval are to be effective, to be ob- *c*
served to the full rigour of the regulations. What the Minister wants, and what the
Minister must have before he approves, are the objections which can be urged so
that there is not lurking around some quite valid objection which he has never heard
of, and he must have some idea of the weight of the objections. For example, if the
method of publicising the notice was such that only five people wrote, the Minister
might erroneously think there was not much weight in the opposition. But any *d*
Minister would take a petition, such as the one put forward in the present case by 287
persons, as showing a degree of opposition to which he ought to pay serious attention.
If there had been more notices, even if—and I do not think there would have been—
the number of objectors had been doubled, it does not seem to me that would be
sufficient to make any real difference to the problem which troubled the Minister
who sat down with the proposals on the one hand and the objections on the other. *e*

If I am entitled to apply common sense and to dismiss these proceedings if I am
satisfied that as a result of a bona fide and reasonable attempt to carry out the duties
imposed by the regulations there was ample public notice of the proposals and of the
rights of those who wished to object, I have no doubt these actions ought to be dismissed. The merits and demerits of the objections and the proposals are, of course,
not in issue in these proceedings. *f*

Counsel for the plaintiffs, who argued, as always, strenuously and persuasively,
submitted that I am not concerned with the merits of the attempt to give publicity
to the notice of the proposal. If, he submits, one single breach of the regulations be
proved, then the approval of the Secretary of State is a nullity. Alternatively, he
says, if the court may turn a blind eye to one or two breaches of the regulations, there
were yet sufficient serious breaches in the present case to invalidate the approval of *g*
the Secretary of State. I must therefore consider whether the letter of the regulations
has been observed.

There was an objection to the newspaper publication, but that was limited to
Worksop. In the cases of all three schools the Nottingham Evening Post was chosen;
and it appears that the Nottingham Evening Post has been used by persons giving
notices in north Nottinghamshire generally. It is conceded that as far as Boughton *h*
was concerned, the Post was a newspaper circulating in the area served by the school.
In the neighbourhood of Worksop, detailed research by the plaintiffs has produced
evidence that the Nottingham Evening Post was only purchased by 26 persons in
Worksop at that time, and by them only by virtue of a specific order; this, it is
submitted, is not circulation.

I should be very sorry to think that it is not left to the judgment of local persons to *j*
select a newspaper bona fide. Or that they can be attacked, and the whole edifice of
proposal and approval come crashing to the ground, if it appears they might have
chosen some paper which had a larger circulation. If a newspaper chosen bona fide
can be bought and is sold in the area in question, then in my judgment that is compliance with the regulations. Of course, if a newspaper were chosen deliberately in

order to attempt to muffle up the publicity, different considerations would apply.
a But, as I say, I should be sorry to think that when in respect of an area in Nottinghamshire there is chosen the Nottingham Evening Post, the ferreting around as to how
many people actually bought it and on what terms would be enough to bring up the
dread spectre of nullity and ultra vires. That deals with the newspaper.

So far as the conspicuous places are concerned, we had a long argument as to what was
and was not conspicuous. It was said that some of the notices were not in fact seen.
b There was evidence that some people said they did not see them, and if the notices
had been there, they would have seen them. There was a contention that a notice
board in a Roman Catholic church is not a conspicuous place, especially as non-Roman
Catholics would not frequent it.

But again it seems to me this is a matter for those who in good faith set out to fulfil
the regulations requiring the posting of notices in some conspicuous place, and if
c against the background of this case they said to themselves: 'The obvious and most
conspicuous place is the Roman Catholic church', it seems to me to be quite wrong
for the court to interfere, especially when the threatened consequences are nullity. I
find as a fact that the requisite notices were displayed at the selected churches.

The objection to notices required to be posted at or near a main school entrance
applied to all the schools, and again we had a long argument as to exactly what was done.
d At St Mary's School, it was said, the main entrance was closed for repairs. The notice
should have been posted at the de facto school entrance; it was posted on the inside of
the door and it ought to have been put on the outside; the parents used some other
entrance and never saw the notice; and the school was closed for holidays part of the
time.

Now again, the task of everybody concerned with education, and of this court, is
e going to be made intolerable if every single action which is taken—bona fide action—
to conform with the regulations is to be attacked in this minute manner. The headmaster gave evidence. Early on he reported that he received the notice and that he
posted it on the main entrance door, and he put that on oath in an affidavit. He had
to be brought here and cross-examined; and then issues were raised as to whether he
was right in thinking that the door was in use until near the end of February, and
f whether the notice was blown down by the wind, and who used the door—and his
recollection even of putting up the notice was attacked, as was the recollection of the
priest in connection with the churches.

I am very sorry he had to be brought here, and I am not going to tell a headmaster
how to post a notice at or near the main entrance of his own school; I accept his
evidence that he put it up and that he complied with the regulations.
g As regards the other two schools, there has never been any question that when
investigation was made it was found that the headmasters at Robert Ludlam and St
Joseph's did not display the notice because they did not know—and there it is.

So I find that the regulations were not complied with in the case of Robert Ludlam,
Worksop, and St Joseph's, Boughton, in respect and in respect only of one matter,
namely, the failure to post the notice at or near the main entrance to the school. I
h have to consider the effect of that. I have also to bear in mind, in considering the effect
of attempted compliance with the regulations, the evidence that though in Worksop,
as I have found, the letter of the regulations was observed with regard to the newspaper, it appears that the choice of newspaper could have been happier and that a
newspaper could have been chosen which had a wider circulation in Worksop than
that which was quite innocently chosen.
j Counsel for the plaintiffs, as I have said, submits that any breach of the regulations
makes the decision a nullity. Alternatively, he says, the breaches are so serious,
particularly in the case of Robert Ludlam, that the decision of the Secretary of State is
a nullity. There has been no approval, and the court must therefore prevent the
implementation of the proposals which have not been approved.

Counsel for the defendants submits that if there was, as there undoubtedly was, a

genuine attempt to comply with the regulations, and if the actual compliance with
the regulations, coupled with any other steps taken to give publicity to the rights of   *a*
the objectors, resulted in the Secretary of State receiving objections, the nature and
weight of which were properly represented, then any decision made after consideration of those objections cannot be a nullity. In the present case there was wide publicity. No objections were omitted from the petition. The Secretary of State had
everything before him which he could possibly have had before him.

For the reasons which I have given, I accept that by and large, putting it shortly, the   *b*
breaches of the regulations did not make any difference.

Counsel for the defendants does not dispute that if this had been a case where the
failure to comply with the regulations had been deliberate; or if the breaches of the
regulations were such that when the Secretary of State purported to approve the
proposals he did not have before him the necessary information regarding the actual
objections, or as to the weight of possible objections, then it would have been impossible   *c*
for the Secretary of State validly to consider the proposals or validly to approve them.
His purported approval would be a nullity, vitiated by the fact that he was never in a
position to do his duty, namely, to consider the proposals in the light of the objections.
But that, says counsel, is not the case here—and I agree.

In those circumstances a suggested test, which counsel for the defendants adopted
and put forward, and with which, as a test, counsel for the plaintiffs did not quarrel—   *d*
although of course he disputed the consequence of applying the test—is to be found in
de Smith's Judicial Review of Administrative Action[1]. After hinting that the law
might have been in a bit of a mess, he continues:

> 'When Parliament prescribes the manner or form in which a duty is to be
> performed or a power exercised, it seldom lays down what will be the legal   *e*
> consequences of failure to observe its prescriptions.'

That describes the present case. Parliament has prescribed the manner in which the
duty of giving public notices is to be performed, but it has not specified the consequences of failure. It has not said if the 1968 regulations are not carried out then the
approval is invalid. It has left the result unspecified, and in those circumstances I go   *f*
back to Mr de Smith, who says[2]:

> 'The courts must therefore formulate their own criteria for determining
> whether the procedural rules are to be regarded as mandatory, in which case
> disobedience will render void or voidable what has been done, or as directory, in
> which case disobedience will be treated as an irregularity not affecting the
> validity of what has been done (though in some cases it has been said that there   *g*
> must be "substantial compliance" with the statutory provisions if the deviation
> is to be excused as a mere irregularity). Judges have often stressed the im-
> practicability of specifying exact rules for the assignment of a procedural pro-
> vision to the appropriate category. The whole scope and purpose of the enact-
> ment must be considered, and one must assess "the importance of the provision
> that has been disregarded, and the relation of that provision to the general object   *h*
> intended to be secured by the Act"[3]. Furthermore, much may depend upon the
> particular circumstances of the case in hand. Although "nullification is the
> natural and usual consequence of disobedience"[4], breach of procedural or formal
> rules is likely to be treated as a mere irregularity if the departure from the terms
> of the Act is of a trivial nature, or if no substantial prejudice has been suffered by
> those for whose benefit the requirements were introduced, or if serious public   *j*

---

1   (3rd Edn 1973), pp 122, 123
2   Ibid, p 123
3   See *Howard v Bodington* (1877) 2 PD 203 at 211
4   Maxwell on the Interpretation of Statutes (11th Edn, 1962), p 364

a inconvenience would be caused by holding them to be mandatory, or if the court is for any reason disinclined to interfere with the act or decision that is impugned.'

I accept that test, and applying it, here is an Act which is concerned with the administration of education in which, as has been seen in the present case, the ramifications can be considerable as regards different areas and as regards a host of children. It would in my judgment be lamentable if the carrying out of the purposes of the *b* Education Act 1944 as amended were hampered by a strict insistence on the letter of the 1968 regulations being carried out subject to the dire penalty of the whole thing being invalid. In my judgment, this is a case where the regulations must be treated as directory. Both the object and the terms of the regulations themselves seem to me to support that, and the consequences of the contrary also seem to me to require it.

I accept there must be substantial compliance with the regulations, and in my judg-*c* ment there has been. Asking myself whether any substantial prejudice has been suffered by those for whose benefit the requirements were introduced, I am quite satisfied the answer is No. The plaintiffs having lost the battle on the merits are now fighting a battle purely on the technicalities. I make no criticism. If the 1944 Act is so full of technicalities that the proposals can be tripped up, the plaintiffs are entitled to do just that. But in my judgment this is not an Act where Parliament *d* intended that the technicalities should rule rather than the spirit of the law. The object of s 13 has been achieved, and in those circumstances it seems to me that it would be quite wrong to hold that the technical defects in compliance with the regulations make the Minister's approval invalid.

Counsel for the defendants had an alternative argument. He said even if there had been breaches, or even serious breaches of the regulations, the only remedy of the *e* plaintiffs was to apply under s 99(1) of the 1944 Act. That provides:

'If the Secretary of State is satisfied either, upon complaint by any person or otherwise, that . . . the managers or governors of any county school or voluntary school, have failed to discharge any duty imposed upon them by or for the purposes of this Act, the Secretary of State may make an order declaring . . . the *f* managers or governors . . . to be in default in respect of that duty, and giving such directions for the purpose of enforcing the execution thereof as appears to the Secretary of State to be expedient; and any such directions shall be enforceable, on an application made on behalf of the Secretary of State, by mandamus.'

There is clear authority to the effect that when Parliament has given one remedy of *g* this sort, then that is the remedy to which aggrieved persons are confined and they cannot go outside to the courts. In the present instance, for example, complaint was made to the Secretary of State, and after consideration the Secretary of State gave the answer which I have already read, namely, that he was not disposed to take any action because he thought, and in my judgment rightly thought, that no prejudice had been caused. Counsel for the defendants admits that s 99 would not save the Secretary of *h* State if in fact there had been substantial non-compliance with the order or some gross breach which clearly amounted to prejudice, even though the Minister purported under s 99 to take no action.

In *Bradbury v London Borough of Enfield*[1] an injunction was granted against a local education authority to restrain it from giving effect to proposals whereby, in breach of a positive obligation imposed by s 31(5) of the London Government Act 1963, the *j* authority ceased to maintain eight schools. In that case no notices had been given because the Minister wrongly thought that they did not have to be given. The Court of Appeal held that notices ought to have been given. Lord Denning MR said[2]:

---

1 [1967] 3 All ER 434, [1967] 1 WLR 1311
2 [1967] 3 All ER at 440, [1967] 1 WLR at 1323

'I hold, therefore, in agreement with the judge, that in regard to the eight schools, the council intend to "cease to maintain" them and "to establish new" *a* schools within s. 13 of the Act of 1944. They ought, therefore, to have given public notices of their proposals, so that people could object. On objections being lodged, the Secretary of State would have to consider them. Not till then could the Secretary of State give his approval. Counsel for the defendant council submitted to us that the Secretary of State's approval would be good, even though public notices were not served, nor objections considered. I cannot agree. It is *b* implicit in s. 13 (3) and (4) that the Secretary of State cannot approve unless he has considered all objections submitted to him.'

In *Bradbury*[1] there were two distinctions from the present case. First, no notices at all had been served, so there could have been no substantial compliance. Secondly, in *Bradbury*[1], s 99 of the 1944 Act plainly did not apply because the requirement of main- *c* taining the schools and not ceasing to maintain them was found in the London Government Act 1963, and s 99 has no application to any Act other than the Education Act itself.

In my judgment, if one approaches the present problem on general principles, the 1968 regulations are directory and only render void a decision if substantially there had been no compliance with the regulations. If one approaches the matter under *d* s 99, which can only avail the Minister if there is substantial compliance with the regulations, I am of the opinion that the same result is obtained. Under the general law, the Minister was entitled to find as he did that the regulations had been sub-stantially complied with; and under the particular law, under s 99, the Minister was entitled to take no action; and in either event there is no cause for this court to inter-fere. Other cases were cited to me, but they do not seem to me to get near the present *e* point which is peculiarly concerned with regulations where an honest attempt has been made to carry them out, where substantially they have been carried out, plus further publicity, and one is left with the bare argument that the technicalities have not been complied with. So that both on the grounds of general approach and on the grounds of s 99, this action fails.

Even if I had been in favour of the plaintiffs on the strict letter of the law, I would *f* have felt disinclined to grant any relief in this case. What is sought is a declaration that the approval is invalid and has no legal effect, and an injunction restraining the defendants from carrying out the proposals. Counsel for the plaintiffs said that if he satisfied me that the Minister's approval was a nullity, then he was entitled to his order as of right. But a declaration and an injunction are both forms of relief which are discretionary, although discretion must of course be exercised in accordance with *g* principle.

In the present case the plaintiffs delayed between November 1972, when they first found out about these defects—or at least one or more of them—and October 1973, when they issued the writ. They knew, one of them was in fact a governor of one of the schools, that the pivot of the scheme, namely the building of the Mansfield School, was driving ahead. They knew as a fact, and I find, that everything is geared round *h* that school. I have heard evidence that as one would expect the viability of the school depends on an orderly intake from proper areas at proper ages. That school is due to open on 1st September. It is going to be the centre of education at the appropriate age in north Nottinghamshire. If the school opens on 1st September, but the pupils from Worksop and Boughton cannot go there, counsel for the plaintiffs says there will be no damage suffered, at any rate not to the children of Boughton and Worksop *j* who, he says, may be better off where they are. But I have to bear in mind, in the exercise of my discretion, that vast sums of money have been spent on this school. It is clearly unsatisfactory that it should operate without having these pupils for the

---

1   [1967] 3 All ER 434, [1967] 1 WLR 1311

time being. And if I make a declaration and injunction to please the plaintiffs, I must
a inevitably be making a declaration and injunction which large numbers of parents,
those who approve the proposals, consider not to be in the best interests of their
children.

There was evidence that in regard to the Boughton and Worksop children, if there
was an injunction in theory that merely meant more notices and two months to
elapse for more objections, but in practice the educational system being what it is,
b and teachers having to be lined up and sent to various places, that would put the entry
of Worksop and Boughton children back for a whole year—because you cannot have
children suddenly popping up in November and being fed into what is a highly
complicated mechanism.

If an injunction and declaration were granted, notices would be put up, objections
would be received, and the Secretary of State would then reconsider the whole
c matter. Of course, if that happened, he would sit down and clear his mind as much
as possible and furrow his brow to decide whether to approve the proposals
or not. But having regard to what has happened, to the fact that this objection
only applies to these two small areas, to the raison d'être of the school which
has been built at enormous expense, and to the fact it is not suggested that any new
objections could be presented to him other than those which were considered some
d years ago now, it seems to me that it would be really perverse of any Minister to
change his mind or disagree with his predecessor. No one can be absolutely certain
what a Minister will do; it is a matter for him. But in considering whether to grant
relief in this case, which would seriously prejudice some children, I think I must bear
in mind the probabilities. The probabilities are that if the plaintiffs succeeded on a
technical ground, it would only avail them for at most a year, and then the whole
e thing would go forward to the prejudice of those who had been delayed for a year,
and to the prejudice, I think, of the whole educational machine in north Nottinghamshire.

It is in my judgment partly the plaintiffs' fault that things have got to this pretty
pass that here we are, on 31st July, and if a decision is made in favour of the plaintiffs
it would have most undesirable repercussions as from 1st September. If the writ had
f been issued earlier this action could have come on earlier and before 1st September
loomed so alarmingly close.

So that in the present instance, if I had been for the plaintiffs on the technicalities,
or for that matter on the merits, I would not have been disposed to grant relief. I
would have left it to the Minister, in the light of my judgment, to decide whether she
ought to order any further action or any postponement of the action which is to
g take place on 1st September. That is an administrative matter for her, and I should
be very slow to introduce the swingeing weapon of an injunction, interfering in
administrative and educational matters of great moment by the sledgehammer of
an injunction which would bring to a grinding halt all the co-operation from these
two places which has been obtained in the course of the last few years.

In the result, it being agreed that the motion shall be treated as the trial of the
h action, I dismiss the action.

Motions by consent treated as trial of actions. Actions dismissed.

Solicitors: *Prentis, Seagrove & Co,* agents for *A E Furniss & Co,* Worksop (for the
j plaintiffs); *Ellis, Wood, Bickersteth & Hazel* (for the defendants).

Jacqueline Metcalfe Barrister.

Practice Directions

a

CHANCERY DIVISION

Patent – Practice and procedure – Extension of patent – Petition – Discontinuance of petition.

(1) If a petitioner for extension of the term of a patent under s 23 of the Patents Act *b*
1949 does not wish to continue the proceedings he may, instead of applying to the
judge, issue a summons before the appropriate master in Group A to dismiss the
petition.

(2) Where the patent has not expired the court will require the petitioner to give
an undertaking not to present a further petition on that patent.

(3) The master may make the order without requiring the attendance of the parties *c*
before him if the original summons is lodged at his chambers with the consent of all
parties and the petitioner's undertaking, if appropriate, endorsed thereon, duly
signed by all the parties or their solicitors.

By the direction of the Vice-Chancellor.

R E BALL *d*

19th March 1975   Chief Master

e

CHANCERY DIVISION

European Economic Community – Reference to European Court – Practice – Chancery
Division – Transmission of judgments of European Court to Chancery Division – Special
file – Duplicates of orders referring questions to European Court.

f

1. The first reference to the European Court (i e the Court of Justice of the European Communities) under RSC Ord 114 was made by the Vice-Chancellor (Sir John
Pennycuick) in the action *Van Duyn v The Home Office*[1].

2. A certified copy of the judgment of the European Court has been transmitted
to the Chancery Division. This judgment, and any others of that court affecting
matters in the Chancery Division, will be kept by the Entry Clerk in the Entry Seat, *g*
in a special file.

3. (a) By RSC Ord 114, r 5, where an order (referring a ruling to the European Court)
has been made, the Senior Master shall send a copy thereof to the Registrar of the
European Court. (b) In the Chancery Division, when such an order has been entered,
a duplicate of the order will be sent by the Entry Clerk to the Senior Master.

h

C M KIDD

17th March 1975   Chief Chancery Registrar

1   [1974] 3 All ER 178

a   # Bracewell and another v Appleby

CHANCERY DIVISION
GRAHAM J
25th, 26th, 27th, 28th, 29th NOVEMBER, 11th DECEMBER 1974

b *Easement – Right of way – Dominant tenement – Adjoining land – Right appurtenant to particular close – Grant of right of way to owner of close – Owner of close subsequently acquiring land adjoining close – Right of way to adjoining land – Whether grant having effect of creating right of way to adjoining land.*

Part of a building estate was laid out as a cul de-sac surrounded by six plots of land. The cul-de-sac was fed by a private road known as Hill Road which led into a public
c highway. The plaintiffs each bought one of the plots and the defendant's predecessors in title bought a third plot. On the sale of each of the six plots there were grants and reservations of rights of way over Hill Road and over portions of each plot. In 1968 the defendant's title to the house which had been built on the third plot was registered and he and his family went to live in the house which had become known as 3 Hill Road. In 1971 the defendant bought a piece of land ('the blue land')
d which adjoined the plot on which 3 Hill Road had been built. There was no access to the blue land except from 3 Hill Road or from the back gardens of houses facing other roads nearby. Despite opposition from the plaintiffs and others the defendant obtained planning permission to build a house partly on the garden of 3 Hill Road and partly on the blue land. The house was built and became known as 2A Hill Road. The defendant sold 3 Hill Road and went to live at 2A Hill Road. He intended to
e obtain access to 2A Hill Road by means of a drive parallel to the north western boundary of 3 Hill Road leading to Hill Road and over those portions of the plaintiffs' plots of land which formed part of Hill Road. The plaintiffs brought an action against the defendant claiming, inter alia, an injunction restraining the defendant from passing over the plaintiffs' land for the purpose of gaining access to the blue land.

f **Held** – The grant of a right of way appurtenant to a particular close for the purpose of access to that close did not have the effect of creating a similar easement appurtenant to land adjoining the close which came into the same ownership as the close at a date subsequent to the making of the grant and which might pass with and on a subsequent assignment of the adjoining land. Since at the time when the grant was made to the defendant's predecessors in title, their property was limited to plot 3,
g so far as that grant was concerned the dominant tenement was, and continued to be, plot 3 and consequently the defendant had never had any right of way to any other than plot 3 as it had been at the date of the grant. In the circumstances however, an injunction would be refused but the plaintiffs would be awarded damages in lieu thereof (see p 994 *j* to p 995 *b*, p 998 *g* and *h* and p 999 *e* and *j* to p 1000 *b*, post).
Harris v Flower (1904) 74 LJCh 127 applied.

h **Notes**
For creation of rights of way by express grant, see 12 Halsbury's Laws (3rd Edn) 571-573, paras 1242-1244, and for cases on the subject, see 19 Digest (Repl) 22, 23, 89-94.

Cases referred to in judgment
Finch v Great Western Railway Co (1879) 5 Ex D 254, 41 LT 731, 44 JP 8, 19 Digest (Repl)
j 125, 783.
Harris v Flower (1904) 74 LJCh 127, 91 LT 816, CA, 19 Digest (Repl) 119, 738.
Johnstone v Holdway [1963] 1 All ER 432, [1963] 1 QB 601, [1963] 2 WLR 147, CA, Digest (Cont Vol A) 496, 144a.
Shannon Ltd (The) v Venner Ltd [1965] 1 All ER 590, [1965] Ch 682, [1965] 2 WLR 718, CA, Digest (Cont Vol B) 231, 636b.   LL

Thorpe v Brumfitt (1873) 8 Ch App 650, 37 JP 742, 19 Digest (Repl) 129, 829.
Wrotham Park Estate Co v Parkside Homes Ltd [1974] 2 All ER 321, [1974] 1 WLR 798.   *a*

Cases also cited
Ackroyd v Smith (1850) 10 CB 164, [1843-60] All ER Rep 512.
Callard v Beeney [1930] 1 KB 353.
Charrington v Simons & Co [1971] 2 All ER 588, [1971] 1 WLR 598, CA.
United Land Co v Great Eastern Railway Co (1875) 10 Ch App 586.   *b*
White v Grand Hotel, Eastbourne Ltd [1913] 1 Ch 113, CA.
Whitwham v Westminster Brymbo Coal and Coke Co [1896] 2 Ch 538, CA.
Woollerton and Wilson Ltd v Richard Costain Ltd [1970] 1 All ER 483, [1970] 1 WLR 411.

Action
By a specially indorsed writ issued on 11th April 1973 the plaintiffs, Colin Derek *c*
Bracewell and Guy Armand Charles Wright, being registered as the freehold owners
of the properties known respectively as 4 and 1 Hill Road, Heath End, Farnham,
Surrey, brought an action against the defendant, Edward Appleby, being the owner
of the property known as 3 Hill Road and being entitled by express grant from a
predecessor in title to the right of way appurtenant to 3 Hill Road over the parts
of the plaintiffs' properties (being part of Hill Road) hatched yellow on the plan *d*
served with the writ and being the owner of property ('the additional land') adjoining
3 Hill Road. The plaintiffs claimed (i) a declaration that the defendant was not
entitled to a right of way over the parts hatched yellow for the purposes of gaining
access to the additional land or any part or parts thereof, (ii) an injunction to restrain
the defendant by himself, his servants or agents or licensees from passing over the
parts hatched yellow for the purpose of gaining access to the additional land or any *e*
part or parts thereof, and (iii) damages for trespass. The defendant served a defence
and by an amended counterclaim he sought (i) a declaration that the owners and
occupiers for the time being of the newly constructed house on the additional land
were entitled to the benefit of the right of way granted by transfer to the defendant's predecessor in title; (ii) alternatively (a) rectification of the transfer by substituting for the words 'of the fullest description' the words 'of the widest description *f*
as if such roads were public highways', and (b) if and so far as necessary rectification
of the contract under which the transfer had been made in the like manner. The facts
are set out in the judgment.

Dirik Jackson for the plaintiffs.
John Monckton for the defendant.   *g*

Cur adv vult

11th December. **GRAHAM J** read the following judgment. This is a dispute
between two neighbours about a right of way and is one which, if there had been
better communication between the parties and no clash of personalities, might well *h*
not have come before this court. The case relates to a situation which must have
occurred many times before and in view of the history of our land law one would
have expected to find a number of clear judicial pronouncements on the precise
point involved. Curiously enough, so far as anything cited to me is concerned, this
does not seem to be so apart from a sentence in the judgment of Romer LJ in *Harris
v Flower*[1].   *j*
 The point may be expressed thus: does the law permit the creation of a right of
way appurtenant to a particular close for purposes of access not only to that close
but also to any adjoining land which is not part of such close at the date of the grant,

---

1   (1904) 74 LJCh 127 at 132

but which may, at some future time, come into the ownership of the owner of such
a close? Can a grant which, if that is its proper construction, purports to do such a
thing, have the effect of creating an easement in the true legal sense so that it is
appurtenant to the adjoining land, creates a relationship of dominant and servient
tenement and passes with and on a subsequent assignment of the adjoining land?
Of course it would be possible by agreement for A to grant to B a right to pass over
A's land not only to land then possessed by B but also to any contiguous land he might
b acquire at a later date. That is not however the question here. We are concerned
here with the question whether such a grant can amount to an easement in the
true sense. Were it not for the fact that in a judgment dated 23rd July 1973, in proceedings for an interlocutory injunction in the action, Pennycuick V-C[1] expressly
said that it would be possible to frame such an easement of right of way, I would
myself have said the answer was clearly 'No'. The words of Pennycuick V-C were:

c
> 'It seems to me that it must be possible to frame an easement of right of way
> that the owner of a dominant tenement has a right not only to enter the dominant
> tenement but also to go through it to the other side. There is no reason why
> this should not be possible.'

d This statement was, of course, made in interlocutory proceedings without full argument and its implications may not have been fully examined. However, as will be
seen hereafter, if it was intended to be taken at its face value in the broadest sense I
cannot accept it.

The facts, as I find them, are simple enough. The plaintiffs and the defendant all
bought houses on part of what is known as the Farnham Heights estate in Surrey
which was developed by Wrotham Estate Ltd about 1962. This particular part of
e the estate was laid out as a cul-de-sac with six plots, fed by a private road known as
Hill Road. Hill Road leads into Alma Way, then also a private estate road but now
a public highway, having been duly taken over by the council. The layout can be
seen from the Wrotham Estate's site layout plan, drawing no 86/19, of October 1961
and the so called 'site plan' no 403/72. The plaintiffs respectively bought plots referred to as no 43 or no 4, and no 40 or no 1. The defendant's predecessors in title,
f Mr and Mrs York, bought plot 42 or 3, and plots 38, 39 and 41 were bought by other
parties. On the sale of each of the six plots there were grants and reservations of rights
of way over Hill Road and portions of each plot. For example, the plan attached
to the statement of claim shows a portion of Hill Road hatched yellow, half of which
belongs to Mr Wright and half to Mr Bracewell, subject to the grants, and reservations of rights of way and obligations to repair in question. These are all in the same
g terms for all the plots and are to be found in the first and the second schedules in
the Land Registry transfers, a typical example being in respect of Mr Wright's
title, no SY252861. It is the construction and effect of the grants and reservations in
these schedules, in the light of the further history of the matter, which in my judgment
is the determining factor in this case.

The defendant's title, no SY293256, to his property, 3 Hill Road, was registered on
h 14th October 1968, and the defendant and his family lived there for some time.
In April 1971 the defendant was able to buy for a nominal sum of £25, which included
legal costs, a piece of land, known in this case as 'the blue land', adjoining his plot
no 3 and shown conveniently on the plan attached to the Land Registry entry for
title no SY404350. As will be seen there was no means of access to this piece of land
except from 3 Hill Road or from the back gardens of houses facing the roads, Elm
j Grove or Hermitage Road. It was for practical purposes land-locked, in very rough
condition, and really of no use to anyone except the owner of 3 Hill Road and this
was, no doubt, why the defendant got it at a bargain price. The defendant, in due
course, cleared the land and incorporated it into his garden at 3 Hill Road. He then

---

1 (23rd July 1973) unreported

had the idea of building a new house, partly on the garden of 3 Hill Road and partly
on the blue land, and of obtaining access to the new house by means of a drive parallel *a*
to the north west boundary of 3 Hill Road and leading to Hill Road and over the
plaintiffs' yellow hatched land to Alma Road. He then proposed to sell and did sell
3 Hill Road and moved into the new house which eventually became known as
2A Hill Road and the whole dispute here turns on whether the original right of way,
which he acquired when he bought 3 Hill Road, also gives him a right of way to the
new house which is partly built on land originally part of 3 Hill Road and partly *b*
on the blue land.

The old boundary line can be seen so marked on the site plan. It was not of course
all quite as simple as appears from the above short summary. The defendant had
to obtain planning permission and his applications were opposed by the plaintiffs
and others. It will be appreciated that there had been no restrictive covenant imposed
by Wrotham Estate Ltd when the original development took place which would *c*
entitle the plaintiffs or any of the defendant's neighbours to object to the new house
for that reason. In fact, planning permission was originally refused but, on reconsideration, was granted in November 1972. The defendant entered into a contract
for the construction of the new house in March 1973 and work started shortly thereafter. The total cost of the work excluding legal charges was some £12,750 the
building contract itself being for some £9,232. *d*

Objection to the defendant's proposal was formally taken in August 1972 on the
basis that the defendant did not have a legal right of way over Hill Road which would
entitle him to access to the new house, such right as did exist being limited to the six
existing houses, and giving notice that an injunction would be sought if he proceeded.
At first the defendant appeared to be reasonably amenable and ready to compromise and to discuss the matter. Later, his attitude hardened, apparently following *e*
receipt of an opinion from counsel, and in effect he challenged the plaintiffs to take
proceedings. The plaintiffs asked to see a copy of the opinion but it was not supplied.
The cold war was hotting up and on 30th January 1973 the defendant announced
he would shortly start operations. This was followed by a threat from the plaintiffs
that they would proceed for an injunction and by the letter of 15th February, confirming this and referring to *Harris v Flower*[1]. After a further short exchange of fire *f*
about costs, the defendant apparently started building in early April 1973, and a
notice of impending proceedings was given by the plaintiffs on 4th April. The writ
followed on 18th April and on 24th April the defendant gave notice that he had
changed his solicitors. The new solicitors, Close and Son, on 26th April asked for further
time to consider the matter generally and to file a defence. This was refused on
15th May on the basis that the defendant was pressing forward with the construction *g*
without any regard to the plaintiffs' claim and on 21st May the plaintiffs' solicitors
stated they were instructed to apply for an interim injunction.

The motion in fact came on for hearing in July and on 23rd July Pennycuick V-C
gave the judgment from which I have already given the above-mentioned important
extract. He refused interlocutory relief mainly, as it appears, because of the conduct
of the plaintiffs. He said[2]: *h*

> 'Having reached this point I have to decide whether this is a case worthy
> of interlocutory relief. I have decided that it is not such a case. A number of
> months have passed since the building began. The writ was issued on the 14th
> April. The motion before me was only brought when the house was finished.
> Therefore I will make no order for interlocutory relief.' *j*

I would myself have come to exactly the same conclusion on conduct, the truth
of the matter being, I think, that neither side really felt sufficiently sure to put the
matter to the test until driven to do so. The plaintiffs kept on threatening to bring

1   (1904) 74 LJCh 127
2   (23rd July 1973) unreported

a proceedings, but in fact stood by until the house was erected and the defendant, whilst insisting that he had a right of way by virtue of the grant, in fact never took any proceedings, for example to obtain a declaration to that effect and pushed ahead until the house was a fait accompli.

Having seen both Mr Wright and the defendant in the witness box there was clearly a clash of personalities and Mr Wright said they have not been on speaking terms since the start of this trouble. I have not much sympathy for the way in which *b* either of them has conducted his affairs. As I say, like Pennycuick V-C, I would not have granted an interlocutory injunction, but furthermore I would not grant an injunction now if otherwise satisfied that the plaintiffs were entitled to relief following the same principles as those enunciated by Brightman J in *Wrotham Park Estate Co Ltd v Parkside Homes Ltd*[1]. Although an injunction here would be against trespassing on the plaintiffs' land and would not go to pulling the house down, it would *c* in effect make the house, no 2A, uninhabitable and would put the plaintiffs into an unassailable bargaining position.

Counsel for the plaintiffs, no doubt realising the difficulty, offered on behalf of his clients that if such an injunction were granted he would not insist on enforcing it but would be prepared to grant a right of way on payment of £1,200 to each of the plaintiffs, that sum being one fifth of £6,000 which, he said, the evidence shows *d* is the amount of the notional profit the defendant has made by his operations. I am not prepared to accede to this suggestion because it seems to me it would be quite wrong to do so, (1) in view of the unwillingness of the plaintiffs in fact to take effective action until the house was finished, which would put them into the bargaining position they could have got into if they had taken action before the defendant had committed himself to his contract, and (2) as being intolerable to render un-*e* inhabitable a house, which is a fait accompli, and is now being lived in by the defendant.

This reduces to a considerable extent the matters which have to be decided and attention will first of all be directed to consideration of the nature and extent of the grant and reservation in question. They are contained in the two schedules and read as follows:

f   'First Schedule (a) A right of way of the fullest description over the road shown and coloured brown on the plan [attached] and the roads and footpaths on the said Estate in common with the Transferor and all other persons so entitled . . . Second Schedule (a) A right of way with or without vehicles over the strip of land shown and coloured yellow on the plan aforesaid in common with the Transferee and his successors in title'.

g   Such consideration should be made in the light of evidence of the surrounding circumstances in the sense of the words of Danckwerts LJ in *The Shannon Ltd v Venner Ltd*[2], i e not evidence by the parties as to what they meant by the words of the deed, which is inadmissible, but for example, if such be the case, evidence that in acquiring the land the purchaser had certain plans for its development, a fact which might *h* explain the form the document took. There is a quotation from Upjohn LJ in *Johnstone v Holdway*[3], where he said[4]:

'In our judgment it is a question of the construction of the deed creating a right of way what is the dominant tenement, for the benefit of which the right of way is granted and to which the right of way is appurtenant. In construing the deed the court is entitled to have evidence of all material facts at the time *j* of the execution of the deed so as to place the court in the situation of the grantor.'

1 [1974] 2 All ER 321, [1974] 1 WLR 798
2 [1965] 1 All ER 590 at 593, [1965] 1 Ch 682 at 691
3 [1963] 1 All ER 432, [1963] 1 QB 601
4 [1963] 1 All ER at 435, 436, [1963] 1 QB at 612

I regard a finding which defines the extent of the dominant tenement at the material date, namely the date of the grant, as the determinative finding in the case. *a*
Evidence was given for the defendant by Mr Rowe, a solicitor who had acted for
Wrotham Estate Ltd at the time of its original development. His evidence that his
draft of the rights over Hill Road contained in the schedules was intended to grant
rights which were as wide as if Hill Road had been a public highway, may be, as
counsel for the defendant contended, admissible on the question of rectification,
the subject of the counterclaim, but it is, I think, clearly inadmissible on the question *b*
of construction of the right granted. The surrounding circumstances were those
one might expect to find on the development of an estate on land, previously farm
land. There was a Highways Act 1959, s 40, agreement concerning the main estate
roads, but clearly Hill Road was intended to remain a private road, otherwise it
would have been included in those roads intended to be taken over.

There is no satisfactory explanation to my mind of why there were differences *c*
between the words used in the grant and reservation, possibly the best being that
of counsel for the plaintiffs, that the rights for practical purposes must be reciprocal
so that development of, and life on the estate could proceed, and that the words
of the grant were wider than those of the reservation to give to the purchaser not
only rights over Hill Road equal to those retained by the vendor over Hill Road,
but in addition rights to go over and use the other roads of the estate which at that *d*
time had not been taken over. Mr Rowe, in answer to my question, where did the
words 'A right of way of the fullest description' come from, unhesitatingly replied
out of his own head. This, however, seems to have been wrong because it is clear
they in fact appear in an old abstract of title of a Mrs Mallan, who in 1931 owned
some part of the land which eventually came into the hands of Wrotham Estate Ltd.
They must, I think, have come from there. *e*

To my mind, however, it does not matter where they came from nor is it in my
judgment essential for the purposes of the present case, even if that were possible,
to be able to define their scope with precision. They were very clearly broad words
and the intention it seems to me was to grant a private right of way of as extensive
a nature as legally possible, having regard to the fact that these were private houses
on a building estate being developed. It cannot, I think, have been intended by the *f*
parties to treat Hill Road as a public right of way and make a grant accordingly,
because there was no real reason for doing so. It was not included in the s 40 agreement and it would have been perfectly simple to have said 'such rights as if Hill
Road were a public highway' if that had been the intention.

Whatever the precise intention, it is, however, perfectly clear that at the time
of the grant to the defendant's predecessors, Mr and Mrs York, in November 1962, *g*
the extent of their property was limited to plot 42 on which the house, 3 Hill Road,
was built and did not include any part of the blue land which the defendant later
acquired. So far as that grant is concerned the dominant tenement was, and
continued to be, 3 Hill Road, and the defendant has never had any right of way giving
him access to any land other than no 3 as it was at the date of grant.

Counsel for the plaintiffs' sheet anchor, *Harris v Flower*[1], justifies his assertion *h*
that the grant of access to 3 Hill Road does not enable the defendant to establish
that he has a right to extend his right of way to the blue land to which it is not appurtenant, thereby in practice doubling the burden on the servient tenements of the
plaintiffs because there are now two houses and families using Hill Road from 3 Hill
Road instead of one as before. The words of Romer LJ were[2]:

j

'If a right of way be granted for the enjoyment of Close A, the grantee, because
he owns or acquires Close B, cannot use the way in substance for passing over
Close A to Close B.'

---

1   (1904) 74 LJCh 127
2   74 LJCh at 132

The circumstances in that case and in the present case are very parallel and in my
a judgment the principles of *Harris v Flower*[1], as expressed above by Romer LJ, govern
this case. His words are quoted in Gale on Easements[2], and it does not appear that
there has ever been any criticism of them as not expressing accurately the true legal
position.

A number of cases were relied on by counsel for the defendant as justifying his
proposition put also to Pennycuick V-C in the interlocutory proceedings and set out
b in the judgment given on 23rd July 1973, but I do not think that they qualify the basic
proposition of Romer LJ. *Finch v Great Western Railway Co*[3], was a case where the easement, when created, was from one piece of agricultural land to another. The railway
later came through the dominant tenement on which the cattle pens were then
built. In fact, the courts seem to have treated the railway as a highway and decided
the case on the basis that the change of user was not unreasonable or excessive.
c In *Thorpe v Brumfitt*[4], where a new right of way was substituted by agreement for
an old one, the position seems to have been looked at rather differently by Mellish LJ
and James LJ respectively. The former seems to treat the small triangle of land
to which the new way went as the dominant tenement and as permitting access
to the yard beyond. This of course supports counsel for the defendant's argument.
James LJ, on the other hand, realistically treats the small triangle and the yard
d together as the dominant tenement, the whole object of the transaction being in
fact to give access to the yard and public house. There was, of course, here no question
of the yard being acquired at a date after the grant, and the continuation of access
to it was the very reason for the agreement. This is really a case which, to my mind,
is concluded by the proper identification at the time of the grant of the dominant
tenement as the public house and its yard.

e For these reasons I do not feel able to accept the proposition of Pennycuick V-C
in his interlocutory judgment insofar as it may have been intended to express a
view of the law different from that clearly stated by Romer LJ. It follows that the
defendant was not granted a right of way which entitled him to pass over Hill
Road to and from his new house, 2A Hill Road. His right of way was limited and
appurtenant to 3 Hill Road only.

f Before considering what is to be done, there are two other matters which must
be mentioned. Counsel for the defendant argued that the plaintiff, Mr Wright,
in bringing this action in conjunction with Mr Bracewell, and later continuing it
on his own, when as appears to be the case, Mr Bracewell ran out of funds, was
guilty of maintenance and/or champerty. Apart from the fact that this charge was
not pleaded there was, in my judgment, no evidence to justify it and in fact it is clear
g that the plaintiffs had a common interest in suing the defendant and brought the
action in support of a legal right. I need say no more about this point.

The second matter is the counterclaim. Counsel for the defendant argued that
Wrotham Estate Ltd, having put in no defence to the counterclaim, his client was
entitled to judgment on his pleading, and that if I was against him on the construction of the grant, he was then entitled to rectification of the land transfer as sought in
h para (ii) of the defendant's claim. I am against him on the grant as set out above,
but I am equally against him, on the evidence, on the claim for rectification. As
stated I do not think it was ever intended to treat Hill Road as if it was a public highway and I see no reason for granting rectification in this case. The counterclaim must
therefore fail.

I come now to the question of relief. As already stated, I am unwilling in the
j circumstances to grant an injunction, but as, in my judgment, the plaintiffs have

---

1 (1904) 74 LJCh 127
2 14th Edn (1972), p 282
3 (1879) 5 Ex D 254
4 (1873) 8 Ch App 650

established their legal right, and by reason of the Chancery Amendment Act 1858 (Lord Cairns's Act) they can ask for, and the court can grant, damages in lieu of an injunction. The defendant accepted that such was the position if I was thus far in the plaintiffs' favour. After consideration I propose to approach the question of damages and assess the amount, which I was requested to do by both parties, along the same lines as those followed by Brightman J in *Wrotham Park Estate Co Ltd v Parkside Homes Ltd*[1]. It seems to me that the defendant must be liable to pay an amount of damages which insofar as it can be estimated is equivalent to a proper and fair price which would be payable for the acquisition of the right of way in question. In dealing with the case before him, Brightman J said[2]:

'In my judgment a just substitute for a mandatory injunction would be such a sum of money as might reasonably have been demanded by the plaintiffs from Parkside as a quid pro quo for relaxing the covenant.'

Then, after rejecting the approach which aimed at obtaining half or a third of the development value, he went on[2]:

'I think that in a case such as the present a landowner faced with a request from a developer which, it must be assumed, he feels reluctantly obliged to grant, would have first asked the developer what profit he expected to make from his operation.'

The profit in that case was large, being of the order of £50,000 and in the end the damages were assessed at £2,500 being five per cent of the profit.

In the present case, the plaintiffs, for amenity reasons, did not want an extra house built in the cul-de-sac and I think it is right to regard them also as 'reluctant', just as Brightman J did in the case of the plaintiffs before him. On the other hand, in all the circumstances, I think that for the purpose of estimating damages they and the other servient owners in Hill Road, albeit reluctant, must be treated as being willing to accept a fair price for the right of way in question and must not be treated as if they were in the extremely powerful bargaining position which an interlocutory injunction would have given them if it had been obtained before the defendant started operations and incurred expense. Such is to my mind the penalty of standing by until the house is built.

On the evidence here the probable figure of notional profit which the defendant has made, being the difference between the overall cost of the new house and its present day value seems to be somewhere between £4,000 and £6,000 and I think it is fair to take £5,000 as about an accurate a figure as one can get. The circumstances here are very different from those in *Wrotham Park Estate Co Ltd v Parkside Homes Ltd*[1] and I think that the proper approach is to endeavour to arrive at a fair figure which, on the assumption made, the parties would arrive at as one which the plaintiffs would accept as compensating them for loss of amenity and increased user, and which at the same time, whilst making the blue land a viable building plot, would not be so high as to deter the defendant from building at all. The defendant was not a speculative builder and in fact wanted to live in, and does now live in, 2A Hill Road himself and I think he would have been prepared to pay what is relatively to his notional profit quite a large sum for the right of way in question and to achieve the building of his new home. This was a time of rising property values and I think he would have been prepared to pay £2,000 to get his right of way and if he had made such an offer, I think the other five owners in Hill Road ought also to have been

---

1 [1974] 2 All ER 321, [1974] 1 WLR 798
2 [1974] 2 All ER at 341, [1974] 1 WLR at 815

prepared to accept it. The plaintiffs are, of course, only entitled to their appropriate
a share of this figure, namely one fifth each, and I therefore award them £400 each by
way of damages for the exercise of a right of way over their respective pieces of land.

*Judgment entered for the plaintiffs for damages in lieu of an injunction in the sum of £400
each. Declaration in terms of the statement of claim refused.*

b Solicitors: *Charles Russell & Co,* agents for *W H Hadfield and Son,* Farnham (for the
plaintiffs); *Slaughter & May* (for the defendant).

Evelyn M C Budd Barrister.

c

Harris v Birkenhead Corporation and another (Pascoe and another third party, Alliance Assurance Co Ltd fourth party)

d
Affirmed CA [1976] 1 All ER 341

QUEEN'S BENCH DIVISION AT LIVERPOOL
KILNER BROWN J
9th, 10th, 11th, 12th, 13th, 16th DECEMBER 1974

e *Occupier – Negligence – Trespasser – Duty owed by occupier to trespasser – Occupation –
House acquired by local authority under compulsory purchase order – Effect of notice of
entry – Local authority serving notice to treat and notice of entry on owner of house – House
let to tenant – Notices accompanied by letter – Letter stating local authority required vacant
possession and proposed to offer to rehouse tenant – Local authority officer visiting tenant
pursuant to letter – Tenant making own alternative rehousing arrangements – Tenant leaving*
f *house in good condition – House subsequently broken into and damaged – Child trespasser
injured in fall from broken window – Liability of occupier – Whether local authority or
owner 'occupier'.*

G owned a house, the entrance to which was in a street that was designated as a
play street. The house was near a children's playground and in an area in which the
g local authority had been engaged for many years on a programme of slum clearance.
The local authority realised that empty slum dwellings awaiting demolition were
likely to be explored by young children and in 1963 they resolved that such properties should be bricked up and made secure. They employed a staff to inspect
those dwellings and to record when they required bricking up. In 1966 G's house
was included in a compulsory purchase order scheme. On 3rd July 1967 G was served
h with a notice to treat and a notice of entry, under the Housing Act 1957, stating that
the local authority would enter the property 14 days from the date of service and
take possession of it. At the time G's property was let, through her agents, to R,
who was an excellent tenant. A letter which accompanied the notices stated that
the local authority needed to secure vacant possession of the property and that one
of their officers would call on the occupier to make arrangements for vacant possession
j and proposals for the rehousing of R. R saw the local authority officer and informed
him, and G's agents, that she did not wish to be rehoused, that she would be making
her own private arrangements about her future accommodation and that she would
be leaving G's house just before Christmas. On 23rd December she left it in good
condition. Shortly afterwards it was broken into and considerable damage was
done to it. In particular a window on the second floor, 30 feet above the ground,

was smashed and a large pane of glass removed from it. The window had a low sill and on 6th March 1968 the plaintiff, a child of four years, who had wandered into the *a* house from the nearby playground, fell from the window and sustained grave injuries. On 11th March the local authority sent their men to brick up all the lower openings of the house. No one had done that before the accident. The house had not been recorded on the local authority's books as one where the occupants had been rehoused. The plaintiff brought an action against, inter alios, G and against the local authority, claiming damages under the Occupiers' Liability Act 1957. Both *b* defendants denied liability.

Held – (1) G was not liable to the plaintiff because (i) she was not the occupier of the premises, and (ii) it was not established that she had, or ought to have had, any knowledge of the relevant facts giving rise to a duty to take appropriate precautions (see p 1005 *c* and p 1006 *g*, post).   *c*

(2) The local authority were liable to pay compensation to the plaintiff for her injuries for the following reasons—

(i) They were the legal occupiers of the house at the time of the accident for the effect of the notice of entry together with their letter and conduct in furtherance of it was to give them on and after 23rd December immediate supervision and control *d* of the premises and the power to permit or prohibit the entry of other persons (see p 1006 *e* and *f*, post).

(ii) They knew that where such properties were left unprotected there was a potentially dangerous situation and they ought to have guarded against the possibility of an accident of the kind that had occurred happening in a building which they should have seen was derelict (see p 1005 *c e* and *f* and p 1006 *c*, post).   *e*

Notes

For the duty owed by occupiers of premises to trespassers, see 28 Halsbury's Laws (3rd Edn) 53, 54, para 49, and for cases on the subject, see 36 Digest (Repl) 70, 71, 376-382.

For the standard of care in relation to trespassing children, see 28 Halsbury's Laws *f* (3rd Edn) 17, 18, para 15, and for cases on the subject, see 36 Digest (Repl) 120, 121, 600-611.

Cases referred to in judgment

Addie (R) & Sons (Collieries) Ltd v Dumbreck [1929] AC 358, [1929] All ER Rep 1, 98 LJPC 119, 140 LT 650, HL, 36 Digest (Repl) 120, 604.   *g*

British Railways Board v Herrington [1972] 1 All ER 749, [1972] AC 877, [1972] 2 WLR 537, HL.

Pannett v P McGuiness & Co Ltd [1972] 3 All ER 137, [1972] 2 QB 599, [1972] 3 WLR 386, CA.

Penny v Northampton Borough Council (19th July 1974) unreported; [1974] Bar Library transcript 260, CA.   *h*

Wheat v E Lacon & Co Ltd [1966] 1 All ER 582, [1966] AC 552, [1966] 2 WLR 581, HL, Digest (Cont Vol B) 451, 135a.

Action

The plaintiff, Julie Harris, a minor suing by her next friend, Christina Westcott, brought an action against (i) Birkenhead Corporation ('the local authority'), and (ii) *j* Jessie Kathleen Gledhill, claiming damages under the Occupiers' Liability Act 1957 in respect of injuries which she received when on 6th March 1968 she fell from a second floor window at 239 Price Street, Birkenhead. The second defendant joined Eric Matthew Pascoe and Douglas McNeill Carson, partners in a firm known as Bailey & Neep, as third party. She also served third party proceedings on her insurers,

the Royal Insurance Co Ltd. The third party joined the Alliance Insurance Co Ltd
a as fourth party. The facts are set out in the judgment.

G P Crowe QC and *David Clarke* for the plaintiff.
Michael Morland QC and *Charles James* for the local authority.
Barry Chedlow QC and *Richard Pickering* for the second defendant.
Gerard Wright QC and *M D Byrne* for the third party.
b *J Franklin Willmer QC* and *Jeffreys Collinson* for the fourth party.

KILNER BROWN J. On 6th March 1968 the plaintiff, a little child of four, fell from
the upper window of a derelict house which was awaiting demolition. She sustained
grave injuries and her brain was permanently damaged. By common consent a
c proper figure for compensation is said to be £20,000. Now nearly seven years
later I am asked to decide whether anyone is to be found liable to pay this very
large sum. It has been a complicated case because quite apart from the problems
which arise when little children trespass on property no one is here prepared to
agree who was the occupier or who was in possession or control of the house. A
further complication is added by the refusal of an insurance company to admit
d liability with reference to the status and behaviour of one of the parties.
The history of this matter begins with the bequest to the second defendant, Mrs
Gledhill, of a number of houses, some of which later became subject to a clearance
order made by the appropriate local authority. The particular house involved in
this case was 239 Price Street, Birkenhead. When the second defendant became the
owner of the various properties bequeathed to her she sensibly engaged a highly
e reputable firm of estate agents to manage the properties on her behalf and in due
course to account to her for the few pounds a year which they brought in after
all expenses had been paid. The firm in question was the third party in this case,
Messrs Bailey & Neep.
239 Price Street strangely enough had no entrance to Price Street but was entered
by a door situate in Moreton Street, which was at right angles. Moreton Street
f was designated as a play street. For hundreds of yards all around the junction of
these two streets the local authority had for many years been engaged on the clearance
of slum properties and the substituted building of modern accommodation. At the
bottom of Moreton Street and also above it they built high rise tower accommodation and maisonettes and flats. Close to where the infant plaintiff lived there was
also constructed a children's playground. As various houses became subject to clear-
g ance orders and before they were demolished the signs of desolation and decay
were plain for all to see. The second defendant's houses, carefully managed by
Mr Pascoe of the third party firm, were a shining example of good husbandry.
The local authority, like their neighbours across the water, recognised the fact
that empty slum dwellings while awaiting demolition were a source of temptation
to evil-minded persons intent on scavenging and looting, and also as must be judi-
h cially noticeable to any judge who makes the journey to St George's Hall, a source
of childhood exploration and enjoyment. Thus it was that the local authority employed a staff to descend on these empty dwellings and to deal with them in an
appropriate manner, signified in their records by the mystic appellation of BUALO
and cows which were interpreted by the initiated as 'Brick up all lower openings'
and 'Cut off water supply'. New bricks had to be resorted to because painful
j experience indicated that boards and corrugated iron were inadequate against
scavengers and vandals and, as I find, against mischievous children.
The local authority on 22nd October 1963 recognised these facts of life by resolution of that date, for they then resolved that properties awaiting demolition should
be boarded up and made secure. In 1966 Price Street became included in a compulsory purchase order scheme. On 26th August 1966 the local authority circulated

a statement of reasons which recognised that it was their duty to ensure that the buildings in a clearance area were to be demolished after the occupants had been   *a* rehoused. On 3rd July 1967 the second defendant and her agents, the third party, were served with a notice to treat and a notice of entry under the terms of the Housing Act 1957. An accompanying letter of the same date stated that the local authority needed to secure vacant possession of the various properties, and that one of their officers would call on occupiers to make arrangements for vacant possession and to make proposals for the rehousing of dispossessed occupiers.   *b*

Now 239 Price Street was occupied by Mrs Jean Redmond whose statement of evidence has been admitted in due course. She was a tenant of the second defendant and an excellent tenant, as the local authority's own records indicate. Mr Rhodes, an officer of the local authority, called on her. She called on Mr Rhodes. She informed him and she also informed Mr Harrison, who was employed by Mr Pascoe of the third party firm to collect rents, that she did not wish to be rehoused, she preferred to make   *c* her own arrangements. She would leave just before Christmas 1967 and would leave the keys at a house in nearby Vittoria Street which subsequently met the same fate as other houses in the area at the hands of the demolition gang. She left on 20th or 23rd December 1967.

Within a few weeks of her leaving her excellently tenanted and managed house it became, like nearly all the others, a prey to vandals and a tempting place for ad-   *d* venturous little children. The evidence is overwhelming on this point. By 6th March 1968 the door had been broken down, the windows smashed, the staircase and rooms a scene of desolation. Upstairs on the second floor was a window 30 feet above the ground. One large pane 18 inches by 12 inches was missing. The sill was low. Out of this window and on to the ground below crashed the body of this little child. Earlier she had been safely left by her mother in the enclosed playground at the bottom   *e* of Moreton Street. She and at least one other child had gone into the adjoining play street and no doubt found the door of this house invitingly open at the top of the play street.

Who was in law the person in control of this house? Was it a potential danger to little children? Is anyone liable to pay compensation for the grievous injuries this child sustained? On 11th March 1968 the local authority, no doubt spurred on by   *f* the shocking news of this accident, sent their men to brick up all lower openings. No one had done so before. Was there an obligation so to do? Was this child's accident something which a humane person exercising common sense could have expected or prevented? Who was the person in law who should have been charged with the exercise of humanity?

The leading case on these issues is *British Railways Board v Herrington*[1]. In *Pannett v*   *g* *P McGuinness & Co Ltd*[2] the Court of Appeal had, as I have had, the advantage of an exhaustive examination of the speeches in *Herrington's* case[1]. Lord Denning MR[3] summarised the effect of their Lordships' opinions and laid down four guide lines for the assistance of trial judges. The first matter to be borne in mind is a common sense assessment of the gravity and likelihood of probable injury. Second, account must be taken of the character of the intrusion by the trespasser and allowance be   *h* made for the thoughtlessness of little children. Third, regard must be made to the nature of the place where the trespass occurred and a derelict house awaiting demo-lition be given more consideration than a place of regular occupation. Lastly, account must be taken of the knowledge which the owner or occupier has or ought to have of the likelihood of trespassers coming on the premises.

Edmund Davies LJ applied the same principles in a pragmatic examination of   *j* the facts of the case. So also did Megaw LJ when giving the leading judgment in

1   [1972] 1 All ER 749, [1972] AC 877
2   [1972] 3 All ER 137, [1972] 2 QB 599
3   [1972] 3 All ER at 141, [1972] 2 QB at 607

Penny v Northampton Borough Council[1]. I have endeavoured to apply the same prin-
a ciples and to adopt the same approach in this case. It is to be observed that the fourth
question as posed by Lord Denning MR does not give full weight to the point made
by some of their Lordships in *Herrington's* case[2], and particularly Lord Diplock,
that whilst pronouncing the obsequies over the burial of the harsh rule in *Robert
Addie & Sons (Collieries) Ltd v Dumbreck*[3] recognition must be made of the added
burdens facing even an infant trespasser.

b   It is not necessarily right to burden an occupier with inferred knowledge of risk
within the ordinary common law doctrine of forseeability. Knowledge of relevant
facts must be proved against an occupier. As Megaw LJ put it[4]:

'Did the defendants in the present case have knowledge of facts which ought
to have led them, on reflection, to anticipate the occurrence of an accident of
c   the general nature of the accident which in fact occurred . . .'

Without rehearsing the arguments so admirably presented, or reciting the facts which
are plainly to be discovered, I am of the opinion that such knowledge is not to be
imputed to the second defendant or her agent or independent contractor. Conversely
I am of the opinion that it is to be imputed to the local authority. Consequently
d the second defendant and the third party are entitled to be absolved from liability
even if they were the persons properly to be considered as occupiers or in control
of the premises.

     The first three questions in my judgment have to be answered adversely to the
local authority. I have considered carefully the able and cogent argument of counsel
for the local authority, assisted on this aspect by other counsel. I recognise the force
e of the submission that this accident did not arise from any breach of duty. There is
of course a difference where there is a live rail or a heap of glowing embers, whereas
an open window is a hazard in an ordinarily occupied house. I am firmly of the opinion
that a derelict house openly available to a little toddler of four with a gaping window
only a few inches above the floor is a potentially dangerous situation against which
any humane or common sense person ought to take precautions.

f   No evidence has been called to dispute this adverse inference. Whenever they
thought they had to brick up an empty house that is precisely what this local authority
did. House after house in this vicinity was given the BUALO treatment. This house
was also dealt with after the accident. The only reason it was not so dealt with before
was in my judgment because no one in the local authority considered that they were
under an owner's obligation so to do. The reason was partly because it had been
g until 23rd December effectively occupied and partly because no one in the local
authority had it on their books as a house the occupants of which had been rehoused.

     This fact leads naturally to the consideration of whether or not the local authority
were legally bound to assume the liability of an occupier in the legal sense. On
3rd July 1967 they served not only a notice to treat but also a notice of entry, and an
accompanying letter of even date which is of great importance. Whereas there is
h authority and editorial comment on the effect of a notice to treat there is, so I am
informed, no such authority or academic exegesis on the effect of a notice of entry.
Consequently I am sailing on uncharted seas but with the comforting knowledge
that I have been piloted with admirable skill.

     Until 3rd July 1967 the second defendant was the legal occupier and was in the per-
j son of her tenant in physical occupation. Her legal rights were plainly invaded by

1   (19th July 1974) unreported
2   [1972] 1 All ER 749, [1972] AC 877
3   [1929] AC 358, [1929] All ER Rep 1
4   In *Penny v Northampton Borough Council* (19th July 1974) unreported

the action of the local authority in serving notices. To what extent were they extinguished? The notice of entry is clear and unambiguous. It states that the local authority give notice that they will on the expiration of 14 days from the service of the notice enter on and take possession of the property. But the notice has to be read in conjunction with the letter, the gist of which is that no action to evict will be taken for the time being and arrangements for giving vacant possession would be discussed by the appropriate officer of the local authority. The governing consideration would be mutually satisfactory arrangements for rehousing.

Now although Mrs Redmond was not a tenant of the local authority she was seen by the appropriate officer. She notified the appropriate officer that she was making private arrangements and would be leaving before Christmas. In fact she left by 23rd December. So the local authority acted in pursuance of the letter and the tenant conducted herself as invited to do by the letter. There was the house vacant and awaiting demolition. In my view the local authority were not only possessed of information that it would be available for demolition, but their officer who recorded the necessity for bricking up must through his subordinates have noticed, if they had kept their eyes open as they toured the area, that there was yet another house ready for treatment.

Counsel for the local authority submits that the effect of the notice of entry and the letter is to create a right which is exercisable after the lapse of 14 days. It is an option to enter. The local authority do not become occupiers in the legal sense until they take some step overtly in exercise of their suspended power. There is no obligation to inspect or to find out the physical presence or absence of the tenant. Counsel for the local authority is a lone voice crying in the wilderness. All other counsel disagreed, particularly counsel for the fourth party who stepped from the wings to deliver a powerful criticism of those contentions.

Whilst it recognised that there may be two notional occupiers (see *Wheat v E Lacon & Co Ltd*[1]) the contrary submissions are that on and after 23rd December the control of these premises was in the hands of the local authority. It was they who had the immediate supervision and control and the power of permitting or prohibiting the entry of other persons. *Wheat v E Lacon & Co Ltd*[1] is to be distinguished in its application, for here there was no physical occupation. But, so it is argued, the principle therein enshrined points firmly to the decision that by the form of the notice, the contents of the letter and conduct in furtherance, the persons who were the legal occupiers at the time of the accident were the local authority. I prefer and accept these contentions.

The effect of my conclusions is that the local authority are liable to the plaintiff. The second defendant avoids liability on two grounds (1) that she was not the occupier of the premises and (2) that she has not been proved to have been aware of the relevant facts giving rise to a duty to take precautions.

In the circumstances I have not found it necessary to deal with the effect of my giving leave de bene esse for the second defendants to proffer an amendment to the defence. If it falls to be considered elsewhere it should be recorded that I would not be minded to permit any course which might have led to the non-suiting of the plaintiff where the case had originally been pleaded on different grounds altogether. This means at this stage I am of the opinion that the plaintiff is entitled to judgment in the sum of £20,000 against the local authority.

Judgment for plaintiff against the local authority for £20,000.

Solicitors: *Percy Hughes & Roberts*, Birkenhead (for the plaintiff); *Weightmans*, Liverpool (for the local authority) ; *Bell & Joynson*, Liverpool (for the second defendant); *Byrne Frodsham & Co*, Widnes (for the third party); *Davis, Campbell & Co*, Liverpool (for the fourth party).

Christine Ivamy Barrister.

1   [1966] 1 All ER 582, [1966] AC 552

a

New Hart Builders Ltd v Brindley

CHANCERY DIVISION
GOULDING J
18th, 19th, 20th, 21st, 22nd NOVEMBER, 5th, 18th DECEMBER 1974

b

Sale of land – Contract – Memorandum – Signature of person to be charged – Alteration to memorandum after signature – Memorandum not signed again following alteration – Alteration modifying terms of agreement – Modification agreed to by parties – Party to be charged not signing memorandum afresh or expressly reviving existing signature by appropriate words or gestures – Whether agreement enforceable – Law of Property Act 1925, s 40(1).

c

The company negotiated with the owner of certain land for an option to purchase the land. One of the two partners in the company prepared a document setting out the terms of the proposed option agreement. The document left blank spaces for the owner's name, the price of the land per acre, and the amount of the payment to be made for the option to be inserted. A fourpenny and a threepenny stamp were *d* affixed to the lower part of the document. The two partners discussed the proposed agreement as typed out with the owner and his son, the defendant. The text of the proposed agreement was completed by the insertion of the appropriate details. The owner signed the document over the two stamps and handed it to one of the partners who in turn gave the owner a cheque for £100, the sum which they had agreed to pay for the option. After some conversation between the parties, the defendant asked for *e* the document, and the attached plan of the land, stating that he wished to check them. The defendant marked out on the plan an area ('the blue land') with a blue pencil and inserted between the end of the typewritten text and the owner's signature further provisions. Those provisions were to the effect that the option on the blue land was to be renewed every 12 months and was to run initially from 1st January to 31st December 1967, that the option on the remainder of the land would terminate on 31st *f* December 1968 on any land for which planning permission had not been granted and that thereafter a new agreement would be needed. The owner and the two partners then agreed to those additional provisions. The owner did not put his signature or initials to the additions, nor was anything further said about his signature. Applications for planning permission were made by the company from 1966 onwards. Permission was obtained in 1970. The applications were assisted by the owner and the defendant. *g* In 1970 the owner died and the defendant became his personal representative. In an action against the defendant the company alleged that by letter of 26th October 1971 the company had accepted the offer to sell contained in the option agreement in respect of the blue land and claimed specific performance of the contract of sale constituted by that acceptance. The defendant contended that the contract was unenforceable on the ground that since the written memorandum of the option *h* agreement had been varied after the owner had signed it, the memorandum could not be relied on as verifying the contract constituted by the acceptance of the offer contained in the option agreement as amended by the additional provisions and that accordingly there was no sufficient writing to satisfy s 40(1)[a] of the Law of Property Act 1925. In reply the company contended that the acts of the owner and his son in assisting the applications by the company for planning permission constituted *j* sufficient part performance.

---

a Section 40(1), so far as material, provides: 'No action may be brought upon any contract for the sale . . . of land . . . unless the agreement upon which such action is brought, or some memorandum or note thereof, is in writing, and signed by the party to be charged or by some . . . person . . . by him lawfully authorised.'

Held – The action would be dismissed for the following reasons—
(i) Where the alteration of a document was not merely for the purpose of correcting *a*
a mistake in a written statement of an agreement but effected or evidenced an
alteration of the terms of a contract already concluded and binding on the parties,
s 40(1) of the 1925 Act was not satisfied unless the party to be charged signed the
document afresh or expressly revived the existing signature by appropriate words or
gestures directed to the signature. Accordingly there was no sufficient writing to
satisfy s 40(1) (see p 1012 *b* to *g*, post); *Bluck v Gompertz* (1852) 7 Exch 862, *Stewart v* *b*
Eddowes (1874) LR 9 CP 311 and *Koenigsblatt v Sweet* [1923] 2 Ch 314 distinguished.
(ii) On the assumption that the doctrine of part performance could apply to an
agreement conferring an option whilst the option remained unexercised, the applications by the company for planning permission could not in any event rank as part performance of the agreement unless by their own character they were referable to the
existence of an agreement between the company and the owner. There was nothing *c*
improbable or unusual in the co-operation of a would-be developer and a landowner
in obtaining planning permission in the hope that both would eventually profit,
without necessarily having bound themselves by contractual terms. The planning
applications did not therefore prove the existence of a contract and the company had
failed to make out the plea of part performance (see p 1012 *j* to p 1013 *c*, post).
d

Notes

For signature of memorandum in writing of contract of sale of land, see 34 Halsbury's
Laws (3rd Edn), 207, 208, para 346, and for cases on the subject, see 40 Digest (Repl)
36, 37, *188-198*.

For the Law of Property Act 1925, s 40, see 27 Halsbury's Statutes (3rd Edn) 399.
e

Cases referred to in judgment

Bird v Bass (1843) 6 Man & G 143, 6 Scott NR 928, 1 LTOS 231, 134 ER 841, 5 Digest (Repl)
987, *7959*.

Bluck v Gompertz (1852) 7 Exch 862, 21 LJEx 278, 19 LTOS 285, 155 ER 1199, 26 Digest
(Repl) 50, *341*.

Holwell Securities v Hughes [1974] 1 All ER 161, [1974] 1 WLR 155, CA. *f*

Household Fire and Carriage Accident Insurance Co v Grant (1879) 4 Ex D 216, 48 LJQB 577,
41 LT 298, 44 JP 152, CA, 12 Digest (Reissue), 81, *420*.

Hughes v Metropolitan Railway Co (1877) 2 App Cas 439, [1874-80] All ER Rep 187, 46
LJQB 583, 36 LT 932, HL, 31(2) Digest (Reissue) 846, *6985*.

Koenigsblatt v Sweet [1923] 2 Ch 314, 92 LJCh 598, 129 LT 659, CA, 12 Digest (Reissue)
190, *1141*. *g*

Stewart v Eddowes, Hudson v Stewart (1874) LR 9 CP 311, 43 LJCP 204, 30 LT 333, 12
Digest (Reissue) 202, *1282*.

Cases also cited

Alexander v Steinhardt, Walker & Co [1903] 2 KB 208.
Bruner v Moore [1904] 1 Ch 305. *h*
Brunning v Odhams Bros Ltd (1896) 75 LT 602, HL.
Caton v Caton (1867) LR 2 HL 127, HL.
City & Westminster Properties (1934) Ltd v Mudd [1958] 2 All ER 733, [1959] Ch 129.
Entores Ltd v Miles Far Eastern Corporation [1955] 2 All ER 493, [1955] 2 QB 327, CA.
Griffiths v Young [1970] 3 All ER 601, [1970] Ch 675, CA.
Holland v Bennett [1902] 1 KB 867, CA. *j*
Joscelyne v Nissen [1970] 1 All ER 1213, [1970] 2 QB 86, CA.
Robinson's Settlement, Re, Gant v Hobbs [1912] 1 Ch 717, CA.
Rudd v Bowles [1912] 2 Ch 60.

Action

The plaintiff company, New Hart Builders Ltd, formerly Dean and Hartley Ltd, a brought an action against the defendant, John Brindley, the personal representative of John Brindley deceased, the defendant's father, in which the plaintiff company, by their statement of claim served on 31st January 1972 and re-served as amended on 27th February 1974, alleged that by letter dated 26th October 1971 addressed to the defendant, they had accepted an offer by the defendant's father, made by an option agreement in writing dated 25th November 1966, to sell land at Allen's Rough Farm, Willenhall, Staffordshire, and claimed (1) specific performance of the contract con-

b stituted by the acceptance of the offer; (2) further or alternatively, damages for breach of contract. The facts are set out in the judgment.

Charles Sparrow QC and *Guy Seward* for the plaintiff company.
Michael Albery QC and *T L G Cullen* for the defendant.

c
Cur adv vult

18th December.   **GOULDING J** delivered the following judgment.   This is an action by New Hart Builders Ltd, against Mr John Brindley.   The plaintiff company has recently changed its name, and at the material times was called Dean and Hartley

d Ltd.   It was in substance a partnership between Mr Albert George Dean, a practical builder, and Mr Jack Hartley, who had been a bank manager before engaging with Mr Dean in the business of builders and developers.   It is clear from the evidence that the office work and financial arrangements of the plaintiff company were chiefly the responsibility of Mr Hartley.   The defendant is sued as representing the estate of his late father, like him named John Brindley.   The defendant is the administrator of such estate and the only person beneficially interested therein.

e
The late Mr Brindley was a farmer.   He owned and lived on Allen's Rough Farm between Wolverhampton and Walsall.   By an agreement in writing which I shall call 'the option agreement', dated the 25th November, 1966, the late Mr Brindley gave the plaintiff company an option to buy the farm for £5,000 an acre.   The option agreement distinguished different parts of the farm by reference to a plan.   The land with which

f the action is concerned, something over 20 acres in extent, is edged blue on the plan and is conveniently referred to as 'the blue land'.   There was at one time a dispute about the identity of the plan referred to in the option agreement.   That point however has been settled by an order of Foster J made on 14th June 1973 in an action between the same parties concerning certain land edged yellow on the option plan.   The option agreement provided that the option in respect of the blue land must be renewed every calendar year.   The company says that it renewed the option in or about December

g 1967, December 1968, December 1969 and December 1970, and finally that it exercised the option by a letter dated 26th October, 1971.

Meanwhile the late Mr Brindley had died on 6th February 1970 and the defendant had become his personal representative on 16th November 1970.   Accordingly the plaintiff company now sues the defendant for specific performance of a contract for

h sale of the blue land constituted by the option agreement and the plaintiff company's written exercise of the option.

At the trial the defence, though previously pleaded in wider terms, was narrowed down to three specific points, each raising an issue or issues of fact and requiring consideration of the law.   First the defendant says that the contract on which the plaintiff company sues is unenforceable because there is no sufficient writing to satisfy s 40(1) of the Law of Property Act 1925.   Secondly he alleges that the plaintiff company

j omitted to renew the option on the first occasion when renewal was required, namely in 1967, and thirdly that it also failed to renew the option in 1969.

The plaintiff company called three witnesses, namely Mr Dean, Mr Hartley and Henry Baker, an officer of the head post office at Wolverhampton.   All three were in my view honest and frank witnesses.   When it comes to remembering conversations that took place many years ago I think that Mr Hartley, by education and experience, is more likely to be accurate than Mr Dean, if and so far as their recollections diverge. The defendant neither gave evidence himself nor called any other witness to support *a* his case. I will examine his three points of defence in their chronological order.

Section 40 of the 1925 Act requires a contract for the sale of land either to be in writing or to be evidenced by a memorandum in writing. In either case the writing must be signed by or on behalf of the party to be charged. The only signature which has been relied on for this purpose by the plaintiff company in pleading or in argu- *b* ment is the signature of the late Mr Brindley on the option agreement, and to under- stand the defendant's contention one must know the history of that document in some detail.

In 1966 Mr Dean had a number of business discussions with the late Mr Brindley and the defendant, with whom he had long been acquainted, and he introduced them to Mr Hartley. The subject of the negotiation was the sale of Allen's Rough Farm, or some part of it, to the plaintiff company with a view to residential development. No *c* planning permission for such development had, as yet, been obtained and so an option, rather than an immediate purchase, was what Mr Dean and Mr Hartley aimed at. When he thought the matter was ripe Mr Hartley had a document typed out in the plaintiff company's office. A 4d and a 3d stamp were affixed to the lower part of the paper shortly after it was typed. The typewritten text I shall now read, indicating by the word 'blank' where blank spaces were left in such text. *d*

> 'I [blank] of Allen's Rough Farm, Essington Lane, Willenhall hereby grant to Dean and Hartley Limited of 27 Pooles Lane, Short Heath, the option to purchase my freehold land situate at Allen's Rough Farm Essington and having an area shown on the attached plan and edged in red. This option to be apportioned as follows:—(a) The area edged yellow and having an approximate area of 18·4 acres *e* or thereabouts at the price of £ [blank] per acre. (b) The remaining area edged red at the price of £[blank] per acre. Such option to be taken up within twenty one days of detailed planning permission for residential development being obtained in respect of the 18·4 acres referred to in Clause A above. The remainder to be taken up as and when such approval as aforesaid is received and I acknowledge receipt of the £[blank] being a payment for this said option . . .' *f*

On 25th November 1966 Mr Dean and Mr Hartley took this document to Allen's Rough Farm. They also took some plans which had been prepared by an architect and previously discussed with the late Mr Brindley and the defendant. At the farm they met the late Mr Brindley and his two sons, namely the defendant and a younger son, George Brindley, who has since died. The five men conferred together in the farm- house kitchen. So far as the verbal discussion was concerned, the business was mainly *g* done between Mr Hartley and the defendant. The typewritten text was modified as follows in Mr Hartley's handwriting. The price of the land left blank under para (a) was completed as £5,000 per acre, and that under para (b) as £4,000 per acre. The words 'twenty one days' were struck out and replaced by 'six months'. The blank indicating the payment to be made for the option was completed with the figure £100.

Through the persuasion of one or more of the Brindleys the figure of £4,000 under *h* para (b) was then altered to £5,000. That last figure is probably in the defendant's handwriting. At some point the three Brindleys retired for a short time to another room. Either while they were out or on their return, the late Mr Brindley signed the document—and this is the vital signature relied on by the plaintiff company—over the two stamps. It looks as though the late Mr Brindley also wrote in his own hand the name 'J. Brindley' in the blank after the pronoun 'I' at the beginning of the *j* document, but so far as I can remember no evidence was given on that last point.

After signature the document was handed to Mr Dean and he gave the late Mr Brindley a cheque for £100. A period of conversation followed. The late Mr Brindley was talking with Mr Dean, and Mr Hartley was talking with the defendant; George Brindley had left the kitchen. Then the defendant asked for the option agreement

and the plans, saying he wanted to check them. When he got them the defendant
a wrote some further provisions on the option agreement in the space between the end
of the typed text and the late Mr Brindley's signature. He also drew with a blue
pencil the blue edging which now appears on the plan referred to in the document.
The provisions thus added in the defendant's handwriting are as follows:

> 'The area edged in blue extending to an area of approximately 23 acres the
> option on this land to be renewed every 12 months and to run from Jan 1st to
b > Dec 31st 1967. The option on the remainder of the land will terminate Dec. 31st
> 1968 on any land [for]which planning permission has not been granted, thereafter
> a new agreement will be needed.'

The defendant, still in the farm kitchen, explained the motives of the alterations
which he had made. I do not think it is necessary for me to go into them now. Mr
c Dean was not at all pleased at what he felt to be a high-handed proceeding but in the
end he and Mr Hartley left the farm taking the amended option agreement and the
plans with them. On the evidence as a whole I find that before they left, Mr Dean
and Mr Hartley on behalf of the plaintiff company and the late Mr Brindley on his
side had agreed to the document as amended. The late Mr Brindley did not sign or
initial the alterations made in the handwriting of the defendant, nor was anything
d said about his signature after it was first affixed. I should mention, although it does
not affect the present dispute, that a counterpart of the option agreement had been
signed on behalf of the plaintiff company. This also was altered by the defendant. It
was retained by the late Mr Brindley.

The defendant's case on s 40 of the 1925 Act is perfectly simple. He says that although
the contract on which the plaintiff company sues is in writing, it is not signed by the
e late Mr Brindley. His signature was affixed to the option agreement as it stood before
alteration by the defendant. The terms of the option agreement in that form were
finally agreed, and became binding, when the cheque for £100 was handed to the late
Mr Brindley. The offer contained in the option agreement as it then stood was never
accepted, because it was shortly afterwards discharged when the parties approved the
amendments made in the defendant's handwriting. Thus, argues the defendant,
f there is no signature of the late Mr Brindley to verify the contract made by acceptance
of the offer contained in the revised option agreement.

This is an unattractive argument in the mouth of the defendant. For one thing he
has maintained by his written defence, and still maintained when that defence was
amended during the course of the trial, that he made the manuscript amendments
prior to the signing of the option agreement. Moreover, it was only at a late date that
g he pleaded s 40 at all. Further, if the plea is truly based, there is no reason why the
defendant should not have asserted it in the previous litigation where he unsuccessfully resisted the enforcement of the option agreement in respect of the land edged
yellow on the plan therein referred to.

However, the plaintiff company has not pleaded any estoppel against the defendant
and the point is one of positive law which must be decided on principle and not on
h general merits. So regarded, the defendant's objection has much intrinsic force. On
the evidence the late Mr Brindley's signature was intended by him, at the instant when
it was written on the paper, to authenticate a different option from that which the
plaintiff company claims to have exercised. If I say that in agreeing orally or by
conduct, to be bound by the subsequent alteration of the document the late Mr
Brindley in effect re-executed his signature, I shall be placing a construction of law on
j the words of s 40. I must therefore see whether such construction is authorised by
judicial precedent.

In *Bluck v Gompertz*[1] Pollock CB, stating the judgment of the Court of Exchequer on
an objection based on the Statute of Frauds, said[2]:

---

1   (1852) 7 Exch 862
2   7 Exch at 868

'. . . we also think that words introduced into paper signed by a party, or an alteration in it, may be considered as *authenticated* by a signature already on the *a* paper, if it is plain that they were meant to be so authenticated. The act of signing *after* the introduction of the words is not absolutely necessary.'

Pollock CB was not given to inacurate expressions, and if read without qualification, his observations would dispose of the defendants' plea in the present action.

Counsel for the defendant concedes that in certain cases an alteration made to a *b* document after signature and approved by the party to be charged is sufficiently authenticated, for the purposes of s 40(1) of the 1925 Act, by the original signature. That is so, he says, where the signed document is altered in order to correct a mistake in the written statement of an existing contract, as apparently in *Bluck v Gompertz*[1] itself. The law is similar where the signed document is altered before the parties are contractually bound at all, as in *Stewart v Eddowes*[2] and *Koenigsblatt v Sweet*[3]. But, *c* counsel submits, the result is different where the alteration of the document effects or evidences an alteration of a contract already concluded at some earlier time and binding on the parties. In such circumstances, he says, s 40 is not satisfied unless the party to be charged signs the document afresh, or expressly revives the existing signature. Merely to accept the altered writing is not specific enough for the latter purpose; appropriate words or gestures must be directed to the signature as a *d* signature.

Counsel's arguments do not commend themselves to my uninstructed reason. It seems to me that the force of oral approval of alterations in a signed document as an acknowledgement or revival of the act of signing should be exactly the same whether the document is an unaccepted offer, a concluded agreement whose inaccurate formulation is to be rectified, or a concluded agreement whose terms are to be varied *e* by consent. The legal results are of course different in the different examples, but for myself I would think it equally right or equally wrong in all cases to treat the approval of the alterations as equivalent to going over the existing signature with a pen. However, Pollock CB in *Bluck v Gompertz*[1], Lord Coleridge, Brett J, and Denman J in *Stewart v Eddowes*[2], and Lord Sterndale and Warrington LJ in *Koenigsblatt v Sweet*[3] were all at pains to show that in those cases there was no variation of a concluded agreement *f* after the time of signature, and I think the terms in which they expressed themselves clearly support counsel's argument.

On the general principle that law is not just unless it is certain, I think it is my duty in such a matter as this to follow a strong current of judicial opinion, even though it may not bind me as direct authority and even though it draws what I conceive (perhaps from some limitation of insight or of learning on my part) to be an illogical *g* distinction. Accordingly I accept the defendant's submission that there is no sufficient writing to satisfy s 40 of the 1925 Act.

I must consequently examine the plaintiff company's alternative contention under the well-known equitable doctrine of part performance. The acts relied on as constituting part performance are the planning applications made and prosecuted by the plaintiff company from December 1966 until planning permission was obtained in *h* June 1970. Particulars of such proceedings are set out in the plaintiff company's reply. They were lengthy, troublesome and expensive. The relevant facts are not in dispute save that the defendant suggests that the first application was made before the date of the option agreement. I do not however find that suggestion established by the evidence.

I see some difficulty in applying the doctrine of part performance at all to an agree- *j* ment conferring an option while the latter remains unexercised. Can the grantee of the option be heard to say that he has effected part performance of an agreement

1 (1852) 7 Exch 862
2 (1874) LR 9 CP 311
3 [1923] 2 Ch 314

which imposes no duty on him whatever? I do not mean to express any opinion on

a that point.

On any view the plaintiff company's planning proceedings cannot in my judgment rank as part performance unless by their own character they are referable to the existence of an agreement between the plaintiff company and the late Mr Brindley. Counsel for the plaintiff company laid much stress on the fact that the Brindleys gave assistance to the plaintiff company in pursuing the applications for planning

b permission. However, I see nothing improbable or unusual in the co-operation of a 'would-be' developer and a landowner to obtain planning permission in the hope that both will eventually profit, without necessarily having bound themselves by contractual terms. Thus the planning activities do not prove the existence of a contract, and the plaintiff company has in my view failed to make out the allegation of part performance. The defence under s 40 of the 1925 Act is accordingly a good answer to

c the plaintiff company's claim.

In case, however, the litigation goes further, I must go on to consider the other two grounds of defence. It will be recalled that they both question the due renewal of the option concerning the blue land, and I had better start off with the construction of the provision requiring renewal. All that the option agreement says about it is that the option on the blue land is to be renewed every 12 months and to run from 1st January

d to 31st December 1967. The case has been argued on the footing that that stipulation on its true construction simply meant that the plaintiff company should notify the late Mr Brindley or his successors in title each year of its current intention so that if the plaintiff company no longer wished to develop the blue land then the landowner would be freed from the option.

The question is: what sort of notification is necessary? Counsel for the plaintiff

e company contends that the option agreement does not require a notice to be served, but I am unable to accept his submission. To say that renewal is to be effected by notifying the landowner means, in the ordinary use of words, that notice is to be served on the landowner. Counsel says that it must have been in the contemplation of the parties that renewal might be by post and that, therefore, posting a notice of renewal is enough, even if the letter is never received. For that proposition he relies

f on a well-known line of authorities relating to acceptance of offers and to some other business communications. To apply the principle invoked it is necessary for counsel to show that renewal of the option by posting a letter was impliedly authorised by reason either of general usage or of the relations between the parties to the particular transaction, or of the terms of the option agreement. (See the judgment of Baggallay LJ in *Household Fire and Carriage Accident Insurance Co v Grant*.[1])

g Taking the alternatives in reverse order, there is nothing material in the option agreement itself, and, secondly, the previous negotiations between the plaintiff company and the late Mr Brindley had proceeded not by postal correspondence but by a succession of personal interviews. No general usage affecting this type of communication was alleged or proved, and counsel for the plaintiff company was driven to rely on the usage of English people at the present time to employ the post for business trans

h actions of all sorts. That in my opinion is too vague. In any case, I find it hardly possible to distinguish a requirement 'to notify' a particular individual (the construction of the option agreement accepted by the plaintiff company) from a requirement of 'notice to' a particular individual. The latter form of words was recently held by the Court Appeal in *Holwell Securities v Hughes*[2] to exclude the artificial construction by which the act of posting is a sufficient communication.

j Deciding then that a notice of renewal was to be served on the late Mr Brindley, was writing necessary or would oral notification be enough? The option agreement discloses no intention on the point or on the mode of service generally. Consequently,

---

1   (1879) 4 Ex D 216 at 228
2   [1974] 1 All ER 161, [1974] 1 WLR 155

in my judgment, s 196 of the 1925 Act applies to the case, and any notice of renewal
must be in writing.   *a*

It is common ground that no written notice of renewal was served in 1967. The
plaintiff company relies on a meeting at the farmhouse between the late Mr Brindley,
Mr Dean and Mr Hartley. It took place probably in the first half of December 1967.
The defendant was not present. The plaintiff company's case is that the option
respecting the blue land was orally renewed at this meeting. If, however, as I have
just held, a written notice was required, then the plaintiff company relies on the   *b*
conversation as an agreement by the late Mr Brindley to forgo formal notice in
consideration of the plaintiff company continuing to pursue its planning applications.
Alternatively, the plaintiff company says that the conversation, coupled with the
subsequent prosecution of planning applications by the plaintiff company, subjected the late Mr Brindley to a so-called promissory estoppel or quasi-estoppel on
the principle of *Hughes v Metropolitan Railway Co*[1], thus precluding the defendant *c*
from now asserting that the option was not renewed in 1967.

At the time of the meeting the parties were awaiting the outcome of a public
inquiry regarding the plaintiff company's appeal against certain refusals of permission
to develop land comprised in the option agreement. The public inquiry had been
held in October 1967. Mr Dean's recollection of the conversation in December is that
Mr Hartley did most of the talking and discussed the public inquiry and future   *d*
procedure with the late Mr Brindley. The late Mr Brindley, Mr Dean remembers,
said he was quite happy with the existing option and did not want a new one. Mr
Hartley says he wanted to make sure that the late Mr Brindley was happy for the
plaintiff company to continue, as the obtaining of planning permission might still
cost a lot of money. He thought it advisable to call at the farmhouse in order to avoid
any possible misunderstanding. The late Mr Brindley, according to Mr Hartley, said *e*
he wanted the plaintiff company to continue and in reliance on that assertion Mr
Hartley went ahead.

Neither Mr Dean nor Mr Hartley professes to remember the very words of the
conversation. Mr Dean was not consciously aware of the need to renew the option.
Mr Hartley is sure that he had the question of renewal in mind and that in effect or
in substance the option was renewed. On the other hand, the main purport of the   *f*
interview was undoubtedly to emphasise the plaintiff company's intention to persevere
with its planning applications and sooner or later to develop not only the blue land,
but also (and perhaps primarily) the land edged with yellow on the option plan. Its
rights under the option agreement were no doubt involved by implication, but I am
not satisfied that the question of renewal was brought to the late Mr Brindley's
attention by express and distinct words.   *g*

Certain matters are relied on as corroboration of the plaintiff company's witnesses
on this question. First of all, there is the course of correspondence during the life of the
late Mr Brindley. On the 10th December 1968, the plaintiff company's solicitors sent
a registered letter to the late Mr Brindley in these terms:

> 'Dear Sir, Re: Land at Allen's Rough Farm, Essington Road, Willenhall. On   *h*
> behalf of our Clients, Dean & Hartley Limited, we enclose by way of service a
> notice of renewal relating to the land edged blue on the plan attached to the
> Option.'

The enclosure, also addressed to the late Mr Brindley and signed by Mr Hartley on
behalf of the plaintiff company, read thus:

> 'Dear Sir, We hereby give you notice of renewal for a further period of 12   *j*
> months from the 31st December 1968 of our Option to purchase the land edged
> blue on the plan attached to the Option Agreement granted by you to us re-
> lating to land at Allen's Rough Farm, Essington Road, New Invention, Willenhall,

---

1   (1877) 2 App Cas 439, [1874-80] All ER Rep 187

a   Staffordshire. You will recall that we have already renewed this part of the Option once before, last year.'

There is a further paragraph which I need not read.

Then on 1st January, 1969, the late Mr Brindley's solicitors, in a long letter to the plaintiff company's solicitors, included the following sentence:

b   'In your communication of the 10th December 1968 you enclosed what purported to be a renewal for a further period of 12 months of an option to purchase land edged blue on the plan attached to the document previously referred to and we have to say that our client cannot accept this renewal as it was not renewed as alleged in the previous period as was required by the option agreement.'

c   To that the plaintiff company's solicitors responded by a letter, dated 13th February 1969, sent both to the late Mr Brindley personally and to his solicitors in which they said:

d   'It has been suggested that the renewal of the land edged blue on the plan attached to the Option Agreement is not valid, and that the exercise of the Option relating to the land edged yellow also is not valid. However, it is our contention that both the renewal and the exercise of the Option were quite valid and we have Counsel's Opinion, which strongly supports our Clients' point of view. Counsel's Opinion says that the penultimate paragraph deals only with the blue land on which the option is to be taken up as and when such approval is received. He says it is renewable every 12 months. It was renewed verbally in the previous period as well as in writing this last time. It need not be in writing and another opinion we have suggests that actual renewal may be unnecessary as it would be *e* automatic.'

I will finally refer to a letter of 1st April 1969 by the late Mr Brindley's solicitors to the plaintiff company's solicitors in which the last paragraph is as follows:

f   'We should emphasise that it is our Client's intention to take proceedings in due course for the removal of the entry so far as the land edged blue is concerned and for a declaration that the option in that context is not subsisting.'

I think the reference to the entry must be a reference to an entry in the Land Charges Register.

Almost a year passed between the letter of 13th February 1969, alleging a verbal renewal of the option in 1967, and the death of the late Mr Brindley, but so far as *g* appears no denial of such renewal was made during that time (except the implied denial in the letter of 1st April 1969) nor were particulars of the plaintiff company's allegation demanded.

Secondly, Mr Dean and Mr Hartley swear that they met the defendant as they came away from the farmhouse in December 1967 and told him the substance of their conversation with his father. The defendant has not thought fit to deny their testi-*h* mony. It is relevant not, of course, as direct evidence of what happened at the interview with the late Mr Brindley but as suggesting consistency in the story told by Mr Dean and Mr Hartley.

I have come to the conclusion on the whole of the evidence that oral renewal of the option has not been proved. The honest hesitations of Mr Dean and Mr Hartley in recalling the vital conversation, and the perfectly obvious prudence (if renewal were *j* consciously contemplated) of writing a letter at the time to put the fact beyond doubt, convince me that I ought not to find renewal established against the representative of a dead man unable to speak for himself. Still less can I infer the facts necessary to support the plaintiff company's alternative allegation of an agreement or representation that would make written notice unnecessary.

I come finally to the question whether the option was effectively renewed in 1969.

The plaintiff company attempted to renew it by means of a registered letter, containing a plainly worded notice of renewal dated 19th December 1969. The letter was **a** posted on the 19th December 1969. What happened to it appears from a letter dated 8th January 1970 written on behalf of the Post Office by the witness Mr Baker and addressed to the plaintiff company's solicitors. I admitted the last mentioned letter in evidence pursuant to s 4 of the Civil Evidence Act 1968, and I have no reason to doubt that it truly reports the history of the registered letter. It reads as follows:

b

'Dear Sir, Thank you for your letter of the 6 January 1970, regarding the registered letter addressed to Mr. J. Brindley, Allens Rough Farm, Essington Road, New Invention, Willenhall, Staffs. Records show that the letter was tendered for delivery 20 December, 22 December and the 31 December; on the 31 December the delivery officer was informed that Mr. J. Brindley was on holiday in Ireland. On the 5 January we were informed that he was still in Ireland, had been taken **c** sick and was thought to be staying on in Ireland. All information was obtained from Mr. Brindley's son who runs a scrap business nearby. The Inspector in charge at our NE Postman Delivery Office endorsed the letter "Unable to Deliver etc" on the 5 January 1970 and returned the item to the senders.'

The letter is signed 'H Baker for Head Postmaster'.

I have already said that renewal of the option could not in my judgment have been **d** effected by the mere posting of a letter. Section 196(4) of the 1925 Act is of no assistance to the plaintiff company because the registered letter in question was returned through the Post Office undelivered. The plaintiff company, however, argues that it was left at the late Mr Brindley's place of abode or business within the meaning of s 196(3) and so was duly served by virtue of that subsection. I shall not attempt a definition or paraphrase of the everyday word 'left'. In my judgment, on the evidence **e** furnished by the Post Office, the registered letter was not in any acceptable sense of the word 'left' on the premises, and s 196 does not help the plaintiff company

That however is not the end of the matter. We have seen the active part played by the defendant in the making of the option agreement. There is also in evidence a document of 13th February 1969 whereby the late Mr Brindley authorised his solicitors to take all instructions from the defendant in connection with his dispute with **f** the plaintiff company, over Allen's Rough Farm. There are other indications in the correspondence of the defendant's activity in his father's affairs.

The defendant did not expose himself to further investigation of his authority during the late Mr Brindley's lifetime, but from the foregoing I infer, on a balance of probabilities, that in December 1969 he was authorised to receive correspondence relating to the option and to deal with it on the late Mr Brindley's behalf. I also infer, **g** from the previous history of the case and from the circumstances, that the defendant knew or strongly suspected that the registered letter contained a notice of renewal in respect of the blue land. On the importance of the last inference see the judgment of Maule J in *Bird v Bass*[1]. In consequence I find that the notice dated 19th December 1969 was in fact served on the late Mr Brindley before the end of the year. My finding is **h** however of no avail to the plaintiff company since I have previously held that it omitted to renew the option in 1967.

The action is dismissed.

Action dismissed.

j

Solicitors: *Bartlett & Gluckstein*, agents for *Talbot & Co*, Burton-upon-Trent (for the company); *Sharpe, Pritchard & Co*, agents for *Haden & Stretton*, Walsall (for the defendant).

Evelyn M C Budd Barrister.

1   (1843) 6 Man & G 143

Re A & BC Chewing Gum Ltd
Topps Chewing Gum Inc v Coakley and others

CHANCERY DIVISION

PLOWMAN J

4th, 5th, 6th, 7th, 10th, 11th, 12th, 13th, 14th, 17th, 18th, 19th, 20th, 21st, 24th, 25th, 26th, 27th, 28th JUNE, 1st, 2nd, 3rd, 4th, 31st JULY 1974

Company – Winding-up – Compulsory winding-up – Contributory's application – Just and equitable – Company in substance a partnership – Management of company – Agreement that petitioners and respondents should have equality of control – Provision in articles entitling petitioners to appoint and remove one director – Provision that decisions at board meetings be unanimous – Petitioners agreeing to scheme whereby petitioners appointed one of respondents director – Petitioners subsequently removing respondent director and appointing new director – Respondents refusing to recognise removal and new appointment – Respondents alleging agreement whereby petitioners' right to nominate director abrogated and respondents having sole right to run company – No such agreement – Whether repudiation of petitioners' right to participate in management of company rendering it just and equitable that company be wound up – Companies Act 1948, s 222(f).

Company – Winding-up – Order – Stay pending appeal – Company carrying on profitable business – Stay hampering Official Receiver in discharge of duties – Business of company to be carried on despite refusal of stay.

In 1967 the petitioners, whose business was that of manufacturing and selling chewing gum, purchased one-third of the shareholding in an English company ('the company') carrying on a similar business in the United Kingdom, on the basis that, although they were minority shareholders, they should have equal control with the individual respondents, Douglas Coakley and Anthony Coakley ('the Coakleys') who were brothers and directors of the company, and who owned the remaining two-thirds of the company's equity. In order to achieve equality of control the company adopted a new set of articles which, inter alia, entitled the petitioners to appoint or remove a director to represent them and which provided that decisions at board meetings should be unanimous. On the same day the petitioners, the Coakleys and the company signed and sealed a shareholders' agreement setting out the way in which the day to day business of the company was to be conducted. The share capital of the company was reorganised so that the petitioners became beneficially entitled to one-third of the issued capital and the Coakleys to two-thirds, the petitioners in the main holding 'A' shares and the Coakleys 'B' shares. By 1970 the company was experiencing a grave liquidity problem. The petitioners and the Coakleys took expert advice independently of each other. There were various meetings between the parties to discuss the situation but the existing arrangement was in no way altered. In March 1971 the petitioners, on advice, appointed Douglas Coakley as their 'A' director to represent them. He continued as 'A' director until March 1973 when, because they were dissatisfied with the way in which the company was being run, the petitioners removed him and appointed S as their 'A' director in his place. The Coakleys refused to recognise the removal of Douglas Coakley and the appointment of S as the 'A' director; they alleged that in March 1971 the parties had made a binding agreement which abrogated the petitioners' right to remove a director and appoint a new director in his place and that, therefore, they had the right to run the company to the exclusion of any director appointed by the petitioners. The petitioners applied for an order that the company be wound up under s 222(f)[a] of the Companies Act 1948 on the ground that it was just and equitable to do so.

---

[a] Section 222, so far as material, provides: 'A company may be wound up by the court if . . . (f) the court is of opinion that it is just and equitable that the company should be wound up.'

Held – There was no binding agreement in March 1971 to abrogate the petitioners'
right to nominate a director. The Coakleys had therefore repudiated the petitioners' *a*
right, established by the company's articles and the shareholders' agreement, to
participate in the management of the company. The repudiation of so fundamental
an obligation on the part of the Coakleys constituted grounds which rendered it
just and equitable that the company should be wound up. An order would be made
accordingly (see p 1027 *h* and *j* and p 1028 *e*, post).

  Ebrahimi v Westbourne Galleries Ltd [1972] 2 All ER 492 applied.   *b*

  Per Plowman J. In general where an order is made to wind up a company carrying
on a profitable business, the order will not be stayed pending an appeal, for the grant
of a stay will hamper the Official Receiver in the discharge of his duties should the
appeal be dismissed, whereas, if a stay is refused, the business can nonetheless be
carried on and handed back as a going concern should the appeal be allowed (see
p 1029 *d* to *f*, post).   *c*

Notes

For meaning of 'just and equitable', see 7 Halsbury's Laws (4th Edn) para 1000, and
for cases on the subject, and when it is just and equitable for an order for winding-up
to be made, see 10 Digest (Repl) 856-866, 5638-5694.
                                                                                       d
  For power to stay winding-up proceedings, see 7 Halsbury's Laws (4th Edn) para
1375, and for the exercise of the power, see ibid, para 1376.

  For the Companies Act 1948, s 222, see 5 Halsbury's Statutes (3rd Edn) 289.

Cases referred to in judgment

Blisset v Daniel (1853) 10 Hare 493, 1 Eq Rep 484, 18 Jur 122, 68 ER 1022, 36 Digest (Repl) *e*
  609, 1703.
Const v Harris (1824) Turn & R 496, [1824-34] All ER Rep 311, 37 ER 1191, 36 Digest
  (Repl) 594, 1526.
Ebrahimi v Westbourne Galleries Ltd [1972] 2 All ER 492, [1973] AC 360, [1972] 2 WLR
  1289, HL.
Wondoflex Textiles Pty Ltd, Re [1951] VLR 458.   *f*

Cases also cited

Broadway Enterprise Ltd, Re [1972] 6 WWR 673.
Davis and Collett Ltd, Re [1935] Ch 693, [1935] All ER Rep 315.
Expanded Plugs Ltd, Re [1966] 1 All ER 877, [1966] 1 WLR 514.
Loch v John Blackwood Ltd [1924] AC 783, [1924] All ER Rep 200, PC.   *g*
Lundie Brothers Ltd, Re [1965] 2 All ER 692, [1965] 1 WLR 1051.
Yenidje Tobacco Co Ltd, Re [1916] 2 Ch 426, [1916-17] All ER Rep 1050, CA.

Petition and action

On 20th September 1973, Topps Chewing Gum Inc ('Topps'), the holders of one-third *h*
of the equity share capital of A & B C Chewing Gum Ltd ('the company'), presented a
petition to wind up the company under s 222(*f*) of the Companies Act 1948 on the
ground that it was just and equitable to do so. Topps also brought an action against
the other shareholders, Douglas Albert Coakley and Anthony Francis Coakley, and
the company for a declaration that the defendant shareholders had acted in breach of
duty as directors of the company. The petition and the action were heard together. *j*
The facts are set out in the judgment.

Allan Heyman QC and *W F Stubbs* for Topps.
Jeremiah Harman QC and *Leonard Hoffmann* for the company and the defendant
  shareholders.

a

31st July. **PLOWMAN J** read the following judgment. There are two related matters before me, a petition and an action. I will deal with the action later in this judgment. The petition is a contributory's petition to wind up A & BC Chewing Gum Ltd ('the company'), the petitioners being Topps Chewing Gum Inc ('Topps'), a public quoted New York corporation which holds one-third of the company's equity.

b Topps's case, in a nutshell, is that the individual respondents, Mr Douglas Coakley and Mr Anthony Coakley, who are brothers and directors of the company and who own the other two-thirds of the equity, have repudiated the contract on the basis of which Topps came into the company as shareholders and that, in those circumstances, it is just and equitable to wind up the company.

The hearing before me lasted 23 days but, in the end, the question which I have to

c decide seems to me to lie within a comparatively narrow compass. It is whether, on 3rd March 1971, a binding oral agreement was made between the Coakley brothers and Mr Eddie Shorin, the vice-president international and a director of Topps, on behalf of Topps, that Topps's right under the articles of association of the company to remove a director of the company appointed by it and appoint a new director in his place was abrogated.

d The Coakleys claim that it was; Topps denies it, and if Topps is right about this then, in my judgment, it is prima facie just and equitable to wind up the company because the whole basis on which Topps went into the company was that while as between the Coakleys on the one hand and Topps on the other the shareholdings should be unequal, there should be equality of control. The Coakleys are now claiming sole responsibility and authority for running the company to the exclusion of any

e director appointed by Topps after 1971.

The facts, in outline, are as follows. Topps's business is that of manufacturing and selling chewing gum. Its products are marketed all over the world; in this country by the company under licence. The company was incorporated in 1949 by the Coakley brothers and a Dr Braun. At all material times until 1967 two-thirds of the equity capital of the company was held by the Coakley brothers, and one-third by Dr Braun.

f The company's business was similar to that of Topps, and on 5th February 1958 Topps granted the company a licence to manufacture, sell and distribute chewing gum under the Topps brands and to use certain of Topps's processes within Great Britain, Ireland and certain African countries for a period which, as subsequently extended, expires in February 1998. Under this licence the company is required to pay Topps a royalty of 5 per cent of its turnover. The licence agreement provides that its proper law shall

g be that of the state of New York and it is currently the subject-matter of litigation between Topps and the company in that state. That litigation is irrelevant to these proceedings, except that its existence emphasises the breakdown of the relationship between the two sides.

Since 1958 the exploitation of the Topps licence has been the company's principal business. In 1967 Topps purchased Dr Braun's shareholding in the company for

h £100,000, the Coakleys giving up certain rights of pre-emption so as to facilitate the purchase. Topps came into the company on the basis, as I have said, that though it was to be a minority shareholder, it should have equal control with the Coakleys. In order to achieve this position, the company, on 30th June 1967, adopted a new set of articles and, on the same day, Topps, the Coakleys and the company signed and sealed an agreement which has been called, and which I will call, 'the shareholders' agree-

j ment'. Both these documents are of prime importance in this case and I must refer to them in some detail. But first I should mention that the share capital of the company was reorganised so that, with effect from 30th June 1967, Topps held 2,834 'A' ordinary shares of £1 each and 5,668 preferred 'A' shares of 5p each, the Coakleys between them held 5,666 'B' ordinary shares of £1 each and 11,332 preferred 'B' shares of 5p each, and Topps executed a deed of trust of 1 'A' ordinary share and 2 'A'

preferred shares for itself and the Coakley brothers. This produced the result that
Topps became beneficially entitled to one-third of the issued capital and the Coakleys *a*
to two-thirds.

I turn first to the new articles. Article 48 requires a special resolution for an increase
of capital, thus ensuring that there can be no increase of capital without Topps's
assent. Article 57 is framed so as to invalidate the proceedings of any general meeting
of which Topps has not actually received notice. Article 60, dealing with quorums at
general meetings, provides as follows: *b*

> 'No business shall be transacted at any General Meeting unless a quorum is
> present. Save as in these Articles otherwise provided two Members present in
> person or by proxy of whom one is or represents a holder of Preferred "A"
> Shares and the other is or represents a holder of Preferred "B" Shares shall be a
> quorum for all purposes.' *c*

In art 85, under the heading 'Directors', appears the following:

> '(i) Unless and until otherwise determined by the Company by Special Resolu-
> tion the Directors shall be not less than two nor more than four in number.
> (ii) The holders for the time being of a majority of the Preferred "A" Shares
> shall be entitled by instrument in writing signed by them to appoint one Director *d*
> (in these Articles called an "A" Director), to remove any Director so appointed
> and to appoint another Director in his place. The first such "A" Director shall be
> Dr. Rudolph Braun. (iii) The holders for the time being of a majority of the
> Preferred "B" Shares shall be entitled by instrument in writing signed by them
> to appoint two Directors (in these Articles called "B" Directors), to remove any
> Director so appointed and to appoint another Director in his place. The first such *e*
> "B" Directors shall be Mr. Douglas Albert Coakley and Mr. Anthony Francis
> Coakley. (iv) Whenever a Director appointed pursuant to paragraph (ii) or (iii)
> of this Article vacates office, whether by death or otherwise the holders of the
> shares conferring the right of appointment of such Director shall be entitled by
> instrument in writing signed by a majority of the holders for the time being of
> such shares to appoint another Director in his place.' *f*

Article 91 deals with alternate directors and provides (in part) as follows:

> 'Each Director (other than an Alternate Director) may at any time appoint any
> person approved by a majority of the Directors for the time being appointed by
> the holders of the same class of shares as appointed him to be an alternate Director
> of the Company, and may at any time remove any alternate Director so appointed *g*
> by him from office and, subject to such approval as aforesaid, appoint another
> person in his place; Provided that an alternate Director appointed by an "A"
> Director shall be deemed to be an "A" Director and an alternate Director
> appointed by a "B" Director shall be deemed to be a "B" Director . . .'

I then refer to arts 112 and 113, under the heading 'Proceedings of Directors': *h*

> '112. The Directors may meet together for the dispatch of business, adjourn
> and otherwise regulate their meetings as they think fit. Except as otherwise
> agreed in writing by all the Directors no resolution shall be passed unless all the
> Directors present at the meeting vote in favour of it. Except as may be otherwise
> prescribed by the Company by Special Resolution the chairman shall not have a
> second or casting vote. A Director who is also an alternate Director shall be *j*
> entitled to a separate vote on behalf of the Director he is representing and in
> addition to his own vote. A Director may, and the Secretary on the requisition of
> a Director shall, at any time summon a meeting of the Directors. Ten days'
> notice of every meeting of the Directors shall be given to each Director in manner
> prescribed by these Articles and every such notice shall be accompanied by the

agenda of the meeting to which it relates. A Director may by instrument in writing sent to the Company waive the right to receive notice in any particular case and shall be deemed to have waived the right in respect of every Board Meeting at which he or his alternate is present.

'113. The quorum necessary for the transaction of the business of the Directors may be fixed by the Directors, and unless so fixed at any other number shall be three, at least one of whom shall be an "A" Director and one a "B" Director. For the purposes of this Article an alternate Director shall be counted in a quorum, but so that not less than two individuals shall constitute the quorum.'

There are other provisions in the articles which are intended to safeguard Topps's position, but I need not refer to them.

At this point I will anticipate events by saying that Dr Braun was at once replaced as the 'A' director by Eddie Shorin, who remained the 'A' director until March 1971. In that month Topps appointed Douglas Coakley as its 'A' director in his place. Two years later Topps removed him and appointed in his place John Sullivan, who was then Topps's international marketing director, but the Coakleys say that Douglas Coakley's removal and John Sullivan's appointment were invalid as Topps had abandoned the right conferred on it by art 85 by an oral agreement made on 3rd March 1971.

I turn now to the Shareholders' Agreement. It recites that Topps and the Coakleys are the beneficial owners of the whole of the issued share capital of the company; that the shares owned by Topps include all the issued preferred 'A' shares and that the holders for the time being of the preferred 'A' shares are entitled under the articles to appoint and remove a director, referred to as the ' "A" director'. It then provides as follows:

'EACH of them Topps and Messrs. Coakley hereby undertakes with each of the others of them to exercise all voting rights attached to all shares in the Company for the time being owned or controlled by him and all other powers and authorities possessed by him in relation to the Company in the following manner that is to say: (i) To ensure that no fees or other emoluments are paid to any Director of the Company without the consent of all the Directors thereof. (ii) To ensure that a committee of the Directors consisting of the Messrs. Coakley or the persons who are for the time being Directors appointed by the holders of a majority of the Preferred "B" Shares of the Company (hereinafter referred to as "B" Directors) shall be constituted for the purpose only of carrying on the routine business of the Company including the appointment and discharge of Executives (other than Directors) whose individual total remuneration shall not exceed £3000 per annum and servants of the Company and fixing their remuneration and entering into ordinary short term contracts which do not involve any policy decisions by the Company. (iii) To ensure that the Board of Directors of the Company shall not make any policy decisions or act thereon without all the "A" and the "B" Directors of the Company voting in favour of such policy decision. (iv) To ensure that the Company shall not make decisions on any of the following matters without unanimity of all the Shareholders.'

There then followed 19 separate matters, some of which are as follows:

'(i) the issue by the Company of any shares debentures or loan capital or the creation by the Company of any mortgages liens or charges (including a floating charge) upon or in respect of the business or undertaking or assets or any part thereof or the grant of any share or stock options; (ii) the lending or borrowing of money the giving of any guarantee or entering into any contract for indemnity or suretyship or for services or agency or any contract for hire or rent or hire purchase or purchase by way of credit sale where the individual amount involved exceeds £3000 . . . (v) the sale otherwise than in the normal course of trading of

any property of the Company or the purchase otherwise than in the normal course
of business of any property by the Company . . . (vii) allocations to reserves; (viii) *a*
payment or recommendations of dividends or any other distribution of capital or
profits; (ix) amounts to be written off assets or against profits in respect of bad
debts redundant obsolete or slow moving stock wear and tear and depreciation;
(x) the writing up or revaluation of any assets or change in the method of valuing
stock . . . (xii) the liquidation of the Company; (xiii) matters of policy affecting
sales . . . (xvii) the grant of any licences in respect of know-how or under any *b*
Letters Patent Trade Mark or similar monopoly rights for the time being owned
or controlled by or licensed to the Company or the acceptance termination or
renewal of any such licence; (xviii) the initiation or abandonment of any litigation
or arbitration.'

Then cl 2 provides:
c
'NOTWITHSTANDING anything in paragraph (viii) of Clause 1 hereof the parties
hereto hereby agree that unless otherwise agreed between them they will procure
that at least 60% of the net profits after tax of the Company available for distribution will be distributed as dividends to the Shareholders in each year.'

Clause 5 provides: 'THIS Agreement shall be read and construed in all respects
according to the law of England'; and the last clause, cl 6: 'THIS Agreement shall *d*
continue in force so long as any of the parties hereto own or control any capital in the
Company.' The Coakleys' case is that the whole of the agreement was nullified by
the alleged agreement of 3rd March 1971.

I can pass over much that is not material to my decision and come to the year 1970.
In that year the company was experiencing a grave liquidity problem. In April Lloyds
Bank, the company's bankers, refused them additional overdraft facilities and, in the *e*
same month, the company borrowed £40,000 from Topps on a short-term loan.
This was repaid in August, a month late.

By the end of 1970 the company's need of additional cash was acute, as Topps well
knew. Associated Industrial Consultants Ltd ('AIC') had been called in by the Coakleys to advise the company on various aspects of its affairs and in December 1970 they
made a report on the company's profit plan for 1970-71. This report showed that an *f*
overdraft of £245,000 would be needed in April 1971, but that by 30th September
1971, so far from being overdrawn, the Company should be in an 'in-hand' position to
the tune of £61,000, and the report forecast a net profit before tax for the year 1970-71
of £157,000. In fact during the year in question there was a change in the company's
financial year, and for the 18 months to 31st March 1971 it made a loss of £146,000 odd,
of which about £70,000 was a trading loss, while for the year ending 31st March 1972 *g*
it made a profit of about £19,000. In the event the AIC report was therefore grossly
over-optimistic, but on the strength of it Mr Douglas Coakley at the beginning of
February 1971 approached the National Westminister Bank on the introduction of
AIC and managed to negotiate a loan. On 12th February 1971 the bank wrote to
Douglas Coakley committing it to advances of up to £220,000 on the terms, inter alia,
that the Coakleys should give a joint and several guarantee for £25,000. That letter *h*
was not disclosed to Topps until the meeting of 3rd March 1971, to which I shall come
presently.

Meanwhile at the end of December or the beginning of January, Topps, who had
been warned by their London solicitors of the dangers of trading with knowledge of
insolvency, were very concerned about the Company's liquidity position and instructed
a firm of accountants, Binder Hamlyn & Co, to make an investigation and report on *i*
certain aspects of the company's affairs. Topps received their report on 17th February
1971. It was an unfavourable report and critical of the Coakleys' management. It
expressed the view that, even with better management, in order to survive the coming
months Topps should be prepared to provide a total of £369,000. A copy of the report
was at once made available to the Coakleys.

On 19th February an executive meeting of Topps considered the report and decided
a to keep the company functioning, and for that purpose to make funds available if, but
only if, it (Topps) had complete management control.

On 21st February 1971 Eddie Shorin came to London from New York, and on the
25th had a meeting with Mr Peter Tanswell, a chartered accountant and a member of
the firm of Charles Stuart & Co, who were the company's accountants and auditors.
John Sullivan was also present. The object of the meeting was to discuss the Binder
b Hamlyn report and to consider the courses of action which Topps felt were open to
the company in the light of the acute need for more working capital.

It was made clear that Topps was not prepared to advance further working capital
within the existing set-up, but that it would do so provided it took over complete
management responsibility and had a larger percentage of the company's equity
capital. On the other hand, if the company could arrange substantial additional capital,
c that would resolve the cash problem. No one at that meeting knew of the National
Westminster Bank's commitment, and Topps never imagined that the Coakleys
would be able to raise the money from any source other than Topps itself.

Peter Tanswell reported the proceedings of this meeting to Douglas Coakley by
letter on the same day. On the following day, the 26th, Eddie Shorin, Douglas Coakley
and John Denny of AIC had a meeting to discuss the Binder Hamlyn Report. John
d Sullivan was there for part of the meeting but left before the end. Denny was concerned to justify the AIC report and to fault that of Binder Hamlyn's.

There was no discussion of the terms on which Topps was prepared to advance
money to the company, nor of the National Westminster Bank facility. A further
meeting was arranged for 9 a m on Wednesday, 3rd March, at the Savoy Hotel, where
Eddie Shorin was staying. This meeting was attended by the Coakleys, Peter Tanswell
e and Eddie Shorin. I have heard accounts of what happened from all four persons who
were present; they differed from each other in a number of important respects. The
Coakleys' accounts were broadly to the same effect, but differed fundamentally from
that of Eddie Shorin. Peter Tanswell's version was somewhere between the two.

To decide where the truth lies is not easy. [His Lordship considered the evidence
and continued:] I do not propose to analyse the details of the evidence. But I say
f straight away that I am satisfied that no binding agreement of any sort was concluded
at the meeting of 3rd March. Eddie Shorin made it quite clear, certainly so far as
Peter Tanswell was concerned, that he had no authority to make any decision on
behalf of Topps and that he would have to communicate with his advisers and with
his brother Joel, the president of Topps, before anything was regarded as settled.
There is a difference of testimony between Peter Tanswell and Eddie Shorin as to the
g purpose for which Eddie Shorin needed to consult his advisers and his brother, but
both agreed that no finality was reached at the meeting.

The Coakleys may have failed to take this in, because their focus of attention was
the success or failure of a plan (I might almost say a trap) devised by Douglas Coakley.
This was to keep the National Westminster Bank commitment well up his sleeve until
he had clarified Topps's terms for putting money into the company and found out
h whether Topps would be prepared to accord to the Coakleys, if they were to find the
necessary finance, the same treatment as Topps was demanding for itself as the price
of finding it, that is to say, complete management responsibility and control. I have
little doubt that at an early stage of the meeting Douglas Coakley put this point to
Eddie Shorin and that Eddie Shorin expressed the opinion that Topps might well be
prepared to concur. Eddie Shorin has no recollection of this, and so far as he was
j concerned I am sure that this was no more than an irrelevancy which made no impression on his mind and which was certainly not intended to have any legal consequences. At this stage he had no knowledge of Douglas Coakley's arrangements with
the National Westminster Bank. But the expression of assent, or qualified assent,
which Douglas Coakley got in answer to his enquiry has been seized on by the Coakleys
and elevated into an oral contract to abrogate the shareholders' agreement and such of

the articles of association as would stand in the way of their exclusive management
control. Having got his answer, Douglas Coakley then announced the National *a*
Westminster Bank commitment.

There was no mention at the meeting, however, of either the shareholders' agreement or of the articles, and the question of what was meant by management control
was not discussed. Douglas Coakley then produced to the meeting a form of debenture
in favour of the National Westminster Bank, and Peter Tanswell, who had been asked
by Douglas Coakley to bring the company's seal to the meeting, produced it and the *b*
seal was affixed. The Coakleys signed the debenture, either then or on the following
day, but Eddie Shorin was not willing to be party to the borrowing on his own responsibility because he was not aware of what representations had been made to the
bank in order to induce the advance, and was very conscious of Binder Hamlyn's
adverse report.

It was left that Eddie Shorin would get in touch with his advisers and with his *c*
brother in New York and communicate Topps's decision whether to approve the
National Westminster Bank loan next day. He at once got in touch with Binder
Hamlyn and Herbert Oppenheimer, Nathan & Vandyk, Topps's London solicitors,
and with Joel Shorin.

Messrs Oppenheimers came up with an entirely new idea which no one had previously thought of and which had not been adumbrated at the meeting. This was that *d*
Eddie Shorin should resign as the 'A' director (that is to say, as Topps's nominee)
and that Topps should appoint Douglas Coakley as its 'A' director in Eddie Shorin's
place. This would place management control in the hands of the Coakleys, who
would then be the only directors, and relieve Topps from the responsibility of having
to turn down the National Westminster Bank loan on account of the risks to which
its approval might expose Eddie Shorin and, through him, Topps. *e*

Having got Joel Shorin's approval to this solution, on the following day, 4th March,
Eddie Shorin telephoned Douglas Coakley, Anthony Coakley and Peter Tanswell and
informed them of Topps's decision. This was accepted by the Coakleys and shortly
afterwards Eddie Shorin resigned from the Board and Topps appointed Douglas
Coakley its 'A' director.

Had it been necessary to decide the question, I should have concluded that nothing *f*
that happened on 4th March operated to abrogate the shareholders' agreement nor
to alter the articles of association of the company, and in particular Topps's right to
remove Douglas Coakley and appoint another 'A' director in his place. But it is not
necessary to decide the question because, as I have already said, the Coakleys rest
their case on what happened on the 3rd and do not suggest that Topps made any
irrevocable commitment on the 4th. *g*

I can pass over the events of the next two years during which Douglas Coakley
continued as 'A' director, but in March 1973, for reasons of dissatisfaction into which
I need not enter, Topps removed him and appointed John Sullivan as its 'A' director
in his place. Notification of this was given to the Coakleys without evoking any protest
on their part. John Sullivan, in turn, appointed Eddie Shorin to be his alternate *h*
director.

Up to that time there had been no clear assertion on the Coakleys' part that the
shareholders' agreement was at an end or that the company's articles were not in full
force, but on 15th June 1973, over two years after the meeting of 3rd March 1971,
they put forward for the first time the categorical claim that the shareholders' agreement was cancelled by mutual agreement on 3rd March 1971. They did this as a *j*
result of changing their solicitors a few days earlier, and they have maintained that
attitude ever since. Hence this petition. It is true that, as early as 21st July 1971,
Douglas Coakley wrote to Joel Shorin a letter drafted for him by his solicitor saying
(and I quote):

'Eddy proposed that if we . . . could obtain the finance we should correspondingly a have the full right and responsibility of running the Company and at the same time I feel sure both Peter [Tanswell] and ourselves and Eddy meant this to abrogate the restrictions of the Stockholders Agreement.'

Douglas Coakley now says that it was he and not Eddie Shorin who made the proposal, but the point which I wish to make is that the passage which I have quoted is to my mind tentative and lacks conviction, and subsequent correspondence and conversa-
b tions lead me to believe that Coakleys were always uncertain what effect the alleged Savoy Hotel agreement had on the shareholders' agreement or the company's articles of association and were unable to make up their minds about it.

On 29th July Joel Shorin replied to Douglas Coakley's letter maintaining that the shareholders' agreement remained in existence. He accepted the possibility of its need for revision and asked Douglas Coakley to tell him what provisions he wanted changed,
c but Douglas Coakley never replied to this invitation.

The petition in this case was presented on 20th September 1973 and the hearing was fixed for 4th June of this year. On 6th May 1974 the Coakleys' solicitors, Messrs Titmuss, Sainer & Webb, wrote a letter containing an open offer of settlement to Topps's solicitors, Messrs Freshfields. Much has been made of this letter and I will read it:

d
  'Dear Sirs, A. & B.C. Chewing Gum Ltd. As a basis for a settlement of the differences between our respective Clients we are instructed to put forward an open offer to dispose of the winding-up petition by the purchase by our Clients of your Clients shares in the Company or, alternatively, by the sale by our Clients of their shares in the Company. In our Clients opinion the net worth of the Company is £495,000. Accordingly, our Clients would be willing to sell their
e two-thirds interest in the Ordinary and Preference share capital to yours at £330,000 or to buy your Clients one-third holding at £165,000. This offer will remain open for acceptance in either form until withdrawn.'

Messrs Freshfields replied on 17th May as follows:

f
  'We refer to your letter of 6 May. We referred this to our Clients and the Board of Directors of our Clients have now been able to give us their instructions. They have asked us to record their surprise that your Clients should, at this stage, decide to put forward such offers, particularly as our Clients are almost completely unacquainted with the current position of the Company. Our Clients regret that, for the time being, they are unable to take any decision with regard
g to either of the offers put forward in your letter on account of their not having available to them the material facts upon which they could judge whether or not the figure of £495,000 which your Clients considered to be the net worth of the Company is realistic.'

I pause there to say that we know now that it was quite unrealistic, being based on the
h ever over-optimistic Douglas Coakley's assessment that the company would make an annual profit of at least £90,000 before tax, and using the arbitrary figure of seven as a multiplier. The letter then goes on:

  'Furthermore, your letter does not indicate whether our Clients are to be given any opportunity of conducting the detailed investigation into the Company's affairs which they would consider necessary in order to be able to evaluate the
j offers indicated in your letter, indeed, your letter does not suggest that our Clients can conduct any investigation, however limited, into the Company's affairs. It also fails to indicate [and there are four specific matters set out, to which I need not, I think, refer].'

On 20th May Messrs Titmuss, Sainer & Webb wrote again saying this:

'Thank you for your letter of 17 May. We are not clear what is meant by the "detailed investigation" which your clients consider necessary to evaluate the *a* offers which have been made, but we are sure that the Company's Auditors should be able to provide sufficient information to enable your clients to assess whether the estimate of net worth is realistic, or if unrealistic, in which direction. You will appreciate that the double nature of the offer exposed our clients to risk if their estimate should be either too high or too low. We suggest that you should tell us in more detail what information is required and we shall forward *b* this to the Company's Auditors or arrange for your Accountants to see them, [and they then deal with the four matters to which I referred].'

Messrs Freshfields replied on 29th May, saying this:

'We refer to your letter of 20th May. It has to be appreciated that our Clients are now virtually unacquainted with the present position of the Company and with *c* respect it is not thought that the auditors are in a position to supply our Clients with all the necessary information, since the most recent accounts which they have audited are those ending in March 1973. Furthermore, our Clients, before coming to any decision on your Clients' offers, would wish to make the same investigations as of those normally made in the case of a transaction involving shares in a private company; these are far wider than the inquiries normally made by accountants *d* for an annual audit. We are therefore instructed that our Clients are unwilling to consider whether to act on your Clients' offers without first being given the full opportunity to inspect the books and the affairs of the Company as would normally be the case. We, of course, appreciate that your Clients' offer is to sell their shares or to purchase our Clients' shares at a corresponding price. You pointed out in your letter that your Clients' offers exposed them to risks if their estimate *e* should be either too high or too low. The relevance of this point escapes us, since the double nature of the offer itself, exposes our Clients if they buy at too high a price or sell at too low a price Your Clients from their own position are indeed able to evaluate the risk to which they are exposing themselves. Our Clients, from their position, which is not a voluntary one, are unable to make a similar evaluation. This position postulated by your Clients, must on any view, be re- *f* garded as unacceptable. Not only would our Clients require full access to the Company's books and affairs, but they would wish to be able to have discussions *)* with management in order to evaluate the present trends of the Company's affairs in the light of the particular circumstances which currently face the confectionery industry, and they would also wish to consider the Company's position in the light of the fire which occurred last autumn. It was stated at the recent *g* Annual General Meeting that there were considerable insurance claims outstanding. The outcome of such must materially affect the net worth of the Company. In the circumstances, we can do no more than to say again that our Clients do not have the information which they consider necessary to form a view as to the acceptability as to either of your two offers. To accept either offer on the basis of the information presently available to our clients would hardly be consistent *h* with reasonable commercial prudence.'

Then the same four points are dealt with. Finally, on 30th May, Messrs Titmuss, Sainer & Webb wrote to Messrs Freshfields:

'Thank you for your letter of 29th May, 1974. Our clients do not wish to conceal any information which your clients may require; our suggestion that your clients *j* or their accountants meet the Company's auditors was intended merely to meet the practical difficulty that when our clients' offer was made, the hearing of the petition was only some four weeks off. Now, of course, there is no chance of even the most cursory inquiries before the proceedings are heard. If your clients consider that there is a reasonable prospect of their proposed investigation producing a sale a   or purchase along the lines we have proposed, we should be prepared to join in an application to stand the hearing out of the list. If not, we must treat our offer as rejected.'

Topps was not willing to have the case stood out of the list for an indefinite and possibly long period, and so the case came on as arranged.

b   In my judgment that offer, which was made very late in the day, and invited a lot of investigation, cannot weigh heavily in the balance. Nor, I think, can the plea made by Mr Douglas Coakley in the last paragraph of his affidavit, where he says this:

'The essence of the dispute between Topps and ourselves is over the effect of the Savoy Hotel agreement. We are of course willing to accept any ruling which this Honourable Court may think it appropriate to make in these or other proceedings and to undertake to give full effect to whatever rights Topps may be
c   declared to have, or to have the question decided by arbitration. But we respectfully submit that it is neither just nor equitable, in the interests of the shareholders or the Company's employees or in the public interest that the Company should be wound up.'

But the damage has already been done, and the relationship between Topps and the
d   Coakleys destroyed, and I am satisfied that it cannot be restored.

Finally, so far as the law is concerned, there is really no dispute. I was referred to what I may call the 'partnership' cases, culminating in *Ebrahimi v Westbourne Galleries Ltd*[1]. In that case it was held by the House of Lords that it is wrong to create categories or headings under which cases must be brought if the 'just and equitable' principle is to apply; the generality of the words 'just and equitable' is not to be reduced in that way. It was also held that although the just and equitable provision
e   did not entitle one party to disregard the obligations he had assumed by entering the company, nor entitled the court to dispense him from them, it did entitle the court to subject the exercise of legal rights to equitable considerations. But as counsel for Topps pointed out in the present case, it is from its legal rights—that is to say, from its contractual rights—that Topps has been excluded by the refusal of the Coakleys to recognise the removal of Douglas Coakley and the appointment of John Sullivan
f   as 'A' director pursuant to the power conferred by art 85.

Counsel for the respondents submitted that the facts in the present case are totally different from those in the *Westbourne Galleries* case[1], as, indeed, they are. He pointed out, for instance, that there is no question of a previous partnership before Topps came into the company; that Topps made no direct investment of capital in the company but merely bought Dr Braun's share; and that Topps could, if it wished, get its money
g   out of the company by accepting the Coakleys' offer to buy its shares. He submitted that a winding-up order would destroy the company's licence, and that the petition was based on that objective and not on any shareholder consideration. He also submitted that, if Topps was right about the so-called Savoy Hotel agreement, other relief in the form of declarations and injunctions was open to them, and that the making of a winding-up order would do damage to the Coakleys far in excess of any damage
h   done to Topps by refusing such an order.

I have considered all these submissions carefully but, in the end, I have to come to the conclusion that I ought to exercise my discretion by making a winding-up order. The fact remains that the Coakleys have repudiated the relationship established by the shareholders' agreement and the articles. The case is, in my judgment, analogous
j   to the expulsion type of case which the House of Lords was considering in the *Westbourne Galleries* case[1], although, as I have said, this is not a case of one side making use of its legal rights to the prejudice of the other. The Coakleys had no legal right to do what they have done. In the *Westbourne Galleries* case[2] Lord Wilberforce said:

1   [1972] 2 All ER 492, [1973] AC 360
2   [1972] 2 All ER at 500, 501, [1973] AC at 380

'My Lords, this is an expulsion case, and I must briefly justify the application in such cases of the just and equitable clause. The question is, as always, whether *a* it is equitable to allow one (or two) to make use of his legal rights to the prejudice of his associate(s). The law of companies recognises the right, in many ways, to remove a director from the board. Section 184 of the Companies Act 1948 confers this right on the company in general meeting whatever the articles may say. Some articles may prescribe other methods, for example, a governing director may have the power to remove (cf *Re Wondoflex Textiles Pty Ltd*[1]). And quite apart *b* from removal powers, there are normally provisions for retirement of directors by rotation so that their re-election can be opposed and defeated by a majority, or even by a casting vote. In all these ways a particular director-member may find himself no longer a director, through removal, or non-re-election: this situation he must normally accept, unless he undertakes the burden of proving fraud or mala fides. The just and equitable provision nevertheless comes to his assistance *c* if he can point to, and prove, some special underlying obligation of his fellow member(s) in good faith, or confidence, that so long as the business continues he shall be entitled to management participation, an obligation so basic that if broken, the conclusion must be that the association must be dissolved. And the principles on which he may do so are those worked out by the courts in partnership cases where there has been exclusion from management (see *Const v Harris*[2]) *d* even where under the partnership agreement there is a power of expulsion (see *Blisset v Daniel*[3] and Lindley on Partnership[4]).'

There Lord Wilberforce speaks of entitlement to management participation as being an obligation so basic that, if broken, the conclusion must be that the association must be dissolved.

In the present case management participation was secured by Topps's right to *e* appoint and remove an 'A' director, and that entitlement has been repudiated. I do not read the passage which I have read from Lord Wilberforce's speech as depriving me of a discretion, but in the exercise of that discretion I propose to make a winding-up order.

It is not for me to say what effect this may have on the company's licence, but it *f* would not, in my judgment, be just or equitable to deprive Topps of its remedy merely in order to preserve the benefit of the licence for the company.

That brings me to the action. It is an action by Topps against the Coakleys and the company, claiming a declaration and certain consequential relief. The declaration which it claims is this.

'A Declaration that any and every payment which has been made out of the *g* funds of the third Defendant in or towards payment of any costs or expenses of, or otherwise for or with a view to financing or assisting, any defence or opposition (by the Defendants or any one or more of them) to the Petition presented by the Plaintiff to this Honourable Court on the 20th September, 1973 for the winding-up of the third Defendant . . . involved a breach by the first and second Defendants and each of them of the Articles of Association of the third Defendant and a breach *h* of their fiduciary duties as directors of the third Defendant.'

It is common ground that if, at all material times, John Sullivan was a director of the company, as I hold him to have been, the action must succeed and I will hear counsel as to the appropriate form of order.

Winding-up order. Respondent directors to pay petitioners' costs. Declaration granted in *j*
petitioners' action.

1 [1951] VLR 458
2 (1824) Turn & R 496 at 525, [1824-34] All ER Rep 311 at 315
3 (1853) 10 Hare 493
4 13th Edn (1971), pp 331, 595

[An application was then made on behalf of the respondents for a stay to be granted
a on the order winding up the company.]

PLOWMAN J. As I understand it, the position is this. First of all, as a matter of
jurisdiction it is quite clear that I have jurisdiction to grant a stay, because the Companies Act 1948 says so. It says I can grant a stay on proof to my satisfaction that
b the proceedings ought to be stayed. But then there is the question of practice,
and as a matter of practice a stay is never granted. The only exception that I think is
known to the Department of Trade is where I myself once went wrong in the *Westbourne Galleries* case[1], and not having been alerted to the position, and not knowing it
before, I granted a stay, with precisely what consequences nobody has ever told me.
But there are very good reasons for the practice of never ordering a stay, and they are
c these: as soon as a winding-up order has been made the Official Receiver has to
ascertain first of all the assets at the date of the order; secondly, the assets at the date
of the presentation of the petition, having regard to the possible repercussions of
s 227 of the 1948 Act; and thirdly, the liabilities of the company at the date of the order,
so that he can find out who the preferential creditors are, and also the unsecured
creditors.
d   Supposing there is an appeal and the winding-up order is ultimately affirmed by
the Court of Appeal, and there has been a stay, his ability to discover all these things
is very seriously hampered; it makes it very difficult for him, possibly a year later, to
ascertain what the position was at different times a year previously. But assuming a
stay is not granted, if the business is being carried on at a profit, as I understand this
business now is, really no additional harm has been done once the winding-up order
e has been made by refusing a stay. As I understand it, if the Official Receiver is given an
indemnity, say by the Coakley brothers, who are running this business, he will allow
it to be carried on, and the Coakley brothers, in this case, could be appointed special
managers and carry on the business as they have been doing. If the business is being
carried on at a profit, creditors of the business, after the date of the winding-up order,
would be paid in priority to the unsecured creditors at the date of the order as part of
f the expenses of the winding-up. Then, if the appeal is allowed, the business is handed
back as a going concern, it has not suffered any loss. Of course, if the business can
only be carried on at a loss—it should not be carried on at a loss, obviously.
Those, I think, are really the reasons why, in practice, a stay is not granted—a
profitable business can be carried on as it was before and handed back as a going
concern if the appeal is allowed. If it is not allowed then, of course, cadit quaestio.

g   [Counsel for the company, Mr D A Williams of the Official Receiver's Department
and counsel for Topps addressed the court. Plowman J, having indicated that the
petitioners might be in difficulty if, in the event of the company being wound up,
they exercised a power to revoke the licence which they had granted to the company
and then the company successfully appealed against the order, refused to grant a
h stay.]

Application refused.

Solicitors: *Freshfields* (for Topps); *Titmuss, Sainer & Webb* (for the company and
defendant shareholders).

i
                                                        Jacqueline Metcalfe Barrister.

---

1   [1972] 2 All ER 492, [1973] AC 360

K v JMP Co Ltd

Dicta of Stephenson LJ at 1039,
1041 applied in Mehmet v Perry
[1977] 2 All ER 529

COURT OF APPEAL, CIVIL DIVISION

CAIRNS, STEPHENSON LJJ AND GRAHAM J

3rd, 20th DECEMBER 1974

Fatal accident – Damages – Assessment – Pecuniary loss – Children – Illegitimate children – Provision made by deceased father for mother – Father and mother living together but unmarried – Cessation of provision for mother representing pecuniary loss to children – Mother entitled to social security benefits – Father having made provision for family holidays – Social security benefits not covering cost of holidays – Cessation of expenditure by father on mother's holidays representing a pecuniary loss to children – Children entitled to recover damages in respect of loss.

Fatal accident – Damages – Assessment – Dependency – Children – Period of dependency – Commencement – Appropriate multiplier – Whether period of dependency starting from date of death or date of trial.

National insurance – Supplementary benefit – Entitlement – Aggregation of requirements and resources – Person having to provide for requirements of another person – Meaning of 'requirements' – Other person child under age of 16 – Mother providing for children – Children having sufficient independent means to provide for necessities of life – Mother not having to provide for children's necessities – Whether 'requirements' limited to payments for necessities of life – Whether mother having to provide for children's 'requirements' – Whether children's resources to be aggregated with mother's for purpose of determining her entitlement to supplementary benefit – Ministry of Social Security Act 1966, Sch 2, para 3(2).

The father and the mother started to live together in 1964. They did not marry. They had three children born in March 1965, April 1966 and December 1968 respectively. The father was the breadwinner of the family, earning on average £70 a week for 40 weeks of the year and nothing for the rest of the year. The father and the mother both looked after the children, the father paying each year certain sums of money on housekeeping, outings, air fares for holidays in Ireland, food during the holidays, rent, electricity, television and washing machine instalments. In 1971 the father was killed in an accident for which the defendants admitted liability. The mother continued to look after the children on her own, drawing social security benefits. The children brought an action, by their mother as next friend, against the defendants for damages under the Fatal Accidents Acts 1846 to 1959 for the loss that they had suffered from their father's death. The defendants accepted that the pecuniary loss suffered by the children as a result of the father's death included the sums of money spent by the father on them in respect of housekeeping and holiday food, and the cost of their own outings etc. The judge held, however, that since the father had, during his lifetime, provided for the children to be looked after in the house, and to be accompanied on holidays and outings by their mother, the loss suffered by the children also included those parts of the father's expenditure provided for the mother's food, air fares, outings and electricity, which formed, indirectly, a provision for the children and that accordingly the children's pecuniary loss included all the father's expenditure on the family other than expenditure on himself. He assessed the combined loss at £1,977 which he apportioned equally between the children but applied different multipliers according to their respective ages on the basis that they would not have been dependent on the father after the age of 16. The multipliers were based on a period of dependency starting from the date of the trial. Making the usual adjustments the judge arrived at multipliers of five for the eldest child, six for the middle child and eight for the youngest resulting in awards of £3,295, £3,954 and £5,272 respectively.

The defendants appealed against those awards and the children cross-appealed,
a contending, inter alia, that, although the mother had been in receipt of supplementary benefits for herself and the children since the father's death, once damages had
been awarded to the children to supply their own immediate needs their resources
would have to be aggregated with those of the mother, under para 3(2)^a of Sch 2 to
the Ministry of Social Security Act 1966, and she would therefore lose her entitlement
to benefits.
b

Held – (i) The mother would not lose her entitlement to social security benefits
following an award of damages to the children, since she would not be a person who
had to 'provide for the requirements of' the children, within para 3(2) of Sch 2 to the
1966 Act; the word 'requirements' meant requirements in respect of payments for
the necessities of life and those had all been provided for by the uncontested part of
c the damages awarded to the children. It followed that the resources of the children
would not have to be aggregated with those of the mother under para 3(2) for the purpose of determining her entitlement to social security benefits and she would therefore be able to draw supplementary benefits at the normal rate for a single person
(see p 1036 e and f, p 1039 a and b and p 1043 d, post).

(ii) (Graham J dissenting) As the mother had continued to look after the children
d after the father's death, the change in her resources only constituted a pecuniary loss
to the children to the extent that the care given by her was diminished by the loss of
the father's support, which depended on the extent to which the mother would be
supported by supplementary benefits. The supplementary benefits received by her
covered her necessary living expenses but did not cover the luxuries provided for
her by the father. Consequently the sums of money spent by the father on her house-
e keeping and holiday food were to be deducted from the sums arrived at by the
judge in assessing the annual loss of the children; on the other hand the air fares
and outings were luxuries which supplementary benefit would not cover. Accordingly
the father's expenditure on the mother's fares were to be regarded as a payment
made to enable the children to enjoy the holidays and outings and the cessation of
those payments represented a pecuniary loss to the children. On that basis the
f annual sum for each child should be reduced from £659 to £548 (see p 1036 b c and g
to j, p 1038 b d g and h and p 1039 h to p 1040 a, post).

(iii) Although there was a slight chance that the children might have continued to
be dependent on their father beyond the age of 16, that age was nonetheless the
appropriate age taking into account the risks of accident, illness or unemployment
which might have occurred to the father before the children reached 16. However,
g the period of dependency ought to have been reckoned from the date of the father's
death and not from the date of the trial. Accordingly the multiplier in each case
should be increased by two, resulting in increased awards of £3,836 for the eldest
child, £4,384 for the middle child and £5,480 for the youngest. The defendants'
appeal would therefore be dismissed and the cross-appeal allowed to that extent
(see p 1036 j to p 1037 e, p 1040 b and j, p 1041 c and p 1045 j to p 1046 a, post).
h

Notes
For the pecuniary loss sustained by claimants under the Fatal Accidents Acts, see 28
Halsbury's Laws (3rd Edn) 101-103, para 111, and for cases on the subject, see 36 Digest
(Repl) 211-214, 1111-1132.

For the aggregation of requirements and resources for the purpose of calculating
j entitlement to supplementary benefit, see Supplement to 27 Halsbury's Laws (3rd
Edn) para 947A, 2.

For the Ministry of Social Security Act 1966, Sch 2, para 3, see 23 Halsbury's Statutes
(3rd Edn) 721.

---

a Paragraph 3(2), so far as material, is set out at p 1036 d, post

Cases referred to in judgments

Daish v Wauton [1972] 1 All ER 25, [1972] 2 QB 262, [1972] 2 WLR 29, CA.　　　　*a*

Hay v Hughes p 257, ante, [1975] 2 WLR 34, CA.

Kelliker v Ground Explorations [1955] CLY 741.

Monarch Steamship Co Ltd v A/B Karlshamns Oljefabriker [1949] 1 All ER 1, [1949] AC 196, [1949] LJR 772, 82 Lloyd LR 137, 1949 SC (HL) 1, 1949 SLT 51, HL, 41 Digest (Repl) 362, 1549.

Parry v Cleaver [1969] 1 All ER 555, [1970] AC 1, [1969] 2 WLR 821, [1969] 1 Lloyd's　*b*
Rep 183, HL, Digest (Cont Vol C) 750, 1061e.

Phipps (suing as next friend of three infants), Setterfield v Cunard White Star Co Ltd [1951] 1 TLR 359, [1951] 1 Lloyd's Rep 54, 36 Digest (Repl) 222, 1185.

Sullivan v Saintey (13th February 1959) unreported.

Watson, Laidlaw & Co Ltd v Pott, Cassels & Williamson (1914) 31 RPC 104, HL.

　　　　c

Case also cited

Donnelly v Joyce [1973] 3 All ER 475, [1974] 1 QB 454, CA.

Appeal

The defendants appealed against the judgment of Forbes J given on 23rd May 1974　*d*
awarding the plaintiffs, the three illegitimate children of the deceased father, the sum of £12,521 damages under the Fatal Accidents Acts 1846 to 1959. The defendants had admitted liability and the sole issue at the trial was the amount of the damages. The appeal related solely to the awards under the Fatal Accidents Acts. By a respondent's notice the plaintiffs sought to have the damages awarded to them increased. The facts are set out in the judgment of Cairns LJ.　　　　　　　　　　　*e*

Michael Wright QC and Stephen Desch for the defendants.
Lord Gifford for the plaintiffs.

　　　　　　　　　　　　　　　　　　　　　　　　　　Cur adv vult

　　　　　　　　　　　　　　　　　　　　　　　　　　　　　f

20th December. The following judgments were read.

CAIRNS LJ. On 23rd May 1974 Forbes J gave judgment for the plaintiffs in an action under the Fatal Accidents Acts. The plaintiffs are the three illegitimate children of a father who was killed in an accident for which the defendants were　*g*
admittedly responsible. The damages as apportioned were: £3,295 for the eldest child, £3,954 for the second one and £5,272 for the youngest, together with interest. Costs were awarded to the next friend (the mother) on a common fund basis. The defendants appeal, contending that the damages are excessive and that the costs awarded should have been party and party costs only. The children cross-appeal, contending that the damages are insufficient.　　　　　　　　　　　　　*h*

The father and the mother lived together without being married from 1964 until the father died in consequence of the accident on 19th July 1971. The three plaintiffs are their children, the eldest born on 10th March 1965, the middle one born on 20th April 1966 and the youngest born on 29th December 1968. The father was an Irish builders' labourer, who was not in the service of an employer but worked as a subcontractor. It was found by the trial judge and is not now in issue that his average　*i*
earnings were £70 a week for 40 weeks in the year; for the other 12 weeks he either could not get work or was on holiday. He was a generous man, providing all the necessaries of life for the mother and the children, together with toys, long holidays in Ireland and trips to relations at Leeds.

The following further figures (based on estimates and averages) are now common

ground: the father handed to the mother each year £1,170 to cover 40 weeks' house-
a keeping; the cost of his own keep for those weeks was £320, leaving a balance of £850
for the mother and children; he paid £180 for food for the family during holidays etc
and of that his own consumption cost £72, leaving a balance of £108; air fares to
Ireland were paid by him and the cost for one adult and three children was £110 a
year; other outings, on a similar basis, cost £150; he paid £150 for the children's
clothes and toys; finally he paid for rent, electricity, television and washing machine
b instalments, the total for all these being £609, of which £130 was for electricity.

Now the defendants have always accepted that the children's pecuniary loss resulting from the death of their father included their share of the housekeeping and holiday
food, the cost of their own air fares and outings, the whole cost of their clothes and
toys and the whole cost of rent, television and washing machine. It was however
claimed on behalf of the children that those parts of the father's expenditure which
c provided for the mother's food, air fares, outings and electricity formed indirectly a
provision for the children and accordingly that the pecuniary loss of the three children
taken together was the total of the aforementioned sums of £850, £108, £110, £150,
£150, and £609, that is, £1,977 altogether. The basis of this claim was that during the
lifetime of the father he provided for them to be looked after in the house, and accompanied on holidays and outings, by their mother. Not having similar provision made
d for them after his death, they suffered a loss which could be measured by the amount
of the payments made to support the mother and enable her to travel with them.
(The mother's clothes seem to have been overlooked.)

This argument was accepted by the learned judge. Accordingly he assessed the
combined loss of the three children at £1,977. He apportioned this equally between
them and to the figure of £659 so arrived at he applied different multipliers according
e to the ages of the children. Their ages at the time of the trial being nine, eight and
five respectively he considered that each child could have expected the support of the
father (barring accidents) up to the age of 16, i e for seven, eight and 11 years respectively, and he adjusted these downward on usual principles to arrive at multipliers of
five, six and eight which produced (though there was a small arithmetical error in
the case of two of the children) the sums mentioned at the beginning of this judgment.
f The defendants contend that there was no justification for treating the sums
expended by the father for the benefit of the mother as a provision for the children or
for treating the discontinuance of those expenditures as a loss to the children. There
was no evidence that the mother had not continued to devote the same care to the
children since the father's death as she had done before (they lived on supplementary
benefit up to the trial). Therefore, it is argued, the figures for the annual losses should
g be reduced by deducting, as attributable to the mother, £334 from the housekeeping
and holiday food, £24 from the air fares, £64 from the expenditure on other outings
and £26 from the electricity account. This would come to a total annual deduction of
£470 and would reduce the apportioned damages by £783, £939 and £1,253
respectively. The defendants do not quarrel with the multipliers.

The children, while contending that the assessment of the annual loss was made on
h the right basis, do not criticise the way in which the defendants arrive at the figures
for deductions if it be held that such deductions must be made. They do, however,
by their cross-appeal, contend that the multipliers are too low because the judge
failed to take into account that any of the children might have continued to be dependent on their father beyond the age of 16 either wholly (during a period of further
education) or partially (while earning a low wage after leaving school). A further
j point which was raised by the court during the hearing of the appeal was whether the
judge was mistaken in considering the period covered by the loss of support as dating
only from the time of the trial in 1974 instead of from the death in 1971.

In approaching the main problem raised by the defendants' appeal we are struck,
as was the learned judge, by the fact that although Parliament in 1934 extended the
benefit of the Fatal Accidents Acts to illegitimate children, the Acts still make no

provision for a woman who, outside matrimony, has lived with a man for many years, depended on him and mothered his children. While recognising the harshness of this state of the law, counsel for the defendants has warned us of the danger of, in effect, putting the mother, contrary to the intention of Parliament, in the same position as if she had been a lawful wife by awarding damages to the children equivalent to her own loss of dependency.

It is strange that in the 40 years since 1934 there appear to have been no reported cases in which a claim has been made on the basis which succeeded in this case. Indeed the industry of counsel has been able to unearth no more than three cases relating to claims under the Fatal Accidents Acts by or on behalf of illegitimate children; and the most that can be said of them is that it is unlikely that a claim in respect of the mother's support was made in any of them.

Two of these cases are briefly noted in Kemp and Kemp on the Quantum of Damages[1]. In *Kelliker v Ground Explorations*[2] Byrne J awarded £500 damages to an illegitimate child who was aged three weeks at the date of the death of the putative father, on the basis that if the father had lived the mother would probably have obtained about £1 a week under an affiliation order. Since the money payable under such an order does not include anything for the support of the mother it is clear that Byrne J did not take that into account as something which the child had lost. In *Sullivan v Saintey*[3], decided by Donovan J on 13th February 1959, the child was aged about ten, the deceased father had lived with the mother for some ten years and there was an affiliation order in the sum of 7s 6d a week, but it had not been enforced because all three had been living together. The child was awarded £165 for the loss of the 'future benefit of the order'. So here again nothing was allowed for the loss of support of the mother, though it would seem probable that she had been dependent on the deceased.

The nearest one can get to a pronouncement on the present issue is in an Admiralty case, *Phipps (suing as next friend of three infants), Setterfield v Cunard*[4] where Willmer J upheld an award by the Admiralty registrar of a total of £500 to the mother of three illegitimate children of a deceased seaman, the mother suing on behalf of the children. While intimating that he might have made a rather larger award if he had been dealing with the case in the first instance, Willmer J quoted without disapproval this passage from the registrar's report[5]:

'"Plaintiff's counsel invited me to deal with the claim on the basis of the plaintiff herself claiming. On the facts it was quite clear that Miss Phipps ran the home and maintained the children and was certainly dependent on the deceased. Unfortunately for her, she is not a dependent within the meaning of the Fatal Accidents Acts, and I [found] it impossible to make an award on the basis of her claiming when in fact she was not claiming and in law could not claim. Nor could I award to the three children such a sum as would include the amount I would have awarded to the plaintiff if she had been entitled to claim. The children, nevertheless, shared in the benefit which their mother derived from the payments made to her by the deceased. The share in the mother's benefit they lost when their father died and by reason of their mother's inability to claim under the Fatal Accidents Acts, were never able to recover. In assessing their awards I took into account the benefit which each of them thereby lost".'

So there the children's damages were assessed on substantially the same basis as that for which the defendants contend here. The 'invitation' made in that case by the

---

1 2nd Edn (1962), vol 2, pp 253, 254
2 [1955] CLY 741, cited in Kemp and Kemp on Damages (2nd Edn, 1962), vol 2, p 253
3 (13th February 1959) unreported; cited in Kemp and Kemp on Damages (2nd Edn, 1962), vol 2, p 254
4 [1951] 1 TLR 359
5 [1951] 1 TLR at 360

plaintiff's counsel was however a bolder one than that made here by the children and accepted by the judge; it has never been suggested in this case that the children could be awarded the full sum which the mother could have claimed as a lawful widow—which would have involved a multiplier much higher than any here used.

There has been a considerable development in recent years both in personal injuries cases and in fatal accident cases, of the principle that a plaintiff can recover damages measured by a figure representing reasonable remuneration for a wife or relative or friend who has voluntarily rendered services to the plaintiff by way of nursing or care made necessary by the injuries or death. None of the decisions is at all near to the present case because here the care which the mother gives to the children is not something made necessary by the death but is a continuation of care which was exercised before the death. There are however some passages in the judgments in the recent decision of this court in *Hay v Hughes*[1] to which reference may be made.

In that case a husband and wife had both been fatally injured in an accident and the action was brought on behalf of their two sons, aged $4\frac{1}{2}$ and $2\frac{1}{2}$, for pecuniary loss caused by both deaths. The claim arising from the mother's death was that after it occurred the boys' grandmother took over their care, without asking for payment. (She did later ask for payment on legal advice but this was treated as irrelevant.) This court (Lord Edmund-Davies, Buckley and Ormrod LJJ) upheld the decision of Reeve J allowing this claim. There was a very full review of the earlier cases. The main grounds of the judgments were that the boys had suffered a pecuniary loss in that they had been deprived of the care of their mother, so that, but for the generosity of the grandmother, it would have been necessary to pay for somebody to look after them; and that the grandmother's intervention could not be treated as a relevant benefit because it had of course not been arranged for before the deaths and there was no good reason to expect it at the time of death. I quote from the judgment of Lord Edmund-Davies[2]:

> 'Broadly speaking, it was considered that payments received as a result of arrangements already set up to meet the eventuality of death did so result [i e did result from the death] . . . But the position was and is less clear where payments are made or services having pecuniary value are rendered in circumstances never foreseen before the death . . . And there is a presumption against deducting the value of unpaid services rendered to a bereaved person . . . in my judgment, while the need for the grandmother's care undoubtedly arose from the mother's death, the view which a reasonable jury would be likely to adopt would be that the children benefited not as a result of the mother's death but simply because the grandmother had taken it on herself to render them services. At the time of their mother's death it was anyone's guess what would happen to them and the defendant had not discharged the onus of establishing that at that time there was a reasonable expectation that the grandmother would act as she subsequently did . . . For these reasons I hold that the learned judge rightly came to the conclusion that the grandmother's services should be ignored in calculating the financial loss sustained by the children as a result of the death of their mother.'

Buckley LJ[3] expressed a similar view. Ormrod LJ[4] dealt with the matter more broadly, expressing the opinion that the court ought 'to hesitate to extend the balancing principle to classes of benefit which are not directly covered by authority which is binding on it'.

Now that was a very different case from the present one but, if it is possible to say in the present case that by the death of the father the children have suffered a

---

1 Page 257, ante, [1975] 2 WLR 34
2 See pp 262, 263, 265, 267, ante, [1975] 2 WLR at 41, 42, 44, 46
3 See pp 270, 271, ante, [1975] 2 WLR at 50, 51
4 See p 275, ante, [1975] 2 WLR at 55

pecuniary loss through the loss of the care of a mother supported by the father, then the
question is: must there be set against that loss the benefit of the care of a mother who   *a*
is supported by supplementary benefit? It can hardly be said that 'at the time of the
father's death it was anybody's guess what would happen to the children'. There had
not, of course, been any arrangement made to provide for that event but if the parents
had directed their minds to the possibility they would obviously have said 'the mother
will continue to look after the children to the best of her ability'.

It seems to me, however, that probably the better way of looking at it is that the   *b*
change in the mother's resources does not constitute a pecuniary loss to the children
unless it can be shown, or inferred from the circumstances, that the care which the
mother can give them is diminished by the loss of the father's support. This must
depend on the extent to which she can be expected to be supported by supplementary
benefit. She had been in receipt of such benefit for herself and the children from the date
of death and the weekly payments at the time of the trial were at the rate of £19·25 a   *c*
week. Now counsel for the children has maintained that once damages are awarded
to the children to supply their own immediate needs in the way of food, lodging,
clothing etc, the mother must lose her entitlement to benefit. He bases this on para
3(2) of Sch 2 to the Ministry of Social Security Act 1966 which provides:

> 'Where a person has to provide for the requirements of another person . . .   *d*
> who is a member of the same household, his requirements may be taken, and if
> that other person has not attained the age of sixteen shall be taken, to include
> the requirements of that other person, and in that case their resources also shall
> be aggregated.'

Counsel for the children says that the mother, as the only surviving parent of illegitimate children, is a person who has to provide for their requirements and therefore   *e*
that the resources of the children (being the damages recovered by them and the
interest thereon) will fall to be aggregated with the means of the mother, which
would result in the family's resources being assessed at a figure which would rule out
supplementary benefit. I am quite unable to accept that argument. It is not correct
to say that the mother 'has to provide for the requirements of the children'. 'Requirements' here must mean requirements in respect of payments for the necessaries of   *f*
life and these are all provided for by the uncontested part of the damages awarded
to the children. It therefore appears to me that the mother is entitled to supplementary benefit (or at least is likely to receive it, because the payments are discretionary) at the normal rate for a single person, which at present is £10·40 a week.
Consequently I consider that her estimated share of the housekeeping and holiday
food money provided by the father, £334 a year, must be deducted from the figures   *g*
arrived at by the judge in assessing the annual loss of the three children.

I do not take the same view about the air fares and outings. These seem to me to be
luxuries which one would not expect supplementary benefit to cover. The payment
of the mother's fares by the father can properly be regarded as a payment which was
made to enable the children to enjoy the holidays and outings and accordingly the
cessation of those payments from the father's pocket constitutes a pecuniary loss to the   *h*
children. I am in more doubt about the small item of electricity but on the whole I
think it is fair to treat it like the rent and not to deduct the £26 which it involves. In
the result I would reduce the annual figure for the three children by £334 and no
more, leaving £1,643 to be divided between them. This would give an annual sum of
£548 for each child. The next question is whether the judge adopted the right
multipliers.   *j*

I am not impressed by counsel for the children's argument that the judge should
have given weight to the possibility of the children remaining wholly or partially
dependent on the father after reaching 16. While there is always some chance of the
children of a man in this man's position being of such academic ability as to enable
them to continue their education after 16, and there is probably a greater chance of

a their receiving some financial support after their education is finished, this can be set off against all the risks of accident, illness or unemployment which might have occurred to the father before the children reached that age. And while those risks would be present throughout the period of their schooldays, any prospect of support after leaving school would be deferred for a substantial number of years for each child.

b I am however bound to say that the period of dependency ought to have been reckoned from the date of the death instead of from the date of the trial and, although nobody thought of this until the middle of the hearing of the appeal, I think it is a factor to which effect must be given in the interests of the children. This does not mean that the multipliers must each be increased by three years (the mother was receiving supplementary benefit for the children during those years and it is convenient to take account of that by adjusting the multipliers). Accordingly I would increase each multiplier by two, resulting in multipliers of seven for the eldest, *c* eight for the second child and ten for the youngest. It follows that I would assess the loss at £3,836 for the eldest, £4,384 for the middle one and £5,480 for the youngest. The interest would then fall to be adjusted in accordance with these figures.

I would not interfere with the judge's order for costs on the common fund basis. That is a basis often adopted on a settlement of a children's claim and I do not consider that it could be said that the judge wrongly exercised his discretion in so ordering *d* in this case.

The total of the three sums I have mentioned, £3,836, £4,384 and £5,480 is £13,700. The total awarded by Forbes J was £12,421; but, as I indicated earlier, there was an arithmetical error and the figure should have been £12,521, apart from interest. The difference is small in proportion to the total, but in my judgment it should be given effect to, since the damages here are a matter of calculation and not merely of *e* broad assessment, as in the case of damages for personal injuries. This means that, as a matter of form, the defendants' appeal should be dismissed and the children's cross-appeal should be allowed to the extent I have indicated.

f **STEPHENSON LJ.** The question raised by this appeal is the jury question: what have these three children lost in terms of money or money's worth as a result of their father's death? We have to balance against their gross loss any gain in money or money's worth which the defendants who are responsible in law for their father's death may prove to have resulted from his death, and so to arrive at their net loss for which the defendants must compensate them. This twofold exercise of ascertaining loss and gain and then striking a balance is usually carried out by the courts for *g* widow and children together. Sometimes it has to be carried out for orphaned children. In the former case what has to be ascertained is the net loss of the family and the apportionment between widow and children is comparatively unimportant, is often a matter of agreement, and need not be as precise as the division of maintenance between a neglected wife and neglected children. In a case where both parents die the net loss resulting from the mother's death has to be considered separately, and *h* the need to replace her services gives rise to difficult questions whether the cost, actual or notional, of replacing her services should be taken into account in assessing the motherless children's loss.

But in the instant case the children are not motherless. They have lost their father but their mother still looks after them. She herself has lost just as much by their father's death as if she had been his widow But she did not marry him and there-*i* fore cannot claim compensation for his death, although their illegitimate children can: Fatal Accidents Act 1959, s 1(2)(*a*).

We have therefore to ascertain their net loss, not hers, and are at once confronted with the difficulty of distinguishing the two, a difficulty which must often have arisen since illegitimate children were brought within Lord Campbell's Act by s 2(1) of the Law Reform (Miscellaneous Provisions) Act 1934, but has apparently been the subject

of only three reported decisions in the intervening 40 years. What the father gave to
these children he gave to the family. Some things, the clothes and toys he bought for *a*
them, he gave them direct. Some things he paid for to benefit her and them—and
himself as well; rent, electricity, television, washing machine, holiday fares. And
he gave her housekeeping money to pay mainly for food for all five of them to eat.

One approach to the problem would be to deduct from every family expense
which he paid, directly or indirectly, a portion attributable to his share of benefit
and a portion attributable to hers. Another would be to select some family expenses *b*
for this equal treatment but to reduce other family expenses by the part of it which
would have been spent on him but not by the part of it which would have been spent
on her. A third would be to ignore any part which would have been spent on her and
to make no reduction except for what would have been spent on him.

The first method has logic to recommend it but nothing else. The last, which was in
effect the judge's method and I understand will have the support of Graham J, is open *c*
to the objection that it confers indirectly on an unmarried mother the statutory right
still denied her by Parliament. But this is not so. Apart from the perhaps unimportant
distinction that no part of the total awarded for the children's net loss will belong in
law to the unmarried mother, that total will be substantially less than would have
been awarded if she had been married because the multiplier of the annual figure for
dependency will be lower for those illegitimate children than it would be for a widow. *d*
I have, however, come to the conclusion, in agreement with Cairns LJ, that the
second is the proper method and the one which the common sense of a jury would
apply to the ascertainment of the real loss resulting to illegitimate children from their
father's death.

The help I get on this question from the cases to which we have been referred is that
maternal services are capable of being measured in money, perhaps by the cost of *e*
replacing them or perhaps by something more, since the benefit of a mother's personal
devotion may have a financial value to children greater than the services of a housekeeper or other substitute mother: see McGregor on Damages[1].

It seems to me that the right question to ask is: will the services which this mother
will be able to render these children be probably less valuable than they were before
the father's death or would have been if he had lived? The children are, broadly *f*
speaking, entitled to enjoy the same material standard of life as they would have
enjoyed if their father had continued to support them, and the defendants are bound
to pay them enough to maintain them in the enjoyment of that standard to which the
financial support of their father has accustomed them. That may not be possible
without maintaining their mother in the same standard; by reducing her standard of
life you may necessarily reduce theirs. If as a result of their loss of the father's support *g*
their mother can no longer maintain them up to that standard without compensation
from the defendants, the compensation the defendants must pay them must be
enough to enable her so to maintain them, just as it would have to be enough to
enable a housekeeper or a grandmother to do so if they had no mother. They have
not lost her services; their father's death has not deprived them of those services
altogether. But insofar as it can be proved to have impaired those services, it has *h*
reduced their value; that reduction is their loss and for it they are entitled to be
compensated. I agree with Cairns LJ that this loss depends on (1) the mother's care
being diminished by the loss of the father's support and (2) the extent to which she
can be expected to be supported by supplementary benefit.

The mother was being paid social security benefit, of which £8·15 per week appears
to have been paid to her as a supplementary allowance to a person over the age of 16 *j*
whose resources were insufficient to meet her requirements and £7·35 per week to
her to discharge her liability to maintain her illegitimate children: Ministry of Social
Security Act 1966, renamed the Supplementary Benefit Act 1966, ss 4(1)(b), 22(1)(b),

1 13th Edn (1972), para 1232

Sch 2, para 9(*b*) and (*c*)(*v*) (as amended by the National Insurance Supplementary
a Benefit Act 1973) and para 5(*b*) and (*c*)(*v*). These sums have now been increased to
£10·40 per week and £8·70 per week by the Supplementary Benefits (Determination
of Requirements) Regulations 1974[1]. I agree with Cairns LJ that when the uncontested part of the damages has been paid to the children to compensate them for
their financial loss resulting from their father's death, the mother will not be a person
who has to provide for their requirements under s 4(2) of and Sch 2, para 3(2) to the
b 1966 Act, and that she is likely to continue to receive the benefit which is now £10·40
per week.

I am satisfied that that benefit is intended to cover the cost of feeding and clothing
herself. She cannot look after the children and so secure their maintenance in their
previous standard of life unless she has food and clothes as well as a roof over her head
and, looked at realistically, the same roof over her head as over their heads, because
c children cannot be expected to live on their own. But social security benefit is not
one of the benefits which s 2 of the Fatal Accidents Act 1959 allows the court to ignore
in balancing dependents' gains against losses. It might not have to be set off against
the losses caused by a tortfeasor to a surviving plaintiff: *Parry v Cleaver*[2]; *Daish v
Wauton*[3]. But it would have to be set off against the loss caused to a widow by her
husband's death, though that loss would include the cost of feeding herself. This
d mother is in a different position. She cannot get payment for her food (or clothes)
directly from the defendants but she does get it from the state. She cannot get it
twice over, once from the state and once from the defendants indirectly through the
children. It is only extras which social security benefits would not cover and which
are incurred by the mother in order to maintain the children's standard of life that
can and should be paid for by the defendants as part of the children's loss. In this
e category of expenses paid out of the father's wages, but now beyond the mother's
means supplied by social security, are her expenses on their outings and her air fares
when she accompanies them on flights to and from Ireland. They cannot be expected
to travel without her and would lose the benefit of those outings and holidays if she
could not afford to go with them. In the same category of family expenses not apportionable between mother and children come the cost of the electricity, television and
f washing machine which the father himself used to pay and the cost of gas and the rent
which she paid out of what he gave her. The defendants concede that the children
should be paid the whole cost of these items except electricity and perhaps gas; but I
would regard it as unreasonable to drive the mother to bed at the same time as the
children by disallowing the estimated cost of any extra light or heat she may use after
they have gone to bed.
g I agree with Forbes J on these points and find support for his decision on them in
Buckley LJ's rejection of the defendant's argument in *Hay v Hughes*[4] that the general
family expenditure should have been apportioned by the judge to the father, the
mother and the children in fractions and the dependency of the children reduced by
the apportioned shares of the father and mother who had been killed in the same
accident. Logically something ought to be deducted for the father's share of these
h items but if it is unrealistic to deduct for his it is also unrealistic to deduct for hers and
a jury would not do so and ought not to be directed to do so. It is, however, the
common sense practice to deduct the father's share of the food and I cannot justify
treating the mother differently and not deducting her share also—particularly as her
supplementary benefit will pay for it. So here I part company with the learned judge.

In the category therefore of family expenses which she paid out of what he gave her
j but which I think should be apportioned between mother and children is the cost of

1 SI 1974 No 854
2 [1969] 1 All ER 555, [1970] AC 1
3 [1972] 1 All ER 25, [1972] 2 QB 262
4 Page 257, ante, [1975] 2 WLR 34

food and, insofar as not paid for separately, clothing. You cannot split the children's home into fractions but you must try to divide this mother into two to this limited   *a* extent, strongly as I sympathise with the learned judge for refusing to make the attempt.

The other factor in the learned judge's judgment, which we are asked to review by the children's cross-appeal, is the multiplier. Was it plainly too low or about right? We have first to consider whether it began at the right point. In my opinion, it did not. The point taken by Cairns LJ in argument is indisputably right. The multiplier   *b* must run from the father's death, as he suggested, not from the date of judgment as the judge clearly thought and both counsel apparently accepted. More doubtful is the point at which it should finish. The judge thought that that was when each child reached the age of 16. He has the support of Willmer J, who in 1951 refused to inter-fere with a registrar's award of £500 in all to three children of an unmarried mother in respect of their father's death: *Phipps v Cunard White Star Co Ltd*[1]. That learned judge   *c* was of the opinion, at a time when the school leaving age was, I think, lower than 16, that a person in the station of life of an able seaman, who had been a lorry driver's mate before the war and would have been a lorry driver if he had survived it, could not be expected to have continued supporting his children after they attained the age of approximately 16 years. The children were a boy of 13 and girls of 11 and nine years old at the date of the trial, but their father's death had occurred more than   *d* eight years earlier, in 1942. Yet they were awarded only £100, £150 and £250 res-pectively. Willmer J seems to have approved the registrar's statement that he could not deal with the children's claim on the basis of their unmarried mother's claiming but could only award them their share in the benefit which she had lost when their father died. He described the family as in relatively humble circumstances and he thought that a fair share of each child in what was coming into the house had the   *e* deceased lived would have been about 15s a week; after allowing for uncertainties he would have arrived at a figure somewhat above the registrar's but not enough above to justify increasing it.

It seems clear that Willmer J did not approach those children's loss as generously as Forbes J approached these children's, but it seems at first sight likely that he agreed with him in dating the multiplier from the trial. For if Miss Phipps's children had been   *f* compensated in full for their losses since 1942 the total award must on my calculation have been over £1,300. But there were not only the usual uncertainties of life to reduce the period of dependency; there were also taken into account actual payments of naval pensions made since the father's death and since the date when he would probably have been demobilised. As the amounts of those pensions are not stated, it is impossible to be certain not only what the multipliers were but when they   *g* started.

It is, however, clear from the judgment of this court in the recent case of *Hay v Hughes*[2] that this court in 1974 found nothing wrong with a multiplier of nine years calculated by Reeve J on the assumption that each of two boys aged 4½ and 2½ when both their parents were killed in 1970 would remain dependent until the age of 18½. That resulted in an average period of 15 years' dependency for each which must have   *h* been calculated from the deaths in January 1970, not from the judgment in October 1973. The father was a trainee welder with a weekly take home pay of £24 and good chances of promotion to a job which would increase that to £40.

I would think, with such help as I get from these authorities and without any evi-dence of what these parents' intentions were, that we should not interfere with the judge's assumption that these children would become independent at about the usual   *j* school-leaving age of 16, although I doubt whether I would have put the age of independence so low. Calculated as they should be from the date of their father's

---

1   [1951] 1 Lloyd's Rep 54
2   Page 257, ante, [1975] 2 WLR 34

death, that would give multipliers of ten, 11 and 14 instead of the judge's seven, eight
a and 11. Some reduction must then be made for the supplementary benefit already
received by the mother on the children's behalf as well as for the chances and uncertainties of life, the chances of the father being out of work in the building trade or
earning less, the chances of his meeting with another accident causing incapacity or
death, the chances of the children themselves not reaching the age of 16 and, I would
add on the other side, the chances of the mother being incapacitated or dying before
b they reach it because that event, like any possible increase in the father's earnings,
might require a counter-balancing increase in the dependency which might be
reflected in the multipliers.

At the end of this balancing act I would come down on Cairns LJ's multipliers of
seven, eight and ten instead of the judge's five, six and eight, and I would assess at the
figures he gives, with the appropriate interest, the damages proportioned to the
c injury resulting from their father's death for these three children respectively. I agree
with the result as stated by Cairns LJ: we should dismiss the appeal and, although the
increase in the damages which the judge awarded is proportionately small, we should
allow the cross-appeal.

I too would dismiss the defendants' appeal on costs. This court should not interfere
with a judge's exercise of his direction over costs unless it must, and it must do so
d only when satisfied that his order is plainly wrong. I cannot see anything wrong with
his ordering the defendants to pay the costs of this action on a common fund basis as
they would have been paid had the suit been compromised.

GRAHAM J. I have not found this appeal from Forbes J easy. This may be due to
e the fact that my familiarity with the Fatal Accidents Acts is certainly not as great as
that possessed by Cairns and Stephenson LJJ. In the circumstances it seemed to me
best to approach the matter from first principles in the hope that by such action I
would be more likely to arrive at a just result. Following such a course I have in fact
arrived at figures which are somewhat larger than theirs, since I support the judge's
basic figures but agree that his multipliers should be increased.

f Historically the legislation goes back to the Fatal Accidents Act 1846, also known as
Lord Campbell's Act, which was introduced to give a right of action for the benefit of
the dependants of a deceased person. The object of the Act was to mitigate the common law rule that no action was maintainable for causing death. Sections 1 and 2 of
the 1846 Act give a right of action when death is caused, for the benefit of certain near
relations only of the deceased, namely the wife, husband, parent or child. Section 2
g states that such action had to be brought by and in the name of the executor or
administrator of the deceased, and that—

> 'the jury may give such damages as they may think proportioned to the injury
> resulting from such death to the parties respectively for whom and for whose
> benefit such action shall be brought'.

h It is clear, therefore, that the classes of persons originally given a right of action were
very strictly limited and there was, for example, no question of a so-called common
law wife or illegitimate children being able to recover, but it is also clear that the
estimation of the amount of damages for those who were entitled to recover, was a
question of fact for the jury. This basic section is in force and the question of damages
is therefore a jury question. That such is the proper view of the matter is emphasised
j by a recent decision of this court in another fatal accident case, *Hay v Hughes*[1]. Lord
Edmund-Davies referred[2] to *Monarch Steamship Co Ltd v Karlshamns*[3] and to Lord du

---

1   Page 257, ante, [1975] 2 WLR 34
2   See p 266, ante, [1975] 2 WLR at 45
3   [1949] 1 All ER 1, [1949] AC 196

Parcq's words emphasising that a question of damages was a jury question and that the court must be careful to see that[1]—

'the principles laid down are never so narrowly interpreted as to prevent a jury or judge of fact, from doing justice between the parties.'

The facts of the Monarch case[2] were of course very different from the present case, but as Lord Edmund-Davies clearly recognised the principles of estimating damage there set out are also applicable to fatal accident cases. Buckley LJ also founded his judgment on the same basis as can be seen clearly from his first few sentences[3].

Since the enactment of the Fatal Accidents Act in 1846, legislation has from time to time enlarged the classes of dependent persons entitled to recover damages for the loss of the person on whom they were dependent and made it easier for them to do so. Thus, the Fatal Accidents Act 1864 enabled actions to be brought by persons beneficially interested where there was no executor or administrator of the deceased. The Law Reform (Miscellaneous Provisions) Act 1934 extended the classes to include illegitimate children and adopted children and the Fatal Accidents Act 1959 provided that an adopted person was to be treated as a child of the person by whom he was adopted and an illegitimate person was to be treated as the legitimate child of his mother and reputed father. Section 2 of the same Act enacted that in assessing damages under the 1846 Act 'there shall not be taken into account any insurance money, benefit, pension or gratuity which has been or will or may be paid as a result of the death.'

It will thus be seen that the original Act of 1846, which was strictly confined within the bounds considered proper by the then, perhaps somewhat narrow, Victorian morality, has by reason of subsequent enactments and by judicial decision been considerably extended and there has frequently been liberalisation in favour of beneficiaries over the years. However, it is clear that a woman who is a common law wife is still excluded from being herself able to recover in that capacity under the Acts. If the Act were being enacted for the first time today it seems quite likely that she might have been included and one may perhaps be pardoned for hoping that in due course Parliament will reconsider the scope of the Acts at least in this respect.

The facts and contentions in this case have already been dealt with fully in the judgments of Cairns and Stephenson LJJ, which I have had the advantage of reading, and it is unnecessary for me to repeat them. It might, however, be useful if I mention shortly those points on which I would like to comment before setting out my conclusions, since they are based on an approach which is slightly more general than theirs.

Apart from the question of the length of the respective multipliers, which I will deal with later, the main argument centered on whether or not the learned judge was right in permitting the inclusion in the awards given to the children of the cost of maintaining their mother. In this connection it was said by the defendants that this was a disguised method of enabling a common law wife to claim under this Act for a loss to herself. This was a loss which, as an unmarried woman, living with the deceased, the Acts clearly did not contemplate. Then, as far as the children themselves are concerned, it was said that they have suffered no loss because their mother was still there, albeit being maintained by social security payments, and ready and willing to look after them. The judge was clearly fully alive to these arguments but he took the view that for purposes of calculating the children's 'gross' loss, to borrow the convenient term coined by Buckley LJ in Hay v Hughes[4], one must, notionally at any rate, regard the mother as having two capacities—one as 'wife' and housekeeper

---

1   [1949] 1 All ER at 19, [1949] AC at 232
2   [1949] 1 All ER 1, [1949] AC 196
3   See p 268, ante, [1975] 2 WLR at 47
4   Page 257, ante, [1975] 2 WLR 34

for the deceased and the other as mother, housekeeper and general guardian of the

a children. He deals with this conception clearly and points out that her husband was undoubtedly supporting her in part as mother of his children. He then goes on to look at the matter realistically and says it is impossible to divide the mother into two and refuses to make any distinction between the cost of her support in her two capacities. He then in effect treats her presence and support in the home on the same basis as her presence and support for the purpose of the children's holidays in Ireland.

b As he says: 'In looking at the matter realistically the mother has to be looked after in order that she should be able to look after the children.'

It was then argued that the position on holidays on the one hand and generally in the home on the other are different because at home it can be expected that she will now be supported by social security payments. The probability, it is said, will be that no such payments will be given in respect of the children as a result of their award in

c this case, but that the mother in her personal capacity can expect to receive, as we are told, a figure of the order of £10·40 per week. Though social security is in fact a matter of entitlement or of right (see Ministry of Social Security Act 1966, s 4), nevertheless entitlement and amount are determined by the commission and, judging by the large number of appeals which occur annually, it is often not easy to ascertain what any individual is entitled to nor to be sure that he will automatically receive his

d entitlement. We may from what we are told, I think, assume that it is likely that the children's 'requirements' under the Act will in principle be considered to be met by their award under the Fatal Accidents Acts but that their mother's 'requirement' may necessitate a payment to her up to a maximum of £10·40 per week, depending on her circumstances after this award and on the date with which one is concerned. So far as her support in the home is concerned, it is argued by the defendants that after

e her husband's death she is likely to be in the same position as, or in a reasonably equivalent position to, that in which she was before. I do not however think it is right at this stage to make any definite assumption as to the amount of any social security which she may receive, except that it is very unlikely to be more than £10·40. I agree with Cairns and Stephenson LJJ that her support in the family holidays is an entirely different matter since it cannot be expected that the social security provisions will

f enable her to receive payments equivalent to those she would have received from her husband for this purpose, and it follows that so far as the children are concerned they will not get their holidays unless she is so supported. The cost of holidays is therefore a proper item to take into account in estimating their loss. This contrast may seem at first sight to be a strong argument for saying that the learned judge, though right to include support during holidays, was wrong to include such support generally for the

g rest of the year when the family was normally at home. To my mind however this way of looking at the matter focuses attention on the mother's loss of support and obscures the real question which must be answered, that is whether the children, not their mother, suffered a loss by the death of the father, in that after his death the services and care which their mother is able to give them, being alone without a husband and not being so well supported, are likely to be less than those which she

h could give before the death. When I say 'loss' I am of course using the word in the sense of 'gross loss' capable of being valued in money terms as defined by Buckley LJ in *Hay v Hughes*[1] at the start of his judgment. In that case he formulated a very similar question in words applicable to the circumstances of that case as follows[2]:

> *j* 'But it would surely be necessary at least to compare and take into account the comparative qualities of the services and benefits afforded in these respects by the parents in their lifetime and by the grandmother since the parents' death.'

---

1 See p 268, ante, [1975] 2 WLR at 47
2 See p 270, ante, [1975] 2 WLR as 50

So here it seems to me that it would be correct to leave to the jury, if the case were being so tried, the question whether the comparative qualities of the services and bene- *a* fits afforded to the children in the family home by their mother in that capacity, supported to whatever extent she may be after their father's death, are likely to be, and to continue to be, equal to or less than those which she was able to provide in the same capacity whilst the father was alive, and supported by him as she then was. If the conclusion is that they are likely to be less, then it is also for the jury, difficult though the task may be, to estimate the monetary value of the loss which the children *b* suffer by the diminution of those services and benefit. If it is right to do this in the case of a grandmother, as in *Hay v Hughes*[1], it must logically also be right in the case of a mother, for, as the learned judge says, in the case of infant children they must have someone to look after them and in order to look after them that person, whoever she may be, must be supported. Thus far it seems to me the judge was perfectly correct in the directions which he gave to himself, trying the matter as he was without *c* a jury. He was quite properly looking at the loss of the children and at the services and benefits given to them by the mother in her capacity as mother of and provider for them, and not in her capacity as 'wife' of the deceased. He appreciated clearly that there might be an overlap between the cost of supporting her in her two capacities, and no doubt realised that if it were possible to draw a clear and certain enough line so as to arrive at the relative cost of supporting her in those two capacities, it *d* would be right to make a deduction of so much as should be attributed to her support as the 'wife' of the deceased rather than as the mother of his children. If in these cases it was always necessary to make such an evaluation, it seems clear that the relative costs involved in supporting the mother in question would vary considerably depending on the circumstances and number of persons in the family. In the end, the global sum attributable to the support of the family as a whole would notionally have *e* to be divided arbitrarily between its members, and such division would be very different in different cases. Here, for example, it might be proper to attribute an equal, or approximately equal, share to each member of the family, which seems not unreasonable in the case of a mother in this social category, and three growing children of the ages we are concerned with. On such assumption that it is right here to attribute a quarter of the global sum to the support of the mother in both her capacities, *f* it would perhaps also be right to make a deduction of half this, that is, one eighth, as representing her support in the capacity of a 'wife'. Although depending on the circumstances, it might be a proper course to make such a deduction in some cases, where for example, as already stated, the deduction is sufficiently significant and can be ascertained with sufficient certainty, the learned judge properly, in my judgment, declined to do so here. He took the realistic view, which a jury would also be entitled *g* to take, that in the circumstances here it was impracticable and of no use to try to divide the mother in two; as he said:

'... if some of her has to be supported as the mother of the three children, the whole of her has to be, and I would make no distinction for the cost of her keep in this case.'	*h*

I would not want to disturb this view of the matter, particularly when, as seen above, if one analyses the figures here, the deduction would only be a small fraction of the total. As Lord Shaw said in *Watson, Laidlaw & Co Ltd v Pott, Cassels & Williamson*[2]:

'In the case of damages in general there is one principle which does not underly *j* the assessment ... The idea is to restore the person who has sustained injury and loss to the condition in which he would have been, had he not sustained it ...

1 Page 257, ante, [1975] 2 WLR 34
2 (1914) 31 RPC 104 at 117, 118

a The restoration by way of compensation is therefore accomplished to a large extent by the exercise of sound imagination and the practice of the broad axe.'

Damages under the Fatal Accidents Acts can never be estimated exactly, as this case clearly illustrates, and the court must do its best in all the circumstances. This is a case where provided the aim is good, it is appropriate, in my judgment, to cleave with a broad axe. This is what Forbes J has done and in my judgment he was right in an era

b of inflation, and when estimating for some years ahead the cost of items such as holidays in Ireland which are unlikely ever to become the subject of social security payments.

In the end I consider the whole case turns on whether it was proper for the judge, as he must have done, to pose to himself, as a jury, the question whether the services and benefits which the children will receive after the death of their father are likely

c to be less by reason of the fact that their mother is now on her own without a husband to help her and is not, if such be the case, as well supported as she was before. The material facts on this last point are clear enough. She used generally to get £30 a week from her husband, though this was reduced for maybe the last six weeks of the year to £25 and nearly all of that went on food and on the family as a whole. The figure is exclusive of other sums paid by the husband which have been taken into account in

d the award and of the cigar box reserve about to be mentioned. The husband often earned large sums per week up to the highest figure which was spoken of, namely £90. He kept £5 for himself and the rest was put in a 'cigar box on top of the wardrobe'. 'There was often £300 in it.' This was used, as the mother said, for 'holidays and that'. By 'and that' I assume she meant 'or any other extra the family might from time to time require'. In trying to ascertain the comparable position now, Forbes J rightly

e deducted £8 for the husband's share of the housekeeping so that the figures of £30 and £25 must be reduced accordingly. She may, on the assumption made, in the future have up to a maximum of £10·40 as her social security payment. She will also have whatever sum she is able to allocate to housekeeping from each of the shares in the award of the respective children. If she receives a social security payment of £10·40 and takes the awards made to the children, she will not be worse off from a money

f point of view and in theory this should be sufficient to support her and each child. There will, however, no longer be the comfortable reserve of £300 in the cigar box available for extras when required. She will be carrying the coal herself, and by saying that I do not of course necessarily mean it to be taken literally, but she will in fact herself be doing all the many and time-consuming jobs which have to be done in a home with three young children, and will clearly have less time and probably less

g energy to devote specifically to the welfare of the children individually. I think no jury could be blamed for taking the realistic view that the children will be worse off now than they were before in respect of the housekeeping services and benefits available to them, and that in any event an amount of money to support their mother should be assessed without assuming that the maximum figure of £10·40 by way of social security will necessarily be paid to her. The commission will no doubt make an

h appropriate decision following this award. This is all the learned judge has done, and in my judgment he was right to do so and has thereby carried out the difficult task laid on him by s 2 of the Fatal Accidents Act 1846.

I would only add that it is quite wrong to say, as was said for the defendants in argument, that in effect the judge's finding has placed the mother in the position of a lawful wife and enabled her to recover on that basis when the Act expressly excludes

j her. If she was a lawful wife she might expect to have been supported by her husband for many years to come and any multiplier used in her case, in that capacity, would be quite different from, and much longer than, any used in the case of her support as a mother until the children reach the age of 16 years.

Finally I should say that I am in entire agreement with Cairns LJ, for the reasons which he gives, that the multipliers in the case of the children should be increased from those used by Forbes J by two years in each case. This results in awards of £4,613, £6,590 and £5,272 for the first, second the third plaintiffs respectively, giving   *a* a total without interest of £16,475. This total would have to be adjusted for interest. I agree with both Cairns and Stephenson LJJ that the defendants' appeal on costs should be dismissed since there is no valid reason for disturbing the judge's discretion in this matter.

Appeal dismissed. Cross-appeal allowed. Leave to appeal to the House of Lords granted.   *b*

Solicitors: *Vizards* (for the defendants); *Gasters* (for the plaintiffs).

A S Virdi Esq   Barrister.

c

Re Calgary and Edmonton Land Co Ltd

CHANCERY DIVISION   *d*
MEGARRY J
25th, 26th, 27th, 28th, 29th NOVEMBER, 3rd, 10th DECEMBER 1974

Company – Winding-up – Voluntary winding-up – Creditors' voluntary winding-up – Application for stay of winding-up – Court's discretion to grant stay – Factors to be considered – Companies Act 1948, ss 256, 301, 307.   *e*

The issued capital of a company consisted of 14 million ordinary shares of which the managing director, H, owned 10,000, his wife nearly 150,000 and B & C Ltd over 13 million. There were over 1,100 other shareholders holding between them 730,000 shares. From May 1970 onwards the company was in a creditors' voluntary winding-up. It was highly probable .that when all the company's assets were realised there   *f* would be enough to discharge the expenses of the liquidation (including the liquidator's remuneration), pay all creditors and leave a substantial balance for the shareholders. B & C Ltd applied for the winding-up to be stayed under s 256(1)[a] of the Companies Act 1948, as extended by ss 301, 307[b]. The registrar dismissed their application. B & C Ltd sought to have his order discharged, but they had to abandon those proceedings as they were no longer in a postion to provide sufficient liquid funds   *g* outside the company's own resources to pay the liquidator's remuneration and expenses. H thereupon applied for a stay of the winding-up. He purported to act on behalf of all the shareholders. He stated that he had called two meetings and that the shareholders and unsecured creditors who attended the meetings had voted unanimously for a stay of the winding-up. There was no scheme of arrangement under s 206 of the 1948 Act, and the views of some of the members had not been ascertained.   *h* Communications sent to some of them had been returned undelivered and no attempt had been made to reach them by advertisement.

Held – H's application would be dismissed for the following reasons—
(i) The court would, in normal circumstances, generally exercise its discretion to grant a stay only where the applicant showed (a) that each creditor had either been   *j* paid in full or that satisfactory provision for him to be paid in full was to be made, or that he consented to the stay or was otherwise bound not to object to it; (b) that the

---

a   Section 256(1) is set out at p 1049 *f*, post
b   Section 307, so far as material, is set out at p 1049 *h* and *j*, post

liquidator's position was fully safeguarded, either by paying him the proper amount
a of his expenses or sufficiently securing payment; and (c) that each member either
consented to the stay, or was otherwise bound not to object to it, or there was secured
to him the right to receive all that he would have received if the winding-up had
proceeded to its conclusion (see p 1050 *b* and *c* and p 1051 *d* to p 1052 *a*, post).

(ii) H had not made out a convincing case for a stay for he had failed to produce any
firm and acceptable proposals for satisfying the creditors and the liquidator and there
b was nothing binding the other shareholders (see p 1053 *h* to p 1054 *g*, post).

Re Trix Ltd [1970] 3 All ER 397 applied.

Notes

For power to stay winding-up proceedings, see 7 Halsbury's Laws (4th Edn) 779, para
1375, and for cases on the subject, see 10 Digest (Repl) 1013, 6964-6969.
c   For the Companies Act 1948, ss 256, 301, 307, see 5 Halsbury's Statutes (3rd Edn) 312,
337, 340.

Cases referred to in judgment

Albert Life Assurance Co Arbitration, Re (1871) 15 Sol Jo 923.
d *Calgary and Edmonton Land Co Ltd v Dobinson* [1974] 1 All ER 484, [1974] Ch 102, [1974] 2
    WLR 143.
Central Sugar Factories of Brazil, Re, Hack's Case [1894] 1 Ch 369, 63 LJCh 410, 70 LT 645,
    42 WR 345, 10 TLR 150, 1 Mans 145, 8 R 205, 10 Digest (Repl) 1012, 6960.
Comr of Stamp Duties (Queensland) v Livingston [1964] 3 All ER 692, [1965] AC 694,
    [1964] 3 WLR 963, [1964] TR 351, 43 ATC 325, PC, Digest (Cont Vol B) 247, *258a.
e *General Rolling Stock Co, Re* (1872) 7 Ch App 646.
Inland Revenue Comrs v Olive Mill Ltd [1963] 2 All ER 130, [1963] 1 WLR 712, 41 Tax Cas
    77, [1963] TR 59, 42 ATC 74, Digest (Cont Vol A) 906, 1634c.
NFU Development Trust Ltd, Re [1973] 1 All ER 135, [1972] 1 WLR 1548.
Oriental Inland Steam Co, Re, ex parte Scinde Ry Co (1874) 9 Ch App 557, 43 LJCh 699, 31
    LT 5, 22 WR 810, LJJ, 10 Digest (Repl) 903, 6137.
f *South Barrule State Quarry Co, Re* (1869) LR 8 Eq 688, 10 Digest (Repl) 1124, 7828.
Telescriptor Syndicate Ltd, Re [1903] 2 Ch 174, 72 LJCh 480, 88 LT 389, 19 TLR 375, 10
    Mans 213, 10 Digest (Repl) 1014, 6965.
Trix Ltd, Re [1970] 3 All ER 397, [1970] 1 WLR 1421.
Walters (Stephen) & Sons Ltd, Re [1926] WN 236, 70 Sol Jo 953, 9 Digest (Repl) 151,
    881.
g *Wigan Coal & Iron Co Ltd v Inland Revenue Comrs* [1945] 1 All ER 392, 173 LT 79, 61
    TLR 231, 9 Digest (Repl) 420, 2721.
Wood (Edward) & Co Ltd, Re (8th April 1974) unreported.
Yagerphone Ltd, Re [1935] Ch 392, [1935] All ER Rep 803, 104 LJCh 156, 152 LT 555, 51
    TLR 226, [1934-5] B & CR 240, 10 Digest (Repl) 1029, 7116.

h ### Cases also cited

Flateau, Re, ex parte Official Receiver [1893] 2 QB 219, CA.
Hester, Re, ex parte Hester (1889) 22 QBD 632, [1886-90] All ER Rep 865, CA.
London Chartered Bank of Australia, Re [1893] 3 Ch 540.
Punt v Symons & Co Ltd [1903] 2 Ch 506.

j ### Motion

By notice of motion dated 14th November 1974, Isaac David Hillman, managing
director and contributory of Calgary and Edmonton Land Co Ltd ('the company'),
applied on behalf of those shareholders and unsecured creditors who voted unanimously for a stay of the winding-up of the company at meetings on 27th September
and 7th September respectively (1) for an order that the order of Mr Registrar Berkeley

made on 5th November 1974 be discharged, (2) for an order that each party pay their own costs or that they be paid out of the assets of the company, and (3) for such *a* further and other relief as might seem just. The facts are set out in the judgment.

The applicant appeared in person.
Mary Arden for the liquidator.

Cur adv vult *b*

10th December. **MEGARRY J** read the following judgment. This motion is a further stage in the tangled and often stormy career of the Calgary and Edmonton Land Co Ltd: I shall call it 'the company'. Since 21st May 1970 the company has been in a creditors' voluntary winding-up. The company is a property development company with assets valued at several millions of pounds, though the present economic *c* climate, together with uncertainties as to planning permissions and prospects of development, have made the valuation and realisation of the assets matters of some difficulty. However, there seems to be at least a high degree of probability that when all the assets are realised there will be enough to pay all the remaining creditors, discharge the expenses of liquidation (including paying the liquidator's remuneration) and leave a substantial balance for the shareholders. What is now before me is a *d* motion by Mr I D Hillman to discharge an order made by Mr Registrar Berkeley on 5th November 1974. There are nearly 14 million issued ordinary shares in the company, and Mr Hillman owns nearly 10,000 of them and his wife a little under 150,000. The major shareholder is another company called Bank & Commercial Holdings Ltd: I shall refer to this as 'B & C'. B & C holds over 13 million of the shares in the company, and this is over 93 per cent of the total. B & C acquired a large part of these shares from *e* Mr and Mrs Hillman under what is popularly called a 'take-over bid'; and since the matter was before Mr Registrar Berkeley earlier in the year B & C have acquired a relatively small number of additional shares in the company, though, as the registrar pointed out, a fall in the value of B & C's shares has now made acceptance of their offer far less advantageous than it once was.

On 16th January 1974 B & C issued a summons seeking a stay of the winding-up, *f* together with certain other relief relating to the remuneration of the liquidator. That summons was argued before the registrar by leading counsel on each side, with counsel for the liquidator neither supporting nor opposing the stay but drawing the registrar's attention to a number of relevant factors. On 23rd July 1974 the registrar delivered a reserved judgment of some length, dismissing the application for a stay and directing that the application for other relief should be stood over generally. B & *g* C then gave notice of motion seeking to discharge the registrar's order, and this was called on before me on 14th October. Counsel for B & C at once said that B & C were abandoning the motion, and I accordingly dismissed it. Mr Hillman, who appeared in person, attempted to be heard in support of the motion, but as B & C had abandoned it and he was not a party to it, I refused to hear him. For some while during the hearing of the present motion this change of front by B & C remained a little *h* mysterious, but on Day 4 the mystery was dispelled when, with the assent of all concerned, Mr Stubbs made a brief appearance on behalf of B & C and made a short and helpful statement. The attitude of B & C, he said, was still in favour of a stay; but in the prevailing economic climate B & C was no longer in a position to provide sufficient liquid funds from outside the company's own resources to cover the liquidator's remuneration and expenses. It was for this reason that B & C had not proceeded *j* further with its application for a stay.

After the B & C application for a stay had been abandoned, Mr Hillman took out his own summons, seeking a stay of the winding-up of the company, and seeking further orders in relation to the remuneration of the liquidator. That summons came on for hearing before the registrar on 5th November, when Mr Hillman appeared in person and the liquidator by counsel. The registrar disposed of the appli-

a   cation very shortly, dismissing the application for a stay merely by reference to his decision on B & C's application for a stay. Mr Hillman now moves before me in person under his notice of motion, which simply seeks that the registrar's order in his case 'may be discharged', and that each party pay their own costs, or that they be paid out of the assets of the company; and there is the familiar prayer for further and other relief. Miss Arden appeared for the liquidator, neither supporting nor opposing Mr

b   Hillman's motion, but drawing the attention of the court to relevant matters both of law and of fact. Such assistance is doubly desirable in a case such as this, as the court's file, consisting mainly of affidavits without their exhibits, is over two inches thick, there are voluminous exhibits, there is a good deal of relevant law, and Mr Hillman is not a lawyer. He has an extensive knowledge of the company's affairs, as he has been managing director of the company for 28 years; but that detailed knowledge has, I

c   think, sometimes made it difficult for him to select and explain the facts which are relevant to his motion. I should say that Mr Hillman opened his motion for a whole day and substantial parts of two others, and his reply took over five hours. I made repeated efforts to direct his attention to what was in issue, and away from the many grievances of his which did not arise on his motion; but such successes as I had were intermittent and short-lived. Ultimately, at the end of Day 5, a Friday, I had to tell

d   him that if when the hearing was resumed on the following Tuesday he wished to continue for more than an hour, he would have to satisfy me first that he intended to say something relevant; and in the end, after generous allowances had been made for minor interruptions to his flow, he sat down at 12.15. By the end of his submissions I think that I had understood what there was in his speeches that was relevant to his motion. I may add that, as he told me more than once, he is a very excitable man:

e   but I would emphasise that he remained courteous throughout, with no more than momentary lapses which I fully accept were due to his excitability. I am indebted to counsel for the liquidator not only for her submissions but also for refusing to be drawn into the many side-issues and non-issues in the case.

I can now turn to the law. First, by s 256(1) of the Companies Act 1948,

f   'The court may at any time after an order for winding up, on the application either of the liquidator or the official receiver or any creditor or contributory, and on proof to the satisfaction of the court that all proceedings in relation to the winding up ought to be stayed, make an order staying the proceedings, either altogether or for a limited time, on such terms and conditions as the court thinks fit.'

g   On the face of it, that has no application to a case where, as here, there has been no order for winding-up but the company is in voluntary liquidation. However, s 301 provides that the next nine sections of the Act 'apply to every voluntary winding up whether a members' or a creditors' winding up'; and one of those nine sections is s 307. By sub-s (1) of this,

h   'The liquidator or any contributory or creditor may apply to the court to determine any question arising in the winding up of a company, or to exercise, as respects the enforcing of calls or any other matter, all or any of the powers which the court might exercise if the company were being wound up by the court.'

j   By sub-s (2),

        'The court, if satisfied that the determination of the question or the required exercise of power will be just and beneficial, may accede wholly or partially to the application on such terms and conditions as it thinks fit or may make such other order on the application as it thinks just.'

The result is that the court can exercise its power under s 256 (as extended to a voluntary winding-up) if 'satisfied that the . . . required exercise of power will be just and   *a*
beneficial', and may do so 'on such terms and conditions as it thinks fit', or make such
other order on the application 'as it thinks just'. Under s 256 itself the court 'may . . .
on proof to the satisfaction of the court that all proceedings in relation to the winding
up ought to be stayed' make an order for the stay 'on such terms and conditions as
the court thinks fit'. Quite apart from any authority (and I may mention *Re Tele-*
scriptor Syndicate Ltd[1]) this language seems to me to make it abundantly clear that the   *b*
jurisdiction is discretionary, and that it lies on those who seek a stay to make out a
sufficient case for it. In particular, the words 'satisfied', 'just and beneficial', 'satisfaction
of the court' and 'ought to be stayed' seem to me to indicate that the applicant for a
stay must make out a case that carries conviction. It may be that where the liquidation has been proceeding for only a short while the court ought to be more ready to
grant a stay than in cases where the liquidation has been proceeding for a considerable   *c*
time and much has been done on the faith of it: but this point has not been argued and
I decide nothing on it.

Second, there is s 302, which by virtue of s 301 applies to every voluntary winding-
up. Section 302 runs:

> 'Subject to the provisions of this Act as to preferential payments, the property   *d*
> of a company shall, on its winding up, be applied in satisfaction of its liabilities
> pari passu, and, subject to such application, shall, unless the articles otherwise
> provide, be distributed among the members according to their rights and interests
> in the company.'

The effect of that section on the rights of members of the company seems to me to be   *e*
very considerable. Before the winding-up, each member has no right to be paid any
sum in respect of his capital, but only the right to such dividends as the directors
recommend and the company votes. Once there is a winding-up, each member
becomes instead entitled to an aliquot share of the company's assets after all liabilities
have been discharged. In her argument, counsel for the liquidator sought to establish
that under the winding-up each member was a beneficiary under a trust, and for this   *f*
she mainly relied on *Re The Albert Life Assurance Company Arbitration, The Delhi Bank's*
case[2], *Re General Rolling Stock Co*[3], *Re Oriental Inland Steam Co*[4], *Re Central Sugar Factories*
of Brazil[5], *Re Yagerphone Ltd*[6], *Wigan Coal & Iron Co Ltd v Inland Revenue Comrs*[7] and
Inland Revenue Comrs v Olive Mill Ltd[8]. Some of these authorities seem to me to do
little or nothing to support the proposition that the members of the company are
beneficiaries under a trust. It is one thing to say that there is a trust or a fiduciary duty,   *g*
and another to say that the members are beneficiaries under a trust. The high water-
mark in the authorities are some words of James and Mellish LJJ in *Re Oriental Inland*
Steam Co[9], spoken in relation to creditors rather than members. An alternative way
of regarding the matter is to treat the company and the liquidator as being bound by
fiduciary or statutory obligations towards the creditors and members to administer
the company's assets in accordance with their respective rights under the law. The   *h*
parallel is with the rights of those entitled under an intestacy or gift of residue, on the

---

1   [1903] 2 Ch 174
2   (1871) 15 Sol Jo 923
3   (1872) 7 Ch App 646   *j*
4   (1874) 9 Ch App 557
5   [1894] 1 Ch 369
6   [1935] Ch 392, [1935] All ER Rep 803
7   [1945] 1 All ER 392
8   [1963] 2 All ER 130, [1963] 1 WLR 712
9   9 Ch App at 559, 560

line of authorities of which *Comr of Stamp Duties (Queensland) v Livingston*[1] is one of

a   the latest.

For the purpose of what I have to decide in this case it does not seem to me necessary to attempt to resolve whether the members of the company have vested in them an actual beneficial interest in any of the assets of the company, or whether they merely have a right to compel the company and the liquidator to administer those assets according to law. In *Calgary v Edmonton Land Co Ltd v Dobinson*[2] I appear to

b   have preferred the latter view, rejecting a contention that the creditors and the contributories had beneficial interests under a trust. In the present case I have had the advantage of considering a number of authorities which were not cited in the *Dobinson* case[3], but I very much doubt whether they suffice to carry the opposite conclusion. However, as I have indicated, it does not seem necessary to resolve the point here, because whichever is the right view, the winding-up of the company

c   plainly brought with it a marked change in the position of its members. They thereupon became entitled, whether as beneficial owners or as persons entitled to enforce a statutory or fiduciary duty, to whatever a due process of liquidation would ultimately throw up as being theirs. It might be nothing, or it might be something far greater than the nominal or market value of their shares when the liquidation began; but at all events they became entitled to require the liquidation to be properly

d   conducted so as to give effect to their rights.

That brings me to the third point, that of the persons whose interests have to be considered on an application for a stay. These must, of course, depend on the circumstances of each case; but where, as here, there is a strong probability, if not more, that the assets of the company will suffice to pay all the creditors and the expenses of the liquidation, and so leave a surplus for the members of the company, there are

e   plainly three categories to consider. First, there are the creditors. Their rights are finite, in that they cannot claim more than 100p in the £. I cannot see that in normal circumstances any objection to a stay could be made on behalf of the creditors if for each of them it is established either that he has been paid in full, or that satisfactory provision for him to be paid in full has been or will be made, or else that he consents to the stay or is otherwise bound not to object to it. Second, there is the liquidator.

f   By s 309, all costs, charges and expenses properly incurred in the winding-up, including the liquidator's remuneration, are made payable out of the assets of the company in priority to all other claims. Where a liquidator has accepted office on this footing, I cannot see that in normal circumstances it would be right to stay the winding-up unless his special position had been fully safeguarded, either by paying him the proper amount for his expenses or by sufficiently securing payment. A liquid-

g   ator who loses control of the assets by reason of a stay ought normally to be properly safeguarded in relation to his expenses. Third, there are the members of the company. No question of satisfying them by immediate payment of all that they are entitled to can very well arise; for unlike the creditors, with their ascertained or ascertainable debts, the rights of the members cannot be quantified until the liquidation is complete. Accordingly, in normal circumstances I think that no stay should be granted

h   unless each member either consents to it, or is otherwise bound not to object to it, or else there is secured to him the right to receive all that he would have received had the winding-up proceeded to its conclusion. Each member has a right of a proprietary nature to share in the surplus assets, and each should be protected against the destruction of that right without good cause.

It will be observed that each of the heads is qualified by the words 'in normal

j   circumstances'. I am not suggesting that in these cases there are hard-and-fast rules;

---

1   [1964] 3 All ER 692, [1965] AC 694. See especially [1964] 3 All ER at 699, 700, [1965] AC at 712, 713
2   [1974] 1 All ER 484 at 490, [1974] Ch 102 at 108
3   [1974] 1 All ER 484, [1974] Ch 102

but I am saying that the circumstances that I have mentioned will usually be at least
highly material in deciding how the court's discretion should be exercised. Cases out **a**
of the normal way, of course, call for special treatment. In some respects, *Re South
Barrule Slate Quarry Co*[1] may be regarded both as an example of the principle and as a
special case. There, the total number of the shareholders had been reduced to 18, and
only one of these, holding less than five per cent of the shares, opposed a stay of the
winding-up. James V-C said[2]: 'I do not think I can allow one man to stand in the way
of the wishes of all his fellow shareholders'; and he held that the winding-up should **b**
be stayed, but that the dissenting shareholder should be given 14 days in which to
elect whether to remain a member of the company, or whether to retire and give
up his shares on the petitioner for the stay paying him the value of his interest in
the company's property, with a reference to chambers to enquire into that value.
There, of course, the attitude of all the shareholders to the proposed stay seems to
have been ascertained.   **c**
    There is one other point that I should mention in relation to members. Apart from
cases where their rights to what they would receive on a winding-up have been secured
to them, I have referred to them as either consenting to a stay or being otherwise
bound not to object to it; and that in due course will lead me to s 206. To make this
intelligible, I must refer to the membership of the company. This is conveniently set
out in the registrar's judgment in the B & C case; and it has not been suggested that **d**
there has been any significant change in the figures over the last five months. The
attitude of over 1,100 contributories holding over 730,000 shares was not known to the
registrar. Of these, nearly 400, holding rather under 500,000 shares, had been sent
communications by the liquidator which have not been returned as undelivered.
The remaining contributories, over 700 in number and holding nearly 250,000 shares,
have been sent communications by the liquidator which have been returned to him. **e**
The attitude of those in this latter category, said the registrar, could not be known
unless and until some attempt was made to reach them by advertisement.
    Now the essence of the registrar's decision in the B & C case, and so presumably in
this, is that in the circumstances of the case any application for a stay ought to have
been preceded by a scheme of arrangement under s 206 so that all members might
have an opportunity of putting forward their views. Members whose present ad- **f**
dresses are not known could at least be given the opportunity of responding to advertisements; and if the scheme obtained the statutory majority, those objecting to it
could still oppose it on the application for the sanction of the court under s 206. The
registrar placed some reliance in this respect on *Re Trix Ltd*[3]. That case is by no
means directly in point. It concerned a compromise under s 245, and not a stay; and
it concerned creditors and not contributories. If sanctioned, the compromise would **g**
have authorised a distribution of the company's assets in a way which might not have
accorded with the creditors' rights, which both in law and mathematics were difficult
to determine with precision. Plowman J said[4]:

> 'I am, therefore, confronted with an important question of principle, namely
> whether it is right to authorise such a distribution as I am asked to do without **h**
> either the consent of every creditor or a scheme of arrangement under s 206
> which would bind apathetic creditors (of whom there are apparently a very
> large number here), and the dissentient minority, which in this case appears to be
> one. In my judgment, it is not right. The matter is one which the creditors
> should decide for themselves and on which they are entitled to express their
> views at a meeting or in court.'   **j**

---

1 (1869) LR 8 Eq 688
2 LR 8 Eq at 691
3 [1970] 3 All ER 397, [1970] 1 WLR 1421
4 [1970] 3 All ER at 398, [1970] 1 WLR at 1423

Towards the end of his judgment he said[1]:

a

> 'In my judgment, it would be unfair to non-assenting creditors to deal with the matter in the way proposed since it deprives them of the opportunity of airing their views and of the protection of the court's control over meetings, advertisement and circular under s. 206.'

b
As I have indicated, the facts in that case were different from those in the case now before me; but I think that there is a useful analogy. Indeed, the registrar took the view that the present case was a fortiori; and I agree with him. In *Re Trix Ltd*[2] the proposal was merely to make a distribution to creditors which might not accord with their strict rights. Here, the proposal is not merely to make a possible variation in the distribution but to cancel it altogether, even though the contributories have long been entitled to it under the winding-up. I may add that the registrar's judgment also

c
referred to an unreported case, *Re Edward Wood & Co Ltd*[3], in which the court sanctioned a scheme which provided for a stay and gave the shareholders the option of being paid the estimated amount which they would have received had the winding-up proceeded.

In the present case, the sole question is whether or not it is right to grant a stay of

d
the winding-up. Mr Hillman contends that it is. His notice of motion purports to be given by him—

> 'on behalf of those shareholders and unsecured creditors who voted unanimously for a stay of winding up at meetings on September 27th and September 7th respectively'.

e
However, as Mr Hillman had taken no steps to obtain any representation order and referred me to no evidence of the persons for whom he sought to speak, the size of their interests, or their desire to be represented by him, I heard him in his personal capacity. When at the outset of Day 2 I asked him whether he wished to proceed on his own account or have an adjournment in order to apply for a representation order under r 157(2) of the Companies (Winding Up) Rules 1949[4], he elected for the

f
former course. He nevertheless made frequent assertions that he was speaking for all the shareholders, a much larger claim than that made by his notice of motion. One of his main points was that he had duly summoned the meetings mentioned in his notice of motion, that all shareholders could have attended, and that those who did not attend must be taken to have assented to what was decided. From time to time I reminded him that, statute apart, he could not rely on any doctrine such as

g
'silence means consent', and that there was a difference between company meetings to decide what course the company should take and meetings for the purpose of affecting the proprietary rights of individual shareholders in the company; but Mr Hillman held to his course. On the view that I take I do not think that it matters much whether or not Mr Hillman appeared in the representative capacity claimed in his notice of motion; and in deciding the case I bear that claim in mind.

h
What I have to consider here is an application for a stay made by a shareholder whose application, let me assume, is favoured by a number of other shareholders. The applicant has put forward no firm and acceptable proposals for discharging the claims of the remaining creditors or the liquidator's expenses, or for giving effect to the rights of any shareholders who do not wish the winding-up to be stayed. Mr Hillman's assertion that he thought that he could provide what the liquidator was

j
legally entitled to by means of second mortgages on the company's properties, and

---

1   [1970] 3 All ER at 399, [1970] 1 WLR at 1424
2   [1970] 3 All ER 397, [1970] 1 WLR 1421
3   (8th April 1974)
4   SI 1949 No 330

that the company's unencumbered properties might be sufficient, obviously falls very far short of what is required. Furthermore, the application now being made   **a** comes after a previous application for a stay made by the holder of over 93 per cent of the shares in the company (namely, B & C) had been dismissed and an appeal abandoned because that shareholder could not provide the liquid funds necessary to satisfy the creditors and the liquidator's expenses. Though that shareholder would still like a stay, it could not effectively prosecute its own application, and it has taken no steps to support Mr Hillman's application.   **b**

In those circumstances, the application made by Mr Hillman seems to me to be made in less favourable circumstances than those attending the application made by B & C. However, let me assume that proper arrangements could be made in one way or another to satisfy all the claims of the creditors and the liquidator, including his proper remuneration. Let me also assume that the liquidator can be indemnified in some suitable way against all claims in respect of his acts and defaults during the   **c** liquidation (if any) in respect of which it would be proper for him to be indemnified. Assume all that, and there still remain the members of the company who have not agreed to a stay. Nothing has been put before me to show how many of them would support a stay, or would oppose a stay, or would remain resolutely indifferent. There has been no scheme under s 206 which would bind the inert or an opposing minority. There is nothing to show how strongly, or on what ground, any shareholder who   **d** opposes a stay wishes the liquidation to continue, perhaps at greater speed, so that he may obtain his share of the value of the company's assets instead of remaining a shareholder subject to the dividend policy of the directors for the time being. All that I have is Mr Hillman's contentions and his unsupported and unsupportable assertions that he speaks for all the shareholders. In those circumstances, I do not see how it could possibly be said that the court is satisfied that it is just and beneficial to   **e** exercise the power to stay the proceedings on the ground that the court is satisfied that they ought to be stayed, whatever combination of the words and phrases in ss 256(1) and 307(2) it is right to adopt. In my judgment, in the B & C case the registrar came to the right conclusion for substantially the right reasons, and the same applies in this case. Let me make it clear that I am not holding that no stay ought to be granted in the present state of the winding-up. What I am holding is that in the   **f** absence of any firm and acceptable proposals for satisfying the creditors and the liquidator and of anything binding the other shareholders it would be wrong to grant a stay.

That suffices to dispose of the motion; but I must add something about s 206. Mr Hillman contended that the section could not be used in this case, and he fastened on a sentence in Palmer's Company Law[1], in a paragraph headed 'Take-overs'. After   **g** explaining what a 'take-over' is, the book states, 'Sections 206 and 287 have no application to such a scheme, which is effected by what is popularly known as a "take-over bid"'. In the present case, there had been a take-over by B & C, and so, Mr Hillman contended, s 206 could not be used in the present case to bind the shareholders. The argument, it will be seen, has only to be stated to be refuted: the proposition that a take-over cannot be effected by s 206 is far removed from any proposition that once   **h** there has been a take-over s 206 cannot be used for other purposes.

Mr Hillman also made other submissions or assertions that s 206 did not apply which I do not propose to attempt to set forth. The word 'arrangement' in sub-s (1) is very wide in its meaning, and if the members of a company in liquidation agree with the company to seek or not to oppose a stay of the winding-up, whereunder the members will give up their existing right to have all the proceeds of the company's   **j** assets distributed among them and instead be remitted to their contractual rights under the articles of the company, I do not see why that cannot be described as an

---

1   21st Edn (1968), p 696

'arrangement' between 'the company and its members' within s 206. I observe that
a in *Re Stephen Walters & Co Ltd*[1] the court approved a scheme of arrangement which
included a stay.   Further, in *Re Edward Wood & Co Ltd*[2], which I have already
mentioned, the scheme included a provision that no ordinary shareholder should
oppose the making of an order staying the winding-up of the company; and Templeman J sanctioned the scheme and ordered the stay. That case, I may say, began with a
summons by the contributory which did not put forward a scheme of arrangement
b but sought to compel the liquidator to do this.   However, as in the present case
nothing of any kind has been done to have any scheme put forward, I need not consider the mechanics. Nor do I think that I need discuss *Re NFU Development Trust Ltd*[3],
where Brightman J was understandably disinclined to regard proposals for the
confiscation or total surrender of shares without compensation as being a 'compromise
or arrangement' which could be sanctioned under s 206: no question of that nature
c arises in this case.   I can also dispose quite shortly of Mr Hillman's contention based
on an agreement under seal dated 5th November 1973, to which both he and B & C
(inter alios) were parties, whereby B & C agreed, among other things, to take all
necessary steps to seek stays of the winding-up of this and other companies. Even if
what B & C has already done is not a sufficient compliance with its obligation and
B & C is consequently liable for breach of contract (a matter upon which I say nothing),
d in the circumstances of this case the contract is of little cogency in relation to the
exercise of the court's discretion to order a stay.

Finally, I must say a word about the liquidator's remuneration, a matter on
which Mr Hillman evidently harbours strong feelings.   As I have mentioned, the
summons in this case sought under various heads that the remuneration of the
liquidator be fixed, with certain ancillary directions. The registrar made no order on
e these matters; indeed, he made no order on any part of the summons, save that Mr
Hillman should pay the liquidator's costs.   In view of what I have decided on the
application for a stay, I do not think that I need say anything about the liquidator's
remuneration except that if the point is to be pursued, it should be pursued in chambers on proper material.   Accordingly, the only order that I make on this motion is
that it be dismissed.
f

Motion dismissed.

Solicitors: *Frere Cholmeley & Co* (for the liquidator).

F K Anklesaria Esq Barrister.

g
---

1   [1926] WN 236
2   (8th April 1974) unreported
3   [1973] 1 All ER 135, [1972] 1 WLR 1548

Hubbard and others v Pitt and others   *a*

QUEEN'S BENCH DIVISION

FORBES J

17th OCTOBER, 8th NOVEMBER 1974

Highway – Public nuisance – Unreasonable use of highway – Circumstances constituting **b**
unreasonable use – Picketing – Plaintiffs' offices picketed by defendants every Saturday for
three hours – Picketing not for purpose of trade dispute – Defendants standing in line on
public footpath in front of offices – Defendants protesting against plaintiffs' activities – Public
able to pass on either side of picket line and between individuals forming it – Whether picketing
by defendants unreasonable use of highway.

c

The defendants were among a group of people who felt deeply about the social
problems caused by the redevelopment of Islington and also about the activities there
of property developers. They considered that estate agents who assisted such developers were acting indefensibly. The group decided to picket the offices of the
plaintiffs, who were a prominent firm of estate agents in the Islington area. On three
consecutive days in March and for three hours each Saturday morning thereafter **d**
some of the group stood in a line along the public footway in front of the plaintiffs'
offices. There was room on either side of that line, and between the individuals
forming it, for members of the public to pass along or across the footpath. The
pickets held placards and also distributed leaflets which stated that, inter alia, until
the plaintiffs formally agreed to bring their activities into line with the group's demands the picketing of their offices would continue. The plaintiffs brought an action **e**
against the defendants (who had all at various times been members of the picket
line) claiming (i) an injunction to restrain the defendants from picketing their premises
and from conspiring to do so; (ii) damages for nuisance and conspiracy. They maintained that the defendants had conspired to do an unlawful act (i e to stand on the
highway in front of their premises with placards), that such an act was an unlawful
use of the highway and that they as occupiers of premises adjoining the highway had **f**
suffered greater damage than other members of the public. In their defence the
defendants pleaded that the picketing was not unlawful in that it had been carried
out in a peaceful and orderly fashion in pursuance of the inalienable right of any
individual who felt deeply about a matter of substantial public interest and concern
to express an opinion about it and to draw public attention to it. The plaintiffs applied
for an interlocutory injunction.   **g**

Held – The application would be granted for the following reasons—
   (i) Any act which was inconsistent with the public right to use every part of a highway
for the purpose for which it was dedicated, i e for passage and repassage, and for any
purpose that was reasonably incidental to that use, was likely to be unreasonable,
and accordingly to amount to a public nuisance unless the act (a) was authorised by **h**
statute, or (b) was so fleeting and unappreciable as to fall within the de minimis rule
(see p 1061 *e* to *g* and p 1063 *d*, post); *Hickman v Maisey* [1900] 1 QB 752, *Hadwell v
Righton* [1907] 2 KB 345 and *Wolverton Urban District Council v Willis* (*trading as
S G Willis & Sons*) [1962] 1 All ER 243 applied.
   (ii) The use of the highway for picketing was not a use for which the highway was
dedicated and was illegal unless it was covered by statute, i e as being in contemplation **j**
or furtherance of a trade dispute, or was insubstantial (see p 1065 *c*, p 1067 *e* and p 1068
c and *e* to *g*, post); *Ward, Lock and Co Ltd v Operative Printers' Assistants' Society* (1906) 22
TLR 327 explained.
   (iii) On the evidence the defendants were not acting in contemplation or furtherance
of a trade dispute and their picketing activities could not be described as insubstantial;

a accordingly their conduct in picketing the plaintiffs' office amounted to a public
nuisance and their agreement to do so, to an unlawful conspiracy (see p 1065 *e* and p
1068 *h*, post).

(iv) The plaintiffs had established that they had suffered substantial, and not merely
fleeting or evanescent, damage as a result of the picketing by the defendants (see
p 1068 *j* to p 1069 *c* and *g*, post); dicta of Lord Hanworth MR in *Harper v G N Haden &*
Sons [1932] All ER Rep at 61 applied.

b (v) An interlocutory injunction was necessary for the preservation of the plaintiffs'
business and the restoration of unimpeded access to their premises for their staff and
customers (see p 1070 *b* to *d*, post); dictum of Kay LJ in *J Lyons & Sons v Wilkins* [1896]
1 Ch at 827 applied.

Per Forbes J. Although, by virtue of art 11^a of the European Convention on
Human Rights, everyone has the right to freedom of peaceful assembly and to freedom
c of association with others, that article does not give a right to assemble in public
anywhere the conveners of a public meeting choose, and in particular does not give
a right to assemble on the highway (see p 1067 *a* and *b*, post).

Notes

d For unreasonable use of the highway, see 19 Halsbury's Laws (3rd Edn) 273-275, para
437, and for cases on nuisance by the assembly of crowds on the highway, see 26 Digest
(Repl) 488, *1738-1741*.

Cases referred to in judgment

Attorney-General v Brighton and Hove Co-operative Supply Association [1900] 1 Ch 276, 69
LJCh 204, 81 LT 762, 64 JP Jo 68, CA, 26 Digest (Repl) 485, *1704*.
e *Dawes v Hawkins* (1860) 8 CBNS 848, 29 LJCP 343, 4 LT 288, 25 JP 502, 7 Jur NS 262, 141
ER 1399, 26 Digest (Repl) 304, *246*.
Educational Co of Ireland Ltd v Fitzpatrick [1961] IR 323, 45 Digest (Repl) 589, *708*.
Hadwell v Righton [1907] 2 KB 345, 76 LJKB 891, 97 LT 133, 71 JP 499, 5 LGR 881, 2
Digest (Repl) 320, *191*.
Harper v G N Haden and Sons Ltd [1933] Ch 298, [1932] All ER Rep 59, 102 LJCh 6, 148 LT
f 303, 96 JP 525, 31 LGR 18, CA, 11 Digest (Reissue) 168, *310*.
Harrison v Duke of Rutland [1893] 1 QB 142, [1891-4] All ER Rep 514, 62 LJQB 117, 68 LT
35, 57 JP 278, 4 R 155, CA, 15 Digest (Repl) 996, *9802*.
Hickman v Maisey [1900] 1 QB 752, 69 LJQB 511, 82 LT 321, CA, 26 Digest (Repl) 327, *449*.
Jacobs v London County Council [1950] 1 All ER 737, [1950] AC 361, 114 JP 204, 48 LGR 323,
HL, 26 Digest (Repl) 472, *1604*.
g *Lewis, Ex parte* (1888) 21 QBD 191, 57 LJMC 108, 59 LT 338, 52 JP 773, 16 Cox CC 449,
DC, 26 Digest (Repl) 327, *458*.
Lowdens v Keaveney [1903] 2 IR 82, 67 JP 378, 26 Digest (Repl) 488, *674*.
Lyons (J) & Sons v Wilkins [1896] 1 Ch 811, 65 LJCh 601, 74 LT 358, 60 JP 325, CA, 15
Digest (Repl) 919, *8824*.
Original Hartlepool Collieries Co v Gibb (1877) 5 Ch D 713, 46 LJCh 311, 36 LT 433, 41 JP
h 660, 3 Asp MLC 411, 26 Digest (Repl) 485, *1709*.
R v Carlile (1834) 6 C & P 636, 26 Digest (Repl) 489, *1747*.
R v Clark (No 2) [1963] 3 All ER 884, [1964] 2 QB 315, [1963] 3 WLR 1067, 62 LGR 99,
CCA, Digest (Cont Vol A) 635, *1566a*.
R v Stephens (1866) LR 1 QB 702, 7 B & S 710, 35 LJQB 251, 14 LT 593, 30 JP 822, 12 Jur
NS 961, 10 Cox CC 340, 47 Digest (Repl) 764, *1009*.
j *R v United Kingdom Electric Telegraph Co Ltd* (1862) 2 B & S 647n, 3 F & F 73, 31 LJMC 166,
6 LT 378, 26 JP 690, 8 Jur NS 1153, 9 Cox CC 174, 121 ER 1212, 26 Digest (Repl) 329, *478*.
Tynan v Balmer [1966] 2 All ER 133, [1967] 1 QB 91, [1966] 2 WLR 1181, DC, Digest
(Cont Vol B) 189, *7369d*.

---

a Article 11 is set out at p 1067 *a*, post

Ward. Lock and Co Ltd v Operative Printers' Assistants' Society (1906) 22 TLR 327, CA, 15
Digest (Repl) 919, 8827.

Wolverton Urban District Council v Willis (trading as S G Willis & Sons) [1962] 1 All ER
243, [1962] 1 WLR 205, 126 JP 84, 60 LGR 135, DC, Digest (Cont Vol A) 1, 346a.

Motion

The plaintiffs, Ronald Frederick Hubbard, Christopher Theodore Hubbard, and
Robert Malcolm Owen, partners in Prebble & Co, a firm of estate agents, brought an
action against the defendants, James Michael Bousfield Pitt, Christopher Fisher,
Thomas Crowe, Martin McEnery, Alan McAskill, Malcolm McAskill, Pauline Gordon,
Jack Arthur Gordon, David Sternberg and Margaret Ryan. The plaintiffs claimed,
inter alia, (i) an injunction to restrain the defendants and each of them by themselves, their servants or agents or otherwise from besetting the plaintiffs' premises
at 108-109 Upper Street, Islington, London N1, 82 Parkway, Camden, London NW1
and 543 High Road, Tottenham, London N17, or any of the premises or otherwise
molesting the plaintiffs, their servants, agents or clients or any tenants of such clients,
or any other person transacting or seeking to transact business with the plaintiffs
or committing any nuisance against the plaintiffs in respect of their premises or any
of them and/or from doing any act calculated to damage the plaintiffs in their business and/or from interfering with the plaintiffs' contractual relations with their
clients and any other persons, and/or from further publishing or causing to be published certain words written on placards and displayed and published by the defendants on various occasions from 13th March to 22nd June 1974 to passers-by at the
plaintiffs' premises at Upper Street, Islington, and/or words contained in a leaflet
headed 'Islington Tenants' Campaign' and distributed and published or caused to be
distributed and published by the defendants on 8th June 1974 to passers-by at the
plaintiffs' premises at Upper Street, Islington, or any similar words defamatory of the
plaintiffs and/or from conspiring with each other or with others to do the acts complained of or any of them or any similar acts; (ii) damages for nuisance; (iii) damages
for libel; (iv) damages for conspiracy. The plaintiffs applied for an interlocutory
injunction to restrain the defendants from continuing the activities complained of.
The facts are set out in the judgment.

A T Hoolahan QC and *Richard Rampton* for the plaintiffs.
Lord Gifford for the fifth, sixth, seventh, eighth, ninth and tenth defendants.
The first four defendants appeared in person.

Cur adv vult

8th November. **FORBES J** read the following judgment. This case is concerned
with the district of Islington in London. Like many other areas of the metropolis,
its dwelling-houses present an interesting social history in miniature. Many of them
are terraced houses built in Victorian days as family homes. Over the years, Islington
became less fashionable. Many of those houses became sub-divided into smaller units
let at low rents. The tenants of these properties were people with low incomes. It
was all they could afford. More recently, however, Islington has returned to fashion.
Terraced houses with many tenants to each house have been converted back to single
family homes. Restored and renovated, they have been sold to people who could
afford to buy such properties. It has become what house agents call an improving
area. In addition, there has also been the usual process of demolition of older properties and their replacement by modern blocks of flats or offices. No doubt the
conversion of down-at-heel tenanted properties to well-maintained owner-occupied
houses improves the aesthetics of the urban scene. It also has the effect of drastically
reducing the stock of dwelling-houses available for letting at low rents. Still other
effects follow. The high prices which restored and renovated houses fetch when they

a can be sold with vacant possession represent a powerful incentive to landlords of tenanted property to obtain possession from their tenants. Many of these tenants have some security under various statutory provisions. Some practices designed to obtain possession from tenants are classed as harassment and are illegal. But there are other ways in which landlords can put pressure on tenants in this situation which are not illegal. Some people regard the use of such practices, though legal, as morally unjustifiable. Many others do not go as far as this but recognise that real social

b problems arise when any large scale renovation of a residential area results in a shortage of cheap property to let. The whole situation then becomes heavily charged with emotional and political overtones.

It is important to see this case against that background, for the defendants here are among a group of people who are concerned at the social problems caused by redevelopment in Islington. This group is a loosely knit collection of individuals who

c call themselves The Islington Tenants' Campaign or Crusade. They felt deeply about the activities of property developers in Islington; they also considered that estate agents who assisted property developers were acting indefensibly. The plaintiff firm of estate agents, Prebble & Co, is prominent in Islington, so the group decided to picket the offices of the plaintiffs. On three consecutive days in March some of the group attended on the public footway in front of the plaintiffs' offices at 108-109

d Upper Street, Islington. They held placards and distributed leaflets. Both the placards and the leaflets referred to the plaintiffs in opprobrious terms. Subsequently, pickets carrying similar placards and leaflets attended at the same place on every Saturday. All the defendants have at various times been on these picket lines.

In these circumstances, the plaintiffs started an action against the defendants. Their statement of claim discloses three main heads of claim; in conspiracy, nuisance

e and defamation The plaintiffs maintain that the picket was the result of a conspiracy, an agreement to do an unlawful act. The unlawful act complained of is standing on the highway in front of the plaintiffs' premises with placards, and so on. This, say the plaintiffs, is an unlawful user of the highway. The claim in nuisance also involves unlawful user of the highway, but the plaintiffs accept that they must prove in the ordinary way that they, as occupiers of premises adjoining the highway, suffered

f greater damage than the generality of Her Majesty's subjects. The claim in defamation is based on the terms of the placards carried by the pickets and of leaflets which they handed out. It is answered in the defences of the defendants by a plea of justification. So far as the other claims are concerned, the defendants maintain that they have a lawful right to do what they are doing. I quote from para 4 of the defence of the six defendants for whom Lord Gifford appears, although the same paragraph appears

g also in the defences of the other defendants:

> 'The said pickets were carried out in a peaceful and orderly fashion in pursuance of the lawful right enjoyed by the defendants and other participants to express their opinions about, and draw public attention towards, a matter of substantial public interest and concern.'

h The plaintiffs applied for an interim injunction to restrain the defendants from continuing the picket, and I was asked by the defendants, in view of the general importance of the subject, to hear that application in open court. This suggestion was opposed, though not vehemently, by counsel for the plaintiffs. I thought it right in those circumstances to hear the argument in chambers but to adjourn into open court. I have been greatly assisted by both counsel, whose industry has produced a

j formidable array of authorities.

Before coming to the main contentions, I should dispose quickly of the claim in defamation. It is well settled law that the court will not grant interim injunctions in defamation cases where justification is pleaded, unless perhaps the case of justification put forward is obviously a sham. This exception cannot really apply in a case where counsel is involved because it is counsel's duty to satisfy himself of the genuineness of any plea of justification before putting it forward. So here, no interim injunction to restrain further publication of the matters complained of will be granted.

On the main issues, counsel's contentions for the plaintiffs are these. First, he says the highway is a piece or strip of land dedicated to the use of the public over which each member of the public has a right to pass or repass and do things reasonably incidental thereto. Secondly, any person who enters on a highway and does, or intends to do, anything which is not within the above right is a trespasser unless he can show either that the special right was given in the grant of dedication or has been authorised by statute. Thirdly, a trespasser may not necessarily incur liability, for instance for public nuisance, unless the trespass constitutes an unreasonable use of the highway. And fourthly, there is no right to use the highway to stand, or to stand in line, or to place placards thereon, or to stop pedestrians, or to picket, nor is there any right to do any act with a view to compelling a shopkeeper, for instance, to comply with the demands of the person using the highway.

Lord Gifford, on the other hand, puts forward four propositions of his own. First, he says, picketing is not unlawful or actionable unless it takes the form of a common law nuisance. Secondly, for this purpose, and so far as relates to user of a highway, common law nuisance is equivalent to or synonymous with unreasonable user of the highway. One can do anything, he says, on a highway as long as it is reasonable. If it is reasonable, it is lawful. Thirdly, the mode of user of these defendants was not unreasonable. And fourthly, even if it was, it did not cause substantial damage to the plaintiffs, and substantial damage must be proved for the plaintiffs to succeed.

Although these were the submissions which Lord Gifford put formally at the outset of his argument, the course of that argument is better represented by the following set of propositions: (1) to amount to common law nuisance on the highway, any conduct has to be unreasonable; (2) picketing is a reasonable user of the highway because there is a special kind of democratic right to picket which is analogous to the right of free speech; (3) picketing only becomes unreasonable, and therefore a nuisance, if it is accompanied by violence or intimidation, or amounts to physical obstruction of the highway.

Before considering the wider implications of these propositions, it may be convenient to examine two general questions: what is the nature of the public right in a highway? and, secondly, what conduct in relation to a highway constitutes a common law or public nuisance?

What is the nature of the public right in a highway? The vital characteristic of a highway is that it is land dedicated for a purpose; that purpose is for use by the public for passage to and fro. 'The King has nothing but the passage for himself and his people'[1]. The editors of the 21st Edition of Pratt and Mackenzie's Law of Highways[2] put it thus: 'The right of the public in a highway is an easement of passage only—a right of passing and repassing.' The third edition of Halsbury's Laws of England[3]:

'The right of the public is a right to "pass along" a highway for the purpose of legitimate travel, not to "be on" it, except so far as their presence is attributable to a reasonable and proper user of the highway as such.'

The position was authoritatively set out by Lopes LJ in *Harrison v Duke of Rutland*[4]:

'... if a person uses the soil of the highway for any purpose other than that in respect of which the dedication was made and the easement acquired, he is a trespasser. The easement acquired by the public is a right to pass and repass at their pleasure for the purpose of legitimate travel, and the use of the soil for any

---

1 1 Roll Abr 392
2 (1967), p 3
3 Volume 19, p 73, para 107
4 [1893] 1 QB 142 at 154, [1891-4] All ER Rep 514 at 518

a other purpose, whether lawful or unlawful, is an infringement of the rights of
the owner of the soil.'

Of course, it may well be that use of a highway for purposes incidental to passage
is a proper use. In *Hadwell v Righton*[1] Phillimore J put it in this way: '. . . members of
the public, in addition to using it eundo et redeundo, are also entitled to use it morando
for a short time.' Thus a tired pedestrian may sit down and rest himself. A motorist
b may attempt to repair a minor breakdown. Because the highway is used also as a
means of access to places abutting on the highway, it is permissible to queue for
tickets at a theatre or other place of entertainment, or for a bus. But wherever a
person is using a highway other than purely as a means of passage, he is only entitled
to use it for a purpose which is reasonably incidental to the right of passage.

The importance of bearing in mind that the primary purpose of the highway is
c passage is underlined by Collins LJ in his judgment in *Hickman v Maisey*[2]:

'. . . although in modern times a reasonable extension has been given to the
use of the highway as such, the authorities shew that the primary purpose of the
dedication must always be kept in view. The right of the public to pass and
repass on a highway is subject to all those reasonable extensions which may from
time to time be recognised as necessary to its existence in accordance with the
d enlarged notions of people in a country becoming more populous and highly
civilised, but they must be such as are not inconsistent with the maintenance of
the paramount idea that the right of the public is that of passage.'

The true position, therefore, is that whether passing or repassing, or exercising the
reasonable extensions spoken of by Collins LJ, the user has to be ordinarily and
e reasonably incidental to the exercise of a right of passage, otherwise it becomes a
trespass and therefore unlawful.

Now, even then, such user must be reasonable in extent. The tired pedestrian or
the motorist with the breakdown can only rest for a reasonable while. Those who
queue for theatre tickets or stop to watch window displays must do so reasonably and
in such a way as not unduly to obstruct other users. If a use of a highway, though
f incidental to the right of passage, is unreasonable in extent, it goes beyond the purpose
for which the highway was dedicated. If it is not incidental to the right of passage at
all, it also goes beyond that purpose. One may therefore define the right of the public
to use a highway as a right to use it reasonably for passage and repassage and for any
other purpose reasonably incidental thereto. I find myself, therefore, accepting counsel
for the plaintiffs' first proposition, which is in almost exactly similar terms.

g His second proposition is effectively that a use of the highway which goes beyond
these public rights is a trespass unless such use is covered specially by the dedication
or authorised by some statute. Lord Gifford does not dissent from this proposition,
and, indeed, it seems to me to be well-settled law. Of course, the trespass is only
actionable at the suit of the owner of the soil of the highway.

So much for the first general question, what is the nature of the public right in the
h highway? The second general question is, what conduct in relation to a highway
constitutes a public nuisance? Here counsel for the plaintiffs' third proposition is that
misuse of the highway which amounts to trespass may not amount to public nuisance
unless it constitutes an unreasonable user. Lord Gifford's proposition is to the same
effect, but he puts it really in this way: to amount to a public nuisance, any action or
conduct on the highway has to be unreasonable. It is here that there is a danger of
j becoming involved in a sterile semantic argument. What is or is not reasonable
is not a matter of knowledge a priori. The term 'unreasonable' can only be interpreted
in a context, and the context in this case is the law of highways. What Lord Gifford is
really saying is that his clients were behaving reasonably in the sense that they were

1   [1907] 2 KB 345 at 348
2   [1900] 1 QB 752 at 757, 758

not resorting to violence or intimidation and did not station themselves so as com-   a
pletely to obstruct the footpath or the entrance to the plaintiffs' office. But one is
not here considering what is the behaviour to be expected of a reasonable picket
(whatever that may be) but whether or not the behaviour of these pickets amounted
to an unreasonable user of the highway. And whether or not a use of a highway is
reasonable can only be determined by reference to the fact that the purpose of
dedication is that the public may pass and repass, a subject I have already dealt with
earlier.   b
There is good authority for the proposition that to amount to public nuisance a use
of the highway must be unreasonable or excessive—*Lowdens v Keaveney*[1] and *R v
Clark (No 2)*[2], two cases to which I shall return later. But as Lord Gifford seeks to
appropriate the term 'reasonable' to a different context, it might be more convenient
to adopt a different definition, and in *Jacobs v London County Council*[3], Lord Simonds
approved and adopted the definition used in the 18th edition of Pratt and Mackenzie[4]. c
That definition still appears in the 21st edition[5]. It is as follows:

> 'Nuisance may be defined with reference to highways, as any wrongful act or
> omission upon or near a highway, whereby the public are prevented from freely,
> safely, and conveniently passing along the highway.'

Leaving aside for the moment Lord Gifford's proposition that there exists a demo-   d
cratic right to picket, he bases his claim that his clients acted lawfully on the assertion
that they conducted themselves without violence or intimidation and in a manner
which did not obstruct the highway. It is necessary to consider these matters as part
of the question, was the conduct of the defendants a reasonable user of the highway?
Let me say at once that I am content to assume that no violence or intimidation was
used by any of these defendants, though there is a conflict about this on the affidavits. e
But it is only necessary to look at the photographs to see that these people, disposed
on the highway in this fashion, by their mere presence might well deter clients and
potential clients of the plaintiffs from entering the plaintiffs' offices. And here I am
being careful to base this view on their presence and not on the allegedly defamatory
nature of the placards being displayed, no remedy for which is, in my view, available
to the plaintiffs at this stage.   f
One must also consider the question of obstruction, for Lord Gifford claims that
there was none. In Hawkins's Pleas of the Crown[6] appears this passage under the
heading 'What shall be said to be a nuisance to a highway at common law':

> 'S.10. There is no doubt but that all injuries whatsoever to any highway as by
> digging a ditch or making a hedge overthwart it, or laying logs of timber in it,   g
> or by doing any other act which will render it less commodious to the King's
> people, are public nuisances at common law'.

The term 'less commodious' is explained further in s 11:

> 'Also it seemeth to be clear that it is no excuse for one who layeth such logs
> in the highway that he laid them only here and there so that people might have   h
> a passage by windings and turnings through the logs.'

In *R v United Kingdom Electric Telegraph Co Ltd*[7] telegraph poles driven into the grass
verge of a country road were held by a court which included Blackburn J to amount

---

1   [1903] 2 IR 82   j
2   [1963] 3 All ER 884, [1964] 2 QB 315
3   [1950] 1 All ER 737 at 744, [1950] AC 361 at 375
4   (1932), p 107
5   (1967), p 112
6   8th Edn (1824), bk 1, c 32, p 700
7   (1862) 2 B & S 647n

to a public nuisance. And in *Wolverton Urban District Council v Willis*[1] the Divisional Court laid down these principles:

'(i) that every member of the public is entitled to unrestricted access to the whole of a footway, save insofar as he may be prevented by obstructions lawfully authorised; (ii) that, subject to the de minimis principle, any encroachment on the footway which restricts him in the full exercise of that right and which is not authorised by law, is an unlawful obstruction; and (iii) that every member of the public so restricted in the use of the footway is necessarily obstructed in that, to the extent of the obstruction, he is denied access to the whole of the footway; that is, he is obstructed in his legal right to use the whole of the footway.'

So it is not sufficient to say that the public could easily get by the obstruction, which is one of the claims made by Lord Gifford on behalf of his clients. They were, he suggested, and as the affidavits and the photographs show, strung out in a line along the length of the footway and not across it. There was room either side of the picket line, and even room between the individual members of it, for members of the public to pass along or across the footpath. The law, however, seems to me to be clear. The public has a right to go on every part of the highway, and any act which makes it less commodious is a public nuisance unless it can be said to be so fleeting and so inappreciable as to fall within the de minimis rule.

The authority on which Lord Gifford chiefly relies in support of his contention that to behave in the way the defendants behaved was a reasonable user of the highway, and therefore not a nuisance, is the judgment of Moulton LJ in *Ward, Lock and Co Ltd v Operative Printers' Assistants' Society*[2]. The headnote reads as follows:

'The defendants stationed pickets to watch the plaintiffs' printing works for the purpose of inducing the workmen employed by the plaintiffs to join the union, and then to determine their employment by proper notices, the object being to compel the plaintiffs to become employers of union men and to abstain from employing non-union men. There was no evidence that the pickets invited the men to break their contracts. This was carried out without causing by violence, obstruction, or otherwise, a common law nuisance.'

I should refer to the passages from Moulton LJ's judgment[3] on which Lord Gifford relies:

'It is inaccurate to say that the masters have a right to employ men on any specific terms. They have only a right to employ such, if any, as are willing to accept those terms, and no wrong is done them by anyone who by lawful means lessens the number of those willing to accept them. The right of the plaintiffs to try to persuade a man to accept, and the right of the defendants to try to persuade a man to refuse, appear to me to be rights of freedom of individual action equally lawful and equally deserving of the protection of the law, so long as the means employed are lawful and right. Both become unlawful if the means employed are wrongful. I am therefore of opinion that in support of the plaintiffs' claim with regard to picketing, it must be shown that the defendants or one of them were guilty of a wrongful act, *i.e.*, that the picketing constituted an interference with the plaintiffs' action wrongful at common law, or, as I think it may accurately be phrased, were guilty of a common law nuisance. The picketing complained of in the statement of claim is during the period of the 8th to the 14th of July. It is common ground that there was picketing during this period, in as much as the defendants admit that they had two shifts of three pickets each in

---

1 [1962] 1 All ER 243 at 246, [1962] 1 WLR 205 at 208
2 (1906) 22 TLR 327
3 22 TLR at 330

the neighbourhood of the plaintiffs' premises . . . in my view that which decides
the question is that there is no evidence of any improper or illegal acts, or, *a*
indeed, of any acts whatever, by any pickets sent by the defendants during this
period. There can, therefore, be no pretence that the plaintiffs have established
anything which would give to them a good cause of action in respect of the
picketing complained of. I wish to add that, in my opinion, there is throughout a
complete absence of evidence of anything in the nature of picketing or besetting
which could constitute a nuisance. It appears that the discharged workmen *b*
loitered about for a day or two after leaving work—a thing which is not unlikely
to happen—and that they were at times joined by others, but there is no suggestion even by the plaintiffs' witnesses that any annoyance or molestation took
place, and the evidence to the contrary is overwhelming.'

And then: *c*

'The defendants called the inspector and the sergeant who had charge of the
matter, and their evidence shows that there was nothing which could give any
ground for complaint, and there was a total absence of evidence (other than the
defendants' admission to which I have referred) [and that was that they were
responsible for two shifts of three pickets] that the plaintiffs, or either of them,
were responsible for the presence of any of the men who actually lingered in the *d*
neighbourhood of the premises. I am therefore of opinion that there was no
evidence to go to the jury in respect of any cause of action against the defendants,
or either of them, based on alleged picketing.'

Vaugham Williams LJ[1] also dealt with the matter as a question of fact:

'The evidence shows this [the picketing] to have been done without causing by *e*
violence, obstruction, or otherwise a common law nuisance, such as that mentioned in question 1.'

In fact, the case is only reported for the observations of the court on s 7 of the Conspiracy, and Protection of Property Act 1875, and in my view it is quite impossible to
say that this case, which depends for its decision on the facts, is authority for the wide *f*
proposition for which Lord Gifford contends. All it really amounts to is that in the
circumstances for that particular case the learned Lords Justices felt that three pickets,
the number for which alone the defendants appear to have been responsible, acting in
the way that those pickets acted, did not amount to a common law nuisance. It might
perhaps be added that this decision was given in the same year as the passing of the
Trades Disputes Act 1906 and dealt with picketing by trade union members in further- *g*
ance of a trade dispute in circumstances which s 2 of that Act declared to be legal. On
the other hand, to quote but one example from an Irish case, it was held in *Educational
Co of Ireland Ltd v Fitzpatrick*[2] that peaceful picketing of premises by relays of pickets
drawn from 15 of the total union strength of 16 members was permitted by the Trades
Disputes Act 1906, but would have been illegal but for the statutory provision.

It might be convenient at this stage to consider the statutory provisions relating to *h*
picketing, for both counsel have referred to them at some length. First, s 7 of the
Conspiracy, and Protection of Property Act 1875 in its original form provided, as the
Ward Lock case[3] shows, a convenient criminal sanction for the conduct set out in that
section. This conduct included picketing for the purpose of compelling anyone to do,
or abstain from doing, something which he had a legal right to do or abstain from doing.
The section made nothing illegal whether in tort or crime which was not illegal before. *j*
The proviso which exempted from the provisions of the section what might be called

---

1   (1906) 22 TLR at 329
2   [1961] IR 323
3   (1906) 22 TLR 327

a picketing for the sole purpose of obtaining or communicating information was repealed by the Trades Disputes Act 1906. That Act itself by s 2, of which the heading is 'Peaceful Picketing', provided as follows:

b 'It shall be lawful for one or more persons, acting on their own behalf or on behalf of a trade union or of an individual employer or firm in contemplation or furtherance of a trade dispute, to attend at or near a house or place where a person resides or works or carries on business or happens to be, if they so attend merely for the purpose of peacefully obtaining or communicating information, or of peacefully persuading any person to work or abstain from working.'

The important words are 'contemplation or furtherance of a trade dispute', for if Lord Gifford's contention is right and peaceful picketing is a lawful exercise when *c* performed by any citizen, it would be unnecessary to pass an enactment which legalises such an exercise only when performed in contemplation or furtherance of a trade dispute. The provisions of the 1906 Act were in their turn repealed by the Industrial Relations Act 1971 and s 134 of that Act provided in somewhat more extended terms an exemption for peaceful picketing from proceedings under the 1875 Act and from civil liability for tort; but again only when the picket was conducted 'in con- *d* templation of furtherance of an industrial dispute'. The statutory position is now governed by the Trades Union and Labour Relations Act 1974, s 15 of which broadly re-enacts the provisions of s 2 of the 1906 Act.

It seems to me in view of all these matters that the defendants' conduct, which was not in furtherance of any trade dispute, was not authorised by statute, amounted to an unreasonable use of the highway, and was therefore unlawful unless it can be *e* justified on some principle other than those I have so far reviewed.

Lord Gifford, however, does seek to justify the defendants' conduct by reference to other principles. It is part, he says, of the inalienable right of anyone in a democratic society who feels deeply enough about a subject, or disapproves strongly enough of someone's behaviour, that he is entitled to picket any place, whether public or private, in order to express those feelings and to draw public attention *f* towards a matter of substantial public interest and concern: see para 4 of the defence of the defendants to which I have already adverted. In support of this proposition, he relies first on an analogy with the principles of freedom of speech, and secondly, on a comparison of the defendants' actions with those who on occasions picket the Houses of Parliament or 10 Downing Street or the Soviet Embassy, or those who by way of demonstration march through the streets before holding a public meeting *g* outside the premises of some organisation or power which has attracted particular approbation or disfavour. These, he says, are manifestations of that democratic right which he postulates, and the fact that they are permitted indicates that they are lawful.

Turning first to the defendants' suggestion that the right to picket is analogous to the right usually referred to as freedom of speech. The latter term is itself misleading. *h* There is no such thing in law as unfettered freedom of speech. One's right to say what one likes is circumscribed by, for instance, the laws relating to sedition, contempt of court, obscenity and defamation. Similarly one's right to be on the highway is subject to the law relating to highways. Whereas the passage of years may make a difference in the utterances which are regarded as obscene, defamatory, contemptuous or even seditious, no such alteration is possible in the law of highways. A judge *j* might well be justified in treating as no longer defamatory a word or description which authority shows to have been so considered many years ago, either because the language or the mores of right-thinking members of society has changed, but the only changes time legitimates in relation to highway law are changes in the modes of user for passage. Where, for instance, it was once permissible to pass with a horse and cart, it may now be legal to use a lorry. Freedom of expression was never one of the attributes of highway dedication, and nothing is better settled than that it is impossible to obtain a prescriptive right to obstruct a highway. Byles J in *Dawes v* **a** *Hawkins* said[1]:

'It is also an established maxim,—once a highway always a highway: for, the public cannot release their rights, and there is no extinctive presumption or prescription.'

Then Lord Gifford refers to the picketing of public buildings, embassies, and so on, **b** and the demonstrations with which all are now familiar. Such manifestations of popular expression are common and are permitted; ergo, says Lord Gifford, they must be lawful. In examining this part of the case, it is necessary, I think, to make a distinction between the march or the procession on the one hand and the assembly on the highway in front of some premises on the other. The law appears to be that it does not amount to a common law nuisance to march or conduct a procession **c** through the streets of a town so long, presumably, as the procession allows other people reasonable room for passage and behaves in a non-violent and sensible manner. In the Irish case of *Lowdens v Keaveney*[2] Gibson J considered this question at common law, and his view of the matter was approved by the Court of Criminal Appeal in *R v Clark (No 2)*[3]. Gibson J put it like this[4]:

d
'Before approaching the statute of 1851 I shall briefly refer to the common law. A public highway is primarily for the free passage of the public for all reasonable purposes of business or pleasure; but persons using such highway may stop on lawful occasions, as, e.g. for the purpose of taking up or discharging persons or goods at adjoining houses, provided that in so doing they do not unreasonably interfere with corresponding rights of others. Where the use of the highway is **e** unreasonable or excessive, that is a nuisance, irrespective of any guilty or wrongful intent on the part of the wrongdoer: *R v Stephens*[5]. Examples of such nuisance from illegitimate use are, where a physical obstruction is placed on the thoroughfare, or where a merchant, by continuously keeping vans before his door, practically appropriates for his business purposes part of the roadway: *Original Hartlepool Collieries Co v Gibb*[6]; *Attorney General v Brighton and Hove Co-operative* **f** *Supply Association*[7]; or where one collects a stationary crowd blocking a substantial part of the street. There are many cases deciding that such unlawful or unreasonable user amounts to a common law nuisance. No authority, however, has been cited in reference to a moving crowd, between which and a stationary assembly there is a marked distinction: *R v Carlile*[8]. Processions may use the streets for passage on lawful occasions and for lawful objects; and provided the **g** user is reasonable there is no nuisance.'

The ratio of this case appears to be that a peaceful procession is only exercising the public right of passage. But there is no law permitting public meetings to be held on the highway. The locus classicus for this proposition is the Trafalgar Square case, *Ex parte Lewis*[9], but before turning to look at that decision I should make it clear that the right of public meeting or assembly has not for many years at any rate been in **h** doubt. There is indeed, it seems to me, a democratic right to public assembly, and any attempt to suppress the meeting together of members of the public merely

---

1 (1860) 8 CBNS 848 at 858
2 [1903] 2 IR 82
3 [1963] 3 All ER 884, [1964] 2 QB 315   **j**
4 [1903] 2 IR at 89
5 (1866) LR 1 QB 702
6 (1877) 5 Ch D 713
7 [1900] 1 Ch 276
8 (1834) 6 C & P 636 at 649
9 (1888) 21 QBD 191

because it is a public meeting would rightly be regarded as tyrannical. The right is, in
a fact, specifically mentioned in art 11 of the European Convention on Human Rights:
'Everyone has the right to freedom of peaceful assembly and to freedom of association
with others.' But this does not give a right to assemble in public anywhere the conveners of a public meeting choose, and in particular does not give a right to assemble
on the highway. The position is made quite clear in the judgment of Wills J in *Ex
parte Lewis*[1]:
b

> 'A claim on the part of persons so minded to assemble in any numbers, and for
> so long a time as they please to remain assembled, upon a highway, to the detri-
> ment of others having equal rights, is in its nature irreconcilable with the right
> of free passage, and there is, so far as we have been able to ascertain, no authority
> whatever in favour of it. It was urged that the right of public meeting, and the
c right of occupying any unoccupied land or highway that might seem appropriate
> to those of her Majesty's subjects who wish to meet there, were, if not synony-
> mous, at least correlative. We fail to appreciate the argument, nor are we at all
> impressed with the serious consequences which it was said would follow from a
> contrary view. There has been no difficulty experienced in the past, and we
> anticipate none in the future, when the only and legitimate object is public
d discussion, and no ulterior and injurious results are likely to happen. Things are
> done every day, in every part of the kingdom, without let or hindrance, which
> there is not and cannot be a legal right to do, and not infrequently are submitted
> to with a good grace because they are in their nature incapable, by whatever
> amount of user, of growing into a right.'

e It seems to me, therefore, that while an orderly procession can be regarded as a use
of the highway for the purpose of passage and therefore, so long as it is reasonable in
extent, a use which falls within the purpose of dedication, the stationing of pickets on
the public highway is not a legal exercise of the right of passage and, if it renders the
highway less commodious, amounts to a public nuisance. Further, it is no use adopting
a colourable pretence at passage by having pickets move round, for instance, in a
f circle, as was done in *Tynan v Balmer*[2]. I think that the true reason why demonstrations involving stationary assemblies on the highway are permitted is not that they
are not illegal; it is that they are matters in respect of which the remedies available
are simply not put into operation. For trespass on the highway the remedy is an
action by the owner of the soil. For common law nuisance there may be statutory
provisions under the Highways Act 1971 and the Towns Police Clauses Act 1847 and
g other statutes which give police authorities power to deal with the matter. Apart
from these there are only two ways in which common law nuisance can be brought
before the courts. One is where one of Her Majesty's subjects can prove that he has
suffered special damage not suffered by the generality of those subjects, and the other
is by the cumbrous procedure of an action brought by or in the name of the Attorney-
General.
h Most of the demonstrations and assemblies to which Lord Gifford refers are political
in origin (using that term, of course, in its widest possible sense) and have as targets
premises occupied by persons operating in the political field. It may well be, therefore, that the occupiers of 10 Downing Street and the Soviet Embassy (two examples
given by Lord Gifford) regard it as politically inexpedient to take action even though
it might be shown that greater damage was suffered by such occupiers. And similarly,
j any Attorney-General asked for his fiat before the start of proceedings for common
law nuisance because some political meeting was held on the highway might well
regard it as a wholly unnecessary suppression of popular expression to do anything

---

1   (1888) 21 QBD at 197
2   [1966] 2 All ER 133, [1967] 1 QB 91

about it. It is quite wrong to argue, as in effect Lord Gifford does, that a disinclination
by those operating in the political field to set proceedings in motion to restrain   *a*
political conduct of a particular kind means that such conduct becomes clothed with
a legality which it would not possess in a non-political context. It is not, and I hope
never will be, the law that the democratic right of political expression is sufficient
warrant for the performance of acts which, in the absence of any political content,
would plainly be illegal. And where a private individual does not feel himself bound
by political considerations, but on the other hand takes the view that he has suffered   *b*
damage and wishes to prevent a use of the highway for which that highway was not
dedicated and which amounts to a common law nuisance, it seems to me that the
courts can and should intervene. A man's right to enjoy his property which abuts on
the highway and to have access to that property both for himself and his invitees is a
right which is fully entitled to the support of the courts if and when the courts are
asked to support it.   *c*

In the result, I am convinced that no such general right to picket as that for which
counsel for the defendants contends exists at all.

I should deal with one other short matter because it was raised by one of the
defendants who appear in person. During his address to me in argument, the defendant Mr Pitt said that he had obtained permission from the local authority for these
pickets and he suggested that this in some way legalised their actions. There is no   *d*
evidence about this, but even if it could be shown by evidence that the local authority
was the owner of the subsoil and had purported to authorise the picketing, the most
that could be said is that no proceedings against the pickets for trespass could thereafter be brought to the local authority. But even the owner of the subsoil cannot
legalise an interference with the public right of passage on the highway.

The law appears to me to be clear. At common law, the use of the highway for   *e*
picketing is illegal as it is a use not responsive to the purposes for which the highway
was dedicated. It is, therefore, at least a trespass. It may also be an unreasonable user
of the highway and therefore a common law nuisance. This will always be a question
of fact, and what is or is not a reasonable user of the highway will be determined by
reference to the purposes for which the highway was dedicated. As picketing is a use
of the highway wholly unconnected with the purposes of dedication and is, in fact,   *f*
designed to interfere with the rights of an adjoining owner to have unimpeded access
from the highway, it is likely to be found to be an unreasonable user unless it is so
fleeting and so insubstantial that it can be ignored under the de minimis rule. By
statute, picketing on the highway is legal so long as it is in contemplation or furtherance of a trade dispute and satisfies the other provisions of s 15 of the Trade Union
and Labour Relations Act 1974. Put shortly, therefore, the use of the highway for   *g*
picketing is illegal unless (1) it is in contemplation or furtherance of a trade dispute
in the circumstances set out in the statute, or (2) it is found as a fact to be insubstantial
in the sense I have mentioned.

The defendants were clearly not acting in contemplation or furtherance of a trade
dispute and, looking at the affidavits and the photographs, I am quite unable to say
that this picketing could be ignored as being de minimis. The photographs show a   *h*
fairly formidable array outside the plaintiffs' offices, and I have no doubt that the
impact was intended to be, and was, considerable. I conclude that the activities of the
defendants in picketing the plaintiffs' offices was itself unlawful as an unreasonable use
of the highway and, further, that their agreement to do so amounted to an unlawful
conspiracy.

There remain to be dealt with two final matters; first, have the plaintiffs sufficiently   *j*
demonstrated that they have suffered damage so that they are entitled to an injunction? And, secondly, should such an injunction be granted as interlocutory relief?

First, then, Lord Gifford suggests that the plaintiffs' damage is unsubstantial. He
points to the affidavit of the plaintiff and says that at most this shows that one or
two people have said that they were frightened to go through the picket lines. He

relies on dicta of Lord Hanworth MR in *Harper v G N Haden & Sons Ltd*[1] to the effect
a that the injury complained of must be of substantial character. In addition, both he
and Mr Pitt suggest that as the pickets now attend only for three hours on a Saturday
morning, this is not a permanent but only a temporary manifestation. I do not think
there is any substance in these contentions. Lord Hanworth MR's dictum contrasts
what is substantial with what is fleeting and evanescent. The picket lines shown on
the photographs would inevitably, in my view, have some substantial effect on the
b resort by customers to the plaintiffs' offices, and the passages in the plaintiff's
affidavit, which describe the effect on several customers, only serve to reinforce that
view. A regular picket for three hours every Saturday cannot properly be called
fleeting or evanescent. The matter is put beyond doubt by the terms of a leaflet used
by the pickets, which is exhibited to the plaintiff's affidavit. The material parts of it
are in these terms, and I should explain two words used in the leaflet as they have
c been explained to me. 'Harassment' refers to illegal pressures put on tenants to give
up possession of their premises; 'winkling' to pressures which, while not illegal, are
regarded by the defendants as unacceptable. It is headed 'Islington Tenants' Campaign' and reads as follows:

'*The Prebble Picket.*
d 'Up until a few years ago, Barnsbury and other areas of South Islington were
solid working-class communities. In recent years there has been an invasion of
professional people, and local working people have been forced out by harassment
and winkling in many cases. Homes have been improved, roads closed to traffic
purely in the interest of the middle-class influx. Many estate agents have made a
lot of money by this process; the most prominent was Prebble & Co. whose
e sale-boards infested the area. At the same time, HARASSMENT AND WINKLING WERE
RIFE. This process is still going on, and earlier this year angered tenants decided
to fight back. Prebble & Co. were picked as the main target. The campaign
began with a public meeting, followed by a week of activity, coming to a head
with a mass march from Stonefield Street to Islington Green which passed five
estate agents' offices on the way. At each office a list of demands of conduct to
f safeguard tenants' interests was handed in. To date, Prebble & Co. have still not
agreed to meet the campaign to discuss the demands. Until Prebble & Co.
formally agree to bring their activities into line with our demands, THE PICKET OF
THEIR OFFICE WILL CONTINUE. Pickets of their offices at Camden and Tottenham
will be starting.'

g The threat to carry on the picket until the plaintiffs succumb to their demands
really is an end to any suggestion that the injury to the plaintiffs is or was intended to
be insubstantial.
Secondly, should an interlocutory injunction be granted? On the material I have
and even on the basis of accepting nearly everything in the defendants' affidavits
where there is conflict with the plaintiffs', it seems to me that the plaintiffs would
h still be entitled to an injunction if this were the trial of the action. The basis on which
the court will grant interlocutory injunctions is well settled. The principle is usually
referred to as that of the balance of convenience, and is covered by the note to RSC
Ord 29, r 1[2]. Counsel for the plaintiffs draws my attention to some words of Kay LJ
in *J Lyons & Sons v Wilkins*[3]:

j '... in all these cases of interlocutory injunctions where a man's trade is affected
one sees the enormous importance that there may be in interfering at once
before the action can be brought on for trial; because during the interval, which

---

1   [1933] 1 Ch 298 at 304, [1932] All ER Rep 59 at 61
2   Supreme Court Practice 1973, p 448
3   [1896] 1 Ch 811 at 827

may be long or short according to the state of business in the courts, a man's trade might be absolutely destroyed or ruined by a course of proceedings which, *a* when the action comes to be tried, may be determined to be utterly illegal; and yet nothing can compensate the man for the utter loss of his business by what has been done in that interval.'

What is the advantage to the plaintiffs in obtaining an interim injunction? Clearly, the preservation of their business and the restoration of unimpeded access to their *b* premises for their staff and customers. What of the defendants? If an injunction were granted they would have to suspend operations outside Prebbles. But they would still be free at some other place, and by legitimate means, to bring their dislike of the plaintiffs' actions before the public. The defendant, Mr McEnery, in the course of an able and persuasive argument, suggested that it was important to demonstrate one's dislike of someone's conduct at the place where that conduct was occurring, other- *c* wise, he said, it would lose impact. But the loss of impact seems to me a small weight to be cast in the balance against the possibility of injury to the plaintiffs' business if the picket continues. In those circumstances, it is right that an interlocutory injunction should issue.

I should not like to leave this matter without saying that no one who heard the arguments put forward by those defendants who appear in person could have failed *d* to be impressed by the obvious sincerity and the depth of feeling with which their views were expressed. But the defendants, besides being sincere, are also intelligent and they will realise, I hope, that I have not been concerned with approval or dis-approval either of their attitudes to housing questions in Islington or those of the plaintiffs. The sole issue before me has been whether or not the use of the highway for picketing which is not in contemplation or furtherance of a trade dispute is a *e* lawful operation. I have concluded that it is not.

Finally, two of the defendants are in a special category. The defendant, Mr Jack Gordon, admits that he attended as a picket up to April 1974 but has not done so since. He had obtained a post in the valuation department of the local authority and considered, sensibly, that, as that department frequently had to deal pro-fessionally with the plaintiffs, it would be inadvisable for him to continue as *f* a picket. There is nothing in his affidavit, however, which indicates that he will not either change his mind or, in the event of his leaving the service of the local authority, resume his former activities. It would be right, therefore, to include him in the injunction.

Mr Crowe, alone of the defendants, denies that he was ever a member of the picket. He has a separate and private war with the plaintiffs. Two strange men, he alleges, *g* attempted to indulge in harassing tactics with a view to forcing him to leave his present home. He believes those men were employed by, or responsible to, the plaintiffs, and he watched the plaintiffs' offices from time to time to see whether those men were habitues. On occasions his watching coincided with the picketing, but he has, so his affidavit avers and so he repeated in argument, no connection with the picketing at all. In this he is supported by Mr Pitt's affidavit. For the purposes of *h* these proceedings, I am not satisfied that Mr Crowe was involved in any way with the picketing, so that I will not grant an injunction in his case.

Injunction granted against all the defendants except Mr Crowe.

Solicitors: *Basil Greenby & Co* (for the plaintiffs); *Clinton, Davis & Co* (for the defendants *j* Alan McAskill, Malcolm McAskill, Pauline Gordon, Jack Arthur Gordon, David Sternberg); *Seifert, Sedley & Co* (for the defendant Margaret Ryan).

E H Hunter Esq   Barrister.

a # Discount Records Ltd v Barclays Bank Ltd
and another
Applied in HARBOTTLE V NATIONAL
WESTMINSTER BANK [1977] 2 All ER
862

CHANCERY DIVISION

MEGARRY J

b 16th JULY 1974

Bank – Documentary credit – Irrevocable credit – Circumstances in which court may restrain bank from paying on presentation of draft – Interlocutory injunction – Need to show sufficiently grave cause – Bank instructed by purchasers of goods to provide irrevocable confirmed credit – Allegation by purchasers that goods supplied not in accordance with order – Allegation of
c *fraud – Whether court should restrain bank from paying on presentation of draft.*

On 6th April 1974 the plaintiffs ordered certain quantities of goods from a company in France. On 17th May they instructed the first defendant bank to open an irrevocable confirmed documentary credit with full cash cover. The beneficiary stated in the credit was the French company and the amount of the credit was the equivalent of
d nearly £4,000 sterling. The goods were stated in the order and they were to be shipped not later than 30th May. The last date on which a draft could be presented was 7th June and the maturity date under the credit was 20th July. The credit was made through the second defendant bank who, on the same day, sent telex instructions to a third bank in France directing the opening of an irrevocable credit with a fourth bank ('the Discount Bank'), also in France. On 20th May the French company
e made out an invoice and on 21st May the shippers' agents received the goods and invoice. In the event the goods were not shipped by 30th May. The third bank sent the second defendants an 'advice on presentation' asking them to authorise the Discount Bank to accept a draft due on 20th July and to authorise the third bank to debit the first defendants at maturity. On 5th June the first defendants notified the plaintiffs of discrepancies between the goods in those documents and the plaintiffs'
f instructions. The first defendants made enquiries and, following discussions with the French company, gave assurances which the plaintiffs accepted. On 6th June the second defendants gave instructions to the third bank to accept bills and on 7th June the first defendants debited the plaintiffs with £4,000 which was placed in a new account in the joint names of the first defendants and the plaintiffs. The goods were eventually shipped on 12th June. According to the plaintiffs, however, the cartons,
g when opened, were found to contain only a small quantity of the goods ordered; otherwise they were empty or contained rubbish and goods not ordered. The plaintiffs brought an action against the defendants, alleging that the French company had been guilty of fraud, and sought an interlocutory injunction restraining them from paying the draft drawn on them by the French company or from paying out any sums to the French company or to any party pursuant to the irrevocable letter of credit.
h
Held – The court would only interfere with bankers' irrevocable credits if a sufficiently grave cause were shown. No such cause had been shown. Even if granted, an injunction would not prevent the French company from being paid. Since a bill of exchange had been accepted by the Discount Bank, it might already have passed into the hands of a holder in due course. Although there might be cases in which the court would
j intervene even though an allegation of fraud had not been substantiated, the plaintiffs' application was, in the circumstances, misconceived. Their real claim against the first defendants was for breach of contract and there was no suggestion that the first defendants would not be good for the money. Accordingly the injunction would be refused (see p 1075 *g* to p 1076 *a*, post).

Sztejn v J Henry Schroder Banking Corpn (1941) 31 NYS 2d 631 distinguished.

Note

For commercial letters of credit, see 3 Halsbury's Laws (4th Edn) 99-104, paras 131-137, *a*
and for cases on the subject, see 3 Digest (Repl) 282-285, 846-858.

Case referred to in judgment

Sztejn v J Henry Schroder Banking Corp (1941) 31 NYS 2d 631.

Motion   *b*

By a writ issued on 11th July 1974 the plaintiffs, Discount Records Ltd, brought an
action against the defendants, Barclays Bank Ltd and Barclays Bank International Ltd,
claiming an injunction, the return of £4,000 held by the first and/or second defendants
to the plaintiffs' use and damages for breach of contract. By notice of motion dated
11th July 1974 the plaintiffs sought an injunction restraining the defendants until
judgment or further order from (i) paying a draft drawn on them or either of them in *c*
the sum of 44,175 French francs being equivalent to or alternatively £4,000 sterling by
Promodisc SA BYG Records and/or (ii) paying out either to Promodisc SA BYG Records
or to Discount Bank or to any party at all any sums pursuant to the irrevocable credit
requested by the plaintiffs to be opened on their behalf by the first and/or second
defendants in favour of Promodisc SA BYG Records. The facts are set out in the
judgment.   *d*

Peter Pain QC and *Michael Burton* for the plaintiffs.
R Neville Thomas for the first and second defendants.

MEGARRY J. This is a motion for an injunction brought by the plaintiffs, Dis- *e*
count Records Ltd. Counsel moves against the two defendants, Barclays Bank Ltd, the
first defendants, and Barclays Bank International Ltd, the second defendants. As will
appear, the case involves two other banks, who are not parties. The motion arises out
of an order given by the plaintiffs by a letter dated 6th April 1974 to a French company,
Promodisc SA BYG Records: I shall refer to it as 'Promodisc'. The order was for 8,625
discs (meaning thereby, I understand, gramophone records) and 825 cassettes, specified *f*
by their numbers in accompanying lists. On 17th May the plaintiffs signed instructions to the first defendants for a documentary credit with full cash cover, the credit
being made through the second defendants. The beneficiaries stated in the credit
were Promodisc, and the amount of the credit was 44,175 francs. The credit was
expressed to be irrevocable, and was stated to be at the 'urgent rate'. The numbers of
discs and cassettes were stated as in the order, and they were to be shipped not later *g*
than 30th May. The document stated: 'This credit to be available for negotiation or
payment abroad until 7.6.1974.' I understand this expression to mean that 7th June
1974 was the last date on which a draft could be presented by Promodisc for acceptance. The maturity date under the credit became 20th July 1974. On the day on
which the credit was taken out, 17th May, the second defendants sent telex instructions to the third bank which comes in to the picture, Barclays Bank SA, a French *h*
bank, directing the opening of an irrevocable credit with the fourth bank, the Discount Bank of Paris, and giving the necessary details as to invoices, and so on.
    On 20th May Promodisc made out an invoice for 825 cartridges (and not cassettes)
and 8,625 records, and also a packing list showing 91 cartons and indicating the
contents of each by numbers. On 21st May the shippers received the goods and
invoice in their Paris agent's warehouse. 30th May, the latest date for shipment *j*
stated in the credit, then came and went. Barclays Bank SA sent the second defendants an 'advice of presentation', asking the second defendants to authorise the Discount Bank to accept a draft due on 20th July and to authorise Barclays Bank SA to
debit Barclays Bank, London, at maturity. The document described the goods as
'Records Cartridges'. On 12th June the goods were at last shipped; there is some

a evidence of delays by Promodisc in releasing the goods. In the meantime, it appears from the evidence that on 5th June the first defendants had told Mr Golovner, an official of the plaintiffs, of discrepancies between the goods in the documents and his instructions. The differences were between records and discs, which is of no importance, between cartridges and cassettes, which is a matter of substance, and between there being 91 cartons instead of 94. The evidence is that Mr Golovner accepted all of these discrepancies except that between cartridges and cassettes; and he asked the

b first defendants to enquire about this. The first defendants were assured by Promodisc that cassettes would be delivered. There may at this time have been some discussion about some indemnity being provided. There is also evidence that the first defendants telephoned Mr Golovner about this state of affairs, and he accepted it.

On 6th June, the second defendants cabled instructions to Barclays Bank SA to accept bills, and on 7th June the first defendants debited the plaintiffs with £4,000,

c which was placed in a new deposit account in the joint names of the plaintiffs and the first defendants. On 12th June, as I have already mentioned, the goods were shipped; and by 16th June they had arrived and were opened by the plaintiffs in the presence of a representative of the first defendants. The plaintiffs' evidence is that there were 94 cartons, but of these two were empty, five were filled with rubbish or packing, twenty-five of the record boxes and three of the cassette boxes were only partly filled,

d and two boxes labelled as cassettes were filled with records; instead of 825 cassettes, as ordered, there were only 518 cassettes and 25 cartridges. Out of the 518 cassettes delivered, 75 per cent were not as ordered; instead of 112 different records as ordered, only 12 different records were despatched; and, in toto, out of the 8,625 records ordered, only 275 were delivered as per order. The rest were not as ordered and were either rejects or unsaleable. There was some evidence from the state of the boxes, one

e of which is before me in evidence, that the numbers indicating the serial number of the records inside which appear on the outside of the box had been pasted over with some semi-transparent material and different numbers had been put on the outside, the outside numbers corresponding with the order and the covered-up numbers not corresponding with the order. In those circumstances, the plaintiffs allege that Promodisc has been guilty of fraud.

f On the next day, 17th June, the plaintiffs instructed the first defendants not to pay on the credit, and on 19th June Promodisc wrote a somewhat curious letter to the plaintiffs. The signatory of the letter says that he had just returned from the USA,

> 'and am very surprised to hear of a delivery of records and cassettes to you and a price quoted for this sale. I wish to point out that I did not come to an agreement
g with you about the selling price of our products and I am extremely shocked by your action jeopardizing a future co-operation between our firms.'

The next word in the letter is the word 'sincerely'. On 21st June the plaintiffs' solicitors wrote a letter to the first defendants setting out the matters complained of, and on 24th June the first defendants replied, saying that the letter was being forwarded to their legal advisers, but also saying that in view of the fact that the credit

h was an irrevocable confirmed credit it appeared that there was no way that the first defendants could avoid making payment. The first defendants refused to give any undertaking not to pay, and on 11th July the writ and notice of motion were issued.

The writ seeks an injunction substantially in the terms of the notice of motion, though there are variations. It also seeks the return of the sum of £4,000 as well as

j damages for breach of contract. The injunction sought by the notice of motion prior to being amended was an injunction restraining the two defendants until judgment or further order from—

> '(i) Paying a draft drawn upon them or either of them in the sum of 44,175 French francs being equivalent to or alternatively £4,000 sterling by Promodisc S.A., B.Y.G. Records their servants or agents and/or (ii) Paying out either to

Promodisc S.A., B.Y.G. Records or to Discount Bank or to any party at all any
sums pursuant to the irrevocable credit requested by the Plaintiffs to be opened *a*
on their behalf by the First and/or Second Defendants in favour of Promodisc
S.A., B.Y.G. Records.'

Counsel for the plaintiffs puts his claim for an injunction on two grounds. First of
all, he says that this is a case where Promodisc has been guilty of fraud, and that
fraud is one of the instances in which the court will intervene even in the case of *b*
bankers' irrevocable confirmed credits. He told me that there was no English authority directly on the point or anywhere near it, but he did put before me *Sztejn v J
Henry Schroder Banking Corpn*[1], a case which is summarised in Gutteridge and Megrah,
The Law of Bankers' Commercial Credits[2]. There, it was alleged that the seller
had shipped rubbish and then passed his draft for collection. Shientag J[3] referred to
the well-established rule that a letter of credit is independent of the primary contract *c*
of sale between the buyer and the seller, so that unless the letter of credit otherwise
provides, the bank is neither obliged nor allowed to enter into controversies between
buyer and seller regarding the quality of the merchandise shipped. However, the
learned judge (and I use the phrase as no empty compliment) distinguished mere
breaches of warranty of quality from cases where the seller has intentionally failed to
ship any of the goods ordered by the buyer. In relation to the latter case, the judge *d*
uttered a sentence[4] (quoted in the book)[5] on which counsel for the plaintiffs placed
great reliance:

'In such a situation, where the seller's fraud has been called to the bank's
attention before the drafts and documents have been presented for payment,
the principle of the independence of the bank's obligation under the letter of
credit should not be extended to protect the unscrupulous seller.'　　　　*e*

During the argument on this point before me, the familiar English phrase 'Fraud
unravels all' was also discussed. However, it is important to notice that in the *Sztejn*
case[1] the proceedings consisted of a motion to dismiss the formal complaint on the
ground that it disclosed no cause of action. That being so, the court had to assume
that the facts stated in the complaint were true. The complaint alleged fraud, and *f*
so the court was dealing with a case of established fraud. In the present case there is,
of course, no established fraud, but merely an allegation of fraud. The defendants,
who were not concerned with that matter, have understandably adduced no evidence
on the issue of fraud. Indeed, it seems unlikely that any action to which Promodisc
was not a party would contain the evidence required to resolve this issue. Accordingly, the matter has to be dealt with on the footing that this is a case in which fraud *g*
is alleged but has not been established. I should also add that on the facts required
to be assumed in the *Sztejn* case[1] the collecting bank there was not a holder in due
course, who would not be defeated by the fraud, but was merely an agent for the
fraudulent seller.

Counsel for the plaintiffs' second ground was that there was a lack of correspondence between the documents and the goods, and that whatever might be said about *h*
the allegation that the plaintiffs had in some way waived the lack of conformity there
remained the fact that the goods were shipped 13 days after the latest day for shipment stated in the documents establishing the credit. However, in claiming the relief
before me, counsel for the plaintiffs accepted that the first head of the notice of motion
might not be entirely appropriate. He relied primarily on the second head, but

j

1　(1941) 31 NYS 2d 631
2　4th Edn (1968), pp 133, 134
3　31 NYS 2d at 633
4　31 NYS 2d at 634
5　Op cit

preferred to leave the precise formulation of that claim until he had heard counsel
a for the defendants.

For his part, counsel for the defendants did not seek to deal with the points on
fraud or a lack of correspondence between the goods and the documents. His case
was that the claim for an injunction was misconceived. He said that what would
happen was this. Somewhere there is a bill of exchange which has already been
accepted by the Discount Bank. That bill may well have been negotiated; it may
b indeed have passed into the hands of a holder in due course. That bill will be presented for payment, and the Discount Bank is bound to pay it on 20th July. The
Discount Bank will then debit Barclays Bank SA. Barclays Bank SA will then debit
the second defendants and the second defendants will then debit the first defendants.
The injunction against the two defendants, if granted, would not achieve counsel for
the plaintiffs' avowed purpose, which was to prevent Promodisc from being paid.
c Promodisc, indeed, may already have been paid by discounting the bill. All that the
injunction would do would be to prevent the banks concerned from honouring their
obligations. As regards the two defendants (as distinct from whatever claim there
might be against Promodisc), the plaintiffs' only real claim, counsel for the defendants
said, was against the first defendants, and the first defendants alone, and there was,
and could be, no suggestion that the first defendants were not good for the money.

d Faced with that, and with an invitation from the bench to reconsider the terms of
the injunction, counsel for the plaintiffs, after a certain amount of hesitation, accepted
that a revised form of injunction against the first defendants alone would sufficiently
protect him. He amended his notice of motion so as to claim an injunction restraining
the first defendants from paying out of the £4,000 deposited on or about 7th June 1974,
in the joint names of the plaintiffs and the first defendants, to any party at all, any sums
e pursuant to the irrevocable credit requested by the plaintiffs to be opened in favour
of Promodisc, and so on. He accepted that he had a money claim against the bank
for breach of contract, but asserted that it was better to have a proprietary claim
against the £4,000 as well. When invited to explain why this was better, he said that
he could not explain it exactly, but that he felt in his bones that it was better; and he
said that in particular he was not satisfied that the same matters must be determined
f however his case was put.

I would not dismiss counsel for the plaintiffs' contentions merely because he failed
to particularise them. The sense of litigation of an experienced silk is not something
to be cast lightly overboard. Nevertheless, I do not think that this is a case for an
injunction at all. It cannot harm the plaintiffs in any way if Promodisc is paid, so
long as the money does not come out of the plaintiffs' funds; and the revised form of
g injunction is, I think, the most that the plaintiffs should ever have sought. Even in
that form I cannot see any real justification for it. If the first defendants have acted in
breach of contract, the plaintiffs will have their claim against them. As I have said,
there is no question of them not being good for the money. I see no need to keep the
£4,000 in any state of security, nor have adequate grounds been put before me for
doing anything except leaving the plaintiffs to their claim in contract. I would be slow
h to interfere with bankers' irrevocable credits, and not least in the sphere of international banking, unless a sufficiently grave cause is shown; for interventions by the
court that are too ready or too frequent might gravely impair the reliance which,
quite properly, is placed on such credits. The *Sztejn* case[1] is plainly distinguishable in
relation both to established fraud and to the absence there of any possible holder in
due course. I do not say that the doctrine of that case is wrong or that it is incapable
j of extension to cases in which fraud is alleged but has not been established, provided
a sufficient case is made out. That may or may not be the case. What I do say is that
the present case falls far short of establishing any ground on which it would be right

---

1   (1941) 31 NYS 2d 631

for the court to intervene by granting the interlocutory injunction claimed, even in its revised form. The motion accordingly fails and will be dismissed.   *a*

Motion dismissed.

Solicitors: *Slowes* (for the plaintiffs); *Durrant Piesse* (for the first and second defendants).

F K Anklesaria Esq   Barrister.   *b*

Miliangos v George Frank (Textiles) Ltd

  c

QUEEN'S BENCH DIVISION
BRISTOW J
2nd, 3rd, 4th DECEMBER 1974

COURT OF APPEAL, CIVIL DIVISION
LORD DENNING MR, STEPHENSON AND GEOFFREY LANE LJJ   *d*
6th, 7th, 10th FEBRUARY 1975

Judgment – Judicial decision as authority – Court of Appeal – Previous decision of Court of Appeal – Decision per incuriam – Circumstances in which decision may be regarded as having been given per incuriam – Not all relevant authorities cited – Only one party represented – Whether grounds for treating decision as having been given per incuriam.   *e*

Judgment – Judicial decision as authority – Stare decisis – Decision on alternative grounds – Whether each ground constituting binding precedent.

Judgment – Payment of sum of money – Foreign currency – Jurisdiction to order payment of sum expressed in foreign country – Contract – Currency of contract foreign currency –   *f* *Currency of country which is not a member of the European Economic Community – Currency of contract Swiss francs – Action for price of goods sold and delivered – Whether court having jurisdiction to give judgment for sum expressed in Swiss francs.*

By an agreement in writing made in May 1971 the defendants, an English company, agreed to buy a quantity of yarn from the plaintiff, a Swiss firm. The contract was   *g* governed by Swiss law and the currency of the contract was Swiss francs. The yarn was duly delivered in the autumn of 1971. Under the contract payment was to be made within 30 days. The defendants failed to pay at all. On 20th April 1974 the plaintiff issued a writ claiming payment of the price of goods sold and delivered. The writ claimed payment of a sum which was the sterling equivalent of the contract price in Swiss francs at the date of the breach of contract. A defence and counterclaim   *h* was put in but on 22nd November the defendants abandoned their defence and counterclaim and informed the plaintiff that they would submit to judgment. On 26th November the Court of Appeal gave judgment in *Schorsch Meier GmbH v Hennin[a]*. In that case the court decided that where the money of a contract for the sale of goods was expressed in the currency of a member state of the European Economic Community the court had jurisdiction to give judgment for a sum expressed in that   *j* currency because that was the effect of art 106 of the EEC Treaty, which was directly enforceable in the United Kingdom. In the alternative the court decided, by a majority, that in any event the English courts had jurisdiction to give a money judgment

---

a   Page 152, ante, [1974] 3 WLR 823

expressed in the currency of any foreign country and that the decision of the House of
a Lords in *Re United Railways of the Havana and Regla Warehouses*[a] was not a binding precedent to the contrary. On 2nd December, when the case came on for hearing, the
judge granted the plaintiff leave to amend the statement of claim so as to claim the
contract price in Swiss francs which, because sterling had been devalued since 1971,
was equivalent to a much larger sterling sum than it had been at the time of the breach
of contract. The judge held, however, that the *Schorsch Meier* case[b], so far as it
b related to countries which were not members of the European Economic Community,
was obiter and had been decided per incuriam in that only one party had been represented and not all the relevant authorities had been cited; he further held that it was
inconsistent with the *Havana* case[a]. Accordingly he gave judgment for the sum
claimed in sterling. The plaintiff appealed.

c **Held** – A decision of the Court of Appeal could not be said to have been decided per
incuriam merely because counsel had not cited all the relevant authorities or because
one of the parties had not appeared and the case had been argued on one side only.
The decision of the Court of Appeal in the *Schorsch Meier* case[b] was binding on the
judge for it had not been given per incuriam and furthermore was not inconsistent
with any subsequent decision of the Court of Appeal or the House of Lords. Where a
d decision of the Court of Appeal was based on alternative rationes decidendi both of
the rationes constituted precedents binding on a judge in the High Court. Accordingly
the judge, and the Court of Appeal, were bound to follow the majority decision in the
Schorsch Meier case[b] to the effect that the decision of the House of Lords in the *Havana*
case[a] did not govern the point and that it was open to the court to give judgment for
a sum of money expressed in a currency other than sterling. The appeal would there-
e fore be allowed (see p 1084 *a* to *g*, p 1085 *h* to p 1086 *b* and *d* to *f*, p 1087 *e* and
p 1088 *a* to *c*, post).
   Schorsch Meier GmbH v Hennin p 152, ante, followed.
   Young v Bristol Aeroplane Co [1944] 2 All ER 293 applied.
   Re United Railways of the Havana and Regla Warehouses [1960] 2 All ER 332
distinguished.
f
Notes
For Court of Appeal decisions as authorities, see 22 Halsbury's Laws (3rd Edn) 799,
800, 801, para 1687, and for cases on the subject, see 30 Digest (Reissue) 269-274, 763-804.
   For damages for breach of contract, the currency of which is a foreign currency, see
8 Halsbury's Laws (4th Edn) 424, 425, para 613.
g For judgments for a sum of money payable in a foreign currency, see 11 Halsbury's
Laws (3rd Edn) 306, 307, para 497.

Cases referred to in judgments
Bagshaw v Playn (1595) 1 Cro Eliz 536, 78 ER 783.
Barrington v Lee [1971] 3 All ER 1231, [1972] 1 QB 326, [1971] 3 WLR 962, CA, 30 Digest
h (Reissue) 271, 779.
Burt v Claude Cousins & Co Ltd [1971] 2 All ER 611, [1971] 2 QB 426, [1971] 2 WLR 930,
CA.
Cassell & Co Ltd v Broome [1972] 1 All ER 801, [1972] AC 1027, [1972] 2 WLR 645, HL, 17
Digest (Reissue) 82, 17.
Celia (Steamship) (Owners) v Owners of Steamship Volturno [1921] 2 AC 544, [1921] All ER
j Rep 173, 90 LJP 385, 126 LT 1, 15 Asp MLC 374, 27 Com Cas 46, HL, 17 Digest
(Reissue) 204, 753.
Davies v Powell (1738) Willes 46, Cooke Pr Cas 146, 7 Mod Rep 249, 125 ER 1048, 18
Digest (Repl) 289, 377.

a [1960] 2 All ER 332, [1961] AC 1007
b Page 152, ante, [1974] 3 WLR 823

Halcyon the Great, The, p 882, ante.

Jacobs v London County Council [1950] 1 All ER 737, [1950] AC 361, 114 JP 204, 48 LGR *a*
323, HL, 30 Digest (Reissue) 255, 610.

Joscelyne v Nissen [1970] 1 All ER 1213, [1970] 2 QB 86, [1970] 2 WLR 509, CA, Digest
(Cont Vol C) 707, 307a.

Jugoslavenska Oceanska Plovidba v Castle Investment Co Inc [1973] 3 All ER 498, [1974] QB
292, [1973] 3 WLR 847, [1973] 2 Lloyd's Rep 1, CA.

Law v Jones [1973] 2 All ER 437, [1974] Ch 112, CA. 　　　　　　　　　　　　　　*b*

Manners v Pearson & Son [1898] 1 Ch 581, [1895-9] All ER Rep 415, 67 LJCh 304, 78 LT
432, CA, 35 Digest (Repl) 201, 90.

Morelle Ltd v Wakeling [1955] 1 All ER 708, [1955] 2 QB 379, [1955] 2 WLR 672, CA, 30
Digest (Reissue) 272, 592.

Rayner v Paskell and Cann (1948) 152 Estates Gazette 314, CA; see [1971] 2 All ER at 628,
[1971] 2 WLR at 939. 　　　　　　　　　　　　　　　　　　　　　　　　　　　*c*

Rastell v Draper (1605) Yelv 80, Moore KB 775, 80 ER 55, sub nom *Draper v Rastel* Cro
Jac 88, 22 Digest (Reissue) 164, 1373.

Rookes v Barnard [1964] 1 All ER 367, [1964] AC 1129, [1964] 2 WLR 269, [1964] 1 Lloyd's
Rep 28, HL, 17 Digest (Reissue) 81, 14.

Schorsch Meier GmbH v Hennin p 152, ante, [1974] 3 WLR 823, [1975] 1 Lloyd's Rep 1, CA.

Tiverton Estates Ltd v Wearwell Ltd [1974] 1 All ER 209, [1974] 2 WLR 176, CA 　　*d*

United Railways of the Havana and Regla Warehouses Ltd, Re [1960] 2 All ER 332, sub nom
Tomkinson v First Pennsylvania Banking and Trust Co [1961] AC 1007, [1960] 2 WLR
696, HL, Digest (Cont Vol A) 231, 862a.

Vionnet (Madeleine) et Cie v Wills [1939] 4 All ER 136, [1940] 1 KB 72, 109 LJKB 22, 161 LT
311, CA, 35 Digest (Repl) 197, 72.

Ward v Kidsim (1662) Latch 77, 82 ER 283. 　　　　　　　　　　　　　　　　　*e*

Young v Bristol Aeroplane Co Ltd [1944] 2 All ER 293, [1944] KB 718, 113 LJKB 513, 171
LT 113, 37 BWCC 51, CA; *affd* [1946] 1 All ER 98, [1946] AC 163, 115 LJKB 63, 174 LT
39, 79 LIL Rep 35, 38 BWCC 50, HL, 30 Digest (Reissue) 269, 765.

Cases also cited

Beswick v Beswick [1967] 2 All ER 1197, [1968] AC 58, HL. 　　　　　　　　　　*f*

Contract & Trading Co (Southern) Ltd v Barbey [1959] 3 All ER 846, [1960] AC 244, HL.

Cousins (H) & Co Ltd v D & C Carriers Ltd [1971] 1 All ER 55, [1971] 2 QB 230, CA.

Cuming v Monro (1792) 5 TR 87.

Di Fernando v Simon Smits & Co Ltd [1920] 3 KB 409, [1920] All ER Rep 347, CA.

Edwards v Porter [1925] AC 1, HL.

Rands v Peck (1622) Cro Jac 618. 　　　　　　　　　　　　　　　　　　　　　*g*

Actions

The plaintiff, Michael Miliangos, brought two actions against the defendants, George
Frank (Textiles) Ltd, in respect of two contracts, claiming under each of them the
price of goods sold and delivered to the defendants. The actions were consolidated.
In each action the claim was for a sum of money expressed in sterling. The judge, *h*
however, gave the plaintiff leave to amend his claim in the first action by the addition
of an alternative claim in Swiss francs. The facts are set out in the judgment.

Stuart McKinnon for the plaintiff.
John Peppitt for the defendants.　　　　　　　　　　　　　　　　　　　　　　　*j*

BRISTOW J. These consolidated actions are brought by the plaintiff, whose place
of residence and business is at Payerne in Switzerland, against the defendants in
respect of sales by the plaintiff of texturised polyester yarn for delivery in England.

a The first contract involved deliveries between 7th September and 18th November 1971 at a price expressed in the contractual documents in Swiss francs, the total amounting to 415,522·45 francs. The price was payable 30 days from invoice. Nothing was paid. In respect of these deliveries the defendants accepted two Swiss bills of exchange drawn by the plaintiff for 201,014·05 Swiss francs, which were dishonoured on presentation.

b The plaintiff claims the price of the goods sold and delivered under the contract, or alternatively, on the bills. Though defences were raised and persisted in, the defendants now submit to judgment for the price of the goods sold and delivered under the first contract.

c In the prayer to the statement of claim the amounts claimed under both heads were quantified in sterling at £41,972, the conversion from Swiss francs being made at the rate of 9·9 francs to the pound, the rate obtaining when payment fell due under the contract and on the bills. There is also a claim for interest under s 3 of the Law Reform (Miscellaneous Provisions) Act 1934.

Following on the decision of the Court of Appeal in *Schorsch Meier GmbH v Hennin*[1] the plaintiff applied for leave to amend his statement of claim to claim judgment in Swiss francs in the alternative to claiming judgment in sterling, and I allowed the amendment. If judgment were given in Swiss francs and the judgment debt were **d** discharged in Swiss francs, the effect would be that the judgment debtor would have to find roughly half as much sterling again to discharge the obligation. Put another way, the creditor will suffer an equivalent reduction in the real fruits of his contract if judgment is given in sterling.

The judgment of the Court of Appeal in *Schorsch Meier GmbH v Hennin*[1] proceeded on two grounds. All three members of the court decided that the effect of art 106 **e** of the Treaty of Rome, incorporated into the municipal law of England by the European Communities Act 1972, was to abrogate the rule of English law that the English courts can only give money judgments expressed in sterling. This ground of the judgment does not affect the plaintiff's claim in this action, for Switzerland is not a member of the EEC. But the majority of the court also decided that the English courts have power to give judgment in a foreign currency irrespective of the Treaty **f** of Rome. They held that the reasons for the rule, unchallenged at least since *Rastell v Draper*[2], restated by Lindley MR in *Manners v Pearson*[3] and restated in plain terms by all the members of the House of Lords who decided *Re United Railways of the Havana and Regla Warehouses Ltd*[4], no longer existed and that they were at liberty to discard the rule itself. Cessante ratione legis cessat ipsa lex.

In the *Schorsch Meier*[1] appeal, the defendant debtor, who had succeeded in the **g** county court, did not appear and was not represented, so that the court did not have the advantage I have enjoyed of hearing argument on both sides.

In this case I find myself in effect in the position of embarrassment foreseen by Lord Hailsham LC in *Cassell & Co Ltd v Broome*[5]. I am faced with a judgment of a majority of the Court of Appeal, which in its application to the issue raised before me says that a rule of English law taken for granted by the Court of Appeal and the **h** House of Lords for some 350 years is no longer a rule of English law.

The judgments of the House of Lords in *Cassell v Broome*[6] constrain me in the circumstances to hold that the rule of law that my judgment can only be expressed in sterling is still of full force and effect, since Parliament has not altered it, nor has the House of Lords itself under its 1966 declaration[7]. Whether I think the rule to be good, bad or

j
1 Page 152, ante, [1974] 3 WLR 823
2 (1605) Yelv 80
3 [1898] 1 Ch 581, [1895-99] All ER Rep 415
4 [1960] 2 All ER 332, [1961] AC 1007
5 [1972] 1 All ER 801 at 809, [1972] AC 1027 at 1054
6 [1972] 1 All ER 801, [1972] AC 1027
7 [1966] 3 All ER 77

indifferent, I am bound to apply it, and for the purposes of this judgment there is no point in expressing my view of the merit or otherwise of the rule.   *a*

I am emboldened in finding, as I must, that the majority of the court in *Schorsch Meier v Hennin*[1] reached their non-Treaty of Rome conclusion per incuriam by the consideration put in argument for the defendants before me, though not before the Court of Appeal, that if you express the principle of law with which I am concerned in Latin it is cessante ratione legis cesset ipsa lex apud senatum. In my judgment, the plaintiff is entitled to recover in sterling and for the sum of £44,440·90. The problem *b* of interest is common to both actions.

The second contract involved two deliveries and the price, due on 20th March and 30th April 1972, was expressed in sterling. The problem raised in the first action, therefore, does not arise. Bills were again accepted by the defendants in respect of the price of these two deliveries, also in sterling, but these were not honoured. The plaintiff elected to treat non-payment as a repudiation of the contract, and sues for *c* damages, namely, the price of the first two deliveries and the loss of profits and cost of storage on the remainder, the total claim being £15,220·75.

Happily, subject to the difficulty raised in the first action by the fact that judgment was claimed in the alternative in Swiss francs, the parties have been able to agree on the order that should be made in this action. It is as follows: that in the first action there shall be judgment for £42,038·49, interest at 7½ per cent from 31st October 1971 *d* to 23rd July 1973, thereafter interest at one per cent over the minimum lending rate on a day to day basis, and I am asked to make it clear—and I do—that the basis of agreement on the rates to be applied for interest is that my judgment that I can only award a figure in sterling stands. If this judgment is appealed, as I have no doubt it will be, and if it is found that I am wrong, then the parties are not to be bound by these interest rates. In the second action, there is to be judgment for £3,517.42, interest on *e* £27,778·37 at 7½ per cent from 10th April 1972 to 23rd July 1973, thereafter interest at one per cent over average minimum lending rate calculated on a day to day basis; judgment for £11,391·20 damages with interest at 7½ per cent from 10th April 1972 to 23rd July 1973, thereafter at one per cent over average minimum lending rate, calculated on a day to day basis. In the computation of interest in both actions, credit is to be given to the defendants for the payments of £14,260·95 on 26th August 1974 *f* and £10,000 on 21st November 1974. There is to be an order for payment out to the plaintiff's solicitors in part satisfaction of a sum of £13,857·38 in court, plus accrued interest thereon, and an order for the payment out to the plaintiff's solicitors of a further sum of £800 paid into court on 15th November 1972 as security for costs, plus accrued interest thereon. The plaintiff is to have the costs of the consolidated action, except for the costs of the second day of the trial on the issue of the form of judgment, *g* that is to say, whether the judgment can be in Swiss francs or must be in sterling. The defendants are to have their costs of the second day on that issue and there is to be a mutual set-off as to costs, and there will be liberty to apply.

Judgment for the plaintiff.

h

Solicitors: *Gosling & Lewis Barnes* (for the plaintiff); *Bower, Cotton & Bower* (for the defendants).

Janet Harding Barrister.

Appeal   *j*

The plaintiff appealed against so much of the judgment of Bristow J as adjudged that the plaintiff was not entitled to judgment in Swiss francs, and sought an order that that part of the judgment be set aside and that judgment be entered for the plaintiff

---

1   Page 152, ante, [1974] 3 WLR 823

in the sum of 415,522·45 Swiss francs plus interest. By a respondent's notice the defen-
a dants gave notice that they would contend that the judgment of Bristow J be affirmed
on the following additional grounds: (i) that the rule requiring a money judgment
of an English Court to be expressed in sterling was based on sound practical and
commercial considerations; (ii) that accordingly the rule should be retained except
insofar as it might have been affected by art 106 of the EEC Treaty and the European
Communities Act 1972; and (iii) that to depart from the rule in the instant case would
b be to ignore the intention of the legislature as expressed in s 74(2) of the Bills of
Exchange Act 1882.

Stuart McKinnon and *David Hunt* for the plaintiff.
John Peppitt for the defendants.

c

LORD DENNING MR. We have further considered this case and we consider
we are bound by the earlier decision. So we do not wish to hear further argument.
    At one time it was thought that judgments and awards could only be given in
sterling. That was when sterling was a stable currency. Now that it floats we have had
to think again. 18 months ago we held that arbitrators could make an award in a
d foreign currency: see *Jugoslavenska Oceanska Plovidba v Castle Investment Co Inc*[1]. Two
months ago we held unanimously that the courts could give judgment in a currency
of a Common Market country: see *Schorsch Meier GmbH v Hennin*[2]. In the same court
we held by a majority that judgment could be given in a currency of other foreign
countries. Those decisions have, I believe, been welcomed in the City of London.
But in this case a challenge has been made. I will state the facts.
e   The plaintiff is a Swiss firm who produces yarn at Zurich in Switzerland. The
defendants are an English company who buy yarn to make knitted garments. In
May 1971 the two firms made an agreement in writing by which the defendants agreed
to buy from the plaintiff 90,718 kilogrammes of textured polyester yarn. The price
was 12·56 Swiss francs per kilogramme to be paid within 30 days of invoice, delivery
to be free of charge at the defendants' works. Any dispute could be referred, at
f sellers' option, to the Tribunal of Arbitration at Zurich. So clearly the contract was
governed by Swiss law. The money of account and money of payment was Swiss
francs.
    In the autumn of 1971 the goods were duly delivered in five consignments. The
five invoices stated the quantities in kilogrammes and the price in Swiss francs. Each
invoice stated: 'Conditions of payment: within 30 days date of invoice to be paid to
g Union Bank Swiss, Lausanne.'
    I regret to say that the defendants, the English company, did not honour the con-
tract. They did not pay the Swiss francs to the bank at Lausanne as they should have
done. Not within 30 days or at all. In November 1971, in order to gain time, the
defendants accepted two bills of exchange drawn in Switzerland for a total of 300,000
Swiss francs payable two months later on 31st January 1972. The plaintiff duly presented
h them for payment but they were dishonoured.
    On 20th April the plaintiff issued a writ in the High Court here claiming payment
of the price for goods sold and delivered or alternatively the sums due on the bills of
exchange, in each case converted into the sterling equivalent. On 29th December 1972
the defendants put in a defence alleging that the yarn was defective and making a
counterclaim. Much time was taken up thereafter in interlocutory matters, such as
j particulars, and so forth. Eventually the action was set down for trial and was due
to come on for hearing on 2nd December 1974. But then, nine days before, on 22nd
November 1974, the defendants wrote a letter saying that they abandoned their

---

1 [1973] 3 All ER 498, [1974] QB 292
2 Page 152, *ante*, [1974] 3 WLR 823

defence and counterclaim and would submit to judgment. Then, four days later, this court, on 26th November 1974 gave its decision in the *Schorsch Meier* case[1]. It *a* was held that, where the currency of a contract was a foreign currency, the English courts could give judgment *in that currency*. Next day that case was reported in The Times. The plaintiff saw that it would operate to his advantage. Five days later, when this case came into the list on Monday, 2nd December, the plaintiff applied to amend the statement of claim so as to claim in Swiss francs. The judge allowed the amendment. The statement of claim was amended so as to claim 415,522·45 Swiss francs, *b* which was the contract price.

Since 1971 sterling had been devalued. At the time when payment became due in 1971 the rate of exchange was 9·9 Swiss francs to the £. But sterling was afterwards allowed to float. At the time when the case was heard in December 1974 it was about six Swiss francs to the £. So that it made a great difference. If the plaintiff could get judgment only in sterling, he would recover some £41,000. But if he could get *c* judgment in Swiss francs, he would recover the equivalent in sterling of over £60,000. It would seem very hard on the Swiss suppliers that, instead of receiving Swiss francs worth over £60,000, as the contract required, they should only get sterling worth £41,000. It would mean that the defendants would be taking advantage of their own wrong. They had made default in their contractual obligations (not paying Swiss francs as they agreed to do). They had put forward an allegation of defective goods *d* (which they afterwards withdrew). Yet when it came to payment, they would be paying in depreciated sterling. Their delay would operate to their own advantage and to the loss to the Swiss supplier.

If the judge had followed the decision of this court in the *Schorsch Meier* case[1], he would have given judgment in Swiss francs and thus avoided this result. But he felt unable to do so. He thought that the *Schorsch Meier* case[1] was wrongly decided and *e* that he must apply the previous law and give judgment in sterling for £41,000.

Two days later, on 6th December 1974, another judge, Brandon J[2], thought better of the *Schorsch Meier* case[1]. He used it so as to do something which had never been done before. The owners of a ship called 'Halcyon the Great' had mortgaged it to secure loans in US dollars of over $20 million. The mortgagees brought an action for the money. The judge ordered the ship to be sold for dollars and for the money to be *f* paid into court in dollars and be placed to a dollar deposit account out of which judgment in dollars, if given, could be satisfied directly. That was an eminently sensible and reasonable course which would probably have never been taken but for the *Schorsch Meier* case[1].

Coming back to our present case, Bristow J held that he could only give judgment in sterling. From his decision the plaintiff appeals to this court. On his behalf counsel *g* put the case in two ways: first, that the *Schorsch Meier* case[1] was rightly decided; second, that in any case it was binding on this court.

On the first point, counsel for the plaintiff put forward a telling argument based on much research. He said that, prior to the *Schorsch Meier* case[1], there was only one reported case in which an English court had ever given judgment in a foreign currency; and that was 380 years ago. It was *Bagshaw v Playn*[3]. The court then said[4] that *h* judgment for the plaintiff 'ought to have been *quod recuperet* the 471.8s.8d. Flemish money, and a writ have been awarded to enquire of the value thereof', that is, of the equivalent in sterling. But that was an isolated case. In all other cases for 380 years the courts had only given judgment in sterling. The contrary was never disputed. Everyone assumed that judgment could not be given in a foreign currency. Everyone, that is, save Lindley MR who suggested that a Court of Chancery might make an order *j*

---

1   Page 152, ante, [1974] 3 WLR 823
2   *The Halcyon the Great*, p 882, ante
3   (1595) 1 Cro Eliz 536
4   1 Cro Eliz at 536

that a defendant do specifically perform his contract to pay in a foreign currency: see
a *Manners v Pearson*[1]. That suggestion was not taken up by anyone until the *Schorsch
Meier* case[2] itself, when it was made one of the grounds of the decision. Meanwhile,
however, the common law courts had proceeded on the antiquated rule dating from
Ward v Kidsim[3], that when a defendant did not pay his debt in foreign currency,
as the contract required, it was just as if he had refused to deliver a cow or a piece of
plate. The remedy was not in debt but in damages. It was for the jury to assess those
b damages and they could only do it in sterling. So the judgment had to be in sterling,
and the writ of execution could only be expressed in sterling. In assessing the damages,
the rate of exchange was to be taken as at the date of the failure to deliver the foreign
currency. This line of reasoning culminated in the decision of the House of Lords in
Re United Railways of the Havana and Regla Warehouses Ltd[4]. But in none of those cases
was there any issue about judgments having to be in sterling. It was assumed or con-
c ceded. So counsel for the plaintiff submitted that none of them formed a binding
precedent. And in none was there considered the possibility of an order for specific
performance. Not in *The Volturno*[5], which was an action for damages for tort. Nor in
the *Havana* case[4], which was a proof in the winding-up of an English company which
had to be in sterling. The first time that specific performance was seriously canvassed
was in the *Schorsch Meier* case[2] itself. It should be made available, said counsel for the
d plaintiff, in these cases because damages would not be an adequate remedy. He relied
on a a passage by Dr F A Mann in his book[6]:

> 'The root of the evil lies in the rule of English law of procedure that an English
> court cannot pronounce judgment otherwise than in terms of pounds sterling.
> If an English court is given power to order the defendant to pay at his option
> either a sum of foreign currency or its sterling equivalent at the date of payment,
e > or to pay the latter sum only, if, therefore, conversion is deferred to the stage of
> execution, then, following the Continental example, and the Carriage of Goods by
> Road Act, 1965, England will have adopted a wholly satisfactory rule.'

That was the rule adopted by this court in the *Schorsch Meier* case[2].
So much for the first way in which counsel for the plaintiff put his case. But it is
f not necessary for us to rule on it, if his second way is right. If the *Schorsch Meier* case[2]
is binding on us, that is an end of the matter in this court.
The judge thought that the *Schorsch Meier* case[2] was not binding on him. If that be
so, it is certainly not binding on us. But why was it not binding on him? He was
constrained he said, by the judgment of the House of Lords in *Cassell & Co Ltd v
Broome*[7]. In that case Lord Hailsham of St Marylebone LC thought[8] that this court
g had greatly erred. It had flouted the decision of the House of Lords in *Rookes v Barnard*[9].
He administered to us a severe rebuke. In the present case the judge must have
thought that in the *Schorsch Meier* case[2] we had fallen into the same error again; and
that we had flouted a rule which had been taken for granted for 380 years and accepted
by the House of Lords in the *Havana* case[4]. Nothing was further from our intention.
It was not our intention in *Cassell & Co Ltd v Broome*[7]; nor was it in *Schorsch Meier*[2].
h In our system it is of the first importance that the decisions of the House of Lords
should be loyally followed and applied by this court and all courts in all cases which
they properly govern. In the *Schorsch Meier* case[2] the majority thought that the

---

1   [1898] 1 Ch 581 at 587, [1895-9] All ER Rep 415 at 417
2   Page 152, ante, [1974] 3 WLR 823
j 3   (1662) Latch 77
4   [1960] 2 All ER 332, [1961] AC 1007
5   [1921] 2 AC 544, [1921] All ER Rep 173
6   Legal Aspects of Money (3rd Edn, 1971), p 372
7   [1972] 1 All ER 801, [1972] AC 1027
8   [1972] 1 All ER at 809, [1972] AC at 1053, 1054
9   [1964] 1 All ER 367, [1964] AC 1129

Havana case[1] did not govern the point; and that it was open to the courts to give
judgment in foreign currency. Whether the majority were right in so holding, I *a*
would not presume to say. The House of Lords will tell us later. But whether right
or wrong, it seems to me that, once this court has given a decision on it, all lower
courts should follow the decision of this court unless and until it is reversed by the
House of Lords. In that way any embarrassment will be avoided. In the present
case, therefore, the judge ought not to have refused to follow the decision in *Schorsch
Meier*[2]. He should have followed it and left the aggrieved party to appeal. *b*
    Now that the matter is before us, it stands differently. The question is whether
this court now should follow the *Schorsch Meier* case[2]. In the *Schorsch Meier* case[2]
there were two grounds for the decision. One, by the majority of the court, was that
the English courts had power to give judgment in a foreign currency, when that was
the currency of the contract. The other, by all three, was that, at any rate, the power
existed within the countries of the Common Market. So two grounds were given for *c*
the decision. In this situation there is high authority for saying that both grounds are
just as binding as one alone would have been. 'If a Judge states two grounds for his
decision and bases his decision upon both, neither of those grounds is a dictum':
see *Jacobs v London County Council*[3]. This was not challenged before us. The only
question was whether the first ground given by the majority was binding.
    The law on this subject has been authoritatively stated in *Young v Bristol Aeroplane* *d*
Co[4] and *Morelle Ltd v Wakeling*[5]. This court is bound to follow its own decisions—
including majority decisions—except in closely defined circumstances. One of these
is where a previous decision of this court, although not expressly overruled, cannot
stand with a subsequent decision of the House of Lords[6]. Note the word 'subsequent'.
It is an essential word. That exception does not apply here because there has been no
decision of the House of Lords subsequent to the *Schorsch Meier* case[2]. Another *e*
exception is where a previous decision has been given per incuriam. 'Such cases', said
Lord Greene MR[7] in *Young v Bristol Aeroplane Co*[4], 'would obviously be of the rarest
occurrence and must be dealt with in accordance with their special facts.' So it has
been held that a decision is not given per incuriam because the argument was not
'fully or carefully formulated' (see *Morelle v Wakeling*[8]), or was 'only weakly or
inexpertly put forward' (*Joscelyne v Nissen*[9]); nor that the reasoning was faulty *f*
(*Barrington v Lee*[10] by Stephenson LJ). To these I would add that a case is not decided
per incuriam because counsel have not cited all the relevant authorities or referred to
this or that rule of court or statutory provision. The court does its own researches
itself and consults authorities; and these may never receive mention in the judgments.
Likewise a case is not decided per incuriam because it is argued on one side only and
the other side does not appear. The duty of counsel in those circumstances, as we all *g*
know, is to put the case on both sides to the best of his ability; and the court itself
always examines it with the utmost care, to protect the interests of the one who is not
represented. That was done in the *Schorsch Meier* case[2] itself.
    The cases in which we have interfered are limited. One outstanding case recently
was *Tiverton Estates Ltd v Wearwell Ltd*[11] where this court in effect overruled *Law v
Jones*[12] on the ground that a material line of authority was not before the court and *h*

1   [1960] 2 All ER 332, [1961] AC 1007
2   Page 152, ante, [1974] 3 WLR 823
3   [1950] 1 All ER 737 at 741, [1950] AC 361 at 369, 370
4   [1944] 2 All ER 293, [1944] KB 718
5   [1955] 1 All ER 708, [1955] 2 QB 379
6   See *Young v Bristol Aeroplane Co* [1944] 2 All ER at 298, [1944] KB at 725
7   [1944] 2 All ER at 300, [1944] KB at 729
8   [1955] 1 All ER at 714, [1955] 2 QB at 399
9   [1970] 1 All ER 1213 at 1223, [1970] 2 QB 86 at 89
10   [1971] 3 All ER 1231 at 1245, [1972] 1 QB 326 at 345
11   [1974] 1 All ER 209, [1974] 2 WLR 176
12   [1973] 2 All ER 437, [1974] Ch 112

j

that the point called for immediate remedy. I have myself often said that this court is not
a absolutely bound by its own decisions and may depart from them just as the House of
Lords from theirs; but my colleagues have not gone so far. So that I am in duty
bound to defer to their view.

Returning to the present case, the first ground of per incuriam was suggested by the
judge himself. He said the majority had got the principle of law wrong. They had
founded themselves on the maxim cessante ratione legis cessat ipsa lex. That maxim
b expresses a principle of the highest authority, going back to Coke on Littleton[1] and
quoted in Broom's Legal Maxims[2]. But the judge thought that the correct principle
was in rather different words: 'cessante ratione legis cesset ipsa lex apud senatum'.
Thus he changed the mood 'cessat' to 'cesset' and added the words 'apud senatum'.
Translating his version, it would run: 'If the reason for a law ceases to be valid, then
let the law itself cease when the Senate [the House of Lords or Parliament] so decides.'
c But when we asked where the judge got his version, we found that counsel for the defendants was himself the first and true inventor of it. Good advocate as he is, I prefer the
original. It is a maxim which can be applied by these courts as well as by the House of
Lords or by Parliament. From time to time they have done so. A good instance is the
Court of Common Pleas in *Davies v Powell*[3], where Lord Willes CJ said: 'When the
nature of things changes, the rules of law must change too.' So when the nature of
d sterling changes, the rule of law may change too.

Before us counsel for the defendants suggested other reasons why the decision was
given per incuriam. He said there were rules not brought to the attention of the court
in the *Schorsch Meier* case[4] which show that specific performance could not be ordered
in a foreign currency. He referred particularly to RSC Ord 42, r 1, introduced in
1971[5], which requires judgment to be in decimal currency. He said also that there
e was no means of enforcing it, now that there was no remedy by attachment or imprisonment. He referred to RSC Ord 45, r 1. Further, there would be difficulty in
applying the rules as to set-off and payment into court. Also that *Madeleine Vionnet
et Cie v Wills*[6] was not referred to; nor some of the relevant Common Market cases;
nor s 72(4) of the Bills of Exchange Act 1882. I was able to assure him that, although
not mentioned in the judgment, we had considered most of these cases and points.
f In any event none of them were such as to come under the heading of per incuriam.
I would however mention particularly the way in which a judgment in foreign
currency is able to be enforced. It is done in the same way as an award by arbitrators
is enforced when given in a foreign currency: see the *Jugoslavenska* case[7]. If the defendant does not pay, the plaintiff should file an application for leave to enforce it,
supported by an affidavit showing the rate of exchange at the time, and the figures
g converted into sterling. Leave can then be given to execute for the sterling equivalent.

Apart from these points, counsel for the defendants indicated that his principal
argument was this: that the House of Lords in the *Havana* case[8] had affirmed the
breach-date rule; and that in the *Schorsch Meier* case[4] this court had outflanked that
rule by allowing judgment to be given in foreign currency. That, he said, was a
course not open to the court. Nothing short of legislation could do it. We realise the
h force of that argument. It is the argument which appealed to Lawton LJ in the
Schorsch Meier case[4]. But it was rejected by the majority there. We are bound by

---

1 Co Litt 70b
j 2 10th Edn (1939), p 97-99
3 (1738) Willes 46 at 51
4 Page 152, ante, [1974] 3 WLR 823
5 SI 1971 No
6 [1939] 4 All ER 136, [1940] 1 KB 72
7 [1973] 3 All ER 498 at 502, [1974] QB 292 at 297
8 [1960] 2 All ER 332, [1961] AC 1007

that decision of the majority to reject it here also. Counsel for the plaintiff urged us a
to hear the argument fully out and to express our views. But I think that the rival
views have already been sufficiently deployed and that no useful purpose would be
served by further discussion.

I would therefore allow the appeal on the ground that the case is governed by the
judgment in the *Schorsch Meier* case[1]. Judgment should be entered for the plaintiff
in the terms that the court do order the defendants to pay 415,522·45 Swiss francs b
(plus interest) or the equivalent in sterling at the time of payment.

STEPHENSON LJ. In *Barrington v Lee*[2] this court had to consider whether it was
bound to follow *Burt v Claude Cousins & Co Ltd*[3], an earlier decision (by a majority)
of its own, which was argued to be inconsistent with a much earlier decision of its own, c
in *Rayner v Paskell and Cann*[4]. This court decided (again by a majority) that it was
bound. I pointed out[5] that the decision in *Burt's* case[3] was given not per incuriam
nor in ignorance of the decision in *Rayner's* case[4], but after the most careful consideration of it; the court had the relevant authorities before it, and even if one of those
authorities had been a decision of the House of Lords, we could not consistently with
Young v Bristol Aeroplane Co Ltd[6] refuse to follow the Court of Appeal's decision just d
because we thought the reasoning faulty or the result unjust. If what I said there was
right—and I still think it was for the reasons I there gave—it concludes this appeal in
favour of the plaintiff. For counsel for the defendants has not satisfied me that there
was any relevant authority, statute or rule which was overlooked by the court in
deciding the *Schorsch Meier* case[1], however much it might have been helped by
argument on both sides. His argument before us has failed to justify the judge's e
description of the part of that decision with which Lawton LJ disagreed as given
per incuriam as that phrase has been interpreted for this court in *Young's* case[7], in
Morelle v Wakeling[8] and in *Joscelyne v Nissen*[9]. That part was no more a decision per
incuriam than it was obiter dictum and no decision at all.

The judge thought also—and perhaps more plausibly—that he was in the position
of embarrassment foreseen by Lord Hailsham of St Marylebone LC in *Cassell & Co Ltd v* f
Broome[10], where a decision of this court ignores or refuses to follow a decision of the
House of Lords which has been brought to its notice. But counsel for the defendants
did not strive to support the judge's decision on that ground, and we do not have to
consider what is the duty of a judge of first instance—or of this court—in that situation,
or whether Lord Hailsham LC and the House of Lords in *Broome's* case[11] have added
another exception to those enumerated in *Young's* case[7]. Without argument I should g
have thought that the principle in *Young's* case[7] that this court should follow the last
considered decision of its own would apply both to the judge and to this court on
appeal from him, so that only the House of Lords—or Parliament—could overrule
such an aberration of the Court of Appeal, as Lord Reid described it in *Broome's* case[10];
and that is what I understand all their Lordships to have there said. We have heard

h

1　Page 152, ante, [1974] 3 WLR 823
2　[1971] 3 All ER 1231, [1972] 1 QB 326
3　[1971] 2 All ER 611, [1971] 2 QB 426
4　[1971] 2 All ER at 628, [1971] 2 WLR at 939
5　[1971] 3 All ER at 1244, 1245, [1972] 1 QB at 345　　　　　　　　　　　　　j
6　[1944] 2 All ER 293, [1944] KB 718; *affd* [1946] 1 All ER 98, [1946] AC 163
7　[1944] 2 All ER 293, [1944] KB 718
8　[1955] 1 All ER 708, [1955] 2 QB 379
9　[1970] 1 All ER 1213 at 1223, [1970] 2 QB 86 at 99
10　[1972] 1 All ER 801, [1972] AC 1027
11　[1972] 1 All ER at 809, [1972] AC at 1054

a from counsel for the plaintiff a submission that the majority of the Court of Appeal in the *Schorsch Meier* case[1] were not ignoring any decision of the House of Lords—or of this court; but were deciding that, as the judge correctly put it, 'a rule of English law taken for granted by the Court of Appeal and the House of Lords for some 350 years is no longer a rule of English law.' Counsel for the plaintiff has called our attention to authorities which show that the rule has indeed been taken for granted at the Bar

b and on the Bench by Lindley MR, Vaughan Williams, Bankes, Scrutton, Salmon, Cairns and Roskill LJJ in the Court of Appeal; by Lords Buckmaster, Sumner, Parmoor, Simonds, Reid and Radcliffe in the House of Lords; and by Lord Denning MR both in the Court of Appeal and in the House of Lords. He has submitted that it was and is open to this court, without ignoring any of the decisions cited to us, to discard a rule which has been accepted without challenge, once it is challenged in argument

c and the reasons for it are shown to be no longer valid, however long and high the standing of the rule—at least, when it is only a rule of procedure. I would understand Lord Denning MR's judgment in the *Schorsch Meir* case[1]—with which Foster J agreed —as regarding those earlier decisions in that way. On that understanding this court has already in the *Schorsch Meier* case[1] accepted the substance of counsel for the plaintiff's submission, and it is not for us to review its decision but to accept it without

d argument, as we have done, whether or not we agree with it; and I would add, as at present advised whether we understand it as distinguishing earlier decisions or as disregarding them.

In my judgment, the first question is not whether the first ground of decision in the *Schorsch Meier* case[1] is right, but whether it is binding on us, right or wrong. To that first question the principle stare decisis, as applied to this court in *Young's* case[2], gives

e an affirmative answer and compels us to allow this appeal.

GEOFFREY LANE LJ. For centuries it had been assumed without argument in decision after decision by the Court of Appeal and the House of Lords (some of them

f very recent) that money judgments in the courts of this country could only be expressed in terms of sterling and not in terms of any foreign currency. That rule was brought into question in *Schorsch Meier GmbH v Hennin*[1], when this court decided (Lawton LJ dissenting) that the basis for the rule having disappeared by reason of changing circumstances, the rule itself could no longer be held to exist. The appeal in the present case comes before this court because Bristow J declined to follow the decision in *Schorsch Meier*[1], on the grounds, first, that this is the sort of situation

g envisaged by Lord Hailsham LC in *Cassell v Broome*[3], because *Schorsch Meier*[1] was inconsistent with the earlier decision in the House of Lords in the *Havana* case[4]. Secondly, he decided that the decision in *Schorsch Meier*[1] was given per incuriam. Thus this court is faced with the problem of deciding how far it is bound by its own earlier decisions. The principles were laid down clearly in *Young's* case[5]. The Court of Appeal is bound by its own decisions save in the following circumstances. First of

h all, where there are two conflicting decisions of its own and this court must decide which one it is to follow. Secondly, where there is a decision of this court which is inconsistent with, though not expressly overruled by a subsequent decision of the House of Lords. Thirdly, where this court is satisfied that the earlier decision was given per incuriam, as defined by Lord Greene MR in *Young's* case[2]. Counsel for the

j defendants was faced here with the formidable task of persuading this court that the

---

1 Page 152, ante, [1974] 3 WLR 823
2 [1944] 2 All ER 293, [1944] KB 718
3 [1972] 1 All ER 801 at 809, [1972] AC 1027 at 1054
4 [1960] 2 All ER 332, [1961] AC 1007

decision of the court in *Schorsch Meier*[1], presided over by Lord Denning MR, was given per incuriam, and, despite his industry and tact, he failed to persuade me that it was. There were certain matters of which the court in that case was not fully apprised, but none of them was of sufficient importance to enable one to say that if the court had been told of them they might have decided the case differently. The result is that this court is bound by *Schorsch Meier*[1], just as it is bound by *Young's* case[2].

It is unnecessary and would be invidious for me to express any concluded view as to the correctness of the majority decision in *Schorsch Meier*[1], save to say that I do not altogether share the enthusiasm for that decision which has been here expressed. The effect of *Young's* case[2] is that this court is not designed or empowered to hear appeals from its own decisions. Flexibility has to this extent to be sacrificed to certainty. We are bound to follow *Schorsch Meier*[1]. So was the learned judge.

For those reasons I consider this appeal should succeed.

Judgment in the first action set aside. Judgment entered for plaintiff in the sum of 416,144.20 Swiss francs. Amount of interest to be remitted to the judge, at the minimum lending rate plus one per cent. Stay of execution pending appeal to the House of Lords.

Solicitors: *Gosling & Lewis Barnes* (for the plaintiff); *Bower, Cotton & Bower* (for the defendants).

M G Hammett Esq Barrister.

---

1   Page 152, ante, [1974] 3 WLR 823
2   [1944] 2 All ER 293, [1944] KB 718

End of Volume One